The Geology of North America
Volume L

The Arctic Ocean Region

Edited by

Arthur Grantz
U.S. Geological Survey
345 Middlefield Road
Menlo Park, California 94025

L. Johnson
Office of Naval Research
800 North Quincy St., Code 1125
Arlington, Virginia 22217-5000

J. F. Sweeney
Geological Survey of Canada
100 West Pender Street
Vancouver, British Columbia V6B 1R8
Canada

1990

Acknowledgment

Publication of this volume, one of the synthesis volumes of *The Decade of North American Geology Project* series, has been made possible by members and friends of the Geological Society of America, corporations, and government agencies through contributions to the Decade of North American Geology fund of the Geological Society of America Foundation.

Following is a list of individuals, corporations, and government agencies giving and/or pledging more than $50,000 in support of the DNAG Project:

Amoco Production Company
ARCO Exploration Company
Chevron Corporation
Cities Service Oil and Gas Company
Diamond Shamrock Exploration
　Corporation
Exxon Production Research Company
Getty Oil Company
Gulf Oil Exploration and Production
　Company
Paul V. Hoovler
Kennecott Minerals Company
Kerr McGee Corporation
Marathon Oil Company
Maxus Energy Corporation
McMoRan Oil and Gas Company
Mobil Oil Corporation
Occidental Petroleum Corporation

Pennzoil Exploration and
　Production Company
Phillips Petroleum Company
Shell Oil Company
Caswell Silver
Standard Oil Production Company
Oryx Energy Company (formerly
　Sun Exploration and Production
　Company)
Superior Oil Company
Tenneco Oil Company
Texaco, Inc.
Union Oil Company of California
Union Pacific Corporation and
　its operating companies:
　　Union Pacific Resources
　　　Company
　　Union Pacific Railroad
　　　Company
　　Upland Industries
　　　Corporation
U.S. Department of Energy

© 1990 The Geological Society of America, Inc.
All rights reserved.

All materials subject to this copyright and included in this volume may be photocopied for the noncommercial purpose of scientific or educational advancement.

Copyright is not claimed on any material prepared by government employees within the scope of their employment.

Published by The Geological Society of America, Inc.
3300 Penrose Place, P.O. Box 9140, Boulder, Colorado 80301

Cover Art: Passage through the ice-June 16, 1818. Drawn by Capt. Ross, R. N., Engraved by R. Havell and Son *in* Captain John Ross, 1919, A Voyage of Discovery in His Majesty's Ships Isabela and Alxender for the Purpose of Exploring Baffin's Bay and Inquiring into the Possibility of a North West Passage: London, John Murray, facing p. 46.

10 9 8 7 6 5 4 3 2

Library of Congress Cataloging-in-Publication Data

The Arctic Ocean region / edited by Arthur Grantz, L. Johnson, J. F.
　Sweeney.
　　　p.　　cm. — (The Geology of North America ; v. L)
　Includes bibliographical references.
　ISBN 0-8137-5211-6
　1. Geology—Arctic Ocean Region.　I. Grantz, Arthur, 1927–
II. Johnson, L. (Leonard)　III. Sweeney, J. F.　IV. Series.
QE71.G48　　1986　　vol. L
[QE350.6]
557 s—dc20
[551.46'08'0932]　　　　　　　　　　　90-34734
　　　　　　　　　　　　　　　　　　　　　　CIP

Contents

Preface vii

Foreword ix

1. *Introduction* 1
   The Editors

2. *Historical background; Exploration, concepts, and
   observations* 5
   J. R. Weber and E. F. Roots

Arctic Ocean Ice Cover

3. *Structure and dynamics of the Arctic Ocean ice cover* 37
   Norbert Untersteiner

4. *Arctic Ocean ice cover; Geologic history and climatic
   significance* 53
   David L. Clark

Bathymetry and Physiography

5. *Bathymetry and physiography* 63
   G. L. Johnson, Arthur Grantz, and J. R. Weber

Geophysical Data

6. *Seismicity and focal mechanisms of the Arctic region and
   the North American plate boundary in Asia* 79
   Kazuya Fujita, David B. Cook, Henry Hasegawa,
   David Forsyth, and Robert Wetmiller

7. *Gravity from 64°N to the North Pole* 101
   L. W. Sobczak, D. B. Hearty, R. Forsberg,
   Y. Kristoffersen, O. Eldholm, and S. D. May

8. *Magnetic anomalies* 119
   R. L. Coles and P. T. Taylor

9. *Geothermal observations in the Arctic region* 133
   M. G. Langseth, A. H. Lachenbruch, and B. V. Marshall

10. *Seismic reflection and refraction* 153
    H. R. Jackson, D. A. Forsyth, J. K. Hall,
    and A. Overton

The North American Plate Boundary

11. *The North American plate boundary* 171
    Olav Eldholm, A. M. Karasik, and P. A. Reksnes

Continental Margins

12. *The East Greenland Shelf* 185
    Hans Christian Larsen

13. *The North Greenland Continental Margin* 211
    Peter R. Dawes

14. *The continental margin northwest of the Queen
    Elizabeth Islands* 227
    J. F. Sweeney, L. W. Sobczak, and D. A. Forsyth

15. *Canadian Beaufort Sea and adjacent land areas* 239
    J. Dixon and J. R. Dietrich

16. *Geology of the Arctic Continental Margin of Alaska* 257
    Arthur Grantz, S. D. May, and P. E. Hart

17. *The Arctic continental margin of eastern Siberia* 289
    Kazuya Fujita and David B. Cook

Ridges, Borderlands, and Basins

18. *Ridges and basins in the central Arctic Ocean* 305
    J. R. Weber and J. F. Sweeney

19. *Chukchi Borderland* 337
    John K. Hall

20. *The Norwegian–Greenland Sea* 351
    Olav Eldholm, Jakob Skogseid, Eirik Sundvor,
    and Annik M. Myhre

21. *Eurasia Basin* 365
    Yngve Kristoffersen

22. *Canada Basin* 379
    Arthur Grantz, S. D. May, P. T. Taylor, and L. A. Lawver

Contents

Arctic Basin Sediments, Fossils, Paleoclimate, and History

23. *Late Mesozoic and Cenozoic paleogeographic and paleoclimatic history of the Arctic Ocean Basin, based on shallow-water marine faunas and terrestrial vertebrates* 403
    Louie Marincovich, Jr., Elisabeth M. Brouwers,
    David M. Hopkins, and Malcolm C. McKenna

24. *Late Mesozoic and Cenozoic paleoceanography of the northern polar oceans* 427
    Jorn Thiede, David L. Clark, and Yvonne Herman

Late Neogene and Quaternary Geology

25. *Late Cenozoic geologic evolution of the Alaskan North Slope and adjacent continental shelves* 459
    David A. Dinter, L. David Carter, and
    Julie Brigham-Grette

26. *The late Neogene and Quaternary stratigraphy of the Canadian Beaufort continental shelf* 491
    S. M. Blasco, G. Fortin, P. R. Hill, M. J. O'Connor,
    and J. Brigham-Grette

Mineral Resources

27. *Sedimentary basins and petroleum resource potential of the Arctic Ocean region* 503
    N. E. Haimila, C. E. Kirschner, W. W. Nassichuk,
    G. Ulmichek, and R. M. Procter

28. *Gas hydrates of the Arctic Ocean region* 539
    Keith A. Kvenvolden and Arthur Grantz

29. *Offshore hard minerals* 551
    Peter B. Hale

Origin of the Arctic Basin

30. *Paleomagnetic and plate-tectonic constraints on the evolution of the Alaskan–eastern Siberian Arctic* 567
    William Harbert, Leah Frei, Richard Jarrard,
    Susan Halgedahl, and David Engebretson

31. *A review of tectonic models for the evolution of the Candian Basin* 593
    L. A. Lawver and C. R. Scotese

Summary

32. *Summary* 619
    J. F. Sweeney, G. L. Johnson, and A. Grantz

Index 627

Plates
(in accompanying slipcase)

Plate 1. Bathymetry of the Arctic Ocean
R. K. Perry and H. S. Fleming

Plate 2. Seismicity and heat flow of the Arctic
R. J. Wetmiller, M. G. Langseth, B. V. Marshall, and A. H. Lachenbruch

Plate 3. Gravity of the Arctic
L. W. Sobczak and D. B. Hearty

Plate 4. Residual magnetic anomaly chart of the Arctic Ocean region
L. C. Kovacs, G. L. Johnson, S. P. Srivastava, P. T. Taylor, and P. R. Vogt

Plate 5. Sedimentary thickness map of the Arctic Ocean
H. R. Jackson and G. N. Oakey

Plate 6. Seismic reflection profiles across the continental margin off East Greenland
H. C. Larsen

Plate 7. Single channel seismic reflection profiles from the Arctic Basin
M. G. Langseth, K. L. Hawkins, H. R. Jackson, and S. M. Blasco

Plate 8. Multichannel seismic reflection profiles from the Canadian margin of the Canada Basin
James Dixon, James Dietrich, and Norman E. Haimila

Plate 9. Multichannel seismic reflection profiles from the Alaska margin of the Canada Basin
Arthur Grantz, S. D. May, and P. E. Hart

Plate 10. East Greenland continental margin
H. C. Larsen, P. E. Holm, and C. Marcussen

Plate 11. Major Phanerozoic tectonic features of the Arctic Ocean region
Arthur Grantz, A. R. Green, D. G. Smith, J. C. Lahr, and Kazuya Fujita

Microfiche
(in pocket inside back cover)

Bibliography of Geology and Geophysics of the North American Plate in the Soviet Arctic (1 card)
K. Fujita and D. B. Cook

Arctic Ocean Bibliography (2 cards)
J. K. Hall

Preface

The Geology of North America series has been prepared to mark the Centennial of The Geological Society of America. It represents the cooperative efforts of more than 1,000 individuals from academia, state and federal agencies of many countries, and industry to prepare syntheses that are as current and authoritative as possible about the geology of the North American continent and adjacent oceanic regions.

This series is part of the Decade of North American Geology (DNAG) Project, which also includes eight wall maps at a scale of 1:5,000,000 that summarize the geology, tectonics, magnetic and gravity anomaly patterns, regional stress fields, thermal aspects, seismicity and neotectonics of North America and its surroundings. Together, the synthesis volumes and maps are the first coordinated effort to integrate all available knowledge about the geology and geophysics of a crustal plate on a regional scale.

The products of the DNAG Project present the state of knowledge of the geology and geophysics of North America through the 1980s, and they point the way toward work to be done in the decades ahead.

In addition to the contributions from organizations and individuals acknowledged at the front of this book, major support has been provided to the editors of this volume by the U.S. Geological Survey, the Geological Survey of Canada, and the U.S. Office of Naval Research.

> A. R. Palmer
> General Editor for the volumes published by
> The Geological Society of America
> J. O. Wheeler
> General Editor for the volumes published by
> the Geological Survey of Canada.

Foreword

This volume is a comprehensive summary of the geology and solid earth geophysics of the Arctic Ocean region. In consequence of the hostile environment, the state of knowledge of this region lags behind that of the more temperate parts of North America. The Arctic, however, is no less important than the more temperate areas: it plays a key role in Northern Hemisphere plate reconstructions and paleoclimate.

Because of the perpetual ice pack, data on the geology and geophysics of the central Arctic Ocean Basin presented or discussed in this volume were acquired mainly from drifting platforms: semi-permanent field stations on ice islands (large, tabular icebergs), and more temporary field camps on ice floes, from which observations were generally extended with fixed-wing aircraft, and more recently, with helicopters. One consequence of the heavy reliance of the volume's contributors on ice station and ice camp data is that, because these platforms are logistically difficult and expensive to establish and operate, data are sparse or lacking from large areas of the Arctic Ocean Basin. Unfortunately, much of the pioneering Soviet ice camp data, which dates back as far as 1937, has not been released to the open literature. A second consequence of reliance on drifting platforms is that, with the exception of reconnaissance aeromagnetic and satellite magnetic surveys, systematic regional geophysical coverage and systematic subseabed sampling are not yet available for the Arctic Ocean Basin.

Data concerning the margins of the basin were acquired principally from ships operating at the periphery of the ice pack and by spot landings on the ice by aircraft. The potential of Soviet nuclear ice breakers is only beginning to be utilized for systematic surveys within the main Polar ice pack. Exploration from submarines also has great potential, but the only data that have entered the public domain are, to a limited extent, incorporated in Plate 1, a bathymetric map of the Arctic Ocean. Because of the barrier that the ice pack presents to systematic regional geophysical surveys from ships, the magnetic field data that have been recorded from aircraft and satellites are especially important to many of the chapters in this volume.

Because of its landlocked character, data from the surrounding continents are especially useful to studies of the Arctic Ocean Basin geology. For example, comparisons of regional geology and of paleomagnetic and paleontologic data across the basin have placed important constraints on Arctic tectonic models, even though these studies are in their infancy. Further, the continental margins of several nations face the Arctic Ocean Basin, which invites, and indeed requires, international cooperation between scientists if many of the basic problems of Arctic geology and solid-earth geophysics are to be solved. It should be noted in this regard that scientists from seven nations contributed to this volume. We regret, however, that *Glasnost* did not sweep the Soviet Union a few years earlier than it did. This volume would have benefited significantly from greater participation by our Soviet colleagues, many of whom pioneered geological and geophysical exploration of the Arctic Ocean Basin at a time when such work required extraordinary vision and daring.

In view of the relatively early stage that has been achieved in our knowledge of Arctic Ocean Basin geology and solid-earth geophysics, the pervasive influence of the pack ice, and the landlocked character of the basin, the organization of this volume differs in important ways from other volumes of *The Geology of North America*. Thus, space was provided in Chapter 2 for an extensive review of the economic, political, and scientific context of exploration, as well as a historical account of the expeditions and studies that have brought us to our present state of understanding. Because of the unique and pervasive role that it has had on Arctic geology, climate, and oceanography, Chapters 3 and 4 examine the structure and dynamics and the geologic history of the Polar ice pack. Because of the major influence that Arctic climate exerts on world climate and the world's oceans, Chapters 23 and 24 are devoted to the late Mesozoic and Cenozoic paleoclimatic and paleoceanographic histories of the Arctic Ocean Basin. The embryonic state of our knowledge of the complex bathymetry of the Arctic Ocean Basin, and the major clues that the bathymetry provides for its geologic origin, led us to devote Chapter 5 to that subject.

The sparseness and uneven distribution of basic Arctic geoscience data led us to solicit two very different types of chapters for the sections of the volume that deal with the solid earth of the Arctic Ocean region. The first type (Chapters 6 to 10) are primarily geophysical. These chapters describe and interpret in broad terms the principal geophysical data sets that now exist for the region. Some of these data are also summarized in Plates 1 to 11. The second type (Chapters 11 to 24) are primarily syntheses and geological interpretations of the geophysical data for specific geologic provinces of the Arctic, supplemented where available by core, dredge, and test-well data, and by generous extrapolation of onshore geologic data. Chapters 25 and 26, on Quaternary geology, carry the geologic framework and evolution of the North American margin of the Arctic forward to the Holocene, and Chapters 27 to 29 summarize the substantial mineral resource potential of the Arctic. In view of the nascent stage of our knowledge of Arctic Basin geology, Chapter 30 was solicited to examine the constraints and insights that the paleomagnetic record of the surrounding landmasses and the ocean basins of the Northern Hemisphere place on the tectonic development of the Arctic Basin. A byproduct of the present state of knowledge is that seriously proposed tectonic models for the Arctic Basin are remarkably diverse. The editors hope that Chapter 31 will serve as a useful "field guide" to the principal generic types of models that have been proposed, and to the principal arguments that have been marshalled for each. In Chapter 32, the editors attempt to summarize the present state of understanding of the solid earth in the Arctic Ocean region and make recommendations for promising areas of future research.

All contributions to this volume were reviewed by the volume editors and by peer reviewers selected by the Geological Society of America, whose editorial policies and standards have been followed. It is a pleasure to acknowledge the guidance and enthusiasm of Allison R. (Pete) Palmer in all aspects of planning, organizing, and producing this volume. The reviewers of individual articles are also thanked. The majority of the chapters in this volume were reviewed by 1986, and in some cases they may not be current regarding recently published work. We apologize for the delay. Much of the end art that adorns this volume, and the drawing on the cover, were photographed from early publications on Arctic exploration in the collections of the Arctic Institute of North America, now housed in the University of Calgary library. We thank Gerald J. Thompson, Assistant Director of the Arctic Institute, for providing the necessary photographic services.

The editors wish to recognize the landmark contributions that one of our contributors, the late Dr. A. M. Karasik of Leningrad, made to Arctic geoscience through his studies of the magnetic field and the plate tectonic history and development of the Eurasia Basin of the Arctic Ocean. We regret that his insight, leadership, and scientific collaboration are no longer available to the Arctic geoscience community.

The Editors
January 1990

The Geology of North America
Vol. L, The Arctic Ocean region
The Geological Society of America, 1990

Chapter 1

Introduction

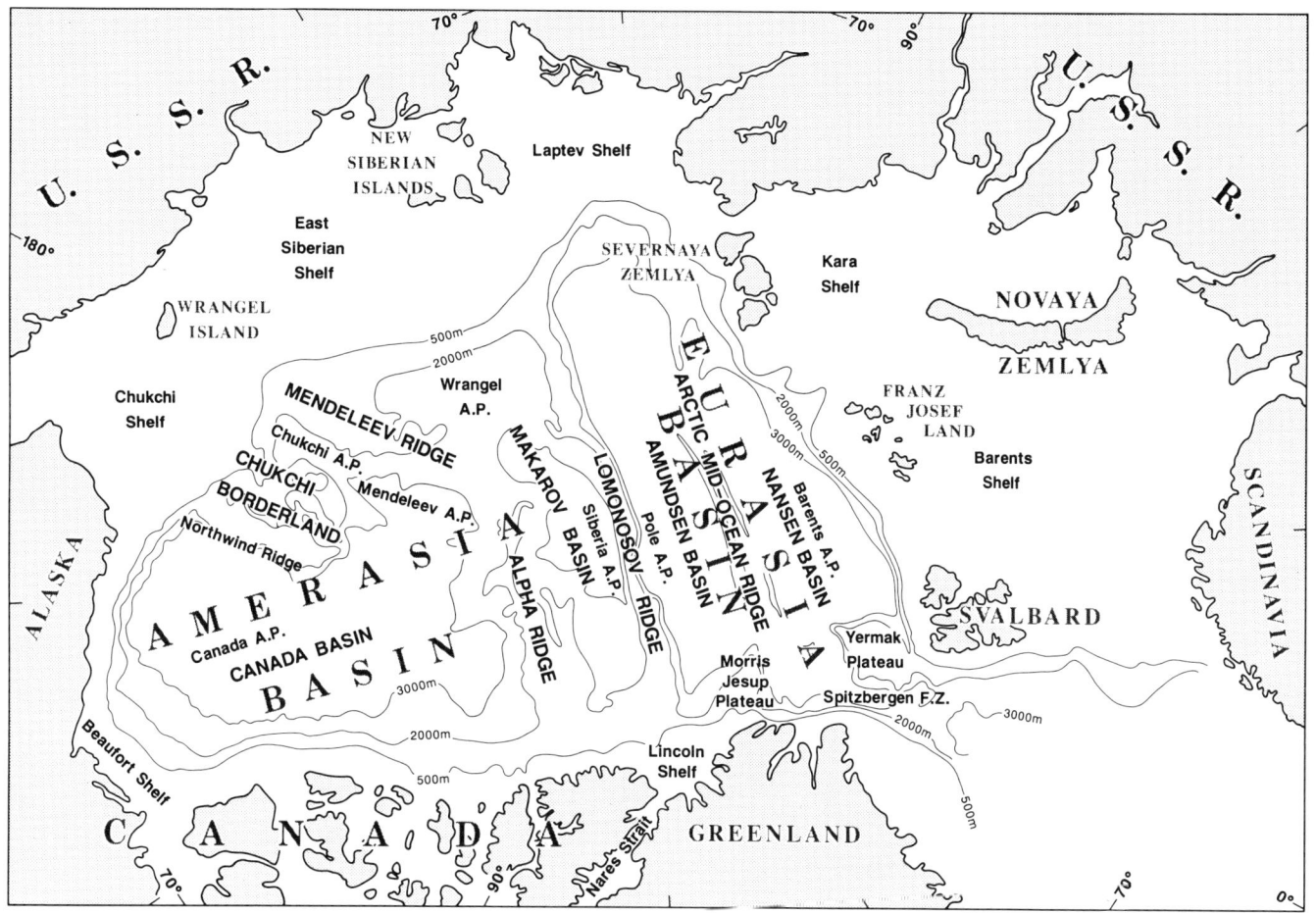

Figure 1. Marine nomenclature of the Arctic Basin. A.P., abyssal plain; F.Z., fracture zone.

Although a sea voyage to ice-infested northern waters was described in antiquity, and repeated attempts to discover a commercial water route to the north of Eurasia and North America were made from the sixteenth century onward, the physical geography of the north polar region was little studied until systematic scientific investigations were undertaken late in the eighteenth century. The International Polar Year in 1882–1883 marked the beginning of coordinated multinational, interdisciplinary scientific studies around the Arctic, and by the end of the nineteenth century, Nansen had demonstrated that a deep ocean exists beneath the ice pack in the central Arctic. Subsequent delineation of the Arctic sea floor has improved gradually; today, although much of the seabed morphology is unknown in detail, the larger physiographic features have been mapped in reconnaissance fashion.

Crustal and marine studies of the area have been underway since the mid-twentieth century. By the 1960s, much new information about these aspects of Arctic science had been acquired and summarized in major volumes such as Raasch (1961). The present volume gives a comprehensive exposition and analysis of geological and geophysical information available from the Arctic Ocean and adjacent seas as of the late 1980s. The information presented is in the public domain. Commercial and military proprietary data are excluded. Also absent is much of the important

The Editors, 1990, Introduction, *in* Grantz, A., Johnson, L., and Sweeney, J. F., eds., The Arctic Ocean region: Boulder, Colorado, Geological Society of America, The Geology of North America, v. L.

Figure 2. Marine nomenclature of the Atlantic region north from Iceland. A.P., abyssal plain; F.Z., fracture zone.

work done in the Arctic by Soviet scientists who, unfortunately, were unable to participate significantly in this synthesis.

This volume covers the Arctic Ocean region and its extension into the Norwegian-Greenland Sea (Figs. 1 and 2). The marine Arctic is composed of the oceanic Eurasia and Amerasia Basins, and it contains large aseismic ridges and plateaus whose origins are, for the most part, enigmatic. There is also an active spreading ridge, thick continental rise sedimentary prisms, and both rifted and sheared continental margins.

The structure and origin of the Arctic region is closely linked to the evolution of the Atlantic and Pacific basins as well as to the history of the surrounding landmasses. An understanding of past and present plate movements and accretionary tectonics in the Arctic will be required before a complete model of even late Mesozoic and Cenozoic worldwide plate motions can be achieved. These motions and the structure, paleontology, and paleoenvironment of Phanerozoic sedimentary rocks in the circum-Arctic and its continental shelves are also highly relevant to exploration for hydrocarbons. Large hydrocarbon discoveries in northern North America and the presence in the Arctic of large sedimentary basins and wide continental shelves suggest that major resources of oil, gas, and coal remain to be discovered in the region.

The evolution of cold polar hydrospheres several million years ago has had a global impact on the world's oceans and biosphere because cold surface waters at high latitudes sink and flow toward the equator to fill the major deep-sea basins. Studies of marine sediments beneath the north polar sea floors have provided important but, so far, fragmentary data about the onset and oscillations of the current climatic regime and the response of indigenous fauna and flora to the cooler temperatures.

There have been many attempts to formalize an Arctic marine nomenclature (e.g., Beal and others, 1966; Treshnikov and others, 1966; Hunkins, 1968; Demenitskaya and Hunkins, 1970; Herman, 1974; Sweeney and Haines, 1978) but several sea-floor features continue to be known by two or more names (Table 1). The scheme adopted for this volume is given in Figures 1 and 2.

Ambiguity in nomenclature derives in part from uncertainty about the extent and morphology of specific features. For example, it is unclear whether the Alpha and Mendeleev ridges are joined or separated. In this volume they are considered separate. Definitions of some other features in Figures 1 and 2 follows: The Chukchi Borderland includes the Northwind Ridge, the Chukchi Abyssal Plain and Arlis Plateau (southeast flank of Mendeleev Ridge). The Borderland is bounded on the south by the continental margin (Chukchi Shelf) and on the north and east by the Mendeleev and Canada abyssal plains, respectively. The Canada Basin contains the Chukchi Borderland and the Canada and Mendeleev abyssal plains. The Makarov Basin takes in the Wrangel and Siberia abyssal plains. The Canada and Makarov basins, together with the Alpha and Mendeleev ridges, make up the Amerasia Basin. The Pole Abyssal Plain and the Morris Jesup Plateau form the Amundsen Basin. The Barents Abyssal Plain and the Yermak Plateau compose the Nansen Basin. The Eurasia Basin includes the Amundsen Basin, the Nansen Basin, and the Arctic Mid-Ocean Ridge. The Lomonosov Ridge separates the Amerasia and Eurasia basins.

The bathymetric map of Perry and others (1985), with bathymetry updated to 1987, is used as the base for the major parameter displays (Plates 1–5, 10, and 11) that accompany this volume. The base map (Plate 1) is a polar stereographic projection, scale 1:6,000,000 at 75°N, with most shoreline and land topography taken from Heezen and others (1975). The north coast of Greenland is provided by the Geodetic Survey of Denmark.

TABLE 1. ARCTIC MARINE NOMENCLATURE; FEATURES WITH ALTERNATE NAMES

This Volume	Other Names
Aegir Ridge	Extinct Axis
Alpha Ridge	Alpha Rise, Alpha Cordillera, Fletchers Ridge, Alpha-Mendeleyev Ridge
Amerasia Basin	Canada Basin, Amerasian Basin, Laurentian Basin
Amundsen Basin	Fram Basin, Fram Deep, Nansen Basin, European Basin
Arctic Mid-Ocean Ridge	Nansen Ridge, Nansen Cordillera, Gakkel Ridge, Nansen-Gakkel Ridge
Canada Abyssal Plain	Canada Basin, Canada Deep
Canada Basin	Hyperborean Basin, Amerasia Basin
Chukchi Borderland	Chukchi Rise, Chukchi Cap, Chukchi Plateau, Chukchi Continental Borderland
Chukchi Cap	Chukchi Plateau
Eurasia Basin	Eurasian Basin, Angara Basin
Knipovich Ridge	Atka Ridge
Kolbeinsey Ridge	Iceland-Jan Mayen Ridge
Lomonosov Ridge	Harris Ridge
Makarov Basin	Central Arctic Basin, Siberia Basin, Markarov Basin
Marvin Spur	Marvin Ridge, Marvin Sea Mounts
Mendeleev Ridge	Mendeleyev Ridge, Alpha-Mendeleyev Ridge, Mendeleev Rise
Morris Jesup Plateau	Morris Jesup Rise, Morris Jessup Rise
Northwind Ridge	Northwind Seahigh
Norway Basin	Norwegian Basin, Norwegian Abyssal Plain
Norwegian-Greenland Sea	Greenland-Norwegian Sea, Nordic Sea
Siberia Abyssal Plain	Fletcher Abyssal Plain
Spitzbergen Fracture Zone	Fram Strait, Lena Trough
Wrangel Abyssal Plain	Makarov Basin, Fletcher Abyssal Plain
Yermak Plateau	Yermak Rise, Nansen Rise, Ermak Plateau

REFERENCES CITED

Beal, M. A., Edvalson, F., Hunkins, K. L., Molloy, A., and Ostenso, N. A., 1966, The floor of the Arctic Ocean; Geographical names: Arctic, p. 215–219.

Blackadar, R. G., Dumych, H., and Griffin, P. J., 1980, Guide to authors: Geological Survey of Canada Miscellaneous Report 29, 66 p.

Demenitskaya, R. M., and Hunkins, K. L., 1970, Shape and structure of the Arctic Ocean, *in* Maxwell, A. E., ed., The sea, Volume 4, Part 2: New York, Wiley Interscience, p. 223–249.

Heezen, B., Tharp, M., and Pinther, M., 1975, Map of the Arctic region: New York, American Geographical Society, World Sheet 14, scale 1:5,000,000.

Herman, Y., 1974, Topography of the Arctic Ocean, *in* Herman, Y., ed., Marine geology and oceanography of the Arctic seas: New York, Springer-Verlag, p. 73–81.

Hunkins, K. L., 1968, Geomorphic provinces of the Arctic Ocean, *in* Sater, J. E., ed., Arctic drifting stations: Washington, D.C., Arctic Institute of North America, p. 365–376.

Perry, R. K., and 6 others, 1985, Bathymetry of the Arctic Ocean: Washington, D.C., Naval Research Laboratory, scale approximately 1:6,000,000.

Raasch, G. O., ed., 1961, Geology of the Arctic, 2 volumes: Toronto, Ontario, University of Toronto Press, 1196 p.

Sweeney, J. F., and Haines, G. V., 1978, Arctic geophysical review; An introduction, *in* Sweeney, J. F., ed., Arctic geophysical review: Ottawa, Ontario, Canada, Earth Physics Branch Publication 45, no. 4, p. 1–6.

Treshnikov, A. F., and 7 others, 1966, Geographic names for the main features of the floor of the Arctic Basin: Problemey Arktiki i Antarktiki, v. 27, p. 1–25 (in Russian).

MANUSCRIPT ACCEPTED BY THE SOCIETY NOVEMBER 22, 1989

Chouette des neiges.
(*Strix nyctea* L.)

Cormoran d'Irkaipij.
(*Graculus bicristatus* Pallas.)

Macareux.
(*Mormon arcticus* L.)

From A. E. Nordenskjold, 1885, Voyage de la Vega Autor de l'Asie et de l'Europe (1878–1879) (Translated from the Swedish by Charles Rabot and Charles Lallemond), Vol. 1: Paris, Libraire Hachette et Cie, p. 119, 405, and 103, respectively).

Chapter 2

Historical background; Exploration, concepts, and observations

J. R. Weber
Geophysics Division, Geological Survey of Canada, 1 Observatory Crescent, Ottawa, Ontario K1A 0Y3, Canada
E. F. Roots
Science Advisor, Department of the Environment, Ottawa, Ontario K1A 0H3, Canada

INTRODUCTION

The first of the four main parts of this chapter presents a short history of the European discovery of circumpolar lands and the Arctic Ocean from the earliest recorded voyages to the twentieth century. The story of geographic exploration of the Arctic regions has been told many times, and there is an enormous literature dealing with expeditions and geographic discoveries. Particularly useful in providing the historical setting for the growth of scientific knowledge of the Arctic Ocean area is the compilation by Kirwan (1959), who provides insights into the economic, strategic, political, and personal motives behind many of the explorations; and the scholarly analyses edited by Rey and others (1984), which trace the development of geographic and scientific knowledge of the Arctic as a result of myths, conjectures, genuine discoveries, and increasingly precise observations from antiquity to the eighteenth century.

The next part deals with the mapping of the Arctic Ocean basin and floor during the last century, from sparse information that led to a shallow, single-basin concept to the complex sea-floor morphology that gradually emerged as a result of the more detailed surveys beginning with the Soviet explorations in 1937. This section ends with a description of the major modern bathymetric maps and charts that have appeared in print, from Bartholomew in 1897 to Perry and others (Plate 1, this volume).

The third section is an outline of the history of the geoscientific work carried out within the Arctic Ocean region, from ships, from drifting stations, and by land-based fixed-wing aircraft and helicopters. Aeromagnetic and satellite magnetic surveys, not included here, have been summarized by Coles and Taylor (this volume). Although much geological, geophysical, oceanographic, and biological data in the Arctic Ocean region has been obtained by Soviet researchers over the past four decades, little of this has been published outside the Soviet Union. Much of the Soviet data and interpretation, if not classified, is scattered throughout the Soviet scientific literature. Therefore, regrettably, the history of the Soviet contribution to Arctic Ocean basin geoscience has been summarized very briefly.

The final section of this chapter discusses the growth of knowledge of the Arctic Ocean basin and surrounding areas during the past 2,300 years of investigation. Speculation on the possible source of some of the cartographic information appearing on sixteenth century prediscovery maps is also presented.

The reader is referred to Plate 1 for geographic place names used in this chapter.

DISCOVERIES AND EXPLORATIONS OF THE ARCTIC LANDS AND SEAS

From antiquity to Mercator and Barents

The first polar explorer on record was Pytheas, from the Greek colony of Massilia, the modern Marseilles. About 320 B.C. he sailed in search of the tin that had mysteriously appeared from time to time in the markets of Massilia, coming, so rumor said, south through Gaul from some remote and unknown northern land. Navigating by sun and stars he steered his square-sailed Greek galley to Brittany and to Cornwall, the source of the tin. After sailing northward from the British Isles for six days, he reached another land, which he identified as Thule, where the nearby sea was frozen. Whether this was Iceland or northern Norway has been much debated; but the consistency with which the wealth of information brought back by Pytheas was reported and used by many contemporaneous sources leaves no doubt that he reached Arctic latitudes and spent some time there. Observations on the relative positions of the stars, the midnight sun, the differing lengths of days and nights as the seasons progressed, the connection between the tides and the phases of the moon, large sea mammals, the unexpected phenomenon of the freezing of the sea, which was mystifying and terrible to warm-ocean sailors— all these were completely new to Mediterranean geographers and scholars, so that the words to describe some of them had to be borrowed from Pytheas' Celtic and Norse contacts. So convincing was his information that this one extended voyage significantly enlarged the known world and brought Arctic phenomena into what was then the mainstream of European scientific knowledge and literature (Chevallier, 1984).

Weber, J. R., and Roots, E. F., 1990, Historical background; Exploration, concepts, and observations, *in* Grantz, A., Johnson, L., and Sweeney, J. F., eds., The Arctic Ocean region: Boulder, Colorado, Geological Society of America, The Geology of North America, v. L.

Figure 1. Grecian conception of the Earth after Pytheas' discoveries and Eratosthenes' calculations: the globe as described by Crates (ca. 150 B.C.). It satisfied symmetry by inventing, in addition to the known inhabited world (the Oecumene), three other populated continents: Perioeci (peoples around the globe from the Oecumene), Antoeci (peoples below the Oecumene), and the Antipodes (peoples on the opposite side of the globe; Raisz, 1948).

Pytheas' observations paved the way for Eratosthenes (220 B.C.) to portray the Earth as a sphere of finite size, and to devise ways to calculate its circumference and axial tilt (Fig. 1). Later geographers and cartographers (Strabo, Ptolemy, etc.) incorporated this information, embellished with fanciful details and reports from various other sources, to develop a European concept of the Arctic regions that remained essentially unchallenged for the next thousand years.

It appears that Iceland was already settled by Irish monks when the Norsemen arrived about A.D. 870. The settlement of Greenland by Eric the Red around A.D. 985 was soon followed by the discoveries of Baffin Island, Labrador, Newfoundland, and possibly Nova Scotia by Norsemen. Norse travelers from West Greenland reached St. Helena Island at the west end of Jones Sound in the central Canadian Archipelago, and Bache Peninsula on Ellesmere Island.

The earliest account of a penetration into the Arctic Ocean basin is in the writings of King Alfred the Great of England, who about 890 A.D. was informed by a Norwegian chieftain named Othere (Ottar), from Halagoland in southern Norway, that some decades earlier he had followed the Scandinavian coast to the north and east: "he was anxious to know how far the land extended, and whether any people lived beyond the wasteland."

(Bosworth, 1855; Sweet, 1883, p. 30). Othere sailed around the North Cape and the Kola Peninsula into the White Sea where he encountered the Finns, from whom he thereafter annually collected produce and tribute (Meriot, 1984). This voyage was followed by considerable coastal trade, and the extension of Norwegian sovereignty from the White Sea to Iceland. Norway's rule became absolute; a royal proclamation in 1294 forbade foreigners to sail north of Bergen and forced English and Dutch merchants to buy produce from all northern waters and lands in the harbor of that town. Even Norwegian ships were subjected to royal restrictions in venturing northward. This principle of *mare clausum* appears to have effectively prevented further exploration of the Arctic Ocean until well into the sixteenth century (Blom, 1984).

Speculation on the geography of northern regions continued, however, and there were several attempts to compile known and imagined records. Early in the fifteenth century, a Dane, Claudius Clavus, made two maps of the North, extending Ptolemy's atlas, which showed only *Terra Incognita* and *Mare Congelatum* north of 63° latitude (which perhaps was Pytheas' northern limit). Presumably using information gathered from traditional Norse mariner's sailing stories, Clavus placed Iceland midway between Norway and Greenland. Norse knowledge of impenetrable sea ice across the northern North Atlantic may also have been the basis for the interpretation that a continuous land bridge between Greenland and Europe closed off *Mare Congelatum*. A map showing both sides of the Atlantic in reasonable scale and proportions based on Norse and English voyages to North America was drawn in Iceland by Sigurdur Stephansson in 1570 (Fig. 2), but it retained the land bridge. Other maps of the time, for example, that of Ortelius published the same year, do not show land connecting Europe and Greenland. Ortelius depicted Greenland as a modest island of realistic shape, and a long marine passage leads around the north of North America to the "Strait of Anian" and the Pacific Ocean.

In 1588, Nicolo Zeno published a story, now considered fiction, of the voyages of two of his ancestors to the Arctic in 1380. He illustrated the story with an imaginative "chart" based partly on the maps of Clavus and later cartographers. The popularity of this drawing was such that "Zenian geography" was accepted as an improvement on previous maps. Genuine contemporary discoveries, such as those of Frobisher, were force-fitted into Zeno's map and thereby falsified (Wallis, 1984).

From the time of the early Greek and Roman globes that showed an all-encompassing ocean beyond the known and unknown lands (Fig. 1), little attention had been given to what lay beyond the traveled world, including the polar region (Rey, 1982). Scandinavian legends told of a polar maelstrom that swirled about a central rock, surrounded by four islands, peopled by pygmies, and between which strong currents of water rushed to the pole. These legends had become known in southern Europe through a widely quoted book, *De Inventione Fortunata qui liber incipit a gradua 54 usque ad polum* (". . . which book begins in the description at latitude 54 degrees and goes as far as the

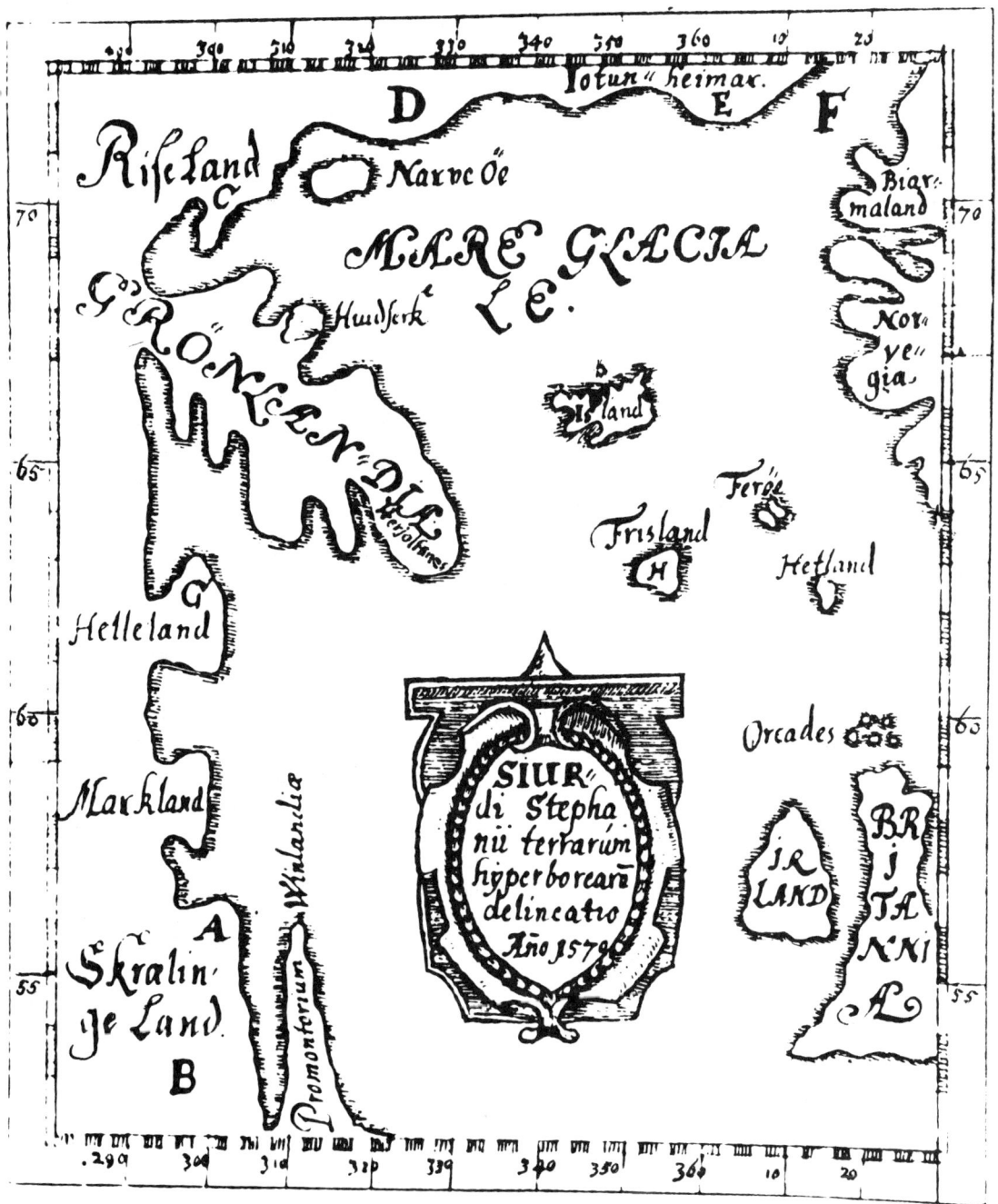

Figure 2. Map of the North Atlantic region drawn in Iceland by Sigurdur Stephansson in 1570. Note the rectangular coordinate system used for latitude and longitude. Stephansson appended explanatory notes to this map, in which he remarks that the Atlantic Ocean was closed by Jotunheiman (the home of giants). Royal Library, Copenhagen.

pole") attributed to Nicholas of Lynne, and which was published in Italy in 1360. Although no copies are known to have been preserved, the book is of interest today because it shows that in the fourteenth century, degrees of latitude were already in widespread use for geographical description, and that the North Pole was a widely understood concept. The partly factual, partly mythical geography of the north polar regions described in this book became a chief source of ideas for cartographers wishing to fill in blanks on the Arctic map.

One of the earliest attempts to draw a map of the polar basin was by Johannes Ruysch of the Netherlands, whose 1507 map is included as Plate 1 in the 1508 edition of *Ptolemy's Geography* published in Rome. Ruysch quotes his authority for the central part of his map by a legend on the map:

"In the book *De Inventione Fortunata* it may be read that there is a high mountain of magnetic stone, 33 German miles in circumference. This is surrounded by flowing 'mare sugenum' which pours out water like a vessel through openings below. Around it are four islands of which two are inhabited. Extensive desolate mountains surround these islands for 24 days' journey, where there is no human habitation" (translation in Nansen, 1911, v. 2, p. 289).

The most influential of the map makers to take their ideas from *De Inventione Fortunata* and similar stories was the Flemish cosmographer and cartographer Gerhard Kremer (Mercator), who in 1569 produced a world chart with a polar projection insert of the Arctic Ocean. This map differs in important ways from his earlier 1538 map (see discussion later in this chapter). Although his 1569 map shows known land and seas as accurately as knowledge then permitted, the central Arctic Ocean is a fanciful cartoon based on *Inventione Fortunata* and the Scandinavian legends. The result was to mislead generations of later explorers. Over the next 30 years, Mercator improved his map and added details from successive discoveries of the known coasts and lands, but never abandoned the imaginary central ocean land masses (Fig. 3). Other well-known world maps of the period, notably that of Ortelius, 1570, also fill the Arctic Ocean with four mythical islands. More cautious map makers, notably the Dutch navigator Willem Barents, produced circumpolar maps depicting only the known and verified lands, at least within the sector of the then-discovered lands, between Davis Strait and Novaya Zemlya (Fig. 4). However, these more accurate renditions had less influence on geographers' concepts of the Arctic Ocean basin.

An interesting detail of Mercator's Arctic maps and of many other European maps of the period, is the inclusion of the "Strait of Anian" that connects the Arctic Ocean with the Kingdom of Japan. The concept of a strait separating Asia from North America was first embodied on maps about 1540, prior to any recorded discoveries in the region (Falk, 1984). Many maps produced during the next 60 years show this strait, and on several of these the geographic position and outlines bear quite close resemblance to Bering Strait. Many modern scholars feel that the representations are pure speculation and the resemblance to actual geography to be coincidental (Fisher, 1984). This conclusion is, however, open to challenge; we will return to this problem later.

The fanciful ideas from the Scandinavian legends and *De Inventione Fortunata* have been very durable. The concept of a magnetic mountain as an attractor for the compass persisted long after William Gilbert showed that the Earth as a whole generated the magnetic forces. The notion of an open north polar sea was a driving force for centuries of later exploration. The concept of an aperture at the pole that led to the interior of the earth developed later into "Symmes Hole," and still further into the idea of a hollow earth, popular with science fiction writers from Jules Verne (*Adventures of Captain Hatteras,* 1864) to Richard Lupoff (*Circumpolar!,* 1984). A number of apparently serious quasi-philosophical tracts that ignore scientific evidence still find a ready popular sale among those wishing to believe in, or be titillated by, a "hole at the Pole" (Bernard, 1976).

Search for the northern sea route to the kingdoms of Cathay

In the sixteenth century, a fresh impetus was given to Arctic exploration: the search for a northern route to the Indies, China, and Japan, or the kingdoms of Cathay as they were called. This search was, in part, the result of the Treaty of Tordesillas in 1494, which divided the right of exploration and acquisition of the then-known world into two domains, the western being granted to Spain, the eastern to Portugal. Although the treaty extended from pole to pole, the Papal bill giving international sanction to the treaty excluded lands already in possession of a Christian power, and did not prevent northern nations from exploring the coasts of lands that they claimed (Theutenberg, 1984). Discovery of a northern route to the Orient would thus circumvent the Spanish and Portugese blockades. Until the eighteenth century, the main motive of voyages in the Arctic remained the search for a northern passage to the Pacific and the oriental kingdoms of Cathay. The concept of a navigable northern trade route to the orient was first strongly promoted in 1527 by the English merchant adventurer Robert Thorne. In addition to political motives, it was bolstered by two misconceptions that, despite growing evidence, were to persist for centuries: (1) that sea ice formed only near coasts, and that continuous Arctic summer sun would maintain an open ice-free polar sea, and (2) a mistaken notion of the distance to China based, apparently, on Marco Polo's erroneous description of the width of Asia (Saladin d'Anglure, 1980). This led to an assumption that a route through the North-West Passage would be much shorter than one to the east.

Figure 3. Gerhard Mercator's revised circumpolar map of the Arctic Ocean, *Septentrionalium terrarum descriptio,* (1595). National Archives of Canada, NMC-29431, Ottawa, 1987.

During the reign of Elizabeth I, in the second half of the sixteenth century, the British ventured both to the northeast and to the northwest. Richard Chancellor sailed as far as the south tip of Novaya Zemlya, where he was forced back by an ice barrier at the entrance to the Kara Sea. In 1576, Martin Frobisher, probing Hudson's Strait and the bays of southeastern Baffin Island, made the first, if dubious, contribution to Arctic economic geology by bringing back pyritiferous mica schist that was mistaken for gold ore. This discovery precipitated two further expeditions in a frantic attempt to find gold—the first Arctic gold rush.

In three carefully documented voyages, 1585 to 1587, John Davis explored the coasts of Greenland along Davis Strait. In 1594, four Dutch ships under the command of Willem Barents managed to penetrate into the Kara Sea. Two years later, another

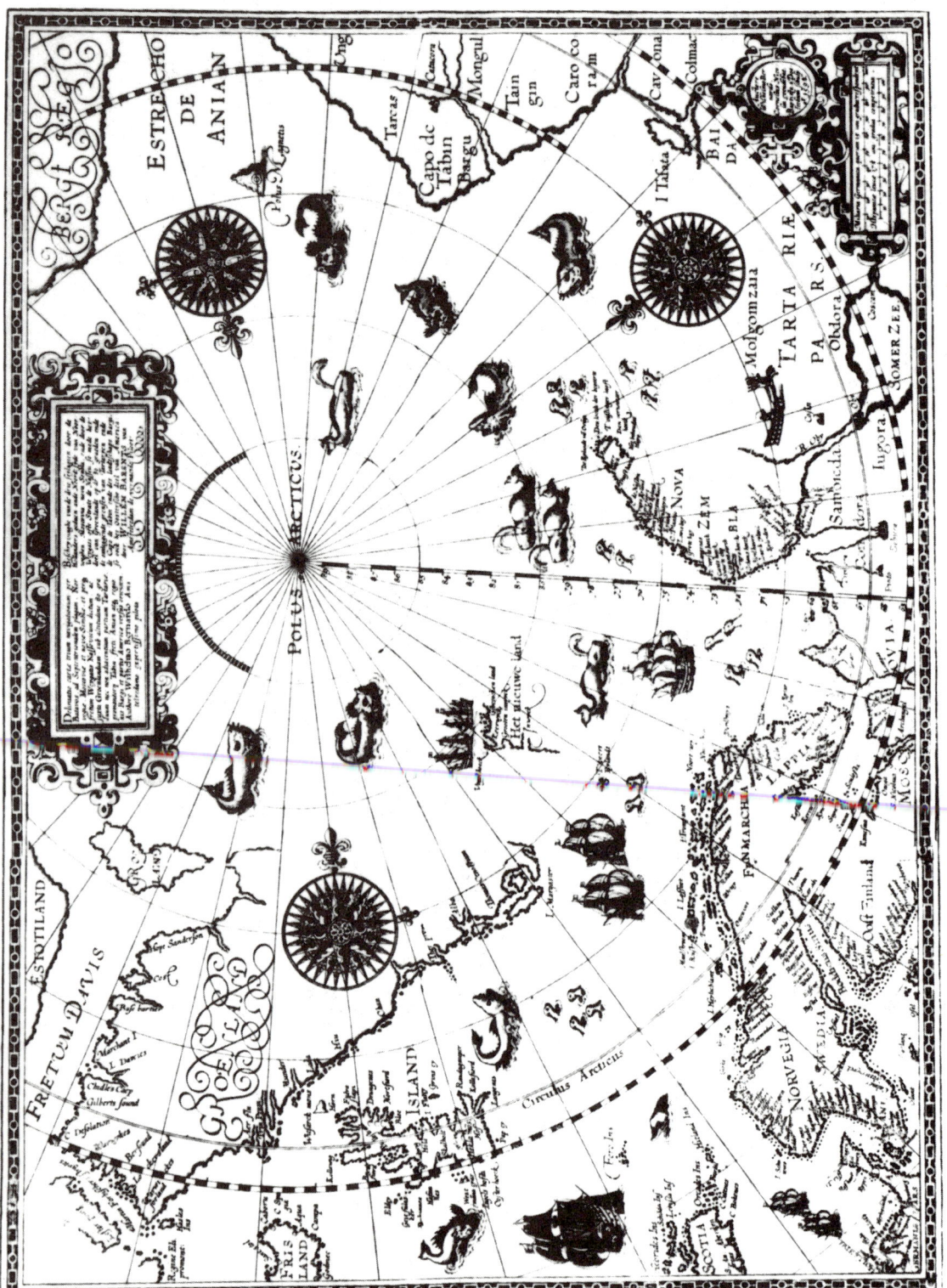

Figure 4. Circumpolar map of the Arctic Ocean drawn by Willem Barents (1598). National Archives of Canada, NMC-10299, Ottawa, 1987.

Dutch expedition, commanded by Jon Rijp and Jacob Heemskerck with Barents as pilot, sailed beyond 80°N. On their way south they discovered Spitzbergen, with its waters abounding with seals, walrus, and whales. Exploring farther to the east, Heemskerck and Barents sailed around the north end of Novaya Zemlya, thus completing the outline of the major land areas north of Eurasia.

In 1609, Holland forced Portugal to grant her full rights to the trade in eastern waters. Thus, Holland had no further need for the Arctic sea route and abandoned its search for a northern route to the Indies. The British, however, were still opposed by Spain and continued the quest, and in 1616 Robert Bylot, with William Baffin as navigator, nearly solved the problem of the North-West Passage. Bylot was by this time on his fifth Arctic exploratory voyage, Baffin on his sixth. They navigated the 50-ton ship *Discovery* along Greenland's west coast to Melville Bay (Melville Bugt), rounded the head of what is now Baffin Bay, crossed Smith Sound at the south end of Nares Strait, and explored the eastern ends of Jones and Lancaster Sounds. Naming all the major land and water features, they established the major geography of West Greenland and the eastern Canadian Arctic Archipelago. Baffin's detailed maps and journals from this voyage, however, were not preserved in public record. The only record of Baffin's surveys that can be identified today is on anonymous Dutch maps in use between 1616 and 1625 (Schilder, 1984) and in the circumpolar chart *Polar Map or Card* produced in 1635 by Luke Foxe, an acquaintance of Baffin, to illustrate his own 1631 to 1632 explorations in Hudson Bay. The map shows in excellent detail the then-known Arctic coastlines of North America, Spitzbergen, and Scandinavia (Taylor, 1955; Wallis, 1984). Otherwise, and in part possibly due to commercial rivalry, Baffin's findings were forgotten or doubted. They were not rediscovered until the nineteenth century.

The seventeenth-century Arctic maritime discoveries, launched by merchant guilds and city companies seeking a trade route to the Orient, were supplemented by the unrecorded voyages of whalers and sealers who followed into sub-Arctic and Arctic waters. The Dutch discovery of rich marine resources in the Barents Sea and around Spitzbergen soon led to a fierce rivalry between English and Dutch whalers and sealers. The extension of whaling grounds into Melville Bay, western Baffin Bay, and Hudson Strait was mainly an English operation, although Dutch, Danish, French, and Portuguese ships are known to have been active. On land the men of the Hudson's Bay Company (founded in 1670), and other trappers, hunters, and voyageurs, had already started to push the North American northern frontier toward the Arctic Ocean. In a similar fashion, the Russian economic empire was expanding eastward across Sibera and along the Asian Arctic coast.

Eighteenth century strategic explorations

With the onset of the eighteenth century, motives and methods of polar exploration changed. Exploration became largely an instrument of government policy, and the national navies of Britain, France, and Russia replaced the private groups and merchant adventurers of former years. In Britain the dominant role of the Royal Navy in the organization and conduct of polar exploration became a tradition that has continued almost to the present day. Most important, however, the eighteenth century saw the beginning of scientific exploration. The new national academies of science that sprang up in England, France, and Russia played a very important part as advisors of governments in all scientific matters, and as initiators of exploration.

The eighteenth century was one of Russian achievement in the Arctic. However, all activities were land based or close to the coast. The question of whether Asia and America are joined had been solved by a Siberian Cossack, Simon Dezhnev. In 1648, he sailed from the Kolyma River on the East Siberian Arctic coast around East Cape (Mys Dezhnev) through Bering Strait to the mouth of Anadyr River. Dezhnev's discovery was reported to the authorities in Yakutsk but remained officially unknown in Europe until well into the first half of the eighteenth century, although rumours of the voyage may have reached the Imperial Court in St. Petersburg earlier. These rumors may have indeed stimulated Tsar Peter the Great to launch a series of grandiose projects of exploration. The first of these, under the leadership of Vitus Bering, was a huge expedition that included 200 horses, which left St. Petersburg in 1725 and crossed Siberia overland. After immense hardships, the expedition reached the coastal town of Okhotsk, on the sea of that name. In 1729 Bering was able to circumnavigate Kamchatka Peninsula and sail up Bering Strait as far as Mys Dezhnev, but due to the lateness of the season and dense fog, he had to return without having sighted the Alaskan coast. In 1732, on a separate expedition, Ivan Fedorov and Mikhail Gvozdev charted the Diomede Islands, Cape Prince of Wales, and King Island, and thus completed the exploration of Bering Strait. It was not until 1740, on a subsequent expedition, that Bering made landfall in Alaska. These expeditions were supplemented by numerous survey activities by the Imperial Admiralty College, and by 1746 the whole of the Siberian Arctic coast from the River Ob to Mys Dezhnev, Bering Strait, and the Anadyr and Kamchatka Peninsulas had been explored and charted.

In eastern Siberia and the Bering Strait, exploration was followed by trade, and by the formation of trading companies. Catherine the Great encouraged a new brand of Russian imperialism across the Bering Strait and down the North American coast during the second half of the eighteenth century. By the first quarter of the nineteenth century, Russia—in the form of the government-sponsored Russian-American Company—was firmly established in Alaska. A rigorous ukase, or ban, proclaimed by Tsar Alexander I in 1818, effectively closed the north Pacific to non-Russians (Roots, 1986b), and the problem of finding a northwest passage around the northern extremity of Canada became a strategic priority for Great Britain. The search for this passage was to preoccupy the British Navy for more than half a century following the Napoleonic Wars.

Among the remarkable advances in science of the eighteenth century, the study of magnetism was one of the most important. The formulation of general laws, or principles, of planetary magnetism and the construction of magnetic charts led to a need for widespread, simultaneous observations of magnetic variation and dip. Consequently, the recording of magnetic observations became a prime duty of naval expeditions. The reemergence of scientific astronomy, and the study of the relation of the Earth to the motions of other planets and "heavenly bodies" became another powerful scientific incentive for global exploration and voyages to distant locations to observe eclipses and make celestial observations.

Advances in technology, such as the invention of John Hadley's reflecting quadrant in 1731, the introduction of John Harrison's chronometer in 1762, the publication by Nevil Maskeleyne in 1767 of the first nautical almanac, the availability of better ships, including rot-resistant rope for rigging, and techniques for preventing scurvy during long voyages, boosted exploration.

Except for Phipps' 1773 voyage north of Spitsbergen in an attempt to sail to the North Pole, no British ships ventured into the high Arctic during the eighteenth century. A number of voyages were undertaken into Hudson's Bay in search of the North-West Passage, motivated primarily by a desire to outflank the French fur trade in the south. During that time, British exploratory interests were mainly preoccupied with the great Pacific and Antarctic voyages of James Cook and with operations to oust the French and secure dominion over Canada.

Between 1770 and 1772, Samuel Hearne of the Hudson's Bay Company, accompanied by Indian guides, made a 2,000-km overland trip from Churchill on Hudson Bay to the Coppermine River on the Arctic coast in search of the source of native copper, and also to determine whether a low-latitude northwest passage could be found north of Churchill. In July 1771, Hearne reached the mouth of the Coppermine River, the first white man to stand on the north coast of the American continent. His explorations showed conclusively that there was no easily navigable passage between eastern North America and the Pacific Ocean (Keating, 1970).

British Royal Navy explorations of the nineteenth century

Following the battle of Waterloo, in 1815, military or territorial goals became closely connected to trade and, except in the North Pacific, the seas were for the first time free to all ships (*mare liberum*). Exploration expanded dramatically. Interest in scientific knowledge among the emerging middle classes, a product of the industrial revolution, found expression in private societies in which scientific aims were followed by a popular, as well as professional, membership. Geographical societies in particular became centers of influence and took a leading role in promoting polar exploration. The first was the Société de Géographie in Paris, founded in 1821, followed by the Gesellschaft für Erdkunde in Berlin (1828), and the Geographical Society of London (1830). Polar exploration during the first half of the nineteenth century was predominantly a naval affair, and naval officers with experience on polar voyages were among the most active members of the new geographical societies. The membership also included owners of whaling and sealing ships. Through them a wealth of practical knowledge accumulated, and the geographical societies became centers of advice on the organization and techniques of polar exploration.

The British Navy was foremost in the revival of polar exploration. The motive was no longer simply a search for a passage to Cathay, but included the delineation of the Arctic coast of British North America and the discovery of new lands or exploitable resources. Britain was keenly aware of its potential rivals, the youthful and ebullient United States to the south, and to the west the Russian Empire. The latter was in control of Alaska and the coasts of the North Pacific from Vancouver Island to Vladivostok, and had spread trading posts as far south as San Francisco. By taking the initiative in northern exploration, the British Admiralty hoped to forestall rival operations in the Arctic.

It is indicative of the politics and mood of the times that British naval interest in Arctic Ocean exploration was sparked by commercial whaling interests and made possible by a surplus of new, well-built, capable vessels and trained officers left at the close of the Napoleonic Wars. The veteran whaling captain William Scorseby, on the basis of experience around Spitsbergen and east Greenland, deduced that polynyas in the pack ice of the North Atlantic were evidence of a "freedom of movement to the north, including open water in the neighborhood of the Pole." (Kane, 1856, v. 1, p. 307). Scorseby, supported by his friend Joseph Banks, president of the Royal Society, was able to revive interest in polar exploration (Taylor, 1955, p. 22). As a result, in 1818, the British government dispatched two major polar expeditions, one under Captain John Buchan, with Lieutenant John Franklin as second in command, to continue the work of Phipps of 45 years earlier (see discussion later in chapter) "to try to reach the Pacific by a northern route across the Pole" (Smith, 1877, p. 41), and the other, led by Commander John Ross, with Edward Parry as second in command, to check on Baffin's findings of 200 years before.

Buchan and Franklin, in the *Dorothea* and *Trent,* barely got north of Spitsbergen before they were, like Phipps, stopped by impenetrable ice. But Ross and Parry, in the *Isabella* and *Alexander,* sailed up Davis Strait and rounded the head of Baffin Bay. Although they did not get as far north as their Elizabethan predecessors Bylot and Baffin, they confirmed Baffin's discoveries and applied his names to the major geographical features of the eastern Canadian Arctic Archipelago. Ross, however, failed to penetrate far into Lancaster Sound and inexplicably turned back, allegedly stopped by a chain of mountains he named Crokers Mountains.

The following year the Admiralty dispatched two ships, the *Hecla* and the *Griper,* under the command of Edward Parry to check on Ross' findings. Parry sailed through Lancaster Sound into Barrow Strait to discover Prince Regent Inlet, Wellington Channel, and Cornwallis Island, and continued into Viscount

Melville Sound until stopped by ice at 110° longitude. The two ships wintered at Winter Harbour on Melville Island, and the following summer, after penetrating a little farther west but finding the ice still barring the way, they returned to England. Parry had with him, as he had also the year before, Captain Edward Sabine of the Royal Artillery, "a gentleman well skilled in Astronomy, Natural History and various branches of knowledge" (Ross, 1819, p. 20). Sabine carried out hydrographic surveys, measured water and air temperatures, studied the movement of tides and currents, made magnetic observations, and observed the effect of the Aurora Borealis on the electrometer and magnetic needle. While wintering on Melville Island, Sabine carried out pendulum measurements from which he subsequently determined the ellipiticity of the Earth (Sabine, 1821). Geological observations were made in Lancaster Sound and on a traverse to the interior of Melville Island.

The experiences of Phipps and Buchan did not dispel the idea of an open polar ocean. In 1827, encouraged by handsome rewards offered by the British Parliament for an attempt to reach the pole, Parry and his crew sailed for Spitsbergen in the *Hecla*. From there, using two ship's boats fitted with iron runners and provisioned for 71 days, they sailed north until they reached solid pack ice. Hauling the boats on foot over the ice and launching them in intervening open water, they toiled for five weeks, but they made very slow progress against the strong Transpolar Current, whose drift rate and direction they carefully recorded. On July 26, 1827, having reached 82° 45′ north latitude, they turned back.

John Ross made another, privately funded attempt to find a passage to the West in 1828. He sailed in the *Victory*, a paddle steamer that had been used in commercial service around the British coast. His second-in-command was his nephew, James Clark Ross, a specialist in the study of magnetism. Sailing south into Prince Regent Inlet, Ross mistook Bellot Strait, the key to the transit to Amudsen Gulf and the North-West Passage, for a bay (Savelle and Holland, 1987), and continued to Boothia Peninsula where the *Victory* was beset by ice. The ship remained icebound for three winters and was finally abandoned. During those years James Clark Ross made long sledging journeys with the Inuit. On one of these trips, to King William Island on May 31, 1831, he determined the location of the North Magnetic Pole.

While shipborne expeditions explored the northern waterways, overland parties, led mostly by naval officers assisted by men of the Hudson's Bay Company, carried out many great journeys in the Arctic mainland. By 1839 the Arctic coasts of Alaska and Canada from Prudhoe Bay to Boothia Peninsula, including the south shores of Victoria and King William Islands, had been explored. During these explorations, the main areas of crystalline rocks (Precambrian Shield) and sedimentary rocks along the North American Arctic coast became known.

The search for the North-West Passage along the southern route, via Coronation Gulf, had narrowed to the gap between Barrow Strait and Queen Maud Gulf. It was Sir John Barrow, who had promoted and organized the Ross and Parry expeditions, who again persuaded the Admiralty to launch yet another expedition in search of the North-West Passage. Approval was motivated in part by the concern that ships of the growing American and Russian fleets might win the honor of finding the passage, in part by the opportunity for testing, under adverse conditions, ships outfitted with the new screw propellors, and in part as a naval training exercise. In 1845, HMS *Erebus* and *Terror,* under the command of Sir John Franklin, left England for Lancaster Sound, where they were last sighted. From Barrow Strait, *Erebus* and *Terror,* after having circumnavigated Cornwallis Island, headed south along Peel Sound and eventually became beset in Victoria Strait. Weakened by scurvy and threatened by starvation, the men abandoned the ships in April 1848 and headed for the mainland in hope of reaching a Hudson's Bay post. None of the 134 men of the original ships' companies was ever seen again, although there is evidence that they may have encountered a small band of Inuit before they perished. As it turned out, Franklin had indeed linked the eastern and western approaches to the North-West Passage.

By 1857, some 40 expeditions had been launched in search of Franklin and his men. The searchers converged by land and by sea from Bering Strait, Lancaster Sound, and Hudson's Bay, with the result that by 1860 almost all of the intricate geography of the Canadian Arctic Archipelago had been mapped. Travelling overland from the south, John Richardson and John Rae (1847, 1848–49, 1851, 1853–54) discovered firm evidence localizing the area where Franklin had disappeared, and added many details to geographic knowledge. In 1852, in the *Isabel,* Commander Inglefield, on a private expedition sponsored by Lady Franklin, advanced into Nares Strait and showed that this channel led northward into the Arctic Ocean, confirming earlier Norse maps and the sixteenth-century charts of Mercator and Ortelius.

Last discoveries of lands and coasts

By 1870, all the circumpolar mainland coasts, Novaya Zemlya, and most of the Canadian Archipelago had been explored. There still remained large unexplored and unmapped areas: the north and northeast coasts of Greenland and its vast interior, Ellesmere Island, the northwestern Queen Elizabeth Islands, much of Spitsbergen, Severnaya Zemlya, and Franz Josef Land. Although the south coast of Ostrov Kotel'nyy had been visited in 1773 (Gorshkov, 1980), the remaining New Siberian Islands had not been explored.

In 1871, the American explorer Kane sledged with Inuit to the northwesternmost limits of the Greenland Ice Cap, discovered Hall Land, and saw Lincoln Sea. He also made a dash for the pole and reached latitude 82°11′N. In 1875, Captain George S. Nares sailed his two ships, *Alert* and *Discovery,* north through Nares Strait to the edge of the Arctic Ocean. One object of the British expedition was to plant the Union Jack beyond America's farthest north. Equally important, however, were scientific objectives. Like their predecessor Parry 50 years earlier, parties of the expedition, led by Lieutenant Albert Markham, man-hauled boats over the pack ice and reached a point a few miles beyond Hall's and Parry's highest latitudes. More significant to science, however, was their exploration and mapping of the northern coasts of Ellesmere Island and Greenland, where they carried out astronomical, geological, magnetic, tidal, meteorological, zoological, botanical, and ethnological studies (Nares, 1876, 1878). The site of their expedition base, Discovery Harbour (later named Fort Conger), was to become an important center for scientific observation in the North American Arctic.

In 1872, two young Austrian scientists, Navy Lieutenant Karl Weyprecht and Army Lieutenant Julius Payer, sailed into the Barents Sea on board the steamer *Tegethoff*. They were going to investigate the claim by the famous German geographer A. H. Petermann of a relatively ice-free approach to the North Pole in this part of the Arctic Ocean—the revival of a 300-year-old idea. Petermann's theories were not substantiated, but the Austrians discovered and mapped part of the archipelago of Franz Josef Land. Weyprecht and Payer put forward the hypothesis that this archipelago might be an outlier of a much greater land mass that included the North Pole. Weyprecht became convinced that scientific study should take precedence over geographic discovery in polar exploration. He began a personal campaign that led to the International Polar Year, 1882 to 1883, with 20 simultaneous expeditions in the polar regions, supported by 11 countries. None of these, however, were in the Arctic Ocean basin.

In 1898, two expeditions attempted to sail into Nares Strait: Robert E. Peary in the USS *Windward*, and Otto Sverdrup in the Norwegian ship *Fram*. Peary's aim was the conquest of the pole, whereas the Norwegians planned to explore and map the north and northeast coasts of Greenland. Ice prevented both ships from penetrating into Kane Basin. The following summer, Sverdrup switched his plans to exploration of western Ellesmere Island and the islands to the west, and sailed into Jones Sound. During the next three years, traveling by ship and by dog team, the Norwegians accurately mapped that part of the Queen Elizabeth Islands now known as Sverdrup Islands (Norsk Videnskaps-Akademi, 1907–1919; Sverdrup, 1903a,b, 1904). Per Schei, the geologist of the expedition, conducted reconnaissance geological surveys and established the first stratigraphic succession in the North American Arctic (Schei, 1903). Peary, in turn, explored north and northeast Greenland, thereby settling any remaining doubts about the insularity of Greenland (Hayes, 1929).

Russian polar expeditions under the leadership of E. Toll explored the New Siberian Islands between 1900 and 1903, and in 1913 the two Russian vessels *Tamir* and *Vaigach* discovered and explored Severnaya Zemlya (Gorshkov, 1980).

A new territorial awareness and interest in her northern frontiers felt by Canada led the Canadian government to sponsor a number of expeditions. In 1903 and 1904, A. P. Low of the Geological Survey of Canada sailed in the steam-powered *Neptune* into Hudson Bay, Smith Sound, and Lancaster Sound; while during the period between 1906 and 1911, Captain J. E. Bernier in the CGS *Arctic* visited most of the islands of the archipelago. The main objective of these expeditions was the establishment of sovereignty, but they also enabled Low on the *Neptune* and J. G. McMillan, geologist on the *Arctic*, to study the geology of the regions traversed by the ships and produce the first regional geological maps of the Canadian Arctic Archipelago.

The Canadian government, through its Geological Survey, also financed Vilhjalmur Stefansson's Canadian Arctic Expedition of 1913 to 1918. An ambitious program was devised in which a northern party, led by Stefansson, would search for new lands in the Beaufort Sea and north of the already discovered islands of the archipelago, while a southern party, under the leadership of R. M. Anderson, would explore and carry out geological field work along the mainland Arctic coast. The *Karluk*, the ship of the northern party, became trapped in the ice near Point Barrow and drifted westward, while Stefansson was hunting on the mainland. Stefansson and his men were unable to get back to the ship, and the *Karluk* drifted across the Chukchi Sea and eventually sank near Herald and Wrangel islands in February 1914. Fewer than half the company of 28 people survived. During this drift, the expedition's oceanographer, James Murray, obtained water depths, dredged bottom sediments, and collected biologic and water samples. The soundings were recorded in the ship's log and preserved, but the samples sank with the *Karluk*, and Murray's notes were lost with him when he attempted to reach the Siberian mainland on foot (W. L. McKinlay, personal communication, 1980). Over the next four years, Stefansson discovered and mapped the remaining of the Queen Elizabeth Islands: Brock, Borden, Mackenzie King, Meighen, and Lougheed. Anderson, meanwhile, surveyed the southwestern islands of the archipelago, initiating a program of geological mapping that has continued, with some interruptions, to the present day. With Stefansson, the last large areas of unknown Arctic lands had been discovered and explored.

EXPLORATION AND MAPPING OF THE ARCTIC SEA FLOOR

Early hydrographic explorations: The single Arctic Basin

Nordenskiöld. Baron A. E. Nordenskiöld was a Swedish chemist and mineralogist who became interested in Arctic science. Starting in 1858, he became engaged in, and later conducted, a number of scientific expeditions to Spitsbergen and Greenland, including the crossing of the ice cap of Northeast Greenland by reindeer team and sledge. In 1872, he turned his attention to the problem of navigation of the North-East Passage. For Russia, Nordenshiöld argued, the navigation of the North-East Passage could be of vital importance; it might open up a commercial highway along the Siberian coast over which the mineral resources of the immense territories of eastern Russia could be brought cheaply to industrial Europe, and in particular to Scandinavia. In addition, there were strong scientific arguments for an expedition: research in geography (including charting), oceanography, geology, and natural history. Nordenskiöld gained the support of the king of Norway and Sweden, his patron Baron Oscar Dickson, and a rich Russian merchant A. Sibiriakov. In 1878, Nordenskiöld sailed from Tromsö in the 357-ton steam and sailing ship *Vega* with scientists from five nations. Sailing close to the coast, and encountering very little ice, the *Vega* made good progress. Off the mouth of the Yenesey River, he found a secure island anchorage, which he named Dickson Island after his Swedish patron. He correctly prophesied that the achorage would "one day be of great importance for commerce of Siberia." (Nordenskjold, 1882, p. 145). The site is the modern port of Dickson. By late fall, the *Vega* came to within 200 km of Mys Dezhneva before becoming beset by winter ice. In July the following year, she sailed through Bering Strait. Soundings were made along the entire track, establishing a shallow-draft shipping route from the White Sea to the Bering Sea. Nordenskiöld's voyage was important for at least two reasons: (1) it reconnoitered the future Soviet Northern Sea Route, and (2) together with the almost simultaneous investigations of the Nares expedition in the Lincoln Sea, it marked a resurgence of serious Arctic Ocean research. Since Phipps' voyage 100 years earlier (discussed later in chapter), polar research had been nearly eclipsed by the attention given to geographical exploration and national prestige.

Fram. In 1880, Lieutenant George De Long of the U.S. Navy, with the financial backing of the *New York Herald,* set off for the North Pole via Bering Strait in the *Jeannette,* only to be almost immediately beset in the ice of the Chukchi Sea. The *Jeannete* then drifted in a westerly direction for 17 months, and on June 13, 1881, was crushed in the ice north of the New Siberian Islands. Her crew managed to reach the estuary of the Lena River, taking their logs and notes along, but hunger and cold killed all but two. For the future of Arctic exploration, nevertheless, this expedition was of greatest significance. Three years later, in 1884, wreckage from the *Jeannette* was found on the southwest coast of Greenland. From this chance discovery and from Siberian driftwood found in Greenland, Norwegian meteorologist Henrik Mohn inferred the existence of a transpolar current across the Arctic Ocean. Fritjof Nansen saw the possibility of using this current to transport a ship across the Arctic Ocean for the purpose of carrying out scientific studies. In the fall of 189 he let his ship, the *Fram,* under the command of Captain Otto Sverdrup, freeze into the pack ice northeast of the New Siberian Islands. Over the next three years the ship became the first scientific station to drift across the Arctic Ocean. The scientists carried out a variety of oceanographic, meteorological, geophysical, and biological studies (Nansen, 1897). Depth soundings taken from the *Fram* at last settled the question of the existence of land in the region of the North Pole and dispelled the idea that the Arctic Ocean was a shallow sea. The *Fram* missed the Lomonosov Ridge and drifted over the Pole Abyssal Plain where depths are in excess of 3,000 m. On the basis of the *Fram* data, many oceanographers concluded that the Arctic Basin was a single oceanic deep. However, the American oceanographer R. A. Harris (1905), on the basis of tidal data alone, postulated that the Arctic Ocean was not a single basin, but was divided by a barrier or ridge into two basins with different periods of oscillation.

Bartlett, Storkerson. During the first decade of the twentieth century the Newfoundlander Robert Bartlett, captain of the *Roosevelt,* while supporting Peary's attempts on the North Pole, made a number of soundings off the north coast of Ellesmere Island and outlined the general shape of part of the continental shelf.

In 1918, Storker Storkerson (Stefansson, 1921), of Vilhjalmur Stefansson's Canadian Arctic Expedition, occupied an ice island for several months, from which he took numerous soundings in the Beaufort Sea. This was the first scientific drifting ice station on record (Weber, 1983).

Wilkins, Sedov, Papanin. In 1927, Sir Hubert Wilkins, flying from Alaska, landed his aircraft on the ice some 1,300 km north of Bering Strait. By setting off an explosive charge and using a stop watch to measure the time it took for the echo to return from the ocean floor, he obtained a depth of 5,440 m (Wilkins, 1928). Wilkin's measurement was later proved to be in error, but for the next 20 years it was much quoted in support of the concept of a single, deep Arctic Ocean basin. Thirty-eight soundings between the North Pole and East Greenland, made in 1937 during the nine-month drift of the Soviet research station *North Pole 1* (Papanin, 1946), seemed to confirm the single-basin idea. Further support came from data collected during the drift, between 1937 and 1940, of the Soviet ice breaker *Sedov* in the Eurasia Basin.

Soviet airborne expeditions. During April 1941, personnel from the Soviet All-Union Arctic Institute, in three successive flights from Wrangel Island in a ski-equipped four-engine aircraft, established three stations between latitudes 78° and 81°N and between longitudes 175° and 170°W in the region of Wrangel and Mendeleev abyssal plains. They occupied each station for four to five days, taking soundings, measuring water temperature and salinity, and sampling the water column and the sea bed. Their measurements of 2,427 m, 1,856 m, and 3,379 m covered a wide range of depths and neither confirmed nor disproved the depth determined by Wilkins (Treshnikov, 1966).

The Soviet expeditions of 1941, which used aircraft exclusively, marked a turning point in Arctic exploration. They demonstrated that aircraft allow a wide choice in station location, simplify logistics, and can decrease costs, compared to occupying an ice station or a frozen-in ship for an extended period of time.

Post-war explorations: The ocean floor reveals its secrets

Soviet activities. In 1948, the All-Union Arctic Institute began a program of systematic exploration of the whole of the Arctic Ocean, carrying out what they called, "High-Latitude Air expeditions." Several aircraft would land parties at a number of points on the floating ice during a period of about six weeks in the spring. While the aircraft waited, salinity, temperature, and depth (STD) measurements, sediment sampling, and magnetic, gravimetric, and meteorological observations were made (Armstrong,

1958). A comprehensive hydrographic station took from six to eight hours to complete.

Between 1948 and 1950, scientists were landed at 87 points on the Arctic Ocean (Gudkovich, 1954–1955). The stations they established were occupied from a few hours to a few days. The Soviet survey revealed that, far from being a flat abyssal plain, the Arctic Basin has a very complicated structure, with depressions, submarine ridges, and plateaus. The most significant discovery was made on April 17, 1948, at lat. 85°26′N, long. 145°E, where a relatively shallow depth of 1,290 m was recorded. Later soundings that year and the following year revealed the outline of a massive submarine mountain range that rises 3,000 m above the sea floor and extends 1,800 km from Ellesmere Island to the New Siberian Islands. It was named after M. V. Lomonosov, the eighteenth-century Russian scientist, grammarian, and poet. The discovery of the Lomonosov Ridge, however, was kept secret at the time.

The aerial work-horses of these Soviet expeditions were the LI-2, the Soviet version of the Douglas DC-3 aircraft, the Antonov AN-2, a large single-engine biplane still used today, and helicopters. These springtime High-Latitude Air Expeditions, later renamed *NORTH*-series, have taken place every year from 1948 to the present.

In 1950, the Soviet *NORTH POLE*-series of operations were initiated (Gordienko and Laktionov, 1960). In contrast to the annual, short-period *NORTH*-series projects, the *NORTH POLE* (NP) stations are occupied from one to several years until they "exit" into the Atlantic via the Greenland Current, or otherwise lose their usefulness. At time of writing (1987), stations *NP-27* and *NP-28* were drifting in the Amerasia Basin.

With the exception of 285 depth soundings (Gudkovich, 1954–1955), released as a contribution to the International Geophysical Year (IGY), Soviet bathymetric data have remained classified.

American activities. Airborne expeditions and drifting ice stations. In April 1951, U.S. scientists joined in the exploration of the Arctic Ocean by mounting two airborne expeditions to the Beaufort Sea. Supported by the U.S. Air Force Cambridge Research Center and using a DC-3 aircraft, they established six stations north of Martin Point, Alaska, between latitudes 73° and 76°N. The observations consisted of seismic soundings, gravity measurements, and determination of the ice drift (Crary and others, 1952). In the same year, *Project Skijump* was inaugurated, sponsored by the U.S. Office of Naval Research (ONR). Twelve landings on the ice north of Point Barrow were made by a Navy DC-3 aircraft. Salinity, temperature, and depth measurements were made at three sites using a winch and Nansen bottles. The following year, refuelling the DC-3 aircraft on the ice from a Navy P-2V aircraft enabled scientists to establish five more hydrographic stations and reach lat. 82°22′N. The observations showed that water temperature and salinity values differed significantly from those obtained by Nansen on the *Fram*. From these observations, Worthington (1953, p. 550, 551) concluded that "there is a submarine ridge, running roughly from Ellesmere Island to the New Siberian Islands, which separates the deepest water of the Beaufort Sea from the remainder of the basin," and that, "the sill depth of the ridge should not exceed 2,300 m." The Americans were unaware of the Soviet *NORTH*- and *NORTH POLE*-series operations and did not know that the Lomonosov Ridge had been discovered five years earlier.

The brief-landing type airborne surveys were replaced in 1952 by year-round occupation of drifting ice floes and "ice islands" (tabular icebergs, up to tens of square kilometers in area). The best known of these ice islands, *Fletcher's Ice Island* or *T-3* (called station *Bravo* during the International Geophysical Year), was occupied at various intervals between 1952 and 1974. Other drifting ice stations were established on the ice floes *Alpha* (1957–1958) and *Charlie* (1959) and on the ice island *ARLIS II* (1961–1965). *T-3* and *Alpha* served as United States stations during the International Geophysical Year (IGY). The stations were equipped with precision depth recorders (Quam, 1966). The *ALPHA* station, during its occupation, drifted over a ridge that lay parallel to the Lomonosov Ridge. Although identified as a general feature on the 1956 Canadian Defence Research Board (DRB) chart (Fig. 5), it was mapped in comparative detail for the first time from station *Alpha,* after which it has been named.

American airborne reconnaissance surveys were resumed in 1960 under the sponsorship of the Office of Naval Research (ONR) and the Geophysical and Polar Research Center of the University of Wisconsin. Using Cessna 180 aircraft, and bases on the north coast of Alaska and on drifting ice stations, they landed on the ice of the Beaufort Sea, Chukchi Sea, and Canada Basin to take soundings and gravity measurements (Ostenso, 1968a). This program was carried out each spring for ten years. By 1969, more than 800 stations had been established (Wold, 1973).

Submarine expeditions and shipborne surveys. The idea that the severe obstacles to Arctic Ocean navigation would be avoided by travelling under the ice arose early in the search for an Arctic route from Europe to Cathay and the Indies. In 1648, Bishop John Wilkins of England proposed to the Royal Society of London that "voyages to the polar regions by submarine vessels would be safe from the uncertainty of tides, the violence of tempests, and from ice and great frosts." (McLaren, 1982, p. 34). Three centuries elapsed until undersea technology was sufficiently advanced to follow up on this idea. In 1931, another Wilkins, Sir Hubert Wilkins, penetrated a short distance under the polar pack in Fram Strait (located between Greenland and Spitsbergen) in a second-hand diesel- and battery-powered submarine which he named *Nautilus*. Largely at his own expense he had it modified and fitted with runners on top of the hull to enable it to slide under what was assumed to be the smooth bottom of the ice. Equipment difficulties prevented Wilkins from going very far, but his idea was shown to be feasible in principle (Wilkins, 1931). However, there was no further private or commercial interest in Arctic submarine traffic until the recent exploration of potential petroleum resources of the Beaufort Sea and Sverdrup Basin that have led to several proposals, so far untried in the Arctic, for under-ice cargo tankers.

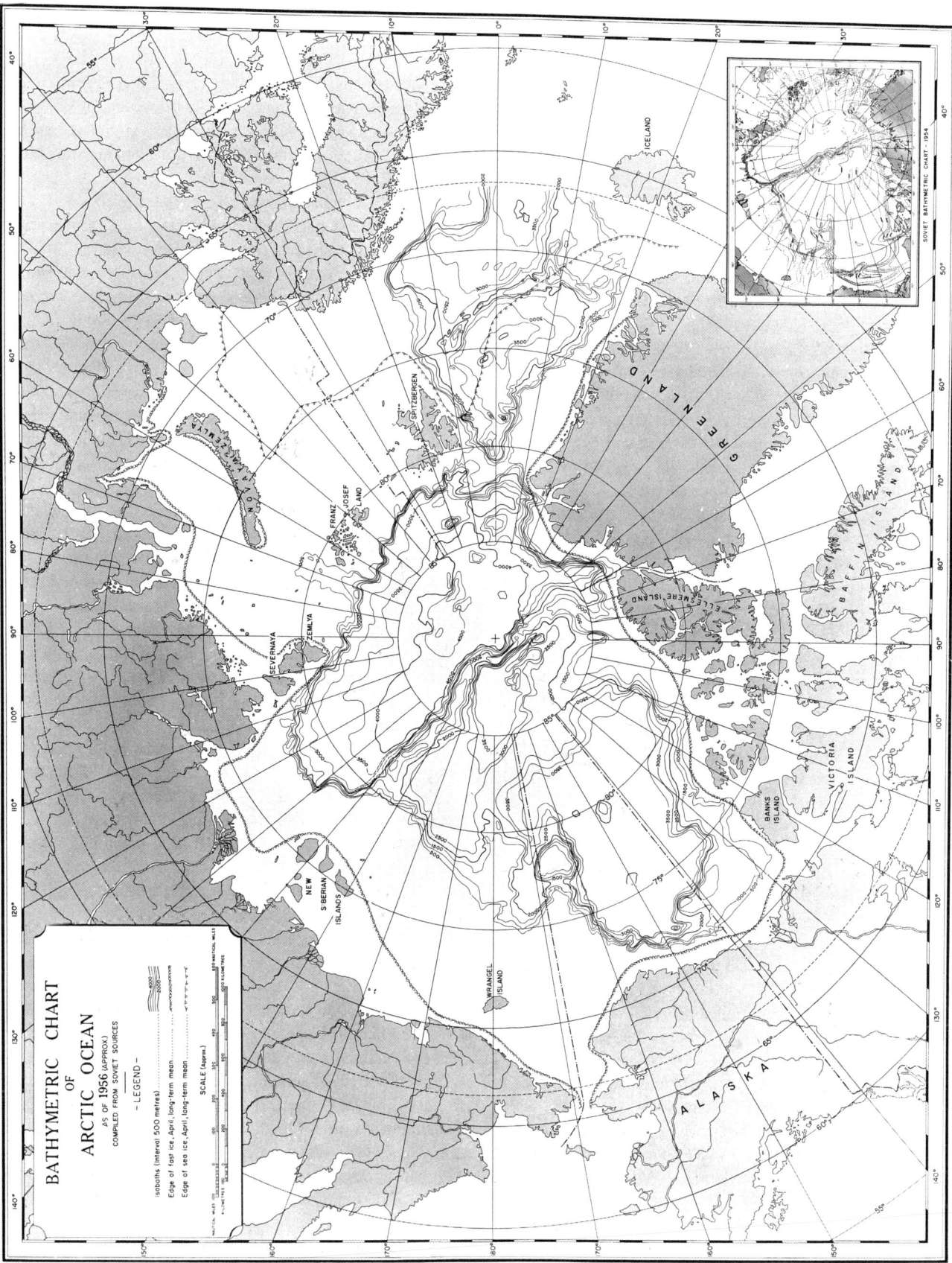

Figure 5. 1956 bathymetric chart of the Arctic Ocean compiled by the Defence Research Board of Canada. Inset depicts the 1954 Soviet map from Burhanov, 1956.

In the 1950s, the U.S., Soviet, and United Kingdom navies became interested in operations under the Arctic ice pack for military purposes, using nuclear-powered submarines. Interestingly, a key proponent and policy authority for the revival of submarine activities under the ice was a third Wilkins, U.S. Navy Admiral C. W. Wilkins (Anderson, 1959). In 1957, the U.S. submarine *Nautilus,* for the first time, entered the Arctic Ocean in the Fram Strait area. A year later, *Nautilus* crossed under the ice from Bering Strait to the Greenland Sea. Other submarines of several navies have operated in the Arctic Ocean since that time.

Echograms from the ocean floor obtained from the USS *Nautilus* (1957, 1958), *Skate* (1958, 1959, 1962), *Sargo* (1960), and *Seadragon* (1960, 1962) were analyzed by Beal (1969). Positioning of the submarines was obtained by dead reckoning, by the ships' inertial navigation systems, and by celestial fixes when possible. The data from these echograms were used extensively in the compilation of bathymetric maps, although the positioning of these early submarine tracks was inaccurate (Beal, 1983), resulting in displacement errors of as much as 70 km (Weber, 1983). All bathymetric data collected since 1963 by U.S. submarines have been under military restriction.

In 1951, the icebreaker USCGC, *Burton Island* and, in 1957, the icebreakers USCGC *Staten Island* and USCGC *Northwind* carried out continuous echo soundings across the continental slope of the Beaufort Sea north of Point Barrow (Fisher and others, 1958; Carsola and others, 1961). In the course of marine seismic reflection surveys, additional bathymetric data were acquired between 1972 and 1978 by the U.S. Geological Survey, and in 1973 by the Geophysical Corporation of Alaska in 1973 (Greenberg and others, 1981).

Based on the data available, including Canadian soundings east of longitude 141°W, Greenberg and others (1981) published a bathymetric map of the continental shelf, slope, and rise of the Beaufort Sea north of Alaska at a scale of 1:500,000. A similar map for the Chukchi Sea (Hill and others, 1984) was also published recently.

Operations in the Eurasia Basin. The U.S. Office of Naval Research began a new program of exploration in the Eurasia Basin in 1978. Four multidisciplinary expeditions, *Fram I* to *IV,* were conducted each spring from 1979 to 1982. During these operations, described in more detail later in this chapter, much bathymetric data from the western Eurasia Basin were collected.

Using ski-equipped aircraft, soundings were taken in the western part of th Eurasia Basin in 1981, in the course of a temperature-salinity mapping program between Spitsbergen and 84°30′N latitude, named Eurasia Basin Experiment (EUBEX; Lewis and Perkins, 1983; Perkins and Lewis, 1984).

In 1983, 1984, and 1987 the Marginal Ice Zone Experiment (MIZEX), with scientists from the United States, Canada, Denmark, England, Finland, France, Germany, Ireland, Norway, Sweden, and Switzerland, studied the interaction of ice, water, and atmosphere at the edge of the pack ice in the East Greenland Sea and Fram Strait. During the course of these studies, additional detail was obtained of the bottom topography of the Atlantic entrance to the Arctic Ocean (Office of Naval Research, 1984; Johannessen, 1987).

Canadian activities. Polar Continental Shelf Project. Forty years after the Arctic expeditions of Low, Bernier, and Stefansson, Canadian exploration of the Arctic Basin was resumed, with the creation, in 1958, of the Polar Continental Shelf Project (PCSP), a multiagency surveying- and research-support organization (Roots, 1968). Since 1960, as part of the PCSP program, the Canadian Hydrographic Service (CHS) and the Earth Physics Branch have been conducting joint bathymetric and gravity surveys over the Arctic continental shelf and interisland channels. To date (1987), all of the continental shelf from the Lincoln Sea to the Yukon-Alaska border has been charted (Weber, 1983, 1987). Between 1969 and 1987 alone, PCSP supported 2,539 research projects (Hobson and Voyce, 1974–1987).

The PCSP has supported four Canadian expeditions to the central Arctic Ocean. The Canadian North Pole expeditions of 1967 and 1969 established some 70 depth soundings and gravity measurements north of 89°20′ latitude, as well as a line of bathymetric and gravity stations across the Lomonosov Ridge and between the Lincoln Sea and the North Pole (Lillestrand and others, 1967; Lillestrand and Weber, 1974). The Lomonosov Ridge Experiment, *LOREX 79,* was a large-scale, multidisciplinary project that included bathymetry and gravity measurements over the Lomonosov Ridge near the North Pole (Weber, 1979, 1983). The Canadian Expedition to Study the Alpha Ridge, *CESAR 83,* similar in scale and nature to *LOREX,* resulted in the bathymetric and gravity coverage over the Ellesmere Island continental shelf and Alpha Ridge as far west as 115° longitude (Weber, 1987).

In 1984 PCSP established a permanent camp for scientific studies on an ice island named *Hobson's Choice.* In March and April 1987, using the ice island as a base, the Canadian Hydrographic Service carried out a bathymetric and gravity survey over the continental shelf west of Axel Heiberg Island. The survey filled in the last gap in the reconnaissance charting of the Canadian Polar continental shelf. The survey was extended beyond the shelf to connect with the 1983 CESAR coverage.

Norwegian, British, and Swedish activities. During the last two decades, Norwegian ships attached to the Polar Institute, Petroleum Directorate, and Institute of Fisheries Research, and equipped with radio navigational aids, have collected bathymetric data in the Barents Sea as far east as Novaya Zemlya. These data have been incorporated in the Perry and Fleming map (Perry and others, 1986) and are included in Plate 1.

In 1975 and 1976 the British nuclear submarine *Sovereign* made a number of cruises into the Arctic Ocean. Some nonclassified bathymetric data from these cruises have been used in the compilation of the 1979 *General Bathymetric Charts of the Oceans* (GEBCO) map (L. W. Sobczak, personal communication, 1980).

In commemoration of Nordenskiöld's first circumnavigation of Asia, between 1878 and 1880, the Swedish icebreaker *Ymer,* in 1980, carried out oceanographic and geophysical studies in Fram Strait and in the Barents Sea. During the voyage, continuous echo soundings were obtained.

Modern maps and charts of the Arctic Ocean

The early maps of the polar regions from antiquity to Mercator were, as described earlier, a mixture of fact and fiction. The first large-area maps that carefully depict the confirmed information and leave most of the unknown areas blank were *Barents' Chart,* published posthumously in 1598 (Fig. 4), and *Foxe's Polar Card,* produced in 1635. They too, however, included unconfirmed sketches of the lands around the North Pacific. Barents' and Foxe's maps remained the most accurate general maps of the Arctic Ocean region until the end of the nineteenth century, although the more complete but partly fanciful productions by Ortelius and Mercator appear to have been in more general use.

Bartholomew's chart of the polar regions of 1897. As an appendix to Fritjof Nansen's book *Farthest North* (Nansen, 1897), J. G. Bartholomew compiled a map of the Arctic Ocean from all sources, including Phipps', Nordenskiöld's, and Nansen's data. This appears to be the first carefully compiled map showing the whole Arctic since those of 300 years earlier. The map is drawn at a scale of 1:14,000,000 and shows the then-known lands that enclose the Arctic Ocean. Of the Canadian Arctic Islands adjoining the Arctic Ocean, only Banks, Prince Patrick, and the eastern and northern part of Ellesmere Islands are shown. In northern Greenland, a channel, named Peary Channel, is shown as separating the main mass of Greenland from Hall Land in the northwest. Missing from the map is the Severnaya Zemlya group of islands. The map shows the track of the *Fram,* the limit of the permanent pack ice, and the directions of the Transpolar and East Greenland currents. Most of the ocean is marked as "unexplored region" except for soundings in the Greenland, Barents, and Kara seas, along the *Vega* track through the North-East Passage, in the Chukchi Sea and Bering Strait, and along *Fram's* track.

Eardley's map of 1948. In the same year that Soviet hydrographers discovered the Lomonosov Ridge, Eardley (1948) published a map that shows the Paleozoic shields and orogenic belts adjacent to the Arctic Ocean. This was the first Arctic Basin map to combine what was known of topography and tectonics. Eardley postulated that the ocean is underlain by subsided continental crustal material of chiefly shield origin. Although he contoured his map from all sources then available to him, the Arctic Ocean is still represented as a single basin. He had virtually no new bathymetric information since Bartholomew's map, published 50 years earlier.

First Soviet map (1954). By 1954, Soviet expeditions had established more than 2,000 soundings, which were used in the compilation of a map of the Arctic sea floor. This map revealed, for the first time, the existence of the Lomonosov Ridge (Burkhanov, 1956) and caused a sensation among Arctic experts outside the Soviet Union, who had been unaware of the scope and magnitude of Soviet exploration. It is interesting to note that the crest of the Lomonosov Ridge, as determined by the *LOREX 79* survey, is accurately positioned on the Soviet map, while on the 25-year younger GEBCO map, the crest is misplaced as much as 34 km. The Soviets used celestial positioning, while the compilers of the GEBCO map relied on early U.S. submarine inertial and celestial navigation (Weber, 1983).

When Stefansson, in 1914, made wire-line soundings during an over-ice journey from Martin Point, Alaska, to Banks Island, many of his soundings, due to a limited amount of wire (911 m and 1,386 m), did not reach seabed. On the map in his book, Stefansson (1921) indicated these soundings as having "no bottom." It appears likely that the Soviet compilers took Stefansson's "no bottom" soundings as actual water depth and thereby created the "Beaufort Terrace" (Beal, 1969; Grantz and Hart, 1984). This feature, giving the Beaufort Sea the appearance of being underlain by a wide continental shelf, has been copied on all later bathymetric maps until 1968.

Defence Research Board chart of 1956. In 1956 the Defence Research Board of Canada (DRB) compiled a bathymetric chart of the Arctic Ocean (Fig. 5). It was compiled by adding United States airborne and *T-3* data to the Soviet map of 1954 (inset) and recontouring Somov's *NP2* soundings (Greenaway, 1983). Here, for the first time, the Alpha-Mendeleev Ridge is outlined as separating the Makarov from the Canada Basin. Note, however, the wide continental shelf in the Beaufort Sea, and Nansen's Sill across Fram Strait. For many years the DRB map remained the best bathymetric chart of the Arctic available to the public.

Second Soviet map (1960). By 1960, the Soviets had established over 20,000 soundings in the Arctic Ocean and published their second bathymetric map (Gordienko and Laktionov, 1960; also in Weber, 1983, Fig. 9). Although generalized because of its small scale and because depth soundings are classified in the Soviet Union, it clearly delineates the Canada Basin, the Alpha-Mendeleev Ridge, and the Makarov Basin, but the Arctic Mid-Ocean Ridge is not clearly defined. No Soviet maps have been published since that show more detail than contemporary western maps.

Heezen and Ewing's Eurasia Basin map of 1961. In 1912, Nansen postulated, based on characteristic differences in the water column of the Arctic Ocean from that of the Greenland Sea, that a shallow east-west submarine ridge connects the shelves off Svalbard and Greenland across Fram Strait, effectively separating the Arctic from the Atlantic water. The existence of Nansen's Sill, as this hypothetical ridge became known, remained unchallenged until 1958, when Soviet hydrographers, sounding from three ice breakers, discovered a narrow, north-south–trending trough more than 4,000 m deep (Laktionov, 1959), now known as Lena Trough.

It has long been known (Linden, 1959) that earthquake epicenters follow a line from Jan Mayen Island through Fram Strait across the Eurasia Basin to the Laptev Sea. Heezen and Ewing (1961) speculated that this seismic belt signifies the continuation of the Mid-Atlantic Ridge and that the Lena Trough is a rift feature. By reexamining the *Fram* and *Sedov* water depths, and by reevaluating published Soviet bathymetric data (Weber, 1983) they revised the chart of the Eurasia Basin to show that the Mid-Atlantic Ridge extends from the Lena Trough to the Laptev Sea, longitudinally bisecting the Eurasia Basin (Heezen and Ewing, 1961). It should be noted that, at that stage, the Arctic Mid-Ocean Ridge was only a hypothesis of Heezen and Ewing, the bathymetric data being too scarce to delineate the ridge to more than a schematic representation. Although the Soviets had far more data available than did Heezen and Ewing, they apparently did not recognize the ridge because they were not looking for it, believing, at that time, that the Arctic Ocean was formed by subsidence of continental platforms (Saks and others, 1955; Gakkel, 1958). Heezen and Ewing did recognize it because, as adherents of the hypothesis that the mid-ocean ridge system girdled the globe, they were expecting it. The existence of the Arctic Mid-Ocean Ridge was not unequivocally confirmed, publicly, until eight years later, with the publication by Beal (1969) of U.S. Navy submarine bathymetry. Virtually no new unclassified depth data from the Eurasia Basin has since become available until the *Fram* and *Ymer* expeditions, when detailed soundings were made near the Atlantic end of the ridge. For most of the Arctic Mid-Ocean Ridge, maps available to the public are based on very little data.

Ostenso's bathymetric map of 1961. In 1961, N. A. Ostenso compiled a map of the Arctic Ocean sea floor based on all available unclassified material (Ostenso, 1962, 1963). The published map is conservatively contoured, and its scale is about 1:18,000,000. The chart is generally similar to the DRB map of 1956 (Fig. 5) with additional detail on the continental shelf of the Queen Elizabeth Islands, in parts of the Chukchi Borderland and Canada Basin, and in Fram Strait.

Canadian bathymetric chart of western half of Arctic Ocean of 1967. In 1967 the Canadian Hydrographic Service (CHS) published two charts of the western half of the Arctic Ocean north of 72°, from longitudes 0° to 90°W, and 90°W to 180° (map sheets 896 and 897). Beyond the 200-m isobath the chart is contoured at 500-m intervals; the scale is 1:2,000,000. Except for the disappearance of Nansen's Sill in Fram Strait and more details on the continental shelf off the Queen Elizabeth Islands, which had been charted by CHS, and the Chukchi Borderland, Alpha Ridge, and Canada Basin, where the University of Wisconsin had been carrying out sounding operations, the chart does not differ significantly from the DRB map of 1956 (Fig. 5).

GEBCO map of 1968. The Canadian Bathymetric Charts of 1967 served as bases for the GEBCO 3rd edition, sheets CI (0° to 90°W) and CII (90° to 180°), which were published in Paris in 1968 by the Institut Géographique National at a scale of 1:3,000,000. Sheet CII, however, differs from CHS map sheet 897 by the disappearance of the "Beaufort Terrace."

The British Admiralty North Polar Chart of 1969. In 1969 the United Kingdom Hydrographic Department published the North Polar Chart, Admiralty Chart No. 4006. It was compiled by Ritchie (1969) at an approximate scale of 1:7,500,000. Beyond the 100-fathom isobath the depth is contoured at 500-fathom intervals. The chart presents no new information, and the contouring appears to be an interpolation, in Imperial depth units, of the GEBCO Chart.

National Geographic Society map of the Arctic Ocean floor of 1971. As part of its series of relief maps of the major ocean basins of the world, the National Geographic Society (U.S.) produced a colored relief drawing of the Arctic Ocean basin and surrounding lands, printed on the reverse side of a detailed geographical-political-historical map of the Arctic regions. The ocean-floor map, drawn at a scale of 1:9,757,000 with spot heights and depths in feet, is based on all data available to 1971. The topography is interpreted by B. C. Heezen and Marie Tharp and is similar to their 1975 *Map of the Arctic Regions* described below. The result is a dramatic detailed drawing with exaggerated vertical scale and ruggedness. Extensive flat continental shelves are bounded by steep escarpments that rim the complex ocean basin. The Mid-Arctic Ocean and Alpha-Mendeleev ridges are depicted as spreading ridges, cut by a multitude of transform faults, giving them a rectangular, blocky appearance. The Lomonosov Ridge, in contrast, is shown as a smooth-sided sinuous wall. The Arctic Mid-Ocean Ridge shows a conspicuous mid-ridge fracture valley leading from the Laptev Continental Shelf to what they call "Nansen Fracture Zone" in Fram Strait.

The map represents the first attempt to portray the floor of the Arctic Ocean in a manner similar to the interpretations then being made of the basins of other oceans in the light of plate-tectonic theory. Although the map is impressionistic and the topography in places differs greatly from what we know today, its wide distribution throughout the world (several million copies to subscribers of the National Geographic Magazine, and many thousands to schools and institutions) has made the Heezen-Tharp interpretation of the Arctic Ocean basin the current norm, familiar to geographers at large and to the public.

Heezen and Tharp's map of the Arctic regions of 1975. In 1975 the American Geographical Society published a map of the Arctic regions, at a scale of 1:5,000,000 (Heezen and Tharp, 1975). It was based on all available unclassified soundings and on extensive use of Beal's (1969) submarine depth profiles. It represents a further development, in larger scale and in contoured form, of their 1971 National Geographic Society relief map. The ocean floor is interpreted in great detail everywhere, regardless of how many or how few data were available for the compilation. A portion of Heezen and Tharp's map with some of the isobaths removed is illustrated in Figure 6a (from Sobczak, 1977). The Arctic Mid-Ocean Ridge is shown with numerous transform faults and flattopped rectangular structures, illustrating the compilers' view of what the bottom topography of an active spreading ridge might look like. Detailed investigations of later aeromagnetic maps suggest that only few, if any, of these transform faults exist (Vogt and others, 1979). The subsequent 1979 GEBCO map, and the latest Perry and Fleming map (this volume; Plate I), still retain some of these controversial transform faults. Commenting on Heezen and Tharp's map and the merit of contouring the ocean floor in detail in areas with little or no data, Kenneth Hunkins (personal communication, 1987) writes, "Heezen's philosophy was that there is only one correct contouring, the one that represents the actual ocean floor. But, of course, we cannot know that from the finite set of soundings available, so the available data must be contoured in terms of theory. Only that contouring done with the correct theory will prevail, and since plate tectonics has been recognized by nearly all geologists as a universal hypothesis, its application to the Arctic Ocean was the correct choice. Details of such contouring may be found in error, but the map will be more correct than one done blindly by contour interpretation using an algorithm without hypothesis."

Sobczak's Arctic bathymetry of 1978. In 1978, the Earth Physics Branch of the Canadian Department of Energy, Mines and Resources published a map of the Arctic Ocean that was compiled by L. W. Sobczak (Sobczak and Sweeney, 1978) at a scale of 1:7,500,000. Nearly 250,000 digitized soundings were used, but the distribution is very uneven. For example, not a single sounding is available from the Laptev Shelf side of the Eurasia Basin south of 85°. Where the contouring is necessarily speculative, the isobaths are represented by broken lines. The data used by Sobczak originate from the same sources as that used earlier by Heezen and Tharp (1975), yet the interpretation is quite different. Compare Figures 6a and 6b (Sobczak, 1977; Monahan, 1979).

GEBCO map of 1979. In 1979, the Canadian Hydrographic Service published GEBCO Chart no. 5.17 under the authority of the International Hydrographic Commission (Johnson and others, 1979). It encompasses the Arctic regions north of 64° and is printed at a scale of 1:6,000,000. The location of the tracks for ships, submarines, and drifting stations, and the locations of individual soundings are plotted, and areas with a high density of soundings, such as the Canadian Polar continental shelf, are delineated. Contouring is conservative, and the Arctic Ocean basin, with the exception of the Arctic Mid-Ocean Ridge, is generally the same as Sobczak's chart.

CESAR map of the central Arctic Ocean of 1986. Using all publicly available sounding data from United States ice stations *T-3, Alpha,* and *ARLIS II,* and United States airlifted stations, CHS stations, Canadian North Pole Expeditions 1967 and 1969, *LOREX 79,* and *CESAR 83,* Weber compiled a 100-m contour bathymetric map of the central Arctic Ocean. Drawn at a scale of 1:500,000, it was published at a reduced scale (Weber, 1986, 1987). The chart, divided into three maps, extends from the Ellesmere Island continental shelf across the Alpha Ridge, Makarov Basin, and Lomonosov Ridge to the north polar area. Sounding locations are indicated by dots.

Perry and Fleming's bathymetry of the Arctic Ocean of 1986. In 1986 the U.S. Office of Naval Research (ONR) published a bathymetric chart of the Arctic Ocean at a scale of 1:4,704,475 (Perry and others, 1986); it includes all of the unclassified bathymetric data collected until 1985. Sounding locations are not shown. The 500-m-interval contours over the uncharted areas of the ocean have been updated on the basis of classified United States submarine data (G. L. Johnson, personal communication, 1984). Plate I, this volume, is a version of this map at a scale of 1:6,000,000.

GEOLOGICAL AND GEOPHYSICAL EXPLORATIONS OF THE ARCTIC BASIN

Phipps' expedition (1773)

The first purely scientific expedition to the Arctic Ocean was the voyage led by the Hon. Captain Constantine John Phipps in 1773. It was outstanding in its scientific preparation and execution, and perhaps the first truly multidisciplinary field research expedition in the modern sense. The plan was proposed by the eminent French round-the-world explorer de Bougainville, who presented it to the French Académie Royale des Sciences. The French turned it down, whereupon de Bougainville took his plan to the Royal Society of London, of which he was a Fellow. Influenced strongly by the urgings and ideas of the Swiss historian and geographer Samuel Engel that there had to be "une mer vaste et libre" around the North Pole, the Royal Society accepted a proposal for "a voyage made towards the north-pole to be of service to the promotion of natural knowledge" (Royal Society, 1782, p. 158). The plan was approved by the Admiralty and King George III. The preparations reveal much about the state of Arctic knowledge and experimental science of the day (Savours, 1984). Elements of the program were navigation, oceanography, hydrography, magnetism, gravity, meteorology, and a full range of biological observations. Prevented by heavy ice from reaching more than a short distance north of Spitzbergen, the two ships explored the ice edge from near Greenland to White Island, and returned with detailed observations on many subjects. Among the better known results of Phipps' expedition were the first scientific descriptions of the polar bear (*Ursus maritimus* Phipps), measurement of the gravity difference between northernmost Spitsbergen and Greenwich, the first measurements of the West Spitzbergen and East Greenland currents, and the first temperature and salinity profiles and depth soundings of Arctic Ocean waters. Although there were no new geographical discoveries, Phipps' voyage provided the first scientific information on the Arctic Ocean and Fram Strait and set the pattern for nineteenth century Arctic and southern ocean expeditions. Equally important, the scientists on the expedition presented their results directly to the Royal Society and scientific bodies, and not as incidental appendices to a commercial or naval operation.

The Fram *Expedition (1893 to 1896)*

During *Fram's* drift across the Eurasia Basin from 1893 to 1896, scientists on board the ship made meteorological (Mohn, 1905), auroral, and astronomical observations (Geelmuyden, 1901), took depth soundings, measured water temperature and

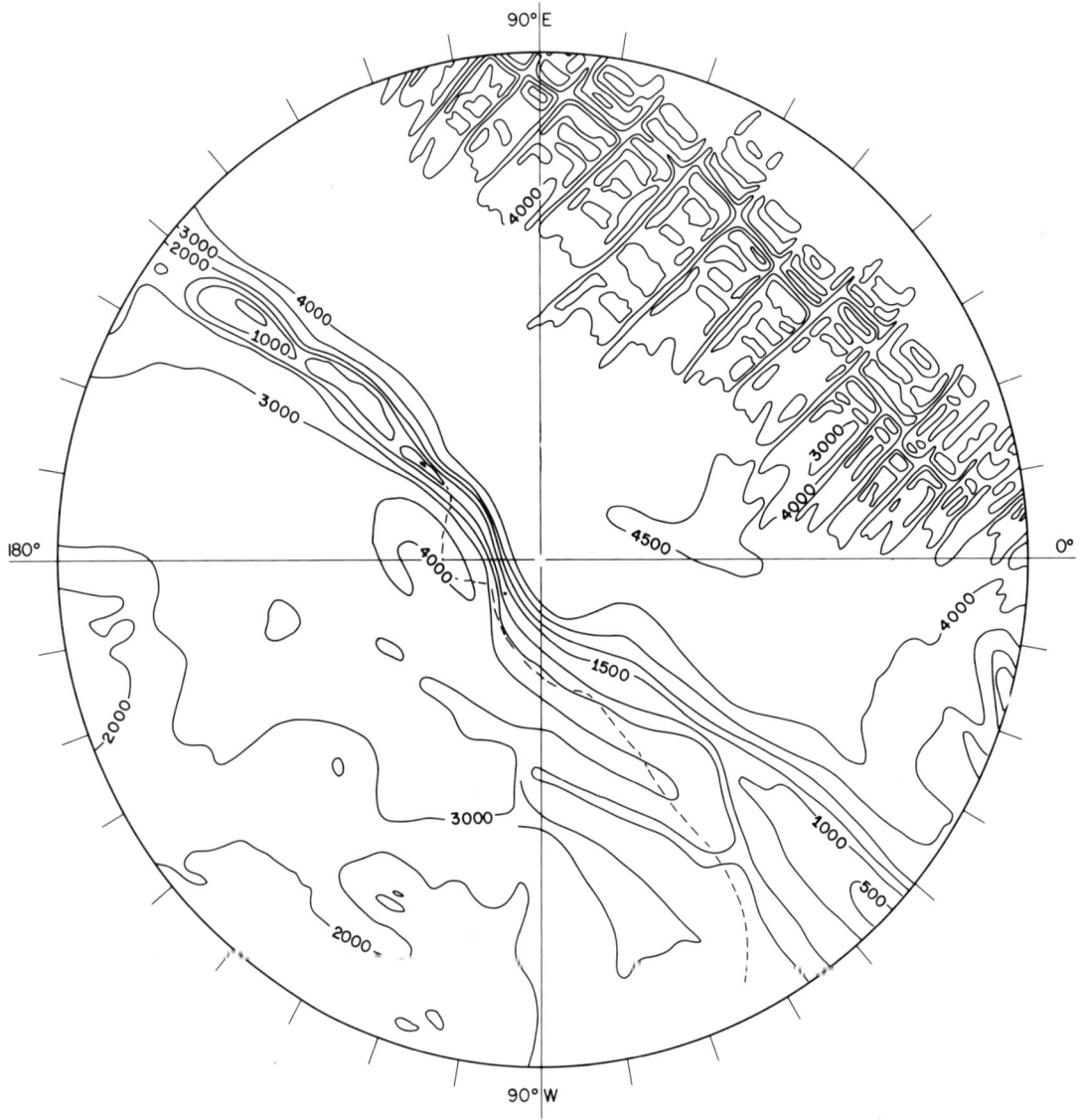

Figure 6a. Interpretative contouring of the Arctic Mid-Ocean Ridge and adjacent areas north of latitude 85° by Heezen and Tharp (1975) indicating numerous transform faults. Only the 500-m contours are shown (Fig. 1 in Sobczak, 1977).

salinity (Nansen, 1897), collected biota, and measured the Earth's magnetic field (Steen, 1901). They also carried two Sterneck four-pendulum gravity apparatus on board. Gravity observations were made in Christiania (Oslo) in 1893 before departure and in 1897 after returning. During the voyage, pendulum observations were made at Khabarovo, south of Novaya Zemlya, at a site whose position had been determined by Nordenskiöld 15 years earlier, and between January 1894 and April 1896, Lieutenant Scott-Hansen carried out ten pendulum measurements on board the *Fram* when she was frozen in the pack ice (Schiötz, 1901). The gravity values were calculated relative to the Vienna value. These are the first gravity measurements made on the open sea. They showed that the free-air anomalies did not significantly differ from those observed on continental lowlands, and Schiötz (1901) reasoned that the mass deficiency of the water must be compensated at depth. These are also, almost a century later, still the only known gravity measurements from that part of the Eurasia Basin.

Soviet drifting stations (1937–)

Over the last four decades, supported by their *NORTH–* and *NORTH POLE*–series operations, Soviet scientists have carried out a multitude of geophysical, geological, oceanographic, and

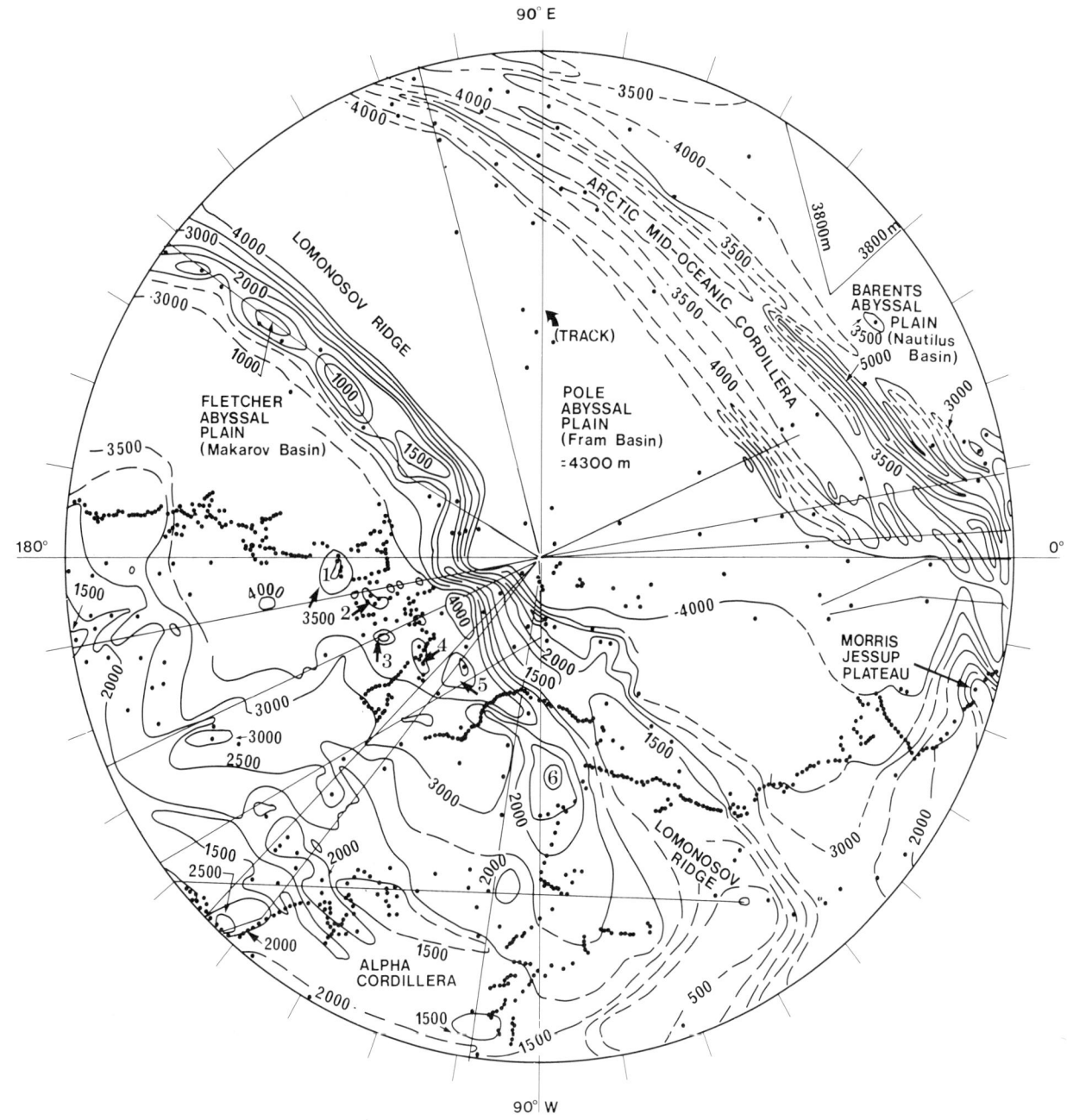

Figure 6b. Bathymetry of the Arctic Ocean floor north of latitude 85° by Sobczak (1977) based on conservative, noninterpretative contouring of the same data as Heezen and Tharp's in Figure 6a. Straight lines indicate location of United States nuclear submarine tracks along which water depth was measured (Beal, 1969). Dots indicate location of spot soundings (Fig. 2 in Sobczak, 1977).

biological investigations in the Arctic Basin. Unfortunately, much of the data collected on these operations, such as bathymetry and gravity, are classified; and the results of other investigations are scattered in the Soviet literature, or have not been translated into western languages, and thus are not easily accessible. Of the geoscientific papers that have appeared in English language journals from time to time, the results and interpretations are often represented in generalized form without back-up data (e.g., Demenitskaya, 1958). There are exceptions, however. In the mid-1960s, Soviet scientists obtained seven heat-flow measurements across the Arctic Mid-Ocean Ridge, which were published (Lubimova and others, 1969a), and 28 observations in the vicinity of the Lomonosov Ridge were also published (Lubimova and others, 1969b; Tomara, 1973). During the 1960s, Soviet scientists conducted aeromagnetic surveys over the eastern parts of the Arctic. Karasik (1973, 1974) published a number of zero-contour charts (i.e., showing positive and negative anomalous field areas), which include much of the Eurasia Basin, the Lomonosov and Mendeleev ridges, and the Eurasian continental shelf. However, cross checks between Soviet and Canadian aeromagnetic charts in areas of overlap showed that the latitude-longitude grid on Karasik's charts was distorted and displaced (Coles and others, 1978). Kiselev (1986) recently summarized Soviet and Western crustal studies in the Arctic Ocean basin and included results of geoscience investigations from Soviet drifting stations previously unknown outside the Soviet Union.

Fletcher's Ice Island (1952 to 1974)

Weather flights over the Arctic Ocean by the U.S. Air Force began in 1947 with trips between Alaska and the North Pole. In 1949, crews of the weather aircraft noticed on their radar screens three large pieces of ice that stood out above the surrounding pack ice (Koenig and others, 1952). These were later designated "ice islands," and since they had been radar targets, were called *T-1*, *T-2* and *T-3*. The Alaskan Air Command decided to set up camp on one of these bodies of ice in order to learn more about their nature and drift paths. *T-3* was selected as it was located well out in the center of the Arctic Ocean. Camp was established in March 1952 under the command of Lieutenant Colonel J. O. Fletcher, and has been known since as *"Fletcher's Ice Island"* or *"T-3."* At that time the ice island was 14 km long, 8 km wide, and between 50 and 60 m thick (Crary and others, 1952).

Before the party settled down for the summer, a trip of historic interest was made. On May 3, 1952, a C-47 aircraft left *T-3* for the North Pole. It landed on an old ice floe and remained at the pole long enough for scientists A. P. Crary and R. D. Cotell to obtain a gravity reading, a seismic depth sounding, and an ice-thickness measurement (Bushnell, 1959a).

In April 1952 a program of geophysical investigations was initiated on *T-3* by A. P. Crary of the U.S. Air Force Cambridge Research Center (Crary and Goldstein, 1957). The program included bathymetry, seismic reflection and refraction, gravity and magnetic measurements, meteorology, oceanography, sediment core studies, ice-drift observations, and ice morphology (Bushnell, 1959a,b; Brown, 1959).

In May 1954, *T-3* was temporarily evacuated because of its proximity to Ellesmere Island but was reoccupied the following spring and operated until the fall of 1961 while the ice island followed the North American polar margin from Ellesmere Island to Alaska. From 1957 to 1959 it served as a U.S. IGY station, during which time it was also known as Station *Bravo*. The geophysical and marine geological work consisted basically of a continuation of Crary's program (Cabaniss, 1962). In addition, the resistivity of sea water as a function of depth was measured, and the thickness of the ice island was determined by electromagnetic methods (Plouff and others, 1961). In March 1960, the ice island became grounded 140 km northwest of Point Barrow. It thereby lost its effectiveness as a drifting platform for geophysical studies and was evacuated in the fall of 1961. Early in 1962, *T-3* was spotted from the air, drifting about 150 km north of where it had been grounded. The old camp was reoccupied, and a geophysical research program was set up by the Lamont-Doherty Geological Observatory (LDGO), which operated for 12 years under the leadership of K. L. Hunkins. Navigational, bathymetric, geomagnetic, gravity, and seismic reflection data from this program were summarized by Hunkins and Tiemann (1977). A total of 580 seabed cores were collected from *T-3*. Some of the seabed coring results have been discussed by Clark (1974), Clark and others (1980), and Minicucci and Clark (1983). Maas (1984) reexamined some of the cores and compared them with the *CESAR* cores. Between 1963 and 1973, some 356 heat-flow measurements were made from *T-3* (Lachenbruch and Marshall, 1966, 1968, 1969; Jessop and others, 1976). Hall (1970) synthesized the geophysical and marine geologic data collected when *T-3* drifted across parts of the Chukchi Borderland, Alpha-Mendeleev Ridge complex, and Canada Basin. His interpretation of the data made him a proponent of the sea-floor spreading origin of the Alpha Ridge (Hall, 1973).

T-3 was abandoned in October 1974 near the coast of Ellesmere Island. With the slow drift and shallow water encountered in this area, the ice island was no longer an efficient research platform. During its 22 years of almost continuous occupation, *T-3* made two complete orbits of the Beaufort gyre. After it was abandoned it completed a third orbit of the Canada Basin before being caught in the Transpolar Current and carried across the Eurasia Basin into the Greenland Sea. Its last confirmed sighting occurred north of the Lena Trough in August 1983, with a possible sighting southeast of Qagssimiut in southern Greenland in March 1984 (D. Barnett, personal communication, 1987).

Alpha (1957 to 1958)

As part of the scientific program of the IGY the U.S. Air Force established a station on a large ice floe in the Canada Basin in June 1957. Over the next 17 months, Station *Alpha* covered some 3,000 km while it drifted across the Mendeleev Plain and part of the Alpha Ridge. LDGO carried out a marine geophysics program consisting of bathymetry, current measurements, magnetic and gravity measurements, coring and dredging, underwater photography, seismic reflection and refraction measurements, and the study of sound propagation in sea ice and sea water (Hunkins, 1960; Hunkins, 1961a,b). Sixteen cores were collected from the seabed. It was from Station *Alpha* that the Alpha Ridge was first delineated (Hunkins, 1961b). The station had to be evacuated in November 1959 because of ice breakup.

Charlie (1959 to 1960)

Station *Charlie* was established on the pack ice 420 km north of Point Barrow with the purpose of continuing Arctic

Ocean research begun during the IGY on Station *Alpha*. From its initial location over the Northwind Ridge on April 13, 1959, the station drifted across the Chukchi Borderland until it had to be abandoned on January 7, 1960, because of ice break up. Geophysical and geological investigations consisted of echo soundings, seismic reflection, magnetic measurements, bottom photography, dredging, and the collection of 22 sediment cores (Hunkins and others, 1962). Other studies included physical oceanography, underwater sound propagation, marine biology, micrometeorology, and ice petrofabrics (Crombie, 1961). After being abandoned, the ice floe apparently made another circuit of the Beaufort Gyre, and in 1969 the remains of the camp were identified and visited on the ice of M'Clure Strait, north of Banks Island.

Arlis II (1961 to 1965)

The last of the "classical" U.S. drifting stations was the ice island *ARLIS II*. It was set up about 200 km north of Barrow, Alaska, by the U.S. Navy Arctic Research Laboratory in May 1961. *ARLIS II* was a fragment of rock-strewn glacier ice that had originated on the west coast of Ellesmere Island. It had been visited by a PCSP party, and served briefly as a gravity station in 1959, when it was off the north end of Ellef Ringnes Island. From 1961 to 1965 it drifted across Northwind Ridge, Chukchi Borderland, Mendeleev Plain, Alpha Ridge, Siberia Plain, Lomonosov Ridge, Amundsen Basin, Morris Jesup Plateau, and through Fram Strait along the East Greenland coast into Denmark Strait, where the camp was abandoned in May 1965. The scientific program, directed by the Lamont-Doherty Geological Observatory and the University of Wisconsin, included seismic reflection; gravity, magnetic, and ocean-bottom seismograph measurements; bathymetry; and coring (Kutschale, 1966; Ostenso, 1968b; Wold, 1973; Ostenso and Wold, 1977; Weber and Sweeney, 1985).

Aidjex (1971, 1972, 1975 to 1976)

Geoscience research from drifting ice stations during the early and mid-seventies was dominated by the Arctic Ice Dynamics Joint Experiment (AIDJEX), a large-scale study of the interaction between the Arctic Ocean water, sea ice, and the atmosphere (Untersteiner, 1979). It was a joint United States–Canadian operation, funded by the National Science Foundation, the Office of Naval Research, and the Polar Continental Shelf Project. Preceeded by pilot studies in 1970 and 1971 and a large-scale pilot study with three manned camps in March and April 1972, the main experiment was conducted from four manned stations between March 1975 and May 1976. Although AIDJEX was primarily concerned with the relationship between large-scale sea ice deformation and the external stress field, the 1970 and 1971 ice camps also served as bases for regional bathymetric and gravity surveys in the Canadian sector of the Beaufort Sea. Recording echo sounders, gravimeters, and magnetometers were operated at the 1972 and 1975/76 main camps;

and in 1976 a crustal seismic refraction survey was conducted using the AIDJEX camp as a base (Mair and Lyons, 1981). The refraction data, which constitute the most useful set of deep seismic data available from the Canada Basin to date, confirmed that the basin is underlain by oceanic crust, as suggested by Oliver and others (1955).

Two years later, Baggeroer and others (1982) conducted a seismic refraction survey in the Beaufort Sea some 200 km to the west of the AIDJEX refraction survey. The operation was dubbed Canada Basin Acoustic Reverberation Experiment (CANBAREX). The results supported Mair and Lyon's findings.

The Canadian North Pole expeditions (1967, 1969)

In the late sixties the Dominion Observatory (later the Earth Physics Branch, now amalgamated with the Geological Survey of Canada), supported by the Polar Continental Shelf Project, conducted two scientific expeditions to the vicinity of the North Pole (Weber, 1983). During the first expedition, May 6–14, 1967, an attempt was made to measure the deflection of the plumbline from visual observation of the satellites *Echo 2* and *Pageos,* and from precise celestial observations. Determination of the precise drift path, which is necessary in order to know the exact position of the station at the time of the satellite transit, was obtained by ranging to a sonar transponder on the ocean floor. A radio data link to a CDC 3600 computer in Minneapolis was used to correct for ice drift and atmospheric refraction (Lillestrand and others, 1967). Although the plumbline deflection experiment could not be carried out because crystal fog obscured the satellites, much was learned about precise navigation in the polar region. It is of historic interest to note that the party landed on an old ice floe at the pole, without previous reconnaissance, in an unmodified heavy commercial Bristol 170 Freighter aircraft on wheels. After a week's observations the party was evacuated to Alert in two single-engine Otter aircraft. A message bottle left on the ice near the pole washed ashore on the east coast of Iceland 18 months later.

Two years later the expedition returned to the vicinity of the North Pole and occupied an ice floe from April 12 to May 3, 1969. The equipment included a commercial transit satellite receiver and an acoustic bottom reference system. Bathymetric and gravity measurements were made, and the deflection of the vertical was determined from star observations and satellite transit data. The deflection measurements and gravity observations suggested that the nearby Lomonosov Ridge had deep, low-density roots and supported the hypothesis (Wilson, 1963; Committee on Polar Research, 1970) that it is a continental fragment broken off the Barents and Kara continental shelves and rafted to its present location by sea-floor spreading (Weber and Lillestrand, 1971; Smith, 1974).

Lorex 79

During the Lomonosov Ridge Experiment (*LOREX 79*; Weber and Sweeney, 1977), which lasted from March 14 to June

10, 1979, a main station and two satellite stations were established updrift of the Lomonosov Ridge, in the vicinity of the North Pole. While the Transpolar Current transported the three stations across the ridge, a variety of investigaions was carried out (Weber, 1979, 1983), including seismic reflection and refraction, magnetic, heatflow and ocean bottom current measurements, sediment core sampling, physical and chemical oceanography, and ice dynamics (Blasco and others, 1979; Mair and Forsyth, 1982). The geophysical investigations confirmed the continental origin of the Lomonosov Ridge (Sweeney and others, 1982).

All three stations were equipped with transit satellite receivers, while the Twin Otter aircraft and helicopters used for spot landings were navigated by Omega Global Navigational System (GNS). Canadian Armed Forces Hercules aircraft dropped fuel, explosives, building materials, and supplies by Low Altitude Parachute Extraction System (LAPES) to the *LOREX* site while a commercial Dash-7 aircraft moved personnel, equipment, and supplies from Alert to the ice station, and also evacuated the expedition back to Alert in June.

The Fram operations (1979-1982)

In 1978 the U.S. Office of Naval Research initiated a program of exploration of the Eurasia Basin north of Fram Strait between 80°N and 87°N. Four expeditions, *Fram I* (Hunkins and others, 1979), *Fram II* (Baggeroer and Dyer, 1982; Duchworth and others, 1982), *Fram III* (Manley and others, 1982), and *Fram IV* (Tiemann and others, 1982) were conducted each spring from 1979 to 1982. Personnel and equipment were flown from Station Nord in North Greenland to the ice by Twin Otter and Tri-Turbo DC-3 aircraft, while fuel was parachuted to the stations by U.S. Air Force planes. From its inception, *Fram* emphasized multidisciplinary research by scientists of several nations (Johnson, 1983). United States, Danish, Norwegian, British, and Canadian scientists carried out geophysical, marine geological, hydroacoustical, physical and chemical oceanographic, marine biological, and sea-ice studies. The main objective of the geoscience studies was to define the nature and geophysical character of the sea floor in the Eurasia Basin. It was found that the crust beneath the sea floor is only 3 km thick, and that the sea floor is accreting at a rate of less than 1 cm per year, more slowly than the apparent motion at any other known spreading ridge (Kristoffersen, 1982).

Cesar 83

Lack of knowledge about the evolution of the Amerasia Basin and of the nature and origin of the Alpha Ridge led, in 1983, to the undertaking of the large-scale, Canadian Expedition to Study the Alpha Ridge (*CESAR 83*) (Weber and others, 1981). The expedition was planned by the Earth Physics Branch, and logistically supported by the Polar Continental Shelf Project. It was assisted by the Canadian Armed Forces, first by parachuting 18 airborne engineers onto the *CESAR* site to build a 1.6-km-long airstrip on the pack ice, and then by deploying, and two months later evacuating, the expedition by military Hercules aircraft. The initial search by Twin Otter aircraft for a suitable camp site was facilitated by an earlier reconnaissance survey of the area, using side-looking airborne radar (SLAR; Weber, 1987). The scientific program, which was similar to that carried out during the *LOREX* expedition, started on April 3 and lasted until May 20 (Jackson and others, 1985; Taylor and others, 1986; Niblett and others, 1987).

Thirty-six gravity and piston cores were collected. One of the cores retrieved from the Cesar Trough (Weber and Sweeney, this volume, Fig. 19-15) contained sediments of Campanian-Maastrichtian age (Mudie and Blasco, 1985). The only other known Late Cretaceous sediments from the Arctic Ocean were found in four sediment cores collected on the Alpha Ridge from *T-3* (Clark and others, 1980). A highly altered and weathered volcanic bedrock sample was also dredged from the Cesar North Ridge (Weber and Sweeney, this volume, Fig. 19; Van Wagoner and others, 1986). Results of the geophysical and marine geological investigations suggest that the eastern part of the Alpha Ridge may be a massive accumulation of volcanic rocks of probable oceanic origin (Weber, 1986; Forsyth and others, 1986b). It is estimated that the Alpha Ridge was formed during the Cretaceous Period between about 120 and 80 Ma (Sweeney and Weber, 1986).

Hobson's Choice (1984-)

In 1983, two large, tabular icebergs, or ice islands, were sighted east of McClintock Inlet, northern Ellesmere Island. They had calved off the Ward Hunt Ice Shelf during the previous year (Jeffries and Serson, 1983) and appear to be the first large pieces of ice discharged from the Ward Hunt Ice Shelf since 1962. If the ice island follows the course of its known predecessors, it can be expected to get caught in the Beaufort Gyre and drift along the North American polar margin to the Chukchi Borderland. The ice island would in that case become an ideal platform from which to carry out scientific investigations (Weber and others, 1984). In the fall of 1984 the ice island was just off Nansen Sound, and PCSP established a year-round camp on it. The island was nicknamed *Hobson's Choice* after Thomas Hobson, who in the seventeenth century, in Cambridge, England, owned livery stables and let horses in strict order according to their position near the door, "a choice of taking what is offered or nothing at all." George Hobson (no known relation) has been PCSP's director since 1972. Scientific work began in the spring of 1985 and continued every spring, summer, and fall. Because the island has so far remained frozen to the land-locked ice during the winter, the camp has been closed during the winter months. Geophysical and marine geological work has included single-shot seismic reflection from an array across the island (Hajnal, 1988), continuous sub-bottom profiling (Jackson, 1986), sediment sampling and bottom biology (Mudie and others, 1985), and navigation.

Cruises of scientific research ships

Hudson 70. In 1970, during a scientific voyage circumnavigating North and South America, the Canadian government research vessel CSS *Hudson* conducted hydrographic, oceanographic, geophysical, and seabed sampling surveys in the Beaufort Sea (Pelletier, 1970). Accompanied by the CSS *Baffin,* the CSS *Parizeau,* and the CSS *Richardson,* the *Hudson* carried out 14 transects at 25 to 30-km spacing across the Beaufort continental shelf and slope. The geophysical investigations consisted of continuous shipborne gravity and magnetics, 1,100 km of side-scan sonar, and 1,600 km of shallow seismic profiling. The seabed studies included coring and dredging (Pelletier, 1984). The sonar and seismic profiling results for the first time revealed the existence of numerous submarine pingos (Shearer and others, 1971) and the effect of ice scouring (Pelletier and Shearer, 1972).

Ymer 80. To commemorate Nordenskiöld's circumnavigation of Asia in the *Vega,* the Swedish government sponsored a scientific expedition into the Arctic Ocean during the summer of 1980. The 7,900-ton Swedish icebreaker *Ymer* served as a platform for an Arctic scientific expedition in the area between Franz Josef Land and northeast Greenland. Scientists from nine countries cooperated in studies ranging from marine biology, physical and chemical oceanography, air chemistry, meteorology, glaciology, land-based physical geography, and Quaternary geology to marine geology and geophysics (Schytt and others, 1981; Schytt, 1982; Kristoffersen and others, 1984).

Polarstern 87. During July and August, 1987, the RV *Polarstern* of the Alfred Wegener Institute for Polar and Marine Research, Bremerhaven, Germany, succeeded in penetrating the pack ice of the Eurasia Basin as far north as 86°11'N. Fifty scientists and technicians from 19 institutions and ten countries carried out a complex program of oceanographic, meteorological, biological, and geoscientific studies (Thiede and others, 1988). This is the first time a modern mobile research platform reached the central part of the Eurasia Basin. Results from the ship's SEABEAM and 3.5 kHz echosounding system along the ship's track showed that the Barents Abyssal Plain is extraordinarily flat, about 200 m deeper than previously known (Perry and others, 1986; Plate I, this volume), and characterized by strongly reflecting, horizontally layered sediments. Preliminary studies of the sediment cores, 7 to 9 m long, revealed a maximum age of about 300 ka and a sedimentation rate of approximately 40 mm/ka. The Arctic Mid-Ocean Ridge was found to be a deeply incised, block-faulted ridge valley, over 5,500 m deep, and more than 2 km below the adjacent ridge crests. Excessively high heat-flow values were measured in the central part of the valley and samples of basaltic bedrock were collected there. These, and the volcanic rock dredged from the Alpha Ridge during *CESAR,* are the only known samples of basement rock from the entire Arctic Ocean (Thiede, 1988; P. Mudie, personal communication, 1988).

Crustal studies over the North American polar margin (1961 to 1986)

While the upper-mid crustal structure beneath the continental shelf between the U.S.-U.S.S.R. border and Banks Island is relatively well known from industry surveys (Thurston and Theiss, 1987; Craig and others, 1985), the deep crustal structure of the Alaskan and Canadian polar margin is still poorly known. To date, six deep seismic studies have been carried out in this region. They are briefly summarized, progressing from west to east.

In 1961, the Office of Naval Research, in cooperation with the University of Minnesota, shot a 320-km-long reversed seismic refraction profile from Point Barrow parallel to the edge of the continental shelf into the Chukchi Sea. The shots were fired from the U.S. *Staten Island.* The inshore end was recorded at Point Barrow, and the offshore end on the ice island *ARLIS II* by personnel from the Lamont-Doherty Geological Observatory. A preliminary interpretation of the data shows a depth of about 30 km to a 7.56 km/s basement layer beneath the inner continental shelf near Point Barrow (D'Andrea and others, 1962; Hunkins, 1966).

In 1965, using the icebreaker USS *Staten Island* as a base, Milne (1966) made unreversed seismic refraction measurements in the Beaufort Sea across the Alaskan continental rise north of Point Barrow and obtained a crustal thickness of 15 km.

In 1977 the U.S. Geological Survey conducted 24-channel common-depth-point seismic reflection surveys on the Alaskan Arctic continental margin from the research vessel *S. P. Lee.* The profiles, spaced at about 20-km intervals over most of the area, covered the continental shelf and slope between the Chukchi Sea and the U.S.-Canada border to the 2,000-m isobath and beyond. The results of the survey suggest an Atlantic-type continental margin north of Alaska (Grantz and May, 1983).

In 1967 an unreversed crustal refraction experiment was carried out from the southwest tip of Prince Patrick Island to a point mid-way down the continental slope, some 220 km from the coast (Berry and Barr, 1971). The interpretation showed that the crustal thickness decreased from about 28 km at the coast to a poorly defined 15 km at the seaward end of the profile near the base of the continental slope.

In 1965, seismologists from the Dominion Observatory conducted an unreversed crustal seismic refraction profile extending northwest from Brock Island 192 km onto the continental shelf. This seismic profile is located parallel and some 280 km northeast of the 1967 profile. Overton (1970) concluded that the depth to the crust-mantle interface decreased from an average of 35 km below Brock Island to a possible 17 km at the northwest end of the line.

In 1961 a seismic party of the Geological Survey of Canada completed seven refraction profiles along the west coast of Ellef Ringnes Island along a line extending from the continental shelf 50 km north of the island to a point in Belcher Channel, 50 km south of the island (Hobson and Overton, 1967). The survey outlined the northern rim and the axis of the Sverdrup Basin.

The thinning of the crust across the margin, observed on the 1965 and 1967 surveys, supported the evidence for an oceanic origin of the Canada Basin (Sobczak and Overton, 1984), first suggested by Oliver and others (1955) based on earthquake surface-wave studies.

Using *Hobson's Choice* as a base, a number of closely spaced seismic refraction profiles (Asudeh and others, 1985, 1986) and gravity profiles (Sobczak and Weber, 1987) were established over the continental shelf off Axel Heiberg and Ellesmere islands in the spring of 1985 and 1986. The refraction models show a passive rifted margin with sedimentary basins containing 5 to 12 km of nominal postrifted sediments. Crustal thickness of 25 km beneath the outer shelf is consistent with a continent-ocean transitional crustal structure.

DISCUSSION

Archeological evidence suggests that intimate and traditional knowledge of the geography and natural history of many parts of the coasts of the Arctic Ocean and surrounding seas has been possessed by successive groups of indigenous and migratory people since late Interglacial or early Würm Glacial times. But the people who possessed this knowledge were mostly isolated, and did not pass it on to other societies. It remained for Greece, the classical center of recorded scholarship, to begin the lengthy process of systematic exploration, observation, and scientific interpretation of the polar regions, which is continuing today.

Growth of knowledge about the Arctic regions has been spasmodic and not always progressive. The obstacles of a harsh environment and great distances have necessitated special efforts, often heroic, to discover and learn about the region. As a result the polar areas have been among the last to be explored, and they remain among the least-known parts of the planet. Three ingredients have had a controlling influence on the course of Arctic exploration and research: (1) strong motivation, either political, economic, or philosophical, in a social climate favorable to risk taking and personal gratification; (2) a recognized advance or change in technology (transport, instrumentation, life support, etc.); and (3) dominant theories or concepts that put previous knowledge into context and point the way for further investigation. Only when all three factors were favorable has Arctic scientific knowledge made its strongest advance.

An additional important factor has been the means by which information and concepts were assembled and distributed. In the Arctic regions, cartographers have played perhaps a stronger role in the development or hampering of scientific knowledge than in any other part of the planet (Saladin d'Anglure, 1984).

The earliest scientific concepts of the Arctic regions were developed from Aristotle's conclusion in the fourth century B.C. that the Earth was spherical in shape. Aristotle cited four lines of evidence: (1) all matter seems to fall as if pulled from a single point; (2) the Earth throws a circular shadow on the moon during an eclipse; (3) ships travelling away from an observer appear to sink below the horizon; and (4) as one travels from south to north, some stars disappear to the south and new ones appear above the northern horizon. These conclusions, and a religious fascination with symmetry, led to ideas of balanced continents in an encompassing ocean that included the north and south poles.

With this intellectual background, motivated by a desire to find precious tin, and equipped with a capable ship and adequate means of navigation, Pytheas, as we have seen, made the first significant Arctic contribution to world science. His findings, although new and spectacular, fitted the ideas of the time—a frozen ocean to balance the torrid zone, a reasonable scale for the convexity of the planet, etc.—and so were incorporated into the pool of knowledge. The globe described by Crates about 150 B.C. (Fig. 1) is easily recognizable as a portrayal of planet Earth, and all we have done since is to refine it.

Through the growth of geographical knowledge from the Norse explorations of the North Atlantic onward, map makers played an important role, not only in recording discoveries, but in interpreting and popularizing scientific theory. Clavus' interpretation of the dense ice pack north of Fram Strait as a land bridge connecting Greenland and Europe (about 1425), and Mercator's embellishment of an otherwise careful map with fanciful islands from Scandinavian mythology (1569) were not likely personal whims of the cartographers, but appear to have reflected prevailing scholarly consensus. Mercator, indeed, went to considerable trouble to explain his need to include a polar projection on his 1595 world chart (drawn on Mercator projection), and to give his sources of information about the central Arctic Ocean basin:

"Since our map could not be extended to the pole, as the degrees of latitude run to infinity, and since we have some description of the north, by no means to be neglected, we have thought it necessary here to give the extreme part of our mapping, and to join what is left as far as the pole. We have taken a figure which best suited that part of the world, and which would represent the position and appearance of the land as if it were on a globe. As for the mapping, we have taken it from the *Itinerium* of Jacobus Cnoyon of the Hague, who cites from the *Gesta* of Arthur of Britain; however, the greater and most important part he learned from a certain priest at the court of the King of Norway in 1364. He was descended in the fifth generation from those whom Arthur had sent to inhabit these islands, and he related that in the year 1360 a certain Minorite from Linna, an Englishman from Oxford, a mathematician, went to these islands; and leaving them, advanced still farther by magic arts and mapped out all and measured them by astrolabe in practically the subjoined figure, as we have learned from Jacobus. The four canals there pictured he said flow with such current to the inner whirlpool, that if vessels once enter they cannot be driven back by any wind; and he said nowhere was there wind strong enough for transporting grain" (G. Mercator, quoted in Nordensköld, 1889, p. 95).

The scholarly care that Mercator applied to the use of available information in the light of the best interpretations of his time, and to revealing the sources of his data, applies equally well today. The inclusion of results from careful navigation, together with ideas from earlier stories, produced charts that were in part reliable and in part fanciful; but they contributed greatly to current geographical awareness and stimulated further research and discovery. These maps appear to have been more influential than the more cautious partial maps of the same period, such as those of Barents and Foxe. A modern illustration of this problem is the need to interpret sparse hydrographic data to produce maps of the central part of the Arctic Ocean floor. The data are so few that unless they are interpreted according to some theory, they would make little sense. Interpretations may differ (compare Figs. 6a and 6b, but each is useful in relating available evidence to current understanding.

One cannot but wonder, however, whether really all of the information depicted on the "pre-discovery" part of Mercator's map (Fig. 3) is based on legends and guesswork alone. There has been much speculation and study concerning whether some of the details on parts of sixteenth century maps, drawn prior to recorded discovery, might represent knowledge or information from earlier sources now lost to us. Some prediscovery features so closely resemble reality that it stretches modern credulity to explain the uncanny likeliness as pure coincidence. Two of these puzzling and instructive examples are the sixteenth century representations of Antarctica on Orontius Finaeus' 1531 map, and South America on Mercator's 1538 map (both National Archives of Canada). Terra Australis on the Finaeus map shows coastal and inland mountains comparable to similar features known today, as well as fjord-like valleys that penetrate the land, where today massive glaciers fill the valleys of the Transarctic Mountains. Yet, the continent of Antarctica was supposedly not discovered until the early 1800s, and the subglacial topography was first explored during the IGY (1957 to 1958; Weihaupt, 1984). Mercator drew South America much as it is known today at a time when exploration of the continent was in its infancy.

A similar situation surrounds the Strait of Anian and the western outlines of what is now Alaska (Falk, 1984). There is a surprising resemblance between Mercator's Asian and American Arctic coasts and the Siberian and Alaskan coasts of modern maps; and the longitude of the Strait of Anian is within a few degrees of that of Bering Strait.

This general likeness between some of the features of sixteenth century and modern maps has led to considerable speculation and controversy (Nordenskjöld, 1889; Hatherton, 1986; Hapgood, 1966; Weihaupt, 1984; Milton, 1984; Liboutry, 1984, and references therein). We are left to conclude that at the time these maps were drawn, before the Asian and American Arctic coasts were "discovered" by a recorded voyage, there may have been available to cartographers a wealth of information from now-forgotten sources (Saladin d'Anglure, 1980, 1984; Wagner, 1931). It is tempting to speculate that Mercator's information on the prediscovery part of the Arctic Ocean is also partly based on this same, possibly pre-medieval knowledge. It appears that he compiled his map of the polar regions based on a variety of sources, including verified discoveries, legends that may have had some basis in fact, and sources now lost to us.

The advent of scientific stations established by aircraft on drifting ice, pioneered by Ivan Papanin in 1937, has marked a revolution in Arctic Ocean research by making all of the basin technically accessible at most seasons of the year. Improved accessibility has also been accompanied by greatly increased budgets for Arctic Basin research, necessitating a change from general reconnaissance to more intensive, short-term, and highly sophisticated investigations on high-priority scientific problems to justify the expenditures (Roots, 1987). The improved technologies for Arctic surface, under-ice, aerial, and satellite exploration have also raised political problems and revived the ideas of *mare nostrum* (our sea) and *mare clausum* (closed sea; a sea under the jurisdiction of a single nation) in the Arctic Ocean (Theutenberg, 1984). Much recent scientific data about the Arctic Basin is today perceived by authorities in several countries to have military significance and is not openly available.

The Arctic Ocean basin has been not only an area for exploration and study for its own sake, but also a testing ground for evolving theories of global evolution and tectonics. The magnetic and pendulum studies of Phipps, Sabine, Ross, Nares, Nordenskjöld, and the International Polar Year provided essential high-latitude information for development of planetary magnetic theory, the shape of the geoid, the axial tilt, and rotational stability of the Earth (Sabine, 1819, 1821, 1863; Heathcote and Armitage, 1959; Roots, 1982).

In his masterful summary of the geologic architecture of the entire planet, Suess (1904–1924) assembled all known information on the geology of the Arctic regions, and interpreted it in the light of the theory of mobile belts and stable continental shields. The circumpolar Arctic structures and the distribution of land masses, sedimentary basins, and "dislocations" in northern regions led Suess to consider that the great bend of the Cordilleran structures in Alaska around the North Pacific was the key to Arctic Ocean geology. He interpreted the Arctic Ocean to be a true ocean, and thus its floor, according to ideas of the time, was "permanent." It is interesting that he postulated the possibility of a folded belt between the Canadian Shield and the Arctic Basin (Suess, 1904–1924, v. IV, p. 249–251), several decades before the existence of the Innuitian orogenic belt was identified in the field. Suess' interpretations were absorbed into the background geological thinking of several generations of earth scientists, and can be seen in the broad Arctic interpretations of Umbgrove (1947), Eardley (1948, 1961), and others.

Nansen's transarctic drift in the *Fram* down the length of the Eurasia Basin replaced the notion of the Arctic Ocean as a shallow sea with the concept of a single, simple basin of oceanic depths. This view was enforced by the accidental drift of the *Sedov* and Papanin's ice station along the same route. Harris' interpretation of the Arctic as a two-basin Arctic Ocean, divided by a submerged central ridge fitted known tidal data and could not be disproved on the basis of the bathymetric observations, but like continental drift a few decades later, it was at variance with fashionable explanations. It remained an unexplained anomaly until the discovery of the Lomonosov Ridge.

Increasing knowledge of the bathymetry of the Arctic led to alternative explanations of the development of parts of the ocean basin (Carey, 1958; Hope, 1959; Eardley, 1961; Yorath and Norris, 1975). Aeromagnetic, gravity, and seismic data, combined with the emergence of the theory of plate tectonics, led to speculation and, as new information accumulated, to increasingly firm evidence for the tectonic evolution of the Eurasia Basin and Lomonosov Ridge (Heezen and Ewing, 1961; Wilson, 1963; Roots, 1966; Sweeney and others, 1982; Forsyth and Mair, 1984) and origin of the Alpha Ridge (Vogt and Ostenso, 1970; Herron and others, 1974; Taylor, 1978; Coles and others, 1978; Coles, 1985; Forsyth and others, 1986a; Weber, 1986). The evolution of the Amerasia Basin as a whole, however, is still a subject of speculation (King and Zietz, 1966; Tailleur, 1973; Grantz and May, 1983; Vogt and others, 1982). The relation of the Arctic Basin to the surrounding continent presented problems of interpretation (Roots, 1969; Committee on Polar Research, 1970) that are not yet satisfactorily resolved.

Advances in world science and research approaches strongly influenced Arctic Basin research. Phipps' priorities in 1773 to study the migration of birds, the fetuses of whales, the variation of the compass, the period of the pendulum, the density and salinity of sea water, the identification of drift wood, and the contraction of metals in high latitudes, reflect a catholic scientific curiosity that was typical of the burgeoning of modern research at the end of the eighteenth century. A century later, the International Polar Year (IPY) of 1882 to 1883 saw a rigorous, synchronized program of observations of preselected subjects at preselected sites around the Arctic Basin. This was the antithesis of geographical exploration, but necessary to put the high-latitude data set on an equal footing with that of more intensively studied regions. A century later still, the *LOREX* and *CESAR* expeditions to the central Arctic represented the modern trend of team research in which scientists from various institutions and disciplines bring their different talents to focus on a common major problem.

A lesson that comes from a review of the history of Arctic Ocean exploration is the importance of ensuring that the observations and data are well recorded and made available to others, who may use them for purposes different from those in mind when the studies were made. Pytheas' observations of the stars in high latitudes, although now lost to us, were used 100 years later in calculation of the diameter of the Earth; the tidal readings of Nares and of the IPY stations were used two decades later by Harris (1905) to postulate the existence of a mid-Arctic ridge. There is no more telling and serious example of the cost to world knowledge of not giving attention to the preservation and dissemination of field data than the deliberate discard of the careful notes and charts of William Baffin. Baffin was an accomplished navigator and surveyor. However, the accounts of his "five recorded voyages" with Robert Bylot (there may have been more) were entrusted to the influential geographical bibliographer and historian, Samuel Purchas. In reference to the 1616 voyage of Bylot and Baffin to the north end of Baffin Bay, and the discovery of the major sounds and islands of the eastern Arctic archipelago, Purchas wrote candidly, "this map of the author (Baffin) for this and the former voyage, with the tables of his journal and sailing, were somewhat troublesome and too costly to insert" (Purchas, 1625, quoted in Taylor, 1955, p. 15). Apparently Purchas, like many bibliographers and data keepers, was short of funds. The wealth of accurate detail apparently produced by Baffin was set aside and lost, whereas shorter and less accurate accounts from other navigators were retained and published because they were less expensive to record (Markham, 1881).

An interesting and important aspect of the history of scientific study of the Arctic Ocean areas, as distinct from the history of its geographical exploration, has been the degree of international cooperation that has been characteristic of Arctic research. The first Arctic Ocean research expedition, that of Phipps, sponsored by the Royal Society of London in 1773, had a genuine international origin and contribution. The concept of international cooperation reached its first full development in the Arctic with the proposals by Weyprecht in 1875 for an International Polar Year. Stating forcibly that "science is not a territory for national possession" Weyprecht argued that national rivalries had no place in the growth of scientific knowledge, and that the quality of science could be maintained only if "the results of the observations were exchanged freely without discrimination" (Wild, 1882, p. 5). The development of the International Polar Commission and the success of the IPY, which it organized, had much to do with the "internationalization" of science. The determination to develop a genuine international program withstood a disruptive European war and discord between many countries. It undoubtedly contributed to the fact that shortly after the IPY, academies of science became international in outlook. International scientific professional societies grew and jealously defended their freedom from political interference. Standards for scientific quality came to be set through review by peers and colleagues rather than approval by sponsors. These concepts, so much part of the ideals of science today, had important origins in Arctic research (Roots, 1982).

Scientific investigations in Arctic regions have contributed to world knowledge and thereby played an important role in developing international scientific cooperation. The open knowledge concepts initiated by Phipps and the IPY have been continued through international programs such as the Second International Polar Year (1932 to 1933; Bartels and others, 1959), and the International Geophysical Year (1957 to 1958) and its many successors with important Arctic geoscience components such as the International Year of the Quiet Sun, the International Magnetosphere Study, and the International Geodynamics Project. Many of the most important Arctic studies of recent years have had an essential international involvement— AIDJEX, *Fram,* MIZEX, *Ymer,* and others. This cooperation is especially important in the context of the increasing political and strategic importance of the Arctic Ocean basin (Roots, 1986a, 1987).

Although the knowledge base and equipment for Arctic Ocean basin research have changed enormously in the 2,300 years since Pytheas first encountered the frozen sea, the motivations for studying the Arctic regions seem to have changed but little. Sponsors have ranged from merchants, to kings, to governments. The actors have included scientists, military men, traders, monks, and philosophers. But each advance in geographic discovery or scientific activity has been characterized by a mixture of political drive, financial incentive, new technology, current scientific or geographical theories, and influential or powerful personalities. The situation is little different today. As Arctic Ocean basin research takes its place in the spectrum of continuing and forthcoming international and national scientific programs, such as the International Geosphere-Biosphere Program and the International Lithosphere Program, it is supported by more than 2,000 years of experience in relating observation, theory, and scientific experimentation to political, economic, and scholarly issues of the day.

Behind all the motives lies curiosity. The history of Arctic Basin exploration and research shows that scientific curiosity is undiminished by Arctic hardships, persistent failure of financial returns, or political setbacks. The words of Thomas Blundeville in 1613 are as timely today as they were for the Elizabethan explorers, or as they were for Pytheas. Of Arctic voyages, he wrote from the comfort of a London fireside (Blundeville, 1613, p. 16B, quoted by Wallis, 1984, p. 489):

". . . notwithstanding I can greatly commend those valient minds that doe attempt such voyages, and the rather when they doe it for knowledge sake, and profit all their countrie, and not altogether for private gaine and lucre."

REFERENCES CITED

Anderson, W. R., 1959, Nautilus 90 North: New York, Signet Books, 144 p.

Armstrong, T. E., 1958, The Russians in the Arctic; Aspects of Soviet exploration and exploitation of the far north, 1937–1957: Fairlawn, New Jersey, Essential Books, Oxford University Press, 182 p.

Asudeh, I., Forsyth, D. A., Jackson, H. R., Stephenson, R., and White, D., 1985, The 1985 ice island refraction survey; Phase 1 report: Ottawa, Geological Survey of Canada Report 1196, 140 p. (Also released as Earth Physics Branch Open-File Report 85-23.)

Asudeh, I., Forsyth, D. A., Jackson, H. R., Stephenson, R., and White, D., 1986, 1986 ice island refraction survey; Phase 2: Ottawa, Geological Survey of Canada Open-File Report 1511, 120 p.

Baggeroer, A. B., and Dyer, I., 1982, Fram 2 in the eastern Arctic: EOS Transactions of the American Geophysical Union, v. 63, no. 14, p. 221–222.

Baggeroer, A. B., Shepard, G. W., and Dyer, I., 1982, Array refraction profiles and crustal models of the Canada Basin: Geophysical Research, v. 87, p. 5461–5476.

Bartels, J., Laurson, V., Brooks, C.E.P., Paton, J., Benyon, W.J.G., Vestine, E. H., and Nagata, T., 1959, The Second International Polar Year: Annals of the International Geophysical Year, v. 1, p. 205–382.

Beal, M. A., 1969, Bathymetry and structure of the Arctic Ocean [Ph.D. thesis]: Corvallis, Oregon State University, 204 p.

——, 1983, Comments on maps of the Arctic Ocean: Arctic, v. 36, p. 372–373.

Bernard, R., 1976, The hollow Earth, 2nd ed.: New York, Citadel Press, 225 p.

Berry, M. J., and Barr, K. G., 1971, A seismic refraction profile across the polar continental shelf of the Queen Elizabeth Islands: Canadian Journal of Earth Sciences, v. 8, no. 3, p. 347–360.

Blasco, S. M., Bornhold, B. D., and Lewis, C.F.M., 1979, Preliminary results of surficial geology and geomorphology studies of the Lomonosov Ridge, Central Arctic Basin: Geological Survey of Canada Current Research Paper 79-1C, part C, p. 73–83.

Blom, G. A., 1984, The participation of the kinds in the early Norwegian sailing to Bjarmeland (Kola Peninsula and Russian waters), and the development of a royal policy concerning the Northern Waters in the Middle Ages: Arctic, v. 37, no. 4, p. 385–388.

Blundeville, T., 1613, A Briefe Description of the Universal Mappes and Cardes and their Use: London, British Library, collected papers.

Bosworth, J., 1855, Description of Europa and the voyage of Othere and Wulfstan by King Alfred the Great: London, Murray, 80 p.

Browne, I. M., 1959, Ice drift in the Arctic Ocean: EOS Transactions of the American Geophysical Union, v. 40, p. 195–200.

Burkhanov, V. F., 1956, New Soviet discoveries in the Arctic: Moscow, Foreign Languages Publishing House, 60 p.

Bushnell, V. C., ed., 1959a, Scientific studies at Fletcher's Ice Island, T-3, 1952–1955: Bedford, Massachusetts, Airforce Cambridge Research Center Geophysical Research Paper 63, Part I, AFCRC-tr-59-232, no. 1, 219 p.; Part II, AFCRC-tr-59-232, no. 2, 117 p.; Part III, AFCRC-tr-59-232, no. 3, 114 p.

——, ed., 1959b, Proceedings, 2nd Annual Arctic Planning Session, October 1959: Bedford, Massachusetts, U.S. Air Force Cambridge Research Center Geophysics Research Note 29, 172 p.

Cabaniss, G. H., ed., 1962, Geophysical data from U.S. Arctic Drifting Stations, 1957–1960: U.S. Air Force Cambridge Research Laboratories Research Note AFCRL-62-683, 234 p.

Carey, S. W., 1958, A tectonic approach to continental drift, in Carey, S. W., ed., Continental drift; A symposium: Hobart, Tasmania University, p. 177–355.

Carsola, A. J., Fisher, R. L., Shipek, C. J., and Shumway, G., 1961, Bathymetry of the Beaufort Sea, in Raasch, G. O., ed., Geology of the Arctic, Vol. 1: Toronto, Ontario, University of Toronto Press, p. 678–689.

Chevallier, R., 1984, The Greco-Roman conception of the North from Pytheas to Tacitus: Arctic, v. 37, no. 4, p. 341–346.

Clark, D. L., 1974, Late Mesozoic and early Cenozoic sediment cores from the Arctic Ocean: Geology, v. 2, p. 41–44.

Clark, D. L., Whitman, R. R., Morgan, K. A., and Mackay, S. D., 1980, Stratigraphy and glacial-marine sediments of the Amerasia Basin, central Arctic Ocean: Geological Society of America Special Paper 181, 57 p.

Coles, R. L., 1985, Magsat scalar magnetic anomalies at northern high latitudes: Journal of Geophysical Research, v. 90, p. 2576–2582.

Coles, R. L., Hannaford, W., and Haines, G. V., 1978, Magnetic anomalies and the evolution of the Arctic: Arctic Geophysical Review, v. 45, no. 4, p. 51–56.

Committee on Polar Research, 1970, Geology and solid-earth geophysics of the polar regions, in Polar research; A survey: U.S. National Academy of Sciences, p. 12–28.

Craig, J. D., Sherwood, K. W., and Johnson, P. P., 1985, Geologic report for the Beaufort Sea planning area, Alaska; Regional geology, petroleum geology and environmental geology: Anchorage, Alaska, U.S. Department of the Interior Mineral Management Service OCS Report MMS 85-0111, 192 p.

Crary, A. P., and Goldstein, N. E., 1957, Geophysical studies in the Arctic Ocean: Deep-Sea Research, v. 4, no. 3, p. 185–201.

Crary, A. P., Cotell, R. D., and Sexton, T. F., 1952, Preliminary report on scientific work on Fletcher's Ice Island, T-3: Arctic, v. 5, no. 4, p. 211–223.

Crombie, W. J., 1961, Preliminary results of investigations on Arctic drift station Charlie, in Raasch, G. O., ed., Geology of the Arctic, Vol. 1: Toronto, Ontario, University of Toronto Press, p. 690–708.

D'Andrea, G., Thiel, E., and Ostenso, N. A., 1962, Seismic crustal studies in the Chukchi Sea: Minneapolis, University of Minnesota, Office of Naval Research Technical Report 1, Contract N-ONR710(44), 21 p.

Dementiskaya, R. M., 1958, Structure of the Earth's crust in the Arctic: Leningrad, Institute of Geology of the Arctic Informational Bulletin 7, p. 42–49 (in Russian).

Duckworth, G. L., Baggeroer, A. B., and Jackson, H. R., 1982, Crustal structure measurements near Fram II in the Polar Abyssal Plain: Tectonophysics, v. 89, no. 1–3, p. 173–215.

Eardley, A. J., 1948, Ancient Arctica: Journal of Geology, v. 56, no. 5,

p. 409–430.

——, 1961, History of geologic thought on the origin of the Arctic Basin, in Raasch, G. O., Geology of the Arctic, Vol. 1: Toronto, Ontario, University of Toronto Press, p. 607–621.

Falk, M. W., 1984, Images of pre-discovery Alaska in the work of European cartographers: Arctic, v. 37, no. 4, p. 562–573.

Fisher, R. H., 1984, The early cartography of the Bering Strait region: Arctic, v. 37, no. 4, p. 574–589.

Fisher, R. L., Carsola, A. J., and Shumway, G., 1958, Deep-sea bathymetry north of Point Barrow: Deep-Sea Research, v. 5, no. 1, p. 1–6.

Forsyth, D. A., and Mair, J. A., 1984, Crustal structure of the Lomonosov Ridge and the Fram and Makarov Basins near the North Pole: Journal of Geophysical Research, v. 89, p. 473–481.

Forsyth, D. A., Asudeh, I., Green, A. G., and Jackson, H. R., 1986a, Crustal structure of the northern Alpha Ridge: Nature, v. 322, p. 349–352.

Forsyth, D. A., Morel-a-l'Huissier, P., Asudeh, I., and Green, A. G., 1986b, Alpha Ridge and Iceland; Product of the same plume?: Journal of Geodynamics, v. 6, p. 197–214.

Gakkel, Ya. Ya., 1958, Signs of recent submarine volcanic activity in the Lomonosov Ridge: Prioroda, v. 4, p. 87–90 (Defense Research Board translation T-296R by E. R. Hope, 1958).

Geelmuyden, H., 1901, Astronomical observations, in Nasen, F., ed., The Norwegian North Polar Expedition 1893–1896; Scientific results: Christiana, Oslo, Jacob Dybwald, 422 p.

Gordienko, P. A., and Laktionov, A. F., 1960, Principal results of the latest oceanographic research in the Arctic Basin: Izvestiya Akademiya Nauk SSSR, Geographic Series 5, p. 22–33 (translated from the Russian by E. R. Hope, for the Directorate of Information Sciences, Defense Research Board translation T-350R, 1961).

Gorshkov, S. G., ed., 1980, World ocean atlas; Vol. 3, Arctic Ocean: U.S.S.R. Ministry of Defence, Department of Navigation and Oceanography, Oxford, Pergamon Press, 203 p.

Grantz, A., and Hart, P. E., 1984, Are there large bathymetric highs near 73°N, 139°W in the Arctic Basin?, Comment on 'Acoustic backscattering from the basin and margins of the Arctic Ocean': Journal of Geophysical Research, v. 89, p. 2105–2108.

Grantz, A., and May, S. D., 1983, Rifting history and structural development of the continental margin north of Alaska, in Watkins, J. S., and Drake, C. L., eds., Studies on continental margin geology: American Association of Petroleum Geologists Memoir 34, p. 77–100.

Grantz, A., Eittreim, S. L., and Whitney, O. T., 1982, Geology and physiography of the continental margin north of Alaska and implications for the origin of the Canada Basin, in Nairn, A.E.M., Churkin, M., Jr., and Stehli, F. G., eds., The Ocean Basins and Margins; Vol. 5, The Arctic Ocean: New York, Plenum Press, p. 439–492.

Greenaway, K. R., 1983, Comments on maps of the Arctic Ocean: Arctic, v. 36, p. 372.

Greenberg, J., Hart, P. E., and Grantz, A., 1981, Bathymetric map of the continental shelf, slope, and rise of the Beaufort Sea north of Alaska: U.S. Geological Survey Miscellaneous Investigations Series Map I-1182-A, scale 1:500,000.

Gudkovich, Z. M., 1954–1955, Depth soundings, in Somov, M. M., ed., Observational data of the scientific research drifting station of 1950–1951: Leningrad, Morskoi Transport, v. 1, article 2, p. 1–28 (translated by D. Kraus, American Meteorological Society, ASTICA document AD-117135).

Hajnal, Z., 1988, Reflection survey on Hobson's Choice ice island, Arctic Ocean [abs.]: Geological Association of Canada/Mineralogical Association of Canada/Canadian Society of Petroleum Geologists Joint Annual Meeting, p. A-50.

Hall, J. K., 1970, Arctic Ocean geophysical studies; The Alpha Cordillera and Mendeleyev Ridge [Ph.D. thesis]: New York, Columbia University, 125 p.

——, 1973, Geophysical evidence for ancient sea-floor spreading from Alpha Cordillera and Mendeleyev Ridge, in Pitcher, M. G., ed., Arctic geology: American Association of Petroleum Geologists Memoir 19, p. 542–561.

Hapgood, C., 1966, Maps of the ancient sea kings; Evidence for advanced civilization in the ice age: Philadelphia, Pennsylvania, Chilton Books, 315 p.

Harris, R. A., 1905, Evidence of land near the North Pole: Washington, D.C., Report of the 8th International Geological Congress, p. 397–406.

Hayes, J. G., 1929, Robert Edwin Peary; A record of his explorations, 1886–1909: London, Richards Tomlin, 448 p.

Hatherton, T., 1986, Antarctica prior to the Antarctic Treaty; A historical perspective, in Antarctic Treaty System; An assessment: Washington, D.C., National Academy Press, p. 15–32.

Heathcote, N. H. deV., and Armitage, A., 1959, The first international polar year: Annals of the International Geophysical Year, v. 1, p. 6–100.

Heezen, B. C., and Ewing, W. M., 1961, The Mid-Oceanic Ridge and its extension through the Arctic Basin, in Raasch, G. O., ed., Geology of the Arctic: Toronto, Ontario, University of Toronto Press, v. 1, p. 622–642.

Heezen, B. C., and Tharp, M., 1975, Map of the Arctic region: New York, American Geographical Society, scale 1:5,000,000.

Herron, E. M., Dewey, J. F., and Pitman, W. C., 1974, Plate tectonics model for evolution of the Arctic: Geology, v. 2, p. 377–380.

Hill, E. R., Grantz, A., May, S. D., and Smith, M., 1984, Bathymetric map of the Chukchi Sea: U.S. Geological Survey Miscellaneous Investigations Series Map I-1182-D, scale 1:1,000,000.

Hobson, G. D., and Overton, A., 1967, A seismic section of the Sverdrup Basin, Canadian Arctic Islands, in Musgrave, A. W., ed., Seismic refraction prospecting: Menasha, Wisconsin, George Banta Company, p. 550–562.

Hobson, G. D., and Voyce, J., 1974–1987, Titles and abstracts of scientific papers supported by Polar Continental Shelf Project: Ottawa, Ontario, Department of Energy, Mines, and Resources, 1974, no. 1, 76 p.; 1975, no. 2, 68 p.; 1977, no. 3, 96 p.; 1980, no. 4, 89 p.; 1983, no. 5, 92 p.; 1985, no. 6, 79 p.; 1987, no. 7, 100 p.

Hope, E. R., 1959, Geotectonics of the Arctic Ocean and the great Arctic magnetic anomaly: Journal of Geophysical Research, v. 64, no. 4, p. 407–427.

Hunkins, K. L., 1960, Seismic studies of sea ice: Journal of Geophysical Research, v. 65, no. 10, p. 3459–3472.

——, 1961a, Seismic studies of the Arctic Ocean floor, in Raasch, G. O., ed., Geology of the Arctic, Vol. 1: Toronto, Ontario, University of Toronto Press, p. 645–665.

——, 1961b, Arctic basin seismic studies from IGY drifting station Alpha; National Academy of Science International Geophysical Year Bulletin 46: EOS Transactions of the American Geophysical Union, v. 42, no. 2, p. 239–243.

——, 1966, The Arctic Continental Shelf north of Alaska, in Poole, W. H., ed., Continental margins and island arcs: Geological Survey of Canada Paper 66-15, p. 197–205.

Hunkins, K. L., and Tiemann, W., 1977, Geophysical data summary for Fletcher's Ice Island (T-3), May 1962–October 1974: Washington, D.C., Office of Naval Research Technical Report CU-1-77, 219 p.

Hunkins, K. L., Herron, T., Kutschale, H. W., and Peter, G., 1962, Geophysical studies of the Chukchi Cap, Arctic Ocean: Journal of Geophysical Research, v. 67, no. 1, p. 235–247.

Hunkins, K. L., Kristoffersen, Y., Johnson, G. L., and Heiberg, A., 1979, Fram 1 expedition: EOS Transactions of the American Geophysical Union, v. 60, no. 52, p. 1043–1044.

Jackson, H. R., 1986, Ice island lab shows petroleum potential: GEOS, v. 15, p. 1–3.

Jackson, H. R., Mudie, P. J., and Blasco, S. M., eds., 1985, Initial geological report on CESAR, the Canadian Expedition to study the Alpha Ridge, Arctic Ocean: Geological Survey of Canada Paper 84-22, p. 19–23.

Jeffries, M. O., and Serson, H., 1983, Recent changes at the front of Ward Hunt Ice Shelf, Ellesmere Island, NWT: Arctic, v. 36, p. 289–290.

Jessop, A. M., Hobard, M. A., and Slater, J. G., 1976, The world heat flow data collection, 1975: Ottawa, Ontario, Department of Energy, Mines and Resources, Earth Physics Branch Geothermal Series no. 5, 125 p.

Johannessen, O. M., 1987, MIZEX, the Marginal Ice Zone Experiment: International Union of Geodesy and Geophysics 19th General Assembly Abstracts, v. 1, p. 140.

Johnson, G. L., 1983, The FRAM expeditions; Arctic Ocean studies from floating ice, 1979–82: Polar Record, v. 21, no. 135, p. 583–589.

Johnson, G. L., Monahan, D., Grolie, G., and Sobzak, L. W., 1979, General bathymetric chart of the ocean (GEBCO): Ottawa, Ontario, Canadian Hydrographic Service Chart 5.17, scale 1:6,000,000 at 75°N.

Kane, E. K., 1856, Arctic explorations—The second Grinnell Expedition in search of Sir John Franklin, 1853, 1854, 1855: Philadelphia, Childs and Peterson, v. 1, 464 p., v. 2, 457 p.

Karasik, A. M., 1973, Anomalous magnetic field of the Eurasian Basin of the Arctic Ocean: Moscow, Akademiya Nauk SSSR Doklady, v. 211, p. 86–89 (in Russian).

—— , 1974, The Eurasia Basin of the Arctic Ocean from the standpoint of plate tectonics, in Problems of the geology of the polar regions: Leningrad, Nedra Publishers, p. 23–31 (in Russian).

Keating, B., 1970, The hard death of Anian, in Keating, B., The Northwest Passage; From the Mathew to the Manhattan: Chicago, Illinois, Rand McNally and Company, p. 51–67.

King, E. R., and Zietz, I., 1966, Magnetic data on the structure of the central Arctic region: Geological Society of America Bulletin, v. 77, p. 619–646.

Kirwan, L. P., 1959, The white road; A survey of polar exploration: London, Hollis and Carter, 374 p.

Kiselev, Yu. G., ed., 1986, Crustal geology of the Arctic BAsin: Moscow, Nedra Publishers, 224 p. (in Russian). (Being translated into English by Translation Bureau, Multilingual Services Division, Secretary of State, Ottawa.)

Koenig, L. S., Greenaway, K. R., Dunbar, M. I., and Hattersley-Smith, G., 1952, Arctic ice islands: Arctic, v. 5, p. 67–103.

Kristoffersen, Y., 1982, The Nansen Ridge, Arctic Ocean: Some geophysical observations of the rift valley at slow spreading rate: Tectonophysics, v. 89, p. 161–172.

Kristoffersen, Y., Milliman, J. D., and Ellis, J. P., 1984, Unconsolidated sediments and shallow structure of the northern Barents Sea: Norsk Polarinstitutt Skrifter no. 180, p. 25–39.

Kutschale, H. W., 1966, Arctic Ocean geophysical studies; The southern half of the Siberia Basin: Geophysics, v. 31, no. 4, p. 683–710.

Lachenbruch, A. H., and Marshall, B. V., 1966, Heat flow through the Arctic Ocean floor; The Canada Basin–Alpha Rise boundary: Journal of Geophysical Research, v. 71, no. 4, p. 1223–1248.

—— , 1968, Heat-flow investigations from drifting stations, in Sater, J. E., coordinator, Arctic drifting stations: Washington, D.C., Arctic Institute of North America, p. 395–417.

—— , 1969, Heat flow in the Arctic: Arctic, v. 22, no. 3, p. 300–311.

Laktionov, A. F., 1959, Bottom topography of the Greenland Sea in the region of Nansen's Sill: Moscow, Priroda, v. 10, p. 95–97 (in Russian; translated by E. R. Hope, Defence Research Board Translation T333R, 5 p.).

Lewis, E. L., and Perkins, R. G., 1983, Supercooling and energy exchange near the Arctic Ocean surface. Journal of Geophysical Research, v. 88, p. 7681–7685.

Lillestrand, R. L., and Weber, J. R., 1974, Plumbline deflection near the North Pole: Journal of Geophysical Research, v. 72, no. 23, p. 3347–3352.

Lillestrand, R. L., Grosch, C. B., and Vanelli, B. D., 1967, Interim technical report on astronavigation during Dominion Observatory polar research project: Minneapolis, Minnesota, Control Data Corporation Technical Report R.D. 1023, 138 p.

Linden, N. A., 1959, Seismic chart of the Arctic 1959 seismological and glaciological researches during the IGY, no. 2: Moscow, Academy of Sciences of the U.S.S.R., p. 7–17 (in Russian).

Lliboutry, L., 1984, Forum; Antarctic ice cover: EOS Transactions of the American Geophysical Union, v. 65, p. 1226.

Lubimova, Ye. A., Tomara, G. A., and Aleksandrov, A. L., 1969a, Heat flux through the floor of the Artic Basin in the region of the Lomonosov Ridge: Akademiya Nauk SSSR Doklady, v. 184, p. 403–405 (in Russian; translated by E. R. Hope, Defence Research Board Translation T 518 R, 1959).

Lubimova, Ye. A., Tomara, G. A., Demenitskaya, R. M., and Karasik, A. M., 1969b, Measurement of heat flow across the Arctic Ocean floor in the vicinity of the median Gakkel Ridge: Akademiya Nauk SSSR Doklady, v. 186, p. 1318–1321 (in Russian; American Geological Institute translation 186, p. 22–24).

Maas, O., 1984, Lithostratigraphy and clay mineralogy of the CESAR cores, central Arctic Ocean [B.Sc. thesis]: Kingston, Ontario, Queen's University, 55 p.

Mair, J. A., and Forsyth, D. A., 1982, Crustal structures of the Canada Basin near Alaska, the Lomonosov Ridge, and adjoining basins near the North Pole: Tectonophysics, v. 89, no. 1–3, p. 239–253.

Mair, J. A., and Lyons, J. A., 1981, Crustal structure and velocity anisostrophy beneath the Beaufort Sea: Canadian Journal of Earth Sciences, v. 18, no. 4, p. 724–741.

Manley, T. O., Codispoti, L. A., Hunkins, K. L., Jackson, H. R., Jones, E. P., Lee, V. E., Moore, S., Morison, J. H., Packard, T. T., and Wadhams, P., 1982, The FRAM 3 expedition: EOS Transactions of the American Geophysical Union, v. 63, no. 35, p. 627–636.

Markham, C. R., 1881, The voyages of William Baffin: London, Haklyut Society, 254 p.

McLaren, A. S., 1982, Exploration under the Arctic ice—Submarine surveys of the polar regions: Explorer's Journal, v. 60, p. 34–39.

Meriot, C., 1984, The Saami People from the time of the Voyage of Ottar to Thomas von Western: Arctic, v. 37, p. 373–384.

Milne, A. R., 1966, A seismic refraction measurement in the Beaufort Sea: Seismological Society of America Bulletin, v. 56, p. 775–779.

Milton, D. J., 1984, Forum; Antarctic ice cover: EOS Transactions of the American Geophysical Union, v. 65, no. 51, p. 1226.

Minicucci, D. A., and Clark, D. L., 1983, A late Cenozoic stratigraphy for glacial-marine sediments of the eastern Alpha Cordillera, central Arctic Ocean, in Molina, B. F., ed., Glacial-marine sedimentation: New York, Plenum Publishing Corporation, p. 331–365.

Mohn, H., 1905, Meterology, in Nansen, F., ed., The Norwegian North Polar Expedition 1893–1896; Vol. 6, part 17, Scientific results: Christiania, Oslo, Jacob Dybwal, 659 p.

Monahan, D., 1979, Comment on 'Bathymetry of the Arctic Ocean north of 85° latitude': Tectonophysics, v. 60, p. 293–302.

Mudie, P. J., and Blasco, S. M., 1985, Lithostratigraphy of the CESAR cores, in Jackson, H. R., Mudie, P. J., and Blasco, S. M., eds., Initial geological report on CESAR, the Canadian expedition to study the Alpha Ridge, Arctic Ocean: Geological Survey of Canada Paper 84-22, p. 59–99.

Mudie, P. J., Mosher, D. C., Van Wagoner, N. A., Aksu, A. E., and Macko, S. A., 1985, Ice island sampling and investigation of sediments: Ice Island Sampling and Investigation of Sediment Program (ISIS) Field Report 1985, 46 p.

Nansen, F., 1897, Farthest North; Being the record of a voyage of exploration of the ship *Fram* 1893–1896: Westminster, Archibald Constable and Company, v. 1, 510 p.; v. 2, 671 p.

—— , 1911, In northern mists; Arctic exploration in early times: London, Heinemann, v. 1, 383 p.; v. 2, 415 p.

Nares, G., 1876, Captain Nares' report, communicated by the Lords Commissioners of the Admiralty, October 27th: Nature, v. 15, p. 24–28.

—— , 1878, Narrative of a voyage to the Polar Sea during 1875–76 in H.M.S. *Alert* and *Discovery*, with notes on the natural history: London, Low, Marston, Searle, and Rivington, v. 1, 395 p.; v. 2, 378 p.

Niblett, E. R., Kurtz, R. D., and Michaud, C., 1987, Magnetotelluric measurements over the Alpha Ridge: Physics of the Earth and Planetary Interiors, v. 45, p. 101–118.

Nordenskjold, A. E., 1882, The voyage of the *Vega* around Asia and Europe with a historical review of previous journeys along the north coast of the old world: New York, Macmillan and Company. Translated by Alexander Leslie. 756 p.

—— , 1889, Facsimile-atlas to the early history of cartography: Stockholm, Norstedt, 121 p.

Norsk Videnskaps-Akademi, 1907–1919, Report of the second Norwegian Arctic Expedition in the *Fram* 1898–1902: Norsk Videnskaps-Akademi, issued in

36 numbers.

Office of Naval Research, 1984, Arctic marginal ice zone experiment (MIZEX): Naval Research Review, v. 36, p. 22–27.

Oliver, J., Ewing, W. M., and Press, F., 1955, Crustal structure of the Arctic regions from the Lg phase: Geological Society of America Bulletin, v. 66, p. 1063–1074.

Ostenso, N. A., 1962, Geophysical investigations of the Arctic ocean basin: Madison, University of Wisconsin Polar Research Center Research Report 62-44, 124 p.

——, 1963, Physiography of the Arctic Ocean Basin, in Proceedings of the 13th Alaskan Science Conference, Alaska Division: American Association for the Advancement of Science, p. 92–114.

——, 1968a, A gravity survey of the Chukchi Sea region and its bearing on westward extension of structures in northern Alaska: Geological Society of America Bulletin, v. 79, p. 241–254.

——, 1968b, Geophysical studies in the Greenland Sea: Geological Society of America Bulletin, v. 79, p. 107–132.

Ostenso, N. A., and Wold, R. J., 1977, A seismic and gravity profile across the Arctic Basin: Tectonophysics, v. 37, no. 1–3, p. 1–24.

Overton, A., 1970, Seismic refraction surveys, western Queen Elizabeth Islands and polar continental margin: Canadian Journal of Earth Sciences, v. 7, no. 5, p. 346–365.

Papanin, I. D., 1946, Life on an ice floe: London, Hutchinson and Company, 240 p.

Pelletier, B. R., 1970, Earth science studies in marine waters, 1970: Bedford Institute Biennial Review 1969/70, p. 11–24.

——, ed., 1984, Marine science atlas of the Beaufort Sea: Geological Survey of Canada Miscellaneous Report 38, 27 maps, various scales.

Pelletier, B. R., and Shearer, J. M., 1972, Sea bottom scouring in the Beaufort Sea of the Arctic Ocean, in Marine geology and geophysics: Proceedings of the International Geological Congress, section 8, p. 251–261.

Perkins, R. G., and Lewis, E. L., 1984, Mixing in the West Spitzbergen Current: Journal of Physical Oceanography, v. 14, p. 1315–1325.

Perry, R. K., Fleming, H. S., Weber, J. R., Kristoffersen, Y., Hall, J. K., Grantz, A., Johnson, G. L., Cherkis, N. Z., and Larsen, B., 1986, Bathymetry of the Arctic Ocean: Washington, D.C., Naval Research Laboratory Acoustics Division, scale 1:4,704,075 at latitude 78°N.

Plouff, D., Keller, G. V., Frischknecht, F. C., and Wahl, R. R., 1961, Geophysical studies of IGY drifting station Bravo, T-3, 1958–1959, in Raasch, G. O., ed., Geology of the Arctic: Toronto, Ontario, University of Toronto Press, p. 709–716.

Purchas, S., 1625, Purchas; His pilgrimes, contayning a history of the world in sea voyages and lande travells by Englishmen and others: London, 14 volumes. (Reprinted 1906 by Maclehose, University of Glasgow.)

Quam, L. O., 1966, Arctic Basin research: Naval Research Reviews, v. 19, no. 10, p. 1.

Raisz, E., 1948, General Cartography, 2nd ed.: New York, McGraw-Hill Book Company, 354 p.

Rey, L., 1982, The Arctic Ocean; A polar Mediterranean, in Rey, L., ed., The Arctic Ocean; The hydrographic environment and the fate of pollutants: London, Macmillan, 515 p.

Rey, L., Upton, C. R., and Falk, M., eds., 1984, Unveiling the Arctic: Anchorage, University of Alaska Press, 292 p. (Reprinted in Arctic, v. 37, no. 4, p. 321–613.)

Ritchie, G. S., 1969, North polar chart: London, Her Majesty's Stationery Office, Hydrographic Chart 4006, scale 1:7,551,000 at 90°N.

Roots, E. F., 1966, The northern margin of North America; A progress report on investigations and problems, in Continental margins and island arcs: Geological Survey of Canada Paper 66-15, p. 188–190.

——, 1968, Canadian polar continental shelf project, 1966: Polar Record, v. 14, p. 192–194.

——, 1969, Arctic margin of Canada: American Association of Petroleum Geologists Bulletin, v. 53, p. 739.

——, 1982, Anniversaries of Arctic investigations; Some background and consequences: Transactions of the Royal Society of Canada, ser. 4, v. 20, p. 373–390.

——, 1986a, International and regional cooperation in Arctic science; A changing situation: Muskox, v. 34, p. 9–28.

——, 1986b, Exclusive economic zones; A brief sketch of historical development and current issues, in Exclusive economic zones; Advances in underwater technology: Ocean Science and Offshore Engineering, v. 8, p. 5–13.

——, chairman, 1987, Canada and polar science: Ottawa, Ontario, Canadian Department of Indian Affairs and Northern Development, 129 p.

Ross, John, 1819, A voyage of discovery, made under the orders of the Admiralty, in his Majesty's ships Isabella and Alexander for the purpose of exploring Baffin Bay, and inquiring into the possibility of a Northwest Passage: London, Murray, 425 p.

Royal Society, 1782, Minutes: Royal Society of London, v. 6 (1769–1782).

Sabine, E., 1819, Observations on the dip and variation of the magnetic needle, and on the intensity of the magnetic force; Made during the late voyage in search of a Northwest Passage: Philosophical Transactions of the Royal Society of London, p. 132–144.

——, 1821, An account of experiments to determine the acceleration of the pendulum in different latitudes: Philosophical Transactions of the Royal Society of London, p. 163–190.

——, 1863, Results of the hourly observations of the magnetic declination made by Sir Francis Leopold McClintock, and the officers of the yacht Fox, at Port Kennedy, in the Arctic Sea, in the winter of 1858–39; and a comparison of these results with those obtained by Captain Rochfort Maquire, in 1852, 1853, and 1854, at Point Barrow: Philosophical Transactions of the Royal Society of London, p. 649–663.

Saks, V. N., Belov, N. A., and Lapina, N. N., 1955, Present concepts of the geology of the central Arctic: Priroda, v. 7, p. 13–22 (in Russian; translated by E. R. Hope, Defence Research Board Translation T196R, 11 p.).

Saladin d'Anglure, B., 1980, Le syndrome chinois de l'Europe nordique ou la demensure de l'Amerasie entre le temps de l'Astrolabe (1480) et l'espace du chronometre (1780): l'Ethnographie, v. 76, p. 81–82.

——, 1984, The route to China; Northern Europe's Arctic delusions: Arctic, v. 37, no. 4, p. 446–452.

Savelle, J. M., and Holland, C., 1987, John Ross and Bellot Strait; Personality versus discovery: Polar Record, v. 23, p. 411–417.

Savours, A., 1984, A very interesting point in geography; The 1773 Phipps expedition towards the North Pole: Arctic, v. 37, no. 4, p. 402–428.

Schei, P. E., 1903, Summary of geological results (of the Norwegian Polar Expedition in the Fram 1898–1902): Geographical Journal, v. 22, p. 55–65.

Schilder, G., 1984, Development and achievements of Dutch northern and Arctic cartography in the sixteenth and seventeenth centuries: Arctic, v. 37, p. 493–514.

Schiötz, O. E., 1901, Results of the pendulum observations and some remarks on the constitution of the earth's crust, in Nasen, F., ed., The Norwegian North Polar Expedition 1893–1896; Vol. 2, part 8, Scientific results: Christiania, Oslo, Jacob Dybwald, p. 1–90.

Schytt, V., 1982, Ymer-80; A Swedish expedition to the Arctic Ocean: Journal of Geography, v. 149, no. 1, p. 22–28.

Schytt, V., Bostrom, K., and Hjort, C., 1981, Geoscience during the Ymer-80 expedition to the Arctic: Geologiska Foreningens i Stockholm Forhandlingar, v. 103, pt. 1, p. 1098–119.

Shearer, J. M., MacNab, R. F., Pelletier, R. B., and Smith, T. B., 1971, Submarine pingos in the Beaufort Sea: Science, v. 174, p. 816–818.

Smith, D. M., 1877, Arctic expeditions from British and foreign shores; from the earliest times to the expedition of 1875–76: Glasgow and Melbourne, Liddell, 824 p.

Smith, P. J., 1974, Plumbing at the North Pole: Nature, v. 251, no. 5477, p. 672–674.

Sobczak, L. W., 1977, Bathymetry of the Arctic Ocean north of 85°N latitude: Tectonophysics, v. 42, no. 1, p. T27–T33.

Sobczak, L. W., and Overton, A., 1984, Shallow and deep crustal structure of the western Sverdrup Basin, Arctic Canada: Canadian Journal of Earth Sciences, v. 21, no. 8, p. 902–919.

Sobczak, L. W., and Sweeney, J. F., 1978, Bathymetry of the Artic Ocean, in Sweeney, J. F., ed., Arctic geophysical review: Canadian Department of Energy, Mines and Resources, Earth Physics Branch, v. 45, no. 4, p. 7–14.

Sobczak, L. W., and Weber, J. R., 1987, Gravity and bathymetry taken along seismic refraction lines from the Canadian Ice Island during 1985 and 1986, in Current research, Part A: Geological Survey of Canada Paper 87–1A, p. 299–404.

Steen, A. S., 1901, Terrestrial magnetism, in Nansen, F., ed., The Norwegian North Polar Expedition 1893–1896; Vol. 2, part 7, Scientific results: Christiania, Oslo, Jacob Dybwald, p. 1196.

Stefansson, V., 1921, The friendly Arctic; The story of five years in polar regions: New York, Macmillan, 784 p.

Suess, E., 1904–1924, The face of the Earth (Das Antlitz der Erde): Oxford, Clarenden Press, v. 1 to 5. (Translated by H.B.C. Sollas.)

Sverdrup, O. N., 1903a, The second Norwegian Polar Expedition in the *Fram*: Scottish Geography Magazine, v. 19, p. 337–353.

—— , 1903b, The Norwegian Polar Expedition in the *Fram* 1898–1902: Geographical Journal, v. 22, p. 38–55.

—— , 1904, New land; Four years in the Arctic regions: London, New York, Longmans, Green, v. 1, 496 p., v. 2, 504 p. (Appendix, Geology, by P. E. Schei.)

Sweeney, J. F., and Weber, J. R., 1986, Progress in understanding the age and origin of the Alpha Ridge, Arctic Ocean: Journal of Geodynamics, v. 6, p. 237–244.

Sweeney, J. F., Weber, J. R., and Blasco, S. M., 1982, Continental ridges in the Arctic Ocean; LOREX constraints: Tectonophysics, v. 89, no. 1–3, p. 217–237.

Sweet, H., ed., 1883, King Alfred's Orosius: London, Early English Text Society, paper 79, 42 p.

Tailleur, I. L., 1973, Probable rift origin of Canada Basin, in Pitcher, M. G., ed., Arctic geology: American Association of Petroleum Geologists Memoir 19, p. 526–535.

Taylor, A., 1955, Geographical discovery and exploration in the Queen Elizabeth Islands: Canada, Geographic Branch Memoir 3, 172 p.

Taylor, A. E., Judge, A. S., and Allen, V., 1986, Terrestrial heat flow from Project CESAR, Alpha Ridge, Arctic Ocean: Journal of Geodynamics, v. 6, p. 137–176.

Taylor, P. T., 1978, Low-level aeromagnetic data across the western Arctic Basin: EOS Transactions of the American Geophysical Union, v. 59, p. 268–269.

Thiede, J., 1988, Scientific cruise report of Arctic Expedition ARK IV/3: Bremerhaven, Germany, Alfred Wegener Institute for Polar and Marine Research Report on Polar Research 43-88, 237 p.

Thiede, J., and ARK IV/3 Scientific Party (SS members), 1988, Breakthrough in Arctic deep-sea-research; *RV Polarstern* Expedition 1987: EOS Transactions of the American Geophysical Union, v. 69, p. 665.

Theutenberg, B. J., 1984, Mare clausum et mare liberum: Arctic, v. 37, no. 4, p. 481–492.

Thurston, D. K., and Theiss, L. A., 1987, Geologic report for the Chukchi Sea planning area, Alaska; Regional geology, petroleum geology, and environmental geology: Anchorage, Alaska, U.S. Department of the Interior Mineral Management Service OCS Report MMS 87-0046, 193 p.

Tiemann, W., Ardai, J., Allen, B., and Manley, T. O., 1982, Geophysical data from drifting ice stations FRAM IV and Tristen: Palisades, New York, Lamont-Doherty Geological Observatory Technical Report LDGO-82-3, 99 p.

Tomara, G. A., 1973, The analysis of records of the geothermal gradient on the floor of the Arctic Basin, in Volkavich, V. E., and Lubimova, E. A., eds., Heat flows from the crust and upper mantle of the Earth; Results of researches on the International Geophysical Project: Moscow, Nauka, v. 12, p. 145–149 (in Russian).

Treshnikov, A. F., 1966, At the poles of the Earth: Moscow, Sovetskaya Rossiya Publishing House (translated by Secretary of State Translation Bureau no. 123842, 30 p.).

Umbgrove, J.H.F., 1947, The pulse of the Earth: The Hague, Martinus Nijhoff, 358 p.

Untersteiner, N., 1979, A review of the AIDJEX project, 1970–77: Polar Record, v. 19, no. 121, p. 363–367.

Van Wagoner, N. A., Williamson, M. C., Robinson, P. T., and Gibson, I., 1986, First samples of acoustic basement recovered from the Alpha Ridge, Arctic Ocean: Journal of Geodynamics, v. 6, p. 177–196.

Vogt, P. R., and Ostenso, N., 1970, Magnetic and gravity profiles across the Alpha Cordillera and their relation to Arctic sea-floor spreading: Journal of Geophysical Research, v. 75, p. 4925–4937.

Vogt, P. R., Taylor, P. T., Kovacs, L. C., and Johnson, G. L., 1979, Detailed aeromagnetic investigation of the Arctic Basin: Journal of Geophysical Research, v. 84, p. 1071–1089.

—— , 1982, The Canada Basin; Aeromagnetic constraints on structure and evolution: Tectonophysics, v. 89, p. 295–336.

Wagner, H. R., 1931, Apocryphal voyages to the northwest coast of America: Proceedings of the American Antiquarian Society, n.s. 41, p. 190–218.

Wallis, H., 1984, England's search for the northern passages in the sixteenth and early seventeenth centuries: Arctic, v. 37, no. 4, p. 453–472.

Weber, J. R., 1979, The Lomonosov Ridge Experiment: LOREX 79: EOS Transactions of the American Geophysical Union, v. 60, no. 42, p. 715–720.

—— , 1983, Maps of the Arctic Basin sea floor; A history of bathymetry and its interpretation: Arctic, v. 36, no. 2, p. 121–142.

—— , 1986, The Alpha Ridge; Gravity, seismic, and magnetic evidence for a homogenous, mafic crust: Journal of Geodynamics, v. 6, p. 117–136.

—— , 1987, Maps of the Arctic Basin sea floor; Part 2, Bathymetry and gravity of the Alpha Ridge; The 1983 CESAR Expedition: Arctic, v. 40, p. 1–15.

Weber, J. R., and Lillestrand, R. L., 1971, Measurement of tilt of a frozen sea: Nature, v. 229, p. 550–551.

Weber, J. R., and Sweeney, J. F., 1977, The Lomonosov Ridge Experiment; A proposal for the study of the Lomonosov Ridge: Ottawa, Ontario, Canadian Department of Energy, Mines and Resources, Earth Physics Branch Internal Report, 46 p.

—— , 1985, Reinterpretation of morphology and crustal structure in the central Arctic Basin: Journal of Geophysical Research, v. 90, p. 663–677.

Weber, J. R., Sweeney, J. F., and Judge, A. S., 1981, CESAR 83 Canadian Expedition to study the Alpha Ridge; A Canadian contribution to the centenary of the First International Polar Year 1882–83: Ottawa, Ontario, Canadian Department of Energy, Mines and Resources, Earth Physics Branch Internal Report 81-47, 71 p.

Weber, J. R., Forsyth, D. A., and Jackson, R. H., 1984, A geoscience program for the Canadian Arctic Ice Island Research Project: Ottawa, Ontario, Canadian Department of Energy, Mines and Resources, Earth Physics Branch Internal Report 85-26, 51 p.

Weihaupt, J. G., 1984, Historic cartographic evidence for Holocene changes in the Antarctic ice cover: EOS Transactions of the American Geophysical Union, v. 65, p. 493–501.

Wild, H., 1882, History of Weyprecht's proposal for international polar scientific research: Bern, Mitteilungen der Internationalen Polarkommission, v. 1, p. 1–12.

Wilkins, G. H., 1928, Flying the Arctic: New York, G. P. Putman and Sons, 336 p.

—— , 1931, Under the North Pole; The Wilkins-Ellsworth submarine expedition: New York, Brewer, Warren, and Putnam, 347 p.

Wilson, J. T., 1963, Hypothesis of the Earth's behaviour: Nature, v. 198, p. 925–929.

Wold, R. J., 1973, Gravity surveys of the Arctic Ocean Basin; Final Report, January 1973: Madison, University of Wisconsin Department of Geological Sciences, 222 p.

Worthington, L. V., 1953, Oceanographic results of Project Skijump I and Skijump II in the Polar Sea, 1951–1952: EOS Transactions of the American Geophysical Union, v. 34, no. 4, p. 543–551.

Yorath, C. J., and Norris, D. K., 1975, The tectonic development of the southern Beaufort Sea and its relationship to the origin of the Arctic Ocean Basin, *in* Yorath, C. J., Parker, E. R., and Glass, D. J., eds., Canada's continental margins: Canadian Society of Petroleum Geologists Memoir 4, p. 589–611.

Manuscript Accepted by the Society April 22, 1988

ACKNOWLEDGMENTS

The authors thank R. L. Christie, D. A. Forsyth, J. F. Sweeney, L. W. Sobczak, and R.A.F. Grieve (Geological Survey of Canada), G. D. Hobson (Polar Continental Shelf Project), A. Grantz (U.S. Geological Survey), N. A. Ostenso (National Oceanic and Atmospheric Administration), and K. Hunkins (Lamont-Doherty Geological Observatory) for critical review of the manuscript. Figure 2 is reproduced with acknowledgement to the Royal Library, Copenhagen. Permission from the National Archives of Canada to reproduce the maps in Figures 3 and 4 is gratefully acknowledged.

Fridtjof Nansen's vessel *Fram* in the Arctic ice, January 10, 1895.

Printed in U.S.A.

Chapter 3

Structure and dynamics of the Arctic Ocean ice cover

Norbert Untersteiner
Graduate Program in Geophysics, University of Washington, Seattle, Washington 98195

INTRODUCTION

At its maximum extent in February/March, sea ice covers about 10% of the total ocean surface in the Northern Hemisphere (Fig. 1). Except for some narrow bands along the North American and Siberian coasts, the Central Arctic Basin is ice covered throughout the year. Seasonal ice (winter only) occurs in the marginal seas: Okhotsk, Bering, Kara, Barents, Baltic, Southern Greenland, Baffin Bay–Davis Strait, Hudson's Bay, and Canadian Archipelago (Plate 1).

The physical constitution of sea ice is that of an aggregate of pieces, ranging in size from small crystals (frazil) and fragments (brash) to solid plates many kilometers in diameter and several meters thick. Winds and ocean currents keep the ice in almost perpetual motion, causing it to diverge, converge, shear, and rotate, thus maintaining its fragmented character. Where thin ice is crushed between two converging heavy floes, pressure ridges are formed with keel depths of up to several tens of meters. Diverging motion exposes the sea surface to the atmosphere and (during the cold season) induces formation of new ice.

SIGNIFICANCE

The most important effect of sea ice is that it suppresses the direct energy exchange between the atmosphere and the ocean, and influences the vertical water structure and circulation. Another feature of the large sea ice fields in both polar regions is their intrinsic positive feedback. When the dark ocean becomes ice covered, much of the incident solar radiation is reflected, thus promoting further cooling and enhancing ice formation (Budyko, 1969; Sellers, 1969; Kellogg, 1975).

The role of the Arctic in the hemispheric circulation of the ocean-atmosphere system is that of a heat sink. The mean net annual transports of energy across 60° and 70°N are directed northward (Oort, 1974). Water masses enter the Arctic Basin warmer than the return currents leaving the Arctic Basin. The seasonal cycle of freezing and melting of sea water in the Arctic Basin produces a net excess amount of ice that is transported to mid-latitudes. That excess ice represents a heat source at the arctic sea surface. In order to maintain a climatic quasi-equilibrium, the heat advected by atmosphere and ocean, and the heat of fusion associated with the positive net ice balance, is lost to space by radiation from the top of the atmosphere.

In a practical sense, sea ice is a severe impediment to human activities, as recently exemplified by the difficulty attending the extraction and transport of hydrocarbons and other natural resources from Arctic coastal regions, both onshore and offshore.

Owing to its effect on the oceanic environment, sea ice is also related to biological productivity (fisheries), especially in the marginal zones of the Bering and Barents seas and the waters around Iceland.

The significance of sea ice in geological studies may be categorized as follows:

a) As a source of moisture for snow deposition and glaciation on the surrounding continents, the central Arctic is insignificant. This is not true of the seasonally ice-covered marginal seas today, and may not have been true for the central Arctic during earlier times when there was less or no ice. However, according to recent studies (Clark and Hanson, 1983), the central Arctic has not been ice-free for at least 5 m.y., making it probable that most of the precipitation available for the nourishment of high-latitude glaciation has been derived from lower latitudes, as it is today.

b) Beach and shallow water processes may be recognized in elevated ancient beaches, thus giving evidence for the presence or absence of sea ice. For instance, ice-shove ridges several meters high have been reported at elevations up to 120 m above present sea level (Washburn, 1973). Sediment scouring by pressure-ridge keels occurs in water depths up to about 70 m (Reimnitz and others, 1984). Scour marks from sea ice seen at greater depths must originate from times of lower sea level, but so far it has not been possible to date them (Barnes and others, 1984). Signs of ice scouring in the sediments of elevated ancient beaches have not been reported.

c) The production of biogenic sediments is controlled by primary production in the upper ocean layers, which is, in turn, determined by the availability of nutrients and light. The light regime under sea ice is sensitive to ice thickness, snow cover, and the percentage area of the ice covered by (transparent) meltwater

---

Untersteiner, N., 1990, Structure and dynamics of the Arctic Ocean ice cover, *in* Grantz, A., Johnson, L., and Sweeney, J. F., eds., The Arctic Ocean region: Boulder, Colorado, Geological Society of America, The Geology of North America, v. L.

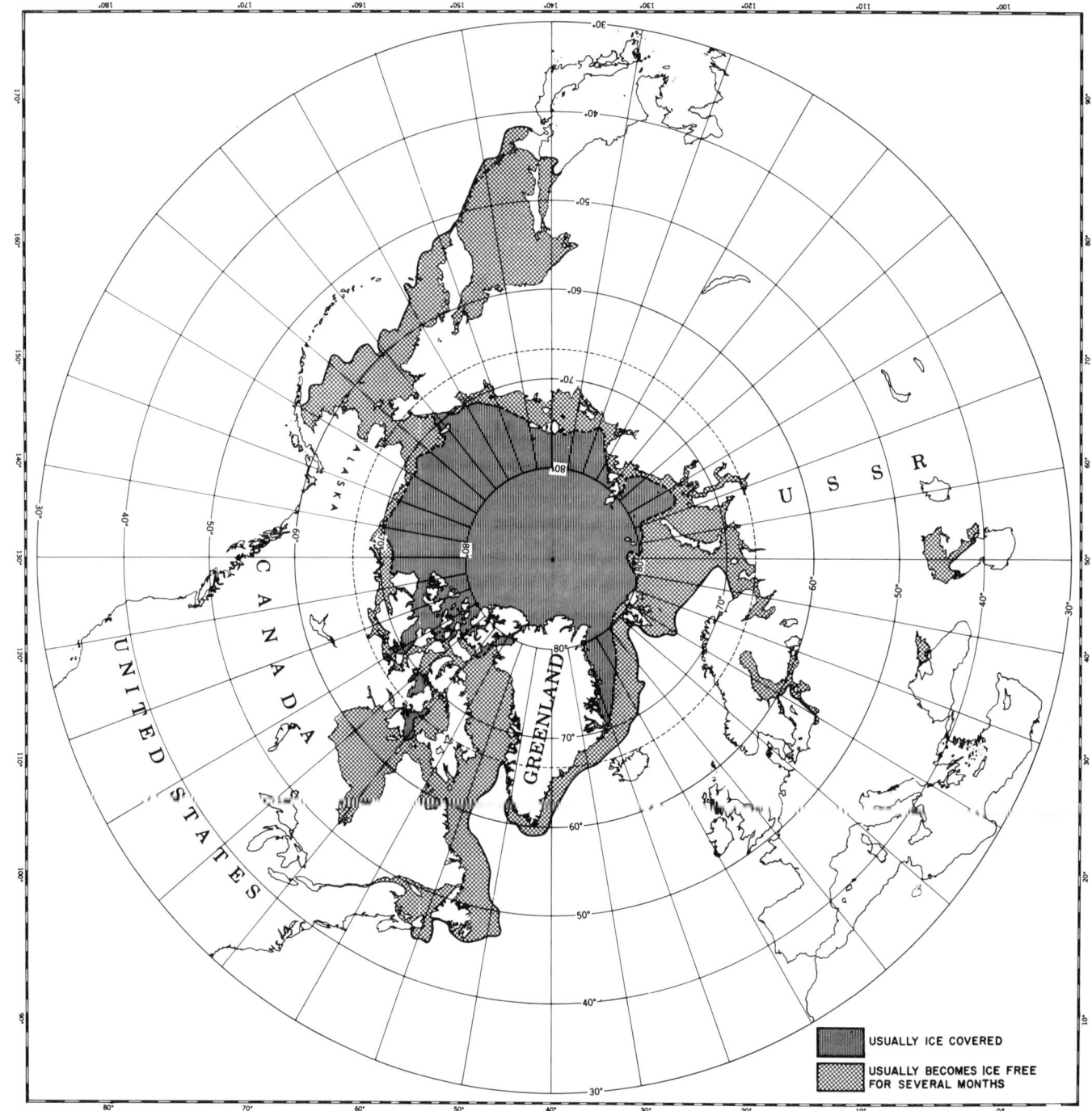

Figure 1. Average minimum (August) and maximum (February) sea ice extent in the Northern Hemisphere.

ponds during summer. Even in today's ice-ocean regime, it is not entirely clear whether the known low rate of primary production is the result of limitations to the available nutrients or the available radiant energy. The availability of nutrients, too, is influenced by the presence of sea ice. The prevailing strong pycnocline suppresses mixing and tends to restrict continental runoff to the upper ocean layer. The ice itself suppresses wind mixing and retards horizontal transport of the upper ocean. More importantly, there is no large-scale upwelling of nutrient-rich water in the Arctic Basin.

d) The most direct connection between sea ice and geology is provided by the coarse material found in Arctic Basin sediment

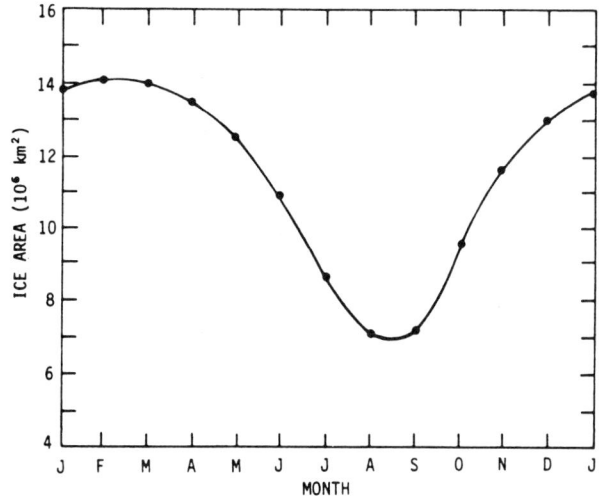

Figure 2. The normal seasonal cycle of Arctic sea ice extent. Dots are 25-year averages of area covered by ice at end of month (from Walsh and Johnson, 1979).

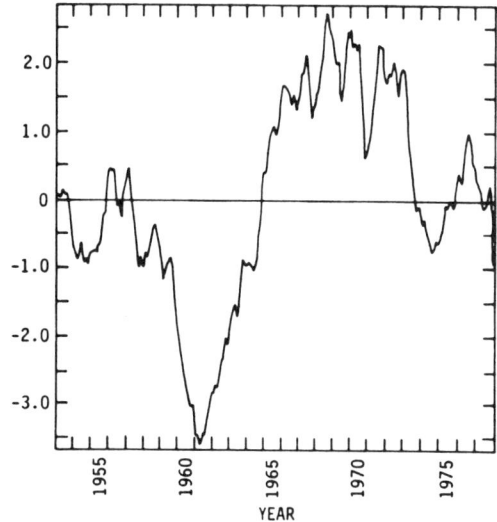

Figure 3. 24-month means of the area covered by Arctic sea ice (from Walsh and Johnson, 1979).

cores at distances from shore where the only feasible mechanism of deposition was rafting by ice, both in the past and at present. Some of that coarse material is clearly of glacial origin, i.e., rafted by ice islands from the north coast of Ellesmere Island at the present stage of land glaciation, and other coastal sources during times of more extensive glaciation. Some of the sand and gravel-size sediment may originate from beaches, where it was incorporated into shore-fast ice during winter or deposited by rivers during spring runoff, and transported out to sea after break-up. The amount of coarse material in the sediment must reflect some general relationship to ice conditions, i.e., ice extent, freeze and thaw cycle, mobility, and drift trajectories (Schwarzacher and Hunkins, 1961). Quantitative connections between climate, sea ice, and the geological record are only now being developed, and the increasing data base and sophistication of the analyses promise rapid progress in the coming decade.

ICE EXTENT

The variability of the extent of Arctic sea ice is largely the result of its large ratio of diameter to thickness, about $10^6:1$. The amount of heat stored in a layer of ice 1 m thick is less than 3% of the total incoming short-wave and long-wave radiation during the course of a year. Given the large seasonal amplitude of incoming radiation, and the general variability of the atmosphere, it is not surprising that the ice cover undergoes large seasonal as well as interannual variations, as shown in Figures 2 and 3.

In the course of an average year, the sea ice cover approximately doubles between minimum and maximum extent. According to Walsh and Johnson (1979), the standard deviation of mean monthly ice extent in individual sectors of 10 degrees longitude is about 20% in summer and 10% in winter. Since the beginning of reliable observations, longer-term deviations (several years) have amounted to about 25% of the average (Fig. 3). Greater deviations from the long-term mean are seen in individual sectors, for instance in the Greenland Sea (Fig. 4). This marginal sea is of particular interest since it is the sink for ice exported out of the Arctic Basin and includes Fram Strait, the only deep water gap through which the Arctic Ocean communicates with the North Atlantic.

According to proxy data obtained by the CLIMAP (Climatic Long-Range Interpretation, Mapping, and Prediction) project (1976), the sea ice cover, 18,000 years B.P. at its seasonal minimum extent in August, reached the shores of the British Isles and the New England States in the Atlantic sector, while in the Pacific sector the summer ice boundary remained well inside the Bering Sea.

ICE MOTION

The main features of sea ice motion in the Arctic Basin are the Beaufort Sea gyre and the transpolar drift. Their existence has been known since the late 19th century, but systematic observations began only with the era of drifting stations.

Since the inception of the Arctic Data Buoy Program in 1979 (Untersteiner and Thorndike, 1982) synoptic observations of ice drift and surface pressure have been gathered over much of the Arctic Basin, adding about 75 buoy-years to the data shown in Figure 5. Colony and Thorndike (1984) computed the overall mean velocity field shown in Figure 6. While their picture confirms earlier data of the Beaufort Sea gyre, both in terms of location and drift velocity, the transpolar drift appears to be less pronounced than it was shown in earlier studies (Gordienko, 1958). Surprisingly, the strongest ice current in Figure 6 is one

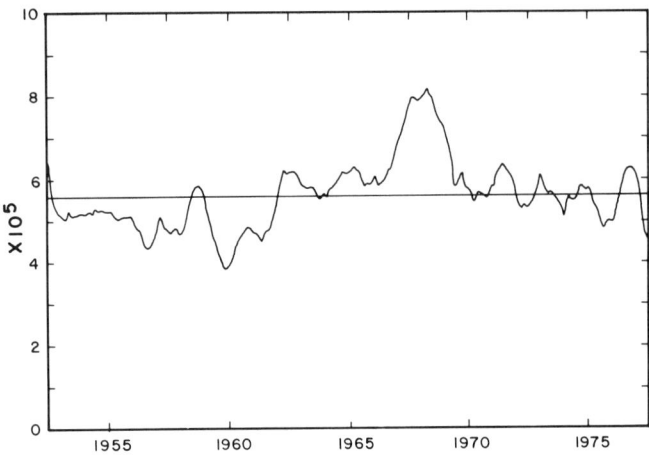

Figure 4. 12-month running means of the ice cover of the Greenland Sea in 10^5 km^2 (from Moritz, 1985).

prisingly large. To illustrate the point (and at the same time to show the large year-to-year variations of the arctic atmosphere) the mean annual surface pressure over the Arctic Basin has been plotted for the years 1979 to 1983 (Fig. 7). Note that, according to well-established dynamic principles (Zubov, 1943) the ice drifts roughly parallel to the geostrophic (frictionless) wind. In any given year, the isobars of surface pressure indicate a variable but pronounced transpolar drift. Most of the temporal variance of sea ice motion is due to variations of the air stress, which is proportional to the geostrophic wind. The standard deviation of the mean annual geostrophic wind (lower right panel in Fig. 7) is highest (1.5 m/s) over the region of the transpolar drift. A multiyear vector average of ice velocity over that region is bound to obscure the strength of the ice current as it exists at shorter time intervals.

transporting ice from the southern Beaufort Sea to the East Siberian Sea.

The apparent weakness of the transpolar drift is the result of vector averaging. In the given data set, the shortest time interval for which ice velocities are computed is one day. Taking the average over increasing time intervals yields values of decreasing variance. But even when averaged over one year, the variance is still sur-

ICE THICKNESS

The only method available for obtaining representative samples of ice thickness and thickness distribution are measurements by upward-looking sonar from nuclear-powered submarines (Lyon, 1961). Such data as have been released from the operators of these submarines provide a rough picture of ice thickness in various regions of the Arctic, but they are too sporadic to allow the establishment of any seasonal or interannual variations. As an example of a thickness distribution, Figure 8

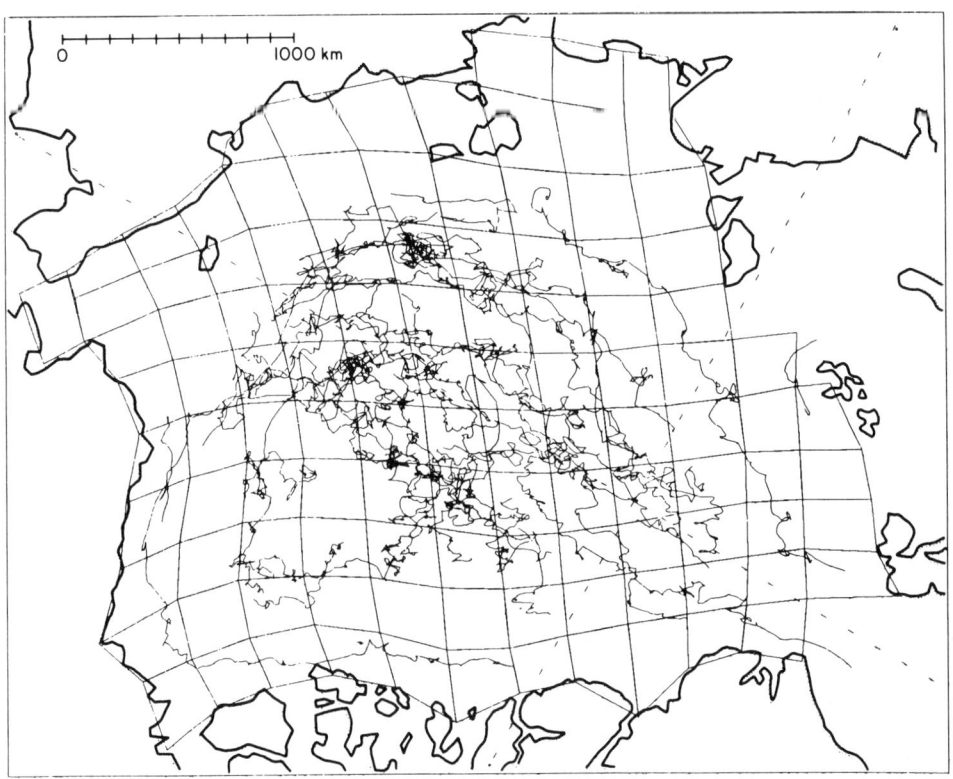

Figure 5. Drift tracks of all manned drifting stations from Nansen's FRAM expedition (1882–1983), representing a total of about 35 stations-years.

shows the probability density of ice draft in the Beaufort Sea in April 1976. The distribution is clearly bimodal, with a preponderance of multi-year ice about 3 m thick and a secondary maximum near 1 m thick, representing ice less than one year old.

The average ice thickness depicted in Figure 9 is obtained from several submarine cruises during a time span of more than 20 years, making the absolute magnitude of the mean thickness a matter of some conjecture. Especially, the ice in the Eurasian Basin may be thicker than shown by the contours. It is certain, however, that the mean ice thickness does increase from the Eurasian coast across the basin toward the north coasts of Greenland and the Canadian Arctic Islands.

ICE THERMODYNAMICS AND PROPERTIES

Sea water freezes at a temperature dependent on its salinity according to the approximate formula $T_f = -0.054 \cdot S$, if the salinity S is expressed in parts per thousand. When the water is cooled to that temperature, a layer of loose ice platelets forms at the surface. Since the crystallographic lattice of ice does not allow the inclusion of significant amounts of other molecules, these platelets are pure ice, separated by water, containing—in addition to its original salt content—the salt rejected by the freezing ice crystals. As the ice continues to freeze and solidify, some brine is extruded upward to form a thin layer of extremely high salinity typically found on freezing leads and polynyas. At thicknesses greater than 5 cm, the ice assumes a structure of vertically standing platelets or lamellae that, at the interface, are separated by thin, vertical layers of brine. As this comb-shaped interface advances downward, most of the salt is rejected but some is trapped in discrete, brine-filled pockets. The slower the growth rate, the lower the bulk ice salinity, and vice versa. At growth rates below 1 cm/day the ice salinity remains nearly constant at about five parts per thousand. For an exhaustive review of sea ice properties, see Weeks and Ackley (1982). Besides the brine pockets, sea ice contains air and vapor bubbles and inclusions of whatever organic and inorganic particles were suspended in the freezing water. But the included brine pockets exert by far the greatest influence on those ice properties of interest here. The thermodynamics of phase equilibrium dictate that the salinity of a brine pocket must attain a certain value determined by the temperature of the surrounding pure ice. Any change of the bulk sea ice temperature is accompanied by freezing or melting on the walls of the brine pocket, increasing or decreasing the brine concentration. Thus the specific heat of sea ice is composed of two parts, one associated with changing the temperature of ice and brine, and another associated with the heat of fusion involved in enlarging or reducing the size of the brine pockets. At temperatures near the freezing point, the specific heat is many times higher than that of pure ice. As sea ice approaches the melting temperature of freshwater ice, its porosity approaches 100% or, in other words, it disintegrates. In summer, porosities of 25% and more are commonly found underneath a disintegrated (granular) surface layer. This dependence of porosity on salt content and temperature has

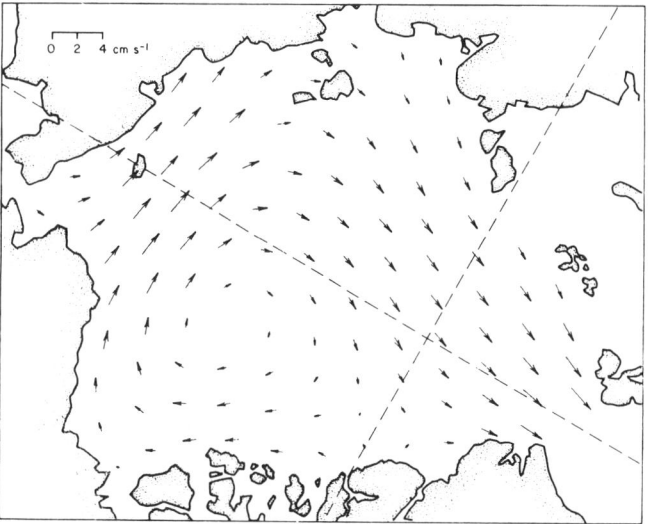

Figure 6. Mean ice velocity field in the central Arctic, based on all available data since the drift of Nansens' *Fram* (1893–1896), other drifting ships, manned stations on sea ice islands, and data buoys (totalling about 100 point years). Owing to the large number of automatic buoys air-dropped in recent years, the velocity field shown here is dominated by data obtained since early 1979 (from Colony and Thorndike, 1984).

a profound effect on all physical properties of the ice: strength, thermal conductivity, dielectric constants, and light scattering and absorption.

Under the present climatic conditions, the average annual cycle may be described as follows: In early September, temperatures begin to drop rapidly, meltwater in ponds on the ice and water in open leads between floes begins to freeze and the surface of the existing ice cools. About 80% of the annual snowfall (10–15 cm water equivalent) is deposited by early November. After that, the atmosphere becomes too cold to carry significant amounts of moisture. The accretion of ice continues until May, slowly under thick ice and more rapidly under thin ice. The ablation of snow begins in early June and that of ice in early July, and continues until late August when the cycle begins anew. Thus every year a certain amount of ice is added at the bottom and melted away at the top. Some ablation occurs also at the bottom when the amount of heat supplied by the ocean is greater than the heat conducted upward within the ice.

The whole process is controlled by the fluxes of radiative, sensible, and latent heat in the atmospheric and oceanic boundary layers adjacent to the ice. With a one-dimensional, time-dependent thermodynamic model of the ice, and using numeric values for the heat balance (Fletcher, 1965), one can calculate ice thickness and temperature. The standard case, representing present climatic conditions, is shown in Figure 10. Barring interannual fluctuations of weather and climate, the annual cycle shown repeats itself and describes an idealized equilibrium. Ablation and accretion depend on the initial ice thickness in such a way that, in the course of several years, they tend toward an equilibrium thickness with a fixed seasonal cycle, as illustrated in Figure 11.

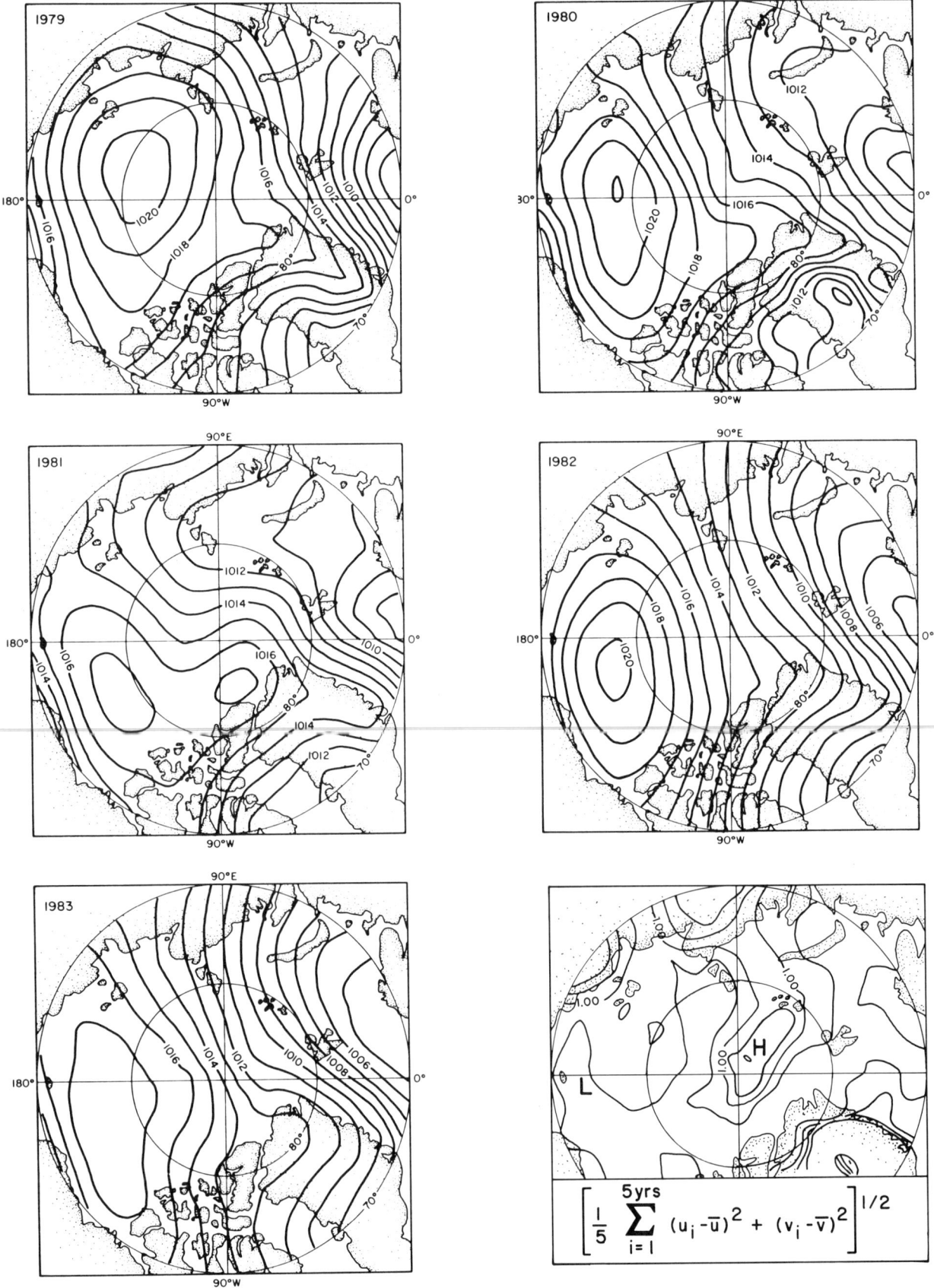

Calculations with a one-dimensional model, although highly idealized, lend themselves to a wide range of informative sensitivity studies (Fig. 12). For instance, the heat flux from the ocean is believed to be 1–2 Wm^{-2}. Doubling it would reduce the equilibrium ice thickness to one-half. Assuming no heat flux from the ocean, the thickness would double from 3 to 6 m. The influence of a varying amount of solar radiation penetrating the ice surface is less pronounced. The effect of snow cover is particularly interesting, showing little effect between zero and 80 cm, but causing the ice to thicken greatly when more snow is added, because the ice remains snow covered throughout the year and reflects most of the incoming short-wave radiation.

For studies of the large-scale ice balance it is desirable to know the age of the ice. Starting from open water in September, as much as 2 m of ice may form in one freezing season. However, growth rate is strongly modified by snow falling on the ice and insulating it from the cold atmosphere. Stipulating the climatological mean show fall (as indicated in Fig. 10) and letting a polynya surrounded by pack ice freeze, starting each first of the month from September to January, one obtains the growth curves (to 100 cm thick) shown in Figure 13. This figure demonstrates that, for instance, ice that is 1 m thick on 1 February may be either one-month or five-months old.

Another important process affecting sea ice properties is the downward migration of brine that invariably happens after the initial, salt-rich layer of ice has formed. The dominant mechanisms of this desalination are believed to be brine expulsion during periods of cooling, and flushing with nearly salt-free meltwater from the surface during the melting period. Both are related to the thermal history of an individual ice particle, schematically shown in Figure 14. If the ice undergoes the cycle shown in Figure 10, mechanically undisturbed for a number of years, then the youngest ice layer will be found at the bottom and the oldest near the top, as indicated by curve B. The thermal history of an individual parcel of ice is curve A. Both the seasonal amplitude in temperature and the maximum temperature reached in summer (and hence the maximum porosity) combine to desalinate the ice. As a result, the salinity of multiyear ice is nearly zero at the top and 5–6 per mil at the bottom. Figure 14 also illustrates how material suspended in the water and becoming incorporated in the ice will migrate toward the surface (following curve B).

As mentioned at the outset, the transmission of light through a sea ice cover is crucial for primary production and the generation of the biotic component of the ocean sediment. As long as there is snow on the ice, it can be considered virtually opaque. As

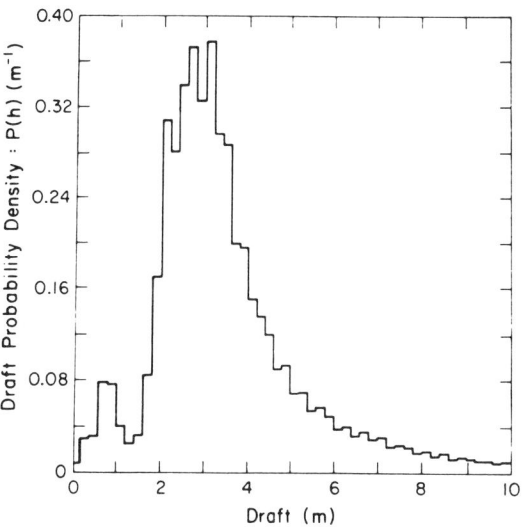

Figure 8. Distribution of ice draft expressed in probability density, observed by narrow-beam upward-looking sonar. The data were taken in April 1976 in the Beaufort Sea along a track 1400 km long (from Wadhams and Horne, 1980). All ice thicker than 4 m is the result of ridging and rafting.

Figure 7. Mean annual surface pressure (1979–1983) (in mb) from daily measurements of an average of 10 drifting data buoys. Since air stress accounts for a large part of the ice displacement, the variability of the geostrophic wind computed from these maps may be taken as an approximate measure of the variability of ice motion. The standard deviation (bottom right frame) shows a maximum over the transpolar drift, suggesting that its weak development in Figure 6 is the result of vector averaging.

indicated in Figure 10, snow melt in the central Arctic begins in early June and the snow disappears by the end of that month. Meltwater ponds form at that time, first large and shallow, covering at least 50% of the surface, and later decreasing in size (20% of area) and increasing in depth. Figure 15 depicts some of the essential information concerning the spectrum of incoming solar radiation, albedo of the ice as a function of pond coverage, and spectral extinction coefficients for various types of ice, and water (Grenfell and Maykut, 1977; Grenfell, 1979). With this information one can determine the amount and spectral composition of radiant energy transmitted by the ice and available for photosynthesis.

MODELING: DYNAMIC-THERMODYNAMIC

One basic approach to modeling sea ice that has evolved during the past several decades is as follows: While a natural sea ice field is clearly not a continuum, it can—to some degree—be treated as such, provided that the scale of spatial resolution is suitably large (usually 100 km or greater). This continuum is driven by horizontal surface tractions at the ice–air and ice–water interfaces. Vertical motions do not occur, except on a subgrid scale where mechanical compression causes the conversion from thin ice to thicker ice. There is no mechanical conversion of thick ice to thin ice (spreading of pressure ridges) except to ice of thickness zero (open water). The two-dimensional aggregate of ice floes is generally assumed to have no strength in extension and some finite strength in compression and shear, so that the local external surface tractions can be transmitted over one or more grid intervals. The composite effects of these forces result in a certain velocity field and thickness distribution, both variable in

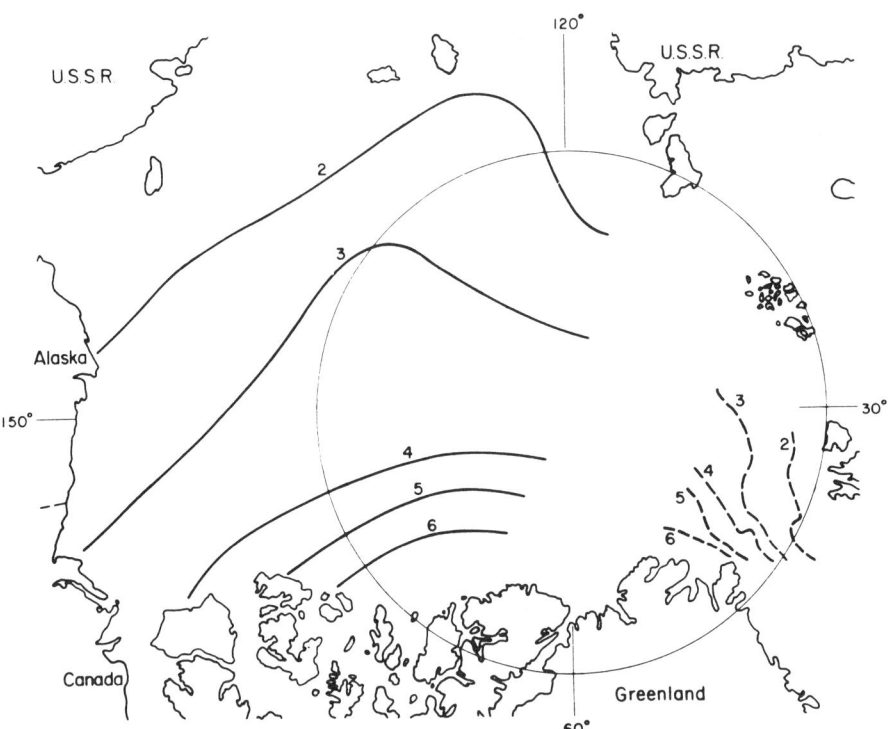

Figure 9. Average ice thickness derived from several upward-looking sonar profiles taken by nuclear submarines over a time span of more than 20 years (figure from Hibler, 1980; data from LeSchack, personal communication, 1985, and Wadhams, 1981).

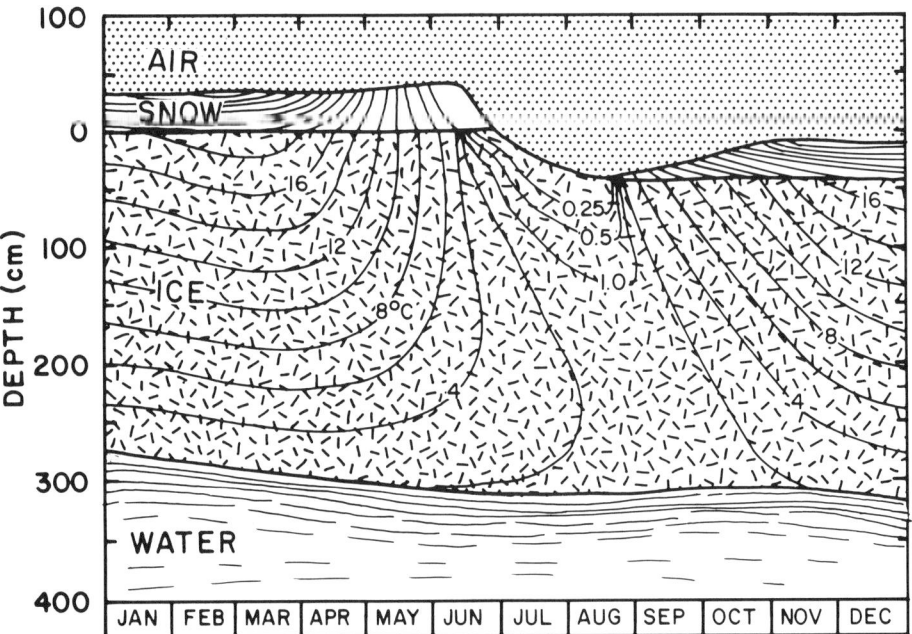

Figure 10. Predicted value of equilibrium temperature and thickness of sea ice, from Maykut and Untersteiner (1971). Isotherms are labelled in negative degrees Celsius. In this simulation, an upward oceanic heat flux of 2 Wm^{-2} is assumed, and 17% of the net short-wave radiation is allowed to pass through the ice surface (when it is snow-free). The albedo of snow-free, melting ice is taken to be 0.64. The snow cover albedos are taken to vary seasonally, as specified by Marshunova (1961). Other heat budget input at the upper boundary was taken from Fletcher (1965). To distinguish between movements of the upper and lower boundary, they are plotted without regard for hydrostatic adjustment.

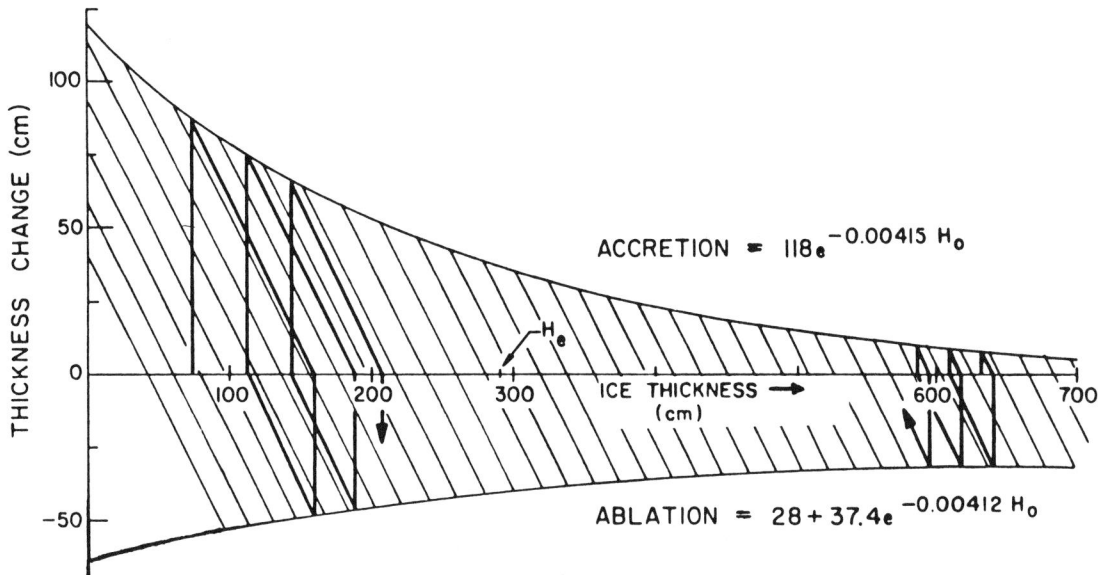

Figure 11. Nomogram of ice accretion (1 Sept.–31 May) and ablation (1 June–31 Aug.), computed from the thermodynamic model and assuming present climatic conditions. Starting from any initial ice thickness H_0 (x-axis) and following the heavy lines as shown in two examples, it is seen how the ice approaches equilibrium thickness H_e, starting from $H_o <$, or $H_o > H_e$ (after Untersteiner, 1962).

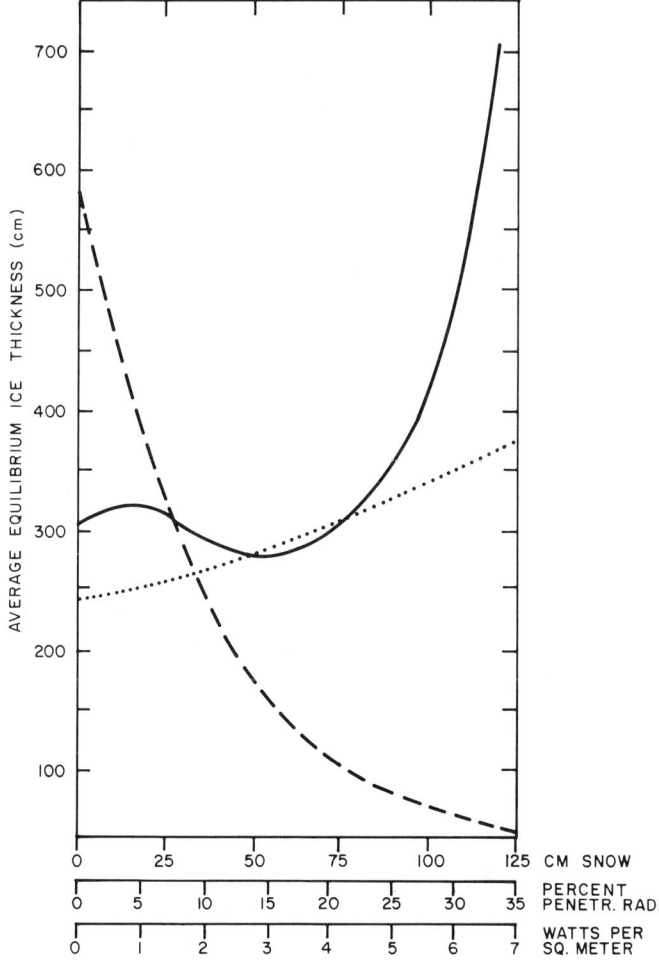

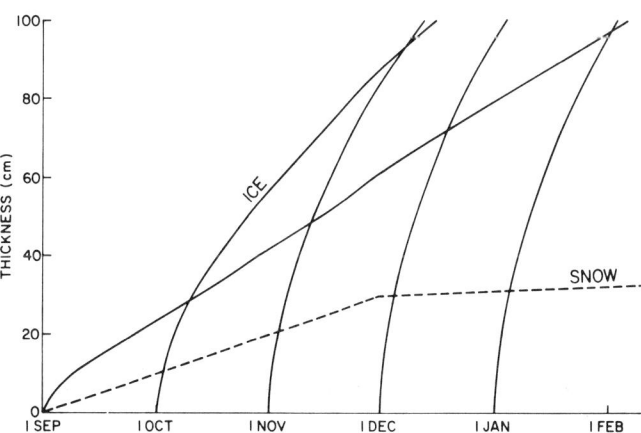

Figure 12. Annual average of the equilibrium ice thickness as a function of snow cover (solid curve), percentage of incoming solar radiation penetrating the surface (dotted curve), and heat influx from the ocean (dashed curve). In each calculation, only one parameter was allowed to vary. All others were kept constant, at the values used in calculating the standard case shown in Figure 10 (from Maykut and Untersteiner, 1971).

Figure 13. Ice thickness as a function of time, beginning on the first of each month from September to January. Snow accumulation (dashed line) is the same as the one used in the standard case thermodynamic model calculation (Fig. 10).

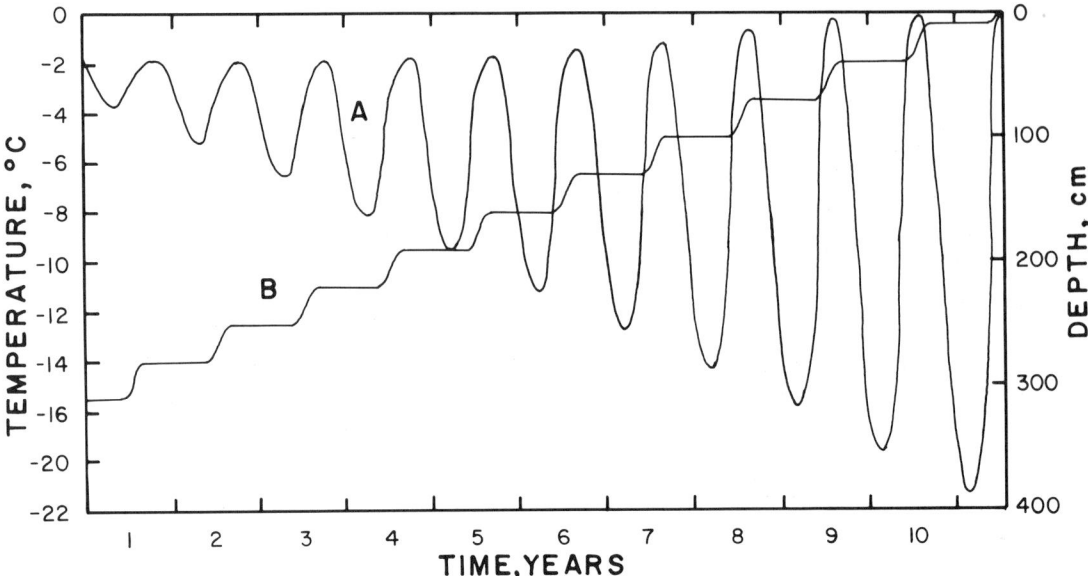

Figure 14. Thermal history of a particle of ice that formed at the bottom of 310-cm-thick ice floe (curve A), and upward migration of that particle during the 11 years of its existence (curve B), assuming the standard case equilibrium cycle shown in Figure 10 (from Untersteiner, 1964).

time. Superimposed on this are the effects of ice thermodynamics, defined as the freezing and melting of ice at both interfaces and the conduction of heat between them. These processes are controlled, in part interactively, by the overlying atmosphere and the underlying ocean. Finally, a process entirely external to this system (specified) is the addition of mass by snowfall from the atmosphere.

In summary, the ice is viewed as a continuum in motion, bounded in part by land and in part by itself (open ocean), and containing sources and sinks both within the region occupied, and along its boundaries.

For the formal representation of this system we use the traditional concepts of momentum balance, continuity, heat balance and fluxes, a constitutive equation (flow law), and a relationship peculiar to the granular structure of sea ice.

The ice velocity $\hat{u}$ in equation 1 is related to its forcing functions by the momentum equation (for a recent review see, for instance, Coon, 1980), usually stated in the form,

$$\rho h \frac{d\hat{u}}{dt} = \tau_a + \tau_w - \rho h f \hat{k} \times \hat{u} + div \sigma - \rho h g \nabla H - h \nabla P. \quad (1)$$

The term $d\hat{u}/dt$ denotes ice acceleration, τ_a and τ_w surface stresses at the top and bottom of the ice, f the Coriolis parameter, $\hat{k}$ the unit vector in the vertical, and σ the horizontal stress in the ice resulting from floe-to-floe stress transmission. The term $-\rho p g \cdot \nabla H$ is a component of the gravitational acceleration, g, along a sea surface with the slope ∇H. This slope is induced by the atmospheric pressure gradient (barometer effect) and by dynamic tilt of the sea surface. The term $-h \nabla P$ is due to the horizontal gradient of the atmospheric pressure at the surface. The surface stresses are generally taken to be proportional to a drag coefficient characterizing the roughness of the ice, and to the square of the relative velocity between ice-air and ice-water.

The term $div\ \sigma$, or internal ice stress, has been the object of intense study. It fundamentally differs from all other terms used in equation (1) insofar as its direct observation is problematic—difficult on small scales and perhaps impossible on large scales.

The conservation of mass is stated (Nikiforov, 1957; Untersteiner, 1963) as the change in time of the volume of ice present in a given area in terms of ice advection and sources (or sinks).

$$\frac{\partial(\rho h)}{\partial t} = -\hat{u} \cdot grad(\rho h) - \rho h \nabla \cdot \hat{u} + \frac{1}{q} Q, \quad (2)$$

where ρ and h denote density and thickness, $\hat{u}$ the velocity, q the heat of fusion, and Q that part of the heat balance available for freezing or melting ice. This term lends itself most readily to direct observations (Zubov, 1943; Untersteiner, 1961; Fletcher, 1965; Vowinckel and Orvig, 1966; Doronin and Kheisin, 1975) and has, therefore, been used most widely in modeling studies (e.g., Untersteiner, 1964; Maykut and Untersteiner, 1971; Parkinson and Washington, 1979; Maykut, 1982). These studies consist, in essence, of evaluations of the last term in equation (2), which can be written in somewhat expanded form as

$$\rho q \frac{dh}{dt} = \Sigma F_s + \Sigma F_b + \int_0^h \rho c \frac{\partial T}{\partial t} dz. \quad (3)$$

ΣF_s and ΣF_b are the sums of all heat fluxes, turbulent and radiative, at the surface and at the bottom of the ice. The last term represents the change of the heat content associated with the change of ice temperature, T, in a slab of thickness $z = h$.

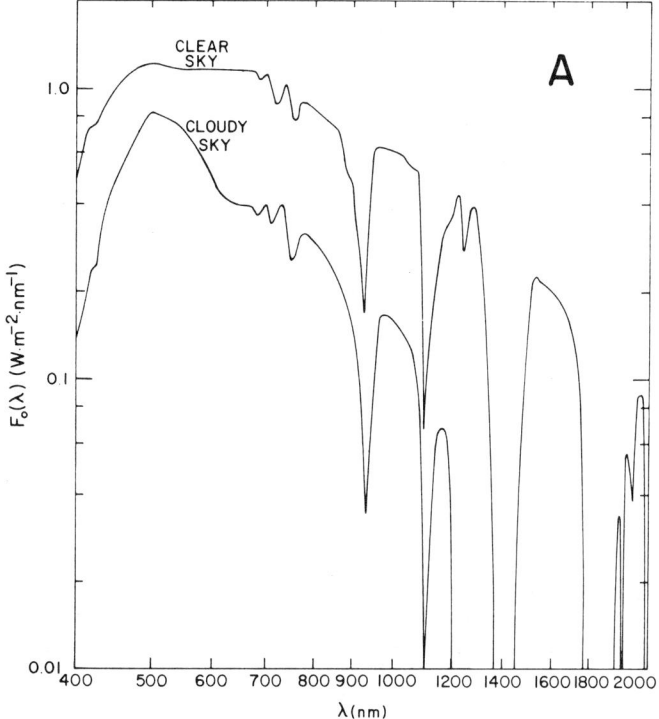
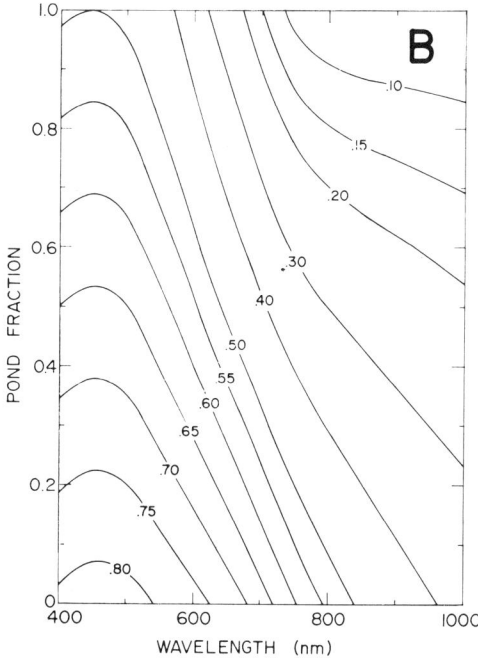
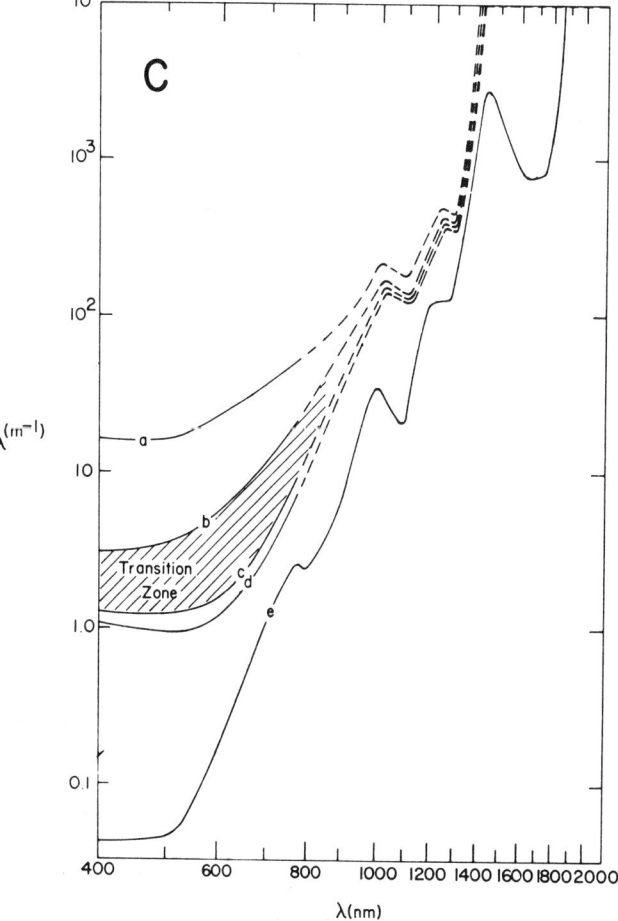

Figure 15. Panel A: Spectrum of incoming solar radiation in the Arctic under clear and cloudy sky at wavelengths between 400 and 2150 nm (from Grenfell, 1979). Panel B: Spectral albedo of multiyear ice as a function of the percentage area covered by meltwater ponds (from Grenfell and Maykut, 1977). Panel C: Spectral extinction coefficients for (a) snow, (b) white ice, scattering surface layer, (c) white ice, interior, (d) blue clear ice, and (e) water. The hatched area between (b) and (c) represents the layer of white highly scattering ice. Note that both ice and water are most transparent for the biologically important blue-green light.

The continuity equation (2) makes no statement about a relationship between the dynamic and thermodynamic terms. They are, of course, related because the ice thickness changes in time by melting and freezing as well as mechanically by ice deformation. An important step toward connecting ice dynamics and thermodynamics was taken by Thorndike and others (1975) in the formulation of an equation relating ice thickness distribution, strain rate, and growth rate:

$$\frac{\partial g}{\partial t} + \hat{u} \cdot \nabla g = -\frac{\partial}{\partial h}\left[\frac{dh}{dt} g\right] + \psi - g\,\mathrm{div}\,\hat{u}. \quad (4)$$

Here g denotes the fractional area covered by ice of a certain range in thickness. The thermodynamic growth rate dh/dt, a function of ice thickness and time, is given by equation (2). The function ψ describes the mechanical redistribution of ice thickness associated with the strain rate. Some principles of formulation for the function ψ have been established, but data available to date have not allowed the choice of a specific form.

These calculations hold great promise as more reliable data

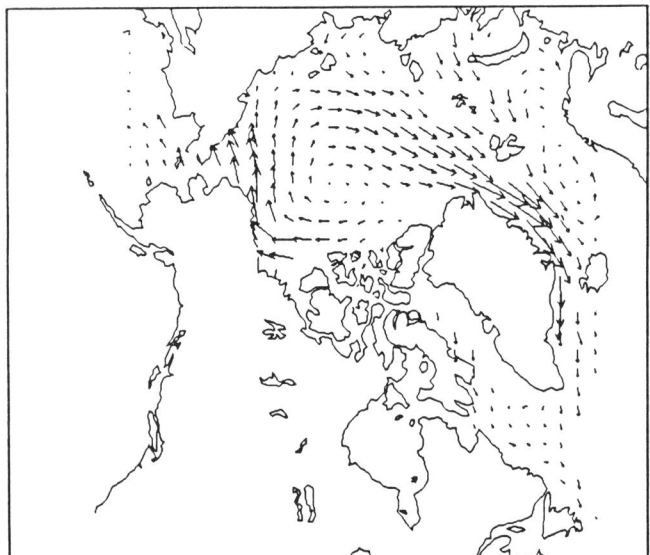

Figure 16. Computed mean ice velocity field (1951–1980) (Walsh and others, 1985). Vectors are scaled to correspond to 40% of the distance travelled in one year (in regions of perennial ice cover). For comparison with the observed velocity field see Figure 6.

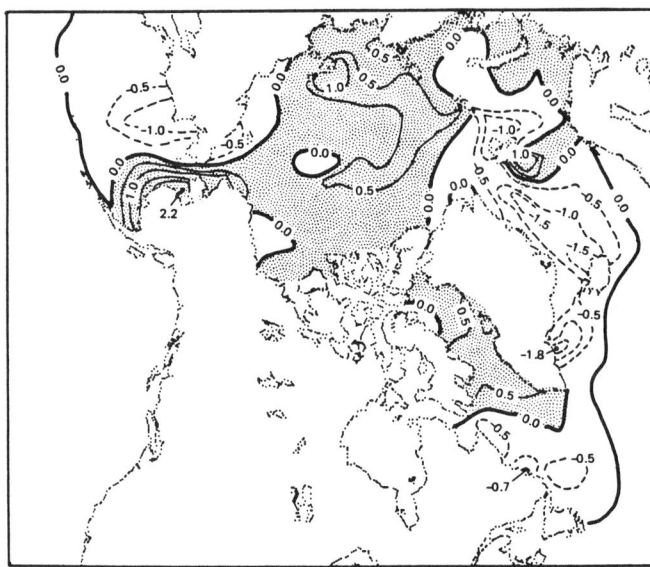

Figure 17. Distribution of ice sources and sinks, in meters per year (from Walsh and others, 1985), computed with a dynamic-thermodynamic sea ice model for the years 1951–1980. Average ice production over the central Arctic Basin is 30–40 cm/a, which equals the estimated ice export through Fram Strait of 3000 km3/a.

on the forcing functions, especially surface wind and oceanic heat flux, become available (WMO-WCRP, 1984). The ultimate goal, of course, is to develop a fully interactive model comprising atmosphere, ice, and ocean. A first step in that direction was taken by Hibler and Bryan (1984) in their study of the ice model coupled to a 14-layer ocean model, with only the atmosphere specified as an external forcing function.

As noted at the outset, equations (1) to (4) presume the ice to be a continuum. The degree to which this assumption yields useful modeling results depends on grid resolution, interpolation schemes, and various circumstances pertaining to the physical constitution of the ice. The processes most closely approximated by a continuum are the thermodynamic ones.

Calculations with a dynamic-thermodynamic model and specified external forcing functions over an entire annual cycle were first carried out by Hibler (1979). Of special interest is a recent modeling study by Walsh and others (1985), who computed Hibler's model for the years 1951 to 1980. Except for the last two years of that interval, wind forcing is, of course, derived by extrapolating coastal atmospheric pressure data into the Arctic Basin. The number used for upward heat flux in the ocean is the $2 Wm^{-2}$ that descended from the International Geophysical Year 1957–1958 (Untersteiner, 1961, 1966; Badgley, 1966) and has not been improved upon since. Even so, the calculations of Walsh and others are a significant step forward in studying the arctic air–sea–ice system. Two sample results are shown in Figures 16 and 17. The mean velocity field agrees well with that of Colony and Thorndike (Fig. 6). Measured and computed ice displacements during short intervals (days) show a median discrepancy of 2.8 km per day, but the long-term (seasonal and annual) ice drifts are virtually identical. Figure 17 depicts the computed net annual ice production (see equation 2). It is about 0.5 m over much of the basin, slightly negative along most of the continental margins and highly negative in the Greenland Sea. The average ice production in the central Arctic Basin is 30–40 cm/a. This seems to confirm the long-held notion that the ice export through Spitzbergen Fracture Zone, estimated to be about 3000 km^3/a (Gordienko and Karelin, 1945; Untersteiner, 1963; Maykut, 1982) originates from a basinwide source, while ice production and melt in most of the near-shore waters are more or less in balance. Recent data evaluated by Vinje and Finnekåsa (1986) indicate an ice export through Spitzbergen Fracture Zone of 4500 km^3/a.

MODELING: STOCHASTIC-KINEMATIC

Deviating from the deterministic approach of ice modeling outlined above, Colony and Thorndike (1985) describe sea ice motion as a random process: an individual ice particle is marked at an initial time and location. Its subsequent motion is described by the probability density of its new location after an arbitrarily chosen time interval. As an example, Figure 18 shows 30-day ice displacements as measured by automatic data buoys at the North Pole (interpolated) during 1979–1982. The future trajectory of the marked ice particle is then described by a succession of such incremental displacements. With this simple model, and using the theory of Markov processes, the statistics of the trajectory can be found analytically. For instance, Figure 19 shows the expected average number of years that it will take a particle of ice to melt

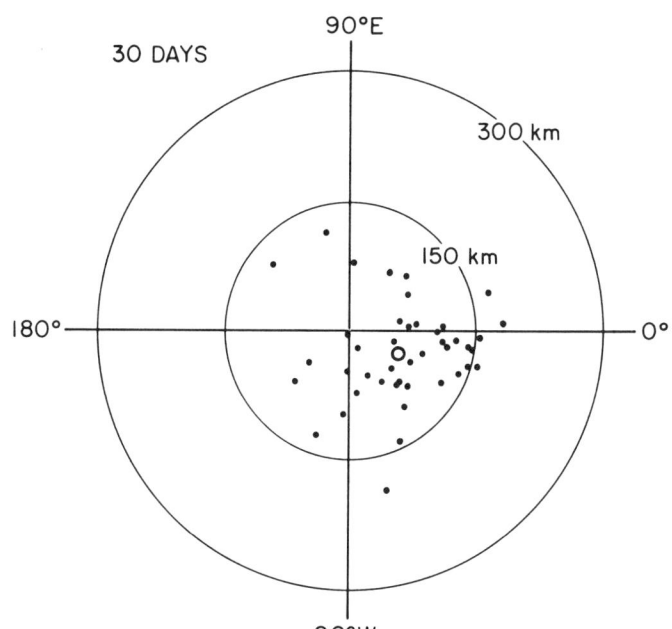

Figure 18. 30-day ice displacements from data buoys (interpolated) at the North Pole during the period 1979–1982. Dots mark the end points of individual displacement vectors. The circle marks the average displacement for the whole period (from Colony and Thorndike, 1985).

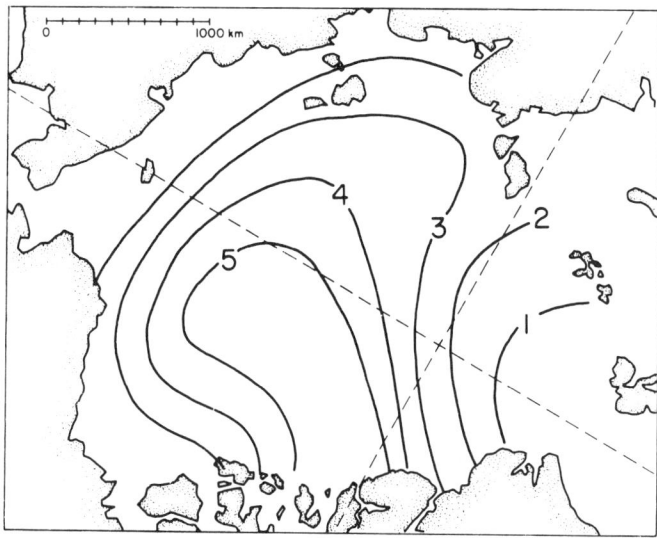

Figure 19. Average expected number of years for the ice to either melt in a marginal sea or exit the domain (from Colony & Thorndike, 1985).

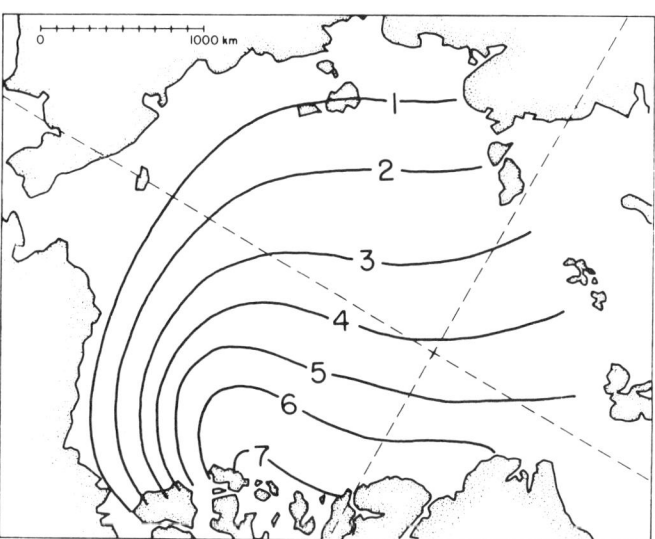

Figure 20. Average age of the ice in years (from Colony & Thorndike, 1985).

in a marginal sea or exit the domain (through Spitzbergen Fracture Zone). The random process thus described can also be used in reverse, tracking a particle of ice backward in time to the region where it was formed. The time elapsed since then is also a random variable defined by a probability distribution. Its average can be interpreted as the average age of the ice, as plotted in Figure 20.

In summary, the stochastic-kinematic model of Colony and Thorndike is purely diagnostic and makes no assumptions about physical processes. The random processes used to characterize ice motion are taken from observations. The model is predictive only to the extent that the statistics of ice motion remain constant in time. The sample results shown in Figures 19 and 20 indicate that casting model output in probabilistic form yields a wealth of information whose derivation from temporally and spatially averaged velocity fields would require a data base far larger than we can expect to have for many years.

Ultimately, of course, the results of dynamic and stochastic representations of the ice should yield compatible results, and the use of one or the other approach will be dictated by the intended use of the model output.

ICE AND SEDIMENT

It is generally accepted that ice rafting is the only way in which the coarse particles found in Arctic Basin sediments could have reached their location. (For a comprehensive review of this issue see Clark and Hanson, 1983.)

Pack ice and icebergs

Only ice originating from the coasts of north Greenland, and Ellesmere and Axel Heiberg islands has a chance to remain in the basin for a number of years, as documented by the drift of ice islands T-3 and ARLIS-II. These ice islands do not appear to sustain much, or any, bottom melting; their thickness decreases due to surface ablation. Therefore, it is not clear whether debris embedded at their underside was released or how much. There is little doubt that surface meltwater streams wash some debris over the side of the ice island, especially when they carry as much debris as ARLIS-II did. Observations on the small number of ice islands studied since the first one was occupied in 1952 indicate that massive melting and release of debris by these islands does not occur until they exit the Arctic Basin. Estimating the transport of coarse material by continental ice is further complicated by the fact that the discharge of such ice into the Arctic Basin may vary on time scales of centuries—too rapidly to allow correlations with the low time resolution of the sedimentary record. The contention that ice islands retain most of their debris load applies only as long as they are perennially surrounded by pack ice, as they are today. In a different setting, for instance during a seasonally ice-free Arctic Ocean and a greater degree of glaciation of the surrounding continents, discharged land ice may have deposited much larger amounts of debris anywhere in the basin.

Transport by formerly shore-fast ice

Each winter, the freezing of water-saturated layers along the beaches incorporates sand and gravel into the shore-fast sea ice. Also, mechanical crushing of ice can churn the sediment in shallow water and incorporate it into pressure ridges and floe bergs (Clark and Hanson, 1983). Some of this material has been seen at widely scattered locations in the Arctic Basin, though generally in small quantities and limited to the smaller grain sizes.

Along those parts of the coast that become seasonally ice-free (see Fig. 1), the shore-fast ice breaks loose some time between mid-April and mid-May. At that time a wide shore lead (typically several tens of km) has already opened and exposed the ocean to warming by solar irradiation. Thus the formerly shore-fast ice has to cross a stretch of relatively warm water before it can join the multiyear polar pack. During its transgression of the shore lead, the ice is subject to melting at its underside, which is bound to release much of the beach material frozen into the bottom layer. Coarse material ground into the ice by thrusting and overturning of blocks is more likely to be retained. The upward flux of ice associated with the seasonal sequence of bottom accretion and surface ablation (see Fig. 14) will move this material to the surface over a number of years. Some of it will be washed into the ocean by meltwater during the summer months, but some will settle into shallow melt pits (due to low albedo and solar absorption) and remain with the ice as long as it remains in the Arctic Basin.

The number of variables participating in this sequence of events is so great that an attempt to estimate the amount of material incorporated into, and transported and deposited by, formerly shore-fast ice does not appear feasible.

Finally, sediment strata devoid of coarse material may signify two extreme circumstances: no ice or immobilized ice. Several authors have speculated that the Arctic Ocean may have been ice-free at times during the past several m.y., even though support for this contention from the sedimentary record is under dispute. These speculations are based primarily on the notion that the Arctic Ocean, once it has become ice-free by gradual climatic warming or by some great short-term anomaly, will remain ice-free even during a subsequent cooling trend, because of the large amount of heat stored in the ocean during the long arctic summer that prevents ice formation during the following winter (positive feedback). While the potential summer heat storage under these circumstances is indeed large, no quantitative analysis has been given as to how the entire interactive air–sea–ice system would react to the absence of sea ice. If the seasonal cycle were reduced to conditions similar to those prevailing in the Antarctic, with ice formation during winter and an ice-free ocean in summer, this would still leave open the possibility of gravel transport by seasonal ice breaking away from the shores in spring. Obviously, such considerations apply only as long as the geographical pole remains inside the Arctic Basin. The most important phenomena to be simulated for an ice-free Arctic Ocean pertain to the cloud-radiation regime and to the density structure and mixing regime in the ocean. Given the difficulties encountered in reproducing even the present-day cloud-radiation regime with partially interactive models of the atmosphere, it is not likely that credible simulations of ice-free regime will be forthcoming in the very near future.

The case of immobilized pack ice raises the question: at what average thickness and thickness distribution does the ice become strong enough to withstand the driving forces of air and ocean currents? During the Arctic Ice Dynamics Joint Experiment (Untersteimer, 1980) there was a period of several weeks in the winter of 1976 when the action of wind stress had completely filled the southeastern Beaufort Sea with ice, presumably crushing all thin ice, and the drift had come to a standstill. The only published analysis of such an event is that by Pritchard (1978). From calculations of the wind stress and the length of the fetch, he found that the large-scale compressive strength of the ice must have been at least $10^5 Nm^{-1}$. It is not likely that the average ice thickness increased by much during that event. Following the normal pattern (Fig. 6), that same ice was in the region north of Point Barrow in the following April, where the thickness distribution shown in Figure 8 was observed by submarine sonar over a 1400-km stretch. Except for the secondary maximum at 1 m thickness, representing new ice formed between February and April due to large-scale stretching of the ice cover, the dominant maximum of the thickness distribution lies at the normal value of about 3 m. In other words, it appears that even the contemporary sea ice is strong enough to withstand compression provided that it is confined by a suitably shaped coastline. This is, of course, not the case in the central basin, nor does the limiting compressive strength readily apply to deformation in shear. It does not seem possible at this stage to estimate at what thickness the entire Arctic ice circulation would come to a halt. A plausible intermediate scenario might be that a band of ice was shorefast and grounded on shallow shelves, while the ice in the interior of the basin was still movable. That scenario, like total stagnation, excludes the rafting of significant amounts of coarse sediment.

In light of the foregoing remarks it seems clear that the only way to distinguish between conditions of no ice or immobilized ice is by way of the biogenic component in the sediment: The ocean under a stagnant sea ice cover should be virtually barren while, in the absence of sea ice, biota should proliferate.

REFERENCES

Badgley, F. I., 1966, Heat budget at the surface of the Arctic Ocean, *in* Proceedings Symposium on the Arctic Heat Budget and Atmospheric Circulation: The Rand Corporation, Santa Monica, California, RM-5233-NSF, p. 267–278.

Barnes, P. W., Rearic, D. M., and Reimnitz, E., 1984, Ice gouging characteristic and processes, *in* The Alaskan Beaufort Sea, Barnes, P. W., Schell, D. M., and Reimnitz, E., eds.: Academic Press, p. 185–212.

Budyko, M. I., 1969, The effect of solar radiation variation on the climate of the earth: Tellus, v. 21, p. 611–619.

Clark, D. L., and Hanson, A., 1983, Central Arctic ocean sediment texture; a key to ice transport mechanisms, *in* Glacial-Marine Sedimentation, Molina, B. F., ed.,: Plenum Publications Corporation, p. 301–330.

CLIMAP Project Members, 1976, The surface of the ice age earth: Science, v. 191, p. 1131–1137.

Colony, R., and Thorndike, A. S., 1984, An estimate of the mean field of Arctic sea ice motion: Journal of Geophysical Research, v. 89, no. C, p. 10623–10639.

—— , 1985, Sea ice motion as a drunkard's walk: Journal of Geophysical Research, v. 90, no. C, p. 965–974.

Coon, M. D., 1980, A review of AIDJEX modeling, *in* Sea Ice Processes and Models, Pritchard, R. S., ed.,: University of Washington Press, p. 12–27.

Doronin, Yu. P., and Kheisin, D. E., 1975, Sea Ice: Gidrometeoizdat Publishers, Leningrad, 323 p. [English translation by American Publishing Company, 1977, TT-75-52088].

Fletcher, J. O., 1965, The heat budget of the Arctic Basin and its relation to climate: The Rand Corporation, Santa Monica, California, R-444-PR, 173 p.

Gordienko, P., 1958, Arctic ice drift, *in* Arctic Sea Ice: National Academy of Science, no. 598, p. 210–220.

Gordienko, P. A., and Karelin, T., 1945, Problems of the movement and distribution of ice in the Arctic Basin: Problemy Arktiki i Antarktiki, no. 3 [In Russian].

Grenfell, T. C., 1979, The effects of ice thickness on the exchange of polar radiation over the Polar oceans: Journal of Glaciology, v. 22, p. 305–320.

Grenfell, T. C., and Maykut, G. A., 1977, The optical properties of ice and snow in the Arctic Basin: Journal of Glaciology, v. 18, p. 445–463.

Hibler, W. D., 1979, A dynamic thermodynamic sea ice model: Journal of Physical Oceanography, v. 9, p. 815–846.

—— , 1980, Modeling a variable thickness sea ice cover: v. 108, p. 1943–1973.

Hibler, W. D., and Bryan, K., 1984, Ocean circulation; its effects on seasonal sea ice simulations: Science, v. 224, p. 489–491.

Kellogg, W. W., 1975, Climatic feedback mechanisms involving the polar regions, *in* Climate of the Arctic, Weller, C., and Bowling, S. A., eds.,: Geophysical Institute, University of Alaska, Fairbanks, Alaska, p. 111–116.

LeShack, L., 1980, Sea ice growth, drift, and decay, *in* Dynamics of Snow and Ice Masses, Colbeck, S. C., ed.,: Academic Press, New York, p. 141–209, [Private communication, Hibler, W. D.].

Lyon, W., 1961, Ocean and sea ice research in the Arctic Ocean via submarine: Transactions, Academy of Science, New York, Ser. II., v. 23.

Marshunova, M. S., 1961, Principal characteristics of the radiation balance of the underlying surface and of the atmosphere in the Arctic, [in Russian]: Proceedings, Arctic and Antarctic Research Institute, Leningrad, 226 p. [Translated by the Rand Corporation, RM-5003-PR, 1966].

Maykut, G. A., 1978, Energy exchange over young sea ice in the Central Arctic: Journal of Geophysical Research, v. 83, p. 3646–3658.

—— , 1982, Large-scale heat exchange and ice production in the Central Arctic: Journal of Geophysical Research, v. 87, no. C, p. 7971–7984.

Maykut, G. A., and Untersteiner, N., 1971, Some results from a time dependent thermodynamic model of sea ice: Journal of Geophysical Research, v. 76, p. 1550–1575.

Nikiforov, Y. E., 1957, Ob izmenenii splochnosti ledyanogo rokrova v svyazi s yego dinamikoy, [A change in the concentration of ice cover in connection with its dynamics]: Problemy Arktiki y Antarktiki, v. 2, p. 59–71.

Oort, A. H., 1974, Year-to-year variations in the energy balance of the Arctic atmosphere: Journal of Geophysical Research, v. 79, p. 1253–1260.

Parkinson, C. L., and Washington, W. M., 1979, A large scale numerical model of sea ice: Journal of Geophysical Research, v. 84, p. 311–377.

Pritchard, R. S., 1978, The effect of strength on simulations of sea ice dynamics: Memorial University of Newfoundland, St. Johns, Proceedings of Arctic 1977, v. 1, p. 494–505.

Reinnitz, E., Barnes, P. W. and Phillips, R. L., 1984, Geological evidence for 60-meter deep pressure ridge keels in the Arctic Ocean: IAHR Ice Symposium Proceedings, v. II, p. 189–206.

Schwarzacher, W., and Hunkins, K. L., 1961: Dredged gravels from the central Arctic Ocean, *in* Raash, G. O., ed., Geology of the Arctic, University of Toronto Press, v. 1, p. 666–677.

Sellers, W. D., 1969, A global climatic model based on the energy balance of the earth atmosphere system: Journal of Applied Meteorology, v. 8, p. 392–400.

Thorndike, A. S., Rothrock, D. A., Makut, G. A., and Colony, R., 1975, The thickness distribution of sea ice: Journal of Geophysical Research, v. 80, p. 4501–4513.

Untersteiner, N., 1961, On the mass and heat budget of Arctic sea ice: Arkiv für Meteorologie, Geophysik und Bioklim atologie, Series A, v. 12, p. 151–182.

—— , 1962, Ice budget of the Arctic Ocean: Proceedings, Arctic Basin Symposium, Arctic Institute of North America, Washington, D.C., p. 219–226.

—— , 1964, Calculations of temperature regime and heat budget of sea ice in the Central Arctic: Journal of Geophysical Research, v. 69, p. 4755–4766.

—— , 1980, AIDJEX review, Sea Ice Processes and Models, Pritchard, R. S., ed.: University of Washington Press, Seattle, p. 3–11.

Untersteiner, N., and Thorndike, A. S., 1982, Arctic data buoy program: Polar Record, v. 21, p. 127–135.

Vinje, T., and Finnekåsa, Ø., 1986, The ice transport through Fram Strait: Oslo, Norsk Polarinstitutt Skrifter 186, 39 p.

Wadhams, P., 1981, Sea-ice topography of the Arctic Ocean in the region 70°W to 25°E: Philosophical Transactions of the Royal Society of London, series A, Mathematical and Physical Sciences, v. 302, p. 45–85.

Wadhams, P., and Horne, R. J., 1980, An analysis of ice profiles obtained by a submarine sonar in the Beaufort Sea: Journal of Glaciology, v. 25, p. 401–421.

Walsh, J. E., and Johnson, C. M., 1979, Interannual atmospheric variability and associated fluctuations in Arctic sea ice extent: Journal of Geophysical Research, v. 84, p. 6915–6928.

Walsh, J. E., Hibler, W. D., and Ross, B., 1985, A model simulation of 20 years of northern hemisphere sea ice fluctuations: Annals of Glaciology, v. 5, p. 170–176.

Washburn, A. L., 1973, Periglacial processes and environments: St. Martin's Press, New York, 320 p.

Weeks, W. F., and Ackley, S. F., 1982, The growth, structure, and properties of sea ice: CRREL monograph, no. 82-1, 130 p.

World Meteorological Organization—World Climate Research Programme, 1984, Report of the meeting of experts on sea ice and climate modeling: WMO-WRCP, WCP-77, Geneva, p. 1–34.

Zubov, N. N., 1943, L'dy Arktiki [Arctic Ice]: Izd. Glasevmorputi, Moscow, 360 p.

MANUSCRIPT ACCEPTED BY THE SOCIETY OCTOBER 8, 1986

ACKNOWLEDGMENTS

I am grateful to Roger Colony, Gary Maykut, David Clark, Robert Pritchard, and Richard Trowbridge for informative discussions during the preparation of this review.

"And now there came both mist and snow, and it grew wondrous cold." From *The Rime of the Ancient Mariner,* S. T. Coleridge. Illustrated by G. Dore.

Chapter 4

Arctic Ocean ice cover; Geologic history and climatic significance

David L. Clark
Department of Geology and Geophysics, University of Wisconsin, Madison, Wisconsin 53706

INTRODUCTION

The Arctic Ocean is unique among the world's oceans because of its perennial ice cover. The geologic and climatologic factors that contributed to development of the Arctic Ocean ice cover are understood in a general way, even though the precise mechanism and time during the Cenozoic that the first ice cover formed are not known. Data concerning climatological processes that encouraged development of an Arctic Ocean ice cover have developed from the general understanding of the paleogeographic sequence of events since the last major time of ice-free conditions during the Cretaceous and early Cenozoic. The lack of facts concerning the precise time, and to some extent the mechanism, of ice cover origin is largely the result of an inadequate data base in the Arctic Ocean. For example, no long sediment core with middle Cenozoic sediment that may represent the time of the initial ice-cover development has been collected. Unfortunately, no research ship with capability for recovery of long sediment cores has been designed for work in the area of year-round Arctic pack ice. Therefore, the only sediment record for the central Arctic Ocean is that recovered from drifting ice stations such as the U.S. T-3 program and the Canadian LOREX and CESAR projects. Offshore drilling on the continental slope of Alaska and Canada has penetrated a more complete Cenozoic section. The sediment is largely nonmarine and, in the shallow Beaufort Sea area, consists of thick deltaic sediment. Detailed paleoclimatologic study of this sediment has not been accomplished, but significant cooling during the middle Cenozoic has been interpreted from palynologic studies (Norris, 1982).

MESOZOIC TO CENOZOIC CLIMATE CHANGE

The transition from the ice-free Earth of the Cretaceous to a middle or late Cenozoic bipolar ice condition can largely be explained in the context of paleogeography and Earth orbital factors. Arrangement and size of continents and ocean basins influenced oceanic and atmospheric circulation and produced climate with a very low thermal gradient during the interval from 65 to 45 Ma. As crustal plate movement progressed toward the present geography, astronomical or orbital forcing became relatively more important in climate production.

Paleogeographic Factors

During most of the Mesozoic, the geography of Earth produced oceanic circulation with a very strong cross-latitude transport, which intensified and enhanced western-boundary current heat transport from low to high latitudes (Fig. 1). The various components of continental placement, paleocirculation, and atmosphere worked together to produce high surface-water temperatures during the Mesozoic, perhaps 15% higher than at present and with a thermal gradient only approximately one-half of that of the present (Berggren, 1982). Certain areas of the Arctic Ocean were the sites of organic-rich sediment accumulation (Clark and Byers, 1984) as well as oceanic upwelling that resulted in accumulation of rich biogenic oozes of Cretaceous diatoms and silicoflagellates (Kitchell and Clark, 1982; Jackson and others, 1985). Upwelling and biogenic siliceous ooze accumulation characterized certain parts of the Arctic Ocean at least sporadically from Late Cretaceous until Middle or Late Eocene (Bukry, 1984). Also, reports of Paleogene vertebrates, terrestrial and aquatic invertebrates, and plants in the Arctic (West and others, 1977; Marincovich and Zinsmeister, 1985; Wolfe, 1985) are consistent with temperate climate conditions during the Eocene. One exception to the idea of a very temperate Cretaceous through Eocene climate is the report of Eocene glacial erratics on Svalbard (Dalland, 1976). Because of the abundant evidence for absence of ice in the Arctic and elsewhere (Clark, 1985), the Svalbard report must be viewed with caution.

As Earth's supercontinents were tectonically rearranged during the Cenozoic, barriers to previous circulation patterns became gateways instead, and the strong cross-latitude heat transport was replaced by a more cross-meridional paleocirculation with less heat transported poleward (Berggren, 1982). Accompanying the change in oceanic circulation, there probably was an almost parallel change in circulation of the atmosphere. There also was a lowering of high atmospheric CO_2 levels from the Mesozoic condition (Berner and others, 1980; Broecker, 1982).

No record of post-Eocene to Late Miocene central Arctic Ocean sediment is known, but there is evidence that by at least the Early Pliocene, glacial-marine sediment was accumulating (Clark and others, 1980; Mudie and Blasco, 1985); this signifies glacial activity in the Arctic. Two-dimensional energy balance

Figure 1. Paleocirculation in the World Ocean, Late Cretaceous. During the Cretaceous, the 180° fetch of the large Pacific permitted heat buildup that was transferred north producing a very low thermal gradient, equator to pole. The Arctic Ocean was ice-free and much warmer than at present. Reconstruction after Crowley, (1983); Luyendyk and others, (1972).

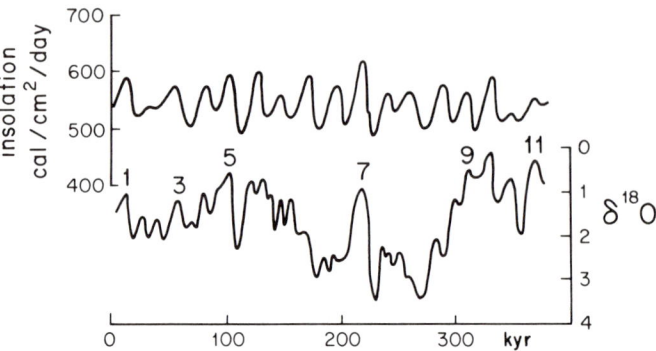

Figure 2. August insolation at 80°N (upper) compared to $\delta^{18}O$ record at 78°N (lower). Major peaks in isotope record (numbered) indicate minimum ice volume and correlate with major insolation highs. Major deglaciations occur at ~100,000 yr intervals. Insolation data from Imbrie and Berger (personal communication). Isotope record of planktonic foraminifer in core F1-124.

climate modeling that stresses the role of seasonality indicates that Arctic ice may have been forming ~40 Ma (Crowley and others, 1986). An analogous sequence of events occurred in Antarctica where glacial ice was forming during the early or middle Cenozoic. The ice was then thermally isolated with the development of the Circum–Antarctic Current by Late Oligocene. The Earth probably had bipolar ice sometime during the Miocene. Because the Antarctic record is better known, it is generally assumed that glaciation in the south polar region preceded that in the north polar area. The accuracy of this will be known when a complete sediment record of the middle Cenozoic is recovered from the Arctic Ocean.

Astronomical Forcing

Additional factors of orbital forcing (the astronomical effects) complement the paleogeographic events leading to the origin of the Arctic ice cover. According to astronomical theory, periodic changes in Earth's orbital parameters influence climatic cycles, and factors of precession, obliquity, and eccentricity are known to account for much of climate cyclicity during the late Cenozoic (Hays and others, 1976; Imbrie and Imbrie, 1980; Berger and others, 1984). The correlation of August insolation at 80°N and the $\delta^{18}O$ record for the past 350,000 years indicates correlation of major insolation peaks with low interglacial $\delta^{18}O$ values in the Arctic at a 100,000-year periodicity (Fig. 2). Figure 2, generated from orbital and fossil data, shows remarkable correlation of most major interglacials (e.g., 1, 5, 7, 9) with insolation highs. The importance of orbital forcing for the Arctic Ocean is also demonstrated by spectral analysis (Fig. 3). This figure illustrates a significant concentration of variance of foraminifera abundance, percent detrital carbonate, and percent coarse-grain sediment at the 100-Ka orbital periodicity for the Arctic Ocean.

Why was orbital forcing a less important factor 65 to 45 m.y. ago? Although orbital forcing has been interpreted for certain Mesozoic sedimentary sequences, no extremely cold climates are known, probably because of the neutralizing effects of high atmospheric levels of CO_2 as well as paleocirculation during that time (Fig. 1). The results of oceanic circulation changes during the Cenozoic were profound (Broecker and others, 1985). The significance of the orbital factors apparently differs at different latitudes (Ruddiman and McIntyre, 1984), but the combined effect of orbital forcing, along with cross-meridional paleocirculation and an atmospheric lowering of CO_2, was the freezing of the Arctic Ocean. Details concerning timing of ice formation and nature of the first ice cover are less well known and this has led to development of diverse theories.

THE LATE CENOZOIC ICE COVER: MODE OF FORMATION AND TIME OF ORIGIN

Nature of Ice Cover

The modern Arctic Ocean is covered by approximately 6×10^6 km² of perennial ice, of which ~99% is frozen sea water (pack ice) (Fig. 4A). Icebergs constitute the remaining 1% and represent a late stage of continental deglaciation occurring in the midst of an interglacial climate (Fig. 4B). The abundance of icebergs has fluctuated with the glacial, deglacial, and interglacial intervals of the high-latitude late Cenozoic climate cycle (Fig. 5). During late glacial and deglacial intervals, the percentage of ice-

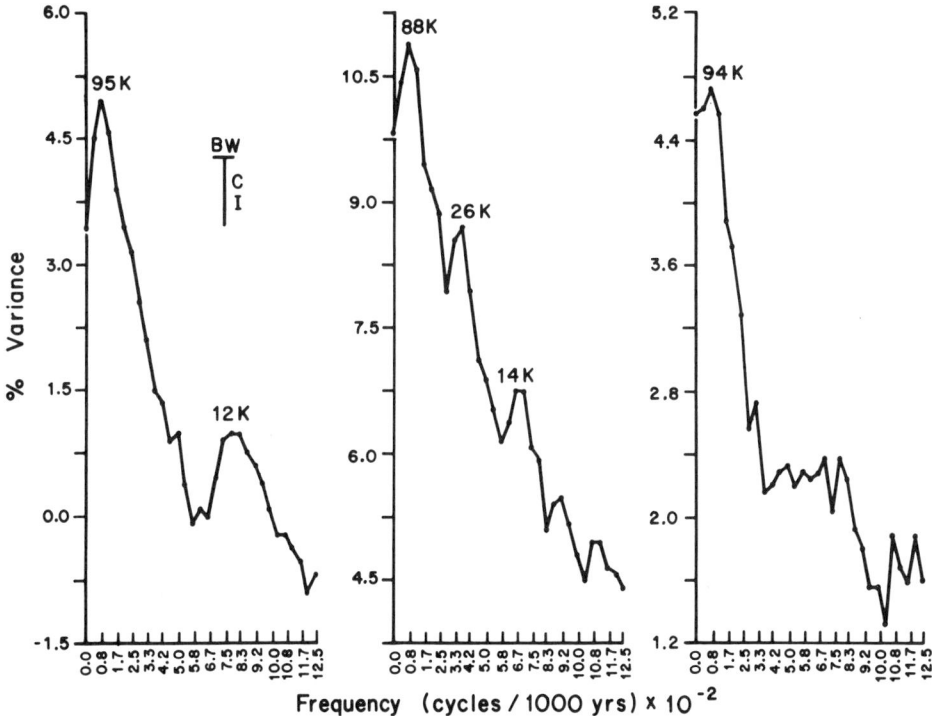

Figure 3. Spectra for F1-124, left, percentage coarse (>62μm); middle, foraminifera abundance; and right, percentage detrital carbonate. CI, confidence interval; BW, band width. Spectra cover past 400,000 yr. Concentrations of variance at periods near 100,000 yr are considered significant. Samples at 1 cm intervals. After Boyd and others, 1984.

bergs in the Arctic Ocean must have been greater than at present. Although the absolute abundance of icebergs present during the height of deglaciation is not known, the relative importance of the two ice types in the Arctic Ocean during the past few m.y. has left a proxy in the sediment record. Icebergs transport a complete range of sediment textures (Fig. 4). The sand to boulder component is of special importance because the deposition of this coarse sediment in the central Arctic Ocean is a fairly certain indicator of iceberg activity. Pack ice generally can only transport clay and fine silt–size material (Fig. 4), because this is the size fraction that commonly is mobilized, put in suspension, and frozen into the ice or transported to the ice by atmospheric processes (Clark and Hanson, 1983). Coarser sediment in shore ice or in river ice is not commonly transported far from shore (Lisitzin, 1972). Thus, for the central Arctic Ocean, coarse- and fine-grain sediment transported by icebergs, and finer-grain sediment transported by pack ice, have recorded the relative abundance of ice types during the late Cenozoic.

The stratigraphic record of several million years of ice rafting in the central Arctic Ocean has been organized into lithostratigraphic units (Clark and others, 1980). The units, designated A through M (from oldest to youngest) are characterized by texture, color, degree of bioturbation, abundance of Fe-Mn micronodules, and microfossils. The A to M stratigraphy represents the Early Pliocene (or Late Miocene) to Holocene Arctic Ocean oceanographic record, and the most important parameter in differentiating the lithostratigraphic units is texture. The textural records of two cores from different parts of the central Arctic Ocean are shown for comparison in Figure 6. For these cores, the textural peaks in excess of 10% coarse sediment probably represent times of major deglaciation in the central Arctic Ocean. In Figure 6, the core texture is illustrated with the Arctic Ocean A to M stratigraphy. The major deglaciation textural peaks (C, F, H, J, L, M) can be correlated across the western Arctic Ocean (Clark and others, 1980). The textural plots (Fig. 6) can be interpreted to suggest that the frequency and/or duration of glacial ice influx into the Arctic Ocean has increased during the past several million years.

The reliability of the A to M lithostratigraphy and age of the Arctic sedimentary units has been widely discussed recently (e.g., Sejrup and others, 1984; Zahn and others, 1985; Jackson and others, 1985). Additional interpretations based on new magnetic, biostratigraphic, ^{18}O and ^{14}C analysis (Aksu and Mudie, 1985; Clark and others, 1986) apparently confirm the traditional age interpretations used in this report.

The effect of increased glacial ice is apparent in the sub-Arctic, as well. Figure 7 is a textural plot from DSDP North Atlantic Leg 49 at 63°N, 30°W. The coarse peaks can be compared with the central Arctic Ocean deglaciation stratigraphy. Independent chronologies are of additional interest. The ~50% coarse peak just above 50 m (Fig. 7) has been interpreted to represent approximately 1.8 Ma (Pliocene-Pleistocene boundary

Figure 4. A. aerial view of pack ice bearing fine-grained sediment (dark ice). Irregular pattern of ice-bearing sediment and cleaner pack ice due to fracturing. B. small iceberg bearing abundant coarse-grained sediment. This iceberg drifted by Barrow, Alaska, in 1971.

(Luyendyk and others, 1979) and correlates with the coarse peaks of stratigraphic unit F of Figure 6. Unit F is dated by extrapolation of sedimentation rates from the Brunhes/Matuyama magnetic boundary to be approximately 2 Ma. Correlation of the coarse peak at ~30 m in Fig. 7 with H in Fig. 6 is also suggested. Recent work in the Norwegian Sea confirms the importance of increased glacial transport during the last 0.5 m.y. (Eldholm and others, 1986).

These correlations suggest that the nature of the Arctic Ocean ice cover during the late Cenozoic can be interpreted from the sediment record and that changes in the nature of the Arctic ice cover may be correlated with climatic events in the North Atlantic, as well.

Theories Based on Climatologic and Oceanographic Factors

Most theories of Arctic ice cover history have attempted to explain the ice in the context of Pleistocene glacial and interglacial cycles with constraints provided by established paleoclimatologic and oceanographic factors (Frakes, 1979; Crowley, 1983). One early theory proposed that a cool but ice-free Arctic Ocean

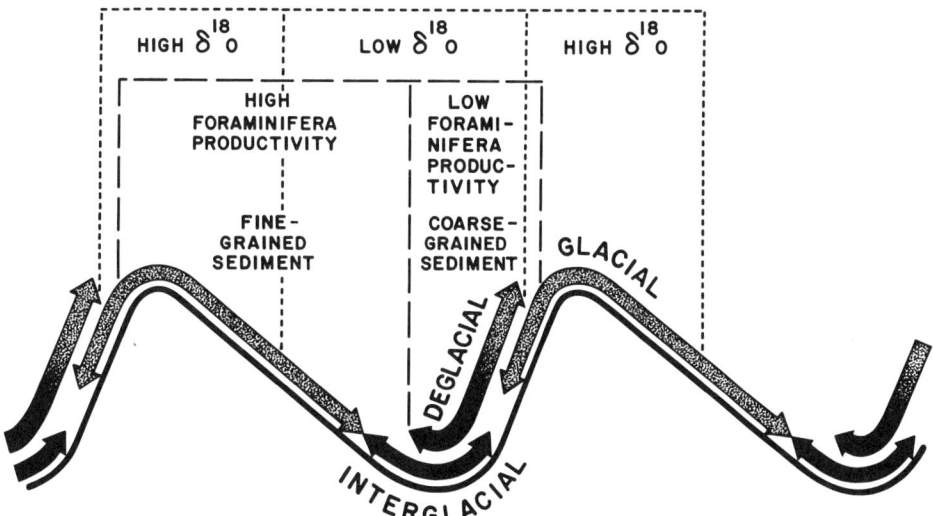

Figure 5. Climate curve with sediment texture, foraminifera productivity and $\delta^{18}O$ values. This model predicts that low foraminifera productivity and coarse-grained sediment should characterize the late glacial stage, all of the deglacial stage, and part of the interglacial stage. Fine-grained sediment and high foraminifera productivity should characterize part of the interglacial and glacial stages. $\delta^{18}O$ values overlap the sedimentary parameters at points on the climate curve.

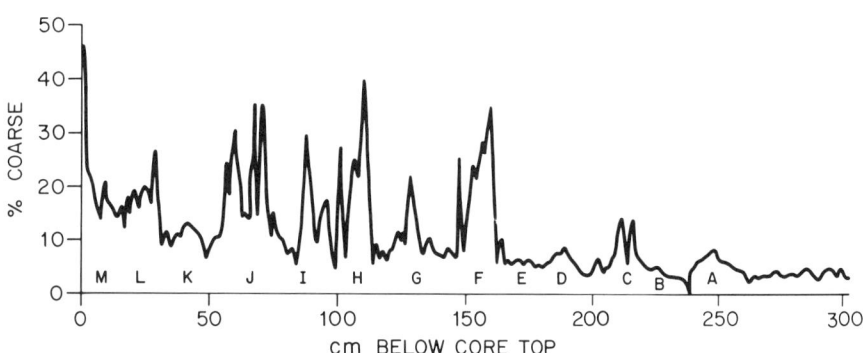

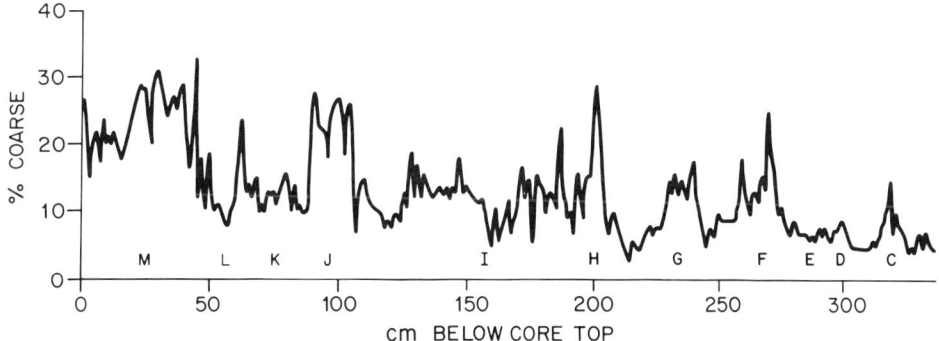

Figure 6. Percent coarse-grained sediment ($>63\mu$) in core F1-286 (upper) and core F1-433 (lower). Stratigraphic units (A to M) indicated. F1-286 from 84°N, 144°W, F1-433 from 85°N, 129°W. Samples at 1-cm intervals.

could provide the moisture necessary for the growth of Pleistocene continental glaciers (Ewing and Donn, 1956). Glacier growth stored water and the resulting lowering of sea level restricted circulation of the Arctic Ocean. Heat loss due to restricted circulation led to development of an ice cover. The ice cover, in turn, restricted moisture flow to glaciers and this resulted in continental glacier reduction. The cycle was repeated as glacial ice melting resulted in sea-level rise and subsequent melting of the Arctic Ocean ice cover. An ice-free Arctic Ocean was the source of moisture for renewed continental glacier growth. Elegant in its simplicity, this theory, formulated before the Arctic Ocean sediments had been studied, proved to be inconsistent with the sediment record (Collinvaux, 1964; Ku and Broecker, 1967; Steuerwald and others, 1968; Clark, 1971).

As additional research in the Arctic Ocean provided a limited but expanded data base, several different interpretations of the ice cover's history were formulated. One of these, the so-called "ice cap" theory, proposed that some of the Pleistocene sea level changes and $\delta^{18}O$ records could be better explained if the Arctic Ocean had developed an Antarctic-size ice cap, perhaps >1000 m thick. Proponents of this theory argued that, for at least the past 160,000 years, a floating ice cap with a thickness close to the mean depth of the Arctic Ocean would be a good explanation for the apparent discrepancy between sea level calculations and the $\delta^{18}O$ records of oceanic ice volume (Mercer, 1970; Broecker, 1975; Hughes and others, 1977; Williams and others, 1981; Keigwin, 1982). The ice cap visualized by proponents of this theory would have been much different from both the ice cover of the modern ocean and the ice cover visualized to have been alternately present and absent by Ewing and Donn (1956). This ice cap theory is not so much a theory of Arctic Ocean ice cover origin as it is an interpretation of possible late Pleistocene Arctic Ocean conditions. The theory requires ice thicknesses and sedimentologic effects that are unsupported by the sediment record.

An elaborate theory that relates Pleistocene glacial-interglacial cycles to Earth's orbital factors and the crust's glacial isostatic adjustment involves geophysical processes ignored by most other theories (Peltier, 1982). This theory explains the periodicity of continental glaciation on the timescale of 10^5 years (and by implication the development of the Arctic Ocean ice) by interacting factors of crustal-mantle deformation due to ice growth and variation in the Earth's rotation caused by ice build-up. Loading and unloading the Northern Hemisphere with ice results in perturbations of the Earth's axis of rotation with important climate consequences, according to this theory.

A recent theory, not directly concerned with the formation of the Arctic Ocean ice cover, is important for the Arctic because it includes a mechanism for high-latitude climate modification. The theory was formulated to explain climate oscillations during glacial times (Broecker and others, 1985). This theory relates fluctuations in the rate of formation of North Atlantic Deep Water (NADW) to rise and fall of Atlantic salinity levels. The higher salinity of the Atlantic Ocean is the result of an excess of evaporation over precipitation for the combined Atlantic and Mediterranean seas. This greater salinity of the Atlantic permits production of North Atlantic water that is very dense and, hence, an important factor in deep cold-water production. Accordingly, a reduction in salinity would reduce the quantity of NADW. Determining the times of higher and lower salinity levels is aided by study of Cd levels in benthic foraminifera. Evidently, high Cd in benthic foraminifera indicates glacial climate with less NADW, and low Cd levels (the present) indicate interglacial climate and greater production of NADW (Boyle and Keigwin, 1982). Taking all of these factors into consideration, the Broecker theory addresses climate oscillations during full glacial stages with the following scenario: At 20,000- or 40,000-year orbital frequencies of increased insolation in the northern latitudes, rate of evaporation of North Atlantic water increases and the resulting oceanic salinity rise supports the production of NADW. The release of excess heat to the atmosphere accompanying the NADW production would enhance orbitally produced insolation and eventually lead to melting of high-latitude ice. The result of ice melting would be a lowering of North Atlantic salinity and a consequent reduction in the production of NADW. This, in turn, would result in less ocean-to-atmosphere heat flux and, when in phase with orbital factors that reduce insolation, ice melting would decrease and climate would eventually return to a full glacial stage. Additional oscillations would follow as new cycles of evaporation and salinity changes affected NADW production.

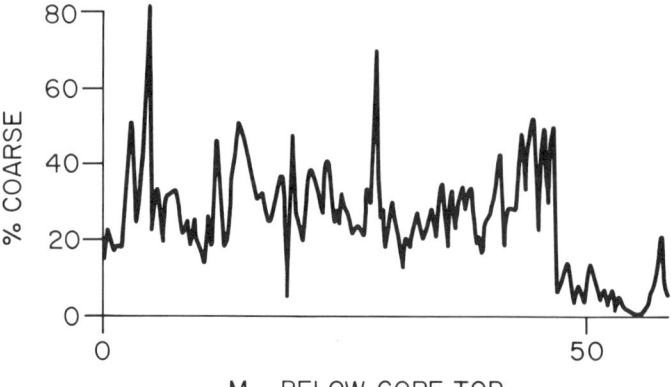

Figure 7. Percent coarse-grained sediment (>63μ) in DSDP Leg 49, core 407, 63°N, 30°W. Samples at 20-cm intervals. Large peak at approximately 46 m is interpreted to represent beginning of North Atlantic deglaciation. 1.8 Ma. Correlation with unit F of Figure 6 is suggested by magnetic dating of F as ~2 Ma. 20% peak below 50 m is thought to correlate with C of Fig. 6 and 70% peak at ~30 m probably correlates with H of Fig. 6 as well.

Fashioned to explain brief Pleistocene climate oscillations, the mechanism may be important in understanding factors that influenced Arctic Ocean ice cover formation. For example, development of the present North Atlantic geography during the Cenozoic should have been accompanied by the production of NADW. If so, the 100,000 year orbital factors that produced major glacial stages probably tempered the ocean-to-atmosphere heat flux of NADW production until ice growth in the Arctic was completed and then, together with ice formation in the North Atlantic, shut off evaporation and related salinity increases. Once formed, the Arctic Ocean ice cover became relatively stable; at least this is suggested by the sediment record (Clark, 1982a). Increased insolation corresponding to 20,000- or 40,000-year orbital frequencies could have been important factors in minor oscillations of glacial climate as well as the initiation of the changes from glacial to interglacial climate when reinforced by as yet poorly understood factors of climate forcing by orbital factors. This hypothesis, while tentative, derives strength from including known factors of orbital forcing (Berger and others, 1984), ocean-to-atmosphere heat flux and NADW formation (Broecker and others, 1985), and the Arctic Ocean sediment record (Clark and others, 1980).

The role of seasonality in Arctic ice formation is stressed in a model described by Crowley and others (1986). This model assumes progressive lowering of summer temperatures in high latitudes until this moderating effect is so great that winter snow and ice does not melt during the summer. According to this model, the Greenland ice cap should have been forming ~40 Ma, and this would be supported by surrounding ocean cooling. This model may be useful in determining time of Arctic Ocean ice formation.

Theories Based on Sediment Factors

Study of the sediment record of the central Arctic Ocean has led to the development of diverse interpretations of the ice cover history. One explanation, dubbed the fluctuating regime theory, proposes that the Pliocene-to-Holocene interval was characterized by three different Arctic Ocean water masses (Herman and Hopkins, 1980; Worsley and Herman, 1980; Margolis and Herman, 1980). The sequence begins with an early (~4 Ma to 2.7 Ma) cold but unfrozen Arctic Ocean with high productivity. The next younger condition, (2.7 to 0.7 Ma) was characterized by stratified saline and fresh water with little vertical mixing that produced a general low-productivity ocean. The final change, beginning approximately 0.7 Ma and extending to the present, was the time of the formation of the first ice cover and also a time of increased water productivity. Some of the details concerning sediment interpretation and times of productivity have been challenged in light of detailed foraminifera and sediment texture study (O'Neill, 1981; Clark, 1982a).

An alternate theory includes consideration of late Cenozoic climate and its relationship to the deglaciation record of the Arctic Ocean (Clark, 1982a; Gilbert and Clark, 1983; Clark and Morris, 1985). This theory proposes that the Arctic Ocean has been in a more or less steady state since the cooling of the World Ocean in the Middle or Late Miocene. By Late Miocene or Pliocene time, oceanic and atmospheric circulation, essentially the same as exists today, was in existence. Decrease in poleward heat transport, coupled with an insolation minimum that correlates with orbital factors, produced the first Northern Hemisphere glaciation, and the products of this glaciation are found in the oldest Neogene sediment recovered to date (Clark and others, 1980). Because growth and decay of continental glaciers has been influenced by orbital forcing and other climate factors (including NADW production) and because the Arctic Ocean–North Atlantic water masses may have a stronger link than previously suggested (Aagaard and others, 1985; Morris and Clark, 1985), the Arctic ice cover may have coexisted with the earliest Northern Hemisphere glaciation.

From the time of ice formation to the present, Arctic Ocean conditions have ranged through a glacial, deglacial, and interglacial cycle (Clark and Morris, 1985). The sediment record for at least the past 4 m.y. shows little variation on a single theme: ice rafting by both pack ice and icebergs. During one interval (from approximately 2 Ma to 1 Ma), an increase in calcareous dinoflagellate and foraminifera abundance may indicate warmer conditions than had existed prior to or since this time (Clark, 1982a; Gilbert and Clark, 1983). Recent confirmation of this warming event has been interpreted from botanical evidence on Greenland (Funder and others, 1985) and from sediment in the Norwegian Sea, as well (Eldholm and others, 1986). The affect of this warming on the permanent ice cover may have been seasonal and related to ice-free conditions only in coastal areas. There is no strong evidence that following the initial freezing, the central Arctic Ocean has ever been ice-free (Untersteiner, 1969).

The sediment-based theories differ in interpretation of timing of initiation of the Arctic ice cover and its permanence. Additional $\delta^{18}O$–$\delta^{13}C$ data, paleoclimatologic modeling, and detailed faunal and sediment studies are needed to provide evidence concerning which of these models is valid.

CLIMATE EFFECTS OF ICE COVER

Because atmospheric circulation is largely generated by the gradients resulting from heat gain at low latitudes and heat loss at polar latitudes, a bipolar ice cover is clearly significant for Earth's climate. The ice cover restricts heat exchange between atmosphere and ocean, suppressing heat loss from the ocean in winter as well as heat gain in the summer. It has been estimated that there is at least three times more atmospheric cooling with bipolar ice than there would be without it (Fletcher and Kelley, 1978). In addition to world climate effects, short-term weather modifications result from a variable-sized Arctic ice pack. Even the variable distribution of snow at high latitude affects weather patterns. The combination of Arctic ice cover and snow cover seasonally may affect up to 40% of Northern Hemisphere land area. The temperature and humidity affected by the resulting radiation balance influences the atmosphere and its movement. The total area seasonally affected can be accurately calculated from satellite imagery, and the resulting weather patterns correlated.

Complete absence of polar ice covers would reduce the Earth's thermal gradient and profoundly affect atmospheric and oceanic circulation. The world climate change that would result from an ice-free Arctic has not been accurately modeled and there is disagreement concerning the magnitude of the change.

Increased precipitation for Canada, India, and the Middle East and China, and a decreased precipitation for most of the United States, Eurasia and northern Africa, has been suggested (Wigley and others, 1980). A generally warmer atmosphere is a certain effect. Both oceanic and atmospheric thermal gradients would decrease, and such changes would introduce new climate patterns (Clark, 1982b). Although rearrangements of continents and a significant rise in atmospheric CO_2 levels would be necessary to recreate a Cretaceous climate, ice-free polar regions would be a certain step in the direction of a more uniform climate. Also, any major change in climate would be expressed first in high latitudes. Atmospheric CO_2 increase, for example, would affect the polar ice covers prior to any equatorial expression; melting of polar ice is one of the most profound effects.

The importance of the Arctic Ocean along with the sub-Arctic Greenland-Labrador sea complex for NADW production, and the relationship of NADW to climate, has already been discussed. Clearly, the Arctic Ocean is a factor in cold deep-water production—an important component of climate modification—and this is in addition to the climatic significance of an ice cover (Aagaard and others, 1985; Morris and Clark, 1985).

BIOLOGIC EFFECTS OF ICE COVER

The high-latitude Arctic Ocean and its ice cover have influenced the evolution of a great variety of organisms as well as their ecosystems. For example, the extremes in seasonal cycles of ice cover and photosynthesis have introduced conditions that have been important in animal and plant behavior and physiology. The lifestyle of Arctic organisms, especially as related to growth and reproduction, is commonly seasonal. Also, the ice cover is used as a platform by Arctic mammals and as an important building medium by ice algae (Polar Research Board, 1985). In addition, behavioral evolution of various Arctic whale species and their adaption to life beneath and adjacent to an ice cover is a good example of coevolution of biological and Arctic physical processes.

The influence of the Arctic Ocean ice cover is well exemplified by the development of *Ursus maritimus* Phipps, the Polar Bear. The Polar Bear is a creature of the ice cover, and its evolution evidently occurred in response to ice development, i.e., the oldest Polar Bear is no older than the formation of the Arctic ice cover.

The cyclic rise and fall of sea level during the late Cenozoic glacial intervals was also of importance for interchange of mammals between North America and Eurasia. At times of glacial ice maxima, the lower sea level exposed the "Beringia" land connection; this permitted exchange of a number of high-latitude mammals (Kurtén and Anderson, 1980). Successive deglaciations resulted in flooding of Beringia, but North America–Eurasia isolation has been temporary during the past few m.y. and insignificant for the homogenization of Arctic land faunas.

The ice cover also provided a unique evolutionary setting for marine flora and invertebrate faunas. Although endemism is a difficult concept to prove without a complete record of biogeography (and this is rare in paleontology), absence of reports from the sub-Arctic of species known to occur in the Arctic Ocean may be taken as evidence of endemism. Low diversity is a product of this Arctic endemism. There are only 25 Arctic Ocean metazoan groups, compared to more than 35 groups that occur in most mid-latitudes (Paul and Menzies, 1973).

The approximately 100 benthic foraminifera described by Lagoe (1977), Paul and Menzies (1973), and Green (1960) from the central Arctic Ocean include approximately 40% endemic forms, species that are adapted to life beneath a perennial ice cover. Of the 19 species of ostracodes, 13 are endemic to the central Arctic Ocean. Larger invertebrates are poorly known and may include more widespread species that are largely unstudied (Clark, 1977). Planktonic protozoans show similar degrees of endemism to that indicated for foraminifera and ostracodes (Tibbs, 1967).

The low diversity probably is a measure of the youthfulness of the Arctic ecosystem. The time of the development of the first ice cover may have been only in the last few million years. All other of the world's major oceans were well developed earlier than this. The youthfulness of the Arctic ecosystem also is related to extreme temperatures.

Of important biologic significance is the fact that the land surrounding the Arctic Ocean is characterized by permafrost and tundra with associated freshwater habitats that are unique. The terrestrial and freshwater organisms that inhabit the area have evolved in response to a frozen Arctic Ocean and the factors that have produced and perpetuated an ice cover.

SUMMARY

The presence (or absence) of the Arctic Ocean ice cover has been a significant factor for world climate as well as specifically affecting sedimentation patterns, biologic evolution and paleobiogeography of North America for the past 100 m.y. Different theories are available to account for time of initiation, size and style, and stability of the ice cover, but all theories agree on the uniqueness of the perennial Arctic Ocean ice cover.

REFERENCES

Aagaard, K., Swift, J. H., and Carmack, E. C., 1985, Thermohaline circulation in the Arctic mediterranean seas: Journal of Geophysical Research, v. 90, no. C3, p. 4833–4846.

Aksu, A. E., and Mudie, P. J., 1985, Magnetostratigraphy and palynology demonstrate at least 4 million years of Arctic Ocean sedimentation: Nature, v. 318, p. 280–283.

Berger, A., Imbrie, J., Hays, J., Kukla, G., and Saltzman, B., eds., 1984, Milankovitch and climate: NATO ASI Series C, Mathematical and Physical Sciences 126, 2 pts., 895 p.

Berggren, W. A., 1982. Role of ocean gateways in climatic change, *in* Climate in Earth history; Studies in Geophysics: National Academy Press, p. 118–125.

Berner, W., Oeschger, H., and Stauffer, B., 1980. Information on the CO_2 cycle from ice core studies: Radiocarbon, v. 22, p. 227–235.

Boyd, R. F., Clark, D. L., Jones, G., Ruddiman, W. F., McIntyre, A., and Pisias,

N. G., 1984, Central Arctic Ocean response to Pleistocene Earth-orbital variations: Quaternary Research, v. 22, p. 121–128.

Boyle, E. A., and Keigwin, L. D., 1982, Deep circulation of the North Atlantic over the last 200,000 years; Geochemical evidence: Science, v. 218, p. 784–787.

Broecker, W. S., 1975, Floating glacial ice-caps in the Arctic Ocean: Science, v. 188, p. 1116–1118.

Broecker, W. S., 1982, Glacial to interglacial changes in ocean chemistry, in Kraus, E. B., and Hanson, H. P., eds., Climatic variability in the oceans: Progress in Oceanography, v. 11, p. 151–197.

Broecker, W. S., Peteet, D. M., and Rind, D., 1985, Does the ocean-atmosphere system have more than one stable mode of operation?: Nature, v. 315, p. 21–26.

Bukry, D., 1984, Paleogene paleoceanography of the Arctic Ocean is constrained by the middle or late Eocene age of U.S.G.S. Core F1-422; evidence from silicoflagellates: Geology, v. 12, p. 122–201.

Clark, D. L., 1971, Arctic Ocean ice cover and its Late Cenozoic history: Geological Society of America Bulletin, v. 82, p. 3313–3324.

—— , 1977, Paleontologic response to post-Jurassic crustal plate movements in the Arctic Ocean, in West, R. M., ed., Paleontology and plate tectonics: Milwaukee Public Museum Special Publications in Biology and Geology, no. 2, p. 55–76.

—— , 1982a, Origin, nature, and world climate effect of Arctic Ocean ice-cover: Nature, v. 300, p. 321–325.

—— , 1982b, The Arctic Ocean and post–Jurassic paleoclimatology, in, Climate in Earth history, Studies in Geophysics: National Academy Press, p. 133–138.

—— , 1985, The Eocene Arctic Ocean and Earth's Early Cenozoic climate: Geological Society of America Abstracts with Programs, v. 17, p. 547.

Clark, D. L., and Byers, C. W., 1984, Cretaceous carbon-rich sediment from the central Arctic Ocean: Geological Society of America Abstracts with Programs, v. 16, p. 472.

Clark, D. L., and Hanson, A., 1983, Central Arctic Ocean sediment texture; A key to ice transport mechanisms, in Molnia, B. F., ed., Glacial–marine sedimentation: New York, Plenum Publishing Corp., p. 301–330.

Clark, D. L., and Morris, T. H., 1985, Arctic Ocean sediment texture and the Pleistocene climate cycle: Geological Society of America Abstracts with Programs, v. 17, p. 547.

Clark, D. L., Whitman, R. R., Morgan, K. A., and Mackey, S. D., 1980, Stratigraphy and glacial-marine sediments of the Amerasian Basin, central Arctic Ocean: Geological Society of America Special Paper 181, 57 p.

Clark, D. L., Andree, M., Broecker, W. S., Mix, A. C., Bonani, G., Hofmann, H. J., Morenzoni, E., Nessi, M., Suter, M. and Woelfli, W., 1986, Arctic Ocean chronology confirmed by accelerator ^{14}C dating: Geophysical Research Letters, v. 13, p. 319–321.

Collinvaux, P. A., 1964, Origin of ice ages; Pollen evidence from Arctic Alaska: Science, v. 145, p. 707–708.

Crowley, T. J., 1983, The geologic record of climate change: Reviews of Geophysics and Space Physics, v. 21, p. 828–877.

Crowley, T. J., Short, D. A., Mengel, J. G., and North, G. R., 1986, Role of seasonality in the evolution of climate during the last 100 million years: Science, v. 231, p. 579–584.

Dalland, A., 1976, Erratic clasts in the lower Tertiary deposits of Svalbard; Evidence of transport by winter ice: Norsk Polarinstitutt Arbok, p. 151–165.

Eldholm, O., 25 co-authors, 1986, Reflector identified, glacial onset seen: Geotimes, v. 31, p. 12–25.

Ewing, M., and Donn, W. L., 1956, A theory of ice-ages: Science, v. 128, p. 1061–1066.

Fletcher, J. O., and Kelley, J. J., 1978, The role of the polar regions in global climate changes, in van Zinderen Bakker, E. M., Balkemann, A. A., eds., Polar Research: Rotterdam, p. 3–13.

Frakes, L. A., 1979, Climates throughout geologic time: New York, Elsevier Publishing Company, 310 p.

Funder, S., Abrahamsen, N., Bennike, O., and Feyling-Hanssen, R. W., 1985, Forested Arctic; Evidence from north Greenland: Geology, v. 13, p. 542–546.

Gilbert, M. W., and Clark, D. L., 1983, Central Arctic Ocean paleoceanographic interpretations based on Late Cenozoic calcareous dinoflagellates: Marine Micropaleontology, v. 7, p. 385–401.

Green, K. E., 1960, Ecology of some Arctic Foraminifera: Micropaleontology, v. 6, p. 57–58.

Hays, J. D., Imbrie, J., and Shackleton, N. J., 1976, Variations in the Earth's orbit; Pacemaker of the ice ages: Science, v. 194, p. 1121–1132.

Herman, Y., and Hopkins, D. M., 1980, Arctic Oceanic climate in Late Cenozoic time: Science, v. 209, p. 557–562.

Hughes, T., Denton, G. H., and Grosswald, M. G., 1977, Was there a late-Würm Arctic ice-sheet?: Nature, v. 266, p. 596–602.

Imbrie, J., and Imbrie, J. Z., 1980, Modeling the climatic response to orbital variations: Science, v. 207, p. 943–952.

Jackson, H. R., Mudie, P. J., and Blasco, S. M., eds., 1985, Initial geological report on CESAR; The Canadian expedition to study the Alpha Ridge, Arctic Ocean: Geological Survey of Canada Paper 84-22, 177 p.

Keigwin, L. D., 1982, An Arctic Ocean ice-sheet in the Pleistocene?: Nature, v. 296, p. 808–809.

Kitchell, J. A., and Clark, D. L., 1982, Late Cretaceous–Paleogene paleogeography and paleocirculation; Evidence of North Polar upwelling: Palaeogeography, Palaeoclimatology, Palaeoecology, v. 40, p. 135–165.

Ku, T. L., and Broecker, W. S., 1967, Rates of sedimentation in the Arctic Ocean: Progress in Oceanography, v. 4, p. 95–104.

Kurtén, B., and Anderson, E., 1980, Pleistocene mammals of North America: New York, Columbia University Press, 442 p.

Lagoe, M. B., 1977, Recent benthic foraminifera from the central Arctic Ocean: Journal of Foraminiferal Research, v. 7, no. 2, p. 106–129.

Lisitzin, A. P., 1972, Sedimentation in the world ocean: Society of Economic Paleontologists and Mineralogists Special Publication 17, 218 p.

Luyendyk, B. P., Forsyth, D., and Phillips, J. D., 1972, Experimental approach to the paleocirculation of the oceanic surface waters: Geological Society of America Bulletin, v. 83, p. 2649–2669.

Luyendyk, B. P., and others, 1979, Initial reports of the Deep Sea Drilling Project, v. 49, 1020 p.

Margolis, S. V., and Herman, Y., 1980, Northern hemisphere sea-ice and glacial development in late Cenozoic: Nature, v. 286, p. 145–149.

Marincovich, L., and Zinsmeister, W. J., 1985, Early Tertiary climates of the Arctic Ocean: Geological Society of America Abstracts with Programs, v. 17, p. 653.

Mercer, J. H., 1970, A former ice-sheet in the Arctic Ocean?: Paleogeography, Palaeoclimatology, Paleoecology, v. 8, p. 19–27.

Morris, T. H., and Clark, D. L., 1985, The calcite lysocline of the central Arctic Ocean and its paleoclimatic significance: Geology Society of America Abstracts with Programs, v. 17, p. 669.

Mudie, P. J., and Blasco, S. M., 1985, Lithostratigraphy of the CESAR cores, in Jackson, H. R., Mudie, P. J., and Blasco, S. M., eds., Initial geologic report on CESAR; The Canadian expedition to study the Alpha Ridge: Geological Survey of Canada Paper 84-22, p. 59–99.

Norris, G., 1982, Spore-pollen evidence for early Oligocene high-latitude cool climate episode in northern Canada: Nature, v. 297, p. 387–389.

O'Neill, B. J., 1981, Pliocene and Pleistocene benthic Foraminifera from the central Arctic Ocean: Journal of Paleontology, v. 55, p. 1141–1170.

Paul, A. Z., and Menzies, R. J., 1973, Benthic ecology of the high Arctic deep-sea; Final report: Department of Oceanography, Florida State University, 337 p.

Peltier, W. R., 1982, Dynamics of the Ice-Age Earth: Advances in Geophysics, v. 24, p. 1–146.

Polar Research Board, 1985, National issues and research priorities in the Arctic: Washington, D.C., National Research Council, 124 p.

Ruddiman, W. F., and McIntyre, A., 1984, Ice-age thermal response and climatic role of the surface Atlantic Ocean, 40°N to 63°N: Geological Society of

America Bulletin, v. 95, p. 381–396.
Sejrup, H. P., Miller, G. H., Brigham-Grette, J., Løvlie, R., and Hopkins, D., 1984, Amino acid epimerization implies rapid sedimentation rates in Arctic Ocean cores: Nature, v. 310, p. 772–775.
Steuerwald, B. A., Clark, D. L., and Andrew, J. A., 1968, Magnetic stratigraphy and faunal patterns in Arctic Ocean sediments: Earth and Planetary Science Letters, v. 5, p. 79–85.
Tibbs, J. F., 1967, On some planktonic Protozoa taken from the track of Drift Station ARLIS 1, 1960–1961: Arctic, v. 20, p. 247–254.
Untersteiner, N., 1969. Sea ice and heat budget: Arctic, v. 22, p. 195–199.
West, R. M., Dawson, M. R., and Hutchinson, J. H., 1977, Fossils from the Paleogene Eureka Sound Formation, N.W.T., Canada; Occurrence, climatic, and paleogeographic implications, in West, R. M., ed., Paleontology and plate tectonics: Milwaukee Public Museum Special Publications in Biology and Geology, no. 2, p. 77–93.
Wigley, T.M.L., Jones, P. D., and Kelly, P. M., 1980, Scenario for a warm, high CO_2 world: Nature, v. 283, p. 17–21.
Williams, D. F., Moore, W. S., and Fillon, R. H., 1981, Role of glacial Arctic Ocean ice-sheets in Pleistocene oxygen isotope and sea level records: Earth and Planetary Science Letters, v. 56, p. 157–166.
Wolfe, J. A., 1985, Probabilities of high-latitude glaciers during the Tertiary: Geological Society of America Abstracts with Programs, v. 17, p. 753.
Worsley, T. R., and Herman, Y., 1980, Episodic ice-free Arctic Ocean in Pliocene and Pleistocene time; Calcareous nannofossil evidence: Science, v. 210, p. 323–325.
Zahn, R., Markussen, B., and Thiede, J., 1985, Stable isotope data and depositional environments in the late Quaternary Arctic Ocean: Nature, v. 314, p. 433–435.

Manuscript Accepted by the Society October 15, 1986

ACKNOWLEDGMENTS

Most of the research on which this compilation is based has been supported by the Office of Naval Research, N00014-82K-003. Early drafts of this chapter were reviewed by G. Leonard Johnson, Jack Sweeney, Art Grantz, Norbert Untersteiner, and Tom Morris although these reviews did not constitute agreement with the chapter content. Almost all that we know concerning the central Arctic Ocean ice cover history is based on sediment cores collected from U.S. ice-island T-3 and from the Canadian LOREX and CESAR projects. Without these projects, this chapter could not have been written. DSDP samples were provided by the East Coast Repository at the Lamont-Doherty Laboratory, Palisades, New York.

NOTE ADDED IN PROOF

Resolution of Arctic Ocean chronology for the past 2 m.y., challenged by early amino acid and isotope studies, is resolved (references 4, 5, and 7). In addition, new data and interpretations, not available when this chapter was submitted in 1986, support the idea that there may have been one or more Arctic Ocean coastal warmings that would have affected the ice cover during the past 3 m.y. (references 1–3, 6).

1. Carter, L. D. and others, 1986, Late Cenozoic Arctic Ocean sea ice and terrestrial paleoclimate: Geology, v. 14, p. 675–678.
2. Clark, D. and others, 1989, The Pleistocene warming of the Arctic Ocean: Tectonophysics (in press).
3. Gartner, S., 1988, Paleoceanography of the Mid-Pleistocene: Marine Micropaleontology, v. 13, p. 23–46.
4. Macko, S. A. and Aksu, A. E., 1986, Amino acid epimerization in planktonic foraminifera suggests slow sedimentation rates for the Alpha Ridge, Arctic Ocean: Nature, v. 322, p. 730–732.
5. Morris, T. H., 1988, Stable isotope stratigraphy of the Arctic Ocean: Palaeogeography, Palaeoclimatology, Palaeoecology, v. 64, p. 201–219.
6. Repenning, C. A. and others, 1987, The Beringian ancestry of *Phenacomys* and the beginning of the modern Arctic Ocean borderland biota: U.S. Geological Survey Bulletin 1687, 31 p.
7. Witte, W. K. and Kent, D. V., 1988, Revised magnetostratigraphies confirm low sedimentation rates in Arctic Ocean cores: Quaternary Research, v. 29, p. 43–53.

Ours blancs.

Dessin de C. Mützel (de Berlin).

From A. E. Nordenskjold, 1885, Voyage de la Vega Autour de l'Asie et de l'Europe (1878–1879), (Translated from the Swedish by Charles Rabot and Charles Lallemond), Vol. 1: Paris, Libraire Hachette et Cie, p. 131.

Printed in U.S.A.

Chapter 5

Bathymetry and physiography

G. L. Johnson
Office of Naval Research, Washington, D.C. 22217
Arthur Grantz
U.S. Geological Survey, 345 Middlefield Road, Menlo Park, Californira 94025
J. R. Weber
Geophysics Division, Geological Survey of Canada, Observatory Crescent, Ottawa, Ontario K1A OY3, Canada

> *Could the waters of the Atlantic be drawn off, so as to expose to view this great sea-gash, which separates continents, and extends from Arctic to the Antarctic, it would present a scene the most rugged, grand, and imposing. The very ribs of the solid earth, with the foundations of the sea, would be brought to light and we should have presented to us at one view, the empty cradle of the ocean.*
>
> *Maury 1855, para 440.*

INTRODUCTION

The oceanic regions located north of the Arctic Circle are the Arctic Ocean, the Norwegian-Greenland Sea, and Baffin Bay (Plate 1). The latter is described in Keen and Williams (1990). Despite the bold isobaths in Plate 1, the bathymetry of the Arctic Ocean is still poorly known. Most of the Norwegian-Greenland Sea, on the other hand, is quite precisely charted. Exceptions are the areas east of Greenland often covered by the pack ice that exits the Arctic Ocean in the East Greenland current.

The names used for the physiographic features in this volume are those shown on Plate 1. Different names that have been applied to these features in the literature are given in Sweeney and others (this volume.)

ARCTIC OCEAN

The Arctic Ocean consists of the deep Arctic Basin, continental shelves, and marginal plateaus (Plate 1). Located on the very wide European and Siberian shelves are five major epicontinental seas, the Barents, Kara, Laptev, East Siberian, and Chukchi seas. The much smaller Beaufort and Lincoln seas overlie part of the generally narrow continental shelves that fringe the North American and Greenland margins of the Arctic Ocean. Three subparallel submarine mountain ranges divide the Arctic Basin into four major subbasins. The Lomonosov Ridge, which crosses the Arctic Basin near the North Pole, divides it into the Eurasia and Amerasia Basins. In turn, the Eurasia Basin is subdivided into Nansen and Amundsen Basins by the Arctic Mid-Ocean Ridge, and the Amerasia Basin is subdivided into Makarov and Canada Basins by the Alpha and Mendeleev Ridges. These submarine features were unknown until well after World War II.

From the Middle Ages until the end of the 19th century, geographers believed that the North Pole was surrounded by land or by an archipelago. Based on the presence of Siberian driftwood in the Norwegian-Greenland Sea, Nansen postulated that the Arctic was a shallow epicontinental sea. This concept was disproved by soundings taken from Nansen's ship, the *Fram*, which drifted across the Arctic while frozen into the polar pack ice from the New Siberian Islands to Svalbard between 1893 and 1896 (Nansen, 1902). This heroic and scientifically significant drift is foremost in the annals of Arctic scientific exploration, and it resulted in the production of a bathymetric chart that showed the Arctic Basin to be a single oceanic deep. However, analysis of tidal data led Harris (1904) to postulate that the Arctic Basin was divided by a barrier or ridge into two basins with different periods of fundamental oscillation.

After World War II, as elsewhere in the world oceans, knowledge of the true character of the Arctic sea floor started to become known. In 1948, the Soviet Union commenced a program of systematic exploration of the entire Arctic Ocean by carrying out ice landings by aircraft on the sea ice (Armstrong, 1958) and by year-round occupation of more permanent ice stations (Weber, 1983). In 1951, U.S. scientists joined in the exploration of the Arctic Ocean Basin by mounting airborne expeditions to the Canada Basin and, in later years, by means of ice island stations and nuclear submarine traverses. In 1959, the

Johnson, G. L., Grantz, A., and Weber, J. R., 1990, Bathymetry and physiography, *in* Grantz, A., Johnson, L., and Sweeney, J. F., eds., The Arctic Ocean region: Boulder Colorado, Geological Society of America, The Geology of North America, v. L.

Canadian Polar Continental Shelf Project started a systematic program of charting the continental shelf from the Canada-Alaska border to the Lincoln Sea (Weber, 1983).

The Lomonosov Ridge was discovered by Soviet scientists in 1948, but was not revealed to the outside world until 1954, with the publication of their first bathymetric map of the Arctic Ocean (Gakkel, 1958; Burkhanov, 1956). The Alpha Ridge was first recognized as a distinct submarine feature by soundings taken from drifting station ALPHA during the International Geophysical Year (Hunkins, 1961). In 1959, Soviet scientists published a second bathymetric map of the Arctic Ocean (Gordienko and Laktionov, 1960), and a number of bathymetric studies published in the 1960s delineated the major physiographic provinces of the Arctic (Heezen and Ewing, 1961; Ostenso, 1962 [Plate 1, Fig. 2]; Gakkel, 1962; Dietz and Shumway, 1961; Dibner and others, 1965; DeLeeuw, 1967; Hunkins, 1968; Johnson, 1969; Ritchie, 1969). The 1970s were marked by the publication of more detailed charts by Heezen and Tharp (1975), Sobczak and Sweeney (1978), Johnson and others (1979), followed by Perry and others (1986).

NORWEGIAN-GREENLAND SEA

The Norwegian-Greenland Sea occupies a rhombohedral basin that extends northward from the Greenland-Iceland-Faroe Ridge to the northern apex between northeastern Greenland and Svalbard (Plate 1, Fig. 1).

A few pre-1960 surveys in the Greenland Sea were conducted by Belgium (DeGerlache, 1907; Helland-Hensen and Koefoed, 1907), Denmark (Boeggild, 1900), Norway (Nansen, 1902), France (Charcot, 1938), the British Admiralty, and the U.S. Naval Oceanographic Office. The first systematic bathymetric survey of the area, however, was a remarkable one made from the S. S. *Veslekari* in 1937–1938, under the leadership of Boyd (1948). Extensive hydrographic surveys in the northern Greenland Sea were conducted by the Arctic and Antarctic Research Institute of the U.S.S.R. between the years 1955 and 1958 (Laktionov, 1959; Volkov, 1961). Eggvin (1963) published a remarkably good synthesis of these data plus much unpublished Norwegian Fisheries Directorate data. Litvin (1964), incorporating about a decade's accumulation of Soviet data, produced an excellent chart of the Norwegian Sea. Johnson and Eckhoff (1966), utilizing icebreaker data from the 1960s, mapped the Greenland Sea, and Johnson and Heezen (1967a) constructed a bathymetric chart of the Norwegian-Greenland Sea. More recently, updated syntheses incorporating newer data for the region have been published by Gronlie and Talwani (1979), Johnson and others (1979), and Perry and others (1977).

PROCESSES OF FORMATION OF OCEANIC RELIEF

The sea floor is generated along the crestal region of a mid-ocean ridge by the upwelling of mantle derivatives. This new crust then moves laterally away from the ridge crest in a conveyor-belt fashion. The new ocean floor is covered by a sedimentary blanket that buries the original igneous surface. The morphology of the sea floor is therefore the result of the generation of igneous topography as a result of faulting and volcanism at the crest of the mid-oceanic ridge and its slow burial by sedimentary processes. Water depths over oceanic crust depend on (1) initial depth at the accretion axis, (2) subsequent thermal subsidence, and (3) effects of sediment loading and its isostatic compensation. Faulting and volcanism become relatively insignificant after newly created sea floor has left the crestal zone of a mid-ocean ridge. The original rifting of continental blocks at a nascent mid-ocean ridge forms pairs of escarpments at which continental slopes are formed.

The thickness of the sedimentary cover reflects (1) the age of the sea floor, (2) its proximity to continents and sediment sources, and (3) the local presence (or absence) of zones of biologic productivity, which may lead to thick deposits of calcareous or siliceous organic material (Plate 5). The contrast in morphology between the mid-ocean ridge and the areas adjacent to the continents (the continental rises and abyssal plains) does not lie in the tectonic processes that formed the ridges, but in the sedimentary material that is subsequently deposited on these areas of the sea floor (Vogt and others, 1969).

MORPHOLOGY OF MID-OCEAN RIDGE SYSTEM IN THE ARCTIC

Kolbeinsey Ridge

The branch of the active mid-oceanic ridge system between Iceland and Jan Mayen is called Kolbeinsey Ridge (Fig. 1), after the island by that name located on its crest at 67°08′N, 18°36′W (Sigurdsson and Brown, 1970). Transform faults created during the last few million years offset the ridge axis at 68°45′N (Spar Fracture Zone [F.Z.]) and at 70°30′N (Johnson and others, 1972; Mayer and others, 1972; Talwani and Eldholm, 1977). Additional fractures of small offset, revealed by detailed aeromagnetic data (Vogt and others, 1980), have formed repeatedly during the last few million years. Between Iceland and the Spar F.Z., the ridge averages only 40 km in width. This segment of the ridge is morphologically similar to the Reykjanes Ridge crest in that it appears as a narrow, elevated block. North of Spar F.Z., the ridge widens to over 100 km, and a small median rift valley with 500 m of relief appears along its axis (Fig. 1, profile 7′). From 70°N to its junction with the Jan Mayen F.Z. at 71°42′N, the bathymetry of the ridge is complex and poorly known. The existence of numerous seamounts and banks in this region, which extends east to volcanically active Jan Mayen Island (Sylvester, 1975), suggests the existence of a Jan Mayen hot spot separate from the Iceland hot spot. At Eggvin Bank, near 71°N, the ridge axis shoals to less than 1,000 m and then descends to below 3,400 m at its junction with Jan Mayen F.Z. This hole, and another at the southeastern end of the active Jan Mayen F.Z. that is 3,845 m deep, may reflect loss of viscous head of the ascending ridge crest magmas (Sleep and Biehler, 1970). Mayer and others (1972) and Johnson and others (1972) have published detailed studies of the ridge.

Mohns Ridge

Profile 6′ in Figure 1 shows that Mohns Ridge has the form of a typical mid-oceanic ridge. A deep axial rift is present on all profiles. The crestal zone averages 75 km in width, and the flanks of the ridge are more than 130 km wide. The crest of the ridge is 1,000 to 2,000 m shallower than the floor of the axial rift valley, which generally lies at depths in excess of 3,000 m. Magnetic anomaly offsets (Fedhynskii and others, 1975) suggest that a number of small axial offsets occur along the ridge, forming a "staircase" of short spreading axes and transform faults (Vogt and others, 1981).

Knipovitch Ridge

The continuation of the mid-oceanic ridge system through the Greenland Sea (Knipovitch Ridge) has been postulated by numerous investigators on the basis of both earthquake epicenters and topography (Heezen and Ewing, 1961; Johnson and Eckhoff, 1966; Deminitskaya and Dibner, 1966) (Plate 1). Morphologically, the Knipovitch Ridge is atypical in that its present rift valley lies asymmetrically on the eastern side of the Greenland Sea. The rift is narrow, generally 1 or 2 km wide at the 3,000 m isobath (Plate 1), and has well-developed structural benches on its walls. The rift mountains generally rise to depths of less than 2,000 m, but are barely discernible to the east due to partial burial by the continental rise sedimentary prism that has built out from Svalbard and the western Barents Shelf. The asymmetry suggests a jump in ridge axis to the east from a more centrally located axis in the past. This would be in keeping with the concept that the ridge axis tends to stay geographically close to a hot spot. Morphologically, the rift valley at the crest of the ridge abruptly terminates at 78°30′N, where it impinges upon the continental slope west of Spitsbergen. Ohta (1982) has described a NW–SE series of transform faults that cause minor offsets to the axis of Knipovich Ridge, and these too may be present beneath the continental margin of Spitsbergen.

Arctic Mid-Ocean Ridge

An extension of the world-encircling mid-ocean ridge system into the Arctic Basin was first suggested on the basis of a well-defined pattern of earthquake epicenters and a few soundings (Heezen and Ewing, 1961; Gakkel, 1962). Our present knowledge of the bathymetric form of the Arctic Mid-Ocean Ridge is revealed by echograms obtained by nuclear submarines operating under the floating ice cap (Dietz and Shumway, 1961; Johnson and Heezen, 1967b). Within 10° of the Greenwich meridian, the ridge has a width of approximately 270 km (Plate 1) (Feden and others, 1979). Here the ridge crest rises 2 km above the median rift valley floor, which lies 5 km below sea level.

The Arctic Mid-Ocean Ridge becomes a relatively subdued feature near the Laptev Sea. The flat portions of the sea floor in this area (Fig. 1, profile 2′) may be segments of the Pole Abyssal Plain elevated by the actively growing and perhaps rising ridge. A more likely interpretation, however, appears to be that sediment poured into the Arctic Basin by the Lena, Ob, and Yenisey rivers has been sufficiently voluminous to bury the Laptev end of the ridge. Indeed, in Figure 2, profiles 3 and 4, sediments from the continental rise are seen to be dammed behind the southern flank of the ridge. Plate 1 indicates that at least two fracture zones offset the ridge between 55° and 85° E (Kovacs and Vink, 1984). These fracture zones may act as conduits for the sediment, which has apparently partially buried the normally high relief of the ridge near 80°E (Fig. 1, profile 2′). The small-scale rough relief shown at 1,000 m in Figure 2, profile 5, may represent the expected amplitude of rugged relief on the Arctic Mid-Ocean Ridge where it intersects the continental slope at the Laptev Sea. The ridge strikes toward the continental margin of Greenland without diminution in width or elevation, which suggests that it is there offset by a fracture zone that is parallel to the nearby Spitsbergen Fracture Zone (Fig. 2).

Mid-Ocean Ridge Elevation Anomalies

It has been known for some time that mid-ocean ridges subside rather uniformly after their formation at axial depths of about 2.5 to 3 km (Sclater and others, 1971). The subsidence appears to be due largely to thermal contraction of the cooling lithosphere, amplified by isostatic adjustment produced by the accompanying increase in thickness of the overlying water column and sediment overburden.

Inspection of Figure 1 shows that almost the entire mid-ocean ridge system in the Arctic is anomalously elevated with respect to the North Pacific, a result which corroborates Sclater and others' (1971) observation that slow-spreading ridges, such as the Mid-Atlantic Ridge, tend to stand persistently higher than fast-spreading ridges. The greatest discrepancy is in the vicinity of Iceland, from which the depth anomaly progressively decreases to both the north and south. Bathymetric profiles suggest that the anomaly persists down the flanks of the ridge, and is therefore not restricted to the most recently formed crust at the ridge crest. Topographically, the most anomalous regions of the ridges are those formed 0–10 Ma and 50–60 Ma. The first region is about 500 m shallower than regions of equivalent age in the North Pacific, and the second is about 700 m shallower. This has been especially well documented between 47 and 51°N by Johnson and Vogt (1973).

CONTINENTAL MARGINS

Continental Shelves

East Greenland. Along the Greenland Sea the continental shelf widens from 60 km off Kong Christian X's Land (71°N) to

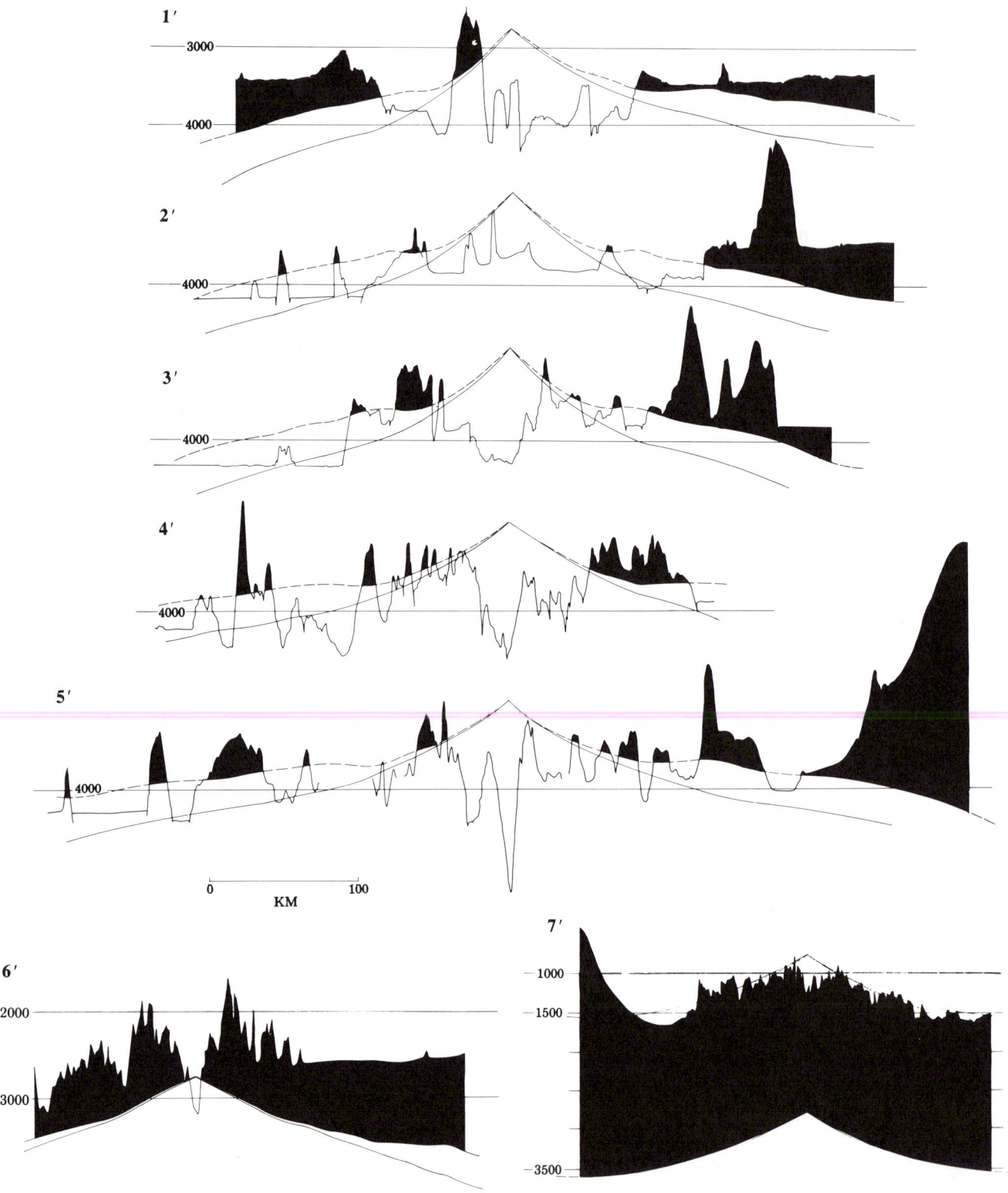

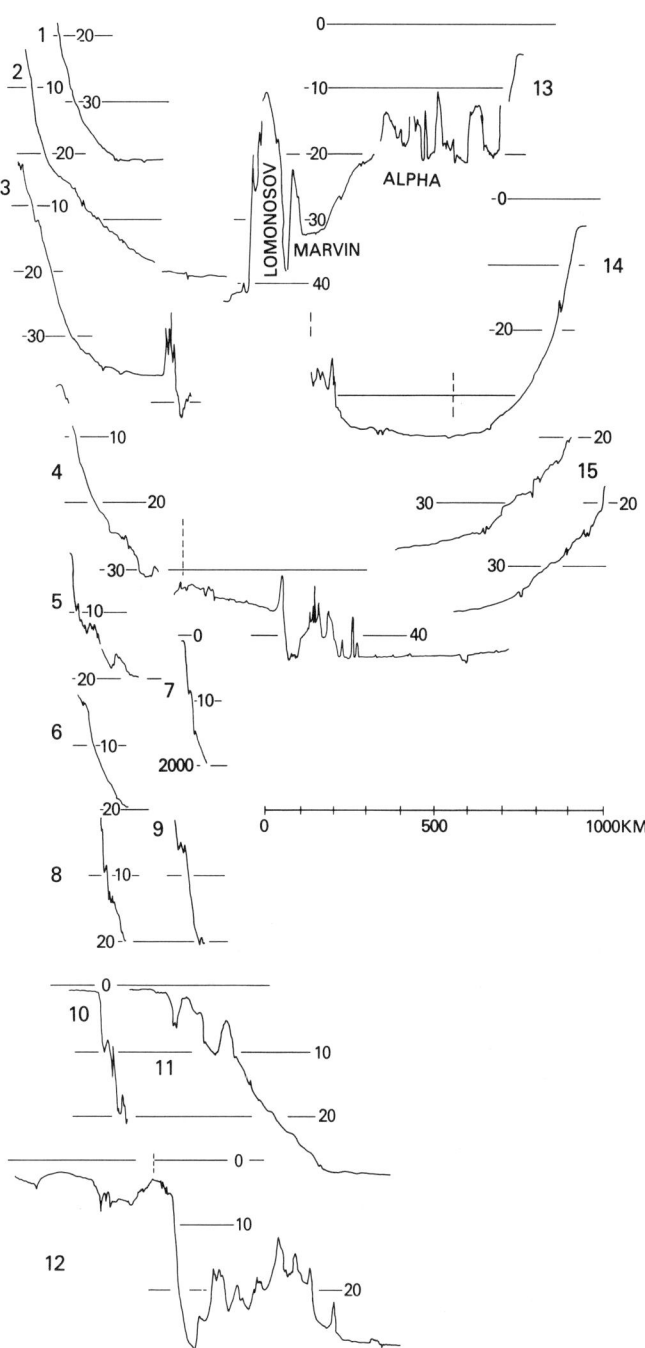

Figure 1. Topographic profiles across representative sections of the mid-ocean ridge system in the Arctic (Johnson, 1984). Depths are given in meters. Profiles 1'–5' are across the Arctic Mid-Oceanic Ridge. The thin line is the theoretical subsidence curve from Sclater and others (1971) for the East Pacific Rise. The upper dashed line assumes an average sedimentation rate as reported by Ruddiman (1972) and thence subtracts for loading and subsequent depression of the crust by the sediments. (See text for explanation.) Profiles were projected perpendicular to assumed spreading rates of .88 cm/yr for 0–10 Ma, .70 cm/yr for 10–21 Ma, .62 cm/yr for 21–38 Ma, .80 cm/yr for 38–49 Ma, and 1.01 cm/yr for 49–60 Ma. Profile 6' is across Mohn's Ridge; NW coordinates are 73°30'N, 3°E, SE coordinates are 71°55'N, 9°E. Profile 7' is across Kolbeinsey Ridge. A spreading rate of .9 cm/yr was assumed. Western coordinates are 69°54'N, 19°30'W; eastern coordinates are 69°54'N, 13°25'W. Profiles are indexed on Figure 4.

Figure 2. Topographic profiles from early submarine cruises. Profiles 1, 2, and 3 are *Skate*, 1959; profiles 4–12 are *Sea Dragon*, 1962; profile 13 is *Sargo*, 1960; profile 14 is *Sea Dragon*, 1960; and profile 15 is *Skate*, 1962. Profiles are indexed on Figure 4. Profiles replotted from Beal, 1969. Depths in meters × 100.

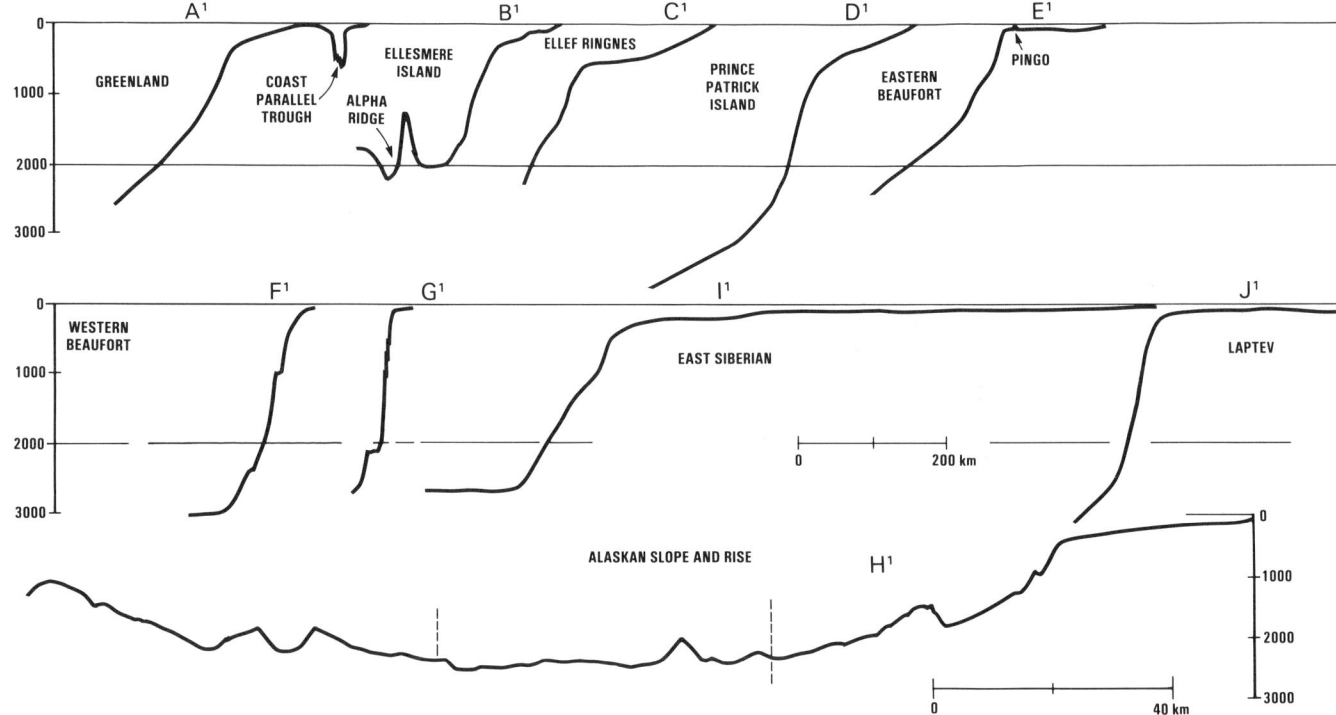

Figure 3. Continental margin profiles. Profile A' is an idealized east Greenland profile from Johnson and others (1979) not indexed; profile B' was constructed from CESAR bathymetric data supplied by J. R. Weber; profile C' and D' are from Weber (personal communication); profile E' was constructed from Canadian Hydrographic Service charts 266602 and 23092-A; and profiles F', and G' were constructed from U.S.G.S. multichannel data from R. V. Lee and profile H' is from seismic reflection data from U.S.C.G. *Burton Island*; profiles I' and J' were constructed from Plate 1. Profiles are indexed on Figure 4. Dashed line shows location of major course change. Depths in meters.

nearly 300 km off Kong Frederik VIII's Land (77°N). Along the northeast coast, seaward of Kronprins Christian Land (83°30'N), the shelf narrows to 20 km, then widens again to some 90 km off the north coast, where it merges with the Morris Jesup Plateau. The depth of the continental shelf break ranges between 350 and 450 m (Table 1).

Morphologically, the east Greenland continental shelf and possibly part of the Ellesmere Island continental shelf are characteristic of shelves along glaciated coasts (Fig. 3). These characteristics include an inner shelf—the strandflat of Nansen (1922)—which, seaward of east Greenland and possibly Ellesmere Island, is generally a submerged continuation of the Paleozoic and Precambrian continental basement (Fig. 3, profiles A' and B'). The outer banks and strandflat are usually separated by relatively long, narrow depressions several hundred meters deep. These marginal channels are generally parallel to the coastline (Holtedahl and Holtedahl, 1961). It has been suggested by Johnson and others (1975 and 1982) that the channels mark a fault or hinge line that separates continental basement from the overlying less resistant prograded Mesozoic and Tertiary sequences that were deposited across the margin after initial rifting. These channels may represent the most landward listric step fault formed during the uplift associated with initial rifting. However, Balkwill and Kyle (1985) suggest that these are the result of Pliocene uplift and/or tension with resultant faulting. This would account for the parallelism of the marginal channels with the coastline. During glacial periods, glaciers tended to flow along these shallow channels, locally breaking seaward to form transverse valleys. The advancing glacial ice abraded the channels, which originally were quite shallow, as well as shallower parts of the outer shelf. In many places the outer shelf is characterized by banks that were presumably constructed by glaciers. These banks, which are thought to be terminal or lateral moraines of glaciers that grounded or terminated on the shelf, have been notched or bevelled by wave action during lower sea-level stands (Fig. 3, profile A').

Canada and Alaska. The Canadian continental shelf ranges in width from 65 to 180 km, and the Alaskan shelf from 50 to 90 km (Table 1). Except for the northernmost part of Ellesmere Island, where the shelf is shallower (Fig. 3, profile B'), the depth of the continental shelf break seaward of the Queen Elizabeth Islands and Banks Island varies between 400 and 650 m (Fig. 3, profiles C' and D'). This is much deeper than the world average of 200 m (Worzel, 1968), suggesting that the present-day subsidence rate there is greater than the sedimentation rate. Ferrand and Gajda (1962) and Patterson (1977) argue that there was never much glacial ice on the Queen Elizabeth Islands, and that glacial rebound since the Pleistocene has been

TABLE 1. ARCTIC CONTINENTAL SHELVES

Region	Depth of Shelf Break	Width (km)	References
East Greenland	350-450	20-300	Johnson and Eckhoff (1966)
Ellesmere	250-400	60-85	Weber (1986)
Canadian Beaufort	400-650	65-180	Canadian Hydrographic Service
Western Beaufort	70-100 (outer shelf 200-800)	70-120	Grantz and others (1981)
Chukchi	65-70 (outer shelf 300-500)	900	Hill and others (1984)
East Siberian	100-400	700-800	Naugler and others (1974) and this chapter
Laptev	100-200	200	Holmes and Creager (1974)

less than 20 m. Therefore, glacial loading apparently cannot be a cause of the depth of the shelf break. At the Mackenzie Delta, where sedimentation is intense, the shelf is much shallower and the inner shelf break lies between 60 and 100 m (Fig. 3, profile E').

The Canada continental shelf is dissected by a number of canyons that head in toward glaciated fiords (Ellesmere and Axel Heiberg Island) or in inter-island channels (Plate 1). Generally, water depths are greatest in the fiords and inter-island channels and shoal as much as several hundred meters toward the continental edge. The nonglaciated coasts of the Queen Elizabeth Islands and mainland do not have the coast-parallel marginal channels found off Greenland, but they have been subjected to scour and gouging by sea ice.

The shelf morphology is particularly well known in the Beaufort Sea (Fig. 3, profiles E' and F'). The continental shelf slopes gently to the shelf edge, which lies between depths of 70 and 100 m. The shelf edge east of 130°W is relatively regular, but to the west the upper continental slope becomes significantly steeper, and the shelf edge is unstable to 137°W (Table 1). Between 132°W and 137°W, the shelf break is characterized by slumping of shelf sediment down the slope. Part of the shelf sea floor in this area is characterized by numerous conical mounds with ice cores similar to pingos onshore (Fig. 3, profile E'). Some of these features are as much as 1,000 m in diameter at the base and rise to within 18 m of the sea surface.

The western Beaufort Sea is characterized by a shallow inner shelf, with a gradient of 1 m/km, that extends from the shore to a slump-controlled break in slope near the 60 m isobath. It is basically a wave-cut surface. The outer portion of the shelf has a steeper gradient of about 16 m/km and extends seaward to the outer shelf break at depths of 200 to 800 m. It apparently reflects a region where slumping and other gravity-controlled processes are causing mechanical erosion on the present shallow shelf.

Eurasia. The bathymetry of both the East Siberian and Laptev Seas is poorly known. The continental shelf of the East Siberian Sea, one of the widest in the world, is a flat, very shallow plain (Plate 1). Only the Indigirka and Kolyma Submarine valleys (Plate 1), which reflect submerged Pleistocene river channels, provide relief. The extreme shoaling is demonstrated by the fact that 350 km from shore west of the Kolyma Valley the shelf is less than 30 m deep. West of Indigirka Valley, depths at 250 km from shore range from 10 to 15 m (Naugler and others, 1974). Profile I' on Figure 3 and Plate 1 indicate that seaward of the shallow shelf a prominent bench is present between 100 and 200 m. Its origin is uncertain, but it may represent an intrashelf delta front.

The Laptev Sea shelf has been described by Holmes and Creager (1974) as consisting of flat, terrace-like features that occur at regular intervals from 10 to 40 m below sea level. Submerged river canyons, similar to those of the East Siberian Sea, are present on the sea bed (Plate 1). The shelf break is at a depth of about 100–200 m (Table 1, Fig. 2, profiles 10 and 11, Plate 1, and Fig. 3, profile J').

Marginal Plateaus

Morris Jesup and Yermak Plateaus. The Morris Jesup Plateau is a poorly known bathymetric feature outlined by the 1,000 m isobath off the northeastern coast of Greenland (Plate 1). It was discovered by Ice Island ARLIS II, which obtained echo soundings, shallow seismic reflection, and gravity measurements over the plateau in 1964 (Ostenso and Wold, 1977). Its counterpart, the Yermak Plateau, which lies northwest of Svalbard, is much better known (Jackson and others, 1984). These plateaus may have related magnetic expressions as shown by Perry and others (1980). The magnetic fields may have a dual origin: oceanic volcanism for the outer section, and continental rocks for the inner one.

Chukchi Borderland. The Chukchi Borderland, which consists of the relatively shallow, flat-topped Chukchi Plateau and Northwind Ridge (Plate 1) and an intervening deep basin containing the Northwind Abyssal Plain and Sea Valley, is 400 km wide and 600 km long. It extends northward from the

Chukchi Shelf between 160° and 170° W longitude (Beal, 1969; Hunkins and others, 1962; Hall, this volume). Arlis Plateau, commonly considered part of Mendeleev Ridge, appears to more closely resemble the flat-topped ridges of the Chukchi Borderland as a relatively shallow marginal plateau. Chukchi Plateau, the largest highstanding feature on the borderland has flat shelves at 270 m and 400–500 m below sea level and rises locally to within 246 m of sea level (Hunkins and others, 1962) (Fig. 2, profile 12). The highest shelf is marked by small-scale relief of 5 to 30 m, which is probably the result of ice gouging during a period when the sea level was lower than at present. The eastern margin of the borderland is the Northwind Escarpment, a steep slope on the east side of the Northwind Ridge that abuts the deep Canada Basin at depths near 3,900 m. Gentler slopes, irregular in plan, characterize the other margins. Bathymetric characteristics suggest that the high-standing parts of the borderland consist of continental crust (Hunkins and others, 1962; Shaver and Hunkins, 1964), in that it is attached morphologically to, and is apparently continuous with, the continental margin.

Continental Slope and Rise

East Greenland. The east Greenland Continental Slope is well developed, with gradients ranging from 20 to 65 m/km. From the slope to the Greenland Fracture Zone, the base of the continental slope generally lies below 2,000 m. South of the fracture zone, the base of the slope is found at depths of 1,500 to 3,000 m. An extensive insular rise bordering the east Greenland slope from 74° to 77°N grades into the Greenland Abyssal Plain. The rise is more than 280 km wide at 74°N, but narrows to the north and is only about 75 km wide on the south side of the Greenland Fracture Zone. It further narrows abruptly at the fracture zone, and averages only 55 km in width to the north of it. This narrowing is probably a reflection of increasing distance from the sediment source. The rise pinches out at about 80°30′N, where the Spitsbergen Fracture Zone impinges upon the Greenland continental block.

Canada. The character of the continental slope in the Lincoln Sea is unknown. To the southwest, however, the continental shelf off Ellesmere Island has been sounded and is known to be marked by a saddle as great as 1,800–2,000 m deep that separates it from the Alpha Ridge (Fig. 2, profile 13; Fig. 3, profile B′; and Fig. 5, profile H). The depth of the continental shelf break north of Ellesmere Island ranges from 250 m to 400 m (Fig. 2). The slope gradient in this area ranges from 10 to 20 m/km, and the slope bottoms out in a saddle at depths of 1,300 to 1,650 m. The continental slope seaward of Ellef Ringnes, Borden, and Prince Patrick islands consists of an inner slope with a gradient of 12 to 30 m/km and an outer, more gentle slope with a gradient of 5 to 15 m/km (Fig. 3, profiles C′ and D′). Off Banks Island (Fig. 2, profile 14), the slope has a gradient that averages 20 m/km, and the base of the slope is slightly deeper than 3,000 m. The end of this profile shows an anomalous area of rough terrain on the continental rise. Johnson and others, 1979, contoured it as an extensive submarine fan and levee complex; however, this interpretation was based on speculation, as sufficient data are not available for a proper determination. Plate 1 contours show a more conservative interpretation. Seaward of Tuktoyaktuk Peninsula the gradient is 12 m/km, and the base of the slope rise to a depth of only 1,500 m. The southward decrease in the depth to the base of the continental slope is a consequence of the abutment of the large Mackenzie Cone continental rise sedimentary prism against the continental slope and rise off Banks Island on the Canadian Beaufort shelf. The surface of this large depositional prism commences in the Mackenzie Delta and merges with the Canada Abyssal Plain (Plate 1) 400–450 km to the west at depths of about 3,600 m.

Alaska. The continental slope north of Alaska follows a gentle arc from Mackenzie Bay to Northwind Ridge of the Chukchi Borderland (Plate 1). Its junction with the continental rise lies at depths of 1,100 to 2,000 m, and its average slope ranges from 7 to 22 m/km. Local steep pitches slope 30 m/km. Numerous slumps, landslides, and incised channels characterize the Alaska continental slope (Fig. 3, profile F′, G′, and H′). The largest slide masses originate at or near the main (outer) shelf break. Along many crossings the vertical drop at the headwall of these slides is 900 to 1,200 m, and the head-to-toe length of some large slides exceeds 35 km (Grantz and others, 1981).

Seismic and bathymetric profiles show that many canyons incise the Alaska continental slope. Some appear to be slump scars; others contain bedded sediments, are bordered by levees, and appear to be turbidity current channels. In these channels, the upper surface of the sedimentary fill is commonly tilted up toward the eastern bank, owing to the Coriolis effect on the depositing current (Grantz and others, 1981). The continental rise north of Alaska is much narrower (about 65 km) than in the Canadian sector (Fig. 3, profile F′).

Eurasia. The Eurasia continental slope, although scarcely known, appears to be typical of other continental slopes. Figure 2, profiles 6–11, are bathymetric profiles across the slope from the Laptev Sea. All show irregularities indicative of either canyons or slumps. The continental rise is well developed landward of the Wrangel Abyssal Plain, and the 2,800 m depth of this plain is at least partially controlled by sediment ponding behind a bedrock sill (Kutschale, 1966).

BASINS AND ABYSSAL PLAINS

Eurasia Basin

The medial Arctic Mid-Ocean Ridge divides the Eurasia Basin into two sub-basins—Nansen Basin to the south and Amundsen Basin to the north. The deepest part of Nansen Basin (3,850 m) lies at its western end, where the relatively small Barents Abyssal Plain (A.P.) is wedged between Barents Shelf, Yermak Plateau, and the Arctic Mid-Ocean Ridge (Plate 1). Sediments originating mainly from the Kara and Laptev shelves have filled the east end of the Nansen Basin, partly buried the eastern part of the bordering Arctic Mid-Ocean Ridge, and restricted the Barents A.P. to the eastern part of the basin. The Lena

River must be the major contributor to this sedimentary fill (Johnson, 1969).

The Pole A.P., first discovered by the U.S. nuclear submarine *Nautilus* (Dietz and Shumway, 1961), is deeper and much larger than the Barents A.P. It is enclosed by the 4,300-m isobath and floors most of the Amundsen Basin. The basin is deepest (a little more than 4,400 m) near the North Pole, suggesting that the primary sources of sediment in the basin are the continental shelves at either end.

Amerasia Basin

Of the five major abyssal plains of the Amerasia Basin, two (Wrangel and Siberia) lie in the Makarov Basin, and three (Canada, Chukchi, and Mendeleev) lie in the Canada Basin (Fig. 2). The Canada A.P., with an area of 25,400 km^2, is by far the most extensive.

The wedge-shaped Makarov Basin lies between the Lomonosov, Alpha, and Mendeleev ridges. It is more than 500 km wide along the East Siberian Shelf and, at the 2,500-m isobath, narrows to a point near Ellesmere Island. The Wrangel A.P., about 2,800 m deep, lies between the East Siberia Shelf and Arlis Gap. Kutschale (1966) reported that a prominent basement ridge underlies Arlis Gap and acts as a dam behind which the sediments of Wrangel A.P. are ponded, and over which they spill onto the deeper (3,900-m) Siberia A.P. The bathymetry suggests that the sediments that incompletely fill the Makarov Basin were deposited from turbidity currents that flowed from the East Siberian Shelf across Wrangel A.P., through Arlis Gap, and onto the Siberia A.P.

The Canada Basin is bounded by the Alpha and Mendeleev ridges, and the Canadian and Alaskan continental shelves. Its deepest area, the Canada A.P. (Plate 1), is remarkably flat, with a uniform depth of about 3,850 m over a great part of its surface. On the east it grades into Mackenzie Cone and the Canadian Continental Rise, which shoal gradually and uniformly upward toward the Mackenzie Delta and the Canadian Arctic Islands. In contrast, the Canada A.P. abuts the Alaska continental slope and rise and the Northwind Escarpment, and rises with marked changes in slope. These morphologic relations indicate that most of the sedimentary fill beneath the Canada A.P. has come from the Mackenzie River Basin and Arctic Islands (Hunkins, 1968).

The Chukchi and Mendeleev Abyssal Plains lie between Chukchi Borderland and Mendeleev Ridge. The Chukchi A.P. (2,100 m depth) is connected via Charlie Gap to the lower-lying Mendeleev A.P. (2,900 m), and a 500 m drop separates the Mendeleev A.P. from the north end of the Canada A.P. Herald Canyon on the western Chukchi Shelf was at least a minor source of sediment to the northern Canada A.P. via the Chukchi A.P., Charlie Gap, and the Mendeleev A.P. (Hunkins, 1968).

Aseismic Submarine Ridges

Lomonosov Ridge. Lomonosov Ridge, an aseismic submarine mountain range, extends 1,700 km from the continental shelf off Ellesmere Island to the continental shelf off the New Siberian Islands (Plate 1). It rises more than 3 km above the Amundsen Basin, which parallels the ridge on the Eurasia Basin side. On the Amerasia Basin side of the ridge lies the shallower Makarov Basin, which separates it from the subparallel Alpha Ridge. The bathymetric gradient of the Makarov-facing slope does not exceed 100 m/km.

The ridge is a relatively narrow, linear, steep-sided, flat-topped feature that parallels the 43°W and 137°E meridians. It is some 200 km wide over most of its length, but near the North Pole is narrows to 65 km. The shallowest depth recorded on top of the ridge is 955 m. Toward Lincoln Sea, the ridge widens considerably and appears to veer southwest toward Ellesmere Island, where it merges with the Alpha Ridge.

Until 1979, the bathymetry of the Lomonosov Ridge was poorly known. Although the Soviets discovered and mapped the ridge (Gakkel, 1958; Karasik and others, 1971), most Soviet bathymetric data remains unavailable to western researchers. As a result, cartographers mapping the Lomonosov Ridge had to rely mainly on generalized contours shown on early, post–World War II, small-scale Soviet maps and on information obtained from U.S. Navy submarines (with questionable navigation) that cruised the area between 1958 and 1962 (Figs. 2 and 5; Beal, 1969). An exception was the bathymetric data collected from U.S. drifting ice station ARLIS II, which, in 1964, obliquely crossed the Lomonosov Ridge from 88°30′N to 86°30′N between the 100°W and 40°W meridians (Ostenso and Wold, 1977). In 1979, the Canadian Department of Energy, Mines, and Resources (EMR) carried out a systematic survey of the Lomonosov Ridge, designated by the acronym LOREX (Lomonosov Ridge Experiment), near the North Pole (Weber, 1983). The LOREX results revealed that the Lomonosov Ridge consists of several slightly tilted en-echelon fault blocks, with scarps facing the Makarov Basin (Blasco and others, 1979). Results from these geophysical studies strengthened the hypothesis (Heezen and Ewing, 1961; Wilson, 1963) that the Lomonosov Ridge is a continental fragment separated from the Kara and Barents shelves during the Late Cretaceous–early Tertiary and transported to its present position by sea-floor spreading (Sweeney and others, 1982; Forsyth and Mair, 1984).

Publicly available bathymetric data on the Lomonosov Ridge outside of the LOREX study area, toward both the Laptev and the Lincoln seas, remains sparse. The junctions of the ridge with the continental shelves on either side are also poorly mapped. On contemporary maps the contours in areas with little or no sounding data are based partly on early Soviet Arctic Basin maps (Burkhanov, 1956; Gordienko and Laktionov, 1960) and partly on classified U.S. Navy submarine data. Without access to the U.S. and Soviet data, assessment of the reliability of the maps in these areas is impossible. Contemporary maps suggest that the Eurasian end of the Lomonosov Ridge is an extension of the New Siberian Islands continental shelf. The North American end of the ridge, on the other hand, merges with the Alpha Ridge near the

Ellesmere Island continental shelf, but it is separated from that shelf by an 1,800- to 2,000-m-deep trough.

Alpha and Mendeleev Ridges. The Alpha and Mendeleev ridges, the largest submarine mountain range complex in the Arctic Ocean, are areally more extensive than the Alps. This complex is about the same length as the Lomonosov Ridge, but slightly deeper, much wider and morphologically more complicated. The ridges separate the Makarov from the Canada Basin. Like the Lomonosov Ridge, they are not seismically active.

Much of the topography of the two ridges is known from the soundings obtained from the United States drifting ice stations ALPHA in 1957–58 (Cabaniss, 1962), T-3 in 1953–57, 1962–63, and 1966–74 (Hunkins and Tiemann, 1977), and ARLIS II in 1962–64 (Wold, 1973), and from echo-grams obtained by U.S. Navy submarines from 1957 to 1962 (Fig. 5, profiles A to H). Hall (1970) carried out a comprehensive study of the Alpha-Mendeleev ridge complex based on the soundings, core samples, and seismic, gravity and magnetic data collected from drifting stations. In 1983 the Canadian Department of Energy, Mines and Resources carried out a multidisciplinary expedition to study the Alpha Ridge: CESAR 83 (Canadian Expedition to Study the Alpha Ridge). In cooperation with the Canadian Hydrographic Service, some 1,300 spot soundings were taken over the continental shelf and Alpha Ridge from the coast of Ellesmere Island to the 120°W meridian. A 100-m contour bathymetric map of the areas of the Lomonosov and Alpha ridges covered by the Canadian LOREX and CESAR surveys, which incorporated all the bathymetric data obtained from the U.S. drifting stations, was compiled by Weber (1986).

The ridge complex is narrowest near 83°N, 180°W in the central Arctic Basin, where the ridge crest is deepest. Belov and Lapina (1958) report this crestal depression to consist of a deep trough with a maximum depth of 2,700 m. This depression, named Cooperation Gap by Treshnikov and others (1966), divides the ridge into two distinct bathymetric features, the Alpha Ridge on the Canadian side, and the Mendeleev Ridge on the U.S.S.R. side of the Amerasia Basin (Plate 1).

The Alpha Ridge is very rugged and consists of ridges and troughs, seamounts and depressions. Although the ridges and troughs are parallel to the overall trend of Alpha Ridge, few continue for long distances (Jackson and Johnson, 1984). Hall (1970) reported sediment thicknesses of from 100 m to 1,200 m on the ridge. A similar range of values was obtained by the CESAR expedition, indicating that relief on the basement is also rugged. Shallow seismic profiles recorded from CESAR (Jackson and others, 1985, 1986) as well as from T-3 show many shortwave length bathymetric features not revealed by the 10-km by 10-km grid of spot soundings used on CESAR to map the ocean floor (Weber and Jackson, 1985). Numerous graben-like troughs bounded by steep faults were reported from the Alpha Ridge by Hall (1970), and a similar structure was traversed by ice station CESAR (Jackson and others, 1985). The physiography of the Mendeleev Ridge is similarly rugged and laced with many fractures. One such area was named by Hall (1970) the Mendeleev Fracture Zone.

Subparallel to the trend of Alpha and Lomonosov Ridges, the Marvin Spur is a relatively small and narrow ridge that juts 120 km into the Siberia A.P. near Greenland. As it trends out of the plain, toward Greenland, the spur becomes strongly asymmetric, and its northern (Lomonosov Ridge–facing) flank becomes a steep scarp. This scarp, which trends 400 km from Siberia A.P. to the Greenland end of Lomonosov Ridge, is parallel to the 40°W meridian. Ice station ARLIS II found a steep scarp with 1,650 m of relief at the north flank of the spur north of 105°W (Ostenso and Wold, 1977). Spot soundings taken during the LOREX and CESAR expeditions along the 160°W and 125°W meridians showed elevation changes of 748 m and 554 m, respectively, at the scarp. This long, steep, continuous escarpment is identified on some older maps (e.g., Heezen and Tharp, 1975) as the Lomonosov Ridge–facing flank of the Marvin spur. Beal and others (1966) proposed that it is an independent feature that bisects the Makarov Basin. Submarine echograms (Figs. 4 and 5, profiles E, F, G, and H), ARLIS II data as reinterpreted by Weber and Sweeney (1985), and preliminary CESAR seismic refraction results (D. A. Forsyth, personal communication, 1984) indicate that this escarpment is the Lomonosov Ridge–facing flank of the Alpha Ridge as first implied by the bathymetric map of Crary (1954). That part of the Siberia A.P. which lies between the escarpment and Lomonosov Ridge is the eastern end of the Makarov Basin. It consists of a wedge-shaped graben that is 70 km wide at its intersection with the Siberia A.P. but narrows to a point where the Alpha and Lomonosov ridges merge near the Lincoln Sea.

A number of diapirs protrude through the sediments of the eastern end of the Makarov Basin. These diapirs, which form knolls that rise as much as 700 m above the abyssal plain (Sobczak and Sweeney, 1978), were referred to as the Marvin Seamounts by Sobczak (1977). However, in order to be called a seamount, a feature needs to have 1,000 m of vertical relief (N. Cherkis, personal communication, 1985). Air-gun seismic reflection profiles (Blasco and others, 1979) show that these diapirs were formed before the basin fill was deposited. Gravity observations indicate that the diapirs consist of rocks higher in density than those exposed in the escarpment (Weber, 1980). The diapirs may represent serpentinized mafic extrusions that originated at the time the Makarov Basin was first formed.

The geophysical and geological aspects and the tectonic origin of the Lomonosov and Alpha ridges are more fully discussed by Weber and Sweeney, Grantz and May, and Harbert and others (this volume).

SUMMARY

The first-order problem in a morphological depiction of the Arctic is that the data base is unevenly distributed. In most areas, even the presence or absence of secondary features, such as canyons in the slopes and rises and glacial scour on the shelves, is unknown. A notable exception is the relatively well-mapped Barents Shelf (Plate 1). The general shape of Alpha Ridge, for exam-

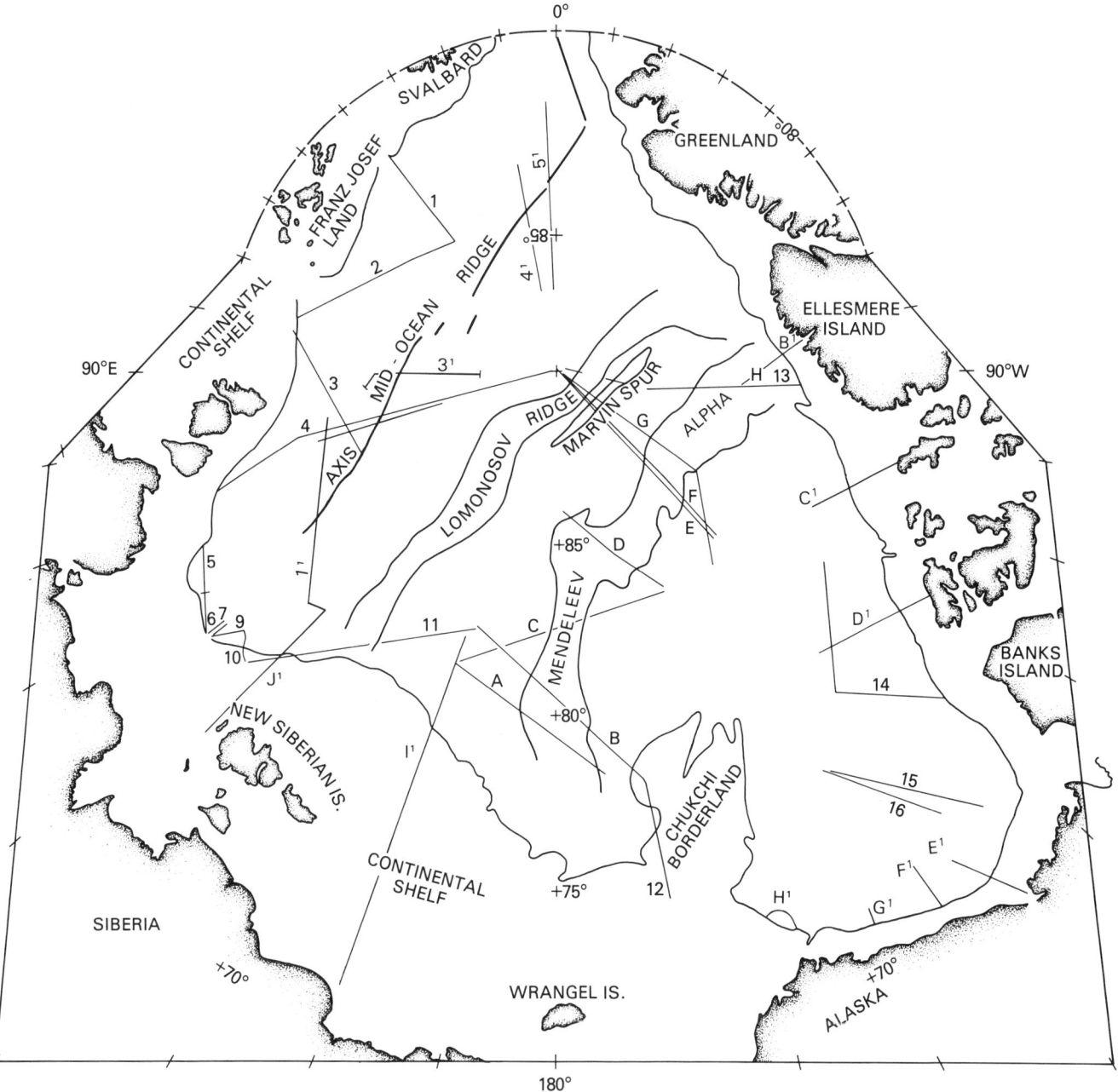

Figure 4. Index for profiles shown in Figures 1, 2, 3, and 5.

ple, is known, but the fabric of individual ridges and valleys is speculative, as is its connection, if any, to the Mendeleev Ridge. Several suggestions have been advanced to correct this deficiency, including surveys by dedicated nuclear research submarines, installation of the SEABEAM seabed scanning system at ice stations, and the deployment of ice-drifting buoys with the capability to acquire and relay seabed soundings to satellites. In the meantime, a large advance in our knowledge of the Arctic would be achieved if classified submarine data were to be declassified and released for scientific purposes beyond that already done for U.S. Navy data, and if classified Soviet data from the North Pole ice floe stations and spot soundings from aircraft would be released for scientific purposes.

In the not-too-distant future it is expected that first-order bathymetric features may be derived from aero-gravimetric and satellite altimeter data (Vogt and others, 1984). To use the latter, algorithms must be constructed to subtract the uneven ice surface. For the former it appears that the Global Positioning System will provide sufficient three-dimensional location accuracy to obtain meaningful gravity data. Magnetic lineations are used now routinely to infer the strike and offset of bathymetric features.

Morphology can be utilized in some cases to infer the gene-

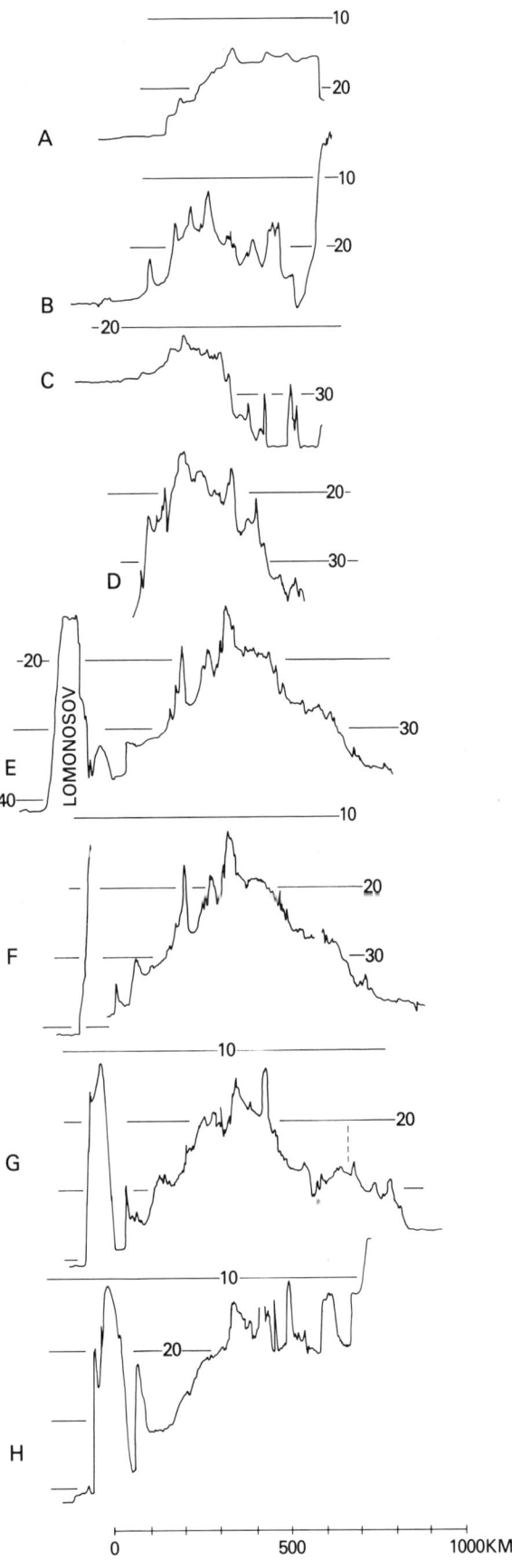

sis of a submarine feature. This is true in several instances in the Arctic. The elevated ridge crest topography and, in the case of Kolbeinsey Ridge, the lack of a rift valley is apparently the result of proximity to the Iceland hot spot (Vogt and others, 1980; Johnson and Jakobssen, 1985).

The Arctic Mid-Ocean Ridge system has a slow-spreading rate of less than 1 cm a year (half-rate). This has created typical Mid-Atlantic Ridge–type, rough, blocky terrain as contrasted with the more subdued relief of faster-spreading ridges. The data base is inadequate to determine whether or not there is a marked change in morphology as one progresses toward the pole of rotation, located in Siberia.

The location of the Iceland hot spot and suspected secondary centers in Svalbard and Jan Mayen (Vogt and others, 1981) may explain the local asymmetry in location of the mid-ocean ridge system. Due to a shift (jump) in the spreading axis (anomaly 6C, 24 Ma), Kolbeinsey Ridge is located in the western section of the Norwegian-Greenland Sea (Vogt and others, 1980). Knipovitch Ridge is situated on the eastern extreme of the basin, probably as the result of a relatively recent ridge relocation (Vogt and others, 1981). In both instances this may be a reflection of the tendency of ridge systems to remain near the heat source.

Bottom currents can sculpt the sea floor, and therefore their presence can be inferred from bottom morphology. Evidence for past or present currents has been reported from the Alpha Ridge region by Hall (1979) and from the crest and flanks of Lomonosov Ridge crest by Aagaard (1981).

In the Arctic, at least two slivers of continental crust which have been transported into oceanic basins by sea-floor spreading are Jan Mayen and Lomonosov ridges. Their relatively smooth, steep sides and rounded tops are quite different from ridges formed entirely by volcanic activity. The bathymetric contours from the pole toward Siberia do, however, suggest a volcanic component to Lomonosov Ridge. This is reinforced by the recent volcanism near Bennett Island (Shabad, 1984) and the Soviet report of volcanism on the Lomonosov Ridge (Gakkel, 1958).

Figure 5. Topographic profiles from early submarine cruises. Profiles A, C, D, and H are from *Sargo,* 1960; profiles B and E are from *Sea Dragon,* 1962; profile F is from *Skate,* 1962; and profile G is from *Sea Dragon,* 1960. Profiles are indexed on Figure 4. Profiles replotted from Beal (1969). Depths in meters × 100.

The spreading rate history and evolution of the Amerasia Basin is obscure, and a number of concepts have been proposed (Grantz and others, ch. 16, and Lawver and Scotese, both this volume). This has created problems in the morphologic interpretation of Alpha Ridge. For example, does the central valley represent a rift valley with orthogonal fractional zones? If Alpha Ridge were a heavily intruded and fractured continental block, its morphology would be quite different.

There is a wide variation in depth of the continental shelves (Table 1) and it is unclear how their depth relates to glacial depression and subsequent rebound, which is thought to be minimal in polar Canada. In general, the deeper shelves are found seaward of the Northwest Territories and Greenland (areas with remnant glacial ice), and the shallowest lie seaward of Alaska and central Siberia where glacial ice is absent. This suggests that glacial rebound is largely complete and that sedimentation rates are high in the latter areas.

Morphological studies of the sea floor thus can complement geophysical studies and in any case, are the base from which geological and geophysical investigations must depart.

REFERENCES CITED

Aagaard, K., 1981, On deep circulation in the Arctic Ocean: Deep-Sea Research, v. 28A, p. 251–268.

Armstrong, T., 1958, The Russians in the Arctic, Aspects of Soviet exploration and exploitation of the Far North, 1937–57: London, Metheun, 182 p.

Balkwill, H. R., and Kyle, R. O., 1985, Seismic evidence for Labrador Shelf Tectonics [abs.]: Calgary, Canadian Society of Exploration Geophysicists/Canadian Geophysical Union, p. 35.

Beal, M. A., 1969, Bathymetry and structure of the Arctic Ocean [Ph.D. thesis]: Corvallis, Oregon State University, 188 p.

Beal, M. A., Edvalson, K., Hunkins, K., Molloy, A., and Ostenso, N., 1966, The floor of the Arctic Ocean: Geographical Names, Arctic, v. 19, p. 215–219.

Belov, N. A., and Lapina, N. N., 1958, New data on the stratification of bottom sediments of the Arctic Basin [In Russian]: Doklady Akademii Nauk SSSR, v. 122, p. 155–218.

Blasco, S. M., Bornhold, B. D., and Lewis, C.F.M., 1979, Preliminary results of surficial geology and geomorphology studies of the Lomonosov Ridge, central Arctic Basin: Geological Survey of Canada Current Research, Paper 79-IC, p. 73–83.

Boeggild, O. B., 1900, The deposits of the sea bottom in the Danish Ingolf expedition, Lono, B., and Dreyer, F., eds., Copenhagen, Printer to the Court, v. 1, Part 3, p. 1–89.

Boyd, L. A., 1948, The coast of northeast Greenland: American Geographical Society Special Publication, 339 p.

Burkhanov, V., 1956, New Soviet discoveries in the Arctic: Moscow, Foreign Languages Publishing House, 60 p.

Cabaniss, G. H., 1962, Geophysical data from U.S. Arctic Drifting Stations, 1957–1960: Air Force Cambridge Research Laboratory, U.S.A.F. Research Note AFCRL—62-683, 234 p.

Charcot, J.B.A., 1938, Dans la mer de Groenland: Paris, les croisères du Pourquoi Pas, Elbeuf, 221 p.

Crary, A. P., 1954, Bathymetric chart of the Arctic Ocean: Geological Society of America Bulletin, v. 65, p. 709–712.

DeGerlache, A., 1907, Carte Bathymetrique de la mer du Groenland, Croisere oceanographique accomple a bord de la Belgica dans la mer du Groenland, 1905: Bruxelles, Charles Bulens, 345 p.

DeLeeuw, M. M., 1967, New Canadian bathymetric chart of the western Arctic Ocean, north of 72°: Deep Sea Research, v. 14, no. 5, p. 489–504.

Deminitskaya, R. M., and Dibner, V. D., 1966, Morphological structure and the Earth's crust of the North Atlantic region, Poole, W. H., ed.: Geological Survey of Canada Paper 66-15, p. 62–79.

Dibner, V. D., Gakkel, Ya Ya, Litvin, V. M., Martynov, V. T., and Shurgayeva, N. D., 1965, Geomorphological map of the Arctic Ocean: Trudy Nauchno-Issledovatel'skogo Instituta Geologii Arktiki, v. 143, p. 341–345. [In Russian], scale 1:5,000,000.

Dietz, R. S., and Shumway, G., 1961, Arctic Basin geomorphology: Geological Society of America Bulletin, v. 72, no. 9, p. 1319–1330.

Eggvin, J., 1963, Bathymetric chart of the Norwegian Sea and adjacent areas: Bergen, Norway, Fiskeridirektorates Havforskningsinstitutt. scale 1:5,000,000.

Feden, R. A., Vogt, P. R., and Fleming, H. S., 1979, Magnetic and bathymetric evidence for the "Yermak" hot spot northwest of Svalbard in the Arctic Basin: Earth and Planetary Science Letters, v. 44, p. 18–38.

Fedhynskii, V. V., Rassokho, A. U., Demintskaya, R. M., Karasik, A. M., and Rozhdestbenskii, S. S., 1975, The structure of the anomalous magnetic field of the southwest part of the Mohns Ridge [In Russian]: Doklady Akademii Nauk, SSSR, v. 223, p. 237–240.

Ferrand, W. R., and Gajda, R. T., 1962, Isobases on the Wisconsin marine limit in Canada: Ottawa, Department of Mines and Technical Services, Geographical Bulletin 17, p. 5–22.

Forsyth, D. A., and Mair, J. A., 1984, Crustal structure of the Lomonosov Ridge and the Fram and Makarov basins near the North Pole: Journal of Geophysical Research, v. 89, p. 473–481.

Gakkel, Ya Ya, 1958, Evidence of recent submarine volcanism on the Lomonosov Ridge: Moscow, Priroda, v. 4, p. 87–90.

—— , 1962, The exploration and development of polar lands, in Harris, C. D., ed., Soviet geography; Accomplishments and tasks: New York, American Geographical Society Occasional Publication no. 1, p. 265–274.

Gordienko, P. A. and Laktionov, A. F., 1960, Principal results of the latest oceanographic research in the Arctic Basin: Akad. Nauk, SSSR, Izvestiya, Geographical series no. 5, p. 22–23.

Grantz, A., Eittreim, S., and Whitney, O.T., 1981, Geology and physiography of the continental margin north of Alaska and implications for the origin of the Canada Basin; in Churkin, M., Nairn, A., and Stehli, F., eds.: The ocean basin and margins, Plenum Press, v. 5, p. 439–492.

Gronlie, G., and Talwani, M., 1979, Bathymetry of the Norwegian-Greenland Sea: Norsk/Polarinsitutt Skrifter, v. 170, p. 3–24.

Hall, J. K., 1970, Arctic Ocean geophysical studies, The Alpha Cordillera and Mendeleyev Ridge: Washington, D.C., Office of Naval Research Technical Report no. CU-2-70, 125 p.

—— , 1979, Sediment waves and other evidence of paleo-bottom currents at two locations in the deep Arctic Ocean: Sedimentary Geology, v. 23, p. 269–299.

Harris, R. A., 1904, Some indication of land in the vicinity of the North Pole: National Geographic Magazine, v. 15, p. 255–261.

Heezen, B. C., and Ewing, M., 1961, The Mid-Oceanic Ridge and its extension through the Arctic Basin, in Raasch, G. O., ed., Geology of the Arctic: University of Toronto Press, p. 622–642.

Heezen, B. C., and Tharp, M., 1975, Bathymetry of the Arctic region: New York, American Geographic Society, scale 1:5,000,000.

Helland-Hanson, B., and Koeford, E., 1907, Croisière Oceanographique accompli a bord de la *Belgica* dans la mer du Gronland 1905, Hydrographie: Bruxelles, Charles Bulens, p. 275–347.

Hill, E. R., Grantz, A., May, S. D., and Smith, M., 1984, Bathymetric map of the

Chukchi Sea: U.S. Geological Survey Miscellaneous Investigations Series Map I-II82-8, scale 1:1,000,000.
Holmes, M. L., and Creager, J. S., 1974, Holocene history of the Laptev Sea Continental Shelf, in Herman, Y., ed., Marine geology and oceanography of the Arctic Seas: New York, Springer-Verlag, p. 211–230.
Holtedahl, O., and Holtedahl, H. W., 1961, On "marginal channels" along continental borders and the problem of their origin: University of Uppsala, Geological Institute Bulletin, v. 40, p. 183–187.
Hunkins, K., 1961, Seismic studies of Arctic Ocean floor, in Raasch, G. O., ed., Geology of the Arctic: University of Toronto Press, p. 646–665.
——, 1968, Geomorphic provinces of the Arctic Ocean, in Sater, J. E., ed., Arctic drifting stations: Arctic Institute of North America, p. 365–376.
Hunkins, K., and Tiemann, W., 1977, Geophysical data summary for Fletcher's Ice Island (T-3) May 1962–October 1974: Washington, D.C., Office of Naval Research Technical Report no. CU-1-77, 219 p.
Hunkins, K., Herron, T., Kutschale, H., and Peter, G., 1962, Geophysical studies of the Chukchi Cap, Arctic Ocean: Journal of Geophysical Research, v. 67, p. 235–247.
Jackson, H. R., and Johnson, G. L., 1984, Structure and history of the Amerasian Basin, Arctic Geology: Moscow, 27th International Geological Congress Proceedings, p. 143–151.
Jackson, H. R., Johnson, G. L., Sundvor, E., and Myhre, A. M., 1984, The Yermak Plateau, formed at a triple junction: Journal of Geophysical Research, v. 89, p. 3223–3232.
Jackson, H. R., Mudie, P. J., and Blasco, S. M., eds., 1985, Initial geological data report on CESAR; Expedition to study Alpha Ridge: Geological Survey of Canada, Paper 84-22, 177 p.
Jackson, H. R., Forsyth, D., and Johnson, G. L., 1986, Oceanic affinities of the Alpha Ridge, Arctic Ocean: Marine Geology, v. 73, p. 237–261.
Johnson, G. L., 1969, Morphology of the Eurasian Arctic Basin: Polar Record, v. 14, p. 619–628.
Johnson, G. L., and Eckhoff, O. B., 1966, Bathymetry of north Greenland Sea: Deep Sea Research, v. 14, p. 755–771.
Johnson, G. L., and Heezen, B. C., 1967a, Morphology and evolution of the Norwegian-Greenland Sea: Deep Sea Research, v. 13, no. 6, p. 1161–1173.
——, 1967b, The Arctic Mid-Oceanic Ridge: Nature, v. 215, p. 724–725.
Johnson, G. L., and Jakobsson, S. P., 1985, Structure and petrology of the Reykjanes Ridge between 62°55'N and 63°48'N: Geophysical Research, v. 90, p. 10073–10083.
Johnson, G. L., and Vogt, P. R., 1973, The Mid-Atlantic Ridge from 47°–51°N: Geological Society of America Bulletin, v. 84, p. 3443–3462.
Johnson, G. L., Southall, J. R., Yound, P. W., and Vogt, P. R., 1972, The origin and structure of the Iceland Plateau and Kolbeinsey Ridge: Journal of Geophysical Research, v. 77, p. 5688–5696.
Johnson, G. L., McMillan, N. J., Rasmussen, M., Campsie, U., and Dittmar, F., 1975, Sedimentary rocks dredged from the southwest Greenland continental margin, in Yorath, C., Parker, E. R., and Glass, D. J., eds., Canadian continental margins and offshore petroleum exploration: Canadian Society of Petroleum Geology Memoir, v. 4, p. 391–410.
Johnson, G. L., Monahan, D., Gronlie, G., and Sobczak, L., 1979, Bathymetric chart of the Arctic, GEBCO Sheet 5:17 : Ottawa, Canadian Hydrographic Service, scale 1:6,000,000.
Johnson, G. L., Vanney, J. R., and Hayes, D., 1982, The Antarctic Continental Shelf, in Craddock, C., ed., Antarctic geoscience,: University of Wisconsin Press, p. 995–1002.
Karasik, A. M., Gurench, N. I., Masalov, V. N., and Shchelovanov, V. G., 1971, Some features of the deep structure and genesis of the Lomonosov Ridge based data of airborne magnetic surveys: Geofiz. Metody Razvedki v. Arktiki, v. 6, p. 9–16.
Keen, M. J. and Williams, G. L., 1990, The Geology of the Continental Margin off Eastern Canada: Ottawa, Geological Survey of Canada, Geology of Canada series, v. 7 (Geological Society of America, The Geology of North America, v. I-1) (in press).
Kovacs, L. C., and Vink, G., 1984, New aeromagnetic data from the high Arctic and Norwegian-Greenland Sea [abs.]: CMOS/CGU 18th Annual Congress, Dalhousie University, p. 127.
Kutschale, H., 1966, Arctic ocean geophysical studies; The southern half of the Siberian Basin: Geophysics, v. 31, p. 683–710.
Laktionov, A. V., 1959, Bottom topography of the Greenland Sea in the region of Nansen's Sill: Priroda, v. 10, p. 95–97.
Litvin, V. M., 1964, Bottom relief of the Norwegian Sea [In Russian]: Trudy Polyarnii, Nauchno-Issledovatelniy Institute Morskoy Rhybnoe Khozyaystvo Okeanografiya (PINRO), v. 16, p. 89–109.
Maury, M. F., 1855, Physical geography of the sea: New York, Harpers, 389 p.
Mayer, O., Voppel, D., Fleischer, U., Closs, H., and Gerke, K., 1972, Results of bathymetric magnetic, and gravimetric measurements between Iceland and 70°N: Deutsche Hydrographische Zeitschsrift, v. 25, p. 193–201.
Nansen, F., 1902, Comparison between North Polar Basin and the Norwegian Sea, Norwegian North Polar expedition, 1893–1896; Scientific results: Christiania, Jacob Dybwad, publisher, v. III, p. 406–407.
——, 1922, The strandflat and isostasy: London, Vidinskapsselskapets Skrifter I, Mat-Naturv. Kl., 313 p.
Naugler, F. P., Silverberg, N., and Creager, J. S., 1974, Recent sediments of the east Siberian Sea, in Herman, Y., ed., Marine geology and oceanography of the Arctic Seas: New York, Springer-Verlag, p. 191–210.
Ohta, Y., 1982, Morpho-tectonic studies around Svalbard and the northernmost Atlantic, in Balkwill, H. R., and Embrey, A. R., eds., Proceedings of Third International Symposium on Arctic Geology: Calgary, Canadian Society of Petroleum Geologists, Memoir 8, p. 415–430.
Ostenso, N. A., 1962, Geophysical investigation of the Arctic Ocean Basin: University of Wisconsin Research, Geophysical and Polar Research Center, Research Report 4, 124 p.
Ostenso, N. A., and Wold, R. J., 1977, A seismic and gravity profile across the Arctic Ocean Basin: Tectonophysics, v. 37, p. 1–24.
Patterson, W.S.B., 1977, Extent of late Wisconsinan glaciation in northwest Greenland and northern Ellesmere Island; A review of the glaciological and geological evidence: Quaternary Research, v. 8, p. 180–190.
Perry, R. K., Fleming, H. S., Cherkis, N. Z., Feden, R. H., and Massingill, J. V., 1977, Bathymetry of the Norwegian-Greenland and western Barents seas: Geological Society of America Map and Chart Series MC-21. Scale 1:2,333,230 at 71°N.
Perry, R. K., and Fleming, H. S., compilers, 1986, Bathymetry of the Arctic Ocean: Geological Society of America Map and Chart Series MC-56.
Ritchie, G. S., 1969, North Polar Chart No. 4006: Taunton, United Kingdom, Hydrographer of the Navy. Scale 1:7,551,000 at 90°N.
Ruddiman, W. F., 1972, Sediment redistribution on the Reykjanes Ridge, Seismic evidence: Geological Society of America Bulletin, v. 83, p. 2039–2062.
Sclater, J. G., Anderson, R. N., and Bell, M. L., 1971, Elevation of ridges and evolution of the central eastern Pacific: Journal of Geophysical Research, v. 76, p. 7888–7915.
Shabad, T., 1984, News Notes: Polar Geography and Geology, v. 8, p. 172.
Shaver, R. H., and Hunkins, K., 1964, Arctic Ocean geophysical studies; Chukchi Cap and Chukchi Abyssal Plain: Deep-Sea Research, v. 11, p. 905–916.
Sigurdsson, H., and Brown, G. M., 1970, An unusual Enstatite-Forsteritic Basalt from Kolbeinsey Island, North of Iceland: Journal of Petrology, v. 11, p. 205–220.
Sleep, N. H., and Biehler, S. H., 1970, Topography and tectonics at the intersections of fracture zones with central rifts: Journal of Geophysical Research, v. 75, p. 2752–2782.
Sobczak, L. W., 1977, Bathymetry of the Arctic Ocean north of 85° latitude: Tectonophysics, v. 42, p. T-27–T-33.
Sobczak, L. W., and Sweeney, J. F., 1978, Bathymetry of the Arctic Ocean, in Sweeney, J. F., ed., Arctic geophysical review: Ottawa, Earth Physics Branch, v. 45, no. 4, p. 7–14.
Sweeney, J. F., and Haines, G. V., 1978, Arctic geophysical review: An introduction, in Sweeney, J. F., ed., Arctic geophysical review: Ottawa, Earth Physics Branch, v. 45, no. 4, p. 1–6.
Sweeney, J. F., Weber, J. R., and Blasco, S. M., 1982, Continental ridges in the

Arctic Ocean; LOREX constraints: Tectonophysics, v. 89, p. 217–238.
Sylvester, A. G., 1975, History and surveillance of volcanic activity on Jan Mayen Island: Bulletin Volcanologique, v. 39, p. 1–23.
Talwani, M., and Eldholm, O., 1977, Evolution of the Norwegian-Greenland Sea: Geological Society of America Bulletin, v. 88, p. 969–999.
Treshnikov, A. F., Balakshin, L. L., Belov, N. A., Demenitskaya, R. M., Dibner, V. D., Karasik, A. M., Shpaikher, A. D., and Shurgaeva, N. D., 1966, Geographic names of the main features of the floor of the Arctic Basin: Problemy Arktiki i Antarktiki, v. 27, p. 1–25 [In Russian] [Naval Electronic Laboratory Translation 116, 1967].
Vogt, P. R., Schneider, E. D., and Johnson, G. L., 1969, The crust and upper mantle beneath the sea in the Earth's crust and upper mantle, in Beloussov, V. V., and Hart, P. J., eds., The Earth's crust and upper mantle: American Geophysical Union Monograph 13, p. 556–617.
Vogt, P. R., Johnson, G. L., and Kristjannson, L., 1980, Morphology and magnetic anomalies north of Iceland: Journal of Geophysics, v. 47, p. 67–80.
Vogt, P. R., Perry, R. K., Feden, R. H., Fleming, H. S., and Cherkis, N. Z., 1981, The Greenland-Norwegian Sea and Iceland environment; Geology and geophysics, in Churkin, M., Nairn, A. E., and Stehli, F. G., eds., The ocean basins and margins: New York, Plenum Press, p. 493–598.
Vogt, P. R., Zondek, B., Fell, P. W., Cherkis, N. Z., and Perry, R. K., 1984, Seasat altimetry, the North Atlantic geoid, and evaluation by shipborne subsatellite profiles: Journal of Geophysical Research, v. 89, p. 9885–9903.
Volkov, P., 1961, New explorations of the bottom topography in the Greenland Sea: Morskoi Flot, v. 3, p. 35–37 [In Russian].

Weber, J. R., 1980, Exploring the Arctic sea floor: Ottawa, Department of Energy, Mines and Resources, GEOS, v. 9, p. 2–7.
——, 1983, Maps of the Arctic basin sea floor; A history of bathymetry and its interpretation: Arctic, v. 36, p. 121–142.
——, 1986, The Alpha Ridge: gravity, seismic and magnetic evidence for a homogenous, mafic crust; in Johnson, G. L., and Kaminuma, K., eds., Polar Geophysics: Journal of Geodynamics, v. 6, p. 117–136.
Weber, J. R., and Jackson, H. R., 1985, CESAR Bathymetry, in Jackson, H. R., Mudie, P. J., and Blasco, S. M., eds., Initial geological data report on CESAR; Canadian Expedition to study the Alpha Ridge: Geological Survey of Canada, Paper 84-22, p. 15–17.
Weber, J. R., and Sweeney, J. F., 1985, Reinterpretation of morphology and crustal structure in the central Arctic Basin: Journal of Geophysical Research, v. 90, p. 663–672.
Wilson, J. T., 1963, Hypothesis of the Earth's behavior: Nature, v. 198, p. 925–929.
Wold, R. J., 1973, Gravity surveys of the Arctic Ocean Basin; Final report: Milwaukee, University of Wisconsin, 222 p.
Worzel, J. L., 1968, Advances in marine geophysical research of continental margins: Canadian Journal of Earth Sciences, v. 5, p. 963–983.

MANUSCRIPT ACCEPTED BY THE SOCIETY NOVEMBER 14, 1986

(Above and page 78) Thule District, Greenland. Photos from Jurgen Taagholt, Commission for Scientific Research in Greenland.

Chapter 6

Seismicity and focal mechanisms of the Arctic region and the North American plate boundary in Asia

Kazuya Fujita and David B. Cook
Department of Geological Sciences, Michigan State University, East Lansing, Michigan 48824-1115
Henry Hasegawa, David Forsyth, and Robert Wetmiller
Geophysics Division, Geological Survey of Canada, Department of Energy Mines and Resources, 1 Observatory Crescent, Ottawa, Ontario K1A OY3, Canada

INTRODUCTION

Although Arctic earthquakes have been recorded since 1908, detailed study of them has been hampered due to the lack of seismograph stations and the infrequent occurrence of large earthquakes north of the Arctic Circle. Detailed analysis of Arctic earthquakes began during the International Geophysical Year (IGY, 1957–1958), and subsequent studies have been facilitated by the development of the World-Wide Standardized Seismograph Network (WWSSN) starting in 1963.

Many authors have published summaries of Arctic seismicity. The pre-IGY state of knowledge is summarized by Hodgson and others (1965), and epicentral coordinates and magnitude estimates of pre-WWSSN seismicity are given in Gutenberg and Richter (1954), Linden (1961), Hodgson and others (1965), and Rothe (1969). Overview summaries of the distribution and magnitude of Arctic seismicity are presented by Sykes (1965) and Wetmiller and Forsyth (1978). Numerous maps of Arctic seismicity have been published (e.g., Veis-Ksenofontova, 1962; Sykes, 1965; Barazangi and Dorman, 1970; Tarr, 1970; Wetmiller, 1978; Avetisov and Sokolova, 1980). Additional details about Arctic seismicity are given in international bulletins, national seismicity summaries, and annual reports.

In this chapter we summarize the development of seismograph stations in the Arctic, the distribution of seismicity in the Arctic, focal mechanisms that have been determined for the Arctic seismic zone, including northeastern Siberia and Baffin Bay, and the implications of the seismic data for plate tectonic models of the region. In addition, we summarize inferences on crustal structure of the Arctic region based on the propagation characteristics of earthquake waves. This chapter covers the seismicity of the Arctic Ocean basins and peripheral continental margins within, and along the margins of, the North American plate.

SEISMIC STATIONS

Prior to the 1950s, only two permanent seismograph stations were operational north of the Arctic Circle: Scoresbysund, Greenland, and Abisko, Sweden (Fig. 1). Except for two stations in Alaska (College and Sitka) and a number of stations in northern Europe, the stations nearest to the study area were south of 55°N. The seismograph station at Resolute, Canada, was established in 1951; detection capability was substantially improved during the IGY, when many stations were upgraded or established (Hodgson and others, 1965). The Soviet Union developed a network in northeast Siberia in the 1970s. The United States established several stations in the Aleutians in the 1950s, and both the United States and Canada expanded their Arctic networks in the early to mid-1960s and 1970s (Poppe, 1980). In addition to permanent stations and networks, several local networks of temporary duration have operated in northeast Siberia, western and north-central Alaska, and Canada.

RELIABILITY AND COMPLETENESS OF THE ARCTIC DATA SET

An understanding of the reliability of hypocentral determinations and the threshold of complete detection is important to the study of Arctic seismicity due to the wide separation and temporal variability in the deployment of seismograph stations. Basham and others (1977) and Leblanc and Wetmiller (1974) consider the implications of the limitations for the continental part of Arctic Canada, and Wetmiller and Forsyth (1978) maintain that their conclusions for northern Canada can be applied to the rest of the Arctic as well.

The above authors conclude that the epicentral coordinates are generally reliable to ±100 km prior to 1962, although some events may have epicentral uncertainties of ±300 km. Since 1962, uncertainties in epicentral locations are about ±50 km for small events, and as low as ±20 km for large, teleseismically recorded events (inset, Fig. 1). Microearthquakes (m < 4 are susceptible to larger epicentral uncertainties, perhaps ±100 km in some instances, especially for events recorded by only a small

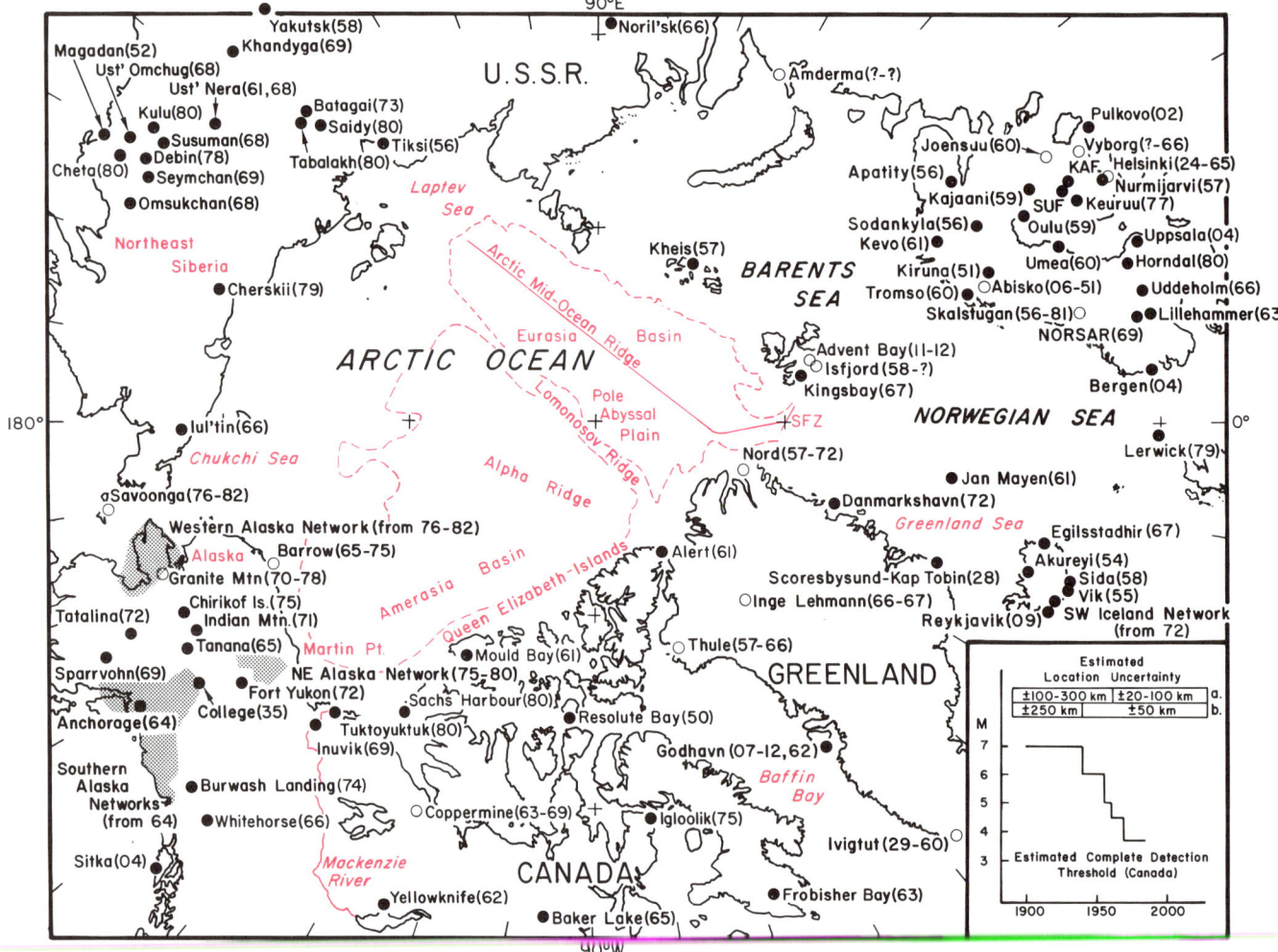

Figure 1. Development of seismic stations in the Arctic. All seismic stations that operated for more than one year are shown; other selected stations are also shown. Solid dots indicate stations presently operating, open circles represent former stations. Dates denote initial year of operation, a terminating date is provided for closed stations. If several stations existed in the same general location, they have been combined with their collective dates of operation shown and the longest operating station name given. Locations and names of several stations in northeast Siberia are approximate. Inset shows the completeness threshold for detection of Arctic earthquakes. Additional geographic and structural features are labelled in red. The dashed red lines outline the major basins of the Arctic Ocean.

number of stations. Kondorskaya and Shebalin (1982) assign epicentral uncertainties of ±250 km to Arctic Ocean basin earthquakes in the early part of the 20th century, and ±50 km after the 1940s. They assign a ±50 km uncertainty for all earthquakes on land until 1964. Microearthquakes detected in Chukotka are also assigned an uncertainty of ±50 km.

Focal depths of Arctic earthquakes are not well constrained except when depth phases have been identified or inversions for centroid depth (the depth of the best-fitting point source) have been performed. In general, focal depths are arbitrarily assigned to the base of the crust; at 10 km in the ocean basins and at 33 km under the continents. Available geophysical data and plate tectonic models support the view that no Arctic earthquakes should occur deeper than 50 km except for those occurring near the subduction zones of Alaska and Kamchatka. A few anomalously deep depths have been reported; however, these are almost certainly mislocations. In general, focal depths determined for most Arctic earthquakes should be viewed as estimates only.

Gutenberg and Richter (1954) suggest that all earthquakes greater than magnitude (M) 7 have been detected since the start of the 20th century and Wetmiller and Forsyth (1978) conclude that this opinion applies to the Arctic as well. With the gradual increase in the number of seismograph stations in the Arctic, the completeness threshold probably decreases to M = 6 in the 1940s and to M = 5 in the mid-1950s (inset, Fig. 1). For the continental part of Arctic Canada, Leblanc and Wetmiller (1974) suggest that all events greater than M 4.5 have been detected since the 1960s. Basham and others (1977) suggest that the completeness

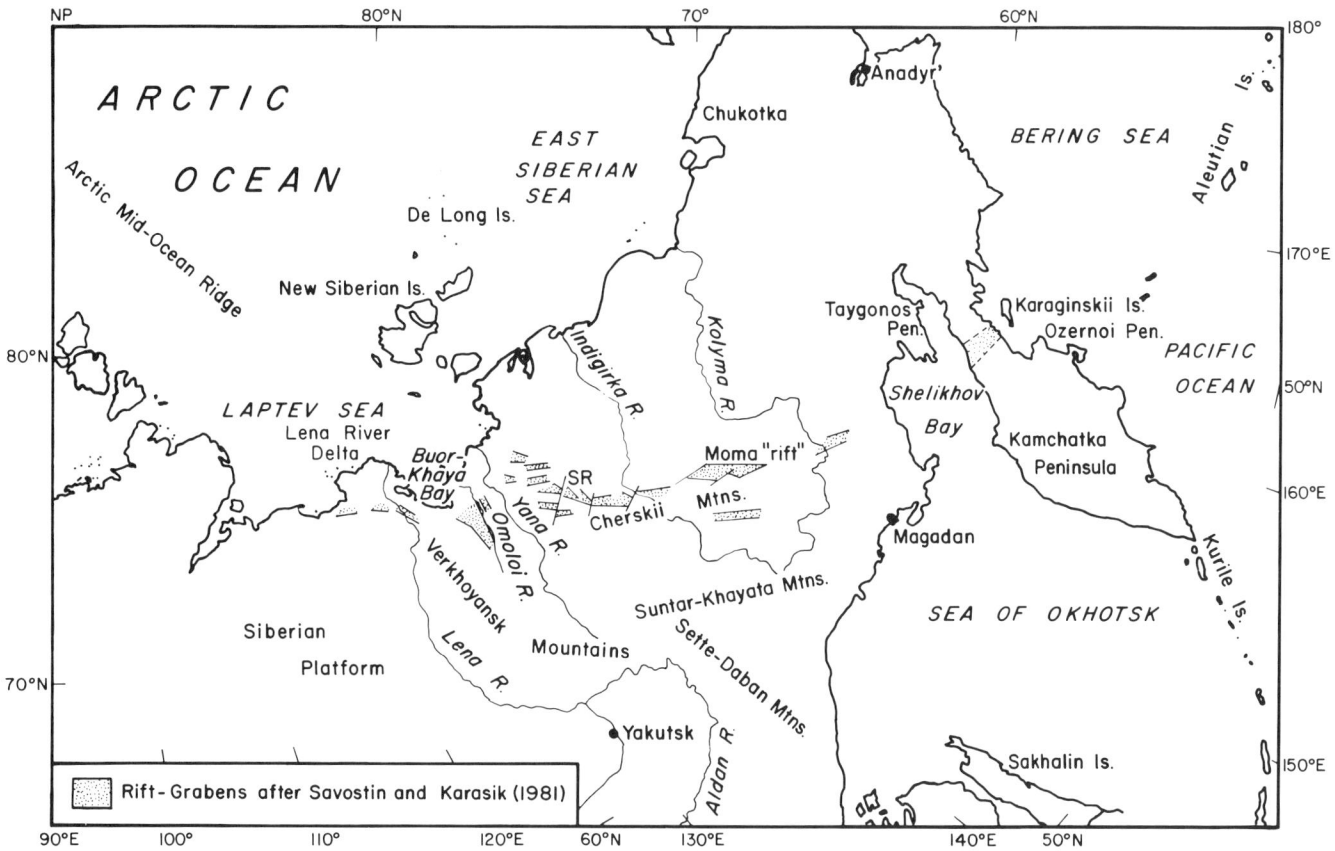

Figure 2. Geographic index map of northeast Siberia. Rift-grabens, as shown by Savostin and Karasik (1981) and Savostin and others (1983), are stippled. SR denotes the Selennyakh Range.

threshold has decreased to 3.7 since 1968. These values are probably also applicable to the continental slope areas bordering Arctic Canada and Alaska.

For the Arctic Ocean, the detection level and completeness threshold magnitudes are certainly higher, particularly near the center of the ocean basin. Using frequency-magnitude relationships, Kristoffersen (1982) suggests that the present completeness threshold along the Arctic Mid-Ocean Ridge may be as high as body wave magnitude (m_b) 5.0–5.2

SEISMICITY

The seismicity of the North American plate in the Arctic (Plate 2) can be partitioned into four regional or tectonic groups. The majority of the events occur along the crest of the Arctic Mid-Ocean Ridge, which forms the boundary between the North American and Eurasian plates and bisects the Eurasia Basin. The seismicity defines a linear trend which may be the longest in the mid-ocean ridge system (Sykes, 1965). On the basis of this trend in seismicity, Emery (1949) and Heezen and Ewing (1961) were the first to postulate that the mid-ocean ridge system extends into the Eurasia Basin. The second group of earthquakes occur along the continuation of the plate boundary onto the Laptev Shelf and into continental Asia (Fig. 2; Plate 2). This zone extends to the northern Sea of Okhotsk, then bends east to northeastern Kamchatka and the junction of the Kurile and Aleutian arcs. A branch of this zone may trend south to Sakhalin and northern Japan from the Cherskii Mountains. The third group consists of intraplate earthquakes, which occur along, and just seaward of, the continental slopes of Greenland, Arctic Canada, Baffin Bay, eastern Greenland, and northeastern Alaska. No similar band of seismicity is noted along the continental slope of northwestern Alaska and northeastern Siberia. In the case of the East Siberian Shelf, however, this observation may be due, in part, to a lack of close-in recording stations. The fourth group consists of intraplate earthquakes that occur in small clusters along the shelves of the Chukchi and East Siberian Seas and form no identifiable trends.

FOCAL MECHANISMS

Many authors have determined focal mechanisms for Arctic earthquakes to investigate the nature of faulting and deviatoric stress orientations. The earliest studies, by Lazareva and Misharina (1965) and Scheidegger (1966), delineate an extensional zone in the Eurasia Basin and a compressional zone in northeast Siberia. Because earthquakes in the Arctic are generally of small magnitude, mechanisms are based primarily on P-wave first motions, usually from short-period records. Soviet authors have determined a number of mechanisms, but have relied primarily on first motions reported in the bulletins of the International Seismological Center (ISC) and the Bureau Central International de Seismologie (BCIS). Both sources may report erroneous first motions that cannot be verified because of the inherent difficulty in checking the data. Due to the lack of regional stations in most of the Arctic, data are primarily from teleseismic distances, and this limitation results in poor constraints on at least one of the nodal planes, in particular for thrust and normal faulting events. The nonuniform station distribution also results in some quadrants with no data, which increases the uncertainty of fault plane solutions.

The radiation patterns of surface waves have been used to further constrain focal mechanisms for larger events (M >5.5); usually Rayleigh waves are studied. Unfortunately, few events of this magnitude occur in the Arctic. For smaller events, surface wave data can sometimes be used to indicate the fault geometry or to place better constraints on the mechanism. Synthetic seismograms can be generated and compared with observed records to determine fault parameters and focal depths. The small magnitudes of Arctic events generally preclude the use of long-period synthetics. Cook and others (1984), however, report some success at modeling short-period records. Since signatures on short-period seismograms are highly sensitive to crustal structure (Seno and Kroeger, 1983), a definitive modeling of short-period records requires the use of a layered medium (e.g., Kroeger and Geller, 1983), and knowledge of the upper crustal structure acquired either from refraction studies or generalized stratigraphic sections. For the largest events, body-wave inversion (Bergman and Solomon, 1984) or moment tensor inversion (Driewonski and others, 1981) have been used for source mechanism studies. Up to the present, fewer than a dozen Arctic earthquakes have been amenable to inversion techniques.

Table 1 summarizes focal mechanism parameters of Arctic earthquakes, regardless of quality or consistency. A reliability estimate of each mechanism is presented by listing the techniques used to determine the mechanism, together with an indication of the degree of constraint of the nodal planes. These constraint levels should be considered in conjunction with the techniques used in assessing the accuracy or reliability of each mechanism.

INTERPLATE SEISMICITY

The Arctic Mid-Ocean Ridge

The seismicity along the Arctic Mid-Ocean Ridge forms a nearly linear band from the northern end of the Spitzbergen Fracture Zone (82°N, 8°W) to the Laptev Sea Shelf (78°N, 125°E) (Fig. 1). On the basis of recent (post-1964) teleseismic epicentral locations (Plate 2), the earthquakes are restricted to a 40–50-km-wide band about the ridge axis. When the accuracy of epicentral locations is considered, the distribution of seismicity indicates no offsets in the ridge axis in excess of 100 km anywhere along the ridge. The largest earthquakes recorded in the oceanic part of the ridge do not exceed magnitude 6.5, with the majority being less than m_b 5.5.

Based on body-waveform inversions, Jemsek and others (1984) determine centroid depths for several large earthquakes along the ridge. The focal depths determined in that study for ridge axis earthquakes are 1–2 km below the seafloor, whereas earthquakes at the northern edge of the Laptev Sea Shelf have focal depths of about 5 km. The reported focal depths for most of the other larger earthquakes along the ridge axis are constrained by depth phases and vary from 5–35 km. There is a strong possibility, however, that the ocean surface reflection, pwP, may be misidentified as pP (Yoshii, 1979) and consequently some of the estimated focal depths may be too great. If it is assumed that the reported pP phases are actually pwP, then revised focal depths of 0–15 km below the sea floor are obtained.

In May, 1979, Kristoffersen and others (1982) operated a sonobuoy array on the ice station Fram 1. The station drifted to within 25 km of the rift valley near the western terminus of the Arctic Mid-Ocean Ridge, and in the course of this journey, over 100 probable small-magnitude (1–2) seismic events were recorded. About 20 of these seismic events were located on the assumption of a shallow focal depth. The epicentral distribution suggests the presence of two linear trends about 10 km apart in the rift valley. Based on the frequency-magnitude dependence of the events, as compared with what normally would be expected for this region, Kristoffersen and others (1982) suggest that the events recorded on Fram 1 represent an earthquake swarm and consequently the recorded activity was more frequent than is the norm for the ridge.

Published focal mechanisms for nine events along the Arctic Mid-Ocean Ridge are listed in Table 1 (#1–9) and shown in Figure 3. Seven of the events indicate almost pure normal faulting with a tension axis perpendicular to the strike of the ridge.

The August 25, 1964 event (#9) is one of the largest earthquakes to occur in the oceanic part of the Arctic (seismic moment, M_o, of 1.35×10^{26} dyne-cm). Jemsek and others (1984) determine that the centroid depth is 4 km and that the rupture propagated from north to south at 2 km/s. The mechanism of this event, as determined by Sykes (1967), has a nonorthoganal orientation of the nodal planes. This is due to the laterally heterogeneous crustal structure at the source, which results in take-off angles to nearby stations that are too small (Solomon and Julian, 1974). The body-wave inversion solution of Jenmsek and others (1984) agrees well with the Sykes (1967) solution and is the preferred solution.

Fault plane solutions for two events, July 31, 1964 (#3) and October 5, 1959 (#7), are different from the above-described normal faulting pattern. Savostin and Karasik (1981) present a predominantly normal faulting mechanism with a sizeable strike-slip component for the 1964 event; however, a pure strike-slip solution would not be inconsistent with the data. The mechanism for the 1959 event is poorly constrained, and plausible interpretations could range from a high-angle dip-slip fault to a strike-slip mechanism. Both of these events can be interpreted as having one

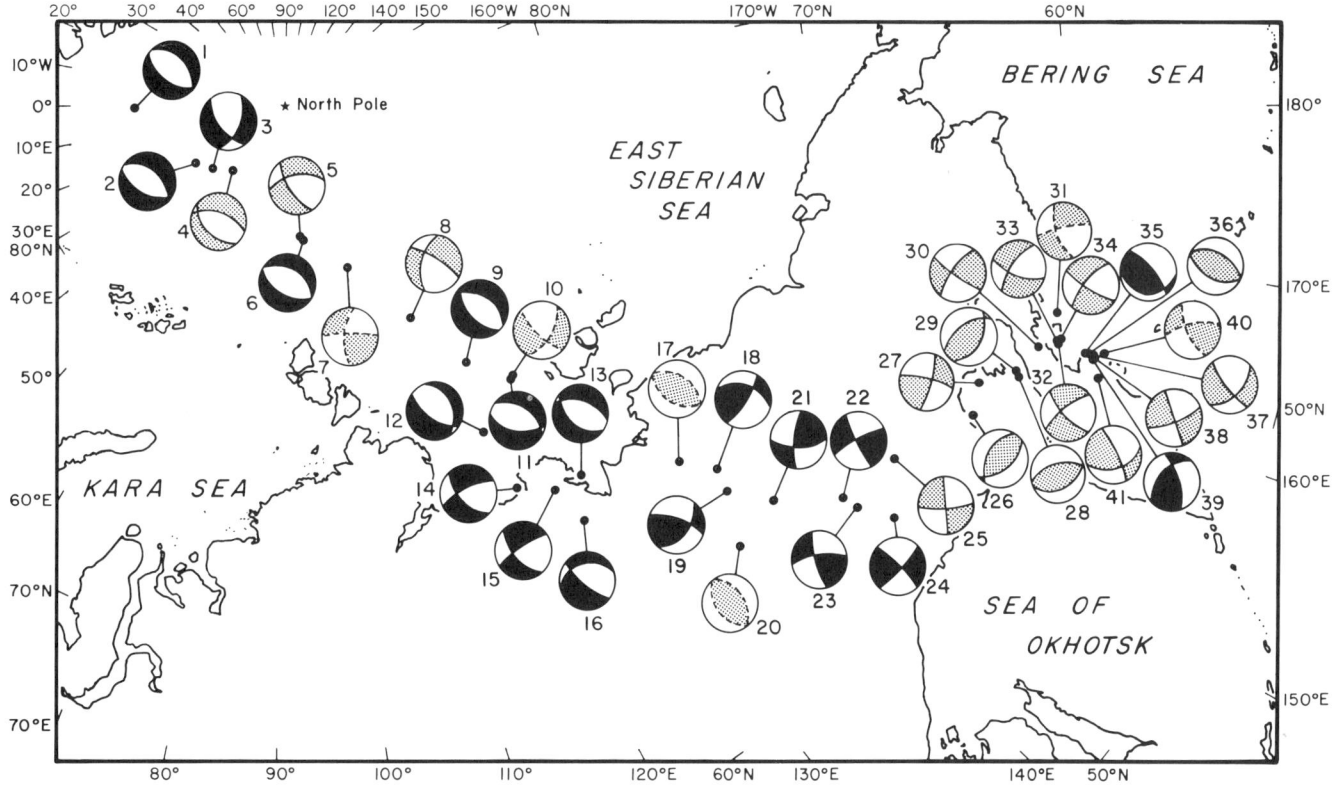

Figure 3. Focal mechanisms of Arctic interplate earthquakes. Lower-hemisphere equal-area projections are shown with compressional quadrants solid; stippled compressional quadrants denote less certain mechanisms and dashed nodal planes indicate that the orientation of the plane is unconstrained. Numbers correspond to Table 1.

nodal plane perpendicular to the strike of the ridge axis, and thus may represent events along short transform faults.

Laptev Sea–Lena River Delta

Along the extension of the North America–Eurasia plate boundary onto the continental shelf of northern Siberia, the seismicity pattern becomes more diffuse (Plate 2). The linear trend of the Arctic Mid-Ocean Ridge seismicity terminates at about 77°N, and the exact location of the plate boundary further south becomes difficult to ascertain. The largest earthquakes appear to occur 300 km west of the linear extrapolation of the ridge axis, and the new trend intersects the coastline of northern Siberia near the Lena River Delta. A diffuse lineation of smaller events occurs along the western side of the New Siberian Islands (see Fig. 8) and may be related to a zone of weakness along a possible suture zone (Fujita and Cook, this volume). Well-constrained focal depths, based on source inversions or depth phases, lie between 10 and 25 km.

Seven focal mechanisms (Table 1, #10–16; Fig. 3) have been determined for earthquakes with epicenters on the Laptev Sea Shelf. Four earthquakes are clear normal faulting events and are related to rifting along an extension of the Arctic Mid-Ocean Ridge (see Grachev, 1982). The April 7, 1969, event (#11), occurred along the extrapolation of the ridge axis into the shelf and has been studied extensively. There is a consensus among the authors who have obtained focal mechanisms for this event that normal faulting predominates. There is, however, disagreement over the relative amount of strike-slip motion. The body-wave inversion solution of Jemsek and others (1984) is the closest of the solutions to a pure normal fault and is the preferred solution. The surface wave radiation pattern (Chapman and Solomon, 1976) suggests a tension axis rotated more to the north than indicated by the body-wave inversion study. A focal depth of 10 km is obtained both from body-wave inversion and waveform modeling.

A m_b 5.6 event (#12) occurred on June 10, 1983, to the southwest of the April 7, 1969, event. Solutions obtained by centroid moment tensor inversion (Dziewonski and others, 1983) and body-wave inversion (Jemsek and others, 1984) agree and show almost pure normal faulting, with only a slight strike-slip component. However, the centroid depths differ, with the body-wave inversion solution 10 km deeper, at 22 km, than the moment tensor solution (Table 1).

The southernmost predominantly normal faulting event occurred on July 21, 1964, in Bour Khaya Bay (#13), off the eastern coast of the Lena River Delta. The focal depth, as determined from waveform modeling, is 12 km, and the focal mecha-

TABLE 1. FOCAL PARAMETERS OF ARCTIC EARTHQUAKES

No	Date H (UTC)	Lat. (°N)	Long. (°)	m_b	M_s	M_o^1	Depth (km)	Dur. (s)	Plane I[2]	Plane II	P-axis[3]	T-axis	Data[4]	T[5]	C[6]	Ref[7]
	Interplate Earthquakes															
1	1976 09 16 03 26 55.4	84.30	0.9 E	5.4	6.5	4.7	1.9¤	3.0	030/51E*	228/40W	248/81	128/06	I	N	-	Jem84
2	1973 11 09 13 42 41.4	86.05	32.8 E	5.4	5.1	5.0	1.3¤	5.0	045/63S*	256/31N	285/68	146/17	I	N	-	Jem84
3	1964 07 31 23 45 55.9	86.47	40.7 E	5.2			7 †		331/53N*	089/59S	303/52	208/04	B	N	F	Sav81
4	1968 06 08 00 41 28.7	87.00	51.4 E	5.2	4.6		32 †		248/54N*	096/40S	105/73	350/07	B	N	P	Sav81
5	1975 03 02 14 23 26.2	85.01	98.0 E	5.1	5.0		27 †		266/56N*	154/60W	119/49	211/02	B	N	F	Sav81
6	1975 02 26 04 48 53.2	84.98	98.5 E	5.3	5.6	4.9	1.9¤	3.0	314/41N* 280/44N*	154/51W 154/62W	120/78 116/57	235/05 221/03	I B	N N	- F	Jem84 Sav81
7	1959 10 05 18 27 45.5	83.53	112.54E	5.6	5.9		20		290/85N	205/60W	065/25	161/15	B[8]	S	P	Laz65
8	1970 04 23 00 55 47.6	80.65	122.0 E	5.2	4.9		27 †		226/50N*	332/72E	197/42	094/14	B	N	P	Sav81
9	1964 08 25 13 47 19.3	78.15	126.65E	6.2	6.5	135.	3.8¤	16.0	346/48E* 338/54E 338/34E	164/42W 184/58W 184/58W	274/87 180/73 127/74	075/03 081/00 263/12	I[9] P[8] P[10]	N N N	- P P	Jem84 Syk67 Sav81
10	1960 12 03 20 20 58.9	76.64	131.24E	5			28		070/60S	175/65W	035/45	300/00	B[8]	N	-	Laz65
11	1969 04 07 20 26 30.5	76.55	130.86E	5.4	5.5	1.9	10.2¤ 11 §	3.0	314/48N* 017/70E 300/64E 016/40E* 330/60E 011/38E	157/45W 120/65S 152/30W 160/50W 195/60W 268/80N	155/77 339/33 180/67 358/85 172/56 213/44	055/02 070/03 040/18 265/05 082/00 329/26	I RPM PR B P[8] B	N N N N N S	- F F F - P	Jem84 Coo84 Cha76 Sav81 Con72 Koz84
12	1983 06 10 02 13 23.2	75.53	122.75E	5.4	5.4	1.4 3.6	21.9¤ 12.1¤	3.0 10.0	144/72W* 142/59W 150/70W	029/39E 008/40E 034/40E	013/50 005/67 018/52	258/19 252/10 265/17	I C B	N N N	- - F	Jem84 Dzi83 Coo84
13	1964 07 21 09 56 17.1	72.10	130.10E	5.4			12 §		170/45W* 274/72N	326/50E 170/52W	177/73 038/13	068/03 139/41	PRM B	N S	G F	Coo84 Koz84
14	1980 02 01 17 30 25	73.06	122.59E	5.4	5.3		22 †		274/71N* 315/55N	168/50W 114/36S	138/43 262/76	036/13 036/10	BPR C	N N	F -	Coo84 D2188
15	1963 05 20 17 01 40.2	72.20	126.25E	5.0			10		174/60W* 154/60W 300/90V	270/80N 261/64N* 030/65E	136/28 120/41 348/17	039/13 028/03 252/17	BP B BP	S N S	F F -	Coo84 Sav81 Laz65
16	1975 08 12 15 00 00	70.76	127.12E	5.1			16		164/72W* 145/43W* 197/68W*	286/30N 286/54N 312/44N	103/56 136/68 260/14	233/23 032/07 152/51	BP B B	N N T	F F F	Coo84 Sav81 Koz84
17	1962 04 19 23 16 04.5	69.80	138.98E	6.2			17		170/40W	350/50E	080/05	260/85	B	T	U	Coo84
18	1984 11 22 13 52 58.9	68.53	140.88E	5.4	4.9	0.6	26.1¤	2.8	087/75S*	341/45E	208/18	316/43	C	T	-	Dzi85

TABLE 1. (CONTINUED)

No	Date H (UTC)	Lat. (°N)	Long. (°)	m_b	M_s	M_o[1]	Depth (km)	Dur. (s)	Plane I[2]	Plane II	P-axis[3]	T-axis	Data[4]	T[5]	C[6]	Ref[7]
Interplate Earthquakes																
19	1976 01 21 06 01 48.5	67.73	140.03E	5.0	4.7		18	†	090/45S* 106/34S* 088/58S*	338/70E 348/72E 180/87W	040/15 055/20 049/24	293/48 292/55 309/20	BP B B	T T S	P F F	Coo84 Sav81 Koz84
20	1959 10 30 04 00 25.7	65.93	137.03E	5.3	6		33		330/50E 260/80N	150/40W 170/75W	060/05 126/03	240/85 036/18	B B	T S	U –	Coo84 Laz65
21	1968 09 09 02 20 59.2	66.17	142.13E	5.0	5.0		5.5§		238/73N* 284/68N* 274/69N	140/65W 174/50W 162/47W	008/04 045/11 034/13	100/30 147/46 139/49	BPM B B	S T T	F F F	Coo84 Sav81 Koz84
22	1971 05 18 22 44 39.3	63.92	146.10E	5.9	6.6	>10.	10	§	300/82N* 313/83N* 325/90V* 308/86N* 327/90V*	210/88W 223/89W 235/90V 218/81W 237/90V	255/04 268/04 280/00 082/00 282/00	165/07 178/06 190/00 173/10 192/00	BPM P PR[9] B BP	S S S S S	G G – F –	McM85 Cha76 Fi172 Koz84 Koz75
23	1970 06 05 10 31 53.9	63.26	146.18E	5.4	5.4		4	§	316/70E* 312/62E* 294/66N* 241/84N	218/72W 211/67W 196/73W 150/84W	268/01 262/03 246/05 196/00	177/27 169/37 154/30 106/09	BPM B B –	S S S S	G F P –	McM85 Sav81 Koz84 Koz73
24	1972 01 13 17 24 23.2	61.94	147.04E	5.3	5.3	5.6	33		100/80S* 140/66W* 135/90V* 260/72N*	010/82E 047/84E 225/88W 358/68E	235/04 096/12 090/01 218/29	325/07 001/12 180/02 310/02	BPR P B B	S S S S	F F F F	McM85 Cha76 Sav81 Koz84
25	1974 06 19 03 09 36	63.14	150.92E	4.9	4.8		17	†	146/77W*	236/90V	102/09	010/09	B	S	P	Koz84
26	1981 05 22 04 59 25.9	61.15	156.62E	5.1	4.5		11	†	278/45N	120/48S	199/02	106/77	BP	T	F	McM85
27	1979 08 19 07 10 07	61.33	159.04E	5.1	5.3	2.3	16	†	082/78S* 315/71N	352/76E 216/65W	214/01 177/22	306/18 084/04	BR B	S S	P F	McM85 Koz84
28	1975 11 04 12 41 12.4	60.02	160.32E	4.7			52		143/33W	323/57E	054/12	234/78	BP	T	F	Koz84
29	1978 06 05 07 05 59	60.13	160.41E	5.1	4.7		13	†	306/50N*	112/40S	029/05	267/85	BP	T	P	McM85
30	1972 08 03 12 36 46.9	59.47	163.15E	5.2	4.9		11	†	287/72N*	197/82W	242/07	150/19	BPR	S	P	McM85
31	1943 03 07 03 01 39.8	59.18	165.57E	6.5			20		235/66N	334/71E	193/33	105/03	B	S	–	Ave73
32	1976 01 21 18 02 04	58.93	163.57E	5.4	5.6		30	†	210/74W* 076/00H 093/64S	304/74N 256/90V 323/38E	167/23 166/45 203/16	257/00 346/45 323/60	BR B B	S N T	F F P	McM85 Sav83 Koz84
33	1976 01 22 22 06 35	58.96	163.73E	5.2	5.1		48	†	184/60W* 103/00H	290/60N 283/90V	149/45 193/45	058/00 013/45	B B	N N	P F	McM85 Sav83
34	1977 02 17 13 32 30.0	58.89	163.82E	5.1	4.1		18		196/80W*	294/70N	151/21	244/07	B	S	F	McM85
35	1969 11 22 23 09 39.2	57.70	163.56E	6.2	7.3		51	†	032/75E 038/73E 010/60E 032/74E	172/19W 225/16W 190/30W 308/50N	112/29 130/28 100/15 176/16	319/58 305/62 280/75 278/42	PS PS BP B	T T T S	G G – –	Sta76 Cor75 Vei74 Zob77

TABLE 1. (CONTINUED)

No	Date H (UTC)	Lat. (°N)	Long. (°)	m_b	M_s	M_o^1	Depth (km)	Dur. (s)	Plane I[2]	Plane II	P-axis[3]	T-axis	Data[4]	T[5]	C[6]	Ref[7]
Interplate Earthquakes																
36	1970 01 27 11 17 30.2	57.64	163.60E	5.0	4.5		51		010/45E	190/45W	100/00	280/90	BP	T	-	Vei74
37	1969 12 02 04 12 31	57.44	163.43E	5.0	4.7		9		215/75W	120/50S	085/40	340/15	B	N	-	Zob77
38	1970 06 19 18 52 33.8	57.38	163.35E	5.2	5.1		33		142/76W	053/90V	096/10	005/10	B	S	-	Zob77
39	1969 12 23 13 22 51	57.34	163.14E	5.4	5.5		13	†	057/64S	293/41N	170/13	281/58	PS	T	F	Cor75
									033/82E	293/41N	154/26	267/39	BP	T	F	McM85
									010/40E	190/50W	280/05	100/85	BP	T	-	Vei74
									050/76S	143/73W	097/03	006/18	B	S	-	Zob77
40	1945 04 15 02 35 20.4	57.17	163.71E	6.8			20		230/64N	332/69E	099/04	192/36	B	T	-	Ave73
41	1969 12 08 05 18 33.1	57.01	162.23E	4.7	5.1		54		049/80S	148/40W	108/26	350/43	B	T	-	Zob77
Intraplate Earthquakes																
42	1978 01 04 14 52 09.7	85.71	23.9 W	4.9	4.6		36	†	222/86W	130/76S	356/07	087/13	BP	S	G	Wet82
									216/80W	124/74S	349/04	080/19	BP	S	G	Gre82
43	1971 11 26 23 07 47.3	79.43	18.0 W	5.1			18	†	190/52W	063/52S	036/61	126/00	P	N	G	Syk74
44	1933 11 20 23 21 34	73.23	70.02W		7.3	4000.	10	§	052/68S	188/36W	124/18	356/57	PM	T	G	Kro87
									088/64S	246/27N	170/19	018/70	PR	T	P	Ste79
45	1976 11 12 14 47 23.7	72.37	70.33W	5.3	5.1		23	†	295/55N	160/45W	046/05	148/65	P	T	G	Ste79
									054/73S	316/66E	183/05	277/30	BP	S	P	Wet78
46	1972 01 21 14 43 40.5	71.91	74.8 W	4.2		0.093	6.0σ		300/30N	120/60S	030/75	210/15	PR	N	F	Has73
47	1963 09 04 13 32 11.1	71.25	72.94W	5.9	6.2	17.	7	§ 2.5	098/66S	308/27N	344/67	198/20	PM	N	G	Liu80
									110/73S	320/20E	006/61	208/27	PR	N	G	Ste79
									093/70S	286/20N	356/65	186/25	P	N	G	Syk70
									292/90V	022/50E	345/27	239/27	P	S	P	Qam74
48	1970 12 02 11 03 10.0	68.50	67.55W	4.9	4.5	0.51	8.6σ		288/80N	195/71W	152/21	060/06	PR	S	G	Has73
49	1975 06 14 20 50 26.9	71.94	132.77W	5.1	4.2	1.4	40	†	035/59E*	135/73W	359/35	263/09	BR	S	F	Has79
50	1975 03 31 12 53 03.5	69.89	142.5 W	3.8			33		158/60W	060/80S	015/30	113/10	P	S	F	Est85
51	1968 01 22 23 44 30.4	70.36	144.0 W	4.4			9		050/60S	315/80N	006/14	269/29	BP	S	F	Bis86
									289/87N*	022/56E	241/26	341/21	BPR	S	F	Fuj83
52	1971 10 05 01 40 41.6	67.38	172.57W	5.2	5.0		33		310/75N*	216/71W	082/03	173/24	BPR	S	P	Col83
									280/90V*	100/00H	010/45	190/45	BPR	S	P	Fuj83
									243/40N	063/50S	333/85	153/05	BP	N	-	Bis86
53	1973 12 15 23 31 43.9	74.11	147.04E	4.9	4.9		33		167/64W*	280/50N	227/08	127/50	BPR	T	G	Coo84
									151/37W*	291/60N	037/12	157/66	B	T	F	Koz84
									264/80N*	355/80E	220/12	310/01	B	S	P	Ave78

¹ Seismic moment in 10^{24} dyne-cm (10^{17} N-m)
² Strike and dip of nodal planes using the convention of Aki and Richards (1980, p. 106)
³ Trend and plunge of principal deviatoric stress axes, trend in degrees east of north
⁴ Data used by author(s) to determine the mechanism: B - P-wave first motions reported in bulletins;
    C - centroid-moment tensor inversion, best fitting double-couple solution; I - P and SH wave
    inversion; M - forward modelling of P-waves; P - P-wave first motions read from seismograms by
    the author(s); R - Rayleigh wave amplitude radiation pattern; S - S-wave polarization angles
⁵ Dominant type of faulting: N - normal; S - strike-slip; T - thrust
⁶ Approximate level of constraint of the mechanism: G - both nodal planes are tightly constrained
    (for mechanisms determined with P-wave first motions, good coverage of the focal sphere and a
    redundancy in similar first motions used to constrain planes is required); F - only one plane
    is well constrained; P - both planes are poorly constrained; U - both planes are unconstrained
    but the type of faulting is apparent; "-" denotes that the degree of constraint is unknown
⁷ Reference: Ave73 - Aver'yanova, 1973; Ave78 - Avetisov, 1978; Bis86 - Biswas and others, 1986; Cha76 -
    Chapman and Solomon, 1976; Col83 - Coley, 1983; Con72 - Conant, 1972; Coo84 - Cook and others,
    1984; Cor75 - Cormier, 1975; Dzi83 - Dziewonski and others, 1983; Dzi85 - Dziewonski and others,
    1985; Est85 - Estabrook, 1985; Fil72 - Filson and Frasier, 1972; Fuj83 - Fujita and others, 1983;
    Gre82 - Gregersen, 1982b; Has73 - Hashizume, 1973; Has79 - Hasegawa and others, 1979; Jem84 -
    Jemsek and others, 1984; Koz73 - Koz'min, 1973; Koz75 - Koz'min and others, 1975; Koz84 - Koz'min,
    1984; Laz65 - Lazareva and Misharina, 1965; Liu80 - Liu and Kanamori, 1980; McM85 - McMullen, 1985;
    Qam74 - Qamar, 1974; Sav81 - Savostin and Karasik, 1981; Sav83 - Savostin and others, 1983; SleIP -
    Kroeger (1987); Sta76 - Stauder and Mualchin, 1976; Ste79 - Stein and others,
    1979; Syk67 - Sykes, 1967; Syk70 - Sykes, 1970; Syk74 - Sykes and Sbar, 1974; Vei74 - Veith, 1974;
    Wet78 - Wetmiller and Horner, 1978; Wet82 - Wetmiller and Forsyth, 1982; Zob77 - Zobin and
    Simbireva, 1977
⁸ Non-orthogonal nodal planes (q.v., Solomon and Julian, 1974)
⁹ Propagating rupture
¹⁰ Adapted from Sykes (1967) by orthogonalizing planes
* Probable or presumed fault plane
¤ Centroid depth from inversion
§ Determined from waveform modelling
† Determined from depth phases (pP)
σ Determined from surface wave analysis

nism is well constrained by Cook and others (1984). The solution proposed by Koz'min (1984) is predominantly strike-slip, with some thrust component, however, this solution cannot be reconciled with the observed waveform and surface wave data.

The Lena River Delta region has been the site of several major earthquakes in the last 75 years. Two damaging earthquakes occurred in 1927 (Kochetkov, 1976; Koz'min, 1984), the larger being of magnitude 6.8. Three smaller (m_b 5.4) events in this region have been studied, although none have well-constrained mechanisms.

The largest event of this group occurred on February 1, 1980 (#14) at the western edge of the Lena River Delta. The waveform character is indicative of a complex rupture and the fault plane solution indicates predominantly normal faulting with a moderate amount of strike-slip motion (Cook and others, 1984). An event (#15) that occurred southeast of the 1980 event on May 20, 1963, is interpreted as a predominantly strike-slip earthquake with a moderate normal faulting component (Savostin and Karasik, 1981; Cook and others, 1984). The southernmost event with a significant normal faulting component occurred on August 12, 1975 (#16), about 100 km south of the Lena River Delta. On the basis of teleseismic data, both Savostin and Karasik (1981) and Cook and others (1984) suggest that this event is a predominantly normal faulting event with a moderate amount of strike-slip motion. Koz'min (1984) obtains a thrust faulting mechanism, probably based on data from local stations in northeast Siberia. The discrepancies between the different proposed mechainsms cannot be resolved on the basis of available data.

All three of these events occurred near the hinge line at the edge of the Siberian Platform (Andreev, 1983) and can be interpreted either as dominantly dip-slip or as dominantly strike-slip events. If the events are considered to be strike-slip events, all three imply consistent left-lateral motion along a north-to-northwest striking nodal plane, parallel to the margin of the Siberian Platform. If they are considered dip-slip events, they may be related to reactivation of basement faults as a result of tensional stresses due to rifting at the southern end of the Arctic Mid-Ocean Ridge.

Cherskii Mountains

The level of seismicity decreases to the south over a 300-km-wide segment of the plate boundary in the lower reaches of the Omoloi and Yana rivers (Fig. 2). The earthquakes that do occur are generally smaller than m_b 4.5 and are recorded only at Soviet stations in northeastern Siberia. This apparent "gap" in seismicity may be due either to a magnitude 6.3 event that released accumulated stresses in this area in 1918, or because of the area's proximity to the North America–Eurasia pole of rotation. The latter explanation is supported by the change in earthquake focal mechanisms from normal faulting in the north to thrust faulting in the south, and also by pole of rotation determinations using only North Atlantic and Arctic data, which indicate a pole near 70°N and 130°E (Pitman and Talwani, 1972; Minster and others, 1974; Cook and others, 1986; DeMets and others, 1990).

The level of seismicity increases south of the Selennyakh Range (Grachev, 1982) and becomes considerably more diffuse. The seismic zone is 300 km wide in the northern Cherskii Mountains and expands to a width of 500 km north of Magadan. The largest events are concentrated along the northeastern edge of this zone and have a maximum magnitude of about 6. Many of the earthquakes appear to be located on or near large faults that both parallel and intersect the Cherskii Mountains (Kochetkov, 1976).

The northern and central Cherskii Mountains are located along the southern boundary of the Moma "rift" system (Fig. 2), a series of depressions that parallel the seismic zone from about 70°N, 138°E to 63°N, 153°E. These depressions are sites of relative subsidence, high heat flow, and limited basaltic volcanism (Argunov and Gavrikov, 1960; Naymark, 1976; Savostin and Karasik, 1981). This combination of geophysical processes has led Soviet investigators to consider this region to be an extension of the Arctic Mid-Ocean Ridge and thus to interpret the depressions as grabens that are offset by transform faults (Demenitskaya and Karasik, 1969; Grachev and others, 1970; Zonenshayn and others, 1978; Savostin and Karasik, 1981; Grachev, 1982).

Contrary to expectations based on the above viewpoint, all focal mechanisms determined for the northern Cherskii Mountains indicate predominantly thrust faulting with the compression axis perpendicular to the strike of the depressions (Figs. 3, 4). The northernmost thrust event occurred on April 19, 1962 (#17), at the northern end of the Selennyakh Range. Although the nodal planes are unconstrained, the fault plane solution must be predominantly thrust, and allows only a minor strike-slip component. On November 22, 1984, an event (#18) occurred in the southern Selennyakh Range, which was determined to be a thrust by Dziewonski and others (1985) using centroid-moment tensor inversion. Near the northern terminus of the Moma depression, a m_b 5.0 earthquake occurred on January 21, 1976 (#19), which both Savostin and Karasik (1981) and Cook and others (1984) determined to be a thrust event. Koz'min (1984) presents a solution, obtained using local network data, with a greater strike-slip component, but all of the local stations are consistent with a thrust mechanism.

The most tightly constrained event with a thrusting component is the September 9, 1968 (#21), event, which was located south of the Moma depression. Cook and others (1984) obtained a strike-slip solution with a thrust component, while Savostin and Karasik (1981) and Koz'min (1984) obtained similar solutions but with a greater thrust component. A fifth event (#20), somewhat to the west of the lineation formed by the four earthquakes discussed above, has a strike-slip mechanism according to Lazareva and Misharina (1965). Given the limitations in the data, however, a thrust mechanism with a northeast-trending compression axis is equally tenable.

These five mechanisms indicate that the northern part of the Moma rift system is currently undergoing northeast–southwest-directed deviatoric compression rather than extension. This view is supported by Rezanov and Kochetkov (1962), who note that recent tectonic movements, as determined by the elevation of the pre-Pleistocene peneplanation surface, indicate uplift throughout the Cherskii Mountains and the Moma rift system. Cook and others (1986) have suggested that the North America–Eurasia pole of rotation was situated to the south in the recent past (2–7 Ma), perhaps in the northern Pacific Ocean basin. Rotation about that pole opened these depressions, as an extension of the Arctic Mid-Ocean Ridge. They then suggest that in the past 1–3 m.y. the pole of rotation again migrated back to the Lena River Delta region (Fig. 4), causing compression in the Cherskii Mountains. The fault planes of recent earthquakes may then be reactivated relict transform faults from the rifting episode.

In the southeastern Cherskii Mountains, three large strike-slip earthquakes with similar focal mechanisms occurred between 1970 and 1972 (Fig. 3). The largest of these was the Artyk earthquake of May 18, 1971 (#22), with a surface wave magnitude (M_s) of 6.6 and a M_o on the order of 10^{25} dyne-cm. The rupture propagated from southeast to northwest at 4.0–5.0 km/s over a fault length of 40 km (Filson and Frasier, 1972). Long-period body-wave modeling indicates a focal depth of 11 km (McMullen, 1985). Several temporary seismic stations, which were deployed following the mainshock, recorded 1200 aftershocks over a three-month period. The zone of aftershocks extended over a length of about 60 km, with a strike of N60°W (Koz'min and others, 1975; Koz'min, 1984), which is nearly parallel to the strike of one of the nodal planes (Filson and Frasier, 1972; Chapman and Solomon, 1976; Savostin and Karasik, 1981; Koz'min, 1984; McMullen, 1985). The focal mechanisms solutions are all well constrained, essentially identical, and indicate left-lateral strike-slip motion along a northwest-striking fault plane.

On June 5, 1970, a m_b 5.4 event (#23) occurred about 75 km to the south of the 1971 event. The solutions of Savostin and Karasik (1981) and McMullen (1985) are nearly identical and indicate primarily left-lateral strike-slip motion, on a fault plane striking N45°W. Another earthquake in the region for which left-lateral strike-slip motion predominates occurred on January 13, 1972 (#24). The surface wave solution (McMullen, 1985) indicates a fault plane somewhat more east-west than determined from P-wave first motions alone (Chapman and Solomon, 1976; Savostin and Karasik, 1981). To the south and west of these events, considerable microseismicity is detected by the local Soviet seismic network (Koz'min, 1984).

Okhotsk Plate

The exact location of plate boundaries south of 68°N is controversial. The extent of active seismicity in the Magadan region is diffuse, with no known earthquakes greater than magnitude 5.5 occurring between the epicenter of the January 13,

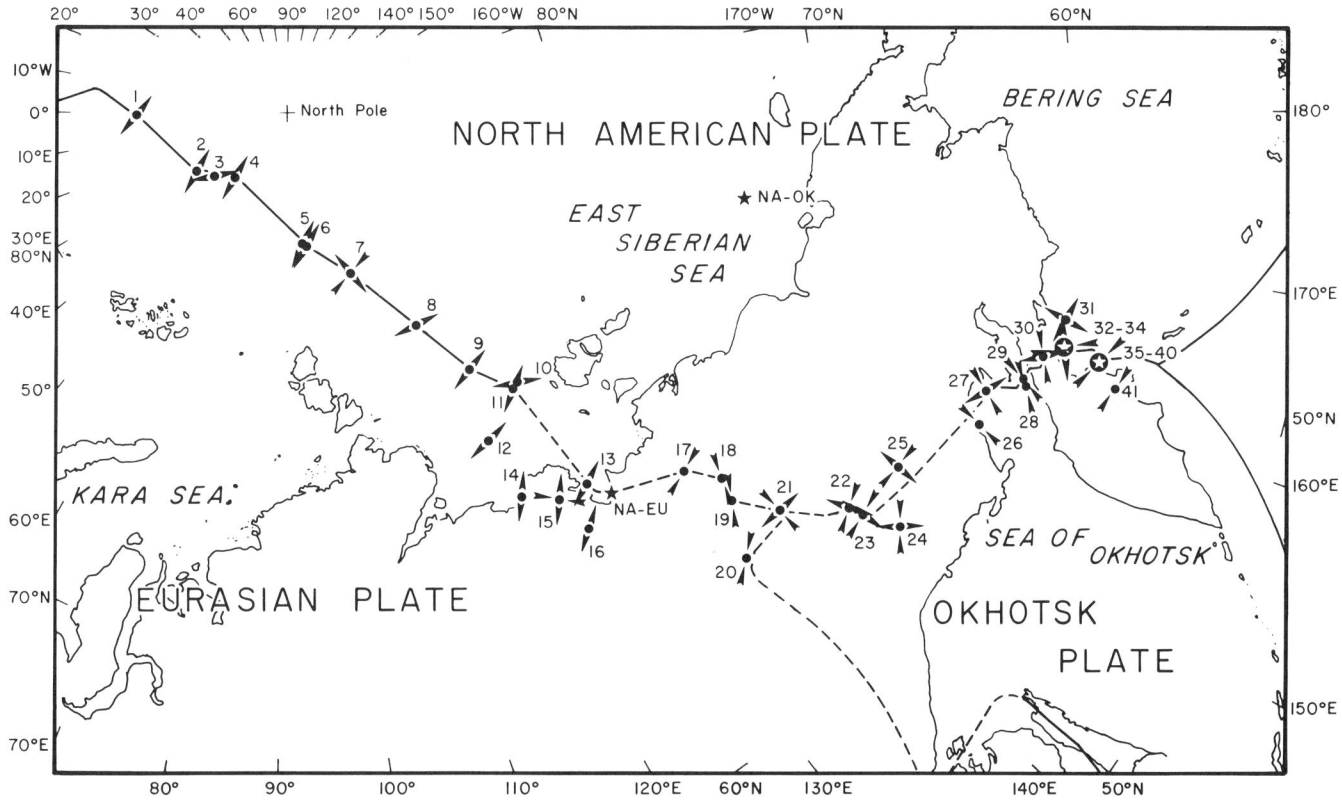

Figure 4. Deviatoric stress orientations (arrows) for Arctic interplate earthquakes, poles of rotation (stars), and present-day plate boundaries (solid lines, dashed where approximate, after Cook and others, 1986). The deviatoric tension direction is shown for dominantly normal faulting events, and the compressional direction for thrust events. Both tension and compression directions shown for strike-slip events. Stress orientations are generalized for two clusters (shown by solid dots with stars) off of northeast Kamchatka. NA–OK denotes the North America–Okhotsk pole of rotation and NA–EU denotes the North America–Eurasia pole according to Cook and others (1986). Numbers for earthquakes correspond to Table 1.

1972, event and northern Sakhalin Island or Karaginskii Island (east of Kamchatka; Fig. 2). Chapman and Solomon (1976) examine several possible plate configurations, including one in which the plate boundary bends south and extends into the seismic zone on Sakhalin Island. They prefer this model because of the consistency of slip-vectors of Sakhalin earthquakes with those the model predicted for a North America–Eurasia boundary in that region. In addition, two m_b 5.5 events have occurred (1951, 1971) near 61°N, 140°E, between the Cherskii Mountains and Sakhalin Island near their proposed boundary. Chapman and Solomon (1976) also note, however, that the slip-vectors for the 1971 and 1972 events (#22 and #24) in the southern Cherskii Mountains do not fit the pattern of faulting predicted by their proposed pole of rotation.

Savostin and Karasik (1981) postulate a Sea of Okhotsk plate that is decoupled from any plate around its periphery, on the basis of zones of seismicity along the northern shores of the Sea of Okhotsk that link the seismicity along the southern Cherskii Mountains to both the seismic zone south of Karaginskii Island and the zone on Sakhalin Island. They note that no earthquakes greater than magnitude 4.5 have occurred on either branch of the seismic zone. However, Cook and others (1986) point out that several earthquakes of m_b 5.1 have occurred recently in Shelikhov Bay (northeastern Sea of Okhotsk). The focal mechanisms, discussed below, are poorly constrained; however, they are consistent with thrusting and strike-slip motion between the North American plate and an eastward-moving plate containing the Sea of Okhotsk. The absence of large earthquakes along either branch of the seismic zone indicates that the relative motions are fairly small. If, however, the North America–Okhotsk and North America–Eurasia poles of rotation are appreciably different, the large discrepancies between observed and predicted slip-vector strikes, computed assuming that these earthquakes are occurring between North America and Eurasia (Chapman and Solomon, 1976), can be explained.

In the aftermath of the May 26, 1983, earthquake off the western coast of northeast Japan (Satake, 1985), several authors (e.g., Nakamura, 1983; Seno, 1985) consider the possibility that northeast Japan may be part of the North American plate. This suggestion is based on the general agreement of slip-vectors off northeast Japan with those predicted for Pacific–North America interaction and the eastward-directed thrusting in the Japan Sea.

Ishikawa and Yu (1984) agree with the proposed plate boundaries in the Japan region, but consider northeast Japan to be part of the Sea of Okhotsk plate. For the purposes of this chapter, we consider the Sea of Okhotsk to be independent of North America; we trace the North American plate boundary through the northern Sea of Okhotsk to Karaginskii Island and southward to the junction of the Kurile and Aleutian island arcs (Fig. 2).

Northern Sea of Okhotsk

Three events which occurred in Shelikhov Bay are large enough for analysis by teleseismic data, and a fourth event has been studied using data primarily from the Soviet network. The westernmost of the events, with m_b 5.1, occurred on May 22, 1981 (#26), along the northwest shore of Shelikhov Bay. McMullen (1985) determines a poorly constrained thrust faulting mechanism for this event; only a minor strike-slip component is possible. On August 19, 1979, a m_b 5.1 event (#27) occurred in the middle of Shelikhov Bay. For this event, both Koz'min (1984) and McMullen (1985) propose a strike-slip mechanism; however, the orientation of the nodal planes and the sense of motion differ. McMullen (1985) suggests left-lateral motion along a nearly east-west-striking fault with the compression axis striking northeast-southwest, consistent with almost all other events in the region. Koz'min's (1984) solution is poorly constrained and indicates right-lateral faulting on a northwest-southeast-striking plane, which is inconsistent with nearby strike-slip mechanisms. Depth phases indicate that both the 1981 and 1979 events are shallow (<20 km).

Two events occurred southeast of Taygonos Peninsula in Shelikhov Bay. Both events are consistent with northeast-southwest-directed thrusting with fault planes striking northwest-southeast (McMullen, 1985; Koz'min, 1984). The nodal planes of the larger event (m_b 5.1, June 5, 1978, #29) are poorly constrained; however, the November 4, 1975 event (m_b 4.7, #28) is fairly well constrained by nearby stations. The 1978 event has a focal depth of 13 km based on depth phases.

On August 3, 1972, a m_b 5.2 event (#30) occurred in northwestern Kamchatka, just west of Karaginskii Island. The focal depth based on depth phases is about 11 km. This event is important because it may represent the eastern terminus of the seismic zone across Shelikhov Bay and northwestern Kamchatka. The data are not inconsistent with a left-lateral strike-slip mechanism with faulting along a nearly east-west plane (McMullen, 1985).

The trend of seismicity and preferred fault planes for all of the above focal mechanisms are transverse to the regional geologic features, which formed in a convergent episode in the Late Cretaceous and strike northeast-southwest (Watson and Fujita, 1985). The present seismicity must, therefore, reflect recently developed tectonic processes (Savostin and others, 1983). Examination of photography from space shuttle missions (STS-9) and aeronautical navigation charts indicates the presence of lineaments in northwest Kamchatka and Taygonos Peninsula with strikes of S25°E and N88°E. Based on a pole of rotation off the coast of Chukotka, these lineaments should correspond to thrust faulting and left-lateral strike-slip motion, respectively (Cook and others, 1986). The epicenter of the 1972 event (#30) falls on one of the east-west lineaments, and the mechanisms for the thrust events in Shelikhov Bay (#25, 27, and 28) are not inconsistent with thrusting along the S25°E striking plane.

Northeast Kamchatka Seismic Zone

A zone of intense seismicity, with magnitudes up to 7, extends south from Karaginskii Island to the junction of the Kurile and Aleutian island arcs (Cormier, 1975). The three largest earthquake sequences occurred in April, 1945 (M ~5.8), November to Decmber, 1969 (M ~7.3), and in January, 1976 (M ~5.8). The 1945 and 1969 events occurred off Ozernoi Peninsula and the 1976 sequence was near Karaginskii Island (Fig. 2).

P-wave nodal plane solutions of three earthquakes of the 1976 sequence are ambiguous and poorly constrained. The January 21, 1976, mainshock (#32) has been interpreted as a north-south-directed thrust (Koz'min, 1984), a dip-slip fault (Savostin and others, 1983), and a left-lateral strike-slip fault on a nearly north-south-striking fault plane (McMullen, 1985). The latter two solutions indicate a northwest-southeast-striking compression axis; the Rayleigh wave radiation pattern, although ambiguous, seems to indicate a north-south-striking node (McMullen, 1985), which supports the strike-slip solution. Aftershocks of this event also align nearly north-south (Fedotov and others, 1980). Savostin and others (1983) and Koz'min (1984) both choose a nearly east-west-striking fault plane.

The largest aftershock (#33) of event #32 occurred the next day. Savostin and others (1983) have proposed a dip-slip mechanism, while McMullen (1985) proposes a strike-slip solution; both mechanisms are admissible from the data. A small (m_b 5.1) event on February 17, 1977 (#34), can also be interpreted as a strike-slip event (McMullen, 1985). All solutions for these events (#32–34) are incompatible with possible plate configurations and relative motions.

The largest event in the northeast Kamchatka seismic zone occurred on November 22, 1969 (#35), and has been assigned a magnitude of 7.3 by Cormier (1975). Relatively well-constrained focal mechanisms indicate a nearly pure thrust mechanism (Cormier, 1975; Stauder and Mualchin, 1976). Local geology allows either the high-angle or low-angle thrust plane to be the fault plane (Cormier, 1975). The aftershock sequence of this event lasted more than six months and covered an area of larger than 1,000 km^2. The largest aftershock occurred on December 23, 1969 (m_b 5.4, #39), and is probably a thrust fault with a small strike-slip component (Veith, 1974; Cormier, 1975). Zobin and Simbireva (1977) interpret this event, as well as those on June 19, 1970 (#38), December 2, 1969 (#37), and December 8, 1969 (#41), as thrust faults with a large right-lateral strike-slip component, assuming the fault plane parallels the coastline. It may be that some of these aftershocks occurred on small en-echelon faults of northwesterly strike and not the plate boundary. Alternatively, given the small size of these events, they may all be poorly constrained thrusts. Veith (1974) also obtains a pure thrust solution for an aftershock on January 27, 1970 (#36).

Just seaward of the 1969 sequence, several events occurred in 1945. Aver'yanova (1973) suggests that the largest event, on April 15 (#40), is a thrust with a moderate strike-slip component. Given the poor data available for this event, it is unlikely that this mechanism is well constrained.

Immediately to the south of these events, the seismic zone intersects the Aleutian and Kurile seismic zones. The tectonics and seismicity of this intersection, which is probably a triple junction, are poorly understood and require further study (Cormier, 1975; Newberry and others, 1986).

Stress Orientations and Implications for Plate Motions

The orientations of the deviatoric stress axes, which are determined from the focal mechanisms, usually lie within ±20° of the true principal stress axes. The stress axes that have been determined are fairly consistent along individual segments of the plate boundary (Fig. 4). Along the Arctic Mid-Ocean Ridge, the tension axis is horizontal and perpendicular to the ridge crest except at possible transform faults. This trend continues to the southern edge of the Laptev Sea. South of the Selennyakh Range, the compression axis is nearly horizontal and strikes northeast–southwest throughout the Cherskii Mountains and the northern Sea of Okhotsk. Finally, compression appears to be east–west to northwest–southeast along the northeast Kamchatka seismic zone. The change from tension to compression perpendicular to the plate boundary occurs near the Lena delta and suggests the possibility of the pole of rotation being in that area.

Slip vectors from earthquakes along the Arctic Mid-Ocean Ridge and in northeastern Siberia can be used to constrain the pole of rotation between North America and the Eurasian and Okhotsk plates. The data set falls into two distinct groups: the first consists of earthquakes along the ridge axis and in the northern Cherskii Mountains (#1–#21), while the second consists of the events from the southern Cherskii Mountains to the Aleutian-Kurile arc-arc junction (#22–#41). The first group, combined with slip-vector and transform fault strike data from the North Atlantic, defines a North America–Eurasia pole near 71°N, 132°E (Cook and others, 1986). This pole is in agreement with pole determinations based on magnetic lineations (anomalies 5, 6, and 13) in the Arctic (Peters and Vink, 1985) and recent global plate inversions (DeMets and others, 1990). The northerly pole determination is discordant with poles computed by Soviet workers (e.g., Savostin and others, 1982) and by Chapman and Solomon (1976), who determined more southerly poles. The difference arises from the use of fault strikes in the Cherskii Mountains by the Soviets, which apparently are no longer acting as transforms, and the use of earthquakes on Sakhalin Island by Chapman and Solomon (1976), which may not reflect motion between North America and Eurasia.

As discussed previously, the northerly poles are in agreement with observed thrusting in the northern Cherskii Mountains (#18–#21); however, they are discordant with the observed geologic structures of the Cherskii Mountains.

INTRAPLATE SEISMICITY

Intraplate seismicity within the Arctic Ocean region of the North American plate is confined, with a few exceptions, to the continental margins and shelves. Most of the known intraplate events are located in several clusters in and around northern Greenland, off Baffin Island (Fig. 5), along the continental slope of the Queen Elizabeth Islands, off the Canadian and Alaskan coasts in the Beaufort Sea (Fig. 6), in the southern Chukchi Sea (Fig. 7), and in the New Siberian Islands region (Fig. 8). Because of the large separation between, and nonuniform deployment of, seismic stations around the Arctic Ocean (Fig. 1), the distribution of epicenters is biased towards the seismic stations and the locations between them, especially in the Soviet Arctic.

Arctic Ocean and Lincoln Sea

A few intraplate events have been reported in the oceanic parts of the Arctic Ocean. The largest of these occurred on January 4, 1978, in the northern Lincoln Sea (Fig. 5), along the continental slope between the Pole Abyssal Plain and Nares Strait. Wetmiller and Forsyth (1982) and Gregersen (1982b) determine a strike-slip focal mechanism for this event (#42) with a nearly horizontal, north–south striking compression axis. The tension axis is perpendicular to the Arctic Mid-Ocean Ridge, located 200 km to the east. A second event (m_b 4.8) occurred in the same region on August 10, 1983, and may have a similar mechanism. These events may be due, in part, to sediment loading of the oceanic crust further south, which creates horizontal compressional stresses perpendicular to the continental margin seaward of the load (Fig. 6; see Basham and others, 1977; Hasegawa and others, 1978), combined with regional tectonic stresses.

A number of very small events ($m_b \sim 4$) have been reported in the vicinity of 87°N, 110°W, the Lomonosov Ridge, and in the Pole Abyssal Plain. These earthquakes are probably mislocations of events occurring on the Arctic Mid-Ocean Ridge or in other parts of the circum-Arctic. No other events of magnitude 4 or greater have been reported away from the continental margins and, at this detection threshold, the Amerasia Basin, Alpha Ridge, and Lomonosov Ridge appear to be aseismic.

Eastern Greenland

A major cluster of seismicity occurs north of Danmarkshavn, Greenland in a region of Caledonian folding (Gregersen, 1982a); the largest event, with a magnitude of 5.1, occurred in 1971 (#43). This event had a focal depth of 19 km, and Sykes and Sbar (1974) have determined a normal faulting mechanism (Fig. 5). Kroeger (1987) suggests that this event is due to stresses related to deglaciation and lithospheric rebound. In November, 1974, a swarm of earthquakes occurred in the same area with magnitudes between 2 and 3 (Gregersen, 1979). A few earthquakes have occurred in a broad zone further south along the eastern coast of Greenland. Although very few instrumentally detected earthquakes have been located near Angmagssalik, well over one hundred felt earthquakes have been reported since 1894, including some with high intensities (Gregersen, 1982b).

Baffin Bay and Nares Strait

Most current seismicity under Baffin Bay is confined to the landward side of the 2,000-m isobath (Fig. 5; Qamar, 1974; Baham and others, 1977; Wetmiller and Forsyth, 1982). The largest event to date in northeastern Canada occurred in 1933 and had a magnitude of 7.3 (#44). Aftershocks of this earthquake were as large as M 6.5. Subsequent events of magnitude 6 occurred in 1945, 1947, and 1957.

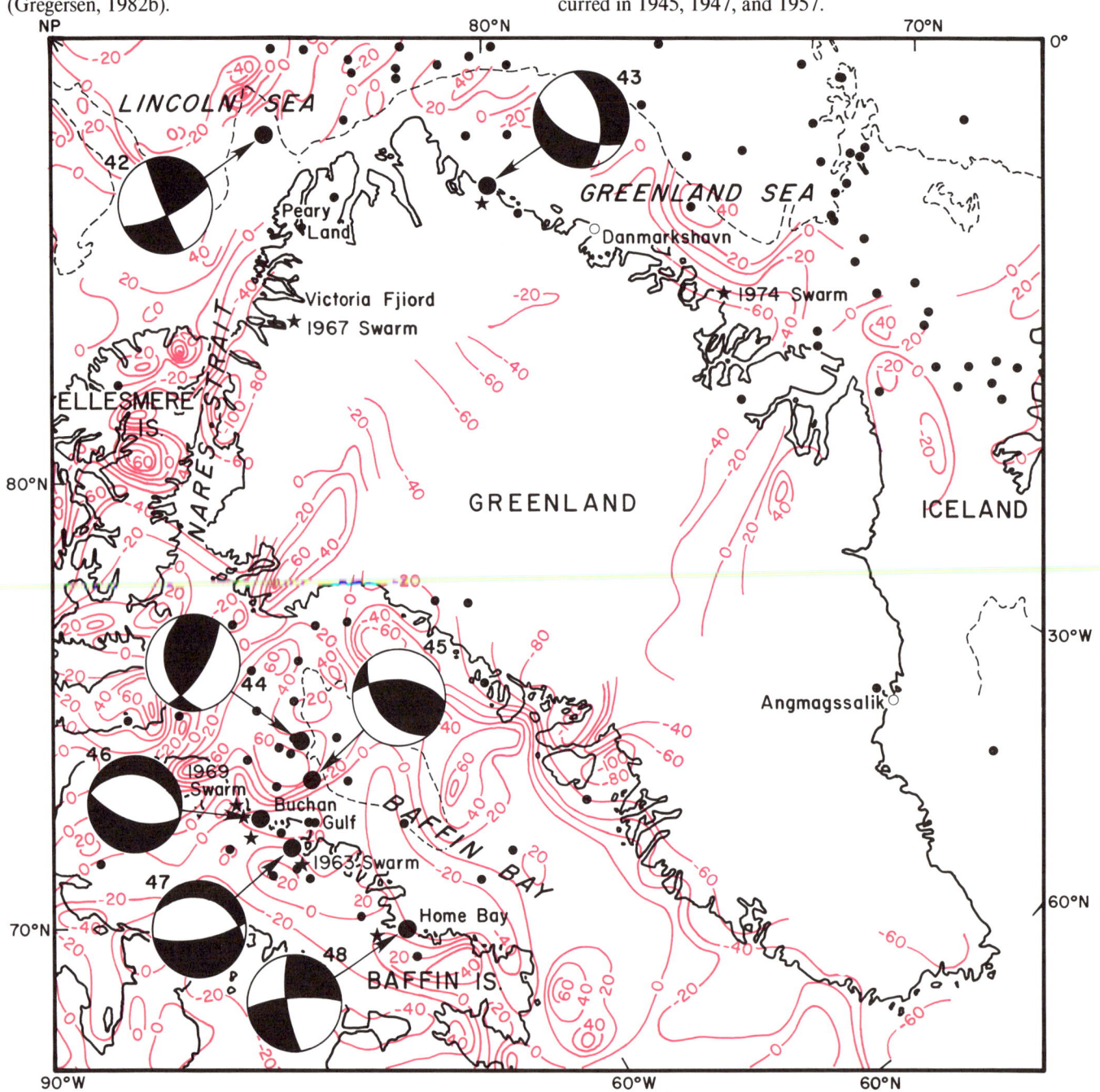

Figure 5. Seismicity (m_b >4.0; after Wetmiller, 1978), focal mechanisms, and residual free-air gravity anomalies (in red, 20-mGal contour interval; after Sobczak, 1978) of Greenland and northern Baffin Bay. Stars denote swarms of clusters of earthquakes. Focal mechanisms are shown using the conventions of Figure 3.

Prior to 1960, only one earthquake (M 5.5–6 event in 1935) was reported on Baffin Island. However, with the expansion of the Canadian seismograph network, increased seismicity, often in the form of clusters, was found along the northeastern coastline of Baffin Island. A clustering of seismic activity occurs in the Home Bay and Buchan Gulf region, but does not extend further inland than the head of the fjiords (Fig. 5). Since 1960, the largest earthquake on Baffin Island is the M_S 6.2 event in 1963 (#47); several events of magnitude near 5 have occurred since then.

Preliminary results indicate that focal depths of the larger Baffin Bay events appear to be shallow. The 1983 event had a focal depth of about 10 km, while the 1976 event is given a depth of 24 km based on pP phases (Kroeger, 1987). Estimates of focal depths of microearthquakes vary, and may extend to depths of 50 km (Reid and Falconer, 1982). In comparison, the focal depths of Baffin Island earthquakes are shallower, about 6–9 km (Hashizume, 1973; Liu and Kanamori, 1980). Microearthquakes also cluster in this depth range (Reid and Falconer, 1982).

Fault plane solutions (Table 1) of two Baffin Bay earthquakes (#44, 45) indicate a predominance of thrust faulting (Stein and others, 1979; Kroeger, 1987), while fault plane solutions of earthquakes on Baffin Island (#46, 47) indicate normal faulting (Fig. 5; Stein and others, 1979; Liu and Kanamori, 1980). One event (#48), shows a combination of strike-slip motion with a normal component (Hashizume, 1973).

Plate tectonic reconstructions suggest that Baffin Bay formed during early Tertiary time due to the rifting of Greenland from Baffin Island (Kristoffersen and Talwani, 1977; Srivastava, 1978). Crustal structures produced by this rifting probably exist throughout the region and may be reactivated by present-day stresses. The area of greatest seismic activity coincides with a generally east–west striking zone of intense shearing and folding, marking the southern edge of the Foxe fold belt in the vicinity of Home Bay (Jackson and Taylor, 1972; Wetmiller and Forsyth, 1982).

There are a number of processes that can generate (1) horizontal deviatoric extension at shallow depths in the upper crust along the northeastern coastline of Baffin Island, and (2) compression in Baffin Bay. These include pronounced topography of mountain ranges (Artyushkov, 1973), the continent-ocean crustal transition in the epicentral region (Bott and Dean, 1972), glacial unloading and rebound (Stein and others, 1979; Quinlan, 1984), and sediment loading.

The free-air gravity map of Baffin Bay (Fig. 5; Ross, 1973; Sobczak, 1978) shows elliptically shaped anomaly contours in the continental slope area. While no individual anomaly shows as clear a correlation with earthquakes as those on the northern continental slope (compare Figs. 5 and 6), there is a strong correlation between steep gradients in the free-air anomalies, uplift isobase contours (Miller and Dyke, 1974; England, 1976), and epicentral trends. The gravity anomalies indicate that the region has not attained isostatic equilibrium. This disequilibrium could be caused by two processes: sediment loading on the continental margin, or rebound due to deglaciation (Peltier and Wu, 1982).

Either process would cause flexural stresses in the lithosphere, which could trigger earthquakes. Computations suggesting shear stresses associated with sediment loading reach a maximum under regions where the gravity gradients reach a maximum (Hasegawa and others, 1979), which is where most of the seismicity is concentrated. However, Kroeger (1987) notes that long-term rates of sedimentation are insufficient to cause the deviatoric stresses required for the seismicity in Baffin Bay, and that stresses associated with sediment loads would be present at all passive margins, while earthquakes appear to preferentially occur along deglaciated ones.

Stresses due to ongoing postglacial uplift may trigger earthquakes and also explain the distribution of deviatoric stresses deduced from focal mechanisms (Stein and others, 1979; Quinlan, 1984; Kroeger, 1987). Stein and others (1979) and Kroeger (1987) model the lithosphere as a thin elastic beam that has been unloaded; they obtain resulting deviatoric horizontal stresses of about 40 MPa. They and Quinlan (1984) also note that spreading stresses at continental margins yield similar magnitudes of stress, but neither process alone can account for the level of stress necessary to cause the 1933 event. Kroeger (1987) notes that a combination of the two processes yields good theoretical results that fit the observed epicentral distributions and focal mechanisms. The correlation of seismicity with high uplift rates and a lack of seismicity in Greenland and southwestern Baffin Island suggests rebound may be a major contributor to the stress field.

Nares Strait, a linear channel separating Greenland from eastern Ellesmere Island, is, at the present time, aseismic at the magnitude 4 level (Fig. 5; Wetmiller and Forsyth, 1982; Gregersen, 1982b) and no historical events have been recorded that can confidently be assigned to that region. It is possible that the present aseismic regime may be a quiescent period in a variable seismic history (Wetmiller and Forsyth, 1982).

Continental Slope of Arctic Canada

The continental slope and the coastal areas of northern Greenland and the Queen Elizabeth Islands are characterized by a moderately high level of seismic activity, including a few historical events that may have reached magnitudes up to 6 (Basham and others, 1977; Gregersen, 1982b). Although a diffuse band of seismicity marks the entire margin, except northwest of Banks Island, there are denser clusters of seismicity in eastern Peary Land and the Victoria Fjord region of Greenland, between Axel Heiberg and Prince Patrick Islands, and northwest of Ellef Ringnes Island (Figs. 5 and 6).

The seismicity of the Victoria Fjord area is dominated by a swarm of 80 magnitude 1.8–2.9 events on July 30, 1967. They may be due to stresses related to uplifting (Gregersen, 1979).

The events clustered in western Ellesmere and Axel Heiberg Islands (Fig. 6) have magnitudes between 3 and 5; the largest event occurred in March, 1975. The events are fairly shallow, probably all within the upper crust, and the 1975 event produced well-recorded surface waves (Basham and others, 1977). The regions of seismicity correlate with steep gradients in post-glacial uplift contours (Wetmiller and Forsyth, 1982).

The group of earthquakes northwest of Ellef Ringnes Island (Fig. 6) includes events of magnitude 2.5–4.5. One event of magnitude 5.5 occurred in the same area on June 3, 1956. The cluster extends over an area of about 4,000 km^2 and is centered on a 100-mGal free-air gravity anomaly. The bathymetric trends in the region are also perturbed and a region of local magnetic highs exist in the northwestern part of the cluster (McGrath and Frazer, 1981). Although the aeromagnetic data are not complete and epicentral uncertainties are greater in the region further offshore, the geophysical fields and bathymetry may indicate the presence of an active tectonic feature in this part of the Arctic Ocean. Alternatively, these events could also be related to stresses associated with uncompensated sedimentary loads.

During a 30-day period in March and April, 1965, an earthquake swarm consisting of approximately 2,000 events, with the largest of local magnitude (M_L) 2.9, occurred on the southeast coast of Prince Patrick Island in an epicentral zone 3 km^2 in area. The events were all shallow, between 5 and 8 km in depth, with the epicentral trend elongated in the north–south direction along a vertical plane, presumed to be the fault plane (Smith and others, 1968). On the basis of consistent compressional first motions observed at Mould Bay, the events are likely to have been the result of right-lateral strike-slip motion (Smith and others, 1968). There is an abrupt termination of this seismicity at the edge of M'Clure Strait, just south of the island. The significance of this apparent termination is not known.

One of the more seismically active regions of the Arctic margins is the southern part of the Beaufort Sea. A magnitude 6.5 event occurred in the region on November 16, 1920, and two other events with magnitude greater than 5 occurred in 1937 and 1975 (Basham and others, 1977). Most of the earthquakes occur between the 200- and 2500-m bathymetric contours (Fig. 6) and are located on the northwest side of a 100-mGal free-air gravity anomaly (Hasegawa and others, 1979). Hasegawa and others (1979) obtain a predominantly strike-slip mechanism for event #49 with a considerable normal faulting component and a focal depth of 40 km, based on depth phases and Love to Rayleigh wave amplitude ratios. The compressional axis strikes nearly north–south, oblique to the continental slope but perpendicular to the Arctic Mid-Ocean Ridge. Based on stress computations, there

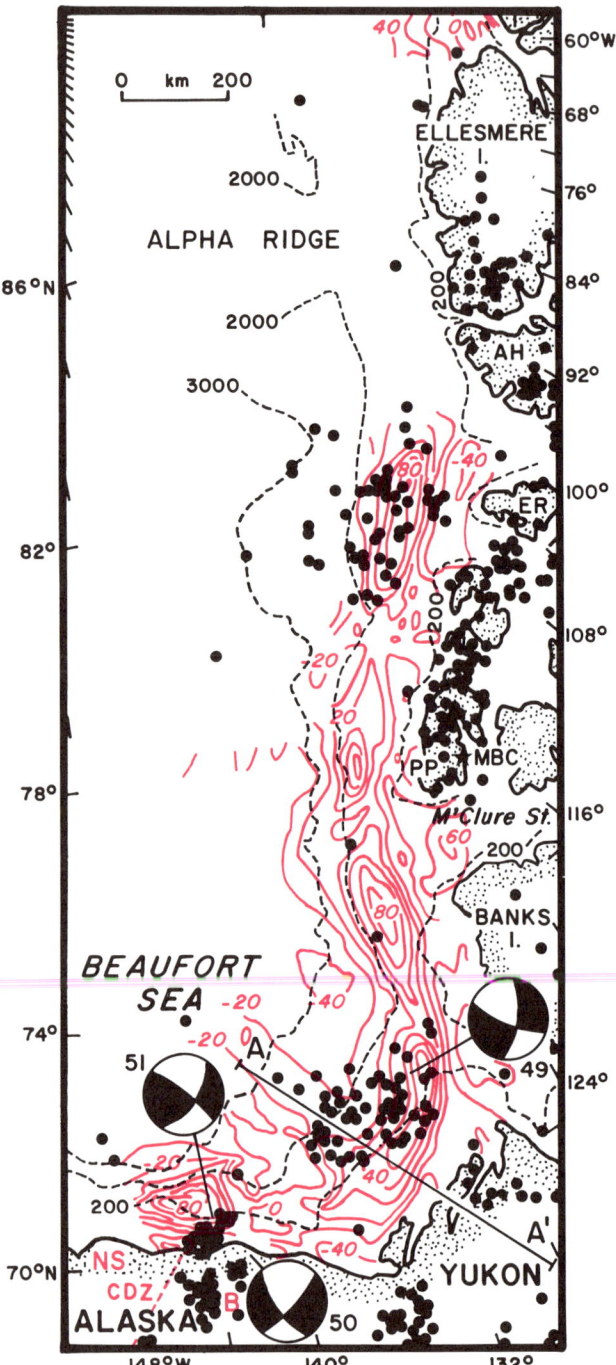

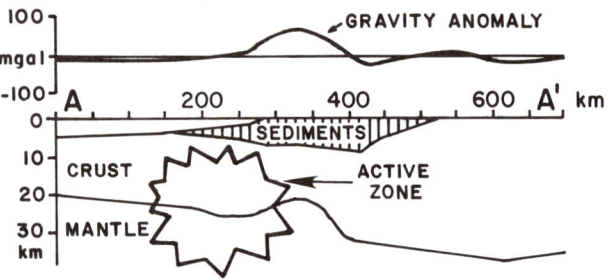

Figure 6. Seismicity (1962–1983) of the continental margin of Arctic Canada. Dots denote epicenters, and dashed lines indicate bathymetry (200-, 2000-, and 3000-m contours). Gravity anomalies (20-mGal intervals) are shown in red. Focal mechanisms shown for events #49–51 with conventions as in Figure 3. Inset at bottom shows the gravity anomaly across the Beaufort Shelf and a schematic cross-section showing relation between the sedimentary load and region of active seismicity. The red dashed line shows the "Canning Displacement Zone" (CDZ) of Grantz and May (1982) and B and NS stand for the northeastern Brooks Range and North Slope of Alaska, respectively.

are two factors that together may contribute to causing the events. First, there may be a weakened zone subjected to deviatoric horizontal extension perpendicular to the continental margin, due to the overlying Quaternary sediment load. Second, there may be compressional stresses resulting from sea floor spreading along the Arctic Mid-Ocean Ridge (Hasegawa and others, 1979). The preferred fault plane is the nodal plane subparallel to the continental slope.

Martin Point

Northeastern Alaska is characterized by a high level of microseismicity (Gedney and others, 1977) with a few small (m <5) teleseismic events. Most of the earthquakes are located east of the "Canning Displacement Zone" suggested by Grantz and others (1983) and Grantz and May (1982) to separate the tectonically active northeastern Brooks Range (Romanzov Mountains) from the North Slope of Alaska (Fig. 6).

On January 22, 1968, a m_b 4.4 earthquake (#51) occurred 30 km northwest of Martin Point, Alaska. It was followed by a series of aftershocks with magnitudes up to 4, which continued for about six months. The main shock is located at the northern limit of detected seismicity of the eastern Brooks Range (Biswas and others, 1977) and at the northern edge of the zone of Neogene age deformation (Grantz and May, 1982; Grantz and others, 1983). The earthquake sequence is located on the southern edge of a 90-mGal free-air gravity anomaly centered about 100 km northwest of Martin Point (Fig. 6). Relatively large surface waves imply a shallow focal depth.

Fujita and others (1983) and Biswas and others (1986) have both obtained strike-slip solutions for this event (#51). Their solutions, however, differ in the orientation of the compression axis. The Biswas and others (1986) solution has a north–south compression axis, while the Fujita and others (1983) solution has a northeast–southwest striking axis. The regional tectonics of northeast Alaska appear to favor the Biswas and others (1986) mechanism, while the probable shallow depth of the earthquake and the consistency of their P-axis with stress measurements from well breakout data from the northern Yukon and Mackenzie River Delta (Gough and others, 1983) favor the Fujita and others (1983) mechanism. A second event (#50) occurred in 1975 for which Estabrook (1985) determined a normal faulting mechanism and an east–west striking tension axis.

Chukchi Sea

The southern part of the Chukchi Sea is seismically active (Fig. 7). The largest known earthquakes occurred in 1928, when four events of magnitude 5.5–7 occurred in an area about 250 km northeast of Kolyuchin Gulf. Since 1960, six additional teleseismically detected events have occurred in the area, the two largest being magnitude 5.5 events that occurred in 1962 and 1971. A number of smaller events (m_b <2) have been recorded at the Soviet seismic station Iul'tin (ILT) 500 km to the west. These events were probably located using P-wave polarization angles (N. H. Sleep, personal communication, 1983).

The October 5, 1971, event (#52) is the only one large enough to have been recorded at many stations of the WWSSN. This event was felt over a wide portion of the Chukchi Peninsula, with maximum intensity reaching 5 at Neshkan. Fifty aftershocks were recorded, but only a few were large enough to be located (Lazareva, 1975). Three possible mechanisms have been proposed, none of which can be excluded. Fujita and others (1983) and Coley (1983) suggest that one nodal plane has a strike of about N60°W, which is nearly identical with the trends of many faults on and near Chukchi Peninsula, one of which may form the northern coast of Chukchi Peninsula, and the strike of Kotzebue Arch. Biswas and others (1986) suggest a normal faulting mechanism with the nodal planes striking northeast–southwest, transverse to the above-mentioned structures. The focal depth of the 1971 event is unknown; however, an event in 1982 had a focal depth of 3 km based on depth phases.

Based on limited data, the 1962 event probably had a mechanism similar to that of the 1971 event. Fujita and others (1983) suggest that all events are due to the continuing uplift on the western part of Kotzebue Arch (Fig. 7). United States Geological Survey single-channel reflection profiles have detected a fault (Eittreim and others, 1979) along which these events may be occurring. No events occur along the eastern end of Kotzebue Arch (Biswas and others, 1980).

Since 1965, a series of four earthquakes has been recorded along the eastern end of the Herald thrust offshore of, and in, the Lisburne Hills, Alaska. All events are small (m <4.5), and additional microearthquakes, forming east–west lineations, have been recorded by the Alaskan network in Kotzebue Sound (Biswas and others, 1980). No events have been recorded further west on Herald Thrust.

Two other clusters of microseismicity have occurred in Chukotka (Fig. 7). One cluster is situated 200 km southeast of Cape Billings in the northern part of the Pegtymel'skii Range and the Kuckvun' River Valley. The other group lies at the northern tip of Kresta Gulf and is in the region of a m_b 3.5 earthquake that occurred on August 22, 1971. Some 20 aftershocks were recorded, and a generally broad, northwest–southeast-striking band of microseismicity is delineated in the region (Kondorskaya and Sheblian, 1982; Koz'min, 1984).

Icequake swarms have also been noted in the southern Chukchi Sea by Biswas and others (1977), usually during times of northerly wind direction and the fracturing of ice sheets. Some of the other events in the Chukchi Sea may also be icequakes.

New Siberian Islands

The New Siberian Islands region appears to be mildly seismic at the magnitude 3 to 4 level. Numerous earthquakes have been recorded using a pair of temporary stations deployed during the summer months (Avetisov, 1975). A few events (m_b <3.8)

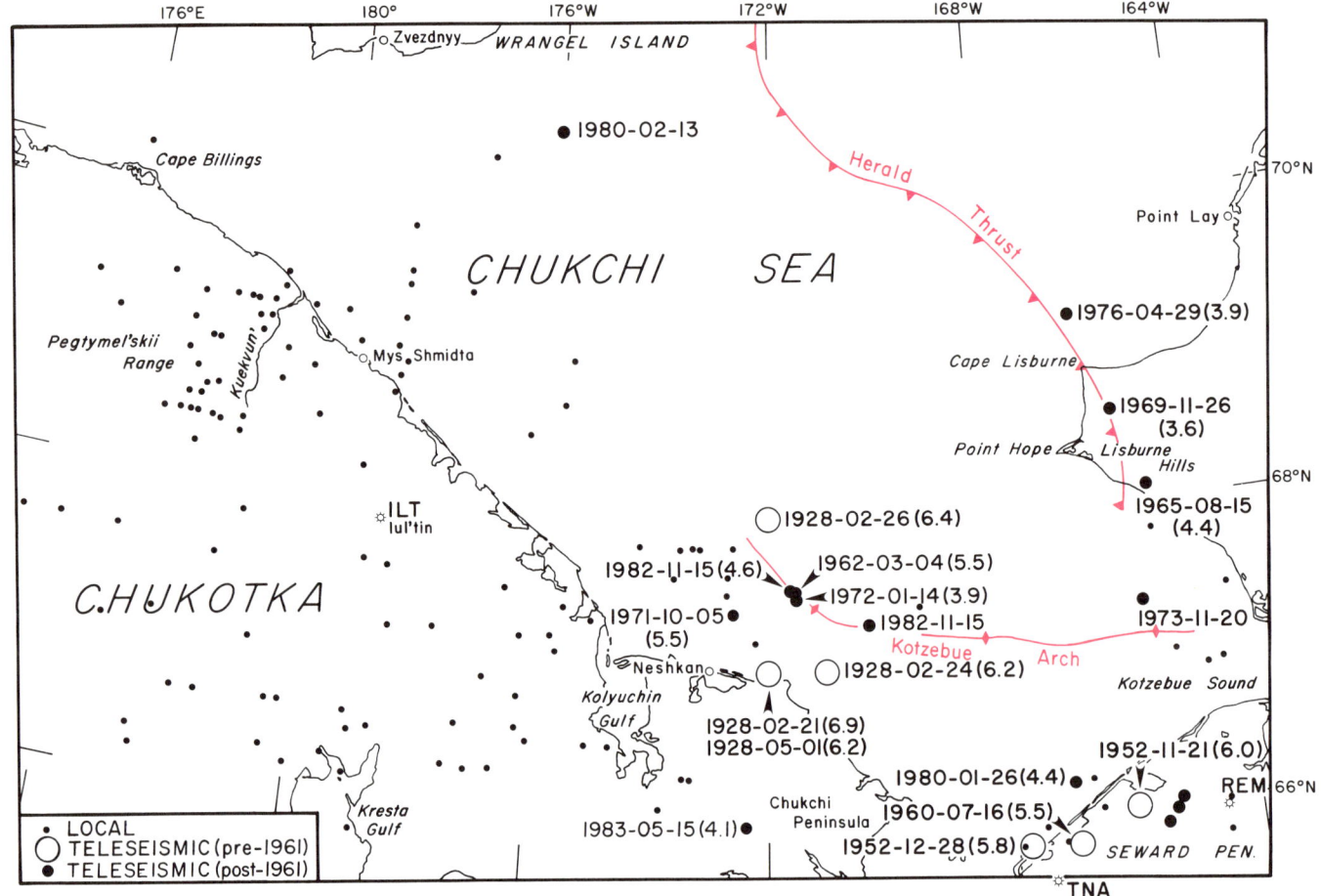

Figure 7. Seismicity (1928–1982) of the Chukchi Sea. Local solutions were obtained from station Iul'tin (USSR events) and the Northwest Alaska Network (USA events). Open circles represent less reliable pre-1961 teleseismic locations. Numbers in parentheses after date are magnitudes. Barbed circles with three-letter codes show locations of seismic stations. Structural features are shown in red.

have been recorded by the seismic network in the northeast USSR and were felt in the New Siberian Islands (Fig. 8; Koz'min and Andreev, 1978, 1980).

The only teleseismically recorded event in the area is the m_b 4.9 event of December 15, 1973 (#53), which occurred south of Novaya Sibir' Island (Fig. 8). Cook and others (1984) and Koz'min (1984) determine a thrust faulting mechanism with a northeast–southwest-striking compression axis. The strike of both nodal planes is approximately 300°, which is roughly coincident with the strike of fold axes on Kotel'nyi and Novaya Sibir' Islands (Koz'min, 1984; Fujita and Cook, this volume). The event is shallow (<15 km). Avetisov (1975) reports the detection of 30 aftershocks in March and April, 1974, and an additional six in April and May, 1975. A continuous occurrence of aftershocks between these intervals must be presumed.

The smaller earthquakes in the region appear to line up along the strike of the south coast of Bol'shoi Lyakhov Island and in a broad band striking northwest–southeast, southwest of Kotel'nyi Island. This second distribution may be an artifact of locations based on data from Tiksi station (Fig. 1). The epicentral distribution may also be due to faults along the margins of the straits between the New Siberian Islands (Avetisov, 1978). One event (April 18, 1974) is reported to have occurred about 75 km north of Novaya Sibir' Island. No activity is reported in the De Long Islands (Avetisov, 1975).

CRUSTAL STRUCTURE FROM EARTHQUAKE SEISMOLOGY

Surface waves from earthquakes have been used by several authors to investigate the crustal structure in the Arctic and northeast Siberia. The oceanic character of the Arctic Ocean basins was first established by Oliver and others (1955), who note that the continental Lg phase is not observed on any records for which ray paths crossed the deep water parts of the Arctic. Lg propagation was also impeded along paths that parallel the continental shelves of both Canada and northeastern Siberia and may indicate that sections of the East Siberian Sea are underlain by noncontinental crust.

Oliver and others (1955) also note that Rayleigh wave dispersion curves for the Arctic Ocean were intermediate, between continental and oceanic, for three paths. Further work by Oborina (1961) concludes that the Arctic Ocean has a crustal thickness of about 10 km. Similar studies by Hunkins (1963) conclude that the crust of the Arctic Ocean basins is between 6 and 15 km thick: Chapman (1973) obtains results indicating a 2-km sedimentary layer overlying a 15-km-thick crust. Chapman (1973) also notes that the Arctic Mid-Ocean Ridge is a typical mid-ocean ridge in terms of surface wave propagation characteristics. The propagation of Lg waves is impeded in the northern part of Baffin Bay, just south of Nares Strait, and suggests the presence of oceanic crust in that region (Wetmiller, 1974; Wetmiller and Forsyth, 1982).

Gregersen (1971) uses surface wave dispersion curves to show that the crustal structure in Greenland is essentially identical to that of the Canadian Shield, except for the ice layer. Subsequent studies suggest that the ice cap contributes to the attenuation of the Lg phase and that attenuation of Lg is also enhanced along paths that cross younger geologic structures (Gregersen, 1982a).

Lander (1984) notes that Rayleigh waves along great circle paths through the Cherskii Mountains and the Moma rift system have particle motions that are polarized at angles up to 50° with respect to the propagation path. Surface waves not traveling through the Cherskii Mountains are not affected; thus Lander (1984) attributes the polarization anomaly to the Moma rift system.

Stewart (1980a, b, 1981) uses the differential travel-time between the P and PP phases to determine the crustal properties at the reflection point of the PP wave. Late reflections occur along the Lomonosov Ridge, Alpha Ridge, and in the central part of the East Siberian Sea. Early reflections occur along the Arctic Mid-Ocean Ridge, except in the Lena River Delta, where reflections tend to be late. Whereas differences in residuals appear to segregate tectonic regimes, they do not always agree with expected anomalies. For example, the Arctic Mid-Ocean Ridge should yield late reflections, due to the high heat flow and hot mantle under the ridge. The Lomonosov Ridge, on the other hand, should have early reflections as is observed for the shields. Buchbinder (1982) notes, however, that the differential residuals need to be computed with reference models that approximate the source-receiver path, and that velocity variations and scattering near the reflection point cause uncertainties in defining the true reflection points of PP. Additional problems could result because of source structure and depth variations of the reflection point.

Avetisov (1983) uses near-receiver P to S conversions in the New Siberian Islands to determine the crustal structure (Fujita and Cook, this volume).

SUMMARY

The increase in the number of seismic stations and the development of analysis techniques have greatly increased our knowledge of Arctic seismicity in recent years. However, the relatively small sizes of the events and the remoteness of much of the circum-Arctic continues to hinder detailed study.

Our present state of knowledge indicates that the seismicity of the Arctic is dominated by activity along the plate boundary between the North American and Eurasian plates along the Arctic Mid-Ocean Ridge and its extension in the Laptev Sea. Almost all events reflect normal faulting and are 1–2 km below the sea floor, slightly deeper near the Laptev shelf. In northeastern Siberia, there is a transition from normal faulting to thrust faulting, with compression in the northern Cherskii Mountains. The pole of rotation between North America and Eurasia probably lies in this transition zone. The seismicity of the southern Cherskii Mountains, the northern Sea of Okhotsk, and the Northeast Kamchatka Seismic Zone appears to reflect relative motion between the North American and Okhotsk plates, with the Okhotsk plate moving counter-clockwise about a pole off Chukotka with respect to a fixed North America. Focal depths of most events in northeastern Siberia are about 10 km and the compressive stress axes align with a northeast–southwest orientation. Due to the reltively small magnitudes of the earthquakes, there is considerable variability in the proposed focal mechanisms.

Almost all intraplate seismicity is confined to the continental margins of Greenland, Arctic Canada, and northeastern Alaska and to the shelves of the Chukchi and East Siberian Seas. Focal mechanisms are not definitive, but suggest that the continental margin earthquakes may be due to a combination of sediment loading and glacial rebound. Crustal studies using surface waves have contributed to determining that the crust of the deepest parts of the Arctic Ocean basins is oceanic in nature and has a mean thickness of about 10 km.

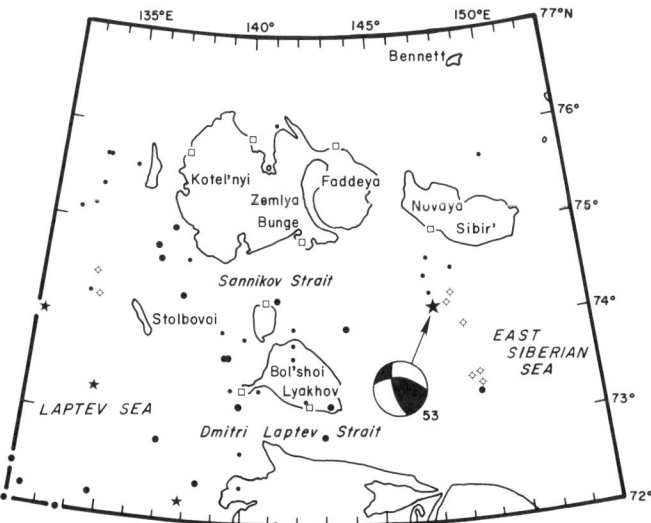

Figure 8. Seismicity (1964–1981) of the New Siberian Islands region. Stars denote teleseismically detected events, large solid dots are from the Soviet regional catalog, small solid dots are locations given by Avetisov (1975), and open circles are less-reliable locations derived from Avetisov (1975). Squares denote locations of temporary seismic stations operated by Avetisov (1975). Focal mechanism of event 53 shown with conventions as in Figure 3.

REFERENCES

Aki, K., and Richards, P. G., 1980, Quantitative seismology, v. 1: San Francisco, W. H. Freeman, 557 p.

Andreev, V. S., 1983, Boguchanskii glubinnyi razlom: Vestnik Moskva Universitet, ser. 4, Geologiya, no. 2, p. 77–80.

Argunov, M. S., and Gavrikov, S. I., 1960, Balagan-Tas, an early Quaternary volcano: Izvestiya Academy of Sciences of the USSR, no. 8, p. 72–74.

Artyushkov, E. V., 1973, Stresses in the lithosphere caused by crustal thickness inhomogeneities: Journal of Geophysical Research, v. 78, p. 7675–7708.

Aver'yanova, V. N., 1973, Seismic foci in the Far East: Jerusalem, Israel Program for Scientific Translation, 207 p.

Avetisov, G. P., 1975, Seismichnost' Morya Laptevykh i ee svyaz' s seismichnost'yu Evraziiskogo basseina: Tektonika Arktiki, v. 1, p. 31–36.

——, G. P., 1978, O mekhanizme ochaga odnogo Arkticheskogo zemletryaseniya, in Geofizicheskie metody razvedki v Arktike: Leningrad, Nauchno-Issledovatel'skii Institut Geologii Arktiki, p. 145–148.

——, 1983, Seismologic data on the deep structure of the New Siberian Islands and adjacent sea areas: International Geology Review, v. 25, p. 651–660.

Avetisov, G. P., and Sokolova, L. G., 1980, Zemletryaseniya i vulkany, in Gorshkov, S. G., ed., Atlas okeanov, Severnyi Ledovityi Okean: Ministry of Defence of the USSR, plate 24-25, scale 1:15,000,000.

Barazangi, M., and Dorman, J., 1970, Seismicity map of the Arctic compiled from ESSA, Coast and Geodetic Survey, epicenter data January 1961 through September 1969: Bulletin of the Seismological Society of America, v. 60, p. 1741–1743.

Basham, P. W., Forsyth, D. A., and Wetmiller, R. J., 1977, The seismicity of northern Canada: Canadian Journal of Earth Sciences, v. 14, p. 1646–1667.

Bergman, E. A., and Solomon, S. C., 1984, Source mechanisms of earthquakes near mid-ocean ridges from body waveform inversion; Implications for the early evolution of oceanic lithosphere: Journal of Geophysical Research, v. 89, p. 11415–11441.

Biswas, N. N., Gedney, L., and Huang, P., 1977, Seismicity studied; (A) northeast Alaska and (B) Norton and Kotzebue Sounds: Environmental Assessment of the Alaskan Continental Shelf, Annual Reports, v. 18, p. 269–315.

Biswas, N. N., Gedney, L., and Agnew, J., 1980, Seismicity of western Alaska: Bulletin of the Seismological Society of America, v. 70, p. 873–883.

Biswas, N. N., Aki, K., Puplan, H., and Tytgat, G., 1986, Characteristics of regional stresses in Alaska and neighboring areas: Geophysical Research Letters, v. 13, p. 177–180.

Bott, M.H.P., and Dean, D. S., 1972, Stress systems at young continental margins: Nature Physical Science, v. 235, p. 23–25.

Buchbinder, G.G.R., 1982, On PP and SS reflection point anomalies: Canadian Journal of Earth Sciences, v. 19, p. 434–437.

Chapman, E. D., 1973, Structure and tectonics of the Arctic region [M.S. thesis]: Cambridge, Massachusetts Institute of Technology, 119 p.

Chapman, M. E., and Solomon, S. C., 1976, North American-Eurasian plate boundary in northeast Asia: Journal of Geophysical Research, v. 81, p. 921–930.

Coley, M. J., 1983, Intraplate seismicity in central Alaska and Chukotka [M.S. thesis]: East Lansing, Michigan State University, 97 p.

Conant, D. A., 1972, Six new focal mechanism solutions for the Arctic and a center of rotation for plate movements [M.A. thesis]: New York, Columbia University, 18 p.

Cook, D. B., Fujita, K., and McMullen, C. A., 1984, Seismotectonics of northern Yakutia and the Laptev Sea (northeast USSR) [abs.]: EOS American Geophysical Union Transactions, v. 65, p. 1016.

——, 1986, Present day plate interactions in northeast Asia; North American, Eurasian, and Okhotsk plates: Journal of Geodynamics, v. 6, p. 33–51.

Cormier, V. F., 1975, Tectonics near the junction of the Aleutian and Kuril-Kamchatka arcs and a mechanism for middle Tertiary magmatism in the Kamchatka basin: Geological Society of America Bulletin, v. 86, p. 443–453.

Demenitskaya, R. M., and Karasik, A. M., 1969, The active rift system of the Arctic Ocean: Tectonophysics, v. 8, p. 345–351.

DeMets, C., Gordon, R. G., Argus, D. F., and Stein, S., 1990, Current plate motions: Geophysical Journal International (in press).

Dziewonski, A. M., Chou, T.-A., and Woodhouse, J. H., 1981, Determination of earthquake source parameters from waveform data for studies of global and regional seismicity: Journal of Geophysical Research, v. 86, p. 2825–2852.

Dziewonski, A. M., Franzen, J. E., and Woodhouse, J. H., 1983, Centroid-moment tensor solutions for April–June, 1983; Physics of the Earth and Planetary Interiors, v. 33, p. 243–249.

——, 1985, Centroid-moment tensor solutions for October–December, 1984: Physics of the Earth and Planetary Interiors, v. 39, p. 147–156.

Eittreim, S., Grantz, A., and Whitney, O. T., 1979, Cenozoic sedimentation and tectonics of Hope Basin, southern Chukchi Sea, in Sisson, A., ed., The relationship of plate tectonics to Alaskan geology and resources, 1977 symposium proceedings: Anchorage, Alaska Geological Society, p. B1–B11.

Emery, K. O., 1949, Topography and sediments of the Arctic basin: Journal of Geology, v. 57, p. 512–521.

England, J., 1976, Late Quaternary glaciation of the eastern Queen Elizabeth Islands, N.W.T., Canada; Alternative models: Quaternary Research, v. 6, p. 185–202.

Estabrook, C. H., 1985, Seismotectonics of northern Alaska [M.S. thesis]: Fairbanks, University of Alaska, 139 p.

Fedotov, S. A., Simbireva, I. G., Feodilaktov, V. D., and Matvienko, Y. D., 1980, Zemletryaseniya Kamchatki, in Gorbunova, I. V., Kondorskaya, N. V., and Shebalin, N. V., eds., Zemletryaseniya v SSSR v 1976 godu: Moskva, Nauka, p. 83–87.

Filson, J., and Frasier, C. W., 1972, The source of a Siberian earthquake [abs.]: EOS American Geophysical Union Transactions, v. 53, p. 1041.

Fujita, K., Cook, D. B., and Coley, M. J., 1983, Tectonics of the western Beaufort and Chukchi seas [abs.]: EOS American Geophysical Union Transactions, v. 64, p. 263.

Gedney, L., Biswas, N., Huang, P., Estes, S., and Pearson, C., 1977, Seismicity of northeast Alaska: Geophysical Research Letters, v. 4, p. 175–177.

Gough, D. I., Fordjor, C. K., and Bell, J. S., 1983, A stress province boundary and tractions on the North American plate: Nature, v. 305, p. 619–621.

Grachev, A. F., 1982, Geodynamics of the transitional zone from the Moma rift to the Gakkel Ridge, in Watkins, J. S., and Drake, C. L., eds., Studies of continental margin geology: American Association of Petroleum Geologists Memoir 34, p. 103–113.

Grachev, A. F., Demenitskaya, R. M., and Karasik, A. M., 1970, The Mid-Arctic Ridge and its continental continuation: Geomorphology, v. 1, p. 30–32.

Grantz, A., and May, S. D., 1982, Rifting history and structural development of the continental margin north of Alaska, in Watkins, J. S., and Drake, C. L., eds., Studies of continental margin geology: American Association of Petroleum Geologists Memoir 34, p. 77–100.

Grantz, A., Dinter, D. A., and Biswas, N. N., 1983, Map, cross sections, and chart showing late Quaternary faults, folds, and earthquake epicenters on the Alaskan Beaufort shelf: U.S. Geological Survey Map I-1182-C, scale 1:500,000.

Gregersen, S., 1971, Surface wave dispersion and crust structure in Greenland: Geophysical Journal of the Royal Astronomical Society, v. 22, p. 29–39.

——, 1979, Intraplate earthquake swarm in Greenland and adjacent continental regions: Nature, v. 281, p. 661–662.

——, 1982a, Seismicity and observations of Lg wave attenuation in Greenland: Tectonophysics, v. 89, p. 77–93.

——, 1982b, Earthquakes in Greenland: Bulletin of the Geological Society of Denmark, v. 31, p. 11–27.

Gutenberg, B., and Richter, C. F., 1954, Seismicity of the Earth and associated phenomena: New York, Hafner, 310 p. (1965 reprint).

Hasegawa, H. S., Chou, C. W., and Basham, P. W., 1979, Seismotectonics of the

Beaufort Sea: Canadian Journal of Earth Sciences, v. 16, p. 816–830.
Hashizume, M., 1973, Two earthquakes on Baffin Island and their tectonic implications: Journal of Geophysical Research, v. 79, p. 5458–5468.
Heezen, B. C., and Ewing, M., 1961, The mid-oceanic ridge and its extension through the Arctic basin, in Raasch, G. O., ed., Geology of the Arctic: Toronto, University of Toronto, p. 622–641.
Hodgson, J. H., Bath, M., Jensen, H., Kvale, A., Linden, N. A., Murphy, L. M., Shebalin, N. V., Tryggvason, E., and Vesanen, E., 1965, Seismicity of the Arctic: Annals of the International Geophysical Year, v. 30, p. 33–66.
Hunkins, K., 1963, Submarine studies of the Arctic Ocean from earthquake surface wave studies, in Proceedings of the Arctic Basin Symposium, October, 1962: Washington, D.C., Arctic Institute of North America, p. 3–8.
Ishikawa, Y., and Yu, L.-W., 1984, Higashi Ajia no tekutonikkusu [abs.]: Programme and Abstracts, Seismological Society of Japan, nr. 2, p. 42.
Jackson, G. D., and Taylor, F. C., 1972, Correlation of major Aphebian rock units in the northeastern Canadian shield: Canadian Journal of Earth Sciences, v. 9, p. 1650–1669.
Jemsek, J. P., Bergman, E. A., Nabelek, J. L., and Solomon, S. C., 1984, Focal depths and mechanisms of large earthquakes on the Mid-Arctic Ridge system [abs.]: EOS American Geophysical Union Transactions, v. 65, p. 273.
Kochetkov, V. M., 1976, The Yakut zone, in Medvedev, S. V., ed., Seismic zoning of the USSR: Jerusalem, Israel Program for Scientific Translations, p. 410–429.
Kondorskaya, N. V., and Shebalin, N. V., 1982, New catalog of strong earthquakes in the USSR from ancient times through 1977: World Data Center A for Solid Earth Geophysics, Report SE-31, 608 p.
Koz'min, B. M., 1973, Zemletryaseniya Yakutii, in Vvedenskaya, N. A., Kondorskaya, N. V., and Shebalin, N. V., eds., Zemletryaseniya v SSSR v 1970 godu: Moskva, Nauka, p. 147–154.
——— , 1984, Seismicheskie poyasa Yakutii i mekhanismy ochagov ikh zemletryasenii: Moskva, Nauka, 126 p.
Koz'min, B. M., and Andreev, T. A., 1978, Zemletryaseniya Yakutii i Severo-Vostoka SSSR, in Gorbunova, I. V., Kondorskaya, N. V., and Shebalin, N. V., eds., Zemletryaseniya v SSSR v 1975 godu: Moskva, Nauka, p. 87–89.
——— , 1980, Zemletryaseniya Yakutii i Severo-Vostoka SSSR, in Gorbunova, I. V., Kondorskaya, N. V., and Shebalin, N. V., eds., Zemletryaseniya v SSSR v 1976 godu: Moskva, Nauka, p. 58–61.
Koz'min, B. M., Emel'yanov, N. P., Emel'yanova, A. A., Zhelinskaya, E. A., Garionov, A. G., and Li, B. F., 1975, Sil'nye zemletryaseniya Yakutii, in Gorbunova, I. V., Kondorskaya, N. V., and Shebalin, N. V., eds., Zemletryaseniya v SSSR v 1971 godu: Moskva, Nauka, p. 133–141.
Kristoffersen, Y., 1982, The Nansen Ridge, Arctic Ocean; Some geophysical observations of the rift valley at slow spreading rate: Tectonophysics, v. 89, p. 61–172.
Kristoffersen, Y., and Talwani, M., 1977, Extinct triple junction south of Greenland and the Tertiary motion of Greenland relative to North America: Geological Society of America Bulletin, v. 88, p. 1037–1049.
Kristoffersen, Y., Husebye, E. S., Bungum, H., and Gregersen, S., 1982, Seismic investigations of the Nansen Ridge during the Fram I experiment: Tectonophysics, v. 82, p. 57–68.
Kroeger, G. C., 1987, Synthesis and analysis of teleseismic body wave seismograms [Ph.D. thesis]: Palo Alto, Stanford University, 135 p.
Kroeger, G. C., and Geller, R. J., 1983, An efficient method for computing synthetic reflection seismograms for plane layered media [abs.]: EOS American Geophysical Union Transactions, v. 64, p. 772.
Lander, A. V., 1984, Anomal'nye yavleniya v poverkhnostnykh volnakh na Severo-Vostoke Evrazii i ikh svyaz' s raionom Momskogo rifta, in Keilis-Borok, V. I., and Levshin, A. L., eds., Matematicheskoe modelirovanie i interpretatsiya geofizicheskikh dannykh, vychislitel'naya seismologiya, v. 16: Moskva, Nauka, p. 127–155.
Lazareva, A. P., 1975, Zemletryaseniya Arktiki v 1970 i 1971 gg, in Gorbunova, I. V., Kondorskaya, N. V., and Shebalin, N. V., eds., Zemletryaseniya v SSSR v 1971 godu: Moskva, Nauka, p. 145–149.
Lazareva, A. P., and Misharina, L. A., 1965, Stresses in earthquake foci in the Arctic seismic belt: Izvestiya Academy of Sciences of the USSR, Physics of the Solid Earth, v. 1, p. 84–87.
Leblanc, G., and Wetmiller, R. J., 1974, An evaluation of seismological data available for the Yukon territory and the Mackenzie valley: Canadian Journal of Earth Sciences, v. 11, p. 1435–1454.
Linden, N. A., 1961, Seismicity of the Arctic region: Annals of the International Geophysical Year, v. 11, p. 375–387.
Liu, H.-L., and Kanamori, H., 1980, Determination of source parameters of mid-plate earthquakes from the waveforms of body waves: Bulletin of the Seismological Society of America, v. 70, p. 1989–2004.
McGrath, P. H., and Fraser, I., 1981, Magnetic anomaly map of Arctic Canada: Geological Survey of Canada Map 1512A.
McMullen, C. A., 1985, Seismicity and tectonics of the northeastern Sea of Okhotsk [M.S. thesis]: East Lansing, Michigan State University, 107 p.
Miller, G. H., and Dyke, A. S., 1974, Proposed extent of Late Wisconsin Laurentide ice on eastern Baffin Island: Geology, v. 2, p. 125–130.
Minster, J. B., Jordan, T. H., Molnar, P., and Haines, E., 1974, Numerical modelling of instantaneous plate tectonics: Geophysical Journal of the Royal Astronomical Society, v. 36, p. 541–576.
Nakamura, K., 1983, Possible nascent trench along the eastern Japan Sea as the convergent boundary between Eurasian and North American plates: Bulletin of the Earthquake Research Institute, v. 58, p. 711–722.
Naymark, A. A., 1976, Neotectonics of the Moma region, northeastern USSR: Doklady Academy of Sciences of the USSR, Earth Sciences Section, v. 229, p. 39–42.
Newberry, J. T., LaClair, D. L., and Fujita, K., 1986, Seismicity and tectonics of the far western Aleutian Islands: Journal of Geodynamics, v. 6, p. 13–32..
Oborina, S. F., 1961, On the crustal structure of the Arctic region: Izvestiya Academy of Sciences of the USSR, Geophysics Series, p. 534–536.
Oliver, J., Ewing, M., and Press, F., 1955, Crustal structure of the Arctic regions from the Lg phase: Bulletin of the Geological Society of America, v. 66, p. 1063–1074.
Peltier, W. R., and Wu, P., 1982, Mantle phase transitions and the free-air gravity anomalies over Fennoscandia and Laurentia: Geophysical Research Letters, v. 7, p. 731–734.
Peters, M. F., and Vink, G. E., 1985, Plate reconstruction poles determined by a least squares algorithm [abs.]: EOS American Geophysical Union Transactions, v. 66, p. 1061.
Pitman, W. C., III, and Talwani, M., 1972, Sea-floor spreading in the North Atlantic: Geological Society of America Bulletin, v. 83, p. 619–646.
Poppe, B. A., 1980, Directory of world seismograph stations, v. 1, The Americas, pt. 1, United States, Canada, Bermuda: World Data Center A for Solid Earth Geophysics, Report SE-25, 465 p.
Qamar, A., 1974, Seismicity of the Baffin Bay region: Bulletin of the Seismological Society of America, v. 64, p. 87–98.
Quinlan, G., 1984, Postglacial rebound and focal mechanisms of eastern Canadian earthquakes: Canadian Journal of Earth Sciences, v. 21, p. 1018–1023.
Reid, I., and Falconer, R.K.H., 1982, A seismicity study in northern Baffin Bay: Canadian Journal of Earth Sciences, v. 19, p. 1518–1531.
Rezanov, I. A., and Kochetkov, V. M., 1962, Recent tectonics and seismic regionalization in the North-Eastern region of the USSR: Izvestiya Academy of Sciences of the USSR, Geophysics Series, p. 1045–1052.
Ross, D. I., 1973, Free-air and Bouguer gravity maps of Baffin Bay and adjacent continental margins: Geological Survey of Canada Paper 73-37.
Rothe, J. P., 1969, Seismicity of the Earth 1953–1965: Paris, UNESCO, 336 p.
Satake, K., 1985, The mechanism of the 1983 Japan Sea earthquake as inferred from long-period surface waves and tsunamis: Physics of the Earth and Planetary Interiors, v. 37, p. 249–260.
Savostin, L. A., and Karasik, A. M., 1981, Recent plate tectonics of the Arctic basin and of northeastern Asia: Tectonophysics, v. 74, p. 111–145.
Savostin, L. A., Verzhbitskaya, A. I., and Baranov, B. V., 1982, Holocene plate

tectonics of the Sea of Okhotsk region: Doklady Academy of Sciences of the USSR, Earth Sciences Section, v. 266, p. 62–65.

Savostin, L. A., Zonenshain, L. P., and Baranov, B., 1983, Geology and plate tectonics of the Sea of Okhotsk, *in* Hilde, T.W.C., and Uyeda, S., eds., Geodynamics of the western Pacific–Indonesian Region: American Geophysical Union, Geodynamics Series, v. 11, p. 189–221.

Scheidegger, A. E., 1966, Tectonics of the Arctic seismic belt in the light of fault-plane solutions of earthquakes: Bulletin of the Seismological Society of America, v. 56, p. 241–245.

Seno, T., 1985, Is northern Honshu a microplate?: Tectonophysics, v. 115, p. 177–196.

Seno, T., and Kroeger, G., 1983, A reexamination of earthquakes previously thought to have occurred within the slab between the trench axis and double seismic zone, northern Honshu arc: Journal of Physics of the Earth, v. 31, p. 195–216.

Smith, W.E.T., Whitham, K., and Piche, W. T., 1968, Microearthquake swarm in 1965 near Mould Bay, N.W.T., Canada: Bulletin of the Seismological Society of America, v. 58, p. 1991–2011.

Sobczak, L. W., 1978, Arctic free-air gravity (residual field), *in* Sweeney, J. F., ed., Arctic geophysical review: Publications of the Earth Physics Branch, v. 45, no. 4, plate 4, scale 1:7,500,000.

Solomon, S. C., and Julian, B. R., 1974, Seismic constraints on ocean-ridge mantle structure: anomalous fault plane solutions from first motions: Geophysical Journal of the Royal Astronomical Society, v. 38, p. 265–285.

Srivastava, S. P., 1978, Evolution of the Labrador Sea and its bearing on the early evolution of the North Atlantic: Geophysical Journal of the Royal Astronomical Society, v. 52, p. 313–357.

Stauder, W., and Mualchin, L., 1976, Fault motion in the larger earthquakes of the Kurile-Kamchatka arc and of the Kurile-Hokkaido corner: Journal of Geophysical Research, v. 81, p. 297–308.

Stein, S., Sleep, N. H., Geller, R. J., Wang, S.-C., and Kroeger, G. C., 1979, Earthquakes along the passive margin of eastern Canada: Geophysical Research Letters, v. 6, p. 537–540.

Stewart, I.C.F., 1980a, Arctic lithospheric structure from delays of teleseismic P-wave reflections: Tectonophysics, v. 69, p. 37–62.

—— , 1980b, Anomalous travel times of teleseismic P-waves reflected under Arctic marine areas: Marine Geophysical Researches, v. 4, p. 291–304.

—— , 1981, Lithospheric structure and teleseismic P-wave reflection delays under Fennoscandia and Siberia: Journal of Geophysics, v. 49, p. 108–114.

Sykes, L. R., 1965, The seismicity of the Arctic: Bulletin of the Seismological Society of America, v. 55, p. 519–536.

—— , 1967, Mechanisms of earthquakes and nature of faulting on the mid-oceanic ridges: Journal of Geophysical Research, v. 72, p. 2131–2153.

—— , 1970, Focal mechanism solutions for earthquakes along the world rift system: Bulletin of the Seismological Society of America, v. 60, p. 1749–1752.

Sykes, L. R., and Sbar, M. L., 1974, Focal mechanism solutions of intraplate earthquakes and stresses in the lithosphere, *in* Kristjansson, L., ed., Geodynamics of Iceland and the North Atlantic area: Boston, D. Reidel, p. 207–224.

Tarr, A. C., 1970, New maps of polar seismicity: Bulletin of the Seismological Society of America, v. 60, p. 1745–1747.

Veith, K. F., 1974, The relationship of island arc seismicity to plate tectonics [Ph.D. thesis]: Dallas, Southern Methodist University.

Veis-Ksenofontova, E. G., 1962, Arktika zemletryaseniya—1908–1958, *in* Savarenskii, E. F., Solov'ev, S. L., and Kharin, D. A., eds., Atlas zemletryasenii v SSSR: Moskva, Akademii Nauk SSSR, map 19, scale 1:20,000,000.

Watson, B. F., and Fujita, K., 1985, Tectonic evolution of Kamchatka and the Sea of Okhotsk and implications for the Pacific basin, *in* Howell, D. G., ed., Tectonostratigraphic terranes of the Circum-Pacific region: Circum-Pacific Council for Energy and Mineral Resources, Earth Science Series, no. 1, p. 333–348.

Wetmiller, R. J., 1974, Crustal structure of Baffin Bay from the earthquake generated Lg phase: Canadian Journal of Earth Sciences, v. 11, p. 123–130.

—— , 1978, Arctic seismicity (1908–1975), *in* Sweeney, J. F., ed., Arctic Geophysical Review: Publications of the Earth Physics Branch, v. 45, no. 4, plate 2, sclae 1:7,500,000.

Wetmiller, R. J., and Forsyth, D. A., 1978, Seismicity of the Arctic, 1908–1975, *in* Sweeney, J. F., ed., Arctic geophysical review: Publications of the Earth Physics Branch, v. 45, no. 4, p. 15–24.

—— , 1982, Review of seismicity and other geophysical data near Nares Strait: Meddelelser om Gronland, Geoscience, v. 8, p. 261–274.

Wetmiller, R. J., and Horner, R. B., 1978, Canadian earthquakes—1976: Seismological Service of Canada, Seismological Series, no. 79, 75 p.

Yoshii, T., 1979, A detailed cross section of the deep seismic zone beneath northeastern Honshu, Japan: Tectonophysics, v. 55, p. 349–360.

Zobin, V. M., and Simbireva, I. G., 1977, Focal mechanism of earthquakes in the Kamchatka-Commander region and heterogeneities of the active seismic zone: Pure and Applied Geophysics, v. 115, p. 284–299.

Zonenshayn, L. P., Natapov, L. M., Savostin, L. A., and Stavskii, A. P., 1978, Recent plate tectonics of northeastern Asia in connection with the opening of the North Atlantic and the Arctic Ocean basins: Oceanology, v. 18, p. 550–555.

Manuscript Accepted by the Society October 20, 1986

ACKNOWLEDGMENTS

We thank V. Vinogradov and B. M. Koz'min for providing copies of Soviet publications. Nirendra Biswas, Michael Coley, Charles DeMets, Arthur Grantz, G. Leonard Johnson, Glenn Kroeger, Cindy McMullen, James Newberry, Norman Sleep, Sean Solomon, David Stone, and Peter Vogt provided data prior to publication and made numerous helpful comments and criticisms. Gary Rogers, Seth Stein, and Jack Sweeney provided many helpful comments. Ken DeMino, Martha Fujita, Michelle Groves, and Theodore Tomczyk provided technical assistance and editorial comments. This work was funded, in part, by Office of Naval Research contract no. N00014-83-K-0693 and a research initiation grant from Michigan State University. Contribution No. 1204 of the Earth Physics Branch.

NOTE ADDED IN PROOF

Additional focal mechanisms and discussions of the seismicity and tectonics of the North America–Eurasia plate boundary are summarized by Fujita and others (in press, Tectonophysics) and Parfenov and others (1987, *in* Recent Tectonic Activity of the Earth and Seismicity: Moskva, Nauka; 1988, Vulkanologiya i Seismologiya). Seno (1987, Seismological Society of Japan, Abstracts, No. 1) obtained a North America–Okhotsk pole of rotation near Sakhalin Island, and Chan (1989, 28th International Geological Congress, Abstracts) has performed a tomographic inversion for Arctic structure.

Chapter 7

Gravity from 64°N to the North Pole

L. W. Sobczak and D. B. Hearty
Geological Survey of Canada, Department of Energy, Mines and Resources, 1 Observatory Crescent, Ottawa, Ontario K1A 0Y3, Canada
R. Forsberg
Geodetic Institute, Gamlehave Alle 22, DK 2920, Copenhagen, Denmark
Y. Kristoffersen
Seismological Institute, University of Bergen, Bergen, Norway
O. Eldholm
University of Oslo, Department of Geology, Postboks 1047, Blindern, 0316 Oslo 3, Norway
S. D. May
U.S. Geological Survey, 345 Middlefield Road, MS 904, Menlo Park, California 94025

INTRODUCTION

Although gravity observations were made prior to 1960, systematic regional gravity coverage in the Arctic began in earnest in the early 1960s on land and sea ice with the advent of helicopters and reliable portable gravimeters, and was extended in the 1970s over the oceans with ships and reliable marine gravimeters. As a result, about half of the polar area north of 64°N latitude is now covered with regional (spacings 12 km or less) gravity observations for which the data are readily available to the public. Permanently ice-covered regions of the Arctic Ocean, as well as mountainous and glacier-covered areas, are still largely unmapped. Except for a few pre-World War II gravity stations from regions within the Soviet Union (USSR), no gravity data from the USSR are displayed on Plate 3.

The observed gravity field of the whole Arctic region north of 60°N was first discussed by Sobczak (1978), who presented maps (scale 1:7,500,000) showing the gravity field derived from mean values based on observed (1/2° latitude × 2° longitude) and predicted (1° latitude × 1° longitude) free-air anomalies and a residual gravity field derived by removing the satellite gravity field (Goddard Earth Model 8, GEM 8) from the observed and predicted fields. These maps indicate anomalous gravitational features of wavelengths in excess of 100 km.

Bowin and others (1982) presented a comprehensive free-air gravity anomaly atlas of the world, including a map of the Arctic region north of 70° at a scale of about 1:14,000,000.

The intent of the present compilation (Plate 3) is to show, in the most informative way, the observed gravity field based on surface measurements, to indicate the density of observations, to update the gravity information, and to minimize distortion of the map due to projection. Plate 3 describes how the observed gravity was checked by plotting the data on large sheets as indexed in

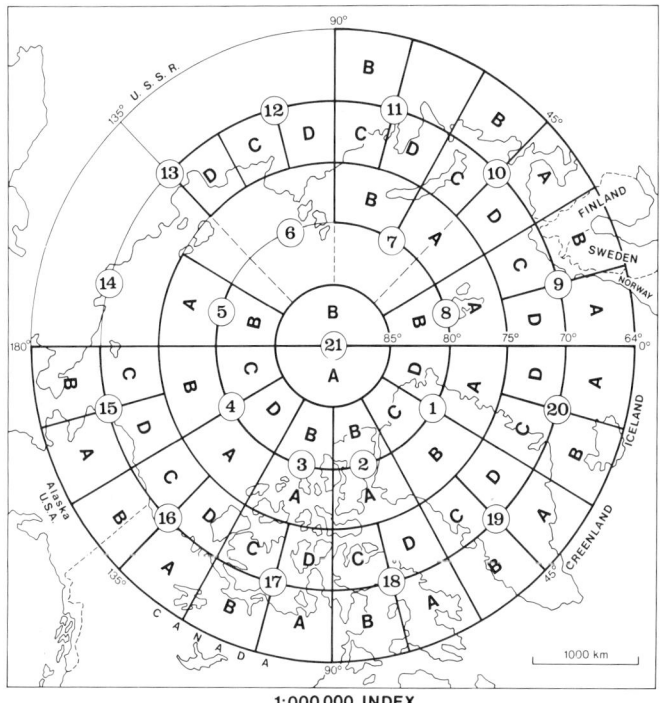

Figure 1. Index to areas of observed gravity plotted at a scale of 1:1,000,000 that were used initially in compiling Figure 2 and Plate 3.

Figure 1 and shown in a simplified form in Figure 2. It also describes the method of reduction and accuracy of the gravity anomalies. Not included in Plate 3 are satellite data or predicted gravity values. Reduced maps of the satellite data are included separately as text figures and discussed briefly for those areas where no observed surface data are available. Predicted gravity anomalies have been discussed earlier by Sobczak (1978).

Sobczak, L. W., Hearty, D. B., Forsberg, R., Kristoffersen, Y., Eldholm, O., and May, S. D., 1990, Gravity from 64°N to the North Pole, *in* Grantz, A., Johnson, L., and Sweeney, J. F., eds., The Arctic Ocean region: Boulder, Colorado, Geological Society of America, The Geology of North America, v. L.

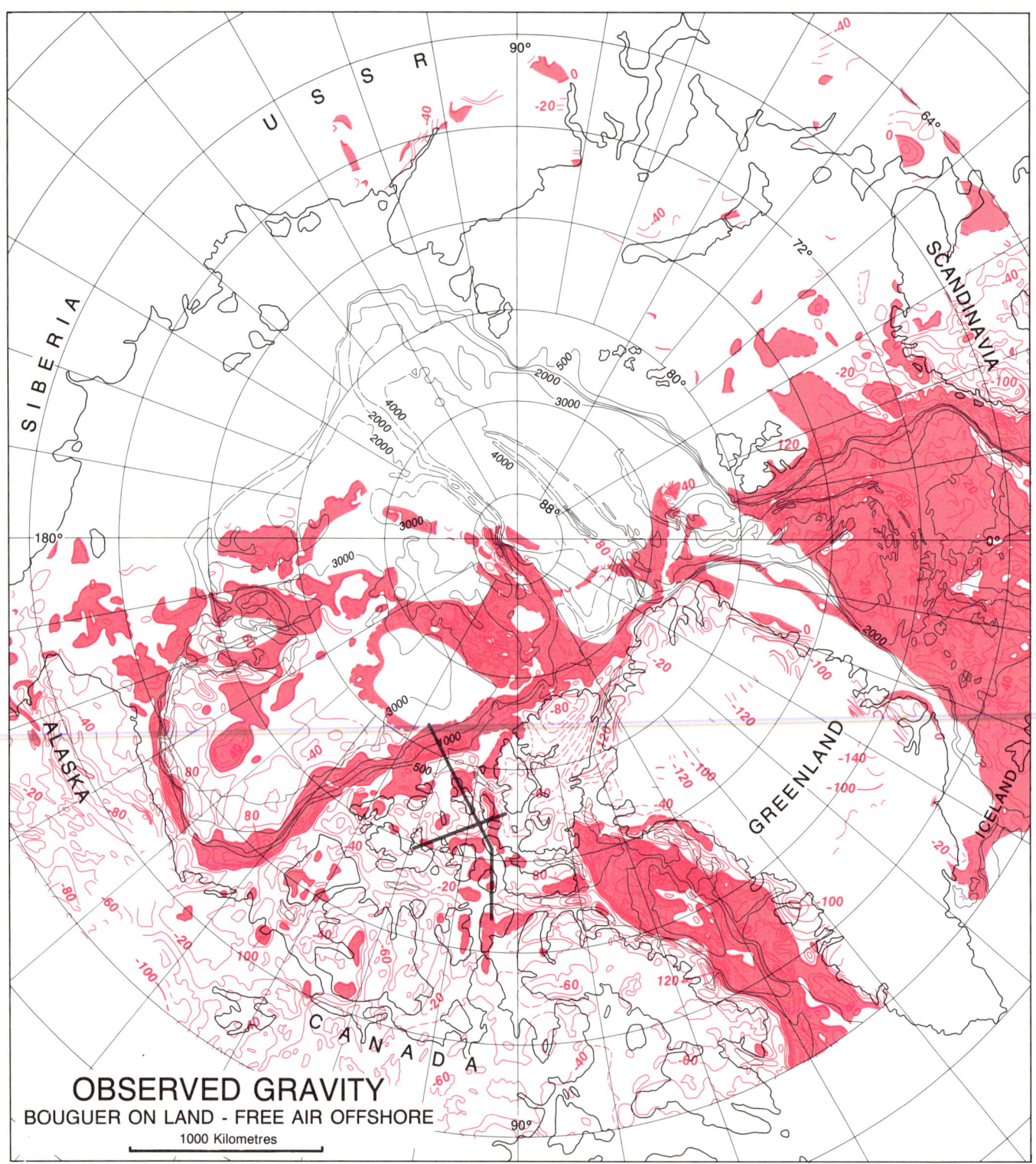

Figure 2. Observed gravity anomalies of the Arctic region, reduced and simplified from 57 sheets (Fig. 1) which were hand contoured. Contour interval is 20 mGal. Red shaded areas are positive. Profile locations for Figures 5 to 7 indicated.

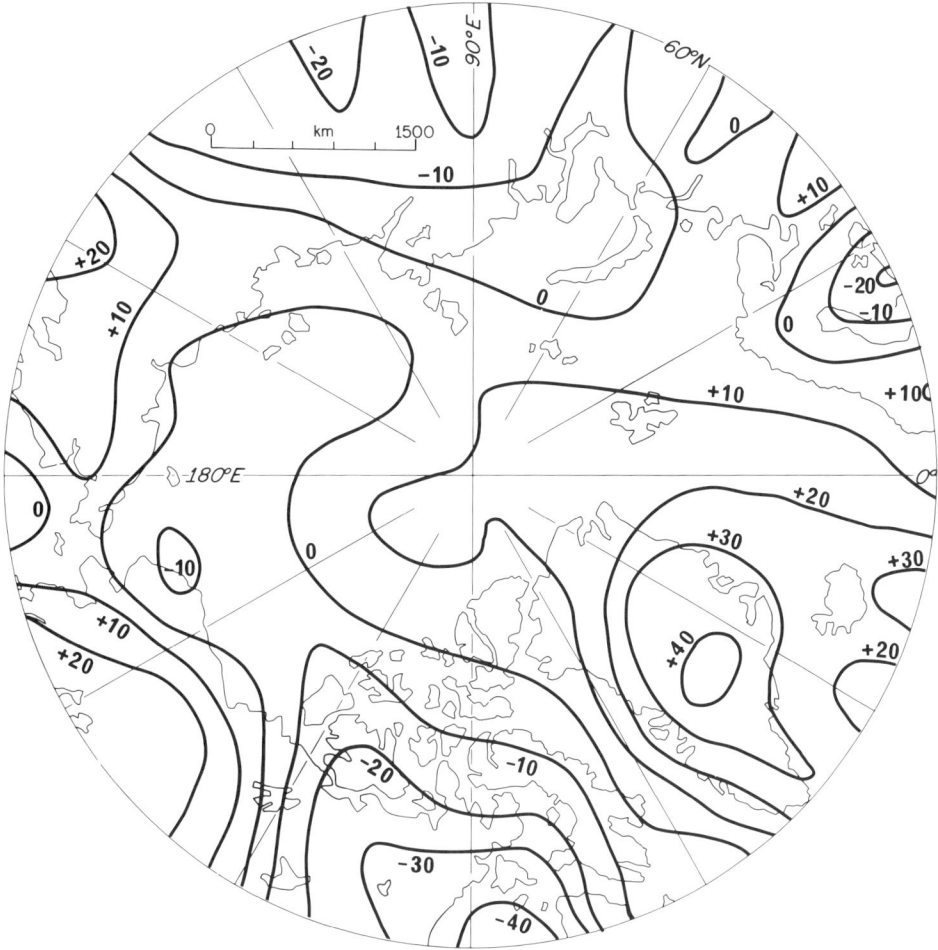

Figure 3. Calculated satellite free-air anomalies of the Arctic region. Map based on the IGSN 1971 and GRS 1967, which were produced from a combination of satellite tracking data using Goddard Earth Model 8 (GEM8) and surface gravity data complete to spherical harmonic degree and order of 25. Contour interval is 10 mGal.

GRAVITY DATA (SATELLITE)

Satellite free-air anomalies (Fig. 3) were calculated and discussed by Sobczak (1978). The United States National Geodetic Satellite Program has produced ten solutions (GEM 1–10, Smith and others, 1976; Wagner and others, 1976; Lerch and others, 1979) for the Earth's gravity field, based on a combination of satellite tracking data and surface gravity measurements using mean gravity anomalies for 5° × 5° areas. New solutions are calculated in pairs as more gravity data become available. The odd-numbered solutions use only satellite tracking data and the even-numbered solutions also take into account gravity data measured on the surface of the earth. As no new surface data have been added to the USSR sector, GEM 8 (at a degree and order of 25) would be similar to later solutions in the Arctic Ocean area within the eastern hemisphere. The satellite gravity field in this area is relatively flat, varying from 0 to 10 mGal. The even-numbered GEM solutions show only anomalies with wavelengths greater than 1,000 km. At this scale the anomaly field probably images very deep mass distribution within the Earth's core and mantle (Bowin and others, 1982).

A more detailed free-air anomaly field (Fig. 4), complete to spherical harmonic degree and order of 180, has been developed at Ohio State University (Rapp, 1981). This field combines satellite tracking data, results from satellite altimetry and terrestrial 1° × 1° mean gravity values. The ocean satellite altimetry coverage only extends northwards to latitude 72°N, and this region is essentially covered by terrestrial data shown in Figure 2 and Plate 3.

Figure 4 shows the gravity field over the Eurasia Basin and adjacent shelves (Barents, Kara, and Laptev) to be at the zero anomaly level. The gravity field over the Norwegian–Greenland Sea and over the Amerasia Basin compares favorably with terrestrial observed gravity except that the field is more generalized. This field is beneficial in filling in areas where there is no terrestrial data and shows fairly detailed free-air anomalies over the land areas, which can complement the Bouguer anomalies shown in Figure 2 and Plate 3. Figure 4, with a few exceptions, shows

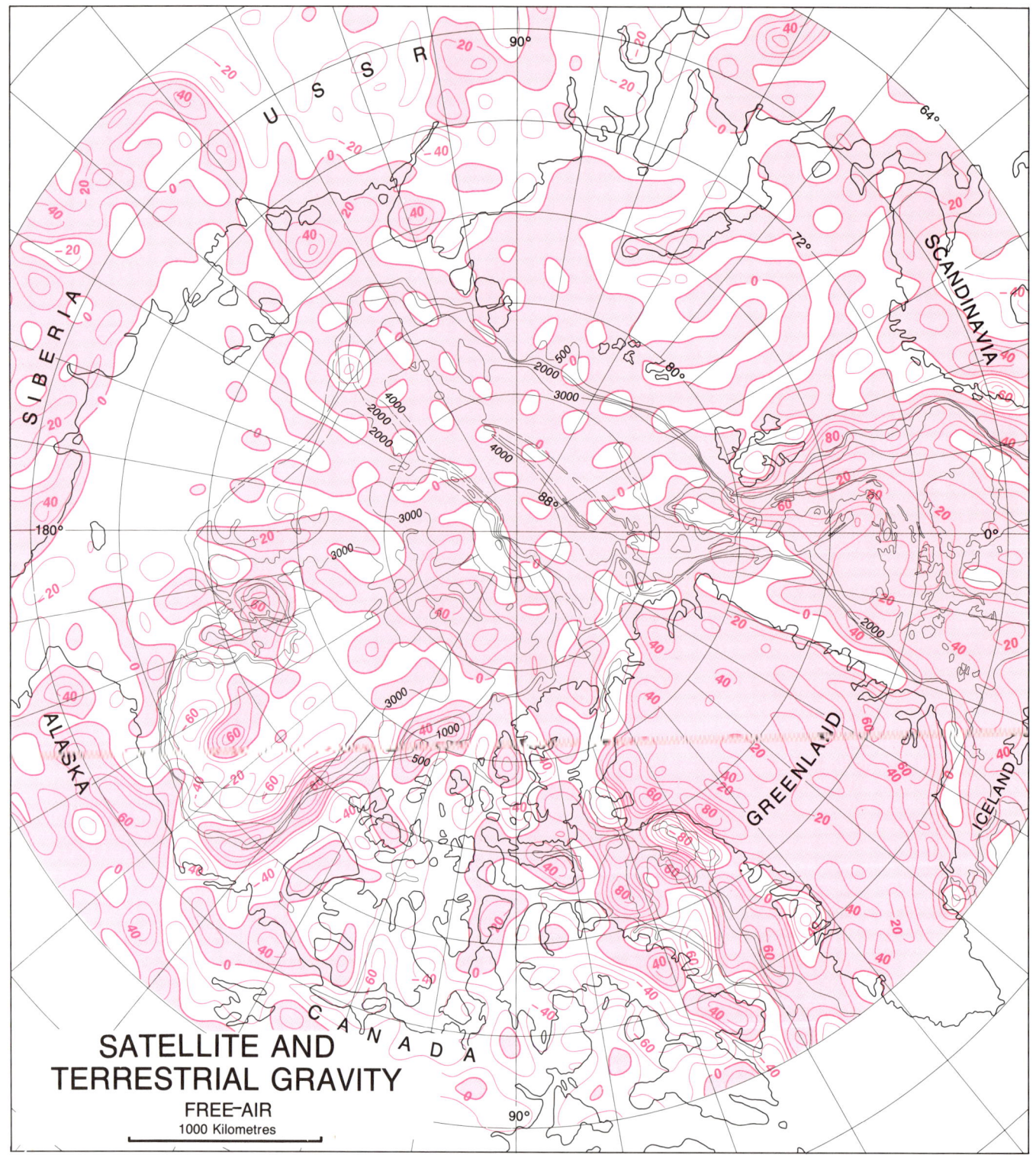

Figure 4. Gravity field of the Arctic region showing free-air anomalies complete to spherical harmonic degree and order of 180 using satellite tracking data, results from satellite altimetry and terrestrial 1° × 1° mean gravity values (after Rapp, 1981). Contour interval is 20 mGal. Red shaded areas are positive.

negative free-air anomalies over northern Canada, the Beaufort Sea, and the central northern USSR region and positive free-air anomalies over Alaska, eastern and western USSR, the Arctic Ocean, the Norwegian-Greenland Sea, Greenland, and Baffin Bay.

OBSERVED GRAVITY ANOMALIES

The observed gravity anomalies are discussed for the land and sea areas by regions. For each region the history of development, accuracy of the measurements, and a brief description of the gravity anomaly field and its relation to the regional geology are presented.

Alaska

Bouguer gravity anomalies over Alaska and adjacent offshore have been shown and discussed by Barnes (1977), whose map was compiled from about 30,000 land gravity measurements and 40,000 line km of surface-ship gravimeter data. In the last decade, data collection in Alaska has been concentrated in the National Petroleum Reserve Alaska (NPRA) and in central northern Alaska, as indicated by a dense concentration of stations on Plate 3.

Because most of the gravity data in Alaska are not available in digital form, the gravity contours from Barnes's (1977) Alaska map were digitized, courtesy of R. Godson, U.S.G.S., Denver, Colorado, and thereby incorporated in Plate 3.

A large, elongated east-west-trending low (minimum –100 mGal) along the Brooks Range extends westward across the Chukchi Sea. In the Brooks Range this low is related by Barnes (1977) to increased crustal thicknesses as great as 40 km.

A belt of pronounced relative highs along much of the southwestern flank of the Brooks Range (about 66°N latitude) parallels a trend of alternating + and – aeromagnetic anomalies and a belt of dense late Paleozoic marine volcanic rocks that crop out along the northern margin of the gravity high. To the east of about 151°W this east-west high weakens considerably and appears to curve or is displaced southward about 125 km before striking eastward again in the region of the Yukon River. This curve appears to line up with the Canning Displacement Zone in the north (Grantz and May, 1983). In the west this belt appears to bifurcate around Seward Peninsula. The northern high culminates in a 50-mGal peak with a steep gradient of 5 mGal/km to an adjacent low to the southwest of –50 mGal (Barnes, 1970; Barnes and Tailleur, 1970), thought to be produced, respectively, by a dense intrusive body with a magnetic relief of 1700 nT and a localized basin of low-density sediments with no magnetic relief (Barnes, 1977).

The Barrow Arch follows the northern coast of Alaska from the Canning Displacement Zone westward through Point Barrow and the Chukchi Shelf (Grantz and May, 1983; Bee and others, 1984) and has a variable but subdued gravity field (+10 to –20 mGal) that is relatively positive compared with lows to the south (minimum –100 mGal) over the Brooks Range and to the north (0 to –20 mGal) along the polar margin of Alaska. On its southern flank a borehole encounters granitic rocks 3.2 km deep (Bee and others, 1984). Gravity lows along the Barrow Arch may indicate the presence of granitic basement.

Northern Canada

Since 1960 gravity in northern Canada has been measured largely by the Earth Physics Branch (EPB), now part of the Geological Survey of Canada, in a series of air-lifted surveys under the aegis of the Polar Continental Shelf Project (PCSP) (Sobczak, 1963; Sobczak and others, 1963; Berkhout and Sobczak, 1967; Picklyk, 1969; Sobczak and Weber, 1970; Hornal and others, 1970; Berkhout, 1970; Stephens and others, 1972; Hornal and Boyd, 1972; Sobczak and others, 1973; Sobczak and Stephens, 1974; Gibb and Halliday, 1975; Sobczak, 1978). Additional surveys were made over Baffin Island, eastern and western sides of Victoria Island, Amundsen Gulf, and western and eastern parts of Viscount Melville Sound, and the results were included on the Gravity Map of Canada (1980).

Bouguer gravity anomalies range from a high of about 100 mGal over Darnley Bay to a low of less than –100 mGal over east-central Ellesmere Island. In general, gravity highs overlie folded, uplifted, and mafic intruded areas and lows overlie basins, interisland channels, and mountainous and evaporite intruded areas. These features have been described by Sobczak (1963), Berkhout and Sobczak (1967), Hornal (1968, 1969), Picklyk (1969), Berkhout (1970), Hornal and others (1970), Stacey (1971), Sobczak and Stephens (1974), Sobczak and Overton (1984), Sweeney and others (1984), and Sobczak and others (1986).

Isostatic conditions prevail regionally for the interisland areas (Sobczak and Weber, 1973) and probably also for the mainland, but there may be local areas of disequilibrium, as indicated by gravity highs and contemporary seismicity along folded and uplifted regions (Sobczak and others, 1986). For the western Queen Elizabeth Islands, Sobczak and Weber (1973) determined an average free-air anomaly of 7.3 mGal, which, corrected to the new datum (IGSN71) and Geodetic Reference System 1967, is –2.7 mGal. This value indicates regional isostatic equilibrium. Mean free-air anomalies averaged by 1° of longitude by ½° of latitude show this area to have values varying from –40 to 40 mGal and, for northern Canada, from –60 to 60 mGal (Sobczak, 1978).

Greenland

Gravity surveying over Greenland has been done largely by the Danish Geodetic Survey (Geodaetisk Institut), concentrating on the ice-free areas along the coast, and by a few international inland ice expeditions. The first large-scale gravity surveys in Greenland date back to the early 1950s, but at present large parts of the ice-free areas and virtually all of the ice cap remain unsurveyed. The gravity data available for the ice-free areas consist of both older, shipborne survey results, and recent results from integrated mapping and gravity surveys using helicopters as the primary mode of transportation. The older surveys, roughly 1,000 gravity stations in western Greenland, have been discussed (Kejlso, 1958; Svejgaard, 1959; Saxov, 1958; Olsen, 1970). A new gravity reference network has been set up by Forsberg (1981). Recent regional surveys have been executed in northern and northeastern Greenland 1978-80 (Forsberg, 1979; Weng, 1980; Forsberg, 1981) and central east Greenland 1982-84 (Forsberg, 1986). For these surveys, a combination of classical triangulation, Dopper satellite positioning, and barometric leveling has been used as primary elevation control, giving Bouguer anomaly accuracies in the range of 0.5-3 mGal. Similar accuracies are probable for the older networks. Actual terrain corrections have been computed for some stations in southern and eastern Greenland (Forsberg, 1986), but have not been used for the compilation of Plate 3. Terrain corrections vary from values less than 1 mGal to 10 mGal, with a few stations above 30 mGal (maximum 47.6 mGal).

In addition to gravity measurements taken by the Geodaetisk Institut, the EPB and the University of London collected gravity data in northern and southern Greenland respectively (e.g., Sobczak and Stephens, 1974; Blundell, 1978).

On the inland ice, gravity measurements have been taken in a northern profile (Bull, 1955), a central profile (Martin and others, 1954; Hoisl, 1965), and at a few sites on the southern part of the ice cap (Jezek and others, 1982). The ice thicknesses used for the Bouguer reductions have been obtained from recent airborne radar soundings by the Greenland Ice Sheet Project (Overgaard, 1983) and by interpolation from ice-thickness maps. For the southern stations, surface radar measurements have been utilized (Jezek and others, 1982). Although the airborne radar measures profile ice thicknesses with an error around 20 m, (Overgaard, personal communication, 1984), the interpolation procedure produces much larger errors, especially along the northern profile, where systematic errors of 100-200 m are possible, corresponding to Bouguer anomaly errors of 10 mGal or more. Even larger errors are possible near the ice margins, where the sub-ice topography generally is not well resolved.

Bouguer anomalies show a general decrease from the outer coast to the edge of the ice cap, with typical values of about +40 mGal at the outer islands to about -60 mGal at the ice margin in northern and western Greenland. This decrease in gravity from the coast area inward expresses general isostatic compensation of the ice and topography (Weidick, 1976).

Regional gravity anomalies over Greenland are poorly defined due to the uneven coverage and the overall lack of measurements. In central west Greenland, near 68°N, a relatively positive anomaly seems to be associated with the Nagssuqtoqidian mobile belt, bordering the Archaean craton to the south. Other major anomalies include relative minima (-40 mGal) associated with Mesozoic sedimentary basins, such as the basin east of the Caledonian Fold Belt in central east Greenland (Jameson Land).

The pattern of free-air anomalies likewise indicates incomplete local isostatic compensation. In the northern profiles the mean free-air anomaly changes from roughly +60 mGal in the west to -30 m Gal in the center and increases to +10 mGal in the east. The central profile shows higher free-air anomalies, with values around +20 mGal to +40 mGal, going from west to east. For the southern inland ice stations at 64°N latitude, rather large free-air anomalies (70-80 mGal) are observed, which Jezek and others (1982) hypothesize are produced by deep-seated mass excess.

Fennoscandia

The first gravity map (free-air) of Fennoscandia was presented by Honkasalo (1963) and later was supplemented by the maps of Kaula (1972). Balling (1980; 1984) constructed a series of regional mean gravity anomaly maps using grids of 0.5 (lat.) × 1 (long.), 1 × 2, 2 × 4, and 4 × 8 degrees, and demonstrated that the Bouguer gravity has a negative correlation with topography (-0.07 mGal/m), and the free-air gravity is positively correlated, exhibiting a value of 0.04 mGal/m. A coastal low of up to -140 mGal is present along the mountains (Plate 3). To the east the gravity field becomes more positive and more chaotic, reaching peak values of +15 mGal at the northern end of Finland. Subparallel and to the east of this latter trend is a belt of lows over the Gulf of Bothnia, ranging from 0 to -60 mGal. This belt trends northeastward toward the Kola Peninsula of the USSR. To the south, at the western end of the White Sea, the gravity field increases in value and becomes more positive, with peak values of +40 mGal.

Arctic Ocean

In the offshore area of Alaska, some 40,000 line km of surface-ship traverses were made by the U.S.G.S. and university groups prior to 1975. These have been described in part by Cady and others (1973); Hanna and others (1974); Ruppel and McHendrie (1975); Boucher (1977); and Dehlinger (1980) and were shown on a gravity map of the Arctic by Sobczak (1978). Since then, the U.S.G.S. obtained approximately 15,000 line km of gravity data, which have been described by May and others (1985a, b), May and Grantz (1985a, b, c), and May (1985).

Analysis of crossovers of shiptracks by May (1985) and Dehlinger (1980) estimate uncertainties within ±2 mGal. The majority of data for Chukchi and Beaufort seas used in Plate 3 comes from these two sources. A regional geologic interpretation of the seismic data throughout much of this region is discussed in Grantz and May (1983, 1984).

To the north of Canada and Greenland, Arctic Ocean gravity surveys have been discussed by Sobczak and Weber (1970, 1973); Wold and others (1970); Hall (1970); Wold and Ostenso (1971); Wold (1973); Sobczak and others (1973); Ostenso and Wold (1977); Hunkins and Tiemann (1977); Sobczak (1978); Weber (1979, 1980); and Sweeney and others (1982). The University of Wisconsin used ski-plane landings from 1960 to 1969 for about 800 gravity measurements and took about 6,000 gravity observations from an ice-island (ARLIS II) from 1961 to 1965 (Wold, 1973). Lamont-Doherty Geological Observatory (L-DGO) took nearly 9,000 gravity observations from Fletcher's Ice Island (T-3) from 1962 to 1974 (Hunkins and Tiemann, 1977). Both groups used the same pendulum control station at Point Barrow, Alaska, but the initial control values were different by 4.9 mGal, which would reduce the accuracy of the anomalies by this value. In 1979, EPB took 260 spot gravity observations and recorded gravity continuously at three separate camps as they drifted over the Lomonosov Ridge and adjacent basins near the North Pole (the Lomonosov Ridge Experiment, LOREX) (Weber, 1979, 1980; Sweeney and others, 1982). In 1983, 860 spot gravity observations were taken at a spacing of 6 km over the continental margin north of Ellesmere Island and 750 at a spacing of 20 km over the Alpha Ridge, during the Canadian Expedition to Study the Alpha Ridge (CESAR). During the U.S. FRAM I and II expeditions north of Greenland in 1979 and 1980, L-DGO monitored gravity along the drift track (Hunkins and others, 1979; Allen and others, 1980). These values were augmented by 221 spot gravity measurements in a joint program with the University of Oslo/Norwegian Polar Research Institute (on FRAM I), which extended the coverage to the Arctic Mid-Ocean Ridge. Accuracy of LOREX, CESAR, and FRAM data is estimated to be about 1 mGal (J. R. Weber, personal communication, 1984; Yngve Kristoffersen, personal communication, 1985).

In the offshore area of Svalbard, Captain Sigurd Scott-Hansen (Schiotz, 1901), during the drift of the FRAM (1893–96), obtained the first gravity readings over water and the Arctic Ocean using pendulums. The pendulum measurements gave values of free-air gravity in the range of –88 to 77 mGal (current gravity datum) over the Nansen Basin (southern side of the Arctic Mid-Ocean Ridge) from which Schiotz concluded that gravity over land is similar to gravity over the ocean. He showed that the ocean area is in general isostatic equilibrium. Almost 90 years passed before more gravity data were collected in the region in 1981 and 1982, during the U.S. FRAM III and IV expeditions along the northern flank of the Yermak Plateau. On FRAM III, L-DGO made 135 gravity readings along the drift track, and on FRAM IV, the University of Oslo/Norwegian Polar Research Institute collected 87 spot readings from remote sites out to 100 km away from camp (Hunkins and others, 1981; Kristoffersen, 1982). Shipborne gravity surveys are usually limited to areas south of 80°N due to prevailing ice conditions (see Gronlie and Talwani, 1982; Faleide and others, 1984).

The gravity map (Plate 3) over the Barents Sea is based on values received from DMAAC and covers the free-air map of Faleide and others (1984) and the Bouguer map of Beskow (1984) west of 35°E. More stations are shown on their contour maps, but the principal facts were not available to us in digital form. Thus these observations are not included in Plate 3.

Gravity anomalies along the margins of the Arctic Basin are most pronounced over relatively narrow continental shelves and appear more subdued over wide shelves. Over the narrow shelves a prominent belt of positive, elliptically shaped free-air anomalies (maximum 100 mGal) straddles the continental break off Alaska, Canada, and Greenland. These highs are typical of passive continental margins (Grow and others, 1979; Sobczak, 1975a; Worzel and Shurbet, 1955). North of Alaska a belt of highs over the shelf break extends westward along the northern side of the North Chukchi Basin, on strike with the Barrow Arch. Another branch of highs splinters off northwest of Point Barrow and follows the south flank of the North Chukchi Basin. This pattern is unusual in that such gravity highs are expected to follow the shelf break, in this case the edges of the Chukchi Borderland. Instead, elliptically shaped gravity lows (–50 to –70 mGal) flank the eastern Northwind Ridge) and northern sides of the Chukchi Borderland.

North of Alaska there is a correspondence between the gravity highs and a rifted or sheared hingeline, which has been mapped beneath the Beaufort Shelf in some detail by Grantz and May (1983). The hingeline controlled the location of post-breakup (post Neocomian) sedimentation on the Beaufort Shelf, resulting in two post-breakup sedimentary basins coincident with peaks in the free-air anomaly field (+90 mGal near 145°W 71°N and +60 mGal near 153°W 71° 40′N). Similarly thick sedimentary basins occur below the gravity highs off Canada (Sobczak, 1975a, b; Sweeney and others, 1984; Sobczak and others, 1986). Seismicity also occurs over the gravity highs in the Beaufort Sea and northwest of Ellef Ringnes Island (Sobczak and others, 1986). Landward and subparallel to these highs lies a subdued belt of lows over the inner continental shelf that touches land in northeastern Alaska, Mackenzie Delta, Banks Island, and elsewhere.

Gravity anomalies over the wide Chukchi and Barents shelves are more subdued and variable. The Chukchi Shelf, where water depths are less than 200 m, has been divided into several distinct structural provinces based on interpretation of reflection seismic data (Grantz and May, 1984); these provinces are usually distinct in their gravity anomaly patterns as well.

A large east–west trough in the gravity field between 166° and 177°W adjacent to 73°N is related to North Chukchi Basin, which contains more than 12 km of Cretaceous and Tertiary sediments (Grantz and May, 1983). The northern flank of the basin is known from gravity data only and its structure can be inferred from the associated relatively steep anomaly gradient that rises northward. Near 168°W, gravity gradients indicate that the northern margin of the basin may be considerably steeper than that seen seismically along the southern margin. It is possible that the steep gradient at the north flank of the basin could mark the northern edge of the unbroken continent, because it is on strike with the shelf-edge anomalies to the east, in the Beaufort Sea. North of this gradient lies the Chukchi Borderland. To the east is a northeast-trending anomaly pattern that overlies part of the Hanna Trough, which has persisted from late Paleozoic through Tertiary time (Grantz and May, 1983). A major north-striking fault, seen seismically near 162°W, 71°40′N, forms part of the eastern boundary of the Hanna Trough. This fault, which places relatively younger strata within the trough against a thick section of early Paleozoic and older strata, may explain the broad positive gravity anomalies of the northeastern Chukchi Sea.

Over the Barents Shelf, water depths are deeper (more than 500 m) and more irregular. The gravity field is more positive than over the Chukchi Shelf. Over the Barents Shelf south of 74°N, the gravity field changes character at about 23°E. To the east, the gravity field is relatively smooth, with values typically ranging from –10 to +20 mGal. The regional trend is northeasterly, and the anomalies reveal a first order correlation with the subsurface structures (Faleide and others, 1984). In the southeast, there are some poorly defined local negative anomalies between 72 and 74°N, associated with salt deposits in the Nordkapp Basin.

West of 23°E the anomaly field has greater amplitudes and steeper gradients, especially in the southwest where gravity highs and lows correspond to shallower and deeper sedimentary basins respectively. North of 74°N, a system of generally positive anomalies is associated with the Svalbard Platform.

Over the Chukchi Borderland the gravity anomalies vary from a high of +60 mGal over the Northwind Ridge to a low of –30 mGal at the south end of this ridge. This low appears to be on strike with a belt of lows (minimum –60 mGal) lying at the base of the slope off the north coast of Alaska. This belt of low anomalies crosses the southern side of the Chukchi Borderland with steep gravity gradients (1.5–4 mGal/km). Gravity lows (minimum –70 mGal) appear to surround the borderland.

Gravity anomalies over the Morris Jesup Plateau vary from 110 to –50 mGal on the Eurasia side of the plateau. The high is restricted to the crest and the lows to the flanks of the plateau, yielding strong gravity gradients (maximum 6.5 mGal/km) over the periphery of the plateau.

Similarly, the free-air gravity field shows strong gradients (6.7 mGal/km) over the eastern end of the Yermak Plateau with values ranging from 60 mGal over the crest to –40 mGal at the base of the slope. The bathymetric spot measurements show the eastern termination of the plateau to be a NNW-trending steep scarp, which may be interpreted as a fracture zone when seen in conjunction with the local low-amplitude aeromagnetic data of Vogt and others (1980).

The character of the gravity field over the Canada Basin is more subdued (longer wavelength anomalies) than that over the Chukchi and Barents shelves and major sedimentary basins. Gravity anomalies over the Canada Basin appear to be divided at about 80°N into a positive northern region and a negative southern region. The latter is divided by a positive (maximum +50 mGal, centered at 74°N, 145°W) belt between the Chukchi Borderland and the Mackenzie Delta. The boundary between the negative southern part of the basin and the positive northern part is on line with a highly anomalous gravity field that extends across the Sverdrup Rim between Prince Patrick and Borden islands and over a fan-like spur that extends from the continental margin into the Canada Basin (Sobczak and Sweeney, 1978).

Gravity anomalies over the Alpha, Mendeleev, Lomonosov, and Arctic Mid-Ocean ridges are regionally positive and chaotic.

Gravity anomalies over the Alpha Ridge vary from –70 to 70 mGal; they mainly reflect the sea bed topography (highs over ridges and lows over valleys) (J. R. Weber, personal communication, 1984), and appear to extend across the Mendeleev Abyssal Plain to the Chukchi Borderland and the eastern side of the Mendeleev Ridge. Unfortunately much of the Mendeleev Ridge and the southwestern part of the Alpha Ridge are unmapped.

Gravity anomalies over the Lomonosov Ridge have much steeper gradients with peak values of 80 mGal over the ridge. Minimum values are –40 mGal on the Amundsen Basin side and –60 mGal on the Makarov Basin side of the ridge. These lows rapidly increase to positive values; 20 mGal over the Amundsen Basin near the North Pole, and a variable field from 0 to 30 mGal over the Makarov Basin. There is a belt of gravity highs near the central axis of the Makarov Basin that appears, from seismic evidence, to be related to basement relief (Sweeney and others, 1982). Free-air gravity over the northern flank of the Arctic Mid-Ocean Ridge shows a strong correlation to basement topography, with a maximum peak-to-peak value of 80 mGal. This is discussed more fully by Kristoffersen (1982).

Baffin Bay–Davis Strait

Gravity data over Baffin Bay and Davis Strait were acquired by the Atlantic Geoscience Centre (AGC) during the 1970s from ships using sea gravimeters mounted on gyro stabilized platforms. Gravity measurements taken along about 18,000 km of track in 1970 and 1971 were described by Ross (1973). Satellite navigation, Loran A, and radar control were used for positioning to an accuracy of ±1 km. A root mean square discrepancy fo all gravity crossovers of 8.8 mGal was obtained (Ross, 1973). The bathymetry was obtained from a much larger number (about 3 times) of ship tracks dating back to the early 1960s, including data from the Ministry of Transport, Canadian Hydrographic Service, and the Danish Hydrographic Service. In addition, other geophysical studies, including gravity, were made by Keen and others (1972), Keen and Barrett (1973), Ross and Henderson (1973), Manchester and Clarke (1973), Keen and others (1974), and Jackson and others (1977, 1979). The Gravity Map of Canada (1980) shows free-air anomalies for all of Baffin Bay, Davis Strait, and Labrador Sea, derived from published contours. These data have been adjusted to a uniform datum at EPB (EPB and AGC, 1986).

Positive free-air highs (peak values up to 140 mGal) straddle the shelf break as along the north polar margin of Canada and Alaska. In the vicinity of the Cape Dyer and Disko Island, these highs touch land. Landward from these highs, around the Bay and Davis Strait, is a ring of lows (minimum values of –80 mGal). The deep water area (Ross, 1973; Menzies, 1982) is characterized by anomalies varying between ±20 mGal, with a narrow belt of lows striking northwest–southeast near the axis of the bay.

Norwegian-Greenland Sea

During the last 15 to 20 years the Norwegian-Greenland Sea has been surveyed extensively using shipboard surface gravimeters. Although a number of institutions have carried out measurements, a major part of the data base, particularly in deeper waters, has been collected by L-DGO. In general, the area is well covered except for the continental margin east of Greenland.

The free-air anomalies south of 73°N on Plate 3 are based mainly on digital data used for the map of Talwani and Gronlie (1976), which has been described and updated by Gronlie and Talwani (1982). Of special regional interest are the 10-mGal free-air maps published by Talwani and Eldholm (1972) and Eldholm and others (1979). Gronlie and Talwani (1982) found that the agreement in gravity values at most track intersections was better than 5 mGal and indicated an accuracy of ±5 mGal in areas with adequate coverage.

North of 73°N (Plate 3), data have been shown on a 10-mGal free-air anomaly map of the Greenland Sea by Faleide and others (1984). It was based on 16 earlier, uncorrected gravity maps with differences of 3 to 15 mGal at track intersections. After corrections were made, Faleide and others estimated the accuracy of the map to be better than 5 mGal for areas with many track cross-overs. They indicated that the main features of the free-air gravity field reveal a first-order correlation with subsurface structures. In general, the Norwegian-Greenland Sea is characterized by free-air anomalies more positive than 25 mGal. The long and intermediate wavelength components of the field were analyzed by Cochran and Talwani (1978), who computed 1 × 2° and 5 × 5° averages from the observed data. They found that the major features in the regional 1 × 2° average anomaly field correlate with the present plate boundary, and that local positive anomaly belts occurred over the continental shelf.

As expected for a young ocean, the main structural features are quite prominent, both topographically and in the short wavelength free-air anomaly field (Plate 3). In particular:

The present spreading axis (Kolbeinsey, Mohn and Knipovich ridges) is well defined by positive anomalies greater than 50 mGal, although an axial minimum is observed where a typical rift valley is developed (e.g., Knipovich Ridge).

The Aegir Ridge in the Norway Basin (Talwani and Eldholm, 1977) exhibits a pronounced linear gravity low (minimum –40 mGal), which is partly ascribed to a large infill of low-density sediments.

The positive and negative anomalies at fracture zones are ascribed to basement topography; lows occur in the troughs or deeper parts, highs over the ridges or shallower portions of the fracture zones.

The positive gravity anomaly over the Jan Mayen Ridge has been explained by elevated bathymetry and a substantial amount of sedimentary rocks, in support of the idea that the ridge is a microcontinent (Gronlie and Talwani, 1982).

Along the continental margin off Norway a relative low over the inner continental slope becomes a gravity high near the base of the slope. These marginal gravity highs and lows have been associated with basement relief bounded landward by escarpment-like features. Talwani and Eldholm (1972, 1973) suggested that the landward gradient of this marginal high, which is maintained also in the isostatic anomaly field (Talwani and Eldholm, 1977), could indicate the location of the continent-ocean boundary.

The elongated positive anomalies on the shelf off Norway have been ascribed to intrabasement high-density bodies. A similar origin is suggested for the anomaly over the Lofoten Islands (Talwani and Eldholm, 1972). New seismic data support this inference (Eldholm and Mutter, 1986).

The elongated positive belt seaward of the shelf edge off the Barents Sea between Svalbard and Norway was interpreted by Talwani and Eldholm (1977) as marking a sheared continent-ocean boundary, although the crustal transition appears to occur at the landward gradient of the anomaly. Furthermore, the positive anomalies at the outer shelf further north (maximum 145 mGal) appear to correlate with elevated basement seaward of the continent-ocean boundary at the rifted margin segments (Myhre, 1984).

The gravity field is poorly mapped over the Chukchi Borderland and the Morris Jesup and Yermak plateaus but well mapped over the Voring Plateau and Iceland. With the exception of Iceland, positive anomalies occur where the sea is shallowest and are negative over the deeper parts. Strong gravity gradients surround the plateaus with the lowest values at the base of the slopes.

The Voring Plateau has gravity features similar to the Chukchi Borderland. Highs (peak value 50 mGal) overlie the crestal seaward part of the plateau, and lows (minimum value –30 mGal) occur over the landward part which is on strike with a belt of lows (minimum –40 mGal) along the base of the slope off Norway. Medium gravity gradients (maximum 3.3 mGal/km) flank the plateau.

The character of gravity anomalies over Iceland is completely different from those over the plateaus. A smooth regional low (minimum value –50 mGal) overlies the interior of the island and becomes more positive (10 to 40 mGal) towards the coastline. A rough (short wavelength), chaotic anomalous gravity field (0 to 60 mGal) surrounds the island. The gravity gradient is relatively uniform and small (about 0.7 mGal/km) and opposite in sign to those over other plateaus.

DISCUSSION

The land areas of the Arctic produce negative gravity anomalies chiefly over the mountains of northern Alaska (Brooks Range), Ellesmere Island, Greenland, and Norway. Generally these long wavelength anomaly lows are inversely related to elevation and indicate areas of greater crustal thickness, assuming Airy isostatic equilibrium. Barnes (1977), using gravity data, estimated crustal thicknesses for Alaska to vary from 25 to 50 km, with the thickest crust below the mountains. Sobczak and Stephens (1974) also suggested a root system (5 km or more of additional crust) below the mountains of northern Ellesmere Island. As yet no direct comparisons have been made between crustal thicknesses determined seismically and gravitationally in

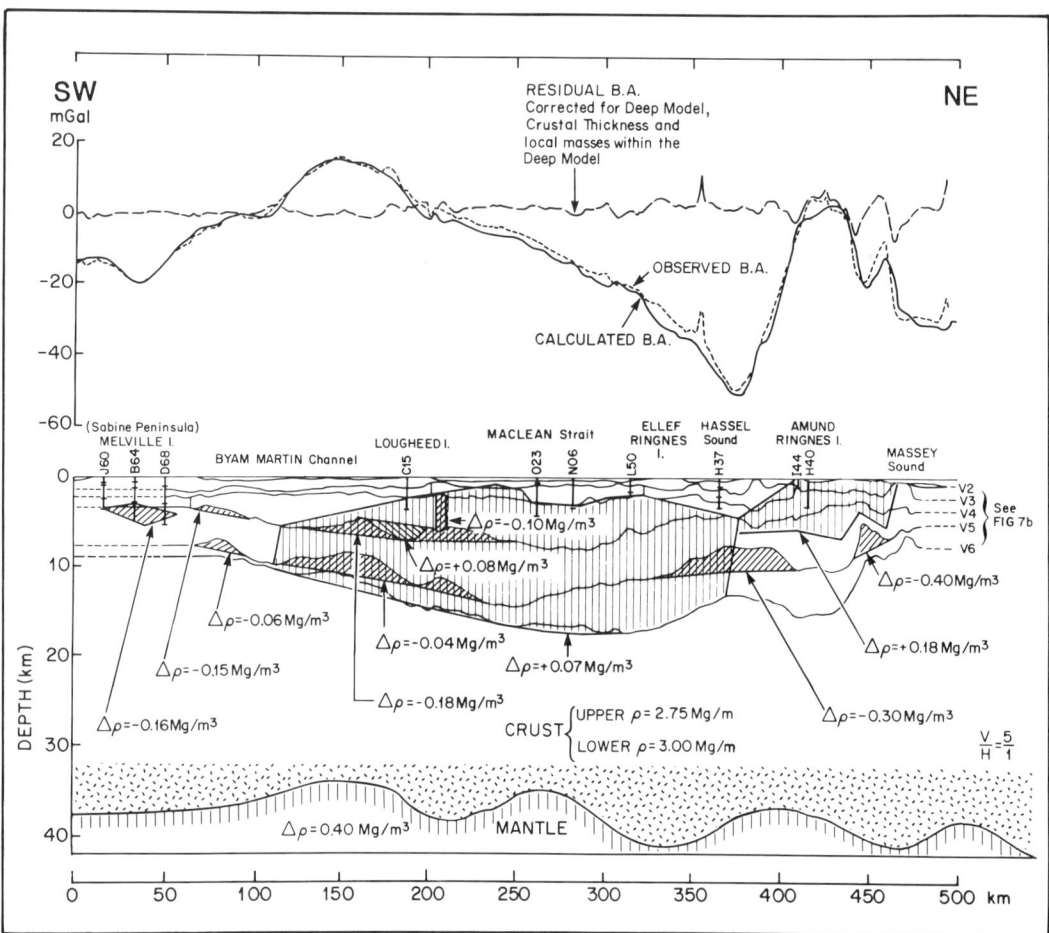

Figure 5. Structural section along northeast-trending profile (location in Fig. 2) taken from Sobzcak and Overton (1984). The crust-mantle and the sedimentary crystalline boundaries were determined seismically by Forsyth and others (1979), Forsyth (personal communication, 1979), and Overton (1982). Because seismic refraction velocities gradually increase with depth the Phanerozoic section was divided into five velocity layers varying between 3.0 and 6.9 km/s. The upper three layers closely approximate the Sverdrup Basin and the lower two layers represent the Franklinian Basin and perhaps some Proterozoic sedimentary basin material. Density contrasts for these layers vary from 0.49 Mg/m^3 for the upper layer to 0.05 Mg/m^3 for the lower layers and were primarily obtained from drill holes indicated by a letter followed by a number. Although the refraction velocity remained the same for a particular layer the density contrasts did vary according to lithological and porosity changes. For example layer 3, second from the surface, varied from 0.36 Mg/m^3 at Sabine Peninsula to a low of 0.23 Mg/m^3 below Maclean Strait to 0.31 Mg/m^3 below Ellef and Amund Ringnes islands. Structural configuration of disturbing masses within the Phanerozoic section was determined from a gravity analysis.

the mountainous areas of the Arctic. However, comparisons have been made in low-lying areas such as the Sverdrup Basin where the gravity anomalies are lower in amplitude and near isostatic equilibrium (Sobczak and Weber, 1973). A detailed seismic-gravity line from Melville Island to Axel Heiberg Island (Fig. 5), within the Sverdrup Basin (Sobczak and Overton, 1984), indicates that the mass deficiency of the sediments is compensated by variations in crustal thickness. This line provided depth control for a 1,300-km-long transect (Figs. 6, 7; after Sobczak and others, 1986) from Somerset Island, where Precambrian crystalline continental rocks crop out, northward to the Arctic Ocean where sediment-covered oceanic crust exists (Sweeney and others, 1986; Sobczak and others, 1986). These reports indicate that the continental crystalline crust probably thins from 48 km at the craton to 8 km below the margin and has been stretched 282 km for the Phanerozoic-covered part of the line from 543 to 825 km, with an apparent stretch factor of 1.5.

The character of the gravity field (Plate 3) over the oceans varies from region to region. For passive continental margins, prominent sinuous belts of elliptically shaped positive gravity anomalies straddle the continental break and are usually flanked landward and seaward by belts of broad, low-amplitude gravity lows. This gravity pattern can be produced in several ways, including edge effects associated with the change in crustal thick-

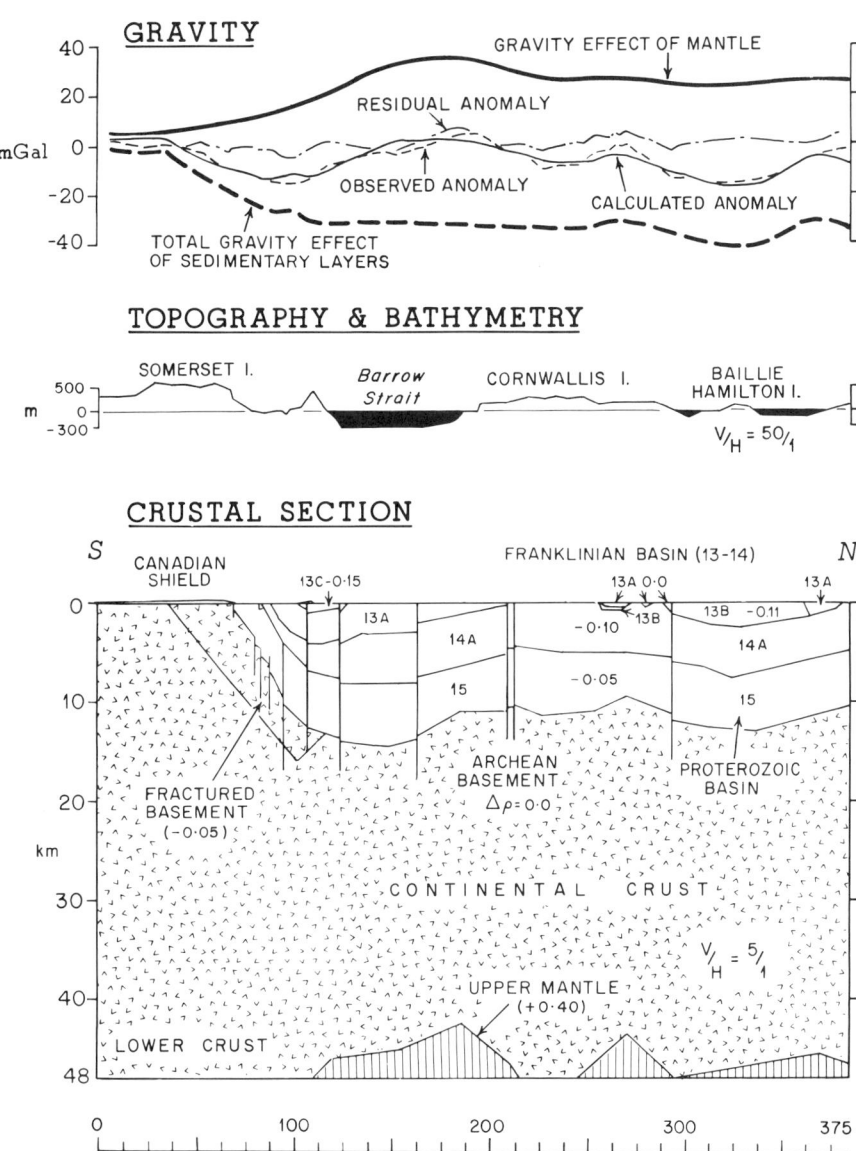

Figure 6. The southern part of a 1300-km north–south transect (location in Fig. 2) from the Canadian Shield to the Arctic Ocean taken from Sobczak and others (1986). The sedimentary layers were determined from geology by U. Mayr (personal communication, 1983; Sweeney and others, 1984). The boundary between sedimentary strata and Precambrian crystalline basement was determined using geology and gravity analysis. The crust-mantle boundary was determined by gravity modeling so that the long-wavelength components of the Bouguer anomalies, after correcting for the sedimentary layers, were compensated by crustal thinning. Density contrasts are in Mg/m^3. Layers 13 and 14 represent the Franklinian Basin. Layer 15 represents the Proterozoic Basin. The Archean basement appears to be lower in density possibly due to fracturing as suggested by lower gravity anomaly values.

ness between continent and ocean, uncompensated loads of sediments, dense intrabasement igneous rocks, and basement rises. Sobczak (1975a, b) suggested that gravity highs in the Mackenzie Delta area can be explained in part (about 20%) by an edge effect in combination with an uncompensated load of sediments (about 3 km thick). The flanking gravity lows can be explained by low-density basin sediments that have not been totally compensated.

Gravity lows that overlie the Baffin Bay shelves may depict the centers of thick sedimentary basins. For example, Keen and Barrett (1972) found, from seismic refraction studies, 4.5 to 7 km of sediments in Smith Sound; Keen and Barrett (1972) and Ross and Henderson (1973) found, from geophysical studies, 7 to 10 km of sediments in Melville Bay; and Keen and Barrett (1973) and Jackson and others (1977) found, from geophysical studies, 8 to 10 km of sediments in Lancaster Sound. Along the North

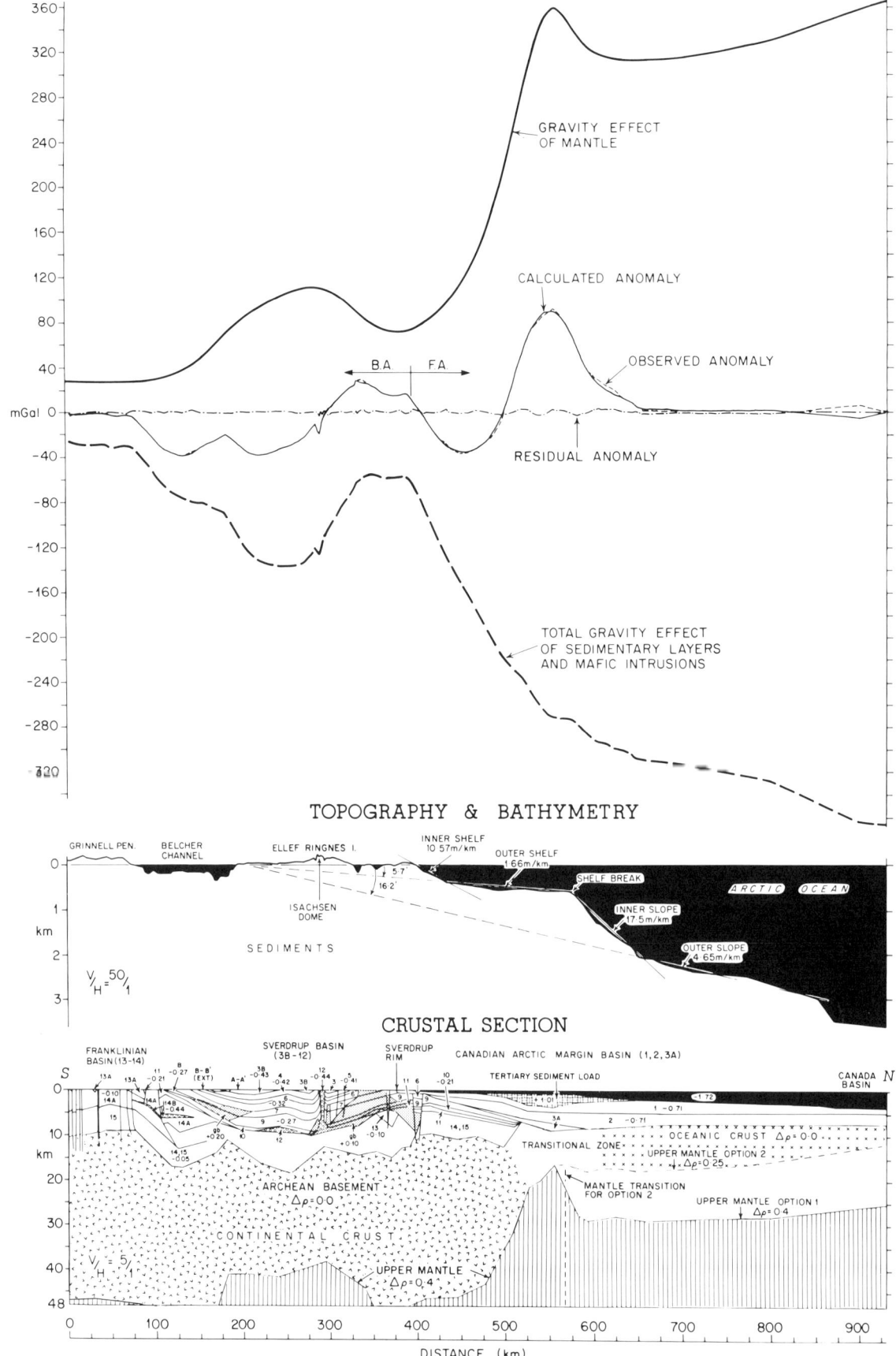

American polar margin, Sobczak and Weber (1973), Sweeney and others (1986), and Sobczak and others (1986) estimate from gravity models about 10 km of sediments below the shelf northwest of Ellef Ringnes Island. Sobczak (1975) estimates from gravity analysis about 10 km of sediments off the Mackenzie Delta and 6 km of sediments below the shelf west of Banks Island. Grantz and May (1983) found from seismic refraction studies over 12 km of sediments in the North Chukchi Basin and about 12.5 km of clastics below the shelf north of Alaska. The gravity lows over these basins indicate only a small part of the mass deficiency of these basins.

North of Alaska the shelf-break highs correspond to the location of a hingeline where post-rift sedimentation created several sedimentary basins (Grantz and May, 1983). This belt of highs extends west to the north and south of the North Chukchi Basin, which contains more than 12 km of Cretaceous and Tertiary sediments (Grantz and May, 1983).

Along the Canadian Arctic margin the depth of the shelf break (Sobczak and others, 1986) between Amundsen Gulf and Ellesmere Island is 300 to 450 m below the world average depth of about 200 m (Worzel, 1968) suggesting that modern sedimentation in this region may not be keeping up with the rate of margin subsidence. The association of contemporary seismicity with shelf-break gravity highs in this region may be related to ongoing isostatic compensation (Basham and others, 1977). Regionally, the mean value of the free-air anomalies over the Canadian polar margin is about 10 mGal (Sobczak and others, 1986), which suggests that the margin overall is near isostatic equilibrium.

The shelf-break gravity highs that surround Baffin Bay and Davis Strait may be related to uncompensated sediments plus the rapid transition to thinner crust towards the middle of the bay (Menzies, 1982) and also to the intrusion of Tertiary volcanics (Park and others, 1970; Keen and others, 1972). Structure sections across the bay and strait have been shown by Keen and others (1971), Jackson and others (1977), and Menzies (1982) who indicated thick (4–6 km) sedimentary basins below the continental margin and adjacent oceanic areas, steep (15°–90°) contact zones between continental and oceanic crusts at the Mohorovicic Discontinuity, and variable depths to the top of the mantle (10–11 km in the center of Baffin Bay and 22–23 km in Davis Strait). Volcanics crop out onshore in the vicinity of Cape Dyer and Disko Island where the positive gravity anomalies of the shelf-break touch land. Gravity lows encircling the belts of highs may indicate the presence of sedimentary basins and grabens (Keen and Barrett, 1972; Ross and Henderson, 1973; Jackson and others, 1977).

Anomaly highs around the Norwegian-Greenland Sea have been associated with buried basement arches and high-density belts and have been used to mark the location of the continent-ocean boundary (Talwani and Eldholm, 1972, 1973). Talwani and Eldholm interpreted a subparallel anomaly high on the shelf off Norway over the Lofoten Islands to be associated with an intrabasement high-density body, which may be similar to the dense volcanics found in Baffin Bay at Cape Dyer and Disko Island and to the dense mafic masses found along the Sverdrup Rim. Talwani and Eldholm (1977) place the continent-ocean transition zone on the landward side of the anomaly highs between Svalbard and Norway, whereas Sobczak and others (1986) place this transition on the seaward side of the high across the Canadian arctic shelf. Although the location of these highs relative to the shelf morphology varies from area to area, the anomaly highs do at least indicate the general location of the transition zone.

Talwani and Eldholm (1977) defined the Senja Fracture Zone on the basis of a prominent positive anomaly (maximum 106 mGal) on the lower continental slope between 71° and 74°N, westward of the Barents Shelf. Myhre (1984) and Myhre and Eldholm (1985) connected the Senja Fracture Zone with the Hornsund Fault Zone partly on the basis of its gravity signature, and claimed that the latter is composed of rifted and sheared segments at the continent-ocean boundary.

The character of the gravity anomalies and their relationship to subsurface structures over the Chukchi and Barents shelves are similar to the gravity signatures over inland coastal basins such as the Sverdrup and Mackenzie basins. Gravity highs indicate arches, horsts, uplifted fault blocks, and mafic intrusions while the gravity lows indicate troughs, grabens, depressions, and intrusions of evaporites. Structures below the Chukchi Shelf discussed by Grantz and May (1983) are outlined in the gravity field. The gravity field over, and the structures below, the Barents Shelf are discussed by Faleide and others (1984, 1985). Some poorly defined negative anomalies between 72° and 73°N in the Nordkapp Basin are explained by salt deposits (Ronnevik, 1981).

The character of the gravity anomalies over oceanic crust (Plate 3) is related to basement morphology and to the age of the crust. Gravity highs are noted over the ridges and lows over the basins. The anomaly level is also more positive over the youngest oceanic crust—the mid-ocean ridge area in the Norwegian-Greenland Sea—than over older crust such as Baffin Bay (about 38–60 Ma; Jackson and others, 1979) and Canada Basin (about

Figure 7. The northern part of a 1300-km transect (location in Fig. 2) taken from Sobczak and others (1986). The sedimentary layering is based on geological, seismic, and proprietary information provided by U. Mayr and H. Balkwill. The boundaries between sediments and crystalline crust and between crust and mantle were determined by gravity modeling from a control line (Fig. 5). Density contrasts are in Mg/m^3. The Tertiary sediment load and layers 1, 2, and 3A form the Canadian Arctic Margin Basin; layers 3–12 form the Sverdrup Basin; layers 13 and 14 form the Franklinian Basin. Combined layers 14 and 15 may be a mix of Paleozoic and Proterozoic sediments with possible inclusions of fractured crystalline basement rocks. Crustal thinning in a seaward direction is based on two options. Option one assumes a constant density contrast (0.40 Mg/m^3) between mantle and lower crustal rocks and option two assumes an abrupt change in the constant density contrast (from 0.40 to 0.25 Mg/m^3) below the zone of assumed transitional crust. Option two assumes a thin oceanic crust below the Canada Basin after Mair and Lyons (1981).

79–118 Ma; Sweeney, 1985). Weber (personal communication, 1984) found the gravity field over the Alpha Ridge to correlate with, and to be explained by, the bottom topography. The structure of the ridge determined by seismic refraction method showed that the mass of the Lomonosov and Alpha ridges above the sea floor is compensated by an Airy model root system (Weber and Sweeney, 1985). Preliminary seismic refraction data across the Lomonosov Ridge indicated a 28-km-thick ridge of continental crustal composition flanked by a 16-km-thick Amundsen Basin crust and a 13-km-thick Makarov Basin crust (including water depths, Mair and Forsyth, 1982; Forsyth and Mair, 1984). However, gravity modeling indicated the Amundsen Basin crust to be thinner (11 km, Weber and Sweeney, 1985), similar to seismic results from the FRAM II operation in 1980 (Duckworth and others, 1982). The thickness of the Alpha Ridge is 35 to 38 km, based on seismic refraction data (Forsyth and Jackson, 1984). To the south over the Canada Basin the oceanic crust is about 15 km thick (Mair and Lyons, 1981) and covered by 4 to 6 km of sediments (Baggeroer and Falconer, 1982).

Free-air gravity over the northern flank of the Arctic Mid-Ocean Ridge shows a strong relation to basement topography with a maximum amplitude change of 80 mGal (Kristoffersen, 1982b). Also, an Airy model of isostatic compensation for the Arctic Mid-Ocean Ridge would require compensation depths in the range of 10 to 20 km (Kristoffersen, 1982b), where seismic refraction profiles show crustal thicknesses of only 6 to 7 km (Jackson and others, 1981; Kristoffersen and others, 1982). This and the spectral ratio between gravity and bathymetry (Kristoffersen, 1982b) suggest that the sea floor topography in this locality is supported by an elastic plate of a thickness (3 to 6 km) even less than the thickness observed on the Mid-Atlantic Ridge (Kristoffersen, 1982b). This preliminary result appears to be at variance with the larger data set from the Atlantic and the Pacific, where the relation between gravity and bathymetry at mid-ocean ridge crests favors an isostatic compensation scheme in which the basement topography is supported by an elastic plate of thickness inversely proportional to spreading rate (Cochran, 1979). Jackson and others (1984) used the FRAM III gravity data to interpolate the crustal structure from seismic refraction data between the Nansen Basin and the central northern part of the Yermak Plateau where crustal thickness is about 20 km. They concluded from aeromagnetic and seismic refraction data a dual origin for the Yermak Plateau, thick oceanic crust north of 81° 55′N and thinned continental crust to the south. To the south of the Yermak Plateau, Guterch and others (1978), using seismic refraction data, concluded that crustal thickness was about 22 km in western Spitsbergen and increased in thickness eastward to 33 km, in accord with the gravity field (lows over thick crust and highs over thinner crust). Gronlie and others (1979), in their discussion of the origin and evolution of the Jan Mayen Ridge, found the gravity anomalies to correlate well with the bottom and basement topography. Also they found, from gravity modeling and from other geophysical data, that this ridge consists of about 7 km of low-density (2.4-Mg/m^3) material at the top and is probably continental, as Talwani and Eldholm (1977) earlier concluded. Talwani and Eldholm (1972) showed a 600-km structural section using gravity analysis across the Norwegian Shelf and Voring Plateau to the Norway Basin. They explained the gravity high over the outer Voring Plateau by a basement escarpment over 5 km high, the gravity low over the inner Voring Plateau by sediments up to 6 km thick, and the gravity high over the shelf break by high-density belts within the basement, which in turn is covered by a sedimentary basin over 8 km thick. These intrabasement high-density belts were extended below the Lofoten and Vesteralen islands as depicted in the positive gravity and magnetic fields. Heier and Compston (1969) relate these high-density belts to granulite and amphibolite facies rocks, which were produced by metamorphism about 1700 to 1800 Ma.

Gravity highs over passive margins usually overlie the shelf break but in some places may be landward or seaward of it. Some subparallel anomalies may also occur. These anomalies and those over the shelf break provide a constraint to any proposed model.

The satellite and terrestrial free-air anomaly map shown in Figure 4 shows the marine Arctic to be mainly overlain by positive anomalies. These anomalies appear to relate to areas that are or have been subjected to recent (i.e., last 100 m.y.) mountain building, plate movements, and glaciation processes. If this relationship is correct, northern Canada and central USSR with Precambrian Shield rocks exposed, or as basement below the sediments, would appear to be the stable areas of the Arctic. Also, for the exception of the regions of highs over the shelf break along the east side of the Beaufort Sea and Chukchi Plateau, a stable area is suggested for the southern Canada Basin (Beaufort Sea), Chukchi Sea, East Siberian Sea, and central USSR region.

Gravity anomalies (Plate 3) also appear to be related to stability, age and type of crust; generally the younger active areas, usually oceanic, have more positive anomalies than the older stable continental areas. The Greenland-Norwegian Sea, Baffin Bay, and northern Canada Basin ridge areas within the Arctic Ocean, and the shelf breaks around the oceans, are more positive regionally than the continental areas. Gravity anomalies over continental areas are also related to elevation: the higher the topography the more negative the anomalies. In oceanic areas, although they are more positive regionally than continental areas, the ridge areas are more positive than the basin areas, which is the reverse of what is observed over land areas.

REFERENCES

Allen, B., Ardai, J., Hunkins, K., Lee, T., Manley, T. O., and Tiemann, W., 1980, Observations of position, ocean depths, and gravity taken from the FRAM-II and Camp I drifting ice stations: Palisades, New York, Lamont–Doherty Geological Observatory, CU-13-80 Technical Report No. 13.

Baggeroer, A. B., and Falconer, R., 1982, Array refraction profiles and crustal models of the Canada Basin: Journal of Geophysical Research, v. 87, p. 5461–5476.

Balling, N., 1980, The land uplift in Fennoscandia, gravity field anomalies, and isostasy, *in* Mörner, N. A., ed., Earth rheology, isostasy, and eustasy: Chichester, John Wiley and Sons, p. 297–321.

Barnes, D. F., 1970, Gravity and other geophysical data from northern Alaska, in Adkinson, W. L., and Brosgé, M. M., eds., Proceedings of the geological seminar on the North Slope of Alaska: Los Angeles, California, Pacific Section American Association Petroleum Geologists, p. 11–20.

——, 1977, Bouguer gravity map of Alaska: Department of the Interior, U.S. Geological Survey Map GP-913, scale 1:2,500,000.

Barnes, D. F., and Tailleur, I. L., 1970, Preliminary interpretation of geophysical data from the lower Noatak River basin, Alaska: U.S. Geological Survey Open-File Report, 15 p.

Basham, P. W., Forsyth, D. A., and Wetmiller, R. J., 1977, The seismicity of northern Canada: Canadian Journal of Earth Sciences, v. 14, no. 7, p. 1646–1667.

Bee, M., Johnson, S. H., and Chiburis, E. F., 1984, Marine seismic refraction study between Cape Simpson and Prudhoe Bay, Alaska: Journal of Geophysical Research, v. 89 (B8), p. 6941–6960.

Berkhout, A.W.J., 1970, The gravity anomaly field of Prince of Wales, Somerset, and northern Baffin islands, District of Franklin, Northwest Territories: Ottawa, Canada, Department of Energy, Mines and Resources, Dominion Observatory, v. 39, no. 7, p. 179–209.

Berkhout, A.W.J., and Sobczak, L. W., 1967, A preliminary investigation of gravity observations in the Somerset and Prince of Wales islands, Arctic Canada, with map: Ottawa, Canada, Department of Energy, Mines and Resources, Dominion Observatory, Gravity Map Series Number 81, 10 p.

Boucher, G., 1977, Gravity measurements on summer sea ice in the Beaufort and Chukchi seas, 1976: U.S. Geological Survey Open-File Report 77-705, 5 p.

Bouguer Anomaly Map of Canada, 1974: Ottawa, Canada, Department of Energy, Mines and Resources, Earth Physics Branch, Gravity Map Series Number 74-1, scale 1:5,000,000.

Bowin, C., Warsi, W., and Milligan, J., 1982, Free-air gravity anomaly atlas of the world: Geological Society of America Map and Chart Series No. MC-46.

Bull, C., 1955, Values of gravity on the inland ice in north Greenland: Meddelelser om Gronland, v. 137, no. 1, part 3, 11 p.

Cady, J., Ruppell, B. D., McHendrie, A. G., and Deas, H. G., 1973, Magnetic and gravity profiles, Part 2, in Grantz, A., Holmes, M. L., Riley, D. G., and Wallace, S. L., eds., Seismic, magnetic, and gravity profiles Chukchi Sea and adjacent Arctic Ocean, 1972: U.S. Geological Survey Open-File Report, 19 sheets.

Cochran, J. R., 1979, An analysis of isostasy in the world's oceans; 2. Mid-ocean ridge crests: Journal Geophysics Research, v. 84, p. 4713–4747.

Cochran, J. R., and Talwani, M., 1978, Gravity anomalies, regional elevations, and the deep structure of the North Atlantic: Journal Geophysical Research, v. 83, p. 4907–4924.

Dehlinger, P., 1980, Gravity and crustal structure in the southern Beaufort Sea (north of Alaska): Office of Naval Research Report, Contract Number NOC 014-75-C-0714, 31 p.

Dehlinger, P., Chiburis, E. F., and Dowling, J. J., 1972, Pacific Seamap 1961–1970 data evaluation summary: U.S. National Oceanic and Atmospheric Administration Technical Report Number 52, 10 p.

Duckworth, G. L., Baggeroer, A. B., and Jackson, H. R., 1982, Crustal structure measurements near FRAM II in the Pole Abyssal Plain: Tectonophysics, v. 89, p. 173–216.

Earth Physics Branch and Atlantic Geoscience Centre, 1986, Integration of Atlantic Geoscience Centre marine gravity data into the National Gravity Database: Department of Energy, Mines and Resources, Earth Physics Branch Open-File 85-32, 48 p.

Eldholm, O., Mutter, D. C., 1986, Basin structure on the Norwegian margins from analysis of digitally recorded sonobuoys: Journal of Geophysical Research, v. 91, p. 3763–3783.

Eldholm, O., Sundvor, E., Myhre, A. M., 1979, Continental margin off Lofoten–Vestaralen: Margin Geophysics Research, v. 4, p. 3–35.

Faleide, J. I., Gudlaugsson, S. T., Johansen, B., Myhre, A. M., and Eldholm, O., 1984, Free-air gravity anomaly maps of the Greenland Sea and the Barents Sea: Polar Research SKR., 180, p. 63–67.

Faleide, J. I., Gudlaugsson, S. T., and Jacquart, G., 1985, Evolution of the western Barents Sea: Marine and Petroleum Geology, v. 1, no. 2, p. 123–150.

Forsberg, R., 1979, A gravity map of Peary Land, north Greenland: Rapp., Gronlands Geologiske Undersogelse, v. 88, p. 93–94.

——, 1981, Preliminary Bouguer anomalies of north-east Greenland: Rapp., Gronlands Geologiske Undersogelse, v. 106, p. 105–107.

——, 1986, Gravity measurements in Jameson Land and central east Greenland: Meddelser om Gronland, Geoscience, v. 15, p. 1–23.

Forsyth, D. A., and Jackson, R., 1984, Alpha and Lomonosov ridge crustal structures: Canadian Geophysical Union, Abstract, p. 86.

Forsyth, D. A., and Mair, J. A., 1984, Crustal structure of the Lomonosov Ridge and the Fram and Makarov Basins near the North Pole: Journal of Geophysical Research, v. 89 (B1), p. 473–481.

Forsyth, D. A., Mair, J. A., and Fraser, I., 1979, Crustal structure of the central Sverdrup Basin: Canadian Journal of Earth Sciences, v. 16, p. 1581–1598.

Geodetic Reference System 1967, 1971: Paris, International Association of Geodesy, Publication Special Number 3, 116 p.

Gibb, R. A., and Halliday, D. W., 1975, Gravity measurements in northern District of Keewatin and parts of District of Mackenzie and District of Franklin, N.W.T. with maps: Ottawa, Canada, Department of Energy, Mines and Resources, Earth Physics Branch, Gravity Map Series Number 139-148, p. 8.

Grantz, A., Eittreim, S., and Dinter, D. A., 1979, Geology and tectonic development of the continental margin north of Alaska: Tectonophysics, v. 59, p. 263–291.

Grantz, A., Eittreim, S., and Whitney, O. T., 1981, Geology and physiography of the continental margin north of Alaska and implications for origin of the Canada Basin, in Nairn, A.E.M., Churkin, M., Jr., and Stehli, F. G., eds., The ocean basins and margins: New York, Plenum Publishing Corporation, v. 5, p. 439–492.

Grantz, A., and May, S. D., 1983, Rifting history and structural development of the continental margin north of Alaska, in Watkins, J. S., and Drake, C. L., eds., Studies in continental margin geology: American Association of Petroleum Geologists Memoir 34, p. 77–100.

Grantz, A., and May, S. D., 1984, Summary geologic report for Barrow Arch outer continental shelf (OCS) planning area, Chukchi Sea, Alaska: U.S. Geological Survey Open-File Report 84-395, 40 p.

Gravity Map of Canada, 1980: Ottawa, Canada, Department of Energy, Mines and Resources, Earth Physics Branch, Gravity Map Series 80-1, scale 1:5,000,000.

Gronlie, G., and Talwani, M., 1982, The free-air gravity field of the Norwegian–Greenland Sea and adjacent areas: Earth Evolution Series, v. 2, p. 79–103.

Gronlie, G., Chapman, M., and Talwani, M., 1979, Jan Mayen Ridge and Iceland Plateau; Origin and evolution: Oslo, Norsk Polarinstitutt, p. 25–47.

Grow, J. A., Bowin, C. O., and Hutchinson, D. R., 1979, The gravity field of the U.S. Atlantic continental margin: Tectonophysics, v. 59, p. 27–52.

Guterch, A., Pajchel, J., Perchue, E., Kowalski, J., Duda, S., Komber, J., Bojdys, G., and Sellevoll, M. A., 1978, Seismic reconnaissance measurements on the crustal structure in the Spitsbergen region, 1976: Bergen, Norway, University of Bergen, 61 p.

Hall, J. K., 1970, Arctic Ocean geophysical studies; The Alpha Cordillera and Mendeleyev Ridge: Palisades, New York, Lamont–Doherty Geological Observatory of Columbia University, Technical Report No. 2, CU-2-70, 125 p.

Hanna, W. F., Ruppell, B. D., McHendrie, A. G., and Sikora, R. F., 1974, Residual magnetic anomaly and free-air gravity anomaly profiles 1973 on continental shelf and slope between Bering Strait and Barrow, Alaska, and Mackenzie Bay Canada: U.S. Geological Survey Open-File Report 74-6, scale 1:1,000,000.

Heier, K. S., and Compston, W., 1969, Interpretation of Rb–Sr age patterns in high-grade metamorphic rocks, North Norway: Norsk Geologisk Tidsskrift, v. 49, p. 257–283.

Hoisl, R., 1965, Gravimetermessungen uber das Gronlandisches Indlandseis auf einer West–Ost Profil (E.G.I.G.) 1959; Dissertation Muchen, Deutsche Geodatische Kommission, Bayerische Akademic des Wesenschaften, Reihe, C, heft 85 (Gravity measurements on the Greenland inland ice on east–west profiles): German Geodetic Commission, 53 p.

Honkasalo, T., 1963, On the use of gravity measurements for investigation of land upheaval in Fennoscandia: Fennia, v. 89, p. 21–23.

Hornal, R. W., 1968, The gravity anomaly field in the Coppermine area of the Northwest Territories: Ottawa, Canada, Department of Energy, Mines and Resources, Dominion Observatory, Gravity Map Series, No. 45, 9 p.

Hornal, R. W., 1969, The gravity field over the northwestern Canadian Shield [abs.]: EOS American Geophysical Union Transactions, v. 50, 321 p.

Hornal, R. W., and Boyd, J. B., 1972, Gravity measurements in the Slave and Bear Structural Provinces, Northwest Territories with Maps: Ottawa, Canada, Department of Energy, Mines and Resources, Earth Physics Branch, Gravity Map Series Numbers 89-95, 12 p.

Hornal, R. W., Sobczak, L. W., Burke, W.E.F., and Stephens, L. E., 1970, Preliminary results of gravity surveys over the Mackenzie Basin and Beaufort Sea with maps: Ottawa, Canada, Department of Energy, Mines and Resources, Dominion Observatory, Gravity Map Series Numbers 117-119, 12 p.

Hunkins, K., Manley, T., and Tiemann, W., 1979, Observations of position, ocean depth, ice rotation, magnetic declination, and gravity taken at the FRAM-I drifting ice station: Palisades, New York, Lamont–Doherty Geological Observatory of Columbia University, CU-1-79 Technical Report Number 1, 56 p.

Hunkins, K., Manley, T. O., Tiemann, W., and Jackson, R., 1981, Geophysical data from drifting ice station FRAM III: Palisades, New York, Lamont–Doherty Geological Observatory of Columbia University, CU-3-81 Technical Report Number 3, 101 p.

Hunkins, K., and Tiemann, W., 1977, Geophysical data summary for Fletcher's Ice Island (T-3), May 1962–October 1974: Palisades, New York, Lamont–Doherty Geological Observatory of Columbia University, Technical Report Number CU-1-77, 219 p.

Jackson, H. R., 1985, Nares Strait; A suture zone; Geophysical and geological implications: Tectonophysics, v. 114, p. 11–28.

Jackson, H. R., Johnson, G. L., Sundvor, E., and Myhre, A., 1984, The Yermak Plateau; Formed at a Triple Junction: Journal Geophysics Research, v. 89, p. 3223–3232.

Jackson, H. R., Keen, C. E., and Barrett, D. L., 1977, Geophysical studies on the eastern continental margin of Baffin Bay and in Lancaster Sound: Canadian Journal of Earth Sciences, v. 14, p. 1991–2001.

Jackson, H. R., Keen, C. E., Falconer, R.K.H., and Appleton, K. P., 1979, New geophysical evidence for sea-floor spreading in central Baffin Bay: Canadian Journal of Earth Sciences, v. 15, p. 2122–2135.

Jackson, H. R., Reid, I., and Falconer, R.K.H., 1981, Crustal structure near the Arctic Mid-Ocean Ridge: Journal of Geophysical Research, v. 87, p. 1773–1783.

Jezek, K. C., Roeloffs, E. A., and Greischar, L. L., 1982, A geological survey of sub-glacial geology around the deep-drilling site at Dye-3, Greenland, in Langway, C. C., Jr., Oeschger, H., Dansgaard, W., eds., Greenland ice core; Geophysics, geochemistry and the environment: American Geophysical Union Geophysical Monograph 3, p. 105–110.

Kaula, W. M., 1972, Global gravity and tectonics, in Robertson, E. C., ed., The nature of the solid earth: McGraw-Hill, p. 385–405.

Kejlso, E., 1958, Gravity measurements in western Greenland 1950–52: Geodaetisk Instituts Skrifter, 3, raekke, 69 p.

Keen, C. E., 1979, Thermal history and subsidence of rifted continental margins; Evidence from wells on the Nova Scotian and Labrador shelves: Canadian Journal of Earth Sciences, v. 16, p. 505–522.

Keen, C. E., and Barrett, D. L., 1972, Seismic refraction studies in Baffin Bay; An example of a developing ocean basin: Geophysical Journal Royal Astronomical Society, v. 30, p. 253–271.

Keen, C. E., and Barrett, D. L., 1973, Structural characteristics of some sedimentary basins in northern Baffin Bay: Canadian Journal of Earth Sciences, v. 10, p. 1267–1278.

Keen, C. E., Barrett, D. L., Manchester, K. S., and Ross, D. I., 1971, Geophysical studies in Baffin Bay and some tectonic implications: Canadian Journal of Earth Sciences, v. 9, p. 239–256.

Keen, M. J., Johnson, J., and Park, I., 1972, Geophysical and geological studies in eastern and northern Baffin Bay and Lancaster Sound: Canadian Journal of Earth Sciences, v. 9, p. 689–708.

Keen, C. E., Keen, M. J., Ross, D. I., and Lack, M., 1974, Baffin Bay; Small ocean basin formed by sea-floor spreading: The American Association of Petroleum Geologists Bulletin 58, p. 1089–1108.

Kristoffersen, Y., 1982a, U.S. ice drift station FRAM-IV; Report on the Norwegian field program: Norsk Polarinstitutt Report Number 11, 60 p.

——, 1982b, The Nansen Ridge, Arctic Ocean; Some geophysical observations of the rift valley at slow spreading rate: Tectonophysics, v. 89, p. 161–172.

Kristoffersen, Y., Husebye, E. S., Bungum, H., and Gregersen, S., 1982, Seismic investigations of the Nansen Ridge during FRAM-I experiment: Tectonophysics, v. 82, p. 57–68.

Lerch, F. J., Klosko, S. M., Laubscher, R. E., and Wagner, C. A., 1979, Gravity model improvements using GEOS 3 (GEM 9 and 10): Journal of Geophysical Research, v. 84, p. 3897–3916.

Mair, J. A., and Forsyth, D. A., 1982, Crustal structures of the Canada Basin near Alaska, the Lomonosov Ridge, and adjoining basins near the North Pole: Tectonophysics, v. 89, p. 139–254.

Mair, J. A., and Lyons, J. A., 1981, Crustal structure and velocity anisotropy beneath the Beaufort Sea: Canadian Journal of Earth Science, v. 18, p. 724–741.

Manchester, K. S., and Clarke, D. B., 1973, Geologic structure of Baffin Bay and Davis Strait as determined by geophysical techniques; Arctic geology: The American Association of Petroleum Geologists Memoir 19, p. 536–541.

Martin, J., Stahl, P., Munch, F., and Joset, A., 1954, Groenland 1948–52: Gravimétrie, 1. partie, Expéditions Polaires Françaises, Résultats Scientifiques, no. 3, p. 27–41.

May, S. D., 1985, Free-air gravity anomaly map of the Chukchi and Alaskan Beaufort Seas, Arctic Ocean: U.S. Geological Survey Miscellaneous Investigations Map I-1182E, 1 sheet, scale 1:1,000,000.

May, S. D., and Grantz, A., 1985a, Digital marine gravity data collected in the Chukchi Sea in 1978: U.S. Geological Survey Open-File Report 85-602, 5 p.

——, 1985b, Digital marine gravity data collected in the Southern Chukchi Sea in 1980: U.S. Geological Survey Open-File Report 85-603, 5 p.

——, 1985c, Digital marine gravity data collected in the Chukchi Sea in 1982: U.S. Geological Survey Open-File Report 85-742, 4 p.

May, S. D., Ruppel, B. D., and Grantz, A., 1985a, Digital marine gravity data collected in the southern Chukchi Sea in 1976: U.S. Geological Survey Open-File Report 85-600, 5 p.

——, 1985b, Digital marine gravity data collected in the Beaufort and Chukchi Seas in 1977: U.S. Geological Survey Open-File Report 85-601, 5 p.

Menzies, A. W., 1982, Crustal history and basin development of Baffin Bay, in Dawes, P. R., and Kerr, J. W., eds., Nares Strait and the Drift of Greenland; A Conflict in Plate Tectonics: Meddelelser om Gronland, Geoscience 8, p. 295–312.

Morelli, C., Gantar, C., Honkasalo, T., McConnell, R. K., Tanner, J. G., Szabo, B., Uotila, U., and Whalen, C. T., 1974, The international gravity standardization net 1971 (I.G.S.N. 71): The International Association of Geodesy Special Publication no. 4, 194 p.

Myhre, A. M., 1984, The western Svalbard margin (74-80°N) [Ph.D. thesis]: Norway, University of Oslo, p. 133–201.

Myhre, A. M., and Eldholm, O., 1985, Evolution of the eastern Greenland Sea continental margin [abs.]: Canadian Society of Exploration Geophysicists–Canadian Geophysical Union–National Convention, Calgary, p. 32.

Olsen, J., 1970, Tyngdemaalinger i kyst-og fjeldstationer i Julianehaab and Godthaab fjord omraderne (Gravity measurements in the Julianehaab and Godthaab fjord areas) [Thesis manuscript]: Copenhagen, Geodaetisk Institut, 40 p.

Ostenso, N. A., and Wold, R. J., 1977, A seismic and gravity profile across the

Arctic Ocean basin: Tectonophysics, v. 37, p. 1–24.

Overgaard, S., 1983, Unpublished maps of the Greenland Ice Sheet: Electromagnetic Institute, Technical University of Copenhagen, scale 1:2,500,000.

Park, I., Clarke, D. B., Johnson, J., and Keen, M. J., 1970, Seaward extension of the west Greenland Tertiary volcanic province: Earth and Planetary Science Letters, v. 10, p. 235–238.

Picklyk, D. D., 1969, A regional gravity survey of Devon and southern Ellesmere Islands, Canadian Arctic Archipelago: Ottawa, Canada, Department of Energy, Mines and Resources, Dominion Observatory, Gravity Map Series Number 87, 10 p.

Rapp, R. H., 1981, The Earth's gravity field to degree and order 180 using Seasat altimeter data, terrestrial gravity data, and other data: Columbus, Ohio State University, Department of Geodetic Science and Surveying, Report no. 322, 53 p.

Ronnevik, H. C., 1981, Geology of the Barents Sea, in Illing, L. V., and Hobson, G. D., eds., Petroleum geology of the Continental Shelf of north-west Europe: London, Institute of Petroleum, p. 395–406.

Ross, D. I., 1973, Free-air and simple Bouguer gravity maps of Baffin Bay and adjacent continental margins: Geological Survey of Canada Paper 73-37, 11 p.

Ross, D. I., and Henderson, G., 1973, New geophysical data on the continental shelf of central and northern west Greenland: Canadian Journal of Earth Sciences, v. 10, p. 485–497.

Ruppell, B. D., and McHendrie, A. G., 1975, Free-air gravity anomaly profiles from the Chukchi Sea, 1974: U.S. Geological Survey Open-File Report 75-343, scale 1:1,000,000, 5 p.

Ruppell, B. D., and McHendrie, A. G., 1976, Free-air gravity anomaly map of the eastern Chukchi and southern Beaufort Seas: U.S. Geological Survey Miscellaneous Field Studies Map MF-785, scale 1:2,000,000.

Saxov, S., 1958, Gravity in western Greenland from 66° to 69°N: Geodaetisk Instituts Skrifter, 3, raekke. 34 p.

Schiotz, O. E., 1901, Results of the pendulum observations and some remarks on the constitution of the Earth's crust, in Nansen, F., ed., The Norwegian north polar expedition 1893–1896; Scientific results: Volume II. p. 1–90.

Smith, D. E., Lerch, F. J., Marsh, J. G., Wagner, C. A., Kolenkiewiez, R., and Khan, M. A., 1976, Contribution to the National Geodetic Satellite Program by Goddard Space Flight Center: Journal of Geophysical Research, v. 81, p. 1006–1026.

Sobczak, L. W., 1963, Regional gravity survey of the Sverdrup Islands and vicinity with map: Ottawa, Canada, Department of Energy, Mines and Resources, Dominion Observatory, Gravity Map Series Number 11, 19 p.

——, 1975a, Gravity anomalies and passive continental margins Canada and Norway, in Yorath, C. J., Parker, E. R., and Glass, D. J., eds., Canada's continental margins: Canadian Society of Petroleum Geologists Memoir 4, p. 743–761.

——, 1975b, Gravity and deep structure of the continental margin of Banks Island and Mackenzie Delta: Canadian Journal Earth Sciences, v. 12, p. 378–394.

——, 1978, Gravity from 60°N to the North Pole, in Sweeney, J. F., ed., Arctic geophysical review: Ottawa, Canada, Department of Energy, Mines and Resources, v. 45, no. 4, p. 67–73.

Sobczak, L. W., and Overton, T., 1984, Shallow and deep crustal structure of the western Svedrup Basin: Canadian Journal of Earth Sciences, v. 21, p. 902–919.

Sobczak, L. W., and Stephens, L. E., 1974, The gravity field of north eastern Ellesmere Island, part of Northern Greenland and Lincoln Sea with map: Ottawa, Canada, Department of Energy, Mines and Resources, Earth Physics Branch, Gravity Map Series No. 114, 9 p.

Sobczak, L. W., and Sweeney, J. F., 1978, Bathymetry of the Arctic Ocean, in Sweeney, J. F., ed., Arctic geophysical review: Ottawa, Canada, Department of Energy, Mines and Resources, v. 45, no. 4, p. 7–14.

Sobczak, L. W., and Weber, J. R., 1970, Gravity measurements in the Queen Elizabeth Islands with maps: Ottawa, Canada, Department of Energy, Mines and Resources, Earth Physics Branch, Gravity Map Series, Numbers 115–116, 14 p.

Sobczak, L. W., and Weber, J. R., 1973, Crustal structure of the Queen Elizabeth Islands and polar continental margin, in Pitcher, M. G., ed., Arctic geology: American Association of Petroleum Geology Memoir 19, p. 517–525.

Sobczak, L. W., Weber, J. R., Goodacre, A. K., and Bisson, J. L., 1963, Preliminary results of gravity surveys in the Queen Elizabeth Islands with maps: Ottawa, Canada, Department of Energy, Mines and Resources, Dominion Observatory, Gravity Map Series Numbers 12-15, 2 p.

Sobczak, L. W., Stephens, L. E., Winter, P. J., and Hearty, D. B., 1973, Gravity measurements over the Beaufort Sea, Banks Island, and Mackenzie Delta: Ottawa, Canada, Department of Energy, Mines and Resources, Earth Physics Branch, Gravity Map Series Number 151, 16 p.

Sobczak, L. W., Mayr, U., and Sweeney, J. F., 1986, Crustal section across the polar continent–ocean transition in Canada: Canadian Journal of Earth Sciences, v. 23, p. 608–621.

Stacey, R. A., 1971, Interpretation of the gravity anomaly at Darnley Bay, N.W.T.: Canadian Journal of Earth Sciences, v. 8, p. 1037–1042.

Stephens, L. E., Sobczak, L. W., and Wainwright, E. S., 1972, Gravity measurements on Banks Island, N.W.T. with map: Ottawa, Canada, Department of Energy, Mines and Resources, Earth Physics Branch, Gravity Map Series Number 150, 4 p.

Svejgaard, B., 1959, Gravity measurements in western Greenland 1953 and 1955: Geodaetisk Instituts Skrifter, 3, raekke, 19 p.

Sweeney, J. F., 1985, Comments about the age of the Canada Basin: Tectonophysics, v. 114, p. 1–10.

Sweeney, J. F. and 7 others, 1986, Transect G Somerset Island to Canada Basin: Boulder, Colorado, Geological Society of America, Centennial Continent/Ocean Transect no. 11, 2 sheets with text, scale 1:500,000.

Sweeney, J. F., Weber, J. R., and Blasco, S. M., 1982, Continental ridges in the Arctic Ocean; LOREX constraints: Tectonophysics, v. 89. LOREX Publication no. 9, p. 217–238.

Talwani, M., and Gronlie, G., 1976, Free-air gravity field of the Norwegian--Greenland seas: Geological Society of America Map and Chart Series, MC-15, scale 1:3,000,000.

Talwani, M., and Eldholm, O., 1972, The continental margin of Norway; A geophysical study: Geological Society of America Bulletin, v. 83, p. 3575–3608.

Talwani, M., and Eldholm, O., 1973, The boundary between continental and oceanic crust of the margin of rifted continents: Nature, v. 241, p. 325–330.

Talwani, M., and Eldholm, O., 1977, Evolution of the Norwegian–Greenland Sea: Geological Society of America Bulletin, v. 88, p. 969–999.

Vogt, P. R., Johnson, G. L., and Kristjansson, L., 1980, Morphology and magnetic anomalies north of Iceland: Journal of Geophysics, v. 47, p. 67–80.

Wagner, C. A., Lerch, F. J., Brown, J. E., and Richardson, J. A., 1976, Improvement in the geopotential derived from satellite and surface data (GEM 7 and 8): Greenbelt, Maryland, NASA Goddard Space Flight Center, Document X-921-76-20.

Weber, J. R., 1979, The Lomonosov Ridge experiment, LOREX 79: EOS Transactions of the American Geophysical Union, v. 60, p. 715–721.

——, 1980, Exploring the Arctic sea floor: GEOS, p. 2–7.

Weber, J. R., and Sweeney, J. F., 1985, Reinterpretation of morphology and crustal structure in the central Arctic Ocean Basin: Journal of Geophysical Research, v. 90, p. 663–677.

Weidick, A., 1976, Quaternary geology, in Geology of Greenland: Copenhagen, Greenland Geological Survey, p. 430–458.

Weng, W. L., 1980, Preliminary Bouguer anomalies of western north Greenland: Rapp. Gronlands Geologiske Undersogelse, v. 99, p. 153–154.

Wold, R. J., 1973, Gravity surveys of the Arctic Ocean Basin: Milwaukee, University of Wisconsin, Department of Geological Sciences, 222 p.

Wold, R. J., and Ostenso, N. A., 1971, Gravity and bathymetry survey of the Arctic and its geodetic implications: Journal Geophysical Research, v. 76, p. 6253–6254.

Wold, R. J., Woodzick, T. L., and Ostenso, N. A., 1970, Structure of the Beaufort Sea continental margin: Geophysics, v. 35, p. 849–861.

Worzel, J. L., 1968, Advances in marine geophysical research of continental margins: Canadian Journal Earth Sciences, v. 5, no. 4, p. 458–469.

Worzel, J. L., and Shurbet, G. L., 1955, Gravity anomalies at continental margins: National Academy of Science Washington Proceedings, v. 41, p. 458–469.

MANUSCRIPT ACCEPTED BY THE SOCIETY OCTOBER 15, 1986

ACKNOWLEDGMENTS

We gratefully acknowledge the support given by Earth Physics Branch (now part of the Geological Survey of Canada) personnel of the Department of Energy, Mines and Resources, Canada, namely J. G. Tanner, M. R. Dence, R. K. McConnell; to J. D. Rupert and R. V. Cooper for format conversions, editing and processing of Atlantic Geoscience Centre data for Baffin Bay and Davis Strait; D. Cleary for hand contouring 57 gravity sheets with overlays; J. F. Halpenny for Applicon gravity plots; and L. A. Warren for drafting of drawings. We also deeply appreciate the assistance given by colleagues from other institutions such as D. Godson of the U.S. Department of the Interior, U.S.G.S., Denver, Colorado, for providing digitized gravity contours for the State of Alaska taken from D. Barnes gravity map (1977); F. Renschen and D. Scheibe of the DMAAC, St. Louis, Missouri, for providing predicted gravity values over the whole area 64 to 90°N latitude and 0 to 360° longitude and for helping in resolving discrepancies in T-3 and Arlis II data over the Arctic Ocean; J. Milligan of Woods Hole Oceanographic Institution; Woods Hole, Massachusetts, who provided gravity data in northern Alaska, assisted in removing some discrepancies, and promptly replied to all correspondence; K. Hunkins of Lamont Doherty Geological Observatory, Columbia University, Palisades, New York, provided us with the gravity datum and control station gravity value he used for the University of Wisconsin pendulum base station in Point Barrow, Alaska, which was used for determining the gravity observed on T-3 and helped resolve the problems with *Fram* I to IV and helicopter station gravity values reduced by Yngve Kristoffersen; D. Metzger of the National Geophysical Data Center, Boulder, Colorado, helped prepare gravity data and provided over 67,000 gravity records for the North Atlantic Ocean. Thanks are also extended to L. C. Kovacs of the Department of the Navy, Naval Research Laboratory, Washington, D.C., who provided a mylar base map of the General Bathymetric Charts of the Oceans (GEBCO, sheet 5.17); J. Kakkuri, Director of the Finnish Geodetic Institute who agreed to release gravity data for Finland and the Gulf of Bothnia; and to G. Balmino of the International Gravity Bureau, Toulouse, France, who provided the gravity data on magnetic tape from their gravity library.

NOTE ADDED IN PROOF:

The gravity map (Plate 3) showing Bouguer anomalies on land and free-air anomalies offshore represents an invaluable data base. These anomalies, however, contain deficiencies arising from isostatic response to topographic loading, which diminish their usefulness for geological and tectonic interpretation. For these purposes, more appropriate representations of the gravity field have been developed, such as isostatic and enhanced isostatic anomaly maps. Derivation and discussion of these maps are presented by Sobczak and Halpenny (1989, 1990). Gravity-density models, using these new anomalies for interpretation, have been determined for the Canadian ice island area off Axel Heiberg and Ellesmere islands (Sobczak, Halpenny and Henderson, in preparation). These new maps enable one to distinguish areas of continental crust within an oceanic domain—such as the Voring Plateau and Jan Mayen Ridge in the North Atlantic Ocean (Sobczak and Halpenny, 1990), the Alpha and Lomonosov Ridges in the Arctic Ocean (Sobczak, 1990), and areas affected by thermal metamorphism—which in turn, may relate to the hydrocarbon potential of an area (Sobczak and Halpenny, 1989).

Sobczak, L. W., 1990, Stratigraphy and tectonic significance of cretaceous volcanism in the Queen Elizabeth Islands, Canadian Arctic Archipelago; A discussion: Canadian Journal of Earth Sciences (in press).

Sobczak, L. W., 1990, Stratigraphy and tectonic significance of cretaceous volcanism in the Queen Elizabeth Islands, Canadian Arctic Archipelago; A discussion: Canadian Journal of Earth Sciences (in press).

Sobczak, L. W., and Halpenny, J. F., 1989, Isostatic and enhanced isostatic anomaly maps of the Arctic at a scale of 1:6,000,000 with notes: Geological Survey of Canada Paper 89–16.

——, 1990, Gravity anomaly maps of the Arctic (free-air, Bouguer, isostatic, and enhanced isostatic): Tectonophysics, Special Issue (in press).

Chapter 8

Magnetic anomalies

R. L. Coles
Geological Survey of Canada, Energy, Mines and Resources, Ottawa, Ontario K1A 0Y3, Canada
P. T. Taylor
NASA Goddard Space Flight Center, Greenbelt, Maryland 20771

INTRODUCTION

Extensive magnetic surveys have been made over the Arctic Ocean since 1946. The survey techniques have varied, as have the methods and forms of data presentation. This chapter reviews the magnetic anomaly information from the Arctic Ocean region and discusses the significant contributions made by magnetic surveys to the understanding of this region of the earth's crust. The magnetic anomaly field is the only geophysical parameter in the Arctic that has been reasonably uniformly measured. It is critical to the study of Arctic structure and evolution.

HISTORICAL OVERVIEW

Several early reconnaissance magnetic surveys were conducted by Soviet agencies from 1946 onward (Demenitskaya and Hunkins, 1970). The first major airborne survey in the central Arctic was made by the U.S. Air Force (USAF) and the U.S. Coast and Geodetic Survey (USCGS) in 1950–52 (King and others, 1966). During the period 1960 through 1963, several flights were made by Project Magnet aircraft over the Arctic Region under the auspices of the U.S. Naval Oceanographic Office (USNOO). In 1961, 1963, and 1964, extensive airborne surveys were conducted by the University of Wisconsin Polar Research Institute (Ostenso and Wold, 1971, 1973). The Earth Physics Branch of the Canadian Department of Energy, Mines and Resources (EPB/EMR), Ottawa, carried out airborne surveys in 1963 (Haines, 1967) and 1970 (Haines and Hannaford, 1974). During the 1960s, surveys by the Canadian Polar Continental Shelf Project (PCSP) were flown over the outer Canadian Arctic Islands and the continental shelf. Karasik and others (1972) and Karasik (1980) summarized the Soviet aeromagnetic surveying techniques, with tracks covering much of the eastern Arctic Ocean.

Since the early 1970s, significant technological advances have permitted more detailed systematic surveys over much of the Arctic Ocean. These have been made primarily by U.S. Navy aircraft. In addition to these major surveys, a number of other surveys by aircraft (Hood and Bower, 1976, 1980), by ice stations (Hunkins and others, 1962; Hall, 1970; Coles, 1980) and, in marginal seas, by ship, have added important information. For a summary of published data up to 1978, see Coles and others (1978).

A new perspective emerged with the advent of satellite data, initially from the Polar Orbiting Geophysical Observatory (POGO) satellites (Langel and others, 1980; Langel and Thorning, 1982) and subsequently from the Magnetic Satellite (Magsat) (Coles and others, 1982; Coles, 1985; Haines, 1985).

MEASURING THE MAGNETIC FIELD IN THE ARCTIC

Temporal Field Variations

One of the more significant problems in magnetic surveying in the Arctic is the avoidance or removal of time variations in the magnetic field resulting from electrical current flow in the ionosphere and magnetosphere. While often present in all regions, rapid external field changes are especially important at high latitudes. These temporal variations present complex, and often not well-understood, noise, which interferes with the crustal anomaly signal and which can exceed the magnitudes of the anomalies themselves. Magnetic storm and diurnal (daily) activity are particularly high in the auroral oval, the instantaneous locus of auroral activity encircling the polar cap region. Figure 1 indicates the manner in which the position of the auroral oval, relative to geographic locations, varies during the course of a day. This variation results from the interaction of the solar wind with the geomagnetic field, whose primary axis is not coaxial with the earth's spin axis. The levels of magnetic activity (given in terms of hourly ranges) are only representative, but give an indication of typical magnetic activity during the northern summer months. For magnetic anomaly surveying, one must wait for intervals when the activity levels are considerably lower than these. Activity tends to be lower during winter months, but of course other problems become more severe at such times. Changes in the

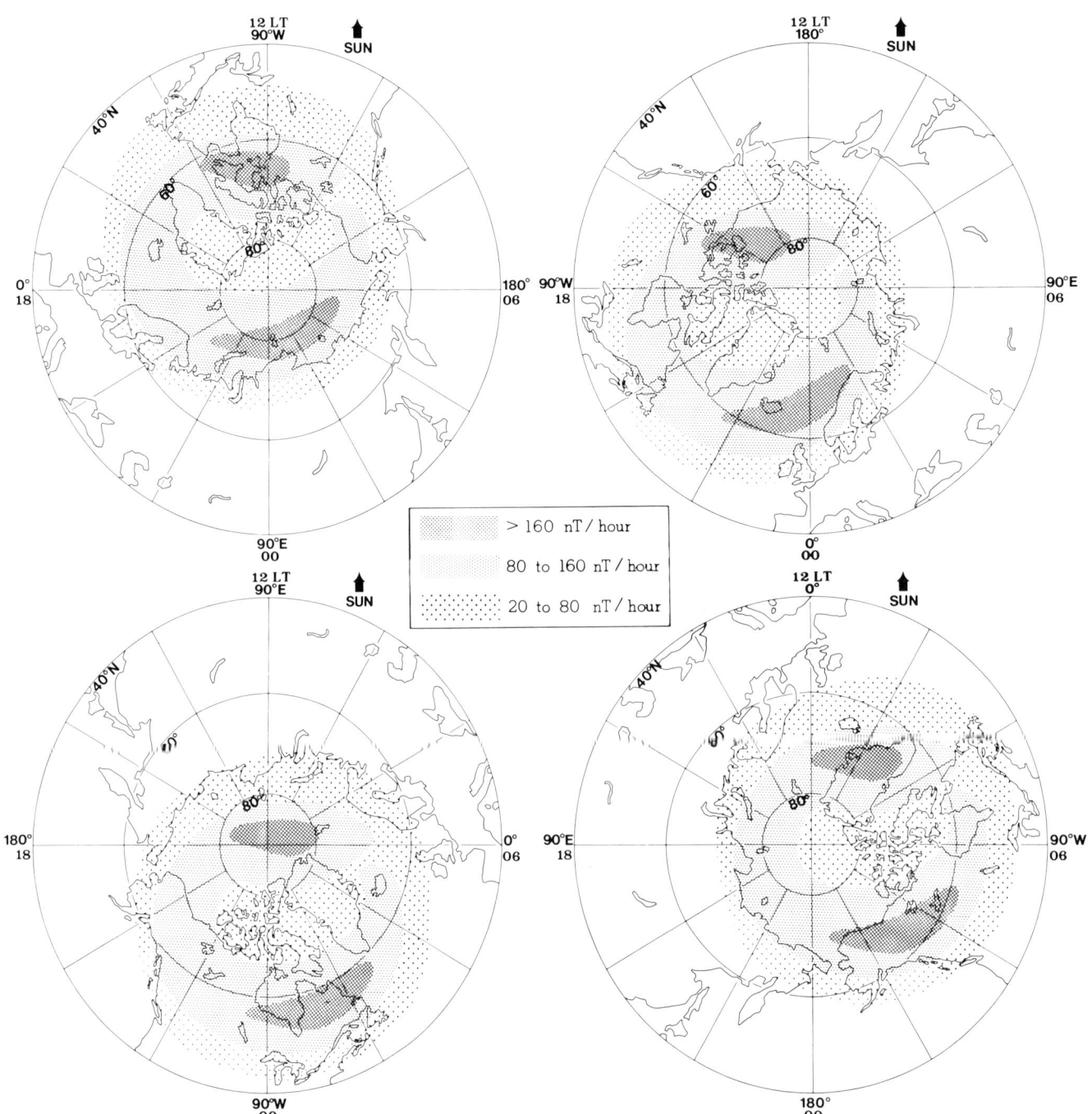

Figure 1. Typical magnetic activity levels during northern summer months, for different times of the day. These patterns are representative of the relative rates of change of disturbance due to external magnetic fields and show maxima in the auroral regions, which at certain parts of the day overlie the Arctic Ocean.

interplanetary magnetic field (IMF), especially during the summer months, can result in large shifts in the quiet level of the magnetic field in the polar cap (Loomer, 1979).

There are major difficulties in removing these temporal effects from the data since there is a scarcity of magnetic observatories or other magnetic recording stations in the Arctic, and due to the lack of spatial coherency in many of these temporal variations. The best that can be achieved in most situations is to use only data acquired during intervals of low external geomagnetic activity.

Survey Planning

Magnetic surveying is considerably more difficult in the Arctic region than at lower latitudes. The vast areas of frozen ocean, the low temperatures and severe weather conditions, the restricted availability of airbases and ports, all contribute to the logistics problems in operating a survey over this part of the earth.

An airborne survey is commonly designed so that flight lines are roughly normal to major structural trends. In the Arctic Ocean, no geological information was available to the early workers to suggest these trends. As evidenced by the almost haphazard patterns of flight lines (Figs. 2 and 3), the early surveys suffered from charting the unknown. Only bathymetric data, when available, could indicate possible geologic trends. Once a preferred flight direction was chosen, this acted as an automatic directional filter for short-wavelength magnetic anomalies and tended to suppress features that are parallel to the flight lines. Thus, the planning of a survey may, to a certain extent, have depended on an *a priori* hypothesis for the nature and evolution of a region, with the possible result that information supporting other hypotheses may have been suppressed. This is a danger anywhere, but it is particularly acute in the Arctic, where many conflicting hypotheses and comparatively little data exist. With the publication of maps such as those by the American Geographical Society (1975), Sobczak and Sweeney (1978), and the General Bathymetric Charts of the Ocean (GEBCO) Arctic sheet (Johnson and others, 1979) and the recent chart by Perry and others (1986), a near-definitive outline of Arctic physiography became available. Weber (1983) has provided a history of bathymetric mapping and its interpretation.

Navigation

An accurate knowledge of geographic location is essential for the proper interpretation of any geophysical measurement. It is particularly critical for magnetic anomaly data since the anomaly field often changes rapidly over relatively short distances. Until recently, there have been major difficulties with navigation in the Arctic. The small number of radio beacons and the great distances involved placed much emphasis on celestial fixes and dead reckoning. Starting in the mid-1970s, more sophisticated navigational aids (including Very Low Frequency [VLF] radio, satellite positioning [GPS] and inertial navigational systems) have become available.

Although the existence of published zero-contour (black and white zebra-stripe) anomaly maps indicates an extensive aeromagnetic coverage of much of the Arctic Ocean by Soviet agencies, specific details of these surveys are not available. Karasik and others (1972) discussed some of the Soviet techniques. The large compilation maps were derived from a combination of data from a number of detailed survey areas tied together by data from reconnaissance flights. These authors discussed the problems inherent in the use of drifting ice as bases for the aircraft support stations and radio navigational beacons. Over shelf areas, Karasik and others claimed a positional accuracy of 1 to 2 km using radio navigation. Where radio navigational installations were used on drifting ice, an accuracy of 1 to 2 km was again claimed for small survey areas (although this may be only relative). For much of the area covered by Soviet surveys, radio aids were not available, and rms errors of 10 to 20 km were quoted. By using comparisons among reconnaissance flights and detailed surveys, Karasik and others considered that many navigational inadequacies were removed from the reconnaissance data. However, Vogt and others (1979) and Coles and others (1978), in their compilations, found discrepancies of the order of 30 to 40 km in trying to match anomaly patterns from the Soviet maps with the U.S. and Canadian data over the Eurasian Basin.

The USAF/USCGS surveys in 1950–52 (King and others, 1966) navigated primarily on celestial fixes, with an estimated accuracy of ±8 km. The Project Magnet flights (1960 to 1963) (USNOO, 1982) and the University of Wisconsin surveys (1961–64) used some radio aids, celestial fixes and dead reckoning, an accuracy of ±15 km being quoted by Ostenso and Wold (1971) for the latter surveys. The EPB survey of 1963 navigated primarily by celestial fixes. The EPB survey of 1970 used a Doppler drift and ground speed unit, radar, and Loran units, in addition to the celestial techniques, and probable errors of ±5 km were quoted (Haines and Hannaford, 1974). The detailed Canadian PCSP surveys (1963–67) used various radio navigational aids with accuracy better than ±1 km.

Since 1972, the U.S. Navy has been engaged in a long-term program of mapping, in a relatively detailed manner, the magnetic field over that portion of the Arctic Basin accessible to their aircraft (Vogt and others, 1979; Vogt and others, 1981b; Taylor and others, 1981). Orion P-3 aircraft were used, with typical speeds of about 440 km/hr. An inertial navigation system (LNT-51) was used with an estimated positioning error of less than 5 km (Taylor and others, 1981), and as good as 1 or 2 km in some areas (Feden and others, 1979).

The North Star aircraft of the Canadian National Aeronautical Establishment (NAE) used by Hood and Bower (1976) carried a GNS 200 VLF navigation system and a Doppler radar unit, with positioning accuracy of ±1 km.

Flight Altitudes

The intensity and spatial extent (wavelength) of an anomaly depend significantly on the distance between the geological

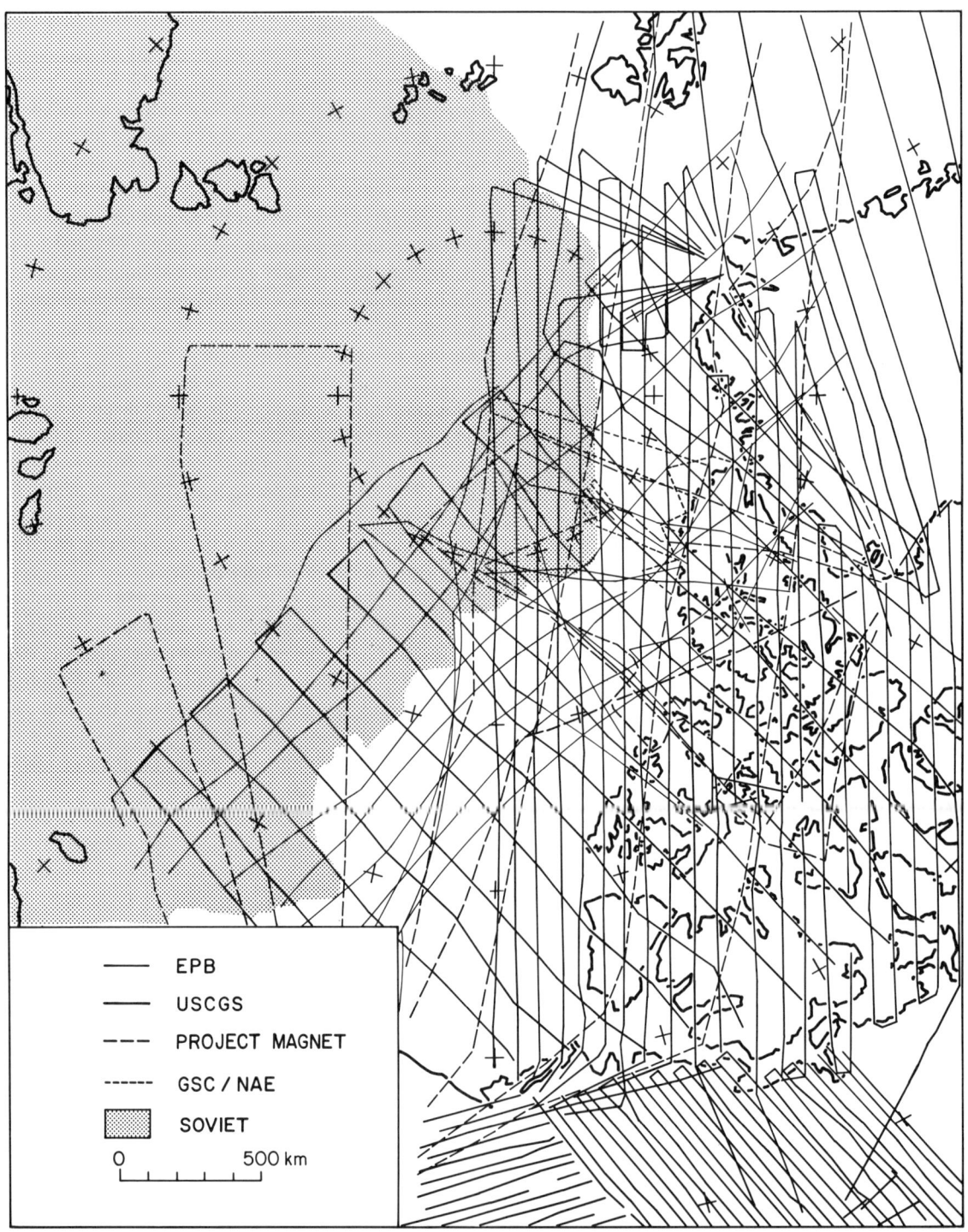

Figure 2. Some Arctic airborne magnetic surveys. Digital position data are plotted for surveys of the Earth Physics Branch (EPB), U.S. Coast and Geodetic Survey (USCGS), Project Magnet, and Geological Survey of Canada/National Aeronautical Establishment (GSC/NAE). Individual track data are not available for Soviet surveys.

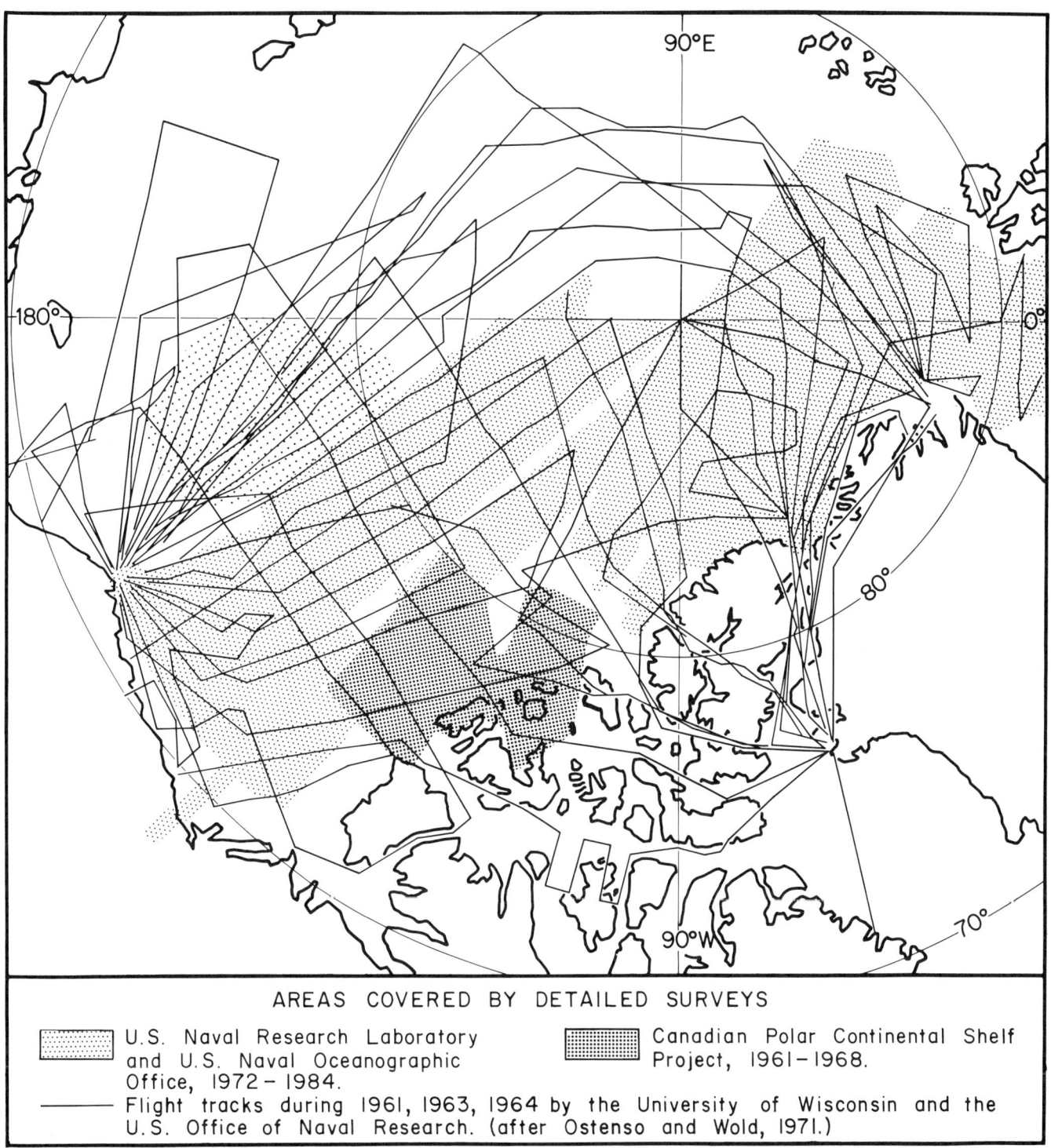

Figure 3. The map shows approximate positions of tracks described by Ostenso and Wold (1971). Densely stippled areas show coverage by low-level surveys at close line spacing. Lightly stippled area indicates the region over and near the Chukchi gap where few aeromagnetic, but numerous ice station magnetic measurements, have been made.

source and the survey instrument. As the distance increases the intensity of the anomaly decreases, and the dominant wavelength increases. For a compilation or interpretative map to be quantitatively useful, some account has to be taken of any flight altitude variations.

Almost all known published aeromagnetic surveys over the Arctic Ocean have been flown at altitudes between 150 m and 600 m. Exceptions are the early USAF/USCGS, surveys (nominally at about 6 km altitude) and the EPB surveys (altitudes 3.5 km and 5 km).

Aeromagnetic Instrumentation

In most aeromagnetic surveys, total field intensity measurements were made either using a proton precession magnetometer or an alkali-vapor magnetometer. The USAF/USCGS, NOO, and EPB surveys, which were flown for main field charting purposes as well, also determined the vector components of the magnetic field, using fluxgate magnetometer systems. For descriptions of the principles of these instruments see, for example, Parkinson (1983).

Aeromagnetic Data

As noted earlier, the wide variety of surveys makes a quantitative compilation of the aeromagnetic data practically impossible. In an attempt to show the broad patterns in the data, Coles and others (1978) produced a composite zebra-stripe (zero contour) map. Subsequently, Vogt and others (1982) produced a more comprehensive zebra-stripe map (Fig. 4), incorporating more recent data. McGrath and Fraser (1981) were successful in compiling a map showing magnetic anomalies over the Canadian Arctic.

Profile plots of recent U.S. Navy aeromagnetic data have been published in several papers (Vogt and others, 1979; Vogt and others, 1982; Taylor and others, 1981) and in the most complete form, along with some data from other agencies, in the Residual Magnetic Anomaly Chart of the Arctic Ocean Region (Kovacs and others, 1985) (Plate 4).

Satellite Surveys

A new era in studies of magnetic anomalies at high latitudes began with the reduction of magnetic data from the POGO satellites during 1965–1971 (Cain and Langel, 1971). The piecewise surveying of often small areas by aircraft with a wide variety of sensors and platforms had all but precluded the study of the longer-wavelength regional anomalies. Now, the global magnetic anomaly field could be studied. Langel and others (1980) made a successful comparison between POGO anomalies and aeromagnetic anomalies for western and Arctic Canada. Subsequently, Langel and Thorning (1982) published a complete polar magnetic anomaly map based on the POGO data. These maps showed some remarkable magnetic contrasts among the major Arctic tectonic regions. The POGO data were obtained at altitudes ranging between 400 and 700 km.

The Magsat mission in 1979–80 (Langel and others, 1981) was dedicated to measurements of the near-earth magnetic field and obtained data at altitudes between about 300 and 565 km. Northern polar maps from Magsat data have been published by Coles and others (1982), Coles (1985), Langel (written communication, 1981), and Haines (1985). These maps confirm the major features of the POGO map and add more detail in some areas.

Figure 5 (derived from Haines, 1985) shows the vertical component magnetic anomalies over the Arctic region, derived from Magsat. As a result of the Magsat orbital parameters (inclination 97°), a region of radius 7° around the geographic North Pole was not covered. However, Haines' (1985) model continues the map through this region in a manner consistent with the available data.

These satellite data provide a new perspective to anomaly studies. They permit maps to be prepared of the regional anomalies that assist the development of regional tectonic models (Taylor, 1983a).

Other Sources of Data

Although the bulk of magnetic anomaly information from the Arctic Basin has been derived from aeromagnetic and satellite surveys, significant information has been recorded by ships and ice stations. The inclement weather conditions, large magnetic disturbance and diurnal fields, and navigational inaccuracies are still present, but in addition the lack of control over the path of ice stations presents problems in data reduction and interpretation. To a considerable degree, the specific region surveyed from an ice station is a matter of chance; as a result, magnetic data from ice stations are often difficult to compile and interpret. Because of the ice conditions, shipborne magnetic surveys have been restricted to marginal seas (e.g., Bassinger, 1968; Cramer and others, 1986). A recent compilation by Godson (1985) shows magnetic data over Alaska and the adjacent Arctic offshore obtained from ship and airborne surveys.

Ice Stations

Hunkins and others (1962) described magnetic and other measurements over the Chukchi Plateau taken from drifting station Charlie. Distinctive magnetic anomalies were observed, but unfortunately several magnetic storms interrupted an otherwise continuous profile over the Chukchi Plateau. Hunkins (1966b) summarizes magnetic data from several ice stations. Hall (1970, 1973) discussed magnetic and other data obtained from Fletcher's Ice Island (T-3) during the period 1962–1970. During this time, the Ice Island traversed the Chukchi Plateau, portions of the Alpha and Mendeleev ridges, and the Chukchi, Mendeleev and Canada plains (Hunkins and Tiemann, 1977). Some magnetic data (unpublished) were also obtained by the British Trans-Arctic Expedition (1968–69) on an ice flow some 140 km

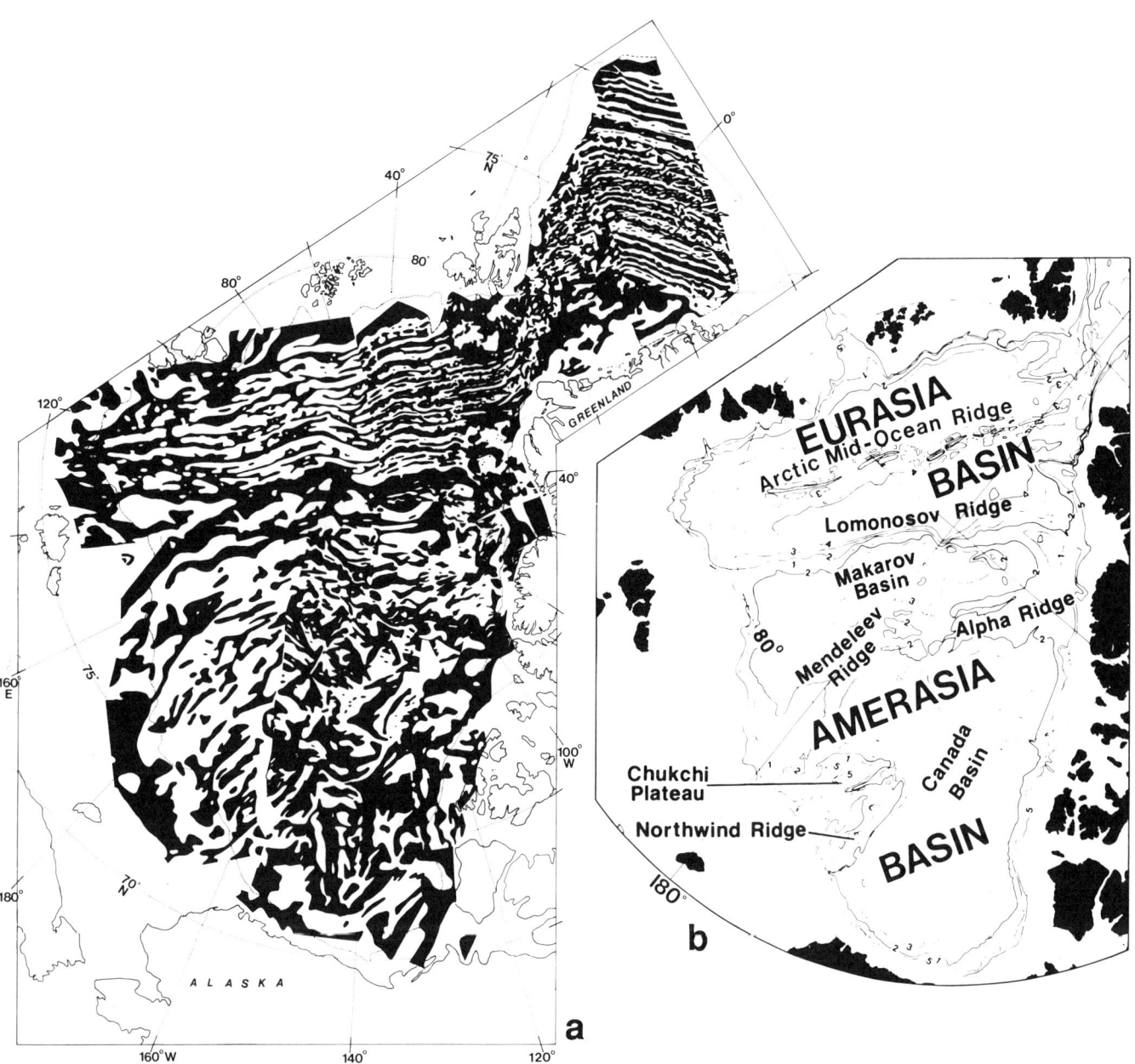

Figure 4. a) Residual (zebra-stripe) magnetic anomaly pattern from aeromagnetic surveys over the Arctic. Black indicates negative. Anomalies to left of line a–b are from Soviet surveys; to the right, from primarily U.S. Navy data plus some data from the Geological Survey of Canada (see Fig 2 and Plate 4). No attempt was made to adjust data at survey boundaries. (After Vogt and others, 1982). b) Simplified bathymetric chart of the Arctic Basin; depths in km. (Modified from Vogt and others, 1982).

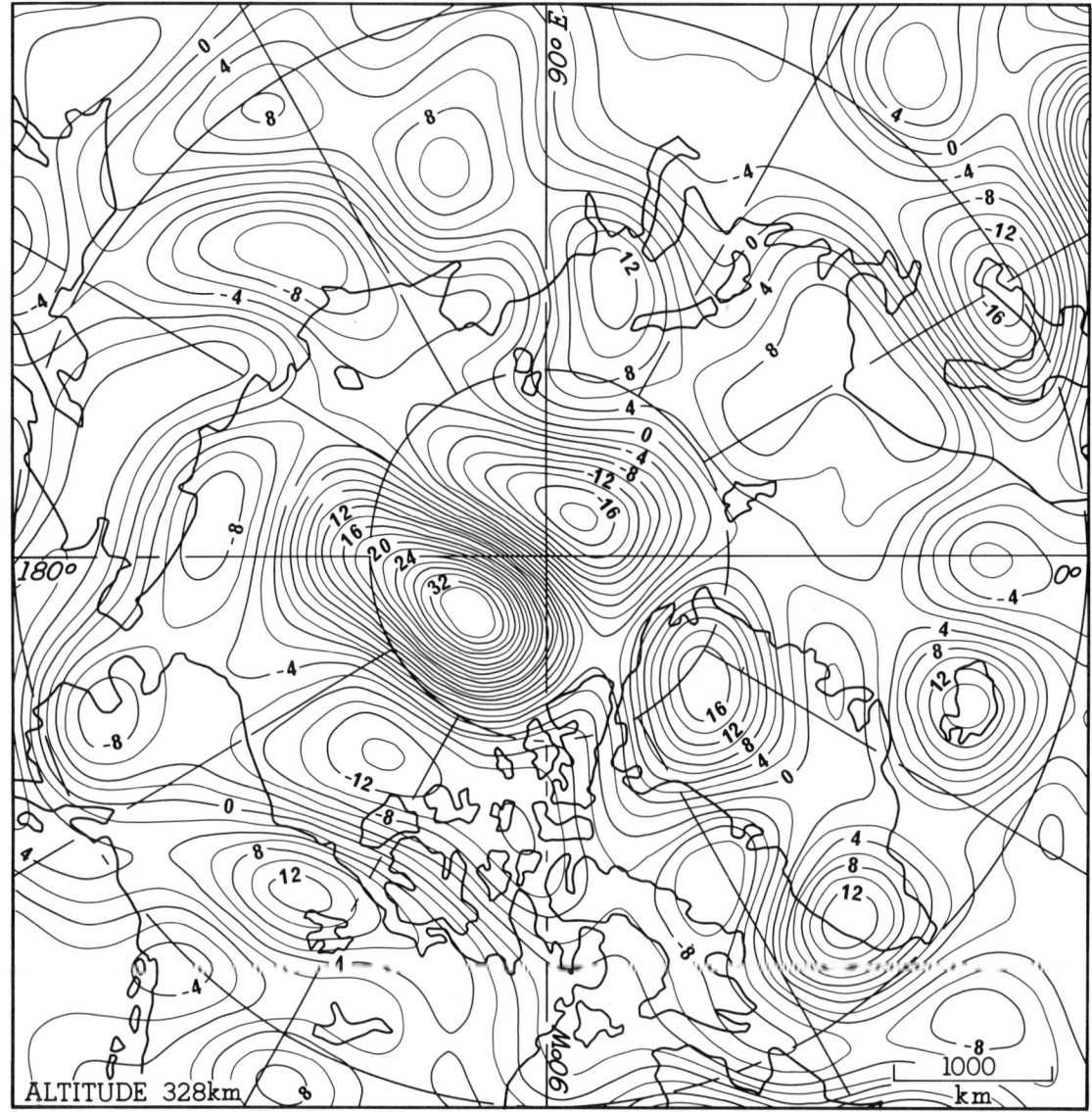

Figure 5. Magnetic anomalies in the vertical field from a spherical cap harmonic analysis of Magsat satellite data (Adapted from Haines, 1985).

from T-3. The ice station data over the Chukchi Plateau are particularly important because of the paucity of other published magnetic data for this region.

Heirtzler (1967) demonstrated a gradiometer technique (using two magnetometers, one above the other, to measure vertical magnetic gradients) for defining crustal magnetic anomalies with measurements from Fletcher's Ice Island. He showed that magnetic anomalies can be detected in the presence of large time variations using this technique.

In 1979, three ice stations, as part of the Lomonosov Ridge Experiment (LOREX), drifted over the Lomonosov Ridge close to the North Pole. Proton procession magnetometers in a vertical gradiometer configuration operated at two of these stations. Despite some problems, significant anomalies associated with the ridge were measured and interpreted (Coles, 1980; Sweeney and others, 1982).

REGIONAL INTERPRETATIONS

During the past 40 years, vast amounts of magnetic data over the Arctic Basin have been acquired by sea, ice, air, and space vehicles, and constitute the best, most extensive, yet detailed data set available for the region. It is appropriate to ask the question, what are the significant contributions to our understanding of the structure and evolution of the Arctic region that have arisen primarily from these magnetic data? What have we learned about the region that would likely not have resulted from other disciplines? Often the acquisition of data not only provides the means of resolving problems or questions, but also has the effect of raising further problems. In Table 1, the data and interpretations available for the major features in the Arctic Basin have been summarized; in a few cases, there is little or no controversy; however, in others there is no consensus of interpretations.

One of the more important concepts that has developed from the availability of relatively detailed magnetic data over large areas is that of magnetic provinces (Hall, 1968). A magnetic province has a distinct characteristic signature of anomalies, whether it be in terms of trend, wavelength, relief, shape, or a combination of these factors. Ultimately, the characteristic signature results from geological processes, and so differences in signature imply differences in geologic processes. Comparisons may well provide clues to the origins of magnetic provinces in the Arctic.

Since it remains the most enigmatic structure in the region, we will discuss the Alpha Ridge in more detail. Over the Alpha Ridge, one of the largest global satellite magnetic anomalies has been recorded. Other global large-amplitude magnetic features are detected over Bangui in central Africa (Regan and Marsh, 1982), Kentucky (Mayhew and others, 1982), Broken Ridge, the Indian Ocean (Johnson, 1985), northern Greenland (Langel and Thorning, 1982; Coles, 1985), and Antarctica (Ritzwoller and Bentley, 1982). In practically every instance of these and other large-amplitude anomalies, the apparent causative body is continental or pseudo-continental in nature. This strongly suggests that the Alpha Ridge is of a continental character (Coles and others, 1978; Taylor, 1983b). While not all continental structures possess large-amplitude magnetic anomalies at satellite altitude, all large-amplitude magnetic anomalies are associated with continental or pseudo-continental features.

The amplitude of the Alpha Ridge anomaly in Figure 5 is consistent with the amplitudes predicted for 300-km and 500-km altitudes on the basis of upward continuation of aeromagnetic data (Coles and Haines, 1979; Langel and others, 1980). Taylor (1983b), using a preliminary Magsat map, modeled the Alpha Ridge using an assumed crustal thickness of 30 km and a magnetization contrast of 2.5 A/m. He concluded on the basis of the Magsat anomalies and the modeling that the Mendeleev and Alpha ridges are separate geological provinces. Coles (1985) noted the magnetic similarities between Iceland and the Alpha Ridge. From gravity data, Weber and Sweeney (1985) computed a thickness of less than 20 km for the crust below the northern (Makarov) flank of the Alpha Ridge. Forsyth and others (1986), on the basis of analyses of seismic refraction data from CESAR (Canadian Expedition to Study the Alpha Ridge), have concluded that beneath the crest of the Alpha Ridge the crust is between 35 and 40 km thick. They consider that the seismic velocities are similar to those of oceanic crust, suggesting an oceanic plateau. The velocity structure has some similarities to that of Iceland. Forsyth and others (1986, in preparation) have proposed that the Alpha Ridge and Iceland might be products of the same plume.

In contrast to the high anomaly over the Alpha Ridge, the Arctic Mid-Ocean Ridge has an associated low magnetic anomaly (Fig. 5). In fact, the low anomaly spans the entire Eurasia Basin and continues into eastern Siberia over the seismically active Cherskiy Mountains. The Eurasia Basin is characterized by an aeromagnetic anomaly pattern that is part of one of the more convincing examples of sea-floor-spreading anomaly patterns, extending from the North Atlantic Ocean to the Siberian Shelf (Vogt and others, 1981a). Although many details of the anomaly field (anomaly amplitudes, axial anomaly, etc.) are not well understood, the overall evolution of this basin is considered to be known.

The southern Canada Basin is characterized by a broad low anomaly (from Magsat data; Fig. 5), which extends westward north of Siberia and eastward into the Canadian Arctic Islands. Aeromagnetic data over this basin (Taylor and others, 1981) reveal low-amplitude broad anomalies, which have been interpreted as sea-floor-spreading lineations. These data were subsequently filtered to attempt the removal of time variations (Taylor, 1983a, 1983b). These interpretations remain controversial (Vogt and others, 1984).

Aeromagnetic data cover much of these regions, with distinct characteristic signatures. The delineation of magnetic provincial boundaries is therefore an important contribution by magnetic studies to the understanding of Arctic geology and structure, where the solid crust is rarely available for direct observation. These magnetic provinces map out the distributions of magnetic properties and structures and do not necessarily correspond directly to known geological and structural/tectonic features. Lack of correspondence may reveal areas for further research.

SUMMARY

In a general discussion of the Arctic, the geologic/geophysical data base cannot be separated from the region's geographic setting or its geopolitical history. For example, if the Arctic were situated at a lower latitude, data would be more readily obtainable. Its inaccessibility, however, makes the acquisition and compilation of vast data sets difficult and often impractical. Political considerations militate against pan-Arctic surveys. If these factors were not enough, the Arctic is a relatively small ocean basin with an abundance of enigmatic features.

In 1982, during a Comité Arctique International meeting, Professor Louis Rey commented that the Arctic was like a polar Mediterranean. Both regions are small ocean basins with geologically puzzling structures and there is only a limited exchange of sea water with the world's oceans. A great deal of data exists for the Mediterranean Sea; however, magnetics represents the only ubiquitous data base for the Arctic. We can but speculate on what our interpretation of the Mediterranean Sea might be if only magnetic data were available.

TABLE 1. SUMMARY OF ARCTIC DATA AND INTERPRETATIONS

Feature	Magnetic Data	Interpretation	Comments (including other data types)
Eurasia Basin (Arctic Mid-Ocean Ridge)	AEROMAGNETIC: linear anomalies, low amplitude (<500 nT), 30-km wavelength, variable intensity axial feature (Vogt and others, 1979); Riddihough and others, 1973; Demenitskaya and Karasik, 1969).	Sea-floor spreading anomalies. Anomaly numbers 0 to 24B. Very slow spreading rate (0.5-1.0 cm/yr) (Coles and others, 1978; Vogt and others, 1979). Variable and low-amplitude ridge axis anomaly: cause unknown.	Continuation of mid-Atlantic Ridge close to pole of rotation (Emery, 1949; Heezen and Ewing, 1961; Wilson, 1963).
Alpha-Mendeleev ridge complex	AEROMAGNETIC: Unlineated high-amplitude (1500-2500 nT) (Vogt and others, 1979; Riddihough and others, 1973). SATELLITE: Extremely large-amplitude (22 nT at 415 km altitude) (Coles, 1985; Langel and Thorning, 1982). ICE ISLAND: T3 profiles amplitude 1300 nT and wavelength 180 km (Hall, 1970, 1973).	Not standard sea-floor spreading. Iceland-like or oceanic plateau, which have similar but not as high amplitude anomalies. Continental possibilities (similar to Lord Howe rise, Seychelles and Broken Ridge). Other very large satellite magnetic anomalies are continental. Uncertain link with Ellesmere Island (Coles and others, 1978; Taylor, 1978; Coles, 1985; Vogt and others, 1979).	Seismic evidence suggests oceanic plateau or continental (Forsyth and others, 1986). Iceland-type feature preferred (Coles, 1985). Mendeleev Ridge may be separate structure (Taylor, 1983a). Ellesmere Island link on basis of depth to basement (Kovacs and Vogt, 1982), not firmly established. Gravity data (Weber and Sweeney, 1985) suggest a less than 20-km-thick crust below northern flank, with volcanics similar to Lord Howe Rise. Herron and others (1974) interpreted this feature to be a relic subduction zone. Vogt and Ostenso (1970) and Kerr (1980) favor former center of sea-floor spreading.
Northern Canada Basin (north of 78°N lat.)	AEROMAGNETIC: Variable (100-1500 nT), longer wavelength (40-150 nT) but similar to anomalies on Alpha ridge (Taylor and others, 1981). ICE STATION: T3 data, amplitude 500 nT, wavelength 70 km (Hall, 1970, 1973).	Similar to Alpha Ridge.	Southern flank of Alpha Ridge buried by sediments.
Southern Canada Basin	AEROMAGNETIC: Low relief (~200 nT) and long wavelengths (40-100 km) (Taylor and others, 1981). SATELLITE: Low relief (Coles, 1985). ICE ISLAND: T3, amplitude 200 nT, wavelength 30 km (Hall, 1970, 1973).	Possibility of fan-shaped sea-floor-spreading anomalies, number M-12 (127 Ma) to M-25 (153 Ma)–Late Jurassic to Cretaceous (Taylor and others, 1981). Spreading during a quiet magnetic interval suggested by Herron and others (1974), Lawver and Baggeroer (1983). Sweeney (1985), Jones (1980) and Vogt and others (1981a) interpret these anomalies to describe a shear pattern for the Alaskan margin-Canada Basin boundary.	Most likely sea floor spreading. Axis, age, orientation uncertain. Seismic evidence favors oceanic crust (Mair and Lyons, 1981; Mair and Forsyth, 1982). Heat flow data support mid-Cretaceous age (Lawver and Baggoerer, 1983). Seismic refraction results (Bee and others, 1984) indicate that the Alaskan continental margin is an Atlantic or passive-type feature, tending to support the fan-rotation model.
Lomonosov Ridge	AEROMAGNETIC: Anomalies range up to 500 nT, wavelengths >100 km; irregular pattern, unlineated (Hood and Bower, 1980; Coles, 1980; Vogt and others, 1979; Karasik and others, 1971). Overall positive anomaly associated with ridge (Coles, 1980).	Lomonosov ridge overlies a tabular region of high susceptibility (0.06 SI) at depth between 7 and 17 km. Short-wavelength anomalies coincide with local bathymetric peaks (Coles, 1980; Sweeney, and others, 1982). Large positive magnetic anomaly along the Makarov Basin facing ridge flank suggests dike-like intrusion (Sweeney and others, 1982).	Seismic refraction results (Mair and Forsyth, 1982) found mantle at depth of 27 km; velocity of ridge core (4.7 km/s) could be basalt or continental rocks. Lomonosov Ridge formed by a strike-slip shear zone from the Eurasian margin (Mair and Forsyth, 1982). Lomonosov Ridge bounded by fractures, with a continental or sub-continental crust (Karasik and others, 1971). Compositional parameters permit Lomonosov Ridge to be "a pile of vesicular basalts overlying a core of basic rocks and therefore oceanic in nature" (Sweeney and others, 1982).

TABLE 1. (continued)

Feature	Magnetic Data	Interpretation	Comments (including other data types)
Chukchi Cap-Northwind Ridge (together with Chukchi Rise are collectively called Chukchi Plateau)	ICE STATION CHARLIE: 1600-nT amplitude anomaly on western margin, wavelength 60 km (Hunkins and others, 1562; Shaver and Hunkins, 1966a).	Large basement ridge of high susceptibility (0.75 SI) and 6 km relief is similar to the East Coast magnetic anomaly (ECMA; Drake and others, 1959; Taylor and others, 1968; Behrendt and Kitgord, 1978). Both induced and remanent magnetization proposed (Hunkins and others, 1962).	Magnetic data indicate Chukchi plateau differs from bordering north Canada Basin. Positive anomalies bordering plateau could be basement ridge, edge effects, or intruding dikes.
	AEROMAGNETIC: Ten profiles cross northern Canada Basin and Chukchi Plateau. High-amplitude anomalies bound this plateau north and south (>1000 nT; wavelength ~30 km). Plateau proper, low-amplitude (<200 nT) long-wavelength anomalies (Vogt and others, 1979; Ostenso, 1963). Magnetic profiles across western border range between 500 and 1500 nT (Ostenso, 1963) with wavelengths of 150 km.	Chukchi of continental origin; present location may be due to counterclockwise rotation from the Alaskan coast east of Barrow (Hunkins, 1966a). Anomaly result of contrasting magnetization (most likely remanent) within the crust, which parallels bathymetric trends (Shaver and Hunkins, 1964).	Chukchi Cap primarily a thick sediment sequence; therefore formerly part of continental shelf, originally from a point east of Pt. Barrow.
Nares Strait	AEROMAGNETIC: Predominantly a magnetic low trending NW (76°30'N to 78°N). On Greenland continental shelf, magnetic field anomalies become short-wavelength positive (Hood and Bower, 1976).	Half graben containing over 20 km of sediments in the east, shallowing to 10 km in the west.	The case for major displacement along Nares Strait is presented by Johnson and Srivastava (1982). The case against major displacement along Nares Strait is presented by Dawes and Kerr (1982).
	Lincoln Sea-Amundsen Basin anomalies (>100 nT; wavelengths ≥60 km), low amplitude and broad (Kovacs, 1982); Kane Basin: Linear anomaly pattern (300 nT; wavelength 25 km) (Hood and others, 1985).	250 km offset along Wegener fracture zone used to account for offsetting (Kovacs, 1982).	
	Very short wavelength (>5 km, >500 nT) anomalies occur along Axel Heiberg, Ellesmere Islands, and Greenland coasts (Kovacs, 1982). Kane Basin: Linear anomaly pattern (300 nT; wavelength 25 km) (Hood and others, 1985).	25-km offset, left lateral (Hood and others, 1985).	
	SATELLITE: Large positive anomaly over northern Greenland (>8 nT at 500 km altitude contrasts with a low (<-2 nT) over Canadian Arctic Islands. Sharp gradient lies parallel to the Nares Strait (Langel and Thorning, 1982).	This suggests a fundamental crustal structure difference across the Nares Strait (Langel and Thorning, 1982).	
Makarov Basin	AEROMAGNETIC: Lineated anomalies (Taylor and others, 1981; Hood and Bower, 1980). Amplitudes >700 nT, wavelengths 20-60 km). ICE STATION: Arlis II: ~600 nT anomaly, wavelength ~50 km (Kutschale, 1966).	Possible sea-floor spreading, anomalies numbers 21-34 (53 Ma to 80 Ma) (Taylor and others, 1981). May be bathymetric control of lineated anomalies (Sweeney and others, 1982; Sweeney, 1985; Kutschale, 1966).	Oceanic origin suggested by 9-km-thick crust (Mair and Forsyth, 1982). Alternately, continental stretching (Sweeney and others, 1982). A 10.5-km thick crust has been derived from Arlis II and Lorex gravity data (Weber and Sweeney, 1985), suggesting crustal extension.
Morris-Jesup Plateau Yermak Plateau	AEROMAGNETIC: (Feden and others, 1979). Large positive anomalies (500-2000 nT; 50-200 km).	Paired aseismic ridges that split apart 60 m.y. ago (Feden and others, 1979). Large anomaly amplitudes due to significant differentiation.	Seismic refraction data yield 8-km-thick crust and 6.7-km/s velocity under Yermak high-amplitude magnetic anomaly (Jackson and others, 1982). Suggests an oceanic hot-spot origin for this feature.

In this section we will summarize our interpretation of the Arctic from the magnetic and other measurements described in this review. (Consult Table 1 for references). We will begin at the Eurasian margin and proceed, across the pole, to the Canadian-Alaskan margin.

The Arctic Mid-Ocean Ridge, with the flanking Nansen and Amandsen basins, is the Arctic extension of the worldwide mid-ocean ridge system. Magnetic data have played a crucial role in these interpretations. Once part of the Eurasian mainland, the Lomonosov Ridge is a slice of continental crust displaced toward the pole. Crossing from the Eurasia to the Amerasia basin, we find the bathymetric depression known as the Makarov Basin. This trough could have been formed by either sea-floor spreading or crustal extension processes. Again, magnetic data are a vital element in the interpretations.

It is not known if the Alpha-Mendeleev ridge complex is one distinct geologic feature or two different but contiguous structures. This structure is the most puzzling physiographic feature of the Arctic. It has been interpreted as continental, as a hot spot (like Iceland), as a subduction zone, and as a former site of sea-floor spreading. Recent seismic refraction work from the CESAR study indicates a crust of variable thickness with values as great as 35–40 km beneath the Alpha Ridge, and a possible origin similar to that of Iceland.

Beneath the northern sector of the Canada Basin (north of 78°N latitude), the Alpha Ridge, identified as such by the magnetic anomaly signature, is buried beneath sedimentary strata. This means that this ridge is an even more dominant physiographic feature than bathymetry reveals. The southern Canada basin is a region of former crustal extension (see Table 1), the age and nature of which remain controversial. There is no agreement as to whether crustal formation had a fan-like or lateral motion (the available magnetic data are still too sparse). Its age has been described as being mid-Cretaceous (118–79 Ma) (Sweeney, 1985). Recent seismic refraction results reveal an Atlantic or passive-type continental margin, which is consistent with a rotation-like origin.

Obviously much more data, of all types, are required if we are to increase our understanding of the Arctic. Magnetic data have played a vital role in our understanding of the Arctic. For example, the Eurasia Basin: symmetric anomalies indicate an origin by sea floor spreading, they bracket the time of origin, they indicate asymmetries and variations of spreading rates with time. The magnetic differences between the Alpha and Lomonosov ridges imply greatly different origins. The magnetic patterns in the northern Canada Basin point out the full extent of the Alpha Ridge structure. The correlations between the Morris Jesup and Yermak plateaus have significantly influenced interpretations of the development of the southern Eurasia Basin. There are many more, referred to in Table 1 and the references. As a result of the handicaps of this region, aeromagnetic data must remain a dominant source of information.

REFERENCES

American Geographical Society, 1975, Map of the Arctic region, (Bathymetry after Heezen and Tharp): New York, scale 1:5,000,000.

Bassinger, B. G., 1968, Marine magnetic study in the northeast Chukchi Sea: Journal of Geophysical Research, v. 73, p. 683–687.

Bee, M., Johnson, S. H., and Chiboris, E. F., 1984, Seismic refraction study between Cape Simpson and Prudhoe Bay, Alaska: Journal of Geophysical Research, v. 89, p. 6941–6960.

Behrendt, J. C., and Klitgord, K. D., 1978, Origin of the East Coast Magnetic Anomaly: EOS American Geophysical Union Transactions, v. 59, p. 390–391.

Cain, J. C., and Langel, R. A., 1971, Geomagnetic surveys by the Polar Orbiting Geophysical Observatories, in Zmuda, A. J., ed., World magnetic surveys 1957–1969: Paris, International Association of Geomagnetism and Aeronomy Bulletin, no. 28, p. 65–75.

Coles, R. L., 1980, The LOREX magnetic gradient and total field experiment, 1979: Ottawa, Earth Physics Branch, Internal Geomagnetic Laboratory Report, 12 p.

——, 1985, Magsat scalar magnetic anomalies at northern high latitudes: Journal of Geophysical Research, v. 90, p. 2576–2582.

Coles, R. L., and Haines, G. V., 1979, Long-wavelength magnetic anomalies over Canada, using polynomial and upward continuation techniques: Journal of Geomagnetism and Geoelectricity, v. 31, p. 545–566.

Coles, R. L., Hannaford, W., and Haines, G. V., 1978, Magnetic anomalies and the evolution of the Arctic, in Sweeney, J. F., ed., Arctic geophysical review: Ottawa, Publication of the Earth Physics Branch, v. 45, p. 51–66.

Coles, R. L., Haines, G. V., Jansen van Beek, G., Nandi, A., and Walker, J. K., 1982, Magnetic anomaly maps from 40°N to 83°N derived from Magsat satellite data: Geophysical Research Letters, v. 9, p. 281–284.

Cramer, C. H., May, S. D., and Hanna, W. F., 1986, Magnetic anomaly map of the Chukchi Sea and adjacent northwest Alaska: U.S. Geological Survey Miscellaneous Investigations, Map J-1182-F, scale 1:1,000,000.

Dawes, P. R., and Kerr, J. W., 1982, The case against major displacement along Nares Strait, in Dawes, P. R., and Kerr, J. W., eds., Nares Strait and the drift of Greenland; A conflict in plate tectonics: Meddelelser om Gronland, Geoscience, v. 8, p. 369–386.

Demenitskaya, R. M., and Hunkins, K., 1970, Shape and structure of the Arctic Ocean, in Maxwell, A. E., ed., The sea, v. 4, part 2: New York, Wiley-Interscience, p. 223–249.

Demenitskaya, R. M., and Karasik, A. M., 1969, The active rift system of the Arctic Ocean: Tectonophysics, v. 8, p. 345–351.

Drake, C. L., Ewing, W. M., and Sutton, G. H., 1959, Continental margins and geosynclines; The east coast of North America north of Cape Hatteras, in Ahrens, L. H., and others, eds., Physics and chemistry of the Earth: v. 3, p. 110–198.

Emery, K. O., 1949, Topography and sediments of the Arctic Basin: Journal of Geology, v. 57, p. 512–521.

Feden, R. H., Vogt, P. R., and Fleming, H. S., 1979, Magnetic and bathymetric evidence for the "Yermak hot spot" northwest of Svalbard in the Arctic Basin: Earth and Planetary Science Letters, v. 44, p. 18–38.

Forsyth, D. A., Asudeh, I., Green, A. G., and Jackson, H. R., 1986, Crustal structure of the northern Alpha Ridge beneath the Arctic Ocean: Nature, v. 322, p. 349–352..

Godson, R. H., 1985, Preparation of magnetic anomaly maps of Alaska and Hawaii, in Hinze, W. J., ed., The utility of regional and gravity anomaly maps: Tulsa, Oklahoma, Society of Exploration Geophysicists, p. 25–32.

Haines, G. V., 1967, A Taylor expansion of the geomagnetic field in the Canadian Arctic: Ottawa, Publication of the Dominion Observatory, v. 35, p. 115–140.

———, 1985, Magsat vertical-field anomalies above 40°N from spherical-cap harmonic analysis: Journal of Geophysical Research, v. 90, p. 2593–2598.

Haines, G. V., and Hannaford, W., 1974, A three-component aeromagnetic survey of the Canadian Arctic: Ottawa, Publication of the Dominion Observatory, v. 44, p. 209–228.

Hall, D. H., 1968, Regional magnetic anomalies, magnetic units, and crustal structure in the Kenora District of Ontario: Canadian Journal of Earth Sciences, v. 5, p. 1277–1296.

Hall, J. K., 1970, Arctic Ocean geophysical studies: The Alpha Cordillera and Mendeleyev Ridge: CU-2-70, Palisades, New York, Lamont–Doherty Geological Observatory, Technical Report No. 2, p. 125.

———, 1973, Geophysical evidence for ancient sea-floor spreading from Alpha Cordillera and Mendeleyev Ridge, in Pitcher, M. G., ed., Arctic geology: American Association of Petroleum Geologists Memoir 19, p. 542–561.

Heezen, B. C., and Ewing, M., 1961, The mid-Oceanic Ridge and its extension through the Arctic Basin, in Rasch, G. O., ed., Geology of the Arctic: Toronto, University of Toronto Press, p. 622–642.

Heirtzler, J. R., 1967, Measurements of the vertical geomagnetic field gradient beneath the surface of the Arctic Ocean: Geophysical Prospecting, v. 15, p. 194–203.

Herron, E. M., Dewey, J. F., and Pitman, W. C., III, 1974, Plate tectonics model for the evolution of the Arctic: Geology, v. 2, p. 377–380.

Hood, P. J., and Bower, M. E., 1976, Arctic Ocean; Low-level aeromagnetic profiles obtained in 1975: Geological Survey of Canada Paper 76-1A, p. 421–424.

Hood, P. J., and Bower, M. E., 1980, Aeromagnetic reconnaissance; Lorex project [abs.]: EOS American Geophysical Union Transactions, v. 61, p. 227.

Hood, P. J., Bower, M. E., Hardwick, C. D., and Teskey, D. J., 1985, Direct geophysical evidence for displacement along Nares Strait (Canada–Greenland) from low-level aeromagnetic data; A progress report: Current Research, Part A, Geological Survey of Canada Paper 85-1A, p. 517–522.

Hunkins, K., 1966a, The Arctic Continental Shelf north of Alaska; Continental margins and island arcs: Geological Survey of Canada Paper 65-15, p. 197–204.

———, 1966b, Geomorphic provinces of the Arctic Ocean, in Sater, J. E., ed., Arctic drifting stations: Arctic Institute of North America, Symposium Proceedings, Warrenton, Virginia, p. 365–376.

Hunkins, K., and Tiemann, W., 1977, Geophysical data summary for Fletcher's Ice Island: Palisades, New York, Lamont-Doherty Geological Observatory Technical Report CU-1-77, p. 219.

Hunkins, K., Herron, T., Kutschale, H., and Peter, G., 1962, Geophysical studies of the Chukchi Cap, Arctic Ocean: Journal of Geophysical Research, v. 67, p. 235–247.

Jackson, H. R., Reid, I., and Falconer, R.K.H., 1982, Crustal structure near Arctic midocean ridges: Journal of Geophysical Research, v. 87, p. 1773–1783.

Johnson, D. B., 1985, Viscous remanent magnetization model for the Broken Ridge satellite magnetic anomaly: Journal of Geophysical Research, v. 90, p. 2640–2646.

Johnson, G. L., and Srivastava, S. P., 1982, The case for major displacement along Nares Strait, in Dawes, P. R., and Kerr, J. W., eds., Nares Strait and the drift of Greenland; A conflict in plate tectonics: Meddelelser om Gronland, Geoscience, v. 8, p. 365–368.

Johnson, G. L., Monahan, D., Gronlie, G., and Sobczak, L., 1979, GEBCO sheet 5.17, Arctic Ocean: Ottawa, Bathymetric map series, Canadian Hydrographic Service.

Jones, P. B., 1980, Evidence from Canada and Alaska on plate tectonic evolution of the Arctic: Nature, v. 285, p. 215–217.

Karasik, A. M., 1980, Basic specifics of the history of development and the structure of the Arctic Basin bottom according to aeromagnetic data: Marine Geology, Sedimentology, Sedimentary Petrography, and Geology of the Ocean, Academy of Sciences of the U.S.S.R., Ministry of Geology of the U.S.S.R., National Committee of Geologists of the Soviet Union, Leningrad, p. 178–193. (Translated 1981: NASA GSFC-07).

Karasik, A. M., Guerevich, V. N., Masolov, V. N., and Shchelovanov, V. G., 1971, Some features of the deep structure and genesis of the Lomonosov Ridge based on data of airborne magnetic surveys: Geofiz. Metody razvedki v Arktike, v. 6, p. 9–19 (in Russian).

Karasik, A. M., Masalov, V. N., and Shchelovanov, V. G., 1972, Methodological problems of aerial magnetic mapping in the Arctic Ocean: Geofiz. Metody razvedki v Arktike, v. 7, p. 74–79 (in Russian).

Kerr, J. W., 1980, A plate tectonic contest in Arctic Canada, in Strangway, D. W., ed., The continental crust and its mineral deposits: Geological Association of Canada Special Paper 20, p. 457–484.

King, E. R., Zietz, I., and Alldredge, L. R., 1966, Magnetic data on the structure of the central Arctic region: Geological Society of America Bulletin, v. 77, p. 619–646.

Kovacs, L. C., 1982, Motion along Nares Strait recorded in the Lincoln Sea; Aeromagnetic evidence, in Dawes, P. R., and Kerr, J. W., eds., Nares Strait and the drift of Greenland; A conflict in plate tectonics: Meddelelser om Gronland, Geoscience, v. 8, p. 105–120.

Kovacs, L. C., and Vogt, P. R., 1982, Depth-to-magnetic source analysis of the Arctic Ocean region: Tectonophysics, v. 89, p. 255–294.

Kovacs, L. C., Bernero, C., Johnson, G. L., Pilger, R. H., Srivastava, S. P., Taylor, P. T., Vink, G. E., Vogt, P. R., 1985, Residual magnetic anomaly chart of the Arctic Ocean region: Geological Society of America Map and Chart Series MC-53, scale 1:6,000,000.

Kutschale, A. W., 1966, Arctic Ocean geophysical studies; The southern half of the Siberian Basin: Geophysics, v. 31, p. 683–710.

Langel, R. A., and Thorning, L., 1982, A satellite magnetic anomaly map of Greenland: Geophysical Journal of the Royal Astronomical Society, v. 71, p. 599–602.

Langel, R. A., Coles, R. L., and Mayhew, M. A., 1980, Comparisons of magnetic anomalies of lithospheric origin measured by satellite and airborne magnetometers over western Canada: Canadian Journal of Earth Sciences, v. 17, p. 876–887.

Langel, R., Ousley, G., Berbert, J., Murphy, J., and Settle, M., 1981, The Magsat mission: Geophysical Research Letters, v. 9, p. 243–245.

Lawver, L., and Baggeroer, A., 1983, A note on the age of the Canada Basin: Journal of the Alaska Geological Society, v. 2, p. 57–66.

Loomer, E. I., 1979, The effect of changes in the interplanetary magnetic field on the reduction of magnetic data from the polar cap: Ottawa, Earth Physics Branch, Geomagnetic Series, no. 17, p. 1–26.

Mair, J. A., and Forsyth, D. A., 1982, Crustal structures of the Canada Basin near Alaska, the Lomonosov Ridge, and adjoining basins near the North Pole: Tectonophysics, v. 89, p. 239–253.

Mair, J. A., and Lyons, J. A., 1981, Crustal structure and velocity anisotropy beneath the Beaufort Sea: Canadian Journal of Earth Sciences, v. 18, p. 724–741.

Mayhew, M. A., Thomas, H. H., and Wasilewski, P. J., 1982, Satellite and surface geophysical expression of anomalous crustal structure in Kentucky and Tennessee: Earth and Planetary Science Letters, v. 58, p. 395–405.

McGrath, P. H., and Fraser, I., 1981, Magnetic anomaly map of Arctic Canada: Geological Survey of Canada Map 1512A, scale 1:3,500,000.

Ostenso, N. A., 1963, Aeromagnetic survey of the Arctic Ocean Basin: Proceedings of Thirteenth Alaskan Science Conference, Juneau, Alaska, p. 115–148.

Ostenso, N. A., and Wold, R. J., 1971, Aeromagnetic survey of the Arctic Ocean; Techniques and interpretations: Marine Geophysical Researches, v. 1, p. 178–219.

———, 1973, Aeromagnetic evidence for the origin of Arctic Ocean Basin, in Pitcher, M. G., ed., Arctic geology: American Association of Petroleum Geologists Memoir 19, p. 506–516.

Parkinson, W. D., 1983, Introduction to geomagnetism: New York, Elsevier Science Publishing Company, 433 p.

Perry, R. K., and others, 1986, Bathymetry of the Arctic Ocean: Geological Society of America Map and Chart Series MC-56, scale 1:4,704,075.

Regan, R. D., and Marsh, B. D., 1982, The Bangui magnetic anomaly; Its geological origin: Journal of Geophysical Research, v. 87, p. 1107–1120.

Riddihough, R. P., Haines, G. V., and Hannaford, W., 1973, Regional magnetic anomalies of the Canadian Arctic: Canadian Journal of Earth Sciences, v. 10, p. 147–163.

Ritzwoller, M. H., and Bentley, C. R., 1982, Magsat magnetic anomalies over Antarctica and the surrounding oceans: Geophysical Research Letters, v. 9, p. 285–288.

Shaver, R., and Hunkins, K., 1964, Arctic Ocean geophysical studies; Chukchi Cap and Chukchi Abyssal Plain: Deep-Sea Research, v. 11, p. 905–916.

Sobczak, L. W., and Sweeney, J. F., 1978, Bathymetry of the Arctic Ocean, in Sweeney, J. F., ed., Arctic geophysical review: Ottawa, Publication of the Earth Physics Branch, v. 45, p. 7–14.

Sweeney, J. F., 1985, Comments about the age of the Canada Basin: Tectonophysics, v. 114, p. 1–10.

Sweeney, J. F., Weber, J. R., and Blasco, S. M., 1982, Continental ridges in the Arctic Ocean; LOREX constraints: Tectonophysics, v. 89, p. 217–237.

Taylor, P. T., 1978, Low-level aeromagnetic data across the western Arctic Basin: EOS American Geophysical Union Transactions, v. 59, p. 268–269.

Taylor, P. T., 1983a, Nature of the Canada Basin; Implications from satellite-derived magnetic anomaly field data: Journal of the Alaska Geological Society, v. 2, p. 1–8.

—— , 1983b, Magnetic data over the Arctic from aircraft and satellites: Cold Regions Science and Technology, v. 7, p. 35–40.

Taylor, P. T., Zietz, I., and Dennis, L. S., 1968, Geologic implications of aeromagnetic data for the eastern continental margin of the United States: Geophysics, v. 33, p. 755–780.

Taylor, P. T., Kovacs, L. C., Vogt, P. R., and Johnson, G. L., 1981, Detailed aeromagnetic investigations of the Arctic Basin, 2: Journal of Geophysical Research, v. 86, p. 6323–6333.

USNOO, 1982, Geomagnetic surveys: Bay St. Louis, Mississippi, U.S. Naval Oceanographic Office, NSTL Station, Reference Publication-23, p. 1–90.

Vogt, P. R., and Ostenso, N. A., 1970, Magnetic and gravity profiles across the Alpha Cordillera and their relation to Arctic sea-floor spreading: Journal of Geophysical Research, v. 75, p. 4925–4938.

Vogt, P. R., Taylor, P. T., Kovacs, L. C., and Johnson, G. L., 1979, Detailed aeromagnetic investigation of the Arctic Basin: Journal of Geophysical Research, v. 84, p. 1071–1089.

Vogt, P., Bernero, C., Kovacs, L., and Taylor, P., 1981a, Structure and plate tectonic evolution of the marine Arctic as revealed by aeromagnetics: Oceanologica Acta, Proceedings of 26th International Geological Congress, Geology of Oceans Symposium, Paris, July 7–17, 1980, p. 25–40.

Vogt, P. R., Perry, R. K., Feden, R. H., Fleming, H. S., and Cherkis, N. Z., 1981b, The Greenland-Norwegian Sea and Iceland environment; Geology and geophysics, in Nairn, A. E., and Stehli, F. G., eds., Ocean basins and margins, v. 5: New York, Plenum Publishing Corp., p. 493–598.

Vogt, P. R., Taylor, P. T., Kovacs, L. C., and Johnson, G. L., 1982, The Canada Basin; Aeromagnetic constraints on structure and evolution: Tectonophysics, v. 89, p. 295–336.

Vogt, P. R., Kovacs, K. C., Perry, R. K., and Taylor, P. T., 1984, Amerasian Basin, Arctic Ocean; Magnetic anomalies and their decipherment: 27th International Geological Congress, Moscow, Colloquium 04, Arctic Geology, Reports, v. 4, p. 152–161.

Weber, J. R., 1983, Maps of the Arctic Basin sea floor; A history of bathymetry and its interpretation: Arctic, v. 36, p. 121–142.

Weber, J. R., and Sweeney, J. F., 1985, Reinterpretation of morphology and crustal structure in the central Arctic Ocean Basin: Journal of Geophysical Research, v. 90, p. 663–677.

Wilson, J. T., 1963, Hypothesis of Earth's behavior; Nature, v. 198, p. 925–929.

MANUSCRIPT ACCEPTED BY THE SOCIETY NOVEMBER 24, 1986

ACKNOWLEDGMENTS

The authors wish to thank the following colleagues for their help, advice, and comments during the preparation of this chapter: M. J. Berry, D. A. Forsyth, A. Grantz, A. G. Green, J. R. Heirtzler, K. Hunkins, G. L. Johnson, R. D. Kurtz, E. R. Niblett, R. P. Riddihough, J. F. Sweeney, P. R. Vogt.

NOTE ADDED IN PROOF

Between March and September 1985, Questar Surveys Ltd., under contract to the Geological Survey of Canada, conducted a precision digital magnetometer (proton) survey in the Canadian Arctic. The survey area was within the boundaries of 68 to 72°N and 124 to 142°W. Flight altitude was 305 m above mean sea level for the over-water portion and 1,829 m for the land. Precise Decca navigation and 0.2 nT anomaly resolution permitted these total field data to be contoured at 5 nT and presented on a scale of 1:250,000. These data are presented in anomaly form on the Magnetic Anomaly Map of North America (DNAG Continental-Scale Map 003). These newer data confirm that the linear fan-like anomaly pattern of the southern Canada Basin has its focus or apex near the Mackenzie River delta.

These magnetic data are published in the Geological Survey of Canada Map Series as Numbers 7951-2G, 7971-73G, 7992-94G, 8012-15G, and 8183-8186G. We thank Peter J. Hood (Geological Survey of Canada) for supplying these data and his help.

From A. E. Nordenskjold, 1885, Voyage de la *Vega* Autour de l'Asie et de l'Europe [1878–1879], (translated from Swedish by Charles Rabot and Charles Lallemond), Vol. 1: Paris, Libraire Hachette et Cie, p. 119, 405, and 103, respectively.

Chapter 9

Geothermal observations in the Arctic region

M. G. Langseth
Lamont-Doherty Geological Observatory of Columbia University, Palisades, New York 10964
A. H. Lachenbruch and B. V. Marshall
U.S. Geological Survey, 345 Middlefield Road, Menlo Park, California 94025

INTRODUCTION

A fundamental goal of geothermal studies in the Arctic region is to determine the rate of heat flow from deep in the earth's crust. Research during the past 25 years has shown heat flux is closely related to the tectonic evolution of a geological province. When combined with other geological and geophysical data, accurate heat-flow measurements can set constraints on crustal temperatures, age and evolution of the lithosphere, and the distribution of radiogenic heat in the crust. At an even more fundamental level, accurate measurements help determine the total rate of heat loss from the Earth and define the global variation of heat flow and its correlation with other long-wavelength geophysical features.

In addition to the fundamental scientific interest, the subsurface thermal regimes of continents and continental margins of the Arctic are of practical concern for natural resource development. Mean annual surface temperatures on land are well below freezing, which results in a permafrost layer hundreds of meters thick in some places; for example Judge and others (1981) reported a permafrost thickness of 726 m on Cameron Island in the Canadian Arctic Archipelago. The ice-bearing permafrost presents many obstacles to the development of resources and the maintenance of facilities in the Arctic, and as a consequence, a considerable effort has been made by the Canadian and United States governments and industry to evaluate the subsurface thermal regime from an engineering perspective. These efforts have provided many drill holes for subsurface temperature and thermal properties data. Many of these holes will provide accurate determinations of terrestrial heat flow.

Sea-floor measurements in the Arctic have no such practical impetus, yet more than 700 observations have been made over the past two decades using oceanographic techniques from ice islands, through pack ice, and from ships in ice-free regions around the perimeter of the Arctic Ocean.

Geothermal studies in the Arctic began shortly after World War II with the measurements by Dominion Observatory of Canada and University of Western Ontario at Resolute Bay, on Cornwallis Island (Misener, 1955; Misener and others, 1956). The measurements were made in holes drilled to explore the Resolute Bay area as a site for a seismological station. These first subsurface temperature measurements revealed many of the important geothermal features of the Arctic region. For example, borehole temperatures in the upper 100 m actually decreased with depth as a result of recent climatic warming. The shallow temperatures in the borehole showed a steady temporal increase over a 4-yr period. At depths below 100 m the gradient reversed and an unusually high rate of increase of temperature with depth (39 mK/m) was observed, which corresponds to a heat flow of about 121 mW/m^2. This value is significantly above the global average of continental values of about 65 mW/m^2. Lachenbruch (1957) showed later that much of this heat came from the nearby ocean floor where bottom temperatures are 15°C warmer than on land.

At about the same time, pioneering geothermal studies had begun in northern Alaska by scientists of the U.S. Geological Survey who instrumented holes drilled on the Naval Petroleum Reserve No. 4 near Point Barrow (MacCarthy, 1952; Brewer, 1958). Measurement in holes close to shore showed relatively high gradients like those at Resolute Bay. Lachenbruch and Brewer (1959) analyzed the return to equilibrium at one of the Point Barrow wells that is far enough inland to avoid the ocean effect and determined a gradient of 30.1 °C/m.

One of the most comprehensive scientific investigations of a region of permafrost and tundra was carried out at Cape Thompson, Alaska. Temperature measurements were made using multisensor cables installed in four holes as part of Project Chariot, a multidisciplinary study of the Cape Thompson environment (Lachenbruch and others, 1966). Measurements in the deepest hole were sufficiently far from shore to attenuate the ocean effect to a negligible level, so that this hole yielded the first accurate measurement of heat flow in Arctic North America: 59 mW/m^2.

The Earth Physics Branch (now the Geological Survey of Canada) of the Department of Energy, Mines, and Resources and

Langseth, M. G., Lachenbruch, A. H., and Marshall, B. V., 1990, Geothermal observations in the Arctic region, *in* Grantz, A., Johnson, L., and Sweeney, J. F., eds., The Arctic Ocean region: Boulder, Colorado, Geological Society of America, The Geology of North America, v. L.

the U.S. Geological Survey have continuing programs to make temperature and thermal-property measurements at boreholes in Arctic Canada and northern Alaska. This work is carried out in close cooperation with commercial companies, particularly petroleum companies, who have made boreholes available for these measurements. The locations of sites where borehole temperatures have been or are being monitored are shown on the map in Figure 3b and on Plate 2B. Interim reports on these observations are available from both agencies, for example, a series of reports by the Canadian Geothermal Data Collection (Taylor and others, 1982, and preceeding volumes referenced therein).

Measurement of heat flow through the sea floor in the Arctic Ocean began in 1963. In that year, the USGS group at Menlo Park initiated a program from a large ice island named T-3. The program continued for ten years as T-3 drifted with the ice pack in the western part of the Arctic Ocean. This effort produced 356 measurements (Lachenbruch and Marshall, 1966, 1969). In 1964, Law and others (1965) and Paterson and Law (1966) made nine sea-floor measurements through the ice in McClure Strait and northwest of Prince Patrick Island using a portable oceanographic system that was carried to sites on pack ice by airplane.

Soviet geophysicists have reported two programs of heat-flow measurement through the ice cover of the Arctic Ocean made in the mid-1960s (Lubimova and others, 1973a, b). One program from the "North Pole 15" station crossed part of the Makarov Basin and traversed the Lomonosov Ridge near the North Pole. The second program produced a heat-flow profile across the axis of the Arctic Mid-Ocean Ridge.

Recently two geophysical programs that included heat-flow measurements through the pack ice were carried out by the Geological Survey of Canada; the LOREX program to explore the Lomonosov Ridge (Judge, 1980), and project CESAR to study the central Alpha Ridge (Taylor and others, 1986).

Measurements from oceanographic ships in Arctic Ocean waters have been made in Baffin Bay by Pye and Hyndman (1972); in Fram Strait between Greenland and Spitzbergen by Crane and others (1982) and Crane and Sundvor (personal communication, 1986) from the Swedish research vessel *Ymer*; and on the Yermak Plateau (Jackson and others, 1984). Sea-floor measurements in the Norwegian-Greenland Sea have been reported by Langseth and Zielinski (1974), Lachenbruch and Marshall (1968), Zielinski (1977), and Haenel (1974).

LAND HEAT-FLOW MEASUREMENTS IN THE ARCTIC

Geothermal data for eight land heat-flow measurements in the Arctic region are presented in Table 1. Seven of the eight reported measurements of heat flow in Arctic North America were made in boreholes; the eighth was made in a deep mine at Eldorado, Saskatchewan. Temperature profiles are measured by a calibrated thermistor that is lowered into the hole on a conducting cable. Alternatively, a prefabricated multisensor cable is implanted and left in the hole for a series of measurements over a period often years in length. For the first technique, boreholes are usually filled with arctic diesel oil to prevent freezing. Figure 1 shows an example of repeated temperature measurements in a borehole at Prudhoe Bay and its equilibration subsequent to drilling.

The ice-bonded permafrost provides an excellent medium for measuring heat flow since the interstitial ice prevents advection of pore fluids. However, the thermal response of the ice-bound layer to drilling and the recovery of the borehole to equilibrium is made complex by latent heat absorbed during drilling and released during refreezing of material around the borehole, as is clearly evident in the evolution of borehole temperatures shown in Figure 1.

Thermal conductivity of the strata in which temperature is measured is estimated from measurements on samples from the drill holes or nearby outcrops. Two techniques of measurement are in common use: the steady-state divided-bar technique (see e.g., Beck, 1965), and the transient heated needle-probe technique (Von Herzen and Maxwell, 1959). For these methods, samples may be intact samples of solid rock, water saturated drill cuttings, or unconsolidated sediments from the borehole (Sass and others, 1971).

Determining the conductivity of the frozen zone in permafrost regions presents unique problems. Usually, the ice is melted during drilling operations or the samples thaw before measurements can be made, and it is often necessary to use a theoretical model of a two-component aggregate material to estimate conductivity. The conductivity of a solidly frozen saturated aggregate will be higher than a water-saturated aggregate because the conductivity of ice near 0° is 2.2 W/m–°c, whereas water is only 0.56 W/m–°c at 0°C. In Figure 1A an increase in temperature gradient below the frozen zone can be clearly seen due to the transition from higher conductivity frozen strata to water-saturated material beneath.

Regional significance of heat-flow measurements at Arctic land sites

Traditionally, publication of a land heat-flow determination at a site implies that the value given is a reliable estimate of heat flux from deep in the crust, and that known near-surface disturbances to heat flow have been avoided or appropriate corrections have been made. Such a determination we refer here to as a "regionally significant value." The term implies that the value obtained can be used confidently to set constraints on subsurface temperature and heat production, the magmatic and tectonic history of a region, and that the values can be used within stated uncertainties to study the global variation of heat escaping from the Earth's interior. The thermal environment and thermal history of the Arctic may introduce many disturbances to subsurface temperatures. Gold and Lachenbruch (1973) present a summary of these effects.

The ocean or lake effect. Proximity of a heat-flow measurement site to the ocean or a lake introduces a large disturbance

TABLE 1. LAND HEAT-FLOW DETERMINATIONS IN ARCTIC NORTH AMERICA

	Lat. (N)	Long. (W)	Elevation (m)	Gradient (°C/km)	Mean Conductivity (W/m-°C)	Heat Flow (mW/m²)
Alaska						
Cape Thompson	68°06'	165°40'	21	19.8	2.93	58.6
Prudhoe Bay*	70°17'	148°40'	9	16.4 (28.2)	3.37 (1.96)	54.4
Canadian Mainland						
Muskox**	66°59'	115°16'	578	---	---	54
Asbestos Hill	61°49'	73°58'	420	12.0	3.2	38
Eldorado	59°34'	108°28'	318	14.7	3.35	56
Whitehorse	60°45'	135°11'	872	18.0	2.94	64
Norman Wells	65°18'	126°52'	---	---	1.70	83
Canadian Arctic Islands						
Resolute Bay	74°41'	94°54'	10	39.5	3.1	53

*Gradient and Mean Conductivity are given for frozen and thawed sections: frozen (thawed).

**Large correction applied for nearby Speers Lake.

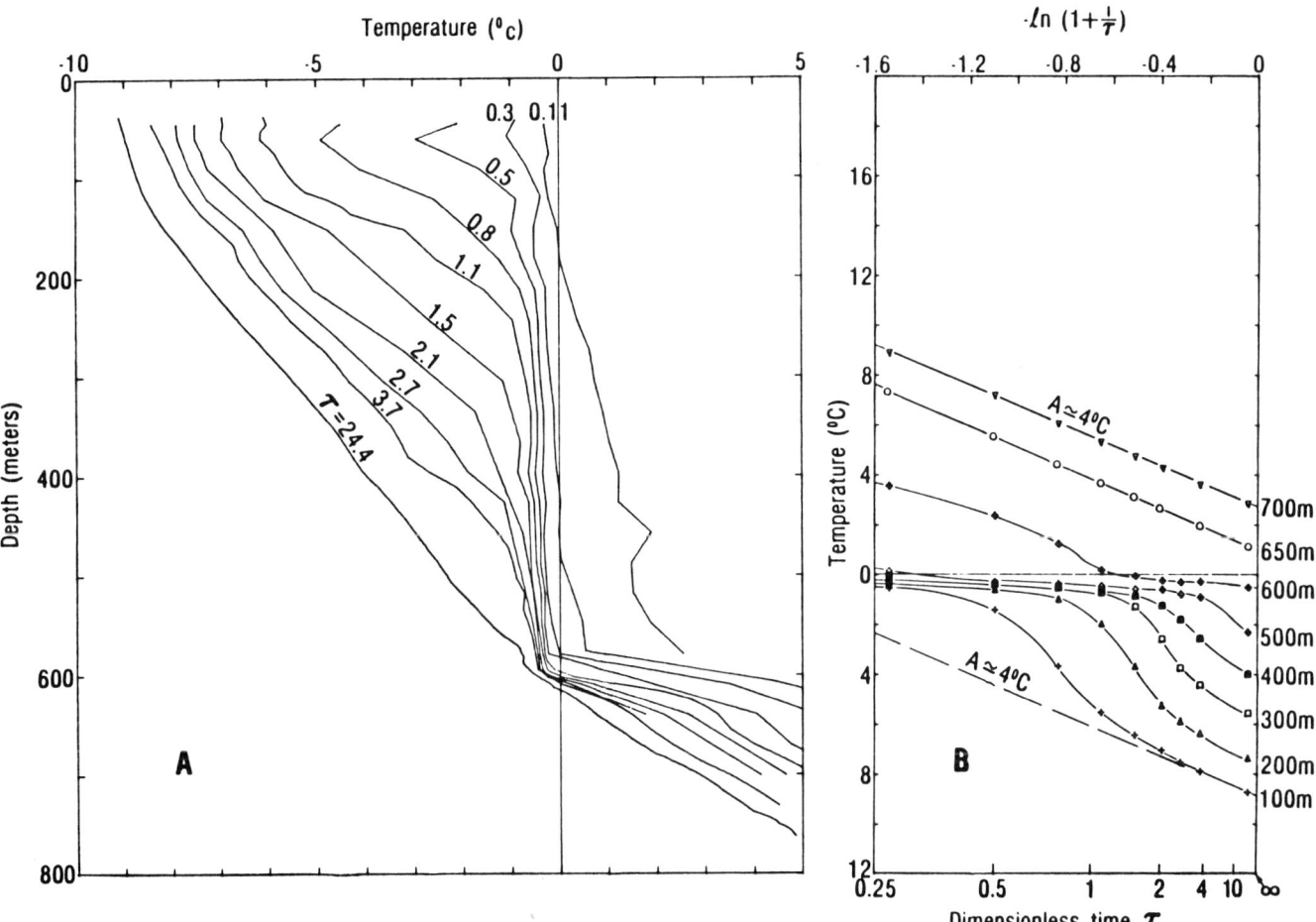

Figure 1. (A) Successive temperature profiles from a borehole at Prudhoe Bay observed over a 3-yr period after completion of drilling, (from Lachenbruch and others, 1982a, Fig. 4.) (B) The dissipation of the drilling disturbance at selected depths as indicated on the right-hand side. τ is the time elapsed since completion of drilling measured in multiples of the drilling period (44 days).

to the subsurface temperatures (see Lachenbruch, 1957). This results from the fact that bottom water offshore or in a lake holds the ground surface temperature at a value that is significantly higher than adjacent subaerial terrain. As a consequence, heat flows into the earth through the ocean and lake bottoms and disturbs subsurface temperatures. Lachenbruch (1957) presents techniques for estimating the amplitude of the ocean effect and calculating corrections to gradient measurements.

Transient surface temperatures. Changes in mean annual surface temperature at or near a site cause transient heat flows near the surface that are superimposed on heat flow from depth. In the Arctic, one of the most important sources of long-term transients is the transgression and regression of the shoreline due to sea-level changes (see, e.g., Taylor and others, 1983). Most Arctic lakes are transient features that formed at the end of Pleistocene glaciation (Beck and Sass, 1966), and the thermal effects of their emplacement are still felt 8,000 yrs later.

Temperature measurements in many boreholes in the Arctic show a substantial decrease of the temperature gradient in the upper 75 to 100 m. This phenomenon results from a substantial increase in mean annual surface temperature during the past century, perhaps due to a climatic warming. The history of this surface temperature change is sparsely documented for the Arctic, and data suggest that its amplitude may vary considerably from one area to another (Lachenbruch and Marshall, 1986). One consequence of this warming is that to obtain a determination of heat flow from depth requires measuring temperature gradients at depths greater than 200 m.

A change in surface temperature accompanies the advance and retreat of the Pleistocene ice sheets; however, the timing and amplitude of the surface changes are not well known. Because of this uncertainty, it is a usual practice not to correct heat-flow values in areas covered by the Wisconsin ice sheet for hypothetical surface temperature histories due to glaciation, even though in some areas the glacial effect may be appreciable. In the Arctic the mean surface temperature usually decreased when the ice sheets retreated, so that corrections for glaciation reduce the observed heat flow.

MARINE HEAT-FLOW DATA IN THE ARCTIC

Sea-floor measurements in the Arctic region have been made with oceanographic-type instruments that measure the temperature gradient in the upper few meters of unconsolidated sea-floor sediment by driving a probe with two to five temperature sensors spaced along it into the bottom. Temperature at each sensor or temperature difference between sensors is recorded while the probe is left undisturbed in the sediment long enough to allow accurate extrapolation of the temperature history of each probe to equilibrium.

Thermal conductivity is measured in sediment core samples taken either with the gradient observation or nearby. In some instances the conductivity is estimated using empirically established relationships between conductivity and water content of

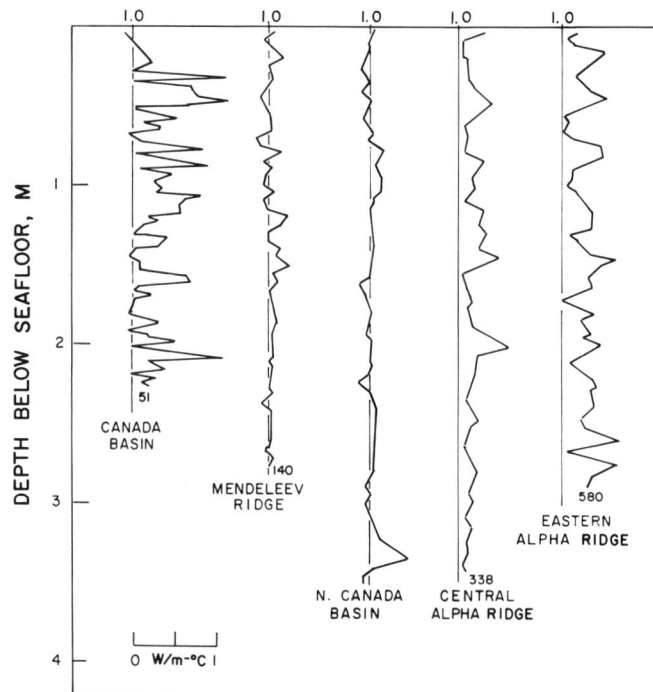

Figure 2. Typical thermal conductivity versus depth profiles for 6 different areas of the Amerasia Basin.

the sediment. Figure 2 shows several typical conductivity-versus-depth profiles for stations in the Amerasia Basin in the Arctic Ocean.

The references of heat-flow measurements in the Arctic Ocean Basin and surrounding oceanic areas are summarized in Table 2, and the locations of all reported heat-flow measurements are shown on the maps of Figure 3a–c and in Plate 2.

The regional significance of marine heat-flow measurements

As part of this review we have examined existing sea-floor measurements in the western Arctic Ocean in terms of their representativeness of heat flow from deep in the crust. Criteria based on data quality, geological and hydrological environment, and the statistics of closely spaced measurements allow an assessment of the regional significance of a set of marine values that is comparable to the evaluations of land measurements described earlier.

Data quality. Most oceanographic instruments measure heat flow across two to five depth intervals at each station, which provides a test of the uniformity of heat flow with depth. A lack of uniformity can indicate experimental errors, transient heat flow, or a significant advective component of heat transfer; however, a uniform heat flow with depth is no guarantee of the absence of long-term transients.

Methods to estimate accurately thermal conductivity of the

TABLE 2. REFERENCES TO MARINE HEAT-FLOW MEASUREMENTS IN THE ARCTIC

Region	Year	Number	References*	Comments
Canadian Arctic Archipelago	1964	10	1, 2	From floe ice using an airplane
Amerasian Basin	1964-1973	356	3, 4	Outrigged sensors on corer from T-3
Alpha Ridge	1983	10	15	Lister-type instrument with in situ conductivity
Baffin Bay and Labrador Sea	1970	11	5	Bullard probe, transients in Baffin Basin
Yermak Plateau	1980	16	6	Outrigged sensors on corer
Arctic Mid-Ocean Ridge	1969	8	7	Highly variable environmental disturbance likely
Lomonosov Ridge and vicinity**	1969	23	7	Bullard-type probe content. USSR North Pole Exp.
Lomonosov Ridge	1980	---	16	Measurements from the pack using Bullard probe
Yermak Plateau	1981	4	9	2.5-m Bullard-type probe. Transients at shallow sites
Mendeleev Ridge**	1969	5	7	Values in agreement with USGS results
Norwegian-Greenland Sea	1974	55	10, 11	Outrigged probes on piston corer
Norwegian-Greenland Sea	1974	7	12	Probe penetrations 3.5 to 5 m
Norwegian-Greenland Sea	1968	9	13	Made from ice island, bottom-water transients observed
Norwegian-Greenland Sea	1973	15	8	Piston corer with probes
Norwegian-Greenland Sea	1977	11	14	Piston corer with probes
Norwegian-Greenland Sea	1986	35	17	Multipenetration probe used

*References:
1. Law and others, 1965
2. Paterson and Law, 1966
3. Lachenbruch and Marshall, 1966
4. Lachenbruch and Marshall, 1969
5. Pye and Hyndman, 1972
6. Crane and others, 1982
7. Lubimova and others, 1976
8. Lubimova and others, 1973a
9. Jackson and others, 1984
10. Langseth and Zielinski, 1974
11. Zielinski, 1979
12. Haenel, 1974
13. Lachenbruch and Marshall, 1966
14. Zielinski, 1977
15. Taylor and others, 1986
16. Judge, 1980
17. Crane and Sundvor, 1986 (personal communication)

**Values and locations vary slightly between available publications.

sea-floor sediments are critical in the Arctic Ocean. Figure 2 illustrates that there is large variability with depth and from region to region. To estimate the average conductivity to better than 10 percent in areas such as the Canada Abyssal Plain or the Alpha Rise requires many measurements (five or more per meter) along sediment cores or a comparable density of in situ measurements (Lister, 1970).

Estimates of conductivity based on results at nearby stations or the water content of sediment can lead to serious errors in the Arctic Ocean Basin due to the high variability of conductivity of the solid constituents (Lachenbruch and Marshall, 1966). An accurate estimate using a simple two-component model of the conductivity of an aggregate material requires accurate information on the mineralogy of the solid component (Matsuda and Von Herzen, 1986).

Geological environment. In many areas of the sea floor, particularly in the vicinity of mid-ocean ridges, water is convecting within a relatively permeable oceanic crust at thermally significant rates (Lister, 1972). This circulation causes variations of heat flow at a scale comparable to the thickness of the oceanic crust (Williams and others, 1974). Vertical advection of water through the sea floor can produce large disturbances of the thermal regime of the upper crust in areas of the sea floor with thin or no sediments. In areas of draw down, cold water flowing into the sea floor absorbs much of the geothermal heat so that the heat flow through the sea-floor sediments is only a fraction of that from depth (Hyndman and others, 1976; Langseth and others, 1984). If convection in the crust is hydraulically decoupled from the ocean bottom water by a continuous blanket of impermeable sediments, there may still be a large spatial variation of sea-floor heat flow. However, the mean of a sufficiently large sample over the region should yield a good estimate of the true heat flow from deep in the crust, since all of the heat must flow through the impermeable sedimentary layer.

The problem of assessing the regional significance of heat-flow averages has been addressed by Sclater and others (1976). They emphasize the importance of the thickness and distribution of sediments at and near the observation sites, since a sufficient cover of low-permeability marine sediments will prevent thermally significant advection through the sea floor. Sclater and others (1976) proposed a simple four-part classification of sedimentary environments that range from type "A"—flat or subdued topography with continuous sediment cover of 150 m or more within an 18 km radius of the site—to a type "D", where the sea floor is predominantly exposed igneous basement. A great deal of experience shows that measurements in an "A"-type environment usually yield a reliable estimate of heat flow from depth. Sclater and others (1976) conclude that only "A"-type environments provide a setting for reliable determinations of regional heat flow.

Thermal stability of bottom water. Temporal variations in bottom-water temperature can produce detectable transients in the sea-floor heat flow. Heat-flow values are not reliable unless the temperature variation of bottom water produces negligible subseafloor disturbances, or the variations are accurately known and can be accounted for. The Arctic Ocean deep water is extremely uniform in temperature and salinity below 500 m, and generally provides an excellent thermal environment for geo-

thermal measurements (Taylor and others, 1986). One possible source of deep bottom water variation in Arctic Ocean basins is episodic spillage over the Lomonosov Ridge, which forms a sill separating cold Eurasia Basin water at −0.8 °C from Amerasia Basin water at −0.45 °C below 1,400 m (Aagaard and others, 1979). Shallower elevations on the western flank of the Lomonosov Ridge are vulnerable to small-amplitude temporal variations.

Interesting examples of spills over a sill in the oceans bordering the Arctic Ocean and their effect on sub–sea-floor temperatures are provided by the surveys of Pye and Hyndman (1972), Lachenbruch and Marshall (1968), and Talwani and others (1971).

Statistical tests. Statistical methods have been used extensively in the past to test the significance of averages of marine heat-flow measurements and correlations with other geophysical parameters. By and large, these methods have not been successful primarily because of the high probability of systematic biases in the heat-flow observations and a lack of knowledge about the spatial distribution of heat-flow variability. However, our understanding of heat transfer in the oceanic crust has increased in the past decade and should be the basis for a more useful statistical approach. A group of measurements of good experimental quality—taken in type "A" geological environments and in areas free from transient disturbances—are unlikely to contain systematic biases. Only under these conditions is it valid to use first-order statistics to evaluate the regional significance of means and establish meaningful confidence limits.

RESULTS OF MARINE HEAT-FLOW MEASUREMENTS IN THE OCEAN BASINS OF THE ARCTIC REGION

Heat flow in the Tertiary basins of the Arctic region

The Norwegian-Greenland Sea and the Eurasia Basin formed during the past 60 m.y. at an active spreading center that is the northernmost segment of the Mid-Atlantic ridge. This spreading center is characterized by a half spreading rate of less than one cm/yr, which is among the slowest observed on the global mid-ocean ridge system.

There are now over 150 published marine measurements of heat flow in these basins (see Table 2 and Fig. 3c). The observations in the Norwegian-Greenland Sea are widely scattered. There are three groups of closely spaced measurements: nine measurements in the Denmark Strait (Lachenbruch and Marshall, 1968), eight measurements across the Kolbeinsey Ridge (Lubimova and others, 1973a), and 10 measurements on the Voring Plateau (Zielinski, 1979; Haenel, 1974). All three areas may be subject to environmental disturbances: either transient temperature variations in bottom water or hydrothermal circulation in the crust.

Measurements in the Eurasia Basin are far too sparse to be definitive. There are several on the Yermak Plateau (Crane and others, 1982; Jackson and others, 1984) and, as reported by

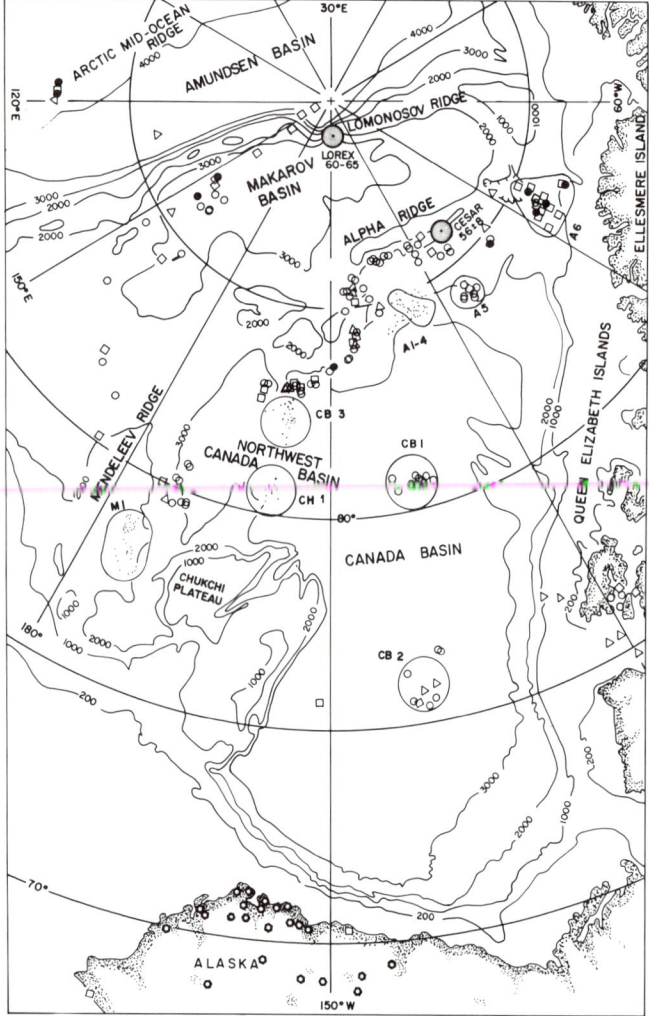

Figure 3a. Map showing locations of heat-flow values in the Amerasia Basin. Values are coded to indicate their range in mW/m²; triangles <40, open circles 40 to 60, squares 60 to 80, and solid circles >80. Hexagons show the location of boreholes instrumented for temperature measurements. Where stations are too close together to code clearly, the locations are shown by small dots; larger scale maps of these regions are presented in Figure 7.

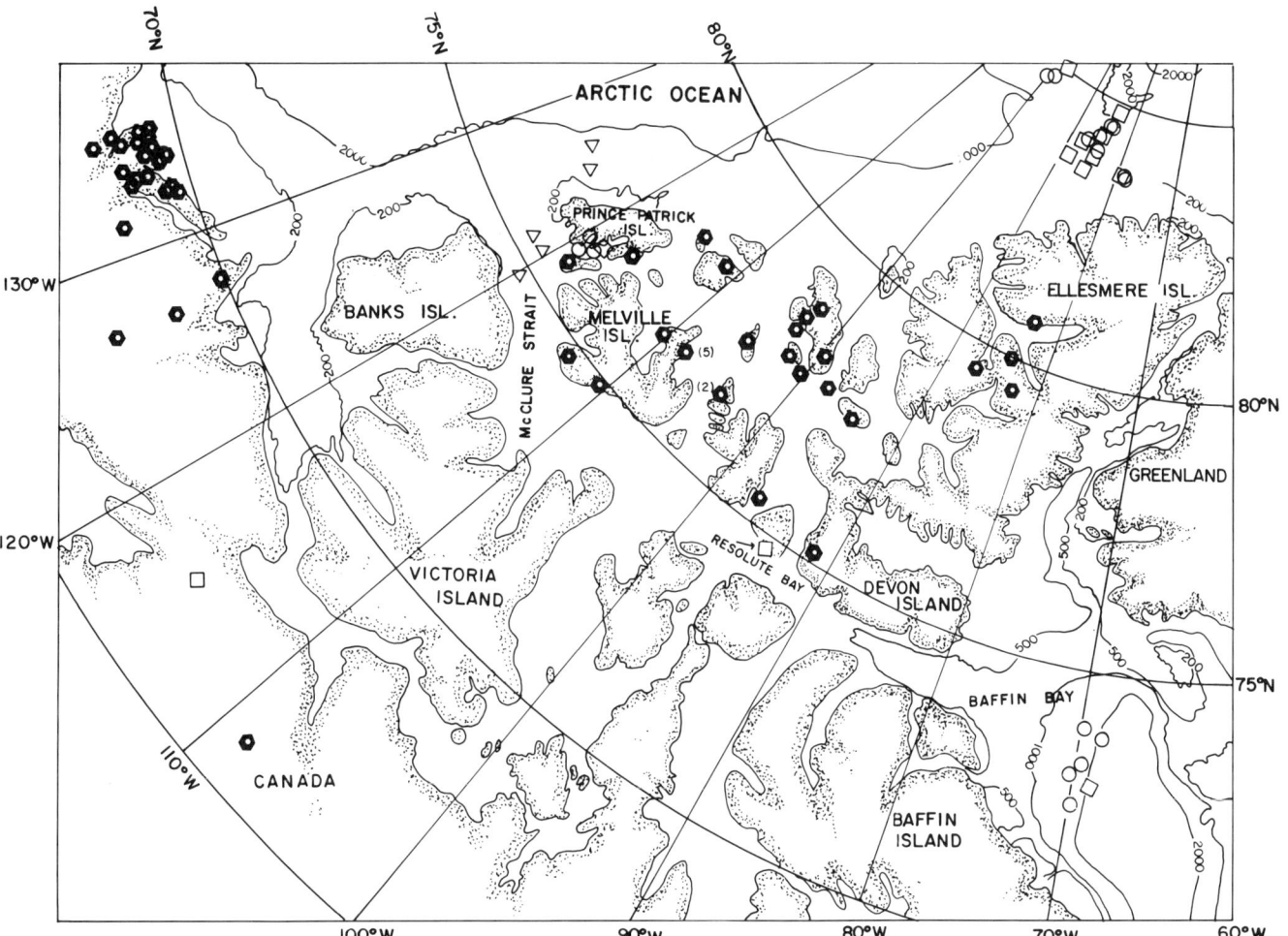

Figure 3b. Map showing the location of heat-flow measurements and instrumented boreholes in the Canadian Arctic Archipelago (coded as in Fig. 3a).

Lubimova and others, (1976), a transect of closely spaced measurements across the Arctic Mid-Ocean Ridge and two isolated values in the Admundsen Basin at the foot of the Lomonosov Ridge.

In Figure 4 the values at stations that are in basins where magnetic lineations can be identified are plotted versus age. The anomaly correlations of Gronlie and Talwani (1978) in the Norwegian-Greenland Sea and the opening history of the Eurasian Basin and Greenland Sea developed by Reksnes and Vagnes (1985) were used to determine age of each station. In Figure 4, we use coded symbols to distinguish between stations with environments favorable for representative observations and those where a disturbance is likely or data to make an assessment is lacking (see Langseth and Zielinski, 1974). The values are compared with curves of predicted heat flow versus age based on two commonly quoted estimators (Parsons and Sclater, 1977; Davis and Lister, 1977).

With the exception of three anomalous measurements, the reliable measurements are in reasonable agreement with the curves for ages greater than 20 Ma. For oceanic lithosphere less than 20 Ma, most values fall 10 to 20 percent below the predicted heat flow. This is probably due to the loss of significant amounts of geothermal heat by pore-water movement through the sea floor. If we disregard values over crust younger than 20 Ma, the variations of heat flow in the Tertiary oceanic basins of the Arctic region are in accord with the estimators derived empirically from data in the world oceans fitted to simple models of the thermal evolution of the lithosphere by upward conductive cooling. Earlier comparisons of Norwegian-Greenland Sea data with data from the Pacific Ocean (see, e.g., Langseth and Zielinski, 1974) had indicated that the ocean basins near Iceland may have anomalously high heat loss, but this new analysis indicates that the heat flow to age relation in the Tertiary basins north of 60° and the parameters that control it can not be distinguished from that in other mid-ocean ridges. It is interesting to note that the values measured in the Norway Basin, where active spreading is believed to have stopped by 25 Ma (Talwani and Eldholm, 1977), appear to fit the general thermal evolution reasonably well.

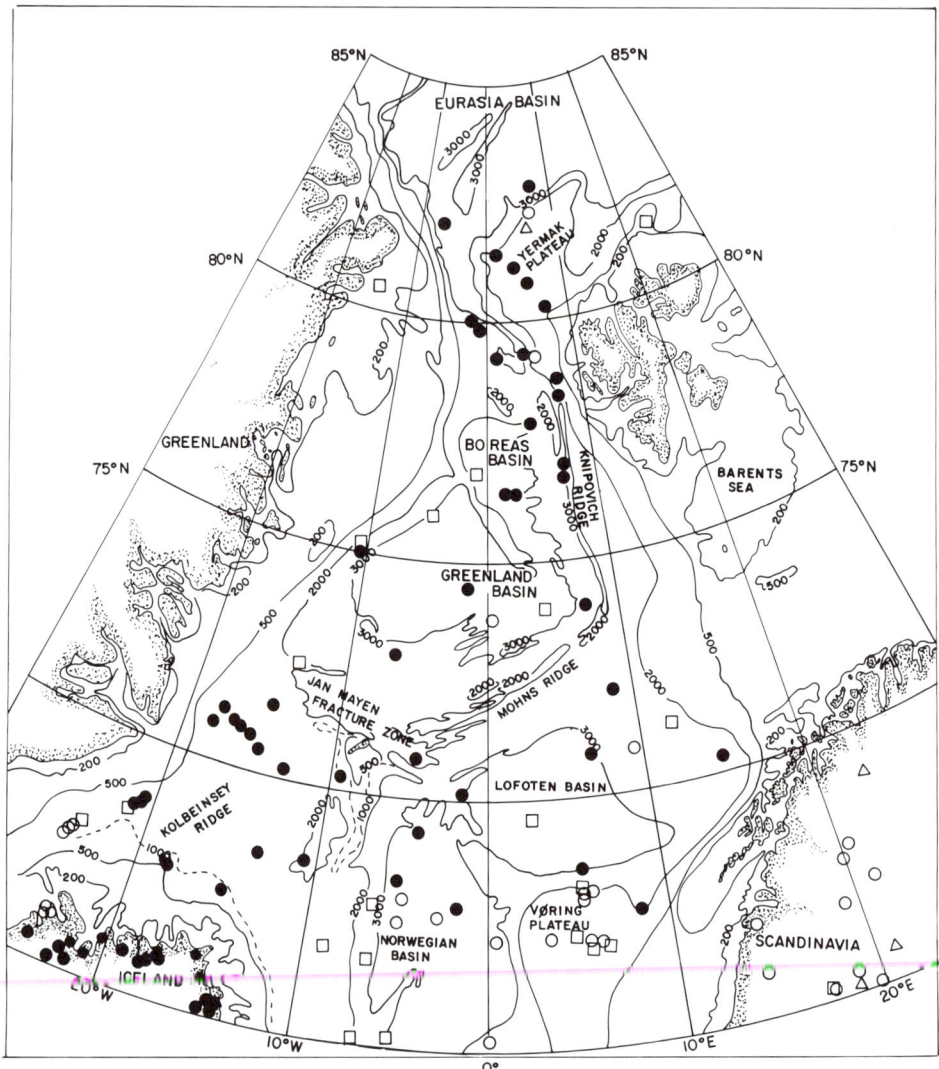

Figure 3c. Map showing the locations of published heat-flow stations in the Norwegian-Greenland Sea. Values are coded as in Figure 3a.

A brief summary of the physiography and current ideas about the evolution of the Arctic Ocean basins

The Arctic Ocean is geographically divided into two major basins: the Eurasia and Amerasia. They are separated by the Lomonosov Ridge, which is a remarkably straight aseismic ridge that transects the deep Arctic Ocean and passes very near the north pole. The two basins are strongly differentiated in terms of their origin and geology. A clear pattern of magnetic anomaly lineations indicates that the Eurasia Basin is a Tertiary oceanic basin that opened contemporaneously with the Norwegian-Greenland Sea at a currently active spreading center, the Arctic Mid-Ocean Ridge.

The origin of the Amerasia Basin is not well understood. Sparse geological and geophysical data suggest that the deep oceanic basins were formed during the Mesozoic. Estimates of the age of the lithosphere underlying the Amerasia Basin vary from Middle Jurassic to Early Cretaceous (Taylor and others, 1981) to Late Cretaceous (Lawver and others, 1981). An analysis reported by Lawver and Baggeroer (1983) suggested that the depth to basement and the heat flow in the Canada Basin are consistent with a middle to Late Cretaceous age (90 to 125 Ma). We will show in the discussion section that age estimates based on heat flow and depth to basement in thickly sedimented basins such as the Canada Basin are strongly dependent on the model of thermal evolution used in the analysis.

Among the most enigmatic features of the Amerasia Basin is the Alpha/Mendeleev Ridge complex. A lack of coherent magnetic lineations confounds a precise determination of the crustal age. The heat flow of about 50 mW/m^2 (Lachenbruch and Marshall, 1969), and the absence of clear Tertiary magnetic anomaly patterns indicate a Mesozoic age for these features perhaps con-

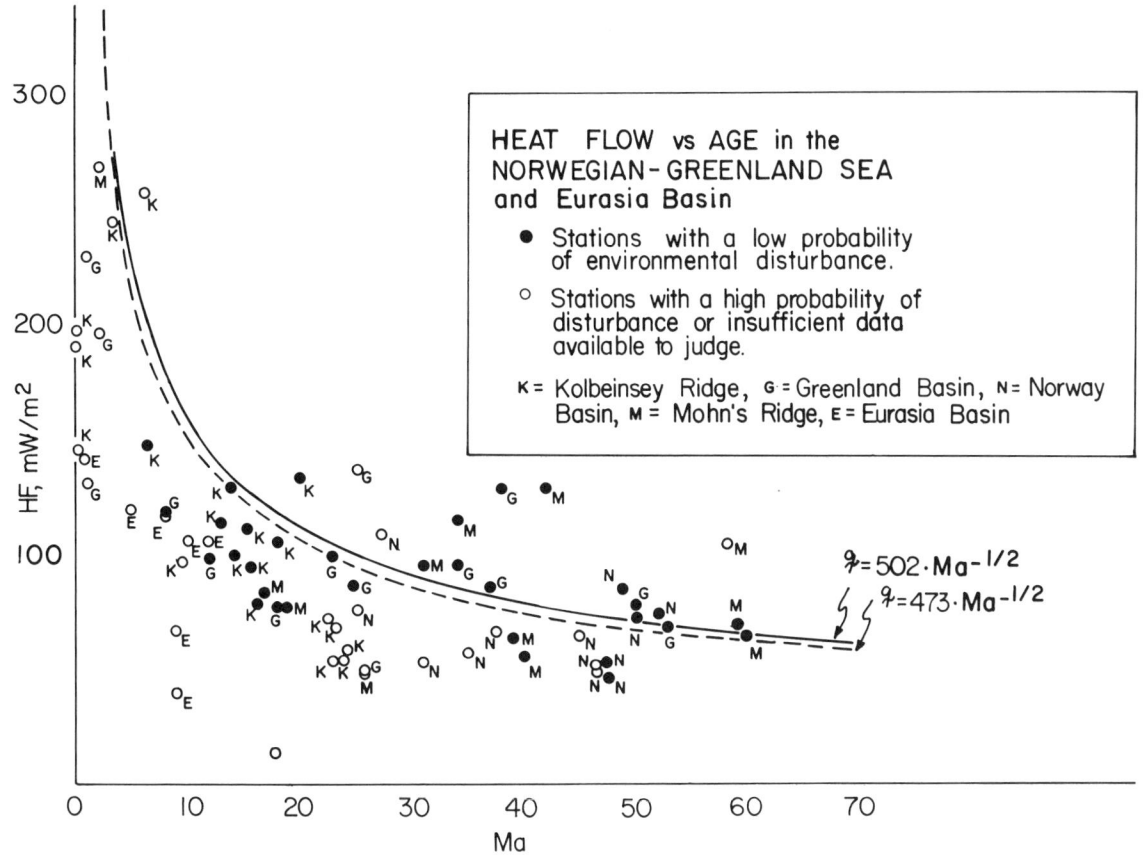

Figure 4. Sea-floor heat flow in the Norwegian-Greenland Sea plotted versus age of the crust. Each point is coded to indicate whether the geological environment is favorable or poor for a representative heat-flow measurement, and labelled to indicate the ridge province or basin in which the measurement was made. The curves represent two commonly used estimators of heat flow versus age over oceanic lithosphere for ages younger than 80 Ma.

temporaneous with the formation of the Canada Basin. More recently, cores containing Late Cretaceous material have been taken from the Alpha Ridge (Taylor and others, 1986). The present elevation of the ridge complex, up to 1,500 m in places, requires that there be a thickened low-density crust below the ridge complex since it is in approximate isostatic equilibrium and has low heat flow. Whether this thickened crust is oceanic, as existing data suggest (Hunkins, 1961), or continental is key to understanding its origin.

Lachenbruch and Marshall (1966) reported a large contrast in heat flow at the boundary between the Alpha Ridge and the Northwest Canada Basin. The heat flow in the Northwest Canada Basin is relatively high and uniform, whereas that in the adjoining ridge flank is relatively low and variable. In their analysis, Lachenbruch and Marshall show that this contrast can be explained if a 15-km-thick crust of relatively low conductivity underlies the Alpha Ridge flank.

Heat flow in the Amerasia Basin

The geological and hydrographic conditions in much of the Amerasia Basin are ideal for geothermal observations. The sedimentary cover is thick and pervasive, and the sea-floor temperature remains stable over long periods of time. The measurements of heat flow made from the ice island T-3 were taken with careful attention to experimental accuracy, and in several areas of the basin the drift pattern of T-3 allowed numerous measurements to be made in a relatively small area, which allows a statistical assessment of local averages and variability between regions. The closely spaced heat-flow measurements made during the CESAR project permit a similar assessment. Regions of the Amerasia Basin where there are closely spaced measurements are indicated on Figure 3a and Plate 2. The statistics of these regions are given in Table 3 and in Figure 5 and 6 in the form of histograms. Larger scale maps showing the station locations in these regions are presented in Figure 7a through c. We have excluded from the statistics in Table 3 stations that have only one interval of gradient measurement or a large difference in gradient between two or more intervals at the same station.

Thirty measurements in the Northwest Canada Basin (area CB3 on Table 3) show very low scatter; the standard deviation from the mean of 67.2 is only 3. The distribution of values in this group is normal, as shown in Figure 5; thus, the mean heat flow

TABLE 3. STATISTICS OF CLOSELY SPACED GROUPS OF HEAT-FLOW VALUES IN THE AMERASIA BASIN*

Region	Mean Latitude North	Mean Longitude West	No.	Mean	Standard Deviation	95% Confidence Limits
Canada Basin						
CB1	80°36'	137°16'	15	55.8	3.0	±1.5
CB2	75°30'	140°00'	5	57.3	5.7	±5.0
CB3	82°22'	157°40'	30	67.2	3.0	±1.0
Chukchi Cap						
CH1	80°31'	158°42'	9	56.7	3.6	±2.4
Mendeleev Ridge						
M1	78°39'	176°01'	21	49.6	3.3	±1.9
Alpha Ridge						
A1	84°57'	130°20'	14	48.0	7.4	±5.0
A2	84°48'	130°53'	19	45.7	6.6	±3.5
A3	84°31'	128°30'	11	49.4	6.7	±4.5
A4	84°30'	125°55'	13	52.7	4.0	±2.7
A1-A4	84°45'	129°55'	57	48.6	6.5	±2.0
A5	84°15'	112°17'	17	54.4	8.5	±5.0
A6	84°07'	85°00'	14	72.5	13.7	±9.0
CESAR**	85°50'	108°40'	10	56.0	6.5	±5.0

*See Figure 3a for area locations.
**Statistics are for values uncorrected for topography and using the conductivity measured on nearby cores (Taylor and others, 1986).

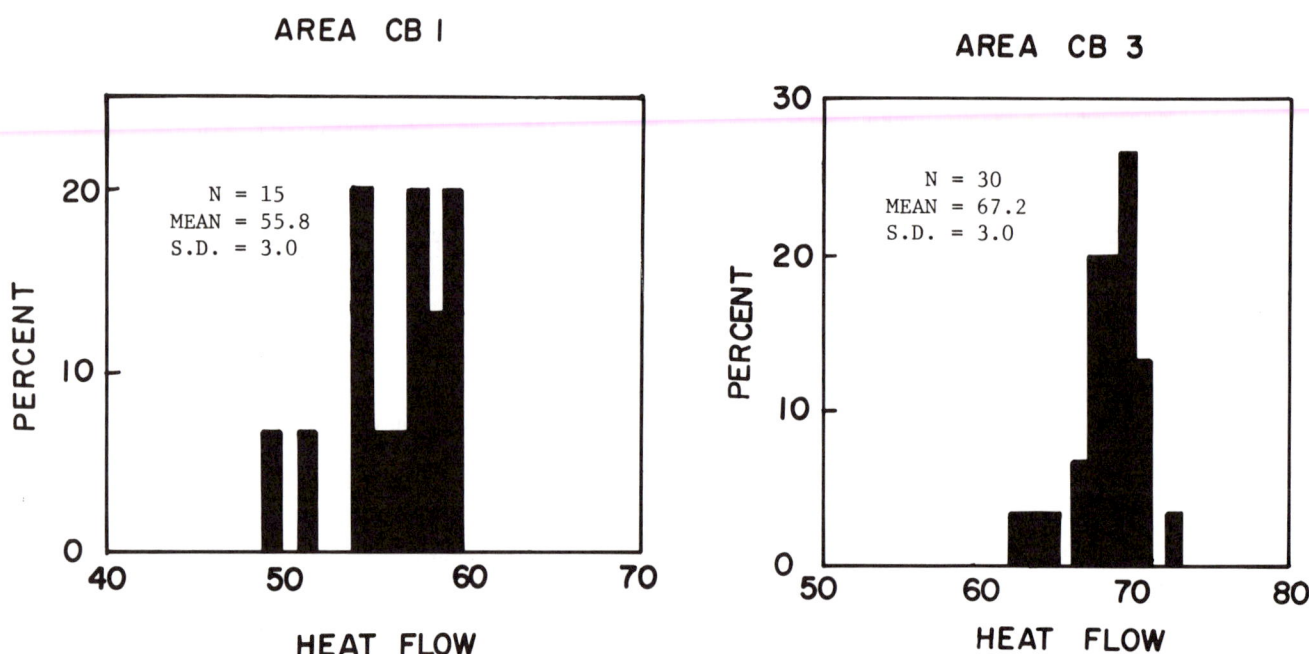

Figure 5. Histograms of heat-flow values in two areas of the Canada Basin; see Table 3. Notice the change in heat-flow scale between the two diagrams.

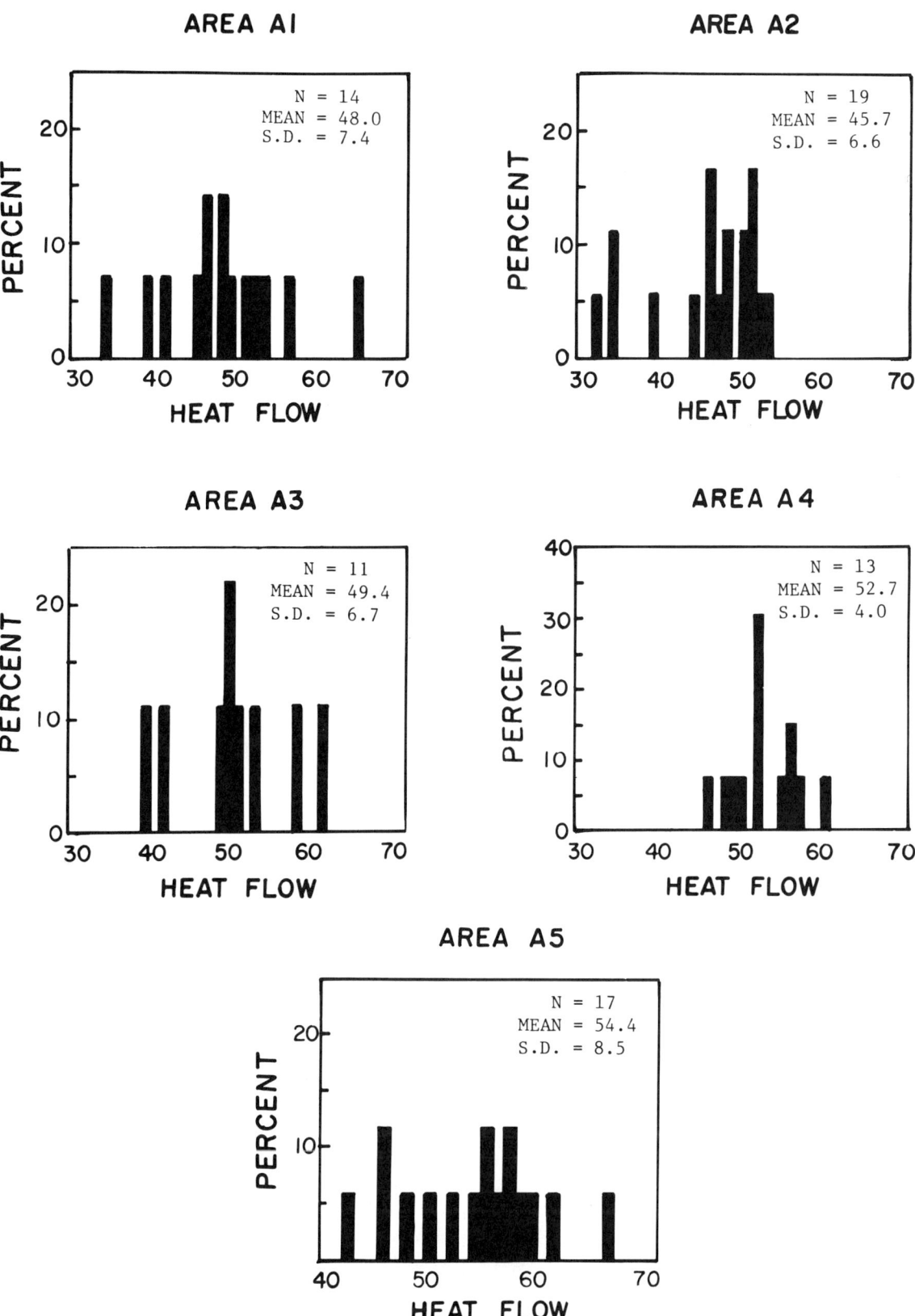

Figure 6. Five histograms of heat-flow values from areas on the southern flank of the Alpha Ridge. See Figures 3a and 7c and Table 3.

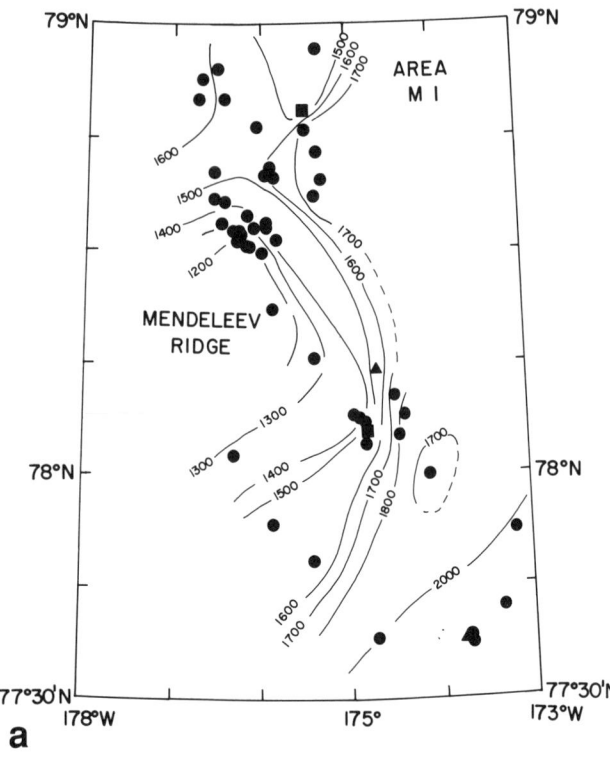

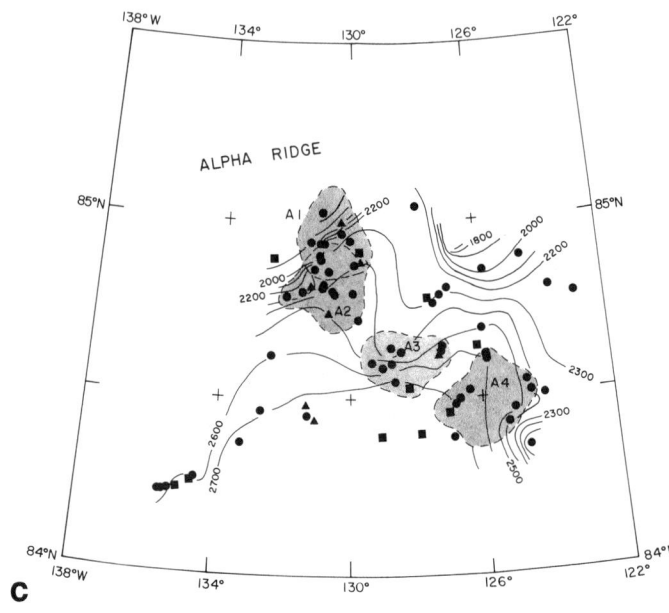

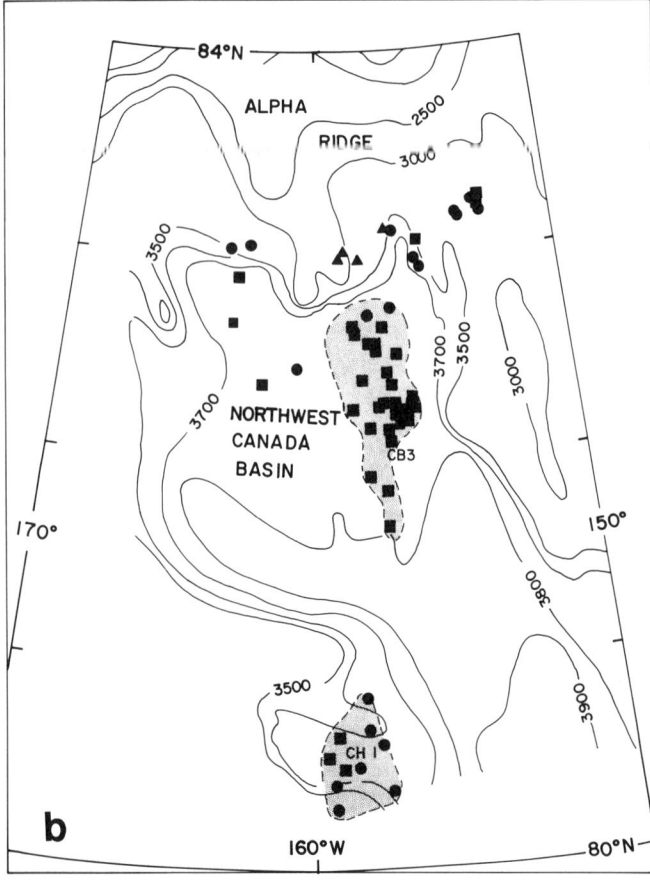

Figure 7. Maps showing the locations of heat-flow stations in the Amerasia Basin: a, Area M1 in Mendeleev Ridge; b, Areas CH1, and CB3 in Northwest Canada Basin; and c, areas A1 to A4 on the Alpha Ridge.

in this basin is 67.2 (±1.0) at the 95 percent confidence level. This small basin is flat-floored and covered by a thick layer of mainly hemipelagic sediments. The likelihood of variability of heat flow due to environmental disturbances is virtually nil, and thus this group of measurements provides an empirical estimate of the random measurement errors of good-quality observations taken from T-3.

A group of 15 good-quality measurements in the north-central part of the Canada Basin (CB1) and a group of 5 in the southern part (CB2) have means of 55.8 (±1.5) and 57.3 (±5.0). (The limits given in parentheses are at the 95 percent confidence level.) Since these measurements were taken in a thickly sedimented abyssal plain, the environmental contribution to the scatter is probably small. A group of stations on the north flank of the Chukchi Rise (CH1) has a similar mean of 56.7 (± 2.4). The CH1 group of stations lies just south of the region CB3, where heat flow is anomalously high compared to the other parts of the Canada Basin that were sampled.

The measurements in the Mendeleev and Central Alpha ridges have a significantly lower average than the basins. Twenty-one measurements on the eastern flank of the Mendeleev Ridge (M1) yield a mean of 49.6 (±1.9). These measurements are in an area where the seismic reflection records show the sea floor to be relatively smooth and the sedimentary cover thick and nearly continuous. From the data available, it appears that the likelihood of environmental disturbance is small.

This does not appear to be the case for a large group of 57 closely spaced measurements on the western flank of the Alpha Ridge (area A1–A4; and see Fig. 7c). The average of this group is

48.6 with a standard deviation of 6.5. The mean is not significantly different from that of the Mendeleev Ridge, but the variance is much higher. The histograms of five subdivisions of the region A1 through A5 in Figure 6, show remarkably flat and nonnormal distributions. This can be ascribed to a significant contribution to the variance by environmental factors. Hall (1970) reported hummocky terrain in this area of the Alpha Ridge. The sea floor has small-scale relief up to 55 m in height and up to a kilometer in wavelength. This topography could contribute significant scatter to randomly positioned heat-flow measurements, and the distribution of values will be much flatter than a normal distribution.

This small-scale topography will also cause a slight reduction in the mean of randomly placed measurements due to the increase in surface area through which the heat can escape (Lachenbruch and Marshall, 1966). This effect could cause a local reduction of 2 to 5 percent (1 to 3 mW/m^2). In area A4 the sea-floor topography has much lower relief, and the standard deviation is lower and the average is higher.

Most of the area of the Mendeleev and Central Alpha ridges appears to be characterized by mean heat-flow values between 49 and 51, but values show a significant increase in the eastern part of the Alpha Ridge adjacent to the Ellesmere Island shelf (areas A5, CESAR, and A6). Some of these stations showed a large difference in gradient between the intervals of measurement, possibly due to recent changes in bottom-water temperature. The observations in this area of the ridge were taken at relatively shallow depths (less than 1,700 m) and thus are more vulnerable to transient disturbances of bottom water. The variance of this group of stations is also large, further indicating the likelihood of environmental disturbances.

In summary, the density and quality of measurements in the Amerasia Basin, combined with a favorable hydrographic and geological environment, allow the determination of regionally significant means of groups of heat-flow values in the basin. These results show: (1) the heat flow in the main part of the Canada Basin is 56 ($\pm$1.5), and (2) over much of their length the Mendeleev and Alpha ridges have a mean heat flow of 49 ($\pm$3), which is significantly less than the basin. A small abyssal plain in the Northwest Canada Basin is characterized by anomalously high heat flow, nearly 20 percent higher than the Canada Basin to the southeast. Values show a tendency toward higher heat flow in an easterly direction along the Alpha Ridge. At the eastern terminus of the ridge, near its intersection with the Ellesmere margin, heat-flow values are anomalously high with a mean of 14 values of 72.5, but there are indications that this area of the ocean floor may be disturbed by recent changes in bottom water temperature.

Heat flow estimates from gas hydrate layers

Pressure and temperature conditions in deep-sea sediments are suitable for the formation of gas hydrates (Stoll and others, 1971), and evidence for them has been widely found, especially in continental margin areas.

The boundary between gas hydrate and gas dissolved in water is temperature and pressure dependent. The phase boundary on a P-T diagram has been presented by several authors (see, e.g., Clayppool and Kaplan, 1974). The pressure at the bottom simulating reflector (BSR) can be estimated from the depth and density of sediment; therefore, the P-T phase diagram can be used to estimate the temperature of the hydrate layer. The temperature combined with the depth gives an estimate of the temperature gradient in the upper few hundred meters of sediment. Yamano and others (1982) have used the BSR in the Nankai Trough to estimate the heat-flow level and variation over this feature.

There is a well-developed BSR in seismic sections made on the continental margin of the Beaufort Sea (Eittreim and Grantz, 1979). MacLeod (1982) has shown that the depth to the BSR in these sections is best explained by a temperature gradient of 50 $\pm$5 mK/m^{-1}. To estimate the heat flow from this gradient requires knowledge of the thermal conductivity. No direct data are available, but an estimate can be made using empirical relations of velocity, V_p, and thermal conductivity, k, versus porosity, P.

Eittreim and Grantz (1979) report velocities that range from 1.6 to 2.2 km/sec, for sediments overlying the BSR, but values between 1.7 and 1.9 km/sec are most prevalent, and the mean is 1.8 km/sec. For velocities less than 2 km/sec, which correspond to porosities greater than 0.5, the slope of empirical fits of experimental data shows a small dependence of V_p on porosity with considerable scatter around the best fitting line, which leads to large uncertainties. Using the best-fitting curves published by Horai (1981), a velocity of 1.8 km/sec corresponds to a porosity of 0.58 $\pm$ 0.1, which in turn predicts a conductivity for the sediment of 1.2 $\pm$ 0.2 W/m-°C.

Combining this estimate of conductivity with MacLeod's estimate of gradient we obtain a heat flow of 60 $\pm$ 15 mW/m^2. The uncertainty limits are large, but the most likely value is in reasonable agreement with values measured in the Southern Canada Basin, which average 56 mW/m^2 (Lachenbruch and Marshall, 1969; and this paper), and continental measurements on the perimeter of the Arctic Ocean Basin.

Acoustic reflectors associated with gas hydrates are likely to be found over other areas of the Arctic Ocean Basin deeper than 500 m. If more accurate determinations of the thermal conductivity were available, then gas hydrates could be used to estimate heat flow over a significant part of the continental margins of the Arctic. Direct measurements of heat flow using oceanographic instruments in the same area would provide an important calibration of the estimates based on the BSR. Mapping the BSR over a region provides an indication of the lateral variation of heat flow at a scale unobtainable by conventional techniques.

HEAT FLOW AND AGE OF PROVINCES IN THE AMERASIA BASIN

Current geological evidence indicates that the floor of the Amerasia Basin formed during the Mesozoic. Debate continues as to whether the lithosphere was emplaced in mid-Mesozoic

(Sweeney and others, 1978; Taylor and others, 1981) or late Mesozoic (Lawver and Baggeroer, 1982). Lawver and Baggeroer made an estimate of the age of the central Canada Basin based on the heat flow of 56 mW/m^2 (Lachenbruch and Marshall, 1969) and the elevation of oceanic basement, about 5,600 m below sea level, after the loading by sediments has been taken into account. They obtained age ranges from 80 to 110 Ma from heat flow and 90 to 125 Ma from basement depth. These estimates included corrections of the observed sea-floor heat flow for the accumulation and compaction of sediments, and for the contribution to the sea-floor heat flow by radiogenic heat in the sediment. The age estimate was obtained by comparing the corrected heat-flow value with the empirical curves of Parsons and Sclater (1977).

The thickness of the sediment in the Canada Basin is important to the analysis. Lawver and Baggeroer (1982) used a sediment thickness of about 4.3 km, based on the interpretation of seismic refraction experiments in the southern part of the Canada Basin reported by Mair and Lyons (1981) and Baggeroer and Falconer (1982). This estimate of thickness depends on interpreting a refracting layer with a velocity between 4.3 and 4.9 km/sec as oceanic basement. Grantz (personal communication, 1984) has suggested that the 4.5 km/s layer, which is about 4 km thick, is instead a consolidated sedimentary layer, which would make the sediments that fill the southeastern part of the Canada Basin 6 to 8 km thick. We shall consider the implications of each of these assumptions.

To analyze the relation between heat flow and age in a region like the Amerasia Basin where there are regionally significant heat-flow determinations, we use a one-dimensional model that includes sedimentation effects in a lithosphere cooling from an initially uniform temperature. The lithosphere is modeled as a plate of finite thickness by holding the temperature at the base of the lithosphere constant at the initial temperature (Parsons and Sclater, 1977). We assume the sediment accumulates on the cooling lithosphere at a uniform rate and that heat is generated in the sediment by radioactivity. The model we use is one described by Hutchison (1985) and includes the thermal effects of compaction of the sediment. The porosity of the sediment is assumed to decrease exponentially with depth according to the expression $P = P_0 \exp(-Z/\lambda)$, where P_0 is the porosity at the sea floor, Z is depth below the sea floor, and λ is the 1/e folding depth. Temperatures and heat flow are calculated using a finite difference scheme that divides the lithosphere into 40 discrete layers that increase in thickness geometrically with depth. The temperatures after each time step are solved implicitly so that solutions are always stable. However, for practical time steps (1 m.y.), errors in the first several million years are a few percent, decreasing to below 1 percent for times greater than 10 m.y.

In Figure 8 we show some typical heat flow versus age curves for six different sedimentation rates. These curves show that for sedimentation rates greater than 100 m/m.y. the predicted sea-floor heat flow shows very little variation for times greater than 100 m.y., because the contribution of radiogenic heat compensates for the effects of continued cooling and sedimentation. Thus, for thickly sedimented Mesozoic basins, estimates of age based on heat flow are entirely dependent on models of sedimentation and thermal parameters assumed for sediment and the cooling lithosphere.

For all of our model calculations we have used the parameters assumed by Parsons and Sclater (1977). This model is widely quoted and has been shown to fit elevation versus age data of the Pacific Plate out to 80 Ma reasonably well. The physical properties and radioactive heat production of the sediment are averages of measurements made on cores taken simultaneously with the T-3 heat-flow stations. Assumed values are given in the legends of Figure 9, where the results are presented in terms of the two measurable parameters; heat flow versus sediment thickness. This presentation shows clearly how the deposition rates and radiogenic heat production affect the heat flow versus age evolution. Curves for six different sedimentation rates are shown as solid lines. The dashed curves connect points of equal time after cooling started. Their intersection with the ordinate axis gives heat flow as a function of time for zero sedimentation rate. The isochrons show that for the first 30 m.y. the heat flow decreases with increasing sediment thickness. Between 40 and 60 m.y. the opposing effect of radiogenic heat production in the thickening sediments offsets the cooling so that the heat flow at a given age in this range is almost insensitive to sediment thickness. After 70 m.y. radioactive heat production begins to dominate, and for a given age the heat flow increases linearly with sediment thickness.

The values of heat flow and sediment thickness for five regions in the Amerasia Basin are superimposed on two graphs. In Figure 9a the thickness of the lithosphere (L) is assumed to be 90 km, and in Figure 9b L = 125 km. The height of each stippled rectangle represents the 95 percent confidence limit for the heat-flow mean, and the width represents the uncertainty in sediment thickness. The thickness of sediment in the Arctic Ocean basins is poorly known due to the paucity of seismic data; thus, we have indicated large uncertainties for these estimates.

The model ages for five provinces in which the heat flow is well determined can be read directly from the plots. These age estimates are listed in Table 4. For heat-flow values less than 60 mW/m^2 the model with L = 90 km yields higher age estimates, but the crowding of isochrons results in larger uncertainty bounds. In addition to the Arctic data, we show the average heat flow, sediment thickness, and ages for four Mesozoic sites in the western Atlantic, where the regional heat flow has been measured with the best attainable accuracy in favorable environments (Davis and others, 1984) and ages are well constrained by magnetic lineations. The thinner lithosphere model is in better agreement with the Atlantic results.

The model age for the Canada Basin, assuming L = 90 km and a sediment thickness of about 6.5 km, is 90 to 110 Ma. A 125-km lithosphere and a sedimentary thickness of 4.5 km yield an estimate of 78 to 92 Ma. The latter agrees well with that proposed by Lawver and Baggeroer (1982), who used the same data and a similar model for their estimates. If we use the greater sediment thickness proposed by Grantz (personal communica-

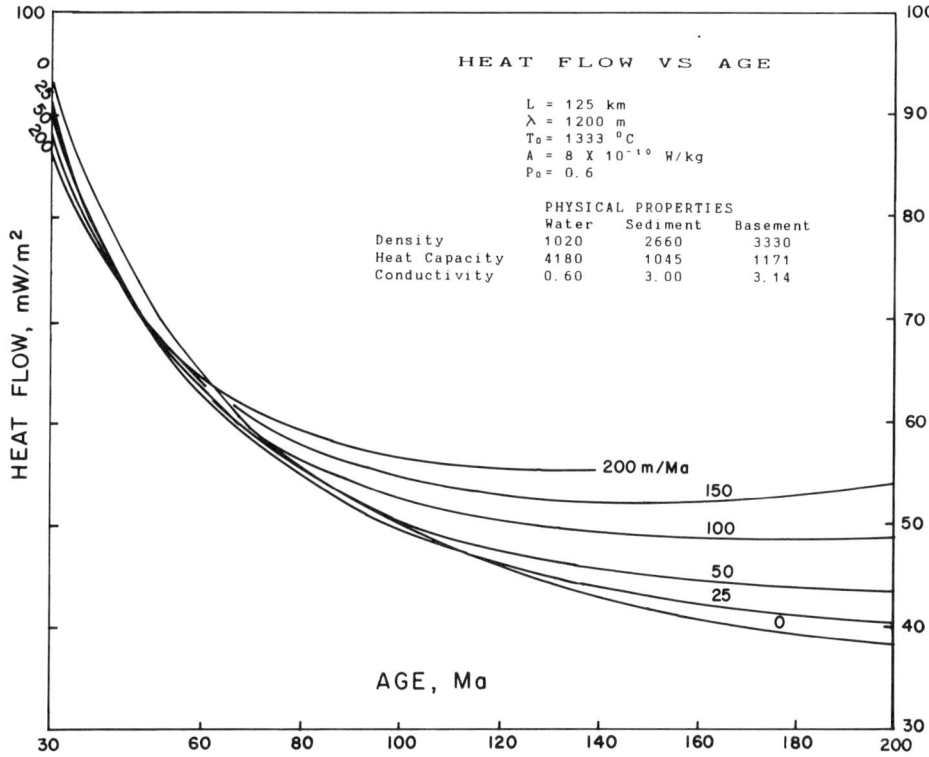

Figure 8. The predicted heat flow for a cooling lithosphere on which sediment is accumulating at a uniform rate. The curves are based on a model that accounts for the compaction of sediment with depth of burial and radioactive heat production in the sediment (Hutchison, 1985). Curves are shown for six different sedimentation rates. Parameters of the model are given in the table on the figure with density in kg/m^3, heat capacity as J/kg–°C, and thermal conductivity as W/m–°C. L is the thickness of the lithosphere; T_o is the initial temperature of the lithosphere, 1,333°C; λ is 1/e folding depth of the porosity versus depth function, A is heat production in the solid component of the sediment, 8×10^{-10} W/kg; and 6×10^{-12} W/kg in the lithosphere; P_o is the porosity of sediment at the sea floor.

TABLE 4. MODEL AGES OF FIVE PROVINCES IN THE AMERASIA BASIN BASED ON HEAT FLOW AND SEDIMENT THICKNESS OBSERVATIONS

Region	Sediment Thickness (km)	Age for Lithospheric Thickness of:	
		125 km	90 km
Central Canada Basin (CB1)	4-5	78-92	80-120
Central Canada Basin (CB1)	5.5-6.5	82-95	90-110
Southern Canada Basin (CB2)	6-7	70-120	>90
Central Alpha and Mendeleev Ridge (A1-A4, M1)	1-2	80-96	90-120
Eastern Alpha Ridge (A6)	1-2	37-60	37-60
Northwest Canada Basin (CB3)	>2	51-55	51-55

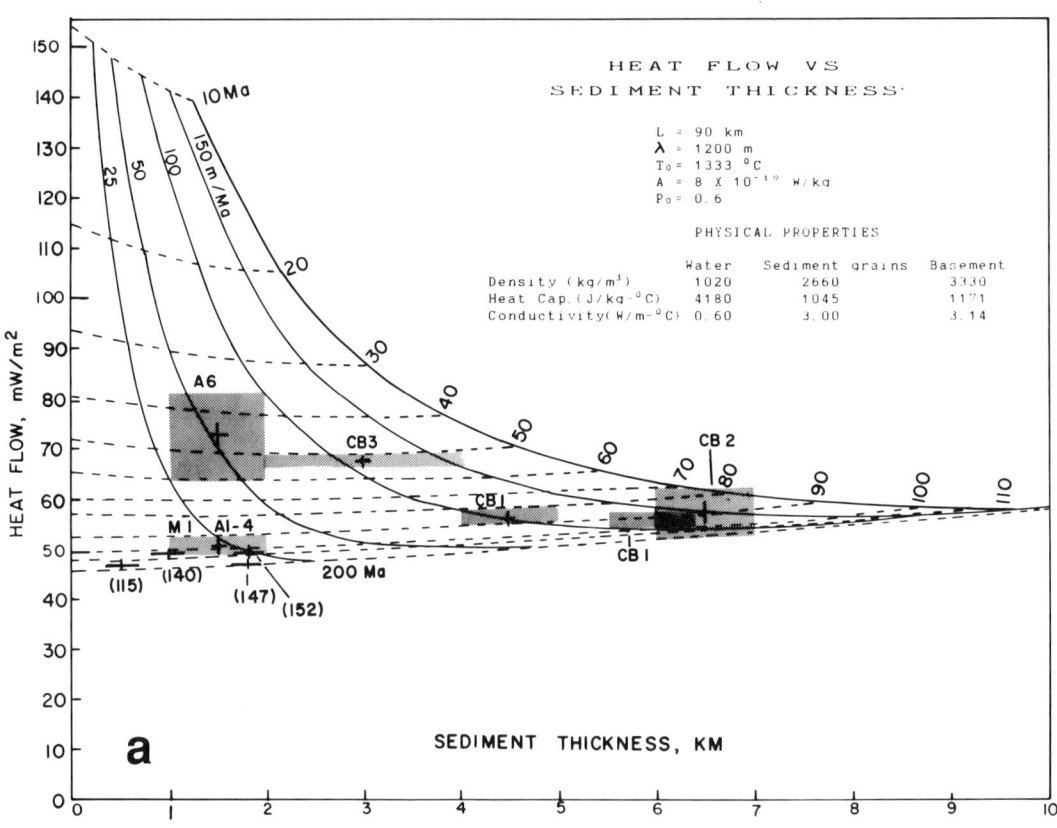

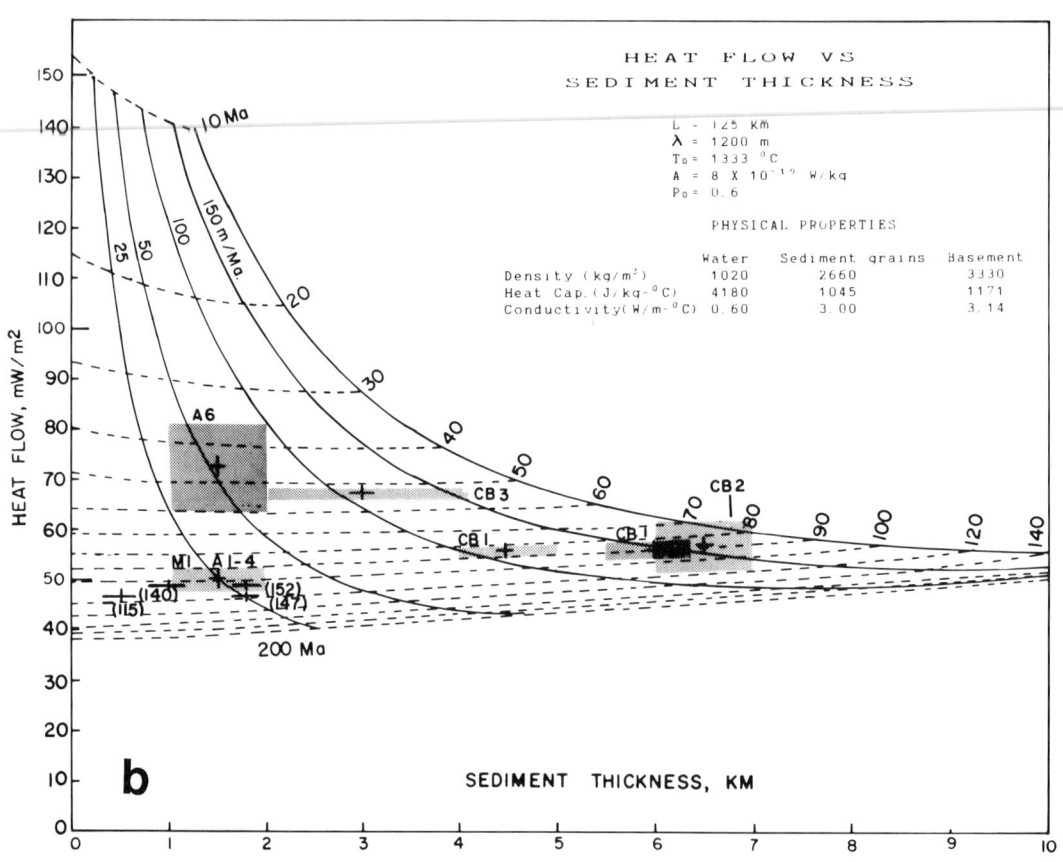

tion, 1984), Figure 9 shows that estimates of age increase only slightly.

The mean heat flow in the Mendeleev Ridge (M1) and central Alpha Ridge (A1–A4) of 49 ± 2 and sediment thickness of 1.5 km predict an age of 80 to 120 Ma (Table 4). The model age is not significantly different from that of the Canada Basin. A minimum age of Cretaceous is supported by cores containing Cretaceous material taken from the Alpha Ridge during the T-3 program (Clark, 1974) and from the CESAR project (Taylor and others, 1986). This age suggests that the lithosphere underlying the central and eastern segments of the Alpha Ridge complex may have been formed at approximately the same time as that below the Canada Basin. According to Figure 9, the difference in heat flow between the ridge and the Canada Basin can be explained by the radioactive heat production in the thick sediments of the Canada Abyssal Plain.

The greater thickness of basaltic crust below the Alpha Ridge (DeLaurier, 1978; Lachenbruch and Marshall, 1966), combined with evidence that the age of the ridge is comparable to the Canada Basin, support the hypothesis that the Alpha/Mendeleev Ridge was formed as an aseismic ridge by anomalously high magma generation at a "hot spot" on the spreading center that formed the Amerasia Basin (Forsyth and others, 1986) in a manner analogous to the formation of the Faroe Island–Greenland Ridge at the Iceland "hot spot."

The anomalously high heat flow in the Northwest Canada Basin (CB3) of 67 ± 1 is consistent with an age between 50 and 55 Ma. This mean heat flow is well determined; it would be difficult to argue for a greater age without invoking some as yet unknown mechanism for generating the extra heat. Heat-flow measurements on the southern end of the Alpha Ridge (A6) near the Ellesmere Island margin also yielded an anomalously high mean (72 ± 9). The 95 percent confidence limits for this mean are large, but the range of predicted ages bracket the age of the Northwest Canada Basin. These results, combined with higher values observed in the Makarov Basin (Lubimova and others, 1973b), suggest that there was an extensional tectonic event in the northwestern Amerasia Basin in the early Paleogene.

The major conclusions that result from our effort to model the thermal evolution of a cooling lithosphere upon which sediment is rapidly accumulating are as follows:

Figure 9. Heat flow versus sediment thickness for a conductively cooling lithosphere on which sediment is accumulating at a uniform rate (solid curves). Dashed curves show equal time after the lithosphere was emplaced and deposition began. Compaction of the sediment with depth and the effects of radiogenic heat in the sediment are taken into account in the model. Parameters of the models are given in the legend and defined in the caption for Figure 8. The stippled rectangles show data from five well-sampled provinces of the Amerasia Basin (Fig. 3a). The bold crosses are data from four sites in the northwestern Atlantic (Davis and others, 1984). The numbers in parentheses are ages of the crust in the Atlantic based on magnetic lineations. (a) Assumes lithosphere is 90 km thick, (b) assumes lithosphere is 125 km thick.

1. Age estimates from heat flow in Mesozoic basins with thick sediment accumulations are almost completely dependent on accuracy of models of the sedimentation effects and of lithospheric cooling.

2. The present-day heat flow indicates that the lithospheres underlying the central and eastern segments of the Alpha/Mendeleev Ridge and central Canada Basin were formed at approximately the same time. The model ages of these provinces, which form a major part of the Amerasia Basin, are between 90 and 120 Ma. The heat-flow values could be consistent with greater ages if one assumes a lithosphere thinner than 90 km.

3. Anomalously high heat flow compared to other regions of the Amerasia Basin are found in the Northwest Canada Basin, the western segment of the Alpha Ridge, and possibly the Makarov Basin, indicating that younger lithosphere underlies these regions, which may have experienced extensional tectonics during the early Paleogene.

FINAL REMARKS

In this review we have concentrated on the marine heat-flow measurements of the Arctic region, primarily because they are more numerous and because the data in the Amerasia Basin provides critical constraints on the tectonic evolution of this basin (which is still the subject of considerable debate). In the next decade we expect the number of regionally significant land heat-flow determinations to increase substantially as data from boreholes now under observation are interpreted and reported.

In addition to the determination of regionally significant heat flow, there are other important phenomena in the subsurface thermal regime of the Arctic region to which the long-term borehole observations will contribute; these include refining the evidence for recent climatic warming, the history of shoreline transgression, establishment of arctic lakes, and the fate of the permafrost beneath the drowned shelf.

We have emphasized the importance of critically examining the marine measurements in terms of their regional significance. In some areas, temperature variations in bottom water and the hydrogeology of the shallow crust preclude the possibility of sea-floor heat flow truly reflecting the thermal regime deep in the crust. However, measurements in such areas may be relevant to the history of bottom-water temperatures, or to understanding heat-transfer mechanisms in the shallow crust, which are scientifically important in their own right. They also provide increased understanding of the submarine hydrothermal regime and a basis for more confident determination of regionally significant measurements.

In the Amerasia Basin, closely spaced groups of carefully made sea-floor measurements in thermally favorable environments provide averages that we believe are regionally significant and set important constraints on the age of the Canada Basin and the Alpha Ridge complex.

REFERENCES CITED

Aagaard, K., and 6 others, 1979, The Arctic Ocean heat budget: Steering Committee for Oceanographic Research (SCOR) Working Group 58, Report 52, 98 p.

Baggeroer, A. B., and Falconer, R., 1982, Array refraction profiles and crustal models of the Canada Basin: Journal of Geophysical Research, v. 87, p. 5461–5476.

Beck, A. E., 1965, Techniques of measuring heat flow on land: American Geophysical Union Monograph 8, p. 24–51.

Beck, A. E., and Sass, J. H., 1966, A preliminary value of heat flow at the Muskox intrusion near Coppermine, Northwest Territories, Canada: Earth and Planetary Science Letters, v. 1, p. 123–129.

Brewer, M. C., 1958, Thermal regime of an Arctic lake: EOS Transactions of the American Geophysical Union, v. 39, p. 278.

Clark, D. L., 1974, Late Mesozoic and early Cenozoic sediment cores from the Arctic Ocean: Geology, v. 2, p. 41–44.

Claypool, G. E., and Kaplan, I. R., 1974, The origin and distribution of methane in marine sediment, *in* Kaplan, I. R., ed., Natural gases in marine sediments: Plenum Press, p. 99–139.

Crane, K., Eldholm, O., Myhre, A. H., and Sundvor, E., 1982, Thermal implications for the evolution of the Spitsbergen Transform Fault: Tectonophysics, v. 89, p. 1–32.

Davis, E. E., and Lister, C.R.B., 1977, Heat flow measured over the Juan de Fuca Ridge; Evidence for widespread hydrothermal circulation in a highly heat transportive crust: Journal of Geophysical Research, v. 80, no. 30, p. 4845–4860.

Davis, E. E., Lister, C.R.B., and Sclater, J. G., 1984, Old ocean heat flow: Geophysical Journal of the Royal Astronomical Society, v. 78, p. 507–545.

DeLaurier, J. M., 1978, The Alpha Ridge is not a spreading centre, *in* Sweeney, J. F., ed., Arctic geophysical review: Ottawa, Canada, Earth Physics Branch, p. 87–90.

Eittriem, S., and Grantz, A., 1979, CDP seismic sections of the western Beaufort Continental Margin, *in* Keen, C. E., ed., Crustal properties across passive margins: Tectonophysics, v. 59, p. 251–262.

Forsyth, D. A., Asudeh, I., and Morel a l'Huissier, P., 1986, Alpha Ridge and Iceland; Products of the same plume?: Journal of Geodynamics, v. 6, p. 197–214.

Gold, L. W., and Lachenbruch, A. H., 1973, Thermal conditions in permafrost; A review of North American literature in permafrost, *in* Permafrost; North American Contribution, 2nd International Conference; Thermal Aspects of Permafrost Formation and Evolution: Washington, D.C., National Academy of Science, p. 3–25.

Gronlie, G., and Talwani, M., 1978, Geophysical atlas of the Norwegian-Greenland Sea: Palisades, New York, Lamont-Doherty Geological Observatory, Vema Research Series 4, scale approximately 1:1,000,000.

Haenel, R., 1974, Heat flow measurements in the Norwegian Sea: "Meteor" Forschungsergebnisse, v. 17, p. 74–78.

Hall, J. K., 1970, Arctic Ocean geophysical studies; The Alpha Cordillera and Mendeleev Ridge: Lamont-Doherty Geological Observatory Technical Report 2, CU-2-70, 125 p.

Horai, K., 1981, Thermal conductivity of oceanic crustal samples collected during DSDP Leg 60 drilling, *in* Hussong, D. M., and Uyeda, S., eds., Initial reports of the Deep Sea Drilling Project: Washington, D.C., U.S. Government Printing Office, v. 60, p. 807–834.

Hutchison, I., 1985, The effects of sedimentation and compaction on oceanic heat flow: Geophysical Journal of the Royal Astronomical Society, v. 82, p. 439–459.

Hunkins, K., 1961, Seismic studies of the Arctic Ocean floor, *in* Geology of the Arctic: University of Toronto Press, p. 645–665.

Hyndman, R. D., Von Herzen, R. P., Erickson, A. J., and Jolivet, J., 1976, Heat flow measurements in deep crustal holes in the mid-Atlantic ridge: Journal of Geophysical Research, v. 81, p. 4035–4060.

Jackson, R. H., Johnson, G. L., Sundvor, E., and Myhre, A. M., 1984, The Yermak Plateau; Formed at a triple junction: Journal of Geophysical Research, v. 89, no. B5, p. 3223–3232.

Judge, A. S., 1980, Heat flow measurements in the vicinity of the North Pole [abs.]: EOS Transactions of the American Geophysical Union, v. 61, p. 277.

Judge, A. S., Taylor, A. E., Burgess, M., and Allen, V. S., 1981, Canadian geothermal data collection; Northern wells, 1978–80: Canadian Earth Physics Branch Geothermal Series no. 12, 190 p.

Lachenbruch, A. H., 1957, Thermal effects of the ocean on permafrost: Geological Society of America Bulletin, v. 68, p. 1515.

Lachenbruch, A. H., and Brewer, M. C., 1959, Dissipation of the temperature effect of drilling a well in Arctic Alaska: U.S. Geological Survey Bulletin 1083-C, p. 73–109.

Lachenbruch, A. H., and Marshall, B. V., 1966, Heat flow through the Arctic Ocean floor; The Canada Basin–Alpha Rise boundary: Journal of Geophysical Research, v. 71, p. 1223–1248.

—— , 1968, Heat flow and water temperature fluctuations in the Denmark Strait: Journal of Geophysical Research, v. 73, p. 5829–5842.

—— , 1969, Heat flow in the Arctic: Journal of the Arctic Institute of North America, v. 22, p. 300–311.

—— , 1986, Changing climate: geothermal evidence from permafrost in the Alaskan Arctic: Science, v. 234, p. 689–696.

Lachenbruch, A. H., Green, G. W., and Marshall, B. V., 1966, Permafrost and the geothermal regimes, *in* Wilimovsky, N. J., and Wolfe, J. N., eds., Environment of the Cape Thompson region, Alaska: Washington, D.C., U.S. Atomic Energy Commission Division of Technical Information, p. 149–163.

Lachenbruch, A. H., Sass, J. H., Marshall, B. V., and Moses, T. H., Jr., 1982a, Permafrost, heat flow, and the geothermal regime at Prudhoe Bay, Alaska: Journal of Geophysical Research, v. 87, p. 9301–9316.

Langseth, M. G., and Zielinski, G. W., 1974, Marine heat-flow measurements in the Norwegian-Greenland Sea and in the vicinity of Iceland, *in* Kristjanson, L., ed., Geodynamics of Iceland and the North Atlantic area: Dordrecht, Holland, Reidel, p. 227–296.

Langseth, M. G., Hyndman, R. D., Becker, K., Hickman, S. H., and Salisbury, M. H., 1984, The hydrogeological regime of isolated sediment ponds in mid-oceanic ridges, *in* Hyndman, R. D., and Salisbury, M. H., eds., Initial report of the Deep Sea Drilling Project: Washington, D.C., U.S. Government Printing Office, v. 78, p. 825–837.

Law, L. K., Paterson, W.S.B., and Witham, K., 1965, Heat-flow determinations in the Canadian Arctic Archipelago: Canadian Journal of the Earth Sciences, v. 2, p. 59.

Lawver, L. A., and Baggeroer, A., 1983, A note on the age of the Canada Basin: Journal of Alaskan Geological Society, v. 2, p. 57–66.

Lawver, L. A., Grantz, A., and Meinke, L., 1981, The tectonics of the Arctic Ocean, *in* Dyer, I., and Chryssostomidis, C., eds., Arctic technology and policy: Washington, D.C., Hemisphere Publishing Corporation, p. 147–1578.

Lister, C.R.B., 1970, Measurement of in situ sediment conductivity by means of a Bullard-type probe: Geophysical Journal of the Royal Astronomical Society, v. 19, p. 521–532.

—— , 1972, On the thermal balance of a mid-ocean ridge: Geophysical Journal of the Royal Astronomical Society, v. 26, p. 515–535.

Lubimova, E. A., Alexandrov, A. L., and Duchkov, A. D., 1973a, Methods of study of the heat flow through the bottom of the ocean: Moscow, Nauka, 176 p.

Lubimova, E. A., and 7 others, 1973b, Review of heat flow in the USSR, *in* Heat flows from the crust and upper mantle of the earth, n. 12: Moscow, Nauka, p. 154–195.

Lubimova, E. A., Nikitina, V. N., and Tomara, G. A., 1976, Thermal fields of the inland marginal seas of the USSR: Moscow, Nauka, 222 p. (in Russian).

MacCarthy, G. R., 1952, Geothermal investigations on the Arctic Slope of Alaska: EOS Transactions of the American Geophysical Union, v. 33, p. 589.

MacLeod, M. K., 1982, Gas hydrates in ocean bottom sediments: American Association of Petroleum Geologists Bulletin, v. 66, p. 2649–2662.

Mair, J. A., and Lyons, J. A., 1981, Crustal structure and velocity anisotrophy beneath the Beaufort Sea: Canadian Journal of Earth Sciences, v. 18, p. 724–741.

Matsuda, J. I., and Von Herzen, R. P., 1986, Thermal conductivity variation in a deep-sea sediment core and its relation to H_2O, Ca, and Si content: Deep-sea Research, v. 33, p. 165–175.

Misener, A. D., 1955, Heat flow and depth of permafrost at Resolute Bay, Cornwallis Island, Northwest Territories, Canada: EOS Transactions of the American Geophysical Union, v. 36, p. 1055–1060.

Misener, A. D., Bremner, P. C., and Hodgson, J. H., 1956, Heat flow measurements in permafrost at Resolute Bay, Northwest Territories: Journal of the Royal Astronomical Society of Canada, v. 50, p. 14–24.

Parsons, B., and Sclater, J. G., 1977, An analysis of the variation of ocean floor bathymetry and heat flow with age: Journal of Geophysical Research, v. 82, p. 803–826.

Paterson, W.S.B., and Law, L. K., 1966, Additional heat-flow determinations in the area of Mould Bay, Arctic Canada: Canadian Journal of Earth Sciences, v. 3, p. 237–246.

Pye, G. D., and Hyndman, R. D., 1972, Heat flow measurements in Baffin Bay and the Labrador Sea: Journal of Geophysical Research, v. 77, p. 938–944.

Reksnes, P. A., and Vågnes, E., 1985, Evolution of the Greenland Sea and Eurasia Basin [Cand. Scient. thesis]: Norway, University of Oslo, Department of Geology, 136 p.

Sass, J. H., Lachenbruch, A. H., and Munroe, R. J., 1971, Thermal conductivity of rocks from measurements on fragments and its application to heat-flow determinations: Journal of Geophysical Research, v. 76, p. 3391–3401.

Sclater, J. G., Crowe, J., and Anderson, R. N., 1976, On the reliability of oceanic heat-flow averages: Journal of Geophysical Research, v. 81, no. 17, p. 2997–3006.

Stoll, R. D., Ewing, J. I., and Bryan, G. M., 1971, Anomalous wave velocities in sediments containing gas hydrates: Journal of Geophysical Research, v. 76, p. 2090–2094.

Sweeney, J. F., Irving, E., and Geuer, J. W., 1978, Evolution of the Arctic Basin: Arctic Geophysical Review, v. 45, no. 4, p. 91–107.

Talwani, M., and Eldholm, O., 1977, Evolution of the Norwegian-Greenland Sea: Geological Society of America Bulletin, v. 88, p. 969–999.

Talwani, M., Windisch, C. C., and Langseth, M. G., 1971, Reykjanes Ridge crest: a detailed geophysical study: Journal of Geophysical Research, v. 76, p. 473–517.

Taylor, A. E., Burgess, M., Judge, A. S., and Allen, V. C., 1982, Canadian geothermal data collection; Northern wells, 1981; Ottawa, Canada, Energy, Mines, and Resources Geothermal Series no. 13, 153 p.

Taylor, A. E., Judge, A. S., and Desrochers, D., 1983, Shoreline regression; Its effect on permafrost and the geothermal regime, Canadian Arctic Archipelago, in Permafrost; 4th International Conference, Proceedings: Washington, D.C., National Academic Press, p. 1239–1244.

Taylor, A. E., Judge, A., and Allen, V. S., 1986, Terrestrial heat flow from Project CESAR; Alpha Ridge, Arctic Ocean Basin: Journal of Geodynamics, v. 6, p. 137–176.

Taylor, P. T., Kovacs, L. S., Vogt, P. R., and Johnson, G. L., 1981, Detailed aeromagnetic investigation of the Arctic Basin, 2: Journal of Geophysical Research, v. 86, p. 6323–6333.

Von Herzen, R. P., and Maxwell, A. E., 1959, The measurement of thermal conductivity of deep-sea sediments by the needle probe method: Journal of Geophysical Research, v. 64, p. 1557–1563.

Williams, D. L., Von Herzen, R. P., Sclater, J. G., and Anderson, R. N., 1974, The Galapagos spreading centre; Lithospheric cooling and hydrothermal circulation: Geophysical Journal of the Royal Astronomical Society, v. 38, p. 587–608.

Yamano, M., Uyeda, S., Aoki, Y., and Shipley, T. H., 1982, Estimates of heat flow derived from gas hydrates: Geology, v. 10, p. 339–343.

Zielinski, G. W., 1977, Thermal history of the Norwegian-Greenland Sea and its rifted continental margin [Ph.D. thesis]: New York, Columbia University, 160 p.

——— , 1979, On the thermal evolution of passive continental margins, thermal depth anomalies, and the Norwegian-Greenland Sea: Journal of Geophysical Research, v. 84, p. 7577–7588.

MANUSCRIPT ACCEPTED BY THE SOCIETY MARCH 31, 1987

ACKNOWLEDGMENTS

Much of the effort to organize and present the data in this chapter was done during a visit by M. Langseth to the U.S. Geological Survey's Menlo Park facility in 1984. This visit and the research were supported by the Arctic Office of the Office of Naval Research, the Polar Programs Office of the National Science Foundation, and the U.S. Geological Survey. Alan Judge, Alan Taylor, Kathy Crane, and Eirik Sundvor kindly provided heat-flow results prior to publication. Discussions with Art Grantz, David Clark, Glen Jones, Leonard Johnson, and Kenneth Hunkins were stimulating and helpful. We are indebted to Alan Taylor, Jack Sweeney, and Alan Beck for thoughtful reviews of the manuscript.

Tupileq carvings from Greenland used to ward off evil spirits. From Tidsskriftet Gronland, No. 5, 1986.

Printed in U.S.A.

Chapter 10

Seismic reflection and refraction

H. R. Jackson
Atlantic Geoscience Centre, Geological Survey of Canada, Bedford Institute of Oceanography, Dartmouth, Nova Scotia B2Y 4A2, Canada
D. A. Forsyth
Lithosphere and Canadian Shield Division, Geological Survey of Canada, Observatory Crescent, Ottawa, Ontario K1A 0Y3, Canada
J. K. Hall
Marine Geological Division, Geological Survey of Israel, 30 Malchei Israel Street, Jerusalem 95 501, Israel
A. Overton
Terrain Science Division, Geological Survey of Canada, 601 Booth Street, Ottawa, Ontario K1A 0E8, Canada

INTRODUCTION

The ice cover of the Arctic Ocean restricts research vessels, limiting the number of miles of seismic reflection and refraction lines in the area. Figures 1 and 2 show the distribution of the lines, and Tables 1 and 2 provide references keyed to those figures. This paper describes the distribution, collection, and processing of the seismic reflection and refraction data available in the deep basins and major ridges in the Arctic Ocean and briefly discusses the salient geological results by region. In addition, the position of seismic surveys on the continental margins and adjacent landmasses of the North American plate have been compiled for completeness. These peripheral areas are documented with recent review papers (Table 1) including Eldholm and others (this volume) and Larsen (this volume).

Most of the seismic reflection information in the Arctic Ocean has been collected on drifting ice stations; thus, the direction of the lines is controlled by the whims of nature. The data set presented here is incomplete due to the inaccessibility of information collected by Soviet scientists. No seismic profiling has been run from the northern margin of Greenland, and only three refraction surveys and one reflection line exist on the Canadian Polar margin from Greenland to the Beaufort Sea. Most of the reflection lines in the Canada Basin were acquired with power sources of insufficient strength to penetrate the sedimentary section. Even with this meager collection of erratically spaced and variable quality information, important trends can be seen, interesting features noted, and in some cases significant new information with global consequences has been acquired (Plate 5).

In the Arctic, environmental factors modify the experimental setup. The extreme cold must be dealt with, both its effect on personnel and equipment (Baggeroer and Falconer, 1982). Special methods are required to get sound into and out of ice-covered waters. In some circumstances the sea ice generates high levels of background noise. Offsetting this are cases where a 5,000 j sparker has penetrated up to 1.5 s with a single hydrophone receiver.

Care must be taken when comparing velocities from independent refraction progarms. Prior to about 1974, refraction data from the Arctic were interpreted using plain layered models. Gradually, ray tracing, amplitude modelling, and other processing techniques were employed that permitted the recognition of velocity gradients within layers and two-dimensional structures.

SEISMIC MEASUREMENTS

Eurasia Basin

Seismic data in the Eurasia Basin are concentrated in the area north of Greenland and Svalbard (Fig. 1) due to the flight range of the aircraft used in the experiments. The southern section of the Yermak Plateau has the densest coverage because ice conditions are light enough in some years to tow seismic equipment behind ships.

For the reflection lines, sparkers and airguns were the sound sources. The sparkers had insufficient energy to consistently penetrate the sedimentary cover and image basement. The only available seismic reflection data on the Morris Jesup Plateau was collected on ice station Arlis II (Ostenso and Wold, 1977) with a 5,000 j sparker as the source. The other sparker line is along the Fram III track (Fig. 1, line 13A) and is of poor quality (Hunkins and others, 1981). Fortunately, higher-quality multichannel data were collected in this region on Fram IV (Fig. 1, line 19). A 2-km-long seismic array of 20 telemetering sonobuoys were the receivers for a 120 in^3 airgun (Kristoffersen and Husebye, 1984). This reflection line is the only one in the Arctic Ocean basins in

Jackson, H. R., Forsyth, D. A., Hall, J. K., and Overton, A., 1990, Seismic reflection and refraction, *in* Grantz, A., Johnson, L., and Sweeney, J. F., eds., The Arctic Ocean region: Boulder, Colorado, Geological Society of America, The Geology of North America, v. L.

Figure 1. The location of seismic reflecton profiles in the Arctic Ocean. The numbers are the indexed references in Table 1. The Amundsen and Nansen basins together are called the Eurasia Basin.

which the shot points were regularly spaced. All other lines have been collected with the sound source firing at equal time intervals, thereby distorting horizontal scales because ice camp drift rates can vary from near zero to 850 m per hour (Kristoffersen, 1982a). In addition, a single-channel line with a 40 in³ airgun as source was collected on Fram I (Fig. 1, line 11). The reflection data recorded from a ship on the Yermak Plateau (Fig. 1, survey 29) employed a DSF-V digital recording unit, a 300 in³ gun, and had 9-fold coverage (Sundvor and others, 1982). In addition, 21 digitally recorded sonobuoys were acquired simultaneously with the reflection measurements.

The crustal seismic refraction data were recorded principally on three types of instruments: a three-sensor ocean-bottom seismometer tethered with light-weight kevlar cable (Jackson and others, 1982); a 6-element 4-km-long sonobuoy array (Kristoffersen and others, 1982a); and a 24-channel two-dimensional hydrophone array 1 km in length (Duckworth and others, 1982; Duckworth and Baggeroer, 1985). All shots were fired by carrying explosives away from the recording instruments by helicopter and detonated by SUS (sound underwater signal) charges at 245 m depth. The lines were up to 100 km long with shot sizes of 25 to 100 kg. Shot spacing was variable due to the irregular distribution of open water and thin ice. The shot spacing was rarely closer than 5 km. As a result the ocean bottom seismometer recorded few seismic arrivals in the sedimentary or upper crustal region. However, the hydrophone array was employed

Figure 2. The location of seismic refraction lines in the Arctic Ocean. The numbers are the indexed references to the data sources in Table 2.

simultaneously with the ocean bottom seismometer on Fram II and alone on Fram IV. Processing techniques used on the array data are sensitive to information in this shallow depth range (Duckworth and others, 1982; Duckworth and Baggeroer, 1985).

The location of the shots was achieved with a variety of positioning systems. The principal navigation system in the helicopter was OMEGA, which was used to fly to within several kilometers of the preplanned shot position. This positioning was augmented by other systems. The water-wave arrivals were used to obtain range information. For the ocean-bottom seismometer data, a constant water wave velocity of 1.47 km/s was used. Overall errors in distance, based on 2-way travel time, are estimated at ± 500 m, which corresponds to an error of ± 0.1 s in seismic arrival times (Jackson and others, 1982). Velocimeter measurements in the water column were done on Fram II and Fram IV, so distance accuracies of ± 50 m are predicted (Duckworth and Baggeroer, 1985). In addition, on Fram I and Fram IV, mini-ranger positions out to about 40 km with ± 10 m accuracy were used. All refraction lines shot in this basin are unreversed; therefore, dipping structures are not readily resolved.

Processing and interpreting the refraction data involved a wide range of methods. The ocean-bottom seismometer data was digitized and plotted in record section format; that is, an X-T plot, where the horizontal axis X is distance and the vertical axis T is the time after the shot. Synthetic seismograms were developed to match the original. The array data were processed to yield veloc-

TABLE 1. REFLECTION REFERENCE INDEX FOR FIGURE 1

Reference	Number
Dietrich and others (1985)	2
Eldholm and others (this volume); Eldholm and Windisch (1974)	39
Grantz and May (1984)	10
Grantz and others (1982)	26
Hall (1970, 1973, 1979); Hunkins and Tiemann (1977)	15
Hunkins and others (1981)	13A
Jackson (1985)	16
Jackson and others (1982)	11
Kristoffersen (1982a), Kristofferson and Husebye (1984)	19
Kutschale (1966)	20
Myhre and Eldholm (1987), Sundvor and Eldholm (1979)	40
Ostenso and Wold (1977)	24
Rønnevik and Jacobsen (1984), Riis and others (1986)	17
Sundvor and others (1982)	29
Sweeney and others (1982)	27
Talwani and Eldholm (1979), Eldholm and others (1979)	32
Weber and Sweeney (1985)	24, 27

TABLE 2. REFRACTION REFERENCE INDEX FOR FIGURE 2

Reference	Number
Asudeh and others (1985)	1
Baggeroer and Falconer (1982)	38
Bee and others (1984)	3
Berry and Barr (1971)	4
Chan and Mitchell (1982)	5
Davydova and others (1985)	31
Duckworth and others (1982)	6
Duckworth and Baggeroer (1985); Ojo (1982)	6, 19
Eldholm and others (1984)	36
Forsyth and others (1985)	7
Forsyth and others (1979)	8
Grachev (1982)	30
Grantz and others (1975); Houtz and others (1981) >100 sonobouys in 10, 26 Figure 1	9
Hobson (1962)	34
Hobson and Overton (1967)	33
Houtz and Windisch (1977)	23
Hunkins (1961)	42
Hunkins (1966)	12
Jackson and others (1977)	18
Jackson and others (1982)	14
Jackson and others (1984)	13
Keen and Barrett (1972)	18
Kristoffersen (1982a)	19
Kristoffersen and others (1982)	14
Mair and Forsyth (1982)	21, 27
Mair and Lyons (1981)	21
Milne (1966)	22
Ojo and others (1986)	6
Overton (1970)	25
Overton (1982)	8, 37
Sander and Overton (1965)	28

ity spectra. The velocity spectra were transformed to tau-slowness and offset-slowness and inverted by a variety of techniques (Duckworth and Baggeroer, 1985).

Nansen and Amundsen basins

The principal sedimentary and crustal structures observed in these basins are summarized in this section. The reflection line from Fram I (Figs. 1 and 3), although of intermediate quality, is the best available cross-section. Sedimentary thickness decreases as the ridge is approached, and irregular basement highs are observed. In the vicinity of the Morris Jesup Plateau (Fig. 2, survey 6), sedimentary sections of 1.5 to 2 km thickness are measured (Ojo and others, 1986). The velocity is estimated to be between 1.6 and 2.1 km/s and the sediments are thought to be poorly consolidated based on the character of the shear-wave arrivals.

In the Nansen Basin, up to 1.5 km of sedimentary material is observed on the multichannel reflection line (Kristoffersen and Husebye, 1984), which is confirmed by the refraction data (Duckworth and Baggeroer, 1985). The crustal structure of the basin, oceanic layers 2 and 3, has been observed to have a thickness between 3 and 5 km (Jackson and others, 1982; Duckworth and others, 1982; Duckworth and Baggeroer, 1985; Ojo and othrs, 1986). This thin crust (average oceanic crust is 6.5 km thick; Christensen and Salisbury, 1975) is clearly illustrated on the ocean bottom seismometer line (Fig. 4). Mantle refractors are first arrivals at a mere 10-km range. The thin crust is thought to be a product of the slow spreading rate of about 5 mm/yr in this area (Jackson and others, 1982).

Shear waves are more strongly developed in the Amundsen Basin than in the Nansen Basin. Duckworth and Baggeroer (1985) attribute this to a more irregular basement topography in the Nansen Basin.

The southern portion of the Arctic Mid-Ocean Ridge is the Yermak H zone (Feden and others, 1979). High-amplitude magnetic anomalies and shallow bathymetry are peculiar to the region and define the H zone. In the H zone the crust is 8 km thick (Kristofferson and others, 1982b) and has more uniform arrivals than in other parts of the basin. The thick and consistent crustal arrivals contrast with seismic refraction events in the rest of the Eurasia Basin (Jackson and others, 1982).

Yermak-Morris Jesup plateaus

These paired aseismic plateaus are believed to have formed in a similar manner (Feden and others, 1979; Jackson and others,

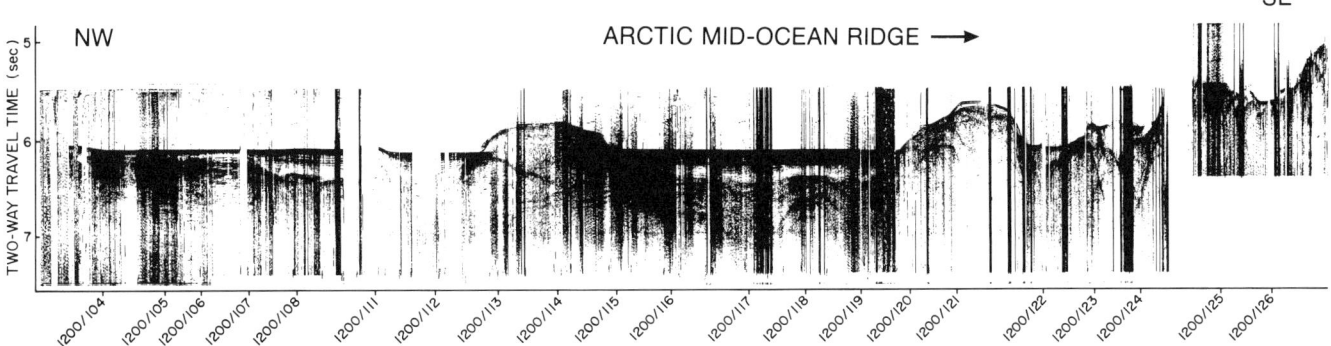

Figure 3. A single channel 655 cm³ (40 in³) airgun line in the Amundsen Basin numbered 11 on Figure 1. Note irregular basement topography increasing in height with decreasing sedimentary covers as the ridge is approached. The line is about 100 km long.

1984). Nevertheless, the Yermak Plateau shows a distinctive change in bathymetric and magnetic trends that indicates care should be taken to distinguish between its northern and southern attributes. The upper right illustration on Figure 5 shows the changing magnetic character and bathymetric trend on the Yermak Plateau.

A high-quality multichannel seismic reflection line (Kristofferson and Husebye, 1984) crosses the Nansen Basin and part of the northern Yermak Plateau. The sedimentary reflectors thin and basement shallows toward the plateau (Fig. 6, line 19). The continuity of basement from the deep sea to the shallow plateau supports an oceanic origin for this portion of the plateau. On the Morris Jesup Plateau's western flank, up to 1.3 s of well-stratified sedimentary rocks are penetrated with the Arlis II sparker. The layering in the sedimentary section terminates against the steep basement rise in the plateau. Basement shallows to the east in an irregular manner. The Morris Jesup Plateau demonstrates a more rugged topography and less sedimentary cover than the Yermak Plateau.

On the southern Yermak Plateau, over 3 s of sedimentary rocks have been deposited on its flanks in a pattern that thickens away from the plateau center (Sundvor and others, 1982). The basement reflector is opaque and smooth in nature and in places highly faulted (Fig. 7). The corresponding refractor determined by sonobuoy measurements has a velocity greater than 5 km/s. This basement reflector can be traced to within 25 km of northwestern Svalbard where the basement is Precambrian gneiss, but the correlation cannot be verified on the reflection records.

Refraction measurements on the flanks of the Morris Jesup Plateau show oceanic crust thickening toward the plateau, in accord with the hypothesis that it is of oceanic origin (Duckworth and Baggeroer, 1985). Refraction measurements on the Yermak Plateau, although not well constrained because the lines are 60 to 100 km long with only 8 to 13 shots, indicate a dichotomous crustal structure. On the northern segment, velocities of 5.0 and 7.2 km/s typical of oceanic crust were recorded (Jackson and others, 1984). These velocities contrast with the 4.3, 6.0, and 8.0 km/s measurements on the southern section. These refraction lines are unreversed, but the differences between them are too large to be produced by dipping layers (Fig. 5).

Amerasia Basin

The majority of the reflection data collected in this region was recorded from the ice island T-3 between 1962 and 1970 (Hall, 1970, 1973, 1979; Hunkins and Tiemann, 1977) and in the early 1950s (Crary and Goldstein, 1957). Shorter but significant lines are reported by Hunkins (1961), Kutschale (1966), Ostenso and Wold (1977), Blasco and others (1979), Overton (1980), and Jackson (1985).

On T-3, from 1962 onward, the sound source for the seismic data was a 9,000 j sparker with a single electrode suspended 8 m below the ice. The receiver consisted of one flexural disk hydrophone suspended 4 m below the ice and separated by 25 m from the source. The signal was recorded on dry paper. This system had insufficient power to penetrate the sedimentary column to basement in the basins. The record quality is poor to fair (Hunkins and Tiemann, 1977). From Arlis II (Fig. 1, line 20), two

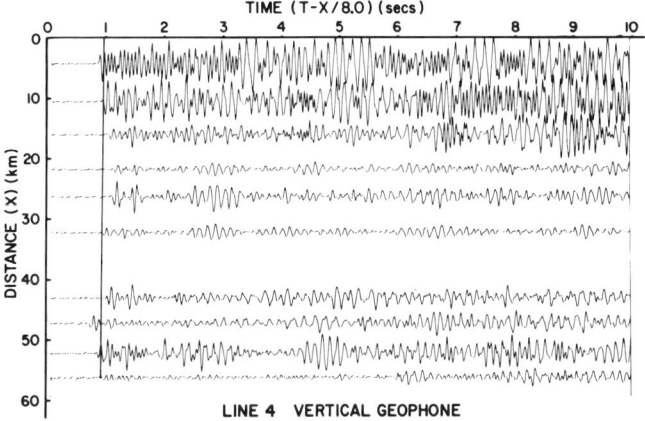

Figure 4. The arrival trains for the seismic refraction experiment labeled 14 on Figure 2. The remarkable early breakover of the mantle velocity of 8.0 km/s that extends across the figure is the salient feature.

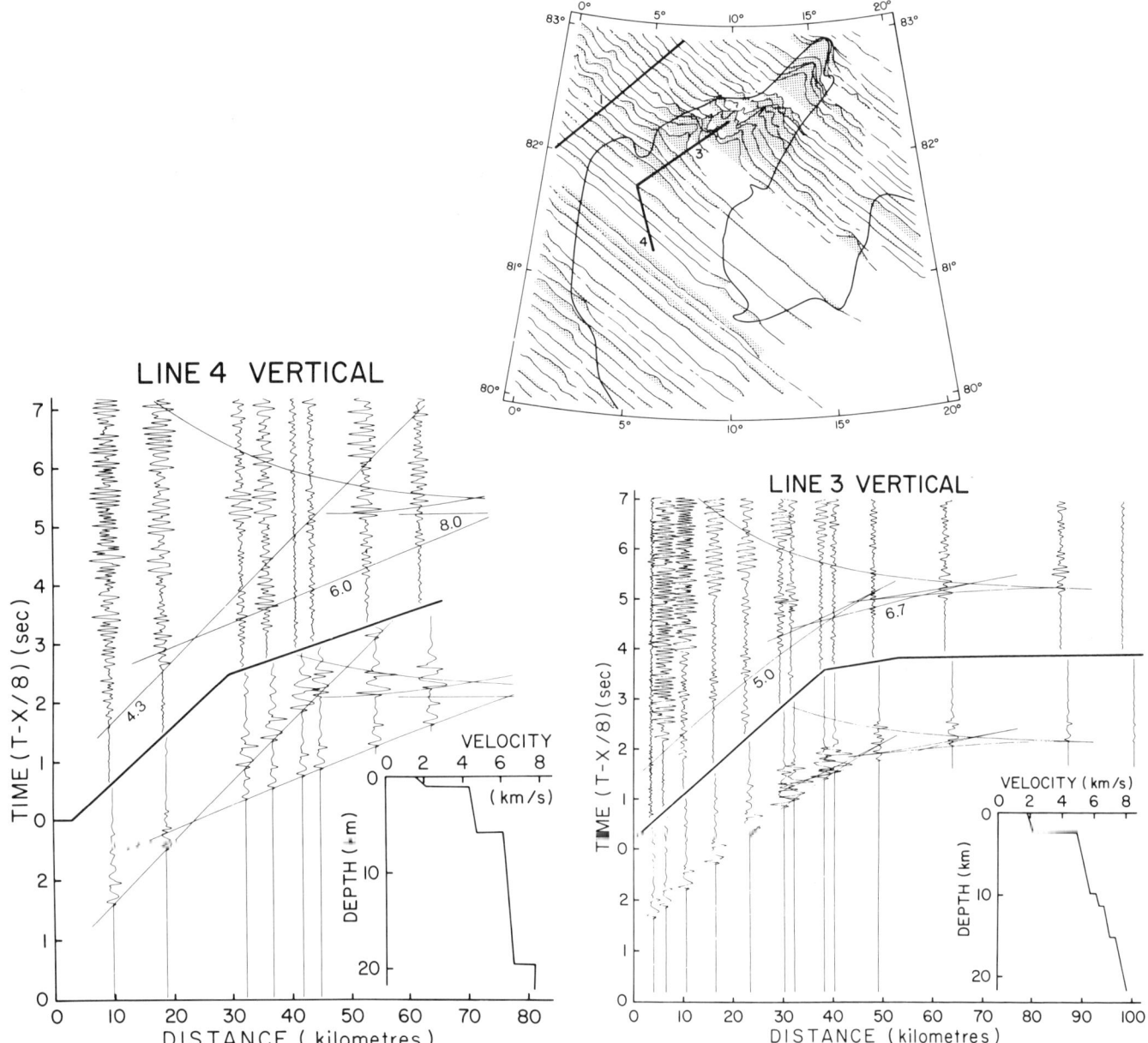

Figure 5. Seismic refraction lines on the Yermak Plateau from Jackson and others (1984). Line 3 is located on the northern segment of the plateau characterized by the high amplitude magnetic anomalies in contrast to line 4 on the southern portion. The upper section of the refraction section is the original data and the lower and synthetic model. The numbers on the upper section are velocities in km/s.

systems for collecting reflection data were employed. From 81°N 173°E to 82°20′N 164°E, primers of 0.45 kg were fired every 10 minutes for an average of 6 hours a day. The seismic data collected with this technique penetrated up to 3.5 s; however, the record is not continuous. From 82°20′N 165°E to 82°30′N 169°E a 5,000 j sparker sound source with single hydrophone receiver was used. Record sections with about 1.5 s penetration were collected, and basement reflectors are glimpsed. Later, on Arlis II (Fig. 1, line 24), the sparker system was operated again. Line drawings of the original records are displayed in Ostenso and Wold (1977). In addition, in this basin, vertical reflections were colleted daily in the winter and twice daily in the summer with ¼-lb charges fired from ice station Alpha (Hunkins, 1961). This recording system produced subbottom reflectors that were classified on a system based on the strength and the number of reflections. Because of the highly discontinuous nature of the data, they are not plotted on Figure 1.

After April, 1967, positioning of these ice stations, except T-3, was based on celestial navigation, sun shots during the summer, and star shots in the winter. Errors of ± 0.5 km in the

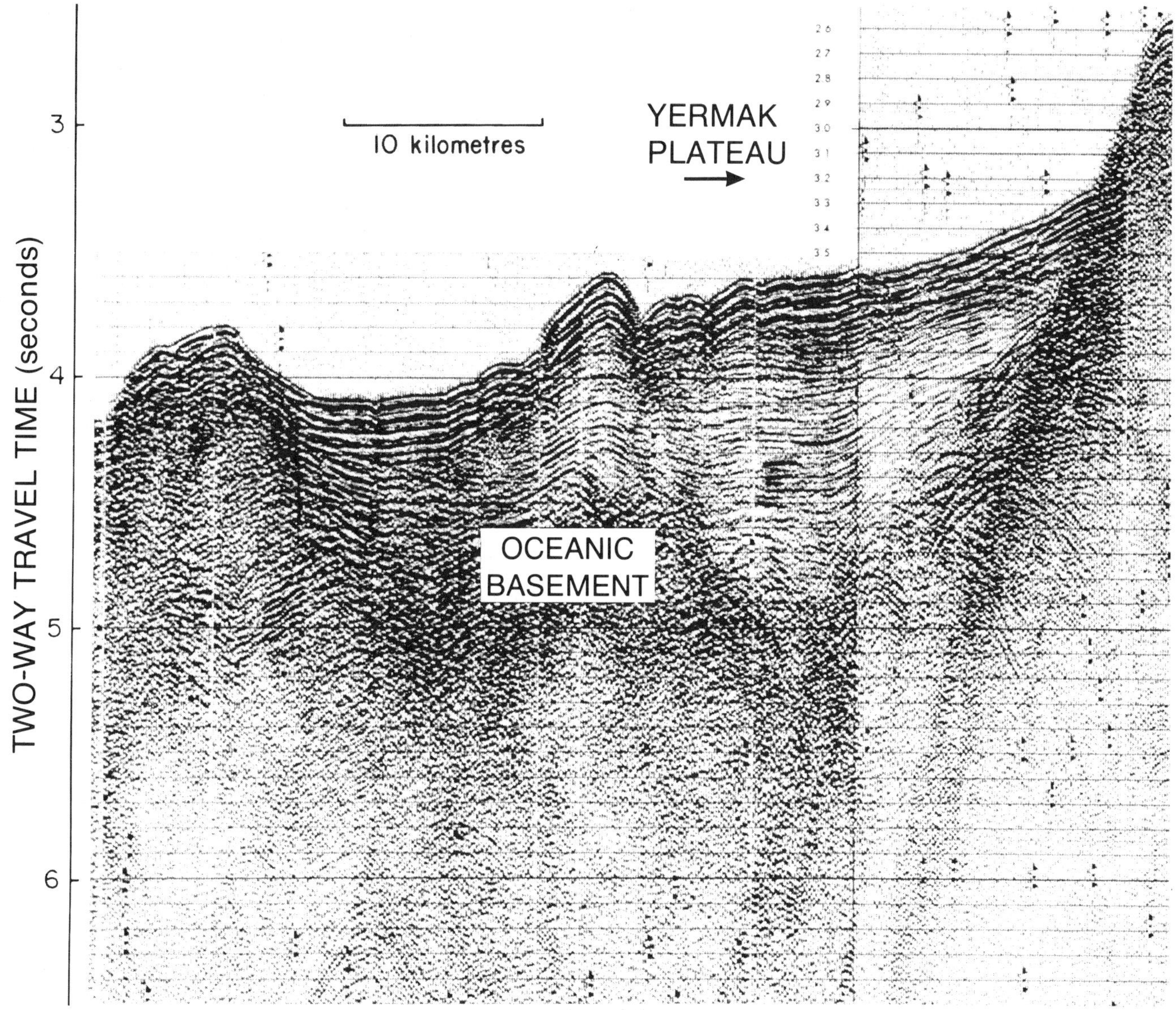

Figure 6. This multichannel seismic reflection profile (19) on Figure 1 displays acoustic basement shallowing from the Nansen Basin as the northern section of the Yermak Plateau is approached. The figure is from Kristoffersen (1982a).

winter and ± 1 km in the summer were usual when meteorological conditions made it possible to take a fix. Wind data were used to determine the most probable track between fixes. On T-3 after April 1967, satellite fixes with maximum errors of ± 0.25 km were general (Hall, 1973).

Less extensive but higher-quality seismic reflection lines with better positioning were collected over the Lomonosov Ridge and on the Alpha Ridge (Fig. 1, lines 15, 27). On ice station LOREX (Lomonosov Ridge Experiment), which drifted for 2.5 months at an average rate of 5 km per day, a range of reflection techniques were used to collect high-resolution as well as deep-penetration profiles. A high-resolution line was collected by firing

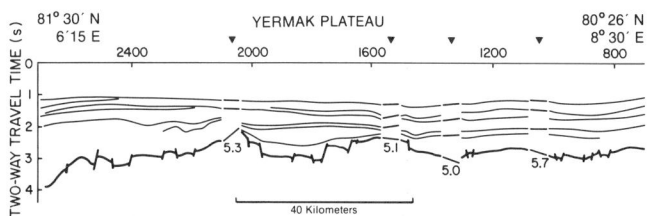

Figure 7. A line drawing of a multichannel seismic line from the southern region of the Yermak Plateau (29) on Figure 1. A thick sedimentary section overlying a block-faulted basement is shown. The numbers beneath the heavy-line reflector are velocities in km/s from sonobuoy measurements (Sundvor and others, 1982).

a 164 cm^3 (10 in^3) airgun at one-minute intervals, which was received by a single hydrophone suspended 5 m below the sea ice. A high-resolution record clearly displaying the sediment structures and basement topography was produced. Additionally, a 24-channel cross-shaped geophone array to which 1 and 10 kg explosive charges were fired at regular time intevals was also in operation. Two hundred seismic sections were recorded in this manner (Overton, 1980). The large charges produced reflections through the crust to the mantle. On CESAR (Canadian Expedition to Study the Alpha Ridge) (Fig. 1, line 16), a 655 cm^3 (40 in^3) airgun fired at five-minute intervals to a single hydrophone was used (Jackson, 1985). Also the multichannel array used at the LOREX expedition was set up. The array data from the CESAR experiment are difficult to process and interpret because of the irregular topography of the ridge and the thinness of the sedimentary cover (A. Overton, personal communication, 1985). Navigation on CESAR and LOREX was accomplished with a Satnav system. Accuracies of ± 20 m for CESAR and ± 100 m for LOREX (J. Popelar, personal communication, 1985) are established.

The seismic refraction experiments on the basin and ridges of the Amerasia Basin have in many cases been collected with the same instruments and interpreted with similar processing techniques. In this region an array of receivers with geophones was placed on the ice with 10 km spacings (Mair and Lyons, 1981; Forsyth and Mair, 1984); this contrasts with the ocean-bottom seismometers and hydrophone array instrumentation employed in the Eurasia Basin. Six to twelve digitally recording cassettes with gain-ranging amplifiers and a 16-element geophone array were the receivers for experiments on the Lomonosov Ridge, Alpha Ridge, and the adjacent basins including the Canada Basin (Fig. 2, surveys 7, 21, 27; Mair and Lyons, 1981; Mair and Forsyth, 1982; Forsyth and Mair, 1984; Forsyth and others, 1985; Forsyth and others, 1986). The sound source was explosive charges from 25 to 1,000 kg. Less open water was available for getting the explosives into the water than in the Eurasia Basin, so holes were augered through the ice and specially manufactured cylindrical charges were used. The explosives were lowered on rope to 100 m depth and electrically detonated. These surveys consisted of reversed lines up to 200 km long. With experience and technological development, the number of seismic events recorded on each experiment increased such that on CESAR in 1983 it was possible to record 48 seismic arrivals a day, 96 arrivals a day on the ice island experiment in 1985 (Asudeh and others, 1985; line 1, Fig. 2), and 207 arrivals a day on the ice island 1986 experiment.

The refraction data were plotted in record section format, and ray tracing and amplitude matching programs are used to interpret the seismic traces.

Several other refraction experiments were conducted in the Canada Basin (Fig. 2, line 38). The Massachusetts Institute of Technology hydrophone array and the Bedford Institute of Oceanography ocean-bottom seismometer were used on one experiment, CANBARX (Canadian Basin Acoustic Reverberation Experiment) (Baggeroer and Falconer, 1982). The instrumentation and processing techniques were similar to those used in the Eurasia Basin. On the CANBARX survey, seven unreversed shots were fired at ranges of 11 to 73 km. The ranges for the shots were determined by water waves to within 200 m. The data were plotted in X-T format and as velocity spectra, and amplitude analysis was done on the arrivals.

Other data in the Amerasia Basin include an unreversed line run by Milne (1966; Fig. 2, line 22) from an ice breaker. The receiver was a single hydrophone, and charges sized to 180 kg were detonated. The data were interpreted with straight-line fits on an X-T plot. Hunkins (1961) reports three unreversed refraction lines up to 15 km long on the Alpha Ridge at 85°02′N 138°31′W. Explosives were sledged and backpacked to their locations; the ice conditions prevented longer lines. Charge sizes were 25 to 75 lbs. The data were again plotted in record sections and interpreted with straight-line fits.

SEISMIC CHARACTERISTICS

Lomonosov Ridge

The Lomonosov Ridge was crossed by ice stations LOREX and Arlis II (Fig. 1, lines 24 and 27, respectively). The LOREX reflection record displays an irregular crest with gentler slopes on the Eurasia Basin flank than on the Makarov Basin flank (Fig. 8). Near the North Pole a 40-m-thick veneer of sedimentary cover is measured on the Eurasia flank of the ridge, compared with 75 m on the Makarov flank (Blasco and others, 1979). On the Arlis II crossing of the ridge nearer the continental margin a 750-m sedimentary section is recorded. The surface of the sedimentary sequence is remarkably flat; however, the horizons within it are hummocky. Both reflection profiles suggest the ridge to be a fault block or a series of en echelon fault blocks (Ostenso and Wold, 1977; Sweeney and others, 1982).

The large-charge multichannel reflection line recorded during LOREX from the bathymetric edge of the Lomonosov Ridge into the Amundsen Basin displays deep structures not previously described (Fig. 9). Three pertinent reflectors are highlighted. The shallowest reflector (1) delimits the sediment/basement interface. This interpretation is based on a difference in frequency content that occurs in the record as well as on the shape of the reflectors. The middle reflector (2) marks the oceanward extent of the Lomonosov Ridge. The continental crust (Forsyth and Mair, 1984) associated with the ridge can be seen to thin and terminate about 80 km from the bathymetric edge of the ridge. The deepest horizon (3) is interpreted to be the mantle reflection. Probable mantle reflections can be traced from beneath the crust of the ridge as it shallows oceanward. Between the sediment/basement interface (1) and the mantle reflections (3) at basinward extent on the eastern end of the profile, 1.5 s of crust is observed. Using the refraction velocities from the nearest experiment (Duckworth and others, 1982), crust is calculated to be between 3.7 and 4.7 km thick. This thickness is consistent with that measured by refraction lines in the Amundsen Basin.

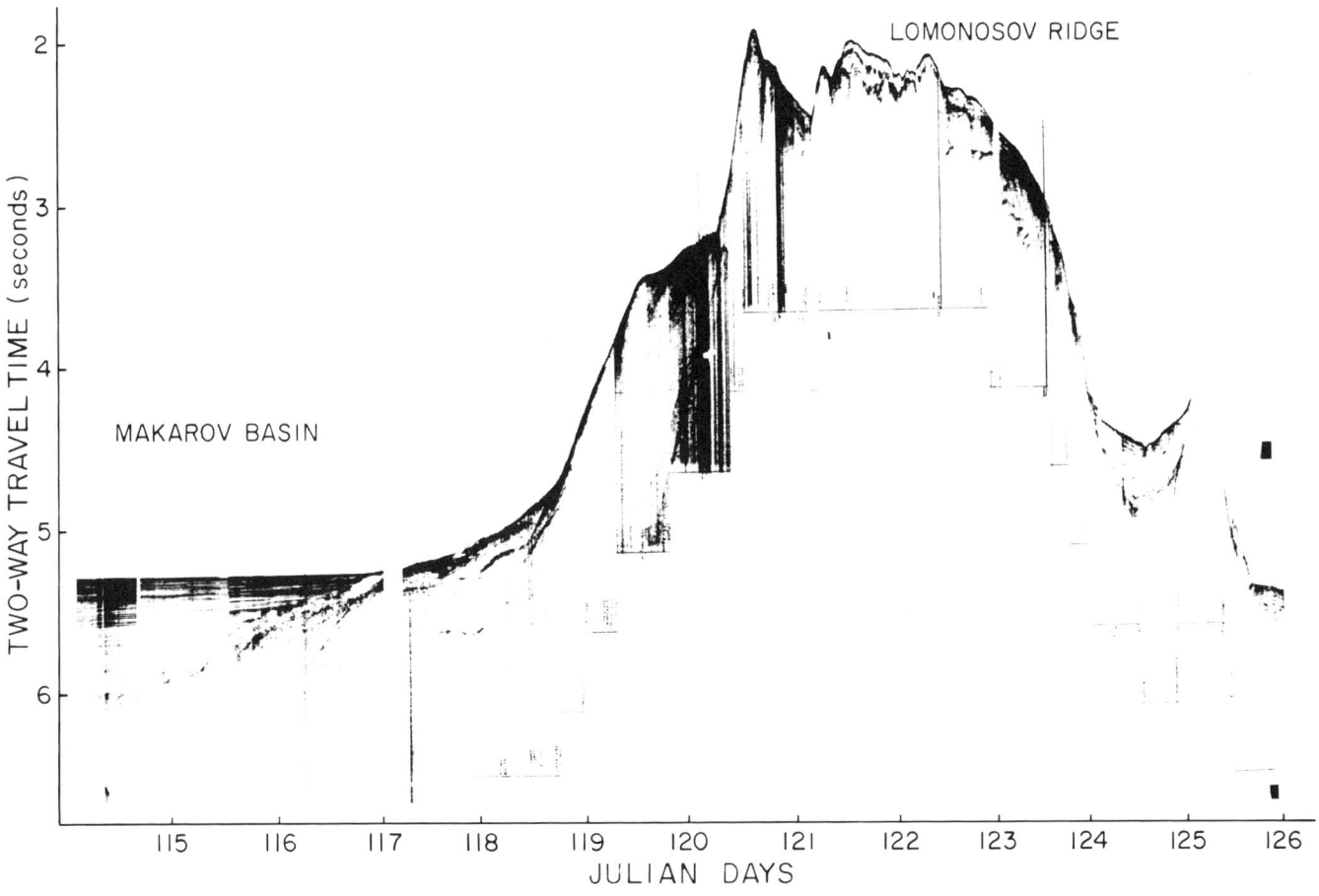

Figure 8. A 164 cm³ (10 in³) airgun high-resolution profile across the Lomonosov Ridge labeled as 27 in Figure 1. The sawtooth character of the ridge is clearly displayed. The ridge is about 70 km wide. The seismic line was provided by S. Blasco, Bedford Institute of Oceanography.

The reversed crustal refraction lines shot on and across the Lomonosov Ridge (Mair and Forsyth, 1982; Forsyth and Mair, 1984) measured a complete section to mantle. A thin low-velocity sedimentary layer consistent with the reflection data was measured. An upper crustal unit with a seismic velocity of 4.7 km/s with a low-velocity gradient and a thickness of 5 km (Fig. 9) overlies a layer with a velocity of 6.6 km/s with a small gradient and a thickness of 15 to 20 km. A mantle velocity of 8.3 km/s was recorded. The regular character of the first arrivals and multiples suggests the structure is continuous along the ridge. The velocity profile is interpreted to represent continental crust consistent with the plate reconstruction for the Eurasia Basin that places the Lomonosov Ridge adjacent to the Barents-Kara Shelf. The refraction profiles on the Lomonosov Ridge and on the margins of the Barents and Kara Seas (Fig. 10) are remarkably similar (Forsyth and Mair, 1984).

A refraction line across the Lomonosov Ridge into the adjacent basins (Forsyth and Mair, 1984) demonstrates that the crust beneath the ridge is thicker than that in the ocean basins and indicates an asymmetric root beneath the ridge. The slope of the root is more gradual into the Amundsen Basin than into the Makarov Basin. The slope on the mantle into the Amundsen Basin is seen on the seismic reflection profile shown in Figure 9. The dip lines are too short to determine the crustal structure below the basins.

Alpha-Mendeleev Ridge Complex

The Alpha and Mendeleev Ridges (Fig. 2) are either a continuous feature that crosses the Arctic Ocean or two separate features that have coterminus ends. In cross section the Mendeleev and Alpha Ridges both exhibit a depth-with-distance symmetry about their respective crestal axes (Fig. 11). Scarcity of data, especially from the Mendeleev Ridge, prevents further comparisons.

Seismic reflection profiles on the broad and topographically complex Alpha Ridge show sedimentary deposits varying in thickness from nil where basement outcrops to about 1.2 km. The generally conformable sequence increases in thickness toward the North American continental margin. Within the sedimentary column, distinct reflectors are observed locally. On the crestal regions of the Alpha Ridge in the area of 85°N 130°W, a series of large overlapping hyperbolae (Fig. 12) were observed by Hall

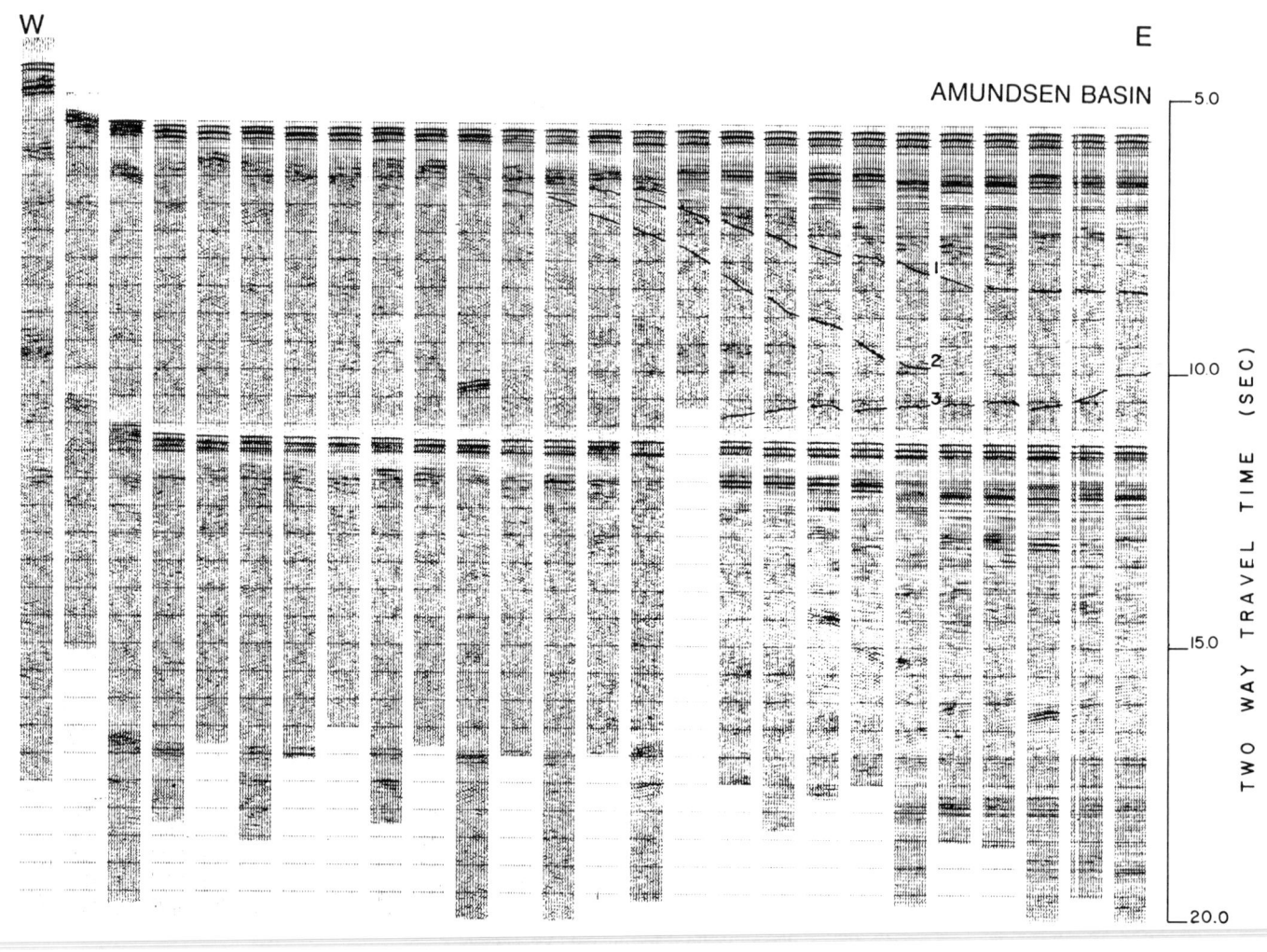

Figure 9. Multichannel reflection line shot with 10 kg explosive charges labeled 27 on Figure 1. The portion of the record shown here extends from the edge of the Lomonosov Ridge 89°35′N 135°W shown in Figure 7 into the Amundsen Basin 89°20′N 165°W. The multiple as well as the first arrival are shown so the labelled horizons can be verified independently. This line was run by A. Overton on ice station LOREX.

(1970). These hyperbolae are best developed on the gentle southern slopes of local highs. In some locations these features are observed as linear features 100 m thick. These probable sediment waves may be due to vigorous former current activity (Hall, 1979).

To the east of the region, where hyperbolic reflectors are observed, seismic profiles are obscured in some localities by a bottom simulating reflector (BSR) (Jackson, 1985). The BSR occurs 0.15 s below the sea-floor reflection. The record immediately above the BSR is transparent (Fig. 13). The temperature/depth range of the BSR is found within the range where gas hydrates can form. Gas hydrates are a possible cause of the BSR and are thought to occur in a number of locations in the Arctic (Kvenvolden, and Grantz, Chapter 28).

An airgun-reflection profile across a graben-like valley on the Alpha Ridge shows a thicker sedimentary section on the valley floor than on adjacent parts of the ridge (Fig. 14; Jackson and others, 1986). One of the valley walls appears to be covered by a chaotic, perhaps slumped, deposit. Similarly shaped valleys with exposed basement rims are observed on large oceanic plateaus such as the Manihiki, but it is not known whether they are strike-slip or tensional features. In addition there are localities on the crest of the Alpha Ridge where faulting has truncated the sedimentary horizons (Fig. 13). Here the reflectors are curved close to the fault plain, and coring in this location recovered Late Cretaceous fossils (Bukry, 1985; Barron, 1985; Mudie, 1985).

On the short excursion of ice island T-3 over the Mendeleev Ridge, up to 1 s of sedimentary cover was observed. Steep slopes

Seismic reflection and refraction 163

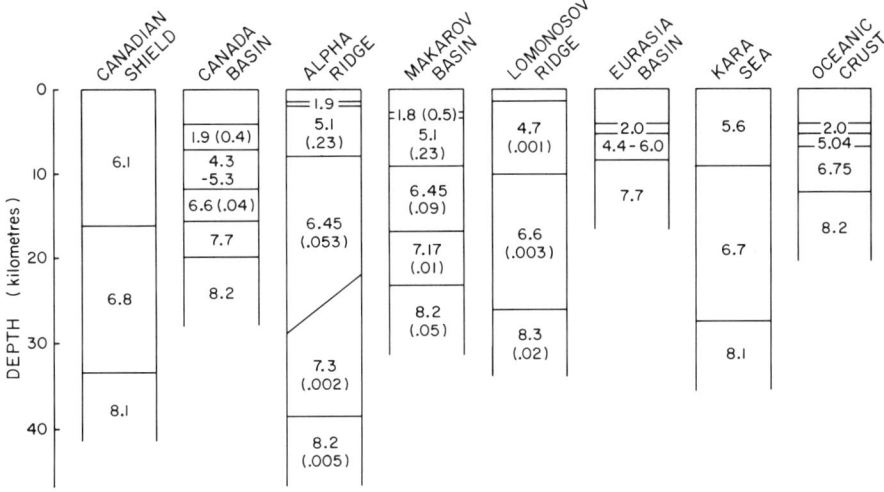

Figure 10. Column diagram summarizing refraction measurements from basins and major topographic features of the Arctic Ocean. The numbers following the velocities in brackets are velocity gradients. Velocity gradients are shown where ray tracing and synthetic seismogram processing techniques required them. Lines without gradients may have been completed before these processing techniques were commonly used or when the processing technique for the data is unknown.

and rough topography are evident even though the sedimentary cover smooths the basement irregularities (Hall, 1970). Along the Mendeleev Ridge an 80-km-long linear scarp and fault trough were examined. Hall (1970) describes the scarp as a buried basement feature enhanced by depositional accumulation. On the high side of the scarp, 100 m of undeformed sediments thicken toward the scarp face. In the trough a similar sequence, 900 m thick, is recorded. The greater accumulation of sedimentary strata in the trough is apparently due to sediment ponding, which implies that the scarp predates the period of deposition (Hall, 1970).

The crustal structure of the Alpha Ridge as determined by Forsyth and others (1986) has a basement velocity of 5.1 km/s with a gradient of 0.23 s^{-1} (Figure 15). The velocity structure below this layer showed lateral variations ranging from 6.45 to 6.8 km/s with both positive and negative velocity gradients. At a depth of 20 km, a more laterally consistent velocity of 7.3 km/s was determined. The 8.05 km/s velocity is not well constrained because few of the seismic rays traveled through this segment of the crust. The crust-mantle interface is at 38 km. The thick crustal structure and the high-velocity lower crust of the Alpha Ridge (Jackson and others, 1986) resemble the crustal structure of plateaus in the oceans believed to be formed of oceanic crust (Carlson and others, 1980). The velocity-depth profile is also similar to that observed beneath Iceland (Forsyth and others, 1986).

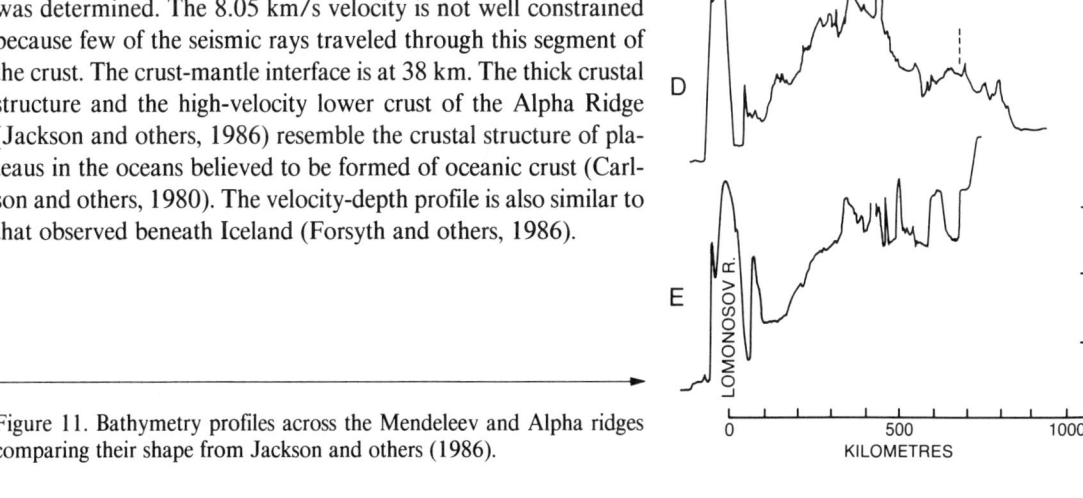

Figure 11. Bathymetry profiles across the Mendeleev and Alpha ridges comparing their shape from Jackson and others (1986).

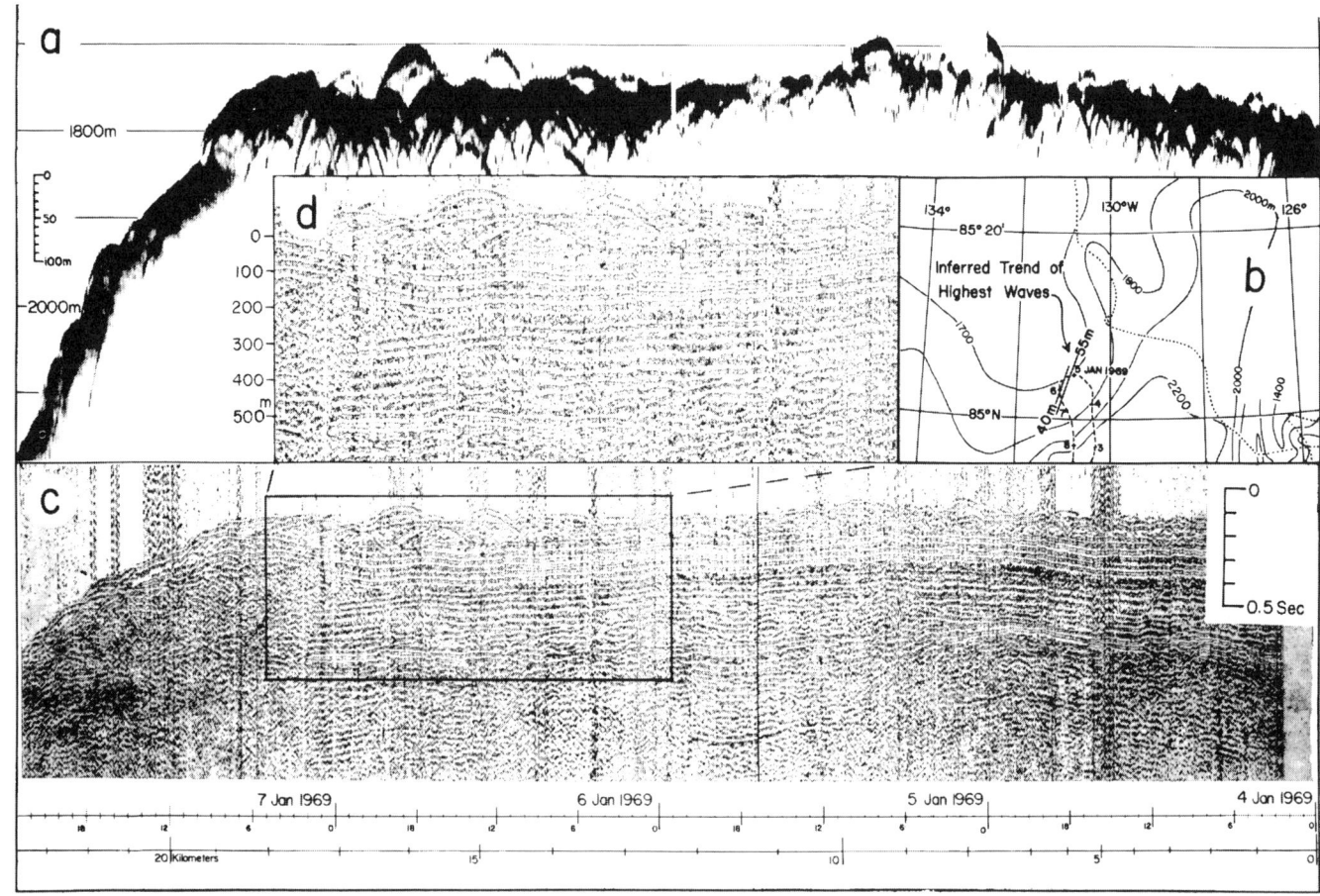

Figure 12. Seismic record from the crestal part of the Alpha Ridge showing overlapping hyperbolae identified as sediment waves: a, 12 Khz profile over the fossil sediment waves; b, location of the profile and the inferred trends of the 40 m and 55 m high sediment waves; c, 9,000 joule sparker profile along the same track as the 12 Khz profile; d, detail of the sediment wave and underlying reflectors taken from c. From Hall (1970, 1979).

Canada and Makarov basins

The sparse and poor-to-fair quality reflection lines in these basins do not penetrate to basement and show only a minimum thickness of sediment of 4 km (Grantz and others, Chapter 22, this volume). The thickness of sedimentary deposits in the various basins probably varies as a function of sediment supply from the bordering shelves. Crustal refraction experiments carried out at three locations on the periphery of the Canada Basin (Milne, 1966; Mair and Lyons, 1981; Baggeroer and Falconer, 1982; 21, 22, 38 on Fig. 2) observed a sedimentary section at least 4 to 5 km thick. The sedimentary column is thicker than that observed in most deep ocean basins because of the landlocked nature of the ocean and its probable Cretaceous age (Sweeney and others, 1982).

The uppermost sedimentary layers' velocity has been determined to be 1.8 km/s by the analysis of multiple water-wave events by Mair and Lyons (1981). The gradient is such that 3.5 km/s was the velocity used at the base of the section. Similarly a mean velocity of 2.7 km/s was used for the sedimentary strata by Baggeroer and Falconer (1982) based on nearby sonobuoy data (Ettreim and Grantz, 1979).

A velocity of 4.3 to 4.9 km/s is recorded as a strong event on all refraction data sets (Fig. 10). The high amplitude of the event suggested it is the sediment-crust interface. Supporting this interpretation, seismic reflection data near the site of CANBARX (Baggeroer and Falconer, 1982) shows indications of basement at the depth this boundary is observed. However, Grantz and others (Chapter 22, this volume) interpret the intersection of the 4.3 km/s reflector with the reflection data to be a sedimentary horizon. Thus the sedimentary secton may be greater than 5 km thick.

If Baggeroer and Falconer's (1982) interpretation of the 4.3 km/s arrivals as basement is correct, oceanic layer 2 is between 5.3 and 5.6 km thick compared to the average worldwide thickness of 1.39 ± 0.5 km (Christensen and Salisbury, 1975). However, the deeper crustal structure of the southern Canada Basin, including the base of layer 2, is poorly defined. Baggeroer

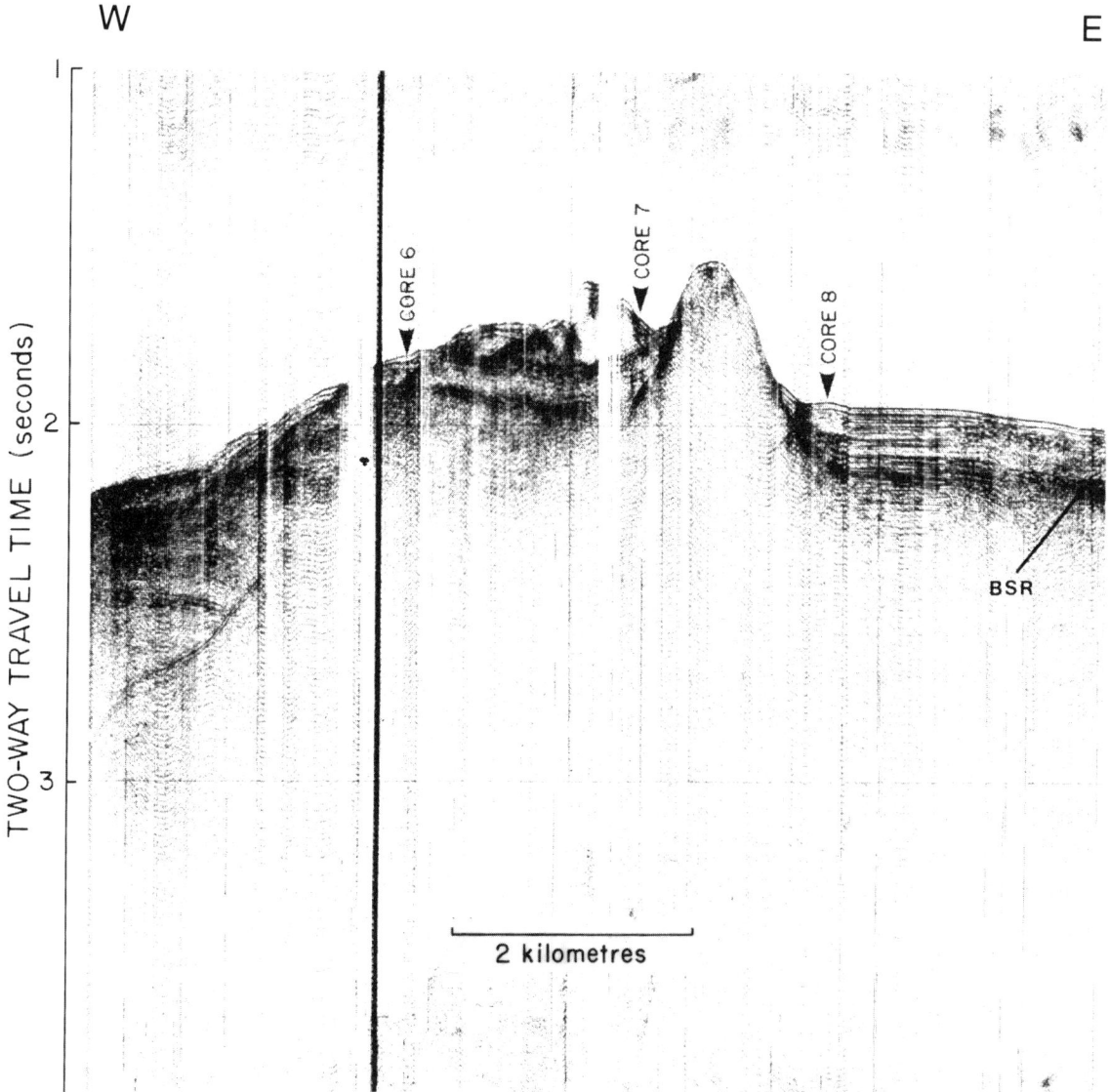

Figure 13. A 655 cm³ (40 in³) airgun single-channel reflection record from CESAR labeled as 16 in Figure 1. Here the sedimentary horizons are disturbed by faulting, and core 6 containing material of Late Cretaceous age verifies this. The bottom-simulating reflector (B.S.R.) is indicated.

and Falconer (1982) and Milne (1966) did not record a layer 3 velocity, and Mair and Lyons (1981) had difficulty finding seismic arrivals from this section of the crust. Oceanic crust having a velocity gradient produces arrivals more distinct than crust with discrete layering. The M discontinuity is identified by a break over to mantle refractors (Fig. 9). Mair and Lyons (1981) observed a velocity anistropy of 3 percent on mantle arrivals.

DISCUSSION

Figures 1 and 2 illustrate the limited seismic reflection and refraction coverage in the Arctic region. The text and the figures indicate the restrictions on the type and the quality of the data. The paucity of information confines the understanding of the sedimentary and crustal structure of the area. It is therefore difficult to deduce a unique origin and history for the area, and multiple hypotheses exist for many of the principal features of the Arctic Ocean.

In spite of the limited data base an attempt has been made to produce a sedimentary thickness map of the region. The seismic information, along with Soviet maps based on a variety of data sources, has been used to develop Figure 16 and Plate 5. This synopsis shows the contrasting sedimentary thicknesses in the Canada and Eurasia Basins. The contouring in the Eurasia Basin is smoother than that in the Norwegin-Greenland Sea because few data are available from the former. Sedimentary thicknesses of greater than 10 km are measured on the Barents and Laptev shelves and on the polar margins of northern Canada and Alaska. The irregular pattern of sedimentary deposits on the Alpha Ridge imitates the basement topography.

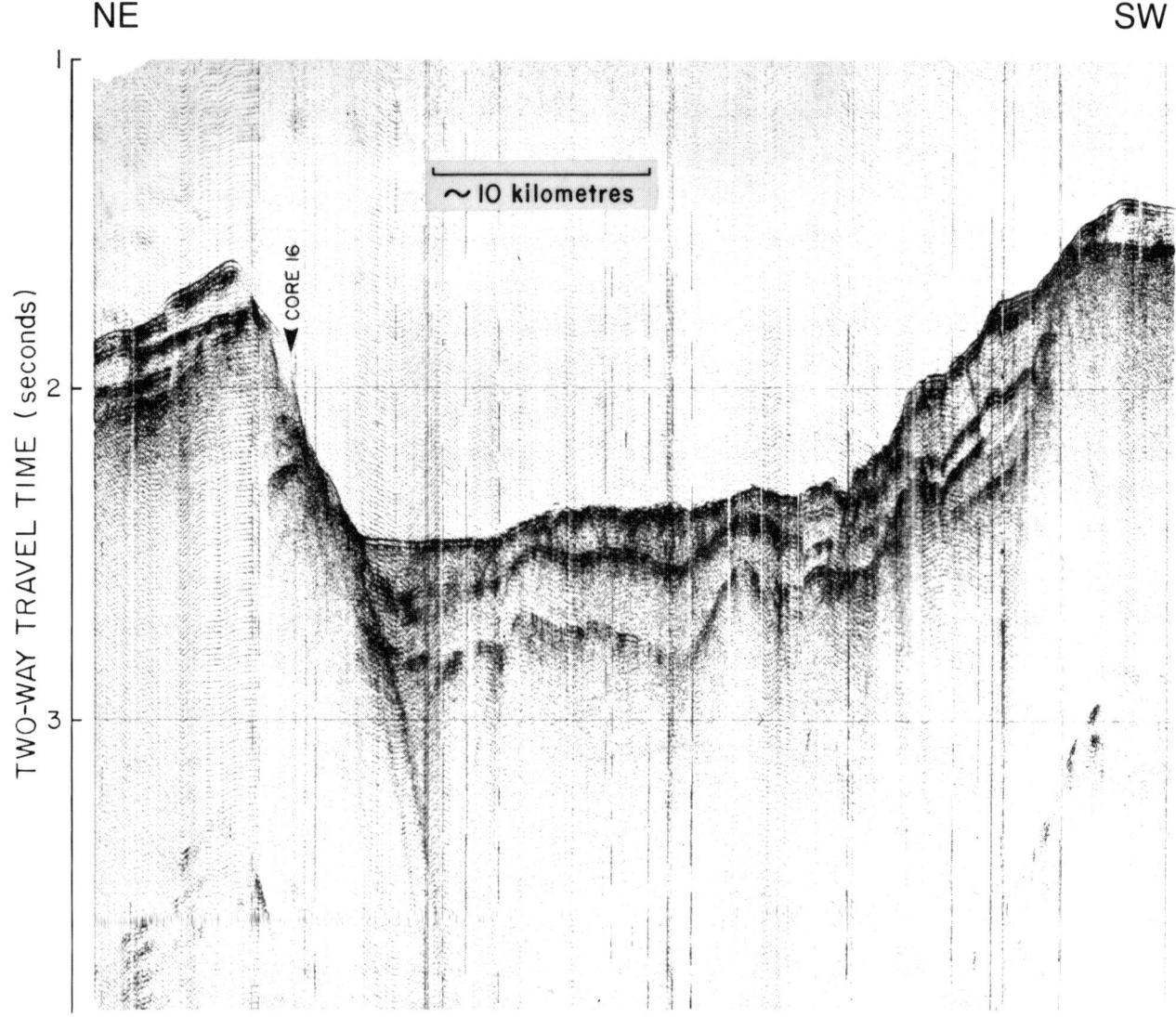

Figure 14. A 655 cm³ (40 in³) airgun single-channel reflection record from CESAR labeled as 16 in Figure 1 showing a cross section of a major valley in the Alpha Ridge.

The sedimentary reflectors in the deep basins and ridges are generally undisturbed by tectonic processes. In the deep basins the sedimentary horizons onlap basement and are commonly flat lying or conformable to basement. The sedimentary section in the Makarov Basin is less stratified than that in the Eurasia Basin. Locally disturbed reflectors occur on portions of the Alpha Ridge, the Lomonosov Ridge near North America, between the Lomonosov Ridge and the Morris Jesup Plateau, and on the Chukchi Plateau. The identified structures on the Alpha Ridge, grabens and faults, suggest that extensional processes occurred early in the depositional history, before much sedimentary accumulation. The lack of reflection profiles that penetrate to basement in the Canada Basin is a serious gap in our knowledge.

The seismic basement in the Makarov Basin exhibits more relief than basement in Amundsen Basin. Within 60 km of the Lomonosov Ridge in the vicinity of the North Pole basement rises through the Makarov Basin sedimentary deposits. Basement reflectors in the Eurasia Basin exhibit characteristics similar to those in most ocean basins. Basement of the Lomonosov Ridge near the North Pole has a sawtooth configuration probably due to block faulting that is not observed near its intersection with North America. On the Alpha Ridge, basement exhibits a complex topography. Seamounts, grabens, and exposed basement rims bordering large valleys are a few of the observed features. Crustal refraction studies in the three large subbasins of the Arctic Ocean demonstrate striking differences (Fig. 10). In the Eurasia Basin the salient character of the crust, oceanic layers 2 and 3, is its thinness, between 3 and 5 km. In contrast, what has been called the Makarov Basin in the vicinity of the Alpha Ridge has a crustal thickness of 23 km that includes a thick high-velocity layer. The

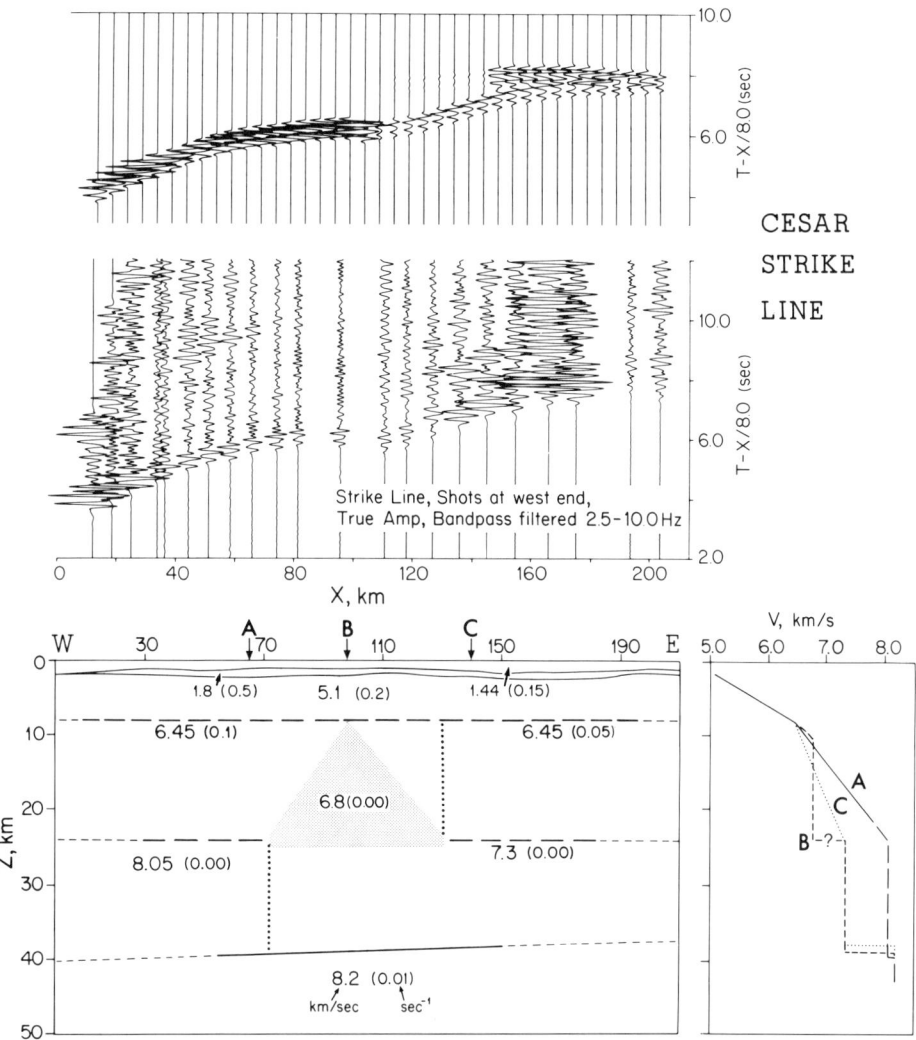

Figure 15. Synthetic seismogram (upper section) compared to seismic arrivals (middle section) from the CESAR strike line, Alpha Ridge. Also shown (bottom of the diagram) is the earth model used to produce the synthetics. The velocity-depth profiles (far right) are shown for three portions of the earth model labeled A, B and C (Forsyth and others, 1986).

crust in this portion of the Makarov Basin is similar to but thinner than the Alpha Ridge and may form part of the ridge. The refraction lines in the Makarov Basin are close to the Alpha and Lomonosov Ridges, and the structures measured may not be indicative of true basin crust. A refraction survey in the deep water of the Makarov Basin is needed to determine uniquely its velocity-depth curve. In the Canada Basin a thick sedimentary section obscures the crustal structure. There is uncertainty about whether the horizon identified as layer 2 near Alaska might be a sedimentary horizon. In this region, layer 3 velocity has proved to be difficult to measure. A refraction survey away from the continental margins is required to clarify these problems.

The Morris Jesup and the Chukchi Plateaus have been poorly surveyed; the Yermak Plateau has been studied in reconnaissance fashion. The southern portion of the Yermak Plateau and Svalbard exhibit similar velocities with continental affinities, while the northern portion of the Yermak and Morris Jesup Plateaus may be thick oceanic crust based on limited refraction data. Refraction and reflection lines are needed on the Chukchi Plateau, where no clearly established crustal or mantle velocities are available.

There remain many unanswered questions. The seismic reflection and refraction data cannot be combined to give sufficient information to define basement structures such as the extent to which the Alpha Ridge extends into the Makarov and Canada Basins and the manner in which the transition takes place. The basement relief on both the ridges and basins is inadequately documented. On the Alpha Ridge, where the densest seismic reflection coverage is available, a complicated basement structure is mapped and is also seen in the bathymetry. Where closely

Figure 16. Sedimentary thickness chart of the Arctic Ocean summarizing the results of the seismic data and incorporating results from other sources from Plate 5 (this volume).

spaced lines exist, an en echelon pattern of valleys can be seen. However, the denser the sounding spacing, the more irregular topography appears (Weber and Jackson, 1985).

Reiterating, there are too few reflection profiles in the Arctic Ocean that penetrate to basement to properly address these problems. The Lomonosov Ridge is crossed by only two reflection profiles; it is simply not enough to adequately describe the basement structures associated with it.

Although significant seismic reflection and refraction data have been collected in the Arctic Ocean, its ice cover restricts the collection of seismic data in a normal shipboard fashion so that there are many gaps in our knowledge that prevent understanding of this ocean in a manner comparable with more southerly seas. The Arctic Ocean continues to be an area where more measurements are needed to improve our understanding of its structure and origin.

REFERENCES

Asudeh, I., Forsyth, D. A., Jackson, H. R., Stephensen, R., and White, D., 1985, 1985 Ice Island refraction survey phase 1 report: Earth Physics Branch Open File 85-23, Geological Survey of Canada Open File 1196, 25 p.

Baggeroer, A. B., and Falconer, R.H.F., 1982, Array refraction profiles and crustal models of the Canada Basin: Journal of Geophysical Research, v. 87, no. 87, p. 5461–5476.

Barron, J. A., 1985, Diatom biostratigraphy of the CESAR 6 core, Alpha Ridge, in Jackson, H. R., Mudie, P. J., and Blasco, S. M., eds., Initial geological reports on CESAR; The Canadian expedition to study the Alpha Ridge: Geological Survey of Canada Paper 84-22, p. 137–148.

Bee, M., Johnson, S. H., and Chiburis, E. F., 1984, Marine seismic refraction study between Cape Simpson and Prudhoe Bay, Alaska: Journal of Geophysical Research, v. 89, no B8, p. 6941–6960.

Berry, M. J., and Barr, K. G., 1971, A seismic refraction profile across the Polar continental shelf of the Queen Elizabeth Islands: Canadian Journal of Earth Sciences, v. 8, p. 347–360.

Blasco, S. M., Bornhold, B. D., and Lewis, C.F.M., 1979, Preliminary results of the surficial geology and geomorphology studies of the Lomonosov Ridge, central Arctic Ocean: Geological Survey of Canada Paper 79-C, p. 73–83.

Bukry, D., 1985, Correlation of Late Cretaceous Arctic silicoflagellates from Alpha Ridge, in Jackson, H. R., Mudie, P. J., and Blasco, S. M., eds., Initial geological report on CESAR: The Canadian expedition to study the Alpha Ridge: Geological Survey of Canada Paper 84-22, p. 125–136.

Carlson, R. L., Christensen, N. I., and Moore, R. P., 1980, Anomalous crustal structures in ocean basins, continental fragments, and oceanic plateaus: Earth and Planetary Science Letters, v. 51, p. 171–180.

Chan, W. W., and Mitchell, B. J., 1982, Synthetic seismogram and surface wave constraints on crustal models of Spitsbergen: Tectonophysics, v. 89, p. 51–76.

Christensen, N. I., and Salisbury, M. H., 1975, Structure and constitution of the lower oceanic crust: Reviews of Geophysics and Space Physics, v. 13, p. 57–86.

Crary, A. P., and Goldstein, N., 1957, Geophysical studies in the Arctic Ocean: Deep-Sea Research, v. 4, p. 185–201.

Davydova, N. I., Pavlenokova, N. I., Tulina, Yu.V., and Zverev, S. M., 1985, Crustal structure of the Barents Sea from seismic data: Tectonophysics, v. 114, p. 213–231.

Dietrich, J. R., Dixon, J., and McNeil, D. H., 1985, Sequence analysis and nomenclature of the Upper Cretaceous to Holocene strata in the Beaufort-MacKenzie Basin: Geological Survey of Canada Paper 85-1A, p. 613–628.

Duckworth, G. L., and Baggeroer, A. B., 1985, Inversion of refraction data from the Fram and Nansen basins of the Arctic Ocean: Tectonophysics, v. 114, p. 55–102.

Duckworth, G. L., Baggeroer, A. B., and Jackson, H. R., 1982, Crustal structure measurements near FRAM II in the Pole Abyssal Plain: Tectonophysics, v. 89, p. 173–215.

Eittreim, S., and Grantz, A., 1979, CDP seismic sections of the western Beaufort continental margin: Tectonophysics, v. 59, p. 251–262.

Eldholm, O., and Windisch, C. C., 1974, Sediment distribution in the Norwegian-Greenland Sea: Geological Society of America Bulletin, v. 85, p. 1661–1676.

Eldholm, O., Sundvor, E., and Myhre, A. M., 1979, Continental margin off Lofoten-Vesteralen, northern Norway: Marine Geophysical Researches, v. 4, p. 3–35.

Eldholm, O., Sundvor, E., and Crane, K., 1984, Sonobuoy measurements during the "Ymer" expedition: Norsk Polarinstitutt Skrifter, v. 180, p. 17–23.

Feden, R. H., Vogt, P. R., and Fleming, H. S., 1979, Magnetic and bathymetric evidence of the "Ymer" hot spot northwest of Svalbard in the Arctic Ocean: Earth and Planetary Science Letters, v. 44, p. 18–38.

Forsyth, D. A., and Mair, J. A., 1984, Crustal structure of the Lomonosov Ridge and the Fram and Makarov basins near the North Pole: Journal of Geophysical Research, v. 89, p. 473–481.

Forsyth, D. A., Mair, J. A., and Fraser, I., 1979, Crustal structure of the Sverdrup Basin: Canadian Journal of Earth Sciences, v. 16, p. 1581–1598.

Forsyth, D. A., Asudeh, I., and Green, A. G., 1985, Crustal structure of the Arctic, Northern Alpha Cordillera, and Makarov Basin [abs.]: Geological Association of Canada, v. 10, p. A18.

Forsyth, D. A., Asudeh, I., Green, A. G., and Jackson, H. R., 1986, Crustal structure of the northern Alpha Ridge: Nature, v. 322, p. 349–352.

Grachev, A. F., 1982, Geodynamics of the Transitional Zone from the Moma Rift to the Gakkel Ridge, in Watkins, J. S., and Drake, C. L., eds., Studies in continental margin geology: American Association of Petroleum Geologists Memoir 34, p. 103–113.

Grantz, A., and May, S. D., 1984, Summary geological report for Barrow Arch outer continental shelf planning area, Chukchi Sea: U.S. Geological Survey Open-File Report 84-395, 40 p.

Grantz, A., Holmes, M. L., and Kososki, B. A., 1975, Geologic framework of the Alaskan Continental Terrace in the Chukchi and Beaufort seas: American Association of Petroleum Geologists Memoir 19, p. 669–700.

Grantz, A., and six others, 1982, Geological framework hydrocarbon potential and environmental conditions for exploration and development of proposed oil and gas lease sale 87 in the Beaufort Sea and northeastern Chukchi Sea: U.S. Geological Survey Open-File Report 82-482, 80 p.

Hall, J. K., 1970, Arctic Ocean geophysical studies; The Alpha Cordillera and Mendeleyev Ridge [Ph.D. thesis]: New York, Columbia University, 125 p.

——, 1973, Geophysical evidence for ancient sea floor spreading from Alpha Cordillera and Mendeleyev Ridge, in Pitcher, M. G., ed., Arctic geology: American Association of Petroleum Geologists Memoir 19, p. 542–561.

——, 1979, Sediment waves and other evidence of paleo-bottom currents at two locations in the deep Arctic ocean: Sedimentary Geology, v. 23, p. 269–299.

Hobson, G. D., 1962, Seismic exploration in the Canadian Arctic Islands: Geophysics, v. 28, p. 253–273.

Hobson, G. D., and Overton, A., 1967, A seismic section of the Sverdrup Basin, Canadian Arctic Islands, in Musgrave, A. W., ed., Seismic refraction prospecting: The Society of Exploration Geophysicists, p. 550–562.

Houtz, R., and Windisch, C., 1977, Barents Sea continental margin sonobuoy data: Geological Society of America Bulletin, v. 88, p. 1030–1036.

Houtz, R. E., Ettreim, S., and Grantz, A., 1981, Acoustic properties of the northern Alaskan shelves in relation to the regional geology: Journal of Geophysics, v.86, p. 3932–3943.

Hunkins, K., 1961, Seismic studies of the Arctic Ocean floor: Palisades, New York, Lamont-Doherty Geological Observatory Scientific Report 1, AFCRCTN60-257, 14 p.

——, 1966, The Arctic continental shelf north of Alaska, in Poole, W. M., ed., Continental margins and island arcs: Geological Survey of Canada paper 66-15, p. 197–205.

Hunkins, K., and Tiemann, W., 1977, Geophysical data summary for Fletcher's Ice Island (T-3) May 1962–October 1974: Palisades, New York, Lamont-Doherty Geological Observatory Technical Report Cu-1-77, 219 p.

Hunkins, K., Manley, T. O., Tiemann, W., and Jackson, H. R., 1981, Geophysical data from drifting ice station Fram III: Palisades, New York, Lamont-Doherty Geological Observatory Technical Report no. 3, Cu-3-81, 106 p.

Jackson, H. R., 1985, Seismic reflection results from CESAR, in Jackson, H. R., Mudie, P. M., and Blasco, S. M., eds., Initial geological report on CESAR; The Canadian expedition to study the Alpha Ridge: Geological Survey of Canada Paper 84-22, p. 19–23.

Jackson, H. R., Keen, C. E., and Barrett, D. L., 1977, Geophysical studies on the eastern continental margin of Baffin Bay and in Lancaster Sound: Canadian Journal of Earth Sciences, v. 14, p. 1991–2001.

Jackson, H. R., Reid, I., and Falconer, R.K.H., 1982, Crustal structure near the Arctic Mid-Ocean Ridge: Journal of Geophysical Research, v. 87, p. 1773–1783.

Jackson, H. R., Johnson, G. L., Sundvor, E., and Myhre, A. M., 1984, The Yermak Plateau, formed at a triple junction: Journal of Geophysical Research, v. 89, p. 3223–3232.

Jackson, H. R., Forsyth, D. A., and Johnson, G. L., 1986, Oceanic affinities of the Alpha Ridge: Marine Geology, v. 73, p. 237–261.

Keen, C. E., and Barrett, D. L., 1972, Seismic refraction studies in Baffin Bay; An example of developing ocean basin: Geophysical Journal of the Royal Astronomical Society, v. 30, p. 253–271.

Kristoffersen, Y., 1982a, United States ice drift station Fram IV; Report on the Norwegian field program, NR-11: Oslo, Norsk Polarinstitutt, 60 p.

——, 1982b, The Nansen Ridge, Arctic Ocean; Some geophysical observations of the rift valley at slow spreading rate: Tectonophysics, v. 89, p. 161–172.

Kristoffersen, Y., and Husebye, E. S., 1984, Multichannel seismic reflection measurements in the Eurasian Basin, Arctic Ocean, from the United States ice station Fram IV: Tectonophysics, v. 114, p. 103–115.

Kristoffersen, Y., Husebye, E. S., Bungum, H., and Gregersen, S., 1982, Seismic investigations of the Nansen Ridge during the Fram I experiment: Tectonophysics, v. 82, p. 57–68.

Kutschale, H., 1966, Arctic Ocean geophysical studies; The southern half of the Siberia Basin: Geophysics, v. 31, no. 4, p. 683–710.

Mair, J. A., and Forsyth, D. A., 1982, Crustal structures of the Canada Basin near Alaska; The Lomonosov Ridge and adjoining basins near the North Pole: Tectonophysics, v. 89, p. 239–253.

Mair, J. A., and Lyons, J. A., 1981, Crustal structure and velocity anistropy beneath the Beaufort Sea: Canadian Journal of Earth Sciences, v. 18, no. 4, p. 724–741.

Milne, A. R., 1966, A seismic refraction measurement in the Beaufort Sea: Seismological Society of America Bulletin, v. 56, p. 775–779.

Mudie, P. J., 1985, Palynology of the CESAR cores, Alpha Ridge, in Jackson, H. R., Mudie, P. J., and Blasco, S. M., eds., Initial geological report on CESAR; The Canadian expedition to study the Alpha Ridge: Geological Survey of Canada Paper 84-22, p. 149–174.

Myhre, A. M., and Eldholm, O., 1988, The western Svalbard margin (74°80°N): Marine and Petroleum Geology: Marine and Petroleum Geology, v. 5, p. 134–156.

Ojo, S. B., Jackson, H. R., and Duckworth, G. L., 1986, Shear wave constraints on the crustal structure of the Pole Abyssal Plain: Journal of Geodynamics, v. 6, p. 71–90.

Ostenso, N. A., and Wold, R. J., 1977, A seismic and gravity profile across the Arctic Ocean Basin: Tectonophysics, v. 37, p. 1–24.

Overton, A., 1970, Seismic refraction surveys western Queen Elizabeth Islands and Polar continental margin: Canadian Journal of Earth Sciences, v. 7, p. 346–365.

——, 1980, Intermediate reflection profiles: EOS Transactions of the American Geophysical Union, v. 61, p. 276.

——, 1982, Seismic reconnaissance profiles across the Sverdrup Basin, Canadian Arctic Islands: Geological Survey of Canada Paper 82-1B, p. 139–145.

Riis, F., Vollset, J., and Sand, M., 1986, Tectonic development of the western margin of the Barents Sea and adjacent areas, in Halbouty, M. T., ed., Future Petroleum Provinces of the World: American Assocation of Petroleum Geologists Memoir 40, p. 661–675.

Ronnevik, H., and Jacobsen, H. P., 1984, Structural high and basins in the western Barents Sea, in Spencer, A. M., and others, eds., Petroleum geology of the northern European margin: London, Graham and Trotman Ltd., p. 19–32.

Sander, G. W., and Overton, A., 1965, Deep seismic refraction investigation in the Canadian Arctic Archipelago: Geophysics, v. 30, p. 87–96.

Sundvor, E., and Eldholm, O., 1979, The western and northern margin off Svalbard, in Keen, C. E., ed., Crustal properties across passive margins: Developments in Geotectonics, v. 15, Amsterdam, Elsevier Scientific Publishing Co., p. 239–250.

Sundvor, E., and five others, 1982, Marine geophysical survey of the Yermak Plateau: The Norwegian Petroleum Directorate/Geophysical Investigations Scientific Report no. 7, 14 p.

Sweeney, J. F., Weber, J. R., and Blasco, S. M., 1982, Continental ridges in the Arctic Ocean, LOREX constraints: Tectonophysics, v. 89, p. 217–238.

Talwani, M., and Eldholm, O., 1974, Margins of the Norwegian-Greenland Sea, in Burk, C. A., and Drake, C. L., eds., The Geology of Continental Margins: New York, Springer-Verlag, p. 361–374.

Weber, J. R., and Sweeney, J. F., 1985, Reinterpretation of morphology and crustal structure in the central Arctic Ocean Basin: Journal of Geophysical Research, v. 90, p. 663–677.

Weber, J. R., and Jackson, H. R., 1985, CESAR bathymetry, in Jackson, H. R., and Blasco, S. M., eds., Initial geological report on CESAR; The Canadian expedition to study the Alpha Ridge: Geological Survey of Canada Paper 84-22, p. 15–17.

Manuscript Accepted by the Society June 16, 1987

ACKNOWLEDGMENTS

We wish to thank Dr. G. L. Johnson for the encouragement he provided to us while writing this paper. Many helpful suggestions for improving the manuscript were given by Drs. A. Baggeroer, A. Grantz, O. Eldholm, and J. Sweeney.

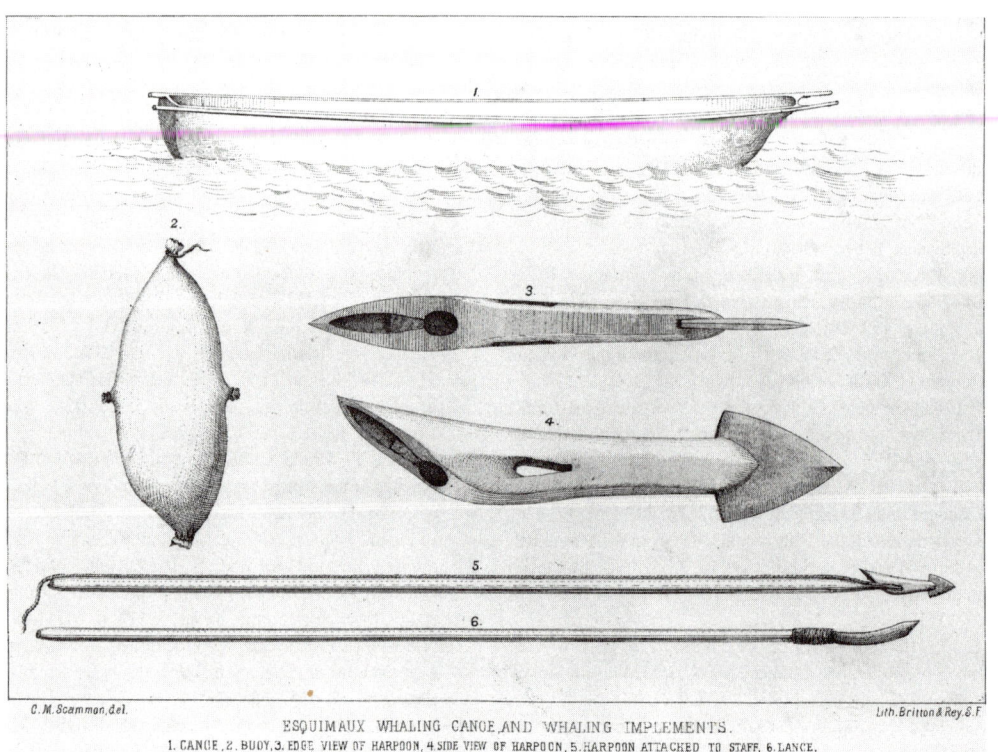

From Charles M. Scammon, 1874, The Marine Mammals of the North-western Coast of North America: San Francisco, John H. Carmany and Company, facing p. 37.

Chapter 11

The North American plate boundary

Olav Eldholm
Department of Geology, University of Oslo, Oslo, Norway
A. M. Karasik (Deceased)
LO ISMIR AN, USSR Academy of Sciences, Leningrad, U.S.S.R.
P. A. Reksnes*
Department of Geology, University of Oslo, Oslo, Norway

INTRODUCTION

In the Norwegian-Greenland Sea and the Arctic Ocean the present-day North American plate boundary exhibits great variety in morphology and structural style. From the neovolcanic rift zone in Iceland the plate boundary extends into the Norwegian-Greenland Sea and the Eurasian Basin of the Arctic Ocean as a system of mid-oceanic ridge segments and transform faults, but becomes less distinct beneath the Siberian continental margin (Fig. 1). The asymmetry in the location of some of the active spreading axes, as well as the existence of extinct spreading centers, microcontinents, and volcanic plateaus and ridges imply a complex structural evolution of the surrounding ocean basins. It is reasonably well documented that the oldest oceanic crust formed by sea-floor spreading between Greenland, Lomonosov Ridge, and Eurasia dates back to the negative polarity interval between magnetic anomalies 24B and 25 (late Paleocene/early Eocene).

In this chapter we focus on a description of the present plate boundary in terms of morphology, relative plate motion, variation in geological and geophysical parameters, and seismicity. For practical purposes we restrict ourselves to the youngest crust and primarily discuss the crust formed during the past 10 m.y. More comprehensive treatments of the ocean basins and their plate tectonic evolution are presented by Eldholm and others (this volume) and by Kristoffersen and others (this volume). Various aspects of the plate boundary north of Iceland have also been discussed in the Western North Atlantic synthesis volume of this series (Einarsson, 1986; Melson and O'Hearn, 1986; Schilling, 1986; Srivastava and Tapscottt, 1986; Vogt, 1986).

During the last few years, sophisticated experiments and mapping techniques have provided detailed information about ridges and fracture zones and have yielded a new dimension to our understanding of geological processes occurring at plate boundaries. However, almost no such data are available in the region covered by this chapter. Therefore, the observations and inferences presented here, based largely on regional track coverage, must be considered as primarily revealing only first-order features and phenomena.

GENERAL DESCRIPTION

In a regional sense the continuation of the mid-Atlantic Ridge system into the Norwegian-Greenland Sea and the Arctic Ocean is well documented (Johnson and Heezen, 1967a, 1967b; Rassokho and others, 1967), with typical axial segments offset by transform faults of varying lengths (Karasik, 1968; Johnson, 1974; Grønlie and Talwani, 1979; Johnson and others, 1979 and this volume; Perry and others, 1980, 1985; Plate 1). However, in terms of the detailed plate boundary configuration, there are still areas where the actual location must be considered tentative. This uncertainty is caused both by inadequate data coverage and by structural complexities.

The plate boundary, as shown in Figures 1–6, is primarily defined by bathymetry and basement relief in seismic profiles. Along the axial segments, it has been plotted in the central rift valley, or at the ridge summit where no axial valley exists. Elsewhere, the positive central magnetic anomaly has been used as a guide.

At present, the spreading rate (half-rate) varies from about 0.3 cm/yr in the eastern Eurasia Basin to 1.1 cm/yr at the southern Iceland Plateau (Fig. 7). According to the definition of Fox and Gallo (1984), we would expect slow-slipping transforms to have developed between the axial segments. These features are characterized by a broad, anomalously deep valley bounded by inward-facing and opposing walls having a relief in the range 1 to 5 km. Fox and Gallo (1984) note that the transform fault relief is

---
*Present address: Norsk Hydro A/S, Oslo, Norway.

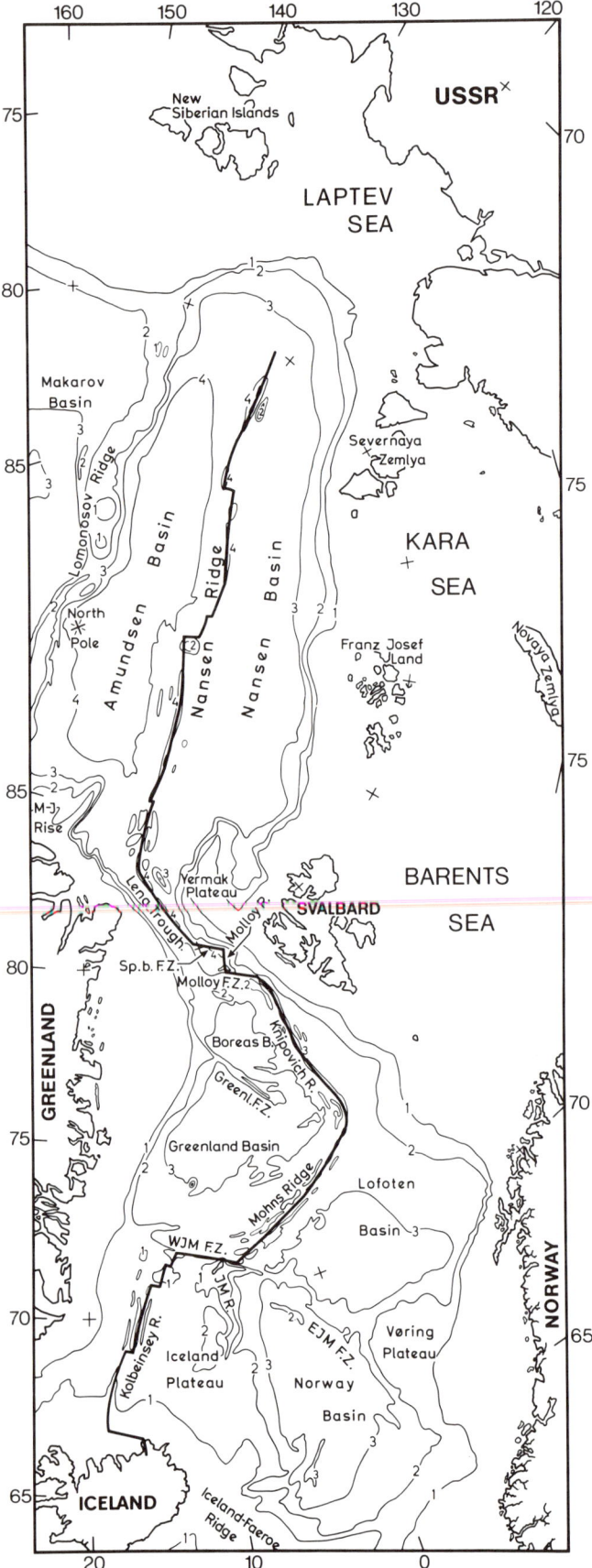

Figure 1. Main physiographic and structural elements in the vicinity of the plate boundary north of Iceland. Selected bathymetry from Perry and others (1980, 1985) and Johnson and others (1979). Contour interval 1 km. M-J Rise: Morris-Jessup Rise. WMJ F.Z. and EJM F.Z.: west and east Jan Mayen Fracture Zone respectively. Sp.b. F.Z.: Spitsbergen Fracture Zone.

relatively small, about 1.5 km, for offsets less than 30 km, increasing to several kilometers for offsets larger than 100 km. A bathymetric depression at the ridge-transform intersection is also quite typical. Sleep and Biehler (1970) explained such nodal depressions as representing areas of additional hydraulic head loss due to the viscosity of the rising asthenospheric material, whereas Parmentier and Forsyth (1985) introduced a pressure gradient associated with horizontal flow in the ridge axis conduit. In general, similar features are observed in the study area where there are prominent nodal deeps at either end of the west Jan Mayen Fracture Zone and the Molloy Ridge and smaller magnitude depressions at other ridge-transform intersections. These criteria have been used to define the transform segments of the plate boundary (Figs. 2–6).

In the following we base our description on a series of five maps (Figs. 2–6) showing the plate boundary and the crust younger than about 10 Ma. The maps are presented in a polar stereographic projection showing the bathymetry of Perry and others (1980, 1985), earthquake epicenters compiled by the International Seismological Center and U.S. Geological Survey, flowlines depicting the relative plate motion since anomaly 5 time, and finally sediment isopachs (Karlstad, 1981; Økern, 1981). The isopachs represent average sediment thickness smoothed over a 37-km moving interval along the seismic profiles and are expressed in two-way reflection time.

Kolbeinsey Ridge (Fig. 2)

The neovolcanic zone in eastern Iceland intersects the coastline between 16 and 17°W in a region where the plate boundary moves offshore and is offset by the Tjørnes Fracture Zone about 75 km westward to the bathymetrically well-defined Kolbeinsey Ridge. The Tjørnes Fracture Zone is not clearly expressed in the bathymetry, but Sæmundsson (1974) defines it as a 60-km-wide zone bounded to the south by the Husavik Fault (Fig. 2). According to McMaster and others (1977), the Tjørnes Fracture Zone is presently in a transient deformational stage. The fracture zone was generated by an eastward jump of the plate boundary about 4.5 Ma. The Husavik Fault is continued offshore by a narrow, elongate, negative free-air gravity anomaly (Palmason, 1974; Talwani and Eldholm, 1977) which may reflect an infilled transform valley. At about 1 Ma the rift in Iceland propagated north (Sæmundsson, 1974) and the present transform probably lies in the vicinity of the northern boundary in Figure 2 extending towards the 700-m-deep nodal depression at the southern end of the Kolbeinsey Ridge. The pattern of linear magnetic anomalies

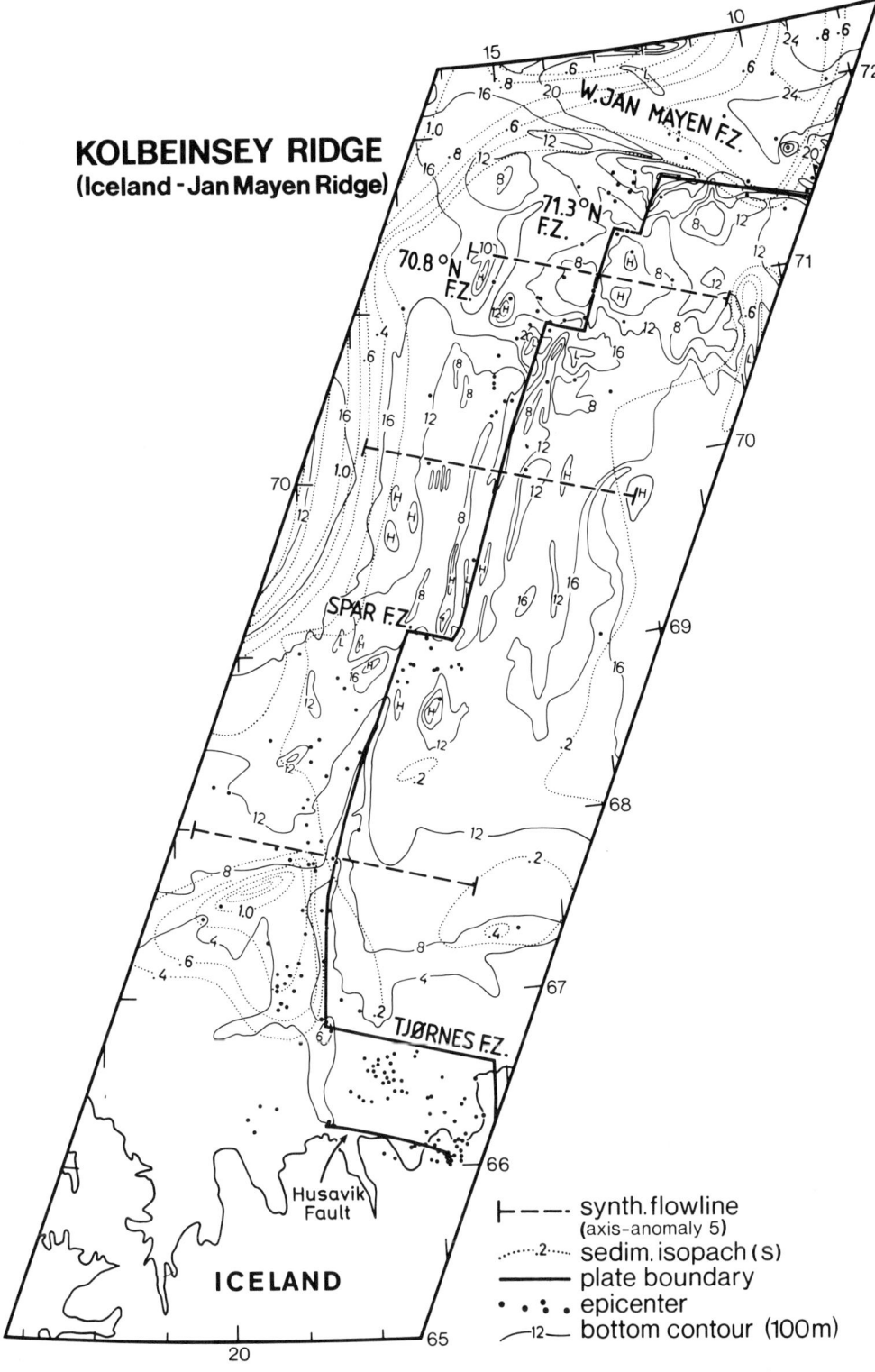

Figure 2. The plate boundary region between Iceland and West Jan Mayen Fracture Zone. Bathymetry, contour interval 400 m, from Perry and others (1980). Earthquake epicenters north of Iceland, sediment isopachs (Karlstad, 1981), and flowlines (Talwani and Eldholm, 1977) also shown.

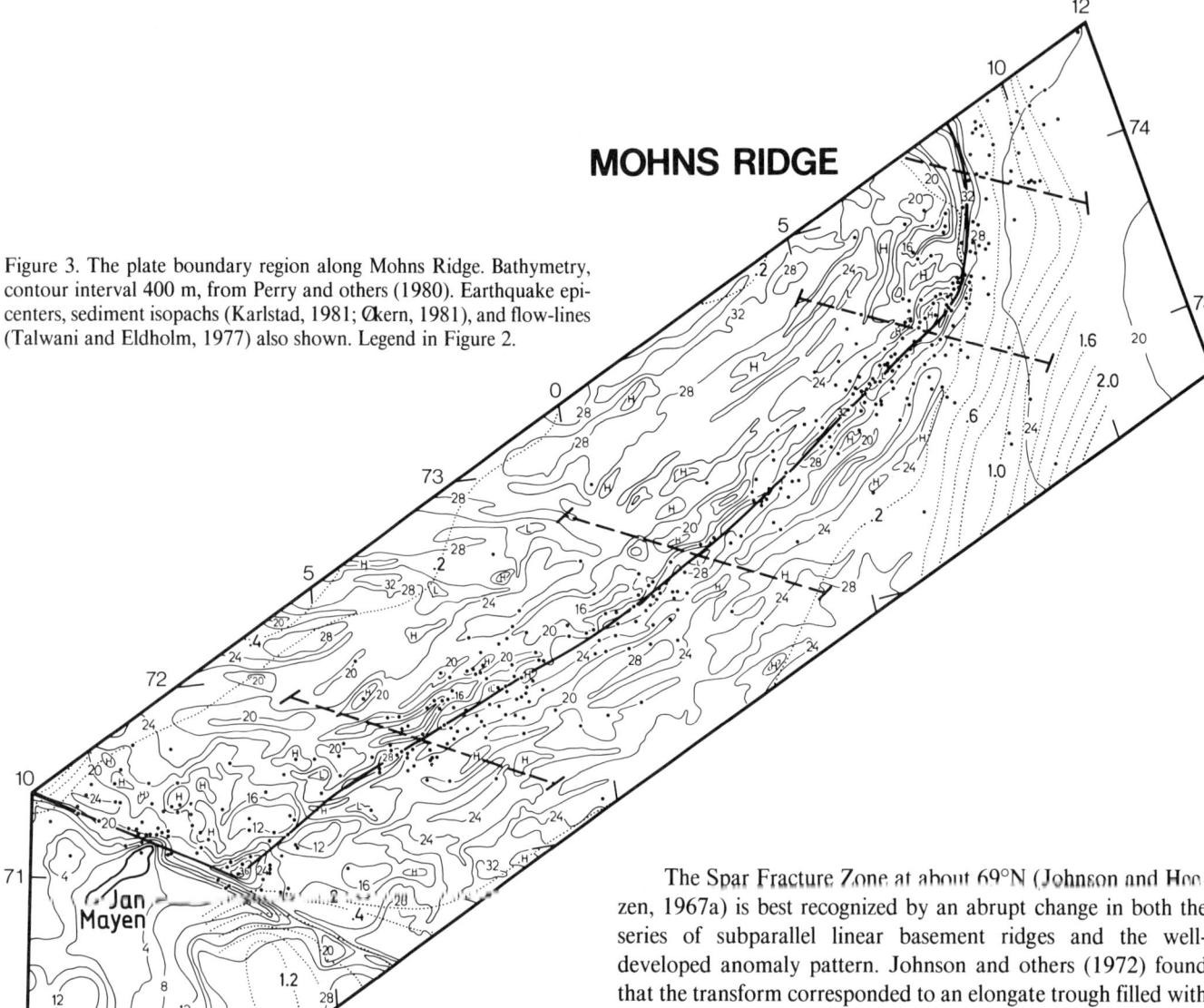

Figure 3. The plate boundary region along Mohns Ridge. Bathymetry, contour interval 400 m, from Perry and others (1980). Earthquake epicenters, sediment isopachs (Karlstad, 1981; Økern, 1981), and flow-lines (Talwani and Eldholm, 1977) also shown. Legend in Figure 2.

along the ridge breaks up at the Tjørnes Fracture Zone (Meyer and others, 1972; Litvin and others, 1978).

The Kolbeinsey Ridge axis comprises several segments that are shifted eastward by small offset fracture zones, which also demarcate changes in the ridge morphology. Vogt and others (1980) suggested that numerous minor fracture zones and bends superimposed on this main pattern may have formed during the last 10 m.y. Apparently, these features are ephemeral, lasting only a few million years, without significant offset and separated by distances of 30–50 km.

From the Iceland shelf the ridge plunges northward toward the Spar Fracture Zone. There is little axial relief on either side of the axial block (Fig. 8). This anomalously shallow spreading ridge segment has not developed a rift valley, thus resembling the Reykjanes Ridge south of Iceland.

The Spar Fracture Zone at about 69°N (Johnson and Heezen, 1967a) is best recognized by an abrupt change in both the series of subparallel linear basement ridges and the well-developed anomaly pattern. Johnson and others (1972) found that the transform corresponded to an elongate trough filled with up to 400 m of sediments. The depositional pattern indicates a westward bottom current flowing along the depression. The offset is about 30 km, and the fracture zone came into existence by an eastward shift of the ridge axis about 3 Ma (Meyer and others, 1972; Talwani and Eldholm, 1977), although an earlier feature was postulated by Vogt and others (1980).

Except for its shallow depth, the ridge morphology between 69.0 and 70.8°N resembles a mid-oceanic ridge. The rift valley lies at a depth of 1,100–1,400 m with axial mountains rising 300–800 m above this level. Here, the western mountains have more accentuated relief and stand somewhat higher than those on the eastern side. This ridge segment terminates at a small, 25-km offset fracture zone at 70.8°N, north of which the basement topography becomes fragmented and complex without a distinct axial zone. North of 70.8°N the plate boundary suggested in Figure 2 is the best fit to the topography, assuming a termination at the pronounced basement depression at the western Jan Mayen Fracture Zone and including a minor fracture zone at 71.3°N (Vogt and others, 1981). The nodal deep at the West Jan

Mayen Fracture Zone, is barren of sediments and reveals recent tectonic activity (Johnson and Campsie, 1976). The fracture zone at 70.8°N, which was earlier placed at 70.5°N based on epicenter information (Johnson and Campsie, 1976), originated by an axial shift not earlier than 4 Ma (Talwani and Eldholm, 1977). Interestingly, this fracture zone lines up with a prominent, bight-like feature at the western margin of the Jan Mayen Ridge.

Disregarding local accumulations, the axial zone has little sediment cover; however, there is a marked asymmetry in sediment distribution on either side of the ridge as the crust becomes older. The thicker sediments on the western flank have been attributed to the fact that the ridge has restricted material from the main source area at the Greenland margin (Eldholm and Windisch, 1974). However, a remarkable feature exists near 67.6°N, 20°W close to the ridge axis. Here, about 1.4 km of low-velocity sediments have been deposited on very young crust.

West Jan Mayen Fracture Zone (Figs. 2 and 3)

The transform part of the West Jan Mayen Fracture Zone is one of the best defined structural elements in the Norwegian-Greenland Sea. It separates the shallow, young Iceland Plateau from the deeper and older Greenland Basin. Its existence was postulated by Sykes (1965) and mapped by Johnson and Heezen (1967a). Both ridge-transform intersections are amplified by the prominent nodal depressions having maximum depths of more than 3.4 and 3.8 km, respectively. In cross section the transform is defined by a steeply dipping east–northeast facing basement escarpment and a parallel basement depression at the foot of the wall. Locally, there are sediment-filled troughs and small ridges that are subparallel to the fracture zone, but the main escarpment is mostly devoid of sediments. Jan Mayen Island with its active Beerenberg volcano just south of the escarpment may be genetically related to the transform, although a hot-spot origin for the island and its surroundings has been suggested (Johnson and Campsie, 1976).

The complex, and still debated, history of the formation of the Iceland Plateau makes the age of the West Jan Mayen Fracture Zone somewhat uncertain. It may date back to anomaly 13 time (36 Ma), but could be younger, possibly initiated at the time of final separation of the Jan Mayen microcontinent from Greenland about 25 Ma.

Mohns and Knipovich ridges (Figs. 3 and 4)

The continuous spreading axis between West Jan Mayen Fracture Zone and the Molloy Fracture Zone is composed of two parts: the northeast-trending Mohns Ridge and the north-trending

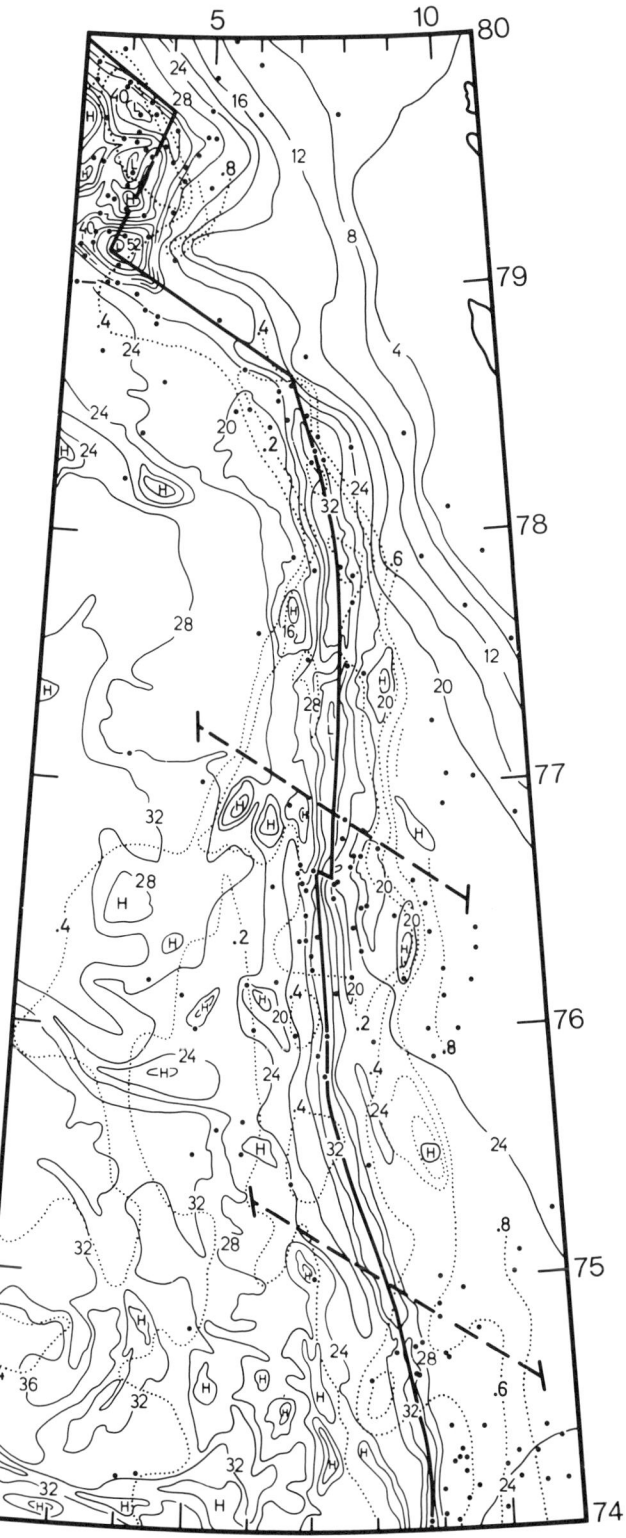

Figure 4. The plate boundary region along Knipovich Ridge. Bathymetry, contour interval 400 m, from Perry and others (1980). Earthquake epicenters, selected sediment isopachs (Eldholm and others, 1980), and flowlines (Talwani and Eldholm, 1977) also shown. Legend in Figure 2.

Knipovich Ridge. These ridges, of which Mohns Ridge is centrally located in the ocean basin and Knipovich Ridge lies on the eastern side approaching the Svalbard continental margin, contrast also in terms of ridge morphology and geophysical parameters.

Mohns Ridge has been the most stable part of the plate boundary in the Norwegian-Greenland Sea since the early Eocene. It is characterized by an axial rift valley with depth generally between 2.8 and 3.2 km increasing to the northeast. The axial mountains rise 1.5 to 2.0 km above the valley floor, but the axial mountains exhibit more relief and rise higher on the northwestern side (Vogt and others, 1982). A central positive magnetic anomaly is associated with the rift valley and is flanked by linear sea-floor spreading type lineations. Although the rift valley appears continuous north of 71.4°N, there may exist very small offset transforms along the ridge, as suggested by Fedynskiy and others (1975). The structurally most complex area is at the southwestern part where various plate boundary configurations have been indicated. A fracture zone is often shown at 71.4°N (Fedynskiy and others, 1975; Vogt and others, 1981; Nunns, 1983), but the bathymetric data of Perry and others (1980) do not require this transform.

An elevated ridge block transected by a prominently developed rift valley characterizes the Knipovich Ridge. The nature of the rift valley changes considerably along its strike. At the transition with Mohns Ridge it is narrow and V-shaped, becoming progressively wider and more U-shaped in cross section at the Knipovich Ridge. In an east–west direction the valley floor is about 10 km wide west of Svalbard (Fig. 8). The rift valley depth, 3.2–3.4 km, is also deeper than at the Mohns Ridge (Fig. 7). Again we notice that the axial mountains stand higher on the western side. On this flank, little sediment has been deposited, whereas large sediment thicknesses are encountered near the axis on the eastern side (Myhre and others, 1983). This is attributed to the proximity to the Svalbard margin, causing damming up of sediments against the ridge flank. Locally, sediments have overflowed the axial mountains and can be observed in the rift valley proper. The asymmetric load of sediments may possibly contribute to the difference in elevation on either side of the rift (Desimon and Karasik, 1979). Bathymetrically, the rift valley ends at 79.5°N but continues as a buried feature turning north–northwest (Eldholm and Windisch, 1974).

Eldholm and Sundvor (1980) noted that the axial block was bounded by small but continuous basement escarpments. These have been interpreted as bounding the crust accreted at the present ridge axis, thus implying earlier shifts in the location of the plate boundary. Desimon and Karasik (1979) and Reksnes and Vågnes (1985), on the other hand, suggest that the Knipovich Ridge south of 77.5°N might have been active at least back to mid-Oligocene time.

Offsets in the plate boundary have been inferred from earthquake and bathymetric data (Husebye and others, 1975; Rozhdestvenskiy and Karasik, 1982; Savostin and Karasik, 1981; Ohta, 1982). Figure 4 shows, as also recognized by Desimon and Karasik (1979), several bathymetric lineaments striking approximately along the flowlines. These features may reflect fossil and active transforms, although the individual offsets are probably less than 10 km long. This suggests an ongoing process of plate boundary adjustment which could, in some way, be related to the wide zone of crustal accretion. For simplicity, only one small offset transform is indicated in Figure 4. On the other hand, a segmented plate boundary could make the spreading process much more orthogonal than indicated in Figure 7.

Spitsbergen Transform (Fig. 5)

The plate boundary between the Knipovich and Nansen ridges must still be considered poorly located, but in a regional sense it is generally considered to be composed of a system of right-lateral transform faults and short ridge axis segments (Tal-

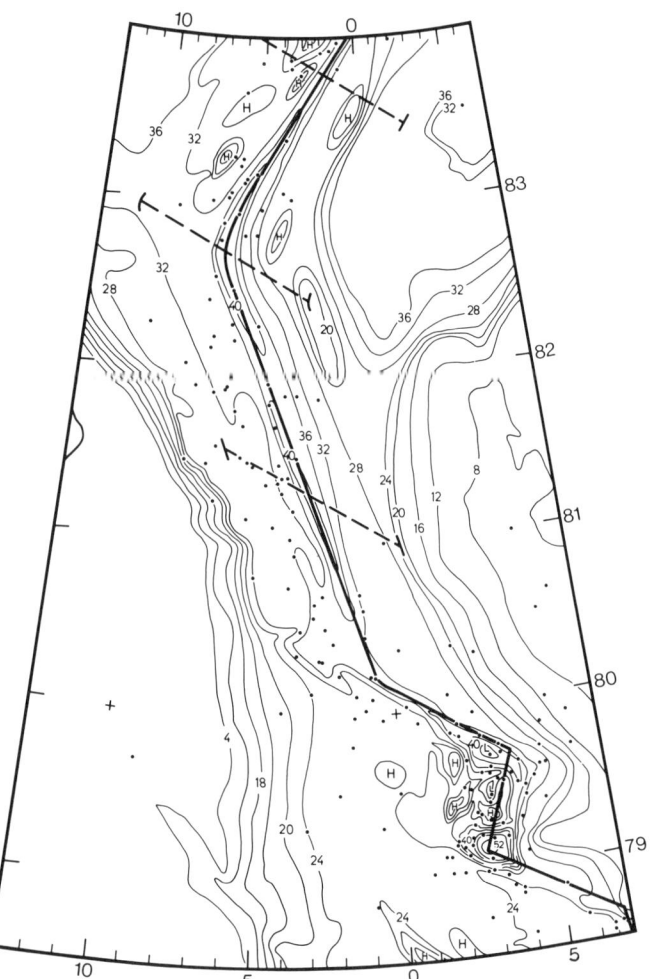

Figure 5. The plate boundary region between Knipovich and Nansen ridges, the Spitsbergen Transform. Bathymetry, contour interval 400 m, from Perry and others (1980; 1985). Earthquake epicenters and flowlines (Talwani and Eldholm, 1977) also shown. Legend in Figure 2.

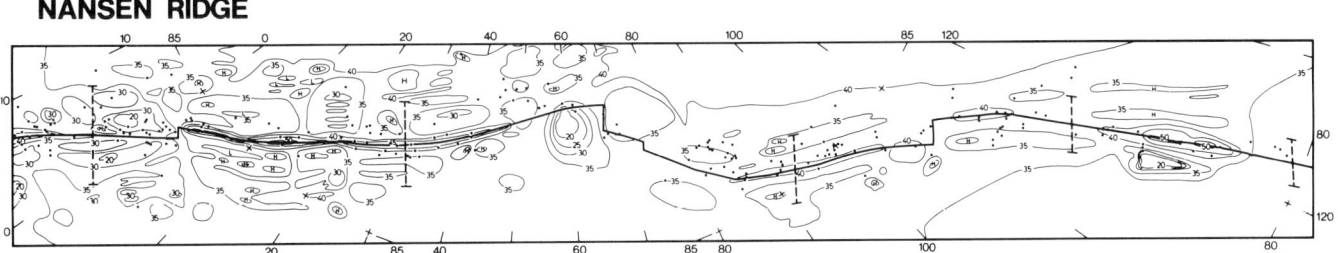

Figure 6. The plate boundary region in the Eurasia Basin. Bathymetry, contour interval 500 m, from Perry and others (1985). Earthquake epicenters and flowlines (Talwani and Eldholm, 1977) also shown. Legend in Figure 2.

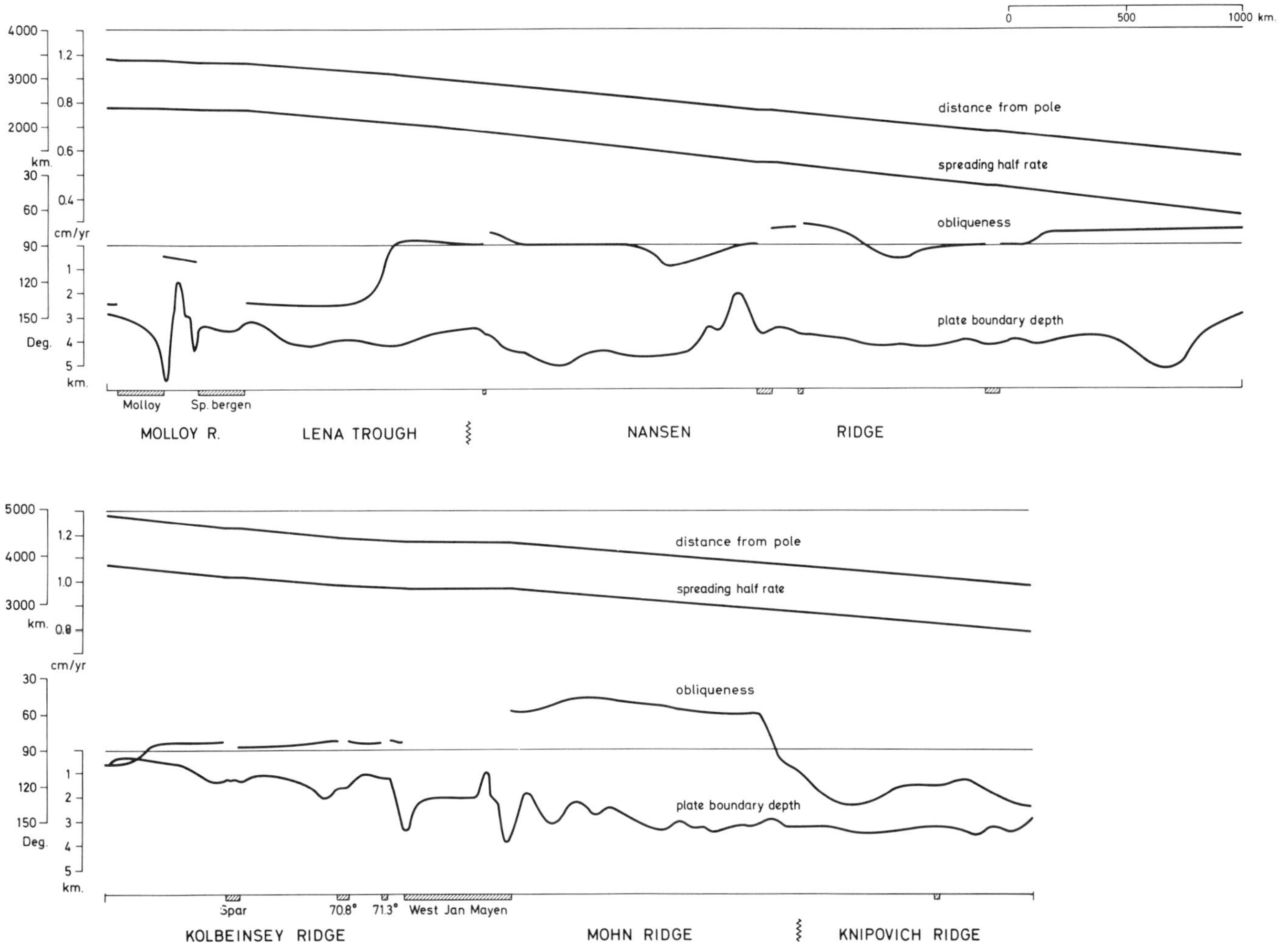

Figure 7. Geophysical and geological parameters plotted according to distance along the plate boundary. From top to bottom: Distance from pole of rotation (68°N, 137°E), spreading rate (half-rate between anomalies 1–5), obliqueness of plate motion measured as the angle between the ridge axis and the 1–5 flowlines, and the maximum depth of the rift valley.

wani and Eldholm, 1977; Vogt and others, 1981; Savostin and Karasik, 1981). Following Crane and others (1982) we denote this system the Spitsbergen Transform. The southern region is best defined and includes the 70-km-long Molloy Ridge between the Molloy and Spitsbergen fracture zones. At either end of the Molloy Ridge lie the greatest depths in the entire Norwegian-Greenland Sea.

The earlier maps have indicated complex bathymetry north of Spitsbergen Fracture Zone and an en echelon pattern is often suggested. In Figure 5, we base the plate boundary on the new map of Perry and others (1985) in which there is a continuous depression, the Lena Trough, between the Spitsbergen Fracture Zone and the Nansen Ridge. The magnetic pattern associated with the ridge segments has not been resolved, although there is a central anomaly over the Molloy Ridge.

The suggested plate geometry at the northern Spitsbergen Transform becomes particularly intriguing in view of the apparent geometrical similarities between the Nansen/Lena and Mohn/Knipovich ridge transitions. The evolution of the continuous and curving ridge axis between axial segments having pronounced differences in azimuths has not yet been worked out. However, it is probably a recent development that has smoothed an earlier complex system of transform faults.

Nansen Ridge (Fig. 6)

The Nansen (Gakkel) Ridge extends across the Eurasia Basin to 79°N, where it ceases to be reflected in the bathymetry (Grachev and Naryshkin, 1978). However, the axial ridge structure has been traced beneath the sediments as a basement ridge reaching the Laptev Sea continental slope (Grachev and Karasik, 1974). The plate boundary passes onto the Laptev Sea continental margin in the region of the Sadko Trough, which is considered to be a rifted structure (Demenitskaya and Hunkins, 1969). For more detailed discussions on the plate boundary continuation beneath the continent we refer to Churkin (1972), Chapman and Solomon (1976), Savostin and Karasik (1981), Grachev (1982), and Fujita and Cook (this volume).

The axial province, which is entirely embraced by anomaly 6 (Karasik, 1974), ranges in width from 180 to 60 km, decreasing toward the Laptev Sea. The regional ridge trend is quite stable with some local changes, particularly between 40 and 82°E. At about 82°E, the width of the axial zone changes abruptly from 180 to 120 km. The axial mountains rise 2–2.5 km above the rift valley floor (Grachev and Naryshkin, 1978). However, a pronounced negative depth anomaly, of the order of 1.5 km, is observed toward the Laptev Margin (Karasik and Pozdnyakova, 1979). Along the western part of the ridge there are a number of parallel troughs and ridges, the northern flank generally being wider and shallower than the southern one. This asymmetry has been attributed to a more extensive burial by sediments in the Nansen Basin (Grachev and Karasik, 1974).

The entire rift valley is delineated by a series of linear troughs, 10–50 km long, separated by blockages and/or small

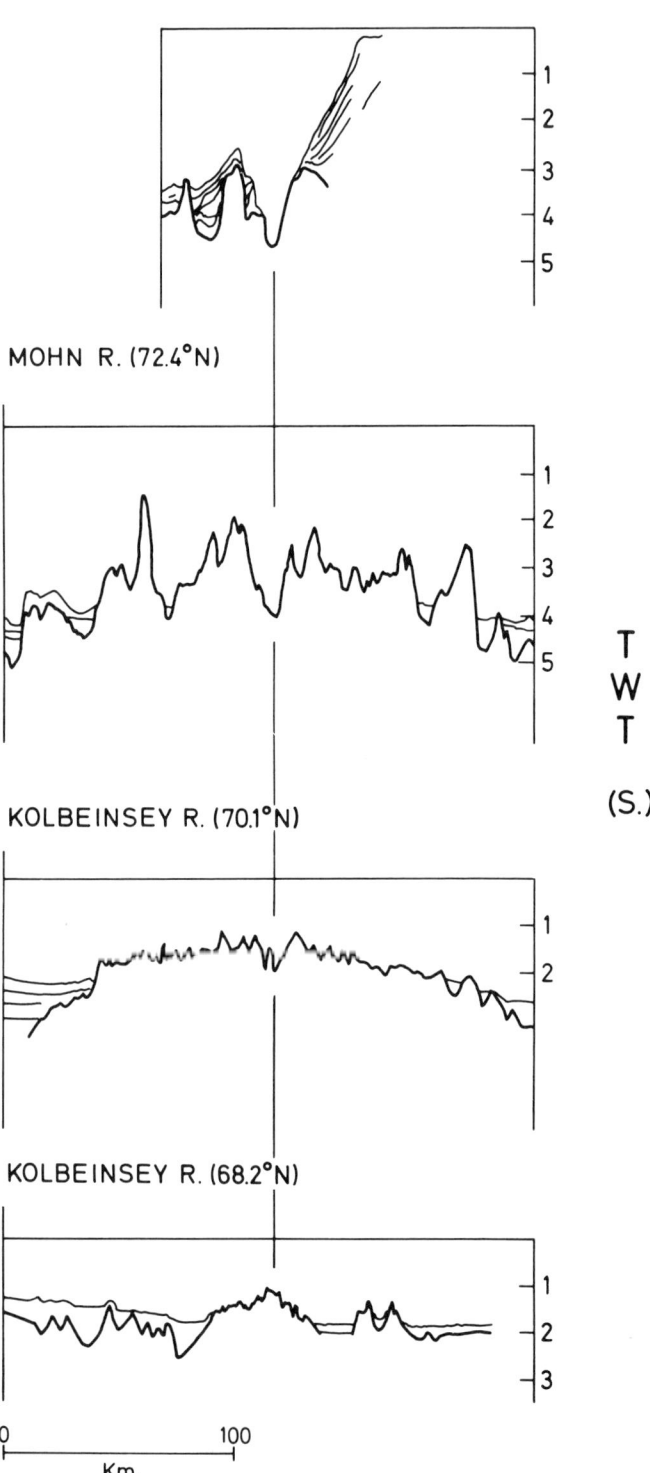

Figure 8. Cross section showing the changing nature of the plate boundary in the Norwegian-Greenland Sea. The sections have been projected along the azimuth of relative plate motion.

offsets. Morphologically, the rift valley changes considerably along the ridge, but the floor is almost flat over large distances. Its width varies from 15 to 40 km and the depth from 4.2 to 5.3 km, revealing one of the deepest rift valleys known (Grachev and Naryshkin, 1978).

The Nansen Ridge appears to have been a stable plate boundary throughout the Cenozoic. The spreading rates estimated from magnetic anomalies suggest asymmetrical spreading, occurring faster in the southern direction (Karasik, 1971, 1974; Vogt and others, 1979b). At present, the axial province is characterized by an abundance of paired volcanoes or even chains of paired volcanoes on either side of the rift valley (Karasik, 1968, 1974) that are parallel to the flow lines (Savostin and Karasik, 1981). Systematic studies have identified a number of fracture zones distinguished both by the magnetic anomaly pattern and the morphology (Karasik, 1968, 1973; Grachev, 1982; Vogt and others, 1979b). Most fracture zones are characterized by offsets up to 10 km, which is less than the width of the rift valley. In the bathymetry, these are expressed as blockages of the rift valley and can be considered as zero-offset transform faults (Karasik, 1973). Some transform faults with larger offsets have also been recognized (Karasik, 1968, 1974; Kovacs and Vink, 1984) as indicated in Figure 6.

The available data have not allowed any precise mapping of the plate boundary along the Nansen Ridge. Thus, the plate boundary as indicated in Figure 6, based on the Perry and others (1985) bathymetric map, must be considered an approximation.

VARIATION OF GEOPHYSICAL AND GEOLOGICAL PARAMETERS

The preceding description has outlined some of the most prominent features related to the plate boundary and its adjacent oceanic crust. We now discuss in more detail various observations relating to this region to elucidate its nature, evolution, and along-strike variations. Some of the information is compiled in Figure 7 in which several key parameters are plotted against the total plate boundary length.

Seismicity

The correlation of seismicity with the plate boundary has been demonstrated in regional studies and in reviews by Husebye and others (1975), Savostin and Karasik (1981), Vogt and others (1981), and Einarsson (1986). The considerable scatter in the distribution of epicenters may, to some extent, originate from poor location parameters, particularly for the small-magnitude events. It appears that a fair number of events do occur within the oceanic plates, and their cause is enigmatic. In general, there are few focal mechanism solutions available, especially at the Nansen Ridge. Most of the available solutions have been compiled by Savostin and Karasik (1981).

The indistinct character of the Tjørnes Fracture is reflected in the seismicity, which is too diffuse to be associated with a simple transform. Einarsson and Bjørnsson (1979) suggested that the plate motion was taken up by a series of parallel faults along which the main faulting is right-lateral strike-slip. No pronounced seismicity relates to the Spar and 70.8°N fracture zones, but their existences are confirmed by focal plane solutions. Lazareva and Misharina (1965) reported sinistral transform motion at the Spar Fracture Zone, and Savostin and Karasik (1981) found strike-slip with a large normal faulting component near the 70.8°N fracture zone.

The transform part of the West Jan Mayen Fracture Zone is characterized by few, but large, events in the west and numerous, but smaller, earthquakes in the east. The latter, often swarm-like events, are associated with the activity of the Beerenberg Volcano at Jan Mayen Island (Navrestad and Sørnes, 1974; Sørnes and Fjeldskaar, 1980; Havskov and others, 1986). The fault planes are mostly within 10 degrees of the transform trend in Figures 2 and 3 (Bungum and Husebye, 1977; Bungum, 1978), and yield left-lateral strike-slip. The variability in slip vectors led Bungum and Husebye (1977) to suggest several en echelon segments within the main transform, whereas Savostin and Karasik (1981) proposed a compressive component based on a small southern dip of the fault planes. On the other hand, Einarsson (1986) indicates there is no need for explanations of these kinds.

Seismically, the Mohns Ridge is the most active ridge segment in the Norwegian-Greenland Sea. In general, the epicenters appear to be located in a narrow continuous belt lying at the central portion of the rift axis. A focal solution by Lazareva and Misharina (1965) may be interpreted in terms of a sinistral strike-slip fault at 1.2°W, but other solutions reveal predominantly normal faulting.

There is a pronounced difference in seismicity between the Mohns and the Knipovich Ridge. Along the Knipovich Ridge the seismicity is diffuse and relatively clustered, with the majority of events centered over the eastern ridge flank. It is possible that the asymmetry in events is related to the effect of sediment loading on the eastern flank, and many events may therefore be of intraplate nature. The limited fault plane data may be interpreted in terms of transform motion along the ridge (Husebye and others, 1975; Savostin and Karasik, 1981).

The Molloy Ridge is associated with a typical seismicity pattern as is the Spitsbergen Fracture Zone and the Lena Trough, where several large-magnitude events allow reliable focal mechanisms (Horsfield and Maton, 1970; Conant, 1972; Savostin and Karasik, 1981) and show a northwest-trending fault plane having dextral motion. We note, however, that there is an event indicative of sinistral motion close to the Nansen Ridge, which led Savostin and Karsik (1981) to propose a complex plate boundary pattern there.

At the Nansen Ridge the seismicity is relatively continuous and closely related to the axial zone, becoming more scattered when the ridge approaches the Siberian margin where one would expect a transition from a narrow oceanic plate boundary to a wider zone of thinned and stretched continental crust. Fault plane solutions yield predominantly normal faulting (Savostin and Karasik, 1981; Fujita and others, this volume).

Oblique and Asymmetric Spreading

The along-strike change in the direction of the spreading axis (Fig. 1) causes a varying angle between the axis and the direction of relative motion, resulting in oblique spreading (Fig. 7). Ideally, one would want to know the direction of spreading at the present time. The earthquake slip vectors provide the information, but the inherit uncertainty is too large for a precise estimate. Another method is based on reconstructions using linear magnetic anomalies and main structural features in the ocean basins. However, even finite difference poles give average directions for time intervals of several million years. Here, we have chosen flowlines, representing the time from present to anomaly 5 (9.5 Ma), to illustrate the relative motion for the youngest part of the two plates (Figs. 2–6). The fault plane solutions indicate that such flowlines yield a reasonable estimate of the present direction. The 0–5 pole at 68°N and 137°E, first calculated by Pitman and Talwani (1972), is used to construct the flowlines.

The various maps show that many bathymetric features line up along the flowlines, as one would expect if the zone of injection has been locally unstable, producing relatively short-lived, small offset transforms. The magnitude of oblique spreading is at a minimum at the Iceland Plateau and along the major part of the Nansen Ridge. However, there are large oblique components at Mohns Ridge, although maximal values occur at either end of the Knipovich Ridge and along the Lena Trough (Fig. 8). Note that the rift valley becomes still wider when measured along the flowlines, a fact that Karasik and Rozhdestvenskiy (1977) interpreted in terms of fragmentation by short transforms.

The predicted spreading rates in Figure 7 compare quite well with rates measured between anomalies 5 on either side of the ridge axis. It has often been noticed that the axis is not entirely symmetrical with respect to anomaly 5. These differences have been studied in detail at the Iceland Plateau (Vogt and others, 1980) and in the Eurasia Basin (Vogt and others, 1979b). The variable along-strike asymmetry at the Kolbeinsey Ridge is most likely attributed to the ridge axis jumps reflected in the generation of the transforms discussed earlier. The .06 cm/yr higher rate of spreading at the Eurasia flank of Nansen Ridge, on the other hand, reflects an asymmetry that has persisted throughout most of the Cenozoic. At the Mohns Ridge the degree of asymmetry varies along strike, being .23 cm/yr at the southern North American plate flank and decreasing to .03 cm/yr in the northeast (Vogt and others, 1982).

Using statistical analysis of zero-age crustal depth (that is, the average basement depth during its formation), elevation of the highest rift mountains, and depth to magnetic basement (as estimated by Kovacs and Vogt, 1982), Vogt and others (1982) showed that there is an obvious difference between the two ridge flanks. The observations (Figs. 2–4 and 6) of a higher elevation and more rugged relief on the North American flank were confirmed. Although the reason for this phenomenon is poorly understood, Vogt and others (1982) attribute it to asymmetry in the crustal accretion process, whereas Karasik and Pozdnyakova (1979) propose anomalous asthenosphere in the Eurasian Basin.

Gravity and Depth Anomalies

There is reasonably good regional gravity coverage of the plate boundary between Iceland and the Molloy Ridge, whereas few data exist further north. The long-wavelength field is centered around Iceland and is composed of a regional high of about +20 mGal extending from Spitsbergen Fracture Zone to 30° N, and an axial high of ±30–40 mGal amplitude decreasing as the crust matures (Cochran and Talwani, 1978).

The local free-air anomaly field along the plate boundary generally reflects the bathymetry (Talwani and Grønlie, 1976; Faleide and others, 1984). In fact it may be considered as representing filtered basement relief, making it particularly useful for defining location and trends of transform faults. The most typical features are axial maxima surrounding a well-defined minimum over the rift valley, and elongate lows associated with the fracture zones. The difference in axial relief at the Mohns and Knipovich ridges is reflected in 0–15 and 10–20 mGal higher values at the North American plate edge respectively. Grønlie and Talwani (1982) modeled representative profiles across the spreading axes and concluded that the local gravity field over the Kolbeinsey Ridge could be explained by bathymetry and its compensations using a local Airy type model. Similar observations were made at the Mohns and Knipovich ridges, but here the model did not account for a −20 to −30 mGal isostatic low below the rift valley. This anomaly was, however, ascribed to low-density basalt near the valley floor and a lighter, partly melted, upper mantle producing the magma.

In terms of depth anomalies, the region south of the Spitsbergen Transform is abnormally shallow with a maximum at Iceland. Except for anomalously deep areas at either end of the Nansen Ridge, the plate boundary in the Eurasia Basin lies at normal basement depth (Vogt and others, 1979a).

Magnetics

The present-day transforms are magnetically indistinct, whereas large parts of the mid-oceanic ridge axis are characterized by a typical central magnetic anomaly. Although there is considerable variability in the amplitude of the central anomaly, most of the changes are ascribed to depth to source, inhomogenous distribution of magnetic minerals, and existence of undetected small offset transforms.

Near the northern coast of Iceland there is lowering of magnetic amplitude despite shallower source depth. Vogt and others (1980) list a number of possible causes such as thermal blanketing effects, erosion during low stands of sea level, and high vesicularity and sulfur concentrations at shallow depths. The most remarkable magnetic pattern occurs, however, over the Knipovich Ridge, where the central anomaly is locally nonexistent or of very small amplitude. The fact that large areas of the Greenland

Sea and parts of the region adjacent to the Spitsbergen Transform also exhibit low-magnetic amplitudes may indicate that the causative process has been active for some time. Even though there is not yet a clear understanding of this phenomenon, several mechanisms have been suggested; e.g., thermal blanketing by sediments in the rift valley, possibly combined with a wider-than-normal zone of injection (Eldholm and others, 1978), high heat flow, fragmentation due to axial shifts and short-lived transforms (Roots and Srivastava, 1984), and slow oblique spreading (Vogt and others, 1981).

Magnetic surveys over the Nansen Ridge show a linear pattern over the axial province and a relatively large variability in the amplitude of the central anomaly (Karasik, 1974; Feden and others, 1979; Vogt and others, 1979b). As no sediment cover could be inferred where the anomaly was anomalously low, Vogt and others (1979b) correlated anomaly amplitude with increased elevation of the rift valley floor and axial mountains, which they related to a thicker oceanic layer 2A. On the other hand, Karasik and Pozdnyakova (1979) found a negative correlation between the axial anomaly and seismically determined basement depth in the rift valley.

Seismic Velocity Structure

The seismic crustal velocity profiles in the Norwegian-Greenland Sea were analysed by Myhre and Eldholm (1981). Although the number of profiles within the axial region are few and normally only penetrate the upper crust, there appears to be a well-defined velocity structure similar to that of the Houtz and Ewing (1976) model. In particular, layer 2A, having an average velocity of 3.9 km/s, was typical for crust younger than 10 Ma. The Houtz-Ewing model does not apply to the Knipovich Ridge, where a more complex velocity structure consisting of average velocities 2.8, 3.7, 4.5, 5.5, 6.2, and 7.3 km/s was reported. These results are, however, quite similar to the axial region of the Reykjanes Ridge south of Iceland (Talwani and others, 1971). Even fewer data exist from the Nansen Ridge. Kiselev (1984), in reviewing Russian data in a generalized manner, describes a pronounced crustal thinning, 3.0–3.5 km, near the axial zone in which the seismic stratification disappears, yielding a more complex velocity distribution than in the older oceanic crust. Results from the FRAM-I experiment show a 2–3 km laterally and vertically heterogeneous crust over a 7.9 km/s mantle at the northern flank near anomaly 5 (Jackson and others, 1982). At the southern flank, Kristoffersen and others (1982) measured velocities of 4.6, 6.1, and 7.9 km/s, and 4.6 and 7.2 km/s in the median valley.

Heat Flow

Langseth and Zielinski (1974) have shown the existence of variable, very high heat flow values in the vicinity of the plate boundary in the Norwegian-Greenland Sea. Similar observations were made by Crane and others (1982) in the Svalbard Transform region. For the entire ocean the average heatflow, 2.7 heat flow units, is higher than in oceans of comparable age, according to Langseth and Zielinski (1974). They did not observe the typical low values at the ridge flanks, which have been recognized at other spreading axes; Zielinski (1979) interpreted this in terms of a less-prevalent hydrothermal circulation in the Norwegian-Greenland Sea. Furthermore, he suggested that thermal expansion in the upper mantle causes the unusually shallow crustal depths, as well as the positive free-air gravity anomalies noted earlier. The only available data from the Nansen Ridge refers to a 50-km traverse across the axial zone near 118°E (Lyubimova and others, 1969). The average values lie in the range for normal mid-oceanic ridges, but are slightly lower than in the Norwegian-Greenland sea, suggesting that the thermal expansion does not extend into the main Eurasian Basin.

Petrology

Petrological and geochemical analyses of dredge samples provide crucial information about the processes generating the oceanic crust, and comprehensive sampling programs have been carried out south of 78°N. The results from the Kolbeinsey Ridge have been summarized by Brooks and Jakobsson (1974), Dittmer and others (1975), and Schilling and others (1983); Neumann and Schilling (1984) discuss the Mohns and Knipovich ridges. The data have also been reviewed by Melson and O'Hearn (1986) and Schilling (1986).

The basalts in the Norwegian-Greenland Sea may be classified into three main types (Brooks and Jakobsson, 1974): mid-oceanic ridge (MORB), Icelandic or hot spot, and alkali basalts. Schilling and others (1983) document that the anomalous morphology and tectonics characterizing such areas as Iceland and the Jan Mayen region, defined as hot spots, are also reflected in the petrology and geochemistry of the basalts at the plate boundary. Compared with the LIL (large ionic lithophile)-depleted mantle normally forming ridge basalts, it is evident that the mantle below the hotspot is enriched in large incompatible elements, H_2O, and halogens. It is further inferred that the hotspot sources have developed separately from those of the mid-oceanic ridge, probably by segregating from partial melting zones that extend deeper than those at the normal spreading ridge.

Between the hot spots, MORB is the dominant rock type at the Kolbeinsey Ridge (Brooks and Jakobsson, 1974) and along the Mohn-Knipovich complex. More subtle along-strike petrological differences within the tholeiites north of Jan Mayen have been recognized and discussed by Neumann and Schilling (1984), although their causes are considered uncertain. They also noted a geochemical gradient northward along Knipovich Ridge that could be indicative of an additional mantle plume north of 77.5°N. Finally, alkali-kindred basalts sampled in the vicinity of Jan Mayen Island and along the very southwestern part of Mohn Ridge were considered to suggest that the present-day volcanism is not confined to the island but is more widespread.

SUMMARY

The North American plate boundary from Iceland to the Laptev Sea continental margin is a 4600-km-long continuation of the Mid-Atlantic Ridge system along which new oceanic crust accretes at half-rates between 1.1 and 0.3 cm/yr. The plate boundary is characterized by great variability and changes in morphology, structural style, and related geophysical and geological parameters from south to north. These changes, we believe, are the manifestations of the complex processes involved in separation of continents and generation of new oceanic crust, some of which may relate to the very low rates of crustal accretion when approaching the pole of plate rotation.

Regionally, the boundary can be separated into three main segments, the Kolbeinsey, Mohns-Knipovich, and Nansen ridges, separated by the West Jan Mayen Fracture Zone and the Spitsbergen Transform. Several small-offset fracture zones are located along the main ridges. The changing strike of the ridge axes creates oblique sea-floor spreading, particularly along the Mohns and Knipovich ridges. However, local fragmentation by a large number of minor transforms cannot be ruled out.

Our knowledge and understanding of the plate boundary also varies considerably. In the Norwegian-Greenland Sea it is reasonably well mapped, but the Eurasia Basin must still be considered largely unexplored. Generally, a well-defined pattern of earthquakes is associated with the spreading ridges and transforms, and the focal mechanisms support the prevailing geodynamic models as do most of the geophysical data. However, there are many intriguing observations. In the Norwegian-Greenland Sea the ridges have unusually shallow depths, the gravity field is more positive, and the heat flow higher than normal. These phenomena may in some way reflect the elevation of Iceland and its associated mantle plume. The style of the spreading axis also changes with distance from Iceland. The rift valley is absent close to Iceland, gradually being developed north of the Spar Fracture Zone, and approaching a more normal mid-oceanic rift at the Mohns Ridge. The Knipovich rift valley is indeed wide and quite deep, whereas the Nansen Ridge again resembles a normal spreading ridge, although local depth anomalies occur north of the Yermak Plateau. At the Knipovich Ridge the central magnetic anomaly, well developed elsewhere, diminishes, possibly due to a wide zone of injection and/or thermal blanketing effects by sediment deposition in the valley proper. Finally, there is a more rugged and high relief of the axial mountains over the North American plate edge, the cause for which is obscure.

In terms of future research, two approaches are advised. First, a continued mapping program is needed to more precisely locate and geophysically characterize the plate boundary north of the Molloy Fracture Zone. Additional mapping of this kind is also needed at the intersections of Mohn and Kolbeinsey ridges with the West Jan Mayen Fracture Zone. Second, detailed, high-resolution bathymetric mapping, geophysical experiments, and sea-floor sampling should be carried out along transects crossing the axial zones along flowlines. The objective should be to select transects across the major types of ridge segments and to interpret the data in terms of the along-strike variability discussed above.

REFERENCES CITED

Brooks, C. K., and Jakobsson, S. P., 1974, Petrochemistry of the volcanic rocks of the North Atlantic Ridge System, *in* Kristjansson, L., ed., Geodynamics of Iceland and the North Atlantic area: Dordrecht, D. Reidel Publishing Co., p. 139–154.

Bungum, H., 1978, Reanalyzation of three focal-mechanism solutions for earthquakes from Jan Mayen, Iceland and Svalbard: Tectonophysics, v. 51, p. T15–T16.

Bungum, H., and Husebye, E. S., 1977, Seismicity of the Norwegian Sea; The Jan Mayen Fracture Zone: Tectonophysics, v. 40, p. 351–360.

Chapman, M. E., and Solomon, S. C., 1976, North American–Eurasian plate boundary in Northeast Asia: Journal of Geophysical Research, v. 81, p. 921–930.

Churkin, M., Jr., 1972, Western boundary of the North American continental plate in Asia: Geological Society of America Bulletin, v. 83, p. 1027–1036.

Cochran, J. R., and Talwani, M., 1978, Gravity anomalies, regional elevation, and the deep structure of the North Atlantic: Journal of Geophysical Research, v. 83, p. 4907–4924.

Conant, D. A., 1972, Six new focal mechanism solutions for the Arctic and a center of rotation for plate movements [M.A. thesis]: New York, Columbia University.

Crane, K., Eldholm, O., Myhre, A. M., and Sundvor, E., 1982, Thermal implications for the evolution of the Spitsbergen Transform Fault: Tectonophysics, v. 89, p. 1–32.

Demenitskaya, R. M., and Hunkins, K. L., 1970, Shape and structure of the Arctic Ocean: *in* Maxwell, A. E., ed., The Sea: Interscience, New York, p. 223–249.

Desimon, A. I., and Karasik, A. M., 1979, Some features of bottom relief and sea-floor spreading on the Knipovich Ridge, Arctic Ocean: [Translated from Doklady Akademia Nauk, SSSR), v. 247, p. 1215–1220.

Dittmer, F., and four others, 1975, Dredged basalts from the Mid-oceanic Ridge north of Iceland: Nature, v. 254, p. 298–301.

Einarsson, P., 1986, Seismicity along the eastern margin of the North American plate, *in* Vogt, P. R., and Tucholke, B. E., eds., The western North Atlantic region: Boulder, Colorado, Geological Society of America, Geology of North America, v. M, p. 99–116.

Einarsson, P., and Bjørnsson, S., 1979, Earthquakes in Iceland: Jøkull, v. 29, p. 37–43.

Eldholm, O., and Sundvor, E., 1980, The continental margins of the Norwegian-Greenland Sea; Recent results and outstanding problems: Royal Society of London Philosophical Transaction, series A, v. 294, p. 77–86.

Eldholm, O., and Windisch, C. C., 1974, Sediment distribution in the Norwegian-Greenland Sea: Geological Society of America Bulletin, v. 85, p. 1661–1676.

Eldholm, O., Vogt, P. R., and Perry, R., 1978, Plate tectonic development of the Mid-Oceanic Ridge System north of the Jan Mayen Fracture Zone, A; Present plate boundaries: EOS, v. 59, p. 371.

Eldholm, O., and four others, 1980, The sediment distribution on oceanic crust in the Norwegian Sea (abs.): 14 Nordisk Geologisk Vintermøte, Bergen, 1980 (in Norwegian).

Faleide, J. I., and four others, 1984, Free-air gravity anomaly maps of the Greenland Sea and the Barents Sea: Norsk Polarinstitutts Skrifter, no. 180, p. 63–67.

Feden, R. H., Vogt, P. R., and Flemming, H. S., 1979, Magnetic and bathymetric evidence for the "Yermak hot spot" northwest of Svalbard in the Arctic Basin: Earth and Planetary Science Letters, v. 44, p. 18–38.

Fedynskiy, V. V., and four others, 1975, The structure of the anomalous magnetic field in the southwestern part of Mohns Rise: Doklady Akademia Nauk SSSR, v. 223, p. 726–729.

Fox, P. J., and Gallo, D. G., 1984, A tectonic model for ridge-transform-ridge plate boundaries; Implications for the structure of oceanic lithosphere: Tectonophysics, v. 104, p. 205–242.

Grachev, A. F., 1982, Geodynamics of the Transitional Zone from the Moma Rift to the Gakkel Ridge: American Association of Petroleum Geologists Memoir 4, p. 525–529.

Grachev, A. F., and Karaski, A. M., 1974, Sea-floor spreading and plate tectonics of the Eurasia Basin of the Arctic Ocean, Geotectonic prerequisite for mineral prospecting on the Arctic Shelf: Leningrad, NIIGA, p. 19–33 (in Russian).

Grachev, A. G., and Naryshkin, G. D., 1978, The main features of sea-bottom topography of the Eurasia Basin, the Arctic Ocean: Proceedings of the Leningrad State University, v. 2, p. 94–102 (in Russian).

Grønlie, G., and Talwani, M., 1979, Bathymetry of the Norwegian-Greenland Sea: Norsk Polarinstitutts Skrifter, no. 70, p. 3–24.

——, 1982, The free-air gravity field of the Norwegian-Greenland Sea and adjacent area: Earth Evolution Series, v. 2, p. 79–103.

Havskov, J., Kvamme, L., and Bungum, H., 1986, Attenuation of seismic waves in the Jan Mayen Island area: Marine Geophysical Researches, v. 8, p. 39–48.

Horsfield, W. T., and Maton, P. I., 1970, Transform faulting along the De Geer line: Nature, v. 226, p. 256–257.

Houtz, R., and Ewing, J., 1976, Upper crustal structure as a function of plate age: Journal of Geophysical Research, v. 81, p. 2490–2498.

Husebye, E. S., and three others, 1975, The seismicity of the Norwegian-Greenland Sea: Tectonophysics, v. 26, p. 55–70.

Jackson, H. R., Reid, I., and Falconer, R.K.H., 1982, Crustal structure near the Arctic Mid-Oceanic Ridge: Journal of Geophysical Research, v. 87, p. 1773–1783.

Johnson, G. L., 1974, Morphology of the Mid-Ocean Ridge between Iceland and the Arctic Basin, in Kristjansson, L., ed., Geodynamics of Iceland and North Atlantic area: Dordrecht, D. Reidel Publishing Co., p. 49–62.

Johnson, G. L., and Campsie, J., 1976, Morphology and structure of the western Jan Mayen Fracture Zone: Norsk Polarinstitutt, Årbok 1974, p. 69–81.

Johnson, G. L., and Heezen, B. C., 1967a, Morphology and evolution of the Norwegian-Greenland Sea: Deep-Sea Research, v. 14, p. 755–771.

Johnson, G. L., Southall, J. R., Young, P. W., and Vogt, P. R., 1972, Origin and structure of the Iceland Plateau and Kolbeinesey Ridge: Journal of Geophysical Research, v. 77, p. 5688–5696.

Johnson, G. L., Monahan, D., Grønlie, G., and Sobczak, L., 1979, Bathymetric chart of the Arctic, Gebco sheet 5:17: Canadian Hydrographic Service, Ottawa, Canada.

Karasik, A. M., 1968, Magnetic anomalies of the Gakkel Ridge and origin of the Arctic Ocean, Geophysical methods of prospecting in the Arctic: Leningrad, NIIGA, p. 8–19 (in Russian).

——, 1971, Marine magnetic anomalies and sea-floor spreading hypothesis: Geotektoniks, n. 2, p. 3–19 (in Russian).

——, 1973, Anomalous magnetic field of the Eurasian Basin, Arctic Ocean: Doklady Akademia Nauk SSSR, v. 211, p. 86–89.

——, 1974, The Eurasia Basin of the Arctic Ocean in terms of plate tectonics, in Problems in geology of the polar regions of the world: Leningrad, NEDRA, p. 24–31 (in Russian).

Karasik, A. M., and Pozdnyakova, R. A., 1979, Basement depth versus its age in Eurasian Basin, Arctic Ocean: Doklady Akademia Nauk SSSR, v. 248, p. 169–174.

Karasik, A. M., and Rozhdestvenskiy, S. S., 1977, Configuration of sea-floor spreading axis and regularities of its formation, The main problems of riftgenesis: Novosibirsk, Nauka, p. 167–175 (in Russian).

Karlstad, B., 1981, The sediment distribution between Jan Mayen and Greenland Senja fracture zones [thesis]: Oslo, University of Oslo, 105 p. (in Norwegian).

Kiselev, Yu G., 1984, Crustal structure and geophysical fields of the deep-sea parts of the Arctic Ocean: Proceedings, 27th International Geological Congress, v. 6, p. 299–319.

Kovacs, L. C., and Vink, G. E., 1984, New aeromagnetic data from the high Arctic and Norwegian-Greenland Sea: EOS, v. 65, p. 199.

Kovacs, L. C., and Vogt, P. R., 1982, Depth-to-magnetic source analysis of the Arctic Ocean region: Tectonophysics, v. 89, p. 255–294.

Kristoffersen, Y., Husebye, E. S., Bungum, H., and Gregersen, S., 1982, Seismic investigations of the Nansen Ridge during the Fram I experiment: Tectonophysics, v. 82, p. 57–68.

Langseth, M. G. and Zielinski, G. W., 1974, Marine heat flow measurements in the Norwegian-Greenland Sea and in the vicinity of Iceland, in Kristjansson, L., ed., Geodynamics of Iceland and the North Atlantic area: Dordrecht, D. Reidel Publishing Co., p. 277–295.

Lazareva, A. P. and Misharina, L. A., 1965, Stresses in earthquake foci in the Arctic seismic belt: Izv. Earth Physical Series, v. 2, p. 5–10.

Litvin, V. M., Suzjumov, A. Ye, and Mirlin, Ye. G., 1978, Results of hydromagnetic and geomorphological investigations of the south part of the Kolbeinsey Ridge: Doklady Akademia Nauk SSSR, v. 240, p. 193–196.

Lyubimova, Ye. A., Tomara, G. A., Deminitskaya, R. M., and Karasik, A. M., 1969, Measurement of heat flow across the Arctic Ocean floor in the vicinity of the median Gakkel Ridge: Doklady Akademia Nauk SSSR, v. 180, p. 22–24.

McMaster, R. L., Schilling, J-G., and Pinet, P. R., 1977, Plate boundary within Tjørnes Fracture Zone on northern Iceland's insular margin: Nature, v. 269, p. 663–668.

Melson, W. G., and O'Hearn, T., 1986, "Zero-age" variations in the composition of abyssal volcanic rocks along the axial zone of the Mid-Atlantic Ridge, in Vogt, P. R., and Tucholke, B. E., eds., The western North Atlantic region: Boulder, Colorado, Geological Society of America, Geology of North America, v. M, p. 117–136.

Meyer, O., and four others, 1972, Results of bathymetric, magnetic, and gravimetric measurements between Iceland and 70°N: Deutches Hydrographische Zeitschrift, v. 25, p. 193–201.

Myhre, A. M., and Eldholm, O., 1981, Sedimentary and crustal velocities in the Norwegian-Greenland Sea: Journal of Geophysical Research, v. 86, p. 5012–5022.

Myhre, A. M., Eldholm, O., and Sundvor, E., 1983, The margin between Senja and Spitsbergen fracture zones; Implications from plate tectonics: Tectonophysics, v. 89, p. 1–32.

Narvestad, T., and Sørnes, A., 1974, The seismicity around Jan Mayen: Norsk Polarinstitutt, Årbok 1972, p. 29–40.

Neumann, E.-R., and Schilling, J.-G., 1984, Petrology of basalts from the Mohns-Knipovich Ridge; The Norwegian-Greenland Sea: Contribution Mineralogy and Petrology, v. 85, p. 209–223.

Nunns, A., 1983, The structure and evolution of the Jan Mayen Ridge and surrounding regions: American Association of Petroleum Geologists Memoir 34, p. 193–208.

Ohta, Y., 1982, Morpho-tectonic studies around Svalbard and the northernmost Atlantic: Canadian Society of Petroleum Geologists Memoir 8, p. 415–429.

Økern, J., 1981, The sediment distribution between the Faeroe-Iceland Ridge and the Jan Mayen Fracture Zone [Cand. real. thesis]: University of Oslo, 90 p. (in Norwegian).

Palmason, G., 1974, The insular margin of Iceland, in Burk, C. A., and Drake, C. L., eds., The geology of continental margins: Springer-Verlag, p. 375–380.

Parmentier, E. M., and Forsyth, D. W., 1985, Three-dimensional flow beneath a slow spreading ridge axis; A dynamic contribution to the deepening of the median valley toward fracture zones: Journal of Geophysical Research, v. 90, p. 678–684.

Perry, R. B., and four others, 1980, Bathymetry of the Norwegian-Greenland and

western Barents seas: Geological Society of American Map and Chart Series MC-21, scale 1:2,333,230.
Perry, R. B., and six others, 1985, Bathymetry of the Arctic Ocean: Washington, D.C., Naval Research Laboratory, Map, scale 1:6,000,000.
Pitman, W. C., and Talwani, M., 1972, Sea-floor spreading in the North Atlantic: Geological Society of America Bulletin, v. 83, p. 619–646.
Rassokho, A. I., and five others, 1967, Submarine Mid-Oceanic Arctic Ridge and its place in the system of Arctic Ocean ridges: Doklady Akademia Nauk SSSR, v. 172, p. 659–662.
Reksnes, P. A., and Vågnes, E., 1985, Evolution of the Greenland Sea and Eurasia Basin [Cand. scient. thesis]: University of Oslo, 136 p.
Roots, W. D., and Srivastava, S. P., 1984, Origin of marine magnetic quiet zones in the Labrador and Greenland seas: Marine Geophysical Researches, v. 6, p. 395–408.
Rozhdestvenskiy, S. S., and Karasik, A. M., 1982, Present-day geometry of the diverging boundary between the North American and Eurasian crustal plates: Doklady Akademia Nauk SSSR, v. 227, p. 208–211.
Saemundsson, K., 1974, Evolution of the axial rifting zone in northern Iceland and the Tjørnes Fracture Zone: Geological Society of American Bulletin, v. 85, p. 495–504.
Savostin, L. A., and Karasik, A. M., 1981, Recent plate tectonics of the Arctic Basin and of northeastern Asia: Tectonophysics, v. 74, p. 111–145.
Schilling, J.-G., 1986, Geochemical and isotopic variation along the Mid-Atlantic Ridge axis from 79°N to 0°N, in Vogt, P. R., and Tucholke, B. E., eds., The western North Atlantic region: Boulder, Colorado, Geological Society of America, Geology of North America, v. M, p. 137–156.
Schilling, J.-G., and six others, 1983, Petrologic and geochemical variations along the Mid-Atlantic Ridge from 29°N to 73°N: American Journal of Science, v. 283, p. 510–586.
Sleep, N. H., and Biehler, S., 1970, Topography and tectonics at the intersections of fracture zones with central rifts: Journal of Geophysical Research, v. 75, p. 2748–2752.
Sørnes, A., and Fjeldskaar, W., 1980, The local seismicity in the Jan Mayen area: Norsk Polarinstitutts Skrifter, n. 12, p. 21–32.
Srivastava, S. P., and Tapscott, C. R., 1986, Plate kinematics of the North Atlantic, in Vogt, P. R., and Tucholke, B. E., eds., The western North Atlantic region: Boulder, Colorado, Geological Society of America, Geology of North America, v. M, p. 379–404.
Sykes, L. R., 1965, The seismicity of the Arctic: Seismological Society of America Bulletin, v. 55, p. 501–518.
Talwani, M., and Eldholm, O., 1977, Evolution of the Norwegian–Greenland Sea: Geological Society of America Bulletin, v. 88, p. 969–999.
Talwani, M., and Grønlie, G., 1976, Free-air gravity field of the Norwegian–Greenland Sea: Geological Society of America Map and Chart Series, MC-15.
Talwani, M., Windisch, C. C., and Langseth, M. G., 1971, Reykjanes ridge crest; A detailed geophysical study: Journal of Geophysical Research, v. 76, p. 473–517.
Vogt, P. R., 1986, The present accreting plate boundary configuration, North Atlantic plate, in Vogt, P. R., and Tucholke, B. E., eds., The western North Atlantic region: Boulder, Colorado, Geological Society of America, Geology of North America, v. M, p. 189–204.
Vogt, P. R., and three others, 1979a, The Eurasian Basin, in Norwegian Sea Symposium: Norwegian Petroleum Society, NSS-3, p. 1–29.
Vogt, P. R., and three others, 1979b, Detailed aeromagnetic investigation of the Arctic Basin: Journal of Geophysical Research, v. 84, p. 1071–1089.
Vogt, P. R., Johnson, G. L., and Kristjansson, L., 1980, Morphology and magnetic anomalies north of Iceland: Geophysical Journal, v. 47, p. 61–66.
Vogt, P. R., and four others, 1981, The Greenland–Norwegian Sea and Iceland environment; Geology and geophysics, in Nairn, A.E.M., and Churkin, M., Jr., eds., The ocean basins and margins, p. 493–598.
Zielinski, G. W., 1979, On the thermal evolution of passive continental margins, thermal depth anomalies, and the Norwegian–Greenland Sea: Journal of Geophysical Reseach, v. 84, p. 7577–7588.

Manuscript Accepted by the Society December 10, 1986

ACKNOWLEDGMENTS

We thank H. Bungum for providing epicenter locations and G. L. Johnson for comments and advice.

Morse (femelle avec son petit).
(Vieille gravure hollandaise.)

From A. E. Nordenskjold, 1885, Voyage de la Vega Artour l'Asie et de l'Europe [1878–1875], (translated from Swedish by Charles Rabot and Charles Lallemand), vol. 1: Paris, Libraire Hachette et Cie, p. 420.

Printed in U.S.A.

Chapter 12

The East Greenland Shelf

Hans Christian Larsen
The Geological Survey of Greenland, Øster Voldgade 10, DK-1350, Copenhagen, Denmark

INTRODUCTION

Geologically, the East Greenland Shelf remained virtually unexplored for many years while the onshore East Greenland Mesozoic basin stratigraphy was intensely studied and served as a reference for the interpretation of the offshore East Greenland and northwest European margins. This development was a natural consequence of the excellent onshore basin exposure while polar pack ice is found almost year-around on the East Greenland shelf. The first geophysical information from the East Greenland shelf was published by Vogt (1970), Eldholm and Windisch (1974), Johnson and others (1975a, b), B. Larsen (1975), H. C. Larsen (1975, 1978), Henderson (1976), and Featherstone and others (1977).

Results of the first multichannel reflection seismic surveying on the shelf were reported by Hinz and Schlüter (1978, 1980). On the basis of this information and initial results from an aeromagnetic survey (H. C. Larsen and Thorning, 1979, 1980), a regional geological model for the East Greenland Shelf was proposed by H. C. Larsen (1980). This model involved early Tertiary oceanic crust thought to be present below parts of the outer shelf off central East Greenland and subsided continental crust thought to be present up to approximately 100 km seaward of the shelf break off southeastern Greenland. The actual position of the shelf edge was found to be controlled mainly by post-rift sedimentation rather than deep crustal features (H. C. Larsen, 1980). It was further suggested that Cenozoic basins might dominate the southern half of the shelf while Mesozoic and Paleozoic basins were likely to be present beneath the northern shelf.

This chapter summarizes the results of a four-year marine geophysical acquisition program conducted by the Geological Survey of Greenland (H. C. Larsen, 1983), which included a regional coverage of high-fold multichannel reflection seismic, refraction seismic, and marine gravity data (Figs. 1, 2). These data provide, in the area south of latitude 72°N, good control of the sediment thickness, the general stratigraphy, and the structure of the sedimentary shelf. The data also provide information on the structure and origin of the basement below the sedimentary shelf. Seismic data are sparse north of latitude 72°N and were never recorded north of latitude 74°N. Hence, the interpretation of the stratigraphy and the basin structures on the northern shelf still remains based on information deduced from aeromagnetic data. A preliminary interpretation of the offshore geology was presented by H. C. Larsen (1984).

One of the main findings of the last six years of geophysical surveying of the East Greenland Shelf is that different structural styles and tectonic development characterize the southern and northern shelf. The transition zone between these two regions is centered around the landward projection of the Jan Mayen Fracture Zone onto the shelf at approximately lat. 72°N (Fig. 1). This superior two-fold subdivision of the East Greenland margin is, in this chapter, related to the diversity in both the preexisting geologic setting and the development along the margin of rifting and sea-floor spreading during the Tertiary (H. C. Larsen, 1988).

Another important observation made from the geophysical data is the widespread presence along the margin of a wedge of seaward-dipping sub-basement reflectors. This wedge is found in regions both landward and seaward of the oldest sea-floor spreading anomaly along the margin (anomaly 24), and is interpreted to be a result of subaerial sea-floor spreading (H. C. Larsen and Jakobsdóttir, 1988). This interpretation of the seaward-dipping sub-basement reflector sequence dramatically reduces the areas of possible continental crust seaward of the shelf break and indicates the start of spreading within the northeast Atlantic during the reverse period 24R, well before anomaly 24.

Limits of the study area

The limits of the present study area are shown in Figure 1. The southern boundary is rather arbitrarily set at lat. 60°N (approximate southern tip of Greenland). The northern boundary follows the approximate position and trend of the Greenland Fracture Zone. This fracture zone probably was part of the Late Cretaceous to early Tertiary transform shear zone between the North Greenland margin and the Barents Sea/Spitsbergen margin (see Dawes, this volume; Eldholm, this volume).

The present chapter includes only limited reference to the onshore geologic development and to the plate-kinematic development since initial formation of the Tertiary oceanic lithosphere to the east of the East Greenland continental margin. Except for

Larsen, H. C., 1990, The East Greenland Shelf, *in* Grantz, A., Johnson, L., and Sweeney, J. F., eds., The Arctic Ocean region: Boulder, Colorado, Geological Society of America, The Geology of North America, v. L.

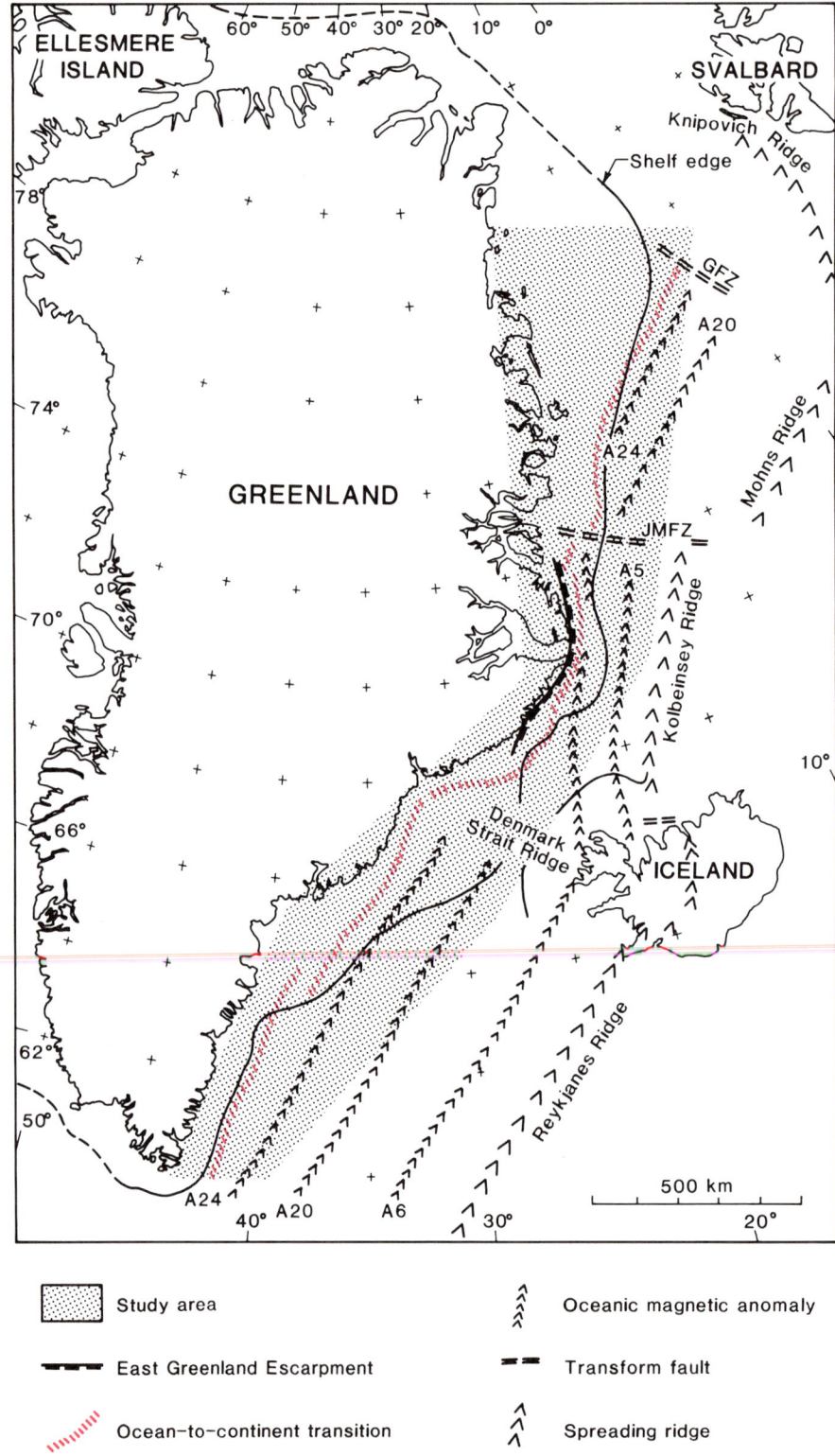

Figure 1. Study area. Present spreading ridges and major transform faults shown along with selected sea-floor spreading anomalies. Crustal rupturing and seaward down-faulting along the prominent East Greenland Escarpment have made the formation of a thick Tertiary basin possible in the area between the Denmark Strait Ridge and the Jan Mayen Fracture Zone (JMFZ). Tertiary subsidence and basin formation is less pronounced south of the Denmark Strait Ridge and is almost absent in the inner shelf north of the JMFZ. GFZ, Greenland Fracture Zone.

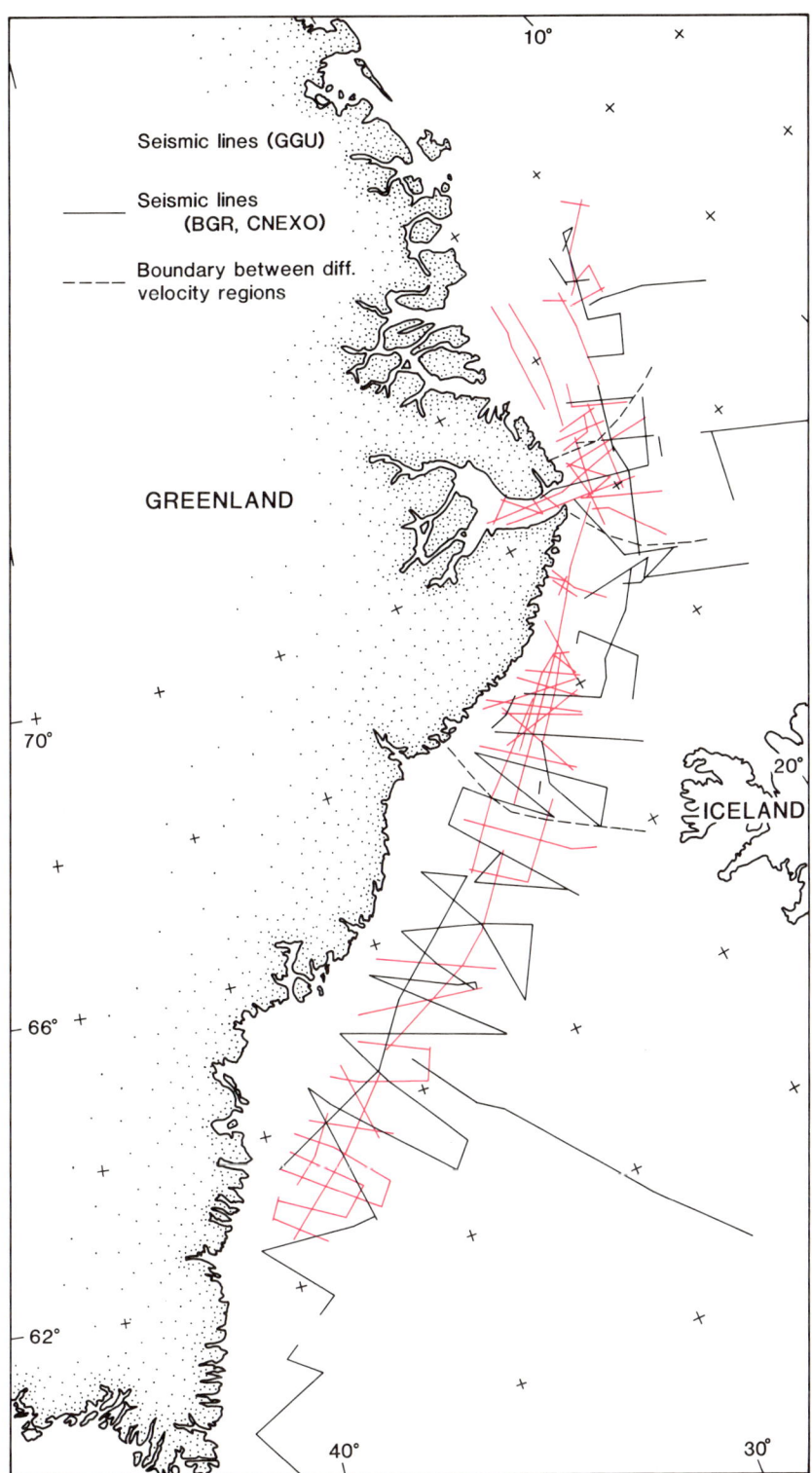

Figure 2. Map of the multichannel seismic coverage off East Greenland used for the compilation of the sediment isopach map (Plate 10). Three different velocity functions have been used for depth conversion. The Geological Survey of Greenland (GGU) seismic data comprise about 8,000 km of data out of a total of about 12,000 km. The GGU data are 24 to 60 fold good quality data. The Bundesanstalt für Geowissenschaften und Rohstoffe (BGR) data are 4 to 24 fold data with poor attenuation of multiple noise. The Centre National pour L'Exploitation des Oceans (CNEXO) data are rather poor quality data of 6 to 12 fold coverage. Selected GGU seismic lines are displayed in Plate 6 (positions shown on Plate 10, in pocket).

the deep-water region seaward of the shelf break off southeast Greenland (Fig. 1), the present chapter is thus restricted to the geologic development and structure of the shelf and slope. The deep-water region off southeast Greenland is included because it earlier was assumed to contain subsided continental crust (Featherstone and others, 1977; H. C. Larsen, 1980) and because it now is a key area for understanding the development of the so-called seaward-dipping reflector sequences and their relation to the earliest spreading phase in the northeast Atlantic (H. C. Larsen and Jakobsdóttir, 1988). In total, the study area comprises around 500,000 km^2.

Setting

A summary of the onshore geology was given by H. C. Larsen (1980) and Surlyk and others (1981). The southern half of the East Greenland coast is made up of Precambrian basement rocks of Early Proterozoic and Archean age. The northern half comprises a coast-parallel mountain belt of Caledonian age and Paleozoic and Mesozoic rift basins along the same trend. At the junction between these two geologically different regions, vast volumes of early Tertiary volcanics have overflooded the margin, and subaerially erupted lavas make up the coast for several hundred kilometers (Fig. 3). Important intrusive and tectonic activity of the same age also took place in even wider regions. A well-known example of the latter is the formation of the East Greenland dike swarm and associated coastal flexure (Wager and Deer, 1938; Nielsen, 1978; H. C. Larsen, 1978). Finally, most of the East Greenland land area was considerably uplifted during the Cenozoic (Fig. 4).

The seaward boundary of the East Greenland continental margin is marked by the western edge of Tertiary oceanic crust formed along the Reykjanes Ridge, the Icelandic spreading center, the Kolbeinsey Ridge, and the Mohns Ridge (Figs. 1 and 3). The type of transition from continental to oceanic crust is believed to be mainly of the passive rifted type (volcanic passive margin), except for the very northern part of the margin (north of the Greenland Fracture Zone). Along this northern boundary (outside the present study area), segments of both sheared-type passive margin and rifted-type passive margin are likely to occur along the general trend of the Greenland Fracture Zone (see also Dawes, this volume).

The precise location of the ocean-to-continent transition is, as it is in many other areas, debatable. H. C. Larsen (1984) proposed a fairly narrow to, in places, virtually absent "true continental" shelf (e. g., an ocean-to-continent transition very close to the present coastline in large areas south of lat. 72°N). This view is only slightly modified in the present chapter (Figs. 1 and 3).

The idea of oceanic crust being present below large parts of the East Greenland Shelf in the area between Iceland and Greenland is not new. Based on magnetic data and general plate-kinematic considerations, both Vogt and others (1980) and H. C. Larsen (1980) made this suggestion. This general ideal was also adopted by Nunns (1983) in proposing a spreading model for the central northeast Atlantic (see also Eldholm, this volume; and H. C. Larsen, 1988).

With the new geophysical data available, additional and partly independent criteria such as tectonic styles/subsidence patterns, regional gravity changes, presence or absence of seaward-dipping basaltic reflectors, and seismic stratigraphic dating and mapping of different seismic sequences can all be used in the attempt to locate and map the ocean-to-continent transition.

The marginal escarpments suggested to form the ocean-to-continent transition on the northwest European margin (Talwani and Eldholm, 1977) are not easily identified off East Greenland. One was reported by Eldholm and Windisch (1974) at approximately lat. 74°N, and a number of apparent escarpments (called pseudo-escarpments in this chapter) have been located through the more recent seismic program. These are believed to consist mainly of interdigitating sediments and volcanics and are thus not necessarily of deep crustal nature (Fig. 5). Some of them show, however, fairly close relationship to the inferred ocean-to-continent transition.

PHYSIOGRAPHY

The detailed bathymetry and morphology of the East Greenland Shelf are poorly known, especially in the northern part, where even information on the regional bathymetry is sparse. Studies of the shelf morphology have been published by Sommerhoff (1973), B. Larsen (1975, 1980, 1983), and Johnson and others (1975b). H. C. Larsen (1980) presented a small-scale compilation of regional shelf and slope bathymetry. The regional bathymetric maps by Perry and others (1977, 1985) and Grønlie and Talwani (1978) also cover all or most of the East Greenland Shelf.

In general, the East Greenland Shelf shows rather great water depths, typically in the range of 250 to 350 m (Johnson and others, this volume; Plate 1). A number of banks, often situated at the outer shelf, show water depths around 200 m; a number of mainly transverse shelf channels originating from the major fiords show water depths between 400 and 600 m on the sedimentary shelf. These channels can be as much as 1,000 m deep where basement is exposed. Some smaller banks situated close to the coast are reported to show water depths of only 20 to 100 m.

The recent bathymetric map by Perry and others (1985) shows the presence on the Northeast Greenland Shelf of fairly large banks with surprisingly shallow water depths, around 100 to 200 m. Shoals with as little as 15 m of water depth occur on the large Belgica Bank (Johnson and others, this volume; see Plate 1).

The average water depth in the north thus seems less than on the southern two-thirds of the shelf. Also, there seems to be some correlation between the deep structure and the present morphology. Shallow shoals are located on top of structural highs between the coast-parallel, rifted basins and exposures of old and

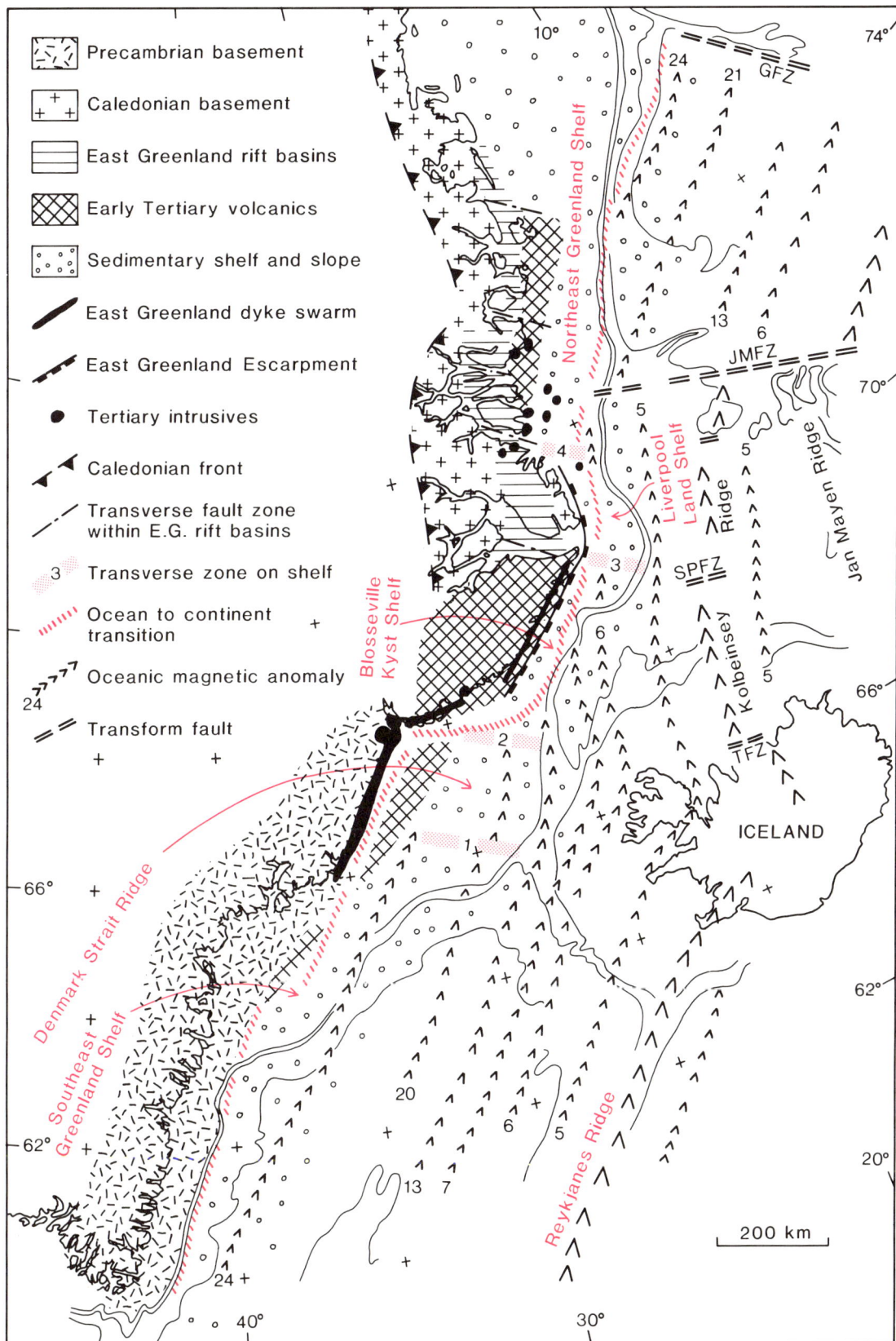

Figure 3. Geological/tectonic sketch map: GFZ, Greenland Fracture Zone; JMFZ, Jan Mayen Fracture Zone; SPFZ, Spar Fracture Zone; TFZ, Tjørnes Fracture Zone. Early Tertiary volcanics only shown where outcropping or at shallow depths.

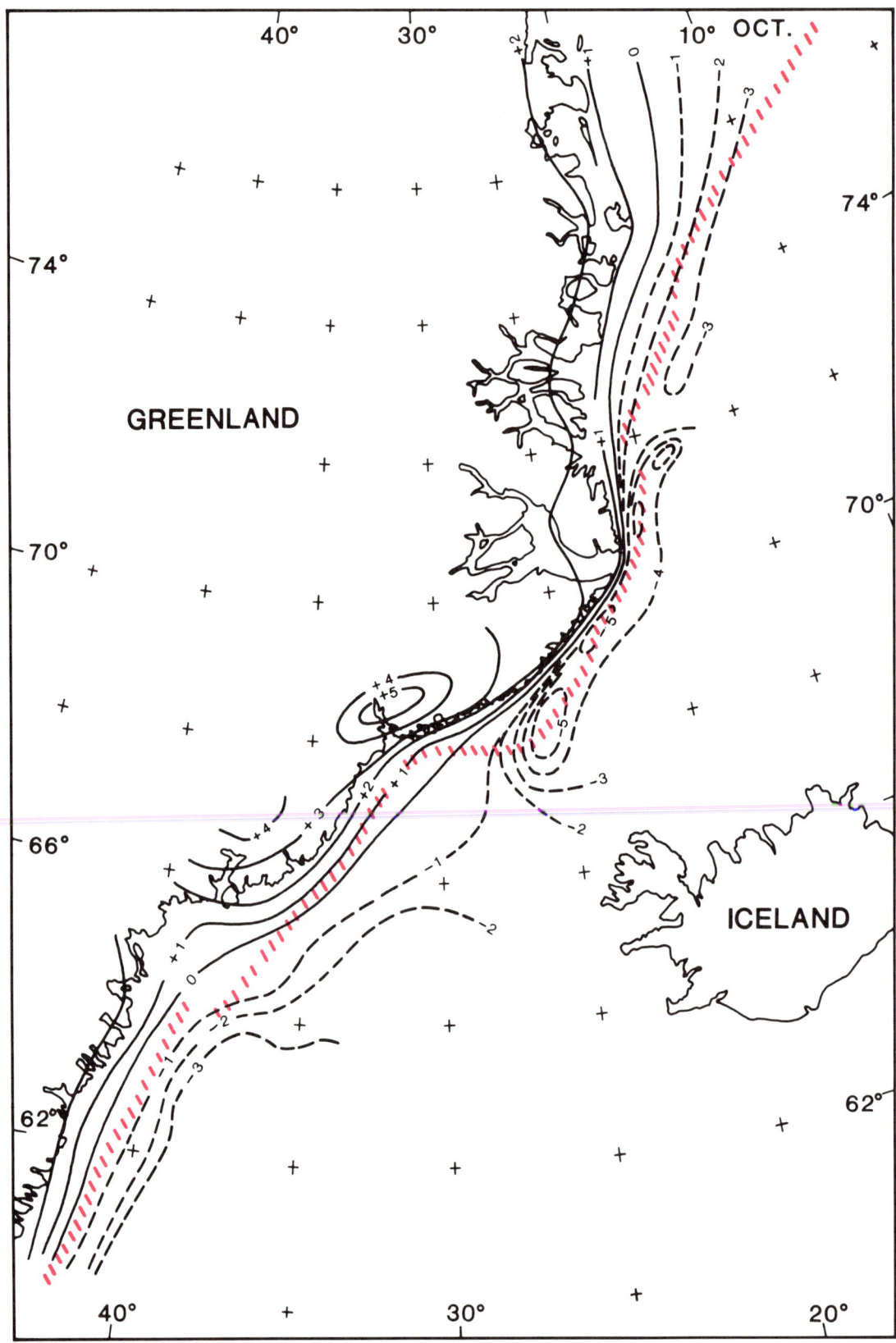

Figure 4. Approximate post-drift (= post-Paleocene) vertical crustal movements along the East Greenland margin constructed from seismic stratigraphy, fission track data, thermal maturity data, geomorphological, and geological investigations. See text for references.

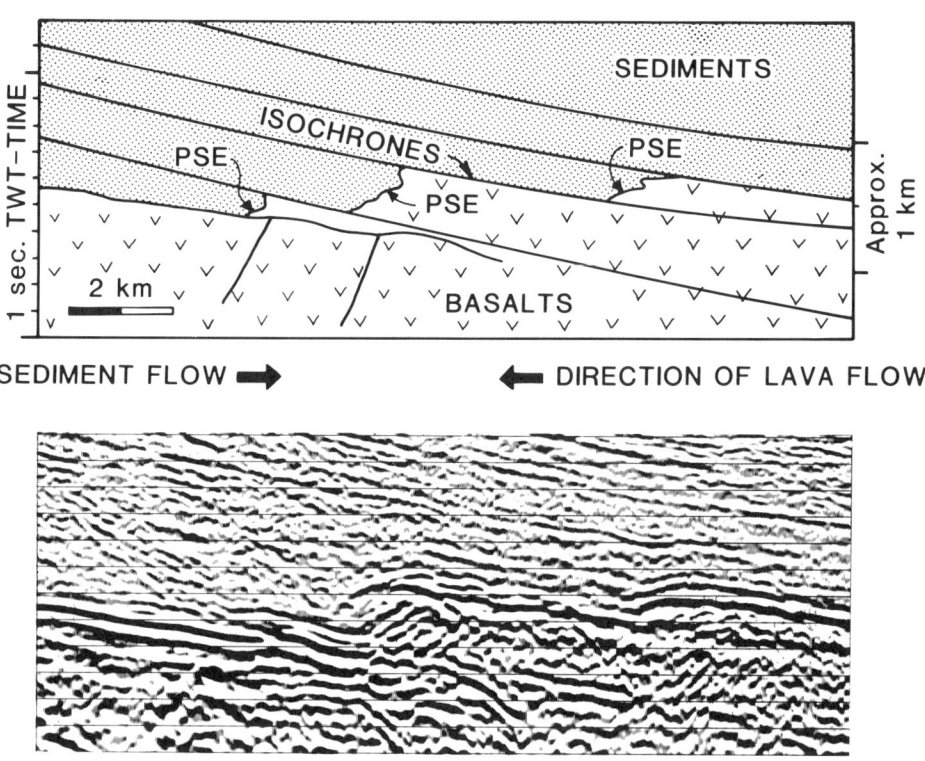

Figure 5. Formation of so-called pseudo-escarpments. The name pseudo-escarpment is applied in order to stress that such escarpments do not necessarily have important tectonic or chronostratigraphic implications, but are merely a gradual to sharp lateral changes in lithostratigraphic composition. On a more detailed scale, components of a pseudo-escarpment are real escarpments.

hard Mesozoic/Paleozoic sediments or basement rocks may therefore occur on the shallow shoals.

Correlation of the deep structure with the present-day morphology of the sedimentary shelf can also be made in the area between northwest Iceland and Greenland. In this region, the Greenland Shelf and the insular shelf of Iceland almost merge. This fairly shallow-water ridge (maximum 800 m water depth) between Iceland and Greenland, the so-called Denmark Strait Ridge, is part of a more extensive ridge system from the Faeroes across Iceland to Greenland (Bott and others, 1983). This ridge is evidently related to a basement ridge (see Plate 10), although later sedimentary and glacial processes contributed to the present-day morphology of the ridge.

Most other parts of the East Greenland sedimentary shelf show less obvious, if any, correlation between present-day water depths and the deep structure; thus, the shelf morphology in these areas is more likely to be controlled mainly by late Cenozoic sedimentation and glacial processes.

The morphology of the sea bed is irregular where basement is exposed. Precambrian basement is characterized by "hilly" topography, whereas the areas of Tertiary lava exposure may show a cuesta-like morphology (B. Larsen, 1983, Fig. 5). The sedimentary shelf is normally fairly flat with just gentle changes in water depth. This monotony is disturbed only by the broad and mainly transverse channels outside the major fiords and by the intense iceberg scouring of the shallower banks (B. Larsen, 1983, Fig. 8).

The sea bed of the sedimentary shelf off East Greenland appears very hard and initiates a sequence of strong water-bottom multiples during seismic work. The lithology of the sea bed on the sedimentary shelf is poorly known. Some dredge samples were described by Sommerhoff (1973) and Johnson and others (1975a). Clastic sediments and volcanics ranging from the Carboniferous to the Oligocene in age were reported, suggesting a major component of glacial drift material.

There has been considerable speculation about why many Arctic shelves, including the East Greenland Shelf, are so deep (Vogt and Perry, 1978). Seismic stratigraphic interpretation of the central East Greenland Shelf outside the Scoresby Sund fiord suggests that the shelf here originated as a shallow-water prograding shelf during the latest Cenozoic (H. C. Larsen, unpublished data). The present shelf depth may thus be of fairly recent (Pleistocene?) origin. Perhaps the present water depth reflects a combination of several factors: termination of shelf platform sedimentation by glacier formation, glacial erosion of the upper surface of the shelf, and crustal subsidence due to earlier sediment loading, later ice-loading, and, in particular, thermal contraction of the lithosphere following the fairly recent (20 Ma) rifting of the area. In order to effect a marked increase in the water depth through such mechanisms, a fairly extensive period of shelf glaciation with strongly reduced vertical sediment aggradation on the shelf platform is required. Evidence for a major glaciation event starting at approximately 2.5 Ma (Shackleton and others, 1984; Eldholm and others, 1986) provides some support for this suggestion.

GEOLOGIC PROVINCES

The main structural subdivision of the East Greenland Shelf is shown in Figure 3. This subdivision is also easily recognized within the sediment isopach map (see Plate 10).

Four transverse zones are believed to separate five different geologic provinces. Important structural and stratigraphic changes take place across these transverse zones, while each of the five geologic provinces appears fairly uniform internally. The tectonic diversity includes changes in crustal type, amount of basin subsidence, contrasting basement tectonics, and different timing of basin formation.

The four transverse zones are located (Fig. 3): (1) in the southern Denmark Strait, (2) in the northern Denmark Strait just outside the mouth of the Kangerdlugssuaq fiord, (3) outside the mouth of the Scoresby Sund fiord, and (4) outside the mouth of Kong Oscars Fiord.

The present-day equivalents to (1) and (2) are the transform zones of southern and northern Iceland (Fig. 3). They are named, respectively, the Denmark Strait Escarpment Zone and the Kangerdlugssuaq Escarpment Zone. A recent equivalent to (3), named the Scoresby Sund Fracture Zone, may be found in the Spar Fracture Zone north of Iceland (Vogt and others, 1980). Transverse Zone (4) is related to the projection of the Jan Mayen Fracture Zone onto the shelf, and is called the Kong Oscars Fiord Fracture Zone (see also Surlyk, 1977b, 1978).

Five regions, discussed below and defined by the four transverse zones, are: the Southeast Greenland Shelf and Rise, the Denmark Strait Ridge, the Blosseville Kyst Shelf, the Liverpool Land Shelf, and the Northeast Greenland Shelf.

A further subdivision of these five regions can be expected should new and more detailed data be gathered. An apparently natural subdivision of the large Northeast Greenland Shelf region into a southern and northern area has thus not been formalized here, owing to a lack of seismic data.

The tectonic and stratigraphic subdivision of the shelf into the five regions is based primarily on the aeromagnetic and reflection seismic mapping done by H. C. Larsen and Thorning (1980) and H. C. Larsen (1983), assisted by marine gravity and refraction seismic data (H. C. Larsen and Jakobsdóttir, 1988). Direct or indirect stratigraphic information from wells or from dredged material of autochthonous origin is simply not present from anywhere on the East Greenland Shelf. Hence, all offshore stratigraphic interpretations in this chapter are based on seismic stratigraphic interpretations (i.e., on seismic sequence and unconformity recognition and correlation with global charts; Vail and others, 1977).

In the four southern subregions, however, this procedure is strongly aided by the presence of a volcanic basement below part of the shelf (Fig. 6), which shows datable sea-floor spreading anomalies of Cenozoic age. Baselap of a regional unconformity onto datable oceanic crust has been used as an independent (maximum) age for the overlying sediments, in addition to the seismic stratigraphic age obtained. In areas of continuous sedimentation and a broad age range within the basement, a fairly precise stratigraphic framework can be established by this integrated method, especially if an interdigitating relationship between sediments and volcanics of the basement can be demonstrated. The Cenozoic stratigraphy, and the Neogene stratigraphy in particular, established within the Blosseville Kyst Shelf and the Liverpool Land Shelf, is thus believed to be fairly precise, with the potential of high stratigraphic resolution.

In basins of relatively incomplete stratigraphic composition and with limited age control from sea-floor spreading anomalies, the seismic stratigraphic interpretations can only provide a tentative stratigraphic framework. The Cenozoic stratigraphy of the Southeast Greenland Shelf and the Denmark Strait Ridge is thus considered less well controlled.

In the southern four areas, pre-Cenozoic sediments are believed to subcrop only below the innermost part of the Liverpool Land Shelf. The seismic coverage of these potential pre-Cenozoic sediments, however, does not qualify for a seismic stratigraphic analysis. As there is virtually no seismic coverage from the fifth and northernmost region, the Northeast Greenland Shelf, the regional stratigraphy tentatively proposed for this area is based merely on extrapolation from onshore basin exposures and regional correlation with the explored Norwegian Shelf.

Estimates of offshore subsidence and subsidence history of the East Greenland margin can only be portrayed in an indirect manner because of the lack of offshore wells. An attempt to regionally reconstruct the approximate net uplift/subsidence of the East Greenland margin since the time of initial rifting and early sea-floor spreading is shown in Figure 4. The basis of this map is the recognition of the widespread late Paleocene volcanic event along the margin. Large parts of the margin were overflooded by basalts that apparently rest on a low-relief regional peneplain. The continental basalt province of late Paleocene age in East Greenland (see H. C. Larsen, 1980 for review; Soper and others, 1976) is found to continue below part of the inner shelf, and it is eventually replaced seaward by the seaward-dipping sub-basement reflector sequence. Both the flat-lying continental basalts and the basalts of the seaward-dipping reflector sequence were deposited subaerially, or perhaps into a shallow sea. Figure 4 is based on the assumption that the top of the syn-rift to early spreading phase extrusive basaltic sequence formed at sea level and has since moved into its present-day uplifted or subsided position.

The Cenozoic offshore basin formation and the tentative stratigraphy erected here provide some control on the offshore subsidence history, whereas on land, fission-track dating, radiometric dating of Tertiary subvolcanic complexes, and geomorphological studies indicate accelerated uplift of the Greenland

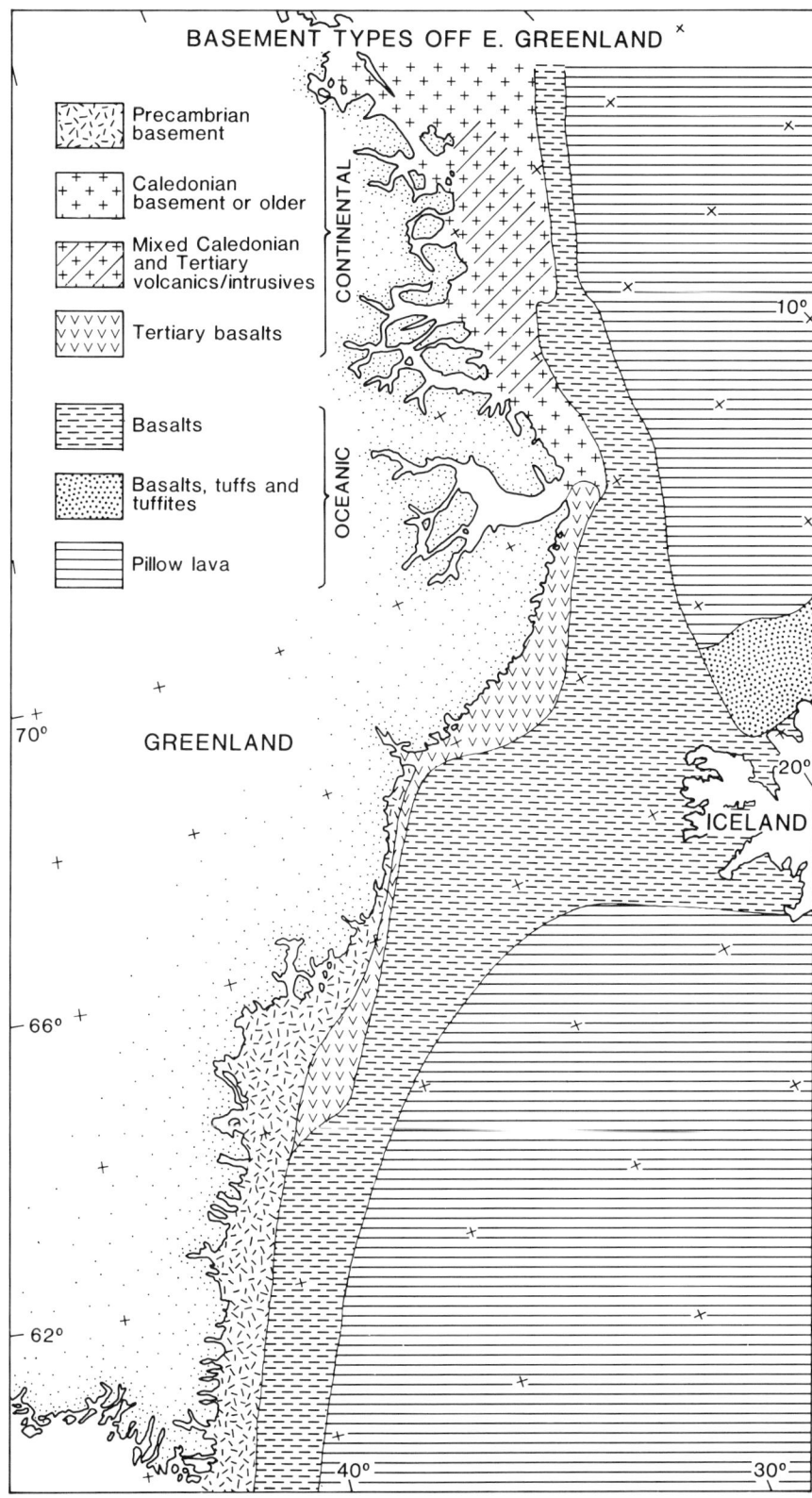

Figure 6. Different basement types along the East Greenland margin. Tertiary volcanics of varying thickness are interbedded within the sedimentary section at shallow to intermediate depth in large parts of the Caledonian basement region (crosshatched in the figure).

mainland during the mid- and late Tertiary (Brooks and Gleadow, 1977; Brooks, 1979; H. C. Larsen, 1980; Hansen, 1985, 1988).

Southeast Greenland Shelf and Rise (SEAS)

A major structural element in the Cenozoic development of this area is the formation of a coast-parallel monoclinal flexure separating relatively uplifted continental crust from relatively subsided oceanic crust (Fig. 4; Plate 10). The inferred ocean-to-continent transition (OCT) and the associated flexure follow the shelf edge in the very southern part of the SEAS, but come very close to the coast in the north. Thus, most of the very southern shelf is made up of exposed continental basement (Precambrian) with some Tertiary volcanics, and the northern part of the SEAS is floored by subsided oceanic crust covered with Tertiary sediments. The southernmost shelf is quite narrow (75 km), but widens northward to about 175 km (Fig. 7).

Sea-floor spreading along this part of the East Greenland margin started along the Reykjanes Ridge under subaerial conditions in the late Paleocene at, or just after, magnetic anomaly 25 and about 80 to 90 km inland of the oldest well-developed magnetic anomaly, 24 A/B (H. C. Larsen, 1980; H. C. Larsen and Jakobsdóttir, 1988). The subaerial sea-floor spreading resulted in a crust characterized in its upper part by seaward-dipping basement reflectors (Fig. 7; see also profile A of Plate 6). The nascent oceanic crust, however, soon began to subside in response to cooling of the oceanic lithosphere, and a depression started to form between the southeast Greenland continental margin in the west and the Reykjanes Ridge in the east. By this means, the coast-parallel monoclinal flexure that separates the relatively uplifted Greenland continental crust from the relatively subsided oceanic crust was initiated. A presumably shallow sea overflooded this depression from the south. The paleoslope of this marine embayment was to the south (see Plate 10; Fig. 8). During the early stages of this basin formation, an eastern basin limit was formed by the Reykjanes Ridge. Following subsidence of the Reykjanes Ridge below sea level during the Eocene (H. C. Larsen and Jakobsdóttir, 1988), a seaway was established to the east, between the marine embayment and Rockall Basin, but the Reykjanes Ridge continued to exist as a ridge between the two basins.

Because the basin started in the Early Eocene as a shallow marine embayment, and the deepest basement is now found at 4 km depth (Plate 10), considerable subsidence, as would be expected, has taken place. Present-day water depth exceeds 2 km in large areas, and hence, the basin clearly developed into a starved, deep-water basin during the Tertiary because of insufficient sediment supply from the Greenland continent.

On a regional scale, three seismic stratigraphic sequences have tentatively been distinguished within the Cenozoic basin of the SEAS area (see profile A of Plate 6). The oldest of these sequences (sequence 1) is assumed to correspond to the initial transgression of the basin during the late Paleocene and Eocene. A total of up to approximately 700 m of presumed marine clastics, shelf carbonates (mainly western and northern part), and volcaniclastic sediments (mainly eastern part) were laid down in the Southeast Greenland Basin during the deposition of sequence 1 (see profile A of Plate 6).

The depositional pattern of sequence 1 changed, however, following subsidence to fairly great depths due to cooling of the oceanic lithosphere in combination with a limited sediment supply to the basin. Turbiditic deposition within the deeper and central parts of the basin most likely took over while an erosional unconformity formed along the western part of the basin (profile A of Plate 6). A deep-water sequence up to 1,000 m thick was laid down in the central part of the basin during this depositional phase (seismic sequence 2). Responding to increased crustal flexuring along the initial line of rifting, including accelerating continental uplift and continued oceanic subsidence, the pattern of basin filling developed further during the Neogene. Deposition of a strongly progradational wedge of clastic sediments across the crustal flexure zone was initiated, while abyssal current deposition/erosion became important within the more distal and deeper parts of the basin (seismic sequence 3). The progradational part of the sequence is locally as much as about 1,500 m thick, but normally only 600 to 800 m thick. The deep-water part of sequence 3 is as much as approximately 1,000 m thick.

The outbuilding clastic wedge making up most of the present-day sedimentary shelf has prograded only 5 to 20 km within the very southern area and between 50 and 70 km along the middle and northern part of the Southeast Greenland Shelf (profiles A, B of Plate 6). The narrow prograded areas show very steep (5° to 10°) sigmoidal clinoforms that apparently prograded into a fairly deep marine basin. They are probably the results of reduced clastic input and more intense contour current activity compared with the wider prograded shelf areas farther north (1° to 3° dipping clinoforms).

Evidence for the existence of pre-rift sediments on this part of the East Greenland margin is virtually absent except for one small, sub-basaltic exposure at the coast (see H. C. Larsen, 1980 for review) and some subvolcanic reflections (Fig. 7). Basement for the post-rift sediments is in most cases flat, seismically well defined and little affected by faulting. It shows widespread presence of seaward-dipping, divergent sub-basement reflectors deep in the crust (5 to 7 km; see profile A, B of Plate 6). The dipping reflectors have been discussed by various authors (Mutter and others, 1982; Hinz, 1981; Hinz and others, 1987; Smythe, 1983; H. C. Larsen and Jakobsdóttir, 1988), and are used in this chapter as an oceanic-crust indicator where they are extensively developed.

The general thickness of the post-rift sediments within the SEAS is less than 2 km, and the maximum thickness of 2.8 km associated with a Neogene depocenter is found close to the shelf edge around lat. 63.5°N, long. 38°W (see Plate 10).

The Denmark Strait Ridge

The southern boundary of the Denmark Strait Ridge is associated with a transverse basement escarpment with about 500

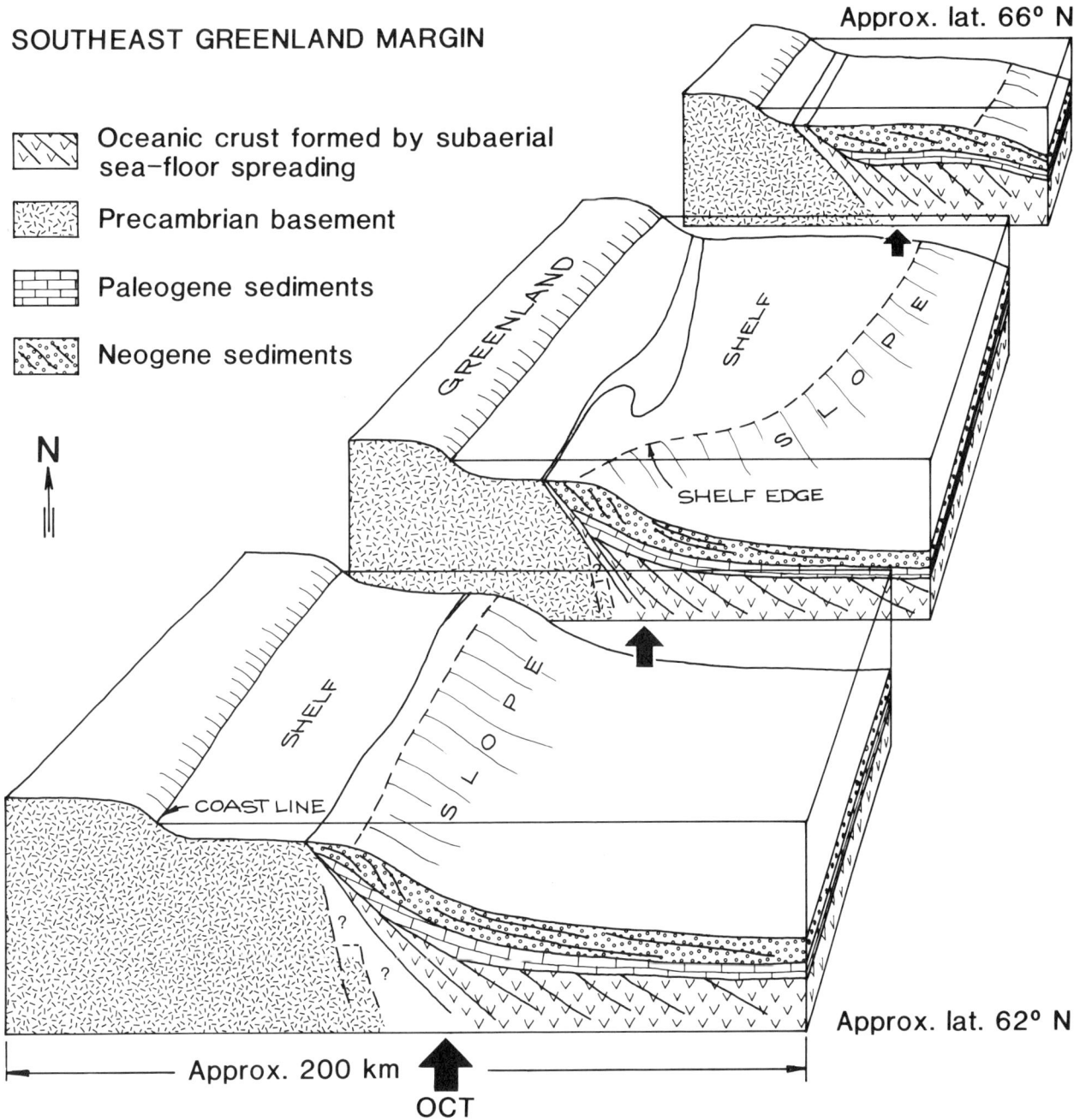

Figure 7. Three-dimensional view of the Southeast Greenland Shelf seen from south. Note how the crystalline basement extends over most of the shelf in the south. The width of the crystalline basement on the shelf slightly narrows to the north and occupies relatively much less of the shelf because the sedimentary shelf has prograded seawards in the northern area. OCT, approximate ocean-to-continent transition. The trend of the OCT is oblique to the coast line and the OCT is very close to the coast in the north. The classic East Greenland dyke swarm can be seen along the coast from about lat. 66°N (Wager and Deer, 1938) and most likely is the start of the oceanic lithosphere as suggested by H. C. Larsen (1978). The coastal dyke swarm is not shown in this figure.

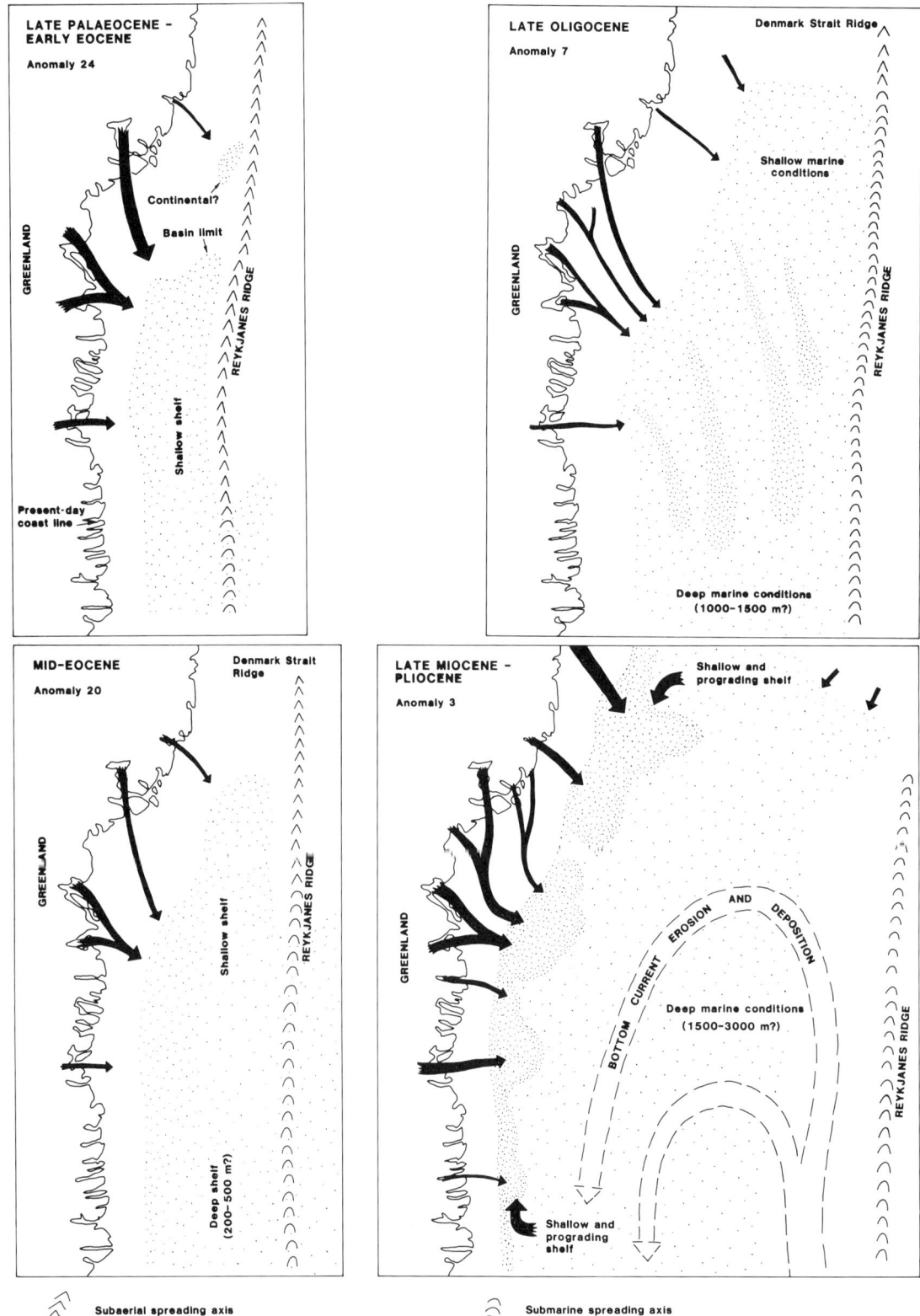

Figure 8. Four stages of the Tertiary basin formation off southeast Greenland. Considerable deepening of the basin took place because of limited sediment supply relative to the fairly rapid thermal subsidence of the oceanic crust below the basin.

m of relief (see Plate 10). The origin and nature of this escarpment is not known. It is here named the Denmark Strait Escarpment Zone. There is no evidence of lateral or vertical movements along the escarpment, and it is thus most likely that the escarpment existed prior to sedimentation in the area; there is also no significant offset of sea-floor spreading anomalies along the escarpment. It might separate less thick oceanic crust in the south from anomalously thick, Icelandic-type crust in the north and below the Denmark Strait Ridge, but sonobouy refraction data indicate that northward crustal thickening actually may start south of the escarpment (H. C. Larsen and Jakobsdôttir, 1988). The thickness of the sediments on the ridge varies from slightly less than 800 m to 1,200 m, and the sediments increase in thickness both north and south of the ridge.

The topographic expression of the so-called Kangerdlugssuaq Escarpment Zone, which forms the northern limit of the Denmark Strait Ridge, is generally less distinct than the southern boundary of the ridge. It is more like a northward-sloping basement flexure rather than an escarpment.

The formation of the ridge and its plate-kinematic development have been a matter for discussion. Complex spreading patterns, including large-scale westward jumps of the spreading axis, have been proposed (see Bott and others, 1983, for review). A new observation made by H. C. Larsen and Jakobsdôttir (1988) is the nearly continuous presence of seaward-dipping reflectors across the ridge (see profile C of Plate 6). These are interpreted as evidence for a continuous and fairly simple sea-floor spreading process above sea level from about anomaly 24 onward. In a spreading model proposed by H. C. Larsen (1988), the Denmark Strait Ridge is, from a plate-kinematic view, simply a northward continuation of the Reykjanes Ridge. The continuous formation of the basement ridge above sea level clearly indicates an excess volcanism to be present in the area (Icelandic hot spot).

The relatively smaller Tertiary subsidence of the oceanic crust below the Denmark Strait, compared to the areas north and south, means that the coast-parallel flexure zone is only weakly developed in this region (Fig. 4). The basement ridge between Iceland and Greenland thus most likely formed an emergent or very shallow-water transverse ridge during large parts of Tertiary time. According to seismic stratigraphic interpretation, the oldest sediments on the top of the ridge are only of late Middle Miocene or younger age (see profile C of Plate 6). A land bridge between East Greenland and northwestern Iceland during most of the Tertiary and until late Miocene is therefore a likely possibility, and one that has independent support from faunal studies in Iceland (Friederich and Simonarson, 1982).

The Blosseville Kyst Shelf (BLKS)

The geologic province called the Blosseville Kyst Shelf stretches northward along the Blosseville Kyst, from the northern boundary of the Denmark Strait Ridge on the south to just south of the Scoresby Sund fiord. This northern boundary toward the Liverpool Land Shelf is somewhat arbitrarily derived along a northwest-to-southeast–striking–basement ridge around lat. 69.6°N (see Fig. 11 and Plate 10). The Blosseville Kyst Shelf is bounded to the west and northwest by a prominent, coast-parallel, monoclinal flexure, which develops into an escarpment in the northern part of the BLKS; it is called the East Greenland Escarpment. East of the shelf break is the west- to northwest-sloping volcanic basement surface of the Icelandic Plateau (see also Eldholm, this volume), which partly extends westward below the slope and outer shelf. The shelf is fairly wide toward the south (about 200 km), but narrows northward to only about 100 km.

The shelf in this region has the same general setting as the Southeast Greenland Shelf. It is made up mainly of post-rift sediments of presumed clastic origin, deposited in front of a pronounced crustal flexure. The BLKS differs from the SEAS, however, by showing much larger subsidence and greater sediment thickness and by having a seismically less well-defined basement. The basement thus displays much relief. Also, there is no clear seismic evidence of seaward-dipping sub-basement reflectors in the deeper part of the basin. The landward-bounding flexure zone is more intensely developed in the BLKS compared with the flexure zone on the southern shelf, and develops northward into a major crustal escarpment (Fig. 9; see also Plate 10 and profile D on Plate 6).

The coast-parallel basin axis is situated on the shelf itself and is fairly close to the coast in front of the coastal flexure zone. The depth-to-basement along this basin axis is generally more than 5 km and locally reaches 6 to 7 km. Basement relief, including the coast-parallel escarpment zone, was mainly established prior to sedimentation by down-faulting and possible erosion of a volcanic plateau into a rifted depression. Further basement topography was introduced by later sedimentation and volcanism associated with the formation of the Icelandic Plateau by sea-floor spreading (see Eldholm, this volume). So-called pseudo-escarpments (Fig. 5) formed as a result of the coexisting sedimentation and volcanism and a major, extrusive volcanic complex formed at the ocean-to-continent transition within the northern part of the BLKS (see Plate 10).

The basement of the Blosseville Kyst Basin is mainly, if not entirely, of volcanic origin. It is not known exactly how much of the basin is underlain by oceanic crust.

The most landward position of the ocean-to-continent transition compatible with the present data would be a transition coinciding with the coastal flexure and escarpment zone. Mapping of some of the oldest seismic sequences, as well as gravity data, however, indicate that the transition in this area is somewhat seaward from this position. The more seaward position is considered the most likely; thus, the deep part of the basin, which shows fairly strong basement relief, is actually floored by rifted and attenuated continental crust, including thick deposits of rift volcanics. The upper surface of these rocks was used as the basement contour horizon in Plate 10. The ocean-to-continent transition cannot, however, be situated very far seaward of the deep part of the basin, and it most likely lies between the 4,000 m and

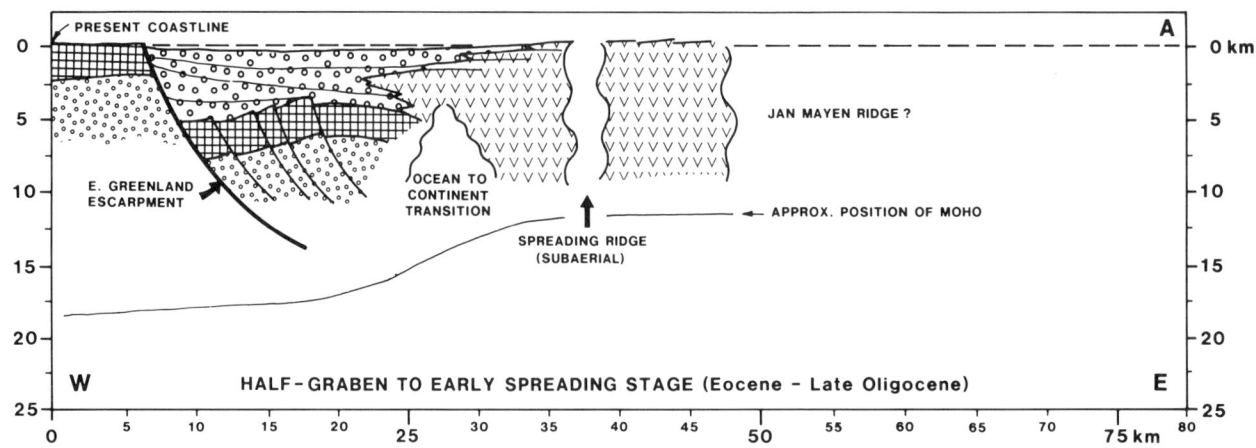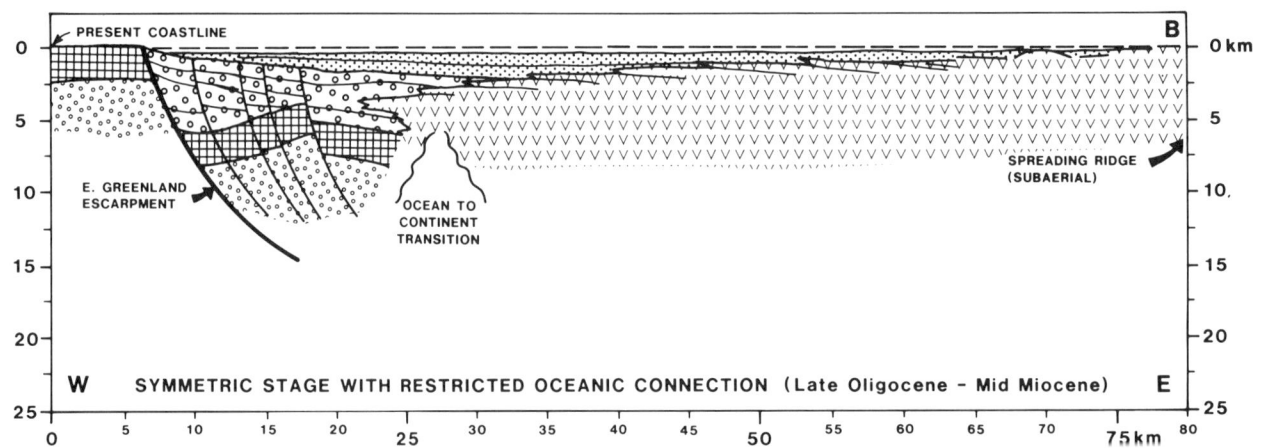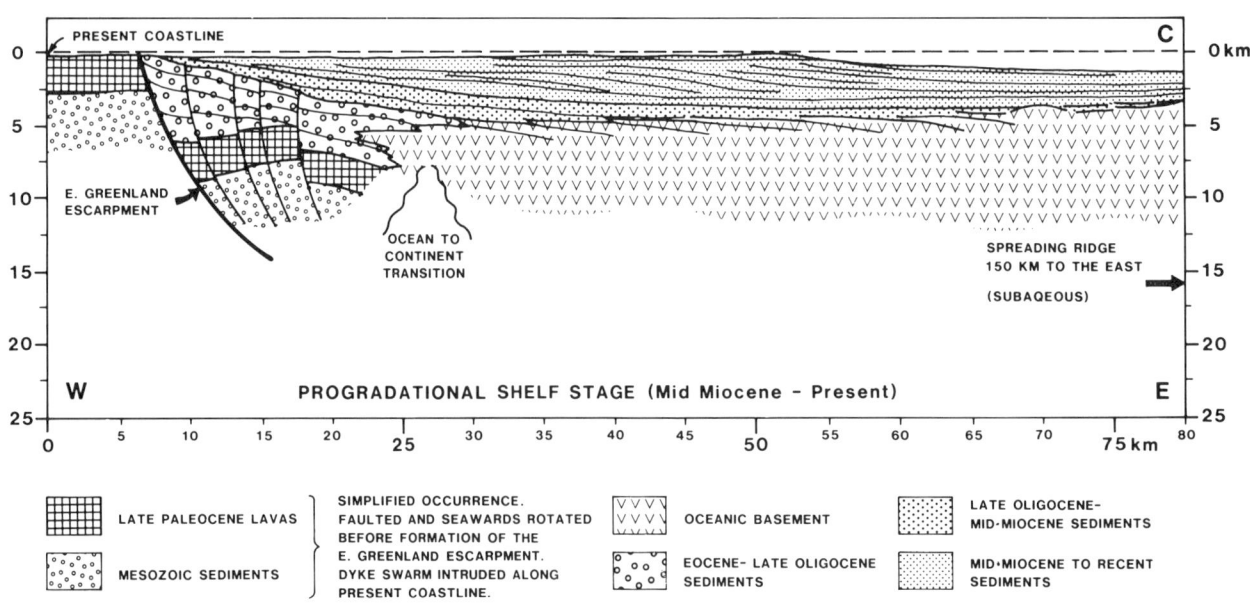

Figure 9. Development of the Blosseville Kyst shelf through initial half-graben stage to open progradational shelf stage.

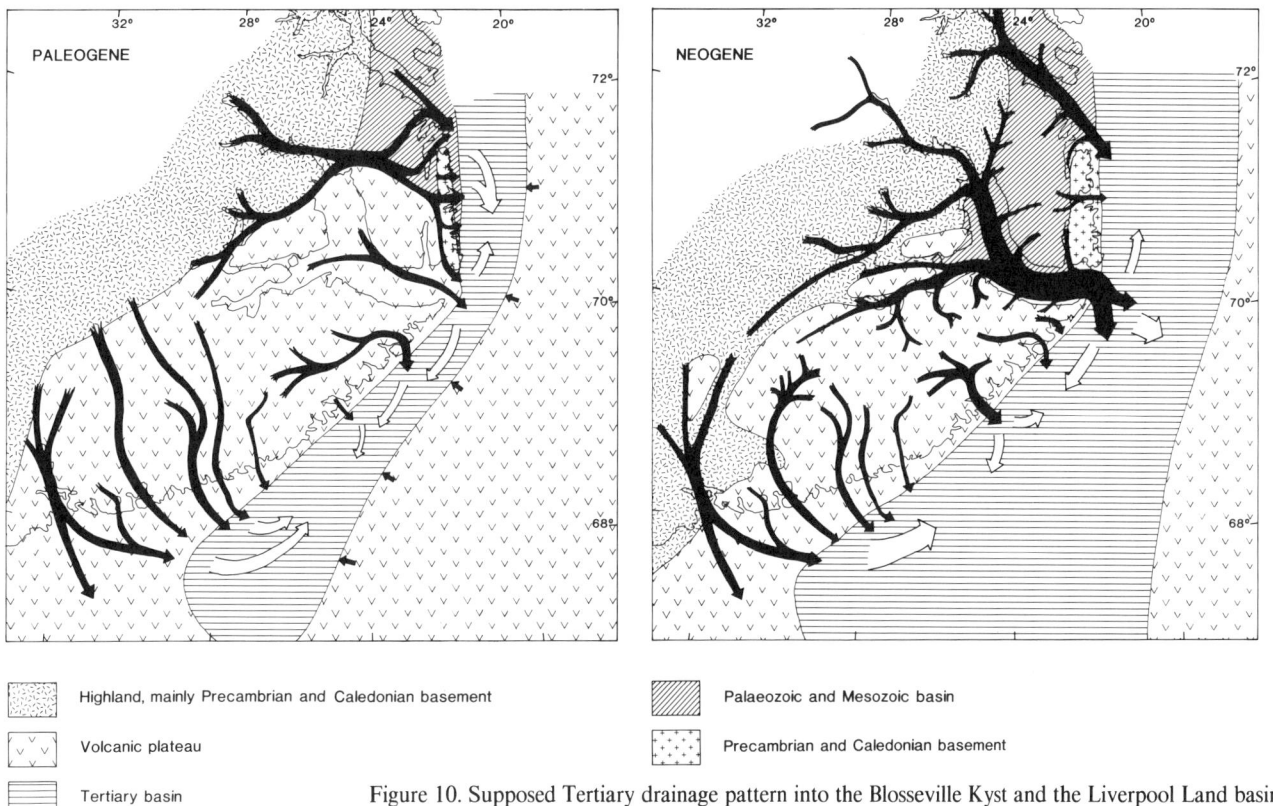

Figure 10. Supposed Tertiary drainage pattern into the Blosseville Kyst and the Liverpool Land basins.

5,000 m contour interval on the sediment isopach map (seaward side of basin axis; see Plate 10).

Sub-basalt, pre-rift sediments of Mesozoic or older age might occur within the central part of the basin. If present, they are likely to be buried by as much as 7 to 9 km of Tertiary sediments and rift volcanic units belonging to the group of East Greenland plateau basalts (Fig. 9).

The Tertiary sedimentary sequence in the Blosseville Kyst Basin is at least 10 km thick and appears very complete (see profile D of Plate 6). Subsidence and sedimentation is assumed to have started in the Eocene, as it did in small down-faulted, depressions along the coast (see H. C. Larsen, 1980, for a review). A deep, but narrow and asymmetrical, half-graben formed along with and in front of the coastal escarpment zone (Fig. 9). The half-graben basin probably had some narrow connection to the Norwegian Sea/Arctic Ocean to the north through the Liverpool Land basins (Figs. 10, 11). By Oligocene time, sea-floor spreading started to propagate from Iceland northward along the eastern flank of the Blosseville Kyst half-graben. As the new spreading ridge north of Iceland moved eastward with reference to Greenland, seaward progradation of the Blosseville Kyst Basin was made possible (Figs. 9, 10). The basin, however, remained bounded on the east by the subaerial spreading ridge north of Iceland until the late Middle Miocene (Fig. 10). At this time, the spreading axis subsided below sea level, and the basin became a wider and open shelf basin (Fig. 9). The depocenter remained seaward of the half-graben during the Neogene, and up to 4.5 km of Neogene sediments accumulated here.

The Paleogene infill of the half-graben was probably dominated by relatively coarse and immature clastic debris from the rising Greenland continent that poured into the basin east of the coast-parallel escarpment. Sedimentation may have started above sea level, but is likely to have changed rather quickly into marine sedimentation.

The basin floor of this Paleogene half-graben was not flat, but showed some high relief. One outstanding feature is the presence of an isolated structural high centered at lat. 68.3°N, long. 26°W (see Plate 10). This large high, a presumed horst block of rifted continental crust, apparently was a seamount within the Paleogene basin and first became buried in the Neogene. Another marked topographical feature within the basement of the basin is the deep, semicircular depression found at approximately lat. 69.4°N, long. 23.3°W. This depression clearly formed as a result of local loading imposed by the formation of a presumed mid-Tertiary extrusive volcanic complex at the approximate ocean-to-continent transition (see Plate 10). The preexisting layered basement can be followed seismically below this younger volcanic feature and has been used for the depth-to-basement mapping. The younger, mid-Tertiary volcanic complex is, of course, not included in the sediment isopach map (see Plate 10).

The Neogene section can be divided into a large number of seismic stratigraphic sequences separated by regional unconformi-

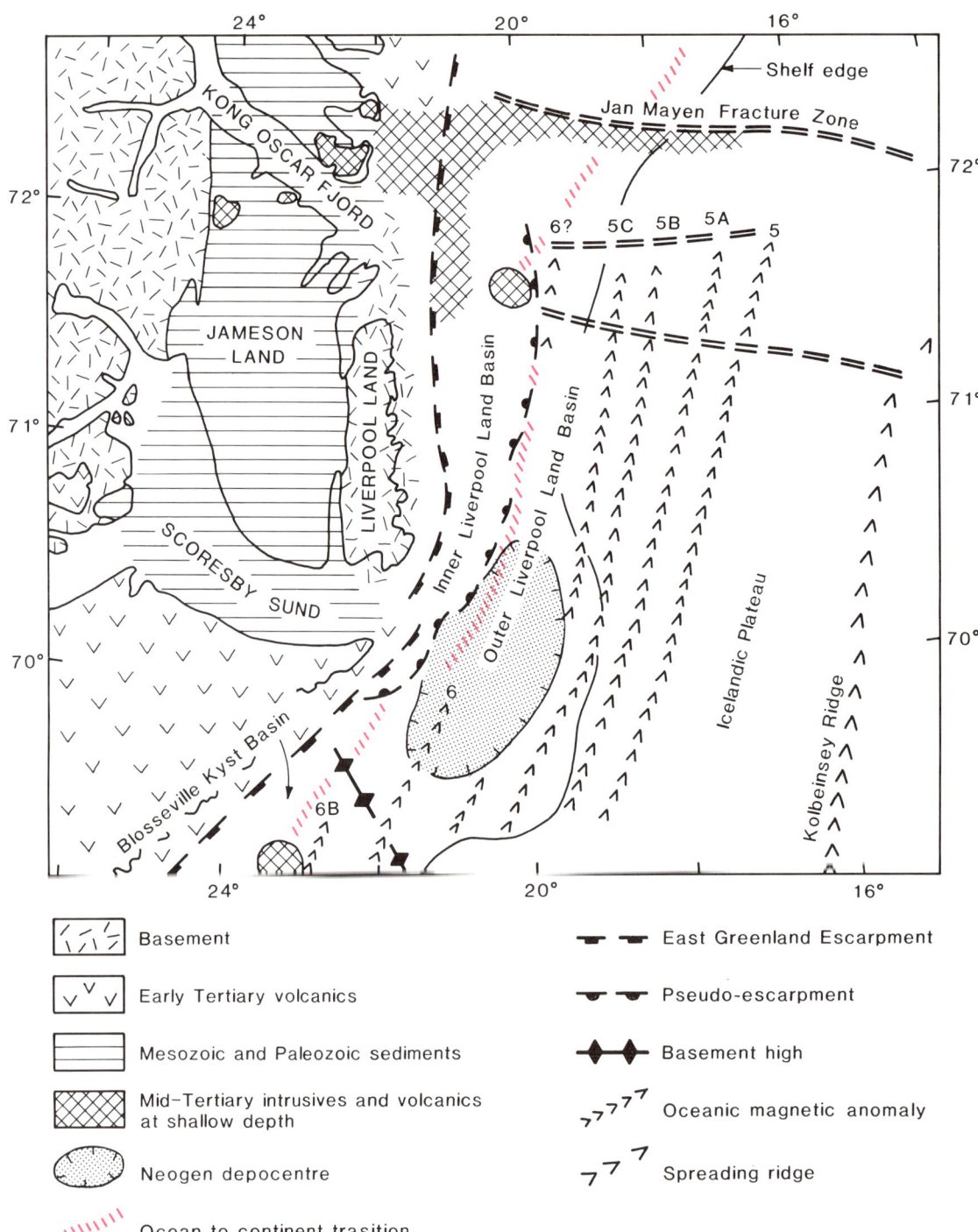

Figure 11. Tectonic sketch map of the Liverpool Land Shelf and adjacent continental and oceanic regions. The two Liverpool Land basins are separated from the southern Blosseville Kyst Basin through a basement high. The high has the character of an open anticlinal structure involving both the stratified basement (volcanics) and part of the overlying sedimentary sequence. The anticlinal structure formed between the two depocenters north and south of it respectively. The northern boundary of the two Liverpool Land basins is related to the Jan Mayen Fracture Zone. Mid-Tertiary intrusives and volcanics are present here within the Tertiary section at shallow to intermediate depth seawards of the East Greenland Escarpment and are exposed on the sea bed or on land landward of the escarpment. The pseudo-escarpment between the two basins is believed to consist of interdigitating sediments and volcanics. The basement of the inner basin is of presumed Caledonian origin. A volcanic, and mainly oceanic basement is present seawards of the pseudo-escarpment.

ties (see profile D of Plate 6). Throughout most of the Neogene, sedimentation alternated between vertical aggradation in a relatively deep shelf environment and major lateral shelf progradation during periods of relatively lower sea-stands. Changes in sedimentation were caused by the integrated effect of sea level changes, varied sedimentary input from the Greenland continent, and the thermally induced subsidence.

In the Late Miocene and the Plio-Pleistocene, increasing fluctuations in sea level, most likely acting in combination with increased input of sediments (climatic effect and/or renewed uplift of the Greenland block?), led to episodes of shelf progradation (Fig. 9). The Upper Miocene and Pliocene sequence locally achieves thicknesses of about 2.5 km, and in some areas the shelf edge advanced seaward between 10 and 30 km during this period.

The main source area for the Tertiary infill of the Blosseville Kyst Basin is the Greenland continent. The continent was uplifted 1 to 2 km, or locally more, through the Tertiary (Fig. 4). The exact timing and history of this uplift is not known, but there is some indication that uplift accelerated in the Late Oligocene (Brooks, 1979; H. C. Larsen, 1980, 1984; Hansen, 1988). Coevally, the Blosseville Kyst Basin was an area of continued subsidence.

The sediment source area for the deep Tertiary basin offshore, below the present-day shelf, includes the Blosseville Kyst volcanic plateau and, most likely, both Precambrian and Caledonian crystalline rocks as well as Mesozoic sediments (Fig. 10).

A major, eastward-flowing river system no doubt existed in the present-day Scoresby Sund during the Neogene (Fig. 10). The erosional detritus from the Jameson Land area and the crystalline basement to the west of Jameson Land was transported through this system and deposited in the Tertiary basin seaward of the coastal escarpment zone. Supplementary drainage may have taken place through relatively minor river systems within the volcanic plateau that were subsequently further eroded and occupied by glaciers.

It is presently difficult to envisage how different the Paleogene drainage pattern was from this scenario. However, the Paleogene equivalent to the Neogene Scoresby Sund river system was most likely situated farther north because at that time the Neogene and present-day position of the Scoresby Sund Fiord was blocked by volcanics. A likely pattern of Paleogene drainage is shown in Figure 10.

The Liverpool Land Shelf (LILS)

The Liverpool Land Shelf extends from just south of the mouth of the Scoresby Sund northward to the Jan Mayen Fracture Zone (Figs. 3, 11). The isopach map (see Plate 10) shows that a thick sedimentary sequence is present below this part of the shelf, with maximum depth to basement lying below the acoustic penetration of the present seismic data. A maximum depth of around 10 km is indicated from aeromagnetic data.

According to H. C. Larsen (1984), two coast-parallel, structural units or subbasins can be recognized in the region (Fig. 11). They are named Inner Liverpool Land basin and Outer Liverpool Land basin, respectively. The two basins are roughly of equal width and underlie the inner and the outer halves of the shelf, respectively.

The Tertiary stratigraphy and development of the two Liverpool Land basins show great similarities to the Blosseville Kyst Shelf (see profile E of Plate 6). The inner basin can be compared with the Paleogene half-graben development, and the outer basin with the Neogene basin development of the Blosseville Kyst Shelf. The main difference is that the Inner Liverpool basin, in addition to thick rift and post-rift Tertiary deposits, contains a fairly thick sequence of pre-rift sediments of presumed late Paleozoic to Mesozoic age. The Cenozoic sediments apparently are separated from the pre-rift sequence only by a tectonic unconformity (see profile E of Plate 6), and not by an extensive, thick sequence of rift volcanics as seen in other places along the East Greenland Shelf south of lat. 72°N. The anomalously large depth-to-basement within the Inner Liverpool Land basin (Plate 10) is thus caused by the inclusion in this region of as much as approximately 4 km of pre-rift section in the depth mapping.

The southern boundary of the two Liverpool Land basins within the Blosseville Kyst Shelf is somewhat arbitrary (see above). Both are bounded to the north by the Kong Oscar Fiord transverse fault zone (landward projection of the Jan Mayen Fracture Zone; see also Fig. 11). The inner basin is bounded to the west, against the Liverpool Land crystalline basement, by a major coast-parallel escarpment or fault. This northern extension of the East Greenland Escarpment (Figs. 3, 11) was named the Liverpool Land Escarpment by H. C. Larsen (1984). The outer basin is bounded to the east by the west sloping volcanic basement surface of the Icelandic Plateau.

The two Liverpool Land basins are separated by a west-facing, presumed pseudo-escarpment that separates the deeper Inner Liverpool Land basin from the shallower Outer Liverpool Land basin (see profile E of Plate 6). This pseudo-escarpment is caused by the landward termination of the volcanic basement units of the outer shelf, and is not believed to be associated with any major vertical crustal offsets. The pseudo-escarpment is not thought of as a well-defined edge of the outer-shelf volcanic basement, but is rather of transitional character, with interdigitating volcanics and sediments (see also Fig. 5). Notable linear, deeply sourced magnetic and gravity anomalies are present, however, parallel to and slightly seaward of the escarpment, suggesting important crustal changes across the escarpment zone. The ocean-to-continent transition is thus placed just seaward of the escarpment.

The outer shelf basin is floored by a flat and in most cases nonfaulted and well-defined acoustic basement, interpreted as being volcanic and oceanic in origin. The interpretation of oceanic basement is based on its layered nature with local development of seaward-dipping reflectors, its simple continuation into young oceanic basement of anomaly 5 age, the presence of weak but linear magnetic anomalies of inferred anomaly 5 to 6 age, and gravity and refraction seismic data (H. C. Larsen and Jakobsdóttir, 1988). The seaward-dipping sub-basement reflectors extend only to shallow depths, as compared to the very deep occurrence off Southeast Greenland.

The seismic character of the outer shelf basement changes seaward of magnetic anomaly 5A into a hummocky-type reflection pattern with no significant or continuous recoverable sub-basement reflections. This very systematic change in reflection pattern is interpreted as a seaward change from pre–anomaly 5 subaerially erupted basalts into post–anomaly 5 pillow lavas erupted under submarine conditions.

The inner shelf area of the Liverpool Land Shelf was most likely continuous with the Jan Mayen Ridge before separation of the ridge from the Greenland block (Talwani and Eldholm, 1977; Hinz and Schlüter, 1980; Vogt and others, 1980; H. C. Larsen, 1980, 1988; Eldholm, this volume). Prior to this separation, rifting and thinning of the crust, landward rotation of fault blocks, and strong subsidence seaward of the coastal escarpment took place.

The main tectonic episode of block faulting and escarpment formation is suggested to be of (early?) Eocene age (H. C. Larsen, 1984). This tectonic episode, therefore, partly overlaps in time the main tectonic episode in the BLKS area and the rifting east of the Jan Mayen Ridge (i.e., within the Norway Basin; Talwani and Eldholm, 1977; Eldholm, this volume). A similar development of block faulting can thus be expected below the Jan Mayen Ridge (see also Eldholm, this volume).

The rifting and associated strong subsidence within the inner basin rapidly changed the setting from a presumed shallow and fairly low-relief area (volcanic plateau) into a deep tectonic depression separated from the present-day land area by a large topographic escarpment. The floor of this tectonic depression also showed tectonically inherited high relief (rotation of fault blocks).

Early post-rift sedimentation may include continental to shallow-water clastic deposits. However, following continued subsidence, sedimentation most likely developed into marine (fan?) sedimentation in front of the coastal escarpment. The more distal parts of this sequence were deposited on the Jan Mayen Ridge as deep-water, complex fan sediments and turbidites (Talwani and others, 1976; Talwani and Udintsev, 1976). Passage of the sediments from the Greenland margin into the Jan Mayen Ridge area thus apparently occurred throughout the Eocene and Early Oligocene, but the scenario changed during the Oligocene. The change was mainly due to incipient formation of a volcanic ridge between the Greenland margin and the Jan Mayen Ridge during the Oligocene, but perhaps also because of the Oligocene sea-level drop (Vail and others, 1977).

The volcanic ridge roughly coincides with the position of the ocean-to-continent transition inferred in this chapter. The western flank of the volcanic ridge constitutes the mid-shelf pseudo-escarpment discussed above and forms the seaward boundary of the inner shelf basin within the LILS area. The volcanism associated with formation of the ridge apparently began before actual sea-floor spreading commenced along the propagating Kolbeinsey Ridge (anomaly 6 time) in this area (Fig. 11; H. C. Larsen, 1988). Volcanism perhaps was submarine during the earlier stages. However, the active Kolbeinsey Ridge was mainly emergent during the early and middle part of the Miocene and first became permanently submarine around anomaly 5 to 5A (late Middle to early Late Miocene).

During the early part of the Neogene, the continued subsidence of the LILS area created a shallow to moderately deep marine embayment with a limited marine opening to the north (Fig. 10). Since the Kolbeinsey Ridge eventually subsided below sea level between anomaly 5 and 5A, increasingly open marine conditions developed. As in the BLKS area, and basically for the same reasons, vertical aggradation predominated throughout the Lower and Middle Miocene, whereas the Upper Miocene and the Plio-Pleistocene show progradational features. Some erosional features, however, can be seen on the present-day slope in this region.

The thickest Neogene section off East Greenland is found within the depocenter of the outer basin. This depocenter is situated off the mouth of the Scoresby Sund (Fig. 11; see also Plate 10). As much as 6,000 m of mid-Miocene to recent sediments have been deposited here within a bowl-shaped depression of the basement. The basement below this thick Neogene section is oceanic crust of Early and Middle Miocene age (i.e., subaerially erupted basalts of anomaly 6 to 5B age). The large and rapid subsidence within this area, averaging up to approximately 300 m/m.y., is not associated with any faulting or crustal thinning, but is due to cooling and contraction of the young oceanic lithosphere in combination with strong loading by the large volumes of sediments from the large Scoresby Sund river system (Figs. 10, 12).

The Northeast Greenland Shelf (NEAS)

The geologic province named the Northeast Greenland Shelf in this chapter stretches northward from the Jan Mayen Fracture Zone in the south (approx. lat. 72°N) to the Greenland Fracture Zone (lat. 78° to 80°N) in the north. The province is about 800 km long in the north-south direction and between 125 km (southern part) and 300 km (northern part) wide. From present data, the area apparently can be subdivided into a southern part affected by Tertiary tectonism and volcanism (approx. lat. 72° to 75°N) and a northern, nonvolcanic part (approx. lat. 75° to 80°N). When more geophysical data, including seismic data, become available from this remote region, a formal subdivision of the Northeast Greenland Shelf into two separate provinces may be applicable. Such a subdivision would depend on the intensity of Tertiary tectonism and volcanism within the southern part of the Northeast Greenland Shelf.

The general stratigraphy and tectonics of the Northeast Greenland Shelf are different from the shelf area to the south. This difference is caused mainly by (a) the limited development or, locally, lack of Tertiary sedimentary rocks and seaward down-flexuring of the lithosphere along a coastal hinge line; and (b) the much more seaward position of the ocean-to-continent transition, and hence the presence of a much wider, truly continental shelf. The wide continental shelf comprises a number of coast-parallel, elongated basins and highs of presumed Paleozoic and Mesozoic age (Fig. 13).

Information on the deep structure of this northern shelf segment has to be derived mainly from aeromagnetic data. Only limited seismic reflection information is available, and that only from the very southern part of the segment and from the ice-free deep-water region seaward of the shelf (this chapter; and Hinz and others, 1987). However, aeromagnetic data coverage is good (H. C. Larsen and Thorning, 1980; H. C. Larsen, 1980) and

provides, along with onshore Mesozoic basin exposures and fault studies (Surlyk, 1977a, b; Surlyk and others, 1981), fairly firm structural/stratigraphic conclusions.

The Tertiary volcanism in the southern area comprises both emplacement of major plutons and extrusion of lavas, as is seen onshore (Noe-Nygaard, 1976). The plutonic activity, of presumed mid-Tertiary age, appears to have been concentrated close to the Jan Mayen Fracture Zone, whereas a partly erratic occurrence of lavas at sea-bed level (Late Paleocene to Eocene age?) has a much wider distribution on the inner shelf. The lavas also appear to be present at greater depth below younger deposits at the outer, southern part of the Northeast Greenland Shelf.

Aeromagnetic depth-mapping of the basement topography

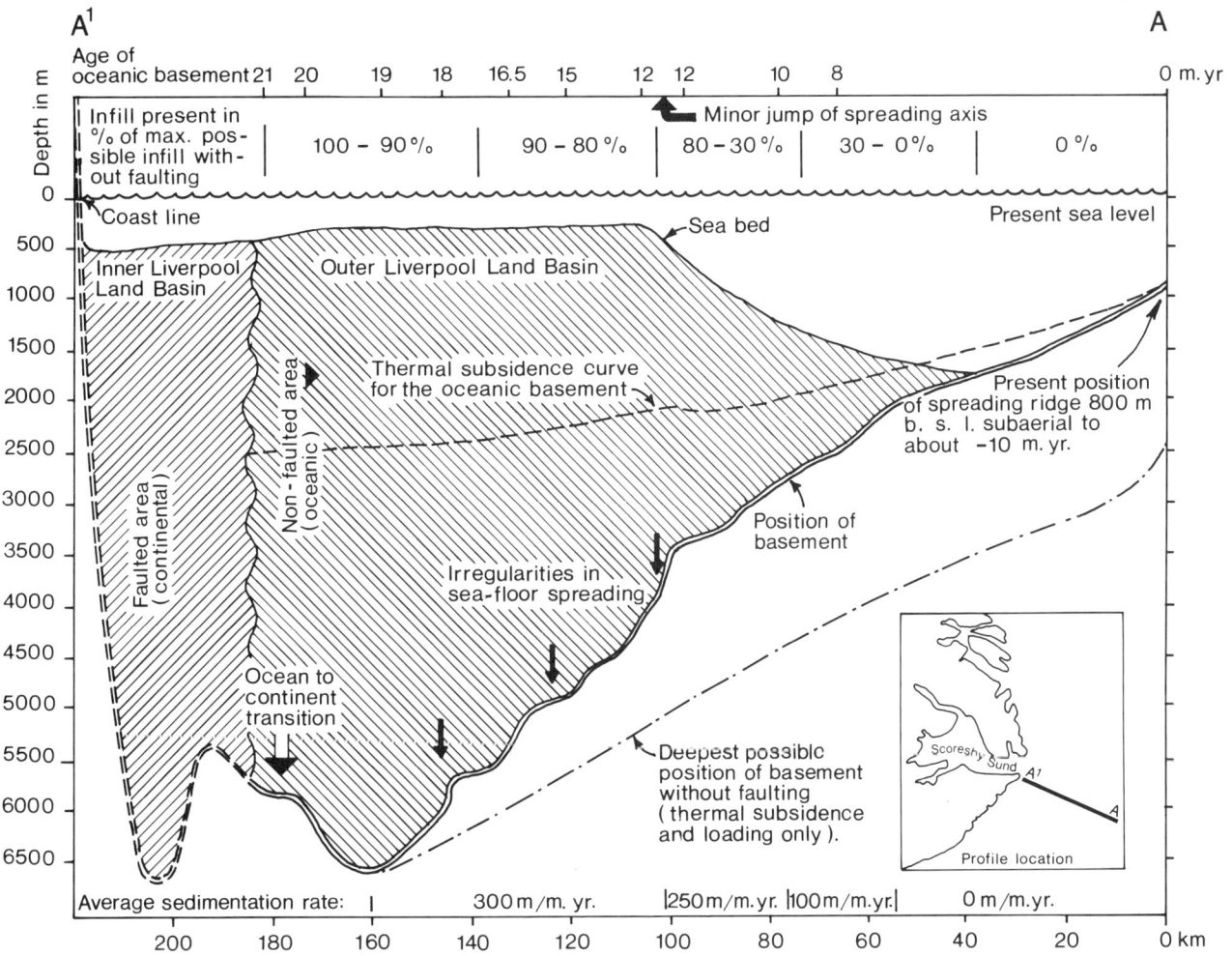

Figure 12. Depth-converted profile from the mouth of Scoresby Sund and across the Inner and Outer Liverpool Land Basins. Note that oceanic crust younger than 20 Ma has subsided up to 6 km without any appreciable faulting. The oceanic crust below the outer basin originated above sea level until 10 Ma at which time the spreading axis north of Iceland became submerged. The thermal subsidence according to Parsons and Schlater (1977) is shown, and assuming simple Airy isostasy, the maximum subsidence due to loading calculated. Note that the deepest possible position of the oceanic basement without faulting has been reached within the depocenter of the outer basin.

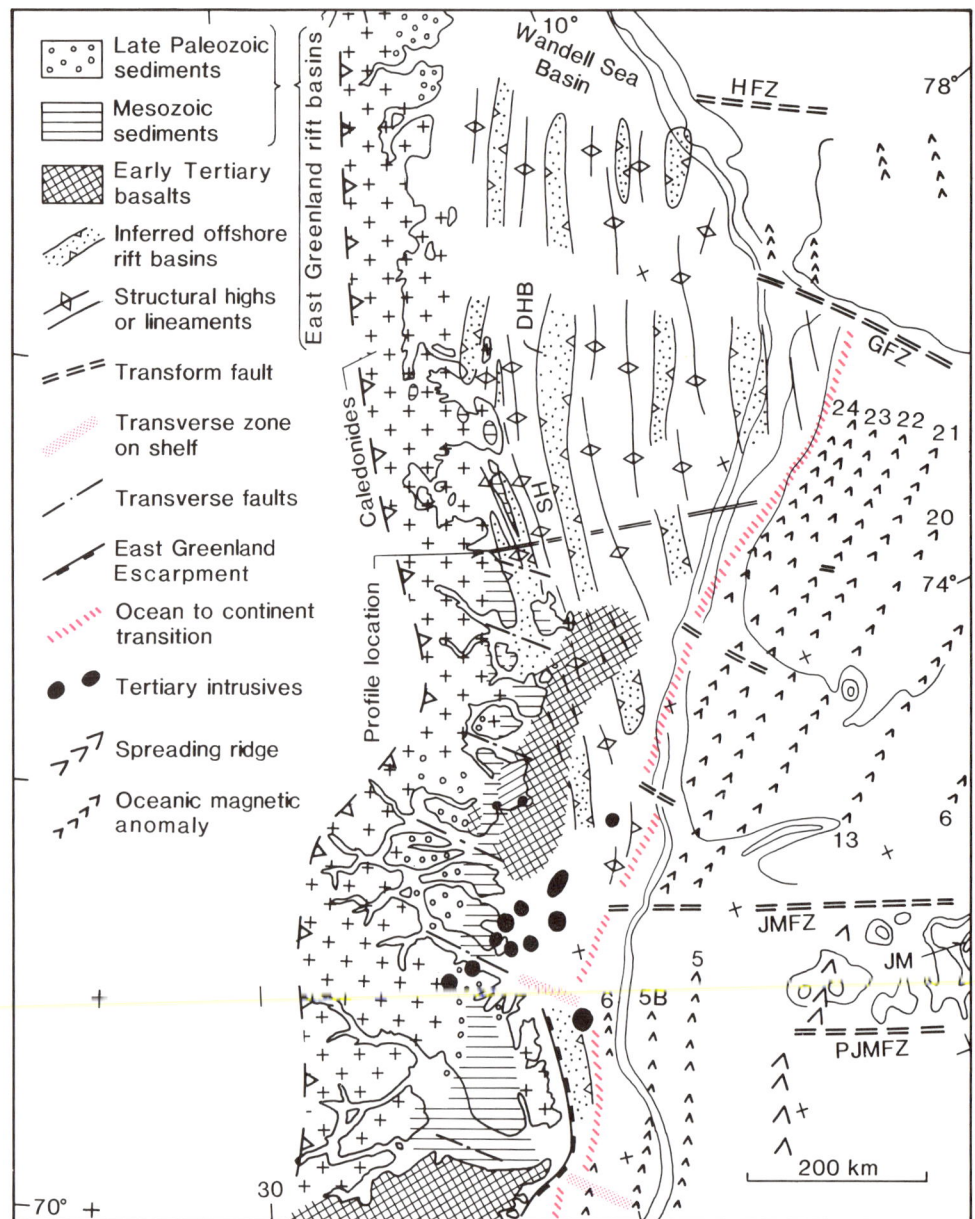

Figure 13. Regional tectonic map of the Liverpool Land shelf area and the Northeast Greenland Shelf. Sediment-filled grabens assumed to contain 6 to 12 km of Paleozoic and Mesozoic sediments; early Tertiary volcanics only shown where outcropping or at shallow depths (see text and Fig. 14). Sediment cover over elongated highs estimated to be approximately 2 to 4 km in thickness. DHB, Danmarkshan Basin; GFZ, Greenland Fracture Zone; HFZ, Hovgaard Fracture Zone; JM, Jan Mayen; JMFZ, Jan Mayen Fracture Zone; PJMFZ. proto-Jan Mayen Fracture Zone; SH, Shannon High.

in this region is impeded by the presence of Tertiary volcanics at different levels within the sedimentary section. Ridge crests at about 2 km depth and basins more than 6 km deep can, however, be interpreted (Geological Survey of Greenland, unpublished). The northern part of the NEAS (75° to 80°N) is, according to the present interpretation, dominated by a number of very long, coast-parallel graben-ridge systems (Figs. 13, 14). Correlation of these structures can be made with onshore basins (H. C. Larsen, 1980, 1984; Surlyk and others, 1981). Basement topography de-

rived from the aeromagnetic depth mapping shows large variations in structural relief ranging from more than 10 km depth within the graben areas to only about 3 km depth over some of the ridges.

Taking the fairly good Mesozoic stratigraphic correlation between Northeast Greenland onshore and the northern Norwegian Shelf (Gowers and Lunde, 1984), and the proximity of the two areas in pre-drift time, a hypothetical cross section bridging the two areas may be constructed. In the absence of seismic

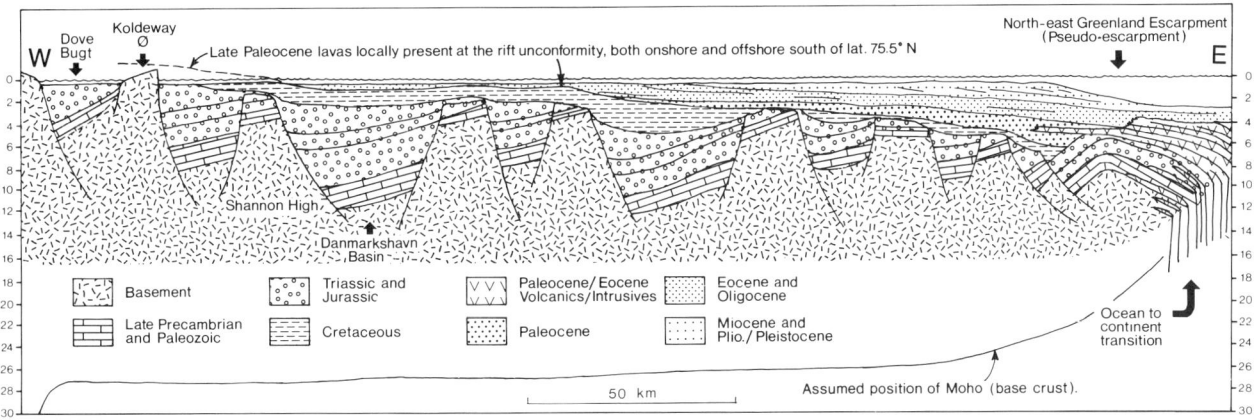

Figure 14. Highly hypothetical cross section of the Northeast Greenland Continental Shelf around lat. 76°N. The cross section is purely based on aeromagnetic data and stratigraphical/tectonic comparisons with basins in East Greenland and on the Norwegian shelf. The aeromagnetic data provide good control on the position and distribution of basins and highs. The lack of seismic data makes the stratigraphical and structural information shown less reliable.

data, this inferred profile of the Northeast Greenland Shelf is by nature speculative (Fig. 14).

TECTONIC DEVELOPMENT

The East Greenland Shelf has been subdivided into five different geologic provinces in this chapter, with a possible subdivision of the northernmost province (Northeast Greenland Shelf) into a southern and a northern part. From a more regional and plate-tectonic viewpoint, these five to six geologic provinces can be grouped into only three superior tectonic realms: a southern tectonic realm comprising the Southeast Greenland Shelf and the Denmark Strait Ridge; an intervening tectonic realm comprising the Blosseville Kyst Shelf and the Liverpool Land Shelf; and a northern tectonic realm comprising the Northeast Greenland Shelf (Fig. 15). For the present purpose, the three different realms are named A, B, and C (from north to south).

It appears that the three-fold tectonic subdivision of the East Greenland margin is the result of a variable Tertiary rifting and sea-floor spreading process superimposed on two regions of differing tectonic character, one in the south consisting of Precambrian cratonic basement that underwent limited (or no?) rifting prior to Cenozoic sea-floor spreading, and another in the north comprising Caledonian basement that underwent extensive late Paleozoic and Mesozoic rifting before sea-floor spreading eventually commenced in the Cenozoic (Haller, 1970; Surlyk, 1978; Surlyk and others, 1973, 1981, 1986; Friend and others, 1983).

In addition to the fundamental inhomogeneity in pre-rift geology along the initial line of Tertiary rifting and sea-floor spreading, the spreading axis itself was subdivided into three segments: (1) the Reykjanes Ridge (including the Denmark Strait Ridge); (2) the paired axes of Aegir Ridge (Paleogene) and Kolbeinsey Ridge (Neogene) between Iceland and the Jan Mayen Fracture Zone; and (3) the Mohns Ridge between the Jan Mayen Fracture Zone and the Greenland Fracture Zone (Eldholm, this volume; H. C. Larsen, 1988). The northern and southern segments correlate with the two fundamentally different geologic realms (A and C) in which spreading started. The middle segment, with its two paired spreading axes, correlates with the transition realm (B) between realms A and C (Fig. 15).

Although not understood in detail, it is likely that the different geologic "boundary conditions" prior to spreading influenced the spreading pattern, and it appears clear that the three different tectonic realms (A, B, and C) off East Greenland are directly connected with each of the three different spreading-axis segments in the northeast Atlantic (Fig. 15). The tectonic development of realms A through C off East Greenland is summarized below.

Tectonic realm A

In many respects, this northernmost tectonic realm of the East Greenland margin appears to possess the typical features of a passive rifted margin (Figs. 14, 16). The outer edge of the Greenland continent in this realm was attenuated through several episodes of rifting prior to spreading. Following continental separation in the early Tertiary, a good coupling developed between this attenuated, and hence less buoyant, outer continental margin and the oceanic lithosphere. This gave rise to a wide flexure zone at the outer continental margin and caused large parts of the (attenuated) continental lithosphere to subside along with the cooling oceanic lithosphere.

Tectonic realm B

Tectonic realm B comprises the Blosseville Kyst Basin and the two Liverpool Land basins (Fig. 15). The main difference between the two areas is that the Blosseville Kyst Basin, in contrast to the Liverpool land basins, is believed to be continuously floored with basalt. The basalt is associated with oceanic crust beneath the outer shelf and in the Blosseville Kyst Basin, it is believed, with attenuated continental crust beneath the inner shelf.

The Tertiary sea-floor spreading pattern in the adjacent southern Norwegian Sea is more complex and less well understood than the development to the south and north (see Eldholm, this volume). It is generally agreed, however, that initiation of spreading in this region took place along the now-extinct axis in the Norway Basin—the so-called Aegir Ridge or Extinct Axis—and that spreading later shifted toward the East Greenland margin (Talwani and Eldholm, 1977; Nunns, 1983; Eldholm, this volume). Recently, H. C. Larsen (1988) interpreted the westward shift of spreading in the southern Norwegian Sea as a mid-Tertiary, northward propagation of the Reykjanes Ridge from the position of the Icelandic hot spot. A continental sliver (Jan Mayen Ridge) was torn from the Greenland continent by the propagating spreading ridge, which eventually overstepped the early Jan Mayen Fracture Zone and established the present-day Jan Mayen Fracture Zone. This development caused the formation of a diachronous ocean-to-continent transition of anomaly 20 to anomaly 6 age along this part of the East Greenland margin.

Perhaps because of the complexity, and in contrast to other parts of the East Greenland margin and the northeast Atlantic in general, strong Tertiary rift-basin formation (half-graben stage in Fig. 9) took place prior to spreading in this region. The Tertiary rift basin was bounded landward by the coast-parallel, East Greenland Escarpment, which caused rupturing rather than flexuring within the transition zone (Fig. 16). This development, in combination with the nascent spreading ridge north of Iceland, created an effective trap for syn- and post-rift sediments in front of the coastal escarpment. The "rupturing transition" also prevented most of the Paleozoic/Mesozoic rifted margin of the Greenland continent from subsiding along with the adjacent cooling oceanic lithosphere. In fact, the opposite took place, perhaps partly as a result of marginal uplift relative to the subsiding offshore basin (Fig. 16).

Tectonic realm C

Tectonic realm C comprises both the Southeast Greenland Basin and the Denmark Strait Ridge. The basin and the ridge obviously have quite different stratigraphic records, and the basin contains both shelf areas and deep-water areas with contrasting

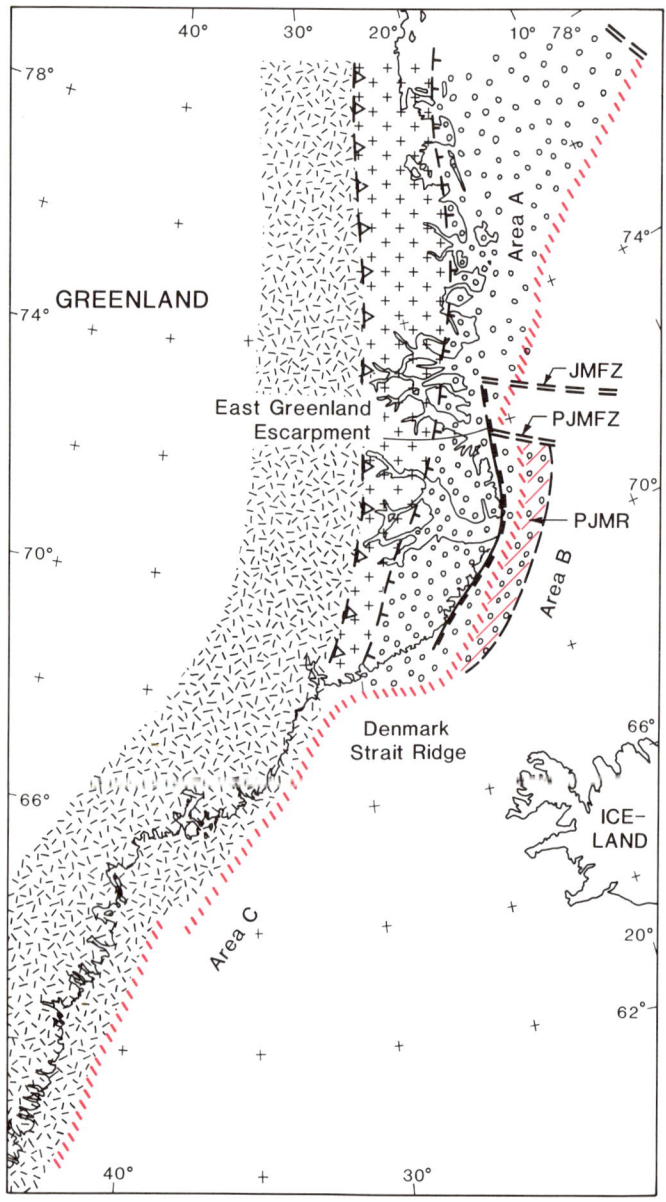

Figure 15. Three tectonic realms A, B, and C along the East Greenland margin. The present ocean-to-continent transition is identical to the initial line of rifting along the margin except for the middle area B. In this area, a mid-Tertiary and westward migration of the spreading axis tore off a continental sliver, the Proto–Jan Mayen Ridge (PJMR), from the Greenland margin and this was moved eastwards relative to Greenland and now forms the Jan Mayen Ridge northeast of Iceland. The Jan Mayen Fracture Zone (JMFZ) was positioned south of its present position until separation of the Jan Mayen Ridge from Greenland (H. C. Larsen, 1980, 1988). The older fracture zone is named the Proto–Jan Mayen Fracture Zone (PJMFZ). Spreading along the initial line of rifting thus took place within a Precambrian craton in the south (area C), and made a large right-lateral bend into a tectonic realm of Paleozoic and Mesozoic rifted Caledonian lithosphere (areas A and B; see also text and Fig. 16).

stratigraphic development. What unifies this diverse area into one regional tectonic realm is the uniform Tertiary plate-kinematic development of the region along one spreading axis operating in a rather uniform geologic setting.

Sea-floor spreading started above sea level in anomaly 24R time along an almost continuous axis (Reykjanes Ridge), and produced strongly layered oceanic crust with characteristic seaward-dipping sub-basement reflectors (see profile A of Plate 6; H. C. Larsen and Jakobsdóttir, 1988). The landward part of this large volcanic, mainly oceanic edifice onlaps the outer edge of the continent. Locally, down-faulted pre-rift high-stand deposits may be found between the cratonic basement and the landward part of the dipping reflector sequence. In general, however, the ocean-to-continent transition is dominated by a narrow flexure zone in which Precambrian crystalline rocks are replaced seaward by the oceanic volcanic edifice (Fig. 16). The little-attenuated continental edge apparently resisted major down-flexuring when the adjacent oceanic crust cooled and subsided and thus caused a narrow flexure zone to develop. The strong seaward crustal down-flexuring along the East Greenland coast was previously noted by Wager and Deer (1938).

Subsidence rates of the oceanic crust along this part of the East Greenland margin show systematic variations from around 80 m/Ma in the south to locally only around 20 to 30 m/Ma in the north below the Denmark Strait Ridge, near the Icelandic hot spot. Along with north-south variations in sediment supply, the variable subsidence pattern caused differential flexure development and variations in stratigraphy along the margin in this area.

The subaerial formation of oceanic crust with seaward-dipping sub-basement reflectors is interpreted by H. C. Larsen and Jakobsdóttir (1988) in terms of an Icelandic spreading model (Pálmason, 1973, 1980; Smythe, 1983; Mutter and others, 1982). The dipping reflectors are interpreted to rise from bedding planes between major flows or groups of flows that acquired their seaward dip through symmetric and differential subsidence about the rift zone. From the study by H. C. Larsen and Jakobsdóttir (1988), it appears that both spreading rate and volcanic productivity rate were about three times these values in present-day Iceland and that the rift zone was only around 3 to 10 km wide.

SUMMARY

Major conclusions

The East Greenland Shelf can be subdivided from north to south into three regional tectonic realms: A, B, and C (Fig. 15). Realm A comprises a wide shelf with coast-parallel pre-drift basins covered by a moderately thick wedge of Cenozoic rift and post-rift sediments. In contrast, realms B and C are both dominated by the intense development of Cenozoic rift and post-rift deposits, including extensive volcanics.

Within realm C, a moderately thick (1 to 3 km) sequence of Cenozoic post-rift sediments was laid down on a smooth basement of rift- and sea-floor spreading volcanics. The basement is characterized by seaward-dipping sub-basement reflectors that

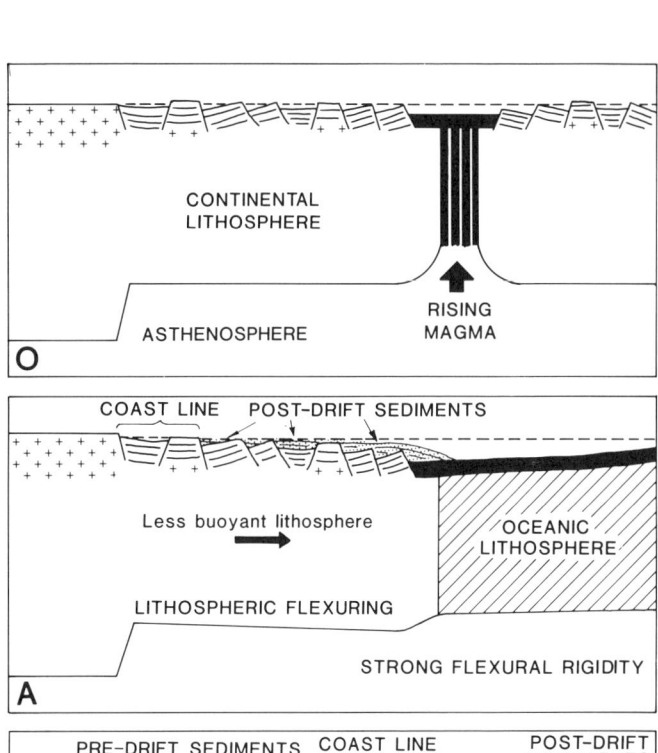
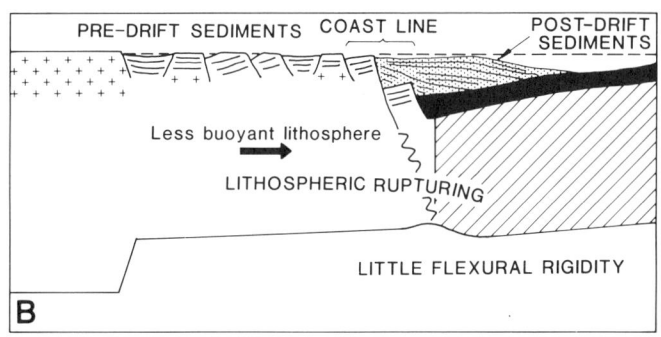
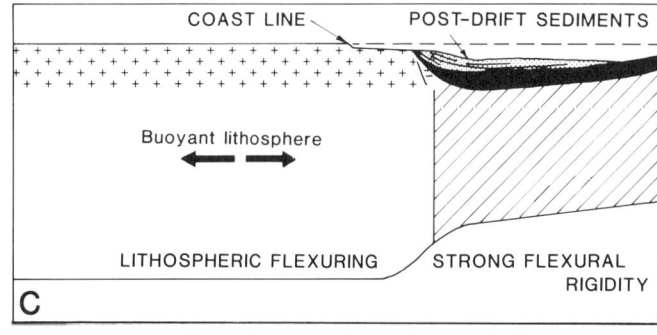

Figure 16. Schematic development of a passive margin from initial drift stage (0) to different and mature stages (A, B, and C, see also Fig. 15). Stage A characterizes the Northeast Greenland Shelf (area A of Fig. 15) and many other rifted margins. A different development characterizing the Blosseville Kyst and the Liverpool Land basins (area B of Fig. 15) is shown in B. The Southeast Greenland margin development (area C of Fig. 15) corresponds to stage C. (See also text and Fig. 15 for further discussion.)

extend deep into the crust (see profile A of Plate 6). The basement has subsided to present depths mainly by thermal subsidence. Loading is relatively less important in this region because sediments were not trapped within a limited basin. Very little subsidence took place within the Denmark Strait area between Iceland and East Greenland, which resulted in a basement ridge with very limited sediment thickness (see Plate 10). The Denmark Strait Ridge apparently stayed above sea level until about the Late Miocene and hence exerted strong influence on the Tertiary paleoceanography of the northeast Atlantic (see Eldholm, this volume).

Sedimentation within realm C started in a presumed shelf environment in Late Paleocene to Eocene time, which developed into a starved deep-water basin during the mid-Tertiary. Considerable shelf progradation into the deep-water basin took place in the late Neogene. Realm C is considered almost devoid of petroleum potential because of the limited sediment thickness (maximum 2.8 km; see Plate 10).

Realm B (Fig. 15) comprises a sequence 5 to 7 km thick of Cenozoic rift and postrift sediments with an integrated stratigraphic thickness of 10 km or more. The region shows anomalously strong Tertiary rifting and basin subsidence seaward of a marked, coast-parallel escarpment—the so-called East Greenland Escarpment (Fig. 15). The effectiveness of the sediment trap forming seaward of the escarpment was aided by the presence of a volcanic ridge seaward of the rift (Figs. 9, 10). This volcanic ridge formed as a result of rift propagation of the spreading Kolbeinsey Ridge, the northward continuation of the Reykjanes Ridge north of the Icelandic hot spot. Following formation of mid- to late Tertiary oceanic crust around this volcanic ridge, the basin prograded seaward over the young oceanic crust and formed a shelf.

Massive sediment supply, limited basin size, and the presence of young oceanic basement (Figs. 9, 10, 11, 12) together provided the setting for a rapidly subsiding basin. Development of the basin was "driven" by tectonic subsidence on the inner shelf (half-graben stage of Fig. 9) and by thermal subsidence and loading of the outer shelf. The region is considered to have moderate to fair petroleum potential (H. C. Larsen, 1985).

Realm A, in the north (Fig. 15), comprises a wide continental shelf underlain by a number of elongate, coast-parallel, rifted basins of Paleozoic and Mesozoic age. Relatively thin Tertiary deposits, locally including volcanics, overlie the older rift basins on the inner shelf, but these deposits increase in thickness seaward to about 3 km. Drawing heavily on the aeromagnetic information, the onshore geologic record and comparisons with the Norwegian margin (Eldholm, this volume; Gowers and Lunde, 1984), a regional tectonic map and a hypothetical cross section with virtually no seismic control have been constructed (Figs. 13, 14).

The northern part of realm A comprises around 100,000 km^2 of continental shelf that is highly prospective for petroleum, but it is hardly accessible with present-day exploration techniques due to drifting ice (H. C. Larsen, 1985).

Comparisons to other margins

Unlike most other passive margins, little rifting and stretching of the continental lithosphere apparently took place prior to spreading along the southern East Greenland margin (realm C).

In realm B, on the middle margin, intense Tertiary rifting and basin subsidence virtually obliterated, at least from the upper crust, possible pre-rift basins and caused the formation of a coast-parallel escarpment. This led to lithospheric rupturing of the shelf region rather than post-drift seaward flexuring of the shelf.

In spite of the many uncertainties caused by lack of seismic data from realm A, in the north, there is no doubt that this northern shelf region—to a much higher degree than the two other tectonic regions—shows the typical characteristics of a passive rifted margin. These include the existence of margin-parallel pre-rift basins, which suffered progressive seaward subsidence in post-drift time and accordingly received a seaward-thickening cover of post-drift sediments.

Opposing passive rifted margins by nature tend to develop some symmetry. The tectonic realms A and C off East Greenland show a fair symmetry with the northern Norwegian margin (Eldholm, this volume; Gowers and Lunde, 1984) and the Rockall margin (Roberts and others, 1979, 1984; White and others, 1987). However, information about structural style and stratigraphy of the northern Norwegian margin was used in the interpretation of the northernmost realm, and hence the fair correlation between these two opposing margin segments may look better than it actually is. Thus, H. C. Larsen (1980, 1984) noted that the initial line of rifting in realm A was oblique to the predominant Paleozoic and Mesozoic rift trend in the area. As a result, the Greenland continental margin widens to the north while the northern Norwegian margin narrow dramatically in the same direction (Eldholm, this volume; Talwani and Eldholm, 1977).

Tectonic realm B, off East Greenland, is different from its opposite and former counterpart, the mid-Norwegian margin (Bøen and others, 1984). Actually, one should not expect too high a degree of symmetry in this region because of its complex and asymmetric sea-floor spreading history. Strictly speaking, the true counterpart to realm B is not the mid-Norwegian margin but the Jan Mayen Ridge, which shows some similarity to tectonic realm B. There is some evidence of rifted structure below the ridge, and the ridge is covered with early Tertiary basalts (Talwani and others, 1976; Talwani and Udintsev, 1976; see also Eldholm, this volume). Very little post-drift sediment accumulated on the ridge, however, because it became detached from Greenland and was isolated from sediment supply in the middle of the ocean.

Unsolved problems

Our understanding of the tectonic and stratigraphic development of the northern part of the East Greenland Shelf is rather weakly based. Good-quality seismic reflection data are needed to further test and develop our present working hypothesis. Seismic working conditions in the area are difficult because of the continuous presence of multiyear pack ice. Nonconventional methods involving icebreakers have to be considered (H. C. Larsen, 1986). The petroleum geological information from such data could prove invaluable.

The Tertiary seismic stratigraphy within the southern two-thirds of the present study area is not tested by, or linked to, any well information. Testing of the proposed stratigraphy within the framework of the Ocean Drilling Program would be a natural suggestion. Especially, testing of some of the conclusions drawn from the seismic stratigraphic interpretations such as the timing of the submergence of the Denmark Strait Ridge and the timing of extensive shelf glaciation in the Late Pliocene and early Pleistocene might provide new data of regional interest. High-resolution seismic mapping of key seismic stratigraphic units, followed by drilling, should be attempted.

Deep crustal features have been inferred from the present, mainly upper crustal, study; however deep seismic profiling is required to test and further develop our ideas about these features.

REFERENCES CITED

Bott, M.H.P., 1983, The crust beneath the Iceland-Faeroe Ridge, *in* Bott, M.H.P., Saxov, S., Talwani, M., and Thiede, J., eds., Structure and development of the Greenland-Scotland Ridge; New methods and concepts: New York, Plenum Press, p. 63–75.

Brooks, C. K., 1979, Geomorphological observations at Kangerdluggssuaq, East Greenland: Greenland Geoscience, v. 1, p. 1–21.

Brooks, C. K., and Gleadow, A.S.W., 1977, A fission-track age for the Skaergaard intrusion and the age of the East Greenland basalt: Geology, v. 5, p. 539–540.

Boen, F., Eggen, S., and Vollset, J., 1984, Structures and basins of the margin from 62° to 69°N and their development, *in* Spencer, A. M., ed., Petroleum geology of the north European margin: Graham and Trotman, p. 253–270.

Eldholm, O., and Windisch, C. C., 1974, Sediment distribution in the Norwegian-Greenland Sea: Geological Society of America Bulletin, v. 85, p. 1661–1676.

Eldholm, O., Thiede, J., and Shipboard Scientific Party, 1986, Ocean drilling at the Vøring Plateau in the Norwegian Sea: Nature, v. 319, p. 360–361.

Featherstone, P. S., Bott, M.H.P., and Peacock, J. H., 1977, Structure of the continental margin of southeastern Greenland: Geophysical Journal of the Royal Astronomical Society, v. 48, p. 15–27.

Friederich, W. L., and Simonarson, L. A., 1982, Acer-Funde aus dem Neogen von Island und ihre stratigraphische Stellung: Palaeontographica, v. 182, sec. B, p. 151–166.

Friend, P. F., Alexander-Marrack, P. D., Callen, K. C., Nicholson, J., and Yeats, A. K., 1983, Devonian sediments of East Greenland; VI, Review of results: Meddelelser om Grønland, v. 206, no. 6, p. 1–96.

Gowers, M. B., and Lunde, G., 1984, Geological history of Traenabanken, *in* Spencer, A. M., ed., Petroleum geology of the North European margin: Graham and Trotman, p. 137–251.

Grønlie, G., and Talwani, M., 1978, Geophysical atlas of the Norwegian Greenland Sea: Palisades, New York, Lamont-Doherty Geological Observatory VEMA Research series 4, 26 p.

Haller, J., 1970, Tectonic map of East Greenland; An account of tectonism, plutonism, and volcanism in East Greenland: Meddelelser om Grønland, v. 71, no. 5, 286 p., scale 1:500,000.

Hansen, K., 1985, Fission track age determinations of vertical movements in the crust caused by continental rifting; A fission track age study of the Scoresby Sund area; Methods and results [Ph.D. thesis]: University of Copenhagen, 119 p.

——, 1988, Preliminary report of fission track studies in the Jameson Land basin, East Greenland: Grølands Geologiske Undersøgelse Rapport 140, p. 85–89.

Henderson, G., 1976, Petroleum geology, *in* Escher, A., and Watt, W. S., eds., Geology of Greenland: Copenhagen, Geological Survey of Greenland, p. 488–505.

Hinz, K., 1981, An hypothesis on terrestrial catastrophes wedges of very thick oceanward dipping layers beneath passive continental margins; Their origin and paleoenvironmental significance: Jahrbuch, E2 Geologie, v. 2, p. 3–28.

Hinz, K., and Schlüter, H.-U., 1978, The North Atlantic; Results of geophysical investigations by the Federal Institute for Geosciences and Natural Resources on North Atlantic continental margins: Erdöl-Erdgas-Zeitschrift, no. 94, p. 271–280.

——, 1980, Continental margin off East Greenland; Proceedings of the 10th World Petroleum Congress; v. 2, Exploration, supply, and demand, Bucharest: London, Heyden, p. 405–418.

Hinz, K., Mutter, J. C., Zehnder, C. M., and the NGT Study Group, 1987, Symmetric conjugation of continent-ocean boundary structures along the Norwegian and East Greenland margins: Marine and Petroleum Geology, v. 4, p. 166–187.

Johnson, G. L., McMillan, J. H., and Egloff, J., 1975a, East Greenland continental margin, *in* Yorath, C. J., Parker, E. R., and Glass, D. J., eds., Canada's continental margins and offshore petroleum exploration: Canadian Society of Petroleum Geology Memoir 4, p. 205–224.

Johnson, G. L., Sommerhoff, G., and Egloff, 1975b, Structure and morphology of the west Reykjanes basin and the southeast Greenland continental margin: Marine Geology, v. 18, p. 175–196.

Larsen, B., 1975, Marine geophysical survey of the East Greenland shelf south of Angmassalik: Grønlands Geologiske Undersøgelse Rapport 75, p. 87–88.

——, 1980, A marine geophysical survey of the continental shelf of East Greenland 60° to 70°N; Project Dana 79: Grønlands Geologiske Undersøgelse Rapport 100, p. 94–98.

——, 1983, Geology of the Greenland-Iceland Ridge in the Denmark Strait, *in* Bott, M.H.P., Saxov, S., Talwani, M., and Thiede, J., eds., Structure and development of the Greenland-Scotland Ridge; New methods and concepts: New York, Plenum Press, p. 425–444.

Larsen, H. C., 1975, Aeromagnetic investigations in East Greenland: Grønlands Geologiske Undersøgelse Rapport 75, p. 88–91.

——, 1978, Offshore continuation of East Greenland dyke swarm and North Atlantic Ocean formation: Nature, v. 274, p. 220–223.

——, 1980, Geological perspective of the East Greenland continental margin: Geological Society of Denmark Bulletin 29, p. 77–101.

——, 1983, Marine geophysical investigations offshore East Greenland: Grønlands Geologiske Undersøgelse Rapport 115, p. 93–100.

——, 1984, Geology of the East Greenland Shelf, *in* Spencer, A. M., ed., Petroleum geology of the North European margin: Graham and Trotman, p. 329–339.

——, 1985, Petroleum geological assessment of the East Greenland Shelf: Grønlands Geologiske Undersøgelse Open-File Report, 78 p., plus appendix.

——, 1986, Project KANUMAS; Proposal for a regional marine seismic survey around Greenland; Geophysical description: Grønlands Geologiske Undersøgelse Open-File Report, 58 p.

——, 1988, A multiple and propagating rift model for the NE Atlantic, *in* Morton, A. C., and Parson, L. M., eds., Early Tertiary volcanism and the opening of the NE Atlantic: Geological Society of London Special Publication 39, p. 157–158.

Larsen, H. C., and Jakobsdôttir, S. J., 1988, Distribution, crustal properties, and significance of seawards-dipping sub-basement reflectors off E. Greenland, *in* Morton, A. C., and Parson, L. M., eds., Early Tertiary volcanism and the opening of the NE Atlantic: Geological Society of London Special Publication 39, p. 95–114.

Larsen, H. C., and Thorning, L., 1979, Project EASTMAR; Planning of an aeromagnetic survey of East Greenland: Grønlands Geologiske Undersøgelse Rapport 95, p. 93–96.

——, 1980, Project EASTMAR; Acquisition of high sensitivity aeromagnetic data off East Greenland: Grønlands Geologiske Undersøgelse Rapport 100, p. 91–94.

Mutter, J. C., Talwani, M., and Stoffa, P. L., 1982, Origin of seaward-dipping reflectors in oceanic crust off the Norwegian margin by "subaerial sea-floor spreading": Geology, v. 10, p. 353–357.

Nielsen, T.F.D., 1978, The Tertiary dike swarm of the Kangerdlugssuaq area, East Greenland: Contributions to Mineralogy and Petrology, v. 67, p. 63–78.

Noe-Nygaard, A., 1976, Tertiary igneous rocks between Shannon and Scoresby Sund, East Greenland, in Escher, A., and Watt, W. S., eds., Geology of Greenland: Copenhagen, Geological Survey of Greenland, p. 386–404.

Nunns, A. G., 1983, Plate tectonic evolution of the Greenland-Scotland Ridge and surrounding regions, in Bott, M.H.P., Saxov, S., Talwani, M., and Thiede, J., eds., Structure and development of the Greenland-Scotland Ridge; New methods and concepts: New York, Plenum Press, p. 11–30.

Pálmason, G., 1973, Kinematics and heat flow in a volcanic rift zone, with application to Iceland: Geophysical Journal of the Royal Astronomical Society, v. 33, p. 451–481.

——, 1980, A continuum model of crustal generation in Iceland; Kinematic aspects: Journal of Geophysics, v. 47, p. 7–18.

Perry, R. K., Fleming, H. S., Cherkis, N. Z., Feden, R. H., and Massingill, J. V., 1977, Bathymetry of the Norwegian-Greenland and western Barents Seas: Washington, D.C., U.S. Naval Research Laboratory, scale 1:2,333,230 at latitude 71°N, polar stereographic projection.

Perry, R. K., Fleming, H. S., Weber, J. R., Kristoffersen, V., Hall, J. K., Grantz, A., and Johnson, G. L., 1985, Bathymetry of the Arctic Ocean: Washington, D.C., U.S. Naval Research Laboratory, scale 1:4,704,075 at 87°N.

Roberts, D. G., Montadert, L., and Searle, R. C., 1979, The western Rockall Plateau; Stratigraphy and structural evolution, in Initial reports of the Deep Sea Drilling Project covering Leg 48: Washington, D.C., U.S. Government Printing Office, v. 48, p. 1061–1088.

Roberts, D. G., Backman, J., Morton, A. C., Murray, J. W., and Keene, J. B., 1984, Evolution of volcanic rifted margins; Synthesis of Leg 81 results on the west margin of Rockall Plateau, in Initial reports of the Deep Sea Drilling Project: Washington, D.C., U.S. Government Printing Office, v. 39, p. 883–911.

Shackleton, N. J., Backman, J., and Shipboard Scientific Party, 1984, Oxygen isotope calibration of the onset of ice rafting and history of glaciation in the North Atlantic region: Nature, v. 307, p. 620–623.

Smythe, D. K., 1983, Faeroe-Shetland escarpment and continental margin north of the Faeroes, in Bott, M.H.P., Saxov, S., Talwani, M., and Thiede, J., eds., Structure and development of the Greenland-Scotland Ridge; New methods and concepts: New York, Plenum Press, p. 109–120.

Sommerhoff, G., 1973, Formenschatz und morphologische Gliederung des südostgrönlandischen Schelfgebietes und Kontinentalabhanges; "Meteor": Forshungs-Ergebnisse, C15, p. 1–54.

Surlyk, F., 1977a, Stratigraphy, tectonics, and palaeogeography of the Jurassic sediments of the areas north of King Oscar Fjord, East Greenland: Grønlands Geologiske Undersøgelse Bulletin 123, 56 p.

——, 1977b, Mesozoic faulting in East Greenland, in Frost, R.T.C., and Dikkers, A. J., eds., Fault tectonics in NW Europe: Geologie en Mijnbouw, v. 56, p. 311–327.

——, 1978, Jurassic basin evolution of East Greenland: Nature, v. 274, p. 130–133.

Surlyk, F., Callomon, J. H., Bromley, R. G., and Birkelund, T., 1973, The stratigraphy of the Jurassic–Lower Cretaceous sediments of Jameson Land and Scoresby Land, East Greenland: Grønlands Geologiske Undersøgelse Bulletin 105, 76 p.

Surlyk, F., Clemmensen, L. B., and Larsen, H. C., 1981, Post-Paleozoic evolution of the East Greenland continental margin, in Kerr, J. S., and Fergusson, A. J., eds., Geology of the North Atlantic borderlands: Canadian Society of Petroleum Geology Memoir 7, p. 611–645.

Surlyk, F., Hurst, J. M., Scholle, P. A., Piasecki, S., Stemmerik, L., Rolle, F., and Thomsen, E., 1986, The Permian of the western margin of the Greenland Sea; A future exploration target, in Halbouty, M. T., ed., Future petroleum provinces of the world: American Association of Petroleum Geologists Memoir 40, p. 629–659.

Talwani, M., and Eldholm, O., 1977, Evolution of the Norwegian-Greenland Sea: Geological Society of America Bulletin, v. 88, p. 969–999.

Talwani, M., and Udintsev, G., 1976, Tectonic synthesis, in Talwani, M., and Udintsev, G., eds., Initial reports of the Deep Sea Drilling Project, Leg 38: Washington, D.C., U.S. Government Printing Office, v. 38, p. 1213–1242.

Talwani, M., Udintsev, G., and the Shipboard Scientific Party, 1976, Sites 346, 347, and 349, in Talwani, M., and Udintsev, G., eds., Initial reports of the Deep Sea Drilling Project, Leg 38: Washington, D.C., U.S. Government Printing Office, v. 38, p. 521–539.

Vail, P. R., Mitchum, R. M., Todd, R. G., Widmier, J. M., Thompson, S., Sangree, J. B., Bubb, J. W., and Hatlelid, W. G., 1977, Seismic stratigraphy and global changes of sea level, in Payton, C. F., ed., Seismic stratigraphy; Applications to hydrocarbon exploration: American Association of Petroleum Geologists Memoir 26, p. 49–212.

Vogt, P. R., 1970, Magnetized basement outcrops on the southeastern Greenland continental shelf: Nature, v. 226, p. 743–744.

Vogt, P. R., and Perry, R., 1978, Post-rifting accretion of continental margins in the Norwegian-Greenland and Labrador seas; Morphologic evidence [abs.]: EOS Transactions of the American Geophysical Union, v. 59, p. 1204.

Vogt, P. R., Johnson, G. L., and Kristjansson, L., 1980, Morphology and magnetic anomalies in north Iceland: Journal of Geophysics, v. 47, p. 67–80.

Wager, L. R., and Deer, W. A., 1938, A dyke swarm and coastal flexure in East Greenland: Geological Magazine, v. 75, p. 39–46.

White, R. S., Spence, G. D., Fowler, S. R., McKenzie, D. P., Westbrook, G. K., and Bowen, A. N., 1987, Magmatism at rifted continental margins: Nature, v. 330, p. 439–444.

Manuscript Accepted by the Society June 8, 1988

ACKNOWLEDGMENTS

This chapter represents a summary of the past seven years of geophysical data acquisition, processing, and interpretation within the Geological Survey of Greenland. I thank the Directorate-General for Energy of the European Economic Communities (EEC), the Danish Ministry of Energy, and the Danish Natural Science Research Council for providing funds for this large project. The following geophysical service companies provided excellent field and processing services: Aero Service, Western Geophysical, Compagnie Generale de Geophysique, Rebbeck Hunter, and Seismic Profilers (now GECO and Merlin Geophysical). I also thank P. E. Holm for his contributions in constructing the isopach contour map, S. Jakobsdóttir for modelling refraction data, and C. Marcussen for his contributions to the seismic data processing and many other data problems. B. S. Hansen did the drawings and V. Hermansen and N. Turner typed the manuscript. Seismic data from the Centre National pour l'Exploitation des Oceans (CNEXO), Brest, and from the Bundesanstalt für Geowissenschaften und Rohstoffe (BGR), Hannover, have been used in the construction of the isopach contour map; their availability is gratefully acknowledged.

During the past ten years, I have benefitted greatly from discussions of the Cenozoic geology of the northeast Atlantic, and the East Greenland margin in particular, with the following persons: M. S. Andersen, C. K. Brooks, O. Eldholm, S. Funder, K. Hinz, G. L. Johnson, B. Larsen, L. M. Larsen, J. Mutter, T.D.F. Nielsen, A. Nunns, D. G. Roberts, D. Smythe, F. Surlyk, and P. Vogt. I thank them all for stimulating discussions each of which, in one way or another, contributed to the present chapter. This text is published with the permission of the Director of the Geological Survey of Greenland.

Printed in U.S.A.

Chapter 13

The North Greenland Continental Margin

Peter R. Dawes
Geological Survey of Greenland, Øster Voldgade 10, DK-1350, Copenhagen, Denmark

INTRODUCTION

Geologic setting

Physiographically, the North Greenland margin is an eastward extension of the passive rifted continental margin of the Canadian Arctic Islands (see Sweeney and Sobczak, this volume); however, geologically it has a very different setting. It is a transform-rifted margin and represents the only part of the margin that borders the relatively young, oceanic, and seismically active part of the Arctic Basin—the Eurasia Basin. This is in contrast to the extensive western margin that faces the older and seemingly more complex Amerasia (Canada-Makarov) Basin (Fig. 1).

Limits of study area

The North Greenland margin is defined here as that part of the continental shelf and slope bordered by the 2,000 m isobath; it forms an area of approximately 120,000 km² (Fig. 2). In the west and northwest the study area is limited by the junction of the Lomonosov Ridge with the continental margin of Ellesmere Island (see Weber and others, this volume); to the east and southeast, where the margin is narrowest, the border is drawn off Kronprins Christian Land to the north of the broad Belgica Bank that forms the northernmost part of the East Greenland margin (see Larsen, this volume).

In addition, Nares Strait, joining Baffin Bay to the Arctic Basin, is briefly considered in the section on tectonic development. Although not described as part of the continental margin of the Arctic Ocean, it forms a prominent associated lineament and holds a key role in plate reconstructions of the Arctic region.

Previous work

Bathymetrically and geologically the offshore part of the North Greenland margin is one of the least known of the entire Arctic Basin. Available data are sporadic and mainly of reconnaissance type; as yet no detailed multidisciplinary studies or traverses aimed at the elucidation of prominent features have been carried out, as is the case with the Alaskan-Canadian part of

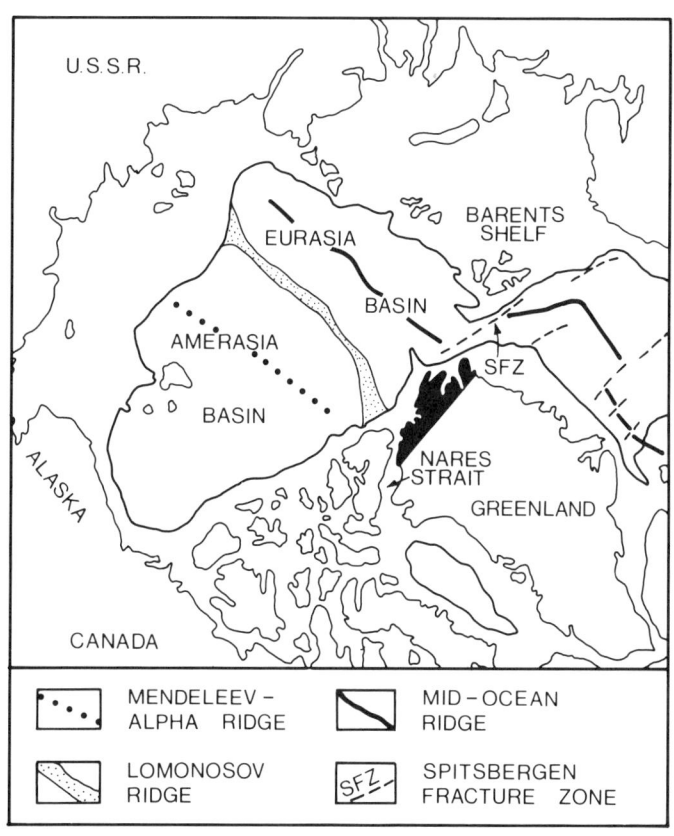

Figure 1. Map of the Arctic region showing the position of the North Greenland margin bordering the Eurasia Basin. The continental shelf is deliminated by the 1,000 m isobath taken from Johnson and others (1979).

the margin. Deep seismic sounding techniques have not been utilized, and information on deep crustal structure is conjectural. For parts of the margin—for example, the inner shelf off Peary Land—bathymetric data are rudimentary or totally lacking (Fig. 2); paradoxically in fact, some of these areas are much better known magnetically than bathymetrically.

Compositional and structural interpretations of the margin

Dawes, P. R., 1990, The North Greenland Continental Margin, *in* Grantz, A., Johnson, L., and Sweeney, J. F., eds., The Arctic Ocean region: Boulder, Colorado, Geological Society of America, The Geology of North America, v. L.

are based on geophysical data alone; no drill or dredge samples have been collected, and no bottom photography is available. The coast north of Greenland is ice-locked throughout the year and most of the available information is derived from airborne surveys. Shipborne work has been carried out only as far north as the Kennedy Channel (81°N) in the west (Kravitz, 1976) and to the northern Greenland Sea in the east (82°N). There, the most recent cruise, that of the *Ymer* in 1980, undertook geophysical measurements (Schytt and others, 1981), including some seismic refraction profiling off Kronprins Christian land, using expendable sonobuoys (Eldholm and others, 1984).

Drifting ice stations have rarely passed near the North Greenland margin (Fletcher, 1968); however, some seismic and gravity data relevant for crustal interpretations of the margin have been collected, for example from ARLIS II (Ostenso and Pew, 1968; Ostenso and Wold, 1977; see Fig. 5). Helicopter-supported offshore operations have been extremely limited; of particular note is the gravity survey carried out in 1967 on the sea ice of Lincoln Sea (Sobczak and Stephens, 1974).

The main geophysical data from the margin are aeromagnetic and gravity. Early data are parts of regional surveys of the Arctic, such as the high-level aeromagnetic studies reported on by King and others (1966), Haines and others (1970), Riddihough and others (1973), and Coles and others (1976), and the low-level surveys of Ostenso (1962) and Ostenso and Wold (1971). Interpretation of these data in terms of detailed structure of the margin is problematic; collection techniques have varied from survey to survey, and it is difficult to correlate data sets and conclusions (Coles and others, 1978). More recent offshore low-level (300 m) aeromagnetic data are available from the main part of the margin, for example, the Lincoln Sea and Morris Jesup Plateau (see Fig. 4); descriptions of these data, including estimated magnetic source depth (EMSD) analysis, and interpretation in terms of modern plate tectonic models are given by Vogt and others (1978, 1982), Feden and others (1979), Kovacs (1982), and Kovacs and Vogt (1982). In addition, low-level magnetic reconnaissance of Nares Strait included flight lines as far north as the Robeson Channel (Hood and others, 1985).

Detailed gravity data have only been collected over the western part of the margin, that is, over the Lincoln Sea. Results are available in the form of a Bouguer anomaly map at 1:500,000 compiled from measurements at more than 700 ground and sea ice stations (Sobczak and Stephens, 1974; see Fig. 6). Regional gravity data exist in the form of map compilations based on observed and predicted free-air anomalies and satellite information (Sobczak, 1978; Bowin and others, 1981).

In addition to the sonobuoy refraction measurements by Eldholm mentioned above, published seismic data are restricted to a single seismic reflection profile across the Morris Jesup Plateau and continental slope to the east collected during the ARLIS II drift (Ostenso and Pew, 1968; Ostenso and Wold, 1977). A single refraction line from FRAM II crossed the northern flank of the plateau (Duckworth and others, 1982), but results have not been published.

Aim

This chapter reviews the gross physiographic and geologic provinces of the North Greenland margin, as presently defined by published bathymetric and geophysical data. Extrapolations of the onshore geology onto the shelf are attempted, and a tentative geological history is outlined.

PHYSIOGRAPHY

The North Greenland margin shows marked changes in width and topography (Fig. 2). Three main physiographic provinces can be defined. A marginal plateau, the Morris Jesup Plateau, projects into the Eurasia Basin from the inner shelf off Peary Land, and separates the narrow and linear Wandel Sea margin in the east from the broad Lincoln Sea margin in the west. The bathymetry of Figure 2 is from the General Bathymetric Chart of the Oceans (GEBCO) sheet by Johnson and others (1979); this differs in important detail from the bathymetric maps of Heezen and Tharp (1975) and Sobczak (1978) (see Plate 1, this volume, for a more recent version of this map.) In the Heezen and Tharp compilation, for example, the Lomonosov Ridge is shown terminating at the North Greenland margin off Peary Land.

The Wandel Sea margin is the narrowest margin of the entire Arctic Basin. Off northern Kronprins Christian Land, the continental shelf is only about 30 km wide; to the northwest off eastern Peary Land, it broadens to about 60 km. The shelf is delimited by a sharp topographic break that forms a linear escarpment at around the 400 m isobath. The continental slope has a steep gradient that falls directly away to the abyssal depths of the Amundsen Basin and Lena Trough, which are more than 4,000 m deep. Sobczak (1978) shows a more complicated slope off eastern Peary Land, with several small plateaus marked as an eastward extension of the Morris Jesup Plateau.

The *Morris Jesup Plateau* is a fairly broad plateau about 200 km wide that trends northeastward into the Amundsen Basin, extending the width of the margin to about 300 km. On present maps the plateau is well defined by the 2,000 m isobath (Figs. 2 and 3). It is characterized by steep, rugged sides, of which the eastern is notably linear and scarplike and about 3 km high, and a fairly flat eastern summit. These features are seen well on the single-channel seismic reflection profile from ARLIS II (see Fig. 5). Reinterpretation of the bathymetry of Johnson and others (1979) based on magnetic and depth-to-source data suggests that the western side of the rise is not a single escarpment descending to the depths of the Amundsen Basin, but rather a complex group of ridges and depressions (Fig. 3).

It should be noted that the name Morris Jesup Plateau is used in the sense of Ostenso and Wold (1977; these authors actually use "Morris Jessup Rise") to include both the fairly narrow, triangular-shaped, flat-topped easternlike plateau, as well as the western segment that is characterized by much more undulating topography. This contrasts with recent usage that tends to

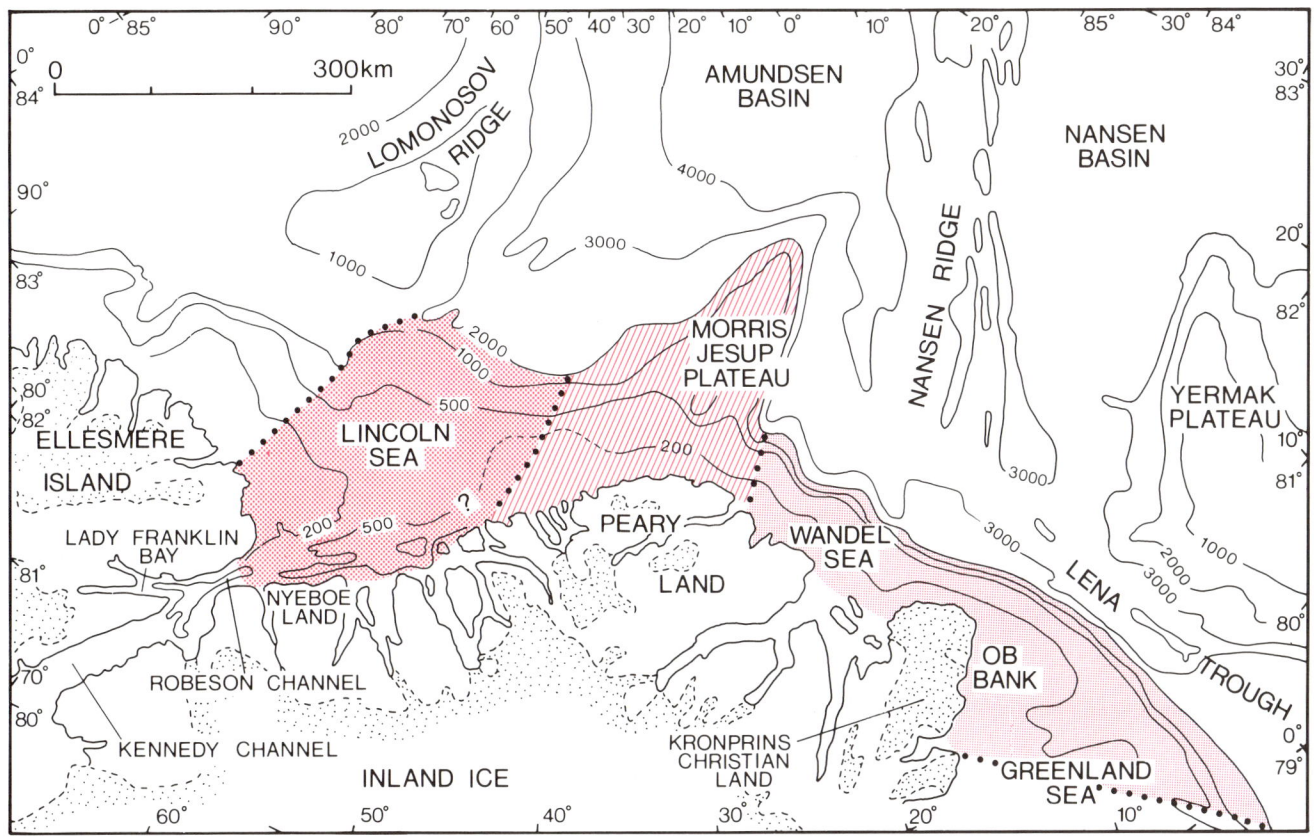

Figure 2. Location map showing the three physiographic-geologic provinces of the North Greenland margin. Bathymetry is mainly taken from Johnson and others (1979), with additions from Sobczak (1978). Isobath detail between 3,000 to 4,000 m around the Nansen Ridge is omitted.

restrict the name to cover only the eastern ridgelike part (e.g., Feden and others, 1979; Kovacs, 1982).

The inner part of the shelf off Peary Land is very poorly known bathymetrically. Early map compilations inferred that the Morris Jesup Plateau was separated from the continental shelf by a narrow linear trough; recent interpretations suggest that the plateau is an intrinsic part of the shelf.

The *Lincoln Sea margin* is characterized by a broad shelf, up to 250 km wide, situated between the Morris Jesup Plateau and the relatively narrow shelf off northern Ellesmere Island facing the Amerasia Basin. Little is known about the topography of the Lincoln Sea shelf other than that it appears to have a gently undulating surface without prominent rises. The continental slope here has a much shallower gradient than in the Wandel Sea margin. Bathymetric data indicate that a very prominent, narrow topographic depression, more than 500 m deep, parallels the Greenland coast for at least 200 km east of Robeson Channel. This feature strikes at an angle to the Nares Strait lineament; it is on direct line with the submarine depression of Lady Franklin Bay in Ellesmere Island. The eastern termination of this depression has not been mapped (Fig. 2).

GEOLOGIC PROVINCES

Northern Greenland is underlain by Precambrian shield that is overlain in the north by a thick Proterozoic-Phanerozoic succession—the remnants of two major sedimentary basins: the Proterozoic–mid-Paleozoic Franklinian Basin and the late Paleozoic–Tertiary Wandel Sea Basin. The shield is exposed in three areas around the margin of the Inland Ice: along Nares Strait in the west, at the head of Victoria Fjord in the north, and facing the Greenland Sea in the east (Fig. 3). Onland geology is well known, having been studied during the extensive mapping program by the Geological Survey of Greenland in the decade up to 1985.

The geologic mapping of the continental shelf is at a rudimentary stage. Based on the bathymetric and geophysical data outlined above, with extrapolations of the onshore lithologies, some interpretations of geologic composition can be made. The large-scale magnetic pattern (flat or nearly flat magnetic profiles) over the thick sedimentary sequences composing the Franklinian Basin (~10 km thick), the Wandel Sea Basin (~7 km), and adjoining Sverdrup Basin of Ellesmere Island, extends over the

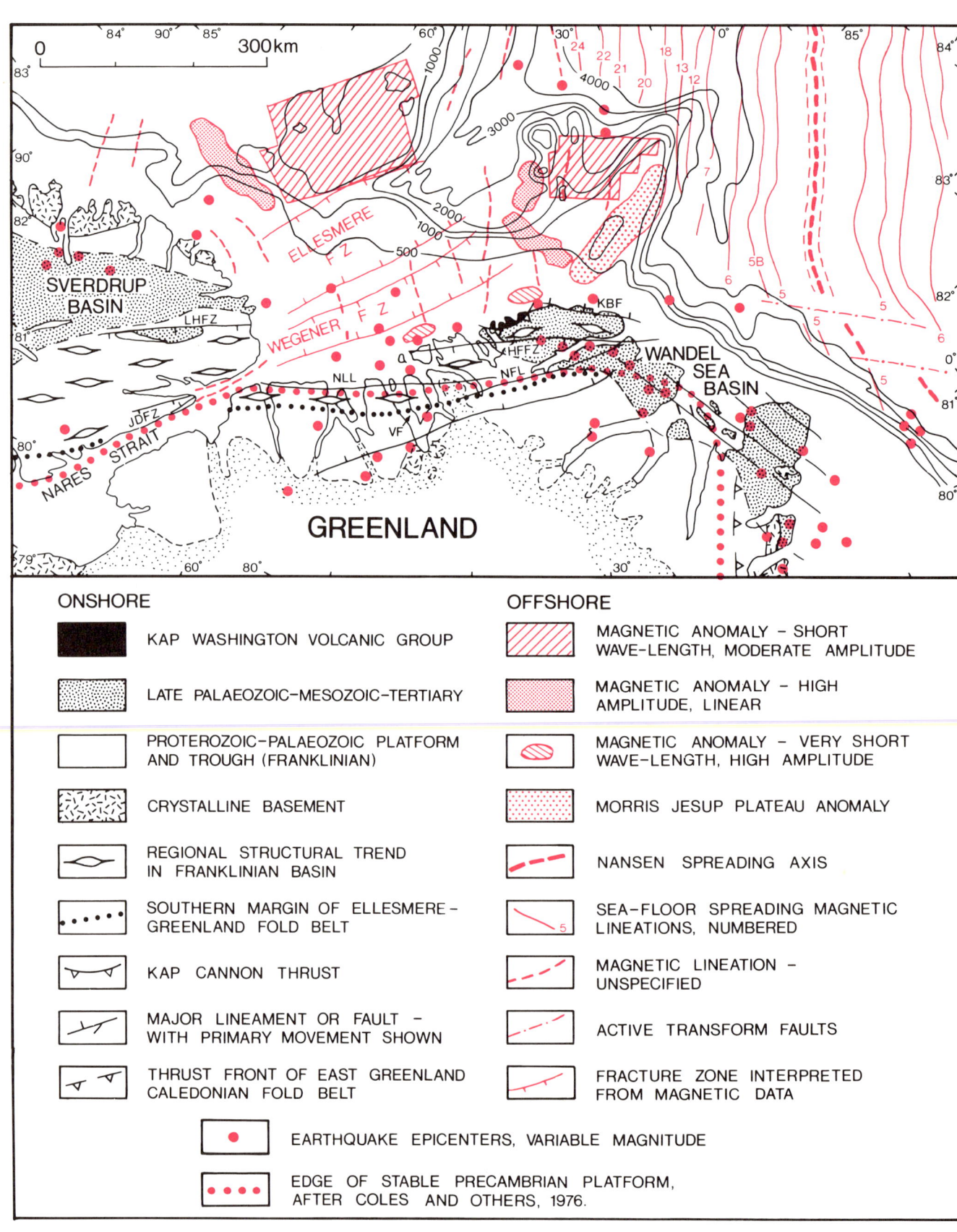

adjacent shelf and suggests that strata of these provinces also underlie the continental shelf (King and others, 1966; Ostenso and Wold, 1971).

Regions where the Greenland-Canadian Shield lies near the surface are characterized by a complex magnetic anomaly pattern. Regional maps presented by Riddihough and others (1973) and Coles and others (1976) show a north-south to northwest-southeast anomaly trend over northern Greenland and adjacent Canada (southern Ellesmere, Devon, and northern Baffin Islands). These authors suggest that the northern boundary of this distinctive magnetic signature, which crosses Greenland from the Robeson Channel to eastern Peary Land (Fig. 3), represents the northern edge of the essentially undisturbed and stable Precambrian craton. However, "granitic" basement outcrops on the shores of the Greenland Sea, and there is evidence that such rocks extend far north of this geophysically defined boundary—at least to the north coast. Firstly, xenoliths of a variety of gneisses, granites, and metabasic rocks occur in volcanic centers and minor intrusions in northernmost Peary Land, suggesting the presence of sialic crust at depth (Soper and others, 1980; Parsons, 1981; Higgins and others, 1985). Secondly, alkaline dykes and peralkaline volcanics (Kap Washington Group), characterized by "within-plate" chemistry and concentrated at the outer coast, are regarded as products of continental rift magmatism (Batten and others, 1981; Soper and others, 1982), suggesting that the region was, at least in early Cenozoic time, composed essentially of continental crust.

Preliminary Bouguer gravity maps over northern Greenland are characterized by roughly coast-parallel contours and a rise in gravity values seaward—features generally interpreted as indicative of crustal thinning toward the continental shelf (Forsberg, 1979, 1981; Weng, 1980). The entire Franklinian basin in Greenland probably evolved on continental crust—a conclusion also reached for the more extensive part of the basin in Ellesmere Island, where crystalline rocks outcrop at the outer coast around 83°N (Trettin and Balkwill, 1979). Kovacs (1982) recognizes high-amplitude linear magnetic anomalies along the continental shelf-slope border off northern Ellesmere Island and Peary Land (Fig. 3), which he interprets as indicative of the continent-ocean boundary. Gravity data over the Lincoln Sea suggest seaward crustal thinning; high anomalies at the outer shelf may represent thin continental or oceanic crust (Sobczak and Stephens, 1974). An alternative model is that such outer-shelf anomalies may be due to uncompensated prisms of young sediments causing mass excesses on the crust (Sobczak, 1975).

It seems most likely that at least the inner part of the continental shelf is underlain by thinned granitic crust, overlain by thick Paleozoic successions and in part by Mesozoic and Cenozoic sequences and volcanic rocks. Within the limits of the available data, it seems that the physiographic provinces described earlier generally correspond to fairly distinctive geological-geophysical provinces; thus, in the following text the same tripartite division of the margin is maintained.

The Wandel Sea margin is considered to be underlain by late Paleozoic-Mesozoic-Cenozoic strata (Dawes and Soper, 1973); islands on the shelf up to 40 km east of the coast of Kronprins Christian Land are composed of Wandel Sea Basin strata (Dawes and Peel, 1981). Recent seismic refraction data over the Ob Bank, which show average velocity structure of 2.2, 3.5, and 5.1 km/s in the upper crust, support the model (Eldholm and others, 1984).

The dominant tectonic grain of the Wandel Sea Basin onshore is northwest-southeast, and a series of major faults with this trend have been interpreted as a Cretaceous-Tertiary strike-slip mobile belt (Håkansson, 1979; Håkansson and Pedersen, 1982). The continental shelf break is parallel to, and presumably controlled by, these major northwest-trending dislocations. Many authors have noted the parallelism between this lineament direction and the main trend of the Lena Trough, which contains the complex Spitsbergen Fracture Zone that separates the spreading axes of the Eurasia Basin (Nansen Ridge) and the North Atlantic Basin (Knipovitch Ridge; Fig. 1). Presumably northwest-southeast structures dominate the continental shelf and slope in the Wandel Sea and are complimentary to structures on the Svalbard shelf. Such structures form a major tectonic zone developed by interaction of the Wandel Sea and Barents Sea margins during the Mesozoic-Cenozoic (Harland, 1965, 1969; Birkenmajor, 1972; Lowell, 1972; Kellogg, 1975; Soper and others, 1982; Håkansson and Pedersen, 1982; see Fig. 7). To what extent this tectonism has obliterated older structures of the margin must remain speculative. However, one steep westward-verging fault, recorded on a seismic profile, some 85 km off the northern coast of Kronprins Christian Land, has been suggested by Ostenso and Pew (1968) to be an offshore expression of the East Greenland Caledonian thrust front.

Wandel Sea Basin strata (late Paleozoic, Mesozoic, Tertiary) probably compose the shelf as far south as 75°N, where aeromagnetic data indicate that a major sedimentary basin char-

Figure 3. Map of the North Greenland margin showing onshore geologic provinces and main structures, and offshore magnetic and interpreted tectonic features. Onshore geology from Dawes and Kerr (1982), Håkansson and Pedersen (1982), and Surlyk and Hurst (1984). Offshore: distinctive magnetic regions from Kovacs (1982); Ellesmere and Wegener Fracture Zones from Vogt and others (1982) and Kovacs (1982); sea-floor spreading type magnetic lineations and Nansen Ridge axis from Kovacs and others (undated); unspecified magnetic anomaly lineations from Kovacs and others (undated) and Vogt and others (1982), except those in Robeson Channel that are from Hood and others (1985). Earthquake epicenters from Wetmiller and Forsyth (1982) and Gregersen (1982, and personal communication, 1985); intense earthquake activity and magnetic lineations 1 to 4 in connection with the Nansen Ridge are not shown. Bathymetry from Johnson and others (1979) with modifications, particularly in area of western Morris Jesup Plateau from Kovacs (1982). Bathymetry of Nansen Ridge is not shown—see Figure 2. JDFZ = Judge Daly fault zone; NLL = Nyeboe Land lineament; NFL = Navarana Fjord lineament; HFFZ = Harder Fjord fault zone; KBF = Kap Bridgman fault; VF = Victoria Fjord.

acterized by coast-parallel sediment-filled grabens underlies the Belgica Bank shelf (Henderson, 1976; Larsen, 1984; see Larsen, this volume).

The Morris Jesup Plateau figures as a discrete geological province in modern plate tectonic scenarios; it is characterized by a very large positive magnetic anomaly, seen on regional charts to impinge on the Peary Land coast (Ostenso and Wold, 1971; Riddihough and others, 1973). There is now general consensus that the structure is fundamentally an oceanic rise formed during the early opening of the Eurasia Basin (Phillips and others, 1978; Feden and others, 1979; Vogt and others, 1979; Kovacs and Vogt, 1982; Jackson and others, 1984). Much emphasis has been placed on the presence of a magnetically similar submarine region on the opposite side of the Nansen Ridge (the Yermak Plateau), and this has led to the conclusion that the Morris Jesup Plateau is a complimentary and coeval feature—the western part of a once-continuous aseismic ridge, formed and subsequently split by seafloor spreading prior to anomaly 13 time (Fig. 7; see Kristoffersen, this volume).

Feden and others (1979) regard the plateau as a manifestation of hot-spot magmatism, and by analogy with Pacific hot-spot/mid-ocean ridge products (e.g. Galapagos, Juan de Fuca) suggest the presence of "exceptionally fractionated Fe-Ti-enriched basalts of high remanence."

The magnetic signature of the Morris Jesup Plateau is dominated by high amplitude, long-wavelength anomalies, with a persistent relief at 700 to 800 nT that locally increases to more than 2,000 nT (Feden and others, 1979). The highest amplitudes occur in the eastern and southeastern part of the plateau, with a second high to the northeast, while amplitudes of over 500 nT occur across the shelf to Peary Land (Fig. 4). Estimated magnetic source depth (EMSD) analyses indicate depths as shallow as 800 to 1,500 m over highs separated by a deep of 5,000 to 6,000 m over low-amplitude anomalies (Kovacs and Vogt, 1982; Kovacs, 1982).

It is important to note that the fairly well developed magnetic stripe pattern in the Amundsen Basin fades out some distance to the north of the Morris Jesup Plateau, and at best only a vague and speculative correlation might be attempted between this pattern and the generally semilinear to disordered magnetic pattern of the plateau itself (Fig. 3). Vogt and others (1982) and Kovacs and others (undated) extend magnetic anomalies 7 to 20 onto the flanks of the plateau, although clear magnetic linear definition is lacking. Furthermore, the sites of some of these numbered anomalies are drawn through magnetically negative terrain.

Interpretations of the high magnetic relief certainly suggest the presence of Fe-Ti–rich magmatic rocks; the only types of "granitic" crust that could create a comparable magnetic signature might be a large granulite facies terrain, large plutons, or perhaps a major ore body. An oceanic origin has gained wide support, convincingly, because in modern plate tectonic reconstructions there is "no room" for continental material when the Eurasia Basin is closed (e.g., Feden and others, 1979; Jackson and others, 1984; Srivastava, 1985). However, we should be

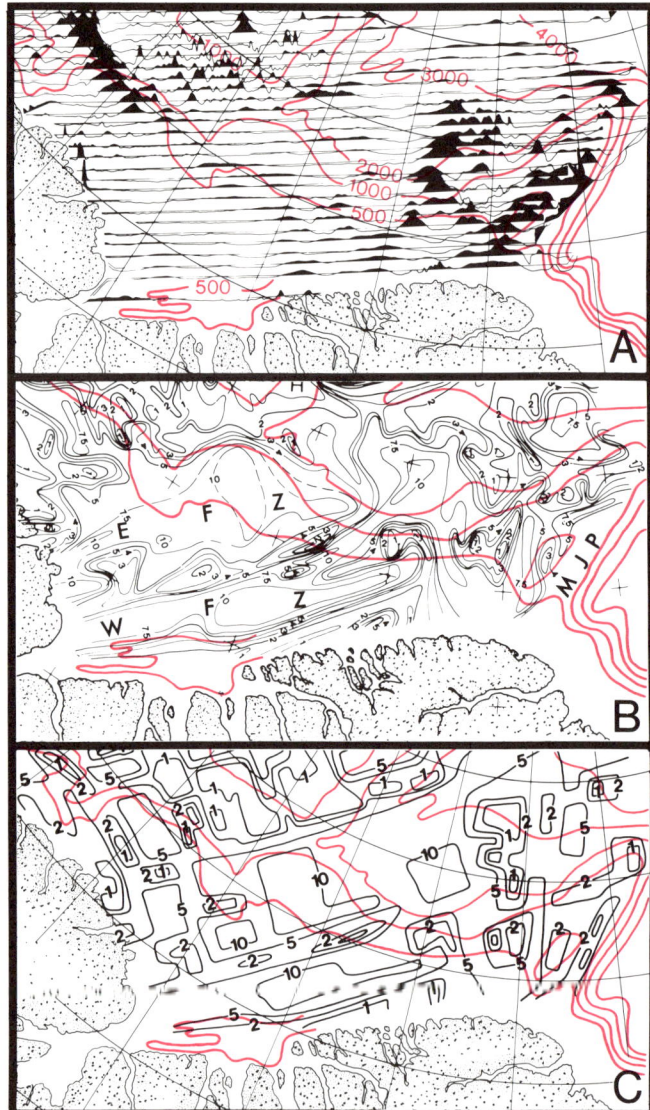

Figure 4. Aeromagnetic data over the North Greenland margin (Lincoln Sea–Morris Jesup Plateau). A. Residual magnetic anomalies (with diurnal variations removed) along low-level flight tracks. Black areas are positive anomalies; vertical exaggeration is 4,000 nT per degree of latitude. Modified from Kovacs (1982). B. Contoured estimated magnetic source depth (EMSD) calculations; contour interval is 1 km from 0 to 5 km, 2.5 km from 5 to 10 km. WFZ = Wegener Fracture Zone, EFZ = Ellesmere Fracture Zone, MJP = Morris Jesup Plateau. Modified from Vogt and others (1982), see also Kovacs (1982). C. Generalized EMSD contours, in kilometers, processed from B above. Modified from Kovacs (1982). All three maps modified by addition of isobath data (in metres) from Johnson and others (1979).

wary that assertions and a consensus of opinion do not lead to acceptance as fact; with present data the nature of the Morris Jesup Plateau is conjectural. Taken in its entirety, the plateau shows considerable magnetic variation, and there are areas of both complex and subdued magnetic signature. For example,

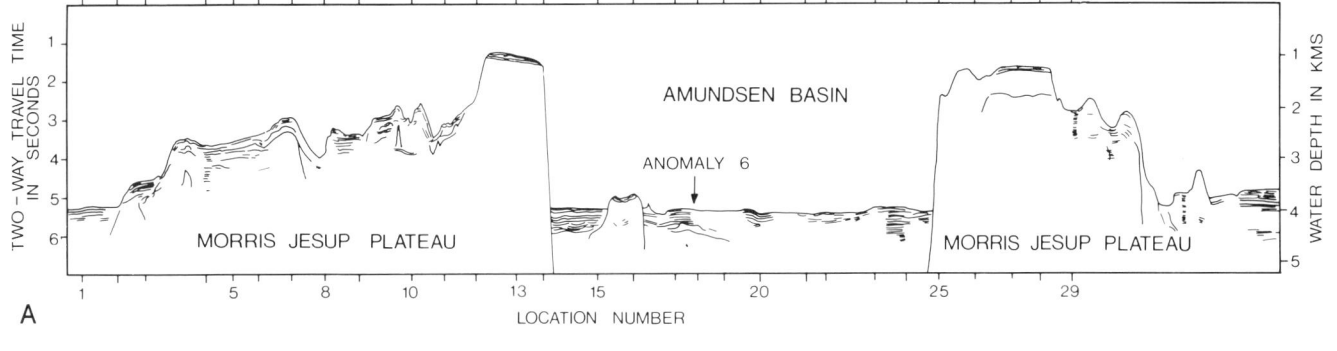

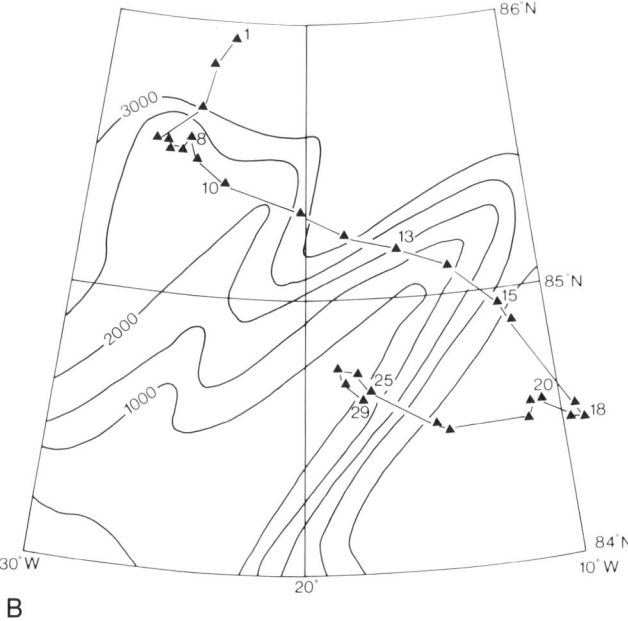

Figure 5. Seismic reflection profile across the northeastern part of the Morris Jesup Plateau. Indicated travel time is two-way in seconds; depth conversion is for water only. Map shows the drift path of ice island ARLIS II and location of profile. Redrawn after Feden and others (1979); original data in Ostenso and Wold (1977).

Kovacs (1982) defines, in addition to the large so-called "Morris Jesup Rise anomaly" that occupies the southeastern part of the plateau, two isolated high-amplitude linear anomalies, as well as a region characterized by high-frequency, moderate-amplitude anomalies (Fig. 3). Furthermore, a group of very short-wavelength (<5 km), moderate- to high-amplitude anomalies occur on the inner shelf. To this author, such magnetic variation (seen together with the available gravity and seismic data) suggests a more complex geologic composition than the oceanic accretion origin publicized in the recent literature quoted above. Gravity and seismic data from the ARLIS II ice drift suggest a faulted horstlike structure, with rugged basement topography, a very pronounced eastern scarp, and a maximum measured sedimentary pile of up to 1.3 km on the plateau surface and up to 1.75 km on the eastern flank (Fig. 5; Ostenso and Wold, 1977). According to these authors, the free-air and Bouguer gravity data indicate the presence of low-density material of a type usually associated with the upper continental crust, although "this does not exclude the alternative possibility that the rise is a thick pile of oceanic basalts" (Ostenso and Wold, 1977, p. 12).

The coincidence of a prominent magnetic high with an onshore volcanic province (Kap Washington Group) led to speculation that volcanics extended across the shelf and onto the Morris Jesup Plateau (Dawes, 1973; Riddihough and others, 1973). This model was also used in the interpretation of the ARLIS II seismic profile (Ostenso and Wold, 1977). It should be noted that the onshore volcanics are now known to be thoroughly alkaline and indicative of continental rift magmatism (Batten and others, 1981; Soper and others, 1982). They are not the products of sea-floor spreading oceanic accretion, but they may well have developed at the intersection of a large transform fault between Svalbard and Greenland and the Nansen accretionary ridge. The magnetic signature of the shelf suggests the presence of magmatic material on the inner shelf (Feden and others, 1979; Kovacs, 1982). From the general geology and gross disposition of the 4- to 5-km-thick volcanic pile of the Kap Washington Group volcanics that forms high coastal cliffs (Brown and Parsons, 1981), it seems almost certain that the volcanic province originally extended far to the north. In the absence of dredge and drill material, however, the precise extent of igneous rocks beneath the shelf, both continental rift volcanics and oceanic basalts, remains a matter of speculation.

Late Cretaceous alkaline basic dykes of several directions occur in northern Peary Land (Soper and others, 1982; Dawes and others, 1983; Friderichsen and Bengaard, 1985). The most dense swarm has a coast-normal trend with a marked concentration of dykes in a 100-km-wide zone in western Peary Land (see Fig. 7). This swarm represents an overall east-west extension of the crust in this zone of about 20 percent, and Friderichsen and Bengaard (1985) note that in some areas crustal extension reaches 50 percent. The north-south swarm dies away southward from the Arctic Ocean. The dykes might reflect the initial continental rift along which the Nansen Ridge developed, and which resulted in the separation of the Lomonosov Ridge from the Barents Shelf (Soper and others, 1982). If so, the dykes might cross the entire continental shelf. Their presence cannot be detected in the available magnetic data, although certain north-south magnetic lineations do occur off western Peary Land (Fig. 3).

Summarizing, the deep structure of the Morris Jesup Plateau is conjectural. Available data are all geophysical. Sea-floor linear magnetic anomalies, essential for the fundamental differentiation between oceanic and continental crust, are lacking. The main arguments for the publicized oceanic origin of the plateau remain the highly magnetic crust and the general plate kinematic setting. Conversely, the plateau, its eastern part in particular, shows a morphology with strong marginal escarpments that is difficult to reconcile with oceanic origin. The same applies to parts of the Yermak Plateau. Seismic refraction data and dredge samples of high-grade gneiss from the southern Yermak Plateau are interpreted to indicate the presence there of thinned continental crust (Jackson and others, 1984; Kristoffersen, this volume). The morphology of the Morris Jesup Plateau may thus indicate appreciable continental remnants below a thick cover of volcanic rocks. Any model involving a complex structure of the Morris Jesup Plateau (e.g., a mixed continental-oceanic origin) demands drastic modification of the conventional spreading model for the southern Eurasia Basin (see below under tectonic development).

The Lincoln Sea margin is considered to be underlain by thick sequences of lower Paleozoic (Franklinian Basin) and Mesozoic-Cenozoic (Sverdrup Basin–Wandel Sea Basin) strata above an attenuated continental basement (Sobczak and Stephens, 1974; Dawes and Peel, 1981; McMillan, 1982). The magnetic signature of the shelf and slope facing the Amundsen Basin is very subdued with amplitudes of 100 nT or less and wavelengths of 60 km or more (Fig. 4; Kovacs, 1982). The shelf is undoubtedly underlain by a large depositional basin filled with detrital material derived from Greenland and northern Ellesmere Island. McMillan (1982) has referred the postulated large volume of mainly nonmagnetic strata to the Lincoln Sea Basin.

Bouguer anomaly data (Fig. 6) indicate a rather uneven gravity field over the Lincoln Sea with primary trends parallel to the east-northeast trends of the lower Paleozoic strata of the Ellesmere-Greenland fold belt (Sobczak and Stephens, 1974). This regional parallelism between gravity and surface geological trends is also evident across northern Greenland (René Forsberg, personal communication, 1985; Dawes, 1986). Anomalies over the Lincoln Sea range from +90 mgal over the outer shelf to a minimum of –50 mgal in the Lincoln Sea Low. This low forms a conspicuous feature across the shelf on line with the onshore

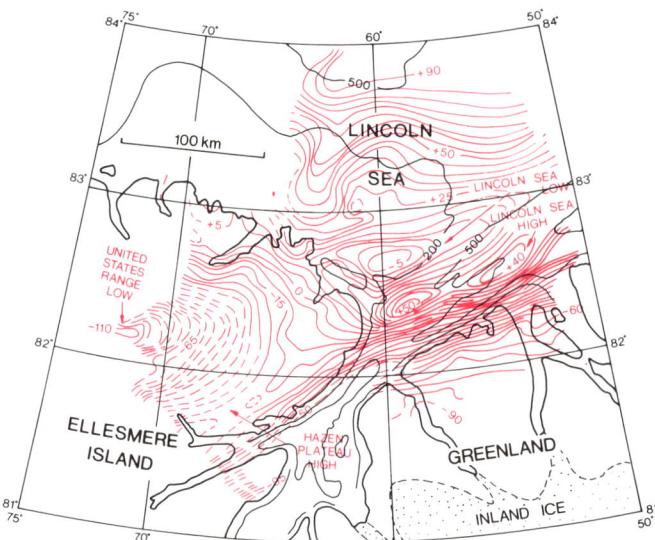

Figure 6. Bouguer anomaly map over the Lincoln Sea and adjacent land. Gravity contours are at 5 mgal intervals. Modified from Sobczak and Stephens (1974); 200 m and 500 m isobaths from Johnson and others (1979).

Sverdrup Basin of Ellesmere Island, with which it invites correlation (Figs. 3 and 6). Using rock densities from onland Mesozoic strata, Sobczak and Stephens (1974) interpret the gravity low as indicative of a "young" sedimentary basin containing at least 2 km of low-density sediments. This is a minimum value; a crustal model given by Sobczak and Weber (1972) suggests a basin with clastic sediments about 7 km thick.

Based on the gravity field and on P-wave earthquake data recorded at Alert, the crustal model favored is one of northward crustal thinning from a normal sialic crust 32 km thick below Greenland, to about 18 km thick at the outer shelf (Sobczak and Stephens, 1974). The steep gravity gradient (max. –3.68 mgal/km) crosses Robeson Channel south of the Lincoln Sea–Hazen Plateau High (+50 mgal; Fig. 6), evidently uninterrupted by structures in Nares Strait. The gradient is considered to represent a steplike thickening of the crust (Sobczak and Stephens, 1974). It coincides with the Nyeboe Land lineament in Greenland (NLL in Fig. 3), which is situated at the early Paleozoic platform margin. This feature may well be governed by a deep-seated change in crustal character or thickness associated with the passage from normal crust in the south to attenuated continental or even to oceanic crust to the north (Dawes, 1982). Sobczak and Stephens (1974), for example, suggest a relation to an ancient plate boundary.

In contrast to gravity trends, which parallel onshore regional structures, magnetic trends derived from estimated magnetic source depth (EMSD) analysis trend generally northeasterly, more or less parallel to Nares Strait (Fig. 4). The main feature of the maps presented by Kovacs (1982) and Kovacs and Vogt

(1982) is a narrow linear trough with a depth of over 10 km that stretches from the Robeson Channel for about 300 km toward the Morris Jesup Plateau (Fig. 4C). This is separated by a narrow ridge of 4 km to less than 1 km depth, from a second, broader basin that extends from northern Ellesmere Island across the outer shelf. The reader is referred to the above papers by Vogt and Kovacs for analytical details of the EMSD method and interpretation of the results in terms of geological features and speculative crustal motions. In essence, the basin and ridge structures are referred to parallel strike-slip fractures—Wegener Fracture Zone and Ellesmere Fracture Zone (WFZ and EFZ in Fig. 4B)—developed on thinned continental crust. Movement along these fracture zones is said to lead to the separation of Greenland and Ellesmere Island along Nares Strait. The narrow, linear, fault-controlled trough (Wegener FZ, or WFZ, Figs. 3 and 4) is regarded as a deep, sediment-filled basin that developed in early Tertiary time due to thinning and foundering of the crust. The broader outer basin (Ellesmere FZ or EFZ) is likewise regarded as thinned and deeply foundered continental crust; however, it could equally represent an area of oceanic crust overlain by a thick sedimentary section.

The EMSD contours lie oblique to the main gravity trends; the sedimentary basin defined by the Lincoln Sea gravity low crosses the narrow EMSD ridge. At present, little correlation can be made between the EMSD contours and gravity data which may be an indication of the complex geologic nature of the shelf. On the other hand, the EMSD contours are calculated on the basis of a single direction of aeromagnetic flight lines that parallel the resultant contours. Several magnetic lineations that strike at right angles to the EMSD contours (Figs. 3 and 4) can be inferred from the residual magnetic anomaly profiles. In the absence of corroborative data, particularly seismic profiles, the geologic significance of the structures delimited by the EMSD analysis must remain speculative.

Two other features of the Lincoln Sea shelf may well be of fundamental geologic significance. These are the prominent lineaments formed by the outer coast of Nyeboe Land and Peary Land and the poorly known, more than 500-m-deep trough that lies parallel to the coast on the inner shelf (Fig. 2). These prominent structures may well have deep crustal control, perhaps reflecting the transition between continental and oceanic crust and/or the site of major dislocations.

The predicted composition of the thick sedimentary section of the Lincoln Sea shelf depends in many ways on the fundamental nature and tectonic history of Nares Strait (see later). McMillan (1982), for example, concluded that if the lineament represents the site of great continental displacement since Late Cretaceous time (~250 km), the predicted geology might be a thick Cretaceous-Cenozoic section (~6 km) overlying a basement of Palaeozoic and older continental crust that probably has been tectonically thinned. If movements along the strait have been minimal (0 to 50 km), a relatively stable shelf is envisaged, and the section might be similar to that onshore, overlying Precambrian granitic crust.

TECTONIC DEVELOPMENT

The three parts of the North Greenland margin show contrasting tectonic characteristics.

The Wandel Sea margin represents a relatively young, sheared continental margin developed in connection with the Spitsbergen Fracture Zone that separates the spreading axes of the Eurasia Basin and the Norwegian-Greenland Sea. According to magnetic anomaly interpretations, formation of oceanic crust commenced in the region at or before anomaly 24 time (52 Ma, early Eocene) and it is still continuing (Vogt and others, 1979, 1982; Srivastava, 1985). Consequently, the Spitsbergen Fracture Zone is seismically active. On Greenland, intraplate earthquake epicenters are concentrated around the Wandel Sea and along linear east-west fractures in Peary Land, such as the Harder Fjord fault zone (Dawes and Peel, 1981; Gregersen, 1982).

The Morris Jesup Plateau, in contrast to the Wandel Sea margin, is aseismic. It is generally assumed to have been generated in connection with the Yermak Plateau as a single oceanic plateau in the period between anomalies 18 and 13 (40–34 Ma, Late Eocene–Early Oligocene). Feden and others (1979) interpret the Morris Jesup Plateau as a product of basalt discharge at the Yermak hot spot. Pearce (1980) and Srivastava (1985) believe it formed at the triple junction of the North American–Greenland–European plates. Major transcurrent fractures as old as the Eurasia Basin itself must occur between the Morris Jesup Plateau and the inner shelf off Peary Land. These dislocations accommodated crustal movements due to spreading on the mid-ocean ridge (Fig. 1).

If the Morris Jesup Plateau is underlain either wholly or in part by continental crust, as is considered possible by this author, then a much more complex tectonic development of the region is required involving a major transform north of the plateau. It also requires another position for the southern segment of the Nansen Ridge in the early Tertiary. The resultant oceanic crust could lie below the western part of the plateau and/or underlie the deeper areas between the plateau and the Lomonosov Ridge. The existence of an early Tertiary transform north of the Morris Jesup Plateau—as well as north of the Yermak Plateau—is consistent with the lack of correlated magnetic anomalies between these marginal plateaus and the Amundsen and Nansen Basins.

The Lincoln Sea margin is the northern extension of the Nares Strait depression, and its geological makeup is tied up with the tectonic history of that lineament—at present a subject of much conjecture (see below). In addition, its development is also dependent on the relationship of the Lomonosov Ridge to the North American plate. Has the ridge occupied a fixed position relative to the Ellesmere Island margin, or has it moved with respect to the Greenland margin during the opening of the Eurasia Basin?

Depending on the tectonic status of Nares Strait, the late Phanerozoic development of the Lincoln Sea margin could have involved rather stable conditions, varying from epeirogenic downwarping of the crust with graben formation to transpressional wrench displacements and pull-apart basins. Conversely, inherent in most conventional plate tectonic models (e.g., Srivastava, 1985) is the idea that the strait represents a zone of continental convergence and collision. Such a scenario suggests that the Lincoln Sea margin has had a much more complex history that could have involved oceanic subduction, magmatic activity, and shortening of continental crust. However, this model gains no support from the available geologic data base. None of the magmatic, tectonic, or metamorphic processes that characterize collision zones are witnessed on land.

The Lincoln Sea shelf is seismically active (Fig. 3). Wetmiller and Forsyth (1982) discuss the record of several significant earthquakes on the shelf and regard the seismicity as related to the active zone of the Sverdrup Basin. Gregersen (1982) shows a concentration of epicenters on the inner shelf off western Peary Land that probably represents the western manifestation of the earthquake activity at the plate boundary in the Lena Trough. Nares Strait is conspicuously aseismic. The intraplate seismicity of the North Greenland margin is connected with a zone that trends oblique to Nares Strait; a clear indication that the present tectonism of the Lincoln Sea margin is not connected with the separation of Greenland and North America along a plate boundary in Nares Strait.

Regional tectonic history

The Phanerozoic stratigraphic record of the North Greenland margin preserves two, now tectonised, sedimentary basins. Inevitably, the early tectonic history deduced from this record and the resultant plate tectonic interpretations are very speculative. Ideas on the Cenozoic development of the margin, which are connected to the formation of the Eurasia Basin and the North Atlantic, are perhaps less speculative.

In early Palaeozoic time, the North Greenland margin was the site of a major east-west–trending sedimentary trough—the Franklinian Basin. Platform carbonates occur in the south and deep-water clastics border the present-day outer coast to the north. This continental margin shelf-basin couplet can be traced to the west across Ellesmere Island (Trettin, 1990). The basin was deformed in mid-Paleozoic (Devonian-Carboniferous) time by north-south compression during the Ellesmerian orogeny, after which the folded and metamorphic sequences were eroded and subsequently overlain with angular unconformity by the Carboniferous-Tertiary Wandel Sea Basin.

In contrast with Ellesmere Island, where perhaps the full width of the Franklinian Basin is preserved (Trettin and Balkwill, 1979), nothing is known about the nature of the northern margin of the basin in Greenland. Clearly this margin lay far to the north of the present Greenland coast and by analogy to Ellesmere Island the basin must have extended at least as far north as the present-day outer shelf. Magnetic data suggest that thick sediments do occur across the shelf (King and others, 1966; Ostenso and Wold, 1971).

The early Paleozoic continental margin strikes approximately east-west, parallel to the present-day margin. Surlyk and Hurst (1984) have suggested that basin evolution was controlled by a series of fault zones and flexures parallel to the ancient margin. The later stages of evolution are characterized by consistent longitudinal transport of detritus from the east, parallel to the margin, suggesting the presence of a restrictive barrier somewhere north of the present-day coast. This may have been an intrabasinal ridge or the opposing shelf area of a northern landmass. Speculations about the nature of this barrier are numerous; a volcanic or magmatic arc, on orogenic welt, a continental block or fragment, and even a mid-ocean spreading ridge, are all possibilities.

Evidence noted earlier suggests that the onshore part of the Franklinian Basin is ensialic. However, the presence of a Paleozoic ocean to the north of Greenland is inferred from the tectonic style of the North Greenland fold belt. The conspicuous northerly overturning of structures seen in the northernmost exposures on Greenland is directed away from the undeformed platform terrain to the south and could be due to structural interaction with ocean floor to the north. Such oceanic crust may have been part of a fairly narrow ocean—for example, a westerly extension of Iapetus—or part of a more extensive proto–Arctic Ocean. One can but speculate as to whether such an ocean completely closed during the Paleozoic. In any case, in late Paleozoic and Mesozoic time the North Greenland and Barents Sea margins were closely associated (Christie, 1979; Håkansson and Pedersen, 1982). Håkansson and Stemmerik (1984) conclude that from Carboniferous time these margins were part of an extensive continental platform that shows a long history of faulting and tectonically controlled transgressions. In the late Mesozoic this platform was split by major wrench dislocations.

In the Cenozoic, Greenland holds a central position in the development of the North Atlantic–Arctic Ocean system. In most plate tectonic models it moved as a separate plate relative to North America and Europe at some time during the Tertiary. Thus the North Greenland margin would appear to have had a complex history having undergone displacements with respect to both adjacent continental blocks. Distribution of earthquake epicenters (Gregersen, 1982; Wetmiller and Forsyth, 1982) indicates that parts of the North Greenland margin are still tectonically active (Fig. 3).

The youngest strata of the Wandel Sea Basin are of Paleocene age; outcrops are isolated and small, and structural data are sparce (Håkansson, 1979, Håkansson and others, 1981). Consequently, details about the extent, nature, and timing of Cenozoic (Eurekan) tectonism in northern Greenland are uncertain. Håkansson and Pedersen (1982) and Birkelund and Håkansson (1983) speculate on the *apparent* lack of post-Cretaceous compressional events in northern Greenland and refer the main structural elements to a Late Cretaceous–Paleocene transpression period. On the other hand Friderichsen and Bengaard (1985) recognize three phases of Eurekan deformation in northernmost Peary Land, including a period of northerly directed Tertiary thrusting that produced the Kap Cannon thrust (Fig. 3).

Soper and others (1982) have summarized the main late Phanerozoic magmatic and tectonic features and attempted explanation in a plate tectonic framework (Fig. 7). Hence, the Late Cretaceous alkaline dykes and peralkaline Kap Washington volcanics are regarded as products of extensional continental magmatism prior to the opening of the Eurasia Basin; the northerly directed thrusting of the margin is regarded as a consequence of the anticlockwise rotation of Greenland in response to sea-floor spreading in the Labrador Sea; the prominent northwest-southeast structures of the Wandel Sea Basin are related to transpressional and extensional (pull-apart) tectonics in connection with large-scale transform shearing between the Wandel Sea and Barents Sea margins. Major uplift is envisaged in Neogene time, with substantial normal displacement (>2 km) on the east-west–trending Harder Fjord fault zone.

Håkansson and Pedersen (1982) have questioned the precise age and timing of some of these events. These authors stress the importance of strike-slip fault systems in the development of the North Greenland margin, and the reader is referred to their work for a highly mobilistic model involving a series of substantial dextral and sinistral movements centered on the Harder Fjord fault zone. These movements include the transport of crustal blocks several hundred kilometers between Peary Land and northern Ellesmere Island. In contrast, Higgins and others (1981) report that no major wrench displacements have taken place along on the Harder Fjord fault zone. Field analysis indicates a maximum of 20 km dextral strike-slip (? Tertiary) on the main fault plane (Friderichsen and Bengaard, 1985; Higgins, 1986).

Nares Strait

Nares Strait is a conspicuous physiographic linear trench, stretching more than 600 km from Baffin Bay to the Lincoln Sea. An obvious tectonic lineament (Fig. 8), it plays a major role in continental drift appraisals of the Arctic. Yet its tectonic character remains the subject of controversy. Is it the site of great sinistral wrench displacement along which Greenland moved 250 km or so relative to North America, or has movement between northern Greenland and Ellesmere Island been of much lesser magnitude, to be measured in tens rather than hundreds of kilometres? Nares Strait is a key to the predrift position of Greenland.

The controversy stems from opposing interpretations: those derived from the onshore geology of the actual strait region versus those derived from plate motions as predicted by conventional plate tectonic theory applied to the surrounding oceans. In 1980 a symposium was directed to the Nares Strait controversy that dealt with many aspects of the onshore and offshore geology and geophysics of the region (Dawes and Kerr, 1982). This symposium and its proceedings have stimulated a reassessment of the problem. Thus, several papers have discussed and reinterpreted selected geologic and geophysical data sets (e.g., Rice and Shade, 1982; Hugon, 1983; Hamilton, 1983; Miall, 1983, 1984; Srivastava, 1985; Jackson, 1985) while others reported new field data (e.g., Wynne and others, 1983; Hood and others, 1985; Jackson and Koppen, 1985; Jackson, 1986). However, the apparent impasse remains. Thus, in plate-tectonic reconstructions, the predrift position of Greenland relative to North America continues to be achieved by restoring substantial left-slip displacement along Nares Strait, more often than not involving a much wider strait than at present (e.g., Jackson and others, 1984; Srivastava, 1985; Srivastava and Tapscott, 1986). In contrast, recent onshore geological field programs, including the comprehensive mapping project in Greenland adjacent to the Lincoln Sea (Dawes, 1984; Henriksen, 1985, 1986; GGU, 1985, 1987), have strengthened the view that northern Greenland and Ellesmere Island have developed as proximal parts of the same crustal block.

There is a tendency to regard Nares Strait as a young transcurrent fault initiated in late Mesozoic–Cenozoic time in connection with the opening of the surrounding oceans. However, some geologic data suggest that some sort of tectonic boundary was situated in the Nares Strait region as early as the Paleozoic (Dawes, 1973; Surlyk, 1982). Like many ancient structural lineaments, the strait may have been the site of repeated tectonic movements. Thus, part of the answer to the enigma may be that Nares Strait represents a tectonic zone along which both dextral and sinistral displacements have occurred. As Christie (1979, p. 284) concludes, "(T)he net movement may thus be incidental rather than a measure of the importance of the zone." However, the land geology indicates that the strait is not the site of all the motion required by conventional plate tectonic models that portray Nares Strait as a zone of oceanic subduction and continental collision. Other lineaments in the Arctic region must have taken up some of the motion traditionally reserved for Nares Strait.

SUMMARY, CONCLUSIONS, FUTURE RESEARCH

The three physiographic-geologic provinces of the North Greenland margin have yet to be investigated in detail. The high magnetic character of the Morris Jesup Plateau—the central aseismic province—is generally thought to represent oceanic basalt discharged during the opening of the Eurasia Basin. However, continental rocks probably form the inner shelf and underlie parts of the plateau. The plateau separates two seismically active provinces. To the east lies the Wandel Sea margin, a narrow, sheared continental margin developed in connection with the Greenland-Barents plate boundary. To the west is the Lincoln Sea margin, a wide, downwarped and faulted region whose depositional regime is connected with that of Nares Strait. Present-day intraplate seismicity occurs in an east-west zone along the North Greenland margin, indicating that recent tectonism is connected to plate boundaries in the Eurasia Basin rather than to interaction of the North American and Greenland plates along Nares Strait.

Gravity data from the Lincoln Sea suggest that the North Greenland margin is underlain by thinned continental crust. The continent-ocean boundary may approximately coincide, in the Lincoln Sea and Wandel Sea, with the continental slope and, off Peary Land, with the inner shelf. However, two important un-

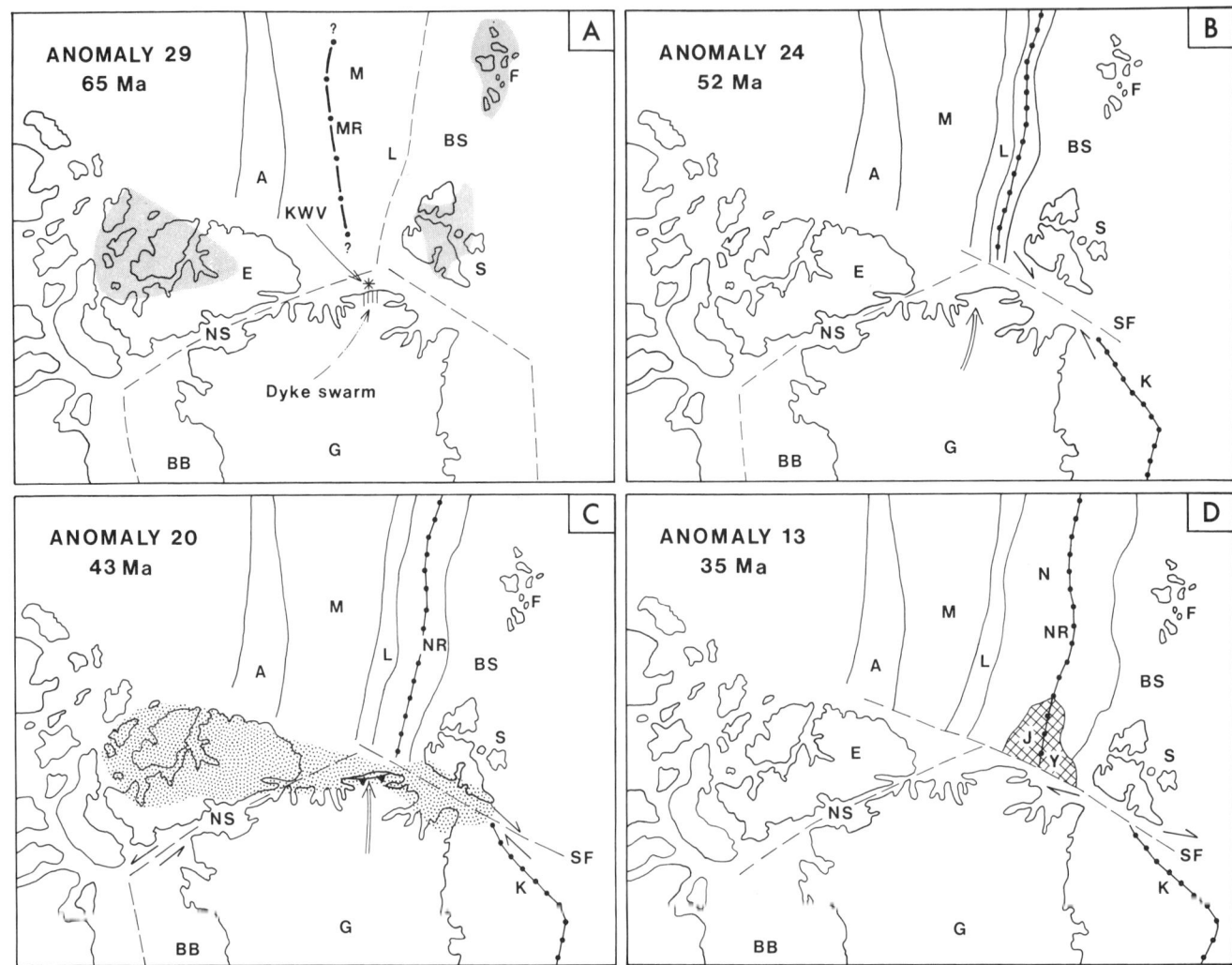

Figure 7. A suggested Cenozoic tectonic history of the North Greenland margin seen in relation to the eastern Canadian Arctic and the Barents Shelf (from Soper and others, 1982). Fracture zones are shown dashed, active-spreading axes are dotted, dot-dash line represents a possible extinct spreading axis, and plate movement direction is shown by single arrows. The fit of northern Greenland and the Barents Shelf approximately follows Phillips and others (1978); fit of Greenland and Ellesmere Island approximately after Le Pichon and others (1977). G, Greenland; E, Ellesmere Island; S, Svalbard; F, Franz Josef Land; BS, Barents Shelf; A, Alpha Ridge; MR, Makarov Ridge; L, Lomonosov Ridge; NR, Nansen (Gakkel) Ridge; K, Knipovitch Ridge; BB, Baffin Bay; M, Makarov Basin; N, Nansen Basin; SF, Spitsbergen Fracture Zone; NS, Nares Strait lineament. A. Reconstruction at anomaly 29 time (Cretaceous-Tertiary boundary) showing main Mesozoic magmatic events; KWV, Kap Washington volcanics (75 to 65 Ma); shaded areas represent mainly basaltic magmatism (Jurassic-Cretaceous). B. Reconstruction at anomaly 24 time (early Eocene). The double arrow represents the inferred compression direction in North Greenland. C. Reconstruction at anomaly 20 time (middle Eocene) showing minor inferred strike-slip displacement along Nares Strait, the Kap Cannon thrust, and the areas affected by the Eurekan orogeny in Canada and Greenland and the West Spitsbergen–Wandel Sea orogenic zone (shaded). D. Reconstruction at anomaly 13 time (early Oligocene). Sea-floor spreading ceases between Greenland and North America. Arrows on Spitsbergen Fracture Zone indicate the inferred extensional displacement. Cross-hatched areas: J, Morris Jesup Plateau; Y, Yermak Plateau.

Figure 8. The Robeson Channel—the northern stretch of Nares Strait—viewed northeastward along the Greenland coast. The steep coastal cliffs suggest fault control, that is, the so-called Wegener fault. Is this the site of great sinistral movement in the Tertiary by which Greenland was displaced 200 to 300 km past Ellesmere Island? This question holds a central place in plate reconstructions of the Arctic region. The hypothesis of great displacement gains no support from the onshore geology of the bordering lands. Photograph T401 L-26 by courtesy of the National Air Photo Library, Canada.

solved factors are (1) the nature of fracture zone(s) along the margin associated with the Spitsbergen Fracture Zone and oceanic accretion in the Lena Trough and Eurasia Basin, and (2) the significance of the pronounced linear trough that occurs along the Greenland coast east of Nares Strait. Such lineaments could reflect significant breaks in crustal structure, separating the continental block of Greenland from the mixed continental-oceanic area of the Arctic Ocean.

A main conclusion must be that the North Greenland margin is both bathymetrically and geologically a relatively poorly known part of the Arctic region. No rocks are available from the shelf and slope, and seaward extrapolation of the well-known land geology is based on limited geophysical information. Apart from low-level aeromagnetic data over the shelf and slope, geophysical data have an irregular distribution. Consequently, the crustal structure of the offshore region is conjectural.

An urgent requirement is the geologic mapping of the shelf area. The Lincoln Sea shelf inferred to overlie a thick sedimentary section, may be a potential petroleum province, and is a principal target area for research. Apart from the very limited data over the Morris Jesup Plateau, no seismic reflection profiles are available across the North Greenland margin. Thus, essential research involves a regional seismic reflection survey coupled with new aeromagnetic data flown normal to the existing coverage, which consists of lines that are more or less parallel to regional geological trends. These and other geophysical disciplines, as well as drilling or dredging programs, should be coordinated with the land geology. Only when such basic geologic and geophysical data are available from the offshore, and fully integrated with the land geology, will it be possible to meaningfully relate the North Greenland margin to the surrounding continental and oceanic regions.

REFERENCES

Batten, D. J., Brown, P. E., Dawes, P. R., Higgins, A. K., Koch, B. E., Parsons, I., and Soper, N. J., 1981, Peralkaline volcanicity of the Eurasia Basin margin: Nature, v. 294, p. 150–152.

Birkelund, T., and Håkansson, E., 1983, The Cretaceous of North Greenland; A stratigraphic and biogeographical analysis: Zitteliana, v. 10, p. 7–25.

Birkenmajer, K., 1972, Tertiary history of Spitsbergen and continental drift: Acta Geologica Polonica, v. 22, p. 193–218.

Bowin, C., Warsi, W., and Milligan, J., 1981, Free-air gravity anomaly map of the world: Geological Society of America Map of Chart Series MC-45, scale 1:22,000,000.

Brown, P. E., and Parsons, I., 1981, The Kap Washington Group volcanics: Grønlands Geologiske Undersøgelse, Rapport no. 106, p. 65–68.

Christie, R. L., 1979, The Franklinian Geosyncline in the Canadian Arctic and its relationship to Svalbard: Norsk Polarinstitutt, Skrifter no. 167, p. 263–314.

Coles, R. L., Haines, G. V., and Hannaford, W., 1976, Large scale magnetic anomalies over western Canada and the Arctic; A discussion: Canadian Journal of Earth Sciences, v. 13, p. 790–802.

Coles, R. L., Hannaford, W., and Haines, G. V., 1978, Magnetic anomalies and the evolution of the Arctic, in Sweeney, J. F., ed., Arctic geophysical review: Publication of the Earth Physics Branch, v. 45, no. 4, p. 51–66.

Dawes, P. R., 1973, The North Greenland fold belt; A clue to the history of the Arctic Ocean Basin and the Nares Strait lineament, in Tarling, D. H., and Runcorn, S. K., eds., Implications of continental drift to the earth sciences, v. 2: London, Academic Press, p. 925–947.

——, 1982, The Nyeboe Land fault zone; A major dislocation on the Greenland coast along northern Nares Strait, in Dawes, P. R., and Kerr, J. W., eds., Nares Strait and the drift of Greenland; A conflict in plate tectonics: Meddelelser om Grønland, Geoscience, no. 8, p. 177–192.

——, 1984, Programme NordGrøn (PNG) 1983–1985; Regional mapping and geological studies in western and central North Greenland: Grønlands Geologiske Undersøgelse, Rapport no. 120, p. 18–24.

——, 1986, The Nares Strait gravity anomaly and its implications for crustal structure; Discussion: Canadian Journal of Earth Sciences, v. 22, p. 2077–2081.

Dawes, P. R., and Kerr, J. W., eds., 1982, Nares Strait and the drift of Greenland; A conflict in plate tectonics: Meddelelser om Grønland, Geoscience no. 8, 392 p.

Dawes, P. R., and Peel, J. S., 1981, The northern margin of Greenland from Baffin Bay to the Greenland Sea, in Nairn, A.E.M., Churkin, M., and Stehli, F. G., eds., The ocean basins and margins; v. 5, The Arctic Ocean: New York and London, Plenum Press, p. 201–264.

Dawes, P. R., and Soper, N. J., 1973, Pre-Quaternary history of North Greenland, in Pitcher, M. G., ed., Arctic geology: American Association of Petroleum Geologists Memoir 19, p. 117–134.

Dawes, P. R., Rex, D. C., and Soper, N. J., 1983, Routine K/Ar age determinations on post-Silurian dolerite dykes, North Greenland fold belt: Grønlands Geologiske Undersøgelse, Rapport no. 115, p. 9–114.

Duckworth, G. L., Baggeroer, A. B., and Jackson, H. R., 1982, Crustal structure measurements near Fram II in the Pole abyssal plain, in Johnson, G. L., and Sweeney, J. F., eds., Structure of the Arctic: Tectonophysics, v. 89, p. 173–215.

Eldholm, O., Sundvor, E., and Crane, K., 1984, Sonobuoy measurements during the "Ymer" Expedition: Norsk Polarinstitutt, Skrifter no. 180, p. 17–23.

Feden, R. H., Vogt, P. R., and Fleming, H. S., 1979, Magnetic and bathymetric evidence for the "Yermak hot spot" northwest of Svalbard in the Arctic Basin: Earth and Planetary Science Letters, v. 44, p. 18–38.

Fletcher, J. O., 1968, Origin and early utilization of aircraft-supported drifting stations, in Sater, J. E., coord., Arctic drifting stations: Washington, D.C., The Arctic Institute of North America, p. 1–13.

Friderichsen, J. D., and Bengaard, H.-J., 1985, The North Greenland fold belt in eastern Nansen Land: Grønlands Geologiske Undersøgelse, Rapport no. 126, p. 69–78.

Forsberg, R., 1979, A gravity map of Peary Land, North Greenland: Grønlands Geologiske Undersøgelse, Rapport no. 88, p. 93–94.

——, 1981, Preliminary Bouguer anomalies of North-East Greenland: Grønlands Geologiske Undersøgelse, Rapport no. 106, p. 105–107.

Gregersen, S., 1982, Earthquakes in Greenland: Geological Society of Denmark Bulletin, v. 31, p. 11–27.

GGU, 1985, Report on the 1984 geological expedition to central and western North Greenland: Grønlands Geologiske Undersøgelse, Rapport no. 126, 128 p.

——, 1987, Report on the 1985 geological expedition to central and western North Greenland: Grønlands Geologiske Undersøgelse, Rapport no. 133, 168 p.

Haines, G. V., Hannaford, W., and Serson, P. H., 1970, Magnetic anomaly maps of the Nordic countries and the Greenland and Norwegian seas: Publications Dominion Observatory Ottawa, v. 39, no. 5, p. 119–149.

Hamilton, W., 1983, Cretaceous and Cenozoic history of the northern continents: Annals of Missouri Botanical Gardens, v. 70, p. 440–458.

Harland, W. B., 1965, Tectonic evolution of the Arctic–North Atlantic region: Philosophical Transactions of the Royal Society of London, v. 258, p. 59–75.

——, 1969, Contributions of Spitsbergen to understanding of tectonic evolution of North Atlantic region, *in* Kay, M., ed., North Atlantic; Geology and continental drift: American Association of Petroleum Geologists Memoir 12, p. 817–851.

Heezen, B. C., and Tharp, M., 1975, Map of the Arctic region (bathymetry): Washington, D.C., American Geographical Society, scale 1:5,000,000.

Henderson, G., 1976, Petroleum geology, *in* Escher, A., and Watt, W. S., eds., Geology of Greenland: Copenhagen, Geological Society of Greenland, p. 180–246.

Henriksen, N., 1985, Systematic 1:500,000 mapping and regional geological studies in central and western North Greenland: Grønlands Geologiske Undersøgelse, Rapport no. 125, p. 9–17.

——, 1986, Completion of field work for the 1:500,000 mapping and regional geological studies in central and western North Greenland: Grønlands Geologiske Undersøgelse, Rapport no. 130, p. 9–17.

Higgins, A. K., 1986, Geology of central and eastern North Greenland: Grønlands Geologiske Undersøgelse, Rapport no. 128, p. 37–54.

Higgins, A. K., Friderichsen, J. D., and Soper, N. J., 1981, The North Greenland fold belt between central Johannes V. Jensen Land and eastern Nansen Land: Grønlands Geologiske Undersøgelse, Rapport no. 106, p. 35–45.

Higgins, A. K., Soper, N. J., and Friderichsen, J. D., 1985, North Greenland fold belt in eastern North Greenland, *in* Gee, D. G., and Sturt, B. A., eds., The Caledonide Orogen; Part 2, Scandinavia and related areas: New York, John Wiley and Sons, p. 1017–1029.

Hood, P. J., Bower, M. E., Hardwick, C. D., and Teskey, D. J., 1985, Direct geophysical evidence for displacement along Nares Strait (Canada-Greenland) from low-level aeromagnetic data; A progress report, *in* Current research, part A: Geological Survey of Canada Paper 85-1A, p. 517–522.

Hugon, H., 1983, Ellesmere-Greenland fold belt; Structural evidence for left-lateral shearing, *in* Friedman, M., and Toksöz, M. N., eds., Continental tectonics; Structure, kinematics, and dynamics: Tectonophysics, v. 100, p. 215–225.

Håkansson, 1979, Carboniferous to Tertiary development of the Wandel Sea Basin, eastern North Greenland: Grølands Geologiske Undersøgelse, Rapport no. 88, p. 73–83.

Håkansson, E., and Pedersen, S.A.S., 1982, Late Paleozoic to Tertiary tectonic evolution of the continental margin in North Greenland, *in* Embry, A. F., and Balkwill, H. R., eds., Arctic geology and geophysics: Canadian Society of Petroleum Geologists Memoir 8, p. 331–348.

Håkansson, E., and Stemmerik, L., 1984, The North Greenland equivalent to Svalbard and the Barents Shelf, *in* The Norwegian Petroleum Society, ed., Petroleum geology of the North European Margin: London, Graham and Trotman, p. 97–107.

Håkansson, E., Heinberg, C., and Stemmerik, L., 1981, The Wandel Sea Basin from Holm Land to Lockwood Ø, eastern North Greenland: Grønlands Geologiske Undersøgelse, Rapport no. 106, p. 47–63.

Jackson, G. D., 1986, Notes on the Proterozoic Thule Group, northern Baffin Bay: Geological Survey of Canada Paper 86-1A, p. 541–552.

Jackson, H. R., 1985, Nares Strait; A suture zone; Geophysical and geological implications, *in* Husebye, E. S., Johnson, G. L., and Kristoffersen, Y., eds., Geophysics of the Polar regions: Tectonophysics, v. 114, p. 11–28.

Jackson, H. R., and Koppen, L., 1985, The Nares Strait gravity anomaly and its implications for crustal structure: Canadian Journal of Earth Sciences, v. 66, p. 1322–1328.

Jackson, H. R., Johnson, G. L., Sundvor, E., and Myhre, A. M., 1984, The Yermak Plateau; Formed at a triple junction: Journal of Geophysical Research, v. 89, p. 3223–3232.

Johnson, G. L., Monahan, D., Grønlie, G., and Sobczak, L. (W.), 1979, General bathymetric chart of the oceans (GEBCO), The Arctic Ocean: Ottawa, Canadian Hydrographic Service, scale 1:6,000,000, sheet 5.17.

Kellogg, H. E., 1975, Tertiary stratigraphy and tectonism in Svalbard and continental drift: American Association of Petroleum Geologists Bulletin, v. 59, p. 465–585.

King, E. R., Zietz, I., and Alldredge, L. R., 1966, Magnetic data on the structure of the Central Arctic Region: Geological Society of America Bulletin, v. 77, p. 619–646.

Kovacs, L. C., 1982, Motion along Nares Strait recorded in the Lincoln Sea; Aeromagnetic evidence, *in* Dawes, P. R., and Kerr, J. W., eds., Nares Strait and the drift of Greenland; A conflict in plate tectonics: Meddelelser om Grønland, Geoscience no. 8, p. 275–290.

Kovacs, L. C., and Vogt, P. R., 1982, Depth-to-magnetic source analysis of the Arctic Ocean region, *in* Johnson, G. L., and Sweeney, J. F., eds., Structure of the Arctic: Tectonophysics, v. 89, p. 255–294.

Kovacs, L. C., Bernero, C., Johnson, G. L., Pilger, R. H., Taylor, P. T., and Vogt, P. R., undated, Residual magnetic anomaly chart of the Arctic Ocean region: Washington, D.C., Naval Research Laboratory and Naval Ocean Research and Development Activities, scale 1:6,000,000.

Kravitz, J. H., 1976, Textural and mineralogical characteristics of the surficial sediments of Kane Basin: Journal of Sedimentary Petrology, v. 46, p. 710–725.

Larsen, H. C., 1984, Geology of the East Greenland Shelf, *in* The Norwegian Petroleum Society, ed., Petroleum geology of the North European Margin: London, Graham and Trotman, p. 329–339.

Le Pichon, X., Sibuet, J.-C., and Francheteau, J., 1977, The fit of the continents around the North Atlantic Ocean: Tectonophysics, v. 38, p. 169–209.

Lowell, J. D., 1972, Spitsbergen Tertiary orogenic belt and the Spitsbergen Fracture Zone: Geological Society of America Bulletin, v. 83, p. 3091–3102.

McMillan, N. J., 1982, Nares Strait and the petroleum explorer, *in* Dawes, P. R., and Kerr, J. W., eds., Nares Strait and the drift of Greenland; A conflict in plate tectonics: Meddelelser om Grønland, Geoscience no. 8, p. 355–361.

Miall, A. D., 1983, The Nares Strait problem; A re-evaluation of some geological evidence in terms of a diffuse oblique-slip plate boundary between Greenland and the Canadian Arctic Islands, *in* Friedman, M., and Toksöz, M. N., eds., Continental tectonics; Structure, kinematics, and dynamics: Tectonophysics, v. 107, p. 227–239.

——, 1984, Sedimentation and tectonics of a diffuse plate boundary; The Canadian Arctic Islands from 80 Ma B.P. to the present: Tectonophysics, v. 107, p. 261–277.

Ostenso, N. A., 1962, Geophysical investigations of the Arctic Ocean Basin: University of Wisconsin, Geophysics and Polar Research Center Report 62-4, 124 p.

Ostenso, N. A., and Pew, J. A., 1968, Sub-bottom seismic profile off the east coast of Greenland, *in* Sater, J. E., coord., Arctic drifting stations: Washington, D.C., The Arctic Institute of North America, p. 345–363.

Ostenso, N. A., and Wold, R. J., 1971, Aeromagnetic survey of the Arctic Ocean; Techniques and interpretations: Marine Geophysical Research, v. 1, p. 178–219.

——, 1977, A seismic and gravity profile across the Arctic Ocean Basin: Tectonophysics, v. 37, p. 1–24.

Parsons, I., 1981, Volcanic centres between Frigg Fjord and Midtkap, eastern North Greenland: Grønlands Geologiske Undersøgelse, Rapport no. 106, p. 69–75.

Pearce, J. W., 1980, The Nares-Nansen triple junction: EOS Transactions of the American Geophysical Union, v. 61, p. 357.

Phillips, J. D., Feden, R. H., Fleming, H. S., and Tapscott, C. R., 1978, Aeromagnetic studies of the Greenland/Norwegian Sea and Arctic Ocean: Unpublished manuscript, 64 p.

Rice, P. D., and Shade, B. D., 1982, Reflection seismic interpretation and seafloor spreading history of Baffin Bay, *in* Embry, A. F., and Balkwill, H. R., eds., Arctic geology and geophysics: Canadian Society of Petroleum Geologists Memoir 8, p. 245–265.

Riddihough, R. P., Haines, G. V., and Hannaford, W., 1973, Regional magnetic anomalies of the Canadian Arctic: Canadian Journal of Earth Sciences, v. 10, p. 157–163.

Schytt, V., Bostrøm, K., and Hjort, C., 1981, Geoscience during the Ymer-80 expedition to the Arctic: Geologiske Föreningens i Stockholm Förhandlingar, v. 103, p. 109–119.

Sobczak, L. W., 1975, Gravity anomalies and passive continental margins, Canada and Norway, in Yorath, C. J., Parker, E. R., and Glass, D. J., eds., Canada's continental margins and offshore petroleum exploration: Canadian Society of Petroleum Geologists Memoir 4, p. 743–761.

—— , 1978, Gravity from 60°N to the North Pole, in Sweeney, J. F., ed., Arctic geophysical review: Publications of the Earth Physics Branch, v. 45, no. 4, p. 67–73.

Sobczak, L. W., and Stephens, L. E., 1974, The gravity field of northeastern Ellesmere Island, part of northern Greenland and Lincoln Sea: Earth Physics Branch, Gravity Map Series, no. 114, 9 p.

Sobczak, L. W., and Weber, J. R., 1972, Deep structure and geophysical characteristics, in Price, R. A., and Douglas, R.J.W., eds., The Innuitian Province, section in Variations in tectonic styles in Canada: Geological Association of Canada Special Paper 11, p. 149–157.

Soper, N. J., Higgins, A. K., and Friderichsen, J. D., 1980, The North Greenland fold belt in eastern Johannes V. Jensen Land: Grønlands Geologiske Undersøgelse, Rapport no. 99, p. 89–98.

Soper, N. J., Dawes, P. R., and Higgins, A. K., 1982, Cretaceous-Tertiary magmatic and tectonic events in North Greenland and the history of adjacent ocean basins, in Dawes, P. R., and Kerr, J. W., eds., Nares Strait and the drift of Greenland; A conflict in plate tectonics: Meddelelser om Grønland, Geoscience no. 8, p. 205–220.

Srivastava, S. P., 1985, Evolution of the Eurasian Basin and its implications to the motion of Greenland along Nares Strait, in Husebye, E. S., Johnson, G. L., and Kristoffersen, Y., eds., Geophysics of the Polar regions: Tectonophysics, v. 114, p. 29–53.

Srivastava, S. P., and Tapscott, C. R., 1986, Plate kinematics in the North Atlantic, in Vogt, P. R., and Tucholke, B. E., eds., The Western North Atlantic Region: Boulder, Colorado, Geological Society of America, The Geology of North America, V. M, p. 379–404.

Surlyk, F., 1982, Nares Strait and the down-current termination of the Silurian turbidite basin of North Greenland, in Dawes, P. R., and Kerr, J. W., eds., Nares Strait and the drift of Greeland; A conflict in plate tectonics: Meddelelser om Grønland, Geoscience no. 8, p. 147–150.

Surlyk, F., and Hurst, J. M., 1984, The evolution of the early Paleozoic deep-water basin of North Greenland: Geological Society of America Bulletin, v. 95, p. 131–154.

Trettin, H. P., ed., 1990, The Innuitian region: Ottawa, Ontario, Geological Survey of Canada, The Geology of North America, v. E (in press).

Trettin, H. P., and Balkwill, H. R., 1979, Contributions to the tectonic history of the Innuition Province, Arctic Canada: Canadian Journal of Earth Sciences, v. 16, p. 748–769.

Vogt, P. R., Feden, R. H., Eldholm, O., and Sundvor, E., 1978, The ocean crust west and north of the Svalbard Archipelago; Synthesis and review of new results: Polarforschung, v. 48, p. 1–19.

Vogt, P. R., Taylor, P. T., Kovacs, L. C., and Johnson, G. L., 1979, Detailed aeromagnetic investigation of the Arctic Basin: Journal of Geophysical Research, v. 84, p. 903–920.

—— , 1982, The Canada Basin; Aeromagnetic constraints on structure and evolution, in Johnson, G. L., and Sweeney, J. F., eds., Structure of the Arctic: Tectonophysics, v. 89, p. 295–336.

Weng, W. L., 1980, Preliminary Bouguer anomalies of western North Greenland: Grønlands Geologiske Undersøgelse, Rapport no. 99, p. 152–154.

Wetmiller, R. J., and Forsyth, D. A., 1982, Review of seismicity and other geophysical data near Nares Strait, in Dawes, P. R., and Kerr, J. W., eds., Nares Strait and the drift of Greenland; A conflict in plate tectonics: Meddelelser om Grønland, Geoscience no. 8, p. 261–274.

Wynne, P. J., Irving, E., and Osadetz, K., 1983, Paleomagnetism of the Esayoo Formation (Permian) of northern Ellesmere Island; Possible clue to the solution of the Nares Strait dilemma, in Friedman, M., and Toksöz, M. N., eds., Continental tectonics; Structure, kinematics, and dynamics: Tectonophysics, v. 100, p. 241–256.

MANUSCRIPT ACCEPTED BY THE SOCIETY FEBRUARY 3, 1987

ACKNOWLEDGMENTS

I am grateful to Anthony K. Higgins, Hans Christian Larsen (Geological Survey of Greenland), and Arthur Grantz (U.S. Geological Survey) for critical reading of the manuscript; J. Wm. Kerr (Consultant Geologist, Calgary) and H. R. Jackson (Bedford Institute of Oceanography) acted as "external" referees. All provided suggestions for improvement of the paper. The aerial photograph used in Figure 8 is reproduced by courtesy of the National Air Photo Library, Ottawa, Canada. Jacob Lautrup and Bente Thomas carried out the technical preparation of the figures; Esben Glendal and Bodil Skall-Jensen typed various drafts of the text. The paper is published with permission of the Director of the Geological Survey of Greenland, Copenhagen, Denmark.

OVER DIFFICULT PRESSURE-MOUNDS, APRIL, 1895
(By A. Eiebakke, from a photograph)

From Fridtjof Nansen, 1900, Farthest North (Popular Edition): New York and London, Harper Brothers, facing p. 386.

Printed in U.S.A.

Chapter 14

The continental margin northwest of the Queen Elizabeth Islands

J. F. Sweeney
Geological Survey of Canada, 100 W. Pender St., Vancouver, British Columbia V6B 1R8, Canada
L. W. Sobczak and D. A. Forsyth
Geological Survey of Canada, 1 Observatory Crescent, Ottawa, Ontario K1A 0Y3, Canada

INTRODUCTION

The polar continental margin described here lies between M'Clure Strait and the Lincoln Sea (Fig. 1). It clearly separates continental sequences of the Queen Elizabeth Islands from presumed oceanic crust beneath the deep Canada Basin and, near Axel Heiberg and Ellesmere Islands, from rocks of the submarine Alpha and Lomonosov Ridges.

Systematic studies in the region began in the late 1940s with Soviet air-lifted spot soundings over the outer continental slope and rise. In the 1950s and 1960s, the Alpha Ridge and adjacent parts of the outer continental shelf and slope were identified by multiparameter measurements from a series of drifting U.S. ice stations. In Canada, onshore geological studies began in 1955, and reconnaissance investigations of the polar shelf and slope were underway by 1960. The reader is referred to Weber (1983) and Weber and Roots (this volume) for further details of early studies.

Comprehensive reviews that include onshore geology adjacent to the polar margin begin with Fortier and others (1963) with later syntheses by Thorsteinsson and Tozer (1970), Trettin and others (1972), Trettin and Balkwill (1979), Hea and others (1980), Miall (1981), and Kerr (1981). Offshore, chiefly geophysical data over the polar shelf and slope are summarized by Trettin and others (1972), Sweeney and others (1978), Vogt and others (1982), Sweeney (1982), and Forsyth and others (1988).

From the information available up to the early 1980s, it was considered that the polar margin formed when the Canada Basin opened in Jurassic or Early Cretaceous time, that the crust thins substantially from the Queen Elizabeth Islands into the Canada Basin and that below the shelf, crystalline, presumably Precambrian, continental crust is present and is overlain by up to 13 km of Phanerozoic strata. Thick sediment loads, particularly prograded latest Cretaceous and younger clastic wedge deposits, were identified as the main sources of contemporary seismic activity, gravity anomaly highs, and magnetic anomaly lows along the polar shelf and slope. This chapter presents an assessment of polar margin structure and development, including the zone north of Ellesmere Island adjacent to the Alpha and Lomonosov Ridges, that places its formation in the late Early Cretaceous to early Late Cretaceous and suggests that significant lateral changes in physical properties and structures are present along the polar margin in Canada.

REGIONAL GEOLOGY AND HISTORY

Geological knowledge of the polar margin northwest of the Queen Elizabeth Islands is inferred by correlating known stratigraphy from boreholes and outcrops onshore with seismic horizons and potential field data from both onshore and offshore (Fig. 1).

Although the existence of Precambrian rocks is unconfirmed below the polar shelf, a complex assemblage of Proterozoic to Upper Silurian units, the Pearya terrane (Trettin, 1987), occupies northernmost Ellesmere Island and presumably extends below the adjoining continental shelf. Phanerozoic stratigraphy of the shelf southwest from Axel Heiberg Island is divided into three main sequences: Devonian and older Paleozoic rocks related to the Franklinian Basin; Early Carboniferous to Late Cretaceous sediments associated with the Sverdrup Basin; and Maastrichtian to Holocene clastics of the Arctic Terrace Wedge (Fig. 1; Meneley and others, 1975; Miall, 1981; Balkwill and others, 1983).

Trettin (1987) defines the Pearya terrane as an amalgam of four largely shallow marine successions that may have been derived from the Caledonide orogen near Svalbard. These successions were transported along sinistral shears to Ellesmere Island where they were sutured to Franklinian rocks in Late Silurian time (Trettin, 1987; Fig. 1). Suturing was accompanied by major compressional deformation, including southwest-directed thrusting, and by granitic plutonism (Trettin and others, 1987).

Both the Sverdrup Basin and Arctic Terrace Wedge sequences could overlie Pearya rocks offshore northwest of Axel

Sweeney, J. F., Sobczak, L. W., and Forsyth, D. A., 1990, The continental margin northwest of the Queen Elizabeth Islands, *in* Grantz, A., Johnson, L., and Sweeney, J. F., eds., The Arctic Ocean region: Boulder, Colorado, Geological Society of America, The Geology of North America, v. L.

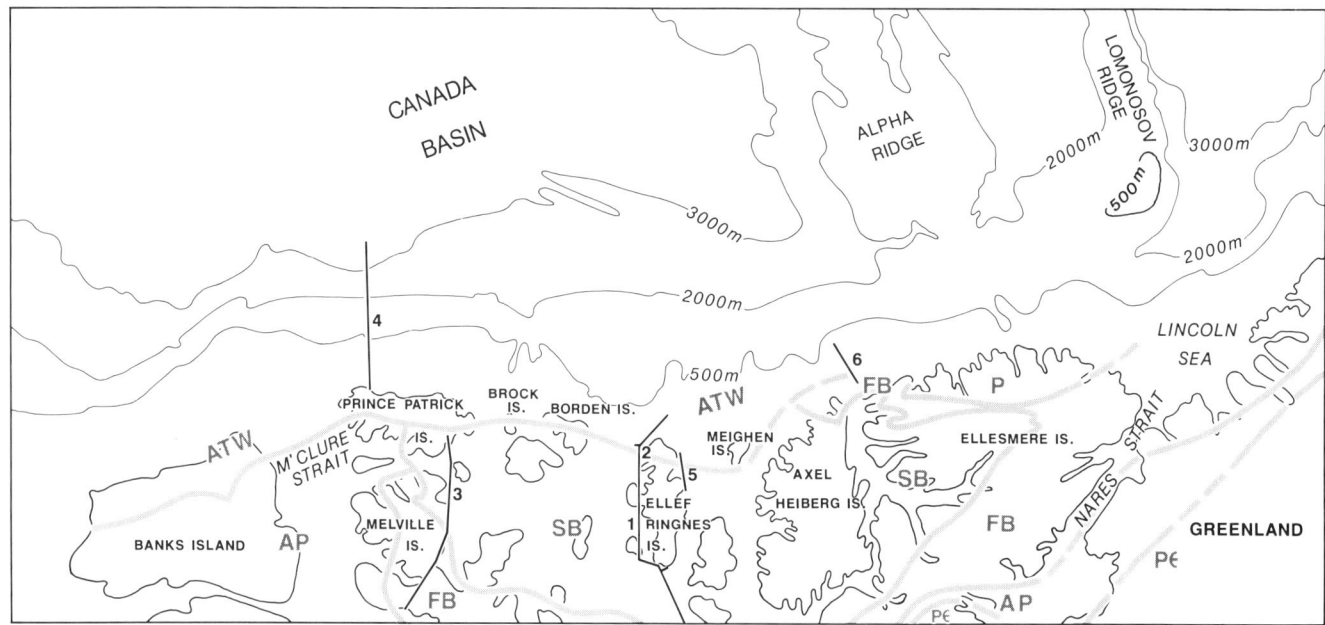

Figure 1. Queen Elizabeth Islands and polar continental margin. Geological provinces are abbreviated as follows: AP, Arctic Platform; ATW, Arctic Terrace Wedge; FB, Franklinian Basin (Ellesmerian orogen); P, Pearya Terrane; PC, Precambrian Shield; SB, Sverdrup Basin. Numbers and locations of the profiles shown in Figures 3 and 4 are indicated.

Heiberg and Ellesmere Islands. Similar Late Paleozoic to Cenozoic sequences are preserved in Svalbard, which was adjacent northeast of Ellesmere Island until the early Tertiary (West and others, 1981; Birkenmajer, 1981). On Ellesmere Island, outliers of Sverdrup Basin rocks are present throughout Pearya (Trettin and Balkwill, 1979).

The Phanerozoic stratigraphy of the Queen Elizabeth Islands is marked by two regional unconformities produced by major tectonic events. The mid-Paleozoic Ellesmerian orogeny deformed and uplifted Franklinian and Pearya rocks with decreasing intensity southwest from Ellesmere Island to Prince Patrick Island (Frisch, 1974; Meneley and others, 1975). In the central and eastern Queen Elizabeth Islands, the latest Cretaceous–early Tertiary Eurekan orogeny produced thrusting and associated folds that ended regional subsidence in the Sverdrup Basin, shed detritus northwestward to form the basal units of the unconformably overlying Arctic Terrace Wedge, and rotated parts of northern Axel Heiberg and Ellesmere Islands (Fig. 2; Balkwill, 1978; Miall, 1981; Ricketts, 1987; Wynne and others, 1988).

Franklinian rocks crop out in northern Ellesmere and Axel Heiberg Islands (Trettin and others, 1972) and are encountered in boreholes at widely spaced points along the inner shelf facing the Canada Basin (Fig. 1). Across northern Ellesmere and Axel Heiberg Islands, shallow-dipping platform rocks extend from the craton northward into dominantly shelf facies. These, in turn, grade northward into rocks of dominantly clastic trough facies that, on Ellesmere Island, are bounded on the north by Pearya (Fig. 1). In the subsurface, Franklinian trough facies are present below northern Ellef Ringnes, Brock (Meneley and others, 1975), and northwestern Banks Islands (Miall, 1976). Trough sediments on both Banks and Ellesmere Islands were derived mainly from cratonic sources to the south and southeast (Miall, 1976; Trettin and others, 1987).

From Late Devonian to Early Carboniferous time, the Ellesmerian orogeny produced regional folding and faulting that was most intense near the present continental margin (Trettin and Balkwill, 1979). Along the margin, tectonic strike varies from northeasterly on northern Ellesmere Island to northwesterly at Prince Patrick Island (Thorsteinsson and Tozer, 1970). The orogeny generated a thick southward-tapering prism of clastic sediments that paleocurrent studies suggest were transported mainly from northeast to southwest across the Queen Elizabeth Islands (Embry and Klovan, 1976). The mobilized belt included northern Ellesmere and Axel Heiberg Islands in early Middle Devonian time. The uplifted zone apparently expanded southwestward during the later Devonian, and by the Early Carboniferous it included northern Prince Patrick Island (Embry and Klovan, 1976, p. 597, 601).

The unconformably overlying Sverdrup Basin sequence is up to 13 km thick and is composed mainly of marine and nonmarine terrigenous clastics with some carbonates and evaporites plus locally abundant gabbro dikes and sills, and basalt flows (Balkwill, 1978). Almost all of the clastics are mature to supermature quartz arenite derived from platform and cratonic source regions to the south and southeast.

To the northwest the basin thins against the Sverdrup Rim, a relatively positive element cored by deformed Franklinian and

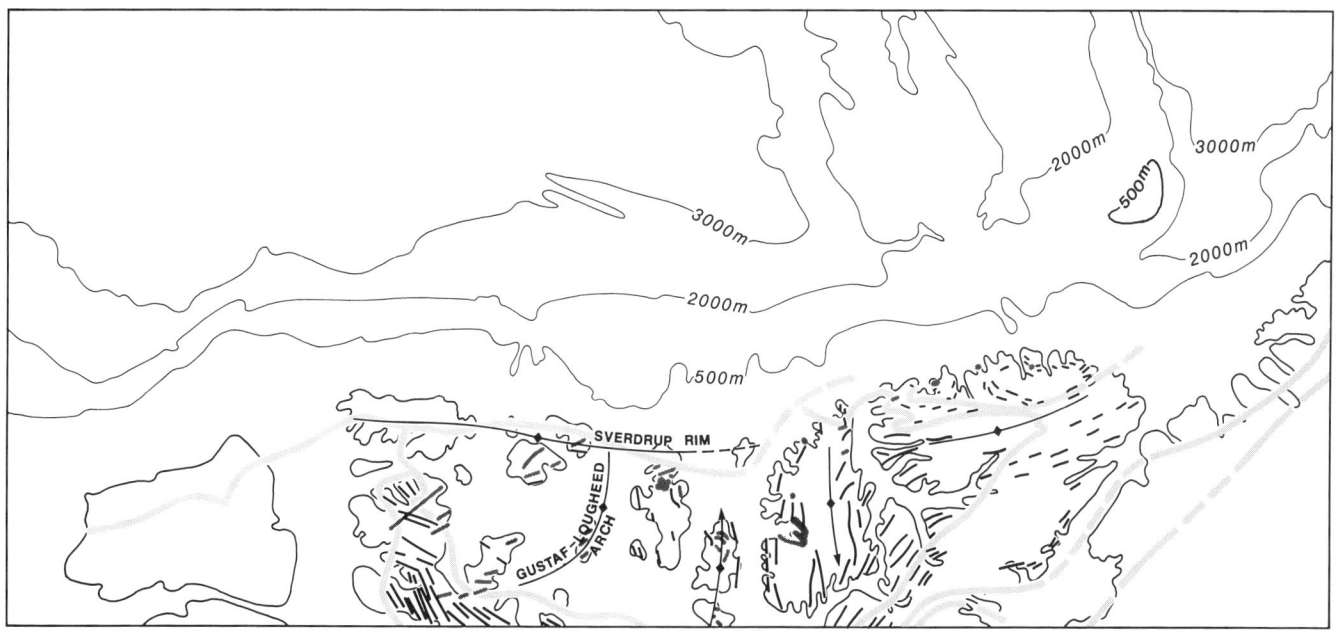

Figure 2. Major structural and igneous features, Queen Elizabeth Islands. Province boundaries as in Figure 1.

possibly pre-Franklinian cratonic rocks (Figs. 2 and 4). In late Paleozoic time the rim subsided more slowly than the basin axis and was fractured, giving access to mafic volcanism on northwestern Ellesmere and northern Axel Heiberg Islands (Balkwill, 1978). During the Mesozoic, the Sverdrup Rim served as a buttress that reduced, and periodically interrupted, the flow of clastic sediments northward across what is now the continental shelf (Thorsteinnson and Tozer, 1970; Meneley and others, 1975; Balkwill, 1978; Hea and others, 1980).

The rim is cut by a northeast-trending system of near-vertical normal faults, some of which served as conduits for mafic intrusions (Stott, 1969; Meneley and others, 1975). Structural offset across individual faults is as much as 1,500 m. The seaward extent of the faulting is unknown, but similar-trending faults and mafic dikes are present within the Sverdrup Basin, particularly along the Gustaf-Lougheed Arch (Forsyth and others, 1979; Hea and others, 1980; Balkwill and Fox, 1982; Fig. 2).

Mafic volcanism and intrusion within the Sverdrup Basin appears to have been concentrated east of the Gustaf-Lougheed Arch; igneous activity is correlated with intervals of rapid basin subsidence (Balkwill, 1978, 1983). One such interval, in Early Cretaceous (late Neocomian–early Aptian) time, has been asso-

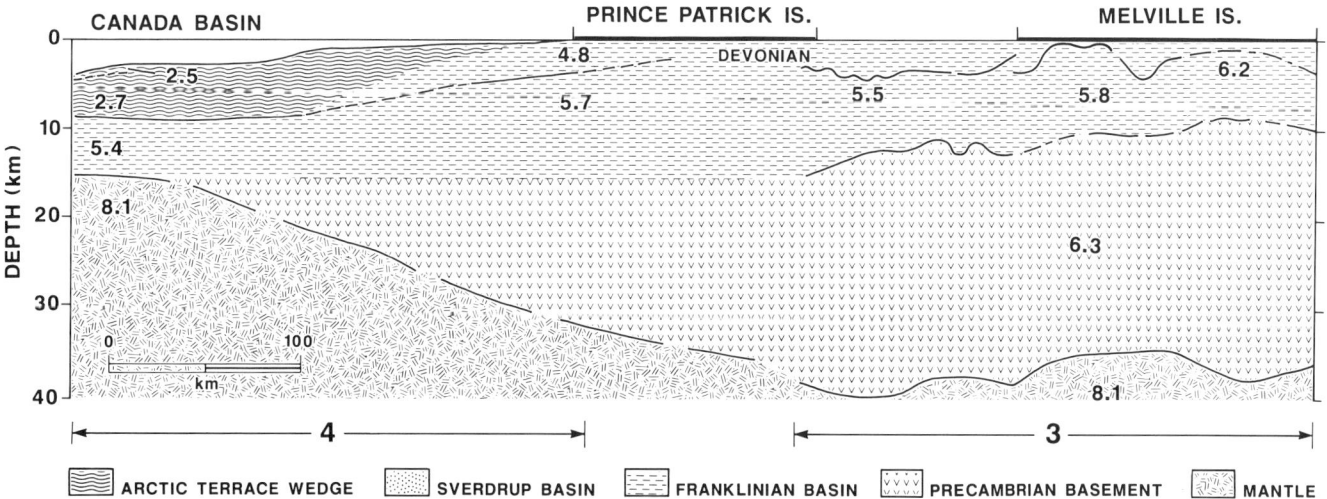

Figure 3. Geological section and crustal P-wave velocity (km/s) across western Queen Elizabeth Islands and polar margin based on references 3 and 4 below. Profile numbers and references for this figure and Figure 4: 1. Sander and Overton (1965); 2. Hobson and Overton (1967); 3. Overton (1970); 4. Berry and Barr (1971); 5. Overton (1982); 6. Asudeh and others (1989). Profile locations on Figure 1.

ciated with an episode of crustal dilation, nearly normal to the present continental margin, that may have generated the northeast-striking system of faults and dikes within the basin (Balkwill, 1983). Near the Sverdrup Rim, exposed mafic rocks are dated as mid-Cretaceous, 110 to 102 Ma, for flows and dikes on northern Ellef Ringnes Island (Larochelle and others, 1965) and 95 to 88 Ma for a northward-thickening volcanic wedge, the Strand Fiord Formation, centered on Axel Heiberg Island (Ricketts and others, 1985). On northernmost Ellesmere Island, mafic flows and intrusions plus anatectic felsic rocks have isotopic ages of 93 to 88 Ma (Trettin and Parrish, 1987).

Regional uplift of the Sverdrup Rim took place in latest Cretaceous (Campanian and Maastrichtian) time (Balkwill and others, 1983). Erosional truncation of Upper Triassic to uppermost Cretaceous beds apparently occurred from M'Clure Strait to Ellef Ringnes Island; Jurassic and Lower Cretaceous rocks are preserved locally in fault-bounded troughs along the rim (Meneley and others, 1975). The northeastern limit of the uplift is indicated by a continuous Upper Cretaceous–lower Tertiary sequence below Meighen Island (e.g., Miall, 1975). These rocks lie unconformably over Upper Triassic sediments, suggesting for Meighen Island a history of pre-Late Cretaceous uplift and erosion that also has been documented for local areas of the Sverdrup Rim to the southwest (Thorsteinsson and Tozer, 1974; Meneley and others, 1975; Miall, 1979).

In late Maastrichtian time the uplifted segment of the Sverdrup Rim began to collapse. At the same time the Eurekan orogeny produced uplift and erosion of Sverdrup Basin fill and older rocks on eastern Ellesmere Island. This was followed by broad folding, reverse faulting, and thrusting in response to northwest-southeast-directed crustal compression that produced at least 60 km of crustal shortening in the eastern Queen Elizabeth Islands during middle Eocene to Oligocene(?) time (Fig. 2; Ricketts and McIntyre, 1986) and produced an episode of erosion throughout the archipelago during the Oligocene (Balkwill, 1978).

Clastic detritus from uplifts produced by Eurekan tectonism migrated mainly northwestward from Maastrichtian time onward, forming the thick deposits of the Arctic Terrace Wedge that cover the present continent–ocean transition. These clastic nonmarine sediments outcrop along the ocean-facing coasts of the northwesternmost Queen Elizabeth Islands (Fig. 2) and are inferred from borehole and seismic refraction information to thicken seaward to at least 5 km below the continental shelf (e.g., Asudeh and others, 1988a).

To summarize, keeping in mind that geologic control is scanty and restricted to onshore areas, the polar margin between M'Clure Strait and the Lincoln Sea is cored by early Paleozoic sedimentary and metasedimentary sequences that are deformed northeast from Prince Patrick Island. They may overlie Precambrian cratonic units. Upper Paleozoic and Mesozoic sediments, unconformable on these older rocks, appear to be less than 4 km thick over the crest of a structural arch, the Sverdrup Rim, below the inner shelf. Over the arch these sediments are cut by normal faults, mafic flows and intrusions and are erosionally truncated.

Faulting and associated igneous activity along the rim is well known from Ellef Ringnes Island northeastward, is oriented strongly northeast and occurred during the Cretaceous Period between late Neocomian and Coniacian time, about 130 to 88 Ma (Embry and Osadetz, 1988; Palmer, 1983, time scale). Erosion, intermittent along the rim throughout the Mesozoic, was most pronounced in Late Cretaceous (Campanian–Maastrichtian) time, about 84 to 70(?) Ma, with the removal of 2,400 m or more of material, chiefly Cretaceous and Jurassic strata, southwest of Meighen Island (Balkwill, 1983). Overlying Maastrichtian and younger clastics form a seaward-thickening wedge that is undeformed where observed and, except below Meighen Island, is unconformable over the truncated Mesozoic rocks of the inner shelf.

GEOPHYSICAL SIGNATURES

Bathymetry, seismic-refraction, potential-field, heat-flow, and seismicity studies have been carried out over the Canadian polar margin since 1959 from land-based stations, floating ice stations, and an ice island. The results of these studies are described below.

Bathymetry

Northwest of the Queen Elizabeth Islands the continental margin trends northeast with few known breaks. The polar shelf is between about 30 and 120 km wide, with the shelf-slope break ranging in depth from about 400 m near Prince Patrick Island to about 700 m close to Axel Heiberg Island to about 500 m north of Ellesmere Island (Plate 1; Johnson and others, this volume). The bathymetric gradient of the shelf is typically less than 4 m/km while that of the slope varies between 9 and 60 m/km (Sobczak and Weber, 1973).

Steep-sided channels between the Queen Elizabeth Islands continue northwestward across the inner shelf as broad, gently sloping valleys that become indistinct along the outer shelf (Plate 1). Narrower, steeper valleys traverse the shelf and upper slope seaward of the rugged topography of Axel Heiberg and Ellesmere Islands (Sobczak and Weber, 1987). Northwest of Ellef Ringnes Island the outer shelf and slope appear to be broadly terraced (Sobczak and others, 1986). North of Ellesmere Island the base of the slope shallows from more than 3,000 m in the Canada Basin to less than 1,600 m where the Alpha and Lomonosov Ridges meet the continent (Fig. 1). In this region the crest of the Lomonosov Ridge rises to within 500 m of the sea surface.

Seismic refraction

The crust below the southern Canada Basin has long been considered as oceanic in character (Oliver and others, 1955). North of Alaska, oceanic crust is about 10 km thick below the continental rise and about 20 km thick at the base of the continental slope (Mair and Lyons, 1981). Moho depths below the

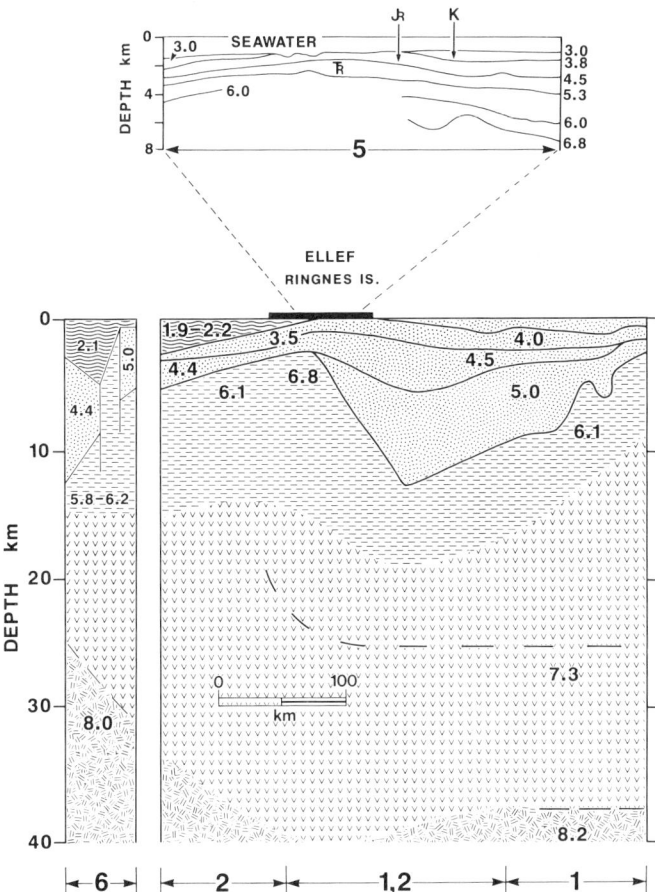

Figure 4. Geological section and crustal P-wave velocity (km/s) across central Queen Elizabeth Islands and polar shelf based on Meneley and others (1975) plus references 1, 2, 5, and 6 given in Figure 3. Profile locations on Figure 1; reference key and lithologic patterns identified in Figure 3.

central part of the Canada Basin have not been measured, but near-zero travel time residuals for teleseismic P-waves reflected below the basin may indicate an absence of unusual crustal thickness (Stewart, 1980). Continental crust below the Queen Elizabeth Islands varies in thickness between about 32 and 40 km (Figs. 3 and 4; Sander and Overton, 1965; Overton, 1970; Forsyth and others, 1979).

Seismic refraction data across the polar margin northwest from Prince Patrick Island indicate that the crust may thin significantly, from 30 ± 7 km beneath the island to an imprecisely defined 11.5 ± 10.5 km near the base of the continental slope about 220 km seaward (Fig. 4) (Berry and Barr, 1971). Offshore of Axel Heiberg Island the crust thins from more than 30 km below the inner shelf to about 25 km near the shelf break about 70 km to the northwest (Fig. 3) (Asudeh and others, 1988a).

P-wave velocity structure across the western Queen Elizabeth Islands (Fig. 3) is complicated by upper crustal carbonate facies and by deformed rocks of the Ellesmerian orogen, but general trends are evident (Overton, 1970). Franklinian Basin rocks have velocities mainly in the range 2.7 to 6.4 km/s and overlie a basement complex with a poorly determined velocity of 6.3 km/s. The top of the basement layer is 10 km below the surface at Melville Island and deepens to about 15 km below Prince Patrick Island. Along the profile, Moho depth appears greatest, at about 40 km, below Prince Patrick Island (Overton, 1970) (Fig. 4).

Overton (1970) associates the surface layer with Ordovician–Silurian carbonates and shales. At Prince Patrick Island, Berry and Barr (1971) indicate that surface units are 2 to 3 km thick with a velocity of 4.8 ± 0.4 km/s. Probably they are Late Devonian clastics that crop out nearby (Fig. 4). They appear to thicken seaward across the inner shelf and overlie a 5.7 ± 0.2 km/s crust. The overlying Arctic Terrace Wedge clastics, apparently too thin to be detected by refracted P-waves near shore, appear below the continental slope as a layered sequence 5 to 6 km thick with a velocity of 2.3 to 2.8 km/s overlying a 5.4 ± 0.1 km/s crust (Berry and Barr, 1971) (Fig. 4).

A more detailed P-wave velocity structure is available across the central Queen Elizabeth Islands. Sander and Overton (1965) show a sequence of velocity horizons down to about 10 km depth, which they associate with Sverdrup Basin strata (Fig. 3). Underlying Franklinian and older rocks, at 6.0 km/s, are exposed south of the basin, and deepen then shallow to the northwest beneath the Sverdrup sequence. Hobson and Overton (1967) revealed this shallowing to be the southeast flank of a basement arch, the Sverdrup Rim, cored by 6.1 km/s rocks that come within 2.5 km of the surface (Fig. 3). Thinning and truncation of lower velocity units over the arch is evident.

Overton (1982) later determined a sequence of velocity horizons across the Sverdrup Rim that shows truncation of a 3.0 km/s layer and the near elimination of a 3.8 km/s layer over the crest of the arch (Fig. 3). The ages associated with these velocity horizons by Sobczak and Overton (1984, Figs. 8 and 13) suggest that Cretaceous and most Jurassic age rocks are truncated over the arch, in accord with the Late Triassic to latest Cretaceous hiatus reported below the Arctic Terrace Wedge by Meneley and others (1975) based on borehole data. North of the arch, Sverdrup Basin strata appear to thicken over the innermost shelf, and the late Mesozoic hiatus apparently diminishes farther seaward (Overton, 1982) (Fig. 3). That is, the unconformity between Sverdrup Basin rocks and Arctic Terrace Wedge clastics may be pronounced only in the vicinity of the Sverdrup Rim.

Northwest of Axel Heiberg Island, Asudeh and others (1989) show a surface layer with a starting velocity of 2.1 km/s thickening from 700 m near shore to about 5 km over a distance of 75 km across the shelf (Fig. 3). This unit, interpreted by Asudeh and others to be the Arctic Terrace Wedge, overlies a seaward-thickening 5.0 km/s layer, about 4.5 km thick near shore, that appears to be truncated below the inner shelf by a complex of faults. The velocity and thickness of this layer suggest that it represents early Mesozoic and older Sverdrup Basin strata. Below the outer shelf, Arctic Terrace Wedge clastics overlie a unit with a starting velocity of 4.4 km/s that is up to 7 km thick. Asudeh and others (1989) suggest that this could be either the continuation of Sverdrup and Franklinian age rocks seaward of the faulted zone or the basal part of the clastic wedge. The time of faulting is crudely bracketed between the early Mesozoic, the presumed age of the youngest truncated rocks, and the latest Cretaceous, the maximum age of clastics that lie undeformed over the faulted zone.

Magnetic field

Aeromagnetic data over this segment of the Arctic margin have been collected at line spacings of 20 km or more at altitudes of 3.5 to 5.0 km (see Coles and others, 1978, for details). There is also low-level (300 m) coverage, at 2 to 3 km line spacing between M'Clure Strait and Ellef Ringnes Island (Bhattacharyya, 1968) and at 12 km line spacing over the Lincoln Sea and north of Ellesmere Island (Kovacs, 1982).

Magnetic anomaly trends over the Lincoln Sea are aligned northeastward, nearly colinear with Nares Strait and the major structural trends across northern Ellesmere Island and Greenland (Fig. 5a). Depth-to-magnetic-source calculations indicate that the Nares Strait channel may continue north of Greenland as a deep trough filled with up to 10 km of nonmagnetic material, presumably sediments (Kovacs and Vogt, 1982).

The crestal portion of the Lomonosov Ridge adjacent to the Lincoln Shelf is characterized by a distinctive high-frequency magnetic anomaly pattern that suggests shallow depths to magnetic source rocks (Fig. 5a). Shallow bathymetry together with near-surface magnetic rocks, presumably mafic volcanics, may cause the observed magnetic anomaly field. If so, volcanic activity could be partly responsible for the high-standing crest of the Lomonosov Ridge in this region.

The intense short-wavelength anomaly pattern associated with the Alpha Ridge appears to cross the slope and shelf adjacent to north-central Ellesmere Island (e.g., Riddihough and others, 1973). Elsewhere along the Queen Elizabeth Islands continental margin the magnetic anomaly pattern is generally negative with low amplitude (<200 nT), from which is inferred deep burial of magnetic basement (Bhattacharyya, 1968; Coles and others, 1978). The negative anomaly axis lies along the outer shelf and slope except between Prince Patrick and Borden Islands where it appears to be displaced seaward by up to 150 km (Fig. 5a; Forsyth and others, 1988).

The reasons for this offset are unclear; Forsyth and others (1988) suggest that Paleozoic structural trends, thought to transect the margin at high angle in this vicinity, locally mask Mesozoic rift geometry below the polar shelf.

Linear anomalies of very low amplitude (10 nT) extend along the outer shelf between Banks and Prince Patrick Islands (Reford, 1967). Similar anomalies lie over the Gustaf-Lougheed Arch and along the Sverdrup Rim at Ellef Ringnes Island (Bhattacharyya, 1968). The latter, and presumably also the former, are associated with late Early Cretaceous extension and dike emplacement (Balkwill and Haimila, 1978). Local magnetic highs over the shelf between Prince Patrick and Ellesmere Islands may represent shallow mafic volcanic centers (Bhattacharyya, 1968), but this is uncertain except offshore of northern Axel Heiberg Island (Fig. 5a; Forsyth and others, 1988).

Gravity

Free-air gravity over the North American polar margin includes a sinuous belt of intense elliptical highs that closely follow the trend of the continental shelf break (Fig. 5b). The anomaly highs, locally greater than 100 mGal, are about 120 km wide, up to 300 km long and are flanked landward and seaward by parallel but more diffuse negative anomaly belts with –20 to –50 mGal amplitudes. A narrow anomaly high along the outer shelf next to north-central Ellesmere Island coincides in part with an intense magnetic high, earlier noted.

The positive anomalies appear to be superimposed on a more subdued but continuous gravity high about 50 km wide with an amplitude of about 30 mGal (Fig. 5b). Northwest of M'Clure Strait the continuous gravity high is displaced seaward by up to 150 km.

Northeast of Ellesmere Island a strong gravity gradient declines southward from 60 mGal along the outer Lincoln Shelf to –80 mGal over the north coast of Greenland (Fig. 5b). Gravity contours are on strike with regional geology onshore; the gradient may be produced by flexural depression of the Greenland crust by the continental ice sheet and/or a crustal root below northern Greenland (Sobczak and Stephens, 1974).

The prominent free-air highs that flank the Canada Basin have been interpreted as the effect of rapid crustal thinning below the outer shelf (Weber, 1963), basement arches (Wold and others, 1970), or belts of dense rock (Weber, 1963) within the crust of the outer shelf and/or regional downflexure of the lithosphere loaded by prograding shelf sediments (Sobczak, 1975).

Arches or large density contrasts within the basement are not evident in P-wave velocity profiles across the margin north of Alaska (Grantz and others, 1979). In Canada, faulted and uplifted basement characterizes the inner shelf (Sverdrup Rim) and is inferred below the central part of the shelf northwest of Axel Heiberg Island by Asudeh and others (1989). Along the outer shelf, available magnetic and seismic data indicate only the presence of thick sediments (Berry and Barr, 1971; Dixon, 1982; Willumsen and Cote, 1982; Asudeh and others, 1989; Figs. 3 and 4). Cenozoic clastics alone are over 3 km thick at several points along the inner shelf (Balkwill, 1978; Grantz and others, 1979; Norris and Yorath, 1981).

The continuous gravity high may correlate with masses of isostatically compensated shelf sediments (Sobczak, 1975); it may also mark the transition to thinner crust and deeper water of the ocean basin. Its displacement seaward near M'Clure Strait occurs in a region of changing continental margin strike (Fig. 5b). The free-air high immediately to the northeast is also displaced seaward, and its northern half, much reduced in amplitude, is coin-

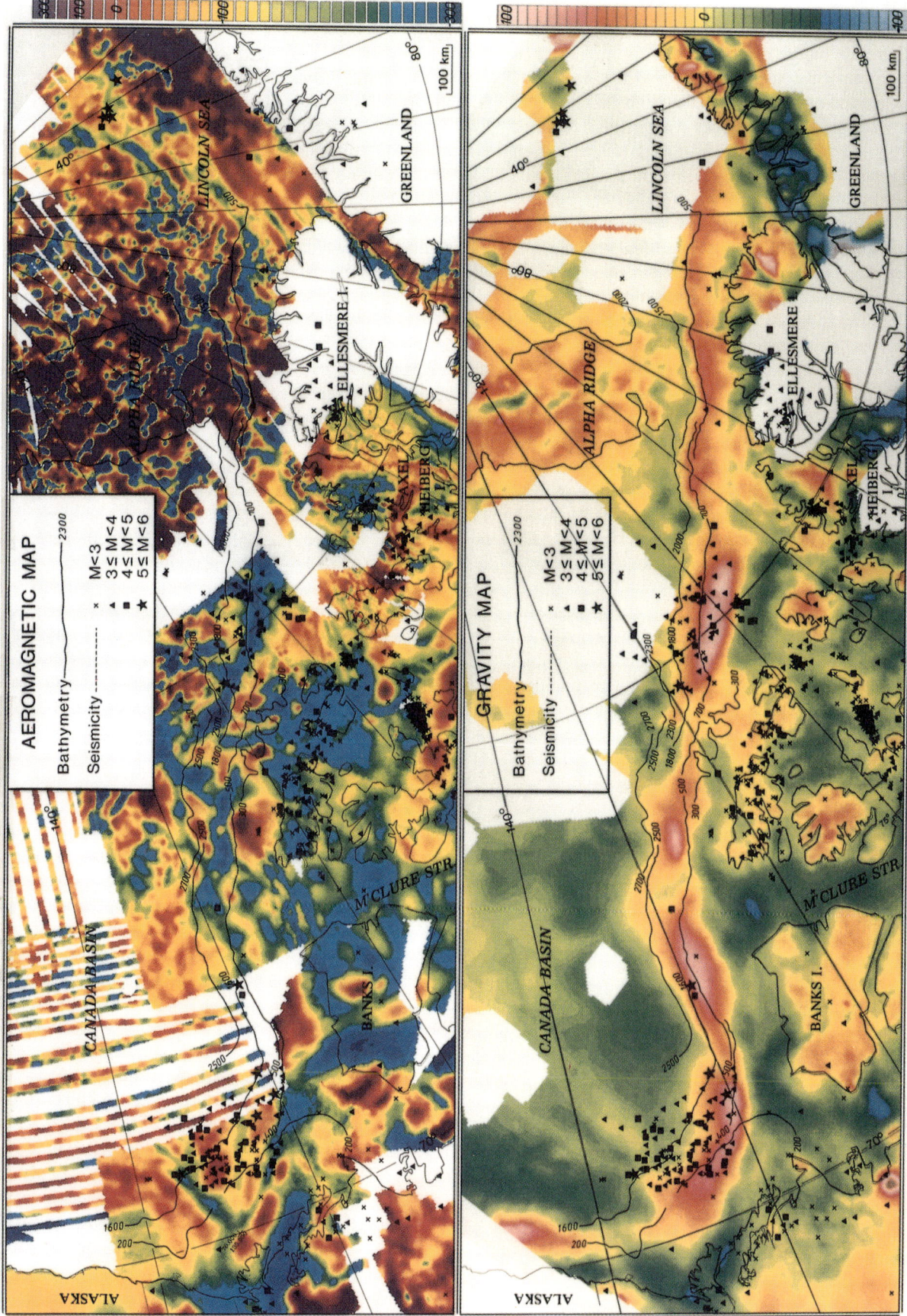

Figure 5a (top). Magnetic anomalies and seismicity along the Canadian polar continental margin (modified from Forsyth and others, 1988). Figure 5b (bottom). Gravity anomalies (Bouguer on land, free air at sea) and seismicity along the Canadian polar continental margin (modified from Forsyth and others, 1988).

cident with the offset in the magnetic negative anomaly axis (Forsyth and others, 1988; Figs. 5a and b).

Density structure models across the polar margin northeast of the Queen Elizabeth Islands interpret up to 8 km of post-breakup sediments and rapid crustal thinning to between 15 and 20 km across the outer shelf and slope (Weber, 1963; Sobczak and others, 1986). In the Sobczak and others (1986) model, Sverdrup and Franklinian strata extend below the Arctic Terrace Wedge sediments to the outer shelf.

Within the continent there appears to be an inverse variation in thickness between combined Sverdrup and Franklinian rocks and the underlying crystalline crust (Sobczak and Overton, 1984). Sobczak and Overton suggest a cause-and-effect relation whereby stretching and thinning of crystalline crust produces subsidence and sediment accumulation above the thinned region.

Heat flow

Three areas have been sampled along the Canadian polar margin, two of which are indicated on Plate 2. Two measurements from the outer shelf near Prince Patrick Island show very low heat flow (20 ± 4 mWm^{-2}; Paterson and Law, 1966). About 30 recent measurements from the shelf near Axel Heiberg Island show similar low heat flows, between 20 and 50 mWm^{-2} (Louden, 1988). High heat flow (73 ± 14 mWm^{-2}; Langseth and others, this volume) is measured at 14 sites off the Ellesmere margin, at the junction of the Alpha Ridge with the continent.

The low heat flows near Prince Patrick Island occur on the landward flank of a major gravity high, where the Berry and Barr (1971) refraction results indicate 5 to 6 km of Arctic Terrace Wedge clastics (Fig. 4). North of Axel Heiberg Island, low-velocity (<3.0 km/s) sediments are much thinner where measured by Asudeh and others (1989; Fig. 3). Low geothermal values along the shelf could be caused mostly by thick young sediments in the former region, and mostly by an absence of Eurekan tectonism in the latter region (e.g., Louden, 1988). High heat flow north of Ellesmere Island, on the other hand, could be related to early Tertiary extension associated with the Eurekan orogeny (Landseth and others, this volume).

Seismicity

Along the polar continental margin, earthquakes occur mainly within the crust and rarely exceed magnitude 5 (Basham and others, 1977; Wetmiller and Forsyth, 1978). Most epicenters offshore lie over the slope along the seaward gradients of the major gravity highs (Fig. 5b). Local trends within the epicenter distribution coincide also with the negative magnetic anomaly axis along the outer shelf (Forsyth and others, 1988). Active areas onshore include the Sverdrup Rim from M'Clure Strait to Borden Island, the zone north of the Sverdrup Basin depoaxis from Ellef Ringnes to north-central Ellesmere Islands, and the north-south zone from eastern Melville Island to the inner shelf. The polar shelf is largely aseismic, as is the Nares Strait region (Figs. 5a and b; Wetmiller and Forsyth, 1982).

The ongoing release of stress associated with deglaciation may produce much of the observed seismicity. This appears to be the case for seismicity associated with the passive margin of Baffin Bay in eastern Canada where over 150 m of post-glacial rebound has already taken place (Stein and others, 1979). However, stresses produced by glacial unloading may not be important along the polar margin and adjacent areas of the Queen Elizabeth Islands because less than 20 m of post-Pleistocene uplift has occurred there (Farrand and Gajda, 1962; Paterson, 1977). The thick sediment loads that apparently are the principal cause of the offshore gravity highs and magnetic lows may also create the deviatoric stress responsible for contemporary seismicity along fault systems beneath the continental slope (Basham and others, 1977; Forsyth and others, 1988).

Shelf-edge gravity highs and clastic wedges are typical features of passive margins. Seismicity is less common. The polar margin structure may have a relatively reduced threshold for seismic activity for two related reasons. First, focal mechanism solutions suggest that the horizontal component of deviatoric tensional stress within the crust is nearly normal to the polar margin between Ellef Ringnes Island and the Beaufort Sea (Hasegawa, 1977; Hasegawa and others, 1979). Second, oceanic crust beneath the Canada Basin is downflexed under an unusually thick sediment cover (4 to 6 km: Hall, 1973; Mair and Lyons, 1981; 6 to 9 km; Grantz and others, 1979 and this volume, ch. 22), and this may induce tensional stresses in the adjacent continental margin, which is mechanically coupled to the oceanic crust. The polar margin may therefore require less additional stress input—by sediment loads along the outer shelf and slope, for example—than typical passive margins to become a locus of seismic activity.

MARGIN STRUCTURE

Axel Heiberg Island to Lincoln Sea

Along this segment of the margin, bathymetric, magnetic, and gravity data are essentially in phase and possess greater short-wavelength variability than is observed along the continent–ocean transition to the southwest. This indicates that sediment cover is probably thin over much of the margin offshore and that the geophysical signatures likely reflect the structure of underlying Franklinian, Sverdrup (?), and igneous rocks (e.g., Forsyth and others, 1988). These inferences are supported by the absence of sediment cover over adjacent Paleozoic strata and Cretaceous plutons exposed on northernmost Ellesmere Island (e.g., Trettin and others, 1987; Figs. 1 and 2), thin sediment cover on the inner shelf near Axel Heiberg Island (Asudeh and others, 1988a) (Fig. 3), and the predominance of short-wavelength anomalies, particularly in the magnetic field, north and northeast of Ellesmere Island (Fig. 5a and b). Potential field trends across the Lincoln Shelf are on line with regional structural boundaries across northern Ellesmere Island, indicating that the boundaries probably continue offshore.

Sediments may be much thicker below the outer shelf and

slope north of Axel Heiberg Island (Asudeh and others, 1989), but to the east a strong magnetic high offshore of north-central Ellesmere Island indicates that magnetic material is close to the surface completely across the continental shelf (Fig. 5a). This anomaly appears to be part of the intense magnetic signature of the Alpha Ridge, which near Canada, is thought to be composed of mafic extrusive rocks (Van Wagoner and Robinson, 1985; Asudeh and others, 1988). Mafic rocks below the adjoining shelf could account for much of the gravity high and its in-phase relation to the magnetic anomaly (Fig. 5b). Elsewhere in this segment, gravity highs along the outer shelf may be caused by the edge effect associated with the continent-ocean transition.

Seismicity in the region is concentrated on northwestern Ellesmere Island. Other parts of Ellesmere Island, including the Pearya terrane, the polar margin to the north and the Nares Strait region to the east, are virtually aseismic (Wetmiller and Forsyth, 1982).

Axel Heiberg Island to M'Clure Strait

Magnetic and gravity data are largely out of phase along this margin segment. Broad, subdued magnetic lows near the shelf break indicate thick accumulations of nonmagnetic material, probably sediments, that refraction data show to be at least 5 km thick northwest of both Prince Patrick and Axel Heiberg Islands (Figs. 3 and 4) (Berry and Barr, 1971; Asudeh and others, 1989). Some of these sediments may act as locally uncompensated loads that generate the strong observed gravity highs, downflex the surrounding lithosphere to produce the broad flanking gravity lows, and contribute to the stress regime responsible for present offshore seismicity (Sobczak, 1975; Basham and others, 1977).

An exception is the shelf region between Borden and Prince Patrick Islands where low-amplitude, short-wavelength gravity and magnetic anomalies are weakly lineated nearly normal to the strike of the shelf edge (Figs. 5a and b). Arctic Terrace Wedge sediments probably are thin in this area, and the potential fields may reflect the continuation across the shelf of Ellesmerian structures that trend northwesterly in this region (e.g., Thorsteinsson and Tozer, 1970; Figs. 1 and 2).

Sverdrup Rim, the broad structural arch below the inner shelf of this margin segment, brings Devonian rocks to the surface on Prince Patrick Island. To the northeast, Sverdrup Basin strata are greatly thinned and partly truncated over the arch. The stratigraphic hiatus at the base of the overlying Arctic Terrace Wedge appears most pronounced over the arch crest, and Sverdrup rocks appear to thicken to the northwest (Fig. 3) (Overton, 1982).

The Sverdrup Rim is partly, and perhaps completely, faultbounded. There is evidence from seismic refraction results (Asudeh and others, 1989) and from depth-to-magnetic-source models (Bhattacharyya, 1968) that steep-sided (faulted?) structures persist across the shelf to the shelf edge below the Arctic Terrace Wedge.

Continental crust below the rim is 35 to 40 km thick (Overton, 1970; Berry and Barr, 1971; Sobczak and Overton, 1984). It thins to about 25 km below the adjacent outer shelf (Asudeh and others, 1989) and to between 10 and 15 km below the outer slope (Berry and Barr, 1971) (Figs. 3 and 4). The rim is seismically active between M'Clure Strait and its junction with the north-trending Gustaf-Lougheed Arch (e.g., Fig. 5a). Northeast from here the rim has little associated seismicity.

AGE AND ORIGIN

The polar continental margin between M'Clure Strait and Ellesmere Island was formed by opening of the Canada Basin during the long Cretaceous interval of normal geomagnetic polarity between about 120 and 80 Ma, a period during which the Alpha Ridge also formed (see Grantz and others, this volume; Weber and Sweeney, this volume). The Lincoln margin northeast of the junction of the Lomonosov Ridge with Ellesmere Island formed much later, during the opening of the Eurasia Basin, beginning in earliest Tertiary time, about 65 to 56 Ma (e.g., Vogt and others, 1979; see Dawes, this volume).

Both margins also possess features that may be related to the Campanian to Oligocene motions of Greenland against the Queen Elizabeth Islands during the Eurekan orogeny. These include uplift and erosion of the Sverdrup Rim, onset of deposition of the Arctic Terrace Wedge (e.g., Balkwill, 1978), and counterclockwise rotation of parts of northern Ellesmere and Axel Heiberg Islands by about 38° (Wynne and others, 1988).

Southwest from Ellesmere Island the time of margin origin is also bracketed by structural and depositional events within the Queen Elizabeth Islands. Along the inner shelf between Brock and Axel Heiberg Islands, basal beds of the Arctic Terrace Wedge, the oldest sediments post-dating continental breakup, are Maastrichtian in age (Meneley and others, 1975; Balkwill, 1978). Continental breakup, therefore, predates about 75 Ma (Palmer, 1983, time scale).

Major crustal extension, an essential feature of continental breakup (e.g., Scrutton, 1982), is evident along the Sverdrup Rim, the Gustaf-Lougheed Arch and the Sverdrup Basin in Early and mid-Cretaceous time. Extensive mantle-derived hypabyssal and extrusive magmas are interbedded within Barremian to Cenomanian strata, or between about 125 to 91 Ma, along the Gustaf-Lougheed Arch and in the Sverdrup Basin (Thorsteinsson and Tozer, 1970; Balkwill and Haimila, 1978; Balkwill and others, 1983). In the central and eastern parts of the basin, subsidence rates increased dramatically during Hauterivian through Albian time, about 131 to 98 Ma (Sweeney, 1977; Balkwill, 1978), presumably in response to a period of crustal dilation, directed almost normal to the present margin, between about 131 and 116 Ma (Balkwill, 1983). Tholeiitic rocks on northern Axel Heiberg Island are dated stratigraphically between 95 nd 88 Ma (Ricketts and others, 1985), and anatectic granites and mafic igneous rocks on northern Ellesmere Island are dated isotopically at 93 to 88 Ma. These ages are evidence for a major thermal event at depth, possibly the intrusion of mantle fluids close to the zone of continental breakup (Trettin and Parrish, 1987). Together, these events put the origin of this part of the margin broadly within the 131 to 88 Ma interval. This overlaps not only the age estimates of other parts of the Canada Basin margin in North America (Dixon and Dietrich, this volume; Grantz and May, this volume) but also the time of formation of both the adjacent deep sea floor (Eittreim and Grantz, 1979; Lawver and Baggeroer, 1983) and the Alpha Ridge (Bukry, 1985; Mudie and others, 1986; Taylor and others, 1986). That is, all parts of the North American polar continental margin could have formed at about the same time, in conjunction with the creation of the Canada Basin and the Alpha Ridge.

The tholeiites observed on Axel Heiberg Island may be related to rocks of the Alpha Ridge (Irving and Sweeney, 1982; Van Wagoner and Robinson, 1985; Ricketts and others, 1985), but preliminary estimates of upper crustal velocity structure below the Arctic Terrace Wedge north of Axel Heiberg Island indicate that, oceanward, layer velocities become significantly lower below the outer shelf (Fig. 3) (Asudeh and others, 1989). One interpretation is that high-velocity tholeiitic rocks are absent within the crust at the continental edge, perhaps because Axel Heiberg rocks have been rotated to the west relative to the Alpha Ridge by Eurekan events, but, as Wynne and others (1988) point out, the paleomagnetic evidence is equivocal.

The Lomonosov Ridge is continental in origin (Wilson, 1963; Sweeney and others, 1982) and was separated from Eurasia in the interval between marine magnetic anomalies 29 and 24 (Vogt and others, 1979), between 65 and 56 Ma (Palmer, 1983),

at least 15 m.y. after the genesis of the Alpha Ridge, the Canada Basin, and the polar margin of Ellesmere Island. Thus, what was about to become the Lomonosov Ridge may have been disconnected from North America long before it pulled away from Eurasia.

CLOSING REMARKS

This chapter has outlined the history of study of the continental margin northwest of the Queen Elizabeth Islands and has sketched what is known about the composition and structure of its crust, the causes of its present geophysical character and its tectonic history. The character and distribution of sediments and underlying basement rocks along the margin are poorly understood, and thus the present knowledge of margin physical properties is rudimentary. Also, the mechanics of margin development are largely unknown.

New multiparameter geostudies of the polar margin clearly are needed to tie the onshore geologic history to that of the adjacent oceanic regions. Studies from the Canadian ice island near Axel Heiberg Island are beginning to achieve this desired end (e.g., Asudeh and others, 1989). It is anticipated that, as the ice island drifts to the southwest over the next several years, the polar margin will continue to be a major research focus, and that new techniques, in particular deep drilling of the shelf, will be employed in future studies.

REFERENCES CITED

Asudeh, I., Green, A. and Forsyth, D. A., 1988, Canadian expedition to study the Alpha Ridge complex—results of the seismic refraction survey: Geophysical Journal of the Royal Astronomical Society, v. 92, p. 283–301.

Asudeh, I., Forsyth, D. A., Stephenson, R., Embry, A., Jackson, H. R. and White, D., 1989, Crustal structure of the Canadian polar margin: Part I: Canadian Journal of Earth Sciences, v. 26, p. 853–866.

Balkwill, H. R., 1978, Evolution of Sverdrup basin, Arctic Canada: American Association of Petroleum Geologists Bulletin, v. 62, p. 1004–1028.

——, 1983, Geology of Amund Ringnes, Cornwall, and Haig–Thomas Islands, District of Franklin: Geological Survey of Canada Memoir 390, 76 p.

Balkwill, H. R., and Fox, F. G., 1982, Incipient rift zone, western Sverdrup Basin, Arctic Canada, in Embry, A. F., and Balkwill, H. R., eds., Arctic Geology and Geophysics: Canadian Society of Petroleum Geologists Memoir 8, p. 171–187.

Balkwill, H. R., and Haimila, N. E., 1978, K/Ar ages and significance of mafic rocks, Sabine Peninsula, Melville Island, District of Franklin, in Current Research, Part C: Geological Survey of Canada Paper 78-1C, p. 35–38.

Balkwill, H. R., Cook, D. G., Detterman, R. L., Embry, A. F., Hakansson, E., Miall, A. D., Poulton, T. P., and Young, F. G., 1983, Arctic North America and northern Greenland, in Moullade, M., and Nairn, A.E.M., eds., The Phanerozoic Geology of the World, II. The Mesozoic: Amsterdam, B. Elsevier, p. 1–31.

Basham, P. W., Forsyth, D. A., and Wetmiller, R. J., 1977, Seismicity of northern Canada: Canadian Journal of Earth Sciences, v. 14, p. 1646–1667.

Berry, M. J., and Barr, K. G., 1971, A seismic refraction profile across the polar continental shelf of the Queen Elizabeth Islands: Canadian Journal of Earth Sciences, v. 8, p. 347–360.

Bhattacharyya, B. K., 1968, Analysis of aeromagnetic data over the Arctic Islands and continental shelf of Canada: Geological Survey of Canada Paper 68-44, p. 1–14.

Birkenmajer, K., 1981, The geology of Svalbard, the western part of the Barents Sea, and the continental margin of Scandinavia, in Nairn, A.E.M., Churkin, M., Jr., and Stehli, F. G., eds., The Ocean Basins and Margins. Volume 5, The Arctic Ocean: New York, Plenum Press, p. 265–329.

Bukry, D., 1985, Correlation of Late Cretaceous Arctic silicoflagellates from Alpha Ridge: Geological Survey of Canada Paper 84-22, p. 125–135.

Coles, R. L., Hannaford, W., and Haines, G. V., 1978, Magnetic anomalies and the evolution of the Arctic, in Sweeney, J. F., ed., Arctic Geophysical Review: Ottawa, Publications of the Earth Physics Branch, v. 45, p. 51–66.

Dixon, J., 1982, Upper Oxfordian to Albian geology, Mackenzie Delta, arctic Canada, in Embry, A. F., and Balkwill, H. R., eds., Arctic Geology and Geophysics: Canadian Society of Petroleum Geologists Memoir 8, p. 29–42.

Eittreim, S., and Grantz, A., 1979, CDP seismic sections of the western Beaufort continental margin: Tectonophysics, v. 59, p. 251–262.

Embry, A. F., and Klovan, J. E., 1976, The Middle-Upper Devonian clastic wedge of the Franklinian geosyncline: Bulletin of Canadian Petroleum Geology, v. 24, p. 485–639.

Embry, A. F. and Osadetz, K. G., 1988, Stratigraphy and tectonic significance of Cretaceous volcanism, Queen Charlotte Islands, Arctic Archipelago: Canadian Journal of Earth Sciences, v. 25, p. 1209–1219.

Farrand, W. R., and Gajda, R. T., 1962, Isobases on the Wisconsin marine limit in Canada: Ottawa, Department of Mines and Technical Surveys Geographic Bulletin 17, p. 5–22.

Forsyth, D. A., Mair, J. A., and Fraser, I., 1979, Crustal structure of the central Sverdrup Basin: Canadian Journal of Earth Sciences, v. 16, p. 1581–1598.

Forsyth, D. A., Broome, J., Embry, A. F., and Halpenny, J., 1988, The Canadian polar margin, aeromagnetic, gravity, and earthquake features: Ottawa, Department of Energy, Mines, and Resources, GEOS, v. 17, p. 12–16.

Fortier, Y. O., and 10 others, 1963, Geology of the north-central part of the Arctic Archipelago, Northwest Territories (Operation Franklin): Geological Survey of Canada Memoir 320, 671 p.

Frisch, T., 1974, Metamorphic and plutonic rocks of northernmost Ellesmere Island, Canadian Arctic Archipelago: Geological Survey of Canada Bulletin 229, 87 p.

Grantz, A., Eittreim, S., and Dinter, D. A., 1979, Geology and tectonic development of the continental margin north of Alaska: Tectonophysics, v. 59, p. 263–291.

Hall, J. K., 1973, Geophysical evidence for ancient seafloor spreading from Alpha Cordillera and Mendeleev Ridge, in Pitcher, M. G., ed., Arctic Geology: American Association of Petroleum Geologists Memoir 19, p. 542–561.

Hasegawa, H. S., 1977, Focal parameters of four Sverdrup Basin, Arctic Canada, earthquakes in November and December of 1972: Canadian Journal of Earth Sciences, v. 14, p. 2481–2494.

Hasegawa, H. S., Chou, C. W., and Basham, P. W., 1979, Seismotectonics of the Beaufort Sea: Canadian Journal of Earth Sciences, v. 16, p. 816–830.

Hea, J. P., and 7 others, 1980, Post Ellesmerian basins of Arctic Canada—their depocentres, rates of sedimentation, and petroleum potential: Canadian Society of Petroleum Geologists Memoir 6, p. 447–488.

Hobson, G. F., and Overton, A., 1967, A seismic section of the Sverdrup Basin, Canadian Arctic Islands, in Musgrave, A. W., ed., Seismic Refraction Prospecting: Society of Exploration Geophysicists, p. 550–562.

Irving, E., and Sweeney, J. F., 1982, Origin of the Arctic Basin: Transactions of the Royal Society of Canada, series 4, v. 29, p. 409–416.

Kerr, J. W., 1981, Evolution of the Canadian Arctic Islands; A transition between the Atlantic and Arctic oceans, in Nairn, A.E.M., Churkin, M., Jr., and Stehli, F.G., eds., The Ocean Basins and Margins; Volume 5, The Arctic Ocean: New York, Plenum Press, p. 105–199.

Kovacs, L. C., 1982, Motion along Nares Strait recorded in the Lincoln Sea—aeromagnetic evidence, in Dawes, P. R., and Kerr, J. W., eds., Nares Strait and the drift of Greenland—a conflict in Plate Tectonics: Meddelelser om Grønland, Geoscience 8, p. 275–290.

Kovacs, L. C., and Vogt, P. R., 1982, Depth-to-magnetic source analysis of the Arctic Ocean region: Tectonophysics, v. 89, p. 255–294.

Larochelle, A., Black, R. F., and Wanless, R. K., 1965, Paleomagnetism of the Isachsen diabasic rocks: Nature, v. 208, p. 179.

Lawver, L. A., and Baggeroer, A., 1983, A note on the age of the Canada Basin, in Mull, C. G., and Reed, K. M., eds., The Origin of the Arctic Ocean (Canada Basin): Journal of the Alaska Geological Society, v. 2, p. 57–66.

Louden, K. E., 1988, Marine heatflow observations on the Arctic continental shelf [abs.]: Geological Association of Canada Joint Annual Meeting, St. John's, v. 13, p. A75.

Mair, J. A., and Lyons, J. A., 1981, Crustal structure and velocity anistrophy beneath the Beaufort Sea: Canadian Journal of Earth Sciences, v. 18, p. 724–741.

Meneley, R. A., Henao, D., and Merritt, R. K., 1975, The northwest margin of the Sverdrup Basin, in Yorath, C. J., Parker, E. R., and Glass, D. J., eds., Canada's Continental Margins: Canadian Society of Petroleum Geologists Memoir 4, p. 531–544.

Miall, A. D., 1975, Post-Paleozoic geology of Banks, Prince Patrick and Eglinton islands, Arctic Canada, in Yorath, C. J., Parker, E. R., and Glass, D. J., eds., Canada's Continental Margins: Canadian Society of Petroleum Geologists Memoir 4, p. 557–587.

—— , 1976, Devonian geology of Banks Island, Arctic Canada, and its bearing on the tectonic development of the Circum-Arctic region: Geological Society of America Bulletin, v. 87, p. 1599–1608.

—— , 1979, Mesozoic and Tertiary geology of Banks Island, Arctic Canada: Geological Survey of Canada Memoir 387, 235 p.

—— , 1981, Late Cretaceous and Paleogene sedimentation and tectonics in the Canadian Arctic Islands, in Miall, A. D., ed., Sedimentation and Tectonics in Alluvial Basins: Geological Association of Canada Special paper 23, p. 221–272.

Mudie, P. J., Stoffyn-Egli, P., and Van Wagoner, N. A., 1986, Geological constraints for tectonic models of the Alpha Ridge: Journal of Geodynamics, v. 6, p. 215–236.

Norris, D. K., and Yorath, C. J., 1981, The North American plate from the Arctic Archipelago to the Romanzof Mountains, in Nairn, A.E.M., Churkin, M., Jr., and Stehli, F. G., eds., The Ocean Basins and Margins; Volume 5, The Arctic Ocean: New York, Plenum Press, p. 37–104.

Oliver, J., Ewing, M., and Press, F., 1955, Crustal structure of the Arctic regions from L_g phase: Geological Society of America Bulletin, v. 66, p. 1063–1074.

Overton, A., 1970, Seismic refraction surveys, western Queen Elizabeth Islands and polar continental margin: Canadian Journal of Earth Sciences, v. 7, p. 346–365.

—— , 1982, Seismic reconnaissance profiles across the Sverdrup Basin, Canadian Arctic Islands, in Current Research, Part B: Geological Survey of Canada Paper 82–1B, p. 139–145.

Palmer, A. R., 1983, The decade of North American geology 1983 geologic time scale: Geology, v. 11, p. 503–504.

Paterson, W.S.B., 1977, Extent of the Late Wisconsin glaciation in northwest Greenland and northern Ellesmere Island—a review of the glaciological and geological evidence: Quaternary Research, v. 8, p. 180–190.

Paterson, W.S.B., and Law, L. K., 1966, Additional heat flow determinations in the area of Mould Bay, Arctic Canada: Canadian Journal of Earth Sciences, v. 3, p. 237–246.

Reford, M. S., 1967, Aeromagnetic interpretation, Sverdrup Basin: Ottawa, Department of Indian Affairs and Northern Development Oil and Gas Technical Reports 1975, 678-7-10-1 to 678-7-10-5.

Ricketts, B. D., 1987, Preliminary structural cross-sections across Fosheim Peninsula and Axel Heiberg Island, Arctic Archipelago, in Current Research, Part A: Geological Survey of Canada Paper 87–1A, p. 369–374.

Ricketts, B. D., and McIntyre, D. J., 1986, The Eureka Sound Group of eastern Axel Heiberg Island—new data on the Eurekan orogeny, in Current Research, Part B: Geological Survey of Canada Paper 86–1B, p. 405–410.

Ricketts, B., Osadetz, K. G., and Embry, A. F., 1985, Volcanic style in the Strand Fiord Formation (Upper Cretaceous), Axel Heiberg Island, Canadian Arctic Archipelago: Polar Research, v. 3, p. 107–122.

Riddihough, R. P., Haines, G. V., and Hannaford, W., 1973, Regional magnetic anomalies of the Canadian Arctic: Canadian Journal of Earth Sciences, v. 10, p. 147–163.

Sander, G. W., and Overton, A., 1965, Deep seismic refraction investigation in the Canadian Arctic Archipelago: Geophysics, v. 30, p. 87–96.

Scrutton, R. A., 1982, Passive continental margins—a review of observations and mechanisms, in Scrutton, R. A., ed., Dynamics of Passive Margins: American Geophysical Union Geodynamics Series, v. 6, p. 5–11.

Sobczak, L. W., 1975, Gravity and deep structure of the continental margin of Banks Island and the Mackenzie Delta: Canadian Journal of Earth Sciences, v. 12, p. 378–394.

Sobczak, L. W., and Overton, A., 1984, Shallow and deep crustal structure of the western Sverdrup Basin, Arctic Canada: Canadian Journal of Earth Sciences, v. 21, p. 902–919.

Sobczak, L. W., and Stephens, L. E., 1974, The gravity field of northeastern Ellesmere Island, part of northern Greenland, and Lincoln Sea, with map: Ottawa, Department of Energy, Mines and Resources Publications of the Earth Physics Branch Gravity Map Series 114, 9 p.

Sobczak, L. W., and Weber, J. R., 1973, Crustal structure of the Queen Elizabeth Islands and polar continental margin, in Pitcher, M. G., ed., Arctic Geology: American Association of Petroleum Geologists Memoir 19, p. 517–525.

—— , 1987, Gravity and bathymetry taken along seismic refraction lines from the Canadian ice island during 1985 and 1986, in Current Research, Part A: Geological Survey of Canada Paper 87–1A, p. 299–304.

Sobczak, L. W., Mayr, U., and Sweeney, J. F., 1986, Crustal section across the polar continent-ocean transition in Canada: Canadian Journal of Earth Sciences, v. 23, p. 608–621.

Stein, S., Sleep, N. H., Geller, R. J., Wang, S-C., and Kroeger, G. C., 1979, Earthquakes along the passive margin of eastern Canada: Geophysical Research Letters, v. 6, p. 537–540.

Stewart, I.C.F., 1980, Arctic lithospheric structure from delays of teleseismic P-wave reflections: Tectonophysics, v. 69, p. 37–62.
Stott, D. F., 1969, Ellef Ringnes Island, Canadian Arctic Archipelago: Geological Survey of Canada Paper 68-16, 44 p.
Sweeney, J. F., 1977, Subsidence of the Sverdrup Basin, Canadian Arctic Islands: Geological Society of America Bulletin, v. 88, p. 41–48.
——, 1982, Structure and development of the polar margin of North America, in Scrutton, R. A., ed., Dynamics of Passive Margins: American Geophysical Union Geodynamics Series, v. 6, p. 17–29.
Sweeney, J. F., and 7 others, 1978, Arctic Geophysical Review—A summary, in Sweeney, J. F., ed., Arctic Geophysical Review: Ottawa, Publications of the Earth Physics Branch, v. 45, p. 101–108.
Sweeney, J. F., Weber, J. R., and Balsco, S. M., 1982, Continental ridges in the Arctic Ocean, LOREX constraints: Tectonophysics, v. 89, p. 217–237.
Taylor, A., Judge, A., and Allen, V., 1986, Terrestrial heat flow from project CESAR, Alpha Ridge, Arctic Ocean: Journal of Geodynamics, v. 6, p. 137–176.
Thorstensson, R., and Tozer, E. T., 1970, Geology of the Arctic Archipelago, in Douglas, R.J.W., ed., Geology and Economic Minerals of Canada, edition 5: Ottawa, Geological Survey of Canada Economic Geology Report 1, p. 548–590.
——, 1974, Carboniferous and Permian stratigraphy of Axel Heiberg Island and western Ellesmere Island, Canadian Arctic Archipelago: Geological Survey of Canada Bulletin 224, 115 p.
Trettin, H. P., 1987, Pearya—a composite terrane with Caledonian affinities in northern Ellesmere Island: Canadian Journal of Earth Sciences, v. 24, p. 224–245.
Trettin, H. P., and Balkwill, H. R., 1979, Contributions to the tectonic history of the Innuitian Province, Arctic Canada: Canadian Journal of Earth Sciences, v. 16, p. 748–769.
Trettin, H. P., and Parrish, R., 1987, Late Cretaceous bimodal magmatism, northern Ellesmere Island—isotopic age and origin: Canadian Journal of Earth Sciences, v. 24, p. 257–265.
Trettin, H. P., and 7 others, 1972, The Innuitian Province, in Price, R. A., and Douglas, R.J.W., eds., Variations in Tectonic Styles in Canada: Geological Association of Canada Special Paper 11, p. 83–179.
Trettin, H. P., Parrish, R., and Loveridge, W. D., 1987, U-Pb determinations on Proterozoic to Devonian rocks from northern Ellesmere Island, Arctic Canada: Canadian Journal of Earth Sciences, v. 24, p. 246–256.
Van Wagoner, N. A., and Robinson, P. T., 1985, Petrology and geochemistry of a CESAR bedrock sample, implications for the origin of the Alpha Ridge: Geological Survey of Canada Paper 84-22, p. 47–57.

Vogt, P. R., Taylor, P. T., Kovacs, L. C. and Johnson, G. L., 1979, Detailed aeromagnetic investigations of the Arctic Basin: Journal of Geophysical Research, v. 84, p. 1071–1089.
——, 1982, The Canada Basin, aeromagnetic constraints on structure and evolution: Tectonophysics, v. 89, p. 295–336.
Weber, J. R., 1963, Gravity anomalies over the polar continental shelf: Contributions from the Dominion Observatory, v. 5, no. 17, p. 3–10.
——, 1983, Maps of the Arctic seafloor, a history of bathymetry and its interpretation: Arctic, v. 36, p. 121–142.
West, R. M., Dawson, M. R., Hickey, L. J., and Miall, A. D., 1981, Upper Cretaceous and Paleogene sedimentary rocks, eastern Canadian Arctic and related North Atlantic areas, in Kerr, J. W., and others, eds., Geology of the North Atlantic Borderlands: Canadian Society of Petroleum Geologists Memoir 7, p. 279–298.
Wetmiller, R. J., and Forsyth, D. A., 1978, Seismicity of the Arctic, 1908–1975, in Sweeney, J. F., ed., Arctic Geophysical Review: Ottawa, Publications of the Earth Physics Branch, v. 45, p. 15–24.
——, 1982, Review of seismicity and other geophysical data near Nares Strait, in Dawes, P. R., and Kerr, J. W., eds., Nares Strait and the Drift of Greenland—a Conflict in Plate Tectonics: Meddelelser om Grønland Geoscience 8, p. 261–274.
Willumsen, P. S., and Cote, R. P., 1982, Tertiary sedimentation in southern Beaufort Sea, Canada, in Embry, A. F., and Balkwill, H. R., eds., Arctic Geology and Geophysics: Canadian Society of Petroleum Geologists Memoir 8, p. 43–53.
Wilson, J. T., 1963, Hypothesis of the Earth's behaviour: Nature, v. 198, p. 925–929.
Wold, R. J., Woodzick, T. L., and Ostenso, N. A., 1970, Structure of the Beaufort Sea continental margin: Geophysics, v. 35, p. 849–861.
Wynne, P. J., Irving, E., and Ozadetz, K., 1988, Paleomagnetism of Cretaceous volcanic rocks of the Sverdrup Basin—magnetostratigraphy, paleolatitudes, and rotations: Canadian Journal of Earth Sciences, v. 25, p. 1220–1239.

MANUSCRIPT ACCEPTED BY THE SOCIETY NOVEMBER 18, 1988

ACKNOWLEDGMENT

We thank H. R. Balkwill, J. Dixon and A. R. Palmer for useful comments and suggestions.

Icebergs near Kosoak, Life Boat Cove. Reproduced from Kane, E. K., 1856, Arctic Explorations: The Second Grinnell Expedition in Search of Sir John Franklin, 1853, '54, '55. Volume 2: Philadelphia, Childs and Peterson, facing p. 57.

Printed in U.S.A.

Chapter 15

Canadian Beaufort Sea and adjacent land areas

J. Dixon and J. R. Dietrich
Geological Survey of Canada, 3303 33rd St. NW, Calgary, Alberta T2L 2A7, Canada

INTRODUCTION

Geographical Setting

The Canadian Beaufort Sea extends from offshore Banks Island to 141°W longitude (Fig. 1). It is rimmed to the south by the Yukon Coastal Plain, the outer Mackenzie Delta, including Richards Island, and Tuktoyaktuk Peninsula. The narrow coastal plain of northern Yukon is bounded to the south by the British Mountains and the Porcupine Plateau (Fig. 1). The broad Amundsen Gulf separates the Anderson and Horton plains of the Northwest Territories mainland from Banks Island and Victoria Island.

The continental margin beneath the Beaufort Sea can be divided into several physiographic regions. The shallow-water shelf is 50–100 km wide and is characterized by low, uniform slope gradients of 1–2 m/km. An abrupt increase in the sea-floor slope gradient marks the shelf edge. Water depths at the shelf break vary from 60 m near 141°W to almost 500 m west of Banks Island. Two channel-like features cut across the Beaufort shelf. Northeast of Herschel Island, the Mackenzie Trough (formerly Mackenzie Canyon) cuts obliquely across the shelf in a northwesterly direction (Fig. 1). Southwest of Banks Island, the broad Amundsen Gulf channel cuts across the shelf in a northwesterly direction. Both of these bathymetric troughs are 100–500 m deep and are geologically recent in origin. The continental slope seaward of the shelf edge is 20–50 km wide and is characterized by variable slope gradients of 5–30 m/km. The outer continental slope north of the Mackenzie Trough is marked by a steep, sea-floor escarpment with local slope gradients of up to 170 m/km (Fig. 1). In Alaskan waters the region between the shelf edge and this outer escarpment has been referred to as the Beaufort Ramp (Grantz and others, 1981). The ramp appears to be the product of Quaternary subsidence and tilting of an upper Tertiary outer continental shelf. The continental slope merges with the continental rise in water depths of 1,100–1,800 m. The continental rise extends for several hundred kilometres into the Canada Basin with typical slope gradients of 10–15 m/km.

The permanent polar ice-pack (Fig. 1) covers much of the area underlain by the continental rise and portions of the shelf and slope offshore from Banks Island. Acquisition of marine reflection seismic data has been concentrated along the southern rim of the Beaufort Sea, where the summer ice-retreat is most extensive and predictable. To date, all of the offshore drilling by the petroleum industry has been located along the southern Beaufort shelf, in water depths up to 80 m. There are 220 exploration wells in the area and approximately 80,000 km of released industry reflection seismic data.

Previous Work

The earliest comprehensive geological synthesis to include the Beaufort Sea was by Lerand (1973), closely followed by Yorath (1973) and Yorath and Norris (1975). However, a lack of data from the Beaufort Sea tended to focus their work more on the adjacent land areas. With the increased availability of data from reflection seismic profiles and exploration drilling, more detailed geological descriptions of Beaufort Sea geology became possible. Most of the offshore data is concentrated in the southern part of the Beaufort Sea, with relatively little information available for offshore Banks Island.

Some of the more notable reports using the newer information are by Hawkings and Hatlelid (1975), Young (1975), and Young and others (1976). As exploration continued and drilling extended further into the offshore, reports on the wells began to appear (Dixon and Snowdon, 1979; Jones and others, 1980; McNeil and others, 1982; Dixon and others, 1984). Young and McNeil (1984) proposed lithostratigraphic nomenclature for the Tertiary succession under the Mackenzie Delta, whereas Dietrich and others (1985) (Table 1) proposed an alternative stratigraphic scheme based, in large part, on the recognition of basin-wide depositional sequences (Mitchum and others, 1977), identified primarily from reflection seismic profiles.

Recent stratigraphic syntheses have included the work of Hea and others (1980), which dealt with the whole of the Beaufort Sea, and Willumsen and Coté (1982), who dealt only with the Mackenzie Delta and the immediately adjacent offshore area.

Dixon, J., and Dietrich, J. R., 1990, Canadian Beaufort Sea and adjacent land areas, *in* Grantz, A., Johnson, L., and Sweeney, J. F., eds., The Arctic Ocean region: Boulder, Colorado, Geological Society of America, The Geology of North America, v. L.

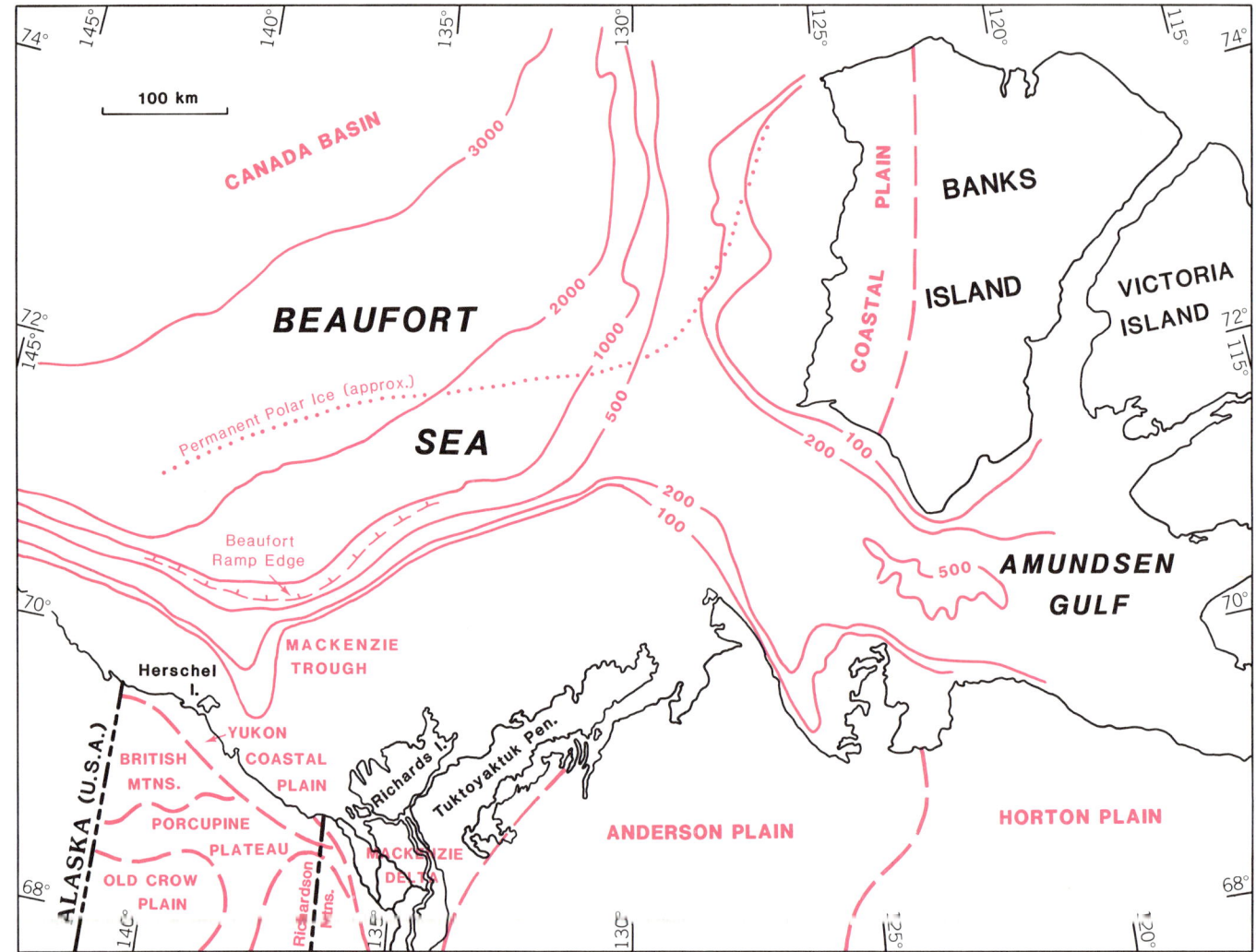

Figure 1. Location map and physiographic regions of the Canadian Beaufort Sea and adjacent land areas (bathymetry in metres).

Norris and Yorath (1981) and Balkwill and others (1983) incorporated the Beaufort Sea into their regional tectono-stratigraphic syntheses, but in both cases most of their data is land based.

Comprehensive studies of Banks Island geology began with Thorsteinsson and Tozer (1962). More detailed studies followed: Hills (1969) on the Tertiary Beaufort Formation, Embry and Klovan (1971) and Klovan and Embry (1971) on Upper Devonian strata, and Plauchut and Jutard (1976) on the Cretaceous and Tertiary. The most recent detailed accounts are by Miall (1975, 1976, 1979). Offshore Banks Island, the least studied part of the Beaufort Sea area, has been briefly mentioned by Lerand (1973) and Miall (1975, 1979).

Regional Tectonic Elements

The Beaufort Sea is bordered on its landward side by a variety of geological terrains (Fig. 2; see also the maps of Norris, 1981a, b, c, d; and Miall, 1979). In northern Yukon the Proterozoic-cored Romanzof Uplift lies only a few kilometers from the shoreline. Southeast of the uplift there are two depressions, defined primarily by their Jurassic to Albian sedimentary fill. These are the Old Crow–Babbage and Rapid depressions, separated in part by the Paleozoic-cored Barn Uplift. The Rapid Depression contains the Rapid Fault Array, a series of north-trending, high-angle faults with substantial vertical and possible right-lateral displacements of Cretaceous and older strata (Yorath and Norris, 1975). Pronounced thickness variations occur in Jurassic and Lower Cretaceous strata within and across the fault array (Young, 1974; Poulton, 1982; Dixon, 1986). The east flank of the Rapid Depression is marked by the Paleozoic-cored Cache Creek Uplift. Northeast of and on trend with the Cache Creek Uplift is the Tununuk High. East of these two positive elements are the northeast-trending Canoe Depression and Kugmallit Trough, separated by a structural-stratigraphic high known as the Napoiak High. The southeast flank of the Kugmallit and Canoe depressions is defined by the Eskimo Lakes Arch (Fig. 2). The

TABLE 1. STRATIGRAPHIC UNITS IN THE CANADIAN BEAUFORT SEA REGION.

Era	Period	Epoch	WEST BEAUFORT SEA AND NORTHERN YUKON	TUKTOYAKTUK PENINSULA AND CENTRAL BEAUFORT SEA	BANKS ISLAND AND OFFSHORE	TE*
CENOZOIC	QUAT.	PLEIST.	SHALLOW BAY SEQUENCE / Glacial-interglacial deposits	SHALLOW BAY SEQUENCE / Glacial-interglacial deposits	Modern deposits / Glacial-interglacial deposits	MINOR TECTONIC ACTIVITY
CENOZOIC	TERTIARY	NEO.	IPERK SEQUENCE	IPERK SEQUENCE	IPERK SEQUENCE (?Worth Point Fm. onshore)	POST-DRIFT / COMPRESSION AND STRIKE-SLIP
CENOZOIC	TERTIARY	PALEOGENE	AKPAK SEQUENCE / MACKENZIE BAY SEQUENCE / KUGMALLIT SEQUENCE / KOPANOAR SEQ. / RICHARDS SEQUENCE / REINDEER SEQUENCE	AKPAK SEQUENCE / MACKENZIE BAY SEQUENCE / KUGMALLIT SEQUENCE / KOPANOAR SEQ. / RICHARDS SEQUENCE / REINDEER SEQUENCE	BEAUFORT FM. / EUREKA SOUND FM.	
MESOZOIC	CRETACEOUS	U	FISH RIVER SEQUENCE (Tent Island and Moose Channel Fms.) / BOUNDARY CREEK SEQ./FM.	FISH RIVER SEQUENCE (Mostly Mason River Fm.) / SMOKING HILLS SEQ./FM. / BOUNDARY CREEK SEQ./FM.	KANGUK FM.	
MESOZOIC	CRETACEOUS	L	Albian flysch / RAT RIVER FM. / MOUNT GOODENOUGH FM.	ARCTIC RED FM. / RAT RIVER FM. / MOUNT GOODENOUGH FM. / ATKINSON POINT FM. / SIKU FM.	HASSEL FM. / CHRISTOPHER FM. / ISACHSEN FM.	DRIFTING
MESOZOIC	JURASSIC	U/M/L	PARSONS GP. / KINGAK FM. / HUSKY FM. / BUG CREEK GP. / unnamed	PARSONS GP. / HUSKY FM. / BUG CREEK GP.	Jurassic shale	RIFTING
MESOZOIC	TRIAS	U/M/L	SHUBLIK FM.			RIFTING
PALEOZOIC	PERMIAN	U/L	SADLEROCHIT FM. (Romanzoff Mts.) / Unnamed (Cache Creek Uplift)			RIFTING
PALEOZOIC	CARB.	MISS./PENN	LISBURNE GROUP / KAYAK FM. / KEKIKTUK FM.			RIFTING
PALEOZOIC	DEVONIAN	U/M/L		IMPERIAL FM. / CANOL FM. / HUME FM.	MELVILLE ISLAND GP. / ORKSUT AND NANUK FMS. / BLUE FIORD FM.	RIFTING
PALEOZOIC	SILURIAN	U/M/L	Unnamed shale, chert, phyllite and quartzite (Road River Fm., in part – Richardson Mts.) Lower-Upper Cambrian volcanics in the Romanzoff Uplift.	Unnamed dolostone / (Offshore may pass laterally into shale)	Unnamed dolostone (Offshore may pass laterally into shale)	RIFTING
PALEOZOIC	ORDOVICIAN	U/M/L			Unnamed dolostone (projected from Victoria Island)	RIFTING
PALEOZOIC	CAMBRIAN	U/M/L		?Clastic unit (projected)	unnamed clastic unit	RIFTING
PREC.	PROT.	He/Ha/Ap	NERUOKPUK FM.	unnamed	SHALER GP.	
			? ?	? ?	? ?	

*TE – Tectonic events related to the development of Canada Basin

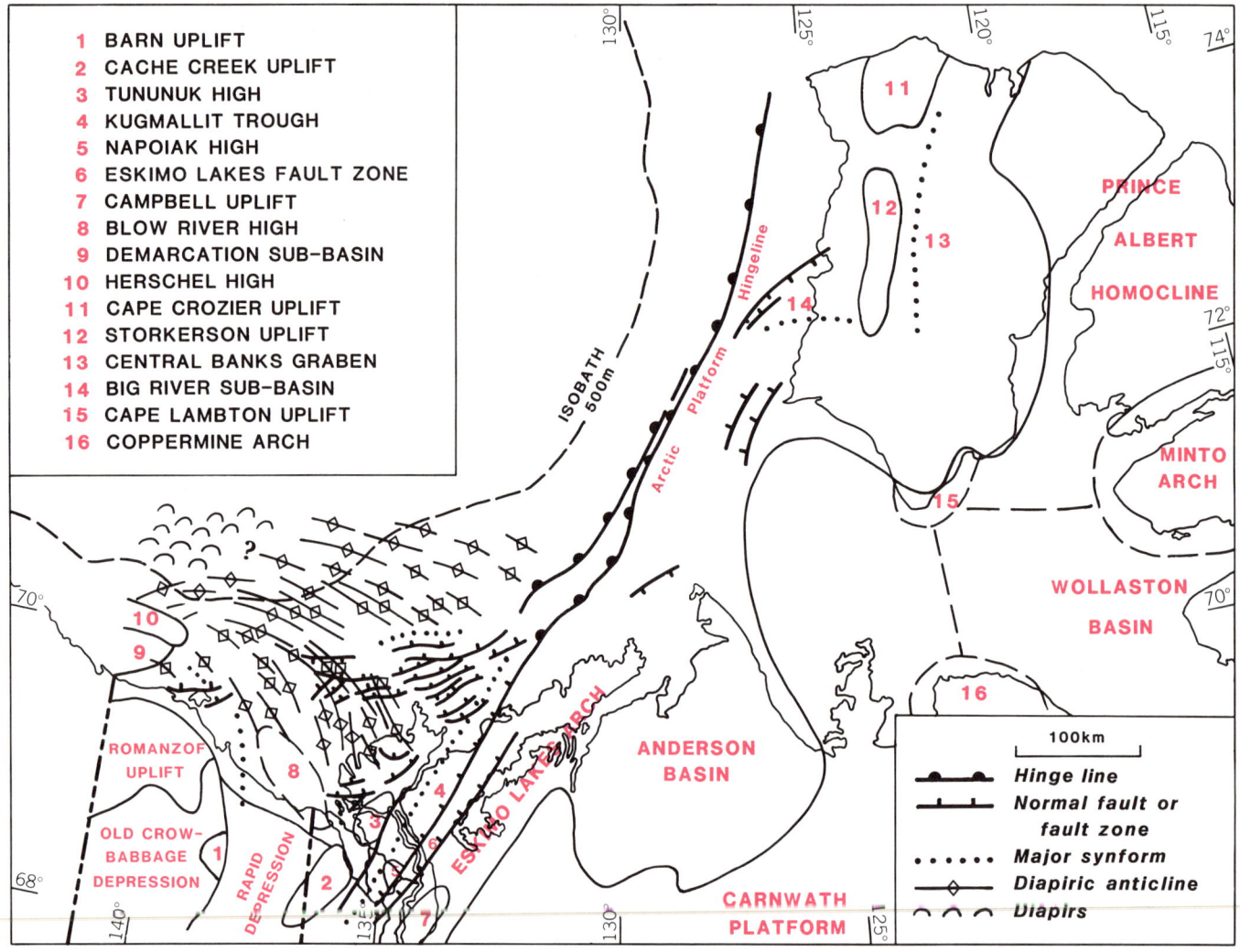

Figure 2. Regional tectonic elements; Canadian Beaufort Sea and adjacent land areas.

northwest flank of this positive element is cut by a series of subparallel, northeast-trending faults. Many of these faults, including the Eskimo Lakes Fault (Coté and others, 1975), have substantial vertical displacements with considerably expanded Lower Cretaceous sections on their downthrown, northwest sides. The magnitude of this faulting generally decreases from southwest to northeast, into the Beaufort Sea shelf area. East of the Eskimo Lakes Arch is the Anderson Basin, a broad, shallow depression containing Cretaceous strata. The basin is bounded to the east and south by Paleozoic rocks of the Carnwath Platform.

Banks Island is underlain by Paleozoic strata of the Prince Albert Homocline, strata which are exposed in the northeastern part of the island and adjacent Victoria Island (Fig. 2). Proterozoic strata are exposed at the extreme southern tip of the island in the Cape Lambton Uplift. A relatively thin cover of Jurassic to Tertiary strata overlies the pre-Mesozoic section over much of Banks Island. The thickest successions of Mesozoic-Cenozoic strata on the island occur in the Big River sub-basin (Fig. 2) and in a north–south-trending graben in the central part of the island. The graben is bounded to the west by the Paleozoic-cored Storkerson Uplift. Other smaller uplifts have been identified on the island by Miall (1979).

Amundsen Gulf is underlain by lower Paleozoic strata of the Carnwath Platform and, locally, Proterozoic rocks of Coppermine and Minto arches and Cape Lambton Uplift. On a more regional scale, the Paleozoic rocks of the Banks Island, Amundsen Gulf, and eastern Beaufort Sea areas collectively constitute the western Arctic Platform.

The Beaufort Sea is underlain by thick successions of Upper Cretaceous to Holocene strata (Fig. 3) deposited in two major depositional basins—the Beaufort-Mackenzie Basin (Young and others, 1976; the Mackenzie Basin of Lerand, 1973), and the Banks Island Basin (Thorsteinsson and Tozer, 1960). In the context of this chapter, it is our intention to limit these terms to depositional basins containing Upper Cretaceous to Holocene strata; this differs from original usage of these terms to describe post-Paleozoic depocentres. We also consider the several basins identified on Banks Island by Miall (1979) to be sub-basins within the larger Banks Island Basin. Similarly, the Demarcation sub-basin (Fig. 2; Hea and others, 1980) is an upper Tertiary depocenter that is part of the Beaufort-Mackenzie Basin. This sub-basin is bounded to the north by the Herschel High. Both the Herschel High and Blow River High (Fig. 2) are positive features within the Beaufort-Mackenzie Basin that appear to be cored by closely spaced Upper Cretaceous–lower Tertiary-cored anticlines. Other structural features within the Upper Cretaceous–Tertiary succession of the Beaufort-Mackenzie Basin include an arcuate array of lower Tertiary-cored anticlines, large-scale growth faults, and mudstone-cored diapirs beneath the present-day continental rise (Fig. 2).

Beneath the eastern Beaufort Sea, upper Mesozoic-Cenozoic sediments overlie pre-Mesozoic strata of the Arctic Platform. The offshore extension of the northwest margin of the Eskimo Lakes Arch is defined by the Arctic Platform hinge line (Fig. 2). This subsidence hinge line is marked by an abrupt increase in the basinward dip of the top of the Arctic Platform. Beneath the Beaufort-Mackenzie Basin, pre-Mesozoic strata extend a short distance basinward of the hinge line to a second, outer hinge zone or fault margin (Fig. 2). Beyond this outer hinge zone the pre-Mesozoic section dips steeply below the resolution of available reflection seismic data.

TECTONIC IMPLICATIONS RELATED TO CONTINENTAL MARGIN DEVELOPMENT

Mesozoic Tectonics

The continental margin beneath the Canadian Beaufort Sea forms the arcuate southeast margin of the deep Canada Basin (Fig. 1). While it is widely accepted that the Canada Basin is underlain by oceanic crust, the timing and tectonic nature of the development of the basin and adjacent continental margins has been the subject of considerable debate (see, for example, the review of Lawver and others, 1984). One of the more commonly

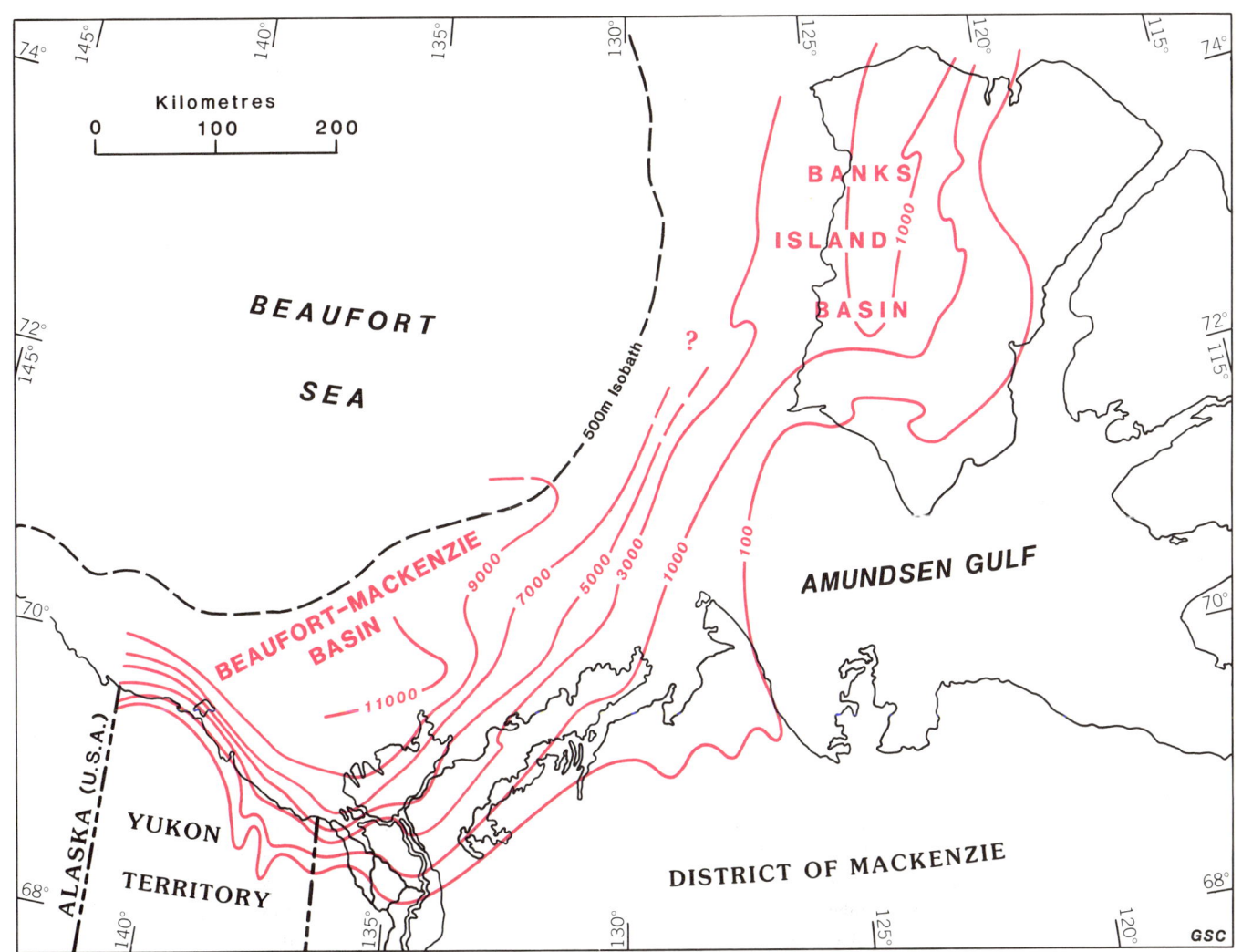

Figure 3. Isopachs of Upper Cretaceous to Holocene strata; Canadian Beaufort Sea.

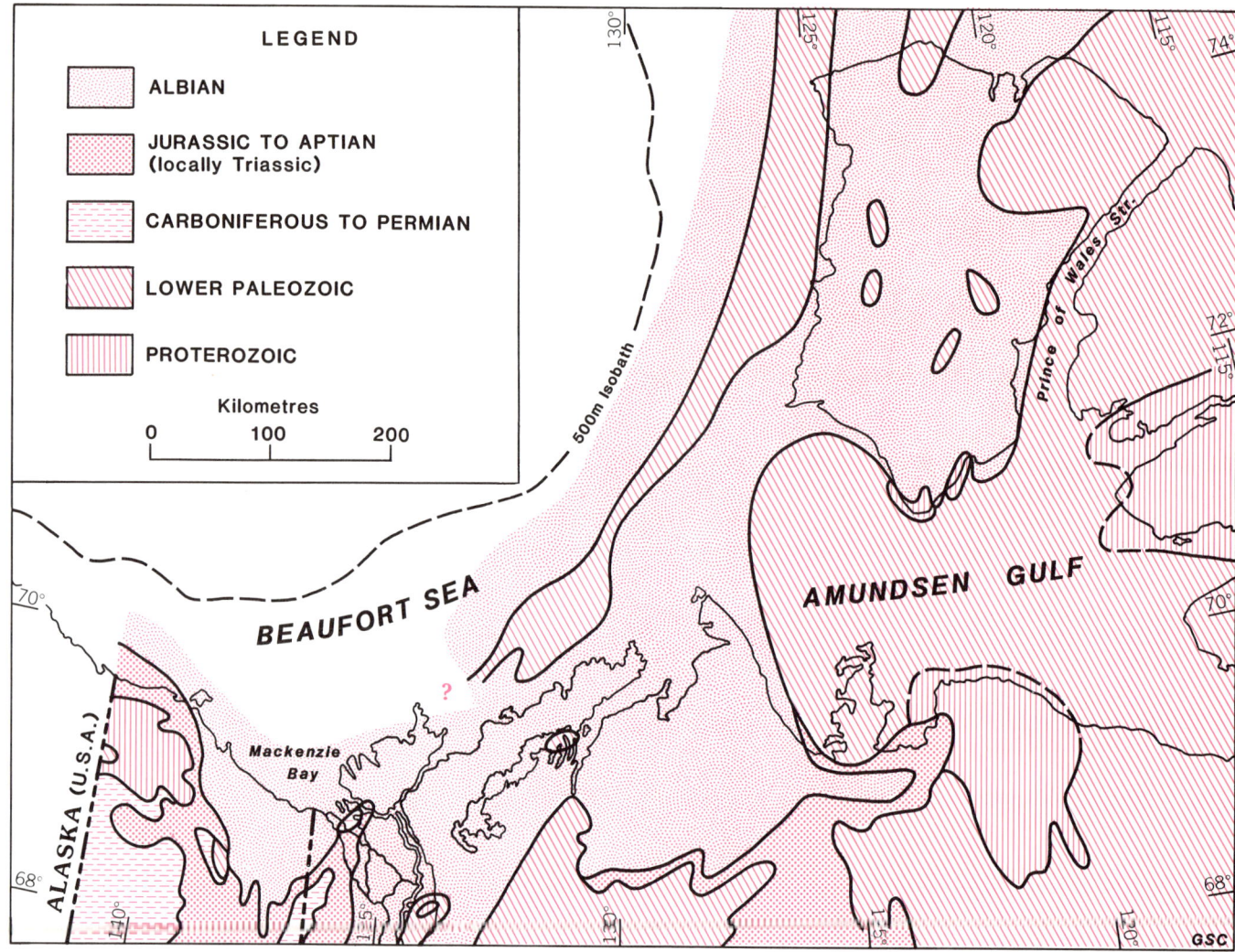

Figure 4. Pre-Upper Cretaceous geology beneath the Canadian Beaufort Sea and adjacent land areas.

proposed plate tectonic models for the region involves the rotational rifting of northern Alaska away from the Canadian Arctic Islands about a pivot point located near the Mackenzie Delta (e.g., Tailleur, 1973; Grantz and others, 1979). Continental breakup and subsequent sea-floor spreading in the Canada Basin are believed to have occurred during part of the Cretaceous period, extending from about 130 to 80 Ma (Sweeney, 1985). In the context of the rotational model, the continental margins bordering the southern Canada Basin are assumed to be passive type, pull-apart margins.

Several aspects of the pre-Cenozoic geology in the Canadian Beaufort Sea region can be cited as evidence in support of a rotational rifting model. Beneath the eastern Beaufort Sea, pre-Mesozoic strata of the Arctic Platform display the effects of Cretaceous uplift and erosion along an outer platform margin, subparallel to a pronounced subsidence hinge line (Figs. 2, 4, 10). Both the subsidence hinge line and remnant marginal high are typical features of rifted, passive margins. Seaward of the hinge line, rapid subsidence and faulting of the outermost Arctic Platform accompanied deposition of a basinward-thickening wedge of sediment of inferred Early Cretaceous age (Figs. 10, 11). The extensional nature of the Early Cretaceous deformation in the area is also evident from the abundance and magnitude of normal faulting along the northwest margin of the Eskimo Lakes Arch beneath Tuktoyaktuk Peninsula. The adjacent Kugmallit Trough is a latest Jurassic–Early Cretaceous half-graben, which resembles the typical rift-valleys commonly found adjacent to pull-apart margins. The central Banks Island graben is a similar extensional feature containing latest Jurassic and expanded Early Cretaceous strata. Although initial subsidence within these grabens began as early as Oxfordian (Husky Formation deposition), the main phase of subsidence and syndepositional faulting appears to have occurred during late Early Cretaceous deposition. In northern Yukon, the Rapid Depression initially developed as an Early Jurassic extensional trough containing a series of south-trending, high-angle normal faults. The southern apex of the

Rapid Depression (located south of the study area, near 138°W and 68°N) has been proposed as the pivot point for the rotational separation of the northern Alaska plate from the Arctic Islands margin (Norris, 1983). North of the rotational pole, stratigraphic and structural patterns indicate that maximum extension and subsidence within the trough occurred during Aptian and Albian deposition (Young, 1974). Concurrent uplift in the adjacent Brooks Range Geanticline may be related to compressional deformation along the leading edge of the rotated northern Alaska–northern Yukon plate.

The onset of continental breakup along the margin north of Alaska is marked by a prominent breakup unconformity at the base of the Hauterivian to Barremian pebble-shale unit (Grantz and May, 1983). In the Mackenzie Delta area the same middle Hauterivian unconformity is recognized at the base of the Mount Goodenough Formation (Dixon, 1982). The widespread erosional nature of this unconformity attests to the intensity of the uplift and tectonism throughout the area during this time. On Banks Island a similarly dramatic unconformity occurs at the base of the Barremian to Aptian Isachsen Formation (Miall, 1979). In both the Banks Island and Mackenzie Delta areas, post-Hauterivian sedimentation is characterized by greatly expanded depositional limits and locally accelerated rates of subsidence and syndepositional faulting. All of these features can be related to the general tectonic instability and downwarping adjacent to a newly formed continental margin.

Two Late Cretaceous unconformities (early Cenomanian and middle Campanian) within the study area developed during major periods of uplift and erosion of parts of the continental margin. Their development may have some relation to the tectonics associated with the final stages and eventual termination of sea-floor spreading in the Canada Basin.

Cenozoic Tectonics

Throughout much of the Beaufort-Mackenzie Basin the record of pre–Late Cretaceous sedimentation and tectonism is masked beneath the thick cover of latest Cretaceous-Tertiary sediments. The Maastrichtian and Tertiary strata above Late Cretaceous unconformities were deposited during periods of rapid sedimentation and subsidence along the entire Beaufort Sea continental margin. The structural deformation within the Tertiary continental margin prism is dominated by growth faulting and shale diapirism. In the western part of the basin there is also a significant component of compressional deformation (including reverse faulting) associated with the development of the array of lower Tertiary–cored diapiric anticlines (Figs. 2, 8). This deformation may be related to gravity flow folding and/or crustal shortening seaward of the front of the Romanzof Uplift. Early to mid-Tertiary deformation within the Rapid Depression in northern Yukon has been interpreted as the result of the northeasterly directed slip of the entire northern Alaska–northern Yukon crustal plate, with the lateral motion accommodated by strike-slip displacement along components of the Rapid Fault Array (Norris, 1972, 1974, 1985b; Collot and others, 1984). The culmination of the tectonism may correlate with the development of a prominent unconformity of middle or late Eocene age in the western Beaufort-Mackenzie Basin.

Tertiary strata within the Beaufort-Mackenzie Basin are also deformed by large-scale growth faults, particularly in the Richards Island and south-central Beaufort Sea areas (Figs. 2, 9). The orientations of these Eocene to mid-Miocene faults are generally oblique to the lower Tertiary-cored diapiric anticlines and their development either postdates, or is kinematically unrelated to most of the development of the anticlinal structures.

A dramatic tectono-stratigraphic break occurs within the Tertiary succession across a late Miocene unconformity. Most of the early to mid-Tertiary structural features are truncated at the unconformity surface and the overlying Plio-Pleistocene sediments are largely undeformed (Fig. 9). The late Miocene unconformity, which may have developed in response to a major eustatic sea level fall, marks the end of significant tectonism and structural instability within the Tertiary continental margin prism.

STRATIGRAPHY

Introduction

The geology of the Beaufort Sea continental margin is known through the interpretation of reflection seismic data, borehole information, and onshore surface geology. The stratigraphy of the area is presented in two subdivisions, pre-Upper Cretaceous and Upper Cretaceous to Holocene strata. A major unconformity between Upper Cretaceous and older strata marks a significant tectono-stratigraphic boundary throughout the region (Table 1; see also Young, 1973; Yorath and Norris, 1975; Hawkings and Hatlelid, 1975). Upper Cretaceous and Tertiary strata are up to 11,000 m thick in the central Beaufort-Mackenzie Basin and are at least 4,000 m thick in the offshore portion of the Banks Island Basin (Fig. 3). In the Beaufort-Mackenzie Basin these strata have been divided into eleven major depositional sequences (Table 1; Dietrich and others, 1985; see Dixon, 1986 for a discussion of possible eustatic influences). Pre-Upper Cretaceous geology is best known from the land areas adjacent to the Beaufort Sea, where the stratigraphy has been described in more conventional terms of formations and groups (Table 1).

PRE–UPPER CRETACEOUS STRATIGRAPHY

Precambrian

Archean crystalline basement is not exposed anywhere near the Beaufort Sea, with the nearest outcrops occurring on the Canadian Shield, several hundred kilometres to the southeast. Proterozoic strata, however, crop out at several sites (Fig. 4). The Hadrynian Glenelg Formation of the Shaler Group crops out on the southern tip of Banks Island, in the Cape Lambton Uplift (Thorsteinsson and Tozer, 1962; Young and Jefferson, 1975;

Miall, 1976). It consists of a lower cherty member and an upper sandstone member.

On the Eskimo Lakes Arch unnamed Proterozoic clastics and carbonates are exposed in the Campbell Uplift (Fig. 2; Dyke, 1975). In the subsurface of Tuktoyaktuk Peninsula, presumed Proterozoic quartzitic sandstones and conglomerates and volcanic rocks occur below Mesozoic strata (Dixon, 1979).

Proterozoic strata in the Romanzof Uplift consist of thrust-faulted and isoclinally folded argillites, feldspathic sandstones, limestones and basic volcanic rocks; all of which are part of the Neroukpuk Formation. The exact age of these strata is not known, although Norris (1985a) suggested a Hadrynian age.

Cambrian to Devonian

Adjacent to and underlying Banks Island Basin and the eastern Beaufort-Mackenzie Basin is a thick succession of Lower Cambrian to Devonian strata (Table 1; Fig. 4). Cratonic-derived Lower and Middle Cambrian clastics grade upward into upper Cambrian to Middle Devonian platform carbonates, which, in turn, are overlain by Upper Devonian clastics. The Devonian clastics occur in the Orksut and Nanuk formations and the Melville Island Group on Banks Island (Klovan and Embry, 1971; Miall, 1976), and the Canol and Imperial formations in the Anderson Plain and Tuktoyaktuk Peninsula area. The Upper Devonian succession on Banks Island represents an overall prograding succession, with deep-water sediments at the base, grading up into shallow-marine and finally nonmarine deposits (Klovan and Embry, 1971; Miall, 1976). On the mainland, the Imperial Formation is predominantly turbidite-like in character. These Late Devonian clastics are related to the final phase of the Franklinian orogeny.

In the northern Yukon, Cambrian to Devonian shales are preserved in the north-south oriented Richardson Mountains (Norris, 1981e). These basinal shales were deposited in the Richardson Trough, which separated platform carbonates to the east and west (Jackson and Lenz, 1962). The trough may have linked up with the Hazen Trough that extends through Banks Island (Miall, 1976) into the Arctic Islands, as well as the Early Paleozoic basinal sediments in northwestern Yukon and northeastern Alaska. The northwest Yukon strata consist of Lower to Upper Cambrian basic volcanics, argillites and limestones, exposed in the core of the Romanzof Uplift (Norris, 1981a) and Ordovician-Silurian shale, chert and quartzite in the Barn Uplift and Hoidahl Dome (Norris, 1981b). In Alaska, sediments similar to those in the Romanzof Uplift are present but are overlain gradationally by chert and phyllite (Dutro and others, 1972). At the northern end of the Richardson Mountains, platform carbonates are locally preserved in the White Uplift (Norford, 1964). In the northern Yukon there are also a number of igneous intrusions (granite, quartz monzonite, and syenite) that appear to have been emplaced during the latest Ordovician or earliest Silurian (Norris and Yorath, 1981).

Carboniferous to Permian

In the subsurface of the southwestern Mackenzie Delta and exposed throughout the northern Yukon are extensive areas of Carboniferous and Permian strata (Fig. 4; Table 1; Norris 1981a, b, d; Bamber and Waterhouse, 1971). Conglomerates of the Carboniferous Kekiktuk Formation rest unconformably on older strata, which, in turn, are overlapped by the Kayak Formation. The latter contains shale and coal in its lower part, gradationally overlain by calcareous shale and limestone. Lisburne Group carbonates gradationally overlie Kayak strata. Carboniferous strata also are exposed on the rims of the Romanzof Uplift and Barn Uplift. Disconformably overlying Carboniferous rocks on the flanks of the Romanzof Uplift are Permian clastics and thin limestone beds of the Sadlerochit Formation. Correlative, but much thicker, unnamed Permian strata occur in the core of the Cache Creek Uplift, where they rest disconformably on the Lisburne Group (Bamber and Waterhouse, 1971).

No Carboniferous or Permian strata are known to underlie Banks Island, Amundsen Gulf, Tuktoyaktuk Peninsula, or the eastern Beaufort Sea. Paleozoic rocks in these areas are entirely Cambrian to Devonian in age. The extent and nature of Paleozoic and older strata beneath the western part of the Beaufort Sea is not known.

Triassic to Albian

Triassic strata are preserved locally in synclinal structures adjacent to the Romanzof Uplift (Norris, 1981a). They consist of up to 150 m of interbedded carbonates and clastics of the Shublik Formation.

Jurassic to Albian strata are exposed extensively throughout the land areas and have cumulative thicknesses of up to 2,500 m in the Kugmallit Trough and possibly 5,000 m in the Rapid Depression (Fig. 2).

The Lower and Middle Jurassic Kingak Formation and Bug Creek Group occur throughout the northern Yukon and Mackenzie Delta (Poulton and others, 1982; Dixon, 1982). The Lower and Middle Jurassic strata reported from Banks Island (Miall, 1979) is based on questionable dating of microfossils (J. H. Wall, personal communication, 1985) and it is probable that the strata there are no older than Oxfordian. The Bug Creek Group consists of a series of westward-prograding, coarsening-upward units that grade laterally into marine shales of the Kingak Formation.

Bug Creek strata are overlapped by, and in abrupt contact with, Oxfordian strata of the Husky Formation, and locally the Porcupine River Formation (Poulton, 1982). On Banks Island, Jurassic shales (Miall, 1979) are facies equivalents of, and co-eval with, the Husky Formation. The Oxfordian to Berriasian Husky Formation and equivalent strata on Banks Island are shale-dominant successions with some sandy horizons in their lower parts (Jeletzky, 1967; Dixon, 1982; Miall, 1979). The upper part of the Kingak Formation in northwestern Yukon probably includes Oxfordian to Berriasian strata. Oxfordian to Berriasian strata are preserved in the Kugmallit Trough, the central Banks Island graben, and in an erosional remnant in the Anderson Basin (Brideaux and Fisher, 1976).

In the Mackenzie Delta and northern Yukon areas, the Husky Formation is gradationally overlain by sandstones of the upper Berriasian to lower Valanginian Martin Creek Formation (Dixon, 1982). Unconformably to disconformably overlying the Martin Creek Formation is the shale-dominant McGuire Formation, which in turn is gradationally succeeded by the sandstone-dominant, upper Valanginian to middle Hauterivian Kamik Formation (Dixon, 1982). The Martin Creek, McGuire, and Kamik formations comprise the Parsons Group (Table 1). Abruptly overlying the Parsons Group is a thin marine shale unit, the Siku Formation (Dixon, 1982), that apparently is only preserved in the deeper parts of the Kugmallit Trough. On Banks Island, there are no equivalent strata to the Parsons Group or the Siku Formation. In the Beaufort-Mackenzie area, Jurassic to Hauterivian sediments were derived from the east and southeast, from the cratonic areas (Dixon, 1986).

In the Mackenzie Delta area, upper Hauterivian strata of the Mount Goodenough Formation rest erosionally on older strata. The unconformity at the base of the formation is a major regional feature that records a significant phase of tectonic activity in the area, probably the onset of rifting in Canada Basin. Above its basal silty to sandy transgressive beds, the Mount Goodenough Formation is shale dominant. Sandstone interbeds increase in number up-section and there is an apparent gradation into the sandstone-dominant, Barremian to Aptian Rat River Formation. On Banks Island, the nonmarine Aptian Isachsen Formation rests unconformably on Jurassic shales (Miall, 1979). In the Anderson Basin, Aptian strata also rest unconformably on older rocks (Yorath and Cook, 1981). On the Eskimo Lakes Arch, Aptian Atkinson Point strata are preserved locally (Dixon, 1979, 1982). Late Hauterivian to Aptian sediments were derived principally from the cratonic areas east and southeast of the Beaufort-Mackenzie and Banks Island basins (Dixon, 1986; Miall, 1979).

Albian strata rest abruptly, and locally unconformably, on Aptian and older rocks. Throughout most of the area east of the Cache Creek Uplift, Albian strata consist of marine shelf shales. These are represented by the Christopher Formation on Banks Island and the Arctic Red Formation in the Mackenzie Delta and Tuktoyaktuk Peninsula regions. In the northernmost Richardson Mountains, Albian strata are represented by ironstone beds of the Rapid Creek Formation (Young and Robertson, 1984). West of the Cache Creek Uplift, the Rapid Depression contains up to 2,000 m of unnamed Albian conglomerates, sandstones, and shales of sediment gravity-flow origin (Young and others, 1976).

Albian sedimentation in northern Yukon marks a significant change in Mesozoic source terrains within the study area. Sediments within the epicontinental, Jurassic to Aptian deposits were derived from the North American craton, south and east of the present-day Mackenzie Delta (Poulton, 1982a; Young and others, 1976; Dixon, 1986). The Albian deposits in the Rapid Depression were derived from a western terrain, the Brooks Range Geanticline (an Albian uplift that includes the present-day Romanzoff Uplift and Old Crow–Babbage Depression: Young and others, 1976). Coarse clastics were shed from this uplifted terrain into the adjacent trough of the Rapid Depression. South of the present study area, in the vicinity of the Peel Trough, Albian and Aptian sediments were shed from the Cordilleran orogen (Dixon, 1986). On Banks Island, most of the Mesozoic sediment appears to have come from the craton to the east.

Lower Cretaceous and Jurassic(?) strata are believed to be widespread beneath the offshore portion of the Beaufort-Mackenzie Basin. The thickest sections probably occur north of the Rapid Depression and in the seaward extension of the Kugmallit Trough (Fig. 2). In the eastern Beaufort Sea area, however, Lower Cretaceous strata (mostly Albian, seaward of Amundsen Gulf) have been removed from along the basinward margin of the Arctic Platform by Late Cretaceous erosion (Fig. 4).

UPPER CRETACEOUS–HOLOCENE STRATIGRAPHY

Boundary Creek Sequence

The Boundary Creek sequence is an unconformity-bounded unit of late Cenomanian to Turonian age that occurs in outcrops and the subsurface along the southwestern margin of the Beaufort-Mackenzie Basin. The unconformable contact between Boundary Creek and underlying Albian strata is exposed along the Fish River in the northern Richardson Mountains (Fig. 5). The Boundary Creek sequence is up to 1,100 m thick and is unconformably overlain by Fish River strata (Young, 1975). The sequence consists of organic-rich shales interbedded with thin bentonite beds and ironstone concretions. The high organic content, common occurrence of concretions, and lack of coarse clastic material indicate deposition in a low-energy, anoxic, outer-shelf to slope environment. Frequent volcanic activity during the late Cenomanian–Turonian is evident from the abundance of bentonite beds.

Boundary Creek strata are progressively truncated in an eastward direction and do not appear to be present in the eastern Beaufort-Mackenzie or Banks Island basins. The erosional nature of the sequence's upper contact indicates that it is unlikely to form an areally extensive deposit beneath the Beaufort Sea. Coarse clastic equivalents of Boundary Creek strata occur well to the south of the study area, in the Eagle Plain and Monster formations (Ricketts, 1988).

Smoking Hills Sequence

The Smoking Hills sequence is present in the Anderson Basin (Yorath and others, 1975), the eastern Beaufort-Mackenzie Basin (Myhr, 1975), and in the Banks Island Basin where it is represented by the basal bituminous zone of the Kanguk Formation (Miall, 1979). The sequence consists of organic-rich marine

Figure 5. Contact between Upper (KU) and Lower (KL) Cretaceous strata, Fish River, northern Richardson Mountains. Note the detached fold in the Upper Cretaceous strata.

shales interbedded with bentonite beds. In the Anderson and Beaufort-Mackenzie basins, Smoking Hills strata rest disconformably to erosionally on older strata. The upper contact with the Fish River sequence (mostly the Mason River Formation) is disconformable in the Anderson Basin and erosional in the Beaufort-Mackenzie Basin. The sequence varies in thickness from less than 100 m in outcrop areas to several hundred metres in the subsurface. A ?late Coniacian to Campanian age is indicated by the contained fossils (Yorath and others, 1975), although McIntyre (1974) restricted the age span to the Santonian-Campanian. On Banks Island, the Turonian age indicated for the basal part of the bituminous zone (Miall, 1979) was based on isolated occurrences of *Haplophragmoides bonanzensis,* which by itself is not wholly age-diagnostic (J. H. Wall, personal communication, 1985). Most of the other faunal data from this interval suggest a younger age.

Smoking Hills strata are lithologically similar to the Boundary Creek strata. Based on this similarity, previous authors implied equivalence between the two units (e.g., Young, 1975; Young and others, 1976; Snowdon, 1980; Dixon, 1982). The distinct age differences between the two units, however, favors their separation into discrete depositional sequences. Also, subsurface correlations (Dixon, unpublished data) strongly suggest two physically separate units.

The upper-bounding surface of both the Boundary Creek and Smoking Hills sequences is the pre–Fish River, mid-Campanian–Maastrichtian unconformity.

Fish River Sequence

The Maastrichtian to mid-Paleocene Fish River sequence consists of the Tent Island and Moose Channel Formations (exclusive of the Ministicoog Member) in the Beaufort-Mackenzie Basin, the Mason River Formation in Anderson Basin, and the Kanguk Formation (exclusive of the basal bituminous beds) in Banks Island Basin. Fish River strata in the Beaufort-Mackenzie Basin outcrop at a series of scattered localities along the Yukon coastal plain and the northernmost part of the Richardson Mountains (Norris, 1981b). In the Anderson and Banks basins, Fish River strata are generally exposed along river or coastal cliffs (Yorath and Cook, 1981; Miall, 1979). In the Beaufort-Mackenzie and Banks Island basins the sequence rests unconformably on Smoking Hills and older strata and is abruptly, and locally unconformably, overlain by the Reindeer sequence. The Fish River sequence is a thick, progradational wedge containing deltaic strata of the Moose Channel Formation, which gradationally overlie prodelta and shelf shales of the Tent Island, Mason River, and Kanguk formations. The sequence depocenter is located in the southwestern Beaufort-Mackenzie Basin, where up to 5,000 m of strata may be present. The deltaic sediments in this area appear to have prograded basinward along an arcuate trend (Fig. 6) with the sediments derived from uplifted terrains in northern Yukon.

Reindeer Sequence

The mid-Paleocene to Middle Eocene Reindeer sequence consists of the Ministicoog Member (Moose Channel Formation) and Reindeer Formation in the Beaufort-Mackenzie Basin, and the Eureka Sound Formation in Banks Island Basin. In the Beaufort-Mackenzie Basin, Reindeer strata outcrop in the Caribou Hills, northernmost Richardson Mountains, and at scattered localities along the Yukon coastal plain (Norris, 1981b). On Banks Island the Eureka Sound Formation is best exposed on the northern part of the island (Miall, 1979). In the Beaufort-Mackenzie Basin the Reindeer succession is up to 4,000 m thick, and is disconformably to unconformably overlain by Richards or younger strata. On Banks Island none of the post-Reindeer, mid-Tertiary sequences are present, and upper Tertiary sediments unconformably overlie the Reindeer sequence (Eureka Sound Formation).

In the western Beaufort-Mackenzie Basin, in the vicinity of the Natsek E-56 well location, a prominent unconformity originally identified as the mid-Paleocene, base-Reindeer sequence boundary (Dietrich and others, 1985, Fig. 73.11) is now considered to be an Early Eocene, intra-Reindeer unconformity (D. McNeil, D. McIntyre, unpublished data on the Natsek E-56 well). This Early Eocene unconformity has not yet been recog-

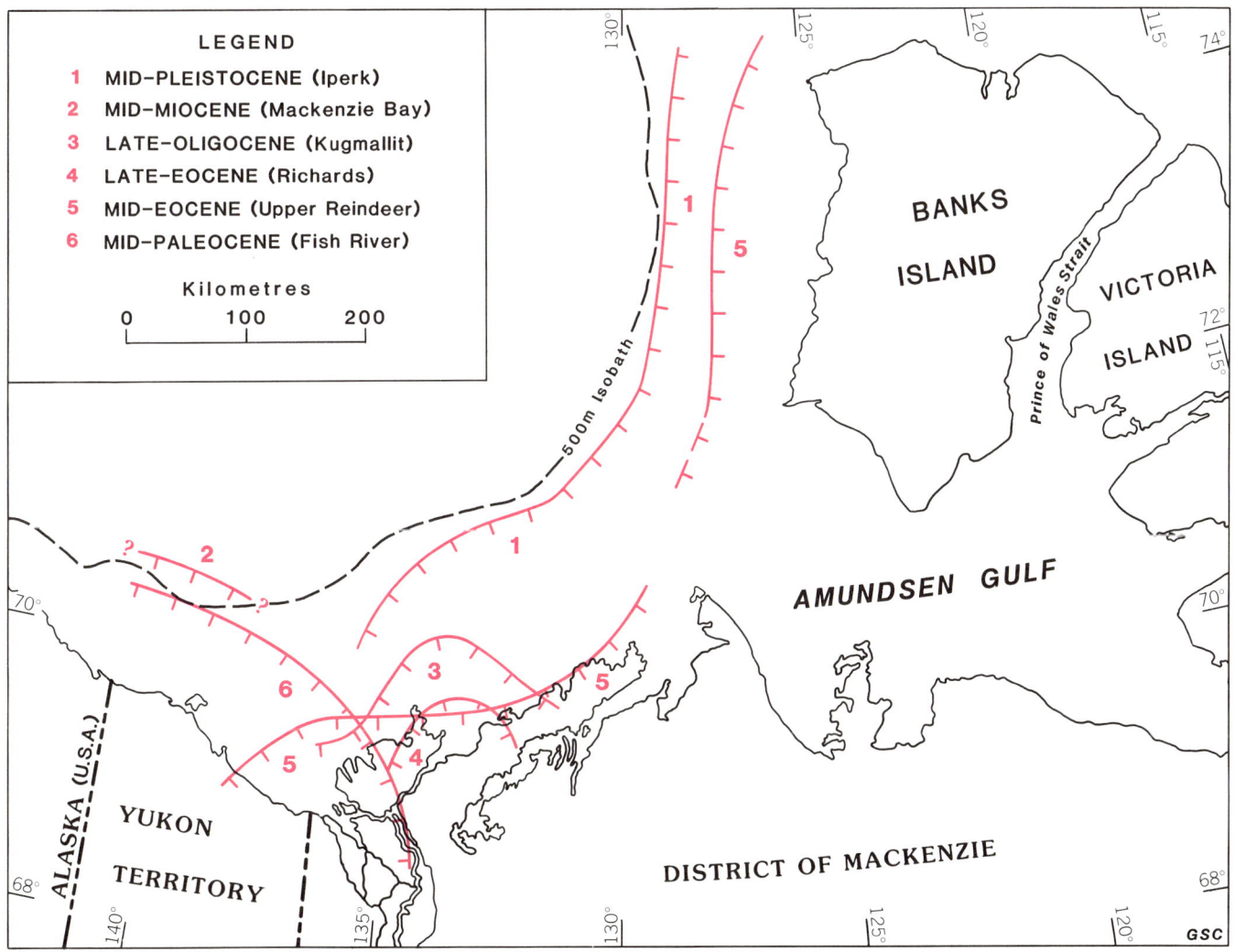

Figure 6. Maximum progradation of the major Cenozoic delta complexes in the Beaufort-Mackenzie and Banks Island basins.

nized in the central or eastern Beaufort-Mackenzie Basin. The maximum known basinward extent of fluviodeltaic strata within the upper part of Reindeer sequence is illustrated in Figure 6.

Richards Sequence

The bulk of the Middle to Upper Eocene Richards sequence consists of prodelta/shelf mudstones with some local sandstone and conglomeratic beds of probable sediment gravity-flow origin (Glaister and Hopkins, 1974). The Richards sequence is up to 2,000 m thick beneath parts of Richards Island and is unconformably to disconformably overlain by strata of the Kugmallit or Mackenzie Bay sequences. Beneath the northeastern part of Richards Island and adjacent offshore areas, the upper-bounding unconformity of the Richards sequence may pass through the lowermost beds of the Kugmallit Formation (sensu, Young and McNeil, 1984). These latter beds consist of sandstone-dominant delta-front deposits, which may be the remnants of a Richards delta (Fig. 6).

A Late Eocene period of uplift and/or sea level fall led to basin margin and paleo-shelf edge erosion of the Richards sequence. As a result, Richards strata may be very thin or absent in many parts of the outer Beaufort-Mackenzie Basin.

Kopanoar Sequence

The Late Eocene-?Early Oligocene Kopanoar sequence is a thick accumulation of deep-water sediments in the central Beaufort-Mackenzie Basin. The sequence is up to 2,000 m thick in a depocenter located between the Kopanoar and North Issungnak well locations (Fig. 7). The sequence thins south and west of this area, and equivalent strata beneath the inner Beaufort shelf have not been identified with certainty. Kopanoar strata are mud-dominent with local sand-rich horizons which are interpreted to be submarine-fan deposits (Dixon and others, 1984). In the vicinity of the Kopanoar well location, the sequence unconformably overlies pre-Late Eocene strata and is abruptly overlain by deep-water sediments of the Kugmallit sequence. A large part

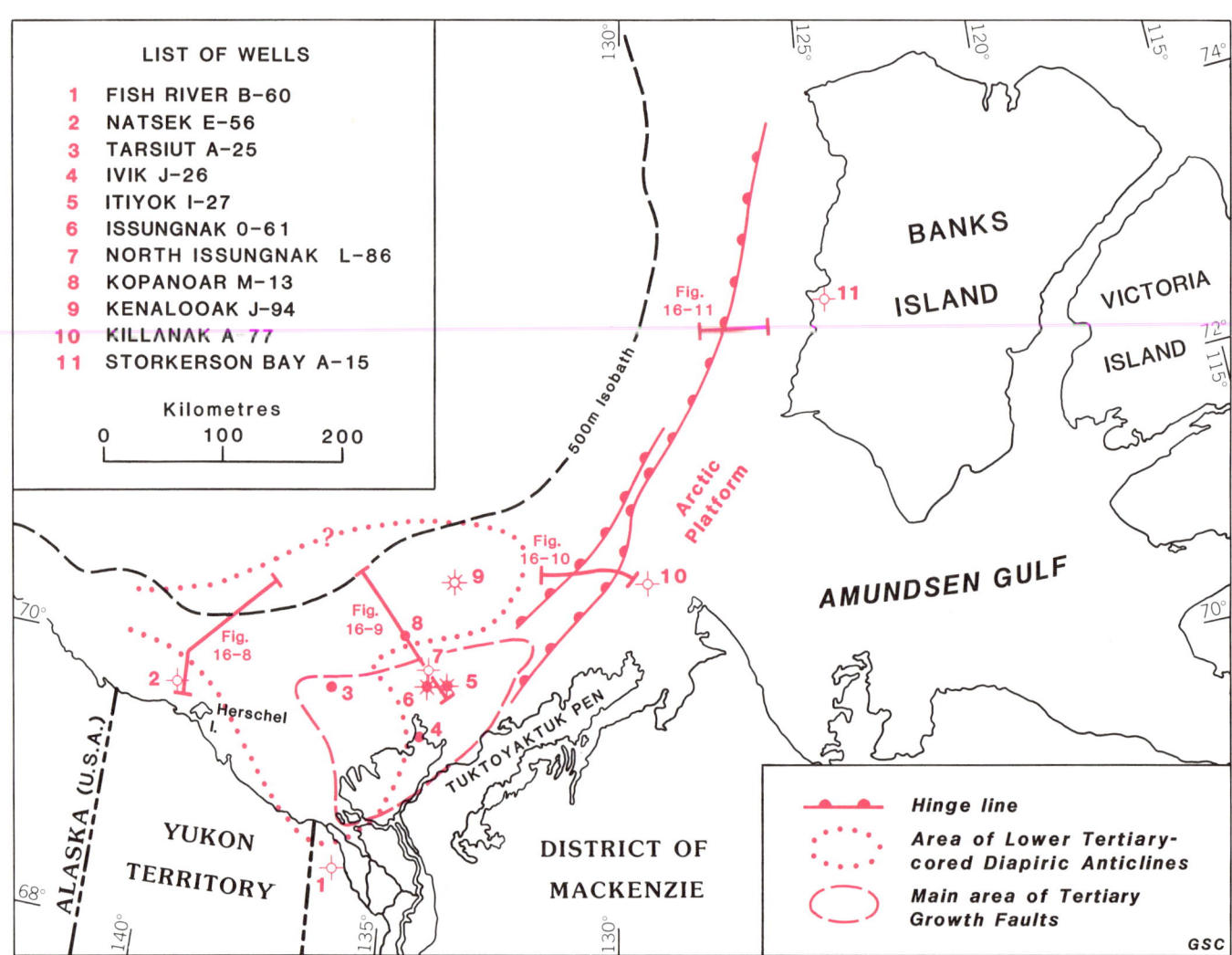

Figure 7. Location of cross-sections and wells referred to in text.

of the Kopanoar sequence is believed to have been deposited during the Late Eocene period of emergence of the margins of the Beaufort-Mackenzie Basin.

Kugmallit Sequence

The Oligocene Kugmallit sequence is up to 2,500 m thick in the vicinity of the depocenter of the Kugmallit delta, between the Ivik and North Issungnak well locations (Figs. 6, 7). East and west of the deltaic deposits are mud-dominant prodelta/shelf sediments. North of the delta are slope and deep-water sediments, similar in character to those of the underlying Kopanoar sequence.

Mackenzie Bay Sequence

The Late Oligocene–Middle Miocene Mackenzie Bay sequence rests abruptly, and locally unconformably, on Kugmallit and older strata. The sequence is up to 1,000 m thick in the central Beaufort-Mackenzie Basin and up to 2,000 m thick in the western part of the basin. Mackenzie Bay strata may be even thicker in the Demarcation sub-basin. The Beaufort Formation on Banks Island may be equivalent to the Mackenzie Bay sequence (Table 1; see also discussion by Dietrich and others, 1985). In the central part of the Beaufort-Mackenzie Basin the sequence is predominantly a mudstone–siltstone succession. The sequence appears to become slightly sandier to the west (toward the Tarsiut well location, Fig. 7), and deltaic strata may be present in the Demarcation sub-basin and adjacent areas (Fig. 6). Both the Mackenzie Bay and overlying Akpak sequence contain deep-water, slope, and basinal sediments in the outer Beaufort-Mackenzie Basin.

Akpak Sequence

Disconformably to erosionally overlying the Mackenzie Bay strata is the Middle to Late Miocene Akpak sequence. The distribution of the sequence is very similar to Mackenzie Bay strata, with the thickness increasing from a few hundred meters in the central part of the Beaufort-Mackenzie Basin to almost 2,000 m in the western part of the basin. Akpak strata probably are present in the Demarcation sub-basin. The sequence is mud-dominant in the central Beaufort Sea area, but may become sandier to the west.

Iperk Sequence

The Upper Miocene to Pleistocene Iperk sequence forms a thick prograding lens of sediment resting unconformably on older units. The Iperk sequence thickens from a few hundred meters beneath the inner Beaufort Sea shelf to almost 5,000 m beneath the outer shelf northeast of the Kenalooak well location (Fig. 7). The Iperk sequence depocenter probably extends to the northeast, beneath the outer shelf and slope seaward of Banks Island. The sequence contains an areally extensive fluvio-deltaic complex, which prograded from the east and southeast into the Beaufort Sea area. The maximum basinward extent of the Iperk delta(s) is close to the present-day shelf edge (Fig. 6).

Shallow Bay Sequence

The Late Pleistocene–Holocene Shallow Bay sequence is a relatively thin unit unconformably overlying Iperk and older strata. In the Mackenzie Trough area of the Beaufort Sea the base–Shallow Bay unconformity is a prominent erosional surface. The sequence is up to 400 m thick in the trough, but thins substantially into the adjacent shelf areas (see Blasco and others, this volume, for more detailed descriptions of the Quaternary deposits of the Canadian Beaufort shelf). Sediments of the modern Mackenzie Delta are part of the Shallow Bay sequence.

STRUCTURAL AND DEPOSITIONAL STYLES ALONG THE CONTINENTAL MARGIN

The sedimentary assemblages that occur beneath the Canadian Beaufort Sea are quite variable in their regional distribution and structure. Some of the geological diversity along the continental margin can be illustrated through a series of regional cross-sections (Figs. 8 to 11). The four sections are geological interpretations of multifold reflection seismic lines from different areas of the Beaufort Sea (Fig. 7; see also Plate 8 for actual reproductions of the seismic profiles interpreted for Figs. 8, 9, and 10).

The western Beaufort Sea profile (Fig. 8) extends some 120 km from the inner shelf north of Herschel Island to the outer continental slope, in 1,000 m of water (Fig. 7). At the south end of the profile, lower Tertiary strata of the Richards, Reindeer, and Fish River sequences overlie deeply buried ?Lower Cretaceous and older strata. North of the Natsek well location the pre-Late Eocene sequences are unconformably overlain by basinward-thickening wedges of Akpak, Mackenzie Bay, and Kugmallit strata. The Mackenzie Bay sequence, in particular, contains well-preserved paleo-continental shelf margins. Unconformably overlying the Akpak sequence are relatively thin assemblages of Iperk and Shallow Bay sediments. Beneath the outer shelf and slope, the pre–Late Eocene sequences (mostly Lower Reindeer and Fish River strata) are deformed into large, shale-cored, diapiric anticlines. These asymmetric anticlines are locally cut by both normal and reverse faults and are oriented in an arcuate trend (Fig. 2). Northwest of the seaward end of the profile, a series of large, symmetrical, diapir-like folds underlie the upper continental rise (Fig. 2; see also Fig. 14 in Grantz and May, 1983). It is uncertain whether these folds are cored by shales of the Fish River sequence or younger Mackenzie Bay and Akpak sediments.

The central Beaufort Sea profile (Fig. 9) extends 120 km from the inner shelf northeast of Richards Island to the continental slope, in 750 m of water. Along this part of the continental margin the Iperk sequence is a much thicker unit, containing

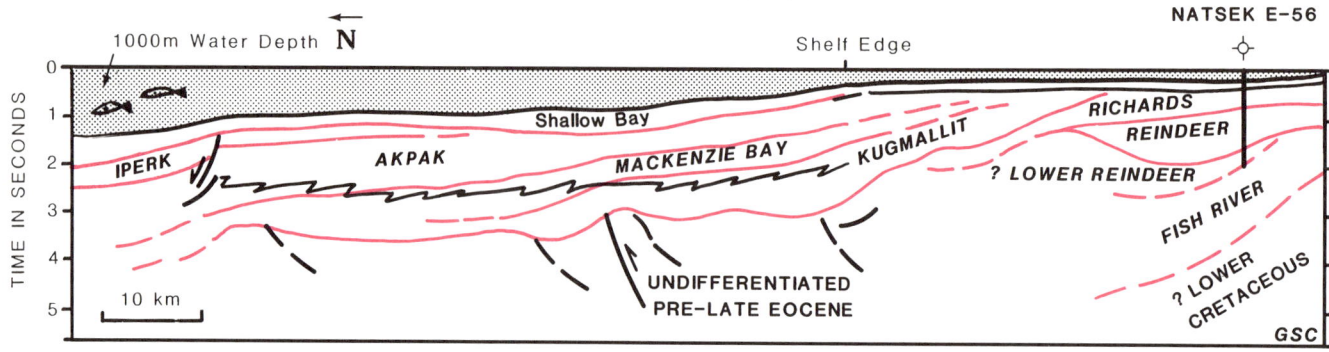

Figure 8. Geological interpretation of a reflection seismic profile across the west Beaufort shelf and slope north of Herschel Island.

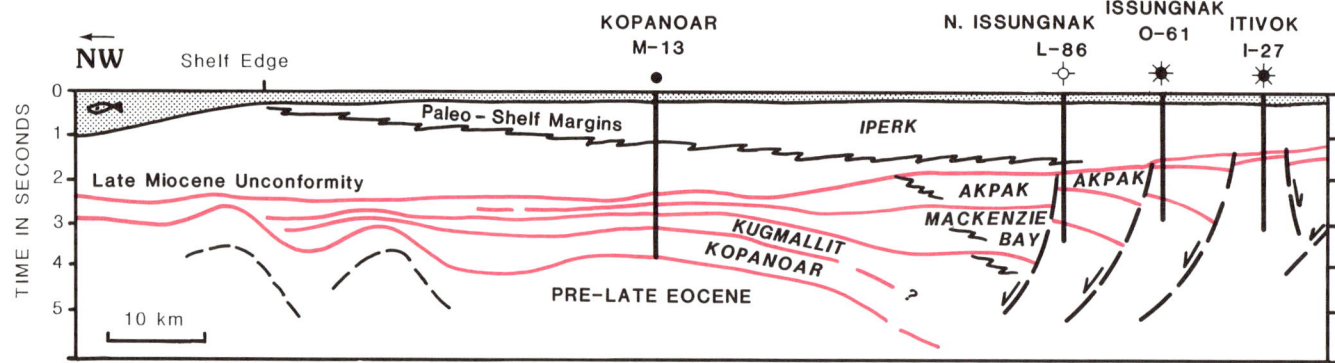

Figure 9. Geological interpretation of a reflection seismic profile across the central Beaufort shelf and slope north of Richards Island.

seismically well-defined paleo-shelf margins. In comparison to the pre–Late Miocene sequences in this area, Iperk deposition was characterized by substantially increased rates of shelf margin progradation. The entire Iperk sequence, in fact, contains very little seismically visible structure, with the exception of local sediment slumping on paleo-continental slopes. Beneath the Iperk strata, at the south end of the profile, topset beds of the Akpak, Mackenzie Bay, and Kugmallit sequences are disrupted by several listric faults, with large, predominantly down-to-basin throws (Fig. 2). The initial development of these faults was probably related to the progradation of the Kugmallit delta across older, unstable shelf margins. Continued "growth" of these faults accompanied the deposition of the Mackenzie Bay and Akpak shelf sediments. Between the Kopanoar and North Issungnak well locations, the Late Eocene to Late Miocene sequences prograde into slope and basinal deposits, with substantial thinning of the entire succession. North of the Kopanoar location the thinned, Late Eocene to Late Miocene wedge onlaps onto Fish River–cored anticlines. Although pre-Tertiary strata have not been identified along the length of this 6.0-sec seismic profile, other seismic data in the vicinity of the Kopanoar location have revealed the presence of a deep (6.5 to 7.0 s; 9 to 10 km) structural discontinuity or detachment surface below many of the lower Tertiary anticlines (Dixon and others, 1984). This detachment surface is believed to separate latest Cretaceous-Tertiary sediments from older strata.

The southeast Beaufort Sea profile (Fig. 10) extends some 75 km across the shelf north of Tuktoyaktuk Peninsula (Fig. 7). Along the eastern end of the profile, Paleozoic clastics of the Imperial Formation disconformably overlie lower Paleozoic carbonates. These units comprise the Arctic Platform, which is unconformably overlain by Albian shales of the Arctic Red Formation. The thin Albian section is unconformably overlain by foreset beds of the Fish River sequence (mostly the Mason River Formation). Beyond the east end of the profile, in the vicinity of the Kilannak well, a thin section of bituminous shales of the Smoking Hills sequence separates the Fish River from Albian strata. Both the Smoking Hills and Albian sections are progressively truncated in a basinward direction by pre–Fish River (Campanian-Maastrichtian) erosion. To the west of the Arctic Platform hinge line, seismically defined dip reversals in the pre-Mesozoic section outline remnants of an uplifted marginal high. Subcrop patterns and structural relationships along the seismic profile (and on other lines in the area) indicate that the outer Arctic Platform was uplifted and eroded during both pre-Albian (possibly Hauterivian) and latest Cretaceous (Campanian-Maastrichtian) tectonism. Toward the west end of the profile, the pre-Mesozoic section appears to be onlapped and abutted by a

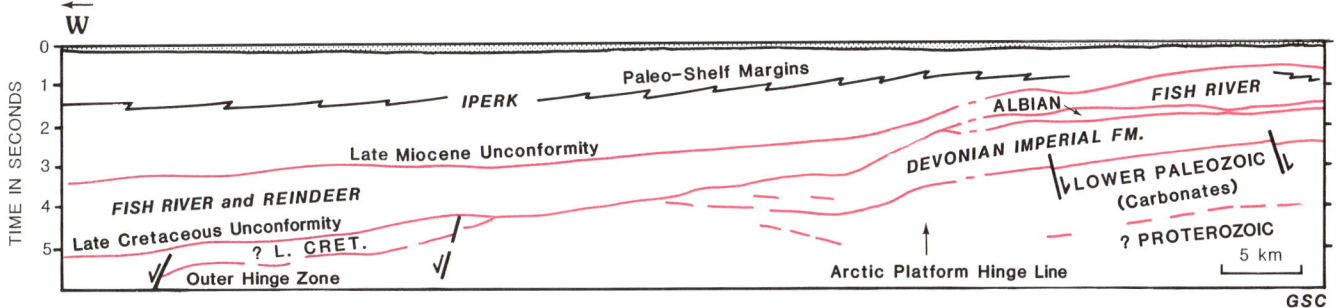

Figure 10. Geological interpretation of a reflection seismic profile across the southeast Beaufort shelf north of Tuktoyaktuk Peninsula.

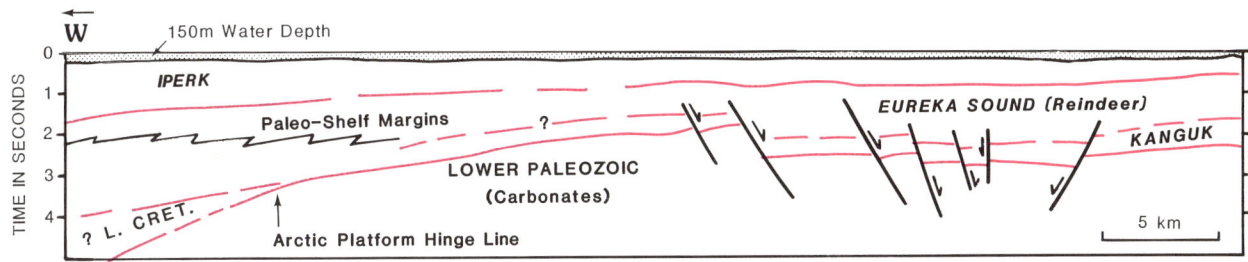

Figure 11. Geological interpretation of a reflection seismic profile across the northeast Beaufort Shelf, west of Banks Island.

thick wedge of sediment of presumed Early Cretaceous age. The ?Lower Cretaceous sediments appear to thicken basinward across an outer hinge line or normal fault, beyond which pre-Mesozoic strata cannot be identified. The unconformity above the ?Lower Cretaceous sediment wedge is believed to be the pre–Fish River (Late Cretaceous) surface. Above the Late Cretaceous unconformity, at the west end of the profile, an estimated 3,000 m of basinal sediments of the Reindeer and Fish River sequences are preserved below a 4,000-m-thick wedge of Iperk strata. The entire Tertiary succession is relatively unstructured beneath this part of the Beaufort Sea shelf (Fig. 2).

The fourth cross-section (Fig. 11) is an interpretation of a seismic profile across the northeastern Beaufort Shelf, offshore from Banks Island (Fig. 7). The control for the interpretation of this line is provided by a tie (via other seismic lines) to the Storkerson Bay well location. Along almost the entire length of the profile, lower Paleozoic carbonates of the Arctic Platform are unconformably overlain by a Late Cretaceous-Tertiary wedge containing topset and foreset beds of the Kanguk and Eureka Sound Formations (Fish River and Reindeer sequences). The lower Tertiary sequences are in turn disconformably overlain by Iperk sediments, which are believed to thicken rapidly basinward, beyond the west end of the profile. The lower Tertiary strata and underlying Arctic Platform are locally disrupted by large-scale normal faults (Fig. 2). The Arctic Platform hinge line is crossed near the west end of the profile. The outer and inner hinge zones described on the southeast Beaufort profile (Fig. 10) appear to have merged northward into one prominent hinge line offshore from Banks Island (Fig. 2). On the basinward side of the hinge zone, a thick wedge of sediment, again of presumed Early Cretaceous age, onlaps the steeply dipping pre-Mesozoic surface (see also Fig. 16 in Lerand, 1973).

REFERENCES CITED

Balkwill, H. R., and seven others, 1983, Arctic North America and northern Greenland, in Mollade, A. M., and Nairn, A.E.M., eds., The Mesozoic, B: Amsterdam, Elsevier Publishing Co., p. 1–31.

Bamber, E. W., and Waterhouse, J. B., 1971, Carboniferous and Permian stratigraphy and paleontology, northern Yukon Territory, Canada: Bulletin of Canadian Petroleum Geology, v. 14, p. 337–381.

Brideaux, W. W., and Fisher, M. J., 1976, Upper Jurassic–Lower Cretaceous dinoflagellate assemblages from Arctic Canada: Geological Survey of Canada Bulletin 259, 53 p.

Collot, B., Hemingson, A. P., Reed, G. L., and Simpson, D. G., 1984, Constraints on the Late Cretaceous to Middle Tertiary tectonics of the Beaufort-Mackenzie Basin of Arctic Canada: Calgary, Canadian Society of Petroleum Geologists–Canadian Society of Exploration Geophysicists, Program with Abstracts, Annual Convention.

Coté, R. P., Lerand, M. M., and Rector, R. J., 1975, Geology of the Lower Cretaceous Parsons Lake gas field, Mackenzie Delta, Northwest Territories, in Yorath, C. L., Parker, E. R., and Glass, D. J., eds., Canada's continental margins: Canadian Society of Petroleum Geologists Memoir 4, p. 613–632.

Dietrich, J. R., Dixon, J., and McNeil, D. H., 1985, Sequence analysis and nomenclature of Upper Cretaceous to Holocene strata in the Beaufort-Mackenzie Basin: Geological Survey of Canada Paper 85-1A, p. 613–628.

Dixon, J., 1979, The Lower Cretaceous Atkinson Point Formation (new name) on the Tuktoyaktuk Peninsula, Northwest Territory; A coastal fan-delta to marine sequence: Bulletin of Canadian Petroleum Geology, v. 27, p. 163–182.

——, 1982, Jurassic and Lower Cretaceous stratigraphy of the Mackenzie Delta-Tuktoyaktuk Peninsula, Northwest Territory: Geological Survey of Canada Bulletin 349, 52 p.

——, 1986, Cretaceous to Pleistocene stratigraphy and paleogeography, northern Yukon and northwestern District of Mackenzie: Bulletin of Canadian Petroleum Geology, v. 34, no. 1, p. 49–70.

Dixon, J. D., and Snowdon, L. R., 1979, Geology and organic geochemistry of the Dome Hunt Nektoralik K-59 well, Beaufort Sea: Geological Survey of Canada Paper 79-1C, p. 85–90.

Dixon, J. D., and four others, 1984, Geology and biostratigraphy of the Dome Gulf et al., Hunt Kopanoar M-13 well, Beaufort Sea: Geological Survey of Canada Paper 82-13, 28 p.

Dutro, J. T., Jr., Brosgé, W. P., and Reiser, H. N., 1972, Significance of recently discovered Cambrian fossils and reinterpretation of Neruokpuk Formation, northeastern Alaska: American Association of Petroleum Geologists Bulletin, v. 56, p. 808–815.

Dyke, L. D., 1975, Structural investigations in Campbell Uplift, District of Mackenzie: Geological Survey of Canada Paper 75-1A, p. 525–532.

Embry, A. E., III, and Klovan, J. E., 1971, A Late Devonian reef tract on northeastern Banks Island, Northwest Territory: Bulletin of Canadian Petroleum Geology, v. 19, p. 730–781.

Glaister, R. P., and Hopkins, J., 1974, Turbidity-current and debris-flow deposits, in Shawa, M. S., ed., Use of sedimentary structures for recognition of clastic environments: Canadian Society of Petroleum Geologists, p. 23–40.

Grantz, A., and May, S. D., 1983, Rifting history and structural development of the continental margin north of Alaska, in Watkins, J. S., and Drake, C. L., eds., Studies in continental margin geology: American Association of Petroleum Geologists Memoir 34, p. 77–100.

Grantz, A., Etrreim, S., and Dinter, D. A., 1979, Geology and tectonic development of the continental margin north of Alaska: Tectonophysics, v. 59, p. 263–291.

Grantz, A., Etrreim, S., and Whitney, O. T., 1981, Geology and physiography of the continental margin north of Alaska and implications of the origin of the Canada Basin, in Nairn, A. E., Churkin, M., Jr., and Stehli, F. G., eds., The ocean basins and margins: New York, Plenum Publishing Corp., p. 439–492.

Hawkings, T. J., and Hatlelid, W. G., 1975, The regional setting of the Taglu gas field, in Yorath, C. L., Parker, E. R., and Glass, D. J., eds., Canada's continental margins: Canadian Society of Petroleum Geologists Memoir 4, p. 633–648.

Hea, J. P., and seven others, 1980, Post-Ellesmerian basins of the Arctic Canada; Their depocenters, rates of sedimentation and petroleum potential, in Miall, A. D., ed., Facts and principles of world oil occurrence: Canadian Society of Petroleum Geologists Memoir 6, p. 447–488.

Hills, L. V., 1969, Beaufort Formation, northwestern Banks Island, District of Mackenzie: Geological Survey of Canada Paper 69-1A, p. 204–207.

Jackson, D. E., and Lenz, A. C., 1962, Zonation of Ordovician and Silurian graptolites of northern Yukon, Canada: American Association of Petroleum Geologists Bulletin, v. 46, p. 30–45.

Jeletzky, J. A., 1967, Jurassic and (?)Triassic rocks of the eastern slope of Richardson Mountains, northwestern District of Mackenzie: Geological Survey of Canada Paper 66-50, 171 p.

Jones, P. B., Brache, J., and Lentin, J. K., 1980, The geology of the 1977 offshore hydrocarbon discoveries in the Beaufort-Mackenzie Basin, Northwest Territories: Bulletin of Canadian Petroleum Geology, v. 28, p. 81–102.

Klovan, J. E., and Embry, A. E., III, 1971, Upper Devonian stratigraphy, northeastern Banks Island, Northwest Territories: Bulletin of Canadian Petroleum Geology, v. 19, p. 705–729.

Lawver, L. A., Grantz, A., and Meinke, L., 1984, The tectonics of the Arctic Ocean, in Dyer, I., and Chryssostomidis, C., eds., Arctic technology and policy: New York, Hemisphere Publishing Corp. (also through McGraw-Hill International Book Co.), p. 147–158.

Lerand, M., 1973, Beaufort Sea, in McCrossan, R. G., ed., The future petroleum provinces of Canada: Canadian Society of Petroleum Geologists Memoir 1, p. 315–386.

McIntyre, D. J., 1974, Palynology of an Upper Cretaceous section, Horton River, District of Mackenzie, Northwest Territories: Geological Survey of Canada Paper 74-14, 56 p.

McNeil, D. M., Ioannides, N. S., and Dixon, J., 1982, Geology and biostratigraphy of the Dome Gulf et al. Ukalerk C-50 well, Beaufort Sea: Geological Survey of Canada Paper 80-32, 17 p.

Miall, A. D., 1975, Post-Paleozoic geology of Banks, Prince Patrick and Eglinton islands, Arctic Canada, in Yorath, C. J., Parker, E. R., and Glass, D. J., eds., Canada's continental margins: Canadian Society of Petroleum Geologists Memoir 4, p. 557–588.

——, 1976, Proterozoic and Paleozoic geology of Banks Island, Arctic Canada: Geological Survey of Canada Bulletin 258, 77 p.

——, 1979, Mesozoic and Tertiary geology of Banks Island, Arctic Canada; The history of an unstable craton margin: Geological Survey of Canada Memoir 387, 235 p.

Mitchum, R. M., Jr., Vail, P. R., and Thompson, S., III, 1977, Seismic stratigraphy and global changes of sea level; Pt. 2, The depositional sequence as a basic unit for stratigraphic analysis, in Payton, C. E., ed., Seismic stratigraphy; Applications to hydrocarbon exploration: American Association of Petroleum Geologists Memoir 26, p. 53–62.

Myhr, D. W., 1975, Markers within Cretaceous rocks as indicated by mechanical logs from boreholes in the Mackenzie Delta area, Northwest Territories: Geological Survey of Canada Paper 75-1B, p. 267–275.

Norford, B. S., 1964, Reconnaissance of the Ordovician and Silurian rocks of northern Yukon Territory: Geological Survey of Canada Paper 63-39, 139 p.

Norris, D. K., 1972, Structural and stratigraphic studies in the tectonic complex of northern Yukon Territory, north of Porcupine River: Geological Survey of Canada Paper 72-1B, p. 91–99.

——, 1974, Structural geometry and geological history of the northern Canadian Cordillera, in Wren, A. E., and Cruz, R. B., eds., Proceedings of the 1973 National Convention: Canadian Society of Exploration Geophysicists, p. 18–45.

——, 1981a, Geology, Herschel Island and Demarcation Point, Yukon Territory: Geological Survey of Canada Map 1514A, scale 1:250,000.

——, 1981b, Geology, Blow River and Davidson Mountains, Yukon Territory: Geological Survey of Canada Map 1516A, scale 1:250,000.

——, 1981c, Geology, Mackenzie Delta, District of Mackenzie: Geological Survey of Canada Map 1515A, scale 1:250,000.

——, 1981d, Geology, Aklavid, District of Mackenzie: Geological Survey of Canada Map 1517A, scale 1:250,000.

——, 1981e, Geology, Trail River, Yukon-Northwest Territories; Geological Survey of Canada Map 1524A, scale 1:250,000.

——, 1983, Porcupine Virgation; The structural link among the Columbia, Innuitian, and Alaskan orogens: Geological Association of Canada–Mineralogical Association of Canada–Canadian Geophysical Union, Program with Abstracts, v. 8, p. A51.

——, 1985a, The Neruokput Formation, Yukon Territory and Alaska: Geological Survey of Canada Paper 85-1B, p. 223–229.

——, 1985b, Eastern Cordilleran foldbelt of northern Canada; Its structural geometry and hydrocargon potential: American Association of Petroleum Geologists Bulletin, v. 69, p. 788–808.

Norris, D. K., and Yorath, C. J., 1981, The North American plate from the Arctic Archipelago to the Romanzoff Mountains, in Nairns, A.E.M., Churkin, M., Jr., and Stehli, F. G., eds., The ocean basin and margins: New York and London, Plenum Press, v. 5, p. 37–103.

Plauchut, B. D., and Jutard, G. G., 1976, Cretaceous and Tertiary stratigraphy,

Banks and Eglinton islands and Anderson Plain, Northwest Territories: Bulletin of Canadian Petroleum Geology, v. 24, p. 321–371.

Poulton, T. P., 1982, Paleogeographic and tectonic implications of the Lower and Middle Jurassic facies patterns in northern Yukon Territory and adjacent Northwest Territories, *in* Embry, A. F., and Balkwill, H. R., eds., Arctic geology and geophysics: Canadian Society of Petroleum Geologists Memoir 8, p. 13–28.

Poulton, T. P., Leskiw, K., and Audretsch, A. P., 1982, Stratigraphy and microfossils of Jurassic Bug Creek Group of northern Richardson Mountains, northern Yukon and adjacent Northwest Territories: Geological Survey of Canada Bulletin 325, 130 p.

Ricketts, B. D., 1988, The Monster Formation; A coastal fan system of Late Cretaceous age, Yukon: Geological Survey of Canada Paper 86-14, 27 p.

Snowdon, L. R., 1980, Petroleum source potential of the Boundary Creek Formation, Beaufort-Mackenzie Basin: Bulletin of Canadian Petroleum Geology, v. 28, p. 46–58.

Sweeney, J. F., 1985, Comments about the age of the Canada Basin, *in* Husebye, E. S., Johnson, G. L., and Kristofferson, Y., eds., Geophysics of the polar regions: Tectonophysics, v. 114, p. 1–10.

Tailleur, I. L., 1973, Probable rift origin of Canada Basin, Arctic Ocean, *in* Pitcher, M. G., ed., Arctic geology: American Association of Petroleum Geologists Memoir 19, p. 526–535.

Thorsteinsson, R. L., and Tozer, E. T., 1960, Summary account of structural history of the Canadian Arctic Archipelago since Precambrian time: Geological Survey of Canada Paper 60-7, 25 p.

——, 1962, Banks, Victoria, and Stefansson islands, Arctic Archipelago: Geological Survey of Canada Memoir 330, 85 p.

Willumsen, P. S., and Coté, R. P., 1982, Tertiary sedimentation in the southern Beaufort Sea, Canada, *in* Embry, A. F., and Balkwill, H. R., eds., Arctic geology and geophysics: Canadian Society of Petroleum Geologists Memoir 8, p. 43–54.

Yorath, C. J., 1973, Geology of Beaufort-Mackenzie Basin and eastern part of Northern Interior Plains, *in* Pitcher, M. G., ed., Arctic geology: American Association of Petroleum Geologists Memoir 19, p. 41–47.

Yorath, C. J., and Cook, D. G., 1981, Cretaceous and Tertiary stratigraphy and paleogeography, Northern Interior Plains, District of Mackenzie: Geological Survey of Canada Memoir 398, 76 p.

Yorath, C. J., and Norris, D. K., 1975, The tectonic development of the southern Beaufort Sea and its relationship to the origin of the Arctic Ocean Basin, *in* Yorath, C. J., Parker, E. R., and Glass, D. J., eds., Canada's continental margins: Canadian Society of Petroleum Geologists Memoir 4, p. 589–612.

Yorath, C. J., Balkwill, H. R., and Klassen, R. W., 1975, Franklin Bay and Malloch Hill map areas, District of Mackenzie: Geological Survey of Canada Paper 74-36, 35 p.

Young, F. G., 1973, Mesozoic epicontinental, flyschoid, and molassoid depositional phases of Yukon's North Slope, *in* Aitken, J. D., and Glass, D. J., eds., Canadian Arctic geology: Geological Association of Canada–Canadian Society of Petroleum Geologists, p. 181–201.

——, 1974, Cretaceous stratigraphic displacements across Blow fault zone, northern Yukon Territory: Geological Survey of Canada Paper 74-1B, p. 291–296.

——, 1975, Upper Cretaceous stratigraphy, Yukon Coastal Plain and northwestern Mackenzie Delta: Geological Survey of Canada Bulletin 249, 83 p.

Young, F. G., and McNeil, D. M., 1984, Cenozoic stratigraphy of Mackenzie Delta, Northwest Territories, NTS 107B, 107C: Geological Survey of Canada Bulletin 336.

Young, F. G., and Robertson, B. T., 1984, The Rapid Creek Formation; An Albian flysch-related phosphatic iron formation in northern Yukon Territory, *in* Stott, D. F., and Glass, D. W., eds., The Mesozoic of middle North America: Canadian Society of Petroleum Geologists Memoir 9, p. 361–372.

Young, F. G., Myhr, D. W., and Yorath, C. J., 1976, Geology of the Beaufort-Mackenzie Basin: Geological Survey of Canada Paper 76-11, 63 p.

Young, G. M., and Jefferson, C. W., 1975, Late Precambrian shallow-water deposits, Banks and Victoria islands, Arctic Archipelago: Canadian Journal of Earth Sciences, v. 12, p. 1734–1748.

MANUSCRIPT ACCEPTED BY THE SOCIETY DECEMBER 3, 1986

NOTE ADDED IN PROOF

Subsequent to completing the text for this chapter, a number of facts and interpretations have been published or reconsidered by the authors and others which change or modify a few items in the chapter:

1. The anticlines in the west Beaufort Sea are considered to be primarily compressional in origin with some possible diapiric reactivation.

2. On the northeast flank of the Romanzof Uplift, strata mapped as Proterozoic Neroukpuk Formation have been identified as lower Paleozoic strata (Lane and Cecile, 1989) and comparable to similar strata in the Barn Uplift to the southeast.

3. Lane (1988) has pointed out that the Rapid Fault Array is as much a foldbelt as it is faulted, and has documented thrust faults and compressional folds in the exposed Albian strata.

4. The Reindeer sequence can be divided into two sequences. These have been documented at the Natsek E-56 well and named the Aklak and Taglu sequences (Dietrich and others, 1989a).

5. The stratigraphy of the Natsek E-56 well has been modified from that illustrated in Figure 8. The well did not penetrate the Richards sequence, and the major unconformity truncating the thrust-cored folds is now identified as the boundary at the base of the Richards sequence (Middle Eocene) (Dietrich and others, 1989a).

6. The Kopanoar sequence was mistakenly identified as a depositional sequence when, in fact, it is a lowstand deposit of the Kugmallit sequence to which it is now relegated. However, because of its mappability, we have retained it as a named unit and now refer to the interval as Kopanaoar subsequence.

7. Acquisition of deep-reflection seismic data within the Beaufort-Mackenzie Basin by the Geological Survey of Canada has given us new data on deep crustal features (Cook and others, 1987a, b; Dietrich and others, 1989b). The landward edge of the southeast margin is underlain by 16 to 20 km of lower Paleozoic and Proterozoic strata which contain Ellesmerian compressional structures. The Moho at the landward edge of the southeast margin is approximately 35 to 39 km deep, rising to 20 to 25 km under the outer Beaufort Shelf and upper slope areas. The southeast margin contains extensional faults that sole out to the north, in presumed Proterozoic strata. Deep crustal structure in the western Beaufort Sea is masked on the deep-reflection seismic profiles by structures in the Tertiary succession.

8. Dixon (1990) has suggested that the breakup unconformity may be between Albian and Cenomanian strata, as opposed to the late Hauterivian unconformity at the base of the Mount Goodenough Formation.

ADDITIONAL REFERENCES

Cook, F. A., Coflin, K. C., Lane, L. S., Dietrich, J. R., and Dixon, J., 1987a, Preliminary interpretations of the Mackenzie-Beaufort Basin deep crustal reflection survey: Geological Survey of Canada Open File Report 1,549, 29 p.

——, 1987b, Structure of the southeast margin of the Beaufort-Mackenzie basin, arctic Canada, from crustal seismic reflection data: Geology, v. 15, p. 931–935.

Dietrich, J. R., and 5 others, 1989a, The geology, biostratigraphy, and organic geochemistry of the Natsek E-56 and Edlok N-56 wells, western Beaufort Sea, Arctic Canada, *in* Current Research, Part G: Geological Survey of Canada Paper 89-1G, p. 133–157.

Dietrich, J. R., Coflin, K. C., Lane, L. S., Dixon, J., and Cook, F. A., 1989b, Interpretation of deep seismic reflection data, Beaufort Sea, arctic Canada: Geological Survey of Canada Open-File Report 2106, 15 p.

Dixon, J., 1990, Cretaceous tectonics and sedimentation in northwest Canada, *in* Caldwell, W.G.E., ed., Evolution of the Western Interior Foreland Basin:

Geological Association of Canada Special Paper (in press).

Lane, L. S., 1988, The Rapid fault array; A foldbelt in the Arctic Yukon, *in* Current Research, Part D: Geological Survey of Canada Paper 88-1D, p. 95–98.

Lane, L. S., and Cecile, M. P., 1989, Stratigraphy and structure of the "Neruokpuk Formation," northern Yukon, *in* Current Research, Part G: Geological Survey of Canada Paper 89-1D, p. 57–62.

THE "FRAM" AFTER AN ICE-PRESSURE, JANUARY 10, 1895
(*From a photograph*)

From Fridtjof Nansen, 1900, Farthest North (Popular Edition): New York and London, Harper Brothers, facing p. 474.

Chapter 16

Geology of the Arctic Continental Margin of Alaska

Arthur Grantz, S. D. May, and P. E. Hart
U.S. Geological Survey, 345 Middlefield Road, Menlo Park, California 94025

INTRODUCTION

Location and physiography

Alaska faces the Canada Basin of the Arctic Ocean along an arcuate continental margin, gently concave to the north, that stretches unbroken from the Mackenzie Delta, near 137°W to Northwind Ridge of the Chukchi Borderland near 162°W. (These and other regional geographic features mentioned below can be found in Plates 1 and 11.) This margin, with an arc-length of about 1,050 km, marks one side of a continental rift along which the Canada Basin opened by rotation about a pole in the Mackenzie Delta region during middle Cretaceous time. The rift-margin structures, which lie beneath the inner shelf and coastal plain in the eastern Alaskan Beaufort Shelf and beneath the outer shelf in the western Beaufort and Chukchi Shelf, are now buried by a thick middle Lower Cretaceous to Holocene progradational continental terrace sedimentary prism.

We divide the Arctic continental margin of Alaska into three sectors of strongly contrasting geologic structure and physiographic expression. In the Barter Island sector (see Figs. 3 and 4) the structure is dominated by the effects of Eocene to Holocene convergence and uplift, and the continental slope is upwardly convex; in the Barrow sector the structure is dominated by the effects of middle Early Cretaceous rifting and continental breakup, and the continental slope is upwardly concave; and in the Chukchi sector the structure is controlled by an easterly trending middle Early Cretaceous rift, and the continental slope abuts the Chukchi Borderland.

Physiographically, the Alaska continental margin is expressed by the Alaska continental rise and slope (Fig. 1), which lies between the oceanic Canada Basin to the north and the flat and shallow continental shelves of the Beaufort and Chukchi Seas to the south. Outer shelf and slope morphology along the margin is dominated by gravity-driven slope failures. These include both surficial slumps and deeply penetrating slope failures related to listric normal faults that dip toward the modern and ancient free face of the continental slope. Some of the listric faults offset Quaternary deposits or the seabed (Grantz and others, 1983a).

A major influence on the physiography of the region is the relative size and age of the sediment sources that built the progradational sedimentary prisms of the narrow Alaska slope and rise and the much more extensive continental rise and abyssal plain of the Canada Basin. The great volume of clastic sediment that poured into the Canada Basin from the Mackenzie River drainage system and from the Canadian Shield via the Amundsen Gulf, in Cretaceous and especially Cenozoic time, overwhelmed that which built the Alaska slope and rise. The extensive Canada Basin fill is banked against the Alaska slope and rise at depths of a little more than 1,000 m at the Mackenzie Delta—the major sediment source for the basin—to almost 4,000 m at the abyssal plain at the foot of the Northwind Escarpment. The disparity in sediment supply is illustrated by the fact that the deepest part of the Canada abyssal plain lies near the foot of the narrow Alaska slope and rise (Plate 1).

Previous studies

Early ideas on the geology of the northern Alaska continental margin were extrapolated from studies of the surrounding landmasses. Carey (1958) originally suggested that the Beaufort Sea margin of Alaska was created by a rift in which northern Alaska was rotated away from the Canadian Arctic Islands by oroclinal bending about a pivot in the Gulf of Alaska. Regional geologic considerations led Tailleur (1969a, b, and 1973) also to postulate that rotational rifting played a crucial role in the tectonic evolution of the region. Based on data acquired during oil exploration, Rickwood (1970) concurred with the rotational rift hypothesis and proposed that rifting was crucial to creation of the trap that holds the supergiant hydrocarbon deposit at Prudhoe Bay.

In the past decade, interpretation of the geology of the Beaufort Shelf has relied heavily on multichannel seismic reflection data, but the first geological cross sections of the region were drawn from other types of geophysical data. Wold and others (1970) published an interpretation of the Beaufort Sea margin based on gravity data collected from light airplane landings on sea ice. A more detailed survey, based on shipborne gravity meter readings, was presented and interpreted by Dehlinger (1980). To date, the most detailed published gravity map of the region, com-

---

Grantz, A., May, S. D., and Hart, P. E., 1990, Geology of the Arctic Continental Margin of Alaska, *in* Grantz, A., Johnson, L., and Sweeney, J. F., eds., The Arctic Ocean region: Boulder, Colorado, Geological Society of America, The Geology of North America, v. L.

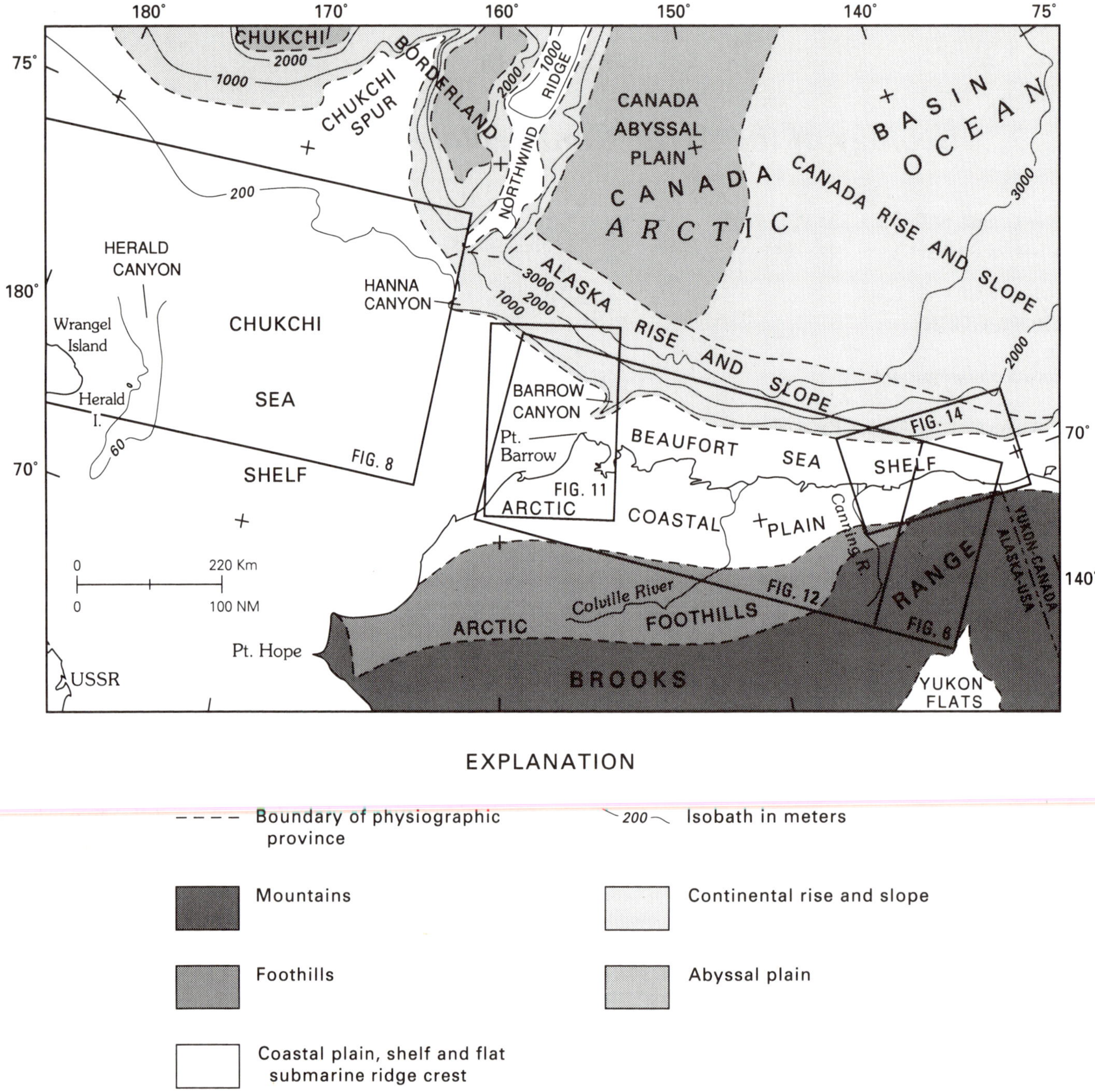

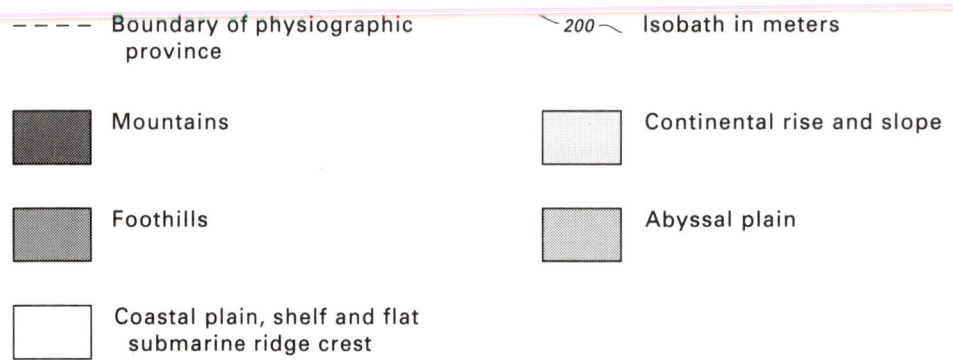

Figure 1. Map of Arctic continental margin of Alaska showing major physiographic features and location of Figures 6, 8, 11, 12, and 14.

piled from shipborne data gathered by the U.S. Geological Survey between 1972 and 1982, was published by May (1985). Extensive proprietary surveys also exist.

Two early seismic refraction studies of the Alaskan continental margin produced reconnaissance profiles. One, across the lower continental slope and upper rise north of Barrow by Milne (1966), is unreversed and of limited usefulness. The other, a long reversed profile from Barrow to the northern Chukchi Shelf (Hunkins, 1966), suggests that the shelf there is underlain by continental crust and that the top of basement deepens from about 1 km near Barrow to about 6 km near the shelf edge. Two studies of the seismic velocity structure of the Beaufort Sea and Chukchi Sea margins were based on sonobuoys. Houtz and others (1981) used more than 100 sonobuoy records from the northern Alaskan shelves to interpret the general velocity structure of the region. A more detailed study of the velocity structure of the

Beaufort Shelf between Prudhoe Bay and Cape Simpson was published by Bee and others (1984).

Published data on both present magnetic field anomalies and paleomagnetic field directions in the region are limited. Extensive proprietary aeromagnetic surveys have been conducted over the Beaufort Shelf, but published data consist primarily of a reconnaissance magnetic anomaly map (Cramer and others, 1986) of the area west of 155°W. Pioneering paleomagnetic studies of upper Paleozoic strata in the Brooks Range were interpreted to agree with the proposed counterclockwise rotation of Arctic Alaska away from the Canadian Arctic Islands (Newman and others, 1979), but Hillhouse and Grommé (1983) showed that the magnetic field direction was overprinted during the Cretaceous. More recently, Halgedahl and Jarrard (1987) have reported that oriented drill cores from the Kuparuk oil field, near the Beaufort Sea coast, apparently escaped overprinting. These cores indicate that Arctic Alaska was rotated counterclockwise with respect to North America since deposition of the cored rocks in middle Early Cretaceous time.

An early discussion of the regional geologic framework of the Beaufort and Chukchi Shelves, based primarily on analog single channel seismic reflection data, was published by Grantz and others (1975). In 1977, 1978, and 1980 the U.S. Geological Survey conducted multichannel seismic reflection surveys of the entire Alaska Beaufort Shelf and the central and eastern parts of the Chukchi Shelf. Regional geological interpretations of these data have been published in several reports (Grantz and May, 1983, 1987; Grantz and others, 1979, 1981, 1987a, b). Craig and others (1985) used proprietary subsurface and seismic reflection data, in conjunction with previously published reports, to summarize the regional geology, petroleum resources, and environmental geology of the Alaskan Beaufort Shelf. An interpretation of the stratigraphy and geologic history of the Beaufort Shelf, also based on proprietary data, was recently presented by Hubbard and others (1987). An important recent contribution is a discussion of the regional geology of the central and northern Chukchi Shelf by Thurston and Theiss (1987).

Time-to-depth conversion functions

The seismic reflection time-to-depth conversion functions used in this study were calculated from regionally averaged multichannel seismic reflection stacking velocities (Fig. 2). These functions enable the reader to determine the generalized depth of seismic horizons in Figures 7A, 7B, 8, 9, 11, 13, and 14. The curves for the Beaufort Shelf and North Chukchi Basin exhibit velocities which are common for Mesozoic and Cenozoic sedimentary strata, whereas the curve for the Chukchi Shelf shows a considerably higher velocity structure. The Chukchi Shelf velocities are higher because lower Mesozoic and Paleozoic strata lie at shallower depths beneath large areas of this shelf than they do beneath the Beaufort Shelf and North Chukchi Basin. Users of the time-to-depth functions of Figure 2 should keep in mind that these are regional averages, and that they become increasingly

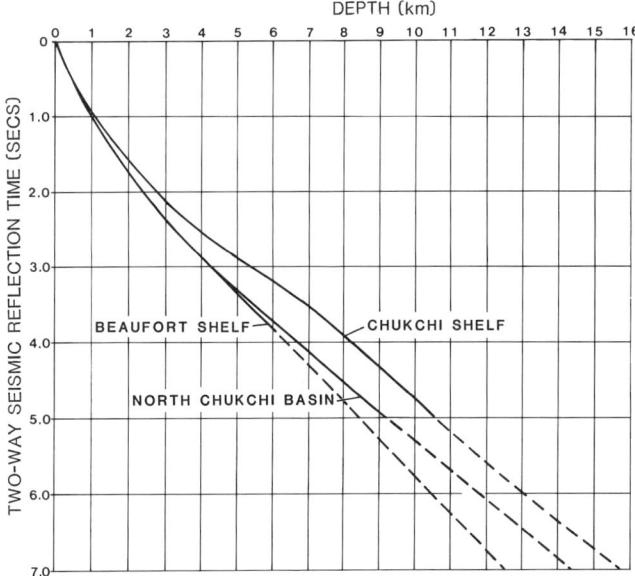

Figure 2. Depth as a function of regionally averaged seismic-reflection time for the Beaufort and Chukchi Shelves and the North Chukchi Basin, derived from seismic-stacking-velocity measurements. Dashed where inferred.

uncertain with depth as a result of the increasing uncertainty of stacking velocities with depth.

GEOLOGIC FRAMEWORK AND REGIONAL STRATIGRAPHY

Major provinces

Three regional tectonic provinces meet at the continental margin north of Alaska: the Canada Basin of the Arctic Ocean, the Arctic Platform of the Arctic Alaska plate of northern Alaska and adjacent shelves, and the Chukchi Borderland of the Arctic Basin north of the Chukchi Shelf (see Plate 1 and Figs. 1, 3, and 4). The geologic character of the margin and the juxtaposition of these first-order features are the result of five distinct, but in part related, tectonic events. (1) Rifting beginning in Early Jurassic time separated the Arctic Platform from the North American craton and produced a series of rifts now located beneath the Alaska Beaufort Shelf and slope and Banks Island of the Canadian Beaufort margin (Fig. 12 in Grantz and others, this volume). This extensional event was almost synchronous with the initiation of major convergence in the Brooks Range orogen in Middle Jurassic time. (2) Rotational rifting beginning in Hauterivian (middle Early Cretaceous) time led to continental breakup and drift of the Arctic Alaska plate away from the Canadian Arctic Islands about a pole of rotation near 68.5°N, 136°W (Fig. 3) and formed the Canada Basin in mid-Cretaceous time. The initiation of this event, in turn, was almost synchronous with the end of major convergence in the Brooks Range orogen in early Albian

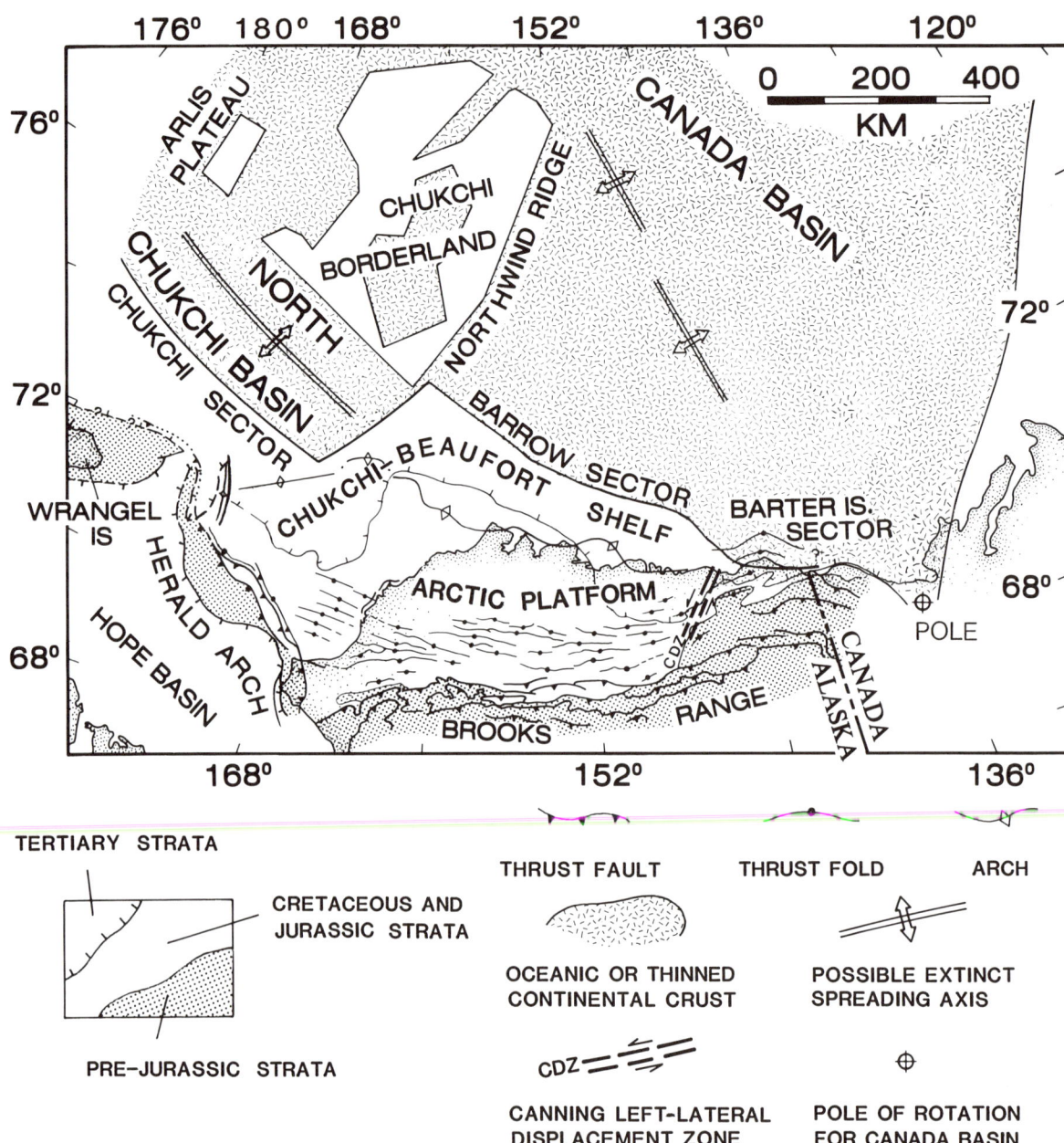

Figure 3. Tectonic model for Alaska segment of Arctic Ocean Basin showing major structural features, inferred distribution of continental versus oceanic or thinned continental crust, and the relation of the Chukchi, Barrow, and Barter Island sectors to the structural features that define them. Possible spreading axis in Canada Basin after Taylor and others (1981), in North Chukchi Basin after Grantz and others (1979).

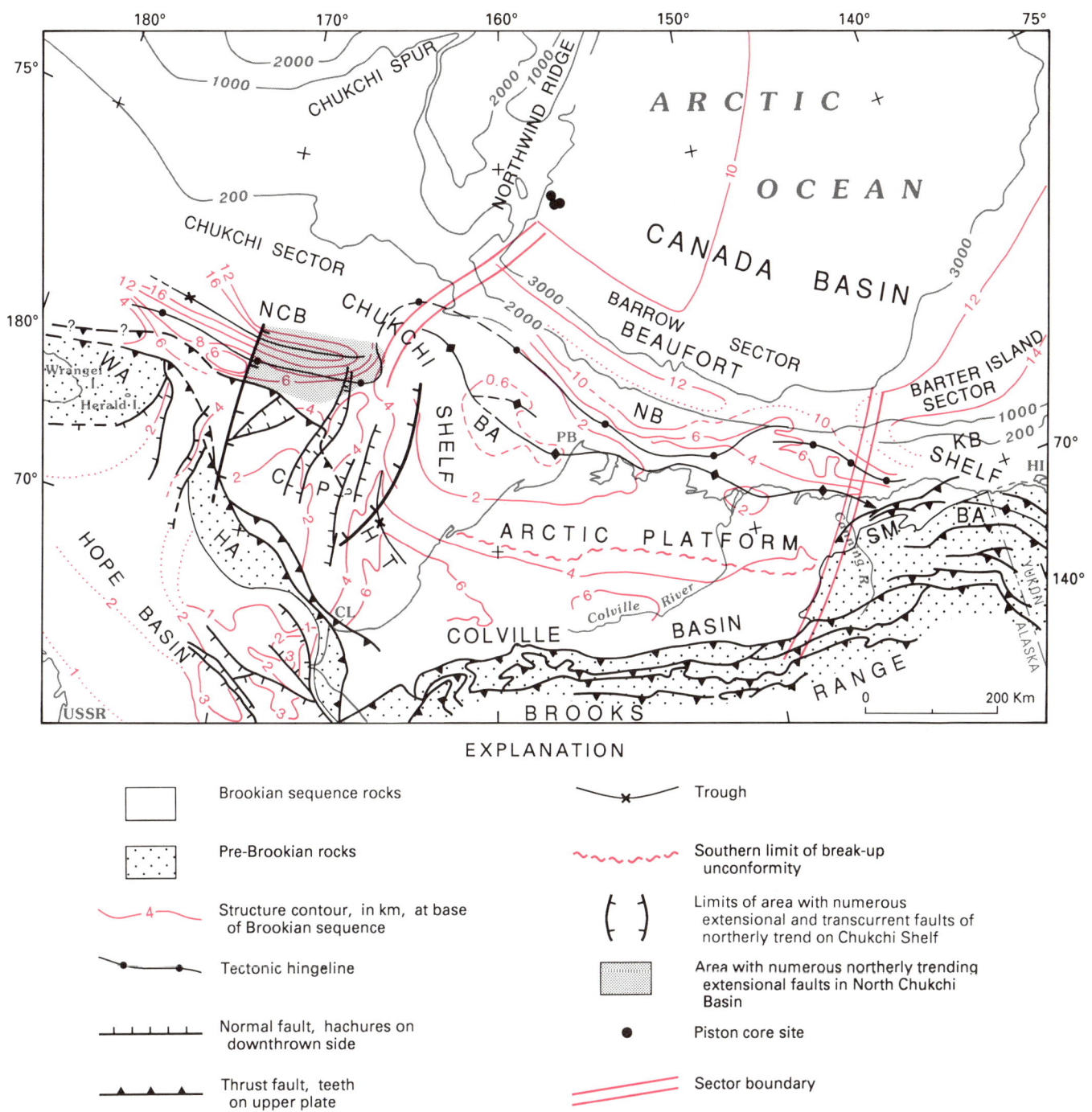

Figure 4. Major geologic features of the Alaska segment of the Arctic continental margin. BA, Barrow arch; BFZ, Barrow fault zone; CDZ, Canning displacement zone; CL, Cape Lisburne; CP, Chukchi Platform; HA, Herald arch; HI, Herschel Island; HT, Hanna trough; KB, Kaktovik Basin; NB, Nuwuk Basin; NCB, North Chukchi Basin; PB, Point Barrow; SM, Sadlerochit and Shublik Mountains; WA, Wrangel arch.

time. (3 and 4) Poorly understood, but more localized rifting in the western Chukchi Shelf and Chukchi Borderland created the North Chukchi Basin during two events—Jurassic to Neocomian and late Early Cretaceous. An oversimplified model for these events shown in Figure 3 is speculative, but it illustrates one possible geometry for the proposed rifting after the added complication of segmentation of the borderland into north-trending ridges and basins by late Late Cretaceous and early Paleogene rifting. (For convenience, events of this general age will hereafter be called "Laramide" in this chapter.) (5) Eocene to Quaternary thrusting in the Brooks Range orogen in northeastern Alaska and the adjacent continental margin.

Arctic Platform

Regional structure. The Arctic platform slopes gently southward from the broad crest of the Barrow arch, near the sea coast, to beneath the northward-thrust nappes of the Brooks Range orogenic belt (Fig. 3). The platform gradient is about 1° beneath the Arctic Coastal Plain and about 2° to 4° beneath the Arctic (Northern) Foothills of the Brooks Range. This gradient developed in two stages. The initial gradient developed in Mississippian to Neocomian time, when the Arctic Platform was the site of clastic and carbonate deposition in a stable shelf environment. The sourceland for the clastic sediments (Barrovia of Tailleur, 1973) lay north of the present continental shelf, and the platform sloped generally southward to a rifted margin of Devonian age south of the present Brooks Range. The initial gradient was augmented in Middle or Late Jurassic and Early Cretaceous time by loading of the southern part of the Arctic Platform by multiple nappes from the Brooks Range orogen to the south and by the weight of sediment deposited in the Colville Basin, a foreland basin on the north side of the orogen.

Brooks Range orogen. Multiple, far-travelled nappes of the Brooks Range orogen override the Arctic Platform beneath the present Brooks Range across the width of Alaska, and related thrust faults and folds extend into the Cretaceous and Tertiary strata of the Colville foreland basin beneath the Arctic Foothills of the Brooks Range. (See Moore and others, 1990, for a recent summary of Brooks Range tectonics.) Nappe emplacement was a response to convergence between the Paleo-Pacific Basin and the southern margin of Arctic Alaska. Convergence began in Middle Jurassic time, and the major displacements, which were northerly directed, were largely completed during Albian time. Mayfield and others (1988) estimate that crustal shortening across the western Brooks Range exceeds 700 to 800 km.

In the eastern Brooks Range, renewed thrusting in Eocene or earlier time was superimposed upon the Jurassic and Cretaceous compressional events. The Cenozoic thrusting is strongest east of a narrow, northeasterly striking zone of earthquake epicenters designated the Canning displacement (fault) zone (Fig. 4 and Plate 11) by Grantz and others (1983a). This zone is a northern extension of Aleutian arc Benioff zone earthquakes from central Alaska to the Beaufort Sea. Some Tertiary thrust displacement also occurred in the foreland west of this zone. Counterclockwise rotation of fold axes, faults, and geologic contacts indicate that the Canning displacement zone was, and continues to be, the site of significant left-lateral deformation. Earthquake epicenters suggest that the zone has a counterpart to the east, along the north-trending Cordilleran front at the east face of the Richardson Mountains, which lie west of the lower Mackenzie River valley north of 66°N (Plate 11). The intervening region, which corresponds to the Barter Island sector of the continental margin, has been uplifted 300 to 500 m above the surrounding plains and plateaus to form the northeastern Brooks Range.

Elevation of the northeastern Brooks Range is related to thickening of the crust by thrusting. Depression of the crust to form the deep Kaktovik Basin (Fig. 4), which lies north of the northeast Brooks Range, resulted from loading by the northward-thrust nappes and by thick accumulations of Upper Cretaceous and Cenozoic detritus derived from accelerated erosion of the new topography generated by nappe emplacement. The amount of Cenozoic displacement of the nappes is uncertain, but total tectonic transport, including that which occurred in late Mesozoic time, is estimated by Rattey (1985) to exceed 400 km. On the basis of rotated fold axes and faults in Upper Cretaceous and lower(?) Tertiary rocks in and adjacent to the Canning displacement zone, Grantz and others (1983a) estimated that Cenozoic tectonic transport in the northeast Brooks Range was at least 25 to 50 km northward with respect to the Arctic Coastal Plain and Foothills to the west.

Barrow arch. A broad structural high known as the Barrow arch (Fig. 4) trends along the Arctic coast of Alaska from the northeastern Chukchi Shelf to Yukon Territory. This feature is the product of multiple Jurassic and Cretaceous events of regional influence rather than the product of a single episode of folding or upwarping. The south flank of the arch is the south-sloping Arctic Platform. The north flank is a collapsed continental margin formed by thermal subsidence and subsequent sedimentary loading adjacent to the rifts that separated northern Alaska from the Canadian Arctic Islands in Jurassic and Early Cretaceous time. The overall slope of the top of Paleozoic basement toward the Canada Basin, including the effects of faulting, is as steep as 12° and locally may exceed 16°.

The western part of the Barrow arch appears to have been uplifted in Tertiary time. Shale compaction studies by Ervin (1981) suggest that west of the Colville River the crest of the arch has been differentially uplifted with respect to areas south and east. The uplift increases westward from about 100 to 200 m near the Colville River to a maximum of 600 to 900 m near Barrow. The uplifted area presumably extends westward beneath the northeastern Chukchi Shelf, where the western limit of uplift is not defined by compaction data. Regional stratigraphy suggests that the uplift was post-Cretaceous in age. Structural relief on the Barrow arch at the meridian of Prudhoe Bay, east of the area of presumed Tertiary uplift, is about 5 km on the south flank and about 10 km on the north flank.

Characteristic stratigraphy permits the Barrow arch to be

recognized even where the position of its crestline is obscured by structural complexity. The most distinctive stratigraphic feature is a Hauterivian breakup unconformity that overlies the crest and upper flanks of the arch. A second characteristic is the absence or patchy occurrence of the otherwise widespread stable shelf clastic and carbonate strata of the Mississippian to Neocomian Ellesmerian sequence from the crestal region and north flank of the arch. A third is the presence of failed rift deposits of probable Jurassic to Neocomian age seaward of the Barrow arch crestline. By these criteria, the Barrow arch can be traced from the northeast Chukchi Sea to Flaxman Island and projected southeast from Flaxman Island beneath the Arctic Coastal Plain to the front of the Brooks Range some 40 or 50 km west southwest of Demarcation Bay. An analogous feature can be traced across the north slope of the British Mountains in northern Yukon Territory. If the position of the arch is correctly projected beneath the Arctic Coastal Plain in northeastern Alaska, its counterpart in coastal Yukon has been offset some 20 or 30 km northward with respect to its position beneath the coastal plain on the frontal thrust faults of the Brooks Range (Fig. 4).

Stratigraphy. Stable shelf deposits of northern provenance and Early Mississippian to Neocomian age that lie beneath and north of the far-travelled nappes of the Brooks Range orogen define the Arctic Platform of northern Alaska. The rocks upon which the platform was developed, and those that were deposited upon it, have been divided into four distinct stratigraphic sequences whose lithologic character reflects their tectonic environment (Fig. 5). The pre-platform rocks, of Ordovician or older through Devonian age, are correlated with the lithologically similar main part of the Franklinian sequence of Lerand (1973). This sequence was named for the Upper Cambrian through Devonian eugeoclinal and miogeoclinal strata of the areally extensive Franklinian geosyncline and adjacent cratonic shelf of the Canadian Arctic Islands.

In Late Silurian to Early Devonian time the Franklinian rocks of northern Alaska were strongly deformed, mildly metamorphosed, and structurally consolidated (cratonized) by an early stage of the Ellesmerian orogeny. Large grabens and half grabens developed in the tectonized Franklinian rocks during probably two cycles of late- and early post–Ellesmerian orogeny extension. Basins of the older cycle were filled by Lower(?) or Middle Devonian nonmarine sediments, now strongly folded but unmetamorphosed, that are assigned to the upper part of the Franklinian sequence. Basins of the younger cycle, well observed on seismic reflection profiles (Plate 9.2 in Kirschner and Rycerski, 1988), were filled by Upper Devonian(?) and Lower Mississippian nonmarine clastic rocks of local derivation, which are here designated the Eo-Ellesmerian sequence. Deep erosion and extensional faulting associated with the formation of these basins constituted the final stage in the development of the Arctic Platform. A measure of the tectonic stability achieved by these Devonian events is the virtual lack of deformation of the 340-Ma Arctic Platform beneath the North Slope in spite of middle Early Cretaceous rifting, which severed the platform from the Canadian Arctic Islands, and Middle Jurassic to Quaternary convergence, which buried its southern part beneath the large nappes of the Brooks Range orogen. Gravity modelling along the Trans-Alaska Pipeline route south of Prudhoe Bay tied to refraction measurements in the Canada Basin suggests (Grantz and others, 1990) that the crust in the area of the Arctic platform is about 34 km thick, and thus of normal continental thickness.

On the Arctic Platform the Eo-Ellesmerian sequence is succeeded by the gently dipping stable-shelf clastic and platform carbonate rocks of the Early Mississippian to Neocomian Ellesmerian sequence, which is of northern provenance (Fig. 5). The term Ellesmerian sequence was proposed by Lerand (1973) for the carbonate and overlying clastic rocks of Mississippian through Jurassic age in the Sverdrup Basin of the Canadian Arctic Islands. In northern Alaska, platformal Neocomian beds of northern provenance have been added to the Ellesmerian sequence as defined by Lerand (1973). Failed rift deposits of inferred Jurassic and Neocomian age beneath the central and eastern Alaskan Beaufort Shelf, the Dinkum succession, are correlative with the upper part of the Ellesmerian sequence of the North Slope. The Ellesmerian and Dinkum beds are overlain by the Brookian sequence. This sequence consists of thick continental-deltaic and shelf clastic deposits of southern (Brooks Range) provenance that prograded across the Arctic Platform and the newly established continental margin in Aptian or Albian to Quaternary time. The Ellesmerian rocks wedge out toward an ancient sourceland (Barrovia) near the present Beaufort Sea coast, but the underlying Franklinian and overlying Brookian sequences extend to the outer shelf and slope. Principal sources for the discussion of the stratigraphy of the Arctic Platform that follows include Moore and Mull (1989), Moore and others (1990), Kirschner and Rycerski (1988), and Molenaar and others (1986).

Franklinian sequence. Outcrops in the northeast Brooks Range and test wells on the North Slope show that the Arctic Platform, and probably the adjacent continental shelf, is underlain by lithologically varied sedimentary and volcanic rocks of Proterozoic and early Paleozoic age. West of the Canning River, deep test wells encounter strongly deformed, mildly metamorphosed argillite, arenite, carbonate rocks, and chert containing graptolites and chitinozoans of Ordovician and Silurian age (Carter and Laufeld, 1975). Lithologically and faunally these beds resemble the Ordovician and Silurian flysch of the Franklinian geosyncline in the Canadian Arctic Islands (Trettin, 1972; Trettin and Balkwill, 1979), Ordovician and Silurian graptolite-bearing argillite in northern Yukon Territory about 50 km south of Herschel Island (Lane and Cecile, 1989), and graptolitic flysch and shale of Ordovician and Silurian age on the Lisburne Peninsula of the westernmost Brooks Range (Grantz and others, 1983b).

In test wells on Flaxman Island, near the mouth of the Canning River, and in outcrops in the Sadlerochit and Shublik Mountains east of the river (Fig. 4) are found Proterozoic to Devonian carbonate rocks with minor amounts of quartzite, argillite, and mafic volcanic rocks (Blodgett and others, 1986; Clough and others, 1988). Only the Cambrian to Devonian beds of this

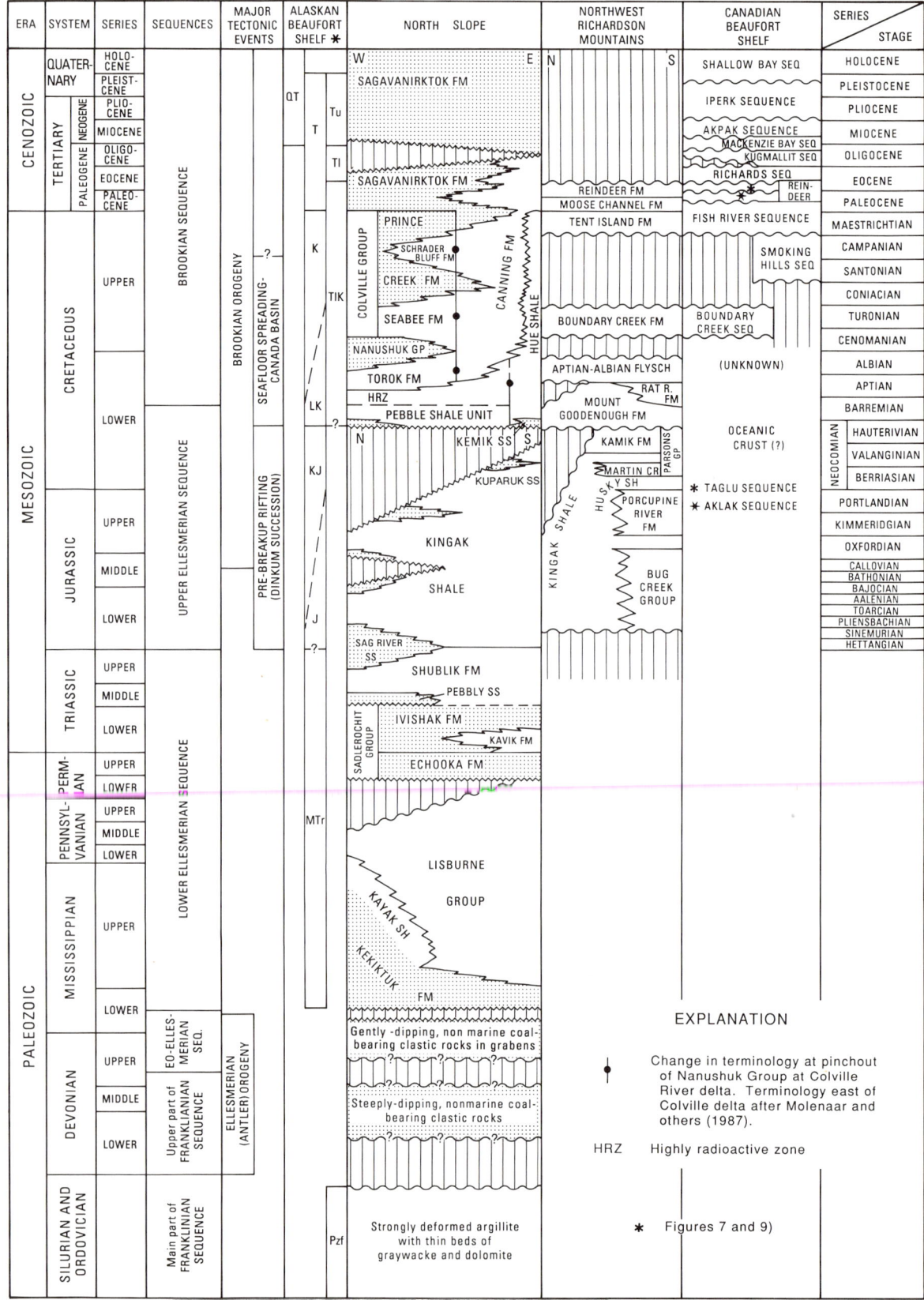

Figure 5. Stratigraphy of Arctic Alaska and adjacent continental shelves after Mickey and Haga (1987), Molenaar and others (1987), Dietrich and others (1989), J. Dixon (personal communication, 1989), and this chapter.

basin plain to carbonate platform assemblage correlate with the Franklinian sequence. Farther east, beneath the narrow Arctic Coastal Plain of northeastern Alaska, seismic reflection data suggest to Fisher and Bruns (1987) the presence of pre-Mississippian rocks there are more than 5 to 7 km thick and possess a simple structure.

Upper part of Franklinian sequence: More than 100 m of strongly folded, but unmetamorphosed nonmarine beds at the bottom of the Topagoruk test well, in the western part of the North Slope, are here placed in the upper part of the Franklinian sequence. These beds are chert-pebble conglomerate and dark gray shale with carbonaceous partings and plant fragments of Middle (possibly Early) Devonian age. As described by Collins (1958), these beds dip 35° to 60° and are overlain unconformably by gently inclined beds that we correlate with the Ellesmerian sequence. Lack of metamorphism in the Middle Devonian rocks indicates that they postdate the main orogeny, which regionally deformed and mildly metamorphosed the underlying Ordovician and Silurian argillite and graywacke. The moderately steep dip of the Lower(?) or Middle Devonian beds indicates that they were, in turn, folded and truncated by erosion before the low-dipping beds of the overlying Ellesmerian sequence were deposited. The Late Devonian structural event that tilted the Lower(?) or Middle Devonian beds correlates with the Late Devonian and Early Mississippian Ellesmerian orogeny of Lerand (1973). Together the stronger Early Devonian event and the weaker Late Devonian or Early Mississippian event constitute the main phases of the Ellesmerian orogeny on the North Slope.

Ellesmerian sequence. Eo-Ellesmerian sequence: Unmetamorphosed Upper Devonian(?) and Lower Mississippian coal-bearing nonmarine strata, the oldest beds of the Ellesmerian sequence on the Arctic Platform, rest nonconformably on Franklinian beds. Seismic reflection records (Kirschner and Rycerski, 1988, Plate 9.2) show that these strata occupy fault-bounded basins (grabens and half grabens) and range in thickness from a knife edge to more than 3,000 m. Kirschner and Rycerski (1988) place these strata in the Endicott Group, but their confinement to grabens isolates them from the Upper Devonian and Lower Mississippian type-Endicott strata of the Brooks Range allochthons, from which the coastal plain rocks also differ greatly in character of substrate, lithology, and depositional environment. In this chapter we refer to these beds as Eo-Ellesmerian in the sense that they are atypical beds in the earliest part of the Ellesmerian sequence that are transitional between the nonmarine beds of the upper Franklinian sequence below and the typical Ellesmerian marine shelfal strata above. The seismic reflection records of Kirschner and Rycerski (1988) show that an erosional unconformity with mild angular discordance overlies the Eo-Ellesmerian strata and that the main body of Ellesmerian rocks oversteps the areally more restricted graben deposits. This Lower Mississippian unconformity represents the waning, final phase of the Ellesmerian orogeny on the North Slope.

Lower part of the Ellesmerian sequence: Ellesmerian strata above the Eo-Ellesmerian graben deposits consist of four transgressive-regressive cycles whose clastic components were derived from the northern sourceland of Barrovia. The sequence as a whole, and many of its constituent units, thins northward to pinch-outs, mainly erosional truncations in paralic facies, near the Beaufort coast and beneath the northern Chukchi Shelf.

Well-bedded sedimentary rocks of shelf facies that in general produce strong seismic reflections characterize the lower part of the Ellesmerian sequence on the North Slope, where they have been divided into three major, partly unconformity-bounded transgressive-regressive sedimentary cycles (Moore and Mull, 1989). The lowest cycle consists of platform carbonate rocks of the Lower Mississippian to Lower Permian Lisburne Group and the partly underlying, partly time-equivalent Kayak Shale and subjacent basal Kekiktuk Conglomerate. The cycle ranges in thickness from a wedge edge near the coast to more than 1,700 m beneath the central part of the coastal plain. The middle cycle is a dominantly clastic deposit, the Lower Permian to Lower Triassic Sadlerochit Group, which overlies the Lisburne Group on a regional unconformity. The Sadlerochit grades from commonly coarse nonmarine facies near the coast to marine lutite and fine-grained sandstone in North Slope wells. Its thickness ranges from a wedge edge near the coast to more than 800 m beneath the central coastal plain. The highest cycle consists of Middle and Upper Triassic marine shelf deposits of the Shublik Formation and its proximal facies, the partly overlying Sag River Sandstone and the coeval Karen Creek Sandstone of the eastern North Slope. The Shublik is as much as 200 m thick and consists of phosphatic shale, siltstone, and coquinoid limestone.

Upper part of the Ellesmerian sequence and the Hauterivian breakup unconformity: Basinal marine lutite with a few thin sandstone bodies of the Jurassic and early Neocomian (Berriasian and Valanginian) Kingak Shale constitutes the lower stratigraphic unit of the upper part of the Ellesmerian sequence beneath the North Slope and the central Chukchi Shelf. Hauterivian and Barremian (Mickey and Haga, 1987) organic-rich marine shale of the informally named pebble shale unit (PSU in this chapter) constitutes the upper stratigraphic unit. An angular unconformity lies between these units on Barrow arch, but south of a middle Neocomian shelf break beneath the northern part of the Arctic Foothills the PSU rests conformably on lower Neocomian clinoforms at the top of the Kingak Shale (Molenaar, 1988).

Foreset beds interpreted from seismic reflection records show that the Kingak prograded south- or southeastward from the Barrow arch onto a subsiding shelf that was about 1 km deep beneath the Arctic Foothills. Neocomian erosion at the base of the PSU has in many places stripped the Kingak from the north flank and crest of the Barrow arch. Total thickness of the Kingak ranges from a knife edge along the crest of the arch to a maximum of 1,200 m in the northern part of the Arctic Foothills (Bird, 1988a).

The PSU consists mainly of highly organic marine shale characterized by floating grains and pebbles of frosted quartz and chert, elevated levels of gamma ray activity, and low seismic velocity. The unit is 60 to 150 m thick on the Barrow arch and

60 to 75 m thick beneath the Arctic Foothills (Bird, 1988a). At several places on the arch, as much as 15 m of locally and northerly sourced sandstone and pebble conglomerate occur at the base of the PSU. According to Witmer and others (1981) and Mickey and Haga (1987) foraminifer and palynomorphs indicate that below a highly radioactive zone (HRZ) in its uppermost 6 to 12 m, the PSU is Hauterivian and Barremian in age. The floating quartz and chert grains that characterize the PSU below the HRZ are thought to have a local source on Barrow arch or its northern flank, as did the more voluminous Kingak Shale.

The HRZ is a condensed organic shale that contains Barremian to possibly lower or middle Albian radiolarians and palynomorphs (Mickey and Haga, 1987), and it lacks the floating quartz and chert grains that characterize the PSU. Its scant thickness (6 to 12 m), modest time span, fine-grained texture, high organic content, and high gamma ray activity demonstrate that the HRZ is a pelagic or hemipelagic deposit largely isolated from sources of terrigenous clastic sediment. If the HRZ were a bottomset basinal deposit at the base of the prograding Brookian sequence, as suggested by Mickey and Haga (1987), it should contain distal turbidites from the adjacent continental terrace, and be thicker. Because the HRZ is a pelagic or hemipelagic deposit with neither Ellesmerian nor Brookian sedimentary contributions, it should be regarded as an independent transitional unit. Because of its thinness, however, and because it cannot ordinarily be separated from the PSU on seismic reflection records, the HRZ is in practice lumped with the PSU and the Ellesmerian sequence (Fig. 5).

The erosional unconformity at the base of the PSU is thought to be the breakup unconformity associated with initiation of continental drift in the Canada Basin. The thin, strongly reflective, highly organic PSU is considered to be the product of feeble, locally sourced, synbreakup or earliest post-breakup sedimentation on the rift-margin high. Like the HRZ, the PSU is a transitional, synrift unit between the Ellesmerian and Brookian sequences. The change from the feeble clastic sedimentation of the PSU to the condensed, pelagic or hemipelagic sedimentation of the HRZ records the early post-breakup subsidence of the rift-margin high below wave base. This subsidence ended the era of rift-margin sedimentation from local (Barrow arch) sources that had nourished the PSU and began the era of condensed sedimentation in a deeper environment, which was isolated from terrigenous sourcelands that produced the HRZ. Overtopping of the Barrow arch by detritus from the Brooks Range orogen terminated HRZ deposition, and initiated south-sourced Brookian sedimentation above the HRZ by Aptian or Albian time.

Dinkum succession (Failed rift deposits of the Beaufort Shelf and slope). On the central Beaufort Shelf north of Barrow arch, the PSU rests unconformably on strata of inferred Jurassic and early Neocomian age in and north of the Dinkum graben (Figs. 6, 7). We interpret these beds to have been deposited in a failed rift system along the continental margin. Hubbard and others (1987) have grouped the graben-filling beds of the Beaufort Shelf and the upper beds of the Ellesmerian sequence (for convenience, herein referred to as the upper Ellesmerian beds) of the North Slope in a new sequence, the Beaufortian, on the premise that both are rift related. In this chapter we place these deposits in separate sequences because, although largely coeval, they were deposited in different tectonic and sedimentary environments and have different stratigraphies. The upper Ellesmerian beds of the North Slope were deposited on an areally extensive stable shelf that subsided and tilted southward in response to tectonic overriding and loading by the early phases of the Brookian orogeny. In contrast the Dinkum graben fill, and the probably related deposits of the outer shelf and slope, were deposited in fault-bounded half grabens or grabens and have much higher ratios of length and thickness to width. We retain the term upper Ellesmerian for the areally extensive Jurassic and Neocomian marine deposits of the tectonically stable Arctic Platform and use Dinkum succession to designate the thick, but elongate and areally limited deposits of Dinkum graben and the tectonically related deposits of the continental margin.

Brookian sequence. The Brookian sequence of the North Slope was deposited in the Colville Basin, a foreland basin, and as a progradational continental terrace sedimentary prism along the continental margin. The stratigraphy of the sequence is complicated by east-west changes in facies and sediment thickness related to the location and timing of local domains of convergent tectonism and uplift in the Brooks Range.

South-sourced syntectonic flysch and molasse of the Aptian(?) and early Albian Fortress Mountain Formation lie at the base of the Colville Basin section in the southern North Slope. These sandstones, lutites, and conglomerates grade laterally northward into the lower part of the Torok Formation, which consists of foreset and bottomset turbidite and hemipelagic clastic deposits of Aptian(?) and Albian age that extend north to the continental shelf. The partly coeval, partly younger Torok Formation is about 6,000 m thick beneath the Arctic Foothills and less than 150 m thick on the Barrow arch. Beneath the central and western parts of the Arctic Coastal Plain the Torok downlaps onto the south-dipping upper surface of the HRZ.

The Fortress Mountain Formation is overlain by the posttectonic (molassoid) Nanushuk Group—regressive shallow marine and deltaic sandstone, lutite, conglomerate, and coal of middle or late Albian to early Cenomanian age. The Nanushuk intertongues with foreset beds in the partly underlying, partly equivalent upper Torok Formation in the central and northern parts of the Colville Basin. By middle or late Albian time, post-rift subsidence of the rift margin permitted Torok sediments to overtop the Barrow arch in many places, and to begin the progradation of a continental terrace sedimentary prism along the then recently formed Beaufort Sea margin of the Canada Basin. The Nanushuk-Torok interval is several thousand meters thick west of the lower Colville River, but east of the river it thins drastically and is represented by condensed bottomset shale, which is no more than a few tens of meters thick on the Barrow arch east of Prudhoe Bay (Molenaar and others, 1986). The post-Nanushuk deposits of the Colville Basin rest on a middle Cenomanian unconformity that is distinct on logs and seismic sections according

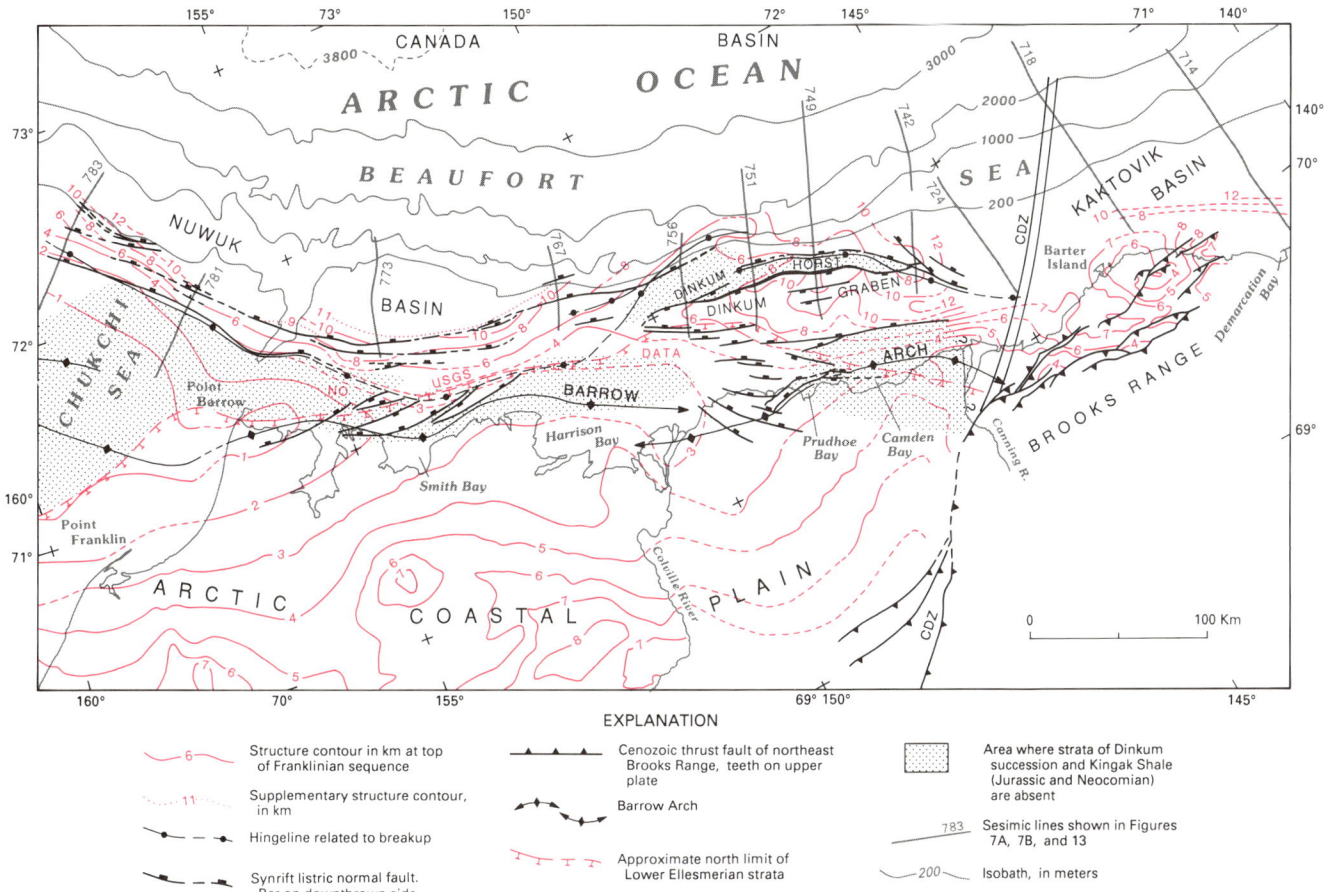

Figure 6. Map of Arctic Alaska continental margin showing depth in kilometers to top of Franklinian sequence, location of synrift structures, and area adjacent to rift stripped of Jurassic and early Neocomian strata in late Neocomian time. Onshore data from Bruynzeel and others (1982), Tailleur and others (1978), Bruns and others (1987), Bird (1988a, b), and Jamison and others (1980). Offshore data from profiles in Grantz and others (1982, 1986) and maps in Hubbard and others (1987), Craig and others (1985), and Pessel and others (1978). Lines dashed where projected or speculative.

to Bruynzeel and others (1982), but correlated well sections by Molenaar and others (1986) suggest that at least in places this contact is a facies boundary. A widespread transgressive marine shale, the late Cenomanian and Turonian Seabee Formation of the Colville Group, rests on the unconformity and is presumably related in origin to the major long-term worldwide rise in sea level that culminated in late Cenomanian and early Turonian time (Haq and others, 1987). Molenaar and others (1986, 1987) apply the name "Hue Shale" to the highly organic and bentonitic basinal marine shale of Aptian(?) to Maastrichtian (and possibly Paleocene) age that constitutes the diachronous basal Brookian unit east of the Colville Delta. The unit is a condensed deposit, 300 m or less thick. It is overlain by prodelta or basin slope marine shale of Aptian or Albian to Eocene or Oligocene age, with turbidites in the lower beds, which Molenaar and others (1986, 1987) named the Canning Formation. The Canning is laterally equivalent to all of the shales of the Torok Formation, Colville Group, and lower Sagavanirktok Formation to the west of the Colville Delta. Between the Canning and Colville Rivers the Canning Formation is 1,500 to 3,000 m or more thick, but east of the Canning River where the formation is Campanian to Eocene or Oligocene in age, its thickness is unknown.

All of the nonmarine and marine deltaic and alluvial plain sandstones, lutites, and conglomerates above the Canning Formation east of the Colville River were placed in the Sagavanirktok Formation by Molenaar and others (1986, 1987). Near the Canning River the unit is 1,800 to 2,300 m thick and Late Eocene through Pliocene in age. The base of the unit becomes older to the west and near the Colville River the basal beds are Campanian. West of the Colville River, where the preexisting stratigraphic terminology is retained, the post-Nanushuk-Torok section is placed into two units: the Colville Group of middle Cenomanian through Maastrichtian age, and the Sagavanirktok Formation of Tertiary age. All of these units extend beneath the continental shelf. The overlying glacial and interglacial deposits, which are no more than a few tens of meters thick beneath the North Slope, thicken to 100 meters or more near the shelf break. These heterogeneous deposits are assigned to the upper Pliocene and Quater-

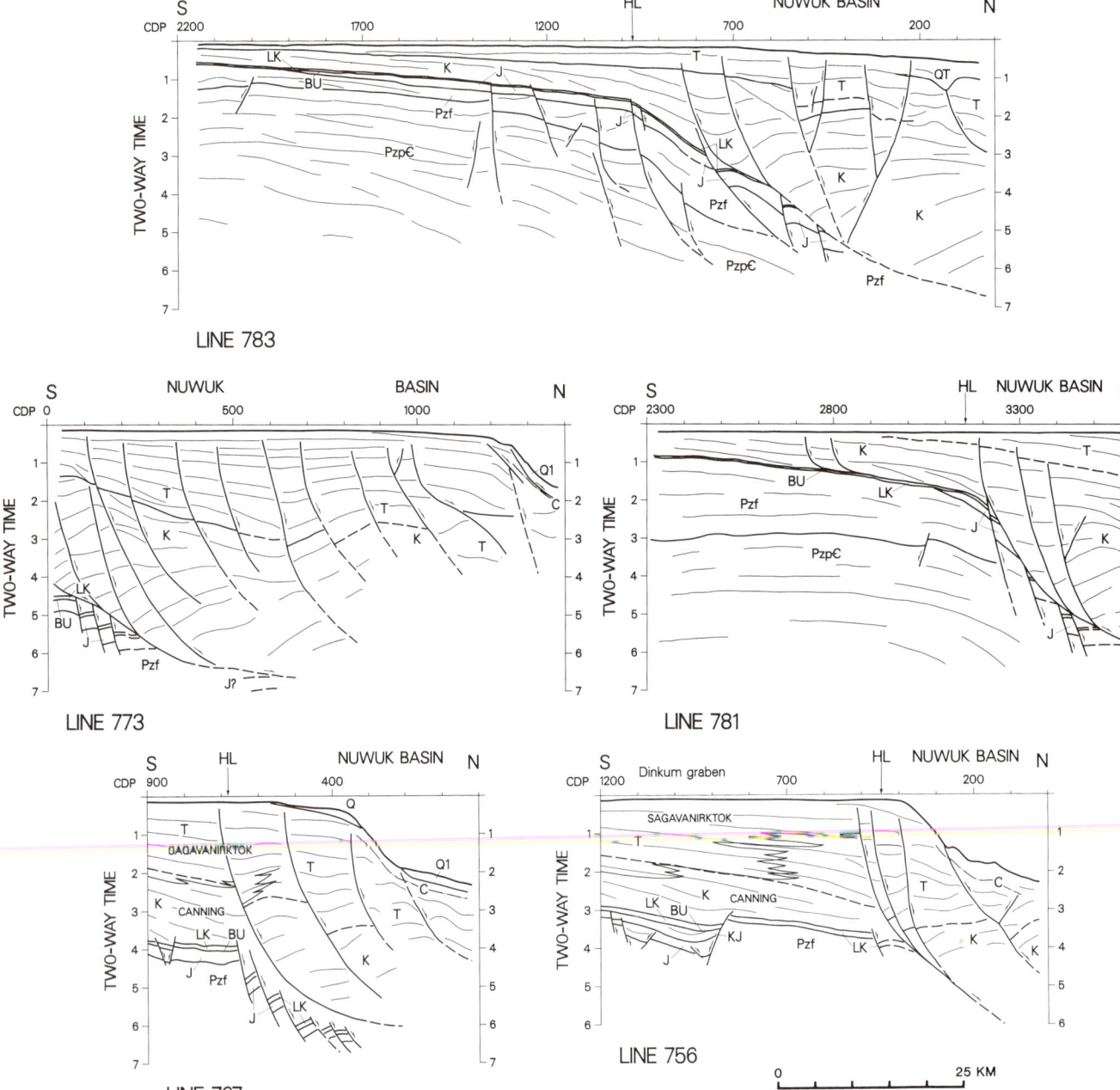

Figure 7. (This and facing page) Line drawings showing geologic structure and stratigraphy on seismic reflection profiles 756, 767, 773, 781, and 783 (shown on A) and 742, 749, and 751 (shown on B) across the Arctic Alaska continental margin. Time sections from Grantz and others (1982). Figure 2 shows approximate equivalence of seismic reflection time and depth, Figures 6 and 12 show location of profiles. Vertical exaggeration in water column is 7; in subsea sediments roughly 3.5, but highly variable. Q1, Quaternary submarine slide deposits; QT, Quaternary and late Tertiary marine sedimentary strata; T, Tertiary strata of the marine and nonmarine Gubik Formation, the dominantly nonmarine Sagavanirktok Formation, and the marine Canning Formation; Tu, upper Tertiary marine and nonmarine strata of the eastern Beaufort Shelf and slope; T1, post–middle Eocene lower Tertiary marine sedimentary strata of the eastern Beaufort Shelf and slope; T1K pre–middle Eocene to Cretaceous, and in places possibly Jurassic, marine sedimentary strata of the eastern Beaufort Shelf and slope; K, Upper to upper Lower Cretaceous strata of the marine and nonmarine Colville Group and Nanushuk Group and the marine Torok Formation and their equivalents beneath the continental slope and rise; LK, Hauterivian to early or middle Albian condensed marine shale with local lenses of sandstone and conglomerate of

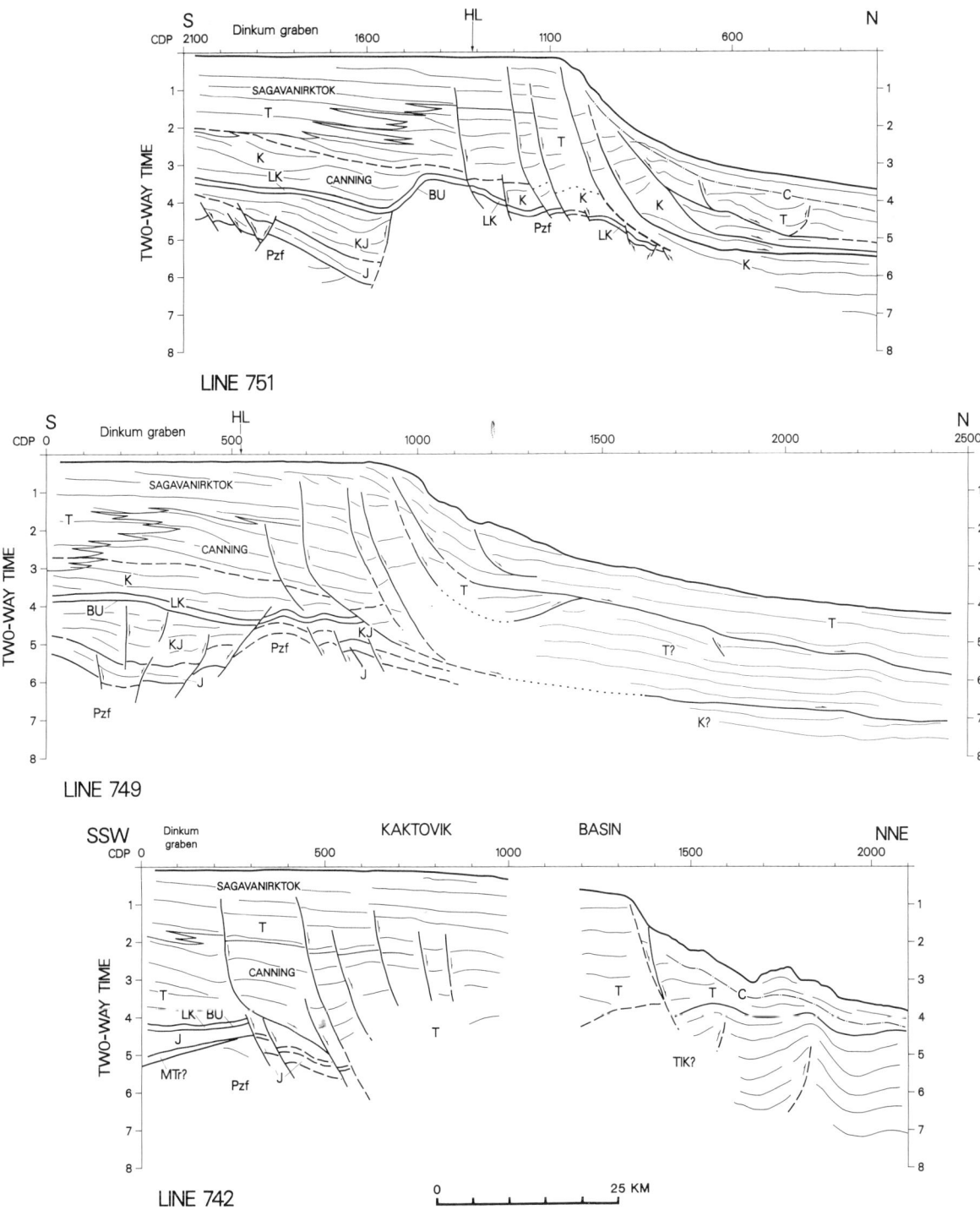

the "pebble shale unit" (PSU) on the western Beaufort Shelf and the Barremian to Maastrichtian Hue Shale on the eastern Beaufort Shelf; KJ, Jurassic and Neocomian synrift marine lutite of Dinkum succession; J, inferred sandstone and possibly conglomerate equivalent to the lower part of the Kingak Shale and possibly lower Ellesmerian sequence marine and paralic stable shelf deposits; MTR, lower Ellesmerian sequence marine and paralic stable shelf deposits; Pzf, lower Paleozoic (pre-Mississippian) eugeoclinal clastic and miogeoclinal carbonate and clastic strata; PzpЄ, lower Paleozoic and Precambrian strata, inferred to include carbonate or possibly quartzite; BU, breakup unconformity; SU, syntectonic unconformity; SU-Teu, middle Eocene syntectonic unconformity; HL, tectonic hinge line related to rifting; D, diapiric core of thrust fold; C, base of solid gas hydrate.

nary Gubik Formation, which is summarized in Dinter and others (this volume).

Canada Basin

The Canada Basin is thought to have formed by rotational rifting during Hauterivian to early Late Cretaceous time. Available data (May and Grantz, 1990; Grantz and others, this volume) suggest that oceanic crust (layers 2 and 3) beneath the southern Canada Basin is of near normal thickness (6 to 8 km) but that it is overlain by an unusually thick sedimentary layer (part 1). The layer 1 sediments are stratigraphically continuous with those of the post-rift sedimentary prism of the Barrow sector of the continental margin. An empirical relation between regional bathymetry and sediment thickness derived from seismic refraction data (Fig. 8 in Grantz and others, this volume) suggests that oceanic crust lies less than 10 km below sea level north of the Chukchi Shelf to 12 km or more off the Mackenzie Delta, and that the overlying sedimentary layer may be a little more than 6 km thick in the former area and 12 km in the latter. The apex of the large continental rise sedimentary prism that fills the southern Canada Basin heads against the Mackenzie Delta and Amundsen Gulf (Plate 1), which indicates that most of the fill originated in the Mackenzie River valley and the glacial drainages entering Amundsen Gulf. Most of the geologic structure in the Canada Basin was imposed by stresses that originated within or south of the Beaufort Shelf. These structures include large submarine slides and, in the Barter Island sector, large thrust faults and thrust-folds related to detachment faults that root beneath the Brooks Range. Grantz and others (this volume) discuss the structure and stratigraphy of the Canada Basin.

Chukchi Borderland

A compact group of aseismic submarine ridges and plateaus and intervening deep basins, the Chukchi Borderland, intersects the continental shelf and slope west of 162°W (Plate 1). The ridges and plateaus are high-standing, flat-topped features with a dominant trend of about N20°E, whose geologic character and mode of origin are poorly known. Present knowledge of Chukchi Borderland geology and geophysics is summarized by Hall (this volume), who concludes that the borderland consists of three or more highstanding continental blocks separated by deep, graben-like basins formed by rifting. The physiography of the borderland suggests that the bounding faults of the continental blocks and grabens have a northerly trend.

Understanding of the character and origin of the borderland is a prerequisite for a complete understanding of the Alaskan Arctic continental margin because the Northwind Escarpment, which forms the eastern boundary of the borderland, is on strike with the eastern boundary of the North Chukchi Basin of the northwestern Chukchi Shelf. This juxtaposition suggests that these features may be genetically linked. Grantz and others (1979) and Vogt and others (1982) proposed that the highstanding ridges of the Chukchi Borderland were rifted from the continental shelf in the western Chukchi and East Siberian Seas, an area now occupied by the North Chukchi Basin.

Some data bearing on the origin of the borderland were collected over the southern part of Northwind Ridge in 1988. A two-channel seismic profile across the eastern half of the ridge showed that it is underlain by 400 to 600 m of flat-lying strata characterized by strong seismic reflectors. The flat-lying strata rest unconformably on moderately dipping to probably strongly deformed beds that are at least 2 km, and possibly 4 km or more thick. Three piston cores from the lower slopes of the Northwind Escarpment near 74°35′N (Fig. 3), at water depths of 3,200 m to 3,700 m, sampled the deformed beds. The lowest unit in the cores consists of bedrock or coarse rubble composed of yellowish brown to light gray, oxidized, foraminifer-bearing marine lutite and dark brown lutite containing abundant palynomorphs. The foraminifers, dated by W. V. Sliter of the U.S. Geological Survey as Albian (personal communication, 1989), resemble forms found in parts of the thick Nanushuk Group of paralic sedimentary rocks of the North Slope. The character and age of the flat-lying upper beds are not known, but their structural position, local deep erosion, and the presence of block faulting that is on strike with that of the eastern North Chukchi Basin suggest that they are no older than latest Cretaceous or Tertiary.

STRUCTURE AND STRATIGRAPHY OF THE ALASKAN MARGIN

Chukchi sector

North Chukchi Basin. The North Chukchi Basin and the Chukchi Borderland are the characterizing features of the Chukchi sector of the continental margin. Principal sources of data on the geologic character of the North Chukchi Basin are eight multichannel and a few single-channel U.S. Geological Survey seismic reflection profiles (Grantz and others, 1972a, b, and 1986) shown in Figures 8 and 9, and Thurston and Theiss (1987), which is based on unpublished proprietary data. We rely mostly on the sparser, but published, Geological Survey data.

The full extent of the North Chukchi Basin is not known. On the east the basin's Brookian strata thin toward the western extension of the Barrow arch (the North Chukchi High of Thurston and Theiss, 1987) beneath the north-central Chukchi Shelf (Fig. 8), and on the southeast they thin toward the Chukchi Platform. To the south the basin is bounded by a south-dipping Cenozoic thrust-fault system near 72°N that extends to the base of the Quaternary cover at the sea floor (Figs. 4 and 8). South of this fault system lies the Wrangel arch, which on Herald and Wrangel Islands (Fig. 8), exposes Proterozoic(?) to Middle Cambrian(?) metavolcanic and metasedimentary rocks and folded and thrust-faulted Paleozoic to Triassic sedimentary rocks (Cecile and Harrison, 1987). Between the Chukchi Platform and Wrangel arch, the south limit of the basin is obscured by thick sequences of Tertiary strata in northerly striking horst and graben structures (Jessup, 1985). Multichannel seismic reflection data extend the

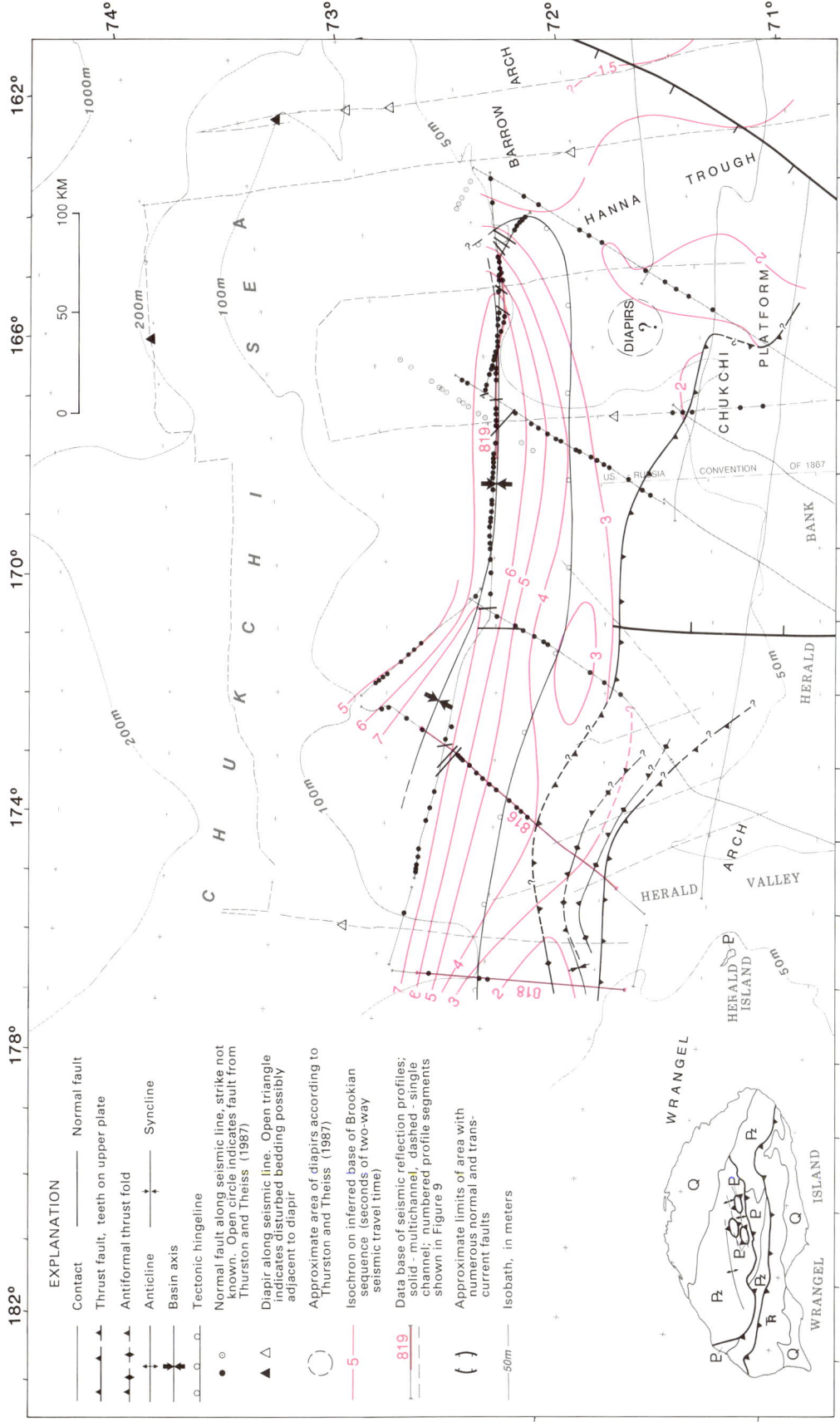

Figure 8. Map of northwestern Chukchi Shelf showing seismic-geologic features and isochrons on base of Brookian sequence in North Chukchi Basin, generalized geology of Wrangel Island after Cecile and Harrison (1987), and location of seismic reflection profiles shown in Figure 9. See Figure 2 for relationship between isochrons and depth. Q, Quaternary deposits; T̄, Triassic flyschoid strata; Pz, Paleozoic fluvial to shelfal clastic and platform to slope carbonate rocks; P, Proterozoic(?) to Middle Cambrian(?) metavolcanic and metasedimentary rocks intruded by granitic sills and dikes (Gromov Complex). Contacts, faults, and axes are dashed where inferred, queried where speculative.

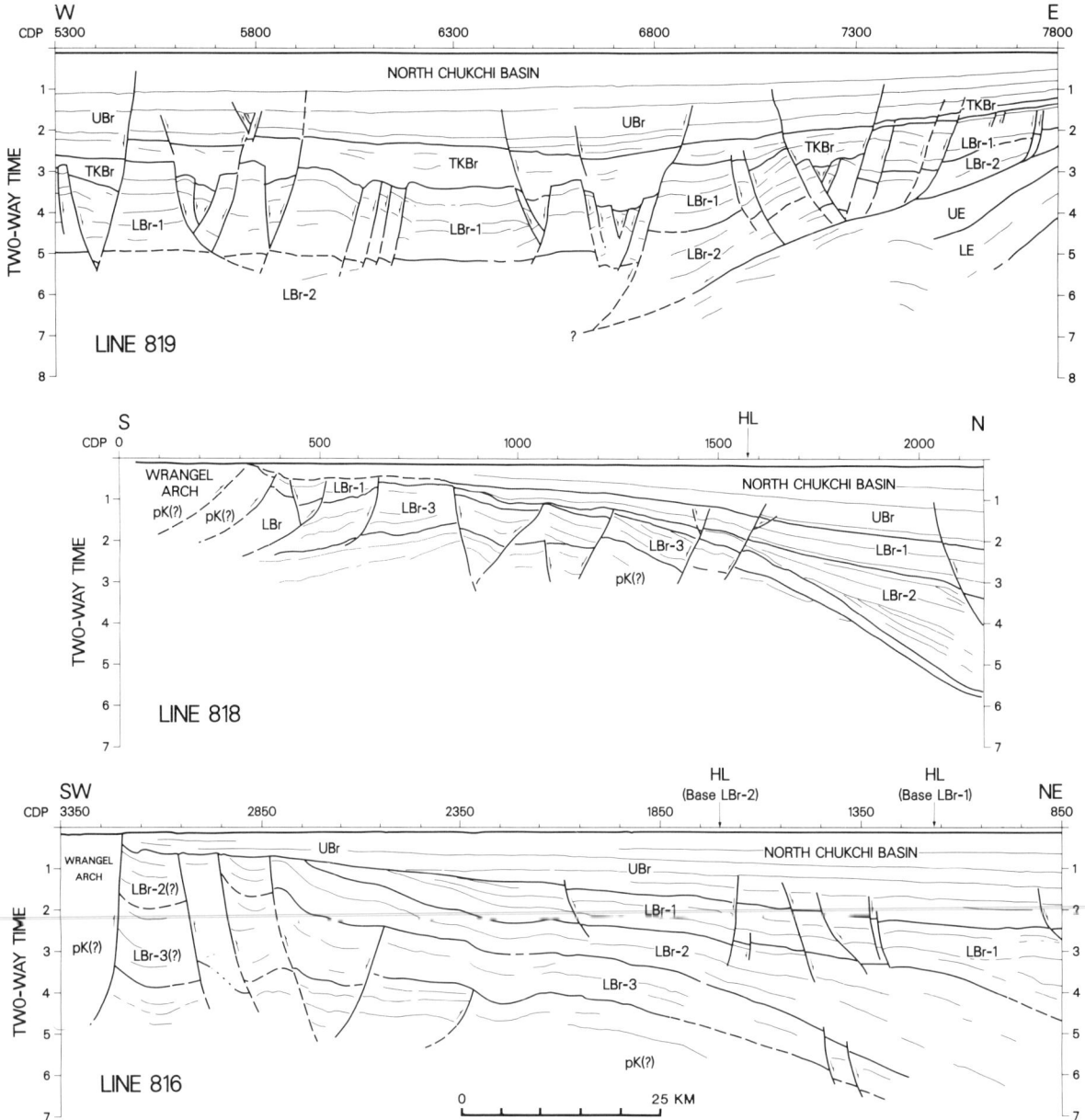

Figure 9. Line drawings showing inferred geologic structure and stratigraphy on seismic reflection profiles 816, 818, and 819 across North Chukchi Basin. Profiles from Grantz and others (1986). See Figure 2 for equivalence of reflection time and depth and Figure 8 for location of profiles. Vertical exaggeration in water column is 7; in subsea sediments roughly 3.5, but highly variable. UBr, upper Brookian (Tertiary) marine strata; TKBr, "Laramide" (uppermost Cretaceous and/or lower Paleogene) marine strata; LBr-1, LBr-2, and LBr-3, seismic-stratigraphic subdivisions of inferred lower Brookian (Cretaceous) marine strata; pK, inferred pre-Cretaceous strata; UE, inferred upper Ellesmerian (Jurassic) marine strata; LE, inferred lower Ellesmerian stable shelf marine strata; HL, tectonic hinge line.

known area of the basin as far north as 73°10′N and as far west as 176°15′W, and single-channel data suggest that the basin extends north of 74°N. The basin axis is incompletely mapped, but it appears to lie near 72°30′ to 73°N and to trend N65° to 85°W.

Stratigraphy and internal structure. We recognize five major seismic-stratigraphic units in the North Chukchi Basin and tentatively correlate them with units in northern Alaska and the Beaufort Shelf. Line drawings in Figure 9 show these units plus pre-Cretaceous (unit pK) strata for which no correlation is apparent. The oldest unit (LE) is interpreted to consist of strata in the lower part of the Ellesmerian sequence that are poorly bedded in the lower part and well bedded in the upper part. These beds appear to lack clinoforms and may be shelf deposits. Unit LE is interpreted to be overlain by Jurassic and Neocomian marine clastic rocks of the upper Ellesmerian sequence (unit UE), which thickens from less than 1 km at the basin edge to more than 2.5 km within the basin 15 km to the west. It may have been a precursor of the North Chukchi Basin, just as the Dinkum succession of the Barrow sector was a precursor to the Hauterivian and younger rift basins of the Beaufort margin. The lower two-thirds or more of unit UE consists of weakly reflective beds thought to be lutites, but the upper third or less on profile 819 (Fig. 9) also contains beds that produce stronger reflections and may include sandstone. These upper beds are gently folded and have been truncated by an angular unconformity at the base of the overlying Brookian sequence. Erosion has locally removed most of unit UE from the east flank of the basin.

A thick sequence of reflections, interpreted to represent clastic rocks in the lower (Cretaceous) part of the Brookian sequence (LBr), unconformably overlies units pK and UE. The internal stratigraphy of unit LBr is hard to define on the basis of our widely spaced profiles, but it may be divisible into three units. Unit LBr-3, the oldest, is shown on profiles 816 and 818 (Fig. 9), where it thins basinward from 1.8 to 3.2 km or more on the paleoshelf at the southern margin of the basin to less than 0.2 to 2.0 km where the unit fades out of our records in the axial deep to the north. The unit consists of weakly to moderately reflective beds, apparently topsets, that have been offset locally by mild folds and at least one thrust fault. These beds were erosionally truncated before unit LBr-2 was deposited upon them.

Units LBr-2 and -1 consist of moderately to strongly reflective, well-bedded rocks that are in topset facies south and east of the tectonic hinge line that separates the paleoshelf regions of the basin from its axial deep (Figs. 8 and 9). On the paleoshelf, unit LBr-2 ranges from 0 to at least 1.7 km, and unit LBr-1 from 0 to at least 1.4 km in thickness. North and west of the hinge line units LBr-2 and -1 increase dramatically in thickness—LBr-2 to more than 6.7 km and LBr-1 to more than 5.4 km. Reflective properties of the constituent beds also are more varied basinward of the hinge line, ranging from weak to strong, and with foreset as well as topset beds present, especially in the lower half of each unit.

The tectonic hinge line at the base of unit LBr-1 (Fig. 9) is about 20 to 30 km farther north than is the hinge line at the base of unit LBr-2, which suggests that subsidence was a multistage event that progressed basinward. On the westernmost profile (818 in Fig. 9), Unit LBr-2 was faulted, uplifted, and eroded on the paleoshelf before overstepping unit LBr-1 was deposited. On the eastern part of line 819 in Figure 9, which crosses the edge of the axial deep, unit LBr-2 can be seen to rest on a glide plane. In consequence, the relation of unit LBr-2 to older units on this profile is not known, and as drawn the unit may include part of unit LBr-3.

An extensional event block-faulted the LBr units in the eastern part of the basin (Fig. 8) and created a spectacular horst and graben paleotopography that was infilled and smoothed by unit TKBr (profile 819, Fig. 9). The extension produced fault scarps with local relief that in places exceeds 2.5 km. The extensional faulting that produced this relief was below wave base because the height of the fault scarps approximates the structural relief on the faults. The area affected is shown on Figures 4 and 8. Unit TKBr, of inferred "Laramide" age, consists of weakly to moderately reflective foreset and bottomset beds that were deposited in local sediment catchments, as well as some topset beds. The unit is as much as 3.2 km thick. A change to markedly better bedded, and more strongly reflective rocks in overlying unit UBr suggests that the deposition of unit TKBr brought the seabed close to wave base and largely filled the depression formed by the extensional faulting.

Unit TKBr thins eastward and southeastward toward a bordering paleoshelf beneath the present central Chukchi Shelf, and it thins over broad structural highs on the shelf such as the Chukchi Platform. It also infills low-lying areas such as the partly erosional, partly structural "Laramide" depression that overlies part of the Hanna trough (Figs. 4 and 8) between the Chukchi Platform and the western part of the Barrow arch. Unit TKBr is about 2 km thick in the trough, is about 2 km deep, and is connected with the main body of unit TKBr in the North Chukchi Basin by two very broad channels. These channels, like the "Laramide-age" depression in the Hanna trough, are partly structural, partly erosional. We postulate that a graded surface originally extended from the depression over the Hanna trough to the deeper North Chukchi Basin during unit TKBr deposition. This surface was uplifted after unit TKBr deposition in the area between the northern part of the Chukchi Platform and the western part of the Barrow arch, and the base of the broad channel now lies above the base of the "Laramide" depression. In the western part of the mapped area of the North Chukchi Basin, beyond the area affected by intense extensional faulting (see Figs. 4 and 8), unit TKBr assumes the geometry of the underlying and overlying formations and has been included in unit LBr-1.

Conformably above unit TKBr in the North Chukchi Basin lies a sequence of well-bedded, moderately to strongly reflective rocks, unit UBr, that is 3.7 km or more thick. The unit was deposited on a generally smooth surface with a long-wavelength structural sag in the eastern part of the basin (profile 819 in Fig. 9). Topset beds are dominant in unit UBr, although it contains some foreset and bottomset beds in the western part of the mapped area. The predominance of topset beds throughout this thick unit indicates that sedimentation generally kept pace with subsidence and that the sediment supply was abundant. Continuing or renewed activity on the larger listric faults that distended units LBr and TKBr has in places offset beds in the lower part of unit UBr (profile 819). Some of the faults that offset lower UBr beds are of moderate displacement and have similar thicknesses of TKBr in their hanging and footwalls. These appear to represent tectonic movement during the early stages of unit UBr deposition. Most of the faults that offset lower UBr beds, however, have displacements of only 100 to 200 m in the UBr, much larger displacements in underlying units, and markedly disparate thicknesses of unit TKBr in their hanging walls and footwalls. These small offsets are thought to have resulted from differential compaction.

Diapirs. Thurston and Theiss (1987) report that a north-trending graben on the northern part of the Chukchi Platform appears to be the source of diapirs, diapir mounds similar to "salt pillows," and associated collapse and withdrawal structures (Fig. 8). The diapirs originate in the upper part, and possibly in the lower part of the Ellesmerian sequence in the graben, and some of them pierce strata as young as upper Brookian (Tertiary).

Several diapirs, and structural features possibly associated with diapirs, were also observed in upper Brookian strata on Geological Survey seismic profiles in and near the North Chukchi Basin. Figure 10 shows two of these diapirs, piercement structures reaching to within 200 m of the seabed, that were identified on a single-channel seismic reflection profiles. A star pattern of seismic profiles across the diapir at 73°21′N shows that this feature is about 2 km in diameter, that its base lies more than 2.5 km below sea level, and that it may be surrounded by a withdrawal syncline. Morphologically these features resemble late-stage salt diapirs, but reconnaissance gravity and refraction measurements (Fig. 10) showed no associated negative density or velocity anomalies. Grantz and others (1975) therefore inferred that these diapirs may be shale cored.

Listric-normal fault province. The eastern part of North Chukchi Basin is underlain by a province of listric faults, horsts, and grabens illustrated in profile 819 (Fig. 9). The faults are mainly of latest Cretaceous or earliest Tertiary age because they disrupt unit LBr, inferred to be of middle Early to Late Cretaceous age, and are overlain by mainly undeformed unit TKBr, of inferred "Laramide" age. A few offset the lower beds of unit UBr of inferred Tertiary age. The extent of the fault province is shown in Figures 4 and 8. Correlation of the faults between U.S. Geological Survey seismic profiles and text figures in Thurston and Theiss (1987) indicate that the strike of the faults is variable, but mainly northerly. Maximum observed displacement on individual fault sets of the listric fault system is about 2.5 km. Extension along our seismic profiles in the listric fault area, as measured by offsets in unit LBr, ranges from 5 to 12 percent. The down-dip terminations of the listric faults in the axial deep lie below our deepest identifiable seismic reflections (6.5 seconds, about 13 km), but the faults can be seen on profile 819 to merge in a detachment, or sole, fault on the eastern slope of the basin Fig. 9). This detachment fault follows the top of unit UE, which underwent some fault truncation of its uppermost beds, from a depth of 3 km near the eastern end of profile 819 to more than 14 km at the east end of the axial deep, 55 km to the west.

The extensional fault terrane lies between a zone of north- to northeast-striking faults to the south and east, and the north-northeast–striking ridges and basins of the Chukchi Borderland to the north (Fig. 4 and Plate 11). The faults to the south of the extensional fault terrane were mapped by Jessup (1985), who reported that they were normal faults that displace upper Brookian (Tertiary) strata. Those to the east and south were mapped by Thurston and Theiss (1987) as the Hanna wrench fault zone. Thurston and Theiss (1987) suggest that many of the faults in the Hanna wrench-fault zone formed in transtensional or transpres-

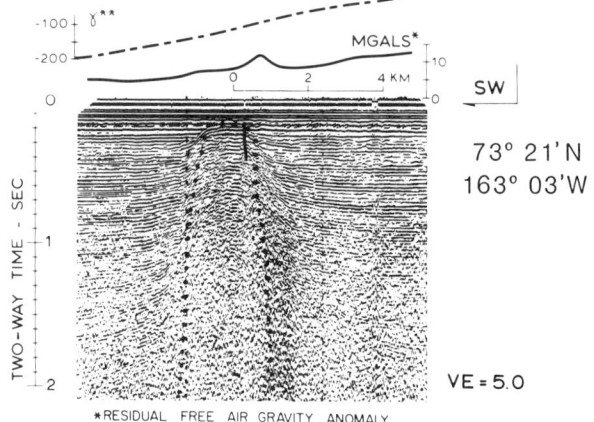

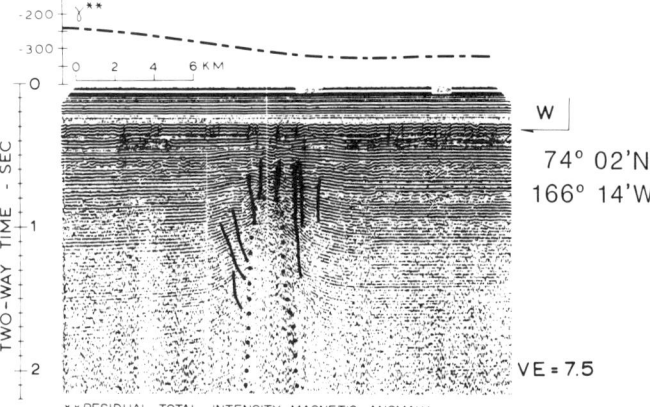

Figure 10. Single-channel air gun seismic reflection, gravity, and magnetic profiles across piercement diapirs in North Chukchi Basin. The upper profile is a central crossing of diapir at 73°21′N, 163°03′W; the lower profile is probably an oblique crossing of diapir at 74°02′N, 166°14′W. See Figure 8 for location.

sional stress fields, but the sense of displacement is not reported. Wrench-fault features are best developed in the eastern part of the Hanna fault zone and may give way to normal faults to the west and in the North Chukchi Basin. The wrench faults reportedly do not extend south of Herald arch and they can not be traced into the North Chukchi high at the west end of the Barrow arch.

Salient features of the listric normal fault province that bear on its origin are the north to northeast trend of its individual faults, the large structural relief on individual fault sets (2.5 km or more), its compactness (fault densities are high within the province and low beyond its boundaries), the significant extension produced by the fault system (5 to 12 percent), and the position of the province at the continental margin opposite the north- to northeast-trending aseismic ridges of the Chukchi Borderland. Restriction of the extensional fault system to only the eastern part of the North Chukchi Basin and the northerly trend of the faults is incompatible with a rift origin above the east-trending axial deep of the North Chukchi Basin or with sliding toward the west-northwesterly striking free face of the adjacent continental margin.

An origin for the listric fault province is suggested by its resemblance to the extensional fault system, which disrupts the Eurasian continental margin where it is impinged by the Arctic Mid-Ocean Ridge of the Eurasia Basin in the Laptev Sea (see Plate 11). Similarities include structural position at the continental margin, trend and character of faulting, and dimensions. Based on this resemblance, we suggest that entry of a "Laramide" spreading center from the Arctic Basin into the continent also created the north-northeast–trending ridge and basin topography of the eastern Chukchi Borderland and the listric normal faults of the eastern North Chukchi Basin. Insufficient data are available to constrain a geometric model, but bathymetry and the regional distribution of extensional features of broadly "Laramide" age in the Arctic region suggest that the normal faults of the western Chukchi Shelf may belong to a regional spreading ridge and transform fault system of latest Cretaceous–early Tertiary age. This system might extend from the Chukchi Shelf to the Mid-Atlantic Ridge via north-south trending structures within the Chukchi Borderland, Mendeleev Ridge, Makarov Basin, and Baffin Bay, and transform faults such as Nares Strait and possibly others, as yet not identified, in the central Arctic Basin (Figs. 1, 3, 4, and Plate 11).

Barrow sector

An arcuate continental margin of simple geometry faces the Canada Basin between Northwind Ridge on the west and the Canning displacement (fault) zone on the east (Figs. 4 and 6). This, the Barrow sector of the Arctic Alaska margin, is characterized by the Dinkum graben, a failed rift of Jurassic and Neocomian age, and the Hauterivian to early Late Cretaceous sea-floor spreading that created the Canada Basin. A syn- and post-rift progradational continental terrace sedimentary prism, the Nuwuk Basin, consists of post-Neocomian (Brookian) clastic sediment that buries the rifts. Cretaceous beds are the principal component of the basin on the west and Tertiary beds to the east. The principal structural features of the Barrow sector are shown in map Figures 3, 4, and 6, seismic reflection profiles 724 to 783 in Figures 7A, B, and 13, and seismic profiles 9D and E in Plate 9.

Stratigraphy. Franklinian rocks. Seismic reflection and refraction data indicate that in many areas the Ordovician and Silurian (Franklinian) argillite and graywacke encountered in many wells on the central and western North Slope extend off shore beneath the Beaufort and Chukchi Shelves. For example, sonobuoy refraction measurements by Bee and others (1984) from the inner Beaufort Shelf from west of Smith Bay to Prudhoe Bay found uppermost basement velocities of 4.24 to 6.08 km/s, which they interpret to represent Franklinian basement composed of argillite and phyllite. These workers, however, also found sonobuoy refraction velocities of 6.4 to 7.07 km/s from the top of basement in a smaller area of the inner shelf adjacent to 153°W, between Smith and Harrison Bays. The measurements suggest to these workers that the top of basement in this area, which is about 30 km in east-west dimension, consists of crystalline rock, probably silicic in composition. This high-velocity basement may be related to granite found immediately below the basal Ellesmerian unconformity at the nearby East Teshekput well (Bird and others, 1978), which lies near 153°W about 20 km west-southwest of Harrison Bay. The granite underlies Late Mississippian beds, and K/Ar dating and correlation with plutonic events in the northeast Brooks Range suggest that it may be Devonian. If a large negative gravity anomaly in the area of the well (Barnes, 1977) is created by the pluton, then the diameter of the pluton may be on the order of 50 km—commensurate in size with the area of the inner shelf underlain by high-velocity basement.

West of Point Barrow, beneath the northeastern Chukchi Shelf, Mississippian strata at the base of the Ellesmerian sequence are underlain by a broadly folded unit, Pzf, that is at least 7 km thick (profiles 781 and 783 in Fig. 7A and Plate 9) and has sonobuoy seismic velocities of 4.15 to 5.35 km/s (Houtz and others, 1981). These beds, inferred to consist of clastic sedimentary rocks, overlie about 5 km of well-bedded, strongly reflective beds with sonobuoy seismic velocities of 5.7 to 7.3 km/s in the upper part of unit Pzp€ (profiles 781 and 783). The lower part of unit Pzp€ consists of conformable, but less reflective strata that may be 6 km or more thick. Some seismic reflection profiles in the eastern part of this region show that a structural detachment zone in places lie between broadly folded areas of unit Pzf and the underlying, nonfolded, unit Pzp€. This detachment zone can be seen in Figure 18A of Haimela and others (this volume) and Plate 3 of Craig and others (1985).

An isopach map of unit Pzf in the northeast Chukchi Shelf (Fig. 11) shows that the unit thins from more than 7 km near Point Barrow and Wainwright to less than 1 km about 160 km to the northwest. Seismic reflection profiles show that the unit consists of two contrasting facies and that the unit was eroded at an angular unconformity at the base of the PSU. Beyond 60 km west northwest of Point Barrow, where the base of the unit dips 6° or 7° east-southeast, the unit consists of southeasterly sloping interlayered strong to weak reflections, which we interpret to represent interbedded sandstone and lutite in foreset facies. Closer to the coast the dip flattens and the foresets grade into weak reflections, which we infer to represent basinal lutites in bottomset facies. The foreset unit thins from more than 5 km on the northwest to approximately 2.2 km where it grades into the basinal facies about 40 km offshore. This geometry indicates that the sourceland of this unit lay to the northwest, toward the sourceland of Barrovia (Tailleur, 1973).

Correlation of units Pzf and Pzp€ of the northeastern Chukchi Shelf with the North Slope section is uncertain due to the structural contrast between the mildly deformed pre-Mississippian units of the Chukchi Shelf and the strongly deformed and mildly metamorphosed pre-Mississippian strata of the western North Slope. A complicating factor is the presence of a northeast-striking structurally disturbed zone along the northwest coast of

Alaska that lies between these areas of contrasting structural intensity. This feature, the Barrow fault zone, is postulated by Craig and others (1985) to be a major northeast-striking, northwest-dipping normal fault with about 10 km of stratigraphic displacement (Figs. 4 and 11).

Craig and others (1985) suggest conditionally that unit Pzf may be "age equivalent to the allochthonous Middle to Upper Devonian rocks of the Baird and Endicott Groups in the west-central Brooks Range." Underlying unit PzpЄ is thought by these workers and by Thurston and Theiss (1987, Fig. 11) to consist of Devonian carbonate and acoustic basement. Grantz and May (1983), on the other hand, suggest that unit Pzf is a mildly structured facies of the Ordovician and Silurian argillite and graywacke of the western North Slope and that the underlying, strongly reflective beds of unit PzpЄ may consist of upper Proterozoic or Cambrian carbonate or metamorphic rocks.

The stratigraphy proposed by Craig and others (1985) requires that the pre-Mississippian section of the northeast Chukchi Shelf be very different than that of the western North Slope. Thus, if offshore unit Pzf consists of Devonian clastic strata, as these authors propose, the correlative units beneath the North Slope would include the Devonian nonmarine clastic rocks encountered at the bottom of the Topagarok test well of the western North Slope (Collins, 1958). The Topagarok rocks can be inferred to rest unconformably on seismically incoherent Ordovician and Silurian argillite and graywacke, whereas unit Pzf rests on a thick section of strongly reflective beds (unit PzpЄ) offshore. A contrast in stratigraphy of this magnitude across the Barrow fault zone would require large transcurrent or thrust displacement, and could not be explained by normal displacement, as proposed by Craig and others (1985).

The stratigraphy suggested by Grantz and May (1983) correlates offshore unit Pzf with the Ordovician and Silurian argillite and graywacke of the North Slope and requires that the mild metamorphism and strong deformation that characterize the North Slope rocks die out at the Barrow fault zone. This contrast in deformation could be explained if the Barrow fault zone is a major splay of a regional detachment fault that thrusts more strongly deformed argillite and graywacke of the North Slope against less strongly deformed argillite and graywacke beneath the northeast Chukchi Shelf. The detachment surface between units Pzf and PzpЄ noted above is thought to be the sole fault at which the Barrow fault zone roots. In support of this hypothesis, we note that seismic velocities of unit Pzf in the northeast Chukchi Sea (Vp = 4.15 to 6.0, average = 4.9 km/s; Houtz and others, 1981) are similar to velocities in the argillite and graywacke of the central North Slope (Vp = 4.3 to 4.9, average = 4.6 km/s; Fisher and Bruns, 1987) and the central Beaufort Shelf (Vp = 4.25 to 6.08 km/s; Bee and others, 1984), and that the argillite and graywacke unit is only mildly metamorphosed beneath the North Slope. In addition there is no subsurface or seismic reflection evidence that a well-bedded, high-velocity bedded section more than 7 km thick, such as unit PzpЄ, lies between the argillite and graywacke and the unmetamorphosed Devonian and Mississippian nonmarine clastic rocks of the central and western North Slope. We consider the possibility that more than 7 km of unit PzpЄ-like rocks once lay between these units on the central and western North Slope, but were subsequently completely removed by erosion, to be unlikely.

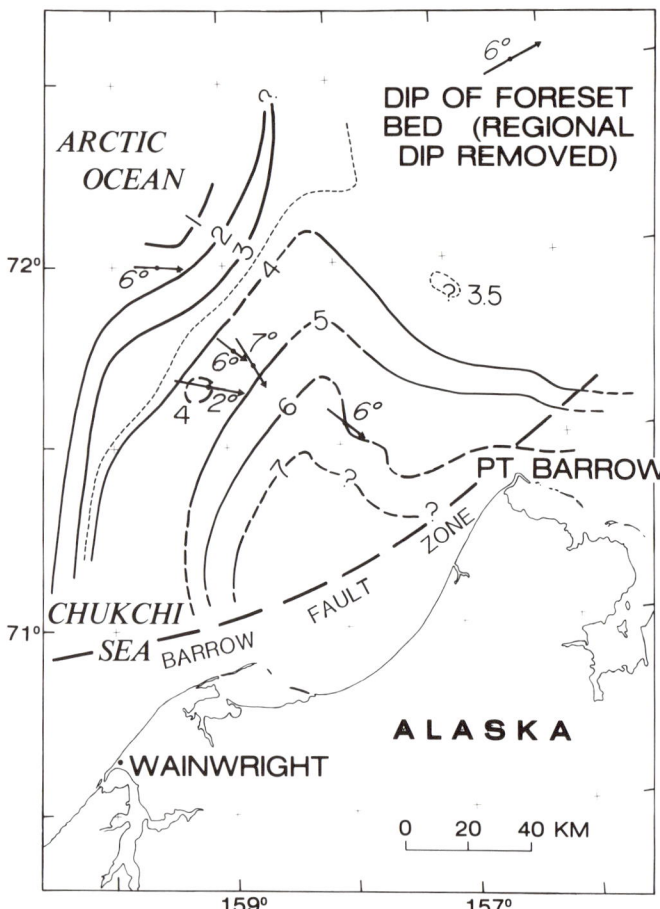

Figure 11. Isopach map of unit Pzf in northeastern Chukchi Shelf showing dip of foreset beds and location of Barrow fault zone (BZF).

Ellesmerian and Brookian rocks. The character of Brookian offshore stratigraphic units in the Barrow sector is shown in profiles 742 to 783 (Figs. 7A, B). Ellesmerian rocks pinch out beneath the inner Beaufort Shelf and the northern Chukchi Shelf to the south of these profiles. Their maximum thickness on the Beaufort Shelf, about 1.3 km, occurs in the Colville Delta–Prudhoe Bay area.

A unit of northward-thickening, moderately strong seismic reflections that is 1.1 km or more thick lies at the base of the sedimentary fill in Dinkum graben (unit J in profiles 742 to 756; Figs. 7A, B). The tectonic setting of these beds at the base of a graben fill suggests that they consist of alternating fine- and coarse-grained clastic materials. The strength of the reflections may corroborate this inference, but other lithologies could also produce such reflections. Near Prudhoe Bay the unit appears to project into upper Ellesmerian strata of the North Slope. We infer that the basal unit of the Dinkum succession in Dinkum graben correlates with the upper Ellesmerian sequence of the North Slope, but it may include lower Ellesmerian beds in paralic facies adjacent to the northern sourceland (Grantz and May, 1983). Overlying the basal beds in Dinkum graben is a unit that produces mainly weak, but some moderate-amplitude seismic reflections. This unit, KJ in Figures 7A and B, is 3.5 km or more thick. Reflection character suggests that the unit consists of topset lutites and some sandstone. Bedding in unit KJ appears to be parallel to that in the underlying, better bedded unit J, and therefore, unit KJ may also consist of topset beds deposited in the subsiding graben. Possible south-dipping foreset beds in the unit on line 751 may indicate that some of these beds are deep-water deposits of northerly provenance. Northward thickening of the Dinkum succession and many of its subunits indicates deposition in a subsiding, north-tilting half graben.

A well-developed angular unconformity, which cuts downsection to the south, forms the upper contact of the Dinkum graben succession (profile 751, Fig. 7B). This is the breakup unconformity of Hauterivian age. The stratigraphic position of this unconformity indicates that the extension represented by the Dinkum succession and graben was an older event than the breakup unconformity and the extension that opened the Canada Basin. A Jurassic and Neocomian age is inferred for the Dinkum succession because it underlies the Hauterivian unconformity; because the succession can be projected into upper Ellesmerian rocks of the North Slope; and because Jurassic marine sedimentary rocks in an analogous stratigraphic and structural position crop out on strike in coastal northern Yukon Territory (Norris, 1984; Poulton, 1978).

A poorly observed, generally deep, northward-thickening seismic reflection unit (J) lies between unit Pzf and the breakup unconformity beneath the outer shelf and slope north of the Dinkum graben. Based on its stratigraphic position and similarities in reflection character, we correlate these beds with unit J in Dinkum graben (Figs. 7A, B). Unit J of the outer shelf produces mainly weak, but some moderately strong seismic reflections with apparent topset morphology. The unit is more uniform in thickness than unit KJ, and is more than 1.3 km thick northwest of Point Barrow and 1.9 km thick north of Prudhoe Bay. We speculate that unit J of the outer shelf was deposited on a subsiding shelf or basin floor in a graben that was tectonically related to, and coeval with, the Dinkum graben. We have, however, identified only north-dipping extensional faults, and the existence of the graben is only inferred from these faults and the position of unit J beneath the continental margin. Correlation of unit J of the outer shelf with that in the Dinkum graben is supported by the proximity of these beds across faults on the north side of the graben on profiles 742 and 749 (Fig. 7B). Unit J is an important marker for measuring the effects of down-to-the-basin rift faulting beneath the outer shelf, and it appears to be the preferred detachment surface for listric normal faults beneath the outer shelf and slope.

Units PSU and HRZ are lumped as seismic unit LK on profiles from the Beaufort and northern Chukchi Shelves (Figs. 7A and 7B). This unit thickens from an average of about 50 m (range 20 to 70 m) beneath the northern Chukchi Shelf (profile 783 in Fig. 7A) to between 400 and 500 m on profiles in the eastern part of the Barrow sector, where it consists of bottomset beds. The age of LK in the western part of the Barrow sector, where it is overlain by the Torok Formation, is Hauterivian to Aptian(?) and possibly early Albian. However, the top of the unit gets progressively younger as it thickens to the east, the direction in which the foreset facies of the Torok and younger formations also pass into bottomset facies. Near the Canning River, in the easternmost part of the Barrow sector, unit LK may include beds as young as Paleocene. Onshore, Molenaar and others (1987, 1987) assign post-PSU bottomset beds, which are equivalent to the upper part of unit LK, to the Hue Shale.

Units K and T in the seismic profiles of Figures 7A and B represent lower Brookian (Cretaceous) and upper Brookian (Tertiary) deposits of the Colville Basin on the North Slope and Chukchi Shelf and the prograding prodelta and intradelta rocks in the continental terrace sedimentary prism of the Nuwuk Basin. The boundary, which was roughly projected from the North Slope, is useful to illustrate structure but it is oblique to the lithologic and facies boundaries in these rocks. The subdivision was effected by roughly projecting the Cretaceous-Tertiary boundary offshore from the North Slope. In both units K and T, topset and foreset facies in the continental shelf pass into bottomset (basinal) facies in the Canada Basin to the north. The approximate position of the interfingering topset-foreset boundary, which is also the contact between the Canning and Sagavanirktok Formations of Molenaar and others (1986), is shown on profiles 742 to 767 (Figs. 7A, B).

On the western North Slope and central Chukchi Shelf, unit K consists of the Torok Formation and the overlying Nanushuk Group. The unit is oldest (Aptian?) in the southern part of the Colville Basin and becomes younger northward by downlap onto unit LK. It is youngest on the crest and north flank of the Barrow arch, where the basal beds are Albian. On the Beaufort Shelf and the northern Chukchi Shelf the uppermost part of unit K also includes topset and foreset beds of the Colville Group. East from Point Barrow, bottomset beds at the base of unit K increase in thickness, the foreset beds at the top of the unit decrease in thickness, and the boundary between these lithofacies becomes younger to the east. Beneath the inner shelf east of Prudhoe Bay the Cretaceous-Tertiary boundary passes from foreset to bottomset facies, and the thickness of unit K is reduced to only about 200 m. Between Prudhoe Bay and Flaxman Island the entire Canning Formation becomes Tertiary (unit T), and unit K is represented only by the condensed bottomset facies of the Hue Shale. The Canning is entirely Tertiary in age beneath the eastern Beaufort Sea.

Sedimentation in unit T of the upper Brookian sequence was a continuation of progressive progradational continental terrace sedimentation established at the beginning of Brookian time. As a result, foreset facies are predominant in unit K, and topset facies

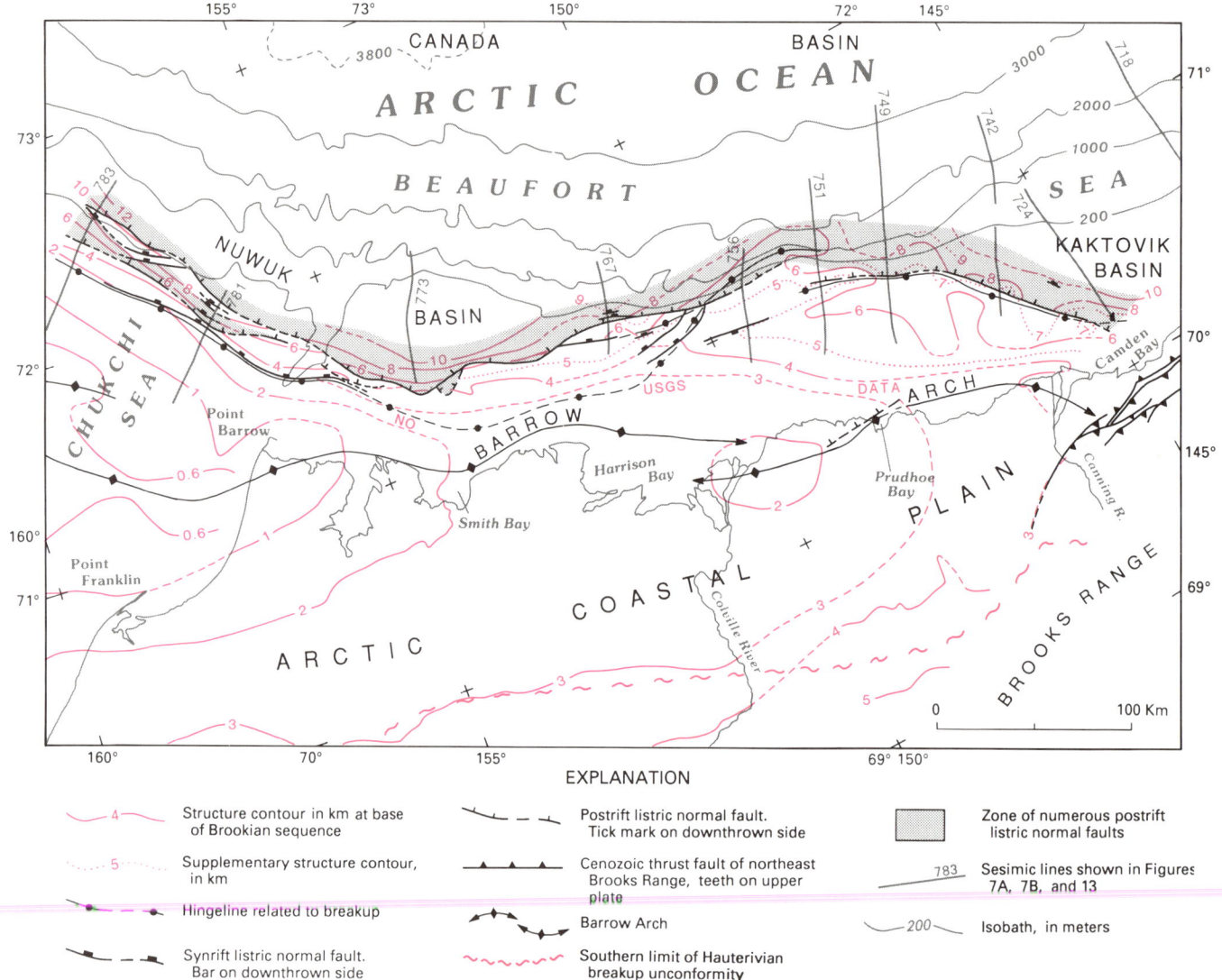

Figure 12. Map of Arctic Alaska continental margin showing depth in kilometers to base of Brookian sequence, which approximates position of Hauterivian breakup unconformity, and synrift and postrift structures. Data sources as for Figure 6. Lines dashed where projected or speculative.

in unit T beneath the continental shelf of the Barrow sector, as suggested by bedding traces in Figures 7A and B. Unit T correlates with the Sagavanirktok Formation of the North Slope west of Prudhoe Bay, but only with its upper part to the east (Molenaar and others, 1986; Kirschner and Rycerski, 1988). The lower part of unit T east of Prudhoe Bay belongs to the Canning Formation, which encloses a thick intertongue of the Sagavanirktok Formation. The Gubik Formation, which caps the section on the Beaufort Shelf, is included in unit T.

Structure. Contours on the top of the Franklinian sequence (Fig. 6) and on the base of the Brookian sequence (Fig. 12) illustrate the regional geologic structure of the Barrow sector. The Franklinian surface slopes seaward with gradients of 30 to 100 m/km from a broad culmination at the crest of the Barrow arch to the tectonic hinge line of Early Cretaceous rifting beneath the outer shelf. At the hinge line the gradient increases abruptly to 250 to 500 m/km, which carries the surface to the lower limit of our seismic data (12 km below sea level) beneath the slope. In places, down-to-basin normal faults of modest displacement offset the Franklinian surface at the hinge line. These faults characteristically are overstepped by the breakup unconformity or extend above it only a short distance into the basal Brookian strata. These faults are therefore related to the rifting events that immediately preceded and accompanied breakup. Seaward of the hinge line the Franklinian surface is offset by down-to-basin normal faults with displacements of 1.5 to 2 km. In places in the eastern part of the Barrow sector, the faults of this set have almost inverted the Dinkum graben by down-dropping rocks on the north flank of this structure below the position of their counterpart units within the graben to the south.

A 50- to 75-km northward excursion of the Early Cretaceous tectonic hinge line at the Colville River delta with respect to its position to the west (Figs. 4 and 6) reflects the influence of extension at the Dinkum graben. Extension at the graben dies out westward in the area of the excursion, suggesting that the excursion is a result of spreading at the graben. The Dinkum fault, which bounds the half graben on the north, has a vertical displacement exceeding 4 km. The principal displacement was pre-breakup (pre–late Hauterivian) but the fault is also the locus of early post-breakup grabenward downflexing and minor faulting (seismic profiles 749 and 751 of Fig. 7B). Dinkum horst, which lies between the graben and the seaward-sloping Franklinian surface north of the hinge line, plunges gently east, as does the floor of the graben, at least as far east as the Canning River. East of the Canning, in the Barter Island sector, the horst and graben pass beneath the thick sedimentary section of the Kaktovik Basin and are lost on our seismic reflection records. The east-southeast trend of the graben would, if not deviated, carry its axis to the coastal plain near Barter Island. Smaller rift features of the same generation as the graben also offset the top Franklinian surface southwest and west of the Dinkum graben, in an area that is shoreward of our seismic coverage (Craig and others, 1985, Fig. 9).

The northward excursion of the hinge line trend (Fig. 4) at the west end of the Dinkum graben forms the east boundary of the middle Early Cretaceous to Tertiary Nuwuk Basin of the central and western parts of the Barrow sector. West of this excursion the width of the sedimentary prism between the hinge line and the shelf break increases from 5 km at profile 756 (Fig. 7A) near the west end of the Dinkum graben to more than 50 km at profile 783 (Fig. 7A), 80 km northwest of Point Barrow. The progradational continental terrace strata of the Nuwuk Basin are virtually undeformed and slope gently seaward south of the hinge line. North of the hinge line these strata are offset by numerous down-to-the-basin listric normal faults, and the structure is dominated by a broad hanging-wall rollover anticline with as much as 1.5 km of structural relief. The rollover formed above a system of north-dipping listric growth faults and some associated south-dipping normal faults that reach nearly to the seabed and sole out at or near the breakup unconformity (see profiles 756 to 783 in Fig. 7A). The growth faults die out within the continental rise sedimentary prism.

North of Dinkum graben, where the hinge-line/shelf-break interval is in places as narrow as 5 to 10 km, the hanging-wall rollover anticline is less well developed and is extensively dismembered by down-to-the-basin listric normal faults. Where the hinge-line/shelf-break interval widens again east of the graben, a broad, high-amplitude rollover anticline is again present beneath the outer shelf (vicinity of CDP 1,500, profile 724, Fig. 13).

Barter Island sector

Large thrust and detachment folds of Cenozoic age with northward vergence characterize the Cretaceous and Cenozoic (Colville Basin) strata of the Barter Island sector (Plates 9 and 11 and Fig. 14; Grantz and others, this volume, Fig. 11). These structures root in thrusts superimposed on the Middle Jurassic to Albian convergent structures that regionally are the dominant features of the Brooks Range orogen. Historic earthquakes along the Camden anticline beneath the continental shelf, folding and faulting of Quaternary sediment beneath the shelf and the Arctic Coastal Plain, and warping of the seabed indicate that this compression is still active.

The thrust and detachment folds developed over a large, multistrand detachment fault system that is projected to lie between 5 and 10 km below sea level beneath the continental slope and that dies out in small folds and back thrusts beneath the continental rise about 170 km north of the coast (Fig. 3 in Grantz and others, this volume; Reiser and others, 1980; Bruns and others, 1987). The western limit of the thrust and detachment folds and related faults, and of the Barter Island sector, is the seismically active Canning displacement zone. The eastern limit is the seismically active eastern front of the Richardson Mountains, in the lower Mackenzie River valley. Note that the Canning displacement zone is a northward extension of the Aleutian Benioff zone (Plate 11), which is of Cenozoic age. This extension and the orientation of the thrust folding and faulting suggest that Cenozoic compression in the Barter Island sector originated in convergence between the Pacific and the North American plates at the Aleutian megathrust. Cenozoic thrusting in the northeast Brooks Range is estimated to have carried older rocks now exposed in the range 25 to 50 km or more northward across the Colville Basin beds of the Barter Island sector. The basin may lie near its original position beneath the thrust sheets, but this has not been documented in seismic reflection profiles across the Arctic Coastal Plain and Foothills (see Bruns and others, 1987). Crustal loading by Cenozoic nappes in the northeast Brooks Range and accelerated erosion and clastic sedimentation from the newly uplifted nappes is also postulated to have depressed the foreland to create the Kaktovik Basin of the Barter Island sector continental margin (Fig. 4).

Stratigraphy. Platform carbonate and clastic strata more than 4.7 to 5.1 km thick, which crop out in south-dipping thrust-fault panels in the Sadlerochit and Shublik Mountains (Blodgett and others, 1986, 1988; Robinson and others, 1989), are the oldest rocks observed in the Barter Island sector. As discussed above under Stratigraphy, Arctic Platform, these beds are Late Proterozoic to Devonian in age. The platform rocks are inferred from outcrop data to rest on a large sole fault system of northern vergence that is rooted in the Brooks Range orogen.

East of the Sadlerochit and Shublik Mountains the oldest strata beneath the Arctic Coastal Plain are pre-Mississippian bedded rocks observed on seismic reflection records (Fisher and Bruns, 1987). These rocks have generally low dips, are 5 to 7 km thick, and are apparently disrupted by low-angle thrust faults. Offshore the pre-Mississippian bedded rocks have been tentatively identified at the south ends of profiles 714 and 718 (Fig. 13), where they have been designated unit Pzf(?). In thickness and reflection character this unit and the pre-Mississippian beds beneath the coastal plain resemble the well-bedded clastic rocks

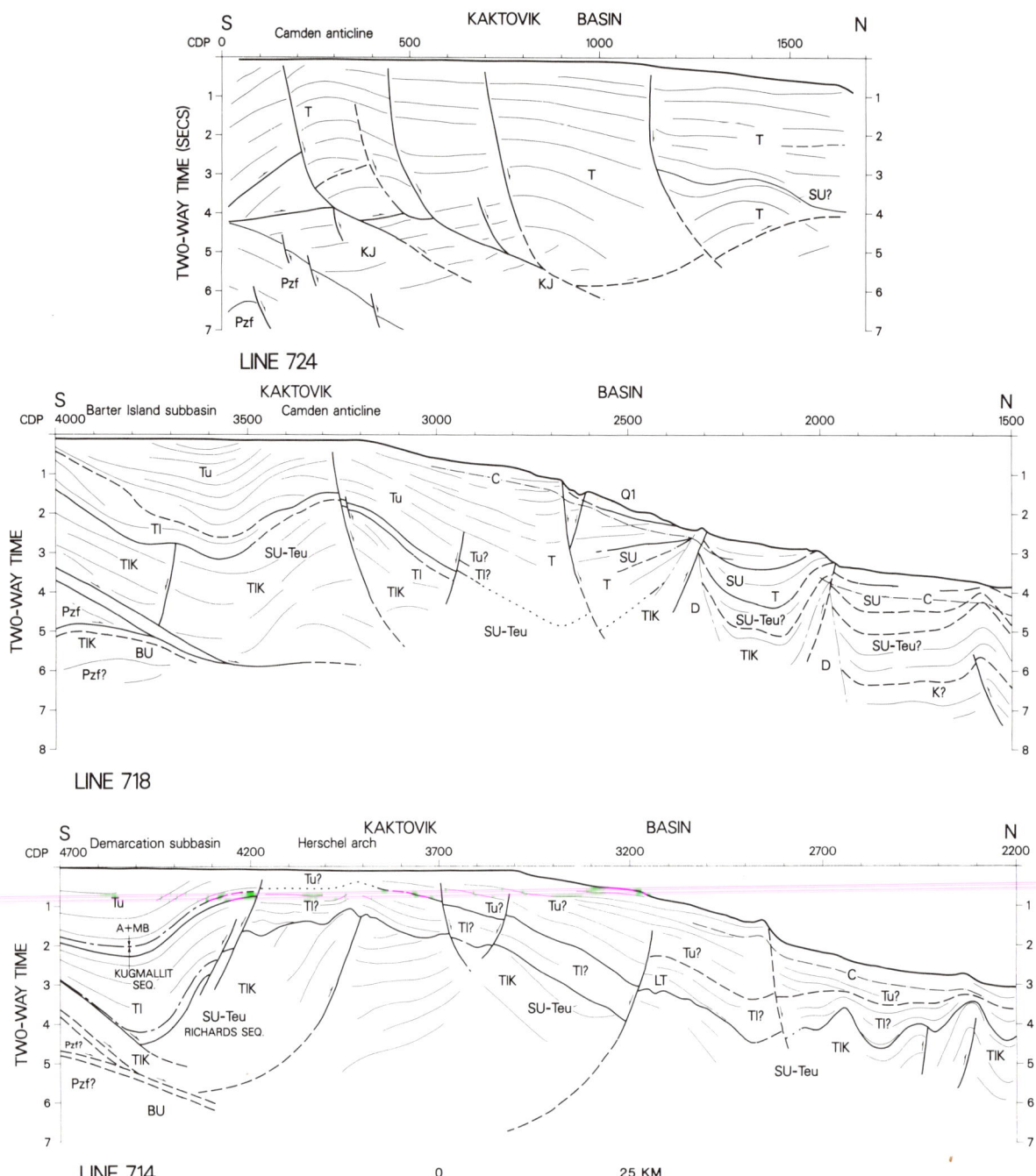

Figure 13. Line drawings showing geologic structures and stratigraphy on seismic reflection profiles 714, 718, and 724 across the Arctic Alaska continental margin. See Figure 7 for explanation and definitions. Sequence names on section 714 extrapolated from Dietrich and others (1989). Time sections from Grantz and others (1982).

of inferred early Paleozoic age in the northeastern Chukchi Shelf (unit Pzf in profiles 781 and 783 in Fig. 7A). We suggest that all of these beds belong to the argillite and graywacke terrane of the central and western North Slope, and that they are a basinal facies of part of the Late Proterozoic to Devonian platformal succession of the Sadlerochit Mountains and vicinity. The north vergence of the platform rocks in the Sadlerochit and Shublik Mountains and their generally high structural position with respect to the argillite and graywacke terrane on either side suggest that the platform rocks have been thrust northward over the argillite and graywacke. The distribution of the platform rocks suggests that they, and any thrust faults that separate them from the argillite and graywacke terrane, extend beneath the continental shelf near Camden Bay and the Canning River.

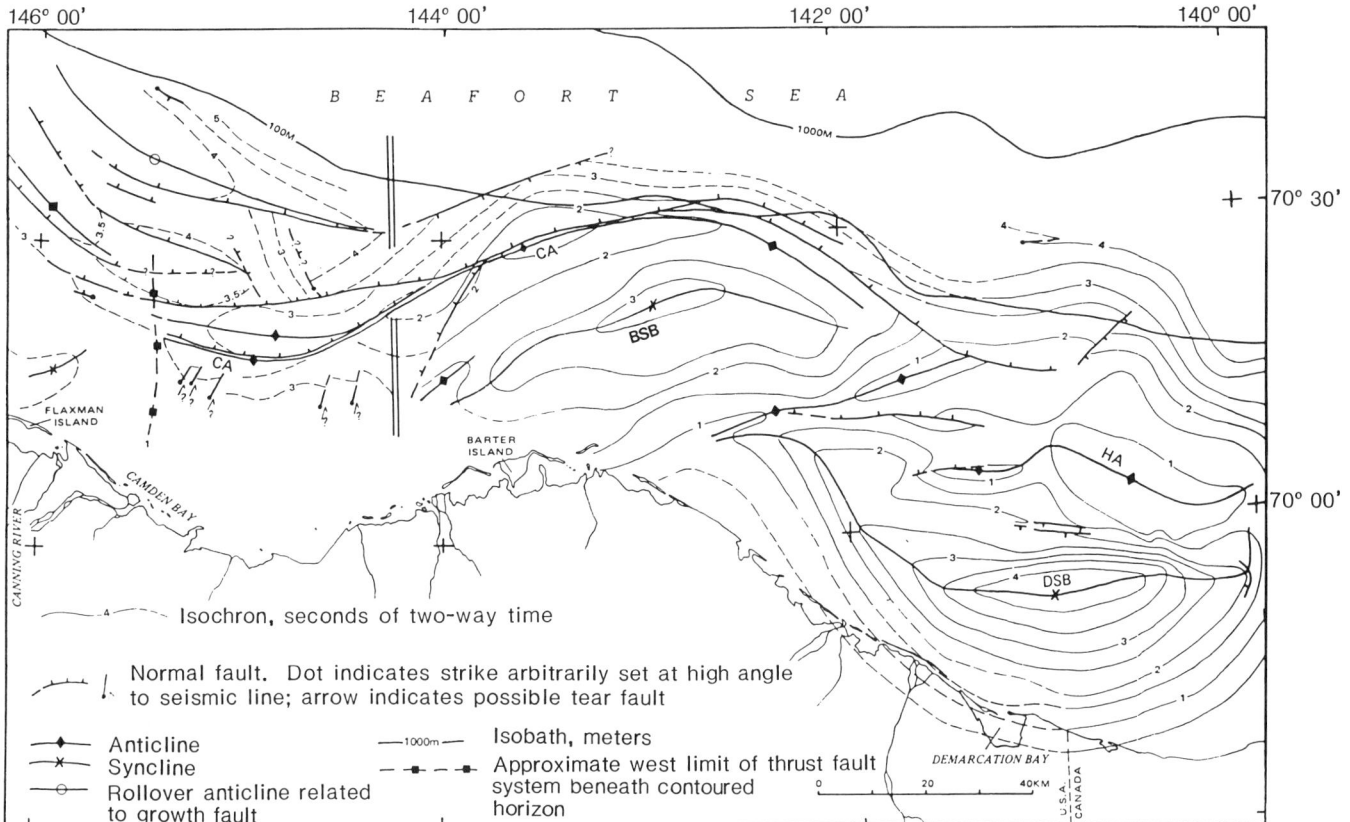

Figure 14. Isochrons (two-way reflection time) on selected surfaces beneath the eastern Alaska Beaufort Shelf; dashed where inferred. See Figure 2 for approximate equivalence of isochrons and depth. Contours are on middle Eocene unconformity east of 144°15′W and on a middle(?) Eocene horizon west of 144°15′W. Contours east of 141°W by James Dixon and James Dietrich (written communication, 1985). CA, Camden anticline; HA, Herschel arch; BSB, Barter Island subbasin; DSB, Demarcation subbasin.

The simple progradational depositional geometry of the Brookian sedimentary prism in the Barrow sector is replaced in the Barter Island sector by a complex of local Tertiary uplifts, erosional unconformities, and local sedimentary subbasins. Figure 14 shows the largest of these features. Camden anticline and Herschel arch are interpreted as large detachment folds, and the Barter Island and Demarcation subbasins as genetically related syndepositional basins. The cross-sectional geometry of these features is shown in profiles 724 to 714 in Figure 13. Growth of the detachment structures began in middle Eocene time, as dated by an erosional unconformity that formed in response to their initial growth. The unconformity, which lies between seismic-stratigraphic units TlK and Tl in profiles 714 and 718, was dated by correlation with a seismic-reflection event dated in test wells on the Canadian Beaufort Shelf (James Dixon and James Dietrich, this volume and personal communication, 1986; Dietrich and others, 1989). It is the major stratigraphic break within the Brookian strata of the Barter Island sector. Above it lie stratigraphically simpler, but more complexly deformed units, and below it stratigraphically more complex, but less deformed units (see profiles 714 to 724 in Fig. 13 and profile 9C in Plate 9).

The character and age of the strata that lie between Franklinian basement and the middle Eocene unconformity (unit TlK in Fig. 13) are uncertain. Reflection character suggests that this unit consists of interbedded shale and sandstone or siltstone, and sonobuoy seismic refraction velocities in the range of 3.0 to 3.8 km/s suggest that the strata are Mesozoic or Paleogene, and not Paleozoic. Regional considerations and comparison with seismic profiles beneath the adjacent coastal plain (Bruns and others, 1987) suggest that near the coast the oldest strata of the unit are basal Brookian. Farther north, however, the oldest strata may, in places, belong to the Dinkum succession and contain Jurassic beds. The uppermost beds of unit TlK are middle Eocene. An unconformity is inferred to lie between unit TlK and the underlying Franklinian basement, but the unconformity is not clearly seen on the seismic profiles and its position in Figure 13 is in part speculative. The thickness of unit TlK may locally exceed 8.6 km, but its true thickness is masked by structural complexity.

Comparison with seismic-reflection profiles tied to test wells on the western Canadian Beaufort Shelf (Dixon and Dietrich, this volume; profile 8E, Plate 8; and Dietrich and others, 1989) suggests that the upper part of unit TlK corresponds to Maastrichtian to middle Eocene strata of intertonguing intradelta and prodelta facies (Fish River and Reindeer depositional sequences on the Canadian shelf; Tent Island, Moose Channel, and Reindeer Formations of northern Yukon—see Fig. 5). The lower part of unit TlK correlates with marine shales of the Jurassic Kingak Formation (Canadian usage), a prodeltaic shale in the late Hauterivian to Aptian Mount Goodenough Formation, Albian flysch composed of detritus from the Brooks Range orogen, and organic-rich shale of the late Cenomanian to Turonian Boundary Creek Formation of northern Yukon. The Boundary Creek contains bentonite beds and ironstone concretions and correlates with lithologically similar beds in the Hue Shale and Seabee Formation of the North Slope.

Dixon and Dietrich (this volume) report that upper Hauterivian strata at the base of the Mount Goodenough Formation rest on a regional unconformity that records a significant tectonic event. The character and age of the unconformity suggest to us that it correlates with the Hauterivian breakup unconformity of the Alaskan margin.

Comparison of unit TlK with the stratigraphic section in coastal wells in the eastern part of the Barrow sector indicate that it corresponds to the condensed shale of the PSU, the condensed distal shale of the Hue Shale, and the lower part of the Canning Formation. If the possible presence of Dinkum succession strata beneath the Beaufort Shelf and slope is excluded, unit TlK ranges in age from Hauterivian to middle Eocene.

Local depocenters and sedimentological complexity characterize the strata that overlie the middle Eocene unconformity in the Kaktovik Basin (units Tl and Tu in profiles 714 and 718 in Fig. 13; profile 9C in Plate 9). The largest local depocenters, the Barter Island and the Demarcation subbasins, lie on the south side of the Camden anticline and the Herschel arch detachment structures (Fig. 14). Narrower and shallower linear depocenters formed behind the ten or more long thrust folds that buckle the Cenozoic strata, and in some places the seabed, beneath the adjacent continental slope and rise. A map of these thrust folds is shown in Figure 11 of Grantz and others (this volume), and the folds are shown in cross section in profiles 714 and 718, Figure 13, and profile 9C, Plate 9.

Angular bedding discordances and thickness changes in the synclinal basins that lie upslope of Herschel arch, Camden anticline, and the thrust anticlines of the shelf and slope indicate that these basin are syntectonic with detachment and thrust folding. Total section in the Demarcation subbasin exceeds 7 km. Of this, 4 km is fill in the initial depression and 3 km is overburden. Thickening of strata into the subbasin, most strongly in the Kugmallit(?) sequence, exceeds 4 km across the south limb and 3 km across the north limb. Fill in the Barter Island subbasin is at least 1.4 km, and the overburden is more than 2.2 km thick. Fill in the basins upslope of the thrust folds of the continental slope is 0.1 to more than 1.0 km thick. The geostatic load created by the trapped sediment appears to have generated soft-sediment flow in underlying unit TlK, causing some of it to move from beneath the Demarcation subbasin, and perhaps the Barter Island subbasin, into the uplifted cores of Herschel arch and Camden anticline (profiles 714 and 718 in Fig. 13).

The basin fills in the Barter Island subbasin, and less clearly in the Demarcation subbasin, are progradational and consist of a lower unit dominated by foreset beds and an upper unit dominated by topset beds. The facies boundary between these units becomes younger to the north. We infer that this boundary, which can be observed on profile 718, Figure 13, corresponds to the similar boundary between the Canning and Sagavanirktok Formations of the Barrow sector. On our seismic records we are unsure whether the inferred Canning beds extend north of Camden anticline or Herschel arch, but locally the Sagavanirktok appears to rest directly on the middle Eocene unconformity over and north of these structures.

Correlation with data in Dixon and Dietrich (this volume) and Dietrich and others (1989) indicates that the Demarcation subbasin contains the Richards and Kugmallit sequences and possibly the Mackenzie Bay, Akpak, and Iperk sequences of the Canadian western Beaufort–Mackenzie Basin (see profile 714 in Fig. 13). The Richards is middle to upper Eocene interbedded nearshore sandstone and mudstone less than 0.3 to more than 0.5 km thick; the Kugmallit about 0.8 to 1.0 km of lower and middle Oligocene mud-dominant prodelta and shelf sediment; the Mackenzie Bay as much as 2.0 km of upper Oligocene and lower Miocene prodelta sediment, and the Akpak middle and upper Miocene prodelta deposits that in places are close to 2.0 km thick. The Pliocene and Pleistocene Iperk sequence, unconsolidated gravel, sand and mud with abundant woody detritus, is about 0.2 km thick. In the Demarcation subbasin the Richards is well bedded, about 0.8 km thick, and appears to consist of topset (shelf) facies deposited on the middle Eocene unconformity. The overlying Kugmallit(?) beds consist of northward prograding topset and foreset beds that are 1.3 km thick about midslope on the south flank of the subbasin, about 2.4 km or less in thickness high on the north flank, and at least 3.8 km thick in the axial region. A correlation based on seismic reflection character suggests that an interval of strong reflections near 2.2 s in the axial region of the Demarcation subbasin (profile 714) may mark the base of the Mackenzie Bay sequence, and the base of an interval of weaker reflections near 1.05 s may mark the base of the Akpak sequence. The Mackenzie Bay(?) interval is about 1.8 km thick and consists of mainly strongly bedded topset beds. The Akpak is about 0.7 km thick and also appears to consist of topset beds, but the reflections are obscured by multiples. If the Iperk sequence is present, it is obscured by multiples.

Structure. Convergent structures of Cenozoic age characterize the Barter Island sector and distinguish it from the Barrow sector, where convergent tectonics are absent. The convergence has also given these continental margin sectors contrasting morphologies, which are illustrated by the superimposed bathymetric profiles shown in Figure 15. The profiles across the slope of the Barrow sector are concave upward, recording the influence of extensional processes, whereas those across the Barter Island sector slope are convex upward, reflecting the influence of conver-

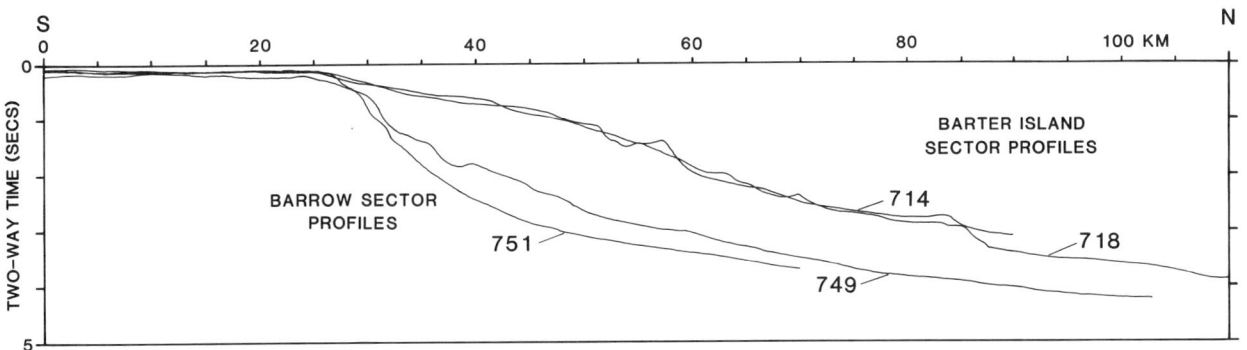

Figure 15. Comparison of seabed morphology across Arctic continental margin in Barter Island sector (profiles 714 and 718 of Fig. 13) and Barrow sector (profiles 749 and 751 of Fig. 7B). Area of prism between the two sets of profiles, equivalent to a tectonic welt almost 1 km high and 60 km wide, is a rough measure of minimum volume of Cenozoic tectonic transport across the convergent continental margin of the Barter Island sector with respect to the extensional (passive) margin of the Barrow sector.

gence. The cross-sectional area between the two sets of profiles extrapolated across the length of the Barter Island sector represent a bulge in the face of the continental terrace equivalent to a tectonic welt almost 1 km high, 60 km wide, and 500 km long. The average horizontal distance between the concave and convex profiles, about 30 km, is a rough measure of the minimum tectonic transport across the convergent Barter Island sector with respect to the extensional Barrow sector in Cenozoic time. An overview of the compressional structures of the Barter Island sector and their relation to regional structure is shown in Plate 11. Maps showing the character of the convergent structures are presented in Figure 14 of this chapter and Figure 11 of Grantz and others, this volume.

Four types of Cenozoic structures, which lie in discrete, east-west–trending belts, are dominant in the upper crust of the Barter Island sector. On the south, beneath the inner and middle shelf, are the deep Barter Island and Demarcation subbasins (Fig. 14, profiles 714 to 724 in Fig. 13, and profile 9C in Plate 9). These basins are paired with broad, northward-convex, en echelon detachment folds, the Camden anticline and Herschel arch, that underlie the middle and outer shelf. North of the detachment folds, beneath the continental slope and rise, is a wide zone of slope-parallel thrust folds of large amplitude. Many of these folds buckle the sea floor and act as sediment traps. Beneath the outer shelf and upper slope are basinward-dipping listric normal faults, which are prominent only in the westernmost part of the sector (Figs. 6 and 12 and profile 724 in Fig. 13). The largest of these dip north and are related to deep slumping of Quaternary age near the present-day continental margin, but a few dip south.

Key to understanding the structure of the continental margin in the Barter Island sector is the character of Herschel arch and Camden anticline (profiles 714, 718, and 724 in Fig. 13, profile 9C in Plate 9). These folds are asymmetric, with a short south limb that dips landward at a large angle to the sea floor and a long north limb that dips seaward only a little more steeply than the sea floor. At the top of unit TlK their cross sections resemble south-facing monoclines at the short south limbs of the folds. The amplitudes of the monoclines at this horizon are 6.75 km for Herschel arch and 3.0 km or more for Camden anticline. The arch, which lies beneath the inner and central shelf, contains structural duplexes within unit TlK. Thrust-fault panels in the core of Herschel arch have a moderate south dip, which suggests that the structure was initiated in the regional, north-vergent compressional fault system of northeastern Alaska. Multiple structural culminations of the unconformity are present at the crest of the arch and must have been uplifted to wave base or the sea surface because they were the source of local sediment aprons. The culminations appear to represent small structural uplifts of the middle Eocene sea floor (see vicinity of CDP 3900, profile 714, Fig. 13). The culminations and the associated sedimentary aprons suggest that thrusting and uplift were penecontemporaneous with erosion and that the unconformity is a product of the early and middle Eocene convergence. The great disparity in thickness of unit TlK between Herschel arch and the basement for the Demarcation subbasin (Fig. 13) suggests that post-unconformity soft sediment flow in unit TlK from beneath the subbasin into the core of the arch may also have contributed to the large structural relief (6.75 km) across its south limb.

Camden anticline, in contrast to Herschel arch, appears to be a relatively simple buckle above a north-sloping detachment fault. In the central part (profile 718 in Fig. 13) the detachment fault has a relatively simple geometry and lies about 10 km below sea level at the fold axis. The amplitude of its south flank here is about 3 km. On the west (profile 724 in Fig. 13) the basal detachment fault system is a little more complex and it lies only about 6 km below sea level at the fold axis. The anticline here has an amplitude at the south flank of 4 km or more, but it is disrupted by several down-to-the-basin listric normal faults that merge with the detachment fault system at depth.

The thrust folds that lie north of Herschel arch and Camden anticline differ greatly from these structures in size and structural character. More than ten thrust folds have been identified beneath the continental slope and rise (profiles 714 and 718 in Fig. 13 and profile 9C in Plate 9; Fig. 11 in Grantz and others, this volume). These structures are slope-parallel, range from a few tens of meters to at least 1.4 km in amplitude, and have wavelengths of 5 to 20 km. The folds are relatively narrow, elongate, and typically separated by broad, flat-bottomed synclines, in which respects they resemble detachment folds. Most are north vergent and appear to be cored by south-dipping thrusts, but a few are unfaulted or have north-dipping back thrusts in the core. Many of the folds have buckled the seabed, and some have acted as sediment traps in which hundreds of meters of sediment has accumulated. Additional discussion of these features can be found in Grantz and others, this volume.

Demarcation and Barter Island subbasins are compact, ovate extensional subbasins that lie en echelon on the landward side of Herschel arch and Camden anticline (Fig. 14). The Demarcation subbasin is 7.5 km deep, and the Barter Island subbasin a little more than 4 km deep (Fig. 13). Their north flanks, which lie against the arch and anticline, are steeper than their south flanks, and the north flank of the Demarcation subbasin is broken by south-dipping normal faults. Bedding is parallel to the subbasin floors or onlaps them in a southerly direction at low angles on the south flanks of the subbasins. In contrast, many beds onlap the floors of the north flanks of the subbasins and do so in a northerly direction and at steeper angles to the subbasin floors. In the Demarcation subbasin the lower part of the subbasin fill (upper Eocene and Oligocene beds of the Richards and Kugmallit sequences) thickens from less than 0.6 km over the south flank and less than 0.2 km over the north flank to 3.5 km at the subbasin axis. Some additional thickening occurred in higher beds, in the central part of the subbasin section, and part of the thinning on the north flank is due to normal faulting.

The regional geologic structure of northeastern Alaska, including the geologic structure of the Arctic Coastal Plain (Bruns and others, 1987), shows that the Cenozoic structures of the shelf in the Barter Island sector formed in a compressional environment. It therefore seems anomalous that the Demarcation and Barter Island subbasins are extensional features, that cross sections of Herschel arch and Camden anticline resemble south-facing monoclines, and that these large features lack the strongly compressional structural overprint of the thrust-fold belt of the adjacent continental slope and rise. Our seismic data do not penetrate deeply enough to fully resolve this anomaly, but the following hypothesis may explain our observations. We suggest that the growth of Herschel arch began in early or middle Eocene time as a compressional structure above a sole fault that extended from beneath the Brooks Range to the continental slope. As the sole fault passed from the Brooks Range to the Eocene shelf and continental margin, we propose that its dip changed from low south to low north. Compressionally thickened unit TlK was unstable where it overlay the northward-sloping portion of the sole fault beneath the continental margin, and we postulate that it began to glide slowly basinward under body forces. The rate of displacement was moderated by the resistance offered by sediment down-slope, in front of the gliding block. The space vacated by the block guide created the proto-Demarcation subbasin in late Eocene and Oligocene time. Thick and rapid Oligocene sedimentation in the subbasin may have mobilized the underlying unit TlK, facilitating the gliding and perhaps transferring some material to the glide block. An angular discordance at the base of the fill beneath the center and south flank of the basin (profile 714, Fig. 13) is interpreted as a detachment fault on which some of the gliding took place. Camden anticline and Barter Island subbasin are thought to be analogous to Herschel arch and the Demarcation subbasin; there was less thinning of unit TlK beneath the Barter Island subbasin, however, and its structure and stratigraphy indicate that this subbasin did not originate until late Cenozoic time.

Most of the thrust folds beneath the slope and rise are Neogene or Quaternary in age, but some were active during mid-Tertiary time. We suggest that these north-vergent compressional structures were formed in consequence of both middle and late Cenozoic movement on the Herschel arch block glide. Large-scale folding of the entire fill in both the Demarcation and Barter Island subbasins indicates that both subbasins were also affected by strong late Cenozoic tectonic movement. The geometry of this movement is not clear from our data. Presumably it would involve continued transmission of north-vergent compression to the rocks above the detachment faults of the Barter Island sector, moderately large displacements on the basal detachment faults where they dip north, and continued thickening and buckling of unit TlK above the detachment faults in both Herschel arch and Camden anticline. Distally, the displacement is transmitted to, and expended within the thrust folds that buckle the sea floor beneath the continental slope. The earthquake and aftershock swarm of 1968 on the Beaufort Shelf in the western part of the Barter Island sector suggest that this activity is continuing (Biswas and others, 1977).

The geometry of Herschel arch and Camden anticline suggest that these large structures formed under similar paleogeographic and structural conditions. If the Demarcation subbasin was created by block gliding, its 30 km width, is a measure of the minimum seaward displacement of the postulated Herschel arch glide block. Likewise, if the Barter Island subbasin was formed by block gliding, its width indicates that horizontal displacement of the Camden anticline glide block was also 30 km or more. The geometry and trend of the anticline indicate that its west end was fixed and that its initial position on the east was parallel to the coast about 10 or 20 km seaward of Barter Island.

TECTONIC HISTORY

The Arctic Ocean Basin is closely surrounded by the major continents of the Northern Hemisphere, which are characterized tectonically by numerous, large convergent orogens of Paleozoic, Mesozoic, and Cenozoic age. Yet, paradoxically, the Arctic Basin was formed by a series of extensional, or rifting events that began at least as early as late Paleozoic time. The best known of the extensional events that preceded formation of the Canada Basin and the Alaskan continental margin during middle Early Cretaceous time occurred in the Sverdrup basin of the western Canadian Arctic Islands (Plates 1 and 11). In the western part of this basin, Balkwill and Fox (1982) describe an incipient rift zone of Carboniferous to Late Cretaceous age marked by aligned normal faults, gabbro dikes, magnetic anomalies, and evaporite diapirs. The incipient rift also has stratigraphic expression in Carboniferous to Upper Cretaceous rocks. The rift strikes N40°E from Melville to northern Ellef Ringnes Island, about 25° counterclockwise from the trend of the adjacent present-day continental margin. Aligned dikes show the location of this feature on Plate 11. Balkwill and Fox (1982) state that the Sverdrup basin rift zone is likely to be the supracrustal expression of a crustal suture in Precambrian basement.

A second failed rift zone (Grantz and May, 1983) occurs along the continental margin from Banks Island to the continental slope west of Point Barrow. Stratigraphic relations in the northern slopes of the British Mountains in northern Yukon Territory indicate that this rift postdated thin, northerly sourced nearshore deposits of Late Triassic age and that the rift contains thick lutites as old as late Early Jurassic (Poulton, 1978). The presence of shale and siltstone of earliest Early to latest Middle Jurassic age in the Bonnet Lake area of the northern Richardson Mountains suggests that the oldest deposits in the rift may date back to the earliest Jurassic. Seismic stratigraphic relations along the Alaskan continental margin, detailed in previous sections of this chapter, indicate that the failed rift system contains as much as 4.7 km of Jurassic and Neocomian strata. The known and inferred distribution of the Jurassic failed rift deposits indicate that the rift was parallel to, and lay along or near the present continental margin along both the Canadian Arctic Islands and Alaskan sectors of the Canada Basin, and that the rift extended southward into the continent in the lower Mackenzie Valley. Restoring the Hauterivian to early Late Cretaceous counterclockwise rotation of Arctic Alaska away from the Canadian Arctic Islands about a pivot in the lower Mackenzie Valley (see Fig. 12 in Grantz and others, this volume) would unite the now-separated fragments of the Jurassic failed rift deposits into a single rift system. This rift system would have lain within the peripheral platform of the Canadian Shield near, and subparallel to, the Carboniferous to Cretaceous failed rift of the Sverdrup basin.

The Jurassic rifting episode was a precursor to the late Neocomian rifting and Hauterivian breakup events that finally separated Arctic Alaska from the Canadian Arctic Islands. The newly formed Canada Basin was sufficiently well developed by Aptian time to receive more than 8.4 km of Albian progradational clastic deposits, and to serve as base level for development of submarine canyons with 1.4 km or more of erosional relief by Turonian time (Collins and Robinson, 1967). Firm evidence for the duration of rifting is not available, but the assumption of moderate rates for the spreading suggests that spreading was completed by middle Late Cretaceous time.

The geometry of the tectonic hinge line created by Hauterivian rifting and breakup (Figs. 4, 6, and 12) shows that this rifting event was the culmination of Jurassic rifting, and not a wholly independent event. Thus, the apparent position and trend of the Jurassic failed rift, as reconstructed from seismic and scattered outcrop data, is close to that of the successful Hauterivian and Barremian rift that produced the present continental margin. At a finer scale, the northward displacement of the Hauterivian hinge line at the mainly older Dinkum graben indicates that the breakup structures followed, rather than cut across, those of the precursor Jurassic rift system.

The southward excursion of the tectonic hinge line near 165°W, in the northwestern Chukchi shelf is associated with the genesis of the North Chukchi Basin. The great depth of this basin, its parallelism to the rifted margin to the east, and the apparent absence of a major transcurrent structure at its eastern margin, suggest that this offset segment of the continental margin also may have originated as a failed Jurassic rift. An intriguing unknown is whether the high-standing, northerly striking aseismic ridges of the adjacent Chukchi Borderland constitute fragments of the former northern margin of the North Chukchi Basin left behind by local complexities in the plate motions and geometry that created the Canada Basin.

A fourth episode of rifting may be represented by the wide zone of northerly trending "Laramide" extensional faults that disrupt the northwestern Chukchi Shelf and the eastern part of the adjacent North Chukchi Basin. This zone enters the continental margin from the north and apparently dies out within the Chukchi Platform of the central Chukchi Shelf. The position, trend, age, and deformational vigor of this event suggest that it may have been responsible for the dismemberment of a formerly compact Chukchi Borderland into its present array of northerly striking ridges and basins. These characteristics also suggest that the rift zone may have been connected, by a route which at present can only be conjectured, with rifting and sea-floor spreading of similar age in Baffin Bay and the Labrador Sea (Plate 11).

Convergent tectonics did not return to the Arctic Basin until Cenozoic time when compression strongly deformed sediments of the continental margin in the Barter Island sector and adjacent parts of the southeastern Canada Basin. Distal effects of the deformation extend as far as 170 km north of the coast line, where water depths are in excess of 3,000 m. This episode of convergence probably began in Eocene time, and historic earthquakes and an abundance of deformed Quaternary sediments demonstrate that the convergence is still active. The tectonic position of the structures and earthquakes produced by this activity indicate that the compressional structures of the Barter Island sector in northeastern Alaska and northwestern Canada are distal effects of convergence between the Pacific Plate and North America at the Aleutian subduction zone.

REFERENCES CITED

Balkwill, H. R., and Fox, F. G., 1982, Incipient rift zone, western Sverdrup Basin, Arctic Canada, *in* Embry, A. F., and Balkwill, H. R., eds., Arctic geology and geophysics: Calgary, Canadian Society of Petroleum Geologists Memoir 8, p. 171–187.

Barnes, D. F., 1977, Bouguer gravity map of Alaska: U.S. Geological Survey Geophysical Investigations Map GP-913, 1 sheet, scale 1:2,500,000.

Bee, M., Johnson, S. H., and Chiburis, E. F., 1984, Marine seismic refraction study between Cape Simpson and Prudhoe Bay, Alaska: Journal of Geophysical Research, v. 89, no. B8, p. 6941–6960.

Bird, K. J., 1988a, Alaskan North Slope stratigraphic nomenclature and data summary for government-drilled wells, *in* Gryc, G., ed., Geology and exploration of the National Petroleum Reserve in Alaska, 1974 to 1982: U.S. Geological Survey Professional Paper 1399, p. 317–354.

—— , 1988b, Structure-contour and isopach maps of the National Petroleum Reserve in Alaska, *in* Gryc, G., ed., Geology and exploration of the National Petroleum Reserve in Alaska, 1974 to 1982: U.S. Geological Survey Professional Paper 1399, p. 355–380.

Bird, K. J., Connor, C. L., Tailleur, I. L., Silberman, M. L., and Christie, J. L., 1978, Granite on the Barrow Arch, northeast NPRA: U.S. Geological Survey Circular 772-B, p. 24–25.

Biswas, N. N., Gedney, L. D., and Huang, P., 1977, Seismicity studies in northeast Alaska by a localized seismographic network: University of Alaska Geophysical Institute Final Report No. 14-08-0001-15220, 22 p.

Blodgett, R. B., and 5 others, 1986, Age revisions for the Nanook Limestone and Katakturuk Dolomite, northeastern Brooks Range, Alaska: U.S. Geological Survey Circular 978, p. 5–10.

Blodgett, R. B., Rohr, D. M., Harris, A. G., and Rong, J., 1988, A major unconformity between Upper Ordovician and Lower Devonian strata in the Nanook Limestone, Shublik Mountains, northeastern Brooks Range, *in* Galloway, J. P., and Hamilton, T. D., eds., Geologic studies in Alaska by the U.S. Geological Survey during 1987: U.S. Geological Survey Circular 1016, p. 18–23.

Bruns, T. R., Fisher, M. A., Leinbach, W. J., and Miller, J. J., 1987, Regional structure of rocks beneath the coastal plain, *in* Bird, K. J., and Magoon, L. R., eds., Petroleum geology of the northern part of the Arctic National Wildlife Refuge, northeastern Alaska: U.S. Geological Survey Bulletin 1778, p. 249–254.

Bruynzeel, J. W., Guldenzopf, E. C., and Pickard, J. E., 1982, Petroleum exploration of NPRA, 1974–1981: Houston, Texas, Tetra-Tech, Inc., prepared for Husky Oil National Petroleum Reserve Operations, Inc., under contract to U.S. Geological Survey, 3 vols., 183 p.

Carey, S. W., 1958, The tectonic approach to continental drift, *in* Carey, S. W., ed., Continental drift; A symposium: Hobart, Tasmania University, p. 177–355.

Carter, C., and Laufield, S., 1975, Ordovician and Silurian fossils in well cores from North Slope of Alaska: American Association of Petroleum Geologists Bulletin, v. 59, p. 457–464.

Cecile, M. P., and Harrison, J. C., 1987, Review of the geology of Wrangel Island, Chukchi and east Siberian Sea, far northeastern Soviet Union: Geological Survey of Canada Open-File Report 1955, 109 p.

Clough, J. G., Blodgett, R. B., Imm, T. A., and Pavia, E. A., 1988, Depositional environments of Katakturuk Dolomite and Nanook Limestone, Arctic National Wildlife Refuge, Alaska [abs.]: American Association of Petroleum Geologists Bulletin, v. 72, p. 172.

Collins, F. R., 1958, Test wells, Topagoruk area, Alaska: U.S. Geological Survey Professional Paper 305-D, p. 265–316.

Collins, F. R., and Robinson, F. M., 1967, Subsurface stratigraphic, structural, and economic geology, northern Alaska: U.S. Geological Survey Open-File Report, 250 p.

Craig, J. D., Sherwood, K. W., and Johnson, P. P., 1985, Geologic report for the Beaufort Sea planning area, Alaska; Regional geology, petroleum geology, environmental geology: Anchorage, Alaska, U.S. Minerals Management Service OCS Report MMS 85-0111, 192 p.

Cramer, C. H., May, S. D., Hanna, W. F., Grantz, A., and Holmes, M. L., 1986, Magnetic anomaly map of the Chukchi Sea and adjacent northwest Alaska: U.S. Geological Survey Miscellaneous Investigations Map I–1182–F, scale 1:1,000,000.

Dehlinger, P., 1980, Gravity and crustal structure in the southern Beaufort Sea (north of Alaska): Final report to the Office of Naval Research on contract N 0014-75-C-0714 with the University of Connecticut, Storrs, September 1980, 31 p.

Dietrich, J. R., and 5 others, 1989, The geology, biostratigraphy, and organic geochemistry of the Natsek E-56 and Edlok N-56 wells, western Beaufort Sea, *in* Current Research, Part G: Geological Survey of Canada Paper 89-1G, p. 133–158.

Ervin, L. D., 1981, The geologic significance of compaction gradient plots of wells in the National Petroleum Reserve; Alaska: Report prepared for Husky Oil NPR Operations, Inc., under contract to U.S. Geological Survey Office of National Petroleum Reserve, Alaska, 21 p.

Fisher, M. A., and Bruns, T. R., 1987, Structure of Pre-Mississippian rocks beneath the Coastal Plain, *in* Bird, K. J., and Magoon, L. B., eds., Petroleum geology of the northern part of the Arctic National Wildlife Refuge, northeastern Alaska: U.S. Geological Survey Bulletin 1778, p. 245–248.

Grantz, A., and May, S. D., 1983, Rifting history and structural development of the continental margin north of Alaska, *in* Watkins, J. S., and Drake, C. L., eds., Studies in continental margin geology: American Association of Petroleum Geologists Memoir 34, p. 77–100.

—— , 1987, Regional geology and petroleum potential of the United States Chukchi Shelf north of Point Hope, *in* Scholl, D. W., Grantz, A., and Vedder, J. G., eds., Geology and resource potential of the continental margin of western North America and adjacent ocean basins; Beaufort Sea to Baja California: Houston, Texas, Circum-Pacific Council for Energy and Mineral Resources, Earth Science Series 6, p. 37–58.

Grantz, A., Hanna, W. F., and Wallace, S. L., 1972a, Chukchi Sea seismic reflection and magnetic profiles, 1971, between northern Alaska and Herald Island: U.S. Geological Survey Open-File Report 72-137, 38 sheets.

Grantz, A., Holmes, M. L., Riley, D. C., and Wallace, S. L., 1972b, Seismic reflection profiles; Part 1, Seismic, magnetic, and gravity profiles; Chukchi Sea and adjacent Arctic Ocean, 1972: U.S. Geological Survey Open-File Report 72-138, 19 sheets.

Grantz, A., Holmes, M. L., and Kososki, B. A., 1975, Geologic framework of the Alaskan continental terrace in the Chukchi and Beaufort Seas, *in* Yorath, C. J., Parker, E. R., and Glass, D. J., eds., Canada's continental margins and offshore petroleum exploration: Canadian Society of Petroleum Geologists Memoir 4, p. 669–700.

Grantz, A., Eittreim, S. L., and Dinter, D. A., 1979, Geology and tectonic development of the continental margin north of Alaska, *in* Keen, C. E., ed., Crustal properties across passive margins: Tectonophysics, v. 59, p. 263–291.

Grantz, A., Eittreim, S. L., and Whitney, O. T., 1981, Geology and physiography of the continental margin north of Alaska and implications for the origin of the Canada Basin, *in* Nairn, A.E.M., Churkin, M., and Stehli, F. G., eds., The ocean basins and margins; Vol. 5, Geology of the Arctic Ocean Basin and its margins: New York, Plenum, p. 439–492.

Grantz, A., Mann, D. M., and May, S. D., 1982, Tracklines of multichannel seismic-reflection data collected by the U.S. Geological Survey in the Beaufort and Chukchi Seas in 1977 for which profiles and stack tapes are available: U.S. Geological Survey Open-File Report 82-735, 1 map sheet with text.

Grantz, A., Dinter, D. A., and Biswas, N. N., 1983a, Map, cross sections, and chart showing late Quaternary faults, folds, and earthquake epicenters on the Alaskan Beaufort Shelf: U.S. Geological Survey Miscellaneous Investigations Series Map I–1182–C, scale 1:500,000.

Grantz, A., Tailleur, I. L., and Carter, C., 1983b, Tectonic significance of Silurian and Ordovician graptolites, Lisburne Hills, northwest Alaska: Geological Society of America Abstracts with Programs, v. 15, p. 274.

Grantz, A., Mann, D. M., and May, S. D., 1986, Multichannel seismic-reflection data collected in 1978 in the eastern Chukchi Sea: U.S. Geological Survey Open-File Report 86-206, 3 p.

Grantz, A., Dinter, D. A., and Culotta, R. C., 1987a, Geology of the continental shelf north of the Arctic National Wildlife Refuge, in Tailleur, I. L., and Weimer, P., eds., Alaskan North Slope geology: Los Angeles, California, Society of Economic Paleontologists and Mineralogists, Pacific Section, and Anchorage, Alaska Geological Society, v. 2, p. 759-762.

Grantz, A., May, S. D., and Dinter, D. A., 1987b, Regional geology and petroleum potential of the United States Beaufort and northeasternmost Chukchi Seas, in Scholl, D. W., Grantz, A., and Vedder, J G., eds., Geology and resource potential of the continental margin of western North America and adjacent ocean basins; Beaufort Sea to Baja California: Houston, Texas, Circum-Pacific Council for Energy and Mineral Resources, Earth Science Series 6, p. 17-35.

Grantz, A., Moore, T. E., and Roeske, S. M., 1990, North American continent-ocean transect A-3; Gulf of Alaska to Arctic Ocean: Geological Society of America Centennial Continent/Ocean Transect: Boulder, Colorado, Geological Society of America, 3 sheets, scale 1:500,000, 49 p. (in press).

Halgedahl, S. L., and Jarrard, R. D., 1987, Paleomagnetism of the Kuparuk River Formation from oriented drill core; Evidence for rotation of the North Slope block, in Tailleur, I. L., and Weimer, P., eds., Alaskan North Slope geology: Los Angeles, California, Society of Economic Paleontologists and Mineralogists, Pacific Section, and Anchorage, Alaska Geological Society, v. 2, p. 581-617.

Haq, B. U., Hardenbol, J., and Vail, P. R., 1987, Chronology of fluctuating sea levels since the Triassic: Science, v. 235, p. 1156-1167.

Hillhouse, J. W., and Grommé, S. C., 1983, Paleomagnetic studies and the hypothetical rotation of Arctic Alaska: Journal of the Alaska Geological Society, v. 2, p. 27-39.

Houtz, R. E., Eittreim, S., and Grantz, A., 1981, Acoustic properties of northern Alaska shelves in relation to the regional geology: Journal of Geophysical Research, v. 86, no. B5, p. 3935-3943.

Hubbard, R. J., Edrich, S. P., and Rattey, R. P., 1987, Geologic evolution and hydrocarbon habitat of the "Arctic Alaska Microplate": Marine and Petroleum Geology, v. 4, no. 1, p. 2-34.

Hunkins, K., 1966, The Arctic continental shelf north of Alaska, in Poole, W. H., ed., Continental margins and island arcs: Geological Survey of Canada Paper 66-15, p. 197-205.

Jamison, H. C., Brockett, L. B., and McIntosh, R. A., 1980, Prudhoe Bay; A 10-year perspective, in Halbouty, M. T., ed., Giant oil and gas fields of the decade 1968-1978: American Association of Petroleum Geologists Memoir 30, p. 289-314.

Jessup, D. D., 1985, Reconnaissance geology of the Chukchi platform; West-central Chukchi shelf, offshore Alaska [M.S. thesis]: East Lansing, Michigan State University, 105 p.

Kirschner, C. E., and Rycerski, B. A., 1988, Petroleum potential of representative stratigraphic and structural elements in the National Petroleum Reserve in Alaska, in Gryc, G., ed., Geology and exploration of the National Petroleum Reserve in Alaska, 1974 to 1982: U.S. Geological Survey Professional Paper 1399, p. 191-208.

Lane, L. S., and Cecile, M. P., 1989, Stratigraphy and structure of the Neruokpuk Formation, northern Yukon, in Current Research, Part G: Geological Survey of Canada Paper 89-19, p. 57-62.

Lerand, M., 1973, Beaufort Sea, in McCrossan, R. G., ed., The future petroleum provinces of Canada; Their geology and potential: Canadian Society of Petroleum Geologists Memoir 1, p. 315-386.

May, S. D., 1985, Free-air gravity anomaly map of the Chukchi and Alaskan Beaufort Seas, Arctic Ocean: U.S. Geological Survey Miscellaneous Investigations Series Map I-1182-E, scale 1:1,000,000.

May, S. D., and Grantz, A., 1990, Sediment thickness in the southern Canada Basin: Marine Geology (in press).

Mayfield, C. F., Tailleur, I. L., and Ellersieck, I., 1988, Stratigraphy, structure, and palinspastic synthesis of the western Brooks Range, northwestern Alaska: U.S. Geological Survey Professional Paper 1399, p. 143-186.

Mickey, M. B., and Haga, H., 1987, Jurassic-Neocomian biostratigraphy, North Slope, Alaska, in Tailleur, I. L., and Weimer, P., eds., Alaskan North Slope geology: Los Angeles, California, Society of Economic Paleontologists and Mineralogists, Pacific Section, and Anchorage, Alaska Geological Society, v. 1, p. 397-404.

Milne, A. R., 1966, A seismic refraction measurement in the Beaufort Sea: Seismological Society of America Bulletin, v. 56, no. 3, p. 775-779.

Molenaar, C. M., 1988, Depositional history and seismic stratigraphy of Lower Cretaceous rocks in the National Petroleum Reserve in Alaska and adjacent areas, in Gryc, G., ed., Geology and exploration of the National Petroleum Reserve in Alaska, 1974 to 1982: U.S. Geological Survey Professional Paper 1399, p. 593-622.

Molenaar, C. M., Bird, K. J., and Collett, T. S., 1986, Regional correlation sections across the North Slope of Alaska: U.S. Geological Survey Miscellaneous Field Studies Map MF-1907, 1 sheet.

Molenaar, C. M., Bird, K. J., and Kirk, A. R., 1987 Cretaceous and Tertiary stratigraphy of northeastern Alaska, in Tailleur, I. L., and Weimer, P., eds., Alaskan North Slope geology: Los Angeles, California, Society of Economic Paleontologists and Mineralogists, Pacific Section, and Anchorage, Alaska Geological Society, v. 1, p. 513-528.

Moore, T. E., and Mull, C. G., 1989, Geology of the Brooks Range and North Slope, in Nokleberg, W. J., and Fisher, M. A., eds., Alaskan geological and geophysical transect, Valdez to Coldfoot, June 24-July 5, 1989, 28th International Geological Congress Field Trip Guidebook T104, Washington: American Geophysical Union, p. 107-131.

Moore, T. E., and 5 others, 1990, Geology of northern Alaska, in Plafker, G., Jones, D. L., and Berg, H. C., eds., The Cordilleran Orogen; Alaska: Boulder, Colorado, Geological Society of America, The Geology of North America, v. G-1 (in press).

Newman, G. W., Mull, G. G., and Watkins, N. D., 1979, Northern Alaska paleomagnetism, plate rotation, and tectonics, in Sisson, A., ed., Relationship of plate tectonics to Alaskan geology and resources; Proceedings, Alaska Geological Society Symposium, Anchorage, Alaska, April, 1977: Alaska Geological Society, p. C-1 to C-7.

Norris, D. K., 1984, Geology of the Northern Yukon and Northwestern District of Mackenzie: Geological Survey of Canada Map 1581A, scale 1:500,000.

Pessel, G. H., Levorsen, J. A., and Tailleur, I. L., 1978, Generalized isopach map of Jurassic and possibly Lower Cretaceous shale, including Kingak Shale, eastern North Slope petroleum province, Alaska: U.S. Geological Survey Miscellaneous Field Studies Map MF-928K, 1 sheet, scale 1:500,000.

Poulton, T. P., 1978, Pre-Late Oxfordian Jurassic biostratigraphy of northern Yukon and adjacent Northwest Territories, in Stelck, C. R., and Chatterton, B.D.E., eds., Western and Arctic Canadian biostratigraphy: Geological Association of Canada Special Paper 18, p. 445-472.

Rattey, R. P., 1985, Northeastern Brooks Range, Alaska; New evidence for complex thin-skinned thrusting: American Association of Petroleum Geologists Bulletin, v. 69, p. 676-677.

Reiser, H. N., Brosgé, W. P., Dutro, J. T., Jr., and Detterman, R. L., 1980, Geologic map of the Demarcation Point Quadrangle, Alaska: U.S. Geological Survey Miscellaneous Investigations Series Map I-1133, scale 1:250,000.

Rickwood, F. K., 1970, The Prudhoe Bay field, in Adkison, W. L., and Brosgé, M. M., eds., Proceedings of the geological seminar on the North Slope of Alaska: Los Angeles, California, American Association of Petroleum Geologists, Pacific Section, p. L1-L11.

Robinson, M. S., and 6 others, 1989, Geology of the Sadlerochit and Shublik Mountains, Arctic National Wildlife Refuge, northeastern Alaska: Alaska Department of Natural Resources, Division of Geological and Geophysical Surveys Professional Report 100, 1 map sheet, scale 1:63,360.

Tailleur, I. L., 1969a, Speculations on North Slope geology: Oil and Gas Journal, v. 67, no. 38, p. 215–220, 225–226.
——, 1969b, Rifting speculation on the geology of Alaska's North Slope: Oil and Gas Journal, v. 67, no. 39, p. 128–130.
——, 1973, Probable rift origin of the Canada Basin, *in* Pitcher, M. G., ed., Arctic geology: American Association of Petroleum Geologists Memoir 19, p. 526–535.
Tailleur, I. L., Enwicht, S. E., Pessel, G. H., and Leverson, J. A., 1978, Maps showing land status and well locations and tables of well data, eastern North Slope petroleum province, Alaska: U.S. Geological Survey Miscellaneous Field Investigations Map MF-928-A, 5 sheets, scale 1:500,000.
Taylor, P. T., Kovacs, L. C., Vogt, P. R., and Johnson, G. L., 1981, Detailed aeromagnetic investigation of the Arctic Basin, 2: Journal of Geophysical Research, v. 86, p. 6323–6333.
Thurston, D. K., and Theiss, L. A., 1987, Geologic report for the Chukchi Sea planning area, Alaska; Regional geology, petroleum geology, and environmental geology: Anchorage, Alaska, U.S. Minerals Management Service OCS Report MMS 87-0046, 193 p.

Trettin, H. P., coordinator, 1972, The Innuitian Province, *in* Price, R. A., and Douglas, R.J.W., eds., Variations in tectonic styles in Canada: Canada Geological Association Special Paper 11, p. 83–180.
Trettin, H. P., and Balkwill, H. R., 1979, Contributions to the tectonic history of the Innuitian Province, Arctic Canada: Canadian Journal of Earth Sciences, v. 16, no. 3, p. 748–769.
Vogt, P. R., Taylor, P. T., Kovacs, L. C., and Johnson, G. L., 1982, The Canada Basin; Aeromagnetic constraints on structure and evolution: Tectonophysics, v. 89, p. 295–336.
Witmer, R. J., Haga, H., and Mickey, M. B., 1981, Biostratigraphic report of thirty-three wells drilled from 1975 to 1981 in National Petroleum Reserve in Alaska: U.S.. Geological Survey Open-File Report 81-1166, 47 p.
Wold, R. J., Woodzick, T. L., and Ostenso, N. A., 1970, Structure of the Beaufort Sea Continental Margin: Geophysics, v. 35, p. 849–861.

MANUSCRIPT ACCEPTED BY THE SOCIETY JANUARY 19, 1990

"The ice was here, the ice was there, the ice was all around." Woodcut by Gustav Doré, from *Rime of the Ancient Mariner,* by Samuel Taylor Coleridge.

Chapter 17

The Arctic continental margin of eastern Siberia

Kazuya Fujita and David B. Cook
Department of Geological Sciences, Michigan State University, East Lansing, Michigan 48824-1115

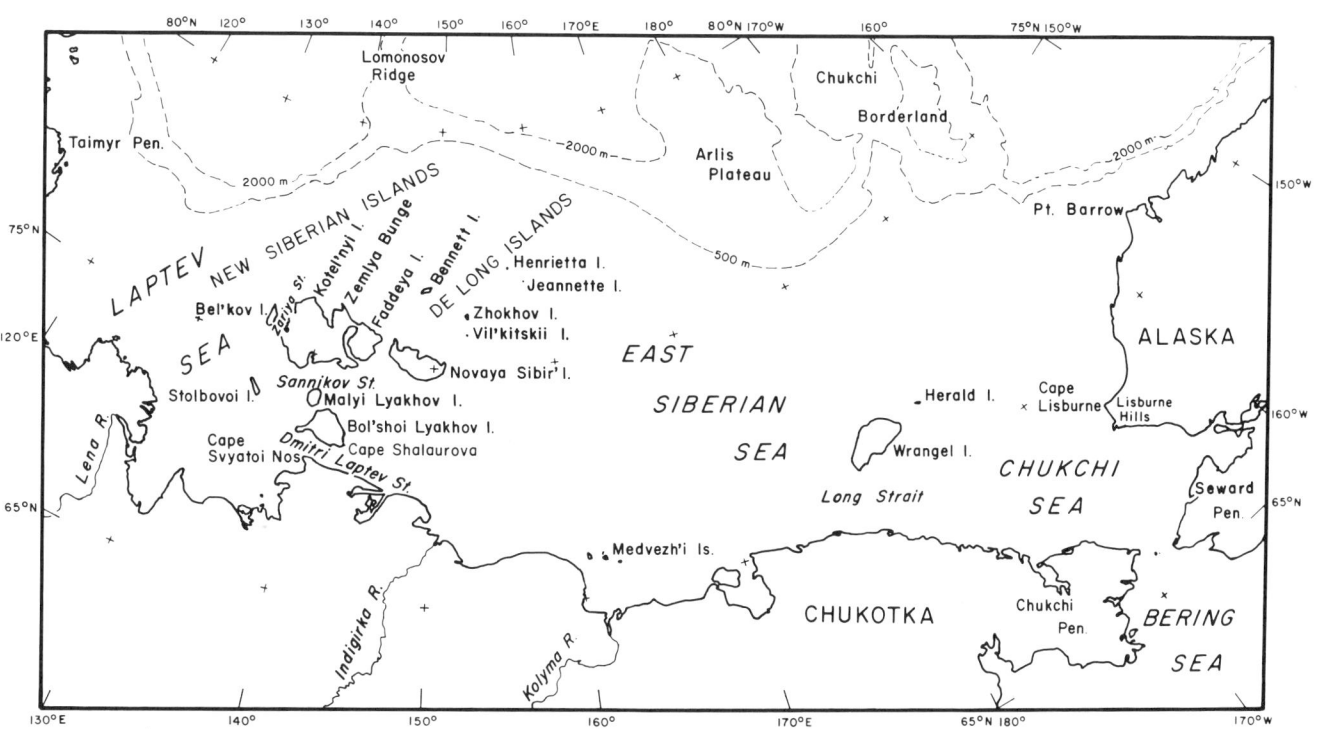

Figure 1. Index map of the East Siberian Shelf and adjacent regions. Bathymetric contours are shown at 2000 and 500 m.

INTRODUCTION

The Arctic Ocean margin of the North American plate in Asia forms a continental shelf up to 800 km wide, which underlies the East Siberia Sea (Fig. 1). The New Siberian Islands separate the East Siberian Sea from the Laptev Sea on the west, and Wrangel Island (Ostrov Vrangelya) separates the East Siberian Sea from the Chukchi Sea on the east. The area of the East Siberian Sea is about 1,500,000 km^2, and it is connected to the Chukchi Sea by Long Strait (Proliv Longa) and to the Laptev Sea by several straits through the New Siberian Islands.

The shelf of the East Siberian Sea is shallow, less than 50 m deep, and flat. The shelf is cut by two valleys, a few tens of meters deeper than the surrounding shelf, which are extensions of the Indigirka and Kolyma rivers (Naugler and others, 1974). The continental slope of the East Siberian Sea is gentle (slope ~1°), and alluvial cones spread out into the adjacent abyssal plain from submarine canyons (Lastochkin, 1980). The shelf appears to be connected to the Arlis Plateau, but is separated from the Lomonosov Ridge by a sediment-filled trough (Dementiskaya and Hunkins, 1971) (Fig. 2).

Since the geology of the East Siberian Shelf is poorly known, most tectonic and geologic models are extrapolations of the geology of the New Siberian Islands, Wrangel Island, and northern Eurasia. Rather than present the details of these speculations, in this chapter we summarize the known geology of the islands and the geophysical data from the region. A brief summary of the principal tectonic models is presented at the conclusion.

Summaries of the geology and models for the tectonic evolu-

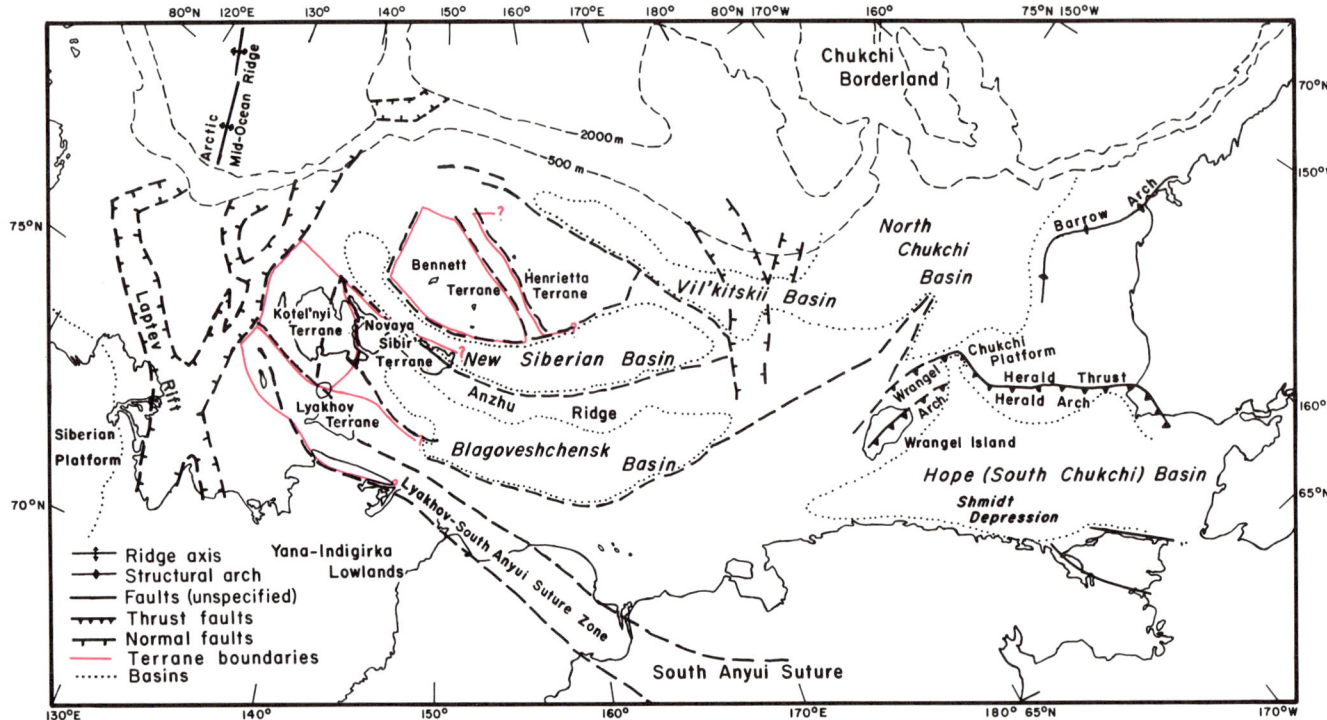

Figure 2. Structural map of the subsurface of the East Siberian Shelf showing faults, terrane boundaries (in red), and basins. Faults are dashed where inferred or uncertain. Bathymetric contours shown at 2000 and 500 m.

tion of the adjacent Eurasian continent, in a plate tectonic context, are given in Fujita (1978), Fujita and Newberry (1982, 1983) and Savostin and others (1984). Similar studies in a less mobilistic context are presented by Parfenov and others (1978), Shilo and Til'man (1981), Kosygin and Parfenov (1981), and Natal'in and Parfenov (1983). Information on the unconsolidated sediments of the East Siberian Shelf, obtained by the USCGC *Northwind* and USCGC *Burton Island,* is presented by Naugler and others (1974).

GEOLOGY OF THE NEW SIBERIAN ISLANDS

The New Siberian Islands comprise three groups of islands (Fig. 1 and Plate 1). The Lyakhov Islands were discovered in 1711 and consist of Bol'shoi (Greater) Lyakhov Island (5,230 km^2), Malyi (Lesser) Lyakhov Island (1,320 km^2), and Stolbovoi Island (320 km^2). The Lyakhov Islands are separated from the mainland of Eurasia by Dmitri Laptev Strait, and from the Anzhu Islands by Sannikov Strait.

The Anzhu (Anjou) Islands, north of the Lyakhov Islands, comprise three islands. They are Bel'kov Island (530 km^2) on the west, Novaya Sibir' (New Siberia) Island (6,500 km^2) on the east, and a large island in the middle, which is divided into three parts: Kotel'nyi Island (10,920 km^2), Zemlya Bunge (6,920 km^2), and Faddeya Island (Ostrov Faddeevskii; 5,000 km^2). Northeast of the Anzhu Islands are the De Long Islands, discovered in 1881. The De Long Islands are small and are named Bennett Island (160 km^2), Zhokhov Island (120 km^3), Henrietta Island (Ostrov Genrietti; 13.5 km^2), Jeannette Island (Ostrov Zhannetti; 4 km^2), and Vil'kitskii Island (1 km^2). The total area of the New Siberian Islands is about 37,000 km^2 (Vol'nov and others, 1970a).

The earliest geologic explorations of the islands were by M. M. Hedenstrom, Y. Sannikov, F. F. Wrangell, and P. F. Anjou in the early 1800s. Detailed geologic information became available through the studies of E. V. Toll', who visited the region between 1885 and 1902, and through the Russian Hydrographic Expedition of B. A. Vil'kitskii in 1913–1914, which visited the De Long Islands (Starokadomskiy, 1976). Detailed mapping and studies have been conducted by the Academy of Sciences since 1945 and by the Scientific Investigations Institute on the Geology of the Arctic (NIIGA) since 1955 (Vakar, 1970). Geophysical data have been collected throughout the region since the 1950s.

Geologically, the New Siberian Islands can be divided into five terranes. The extent of each terrane is unknown; however, tentative boundaries based in part on Soviet tectonic maps are shown in Figure 2. Most of the geologic information summarized below is from Vol'nov and others (1970a) and Vol'nov (1975) and only additional references are cited. Stratigraphic columns

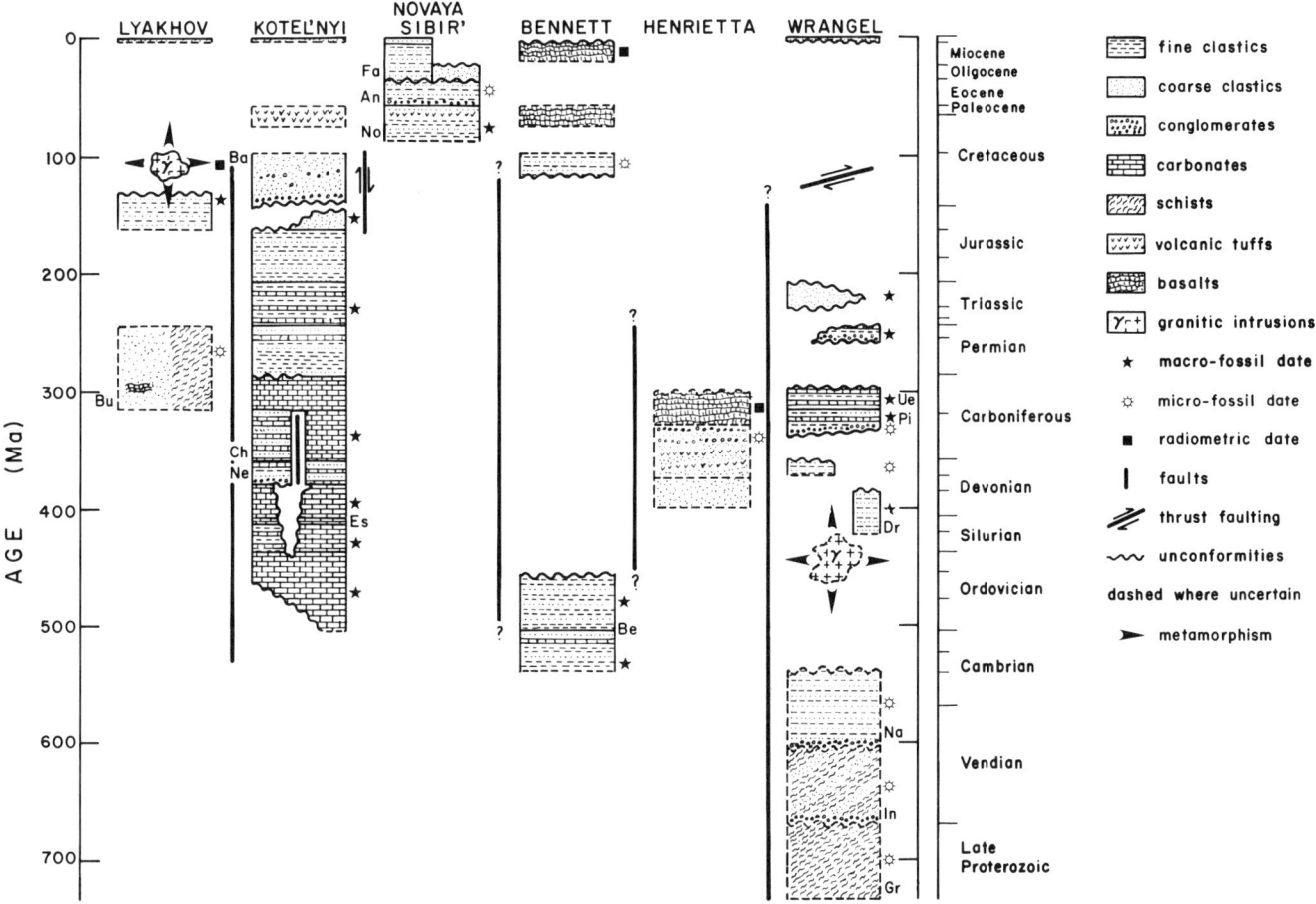

Figure 3. Geologic columns for the terranes of the New Siberian Islands and Wrangel Island. Lithologic key is given at right. Two letter codes refer to formation names: An, Anzhu series; Ba, Balyktakh suite; Be, Bennett complex; Bu, Burustas suite; Ch, Chekurian suite; Dr, Dremkhedian suite; Es, Eselekhian suite; Fa, Faddeya complex; Gr, Gromovian suite; In, Inkalinian suite; Na, Naskhokian series; Ne, Nerpalakhian suite; No, Novosibirsk complex; Pi, Pillar suite; Ue, Uering suite.

are summarized in Figure 3 and a geologic map is presented in Figure 4.

Lyakhov Terrane

The Lyakhov terrane comprises Bol'shoi Lyakhov Island, Stolbovoi Island, and, probably, part of Malyi Lyakhov Island. It is characterized by a metamorphic complex overlain by Mesozoic terrigenous sediments and intruded by granites. Gravity and magnetic data suggest the extension of this terrane to the southeast and northwest.

The most highly metamorphosed rocks are found in small exposures on the southeastern part of Bol'shoi Lyakhov Island. They consist of crystalline schists with a gneissoid appearance and have pyroxene-plagioclase-amphibole, amphibole, epidote-amphibole, plagioclase-amphibole, and plagioclase-epidote compositions. The schists have a total thickness of about 2,000 m and have a northwesterly striking schistosity. While no contacts with over- or underlying rocks are exposed, the schists are intruded by Early Cretaceous granodiorites with contact metamorphism along their margins.

Initially, M. M. Ermolaev considered some of these schists to be Paleozoic carbonaceous formations that had been metamorphosed by the intrusions, but the discovery of the metamorphic aureoles led Voitsekhovskii and Mikhalyuko to postulate that the schists were the product of deep regional metamorphism. On the basis of metamorphic grade and similarities to formations elsewhere in northeast Siberia, they considered them Early Proterozoic in age. Some still accept this dating due to the purported discovery of Proterozoic acritarchs in the schist by L. I. Il'chenko. These schists are only found adjacent to large granitic intrusions on Bol'shoi Lyakhov Island (Gnibidenko, 1969; Vol'nov and others, 1970b), and thus it is suggested that the schists were formed as a result of the metamorphism of Paleozoic or Mesozoic

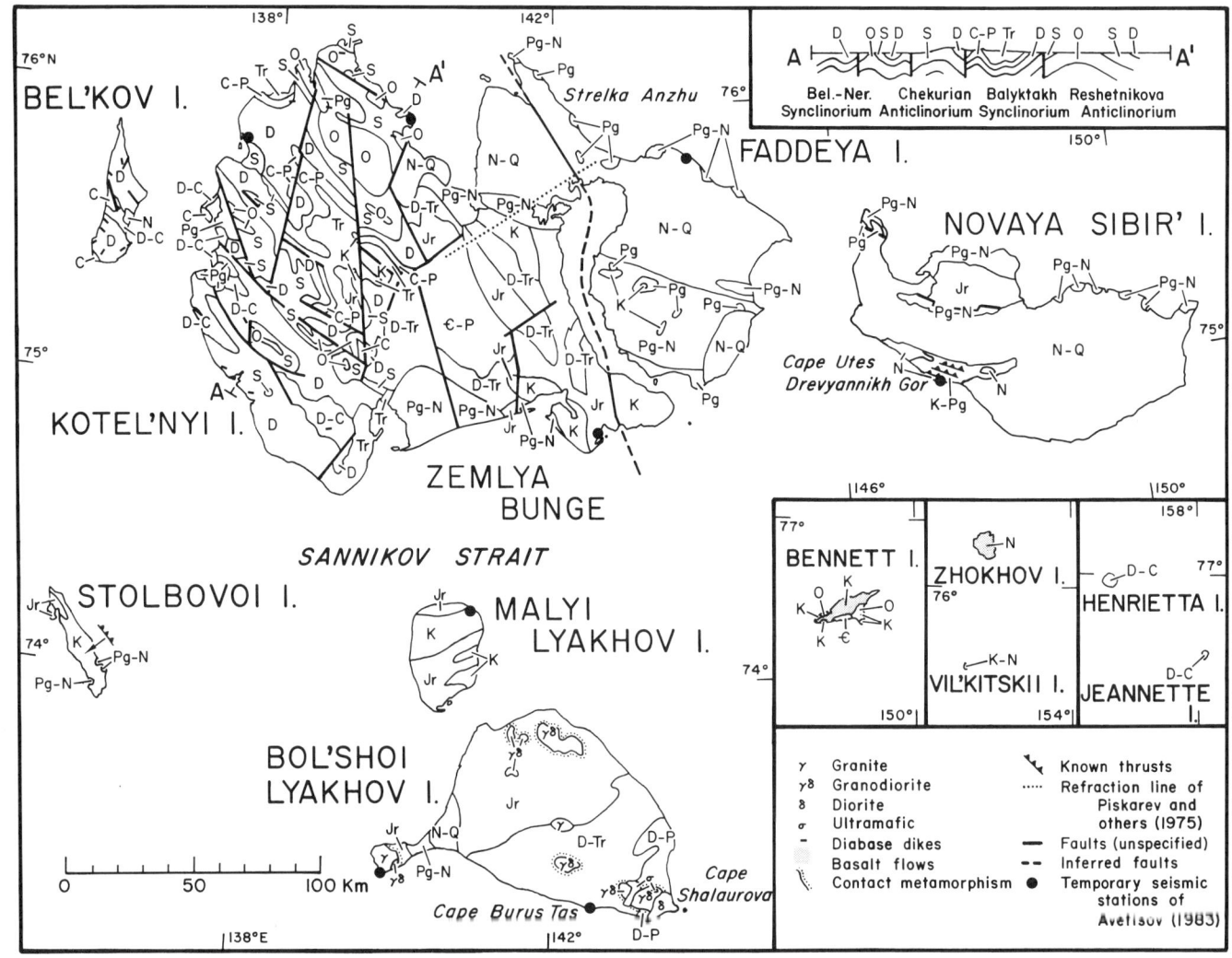

Figure 4. Bedrock geology map of the New Siberian Islands after Vol'nov and others (1970b) and Nalivkin (1983). Inset at upper right shows a cross section across Kotel'nyi Island and the De Long Islands are shown in the inset at the lower right. Letters are unit ages given using standard abbreviations for geologic systems except for Pt, Proterozoic eon, and Pg, Paleogene subsystem. Lithologies of these units can be inferred from Figure 3.

host rocks by the Cretaceous intrusions (Gnibidenko, 1969). Vinogradov and others (1977) consider the schists to be Proterozoic, but note that they are similar to remnants of oceanic crust found in the Urals and Appalachians.

The Burustas suite (Bu; see Fig. 3), composed of alternating units of feldspathic-quartzose schistose sandstone and phyllitic sericite-quartz schist, is thought to be stratigraphically younger than the crystalline schist. Minor units of carbonaceous schist are also present. In the western part of the island, these rocks are encountered in complex folds with a west–northwest strike and axial planes dipping to the southwest at angles of 20°–30°, which is similar to the orientation of structures observed on Cape Svyatoi Nos. The strike changes to northeast in the eastern part of the island (Genin and others, 1977). The total thickness of the Burustas suite is about 1,200 m (Vinogradov and others, 1974a).

A Mesozoic age for these metasediments was proposed by Vollosovich and Ermolaev; however, Voitsekhovskii and Mikhalyuko considered them late Paleozoic. In the 1950s, microfossils identified by Timofeyev as Proterozoic in age were reported in these rocks. Gnibidenko (1969) questions this dating since such microfossils have been reported from macrofaunally dated Mesozoic rocks elsewhere. In the late 1960s and early 1970s, miospores similar to those of the Siberian platform were found in the Burustas suite, and were identified as Permian, and possibly Carboniferous, in age (Vinogradov and others, 1974a). Vinogradov and others (1974a) also note the presence of coal in the carbonaceous sections of the metasediments and the imprint of a macrofossil. These findings support the dating of the Burustas suite as late Paleozoic (Pushcharovskiy, 1976). The Burustas suite was metamorphosed in the Mesozoic by the intrusion of granites.

Near Cape Burus Tas there is a 50-m-thick layer of spilite. The pillows become smaller toward the top of the flow, and major element chemistry indicates that the flow is a tholeiitic basalt with oceanic affinities. Also associated with the metamorphic rocks of Bol'shoi Lyakhov Island are peridotite and pyroxenite found as fragments in talus, as intrusions penetrating the crystalline schist, and in drill cores off Cape Shalaurova (Nalivkin, 1983; L. Z. Lipkov, personal communication, 1986). Based on gravity data, Genin and others (1977) suggest that the basement of Bol'shoi Lyakhov Island is composed of mafic rocks.

On Stolbovoi Island, Late Jurassic to Lower Cretaceous terrigenous, rhythmic, flyschoid strata are known. The Jurassic part of the section is about 1,200 m thick, while the Cretaceous (Valanginian) section, dated by pelecypod fossils, is 600 m thick. The sections form part of a large northwest-striking synclinal structure with northwesterly striking thrusts and other faults with offsets in the tens of meters. These strata are also intruded by small quartz dolerite dikes (Ivanov and others, 1974, 1977). Ivanov and others (1977) report paleomagnetic data from the Jurassic deposits that show the Jurassic mixed-polarity superchron and yield a paleomagnetic pole position for the Late Jurassic and Early Cretaceous of 30°N, 170°W. This position is discordant to pole positions determined for neighboring areas.

On Malyi Lyakhov Island is a similar, probably Late Jurassic to Early Cretaceous, sand-clay formation with a thickness of 200 m. The formation is folded into a syncline with a northeasterly strike (Nalivkin, 1983). Drill hole data suggest that the deeper structure of Malyi Lyakhov Island is similar to Zemlya Bunge (Genin and others, 1977); thus part of Malyi Lyakhov Island may be part of the Kotel'nyi terrane.

On northern and western Bol'shoi Lyakhov Island, a possibly Jurassic sequence, similar in lithology to the rocks on Stolbovoi Island, has a thickness of 800 m. This sequence on Bol'shoi Lyakhov Island is nearly isoclinally folded, and has been contact metamorphosed. Thrusts have been reported from the westernmost part of the island (Byalobzheskii and Ivanov, 1971).

The pre-Cretaceous deposits on Bol'shoi Lyakhov Island have been intruded by granodiorites, granites, and diorite porphyries of two phases, closely spaced in time (L. Z. Lipkov, personal communication, 1986). A biotite granite has been radiometrically dated as 112 Ma (Aptian–Albian).

Based on the available data, we interpret the stratigraphic section of the Lyakhov terrane to be post-middle Paleozoic in age. The section can be interpreted as terrigenous flyschoid formations that incorporate some fragments of oceanic crust (Genin and others, 1977). The formations have been metamorphosed more than once, the last time during the intrusion of the granites. The age of one phase of folding is post-Valanginian, and post-deformational granites are dated as Aptian–Albian. These dates correspond with the Valanginian–Hauterivian collisional episode known in the South Anyui suture zone of Chukotka (Seslavinskiy, 1970, 1979), and, based on magnetic anomalies that connect the two regions (Ivanov and Belyayev, 1973; Vinogradov and others, 1974b), the deformation is suggested to be due to the same collisional event (Genin and others, 1977; Savostin and others, 1984).

Kotel'nyi Terrane

The Kotel'nyi terrane comprises Kotel'nyi Island, Bel'kov Island, and underlies most of Zemlya Bunge and Malyi Lyakhov Island. It is characterized by an extensive Paleozoic carbonate and terrigenous section. There are similarities between the stratigraphic section of Kotel'nyi Island and the section of Taimyr Peninsula (K. Burke, personal communication, 1985).

The oldest exposed formations are Ordovician carbonates with a total thickness of 1,500 m. The presence of older rocks, including Cambrian carbonates and terrigenous rocks, is surmised from subsurface thickness estimates based on converted wave data from earthquakes (Avetisov, 1983). The Ordovician formations are rich in macrofauna similar to those found on the Siberian platform and on Taimyr Peninsula (Zhizhina, 1959).

Conformably overlying the Ordovician are Lower to Middle Silurian formations, which are divided into two facies zones. The southwest (deep-water) facies zone is composed of carbonates with fine clastics and contains abundant remains of graptolites and pelecypods. The northwest (shallow, lagoonal) zone is represented by limestones and dolomites with brachiopod and coral remains. The transition between the two zones is gradual (Kos'ko and others, 1975; Kos'ko, 1977). In both regions the Upper Silurian is composed of dolomite (Eselekhian suite, Es). The total thickness of the Silurian is 1,500 m, decreasing to the southwest (Zhizhina, 1959). Early and Middle Devonian formations, 1,600 m thick, conformably overlie the Silurian and are a continuation of the platform carbonates with abundant faunal remains.

The late-Middle and Upper Devonian form two distinctly different facies. In the southwestern part of Kotel'nyi Island and on Bel'kov Island, a thick section of clayey carbonate and interbedded sandstone, limestone, and conglomerate (Nerpalakhian, Ne, and Chekurian, Ch, suites) lies unconformably (Kos'ko and Nepomiluev, 1975) on the Ordovician through Middle Devonian. These formations have a maximum thickness of about 8 km and fill the Bel'kov-Nerpalakh depression; the thickness varies greatly, decreasing to the east and west. Based on faunal remains, deeper water existed to the west, with near-shore conditions prevalent to the east (Kos'ko and Nepomiluev, 1975). The Lower Carboniferous is 1,600 m thick and has a similar lithology except with a greater proportion of carbonates and abundant brachiopod remains.

In contrast, the Upper Devonian in the central and northeastern Kotel'nyi Island lies conformably on older rocks and is composed of red-colored sandstone and carbonate only 300 m thick. The overlying Lower Carboniferous is composed of limestone with brachiopod remains and is up to 400 m thick. Subsidence in the western part of the island diminished by Late Carboniferous time, resulting in the formation of carbonates and terrigenous deposits only 125 m thick. Limestone deposits, 15 m thick, are found in the central part of the island.

The transition from the thick deposits of the Bel'kov–Nerpalakh depression to the platformal deposits of east-central Kotel'nyi Island is abrupt and may be along a fault zone (Vol'nov, 1975). The Late Devonian and older deposits of the Bel'kov–Nerpalakh depression are intruded by thin (tens of meters) dikes and sills of diabase and gabbro-diabase.

The Permian, exposed in northern and central Kotel'nyi Island, is composed of mudstone, siltstone, and sandstone with a thickness of 200 m. In the central part of the island, the Permian lies unconformably on Carboniferous strata, is thinner, and contains proportionally more carbonate. The Permian is overlain unconformably by Triassic mudrock and limestone, which increase in thickness to the north and northeast from 300 to 1,200 m. The Permian and Triassic contain an abundant fauna and are intruded in northwestern Kotel'nyi Island by thin (2-m) diabase dikes.

Jurassic formations are exposed on Kotel'nyi Island and consist of mudstone, siltstone, and sandstone, which thicken to the east up to 300 m. The Upper Jurassic is found only in eastern Kotel'nyi Island and includes a glauconitic sandstone with remains of microfauna and ammonites.

Zemlya Bunge is believed to be composed of similar formations under 400–900 m of Neogene to Quaternary sedimentary cover. Based on seismic refraction and electric resistivity studies, Piskarev and others (1975) and Genin and others (1977) suggest that there is a 2–2.5-km-thick Triassic(?) clastic layer underlying much of northern Zemlya Bunge. Nalivkin (1983) considers bedrock to be much more heterogeneous (Fig. 4).

All of the above-described Paleozoic and Mesozoic deposits are folded in complex anticlines and synclines that strike northwest–southeast and have decreasing amounts of deformation to the northeast. The Chekurian anticlinorium (Fig. 4, inset) is located in southwestern Kotel'nyi and Bel'kov Islands and deforms Ordovician through Carboniferous deposits. The limbs of the folds have dip angles rarely exceeding 60°, and faults of considerable offset are known. The Balyktakh synclinorium forms the central part of Kotel'nyi Island and deforms Devonian to Triassic formations. The dip angles of the fold limbs here are about 30°, except in the southeast where dips of 60° are common. The Reshetnikova anticlinorium is located in northern Kotel'nyi Island. The fold axes appear fan-shaped in map view and the majority of the folds are symmetric and have dip angles on their limbs of 50° or less. The strikes of the fold axes and the decreasing deformation to the north suggest that this deformation is related to the closing of the Lyakhov–South Anyui suture.

On Kotel'nyi Island, 300 m of Lower Cretaceous coal-bearing deposits (Balyktakh suite, Ba) lie transgressively on the Upper Triassic and Lower Jurassic. These are composed of poorly compacted sandstone, conglomerate, siltstone, clay, and mafic and felsic extrusives. The deposits dip to the east at angles of 5° to 15°. The felsic extrusives, also found in Zemlya Bunge, are composed of rhyolites and their tuffs and may be as young as Oligocene. Unconsolidated deposits, ^{14}C dated around 30,000 years, overlie the Mesozoic and are composed of peat and gravel containing spores and pollen (Lozhkin, 1977). Based on the distribution of permafrost, Genin and others (1977) suggest that Zemlya Bunge has only recently been uplifted above sea level.

Kotel'nyi Island and Zemlya Bunge are cut by faults of two orientations. One set, with a west–northwest strike, is parallel to the fold axes of the major structures of the region and is thus associated with pre-Cenozoic deformations. The second set has a north–south strike and is believed to be younger and related to the present-day tectonics of the East Siberian Shelf (Kos'ko and Nepomiluev, 1975). Normal faults have a displacement of 500–700 m, and strike-slip faults have displacements up to 2 km (Mokshantsev and others, 1964). Bel'kov Island is cut by high angle faults with brecciated zones 30 m thick (Vinogradov, 1984). Geophysical data suggest that a zone of intrusions, possibly including ultramafics, may lie along the eastern boundary of Zemlya Bunge (Genin and others, 1977).

The stratigraphic section appears to represent a platformal regime during the early Paleozoic with the formation in the Late Devonian of a deep basin, accompanied by intrusions, in the southwest. The region was uplifted thereafter and was the site of clastic deposition through the Mesozoic. The region was folded in Early Cretaceous time, probably due to a collision along the Lyakhov–South Anyui suture, although Kos'ko and Nepomiluev (1975) suggest that the deformation may have initiated as early as the Carboniferous. In the Cenozoic, the region was uplifted, and extrusives were deposited similar to those found on Faddeya Island.

Novaya Sibir' Terrane

The Novaya Sibir' terrane comprises the islands of Novaya Sibir' and Faddeya, and probably underlies an extensive part of the East Siberian Sea to the south and east of the Anzhu Islands. The terrane is characterized by extensive Paleogene coal-bearing terrigenous formations. The Novaya Sibir' terrane is separated from the Kotel'nyi terrane by a fault zone located in eastern Zemlya Bunge.

The oldest exposed rocks form the Novosibirsk complex (No) of Senonian (Late Cretaceous) to Eocene age. On Novaya Sibir' Island, the complex is composed of sandstone, tuffaceous sandstone, mudrock, clay, and brown coal. The Cretaceous part of the section has a thickness of 300 m and contains plant remains. The Paleocene and Eocene have a thickness of 600–1,300 m and are also found on Faddeya Island (Klubov and others, 1976; Vinogradov and others, 1977). The Novosibirsk complex is extensively deformed into folds with axial planes striking west–northwest and dipping south. Overturned folds are common, and thrusts with dip angles of 40° to 70° are found throughout the exposures at Cape Utes Drevyannikh Gor. Towards the east, the strike of the rocks changes to east–west. On the northern coast of

Novaya Sibir' Island, the deformation is less, and dip angles do not exceed 60°. On Faddeya Island, similar formations are exposed on Strelka Anzhu (Anjou Spit) and have dip angles of only 20° to 40° (Kos'ko, 1984). Felsic tuffs are exposed in small isolated outcrops on Strelka Anzhu. These have been provisionally dated as either Early Cretaceous or Late Cretaceous to Paleogene.

The weakly deformed Anzhu series (An), of Eocene age, overlies, or is the uppermost unit of, the Novosibirsk complex. The series is composed of clay and sand with lenses of brown coal, gravel, and pebbles, and contains abundant spores and pollen similar to those found in the Yana-Indigirka lowland of mainland Eurasia. The series is about 70 m thick on Strelka Anzhu. On Novaya Sibir' Island the series is overlain transgressively by 50 m of Oligocene sand containing poorly sorted material, probably fragments of locally derived rocks (Trufanov and Bakulenko, 1978).

On Faddeya Island, the Oligocene and Miocene are represented by the Faddeya complex (Fa), which consists of clay, sand, and coal-bearing terrigenous rocks, which in turn is overlain by Pleistocene sand and clay. The combined thickness on the island is about 100–200 m, but is assumed to reach 1,000 m in off-shore troughs (Vinogradov and others, 1977). A few hundred meters of Quaternary sand covers the entire terrane.

The Novaya Sibir' terrane seems to represent a region of early Paleogene subsidence, which underwent deformation in Late Oligocene time particularly along the southern coasts of the Anzhu Islands. The tuffs found on the islands may be a result of volcanism in the nearby De Long Islands.

Bennett Terrane

The Bennett terrane consists of Bennett Island and may also include Zhokhov and Vil'kitskii islands and the adjoining continental shelf. The terrane is characterized by weakly deformed lower Paleozoic clastic deposits and Cretaceous to Cenozoic basalts. The extent of the terrane in the oceanic regions is estimated by the characteristic magnetic anomalies associated with the volcanics.

The oldest exposed formations are combined into the Bennett complex (Be; Vinogradov and others, 1977). The complex begins with argillaceous strata with traces of carbonate, which contain Middle Cambrian trilobite remains. The thickness of the exposed Cambrian is about 500 m. The Cambrian is unconformably overlain by Lower to Middle, and perhaps Upper, Ordovician mudstone, siltstone, and sandstone, which contain graptolites. The Lower Ordovician has a thickness of 870 m, while the Middle and Upper Ordovician total 200 m. The Cambrian and Ordovician deposits are folded into gentle, north-northwesterly striking anticlines with dips of the limbs seldom exceeding 10°.

On the eroded surface of the Ordovician is a thin (20 m) layer of poorly cemented sandstone, mudrock, and coal similar to the Balyktakh suite of Kotel'nyi Island. Spores and pollen remains from this layer are thought to date from the upper half of the Early Cretaceous.

Overlying these clastics are two units composed primarily of horizontally layered alkali-rich basalt flows. The lower unit, 60 m thick, consists of a series of thin (less than 15 m) flows of altered basalt and basalt porphyry with lenses and thin (2 m) layers of tuff and tuff-derived mudrock. From this mudrock a spore-pollen complex similar in composition to that in the underlying clastics has been found. The upper unit is 300 m thick, less altered, and consists of five sheets of olivine basalt varying in thickness from 40 to 100 m. The age of the basalts is thought to be Cenozoic, although they may be as old as late Early Cretaceous.

On February 17, 1983, a high-altitude plume was observed off the eastern coast of Bennett Island (Kienle and others, 1983), the largest of more than 150 plumes recorded in the area since 1974. The plumes are cold, as low as –45°C, and are suggested to be the result of methane release during permafrost breakups (Clarke and others, 1986). A Soviet expedition to the island is reported to have found a 15-m-high cone offshore, which is the presumed source of the 1983 plume (Shabad, 1984).

Zhokhov and Vil'kitskii islands are also composed of extrusive basalt flows. The basalts of Zhokhov Island are much fresher than those on Bennett Island and are alkalic tholeiites. Overlying the basalts is a layer of friable volcanic tuff and volcanic ash capped by a massive basalt flow. The total thickness of the section is about 400 m. The basalts have been radiometrically (K-Ar) dated as 3–10 Ma, and as 10–20 Ma based on the very high value of the natural remanent magnetization (Vinogradov and others, 1977). Some rocks obtained from Zhokhov Island are similar to the Ordovician sandstones on Bennett Island. Kos'ko (1984) suggests that the upper basalt flow on Bennett Island may be the equivalent of the Zhokhov flows and, therefore, of Neogene age.

Vil'kitskii Island is composed of nepheline basalt flows with a high alkali content. Basalts similar to those found on Zhokhov, Bennett, and Vil'kitskii islands are also known on Axel Heiberg Island in the Canadian Arctic. Burke (1984) suggests that they are contemporaneous and related to Late Cretaceous rifting of the New Siberian Islands from the Canadian Arctic Archipelago. Alternatively, some of the extrusives in the De Long Islands may be due to intraplate volcanism. Based on the reconstruction of Morgan (1983), the absolute motion of the De Long Islands has been very small in the last 60 m.y., which would allow the volcanism to be concentrated in a small area through the time interval.

Henrietta Terrane

The Henrietta terrane consists of Henrietta and Jeannette islands and is characterized by a tuffaceous clastic sequence overlain by a basalt flow. The ages of the formations on Henrietta Island are not clear; however, altered foraminifera of Carboniferous age are reported from welded tuffs and in the clastic formations (Vinogradov and others, 1975). Radiometric dating (K-Ar) of the basalt yields ages of 310 and 375 Ma, supporting the Paleozoic age of the formations (Vinogradov and others, 1977).

The stratigraphy of Henrietta Island can be divided into five units. The lowest unit is composed of a massive quartzite, sandstone, and a hornfelsic slate and is 170 m thick. Above this unit lies a tuffaceous sandstone with layers of diabase and augite porphyry. This is overlain by a coarse graywacke sandstone with local conglomerates. The section is capped by a conglomerate composed of well-rounded pebbles from the underlying strata as well as from crystalline schists of the greenschist facies, gneiss, and granite. The total thickness of the tuff and coarse clastic deposits ranges from 500 to 900 m. The top-most unit on Henrietta Island is composed of 200 m of basalt and andesitic basalt. The individual flows are about 8 m thick and, in the upper part of the section, there is an argillaceous layer 18 m thick. The volcanic part of the section is intruded by dikes and sills of diorite porphyry less than 6 m thick. The rocks form a monocline dipping up to 65° to the west–southwest, decreasing to the east (Vinogradov and others, 1975, 1977).

On Jeannette Island, the lower part of the section is similar to the graywacke on Henrietta Island. These are unconformably overlain by a conglomerate with pebbles of metamorphic and sedimentary rocks similar to the conglomerate on Henrietta Island. These formations dip to the east–northeast at angles less than 60°.

The deposits of Henrietta Island have been interpreted by Soviet scientists as either an aulocogen (Vinogradov and others, 1977) or as the late stage of geosynclinal development (Vol'nov and others, 1970a).

GEOLOGY OF WRANGEL AND HERALD ISLANDS

Wrangel and Herald (Geral'd) islands were discovered by H. Kellett in 1849. Wrangel Island was first explored in 1881 by American geologists. Russian investigations began in 1911, and detailed geologic work was initiated by L. V. Gromov in 1935 (Vakar, 1970). Wrangel Island has an area of 7,600 km² and is elongated in an east–west direction. The northern half of the island is largely a flat coastal plain, and the topography of the island is dominated by the Central Range. Most of the geologic description given below is after Kameneva (1975, 1977); other references are cited as necessary.

The oldest formations (Fig. 3) on the island are metamorphosed sedimentary and igneous rocks (Wrangel complex of Ivanov, 1973) exposed in the Central Range in a large thrust sheet (Fig. 5). The Gromov suite includes in excess of 2,800 m of felsic, intermediate and mafic metavolcanic rocks, metavolcaniclastics, sericite and chlorite phyllite, and minor gray slaty phyllite and conglomerate; minor carbonates have also been reported by Kameneva and Il'chenko (1976). The Gromovian suite is intruded by now tectonized quartz-feldspar porphyry, metadiabase, actinolite amphibolite rock, and aplitic and peraplitic dikes and small intrusive bodies (M. P. Cecile and C. J. Harrison, personal communication, 1987). These rocks have been metamorphosed to greenschist and locally lower amphibolite facies levels of metamorphism. Kameneva and Il'chenko (1976) report acritarchs and microphytoliths from the marbles and schists similar to

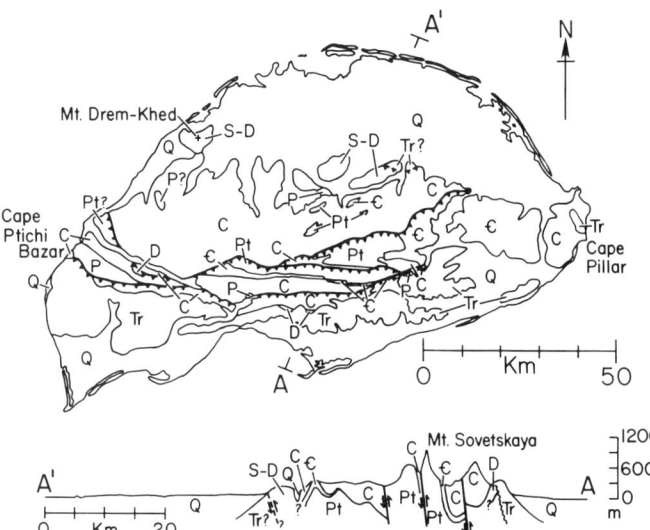

Figure 5. Geologic map (top) and structural section (bottom) of Wrangel Island after Til'man (1970), Kameneva (1975), Nalivkin (1983) and M. Cecile and C. Harrison (personal communication). Letter abbreviations as in Figure 4. Lithologies of the units can be inferred from Figure 3. The toothed lines are thrust faults and are dashed where uncertain. The region between the thrust faults forms the Central Range.

those found in the Ural and Baikal regions, where they are considered Middle to Late Riphean in age. The igneous rocks are suggested to be pre-Ordovician in age by Ivanov (1973) based on radiometric (K-Ar) dating; however, they may be as young as Mesozoic (Til'man and others, 1970).

The Inkalinian (In) suite of Kameneva and Il'chenko (1976) is essentially indistinguishable from the Gromovian suite (M. P. Cecile and J. C. Harrison, personal communication, 1986). It is also reported to contain abundant acritarchs similar to those found in the Vendian of Siberia (Kameneva and Il'chenko, 1976). Intrusions are restricted to these two suites only.

The Naskhokian series (Na) directly overlies the Inkalinian suite and consists of a basal conglomerate overlain by phyllite, quartzite, and quartzitic sandstone. The series is 800 m thick and is reported to contain remains of acritarchs, microphytoliths, and algae of Early Cambrian age (Kameneva and Il'chenko, 1976). The upper part of the Naskhokian series was formerly assigned to the Berri suite (see also Gnibidenko, 1969; Til'man and others, 1970).

These three formations are suggested to have formed through the metamorphism of Late Proterozoic volcanic, clastic, and terrigenous geosynclinal formations (Kameneva, 1975). Gnibidenko (1969), however, considers them to be Late Devonian or older formations that were metamorphosed during the intrusion of Carboniferous and Triassic granites. All three units are deformed in isoclinal folds that strike nearly east–west. Klippen(?) containing Precambrian formations are found on the upper parts of mountains 8–10 km north of the main thrust fault. Parts of the

Drem-Khed Mountains, described by Ivanov (1973), are also probably of Late Precambrian to Early Cambrian age and may be another klippe (Fig. 5). The contact between the Wrangel complex and the Paleozoic is almost everywhere tectonic (Byalobzheskii and Ivanov, 1971; Ivanov, 1973; Kameneva, 1975).

The next younger formations are of Late Silurian to Early Devonian age and form the Dremkhedian suite (Dr). The suite consists of 400 m of mudstone, siltstone, and quartzose sandstone with remains of brachiopods, ostracods, bryozoa, corals, and pelecypods. These deposits are found in the northwestern and north-central parts of the island. South of the Central Range, small sections (150 m) of the Upper Devonian are known and consist of limestone, sandstone, and shale. Frasnian microfauna and pollen are found in these rocks.

Carboniferous deposits are widely distributed in the central and southern parts of Wrangel Island. They are often present in tectonic contact with underlying metamorphic rocks and have undergone extensive deformation, resulting in confusion about the actual thickness, internal stratigraphy, and their relationship to the underlying formations.

South of the Central Range, Carboniferous deposits form a narrow band from Cape Pitchi Bazar to Cape Pillar. The Lower Carboniferous transgressively overlies the Upper Devonian and is composed of a basal conglomerate overlain by clayey limestone and alternating limestone and shale. The total thickness is at least 500 m. Tournaisian to Serupkhovian (Mississippian) brachiopods, corals, and crinoids are found in this unit, which appears to correspond to the Pillar series (Pi) of Ivanov (1973). Gradationally overlying the Serupkhovian deposits is a 300-m-thick section of interbedded limestone and shale with foraminifera of early Bashkirian age, at the bottom, and of late Bashkirian to Moscovian (Pennsylvanian) age at the top (Chernyak and Kameneva, 1976).

North of the Central Range, Carboniferous deposits unconformably overlie Lower Cambrian deposits. The base of the sequence is represented by a conglomerate, 25 m thick, overlain by 100–150 m of limestone and clayey shale that contain abundant Serupkhovian brachiopods and corals (Chernyak and Kameneva, 1976). These formations are probably also part of the Pillar series. The next unit consists of 200–250 m of barren clayey shale and minor amounts of limestone. Above this is a 250-m-thick limestone with a few layers of coarse clastics which appear to correspond to the Uering suite (Ue) of Ivanov (1973), although this reverses the stratigraphic succession of the suites proposed by Ivanov (1973). At the base of this section are strongly silicified bryozoan-algal bioherms; toward the top are remains of late Bashkirian to Moscovian foraminifera (Chernyak and Kameneva, 1976). At the eastern end of the island, near Cape Pillar, the Pillar series is composed of a thick (perhaps 1400 m) section of siltstone, sandstone, and minor amounts of conglomerate with corals, which date the series as Serupkhovian (Ivanov, 1973). The Carboniferous formations are 600–1400 m thick, greater in the southern half of the island.

Middle Carboniferous limestones also form synclinal structures in small outcrops in the midst of metamorphic rocks. However, mylonitization and brecciation of the limestones indicate that the contacts between the carbonates and the metamorphics are tectonic (Gnibidenko, 1968; Ivanov, 1973; Kameneva, 1975). The Carboniferous is also found as inliers in erosional windows through overlying rocks and may have thrusts within it (Byalobzheskii and Ivanov, 1971). Parts of the Carboniferous were included in the Berri suite by Til'man and others (1970).

The Upper Permian is exposed primarily in the northern part of the island and is composed of a basal conglomerate, 15 m thick, overlain by about 150 m of mudrock and limestone, which contain remains of foraminifera and a pelecypod of the genus *Kolymia*. Small outcrops of the Upper Permian are also found in the southern part of the island (Chernyak and Kameneva, 1976; M. P. Cecile and J. C. Harrison, personal communication, 1986).

Upper Triassic deposits are thrust or unconformably overlap older deposits of various ages at an angle of 15–20° and are primarily exposed on the southern coast of the island. They are composed of a lower clayey shale and limestone overlain by an immature graywacke which coarsens upward. The total thickness is 800 to 1,500 m and is dated using pelecypods as Carnian to Norian (Byalobzheskii and Ivanov, 1971; Ivanov, 1973; M. P. Cecile and J. C. Harrison, personal communication, 1986).

Unconsolidated Quaternary deposits overlie a large part of the northern part of the island and a small coastal strip along the southern coast. The deposits are alluvial, except in the mountains where they form talus deposits.

The dominant structure of Wrangel Island is a thrust with the central and southern parts of the island forming the upper plate (Fig. 5). The main thrust strikes nearly east–west and dips 30° to the south. It can be traced for about 65 km along the northern slopes of the Central Range. From the location of the klippen, 10 to 20 km north of the thrust, the thrust plane must become nearly horizontal toward the north. The lower plate is crumpled into corrugated folds, and the thrust plane is marked by extensive mylonitization, brecciation, and silicification. The upper plate is cut by east–west-striking thrust faults, the largest of which can be traced along the southern slopes of the Central Range and forms the southern boundary of the metamorphic complex (Bogdanov and Til'man, 1964; Kameneva, 1975). Many folds near the thrust plane are overturned.

The region to the south of the metamorphic complex is strongly deformed into linear folds with an east–west strike. The folds have a width of 3–8 km with steeply dipping limbs on the north and more gently dipping limbs on the south. Axial planes dip to the south to southeast at an angle of 35–40°, the same as the schistosity in the Wrangel complex. Small thrusts, reverse faults, and overturned folds are also present. A pervasive cleavage, dipping south, penetrates all rocks Triassic and older (Byalobzheskii and Ivanov, 1971). A third large thrust occurs within the Phanerozoic section, and the Devonian to Permian section is repeated south of it (M. P. Cecile and J. C. Harrison, personal communication, 1986). The age of the thrusting is post-Triassic and, if K-Ar dates on extrusive rocks penetrated by the cleavage are from the time of extrusion, post-Jurassic (Bogdanov and Til'man, 1964; Byalobzheskii and Ivanov, 1971).

North of the main thrust, folds in the lower plate are much gentler and form short, broad synclines separated by narrow, ridge-like anticlines. The fold axes strike northeast and are discordant from the east–west fold axes on the upper plate. Byalobzheskii and Ivanov (1971), however, suggest that thrusting is also present north of the Central Range. In particular, they propose that Triassic(?) rocks found at the northern end of the foothills are in thrust contact with Paleozoic rocks both above and below them.

Radiometric (K-Ar) dates have been obtained from a variety of igneous, sedimentary, and metamorphic rocks from the upper thrust sheet. These rocks represent a wide span of ages, from 575 Ma to 115 Ma. Clusters of ages occur near 400 Ma, 270 Ma, and 120 Ma (Ivanov, 1973). The last age is a likely time for the thrusting and resetting of K-Ar systems. The 120 Ma date falls only somewhat earlier (Aptian) than the time of thrusting of Herald arch (late Albian), as mapped by Grantz and others (1981), and is contemporaneous with some thrusting in the Brooks Range. A thrust surface observed on seismic reflection profiles in the Chukchi Sea (Grantz and others, 1981) may also underlie Wrangel Island.

Northwest to north striking strike-slip faults, transverse to the strike of the thrust zone, cut the thrust and all older deposits, and thus may be dated as post-middle Cretaceous. Rivers follow some of these fault traces.

The stratigraphy of Wrangel Island has been compared to that of northwestern Alaska by numerous authors (Bogdanov and Til'man, 1964; Churkin, 1973; Tailleur, 1973). In particular, the Carboniferous to Triassic of Wrangel Island is very similar to sequences of the same age exposed on an allochthonous sheet in the Lisburne Hills, Alaska (Martin, 1970), the on-land continuation of Herald arch and thrust (Grantz and others, 1981).

Herald Island is located 60 km east of Wrangel Island on the eastern end of Wrangel arch. The island is elongated in a northwesterly direction and has an area of about 20 km^2. The northwest tip of the island is composed of sandstone, phyllite, quartzose sandstone, quartz-chlorite-sericite schist mylonite, and cataclastic quartz syenite, with a thickness of 600 m. By analogy with similar rocks on Wrangel Island, the age of this complex is thought to be Proterozoic to early Paleozoic (Lobanov, 1957; Egiazarov, 1970). The mylonite and cataclastics suggest the presence of faulting, and the main thrust of Wrangel Island may pass through Herald Island. The rest of the island is composed of a granitic pluton (Lobanov, 1957; Til'man, 1970) that is reportedly Jurassic in age (Grantz and others, 1981). Pending subsequent investigations, the island can be postulated as an extension of the central zone of Wrangel Island.

GEOPHYSICAL STUDIES OF THE EAST SIBERIAN SEA AND THE NEW SIBERIAN ISLANDS

Aeromagnetic Surveys

Soviet aeromagnetic surveys have been conducted over the entire East Siberian Shelf since the early 1960s. One American survey line crosses the north-central part of the East Siberian Sea (Ostenso and Wold, 1971). Although neither tracklines nor profiles of the Soviet surveys have been published, general trends have been summarized.

The southern boundary of the East Siberian Sea is marked by a west–northwest-striking band of anomalies, which trend from Bol'shoi Laykhov Island to the South Anyui suture (Shilo and others, 1973; Meyerhoff, 1973; Kos'ko, 1984) (Fig. 2). The anomalies have amplitudes of up to 1,500 nanotesla (nT) and are ascribed to magnetic granites, gabbros, and extrusives (Ivanov and Belyayev, 1973; Vinogradov and others, 1974b). Vol'nov and others (1970a) state that the axis of the Lyakhov terrane extends northwest off the coasts of Kotel'nyi and Bel'kov islands and is defined by "frequently changing positive and negative anomalies," which change in strike in the Laptev Sea to a more north–south orientation (Vinogradov and others, 1974b).

The Kotel'nyi Terrane is characterized by a broad, weak (300 nT), northwesterly striking anomaly on which isometric or northwest-striking, high-frequency anomalies are superimposed, particularly along the edge of the terrane (Vinogradov and others, 1974b; Genin and others, 1977). The anomalies damp out to the north and do not extend to the continental slope. The anomalies also damp out toward the southeast, due to the subsidence of the magnetic layer in the Blagoveshchensk Basin. West–northwest to east–west striking anomalies are found over eastern Faddeya and Novaya Sibir' islands; they damp out, with the magnetic field becoming nearly constant (anomalies of less than 50 nT), over the New Siberian Basin (Vol'nov and others, 1970a; Vinogradov and others, 1974b). A series of linear magnetic anomalies is also associated with Anzhu Ridge (L. Z. Lipkov, personal communication, 1986), and a zone of irregular anomalies is found east and south of Malyi Lyakhov Island (Genin and others, 1977).

The magnetic field in the region of the De Long Islands is varied. Near Bennett, Zhokhov, and Vil'kitskii islands, the field varies in polarity without any clearly defined linear trends. The anomalies have an amplitude of 800–1,000 nT with the greatest anomalies associated with the islands. This field is assumed to represent the extent of the Cretaceous to Cenozoic basalt flows, which are exposed on the islands (Vol'nov and others, 1970a; Vinogradov and others, 1974b). Near Henrietta and Jeannette islands, linear anomalies strike northwest or nearly north–south (Vol'nov and others, 1970a) with amplitudes around 300 nT (Ostenso and Wold, 1971). These anomalies are truncated to the south by large amplitude (800–1,000 nT), nearly east–west-striking anomalies thought to be due to intrusions located along faults at the northern edge of the New Siberian Basin (Vol'nov and others, 1970a; Vinogradov and others, 1974b, 1977). These anomalies become more north–south to the east.

The anomalies in the eastern half of the East Siberian Sea are less well described; however, wide, linear, nearly east–west-striking anomalies of 250–500 nT are found northwest of Wrangel Island. These anomalies are discordant, in strike, to structural trends on the island itself (Vinogradov and others, 1974b, 1977).

North of Wrangel Island, there is a zone of high-intensity anomalies presumed to be due to basalts, speculated to be of late Paleogene to Neogene age (Pol'kin, 1984). Eastern Vil'kitskii Basin has a generally negative anomaly (Coles and others, 1978). West of Wrangel Island, between the Blagoveshchensk and Hope basins, the magnetic field is generally quiet, with broad anomalies of up to 200 nT (Vinogradov and others, 1974b).

MAGSAT data, taken at a mean height of 400 km, indicate generally negative scalar magnetic anomalies over the East Siberian Sea with a high near zero nT in the New Siberian Islands area, decreasing to –4 nT in the Blagoveshchesk Basin (Coles and others, 1982).

The subsurface structure of the East Siberian Sea has been estimated by the computation of depth to magnetic basement. Maps of the thickness of sedimentary cover in the East Siberian Sea consistently show three roughly east–west striking basins, with some variation in the details (e.g., Egiazarov, 1978; Pogrebitskii, 1984). The analyses performed are not known, but may be similar to those presented by Kovacs and Vogt (1982). All of the basins are assumed, by Soviet geologists, to be underlain by Precambrian continental crust (Vinogradov and others, 1977; Kos'ko, 1984), and their analyses are based on this assumption. Thus the results discussed below must be interpreted with caution. Kos'ko (1984) names the basins, from south to north (Fig. 2), the Blagoveshchensk, New Siberian, and Vil'kitskii. The Blagoveshchensk and New Siberian basins are sometimes combined into the East Siberian Basin, and other names have been used by some authors (see also Meyerhoff, 1982). The Anzhu Ridge separates the Blagoveshchensk and New Siberian basins.

The Blagoveshchensk and New Siberian basins are believed to be filled primarily with Paleozoic to Mesozoic—and possibly some Cenozoic—sediments analogous to those found in the Kotel'nyi and Novaya Sibir' terranes. Kos'ko (1984) considers Faddeya Island and southwest Novaya Sibir' Island as on-land extensions of the Blagoveshchensk Basin, and northeastern Novaya Sibir' Island and Strelka Anzhu as extensions of the Anzhu Ridge. Anzhu Ridge is presumed to be composed of Late Proterozoic to Jurassic sediments, folded in Late Jurassic to Early Cretaceous time (Kos'ko, 1984), and may be a basement uplift similar to Herald arch. The Vil'kitskii Basin is the northwest continuation of the North Chukchi Basin of Grantz and others (1981) and is assumed to have the same structure and composition. Kos'ko (1984) suggests that the basin is filled with Cenozoic sediments and has clay diapirs as observed in the North Chukchi Basin. The westward extent of the Vil'kitskii Basin is uncertain. Kos'ko (1984) extends the basin to the northern edge of the De Long Islands, while Pogrebitskii (1984) terminates it near 170°E.

The thickness of the sedimentary cover is estimated by Demenitskaya and others (1973b) to exceed 5 km throughout most of the East Siberian Sea and to be between 2 and 5 km in the De Long Islands. Egiazarov (1978) and Pogrebitskii (1984) show maximum thicknesses of 5 km in the Blagovshchensk and New Siberian Basins and up to 6 km in the eastern Vil'kitskii Basin. Volk and others (1984) computed sediment thicknesses for two sites in the Blagoveshchensk Basin and obtained a maximum sedimentary thickness of about 9 km, underlain by an additional 5–10 km of deformed Paleozoic sediment, with the top of crystalline basement lying 10–15 km below the surface.

The region northwest of Wrangel Island is considered a terrace with basement rocks lying at 1–2 km depth. This region may be an analog of the Chukchi Platform identified to the east of Wrangel Island by Grantz and May (1984).

An extensive study using aeromagnetic data to determine crustal structure has been performed by Volk and others (1984). The authors show crustal models along 77°N and 160°E. Assuming the crust of the East Siberian Sea to be continental, they divide it into a sedimentary layer (intensity of magnetization, J, of 0.2–1.0 Ampere/meter), a folded basement complex (J = 0.3–1.5 A/m), and a granitic layer (J = 0.3–2.0 A/m). Where the De Long Islands basalts are present, a top layer with J = 3 A/m is shown. The total thickness of the crust is nearly constant at 30–35 km, with granitic and basaltic layers having mean thicknesses of 10 and 15 km, respectively (Volk and others, 1984; Volk and Gaponenko, 1984). This agrees with earlier work by Demenitskaya and others (1973b) who obtained a crustal thickness of 30–35 km, increasing to 40 km under Wrangel Island and dropping to 25 km in the northern De Long Islands.

Gravimetric Surveys

The Lyakhov Islands, Dmitri Laptev Strait, and Cape Svyatoi Nos coincide with gravity highs and are also surrounded by a 100–150-km-wide positive gravity anomaly, as is Kotel'nyi Island (Vol'nov and others, 1970a). Isolated gravity highs are associated with the ultramafic rocks found in southwest Bol'shoi Lyakhov Island and off Cape Shalaurova. Gravity lows are found over granitic intrusions in northern and western Bol'shoi Lyakhov Island (Andreev and others, 1975). Sharp positive anomalies, the amplitudes of which correlate with elevation, occur over Stolbovoi, and Bel'kov islands and are thought to reflect uncompensated recent uplifts. Gravity lows exist in parts of Dmitri Laptev Strait and bracket Bel'kov Island. They are presumed to represent Paleogene to Neogene grabens 2.5–3 km deep (Genin and others, 1977; Vinogradov, 1984). Gravity anomalies strike northwest–southeast over Kotel'nyi Island, have varying strikes in Zemlya Bunge, and are interpreted as representing a blocky subsurface structure. Gravity lows are also found over the Nerpalakh depression and the eastern part of the Balyktakh synclinorium (Genin and others, 1977). Most of Zemlya Bunge has a negative gravity anomaly, with sharp gradients on its border with Kotel'nyi Island and just west of Strelka Anzhu, which suggest that the depth to basement (ρ = 2.95 gm/cm^3) increases to 11 km, from 9 km under Kotel'nyi Island. The overlying folded sedimentary complex is modeled with ρ = 2.75 gm/cm^3 (Piskarev and others, 1975). A gravity gradient is also found along the north coast of Faddeya and Novaya Sibir' islands (L. Z. Lipkov, personal communication, 1986) and probably reflects faults along the western extrapolation of Anzhu Ridge. Although the gravitational field is generally positive over the Blagoveshchensk Basin (Kos'ko, 1984), it smoothly becomes negative over the New Siberian Basin and indicates a depth to basement of 10 km (Vol'nov and others, 1970a).

The De Long Islands have a uniformly positive gravity anomaly, the boundary of which correlates with the magnetic field associated with the basaltic extrusives (Vol'nov and others, 1970a). Anzhu Ridge shows a slightly more positive anomaly than the Blagoveshchensk Basin (Kos'ko, 1984).

A steep gravity gradient exists along the northern coast of Chukotka, and there is a local gravity minimum, attributed to granitic rocks, in the middle of Long Strait (Shilo and others, 1982).

Seismic Refraction and Earthquake Studies

One seismic refraction line has been obtained in the New Siberian Islands. The line extends for 76 km/s across Zemlya Bunge from east–central Kotel'nyi Island to northeastern Faddeya Island. The resulting velocity model indicates that Kotel'nyi Island is composed of a surficial layer with an interval velocity of 6.2–6.6 km/s, while most of Zemlya Bunge has a surficial layer with a P-wave velocity of 3.5 km/s. A 6.7 km/s layer in the west (presumed to be carbonates) and a 4.5 km/s layer in the central and eastern sections of Zemlya Bunge underlies the 3.5 km/s layer at a depth of about 600 m. Near the boundary between Zemlya Bunge and Faddeya Island, there is a zone of elevated seismic velocities, up to 4.8 km/s, proposed to be a result of terrigenous rocks with granitic intrusions. The surface terrigenous layer on Faddeya Island has a velocity of 3.3 km/s, but is also underlain by the 4.5 km/s layer (Piskarev and others, 1975).

Avetisov (1983) studied the crustal structure of the Anzhu and Lyakhov islands using the emergence angles of seismic waves from earthquakes and near-receiver P to S conversions. His results indicate three crustal blocks in the region that correlate roughly to the Lyakhov, Kotel'nyi, and Novaya Sibir' terranes. The Lyakhov terrane has three layers above the Moho, with velocities of 5.3–5.9 km/s (at 0–12.5 km depth), 6.0–6.2 km/s (12.5–22.5 km), and 6.2–6.4 km/s (22.5–34 km). The Kotel'nyi terrane appears to be more complicated with more layers in the crustal section. The surface velocity is 6.2–6.6 km/s and corresponds to the carbonates. Locally, in Zarya strait, 2.5 km of 4.0 km/s terrigenous sediment is present. Basement rocks with a seismic velocity of 6.3–6.5 km/s occur at depths of 15–32.5 km.

The Novaya Sibir' terrane is subdivided into five layers, the topmost being a thin (<0.5 km) layer of 3.3–3.5 km/s material (Cretaceous and Cenozoic deposits). Underlying this is a layer of 4.2–4.8 km/s material, presumed to be terrigenous sediments (base at 4 km). The next layer is a 5.5–5.6 km/s layer (base at 10 km), which may be folded basement rocks. Underneath this is a 5.7–6.0 km/s layer of the granitic basement (base at 20 km), and a final basaltic layer with velocities of 5.9–6.3 km/s (20–33 km). The uppermost mantle appears to have an anomalous layer with a velocity of 6.3–6.6 km/s underlying the entire region (Avetisov, 1983).

Demenitskaya and others (1973a) cite seismic velocities and layer thicknesses from various parts of the East Siberian Shelf, probably obtained from refraction studies run from ice islands. They consider the shelf to consist of four layers. The uppermost is probably composed of unconsolidated sediments with a refraction velocity of 1.8–2.5 km/s and a thickness of 0.5 km in the northwestern East Siberian Sea, 1.5 km in the central part of the shelf, and 2 km in the eastern Vil'kitskii Basin. Consolidated sediments with a velocity of 3.5–4.0 km/s (northwestern Vil'kitskii Basin) are presumed to underlie this layer. Their thickness reaches 5–7 km in the New Siberian and Blagoveshchensk basins, and 4 km in the Vil'kitskii Basin. The third layer is assumed to consist of folded basement rocks and has a seismic velocity of 5.5–5.7 km/s. Finally, the crystalline basement is reported to have a seismic velocity of 6.0–6.3 km/s and lie at a depth of 9 km in the northwestern East Siberian Sea and 12 km in the Blagoveshchensk and New Siberian basins. Some of the data reported for the East Siberian Sea may be derived from studies by Grantz and others (1975) in the North Chukchi Basin.

Seismic refraction data have been obtained by American and Soviet workers in the western part of Hope Basin (western South Chukchi Basin of Kos'ko, 1984). The Soviet results are summarized below and derived from Kos'ko (1984) and Pol'kin (1984). The top-most layer has a seismic velocity of 1.8 km/s and a thickness of 750 m, presumably composed of Neogene to Quaternary unconsolidated sediments. Underlying this is a layer, assigned to the Paleogene, with a velocity of 2.2 km/s and a thickness of 437 m, thinning on the crests of anticlines. The third horizon is identified by a refraction velocity of 3.5–3.6 km/s and has a thickness of more than 700 m, thinning to 300–350 m at the edges of the basin. Below this is a low-velocity layer, 150–400 m thick, found only in the western part of Hope Basin, with a seismic velocity of 2.5 km/s. Kos'ko (1984) considers this to represent a layer of clay, as found at the base of the Cretaceous in the New Siberian Islands. The fifth layer, probably composed of Early Cretaceous coal-bearing molasse, is characterized by a velocity of 4.5 km/s and has a thickness of up to 1.5 km. The complex is underlain by basement, which corresponds to magnetic basement, with a seismic velocity of 6.1 km/s. The total thickness of the sedimentary cover in the Shmidt depression of Hope Basin is 3 km.

Magnetotelluric Surveys

Magnetotelluric data obtained from ice islands near the eastern De Long Islands in 1962 (Novysh and Fonarev, 1966) were interpreted by Deniskin and Lipskaya (1967) to represent sedimentary thicknesses of 300–800 m. DeLaurier (1978) recomputed these values using a different model and obtained sediment thicknesses of 700–1,200 m, depending on the assumed thermal gradient. Deniskin and Lipskaya (1967) also reported data gathered in the northwestern Vil'kitskii Basin and obtained sediment thickness of 2,000–4,000 m, thickening to the east. DeLaurier (1978) recomputed these values to 1,700–4,300 m.

TECTONIC EVOLUTION AND SETTING

Due to the lack of data on the East Siberian Sea, its structure and history are poorly understood. Most Soviet summaries (e.g., Vinogradov and others, 1977; Kos'ko, 1984) extrapolate the geology of the New Siberian Islands, Wrangel Island, and the continental part of Eurasia to the East Siberian Shelf. Given the strong evidence for a suture zone between Eurasia and the shelf (Lyakhov–South Anyui suture), and distinct terranes in the islands, these extrapolations may not be valid.

In the 1930s, Shatskii and others proposed that the northern part of the East Siberian Shelf and Chukotka Peninsula were the remnants of a Precambrian shield, most of which now underlies the deep basin of the Arctic Ocean. This was named the Hyperborean platform by the Soviets (Churkin, 1973) and Ancient Arctica by Eardley (1948). As the structures and geology of the New Siberian Islands and Wrangel Island were studied and interpreted as remnants of geosynclines between the platform and the Mesozoic folded regions of continental Eurasia and the Siberian platform, the size of the Hyperborean platform was reduced (Pushcharovskiy, 1960). Most Soviet analyses still lean toward this interpretation (Pushcharovskiy, 1976; Vinogradov and others, 1977; Markov and others, 1978; Til'man and Byalobzhesky, 1984) despite evidence of structures unusual for a Precambrian platform, for example, the geosynclinal deposits of Henrietta Island, and the oceanic nature of the Arctic Ocean basins.

Friedman and others (1984) and Rowley and others (1985) suggest that the East Siberian Shelf has been connected to both Alaska and Siberia since mid-Paleozoic time in its present configuration. This is based partially on the similarity of Paleozoic rocks on Kotel'nyi Island to the Siberian platform on one hand, and of Wrangel Island to the north slope of Alaska on the other, as well as on the lack of evidence for a suture zone between them.

Fujita and Newberry (1982) suggest that the Blagoveshchensk and New Siberian basins may be underlain by oceanic or thinned continental crust in a manner similar to that proposed for the North Chukchi Basin by Grantz and others (1979). They assign the New Siberian Islands to the Siberian platform and Wrangel Island to Alaska, leaving a now sediment-filled gap between them. They also note that including the New Siberian Islands in the Arctic Alaska plate results in geometric problems with rotation-based reconstructions for Alaska.

Fujita (1978), Burke (1984), and Savostin and others (1984) suggest that the New Siberian Islands, or parts thereof, represent an independent plate which rifted from the Canadian Arctic Islands in the Cretaceous, and collided with Eurasia along the Lyakhov–South Anyui suture. Burke (1984) places the western boundary of the plate at the junction of Kotel'nyi Island and Zemlya Bunge and considers it a transform fault. Burke also notes the similarities in age and composition of the De Long Islands volcanics to volcanics in the Canadian Arctic. Savostin and others (1984) and Fujita (1978) place the western boundary of the New Siberian plate in the Laptev Sea and postulate a Khroma plate on the southern side of the Lyakhov–South Anyui suture zone, incorporating Cape Svyatoi Nos (Fig. 1).

All of the above models have aspects that are both supported and refuted by the geology of the islands and the limited geophysical data available. At this time, it seems reasonable to interpret the Lyakhov terrane as lying along the northern margin of the Lyakhov–South Anyui suture and to consider Wrangel Island as a part of the thrust system found in the Chukchi Sea. The extension of the Lyakhov terrane to the west, based on geophysical data, suggests that a suture lies west of Kotel'nyi Island in the Laptev Sea. However, lithology and paleofauna are similar on both sides of this boundary. The geology of the New Siberian Islands also bears gross similarities to northern Alaska, with the Lyakhov terrane corresponding to the southern Brooks Range, the Kotel'nyi terrane to the central Brooks Range, the Novaya Sibir' terrane to the north slope basins, and the Bennett terrane to the Barrow Arch basement uplift. This suggests a possible link, at some points in time, between the New Siberian Islands and Alaska.

Unfortunately, the crucial structures are buried deep beneath the sedimentary cover of the eastern East Siberian Sea and in the rift-dissected water-covered areas of the Laptev Sea. It is hoped that additional seismic reflection and refraction work, as well as detailed gravimetric modeling, can be conducted to help determine the structures of this region.

REFERENCES

Andreev, S. I., Ushakov, V. I., Genin, B. L., Lipkov, L. Z., and Piskarev, A. L., 1975, Geologic-geophysical prerequisites in the search for solid commercial minerals on the shelf of the eastern part of the Laptev Sea: Geologiya Morya, v. 4, p. 5–14 [in Russian].

Avetisov, G. P., 1983, Seismological data on the deep structure of the New Siberian Islands and adjacent sea areas: International Geology Review, v. 25, p. 651–660.

Bogdanov, N. A., and Til'man, S. M., 1964, Similarities in the development of the Paleozoic structures of Wrangel Island and the western part of the Brooks Range (Alaska), in Conference on tectonic problems, Moskva, 1963, Folded regions of Eurasia, materialy: Moskva, p. 219–230 [in Russian].

Burke, K., 1984, Plate tectonic history of the Arctic, in Arctic geology, reports, v. 4, 27th International Geologic Congress, Moscow: Moskva, Nauka, p. 189–198.

Byalobzheskii, S. G., and Ivanov, S. M., 1971, Thrust structures on Wrangel Island, in Shilo, N. A., ed., Mesozoic tectonogenesis: Magadan, Akademiya Nauk SSSR, Dal'negovostochnyi Tsentr Severo-Vostochnyi Kompleksnyi Institut, p. 73–80 [in Russian].

Chernyak, G. Y., and Kameneva, G. I., 1976, Carboniferous and Permian sediments of Wrangel Island: Doklady Academy of Sciences of the USSR, Earth Science Sections, v. 227, p. 93–95.

Churkin, M., Jr., 1973, Geologic concepts of Arctic Ocean basin, in Pitcher,

M. G., ed., Arctic geology: American Association of Petroleum Geologists Memoir 19, p. 485–499.
Clarke, J. W., St. Amand, P., and Matson, M., 1986, Possible cause of plumes from Bennett Island, Soviet Far Arctic [abs.]: American Association of Petroleum Geologists, v. 70, p. 574.
Coles, R. L., Hannaford, W., and Haines, G. V., 1978, Magnetic anomalies and the evolution of the Arctic, in Sweeney, J. F., ed., Arctic geophysical review: Publications of the Earth Physics Branch, v. 45, no. 4, p. 51–66.
Coles, R. L., Haines, G. V., van Beek, G. J., Nandi, A., and Walker, J. K., 1982, Magnetic anomaly maps from 40°N to 83°N derived from MAGSAT satellite data: Geophysical Research Letters, v. 9, p. 281–284.
DeLaurier, J. M., 1978, Arctic Ocean sediment thicknesses and upper mantle temperatures from magnetotelluric soundings, in Sweeney, J. F., ed., Arctic geophysical review: Publications of the Earth Physics Branch, v. 45, no. 4, p. 35–49.
Demenitskaya, R. M., and Hunkins, K. L., 1971, Shape and structure of the Arctic Ocean, in Maxwell, A. E., ed., The sea, v. 4; New concepts of sea floor evolution, pt. 2; Regional observations, concepts: New York, Wiley-Interscience, p. 223–249.
Demenitskaya, R. M., Gaponenko, G. I., Kiselev, Y. G., and Ivanov, S. S., 1973a, Features of sedimentary layers beneath Arctic Ocean, in Pitcher, M. G., ed., Arctic geology: American Association of Petroleum Geologists Memoir 19, p. 332–335.
Demenitskaya, R. M., Ivanov, S. S., and Volk, V. E., 1973b, Crust of the Arctic seas of Eurasia: Tectonophysics, v. 20, p. 97–104.
Deniskin, N. A., and Lipskaya, N. V., 1967, Results of magnetotelluric probing in the station Severnyy Polyus 13 drift area: Doklady Academy of Sciences of the USSR, Earth Science Sections, v. 177, p. 28–30.
Eardley, A. J., 1948, Ancient Arctica: Journal of Geology, v. 56, p. 409–436.
Egiazarov, B. K., 1970, Medvesh'i, Aion, Routan, and Herald Islands, in Tkachenko, B. V., and Egiazarov, B. K., eds., Geology of the USSR, v. 26, Islands of the Soviet Arctic: Moskva, Nedra, p. 375–377 [in Russian].
Egiazarov, B. K., ed., 1978, Tectonic map of the North Polar regions of the Earth: Moscow, Ministry of Geology of the USSR, 6 sheets, scale 1:5,000,000.
Friedman, R., Lottes, A. L., Rowley, D. B., Scotese, C. R., and Ziegler, A. M., 1984, Paleogeographic evolution of Alaska and adjacent regions [abs.]: Geological Society of America Abstracts with Programs, v. 16, p. 284.
Fujita, K., 1978, Pre-Cenozoic tectonic evolution of northeast Siberia: Journal of Geology, v. 86, p. 159–172.
Fujita, K., and Newberry, J. T., 1982, Tectonic evolution of northeastern Siberia and adjacent regions: Tectonophysics, v. 89, p. 337–357.
Fujita, K., and Newberry, J. T., 1983, Accretionary terranes and tectonic evolution of northeast Siberia, in Hashimoto, M., and Uyeda, S., eds., Accretion tectonics in the Circum-Pacific region: Tokyo, Terra Scientific, p. 43–57.
Genin, B. L., Lipkov, L. Z., and Piskarev, A. L., 1977, On the structure of the basement of the East Siberian shelf in the region of the New Siberian Islands archipelago in Pogrebitskii, Y. E., and Kos'ko, M. K., eds., Tectonics of the Arctic. Folded basement of the shelf sedimentary basins: Leningrad, Nauchno-Issledovatel'skii Institut Geologii Arktiki, p. 86–97 [in Russian].
Gnibidenko, G. S., 1968, More information on the Paleozoic stratigraphy of Wrangel Island: Doklady Academy of Sciences of the USSR, Earth Science Sections, v. 179, p. 37–39.
Gnibidenko, G. S., 1969, Metamorphic complexes in the structure of the northwest sector of the Pacific Ocean belt: Moskva, Nauka, 134 p. [in Russian].
Grantz, A., and May, S. D., 1984, Summary geologic report for Barrow Arch outer continental shelf (OCS) planning area, Chukchi Sea, Alaska: U.S. Geological Survey Open-File Report 84-395, 39 p.
Grantz, A., Holmes, M. L., and Kososki, B. A., 1975, Geologic framework of the Alaskan continental terrace in the Chukchi and Beaufort seas, in Yorath, C. J., Parker, E. R., and Glass, D. J., eds., Canada's continental margins: Canadian Society of Petroleum Geologists Memoir 4, p. 669–700.
Grantz, A., Eittreim, S., and Dinter, D. A., 1979, Geology and tectonic development of the continental margin north of Alaska: Tectonophysics, v. 59, p. 263–291.
Grantz, A., Eittreim, S., and Whitney, O. T., 1981, Geology and physiography of the continental margin north of Alaska and implications for the origin of the Canada Basin, in Nairn, A.E.M., Churkin, M., Jr., and Stehli, F. G., eds., The ocean basins and margins, v. 5, The Arctic Ocean: New York, Plenum, p. 439–492.
Ivanov, O. N., 1973, The stratigraphy of Wrangel Island: Izvestiya Akademii Nauk SSSR, Seriya Geologicheskaya, no. 5, p. 104–115 [in Russian].
Ivanov, V. V., and Belyayev, I. V., 1973, Tectonics and oil and gas potentials of the Kolyma and Primor'ye lowlands and adjacent shelves: International Geology Review, v. 15, p. 526–533.
Ivanov, V. V., Ivanov, B. A., and Pokhialaynen, V. P., 1974, New data on the geology of Stolbovoi Island, New Siberian Archipelago: Doklady Academy of Sciences of the USSR, Earth Science Sections, v. 216, p. 74–75.
Ivanov, V. V., Klubov, B. A., Lozhkina, N. V., and Pokhialainen, V. P., 1977, Stratigraphy and paleomagnetic characteristics of the Upper Jurassic and Lower Cretaceous deposits of Stolbovoi Island (Novosibirskii Archipelago): Soviet Geology and Geophysics, v. 18, p. 84–89.
Kameneva, G. I., 1975, The structure of the central part of Wrangel Island, in Geology and mineral resources of the New Siberian Islands and Wrangel Island: Leningrad, Nauchno-Issledovatel'skii Institut Geologii Arktiki, p. 72–77 [in Russian].
——, 1977, On the question of the tectonic setting of Wrangel Island and its structural ties to Alaska in the Paleozoic, in Pogrebitskii, Y. E., and Kos'ko, M. K., eds., Tectonics of the Arctic. Folded basement of the shelf sedimentary basins: Leningrad, Nauchno-Issledovatel'skii Institut Geologii Arktiki, p. 122–131 [in Russian].
Kameneva, G. I., and Il'chenko, L. N., 1976, New data on the age of the metamorphic complex of Wrangel Island: Doklady Academy of Sciences of the USSR, Earth Science Series, v. 227, p. 51–53.
Kienle, J., Roederer, J. G., and Shaw, G. E., 1983, Volcanic event in Soviet Arctic?: Eos (American Geophysical Union Transactions), v. 64, p. 377.
Klubov, B. A., Korshunov, A. A., and Badera, I. G., 1976, New data on coal measures of Novaya Sibir' Island, New Siberian Islands: Doklady Academy of Sciences of the USSR, Earth Science Sections, v. 231, p. 58–60.
Kos'ko, M. K., 1977, Structural-facial zonation of the Ordovician–Middle Devonian carbonate complex of the Anzhu Islands, in Pogrebitskii, Y. E., and Kos'ko, M. K., eds., Tectonics of the Arctic. Folded basement of the shelf sedimentary basins: Leningrad, Nauchno-Issledovatel'skii Institut Geologii Arktiki, p. 55–85 [in Russian].
Kos'ko, M. K., 1984, The East Siberian Sea, in Gramberg, I. S., and Pogrebitskii, Y. E., eds., Geology of the USSR and distribution of mineral resources, v. 9, Seas of the Soviet Arctic: Leningrad, Nedra, p. 60–67 [in Russian].
Kos'ko, M. K., and Nepomiluev, V. F., 1975, Towards the reconstruction of Paleozoic structural-formational zones in the region of the Anzhu Islands: Tektonika Arktiki, v. 1, p. 26–30 [in Russian].
Kos'ko, M. K., Sobolevskaya, R. F., Nepomiluev, V. F., and Vol'nov, D. A., 1975, Cambrian–Middle Devonian deposits of the New Siberian islands, in Geology and mineral resources of the New Siberian Islands and Wrangel Island: Leningrad, Nauchno-Issledovatel'skii Institut Geologii Arktiki, p. 8–21 [in Russian].
Kosygin, Y. A., and Parfenov, L. M., 1981, Tectonics of the Soviet Far East, in Nairn, A.E.M., Churkin, M., Jr., and Stehli, F. G., eds., The ocean basins and margins, v. 5, The Arctic Ocean: New York, Plenum, p. 377–412.
Kovacs, K. C., and Vogt, P. R., 1982, Depth-to-magnetic source analysis of the Arctic Ocean region: Tectonophysics, v. 89, p. 255–294.
Lobanov, M. F., 1957, Geologic structure of Wrangel and Herald Islands, in Markov, F. G., and Nalivkin, D. V., eds., Geology of the Soviet Arctic: Moskva, Gosgeoltekhizdat, p. 504–520 [in Russian].
Lastochkin, A. N., 1980, Orographic boundaries and some morphological features of the northern continental slope of Eurasia: Oceanology, v. 20, p. 179–182.
Lozhkin, A. V., 1977, Radiocarbon dating of Upper Pleistocene sediments of the New Siberian Islands and the age of the "Yedoma" suite of the northeast USSR: Doklady Academy of Sciences of the USSR, Earth Science Sections,

v. 235, p. 57–59.

Markov, M. S., Pushcharovskiy, Y. M., and Til'man, S. M., 1978, Tectonics of the shelf zones of the eastern Arctic and Far Eastern Seas: International Geology Review, v. 20, p. 867–874.

Martin, A. J., 1970, Structure and tectonic history of the western Brooks Range, De Long Mountains and Lisburne Hills, northern Alaska: Geological Society of America Bulletin, v. 81, p. 3605–3622.

Meyerhoff, A. A., 1973, Origin of Arctic and North Atlantic Oceans, *in* Pitcher, M. G., ed., Arctic geology: American Association of Petroleum Geologists Memoir 19, p. 562–582.

Meyerhoff, A. A., 1982, Hydrocarbon resources in Arctic and Subarctic regions, *in* Embry, A. F., and Balkwill, H. R., eds., Arctic geology and geophysics: Canadian Society of Petroleum Geologists Memoir 8, p. 451–522.

Mokshantsev, K. B., Gornshtein, D. K., Gusev, G. S., Den'gin, E. V., and Shtekh, G. I., 1964, Tectonic structure of Yakut ASSR: Moskva, Nauka, 240 p. [in Russian].

Morgan, W. J., 1983, Hot spot tracks and the early rifting of the Atlantic: Tectonophysics, v. 94, p. 123–129.

Nalivkin, D. V., ed., 1983, Geological map of the USSR: Moscow, Ministry of Geology of the USSR, 16 sheets, scale 1:2,500,000.

Natal'in, B. A., and Parfenov, L. M., 1983, Accretional and collisional eugeosynclinal folded systems of the northwestern Pacific rim, *in* Hashimoto, M., and Uyeda, S., eds., Accretion tectonics in the Circum-Pacific regions: Tokyo, Terra Scientific, p. 59–68.

Naugler, F. P., Silberling, N., and Creager, J. S., 1974, Recent sediments of the East Siberian Sea, *in* Herman, Y., ed., Marine geology and oceanography of the Arctic seas: New York, Springer-Verlag, p. 191–210.

Novysh, V. V., and Fonarev, G. A., 1966, Some results of electromagnetic investigations in the Arctic Ocean: Geomagnetism and Aerenomy, v. 6, p. 325–327.

Ostenso, N. A., and Wold, R. J., 1971, Aeromagnetic survey of the Arctic Ocean; Techniques and interpretations: Marine Geophysical Researches, v. 1, p. 178–219.

Parfenov, L. M., Voivona, I. P., Natal'in, B. A., and Semenov, D. F., 1978, Geodynamics of the north-eastern Asia in Mesozoic and Cenozoic time and the nature of volcanic belts: Journal of Physics of the Earth, v. 26, p. S503–S525.

Piskarev, A. L., Avetisov, G. P., Genin, B. L., and Larin, S. M., 1975, Structure of Zemlya Bunge and its zones of articulation with Kotel'nyi and Faddeya Islands: Geofizicheskie Metody Razvedki v Arktike, v. 10, p. 35–40 [in Russian].

Pogrebitskii, Y. E., 1984, Tectonic map of the Arctic Ocean and adjacent territories, *in* Gramberg, I. S., and Pogrebitskii, Y. E., eds., Geological structure of the USSR and distribution of mineral resources, v. 9, Seas of the Soviet Arctic: Leningrad, Nedra, scale 1:15,000,000.

Pol'kin, Y. I., 1984, Chukchi Sea, *in* Gramberg, I. S., and Pogrebitskii, Y. E., eds., Geologic structure of the USSR and distribution of mineral resources, v. 9, Seas of the Soviet Arctic: Leningrad, Nedra, p. 67–79.

Pushcharovskiy, Y. M., 1960, Some general problems of the Arctic zone: Izvestiya Academy of Sciences of the USSR, Geology Series, no. 9, p. 11–24.

Pushcharovskiy, Y. M., 1976, Tectonics of the Arctic Ocean Basin: Geotectonics, v. 10, p. 85–91.

Rowley, D. B., Lottes, A. L., and Ziegler, A. M., 1985, North America–Greenland–Eurasia relative motions; Implications for circum-Arctic tectonic reconstructions [abs.]: American Association of Petroleum Geologists Bulletin, v. 69, p. 303.

Savostin, L. A., Natapov, L. M., and Stavsky, A. P., 1984, Mesozoic paleogeodynamics and paleogeography of the Arctic region, *in* Arctic geology, reports, v. 4, 27th International Geological Congress, Moscow: Moskva, Nauka, p. 217–237.

Seslavinskiy, K. B., 1970, Structure and development of the South Anyui fault trough, west Chukotka: Geotectonics, v. 4, p. 311–317.

——, 1979, The South Anyui geosuture, western Chukotka: Doklady Academy of Sciences of the USSR, Earth Science Sections, v. 249, p. 78–81.

Shabad, T., 1984, New notes: Polar Geography and Geology, v. 8, p. 166–172.

Shilo, N. A., and Til'man, S. M., 1981, The tectonic zones of northeastern USSR and the formation of its continental crust, *in* Nairn, A.E.M., Churkin, M., Jr., Stehli, F. G., The ocean basins and margin, v. 5, The Arctic Ocean: New York, Plenum, p. 413–438.

Shilo, N. A., Merzlyakov, V. M., Terekhov, M. I., and Til'man, S. M., 1973, The Alazeya-Oloy geosynclinal system, a new structure in the Mesozoides of the northeastern USSR: Doklady Academy of Sciences of the USSR, Earth Science Sections, v. 210, p. 99–101.

Shilo, N. A., Vashchilov, Y. Y., Maksimov, V. Y., Malinovskiy, S. B., and Senetarov, Y. Y., 1982, New data on abyssal structure of the southwestern Chukchi Sea based on gravimetric surveys: Doklady Academy of Sciences of the USSR, Earth Science Sections, v. 265, p. 79–81.

Starokadomskiy, L. M., 1976, Charting the Russian northern sea route: Montreal, McGill-Queens University Press, 332 p.

Tailleur, I. L., 1973, Probable rift origin of Canada Basin, Arctic Ocean, *in* Pitcher, M. G., ed., Arctic geology: American Association of Petroleum Geologists Memoir 19, p. 526–535.

Til'man, S. M., 1970, Wrangel Island [Geologic Map], *in* Tkachenko, B. V., and Egiazarov, B. K., eds., Geology of the USSR, v. 26, Islands of the Soviet Arctic: Moskva, Nedra, scale 1:1,500,000.

Til'man, S. M., Bogdanov, N. A., Byalobzheskii, S. G., and Chekhov, A. D., 1970, Wrangel Island, *in* Tkachenko, B. V., and Egiazarov, B. K., eds., Geology of the USSR, v. 26, Islands of the Soviet Arctic: Moskva, Nedra, p. 377–404 [in Russian].

Til'man, S. M., and Byalobzhesky, S. G., 1984, Tectonic evolution of the East Arctic system, *in* Arctic geology, reports, v. 4, 27th International Geological Congress, Moscow: Moskva, Nauka, p. 103–109.

Trufanov, G. V., and Bakulenko, A. S., 1978, Eocene coal measures on the Novosibirsk Islands: Soviet Geology and Geophysics, v. 19, p. 119–121.

Vakar, V. A., 1970, History of geologic investigations in the islands of the Soviet Arctic, *in* Tkachenko, B. V., and Egiazarov, B. K., eds., Geology of the USSR, v. 26, Islands of the Soviety Arctic: Moskva, Nedra, p. 9–21 [in Russian].

Vinogradov, V. A., 1984, Laptev Sea, *in* Gramberg, I. S., and Pogrebitskii, Y. E., eds., Geologic structure of the USSR and distribution of mineral resources, v. 9, Seas of the Soviet Arctic: Leningrad, Nedra, p. 50–60 [in Russian].

Vinogradov, V. A., Dibner, A. F., and Samusin, A. I., 1974a, Identification of Permian sediments on Bol'shoy Lyakhov Island: Doklady Academy of Sciences of the USSR, Earth Science Sections, v. 219, p. 84–86.

Vinogradov, V. A., Gaponenko, G. I., Rusakov, I. M., and Shimaraev, V. N., 1974b, Tectonics of the eastern Arctic shelves of the USSR: Leningrad, Nedra, 144 p. [in Russian].

Vinogradov, V. A., Kameneva, G. I., and Yavshits, G. P., 1975, On the Hyperborean platform in light of new data on the geologic structure of Henrietta Island: Tektonika Arktiki, v. 1, p. 21–25 [in Russian].

Vinogradov, V. A., Gaponenko, G. I., Gramberg, I. S., and Shimarayev, V. N., 1977, Structural-associational complexes of the Arctic shelf of eastern Siberia: International Geology Review, v. 19, p. 1331–1343.

Volk, V. E., and Gaponenko, G. I., 1984, Analysis of physical fields and the deep regionalization of the Earth's crust, *in* Gramberg, I. S., and Pogrebitskii, Y. E., eds., Geological structure of the USSR and distribution of mineral resources, v. 9, Seas of the Soviet Arctic: Leningrad, Nedra, p. 98–110 [in Russian].

Volk, V. E., Gaponenko, G. I., Zatzepin, E. N., Kiselev, Y. G., Lastochkina, N. N., Malyavkin, A. M., Shimaraev, V. N., Shchelovanov, V. G., and Kraev, A. G., 1984, Crustal structure of the Arctic inferred from geophysical data, *in* Arctic geology, reports, v. 4, 27th International Geological Congress, Moscow: Moskva, Nauka, p. 30–41.

Vol'nov, D.A., 1975, History of the geologic development of the New Siberian Islands region, *in* Geology and mineral resources of the New Siberian Islands and Wrangel Island: Leningrad, Nauchno-Issledovatel'skii Institut Geologii Arktiki, p. 61–71 [in Russian].

Vol'nov, D. A., Voitsekhovskii, V. N., Ivanov, O. A., Sorokov, D. S., and Yashin,

D. S., 1970a, New Siberian Islands, *in* Tkachenko, B. V., and Egiazarov, B. K., eds., Geology of the USSR, v. 26, Islands of the Soviet Arctic: Moskva, Nedra, p. 324–374.

Vol'nov, D. A., Sorokov, D. S., and Ivanov, O. A., 1970b, Geological map of the New Siberian Islands, *in* Tkachenko, B. V., and Egiazarov, B. K., eds., Geology of the USSR, v. 26, Islands of the Soviet Arctic: Moskva, Nedra, scale 1:1,500,000.

Zhizhina, M. S., 1959, Age of Paleozoic deposits on the Kotel'nyy Island: Izvestiya Academy of Sciences of the USSR, Geologic Series, no. 4, p. 90–91.

MANUSCRIPT ACCEPTED BY THE SOCIETY NOVEMBER 24, 1986

ACKNOWLEDGMENTS

We thank A. M. Ziegler and M. Churkin, Jr., for their encouragement and for stimulating our interest in northeastern Siberia. V. Vinogradov, A. Grantz, A. Green, and D. W. Scholl provided copies of Soviet papers, which were of great assistance. W. Muehlberger and S. Adamek helped to obtain copies of Soviet maps. J. T. Wilband, F. W. Cambray, and D. D. Jessup helped us to sort out some of the petrologic and structural data. We thank C. S. Cameron and J. W. Clarke for their comments and M. Churkin, Jr., and L. Z. Lipkov for their reviews and comments. R. G. Gordon, G. L. Johnson, and E. R. Wicander helped us with problems in interpreting Soviet data. M. P. Cecile and K. Burke provided us with data prior to publication and with very helpful comments and criticisms. M. J. Fujita and M. A. Velbel helped to edit the text. This research was supported in part by Office of Naval Research contract N00014-83-K-6093.

NOTE ADDED IN PROOF

Subsequent to the submission of this manuscript, several summary papers of the geology of the region, as well as new data, have been published, and additional data have been called to my attention. A Soviet overview of the region, with detailed geologic maps of Kotel'nyi and Wrangel Islands, has been prepared by Kos'ko and others (1990). A detailed review of the geology of Wrangel Island, including the results of their visit, was summarized by Cecile and Harrison (1987), and an overview of the tectonic problems of Wrangel Island was published by Kos'ko (1986). Savostin and others (1988) published geochemistry and descriptions of the basalts of Zhokhov Island (similar to oceanic islands).

The western margin of the North American plate, within the Laptev Sea, was suggested by Fujita and others (1990) to be a region of asymmetric simple-shear rifting, and Grachev and others (1985) quantified the post-Pliocene uplift on Kotel'nyi Island as 100 m.

Savostin and Drachev (1988) identified compressional structures along Strelka Anzhu and on Novaya Sibir' Island and ascribed them to compression between North America and Eurasia in the Oligocene and the earliest Miocene, while Grosval'd (1988) has suggested that the arcuate topographic and bathymetric features in and around the New Siberian Islands were due to shelf-based glaciers that nucleated in the region of the De Long Islands.

Dudko and Spektor (1989) interpreted potential field data to the west of the Kolyma River and suggested that several island arcs and collisional zones are present under one to two kilometers of terrigenous Cenozoic sediments, forming the continuation of the South Anyui suture zone. The existence of an ophiolite zone on Bolshoi Lyakhov Island is confirmed by Spektor and others (1981) and also inferred by them to underlie the entire northern edge of the buried part of the South Anyui zone.

A "zebra stripe" magnetic anomaly map, including the continental shelf of eastern Siberia, was published by Verba and others (1986), and Gusev and Rakhin (1977) presented paleomagnetic pole data from the Devonian and Carboniferous of Kotel'nyi suggesting a pole around 65°N, 158°W.

Finally, Zonenshain and Natapov (1987) have proposed a model for the evolution of the Arctic suggesting the Cretaceous breakup of an "Arctida" continent, which included the present day East Siberian shelf, while a more recent vertical tectonic interpretation of the shelf is presented by Gramberg and others (1986).

REFERENCES CITED

Cecile, M. P., and Harrison, J. C., 1987, Review of the geology of Wrangel Island, Chukchi and East Siberian Sea, far northeastern Soviet Union: Geological Survey of Canada, Open-File Report 1655, 109 p.

Dundo, E. A., and Spektor, V. B., 1989, Northwestern continuation of the South Anyui folded zone in the lower course of the Kolyma: Geologiya i Geofizika, no. 2, p. 21–31 (in Russian).

Fujita, K., Cambray, F. W., and Velbel, M. A., 1990, Tectonics of the Laptev Sea and Moma rift systems, northeast USSR: Tectonophysics (in press).

Grachev, A. F., Kulakov, Y. N., and Puminov, A. P., 1985, Neotectonic map, *in* Treshnikov, A. F., ed., Atlas of the Arctic: Moskva, GUGK, p. 62–63, scale 1:10,000,000 (in Russian).

Gramberg, I. S., Kos'ko, M. K., and Pogrebitskii, Y. E., 1986, Tectonic evolution of the Arctic shelf of Siberia from Riphean through Mesozoic time: International Geology Review, v. 28, p. 943–954.

Grosval'd, M. G., 1988, Priznaki pokrovnogo oledeneniya New Siberian Island and okruzhayuschchesgo shelf: Doklady AN CCCP, v. 302, p. 654–659 (in Russian).

Gusev, B. V., and Rakhin, V. A., 1977, Geologic results of paleomagnetic investigations in the New Siberian Islands, *in* Gaponenko, G. I., ed., Problems of geophysical investigations in the Polar regions of the Earth: Leningrad, Nauchno-Issledovatel'skii Institut Geologii Arktiki, p. 24–34 (in Russian).

Kos'ko, M. K., 1986, Basic problems of the geology of Wrangel Island, *in* Egiazarov, B. K., and Kazmin, Y. B., eds., Structure and history of development of the Arctic Ocean: Leningrad, PGO Sevmorgeologiya, p. 87–103 (in Russian).

Kos'ko, M. K., Lopatin, B. G., and Ganelin, V. G., 1990, Major geological features of the islands of the East Siberian and Chukchi Seas and the northern coast of Chukotka: Tectonophysics (in press).

Savostin, L. A., and Drachev, S. S., 1988, Cenozoic compression in the region of the New Siberian Islands and its relationship to the opening of the Eurasia basin: Okeanologiya, v. 28, p. 775–781 (in Russian).

Savostin, L. A., Silant'ev, S. A., and Bogdanovskii, O. G., 1988, New data about the volcanism of Zhokhov Island (De Long Archipelago, Arctic basin): Doklady Akademii Nauk SSSR, v. 302, p. 1443–1447 (in Russian).

Spektor, V. B., Andrusenko, A. M., Dunko, E. A., and Kareva, N. F., 1981, Continuation of the South Anyui suture in the Primorya lowlands: Doklady Akademii Nauk SSSR, v. 260, p. 1447–1450 (in Russian).

Verba, V. V., Volk, V. E., Kiselev, Y. G., and Kraev, A. G., 1986, Deep structure of the Arctic Ocean according to geophysical data, *in* Egiazarov, B. K., and Kazmin, Y. B., eds., Structure and history of development of the Arctic Ocean: Leningrad, PGO Sevmorgeologiya, p. 54–71 (in Russian).

Zonenshain, L. P., and Natapov, L. M., 1987, Tectonic history of the Arctic, *in* Timofeev, P. P., ed., Present-day problems of the tectonics of oceans and continents: Moskva, Nauka, p. 31–57 (in Russian).

The Geology of North America
Vol. L, The Arctic Ocean Region
The Geological Society of America, 1990

Chapter 18

Ridges and basins in the central Arctic Ocean

J. R. Weber
Geophysics Division, Geological Survey of Canada, 1 Observatory Crescent, Ottawa, Ontario K1A 0Y3, Canada
J. F. Sweeney
Geological Survey of Canada, 100 West Pender, Vancouver, British Columbia V6B 1R8, Canada

INTRODUCTION

This chapter describes the physiography plus the geological and geophysical character of the central Arctic. The available information is chiefly from work done on several ice station transits of the area together with aeromagnetic and satellite magnetic investigations. The data provide crude constraints on the nature and ages of the main sea-floor features of the central Arctic Ocean.

The central area of the Arctic Ocean contains abyssal depths that are traversed by two subparallel submarine mountain ranges, the Lomonosov Ridge and the Alpha-Mendeleev Ridge complex. The wedge-shaped Makarov Basin separates these adjacent ranges, which are close to North America and are more than 500 km apart at their junction with the East Siberian continental margin (Fig. 1). Significant difference in overall morphology and geophysical properties between the Lomonosov and Alpha Ridges, despite their juxtaposition near North America, suggests a complex structural evolution for the central Arctic, whose origins are constrained loosely within the late Early Cretaceous–earliest Tertiary interval.

PHYSIOGRAPHY

Lomonosov Ridge

The Lomonosov Ridge is an aseismic submarine mountain range that bisects the Arctic Ocean basin into the Eurasia and Amerasia basins. It extends over a distance of 1,700 km from the Lincoln Sea continental shelf to the continental shelf off the New Siberian Islands (Fig. 1). The Lomonosov Ridge rises over 3 km above the adjacent Amundsen Basin, which flanks the ridge on the Eurasia side, and rises 2 km above the Makarov Basin on the Amerasia side. The ridge is a relatively narrow, linear, steep-sided, flat-topped feature paralleling the 43°W/137°E meridians. Above the 3,500 m isobath it is some 200 km wide over most of its length except near the North Pole where it narrows to 65 km. Toward the Lincoln Sea the ridge widens considerably and appears to veer to the southwest, apparently merging with the Alpha Ridge toward Ellesmere Island.

The Lomonosov Ridge was discovered by the Soviets in 1948 during the High Latitude Air Expeditions. Systematic soundings during the same and the following year revealed the outline of a massive mountain range (Burkhanov, 1956). Gakkel compiled the first contour map of the ridge in 1949, but the information was kept secret until 1954 (Weber, 1983). Unaware of the Soviet exploration, Worthington (1953) speculated, based on water temperature and salinity measurements, that there was a submarine ridge running roughly from Ellesmere to the New Siberian Islands. During 1952, U.S. scientists on board the ice island T-3 mapped part of the south flank of the Lomonosov Ridge between 90° and 165°W. Crary (1954) speculated that the ridge might well rise to within 1,000 m of sea level. With the exception of 285 soundings that were released as a contribution to the 1957 to 1958 International Geophysical Year (IGY; Gudkovich, 1955), Soviet bathymetric data remains highly confidential. As a result, cartographers mapping the Lomonosov Ridge had to rely on generalized contours of early small-scale Soviet maps and on information obtained from early U.S. submarines that cruised in the polar area between 1958 and 1962 and whose navigation was questionable (Dietz and Shumway, 1961; Beal, 1969). The only reliable early bathymetric data available were from the U.S. drifting ice station ARLIS II, which in 1964 crossed the Lomonosov Ridge obliquely from 88°30′N to 86°30′N latitude between the 100°W and 40°W meridians (Ostenso and Wold, 1977). In 1979 the Canadian Department of Energy, Mines, and Resources (EMR) carried out a systematic survey of the Lomonosov Ridge in the polar area (Weber, 1979). The operation was code-named LOREX 79 (Lomonosov Ridge Experiment) and it resulted in the compilation of a 100-m-contour map of the central part of the Lomonosov Ridge (Fig. 2). The LOREX results revealed that the Lomonosov Ridge consists of several slightly tilted, en echelon fault blocks with scarps facing the Makarov Basin (Blasco and others, 1979). The Makarov-facing slope (up to 14°) is much steeper than the Amundsen-facing slope (not exceeding 6°). The shallowest depth recorded on top of the ridge was 955 m.

Weber, J. R., and Sweeney, J. F., 1990, Ridges and basins in the central Arctic Ocean, *in* Grantz, A., Johnson, L., and Sweeney, J. F., eds., The Arctic Ocean region: Boulder, Colorado, Geological Society of America, The Geology of North America, v. L.

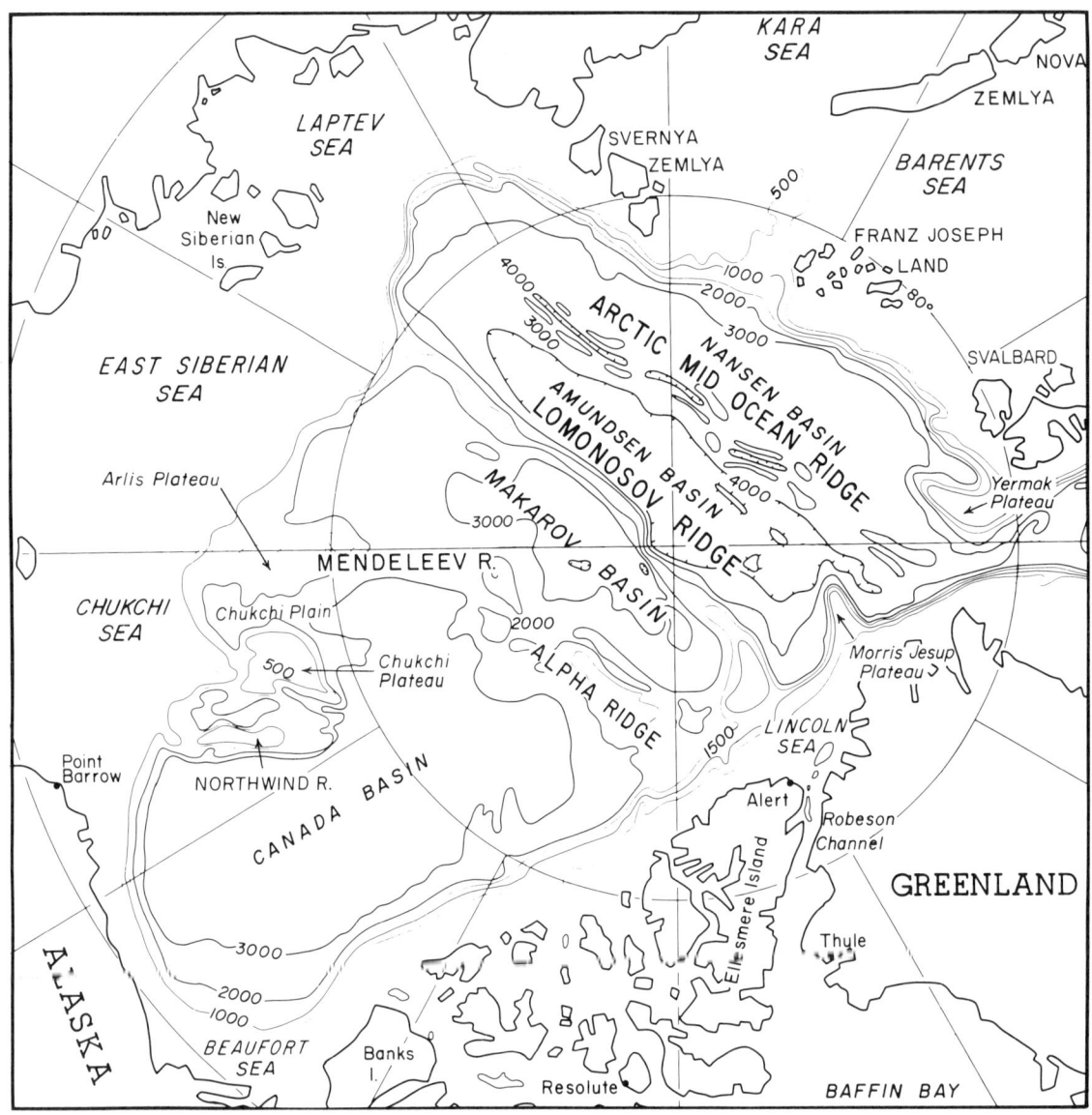

Figure 1. Overview map of the Arctic Ocean.

Publicly available bathymetric data on the remainder of the Lomonosov Ridge toward Siberia and toward Lincoln Sea, including the junctions with the continental shelves, are very scarce. On contemporary maps the contours in areas with little or no sounding data are based partly on early Soviet maps (Burkhanov, 1956; Gordienko and Laktionov, 1960) and partly on unpublished U.S. submarine data. The reliability of the maps in these areas is therefore difficult to assess. Contemporary maps suggest that the Siberian end of the Lomonosov Ridge is an extension of the continental shelf north of the New Siberian Islands while the North American end of the Lomonosov-Alpha Ridge complex appears to be separated from the continental shelf off Ellesmere Island by a trough of between 1,500 and 2,000 m depth (Plate 1).

Makarov Basin

Between the Lomonosov Ridge and the Alpha-Mendeleev Ridge complex lies the Makarov Basin. It contains two abyssal plains: The Wrangel Plain at 2,825 m depth adjoins the East Siberian Shelf; it connects, via Arlis Gap, with the deeper Siberia Plain at a depth of 3,940 m (Kutschale, 1966). The Makarov Basin is wedge shaped and narrows toward Ellesmere Island from a width of more than 500 km along the East Siberian Shelf.

The Marvin Spur (Fig. 3) juts out some 120 km (at the 3,000 m isobath) into the Siberia Plain. The flank facing the Lomonosov Ridge extends toward Ellesmere Island for at least 400 km, paralleling the 40°W/140°E meridian. Crary (1954)

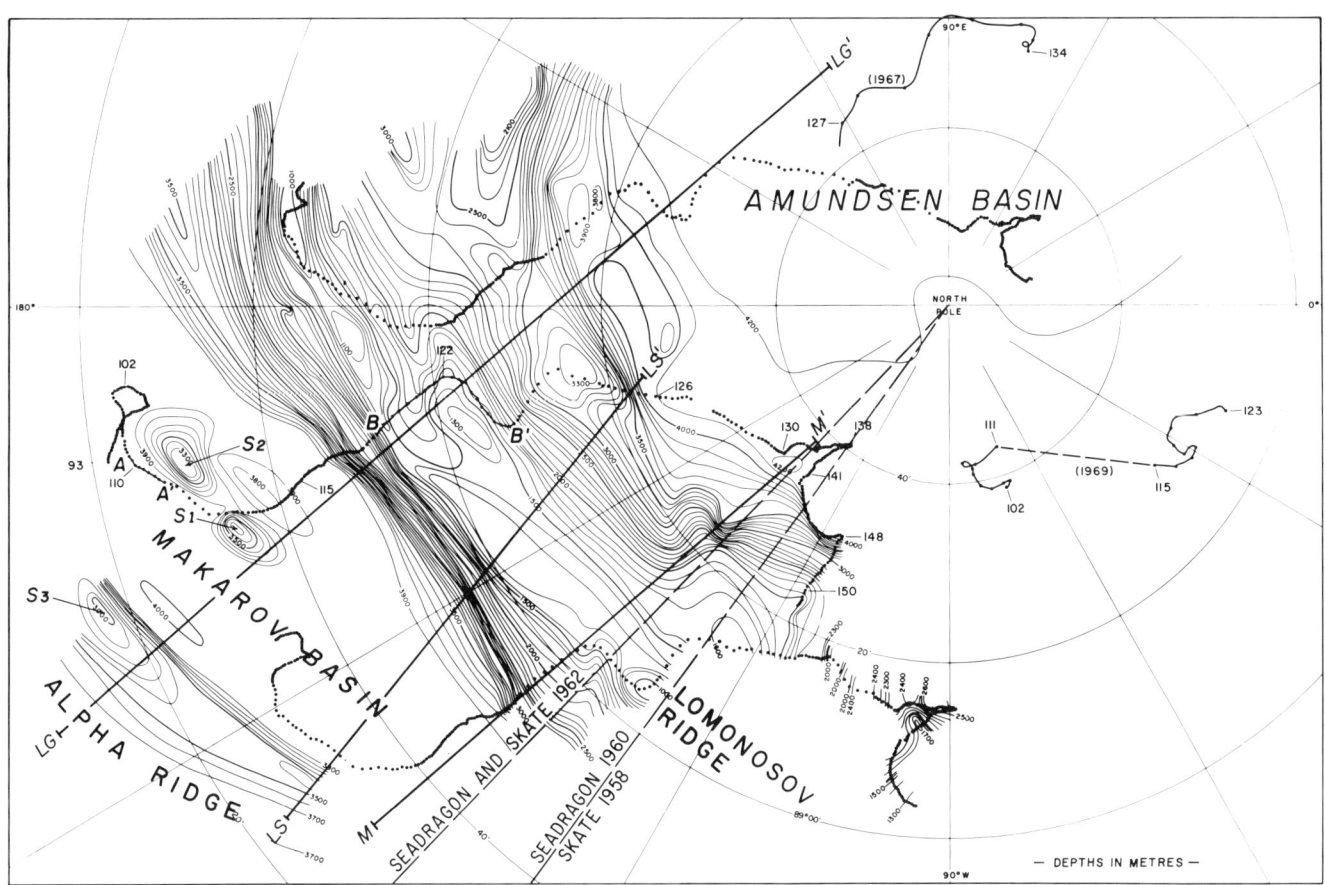

Figure 2. LOREX bathymetric map. Contour interval 100 m. Dotted lines represent drift tracks of the LOREX main camp and two satellite camps with 3-hr intervals between dots; numbers represent Julian days. Drift track portions A–A' and B–B' represent sections of the subbottom profiles of Figures 7a, b. LG–LG', LS–LS', and M–M' represent locations of gravity, seismic refraction, and magnetic models, respectively. For description of bathymetric features S_1, S_2, and S_3 see text. Also shown are the tracks of the submarines whose echograms are illustrated in Figure 7 of Johnson and others, this volume (profiles E, F, G).

compiled a remarkably good sea-floor map, which delineates 300 km of the Marvin Spur as a long, steep, continuous, and northerly facing escarpment with scarps that rise from 500 to 1,500 m and slopes of up to 23°. From 1962 to 1964, ice island ARLIS II drifted the length of the Makarov Basin from the East Siberian Shelf across Wrangel and Siberia plains and obliquely across the Lomonosov Ridge to Morris Jesup Plateau. A steep drop of 1,650 m was recorded when it traversed the escarpment drifting north on the 105°W meridian (Ostenso and Wold, 1977). The Marvin Spur was described by Beal and others (1966) as a feature bisecting the Makarov Basin between the Alpha and Lomonosov ridges. Weber and Sweeney (1985) have suggested that this escarpment is the Lomonosov-facing flank of the Alpha Ridge. Between the escarpment and the Lomonosov Ridge, the Makarov Basin is a wedge-shaped grabenlike trough initially 70 km wide and narrowing to an area where the Alpha and Lomonosov ridges merge. This trough is infilled with at least 2 km of horizontally stratified sediments (Overton, 1982).

Alpha-Mendeleev Ridge complex

The Alpha-Mendeleev Ridge complex is the largest submarine mountain complex in the Arctic Ocean. In areal extent it exceeds that of the Alps. It is about the same length, slightly deeper, much wider, and topographically much more complicated than the Lomonosov Ridge and it separates the Makarov Basin from the Canada Basin.

Although isolated areas of the ridge had first been discovered earlier by the Soviets (Gordienko and Laktionov, 1960), the Alpha Ridge was first recognized as a distinct submarine feature by U.S. scientists aboard the drifting station ALPHA during the IGY (Hunkins, 1961).

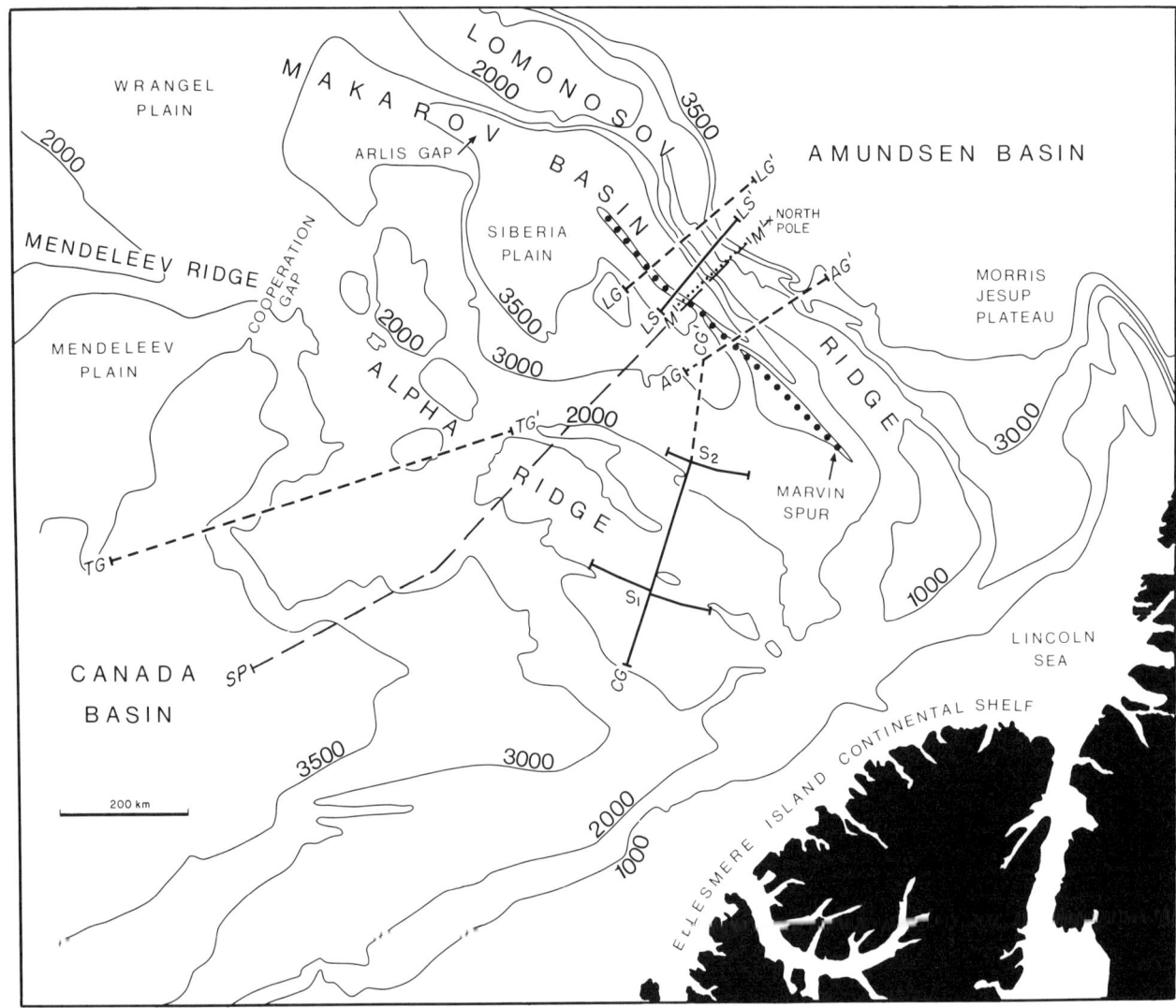

Figure 3. Overview map of the central Arctic Ocean. Dotted line shows location of Marvin Spur. Lines LG–LG', CG–CG', AG–AG', and TG–TG' indicate locations of LOREX, CESAR, ARLIS II, and T-3 gravity profiles, respectively. LS–LS' shows location of LOREX seismic refraction profile. Solid lines across and along Alpha Ridge show locations of CESAR seismic refraction dip and strike profiles. M–M' is the location of the magnetic profile. S_1 and S_2 are the locations of the seismic crustal depth determinations shown in Figure 12. Broken line SP shows submarine track of *Skate* and *Seadragon* of Figure 5. Contour lines are taken from Perry and others (1985).

The Alpha Ridge is a rugged, broad, fractured arch with long ridges and valleys striking in the direction of its axis. Where the sounding density is high, many short-wavelength topographic features in the form of seamounts and depressions appear. The ridge has a symmetrical appearance with the highest elevation at the center (see Fig. 5, Johnson and others, this volume). The CESAR station drifted over two ridge crests and a large intervening valley that was identified by Hall (1970) and referred to by him as Alpha Ridge Graben (Weber and Jackson, 1985).

The physiography of the Mendeleev Ridge shows a similar broad fractured arch, although perhaps not so rough as the Alpha Ridge crestal region.

Much of the topography of the ridge complex is known from the soundings carried out from U.S. drifting ice stations: ALPHA 1957 to 1958 (Cabaniss, 1962); T-3 in 1953 to 1957, 1962 to 1963, and 1966 to 1974 (Hunkins and Tiemann, 1977); and ARLIS II 1962 to 1964 (Wold, 1973); and from early submarine echograms (see profiles A to H in Fig. 5, Johnson and others, this volume). Hall (1970) carried out a comprehensive study of the Alpha and Mendeleev ridges based on the sounding, seismic, gravity, magnetic, and coring results collected on board these drifting stations. In 1983 the Canadian Department of Energy, Mines, and Resources (EMR) carried out a multidisciplinary expedition to study the Alpha Ridge, code-named CESAR 83. In cooperation with the Canadian Hydrographic Service (CHS), some 1,300 spot soundings were taken from the coast of Ellesmere Island over the continental shelf and Alpha Ridge to the 120°W meridian. Figure 4 incorporates all publicly available sounding data from U.S. stations T-3, ALPHA, ARLIS II, U.S. airlifted stations, CHS stations, Canadian North Pole Expeditions 1967 and 1969, LOREX 79, and CESAR 83.

Morphologically, the Alpha Ridge merges with the Lomonosov Ridge some 350 km off the coast of Ellesmere Island. At the junction with the Ellesmere Island Continental Shelf, the Alpha-Lomonosov complex is about 700 km wide above the 3,000 m isobath. It is separated from the continental shelf by a relatively smooth trough between 1,500 and 2,000 m deep. The Alpha Ridge narrows to 120 km midway between North America and Eurasia, where Belov and Lapina (1958) report the crest to consist of a long, deep trough with a maximum depth of 2,700 m. This depression, named Cooperation Gap by Treshnikov and others (1966), divides the ridge into two distinct topographic features, the Alpha Ridge on the Canadian side and the Mendeleev Ridge on the Siberian side. The Mendeleev Ridge widens southward and joins the East Siberian Shelf via the Arlis Plateau. The transition from ridge to shelf appears smooth, with no apparent trough separating the two.

The echograms of the U.S. nuclear submarines *Skate* and *Seadragon*, which sailed from the North Pole across the Lomonosov and Alpha ridges along the 135° meridian in 1962, are reproduced from Beal (1969) in Figure 5, top. Their cruise tracks are shown in Figures 2 and 3 and also as profiles E and F in Figure 5 of Johnson and others (this volume). These submarines were equipped with an early inertial navigation system that was quite inaccurate, and they had to surface from time to time to obtain celestial position fixes (Beal, 1983; Lyon, 1984). In these echograms, echo travel time is converted to depth without correction for the variation of water velocity with depth. The bathymetric profile at the bottom of Figure 5 has been obtained from the *Skate* echogram by correcting depth values and by adjusting for apparent errors in navigation to fit the newly compiled bathymetric data.

GEOLOGICAL AND GEOPHYSICAL CHARACTER

Lomonosov Ridge and Makarov Basin

Early studies. In 1952 the ice island T-3 made four complete traverses of the Makarov Basin between the Marvin Spur and the southern flank of the Lomonosov Ridge (Crary and Goldstein, 1957). Seismic reflection and refraction measurements revealed that the ocean floor on either side of the Marvin Spur consists of 250 to 300 m of undisturbed sediments with a seismic velocity of about 2 km/s. The most northerly profile, approximately along the 167° meridian across the Makarov Basin (Fig. 8 in Crary and Goldstein, 1957), shows 1.8 km of horizontally stratified sediments abutting the Lomonosov Ridge flank, very similar to Overton's reflection profile located a few degrees further west (Fig. 6).

Carrying out seismic reflection and shallow seismic refraction measurements, gravity observations, magnetic measurements, and coring from ice station ARLIS II, Kutschale (1966) reported the discovery of a prominent subbottom basement ridge in the vicinity of Arlis Gap (Fig. 3) running in a direction subparallel to the East Siberian Continental Slope. It appears to form a dam that has permitted the accumulation of a thick sequence of at least 3.5 km, and possibly 5 to 7 km, of horizontally stratified sediments under the higher level Wrangel Plain. Turbidity currents may have transported the overflow of pelagic sediments through Arlis Gap into the lower-level Siberia Plain where they are interspersed with glacial marine material (Ericson and others, 1964). A crustal model based on bathymetry, seismic reflection, gravity, ice station magnetic, and airborne magnetic (Ostenso, 1962) measurements yields a crustal thickness (including water depth) of 22 km under the buried ridge and 15 km in the Wrangel Plain south of the ridge. Kutschale postulated that the Wrangel Plain sediments were deposited on a 6- to 8-km-thick oceanic crust.

In the 1960s Soviet scientists carried out heat-flow measurements from the drift station North Pole 15 in the area between 85°50′ to 89°40′N and 145° to 158°W (Lubimova and others, 1969; Tomara, 1973). The observed values were inconclusive, ranging from 43 to 105 mWm^{-2}, and no consistent pattern emerges from their 13 casts (Judge and Jessop, 1978).

Sykes (1965) relocated all well-recorded earthquakes in the Arctic for the previous ten years. This study indicated that for the Lomonosov Ridge, Alpha Ridge, and intervening Makarov Basin the seismicity is below the detection threshold of about 3.5 on the Richter scale.

During the Second Canadian North Pole Expedition in 1969, plumb-line deflection measurements and gravity observations were carried out in the vicinity of the North Pole and across the nearby Lomonosov Ridge (Lillestrand and Weber, 1974). The observed plumb-line deflections were in good agreement with the values predicted from a model constructed assuming the ridge to be in isostatic equilibrium and composed of sedimentary rocks (densities between 2.2 and 2.5 Mg/m^3) underlain by a continental-type crust 27 km thick and a crust-mantle density contrast of 0.22 Mg/m^3. Gravity measurements were consistent with the free-air gravity anomaly computed from the same model. These early measurements supported the view, first put forward by Heezen and Ewing (1961) and later expanded by Wilson (1963), that the Lomonosov Ridge represents a rafted sliver of the Kara and Barents continental shelves (Smith, 1974).

During 1964 the ice island ARLIS II drifted across the Lomonosov Ridge some 450 km north of Ellesmere Island. Shallow seismic reflection and gravity measurements carried out over the ridge from ARLIS II indicated that the ridge was made up of

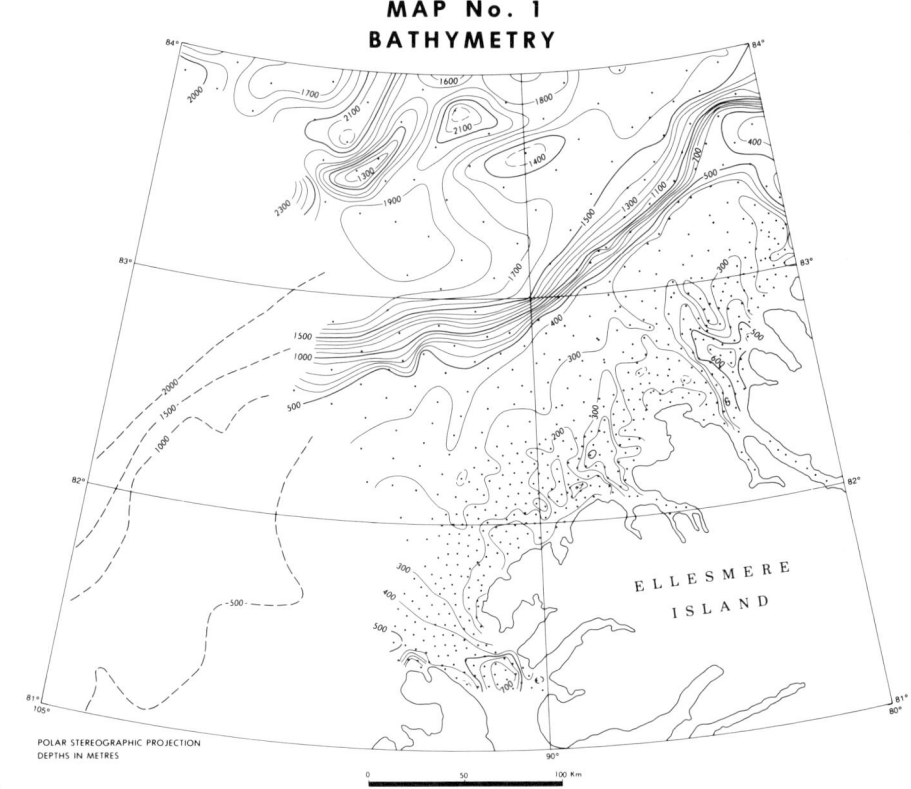

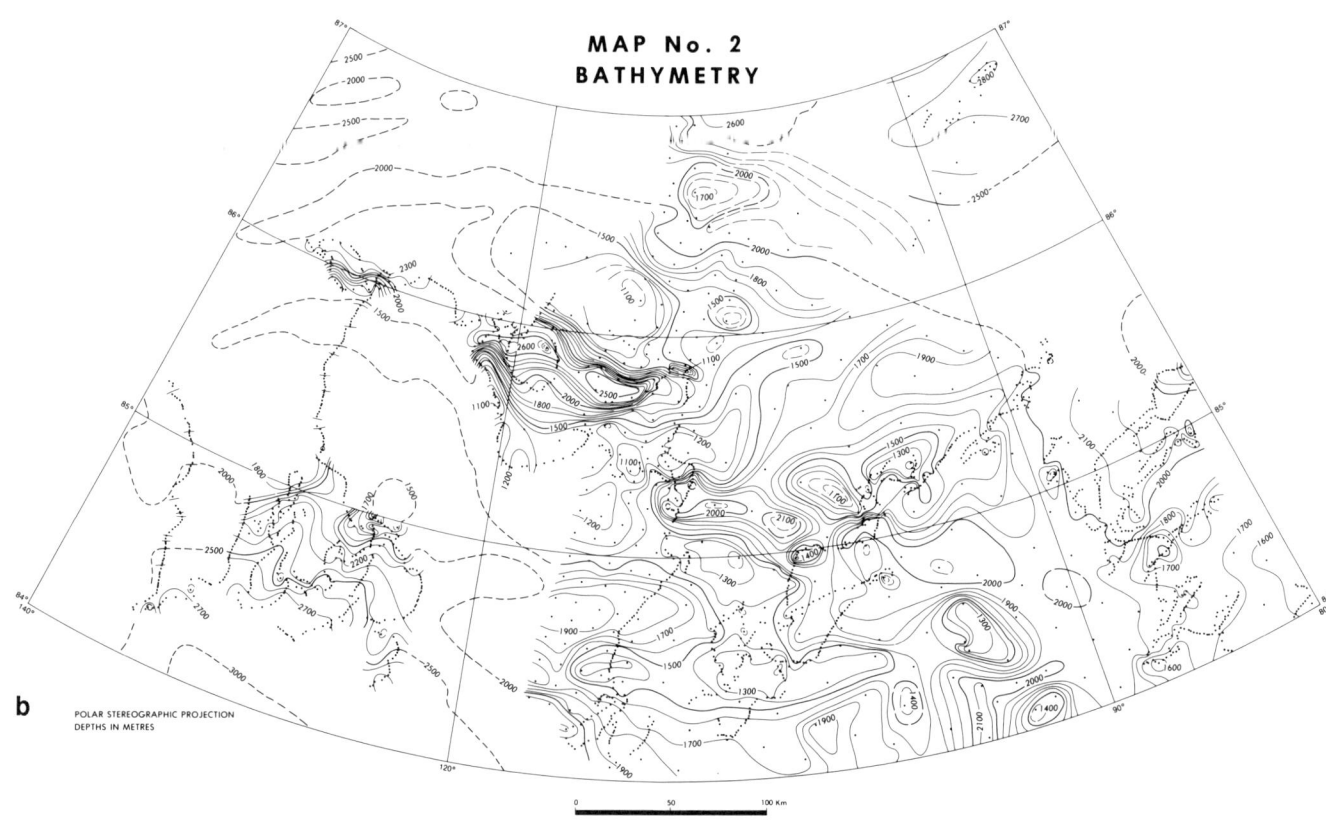

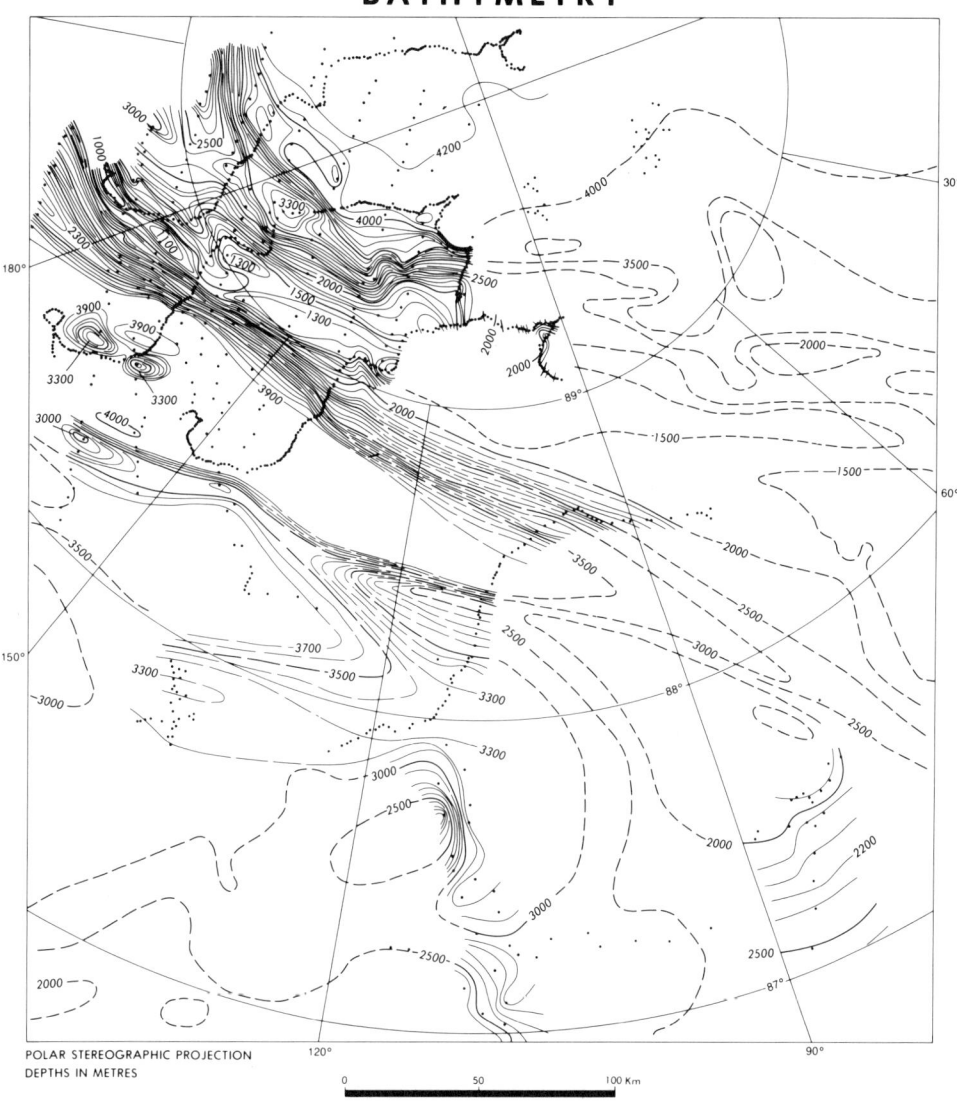

Figure 4a–c (this and facing page). Bathymetric map of the Alpha and Lomonosov ridges compiled from LOREX, CESAR, T3, ARLIS II, and ALPHA data. Contour interval 100 m. Consecutive dots are drift tracks of ice stations, individual dots are locations of spot soundings. Uncharted areas have been filled in by 500 m dashed contour lines taken from "Bathymetry of the Arctic Ocean" by Perry and others (1985).

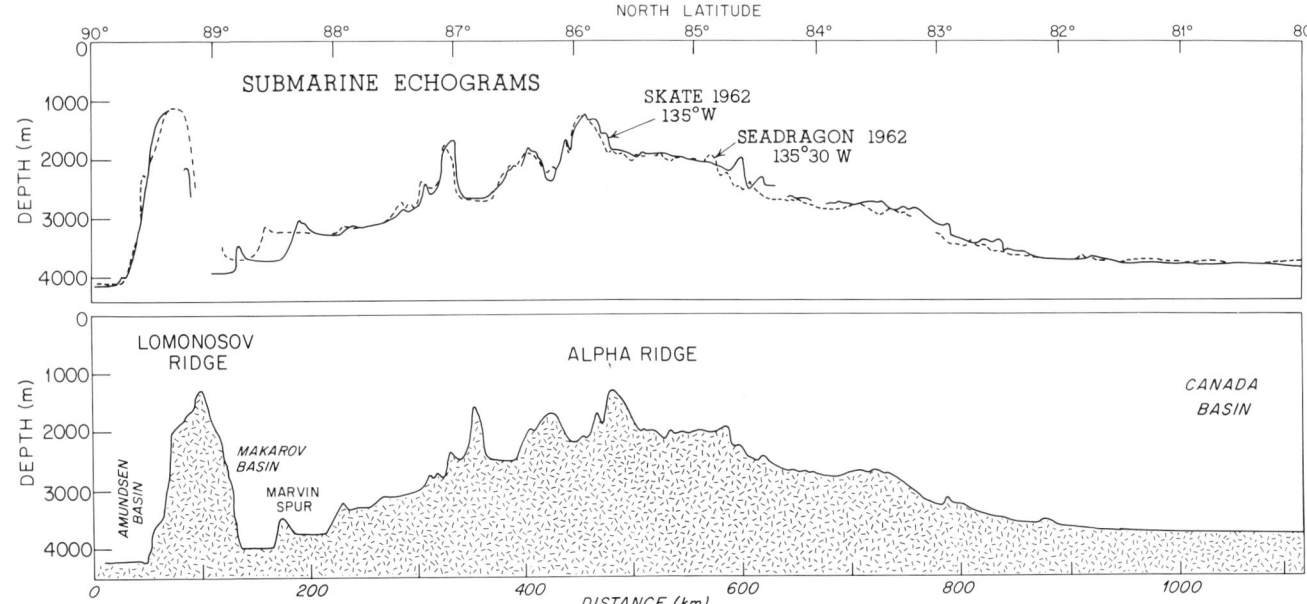

Figure 5. Top: Echograms from the U.S. nuclear submarines *Skate* and *Seadragon* that sailed from the North Pole along the 135°W meridian in 1962. Track is shown in Figure 3. Bottom: Depth profile compiled from the *Skate* corrected vertically and horizontally to fit the bathymetry on maps 2 and 3 in Figures 4b and c.

thick sedimentary sequences leaving "little doubt as to its continental origin." (Ostenso and Wold, 1977, p. 17). This was the first direct evidence for the continental nature of the Lomonosov Ridge.

Recent studies. The two-month-long LOREX survey constituted the first systematic, multidisciplinary study of the Lomonosov Ridge and adjoining Makarov Basin (Weber, 1979). While the main camp drifted with the Transpolar Current from the Makarov Basin across the Lomonosov Ridge into the Amundsen Basin, studies were carried out that included bathymetry and gravity measurements (Sweeney and others, 1982; Weber and Sweeney, 1985), high-resolution shallow seismic reflection profiling (Blasco and others, 1979) and intermediate depth reflection profiling of the sediment column and basement (Overton, 1982), crustal seismic refraction measurements (Mair and Forsyth, 1982; Forsyth and Mair, 1984), heat-flow measurements (Judge, 1980), magnetic induction and magnetotelluric observations (Camfield and others, 1980), an aeromagnetic reconnaissance survey (Hood and Bower, 1980), coring, dredging, and bottom photography (Blasco and others, 1979; Morris, 1983), and near-bottom current measurements (Aagaard, 1981).

Seabed geology. 1. Reflection seismic. Close to the Lomonosov Ridge, high-resolution seismic air-gun profiles reveal that both the Makarov and Amundsen basins are floored by horizontal layers of well-stratified, unconsolidated sediments, up to 1 km thick, which abut unconformably against the ridge flanks (Blasco and others, 1979). On the ridge, sediments are absent from the Makarov-facing flank where the average slope is as steep as 14°. The crest and the Amundsen-facing flank, whose slope does not exceed 6°, are covered with a thin veneer of stratified, unconsolidated sediments that lie conformably upon the underlying bedrock and appear to be slowly eroding by current scour. This is illustrated in the shallow seismic profiles A–A' in the Makarov Basin (Fig. 7a) and B–B' on the top of the ridge (Fig. 7b). The saw-toothed appearance of the crestal region, with Amundsen Basin–facing slopes covered by thin stratified sediments truncated by what appear to be scarps, suggests that the ridge consists of en echelon fault blocks (see also Fig. 4, p. 667, in Sweeney and others, 1982).

Below the Makarov Basin, results of the intermediate depth reflection seismic experiment (Overton, 1982) show an over 20-km-wide trough containing at least 2.1 km of sediments with a well-defined subhorizontal reflector, detected also by air-gun profiling, at about 1 km below the seabed (Fig. 6). The reflector appears conformable with the underlying sequences, and it may represent a temporary change in depositional environment.

2. Coring and dredging. Near-surface samples of the seabed were obtained by gravity coring, grab sampling, and dredging along the drift track of the LOREX Main Camp (Fig. 2). Overall, sediments recovered from abyssal depths are much finer grained than those retrieved from the ridge itself. Makarov Basin sediments, however, contain far more silt-rich interbeds than Amundsen Basin sediments, which are composed mainly of firm clay layers. Sediments recovered from the Lomonosov Ridge

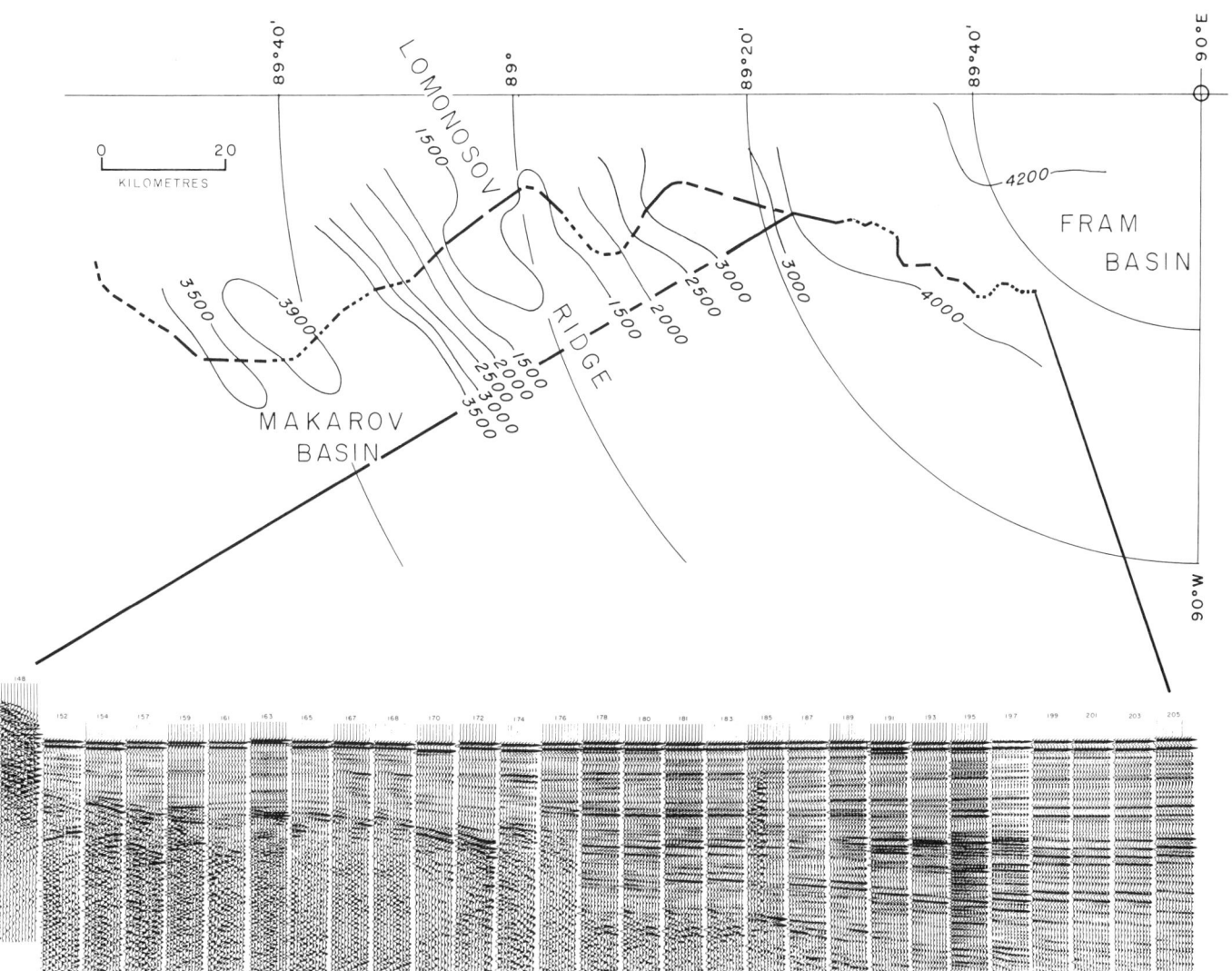

Figure 6. Intermediate depth reflection seismic profile across the Makarov Basin (from Overton, 1982). The depth from sea floor to end of records corresponds to about 2 seconds of two-way travel time.

contain almost no recognizable turbidites and have a large sand-sized fraction, dominantly quartz with minor feldspar (Blasco and others, 1979). Dredge samples from the ridge included fingernail-sized pieces of recrystallized dolomitized chalk, a manganese nodule, and a fragment of biotite schist. Bottom photographs show a coarse gravel pavement over much of the crest and Makarov flank of the ridge. Three types of microfossil populations have been recognized within the top few centimeters of a core recovered from the Amundsen flank of the ridge in 1,721 m of water: late Cenozoic pollen, mid-Cretaceous dinoflagellates, and Upper Devonian spore fragments that have been reworked several times (Blasco and others, 1979). The dinoflagellates and spores have undergone significant thermal alteration.

The 16 short sediment cores include most of the same stratigraphic units as those described from the Alpha-Chukchi areas, some 300 km distant. The LOREX cores include at least 12 sedimentary units differentiated by texture, color, and carbonate content. The units are silty and arenaceous lutites and are principally glacial-marine. Benthic and planktonic foraminifera, degree of bioturbation, and Fe-Mn micronodule abundance generally are positively correlated. Foraminifera in a core from 3,956 m in the Makarov Basin, have been affected by carbonate compensation depth (CCD) fluctuations that did not affect a core from 1,600 m on the crest of the Lomonosov Ridge (Clark and Hanson, 1983).

A stratigraphy for late Pleistocene sediments of the Makarov Basin and Lomonosov Ridge has been recognized (Clark and others, 1980). Makarov Basin sequences cannot be correlated

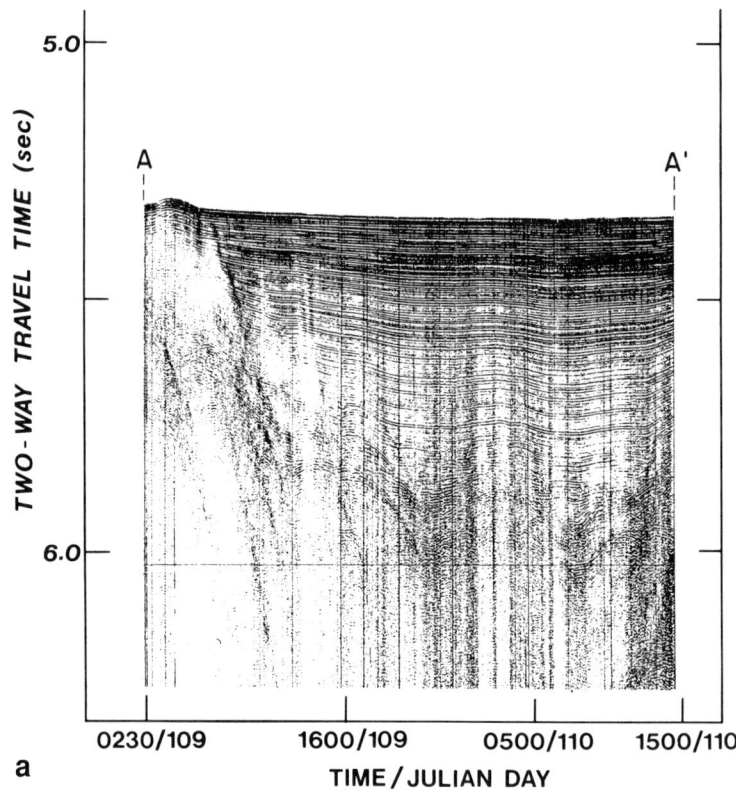

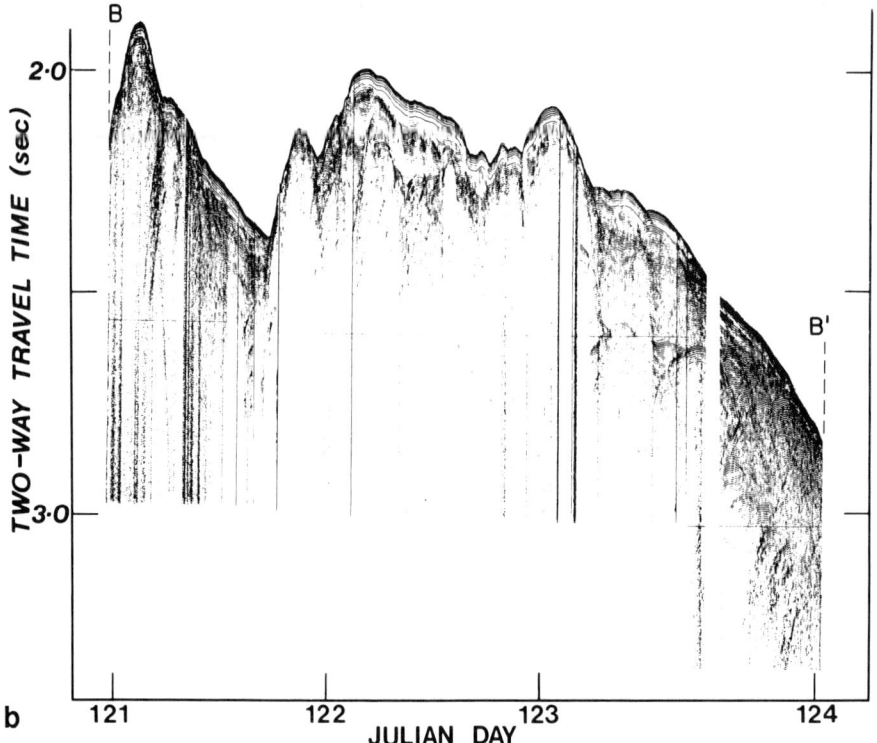

Figure 7. a) Subbottom profile in the Makarov Basin along section A–A' in Figure 2. Profile length approximately 13 km. b) Subbottom profile across the crest of the Lomonosov Ridge along section B–B' in Figure 2. Profile length approximately 28 km.

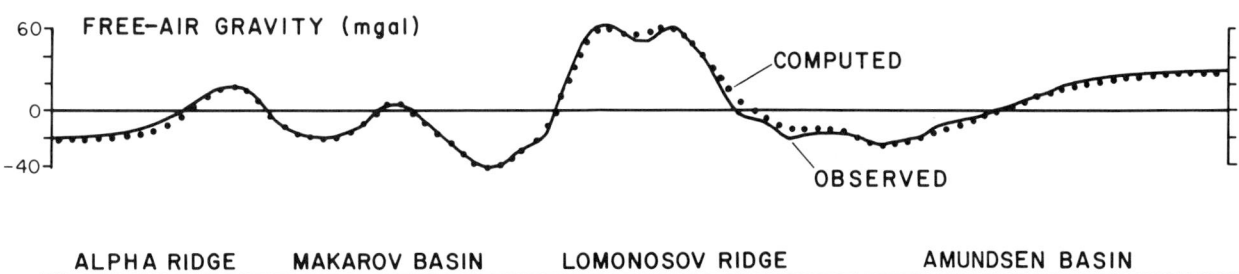
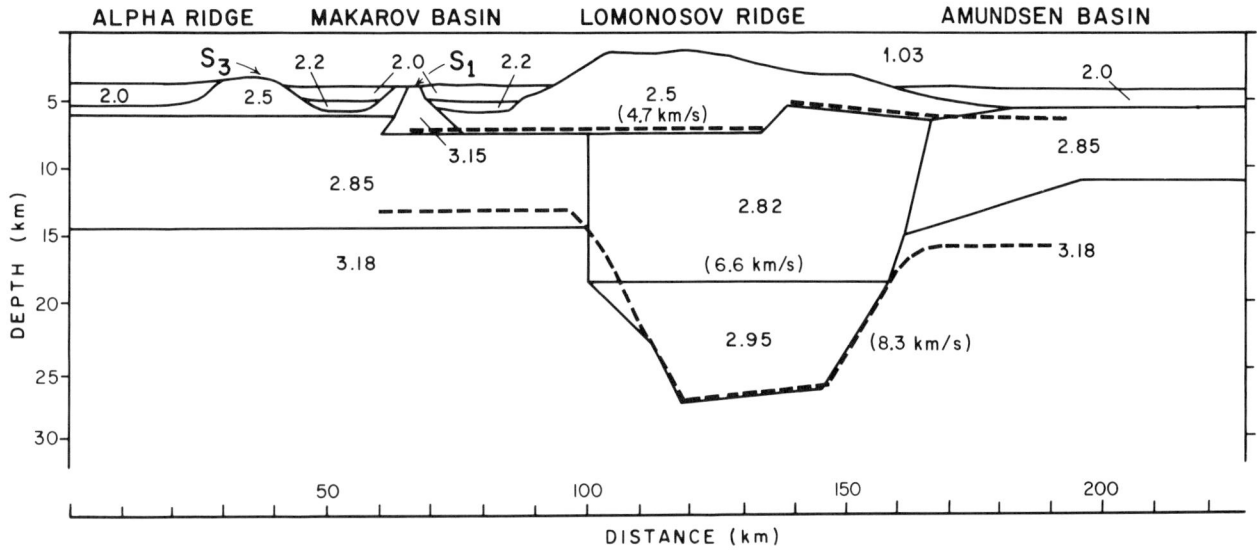

Figure 8. Two-dimensional crustal density model along profile LG–LG' of Figures 2 and 3. Densities are in Mg/m^3. Broken lines represent Mair and Forsyth's (1982) seismic refraction results with an upper crustal velocity of 4.7 km/s, a lower crustal velocity of 6.6 km/s and an upper mantle velocity of 6.3 km/s.

with the sediments of the Amundsen Basin but can be correlated with the stratigraphy of the Alpha Ridge–Chukchi Plateau area, some 300 kilometers distant (Morris, 1983).

Fluctuations in current velocity have occurred over the Lomonosov Ridge during the late Pleistocene causing variation in ridge crest and basin stratigraphic units. Near the top of the ridge, bottom current speeds in excess of 12 cm/s have been measured. The currents are pulsed and appear to flow toward Ellesmere Island diagonally across the ridge into the Makarov Basin (Aagaard, 1981). The Makarov Basin is the depositional sink for silt- and clay-sized particles swept off the Lomonosov Ridge. Ferromanganese micronodules are correlated to silty lutite and bioturbated silty lutite. Paleo CCD levels are interpreted to be between 3,956 m and 1,600 m for much of the late Pleistocene as evidenced by calcareous foraminifera abundance differences between the Lomonosov Ridge crest and the Makarov Basin (Morris, 1983).

Seismic refraction structure. Results of partially reversed seismic refraction profiles (Forsyth and Mair, 1984) across the Lomonosov Ridge show a 5-km-thick upper crustal layer with a velocity of 4.7 km/s succeeded by a 6.6 km/s layer extending to a depth of 28 km under the ridge, near 13 km beneath the Makarov Basin, and near 16 km beneath the Amundsen Basin (Fig. 8).

Figure 9 shows a comparison of the crustal section for the Lomonosov Ridge with other crustal sections. The two 6.3 km/s sections shown in Figure 9a for the Sverdrup Basin indicate that limestone, encountered by deep drilling in this area and known to have this velocity, may overlie granitic rocks of similar velocity. Figure 9b indicates that the structures beneath the now-shallow Barents and Kara seas and the Lomonosov Ridge appear to be related neither to ancient continental shields nor to modern ocean basins; that is, while the crusts are thick enough to be considered continental, they do not exhibit velocities typical of the acidic rocks. The Barents and Kara shelves 78°N sections may then represent an intermediate or "old shelf" type of crustal structure characterized by a 20-km-thick sedimentary section (P-wave velocities near 5.5 km/s) deposited on an older oceanic crust. The structures below the Barents and Kara shelves may be the result of a very thick sedimentary section deposited upon a pre-Jurassic oceanic crust. The resemblance between the structure below the Kara Sea at 82°N and that of the Lomonosov Ridge at 90° in Figure 9b is striking, granted that upper crustal velocity control is poor. (The upper layer velocity of 4.7 km/s was not well con-

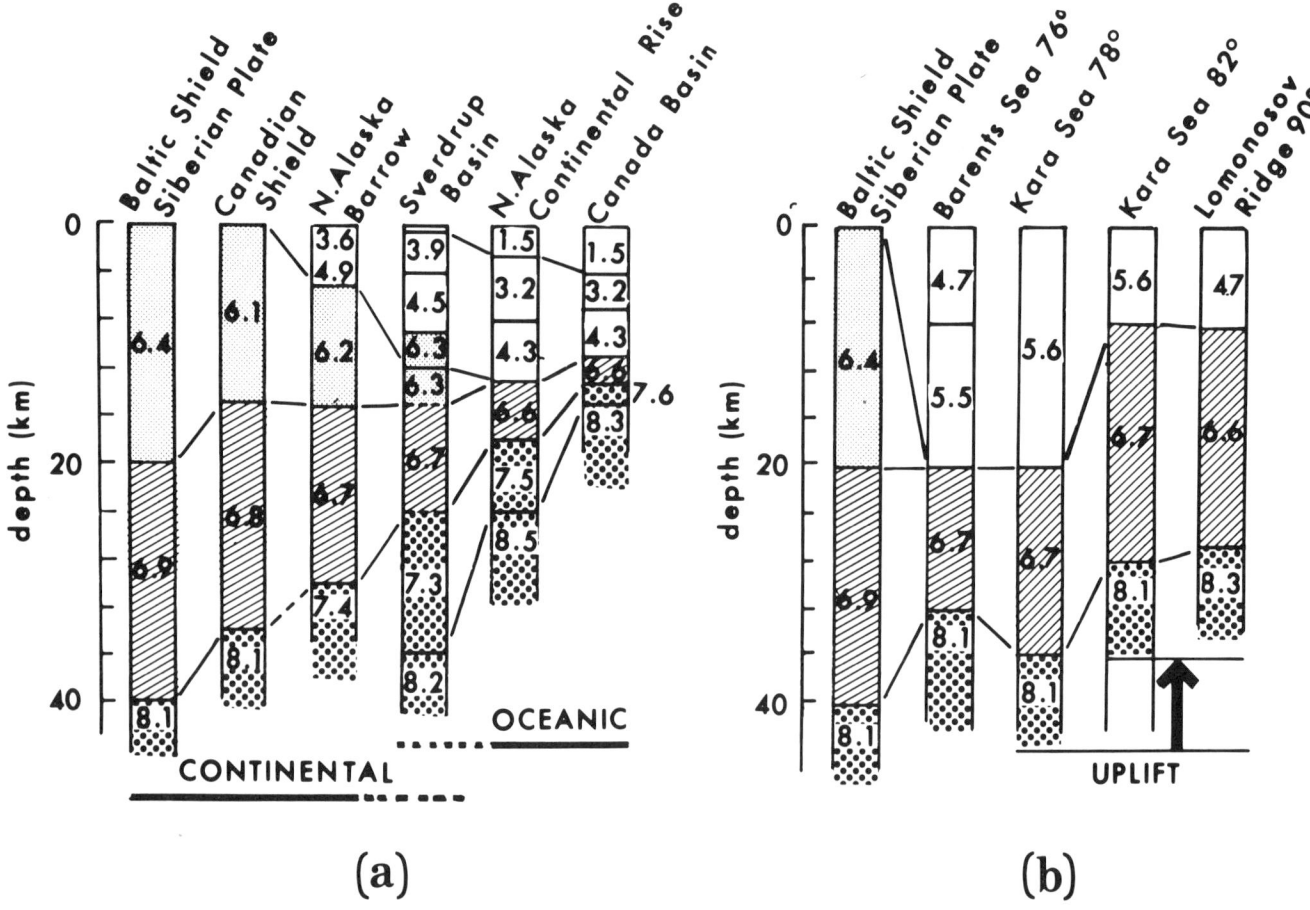

Figure 9. Comparison of crustal structures grading into the Canada Basin with structures from the Lomonosov Ridge and Baltic Shield (from Forsyth and Mair, 1984).

strained by LOREX data and is based largely on T-3 data [Hunkins, 1961]. The better constrained CESAR data [Forsyth and others, 1983] suggest an upper crustal velocity of 5.2 km/s [Forsyth, personal communication, 1985]). Closing of the Amundsen and Nansen basins would place these structures together, and their similar P-wave velocity structure supports the suggestion (see, e.g., Wilson, 1963) that the Lomonosov Ridge is a fragment that was once joined with the Kara and Barents shelves.

Magnetic and conductivity structure. 1. Aeromagnetics. Previous high-level reconnaissance surveys show the Lomonosov Ridge to be associated with an irregular magnetic anomaly pattern of low relief save for local highs along its crest and Makarov flank close to the North Pole (e.g., Coles and others, 1978). The low-level aeromagnetic data (Hood and Bower, 1980) support this regional picture and, in addition, show a spatial correlation in the Makarov Basin between positive magnetic anomalies and basement relief as determined from LOREX bathymetric, gravity, and shallow seismic work (Figs. 6 and 7). A zone of linear magnetic highs in excess of 1,000 nT lies parallel to the ridge crest along the Makarov flank just south of the LOREX traverse (Hood and Bower, 1980). A series of U-shaped anomalies adjacent to the southern flank of the Lomonosov Ridge are reminiscent of those due to grabenlike features such as have been observed in the Melville Bay area of northwestern Greenland and elsewhere (Hood and Bower, 1980).

Coles (1980) showed that a strongly positive magnetic anomaly of up to 400 nT is present over the ridge along the LOREX drift path. A preliminary magnetic crustal model shows that a tabular region of highly susceptible rocks (0.06 SI) at depths between 7 and 17 km can account for the observed anomaly data (Fig. 10). This tabular zone extends, at depth, well into the Makarov Basin. The base of the model is loosely constrained and could be extended to include the crustal root beneath the ridge with appropriate lowering of the rock susceptibility. A shallower model top, however, appreciably degrades the fit to the observed field (R. L. Coles, personal communication, 1981). Shallower magnetic sources within the ridge (Coles, 1980) are indicated by the presence of small short-wavelength positive

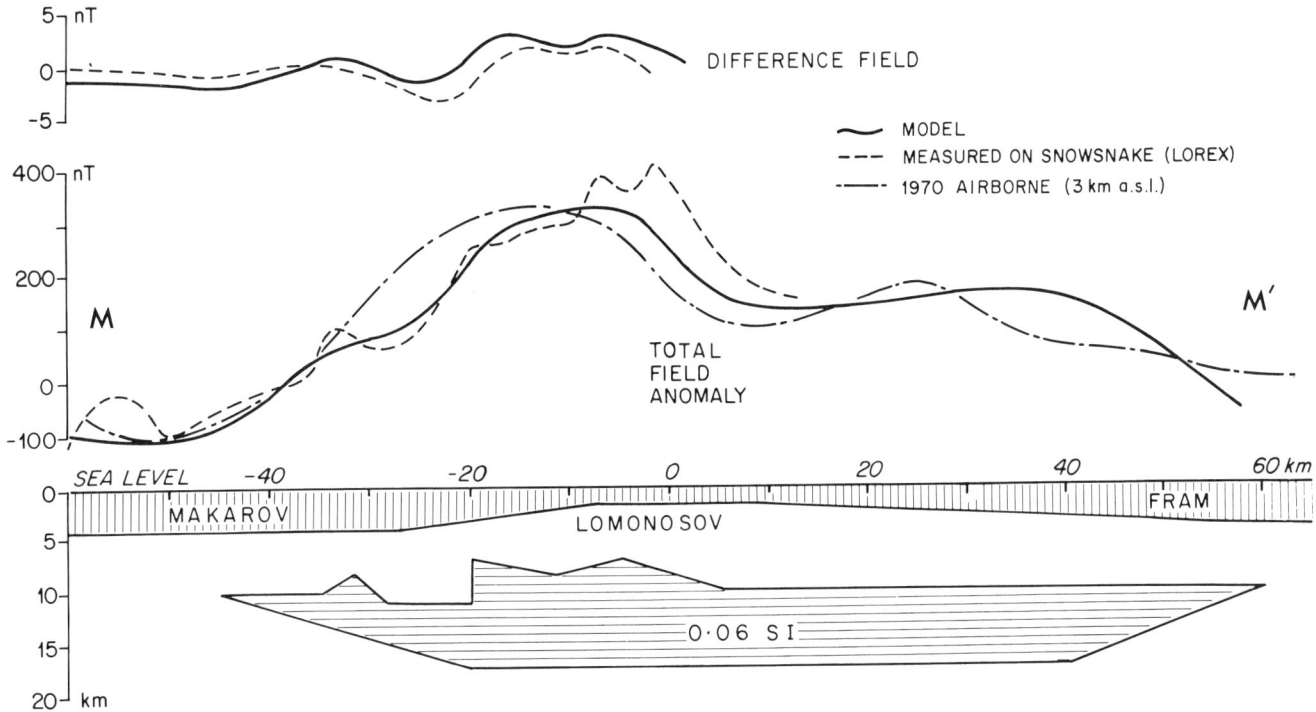

Figure 10. Proposed magnetic source within the crust below the Lomonosov Ridge (modified from Coles, 1980). The model total field (solid line) is compared with LOREX data (dashed line) and 1970 airborne measurements (dot-dash line). Profile location M–M' in Figure 2.

anomalies that coincide, in two instances, with the local topographic maxima on the Amundsen flank near the crestal region (Fig. 7b).

During 1977–1978, twelve low-level magnetic profiles were flown across Siberia Plain by the U.S. Navy. Maximum peak-to-trough anomaly amplitudes extending over 700 nT and wavelengths varying between 20 and 60 km were recorded. Taylor and others (1981) matched these anomalies with a Cretaceous sea-floor spreading time scale and hypothesized that the Makarov Basin in this region was opening from the Late Cretaceous to the Paleocene.

2. Magnetotellurics. Electrical conductivity anomalies are typically attributed to variations in rock temperature, to changes in rock porosity, or to the concentration and continuity of conducting minerals within the earth.

When Camfield and others (1980) reduced the time varying component of the geomagnetic and geoelectric fields to transfer functions and apparent resistivities, two points became evident. First, the ridge does not have a conducting core; induced electrical currents flow parallel to the ridge in the adjacent deep seas rather than within the ridge. Second, spatial changes in magnetotelluric apparent resistivities appear to correlate with the depth of the highly conductive seawater. A simple two-layer two-dimensional model of the ridge involving seawater and the underlying rock was constructed from LOREX bathymetric data. The modeled electrical response agrees reasonably well with measured variations except in the Amundsen Basin adjacent to the base of the ridge where the model response falls off more rapidly than the observations. It has not proved possible to decrease this mismatch by adding model inhomogeneities of reasonable conductivity beneath the Amundsen Basin. The large observed response over the basin may arise from the three-dimensional form of the ridge on the Amundsen side or from problems of incomplete separation of variation fields from internal and external currents (P. A. Camfield, personal communication, 1981; R. D. Kurtz, personal communication, 1982).

3. Geothermics. Lomonosov Ridge heat-flow values from 21 measurements along the Main Camp drift path show gradients linear with depth and a rather uniform pattern of heat-flow variations: 60 to 70 mWm^{-2} in Makarov Basin, 60 to 65 mWm^{-2} on the ridge flanks and crest, 75 to 85 mWm^{-2} in Amundsen Basin (A. S. Judge, 1980, personal communication, 1981). That is, the present thermal regime appears to have a rather deep-seated subcrustal source. Electrical inhomogeneity beneath the Amundsen Basin, if any, may therefore be unrelated to temperature variations within the earth. The Amundsen Basin heat flow, although measured only close to the flank of the Lomonosov Ridge, is consistent with the age ascribed to the formation of the basin.

MAP No. 1
FREE-AIR ANOMALIES
ELLESMERE ISLAND
POLAR STEREOGRAPHIC PROJECTION
CONTOUR INTERVAL 5 MILLIGALS
0 50 100 Km

a

MAP No. 2
FREE-AIR ANOMALIES
POLAR STEREOGRAPHIC PROJECTION
CONTOUR INTERVAL 5 MILLIGALS
0 50 100 Km

b

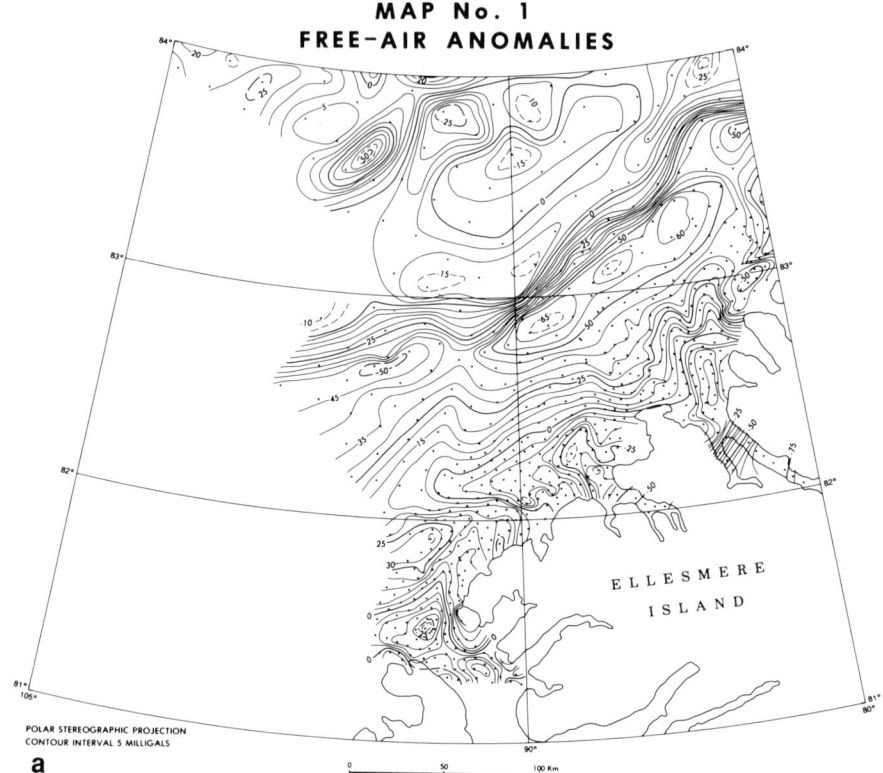

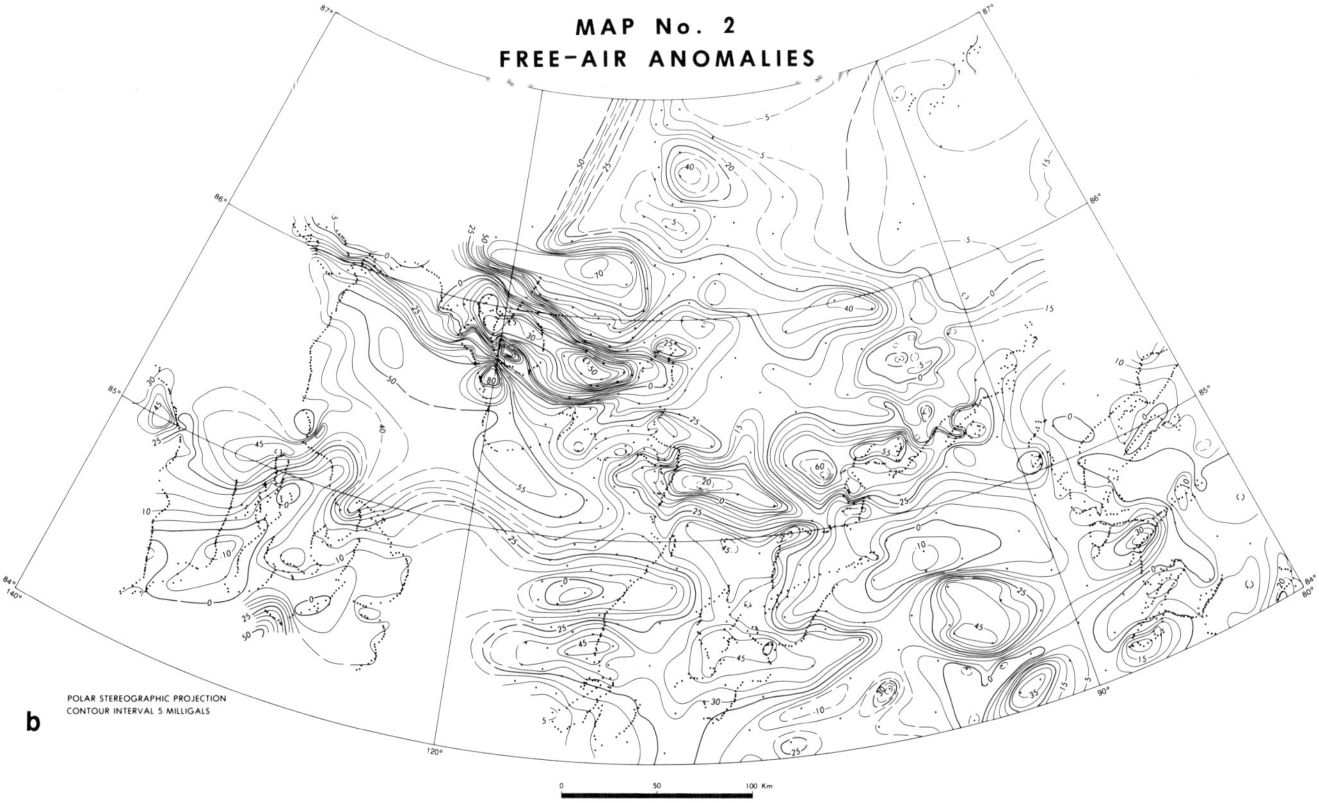

MAP No. 3
FREE-AIR ANOMALIES

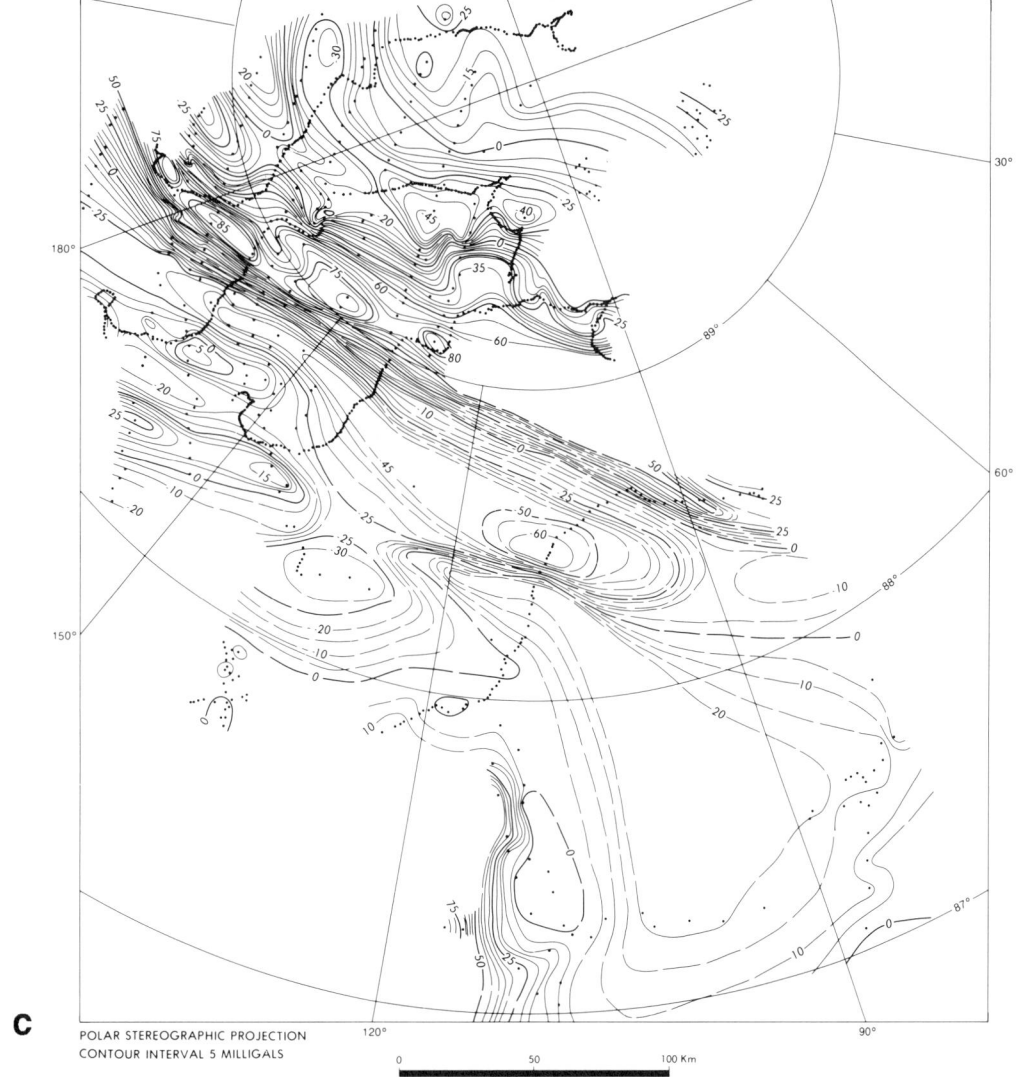

Figure 11a–c (this and facing page). Free-air gravity maps from northern Ellesmere Island to the polar region, across the Alpha and Lomonosov ridges, compiled from LOREX, CESAR, T-3, ARLIS II, and ALPHA data. Contour interval 5 mgal. Dots show location of all points used for contouring. Data base is same as used for compiling "Gravity map of the Arctic north of 64° latitude" (Plate 3, this volume). Map covers same area as bathymetric map of Figures 4a to c except that unexplored regions are left blank.

Gravity structure. The free-air gravity anomaly field is dominated by a prominent positive anomaly of between 60 to 90 mGal centered along the crest of the Lomonosov Ridge (Fig. 11a to c). It is flanked by negative anomalies of between –20 and –50 mGal centered approximately along the 3,900-m isobaths on either side of the ridge. Farther away from the ridge the free-air anomaly field is generally positive over the Amundsen abyssal plain and negative over the Makarov Basin.

A generalized two-dimensional crustal density model was constructed from bathymetry, gravity, and seismic information (Fig. 8). This profile parallels closely the drift path of the main camp from the Makarov Basin across the Lomonosov Ridge, which provides control for crustal density horizons from the LOREX seismic refraction results.

This LOREX gravity model was constructed to be consistent with the hypothesis that the Lomonosov Ridge is a fragment of continental crust flanked by an oceanic Amundsen Basin crust to the north and a thicker Makarov Basin crust of uncertain character to the south. Beneath the ridge the depth and shape of intracrustal boundaries and the Moho were taken from the P-wave velocity model of Mair and Forsyth (1982) and Forsyth and others (1983) except in the Amundsen Basin, as discussed below. Basement cover was modeled from shallow (Blasco and others, 1979) and intermediate (Overton, 1982) reflection data (Figs. 7 and 6). The upper crust beneath the ridge is assigned an average density of 2.50 Mg/m^3 based on gravity model calculations using ridge topography (Sweeney, 1980).

The gravity and seismic data agree reasonably well for the ridge and adjoining Makarov Basin. For the latter, a depth to Moho of 13 km (seismically) and 14.6 km (gravitationally) were obtained. For comparison, Kutschale (1966) estimated the depth to Moho of the Makarov Basin in the Wrangel Abyssal Plain, just south of Arlis Gap, at 15 km. For the Amundsen Basin, however, the refraction crustal thickness appears to be too great (near 16 km compared with the gravitationally determined 11 km). Weber and Sweeney (1985) and Forsyth and Mair (1984) in discussing the discrepancy concluded that the thinner crust is a better estimate.

The basement relief at kilometers 35 and 65 of the crustal density model (Fig. 8) corresponds to S_3 and S_1 of Fig. 2. Both features antedate the sedimentation process, as indicated earlier. From gravity data analysis, however, it appears that the rocks beneath each have quite different densities, namely, 2.5 and 3.15 Mg/m^3, respectively. S_1 may represent an extinct volcano, while S_3 represents the Marvin Spur, which may be composed of the same density material as the sedimentary or metasedimentary rocks of the Lomonosov Ridge.

Examination of the submarine echograms (profiles F, G, and H, Fig. 5 of Johnson and others, this volume) suggest that much of the Marvin Spur is not a separate structure but belongs, morphologically, to the Alpha Ridge, forming its Makarov-facing boundary. It is, in part, a north-facing escarpment that is separated from the Lomonosov Ridge by a grabenlike abyssal trough, up to 60 km wide, which between 140° to 150°W is underlain by thin (9 km) crust (Forsyth and Mair, 1984). The sea floor to the south of the escarpment appears to rise irregularly toward the crest of the Alpha Ridge. The escarpment is distinct from Sobczak's (1977) Marvin Seamounts to which S_1 and S_2 of Figure 2 belong. The LOREX gravity model (Fig. 8) suggests that S_1 and S_2 are composed mainly of high-density rock. If this is so, then we may infer from their basement sediment contacts (Fig. 7a) that the Marvin Seamounts are volcanic features that were in place within the Makarov Basin early in its history before the onset of sediment deposition.

The bathymetric, shallow seismic reflection and gravity measurements carried out from the ice island ARLIS II when it drifted across the Marvin Spur, Makarov Basin, and the Lomonosov Ridge during 1964 (Ostenso and Wold, 1977) were reinterpreted by Weber and Sweeney (1985) in the light of the LOREX studies, and a composite gravity-density structural model was compiled along profile AG–AG' (Fig. 3). Block densities and depths are derived from the LOREX refraction and reflection seismic studies. Water depths over the Lomonosov Ridge and adjacent basins and the distribution of unconsolidated sediments are similar to those found in the LOREX area except that along AG–AG' the ridge is much wider (220 km compared to LOREX's 65 km) and the Makarov Basin is about half as wide. This crustal model (Fig. 12 in Weber and Sweeney, 1985) is incorporated in kilometers 0 to 360 of the crustal density section across the central Arctic Ocean (Fig. 12) as discussed below.

ALPHA-MENDELEEV RIDGE COMPLEX

Early studies

During the crossing of the Alpha Ridge from 1957 to 1958 the ice station ALPHA carried out seismic reflection and refraction studies (Hunkins, 1961). Several short unreversed refraction profiles indicated an average of 380 m of unconsolidated sediments, covering a 2.8-km-thick layer of 4.7 km/s velocity that overlies a 6.44 km/s "oceanic" layer of undetermined thickness.

In 1961 some 66,000 km of aeromagnetic lines were flown (Ostenso, 1961, 1962). Depth-to-source computations suggested that the high-amplitude anomalies associated with the Alpha Ridge were of shallow origin. King and others (1964) and King and Zietz (1966) designated these anomalies, which parallel and extend beyond the flanks of the Alpha Ridge as the "central magnetic zone." They noted that the magnetic signatures closely resemble those observed over Precambrian shields and basement complexes.

Lachenbruch and Marshall (1966) measured the heat flow at twenty stations over the Alpha Ridge flank and in the adjacent Canada Basin from T-3 in 1963 and found the flux over the ridge to be about one-half that of the normal and uniform (59 mWm/m^2) flux measured in the basin. Using models, they concluded that their measurements were best explained by a zone of low-conductivity rock extending below the ridge to a depth of at least 15 km, and projecting out at this depth for some distance beneath the adjacent basin.

Ostenso and Wold (1971, 1973) and Vogt and Ostenso (1970) examined the existing geological and geophysical data, including additional low-level aeromagnetic profiles flown in 1963 and 1964, and found it to be consistent with the hypothesis that the Alpha Ridge is a mid-ocean ridge that became inactive in the Tertiary. The authors suggested a link between the Alpha Ridge and the Mid-Labrador Sea Ridge through Nares Strait.

In his Ph.D. thesis, Hall (1970) expanded on the dormant spreading-center hypothesis for the Alpha and Mendeelev ridges. He identified at least five fracture zones that cut through the Alpha-Mendeleev complex and he inferred 24 offsets of the ridge axis in the crestal region (transform faults). Seismic reflection studies suggested a buried basement topography similar to that found on the Mid-Atlantic Ridge. An example of a seismic reflec-

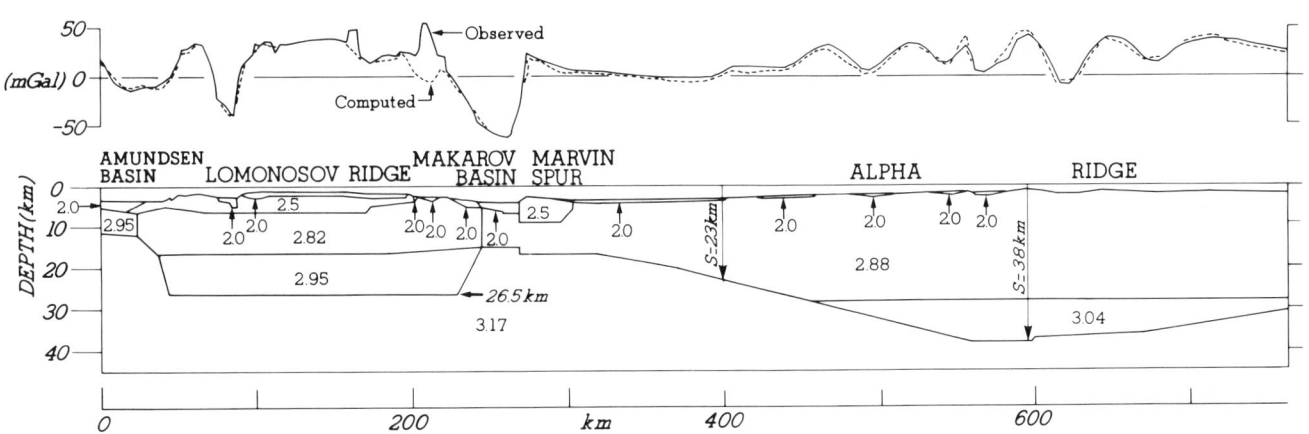

Figure 12. Gravity density model across Lomonosov Ridge, Makarov Basin, and part of the Alpha Ridge along profiles AG′–AG and LG′–LG (Fig. 3). The section from kilometers 0 to 360 across the Lomonosov Ridge is derived from ARLIS II data and taken from Weber and Sweeney (1985). The model across the Alpha Ridge is derived from CESAR data and reproduced from Weber (1986). Densities are in megagrams per cubic meter. S_1 and S_2 are depths determined from seismic refraction measurements (Forsyth and others, 1986a). Over the Alpha Ridge the observed gravity anomaly can be almost completely explained in terms of the effect of water depth and sedimentary fill in the valley troughs.

tion profile across a fracture zone in the Mendeleev Ridge with free-air gravity and magnetic anomalies is shown in Figure 13. Figure 14 illustrates a crustal density model (from Hall, 1970, Fig. 23) based on a continuous 600-km-long gravity and bathymetric profile and one unreversed seismic refraction measurement. It shows a sedimentary layer underlain by a 5-km-thick "oceanic" crust. In order to maintain isostatic equilibrium, a root of low-density mantle material, up to 27 km thick, had to be introduced below the ridge and flank.

Between 1953 and 1970 the Earth Physics Branch (formerly the Dominion Observatory) flew a number of aeromagnetic surveys over the Canadian Arctic Islands, northern Greenland, and adjoining Arctic Ocean. The measurements were made from an altitude of 3.5 km or greater above sea level. From these data, Riddihough and others (1973) compiled a preliminary residual magnetic anomaly map.

Between 1957 and 1973 more than 600 sediment cores were recovered from the Amerasia Basin from the ice stations ALPHA (Hunkins and Kutschale, 1967), CHARLIE (Crombie, 1960), ARLIS II (Herman, 1974), and T-3 (Clark and others, 1980). With two exceptions, the cores studied are of Pliocene and Pleistocene age (Clark, 1969). Only two cores taken from T-3 over the Alpha Ridge have material older than Pliocene age. One of these cores includes a late Campanian–Maastrichtian silicoflagellate assemblage contained in tuffaceous sediment; the other is of Paleocene to Eocene age, containing abundant phytoplankton in tuffaceous sediment. The two cores represent displaced Cretaceous and early Cenozoic masses within a Pliocene-Pleistocene sequence.

These cores provide evidence that a deep-marine environment existed over the Alpha Ridge at least by the Late Cretaceous, a time during which the Arctic Ocean had no ice cover and was a much warmer ocean than it is now (Clark, 1974).

Recent studies. The 1983 CESAR expedition was the first systematic attempt to study the nature and origin of the Alpha Ridge (Weber, 1987). As on the LOREX expedition, the interdisciplinary studies included bathymetry and gravity (Weber and Jackson, 1985; Weber, 1986), high-resolution shallow seismic reflection profiling (Jackson, 1985), and intermediate depth reflection profiling (Overton, 1984), crustal refraction measurements (Forsyth and Jackson, 1984; Asudeh and others, 1985), geothermal measurements (Judge and others, 1984), magnetotelluric measurements (Niblett and others, 1987), coring (Mudie and Blasco, 1985; Aksu, 1985a, 1985b; Bukry, 1985; Barron, 1985; Mudie, 1985), dredging (Van Wagoner and Robinson, 1985), bottom photography (Amos, 1985), and near-surface to near-bottom current measurements.

Seabed geology. 1. Reflection seismic. Fig. 15 shows a bathymetric map of part of the Alpha Ridge crest with the track of ice station CESAR as it drifted in a clockwise direction from March 29 to May 23, 1983. Dots along the drift track are plotted at 3-hr intervals. The ice station drifted over two ridge crests

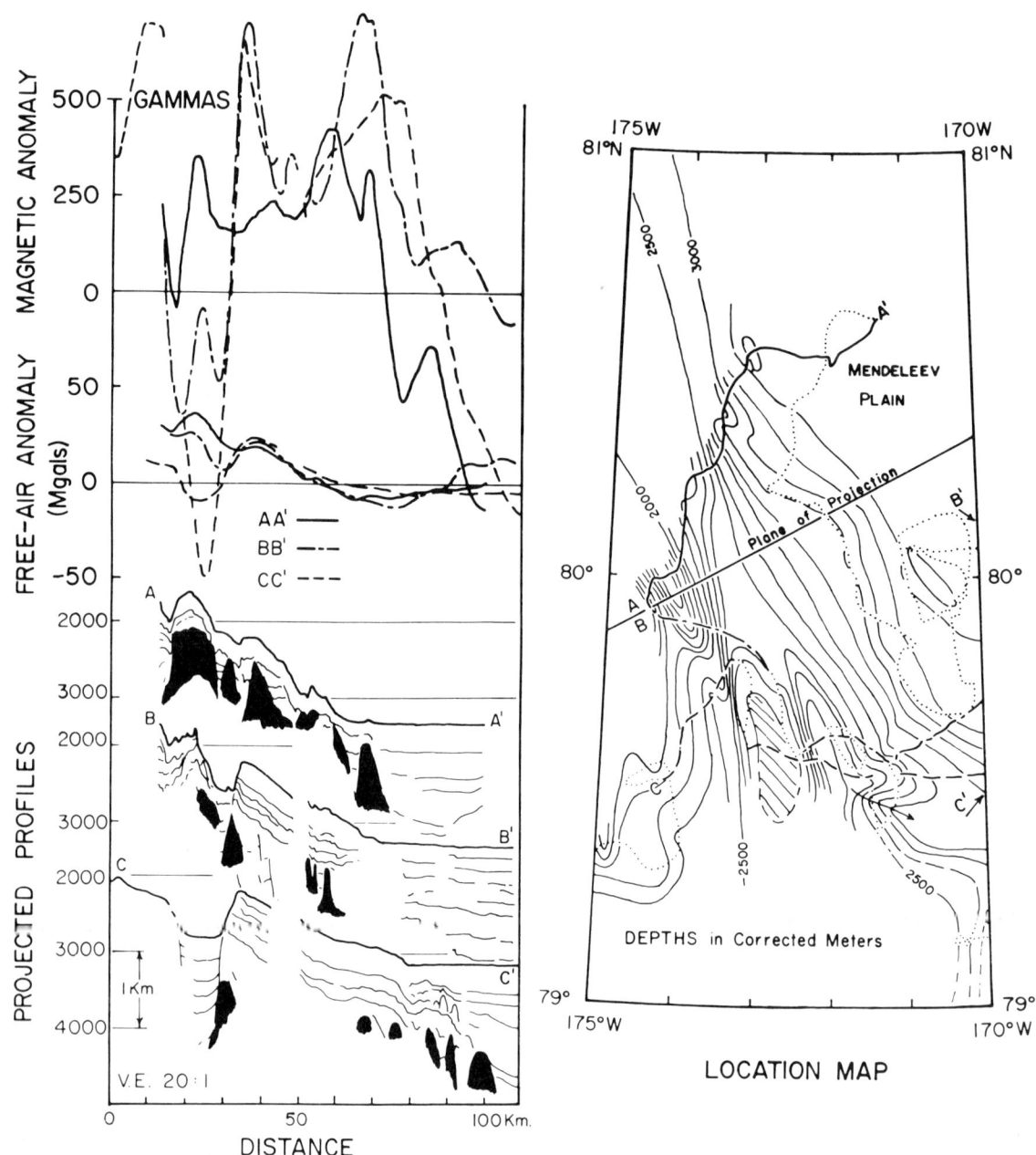

Figure 13. Geophysical profile across the east flank of the Mendeleev Ridge (Fig. 13 in Hall, 1970).

separated by a large, steep-sided valley referred to as a graben by Hall (1970) and named Central Trough by Vogt and others (1979).

The CESAR ice station was equipped with a 0.66 dm^3 air gun, which provided a relatively high resolution acoustic-stratigraphic record of the sedimentary environment from which Alpha Ridge cores and dredge samples were obtained (Figs. 13 and 14, Jackson and others, this volume). The CESAR seismic reflection record shows that the sediment cover on the ridges is layered and is mostly flat lying or conformable to basement structures. Sediment thickness varies from about 0.2 to 0.5s on the ridges. Fig. 16 shows the section across the Central Trough (Julian days 133 to 140, 1983). A thicker sequence of less regularly bedded sediments occurs in the trough; much of this sediment was probably deposited by slumping. Faulting of the ridge sediments suggests a recent tensional regime for the Alpha Ridge. Sediments in the Central Trough, however, onlap the basement, thereby indicating that the tectonic formation of this valley pre-

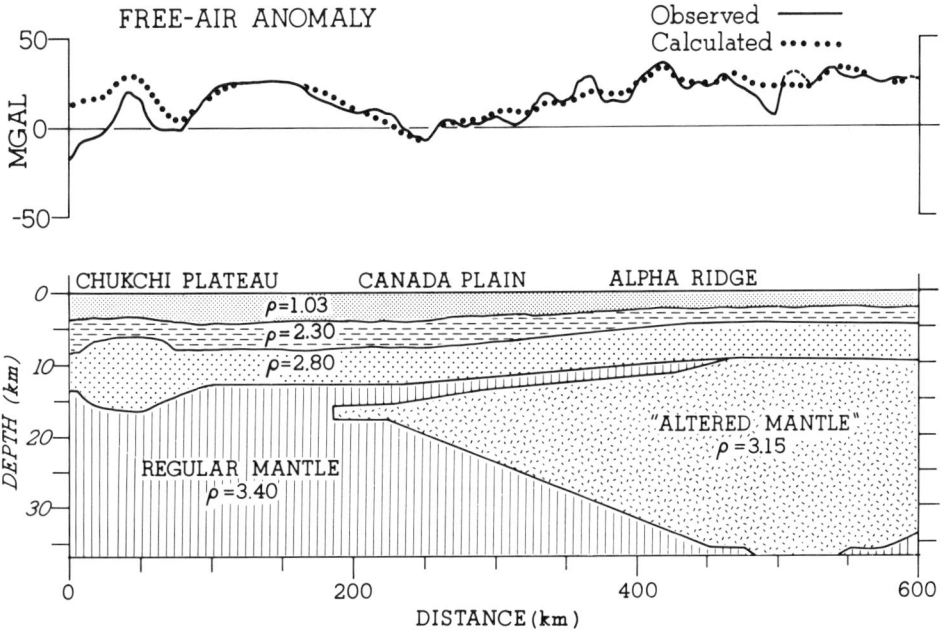

Figure 14. Gravity-derived crustal section from Chukchi Plateau across Canada Plain to Alpha Ridge along profile TG–TG' (Fig. 3); (redrawn from Hall, 1970, Fig. 23). Densities are in Mg/m^3 units.

dated the sediments. Basement structure is rough and irregular on the ridges, and the grabenlike major valley is bounded by scarps (Jackson, 1985).

Seismic reflection results (Overton, 1984) from a fixed geophone array using small explosive charges as the energy source show stratified sediments of less than 1 km thickness in valley floors, but no distinctive acoustic reflectors were observed.

2. Bottom photography and dredging. Most sites investigated show bioturbation features and a strong biomodality of sediment texture that reflect two main sediment sources: (1) a compact matrix of well-sorted clayey mud derived from local bedrock weathering and advective water transport, and (2) a poorly sorted coarse fraction of fine sand to boulder-sized material that could only be transported to the Alpha Ridge by ice. The sediment is well compacted throughout the area, suggesting a very low deposition rate. This interpretation is substantiated by a sediment budget calculated from suspended sediment concentrations in water samples collected during CESAR, which yielded a deposition rate of about 3×10^{-3} mm y^{-1}. Bottom currents below 1,600 m water depth are weak (<2 cm/s) as indicated by drift rates of plumes generated during camera drops. Percentage gravel increases upslope, however, and the shallowest site (1,160 m) showed starved ripples of sand-size material and scouring around cobbles. These bedforms suggest periodic erosion by storm-generated bottom currents.

Bottom mud, bedrock, ice, and water samples were analyzed for grain size, particle shape, biogenic content, and chemical composition. Comparison of the chemistry and quantity of sedimentary components in these different sources reveals that most of the fine sediment on the Alpha Ridge and flank is probably derived from winnowing of weathered local bedrock and not from sea ice as reported in other studies (Amos, 1985). Some coarse silt to sand-size material, however, probably reflects aeolian transport onto the sea ice and subsequent melt-out. Ice-rafted dropstones are present over the entire seabed; their dolomitic or limestone composition indicates a source on the coast of Ellesmere Island, North Greenland, or Axel Heiberg Island. Biogenic debris consists almost entirely of calcareous tests; these are more abundant in deeper water, suggesting some downslope transport following winnowing of the ridge-crest areas. Post-depositional erosion in deeper water, however, is rare as indicated by well-preserved delicate sponge spicules (Amos, 1985).

The rock samples dredged from the scarp of the Central Trough are fragmental volcanics that are highly altered. The fragments are vesicular. The high vesicularity and very fine grained nature of the clasts suggest a shallower water environment for the ridge than its present bathymetric expression. No minerals have been found in the rocks that might be used to obtain a radiometric age for the bedrock. Therefore, dating of the Alpha Ridge bedrock must rely on biostratigraphic age correlation of the basal overlying sediments (Van Wagoner and Robinson, 1985).

3. Coring. Sixteen piston cores and 12 gravity cores were recovered from Cesar North and South ridges and Cesar Trough. Reporting on the preliminary lithologic studies of the CESAR cores, Mudie and Blasco (1985) note that all but one core contain

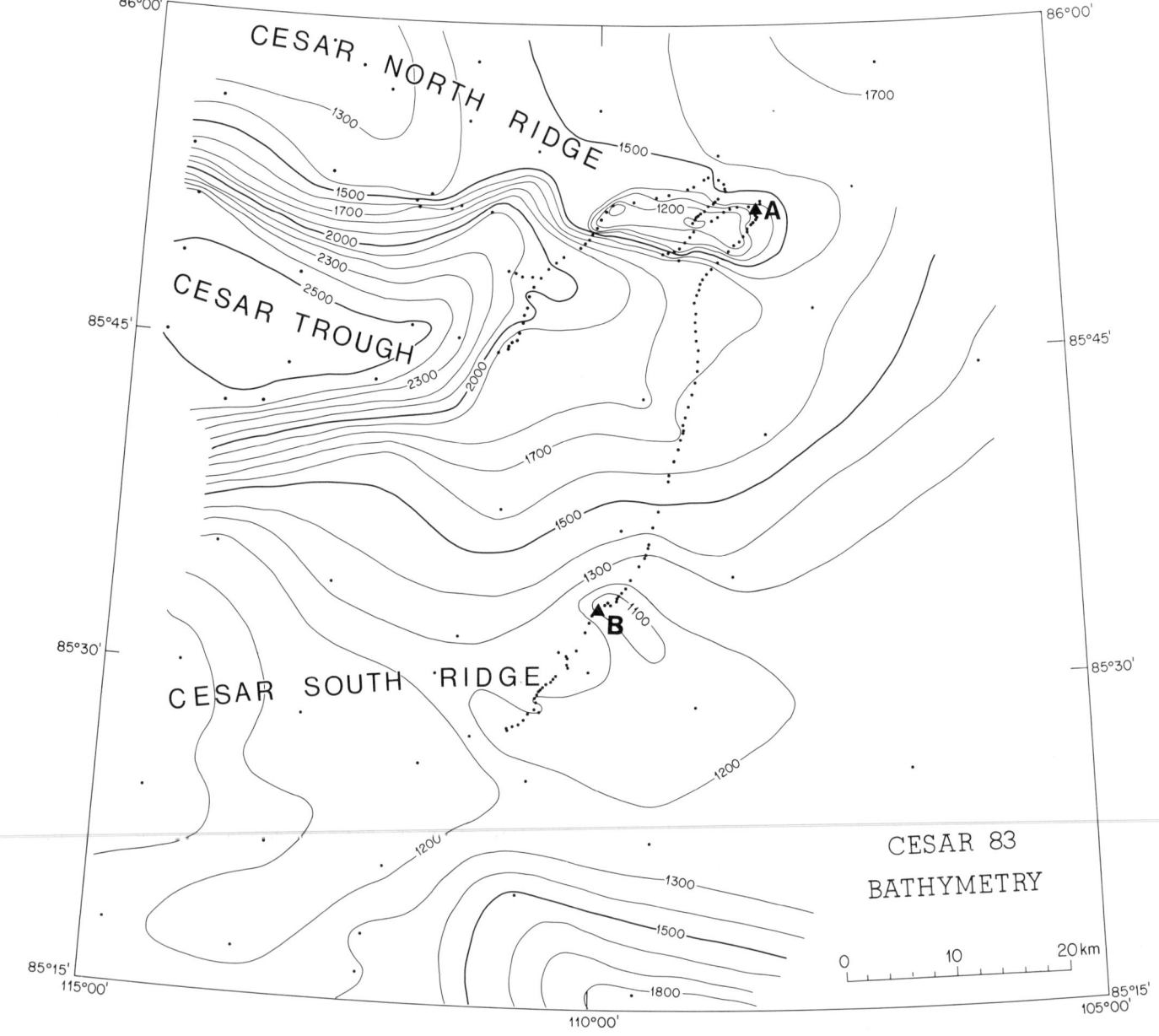

Figure 15. Bathymetric chart with drift track of CESAR Camp. Dots along track are plotted at 3-hr intervals. Remaining dots show location of sounding and gravity measurements.

late Cenozoic muds with variable amounts of sand- to pebble-sized clastic material that probably reflects transport by ice during the past 4 to 5 m.y. Sixteen Cenozoic-Holocene lithostratigraphic units have been delimited on the basis of sediment texture, structure, colour, detrital carbonate, and authigenic ferromanganese content. The composition of the upper 13 units in the CESAR cores is similar to the T-3 cores; hence most units can be broadly correlated over most of the central Arctic Ocean. Three new lithostratigraphic units (A1 to A3) occur at the base of CESAR cores from the Cesar North Ridge. Paleomagnetic and palynological data indicate a Late Miocene–Early Pliocene age for unit A3, which confirms previous reports of a slow sedimentation rate during the Cenozoic.

CESAR core 6 was obtained from an erosional surface on top of a fault block at the north edge of the Cesar Trough. This core contains some 2 m of laminated diatom ooze of Campanian-Maastrichtian age and possibly two Paleogene volcanic ash units below a brown mud unit, which probably correspond to units A2 and A3. The biosiliceous ooze contains no foraminifera or silicoflagellates and only few dinoflagellates. There is little difference in

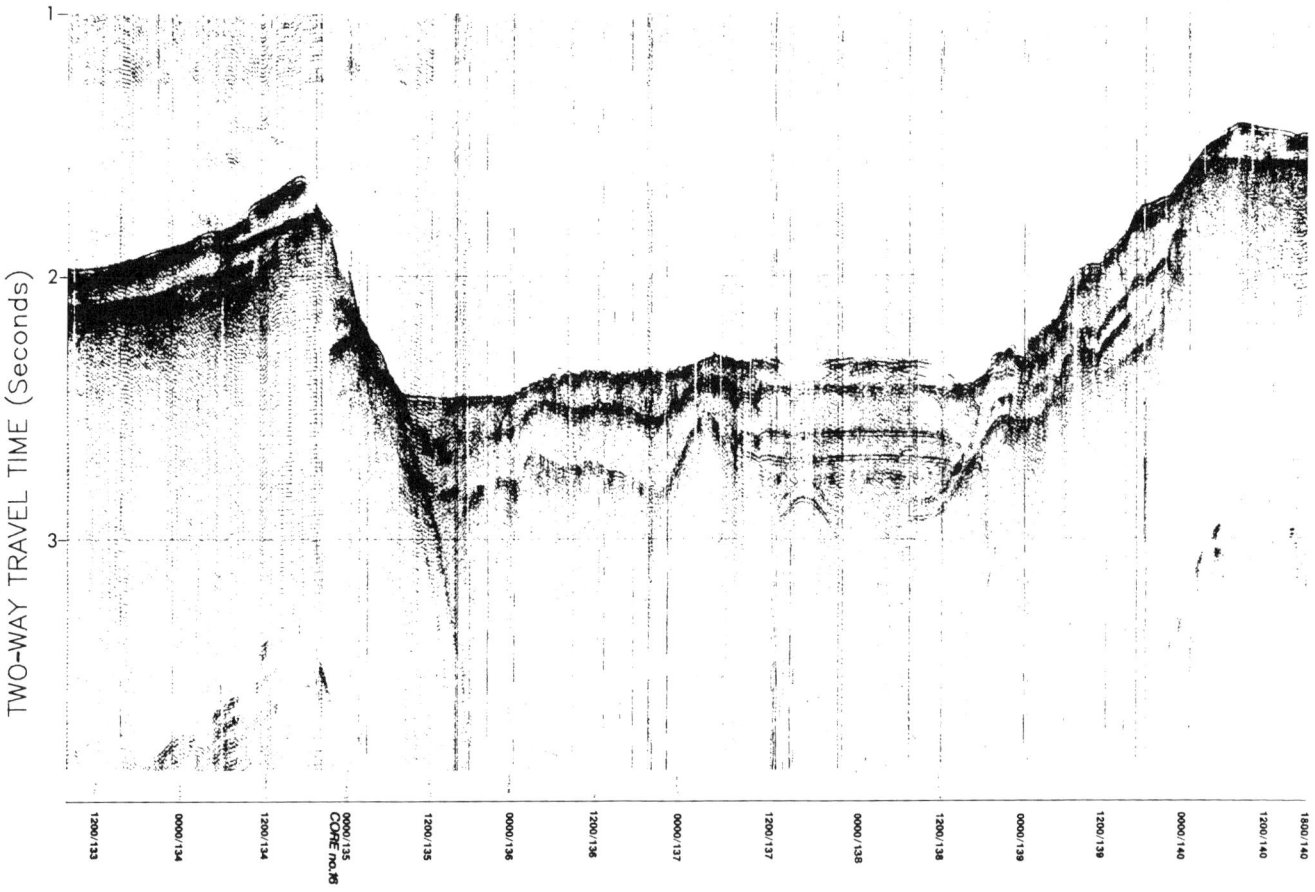

Figure 16. Shallow seismic airgun reflection recorded when ice station CESAR drifted across the Cesar Trough from May 13 to 20, 1983. Depth is in two-way travel time (3-second sweep) and the abscissa is in time units of drift.

biogenic or clastic sediment content between light and dark laminae, and the rhythmites do not appear to be annual varves produced in an upwelling environment. Rather, it appears to reflect cyclical variations in the formation and/or accumulation of particulate iron, probably due to periodic hydrothermal venting (Mudie and others, 1986).

Seismic refraction structure. Some 700 km of reversed crustal refraction data were collected during the CESAR survey, consisting of a dip profile across the center and northern part of the ridge, a strike profile along the ridge crest, and a profile on the northern flank parallel to the ridge (Fig. 3).

Figure 17a illustrates the seismic structure along the crestal strike profile where the crust-mantle boundary is at a depth of 38 to 40 km. Also shown on the figure is the compressional velocity versus depth function. Figure 17b illustrates the corresponding seismic structure along the north flank of the ridge where a crustal depth of 23 km was determined. Perhaps the most striking features are the facts that (1) the velocity versus depth functions down to 23 km are identical for the two profiles, (2) that there is no evidence of a significant reflector in the upper crust, and (3) that the P-waveform is uniform and undisturbed for distances up to 100 km (Asudeh and others, 1985).

Gravity structure. Figure 11a to c shows free-air gravity maps from northern Ellesmere Island to the Polar region, across the Alpha and Lomonosov ridges, compiled from all publicly available data. The positive elliptical anomaly centered over the Ellesmere Island continental break opposite the Alpha Ridge appears to be the northeastern continuation of a string of positive elliptical anomalies located all along the Polar continental margin from Ellef Ringnes Island to Alaska (see Plate 3). These anomalies are a typical feature of passive continental margins and are believed to be caused by the combined gravitational effect of the thickening of the sediments and thinning of the crust across the margin (Weber, 1963). The implication for the Alpha Ridge is that the adjoining continental shelf appears to be a normal passive continental margin structurally not connected to the ridge. Over the Alpha Ridge itself the free-air anomalies mirror the bathymetry. Figure 18 shows a density model of the Cesar Trough. The

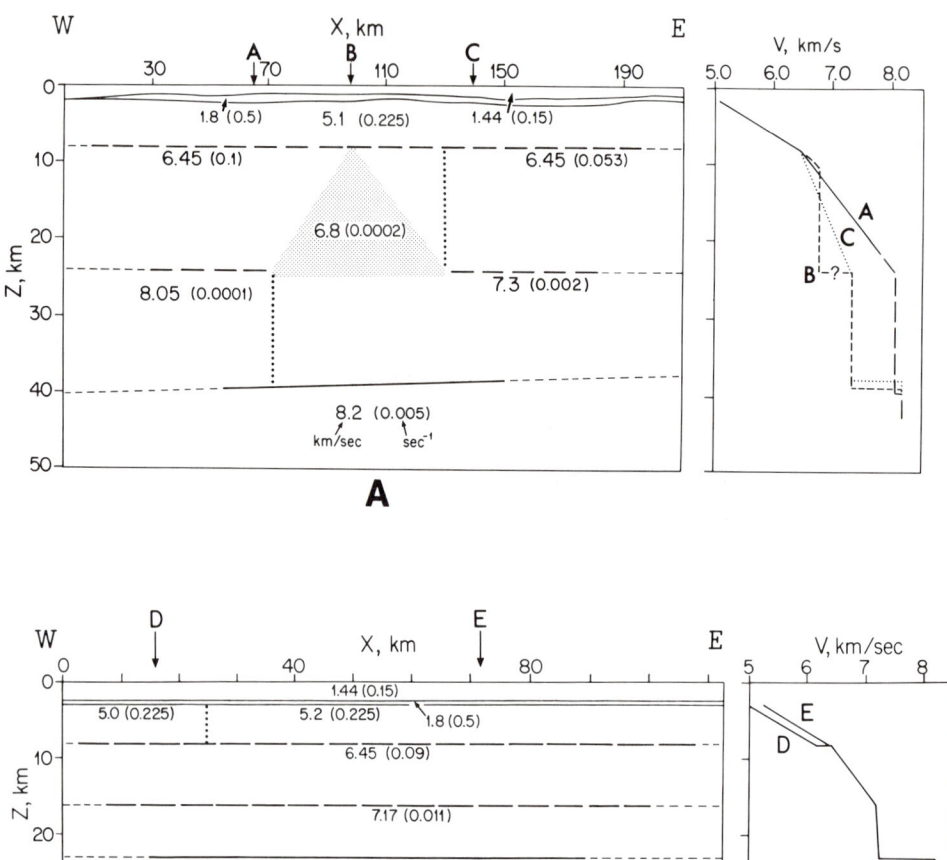

Figure 17. Seismic crustal refraction profiles and velocity-depth function; A, along strike line on Alpha Ridge crest (S_1, Fig. 3); B, along north flank of Alpha Ridge (S_2, Fig. 3).

compilation is based on the observed gravity, bathymetry, and on the airgun profile from Julian days 134 to 140 (Fig. 16), which shows up to four acoustic sedimentary reflectors and a basement reflector. The observed and computed free-air gravity profiles are shown. The best fit between observed and computed gravity is obtained using a density contrast of 0.35 Mg/m³, suggesting that if the density of the consolidated sediments is, for example, 2.15 Mg/m³, the density of the basement rock below is 2.5 Mg/m³ (Weber, 1986).

If the Cesar Trough is a major tectonic feature, as has been postulated by Hall (1970), then one would expect to see a gravity signature caused, for example, by faulting or intrusions of mafic material. However, the free-air anomaly appears as the effect of bathymetry and sediment fill only. That is typical of the whole cross section across the Alpha Ridge (Fig. 19). Figure 12, kilometers 235 to 680, shows the gravity-density model of the Alpha Ridge along the CESAR gravity and seismic refraction dip profile (Fig. 3). The model is derived from CESAR gravity measurements and the two seismically determined depths of 23 km and 38 km. The observed free-air gravity anomaly can be almost completely accounted for by the introduction of a thin (up to 500 m thick) layer of unconsolidated sediments in the valley troughs, of an upper crust of average density of 2.88, a lower crust of average density 3.04, and a mantle density of 3.17 Mg/m³ (Weber, 1986).

When Hall (1970) compiled his gravity-density model from the Chukchi Borderland to the Alpha Ridge (Fig. 14), he assumed that the Alpha Ridge was a former spreading center with a thin oceanic crust, a hypothesis widely held at the time (Vogt and Ostenso 1970). But he could not reconcile the thin crust with the observed gravity. He had to introduce an altered mantle of density 3.15 compared to 3.4 Mg/m³ for the normal mantle. This altered mantle in reality represents the Alpha Ridge crust with a crust-mantle density contrast of 0.25 Mg/m³. This crustal section, representing the south flank of the Alpha Ridge crustal root (albeit some 300 km further west) has the same shape and depth as

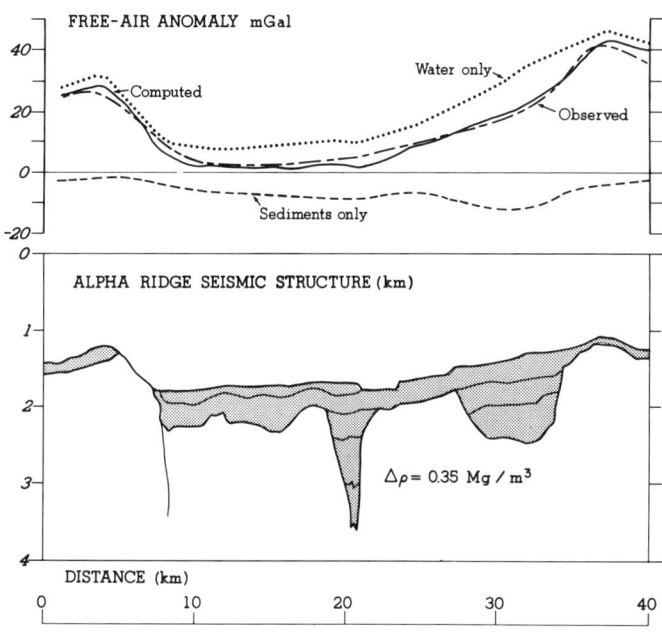

Figure 18. Section across Cesar Trough along drift track (Fig. 15) projected on a plane. Depth has been converted to kilometers assuming a sedimentary seismic velocity of 2 km/s. The abscissa units have been converted from time to distance (km), thus removing the effect of variable drift velocity. Shown are the acoustic basement reflector and up to three acoustic sediment reflectors. Observed and computed gravity anomaly are shown above, assuming a basement-to-sediment density contrast $\Delta\rho$. Also shown are the gravitational effect of water depth and sediment thickness alone. A density contrast $\Delta\rho = 0.35$ Mg/m^3 gives the best fit between observed and computed values.

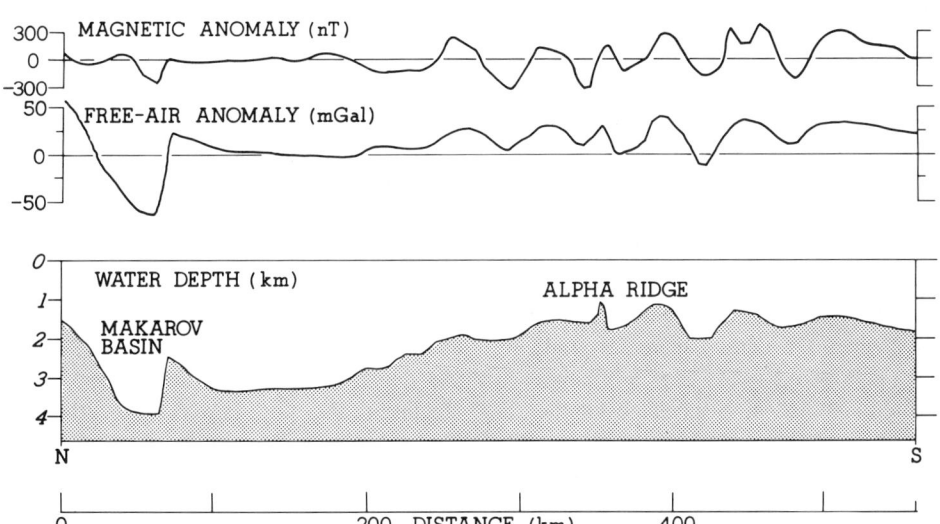

Figure 19. Water depth, free-air gravity anomaly, and aeromagnetic anomaly along southwestern half of profile AG'–AG and along profile CG'–CG (Fig. 3). Bathymetry and gravity are derived from CESAR data (Weber, 1986) and magnetic data are taken from Perry and others (1985).

the corresponding crustal section along the CESAR profile) (Fig. 12), increasing in depth from 20 km to 37 km toward the ridge axis. Using the updated bathymetric and gravity data (Figs. 4b, c, and 11b, c) and using the density structures determined for the Alpha Ridge on CESAR, Hall's gravity-density model was recompiled with the same crust-mantle density contrast of 0.25 Mg/m^3 (Fig. 20). Since the sedimentary thickness of the Canada Plain is unknown, an arbitrary value of 3 km was assumed with an average density of 2.25 Mg/m^3 against a near-surface basement density of 2.75 Mg/m^3. The observed free-air anomaly is not quite the same as Hall's T-3 data indicated. Keeping the model as simple as possible, it was found that the crustal thickness decreases from 30 km under the Alpha Ridge to 13 km under the Canada Plain, some 7 km shallower than Hall's model indicated. The crust appears to thicken again toward the Chukchi Borderland.

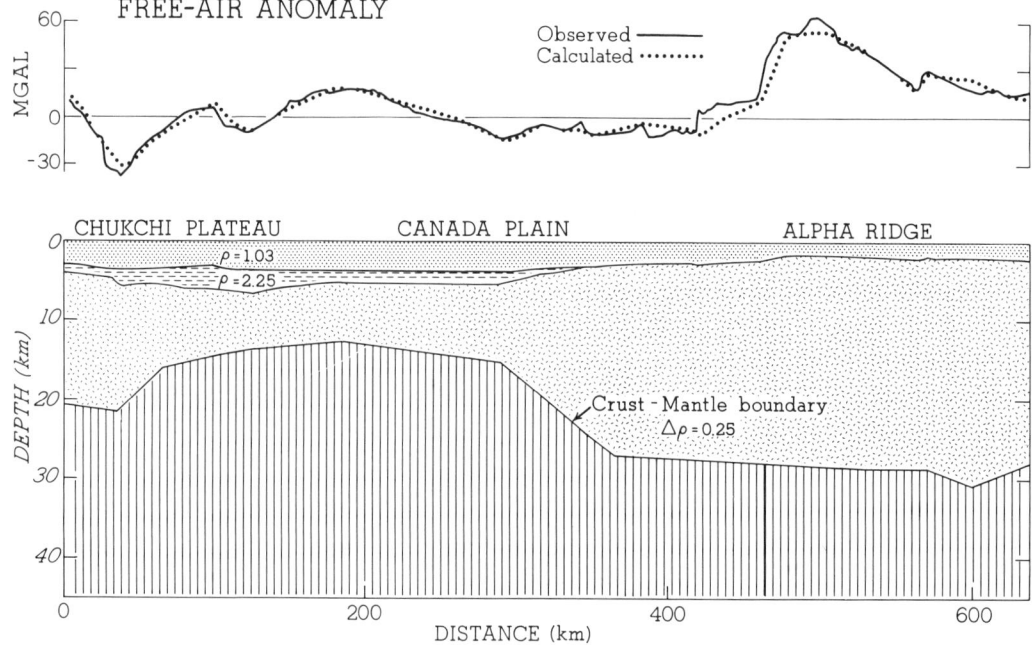

Figure 20. Gravity-derived crustal section from Chukchi Plateau across Canada Plain to Alpha Ridge along profile TG–TG′ (Fig. 3). Updated version of Figure 14 prepared in 1985.

In Figure 21, seismic and gravity structures are compared. Also shown are the average crustal densities excluding water. Note that for the Alpha Ridge the three crustal velocity layers between sediment and Moho represent average velocities used for computation. As mentioned above there is no indication of distinct midcrustal acoustic reflectors. The velocity appears to increase gradually with depth. The same argument may be made for the gravity sections where the density increases gradually starting from a basement density of, say, 2.5 Mg/m^3.

The average density (2.79 Mg/m^2) calculated for the 25-km-thick Lomonosov crust is considerably less than the density (2.86 Mg/m^3) of the 20-km-thick crust under the Alpha Ridge flank or the density (2.91 Mg/m^3) of the 37-km-thick crust below the Alpha Ridge crest (Weber, 1986).

Magnetic and conductivity structure. 1. Aeromagnetics. Adding aeromagnetic data collected in 1972 (Riddihough and others, 1973) to the data collected earlier, Coles and others (1976) prepared a vertical-component magnetic field residual map. In 1978, as a contribution to the Arctic Geophysical Review, Coles and others (1978) summarized all the available aeromagnetic information and discussed the various interpretations. They noted that there is no persistent anomaly pattern associated with the Lomonosov Ridge and that the evidence suggested that the ridge is of continental character. On the other hand, they confirmed the observation by King and others (1966) that the amplitudes and character of the anomalies over the Alpha Ridge are similar in some respects to continental shield anomalies; they also noted that the magnetic pattern of the ridge might equally well be the result of imbricate subduction zones and associated island areas.

During 1974 and 1975, low-level aeromagnetic surveys were flown across the northern Canada Basin and Alpha Ridge by the U.S. Navy (Vogt and others, 1979). The Alpha Ridge magnetic pattern is characterized by extremely variable amplitudes and wavelengths (see Plate 4). The largest observed anomaly, peak to trough, is some 2,000 nT, while the smallest are less than 100 nT (Taylor and others, 1981). Anomaly wavelengths are also quite variable, from 20 to 75 km to an essentially flat field. This high-amplitude, short-wavelength anomaly pattern extends some distance into the Canada Basin, indicating that the ridge may extend beneath the sediments of the Canada Basin further to the south than is indicated by its bathymetric expression. Furthermore, the transition from high-amplitude, short-wavelength anomalies over the Alpha Ridge to low-amplitude, long-wavelength anomalies over the Canada Basin is gradual. There is no boundary between the domains (Taylor and others, 1981). In the area surveyed, the Alpha Ridge has a highly magnetic basement (20 to 30 A/m) below the sediment cover (Vogt and others, 1979). There is also a strong correlation between the regional magnetic anomalies and bathymetry over the Alpha Ridge as illustrated in Figure 19. This suggests that the anomalies are related to the variations in depth to magnetic basement rather than to geomagnetic polarity reversals or internal structures.

During 1977 and 1978, the U.S. Navy flew another aeromagnetic survey over part of the Alpha Ridge. Taylor and others (1981) confirmed the magnetic signatures derived from earlier

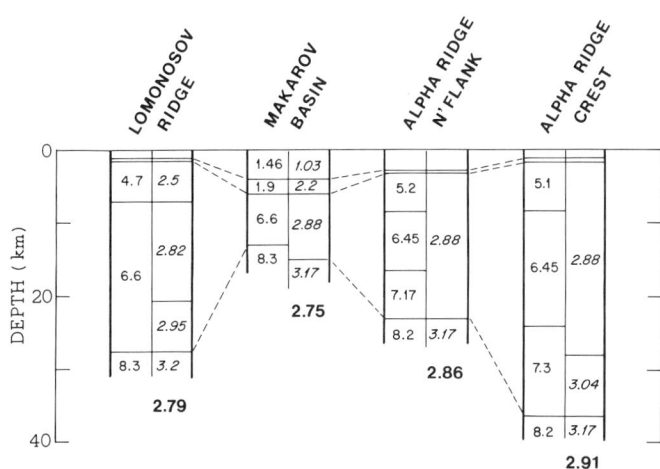

Figure 21. Comparison of seismic and gravity crustal structures for Lomonosov Ridge, Makarov Basin, Alpha Ridge north flank, and Alpha Ridge crest. The left-hand sections show compressional velocities in km/s while the right-hand sections indicate densities in Mg/m^3. All sedimentary velocities are taken as 1.9 km/s and, except for the Makarov Basin, all sediment densities are 2.0 Mg/m^3. Figures in italics denote average density of crust between sea floor and Moho.

work and extended the region over which the signature is known to exist.

Using all the high-quality low-level Arctic aeromagnetic data collected from 1972 to 1978, Kovacs and Vogt (1982) analyzed depth-to-magnetic sources for the Arctic Ocean region. They found that the Alpha Ridge appears as regional high in the calculated magnetic basement topography. Shallow magnetic basement was found under the Greenland-Ellesmere Island end of the Lomonosov Ridge. Regional magnetic source deeps are associated with the Canada and Makarov basins. A sharp drop in the regional magnetic source depths to the southeast of the Alpha Ridge suggest the Alpha Ridge is not presently connected to structures in northwest Ellesmere Island.

2. Satellite magnetics. Magnetic anomalies have been measured by two satellite systems, the POGO (Polar Orbiting Geophysical Observatory), and more recently the Magsat (Magnetic Satellite). Satellite magnetic anomalies over the Arctic have been shown to be in good quantitative agreement with aeromagnetic anomalies upward computed at satellite altitude (Coles and Haines, 1979; Langel and others, 1980; Taylor, 1983). In the most recent scalar magnetic anomaly maps compiled from Magsat data (Plate 4; Coles, 1985; Haines, 1985), the most outstanding anomaly high occurs over the Alpha Ridge. It is more intense (16 nT) than almost all other anomalies seen by the satellites around the earth. Interestingly, a positive anomaly also occurs over Iceland (Coles, 1985). Taylor (1983) modelled the Alpha-Mendeleev Ridge complex using two 30-km-thick rectangular blocks with a magnetization of 4 A/m to simulate the ridge. There is agreement between observed and predicted data only for the Alpha Ridge while the Mendeleev Ridge appears to be essentially nonmagnetic. Taylor (1983) argues that the Alpha Ridge is more likely of a continental nature for the reason that, "While not all continental structures possess extreme (greater than 10 nT) magnetic anomalies at satellite altitude, every extreme magnetic anomaly is associated with a continental or pseudocontinental feature" (p. 5). Taylor suggests that the Mendeleev Ridge is composed of nonmagnetic material—either sediments or rock of low-magnetization such as gneisses and schists.

3. Magnetic variations and magnetotellurics. Analysis of magnetic variation data collected near the CESAR base camp indicates that the in-phase transfer functions are very small (< 0.1) in the period range from 100 to 10,000 s while the quadrature functions are essentially zero. However, the directions of the in-phase induction arrows were well determined at four locations along the drift path. In each case the induction arrow points directly toward deep water and away from topographic highs on the sea floor. Two- and three-dimensional models have been fitted to magnetotelluric data acquired over part of the drift. The results indicate that the lithosphere is about 87 km thick in this region and is underlain by a conductive layer ($\rho \sim 10$ Ωm), which could be associated with partial melt in the asthenosphere. Structural contrasts within the lithosphere could not be resolved because of the screening effect of the seawater (Niblett and others, 1987).

4. Geothermics. Lachenbruch and Marshall (1966) reported an abrupt change of 30 percent in the heat flow from 76 measurements over a distance of 60 km across the transition between the Canada Basin and the Alpha Ridge at 83°N, 160°W. The conductivity contrast needed to account for these data can be produced either by a ridge composed of relatively low-conductivity crust with a low-dipping contact beneath the adjacent ocean basin or by the intrusion of a deep, near-vertical dike parallel to the ridge. The former option is supported by the continuation into the Canada Basin of the magnetic anomaly field associated with the Alpha Ridge. Both of these interpretations are consistent with a heat-flow anomaly caused by an accumulation of basalt, but the low average value (50 ± 7 mWm^2) does not suggest elevated temperatures at present (Judge and Jessop, 1978).

Heat-flow measurements using a 3-m probe and measurements of physical properties made on CESAR piston and gravity cores yielded thermal conductivities that are higher in the upper meter of each core, decreasing somewhat deeper in the sediments, and are in qualitative agreement with core descriptions from the CESAR geology program (Judge and others, 1984). Ninety percent of the conductivities lie between 1.2 and 1.8 WmK^{-1}; these values are at least 50 percent higher than those typical of deep-ocean sediments. Only one core had more typical deep-ocean conductivities of 0.8 WmK^{-1} in the lower few meters.

Using these thermal conductivity determinations and the temperature gradient, estimates of the terrestrial heat flow have been calculated. These heat-flow measurements are low to moderate in value, ranging from 40 to 60 mWm^{-2}. At most stations, however, the heat flow varies measurably with depth in the 3-m-sediment section; this variation may arise from several effects but is consistent with a change in bottom-water temperature by several tenths of a degree during the preceeding few months. If the measured heat flow is corrected for this transient effect, a more constant and generally lower heat flow of about 54 mWm^{-2} is obtained (Judge and others, 1984).

The CESAR heat-flow values are comparable to the values obtained more than a decade ago on the Alpha Ridge from ice island T-3. The low-to-moderate heat flow values determined during CESAR suggest several plausible origins for the Alpha Ridge. Such values would be typical of a fragment of continental crust or of an island arc remnant sufficiently old that any thermal signature has dissipated. Options such as a recent volcanic origin or spreading center may be discarded because elevated heat-flow values were not encountered during CESAR or the T-3 transects across the ridge. Comparison with the plate models for the ocean basins (Sclater and others, 1980) predicts an age of greater than 60 Ma for the Alpha Ridge. Comparison with other back-arc basins (Watanabe and others, 1977) suggests an age of 75 to 125 Ma. Other cooling models such as hot-spot tracks are currently being evaluated. Aseismic ridges in other parts of the oceans typically exhibit mean heat-flow values of 50 to 57 mWm^{-2} (Judge and Jessop, 1978).

TECTONIC EVOLUTION

Lomonosov Ridge: A continental fragment

Origin and age. Wilson's (1963) suggestion that the Lomonosov Ridge is a continental fragment originating from the Barents and Kara continental shelves is generally accepted today. It is postulated that the ridge was transported to its present location by sea-floor spreading central about the Arctic Mid-Ocean Ridge.

The continental nature of the ridge is characterized by the following compositional and geophysical constraints: southerly tilting en echelon fault blocks; conformal sedimentary layer on the ridge crest (Fig. 7b); resemblance between the seismic structure below the Kara Sea and that of the Lomonosov Ridge (Fig. 9); absence of high P-wave velocity (7.3 to 7.6 km/s) basal layer usually associated with oceanic crust; relatively deep crustal root for the narrow width where measured (Fig. 8); average density of 2.5 Mg/m^3 for ridge structure protruding above sea floor suggesting clastic sedimentary or low-grade metasedimentary rocks (Sweeney and others, 1982); average crustal density of 2.79 Mg/m^3 typical of continental crust (Fig. 21); and low-amplitude magnetic anomalies except for local areas (Coles and others, 1978).

The compositional constraints taken by themselves, however, allow that the Lomonosov Ridge crust could be a pile of vesicular basalts overlying a core of basic rocks and therefore oceanic in nature. Hood and Bower (1980) interpreted the zone of high-intensity magnetic anomalies over the southern flank of the ridge near the North Pole as corresponding to those associated with basic rocks such as oceanic basalt. However, the morphology of the ridge and the correspondence between the measured properties of its crust and those of the outer polar shelves of western Eurasia make this possibility less likely, especially when one considers that, before the Eurasia Basin existed, the Lomonosov Ridge was juxtaposed with the Barents and Kara shelves.

Given that the Lomonosov Ridge is a continental sliver, when did the separation occur? Anomaly 24 is the oldest magnetic reversal that can be positively identified in the Eurasia Basin. Although there is 'room' for anomalies 25 to 28 on the deep-sea floor beyond anomaly 24, a broad magnetic negative exists in their place. Either anomalies 25 to 28 were suppressed or erased by either thick sediment cover or some other process associated with initial rifting, or the associated crust is subsided continental material (Vogt and others, 1979). This puts the initiation of oceanic crust in the Eurasia Basin, and hence the separation of the Lomonosov Ridge from the Barents and Kara shelves, within the interval between magnetic anomalies 29 and 24, or sometime between 65 and 56 Ma ago (Palmer, 1983).

Alpha-Mendeleev Ridge complex

Geophysical, geological, and geochemical constraints. The Alpha-Mendeleev Ridge complex is one of the few large-scale geological structures on earth whose tectonic evolution is still unknown. Many hypotheses have been proposed concerning its origin ranging from subsided continental crust (Eardley, 1948; Saks and others, 1955; King and others, 1966), rafted continental fragment (Coles and others, 1978; Sweeney and others, 1982), extinct spreading centre (Vogt and Ostenso, 1970), extinct island arc/subduction zone (Herron and others, 1974), trace of a hot spot (Vogt and others, 1979; Irving and Sweeney, 1982; Van Wagoner and Robinson, 1985), to aseismic oceanic ridge or plateau (Vogt and others, 1979; Jackson and others, 1986).

Refinements of aeromagnetic analyses in recent years and the results of the CESAR expedition have greatly increased the number of constraints imposed on the possible evolutionary history of the Alpha Ridge. Listed below are the known morphological, geological, and geophysical constraints today:

Rugged, broad, fractured arch with long ridges and valleys striking parallel to axis. Symmetrical appearance about axis. Highest elevation less than 1,100 m. Separated by an 1,800- to 2,000-m-deep trough from Ellesmere Island Continental Shelf.

Magnetic anomalies are of high amplitude (ranging from less than $-1,000$ nT to over $+2,000$ nT) and rather irregular, with long-wavelength (30 to 50 km crest to crest, $\pm 1,000$ nT amplitude) and superposed shorter wavelength (~ 10 km crest to crest, ± 100 to 200 nT amplitude) components. The high-amplitude, short-wavelength anomaly pattern extends into the Canada Basin. The transition is gradual; there is no sharp boundary between basin and ridge. Despite the complexity of this pattern, many of these long wavelengths and at least some of the shorter wavelength magnetic features are demonstrably lineated in a direction paralleling the regional strike axis.

Highly magnetized (20–30 A/m) basement rock below sediment cover.

Estimated depth to magnetic source shows a magnetic basement trough separating the Alpha Ridge from North America.

Strong correlation between magnetic anomalies and bathymetry. This and the high intensity of magnetic anomalies imply that if the Alpha Ridge was formed by processes originating in the ocean crust, it was formed during a period dominated by normal geomagnetic polarity such as the mid-Cretaceous interval between 122 and 84 Ma or the later period between 80 and 72 Ma (Palmer, 1983).

Magsat and POGO anomaly maps show an extreme anomaly high over the Alpha-Mendeleev Ridge complex and Makarov Basin.

Reflection seismic indicates some 200 to 500 m of stratified sediments lying partly flat, partly conformable over the Alpha Ridge basement implying that at least some of the basement structures were already formed when the sedimentation process started. Bathymetric depressions are partly filled by slumping. Morphology and shallow seismic structure are similar to those observed on oceanic plateaus such as the Manihiki Plateau.

Faulting of the ridge sediments suggests recently active tensional forces.

No distinctive acoustic reflectors were observed below the basement.

Bedrock samples dredged from the flank of the Cesar North Ridge consist of highly altered, very fine grained, volcanoclastic, vesicular, alkali basalts that originated in shallower water.

CESAR core 6 contains perfectly preserved microfossil assemblages that were never deeply buried or greatly heated since their deposition and that range in age from late Campanian to middle Maastrichtian (~77–70 Ma). This implies that at least part of the ridge escaped deformation by later (Cenozoic) tectonic processes.

The crustal root of the ridge is thickest under the ridge axis and appears to thin on either side, to the north from 37 to 40 km in the CESAR survey area to 17.5 km under the Marvin Spur, and to the south (but some 300 km farther west along the ridge) from 30 km to 13 km under the Canada Basin. These latter depths, based on gravity data alone, are less well constrained.

Seismic refraction indicates the P-wave velocity between basement and Moho increases smoothly from 5.1 to 7.3 km/s with no evidence of significant acoustic reflectors. The P-waveform is uniform and undisturbed for distances up to 100 km.

Gravity anomalies along an early 500-km-long profile across the ridge can be almost completely accounted for by the effect of sea-floor topography, crustal depth variation, and a veneer of 500 m or less of unconsolidated sediments in the topographic lows. This implies a gradual increase of density with depth, combined with an extraordinary lateral uniformity. There is little evidence of gravity signatures caused by faults or mafic intrusions that woulud indicate tectonic activity within the ridge after its construction, not even across the Cesar Trough.

An elliptically shaped positive free-air anomaly over the Ellesmere Island Continental Shelf break opposite the ridge indicates the continental margin is similar in morphology and crustal density structure to the remaining Queen Elisabeth Island and Beaufort Sea continental polar margins. This implies that the Alpha Ridge is structurally separated from the margin.

At the same thickness of 25 km the average crustal density is denser by 0.08 Mg/m^3 for the Alpha Ridge crust than for the Lomonosov Ridge crust.

Heat-flow values over the Alpha Ridge are low to moderate, 50 to 54 mW/m^{-2}, and extend into the Canada Basin.

An electrically conductive zone 90 km below the Alpha Ridge could be associated with partial melt in the asthenosphere.

Hypothesis. The long list of geophysical and geological constraints considerably narrows the field of possible scenarios to explain the evolution of the Alpha Ridge. In spite of the continent-like crustal thickness, seismic velocity structure, gravity structure, morphology, shape of the root, and geological sample evidence, all point to an oceanic origin. Forsyth and others (1986b) point out the similarity between the seismic velocity profiles beneath the Alpha Ridge strike line and the thickened "anomalous crust" beneath the active area of Iceland. The extraordinary lateral density uniformity is not characteristic of continental crust, and the average crustal density appears to be about 0.08 Mg/m^3 greater than that of the continental crust of the Lomonosov Ridge (Fig. 21). The arch-shaped, somewhat symmetrical appearance of the ridge, with its long valleys striking parallel to its axis, contrasts sharply with the flat-topped, block-faulted Lomonosov Ridge. Similarly, the shallowing of the crustal root toward the Makarov and Canada basins is gradual and also contrasts with the slab-shaped Lomonosov Ridge root (Fig. 12).

Jackson and others (1986) compared the topography and sedimentary and basement structure of the Alpha Ridge to that observed on the Manihiki Plateau. The Manihiki Plateau is a large area (0.5 × 10^6 km^2) of shallow water depth in the Pacific. The plateau has a system of deep internal troughs that are oriented roughly parallel to one of the boundaries of the plateau. In cross section, the troughs are similar to those observed on the Alpha Ridge. The average crustal seismic velocities are similar to those observed on the Manihiki and Otong-Java plateaus and other mid-Pacific features. The resemblance of crustal velocities and of many features from the reflection profile of the Alpha Ridge to those observed on records from the Manihiki Plateau provides an analogue for comparison and insight into the structure of the Alpha Ridge. Although even the better studied Manihiki Plateau is not well understood, it is considered to be oceanic crust of Cretaceous age (Winterer and others, 1974).

Although the marine origin of the Alpha Ridge appears probable, the mechanism of its evolution is not clear. Vogt and others (1979) noted the similarity between the high magnetization of the Alpha Ridge and that of the Juan de Fuca, Galapagos, and other hot spots and suggested, on the basis of the magnetic signature, that the accretion process may have been affected by Iceland-type hot-spot activities located near the ridge axis. The petrological and geochemical similarity inferred between the highly weathered volcanic rocks dredged from the Cesar South Ridge and the mafic igneous rocks occurring on Axel Heiberg and Ellesmere islands led Van Wagoner and Robinson (1985) to propose that the Alpha Ridge is the trace of a Hawaii-like intraplate hot spot that penetrated into the Arctic Islands.

Herron and others (1974) and DeLaurier (1978) concluded that the Alpha Ridge could not be a Cretaceous spreading center inactive for as long as 40 m.y. because its present sediment-compensated relief is 2,900 ± 500 m. DeLaurier predicted that, if it represents a typical former spreading center, its relief would have decayed to 500 m or less due to thermal cooling. Jackson and others (1986) argue that if the Alpha Ridge was formed near sea level then about 100 m.y. of thermal subsistence would place the present relief at the current level of about 3,000 m. Jackson and others (1986) proposed, based on the magnetic patterns of the Amerasia Basin and on plate reconstructions by Srivastava (1985), that the Alpha Ridge was formed by accretion of mantle material originating from a hot spot. According to this hypothesis, an incipient spreading axis was originally located between the Arctic Islands and Alaska and subsequently opened up the Canada Basin when Alaska rotated some 70° anticlockwise away from the Arctic Islands to its present location (Carey, 1958; Hamilton, 1970; Tailleur, 1973; Grantz and others, 1979; Irving and Sweeney, 1982). As the spreading axis rotated some 35°, with its pole of rotation located near present-day Mackenzie Delta, a mantle plume located close to the spreading center produced a lot of magma and left a thick crust, the Alpha Ridge, in its wake. Forsyth and others (1986b) proposed that the Alpha Ridge and Iceland were affected by the same mantle plume and that the Alpha Ridge was formed by within-plate volcanism.

The above discussion suggests that the Alpha Ridge crust is oceanic in character and was formed, in one of three ways: (1) similar to Iceland by a combination of sea-floor spreading and plate-margin hot-spot activities, or (2) similar to Hawaii by intraplate hot-spot activities, or (3) by complex sea-floor accretion associated with a migrating rift-rift-shear triple junction that produced the Canada Basin sea floor behind the rotating Arctic-Alaska block.

If the ridge is oceanic in nature and a thermal origin is assumed, the time of its formation can be bracketed from magnetic measurements plus studies of heat flow, biostratigraphy, and palynology of sediment cores recovered from the crustal area. The strong, mainly positive magnetic anomalies over the Alpha Ridge indicate that it formed during an interval dominated by normal geomagnetic polarity. Assuming the construction period lasted much more than 2 or 3 m.y., as seems likely given the large dimensions of the ridge, the reversal record contains two candidate time spans within the Cretaceous period, 122–84 and 80–72 Ma (Palmer, 1983). As previously mentioned, heat-flow values determined from T-3 and CESAR sediment cores indicate a basement age between about 60 and 120 Ma for the Alpha Ridge. Paleontological studies indicate that the retrieved shallow seabed samples are late Campanian and younger in age (Bukry, 1985; Barron, 1985; Mudie, 1985). If volcanic activity built the ridge, it must have happened before the overlying sediment blanket was laid down. The Alpha Ridge basement would therefore be pre-late Campanian, or at least 78 Ma, in age (Palmer, 1983).

The combined age constraints put the construction of the Alpha Ridge within the Cretaceous period between about 122 and 84 Ma. A ridge built rapidly, within 2 or 3 m.y., would render the magnetic age constraints ambiguous as most any period of normal geomagnetic polarity would suffice. But the effect on the time estimate is slight. The age brackets are 120 and 78 Ma, using only the CESAR and T-3 information.

Makarov Basin

Geological and geophysical constraints. Most of the geological and geophysical data on the Makarov Basin are limited to the Canadian side of the basin between Marvin Spur and Lomonosov Ridge, where the basin narrows to a grabenlike trough between 60 and 25 km wide, and were collected from ice islands ARLIS II (Wold, 1973) and on the LOREX expedition. The trough is filled with well-defined horizontally stratified sediments thickening to over 2 km toward the center (Fig. 6). A pronounced reflection from a synclinal structure about 1 km below the sea floor suggests a marked change in depositional environment. The sediments of the graben abut unconformably against the ridge on one side and against a buried seamount, which barely penetrated the sea floor on the south side, indicating that basement topography was formed before the sediments were laid down (Overton, 1982). This same seamount, also visible on the seismic airgun profile of Figure 5a, has been interpreted by Weber (1980) as consisting of high-density rock, and belonging to the Marvin Seamounts (Sobczak, 1977). Weber and Sweeney (1985) suggested the Marvin Seamounts are volcanic features that were in place within the Makarov Basin early in its history before onset of sediment deposition, and are distinct from the Marvin Spur, which, they argued, represents the Lomonosov-facing flank of the Alpha Ridge.

Gravity (Weber and Sweeney, 1985) and seismic refraction studies (Forsyth and Mair, 1984) on LOREX indicated a Moho depth of 14 km under the Makarov Basin between Lomonosov Ridge and Marvin Spur. Further to the south CESAR seismic refraction (Forsyth and others, 1986a) and gravity (Weber, 1986) results halfway between Marvin Spur and Cesar North Ridge (Figs. 3 and 12) revealed a Moho depth of 23 km and a very similar seismic velocity and density structure to that of the Alpha Ridge crest. That is in an area shown on bathymetric maps prior to 1985 as being part of the Makarov Basin. The CESAR results are therefore in agreement with Weber and Sweeney's (1985) hypothesis that the Alpha Ridge may extend to the Marvin Spur.

Aeromagnetic data to the west, which includes the Siberia

Plain, appear to be the only publicly available data on the Makarov Basin. In discussing the aeromagnetic anomalies, Taylor and others (1981) note that the maximum peak-to-trough anomalies extend over 700 nT, while wavelengths vary between 20 and 60 km. Using the same aeromagnetic data, Kovacs and Vogt (1982) found the Makarov Basin to be associated with a depth-to-magnetic source deep.

Age and origin. Little is known about the age and origin of the Makarov Basin. We have seen that the creation of the Alpha Ridge, between about 120 and 78 Ma, and of the Canada Basin, between about 120 and 80 Ma (Sweeney, 1984), could be genetically linked. The Lomonosov Ridge is continental in origin and began to separate from Eurasia between 64 and 56 Ma, or at least 15 to 20 m.y. after the Alpha Ridge and Canada Basin had formed. The Makarov Basin crust, where bounded by Alpha and Lomonosov ridges, may have formed by extension and, at least on the Canadian side, is not truly oceanic (Weber and Sweeney, 1985). Both the Makarov Basin and the Alpha Ridge experienced tensional faulting during or shortly after their formation before most of the overlying sediments were deposited. Down-to-basin faulting along the south flank of the Lomonosov Ridge is probably related to the formation of the Makarov Basin. From the above summary it appears, therefore, that the Makarov Basin formed in the interval bracketed by the opening of the Canada Basin and the initiation of the Eurasia Basin, or sometime between 118 and 56 Ma. It was created by crustal stretching that may have included sea-floor spreading, as suggested by Taylor and others (1981). In interpreting the aeromagnetic data, the authors matched the anomalies with a Cenozoic sea-floor-spreading time scale and identified anomalies 34 to 21 (84 to 49 Ma; Palmer 1983). They hypothesized that the basin was opening from Late Cretaceous through the Paleocene, postulated an axis of symmetry about coincident with the 87°N parallel of latitude, and calculated an average opening rate of 0.017 m/a.

CESAR-based scenarios tie the Makarov Basin genesis to the formation of the Canada Basin–Alpha Ridge. This would mean that the south flank of the Lomonosov Ridge formed at least 15 to 20 m.y. before the north flank was created. If this is so, it implies a change in style of sedimentation in the Makarov Basin, from slope-rise passive margin–type sedimentation the first 15 to 20 m.y., to pelagic sedimentation thereafter. This may explain the pronounced subhorizontal reflector, 1 km below the seabed, identified from LOREX intermediate reflection seismic and airgun profiling (Fig. 6).

CONCLUSIONS

The Lomonosov Ridge is continental in origin and was separated from Eurasia in the interval between marine magnetic anomalies 29 and 24, 65 to 56 Ma, at least 15 m.y. after the Alpha Ridge and the Canada Basin formed.

The creation of the Alpha Ridge is broadly contemporary with Canada Basin sea-floor formation, which probably took place between about 120 and 80 Ma (Sweeney, 1985). Their evolution could be genetically linked although the age determinations are imprecise. Whether the Alpha Ridge formed in an interplate or an intraplate setting is unresolved by CESAR. The rotation scenario for opening the Canada Basin about a pivot near the Beaufort Sea is supported by correlations between Mesozoic rocks in northern Alaska and the Canadian Arctic Islands and by the apparent increase with distance from the presumed pivot of the rate and/or amount of crustal stretching during continental breakup. In this scheme the Alpha Ridge could be a volcanic accumulation that represents the oceanic continuation of the zone of rapid pull-apart behind the rotating block. This would tie the ridge to the formation of the Canada Basin and favor its origin in a plate margin setting as proposed by Jackson and others (1986). Given the loose age constraints, the suggestion of an intraplate, or hot-spot trace, origin—as proposed by Vogt and others (1979), Van Wagoner and others (1986), Forsyth and others (1986a), and Taylor and others (1986)—is viable also. The earlier and late history of the presumed hot spot needs to be examined more closely.

CESAR has provided sufficient new information about the morphology, gross structure, thickness, composition, and bulk density of the Alpha Ridge to permit a preliminary correlation with like aspects of oceanic plateaus and marine volcanic features, in so far as they are known, in other parts of the world. The comparisons apply to the ridge segment between 90°W and 120°W, near Canada where CESAR operated. The western part of the ridge, west of 120°W, differs from the eastern segment in that it possesses slightly lower heat flow (Taylor and others, 1986), has somewhat less rugged subbottom topography, and exhibits less distinct reflections from the basement-sediment interface. Regional variations in ridge composition or structure may be indicated. Satellite magnetic measurements mentioned earlier suggest that continental elements may form part of the ridge. Many uncertainties remain (Sweeney and Weber, 1986).

The Makarov Basin crust, where bounded by the Alpha and Lomonosov ridges, was created by crustal stretching and may have included sea-floor spreading west of 160°W. The place of the Makarov Basin in the tectonic chronology of the central Arctic is enigmatic; it is presumed to have formed in the interval bracketed by sea-floor formation in the Canadian Basin and the initiation of the Eurasia Basin, or sometime between about 120 and 56 Ma.

The Canadian ice island (Weber and others, 1984) may, as did the ice island T-3 between 1948 and 1983, circle the Canada Basin completely and traverse the Alpha Ridge axis, and possibly the Makarov Basin, five to ten years from now. This will likely be Canada's next opportunity to improve upon the constraints established by CESAR regarding the nature and origin of the Alpha Ridge (Sweeney and Weber, 1986).

REFERENCES

Aagaard, K., 1981, On the deep circulation in the Arctic Ocean: Deep-Sea Research, v. 28A, p. 251–268.

Aksu, A. E., 1985a, Paleomagnetic stratigraphy of the CESAR cores, in Jackson, H. R., and others, eds., Initial geologic report on CESAR; The Canadian expedition to study the Alpha Ridge, Arctic Ocean: Geological Survey of Canada Paper 84-22, p. 101–114.

—— , 1985b, Planktonic foraminiferal and oxygen isotopic stratigraphy of CESAR cores 102 and 103; Preliminary results, in Jackson, H. R., and others, eds., Initial geological report on CESAR; The Canadian expedition to study the Alpha Ridge, Arctic Ocean: Geological Survey of Canada Paper 84-22, p. 115–124.

Amos, C. L., 1985, Bottom photography and sediment analysis, in Jackson, H. R., and others, eds., Initial geological report on CESAR; the Canadian expedition to study the Alpha Ridge, Arctic Ocean: Geological Survey of Canada Paper 84-22, p. 25–46.

Asudeh, I., Green, A. G., and Forsyth, D. A., 1985, The uniform waveforms of Arctic crustal data from CESAR 1983; An extensive study of multiple reflections and P to S converted phases [abs.]: Geophysics, v. 50, p. 1362–1363.

Barron, J. A., 1985, Diatom biostratigraphy of CESAR 6 core, Alpha Ridge, Arctic Ocean, in Jackson, H. R., and others, eds., Initial geological report on CESAR; The Canadian expedition to study the Alpha Ridge, Arctic Ocean: Geological Survey of Canada Paper 84-22, p. 137–148.

Beal, M. A., 1969, Bathymetry and structure of the Arctic Ocean [Ph.D. thesis]: Corvallis, Oregon State University, 205 p.

—— , 1983, Letters to the editor: Arctic, v. 36, p. 372–373.

Beal, M. A., Edvalson, F., Hunkins, K., Molloy, A., and Ostenso, N. A., 1966, The floor of the Arctic Ocean: Geographic names, Arctic, v. 19, p. 215–219.

Belov, N. A., and Lapina, N. N., 1958, Bottom sediments in the central portion of the Arctic Ocean: Leningrad, Transactions of the Arctic Geology Institute, v. 85, no. 9, p. 90–116 (in Russian).

Blasco, S. M., Bornhold, B. D., and Lewis, C.F.M., 1979, Preliminary results of surficial geology and geomorphology studies of the Lomonosov Ridge, Central Arctic Basin: Current Research, Geological Survey of Canada Paper 79-1C, p. 73–83.

Bukry, D., 1985, Correlation of Late Cretaceous Arctic silicoflagellates from Alpha Ridge, in Jackson, H. R., and others, eds., Initial geological report on CESAR; The Canadian expedition to study the Alpha Ridge, Arctic Ocean: Geological Survey of Canada Paper 84-22, p. 125–136.

Burkhanov, V., 1956, New Soviet discoveries in the Arctic: Moscow, Foreign Languages Publishing House, 60 p.

Cabaniss, G. H., 1962, Geophysical data from U.S. Arctic drifting stations, 1957–60: Air Force Cambridge Research Laboratory U.S.A.F., Research Note AFCRL-62-683, 234 p.

Camfield, P. A., Kurtz, R. D., Drury, M. J., and Niblett, E. R., 1980, Magnetovariational and magnetotelluric studies over the Lomonosov Ridge and the Makarov and Fram basins of the Arctic Ocean; Operation LOREX: EOS American Geophysical Union Transactions, v. 61, p. 277.

Carey, S. W., 1958, The orocline concept in geotectonics: Royal Society of Tasmania Paper, Proceedings, v. 59, p. 255–288.

Clark, D. L., 1969, Paleoecology and sedimentation in part of the Arctic Basin: Arctic, v. 22, p. 233–245.

—— , 1974, Late Mesozoic and Early Cenozoic sediment cores from the Arctic Ocean: Geology, v. 2, p. 41–44.

Clark, D. L., and Hanson, A., 1983, Central Arctic Ocean sediment texture; A key to ice transport mechanisms, in Moinia, B. F., ed., Glacial marine sedimentation: Plenum Publishing Company, p. 301–329.

Clark, D. L., Whitman, R. R., Morgan, K. A., and Mackey, S. D., 1980, Stratigraphy and glacial-marine sediments of the Amerasian Basin, central Arctic Ocean: Geological Society of America Special Paper 181, 57 p.

Coles, R. L., 1980, The LOREX magnetic gradient and total field experiments, 1979: Ottawa, Earth Physics Branch, Geomagnetic Laboratory Report, 12 p. (unpublished).

—— , 1985, Magsat scalar magnetic anomalies at northern high latitudes: Journal of Geophysical Research, v. 90, p. 2576–2582.

Coles, R. L., and Haines, G. V., 1979, Long-wavelength magnetic anomalies over Canada, using polynomial and upward continuation techniques: Journal of Geomagnetism and Geoelectricity, v. 31, p. 545–566.

Coles, R. L., Haines, G. V., and Hannaford, W., 1976, Large scale magnetic anomalies over western Canada and the Arctic: A discussion: Canadian Journal of Earth Sciences, v. 13, p. 790–802.

Coles, R. L., Hannaford, W., and Haines, G. V., 1978, Magnetic anomalies and the evolution of the Arctic: Publication of the Earth Physics Branch, v. 45, p. 51–66.

Crary, A. P., 1954, Bathymetric chart of the Arctic Ocean along the route of T-3, April 1952 to October 1953: Geological Society of America Bulletin, v. 65, p. 709–712.

Crary, A. P., and Goldstein, N., 1957, Geophysical studies in the Arctic Ocean: Deep-Sea Research, v. 4, p. 185–201.

Crombie, W. J., 1960, Preliminary results of investigations on Arctic Drift Station Charlie, in Raasch, G. O., ed., Geology of the Arctic: University of Toronto Press, p. 690–708.

DeLaurier, J. M., 1978, The Alpha Ridge is not a spreading center: Publication of the Earth Physics Branch, v. 45, p. 87–90.

Dietz, R. S., and Shumway, G., 1961, Arctic Basin geomorphology: Geological Society of America Bulletin, v. 72, p. 1319–1329.

Eardley, A. J., 1948, Ancient Arctica: Journal of Geology, v. 56, p. 409–436.

Ericson, D. B., Ewing, M., and Wolling, G., 1964, Sediment cores from the arctic and subarctic seas: Science, v. 144, p. 1183–1192.

Forsyth, D. A., and Jackson, H. R., 1984, Alpha and Lomonosov Ridge crustal structures [abs.]: Canadian Geophysical Union, 11th Annual Meeting, Halifax, p. 86.

Forsyth, D. A., and Mair, J. A., 1984, Crustal structure of the Lomonosov Ridge and the Fram and Makarov basins near the North Pole: Journal of Geophysical Research, v. 89, p. 473–481.

Forsyth, D. A., Dufresne, D., Jackson, R., and Pilon, C., 1983, Crustal structure of Arctic Ocean-floor ridges near the North Pole [abs.], EOS American Geophysical Union Transactions, v. 64, p. 760.

Forsyth, D. A., Asudeh, I., Green, A. G., and Jackson, H. R., 1986a, Crustal structure of the northern Alpha Ridge beneath the Arctic Ocean: Nature, v. 322, p. 349–352.

Forsyth, D. A., Morel-a-l'Huissier, P., Asudeh, I., and Green, A. G., 1986b, Alpha Ridge and Iceland; Product of the same plume?: Journal of Geodynamics, v. 6, p. 197–214.

Gordienko, P. A., and Laktionov, A. F., 1960, Principal results of the latest oceanographic research in the Arctic Basin: Akademii Nauk SSSR., Isvestiya, Geographical Series, no. 5, p. 22–23.

Grantz, A., Eittreim, S., and Dinter, D. A., 1979, Geology and tectonic development of the continental margin north of Alaska: Tectonophysics, v. 59, p. 263–291.

Gudkovich, Z. M., 1954–1955, Depth soundings. In Observational data of the scientific-research drifting station of 1950–1951, M. M. Somov, (ed.): Leningrad, Morskoi Transport, v. I, article 2, p. 1–28. Translated by D. Kraus, American Meteorological Society, ASTICA Document No. AD 117135.

Haines, G. V., 1985, Magsat vertical field anomalies above 40°N from spherical cap harmonics analysis: Journal of Geophysical Research, v. 90, p. 2593–2598.

Hall, J. K., 1970, Arctic Ocean geophysical studies; The Alpha Cordillera and Mendeleev Ridge: Washington, D.C., Office of Naval Research Technical Report CU-2-70, 125 p.

Hamilton, W., 1970, The Uralides and the motion of the Russian and Siberian platforms: Geological Society of America Bulletin, v. 81, p. 2553–2576.

Heezen, B. C., and Ewing, M., 1961, The mid-oceanic ridge and its extension through the Arctic Basin, *in* Raasch, G. O., ed., Geology of the Arctic: University of Toronto Press, p. 622–642.

Herman, Y., 1974, Arctic Ocean sediments, microfauna, and the climatic record in late Cenozoic time, *in* Herman, Y., ed., Marine geology and oceanography of the Arctic seas: New York, Springer-Verlag, p. 223–348.

Herron, E. M., Dewey, J. F., and Pitman, W. C., 1974, Plate tectonics model for evolution of the Arctic: Geology, v. 2, p. 377–380.

Hood, P., and Bower, M., 1980, Aeromagnetic reconnaissance; LOREX project: EOS American Geophysical Union Transactions, v. 61, p. 277.

Hunkins, K., 1961, Seismic studies of Arctic Ocean floor, *in* Raasch, G. O., ed., Geology of the Arctic: University of Toronto Press, p. 646–665.

Hunkins, K. L., and Kutschale, H. W., 1967, Quaternary sedimentation in the Arctic Ocean, *in* Sears, M., ed., Progress in oceanography, v. 4: New York, Pergamon Press, p. 89–94.

Hunkins, K., and Tiemann, W., 1977, Geophysical data summary for Fletcher's Ice Island (T-3) May 1962–Oct. 1974: Washington, D.C., Office of Naval Research Technical Report CU-1-77, 219 p.

Irving, E., and Sweeney, J. F., 1982, Origin of the Arctic: Transactions of the Royal Society of Canada, Series IV, v. 20, p. 409–415.

Jackson, H. R., 1985, Seismic reflection results from CESAR, *in* Jackson, H. R., and others, eds., Initial geological report on CESAR; The Canadian Expedition to study the Alpha Ridge, Arctic Ocean: Geological Survey of Canada Paper 84-22, p. 19–23.

Jackson, H. R., Forsyth, D. A., and Johnson, G. L., 1986, Oceanic affinities of the Alpha Ridge: Marine Geology, v. 73, p. 237–261.

Judge, A. S., 1980, Heat flow measurements in the vicinity of the North Pole [abs.], EOS American Geophysical Union Transactions, v. 61, p. 277.

Judge, A. S., and Jessop, A. M., 1978, Heat flow north of 60°N: Arctic Geophysical Review, Publication of the Earth Physics Branch, v. 45, p. 25–34.

Judge, A. S., Allen, V. S., and Taylor, A. E., 1984, Geothermal measurements on the Alpha Ridge during CESAR [abs.], Canadian Geophysical Union, 11th Annual Meeting, Halifax, p. 84.

King, E. R., Zietz, I., and Alldredge, R., 1964, Genesis of the Arctic Ocean Basin: Science, v. 144, p. 1551–1557.

—— , 1966, Magnetic data on the structure of the Central Arctic Region: Geological Society of America Bulletin, v. 77, p. 619–646.

Kovacs, L. C., and Vogt, P. R., 1982, Depth to magnetic source analysis of the Arctic Ocean region; Tectonophysics, v. 89, p. 255–294.

Kutschale, H., 1966, Arctic Ocean geophysical studies; The southern half of the Siberia Basin: Geophysics, v. 21, p. 683–709.

Lachenbruch, A. H., and Marshall, B. V., 1966, Heat flow through the Arctic Ocean floor; The Canada Basin–Alpha Rise boundary: Journal of Geophysical Research, v. 71, p. 1223–1248.

Langel, R. A., Coles, R. L., and Mayhew, M. A., 1980, Comparisons of magnetic anomalies of lithospheric origin measured by satellite and airborne magnetometers over western Canada: Canadian Journal of Earth Sciences, v. 17, p. 876–887.

Lillestrand, R. L., and Weber, J. R., 1974, Plumbline deflection near the North Pole: Journal of Geophysical Research, v. 23, p. 3347–3352.

Lubimova, E. A., Tomara, G. A., and Alexandrov, A. L., 1969, Measurement of heat flow through the Arctic Ocean floor in the vicinity of the Lomonosov Ridge: Doklady Akademii Nauk SSSR., v. 184, p. 403–405.

Lyon, W. K., 1984, The navigation of Arctic polar submarines: Journal of Navigation, v. 37, p. 155–179.

Mair, J. A., and Forsyth, D. A., 1982, Crustal structures of the Canada Basin near Alaska, the Lomonosov Ridge, and adjoining basins near the North Pole: Tectonophysics, v. 89, p. 239–254.

Morris, T. H., 1983, The stratigraphy and late Pleistocene sedimentological history of the Lomonosov Ridge–Makarov Basin, Central Arctic Ocean [M.S. thesis]: Madison, University of Wisconsin, 100 p.

Mudie, P. J., 1985, Palynology of the CESAR cores, Arctic Ocean, *in* Jackson, H. R., and others, eds., Initial geological report on CESAR; The Canadian expedition to study the Alpha Ridge, Arctic Ocean: Geological Survey of Canada Paper 84-22, p. 149–174.

Mudie, P. J., and Blasco, S. M., 1985, Lithostratigraphy of the CESAR cores, *in* Jackson, H. R., and others, eds., Initial geological report on CESAR; The Canadian expedition to study the Alpha Ridge, Arctic Ocean: Geological Survey of Canada Paper 84-22, p. 59–100.

Mudie, P. J., Stoffyn-Egli, P., and Van Wagoner, N. A., 1986, Geological constraints for tectonic model of the Alpha Ridge: Journal of Geodynamics, v. 6, p. 215–236.

Niblett, E. R., Kurtz, R. D., and Michaud, C., 1987, Magnetotelluric measurements over the Alpha Ridge: Physics of Earth and Planetary Interior, v. 45, p. 101–118.

Ostenso, N. A., 1961, Reconnaissance residual regional magnetic maps of the Arctic Ocean Basin: University of Wisconsin, Geophysical and Polar Research Center Research Report Series 61-2, 14 p. (unpublished manuscript).

—— , 1962, Geophysical investigations of the Arctic Ocean Basin: University of Wisconsin, Geophysical and Polar Research Center Research Report Series 62-4, 124 p. (unpublished manuscript).

Ostenso, N., and Wold, R. J., 1971, Aeromagnetic survey of the Arctic Ocean; Techniques and interpretation: Marine Geophysical Research, v. 1, p. 178–219.

—— , 1973, Aeromagnetic evidence for origin of Arctic Ocean Basin; Arctic geology: American Association of Petroleum Geologists Memoir 19, p. 506–516.

—— , 1977, A seismic and gravity profile across the Arctic Ocean Basin: Tectonophysics, v. 37, p. 1–24.

Overton, A., 1982, A seismic reflection profile across the Lomonosov Ridge, Central Arctic Ocean: Society of Exploration Geophysicists, Technical Program Abstracts and Biographies, 52nd Annual Meeting, Dallas, p. 87–89.

—— , 1984, Seismic reflection profiles across the Lomonosov Ridge and on the Alpha Ridge, Arctic Ocean Basin [abs.]: Canadian Geophysical Union, 11th Annual Meeting, Halifax, p. 85.

Palmer, A. R., 1983, The decade of North American geology 1983 geologic time scale: Geology, v. 11, p. 503–504.

Perry, R. K., Fleming, H. S., Weber, J. R., Kristoffersen, Y., Hall, J. K., Grantz, A., and Johnson, G. L., compilers, 1985, Bathymetry of the Arctic Ocean: Washington, D. C., Naval Research Laboratory, scale 1:4,704,075.

Riddihough, R. P., Haines, G. V., and Hannaford, W., 1973, Regional magnetic anomalies of the Canadian Arctic: Canadian Journal of Earth Sciences, v. 10, p. 157–163.

Saks, V. N., Belov, N. A., and Lapina, N. N., 1955, Our present concepts of the geology of the Central Arctic: Priroda, v. 7, p. 13–22; translated by E. R. Hope, Defence Research Board, Canada, translation T 196 R.

Sclater, J. G., Jaupart, C., and Galson, D., 1980, The heat flow through oceanic and continetnal crust and the heat loss of the earth: Reviews in Geophysics and Space Physics, v. 18, p. 269–311.

Smith, P. J., 1974, Plumbing at the North Pole: Nature, v. 251, p. 673–674.

Sobczak, L. W., 1977, Bathymetry of the Arctic Ocean north of 85° latitude: Tectonophysics, v. 42, p. T-27-33.

Srivastava, S., 1985, Evolution of the Eurasia Basin and its implications to the motion of Greenland along Nares Strait: Tectonophysics, v. 114, p. 29–53.

Sweeney, J. F., 1980, LOREX Gravity; Implications for Lomonosov Ridge composition and compensation [abs.]: EOS American Geophysical Union Transactions, v. 61, p. 277.

—— , 1984, Arctic tectonics; What we know today; GEOS (Publication of Energy, Mines, and Resources Canada), v. 13, no. 4, p. 7–10.

—— , 1985, Comments about the age of the Canada Basin: Tectonophysics, v. 114, p. 1–10.

Sweeney, J. F., and Weber, J. R., 1986, Progress in understanding the age and origin of the Alpha Ridge, Arctic Ocean: Journal of Geodynamics, v. 6, p. 237–244.

Sweeney, J. F., Weber, J. R., and Blasco, S. M., 1982, Continental ridges in the Arctic Ocean; LOREX constraints: Tectonophysics, v. 89, p. 217–238.

Sykes, L. R., 1965, The seismicity of the Arctic: Seismological Society of America Bulletin, v. 55, p. 501–518.

Tailleur, I. L., 1973, Probable rift origin of Canada Basin, in Pitcher, M. G., ed., Arctic geology: American Association of Petroleum Geologists Memoirs, v. 19, p. 526–535.

Taylor, A. E., Judge, A. S., and Allen, V., 1986, Terrestrial heat flow from Project CESAR, Alpha Ridge, Arctic Ocean 1986: Journal of Geodynamics, v. 6, p. 137–176.

Taylor, P. T., 1983, Nature of the Canada Basin; Implications from satellite-derived magnetic anomaly data: Journal of the Geological Society of Alaska, v. 2, p. 1–8.

Taylor, P. T., Kovacs, L. C., Vogt, P. R., and Johnson, G. L., 1981, Detailed aeromagnetic investigation of the Arctic Basin 2: Journal of Geophysical Research, v. 86, p. 6323–6333.

Tomara, R. A., 1973, The analysis of records of the geothermal gradient on the floor of the Arctic Basin, in Vlokavich, V. E., and Lubimora, E. A., eds., Heat flows from the crust and upper mantle of the earth; Results of research on the International Geophysical Project: Nauka, Moscow, v. 12, p. 145–149 (in Russian).

Treshnikov, A. F., Balakshin, L. L., Belov, N. A., Demenitskaya, R. M., Dibner, V. D., Karasik, A. M., Shpaikher, A. D., and Shurgaeva, N. D., 1966, Geophysical names of the main relief section of the seafloor in the Arctic Basin: Problemey Arktiki i Antarktiki, v. 27, p. 1–25.

Van Wagoner, N. A., and Robinson, P. T., 1985, Petrology and geochemistry of the CESAR bedrock sample; Implications for the origin of the Alpha Ridge, in Jackson, H. R., and others, eds., Initial geological report on CESAR; The Canadian expedition to study the Alpha Ridge, Arctic Ocean: Geological Survey of Canada Paper 84-22, p. 47–58.

Van Wagoner, N. A., Williamson, M. C., Robinson, P. T., and Gibson, I., 1986, First samples of acoustic basement recovered from the Alpha Ridge, Arctic Ocean; New constraints for the origin of the ridge: Journal of Geodynamics, v. 6, p. 177–196.

Vogt, P. R., and Ostenso, N., 1970, Magnetic and gravity profiles across the Alpha Cordillera and their relation to Arctic sea-floor spreading: Journal of Geophysical Research, v. 75, p. 4925–4937.

Vogt, P. R., Taylor, P. T., Kovacs, L. C., and Johnson, G. L., 1979, Detailed aeromagnetic investigation of the Arctic Basin: Journal of Geophysical Research, v. 84, p. 1071–1089.

Watanabe, T., Langseth, M. G., and Anderson, R. W., 1977, Heatflow in back-arch basins of the Western Pacific: American Geophysical Union special volume on Island arcs, deep sea trenches, and back-arch basins, p. 137–162.

Weber, J. R., 1963, Gravity anomalies over the Polar Continental Shelf: Contribution of the Dominion Observatory, v. 5, no. 17, p. 3–10. Also in Proceedings of the Arctic Basin Symposium, October 1962, Arctic Institute of North America, p. 41–45.

———, 1979, The Lomonosov Ridge experiment; "LOREX 79": EOS American Geophysical Union Transactions, v. 60, p. 715–721.

———, 1980, Exploring the Arctic seafloor: GEOS (Publication of Energy, Mines, and Resources Canada), v. 9, no. 3, p. 2–7.

———, 1983, Maps of the Arctic Basin sea floor; A history of bathymetry and its interpretation: Arctic, v. 36, p. 121–142.

———, 1986, The Alpha Ridge; Gravity, seismic, and magnetic evidence for a homogeneous, mafic crust: Journal of Geodynamics, v. 6, p. 117–138.

———, 1987, Maps of the Arctic Ocean seafloor; Part II, Bathymetry and gravity of the Alpha Ridge; The 1983 CESAR Expedition: Arctic, v. 40, p. 1–15.

Weber, J. R., and Jackson, H. R., 1985, CESAR bathymetry, in Jackson, H. R., and others, eds., Initial geological report on CESAR; The Canadian expedition to study the Alpha Ridge, Arctic Ocean: Geological Survey of Canada Paper 84-22, p. 15–17.

Weber, J. R., and Sweeney, J. F., 1985, Reinterpretation of morphology and crustal structure in the Central Arctic Ocean Basin: Journal of Geophysical Research, v. 90, p. 663–677.

Weber, J. R., Forsyth, D. A., Judge, A. S., and Jackson, H. R., 1984, A geoscience program for the Canadian Arctic Ice Island Research Project: Earth Physics Branch, Internal Report 85-26, 57 p.

Wilson, J. T., 1963, Hypothesis of the Earth's behaviour: Nature, v. 198, p. 925–929.

Wold, R. J., 1973, Gravity surveys of the Arctic Ocean Basin; Final Report: Milwaukee, University of Wisconsin, Department of Geological Sciences, 222 p.

Winterer, E. L., Lonsdale, P. F., Matthews, J. L., and Rosendahl, B. R., 1974, Structure and acoustic stratigraphy of the Manihiki Plateau: Deep-Sea Research, v. 21, p. 793–814.

Worthington, L. V., 1953, Oceanographic results of Project Skijump I and Skijump II in the Polar Sea, 1951–1952: EOS Transactions of the American Geophysical Union, v. 34, p. 543–551.

MANUSCRIPT ACCEPTED BY THE SOCIETY MARCH 31, 1987
GEOLOGICAL SURVEY OF CANADA CONTRIBUTION NO. 34886
CESAR CONTRIBUTION NO. 37

Crossing the ice belt at Coffee Gorge. Reproduced from Kane, E. K., 1856, Arctic Explorations: The Second Grinnell Expedition in Search of Sir John Franklin, 1853, '54, '55. Volume 1: Philadelphia, Childs and Peterson, facing p. 92.

Printed in U.S.A.

Chapter 19

Chukchi Borderland

John K. Hall
Marine Geology, Mapping, and Tectonics Division, Geological Survey of Israel, Jerusalem 95 501, Israel

INTRODUCTION

The Chukchi Borderland occupies a rectangular area about 600 by 700 km, or some 4 percent of the Arctic Ocean. It juts out into the deep Amerasia Basin north of the Chukchi Sea, between eastern Siberia and western Alaska (Fig. 1). This area encompasses three approximately north-south–trending segmented ridges: the Northwind Ridge, the Chukchi Cap and Rise, and the western (Arlis, Sargo, and T3) plateaus. Their plateau-like crests rise, in some cases, as much as 3,400 m above their surroundings and they are relatively shallow (depths between 246 and 1,000 m). The ridges have steep flanks, which in some places exhibit remarkable linearity over hundreds of kilometers, especially along the east side of the Northwind Ridge. Between these ridges lie the Northwind, Chukchi, and Mendeleev abyssal plains. These lie at depths between 2,100 and 3,850 m. To the south, the Chukchi Borderland is bounded by the broad and shallow Chukchi Shelf.

Although Figures 1a and b show the Chukchi Borderland to be one of the better-mapped features in the Arctic Basin, its existence was unknown until the 1950–1951 drift of the Soviet ice station North Pole-2 (NP-2; Somov, 1954–1955), when it was discovered by wire soundings. In fact, in the map of Emery (1949), the borderland appears as the deepest part of the Arctic Basin, primarily as a result of an erroneous sounding of 5,455 m from an aircraft landing in 1927, reported by Wilkins (1928). Following its initial discovery in 1950, the general morphology of the plateau was rapidly filled in. In the south, echo soundings in 1950 and 1951 from the icebreaker USS *Burton Island* and in 1957 by the USCGC *Northwind* allowed Fisher and others (1958) to map out the Northwind Ridge where it abuts the continental shelf. In June 1957 the United States ice station Alpha began its northward drift from the deep northern extension of the Chukchi Cap. In August 1958 the nuclear submarine *Nautilus* crossed the northern extension of the Northwind Ridge, which was mistaken for the Chukchi Cap (Dietz and Shumway, 1961). Then, in March 1959, the nuclear submarine USS *Sargo* sounded along the western plateaus adjacent to the Mendeleev Ridge (Beal, 1968), while in 1959–1960 Ice Station Charlie made an east-west crossing of the Chukchi Cap (Hunkins and others, 1962), previously mapped by NP-2. In 1962–1963 Ice Station Arlis II crossed the southern part of the area from southeast to northwest, discovering the Arlis Plateau. Ice Station T-3 (Fletcher's Ice Island, Station Bravo) crossed the Chukchi Cap in 1962 (Shaver and Hunkins, 1964), and in late 1966 made a complete east-west geophysical profile across the southern third (Hall and Hunkins, 1968). Those findings are published here for the first time.

Simultaneously, the Soviet ice stations NP-2, 4, 6, 8, 11, 13, 14, 16, 19, 22, and 23 drifted over parts of the area (Gorshkov, 1980, Plates 12 through 15) between 1950 and 1978. Data from these sources are for the most part not reflected in the bathymetric maps presented here. Of the 29 announced nuclear operations carried out in the Arctic Basin, a number of submarine tracks (Lyon, 1984) have provided additional profiles of the Northwind Ridge and the borderland's southern junction with the Chukchi Shelf. A number of spot soundings have also been made in this area from U.S. and Soviet airlifted gravity stations (Ostenso, 1962, Fig. 5). Numerous aeromagnetic flight lines also cross the area. They consist of U.S. surveys in 1961–1964 (Ostenso, 1962; Ostenso and Wold, 1970), and 1977–1978 (Taylor and others, 1981, Fig. 1b; Vogt and others, 1981, Figs. 2 and 8; Vogt and others, 1982, Fig. 5), and Canadian surveys in 1963 (Haines, 1967). The borderland has also been investigated by teleseismic means that show it to be the northern extension of a zone with large delays (1 to 4 sec) for teleseismic P-wave surface reflections (Stewart, 1980a, b).

This review has three objectives. They are: (1) to summarize information retrieved from the Chukchi Borderland over the past 35 years in diverse investigations; (2) to present previously unpublished data and interpretations from the 1966 traverse of T-3; and (3) to review and evaluate genetic models for the borderland in light of the available data.

PHYSIOGRAPHY

The bathymetry of the Chukchi Borderland is summarized in Figures 1 and 2, and shown on Plate 1. Figure 3 shows a profile across the southern third of the area, based on geophysical data obtained from T-3 in 1966.

Hall, J. K., 1990, Chukchi Borderland, *in* Grantz, A., Johnson, L., and Sweeney, J. F., eds., The Arctic Ocean region: Boulder, Colorado, Geological Society of America, The Geology of North America, v. L.

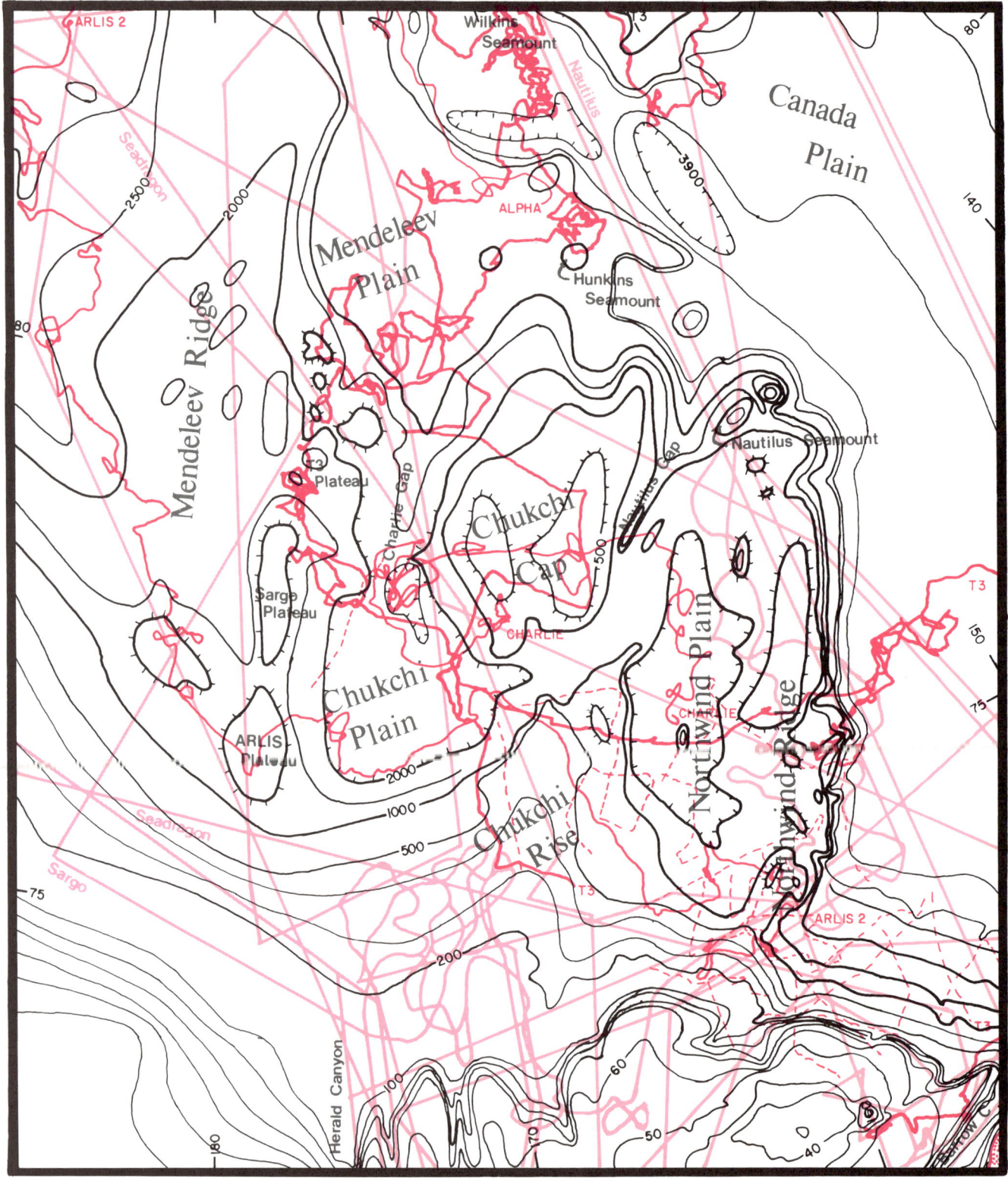

Figure 1. Data location map of the Chukchi Borderland. The bathymetric contours of Plate 1 are shown in dark gray. (a) Light red lines are U.S. nuclear submarine tracks from Lyon (1984). Solid red lines are U.S. ice station tracks. Dashed red lines are American icebreaker tracks. (b) Solid red lines are drift tracks of Soviet North Pole (Severnaya Polya) stations after Gorshkov (1980). Red dots are Soviet airlifted gravity stations after Ostenso (1962).

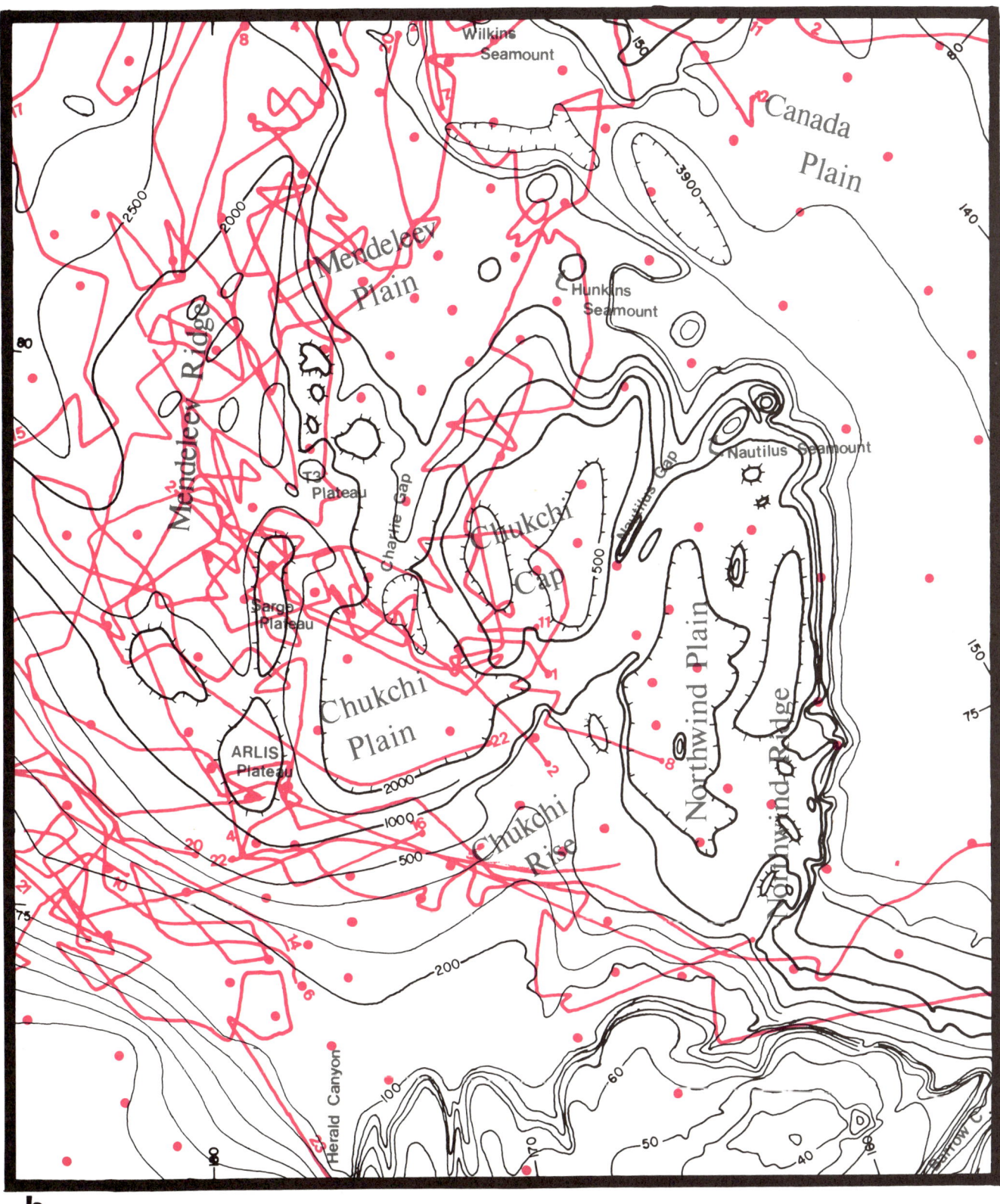

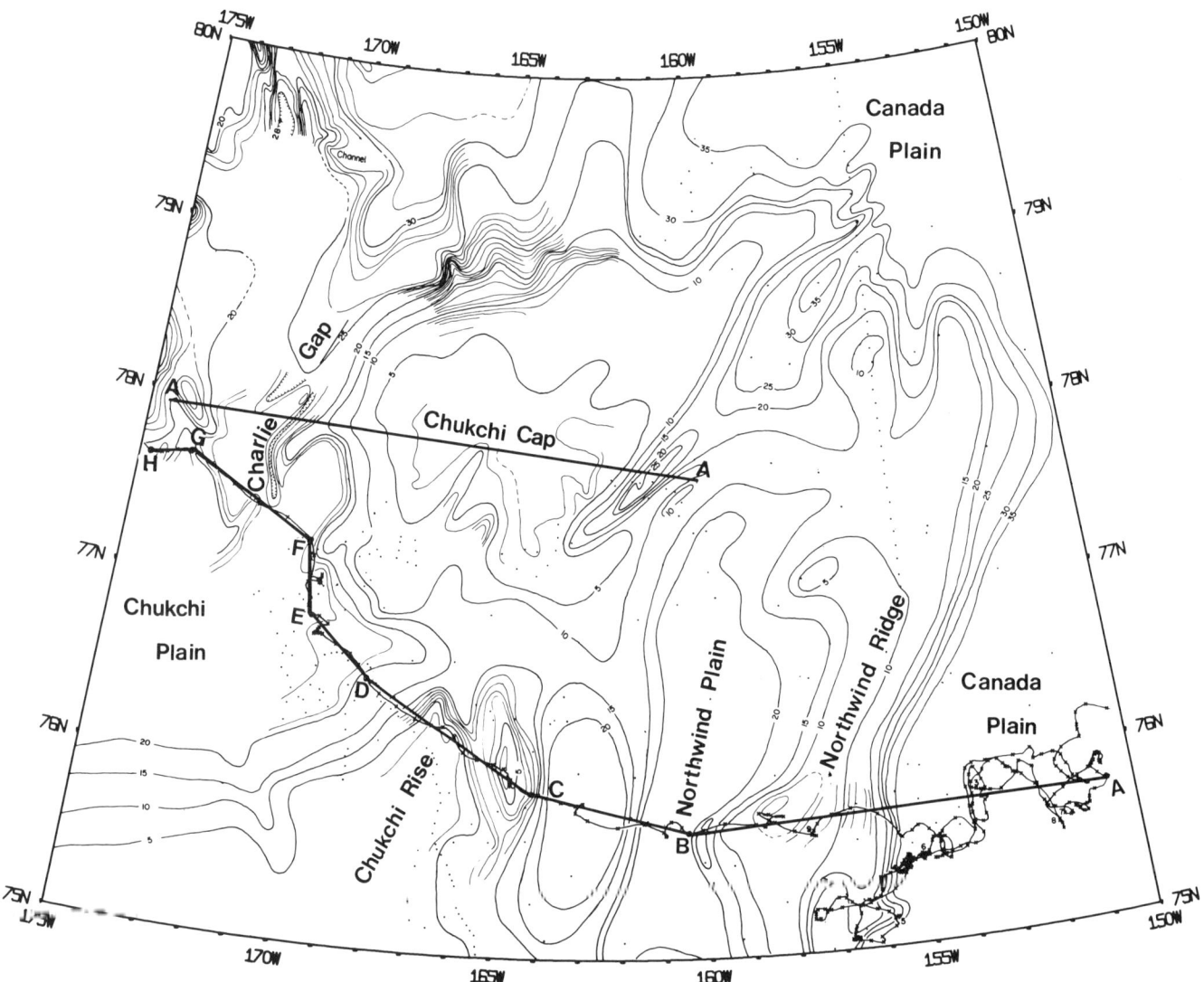

Figure 2. Bathymetric chart of the Chukchi Borderland with 100-m contours along the Ice Station T-3 drift areas (after Hall, 1970). The location of the 1959 Station Charlie profile A-A of Hunkins and others (1962) in Figure 4 and the 1966 T-3 profile A-H of Hall and Hunkins (1968) in Figures 3 and 5 are indicated. Black dots indicate supplementary spot soundings.

Northwind Ridge

The Northwind Ridge is about 500 km long and 100 km wide. Its crest lies at depths between 700 and 1,000 m, with a minimum recorded depth of 485 m. The crest is covered by 700 m or more of sediments that have been penetrated seismically on the eastern half of the ridge. Structural relief on the deepest reflectors indicates the presence of a rough basement immediately below, but no definite acoustic basement has been observed. Rising up to 3,400 m above the Canada Abyssal Plain, the eastern flank of the Northwind Ridge has been characterized as an escarpment, reflecting its steepness and linearity (Fig. 3). This escarpment is especially prominent in acoustic backscattering experiments carried out by Dyer and others (1982).

The Northwind Abyssal Plain

The T-3 geophysical profile (Fig. 3) shows that the western flank of the Northwind Ridge drops precipitously into a broad, flat valley—the Northwind Plain—at 1,820-m depth. This valley covers an irregular area about 300 by 100 km between the Northwind Ridge and the Chukchi Rise and Cap. The northern part of this plain, mapped by Ice Station Charlie (Hunkins and others, 1962), has depths of around 2,110 m. In the south the T-3 profile 9 (Figs. 2 and 3) shows the plain to be divided by a central high about 15 km wide rising to 1,316 m. The eastern half of the plain is very level at around 2,110 m, while the western half is about 50 m higher, and exhibits some bottom roughness. This depth difference suggests that the central high may be ridge-like

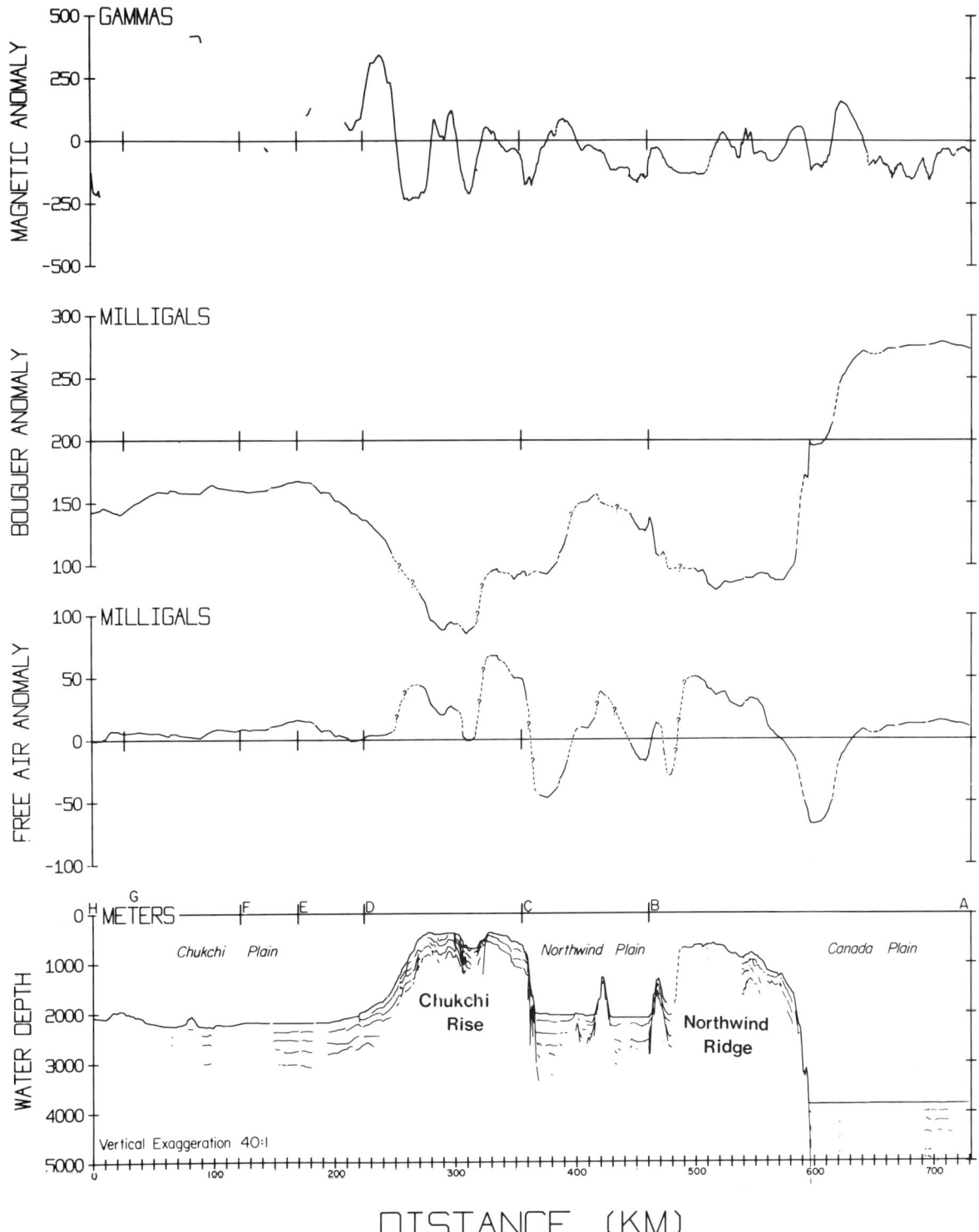

Figure 3. Geophysical profile across the Chukchi Borderland made from drifting Ice Station T-3 between August and November 1966. Data along the curved track (see Fig. 2) are projected onto the straight-line segments A-H at a fixed vertical exaggeration of 40:1. See Hall and Hunkins (1968) and Hall (1970, 1973) for details.

rather than seamount-like. More than 700 and 1,300 m of sediment fill are present beneath the eastern and western half of the plain, respectively, with only intermittent indications of acoustic basement. Just to the west of the central high the basement appears to rise to within 200 m of the sea floor and to be responsible for the minor topography observed there.

It is unlikely that there is any gap-like connection between the northern Northwind Abyssal Plain and the Canada Abyssal Plain to the north. A number of submarine tracks cross the northern part of the Northwind Ridge (Lyon, 1984), and Ostenso (1962) shows several Soviet airlifted gravity stations on the western margin of the Canada Abyssal Plain, which presumably would have identified any such connection.

The Chukchi Rise and Cap

Chukchi Rise is the name given to that part of the Chukchi Shelf that projects up to 200 km offshore toward the Chukchi Cap (DeLeeuw, 1967). In the T-3 profile (Fig. 3) the Chukchi Rise has a width of around 150 km and a minimum depth of 349 m, somewhat shallower than the Northwind Ridge, and displays a similar overall roughness, which appears to reflect structure within the sedimentary cover. The crestal plateau (Figs. 1 through 4) is cut by a 25-km-wide depression oriented northwest-to-southeast. This depression is about 300 m deep and contains more than 500 m of sedimentary fill with no indication of basement. The western edge of this depression consists of an east-dipping fault, which can be traced to a sub-bottom depth of 600 m. The observed dip is 17°, but an actual dip of 25 to 30° may be possible if an oblique crossing is considered. The eastern edge of the depression is bounded by apparent basement, which dips steeply to a recorded sub-bottom depth of 800 m. The eastern half of the Chukchi Rise is underlain by 200 to 500 m of sediment with one or two prominent reflectors overlying eastward-dipping basement. Its eastern flank drops more than 1,500 m to the Northwind Abyssal Plain in a series of very steep scarps. The western half of the Chukchi Rise crest is underlain by up to 600 m of slightly contorted sediment with no indication of basement. Its western flank smoothly joins the Chukchi Abyssal Plain at about 2,200 m. This smooth concave transition is in marked contrast to the abrupt Northwind Ridge–Canada Abyssal Plain transition. The seismic profile shows some low-angle westward-dipping reflectors on the western flank of the Chukchi Rise, and nearly 1 km of sediment beneath the Chukchi Abyssal Plain, again without indication of acoustic basement.

Figure 4 compares an east-west bathymetric profile across the Chukchi Cap, made during the 1959 drift of Station Charlie (Hunkins and others, 1962), with the T-3 sparker profile taken nearly 200 km to the south. Note the remarkable similarity of form between the two features, from the 25-to-30-km-wide central depression to the slopes on both east and west flanks. Seismic soundings at points along the northern track of Station Charlie also indicate a relative sediment thickness pattern beneath the Chukchi Cap that is similar to that beneath the Chukchi Rise to

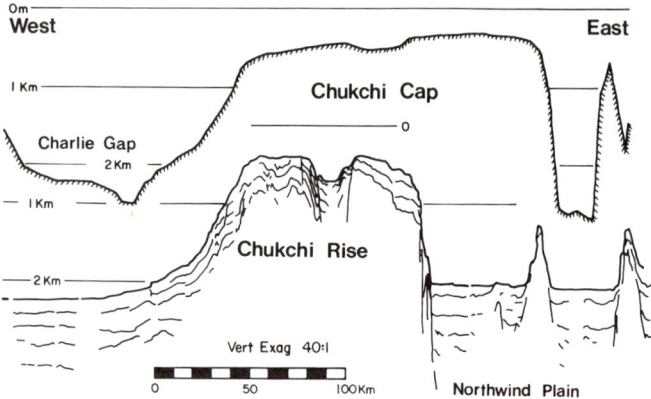

Figure 4. Comparison of the 1966 T-3 profile across the Chukchi Rise with the 1959 east-west bathymetric profile from Station Charlie across the Chukchi Cap (Hunkins and others, 1962, Fig. 3). See Figure 2 for profile locations. Both profiles are at a vertical exaggeration of 40:1. Note the similarities in crestal depressions, slope of the flanks, convex bulge of the lower western flank, and eastern pinnacles (ridges?).

the south. In both areas there is little or no sediment east of the central depression, and progressively increasing sediment thickness from the crest of the borderland west to Charlie Gap. On the crest of the Chukchi Cap, Hunkins and others (1962) noted a smooth, 3°, western dip; but the T-3 profile shows no such dip over the crest of the Chukchi Rise.

The crests of both the Chukchi Rise and Cap have micro-relief. Over the Chukchi Cap, Hunkins and others (1962) observed undulating relief of 5 to 30 m over distances of several hundreds of meters. The micro-relief is best developed on the level eastern areas of the crest. These authors preferred iceberg gouging to debris dumping or small-scale slumping as a cause. Another possibility, because of the regularity of the observed micro-relief, is the existence of sediment waves. Similar bedforms were reported by Hall (1979) for the crestal areas of the Alpha Ridge.

The Chukchi Cap is separated from the Chukchi Rise by a saddle about 75 km wide that lies 1,150 m below sea level. Little information is available for this area beyond one unidentified submarine track, the initial NP-8 drift track, and a few spot soundings. However, the saddle appears to preclude a connection between the western Northwind Plain at 2,080 m and the eastern Chukchi Plain at 2,070 m.

Some 150 km north of the Chukchi Cap lies Hunkins Seamount, whose concave crest rises some 600 m above its surroundings to a depth of about 2,150 m (Hall, 1973, Fig. 7, Profile X-Y-Z). According to Smith (1971), in August 1960 the Soviet drift station NP-8 reported an "active submarine volcano in the northeastern parts of the Chukchi Sea and the Beaufort Sea." At that time, NP-8 was drifting from west to east along the crest of the Mendeleev Ridge. It is not known whether this eruption was from a volcano on the southern flank of the Alpha-Mendeleev ridge complex (perhaps Wilkins or Harris Seamounts), or the north flank of Chukchi Borderland (perhaps Hunkins Seamount).

Chukchi and Mendeleev Abyssal Plains and Charlie Gap

Between the marginal plateaus of the Mendeleev Ridge and the Chukchi Rise and Cap lie two perched abyssal plains connected by an abyssal gap (Fig. 1). The Chukchi Abyssal Plain was first described by Shaver and Hunkins (1964). It has a flat floor at about 2,230 m and covers an area of about 150 by 150 km. To the north, it leads down via the doglegged Charlie Gap to the Mendeleev Abyssal Plain. Charlie Gap is some 200 km long, 100 to 500 m deep, and 2 to 10 km wide in its upper reaches (Hunkins and others, 1962; Shaver and Hunkins, 1964; Hall, 1970). It begins in the south as a narrow feature some 40 km wide and 500 m deep where it joins the Mendeleev Abyssal Plain. This plain, first described by Hall (1970), lies at a depth of about 3,300 m and declines very gently (about 1 m/km) to the northeast. While this gradient barely qualifies it as a true abyssal plain, it is considerably flatter than either the Northwind or Chukchi Abyssal Plains. The relative roughness of the three abyssal plains of the borderland is probably a function of the balance between basement deformation caused by tectonic movement and the amount of overlying sediment in place at the time(s) of deformation. Hall (1970, 1979) reported that more than 2,500 m of stratified sediment underlies the southern part of the Mendeleev Abyssal Plain. A layer of hyperbolic reflections occurs 300 to 500 m below the seabed, similar to those seen below the crestal region of the Alpha Ridge (Jackson and others, this volume, Fig. 12).

The western marginal plateaus—
Arlis, Sargo, and T-3 Plateaus

West of the Chukchi Abyssal Plain, along the southeastern flank of the Mendeleev Ridge, lie three marginal plateaus that are combined on Plate 1 as the Arlis Plateau. From south to north on Figure 1, these are: (1) the Arlis Plateau, discovered 22–23 October 1962 by Ice Station Arlis II, about 20 by 30 km with a minimum depth of 750 m (Black and Ostenso, 1962); (2) the Sargo Plateau, crossed by the nuclear submarine *Sargo* in 1960, with minimum depths of 700 to 900 m (DeLeeuw, 1967; Fig. 1); and (3) the T-3 Plateau, discovered in April 1967, 10 by 20 km with a minimum depth of about 1,100 m (Hall, 1970). Of these, only the T-3 Plateau has been investigated seismically. It appears to be covered by a kilometer or more of gently folded sediments overlying a basement that, where seen, has a rough upper surface (Hall, 1970, Fig. 14, Profile j-k-l).

Very little is known about the relationship of the marginal plateaus to the enigmatic Mendeleev Ridge immediately to the west. They are included within the Chukchi Borderland because of their relatively flat tops, shallow depths, and relief of 500 m or more above their immediate surroundings.

GEOLOGY AND GEOPHYSICS

Little is known about the geology of the Chukchi Borderland. Observations from U.S. drifting stations have provided some information about its surficial sediments, but no refraction, CDP seismic reflection, core, or dredge samples of its underlying deep strata or basement have been obtained. This section summarizes the known observations from the borderland beyond the morphological and seismic reflection data presented above.

Geology

The surficial geology of parts of the borderland is known from bottom photographs and short cores. Cromie (1961) reported on 110 photographs taken at relatively shallow depths on the Chukchi Cap from Station Charlie. These showed ice-rafted rocks, bottom fauna, and lebensspuren (life marks). Hunkins and others (1970) and Kitchell and Clark (1979) reported on 7 bottom-camera stations over the Northwind Ridge and Northwind Abyssal Plain, taken along the T-3 profile in Figure 3. The findings on the ridge are similar to those reported for the Chukchi Cap. Those for the Northwind Abyssal Plain showed no ice-rafted rocks, large pits, or mounds, suggesting that turbidity currents occur with sufficient frequency there to bury such features.

Short (less than 2 m) sediment cores were obtained over the Northwind Ridge and on the western flank of the Chukchi Rise during the 1966 traverse of Ice Station T-3. Later, as part of the U.S. Geological Survey (USGS) heat-flow program, many cores were recovered by T-3 from the western margin of the borderland and the Mendeleev Abyssal Plain to the north (Clark, 1969). Earlier, 22 short (less than a meter) cores were obtained from Station Charlie on the Chukchi Shelf (Cromie, 1960) and Chukchi Cap (Hunkins and others, 1962). A synthesis of these results by Clark (1969, 1981) shows the following: (1) Sedimentation rates on the Chukchi Cap and Plain are 1 to 2 mm/1,000 yr, approximately half the rate for the Canada Abyssal Plain, where density flows deliver considerable sediment. For the Chukchi Borderland, as much as 1 mm/1,000 yr may be of aeolian origin, with the rest largely ice-rafted and pelagic. (2) The upper 2 to 3 m of sediment is grayish brown lutite, sometimes with pinkish zones probably associated with a decrease in free iron and manganese oxide. The coarse fraction makes up 5 to 16 percent of the sediment by weight, with 30 to 90 percent of this consisting of foraminifera. This coarse fraction is about five times more abundant than that found in the Canada Abyssal Plain. (3) The gross mineralogy of the sediments from the ridges and plains of the Chukchi Borderland is more variable than for those found on the Canada Abyssal Plain. Carbonate makes up 9 to 16 percent by weight, with 20 to 40 percent quartz, 15 to 25 percent kaolinite, 15 to 25 percent illite, and less than 10 percent chlorite. Feldspar is also abundant. Thus, the Chukchi Borderland is sedimentologically similar to the rest of the Arctic Basin, except that its height and proximity to a continental margin produce a larger coarse fraction.

Belov and Lapina (1962) reported in general terms on some 500 cores, 1 to 4 m in length, raised between 1948 and 1960 by Soviet drift stations. Unfortunately, western investigators have been unable to use the results, which have been discussed in more than a dozen articles, because the findings are presented in only the most general way.

Heat-flow measurements

Sixty-four heat-flow measurements exist for the area of the western plateaus and the Mendeleev Ridge, and 11 more for the Mendeleev Abyssal Plain and seamount area north of the Northwind Ridge (see Langseth and others, this volume). On the western plateaus, Lachenbruch and Marshall (1969) report average values of around 50.2 mWm^{-2}, which are transitional between the higher values of 56.1 to 62.0 mWm^{-2} measured in the deep (>3,000 m) basins, and the average value of 44.0 mWm^{-2} measured on the adjacent Alpha Ridge (Plate 2).

Seismic refraction

A single, 426-km-long, reversed seismic refraction profile was shot in 1961 between Ice Station Arlis II and the U.S. icebreaker *Staten Island* (Kutschale and others, 1963). The profile extends from the northwest coast of Alaska to the northern North Chukchi Basin on the continental margin adjacent to the Northwind Abyssal Plain (Profile K in Fig. 6). The results indicate a layer with compressional wave velocity of 7.4 km/sec that rises from a depth of 32 km near the Alaskan coast to a depth of 20 km below the shelf edge to the northwest. The overlying, mainly Cretaceous sediments are interpreted to thicken across the Chukchi Shelf from 1.1 km at the Alaskan coast to 6 km near the edge of the shelf (Hunkins, 1966).

Demenitskaya and others (1973) indicated that no Soviet crustal refraction data had been retrieved from the Arctic Basin up to that time, and therefore, crustal modeling must depend on analysis of aeromagnetic data.

Seismology and seismicity

Wetmiller and Forsyth (1978) show no earthquake epicenters within the Chukchi Borderland for the period from 1908 to 1975. Considering that the threshold for complete detection is magnitude 4.5 in this part of the world, the area appears to have very low seismicity (see Fujita and others, this volume; Plate 2). However, a hint of some seismicity is indicated by Hakkel (1962, p. c-9), who states "the Chukchi Trench [Chukchi Plain/Charlie Gap] is the southern extension of this [deformation] axis into the Chukchi Sea shelf and epicenters of earthquakes are located in the trench (Linden, 1959)." Just to the north of the borderland, beneath the Mendeleev Plain at 80°40′N,167°W and in line with the trend of Hakkel (1962), lie two epicenters of magnitude 3 to 3.9 (Wetmiller and Forsyth, 1978).

Earthquake surface waves have also been used to study the crust of the Arctic. However, the position of the Chukchi Borderland, surrounded on three sides by abyssal plains, does not provide suitable travel paths for determining whether it is composed of continental crust.

Gravity

Wold and Ostenso (1971) published maps of free-air and Bouguer anomalies over the Chukchi Borderland, based on U.S. ice station and airlifted gravity station data. For a more complete discussion of the gravity field over the region see Sobczak and others (this volume) and Plate 3.

A crustal model (Fig. 5) was developed for the T-3 gravity profile (Fig. 3) of Hall and Hunkins (1968). The two-dimensional method of Talwani and others (1959) was used because the nearly linear profile lies approximately perpendicular to the general trend of the ridges. A simplified section consisting of four layers was used because of the absence of refraction data in the area. Fortunately, reflection data (Fig. 3) provided an indication of depth to basement over part of the profile, and good correlation of the free-air anomaly with depth to basement allowed extrapolation over the remainder.

With few exceptions, the model provides good agreement with the measured gravity. The steep free-air gradients appear to result from steep slopes in the sediment–basement contact. The calculated model indicates slopes of 25° and 50° for the western and eastern Chukchi Rise basement/sediment interfaces respectively, and 20° for the western Northwind Ridge interface. The profile morphology suggests a series of down-dropped blocks or grabens, bounded by faults.

It is worthwhile to note that the sharp, −70-mGal, free-air anomaly adjacent to the Northwind Ridge in Figure 3 continues along the ridge in Plate 3. It is modeled by a basement offset, probably a fault scarp, that bounds the east side of the ridge.

Aeromagnetics

Many aeromagnetic profiles have been obtained across the Chukchi Borderland. Ostenso and Wold (1970), characterizing the results of 15 low-level (450 m) overflights from 1961 and 1963–1964, describe the central area as having low-amplitude magnetic anomalies, with the margins on the west, north, and east having large amplitude anomalies. Taylor and others (1981) reported on 12 additional low-level (152 m) overflights of the northeast third of the borderland during U.S. Navy operations in 1977–1978. Vogt and others (1981) characterize these profiles as showing "relatively irregular, short to moderate wavelength anomalies similar to those mapped over other continental borderlands and fragments, such as the Lomonosov Ridge. Higher amplitude anomalies of positive sign are found at several sites along the margins of the Chukchi [Borderland]. These anomalies may be associated with the boundary between continental and oceanic crust."

Ostenso and Wold (1970, Fig. 18) have compared 21 of

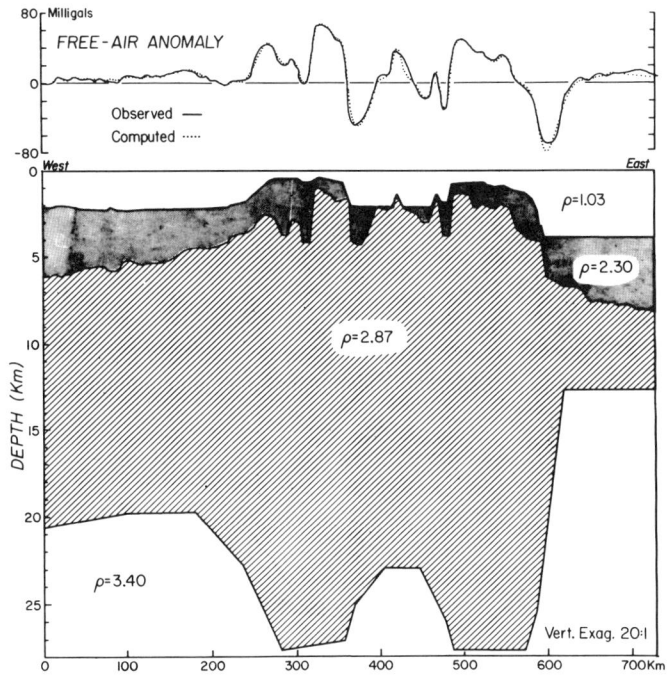

Figure 5. Composite gravity density model across the southern third of the borderland, corresponding to the 1966 T-3 geophysical profile A-H in Figure 3. Vertical exaggeration 20:1. Densities are in gcm^{-3}. The basement-sediment interface is based partly on acoustic basement from the 9,000 joule sparker seismic profiles, with the remainder extrapolated from the high-frequency component of gravity, which appears to correlate well with this interface. The dips of the steep contacts range from 20° to 50°.

these boundary anomalies. The amplitudes vary from 400 to 500 nT in the south over the western Chukchi Rise and eastern Northwind Ridge (Fig. 3) to 1,200 nT over the northern margin, with a maximum of 1,600 nT over the western Chukchi Cap, where Shaver and Hunkins (1964) inferred a basement ridge beneath the foot of the slope.

The zebra-stripe anomaly pattern, reproduced by Vogt and others (1981) from Soviet sources, shows general alignment of the magnetic stripes with the north-south structural grain of the borderland.

Ostenso (1962, Fig. 27) estimated depth-to-source from the magnetic anomalies over the Chukchi Borderland. The results appear to be generally consistent with the findings presented here from the T-3 seismic profile. Estimated depths are 1 to 1.75 km to magnetic material below the ridge crests, 2.25 to 3 km below the ridge flanks, and up to 4.25 to 8.5 km below the intervening abyssal plains.

Shaver and Hunkins (1964) used magnetic and gravity data to arrive at an estimate of 12 km of sediments below the Chukchi Cap. Based on the T-3 seismic data for the Chukchi Rise to the south (Fig. 3) and the spot reflection measurements from Ice Station Charlie over the Chukchi Cap (Hunkins and others, 1962), these "sediments" would have to include acoustic basement. This is a distinct possibility if the underlying "basement" represents old pre-Cretaceous (Franklinian?) rocks, as suggested for the adjacent continental margin by Grantz and others (1981).

Shimarayev (1969) used aeromagnetic data to compile a crustal section along the 173°W meridian btween 66° and 76°N (Profile S in Fig. 6). This profile indicates a continental crust some 31 to 40 km thick below the shelf break and a much thinner crust of 22 km at the edge of the Chukchi Abyssal Plain (Demenitskaya and others, 1973, Fig. 4). In sharp contrast to all other presently available data, the interpretation of Demenitakaya and others shows sediment cover thinning from 10 km at the shelf break to almost nothing at the edge of the Chukchi Abyssal Plain.

Magnetotelluric measurements

The Chukchi Borderland is the location of three of the eight published magnetotelluric measurements for the Arctic Ocean (DeLaurier, 1978). These measurements offer an indirect method of determining sediment thickness, upper mantle temperatures, and depth to conducting mantle. Measurements were made: (1) from NP-8 in 1,100 m of water on the saddle between the Chukchi Rise and Cap in 1959 (Trofimov and Fonarev, 1972); (2) by Swift and Hessler (1964) from Ice Station Charlie in 2,250 m of water over the Charlie Gap in the winter of 1959–1960; and (3) from Station Arlis I in 425 m of water on the Chukchi Shelf and Rise in 1960 (Circles MT-1, C, and A, respectively, in Fig. 6). From these data the thickness of conducting sediment and the depth to mantle conductors are estimated to be, respectively, 3.8 to 2.1 km and 165 to 230 km at location MT-1, 1.4 to 1.0 km and 100 to 400 km at location C, and 2.3 to 1.5 km and 100 to 400 km at location A. Temperatures at upper mantle depths are estimated to be between 1,100° and 2,000°C (DeLaurier, 1978). The sediment thickness estimates generally agree with estimates based on potential field data presented previously.

TECTONIC DEVELOPMENT

The Chukchi Borderland is an important element in the tectonic framework of the Amerasia Basin. It has been generally thought that the Chukchi Borderland consists of continental blocks that were somehow displaced from one of the margins of the Amerasia Basin, but there is little agreement as to which margin this might be or how the blocks moved. Because of its presumed continental nature, and because limited geophysical measurements suggest that its composition may be relatively uniform over large areas (i.e., it is probably not composed of allochthonous terranes), identification of borderland crustal rocks would likely determine its original position relative to the surrounding continental margins and, hence, severely constrain models for the origin of the Amerasia Basin itself.

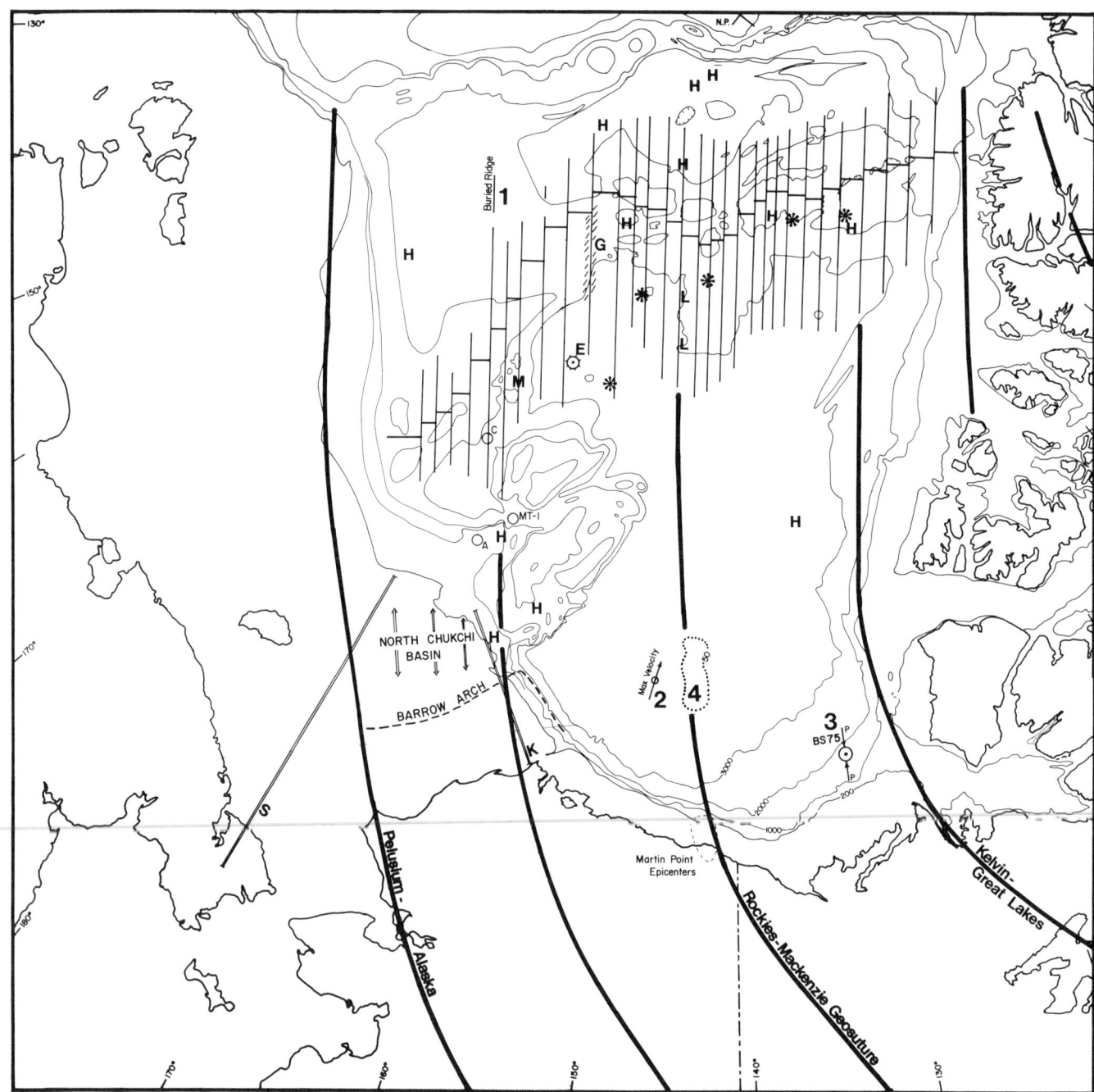

Figure 6. Location of various features mentioned in text. E—two co-located earthquake epicenters reported by Wetmiller and Forsyth (1978); A, C, MT-1—locations of Arlis, Charlie, and NP-8 magnetotelluric measurements; G—location of the Sotrudnichestva (Cooperation) Gap reported by Belov and Lapina (1958) and named by Treshnikov and others (1967); H—locations of basaltic hornblende detritus indicated on the map of Hakkel (1958). L-L—position of the 200-km-long Lamont Ridge, crossed seven times by T-3; M—Mendeleev Fracture Zone of Hall (1970, 1973); K—refraction profile of Kutschale and others (1963); snowflake symbol indicates seamounts with volcanic appearance. 1—location of buried ridge beneath the Siberia Plain (Kutschale, 1966); 2—location of anisotrophy measurement and direction of maximum upper-mantle velocity in the western Beaufort Sea (Mair and Lyons, 1981); 3—location of the BS-75 epicenter and direction of maximum stress inferred by Hasegawa and others (1979) for that earthquake; 4—zone of high free-air gravity anomaly cited by Vogt and others (1982, Fig. 9) as evidence for an extinct spreading axis. Note also the fracture zone and ridge axis pattern for the Alpha and Mendeleev Ridges proposed by Hall (1970, 1973), and the locations of geosutures proposed by Neev and Hall (1982).

Discussion of the various models

Because so few constraints exist, a number of often conflicting speculative models have been proposed for the origin of the Chukchi Borderland. In the sections below, these models are lumped into three classes.

(1) Rifted-translational models. (a) Heezen and Ewing (1961) were the first to speculate on the origin of the then-recently-discovered Chukchi Cap. On the basis of its topography, they suggested that it might be a "semi-detached piece of continental shelf," and compared it with the Flemish Cap off Newfoundland in the North Atlantic. No mechanism was given for its emplacement.

More recent models have been more specific, and have been concerned with either east-west or north-south translations.

(b) Herron and others (1974) proposed a model in which the Chukchi Borderland is part of the rifted trailing edge of the Kolymski Block that pulled away from polar Canada as the Amerasia Basin opened (see Lawver and Scotese, this volume, Fig. 5). The borderland may have been subsequently deformed by north-directed movement of the Canada Basin sea floor, which Herron and others (1974) thought was subducted along the Alpha-Mendeleev ridge complex.

(3) Hall (1970, 1973) proposed a fracture pattern model for the origin of the Amerasia Basin by spreading from the Alpha and Mendeleev ridges (see fracture pattern in Fig. 6). While not directly addressing the origin of the Chukchi Borderland, this interpretation provides geometric constraints, which form the basis for the model in the third class below. The model is based on the identification of many lineaments and several prominent basement fractures oriented parallel to the 142°W meridian. These fractures were mapped onto the western and northern parts of the Chukchi Borderland, and coincide with the steep lineations, basement ridges, and seamounts seen there.

(d) Jones (1980) proposed a similar model in which north-south spreading from the Alpha and Mendeleev ridges expands the Amerasia Basin. Concurrent transform motion along the Alaska-Siberia polar shelf-edge represents an extension of dextral slip of the Tintina Fault into the Beaufort Sea (see Lawver and Scotese, this volume, Fig. 16). Although the Chukchi Borderland is not discussed by Jones (1980), it would presumably have been rifted and translated by this spreading episode.

(e) Vogt and others (1982) proposed a model in which east-west-oriented sea-floor spreading north of Alaska breaks up the Chukchi Borderland and separates it from continental crust of the Siberian Shelf (see Lawver and Scotese, this volume, Fig. 15). This model is based on an analysis of magnetic lineations in the Canada Basin (Taylor and others, 1981), which were interpreted as indicating an approximately north-south-spreading axis. It suggests that the Chukchi Borderland was originally the bridge between the MacKenzie Delta–Banks Island and Siberian continental margins.

(2) Rifted-rotational models. This class of models is primarily based on the sphenochasm concept of Carey (1958), in which rotational movements produce wedge-shaped rifts. Although a number of authors (e.g., Boucher, 1978; Newman and others, 1977; Rickwood, 1970; Tailleur, 1969, 1973) have invoked this model to explain the origin of the Canada Basin, only those specifically addressing the Chukchi Borderland and its immediate surroundings are discussed.

(a) Shaver and Hunkins (1964) first proposed application of this concept to the Chukchi Borderland. Basing their model on the presence of a strong magnetic anomaly along the margin of the borderland, a feature often associated with continental margins, and the thick sequence of sediments interpreted from gravity and magnetic modeling, they suggested that the Chukchi Borderland was originally part of the Alaskan continental margin and had rotated counterclockwise 90° from the margin about a pivot located at 75°N,165°W. According to this model the Northwind Ridge represents an integral part of the ancient Alaskan shelf, while the Chukchi Rise and Cap represents the original continental shelf-edge, slope, and rise.

(b) Hall and Hunkins (1968) supported Shaver and Hunkins' (1964) model. This support was based on sedimentary asymmetry in the T-3 seismic profile (Fig. 3), which could suggest rifted basement with a thin sediment cover in the east over the Northwind Ridge and the eastern half of the Chukchi Rise, contrasting with a thick, shelf-like, sedimentary sequence on the western half of the Chukchi Rise and the edge of the Chukchi Plain.

(c) Mair and Lyons (1981) also supported this model on the basis of refraction measurements in the western Beaufort Sea, which showed an anisotropic upper mantle with maximum velocity in an approximate north-south direction (Fig. 6). This was in line with the observation that the directions of maximum velocity generally coincide with the direction of oceanic spreading (c.f., Whitmarsh, 1968).

(d) Grantz and others (1979) introduced a similar model that operated at right angles to that of Shaver and Hunkins (1964). Based mainly on their seismic investigations of the North Chukchi Basin, Grantz and others proposed that the Chukchi Borderland originated by rifting northward out of the North Chukchi Basin when the Canada Basin opened about a pivot point at 69.1°N,130.5°W in the Mackenzie Delta area. The steep contact between the Northwind Ridge and Canada Basin represents a fracture zone trace of this rifting event in their model (see Lawver and Scotese, this volume, Fig. 3).

(e) Vogt and others (1982, Fig. 12), in the form of an "alternative scenario" to model 1e above, presented a model similar to that of Grantz and others (1979). It is again primarily based on the new magnetic data of Taylor and others (1981). In this case, rifting and spreading also separated the broken-up borderland from the ancient Chukchi Shelf.

(3) Translation (rotational) models. (a) Neev and Hall (1982) presented a speculative tectonic model for the Earth in which a global system of subparallel spiraling geosutures was identified, based on alignments of major structural and stratigraphic discontinuities. In the Arctic, these include the Alpha and

Mendeleev ridge lineaments of Hall (1970, 1973), the margins of the deep basins, and others features indicated in Figure 6.

In this model, differential movement along adjacent geosutures can produce a broad range of rotations within the intervening crustal "slice." The Chukchi Borderland might, thereby, have been pulled out from the North Chukchi Basin by differential movements between the nearby geosutures, and rotated or translated into its present configuration.

SUMMARY

The Chukchi Borderland consists of three or more north-trending crustal blocks, with relatively flat tops and steep sides that rise between 1.5 and 3.5 km above the surrounding seabed. Both the blocks and intervening deep troughs are covered with sediments that seismic reflection, gravity, and magnetic data indicate are typically less than 2 km thick over the high blocks and generally more than 4 km thick below the troughs. There is some indication that this sediment blanket thickens to the west.

Free-air gravity anomalies and bathymetry are in phase over the borderland, whereas the magnetic anomaly field is generally subdued and tracks the other parameters only over the Chukchi Rise (Fig. 3). The magnetic character and morphology of the borderland crustal blocks are like those of the Lomonosov Ridge, considered to be a continental fragment. In contrast, the average density of the Chukchi Borderland crust (2.87 gcm^{-3}, Fig. 5) is much higher than that of the Lomonosov Ridge (2.50 gcm^{-3}), but similar to the average crustal density (2.88 gcm^{-3}) of the Alpha Ridge segment near Canada, thought to be marine volcanic in character (see Weber and Sweeney, this volume). This ambiguity about the nature of the crust below the Chukchi Borderland is unresolved by the existing geophysical and geological information.

The Chukchi borderland was created by processes associated with the formation of the Amerasia Basin. The classes of evolutionary models presented above for the borderland reflect the variety of schemes proposed for the creation of the adjacent ocean basin. The horst and graben appearance of the borderland (Figs. 3 and 4) suggest that a tensional regime played a major role in its development. An origin by pull-apart (model 1a) or by rifting (model 2d) from the northwest-trending Chukchi Shelf or by shearing parallel to 142°W (model 1c) does not explain the present northeast orientation of the "horst" blocks. Consistent with this orientation is an origin of the borderland by counterclockwise rotation from the Alaskan polar shelf (models 2a, 2b, and 2c), by rifting from the Canadian Beaufort Shelf (models 1b and 1e), by rifting from the vicinity of the Lomonosov Ridge (model 1d), or by differential movement along adjacent geosutures (model 3a).

This simple evaluation does not consider the larger question of how the adjacent sea floor formed. A more rigorous treatment of the proposed evolutionary models must await new information from the Chukchi Borderland and also a better understanding of the origin of the Amerasia Basin.

FUTURE RESEARCH

Future research targets should concentrate on solving two crucial questions: Where on the adjacent margins did the borderland originate? How was the borderland broken up and moved to its present location? Because of its remote location under ice-covered waters, answers will be difficult to obtain. However, there are several field experiments that could provide pertinent data. These are:

(1) High-resolution refraction and possibly CDP reflection measurements. As with the enigmatic Alpha Ridge, these would be the single most valuable type of new measurements for determining the nature of the crust below the borderland and for providing velocity/structural data to compare with the geology of the adjacent shelves. This could be accomplished by ice stations with satellite camps and icebreakers in times of favorable ice conditions. Refraction data would also be able to determine whether the western marginal plateaus near the Mendeleev Ridge are fragments of continental crust or erosionally truncated volcanic ridges.

(2) Preparation of more precise and detailed compilations and mappings of the morphology, gravity, magnetics, and sediment cover of the borderland. Sparse profile data must now be improved by detailed mapping capable of showing the geophysical "texture" for comparison with adjacent areas, and showing the block boundaries in order to reconstruct the breakup process. There remains much uncompiled data from submarines and a vast quantity of Soviet data from ice pack drift stations. These data sets should be merged, with unsurveyed areas filled in, preferably by additional submarine data. Submarines could be used to acquire gravity and sparker or low-frequency reflection data. Magnetics could be reflown in problematic areas with high-precision GPS navigation. Wide-area acoustic mapping of seabed morphology should be possible by swath-type techniques from submarines or drifting stations. Detailed mapping of the Arctic gravity field might also be accomplished using polar-orbiting, altimeter-equipped, SEASAT-type satellites and new algorithms for determining sea level from sea-ice height measurements, or the U.S. Navy's new P3V-mounted airborne gravity system (P. R. Vogt, personal communication, 1985).

(3) Although no bedrock exposures are known, it is quite likely that some exist on the steep flanks of the Northwind Ridge, the northern seamounts, and perhaps on the Cap and near the western marginal plateaus. These offer the possibility of sampling several kilometers down in the crustal section. These could be dredged by icebreakers or temporary ice stations as the opportunity arose, or as planned by the U.S. Geological Survey for the near future (G. L. Johnson, personal communication, 1985). Or perhaps they could be examined and sampled directly by a long-endurance submersible.

REFERENCES CITED

Beal, N. A., 1968, Bathymetry and structure of the Arctic Ocean [Ph.D. thesis]: Corvallis, Oregon State University, 204 p.

Belov, N. A., and Lapina, N. N., 1958, Bottom sediments in the central part of the Arctic Ocean: Leningrad, Transactions of the Arctic Geology Institute, v. 85, no. 9, p. 90–116 (in Russian).

——, 1962, Geologic investigations of the Arctic Ocean bottom during 25 years: Problemy Arktiki i Antarktiki Sbornik statei, v. 11, p. 97–104 (in Russian). Also in Ostenso, N. A., ed., Arctic Institute of North America Translation to English, 1966, p. l-1–16.

Black, D. J., and Ostenso, N. A., 1962, Gravity observations from Ice Island Arlis II, 6 October, 1961, to 3 April, 1962: Madison, University of Wisconsin Geophysical and Polar Research Center Research Report No. 62-8, 26 p.

Boucher, G. E., 1978, Rotation of Alaska and the opening of the Canada Basin: U.S. Geological Survey Open-File Report 78–96, 12 p.

Carey, S. W., 1958, A tectonic approach to continental drift, in Carey, S. W., ed., Continental Drift; A Symposium: Hobart, University of Tasmania, p. 177–355.

Clark, D. L., 1969, Paleoecology and sedimentation in part of the Arctic Basin: Arctic, v. 22, no. 3, p. 233–245.

——, 1981, Geology and geophysics of the Amerasia Basin, in Nairn, A.E.M., Churkin, M., Jr., and Stehli, F. G., eds., The Ocean Basins and Margins; Volume 5, The Arctic Ocean: New York, Plenum Publishing Corporation, p. 599–634.

Cromie, W. J., 1960, Preliminary results of investigations on Arctic drift station Charlie: Palisades, New York, Lamont-Doherty Geological Observatory Scientific Report 3, 33 p.

——, 1961, Preliminary results of investigations on Arctic drift station Charlie, in Raasch, G. O., ed., Geology of the Arctic, Volume 1: University of Toronto Press, p. 690–708.

DeLaurier, J. M., 1978, Arctic Ocean sediment thicknesses and upper mantle temperatures from magnetotelluric soundings, in Sweeney, J. F., ed., Arctic Geophysical Review: Ottawa, Publications of the Earth Physics Branch, Department of Energy, Mines and Resources, v. 45, no. 4, p. 35–50.

DeLeeuw, M. M., 1967, New Canadian bathymetric chart of the Western Arctic Ocean, north of 72°: Deep-Sea Research, v. 14, no. 5, p. 489–504.

Demenitskaya, R. M., Ivanov, S. S., and Volk, V. E., 1973, Crust of the Arctic Seas of Eurasia: Tectonophysics, v. 20, no. 1/4, p. 97–104.

Dietz, R. S., and Shumway, G., 1961, Arctic basin geomorphology: Geological Society America Bulletin, v. 72, no. 9, p. 1319–1330.

Dyer, I., Baggeroer, A. B., Zittal, J. B., and Williams, R. J., 1982, Acoustic backscattering from the basins and margins of the Arctic Ocean: Journal of Geophysical Research, v. 87, no. C12, p. 9477–9488.

Emery, K. O., 1949, Topography and sediments of the Arctic Ocean: Journal of Geology, v. 57, no. 5, p. 512–521.

Fisher, R. L., Carsola, A. J., and Shumway, G., 1958, Deep-sea bathymetry north of Point Barrow: Deep-Sea Research, v. 5, no. 1, p. 1–6.

Gorshkov, S. G., editor-in-chief, 1980, World Ocean Atlas; Volume 3, Arctic Ocean; Department of Navigation and Oceanography, Ministry of Defence, USSR: Oxford, Pergamon Press, 203 p.

Grantz, A., Eittreim, S., and Dinter, D. A., 1979, Geology and tectonic development of the continental margin north of Alaska, in Keen, C. E., ed., Crustal Properties across Passive Margins: Tectonophysics, v. 59, no. 1/4, p. 263–291.

Grantz, A., Eittreim, S., and Whitney, O. T., 1981, Geology and physiography of the continental margin north of Alaska and implications for the origin of the Canada Basin, in Nairn, A.E.M., Churkin, M., Jr., and Stehli, F. G., eds., The Ocean Basins and Margins; Volume 5, The Arctic Ocean: New York, Plenum Press, p. 439–492.

Haines, G. V., 1967, A Taylor series expansion of the geomagnetic field in the Canadian Arctic: Publications of the Dominion Observatory, v. 35, no. 2, p. 119–140.

Hakkel, Ya. Ya., 1958, Signs of recent submarine volcanic activity in the Lomonosov Ridge: Priroda, v. 4, p. 87–90. (Defense Research Board Translation T-296R by E. R. Hope, June 1958.)

——, 1962, Structural and tectonic features of the Arctic Basin, in Problems of the Arctic and Antarctic; Collection of articles, v. 11 (in Russian). Also in Ostenso, N. A., ed., Arctic Institute of North America Translation to English, 1966, p. c-1–13.

Hall, J. K., 1970, Arctic Ocean geophysical studies; The Alpha Cordillera and Mendeleyev Ridge [Ph.D. thesis]: New York, Columbia University, 125 p. and Lamont-Doherty Geological Observatory Technical Report 2, CU-2-70, Contract N-00014-67-A-0108-0016, November 1970, 125 p.

——, 1973, Geophysical evidence for ancient sea-floor spreading from Alpha Cordillera and Mendeleyev Ridge, in Pitcher, M. G., ed., Arctic Geology: American Association of Petroleum Geologists Memoir 19, p. 542–561.

——, 1979, Sediment waves and other evidence of paleo-bottom currents at two locations in the deep Arctic ocean: Sedimentary Geology, v. 23, no. 1/4, p. 269–299.

Hall, J. K., and Hunkins, K. L., 1968, A geophysical profile across the southern half of the Chukchi Rise, Arctic Ocean [abs.]: EOS Transactions of the American Geophysical Union, v. 49, no. 1, p. 207.

Hasegawa, H. S., Chou, C. W., and Basham, P. W., 1979, Seismotectonics of the Beaufort Sea: Canadian Journal of Earth Sciences, v. 16, no. 4, p. 816–830.

Heezen, B. C., and Ewing, M., 1961, The Mid-Oceanic Ridge and its extension through the Arctic Basin, in Raasch, G. O., ed., Geology of the Arctic, Volume 1: University of Toronto Press, p. 622–642.

Herron, E. M., Dewey, J. F., and Pitman, W. C., III, 1974, Plate tectonic model for the evolution of the Arctic: Geology, v. 2, no. 8, p. 377–380.

Hunkins, K. L., 1966, The Arctic continental shelf north of Alaska, in Poole, W. M., ed., Continental Margins and Island Arcs: Geological Survey of Canada Paper 66-15, p. 197–205.

Hunkins, K. L., Herron, E., Kutschale, H. W., and Peter, G., 1962, Geophysical studies of the Chukchi Cap, Arctic Ocean: Journal of Geophysical Research, v. 67, no. 1, p. 235–247.

Hunkins, K. L., Mathieu, G., Teeter, S. R., and Gill, A., 1970, The floor of the Arctic Ocean in photographs: Arctic, v. 23, no. 3, p. 175–189.

Jones, P. B., 1980, Evidence from Canada and Alaska on plate tectonic evolution of the Arctic Ocean Basin: Nature, v. 285, no. 5762, p. 215–217.

Kitchell, K. A., and Clark, D. L., 1979, A multivariate approach to biofacies analysis of deep-sea traces from the central Arctic: Journal of Paleontology, v. 53, no. 5, p. 1045–1067.

Kutschale, H. W., 1966, Arctic Ocean geophysical studies; The southern half of the Siberia Basin: Geophysics, v. 31, no. 4, p. 683–710.

Kutschale, H. W., Thiel, E., D'Andrea, D., Hunkins, K. L., and Ostenso, N. A., 1963, A long refraction profile on the Arctic continental shelf [abs.]: Proceedings, 13th General Assembly International Union of Geodesy and Geophysics, Berkeley, Paper B36, v. III, p. III-54.

Lachenbruch, A. H., and Marshall, E. V., 1969, Heat flow in the Arctic: Arctic, v. 22, no. 3, p. 300–311.

Linden, N. A., 1959, Seismic chart of the Arctic 1959; Seismological and glaciological researches during the IGY, No. 2: Moscow, Academy of Sciences, p. 7–17.

Lyon, W. K., 1984, The navigation of Arctic polar submarines: Journal of Navigation, v. 37, no. 2, p. 155–179.

Mair, J. A., and Lyons, J. A., 1981, Crustal structure and velocity anisotropy beneath the Beaufort Sea: Canadian Journal of Earth Sciences, v. 18, no. 4, p. 724–741.

Neev, D., and Hall, J. K., 1982, A global system of spiraling geosutures: Journal of Geophysical Research, v. 87, no. B13, p. 10689–10708.

Newman, G. W., Mull, C. G., and Watkins, N. D., 1977, Northern Alaska paleomagnetism, plate rotation, and tectonics [abs.]: Proceedings, Alaska Geological Society Symposium, April 4, 1977, Anchorage, Alaska, p. 16–19.

Ostenso, N. A., 1962, Geophysical investigations of the Arctic Ocean basin: Madison, University of Wisconsin Polar Research Center Research Report 62-4, 124 p.

Ostenso, N. A., and Wold, R. J., 1970, Aeromagnetic survey of the Arctic Ocean; Techniques and interpretations: Marine Geophysical Researches, v. 1, no. 2, p. 178–219.

Rickwood, F. K., 1970, The Prudhoe Bay field, in Atkinson, W. C., and Brosge, M. M., eds., Proceedings of the Geological Seminar on the North Slope of Alaska, Los Angeles: Pacific Section of the American Association of Petroleum Geologists, p. L1–L11.

Shaver, R., and Hunkins, K. L., 1964, Arctic Ocean geophysical studies; Chukchi Cap and Chukchi Abyssal Plain: Deep Sea Research, v. 11, no. 6, p. 905–916.

Shimarayev, V. N., 1969, Crustal structure of East Siberian and Chukchi Seas from aeromagnetic data: Uch. Zap. NIIGA, Regional Geology, v. 16, p. 26–29 (in Russian).

Smith, C. L., 1971, A comparison of Soviet and American drifting ice stations: The Polar Record, v. 15, no. 99, p. 877–885.

Somov, M. M., ed., 1954–1955, Observational data of the scientific-research drifting station of 1950–1951: Morskoi Transport, v. 1, no. 3, p. 180–403; v. 7, no. 2, p. 48–170 (in Russian). Vol. 1, Sec. 4, Translated by D. Kraus, American Meteorological Society, ASTIA Document No. AD 117135, 59 p.

Stewart, I.C.F., 1980a, Anomalous travel times of teleseismic P-waves reflected under Arctic marine areas: Marine Geophysical Researches, v. 4, no. 3, p. 291–304.

——, 1980b, Arctic lithospheric structure from delays of teleseismic P-wave reflections: Tectonophysics, v. 69, no 1/2, p. 37–62.

Swift, D. W., and Hessler, V. P., 1964, A comparison of telluric current and magnetic field observations in the Arctic Ocean: Journal of Geophysical Research, v. 69, no. 9, p. 1883–1893.

Tailleur, I. L., 1969, Rifting speculation on the geology of Alaska's North Slope, part 2: Oil & Gas Journal, v. 67, no. 39, p. 128–130.

——, 1973, Probable rift origin of Canada basin, in Pitcher, Max G., ed., Arctic Geology: American Association of Petroleum Geologists Memoir 19, p. 526–535.

Talwani, M., Worzel, J. L., and Landisman, M., 1959, Rapid gravity computations for two-dimensional bodies with application to the Mendocino submarine fracture zone: Journal of Geophysical Research, v. 64, no. 1, p. 49–59.

Taylor, P. T., Kovacs, L. C., Vogt, P. R., and Johnson, G. L., 1981, Detailed aeromagnetic investigation of the Arctic Basin, 2: Journal of Geophysical Research, v. 86, no. B7, p. 6323–6333.

Treshnikov, A. F., Balakshin, L. L., Belov, N. A., Demenitskaya, R. M., Dibner, V. D., Karasik, A. M., Shpaikher, A. O., and Shurgaeva, N. D., 1967, Geographic names for the main features of the floor of the Arctic Basin: Problems of the Arctic and Antarctic, v. 27, p. 5–15 (in Russian). NEL Translation 116, 1967.

Trofimov, I. L., and Fonarev, G. A., 1972, Some results of magnetotelluric profiling in the Arctic Ocean: Izvestia Akademi Nauk SSSR, Physics of Solid Earth (in Russian). American Geophysical Union English Translation, p. 81–82.

Vogt, P. R., Bernero, C., Kovacs, L. C., and Taylor, P. T., 1981, Structure and plate tectonic evolution of the marine Arctic as revealed by aeromagnetics; Proceedings 28th International Congress on Geology of Oceans Symposium, Paris, July 7–17, 1980: Oceanologica Acta, no. SP, p. 25–40.

Vogt, P. R., Taylor, P. T., Kovacs, L. C., and Johnson, G. L., 1982, The Canada Basin; Aeromagnetic constraints on structure and evolution: Tectonophysics, v. 89, no. 1/3, p. 295–336.

Wetmiller, R. J., and Forsyth, D. A., 1978, Seismicity of the Arctic, 1908–1975, in Sweeney, J. F., ed., Arctic Geophysical Review: Ottawa, Publications of the Earth Physics Branch, Department of Energy, Mines and Resources, v. 45, no. 4, p. 15–24.

Whitmarsh, R. B., 1968, Seismic anisotrophy of the uppermost mantle beneath mid-ocean ridges: Nature, v. 218, no. 5141, p. 558–559.

Wilkins, G. H., 1928, Polar exploration by airplane, in Problems of polar research: American Geographical Society Special Publication 7, p. 396–417.

Wold, R. J., and Ostenso, N. A., 1971, Gravity and bathymetry survey of the Arctic and its geodetic implications: Journal of Geophysical Research, v. 76, no. 26, p. 6253–6264.

Manuscript Accepted by the Society May 26, 1988

ACKNOWLEDGMENTS

The original field work and analysis were part of my unpublished doctoral studies, carried out at Columbia University and the Lamont-Doherty Geological Observatory from 1965 to 1970 under the supervision of Dr. Kenneth L. Hunkins, whose guidance, support, and encouragement is greatly appreciated. The work was funded by Contracts NONR-266(82) and N00014-67-A-0016 with the U.S. Office of Naval Research. I thank J. F. Sweeney, A. Grantz, and an anonymous reviewer for many constructive comments and criticisms, and gratefully acknowledge the time given to me by the Geological Survey of Israel (Israel Ministry of Energy and Infrastructure) to participate in the DNAG project.

Ours blancs.
(D'après Olaüs Magnus, 1555.)

From A. E. Nordenskjold, 1885, Voyage de la Vega Autour de l'Asie et de l'Europe [1878–1879], (translated from Swedish by Charles Rabot and Charles Lallemond). Vol. 1: Paris, Librairie Hachette et Cie, p. 131.

Chapter 20

The Norwegian-Greenland Sea

Olav Eldholm and Jakob Skogseid
Department of Geology, University of Oslo, Oslo, Norway
Eirik Sundvor
Seismological Observatory, University of Bergen, Bergen, Norway
Annik M. Myhre
Department of Geology, University of Oslo, Oslo, Norway

INTRODUCTION

Generation of oceanic crust at the boundary between the Greenland/North American and the northwestern part of the Eurasian plates has created the Norwegian-Greenland Sea. This relatively young ocean comprises a number of separate basins, plateaus, and ridges revealing that the break-up and separation of the two major plates have not, in geological terms, been a simple process.

In this context we define the Norwegian-Greenland Sea as the deep ocean between Europe and Greenland, bounded in the south by the Greenland-Iceland-Faeroe shallow transverse and in the north by the Spitsbergen Fracture Zone (Fig. 1). Geographically, the term Greenland Sea has been used for the ocean between Svalbard and northeast Greenland, but here we have adopted the geologically accepted usage in which it relates to the deep ocean between the Greenland-Senja and Spitsbergen fracture zones.

Passive continental margins consisting of well-developed shelves and slopes separate the Norwegian-Greenland Sea from the adjacent continental masses of Greenland, Svalbard and Fennoscandia. The two adjacent shallow seas, the North Sea and the Barents Sea were, prior to the formation of the deep ocean in early Cenozoic time, part of a much larger contiguous epicontinental sea between the continental masses.

The scientific exploration of the deep ocean, which started late in the last century, was until the 1950s focused on physical oceanography and marine biology. It was not before the mid-1960s that systematic research programs in marine geology and geophysics were initiated. These investigations were pioneered by regional surveys carried out by Lamont-Doherty Geological Observatory and the U.S. Navy, as well as surveys at the eastern margin by Norwegian institutions. The scientific activity gradually expanded, involving institutions in France, West Germany, and the UK. In 1974, deep water scientific drilling was carried out during Leg 38 of the Deep Sea Drilling Project (DSDP). Additional sites were drilled in 1985 by the Ocean Drilling Program (ODP), Leg 104. The commercial exploration in the North Sea has also led to detailed surveying of the margins on either side of the Norwegian-Greenland Sea. These programs have resulted in commercial drilling in several localities at the eastern margin; hydrocarbon accumulations have been found. As of today, a good understanding of the regional geological evolution of the Norwegian-Greenland Sea and its margins has been achieved. However, the recent research activity has also highlighted many unsolved problems, particularly relating to processes involving deep ocean and passive margin formation.

The objective of this chapter is to describe the various regional structural elements and geological provinces of the Norwegian-Greenland Sea, to review the plate tectonic evolution of the region and to discuss the important unsolved problems. Vogt and others (1981), Eldholm and others (1984), and Vogt (1986a, b,) have published comprehensive reviews of the Norwegian-Greenland Sea.

PHYSIOGRAPHY

As new data have become available, more detailed and accurate bathymetric maps have been produced. In this paper, we have used the map of Perry and others (1980), which outlines the physiography in an excellent way, as a base map. As thorough descriptions exist elsewhere (Vogt and others, 1981; Perry, 1986), we here review only the main elements. The primary features are the Mid-Oceanic Ridge, the continental margins and the deep basins (Fig. 1).

The Mid-Oceanic Ridge consists of three main segments: the Kolbeinsey, Mohns, and Knipovich ridges. The morphology of these ridges, which constitute the present plate boundary, varies along strike, although they exhibit most of the features associated with spreading mid-oceanic ridges. However, only Mohns Ridge is symmetrically located with respect to the adjacent basins. The

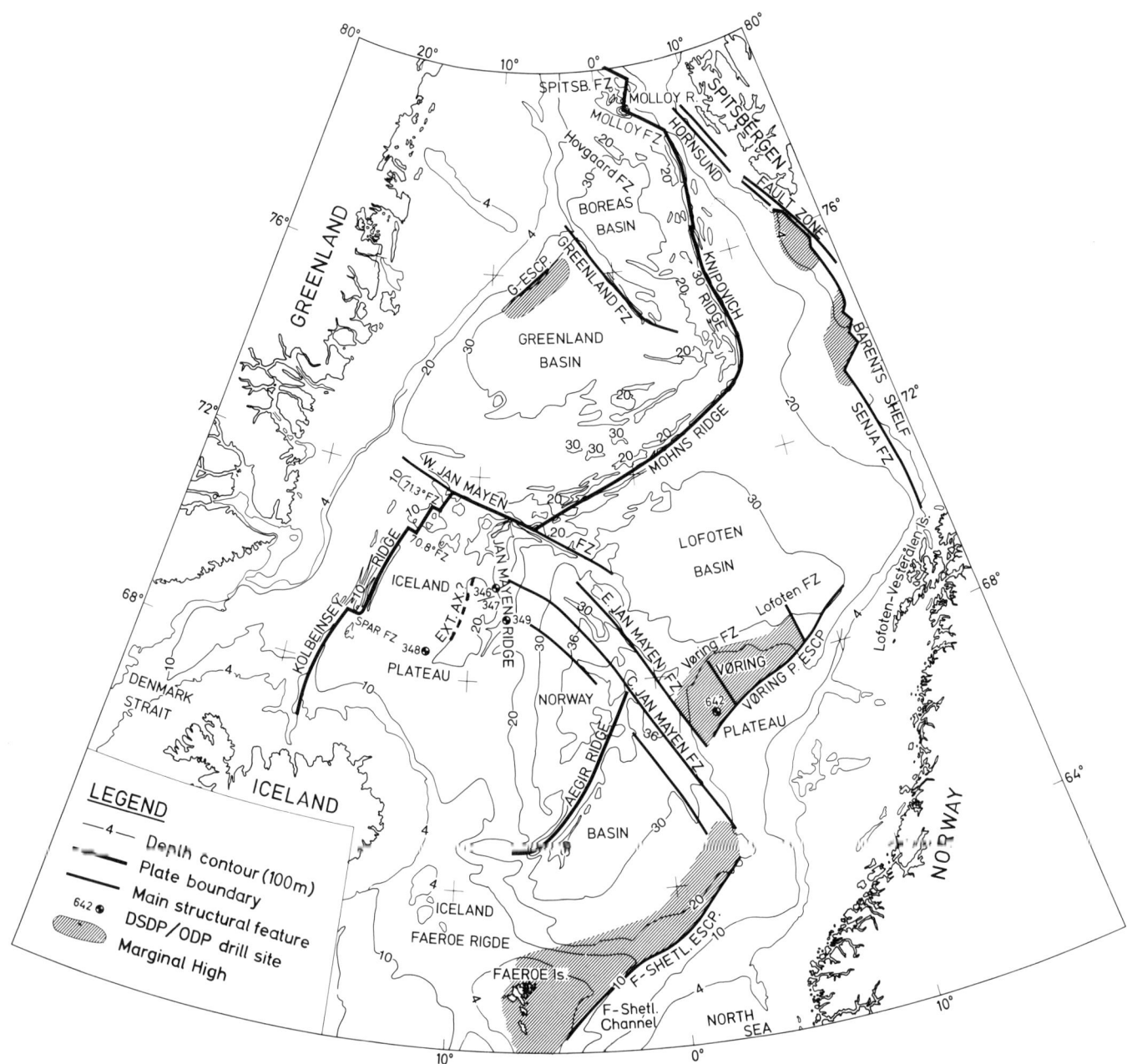

Figure 1. Main physiography and structural features in the Norwegian–Greenland Sea. Selected Deep Sea Drilling Project and Ocean Drilling Program drill sites shown. Simplified bathymetry from Perry and others (1980).

asymmetrical location of the plate boundary north and south of Mohns Ridge is related to complex plate tectonics, which have influenced both the ridge morphology and the general physiography of the entire Norwegian-Greenland Sea. Together with the short Molloy Ridge in the north, the Western Jan Mayen Fracture Zone, and some small-offset fracture zones, the main ridge segments form the boundary between the North American and Eurasian plates.

The nature of the continental margin varies considerably (Fig. 1). Most places exhibit a wide, deep shelf and slope, as is often found at high latitudes. In contrast, a very narrow shelf and steep slope are particularly well developed at the eastern margin off the Lofoten-Vestarålen Islands and central Spitsbergen. The local margin morphology reflects glacial and fluvio-glacial activity and sea level changes on the shelf, and mass movements such as slides and slumps on the slope. Off central Norway, a prominent marginal plateau—the Vøring Plateau—breaks the continental slope at a depth of about 1,500 m.

Physiographically, the deep ocean divides naturally into three regions separated by first-order fracture zone systems. The southern region lies between the Greenland-Iceland-Faeroe transverse and the Jan Mayen Fracture Zone, the central region is bounded by the Jan Mayen and the Greenland-Senja fracture zones, whereas the northern area lies between the Greenland-Senja and Spitsbergen fracture zones (Fig. 1).

The Greenland-Iceland-Faeroe transverse is a broad, shallow, and partly emerged volcanic ridge transecting the ocean. It is bounded by the 900 to 1,000 m deep Faeroe-Shetland Channel in the east and comprises the Faeroe Islands, the 400–600 m deep Iceland-Faeroe Ridge, Iceland, and the Denmark Strait with a sill depth of about 600 m between Iceland and the Greenland continental margin. Apparently, the ridge, which is almost devoid of sediments, is underlain by Icelandic-type oceanic crust that accreted subaerially and then subsided in a way similar to normal oceanic crust (Detrick and others, 1977; Thiede and Eldholm, 1983).

The region north of the ridge includes the Iceland Plateau and the Norway Basin. The Iceland Plateau, which is defined by the 1,800 m contour, increases gently in depth away from the Kolbeinsey Ridge. The northeastern plateau comprises the Jan Mayen Ridge. This flat-topped ridge, which plunges and decreases in width southward from the island of Jan Mayen, is bounded by a steep narrow slope toward the Iceland Plateau and a gentle slope toward the Norway Basin (Talwani and others, 1978; Myhre and others, 1984). The Norway Basin is characterized by an elongate central seamount chain with a continuous central depression believed to be an extinct rift valley, outlined by the 3,600-m contour (Fig. 1). A former spreading ridge (named Aegir Ridge or the Extinct Axis) in this region was postulated by Johnson and Heezen (1967), and further substantiated by Vogt and others (1970), LePichon and others (1971), and Talwani and Eldholm (1977). Recent studies have shown that the former spreading ridge may be offset by fracture zones in the northern Norway Basin (Nunns, 1983a; Skogseid and Eldholm 1986).

Jan Mayen Fracture Zone is composed of two segments. The western segment, which includes the present transform fault, trends west–northwest and is seen as a prominent bathymetric escarpment separating the Iceland Plateau from the Greenland Basin. The eastern part comprises a series of subparallel seamounts and basement depressions that trend southeast and approach the Norwegian margin along the southeastern flank of the Vøring Plateau. The eastern segment is structurally more complex than earlier anticipated and appears to be composed of two parallel features, the Central and East Jan Mayen fracture zones (Skogseid and Eldholm, 1986) (Fig. 1).

The central region of the Norwegian-Greenland Sea has developed from a relatively stable Mohns Ridge spreading axis, separating the Lofoten and Greenland basins whose deepest parts may be classified as abyssal plains. The Greenland Basin is 400 m deeper than its eastern counterpart, probably because of differences in the influx of sediments. Some local seamounts in the southern Greenland Basin might reveal recent volcanic activity.

The Senja Fracture Zone is buried beneath a huge thickness of sediments derived from the Barents Sea region. The Greenland Fracture Zone, on the other hand, has a distinct bathymetric expression as a monolithic elongate ridge. A slight change in trend is noticed at its southeastern end before it loses distinction at the flank of the Knipovich Ridge. The fracture zone separates the Boreas and Greenland basins; the 600 m difference in water depth on either side has been ascribed to a younger crustal age of the Boreas Basin (Eldholm and Windisch, 1974). However, we would like to stress two observations. First, as there presently is no offset between the Mohns and Knipovich ridges, the Greenland-Senja Fracture Zone is no longer active; second, its physiographic expression does not resemble typical oceanic fracture zones, but is more similar to an oceanic aseismic ridge.

The northern region is dominated by the Knipovich Ridge and the Boreas Basin. East of the ridge, there is a small basin between the continental slope and the ridge flank to the south, whereas the slope continues right onto the axial mountains in the north (Myhre and others, 1982). To the north of the Boreas Basin lies the Hovgaard Fracture Zone first mapped by Johnson and Eckhoff (1966). It consists of a western ridge block and an eastern seamount-like feature (Eldholm and Myhre, 1977). We note that the western ridge, although smaller, resembles the Greenland Fracture Zone both physiographically and geophysically. Finally a small, poorly known, ocean basin exists between the Hovgaard and Molloy fracture zones.

MAIN GEOLOGICAL FEATURES

The Sediments

The regional sediment distribution over the oceanic crust of the Norwegian-Greenland Sea shows that the acoustic basement in the seismic record generally corresponds to the top of oceanic crust formed at the ridge axis characterized by oceanic layer 2 velocities (Myhre and Eldholm, 1981), rough topography, and opaque acoustic character. In some areas, however, particularly at the marginal highs (Fig. 1) and parts of the Iceland Plateau, the apparent basement becomes shallow and quite smooth, possibly indicating basalt flows or other highly reflective horizons masking a true basement below. The sediment thickness map (Fig. 2) reveals the following regional features:

• Despite local complexities, there is a first-order relationship with the plate tectonic evolutionary pattern, in that the thickness increases with crustal age. Except for the Knipovich Ridge, the axial region is almost devoid of sediments, and the Aegir Ridge in the Norway Basin is clearly recognized.

• Superimposed on the first-order pattern are the effects of proximity to continents, major drainage systems, and structural elements in the sea floor. For example, outbuilding of material from the Barents Shelf, which was emergent during most of the

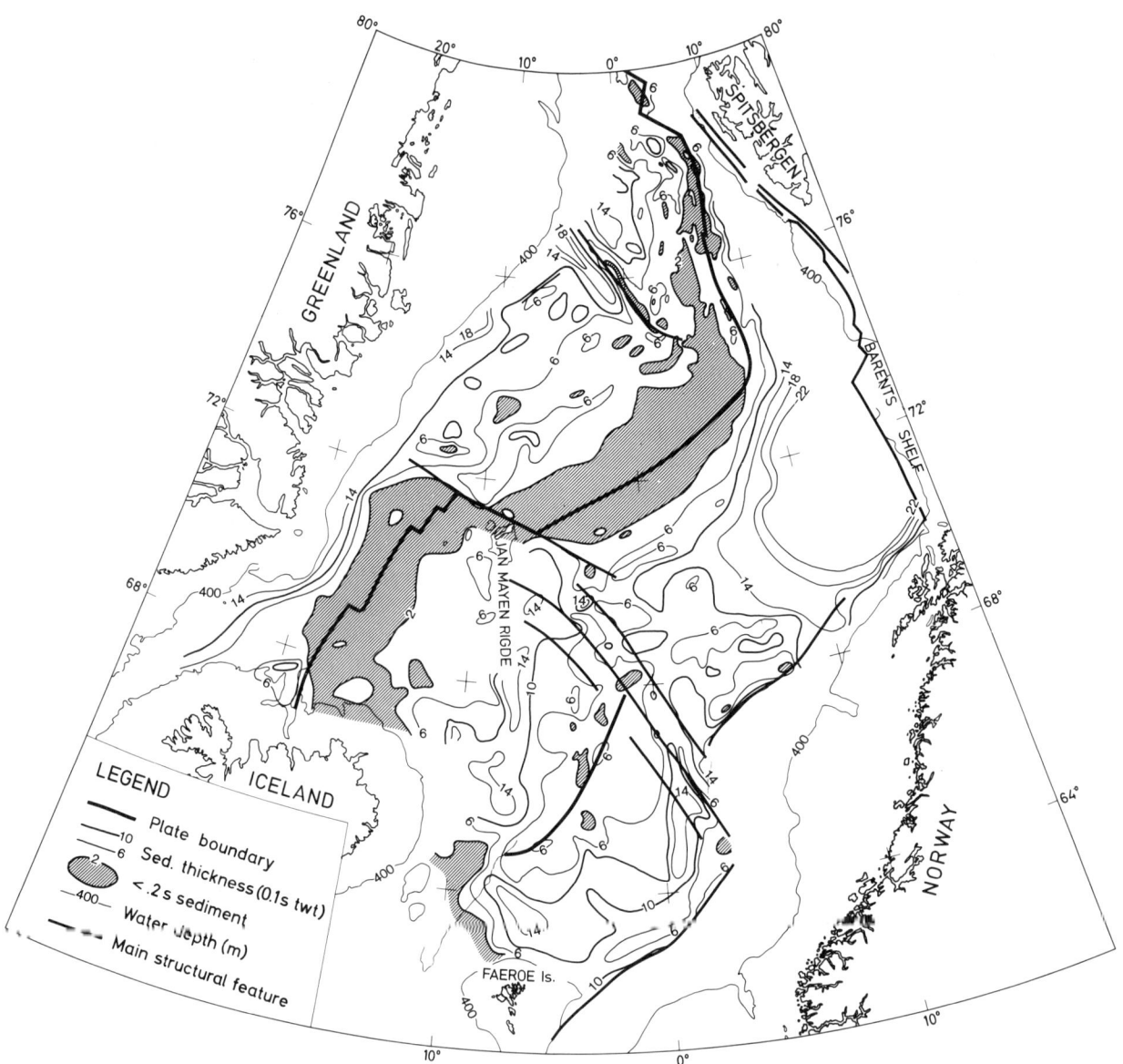

Figure 2. Sediment thickness over oceanic crust expressed in two-way reflection time. Assuming a velocity of 2.0 km/s, 1 s equals 1 km. Compiled from Eldholm and Windisch (1974), Eldholm and others (1980), Karlstad (1981), and Økern (1981).

Tertiary (Eldholm and Ewing, 1971; Faleide and others, 1984), is well demonstrated. Moreover, the active Kolbeinsey and Knipovich ridges, and at earlier times also the marginal escarpments, have acted as major barriers to the flow of terrigenous material.

• Compared with the Atlantic Ocean to the south, the average sea-floor sediment thickness in this region is large and reflects the relative immaturity of the Norwegian-Greenland Sea with its proximity to major source areas of terrigenous sediments.

The primary objective of DSDP Leg 38 was to obtain data relating to the tectonic evolution of the basin (Talwani, Udintsev, and others, 1976). Because most sites were drilled at structural highs and volcanic plateaus, a complete record of the stratigraphy of the Norwegian-Greenland Sea is lacking. However, the samples obtained have provided key information, as demonstrated by Nilsen (1978) and White (1978) who conclude that the sedimentary history is typical for a rifted ocean basin in which the stratigraphic sequences were deposited at increasing water depth with time as the ocean subsided and matured. Moreover, the deposited sediments became finer grained and contained increasing biogenic components through time as the ocean widened. The oldest sediments, formed during rifting, are nonmarine red beds over subaerially weathered basalts. Subsequently, as the ocean became

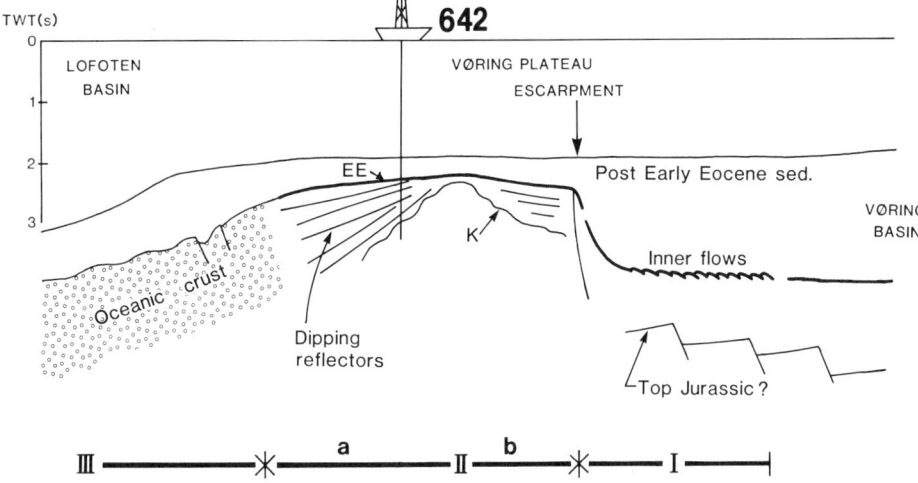

Figure 3. Schematic profile across the Vøring Plateau Escarpment showing the crustal zonation described in the text (Eldholm and others, 1984). Structural position of ODP drill site 642 is also shown.

wider and deeper, the deposited sediments gradually changed from turbidites to hemipelagic mudstones. As the influence of the continental margins diminished, biogenic, calcareous, and siliceous oozes dominated deposition. Finally, there is a blanket of ice-rafted glacial deposits covering the entire sea floor except for the very youngest crust. Analyses of a large number of piston cores yield, with the exception of two locations at the Norwegian margin (Saito and others, 1967; Bjørklund and Kellogg, 1972), only Pleistocene sediments of glacial to interglacial origin (Kellogg, 1980). According to Warnke (1982), the initiation of the northern hemisphere glaciation took place close to the Miocene-Pliocene boundary, at about 5 Ma.

Using 3.5 kHz echograms, as well as bottom photographs and piston cores, Damuth (1978) concluded that large-scale contour current activity has not been a regionally important sedimentary process. He further suggested that the recent terrigeneous deposition is dominated by downslope processes and ice-rafting, and that glacial/interglacial climate fluctuations control the sediment influx. Presently, there are tranquil bottom conditions. Strong bottom current activity is only observed at the top and southern flank of the Iceland-Faeroe Ridge and in the Denmark Strait.

Marginal Highs

Figure 1 shows buried acoustic basement highs beneath the outer Vøring Plateau and the lower slope south of the East Jan Mayen Fracture Zone (Talwani and Eldholm, 1972), as well as below the Greenland margin between 75.3°N and the Greenland Fracture Zone (Eldholm and Windisch, 1974). Similar features have recently been found at the rifted (pull-apart) segments of the Svalbard and Barents Sea continental margin (Myhre, 1984). These highs are bounded landward by escarpment-like features (Fig. 1) often associated with the continent-ocean boundary. The marginal highs mark the seaward termination of very prominent regional sedimentary basins and also separate areas with differing geophysical character. DSDP drilling proved that the acoustic basement reflector beneath the Outer Vøring Plateau is composed of basalts of early Eocene age (Talwani and Udintsev, 1976b).

Results from multichannel seismic surveys show complex structures near the marginal highs. There are local zones of seaward-dipping reflectors beneath the Faeroe-Shetland and Vøring basement highs, and near the base of the slope in the Lofoten Basin (Hinz and Weber, 1976; Hinz and Schlüter; 1978; Talwani, 1978; Eldholm and others, 1979; Talwani and others, 1981). Similar reflectors have recently been found beneath the Greenland marginal high (Mutter and others, 1985) and at the eastern flank of the Jan Mayen Ridge (Skogseid and Eldholm, 1986). Eldholm and Sundvor (1980) noted that the dipping reflectors always occur landward of anomaly 23, beneath the smooth reflectors earlier identified as acoustic basement.

Off Norway, the Vøring Plateau has been most thoroughly investigated. From subsurface seismic data, Hinz and others (1984) and Talwani and others (1983) divided the area into the zones shown schematically in Figure 3. Zone III is underlain by normal oceanic crust formed by sea floor spreading. Zone II, between the escarpment and the oceanic crust, consists of an outer part characterized by a dipping reflector sequence, the early Eocene basalt, and an inner part, where the subbasalt reflectors are horizontal or subhorizontal. The subbasalt reflectors rest on an acoustically homogeneous basement complex, the top of which is the base reflector, K. The width of the two subzones varies along the margin. Zone I marks the extent of a distinct seismic horizon believed to represent flows of the same age as the smooth volcanic reflector in Zone II. These inner flows are underlain by thick sequences of pre-opening sediments in the Vøring Basin (Fig. 3).

The series of dipping reflectors of Zone II appears to be composed of individual seaward-dipping divergent beds, which are slightly convex upward. In this zone, Mutter and others (1984) have found a seismic velocity distribution yielding an approximately normal oceanic layer 3 sequence, whereas the thickness of the layer 2 sequence is greatly expanded relative to normal oceanic crust. This velocity structure is similar to that of eastern Iceland.

The complexity of the marginal highs has initiated a debate as to the nature and composition of the underlying crust. This question is particularly important because similar seaward-dipping sequences have been observed along many rifted margins (Hinz, 1981), indicating that they may have originated from a distinct event that is common to the history of many passive margins. The origin of these features is not resolved. For the Vøring Plateau, several models of emplacement have been suggested:

- The Icelandic type in which generation of the oceanic crust occurs subaerially during the early phase of sea-floor spreading (Mutter and others, 1982).
- An event of intense volcanic activity during early sea-floor spreading (at about anomaly 23 time) associated with a seaward shift of the plate boundary. The volcanic material also overflowed the adjacent continental crust (Eldholm and others, 1979).
- Volcanic material extruded over highly thinned continental crust during the late phase of rifting (Hinz, 1981).
- Sedimentary layers filled into a half-graben bounded by a continentward-dipping listric fault (Bally, 1983).

In the first two models the continent-ocean transition lies in the vicinity of the escarpment, whereas the latter models imply a crustal boundary farther west. Neither of these interpretations was entirely substantiated by the recent ODP Leg 104 drilling at Site 642 (Figs. 1 and 3) (Eldholm and others, 1987, 1989). The drilling proved that the seaward-dipping reflector sequence at the Vøring Plateau consists of cyclic tholeiitic basalt flows and interbedded volcaniclastic sediments. Below reflector K another distinctly different volcanic series of flows and interbedded sediments was encountered. The lower series is dominantly of dacitic nature with evidence of continental contamination. The entire volcanic section appears to have been deposited terrestrially.

In terms of the crustal nature of the outer plateau, Skogseid and Eldholm (1986) note that sea-floor spreading anomalies overlie part of the dipping sequence and that the zone IIa/IIb boundary (Fig. 3) lies at a fixed distance landward of anomaly 24B. This may indicate that the change to oceanic crust occurs beneath the inner seaward-dipping wedge landward of anomaly 24B, and that the region between 24B and the Vøring Plateau Escarpment is underlain by continental crust contaminated by sills and dikes.

Iceland Plateau

Large areas of the Iceland Plateau east of the Kolbeinsey axial province are underlain by an exceptionally smooth and opaque apparent acoustic basement reflector. The reflector is continuous below most of the southern plateau, but breaks up to the north where it is observed locally. This reflector, which was named the "opaque" horizon by Eldholm and Windisch (1974), also extends discontinuously onto the slope toward the Norway Basin. In places, the level of the horizon changes rather abruptly although the overlying sediments, in most places acoustically transparent, appear undisturbed.

Generally, only indistinct reflectors have been observed below the opaque horizon. In places, it is interrupted by small peaks, which appear to originate from deeper levels. This led Eldholm and Windisch (1974) to suggest that the real oceanic basement was buried by the opaque horizon. This is further suggested by the fact that the sea-floor-spreading-type magnetic anomalies show little correspondence with the occurrences of the horizon, which also exhibits no obvious age-depth relationship as expected for young oceanic crust. Finally, Myhre and Eldholm (1981) determined the seismic velocity of the opaque horizon to be 3.3 km/s, noting that the refracted arrivals were weak and indistinct. On the other hand, DSDP Site 348 was drilled near anomaly 6 and reached 19-Ma basalt at the level of the opaque horizon. However, it cannot be determined if the opaque layer drapes an underlying basement high at this site.

Although it is probable that the opaque horizon represents a layer of volcanic extrusives such as flows or pyroclastics, its nature remains enigmatic. The deposition may be related to a major event in the geological history of the Iceland Plateau and/or Iceland, and it is not unreasonable to believe that volcanic remnants of such an event exist in the sedimentary record elsewhere in the ocean.

Microcontinents

The Jan Mayen Ridge block, which becomes fragmented south of 68.5°N, loses its bathymetric signature south of 67.6°N. It has been suggested that the ridge continues farther southward as a buried series of subparallel basement troughs and ridges (Talwani and Eldholm, 1977). Because of its bathymetric character, Johnson and Heezen (1967) indicated that the ridge could be underlain by a fragment of continental crust.

Multichannel seismic surveys (Gairaud and others, 1978; Garde, 1978; Myhre and others, 1984) have made it possible to characterize the northern ridge segment by two regional unconformities (A and O) and the basement surface, as shown by the type section in Figure 4A. In the flanking basins, varying thick-

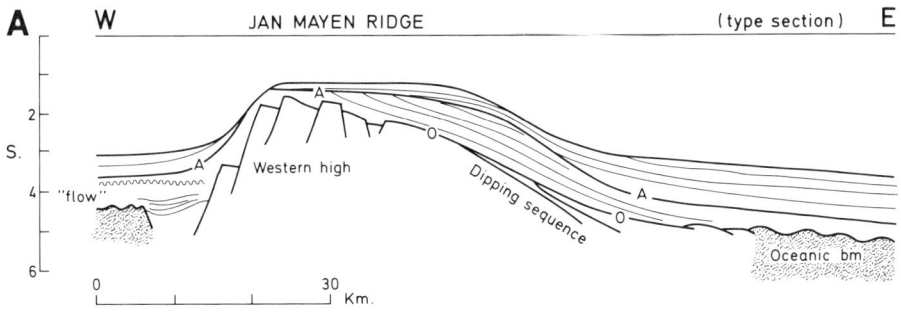

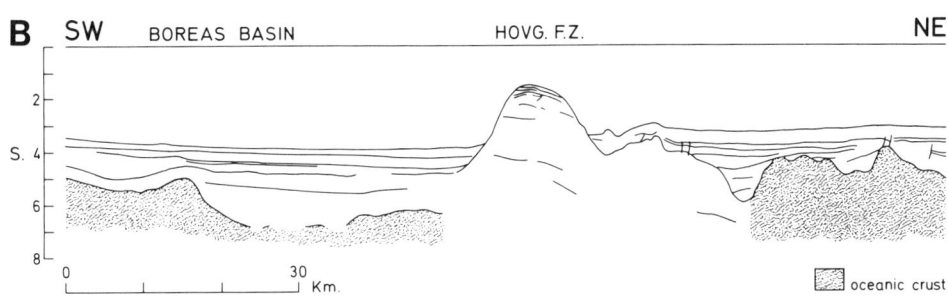

Figure 4. A: Schematic east-west-type section across the northern Jan Mayen Ridge. B: Line drawing of a seismic multichannel profile (BGR-31) crossing the western segment of the Hovgaard Fracture Zone (Myhre, 1984).

nesses of relatively transparent sediments overlie oceanic basement, whose exact termination against the ridge is sometimes obscure. On the western side, the termination of the oceanic crust is normally constrained to a 10-km-wide zone, although the opaque horizon or other volcanic units locally mask the rocks below. Toward the Norway Basin it is probable that early Tertiary lava flows mask the oldest oceanic basement and part of the ridge itself. The upper sediment sequence consists of a few hundred meters of horizontally stratified sediments, increasing in thickness downslope and onlapping oceanic basement. Between reflectors O and A there is a sequence of eastward-dipping layers. Except for a zone of seaward-dipping sub-O reflectors (Skogseid and Eldholm, 1986), only poorly defined layering exists below O. The western part of the ridge is composed of a structurally deformed block, the Western High, indicating an extensional tectonic regime forming horsts and grabens and rotated fault blocks. In Figure 4 it has been shown as a separate unit, but the relationship of this high and the smooth opaque reflector O is unclear.

DSDP sites 346, 347, and 349 (Fig. 1) penetrated reflector A, confirming the existence of an erosional unconformity at this level. The above-lying sediments consist of glacial deposits as well as sandy muds and biogenic siliceous oozes of middle Miocene to middle Oligocene age. Below reflector A, a massive terrigenous sand-mudstone was recovered and dated as early Oligocene to late (and middle?) Eocene (Talwani and Udintsev, 1976). In terms of seismic velocities for the upper sequence, the range is 1.7–2.0 km/s, 2.2–3.3 km/s for the sediments between A and O, and 4.0–4.5 km/s just below O. A 5.6-km/s refractor exists at deeper levels (Myhre and others, 1984).

Gairaud and others (1978) interpret the lower unit to be of early Oligocene to Paleocene age, assuming that reflector O represents a rift unconformity associated with the opening of the Norwegian-Greenland Sea. The rocks below reflector O are interpreted to be Mesozoic–Paleozoic sediments, or possibly Caledonian granitic or metamorphic rocks under the western ridge flank. Hinz and Schlüter (1978), however, indicate the possibility that reflector O may represent a volcanic, possibly pyroclastic, horizon. Noting that no early Tertiary rift unconformity exists elsewhere along the margins of the Norwegian-Greenland Sea, and that there exist similarities in structural style and velocity distribution with the major basins off Norway, Myhre and others (1984) suggested that O might be of pre-opening age. On the other hand, Skogseid and Eldholm (1986) have recently suggested an evolutionary model in which reflector O is similar to reflector EE off Norway, representing the top of flow units laid down during the time of early sea-floor spreading when the Jan Mayen Ridge and the Vøring Plateau were contiguous.

From analysis of geophysical data as well as plate tectonic

considerations Eldholm and Talwani (1973) suggested that the Jan Mayen Ridge was a microcontinent. In particular, they noted the existence of a magnetic quiet zone over the ridge and that the seismic velocity-depth function was quite different from that in the adjacent basin. Gravity modeling also suggests a different crustal composition beneath the ridge proper (Grønlie and Talwani, 1982), an observation which is consistent with seismic crustal experiments (B. Johansen, personal communication, 1986). Presently, most investigators subscribe to the idea that the Jan Mayen Ridge is underlain by continental crust (Talwani and Udintsev, 1976; Talwani and Eldholm, 1977; Gairaud and others, 1978; Garde, 1978; Unternehr, 1982; Nunns, 1983b). However, a note of caution is appropriate, as no rocks predating the Paleocene/Eocene opening of the Norwegian-Greenland Sea have been recovered. Nevertheless, the nature and composition of the rocks below the lower unconformity and the Western High are fundamental in terms of the origin of the ridge. Although it seems reasonable that the northern Jan Mayen Ridge block is underlain by rocks predating the opening of the Norwegian-Greenland Sea, the exact boundaries of the continental fragment, and in particular its southern extension, must still be considered poorly defined.

Investigations of the continental margin off Svalbard have led to speculations that the western segment of the Hovgaard Fracture Zone also may be a microcontinent (Myhre and others, 1982; Myhre, 1984). As noted earlier, the fracture zone consists of two morphologically different ridges separating the Boreas Basin from a smaller and 700-m-shallower basin to the north. The free-air gravity anomalies, which in general reflect the bathymetry, also show differences between the two ridge segments. For example, the deeper eastern segment exhibits much larger gravity and magnetic anomalies than the western shallower segment. This led Eldholm and Myhre (1977) to propose a difference in the composition of the underlying rocks. Moreover, Grønlie and Talwani (1982), using gravity data, were not able to model the western segment as a typical oceanic fracture zone. The single channel seismic lines (Eldholm and Myhre, 1977) revealed a thin sequence of horizontal layers resting unconformably on acoustically opaque basement below the western segment.

A multichannel seismic line crossing the western segment (Fig. 4B) shows that the seismic signature beneath the ridge is distinctively different from the basement peaks and ridges elsewhere in this area. Approaching from the southwest, oceanic basement can be traced rather close to the ridge, whereas the crustal nature is uncertain under the buried high to the north. Except for the top sequence, only a few reflectors can be identified beneath the ridge proper. This seismic signature is indeed similar to that of the Svalbard margin east of the Hornsund Fault (Myhre, 1984). These observations are further supported by recent multichannel data and velocity measurements at the Hovgaard Fracture Zone (Johansen, 1985). Although the geophysical data are not entirely conclusive, they lend credence to the proposition that the western Hovgaard Ridge segment could be a continental sliver split off from the Svalbard Platform. The eastern peak-like ridge segment, on the other hand is believed to be of oceanic origin. We also note that the typical contrast in basement elevation and sediment thickness on either side of the western segment indicates considerably younger crust to the north.

PLATE TECTONIC EVOLUTION

It is commonly accepted that Cenozoic sea-floor spreading in the Norwegian-Greenland Sea was initiated during the time period between magnetic anomalies 25 and 24B (Figs. 5 and 6). With reference to the DNAG geologic time-scale (Palmer, 1983), the opening occurred in the period 56–58.5 Ma, at the Paleocene/Eocene transition.

Seismic data tied to drill-site information indicate that the region between Norway and Greenland has been a depositional area at least since the Carboniferous (Jørgensen and Navrestad, 1981; Rønnevik and others, 1983; Bøen and others, 1984; Bukovics and Ziegler, 1985). Sedimentation started in an epeirogenic setting on a subsiding post-Caledonian surface. In late Paleozoic time, a tectonic phase created a system of rotated fault blocks with sedimentation filling in the fault-bounded basins. From late Paleozoic to early Mesozoic time, sedimentation gradually smoothed the relief, forming a large regional basin in early Jurassic times. A new main phase of extensional tectonics, Kimmerian, in mid- and late Jurassic time, formed a system of basins and ridges. During Cretaceous and into Paleocene time, the relief was again smoothed by marine sedimentation and regional subsidence in large epicontinental basins.

Various episodes of sea-floor spreading within these regional basins have been proposed. The arguments are reviewed by Eldholm and others (1984), who found that such events have not been convincingly documented along the Norwegian-Greenland Sea margins.

In earliest Tertiary time, sea-floor spreading took place along a plate boundary in the North Atlantic and continued into the Labrador Sea (Srivastava and Tapscott, 1986). The continental crust between Norway and Greenland, which had been stretched by several tensional episodes in Mesozoic time, was further thinned, and oceanic crust was generated in Paleocene/Eocene time.

Subsequent to the start of sea-floor spreading, the incipient ocean between Norway and Greenland gradually widened and deepened. However, the present distribution of oceanic ridges and fracture zones reflects a rather complex history of development. A model for Cenozoic plate tectonic history was proposed by Talwani and Eldholm (1977). In terms of sedimentary history, stratigraphy and paleo-oceanography (Schrader and others, 1976; Talwani and Udintsev, 1976; Nilsen, 1978), the DSDP Leg 38 drilling results are in a regional sense consistent with this plate tectonic model. Later work has added new information and suggested changes in the model, particularly relating to the formation of the Norway Basin, the oldest part of the Iceland Plateau (Vogt and others, 1980; Nunns and Peacock, 1982; Unternehr, 1982;

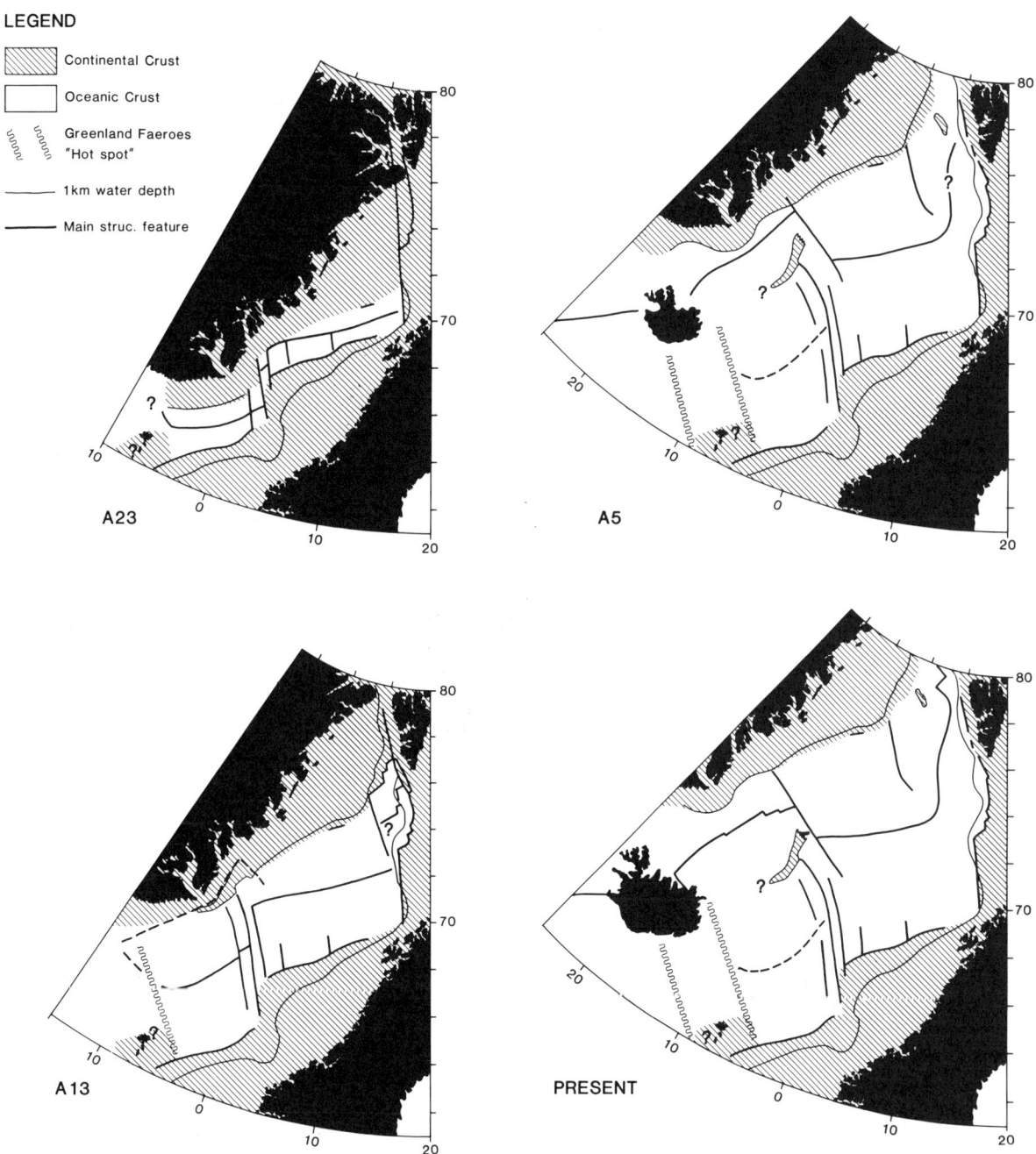

Figure 5. Simplified diagram of the main events in the plate tectonic evolution of the Norwegian–Greenland Sea. Based on Talwani and Eldholm (1977), Nunns (1983), Myhre (1984), Reksnes and Vågnes (1985), and Skogseid and Eldholm (1986). For simplicity the oceanic crust is extended to the marginal escarpments. Possibly, the actual ocean-continent boundary is found at a small, but varying, distance seaward of the escarpments.

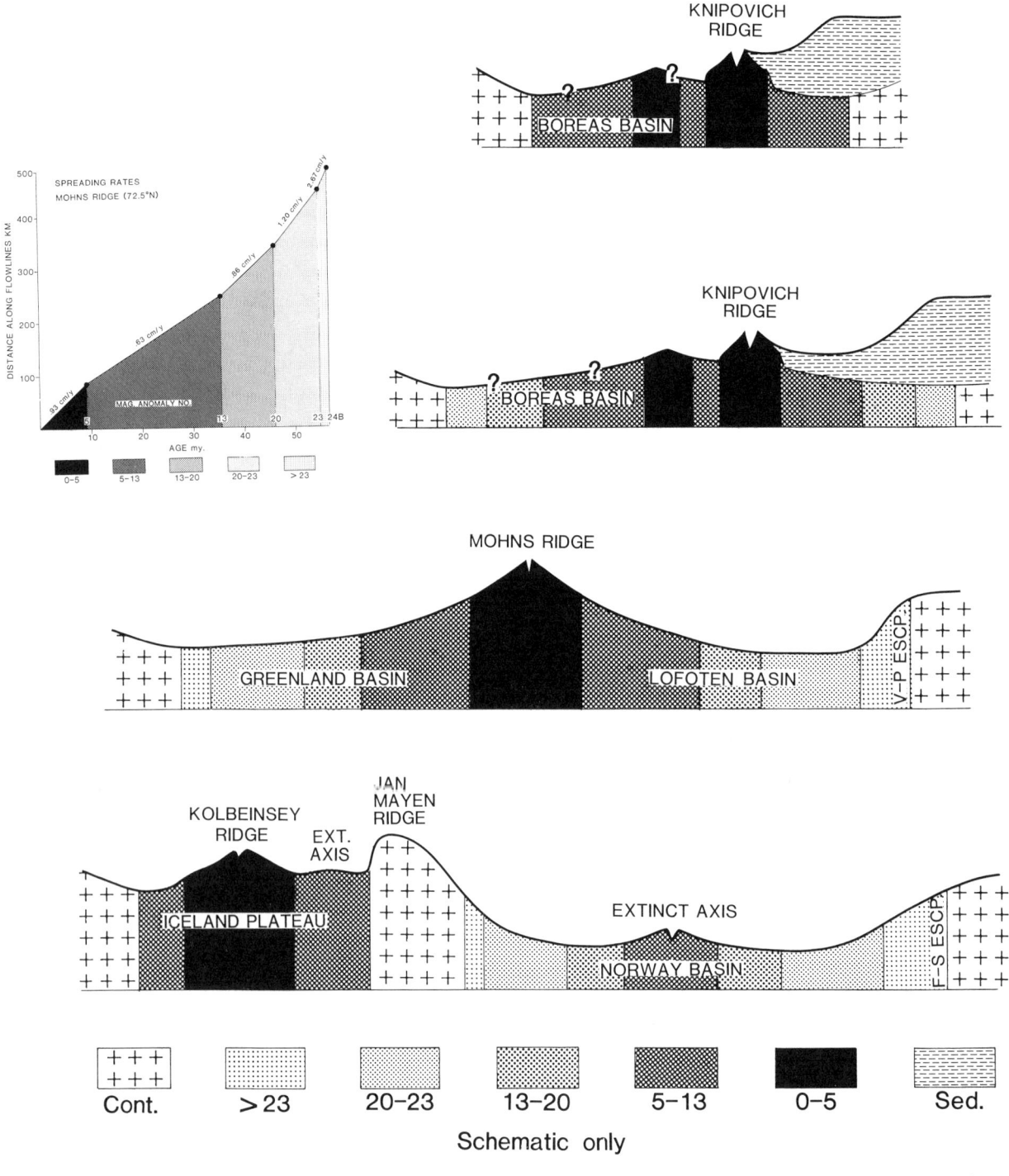

Figure 6. Schematic evolutionary diagrams across the main basins of the Norwegian–Greenland Sea. Based on Talwani and Eldholm (1977) and Myhre and others (1982). There is little conclusive information as to the time of opening in the southern Greenland Sea. Alternative models without an extinct axis at the Iceland Plateau have been proposed for the area south of the Jan Mayen Fracture Zone. Average spreading rates measured along flow lines at the central Mohns Ridge also shown.

Nunns, 1983a; Bott, 1985; Skogseid and Eldholm, 1986), and the evolution of the Greenland Sea (Myhre and others, 1982).

The Cenozoic plate tectonic development is characterized by two major evolutionary phases and local migration of the plate boundary (Figs. 5 and 6). During the first main evolutionary phase, between magnetic anomaly 25/24 and 13 time, Greenland moved in a northwest direction relative to Eurasia. A major change in the pole of rotation at about the time of anomaly 13 caused this relative movement to become almost west–northwest. This change is clearly expressed in the azimuths of fracture zones. The change in the relative direction of spreading in the North Atlantic is associated with the cessation of spreading in the Labrador Sea. At anomaly 13 time the plate geometry in the region changed from a three-plate to a two-plate configuration, with Greenland becoming part of the North American Plate (Kristoffersen and Talwani, 1977; Srivastava, 1978). This event is highly significant for the development of the sea floor and margins north of the Greenland-Senja Fracture Zone. Prior to the time of anomaly 13, Greenland slid along Svalbard with formation of oceanic crust only in the southern Greenland Sea. Since anomaly 13 time, however, sea-floor spreading has taken place along the entire plate boundary between Svalbard and Greenland (Fig. 5).

The two major fracture zone systems, Jan Mayen and Greenland-Senja, separate regions that have evolved differently in terms of plate tectonics (Figs. 5 and 6). In the central region, the initial plate boundary had minor offsets that were eliminated by anomaly 23 time (Hagevang and others, 1983). Subsequently, the plate boundary has been quite stable, with nearly symmetrical generation of oceanic crust along the Mohns Ridge.

The location of the presently active Knipovich Ridge suggests changes in the location of the plate boundary north of the Greenland-Senja Fracture Zone. Eldholm and Sundvor (1980) suggested that the present axis was not older than 5–6 Ma, and even more recent changes may have occurred. A two-stage model for the formation of the Greenland Sea, in which the southern part opened in early Eocene and the northern part at anomaly 13 time, has been proposed by Myhre and others (1982). They also indicated that the Hovgaard Fracture Zone may be a continental fragment split off from the Svalbard margin at about anomaly 13 time. Myhre and others (1982) tentatively suggested opening of the southern Greenland Sea at anomaly 21 time. Reconstructions by Unternehr (1982) and Reksnes and Vågnes (1985) accommodate a slightly older basin, possibly initiated at around anomaly 23 time. It should be borne in mind, however, that no pattern of plate-boundary migration has yet been deciphered and no linear magnetic anomalies confidently identified in the Greenland Sea. In addition, the lack of structural data from the Greenland margin further inhibits any plate tectonic reconstruction. Off Svalbard and the Barents Sea, on the other hand, the ocean-continent transition is reasonably well confined. New seismic data have shown it lies beneath the landward flank of the gravity anomaly associated with the Senja Fracture Zone (J. I. Faleide, personal communication, 1986). Between the Senja Fracture Zone and the Hornsund Fault Zone there is a system of rifted and sheared margin features overlain locally by smooth volcanic horizons. Off Svalbard the ocean-continent boundary is located a short distance west of the Hornsund Fault Zone (Myhre, 1984) (Fig. 1).

The area south of the Jan Mayen Fracture Zone is structurally very complex, including both the active Kolbeinsey Ridge and the extinct spreading axis (Aegir Ridge, Fig. 1) with its fan-shaped anomaly pattern in the Norway Basin. Between these main spreading centers there may have existed relatively short-lived spreading axes at the eastern Iceland Plateau, representing a period of adjustment associated with the major westward shift of the plate boundary. Tentatively, the tectonic history (Talwani and Eldholm, 1977) may be divided into the following stages (Figs. 5 and 6):

1) Pre-anomaly 23 spreading west of the Faeroe–Shetland Escarpment.

2) Spreading along the Aegir Ridge in the Norway Basin (anomaly 23–20 time). Nunns and Peacock (1982) postulate spreading from this axis also prior to anomaly 23.

3) Spreading in the Norway Basin and/or Iceland Plateau, characterized by complex westward axial migration (anomaly 20–7 time). A part of the Greenland margin, what is now the Jan Mayen Ridge, was completely separated just prior to anomaly 6 time. Unternehr (1982) and Nunns (1983b) proposed that the Jan Mayen Ridge acted as an independent plate during the interval between the formation of anomalies 20–7 and 13–7, respectively. The models of Vogt and others (1980) and Nunns (1983b) do not require an intermediate axis at the Iceland Plateau.

4) The present plate boundary came into existence just prior to anomaly 5 time (Eldholm and Talwani, 1977), or at anomaly 6C to 7 time (Vogt and others, 1980; Nunns, 1983a).

The existence of oceanic areas of unusual high elevation has often been associated with hot spots or mantle plumes. Talwani and Eldholm (1977) pointed out that a simple mantle plume model for the elevated crust in the Norwegian-Greenland Sea did not satisfy the geophysical data. Therefore, they suggested a hot spot of large areal extent being responsible for the Greenland-Iceland-Faeroe transverse, and the early Tertiary North Atlantic Volcanic Province. Moreover, the regional trend of the transverse follows the flow lines, which describe the relative plate motion indicating that the presently emergent part of the plate boundary, the Iceland hot spot, has been in existence throughout the history of the ocean. Vink (1984) further expanded the hot spot concept. Assuming a hot spot reference frame fixed with respect to the relative plate motion, he was able to predict the location and age progression of the Greenland-Iceland-Faeroe transverse and the Vøring Marginal High.

With the exception of the first few million years, when generation of crust was most rapid (2.7 cm/yr), the rate of sea-floor spreading has been relatively slow through Cenozoic times, with a somewhat increased rate since anomaly 5 time (Fig. 6).

SUMMARY

Despite an intensive marine geophysical and geological

research effort over the last 10 to 15 years, there are still areas of the Norwegian-Greenland Sea that are poorly mapped. These areas, located along the Greenland margin and in the northwestern Greenland Sea, are normally ice covered. However, in a regional sense the geological history must be considered relatively well understood.

The region between Greenland and Eurasia has experienced several phases of crustal extension since the closing of the proto-Atlantic Ocean in late Paleozoic times. The latest period of crustal tension, starting at the end of the Cretaceous, broke up the continent and generated oceanic crust by the process of sea-floor spreading, which began at the end of the Paleocene Epoch. Since then, the ocean has gradually widened and deepened, but its plate tectonic history is complex, including a major change in relative plate motion and a locally unstable plate boundary, which led to the formation of microcontinents. The change of relative plate motion occurring about 36 Ma is related to termination of spreading in the Labrador Sea. One consequence was that northeast Greenland and Svalbard, which had not been completely separated earlier, now moved apart opening a seaway between the Arctic Ocean and the main Atlantic Ocean. The plate boundary appears to have been particularly unstable, migrating successively westward, south of the Jan Mayen Fracture Zone; however, the evolution of Greenland Sea is poorly understood. The main structural features, as well as the sediment distribution, reflect the plate tectonic development.

The earliest period of sea-floor spreading may have occurred above sea level, forming marginal highs at parts of the rifted segments of the passive continental margin. The marginal highs appear to be associated with Cenozoic margin subsidence, which is mainly flexural in character, whereas the margin is typically block faulted where the highs are absent.

Because of its young age and thin sediment cover, the Norwegian-Greenland Sea is well suited for the study of many of the phenomena that relate to the rifting, and subsequently the drifting, phase of oceanic development and the evolution of passive margins. The present state of knowledge has made it possible to address a number of fundamental problems with both conventional and new sophisticated surveying techniques. A major objective for future research is to focus progressively more on the processes that cause the features observed at and below the sea floor. We anticipate that research of this kind will include:

• Detailed studies of the history of vertical motion for both the oceanic crust and the adjacent margins. Particularly, how the Icelandic and "normal" types of sea-floor spreading occur and interact.

• Mapping the structure and determining the composition of the marginal highs as important elements in the early ocean and passive margin formation.

• Investigations to decipher the details of plate boundary migration, including the temporal and spatial evolution of possible microcontinents. In turn, such information may yield constraints for the motion and thermal history of the underlying lithosphere and asthenosphere.

REFERENCES

Bally, A. W., 1983, Seismic expression of structural styles: American Association Petroleum Geologists Studies in Geology no. 15, v. 2.

Bjørklund, K., and Kellogg, D., 1972, Five new Eocene radiolarian species from the Norwegian Sea: Micropaleontology, v. 18, p. 386–396.

Bøen, F., Eggen, S., and Vollset, J., 1984, Structures and basins of the margin from 62–69°N and their development, in Spencer, A. M. and 5 others, eds., Petroleum Geology of the North European Margin: London, Graham & Trotman, p. 253–270.

Bott, H.M.P., 1985, Plate tectonic evolution of the Icelandic transverse ridge and adjacent regions: Journal of Geophysical Research, v. 90, p. 9953–9960.

Bukovics, C., and Ziegler, P. A., 1985, Tectonic development of the mid-Norway continental margin: Marine and Petroleum Geology, v. 2, p. 2–22.

Damuth, J. E., 1978, Echo character of the Norwegian-Greenland Sea; Relationship to Quaternary sedimentation: Marine Geology, v. 28, p. 1–36.

Detrick, R. S., Slater, J. G., and Thiede, J., 1977, Subsidence of aseismic ridges: Earth and Planetary Science Letters, v. 34, p. 185–196.

Eldholm, O., and Ewing, J., 1971, Marine geophysical survey in the southwestern Barents Sea; Journal of Geophysical Research, v. 76, p. 3832–3841.

Eldholm, O., and Myhre, A. M., 1977, Hovgaard Fracture Zone: Norsk Polarinstitutt, Årbok, 1976, p. 195–208.

Eldholm, O., and Sundvor, E., 1980, The continental margins of the Norwegian-Greenland Sea; Recent results and outstanding problems: Philosophical Transactions Royal Society London, ser. A, p. 77–86.

Eldholm, O., and Talwani, M., 1973, Structure and development of the Jan Mayen Ridge: EOS American Geophysical Union Transactios, v. 54, p. 234.

Eldholm, O., and Windisch, C. C., 1974, Sediment distribution in the Norwegian-Greenland Sea: Geological Society of America Bulletin, v. 85, p. 1661–1676.

Eldholm, O., Sundvor, E., and Myhre, A. M., 1979, Continental margin off Lofoten-Vesterålen: Marine Geophysical Researches, v. 4, p. 3–35.

Eldholm, O., Johansen, B., Karlstad, B., Vogt, P. R., and Økern, J., 1980, Sedimentmektigheter på osean skorpe i Norskehavet [abs.]: Nordiske Geologiske Vintermøte, v. 14, p. 19.

Eldholm, O., Sundvor, E., Myhre, A. M., and Faleide, J. I., 1984, Cenozoic evolution of the continental margin off Norway and western Svalbard, in Spencer, A. M., and 5 others, eds., Petroleum Geology of the North European Margin: London, Graham & Trotman, p. 3–18.

Eldholm, O., Thiede, J. and Taylor, E., eds., 1987, Proceedings, Initial reports of Ocean Drilling Program, Leg 104, Part A: College Station, Texas, Ocean Drilling Program, 783 p.

—— , 1989, Proceedings, Scientific Results, Leg 104: College Station, Texas, Ocean Drilling Program, 1110 p.

Faleide, J. I., Gudlaugsson, S. T., and Jacquart, G., 1984, Evolution of the western Barents Sea: Marine and Petroleum Geology, v. 1, p. 123–150.

Gairaud, H., Jacquart, G., Aubertin, F., and Beuzart, P., 1978, The Jan Mayen Ridge; Synthesis of geological knowledge and new data: Oceanologica Acta, v. 1, p. 335–358.

Garde, S. S., 1978, Zur Geologischen entwicklung des Jan Mayen Ruckens nach Geophysikalischen daten [thesis]: Clausthal, University Clausthal, 74 p.

Grønlie, G., and Talwani, M., 1982, The free-air gravity field of the Norwegian-Greenland Sea and adjacent areas: Earth Evolution Series, v. 2, p. 79–103.

Hagevang, T., Eldholm, O., and Aalstad, I., 1983, Pre-23 magnetic anomalies between Jan Mayen and Greenland-Senja Fracture Zones in the Norwegian Sea: Marine Geophysical Researches, v. 5, p. 345–363.

Hinz, K., 1981, A hypothesis on terrestrial catastrophes; Wedges of very thick oceanward and dipping layers beneath passive continental margins; Their origin and paleoenvironment significance: Geologische Jahrbuch, v. E22, p. 3–28.

Hinz, K., and Schlüter, H–U., 1978, Der Nordatlantik; Ergebnisse Geophysikalischer untersuchungen der Bundesanstalt für Geowissenschaften und Rohstoffe an Nordatlantischen Kontinentalrändern: Erdoel–Erdgas–Zeitschrift, v. 94, p. 271–280.

Hinz, K., and Weber, J., 1976, Zum Geologischen aufbau des Norwegischen Kontinentalranders und der Barents-See nach Reflexionsseismischen messungen: Erdöl und Kohle, Erdgas, Petrochemie, p. 3–29.

Hinz, K., Dostman, H. J., and Hanisch, J., 1984, Structural elements of the Norwegian continental margin: Geologische Jahrbuch, v. A75, p. 193–221.

Johansen, S. E., 1985, Hovgaardbruddsonen [Cand. Scient. thesis]: Bergen, University of Bergen, 145 p.

Johnson, G. L., and Eckhoff, O. B., 1966, Bathymetry of the north Greenland Sea: Deep–Sea Research, v. 13, p. 1161–1173.

Johnson, G. L., and Heezen, B. C., 1967, Morphology and evolution of the Norwegian–Greenland Sea: Deep–Sea Research, v. 14, p. 755–771.

Jørgensen, F., and Navrestad, T., 1981, The geology of the Norwegian shelf between 62°N and the Lofoten Islands, in Illing, L. V., and Hobson, G. D., eds., Petroleum geology of the continental shelf of NW Europe: London, Institute of Petroleum, p. 407–413.

Karlstad, B., 1981, Sedimentfordelingen i Norskehavet mellom Jan Mayen og Grønland–Senja bruddsonene [Cand. Real. thesis]: Oslo, University of Oslo, 105 p.

Kellogg, T. B., 1975, Late Quaternary climatic changes in the Norwegian and Greenland Seas, in Weller, G., and Bowling, S., eds., Climatic of the Arctic: Fairbanks, Geophysical Institute, University of Alaska, p. 3–36.

—— , 1980, Paleoclimatology and paleo-oceanography of the Norwegian and Greenland Seas; Glacial–interglacial contrasts: Boreas, v. 9, p. 115–137.

Kristoffersen, Y., and Talwani, M., 1977, Extinct triple junction south of Greenland and the Tertiary motion of Greenland relative to North America: Geological Society of America Bulletin, v. 88, p. 1037–1049.

LePichon, X., Hyndman, R. D., and Pautot, G., 1971, Geophysical study of the opening of the Labrador Sea: Journal of Geophysical Research, v. 76, p. 4724–4723.

Mutter, J. C., Talwani, M., and Stoffa, P. L., 1982, Origin of seaward dipping reflectors in oceanic crust off the Norwegian margin by "subaerial sea-floor spreading": Geology, v. 10, p. 353–357.

Mutter, J. C., Buhl, P., Zehnder, C. M., and Hinz, K., 1985, Two-ship MCS investigations of the conjugate margins of Norway and east Greenland; Part I, Wide aperture CDP profiling: EOS American Geophysical Union Transactions, v. 66, p. 1106.

Myhre, A. M., 1984, The western Svalbard margin (74-80°N) [Dr. scient. thesis]: Oslo, University of Oslo, p. 133–201.

Myhre, A. M., and Eldholm, O., 1981, Sedimentary and crustal velocities in the Norwegian–Greenland Sea: Journal of Geophysical Research, v. 86, p. 5012–5022.

Myhre, A. M., Eldholm, O., and Sundvor, E., 1982, The margin between Senja and Spitsbergen fracture zones; Implication from plate tectonics: Tectonophysics, v. 89, p. 1–32.

—— , 1984, The Jan Mayen Ridge; Present status: Polar Research, v. 2, p. 47–59.

Nilsen, T. H., 1978, Turbidites, red beds, sedimentary structures, and trace fossils observed in DSDP Leg 38 cores and the sedimentary history of the Norwegian–Greenland Sea, in Talwani, M., and Udintsev, G., eds., Initial reports Deep Sea Drilling Project, v. 38 (suppl.): Washington, D.C., U.S. Government Printing Office, p. 259–287.

Nunns, A. G., 1983a, Plate tectonic evolution of the Greenland–Scotland Ridge and surrounding regions, in Bott, M.H.P., Saxov, S., Talwani, M., and Thiede, J., eds., Structure and development of the Greenland–Scotland Ridge: New York, Plenum Press, p. 11–30.

—— , 1983b, The structure and evolution of the Jan Mayen Ridge and surrounding regions: American Association Petroleum Geologists Memoir 34, p. 193–208.

Nunns, A. G., and Peacock, J. H., 1982, Correlation, identification, and inversion of magnetic anomalies in the Norway Basin: Earth Evolution Series, v. 2, p. 130–138.

Økern, J., 1981, Sediment fordelingen i Norskehavet mellom Færøy–Island ryggen og Jan Mayen Fracture Zone [Cand. Real. thesis]: Oslo, University of Oslo, 90 p.

Palmer, A. R., 1983, The decade of North American geology 1983 geologic time scale: Geology, v. 11, p. 503–504.

Perry, R. K., 1986, Bathymetry, in Hurdle, B. G., ed., The Nordic seas: New York, Springer-Verlag, p. 211–234.

Perry, R. K., Fleming, H. S., Cherkis, N. Z., Feden, R. H., and Vogt, P. R., 1980, Bathymetry of the Norwegian–Greenland and western Barents seas: Map, Washington, D.C., U.S. Naval Research Laboratory.

Reksnes, P. A., and Vågnes, E., 1985, Evolution of the Greenland Sea and Eurasia Basin [Cand. Scient. thesis]: Oslo, University of Oslo, 136 p.

Rønnevik, H. C., Eggen, S., and Vollset, J., 1983, Exploration of the Norwegian Shelf, in Brooks, J., ed., Petroleum geochemistry and exploration of Europe: Oxford, Blackwell, p. 171–194.

Saito, T., Burckle, L. H., and Horn, D. R., 1967, Paleocene core from the Norwegian basin: Nature, v. 216, p. 357–359.

Schrader, J. H., Bjørklund, K., Manum, S. B., Martini, E., and van Hinte, J., 1976, Cenozoic biostratigraphy, physical stratigraphy, and paleooceanography in the Norwegian–Greenland Sea, DSDP Leg 38 Paleontological synthesis, in Talwani, M., and Udintsev, G., eds., Initial reports Deep Sea Drilling Project, v. 38: Washington, D.C., U.S. Government Printing Office, p. 1197–1211.

Skogseid, J., and Eldholm, O., 1986, Early Cenozoic crust at the Norwegian continental margin and the conjugate Jan Mayen Ridge (in press).

Srivastava, S. P., 1978, Evolution of the Labrador Sea and its bearing on the early evolution of the North Atlantic: Geophysical Journal of the Royal Astronomical Society, v. 52, p. 313–357.

Srivastava, S. P., and Tapscott, C. R., 1986, Plate kinematics in the North Atlantic, in Vogt, P. R., and Tucholke, B.E., The western North Atlantic region: Boulder, Colorado, Geological Society of America, The Geology of North America, v. M, p. 379–404.

Talwani, M., 1978, Distribution of basement under the eastern North Atlantic, Ocean and the Norwegian Sea: Geological Journal, special issue, no. 5, p. 347–376.

Talwani, M., and Eldholm, O., 1972, The continental margin off Norway; A geophysical study: Geological Society of America Bulletin, v. 83, p. 3575–3608.

Talwani, M., and Eldholm, O., 1977, Evolution of the Norwegian–Greenland Sea: Geological Society of America Bulletin, v. 88, 969–999.

Talwani, M., and Udintsev, G., 1976a, Tectonic synthesis, in Talwani, M., and Udintsev, G., eds., Initial reports Deep Sea Drilling Project, v. 38: Washington, D.C., U.S. Government Printing Office, p. 1213–1242.

Talwani, M., and Udintsev, G., eds., 1976b, Initial reports Deep Sea Drilling Project, v. 38: Washington, D.C., U.S. Government Printing Office, 1256 p.

Talwani, M., Udintsev, G., Mirlin, E., Beresnev, A. F., Kanayev, V. F., Chapman, M., Grønlie, G., and Eldholm, O., 1978, Survey at sites 346, 347, 348, 349, and 350; The area of the Jan Mayen Ridge and the Icelandic Plateau, in Talwani, M., and Udintsev, G., eds., Initial reports Deep Sea Drilling Project, v. 38 (suppl.): Washington, D.C., U.S. Government Printing Office, p. 95–100.

Talwani, M., Mutter, J. C., and Eldholm, O., 1981, The initiations of opening of the Norwegian Sea: Oceanologica Acta 4 (suppl.), p. 23–30.

Talwani, M., Mutter, J. C., and Hinz, K., 1983, Ocean continent boundary under the Norwegian Continental margin, in Bott, M.H.P., Saxov, S., Talwani, M., and Thiede, J., eds., Structure and development of the Greenland–Scotland Ridge: New York, Plenum Press, p. 121–131.

Thiede, J., and Eldholm, O., 1983, Speculations about the Greenland–Scotland Ridge during Late Mesozoic and Cenozoic times, in Bott, M.H.P., Saxov, S., Talwani, M., and Thiede, J., eds., Structure and development of the Greenland–Scotland Ridge: New York, Plenum Press, p. 445–456.

Unternehr, P., 1982, Etude structurale et cinematique de la mer de Norvege et du Groenland; Evolution du microcontinent de Jan Mayen [Ph.D. thesis]: France, University of Bretagne, 227 p.

Vink, G. E., 1984, A hot spot model for Iceland and the Vøring Plateau: Journal of Geophysical Research, v. 89, p. 9949–9959.

Vogt, P. R., 1986a, Sea-floor topography, sediments, and paleoenvironments, *in* Hurdle, B.G., ed., The Nordic Seas: New York, Springer-Verlag, p. 237–410.

——, 1986b, Geophysical and geochemical signatures and plate tectonics *in* Hurdle, B. G., ed., The Nordic Seas: New York, Springer-Verlag, p. 413–662.

Vogt, P. R., Ostenso, N. A., and Johnson, G. L., 1970, Magnetic and bathymetric data bearing on sea-floor spreading north of Iceland: Journal of Geophysical Research, v. 75, p. 903–920.

Vogt, P. R., Johnson, G. L., and Kristjansson, L., 1980, Morphology and magnetic anomalies north of Iceland: Geophysical Journal, v. 47, p. 61–66.

Vogt, P. R., Perry, R. K., Feden, R. H., Fleming, H. S., and Cherkis, N. Z., 1981, The Greenland–Norwegian Sea and Iceland environment; Geology and geophysics, *in* Nairn, A.E.M., and Churkin, M., eds., The ocean basin and margins: New York, Plenum Press, v. 5, p. 493–598.

Warnke, D. A., 1982, Pre-middle Pliocene sediments of glacial and periglacial origin in the Norwegian–Greenland Seas; Results of DSDP, Leg 38: Earth Evolution Series, v. 62, p. 69–78.

White, S. M., 1978, Sediments of the Norwegian–Greenland Sea, DSDP Leg 38, *in* Talwani, M., and Udintsev, G., eds., Initial reports Deep Sea Drilling Project v. 38 (suppl.): Washington, D.C., U.S. Government Printing Office, p. 193–254.

ACKNOWLEDGMENTS

We thank Per A. Reksnes for assisting in preparing the paper and Jack Sweeney for comments and advice.

NOTE ADDED IN PROOF

The results of Ocean Drilling Program Leg 104 at the Vøring Plateau have added much to the understanding of early opening of the Norwegian-Greenland Sea, particularly with respect to the formation of the volcanic passive margin and the Cenozoic paleoenvironment. For these results we refer to Eldholm and others (1987, 1989).

MANUSCRIPT ACCEPTED BY THE SOCIETY NOVEMBER 3, 1986

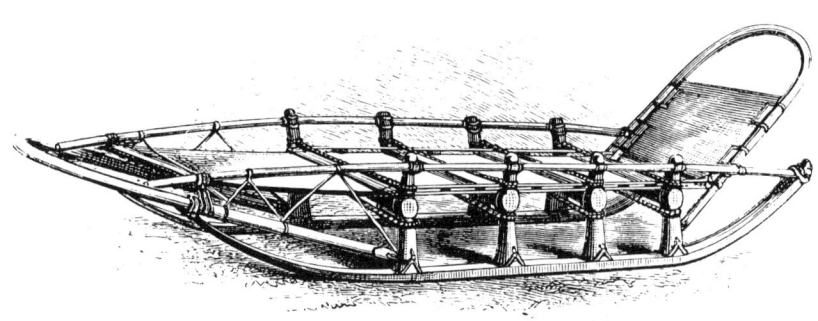

Printed in U.S.A.

# Chapter 21

Eurasia Basin

Yngve Kristoffersen
Seismological Observatory, University of Bergen, Bergen, Norway

INTRODUCTION

The Arctic Ocean is divided into the Eurasia Basin and the Amerasia Basin by the submarine transpolar Lomonosov Ridge (Fig. 1; Plate 1). This chapter provides current knowledge about the geology and geophysics of the Eurasia Basin and its surroundings, derived primarily from ice station and polar expedition data obtained during the past 25 years.

Nansen's pioneering drift with FRAM in 1893 to 1896 (Fig. 2) provided the first soundings, pendulum gravity, and magnetic measurements together with geological samples from the Eurasia Basin (Nansen, 1906). The deployment of the Soviet ice station Northpole-I in 1937 set an operational strategy in Arctic research still followed today, and many Soviet drifting ice camps have entered the Eurasia Basin carrying out a wide range of scientific observations (Fig. 2).

Arlis-II in 1964 was the first United States ice station to traverse the southern end of the Eurasia Basin. With the FRAM I–IV temporary ice stations in 1979 to 1982 and the Canadian LOREX Expedition and two smaller expeditions in 1966 and 1969, the data base in the Eurasia Basin comprises more than 1,700 km of seismic reflection, depth, and gravity measurements. In addition, 22 seismic refraction experiments have been carried out, about two dozen short sediment cores have been recovered, and a dozen heat-flow measurements have been made. The data collected by Soviet scientists has to be added to this inventory.

Traverses by nuclear submarines since 1957 have contributed to mapping of the major bathymetric features in the Arctic Ocean (Dietz and Shumway, 1961). A significant advance in our understanding of the geologic history of the Eurasia Basin has come from Canadian, Soviet, and U.S. aeromagnetic surveys (Coles and Taylor, this volume, Chapter 6), but the difficult Arctic operating conditions have retarded our progress in obtaining geologic "ground truth" information.

PHYSIOGRAPHY

The morphology of the Eurasia Basin, today considered the best understood of the Arctic ocean basins, is the product of its tectonic evolution and sedimentation history (Johnson and others, this volume). The active Arctic Mid-Ocean Ridge, flanked by abyssal plains, further divides the Eurasia Basin into the Amundsen Basin (water depths >4,000 m) on the poleward side and the slightly shallower (by 500 to 900 m) Nansen Basin to the south.

The Arctic Mid-Ocean Ridge crest is shallowest (<2,200 m) in its westernmost part and deepens to 3,000 m or more east of 5°E. Rift valley depths below 4,000 m are observed along three 200- to 400-km-long segments of the ridge. East of 60°E the ridge crest is buried progressively by sediments and merges with the abyssal plain in places.

The continental shelves and slopes bordering the Eurasia Basin show large variation in size and morphology. The Laptev Shelf is more than 300 km wide with water depths less than 50 m in most areas bordering a gentle continental slope and rise. The Barents-Kara Shelf is one of the world's broadest. Across it, several large, glacially eroded troughs cut a relatively steep continental slope. The margin of northeastern Greenland is characterized by a shelf less than 100 km wide and a particularly steep slope, which probably relates to its history as a sheared margin.

Two marginal plateaus—Morris Jesup Plateau and the northern part (north of 82°N) of Yermak Plateau—are symmetric with respect to the rift axis and have basinward-facing steep slopes. The Lomonosov Ridge, which bounds the Eurasia Basin, is a nearly linear 50- to 80-km-wide structure that extends for 1,500 km across the Arctic Ocean. Its crestal water depths range from 500 to 2,000 m. In the central area near the pole, average slopes on the flank of the Amundsen Basin (<7°) are less than those on the Makarov Basin flank (<14°; Weber, 1980); however, this is reversed toward either of the continental margins (Fig. 1).

SEDIMENTS OF THE EURASIA BASIN

Sediment distribution

A compilation of sediment thickness in the Eurasia Basin by Pogrebitskii (1983), Vogt and others (1979a), and Grachev and Karasik (1974) has been updated with seismic reflection data from LOREX and the FRAM series ice stations (Fig. 3).

Cenozoic sediment distribution is broadly symmetric with respect to the active Arctic Mid-Ocean Ridge where sediments are thin or absent, increasing to more than 3 km at the basin margins. Sediment thickness is locally modulated by basement

Kristoffersen, Y., 1990, Eurasia Basin, *in* Grantz, A., Johnson, L., and Sweeney, J. F., eds., The Arctic Ocean region: Boulder, Colorado, Geological Society of America, The Geology of North America, v. L.

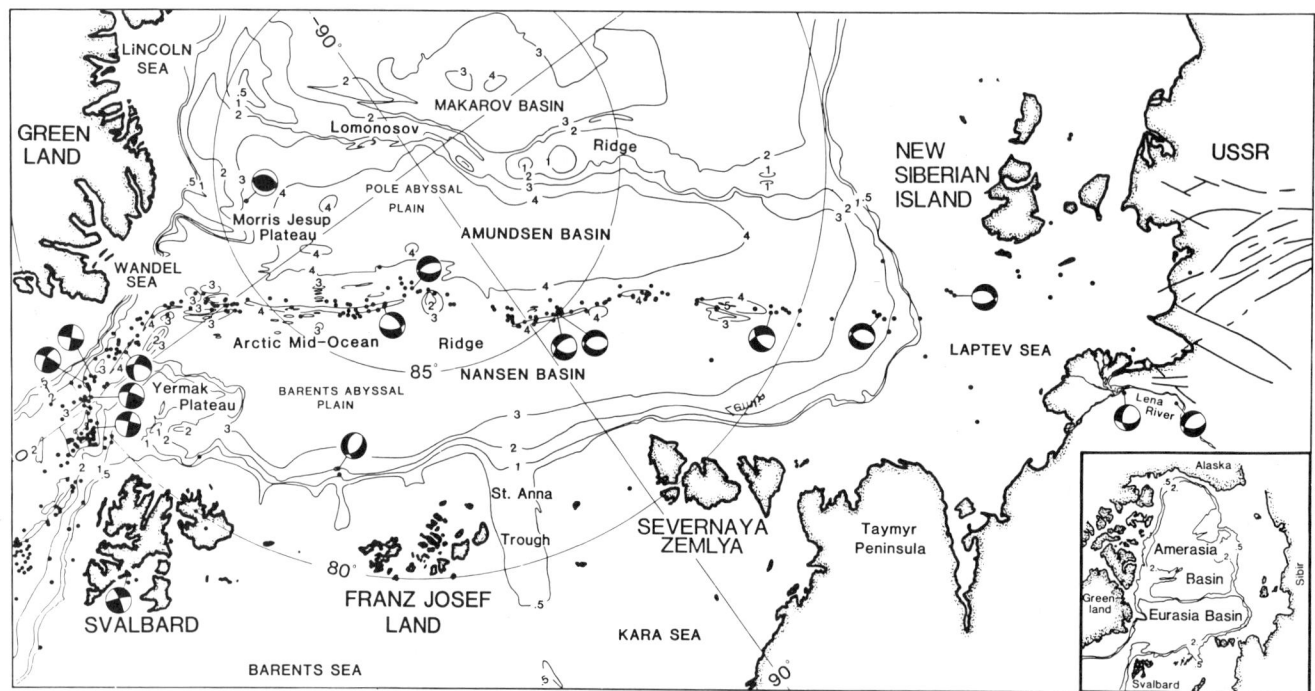

Figure 1. Bathymetry of the Eurasia Basin after Johnson and others (this volume) together with seismicity from 1964 to 1986. Magnitudes Mb >4.0 and minimum 10 stations reporting. Epicenter locations reported by the International Seismological Centre and Preliminary Determination of Epicenters, U.S. Geological Survey. Epicenter file kindly provided by H. Bungum, NTNF/NORSAR, Norway. Focal mechanisms compiled from Bergman and Solomon (1980), Bungum (1977), Chapman and Solomon (1976), Conant (1972), Horsfield and Maton (1970), Lazareva and Misharina (1965), Savostin and Karasik (1981), and Sykes (1967). Major geologic fault structures associated with the extension of the Arctic Mid-Ocean Ridge across the Laptev Shelf into the continent after Grachev (1982) and Patyk-Kara and Grishin (1972). Polar stereographic projection.

topography (Fig. 4). In the western part of the Arctic Mid-Ocean Ridge (5°W to 40°E) where crestal elevations reach up to 2,000 m above the abyssal plain, sediments are present as irregular patches banked up against basement topography (Fig. 4). Local thicknesses are more than 100 m. No significant sediments appear to be present within the rift valley in this area. Farther east (70°E to 130°E), crestal elevations are only of the order of 500 m above the adjacent deep sea floor, and sediment thickness within the axial rift zone ranges from 0.1 km to 1.3 km (Grachev and Karasik, 1974).

Sediment thickness below the abyssal plains varies between 0 and more than 2 km due to buried basement topography (Fig. 4). In the oldest part of the Amundsen Basin, along the base of the Lomonosov Ridge, maximum thickness may exceed 2 km near the pole (Overton, 1982) with an expected increase within 200 to 300 km of the continental shelf at the western and eastern end of the basin. Toward the Laptev Shelf, Cenozoic sediments gradually become thicker and may reach 4 to 5 km (Grachev and Karasik, 1974). However, the most recent compilation by Pogrebitskii (1983) indicates an abrupt basinward increase and a maximum thickness of more than 3 km seaward of a basement block straddling the projection of the Arctic Mid-Ocean Ridge toward the Laptev Shelf.

The Nansen Basin has received more sediments than the Amundsen Basin. This is mainly inferred from the shallower (300 to 700 m) abyssal plain and magnetic depth-to-source estimates (Kovacs and Vogt, 1982; Rzhevsky, 1975). Locally more than 1.5 km of sediments are present beneath the Barents Abyssal Plain, overlying crust of early Oligocene age (Kristoffersen and Husebye, 1985). North of Svalbard, a 3-km-thick Cenozoic section is present beneath the continental slope (Sundvor and others, 1982). Maximum sediment thickness beneath the continental slope may be more than 6 km between Severnaya Zemlya and Franz Josef Land (Pogrebitskii, 1983). Plate 5 shows sediment thickness above basement for all Arctic marine areas.

Stratigraphy

Segments of single and multichannel seismic data obtained by Arlis II, LOREX, and the FRAM I–IV ice stations give some insight into the stratigraphy of the Eurasia Basin.

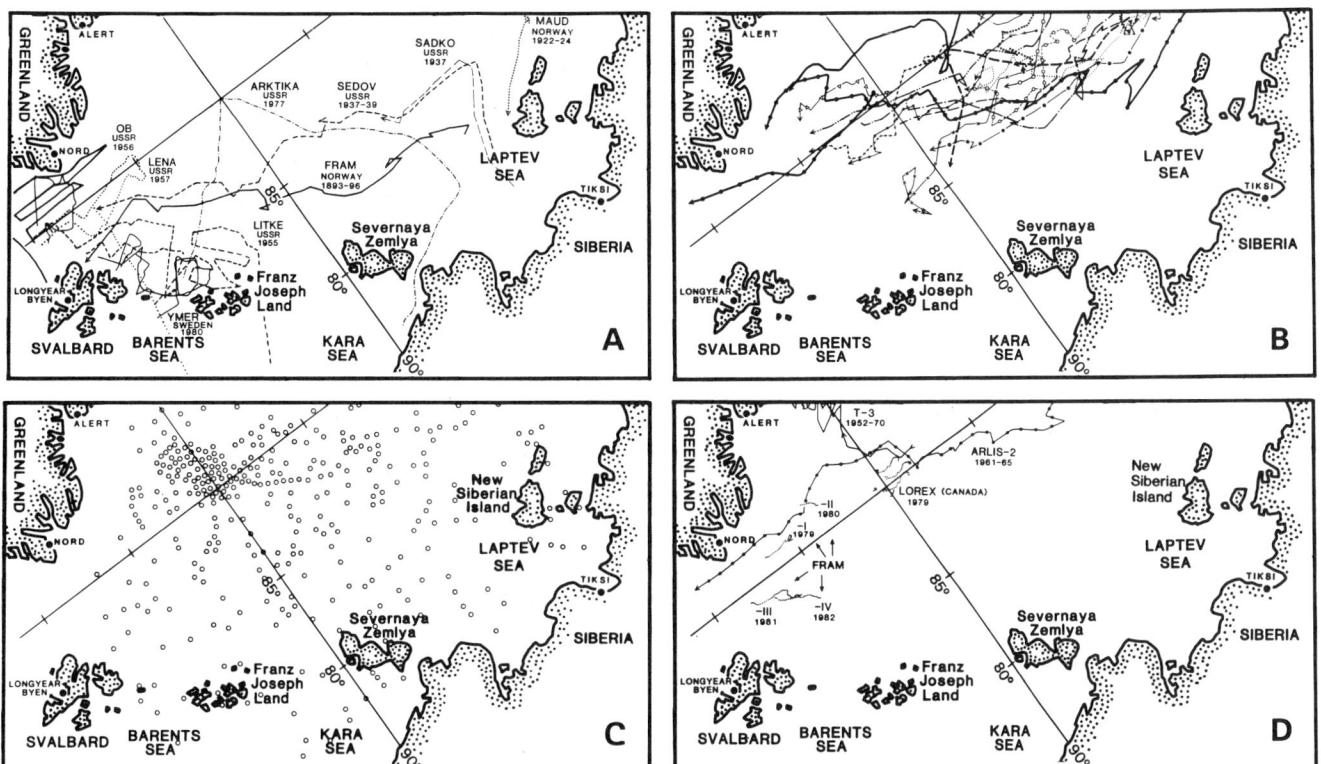

Figure 2. Scientific platforms used in exploration of the Eurasia Basin. A. Ships drifting passively with the ice (Anonymous, 1976) and ice breakers under power (Anonymous, 1978; Bostrøm and Thiede, 1984; Laktionov, 1959); B. Soviet drifting ice stations Northpole 1–22 (Anonymous, 1976); C. Soviet High Latitude Air Expeditions, 1937 to 1956 (Burkhanov, 1956); and D. United States drifting ice stations (Anonymous, 1976).

In the western end of the Nansen Basin, Kristoffersen and Husebye (1985) recognized three seismic sequences below the abyssal plain (Fig. 4). The upper sequence NB-1, is acoustically transparent and shows an apparent uniform thickness (0.3 s two-way travel time) also over areas elevated (300 m) with respect to the deepest part of the abyssal plain (Fig. 4, line 5). In the vicinity of seamounts, there is evidence of current-deposited sediments (Fig. 4, line 2). The corresponding upper sequence (AB-1) in the Amundsen Basin shows a number of closely spaced reflection events. The difference may in part be an artifact of different source and instrument responses. The degree of draping over topography within the abyssal domain is difficult to ascertain because of strong diffractions present in the seismic records. Sequence NB-1 is interpreted to be predominantly hemipelagic clays, although turbidite deposition is probably also important (Kristoffersen and Husebye, 1985). NB-1 may mark the establishment of an effective seaway between the Arctic Ocean and the Norwegian Sea in the middle/late Miocene. The glacial part of the sedimentary section in the Nansen Basin is not resolved by the available seismic data.

The underlying seismic sequence NB-2, bounded by minor local unconformities a and b, is characterized by interfingering and truncations of internal reflectors below the Barents Abyssal Plain, but show better continuity over slightly elevated abyssal areas (Fig. 4, line 5). In the Amundsen Basin, on the other hand, sediments in the corresponding stratigraphic position (AB-2) appear acoustically transparent and grade into a more laminated section 0.7 s below the seabed (Fig. 4). Turbidite deposits are likely to dominate sequence NB-2. The numerous local pinch-outs below the Barents Abyssal Plain is indicative of erosion/deposition by gravity-controlled mass flows.

The basal sequence NB-3 infills basement lows below the Barents Abyssal Plain and also shows evidence of draping over basement highs (Fig. 4). Differential thickening toward the Yermak Plateau suggests that this area was a local source for NB-3 sediments in late Oligocene–early/middle Miocene time.

Local average sedimentation rates in the abyssal domain accessible to turbidite deposition reach a maximum value of 60 m/m.y. along the FRAM I track and 30 m/m.y. along the FRAM IV track using the age of oceanic basement inferred from

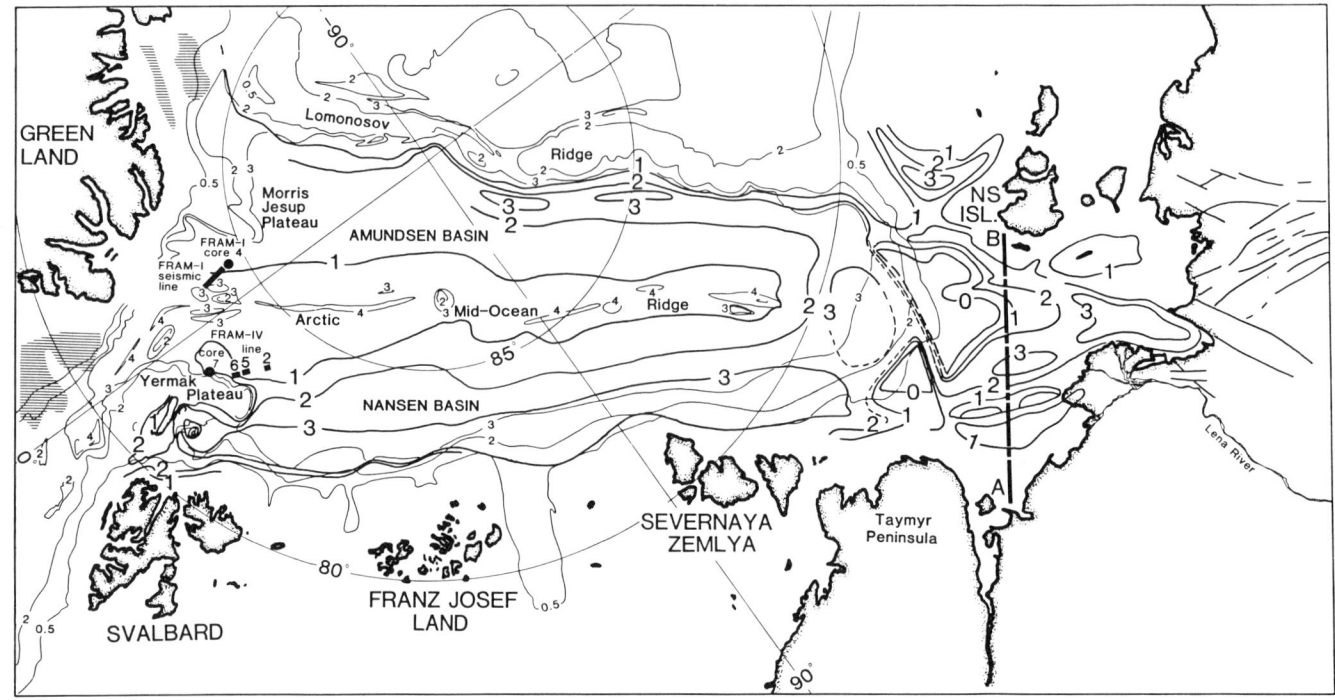

Figure 3. Distribution of Cenozoic sediments in the Eurasia Basin. Data from the eastern basin modified from Pogrebitskii (1983) and from the western part of Amundsen Basin after Jackson and others (1982), Ostenso and Wold (1977), and Overton (unpublished). Sediment thickness in the western Nansen Basin after Kristoffersen and Husebye (1985) and on the Svalbard margin after Sundvor and others (1982). Areas on the shelf and upper continental slope of North Greenland where estimated depth to magnetic basement is more than 5 km are shaded. Locations of short sediment cores (Markussen and others, 1985) shown by large dots. Major geologic faults in the Lena River region after Grachev (1982) and Paty-Kara and Grishin (1972). Crustal section A–B shown in Figure 5. Polar stereographic projection.

magnetic anomalies (Vogt and others (1979a) to constrain the age of the oldest sediments. Recent oxygen isotope dating of a sediment core from abyssal depths in each of the basins (core FRAM I-4 and FRAM IV-7) have yielded late Quaternary sedimentation rates of 1 to 3 cm/kyr (Markussen and others, 1985), which compares well with the seismic evidence. We note that these rates are an order of magnitude larger than current estimates for the Makarov Basin and Lomonosov Ridge (Morris and others, 1985) as well as the Canada Basin and Alpha-Mendeleev Ridge (Clark and others, 1980).

The abyssal plains bordering the Alpha-Mendeleev Ridge show definite similarities in their seismic stratigraphy (Hall, 1979). An upper 0.5-s-thick layer overlies two more closely spaced reflectors (A and B of Hall, 1979). Any correlation with the Makarov or Amundsen Basins has not been attempted yet. Generally, sediments on the Eurasia side of the Lomonosov Ridge show more pronounced seismic stratification (Overton, 1982). Also, the upper sediments recovered by gravity cores in the Amundsen Basin are mainly firm clays, whereas numerous silt-rich interbeds are found in the Makarov Basin (Blasco and others, 1979), making a lithologic correlation very difficult (Morris and others, 1985).

CRUSTAL STRUCTURE

Analysis of earthquake wave trains traversing or originating in the lithosphere below the Arctic Ocean were the first contributions to our understanding of the nature of the underlying crust (Gutenberg and Richter, 1954; Oliver and others, 1955). Geophysical experiments from drifting ice stations since 1979 have provided most of our current information on the crustal structure of the western Eurasia Basin (Johnson, 1983; Weber, 1979). Few experiments have been reported from the eastern part of the basin (Kogan, 1974; Demenitskaya and others, 1964).

Figure 5 is a composite crustal structure section across the Eurasia Basin from seismic refraction measurements carried out to date. Most of the lines are unreversed, and information on

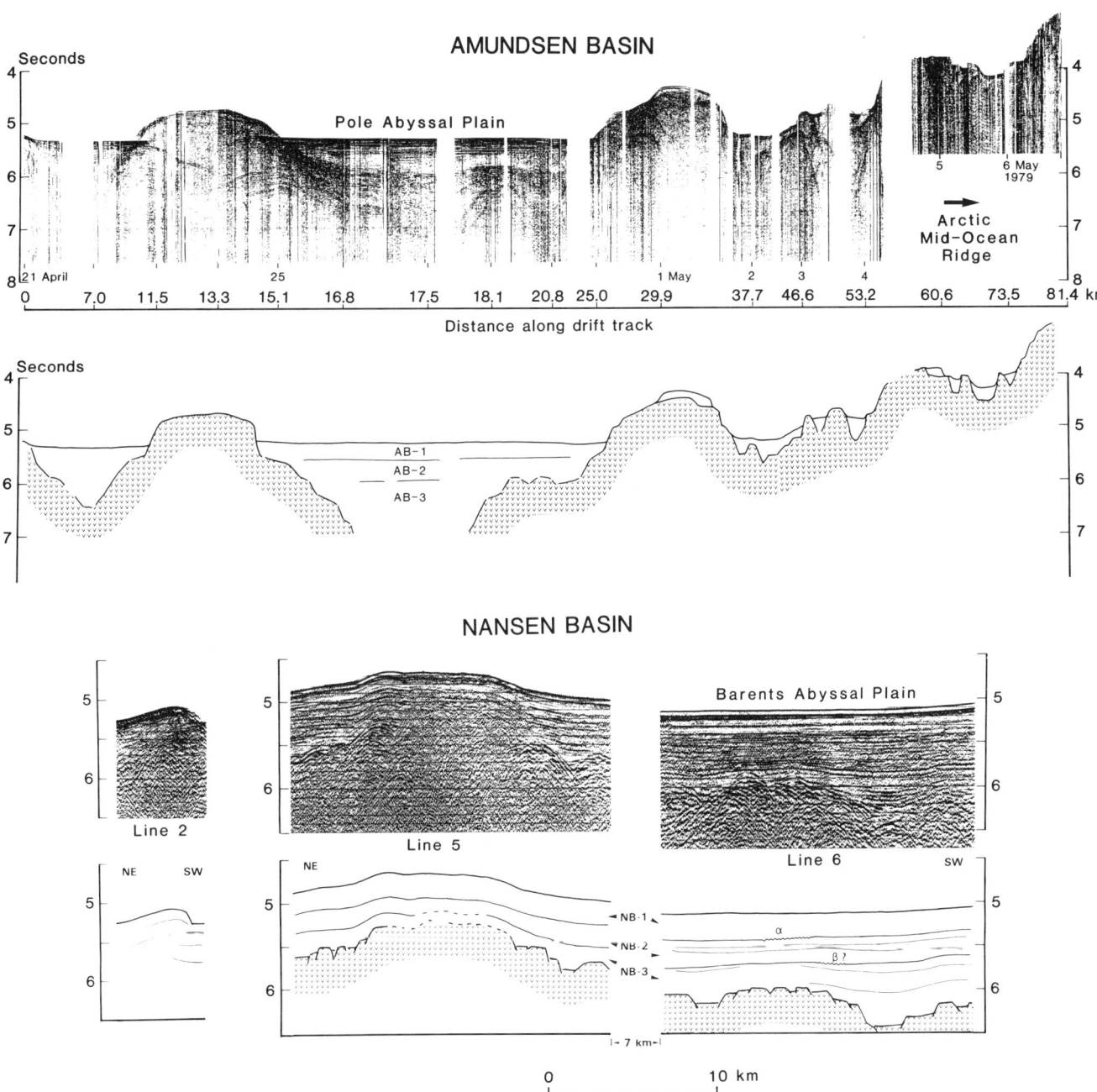

Figure 4. Seismic reflection profiles from western part of Eurasia Basin. Single channel data from Amundsen Basin after Jackson and others (1982) and multichannel data from Nansen Basin after Kristoffersen and Husebye (1985).

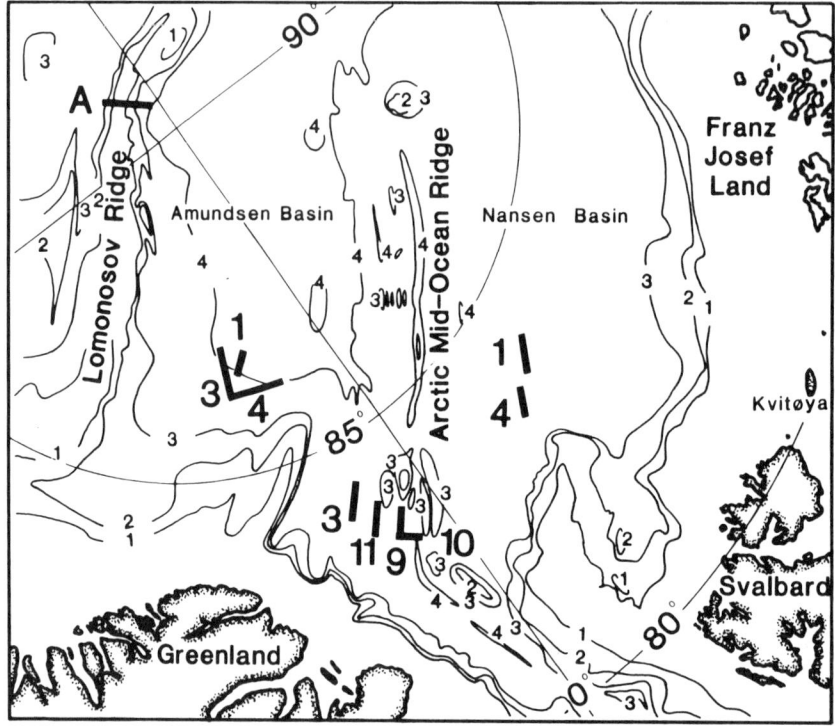
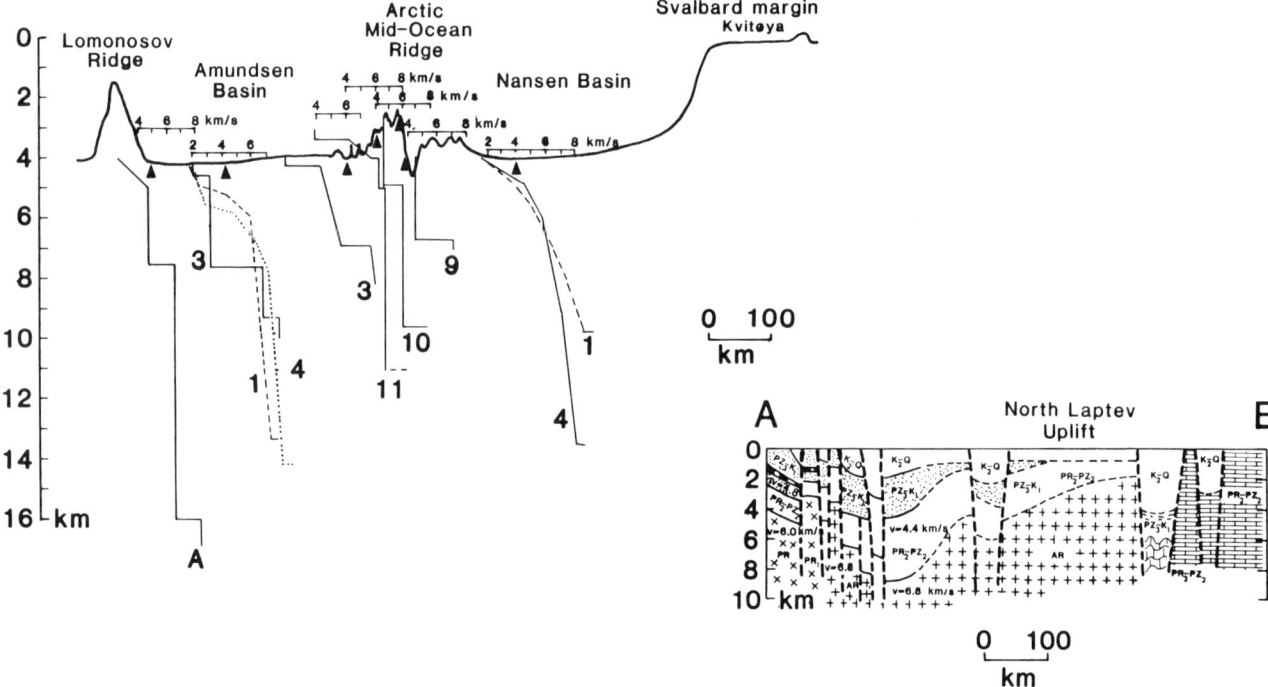

Figure 5. Composite crustal structure section across Eurasia Basin. Compiled from seismic refraction measurements across Lomonosov Ridge after Forsyth and Mair (1984); in the Amundsen Basin (FRAM-II, line 1, 3, and 4) after Duckworth and Baggeroer (1985) and Duckworth and others (1982); on the northern flank of the Arctic Mid-Ocean Ridge (FRAM-I, line 3 and 11) after Jackson and others (1982) and (FRAM-I, line 9 and 10) after Kristoffersen and others (1982); and in the Nansen Basin (FRAM-IV, line 1 and 4) after Duckworth and Baggeroer (1985). Inverted triangles show projected locations of refraction lines. Structure section A–B from the Laptev Shelf after Vinogradov (1984) based on seismic refraction data (continuous interfaces) and gravity and magnetic data (dashed interfaces). Location of section A–B shown in Figure 3.

sediment thickness along some segments are available from continuous seismic reflection measurements.

Severe pack-ice conditions generally inhibit adequate shot range distribution for seismic refraction experiments in the Arctic Ocean. However, array recording and advanced processing techniques can greatly enhance the information potential of a less than ideal data set (Duckworth and Baggeroer, 1985). Synthetic seismogram sections have only been used to a limited extent as a check on the velocity-depth solutions.

Velocity-depth solutions generally show an upper 1-km-thick interval of vertical velocity gradients characteristic of oceanic layer 2 (Spudic and Orcutt, 1980) above more gentle velocity increases designated as layer 3 (Fig. 5). Layer 2 structure of the Arctic oceanic crust is not well determined due to sparse shot coverage in the 5 to 15 km offset range and complex basement topography.

At the Arctic Mid-Ocean Ridge a single seismic line has been shot in rough topography into the rift valley and been interpreted in terms of homogenous layering (Kristoffersen and others, 1982). The depth below the seabed (~3 km) to a 7.3 km/s refractor in the rift valley here appears greater than the depth observed in the FAMOUS area (2 km; Fowler, 1976). This may reflect the relative importance of lateral heat conduction at slow spreading ridges. The thickness (6 to 7 km) and velocity structure of the crust out to 60 km north from the ridge axis (magnetic anomaly 5) appear similar to oceanic crust at other slow spreading ridges (Jackson and others, 1982; Kristoffersen and others, 1982). However, farther into the Amundsen Basin (130 km; anomaly 7), modeling of seven refraction data sets consistently requires anomalously thin (2 to 3 km) crust, the primary evidence being upper-mantle P-wave first arrivals observed at offset ranges less than 15 km (Jackson and others, 1982). At 280 km from the ridge (anomalies 21 to 22; FRAM II, line 1), the observed crustal thickness is 7 km, while FRAM II, line 3, at 330 km from the ridge axis, shows anomalously thin oceanic crust (Duckworth and others, 1982).

Crustal models based on gravity data across the Lomonosov Ridge near the North Pole cannot be reconciled with the relatively thick (~10 km) oceanic crust in the Amundsen Basin interpreted from an unreversed refraction dip line (Forsyth and Mair, 1984) unless anomalously high density values are assigned to the lowermost 4 km of the crust (Weber and Sweeney, 1985).

On the southern flank of the Arctic Mid-Ocean Ridge, seismic refraction measurements have been carried out along the isochron of magnetic anomaly 12-13. Velocity-depth inversions of the FRAM IV line 1 data set give a 4 to 5-km-thick crust, whereas the solutions for line 4 immediately to the south (Fig. 5) indicate an approximately 3-km increase in crustal thickness (Duckworth and Baggeroer, 1985).

Although limited, the seismic refraction measurements in the Eurasia Basin available to date indicate apparent lateral variation in crustal structure. Crustal thickness varies along an isochron as well as perpendicular to it, and symmetry with respect to the ridge axis cannot be established with the available data. It should be pointed out that the observations of anomalously thin (2 to 3 km) crust are based solely on interpretation of first-arrival data. As demonstrated by Orcutt and others (1977) and stressed by Spudic and Orcutt (1980), velocity-depth models ranging from no crust-mantle transition zone to sharp discontinuities can satisfy a particular first-arrival data set unless further constraints from reflected arrivals are available. Therefore, the seismic evidence for true anomalously thin crust in parts of the Eurasia Basin is still ambiguous. On the other hand, detailed work on ophiolite complexes has shown that reconstructed crustal thicknesses may vary from 3 to 4 km to 6 to 7 km over distances of 10 km (Karson and others, 1984).

Compilation of seismic refraction measurements of crustal thickness in the world oceans in relation to spreading rate reveals a possible correlation at rates <2 cm/a (Reid and Jackson, 1981). Theoretical models of lithospheric flow and melting at slow spreading ridges can predict the observed relationship if sublithospheric flow beneath the surface thermal boundary layer is assumed.

The extremely low total opening rate (1.5 to 0.85 cm/a) in the Eurasia Basin offers end-member constraints on spreading-rate-dependent numerical models of rift valley morphology (Kristoffersen, 1982; Sleep and Rosendahl, 1979). For slow spreading ridges (half rate <3 cm/a), the width of the inner rift valley floor appears to be directly related to spreading rate (Ramberg and others, 1977). However, to a first approximation, the observed rift valley width tends to a minimum value with decreasing spreading rate (Kristoffersen, 1982). This minimum rift-valley dimension may reflect the flexural strength of the fractured cooling crust. At slow spreading rates, lateral heat transport will contribute to faster cooling of the axial region (Sleep, 1975).

MARGINAL PLATEAUS

Yermak Plateau

The crustal structure of the conjugate Yermak and Morris Jesup marginal plateaus is considered to be grossly similar and oceanic, although the former may be of dual origin. Based on morphology and aeromagnetic data, the Yermak Plateau can be divided into a northern part (north of 82°N) and a southern part (Fig. 1). A seismic refraction line on the north-northwest-trending southern portion of the plateau shows a velocity of 4.3 km/s at the sea floor and refracting horizons of 6.0 km/s and 8.0 km/s at 5 km (Plate 5) and 20 km, respectively, below the seabed (Jackson and others, 1984). From sonobuoy measurements, compressional velocities are 1.7 to 4.4 km/s within the sedimentary cover and from 5.1 to 5.8 km/s within basement (Austegard, 1982). The observed velocity structure shows gross similarity to refraction results from central Spitsbergen, although the crust is thicker there (Chan and Mitchell, 1982; Gutrecht and others, 1982). Also a smooth magnetic field over this part of the plateau and dredged gneiss boulders of unknown provenance argue in favor of crustal material of continental affinity (Jackson and others, 1984). On the other hand, high heat flow (74 to 196 mW) along the western plateau margin may indicate that part of the southern plateau is formed by oceanic crust (Crane and others, 1982) or renewed volcanic activity (Jackson and others, 1984).

The northeast-trending northern part of the Yermak Plateau is associated with high amplitude (>1,000 nT) magnetic anomalies (Feden and others, 1979). A single refraction line shows a basement velocity of 5.0 km/s, deeper refractors in the range 6.0 to 7.2 km/s, and a minimum crustal thickness of 18 km (Jackson and others, 1984). This velocity-depth structure is marginally different from that of the southern part of the plateau and has been interpreted as oceanic crust.

Morris Jesup Plateau

The crustal structure of Morris Jesup Plateau is inferred from an Arlis-II single-channel seismic reflection profile (Ostenso and Wold, 1977) and from aeromagnetic data, which show high-amplitude anomalies associated with the rise (Kovacs and Vogt, 1982; Feden and others, 1979). The plateau has a flat top, bounded to the east by a steep scarp and to the west by a series of progressively deepening sediment covered fault blocks (Fig. 1). Its geophysical characteristics and conjugate position with respect to the northern part of Yermak Plateau argue for it being a volcanic constructional feature (Feden and others, 1979; Dawes and Soper, 1973).

Lomonosov Ridge

Seismic refraction measurements on the Lomonosov Ridge near the North Pole show an upper crustal layer 5 km thick with a velocity of 4.7 km/s and a lower layer (below a 6.6 km/s refractor) with a thickness of 15 to 20 km (Forsyth and Mair, 1984). On the ridge at 85°N 150°E, Demenitskaya and Kiselev (1968) report a sediment thickness of 3 km (Plate 5) overlying crust with a velocity of about 6.4 km/s. Models assuming a nonmagnetic upper layer and a strongly magnetized lower layer (7 to 17 km depth) are preferred because they account for the observed magnetic anomalies near the North Pole (Coles, 1980). Local short-wavelength magnetic anomalies indicate some shallower magnetic sources, possibly volcanics within the ridge (Hood and Bower, 1980).

A structural high appears to bridge the Lomonosov Ridge to the largest of the New Siberian Islands (Fig. 3), although truncation by a large structural trough has been reported (Demenitskaya and Kiselev, 1968; Plate 5). The trough apparently was formed and filled with sediments in pre-Cenozoic time.

On the Canadian side, the Lomonosov Ridge is separated from Ellesmere Island by a bathymetric depression (Fig. 1), but estimated depths to magnetic basement show a more landward trough of similar trend buried below the present shelf and upper continental slope (Fig. 3). The bulk of the geophysical and geological data support the idea that Lomonosov Ridge is a continental fragment, as first advocated by Heezen and Ewing (1961) and Wilson (1963).

The continental extension of the Arctic Mid-Ocean Ridge

On the Laptev Shelf, colinear with the Arctic Mid-Ocean Ridge, a rift zone is fault bounded to the west of the New Siberian Islands and to the east of the Taimyr Peninsula (Progrebitskii, 1983). A triangular-shaped basement block, the North Laptev Uplift, is isolated within the rift zone near the shelf edge by sediment-filled (2 to 3 km) grabens to the east and west (Figs. 3 and 5). The seismicity indicates an extensional regime (Savostin and Karasik, 1981; Avetisov, 1975). Farther south, epicenter locations can be related to fault traces within a 100-km-wide continental rift zone (Grachev, 1982; Patyk-Kara and Grishin, 1972). A series of horsts, 50 to 70 km long and 10 to 12 km wide, are present within the graben system, and vertical displacements along high-angle faults are up to 2 km. Paleocene-Eocene deposits are coastal plain facies whereas the continental Oligocene-Neogene section is represented by sands, gravels, silts, sandy loams, and brown coal (Vinogradov, 1984).

Kogan (1974) carried out a seismic refraction experiment along a 200-km-long profile southwestward from the delta of the Lena River. Reflected and refracted arrivals from interfaces at 12 km (v = 5.5 to 6.5 km/s) and at 30 to 33 km depth were interpreted as crystalline basement and Moho, respectively, with an upper mantle velocity of 7.5 km/s. This crustal thickness is substantial, considering that about 400 km of Tertiary crustal extension must have taken place within this zone from plate tectonic considerations.

The transition from an oceanic spreading center to stretched and thinned continental crust along the North America-Eurasia plate boundary takes place about 1,000 km from the pole of rotation. This transition probably reflects a threshold in strain rate during continental rifting necessary for development of a mid-ocean ridge (LePichon and others, 1982).

PLATE TECTONIC EVOLUTION OF THE EURASIA BASIN

A mid-ocean rift system extending into the Arctic Ocean was postulated from its presence throughout the Atlantic Ocean, a few earthquake epicenters, and re-evaluation of scattered Soviet depth soundings by Heezen and Ewing (1961). Later, systematic Soviet (Rassokho and others, 1966; Karasik, 1968), United States (Vogt and others, 1979b), and Canadian (Coles and others, 1978) aeromagnetic surveys revealed magnetic lineations that were symmetric with respect to the axial rift of the Arctic Mid-Ocean Ridge wherever bathymetric data existed (Fig. 6). Furthermore, the pattern was strikingly simple compared to the other arctic deep-ocean basins. Observed lineation offsets are minor (<50 km), and the bend in the axial anomaly at about 60°E (Fig. 6) seems to have been inherited from the initial opening (Vogt and others, 1979b).

Interpretation of the magnetic anomalies in terms of sea-floor spreading and their correlation with the geomagnetic time scale have left little ambiguity as to the evolution of the Eurasia

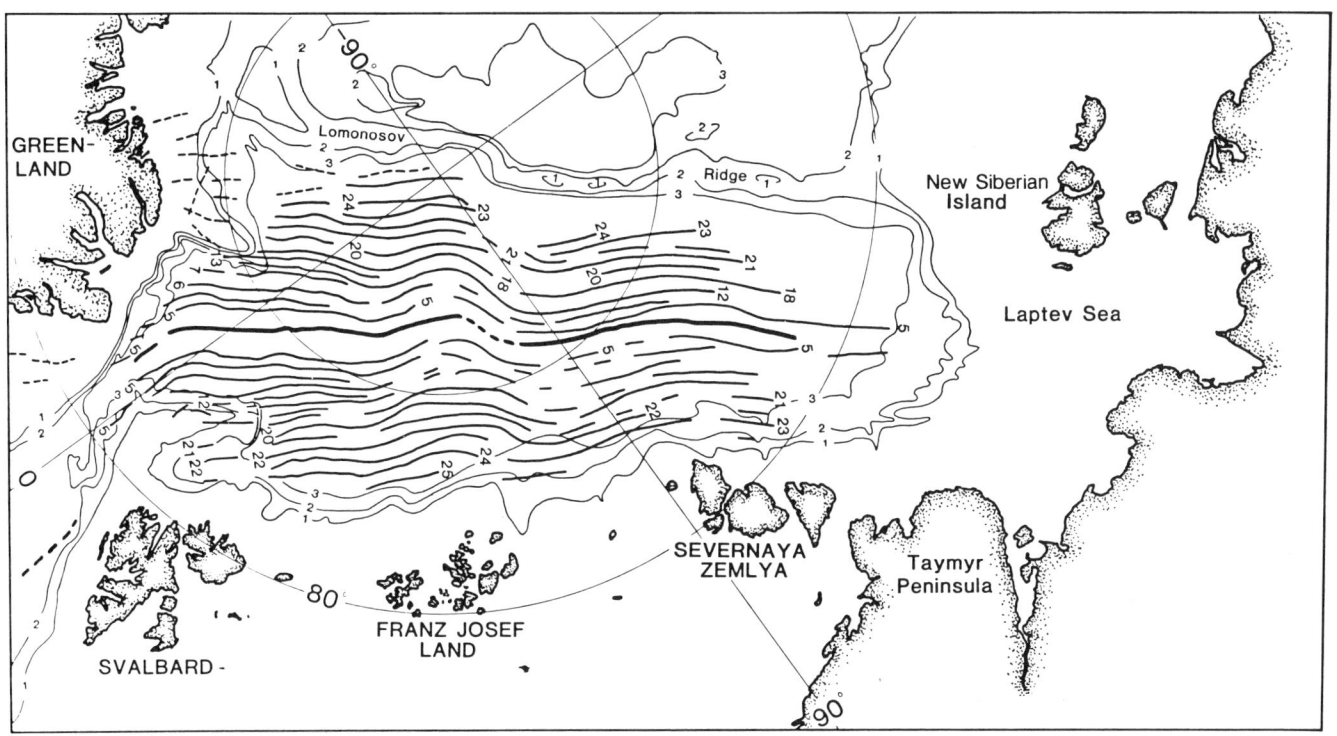

Figure 6. Magnetic lineations in the Eurasia Basin. Modified after Kovacs and others (1983). Polar stereographic projection.

Basin and its ties with the opening of the Norwegian-Greenland Sea (Vogt and others, 1979b; Karasik, 1974; Pitman and Talwani, 1972). Anomaly 24 is the oldest identifiable magnetic lineation observed at the base of the Lomonosov Ridge and along the Barents-Kara Sea continental slope, but an older trend is also present particularly along the foot of the Lomonosov Ridge north of Greenland (Fig. 6).

By analogy with the Norwegian-Greenland Sea (Eldholm and others, 1984), sea-floor spreading in the Eurasia Basin was probably initiated in the time period between anomaly 25 and 24 B at 58 Ma in the late Paleocene (LaBrecque and others, 1977). Along the outer shelf of the Barents-Kara Sea, a long sliver of fault blocks, the proto–Lomonosov Ridge, was severed off with the development of an embryonic ocean basin (Fig. 7). From the late Paleocene onward, the Eurasia Basin opened at an initial rate of 2 cm/yr, steadily decreasing to half this value in Oligocene/early Miocene time and later increasing to 1.5 cm/yr (Vogt and others, 1979b; Karasik, 1974). Greenland moved as a separate plate from the time sea-floor spreading was initiated in the Norwegian-Greenland Sea until Chron 13 (early Oligocene; Srivastava, 1978; Kristoffersen and Talwani, 1977). Strike-slip motion along the Spitsbergen Fracture Zone connected the Mohns Ridge in the Norwegian-Greenland Sea with the Arctic Mid-Ocean Ridge. However, the relative motion between Greenland and North America is ambiguous in that the apparent continuity of geologic structures across Nares Strait does not support any significant left-lateral motion (Dawes and Kerr, 1982). Aeromagnetic data have delineated a 300-km northeastward extension of the Nares Strait basement depression, which underlines its possible role as a tectonic lineament (Kovacs, 1982). Alternatively, a major component of the motion of Greenland, related to sea-floor spreading in the Labrador Sea, may have been accommodated by thrusting in the Canadian Arctic Islands (Kristoffersen and Talwani, 1977) or compression in the Strait itself (Jackson, 1985).

Intraplate Upper Cretaceous explosive volcanism in northeastern Greenland, the Kap Washington Group (Soper and others, 1982), was followed in early Eocene time (Chron 21) by offshore extensive volcanic activity at the adjacent end of the Arctic Mid-Ocean Ridge. This formed the Morris Jesup Plateau and at least the northern end of the Yermak Plateau by early Oligocene or Chron 13 (Feden and others, 1979). The volcanism must, in part, have been subaerial, as present water depths are less than 1,000 m. Feden and others (1979) have related this event to a Yermak hot spot. We note, however, that the timing of this volcanic activity corresponds closely to changes in the motion of Greenland in the waning stages of sea-floor spreading in the Labrador Sea (Kristoffersen and Talwani, 1977). Furthermore,

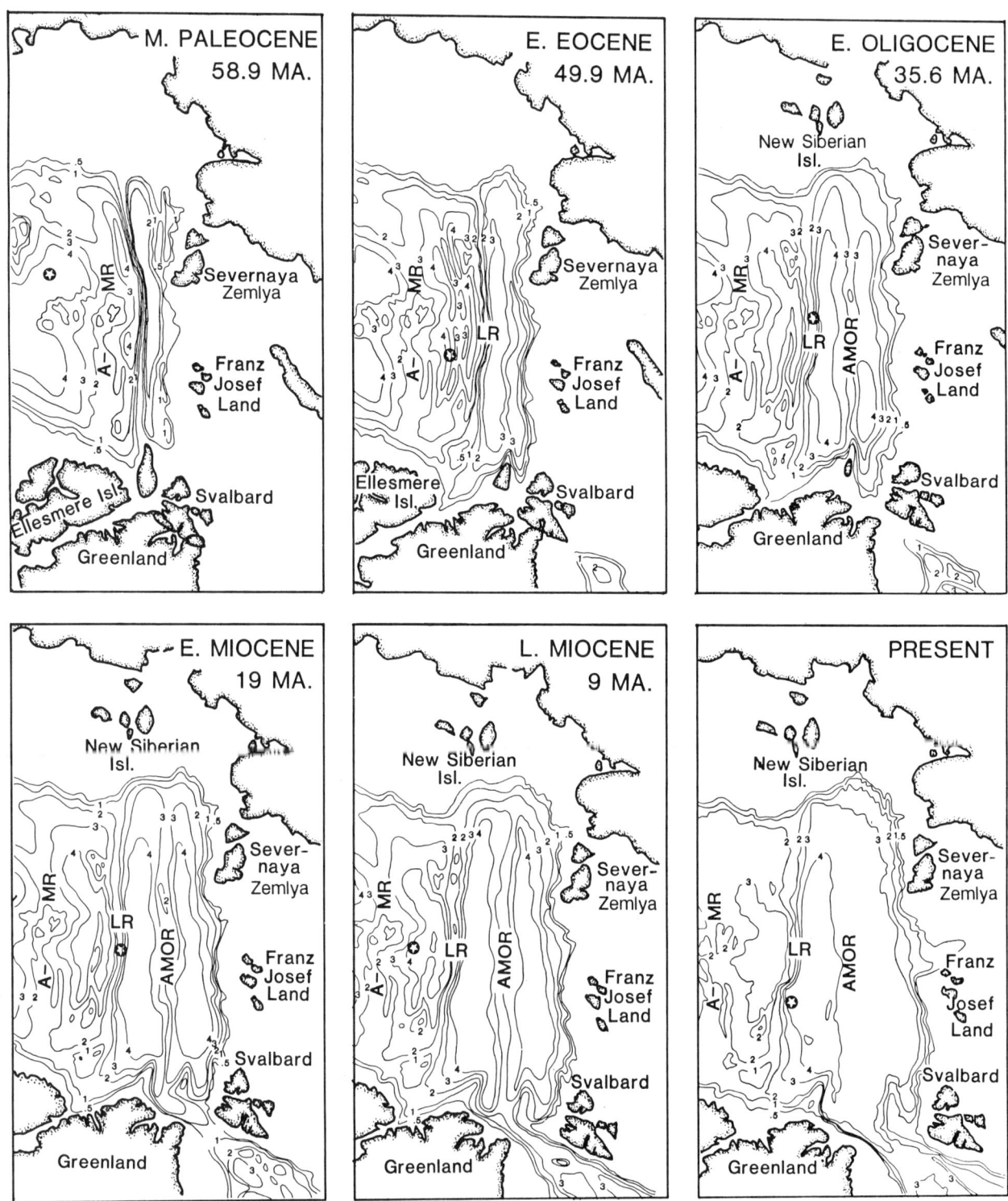

Figure 7. Plate-tectonic reconstructions of Eurasia Basin evolution. Modified after Bernero and others (1983). Polar stereographic projection. AMOR is Arctic Mid-Ocean Ridge, A-MR is Alpha-Mendeleev Ridge and LR is Lomonosov Ridge.

there are several examples of excessive volcanism at ridge segments adjacent to large fracture zones during changes in plate motion: (1) the J-anomaly ridge abutting the Newfoundland Fracture Zone and its timing with the opening between Spain and Newfoundland (Tucholke and Ludwig, 1982); (2) the West and East Thulean basement ridges (Vogt and Avery, 1974) adjacent to the Charlie-Gibbs Fracture Zone and its timing with the opening of the Norwegian Sea. Thus, changes in plate motion may induce excessive deviatoric stresses at ridge-fracture zone intersections and lead to anomalous volcanism as was apparently the case for the Morris Jesup and Yermak Plateaus.

In the early Oligocene, Greenland became part of the North American plate, and the relative motion between Svalbard and Greenland changed from strike-slip to oblique spreading and initiated the opening of a future seaway between the Arctic Ocean and lower-latitude water masses. No significant changes in plate motion have affected the steady evolution of the Eurasia Basin since mid-Cenozoic time.

THE CENOZOIC EURASIA BASIN PALEOENVIRONMENT

Devonian and older structures of the Svalbard Archipelago trend north-northwest and perpendicular to the Barents-Kara Sea margin (Hjelle, 1977). Extensive intrusions of dolerites occurred in the Svalbard archipelago at 145 ± 5 Ma and at 105 ± 5 Ma at a distance of about 250 km from the margin (Burov and others, 1977). Franz Josef Land, situated 100 to 300 km from the margin, was the site of subaerial basalt extrusions beginning in the Hauterivian and culminating in Albian time (Tarachovskii and others, 1980).

Crust that eventually formed the Lomonosov Ridge has been in a complex tectonic environment, as this margin was presumably formed by opening of the Canada Basin, which involved predominantly shear motion (Sweeney, 1985; Green and others, 1984). Later, the Makarov and Eurasia Basins formed by rifting either in one (Sweeney and others, 1982) or as two separate events (Taylor and others, 1981; Herron and others, 1974).

The margin north of Svalbard was a structural high in Late Cretaceous/Early Tertiary time (Steel and Worsley, 1984; Hjelle and Lauritzen, 1982). During the Paleocene rifting, the Lomonosov Ridge may have been at or near sea level. Synrift sediments must have originated mainly from the Barents-Kara Sea margin, and little would have bypassed the spreading center to reach the proto-Amundsen Basin. A shallow seaway through the Kara Sea connected the West Siberian basin with the polar ocean in the early Tertiary (Green and others, 1984). However, at depth, the young Eurasia Basin was a closed basin bounded by the subsiding Lomonosov Ridge and a compressive regime between Svalbard and Greenland through Eocene time (Kellogg, 1975). Anoxic conditions may therefore have occurred.

With the early Oligocene change in relative motion between Greenland and Svalbard, block faulting and infilling of grabens occurred west of Spitsbergen (Birkenmajer, 1972; Harland, 1969) and in the Wandel Sea (Håkansson and Pedersen, 1982). The excessive basalt production that formed the northern Yermak Plateau terminated by early Oligocene, and the cooling ridge probably subsided below sea level in the mid-Miocene (Kristoffersen and Husebye, 1985).

Shear motion along the Spitsbergen Fracture Zone changed to oblique spreading, and a seaway in the Fram Strait began to evolve. The establishment of a deep-water connection between the Arctic Ocean and lower-latitude water masses has been related to a change in the depositional environment in the Nansen Basin from predominantly turbiditic sediments to overlying deposits characteristic of hemipelagic drape (Kristoffersen and Husebye, 1985). Post-Oligocene bottom currents in this basin have been remarkably stable, and the sluggish bottom circulation has had no significant effect on sediment deposition except for local topographically induced turbulence.

During the late Cenozoic northern hemisphere glaciations, several ice caps that were probably present in the Barents and Kara Seas accelerated erosion (Grosswald, 1980). The morphology of the large Vorinin and St. Anna troughs as well as two troughs between Franz Josef Land and Svalbard, are characteristic erosional features of former major glacial ice streams (Sugden and John, 1976), which must have brought large quantities of sediments onto the continental slope. On the western Barents Sea margin, deposits of mainly glacially derived sediments reach a thickness of more than 0.5 km at the head of the major troughs (Solheim and Kristoffersen, 1984).

Both sea ice and glacial ice can transport a significant sediment load, but with differences in grain size distribution (Clark and Hanson, 1983). As noted by Kiær (1906), sea ice that forms on the shallow Laptev Shelf carries fine sediments over the entire Eurasia Basin as it moves with the Transpolar Current. Thus, the reduced biogenic sediment input in an ice-covered ocean is partly counterbalanced by new transport mechanisms of terrigenous sediments to maintain the level of total sediment influx.

REFERENCES

Anonymous, 1976, Scientific plan for the proposed Nansen Drift Station: Washington, D.C., National Academy of Science, 247 p.
——, 1978, Icebreaker voyage to the North Pole: Polar Record, p. 67–78.
Austegard, A., 1982, Velocity analysis of sonobuoy data from the northern Svalbard margin: Bergen, Norway, University of Bergen Seismological Observatory Scientific Report no. 9, 25 p.

Avetisov, G. A., 1975, Seismicity of the Laptev Sea and its connection with that of the Eurasia Basin: Tectonics of the Arctic: Leningrad, USSR, Nauchno-Issledovatel'skiy Institut Geologii Arktiki no. 1, p. 31–36 (in Russian).
Bergman, E., and Solomon, S. E., 1980, Oceanic intraplate earthquakes; Implications for local and regional intraplate stress: Journal of Geophysical Research, v. 85, p. 5389–5410.

Bernero, C., Kovacs, L. C., Vogt, P. R., and Pilger, R. H., Jr., 1983, Paleobathymetry and plate reconstructions, *in* Kovacs, L. C., and others, eds., Residual magnetic anomaly chart of the Arctic Ocean region: U.S. Naval Research Laboratory and Naval Ocean Research and Development Activity, scale 1:6,000,000.

Birkenmajer, K., 1972, Tertiary history of Spitsbergen and continental drift: Acta Geologica Polonica, v. 22, p. 193–218.

Blasco, S. M., Bornhold, B. D., and Lewis, C.F.M., 1979, Preliminary result of surficial geology and geomorphology studies of the Lomonosov Ridge, central Arctic Basin: Geological Survey of Canada Paper 79-1C, p. 73–83.

Bostrøm, K., and Thiede, J., 1984, Ymer-80, Swedish Arctic expedition: Meddelanden Stockholms Universitet Geologiska Institution, no. 260, 123 p.

Bungum, H., 1977, Two focal-mechanism solutions for earthquakes from Iceland and Svalbard: Tectonophysics, v. 41, p. T15–T18.

Burkhanov, V., 1956, New Soviet discoveries in the Arctic: Moscow Foreign Languages Publishing House, 60 p.

Burov, Yu.P., Krasil'scikov, A. A., Firsov, L. V., and Klubov, B. A., 1977, The age of the Spitsbergen dolerites: Norsk Polarinstitutt Arbok 1975, p. 101–108.

Chan, W. W., and Mitchell, B. J., 1982, Synthetic seismogram and surface wave constraints on crustal models of Spitsbergen: Tectonophysics, v. 89, p. 51–76.

Chapman, M. E., and Solomon, S. C., 1976, North American-Eurasian plate boundary in northeast Asia: Journal of Geophysical Research, v. 81, p. 921–929.

Clark, D. L., and Hanson, A., 1983, Central Arctic ocean sediment texture; A key to ice transport mechanisms, *in* Molnia, B. F., ed., Glacial-marine sedimentation: New York, Plenum Publishing Corporation, p. 301–330.

Clark, D. L., Whitman, R. R., Morgan, K. A., and Makey, S. D., 1980, Stratigraphy and glacial-marine sediments of the Amerasian Basin, central Arctic Ocean: Geological Society of America Special Paper 181, 57 p.

Coles, R. L., 1980, The LOREX magnetic gradient and total field experiment: Ottawa, Ontario, Earth Physics Branch Geomagnetic Laboratory Report, 12 p. (internal report).

Coles, R. L., Hannaford, W., and Haines, G. V., 1978, Magnetic anomalies and the evolution of the Arctic, *in* Sweeney, J. F., ed., Arctic Geophysical Review: Ottawa, Ontario, Earth Physics Branch, v. 45, p. 51–66.

Conant, D. A., 1972, Six new focal mechanism solutions for the Arctic and a center of rotation for plate movements, [M.S. thesis]: New York, Columbia University, 17 p.

Crane, K., Eldholm, O., Myhre, A. M., and Sundvor, E., 1982, Thermal implications for the evaluation of the Spitsbergen transform fault: Tectonophysics, v. 89, p. 1–32.

Dawes, P. R., and Kerr, J. W., 1982, The case against major displacement along Nares Strait, *in* Dawes, P. R., and Kerr, J. W., eds., Nares Strait and the drift of Greenland; A conflict in plate tectonics: Meddelser om Grønland, Geoscience, v. 8, p. 369–388.

Dawes, P. R., and Soper, N. J., 1973, Pre-Quaternary history of North Greenland, *in* Pitcher, M. G., ed., Arctic geology: American Association of Petroleum Geologists Memoir 19, p. 117–134.

Demenitskaya, R. M., and Kiselev, Yu.G., 1968, The characteristic features of the structure, morphology and sedimentary cover of the central part of the Lomonosov Ridge from seismic investigations: Geofizicheskie metody razvedki i Arktike, v. 5, p. 33–46 (in Russian).

Demenitskaya, R. M., Karasik, A. M., and Kiselev, Yu.JG., 1964, Crustal structure of the Arctic; Geology of the bottom of seas and oceans: Moscow, Nauka, p. 114–121 (in Russian).

Dietz, R. S., and Shumway, G., 1961, Arctic basin geomorphology: Geological Society of America Bulletin, v. 72, p. 1319–1330.

Duckworth, G. L., and Baggeroer, A. B., 1985, Inversion of refraction data from the Fram and Nansen Basins of the Arctic Ocean: Tectonophysics, v. 114, p. 55–102.

Duckworth, G. L., Baggeroer, A. B., and Jackson, H. R., 1982, Crustal structure measurements near FRAM II in the Pole Abyssal Plain: Tectonophysics, v. 89, p. 172–215.

Eldholm, O., Myhre, A. M., and Faleide, J. I., 1984, Cenozoic evolution of the margin off Norway and Svalbard, *in* Spencer, A. M., and others, eds., Petroleum geology of the north European margin: London, Graham and Trotman, Limited, p. 3–19.

Feden, R. H., Vogt, P. R., and Fleming, H. S., 1979, Magnetic and bathymetric evidence for the "Yermak" hot spot northwest of Svalbard in the Arctic basin: Earth and Planetary Science Letters, v. 44, p. 18–38.

Forsyth, D. A., and Mair, J. A., 1984, Crustal structure of the Lomonosov Ridge and the Fram and Makarov Basins near the North Pole: Journal of Geophysical Research, v. 89, p. 473–481.

Fowler, C.M.R., 1976, Crustal structure of the Mid-Atlantic Ridge crest at 37°N: Geophysical Journal of the Royal Astronomical Society, v. 47, p. 459–491.

Grachev, A. F., 1982, Geodynamics of the transitional zone from the Moma Rift to the Gakkel Ridge, *in* Watkins, J. S., and Drake, C. L., eds., Studies in continental margin geology: American Association of Petroleum Geologists Memoir 34, p. 103–113.

Grachev, A. G., and Karasik, A. M., 1974, Sea-floor spreading and tectonics of the Eurasia Basin; Geotectonic implications to the prospects of mineral resources on the Arctic shelf: Leningrad, Nauchno-Issledovatel'skiy Institut Geologii Arktiki, Trudy, p. 19–33 (in Russian).

Green, A. R., Kaplan, A. A., and Vierbuchen, R. C., 1984, The geological framework and hydrocarbon potential of sedimentary basins in northern seas: Stavanger, Norway, 1982 Proceedings, Offshore Northern Seas Conference, p. E/1-1-E/1-53.

Grosswald, M. G., 1980, Late Weichselian ice sheet of northern Eurasia: Quaternary Research, v. 13, p. 1–32.

Gutenberg, B., and Richter, C. F., 1954, Seismicity of the Earth: Princeton, New Jersey, Princeton University Press, 310 p.

Gutrecht, A., Pajchel, J., and Perchuc, E., 1982, Seismic crustal studies on Spitsbergen, *in* Sellevoll, M. A., ed., The central profile: University of Spitsbergen, Geophysical Research on Spitsbergen Seismological Observatory, p. 33–61 (internal report).

Hall, J. K., 1979, Sediment waves and other evidence of paleobottom currents at two locations in the deep Arctic Ocean: Sedimentary Geology, v. 23, p. 269–299.

Harland, W. B., 1969, Contribution of Spitsbergen to understanding of tectonic evolution of North Atlantic region, *in* Kay, M., ed., North Atlantic geology and continental drift: American Association of Petroleum Geologists Memoir 12, p. 817–851.

Heezen, B. C., and Ewing, M., 1961, The Mid-Oceanic Ridge and its extension through the Arctic Basin, *in* Raasch, G. O., ed., Geology of the Arctic: Toronto, University of Toronto Press, v. 1, p. 622–642.

Herron, E. M., Dewey, J. F., and Pitman, W. C., III, 1974, Plate tectonics model for the evolution of the Arctic: Geology, v. 2, p. 377–380.

Hjelle, A., 1977, An outline of the pre-Carboniferous geology of Nordaustlandet: Polarforschung, v. 48, p. 62–77.

Hjelle, A., and Lauritzen, O., 1982, Geological map of Svalbard, Sheet 3G, northern part: Norsk Polarinstitutt Skrifter no. 154C, 15 p.

Hood, P. J., and Bower, M. E., 1980, Aeromagnetic reconnaissance, LOREX Project [abs.]: EOS American Geophysical Union Transactions, v. 61, p. 277.

Horsfield, W. T., and Maton, P. I., 1970, Transform faulting along the De Geer line: Nature, v. 226, p. 256–257.

Håkansson, E., and Pedersen, S.A.S., 1982, Late Paleozoic to Tertiary tectonic evolution of the continental margin in North Greenland, *in* Embry, A. F., and Balkwill, H. R., eds., Arctic geology and geophysics: Canadian Society of Petroleum Geologists Memoir 8, p. 331–348.

Jackson, H. R., 1985, Nares Strait—A suture zone; Geophysical and geological implications: Tectonophysics, v. 114, p. 11–29.

Jackson, H. R., Reid, I., and Falconer, R.K.H., 1982, Crustal structure near the Arctic Mid-Ocean Ridge: Journal of Geophysical Research, v. 87, p. 1773–1783.

Jackson, H. R., Johnson, G. L., Sundvor, E., and Myhre, A. M., 1984, The Yermak Plateau, formed at a triple junction: Journal of Geophysical Research, v. 89, p. 3223-3232.

Johnson, G. L., 1983, The FRAM expeditions; Arctic Ocean studies from floating ice: Polar Record, v. 21, p. 583-589.

Karasik, A. M., 1968, Magnetic anomalies of the Gakkel Ridge and the origin of the Eurasia Subbasin of the Arctic Ocean: Geofizicheskie metody razvedki i Arktike, v. 5, p. 8-19 (in Russian).

——, 1974, The Eurasia Basin of the Arctic Ocean from the point of view of plate tectonics; Problems in geology of polar areas of the earth: Leningrad, Nauchno-Issledovateliskiy Institut Geologii Avktiki, p. 23-31 (in Russian).

Karson, J. A., Collins, J. A., and Casey, J. F., 1984, Geologic and seismic velocity structure of the crust/mantle transition in the Bay of Islands ophiolite complex: Journal of Geophysical Research, v. 89, p. 6126-6138.

Kellogg, H. E., 1975, Tertiary stratigraphy and tectonism in Svalbard and continental drift: American Association of Petroleum Geologists Bulletin, v. 59, p. 465-485.

Kiær, H., 1906, Thalamophora of the bottom deposits and mud from the ice surface, in Nansen, F., ed., The Norwegian North Polar Expedition 1893-1896; v. 5: New York, Longmans, Green & Co., p. 58-62.

Kogan, A. L., 1974, Seismic studies using CMRW and DSS method from sea ice on the shelf of Arctic Seas (experiment from work in the Laptev Sea): Geofizicheskie metody razvedki i Arktike, v. 9, p. 33-38 (in Russian).

Kovacs, L. C., 1982, Motion along Nares Strait recorded in the Lincoln Sea, aeromagnetic evidence, in Dawes, P. R., and Kerr, J. W., eds., Nares Strait and the drift of Greenland; A conflict in plate tectonics: Meddelelser om Grønland, Geoscience, v. 8, p. 275-290.

Kovacs, L. C., and Vogt, P. R., 1982, Depth-to-magnetic source analysis of the Arctic Ocean region: Tectonophysics, v. 89, p. 255-294.

Kovacs, L. C., and five others, 1983, Residual magnetic anomaly chart of the Arctic Ocean region, U.S. Naval Research Laboratory and Naval Ocean Research and Development Activity, scale 1:6,000,000.

Kristoffersen, Y., 1982, The Nansen Ridge, Arctic Ocean, some geophysical observations of the rift valley at slow spreading rate: Tectonophysics, v. 89, p. 161-172.

Kristoffersen, Y., and Husebye, E. S., 1985, Multi-channel seismic reflection measurements in the Eurasia Basin, Arctic Ocean, from U.S. ice station FRAM IV: Tectonophysics, v. 114, p. 103-115.

Kristoffersen, Y., and Talwani, M., 1977, Extinct triple junction south of Greenland and the Tertiary motion of Greenland relative to North America: Geological Society of America Bulletin, v. 88, p. 1037-1049.

Kristoffersen, Y., Husebye, E. S., Bungum, H., and Gregersen, S., 1982, Seismic investigations of the Nansen Ridge during the FRAM-1 experiment: Tectonophysics, v. 82, p. 57-68.

LaBrecque, J. L., Kent, D. V., and Cande, S. V., 1977, Revised magnetic polarity time scale for Late Cretaceous and Cenozoic time: Geology, v. 5, p. 330-335.

Laktionov, A. F., 1959, Bottom topography of the Greenland Sea in the region of Nansen's sill: Priroda, v. 10, p. 95-97 (in Russian).

Lazareva, A. P., and Misharina, L. A., 1965, Stresses in earthquake foci in the Arctic seismic belt: Academy of Science USSR Bulletin, Geophysical series no. 2, p. 84-87 (in Russian).

LePichon, X., Angelier, J., and Sibuet, J-C., 1982, Plate boundaries and extensional tectonics: Tectonophysics, v. 81, p. 239-256.

Markussen, B., Zahn, R., and Thiede, J., 1985, Late Quaternary sedimentation in the eastern Arctic Basin, stratigraphy and depositional environment: Palaeoceanography, Palaeoclimatology, Palaeoecology, v. 50, p. 271-284.

Morris, T. H., Clark, D. L., and Blasco, S. M., 1985, Sediments of the Lomonosov Ridge and Makarov Basin; A Pleistocene stratigraphy for the North Pole: Geological Society of America Bulletin, v. 96, p. 901-910.

Nansen, F., ed., 1906, The Norwegian North Polar Expedition 1893-1896: New York, Longmans, Green & Co., v. I-V.

Oliver, J., Ewing, M., and Press, F., 1955, Crustal structure of the Arctic regions from the Lg Phase: Geological Society of America Bulletin, v. 66, p. 1063-1074.

Orcutt, J. A., Dorman, L. M., and Spudich, P.K.P., 1977, Inversion of seismic refraction data, in Heacock, J. G., ed., The Earth's crust: Washington, D.C., American Geophysical Union Geophysical Monograph, v. 20, p. 371-384.

Ostenso, N. A., and Wold, R. J., 1977, A seismic and gravity profile across the Arctic Ocean Basin: Tectonophysics, v. 37, p. 1-24.

Overton, A., 1982, A seismic reflection profile across the Lomonosov Ridge, central Arctic Ocean [abs.]: Dallas, Texas, 52nd meeting, Society of Exploration Geophysicists, p. 426.

Patyk-Kara, N. G., and Grishin, M. A., 1972, A location of the Polyusny Ridge in the structure of the northeast USSR and its recent tectonics: Geotektonika, v. 4, p. 90-98 (in Russian).

Pitman, W. C., III, and Talwani, M., 1972, Sea-floor spreading in the North Atlantic: Geological Society of America Bulletin, v. 83, p. 619-646.

Pogrebitskii, Yu.E., 1983, Tectonic map of the Arctic Ocean and of contiguous territories; Geological structure of the USSR and the patterns of disposition of useful minerals: Leningrad, Seas of the Soviet Arctic, v. 9, scale 1:5,000,000.

Ramberg, I. B., Gray, D. F., and Raynolds, R.G.H., 1977, Tectonic evolution of a segment of the Mid-Atlantic Ridge, the FAMOUS area between 35°50' and 37°20'N: Geological Society of America Bulletin, v. 88, p. 609-620.

Rassokho, A. I., and five others, 1966, Submarine Mid-Arctic Ridge and its place in the Arctic Ocean ridge system: Doklady Academia Nauk SSSR, v. 172, p. 659-662 (in Russian).

Reid, I., and Jackson, H. R., 1981, Oceanic spreading rate and crustal thickness: Marine Geophysical Researches, v. 5, p. 165-172.

Rzhevsky, N. N., 1975, On the question of anomalous magnetic field on the southern part of the Gakkel Ridge; Tectonics of the Arctic: Leningrad, Navchno-Issledavatel'skiy Institut Geologii Avktiki, v. 1, p. 18-20 (in Russian).

Savostin, L. A., and Karasik, A. M., 1981, Recent plate tectonics of the Arctic Basin and the northeastern Asia: Tectonophysics, v. 74, p. 111-145.

Sleep, N. H., 1975, Formation of oceanic crust; Some thermal constraints: Journal of Geophysical Research, v. 80, p. 4037-4042.

Sleep, N. H., and Rosendahl, B., 1979, Topography and tectonics of ridge areas: Journal of Geophysical Research, v. 84, p. 6831-6840.

Solheim, A., and Kristoffersen, Y., 1984, Sediments above the upper regional unconformity; Thickness, seismic stratigraphy, and outline of the glacial history, in The physical environment of the western Barents Sea, Sheet B: Norsk Polarinstitutt Skrifter no. 179 B, p. 1-26.

Soper, N. J., Dawes, P. R., and Higgins, A. K., 1982, Cretaceous-Tertiary magmatic and tectonic events in North Greenland and the history of adjacent ocean basins, in Dawes, P. R., and Kerr, J. W., eds., Nares Strait and the drift of Greenland; A conflict in plate tectonics: Meddelelser om Grønland, Geoscience, v. 8, p. 205-220.

Spudic, P., and Orcutt, J., 1980, A new look at the seismic velocity structure of oceanic crust: Reviews of Geophysics and Space Physics, v. 18, p. 627-645.

Srivastava, S. P., 1978, Evolution of the Labrador Sea and its bearing on the early evolution of the North Atlantic: Journal of the Royal Astronomical Society, v. 52, p. 313-357.

Steel, R. J., and Worsley, D., 1984, Svalbard's post-Caledonian strata; An atlas of sedimentological patterns and paleogeographic evolution, in Spencer, A. M., and others, eds., Petroleum geology of the north European margin: London, Graham and Trotman, Limited, p. 109-137.

Sugden, D. E., and John, B. S., 1976, Glaciers and landscape: London, Edward Arnold Publishers, Limited, 376 p.

Sundvor, E., and five others, 1982, Marine geophysical survey on the Yermak Plateau: Bergen, University of Bergen Scientific Report no. 7, 30 p.

Sweeney, J. F., 1985, Comments about the age of the Canada Basin: Tectonophysics, v. 114, p. 1-10.

Sweeney, J. F., Weber, J. R., and Blasco, S. M., 1982, Continental ridges in the Arctic Ocean, LOREX constraints: Tectonophysics, v. 89, p. 217-237.

Sykes, L. R., 1967, Mechanisms of earthquakes and nature of faulting on the mid-oceanic ridges: Journal of Geophysical Research, v. 72, p. 2131-2353.

Tarachovskii, A. N., Skola, I. V., Spektor, V. M., and Ditmar, A. V., 1980, To the question of the stratigraphy of the sedimentary-volcanogenic succession of

Franz Joseph Land; Stratigraphy and paleogeography of the North Atlantic in the Cretaceous Period; Collection of scientific papers: Leningrad, Navchno-Issledovatel'skiy Institut Geologii Arktiki, p. 130–134 (in Russian).

Taylor, P. T., Kovacs, L. C., Vogt, P. R., and Johnson, G. L., 1981, Detailed aeromagnetic investigation of the Arctic Basin, 2: Journal of Geophysical Research, v. 86, p. 6323–6333.

Tucholke, B., and Ludwig, W. J., 1982, Structure and origin of the J Anomaly Ridge, western North Atlantic: Journal of Geophysical Research, v. 87, p. 9389–9407.

Vinogradov, V. A., 1984, Laptev Sea: Marja Sovetskoj Arktiki, p. 50–56 (translated from Russian).

Vogt, P. R., and Avery, O., 1974, Detailed magnetic surveys in the northeast Atlantic and Labrador Sea: Journal of Geophysical Research, v. 79, p. 363–390.

Vogt, P. R., Taylor, P. T., Kovacs, L. C., and Johnson, G. L, 1979a, Detailed aeromagnetic investigations of the Arctic Basin: Journal of Geophysical Research, v. 84, p. 1071–1089.

Vogt, P. R., Kovacs, L. C., Johnson, G. L., and Feden, R. H., 1979b, The evolution of the Arctic Ocean with emphasis on the Eurasia Basin: Oslo, Norwegian Petroleum Society, Proceedings Norwegian Sea Symposium, p. 1–29.

Weber, J. R., 1979, The Lomonosov Ridge experiment, LOREX 79: EOS American Geophysical Union Transactions, v. 60, p. 715–721.

——, 1980, Exploring the Arctic seafloor: Ottawa, Ontario, GEOS, Department of Energy, Mines, and Resources, summer, p. 2–7.

Weber, J. R., and Sweeney, J. F., 1985, Reinterpretation of morphology and crustal structure in the central Arctic Ocean Basin: Journal of Geophysical Research, v. 90, p. 663–677.

Wilson, J. T., 1963, Hypothesis of the Earth's behavior: Nature, v. 198, p. 925–929.

Manuscript Accepted by the Society June 16, 1987

ACKNOWLEDGMENT

I thank Peter Hagevold, of the Norwegian Polar Research Institute, for his tireless effort in translating some of the Russian literature.

Knife with 17-cm-long blade of slate. 17th century. Clavering Island, northeast Greenland. From Claus Andreason, undated, Historical artifacts in the National Park, *in* The National Park in North-east Greenland, Greenland Newsletter: Nuuk (Greenland), Tusarliivik, p. 14.

Chapter 22

Canada Basin

Arthur Grantz and S. D. May
U.S. Geological Survey, 345 Middlefield Road, Menlo Park, California 94025
P. T. Taylor
NASA Goddard Space Flight Center, Greenbelt, Maryland 20771
L. A. Lawver
Institute for Geophysics, University of Texas, Austin, Texas 78751

INTRODUCTION

Location, physiography, and geologic setting

The Canada Basin, 1,600 km long and 650 to 1,050 km wide, is an extensive area of moderately deep water lying in the Amerasia sector of the Arctic Ocean (Fig. 1 and Plate 1). Unlike many other ocean basins, it is poorly understood. The tectonic processes that formed it are thought to have played an important role in the structural development and configuration of Alaska and the northeastern USSR, and in the development of the large hydrocarbon resources that have been discovered around the margins of the basin.

The borders of the Canada Basin are North America on the east and south and a complex of submarine ridges and plateaus on the north and west that may have diverse origins. The submarine ridge features include the Northwind Ridge and Chukchi Cap of the Chukchi Borderland on the southwest, and the Mendeleev and Alpha Ridges on the northwest and north respectively. Much of the basin has an extensive continental rise that slopes westward from the Canadian Arctic Islands toward the deep Canada Abyssal Plain. This abyssal plain, which underlies the western Canada Basin, is its deepest part. The Mendeleev Abyssal Plain (Fig. 1) lies to the west of the northern part of the Canada Abyssal Plain and is separated from it by a scarp 300 m to more than 500 m high. This scarp and the Northwind Escarpment (the east face of Northwind Ridge) together form the west boundary of the Canada Abyssal Plain; and their continuity may have structural significance.

The steep-sided, almost straight Northwind Ridge is the most easterly of three generally flat-topped, high-standing ridges that lie in the Amerasia Basin immediately north of the Chukchi Shelf (Fig. 1). These ridges and intervening deep basins constitute the Chukchi Borderland, which is discussed by Hall (this volume). The character of the borderland is uncertain, but it may consist of continental fragments or erosionally truncated volcanic ridges.

In contrast to the steep and planimetrically straight to gently curved slopes that bound the Canada Basin opposite Canada, Alaska, and the Northwind Ridge, the basin-facing slopes of the Alpha and Mendeleev Ridges are bathymetrically complex. The summit elevations of these ridges are also considerably lower than those of the Chukchi Borderland, and probably as a consequence, they lack the flat tops that typify the ridges of the borderland. Recent work (Weber and others, this volume) suggests that Alpha Ridge is of volcanic origin.

Canada Basin abuts North America at margins that appear to be of rift origin (Sweeney and Sobczak, this volume; Dixon and Dietrich, this volume; and Grantz and May, this volume). The projection of these basin margins meet within the Mackenzie Delta at an acute angle. This geometry has suggested to many workers, beginning with Du Toit (1937) and Carey (1958), that the basin owes its origin to rotational rifting, and the basin is one of Carey's type spenochasms. Presently available evidence appears to us to favor this hypothesis, but other views are widely held. Scotese and Lawver (this volume) review many of the hypotheses that have been proposed.

Acquisition of solid-earth data in Canada Basin

Advances in knowledge of the solid earth beneath the Canada Basin have paralleled advances in the technology of conducting scientific investigations over, on, or under the polar ice. The first endeavor was apparently made by Mikkelsen and Leffingwell in 1907 (Mikkelsen, 1955), at the end of an over-ice trek by dog sled in search of "Keenan Land," which supposedly lay about 300 km north of Flaxman Island, on the eastern Alaska Beaufort Sea coast. Instead of land, they found that the Arctic Ocean 380 km north of Flaxman Island was more than 1,980 m deep.

Formal scientific observations in the Canada Basin were initiated by the Canadian Arctic Expedition of 1913 to 1918, under the direction of Vilhjalmur Stefansson (McKinlay, 1976). In 1913–1914, the expedition's ship *Karluk* drifted for five

Grantz, A., May, S. D., Taylor, P. T., and Lawver, L. A., 1990, Canada Basin, *in* Grantz, A., Johnson, L., and Sweeney, J. F., eds., The Arctic Ocean region: Boulder, Colorado, Geological Society of America, The Geology of North America, v. L.

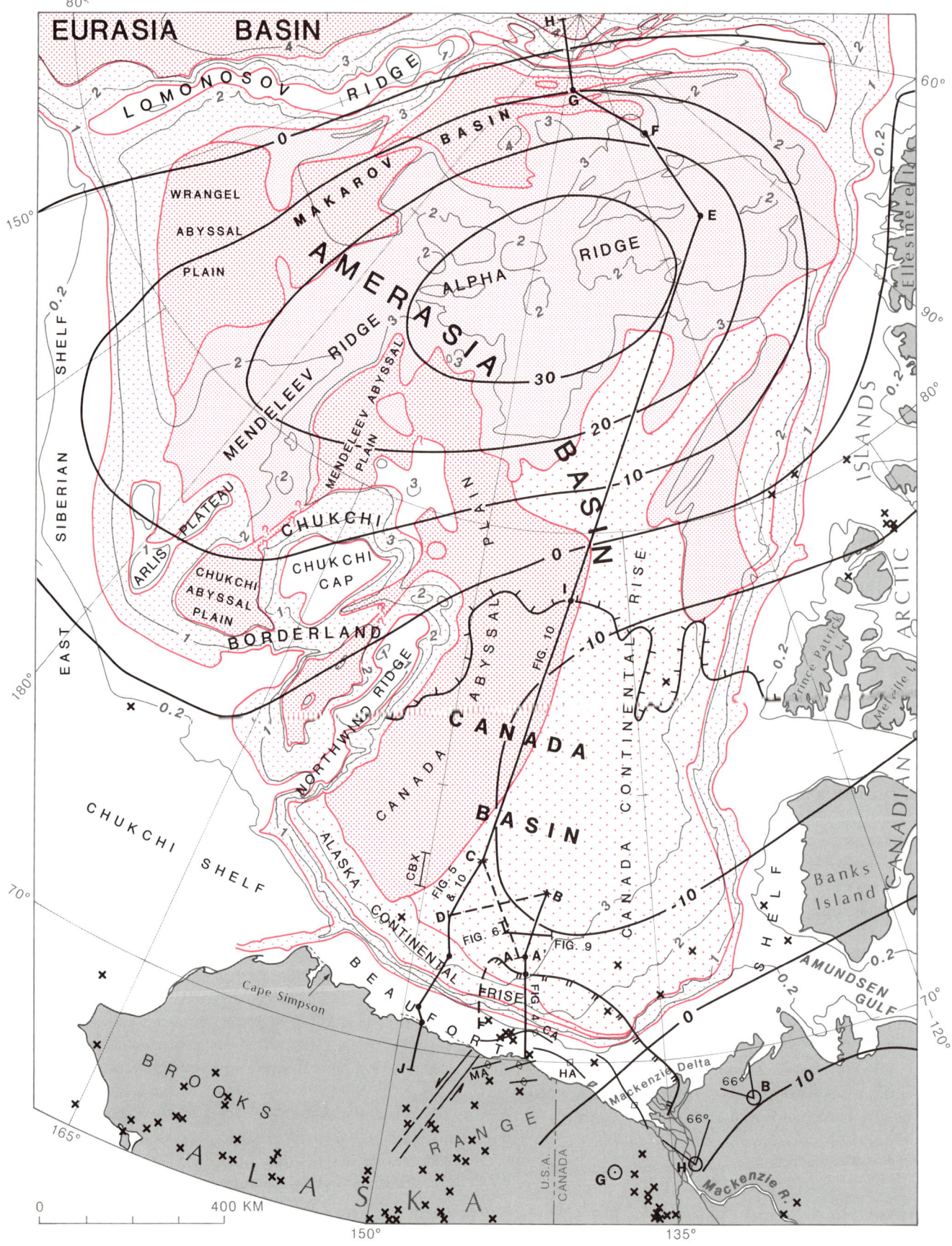

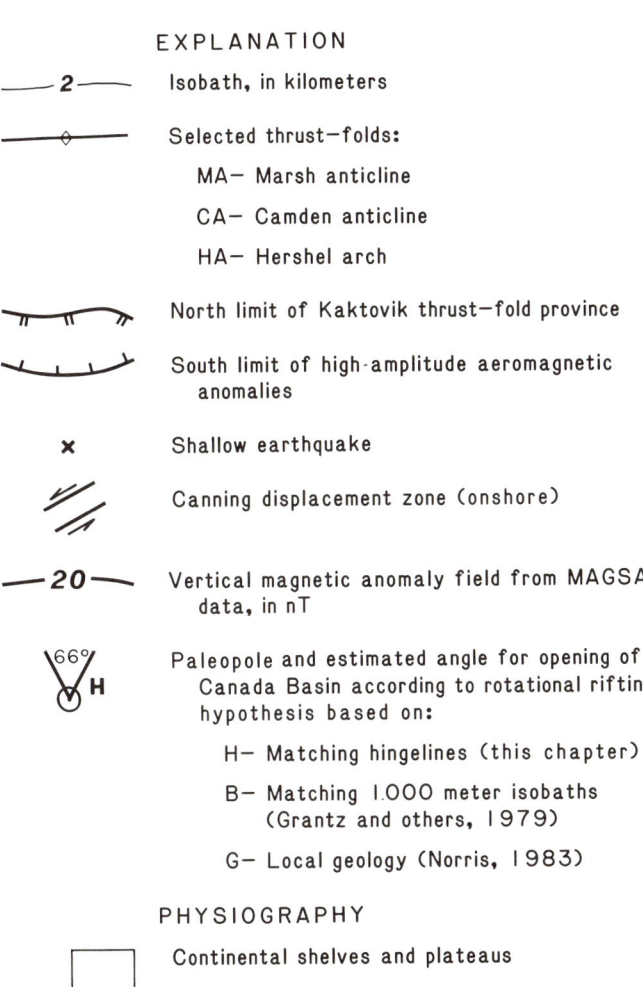

EXPLANATION

— 2 — Isobath, in kilometers

——◆—— Selected thrust-folds:
  MA— Marsh anticline
  CA— Camden anticline
  HA— Hershel arch

North limit of Kaktovik thrust-fold province

South limit of high-amplitude aeromagnetic anomalies

× Shallow earthquake

Canning displacement zone (onshore)

—20— Vertical magnetic anomaly field from MAGSAT data, in nT

Paleopole and estimated angle for opening of Canada Basin according to rotational rifting hypothesis based on:
  H— Matching hingelines (this chapter)
  B— Matching 1,000 meter isobaths (Grantz and others, 1979)
  G— Local geology (Norris, 1983)

PHYSIOGRAPHY

Continental shelves and plateaus

Continental slopes and narrow continental rises

Broad continental rises

Abyssal plains

Submarine highlands and abyssal hills

Figure 1 (facing page, explanation above). Physiographic map of Amerasia Basin of Arctic Ocean showing Canada Basin and selected magnetic features, earthquake epicenters, late Cenozoic geologic structures, seismic refraction stations, and location of Figures 4, 5, 6, 9, and 10. Bathymetry and physiography from Plate 1, Johnson and others (this volume), Hall (1970, 1973) and Beal (1969); satellite magnetic data from Haines (1985); and aeromagnetic data and earthquake epicenters from Kovacs and others (1985). A to D mark locations of Mair and Lyons (1981) refraction stations A to D; CBX marks refraction station of Baggeroer and Falconer (1982); E and F mark refraction stations from Forsyth and others (1986a); and G is a refraction station from Mair and Forsyth (1982).

months in the pack ice of the Beaufort and Chukchi seas before being crushed near Wrangell Island. James Murray, the expedition's oceanographer, took numerous soundings, bottom samples, and water samples during this drift, but only the soundings, recorded in the ship's log, survived his attempt to reach the mainland on foot. Additional soundings during this expedition were made by Stefansson and Storkerson in 1914 during a sledge journey across the southeastern Canada Basin from northeastern Alaska to Banks Island, and by Storkerson from a drifting ice-island north of Prudhoe Bay (Stefansson, 1921).

A major advance in knowledge of the crust beneath the Canada Basin was made possible by the establishment of ice stations by Soviet aircraft over many areas of the Arctic, including the Canada Basin, beginning in 1937 (Somov, 1955; Armstrong, 1958; Treshnikov, 1966). Seabed samples, bathymetric observations, and geophysical data were collected by this pioneering effort. More widely available results from the Canada Basin, however, were gathered from temporary aircraft-established ice camps and permanent ice-island (tabular iceberg) stations (T-3, ALPHA I, CHARLIE, and ARLIS I and II) operated by the United States from 1951 to 1974. These ice-island stations gathered a wide variety of geological and geophysical data, including piston cores and bathymetric, heat-flow, single-channel seismic reflection, seismic-refraction, gravity, and magnetics data from the Canada Basin. Some of these data are presented by Hunkins and Tiemann (1977) and Langseth (1986); while Hall (1970, 1973) summarized much of the earlier data and literature on the Canada Basin in the course of presenting his own ideas on the origin of the Alpha and Mendeleev Ridges. A comprehensive discussion of the late Cenozoic geology of the basin, based mainly on the piston cores obtained from the ice islands, is given by Clark and others (1980).

Reconnaissance networks of gravity and bathymetry observations were established by aircraft over large areas of the Canada Basin by groups from Canada (Weber, 1983) and the United States (Wold, 1973) beginning in 1960. The aeromagnetic field was investigated by workers from the United States and Canada (Vogt and others, 1979, 1982; Taylor and others, 1981; Coles and others, 1978). The results of these efforts are presented in Plates 3 and 4, which show the gravity and total intensity magnetic anomaly fields over the Arctic Basin. The magnetic-anomaly field, as observed from orbiting earth satellites beginning in 1965 (Langel and Thorning, 1982; Haines, 1985), has also proved useful.

Major advances in our understanding of the geologic structure of the Canada Basin came from seismic-refraction measurements made from ice stations established by aircraft in 1976 (Mair and Lyons, 1981) and in 1978 (Baggeroer and Falconer, 1982). Similar data, plus gravity observations and bedrock samples obtained over Alpha Ridge by CESAR (Canadian Expedition to Study the Alpha Ridge) in 1983 (Forsyth and others, 1986a, 1986b; Weber and Sweeney, this volume) have also provided important insights into the nature of the Canada Basin. Seismic reflection, sonobuoy refraction, and gravity data gathered by ship from the margins of the Canada Basin (Grantz and May, 1983; Grantz and others, 1982; Dixon and Deitrich, this volume) provided information on the thickness and structure of sedimentary rocks in the southern Canada Basin, the character of the basin margin, and the origin and age of the basin.

STRATIGRAPHY

Depth and seismic velocity of upper mantle

Measurements of the crustal layers that underlie Canada Basin are sparse and unevenly distributed, and the description of the stratigraphy which follows is in part speculative.

Five measurements of the depth and seismic velocity of the uppermost mantle have been made in the Canada Basin and three in adjacent areas that lie within the proposed proto–Canada Basin, which is discussed in the section "Tectonic Development," at the end of this paper. The largest body of data is that of Mair and Lyons (1981), which is reported as a cluster of four refraction columns 200 to 370 km north of Alaska (A to D in Fig. 1). An additional measurement by Baggeroer and Falconer (1982), was made about 110 km west of the Mair and Lyons study (CBX in Fig. 1). Two refraction profiles in the Amerasia Basin north of the Canada Basin were made by Forsyth and others (1986a). These latter profiles strike parallel to the trend of Alpha Ridge and lie near its crest and on its north flank (E and F in Fig. 1). A third, by Mair and Forsyth (1982), is in the Makarov Basin, which lies between the Alpha and Lomonosov Ridges (G in Fig. 1).

Depth to Moho at stations A to D ranges from 15.5 to 23 km, and a depth of 13.5 to 14.5 km is reported at station CBX (Fig. 2). The relatively shallow measurement at CBX also has the lowest upper mantle velocity. An attempt to project these measurements across the southern Canada Basin, based on a "best-fit" line between values of water depth and depth to mantle at points A to D, is shown in Figure 3. A value of 19.5 km for depth to Moho at point A was used, rather than the reported value of 23.5 km, because such a mantle depth permitted us to match calculated and observed gravity along a crustal section that includes points A and B (Fig. 4). This adjustment also reduced the variability in the reported thickness of layers 2 and 3 across the Mair and Lyons survey. A similar adjustment of the depth to mantle to accommodate the gravity data was made at Mair and Lyons (1981) station "C" in constructing the crustal section near longitude 149° (Fig. 5). (Station "C" lies about 145 km north of station "D" along the projection of the crustal section in Fig. 5.) The adjustment, which consisted of increasing the depth of Moho from 15.5 km to 17.2 km at station "C", had the effect of reducing the variability in the depth to Moho and the thickness of layer 3 in the refraction data. This adjustment was made only in the cross section; it was not used in estimating the depth to Moho in the southern part of the Canada Basin (Fig. 3) or for calculating the mean depth to Moho and the thickness of layer 3 given in the text.

According to the best-fit function, depth to Moho in the southern Canada Basin ranges from a little less than 16 km beneath the abyssal plain to more than 22 km beneath the head of the continental rise at the Mackenzie Delta. In Makarov Basin, a somewhat comparable value (12.6 km at station G, Fig. 1) was measured in 3.4 km of water, and greater values (23.5 and 39.5 km) were obtained beneath the flank and crest of Alpha Ridge. Makarov Basin and Alpha Ridge lie within the proposed proto–Canada Basin.

The mean of the five upper mantle values of seismic velocity (Vp) obtained in the present-day Canada Basin is 8.2 km/s (range 7.9 to 8.5 km/s), and the median value is 8.3 km/s (Fig. 2). Measurements over Alpha Ridge and Makarov Basin in the area of the proposed proto–Canada Basin are 8.2 to 8.3 km/s. These velocities are typical of suboceanic mantle away from modern spreading centers (Christensen and Salisbury, 1975, p. 59). Mair and Lyons (1981) also report that the upper mantle at stations A to D (Fig. 1) is anisotropic by 3 percent, with the direction of maximum velocity being approximately north-south.

Thickness and velocity structure of lower crust

Layer 3. The thickness of layer 3 beneath the Canada Basin was determined by Mair and Lyons (1981) to range from 4.4 to 10.5 km (stations A to D, Fig. 1). If Moho beneath station A is 19.6 km, rather than 23.4 km below sea level, as we suggest, then layer 3 may be only 4.4 to 6.7 km thick. Seismic velocity in the upper unit of layer 3 was found to be 6.6 km/s, and in the lower part 7.5 to 7.7 km/s. These apparently increase to mantle velocities in a 0.5- to 1.0-km-thick zone of high-velocity gradient in the lower part of layer 3. Baggeroer and Falconer (1982), on the other hand, report that layer 3 at station CBX (Fig. 1) is either absent, or no more than about 2.1 km thick if a velocity of 6.8 km/s is assumed. Additional data are needed to choose between these and other possible interpretations.

Layer 2. The reported depth of layer 2 beneath the Canada Basin at stations A to D (Fig. 1) ranges from 7.3 km to 7.6 km below sea level where the seabed is 3.1 to 3.75 km deep. These water depths are from Mair and Lyons (1981) except that their Figure 20 shows the water depth at their station A to be 2.8 km rather than 3.1 km, which is the depth beneath the reported position of the station on the most recent bathymetric maps of the area. The seismic velocity of layer 2 is reported to range from 4.3 km/s at the top to 4.5 km/s at the base, and the thickness from 3.9 to 5.2 km. At station CBX (Fig. 1) Baggeroer and Falconer (1982) report that, where the water depth is 3.8 km, layer 2 is 8.1 km below sea level, 4.4 to 5.6 km thick, and has a seismic velocity of 4.9 km/s.

Both Mair and Lyons (1981) and Baggeroer and Falconer (1982) suggest that layer 2 is 3.9 km to either 5.2 or 5.6 km thick, which is 2.8 to 4 times greater than the average for layer 2 in normal oceanic crust (Christensen and Salisbury, 1975). Multichannel seismic reflection profiles (Grantz and others, 1982) near the Mair and Lyons (1981) refraction study area (Fig. 1) indicate, however, that all of the 4.3 to 4.5 km/s refraction unit above the

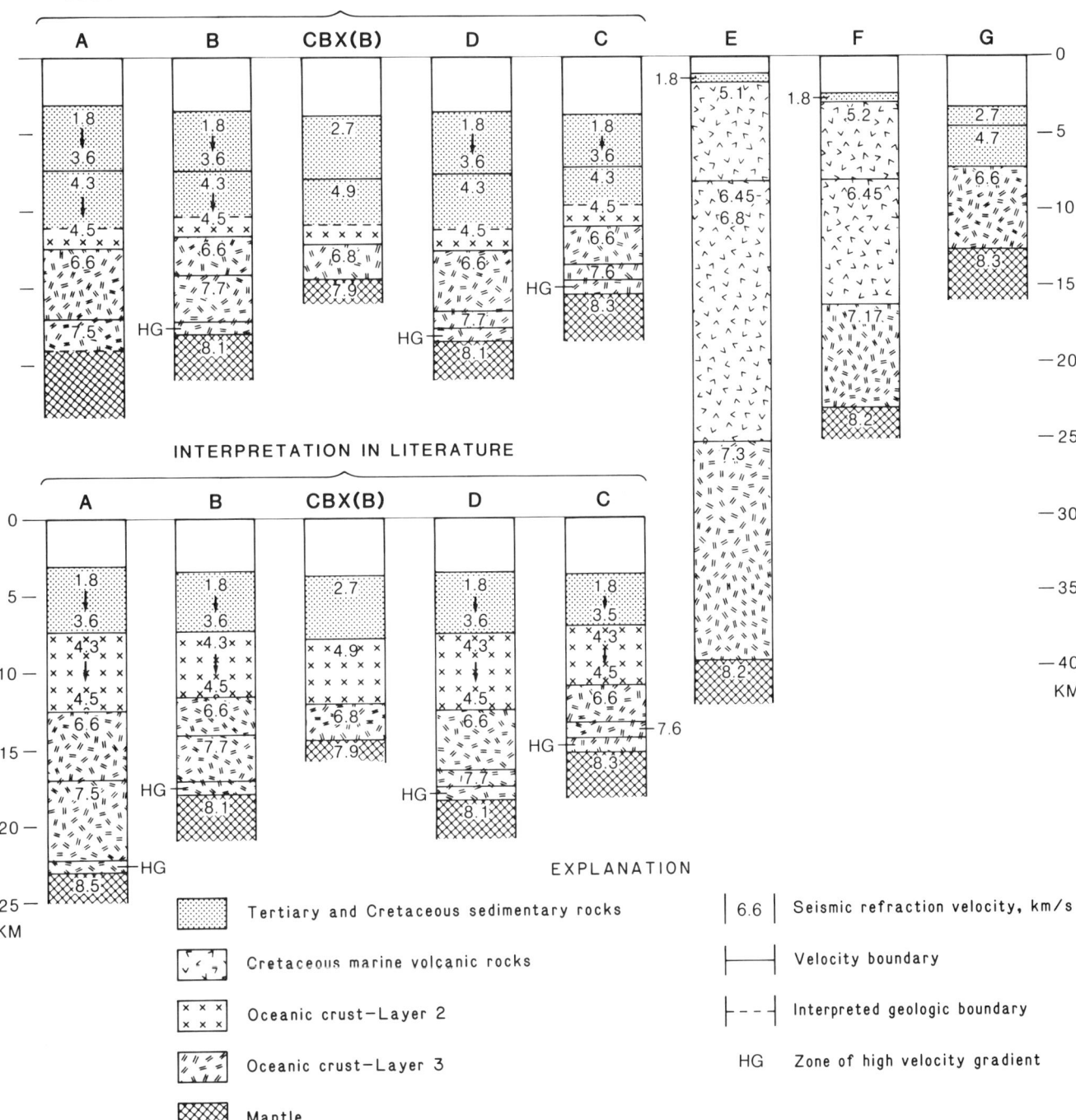

Figure 2. Seismic refraction velocity measurements (Vp) from the Canada Basin and vicinity. Sections A to D from Mair and Lyons (1981); CBX from Baggeroer and Falconer (1982); E and F from Forsyth and others (1986a); and G from Mair and Forsyth (1982). The refraction stratigraphy of Mair and Lyons (1981) and Baggeroer and Falconer (1984) are shown both as reported in the literature and as modified on the basis of seismic reflection and gravity data. See Figure 1 for location of seismic refraction stations.

water-bottom multiple at about 9.2 sec (10.8 km) below sea level consists of sedimentary rocks. One of these reflection profiles, plotted in depth, is shown in Figure 6. Note that the top of the 4.3 to 4.5 km/s refraction unit lies 4.4 km below the sea floor and coincides with a reflector of moderate strength, underlain by at least 3.2 km of reflectors that resemble those produced by well-bedded sedimentary rocks. A rough, hyperbolic reflector, as is typically found at the top of layer 2 on seismic reflection profiles from ocean basins, is clearly absent at the position of the 4.3 to 4.5 km/s refractor on profile 711 of Figure 6, and is also absent on all of the other profiles that extend over the Canada Basin. In addition, Figure 6 shows that the average interval velocity computed from all of the USGS seismic reflection data over the Canada Basin shows no increment near the top of the 4.3 to 4.5 km/s refractor that might indicate a transition from oceanic layers 1 to 2 at that horizon.

An alternative estimate of the depth to layer 2 is an estimated magnetic source depth (EMSD) analysis of low-level aeromagnetic data by Kovacs and Vogt (1982). Their results indicate that magnetic basement (top of layer 2) lies 1.8 to 1.6 km below the seabed at the northwest and southeast ends of profile 711 (see Fig. 6). This depth estimate is 2.5 to 3 km above the top of layer 2 as delineated by the refraction data, and well within sedimentary layer 1 as interpreted from the reflection data. The seismic-interval velocity at this depth is about 2.6 to 2.7 km/s, which is appropriate for layer 1. Similar mismatches between the reflection results and the EMSD are found locally in other areas of the southern Canada Basin and Alpha Ridge where the data sets overlap. The meaning of these mismatches is not clear. The absence in the seismic reflection profiles of features commonly associated with igneous rocks or basement suggests that the magnetic anomalies may be generated at greater depths than those estimated by Kovacs and Vogt (1982), or possibly that they are generated by relatively weak magnetic beds within the sedimentary prism. Uncorrected temporal field variations, however, could explain the relatively shallow EMSD values obtained by Kovacs and Vogt (1982). These high-frequency external magnetic field fluctuations, which are extremely common at high latitudes, could have biased the anomaly field to produce shallow source estimates.

Kovacs and Vogt (1982) conducted their depth-to-source analysis in the Canada Basin on the aeromagnetic data of Taylor and others (1981). These profiles reveal relatively broad (110- to 44-km wavelength) and low-amplitude (200 to 325 nT, peak to trough) anomalies south of 78°N latitude. While not diagnostic, this magnetic anomaly field is consistent with other regions with "typical" oceanic crust. This anomaly field has been interpreted to define a linear sea-floor spreading pattern, which would require that it originate below the sedimentary prism of the southern Canada Basin, at a greater depth than estimated by Kovacs and Vogt (1982). A possible alternative interpretation for the anomaly field, if it was generated below the sedimentary prism, is that the anomalies are the result of a uniformly magnetized layer

Figure 3. Estimated depth to mantle in southern Canada Basin extrapolated from refraction measurements in Mair and Lyons (1981) on the basis of the following empirical relationship between refraction depth and water depth. Depth to mantle (km) = $34.25 - 4.75 \times$ water depth (km). Correlation coefficient = 0.88. See text and Figures 2 and 4 for rationale for modifying one of Mair and Lyons (1981) data points.

2 with topographic relief. If this relief were significant, it might be apparent in the free air gravity anomaly field of this region (see Plate 3). While there appear to be crude lineations in the gravity-anomaly field that in part coincide with the magnetic-field lineations (Plate 3), these are too poorly defined in this admittedly sparse data set to be diagnostic.

The relationships outlined above suggest to us that the top of the 4.3 to 4.5 km/s refractor of Mair and Lyons (1981) lies within layer 1. If it does, then layer 2 lies undetected in the lower part of their 4.3 to 4.5 km/s unit and possibly in the lower part of the 4.9 km/s layer of Baggeroer and Falconer (1982). The velocity of the underlying refractor, 6.6 km/s, is appropriate for layer 3 and presumably forms the base of layer 2. We arbitrarily assume that layer 2 is 1.4 km thick, which is the approximate average thickness of layer 2 in normal oceanic crust (Christensen and Salisbury, 1975). The seismic velocity could be 4.5 km/s, as reported for the lower part of the 4.3 to 4.5 km/s unit by Mair and Lyons. We used the assumed thickness of 1.4 km to construct our crustal sections (Figs. 4 and 5) and the revised crustal columns in Figure 2. A rough projection of the postulated position of the top of layer 2 beneath the southern Canada Basin is shown in Figure 7. The projection is based on a "best-fit" line between values for the postulated position of the top of layer 2 and water depth.

Sediments and sedimentary rocks (Layer 1)

Thickness. An estimate of regional sediment thickness in the southern Canada Basin was calculated from a least squares "best fit" between values for the modified refraction unit thicknesses of Mair and Lyons (1981) and water depth. Contours of the estimated position of the base of the sedimentary fill, and isopach lines showing fill thickness, are shown on Figures 7 and 8, respectively. The sedimentary thickness is roughly estimated to range from about 6 km near Northwind Ridge to more than 12 km near the Mackenzie Delta. The estimate assumes that the underlying oceanic crust is of uniform thickness and that the sedimentary load is isostatically compensated.

The estimate of sediment thickness given in Figure 8 is in part corroborated by other measurements. Seismic reflection data (Grantz and others, 1982) show that near 73°30′N, 145°W (C in Fig. 1), where the water column is 3.4 km deep, the sedimentary prism beneath Canada Basin is more than 7.3 km thick. The correlative sedimentary section beneath the adjacent progradational Beaufort Shelf is more than 12.6 km thick (Grantz and May, 1983). Refraction data by Mair and Lyons (1981) and Baggeroer and Falconer (1982), as reinterpreted above, indicate that the sedimentary fill is 6 to 8 km thick and that its base lies 9.7 to 11.3 km below sea level. In addition, ice-island reflection seismic data (Hall, 1973, Figs. 6, 7) indicate that the sedimentary fill beneath the northern Canada Basin and nearby Mendeleev Abyssal Plain is more than 2 km thick.

A minimum average sedimentation rate for the Canada Basin can be calculated from the estimated thickness of sediment shown in Figure 8 and the inferred age of initial opening of the basin about 125 Ma (see section "Evidence on Age and Origin of Canada Basin" below). Sedimentation rates beneath the Canada Abyssal Plain, where the sedimentary fill is estimated to be about 6 km thick, would be approximately 50 m/m.y. Near the Mackenzie Delta, where the fill may be as much as 12 km thick, the sedimentation rate would be approximately 100 m/m.y. These average rates probably encompass periods of more rapid sedimentation during and shortly after initial rifting and during late Cenozoic glaciation, and of less rapid sedimentation during Late Cretaceous and Paleogene time. They also ignore changes in sediment thickness due to compaction. Calculation of the actual average sedimentation rate would require knowledge of the time that sea-floor spreading in the basin ceased, which is not known.

Velocity structure and age. Refraction measurements show a relatively restricted range of thickness and velocity for the two uppermost refraction-defined stratigraphic units in the southern Canada Basin (Fig. 2). Mair and Lyons (1981) interpret the upper unit to be 3.5 to 4.8 km thick, to have velocities that range from 1.8 km/s at the seabed to 3.5 or 3.6 km/s at the base, and to represent sedimentary strata. The interpretation of Baggeroer and Falconer (1982) falls within these ranges. Correlation of these units with stratigraphy in seismic reflection profiles that extend from land ties on the Beaufort Shelf to the southern Canada Basin (Figs. 4 and 5) suggests that the upper unit is mainly Cenozoic.

The second refraction unit has been interpreted by Mair and Lyons (1981) and Baggeroer and Falconer (1982) to be oceanic layer 2 (oceanic basalt). For reasons proposed in the section "Layer 2" above, we consider this refraction-defined unit to be sedimentary, and we assume that only its lowermost 1.4 km represents layer 2. In the Mair and Lyons survey this sedimentary unit, less the arbitrarily subtracted 1.4 km for layer 2, is 2.5 to 3.8 km thick and has seismic velocities of 4.3 to 4.5 km/s. The thickness of this sedimentary unit is uncertain in the Baggeroer and Falconer survey, but its velocity is 4.9 km/s. Projection of this refraction sedimentary unit from the Mair and Lyons (1981) survey into seismic reflection lines that extend basinward from the Beaufort Shelf (see, e.g., Fig. 4) suggest that the unit corresponds with the lower part of the stratigraphic section of the outer Beaufort Shelf. This section is mainly Cretaceous, but in the eastern Beaufort Sea it may also include lower Paleogene beds.

The differing interpretations of the 4.3 to 4.5 km/s refraction unit may originate in the analogs selected for comparison. Refraction surveys in deep ocean basins (water depth 4 to 5 km) with normal oceanic crustal structure show seismic velocities for layer 2 of 5.04 ± 0.69 km/s (Christensen and Salisbury, 1975). This range encompasses the 4.3 to 4.5 km/s unit. The lower part of thick continental rise sedimentary prisms, however, also have interval velocities in this range. (See, e.g., Grow and others, 1979, Fig. 2). Interval velocities for the upper 8.5 km of sedimentary section in the southern Canada Basin, derived from reflection seismic stacking (RMS) velocities, show no velocity break near 4.5 km sub-seafloor where the refraction data indicate an increase in velocity from 3.6 to 4.3 km/s (Fig. 6). Rather, the reflection-derived interval velocities increase smoothly, but with a decreasing velocity gradient, from 1.7 km/s at the seabed to 5.0 km/s at a depth of 8.5 km subseabed. This kind of velocity-depth function is typical of thick submarine clastic sedimentary prisms on conjugate margins (Houtz, 1981).

Reflection character. Seismic reflection profiles in the southern Canada Basin suggest that the entire section above the water-bottom multiple to depths of at least 10.8 km (9.2 sec) below sea level consists of well-bedded sedimentary rocks (Fig. 6, Plate 9). If a strong, hyperbolated reflector, such as typically marks the top of layer 2 in ocean basins, is present in the Canada Basin it lies below the water-bottom multiple, and is obscured. The geometry of the reflectors and their velocity structure, the morphology of the seabed, the presence of competent nearby detrital sediment sources in North America, and shallow sediment core studies (Clark and others, 1980) suggest that the sedimentary section consists mainly of hemipelagic sediments and turbidites.

Near 72°N, 141° to 146°W, in the deepest part of Canada Basin surveyed by multichannel seismic reflection profiles (Figs. 6 and 9, and Plate 9), the sedimentary section down to the water-bottom multiple can be divided into four seismic-stratigraphic units. These are distinguished by variations in the proportion of strong and weak reflectors and by the presence of gentle angular discordances between some of the units. The lowest unit above

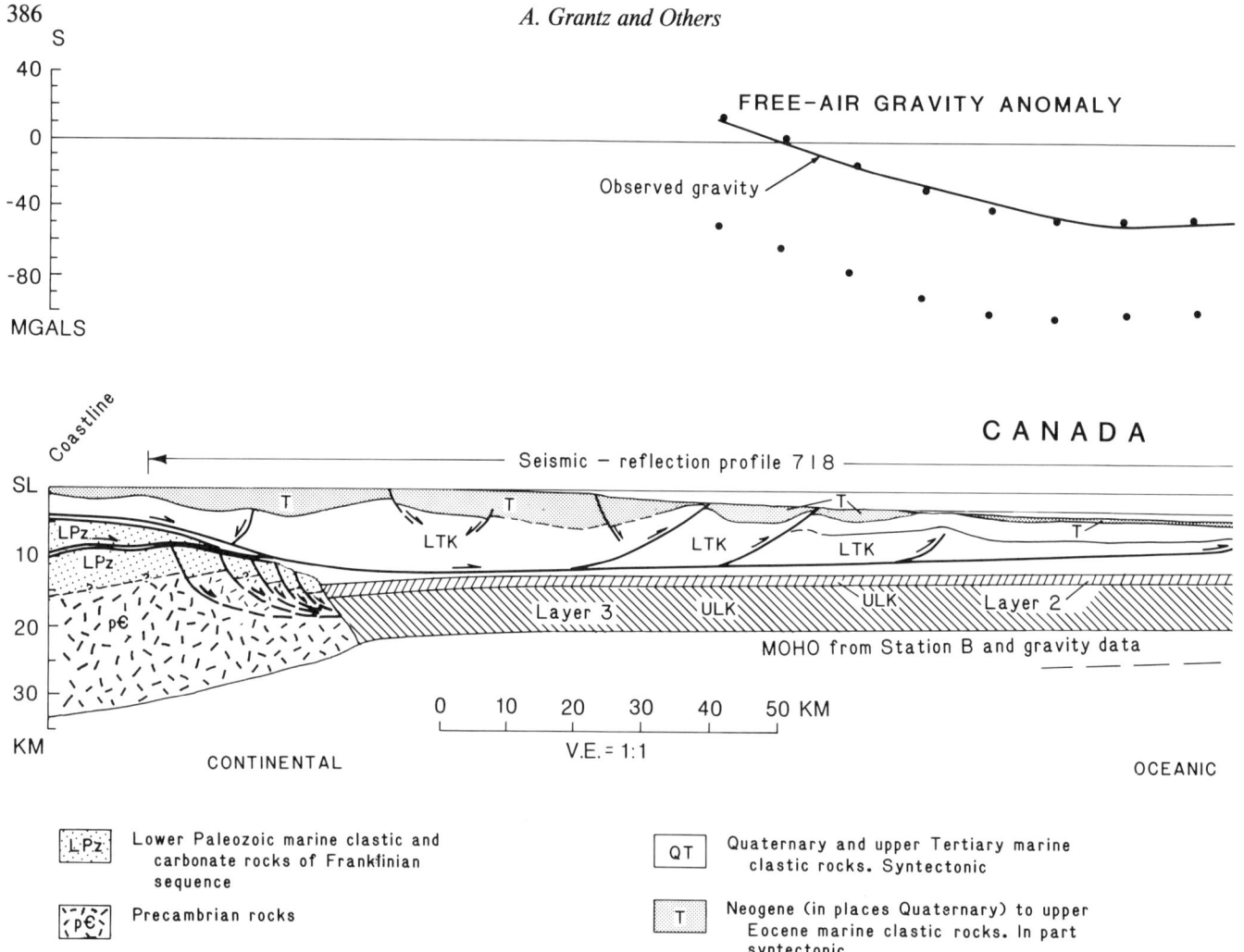

Figure 4. Crustal cross section from the Alaskan coast to the southern Canada Basin near 143° W longitude constructed from seismic refraction data in Mair and Lyons (1981); seismic reflection data (profile 718) in Grantz and others (1982); and gravity data in May (1985) and Sobczak and others (this volume). Geologic boundaries below the deepest seismic reflections (about 10 km, but variable) in the region south of the refraction measurements are speculations that satisfy the gravity data. See Figure 1 for location.

the water-bottom multiple (unit IV in Fig. 6), has both low- and moderate-amplitude reflectors. An extensive, commonly strong reflector, which locally correlates with the top of a refractor that Mair and Lyons (1981) assign to oceanic layer 2A (4.3 to 4.5 km/s refractor in Fig. 2), marks the top of this reflection unit. As noted above, this refractor may lie near the Cretaceous-Tertiary boundary. Unit III has stronger, but fewer and less regularly distributed reflectors than unit IV and the stronger reflections tend to occur in packets. Still fewer and more widely separated strong reflectors characterize unit II. Locally on line 712 (Fig. 9), the base of unit II corresponds with a change from beds with many small normal faults below to beds with few faults above. Unit I can be recognized on all of the reflection profiles from the southeastern part of the basin. It rests on a gentle angular unconformity at which underlying beds are truncated by erosion and against which the basal beds of the unit onlap. The unit itself consists of single strong reflectors or thin packets of such reflectors separated by much thicker units with weak reflectors and a few irregular strong reflectors of limited extent. Locally occurring mounded and downlapping reflectors, small-scale channeling, and pinchouts suggest that unit I contains distal fan deposits as well as continental-rise turbidites. A few mass-movement (landslide) deposits also appear to be present. Unit I is syntectonic. The unconformity at its base resulted from late Cenozoic uplift produced by shortening and thickening of the sedimentary prism in the southeast Canada Basin east of the Canning River by northward-directed thrust faulting and thrust folding, as is discussed in the section on "Structure" below.

Morphology and provenance of upper sedimentary section. The sourceland of the upper part of the sedimentary section in the Canada Basin is suggested by the morphology of the sea floor, predominantly a gently sloping surface of sedimentation (Fig. 1). On the southeast, between the Mackenzie River and Amundsen Gulf, this surface abuts the continental slope near the

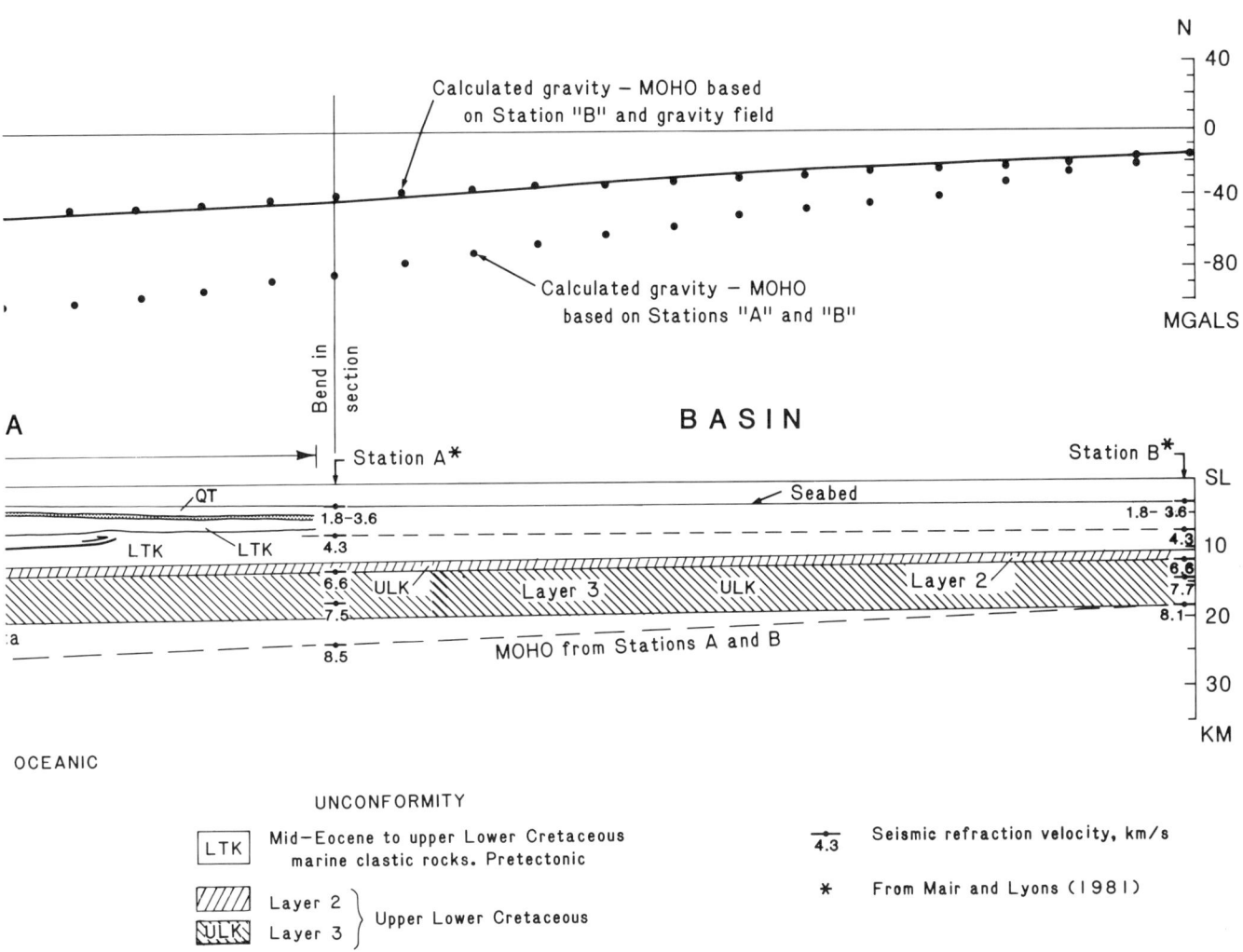

1,000 m isobath. From this area it slopes west-northwest with initial gradients of 25 to 30 m/km near the Mackenzie Delta. These decrease to less than 1.0 m/km where the surface merges with the Canada Abyssal Plain, which lies at depths exceeding 3,700 m, in the western part of the basin. The surface continues to deepen westward to the foot of the steep eastern escarpment of Northwind Ridge. Similarly, the northern part of the abyssal plain lies at the foot of the low, northeast-facing scarp that separates the Mendeleev from the Canada Abyssal Plain in the northwest corner of the Canada Basin (Plate 1 and Fig. 1).

The depth at which the sea floor of the Canada Basin intersects the bordering continental slopes increases uniformly westward from the Mackenzie Delta off Alaska and northward from the delta off Banks Island. The uniform increase in depth of this intersection and the absence of large sediment cones on the continental slope and rise off Alaska and Banks Island indicate that large volumes of sediment did not enter the Canada Basin across these slopes in late Cenozoic time. Rather, the morphology of the sea floor indicates that most of the great volume of young sediment beneath the basin was brought to it by the Mackenzie River and continental glaciers in the broad Mackenzie Valley and Amundsen Gulf.

Northwest of Banks Island the uniform seaward slope of the seabed is interrupted by large ridges and terraces on the lower slope and upper rise (see Plate 1 and Fig. 1). These features suggest that greater structural complexity exists there than to the south. Basinward from these ridges the lower continental rise slopes uniformly westward to the Canada Abyssal Plain, as it does in the southern Canada Basin. Easterly sources must therefore have supplied most of the detrital component of the sediment that underlies the continental rise north of Banks Island. The fiord-bound character of the adjacent coast and the heavily glaciated hinterland indicate that in this area, glaciers rather than rivers supplied the detritus that constitutes the upper part of the rise sedimentary prism. In post-glacial times the fiords presumably acted as sediment traps for most of the detritus that originated in the interior of the Arctic Islands province.

Clark and others (1980) have shown that rafting by glacial icebergs was the dominant mechanism of late Cenozoic sediment transport and deposition in highland areas of the Amerasia Basin. The oldest ice-rafted material is as old as late Miocene. In deepwater areas of the Canada Basin, the ice-rafted component is masked by turbidites.

Detrital sediment may also have reached the Canada Basin

388 A. Grantz and Others

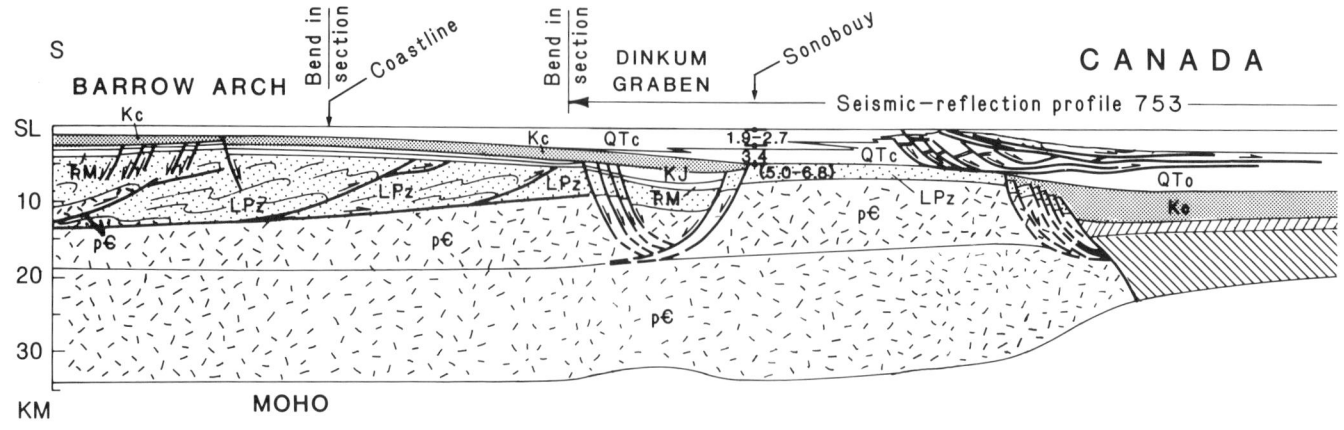

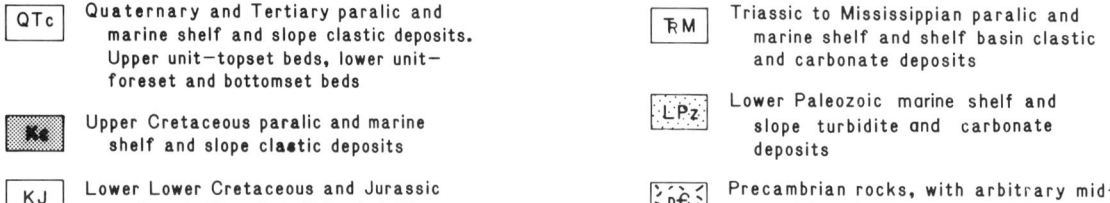

QTc	Quaternary and Tertiary paralic and marine shelf and slope clastic deposits. Upper unit—topset beds, lower unit—foreset and bottomset beds
Kc	Upper Cretaceous paralic and marine shelf and slope clastic deposits
KJ	Lower Lower Cretaceous and Jurassic marine shelf and shelf basin lutite
ŘM	Triassic to Mississippian paralic and marine shelf and shelf basin clastic and carbonate deposits
LPz	Lower Paleozoic marine shelf and slope turbidite and carbonate deposits
pЄ	Precambrian rocks, with arbitrary mid-crust boundary

Figure 5. Crustal cross section from the North Slope of Alaska to the southern Canada Basin near 149° W longitude constructed from seismic refraction data in Mair and Lyons (1981); seismic reflection data (profile 753) in Grantz and others (1982); and gravity data in May (1985) and Sobczak and others (this volume). Geological boundaries below the deepest seismic reflections (about 10 km, but variable) in the region south of the refraction measurements are speculations that satisfy the gravity data. See Figure 1 for location.

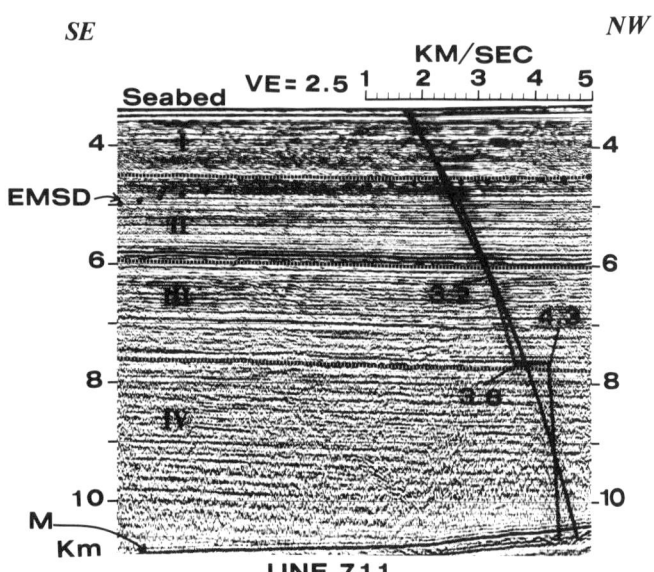

Figure 6. Seismic reflection profile 711 from the southeastern Canada Basin, plotted in depth, showing relation between seismic stratigraphy and the upper refractors at Mair and Lyons (1981) station A. Velocity-depth curves derived from reflection seismic data stacking velocities (smooth curve) and from refraction seismic data in Mair and Lyons (1981; stepped curve). Estimated magnetic source depth curve (EMSD) from data in Kovacs and Vogt (1982). See Figure 1 for location. M = water-bottom multiple.

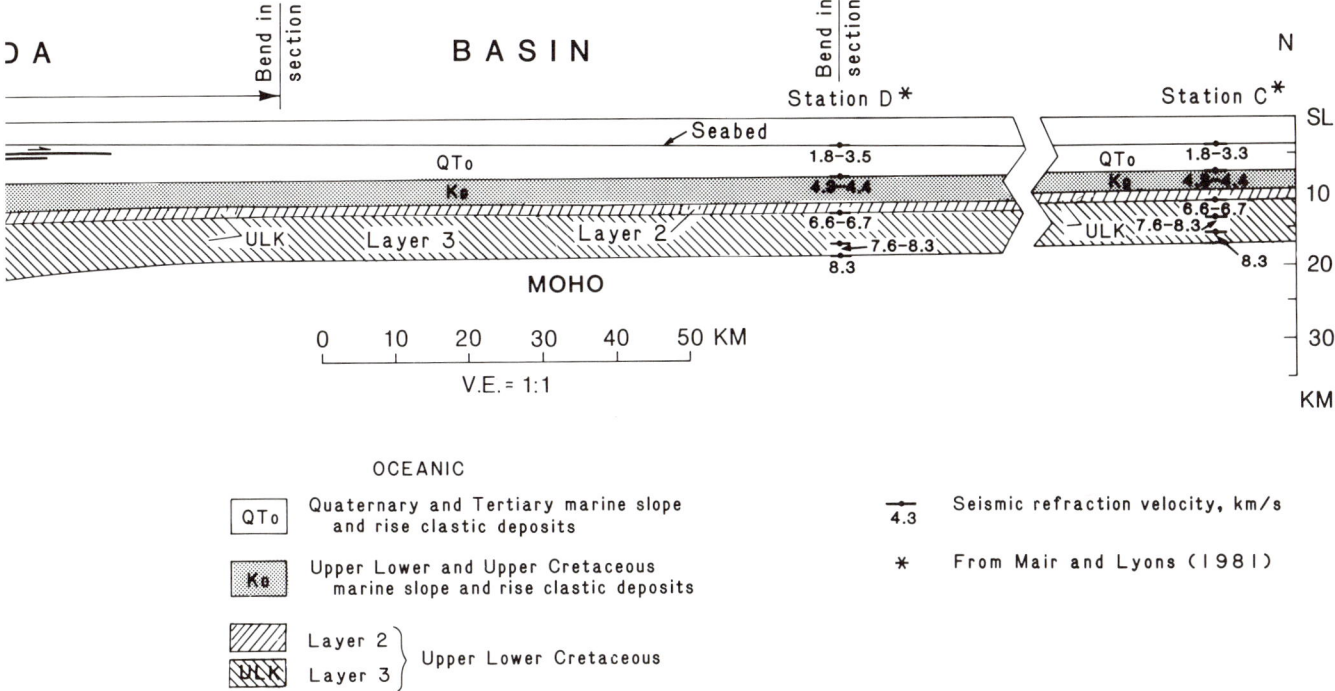

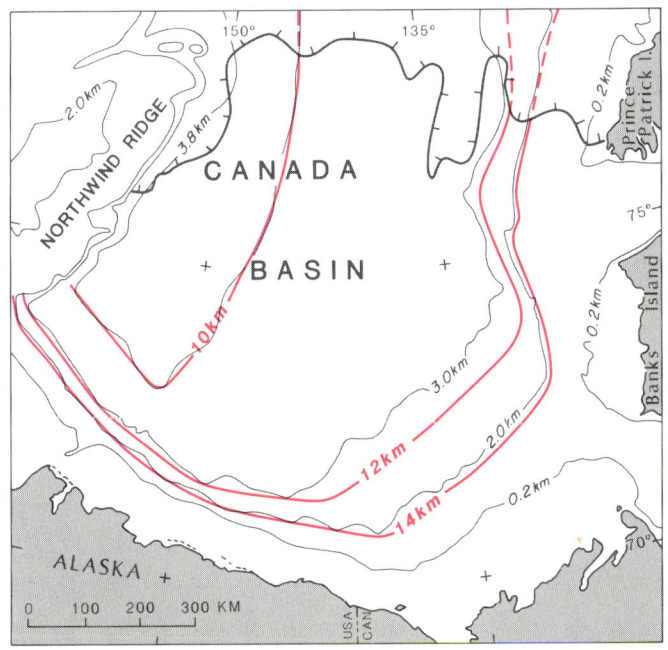

Figure 7. Estimated depth to top of oceanic layer 2 (base of sedimentary fill) in southern Canada Basin extrapolated from refraction measurements in Mair and Lyons (1981) on the basis of the following empirical relationship between modified depth to layer 2 and water depth. Depth to layer 2 (km) = 17.19 − 1.89 × water depth (km). Correlation coefficient = 0.75. See text and Figures 2, 4, and 5 for relation of modified position of layer 2 to that given by Mair and Lyons (1981).

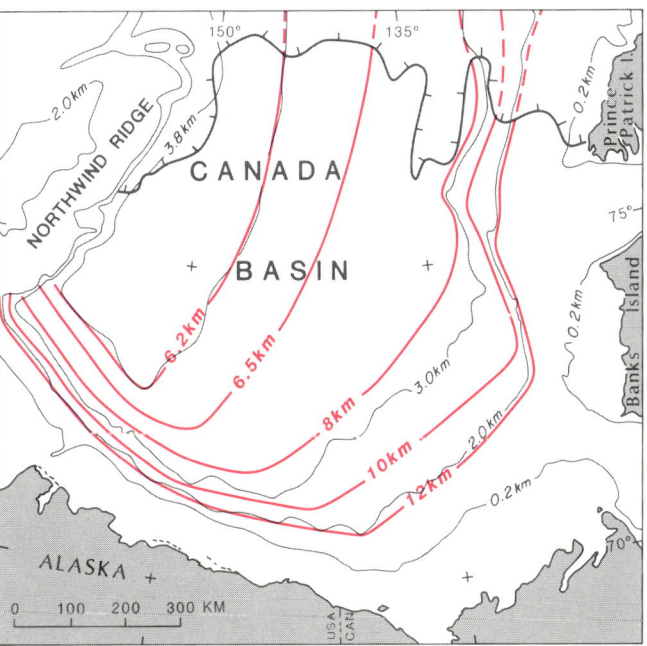

Figure 8. Estimated thickness of sedimentary fill in southern Canada Basin extrapolated from refraction measurements of Mair and Lyons (1981), as modified in this report, on the basis of the following empirical relation between water depth and modified sediment thickness. Sediment thickness (km) = 17.19 − 2.89 × water depth (km). Correlation coefficient = 0.86. See text and Figures 2, 4, 5, and 6 for relation of modified thickness of sedimentary fill to that given by Mair and Lyons (1981).

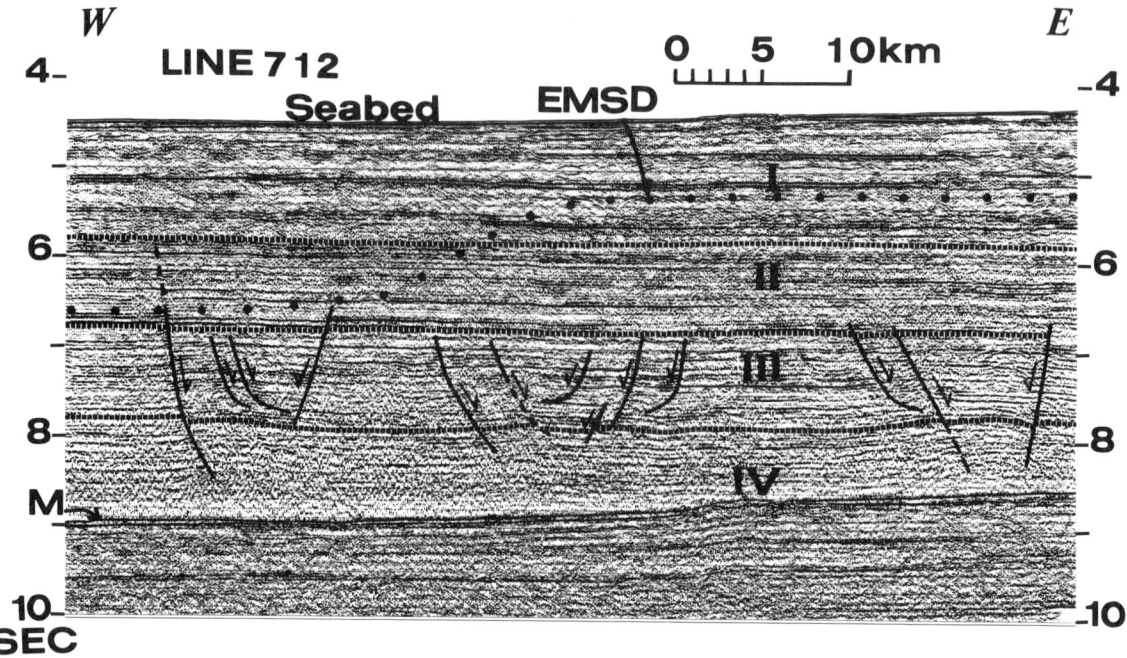

Figure 9. Seismic reflection profile 712 from the southern Canada Basin, plotted in time, showing seismic stratigraphy and normal faulting in the lower beds. See text under Sediments and Sedimentary Rocks, Reflection Character for description of seismic-stratigraphic units. Estimated magnetic source depth curve (EMSD) from data in Kovacs and Vogt (1982). See Figure 1 for location. M = water-bottom multiple.

from Herald Canyon, on the western Chukchi Shelf, and from Kolyma Valley, on the East Siberian Shelf (Plate 1). In times of glacioeustatically lowered sea level, these valleys are inferred to have brought large volumes of glacial outwash from the Noatak-Kobuk valley system of northwest Alaska and the Kolyma River valley of the northeast USSR to the shelf edge north of Wrangell Island (Creager and McManus, 1965; Naugler and others, 1974). The presence of a shallow embayment, rather than a progradational sedimentary body, at the outer shelf and upper slope northeast of Wrangel Island (Plate 1) suggests that much of the outwash may have bypassed the shelf and been deposited on the adjacent Chukchi Abyssal Plain as turbidites. Shaver and Hunkins (1964) estimate from ice-island gravity and magnetic data that this plain, 2.0 to 2.2 km deep, is underlain by about 2.8 km of sediment. Seismic reflection profiles (Hall, 1970, 1973) independently confirm that the sediment is at least 1 km thick. Bathymetry suggests that turbidity flows crossed this plain and passed through the constriction of Charlie Gap to the Mendeleev Abyssal Plain. The latter is 3.3 km deep and is underlain by more than 2 km of sediment (Hall, 1973). It is likely that a few of the turbidity flows also crossed the Mendeleev Plain and the 300- to 500-m scarp that bounds it on the northwest and came to rest on the northern part of the Canada Abyssal Plain. This area, locally more than 3,900 m deep, is the deepest part of the Canada Basin.

Volcanic rocks

Volcanic rocks have been documented within the Canada Basin only along the Canadian end of the Alpha Ridge. Recently acquired geophysical data and seabed samples there (Weber and others, this volume; Van Wagoner and Robinson, 1985; Forsyth and others, 1986a) suggest that this part of the ridge consists of oceanic rocks that are in part alkali basalt, and that the ridge is analogous to Iceland. A thin veneer of pelagic and hemipelagic sediment mantles the volcanic rocks (Mudie and Blasco, 1985). These volcanic rocks may be late Cenomanian to Coniacian or possibly early Campanian in age. If so, they correlate with the middle part of the late Neocomian to Cenozoic sedimentary fill in Canada Basin, and sedimentary strata equivalent to the lower part of the fill may underlie Alpha Ridge. Such relatively low velocity rocks were not recorded by the refraction surveys of Forsyth and others (1986). Even if they escaped significant thermal and pressure densification beneath the volcanic pile, sediments would be difficult to detect beneath the thick, moderately high velocity volcanic rocks of Alpha Ridge.

There is a complex magnetic anomaly pattern across the Alpha Ridge (Vogt and others, 1979; Taylor and others, 1981). The anomalies are of high amplitude (−1,000 to +2,500 nT) and variable wavelength (20 to 100 km). Whether or not these anomalies are lineated is a matter of conjecture. They have been proposed to be caused by normally magnetized basement topography, but they require an extremely large intensity of magnetization (20 to 30 A/m; Vogt and others, 1979). A large magnetic anomaly over Alpha Ridge is also observed at satellite altitude (Haines, 1985). This anomaly, centered at 85°N, 150°W, overlies the ridge and mimics it in map plan and trend (Fig. 1). The aeromagnetic anomaly signature of Alpha Ridge is consistent with a volcanic source, but other sources have been proposed for this feature on the basis of the magnetic data (see Coles and Taylor, this volume).

Aeromagnetic data in Perry and Fleming (1985) shows that the magnetic-anomaly field decreases markedly in amplitude near 78°N (turning point I on cross section H–J in Figs. 1 and 10). If the Alpha Ridge is a volcanic feature, the boundary between large- and small-amplitude aeromagnetic anomalies at turning point I probably approximates the southern edge of substantial thicknesses of volcanic rocks. This indicates that Alpha Ridge rocks extend some 330 km further south than is indicated by the bathymetry (Figs. 1 and 10).

STRUCTURE

Basin margins

Multichannel seismic reflection profiles (Plate 9, Grantz and May, 1983, Grantz and others, ch. 22, this volume; and Dixon and Dietrich, this volume) indicate that the margin of the Canada Basin along the Beaufort Shelf is of passive (Atlantic) type. It was formed by rifting in Jurassic time followed by renewed rifting, breakup, sea-floor spreading, and creation of oceanic crust in the Canada Basin beginning near the close of Hauterivian time (125 Ma). Rotational slumps (rollover anticlines) occur beneath the slope and rise along this margin, and large landslide masses and related slip surfaces have been traced beneath the rise as much as 50 km beyond the shelf break (Fig. 5). Evidence for a similar, but west-facing passive margin has been found between the Mackenzie River and northern Banks Island in the eastern Beaufort Sea (Dixon and Dietrich, this volume). Stratigraphic relations indicate that rifting here was middle Hauterivian to Barremian, which is close to the late Hauterivian or early Barremian age of rifting found along the Alaskan Beaufort Shelf, on the far side of the pole of rotation for opening of Canada Basin according to the rotational rifting model (Grantz and others, 1979). The character of the margin farther north, off the Queen Elizabeth Islands, can not be determined because of a paucity of critical outcrops near the coast and the lack of seismic reflection data offshore. Onland outcrops and potential field data offshore are at least compatible, however, with a rifted origin in late Neocomian time, as is inferred from the better known Beaufort Shelf and Mackenzie Delta (Sweeney and others, this volume).

The margins of the Canada Basin that adjoin oceanic plateaus or ridges are known only from relatively shallow-penetration (nine kilojoule sparker) single-channel seismic-reflection profiles (Hall, 1970, 1973; Hunkins and Tiemann, 1977; and Langseth, 1986). In the southwestern part of the Canada Basin the profiles show that flat-lying, undeformed sediments in the upper part of the basin fill buttress against (onlap) acoustically opaque rocks in the Northwind Escarpment. The ridge was therefore in place before these sediments were deposited. A sparker profile across the north-facing scarp and an abyssal hill that lie between the Mendeleev Abyssal Plain and the northern Canada Abyssal Plain (Hall, 1973, Fig. 7) shows that the youngest sedimentary unit beneath the Canada Abyssal Plain buttresses against the scarp, which therefore predates the fill. Older sedimentary units may also buttress against the scarp, but the records are less clear. This scarp is roughly on strike with the Northwind Escarpment and could be structurally related to it. The sparker profile shows that the upper 0.8 km of sedimentary fill beneath the northern Canada Abyssal Plain is flat lying and buttresses against unconformably underlying, northward-dipping strata. The dipping strata steepen and rise to the seabed beneath the scarp and northern part of the abyssal hill. The folded strata consist of an upper unit about 0.5 km thick and an underlying, more steeply dipping unit more than 1 km thick. These relationships suggest that the scarp between the northern part of the Canada and the Mendeleev Abyssal Plains marks a fault or flexure. If the upper sedimentary unit was deposited at rates comparable to those found for the entire section in the Eurasia Basin (30 to 60 m/m.y., Kristoffersen, this volume) or the deeper (western) part of the Canada Basin (50 m/m.y., this chapter) then the scarp was formed by Early Miocene time, but it could be older.

On the north, the Canada Basin meets the Alpha and Mendeleev Ridges at slopes that sparker records (Hall, 1973, Figs. 6 and 9) show to be bathymetrically irregular and underlain by complex geology. Acoustically opaque rocks are shown to lie near the surface in many places, and faults, fault scarps, and downdropped and rotated fault blocks are abundant. Similar terrain encountered on the crest of the Alpha Ridge by the CESAR expedition (Jackson, 1985; Forsyth and others, 1986a) has been interpreted to mark irregular thicknesses of largely pelagic sediment resting on faulted volcanic rocks. A seismic profile (C–C' in Fig. 6 of Hall, 1973) shows that similarly structured rocks extend from the east flank of the Mendeleev Ridge beneath the uppermost, undeformed sedimentary prism of the Mendeleev Abyssal Plain. The flat-lying beds of the uppermost prism appear to buttress against the structured rocks of Mendeleev Ridge in the same manner that the uppermost, flat-lying beds of the Canada Abyssal Plain buttress against the Northwind Escarpment and against the underlying folded beds in the scarp that separates the Canada Abyssal Plain from the Mendeleev Abyssal Plain. These structural relationships indicate that the tectonic evolution of the Alpha and Mendeleev Ridges included a stage of late (but pre-Middle Miocene) structural deformation.

Basin fill

The ice-island sparker data (Hall, 1973; Hunkins and Tiemann, 1977; Langseth, 1986) and ship-borne multichannel seis-

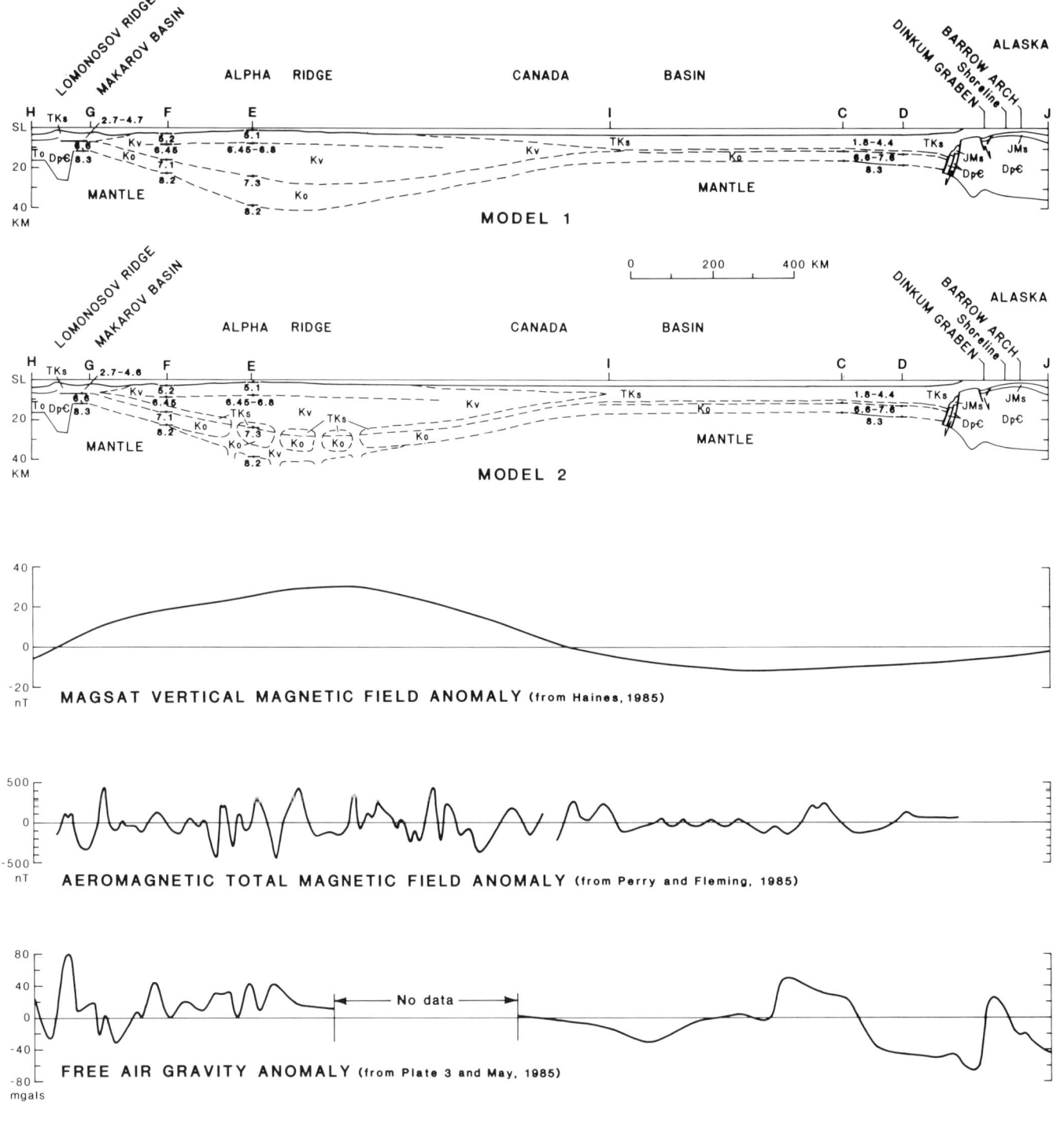

Figure 10. North-south model cross sections through Canada Basin from Lomonosov Ridge to northern Alaska, illustrating alternative hypotheses for origin of Alpha Ridge and its genetic relation to Canada Basin. Cross section based on seismic refraction data from Mair and Lyons (1981), Mair and Forsyth (1982), and Forsyth and others (1986a); seismic reflection data from Grantz and others (1982); and aeromagnetic data from Kovacs and others (1985). See Figure 1 for location.

mic reflection lines in the southeastern part of the Canada Basin (Grantz and others, 1982) provide a partial characterization of the geologic structure of sedimentary rocks in Canada Basin. In most areas the sediments are undeformed. Beneath the Mendeleev Abyssal Plain, however, near-surface, flat-lying sediments 0.8 to 1.0 km thick rest with angular unconformity on tilted beds or acoustic basement (Hall, 1973, Fig. 6). In the northern part of the Canada Abyssal Plain, structurally analogous, and probably correlative flat-lying beds 0.7 km thick are underlain unconformably by gently north-dipping beds about 0.4 km thick (Hall, 1973, Fig. 7). A second angular unconformity about 1.2 km beneath the seabed separates these beds from a somewhat more steeply dipping sequence that is at least 1.2 km thick. Assuming a minimum average sedimentation rate of 50 m/m.y. for the western Canada Basin, the structural event that produced the lower unconformity would be about 28 m.y. old (Late Oligocene) and the younger event about 16 m.y. old (Early Miocene). Deformation of the strata beneath the flat-lying beds of the Mendeleev Abyssal Plain and the northern Canada Basin could be related to the anomalously high heat flow reported from this area by Langseth and others (this volume). These workers suggest that the anomalously high heat flow may be the result of early Paleogene extensional tectonics.

Faulting within the span of time represented by the sedimentary prism is also shown on multichannel seismic reflection profile 712 (Fig. 9), as noted in the section "Sedimentary Rocks—Reflection Character and Stratigraphy." Profile 712 shows that seismic-stratigraphic unit III, of probable Paleogene age, is broken by many normal faults of small displacement that, with a few exceptions, are truncated by the overlying unit II. The top of the more strongly faulted unit III is 3 km below the sea floor. If our minimum average sedimentation rate of 100 m/m.y. for the thicker parts of the sedimentary prism in the southeastern Canada Basin is applied, then the episode of normal faulting that disrupted unit III occurred about 30 Ma, in Late Oligocene time. This episode may therefore correlate with the older deformation event shown in the sparker records from the northern Canada Basin. Although the correlation is not firmly based, it suggests the possibility that a significant tectonic event affected the Canada Basin in mid-Tertiary time.

Tertiary, and in many places Holocene structural deformation has been identified on multichannel seismic reflection records from the southern Canada Basin between Canning River and the International Boundary (Fig. 11) and it undoubtedly extends eastward into the Canadian sector (Grantz and May, 1987; Grantz and others, 1987). The deformation consists of large, northward-verging, slope-parallel thrust-folds of Cenozoic age that have amplitudes as large as 1.4 km and wavelengths of 5 to 20 km. The cores of the folds commonly contain south-dipping thrust-fault splays or north-dipping backthrusts that are inferred to rise from an underlying master (basal) thrust fault system with roots in or south of the Brooks Range (Figs. 1, 4, and 11, and Plate 9). The master fault system may lie 12 to 13 km below sea level beneath the outer shelf and slope and appears to die out in small thrust-folds and backthrusts about 8 or 9 km below sea level at distances of 150 to 180 km north of the Alaskan coast. Beneath the slope and upper rise, and in places beneath the shelf, the thrust-folds deform the entire sedimentary section above the basal fault, shorten and thicken the overlying sedimentary section, and uplift the seabed. Earthquakes in this region provide additional evidence that some of the folds may still be active. Activity on the more distal parts of the fault system, beneath the continental rise, appears to have been pre-Neogene. The earliest episode of faulting may have been pre–Late Eocene because an unconformity of this age separates underlying beds that were more strongly deformed by northward-directed thrust faulting from less strongly deformed beds above.

SEISMICITY

Three centers of seismicity have been observed in or marginal to the Canada Basin (Fig. 1; Fujita and others, this volume; and Plate 2). Earthquakes off Ellef Ringnes Island may be due to activity of unknown tectonic character along the Canadian Arctic Islands margin or to uncompensated sedimentary loads in the continental terrace sedimentary prism (Basham and others, 1977). Others, in the Mackenzie Delta area, may be due to the differential load across the steep southeast margin of the thick, and in part very young sedimentary prism that is accumulating in the southeast Canada Basin (Sobczak, 1975). Hasegawa and others (1979) suggest that these earthquakes may, in addition, be related to remanent (tectonic) stresses and north-south compression generated by extension normal to the Arctic Mid–ocean Ridge. A third center, on the Beaufort Shelf east of Barter Island, consists of shallow earthquakes that are spatially and probably tectonically related to the Cenozoic folds of the southeastern Canada Basin. Some of these events are plotted with the Cenozoic thrust folds on Figure 1. Note that they extend only as far west as the Canning displacement, or fault, zone (Plate 11) (Grantz and May, 1983; Grantz and others, 1983), which is also the west limit of the thrust-fold province. The east limit of this seismic center is not well documented, but it may lie in the belt of earthquakes that trends along the Cordilleran front southeast of the Mackenzie Delta (Fig. 1). A focal mechanism study of a July 26, 1972, earthquake in this area yielded a preferred solution of a near-vertical right-lateral fault striking N32°W (Leblanc and Wetmiller, 1974), but it was felt that other solutions are needed before tectonic interpretations can be drawn. Focal mechanisms for a shallow earthquake beneath the Camden anticline on the Beaufort Shelf (Figs. 1 and 11) by Fujita and others (1983) and Biswas and others (1986) yielded strike-slip solutions with low-dipping north or northeast-striking compression axes. A magnitude 5.1 (mb) earthquake at the foot of the continental slope north of the Mackenzie Delta about 400 km east northeast of Camden anticline (Figs. 1 and 11) also had a northerly directed, near-horizontal compression axis (Hasegawa and others, 1979). The epicenter of this earthquake, however, lies about 200 km northeast of the northeast Brooks Range thrust-and-fold belt

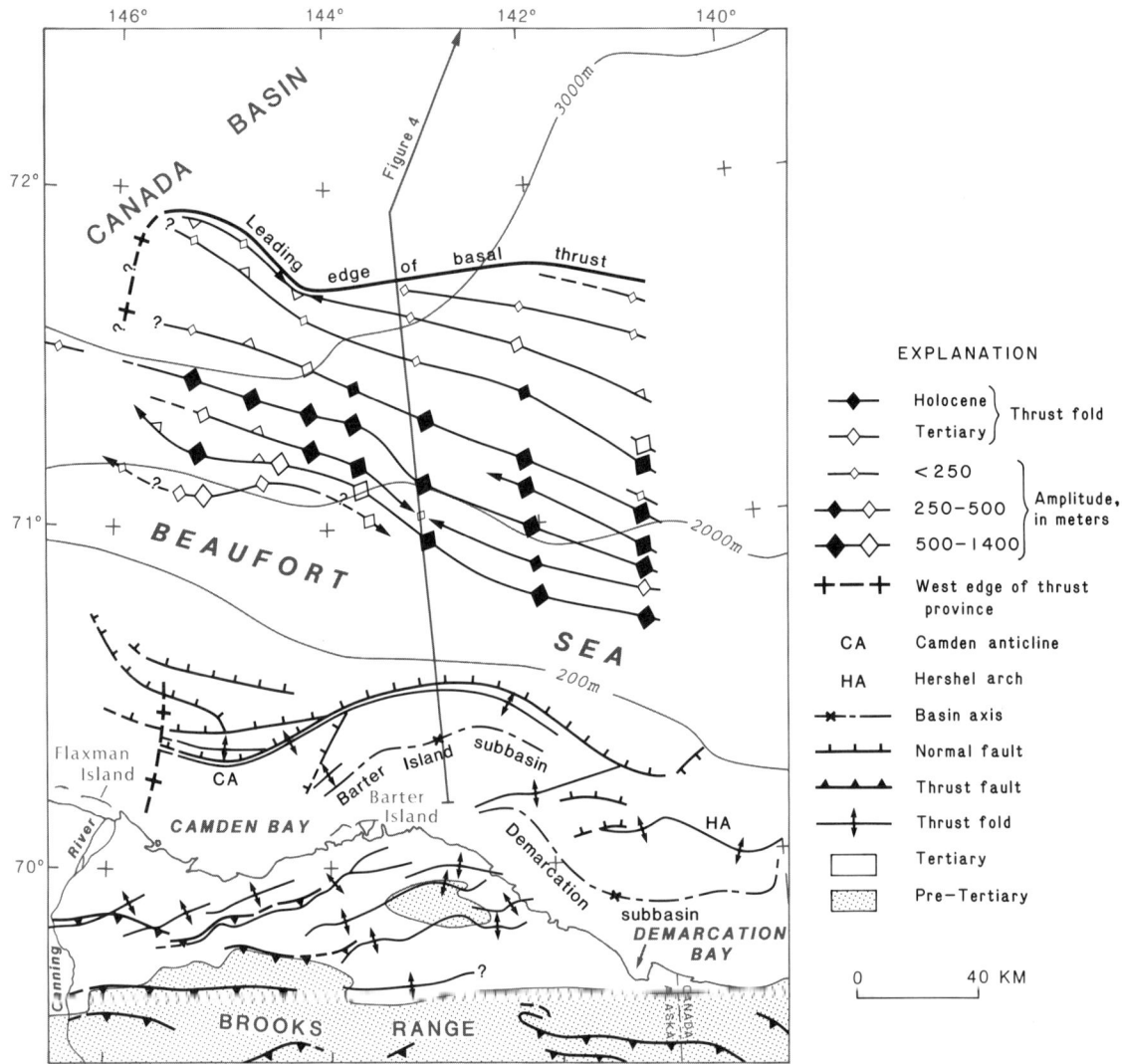

Figure 11. Thrust folds and faults of Cenozoic age in the southeastern Canada Basin and Beaufort Shelf between the Canning River and 141° W longitude. The thrust folds and faults are thought to underlie the shelf as far east as 132° W longitude on the basis of data presented in Dixon and Deitrich (this volume, Fig. 2). West edge of the thrust-fault province is the offshort extension of the Canning displacement, or fault, zone (see Plate 11).

(Fig. 1), and it is not clear that these events are tectonically related.

EVIDENCE ON AGE AND ORIGIN OF CANADA BASIN

Models for the origin of the Amerasia Basin and its major subbasin, the Canada Basin, fall into three broad categories. The first contends that these basins were formed by the foundering, or oceanization of continental crust, the ancient Hyperborean Shield of Shatsky (1935) and "Ancient Arctica" of Eardley (1948). The second contends that the basins consist of either Paleozoic oceanic crust that has been in place for a long time (Churkin, 1969) or Cretaceous oceanic crust (Kula plate?) that was introduced from the Pacific and isolated by a belt of exotic tectonostratigraphic terranes emplaced along the north Pacific rim in late Mesozoic time (Churkin and Trexler, 1980). The third category consists of models that form the basins in situ by sea-floor spreading, for which a rich variety of geometries has been proposed. Some of these models suggest rotational rifting about poles in one of the corners of this triangular basin (e.g., Carey, 1958; Rickwood, 1970; Tailleur, 1969 and 1973; and Rowley and others, 1985). Other models use nonrotational spreading along axes that are normal to pairs of transform faults along the Canadian Arctic Islands and Siberian margins (Crane, 1987; Smith, 1987) or the Alaskan Beaufort slope and parallel faults to the north (Herron and others, 1974; Vogt and others, 1982, Fig. 11). Opening by rotation of smaller tectonic units within the Amerasia Basin (Mair and Lyons, 1981) and by the interaction of intersecting dextral strike-slip faults and associated nonrotational spreading (Jones, 1980) have also been suggested. Although the hypotheses are quite diverse, there appears to be something of a convergence on an origin by sea-floor spreading in late Mesozoic (mainly late Early Cretaceous) time. Major controversy, however, concerns the geometry of spreading.

Any of the proposed models must take into account the Alpha and Mendeleev Ridges, the Chukchi Borderland, and Arlis Plateau. Alpha Ridge has been held to be: (a) a hot-spot trail (Forsyth and others, 1986b; Jackson and others, 1986); (b) an extinct sea-floor spreading axis (Hall, 1970 and 1973; Ostenso, 1972); (c) a subduction zone (Herron and others, 1974); and (d) foundered continental crust (King and others, 1966). The ridges of the Chukchi Borderland have been proposed to consist of continental fragments (Hunkins and others, 1962) or they may be erosionally truncated volcanic ridges. The following sections summarize the data and hypotheses that bear most directly on the age and origin of the Canada Basin.

Morphology

The crustal velocity structure and depth (more than 3.9 km) of the Canada Basin indicate that it is a small ocean basin with an unusually thick sedimentary fill. The shape of the basin (Figs. 1 and 12, Plate 1) may also provide an important clue to its origin. In outline, the modern basin and the proposed proto–Canada Basin form isosceles triangles with apices on the southeast, in the Mackenzie Delta region, and bases on the north, along the Amerasia flank of the Alpha or the Lomonosov Ridges, respectively. This geometry suggested first to Du Toit (1937) and Carey (1958), and then to many others, that the Amerasia Basin is a sphenochasm, which opened by counterclockwise rotational rifting of Arctic Alaska and the northeastern USSR away from the Canadian Arctic Islands. Matching the 1,000 m isobaths on opposite sides of the southeastern Canada Basin suggests that the angle of rotation was 66° (Grantz and others, 1979). A requirement of this hypothesis is that the base of the isosceles triangle be a right-lateral transform fault.

Continental margins

As noted in the section "Basin margins", above, seismic reflection profiles suggest that the continental margin north of Alaska was formed by rifting in Jurassic time, followed by rifting, breakup, and formation of the Canada Basin by sea-floor spreading beginning in Hauterivian time, about 125 Ma (Grantz and May, 1983). Similar data in the Mackenzie Delta region (Dixon and Deitrich, this volume) indicate that the continental margin between the Mackenzie River and northern Banks Island was also formed by rifting initiated in middle Hauterivian to Barremian time. As these two rifted continental margin segments face each other across the Mackenzie Delta and the location of the paleopole for opening of the Canada Basin by rotational rifting as suggested by its bathymetry, their juxtaposition supports the rotational-rifting hypothesis.

Where complications from later structural events are absent, seismic-reflection profiles from the Beaufort and Chukchi Shelves show that the breakup unconformity extends northward as an almost flat surface to a tectonic hinge line beneath the inner or midshelf (Plate 9; Grantz and May, 1983). Small down-to-the-basin normal faults offset the breakup unconformity and the condensed deposits that were deposited upon it after breakup, but not the thick overlying clastic deposits of Brooks Range provenance that overstep them. North of the hinge line the unconformity slopes rather uniformly seaward at a low-to-moderate angle, offset only by small normal faults, to the limits of seismic resolution at depths of 8 to 12 km; and the unconformity is overlain by a thick Albian and younger progradational sedimentary prism. This structural configuration is typical of rifted margins (see, e.g., Falvey, 1974). The presence of a mid-Cretaceous submarine canyon near Cape Simpson that is incised at least 1.2 km, and perhaps more than 1.8 km, into Albian strata and filled with late Cenomanian or Turonian strata (Kirschner and Rycerski, 1987) demonstrates that deep water existed in the southern Canada Basin by early Late Cretaceous time.

A reasonable juxtaposition of the rift-related tectonic hinge lines on opposite sides of the southeast Canada Basin is achieved if northern Alaska (which, with northeasternmost Siberia, forms the Arctic Alaska plate; Fujita and Newberry, 1982), is rotated 66° clockwise about a pole at 68.5°N, 135°W. Such a rotation would place the Arctic Alaska plate against the Canadian Arctic Islands (Figs. 12 A and 12 B). In the absence of clearly identifiable tie points on the respective hinge lines, a geometrically rigorous rotation was not made. The rotation agrees with that obtained by matching the 1,000 m isobaths across the southeast Canada Basin, and appears to be the best current estimate of the counterclockwise rotation required to open the Canada Basin according to the rotational rifting hypothesis.

Comparison of geology across basin

The Sverdrup Basin of the Canadian Arctic Islands and the Arctic Alaska Basin of northern Alaska, on opposite sides of the Canada Basin, contain closely correlative and lithologically similar sedimentary sequences of Mississippian to Neocomian age (Grantz and others, 1979) that have been referred to the Ellesmerian sequence of Lerand (1973). The basins also have similar tectonic histories (Fig. 13). Closing the Canada Basin by rotational rifting about a paleopole in the Mackenzie Delta region would not only bring these basins together but would juxtapose major stratigraphic features within them (Fig. 12 A to C). Restoration would place the northerly-sourced paralic deposits and paleoshorelines of Arctic Alaska against a sourceland, the North American craton, at Banks Island and align them with lithologically similar and correlative paralic strata and paleoshorelines on the cratonward side of the Sverdrup Basin. The axis of maximum sedimentary thickness of the Sverdrup Basin (Fig. 12) would also be aligned with Hanna Trough (Grantz and May, 1987), which is an axis of maximum sedimentary thickness in correlative rocks

SIBERIAN PLATFORM
Indigirka
River
Kolyma
River
COLLAGE OF ALLOCHTHONOUS PALEO-PLATES
EURASIA BASIN
LOMONOSOV RIDGE
N.P.
LR
AR
ALPHA RIDGE
CANADA BASIN
CHUKCHI BORDERLAND
SVERDRUP BASIN
Ellesmere Island
GREENLAND
ARCTIC ALASKA PLATE
Wrangel Island
Anadyr River
BERING SEA
BERING STRAIT
HANNA TROUGH
ARCTIC ALASKA BASIN
Banks Island
NORTH AMERICAN PLATE
ALASKA
YUKON
Yukon River
Mackenzie River
G
H
B
A)
0
500 KM
70°
80°
120°
90°
60°
30°
0°
150°
60°
180°
60°
150°
120°
70°
80°
90°
66°
66°
1000
2000
3000
3
6
9
12
U.S.S.R. PLATE
GREENLAND
Wrangel Island
BERING STRAIT
ALASKA
HANNA TROUGH
ARCTIC
SVERDRUP BASIN
Ellesmere Island
270 Km
AMERICAN PLATE
Banks Island
CANADA
NORTH
ALASKA
YUKON
B)
G
H
B
U.S.S.R. PLATE
GREENLAND
Wrangel Island
BERING STRAIT
ALASKA
HANNA TROUGH
ARCTIC
SVERDRUP BASIN
Ellesmere Island
AMERICAN PLATE
Banks Island
CANADA
NORTH
ALASKA
YUKON
H
H
C)

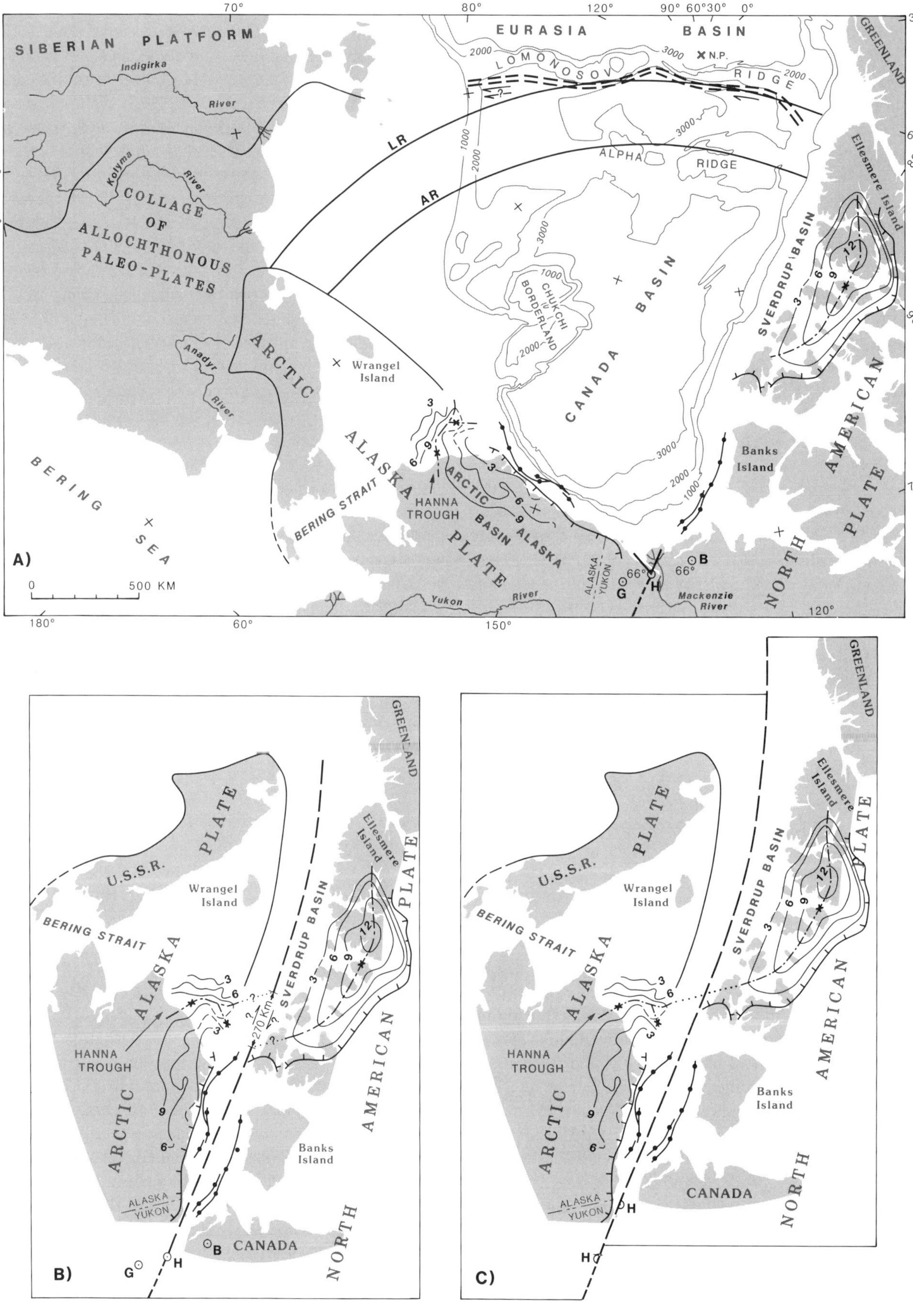

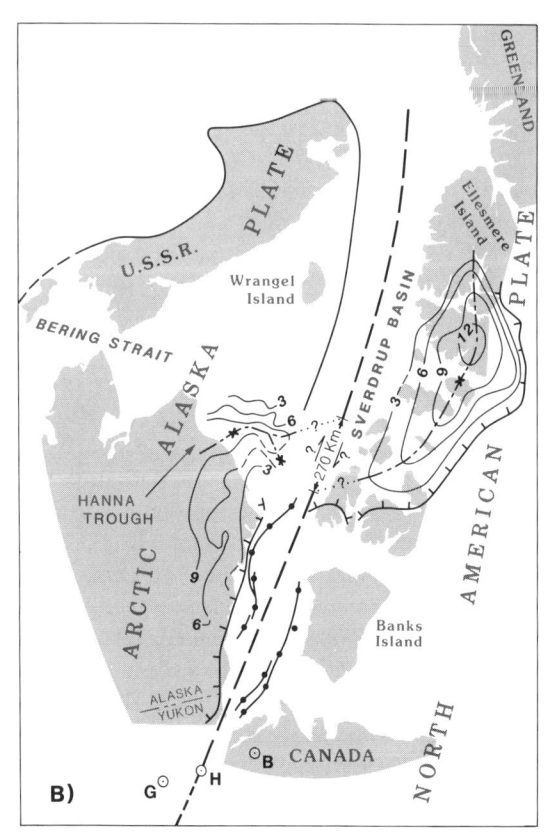

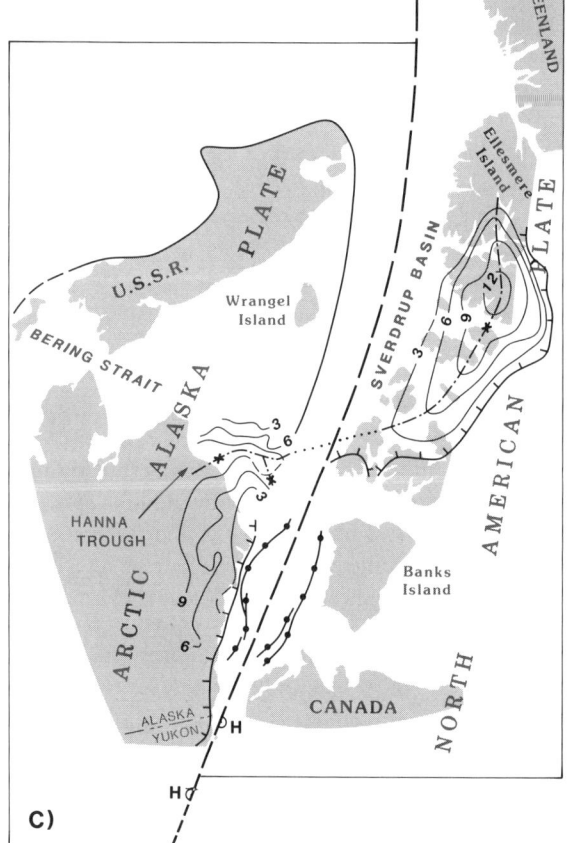

beneath the Chukchi Shelf. Both the Sverdrup Basin and Hanna Trough are sedimentary basins in the sense that they are flanked on opposite sides by marginal facies and shoreward or shelfward merging unconformities. Details of the stratigraphy of the Sverdrup and Arctic Alaska Basins, summarized in Grantz and others (1979), can be found in Balkwill (1978), Balkwill and Fox (1982), Detterman and others (1975), and Bird (1985).

Closing the Canada Basin by a 66° clockwise rotation of the Arctic Alaska plate about a pole at 68.5°N, 135°W, as proposed above, brings the axes of the Sverdrup Basin and Hanna Trough near and parallel to each other, but offset by about 270 km (Figs. 12B and C). The offset suggests that rotation was accompanied or followed by nonrotational motion that can be described as 270 km of right slip along the suture between the rotated blocks. It is possible, however, that the nonrotational motion of Arctic Alaska relative to the Arctic Islands took place west of the proposed suture, had a different orientation, and even predated rifting.

Important differences between the Sverdrup and Arctic Alaska Basins also exist. For example, Carboniferous evaporites, Permian carbonates, and basalt flows of Carboniferous, Permian, and Cretaceous age, which are well developed in the deeply subsided, central part of the Sverdrup Basin, have not been found to date in the Arctic Alaska Basin. Their presence in the Sverdrup Basin would be explained if it was the site of an incipient, or failed rift as suggested by Balkwill and Fox (1982). It is proposed here that the incipient rift was located over only part of a single, regionally extensive Arctic Alaska–Sverdrup Basin (Fig. 12) and that the similar paralic and shelf facies of this now dismembered sedimentary basin can be correlated across the southeastern Canada Basin.

Heat flow

The first heat-flow measurements in the Canada Basin were taken from Ice Island T-3 by U.S. Geological Survey personnel (Lachenbruch and Marshall, 1966, 1969). These and more recent data, upon which the following discussion is based, are summarized by Langseth and others (this volume). If the central part of the Canada Basin is assumed to have a heat flow of 56.5 mW/m^2 (the average of the values presented by Langseth and others, this volume) then an uncorrected age versus heat-flow determination from Parsons and Sclater (1977) would give an age of about 70 Ma for the Canada Basin. This value should, however, be

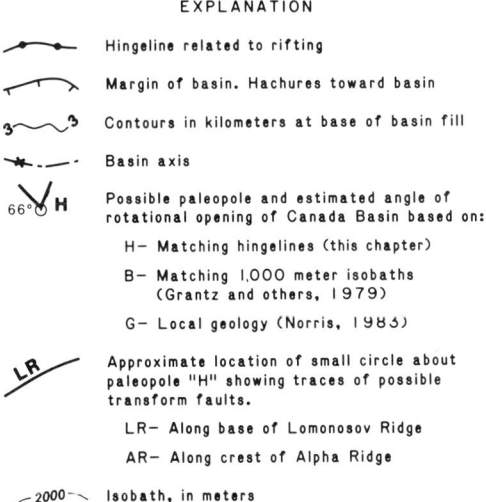

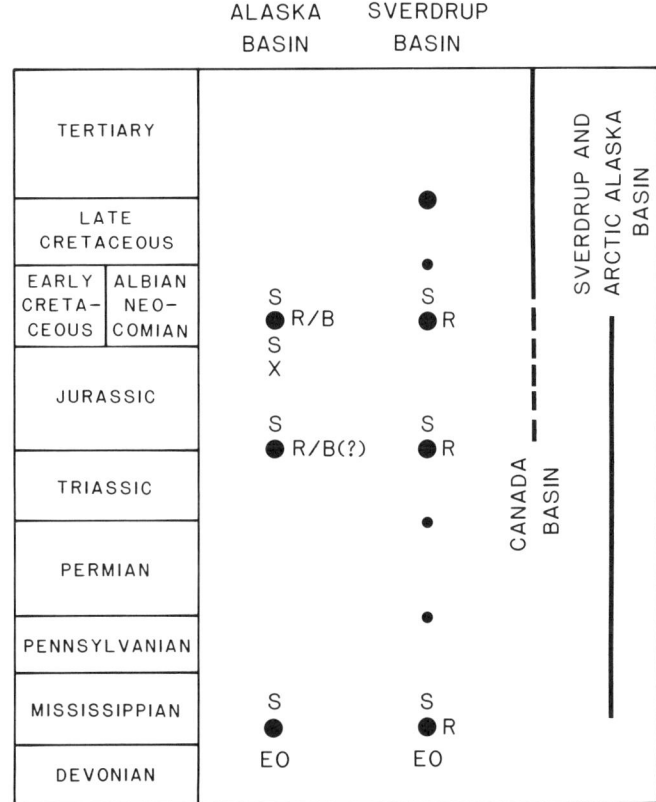

Figure 12 (facing page, explanation above). Selected major tectonic features of Canada Basin and vicinity. A, shows the tectonic features in their present configuration. B, shows the position of the Arctic Alaska plate with 66° of postulated mid-Cretaceous counterclockwise rotation restored. C, shows the position of the Arctic Alaska plate with both 66° of postulated counterclockwise rotation and 270 km of postulated right-lateral transcurrent motion restored. Configuration of paleoplates in northeast USSR from Fujita and Newberry (1982). Tectonic features in eastern Beaufort Shelf from Dixon and Deitrich (this volume) and in western Beaufort and Chukchi Shelves from Grantz and others (ch. 22, this volume). Contours in Sverdrup Basin after Drummond (1973).

Figure 13. Correlation of major tectonic events in the Sverdrup Basin of the Canadian Arctic Islands and the Arctic Alaska Basin of northern Alaska showing the close similarity in their tectonic histories.

corrected for both sedimentation rate and radioactive heat generation. For crustal ages older than 70 Ma, radioactive heat production dominates, and for a given age the heat flow increases linearly with sediment thickness. For a lithospheric thickness of 90 km and a sediment thickness of 6.5 km, Langseth and others (this volume) calculated a model age from heat flow of 90 to 120 Ma, and for a lithospheric thickness of 125 km and a sediment thickness of 4.5 km, a model age of 78 to 92 Ma. Lawver and Baggeroer (1983), using the same data and a similar model, calculated an age of 80 to 110 Ma. Although they corrected for sedimentation rates, they were only able to estimate the heat generated by the sediment.

Paleomagnetism

Opening of the Canada Basin is an ideal problem for paleomagnetic analysis. In particular, the rotational rifting hypothesis is very similar to that proposed for the opening of the Bay of Biscay, for which paleomagnetism provided critical support. Newman and others (1977) were the first to use paleomagnetic data in the search for evidence of rotation of Arctic Alaska. Their data, from Upper Devonian and Mississippian sedimentary rocks in the Brooks Range, gave paleopoles located in the central Pacific Ocean. Their results were interpreted to have been produced by a 70° counterclockwise rotation of Arctic Alaska. Hillhouse and Grommé (1983) questioned these results, suggesting that these data contain a postdeformation magnetic overprint. Their own paleomagnetic studies of Brooks Range rocks revealed a strong magnetic overprint that postdated opening of the Canada Basin. Some of their data, however, were from two oriented cores in test wells drilled near the Beaufort Sea coast, in northern Alaska. In one of these cores they found stable magnetic components that agree with a counterclockwise rotation of Arctic Alaska. Because of uncertainties in these data, however, Hillhouse and Grommé (1983) suggested that confirmation of their results is needed before they can be used to support the rotation hypothesis.

Recently, Jarrard and Halgedahl (1987; also in Harbert and others, this volume) have summarized previous paleomagnetic results from northern Alaska and presented new paleomagnetic data from oriented drill cores from the Kuparuk River oil field of northern Alaska. (The field lies near the Beaufort Sea coast near 150°W longitude). Their data are from beds of Berriasian to Valanginian age in the lower member of the Kuparuk River Formation, which may have been the last beds deposited prior to the proposed rifting of Arctic Alaska away from the Canadian Arctic Islands. Although reversal and fold tests are inconclusive, the mean paleomagnetic pole determined from cores in two of the wells is compatible with the approximately 66° of post-Valanginian (late Early Cretaceous) counterclockwise rotation of Arctic Alaska away from the Canadian Arctic Islands suggested by Tailleur (1969), Rickwood (1970), and Grantz and others (1979). The fact that both polarities are present in the beds studied, and that these beds are essentially flat lying, makes it unlikely that they were remagnetized after Valanginian time (Jarrard and Halgedahl, 1987).

Magnetic Anomalies

In 1977 and 1978, aeromagnetic profiling was done across the Canada Basin (Taylor and others, 1981) in an effort to decipher a sea-floor spreading pattern. The relatively low-amplitude anomalies that were found were interpreted by Taylor and others (1981) to support a Carey-type rotation of Arctic Alaska away from the Canadian Arctic Islands beginning in Late Jurassic time (anomaly M-25) and continuing until Early Cretaceous time (anomaly M-12). These results have been reinterpreted by Vogt and others (1982) to indicate nonrotational rifting of this basin. Herron and others (1974) and Lawver and Baggeroer (1983) proposed that the Canada Basin opened during magnetic quiet periods, when there were no strong magnetic field reversals. The former suggested opening occurred during the Middle Jurassic quiet period, the latter during the mid-Cretaceous (Aptian to Santonian) quiet period.

The magnetic anomalies of the southern Canada Basin are difficult to analyze because of their relatively low amplitude, averaging about 200 nT. This would require a much more closely spaced, grid-type survey to adequately define the anomaly pattern. The fan-shaped pattern, if not the age, of magnetic anomalies suggested by the Taylor and others (1981) magnetic survey may never-the-less be valid. The pattern somewhat resembles that of magnetic anomalies over the Bay of Biscay (Ries, 1978), and in places there appears to be a spatially correlative, albeit poorly developed and defined lineation in the gravity field of the southern Canada Basin (compare Plates 3 and 4).

Recently, satellite magnetic anomaly maps of the entire Arctic have become available (for the latest version, see Haines, 1985). These maps show that a broad negative magnetic anomaly overlies the region south of 80°N latitude (Fig. 1), which encompasses most of the Canada Basin. This negative anomaly suggests that the region is underlain by crust with very low or zero magnetic susceptibility—consistent with the large sedimentary prism that is inferred from other evidence to underlie the Canada Basin. The Alpha Ridge, in contrast, possesses a very large (48 nT, peak-to-trough) positive anomaly at satellite altitude. Both northern Greenland and Iceland have similar positive anomalies, although of lesser amplitude (16 and 14 nT, respectively). These results are consistent with the hot-spot trail interpretation of the Alpha Ridge of Forsyth and others (1986b).

TECTONIC DEVELOPMENT

Proto-Canada Basin

Recent Canadian work over the Alpha Ridge (Weber and Sweeney, this volume; Forsyth and others, 1986a, 1986b; Jackson and others, 1986) provides evidence of a volcanic origin that has important implications for the initial configuration of the Canada

Basin. This work suggests the Canadian end of the ridge is a volcanic feature that is in part alkalic and perhaps analogous to Iceland in lithology and origin; and that it is not a displaced fragment of continental crust (King and others, 1966), a subduction zone (Herron and others, 1974), or a spreading center (Ostenso, 1972; Hall, 1973). However, variations in trans-Arctic teleseismic PP wave travel-time residuals along the Alpha Ridge (Stewart, 1980) suggest that all parts of the ridge may not have a common origin. Forsyth and others (1986a, 1986b) and Jackson and others (1986) suggest that the Alpha Ridge volcanic rocks are the product of a hot-spot plume initially localized in the vicinity of northwestern Ellesmere and northern Axel Heiberg Islands, at the site of the initial rift that eventually opened the Canada Basin by rotational rifting. Synrift hot-spot volcanism is proposed to have built the Alpha Ridge on the newly created oceanic crust on both sides of the rift in the manner proposed for Iceland. The hot-spot activity is correlated with the volcanic rocks of the Strand Fiord Formation in the Sverdrup Basin on northwest Axel Heiberg Island. These rocks are tholeiitic icelandite flows and pyroclastic rocks of approximately late Cenomanian to Coniacian age that thicken northward toward the continental margin (Ricketts and others, 1985). Model 1 of Figure 10 assumes the Canada Basin has had its present size and configuration since it was formed in early Late Cretaceous time and that its northern margin was, and has remained, the south flank of the Alpha Ridge. The model also implies that the Makarov Basin, on the northern side of the Alpha Ridge, has the same age, nature, and origin as the Canada Basin.

An alternative hypothesis for the origin of Alpha Ridge is suggested by the apparent discrepancy in age between the Alpha Ridge volcanic rocks and the floor of the Canada Basin off Alaska and the Mackenzie Delta. If the Alpha Ridge volcanics correlate with the Strand Fiord Formation, they are of late Cenomanian to Coniacian age. Piston cores from biosiliceous ooze above a prominent seismic reflector at the top of the Alpha Ridge volcanics contain some volcanic detritus and silicoflagellates, diatoms, and palynomorphs of late Campanian or of middle or late Maestrichtian age (Ling and others, 1973; Mudie and Blasco, 1985). The cores therefore confirm that the Alpha Ridge volcanics are no younger than latest Cretaceous. A late Cenomanian to Coniacian age for the volcanics may be significantly younger (27 Ma or more) than the Hauterivian age of continental breakup that initiated development of the Canada Basin, as suggested by geologic evidence along its southern margins (Grantz and others, and Dixon and Dietrich, this volume). This difference in age suggests that the Alpha Ridge volcanics could have formed over a hot-spot trace that was younger than the oceanic crust beneath Canada Basin (model 2 of Fig. 10). In this case, the Makarov and Canada Basins would have had a common origin in the same spreading ridge system, and the pre–Alpha Ridge Makarov and Canada Basins would have extended north of Alpha Ridge as a single basin to the foot of the Lomonosov Ridge, then part of the Barents Shelf. By this model, both the volcanic rocks of Alpha Ridge and the sedimentary rocks of Canada and Makarov Basins were deposited in an ancestral (proto–) Canada Basin.

Modern Canada Basin

The refraction work of Mair and Lyons (1981), Baggeroer and Falconer (1982), and Forsyth and others (1986a) have shown that the Canada and Makarov Basins are underlain by oceanic crust; and seismic reflection data in the Mackenzie Delta (Dixon and Dietrich, this volume) and the Alaskan Beaufort Shelf (Grantz and others, ch. 22, this volume, 1983) indicate that these margins of the Canada Basin are of rifted (passive) type and Hauterivian age. Taken together, these observations indicate that the Canada Basin formed by sea-floor spreading beginning in mid-Early Cretaceous (Hauterivian) time. The geometry of the magnetic lineations interpreted to occur in the Canada Basin by Taylor and others (1981), the local and possibly spatially correlative (but poorly developed and defined) gravity lineations, the shape of the basin (exclusive of the Chukchi Borderland), and the correlation of Ellemerian sedimentary basins across the southern Canada Basin support the hypothesis that the basin opened by rotational rifting about a pole in the Mackenzie Delta region. The paleomagnetic results of Jarrard and Halgedahl (1987; Harbert and others, this volume), which are compatible with a 66° counterclockwise rotation of Arctic Alaska away from the Canadian Arctic Islands, provide additional support for, but not conclusive proof of the rotation model.

Three types of data are presently available for estimating the position of the paleopole for the rotational rifting model: bathymetry in the Canada Basin, the position of the tectonic hinge line associated with rifting at the Alaskan and Canadian Beaufort Shelves, and geology in the Mackenzie Delta region. Matching the 1,000 m isobaths across the southeastern Canada Basin suggests a rotation of 66° about a paleopole at 69.1°N, 130.5°W in the eastern Mackenzie Delta (Grantz and others, 1979). Matching the tectonic hinge lines in the eastern and western Beaufort Shelves (Fig. 12) places the paleopole near 68.5°N, 135°W. Regional geology in the lower Mackenzie Valley (Norris, 1983) places the paleopole 135 km to the west-southwest, at the south apex of the Rapid Depression near 68°N, 138°W. This feature is a north-striking, fault-bounded graben-like structure on the west flank of the Richardson Mountains in northern Yukon Territory. Given the current lack of precision in locating the pole of rotation from the shape and position of the hinge lines and the uncertainty introduced by the 270 km of nonrotational motion that apparently accompanied rotation, the paleopole proposed by Norris (1983) on geologic criteria and the paleopole that we propose from the relative position of the hinge lines are equally valid approximations.

If the Alpha Ridge and perhaps the northern part of the Mendeleev Ridge are hot-spot trails, as proposed by Forsyth and others (1986b), then the development of these ridges could have been part of the process that formed the Makarov and Canada Basins. The origin of Chukchi Borderland, Arlis Plateau, and

Mendeleev Ridge, if it is an extension of Arlis Ridge, is more speculative because of a paucity of data. They could be related in origin to the Makarov and Canada Basins if they are fragments of continental crust rifted by local spreading centers from the present sites of deep Late Cretaceous and Tertiary sedimentary basins on the North Chukchi and East Siberian Shelves during or after opening of the Canada Basin. Such a deep and extensive sedimentary basin, the North Chukchi Basin (Grantz and others, 1979), underlies the northwestern Chukchi Shelf and at least the northeastern part of the East Siberian Shelf (Fig. 1). If the flat-topped ridges of the Chukchi Borderland consist of volcanic rocks that were emplaced after rifting and subsequently truncated by marine planation, they could be compatible in origin with rifting, but not necessarily part of the rifting process. Until the origin of these ridges is determined, no fully satisfactory hypothesis for the origin of the Makarov and Canada Basins can be constructed. Their mere presence, however, does not invalidate the rotational rifting or some other hypotheses that have been proposed.

A special requirement of the rotational rifting hypothesis, if it is applied to the entire Amerasia Basin, is that a large right-lateral transform fault system must lie along the base of the Lomonosov ridge, a fragment of continental crust formerly attached to the Barents Shelf (Forsyth and Mair, 1984). The trend of magnetic anomalies in the Canada Basin has been interpreted in a manner that supports this hypothesis (Taylor and others, 1981), but other interpretations, such as nonrotational rifting (Vogt and other, 1982), have been proposed. The anomalies over Fletcher Abyssal Plain, which is the deepest part of the relatively narrow Makarov Basin, and the part least likely to be perturbed by topographic or upper crustal magnetic anomalies, trend at about a 45° angle to the expected direction (see magnetic contours in Perry and Fleming, 1985). These anomalies also trend at about 45° to the Alpha and Lomonosov Ridges. If the anomalies are related to rotational opening of the Canada Basin, they should trend normal to the Lomonosov and Alpha Ridges, and if they are related to spreading along the Alpha Ridge, they should trend parallel to these ridges. Perhaps the magnetic anomalies over the Fletcher Abyssal Plain are of upper crustal origin, or related to sea-floor spreading in a manner that is not yet understood.

The large transform fault system along the base of the Lomonosov Ridge required by the rotational rifting hypothesis must cross the western part of the East Siberian Sea and extend into the northeastern USSR near 155°E longitude, between the Indigirka and Kolyma Rivers (Fig. 12A). This trend places the projected transform fault between the Cherskiy Mountains of the Siberian Platform and a collage of microplates (lithotectonic terranes) that accreted to the northeastern USSR in late Mesozoic time (Fujita and Newberry, 1982). A small circle drawn along the foot of Lomonosov Ridge about the paleopole derived from the position of the tectonic hinge lines strikes into the middle of the collage of microplates (Fig. 12A). A similar circle drawn along the crest of the Alpha Ridge strikes into the western part of the Arctic Alaska plate as defined by Fujita and Newberry (1982), a circumstance that lends some support to the hypothesis that the proto–Canada Basin extended beyond the crest of the Alpha Ridge to the foot of the Lomonosov Ridge. It is possible that the transform reached the paleo–Pacific Ocean along the boundary between the accreted microplates and the Siberian Platform or that the trace of the transform lay within the area of microplates but was later obscured by the processes that emplaced the microplates. In either case, the presence and position of the accreted microplate province is permissive, if not indeed supportive of the rotational-rifting hypothesis.

REFERENCES CITED

Armstrong, T., 1958, The Russians in the Arctic; Aspects of Soviet exploration and exploitation of the Far North, 1937-57: London, Methuen, 182 p.

Baggeroer, A. B., and Falconer, R., 1982, Array refraction profiles and crustal models of the Canada Basin: Journal of Geophysical Research, v. 87, p. 5461-5476.

Balkwill, H. R., 1978, Evolution of Sverdrup Basin, Arctic Canada: American Association of Petroleum Geologists Bulletin, v. 62, p. 1004-1028.

Balkwill, H. R., and Fox, F. G., 1982, Incipient rift zone, western Sverdrup Basin, Arctic Canada, in Embry, A. F., and Balkwill, H. R., eds., Arctic geology and geophysics: Calgary, Canadian Society of Petroleum Geologists Memoir 8, p. 171-187.

Basham, P. W., Forsyth, D. A., and Wetmiller, R. J., 1977, Seismicity of northern Canada: Canadian Journal of Earth Science, v. 14, p. 1646-1667.

Beal, M. A., 1969, Bathymetry and structure of the Arctic Ocean [Ph.D. thesis]: Corvallis, Oregon State University, 204 p.

Bird, K. J., 1985, The framework geology of the North Slope of Alaska as related to oil-source rock correlations, in Magoon, L. B., and Claypool, G. E., eds., Alaska North Slope oil-rock correlation study: Tulsa, American Association of Petroleum Geologists Studies in Geology, no. 20, p. 3-29.

Biswas, N. N., Aki, K., Puplan, H., and Tytgat, G., 1986, Characteristics of regional stresses in Alaska and neighboring areas: Geophysical Research Letters, v. 13, p. 177-180.

Carey, S. W., 1958, The tectonic approach to continental drift, in Carey, S. W., ed., Continental drift; A symposium: Hobart, Tasmania University, p. 177-355.

Christensen, N. I., and Salisbury, M. H., 1975, Structure and constitution of the lower oceanic crust: Reviews of Geophysics and Space Physics, v. 13, no. 1, p. 57-86.

Churkin, M., Jr., 1969, Paleozoic tectonic history of the Arctic basin north of Alaska: Science, v. 165, no. 3893, p. 549-555.

Churkin, M., Jr., and Trexler, J. H., Jr., 1980, Circum-Arctic plate accretion—isolating part of a Pacific plate to form the nucleus of the Arctic Basin: Earth and Planetary Science Letters, v. 49, p. 356-362.

Clark, D. L., Whitman, R. R., Morgan, K. A., and Scudder, D. M., 1980, Stratigraphy and glacial-marine sediments of the Amerasian Basin, central Arctic Ocean: Geological Society of America Special Paper 181, 57 p.

Coles, R. L., Hannaford, W., and Haines, G. V., 1978, Magnetic anomalies and the evolution of the Arctic, in Sweeney, J. F., ed., Arctic geophysical review: Ottawa, Earth Physics Branch, Department of Energy, Mines, and Resources, v. 45, p. 51-66.

Crane, R. C., 1987, Arctic reconstruction from an Alaskan viewpoint, in Tailleur, I. L., and Weimer, P., eds., Alaskan North Slope geology: Los Angeles, Pacific Section, Society of Economic Paleontologists and Mineralogists, and Anchorage, Alaska Geological Society, p. 769-784.

Creager, J. S., and McManus, D. A., 1965, Pleistocene drainage patterns on the floor of the Chukchi Sea: Marine Geology, v. 3, p. 279–290.

Detterman, R. L., Reiser, H. N., Brosgé, W. P., and Dutro, J. T., Jr., 1975, Post-Carboniferous stratigraphy, northeastern Alaska: U.S. Geological Survey Professional Paper 886, 46 p.

Drummond, K. J., 1973, Canadian Arctic Islands, in McCrossan, R. G., ed., The future petroleum provinces of Canada: Canadian Society of Petroleum Geologists Memoir 1, p. 443–472.

Du Toit, A. L., 1937, Our wandering continents: Hafner Publishing Company, 366 p.

Eardley, A. J., 1948, Ancient Arctica: Journal of Geology, v. 56, no. 5, p. 409–536.

Falvey, D. A., 1974, The development of continental margins in plate-tectonic theory: Australian Petroleum Exploration Association Journal, v. 14, p. 95–106.

Forsyth, D. A., and Mair, J. A., 1984, Crustal structure of the Lomonosov Ridge and the Fram and Makarov basins near the North Pole: Journal of Geophysical Research, v. 89, no. B1, p. 473–481.

Forsyth, D. A., Asudeh, I., Green, A. G., and Jackson, H. R., 1986a, Crustal structure of the northern Alpha Ridge: Nature, v. 322, p. 349–352.

Forsyth, D. A., Morel-a-l'Huissier, P., Asudsen, I., and Green, A. G., 1986b, Alpha Ridge and Iceland; Products of the same plume?: Journal of Geodynamics, v. 6, p. 197–214.

Fujita, K., and Newberry, J. T., 1982, Tectonic evolution of northeastern Siberia and adjacent regions: Tectonophysics, v. 89, p. 337–357.

Fujita, K., Cook, D. B., and Coley, M. J., 1983, Tectonics of the western Beaufort and Chukchi seas [abs.]: EOS American Geophysical Union Transactions, v. 64, p. 263.

Grantz, A., and May, S. D., 1983, Rifting history and structural development of the continental margin north of Alaska, in Watkins, J. S., and Drake, C., eds., Studies in continental margin geology: American Association of Petroleum Geologists Memoir 34, p. 77–100.

—— , 1986, Cenozoic thrusting across a Mesozoic passive margin, eastern Beaufort Sea, Alaska, in Canadian Society of Petroleum Geologists 1986 Convention; Program and Abstracts: Calgary, Canadian Society of Petroleum Geologists, p. 47.

—— , 1987, Regional geology and petroleum potential of the United States Chukchi Shelf north of Point Hope, in Scholl, D. W., Grantz, A., and Vedder, J. G., eds., Geology and resource potential of the continental margin of western North America and adjacent ocean basins; Beaufort Sea to Baja California: Circum-Pacific Council for Energy and Mineral Resources, Earth Science Series No. 6, p. 37–58.

Grantz, A., Eittreim, S., and Dinter, D. A., 1979, Geology and tectonic development of the continental margin north of Alaska: Tectonophysics, v. 59, p. 263–291.

Grantz, A., Mann, D. M., and May, S. D., 1982, Tracklines of multichannel seismic-reflection data collected by the U.S. Geological Survey in the Beaufort and Chukchi seas in 1977 for which profiles and stack tapes are available: U.S. Geological Survey Open-File Report 82-735, 1 map sheet with text, scale 1:500,000.

Grantz, A., Dinter, D. A., and Biswas, N., 1983, Holocene faulting, warping, and earthquake epicenters on the Beaufort Shelf north of Alaska: U.S. Geological Survey Map I-1189-C, 7 p., 3 map sheets, scale 1:500,000.

Grantz, A., Dinter, D. A., and Culotta, R. C., 1987, Geology of the continental shelf north of the Arctic National Wildlife Refuge, in Tailleur, I. L., and Weimer, P., eds., Alaskan North Slope geology: Los Angeles, Pacific Section, Society of Economic Paleontologists and Mineralogists and Anchorage, Alaska Geological Society, p. 759–764.

Grow, J. A., Mattick, R. E., and Schlee, J. S., 1979, Multichannel seismic depth sections and interval velocities over outer continental shelf and upper continental slope between Cape Hatteras and Cape Cod, in Watkins, J. S., Montadert, L., and Dickerson, P. W., eds., Geological and geophysical investigations of continental margins: Tulsa, Oklahoma, American Association of Petroleum Geologists, p. 65–83.

Haines, G. V., 1985, Magsat vertical-field anomalies above 40° N from spherical-cap harmonic analysis: Journal of Geophysical Research, v. 90, p. 2593–2598.

Halgedahl, S., and Jarrard, R., 1987, Paleomagnetism of the Kuparuk River Formation from oriented drill core—evidence for rotation of the Arctic Alaska plate, in Tailleur, I. L, and Weimer, P., eds., Alaskan North Slope Geology: Los Angeles, Pacific Section, Society of Economic Paleontologists and Mineralogists, and Anchorage, Alaska Geological Society, p. 581–620.

Hall, J. K., 1970, Arctic Ocean geophysical studies; The Alpha Cordillera and Mendeleyev Ridge: Palisades, New York, Lamont-Doherty Geologic Observatory Technical Report 2, 125 p.

—— , 1973, Geophysical evidence for ancient sea-floor spreading from Alpha Cordillera and Mendeleyev Ridge, in Pitcher, M. G., ed., Arctic geology: American Association of Petroleum Geologists Memoir 19, p. 542–561.

Hasegawa, H. S., Chou, C. W., and Basham, P. W., 1979, Seismotectonics of the Beaufort Sea: Canadian Journal of Earth Sciences, v. 16, p. 816–830.

Herron, E. M., Dewey, J. F., and Pitman, W. C., III, 1974, Plate-tectonics model for the evolution of the Arctic: Geology, v. 2, p. 377–380.

Hillhouse, J. W., and Grommé, S., 1983, Paleomagnetic studies and the hypothetical rotation of Arctic Alaska: Journal of the Alaska Geological Society, v. 2, p. 27–39.

Houtz, R. E., 1981, Comparison of sediment sound-velocity functions from conjugate margins: Geological Society of America Bulletin, v. 92, p. 262–267.

Hunkins, K., and Tiemann, W., 1977, Geophysical data summary for Fletchers Ice Island (T-3) May 1962-Oct. 1974: Lamont-Doherty Geologic Observatory Technical Report CU-1-77, p. 219.

Hunkins, K., Herron, T., Kutschale, H., and Peter, G., 1962, Geophysical studies of the Chukchi Cap, Arctic Ocean: Journal of Geophysical Research, v. 67, no. 1, p. 235–247.

Jackson, H. R., 1985, Seismic reflection results from CESAR: Geological Survey of Canada Paper 84–22, p. 19–23.

Jackson, H. R., Forsyth, D. A., and Johnson, G. L., 1986, Oceanic affinities of the Alpha Ridge, Arctic Ocean: Marine Geology, v. 73, p. 237–262.

Jones, P. R., 1980, Evidence for Canada and Alaska on plate-tectonic evolution of the Arctic Ocean Basin: Nature, v. 185, p. 215–217.

King, E. R., Zietz, I., and Alldredge, L. R., 1966, Magnetic data on the structure of the central Arctic region: Geological Society of America Bulletin, v. 77, p. 619–646.

Kirschner, C. E., and Rycerski, B. A., 1987, Petroleum potential of representative stratigraphic and structural elements in NPRA in Alaska, in The National Petroleum Reserve in Alaska; A series of research papers: U.S. Geological Survey Professional Paper 1399, Chapter 9, p. 191–208..

Kovacs, L. C., and Vogt, P. R., 1982, Depth-to-magnetic source analysis of the Arctic Ocean region, in Johnson, G. L., and Sweeney, J. F., eds., Structure of the Arctic: Tectonophysics, v. 89, p. 255–294.

Kovacs, L. C., Bernero, C., Johnson, G. L., Pilger, R. H., Srivastava, S. P., Taylor, P. T., Vink, G. E., and Vogt, P. R., compilers, 1985, Residual magnetic anomaly chart of the Arctic Ocean region: Geological Society of America Map and Chart Series MC–53, scale 1:6,000,000, at 75° N latitude.

Lachenbruch, A. H., and Marshall, B. V., 1966, Heat flow through the Arctic Ocean floor; The Canada Basin–Alpha Rise boundary: Journal of Geophysical Research, v. 71, p. 1223–1248.

—— , 1969, Heat flow in the Arctic: Journal of the Arctic Institute of North America, v. 22, p. 300–311.

Langel, R. A., and Thorning, L., 1982, A satellite magnetic anomaly map of Greenland: Geophysical Journal of the Royal Astronomical Society, v. 71, p. 599–602.

Langseth, M., 1986, Single-channel seismic records from the T-3 Ice Island (June 1967–April 1970): Palisades, New York, Lamont-Doherty Geological Observatory, March 1986 unpublished supplement to Hunkins and Tiemann, 1977.

Lawver, L. A., and Baggeroer, A., 1983, A note on the age of the Canada Basin: Journal of the Alaska Geological Society, v. 2, p. 57–66.

Leblanc, G., and Wetmiller, R. J., 1974, An evaluation of seismological data available for the Yukon Territory and the Mackenzie Valley: Canadian Journal of Earth Sciences, v. 11, p. 1435–1454.

Lerand, M., 1973, Beaufort Sea, in McCrossan, R. G., ed., The future petroleum provinces of Canada; Their geology and potential: Canadian Society of Petroleum Geologists Memoir 1, p. 315–386.

Ling, H. Y., McPherson, L. M., and Clark, D. L., 1973, Late Cretaceous (Maastrichtian?) silicoflagellates from the Alpha Cordillera of the Arctic Ocean: Science, v. 180, p. 1360–1361.

Mair, J. A., and Forsyth, D. A., 1982, Crustal structures of the Canada Basin near Alaska, the Lomonosov Ridge, and adjoining basins near the North Pole: Tectonophysics, v. 89, p. 239–253.

Mair, J. A., and Lyons, J. A., 1981, Crustal structure and velocity anisotropy beneath the Beaufort Sea: Canadian Journal of Earth Science, v. 18, p. 724–741.

May, S. D., 1985, Free-air gravity anomaly map of the Chukchi and Alaskan Beaufort seas, Arctic Ocean: U.S. Geological Survey Miscellaneous Investigations Series Map I-1182-E, scale 1:1,000,000.

McKinlay, W. L., 1976, Karluk, the great untold story of Arctic exploration: London, Weidenfeld and Nicholson, v. 14, 170 p.

Mikkelsen, E., 1955, Mirage in the Arctic: London, Rupert Hart-Davis, p. 9, 24–27, 88–89.

Mudie, P. J., and Blasco, S. M., 1985, Lithostratigraphy of the CESAR cores: Geological Survey of Canada Paper 84-22, p. 59–99.

Naugler, F. P., Silverberg, N., and Creager, J. S., 1974, Recent sediments of the East Siberian Sea, in Herman, Y., ed., Marine geology and oceanography of the Arctic seas: New York, Springer-Verlag, p. 191–210.

Newman, G. W., Mull, C. G., and Watkins, N. D., 1977, Northern Alaska paleomagnetism, plate rotation, and tectonics [abs.]: Anchorage, Alaska Geological Society Symposium, p. 16–19.

Norris, D. K., 1983, Porcupine virgation; The structural link among the Columbia, Innuitian, and Alaskan orogens: Geological Association of Canada–Mineralogical Association of Canada–Canadian Geophysical Union, Program with Abstracts, v. 8, p. A51.

Ostenso, N. A., 1972, Seafloor spreading and the origin of the Arctic Ocean Basin, in Implications of continental drift to the Earth Sciences: New York, Academic Press, p. 165–173.

Parsons, B., and Sclater, J. G., 1977, An analysis of the variation of ocean floor bathymetry and heat flow with age: Journal of Geophysical Research, v. 82, p. 803–827.

Perry, R. K., and Fleming, H. S., compilers, 1985, Bathymetry of the Arctic Ocean: Geological Society of America Map and Chart Series MC-56, scale 1:4,704,075 at latitude 78°N.

Ricketts, B., Osadetz, K. G., and Embry, A. F., 1985, Volcanic style in the Strand Fiord Formation (Upper Cretaceous), Axel Heiberg Island, Canadian Arctic Archipelago: Polar Research, 3 n.s., p. 107–122.

Rickwood, F. K., 1970, The Prudhoe Bay field, in Adkison, W. L., and Brosgé, W. P., eds., Proceedings of the geological seminar on the North Slope of Alaska: American Association of Petroleum Geologists, Pacific Section, p. L1–L11.

Ries, A. C., 1978, The opening of the Bay of Biscay; A review: Earth-Science Reviews, v. 14, p. 35–63.

Rowley, D. B., Lottes, A. L., and Ziegler, A. M., 1985, North American–Greenland–Eurasian relative motions; Implications for Circum-Arctic tectonic reconstructions: American Association of Petroleum Geologists Bulletin, v. 69, p. 303.

Shatsky, N. S., 1935, Tectonics of the Arctic, in Geologiya i poleznye iskopaemye Severa SSSR: Glavsevmorputi, v. 1, Geologiya, p. 149–168 (in Russian).

Shaver, R., and Hunkins, K., 1964, Arctic Ocean geophysical studies; Chukchi Cap and Chukchi Abyssal Plain: Deep-Sea Research, v. 11, p. 905–916.

Smith, D. G., 1987, Late Paleozoic to Cenozoic reconstructions of the Arctic, in Tailleur, I. L., and Weimer, P., eds., Alaskan North Slope geology: Los Angeles, Pacific Section, Society of Economic Paleontologists and Mineralogists, and Anchorage, Alaska Geological Society, p. 785–796.

Sobczak, L. W., 1975, Gravity and deep structure of the continental margin of Banks Island and Mackenzie Basin: Canadian Journal of Earth Science, v. 12, p. 378–394.

Somov, M. M., 1955, Observational data of the scientific research drifting station of 1950–1951: Leningrad, Moroskoy Transport, v. 1, sec. 4 (translated by D. Kraus, American Meteorological Society, Boston, ASTIA Document no. AD 117135, 59 p.

Stefansson, V., 1921, The friendly Arctic: New York, Macmillan, 784 p.

Stewart, I.C.F., 1980, Anomalous travel times of teleseismic P-waves reflected under Arctic marine areas: Marine Geophysical Researches, v. 4, p. 291–304.

Tailleur, I. L., 1969, Rifting speculation of the geology of Alaska's North Slope: Oil and Gas Journal, v. 67, no. 39, p. 128–130.

—— , 1972, Probable rift origin of Canada Basin, in Fitcher, M. G., ed., Arctic geology: American Association of Petroleum Geologists Memoir 19, p. 526–535.

Taylor, P. T., Kovacs, L. C., Vogt, P. R., and Johnson, G. L., 1981, Detailed aeromagnetic investigations of the Arctic Basin, 2: Journal of Geophysical Research, v. 86, p. 6323–6333.

Treshnikov, A. F., 1966, At the poles of the Earth: Moscow, Sovetskaya Rossiya Publishing House (translated from the Russian, Secretary of State Translation Bureau no. 123842, 30 p.).

Van Wagoner, N. A., and Robinson, P. T., 1985, Petrology and geochemistry of a CESAR bedrock sample; Implications for the origin of the Alpha Ridge: Geological Survey of Canada Paper 84-22, p. 47–77.

Vogt, P. R., Taylor, P. T., Kovacs, L. C., and Johnson, G. L., 1979, Detailed aeromagnetic investigations on the Arctic Basin: Journal of Geophysical Research, v. 84, p. 1071–1089.

Vogt, P. R., Kovacs, L. C., Bernero, C., and Srivastava, S. P., 1982, Asymmetric geophysical signatures in the Greenland-Norwegian and southern Labrador seas and the Eurasian Basin, in Johnson, G. L., and Sweeney, J. F., eds., Structure of the Arctic: Tectonophysics, v. 89, p. 95–160.

Weber, J. R., 1983, Maps of the Arctic Basin sea floor; A history of bathymetry and its interpretation: Arctic, v. 36, no. 2, p. 121–142.

Wold, R. J., 1973, Gravity surveys of the Arctic Ocean Basin. Final report, January, 1973: University of Wisconsin, Department of Geological Sciences, 222 p.

MANUSCRIPT ACCEPTED BY THE SOCIETY AUGUST 28, 1987

Chapter 23

Late Mesozoic and Cenozoic paleogeographic and paleoclimatic history of the Arctic Ocean Basin, based on shallow-water marine faunas and terrestrial vertebrates

Louie Marincovich, Jr.
Branch of Paleontology and Stratigraphy, U.S. Geological Survey, 345 Middlefield Road, Menlo Park, California 94025
Elisabeth M. Brouwers
Branch of Paleontology and Stratigraphy, U.S. Geological Survey, Box 25046, Denver Federal Center, Denver, Colorado 80225
David M. Hopkins
Department of Geology and Geophysics, University of Alaska, Fairbanks, Alaska 99701
Malcolm C. McKenna
Department of Vertebrate Paleontology, American Museum of Natural History, New York, New York 10024

INTRODUCTION

The paleogeography and marine paleoclimate of the Arctic Ocean Basin have evolved considerably during the past 100 million years, since the beginning of the Late Cretaceous. The shallow-water marine faunas that are needed to understand much of this history have recently been found, so that paleontologic studies of the Arctic Ocean Basin and its margins are presently in their early stages. The paleogeographic history of the Arctic Ocean may be divided conveniently into four intervals, each characterized by different marine connections to the world ocean. The first interval extended through most of the Mesozoic, when the Arctic Ocean was a northern gulf of the Pacific Ocean and subsequently developed seaway connections to other oceans. The second interval was during the Late Cretaceous and early Paleogene, when the Arctic Ocean was more or less completely isolated geographically from the world ocean. The third interval lasted from the late Paleogene to the middle Pliocene, during which the Arctic Ocean was connected to the Atlantic but not to the Pacific; and the fourth interval, lasting to the present day, was ushered in at about 3.0–3.5 Ma by the opening of the Bering Strait. The marine paleoclimate of the Arctic Ocean during the Late Cretaceous and early Tertiary was remarkably warm and equable until the onset of gradual cooling that culminated in late Neogene and Pleistocene ice cover.

BACKGROUND

Considerable progress has been made during the past decade in unraveling the geologic history of the Arctic Ocean Basin (Fig. 1), although most studies have had a tectonic, structural, or geophysical focus. These investigations, together with data obtained from the Deep Sea Drilling Program and other geologic studies in the North Atlantic, have greatly increased our understanding of the sequence, timing, and character of the major geologic events of the Mesozoic and Cenozoic that formed the Arctic Ocean Basin and the North Atlantic. The history and significance of major tectonic features of the Arctic Ocean Basin, such as the Lomonosov Ridge and Alpha Ridge, are now better known. However, although these geologic features are of utmost importance to understanding the geologic history of the Arctic Ocean Basin, they are deep sea features and of only secondary importance to the distribution of shallow-water marine faunas.

Until recently, little effort had been directed toward understanding the effects of major geologic events on the Arctic marine biota. Although data from middle-latitude biotas of Europe, Asia, and North America indicate that the Arctic region played a significant role as an avenue of dispersal for both terrestrial vertebrates (McKenna, 1975, 1980, 1983, 1984; Estes and Hutchison, 1980) and marine invertebrates (Durham and MacNeil, 1967; Strauch, 1972) at different times during the Cenozoic, few data were available from Arctic regions to support inferences about these biotic interchanges, especially between the Arctic Ocean and other oceans. Recent finds of well-preserved early Tertiary shallow-water marine mollusks and microfossils from the Arctic Ocean Basin (Fig. 2; Marincovich and others, 1983, 1984, 1985; Brouwers and others, 1984a; Marincovich and Zinsmeister, 1985) shed light on the geologic events and features along the

Marincovich, L., Jr., Brouwers, E. M., Hopkins, D. M., and McKenna, M. C., 1990, Late Mesozoic and Cenozoic paleogeographic and paleoclimatic history of the Arctic Ocean Basin, based on shallow-water marine faunas and terrestrial vertebrates, *in* Grantz, A., Johnson, L., and Sweeney, J. F., eds., The Arctic Ocean region: Boulder, Colorado, Geological Society of America, The Geology of North America, v. L.

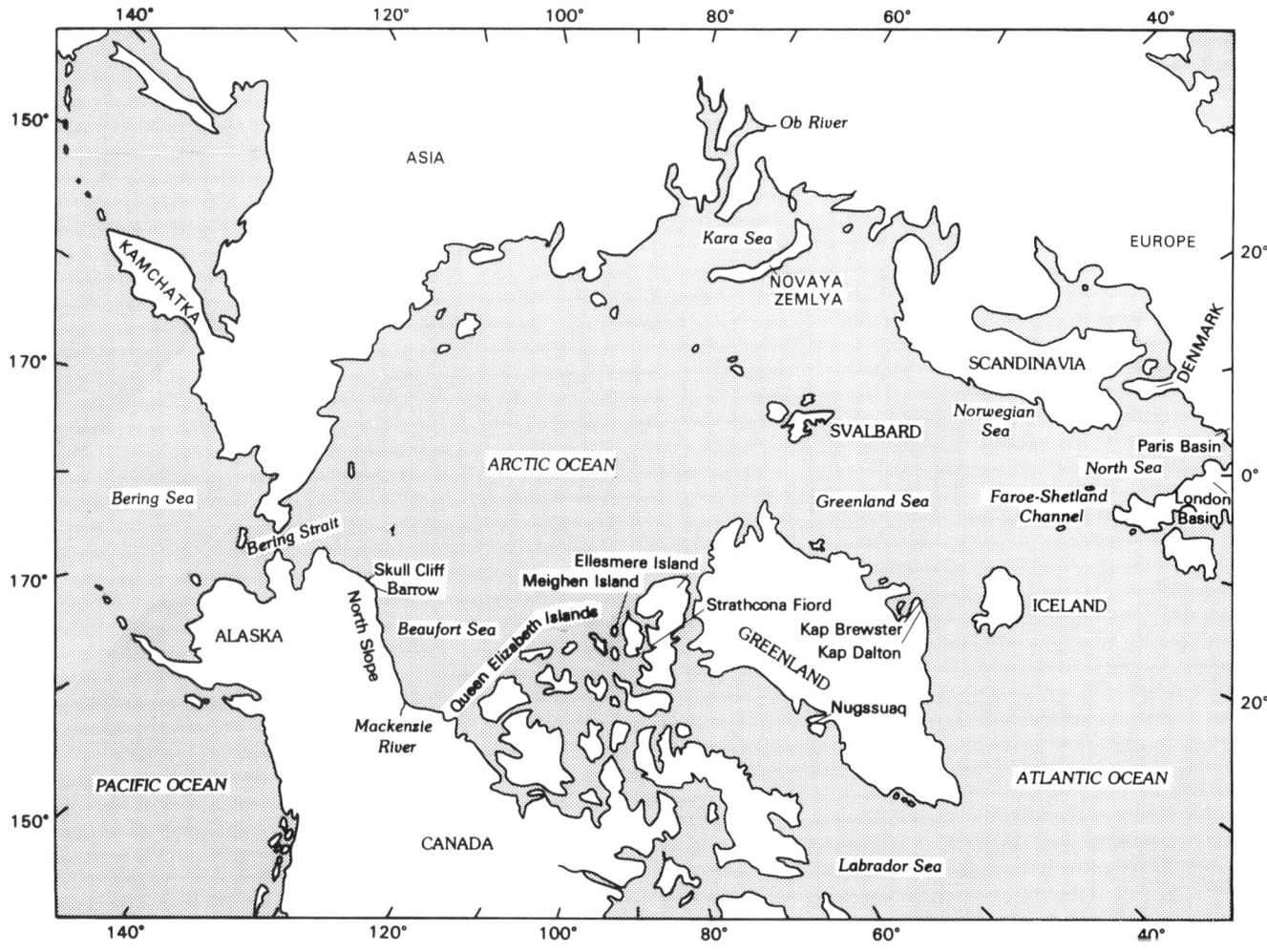

Figure 1. Location map of places mentioned in text.

Arctic Ocean Basin and North Atlantic margins that were important to the development and distribution of the faunas.

This chapter deals with Late Mesozoic and Cenozoic shallow-water marine faunas and terrestrial vertebrates, especially those occurring in outcrop sections along the Arctic Ocean margin. These faunas are few in number and occur at outcrops that are separated by large temporal and geographic gaps. Our discussion focuses on these isolated faunas and necessarily includes speculation in instances where the stratigraphic or faunal record is incomplete or missing. Genus- and species-level paleozoogeographic affinities of Arctic Ocean marine molluscan and ostracode faunas with approximately coeval faunas in northern mid-latitudes provide the main basis for our paleogeographic reconstructions. The data from the marine realm are supplemented by data on terrestrial vertebrate faunas (Dawson and others, 1976; West and others, 1977, 1981; McKenna, 1980; Estes and Hutchison, 1980). Where sufficient faunal data exist,

we infer the nature of Arctic Ocean paleoclimatic regimes at various time intervals.

THE MESOZOIC ARCTIC OCEAN: RESTRICTED CONNECTIONS TO THE WORLD OCEAN

The early Mesozoic

In Triassic time, an ocean basin occupied part of the site of the present-day Amerasian Basin and was joined to the Pacific (Fig. 3) by a broad seaway across northeastern Asia (Fujita and Newberry, 1982). This precursor of the modern Arctic Ocean thereby formed a northern embayment of the Pacific Ocean, whose Late Triassic shores are now delineated by the distribution (Fig. 3) of the distinctive bivalve *Monotis* (Westermann, 1964, 1973).

During the Jurassic and Early Cretaceous, microplates now

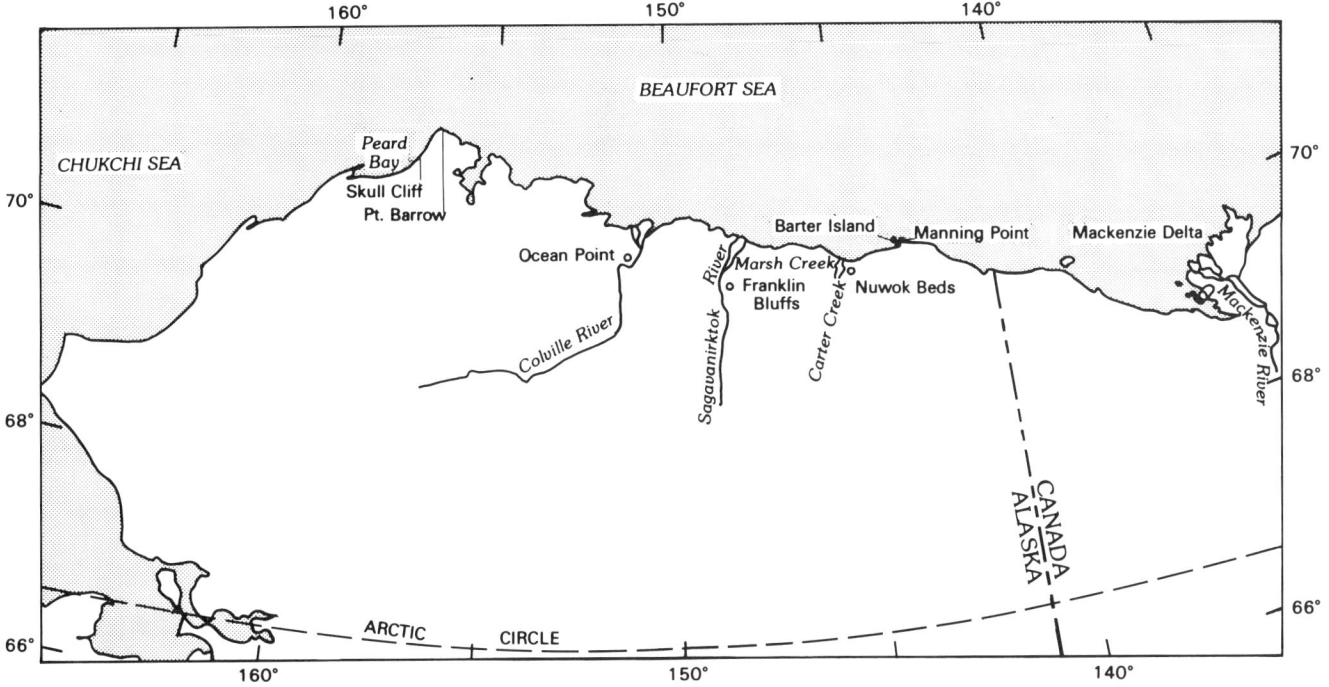

Figure 2. Location map of places in northeastern Alaska and northwestern Canada mentioned in text.

represented by the Siberian Prikolyma and Omolon massifs accreted to the Siberian shield (Fujita and Newberry, 1982). This combined land mass then converged upon arctic Alaska, gradually constricting the seaway between the ancestral Arctic Ocean and the North Pacific (Fig. 4). A later reconstruction by Fujita and Newberry (1983) suggests that no broad opening from the Arctic Ocean to the Pacific Ocean could have existed after the end of the Neocomian, about 125 Ma. However, more limited seaways were at least occasionally present. For example, the co-occurrence of North Pacific and Arctic Ocean ammonites in late early Albian faunas of southern Alaska is evidence for a Pacific-Arctic connection about 110 to 105 Ma (Williams and Stelck, 1975). The time at which shallow-water Pacific-Arctic connections ceased is not known with certainty, because of a lack of appropriate fossil evidence, but is thought to have been before the end of the Cretaceous (Lillegraven and McKenna, 1986).

Western Interior Seaway

Although lacking a broad connection with the Pacific Ocean after the mid-Albian, the Arctic Ocean remained in contact with the world ocean through two epicontinental seaways (Fig. 4): the Western Interior Seaway in North America, and Turgai Strait in western Siberia. Sporadically during the late Albian and continuously from the Cenomanian through the early Maastrichtian, the Western Interior Seaway connected the Arctic Ocean with the tropical to subtropical Gulf of Mexico (Williams and Stelck, 1975; Balkwill and others, 1983). This connection is shown by strong Gulf of Mexico affinities of the Late Cretaceous marine microfaunas of arctic North America (Tappan, 1962; Bergquist, 1966). The Western Interior Seaway was closed by the late Maastrichtian (Williams and Stelck, 1975), as a result of a major drop in eustatic sea level (Vail and others, 1977; Matthews, 1984) and of active tectonism in the rising Rocky Mountain region that caused sedimentary infilling of the seaway from the west.

The Western Interior Seaway extended some 7,000 km from the Arctic Ocean to the Gulf of Mexico and was of variable but substantial width and depth for most of its existence (Fig. 4). However, this seaway sometimes contained barriers to marine faunal dispersal in the form of increased or decreased salinity, increased temperature, and reduced oxygen content. Marked deviations from normal salinity conditions affected the shelf regions, as indicated by the poor representation of normal marine groups such as echinoderms, corals, bryozoans, sponges, brachiopods, planktonic foraminifers, and radiolarians. There is well-documented faunal and lithologic evidence for shoaling and increasingly brackish environments upsection in the Maastrichtian Fox Hills Formation of South Dakota (Waage, 1968; Speden, 1970), indicating that water depth and salinity were barriers to marine dispersal during the later stages of the seaway's existence. However, the Fox Hills Formation still contains some bivalves and cephalopods clearly related to faunas of the Gulf and Atlantic Coastal Province some 2,000 km to the south (Waage, 1968; Speden, 1970).

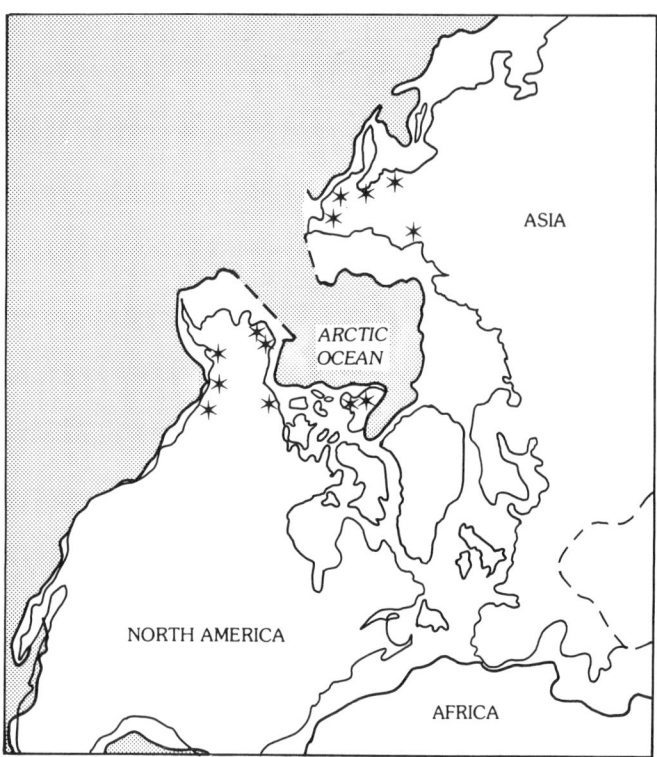

Figure 3. Paleogeographic reconstruction of the Arctic Ocean in the Late Triassic. Stars indicate occurrences of the marine bivalve *Monotis*, after Westermann (1973). Paleocontinental outlines after Smith and Briden (1977).

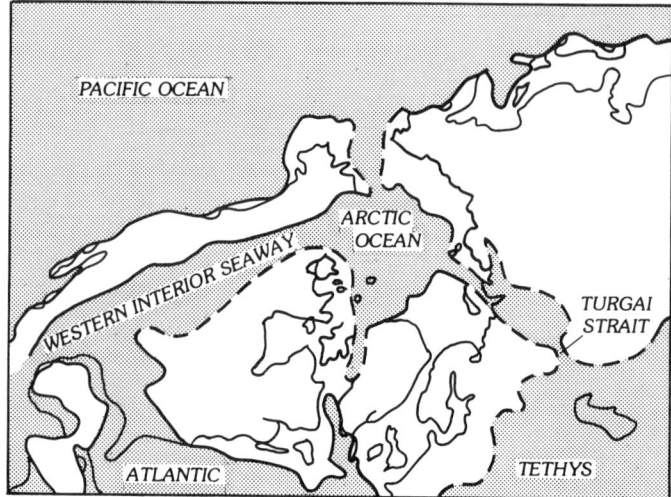

Figure 4. Paleogeographic reconstruction of the Arctic Ocean in the Late Cretaceous, just prior to sealing of the Pacific–Arctic Ocean connection, showing seaway connections to the world ocean (stippled). Adapted from Smith and Briden (1977), Sohl (1971), and Vinogradov and others (1968).

The close similarity between Late Cretaceous ammonite faunas of the Western Interior Seaway and of central West Greenland (Birkelund, 1965) indicates that an arm of the Arctic Ocean extended into the present-day Baffin Bay region (Balkwill and others, 1983) but possibly not much farther south of there. If it did, the southern connection probably did not survive very long into the Tertiary. As noted below, there are profound differences between Paleocene molluscan faunas of central West Greenland and the Arctic Ocean, which suggests that in Paleocene time there was a land barrier between the Arctic Ocean and the warm waters indicated by the marine deposits of central West Greenland.

Global climate during the Cretaceous was significantly warmer and more uniform than today, with less seasonality and a greatly reduced marine temperature gradient between deep and shallow water and between the equator and the poles. Consequently, marine climatic provinces, as defined by faunal distributions, were fewer in number, broader in geographic extent, and more enduring, with gradational boundaries between provinces (Kauffman, 1975). The northern polar oceanic areas (including northern Alaska, Ellesmere Island, and Svalbard) are believed to have had a mild- to cold-temperature marine climate and to have endured lowered light levels in winter. Kauffman (1975) provided a reconstruction of the major Cretaceous current systems of the world based on molluscan distributions and their larval dispersal patterns. He proposed a major circumpolar current system that flowed eastward along the northern continental shelf of North America, around northern Greenland, and across northern Europe to Russia (Fig. 5), with strong south-flowing offshoots entering the Western Interior Seaway and northern Europe. This model is accepted herein, even though it contrasts with that of Fairbridge (1966), who postulated clockwise motion of both shallow- and deep-water Arctic Ocean currents based upon more generalized data.

Water circulation within the Western Interior Seaway was more complex than that of the Arctic Ocean, because the seaway had constricted northern and southern openings that probably had major inflowing current systems. The southern entrance was dominated by a warm proto–Gulf Stream, while the northern entrance was influenced by the incursion of a mild- to cold-temperate circumpolar current. The interplay of currents in the Cretaceous Western Interior Seaway resulted in a complex stratigraphic record with rich biotas containing a mixture of northern cool-water and southern warm-water Cretaceous taxa (Obradovich and Cobban, 1975).

New data on the Late Cretaceous terrestrial climate of northern Alaska are provided by the recent discovery along the Colville River in northeastern Alaska of an abundant dinosaur bone deposit believed to be of Campanian or Maastrichtian age (Davies, 1987; Brouwers and others, 1987). The bone-bearing

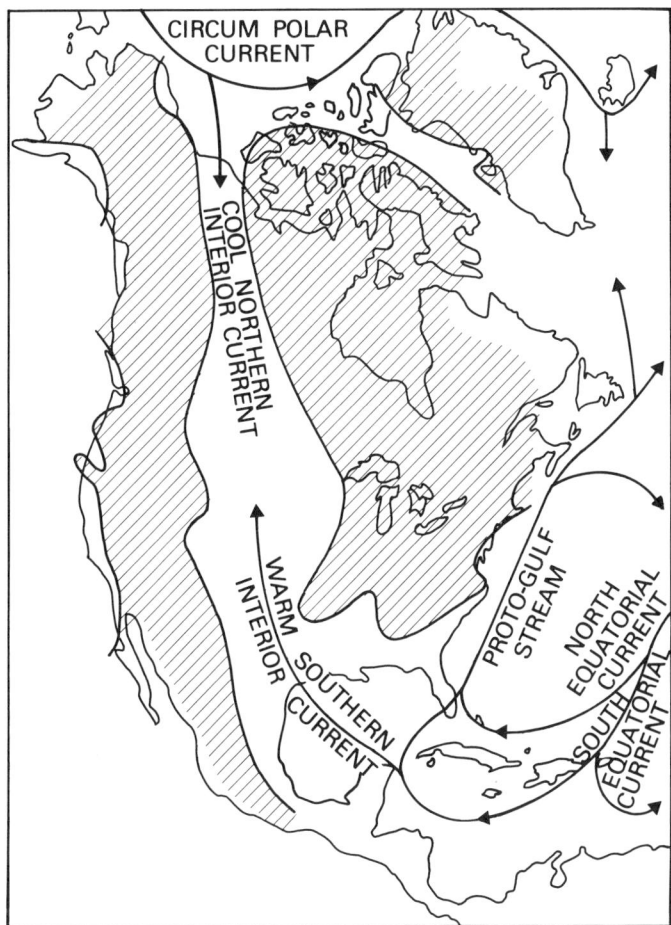

Figure 5. Inferred paleocurrents in the Western Interior Seaway, the North Atlantic, and the Arctic Ocean during the Late Cretaceous, after Kauffman (1975). Paleocontinental outlines after Obradovich and Cobban (1975).

deposit is within the upper part of the Prince Creek Formation in the vicinity of Ocean Point and is less than 200 m stratigraphically below the late Paleocene marine fauna near Ocean Point that is discussed at length below. It consists of carbonaceous siltstone with limestone concretions, both lithologies containing fluvial ostracode and charophyte assemblages. The bone beds contain mainly hadrosaurs (duck bills) but also tyrannosaurids and troodontids, both carnivorous dinosaurs. A fluvial-deltaic environment is indicated by an immediately underlying assemblage of marginal marine arenaceous benthic foraminifers (Brouwers and others, 1987) and by overlying organic-rich nonmarine sands and silts. The presence of such an abundant assemblage of several large reptiles in high paleolatitudes (70°–80° N.) near the end of the Cretaceous provides minimum-temperature constraints on the environment at that time. Because large reptiles presumably could not reproduce in a regime involv-

ing prolonged periods of freezing, their presence, if it were continuous, implies a terrestrial climate that was mild temperate or warmer. In addition, megafloral and palynological data indicate a diverse deciduous coniferous flora that implies no prolonged freezing (Brouwers and others, 1987).

Turgai Strait

In contrast to the environmental barrier of the Western Interior Seaway of North America, Turgai Strait in western Asia was a physical barrier alternately to marine and terrestrial migrations, because this seaway was not continuously present. Beginning in the late Jurassic and for much of Cretaceous and Paleogene time, Turgai Strait extended across western Siberia from the vicinity of the present Aral Sea northward to the area of the modern Kara Sea (Fig. 4), providing a connection between the Arctic Ocean and Tethyan faunal realms (Vinogradov and others, 1967, 1968; Beznosov and others, 1978). It has been suggested, based on the distribution and character of marine sediments, that Turgai Strait was fully open throughout the Late Cretaceous (Vinogradov and others, 1968; Beznosov and others, 1978) but not fully and consistently open during the Paleogene. The Turgai Strait area has been described as a coastal plain that was intermittently flooded by the sea during the Paleocene but was more openly and persistently marine during the Eocene until its closure by marine regression in the late Eocene or Oligocene (Vinogradov and others, 1967). During the Paleocene, Turgai Strait was at times as little as 120 km wide and thus was the narrowest part of a seaway some 5,000 km long (Vinogradov and others, 1967). Because of its intermittent nature, this strait was at times a barrier to north-south dispersals of marine species, just as it was a barrier, when present, to east-west exchanges of terrestrial animals (McKenna, 1975, 1983, 1984). Gradients in temperature, salinity, and oxygen content, although not yet documented, probably also hampered marine dispersals just as they did in the Western Interior Seaway. Turgai Strait Paleogene deposits are entirely subsurface, and no mollusks are known from them. There are no faunal similarities between Paleogene megafaunas now known from the Arctic Ocean realm and those from the Tethyan realm at the southern terminus of Turgai Strait (Marincovich and others, 1985). However, there is at least genus-level similarity between several Paleogene marine ostracodes of the Prince Creek Formation of northern Alaska (Marincovich and others, 1985) and ostracodes in deposits at the northern part of the Turgai Strait region (Khokhlova, 1968; Nikolaeva, 1977) (Fig. 6).

Paleogene ostracode faunas described from the northern Turgai Depression by Khokhlova (1968) are dominated by taxa that are holdovers from Late Paleozoic and Early Mesozoic faunas and include genera in groups such as cytherellids, healdiids, cytherids, bairdiids, and cyprids, which indicate a warm, shallow-water environment. The assemblage also contains some early Cenozoic genera such as *Leptocythere, Paijenborchella, Cytheropteron,* and *Trachyleberis*. The late Paleocene Ocean Point fauna of northern Alaska, discussed at length below, has a 4 percent

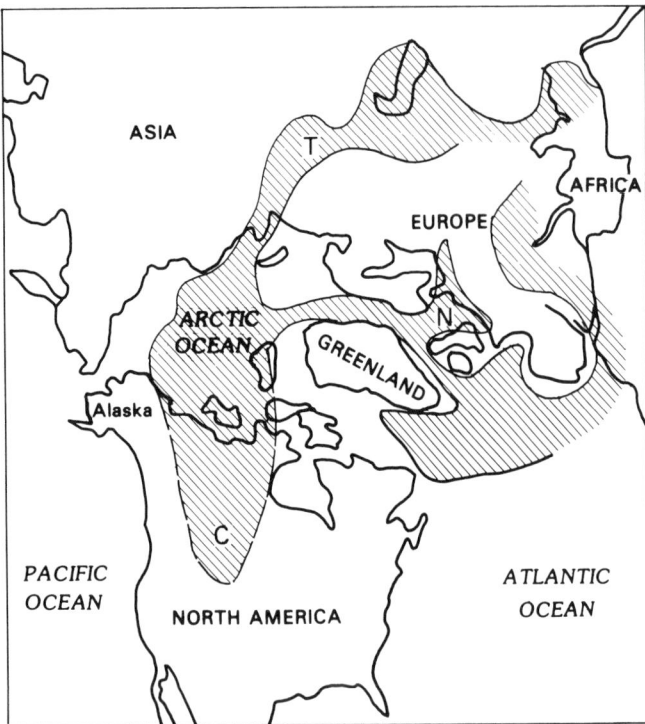

Figure 6. Paleogeographic reconstruction of the Arctic Ocean in the Paleocene, showing restricted connection to the world ocean and an embayment extending into North America. The narrow seaway joining the North Sea Basin with the North Atlantic was blocked at times, especially during part of the Thanetian, by the proto-Iceland volcanic pile. C = Cannonball Formation of North and South Dakota; N = North Sea Basin; T = Turgai Strait. From Marincovich and others (1985).

similarity to the Turgai Province (Fig. 7), with only the genus *Loxoconcha* in common. However, several genera reported by Russian workers to be endemic to the Turgai deposits have ornament morphologies similar to—and perhaps identical to— genera from Ocean Point (based upon illustrations of taxa in Russian publications, for lack of Turgai Strait specimens to examine). Such Turgai Strait genera (and their Ocean Point equivalents) include *Lutkevichinella* (similar to *Patellacythere*), *Paijenborchella* (similar to *Brachycythere*) and *Bakunella* (similar to *Paracypris*). Nikolaeva (1977) described a northern Turgai assemblage that is lower in species diversity but without the unusual Paleozoic holdovers found by Khokhlova. Nikolaeva (1977) also recorded the presence of three taxa (*Bythocypris, Phacorhabdotus,* and *Aulocytheridea*) that occur commonly in upper Cretaceous and lower Tertiary sediments in Europe and the U.S. Gulf Coast.

THE LATEST CRETACEOUS AND PALEOGENE ARCTIC OCEAN: ISOLATION

The Arctic Ocean is thought to have been almost completely isolated from the world ocean during the early Paleogene (Marincovich and others, 1985). The Western Interior Seaway had disappeared in the late Maastrichtian, owing to marine regression and tectonic activity of the Laramide Orogeny. The only two early Paleogene marine connections with the Arctic Ocean were the intermittent seaway of Turgai Strait in western Siberia, which had persisted from the Cretaceous, and an intermittent seaway that extended to the North Sea Basin of northwestern Europe (Brouwers and others, 1984a; Marincovich and others, 1985) (Fig. 6). The exact times in the Paleogene during which these two seaways were submerged or emergent are not known from marine invertebrates. One or both seaways may have been open or closed at a given time, but both were evidently intermittent and shallow and therefore provided a substantial degree of isolation for the arctic marine realm (Hopkins and Marincovich, 1984).

The northern end of the North Sea Basin in turn had a substantial though probably intermittent connection with the Labrador Sea by way of the North Atlantic until the latter half of the Paleocene. The presence of identical species of marine mollusks (Rosenkrantz and Pulvertaft, 1969; Rosenkrantz, 1970; Kollmann and Peel, 1983), ostracodes (Szczechura, 1971), coccoliths (Perch-Nielsen, 1973), planktonic and benthic foraminifers (Hansen, 1970), corals (Floris, 1972), and fishes (Bendix-Almgren, 1969) at Nûgssuaq, West Greenland (i.e., the Labrador Sea) (Fig. 1) and at many sites in the North Sea Basin demonstrates a direct marine connection during both the early and late Danian. However, this connection did not persist throughout the entire Paleocene. The likelihood that this North Sea–Labrador Sea connection was intermittent is supported by geologic and vertebrate paleontologic evidence that proto-Iceland began to form and blocked the way in the late Paleocene (Grønlie, 1979; McKenna, 1983, 1984). During the Thanetian and earliest Ypresian, there was a broad and substantial land connection across the Atlantic that permitted European and North American terrestrial biotas to mingle freely (McKenna, 1984). This barrier separated the North Sea Basin from the Atlantic.

An Arctic Ocean–North Sea Basin seaway is indicated by the presence in arctic marine faunas of mollusks and ostracodes previously known only in post-Danian Paleocene (Thanetian) to early Eocene (Ypresian) North Sea Basin faunas (Brouwers and others, 1984a; Marincovich and others, 1985). This Paleocene or Eocene seaway probably existed only during times of high sea level; it would have prevented the interchange of terrestrial vertebrates between Scandinavia and North America via Svalbard and northern Greenland, while still allowing terrestrial migrations by way of Iceland and Scotland in Thanetian to early Ypresian time. Low sea-level stands would have exposed land bridges and permitted dispersals of terrestrial animals. The proto-Iceland volcanic pile closed the Atlantic–Greenland Sea marine corridor for a while during this interval (Grønlie, 1979). A land bridge connecting North America with Europe south of Scandinavia, isolating the Arctic Ocean and North Sea Basin from the North Atlantic, must have existed as an unbroken barrier during only a short interval at the very end of Paleocene and beginning of

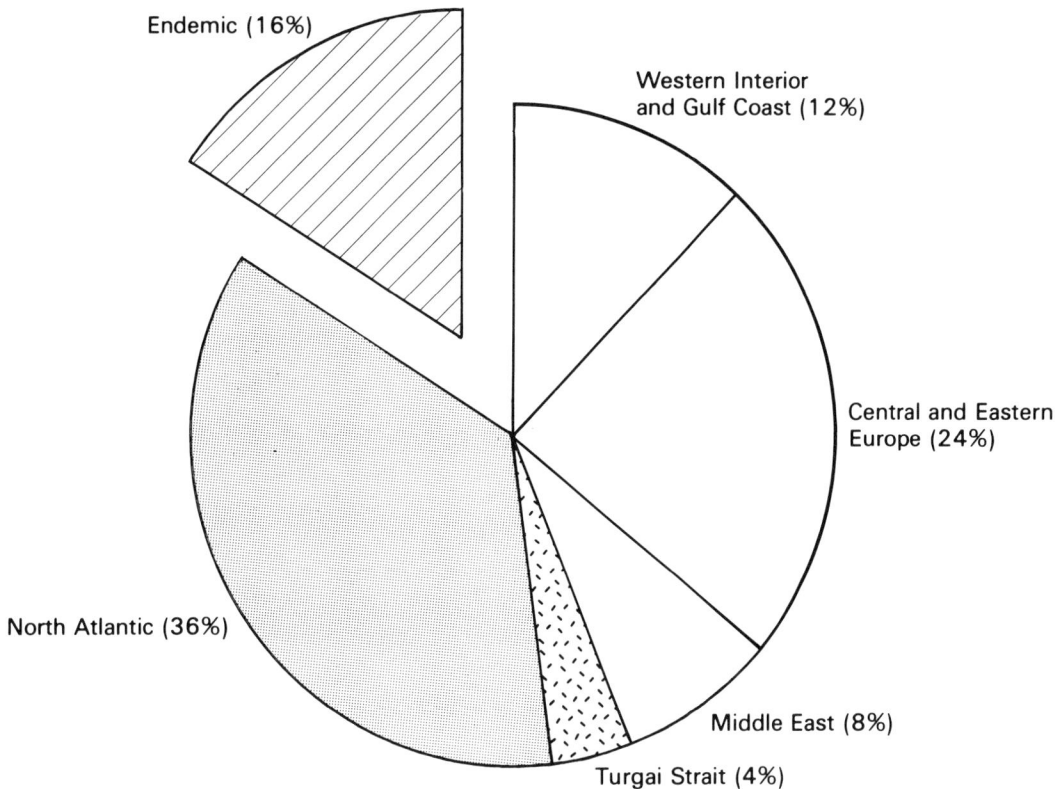

Figure 7. Percent similarity at the genus level of the Ocean Point ostracode assemblage and Paleogene provinces of the Northern Hemisphere. The most similar faunal provinces are the mild- to cold-temperate North Atlantic province (including Greenland, Denmark, the London Basin, and Germany) and the subtropical central and eastern European province (including the Paris Basin, Poland, Turkey, and Belgium). Endemic Arctic Ocean genera make up 16 percent of the Ocean Point assemblage. Genera with affinities to the Western Interior and Gulf Coast province comprise 12 percent of the Ocean Point assemblage. Tropical Middle Eastern and subtropical to temperate Turgai Strait faunas make up the remainder (12 percent) of the assemblage.

Eocene time, based on comparisons of late Paleocene and early Eocene (Ypresian) terrestrial vertebrates (McKenna, 1975, 1983, 1984). The great similarity of North American and European terrestrial vertebrate faunas (south of the inundated Danish-Polish corridor) only during the late Paleocene and early Eocene indicates a short interruption of this increasingly persistent marine corridor as the opening of the North Atlantic progressed.

It is important to keep in mind that the Late Cretaceous and Tertiary marine biotas of the Arctic Ocean are known from exposures representing only very short periods of geologic time. Only three known stratigraphic sequences contain well-preserved shallow-water marine faunas that are thought to have lived in the early Tertiary Arctic Ocean: (1) strata in the upper part of the Prince Creek Formation near Ocean Point, northern Alaska (70°04′N., 151°22′W.); (2) "Member III" (Mount Moore Formation) of the Eureka Sound Group at Strathcona Fiord, Ellesmere Island (78°45′N., 82°30′W.); and (3) the Cannonball Formation (in the sense of Cvancara, 1966) of North and South Dakota (46°N., 102°W.). Marine faunas occur elsewhere in the Eureka Sound Group of the Queen Elizabeth Islands, in arctic Canada, (Miall, 1981; Marincovich and Zinsmeister, 1985) but remain largely unstudied. Relatively sparse early Tertiary molluscan and microfossil faunas of Paleocene or Eocene (Danian to Ypresian) age also occur on Svalbard and in East Greenland, as noted below.

Marine strata near Ocean Point, northern Alaska

Marine mollusks and ostracodes in northern Alaska provided the first evidence for an early Tertiary Arctic Ocean–North

TABLE 1. MOLLUSKS FROM OCEAN POINT, NORTHERN ALASKA

Bivalves:

Arctica	Integricardium
Argyromya	Lahillia?
Chlamys	Neilo
Corbula (Bicorbula)	Neilonella
Crenella	Nucula (Nucula)
Cyrtodaria rutupiensis (Morris, 1852)	Oxytoma (Hypoxytoma)
	"Pecten"
Cyrtodaria n. sp.	Tancredia
Eburneopecten?	Tellinimera
Gari (Garum)	Yoldia

Gastropods:

Amauropsis	Cylichna
Buccinidae?	Genus indeterminate

TABLE 2. OSTRACODES FROM OCEAN POINT, NORTHERN ALASKA

Brachycythere spp.	Loxoconcha spp.
Bythoceratina spp.	Paracyprideis spp.
Crassacythere spp.	"Paracyprideis" spp.
Cytheridea spp.	"Paracyprideis" similis Triebel, 1941
Cytheromorpha spp.	
Cytherura sp.	Paracypris spp.
Eucythere sp.	"Paradoxostoma" sp.
Eucytheridea sp.	Patellacythere sp.
"Eucytheridea" spp.	"Roundstonia" sp.
Haplocytheridea spp.	Sarsicytheridea sp.
"Haplocytheridea" sp.	Schuleridea sp.
"Heterocyprideis" sp.	

Sea Basin connection (Brouwers and others, 1984a; Marincovich and others, 1983, 1985). Strata within the upper part of the Prince Creek Formation near Ocean Point (Fig. 2) contain the only diverse early Tertiary shallow-water marine biota known from northern Alaska. The mollusks, ostracodes, benthic foraminifers, brachiopods, bryozoans, and palynomorphs in this association also make up the most diverse early Tertiary marine biota yet known from the Arctic Ocean Basin. Mollusks (Table 1) and ostracodes (Table 2) indicate a post-Danian Paleocene to early Eocene (Thanetian to Ypresian) age for these beds (Fig. 8) and suggest correlation not only with faunas of the North Sea Basin, as noted above, but also with faunas of the Eureka Sound Group on Ellesmere Island, Canada (Marincovich and Zinsmeister, 1985). The cool-temperate Ocean Point molluscan fauna also has genus-level affinities with the similarly cool-temperate Danian fauna of the Cannonball Formation of North and South Dakota but lacks similar ties to the subtropical Danian molluscan fauna of West Greenland.

The lower Tertiary beds near Ocean Point are about 20 m thick and consist of nearly unconsolidated sandstone and more abundant, weakly consolidated shaley siltstone (Fig. 9). In addition to the paleontological evidence for shallow-water conditions, the presence of numerous carbonaceous laminae throughout these deposits implies a shallow, nearshore site of deposition. These beds dip 1° to 3° to the northeast, form bluffs along the Colville River that extend from near Ocean Point northwestward for 2.3 km (Fig. 2), and are assigned to the Prince Creek Formation (Brosgé and Whittington, 1966; Marincovich and others, 1985). These Paleogene beds also have been referred to as "unnamed marine deposits" within the Sagavanirktok Formation (Carter and Galloway, 1985), which is of Tertiary age and has its principal outcrop area well to the east of Ocean Point (Detterman and others, 1975). The Prince Creek and Sagavanirktok Formations both contain marine and nonmarine sediments, and the contact between the formations is conformable and apparently gradational (Detterman and others, 1975, p. 38). Because the Ocean Point outcrop lies within the areal extent of the Prince Creek Formation, these Paleogene strata are referred to herein as part of the Prince Creek Formation. The Ocean Point Paleogene strata are unconformably overlain by upper Pliocene marine sediments of the Gubik Formation (Repenning, 1983; Carter and Galloway, 1985). Several horizons containing abundant dinosaur bones, noted earlier, are less than 200 m stratigraphically below the early Tertiary Ocean Point marine beds (R. L. Phillips, E. M. Brouwers, and L. Marincovich, Jr., unpublished field data, 1986).

Recognition of the early Tertiary age and biogeographic affinities of the Ocean Point fauna has placed it within the context of the paleogeographic-tectonic events that caused the early Tertiary interactions of the North Atlantic Ocean, the Norwegian-Greenland Sea/North Sea Basin, and the Arctic Ocean. Benthic foraminifers from the Ocean Point marine deposits have been studied by Macbeth and Schmidt (1973), who assigned them a late Campanian age that now requires confirmation; the foraminifers are currently being restudied by W. V. Sliter (personal communication, 1987). The degree to which reworking might have affected the presence and composition of the benthic foraminifer fauna is not yet known.

Palynomorphs from the Ocean Point marine beds provide a variety of ages. Dinoflagellate floras of Jurassic, early Late Cretaceous, and Campanian to Maastrichtian ages occur together with pollen and spores of Berriasian to Turonian and probable Maastrichtian age, according to the studies of different workers (summarized in Marincovich and others, 1985). The mixture of ages suggests that significant reworking has occurred among the palynomorphs within these sediments. In fact, large-scale reworking, as evidenced by features ranging from Cretaceous river channels to Paleocene storm-wave deposits, has clearly taken place in this stratigraphic sequence (R. L. Phillips, E. M. Brouwers, and L. Marincovich, Jr., unpublished field data, 1986). No exclusively Paleocene palynomorphs are known from the Ocean Point beds,

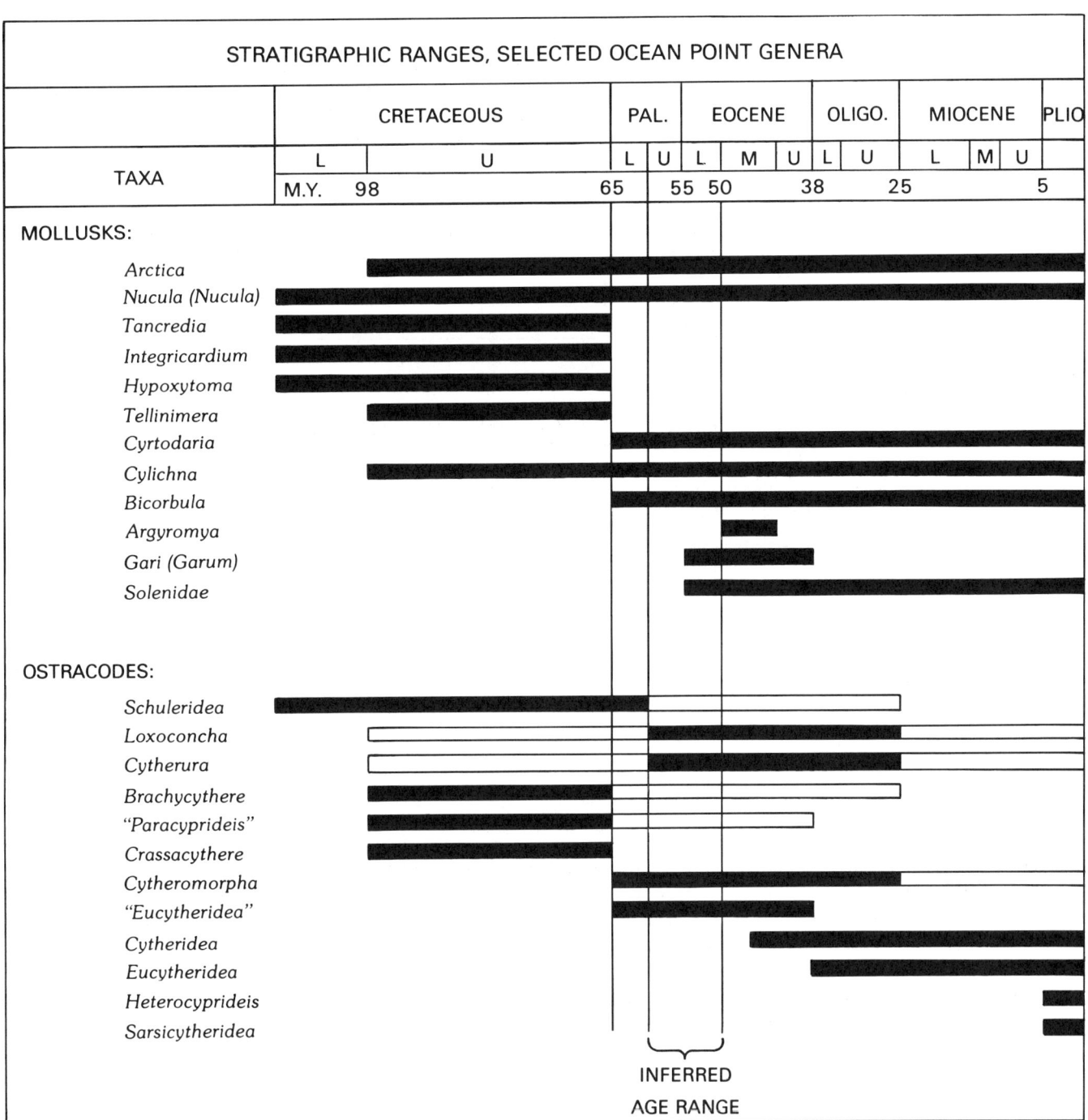

Figure 8. Stratigraphic ranges and inferred age of selected molluscan and ostracode genera from Ocean Point, northern Alaska. Modified from Marincovich and others (1985).

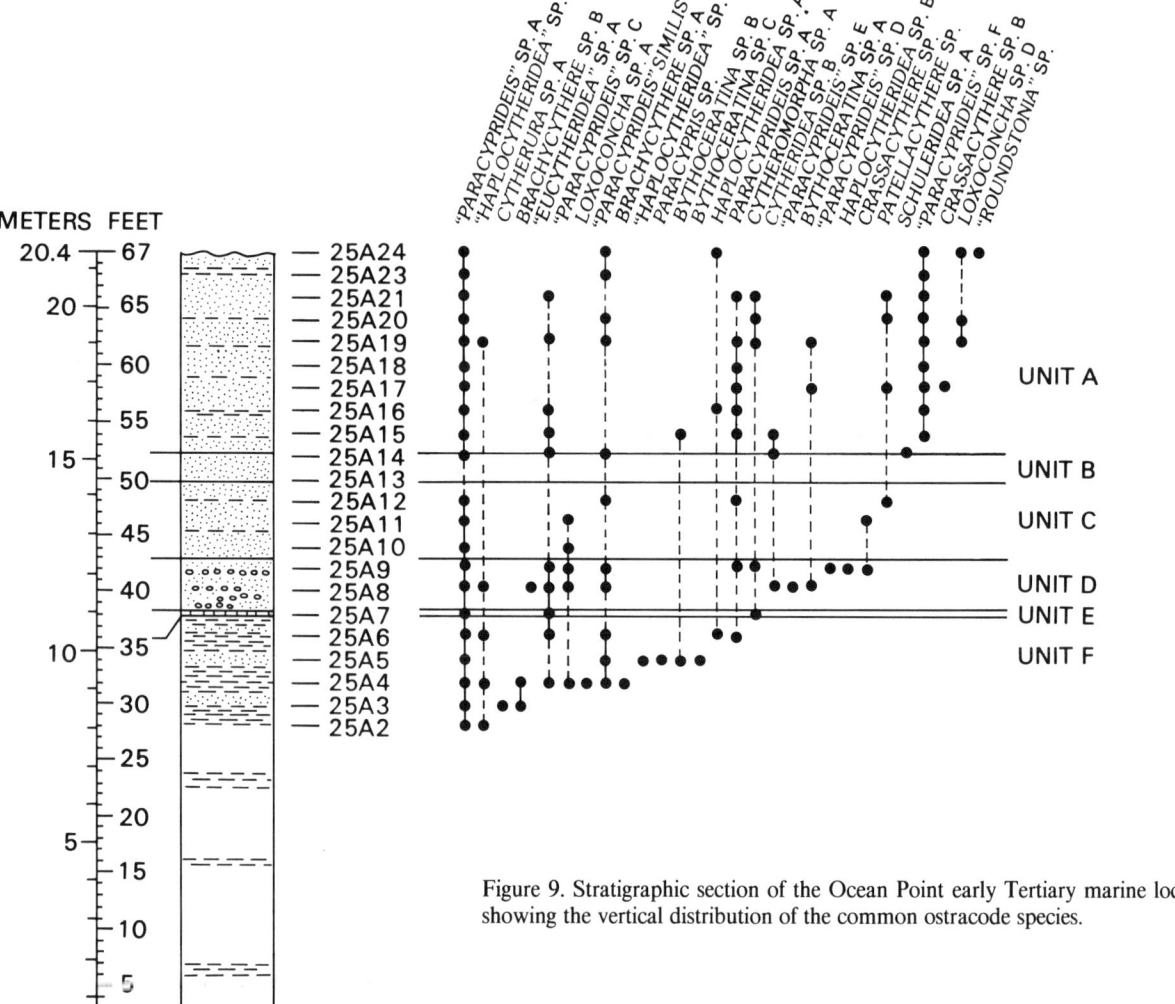

Figure 9. Stratigraphic section of the Ocean Point early Tertiary marine locality, showing the vertical distribution of the common ostracode species.

although taxa ranging into the Paleocene are present (Frederiksen and others, 1985, 1986). These palynological data seem to eliminate a possible early Eocene age for the Ocean Point beds. Further evaluation of Ocean Point palynological ages must take into account convincing evidence that major floral groups of the Cretaceous and early Tertiary appeared later in Alaska than in lower latitudes (Spicer and others, 1987). Considered together with the marine faunal data, palynological evidence narrows the most likely age range of the Ocean Point beds to post-Danian Paleocene. We note below the strong evidence against reworking of most of the mollusk shells and ostracodes at Ocean Point.

Twenty-three species of mollusks and 44 species of ostracodes are known in this marine fauna (Tables 1 and 2), with only one described species from each group known in faunas elsewhere. This strongly endemic composition is inferred to be the result of geographic isolation of the Arctic Ocean Basin lasting from about the end of the Cretaceous to sometime in the Eocene. The bivalve *Cyrtodaria rutupiensis* (Morris, 1852) is known from upper Paleocene and lower Eocene (Thanetian and Ypresian) strata of the London Basin and from approximately coeval strata on Svalbard (Strauch, 1972). Similarly, the ostracode *"Paracyprideis" similis* Triebel, 1941, is known from upper Paleocene and lower Eocene (lower Thanetian to lower Ypresian) strata of the London Basin and Denmark (Keen, 1978).

The age data for the mollusks and ostracodes of the Ocean Point beds further support the concept of an isolated Paleogene Arctic Ocean (Brouwers and others, 1984a; Marincovich and others, 1983, 1985). Marine taxa that have well-documented, exclusively Mesozoic or Cenozoic ages in middle latitude faunas occur in a life assemblage at Ocean Point and include "Cretaceous" and "Paleogene" mollusks and ostracodes and "Neogene" ostracodes (Fig. 8). Their excellent preservation is strong evidence that at least the mollusks of this deposit represent a biocoenosis. "Mesozoic" bivalves such as *Integricardium, Tancredia,* and *Tellinimera* and "Cenozoic" bivalves such as *Argyromya, Cyrtodaria,* and *Gari (Garum)* occur commonly together in inferred living positions, with closed and articulated valves in parallel alignment approximately normal to bedding. Valves of the pectinid *Eburneopecten*? are commonly found articulated and closed and lying parallel to bedding. Many bivalves show well-preserved fine shell sculpture, intact periostraca, and even remnants of ligaments. The lack of abrasion and breakage is especially noteworthy among very fragile shells such as *Hypoxytoma* and *Amauropsis*. There are no known mollusk-bearing Upper Cretaceous marine deposits in the vicinity of Ocean Point from which mollusks preserved like these could have been reworked. Cosmopolitan Mesozoic mollusks such as ammonites and Inoceramidae are conspicuously absent.

Low molluscan species diversity (15 to 30 species) characterizes Arctic Ocean Paleocene faunas of the Eureka Sound Group on Ellesmere Island, the Cannonball Formation of North and South Dakota, and Paleogene formations on Svalbard. In contrast, the Danian warm-water molluscan fauna of central West Greenland consists of several hundred species (Rosenkrantz, 1970; Kollmann and Peel, 1983). This difference in diversity might be due to environmental barriers, geographic separation between the localities, or some combination of each. The central West Greenland Danian deposits are situated farther north than the London Basin Thanetian deposits, but the Greenland site was connected to warmer Atlantic and Tethyan waters and therefore represents a much warmer marine environment. The Paleocene, even though it was cooler than the Cretaceous, is thought to have been a relatively warm period throughout, so it is likely that the difference in species diversity reflects geographically separate faunal provinces rather than parts of a contiguous marine realm.

Ostracode genera characteristic of three ages elsewhere are present at Ocean Point and therefore show a greater degree of age disparity than do the mollusks (Fig. 8). Among these ostracodes, with age ranges based upon occurrences in other (i.e., lower latitude) regions, are Cretaceous to early Paleocene taxa such as *Crassacythere* and *Brachycythere;* late Paleocene-Oligocene taxa such as *"Eucytheridea," Cytheromorpha,* and *"Paracyprideis";* and Neogene to Quaternary taxa such as *Sarsicytheridea, "Roundstonia," "Heterocyprideis", Paracyprideis,* and *Eucytheridea.* Genera such as *Loxoconcha, Cytherura,* and *Cytheromorpha* have long stratigraphic ranges, but each displays distinctive morphologic trends through time that are suggestive of a general age range (Fig. 8; Morkhoven, 1963; E. Brouwers, personal observations). *Loxoconcha,* for example, has three morphotypes: a small, laterally compressed, generally reticulate morphotype known only in Late Cretaceous to earliest Paleocene faunas (illustrated in Howe and Laurencich, 1958; Hazel, 1968); a slightly larger, more inflated morphotype with more varied ornamentation, which is known only in Paleogene faunas including Ocean Point (Keen, 1978); and a large, inflated, elongate-quadrate morphotype with a broad range of strong ornamentation, which is reported only in Neogene faunas (Morkhoven, 1963). *Loxoconcha, Cytherura, Cytheromorpha,* and *Brachycythere* are represented at Ocean Point by morphotypes that are elsewhere characteristic of the Paleogene.

The Ocean Point ostracode assemblage represents a thanatocoenosis, based on the skewed, nonlife proportion of juveniles to adults. However, the abundance and diversity of individuals, the excellent preservation of very fine ornament features, a preservation state of mostly intact carapaces with few broken valves and fragments, and the presence of very early instars of the more common species are evidence against major reworking of the ostracodes (Marincovich and others, 1985).

Paleocene to Eocene ostracode faunas of Europe can be divided into several provinces and subprovinces: the northern shore of Tethys, including a northern offshoot in the Aquitaine Basin; the North Sea Basin, with southern extensions in England, Belgium, and the Paris Basin; and a boreal province, extending from Germany to Russia (Keen, 1983). Limited communication between these different provinces existed at various times in the Paleogene (Keen, 1983). The Ocean Point assemblage shows similarities to both the North Sea Basin province and the boreal province. The North Sea Basin province and the Ocean Point assemblage are dominated by smooth to punctate cytherideid genera, which are typical of shallow water conditions, especially where stressed or fluctuating physical-chemical environmental factors prevail. Those cytherideid genera that are present in the Ocean Point fauna imply a mild- to cold-temperate marine environment and inner to middle sublittoral water depths.

Gulf Coast Paleocene to Eocene assemblages show a slight similarity to the Ocean Point ostracode fauna, with three genera in common (Fig. 7). The Gulf Coast province is also dominated by shallow-water cytherideids but additionally contains large numbers of hemicytherids and trachyleberids and some buntoniids that occur in deeper inner sublittoral to middle sublittoral water depths. The environment can be characterized as subtropical to tropical, with generally slightly deeper water than at Ocean Point.

Coeval Tethyan ostracodes show essentially no similarity to those from Ocean Point. Tethyan assemblages are dominated by tropical taxa, including buntoniids, *Kaesleria,* and endemic hemicytherid and trachyleberid genera, which evidently did not disperse out of the Tethyan realm.

The above-noted presence of relict Cretaceous mollusk and ostracode taxa at Ocean Point implies that, at least for these faunal groups, terminal Cretaceous extinction processes were only partly effective in the Arctic Ocean. The mollusk and ostracode species that characterize the Ocean Point assemblage make up a group of temperate, shallow-water taxa that were capable of surviving fluctuations or instability in their environment. Further, both types of organisms are benthic in habit and therefore are not subject to phenomena that affect the uppermost part of the water column. Terminal Cretaceous time has been characterized as being one of major ocean regression, massive volcanism, and declining temperatures. The postulated latest Maastrichtian bolide impact is thought to have created a suspension of dust and smoke, thereby blocking sunlight and resulting in a net worldwide cooling and darkness for an unknown, but geologically short, period of time. The shallow-water Arctic Ocean ostracodes and mollusks were already adapted to relatively cool conditions and winter darkness. We speculate that these high-latitude invertebrates were able to endure the postulated terminal Cretaceous changes and that some of them survived the events that devastated most planktonic and nektonic organisms living in lower latitudes.

Reflecting its inferred early Tertiary isolation from the world ocean, the Arctic Ocean marine fauna seems to have been one in which new taxa evolved. The ostracodes in particular show the first appearance of some genera that are evidently the Paleogene ancestors of Neogene through Holocene circumpolar genera such as *"Heterocyprideis," "Roundstonia,"* and *Eucytheridea.* Some of the cytherideid genera, including *Eucytheridea* and *Sarsicytheridea,* may have originated in the isolated Arctic Ocean Basin and subsequently dispersed through the new, intermittent connection to the North Atlantic during the late Paleocene and Eocene. Similarly, the occurrence of the bivalves *Argyromya* and *Gari* (*Garum*) at Ocean Point predates their Eocene appearance in European Tethyan faunas. Both the relict Cretaceous and the Tertiary mollusks and ostracodes from Ocean Point are essentially marine in nature, although they allow the possibility of somewhat lowered salinity. They are conclusive evidence against a freshwater Arctic Ocean that has been postulated (Gartner and Keany, 1978) for terminal Cretaceous time.

The Eureka Sound Group on Ellesmere Island, northern Canada

The Eureka Sound Group encompasses marine and nonmarine strata of latest Cretaceous (Maastrichtian) to Eocene and Oligocene(?) age that crop out on several of the Queen Elizabeth Islands of northern Canada (Miall, 1981, 1986; Ricketts, 1986) (Fig. 1). These strata may be as much as 4,000 m thick and represent environments ranging from shallow marine to marginal marine and terrestrial. Some of the best-studied outcrops occur along the margins of Strathcona Fiord and Bay Fiord (78°45′N) in west-central Ellesmere Island (Fig. 1), where about 3,000 m of marine and nonmarine sediments are exposed in a broad syncline (West and others, 1981; Hickey and others, 1983). The central portion of this sequence, the Mount Moore Formation of Miall (1986), consists of about 1,000 m of marine sandstone with well-preserved and locally abundant mollusks (West and others, 1981; Marincovich and Zinsmeister, 1985).

The known Strathcona Fiord molluscan fauna is of low diversity, containing eight bivalves, four gastropods, and one scaphopod (Table 3; L. Marincovich, Jr., and W. Zinsmeister, unpublished data, 1987). The most abundant taxa throughout the marine beds are the bivalves *Arctica, Astarte,* and *Corbicula,* whereas the scaphopod *Dentalium* and the gastropod *Amauropsis* are abundant in thin, widely spaced stratigraphic intervals. Most bivalves occur as single valves, and broken and abraded specimens predominate at many localities. However, intact, articulated, and sometimes closed individuals of *Arctica, Astarte,* and *Cyrtodaria* are common at several localities. The presence of these three shallow-water taxa, together with the occasional presence of the predominantly brackish-water bivalve *Corbicula,* ter-

TABLE 3. MOLLUSKS AND OSTRACODES FROM THE EUREKA SOUND GROUP ON ELLESMERE ISLAND, NORTHERN CANADA

Bivalves:	Gastropods:
Arctica	Amauropsis
Astarte	Aporrhaidae
Corbicula	Genus A
Cyrtodaria rutupiensis	Genus B
(Morris, 1852)	Nonmarine genus A
Pholadidae	Nonmarine genus B
Genus A	Nonmarine genus C
Genus B	
	Ostracodes:
Scaphopod:	Acanthocythereis
Dentalium	Cytheromorpha
	"Paracyprideis"

restrial gastropods, and numerous thin coal beds and abundant plant debris throughout this marine sequence, implies very shallow-water deposition, alternating with nonmarine deposition. This agrees with the conclusions of earlier workers, who described Eureka Sound paleoenvironments as ranging from marine through marginal marine to terrestrial (West and others, 1975, 1977, 1981; Miall, 1979, 1981, 1986). Microfossils are uncommon in the Eureka Sound sediments; to date, only three ostracode species (Table 3; E. Brouwers, 1987) and rare arenaceous and calcareous foraminifers (J. H. Wall, written communication, 1986) have been found. The ostracodes and arenaceous foraminifers imply a nearshore, shallow marine to marginal-marine environment. The inferred early Tertiary geographic isolation of the Arctic Ocean Basin, combined with the inflow from major rivers such as the Mackenzie and Ob, presents the possibility that the Arctic Ocean had below-normal salinities. The Paleocene mollusks and ostracodes from Strathcona Fiord are basically marine in aspect but include taxa that tolerate the lower salinities expected in the nearshore environments indicated in this and other Eureka Sound localities.

The single Mount Moore mollusk identified to species is the bivalve *Cyrtodaria rutupiensis* (Morris, 1852), which is also the only mollusk identified to species in the Ocean Point post-Danian Paleocene fauna (Marincovich and others, 1985). It is best known from upper Paleocene to lower Eocene (Thanetian and Ypresian) strata of the London Basin and from approximately coeval beds on Svalbard (Strauch, 1972). At Strathcona Fiord, *C. rutupiensis* is found within the Paleocene part of this stratigraphic sequence (Hickey and others, 1983), several hundred meters stratigraphically below early Eocene mammalian faunas (W. Zinsmeister and L. Marincovich, Jr., unpublished data, 1987). The occurrence of *C. rutupiensis* in approximately coeval faunas of Alaska, Ellesmere Island, Svalbard, and the London Basin not only aids in correlation but also supports the concept of a distinct early Tertiary northern high-latitude marine realm largely isolated from the world ocean (Brouwers and others, 1984a; Hopkins and Marincovich, 1984). Fossil mammalian evidence suggests a land-bridge barrier to marine faunas during part of Thanetian and early Ypresian time, extending from North America via Greenland, proto-Iceland, and the British Isles to France (McKenna, 1983, 1984). The Paleocene marine fauna geographically closest to Strathcona Fiord is at Nûgssuaq, central West Greenland (70°30′ N.), 1,200 km to the southeast, where the highly diverse, subtropical Danian molluscan fauna does not contain *C. rutupiensis* (Rosenkrantz, 1970). However, the absence of *C. rutupiensis* at Nûgssuaq could have been due to the greater age of those deposits or the presence of an environmental or geographic barrier. Among the few Strathcona Fiord ostracodes present is *"Paracyprideis"* sp., which also is the dominant genus at Ocean Point.

The Strathcona Fiord mollusks are of mild temperate aspect. $^{18}O/^{16}O$ ratios determined from a scaphopod from the Mount Moore Formation indicate a shallow-water temperature of 15°C, provided that paleosalinity was normally marine (W. L. Donn, personal communication, 1978, *in* McKenna, 1980, p. 350–351). Known scaphopods require normal marine salinity. This molluscan fauna represents a marine climate much warmer than prevails at that latitude today but much cooler than that inferred for older Paleocene (Danian) warm-temperate to subtropical marine faunas of northeastern North America (Govoni, 1983), West Greenland (Rosenkrantz, 1970), and the North Sea Basin region (Buchardt, 1978). The low similarity between Paleocene marine faunas of Ellesmere Island and West Greenland is also shown by benthic foraminifers (J. H. Wall, written communication, 1986). The few ostracode taxa known from Strathcona Fiord similarly indicate a mild temperate marine climate and probably rule out a cold temperate climate. These ostracode genera prefer relatively normal marine salinities and indicate water depths within the deeper inner sublittoral zone.

The vertebrate fauna of the upper part of the Eureka Sound Group was discovered in 1973. It occurs primarily in "Member III" and "Member IV" of the Eureka Sound (West and others, 1975, 1977; Estes and Hutchison, 1980; McKenna, 1980; West and others, 1981). At first, only otoliths from about half a dozen species of marine teleost fishes and some sand shark teeth of the genus *Odontaspis* were known from marine sediments of "Member III," but in 1975 and subsequently, terrestrial and fresh-water vertebrates were recovered from "Member IV" and correlated sediments. "Member III" has been called the Mount Moore Formation by Miall (1986) and has also been correlated with the lower part of the type Iceberg Bay Formation of Axel Heiberg Island by Ricketts (1986), whose terminology was proposed independently. Although the nomenclature of the Eureka Sound Group (or Formation) is currently muddled, the age of "Member III," whatever its formal name, in the Strathcona and Bay Fiord areas of Ellesmere Island is approximately late Paleocene (Norris and Miall, 1984), possibly also including medial Paleocene and/or early Eocene sediments.

In the upper part of the Eureka Sound Group (or Formation) above "Member III" of West and others (1981), abundant terrestrial vertebrates of two discernible ages occur in "Member IV," which on lithologic and cartographic criteria is itself potentially subdivisible. "Member IV" has been included in the Margaret Formation of Miall (1986) but left out of his Mokka Fiord Formation (which it closely resembles). Ricketts (1986), on the other hand, regards "Member IV" as the upper part of his Iceberg Bay Formation. Because the Margaret, Mokka Fiord, and Iceberg Bay formations all have their type sections on Axel Heiberg Island rather than on Ellesmere Island, the application of any of these names to rocks on Ellesmere Island is a matter of correlation and interpretation. Whatever its formal name, the lower part of "Member IV" contains a Wasatchian (early Eocene) fauna; the upper part has a Bridgerian (medial Eocene) fauna. In addition to "Member IV" of the Strathcona and Bay Fiord areas, Wasatchian vertebrates have been recovered from similar sediments at Stenkul Fiord and Swinnerton Peninsula on Ellesmere Island and from the type section of the Mokka Fiord Formation on Axel Heiberg Island.

The complete sequence of Eureka Sound vertebrate assemblages has yet to be monographed formally, but a tentative list of taxa from work in progress by Dawson, Hutchison, and McKenna (Table 4) shows that the faunas are extensive, are useful in correlation, and have a strong bearing on any theory of Paleogene paleogeography or climate (McKenna, 1980).

The Wasatchian vertebrates from low in "Member IV" of the Eureka Sound and in correlated deposits occur slightly later in time than the initial break early in the Wasatchian (early Ypresian) of the Thulean land bridge that still connected North America with Europe (south of the Baltic). They therefore probably do not represent the actual species that were distributed across the Thulean Bridge, but the genera represented are, for the most part, known from both sides of the Atlantic; several, such as *Coryphodon, Dissacus,* and *Pachyaena,* are known from Asia as well. The Wasatchian vertebrates of "Member IV" and correlated deposits had not changed very much since the break in North Atlantic terrestrial continuity and therefore are minimally "North American." The faunal composition suggests a temperate climate, far different from that prevailing in the Arctic today.

The few Bridgerian terrestrial vertebrates found thus far high in "Member IV" of the Eureka Sound are wholly unlike members of contemporary European Lutetian terrestrial faunas, reflecting the widening gap between the fragments of the Thulean Bridge and also the length of time since the initial break in the bridge, which would have permitted taxonomically significant differences to accumulate as the member lineages of the two now-isolated faunas evolved.

The Cannonball Formation of North and South Dakota

The Cannonball Formation consists of Danian sandstone and mudstone up to 117 m thick that crops out in portions of western North Dakota and South Dakota (Lemke, 1960; Cvancara, 1966; Fig. 1). These strata contain the only diverse early

TABLE 4. VERTEBRATES FROM THE EUREKA SOUND GROUP, NORTHERN CANADA

Marine late Paleocene, "Member III" = Mount Moore Formation

Class CHONDRICHTHYES
    Family Odontaspididae
        Odontaspis sp. (sand shark).

Class OSTEICHTHYES
    Family Argentinidae
        Genus and species unidentified (argentines—related to smelts).
        2nd species, unidentified.
    Family Gadidae
        Genus and species unidentified (cods and hakes).
    Family Macrouridae
        Genus and species unidentified (grenadiers or rat-tails).

Terrestrial and fresh-water Wasatchian (early Eocene) and Bridgerian (medial Eocene), Lower part of "Member IV"

Class OSTEICHTHYES
    Family Lepisosteidae
        ?*Lepisosteus* sp. (gar). Wasatchian.
    Family Amiidae
        Amia fragosa (bowfin). Wasatchian.
        Amia cf. *A. uintaensis* (bowfin). Wasatchian.
    Family Esocidae
        Esox sp. (pike). Wasatchian.
    Family Ictaluridae
        Ictalurus sp. (catfish). Wasatchian.

Class AMPHIBIA
    Subclass LISSAMPHIBIA
        Family ?Scapherpetontidae
            Piceoerpeton cf. *P. willwoodense* (salamander). Wasatchian.

Class REPTILIA
    Order CRYPTODIRA
        Family Emydidae
            Subfamily Emydinae
                Genus and several species unidentified (pond turtles). Wasatchian and Bridgerian.
            Subfamily Batagurinae
                Echmatemys sp. (pond turtle).
            Subfamily unidentified
                Genus and species unidentified (pond turtle). Wasatchian and Bridgerian.
        Family Testudinidae
            Geochelone sp. (tortoise). Wasatchian and Bridgerian.
        Family Kinosternidae
            Subfamily Kinosterninae
                Genus and species unidentified (turtle). Wasatchian.
        Family Carettochelyidae
            Subfamily Anosteirinae
                Genus and species unidentified (turtle). Bridgerian.
        Family Trionychidae
            Trionyx sp. (turtle). Wasatchian and Bridgerian?
        Family Baenidae
            Baena sp. (turtle). Wasatchian.
        Family Chelydridae
            Genus and species unidentified (snapping turtle). Wasatchian.

Table 4 continues on next page.

TABLE 4. (CONTINUED)

```
Order SQUAMATA
   Suborder LACERTILIA
      Infraorder ANGUIMORPHA
         Family Anguidae
            Subfamily Glyptosaurinae
               Genus and species unidentified (lizard). Wasatchian.
            Subfamily incertae sedis
               Genus and species unidentified (lizard). Wasatchian.
         Family Varanidae
            Genus and species unidentified (monitor lizard). Wasatchian or
               Bridgerian.
   Suborder OPHIDIA
      Family Boidae
         Subfamily Erycinae
            Genus and species unidentified (snake). Wasatchian.
Order CROCODILIA
   Family Crocodylidae
      Subfamily Alligatorinae
         Allognathosuchus sp. Wasatchian and Bridgerian.
         Genus and species unidentified (alligator). Bridgerian.

Class MAMMALIA
   Infraclass ALLOTHERIA
      Order MULTITUBERCULATA
         Family Neoplagiaulacidae
            Neoplagiaulax sp. Wasatchian.
   Infraclass TRECHNOTHERIA
      Grandorder ICTOPSIA
         Family Leptictidae
            Genus and species unidentified. Wasatchian or Bridgerian.
      Grandorder FERAE
         Order CIMOLESTA
            Suborder PANTOLESTA
               Family Pantolestidae
                  Genus and species unidentified. Wasatchian.
            Suborder TAENIODONTA
               Family Stylinodontidae
                  Genus and species unidentified. Bridgerian.
            Suborder PANTODONTA
               Family Coryphondontidae
                  Coryphodon sp. Wasatchian.
         Order CREODONTA
            Family Hyaenodontidae
               Subfamily Hyaenodontinae
                  Genus and species unidentified.
               Subfamily Limnocyoninae
                  Prolimnocyon sp. Wasatchian.
         Order CARNIVORA
            Family Viverravidae
               Viverravus sp. Wasatchian.
            Family Miacidae
               Uintacyon or Vulpavus sp. Wasatchian.
      Grandorder GLIRES
         Order RODENTIA
            Family Ischyromyidae
               Genus and species unidentified. Wasatchian.
               Genus and species unidentified. Wasatchian.
               Genus and species unidentified. Wasatchian.
```

Table 4 continues on next page

TABLE 4. (CONTINUED)

 Grandorder ARCHONTA
  Order PRIMATES
   Family Paromomyidae
    Subfamily Paromomyinae
     Ignatius-like genus and species, undescribed. Wasatchian.
     Second *Ignatus*-like species. Wasatchian.
  Order DERMOPTERA
   Family Plagiomenidae
    cf. *Plagiomene*, several undescribed species ("flying lemur").
    Wasatchian.
 Grandorder UNGULATA
  Order CONDYLARTHA
   Family Phenacodontidae
    Phenacodus sp. Wasatchian.
  Order PERISSODACTYLA
   Superfamily Equoidea
    Family Equidae
     ?*Hyracotherium* sp. (horse). Wasatchian.
   Superfamily Brontotherioidea
    Family Brontotheriidae
     Subfamily Lambdotheriinae
      ?*Lambdotherium* sp. Wasatchian.
     Subfamily Brontopinae
      cf. *Manteoceras* sp. Bridgerian.
   Superfamily Rhinocerotoidea
    Family Hyracodontidae
     Subfamily Hyrachyinae
      ?*Hyrachyus* sp. (primitive tapir-like rhinoceros).
      Wasatchian.
  Order ACREODI
   Family Mesonychidae
    Dissacus sp. Wasatchian.
    Pachyaena sp. Wasatchian.
    Genus and species unidentified. Wasatchian.

Tertiary marine biota known in the central midcontinent of North America and provide an important data point for speculations on early Tertiary Arctic Ocean paleogeography. The paleogeographic importance of these Tertiary marine beds, completely surrounded as they are on all sides by extensive deposits of nonmarine Upper Cretaceous sediments, was first recognized by Stanton (1920).

Early work on Cannonball mollusks suggested affinities with Gulf of Mexico faunas (Stanton, 1920), and the Cannonball deposits were thought to represent the final northward incursion of warm water taxa into the Western Interior Seaway late in the Cretaceous. However, later studies indicated a Danian age for the Cannonball based on planktonic foraminifers (Fox and Olsson, 1969) and suggested faunal ties mostly to the north or east (Feldmann, 1972). The Cannonball deposits are now regarded as the southernmost known extent of the early Tertiary Arctic Ocean; they provide evidence that the Arctic Ocean once flooded a substantial portion of the northern midcontinent of North America (Marincovich and others, 1985).

Cvancara (1966) concluded that Cannonball bivalve mollusks are more similar to late Paleocene (Thanetian) species of the London and Paris Basins than to coeval species of the geographically closer Midway Group of the Gulf of Mexico. However, most workers consider the Cannonball beds to be of Danian age. Boreal North Atlantic affinities have also been observed among Cannonball benthic foraminifers (Lemke, 1960) as well as among dinoflagellates and hystrichosphaerids (Stanley, 1965). Rare planktonic foraminifers were reported to be a mixture of Danian species with inferred Gulf of Mexico affinities and Cretaceous taxa with speculative "eastern" ties (Fox and Olsson, 1969). However, Fox (*fide* Lemke, 1960) also noted that these foraminifers more closely resemble "arctic" taxa from northern Europe than Gulf Coast taxa. Lemke (1960) suggested Cannonball marine connections to both the Arctic Ocean and the Gulf of Mexico, whereas the sum of paleontologic evidence suggested to Cvancara (1966) and to Feldmann (1972) only a northern connection, either to the Arctic Ocean or the North Atlantic Ocean.

The Cannonball molluscan fauna has no known species in

common with the Paleocene faunas of northern Alaska or the Eureka Sound Group on Ellesmere Island. The absence of the bivalve *Cyrtodaria rutupiensis* from the Cannonball fauna might be due to the possible greater age of this fauna compared to the Ocean Point, Ellesmere Island, or London Basin Paleocene faunas that contain the earliest records of this genus and species. Alternatively, *C. rutupiensis* might have been excluded from the Cannonball fauna for ecological or environmental reasons. In light of the known wide distribution of this species, from northern Alaska through northern Canada and Svalbard to northwestern Europe, geographic distance alone probably would not have prevented it from living in the Cannonball fauna.

The Cannonball molluscan fauna consists of 20 species of bivalves (Cvancara, 1966), about 30 species and subspecies of gastropods, and one species of scaphopod (Stanton, 1920). The Cannonball bivalves *Arctica, Corbula (Bicorbula), Crenella, Neilonella,* and *Nucula (Nucula)* also occur in the Ocean Point fauna of northern Alaska (Marincovich and others, 1985); the Cannonball bivalves *Arctica, Corbicula,* and *"Teredo,"* one aporrhaid gastropod, and the scaphopod *Dentalium* are also present in the Eureka Sound Group of Ellesmere Island (Table 3). These genera range throughout the Cenozoic, so their co-occurrence does not establish precise age correlations between these three early Tertiary Arctic Ocean faunas, but it does suggest roughly similar environmental conditions. The low species diversity of these three faunas is also a significant shared characteristic, because it sets them apart from nearly coeval mollusk faunas of high diversity and warm-temperature to subtropical aspect that are found in northwestern Europe and West Greenland.

With the possible exception of the recently collected marine fauna in the Eureka Sound Group at Strathcona Fiord, Ellesmere Island (W. Zinsmeister and L. Marincovich, Jr., unpublished data, 1987), there is no known marine fauna of Cannonball age in Canada. However, Lemke (1960) evidently was the first to speculate that the "Cannonball sea" was an arm of the Arctic Ocean that extended across the midcontinent of Canada south to the Dakotas. The broad similarities of the Cannonball, Ocean Point, and Strathcona Fiord molluscan faunas, and their differences from Paleocene Gulf Coast and North Atlantic faunas, support this marine paleogeographic scenario.

Svalbard and East Greenland

Early Tertiary mollusks and microfossils occur on Svalbard (Fig. 1) within a sedimentary sequence up to 3,500 m thick that consists mainly of marine, brackish-water, and fluvial sandstones (Vonderbank, 1970; Livsic, 1974). The generally poorly preserved fauna includes mollusks, crabs, and benthic foraminifers. Thirty-six species-level bivalve and gastropod taxa have been proposed (Ravn, 1922; Hägg, 1925-1927; Gripp, 1927), but Vonderbank (1970) considered only 19 of these to be distinct. Based upon similarities with molluscan and foraminiferal faunas at Nûgssuaq, West Greenland, and Faxe, Denmark, Vonderbank (1970) inferred an age range of early to middle Paleocene (Danian to Montian). However, Livsic (1974) concluded that mollusks and microfossils of the Svalbard Paleogene sequence range in age from late Paleocene (Thanetian) to perhaps as young as late Eocene or Oligocene. More recently, Feyling-Hansen and Ulleberg (1984) described a middle to late Oligocene benthic foraminiferal fauna from one outcrop on Svalbard (see below).

The low diversity of the Svalbard early Tertiary molluscan fauna probably resulted as much from diagenesis as from original environmental conditions. Nevertheless, the preservation of complete, if imperfectly preserved, benthic foraminiferal tests and the presence of adult and juvenile mollusk shells suggest that the composition of the preserved fauna is fairly representative of the original one. The evident low diversity of the Svalbard fauna is in accord with that noted for other arctic Paleogene molluscan faunas.

The presence on Svalbard of two bivalves that occur at Nûgssuaq, West Greenland, and of two gastropods from Faxe, Denmark (Vonderbank, 1970), is evidence for a direct marine connection between these areas. The occurrence of the bivalve *Cyrtodaria rutupiensis* ties the Svalbard fauna to faunas at Ocean Point in northern Alaska, at Strathcona Fiord on Ellesmere Island, and in the London Basin, England. That 14 of 19 Svalbard molluscan species are endemic, but taxa from adjacent regions are present, suggests that this fauna may be transitional in composition between Paleocene faunas of the Arctic Ocean Basin, the Norwegian-Greenland Sea/North Sea Basin, and the North Atlantic (Tethyan) realm. Both the mollusks and benthic foraminifers indicate a temperate climate for the Svalbard fauna.

There is no evidence for a direct Paleocene marine connection from the southern margin of the North Sea Basin to the North Atlantic (Pomerol, 1982), but one must have existed in the area that was to become Iceland. The first such connection may have occurred in the middle Ypresian at about 54 Ma (the middle of planktonic zone P6), when planktonic foraminifers became abundant and diverse throughout the southern North Sea Basin and when similarity between the North American and European terrestrial vertebrate faunas began to drop. This early Eocene datum is believed to reflect the opening of a southern North Sea Basin–North Atlantic connection, after a brief interval in which proto-Iceland choked the entire gap between Greenland and the British Isles. Immigration of new planktonic species (Keen, 1983) became possible as marine continuity was re-established. The distance from Svalbard of these other Paleocene faunas, and perhaps the presence of intervening ecological and geographic barriers, prevented a greater degree of species commonality. However, the occurrence of at least some species common to localities extending from the western Arctic Ocean Basin to Svalbard, the North Sea Basin, and West Greenland verifies that shallow seaways of very early Tertiary age connected the Arctic Ocean, the Norwegian-Greenland Sea/North Sea, and the North Atlantic.

In addition to the early Paleogene faunas noted above, several much less diverse Paleogene mollusk and microfossil faunas occur around the margin of the Norwegian-Greenland Sea (Buchardt, 1981). The two most notable localities are Kap

Dalton and Kap Brewster in East Greenland (Fig. 1). The stratigraphic sequence at Kap Dalton is less than 100 m thick and consists mainly of upward-fining, relatively coarse clastics. The stratigraphically lowest Tertiary fossils are earliest Eocene (early Ypresian) dinoflagellates (Soper and Costa, 1976). An overlying stratigraphic horizon, referred to as the *Cyrena* beds, contains either early to middle Eocene (Ravn, 1904, 1933) or late Eocene (Hassan, 1953) mollusks and early Eocene (late Ypresian) dinoflagellates (Soper and Costa, 1976). Higher still are the *Coeloma* beds, which contain mollusks of early Oligocene age, discussed below.

The strata at Kap Brewster are about 200 m thick and consist of relatively coarse clastics that contain probable middle or late Eocene mollusks at one horizon and probable early Oligocene mollusks at another (Hassan, 1953). These two horizons are correlated with the Kap Dalton sequence and also are termed the *Cyrena* and *Coeloma* beds, respectively. The early Oligocene benthic foraminifers that also occur in the upper unit (Birkenmajer and Jednorowska, 1977) are discussed below.

Paleogene mollusks from both Kap Dalton and Kap Brewster indicate a very shallow, temperate marine environment and are correlative with faunas in the North Sea Basin (Hassan, 1953). Superjacent Neogene beds at Kap Brewster are discussed later.

Mackenzie Delta

There are no known Arctic Ocean Basin molluscan faunas correlative with the Eocene faunas from Kap Dalton and Kap Brewster, although the presence of temperate Eocene mollusks at high latitudes (now 70°N) in east Greenland allows us to infer a probable temperate marine climate for the adjacent Arctic Ocean at that time. This inference is substantiated by the presence of temperate Eocene microfossil faunas in northwestern Canada that can be correlated with northwestern European biotas. Benthic foraminiferal and marine dinoflagellate assemblages in the Mackenzie Delta indicate an age of late early or middle Eocene to late Eocene for the *Haplophragmoides* assemblage of Young and McNeil (1984). This shallow-water assemblage includes a few foraminifers and dinoflagellates in common with northwestern European biotas and establishes the existence of a seaway connection with the North Sea Basin. However, Young and McNeil (1984) note that most foraminiferal species in this assemblage are apparently undescribed and endemic to the Arctic Ocean Basin, suggesting relative isolation from the Atlantic and Pacific. The low-diversity, agglutinated composition of the *Haplophragmoides* assemblage also suggests a low-salinity marine environment (Young and McNeil, 1984), which may also have been related to the geographic isolation of the Arctic Ocean.

THE LATE PALEOGENE AND EARLY NEOGENE ARCTIC OCEAN: OPEN TO THE ATLANTIC

Although sea-floor spreading during the late Paleogene and Neogene provided an increasingly open marine connection between the Arctic Ocean, the Norwegian-Greenland Sea and North Sea Basin, and the northeastern Atlantic, the exact series of faunal, paleogeographic, and sea-floor spreading events and their interrelations are not well understood. A middle or late Eocene connection to the world ocean is suggested by silicoflagellates from one Arctic Ocean core (Bukry, 1984) and by probable late middle Eocene diatoms and silicoflagellates from sparse marine to marginal-marine beds within the Franklin Bluffs Member of the Sagavanirktok Formation in northeastern Alaska (J. Barron, written communication, 1976). The reduced similarity of North American and European land vertebrates at that time (McKenna, 1983) also could have resulted from the presence of a seaway barrier to land-animal dispersals. Deep-water exchange between the Arctic Ocean and the Norwegian-Greenland Sea evidently began in the early Oligocene, although deep-water communication with the North Atlantic was not established until mid-Miocene time (Eldholm and Thiede, 1980).

Pollen and estuarine dinoflagellate assemblages recovered from Franklin Bluffs, northeastern Alaska (Ager and others, 1985) (Fig. 2), suggest an early to middle Eocene age for these predominantly nonmarine silt and clay deposits, based on comparisons with biostratigraphically dated material from arctic Canada. The pollen assemblages indicate a warm-temperate, moist climate and a forest cover composed primarily of deciduous broad-leaved tree taxa. The presence of estuarine dinoflagellates in the mostly nonmarine section suggests that a marine or marginal-marine environment was nearby.

As noted above, mollusks of inferred early Oligocene age are known from Kap Brewster and Kap Dalton, East Greenland, and are correlative with northwestern European faunas. Feyling-Hansen and Ulleberg (1984) described a benthic foraminiferal fauna from Svalbard that is of middle to late Oligocene age and has numerous species in common with mild-temperate faunas of the North Sea Basin as well as with some Mediterranean faunas. Three of these species, including *Asterigerina guerichi* (Franke), *Cibicides* cf. *C. tenellus* (Reuss), and *Turrilina alsatica* Andreae, are also reported in the *Cibicides* assemblage of middle Oligocene to Miocene age in the subsurface Mackenzie Delta of northwestern Canada (Young and McNeil, 1984). This group of species suggests a temperate, perhaps mild-temperate, Arctic Ocean marine climate during the middle and late Oligocene as well as full communication with the North Sea Basin and the North Atlantic.

One species in the Mackenzie Delta *Cibicides* assemblage, *Turrilina alsatica*, also occurs in the Carter Creek outcrop of the Nuwok Member of the Sagavanirktok Formation, northeastern Alaska, about 400 km to the west, and suggests a late Oligocene age for the latter (Young and McNeil, 1984). The stratigraphic relationship of this fauna with the better-known mollusk-bearing Neogene beds of the Nuwok Member at Carter Creek is not known, although the *Cibicides* assemblage presumably is stratigraphically lower.

The two main outcrop exposures of the Nuwok Member of the Sagavanirktok Formation are at the type section at Carter Creek and on Barter Island (Fig. 2). The type Nuwok strata are 81 m thick, made up of sandstone, siltstone, and claystone, and are the topmost portion of a Tertiary sequence that may be as much as 1,800 m thick and may range in age from Paleocene to Pliocene (Detterman and others, 1975). The Nuwok shallow-water mollusk fauna contains 26 species (Leffingwell, 1919; Dall, 1920; MacNeil, 1957) and is related biogeographically to North Atlantic faunas. The complete absence of Pacific mollusks clearly indicates that the Nuwok fauna lived before the Pliocene opening of Bering Strait at about 3.0 Ma (Gladenkov and others, 1980). The Nuwok mollusks, from the upper 64 m of the stratigraphic section, were thought to be of Pliocene age by Dall (*in* Leffingwell, 1919; Dall, 1920). Mollusks from the immediately underlying 17 m were thought to be of probable late Miocene age by MacNeil (1957), who conceded that narrowly age-diagnostic mollusks were absent. The Nuwok marine beds were tentatively assigned to the late Miocene or early Pliocene by Todd (1957) and MacNeil and others (1961) and considered to be of late Miocene(?) and Pliocene age by Detterman and others (1975). Pollen from these beds have been tentatively assigned a middle Miocene age (J. Wolfe, oral communication, 1985).

Nuwok benthic foraminifers (Todd, 1957) and mollusks (Dall, 1920; MacNeil, 1957) suggest a marine environment that was distinctly cold but warmer than that which prevails along the adjacent Beaufort Sea today. One of the paleoclimatically more important Nuwok bivalves, *Arctica*, has modern northern range limits in central Norway and northern Iceland. Sea ice was likely absent, based on estimates of the first occurrence of perennial Arctic Ocean sea ice no earlier than 5 Ma (Clark, 1982; Clark and others, 1980) and perhaps as recently as 0.73 Ma (Herman, 1974; Carter and others, 1986).

Climatic inferences based on ostracodes from the Nuwok Member at Carter Creek and on Barter Island (Fig. 2) indicate that this unit might span the Miocene-Pliocene boundary. As with the mollusks, the ostracodes have entirely North Atlantic affinities. Further, the ostracodes can be tentatively subdivided into a warm or mild temperate assemblage that has affinities with U.S. Atlantic Coastal Plain Miocene to early Pliocene faunas, and a cold-temperate to subfrigid assemblage with low similarity to North Atlantic and Alaskan late Pliocene faunas. The lack of knowledge about ostracode faunas from colder water Pliocene sediments in the North Atlantic precludes any determination of the geographic limits of the early and middle Pliocene Arctic Ocean ostracode fauna. The ostracode assemblages that indicate a probable middle or late Miocene age for the lower part of the Nuwok include *"Muellerina," Cytheretta,* and an aurilid, which are characteristic of temperate marine climates. The ostracode assemblages in the upper Nuwok that indicate an early to middle Pliocene age have many species in common with upper Pliocene Colvillian sediments of the Gubik Formation, eastern North Slope, including *Pterygocythereis vannieuwenhuisei* Brouwers, 1987, *Rabilimis paramirabilis* (Swain, 1963), *Sarsicytheridea, Roundstonia, Heterocyprideis,* and several *Cytheropteron* taxa (Table 5). These Pliocene taxa indicate colder water conditions than existed for the lower Nuwok assemblage, most probably cold-temperate to subfrigid. The extant ostracode species indicate that water depths for the Nuwok Member ranged from deeper inner sublittoral at Carter Creek to middle sublittoral at Barter Island and Manning Point (Fig. 2).

Strata in northern Canada that are partly correlative with the Nuwok Member are assigned to the Beaufort Formation, which is speculated to range in age from Miocene to Pleistocene. The Beaufort Formation consists largely of deltaic sediments that mantle much of the western Arctic coastal plain of Canada and underlie the southeastern Beaufort Sea with thicknesses as great as 3,000 m (Young and McNeil, 1984; Willumsen and Cote, 1982). Occasional tongues of marine sediments within the Beaufort contain sparse mollusks and microfossils. Most of the few known Beaufort mollusks still live in the Arctic Ocean, although the presence of the Atlantic bivalve *Arctica* in Beaufort deposits at 80°N on Meighen Island (Fig. 1) (Brigham-Grette and others, 1987) indicates an age for one outcrop of greater than 3.0 Ma. Modern *Arctica* lives in the North Atlantic in water not less than 3 to 4°C, with a northern geographic limit in central Norway and northern Iceland. Benthic foraminifers from the middle part of the formation in the subsurface Mackenzie Delta suggest a probable Miocene age (Young and McNeil, 1984).

Precise correlations between the Beaufort Formation and the Nuwok Member of the Sagavanirktok Formation in Alaska, some 300 km to the west, have not been established on the basis of paleontologic evidence. However, general age relations based upon mollusks, ostracodes, pollen, and amino acid racemization studies suggest correlation of the Nuwok beds with the middle or upper part of the Beaufort Formation (Brigham-Grette and others, 1987; E. Brouwers and L. Marincovich, Jr., unpublished data, 1987). Faunas of both stratigraphic units are thought to represent a cold but not frigid marine environment. The presence of the ostracode *Pterygocythereis vannieuwenhuisei* in the Beaufort at a depth of 540 m in one Mackenzie Delta well suggests that a portion of this formation is correlative with the stratigraphic interval in Alaska, ranging from the upper part of the Nuwok Member (middle or upper Miocene to lower Pliocene) to Colvillian (upper Pliocene) sediments of the Gubik Formation. This species is absent from the lower part of the Nuwok and from the younger parts of the Gubik Formation.

The single molluscan fauna of Neogene age on Greenland occurs at Kap Brewster, East Greenland (Hassan, 1953). A small fauna from a unit termed the *Chlamys* beds consists of species with northwest European affinities, some of which also range as far south as the West Indies, and suggests a mild- to warm-temperate marine climate. The absence of Pacific-Arctic mollusks indicates that this fauna, like that of the Beaufort Formation, formed before the Pliocene opening of Bering Strait at about 3.0 Ma. The correlations made by Hassan (1953) suggest a probable Miocene age but are imprecise. If this temperate fauna is coeval with the much cooler water Nuwok and Beaufort strata, as we suspect from preliminary evidence, then a well-developed north-south marine climatic zonation was present in the Neogene.

TABLE 5. LIST OF OSTRACODE TAXA IN MIOCENE AND PLIOCENE SEDIMENTS OF THE
NUWOK MEMBER OF THE SAGAVANIRKTOK FORMATION AT THREE LOCALITIES,
NORTHEASTERN COASTAL PLAIN OF ALASKA
(Localities shown in Fig. 2)

	Barter Island	Manning Point	Carter Creek
Probable middle to late Miocene			
Argilloecia n. sp.	X	X	X
Aurilid			X
Cytheretta n. sp.		X	X
Cytheropteron paralatissimum	X		X
Cytheropteron sedovi	X		
Cytherura n. sp.			X
Eucythere n. sp.	X		
Krithe n. sp.			X
Loxoconcha aff. *venepidermoidea*	X		X
"*Muellerina*" sp.	X		
Paracyprideis aff. *pseudopunctillata*	X	X	
Rabilimis paramirabilis			X
Rabilimis sp.			X
Sarsicytheridea n. sp.			X
Probable early Pliocene			
Acanthocythereis dunelmensis		X	
Cytheromorpha curta		X	
Cytheropteron arcuatum		X	
Cytheropteron paralatissimum		X	X
Cytheropteron simplex		X	
Cytheropteron? n. sp.	X		X
Heterocyprideis sorbyana	X	X	
Krithe sp.	X	X	X
Paracyprideis pseudopunctillata	X		
Pterygocythereis vannieuwenhuisei	X		X
Rabilimis paramirabilis		X	X
Rabilimis septentrionalis		X	
Roundstonia globulifera		X	
Sarsicytheridea bradii			X
Sarsicytheridea n. sp.		X	
Semicytherura complanata		X	

THE LATE NEOGENE AND PLEISTOCENE: AN OPEN BERING STRAIT

The Pliocene opening of Bering Strait produced a dramatic change in the composition of Arctic Ocean shallow-water marine faunas. This shallow-water passage allowed a northward flood of North Pacific marine invertebrates and marine mammals that became and have remained the largest biogeographic element in the Arctic Ocean fauna. Durham and MacNeil (1967) noted that 125 invertebrate species of North Pacific origin, mostly gastropods and bivalves, invaded the Arctic-Atlantic region but that only 16 species or species-groups of Atlantic origin entered the Pacific via Bering Strait. As a result of the scouring action of Late Cenozoic glaciation, there are no known stratigraphic intervals in Alaska or Canada that clearly record this abrupt faunal change. However, the arrival of high-latitude North Pacific mollusks is recorded in Iceland, where the faunal changes produced by Bering Strait are preserved in the stratigraphic sequence at Tjörnes.

The Pliocene and Pleistocene Tjörnes sequence, which consists of about 500 m of fossiliferous marine and nonmarine sediments and of basaltic lava flows yielding paleomagnetic signatures (Einarsson and others, 1967), is divided into four assemblage zones that are characterized by their molluscan faunas (Durham and MacNeil, 1967; Gladenkov and others, 1980). The faunal composition of the molluscan assemblage-zones changes from mostly south boreal and boreal in the lowest beds, through boreal in the *Serripes* Zone, to north boreal, and finally to modern arctic in the uppermost assemblage-zone (Gladenkov, 1981). This upward progression of colder-water molluscan species presumably reflects climatic cooling beginning in the late Neogene and intensifying in the Pleistocene. The youngest mollusk-bearing beds at Tjörnes, associated with basalts and tillites, are less than 0.7 m.y. old (Gladenkov, 1981). Mollusks such as *Serripes groenlandicus* (Bruguiére, 1789), *Clinocardium ciliatum* (Fabricius) *Mya, Musculus, Natica clausa* (Broderip and Sowerby) and *Neptunea,* which have well-documented Miocene or older histories in the North Pacific (Durham and MacNeil, 1967), first appear in Atlantic faunas within the Tjörnes sequence in the basal part of the *Serripes* Zone (Akhmet'yev and Gladenkov, 1979; Gladenkov and others, 1980). Pillow lavas within the *Serripes* Zone occur stratigraphically just above the first appearance of North Pacific mollusks and are inferred to have an age of about 3.0 Ma, based on their placement within the paleomagnetic sequence developed for the Tjörnes region (Einarsson and others, 1967; Gladenkov, 1981). The time of opening of Bering Strait evidently is slightly older than these pillow basalts (Gladenkov, 1981).

Pleistocene glacial sediments and cold-water marine faunas similar to those in the upper beds at Tjörnes occur extensively in Alaska. Most of the Pliocene and Pleistocene sediments that mantle the northern and western coastal lowlands of Alaska are assigned to the Gubik Formation, which records the occurrence of several marine transgressions and regressions (Hopkins, 1967). The great majority of mollusks (Dall, 1920; MacNeil, 1957) and ostracodes (E. Brouwers, unpublished data, 1987) in the Gubik are extant. However, the occurrence of a few extinct species, together with the periodic north-south dispersals of species in response to climatic changes, have made mollusks and ostracodes useful for paleoclimatic studies and for approximate age-dating and correlation (Hopkins, 1967). At present, six to eight separate marine transgressions are recognized on the coastal plains of western (Hopkins, 1967; Hopkins, in Brouwers and others, 1984b) and northern (Carter and Galloway, 1985) Alaska.

The recent introduction of amino acid geochronology has enhanced study of the Gubik Formation by providing a tool for establishing relative stratigraphic position and for correlating deposits that are lithologically and faunally very similar (Brigham, 1985, and references therein). A summary of Gubik stratigraphy, correlations, and paleoclimatic inferences, based on faunal occurrences and amino acid data, is given by Dinter and others (this volume).

SUMMARY

The geographic and stratigraphic occurrences of marine mollusks and microfossils in the Arctic Ocean Basin, and of terrestrial vertebrates around the margins of this basin, support the concept of an Arctic Ocean that was geographically isolated or nearly isolated from the world ocean from the Late Mesozoic until the early Tertiary. The taxonomic composition of Arctic Ocean molluscan and microfossil faunas was strongly influenced by the presence or absence of seaway connections to the Pacific, Atlantic, and Tethyan oceans. When the Arctic Ocean was sealed off from the North Pacific by plate movements in the Late Mesozoic, its remaining marine connections to mid-latitudes were through the Western Interior Seaway in North America and Turgai Strait in western Siberia. The Western Interior Seaway connection disappeared by the late Maastrichtian, and Turgai Strait developed into an intermittent seaway, leaving the Arctic Ocean Basin virtually isolated from the world ocean until the progressive opening of the North Atlantic produced an Arctic-Atlantic seaway in the Paleocene. During this interval of geographic isolation, Cretaceous marine invertebrates in the Arctic Ocean evidently continued to live into Tertiary time, while new species of exclusively Cenozoic provenance evolved.

The length of time during which the Arctic Ocean was a paleogeographically isolated and distinct faunal realm is not known. During this interval, the Arctic Ocean extended southward in North America as an epeiric embayment as far as the present outcrop area of the Cannonball Formation in North and South Dakota. Faunal evidence supports the concept of a fully marine Arctic Ocean during the latest Cretaceous and earliest Tertiary. The first evidence of an Arctic-Atlantic seaway is the occurrence in northern Alaska and Ellesmere Island of late Paleocene mollusks and ostracodes previously known only in northwestern Europe, particularly the London Basin. The well-documented dispersals of late Paleocene (Thanetian) and early Eocene (Ypresian) terrestrial vertebrates between Europe and North America require that the Arctic-Atlantic seaway connection was, at least initially, an intermittent one. Continued opening of the North Atlantic ended east-west dispersals of terrestrial vertebrates but allowed a greater interchange of marine taxa between the Arctic and North Atlantic. The Arctic Ocean marine invertebrate biota was dominated by taxa of Atlantic affinities until the opening of Bering Strait at about 3.0 Ma, at which time Pacific taxa flooded north and largely displaced the Atlantic-Arctic biota. The modern Arctic Ocean invertebrate biota is dominated by taxa of Pacific origin.

Paleocene molluscan and ostracode faunas from northern Alaska, northeastern Canada, and North and South Dakota are of temperate aspect and differ strongly in inferred paleoclimate from approximately coeval warm-temperate to subtropical marine faunas in the North Atlantic realm. The absence of diverse Eocene through Oligocene Arctic Ocean fossil assemblages prevents comparisons with middle latitude faunas. However, probable Miocene molluscan and microfossil faunas from northeastern Alaska and northern Canada indicate paleoclimates distinctly cooler than those at lower latitudes. Progressive late Cenozoic climatic cooling is well documented in a series of marine-transgressive faunas of the Gubik Formation in western and northern Alaska.

REFERENCES CITED

Ager, T. A., Edwards, L. E., and Oftedahl, O., 1985, Eocene palynomorphs from the Franklin Bluffs, Arctic Slope, northeast Alaska: American Association of Stratigraphic Palynologists Program and Abstracts, Annual Meeting, p. 7.

Akhmet'yev, M. A., and Gladenkov, Y. B., 1979, A stratigraphical scheme for the Cenozoic of Iceland and its paleontologic basis: International Geology Review, v. 21, no. 7, p. 769–773.

Balkwill, H. R., Cook, D. G., Detterman, R. L., Embry, A. F., Hakansson, E., Miall, A. D., Poulton, T. P., and Young, F. G., 1983, Arctic North America and northern Greenland, in Moullane, M., and Nairn, A.E.M., eds., The Phanerozoic geology of the world; II, The Mesozoic, B: Amsterdam, Elsevier, p. 1–31.

Bendix-Almgren, S. E., 1969, Notes on the Upper Cretaceous and Lower Tertiary fish faunas of northern West Greenland: Geological Society of Denmark Bulletin, v. 19, p. 204–217.

Bergquist, H. R., 1966, Micropaleontology of the Mesozoic rocks of northern Alaska: U.S. Geological Survey Professional Paper 302-D, p. 93–227.

Beznosov, N. V., Gorbatchik, T. N., Mikhailova, I. A., and Pergament, M. A., 1978, Soviet Union, in Moullade, M., and Nairn, A.E.M., eds., The Phanerozoic geology of the world; II, The Mesozoic, A: Amsterdam, Elsevier, p. 5–53.

Birkelund, T., 1965, Ammonites from the Upper Cretaceous of West Greenland: Meddelelser om Grønland, v. 179, no. 7, 192 p.

Birkenmajer, K., and Jednorowska, A., 1977, Foraminiferal evidence for the East Greenland current during the Oligocene: Grønlands Geologiske Undersøgelse, Rapport 85, p. 86–89.

Brigham, J. K., 1985, Marine stratigraphy and amino acid geochronology of the Gubik Formation, western Arctic coastal plain, Alaska: U.S. Geological Survey Open-File Report 85-381, 218 p.

Brigham-Grette, J., Matthews, J. V., Jr., and Marincovich, L., Jr., 1987, Age and paleoenvironmental significance of *Arctica* in the Neogene Beaufort Fm. on Meighen Island, Queen Elizabeth Islands, Canada: Abstracts of the 16th Arctic Workshop, Edmonton, Alberta, April 30–May 2, 1987: Edmonton, University of Alberta, Boreal Institute for Northern Studies, p. 12–14.

Brosgé, W. P., and Whittington, C. L., 1966, Geology of the Umiat-Maybe Creek region, Alaska: U.S. Geological Survey Professional Paper 303-H, p. 501–638.

Brouwers, E. M., 1987, On *Pterygocythereis vannieuwenhuisei* sp. nov.: Stereo-Atlas of Ostracod Shells, v. 14, pt. 1, p. 17–20.

Brouwers, E. M., Marincovich, L., Jr., and Carter, L. D., 1984a, Paleogeographic affinities and evolutionary significance of a Paleogene marine fauna from northern Alaska: Geological Society of America Abstracts and Program, v. 16, p. 455–456.

Brouwers, E. M., Marincovich, L., Jr., and Hopkins, D. M., 1984b, Paleoenvironmental record of Pleistocene transgressive events preserved at Skull Cliff, northern Alaska: U.S. Geological Survey Circular 939, p. 9–12.

Brouwers, E. M., Clemens, W. A., Spicer, R. A., Ager, T. A., Carter, L. D., and Sliter, W. V., 1987, Dinosaurs on the North Slope, Alaska; High latitude, latest Cretaceous environments: Science, v. 237, p. 1608–1610.

Buchardt, B., 1978, Oxygen-isotope palaeotemperatures from the Tertiary period in the North Sea area: Nature, v. 275, no. 5676, p. 121–123.

——, 1981, Tertiary deposits of the Norwegian-Greenland Sea region (Svalbard, Northeast and East Greenland, Iceland, the Faeroe Islands, and the Norwegian-Greenland Sea) and their correlation to northwest Europe, in Kerr, J. W., and Fergusson, A. J., eds., Geology of the North Atlantic Borderlands: Calgary, Canadian Society of Petroleum Geologists Memoir 7, p. 585–610.

Bukry, D., 1984, Paleogene paleoceanography of the Arctic Basin is constrained by middle or late Eocene age of USGS core F1-422; Evidence from silicoflagellates: Geology, v. 12, p. 199–201.

Carter, L. D., and Galloway, J. P., 1985, Engineering-geologic maps of northern Alaska, Harrison Bay Quadrangle: U.S. Geological Survey Open-file Report 85-256, p. 1–47, 2 map sheets.

Carter, L. D., Brigham-Grette, J., Marincovich, L., Jr., Pease, V. L., and Hillhouse, J. W., 1986, Late Cenozoic Arctic Ocean ice and terrestrial paleoclimate: Geology, v. 14, p. 803–804.

Clark, D. L., 1982, Origin, nature, and world climate effect of Arctic Ocean ice-cover: Nature, v. 300, p. 321–325.

Clark, D. L., Whitman, R. R., Morgan, K. A., and Mackey, S. D., 1980, Stratigraphy and glacial-marine sediments of the Amerasian Basin, central Arctic Ocean: Geological Society of America Special Paper 181, 57 p.

Cvancara, A. V., 1966, Revision of the fauna of the Cannonball Formation (Paleocene) of North and South Dakota: Ann Arbor, University of Michigan, Contributions from the Museum of Paleontology, v. 20, no. 10, p. 1–97.

Dall, W. H., 1920, Pliocene and Pleistocene fossils from the Arctic coast of Alaska and the auriferous beaches of Nome, Norton Sound, Alaska: U.S. Geological Survey Professional Paper 125-C, p. 23–37.

Davies, K. L., 1987, Duck-bill dinosaurs (Hadrosauridae, Ornithischia) from the North Slope of Alaska: Journal of Paleontology, v. 61, no. 1, p. 198–200.

Dawson, M. R., West, R. M., Langston, W., Jr., and Hutchison, J. H., 1976, Paleogene terrestrial vertebrates; Northernmost occurrence, Ellesmere Island, Canada: Science, v. 192, p. 781–782.

Detterman, R. L., Reiser, H. N., Brosgé, W. P., and Dutro, J. T., Jr., 1975, Post-Carboniferous stratigraphy, northeastern Alaska: U.S. Geological Survey Professional Paper 886, 46 p.

Durham, J. W., and MacNeil, F. S., 1967, Cenozoic migrations of marine invertebrates through the Bering Strait region, in Hopkins, D. M., ed., The Bering land bridge: Stanford, California, Stanford University Press, p. 326–349.

Einarsson, T., Hopkins, D. M., and Doell, R. R., 1967, The stratigraphy of Tjörnes, northern Iceland, and the history of the Bering land bridge, in Hopkins, D. M., ed., The Bering Land Bridge: Stanford, California, Stanford University Press, p. 312–325.

Eldholm, O., and Thiede, J., 1980, Cenozoic continental separation between Europe and Greenland: Palaeogeography, Palaeoclimatology, Palaeoecology, v. 30, p. 243–259.

Estes, R., and Hutchison, J. H., 1980, Eocene lower vertebrates from Ellesmere Island, Canadian Arctic Archipelago: Palaeogeography, Palaeoclimatology, Palaeoecology, v. 30, p. 325–347.

Fairbridge, R. W., 1966, The encyclopedia of oceanography: New York, Reinhold Publishing Co., 1021 p.

Feldmann, R. M., 1972, First report of *Hercoglossa ulrichi* (White, 1882) (Cephalopoda: Nautiloida) from the Cannonball Formation (Paleocene) of North Dakota, U.S.A.: Malacologia, v. 11, no. 2, p. 407–413.

Feyling-Hansen, R. W., and Ulleberg, K.K, 1984, A Tertiary-Quaternary section at Sarsbutka, Spitsbergen, Svalbard, and its foraminifera: Polar Research, n.s., v. 2, no. 1, p. 77–106.

Floris, S., 1972, Scleractinian corals from the Upper Cretaceous and Lower Tertiary of Nûgssuaq, West Greenland: Grønlands Geologiske Undersøgelse Bulletin 100, 132 p.

Fox, S. K., and Olsson, R. K., 1969, Danian planktonic foraminifera from the Cannonball Formation in North Dakota: Journal of Paleontology, v. 43, no. 6, p. 1397–1404.

Frederiksen, N. O., Ager, T. A., Oftedahl, O. G., and Edwards, L. E., 1985, Palynological samples near the Cretaceous/Tertiary boundary, North Slope of Alaska: Golden, Colorado, Society of Economic Paleontologists and Mineralogists, Annual Midyear Meeting, 2nd, Abstracts, v. 2, p. 31.

Frederiksen, N. O., Ager, T. A., and Edwards, L. E., 1986, Comment on 'Early Tertiary marine fossils from northern Alaska; Implications for Arctic Ocean paleogeography and faunal evolution': Geology, v. 14, no. 9, p. 802–803.

Fujita, K., and Newberry, J. T., 1982, Tectonic evolution of northeastern Siberia and adjacent regions: Tectonophysics, v. 89, p. 337–357.

——, 1983, Accretionary terranes and tectonic evolution of northeast Siberia, in Hashimoto, M., and Uyeda, S., eds., Accretion tectonics in the Circum-Pacific regions: Tokyo, Terra Scientific Publishing Co., p. 43–57.

Gartner, S., and Keany, J., 1978, The terminal Cretaceous event; A geologic problem with an oceanographic solution: Geology, v. 6, p. 708–712.

Gladenkov, Y. B., 1981, Marine Plio-Pleistocene of Iceland and problems of its correlation: Quaternary Research, v. 15, p. 18–23.

Gladenkov, Y. B., Norton, P., and Spaink, G., 1980, Upper Cenozoic of Iceland: U.S.S.R. Academy of Sciences Transactions, v. 345, 115 p.

Govoni, D. L., 1983, Gastropod molluscs from the Brightseat Formation (Paleocene: Danian) of Maryland [Ph.D. thesis]: Washington, D.C., The George Washington University, 271 p.

Gripp, K., 1927, Beiträge zur Geologie von Spitsbergen: Abhandlungen Naturwissenschaften Verein, v. 21, p. 1–38.

Grønlie, G., 1979, Tertiary paleogeography of the Norwegian-Greenland Sea: Norsk Polarinstitute Skrifter, v. 170, p. 49–61.

Hägg, R., 1925–1927, A new Tertiary fauna from Spitsbergen: University of Uppsala, Geological Institute Bulletin 20, p. 39–56.

Hansen, H. J., 1970, Danian Foraminifera from Nûgssuaq, West Greenland, with special reference to species occurring in Denmark: Grønlands Geologiske Undersøgelse Bulletin 93, 132 p.

Hassan, M. Y., 1953, Tertiary faunas from Kap Brewster, East Greenland: Meddelelser om Grønland, v. 111, no. 5, p. 1–42.

Hazel, J. E., 1968, Ostracodes from the Brightseat Formation (Danian) of Maryland: Journal of Paleontology, v. 42, p. 100–142.

Herman, Y., 1974, Arctic Ocean sediments, microfauna, and the climatic record in late Cenozoic time, in Herman, Y., ed., Marine geology and oceanography of the arctic seas: New York, Springer-Verlag, p. 283–348.

Hickey, L. J., West, R. M., Dawson, M. R., and Choi, D. K., 1983, Arctic terrestrial biota; Paleomagnetic evidence of age disparity with mid-northern latitudes during the late Cretaceous and early Tertiary: Science, v. 221, p. 1153–1156.

Hopkins, D. M., 1967, Quaternary marine transgressions in Alaska, in Hopkins, D. M., ed., The Bering land bridge: Stanford, California, Stanford University, p. 46–90.

Hopkins, D. M., and Marincovich, L. Jr., 1984, Whale biogeography and the history of the Arctic Basin: Netherlands, Groningen Rijksuniversitet, Works of the Arctic Centre, no. 8, p. 7–24.

Howe, H. V., and Laurencich, L., 1958, Introduction to the study of Cretaceous Ostracoda: Baton Rouge, Louisiana State University Press, 536 p.

Kauffman, E. G., 1975, Dispersal and biostratigraphic potential of Cretaceous benthonic Bivalvia in the Western Interior, in Caldwell, W.G.E., ed., The Cretaceous System in the Western Interior of North America: Geological Association of Canada Special Paper 13, p. 163–194.

Keen, M., 1978, The Tertiary-Palaeogene, in Bate, R. H., and Robinson, E., eds., A stratigraphic index of British Ostracoda: Liverpool, Seel House Press, p. 385–450.

—— , 1983, Ostracods and Tertiary biogeography, in Maddocks, R. F., ed., Applications of Ostracoda, Proceedings, Eighth International Symposium on Ostracoda: Houston, Texas, University of Houston, Department of Geosciences, p. 78–95.

Khokhlova, I. A., 1968, New Paleogene cytherids of the Turgai Depression and the northern Aral region, in New species of ancient plants and invertebrates of the U.S.S.R., no. 2, pt. 2: Moscow, U.S.S.R. Academy of Science, p. 248–277.

Kollmann, H. A., and Peel, J. S., 1983, Paleocene gastropods from Nûgssuaq, West Greenland: Grønlands Geologiske Undersøgelse Bulletin 146, p. 1–115.

Leffingwell, E. de K., 1919, The Canning River region, northern Alaska: U.S. Geological Survey, Professional Paper 294-C, p. 99–126.

Lemke, R. W., 1960, Geology of the Souris River area, North Dakota: U.S. Geological Survey Professional Paper 325, p. 1–138.

Lillegraven, J. A., and McKenna, M. C., 1986, Fossil mammals from the "Mesaverde" Formation (Late Cretaceous, Judithian) of the Bighorn and Wind River basins, Wyoming, with definitions of Late Cretaceous North American land-mammal "ages": American Museum of Natural History Novitates, no. 2840, p. 1–68.

Livsic, J. J., 1974, Palaeogene deposits and the platform structure of Svalbard: Norsk Polarinstitutt Skrifter 159, p. 1–51.

Macbeth, J. I., and Schmidt, R.A.M., 1973, Upper Cretaceous foraminifera from Ocean Point, northern Alaska: Journal of Paleontology, v. 47, p. 1047–1061.

McKenna, M. C., 1975, Fossil mammals and early Eocene North Atlantic land continuity: Annals of Missouri Botanical Garden, v. 62, p. 335–353.

—— , 1980, Eocene paleolatitude, climate, and mammals of Ellesmere Island: Palaeogeography, Palaeoclimatology, Palaeoecology, v. 30, p. 349–362.

—— , 1983, Cenozoic paleogeography of North Atlantic land bridges, in Bott, M.H.P., Saxov, S., Talwani, M., and Thiede, J., eds., Structure and development of the Greenland-Scotland Ridge: New York, Plenum, p. 351–399.

—— , 1984, Holarctic landmass rearrangement, cosmic events, and Cenozoic terrestrial organisms: Annals of the Missouri Botanical Garden, v. 70, p. 459–489.

MacNeil, F. S., 1957, Cenozoic megafossils of northern Alaska: U.S. Geological Survey Professional Paper 294-G, p. 99–126.

MacNeil, F. S., Wolfe, J. A., Miller, D. J., and Hopkins, D. M., 1961, Correlation of Tertiary formations of Alaska: Bulletin of the American Association of Petroleum Geologists, v. 45, no. 11, p. 1801–1809.

Marincovich, L., Jr., and Zinsmeister, W. J., 1985, Early Tertiary climates of the Arctic Ocean: Geological Society of America Abstracts with Programs, v. 17, no. 7, p. 653.

Marincovich, L., Jr., Brouwers, E. M., and Hopkins, D. M., 1983, Paleogeographic affinities and endemism of Cretaceous and Paleocene marine faunas in the Arctic: U.S. Geological Survey Circular 911, p. 45–46.

Marincovich, L., Jr., Brouwers, E. M., and Carter, L. D., 1984, Early Tertiary marine fossils from Ocean Point, Arctic Coastal Plain, and their relation to Arctic Ocean paleogeography: U.S. Geological Survey Circular 939, p. 15–17.

—— , 1985, Early Tertiary marine fossils from northern Alaska; Implications for Arctic Ocean paleogeography and faunal evolution: Geology, v. 13, no. 7, p. 770–773.

Matthews, R. K., 1984, Oxygen isotope record of ice-volume history; 100 million years of glacio-eustatic sea-level fluctuation, in Schlee, J. S., ed., Interregional unconformities and hydrocarbon accumulation: American Association of Petroleum Geologists Memoir 36, p. 97–107.

Miall, A. D., 1979, Mesozoic and Tertiary geology of Banks Island, Arctic Canada; The history of an unstable craton margin: Geological Survey of Canada Memoir 387, 235 p.

—— , 1981, Late Cretaceous and Paleogene sedimentation and tectonics in the Canadian Arctic Islands, in Miall, A. D., ed., Sedimentation and tectonics in alluvial basins: Geological Association of Canada Special Paper 23, p. 221–272.

—— , 1986, The Eureka Sound Group (Upper Cretaceous–Oligocene), Canadian Arctic Islands: Bulletin of Canadian Petroleum Geology, v. 34, no. 2, p. 240–270.

Morkhoven, F.P.C.M. van, 1963, Post-Paleozoic Ostracoda, v. 2: Amsterdam, Elsevier, 478 p.

Morris, J., 1852, Description of some fossil shells from the lower Thanet Sands: Geological Society of London Quarterly Journal, v. 8, p. 264–268.

Nikolaeva, I. A., 1977, New ostracode species from the Paleogene of the Turgai Basin: Moscow, U.S.S.R., Paleontological Society, Annual Yearbook Editorial Volume, p. 191–199.

Norris, G., and Miall, A. D., 1984, Arctic biostratigraphic heterochroneity: Science, v. 224, p. 174–175.

Obradovich, J. D., and Cobban, W. A., 1975, A time-scale for the Late Cretaceous of the Western Interior of North America, in Caldwell, W.G.E., ed., The Cretaceous System in the Western Interior of North America: Geological Association of Canada Special Paper 13, p. 31–54.

Perch-Nielsen, K., 1973, Danian and Campanian/Maastrichtian coccoliths from Nûgssuaq, West Greenland: Geological Society of Denmark Bulletin, v. 22, p. 79–82.

Pomerol, C., 1982, The Cenozoic Era, Tertiary and Quaternary: Chichester,

England, Ellis Horwood, Ltd., 272 p.

Ravn, J.P.J., 1904, The Tertiary fauna at Kap Dalton in East Greenland: Meddelelser om Grønland, v. 29, no. 3, p. 94–140.

—— , 1922, On the Mollusca of the Tertiary of Spitsbergen: Det Norske Videnskaps-akademi i Oslo, Resultater av de norske statsunderstøttede spitsbergenekspeditioner, v. 1, no. 2, p. 1–28.

—— , 1933, New investigations of the Tertiary of Cape Dalton, East Greenland: Meddelelser om Grønland, v. 105, no. 1, 15 p.

Repenning, C. A., 1983, New evidence for the age of the Gubik Formation, Alaskan North Slope: Quaternary Research, v. 19, p. 356–372.

Ricketts, B. D., 1986, New formations in the Eureka Sound Group, Canadian Arctic Islands: Geological Survey of Canada Paper 86–1B, Current Research, part B, p. 363–374.

Rosenkrantz, A., 1970, Marine upper Cretaceous and lowermost Tertiary deposits in West Greenland: Geological Society of Denmark Bulletin, v. 19, no. 4, p. 406–453.

Rosenkrantz, A., and Pulvertaft, T.C.R., 1969, Cretaceous-Tertiary stratigraphy and tectonics in northern West Greenland, in Kay, M., ed., North Atlantic; Geology and continental drift: American Association of Petroleum Geologists Memoir 12, p. 883–898.

Smith, A. G., and Briden, J. C., 1977, Mesozoic and Cenozoic paleocontinental maps: Cambridge, Cambridge University Press, 63 p.

Sohl, N. F., 1971, North American Cretaceous biotic provinces delineated by gastropods: Proceedings of the North American Paleontological Convention, part L, p. 1610–1638.

Soper, N. J., and Costa, L. I., 1976, Palynological evidence for the age of Tertiary basalts and post-basaltic sediments at Kap Dalton, central east Greenland: Grønlands Geologiske Undersøgelse Rapport 80, 150 p.

Speden, I. G., 1970, The type Fox Hills Formation, Cretaceous (Maestrichtian), South Dakota; Part 2. Systematics of the Bivalvia: New Haven, Connecticut, Yale University, Peabody Museum of Natural History Bulletin 33, 222 p.

Spicer, R. A., Wolfe, J. A., and Nichols, D. J., 1987, Alaskan Cretaceous-Tertiary floras and Arctic origins: Paleobiology, v. 13, no. 1, p. 73–83.

Stanley, E. A., 1965, Upper Cretaceous and Paleocene plant microfossils and Paleocene dinoflagellates and hystrichosphaerids from northwestern South Dakota: Bulletins of American Paleontology, v. 49, no. 222, p. 177–384.

Stanton, T. W., 1920, The fauna of the Cannonball marine member of the Lance Formation: U.S. Geological Survey Professional Paper 128–A, 60 p.

Strauch, F., 1972, Phylogenese, Adaptation und Migration einiger nordischer mariner Molluskengenera (*Neptunea, Panomya, Cyrtodaria,* und *Mya*): Abhandlungen der Senkenbergischen Naturforschenden Gesellschaft, no. 531, 211 p.

Szczechura, J., 1971, Paleocene Ostracoda from Nûgssuaq, West Greenland: Grønlands Geologiske Undersøgelse Bulletin 94, 42 p.

Tappan, H., 1962, Cretaceous Foraminifera; Part 3, Foraminifera from the Arctic slope of Alaska: U.S. Geological Survey Professional Paper 236–C, p. 91–209.

Todd, R., 1957, Foraminifera from Carter Creek, northeastern Alaska: U.S. Geological Survey Professional Paper 294–F, p. 223–234.

Vail, P. R., Mitchum, R. M., Jr., and Thompson, S. III, 1977, Seismic stratigraphy and global changes of sea level; Part 4, Global cycles of relative changes in sea level, in Payton, C. E., ed., Seismic stratigraphy; Applications to hydrocarbon exploration: American Association of Petroleum Geologists Memoir 36, p. 83–87.

Vinogradov, A. P., Vereshchagin, V., Nalivkin, V., Ronov, A., Khabakov, A., and Khain, V., 1967, Atlas of the lithological-paleogeographical maps of the U.S.S.R., Paleogene, Neogene, and Quaternary: Moscow, U.S.S.R. Ministry of Geology and Academy of Science and Ministry of Geology, 15 maps, scale 1:5,000,000.

—— , 1968, Atlas of the lithological-paleogeographical maps of the U.S.S.R., Triassic, Jurassic, and Cretaceous: Moscow, U.S.S.R. Ministry of Geology and Academy of Science, 20 maps, scale 1:5,000,000.

Vonderbank, K., 1970, Geologie und Fauna der Tertiären Ablagerungen Zentral-Spitsbergens: Norsk Polarinstitutt Skrifter 153, 119 p.

Waage, K. M., 1968, The type Fox Hills Formation, Cretaceous (Maestrichtian), South Dakota; Part 1, Stratigraphy and paleoenvironments: New Haven, Connecticut, Yale University, Peabody Museum of Natural History Bulletin 27, 171 p.

West, R. M., Dawson, M. R., Hutchison, J. H., and Ramaekers, P., 1975, Paleontologic evidence of marine sediments in the Eureka Sound Formation of Ellesmere Island, Arctic Archipelago, N.W.T., Canada: Canadian Journal of Earth Science, v. 12, p. 574–579.

West, R. M., Dawson, M. R., and Hutchison, J. H., 1977, Fossils from the Paleogene Eureka Sound Formation, N.W.T., Canada; Occurrence, climatic, and paleogeographic implications, in West, R. M., ed., Paleontology and plate tectonics: Milwaukee, Wisconsin, Milwaukee Public Museum Special Publications in Biology and Geology 2, p. 77–93.

West, R. M., Dawson, M. R., Hickey, L. J., and Miall, A. D., 1981, Upper Cretaceous and Paleogene sedimentary rocks, eastern Canadian Arctic and related North Atlantic areas, in Kerr, J. W., and Ferguson, A. J., eds., Geology of the North Atlantic borderlands: Canadian Society of Petroleum Geologists Memoir 7, p. 279–298.

Westermann, G.E.G., 1964, Species distribution of the world-wide Triassic pelecypod *Monotis* Brown: New Delhi, 22nd International Geological Congress, Proceedings of Section B, Paleontology and Stratigraphy, p. 374–389.

—— , 1973, The Late Triassic bivalve, *Monotis,* in Hallam, A., ed., Atlas of biogeography: Amsterdam, Elsevier, p. 251–258.

Williams, G. D., and Stelck, C. R., 1975, Speculations on the Cretaceous paleogeography of North America: Geological Association of Canada Special Paper 13, p. 1–20.

Willumsen, P. S., and Cote, R. P., 1982, Tertiary sedimentation in the southern Beaufort Sea, Canada, in Watkins, J. S., and Drake, C. L., Studies in continental margin geology: American Association of Petroleum Geologists Memoir 34, p. 283–294.

Young, F. G., and McNeil, D. H., 1984, Cenozoic stratigraphy of the Mackenzie Delta, Northwest Territories: Geological Survey of Canada Bulletin 336, 63 p.

Manuscript Accepted by the Society November 4, 1987

ACKNOWLEDGMENTS

We acknowledge with great thanks the reviews of this work by Thomas M. Cronin and William V. Sliter, U.S. Geological Survey; Mary R. Dawson, Carnegie Museum of Natural History; and John H. Wall and David H. McNeil, Geological Survey of Canada.

Hudson Bay sledge pattern. Relief expedition, 1884. From Adolphus W. Greeley, Three years of Arctic service, an account of the Lady Franklin Bay expedition of 1881–1884: New York, Charles Scribner's Sons, v. 1, p. 196.

Printed in U.S.A.

Chapter 24

Late Mesozoic and Cenozoic paleoceanography of the northern polar oceans

Jörn Thiede
GEOMAR Research Center for Marine Geosciences, Wischofstrasse 1-3, Building 4, D-2300 Kiel, Federal Republic of Germany
David L. Clark
Department of Geology and Geophysics, University of Wisconsin, Madison, Wisconsin
Yvonne Herman
Department of Geology, Washington State University, Pullman, Washington 99164

INTRODUCTION

High-latitude polar regions of the Earth have experienced cold, cool, and temperature paleoclimates in the course of their geologic history, but they have probably always been colder than low-latitude continents and oceans. Extreme climates leading to development of extensive frozen and ice-covered regions at high latitudes can, however, only be documented for a few, relatively short intervals of the Earth's history, separated by long time spans with little or no ice (Frakes, 1979). The Cenozoic evolution of glacial-type climates during the past 30 to 40 m.y. is the most recent period of extreme climate, and differs from the preceding ones. During the Cenozoic, plate-tectonic processes generated climatically isolated land areas and ocean basins in both the Southern and Northern Hemispheres, which were repeatedly affected by glaciations. For glacial-type paleoclimates older than the Cenozoic, we have only been able to document unipolar glaciation because the opposite high-latitude area was situated in wide and deep ocean basins and was probably relatively ice free due to advection of warmer surface water from lower latitudes.

Despite the apparent similarity of Quaternary high-latitude paleoclimates, the development of glacial-type paleoceanographies of the northern and southern polar oceans have revealed important differences, and they are not easily compared with each other. Our understanding of Cenozoic Southern Hemisphere paleoclimates is much more advanced than it is for the Northern Hemisphere. It is particularly intriguing that the available data appear to indicate that the Southern Hemisphere may have become cold more than 20 m.y. earlier than its northern counterpart.

There are numerous reasons why it is more difficult to achieve progress in studying the late Mesozoic and Cenozoic history of the northern polar oceans. The major obstacles are (1) the difficulty in obtaining long, high-quality deep-sea sediment cores that can be dated easily and efficiently, and (2) the lack of sufficient sample material documenting the early phase (e.g., pre-Pliocene) of development of cold surface waters in the Arctic Ocean proper. In Figure 1 we have compiled evidence from all presently available deep-sea sediment cores from the Arctic Ocean, and it is clear that this attempt to synthesize properties and changes of the Late Mesozoic and Cenozoic depositional environments of the northern polar oceans is rather incomplete. Although important evidence on the evolution of Cenozoic Northern Hemisphere paleoceanography and paleoclimate has been collected from sediment sequences of shelves and land areas adjacent to the Arctic Ocean (Funder and others, 1985), in this paper, we will mostly use data collected in the deep-sea basins proper.

The morphology of the modern northern polar ocean basins (Fig. 2 and Plate 1) is dominated by the large Arctic Ocean with its deep-water connection through the Lena Trough into the Norwegian-Greenland Sea. Important sills such as the Greenland-Scotland Ridge (Bott and others, 1983), Bering Strait (Hopkins, 1967), and relatively minor seaways through the Canadian Arctic archipelago (Kerr, 1982) separate this continuous deep-sea area from the adjacent basins of the world ocean (North Pacific and Atlantic oceans). The deep Bering Sea is really outside the area that can be called truly Arctic. The northern deep-sea basin of Baffin Bay is connected to the Arctic Ocean mainly through the Nares Strait and Lancaster Sound. However, because of its isolation and its small size, its impact on northern polar ocean properties now, as well as in the geologic past, probably has been quite limited.

The basement age of the Canada Basin of the Arctic Ocean documents sea-floor spreading since late Mesozoic times (Green and others, 1982), and since early Tertiary times in the

---

Thiede, J., Clark, D. L., and Herman, Y., 1990, Late Mesozoic and Cenozoic paleoceanography of the northern polar oceans, *in* Grantz, A., Johnson, L., and Sweeney, J. F., eds., The Arctic Ocean region: Boulder, Colorado, Geological Society of America, The Geology of North America, v. L.

Norwegian-Greenland Sea (Talwani and Eldholm, 1977). Because of the plate-tectonic evolution of a larger continuous deep-sea area in the northern polar oceans during the past 80 m.y., and the available sample material from the Arctic Ocean (Figs. 1 and 5), we will concentrate on a synthesis of the properties of the northern polar ocean depositional environments during the past 80 to 100 m.y.

Present physiography, oceanography, and depositional environment

The modern physiography of the northern polar oceans is mainly the result of plate-tectonic processes still in progress. The major physiographic provinces consist of the Norwegian-Greenland Sea, with four deep-sea basins, and the Arctic Ocean proper, with three major subbasins. The two provinces are separated by the volcanic Alpha-Mendeleyev and the continental Lomonosov ridges (Plate 1).

The sills that separate the Arctic Ocean from the North Pacific (Bering Strait), from Baffin Bay (Nares Strait and Barrow Strait), from the Labrador Sea (Davis Strait); and the Norwegian-Greenland Sea from the main North Atlantic Ocean (Greenland-Scotland Ridge, with approximately 900 m water depth in the Faeroe-Shetland Channel), exert a controlling influence on the oceanography of the modern northern polar oceans. The straits direct the flow of surface-water currents into and out of the northern polar deep-sea basins, and the Greenland-Scotland Ridge channels the deep-water outflow from the Norwegian-Greenland Sea into the main North Atlantic Ocean (Meincke, 1983).

The Arctic Ocean is covered by permanent pack ice whose extent and borders fluctuate widely in response to seasonal changes in wind patterns, insolation, and resulting surface water temperatures. True icebergs are rare or absent in most regions due to the absence of large ice shelves or glaciers. Patterns of surface and bottom-water circulation are illustrated schematically in Figure 3. Relatively warm North Atlantic surface water enters the northern polar deep-sea basins across the eastern section of the Greenland-Scotland Ridge. These waters continue northward, paralleling the Norwegian continental margin as the Norwegian Current, which divides north of Norway into a branch entering the Barents Sea and a branch (Vestspitsbergen Current) following the Vestspitsbergen continental margin into the eastern Arctic Basin. Pacific surface waters also enter the western Arctic basin through the Bering Strait, but they are quantitatively much less important than the influx from the North Atlantic Ocean.

The advection of relatively warm surface-water masses into the northern polar deep-sea basins is balanced by cold, partly ice-covered, southward flowing surface waters trailing the East Greenland continental margin (the East Greenland Current, Aagaard and others, 1985), and by deep cold bottom waters flowing over the Greenland-Scotland Ridge into the North Atlantic Ocean (Meincke, 1983).

Salinities of the upper few meters of the surface waters in the

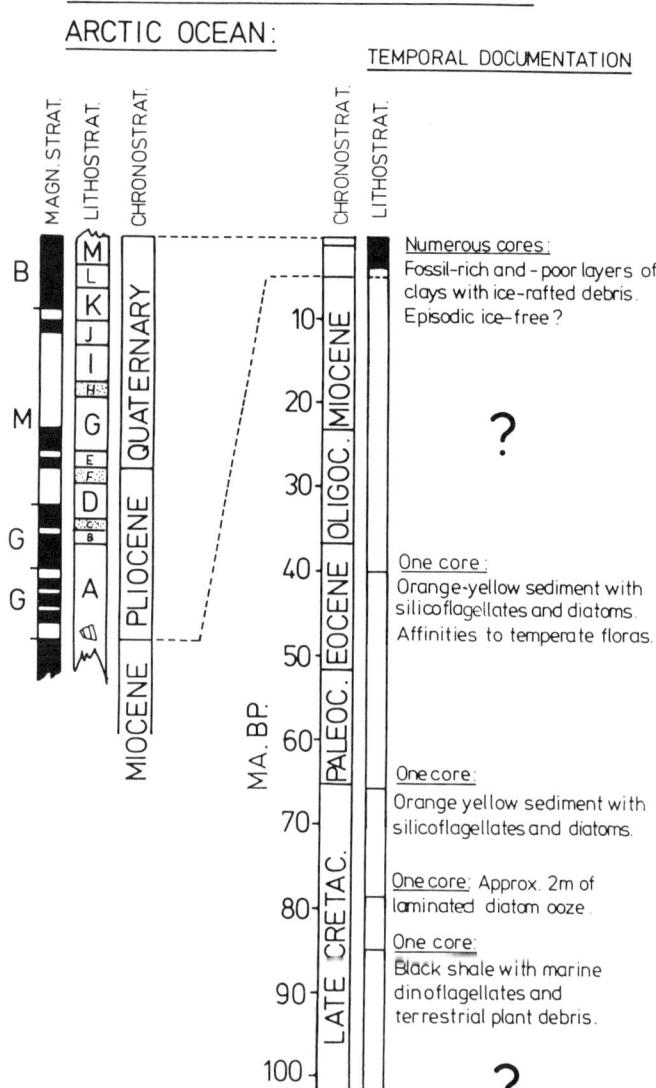

Figure 1. Temporal coverage and composition of all presently available Arctic deep-sea cores (compiled from various sources).

Arctic Ocean proper and in the area of the East Greenland Current are reduced because of the important input of fresh water from Siberian, and to a lesser degree, North American and European rivers into the Arctic Ocean. Reduced surface salinities, together with the cold northern climate, help to maintain the Arctic Ocean pack-ice cover. Structure and properties of the deeper parts of the northern polar deep-sea water column are illustrated on a profile from the Norwegian Basin through the Greenland and Eurasia Basins, to the Canada Basin (Fig. 4). Differences in the deep-water properties between basins demonstrate the importance and impact of sills on the deep-water exchange.

Relatively recently the importance of brine formation on polar shelves has been recognized (Aagaard and others, 1985).

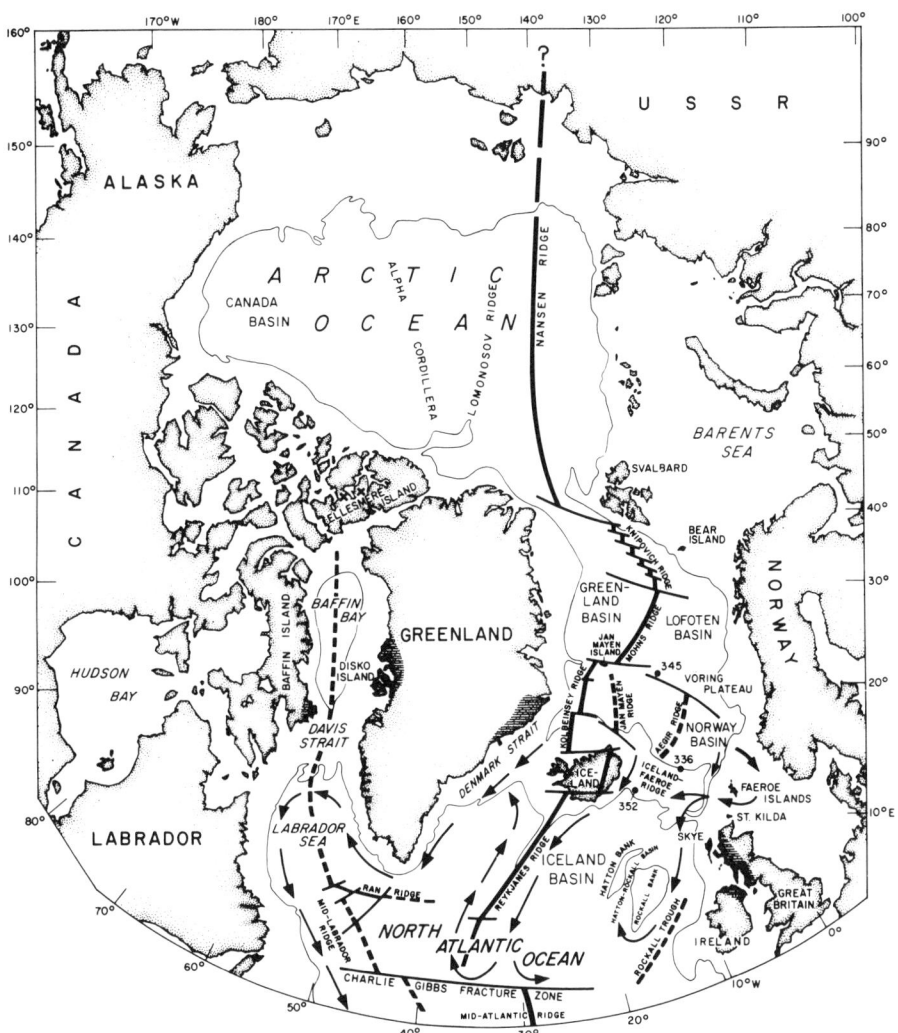

Figure 2. Index map of Norwegian-Greenland Sea, Arctic Ocean, and North Atlantic Ocean. Light line represents 1,000 m depth contour; heavy lines represent spreading centers, dashed where distinct; intermediate lines are transform faults; darkened areas are outcrops of basalt of Early Tertiary North Atlantic igneous province; bottom flow of Norwegian-Greenland Sea overflow water. After Nilsen (1983).

These cold, dense, and well oxygenated brines cascade over the continental margin into the adjacent deep-sea basins, possibly causing locally deep erosion. This type of deep-water renewal is different from the postulated overturn of waters in the open Norwegian-Greenland Sea (Fig. 3). Downwelling of the oxygenated brines over the polar continental margins might well result in the very important color difference between the orange to brownish-reddish deep-sea deposits in the Arctic Ocean and the light brown-grayish-greenish deposits in the Norwegian-Greenland Sea (Holtedahl, 1959; Clark and others, 1980; Markussen and others, 1985).

Plate-tectonic evolution

Magnetic surveys of the ocean floor of the Norwegian-Greenland Sea (Talwani and Eldholm, 1977) and of the Arctic Ocean (Taylor and others, 1981; Taylor, 1983) document linear sea-floor spreading-type magnetic anomalies under major parts of the northern polar deep-sea basins (Plate 4). Sweeney (1985) suggested that the Canada Basin experienced continental breakup from Hauterivian through Aptian time (113 to 131 Ma), with active sea-floor spreading following up to the Campanian. The Makarov Basin probably evolved during Late Cretaceous and very early Tertiary time, and the Eurasia and Norwegian-Greenland Sea basins opened from Early Eocene to Holocene time.

The northern polar deep-sea basins are separated and partly limited by a number of structural highs whose origin and nature are much less clearly defined than the adjacent deep-sea floors. The Greenland-Scotland Ridge (Bott and others, 1983) and the Alpha-Mendeleyev Ridge (Van Wagoner and Robinson, 1985) are of volcanic origin. Nares Strait and Lancaster Sound probably trace old and complex tectonic lineaments (Jackson, 1985), whereas Lomonosov Ridge (Weber, 1979) and Bering Strait

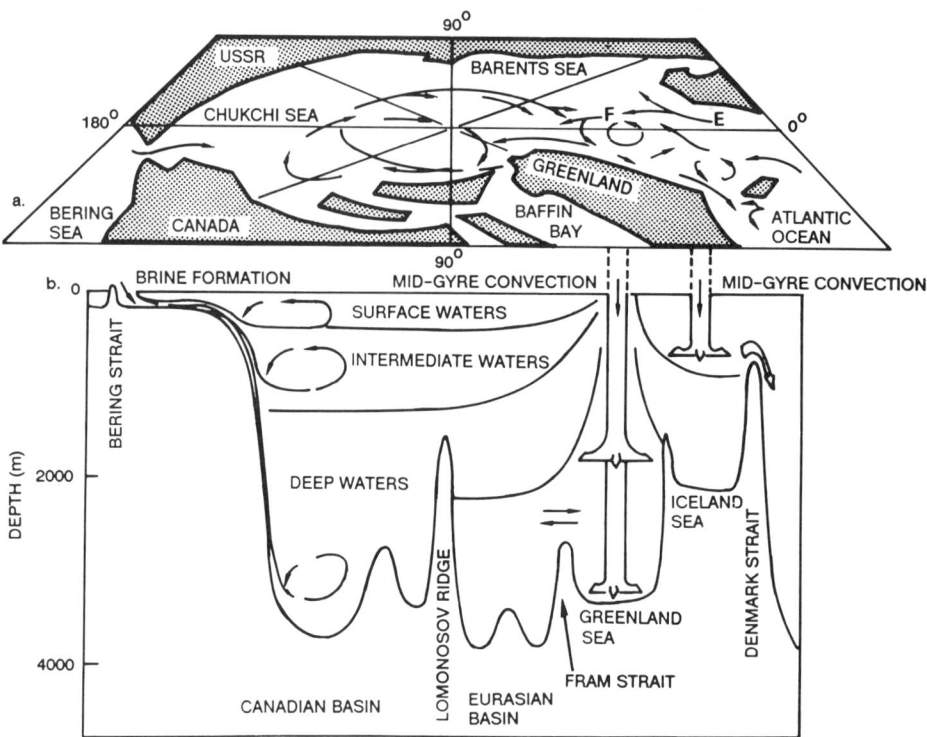

Figure 3. Schematic illustration of surface-water circulation and water-mass structure in the Arctic Ocean and in the Norwegian-Greenland Sea. From Aagaard and others (1985).

(Grantz and others, 1981) are believed to be complex structural units composed of continental crust. The present understanding of the plate tectonic and paleophysiographic evolution of the northern polar deep-sea basins is addressed by Harbert and others as well as Lawver and Scotese (both this volume).

Today we believe that the deep connection between the Arctic Ocean proper and the Norwegian-Greenland Sea (Lena Trough) began to develop since magnetic anomaly 13 (approximately 35 Ma), but a ridge composed of the Yermak Plateau and the Morris-Jessup Rise might have inhibited deep-water flow until much later, possibly into Miocene and/or Pliocene time (Kristoffersen and Husebye, 1985a). The Greenland-Scotland Ridge might have subsided below sea level only during Neogene time (Thiede and Eldholm, 1983), but it might have been partially foundered considerably earlier (Berggren and Schnitker, 1983). Although Mesozoic Arctic planktonic floras suggest a free exchange of pelagic water masses between the Arctic and North Pacific oceans, little is known about how and when pathways across the Bering Strait developed. It is also unknown if and how the Lomonosov and Alpha-Mendeleev Ridges subsided, but both of them might once have had positions close to, or even above, the sea surface.

Available samples and data

The development of a revised interpretation of the paleoceanography of the northern polar oceans is largely due to a number of very successful expeditions to the Arctic Ocean, numerous cruises to the Norwegian-Greenland Sea, and the combined efforts of scientists from a number of North American and European countries. Although Scandinavian researchers recovered and described the first deep-sea sediment samples from the Arctic Ocean proper more than 80 years ago (Düggild, 1906), most progress has only been achieved over the past two decades. American ice-island expeditions explored and sampled the central Arctic region (Fig. 5; Clark and others, 1980); the Canadians launched the CESAR and LOREX expeditions (Jackson and Johnson, 1986; Morris and others, 1985); and several European nations conducted research in the eastern Arctic basins (Fig. 6), including the Swedish YMER-80 expedition (Boström and Thiede, 1981, 1984), the FRAM-I and FRAM-IV ice islands (in close cooperation with North American colleagues, see Kristoffersen, 1979), the Norwegian RV *Polarsirkel* expedition (Markussen and others, 1982), and finally the German expeditions on RV *Polarstern* (Augstein and others, 1984).

The greatest number of sediment cores from the Amerasia Basin was obtained from ice island T-3 (Fig. 5). About 580 cores were collected and curated at the University of Wisconsin, Madison. Additional cores were also taken from T-3 during the time of its occupancy (1954 to 1974) by the Lamont group, and these cores reside at the Lamont-Doherty Geological Observatory. Most of the T-3 cores have been cataloged and are part of the NOAA Ocean Core Repository Library System. Details such as location, sediment type, and age are available by the NOAA office in Boulder, Colorado.

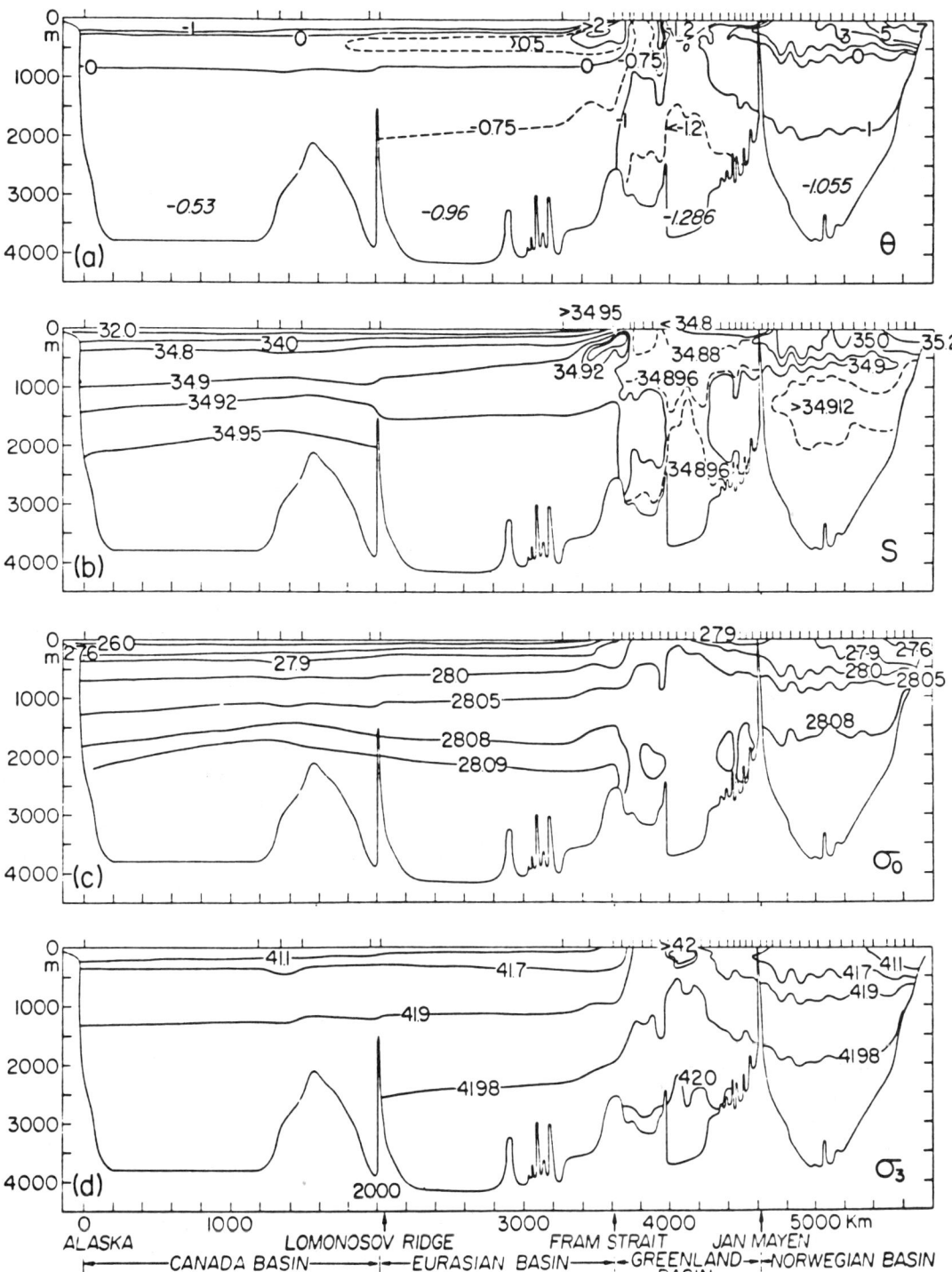

Figure 4. Distribution of hydrographic properties along a profile from the Norwegian Basin across the Arctic Ocean to the Alaskan continental margin. a, potential temperature; b, salinity; c, density relative to the surface; d, density relative to 3,000 m. From Aagaard and others (1985).

The Canadian CESAR project (Jackson, 1985a) recovered 16 sediment cores from the drifting pack ice during spring of 1983. The Lomonosov Ridge and Makarov Basin cores show a similar, but slightly different, lithologic sequence to that of the Alpha Ridge. Nonetheless, stratigraphic correlation of units is possible (Morris and others, 1985), indicating that the cores are upper Pleistocene (less than 730 ka). Sediments from the Fram Basin include turbidites and glacial-marine deposits and have not yet been studied.

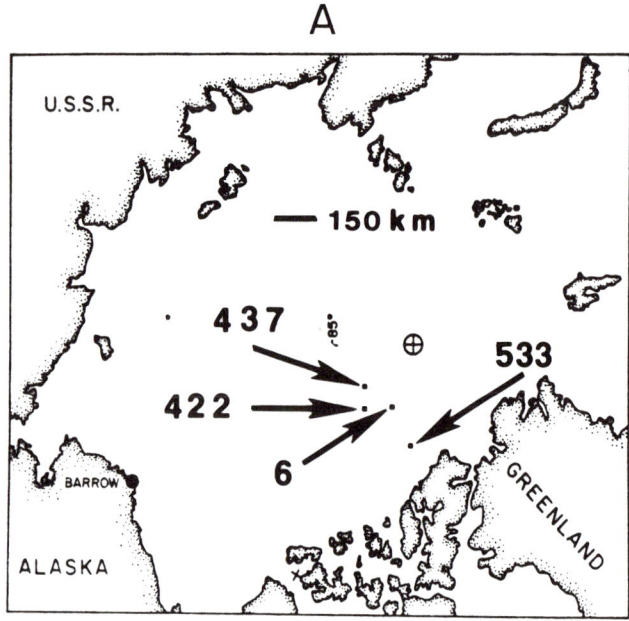

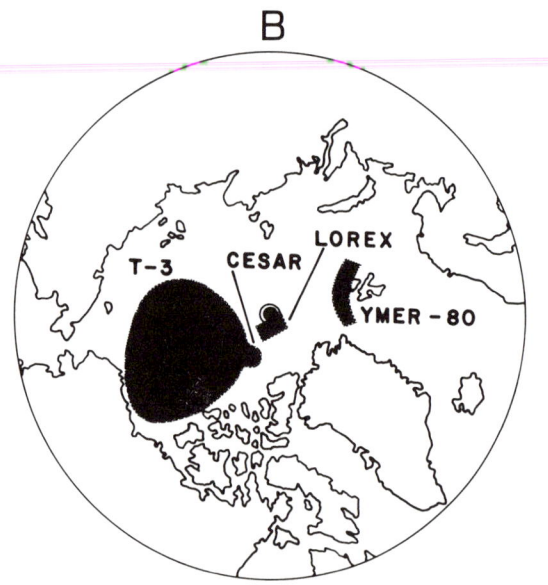

Figure 5. A. Index map of the four pre-Late Cenozoic cores known from the central Arctic Ocean. Core 422 (Middle Eocene), and cores 437 and 533 (Late Cretaceous) are from ice island T-3; core 6 (Late Cretaceous) is from the Canadian CESAR expedition. B. Areas of the Arctic Ocean covered by various scientific projects that included recovery of sediment cores (see project descriptions in text, and Fig. 6 for detail of eastern Arctic Basin).

As far as is currently known, sediment cores from the eastern Arctic basins comprise, without exception, upper Cenozoic, probably Quaternary deposits (Markussen and others, 1985; Zahn and others, 1985), which resemble in many details those of the central and western Arctic basins (Clark and others, 1980). They are stored in the collections of the Departments of Geology of the universities of Oslo (Norway), Stockholm (Sweden), and Kiel (F.R. Germany) as well as in the German Polar Institute (AWI) in Bremerhaven.

In total, these core collections contain several hundred sediment cores of lengths varying between a few centimeters to about 10 m of Neogene and Quaternary sediments, with only four cores from older deposits (Fig. 1). The T-3 ice-island cores contained two Cretaceous cores and one Paleogene core (Kitchell and Clark, 1982; Clark and Byers, 1984; Bukry, 1984); the CESAR expedition succeeded in recovering one Upper Cretaceous laminated diatomite (Mudie and Blasco, 1985).

In contrast to the sparse Arctic Ocean record, the history of the Norwegian-Greenland Sea is documented by numerous sediment cores. They are found in several North American and European core collections. The Deep-Sea Drilling Project (DSDP) and the Ocean Drilling Program (ODP) each devoted one entire leg to this area, drilling a total of 18 sites, which penetrated Paleogene, Neogene, and Quaternary sediment (Talwani and others, 1976; Eldholm and others, 1986a, 1987). Besides a few cores with Tertiary sediments taken from other vessels (Björklund and Kellogg, 1972), numerous cores from Quaternary deposits permit detailed studies of the Cenozoic (Quaternary?) paleoclimatic and paleoceanographic history of the central and southeastern Norwegian Sea and of the Norwegian continental margin (Kellogg, 1976; Jansen and others, 1983; Jansen and Erlenkeuser, 1985). Most of these cores can be dated by conventional methods and correlated to the North Atlantic sedimentary record; however, detailed, high resolution $\delta^{18}O$ curves are published for only a limited number of sediment cores (Thiede and others, 1986).

STRATIGRAPHY OF THE SEDIMENT COVER: AVAILABLE STRATIGRAPHIC METHODS

The stratigraphy of sediment cores from the Norwegian-Greenland Sea (both Tertiary and Quaternary deposits) are dated with reasonable detail and correlated to the record of the adjacent North Atlantic Ocean. The Paleogene and upper Mesozoic deposits of the Arctic Ocean have been dated by means of biostratigraphy only (Ling and others, 1973; Bukry, 1984, 1985; Clark and Byers, 1984) and are correlated to North Pacific and western North American stratigraphic records. The numerous upper Cenozoic Arctic sediment cores, however, pose very serious stratigraphic problems; these problems are not yet resolved, but they have led to controversial opinions on the detailed temporal framework of the Late Cenozoic Arctic Ocean depositional history. Therefore, the stratigraphic methods that have been used to date the cores will be briefly discussed.

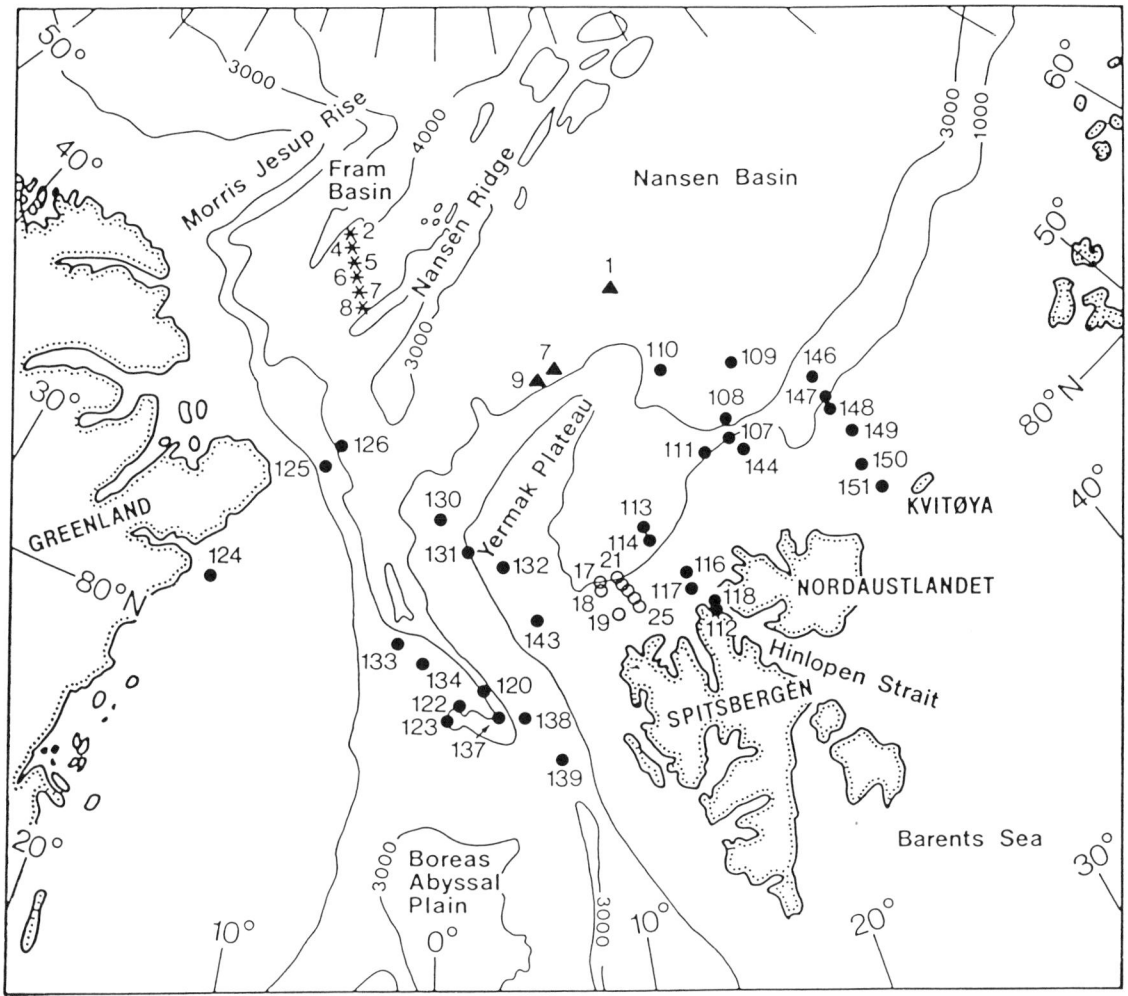

Figure 6. Bathymetric map of the eastern Arctic Ocean between and north of Greenland and Svalbard showing locations of sediment cores: FRAM-I (asterisks), FRAM-IV (closed triangles), RV *Polarsirkel* (open circles), and YMER-80 (closed circles).

Lithostratigraphic methods. Detailed lithostratigraphic descriptions of many upper Cenozoic Arctic sediment cores revealed at an early stage of the investigations that the upper few meters of the Arctic Ocean sediment cover consist of a series of distinct lithological units a few centimeters to decimeters thick (Fig. 7). These units can be discerned from each other based on their composition, texture, structures, and paleontological, sedimentological, and chemical properties. Herman (1974a), Clark and others (1980), and more recently, Morris and others (1985) and Markussen and others (1985) have shown that, although regional variability is observed, these lithologic units can be correlated over wide distances and across different morphological features; they obviously document changes of wide regions of the Arctic Ocean depositional environment.

Biostratigraphic methods. Biostratigraphic data help to resolve the ages of the Paleogene and upper Mesozoic Arctic Ocean cores, but establishing detailed age assignments on the large number of cores from younger sediments is much more difficult. The dominant planktonic foraminifer in all of these upper Cenozoic cores is *Neogloboquadrina pachyderma,* which occurred since early late Miocene (Kennett and Srinivasan, 1983). Although planktonic and benthic foraminifers are not distributed evenly throughout the Arctic Ocean sediment cover (Fig. 7), they have a zonation and they occur enriched in some horizons that can be correlated over wide areas (Herman, 1974a). Many authors believe that the fluctuating concentrations of these fossil groups might reflect productivity changes in Arctic Ocean surface waters; however, the presently available stratigraphic resolution does not yet permit confirmation of this interpretation.

Ostracods, echinoderms, molluscs, and sponge spicules are found in Arctic Ocean sediments in addition to foraminifers, but these have not proven to have stratigraphic value. Diatoms and radiolarians are completely lacking in upper Cenozoic sediments. Noncalcareous dinoflagellates and palynomorphs had been observed only rarely until Mudie (1985) succeeded in establishing detailed biostratigraphic zonations of central Arctic CESAR

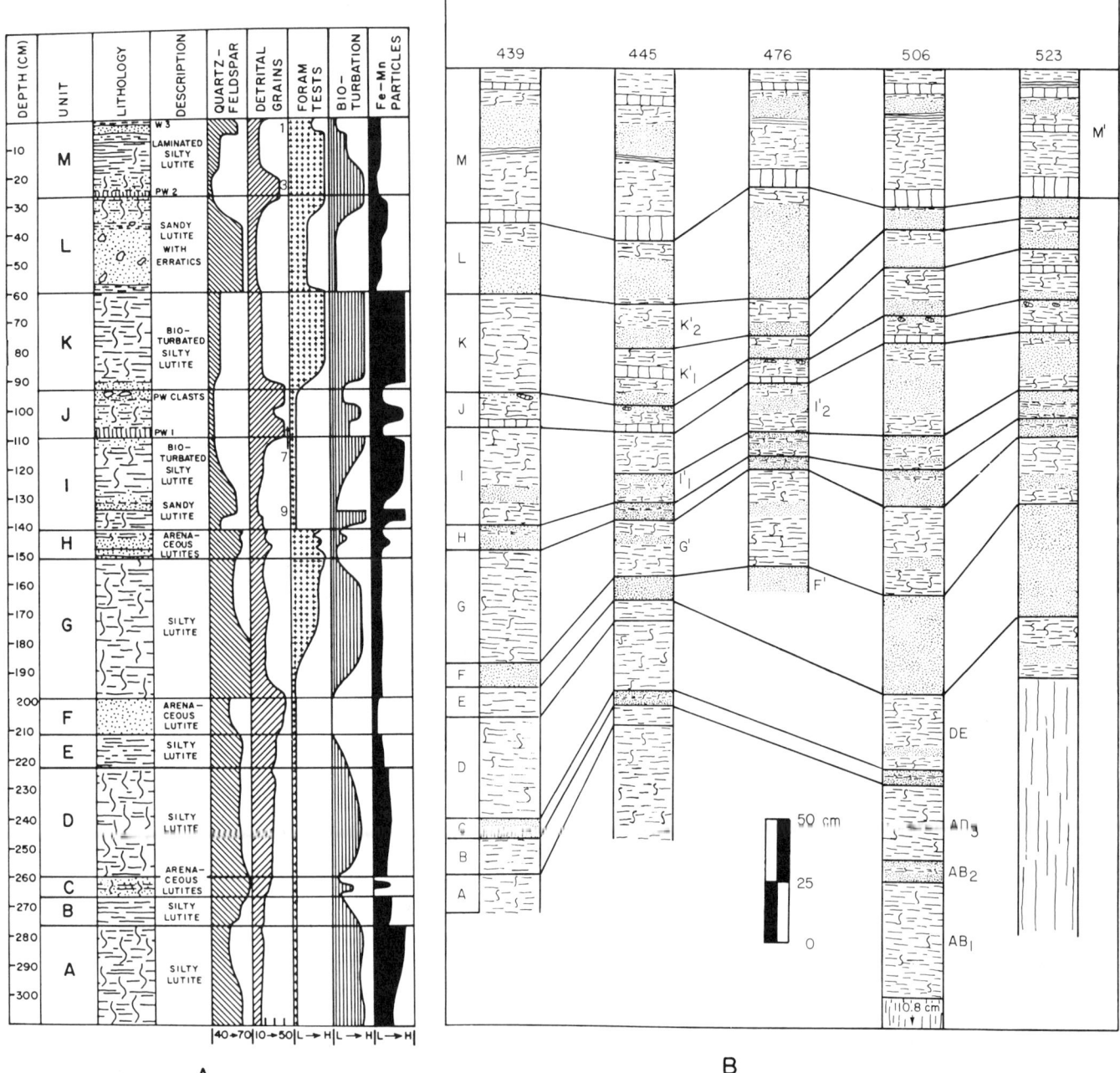

Figure 7. A. Lithostratigraphic units A to M in central Arctic Ocean. Sedimentary parameters include percentages of quartz-feldspar and total detrital grains. L to H indicates low to high abundance. Numbers in "detrital grains" column refer to carbonate maxima peaks. After Clark and others (1980). B. Correlation of Alpha Rise stratigraphy (Clark and others, 1980) with the "eastern" Alpha Ridge area described by Minicucci and Clark (1983).

cores (see also Aksu, 1985a). Contrary to previous expectations, however, coccoliths are found in the young eastern Arctic Ocean sediments, and they help to define a rough, but useful biostratigraphic frame (Worsley and Herman, 1980; Gard, 1986; Knudsen, 1985). The coccolith data aid in establishing maximum ages (Fig. 8) to help verify new interpretations of magnetostratigraphic eastern Arctic sediment-core data.

Magnetostratigraphic methods. The earliest studies of Arctic Ocean sediment cores utilized magnetostratigraphic data to provide a base for stratigraphic interpretations (Fig. 9). Most of the cores seemed to document a time span from late Miocene to modern times (Herman, 1974a; Clark and others, 1980; Steuerwald and others, 1968; Aksu and Mudie, 1985). The actual measurements upon which the interpretations of the pre-1985 studies

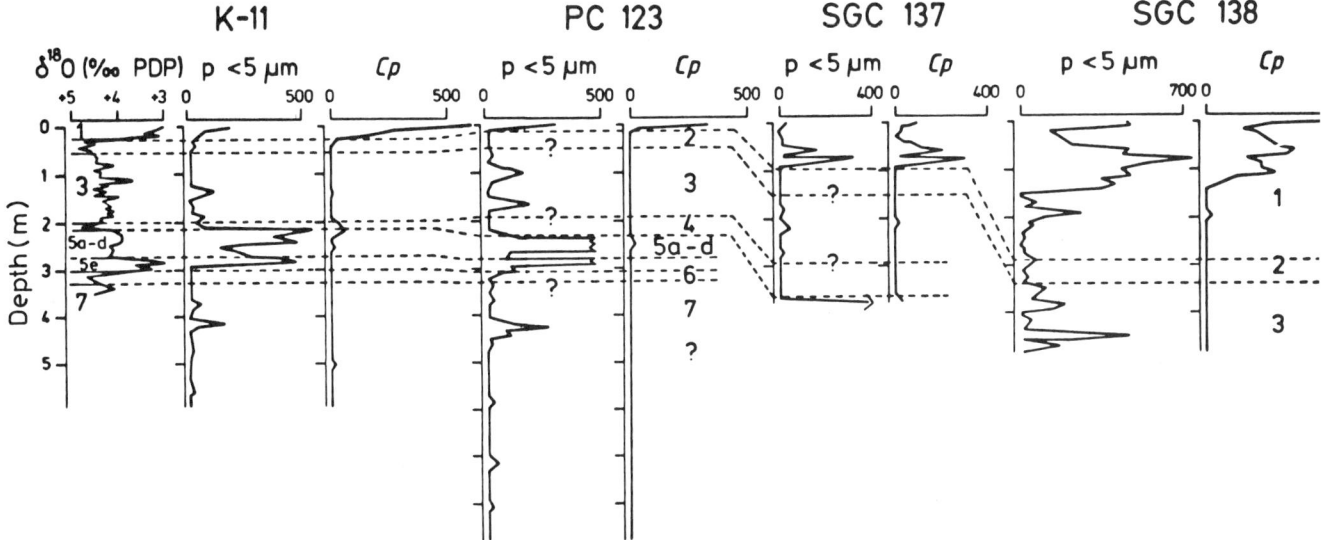

Figure 8. Correlations between K-11 (Norwegian-Greenland Sea) and YMER-80 PC 123, SGC 137, and SGC 138 cores with suggested oxygen-isotope stage boundaries. p, placoliths; Cp, *Coccolithus pelagicus*. After Gard (1986).

are based have never been published. The part of the data that is still accessible is presently under reevaluation, however (Jones, 1987), and the following revised, but still preliminary, ages have been made available for boundaries of the lithological units of Clark and others, 1980: M/L 0.45 Ma, L/K 0.62 Ma, K/J 0.82 Ma, J/I 0.91 Ma, I/H 1.08 Ma, H/G 1.15 Ma, G/F 1.43 Ma, F/E 1.50 Ma, E/D 1.55 Ma, D/C 1.75 Ma, C/B 1.78 Ma, B/A 1.83 Ma.

Recently, Lövlie and others (1986) and Bleil (Bremen, personal communication, 1985) carried out very detailed magnetostratigraphic studies of sediment cores from the Fram Strait and from the continental margin north of Svalbard (Figs. 10A and B), which suggest ages much younger than those in the central Arctic Ocean. They interpreted the intervals of reversed global magnetic field to be correlative to the Blake, Biva I, or Lachamp events within the Brunhes epoch, which suggested that sedimentation rates in the eastern Arctic Basin were one to several orders of magnitude higher than in the central Arctic Ocean.

O-isotopic methods. Measurements of O-isotope ratios in Arctic sediments for stratigraphic purposes have been carried out for many years (Herman and O'Neil, 1975; Minicucci and Clark, 1983). Usually, shell material has been used from the planktonic foraminifer *Neogloboquadrina pachyderma*. However, many of these data series were not satisfying because of the spotty and incoherent distribution of the fossil material. More recently, complete O-isotope curves (Fig. 11) have been established for eastern Arctic Ocean Upper Quaternary sediment sections (Zahn and others, 1985; Markussen and others, 1985), and these data were correlated unequivocally to corresponding O-isotope records of low-latitude ocean basins. It is now expected that detailed O-isotope stratigraphies based both on planktonic and benthic foraminifers have great potential for resolving some of the important stratigraphic problems of Arctic Ocean cores. Arctic O-isotope curves also suggest that at least some of the sediment in the eastern Arctic Ocean accumulated at sedimentation rates much higher than in the central Arctic Ocean. Recently, Aksu (1985b) published planktonic foraminiferal distributions and O-isotope ratios, and attempted a correlation of Arctic magnetic data and O-isotope ratios with those from the tropical Pacific (Shackleton and Opdyke, 1976). These data also appear to support slow sediment accumulation in the central Arctic.

Amino-acid epimerization methods. Recently, amino-acid epimerization techniques have been applied to sample material from several T-3 ice-island cores previously dated by magnetostratigraphic methods (Sejrup and others, 1984). Although amino-acid epimerization data are not easily translated into absolute ages, the ratios obtained from the Arctic fossil material do suggest that these cores document a depositional history of only a few hundred thousand years, which is in conflict with earlier estimates of approximately 3 m.y. (Herman, 1974b; Clark and others, 1980).

Radiometric methods. Reliable radiocarbon ages have been obtained from only a few central Arctic sediment cores (Ku and Broecker, 1967). Since ages at the 7 to 10 cm interval below the sediment surface in the central Arctic were in the range of 25 to 30 ka, much hope cannot be placed on this method even if technical advances (Clark and others, 1986) allow dating of somewhat older sediments. Other radiometric methods have not yet been demonstrated to be easily and economically applicable to Arctic Ocean sediments, and absolute dating of Arctic Ocean sediments has remained an enigma (Herman and Osmond, 1984).

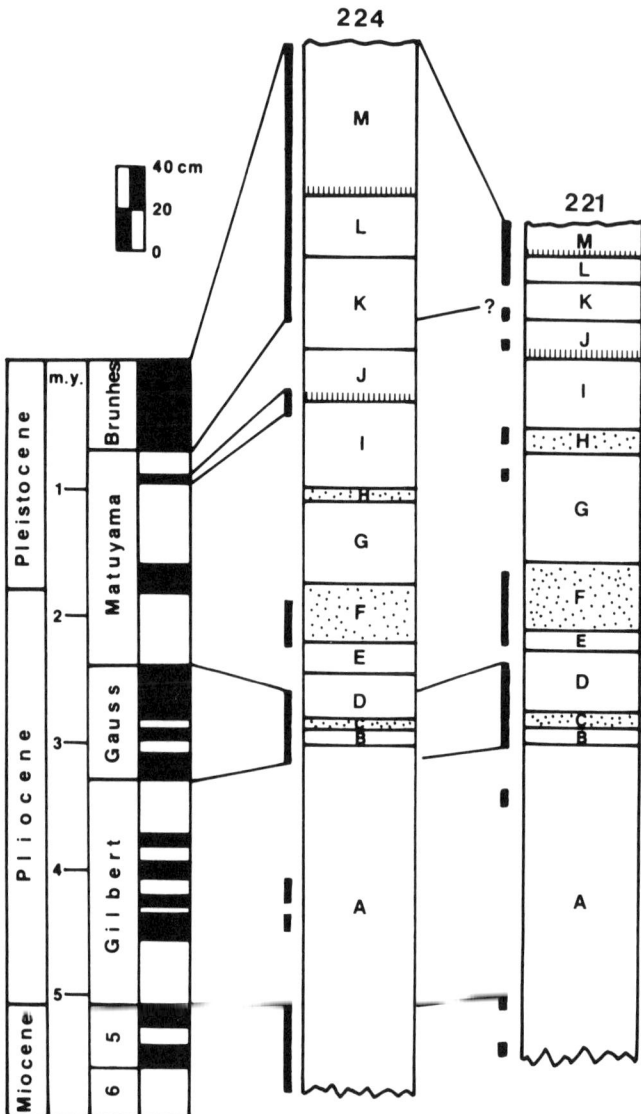

Figure 9. Lithostratigraphic units in two cores from the Alpha Ridge. Correlation with magnetic reversal stratigraphy and classification indicated. Strongest evidence of Late Miocene age is from extrapolation of sedimentation rates from the Gauss-Gilbert and Matuyama-Gauss boundaries. Stippled units are key arenaceous lutite beds in lower part of section. Hachures are key pink-white layers in upper part of section From Clark and others (1980).

LATE MESOZOIC–EARLY CENOZOIC DEPOSITIONAL ENVIRONMENT: THE WARM ARCTIC OCEAN

Most Late Cretaceous paleogeographic reconstructions suggest that the Arctic Ocean was only about one-half as large as it is today but that it had almost the same shape and orientation (Harbert and others, and Lawver and Scotese, both this volume). Its relationship to the world ocean is not fully understood. Most reconstructions suggest a strong Pacific link, a restricted, less developed Atlantic connection, and one or two shelf sea connections. One of these, the Obik Sea, may have connected the Tethyan Sea with the Arctic Ocean through modern Siberia. The North American seaway from the Gulf Coast to the Arctic is better documented. Paleomagnetic reconstructions indicate that the Cretaceous North Pole was only a few hundred kilometers away from the modern pole. In spite of this pole position, all evidence suggests that Cretaceous climates were not like those of the present and a strong equator-to-pole thermal gradient did not exist. This conclusion is based on a wealth of floral, faunal, paleogeographic, and climate modeling data concerning Cretaceous climates that have been generated during the past few years (Frakes, 1979; Barron and others, 1981; Crowley, 1983). Extensive flooding of the continents and increased CO_2 levels of the atmosphere are only two of the parameters that contributed to moderate climates everywhere on earth. Although theoretical considerations had led to the assumption of a cool polar climate (Donn, 1982), no glaciation of any size has been proved at any latitude during this time.

Late Mesozoic environments

The oldest sediment known from the deep Arctic Ocean is Upper Cretaceous (Campanian) black mud. This is recognized in a single core (Fig. 1) recovered from the same general area as upper Mesozoic sediment cores (Fig. 5). The black mud has 15 percent organic carbon, and carbon isotopes indicate that most of the material is from terrestrial plants that have experienced little change since their time of deposition (Clark and Byers, 1984). The source area for the terrestrial plant material is of major interest. Presently, two source areas can be envisioned. Upper Cretaceous coals are known in Svalbard where they occur in large quantities and where they have been mined for several decades. However, it is difficult to imagine how this material could have reached the site of core FL 533, since the Alpha Ridge must have been a structural high that was separated by an ocean basin from the Lomonosov "continental" margin. An alternative source region is offered by considering the subsidence of the Alpha Ridge itself, whose crest is located now at 1,500 to 2,000 m water depth. Since this ridge is composed of volcanic basaltic rocks (van Wagoner and Robinson, 1985), it can be assumed that it subsided like other aseismic rises (Detrick and others, 1977), approximately 2 to 3 km after its formation in late Mesozoic time. If this is true, the Alpha Ridge may have formed in place as a spreading center crossing the Arctic Ocean during Cretaceous time, and it would have been a large, elongated land mass or archipelago that later subsided.

Slightly younger Upper Cretaceous biogenic silica has been identified in 2 cores (Fig. 5) collected approximately 150 km apart from the flanks of Alpha Ridge in the central Arctic Ocean. The sediment consists of diatoms, silico-flagellates, ebridians, and archaemonads with densities up to 400×10^6 specimens g^{-1} bulk sediment. These abundances are similar or even higher than those reported from areas of oceanic upwelling in the Gulf of Califor-

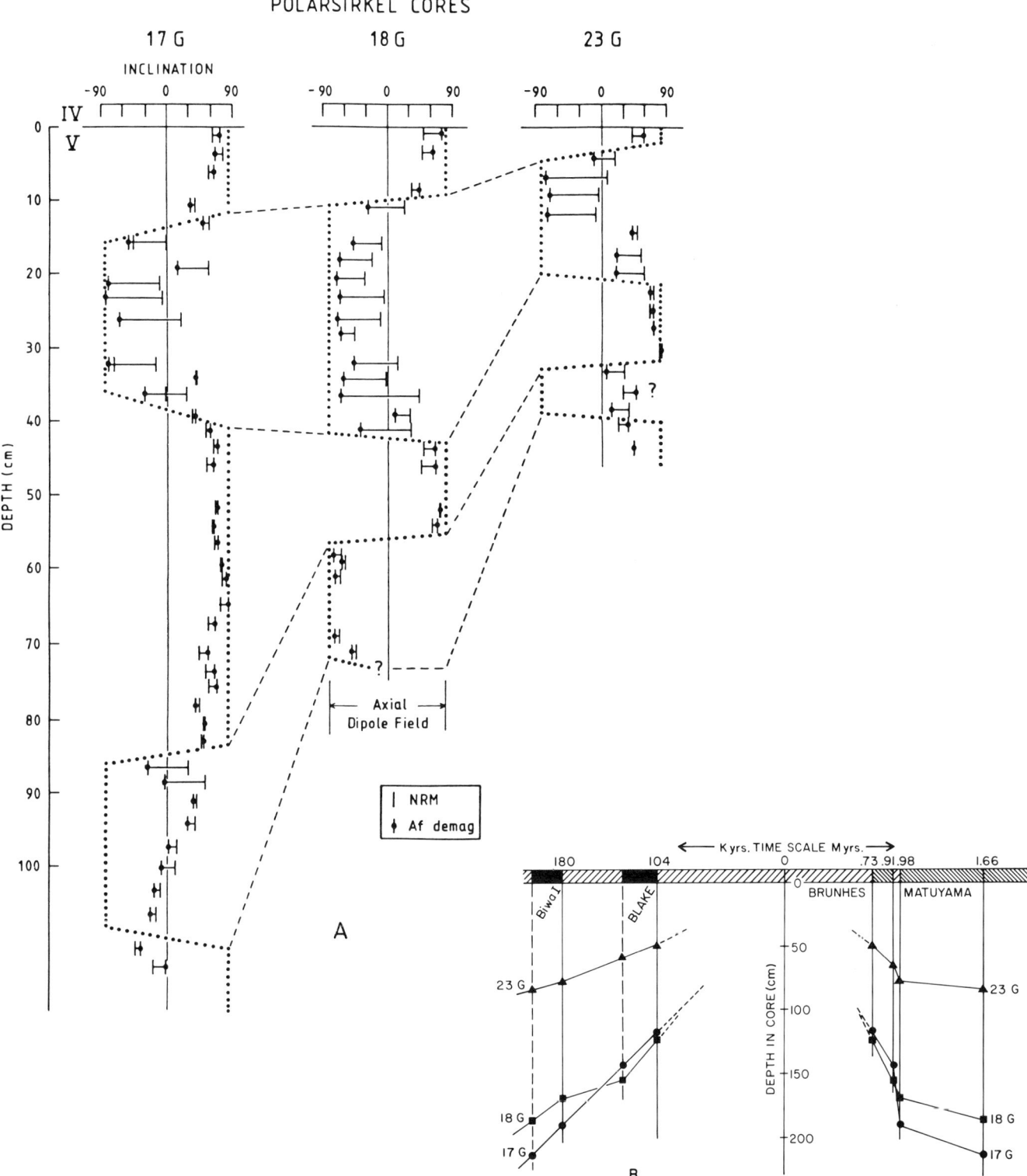

Figure 10. Stratigraphic plots of NRM (bar) and 50 mT (bar with dot) inclination for RV *Polarsirkel* cores 17G, 18G, and 23G. Vertical dotted line indicates expected inclination for the axial geomagnetic field at the sampling localities. Broken lines show proposed magnetostratigraphic correlation with proposed geomagnetic excursions (A) and established geomagnetic reversal time scale (B). Dotted parts of polarity time scale on B indicate duration of the inferred Blake and Biwa I events based on the present results. Both from Lövlie and others (1986).

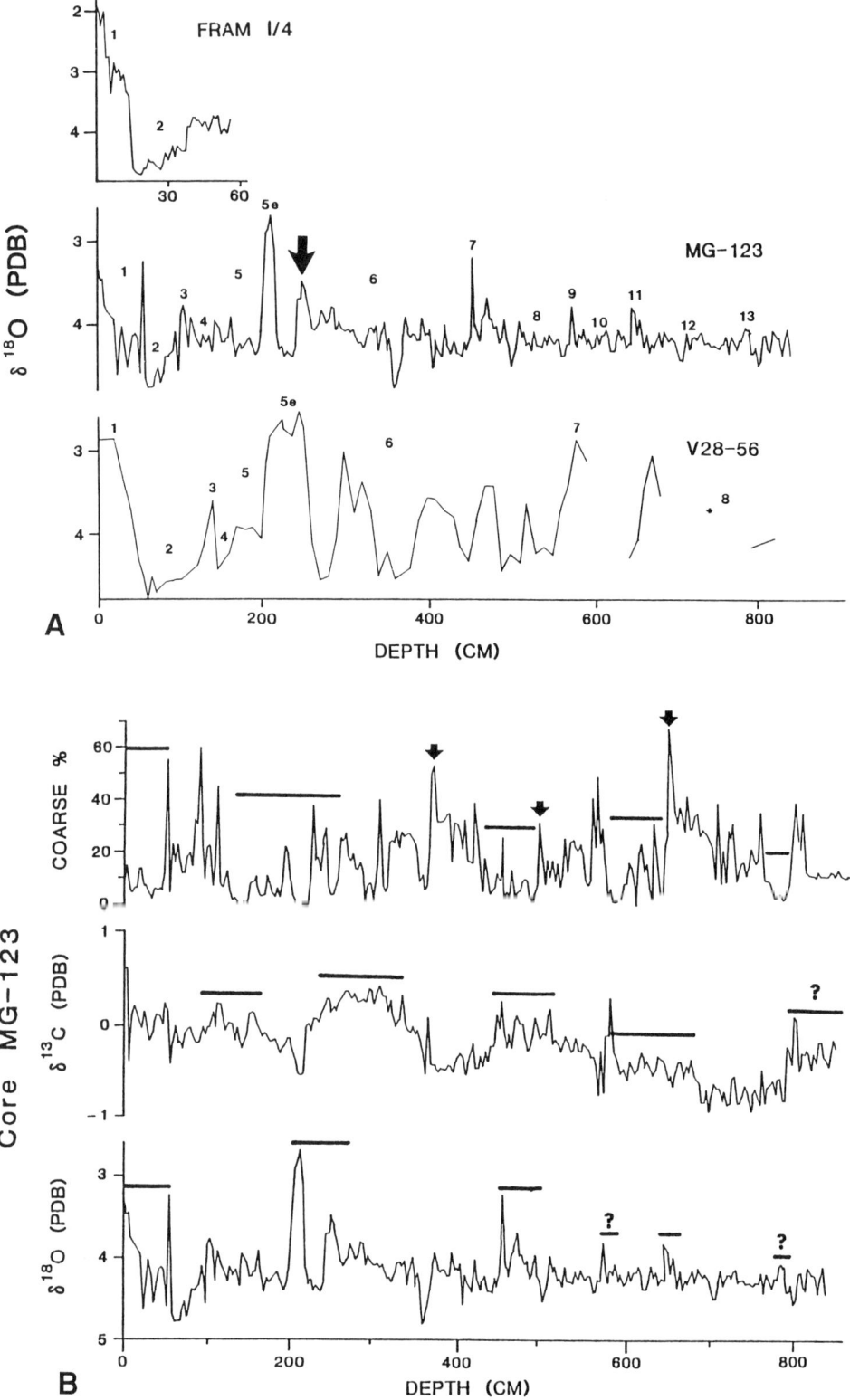

Figure 11. A. O-isotope curves for cores MG—123 (Fram Strait), FRAM-1/4 (Arctic Ocean), and V 28-56 (Norwegian-Greenland Sea), from D. L. Clark (personal communication, 1986). Numbers along curve refer to O-isotope stages. B. O-isotope, C-isotope, and coarse fraction curves for core MG-123 (Fram Strait), from D. L. Clark (personal communication, 1986).

nia, off the coast of southwest Africa, and the Antarctic Convergence (Kitchell and Clark, 1982). The sediment shows little or no terrestrial influx, lacks burrowing, and is laminated.

The sediment of core 6 of the CESAR project (Fig. 12) has very well-defined laminae of light and dark shades of yellow-gray. Lighter colored layers have several different kinds of sizable phytoplankton (diatoms and silicoflagellates), while the darker layers have smaller and more diverse microplankton. If these layers are seasonal, the sedimentation rate could exceed 50 m/m.y. Even in upwelling areas, this sedimentation rate seems excessive. The layers may represent productivity cycles responding to longer periods of orbital forcing (Kitchell and Clark, 1982).

Early Cenozoic paleoenvironments

A third core, containing biogenic siliceous skeletons of Eocene phytoplankton (Bukry, 1984), was recovered in the vicinity of CESAR core 6 (Fig. 5). Although it is possible that upwelling was continuous from at least Late Cretaceous to the middle Eocene, no record of earliest Cenozoic sediment has been recovered to confirm this possibility. The pre-Neogene core data support the idea that the Late Cretaceous–early Cenozoic Arctic Ocean was estuarine in the sense of Berger (1970), with deep-water inflow, winter cyclonic circulation, and mid-ocean upwelling. Anticyclonic circulation, with oceanic convergence and probably coastal upwelling, occurred during the Cretaceous summer. Except for the presence of glendonites (R. Spielhagen, personal communication, 1985) and the occurrence of possibly ice-rafted coarse clastics (Dalland, 1976) in the Paleogene sequence of Svalbard, there is no evidence of glaciation or ice of any kind in the Arctic, which is quite different from the Antarctic record (Kerr, 1981). The flora of the Arctic Ocean and surrounding land, as well as the vertebrate fauna reported to date (Hickey and others, 1983), support the idea of moderate climate with perhaps a shorter and much warmer winter than that of the present.

The Late Cretaceous–Eocene Arctic Ocean was the most northerly site of biogenic silica accumulation for any geologic time period. Accumulation of abundant silica in the Arctic preceded its deposition in similar quantities in the Norwegian-Greenland Sea, Bering Sea, or the circum-Antarctic seas. The shift in the locus of silica accumulation must have accompanied a change in the Arctic Ocean from an estuarine condition with "deep" water spillover into the Arctic Ocean (Berger, 1970) to a lagoonal environment with "deep" spillover out of the Arctic Ocean.

LATE CENOZOIC PALEOENVIRONMENTS: THE COLD ARCTIC OCEAN

Post-Eocene to pre-upper Miocene sediment has not been identified in the central Arctic Ocean. During this interval, glaciation initiated in high latitudes, and a strong thermal gradient developed both in the oceans and the atmosphere. Although this transition cannot be documented in the Arctic proper, the devel-

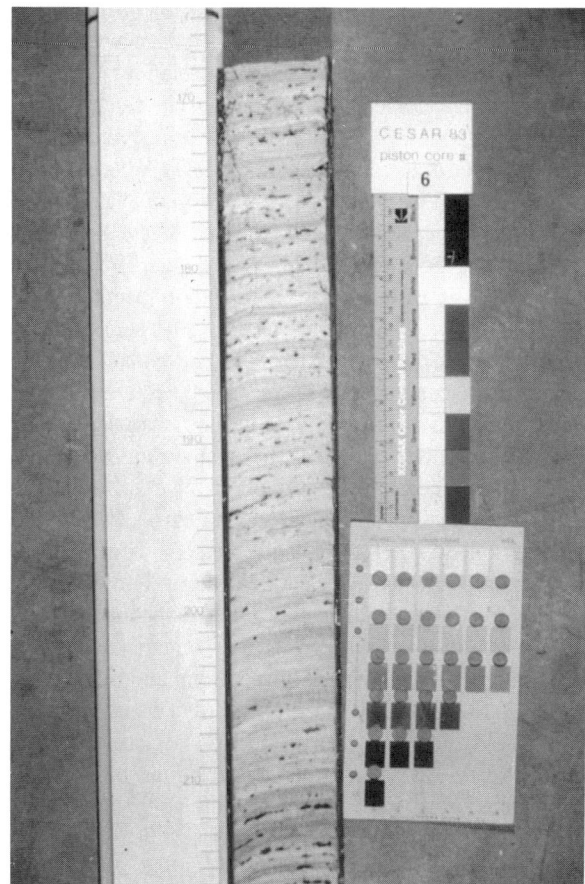

Figure 12. CESAR core 6. Upper Cretaceous laminated diatomites (see Fig. 5 for location).

opment of Northern Hemisphere glacial climates is indicated by the world ocean $\delta^{18}O$ record. The upper Cenozoic sediment record of the central Arctic Ocean documents only glacial depositional environments.

O-isotope records

A number of $\delta^{18}O$ investigations during the past decade suggest that the surface water temperature of the world ocean was reduced by 15° to 20° C from a Cretaceous high to a middle Cenozoic low (Shackleton and Kennett, 1975). Unfortunately, no Arctic sediment record for the critical cooling interval is available, and lower Cenozoic temperate upwelling deposits are separated from paleomagnetically dated upper Neogene glacial-marine deposits by an unknown (not yet recovered!) interval of sediment. In contrast, the available lower-latitude ocean record provides dramatic evidence of significant surface-water cooling worldwide, at least for the interval from the Miocene to Recent. Both glacial ice volume and surface-water temperatures contributed to changes in the $\delta^{18}O$ values.

Did ice form first in Antarctica, producing unipolar glaciation, or was the initiation of Northern Hemisphere glaciation penecontemporaneous with Antarctic glaciation? The oldest known glacial-marine deep-sea sediment in the central Arctic is upper Neogene, recently interpreted to be approximately 2 Ma (G. A. Jones, personal communication, 1987), whereas the new ODP Leg 104 data from the eastern Norwegian Sea suggest that sub-Arctic regions episodically experienced severe glaciation by 2.9 to 3.0 Ma at the latest (Eldholm and others, 1987). There is also evidence of an earlier Antarctic glaciation (Mercer and Sutter, 1982). Based on Cenozoic glacial sediments studied in South America, they concluded that the Miocene global ice volume necessary to explain anomalous sea level, temperature, and precipitation patterns did not accumulate in the Antarctic, but in the Northern Hemisphere. This may be a minimum age, because Dalland (1976) reported—albeit questionably—ice-rafted debris from possible Eocene sediment on Svalbard. This sequence also contains glendonites (Spielhagen, personal communication, 1985). In contrast, firm evidence for Northern Hemisphere glaciation, based on North Atlantic glacial-marine sediment has only been found in mid-Pliocene deposits (e.g., Berggren and Hollister, 1974; Shackleton and others, 1984; Eldholm and others, 1986a; however, see Schaeffer and Spiegler, 1986). This latter date may represent the earliest time that products of deglaciation reached the main North Atlantic; earlier deglaciations may not have greatly affected areas south of 75° N if the volume of ice or the volume of glacial-marine sediment was significantly less than during younger glaciations (Eldholm and others, 1986b, 1987). There is strong evidence that the volume and magnitude of deglaciation has changed through the Late Cenozoic. Cores of the interval under discussion from positions higher than 75° N have not been obtained.

Sedimentary record: regional patterns

Short sediment cores containing a glacial-marine record have been recovered from the Canada Basin, the Chukchi Rise, the Alpha Ridge, the adjacent Makarov Basin, the Lomonosov Ridge, and the adjacent Fram Basin. At least during the Late Cenozoic, glacial-marine sedimentation dominated all parts of the Amerasia Basin, with the exception of the Canada Basin, where turbidites partially masked glacial-marine accumulation.

Canada Basin. Sedimentation in the deep Canada Basin is dominated by turbidites (Campbell and Clark, 1977). Approximately 100, 3- to 4-m-long cores have been recovered from this region. Ages of the Canada Basin sediments are based on a few ^{14}C dates in the uppermost part of several cores. Accumulation rates up to 50 cm/k.y. have been calculated. The sediment consists of turbidites and interbedded glacial-marine (ice-rafted) sediments. Evidently, ice-rafted sedimentation rates are relatively low and turbidite accumulation rates are high in the central abyssal Arctic. Significant accumulations of ice-rafted sediment probably represent long periods between turbidite events (Goldstein, 1983).

Turbidites have flooded the Canada Basin during the very recent geolgoic past, due at least in part to buildup of sediment carried by Arctic rivers to the Canadian and Alaskan continental shelves. For example, the area of the Mackenzie River Delta receives in excess of 30 million tons of sediment per year (Ritchie and Walker, 1974). Generation of turbidity flows in this and similar areas may have been active for most of the late Cenozoic. At least 6 km of unconsolidated sediment is present in the Canada Basin (Jackson, and Grantz and others, this volume). Most of the sediment transported north during the Northern Hemisphere deglaciation has accumulated on the continental slope and shelf of the eastern Canada Basin.

A stratigraphy for the interbedded glacial-marine and turbidity layers of the Canada Basin has been recognized, but only for small areas. Goldstein (1983) concluded that the stratigraphic sequences of turbidites and glacial-marine sediments are similar from core to core in local areas but that major differences can be correlated between the sedimentary sequences in different parts of the Canada Basin (Hunkins and others, 1971).

The Canada Basin sediments accumulate at a much higher rate than sediment elsewhere in the Amerasian Basin and are essentially undated because the cores are too short to include the last major magnetic reversal (720 ka). Fossils are poorly represented except in the glacial-marine layers of Canada Basin, and these fossils are of long-ranging Plio-Pleistocene types.

Chukchi–Alpha Ridge sedimentation. Some 13 lithostratigraphic units (Fig. 7) are defined for the upper Miocene to Holocene sediment of the ridge areas of the Amerasian Basin (Clark and others, 1980). The sedimentary units correlate over 400,000 km^2, and also correlate with the slightly different sedimentary units of the Makarov Basin and Lomonosov Ridge. The sediments of this area consist of interbedded silty and sandy units containing well-preserved fossil assemblages dated from magnetic reversal stratigraphy. The finer grained units are interpreted to represent principally pack-ice deposition. The coarser units result from pack ice and iceberg transported sediment and represent deglaciation events (Herman, 1974a; Clark and Hanson, 1983; Gilbert and Clark, 1983). Geologicallly significant invertebrate faunas developed in this glacial-marine environment, including a predominantly arenaceous (textulariid) biofacies in the late Miocene to Pliocene, and calcareous biofacies (milioliids and rotaliids) in the Pliocene and Pleistocene (O'Neill, 1981). Foraminifers are more abundant in the finer grained sediments of the Miocene and Pliocene (Fig. 7) and are negatively correlated with the coarse-grained sediment. In the younger Pleistocene sediment, foraminiferal abundances and coarse- and fine-grained layers are both in and out of phase. The $\delta^{18}O$ record based on foraminifers gives good evidence that the greatest number of specimens correlate with $\delta^{18}O$ enrichment (glacial ice maxima), while fewer numbers commonly correlate with deglaciation (Fig. 13), times of glacial ice minima, and iceberg calving.

Minicucci and Clark (1983) described the sedimentary units on the eastern margin of the Alpha Ridge and have noted a correlation with the stratigraphic units of the central Chukchi–

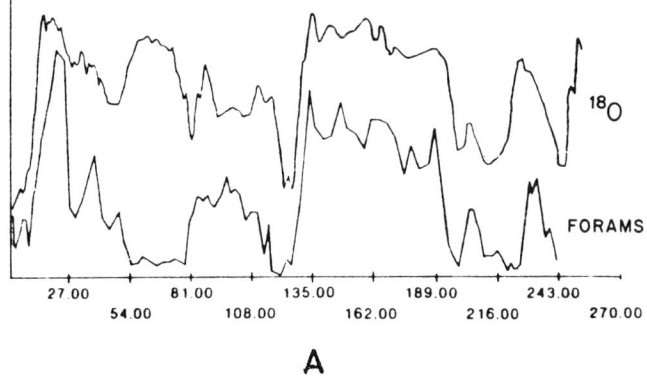

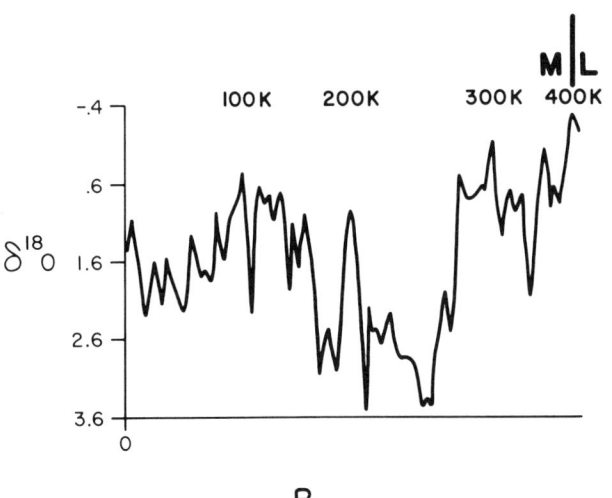

Figure 13. A. Generalized foraminiferal abundance and isotope stratigraphy correlation in the central Arctic. Peaks represent greater $\delta^{18}O$ ratios and more abundant foraminifers in core FL 124. Approximate age in thousands of years is indicated. From Minicucci and Clark (1983). B. Detailed plot of age-interpreted O-isotope data from core FL 124.

Alpha Ridge area. The recent CESAR expedition recovered additional sediment cores from nearly the same area. Examination of the cores indicates that the only differences with the sedimentary units described by Minicucci and Clark (1983) are in the older parts of the cores (Mudie and Blasco, 1985). All of the sediment appears to be glacial marine.

Lomonosov Ridge-Makarov Basin area. Correlatable and more-or-less identical sedimentary sequences are developed over the Lomonosov Ridge and adjacent Makarov Basin, some 300 km from the Alpha Ridge. Most significant local differences in sedimentation in the Lomonosov Ridge-Makarov Basin area are related to local current patterns (Clark and others, 1983; Morris and others, 1985). Currents sweeping over the Lomonosov Ridge from the Fram Basin mobilize and transport silt and clay-size particles and deposit the sediment in the Makarov Basin. Consequently, sedimentary units are thicker and finer grained in the Makarov Basin than on the Lomonosov Ridge crest. The sediment consists of alternating layers of pack ice and iceberg transported materials, and the major lithologies can be correlated with those of the Chukchi-Alpha Ridge area (Fig. 7).

Eastern Arctic Basin. Sediment cores of the eastern Arctic Basin (Fig. 6) have been available only since the late 1970s, and our understanding of their stratigraphy is preliminary. However, studies of the YMER-80, RV *Polarsirkel,* and FRAM-I and -IV cores (Boström and Thiede, 1984; Zahn and others, 1985; Markussen and others, 1985; Lövlie and others, 1986) reveal marked lithostratigraphic similarities with the central and western Arctic cores (Herman, 1974a; Clark and others, 1980). Cores taken from the continental rise and abyssal plain north of Svalbard are poorly suited for stratigraphic studies because of the presence of turbidites, whereas the cores from abyssal hills and continental slopes consist of relatively fine-grained, reddish, brownish or greyish, dominantly clastic materials. These cores also include a substantial proportion of coarse ice-rafted clastic components, and they may be subdivided into similar lithologic units of several centimeters to decimeters in thickness. The presently available stratigraphic resolution of Arctic sediments does not permit a detailed correlation of eastern with central and western Arctic cores.

As in the central and western Arctic, eastern Arctic sediment cores also consist of sedimentary units relatively rich in coarse ice-rafted material alternating with intervals lacking such components. They also have fossil concentrations, which fluctuate throughout the cores. Both benthic and planktonic fossils are enriched in certain horizons that can be traced from core to core. These observations confirm that the eastern Arctic Basin was affected throughout the late Cenozoic by regional changes in the depositional environment similar to those which affected the central and western Arctic basins. Surface sediments in the western and central Arctic basins are rich in (mainly planktonic) foraminifers (Clark, 1971; Herman, 1969), and only some meters below the sea floor does ice-rafted material constitute a higher proportion of the coarse fraction. In contrast, eastern Arctic surface sediments are relatively poor in foraminifers, and their concentration increases some centimeters below the surface (Markussen and others, 1985). If such apparent differences do exist, they can only be resolved once a better understanding of the detailed stratigraphies of long Arctic Ocean sediment cores is reached.

Late Neogene and early Pleistocene depositional environments

Late Cenozoic sediment cores from the area of the Lomonosov Ridge and the Canada Basin represent distinctly different sedimentary environments. Most of the sediments accumulating on the Lomonosov Ridge, Makarov Basin, and the Alpha and Chukchi Ridges are glacial marine. They consist of alternating silty and sandy layers that apparently originated from both iceberg and pack-ice transport. Some of the turbidites (the dominant sediment of the Canada Basin) are interbedded with glacial-marine sediments. Deglaciation on the continents furnished enormous quantities of sediments that were transported to the adjacent Canada Basin by turbidity currents.

Climate interpretations. The record for the Arctic Ocean shows a dramatic change from open water, probably temperate conditions during the Late Cretaceous and early Cenozoic, to glacial-marine sedimentation and a permanent ice cover by the late Cenozoic. What are the reasons for this remarkable climatic change in the Arctic? How did the Arctic Ocean respond to this climatic change? These questions have been discussed by a number of investigators (Clark, 1971, 1977; Herman, 1974a; Hughes and others, 1977; Herman and Hopkins, 1980; Williams and others, 1981; Keigwin, 1982) and summarized by Clark (1982).

Of the various theories of Earth climate that concern the Arctic Ocean, none has been more imaginative than the Ewing-Donn theory (1956). The main thesis of this theory was that the Arctic Ocean provided central control of periodic Northern Hemisphere glaciations. An isolated Arctic Ocean, restricted from water interchange with the world ocean, would develop an ice cover, which in turn, would put a tight lid on evaporation and precipitation. Northern Hemisphere glaciers, deprived of their principal source for growth, would melt and cause sea-level rises, and this would reestablish circulation between the warmer, lower latitude ocean and the Arctic Ocean. From the newly established circulation, the Arctic ice cover would melt, permitting increased evaporation and precipitation in the Northern Hemisphere, and this would lead to renewed glaciation. Glaciation would continue until sea level was lowered enough to isolate the Arctic Ocean. Circulatory isolation would lead to freezing of the surface; this would limit glacial growth, and a new cycle of melting and interglacial conditions would develop, eventually leading to glacial conditions again. Sedimentary evidence from the Arctic Ocean, however, has shown no indication of ice-free and ice-covered conditions that would correlate with known glacial and interglacial cycles (Clark, 1971). Other objections to this elegant theory were equally damaging (Collinvaux, 1964; Ku and Broecker, 1967), and the Arctic Ocean, at least temporarily, lost its role in explaining glacial climate formation.

A considerable body of data has accumulated during the past decade regarding Pleistocene glaciation, including: a detailed description and chronology for the most recent major glaciation (CLIMAP, 1981); identification of a glacial chronology for the Plio-Pleistocene based on $\delta^{18}O$ data (e.g., Shackleton and Opdyke, 1973); and identification of the relationship of Earth climate to orbital forcing (Berger and others, 1984). Additional knowledge of the climatology of the Arctic Ocean, interpreted from sediment cores (Herman, 1974a; Clark and others, 1980; Clark, 1982; Gilbert and Clark, 1983; Boyd and others, 1984), adds to this data base. All of these data indicate that the Arctic Ocean is not pivotal for glacial climate. Rather, the Arctic Ocean responded to orbital forcing along with the Earth as a whole (Boyd and others, 1984) and then by various feedback mechanisms made a significant impact on maintaining world climate.

Spectral analysis of sedimentary parameters of Arctic Ocean cores gives strong evidence that orbital forcing can explain most of the climatic changes interpreted for the Arctic Ocean. This interpretation confirms that the Arctic Ocean responded to climate forcing in much the same manner as all other parts of the world. The dominant signal produced by spectral analysis occurs at a frequency of 100,000 yrs and is associated with the final stages of major deglaciations and interglacial conditions, such as the present (Broecker and van Donk, 1970; Shackleton and Opdyke, 1973; Hays and others, 1976). After Northern Hemisphere ice sheets disintegrate, and before the next insolation minimum initiates another glaciation cycle, the Arctic climate is sufficiently temperate, and subject to sufficiently high insolation, to produce thin, more mobile ice. During this interval, coarse glacial sediments originated from glacier calving are mixed with products of limited biologic productivity in the Arctic Basin itself before a new cycle of ice production occurs.

The spectral interpretations are consistent with patterns of oceanic response farther south. Ruddiman and McIntyre (1984) record a latitudinal shift from strong 23,000 and 100,000 yr power at 40° to 50° North, to dominant 100,000 and 41,000 yr power at 50° to 55° North, and then to dominant 100,000 yr power at 55° to 63° North. At the higher latitudes the oceanic signal is in phase with $\delta^{18}O$ (ice volume), and this part of the ocean reacts passively to fluctuations in ice-sheet size. This geographic progression and line of reasoning predict that the 100,000-yr signal directly associated with full interglaciations will be the strongest record to survive in the central Arctic Ocean (Boyd and others, 1984).

THE LATE PLEISTOCENE ARCTIC OCEAN AND THE LAST DEGLACIATION

Beyond the rather general discussion of the evolution of the Arctic Ocean's depositional environment presented above, recent advances in studies of sediment cores from the eastern Arctic Basin allow a detailed discussion of the late Pleistocene Arctic Ocean and some of its properties during the last deglaciation (Zahn and others, 1985; Markussen and others, 1985; Knudsen, 1985). The major achievement of these studies is progress in stratigraphic resolution, which for the first time permits subdivision of sediment cores into stratigraphic intervals corresponding to O-isotope stages 1, 2, and 3. In addition to observations from the pelagic realm, detailed upper Quaternary sedimentary records of Arctic shelf sedimentation provide evidence on late glacial developments of the adjacent continental platforms (Schytt, 1984; Vorren and others, 1984) that correlate with the Arctic deep-sea basins.

The sedimentary record of the pelagic realm

The sediments found in the cores from the eastern Arctic Basin consist of yellowish brown to greyish red, largely terrige-

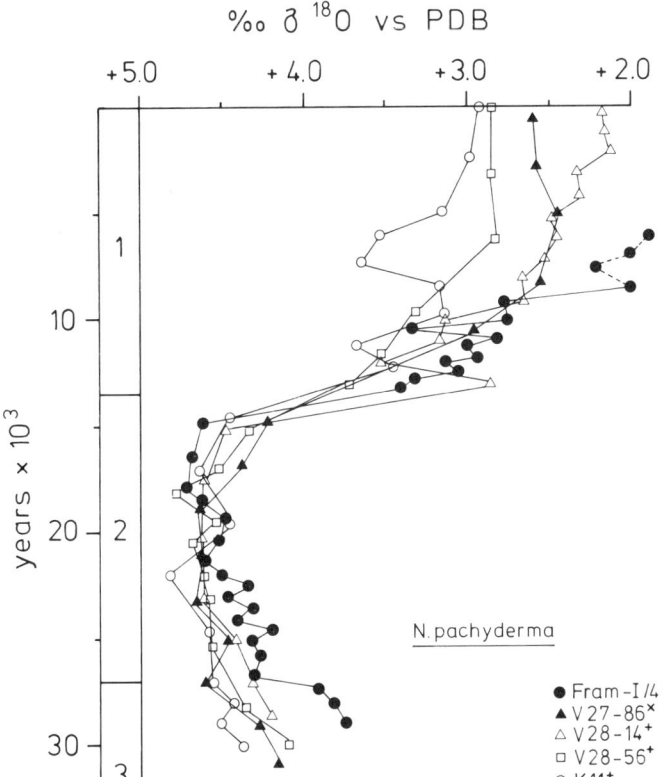

Figure 14. O-isotope curves of cores from Norwegian-Greenland Sea and of core FRAM 1/4. A better comparison has been obtained by replotting the O-isotope data on a timescale defined by well established radiocarbon ages. From Zahn and others (1985).

oppose the hypothesis of Olausson (1985) and Ewing and Donn (1956) who had assumed ice-free or nearly ice-free conditions for the glacial Arctic Ocean. Sediment-laden icebergs and/or coastal ice must have reached the Arctic Ocean throughout the time span documented by these cores and must have at least partially melted and released their sediments there. However, this process clearly fluctuated in intensity, reaching its maximum during times of deglaciation.

Frequencies of coccoliths (Worsley and Herman, 1980; Gard, 1986) and planktonic foraminifers suggest that the thickness and completeness of the ice cover, and possibly its seasonal variability, have fluctuated considerably with time. The presence of these fossil groups documents productivity under glacial as well as interglacial conditions. However, the Fram Strait data (Knudsen, 1985) seem to suggest that the productivity of these polar surface (?) water masses was highest during interglacial times (Fig. 15).

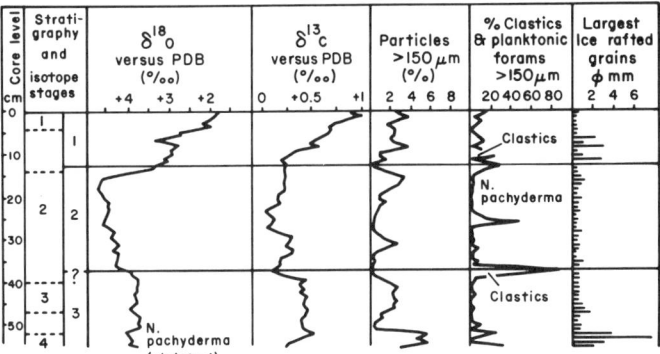

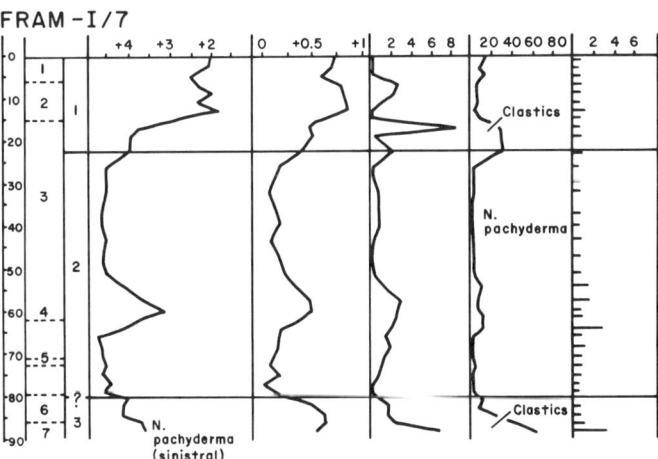

Figure 15. Stable isotope records and lithostratigraphies of cores FRAM-1/4 and 1/7. Numbers 1-4 and 1-7 in left column of "stratigraphies and isotope stage" section indicate the following sediment colors: For FRAM-1/4, 1 = brown, 2 = grayish-red, 3 = dark yellowish-brown, and 4 = yellowish. For FRAM-1/7, 1 = yellowish-brown, 2 = brown, 3 = grayish-red, 4 = brown, 5 = grayish-red, 6 = dark yellowish, and 7 = brown. From Zahn and others, 1985.

nous, and mostly fine-grained muds (Markussen and others, 1982). According to a correlation of two cores obtained during FRAM-I (Kristoffersen, 1979) with sediment cores from the Norwegian-Greenland Sea (Zahn and others, 1985), the planktonic foraminiferal O-isotope record of stages 1 through 3 could also be observed in the Arctic (Fig. 14). Therefore, a number of litho- and biostratigraphic features of the Arctic Ocean can be discussed in a precisely defined temporal framework. Sedimentation rates appear to be 10 to 30 cm/k.y., an order of magnitude higher than those reported from the central Arctic basins (Clark, 1982; Herman and Hopkins, 1980). Sediment cores from the Fram Strait area have recently been shown to have accumulated at sedimentation rates of up to 80 cm/k.y. (Knudsen, 1985), henceforth exceeding those of the central Arctic basins by several orders of magnitude.

The available O-isotope–dated sediment cores clearly document coarse ice-rafted material in the eastern Arctic Basin throughout the past 30 to 40 k.y. Larger particles and more abundant ice-rafted material than usual reached the Lena Trough and the Arctic Ocean during the last deglaciation, in particular during Termination IA (Figs. 15 and 16). These results clearly

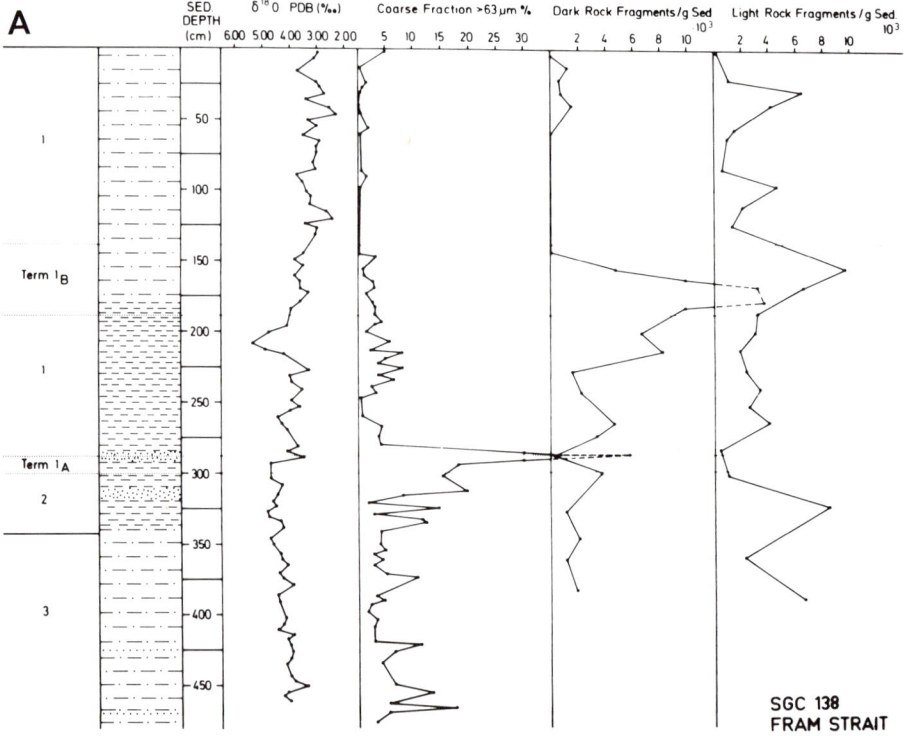
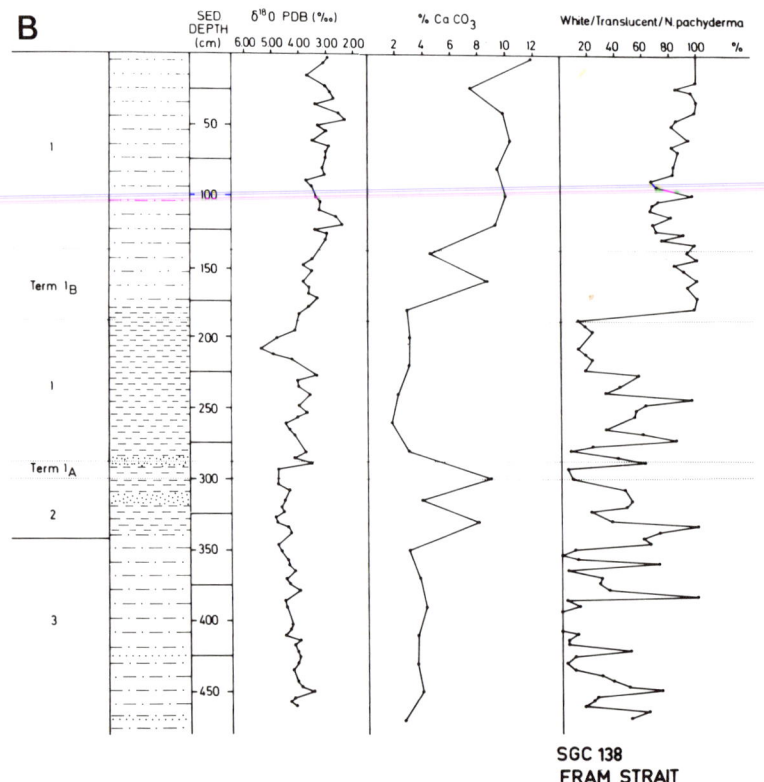

Figure 16. O-isotope stratigraphy, lithology, and distribution of coarse sediment components in the YMER-80 core SGC 138 from the central Fram Strait. From Knudsen, 1985.

Response to glaciations of the surrounding epicontinental seas

The northern polar deep-sea basins are surrounded by some of the world ocean's widest epicontinental seas, whose glacial and postglacial history is poorly known. However, those seas are clearly deeper in areas that were glaciated than in adjacent regions that were not glaciated, or in regions situated outside the polar realm which did not experience repeated Cenozoic glaciation. The distribution of ice shields surrounding the northern polar deep-sea basins during the last glacial maximum (Andersen, 1981) is well understood as far as their southern boundaries on land are concerned; however, their seaward boundaries toward the Norwegian-Greenland Sea and the Arctic Ocean proper are only vaguely known, because it is difficult to map and date the oldest moraines on the continental shelves. Nonmarine glacial shelf deposits are in most cases separated from overlying Holocene marine sediments by a hiatus of variable length (Vorren and others, 1984; Spiridonov, 1982). Results of studies of the Quaternary geology of the northern Barents Sea many years ago showed (de Geer, 1900) that glacial ice shields flowed across the shelf and that wide shelf areas were once ice covered. Reconstructions of isobases also demonstrated that Svalbard and a large part of the Barents Sea during the last glacial age were the center of one of these ice shields (Schytt, 1984; Mangerud and others, 1984). With the onset of the last deglaciation and eustatic sea-level rise, the sea again transgressed the wide northern polar shelf, and in many areas a post-glacial marine stratigraphic record can be documented (Kulikov and others, 1982; Elverhöj, 1984; Dinter and others, and Blasco and others, this volume). Composition and stratigraphic completeness of these marine sedimentary sequences depend on their depositional water depths, but usually morainal (often compacted) deposits grade into glaciomarine deposits. Shallow bank areas are extensively reworked and are covered by pebble fields and bioclastic deposits, while muddy sediments accumulate in depressions. A particular feature of the Barents and Norwegian Sea shelves are bathymetrically controlled regions of iceberg plow marks (Lien, 1983) generated during the last deglaciation and which are found in regions not reached by icebergs today (e.g., off Norway). Evolution of depositional environments similar to that of the Barents Sea also occurred in other northern polar shelf regions.

Glacial history of Arctic shelf areas

Because of the eustatic sea-level drop during glacial stages and the erosive activity of ice shields, it is difficult to relate directly the depositional record of the northern polar deep-sea regions to the glacial history of Arctic shelf regions. However, there is hope in tracing coarse terrigenous ice-rafted sediment components from deep-sea cores to specific source regions, thereby documenting transport paths and times of ice discharge from the shelves into the adjacent deep-sea regions. Although glacial marine sedimentation (Molnia, 1983a) and the properties of ice-rafted materials (Clark and Hanson, 1983) have been studied by numerous colleagues, it is extremely difficult to pinpoint specific source regions. In general, these studies are confined to descriptions of the regional and temporal distribution patterns of such sediment components. Lithostratigraphic correlations of horizons enriched in coarse ice-rafted terrigenous components in Arctic Ocean cores (Clark and others, 1980) and in the North Atlantic Ocean (Molnia, 1983a) have remained ambiguous. Detailed petrographic descriptions of the ice-rafted components have been used to document the regional nature and paleoclimatic significance of the ice-rafting events, but usually did not succeed in defining particular source regions.

Recent studies of coarse, terrigenous ice-rafted components in sediment cores north and west of Svalbard (Snaare, 1984; Knudsen, 1985) for the first time reveal systematic temporal compositional changes of ice-rafted particle assemblages. These studies also pinointed potential source regions for ice-rafted material in the Svalbard archipelago, where very specific lithologies occur in limited areas. As shown previously (Fig. 14), the stratigraphic records of these cores (Markussen and others, 1985; Knudsen, 1985) reveal that modest amounts of coarse ice-rafted components reached the Arctic Ocean floor throughout the past 30 to 40 k.y., whereas in the eastern Fram Strait the supply decreased drastically before, as well as after, Termination IA. In both areas, however, the time span of Termination IA represents a peak event in size and amount of coarse terrigenous ice-rafted components.

Sediment cores north of Svalbard (Fig. 16) contain granitic pebbles originating from limited outcrops on the "Sjuøyane" (Seven Islands) north of Svalbard, and black shales from the Phanerozoic sedimentary sequence of Svalbard (Snaare, 1984). Based on these findings, a northward transport path of sediment-laden ice across the shelf area north of Svalbard was suggested. This transport direction is almost opposite to the general movement of the pack ice in this area of the modern Arctic Ocean (Gorshkov, 1983), although gyres of the Vestspitsbergen Current may flow around the northwest edge of the Svalbard archipelago under certain climatic conditions, resulting in a temporal reversal of the ice drift. During glacial and in early post-glacial times, however, this current did not exist; therefore, it is not clear what the documented transport paths of these ice-rafted pebbles might mean in terms of general ice drift during their time of deposition.

The situation west of Svalbard (Knudsen, 1985) is more easily understood because the sediments there have a much better stratigraphic resolution than cores from the Norwegian-Greenland Sea or even the Arctic Ocean itself. Black shale fragments forming the dominant component of the coarse, ice-rafted particle assemblages have been correlated to the Janusfjell Formation on Svalbard, with a possible source area in Isfjorden. Peak of abundance of these black shale fragments correlates with coccolith frequencies (Gard, 1986) and occurrences of relatively warm planktonic foraminifers (Knudsen, 1985). The black shales are relatively fragile and probably have not been transported over long distances. Sedimentation of black shale fragments in the area west of Svalbard stopped rather abruptly close to Termination IA. They stopped because the source region of the coarse ice-rafted components changed as a consequence of withdrawal of calving glaciers to the inner fjords of Spitsbergen, much like their position under modern conditions. This situation has continued to control the depositional environment throughout post-glacial time.

HOLOCENE AND MODERN DEPOSITIONAL ENVIRONMENTS

The polar ice pack is the most distinctive feature of the Arctic Ocean, determining biologic processes and hydrologic conditions as well as sediment distribution. The maximum ice cover, which is estimated at about 15,106 km^2, can be reduced down to 50 percent in the summer, and the regional extent varies substantially from year to year (Hibler, 1980, and references therein).

Exciting new data relevant to the problem of modern sediment formation in the Arctic presently are being gathered by means of moored sediment traps in the Fram Strait area and in the Norwegian-Greenland Sea (S. Honjo, Woods Hole, and G. Wefer, personal communication, 1986). Preliminary results from these traps show strong seasonality of the terrigenous and biogenic sediment fluxes.

Figure 17. Comparison and composition of coarse, terrigenous ice-rafted pebble in sediments from the continental slope north of Svalbard (top) and from outcrops on Svalbard (bottom). After Snaare (1984).

Sediment source, transport, and composition

The main sedimentary components deposited today are of lithogenous, biogenous, and hydrogenous (formed in the seawater) origin. Supply rates of sediments, topography, postdepositional transport, and solution control the composition of sea floor deposits.

Ice transport. Detrital sediments are incorporated into icebergs and sea ice. Icebergs originate in glaciers and shelf ice. Although the Greenland ice sheet is the main producer of icebergs, the majority of Arctic Ocean icebergs originate from the Ellesmere Island ice shelves, and generally remain in the Beaufort Sea gyre (Weeks and Campbell, 1973). These icebergs drift westward along the Canadian Archipelago, then turn toward the pole north of Bering Strait; after approximately ten years, they return to their point of origin. Carried by winds and currents, and also under the influence of the Coriolis Force, the icebergs gradually decay, releasing incorporated debris onto the sea floor (Robie, 1980; see also Figs. 17 and 18). Some of the icebergs, however, are caught in the East Greenland Current and are carried south. The East Greenland Current also carries vast amounts of Arctic pack ice as far south as the southern tip of Greenland (Robie, 1980).

Sea ice formed in shallow water incorporates significant amounts of lithogenous and biogenous debris (Larsen and others, 1984), mainly of silt and clay size, although sand- and gravel-size detritus is occasionally encountered (e.g., Carsola, 1952). These poorly sorted rock and mineral fragments usually are of variable lithologies (Carsola, 1952; Schwarzacher and Hunkins, 1961). Sediment-laden ice may be carried great distances, gradually melting and dropping the entrapped debris to the sea floor (Schwarzacher and Hunkins, 1961). The general circulation of sea ice consists of a gyre in the Beaufort Sea and a transpolar drift stream. The latter transports ice from the Chukchi and East Siberian Seas, crosses the North Pole and drifts southward along the east coast of Greenland (Hibler, 1980). Beaufort Sea ice may survive in the Beaufort Sea gyre for many years where drift rates are variable, but average 6 km day^{-1} (Hibler, 1980).

Currents. With the exception of the Mackenzie, all major rivers flow into shallow, wide marginal seas (Barents, Kara, Laptev, East Siberian, and Chukchi), covering shelves that are incised by numerous canyons (Andrew and Kravitz, 1974; Naugler and others, 1974; Coachman and Aagaard, 1974). Sediments carried by rivers and discharged onto these shelves may be transported by currents to the Arctic basin floor via the canyons (Coachman and Aagaard, 1974). Shallow-water biogenic materials are transported along with the detrital sediments to the deep-sea floor. Clay-size particles have a long residence time in water and are carried in suspension over great distances by currents before settling to the sea floor (Griffin and others, 1968). They constitute important but variable percentages of the Arctic seafloor detrital minerals (Carsola, 1952; Berry and Johns, 1966; Carrol, 1970; Darby, 1971; Naidu, 1974; Clark and others, 1980). In the Canada Abyssal Plain, bottom currents range from less than 1 to 2.6 cm/sec (Galt, 1967; Hunkins and others, 1969), while on the

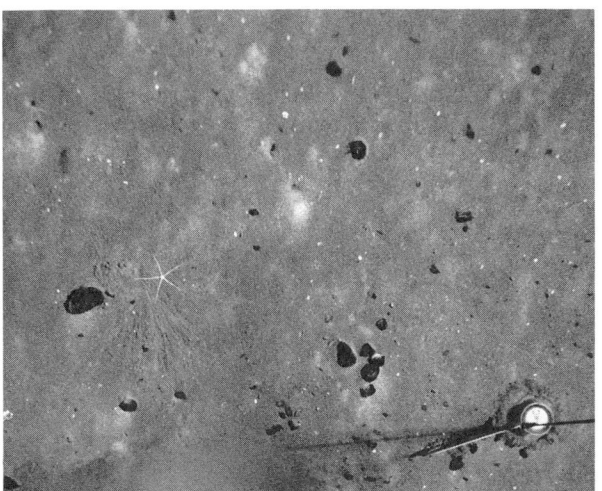
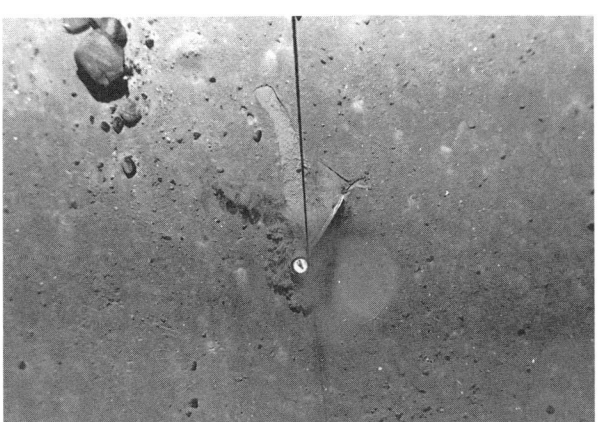

Figure 18. A. Iceberg containing layers of coarse-grained sediment. This iceberg was fused to pack ice that drifted past Barrow, Alaska, as part of general icepack drift. Melting of this iceberg furnished coarse-grained sediment to the Arctic Ocean sea bed. B and C. Pebble and cobble fields on floor of Arctic Ocean. Striations and other glacially derived marks indicate origin of this coarse-grained sediment from icebergs. Bottom photo shows glacial dropstones (erratics) in coarse to fine-grained matrix. Notice ophiuroid in B and faint ichnofauna in B and C. Photos are from Makarov Basin (provided by D. Clark).

Alpha-Mendeleev Rise they range from 4 to 6 cm/sec. In the vicinity of the North Pole, the current pulsates, and peak speeds exceed 12 cm/sec. It runs diagonally up the Eurasian side of the Lomonosov Ridge, overtops it, and then flows down its Canadian flank (Aagaard, 1981).

Eolian dust. From a limited number of samples, it is estimated that airborne dust constitutes between 1 and 10 percent of total Arctic Basin sediment (Darby, 1971; Mullen and others, 1972; Darby and others, 1974).

Lithogenous components. Land-derived clasts transported by ice, winds, surface, and deep currents range in size from gravel to clay; they are of variable lithologies, as mentioned in previous paragraphs.

Hydrogenous (authigenic) materials. Ferro-manganese films cover rock and mineral fragments (Schwarzacher and Hunkins, 1961) and fill and/or cover the empty tests of foraminifers as well (Herman, 1974a).

Biogenous components. Although radiolarians and diatoms are common in the overlying water masses (Zenkevitch, 1963; Herman, unpublished data), their skeletons are rarely preserved in sediments (Herman, 1974a; S. Kruglikova and E. Poliakova, personal communication, 1983). Although coccoliths were recently observed in eastern Arctic Ocean surface sediments (Gard, 1986), calcareous tests of planktonic foraminifers constitute the bulk of faunal remains settling from the water column (Herman, 1969; Herman and Hopkins, 1980). Aragonitic pteropod tests represented by one species (*Limacina helicina*) are preserved in cores shallower than 2,500 m (Herman, 1974a) and are encountered occasionally at much greater depths, probably in displaced, rapidly accumulating sediments (Herman, unpublished). Calcareous foraminifers dominate the benthic assemblages in most Amerasia Basin sediments (Green, 1960; Fetter, 1973; Herman, 1974a; Lagoe, 1977), while arenaceous tests prevail on shelves, slopes, and continental-rise sediments (Cushman, 1948; Loeblich and Tappan, 1953; Vilks, 1969). Gorbunov (1946) and Shedrina (*in* Somov, 1955) report abundant and varied arenaceous foraminifers, composing 41 percent of the benthic foraminiferal fauna recovered from water depths of 512 to 3,800 m along the "Russian side of the Arctic" basin. Ostracods, pelecypods, sponge spicules, and calcareous holothurian sclerites are minor components (Fetter, 1973; Herman, 1974a). Species composition, degree of fragmentation, and ratio of planktonic to benthic species are discussed elsewhere (Herman, 1969, 1974a).

Ice-rafted Carboniferous and Permian fossils have been dredged from the Alpha Ridge (Scharzacher and Hunkins, 1961). Ice rafting also accounts for the scattered occurrence of shallow-water foraminifers and other skeletal remains of shelf organisms (Herman, 1970), and of rare warm-water foraminifers (e.g., Herman and Hopkins, 1980) on the Alpha-Mendeleev Ridge.

More than 2,500 sea-floor photographs (Fig. 18) and numerous samples have been collected with biological trawls and cores, mainly from the Amerasia Basin, and Alpha-Mendeleev Ridge, but much less on the adjacent plains (Carsola, 1952; Schwarzacher and Hunkins, 1961; Cromie, 1961; Paul and Menzies, 1973; Kitchell and others, 1978). Bottom currents, indicated by ripple marks or bending of stalked animals, can be seen on the rise. The impoverished condition of large epifaunal benthos has been discussed by Paul and Menzies (1973) and Kitchell and others (1978). It is the most impoverished condition reported from photographic surveys to date: the average density of organisms is 0.02 organisms m^{-2}. Animal tracks and burrowers were also observed in photographs (Kitchell and others, 1978).

THE ROLE OF THE NORWEGIAN-GREENLAND SEA

Today the Norwegian-Greenland Sea and the eastern Arctic Basin are contiguous deep-sea basins connected by the deep and narrow Fram Strait between the western Svalbard and the eastern Greenland continental margins (Fig. 1 and Plate 1). Although a large portion of the Norwegian-Greenland Sea is located outside the actual polar climatic realm, it influences properties of the Arctic Ocean surface and bottom water masses today and did so during the later part of the Cenozoic. Therefore the history of the Norwegian-Greenland paleoenvironment (Vogt and others, 1981; Vogt, 1986) has to be briefly discussed in this chapter. In addition, it is today one of the most important downwelling areas for modern bottom-water formation in the oceans due to its location adjacent to the cold Arctic region.

The Norwegian-Greenland Sea has been connected with the main North Atlantic Ocean throughout the entire Cenozoic (Bott and others, 1983), although the width and paleodepth of the straits across the Greenland-Scotland Ridge are disputed (Thiede and Eldholm, 1983). The deep-water passage between the Greenland Sea and the eastern Arctic Basin (Lena Trough) appears to have started opening only after magnetic anomaly 13 time, but due to the construction of the aseismic volcanic marginal Yermak Plateau and Morris Jessup Rise, the actual exchange of water might have intensified much later, for example, in Miocene or Pliocene time (Kristoffersen and Husebye, 1985a). The origin and evolution of the Norwegian-Greenland Sea as a group of deep-sea basins after magnetic anomaly 24 time (approximately 56 Ma; Talwani and Eldholm, 1977), is however, well known. Reasonable assumptions about changes of size and shape of these deep-sea basins in the course of the Cenozoic can be made today (Thiede, 1979; Eldholm and Thiede, 1980).

Consideration of relevant aspects of the Norwegian-Greenland Sea paleoenvironment will be subdivided into 2 parts: Tertiary and Quaternary. Evidence for this discussion comes mostly from locations crowded in the ice-free southeastern and eastern parts of this deep-sea region. Because of their ice cover, vast areas, mainly in the Greenland Sea, remain virtually unexplored with respect to their sediment cover and depositional paleoenvironment.

The Tertiary paleoenvironment

Evidence for Norwegian-Greenland Sea Tertiary paleoenvironments comes mostly from deep-sea drilling (Talwani and

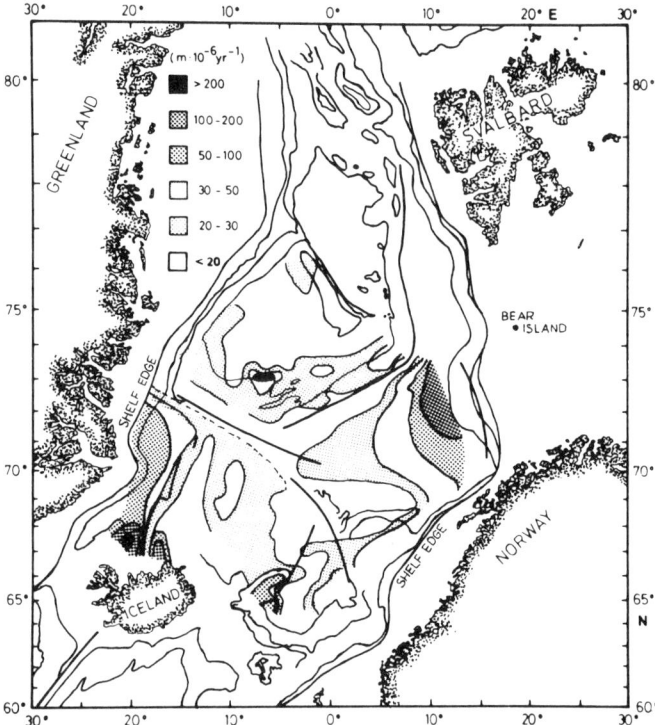

Figure 19. Distribution of linear sedimentation rates (LSR) in the Norwegian-Greenland Sea. The rates (expressed in m $10^{-6}y^{-1}$) have been calculated dividing sediment thicknesses by age of basement. Values from a grid of sample points at the intersections of full degrees of longitude and latitude were used for contouring. From Thiede and others (1986).

others, 1976), although sediment cores with pre-Quaternary pelagic sediments and pelagic deposits have been collected occasionally (Björklund and Kellogg, 1972). The oldest sediment taken during DSDP (Deep Sea Drilling Project) Leg 38 is of early Eocene age (Schrader and others, 1976), documenting fully pelagic and relatively warm environments for that time. It is difficult to imagine that the once high (mostly subaerial) Greenland-Scotland Ridge did not have an important impact on the water exchange between the main North Atlantic Ocean and the Norwegian-Greenland Sea. Most pelagic fossil assemblages, however, do not appear to have been affected severely by this sill (Berggren and Schnitker, 1983). This ridge probably was discontinuous, maybe interrupted in the area of the Faeroe-Shetland Channel.

When reconstructing sediment source regions of Tertiary deposits based on patterns of sedimentation rates (Thiede and others, 1986), it becomes obvious that the dominant share of the Paleogene, and possibly also the lower Neogene, deposits of the Norwegian-Greenland Sea have been delivered from a few, very limited source regions on the adjacent shelves (Fig. 19). The most important one was located to the east of the Senja Fracture Zone in a possibly once-emerged part of the Barents Sea between Bear Island and the Norwegian coast (Eldholm and others, 1984).

Extraordinarily high sedimentation rates in areas that are today located to the north of Iceland and Denmark Strait originated at least partly from source regions along the East Greenland continental margin, where thick sections of lower Tertiary sediment have been found (Larsen, 1983).

Mid-Tertiary depositional environments in the Norwegian-Greenland Sea are poorly known because of the development of an important lower Neogene hiatus that separates "preglacial"- and "glacial"-type deposits. The onset of glacially influenced sedimentation south of the Greenland-Scotland Ridge has been dated as 2.3 to 2.4 Ma (Shackleton and others, 1984). It is known, however, from DSDP Sites 344 (Schrader and others, 1976) and 341 (Nordaa, 1984), and from central Arctic cores (Clark and others, 1980), that glacial conditions had already evolved during late Miocene or early Pliocene times, about 4 to 6 Ma.

Recent drill holes of Ocean Drilling Program (ODP) Leg 104 (Eldholm and others, 1986a, 1986b) have provided important new evidence for the initiation of late Cenozoic Northern Hemisphere cold climates. Cold faunas and floras appeared as early as approximately 4.5 Ma over the Vøring Plateau, but the first well-developed sediment horizons with coarse, ice-rafted terrigenous debris occur only in sediments of 2.9 to 3 Ma.

Quaternary paleoenvironments

With the onset of "glacial"-type depositional environments in the Norwegian-Greenland Sea, the regional patterns of sediment flux to the deep-sea floors changed considerably. Isopachs of sediment with ice-rafted components (Warncke and Hansen, 1977) and isopleths of Quaternary sedimentation rates (Fig. 20) seem to parallel the continental margin along the eastern boundary of this deep-sea region and appear to have been controlled by the major patterns of surface-water circulation. This applies to glacial as well as to interglacial time slices.

The Norwegian-Greenland Sea depositional environment has also responded intensively to the glacial-interglacial paleoclimatic fluctuations of the Quaternary. This applies to parameters that have been generated in the surface waters as well as in the bottom waters. Detailed stratigraphic studies (Kellogg, 1976; Björklund and Goll, 1979) have shown that a relatively warm Norwegian Current reached the Norwegian Sea only during a few selected peak interglacials (Fig. 21), such as during O-isotope stage 5e, whereas the Norwegian Sea surface waters remained polar or even ice covered for most of the Quaternary. The nature, variability, and completeness of these ice covers remain poorly known, but the presence of late glacial iceberg plow marks along the Norwegian continental margin (Lien, 1983) suggests that the surface waters were covered by pack ice mixed with icebergs.

The history of bottom-water properties and bottom-water formation is still the subject of much discussion (Jansen and Erlenkeuser, 1985). O- and C-stable isotope data from outer Norwegian continental margin sediment cores (Sejrup and others, 1984) suggest that the glacial bottom water prior to Termination IA in the deep Norwegian Sea was a bit warmer than today, but lower in oxygen. Between Termination IA (at 13 Ka) and IB (at 10 Ka), a seasonal ice cover is thought to have existed, whereas oxygen-enriched waters filled the deep basin. After Termination IB a situation analogous to the modern one may have been established. The two-tier stepwise transition from the last glaciation to Holocene conditions (Jansen and others, 1983) has also been observed in the Greenland Sea (Grousset and Duplessy, 1983), but Greenland Sea Quaternary depositional environments appear to require further refinement.

MAJOR SOURCE AREAS FOR THE ARCTIC OCEAN SEDIMENT COVER

Bulk sedimentation rates based on geophysical data

Gross average sedimentation rates of a sediment section can be easily obtained if the thickness of the sediment cover above basement and basement age are known. In the Arctic Ocean proper, sufficient geophysical data are available only for the eastern Arctic Basin (Vogt and others, 1981). Estimated sedimentation rates are on the order of 10 to 30 m/m.y. (Y. Kristoffersen, personal communication, 1984), approximately the same value as obtained from reconstructions of sedimentation rates of upper Quaternary sediment cores (Markussen and others, 1985). The data suggest that large quantities of Tertiary sediments fill portions of the eastern Arctic Basin. The fact that they are found asymmetrically distributed on both sides of Nansen Ridge, with the greater thickness in the basin between Nansen Ridge and the Eurasian continental margin, suggests that the dominant share of these sediments are of terrigenous origin, with a provenance region on the Eurasian shelf area (Plate 5).

Bulk sedimentation rates based on sediment cores

Because of the variable composition of the sediment, the discussion of Arctic Ocean bulk sedimentation rates has to be divided into two parts: the upper Mesozoic and Paleogene deposits; and the upper Cenozoic, mostly Quaternary deposits.

The dominantly biogenic siliceous upper Mesozoic and Paleogene deposits of the central Arctic Basin have been dated, but do not provide enough stratigraphic section to estimate sedimentation based on top and bottom ages. At the present time, we can only assume that the lamination in the range of 1 to 2 mm thickness found in three of these cores represents a signal of seasonal changes, thus suggesting that they accumulated at rates of 100 to 200 cm/k.y. This corresponds to the range of similar deposits elsewhere in the world ocean, but it is extraordinarily high for the central Arctic Ocean and can only be explained by their biogenic nature.

Sediment fluxes to different parts of the Arctic region, as determined by sediment core stratigraphies, differ widely depending on region and setting. The Canada Basin received extraordinarily high sediment inputs because of a large proportion of turbidites (Clark and others, 1980). Upper Cenozoic sediments

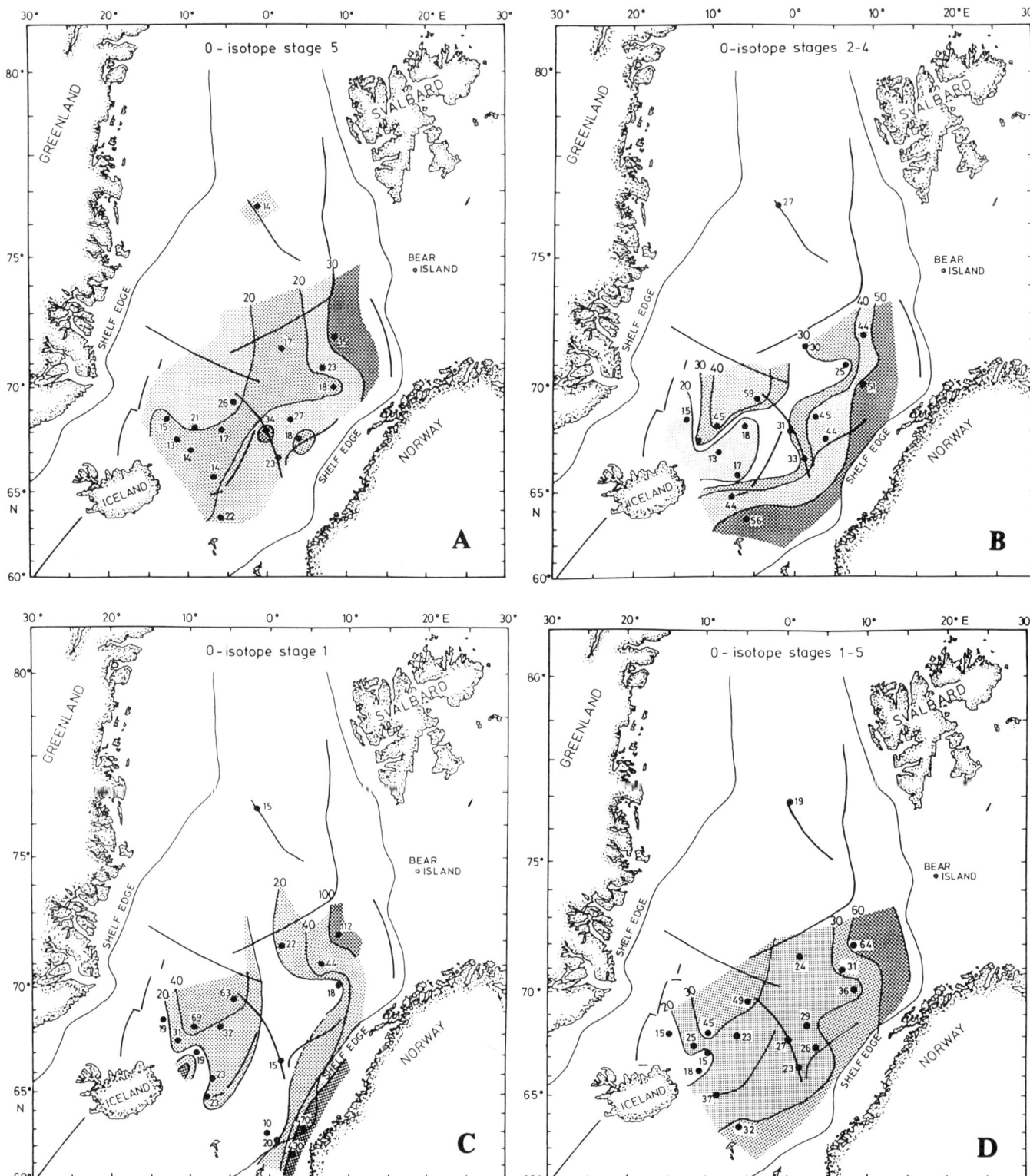

Figure 20. Sedimentation rates (LSR, in $10^{-6} y^{-1}$) in upper Quaternary Norwegian-Greenland Sea sediment cores. A, O-isotope stage 5; B, O-isotope stages 2 to 4; C, O-isotope stage 1; D, average O-isotope stages 1 to 5. From Thiede and others (1986).

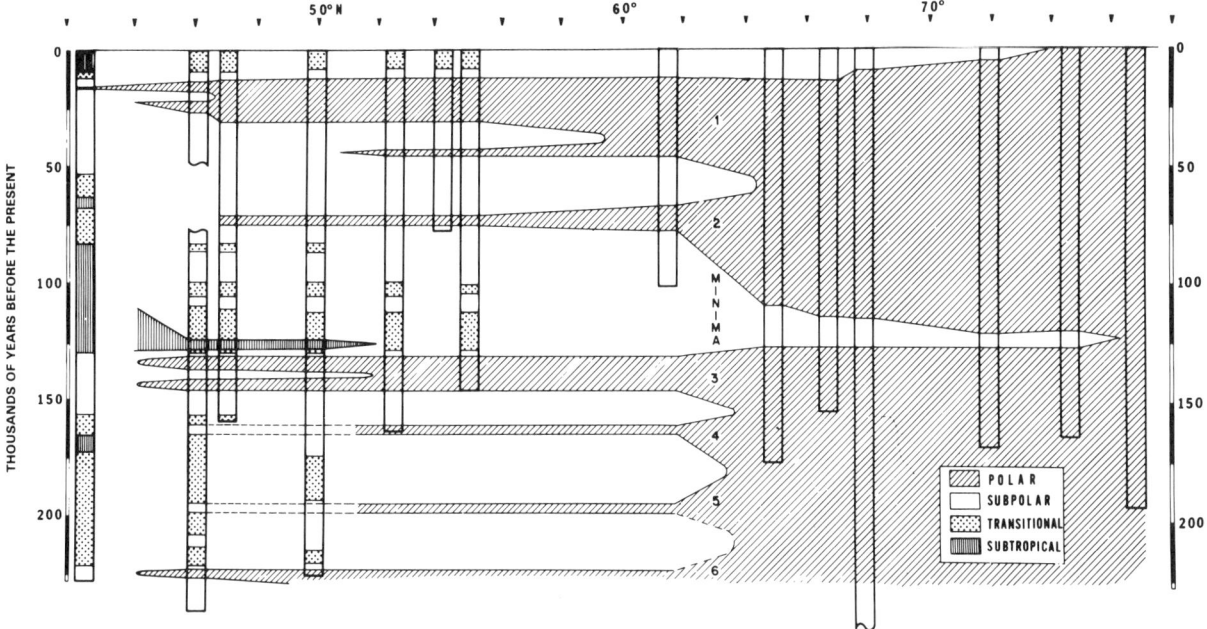

Figure 21. Variations in composition of the fauna and flora of the northern North Atlantic and Norwegian-Greenland Sea. From Kellogg (1976, Fig. 23).

from the central Arctic region accumulated very slowly, on the order of 1 to 3 mm/k.y., based on the magnetic stratigraphy available for most of the cores (however, see Sejrup and others, 1984). In the eastern Arctic Basin, sedimentation rates (based on O-isotope stratigraphies, see Markussen and others, 1985; Zahn and others, 1985) appear to be an order of magnitude higher than in the central Arctic, although lithostratigraphy and thickness of individual lithological units, especially of horizons enriched in coarse, ice-rafted material, seem to be similar. No further progress in these problems can be achieved before a more detailed stratigraphy of central Arctic Ocean sea-floor sediment becomes available.

The sediment core from Fram Strait (Knudsen, 1985) indicates much faster sediment accumulation than any other comparable cores in the Arctic (up to 80 cm/k.y., according to its O-isotope stratigraphy; see Knudsen, 1985). It represents a depositional environment close to an area where an ice shield had existed on Svalbard during the last glaciation (Schytt, 1984) and which delivered high amounts of glacial flour to the ocean floor.

Provenance and source regions of most Arctic deep-sea floor sediment components have been discussed in previous chapters, and it is quite clear that major progress in dating Arctic deep-sea cores is necessary to establish a sediment budget for the entire Arctic Ocean.

The enigma of ice-rafted material

The most characteristic sediment component of young Arctic Ocean deposits is coarse, terrigenous grains or pebbles of highly variable lithology, commonly believed to be ice rafted. They are typical of almost all glaciomarine sediments in the periglacial and glacial-marine areas, and are very easy to identify. Even though they seem to represent components carried under a clearly defined sedimentation mode, many uncertainties remain about how, and from where and when, this material reached the Arctic sea floor. In addition, a considerable amount of fine-grained material is transported with the coarse components by ice rafting. The proportions of coarse- and fine-grained ice-rafted material remain to be determined.

Coarse, terrigenous sediment components can be carried into polar deep-sea basins in a number of ways, the most common of which is by being frozen into sediment-laden ice. Although driftwood timbers in the Arctic have also been reported (Häggblom, 1982) to carry considerable quantities of coarse- and fine-grained material in their roots, their contribuion vis-a-vis ice rafting has never been quantified. In addition, the oceanwide distribution of ice-rafted material has been interpreted to be indicative of iceberg transport, but one has to be aware that river ice, coastal ice, and pack ice can also contain frozen-in fine- and coarse-grained terrigenous material. Furthermore it is poorly known how this material is released from the melting ice. Recent studies of the composition of the ice-rafted coarse sediment component in cores north and west of Svalbard (Knudsen, 1985; Snaare, 1984) are promising to identify restricted source regions for this ice-rafted material, making it possible to map temporal as well as spatial patterns of this mode of sediment transport.

HISTORY OF THE ARCTIC OCEAN

Temporal patterns of Arctic Ocean productivity have changed drastically through time, as observed in composition and sedimentation rates of its upper Mesozoic and Cenozoic deposits. The polar position of the Arctic Ocean led to important seasonal changes in productivity when the Arctic Ocean was relatively warm, as during the late Mesozoic and early Cenozoic, or when it was cold, as it has been since late Miocene time. All of the few upper Mesozoic and lower Cenozoic sediment cores recovered from the Arctic Ocean are laminated, probably reflecting seasonal changes. They are also extraordinarily enriched in siliceous microfossils (diatoms and silicoflagellates), suggesting highly productive surface water related to a seasonal variation in intensity of an upwelling system (Kitchell and Clark, 1982).

The upper Cenozoic deposits mainly contain remains of zooplankters (planktonic foraminifers) and a number of benthic animals. The latter are enriched in certain thick beds (see above), but due to the generally low sedimentation rates, these cannot have accumulated very rapidly. Therefore it is interesting to note that apart from scarce coccoliths, remains of primary producers such as diatoms are lacking in the upper Cenozoic beds. This is surprising because short, but important, plankton blooms have been observed in the modern Arctic Ocean in late spring. Therefore, most of the skeletal materials produced by these diatoms are obviously remobilized before they reach the sea floor. The habitat of Arctic planktonic foraminifers is also poorly known. The problem of Arctic Ocean productivity and its variability through time will have to be considered again once the necessary data have been collected.

EVOLUTION OF MARINE FLORAS AND FAUNAS

The development of geologically significant organisms in the Arctic Ocean involved at least five steps: (1) establishment of the oldest known indigenous floras (phytoplankton) in the Late Cretaceous; (2) replacement of these floras by younger Eocene phytoplankton; (3) development of a primitive arenaceous foraminiferal fauna prior to late Miocene time; (4) appearance of milioliids and rotaliids in the middle Pliocene; and (5) the dramatic early Pleistocene ascendance of planktonic foraminifers together with calcareous dinoflagellates (Gilbert and Clark, 1983) and introduction of additional new rotaliid species.

No data are available for the post-Eocene to pre–late Miocene interval. During this time, siliceous microfloras were replaced by textulariid foraminifers, a step that probably involved development and extinction of several floras and faunas.

Oldest Arctic Ocean fossils

An abundance of pollen and terrestrial plant material in a rich assemblage of marine dinoflagellates are the oldest known Arctic Ocean fossils. These Campanian fossils have been found in core FL-533, taken at 85°N (Clark and Byers, 1984).

Some 20 species or varieties of normal marine silicoflagellates were described from core FL-437 at approximately 86°N (Ling and others, 1973; Bukry, 1981). Additional species of silicoflagellates and diatoms for CESAR 6, of the same age, have been described (Bukry, 1985; Barron, 1985). The assemblage is Maastrichtian in age and interpreted to represent north polar upwelling (Kitchell and Clark, 1982). The dominance of *Vallacerta siderea* is considered unique, particularly at this high latitude. Diatoms occur in great abundance and are of the same genera as those described from Late Cretaceous marine deposits in other parts of the world (Barron, 1985). Ebridians and archaeomonads are also present, along with dinoflagellates (Mudie, 1985).

Eocene phytoplankton

An assemblage of siliceous skeletal fossils, similar in composition to that of the Late Cretaceous but of early Cenozoic age, has been obtained from a single core (FL-422) taken at 85°N, approximately 100 km from the Cretaceous core FL-437. Silicoflagellates and diatoms in abundance equal to that of core FL-437 are present. Taxonomic work is incomplete, but an age of middle Eocene has been determined (Bukry, 1984). There are important taxonomic differences distinguishing the Cenozoic phytoplankton, but the environment of accumulation of siliceous material was very similar to that of the Cretaceous fossils (Kitchell and Clark, 1982). Evolutionary changes along with migration of species account for the change in phytoplankton and are assumed to correspond with the environmental conditions prevailing during the entire interval of about 15 m.y., from Late Cretaceous to early Cenozoic time. It is apparent that a continuous core record, instead of two discontinuous core records (FL-437 and -422) would provide important details of additional taxa and mechanisms of replacement. FL-422 present provides the last look at Arctic Ocean life until the late Miocene.

Late Miocene arenaceous foraminifers

Sometime prior to the late Miocene, some 19 species of textulariid foraminifers became established in the central Arctic Ocean (O'Neill, 1981). The fact that no Oligocene to late Miocene sediment has been recovered from the Arctic Ocean precludes determination of the middle Cenozoic floras or faunas, particularly the precise development of the late Miocene faunas. O'Neill (1981) has described this fauna as the Arctic Ocean textulariid biofacies. The species are not abundant in any of the cores studied, and rarely have more than 5 to 10 specimens per gram of coarse weight been found. The planktonic *Neogloboquadrina pachyderma* is absent in the oldest samples, as are other calcareous tests. The few *N. pachyderma* that occur in the older parts of the record are poorly preserved; together with the absence of any calcareous benthic species, these factors suggest that carbonate concentration depth (CCD) levels may have been higher at this time than during the Pliocene (Herman, 1970). O'Neill (1981) addressed this problem and concluded that the central Arctic Ocean at this time was characterized by harsh, possibly poorly oxygenated bottom waters, with extremely low sedimentation rates. Herman's interpretation of an elevated CCD, very low sedimentation rates, and well-oxygenated bottom water (Herman, 1974) differs from O'Neill (1981) in several aspects.

Middle Pliocene foraminiferal faunas

During late, early, or middle Pliocene time the foraminiferal faunas significantly changed. Three milioliid species and 20 rotaliid species (benthic) appeared in a relatively short period of time and joined the Miocene textulariid fauna. The appearance of a calcareous fauna is rather abrupt and synchronous in all cores studied. Eighteen of the species survive in the modern Arctic Ocean. *N. pachyderma* is relatively rare in the interval where the calcareous benthic fauna appears. O'Neill (1981) referred to this fauna as the Arctic "transitional biofacies". Because longer residence time of bottom water in the Arctic causes oxygen depletion and CO_2 enrichment, O'Neill (1981) suggested that the mixed textulariid and calcareous fauna of the transitional biofacies may indicate increased circulation of Arctic and North Atlantic layer bottom water. This is in apparent accord with the ideas of Vilks (1969) on Atlantic layer interchange and also of Greiner (1969) on co-occurrence of textulariids and rotaliids. As the calcareous benthic forms became established, textulariid species should disappear; this is the record of the middle Pliocene transitional biofacies. During this interval a few ostracods appear that are of the same species as those found in the modern Arctic (Joy and Clark, 1977).

Early Pleistocene calcareous fossils

O'Neill (1981) used the appearance of abundant planktonic *N. pachyderma* along with another dozen species of benthic rotaliids to mark the base of his "Rotaliid Biofacies". The dominance of *N. pachyderma* in unit G and higher in the Arctic Ocean sediment cores (Clark and others, 1980) must have accompanied a significant change in water or preservational conditions, or both. Also, the Arctic calcareous dinoflagellate, *Thoracosphaera arctica* becomes important at the same level. Thus, at approximately the base of the Pleistocene, planktonic foraminifers become abundant and dominate all fossil assemblages. Also, new species of calcareous benthic foraminifers are introduced that, along with the middle Pliocene calcareous benthic fauna, have continued to the present. During this interval, further new foraminiferan species are introduced, and all except three textulariid species disappear in the Arctic Ocean. Ostracods (Joy and Clark, 1977) appear sporadically throughout the interval, as do holothurian sclerites, various bivalve species, and sponge spicules (Gamber and Clark, 1978).

The recent documentation of calcareous dinoflagellates in the Arctic Ocean is of particular importance for the fossil assemblage of this time interval. Although the life cycle of the dinoflagellate that produces the calcareous fossil is unknown, related studies on the North Atlantic *Thoracosphaera heimii* (Tangen and others, 1982) suggest that the Arctic fossil may represent a vegetative cell that was part of the motile life cycle. If this is correct, the ecological conditions during times that the organism produced a calcareous skeleton were probably more moderate during this time interval of approximately 2.0 to 0.7 m.y.; the abundance of calcareous dinoflagellates and planktonic foraminifers also shows a positive correlation. Before and after this interval, calcareous dinoflagellate are rare to absent. Thus, during this part of the Pleistocene, calcareous phytoplankton and zooplankton responded to the same ecological stimulus. Because calcareous dinoflagellates are rare in the modern Arctic (with an average ice cover of 3 m), we suspect that the limiting factor for appearance of calcareous dinoflagellates may be related to photosynthesis beneath an ice cover. Probably during the interval 1.0 to 0.7 Ma, ice cover was thinner or even periodically absent during deglaciations (Herman, 1974). This could encourage the productivity of phytoplankton seen in the record of the Early Pleistocene. During times of relative abundance of calcareous phytoplankton, glacial-marine sediment accumulated in the central Arctic Ocean as they had since the Miocene. During times of initial glaciation (peak deposition of coarse sediment) both phyto-and zooplankton were rare, but following intensive deglaciation the productivity of both organisms increased and was maintained until the next deglaciation (Gilbert and Clark, 1983).

During the present deglaciation, the modern Arctic fauna, which is the richest known in the Arctic for any time, has been established. In general, there has been a decrease in relationship of Arctic forms to North Pacific species and an increase in the relationship to faunas and floras of the North Atlantic (Clark, 1977; O'Neill, 1981; Gilbert and Clark, 1983), suggesting late Cenozoic circulation of Arctic and North Atlantic water. The modern Arctic Ocean has a well-developed fauna and flora of geologically significant organisms, many of which are endemic. This includes at least 86 benthic and 3 planktonic species of foraminifers, 19 species of ostracods, 10 species of bivalves, 8 species or varieties of sponges, 3 holothurians, 2 gastropods, and at least a single species each of echinoids, crinoids, and ophiuroids (Clark, 1977). Phytoplanktons include one silicoflagellate, at least 17 radiolarians, 3 tintinnids, and 4 dinoflagellates, as well as a number of diatom species. These are all minimum figures. The modern siliceous phytoplankton is not as well preserved in the Arctic sediment as the calcareous fossils. Undersaturation of SiO_2 may be a partial explanation for the bias in the sediment record.

SUMMARY AND FUTURE PERSPECTIVES

Mesozoic and Paleogene Arctic Ocean sediment cores, consisting of Campanian black muds and uppermost Cretaceous and Paleogene laminated siliceous oozes, document a relatively warm, stagnant northern polar deep-sea basin. However, paleophysiography of the basin, water depths, and distribution of the oxygen-deficient waters are poorly known, and it is not clear if the entire Arctic Ocean or only the flanks of Alpha Ridge were covered by oxygen-deficient bottom waters.

All upper Cenozoic Arctic Ocean deep-sea sediment cores

document a cold, more or less ice-covered northern polar deep-sea basin, which occasionally received large amounts of ice-rafted coarse terrigenous sediment from the adjacent continents. This happened mainly during times of deglaciation: the last time occurred during Termination IB, when large numbers of icebergs were discharged into the Arctic Ocean.

O-isotope–dated sediment cores from the eastern Arctic Basin allow correlation of upper Quaternary Arctic deep-sea deposits to corresponding sediments in the Norwegian-Greenland Sea. O-isotope stages 1, 2, and 3 have been identified. Bulk sedimentation rates in the eastern Arctic are on the order of 1 to 3 cm/k.y., while in the central Arctic, sedimentation rate is only 1 to 3 mm/k.y.

There is no doubt that the Arctic Ocean has been ice covered during the late Cenozoic, although the extent, completeness, and thickness of the ice cover may have varied widely. The record of the Arctic Ocean ice cover can be traced back to the late Miocene. The lack of samples covering the time span from early Eocene to late Miocene has prevented a more precise definition of the advent of Northern Hemisphere glacial-type climates.

Major progress in our understanding of Arctic Ocean paleoceanography can only be achieved if the following means become available, which are not as much a question of available methodology as a question of financial resources and international resolve to act on these needs: systematic shallow reflection seismic profiling to map sediment distribution and potential sampling sites; a grid of long sediment cores (up to 50 m), to be collected by ultraheavy piston corers from large ice breakers that can crisscross the Arctic Ocean ice cover at will to predetermined sampling sites; deep-sea drilling, from the ice pack or floating platforms (ice breakers), to obtain long, large-diameter, continuous sediment cores in a few regions with extensive site surveys; and refinement of the presently available dating techniques for Arctic Ocean deep-sea sediment.

The history of the northern polar deep-sea water masses is one of the last almost completely unsolved epics of paleoceanography. Its detailed understanding will have wide implications in many fields of marine and continental geoscience.

REFERENCES CITED

Aagard, K., 1981, On the deep circulation in the Arctic Ocean: Deep-Sea Research, v. 28, p. 215–268.

Aagaard, K., Swift, J. H., and Cormack, E. C., 1985, Thermohaline circulation in the Arctic Mediterranean Sea: Journal of Geophysical Research, v. 90, no. C3, p. 4833–4846.

Aksu, A. E., 1985a, Paleomagnetic stratigraphy of the CESAR cores: Geological Survey of Canada Paper 84-22, p. 101–114.

——, 1985b, Planktonic foraminiferal and oxygen isotope stratigraphy of CESAR cores 102 and 103; Preliminary results: Geological Survey of Canada paper 84-22, p. 115–124.

Aksu, A. E., and Mudie, P. J., 1985, Magnetostratigraphy and palynology demonstrate at least 4 million years of Arctic Ocean sedimentation: Nature, v. 318, p. 280–283.

Andersen, B. G., 1981, Late Weichselian ice-sheets in Eurasia and Greenland, in Denton, G. H., and Hughes, T. J., eds., The last great ice sheets: New York, John Wiley and Sons, p. 1–65.

Andrew, J. A., and Kravitz, J. H., 1974, Sediment distribution in deep areas of the northern Kara Sea, in Herman, Y., ed., Marine geology and oceanography of the Arctic seas: New York, Springer-Verlag, p. 231–256.

Augstein, E., Hempel, G., Schwarz, J., Thiede, J., and Weigel, W., 1984, Die Expedition ARKTIS II des FS *Polarstern* 1984: Berichte zur Polarforschung, v. 20, 192 p.

Barron, E. J., Thompson, S. L., and Schneider, S. H., 1981, An ice-free Cretaceous? Results from climate model simulations: Science, v. 212, p. 501–508.

Barron, J. A., 1985, Diatom biostratigraphy of the CESAR-6 core, Alpha Ridge: Geological Survey of Canada Paper 84-22, p. 137–148.

Berger, A., Imbrie, J., Hays, J., Kukla, G, and Saltzman, B., eds., 1984, Milankovitch and climate; NATO ASI series C, Mathematical and physical sciences: Dordrecht, Reidel Publishing Company, v. 126, parts 1 and 2, 895 p.

Berger, W. H., 1970, Biogenous deep-sea sediments; Fractionation by deep-sea circulation: Geological Society of America Bulletin, v. 81, p. 1385–1402.

Berggren, W. A., and Hollister, C. D., 1974, Paleogeography, paleobiogeography, and the history of circulation in the Atlantic Ocean: Society of Economic Paleontologists and Mineralogists Special Publication 20, p. 126–186.

Berggren, W. A., and Schnitker, D., 1983, Cenozoic marine environments in the North Atlantic and Norwegian-Greenland Sea, in Bott, M.H.P., Saxov, S., Talwani, M., and Thiede, J., eds., Structure and development of the Greenland-Scotland Ridge; New methods and concepts: New York, Plenum Press, p. 495–548.

Berry, R. W., and Johns, W. D., 1966, Mineralogy of the clay-sized fractions of some North Atlantic bottom specimens: Geological Society of America Bulletin, v. 7, p. 183–195.

Björklund, K. R., and Goll, R. M., 1979, Ice age climates of the Norwegian-Greenland Sea: GeoJournal, v. 3, no. 3, p. 273–283.

Björklund, K. R., and Kellogg, D. E., 1972, Five new Eocene radiolarian species from the Norwegian Sea: Micropaleontology, v. 1, p. 386–396.

Böggild, O. B., 1906, On the bottom deposits of the north polar seas: Scientific results of the Norwegian North Polar Expedition 1893–1896, v. 5, p. 1–62.

Boström, K., and Thiede, J., 1981, Marin geologi och geofysik i Arktiska oceanen-problem och preliminaera resultat: YMERAarsbok 1981, p. 90–109.

——, 1984, YMER-80, Swedish Arctic Expedition, Cruise report for marine geology and geophysics; Sediment core descriptions: Meddelelser Stockholms Universitetets Geologiska Institutionen, v. 260, 123 p.

Bott, M.H.P., Saxov, S., Talwani, M., and Thiede, J., eds, 1983, Structure and development of the Greenland-Scotland Ridge: New York, Plenum Press, 685 p.

Boyd, R. F., Clark, D. L., Jones, G., Ruddiman, W. F., McIntyre, A., and Pisias, N. G., 1984, Central Arctic Ocean response to Pleistocene earth-orbital variations: Quaternary Research, v. 22, p. 121–128.

Broecker, W. S., and van Donk, J., 1970, Insolation changes, ice volumes, and ^{18}O record in deep-sea sediments: Reviews of Geophysics and Space Physics, v. 8, p. 169–198.

Bukry, D., 1981, Cretaceous Arctic silicoflagellates: Geo-Marine Letters, v. 1, p. 57–63.

——, 1984, Paleogene paleoceanography of the Arctic Ocean is constrained by the middle or late Eocene age of U.S.G.S. Core Fl-422; Evidence from silicoflagellates: Geology, v. 12, p. 199–201.

——, 1985, Correlation of Late Cretaceous Arctic silicoflagellates from Alpha Ridge: Geological Survey of Canada Paper 84-22, p. 125–135.

Campbell, J. S., and Clark, D. L., 1977, Pleistocene turbidites of the Canada Abyssal Plain of the Arctic Ocean: Journal of Sedimentary Petrology, v. 47, p. 657–670.

Carroll, D., 1970, Clay minerals in Arctic Ocean sea-floor sediments: Journal of Sedimentary Petrology, v. 40, p. 814–821.

Carsola, A. J., 1952, Marine geology of the Arctic and adjacent seas of Alaska and northwestern Canada [Ph.D. thesis]: Los Angeles, University of California, 226 p.

Clark, D. L., 1971, Arctic Ocean ice cover and its Late Cenozoic history: Geological Society of America Bulletin, v. 82, p. 3313-3324.
—— , 1977, Paleontological response to post-Jurassic crustal plate movements in the Arctic Ocean: Journal of Paleontology, v. 51, p. 6-7.
—— , 1982, Origin, nature, and world climate effect of Arctic Ocean ice cover: Nature, v. 300, p. 321-325.
Clark, D. L., and Byers, C. W., 1984, Cretaceous carbon-rich sediment from the central Arctic Ocean: Geological Society of America Abstracts with Programs, v. 16, p. 472.
Clark, D. L., and Hanson, A., 1983, Central Arctic Ocean sediment texture; A key to ice transport mechanism, in Molnia, B. F., ed., Glacial-marine sedimentation: New York, Plenum Press, p. 301-330.
Clark, D. L., Whitman, R. R., Morgan, K. A., and Mackey, S. D., 1980, Stratigraphy and glacial marine sediments of the Amerasian Basin, central Arctic Ocean: Geological Society of America Special Paper 181, 57 p.
Clark, D. L., Morris, T. H., and Blasco, S. M., 1983, Pleistocene sedimentation patterns for the Lomonosov Ridge and Amerasian Basin, central Arctic Ocean: Geological Society of America Abstracts with Programs, v. 15, p. 54.
Clark, D. L., Byers, C. W., and Pratt, L. M., 1986, Cretaceous black mud from the central Arctic Ocean: Paleoceanography, v. 1, no. 3, p. 265-271.
CLIMAP Project Members, 1981, Seasonal reconstructions of the earth's surface at the last glacial maximum: Geological Society of America Map and Chart Series MC-36.
Coachman, L. K., and Aagaard, K., 1974, Physical oceanography of Arctic and Subarctic seas, in Hermany Y., ed., Marine geology and oceanography of the Arctic seas: New York, Springer-Verlag, p. 1-72.
Collinvaux, P. A., 1964, Origin of ice age; Pollen evidence from Arctic Alaska: Science, v. 145, p. 707-708.
Cromie, W. J., 1961, Preliminary results of investigations on Arctic drift station "Charlie", in Raasch, G. O., ed., Geology of the Arctic: Toronto, Ontario, University of Toronto Press, p. 690-708.
Crowley, T. J., 1983, The geologic record of climate changes: Reviews in Geophysics and Space Physics, v. 21, p. 808-877.
Dalland, A., 1976, Erratic clasts in the lower Tertiary deposits of Svalbard; Evidence of transport by winter ice: Norsk Polarinstitutt Aarbok, p. 151-165.
Darby, D. A., 1971, Carbonate cycles and clay mineralogy of Arctic Ocean sediment cores [Ph.D. thesis]: Madison, University of Wisconsin, 117 p.
Darby, D. A., Burckle, L. H., and Clark, D. L., 1974, Airborne dust on the Arctic pack ice; Its composition and fallout rate: Earth and Planetary Science Letters, v. 24, p. 166-172.
de Geer, G., 1900, Om oestra Spetsbergens glaciation under istiden: Geologiska Foereningen i Stockholm Forhandlingar, v. 22, p. 427-436.
Detrick, R., Sclater, J. C., and Thiede, J., 1977, Subsidence of aseismic ridges: Earth and Planetary Science Letters, v. 34, p. 185-196.
Donn, W. L., 1982, The enigma of high-latitude paleoclimate: Palaeogeography, Palaeoclimatology, Palaeoecology, v. 40, p. 199-212.
Eldholm, O., and Thiede, J., 1980, Cenozoic continental separation between Europe and Greenland: Palaeogeography, Palaeoclimatology, Palaeoecology, v. 30, p. 243-259.
Eldholm, O., Thiede, J., and Shipboard Scientific Party Offshore Drilling Project Leg 104, 1986a, Formation of the Norwegian Sea: Nature, v. 319, p. 360-361.
—— , 1986b, Reflector identified, glacial onset seen: Geotimes, v. 31, p. 12-15.
—— , 1987, Norwegian sea: Proceedings of Ocean Drilling Program, v. 104A, 783 p.
Elverhöj, A., 1984, Glacigenic and associated marine sediments in the Weddell Sea, fjords of Spitsbergen, and the Barents Sea; A review: Marine Geology, v. 57, p. 53-88.
Ewing, M., and Donn, W. L., 1956, A theory of ice-ages: Science, v. 128, p. 1061-1066.
Fetter, F. C., 1973, Recent deep-sea benthic foraminifera from the Alpha Ridge Province of the Arctic Ocean [M.S. thesis]: Tallahassee, Florida State University, 121 p.

Frakes, L. A., 1979, Climates throughout geologic times: New York, Elsevier Publishing Company, 310 p.
Funder, S., Abrahamsen, N., Bennike, O., and Feyling-Hanssen, R. W., 1985, Forested Arctic; Evidence from North Greenland: Geology, v. 13, p. 543-546.
Galt, J. A., 1967, Current measurements in the Canada Basin of the Arctic Ocean, summer 1965: Seattle, University of Washington Department of Oceanography Technical Report 184, 17 p.
Gamber, J. H., and Clark, D. L., 1978, Distribution of microscopic mollusks, echinoderms, and sponges in the central Arctic Ocean: Micropaleontology, v. 24, p. 422-431.
Gard, G., 1986, Calcareous nannofossil biostratigraphy of late Quaternary Arctic sediments: Boreas, v. 15, p. 217-229.
Gilbert, M. W., and Clark, D. L., 1983, Central Arctic Ocean paleoceanography interpretations based on Late Cenozoic calcareous dinoflagellates: Marine Micropaleontology, v. 7, p. 385-401.
Goldstein, R. H., 1983, Stratigraphy and sedimentology of ice-rafted and turbidite sediment, Canada Basin, Arctic Ocean, in Molnia, B. F., ed., Glacial marine sedimentation: New York, Plenum Press, p. 367-400.
Gorbunov, G., 1946, Bottom life of the Novosiberian shoal-waters and the central part of the Arctic Ocean, in Compendium of results of Drifting Expedition of Ice-Breaker Sedov, 1937-1940: Moscow, Chief Office of North Road, v. 3, 138 p.
Gorshkov, S. G., 1983, Arctic Ocean, in World ocean atlas: London, Pergamon Press, v. 3, 184 p.
Green, A. R., Kaplan, A. A., and Vierbuchen, R. C., 1982, The geological framework and hydrocarbon potential of sedimentary basins in northern seas: Stavanger, Norway, Offshore Northern Seas, Aug. 24-27, E/1, 53 p.
Green, E., 1960, Ecology of some Arctic foraminifera: Micropaleontology, v. 6, p. 57-78.
Greiner, G.O.G., 1969, Recent benthic foraminifera; Environment factors controlling their distribution: Nature, v. 223, p. 168-170.
Griffin, J. J., Windom, H., and Goldberg, E. D., 1968, The distribution of clay minerals in the world ocean: Deep-Sea Research, v. 15, p. 433-459.
Hays, J. D., Imbrie, J., and Shackleton, N. J., 1976, Variations in the earth's orbit; Pacemaker of the ice ages: Science, v. 194, p. 1121-1132.
Herman, Y., 1969, Arctic Ocean Quaternary microfauna and its relation to paleoclimatology: Palaeogeography, Palaeoclimatology, Palaeoecology, v. 6, p. 251-276.
—— , 1970, Arctic paleoceanography in late Cenozoic time: Science, v. 169, p. 474-477.
—— , 1974, Arctic Ocean sediments, microfauna, and the climatic record in late Cenozoic time, in Herman, Y., ed., Marine geology and oceanography of the Arctic seas: New York, Springer-Verlag, p. 283-348.
Hermany, Y., and Hopkins, D. M., 1980, Arctic Ocean climate in late Cenozoic time: Science, v. 209, p. 557-562.
Herman, Y., and O'Neill, J. B., 1975, Arctic paleosalinities during late Cenozoic time: Nature, v. 258, p. 591-595.
Herman, Y., and Osmond, J. K., 1984, Late Neogene Arctic paleoceanography; Micropaleontology and chronology, in Berger, A., Imbrie, J., Hays, J., Kukla, G., and Saltzman, B., eds., Milankovitch and climate: Dordrecht, Reidel Publishing Company, p. 241-250.
Hibler, W. D., III, 1980, Sea Ice growth, drift, and decay, in Colbeck, S. C., ed., Dynamics of snow and ice masses: London, Academic Press, p. 141-209.
Hickey, L. J., West, R. M., Dawson, M. R., and Choi, D. K., 1983, Arctic terrestrial biota; Paleomagnetic evidence of age disparity with mid-northern latitudes during the Late Cretaceous and early Tertiary: Science, v. 221, p. 1153-1156.
Holtedahl, H., 1959, Geology and paleontology of Norwegian Sea bottom cores: Journal of Sedimentary Petrology, v. 29, p. 16-29.
Hopkins, D. M., ed., 1967, The Bering land bridge: Stanford, California, Stanford University Press, 495 p.
Hughes, T., Denton, G. H., and Grosswald, M. G., 1977, Was there a late warm Arctic ice sheet?: Nature, v. 266, p. 596-602.

Hunkins, K. E., Thorndike, E. M., and Mathieu, G., 1969, Nepheloid layers and bottom currents in the Arctic Ocean: Journal of Geophysical Research, v. 74, p. 6995–7008.

Hunkins, K., Bé, A.W.H., Opdyke, N. D., and Mathieu, G., 1971, The late Cenozoic history of the Arctic Ocean, in Turekian, K. K., ed., The late Cenozoic glacial ages: New Haven, Connecticut, Yale University Press, p. 215–237.

Jackson, H. R., 1985a, Seismic reflection, in Jackson, H. R., Mudie, P. J., and Blasco, S. M., eds., Initial geological data report of CESAR; Canadian expedition to study Alpha Ridge: Geological Survey of Canada Paper 84-22, p. 19–23.

Jackson, H. R., 1985b, Nares Strait—A suture zone; Geophysical and geological implications: Tectonophysics, v. 114, p. 11–28.

Jackson, H. R., and Johnson, G. L., 1986, Summary of Arctic geophysics, in Johnson, G. L., and Kaminuma, K., eds., Polar geophysics: Journal of Geodynamics, v. 6, p. 245–262.

Jansen, E., and Erlenkeuser, H., 1985, Ocean circulation in the Norwegian Sea during the last deglaciation; Isotopic evidence: Palaeogeography, Palaeoclimatology, Palaeoecology, v. 49, p. 189–206.

Jansen, E., Sejrup, H. P., Fjaeran, T., Hald, M., Holtedahl, H., and Skarboe, O., 1983, Late Weichselian paleoceanography of the southeastern Norwegian Sea: Norsk Geologisk Tidsskrift, v. 63, p. 117–146.

Jones, G. A., 1987, The central Arctic Ocean sediment record; Current progress in moving from a litho- to a chronostratigraphy: Polar Research, v. 5, p. 309–311.

Joy, J. A., and Clark, D. L., 1977, The distribution, ecology, and systematics of the benthic ostracoda of the central Arctic Ocean: Micropaleontology, v. 23, p. 129–154.

Keigwin, L. D., 1982, An Arctic Ocean ice sheet in the Pleistocene?: Nature, v. 296, p. 808–809.

Kellogg, T. B., 1976, Late Quaternary climatic changes; Evidence from deep-sea cores of Norwegian and Greenland seas: Geological Society of America Memoir 145, p. 77–110.

Kennett, J. P., and Srinivasan, M. S., 1983, Neogene planktonic foraminifera: Stroudsburg, Pennsylvania, Hutchinson Ross Publishing Company, 165 p.

Kerr, W. J., 1981, Evolution of Canadian Arctic islands; A transition between the Atlantic and Arctic oceans, in Nairn, A.E.M., Churkin, M., and Stehli, F. G., eds., The ocean basins and margins; Vol. 5, The Arctic Ocean: New York, Plenum Press, p. 105–199.

—— , 1982, History and implications of the Nares Strait conflict: Meddelelser om Grönland, Geoscience, v. 8, p. 37–49.

Kitchell, J. A., and Clark, D. L., 1982, Late Cretaceous–Paleogene paleogeography and paleocirculation; Evidence of North Polar upwelling: Palaeogeography, Palaeoclimatology, Palaeoecology, v. 40, p. 135–165.

Kitchell, J. A., Kitchell, J. F., Johnson, G. L., and Hunkins, K. L., 1978, Abyssal traces and megafauna; Comparison and productivity, diversity and density in the Arctic and Antarctic: Paleobiology, v. 4, p. 171–180.

Knudsen, B.-E., 1985, Sen-Kartaert paleomiljoe i Framstredet [cand. scient. thesis]: Oslo, Norway, University of Oslo, Department of Geology, 60 p.

Kristoffersen, Y., 1979, Isdriftstasjonen FRAM-I, Ekspedisjonsrapport: Oslo, Norway, Norsk Polarinstitutt, 88 p.

Kristoffersen, Y., and Husebye, E., 1985, The Arctic Ocean; Outline of the submarine geology and geologic evolution of a polar region: Geofysiske publikasjoner, Det norske vitenskapsakademi, Oslo.

Ku, T. L., and Broecker, W. S., 1967, Rates of sedimentation in the Arctic Ocean: Progress in Oceanography, v. 4, p. 95–104.

Kulikov, N. A., Lapina, N.N., Semenov, Yu. P., Belov, N. A., and Spiridonov, M. A., 1982, Stratification and rate of accumulation of floor sediments of the Soviet Arctic seas, in Tolmachev, A. I., ed., The Arctic Ocean and its coast in the Cenozoic Era: New Delhi, Amerind Publishing Company, p. 26–33.

Lagoe, M. B., 1977, Recent benthic foraminifera from the central Arctic Ocean: Journal of Foraminiferal Research, v. 7, p. 106–129.

Larsen, B., 1983, Geology of the Greenland-Iceland Ridge in the Denmark Strait, in Bott, M.H.P., Saxov, S., Talwani, M., and Thiede, J., eds., Structure and development of the Greenland-Scotland Ridge, New York, Plenum Press, p. 425–444.

Larsen, B. B., Elverhöj, A., and Aagaard, P., 1984, Particulate material in the sea ice in the Fram Strait: Oslo, Voksenaasen, p. 74–75.

Lien, R., 1983, Plöyemerker efter isfjell paa norsk kontinentalsokkel: Trondheim, Continental Shelf Institute Publication 109, 147 p.

Ling, H. Y., McPherson, L. M., and Clark, D. L., 1973, Late Cretaceous (Maastrichtian?) silicoflagellates from the Alpha Cordillera of the Arctic Ocean: Science, v. 180, p. 1360–1361.

Loeblich, A. R., Jr., and Tappan, H., 1953, Studies of Arctic foraminifera: Smithsonian Miscellaneous Collections, v. 121, 150 p.

Lövlie, R., Markussen, B., Sejrup, H. P., and Thiede, J., 1986, Magneticstratigraphy in three Arctic Ocean sediment cores; Argument for geomagnetic excursions within oxygen isotope state 2-3: Physics of the Earth and Planetary Interiors, v. 43, p. 173–184.

Mangerud, J., Elgersma, A., Helliksen, D., Landvik, J., and Salvigsen, O., 1984, The late Weichselian glaciation in Isfjorden and van Mijenfjorden, Svalbard: Oslo, Voksenaasen, p. 16–17.

Markussen, B., Lövlie, R., and Thiede, J., 1982, FRAM-I, Senkvartaere avsetninger i den östlige delen av Polhavet (Framstredet): Institutt for geologi Oslo, Intern skriftserie, v. 40, 29 p.

Markussen, B., Zahn, R., and Thiede, J., 1985, Late Quaternary sedimentation in the eastern Arctic basin; Stratigraphy and depositional environment: Palaeogeography, Palaeoclimatology, Palaeoecology, v. 50, p. 271–284.

Meincke, J., 1983, The modern current regime across the Greenland-Scotland Ridge, in Bott, M.H.P., Saxov, S., Talwani, M., and Thiede, J., eds., Structure and development of the Greenland-Scotland Ridge: New York, Plenum Press, p. 637–650.

Mercer, J. H., and Sutter, J. F., 1982, Late Miocene–earliest Pliocene glaciation in southern Argentina; Implications for global ice-sheet history: Palaeogeography, Paleoclimatology, Palaeoecology, v. 38, p. 185–206.

Minicucci, D. A., and Clark, D. L., 1983, A late Cenozoic stratigraphy for glacial-marine sediments of the eastern Alpha Cordillera, central Arctic Ocean, in Molnia, B. F., ed., Glacial-marine sedimentation: New York, Plenum Press, p. 331–365.

Molnia, B. F., 1983, Distal glacial-marine sedimentation: Abundance, composition, and distribution of North Atlantic Ocean Pleistocene ice-rafted sediment, in Molnia, B. F., ed., Glacial-marine sedimentation: New York, Plenum Press, p. 593–626.

Morris, T. H., Clark, D. L., and Blasco, S. M., 1985, Sediments of the Lomonosov Ridge and Makarov Basin; A Pleistocene stratigraphy for the North Pole: Geological Society of America Bulletin, v. 96, p. 901–910.

Mudie, P. J., 1985, Palynology of the CESAR cores, Alpha Ridge: Geological Survey of Canada Paper 84-22, p. 149–174.

Mudie, P. J., and Blasco, S. M., 1985, Lithostratigraphy of the CESAR cores: Geological Survey of Canada Paper 84-22, p. 59–99.

Mullen, R., Darby, D. A., and Clark, D. L., 1972, Significance of atmospheric dust and ice-rafting for Arctic Ocean sediment: Geological Society of America Bulletin, v. 83, p. 205–212.

Naidu, A. S., 1974, Sedimentation in the Beaufort Sea; A synthesis, in Herman, Y., ed., Marine geology and oceanography of the Arctic seas: New York, Springer-Verlag, p. 173–190.

Naugler, P. F., Silverberg, N., and Creager, J. S., 1974, Recent sediments of the East Siberian Sea, in Herman, Y., ed., Marine geology and oceanography of the Arctic seas: New York, Springer-Verlag, p. 191–210.

Nordaa, A., 1984, Neogen stratigrafi og sedimentasjonsmiljö fra DSDP hull 341, Vöringplataet, Norskehavet [cand. scient. thesis]: Oslo, Norway, University of Oslo, Department of Geology, 132 p.

Olausson, E., 1985, The glacial oceans: Palaeogeography, Palaeoclimatology, Palaeoecology, v. 50, p. 291–301.

O'Neill, B. J., 1981, Pliocene and Pleistocene benthic foraminifera from the central Arctic Ocean: Journal of Paleontology, v. 55, p. 1141–1170.

Paul, A. Z., and Menzies, R. J., 1973, Benthic ecology of high Arctic deep sea:

Tallahassee, Florida State University Technical Report, 195 p.

Ritchie, W., and Walker, H. J., 1974, Rivers in the frozen north: Geographical Magazine, August, p. 634–640.

Robie, R. Q., 1980, Iceberg drift and deterioration, in Colbeck, S. C., ed., Dynamics of snow and ice masses: London, Academic Press, p. 211–259.

Ruddiman, W. F., and McIntyre, A., 1984, Ice-age thermal response and climatic role of the surface Atlantic Ocean, 40°N to 63°N: Geological Society of America Bulletin, v. 95, p. 381–396.

Schaeffer, R., and Spiegler, D., 1986, Neogene Kälteeinbrüche und Vereisungsphasen im Nordatlantik: Zeitschrift deutsche geologische Gesellschaft, v. 137, p. 537–552.

Schrader, H.-J., Björklünd, K. R., Manum, S., Martini, E., and van Hinte, J., 1976, Cenozoic biostratigraphy, physical stratigraphy, and paleoceanography in the Norwegian-Greenland Sea, DSDP Leg 38; Paleontological synthesis, in Initial reports of the Deep Sea Drilling Project: Washington, D.C., U.S. Government Printing Office, v. 38, p. 1197–1211.

Schwarzacher, W., and Hunkins, K. L., 1961, Dredged gravels from the central Arctic Ocean: Proceedings of the International Symposium on Arctic Geology, 1960, v. 1, p. 666–667.

Schytt, V., 1984, The Barents Sea ice-sheet; Some introductory remarks: Oslo, Voksenaasen, p. 8–15.

Sejrup, H.-P., Miller, G. H., Brigham-Grette, J., Lövlie, R., and Hopkins, D., 1984, Amino acid epimerization implies rapid sedimentation rates in Arctic Ocean cores: Nature, v. 310, p. 772–775.

Shackleton, N. J., and Kennett, J. P., 1975, Paleotemperature history of Antarctic glaciation; Oxygen and carbon isotope analysis in DSDP sites 277, 279, and 281, in Initial reports of the Deep Sea Drilling Project: Washington, D.C., U.S. Government Printing Office, v. 29, p. 743–755.

Shackleton, N. J., and Opdyke, N. D., 1973, Oxygen isotope and paleomagnetic stratigraphy of equatorial Pacific core V28-238; Oxygen isotope temperatures and ice volumes on a 10^5 and 10^6 year scale: Quaternary Research, v. 3, p. 39–55.

—— , 1976, Oxygen isotope and paleomagnetic stratigraphy of Pacific core V28-239; Late Pliocene to latest Pleistocene: Geological Society of America Memoir 145, p. 449–464.

Shackleton, N. J., and 16 others, 1984, Oxygen isotope calibration of the onset of ice-rafting and history of glaciation in the North Atlantic region: Nature, v. 307, p. 620–623.

Snaare, T. W., 1984, Ice-rafted material in the Arctic: Oslo, Voksenaasen, p. 76.

Somov, M. M., 1955, Observational data of scientific research, drifting station of 1950–1951: Leningrad, Morskoy Transport, v. 1, sec. 4 (Translated by the American Meteorological Society, Boston, ASTIA Document AD 117135, 59 p.).

Spiridonov, M. A., 1982, Geologic structure of glacial shelves of the Atlantic province of the Arctic basin, in Tolmachev, A. I., ed., The Arctic Ocean and its coast in the Cenozoic Era: New Delhi, Amerind Publishing Company, p. 39–44.

Steuerwald, B. A., Clark, D. L., and Andrew, J. A., 1968, Magnetic stratigraphy and faunal patterns in Arctic Ocean sediments: Earth and Planetary Science Letters, v. 5, p. 79–85.

Sweeney, J. F., 1985, Comment about the age of the Canadian Basin: Tectonophysics, v. 114, p. 1–10.

Talwani, M., and Eldholm, O., 1977, Evolution of the Norwegian-Greenland Sea: Geological Society of America Bulletin, v. 88, p. 969–999.

Talwani, M., and Udintsev, G., eds., 1976, Initial reports of the Deep Sea Drilling Project: Washington, D.C., U.S. Government Printing Office, v. 38, 1256 p.

Tangen, K., Brand, L. E., Blackwelder, P. L., and Guillard, R.R.L., 1982, *Thoracosphaera heimii* (Lohmann) Kamptner is a dinophyte; Observations on its morphology and life cycle: Marine Micropaleontology, v. 7, p. 193–212.

Taylor, P. T., 1983, Magnetic data over the Arctic from aircraft and satellites: Cold Regions Science and Technology, v. 7, p. 35–40.

Taylor, P. T., Kovacs, L. D., Vogt, P. R., and Johnson, G. L., 1981, Detailed aeromagnetic investigation of the Arctic Basin, 2: Journal of Geophysical Research, v. 86, no. B7, p. 6323–6333.

Thiede, J., 1979, History of the North Atlantic Ocean; Evolution of an asymmetric zonal paleoenvironment in a latitudinal ocean basin: American Geophysical Union, Maurice Ewing Series, v. 3, p. 275–296.

Thiede, J., and Eldholm, O., 1983, Speculations about the paleodepth of the Greenland-Scotland Ridge during late Mesozoic and Cenozoic times, in Bott, M.H.P., Saxov, S., Talwani, M., and Thiede, J., eds., Structure and development of the Greenland-Scotland Ridge: New York, Plenum Press, p. 445–456.

Thiede, J., Diesen, G. W., Knudsen, B.-E., and Snaare, T., 1986, Patterns of Cenozoic sedimentation in the Norwegian-Greenland Sea: Marine Geology, v. 69, p. 323–352.

Tolmachev, A. I., ed., 1982, The Arctic Ocean and its coast in the Cenozoic Era: New Delhi, Amerind Publishing Company, 564 p.

Van Wagoner, N. A., and Robinson, P. T., 1985, Petrology and geochemistry of a CESAR bedrock sample; Implications for the origin of the Alpha Ridge: Geological Survey of Canada Paper 84-22, p. 47–57.

Vilks, G., 1969, Recent foraminifera in the Canadian Arctic: Micropaleontology, v. 15, p. 35–60.

Vogt, P. R., 1986, Sea-floor topography, sediments, and paleoenvironments, in Hurdle, B. G., ed., The Nordic seas: New York, Springer-Verlag, p. 237–410.

Vogt, P. R., Perry, R. K., Feden, R. H., Fleming, H. S., and Cherkis, N. Z., 1981, The Greenland-Norwegian Sea and Iceland environment; Geology and geophysics, in Nairn, A.E.M., Churkin, M., and Stehli, F. G., eds., The ocean basins and margins; Vol. 5, The Arctic Ocean: New York, Plenum Press, p. 493–598.

Vorren, T. O., Hald, M., and Thomsen, E., 1984, Quaternary sediments and environments on the continental shelf of northern Norway: Marine Geology, v. 57, p. 229–257.

Warncke, D. A., and Hansen, M. E., 1977, Sediments of glacial origin in the area of operations DSDP Leg 38, Norwegian-Greenland Seas; Preliminary results from sites 336–344: Berichte der naturforschenden Gesellschaft in Freiburg im Breisgau, v. 67, p. 371–392.

Weber, J. R., 1979, The Lomonosov Ridge; Experiment LOREX 79: EOS Transactions of the American Geophysical Union, v. 60, p. 715–721.

Williams, D. F., Moore, W. S., and Fillon, R. H., 1981, Role of Arctic Ocean ice sheets in Pleistocene oxygen isotope and sea level records: Earth and Planetary Science Letters, v. 56, p. 157–166.

Worsley, T., and Herman, Y., 1980, Episodic ice-free Arctic Ocean in Pliocene and Pleistocene time; Calcareous nannofossil evidence: Science, v. 210, no. 4467, p. 323–325.

Zahn, R., Markussen, B., and Thiede, J., 1985, Stable isotope data and depositional environments in the late Quaternary Arctic Ocean: Nature, v. 314, p. 433–435.

Zenkevitch, L., 1986, Biology of the seas of the USSR: New York, Interscience Publishers, 955 p.

MANUSCRIPT ACCEPTED BY THE SOCIETY AUGUST 15, 1987

ACKNOWLEDGEMENTS

This study is based upon the efforts of numerous colleagues who supported the expeditions into the harsh Arctic realm. The authors are also grateful for support from U.S. Office of Naval Research, contracts N00014-76-C-0005 and N000 (Thiede). The manuscript has benefited greatly from the comments of L. Johnson, S. Pfirman, H.-J. Schrader, and W. Berggren. Figure 6 has kindly been provided by B. Markussen (Stavanger), Figure 11 by T. Morris (Woods Hole Oceanographic Institution). I thank O. Runze, M. Weinelt, and T.C.W. Wolf for editional help; N. Sucic and G. Thiel for typing the manuscript.

NOTE ADDED IN PROOF

Central Arctic Ocean sedimentation rates and the chronology for the past 2 m.y. were actively debated when this chapter was submitted. These questions have now been clarified (references 2, 4, and 6). References 1, 3, and 5 include important new information related to Arctic paleoceanography.

1. Dalrymple, R. W., and Maass, O. C., 1987, Clay mineralogy of the Late Cenozoic sediment in the CESAR cores, Alpha Ridge, central Arctic Ocean: Canadian Journal of Earth Sciences, v. 24, p. 1562–1569.
2. Macko, S. A., and Aksu, A. E., 1986, Amino acid epimerization in planktonic foraminifera suggests slow sedimentation rates for the Alpha Ridge, Arctic Ocean: Nature, v. 322, p. 730–732.
3. Marquard, R. S., and Clark, D. L., 1987, Pleistocene paleoceanographic correlations; Northern Greenland Sea to central Arctic Ocean: Marine Micropaleontology, v. 12, p. 325–341.
4. Morris, T. H., 1988, Stable isotope stratigraphy of the Arctic Ocean: Palaeogeography, Palaeoclimatology, Palaeoecology, v. 64, p. 201–219.
5. Ostlund, H. G., and others, 1987, Ventilation rate of the deep Arctic Ocean from Carbon 14 data: Journal of Geophysical Research, v. 92, p. 3769–3777.
6. Witte, W. K., and Kent, D. V., 1988, Revised magnetostratigraphies confirm low sedimentation rates in Arctic Ocean cores: Quaternary Research, v. 29, p. 43–53.

From Charles M. Scammon, 1874, The marine mammals of the northwestern coast of North America: San Francisco, John H. Carmany and Company, facing p. 32.

Chapter 25

Late Cenozoic geologic evolution of the Alaskan North Slope and adjacent continental shelves

David A. Dinter
U.S. Geological Survey, 345 Middlefield Road, Menlo Park, California 94025
L. David Carter
Branch of Alaskan Geology, U.S. Geological Survey, 4200 University Drive, Anchorage, Alaska 99508
Julie Brigham-Grette
Department of Geology and Geography, University of Massachusetts, Amherst, Massachusetts 01003

INTRODUCTION

The Alaskan Arctic Coastal Plain and its submerged extensions to the north and west, the Beaufort and Chukchi continental shelves, are underlain by a broad, low-relief bedrock surface, the North Beringian Marine Abrasion Platform, which dips gently seaward from the Arctic foothills of the Brooks Range northward to the continental shelf break of the Arctic Basin (Fig. 1). During late Cenozoic time the sea repeatedly transgressed and receded across the North Beringian Platform in response to glacioeustatic sea level fluctuations. A thin veneer of unconsolidated, interfingering marine and nonmarine deposits mantles the bedrock surface and records the succession of geologic environments that have prevailed there during the last 3 m.y. All of these unconsolidated deposits are presently assigned to the Gubik Formation, which has a maximum measured thickness of about 60 m onshore, and thickens to perhaps a few hundred meters in places beneath the Beaufort shelf. In this chapter, we summarize and discuss the depositional history of the Gubik Formation and its bearing on the late Cenozoic geologic and climatic history of the Arctic region. The discussion begins with the onshore exposures, which have been studied in detail over many years, and for which a coherent stratigraphic framework has begun to emerge, and then moves to the offshore deposits, which, though thicker and better preserved, have only recently become the target of stratigraphic investigations.

The marine deposits of the Gubik Formation on the Arctic Coastal Plain have intrigued researchers since the early years of this century, when Leffingwell (1919) observed that glacially striated boulders and gravel scattered along the Alaskan Beaufort coastline are lithologically unlike any known Brooks Range rocks, and so suggested—correctly—a source in Arctic Canada. Subsequent work, mainly detailed mapping supported by amino acid racemization correlation techniques, has resulted in a resolution of Gubik Formation marine deposits onshore into discrete subunits assignable to successive late Cenozoic marine transgressions. At least six, and possibly eight marine submersions of the Arctic Coastal Plain have occurred since middle Pliocene time. Evidence of several additional transgressions that presumably did not reach present sea level is preserved in Gubik Formation subunits now submerged beneath the Beaufort continental shelf. High-resolution reflection seismic studies of those deposits have also revealed what appears to be a unique record of successive late Pleistocene lowstands.

In addition to the marine submersions, a number of nonmarine environments—notably fluvial, glaciofluvial, deltaic, eolian, and lacustrine—are represented in the Gubik Formation. Large areas of old fluvial and glaciofluvial clastic sediments are preserved on the coastal plain, but complex stratigraphic geometries, patchy preservation, and a paucity of datable material make detailed interpretations difficult. Nonmarine sediments deposited during and since the last (Sangamon) Interglacial have proven more amenable to study, at least locally. Paleontologic, stratigraphic, and geochemical analyses have led to a division of the last 75,000 years or so into several periods of contrasting temperature/moisture regimes, which resulted in distinctive depositional environments.

Active tectonic processes affect the North Beringian Platform only from the Canning River east to Herschel Island, and from central Harrison Bay west to Barrow Sea Valley (Fig. 1). In the eastern area the platform is underlain at depth by active thrust faults rooted beneath the Brooks Range. East-northeast-trending detachment folds forming above these thrusts, and tear faults developed where the thrusts die out near the Canning River mouth, have disrupted Gubik Formation deposits throughout their period of accumulation, and continue to influence depositional geometries today. In the western area, thick post-rift sediments underlying the continental shelf, including a thin mantle of

Dinter, D. A., Carter, L., and Brigham-Grette, J., 1990, Late Cenozoic geologic evolution of the Alaskan North Slope and adjacent continental shelves, *in* Grantz, A., Johnson, L., and Sweeney, J. F., eds., The Arctic Ocean region: Boulder, Colorado, Geological Society of America, The Geology of North America, v. L.

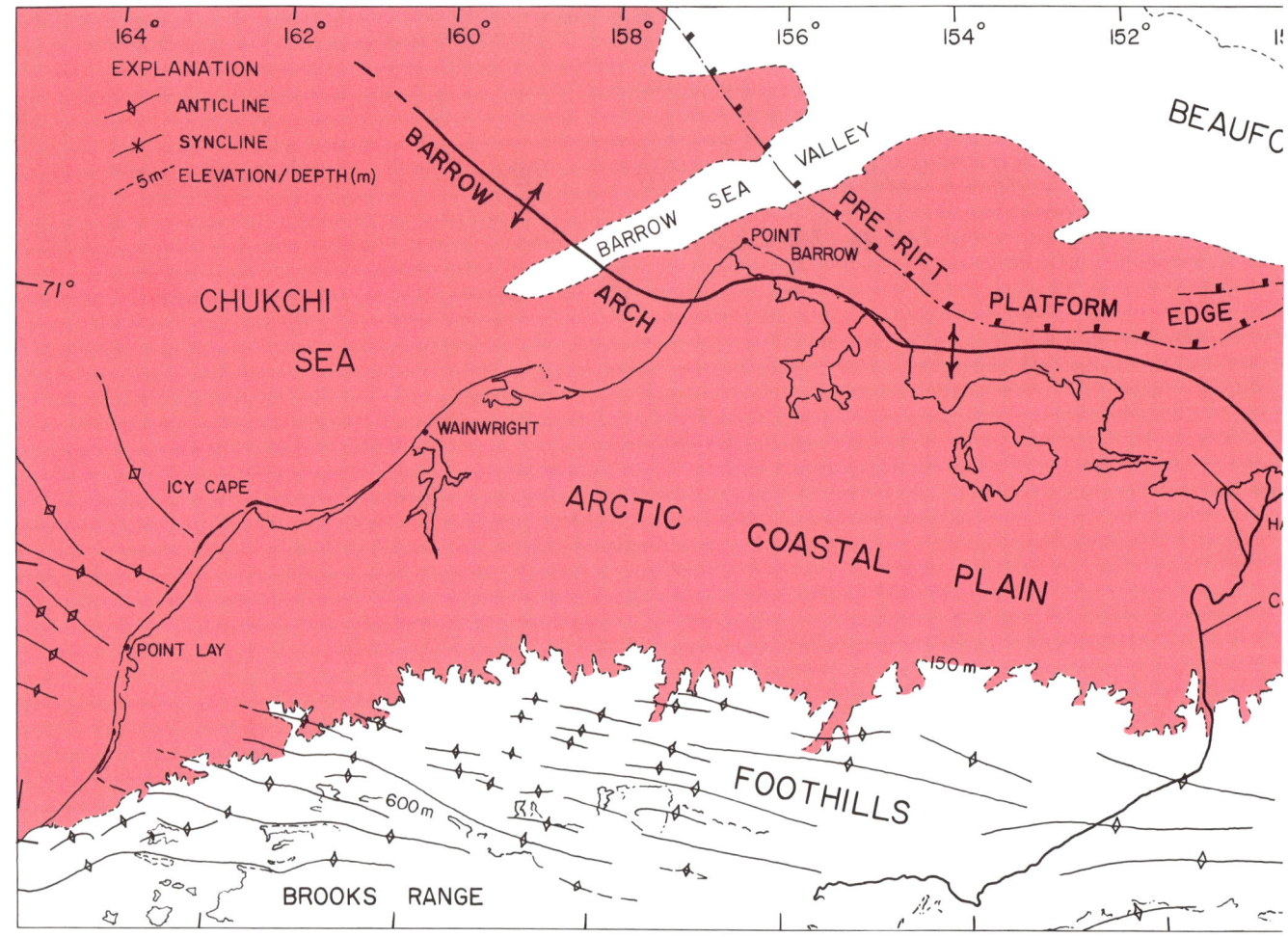

Figure 1. Location map of northern Alaska with major bedrock structural elements. Folds shown west of the Canning River are mainly late Mesozoic, and believed to be currently inactive. Folds east of the Canning have been active throughout Cenozoic time. Barrow Arch separates pre-rift bedrock that dips south toward the Brooks Range thrust sheets from that which dips north toward the pre-rift platform edge. The late Cenozoic North Beringian Marine Abrasion Platform (in light red) extends from the base of the foothills north to the Beaufort/Chukchi continental shelf break.

Quaternary deposits, are disrupted by down-to-the-basin growth faults with long displacement histories.

THE GUBIK FORMATION ONSHORE

Early interpretations of Gubik deposits exposed on the Alaskan Arctic Coastal Plain appear in O'Sullivan (1961), Black (1964), McCulloch (1967), Hopkins (1967), and Sellmann and Brown (1973). Both O'Sullivan (1961) and Black (1964) attempted to subdivide the Gubik Formation and to correlate their subdivisions in scattered exposures based on sedimentary facies distinctions, and by mapping major topographic breaks, which they assumed to be paleoshorelines. Black's (1964) lithologic subdivisions are the Skull Cliff unit, consisting mainly of clay; the Meade River unit, predominantly of sand; and the Barrow unit, consisting of clay, silt, sand, and gravel admixtures. He hypothesized Illinoian, Sangamon, and Wisconsinan ages, respectively, for these units. During more recent investigations (e.g., Williams, 1979, 1983a and b; Carter and others, 1979; Nelson, 1981; Brigham, 1984, 1985; Carter and others, 1986a), the exposures examined in previous studies were reexamined in detail and new exposures identified, resulting in a clearer and substantially revised understanding of the depositional environments of these deposits, the number of marine submersions and subaerial exposures recorded, and the geochronology of these events. A key to these revised interpretations has been the recognition that in many Gubik Formation exposures, superposed shallow marine deposits of widely differing ages are lithologically indistinguishable, and moreover, transgressive shoreface erosional surfaces are not always obvious as unconformities. In such cases, the extent of isoleucine (amino acid) epimerization of fossil mollusks has been instrumental in distinguishing deposits representing different marine transgressions and correlating them in disjunct stratigraphic sections across the coastal plain.

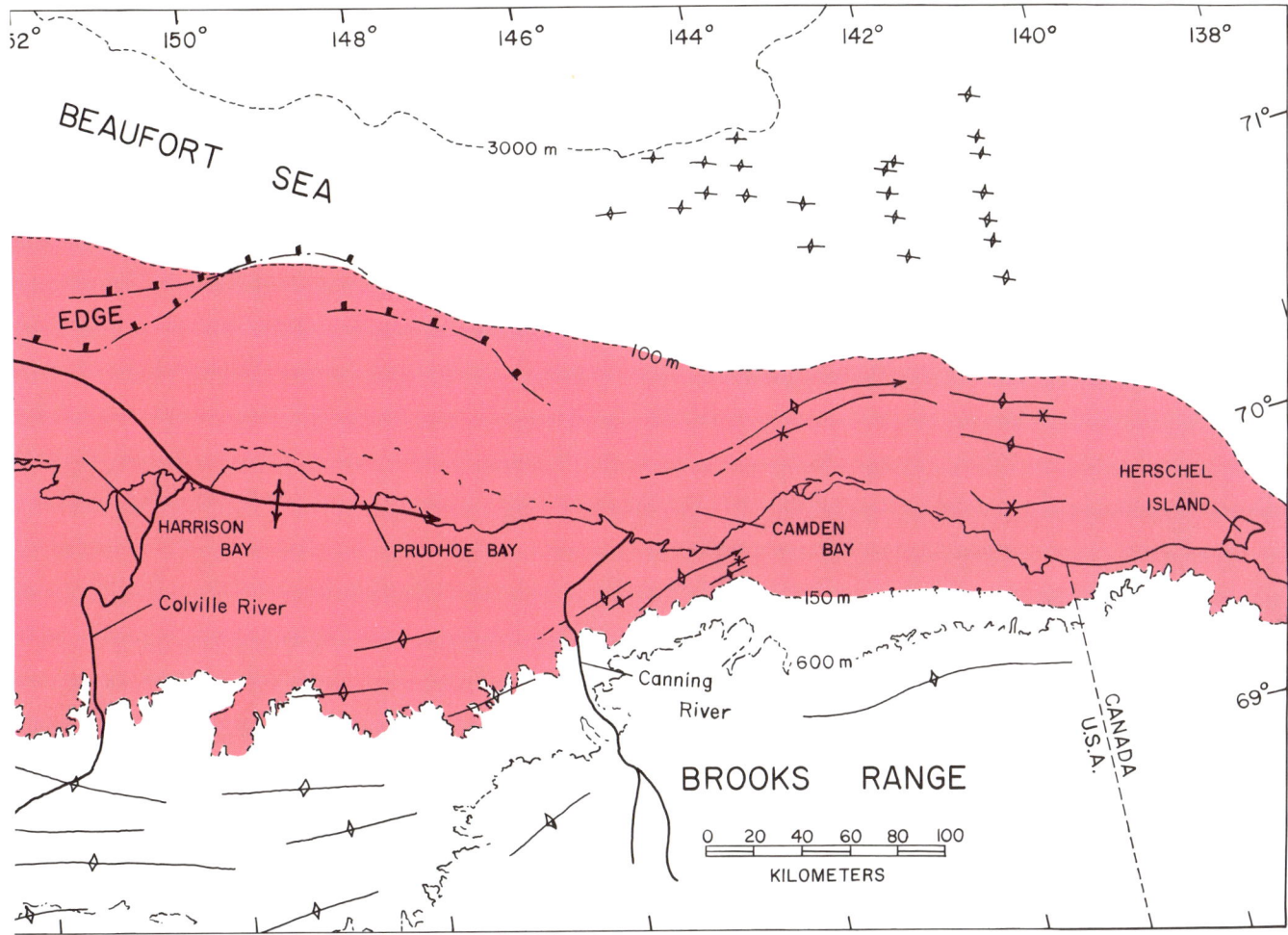

The discussion of Gubik Formation exposures onshore begins with the marine deposits, which represent, in general, relatively warm periods—interglacials or interstadials—when sea levels were high and the Bering Strait provided a marine connection between the Arctic and Pacific Oceans, and proceeds to the nonmarine deposits, which record a wide diversity of climatic regimes that prevailed during subaerial exposures of the coastal plain.

Late Cenozoic marine sediments

At least six and possibly seven or eight late Cenozoic marine transgressions are represented by deposits of the Gubik Formation beneath the coastal plain. The six that are presently defined have been informally named from oldest to youngest the Colvillian, Bigbendian, Fishcreekian, Wainwrightian, Pelukian, and Simpsonian transgressions (Table 1; Carter and others, 1986a). Colvillian and Bigbendian deposits are of Pliocene age (Carter and Galloway, 1985), whereas Fishcreekian beds may be Pliocene (Carter and Galloway, 1985; Carter and others, 1986b; Repenning and others, 1987) or early Pleistocene (Brigham, 1985). Sediments deposited during each of these three transgressions can be correlated across the coastal plain on the basis of alle/Ile ratios in fossil mollusks (Table 1; Fig. 2; Brigham, 1984, 1985; Carter and others, 1986a). Marine beds currently assigned to the Wainwrightian transgression may actually represent two or even three transgressive events. The reference section near Wainwright is believed to be middle Pleistocene, based on amino acid age estimates and a single uranium-trend date of about 500 ka (Brigham, 1985). Possibly correlative beds exposed farther east, however, have yielded younger TL dates. Deposits of the Pelukian and Simpsonian transgressions, which are too old to be dated by radiocarbon methods (Brigham, 1985), have been dated by thermoluminescence (TL) techniques as late Pleistocene (Carter and others, 1986a).

The late Cenozoic marine section of the Arctic Coastal Plain is most complete west of the Kuparuk River (Fig. 3), where sediments representing each transgressive event listed above have been preserved. Between the Kuparuk and Canning Rivers, the only known Gubik Formation marine deposits exposed onshore are those of the Simpsonian (Rawlinson, 1986) and perhaps the Wainwrightian transgressions, which occur primarily in low coastal bluffs. From the Canning River eastward to the Canada–United States border, only Colvillian, Fishcreekian, and Simpsonian beds have so far been recognized.

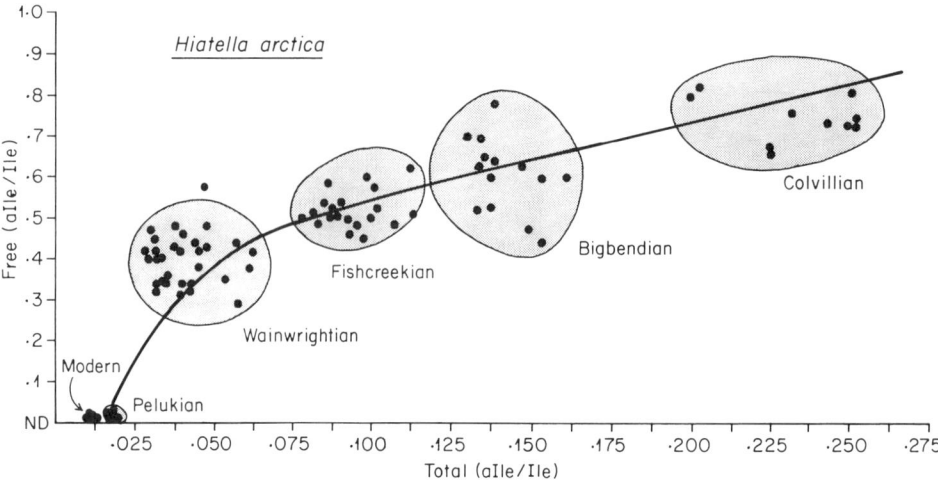

Figure 2. Plot of the free versus total aIle/Ile ratio in all samples of *Hiatella arctica,* from the Gubik Formation. This species yields the best results for use in distinguishing different-aged marine deposits based on amino acid racemization techniques.

The southern limit of Gubik Formation marine deposits between the Colville and Kuparuk Rivers appears to be a highly degraded bluff that truncates a Tertiary gravel unit informally referred to as the Kuparuk gravel (see below). The break in slope at the base of this bluff occurs at an altitude of about 60 m and is inferred to mark the maximum altitude reached by any late Cenozoic marine transgression on this part of the coastal plain (Carter, 1983a; Carter and Galloway, 1985). Present data suggest that this limit was reached during the Colvillian transgression. Along the Kukpowruk River on the westernmost part of the coastal plain the inner limit of marine deposits is also at an altitude of about 60 m (McCulloch, 1967); however, the age of these deposits is unknown. East of the Canning River the coastal plain has been deformed by late Cenozoic tectonism, and the southern limit of marine Gubik Formation deposition there has not yet been determined.

The Colvillian transgression. The Colvillian transgression is defined based on marine deposits that are well exposed in bluffs along the Colville River from its confluence with the Kikiakrorak River north for about 10 km, and upstream along the Kikiakrorak River from the confluence for 5 km (Fig. 3; Carter and others, 1986a). The Colvillian deposits, which appear at altitudes of at least 40 m here, generally consist of a basal gravelly sand up to 1 m thick overlain by up to 2.5 m of silty clay or clayey silt. Cobbles and small boulders from the basal beds include indurated sandstone and chert-pebble conglomerate clasts that are also common as glacial erratics of similar size in the nearby Kuparuk gravel, and metamorphic, intrusive, and volcanic clasts similar to those that occur in Paleocene boulder-bearing beds that underlie the Kuparuk gravel east of the Colville River (Carter and Galloway, 1985). It is likely that the Colvillian cobbles were derived by erosion from the two older units during the Colvillian transgressions. *Hiatella arctica* shells from the Colvillian beds yielded aIle/Ile ratios of 0.236 ± 0.022 (Table 1). Throughout these exposures the Colvillian deposits unconformably overlie Cretaceous or lower Tertiary strata. They are overlain locally by 1.0 to 1.5 m of Bigbendian deposits (see below), and everywhere by 11 to 12 m of much younger fluvial and eolian sediment.

Other sediments deposited during the Colvillian transgression, as determined by amino acid geochemistry and superposition, are exposed east of the Colville River along the Miluveach River, on the north flank of Marsh anticline on the eastern part of the coastal plain, and at Skull Cliff along the Chukchi Sea coast (Figs. 3 and 4), where they have been called the Nulavik beds (Brigham, 1985). The Nulavik beds are mostly inner shelf facies occurring as thin patches of basal cobbly gravel, cross-bedded ripply sand, and silty sand with interbedded sand and silt. They lie unconformably on either Cretaceous bedrock or the Tertiary Papigak clay (Brigham, 1985). *Hiatella arctica* from these beds yield aIle/Ile ratios of 0.235 ± 0.017, nearly identical to those of similar shells from the Colville River exposures.

Faunas of the Colvillian transgression have not been studied in detail, but the mollusks form a diverse assemblage that includes the extinct whelk *Neptunea lyrata leffingwelli* (L. Marincovich, Jr., written communication, 1984). The fauna includes taxa of Pacific origin and thus post-dates the opening of Bering Strait, which occurred shortly before 3 m.y. ago (Hopkins, 1972; Gladenkov, 1981). The Colvillian transgression may be correlative with Hopkins' (1967) Beringian transgression as defined at the type locality near Nome.

The Bigbendian transgression. The Bigbendian transgression is defined based on deposits exposed in bluffs along the big bend of the Colville River from near Ocean Point and the Big Bend benchmark upstream for about 10 km, where they occur at altitudes up to about 35 m (Carter and others, 1986a). The Bigbendian beds here generally consist of a basal, transgressive, gravelly beach sand about 1 m thick overlain by about 4 m of well-bedded sandy silt. The basal bed contains cobbles and

TABLE 1. MARINE TRANSGRESSION OF THE ALASKAN ARCTIC COASTAL PLAIN

Transgression	Maximum Elevation Reached (m)	Age	Ale/Ie* Colville River/ Fish Creek Area	Ale/Ie* Chukchi Sea Coast Area[†]	Possible Correlation With Hopkins (1967)
Simpsonian (Flaxman Member Gubik Formation**)	7	70 to 80 ka	—	—	—
Pelukian (Walakpa beds[‡])	10	120 to 130 ka	—	0.014 ±0.002 (20)[§]	Pelukian
Wainwrightian (Karmuk beds[‡])	20–25	>158 ka, ?210 ka, 540 ka	—	0.038 ±0.007 (28)[§]	Kotzebuan
Fishcreekian (Tuapaktushak beds[‡])	25–35	>1.5, <2.48	0.086 ±0.004 (6)[§]	0.090 ±0.018 (1)[§]	—
Bigbendian (Killi Creek beds[‡])	>35, <60	>2.4 Ma	0.136 ±0.14 (12)[§]	0.15 ±0.025 (8)[§]	Anvilian
Colvillian (Nulavik beds[‡])	>40, <60	<3.5 Ma	0.236 ±0.022 (8)[§]	0.235 ±0.017 (4)[§]	Beringian

*Ratios for total fraction for *Hiatella arctica*.
[†]From Brigham, 1985.
[§]Number of analyses.
**Formal name of Simpsonian transgressive deposits on the North Beringian Platform.
[‡]Informal name of transgressive deposits at Skull Cliff.

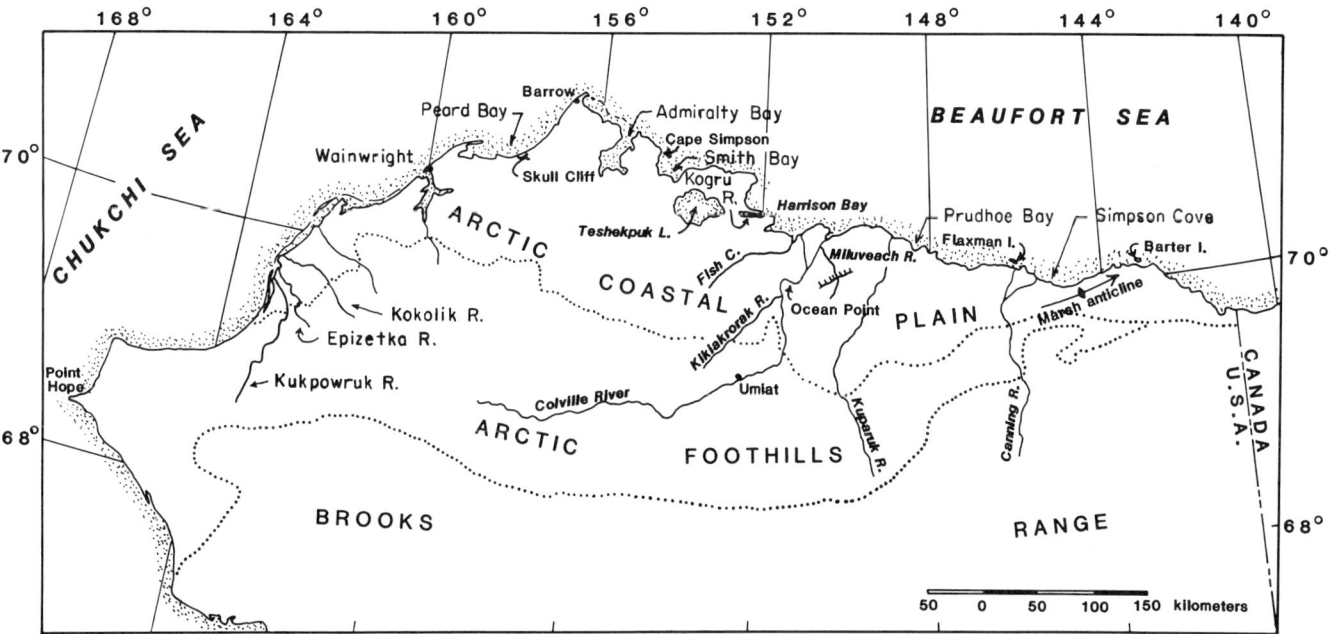

Figure 3. Map of northern Alaska showing localities mentioned in relation to Quaternary deposits.

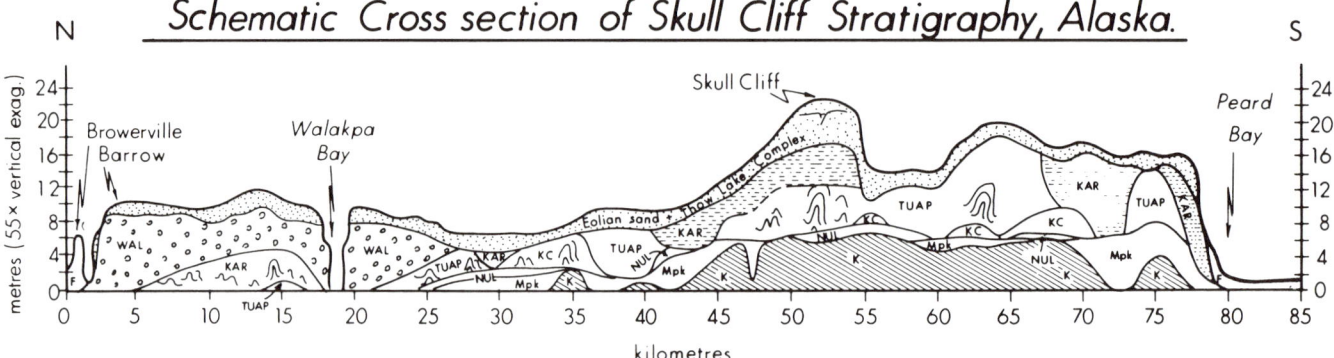

Figure 4. Schematic cross section of Skull Cliff stratigraphy. (See Fig. 3 for location.)

boulders like those described for Colvillian deposits in the Colville River bluffs, and a similar origin is likely. *Hiatella arctica* from these deposits yield aIle/Ile ratios of 0.136 ± 0.014 (Table 1). Bigbendian beds generally rest unconformably on Cretaceous and lower Tertiary strata, but in places are separated from them by a few centimeters of Colvillian deposits.

Bigbendian deposits are also exposed at altitudes up to about 20 m at Skull Cliff, where they are known as the Killi Creek beds (Fig. 4; Brigham, 1985), along the Miluveach River, and possibly at Fish Creek (see below). At Skull Cliff their distribution is patchy and discontinuous due to extensive erosion during younger transgressive events. The Killi Creek beds there include inner shelf facies of gravel, sand, silt, and silty sand, and some basal gravel lags containing cobble-sized clasts. Locally the horizontal bedding is contorted and deformed, perhaps by iceberg scour or soft sediment slides. At present the Killi Creek beds can be distinguished from the Nulavik beds in the Skull Cliff section only by their contrasting aIle/Ile ratios from the enclosed mollusks. *Hiatella arctica* from the Killi Creek beds yielded aIle/Ile ratios of 0.150 ± 0.025 (based on eight individuals), significantly lower than those determined on similar shells from the Nulavik beds. Limited paleontologic studies have identified the extinct mollusk *Astarte leffingwelli* in the Killi Creek beds (L. Marincovich, written communication, 1984).

Permafrost during deposition of the Bigbendian sediments was at most discontinuous, and probably limited to north-facing slopes. This is based on a pollen suite from the Colville River section, which indicates that the nearby coastal plain probably supported a spruce-dominated coniferous forest with significant birch and minor pine and fir, somewhat similar to the modern vegetation surrounding the Anchorage area (Nelson, 1981; Nelson and Carter, 1985). A relatively mild climate is also suggested by the presence of sea otter (*Enhydra?*) remains (Repenning, 1983), and by a mollusk fauna that is richer than the Colvillian fauna and includes the gastropod *Littorina squalida* and the bivalve *Clinocardium californiense* (Deshayes) (Carter and others, 1986b). The modern northern limit of both these mollusk taxa is the Bering Strait. Moreover, modern sea otters cannot tolerate severe seasonal sea ice conditions (Schneider and Faro, 1975); hence, the presence of sea otter remains suggests that the limit of seasonal ice on the Beaufort Sea was north of the Colville River fossil site during the Bigbendian transgression (Carter and others, 1986b). Repenning (1983) suggested a possible age of between 1.7 and 2.6 Ma for the Bigbendian deposits near Ocean Point based on the stage of evolution exhibited by the fossil sea otter remains, but given the otters' antipathy to sea ice, considered the period from 2.2 to 2.6 Ma an unlikely time for the Bigbendian transgression because the first major continental ice accumulation in the northern hemisphere apparently occurred between about 2.2 and 2.4 Ma (Shackleton and Opdyke, 1977). More recently, Carter and Galloway (1985) considered it more probable that the Bigbendian transgression preceded this climatic deterioration, a conclusion now also accepted by Repenning and others (1987).

The Fishcreekian transgression. The Fishcreekian transgression is defined based on folliliferous marine beds exposed along the north side of Fish Creek (Fig. 5; Carter and others, 1986b). Tidal channel deposits near the top of the Fish Creek beds are interpreted to record a sea level about 25 m higher than at present (Carter and Galloway, 1985). This is also the altitude of the base of a wave-cut scarp 30 km east of Fish Creek and 5 km west of the Colville River delta (Fig. 5). The scarp truncates a landform beneath which Bigbendian and Colvillian deposits are preserved (Terrace I of Carter and Galloway, 1982), and is interpreted to have formed during the Fishcreekian transgression (Carter and others, 1979).

Carter and others (1979) divided the Fish Creek beds into two lithologic units. The lower, unit 1, represents a bay or estuary-mouth environment, and consists of 3 to 4 m of indistinctly bedded dark gray silt with sparse sand interbeds, mollusk fragments, sand-filled burrows, and scattered granules of chert and quartz. Carter and Galloway (1985) proposed a Fishcreekian age for unit 1; however, preliminary results of amino acid analyses on *Portlandia arctica* from these deposits suggest that they may, instead, be Bigbendian.

Unit 2 of the Fishcreekian beds, interpreted to be a tidal channel deposit, consists of 5 to 9 m of predominantly trough cross-bedded, fossiliferous, brown to gray sand, pebbly sand, and silt, commonly with detrital wood and organic debris.

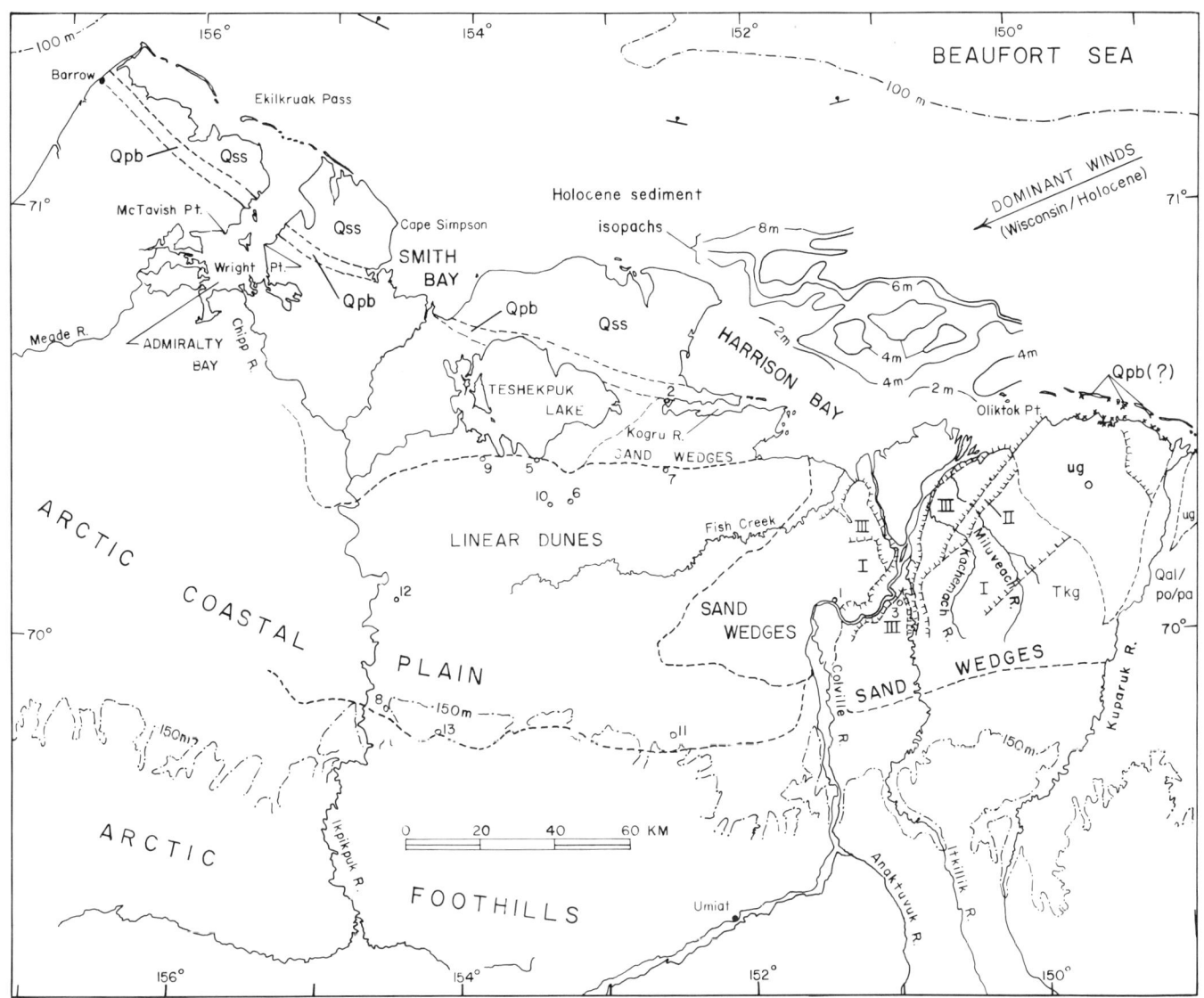

Figure 5. Quaternary geologic features of part of the western Arctic Coastal Plain and Beaufort shelf. See Figure 10 for explanations of Qsm; terraces I, II, and III; Tkg, ug, po, pa, and Qal. Qpb is a Pelukian beach or barrier bar deposit (Carter and Galloway, 1985). Hachured lines are terrace edges or low erosional scarps, lower on the hachured side. "x" along coastline indicates exposures of glacial erratic-bearing marine silt similar in appearance to the Flaxman Member of the Gubik Formation, but not necessarily of Simpsonian age (from Rawlinson, 1986). Wisconsinan linear sand dunes and sand wedges occur in the patterned areas as shown (Carter, 1983c). Open circles locate samples referred to in Table 2.

Hiatella arctica from those sediments yielded AIle/Ile ratios of 0.086 ± 0.004 (Table 1). The Fishcreekian deposits at this location are overlain by up to 17 m of younger nonmarine sediments.

Sediments correlated with the Fishcreekian transgression on the basis of their amino acid geochemistry also occur at Skull Cliff on the western coastal plain, where they are known as the Tuapaktushak beds (Brigham, 1985), and in folded beds on the north flank of Marsh anticline on the eastern coastal plain (Figs. 3 and 4). South of the Kokolik River, Tuapaktushak beds have been mapped to an elevation of 33 to 36 m above sea level, where they intersect the base of a prominent break in slope that was presumably once a wave-cut scarp (Fig. 3). Four to 5 km seaward of this break in slope, between the Kukpowruk and Epizetka Rivers, are beach ridges (cf. McCulloch, 1967) thought to represent contemporaneous offshore barrier islands (Brigham, 1985). The Tuapaktushak beds consist largely of inner-shelf facies of interbedded sand, silty sand, silt, and some clay and pebbly layers overlying a basal gravel lag. Erratic cobbles and boulders, commonly similar in lithology to those of the Flaxman Member of the Gubik Formation (see below) are dispersed sparsely throughout the unit, but are most common at the base. Severely contorted bedding, including isoclinal and overturned folds, is common in those deposits. The origins of these structures are unknown, but possible causes are iceberg scouring and low-angle sliding. *Hiatella arctica* from the Tuapaktushak beds yield aIle/Ile ratios of 0.090 ± 0.018 (Table 1).

Fishcreekian sea surface temperatures warmer than present are indicated by the presence in the Fish Creek beds of the bivalve *Clinocardium californiense,* whose modern northern limit is Norton Sound, and the gastropods *Aforia circinata,* and *Littorina squalidia,* which presently range no farther north than the Bering Sea (Repenning and others, 1987), and also by the presence in the Tuapaktushak beds of the gastropod *Natica (Tectonatica) janthostoma* (Broderip and Sowerby), which is presently limited to the waters adjoining Japan, Kamchatka Peninsula, and the Commander Islands (Carter and others, 1986b). Collections from the Tuapaktushak beds also include the extralimital elements *Clinocardium californiense* and *Aforia circinata* along with extinct forms including *Neptunea lyrata leffingwelli* (Dall) and *Astarte leffingwelli* (Dall) and the extinct ostracode *Rabilimus paramirabilis* Swain (E. M. Brouwers, written communication, 1986). Sea otter remains from unit 2 at Fish Creek suggest that perennial sea ice was absent or severely restricted during the Fishcreekian transgression (Carter and others, 1986b).

In contrast to the relatively warm marine conditions, the Fishcreekian terrestrial climate was apparently harsh. Pollen assemblages from the tidal channel deposits of unit 2 at Fish Creek are similar to those from the late Pliocene or early Pleistocene Cape Deceit Formation of the northern Seward Peninsula (Giterman and others, 1982), and suggest that the nearby coastal plain then supported a shrub-herb tundra with scattered larch trees, or a larch taiga similar to that now found in parts of northeastern Siberia.

A relatively warm ocean adjacent to a cold land surface provides conditions favorable for the build-up of ice sheets (Ruddiman and McIntire, 1979), and it is possible that the Fishcreekian transgression, even though it occurred during an interglacial interval, was coincident with glaciation in the Brooks Range and in other parts of the high Arctic (Carter and Galloway, 1985). Such an event might have produced icebergs that are possibly responsible for the deformational structures, dropstones, and striated boulder pavements observed in the Tuapaktushak beds at Skull Cliff. Hamilton (1981) proposed that a northern moisture source nourished glaciers in the Brooks Range during the Gunsight Mountain glacial interval. Possibly this ice advance was closely related in time to the Fishcreekian transgression.

The age of the Fishcreekian transgression is controversial. Brouwers and others (1984) proposed that it occurred at about 1.2 Ma, based on a tenuous correlation with unfossiliferous marine deposits on the Pribilof Islands and on a calculation based on tentative amino acid epimerization rates obtained from J. Brigham-Grette. Using equations outlined by Brigham and Miller (1983) that define the relationship between the extent of isoleucine epimerization, age, and the effective diagenetic temperature (thermal history) of the sample, Brigham (1985) also estimated an age in the range of 1.0 to 1.4 Ma.

Evidence from the Arctic Coastal Plain suggests that the Fishcreekian transgression occurred much earlier, between 2.4 and 2.48 Ma. The minimum age is provided by a primitive microtine rodent fauna (Repenning and others, 1987). The maximum age is suggested based on the occurrence of tundra-derived pollen in the unit. The earliest known tundra pollen in the Arctic is preserved in the upper Kutuyakh beds of Siberia (Wolfe, 1985), which span the 2.48 Ma Gauss-Matuyama normal/reversed boundary (Sher and others, 1979). Because the Fishcreekian beds have magnetically reversed polarity, are older than 2.4 Ma, and contain tundra pollen, they must be of Matuyaman age, and so cannot be older than 2.48 Ma (Carter and others, 1986b). The suggested age can be refined further if it is assumed that the Fishcreekian transgression corresponds to some ^{18}O minimum recorded in deep sea cores. In the Northern Atlantic, the only significant ^{18}O minimum within the Matuyama Superchron and prior to 2.4 Ma occurs about 2.41 Ma (Shackleton and others, 1984). Carter and others (1986b) tentatively correlated the Fishcreekian transgression with that minimum, which postdates the first evidence of northern hemisphere climatic cooling and immediately predates the first major northern hemisphere glacial episode (Shackleton and others, 1984).

Assuming an age of about 2.41 Ma for the Fishcreekian transgression, the extent of amino acid diagenesis in Fishcreekian mollusks suggests that since their deposition the effective diagenetic temperature (EDT) in the deposits has been about –16°C, or about 7°C colder than modern values, and slightly colder than the EDT calculated for the past 125,000 yr (Carter and others, 1986b; Brigham and Miller, 1983). Such a low EDT suggests that permafrost and perennial sea ice have been present nearly contin-

Figure 6. (a) Glacial marine sediments of the Simpsonian transgression. (b) Marine sand of the Pelukian transgression. (c) Marine silt and clay of the Wainwrightian(?) transgression.

uously since this transgression. However, as noted above, permafrost was probably absent during the Bigbendian transgression, and sea otter fossils suggest that perennial sea ice was either severely restricted in extent or absent during both the Bigbendian and Fishcreekian transgressions. Furthermore, the earliest unequivocal record of permafrost coincides with the first evidence of low-elevation tundra and consists of ice-wedge casts in fluvial and lacustrine deposits of the upper part of the Siberian Kutuyakh beds (Sher and others, 1979). Accordingly, Carter and others (1986b) proposed that permafrost and extensive perennial sea ice were initiated during the late stages of climatic cooling that spanned the Gauss-Matuyama boundary and led into the first major late Cenozoic glaciation of the northern hemisphere. This opinion conflicts with interpretations of sea ice history based on the study of Arctic Ocean deep sea cores (Clark, 1982).

The Wainwrightian transgression. The Wainwrightian transgression is defined as the depositional period of the Karmuk beds of the Gubik Formation, a sequence of basal gravel lag, inner-shelf, barrier beach, and lagoonal sediments exposed intermittently along the Chukchi coastline southwest of Barrow (Figs. 3 and 4; Williams, 1983b; Brigham, 1985). South of Peard Bay to the Kukpowruk River, the paleoshoreline of the Wainwrightian transgression lies at an altitude of about 23 m, commonly coincident with the base of a wave-cut scarp, below which the Karmuk beds are typically of lagoonal and offshore barrier bar facies. Along Skull Cliff between Barrow and Peard Bay, the Karmuk beds are largely inner-shelf deposits, but locally include contemporaneous tidal channel facies. *Hiatella arctica* shells from Wainwrightian deposits on the western coastal plain yield aIle/Ile ratios of 0.038 ± 0.007. The Karmuk beds unconformably overlie either the Fishcreekian Tuapaktushuk beds, older Cenozoic marine beds, or Cretaceous bedrock.

The shelf environment during the Wainwrightian transgression was similar to, but perhaps slightly milder than, at present. Mollusk, ostracode, and foraminiferal faunas are similar to those found on the Arctic shelf today. No extinct species have been found, and only two extralimital ostracode species, *Cythere cf. C. lutea* (Brady) and *Baffinicythere emarginata* (Sars), which now inhabit subfrigid waters from the southern Chukchi Sea to the Aleutian Islands (E. Brouwers, personal communication, 1986).

The absolute age of the Karmuk beds is not precisely determined; however, a uranium-trend date on fine-grained sediments at Skull Cliff suggests an age of 540 ± 60 ka (John Rosholt, personal communication, 1983), and kinetic model age estimates based on amino acid ratios suggest an age around 475 ka (Brigham, 1985).

Other Gubik Formation deposits exposed along the Beaufort Sea coast east of Point Barrow have been tentatively assigned to the Wainwrightian transgression, but may actually represent as many as two additional transgressions. At Cape Simpson, near the western edge of the entrance to Smith Bay (Fig. 5), clayey silts and silty clays underlying deposits of the Pelukian and Simpsonian transgressions yielded a TL age of 209 ± 15 ka, regarded as inconclusive pending the dating of further samples (Carter and others, 1986a). Fine-grained marine sediments also occur beneath Pelukian deposits at McTavish and Wright Points, on the western and eastern shores, respectively, of Admiralty Bay, and along the south shore of Kogru River, which empties into southwest Harrison Bay (Fig. 5). The Wright Point and Kogru River deposits contain ice-rafted stones of Canadian provenance, whereas those at McTavish Point do not. Possible correlations among these deposits or with the Karmuk beds have not yet been tested by amino acid studies. A single sample from the Kogru River area has been dated by TL as older than 158 ka (Carter and others, 1986a).

The Pelukian transgression. The Pelukian transgression was defined by Hopkins (1967) as a high-sea-level event that occurred during the last (Sangamon) interglacial and produced shoreline features and deposits a few meters above present sea level that can be traced discontinuously around the coast of western and northern Alaska. Beach, nearshore, and barrier bar deposits of Sangamon age on the Arctic Coastal Plain are exposed in bluffs along the north shore of Teshekpuk Lake and can be traced eastward to Harrison Bay and northwestward to Barrow (Figs. 5 and 6; Carter and Robinson, 1981). Correlative deposits along the Chukchi Sea coast have been informally named the Walakpa beds (Brigham, 1984). Pelukian deposits are exposed at altitudes ranging from 1 m at the base to perhaps as much as 10 m at the top. East of Barrow, they overlie marine mud and disconformably underlie lacustrine or deltaic deposits and eolian sand. Spruce driftwood is common locally in the Pelukian nearshore sands, and the enclosed foraminifera and ostracode faunas indicate more open water and warmer climatic conditions than presently prevail (Hopkins and others, 1981a).

Amino acid ratios of 0.014 ± 0.003 in the total fraction determined for the bivalve *Hiatella arctica* collected from the Walakpa beds are barely distinguishable from those determined for modern specimens (aIle/Ile of 0.0115 ± 0.0015) (Brigham,

1985), and preclude an age greater than Sangamon. Radiocarbon dates on driftwood from the Walakpa beds between Walakpa Bay and Barrow have all yielded infinite dates (Coulter and others, 1960, 38 ka, W-380; Sellmann and Brown, 1973, 39.9 ka, I-3628; Brigham and Miller, 1983, 36 ka, Beta-1766). Similarly, a finite date on marine shells collected near Barrow (31.2 ± .819/.900 ka, DIC-2569) is considered to be a minimum estimate. Oxygen isotope analyses of the bivalve *Astarte borealis* show that their ^{18}O content is about the same as that of modern *A. borealis* shells (J. R. O'Neil, written communication, 1984), suggesting a correlation with oxygen isotope stage 5e. This correlation is supported by seven TL dates on the beach deposits and underlying muds that range from 108.5 ka to 140 ka and average 123.5 ka (Carter and others, 1986a). The altitude of beach deposits formed during the Pelukian transgression is about the same as that estimated for the eustatic high-stand during isotope stage 5e based on evidence from oceanic islands and other continental shelves (Cronin and others, 1981), suggesting that this part of the western Arctic Coastal Plain has been tectonically stable for at least the past 125,000 years.

The Simpsonian transgression. The Simpsonian transgression is defined as the period during which the Flaxman Member of the Gubik Formation was deposited (Carter and others, 1986a). The Flaxman Member (Dinter, 1985) consists of a few meters of glaciomarine erratic-bearing silt, clayey silt, and silty sand, occurring locally along the Beaufort Sea coast to altitudes of about 7 m; it is especially well exposed at Cape Simpson and at Simpson Cove (Figs. 3, 5, and 6). The Simpsonian transgression may also be represented by several features preserved along the Chukchi Sea coast. These include a curved spit near Point Barrow similar to the modern one there (cf. Sellmann and Brown, 1973; Brigham, 1985), erosional benches at about 6-m altitudes around the shores of Walakpa Bay and other drainages along Skull Cliff, and a planed surface graded to a 5- to 6-m level below the abandoned DEWline site at Peard Bay (Fig. 3). Simpsonian deposits are locally overlain by regressive sandy, beach, deltaic, or fluvial sediments.

The erratic stones of the Flaxman Member are foreign to northern Alaska. Rock types include dolomite, diabase, pyroxenite, red granite, and quartzite (Leffingwell, 1919; MacCarthy, 1958; Mowatt and Naidu, 1974; Rodeick, 1975, 1979), with a most likely source in the Coronation Gulf region of the Canadian Arctic (Rodeick, 1975, 1979). Erratics occur to within a few hundred meters of the southern limit of the deposit, and so were being supplied at the peak of the transgression (Hopkins, 1982a). Their transport to the Beaufort Sea coast by icebergs records the ablation of an ice sheet in the Canadian Arctic. Remains of Pacific marine mammals, including ribbon seal (*Histriophoca fasciata*) and gray whale (*Eschrichtius sp.*) (Repenning, 1983), indicate that a connection with the Bering Sea existed during at least part of this transgression. Mollusk, ostracode, and foraminifera faunas are depauperate and include no extralimital species (Hopkins and others, 1981a).

A uranium series date on whale bone from Flaxman deposits is 75 ka, and ten TL dates on sediment of the Flaxman Member average 72.4 ka (Carter and others, 1985). However, the spread of TL ages is large and the dating program is incomplete. Finite radiocarbon dates previously obtained for organic remains from Flaxman deposits (Carter, 1983a) are apparently erroneous.

Because the western part of the Arctic Coastal Plain has been tectonically stable for at least the past 125 kyr, the altitude of the Flaxman deposits cannot be attributed to tectonism. Furthermore, marine deposits exposed near sea level on the Atlantic Coastal Plain were deposited about 75 ka (Cronin and others, 1981, 1984), suggesting that at least part of the Simpsonian transgression was not a local event but records a eustatic sea level several meters higher than today.

During this high-sea-level event, global ice volumes may have been greater than at present. Biota from deep-sea cores are enriched in ^{18}O during this period (Ruddiman and McIntire, 1979). Chappell and Shackleton (1986) proposed that much of this enrichment might have resulted from temperature changes in South Pacific bottom water. However, marine mollusk shells from shallow-water Flaxman deposits are also enriched in ^{18}O relative to modern values, which is not likely a bottom-water effect, and may indicate high glacial ice volumes.

Cronin and others (1984) proposed that the paradox of a sea-level high occurring simultaneously with extensive glacial ice at 75 ka could be explained by large volumes of floating glacial ice in polar regions. The Flaxman Member attests that floating glacial ice was present in the Arctic Ocean, but the discrepancy between the sea-level and isotope records is so large that an extraordinary ice volume would be required to reconcile them. Broecker (1975) and Fillon and Williams (1983) suggested that thick, largely floating Arctic Ocean ice sheets may have been present during some glacial intervals. If such ice existed, we believe (with J. Brigham-Grette dissenting) that it may partially account for the Simpsonian oxygen isotope values. Another possible mechanism to provide an enormous amount of floating glacial ice would be a surge of the Antarctic ice sheet (Carter and others, 1985). Such a surge would cause a rapid rise in sea level (Davies, 1981) and might lead to the catastrophic breakup of unstable marine-based ice over the central Canadian Shield (Denton and Hughes, 1983). Assuming that the Bell Sea sediments of the Hudson Bay region are 125 kyr old, the amino acid geochemistry of marine mollusk shells in post–Bell Sea deposits from the same area indicate that the Hudson Bay Lowlands were indeed evacuated by Laurentide ice and inundated by marine waters about 75 ka (Andrews and others, 1983).

Late Cenozoic nonmarine sediments

Late Cenozoic terrestrial environments on the Alaskan Arctic Coastal Plain are recorded in glacial drift, fluvial and glaciofluvial sediment, eolian silt and sand, and thaw lake deposits, all assigned to the Gubik Formation except the drift, which is discussed because of its bearing on the depositional history of the other sediments. Most of the pre–late Pleistocene fluvial and glaciofluvial deposits of the coastal plain are undated, and their relationships with the marine transgressions discussed above have been determined only locally by superposition. The eolian and thaw lake deposits, however, are all younger than the youngest (Simpsonian) marine transgression recorded on the coastal plain, and, where they occur, blanket all other Gubik Formation deposits except the Holocene and latest Wisconsin alluvium.

Glacial deposits. Ice from Brooks Range glaciers advanced onto the Arctic Coastal Plain in two areas during several glacial episodes that were widely separated in time. Erratics from the oldest advance appear in a gravel sheet informally referred to as the Kuparuk gravel that lies between the Kuparuk and Itkillik Rivers (Fig. 5; Carter, 1983a; Carter and Galloway, 1985). The gravel is poorly exposed and may be either drift or alluvium into which the erratics have been incorporated by redeposition. Erratics up to a few meters in diameter are composed of rock types common in nearby parts of the Brooks Range, including chert-pebble conglomerate, chert, quartz, and sandstone. The northern limit of the Kuparuk gravel is presently the bluff that marks the southern limit of the most extensive late Cenozoic marine transgression; however, erratics occur in erosional lags at least 10 km north of the bluff, so that ice of this oldest advance must have reached to within 30 km of the modern coast. The age of this glaciation is poorly known. The Kuparuk gravel overlies Paleogene deposits (Carter and Galloway, 1985), and it is older than the Colvillian transgression. Also, the Kuparuk gravel is older than fluvial terraces associated with the late Tertiary Gunsight Mountain glacial interval described by Hamilton (1986).

Younger glacial ice advanced onto the eastern coastal plain on four occasions. The oldest of these advances is recorded by isolated patches of formless drift that may correlate with the Gunsight Mountain glacial interval of the central Brooks Range (Hamilton, 1986). The younger advances retain distinct morainal topography along the Canning, Hulahula, Jago, and Aichilik River drainages (Fig. 3). If the sequence of ice advances there is comparable to that recognized for the central Brooks Range (Hamilton, 1986), then they probably correlate with the early(?) Pleistocene Anaktuvuk River, middle Pleistocene Sagavanirktok River, and late Pleistocene Itkillik River glacial episodes.

Fluvial deposits. East of Oliktok Point, the eastern point of entrance to Harrison Bay, fluvial deposits of the coastal plain are mainly gravel and sandy gravel, whereas to the west they are primarily sand with minor gravelly sand (Fig. 5). Coarser-grained deposits are concentrated in the east because the main streams there originate in Brooks Range valleys that were repeatedly glaciated during Quaternary time and shed much coarse sediment downstream during periods of ice ablation. Most of the streams crossing the western coastal plain, by contrast, head in the northern Arctic foothills, which have not been glaciated.

The Colville and Itkillik Rivers, both of which head in formerly glaciated valleys and traverse the coastal plain west of Oliktok Point, are exceptions. However, these rivers have only flowed in their present western courses since their capture by smaller streams that flowed coastward northeast of Umiat (Fig. 5). A gravel terrace traceable from the Colville River near Umiat eastward to the present floodplain of the Kuparuk River (unit Qus_2; Carter and Galloway, 1986), is evidence that the Colville and Itkillik Rivers formerly followed a more easterly course. This drainage is now occupied by the Kuparuk, Sagavanirktok, and other rivers that enter the Beaufort Sea in the vicinity of Prudhoe Bay (Fig. 7). The time of capture is uncertain, but likely postdates the Anaktuvuk River glaciation because major downcutting—probably initiated by the capture—on tributaries of the Colville west of the Anaktuvuk River did not occur until after this glacial advance (Hamilton, 1986).

The fluvial deposits of the Arctic Coastal Plain bear a rich record of Quaternary terrestrial paleoenvironments there; however, for those deposits older than the limit of radiocarbon dating the ages of deposition are still poorly known. Results of the few detailed studies completed to date are summarized below.

Western Coastal Plain. Middle and late Pleistocene fluvial deposits on the coastal plain from the Colville River west to the Chukchi Sea generally occur within terraces exposed along modern stream and river beds. In the Colville River region, these late Quaternary watercourses are separated by middle and early Pleistocene alluvial plains not related to the modern river valleys. The older alluvial plain sediments are poorly exposed and stratigraphically complex. Pollen studies show that some were deposited during glacial intervals (Nelson, 1981), and spruce (*Picea*), larch (*Larix*), and poplar (*Populus*) macrofossils indicate that others were deposited during interglacial episodes (Carter and Galloway, 1982).

Younger fluvial terraces confined to modern river valleys are also stratigraphically complex and represent a long span of Quaternary time. The oldest such deposits underlie ancient flood plains of the Miluveach and Kachemach Rivers, which are graded to the base of a scarp that trends perpendicular to the two rivers at the southeast margin of terrace II (Fig. 5; Carter and Galloway, 1982). The scarp may be of either fluvial or marine origin. If it marks an ancient beach bluff, it was probably cut during the Fishcreekian transgression.

Younger Pleistocene fluvial deposits crop out beneath several fluvial terrace surfaces on both sides of the Colville and Itkillik Rivers (Fig. 5). Although their ages are as yet undetermined, fossil spruce logs at several localities (Carter and Galloway, 1982) are evidence that these deposits formed during interglacial intervals.

Holocene and latest Pleistocene alluvium forming flood plains and low terraces along modern streams has not been studied in detail, but radiocarbon dating indicates that many of the terraces formed between 8 and 14 ka. This suggests that the streams were not deeply entrenched during late Wisconsin low stands of sea level.

Extensive deltas of silt and sand have formed at the mouths of the Colville River, Fish Creek, Ikpikpuk River, and Meade River since sea level reached its present position during middle or late Holocene time. The thickness of these deposits has not been determined, but may be no greater than 15 m, which is the

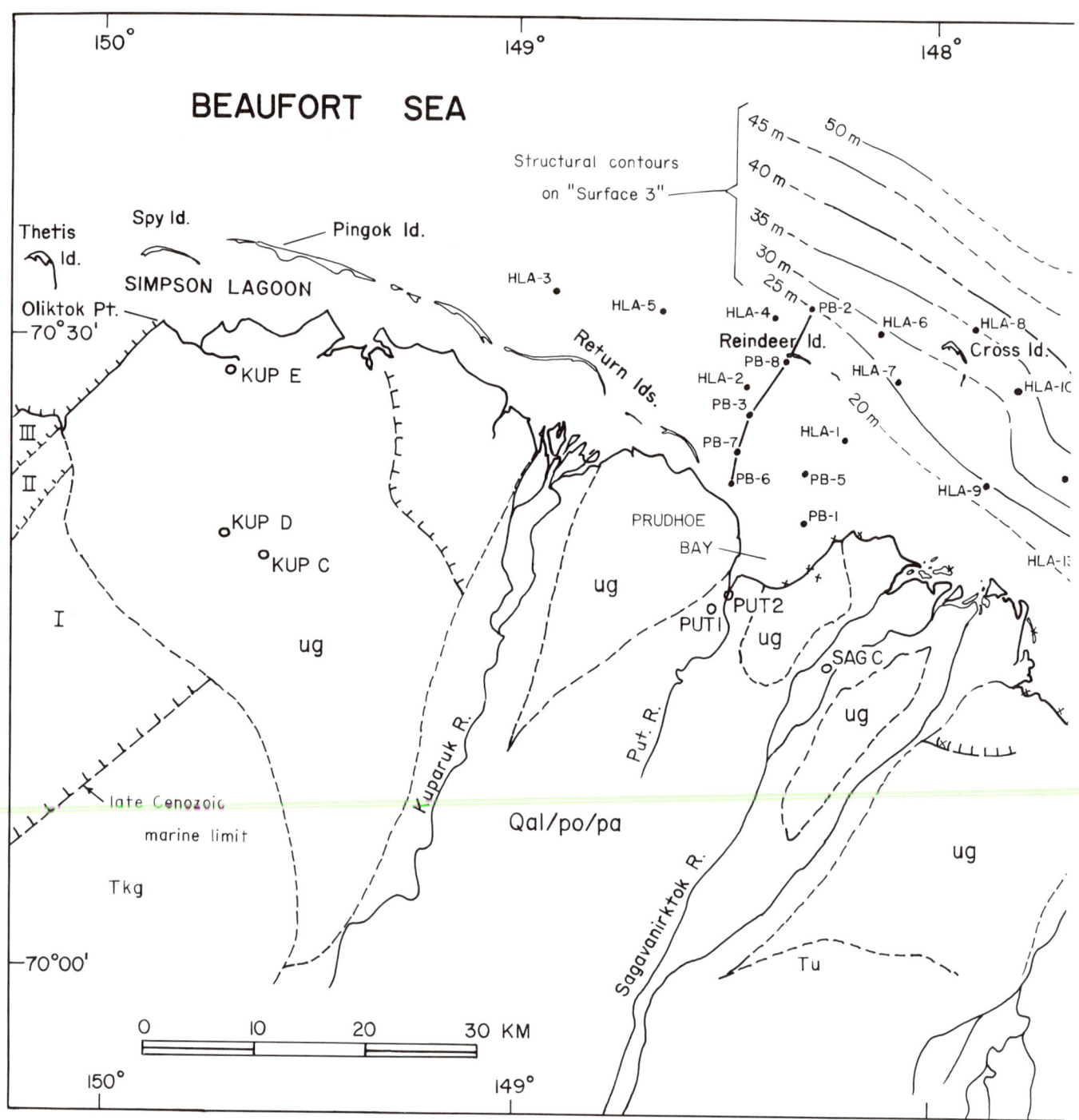

Figure 7. Quaternary geologic features of the central Arctic Coastal Plain and inner Beaufort shelf. Closed circles are borehole locations. Open circles are gravel pit locations. Contours offshore indicate depth beneath present sea level to "surface 3," which may coincide with the base of Pelukian deposits. Hachured lines are terrace boundaries or low erosional scarps, lower on the hachured side. Dashed lines are informal lithologic unit boundaries. I, II, and III are the Colville valley terraces of Carter and Galloway (1982). Tkg = glacial erratic-bearing Kuparuk gravel of Carter (1983a). ug = Sangamon(?)

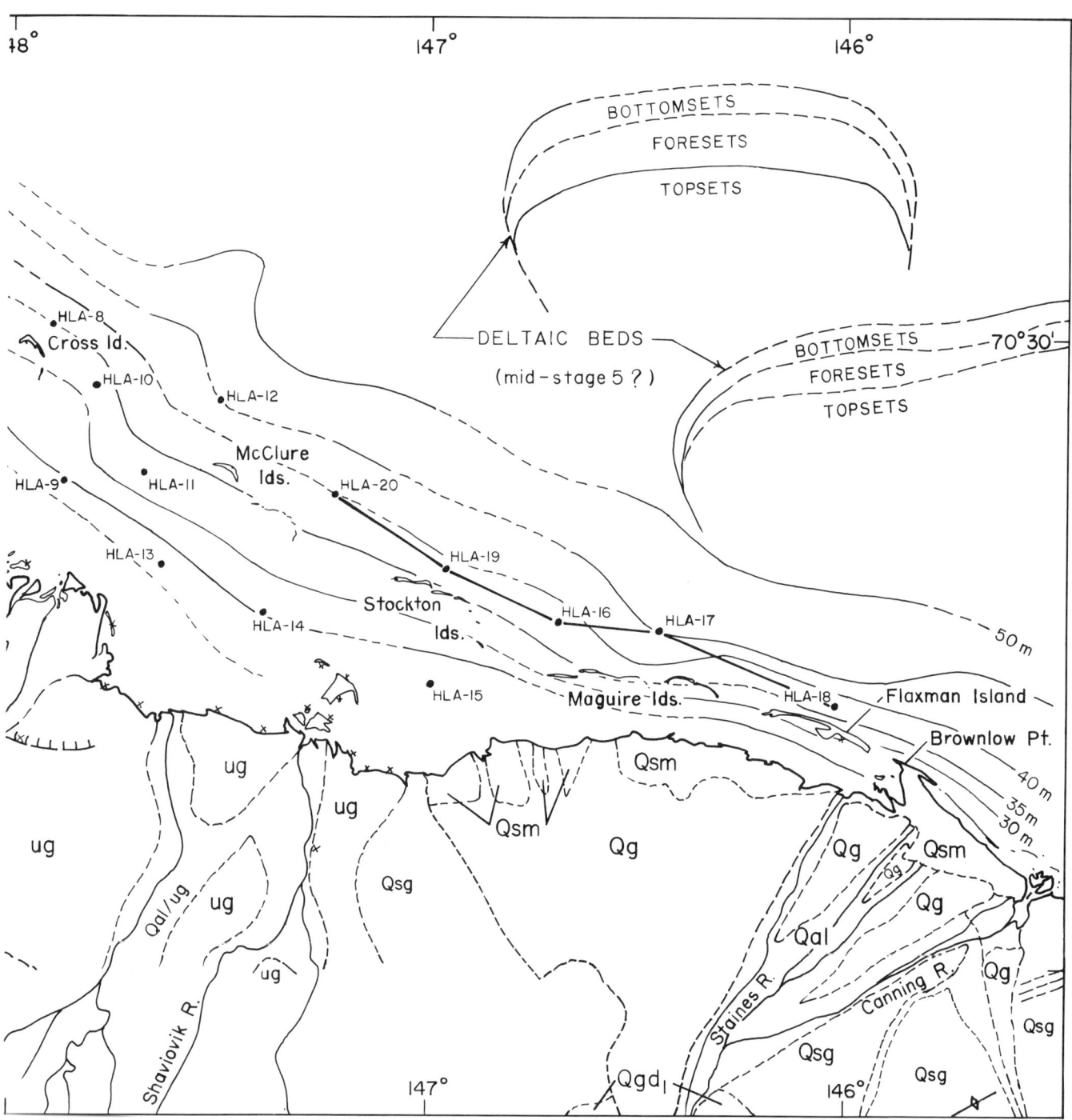

and Illinoian(?) Ugnaravik gravel of Rawlinson (1986), po and pa = the mostly Wisconsinan Put outwash and Put alluvium, respectively, of Rawlinson (1986). Tu = undifferentiated Tertiary deposits. Qal = Quaternary alluvium. Qsm and x along coastline = Simpsonian glaciomarine silts (Rawlinson, 1986; Carter and others, 1986c). Qg and Qsg = fluvial gravel and eolian silt over fluvial gravel, respectively. Qgd_1 = a glacial drift sheet.

approximate depth of the thalweg of the main distributary of the Colville River delta.

Central Coastal Plain. The Kuparuk C, D, and E gravel pits between the Colville and Kuparuk Rivers (Fig. 7) expose up to 17 m of fluvial or glaciofluvial gravel and gravelly sand containing ice wedges, sand-filled ice wedge pseudomorphs, and *Larix* wood, overlain by 1.5 m of eolian sand and 0.5 m of lacustrine deposits (Rawlinson, 1986). Silt samples from the fluvial beds yielded TL ages of 150.2 ± 11 ka (Kup C) and 221.3 ± 17 ka (Kup E). Rawlinson (1986) informally named these fluvial deposits, and probably correlative ones at least as far east as the Canning River fan, the Ugnuravik gravel, and suggested that its depositional period spanned the Sangamon interglacial and Illinoian glacial episodes. He now believes, however, that the TL dates may represent minimum ages, and that the Ugnuravik gravel might be as old as early Pleistocene (S. Rawlinson, oral communication, 1987).

In much of the area between the Kuparuk and Sagavanirktok Rivers, the Ugnuravik gravel has been eroded away and replaced by younger nonmarine sediments referred to informally by Rawlinson (1986) as the Put outwash and alluvium. Detrital wood and peat from the Put deposits have yielded middle Wisconsin (Hopkins and Robinson, 1979; Hopkins and others, 1981b; Rawlinson, 1986) and Holocene (Rawlinson, 1986) radiocarbon ages, indicating that the channels or embayments they fill must have been eroded during or prior to middle Wisconsin time. In the Prudhoe and Harrison Bay areas, Simpsonian (Flaxman) and older marine deposits may have been removed in this erosional event, and if so, it must have happened some time later than about 70 ka. The generally broad extent of the eroded area may suggest that it resulted not from localized downcutting during a sea-level lowstand, but from shoreface erosion during a marine transgression.

Gravel composing the inactive part of the Canning River alluvial fan was informally named the Canning gravel by Rawlinson (1986), who proposed a late Wisconsin age for the surficial fan deposits. Most of the fan gravel, however, probably formed over a broader time span, perhaps beginning in the early Pleistocene.

Eastern Coastal Plain. Little is known of the fluvial history east of the Canning River. The deposits there consist of alluvial fans at the front of the Brooks Range, sheets of silt-covered fluvial or glaciofluvial gravel on coastal plain interfluves (unrelated to modern river valleys), alluvial terrace deposits of gravel and gravelly sand within modern river valleys, and deltas of sand and silt at major river mouths (Carter and others, 1986c). The interfluve gravels and alluvial terraces have been folded in places, reflecting active Quaternary tectonism. Fossil wood from some of the oldest interfluve gravel, which may be Pliocene, has been identified as either *Chamaecyparis nootkaensis* (Alaskan yellow cedar) or *Tsuga* sp. (hemlock) (J. T. Quirk, written communication, 1983). The nearest modern occurrences of these trees are in southeastern and south central Alaska, which suggests that the climate of the North Slope was considerably warmer than that of today during deposition of this gravel.

Eolian deposits and paleoclimates. Eolian deposits consist of silt and very fine sand (loess), which occur as a blanket along much of the inner edge of the Arctic Coastal Plain and on adjacent parts of the Arctic foothills, and of eolian sand, which forms stabilized dunes, sand sheets, and fossil sand wedges elsewhere. Stratigraphic and paleontologic studies of the eolian deposits and assocated fluvial sediments have yielded information sufficient to delineate the major features of the Wisconsin and Holocene paleoclimatic history of the coastal plain.

Loess. The eolian silt of the Alaskan Arctic has been referred to as the foothill silt (O'Sullivan, 1961) and as upland silt (Williams and others, 1977). It is locally thicker than 30 m, but generally poorly exposed, and except for studies by O'Sullivan (1961) and Nelson (1982) has been examined in reconnaissance fashion only. West of the Colville River, the upper part of the deposit has a grain-size distribution like that of eolian silt (O'Sullivan, 1961), but the lower part contains thin-bedded very fine to fine sand, felted detrital peat, and at the base, gravelly sand of fluvial origin. Despite the grain-size characteristics, O'Sullivan and Hussey (1960) argued for a marine-fluviatile origin for the upper part. Williams and others (1977) and Carter (1983b), however, consider the silt to be eolian and to have been deposited during several episodes of eolian sediment transport. During and between these episodes, the eolian silt and very fine sand was eroded and redeposited by fluvial and lacustrine processes. The time of initial eolian silt deposition is unknown, but the most recent depositional periods are Wisconsin and Holocene (Carter, 1983c).

The silt is exceptionally ice-rich (Livingstone and others, 1958), with a total ice content, including interstitial and wedge ice, that in places approaches 80 percent of the sediment volume to depths as great as 21 m below surfaces that have never been affected by thaw lake activity (Williams and Yeend, 1979). The high proportions of ice persist so deeply in part because ice wedge growth has kept pace with the accumulation of eolian silt (Fig. 8).

Sand. Eolian sand ranging in thickness from a few centimeters to tens of meters is generally present on the coastal plain north of the eolian silt accumulations, except on middle and late Holocene stream terraces, and in the low-lying coastal zone underlain by the Flaxman Member of the Gubik Formation west of Harrison Bay. The thickest eolian sand deposits compose stabilized linear dunes that are as much as 30 m high, 1 km wide, and 20 km long, and occupy more than 11,000 km^2 west of the Colville River (Figs. 5 and 9; Carter, 1981). This sand sea is informally called the Ikpikpuk dunes (Carter and others, 1984).

Studies of the Ikpikpuk dunes and adjacent areas by Carter and others (1984) led to a division of middle Wisconsin through early Holocene time into four periods of contrasting seasonal climate. These periods can be broadly related to climatic periods defined by Hopkins (1982b) for the whole of Beringia. The divisions emphasize intervals of eolian sediment transport, soil development, and contrasting fluvial regimes delineated by radiocarbon and thermoluminescence dating, and faunal and floral assemblages.

The oldest period, which was of unknown duration and ended about 36 ka, probably corresponds to the middle part of Hopkins' (1982b) Boutellier interval. Although the Ikpikpuk dunes were active during this period (Table 2), coeval fluvial deposits containing abundant detrital wood and other organic debris crop out at modern stream levels south of the dunes. This period is also represented south of the dunes by ice wedges, paleosols, and ice wedge casts. Eight radiocarbon dates on paleosols and detrital wood from these deposits are between 36 and 46 ka, but others are "infinite." All of the dates might be interpreted as minimum ages; however, concordant radiocarbon and TL dates of about 41 ka on sedges and sediment associated with a buried ice wedge suggest that some of the finite dates in this range may truly represent the age of the latter part of this climatic interval. One fluvial deposit that yielded radiocarbon dates of 43 to 44 ka contains the beetle *Blethisa catenaria* (Nelson, 1982), which indicates mean July temperatures of at least 9.5°C, consistent with insolation values for this time interval and latitude predicted by the Milankovitch orbital theory (Berger, 1978). Pollen spectra and plant and insect macrofossil assemblages from the same deposit indicate generally discontinuous shrub-tundra vegetation on interfluves, with local areas of stable plant communities (Nelson, 1982). Summer surface conditions were probably drier than at present, but wetter than in the succeeding climatic regime. The presence of sparse dwarf birch may indicate that winter snow cover in the Arctic foothills was locally sufficient to protect this low shrub (Carter and others, 1984).

During the second period (36 to 13.5 ka), eolian sediment transport dominated landscape development across much of Alaska north of the Brooks Range. The eolian regime extended about 400 km from sediment sources on outwash plains and fans in the east to where waning winds deposited loess along the margin of the Arctic foothills south and west of the Ikpikpuk dunes (Fig. 5). Bedding attitudes, dune-ridge orientations, and

Figure 8. Syngenetic ice wedges in eolian silt.

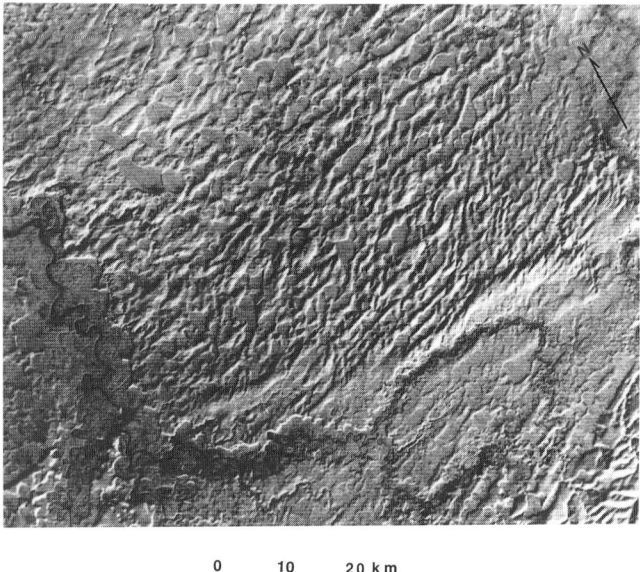

Figure 9. Portion of a Landsat-1 multispectral scanner, band 7, enhanced image (ID1237-2153). Location shown on Figure 5. Low sun angle emphasizes the relief of the ridge and thermokarst-basin terrain of the Ikpikpuk dunes. The ridges are linear dunes. From Carter (1981).

measurements of pseudocrosslamination formed by climbing adhesion ripples demonstrate a wind regime similar to that of the present and indicate that the dominant sand-moving winds were easterly to northeasterly (Figs. 10 and 11). Stratification types within the dunes indicate deposition under predominantly dry conditions. Few interdunal pond deposits have been identified, suggesting that rainfall and snowmelt were insufficient to regularly inundate interdunal depressions. Buried snow or ice has not been observed in the dune sand, and deformational structures that could be attributed to the melting of snow or ice are rare. Snow cover over the dunes is inferred to have been patchy at most.

Downwind of the Ikpikpuk dunes, loess was deposited on interfluves of the northern Arctic foothills, and syngenetic ice wedges formed. Streams aggraded their valleys during this period, forming alluvial deposits up to 20 m thick that are nearly devoid of detrital wood. Drainage was largely blocked by the dunes, and short-lived lakes formed between the dunefield and the Arctic foothills.

Insect and plant macrofossil assemblages and pollen spectra from the aggradational fluvial sequence in the Arctic foothills indicate a progressive drying of the landscape during the first few thousand years of this climatic regime. Dwarf birch was nearly eliminated from the landscape at the beginning of this period, perhaps because of decreased snow cover. If so, then snow cover in the northern foothills was probably less than 15 cm, or less than half the modern average of 30 to 40 cm. Snowfall was probably also less than half of the present 19 to 25 cm (water

TABLE 2. RADIOCARBON DATES BEARING ON THE TIMING OF LINEAR DUNE ACTIVITY
AND SAND WEDGE DEVELOPMENT ON THE WESTERN COASTAL PLAIN
(from Carter, 1983c)

Site	Longitude N and Latitude W	Material	Occurrence	Age and Laboratory Number	Significance
1	70° 04.35' 151° 22.9'	Peat	Involution intruding sand wedge	9,330 ±90 (Beta-5384)	Minimum limiting age of cessation of sand wedge development
1	"	"	"	9,600 ±100 (Beta-5383)	"
2	70° 34.72' 152° 31.38'	Herbaceous plants	Growth position in sand overlying sand wedge	9,680 ±110 (USGS-1377)	"
2	"	"	"	10,200 ±90 (USGS-1378)	"
5	70° 26.7' 153° 28.9'	Peat	Paleosol separating eolian sand sheet from linear dunes	11,230 ±170 (I-10,814)	Minimum limiting age for cessation of activity of linear dunes
6	70° 23.3' 153° 12.2'	Wood	Rooted in paleosol separating eolian sand sheet from linear dunes	11,430 ±170 (I-11,675)	"
7	70° 25.7' 152° 34.23'	Peat	In ice-wedge cast developed in linear dunes	11,700 ±180 (I-12,177)	"
8	69° 49.37' 154° 24.85'	"	Paleosol separating eolian sand sheet from linear dunes	12,070 ±100 (USGS-823)	"
9	70° 27.5' 153° 53.1'	Herbaceous plants	Growth position in dune sand	13,140 ±60 (USGS-1154)	Dates activity of linear dunes
10	70° 18.4' 153° 26.4'	"	Growth position in interdunal pond or lake	13,610 +130 (USGS-624)	"
11	69° 48.8' 152° 37.35'	"	Growth position in dune sand	16,490 ±130 (USGS-1376)	"
8	69° 49.37' 154° 24.51'	"	Growth position in interdunal pond or lake	18,600 ±210 (USGS-824)	"
12	70° 08.1' 154° 28.6'	"	"	25,200 ±180 (USGS-1029)	"
11	69° 48.8' 152° 37.35'	"	"	35,900 ±1,200 (USGS-825)	"
13	69° 48.62' 154° 12.5'	Wood	Detrital wood in alluvium beneath dunes	49,400 +3,000 −2,200 (USGS-826)	If not redeposited, is most likely minimum limiting age for alluvium beneath linear dunes

equivalent) average. Radiocarbon dating of fossil bones indicates that despite these severe conditions the Arctic foothills supported such large herbivores as mammoth, horse, and bison previous to 28 ka. However, none of the dates on these mammal remains is younger than 28 ka, and indeed, few organic remains of any kind have been found in deposits between 14.5 and 28.0 ka, in contrast to both older and younger deposits. Cold, arid conditions evidently intensified during late Wisconsin time coincident with the expansion of glaciers in the Brooks Range.

Inactive sand wedges as much as 7 m deep and 3 m wide extend upwind of the dunes for more than 100 km (Figs. 5 and 12; Carter, 1983c). Sand wedges are forming today in the drier

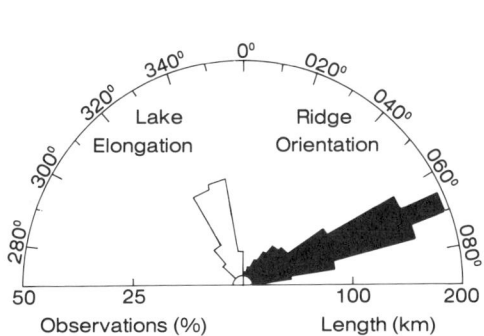 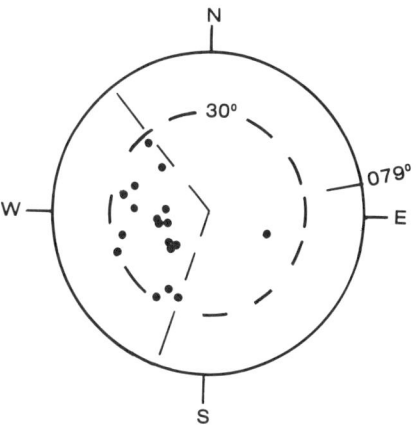

Figure 10. Polar histogram showing (1) total ridge length for linear dunes within each 5° increment of orientation (shaded) as measured from Landsat image of Figure 9, and orientation of elongate axes (unshaded) of thermokarst lakes for that part of the L$_4$ lake unit of Sellmann and others (1975) in the Teshekpuk Quadrangle, plotted as a percentage of 325 observations. Ridge trends are roughly perpendicular to lake elongation and are therefore parallel to the dominant modern regional winds. From Carter (1981).

Figure 11. Stereographic projection of dip measurements on 18 sets of cross-strata from the Ikpikpuk dunes. Azimuth of dot represents dip direction; distance from center indicates degree of dip. The attitudes indicate westerly sand movement and are explainable in terms of net sand transport parallel to the ridge axes. From Carter (1981).

Figure 12. Large sand wedges (A and B) at site 1 of Figure 11. Man is about 1.7 m tall. From Carter (1983c).

parts of Victoria Land, Antarctica (Péwé, 1959; Black and Berg, 1963; Berg and Black, 1966), in some parts of the Sverdrup Islands of Arctic Canada (Hodgson, 1982), and in northern Greenland (C. Hjort, written communication, 1983). Both sand and ice wedges grow as a result of repeated formation and filling of thermal-contraction cracks in permafrost; ice wedges form when the cracks fill with snow, hoar frost, or meltwater (Leffingwell, 1915; Lachenbruch, 1962), whereas sand wedges form when the cracks fill with sand that trickles down from the surface.

Sand wedges developed on the Arctic Coastal Plain as wind-driven sand moving across the coastal plain toward the dunes dropped into open thermal-contraction cracks. The sand wedges record barren ground and document an absence of surface water from the time the thermal contraction cracks formed in middle and late winter until they filled with eolian sand. This suggests that significant sand movement occurred before spring and that snow cover was patchy or absent, as inferred for the dunes. Also like the dunes, the sand wedges may have been active throughout

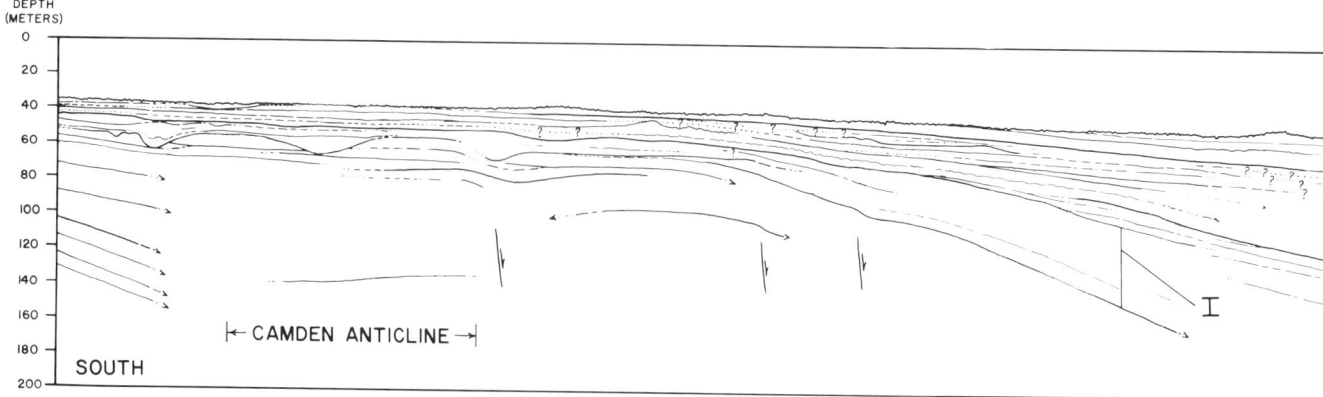

Figure 13. Line drawing of a Uniboom profile from the Western Wedge terrane (from Dinter, 1985). Arrows at reflector terminations indicate that disconformities may persist deeper than shown, but cannot be traced farther on the seismic profile owing to overprint by multiples, or depths exceeding the range of seismic penetration. See Figure 14 for location.

the Wisconsin stage, but are presumed to have been most active during late Wisconsin time (Carter, 1983c).

Streams draining the Arctic foothills south of the Ikpikpuk dunes became throughflowing again at the beginning of the third climatic period (13.5 ka), which corresponds to the beginning of Hopkins' (1982b) "birch zone." Detrital wood and organic debris again became common in fluvial deposits, roughly coincident with a rise in the percentage of birch pollen recorded in lake cores from across east Beringia (Hopkins, 1982b). At about 12 ka the Ikpikpuk dunes were stabilized, organic soil development began across the coastal plain, and ice wedge growth was initiated locally on the previously barren plains north and east of the Ikpikpuk dunes (Table 2; Carter, 1983c). At the same time, streams draining the Arctic foothills south of the Ikpikpuk dunes began downcutting. These relations suggest that at about 13.5 ka, climatic warming began and stream discharge increased from previously low levels. Fossil ostracode assemblages that include temperature- and solute-sensitive taxa suggest that by 12 ka, summers were warmer and wetter than those of today (Carter and others, 1984).

During the fourth period, which lasted from 11 to 8 ka, a new phase of eolian sand movement was initiated that resulted in the formation of an eolian sand sheet 1 to 7 m thick that blanketed the older Ikpikpuk dunes and extended across much of the Arctic Coastal Plain (Carter, 1981, 1983c). Streams draining the Arctic foothills south of the Ikpikpuk dunes continued downcutting, however, to form a series of terraces that range in height from 8 to 10 m above modern stream levels. Climatic conditions during this episode of eolian sand movement were warmer and drier than those of today (Carter and others, 1984). Eolian sand movement ceased about 8 ka when the development of organic soils stabilized the sand surface.

Small parabolic and longitudinal dunes up to 1 km long and a few meters thick (Black, 1951) developed over the area of the sand sheet during late Holocene time. This episode of eolian sand movement was probably coincident with the neoglacial expansion of glaciers in the Brooks Range. If so, then destabilization of the sand surface was probably initiated by cooler and drier climatic conditions than those of today.

Thaw lake deposits. Thaw lakes and thaw lake deposits are widespread on the Arctic Coastal Plain, especially west of the Canning River. They began developing at about 12 ka, following the climatic amelioration that terminated the late Wisconsin glaciation (Lewellen, 1972; Sellmann and others, 1975; Brown and others, 1980). Since stabilization of the eolian sand sheet about 8 ka, the thaw lake cycle has perhaps been the dominant landscape modifier away from rivers and streams. The origin and mechanisms of elongation of thaw lakes have been extensively studied in the Barrow area (Black and Barksdale, 1949; Britton, 1957; Brewer, 1958; Livingstone and others, 1958; Carson and Hussey, 1960, 1962, 1963; Brown, 1965; Hussey and Michelson, 1966; Carson, 1968; Black, 1969, 1976; Morrissey, 1979). Sellmann and others (1975) subdivided the coastal plain into areas containing thaw lakes of similar size, shape, and development of orientation. Their map unit boundaries approximate the boundaries of the lithologically defined Quaternary map units for the western part of the Arctic Coastal Plain (Williams and others, 1977).

THE GUBIK FORMATION OFFSHORE

The Gubik Formation is thicker and more continuous laterally beneath the Beaufort continental shelf than it is to the south beneath the coastal plain. The submerged Gubik deposits generally thicken seaward from at most a few tens of meters near the coastline to more than 100 m locally near the shelf break (Fig. 13). 3.5 kHz and boomer-type high-resolution seismic reflection profiles reveal the offshore Gubik section to be composed of numerous seaward-thickening, wedge-shaped stratal units with thin topset, foreset, bottomset, and channel-fill deposits intercalated locally. The wedge units have been interpreted as marine deposits, each representing a distinct glacioeustatic sea-level highstand, and the intercalated units as deltaic and fluvial sediments deposited during relative lowstands (Dinter, 1985).

The onshore and offshore sections of the Gubik Formation

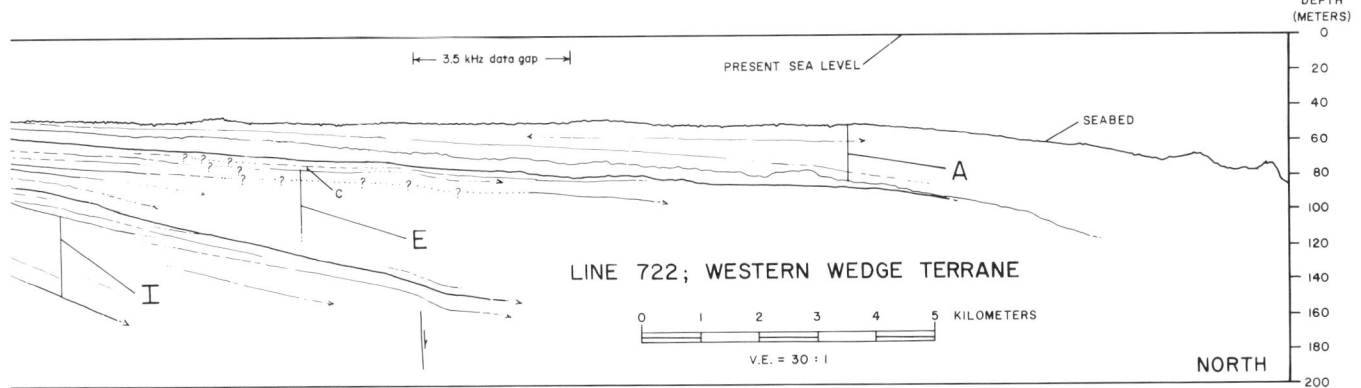

largely record different—and complementary—periods of late Cenozoic geologic history. On the coastal plain the marine deposits represent extreme highstands of sea level, mostly associated with interglacial stages, whereas glacial stages and most interstades are recorded only by nonmarine sediments that commonly yield little information on contemporary marine environments. The submerged Gubik deposits, on the other hand, include marine units deposited during interstades, and apparently provide—in the form of nested, well-preserved disconformities—a record of successive late Quaternary glacioeustatic lowstands.

Seismic stratigraphy, middle and outer Beaufort Shelf

Individual marine wedges beneath the middle and outer Beaufort Shelf are typically bounded by disconformities, several of which are especially pronounced and laterally persistent, and have led to groupings of the wedge deposits into composite wedge units. Three such units—A, E, and I—are evident on Figure 13, a cross-section extending seaward from Camden Bay to the shelf break. Units A and E have prominent basal disconformities, suggested by Dinter (1985) to have formed during transgressions subsequent to major glacioeustatic sea-level lowstands. Unit I, the oldest composite wedge, is incompletely profiled, and will not be further discussed.

Composite unit A. Composite wedge A is thin or absent on the inner and middle shelf, but thickens seaward to more than 40 m locally near the shelf break (Fig. 14). It has accumulated most thickly and extensively on the eastern third of the Alaskan Beaufort Shelf in two structural troughs—the Eastern and Western Wedge Terranes—separated by an arch known as Camden Anticline (Dinter, 1985). To the west as far as Harrison Bay, unit A is thinner, with its wedge shape retained only on the outermost shelf. Possibly correlative deposits underlie the middle shelf, but gaps in seismic coverage preclude firm correlations.

Dinter (1982) inferred unit A to be dominantly marine because of its uniformity along strike, its homogeneous acoustic signature, and because samples from its top at the sea floor are marine. This interpretation is supported by recent paleontological studies of a core obtained from the extension of the Eastern Wedge Terrane onto the Canadian Beaufort Shelf (Fig. 14). Clays and silty clays from this core that probably correlate with unit A contain dominantly marine foraminiferal and ostracode assemblages (Blasco and others, this volume). Unit A contains a few weak, but laterally persistent, internal reflectors subparallel to either the sea bed or the basal disconformity. Much of the incident high-frequency seismic energy, however, was transmitted through unit A to profile deeper reflectors, a fact that may indicate low proportions of sand and coarser-grained sediment beds (e.g., Damuth, 1975).

The age of unit A is still at issue. Its basal disconformity dies out near the shelf break in the Eastern and Western Wedge Terraces at depths ranging from 99 to 116 m below present sea level. Noting the similarity of those values to those of late Wisconsin sea-level minima estimated from data on many other stable continental shelves (Cronin, 1983), Dinter (1982) suggested that the basal disconformity may have formed as a result of the late Wisconsin subaerial shelf exposure, so that all of unit A might be late Wisconsin or Holocene. Faint internal reflectors in unit A were tentatively ascribed to fluctuations in either sea level or depositional regime during the overall rise to present sea level (Dinter, 1985). This age interpretation is consistent with the observation that most sea-bed exposures of unit A are normally consolidated (Reimnitz and others, 1980), indicating little possibility that they have been subaerially exposed since deposition (Chamberlain and Gow, 1979).

The new core data from the Canadian outer shelf, however, and new work on seismic profiles of the Alaskan Beaufort continental slope may necessitate a revised age interpretation for unit A. Core GSC 01 was collected near the Alaska/Yukon border at a site about 20 km east along strike from the last mapped extent of unit A on the Alaskan shelf (Fig. 14). Three TL dates, in descending stratigraphic order, of 53 ka, 66 to 96 ka, and 78 to 117 ka are from fine-grained sediments in that core that probably correlate with unit A (Blasco and others, this volume). Shell fragments from near the top of the core yielded finite radiocarbon dates of $29,900 \pm 600$ and $33,200 \pm 600$, which are interpreted to be minimum age estimates. Moreover, new interpretations of seismic profiles from the Alaskan Beaufort margin north of unit A suggest that significant deposition subsequent to the late Wisconsin lowstand may have been largely limited to the continental slope, with relatively little occurring on the shelf. These new constraints imply that unit A is probably older than late Wisconsin. A tentative maximum age for the base of unit A is provided by information in Smith (1985a, b), who proposed that erratic-bearing glaciomarine deposits exposed at the sea bed on the inner Beaufort shelf correlate with the Flaxman Member of the Gubik Formation, interpreted to be about 70 to 80 ka based on uranium series and preliminary TL data (Carter and others, 1985). Unit A appears to be stratigraphically higher than these deposits, and if so, is younger (Dinter, 1985).

Perhaps the most plausible period for the formation of the unit A basal disconformity in the 18 to 70 ka interval is during the transgression subsequent to the early Wisconsin lowstand (c. 65 to 70 ka). Oxygen isotope ratios at this time (e.g., Shackleton and Opdyke, 1973) do not preclude the possibility that sea level may have dropped nearly as low as the late Wisconsin minimum, thus accommodating the 100-m termination depth of the basal disconformity (Fig. 15). An early Wisconsin origin for this surface may also be favored on climatic grounds: Unit A is thought to be underlain by extensive nearshore(?) and/or fluvial(?) beds (unit B of Dinter, 1982, 1985). These are more likely to have accrued in a relatively wet climate, when streams were transporting sediment to the coast, than during an arid period. An arid climate spanning the late Wisconsin on the Arctic Coastal Plain was already established by 36 ka (Carter, 1983c). During the early Wisconsin, however, much wetter conditions prevailed, as evidenced by the extensive Itkillik IB glacial advance in the northern Brooks Range (Hamilton, 1986). Unit B might be partly composed of outwash from this glaciation.

Unit A in this revised model would presumably record mainly marine deposition during one or more middle Wisconsin interstades. Deposition was concentrated in embayments overly-

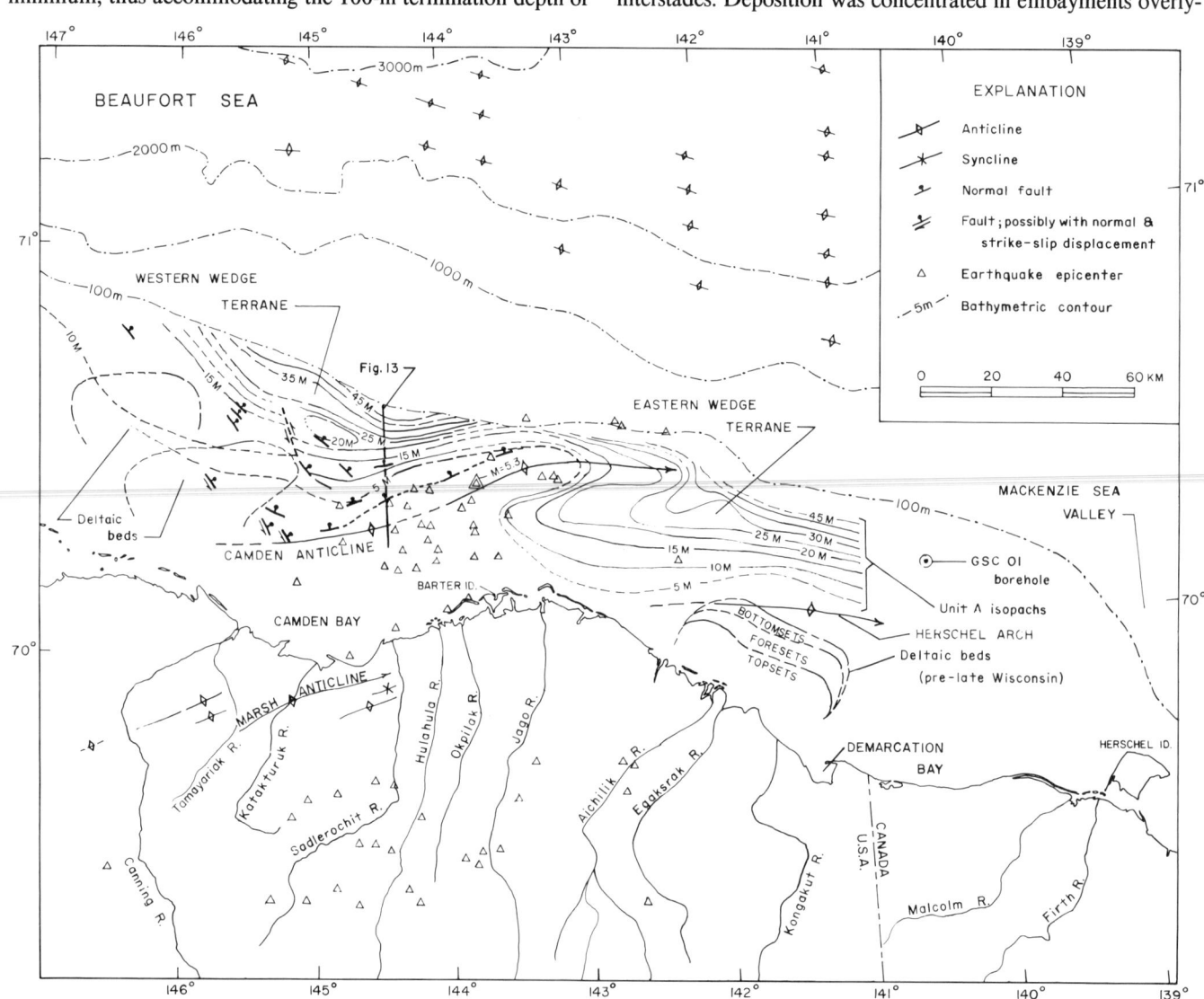

Figure 14. Quaternary geologic features of the eastern Alaskan Beaufort continental margin and coastal plain. All the indicated faults and folds have been active during late Quaternary time. Fold axes onshore are from Carter and Galloway (1986); offshore fold axes on the shelf, faults, and locations of deltaic beds are from Dinter (1985); earthquake epicenters are from Grantz and others (1983); and fold axes beneath the continental rise from Grantz and others (1987).

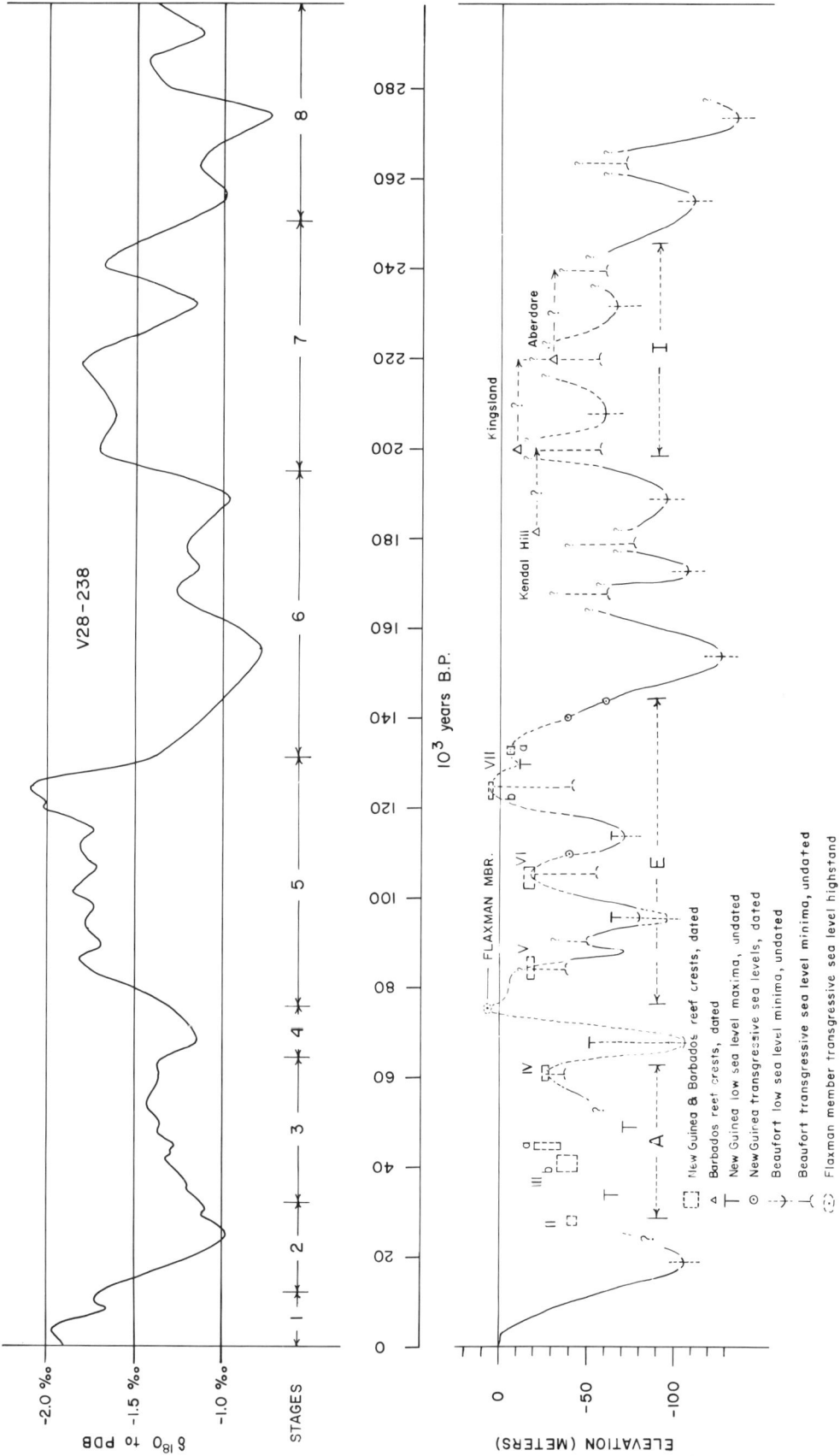

Figure 15. Tentative sea level curve incorporating lowstands and transgressive minima measured from the Westerr Wedge terrane, modified from Dinter (1985), based on first-order correlations of prominent disconformities beneath composite Units A, E, and I with the ^{18}O enrichment maxima of oxygen isotope stages 2, 6, and 8, respectively, of Shackleton and Opdyke (1973). New Guinea reef crest data are from Bloom and others (1974); Barbados reef crest data from Broecker and others (1968) and Fairbanks and Matthews (1978); New Guinea low-sea-level maxima from Chappell (1974); and New Guinea transgressive sea levels from Aharon and others (1980). Elevations of Flaxman glaciomarine boulders are from Leffingwell (1919), and tentative assignment to oxygen isotope stage 5a from Hopkins (1982a). Dashed and solid bars, squares, and ovals indicate uncertainties in data measurements and interpretations.

ing the subsiding Eastern and Western Wedge Terranes, and melting icebergs may have provided a significant fine-grained sediment source, possibly with additional input of outwash from Mackenzie Valley and the Brooks Range. The fact that most surficial samples of unit A are normally consolidated, however, probably indicates that at least a thin veneer of late Wisconsin and/or Holocene deposits is present at the top of unit A. This view is consistent with the interpretation of Redeick (1979), who proposed that glacially striated gravels exposed at the sea bed (at the surface of unit A) on the outer Beaufort shelf were—like the Flaxman Member of the Gubik Formation—derived by ice-rafting from the Coronation Gulf area of the Canadian Arctic Islands. Sediment-laden bergs are inferred to have floated out through Amundsen Gulf into the Arctic Ocean during the decay of the late Wisconsin/early Holocene Laurentide Ice Sheet, and then to have been entrained by the Beaufort Gyre and carried westward to ground and melt on the newly reinundated outer shelf.

Composite unit E. Like unit A, unit E is a seaward-thickening sediment wedge composed of several thinner wedge-shaped strata (Fig. 13). In the Western Wedge Terrane, its total thickness beneath the outer shelf locally exceeds 60 m. Unit E is inferred to be dominantly marine because of its flat, regular bedding, lateral continuity, and acoustic homogeneity observed on seismic profiles, and because it appears to correlate with marine deposits cored beneath the inner shelf. Dinter (1985) divided composite unit E into five marine(?) subunits, C, E_1, E_2, E_3, and E_4, in order of increasing age, based on the interpretation of one representative seismic profile from the Western Wedge Terrane (Fig. 13). The seaward termination depths of disconformities separating these subunits were inferred to record approximate magnitudes of relatively minor (other than full glacial) glacioeustatic sea-level lowstands.

Units E_2 and E_3 are mostly restricted to the outer shelf, and their bounding disconformities cannot be traced laterally over any great distance. The disconformity separating unit E_1 from unit E_4 on the middle shelf, however, is an important one, and it persists from the west flank of Camden anticline west to at least the longitude of central Harrison Bay. In this area, it typically is the youngest, prominent, laterally persistent sub-sea floor reflector evident beneath the inner and middle shelf. In 25- to 30-m water depths the E_1/E_4 disconformity lies about 5 to 12 m below the sea bed. It is generally a flat and featureless surface, probably cut by waves during a transgressive event following a glacioeustatic lowstand. Channels were cut locally into the lower marine unit, and filled prior to the formation of the disconformity. There are also foreset deposits as thick as 8 m intercalated locally between the two broadly marine intervals of composite unit E (Fig. 14). The top of one such deposit north of the Canning River lies 57 m below present sea level.

Unit E's basal disconformity is also strongly reflective and laterally persistent, and can be traced fairly continuously beneath the same portion of the shelf as the E_1/E_4 disconformity. A correlative surface probably exists beneath the shelf west of Harrison Bay, but has not yet been identified on seismic profiles owing to stratigraphic discontinuities and wide line spacings. Nor has a correlative surface been recognized east of Camden Anticline in the Eastern Wedge Terrane, where the appropriate reflector may lie mostly below the limit of seismic penetration.

The seaward stratigraphic termination of unit E's basal disconformity—inferred to record a position near the shoreface during the associated lowstand of sea level—has been profiled on only two lines, both from the Western Wedge Terrane, an area of active normal and tear faulting (Grantz and others, 1983). Corrected approximately for fault displacement since deposition, the termination depth of the basal reflector is about 127 m below present sea level, more than 40 m deeper than the termination of any disconformity within unit E (Dinter, 1985). Ice volume is still generally believed to be the dominant factor influencing the benthic ^{18}O record. Although that record is not a reliable indicator of the absolute magnitudes or timing of glacioeustatic sea level events, it is probably still useful as an indicator of general trends (Mix and Ruddiman, 1984). Assuming that to be so, Dinter (1985) suggested that the most recent time prior to the Wisconsin glacial stage that sea level might have dropped as low as –127 m was during oxygen isotope stage 6 (Fig. 15; Shackleton and Opdyke, 1973; Shackleton, 1977). If the unit E basal disconformity was created during the ensuing transgression to the Sangamon Interglacial sea-level maximum, and if the unit A basal disconformity formed just after the stage 4 minimum as hypothesized above, then composite unit E must represent oxygen isotope stage 5 (Fig. 15).

Age assignments that apparently conflict in some respects with a stage 5 age for unit E have resulted from recent studies of cores and seismic records from the inner shelf that sampled deposits that are probably continuous with unit E (Smith, 1985a and b; Wolf and others, 1985b; K. McDougall, written communications, 1987, 1989). These differences in interpretation are discussed in the following section.

Seismic stratigraphy and cores, inner Beaufort Shelf

High-resolution seismic profiles from the inner Beaufort shelf between the Kuparuk and Canning Rivers delineate two prominent, laterally continuous, slightly seaward-dipping, sub-sea-bed reflectors, surfaces 3 and 4 of Wolf and others (1985a). Structural contours on the lower reflector, surface 3, are reproduced in Figure 7. Contours on surface 4 are similar in shape, but depths average about 8 m shallower. A comparison of these contours with seismic profiles from just offshore reveals an apparent correlation of surface 3 with the basal disconformity of composite unit E, and of surface 4 with the disconformity separating the two dominantly marine subunits of unit E.

In addition to the seismic data, 27 shallow cores have been collected from the inner shelf between the Kuparuk and Canning Rivers at an average spacing of about 12 km (Fig. 7). Although a core-by-core discussion is beyond the scope of this text, two subregions of the inner shelf, each containing a number of cores,

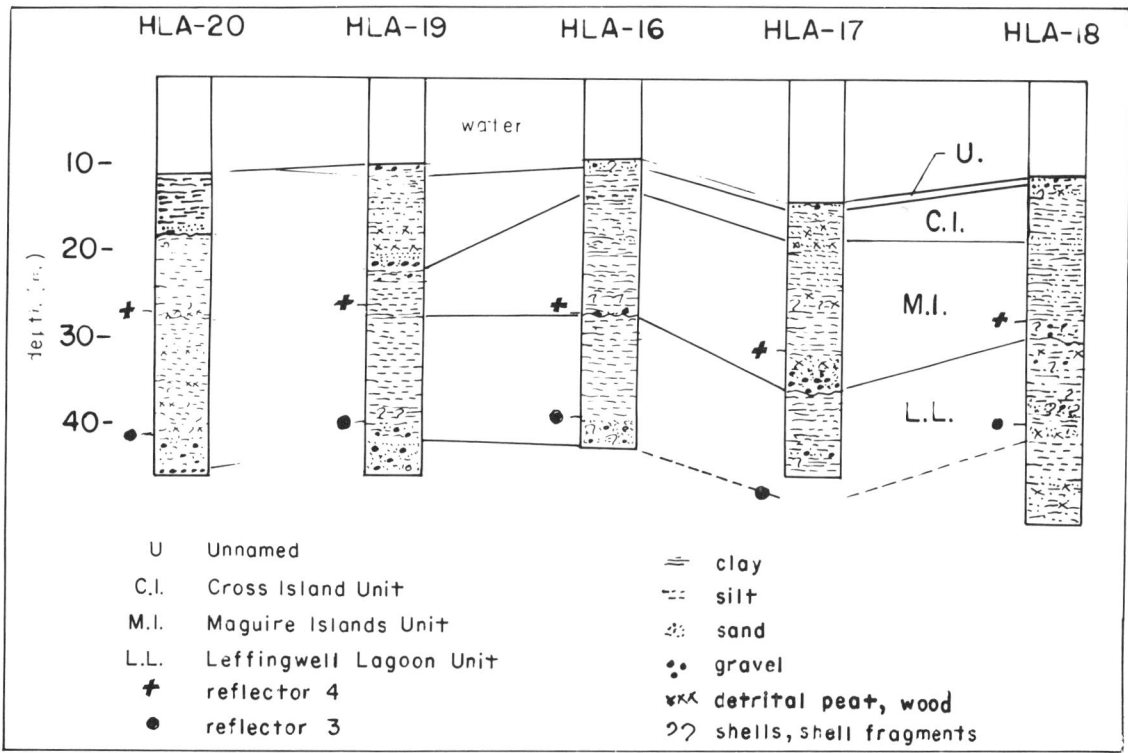

Figure 16. Correlation diagrams, from west to east, of boreholes HLA 16-20, showing generalized sedimentary character, position of prominent reflectors, and unit designations (from Smith, 1985a). See Fig. 7 for location.

have stratigraphic geometries that are sufficiently regular to be summarized briefly.

Core stratigraphy, Kadleroshilik to Canning River. HLA cores 20, 19, 16, 17, and 18 lie on a transect parallel to and about 1 to 2 km seaward of a barrier island chain that extends from the McClure Islands on the west to Flaxman Island on the east (Figs. 7 and 16). Along this transect, surface 3 of Wolf and others (1985a) is underlain by a nonmarine (outwash or alluvial) unit and(or) beach and nearshore deposits, and overlain by at least three successive shallow marine sequences (Smith, 1985a, b; K. McDougall, written communications, 1987, 1989). The oldest of these, approximately bounded below by surface 3 and above by surface 4, is the Leffingwell Lagoon unit, a clayey, sandy marine silt containing no extinct microfaunal species (Fig. 16). The foram and ostracode assemblages from this unit typically document a cold, shallow, nearshore Arctic environment at the base, grading upward into deep, open-water, midshelf conditions, sometimes with Atlantic ostracode immigrants, and then gradual shoaling conditions toward the top. Total thickness is about 15 m along the borehole transect.

Overlying surface 4, which seems to correlate with a thin sand or shell bed or a nearshore lag deposit, is a dominantly marine silt and clay sequence, the Maguire Islands unit, which ranges from about 10 to 15 m thick along the transect. A few meters of inner to middle shelf deposits at its base are overlain in three of the boreholes by silty clays with very low foram numbers, and an ostracode fauna indicative of fluctuating salinities (K. McDougall, written communication, 1987). Seismic profiles show seaward-dipping foreset beds in this interval, which is interpreted as deltaic (Wolf and others, 1985a). The delta top lies at about 14 m below present sea level, which probably approximates sea level during the period of delta construction. The foreset beds at −57 m within composite unit E farther out on the shelf also appear to be younger than surface 4. In HLA-17 and HLA-20 there are no deltaic beds in the Maguire Islands unit, which is characterized instead by very high numbers of forams typical of a stable, inner Arctic shelf environment. Thin, shallow marine deposits also overlie the deltaic beds in the other boreholes (K. McDougall, written communications, 1987, 1989).

Overlying the Maguire Islands unit is a stiff, black, shallow marine silt, the Cross Island unit, which is at most a few meters thick (Smith, 1985a, b). Sparse pebbles in the silt have lithologies typical of the Flaxman Member of the Gubik Formation. The Cross Island unit is overlain by at most one meter of unconsolidated Holocene marine deposits.

Smith (1985a, b) and McDougall (written communication, 1987) correlate the Leffingwell Lagoon, Maguire Islands, and Cross Island units with onshore deposits of the Wainwrightian (older than oxygen isotope stage 5), Pelukian (stage 5e), and Simpsonian (70 to 80 ka) transgressions, respectively. If, however, the correlations between the inner and outer shelf seismic data are correct as stated above, then the stratigraphic model of

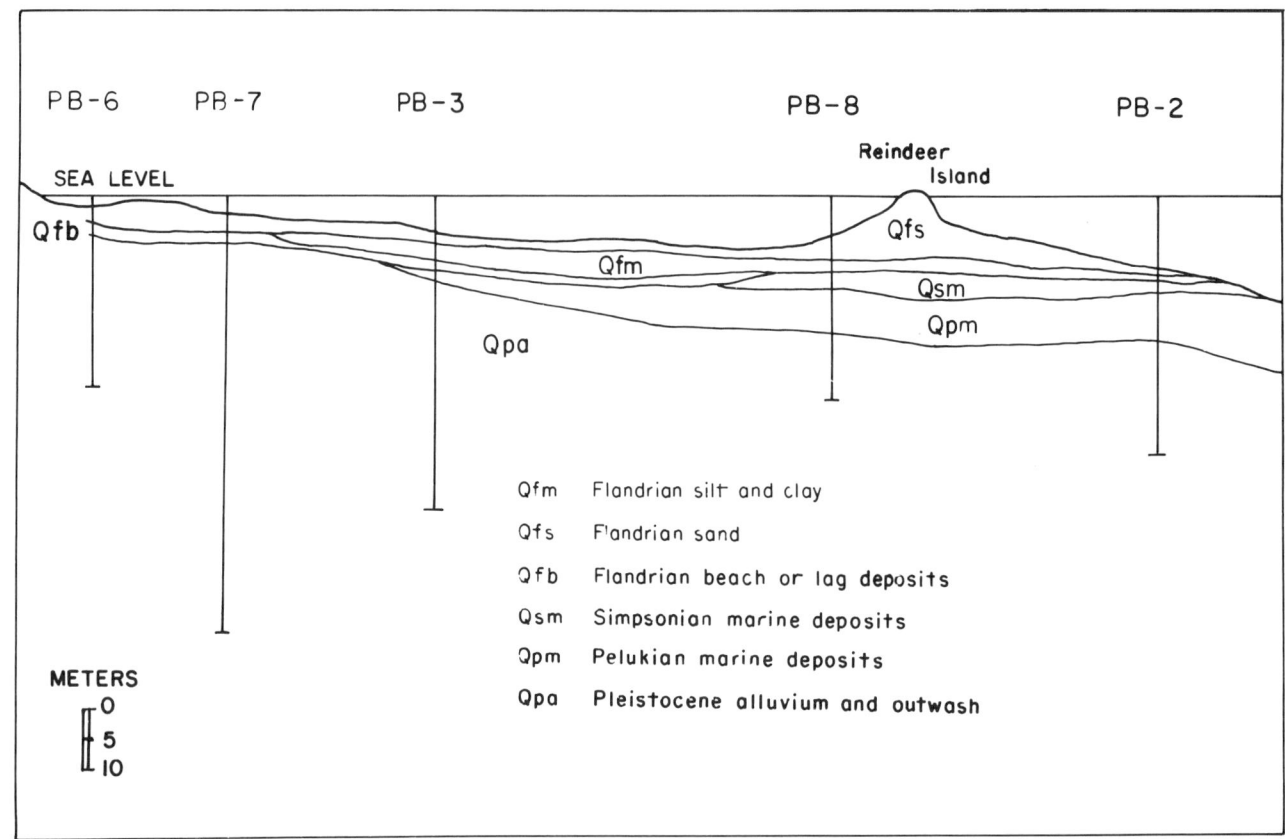

Figure 17. Tentative cross section through boreholes PB-6, -7, -3, -8, and -2 from McDougall and others, 1986. See Figure 7 for location.

Dinter (1985) implies a stage 5 age for both the Leffingwell Lagoon and Maguire Islands units. The seismic based correlation scheme relies on a speculative interpretation of the oxygen isotope curve (Dinter, 1985), whereas the reliability of the paleontologic-based correlations is limited by the fact that no extinct species occur in any of the three marine core units (Smith, 1985a and b; McDougall, written communication, 1987). Unit distinctions in the cores therefore depend on environmentally controlled differences in faunal suites. Ages were assigned to the core units based on assumptions as to what the shelf environments might have been during the Wainwrightian, Pelukian, and Simpsonian transgressions. Those shelf environments are unknown, however, because there are no dated reference sections for the specified transgressions offshore, and no stratigraphic continuity between the core units and the onshore deposits from which the transgressions were defined.

Core stratigraphy, Prudhoe Bay to Reindeer Island vicinity. Seven shallow cores (PB-1, -2, -3, -5, -6, -7, and -8) taken from the inner shelf in and north of Prudhoe Bay (Fig. 7) contain an important record of the shelf environment during the Holocene transgression to present sea level. Several meters of variably sandy, marine silt and clay at the top are underlain by nonmarine gravel and sand deposits (Chamberlain and others, 1978; Chamberlain, 1979; Sellmann and Chamberlain, 1979). The marine section thickens seaward from less than 2 m near shore to about 12 m near Reindeer Island (Fig. 17).

The entire marine sections in cores PB-1, -3, -6, and -7, and all but the lower meter or so of marine deposits in PB-5, are soft and normally consolidated. They have probably, therefore, been deposited during the most recent inundation of the shelf, subsequent to the late Wisconsin sea level lowstand, because subaerial exposure of silts and clays to freeze/thaw cycles is known to cause marked stiffening or overconsolidation (Chamberlain and Gow, 1979; Chamberlain, 1979). A late Wisconsin or Holocene age for these marine deposits is also suggested by radiocarbon dates on organic debris in the underlying gravels (McDougall and others, 1986), and in correlative gravels in the Putuligayuk River drainage just inshore (Rawlinson, 1986). These dates are finite middle Wisconsin values ranging from about 26 to 43 ka.

McDougall and others (1986) note also that the normally consolidated marine deposits in these cores have foraminifera and ostracode assemblages similar to those of modern Prudhoe Bay. Estuarine, deltaic, and shallow (approximately 10 m) open shelf environments are all represented. A dramatic increase in abundance of microfaunal tests is typical near the base of the Holocene marine section.

In cores PB-8 and PB-2, from just south and north of Reindeer Island, respectively, much of the marine section is overconsolidated, and so has been exposed subaerially at least once (Chamberlain, 1979). If this were true only of the northern core, PB-2, it might be explained simply by a southwestward Holocene migration of Reindeer Island over the site (Fig. 7; Chamberlain and others, 1978). The PB-8 occurrence of overconsolidated deposits, however, suggests that the marine sediments in these outer cores must be, at least in part, older than those preserved closer to shore. McDougall and others (1986) divided the marine sections in cores PB-2 and PB-8 into three subunits, units I, II, and III, based on contrasts in depositional environment reflected both in the ostracode and foraminiferal suites, and in lithologies. The youngest subunit, unit III, is sandy in both cores, has faunal assemblages typical of modern, shallow water Arctic environments, and was assigned a Holocene age. Unit II is dominantly clay in both cores, and has a faunal assemblage similar to parts of the modern Prudhoe Bay. McDougall and others (1986) correlate unit II with the Simpsonian transgression in their summary cross-section, reproduced here in Fig. 17. Unit I in both cores is mostly clay in the upper half and coarser grained toward the base. The faunal assemblages fluctuate, but appear to document a transgressive cycle, with a shallow water environment similar to present-day Prudhoe Bay at the base yielding upsection to deeper water, open-shelf conditions. McDougall and others (1986) assign unit I to the Pelukian (Sangamon) transgression.

These age calls should be regarded as tentative, except for those on the Holocene deposits. There are several problems in the correlations between PB-2 and PB-8. In PB-2, unit II is assigned a Simpsonian (c. 75 ka) age, but yielded an 18 ka radiocarbon date, and a relatively high abundance of microfauna. Unit III in that core is impoverished in microfaunal tests. In PB-8, however, unit II is relatively impoverished in specimens, whereas a dramatic increase in abundance occurs at the base of unit III. The primary limitation in the age interpretations, however, is again the lack of well-dated offshore reference sections for any of the transgressions but the Holocene.

Seismic stratigraphy, Harrison Bay

Isopachs of an "acoustically transparent" Holocene(?) marine stratum in and north of Harrison Bay appear in Craig and Thrasher (1982), and are reproduced in part in Figure 5. As in the Prudhoe Bay area, deposits of the Simpsonian and Pelukian transgressions appear to have been removed from the vicinity of Harrison Bay during an important erosional event sometime after 70 ka.

Craig and Thrasher (1982) show the Holocene(?) marine stratum thickening gradually seaward from 2 m near the Colville delta to about 10 m beneath the present 20-m isobath, and then thickening abruptly to 18 m or more at a feature they interpret as a shoreline bluff. From their published seismic profiles, however, it is apparent that several stratigraphic reflectors project through the "bluff," which must, therefore, have a nonstratigraphic origin. Contours seaward of that feature have accordingly been omitted in Figure 5.

Shoreward of the "bluff," the basal Holocene(?) reflector has sharp, irregular relief, which Craig and Thrasher (1982) ascribe to thermokarst topography and stream channels. Another possibility is that this reflector records the top of ice-bonded permafrost, which may locally coincide with the base of post–late Wisconsin marine deposits. In that case, the Holocene(?) isopachs shoreward of the "bluff" may, although erroneous in detail, give a generally correct notion of Holocene marine sediment thickness.

Island chains, inner Beaufort shelf

Rodeick (1975, 1979) divided the gravels of the Beaufort Sea coastline, barrier islands, and shelf into two distinct facies. The chert facies, with a Brooks Range provenance, includes green, brown, gray, and black chert, as well as sandstone, siltstone, shale, coal, limestone, and rare igneous clasts, dominantly of granitic composition. The dolomite facies, containing sandy to microcrystalline dolomite, orthoquartzite, red granite, diabase, pyroxenite, and various metamorphic clasts, is typical of the Flaxman Member of the Gubik Formation, deposited by melting icebergs during the Simpsonian transgression.

The island chain that extends northwest from Brownlow Point, at the western margin of Camden Bay, through Flaxman Island and the Maguire, Stockton, and McClure Islands, to Cross and Reindeer Islands is entirely of the dolomite facies (Fig. 7; Hopkins and Hartz, 1978; Rodeick, 1979). A clue to the origin of most of the islands of this chain is provided by Flaxman Island, part of which is simply a high-standing coastal plain remnant that has survived since the deposition of the Flaxman Member. The remainder of the island was created by coastal drift from the Flaxman core (Hopkins and Hartz, 1978). Most other islands of the chain probably have a similar origin and have migrated south and west from their former positions. Some of the cores have been completely destroyed, leaving only submerged gravel and boulder lags as evidence they once existed (Rodeick, 1979).

Another island chain, closer to shore, extends from Stump Island, west of Prudhoe Bay, through the Return Islands to Spy and Thetis Islands near the eastern margin of Harrison Bay (Fig. 7). These islands, too, likely originated as high-standing coastal plain remnants, but they contain gravel composed dominantly of chert-facies clasts rather than dolomite-facies clasts (Hopkins and Hartz, 1978). They were possibly derived from deposits that were once continuous with the Pelukian beach or barrier ridge that extends from near Barrow across the north shores of Teshekpuk Lake and Kogru River and has a similar gravel composition (Figs. 5 and 6). If so, the connection was removed by a post-Simpsonian erosional event, possibly the same erosional event that created Harrison Bay.

Although the island chain contains dominantly chert-facies clasts, it includes a 10 to 25 percent admixture of dolomite-facies lithologies (Hopkins and Hartz, 1978), as does the Pelukian beach or barrier ridge west of Harrison Bay. This means that exotic, Flaxman-type deposits must have been present on the coastal plain prior to the Pelukian transgression, as was also suggested by the 158-ka TL date on Flaxman-like erratic-bearing silts on the south shore of Kogru River (Carter and others, 1986b), and by basal gravel lags of exotic lithologies in pre-Pelukian deposits at Skull Cliff (Brigham, 1985). Undated Flaxman-like glaciomarine deposits similar to those at Kogru River occur in an analogous position across Harrison Bay along the south shore of Simpson Lagoon, facing the Pelukian barrier-ridge-cored island chain. Although such deposits litter the shoreline, they do not appear in a gravel pit just 2 km inshore, which may suggest that the pit gravels are older than the marine unit. Rawlinson (1986) reported a TL date of 221 ± 17 ka from a silty sand within the alluvial pit gravels in the Kup E pit (Fig. 7). Possibly, then, pre-Pelukian, Flaxman-like, glaciomarine pebbly silts were deposited along the Beaufort coastline in the course of a transgression—similar in character to the Simpsonian transgression—that occurred during oxygen isotope stage 6 or the latter half of stage 7.

A third coastal island chain extends east from Point Barrow toward Smith Bay (Fig. 5). From Ekilkruak Pass east, the islands are all dolomite facies and may have an origin similar to the Flaxman-derived chain farther east. West of that pass the gravels are a mixture of dolomite and chert facies, indicating a dual source (Hopkins and Hartz, 1978).

NEOTECTONICS

Throughout the period of Gubik Formation deposition, most of the North Beringian Marine Abrasion Platform has been structurally quiescent, owing largely to its position above a stable, pre-rift bedrock platform. The northern edge of this platform, beyond which continental crust dips steeply toward the Arctic Basin, roughly underlies the shelf break between central Harrison Bay and the Canning River fan (Fig. 1; Grantz and others, 1982; Grantz and May, 1983). To the east and west, however, the platform edge swings southward, and in those areas the Beaufort shelf is underlain by thick post-rift sediments not nearly so stable as the platform rocks (Fig. 1). Both areas have had a long and continuous history of tectonic deformation.

Eastern Beaufort structural province

The shelf and coastal plain east of the Canning River lie within the active foreland fold and thrust province of the eastern Brooks Range, and are thought to be underlain by at least one major detachment thrust (Grantz and others, 1987). The detachment surface is rooted to the south beneath the mountains and is inferred from multichannel seismic profiles to extend beneath the entire continental margin and to die out beneath the continental rise. It deepens and steepens eastward from Camden Bay, and the intensity of surficial deformation correspondingly decays in that direction. Thrust splays rise from the detachment zone in several places, and have determined the positions and magnitudes of surficial structures.

Folds. The Quaternary expression of this foreland province is dominated by two long, east-northeast-trending arches, Camden and Marsh anticlines, and three associated synformal subbasins (Grantz and others, 1983; Dinter, 1985), all of whose axes appear to plunge eastward (Fig. 14). Camden and Marsh anticlines are both probably thrust-cored, and both have crestal regions underlain by complexly folded strata that record a history of either long, continuing deformation, or of multiple deformational episodes. The axis of the synformal basin developed off the south flank of Camden anticline has been migrating landward throughout most of Cenozoic time. In addition to the major folds, a number of subparallel subsidiary folds have been mapped on shore in fluvial and glacial deposits east of the Canning River (Fig. 17; Carter and others, 1986c).

Camden anticline lies entirely offshore. Its axis, which is delineated by isopach contours on Unit A, cannot be discretely traced west of about the Canning River mouth, and appears to die out to the east near its intersection with the shelf break (Fig. 14). Beds tentatively interpreted to be no older than Pelukian (Sangamon) can be traced on seismic profiles from areas where they are flat-lying and undeformed, to the crestal region of the arch, where they have been warped since deposition, suggesting youthful activity on the fold.

Marsh anticline has been mapped between the Tamayariak and Sadlerochit Rivers on the coastal plain south of Camden Bay, where Miocene or Pliocene beds near its crest dip up to 60°, and Pliocene and Pleistocene beds on its flanks dip 18° (Morris, 1957; Reiser and others, 1971). The fold axis may continue eastward parallel to the shoreline of eastern Camden Bay to connect with Herschel Arch offshore, but this hypothesis has not yet been tested in the field (Dinter, 1985). Smaller folds parallel to Marsh Anticline appear west of its northern flank as far as the Canning River, and east of its southern flank (Fig. 14; Carter and others, 1986c).

The three Cenozoic synformal subbasins associated with the arches are presently expressed as Quaternary depocenters. The Western Wedge Terrane of Dinter (1985) overlies an unnamed subbasin bounded to the southeast by the north flank of Camden anticline, and to the west by the edge of the pre-rift bedrock platform (Grantz and others, 1987). Between the two offshore arches, the east-facing, scoop-shaped Eastern Wedge Terrane overlies Barter Island subbasin, and south of Herschel Arch an unnamed scoop-shaped depocenter overlies Demarcation subbasin (Dinter, 1982; Grantz and May, 1983). Anomalously thick Quaternary sediment and subtle topographic depressions above the basin axes are evidence of youthful basin subsidence (Grantz and others, 1983).

Faults. Active faults of two types disrupt late Quaternary and older deposits in the vicinity of Camden Bay. Those that are parallel to Camden anticline and offset its northern flank toward the Arctic Basin appear to be simple normal failures, formed in response to extension near the arch crest (Fig. 14). Offsets of inferred Wisconsin or younger beds range up to about 6 m along those features, and of inferred Pelukian (Sangamonian) beds, up to about 12 m (Grantz and others, 1983).

The remaining faults in this area are clustered above the

edge of the pre-rift bedrock platform near the western margin of the Western Wedge Terrane. Many may have formed originally as normal failures in the thick post-rift sediments accumulating east of that boundary. Indeed, the faults of this group that lie closest to the shelf edge have normal, down-to-the-basin offsets. Those that lie near the western termination of Camden anticline, however, are inferred to have significant strike-slip offsets, because correlative reflectors typically cannot be identified across the fault traces. These features may have formed or been reactivated as tear faults to accommodate the splaying and dying out of eastern Brook Range thrust surfaces (Grantz and others, 1987). A broad, roughly northeast-trending belt in which this left-lateral tearing and splaying is inferred to be distributed was defined by Grantz and others (1983) as the Canning Displacement Zone.

Earthquakes. Earthquake epicenters shown in Figure 14 include all those recorded from the eastern North Beringian Platform region during the period 1968 to 1978 (Biswas and Gedney, 1978) (Plate 2). Magnitudes range from 0.5 to 5.3, and hypocentral depths were constrained to 10 km. Location errors are typically 15 to 20 km.

A clustering of epicenters coincides with the crestal region of Camden anticline, corroborating the notion of modern activity on that fold suggested by seismostratigraphic interpretations. Although no focal plane solutions are available, the inferred source might be the thrust splay thought to core the anticline. No such clustering coincides with the mapped extent of Marsh anticline, but given the brevity of the seismic record, and the fact that Pleistocene fluvial terraces are warped where they cross the structure (Carter and others, 1986c), it is probably not justified to conclude that the fold is inactive. No earthquakes were recorded west of the Canning Displacement Zone, which supports the interpretation that modern tectonic features die out in that vicinity (Grantz and others, 1983).

Western Beaufort structural province

From the longitude of central Harrison Bay west to Barrow Sea Valley, the middle and outer shelf are underlain by thick, mainly Cretaceous, post-rift sediments (Grantz and May, 1983). Although these deposits are relatively little deformed, they have been disrupted by down-to-the-basin normal and growth faults, some of which are still active (Fig. 5; Grantz and others, 1983). Maximum displacements along these faults of beds inferred to be late Pleistocene range from 1 to 10 m. No Holocene displacements have yet been observed.

SUMMARY

The North Beringian Marine Abrasion Platform is a broad, low-relief plain extending from the Arctic foothills of the Brooks Range north and west to the shelf breaks of the Beaufort and Chukchi Seas. During Pliocene and Quaternary time, the coastline repeatedly transgressed and receded across this platform in response to global glacioeustatic sea-level fluctuations. The successive periods of marine submersion and subaerial exposure are patchily recorded in the unconsolidated clastic deposits of the Gubik Formation, which mantle the bedrock platform to thicknesses no greater than a few tens of meters onshore, and perhaps 100 m or more beneath the continental shelf.

Detailed stratigraphic, paleontologic, geochemical, and radiometric studies of onshore Gubik Formation exposures have resulted in the recognition and regional correlation of marine deposits left by at least six distinct late Cenozoic transgressions. Sediments deposited during the oldest (Colvillian) transgression are found at elevations as high as 40 to 60 m on the coastal plain. They include fossil faunas of Pacific origin, and must therefore be younger than the opening of the Bering Strait just prior to 3 Ma.

Bigbendian transgressive deposits occur at a maximum elevation of about 35 m. Their age is uncertain, but may be between 2.4 and 2.6 Ma. The contemporary climate was relatively mild, as indicated by a pollen suite indicative of a floral community similar to that now surrounding Anchorage, and by the presence of sea otters, whose modern descendants cannot tolerate severe seasonal sea ice.

Fishcreekian transgressive deposits are found up to 36 m above present sea level on the coastal plain, and include probable ice-rafted clasts similar in lithology to those of the much younger Flaxman Member of the Gubik Formation. Relatively warm sea temperatures are suggested by the presence of sea otter remains, and of mollusks that now live only south of Bering Strait. Pollen suites, however, suggest that the terrestrial climate may have been severe during this transgression, supporting only a shrub-herb tundra. Tundra vegetation is thought to have first developed in the Arctic about the time of the 2.48-Ma Gauss-Matuyama geomagnetic reversal. Because Fishcreekian beds have reversed polarity, they must be younger than 2.48 Ma. A minimum age of about 2.4 Ma has been suggested based on the presence of a primitive rodent fauna. Amino acid ratios from Fishcreekian specimens are significantly lower than Bigbendian values.

The Wainwrightian transgression as presently defined may comprise as many as three transgressive events, but data now available do not sufficiently support such distinctions. Wainwrightian beds exposed at elevations up to 23 m along the Chukchi coastline yielded a uranium-trend date of about 540 ka. Enclosed fossil invertebrate fauna are similar to those living presently in nearby Arctic shelf waters. Other possibly Wainwrightian deposits include clayey silts exposed from 1 to 10 m above present sea level along the Beaufort coast west of Harrison Bay. These have yielded a TL date of about 209 ka, and one greater than 158 k.

Pelukian transgressive deposits compose a former beach or barrier ridge exposed discontinuously at elevations up to 10 m from near Barrow east to at least Harrison Bay, and possibly nearly to Prudhoe Bay. Dates and amino acid ratios determined for these deposits support a firm correlation with the Sangamon Interglacial at about 125 ka. The enclosed invertebrate faunal suite is indicative of a slightly warmer, more stable oceanic environment than presently prevails.

The Simpsonian transgression, tentatively TL dated at about 70 or 80 ka, was different in character from the older transgressions discussed above. It is represented on the coastal plain principally by deposits of glaciomarine silt exposed along the Beaufort coast to altitudes as high as about 7 m. Abundant ice-rafted stones contained in the silt originated in the Canadian Arctic Islands, and were transported to Alaska during a high-sea-level event that was extraordinary because it occurred while global ice volumes reamined high. Possible explanations for this event include an Antarctic ice sheet surge, and the presence of a thick, largely floating Arctic ice sheet.

The history of nonmarine deposition on the coastal plain is not regionally as well known as that of the marine beds, owing largely to patchy preservation, complicated stratigraphic geometry, and a paucity of applicable dating techniques. Detailed local studies of fluvial and eolian deposits, however, have elucidated the main features of the late Quaternary paleoclimatic history and contemporary depositional environments. Alluvial and outwash plains older than about the Fishcreekian transgression are probably mostly in positions unrelated to modern river valleys. Younger fluvial deposits typically compose terraces perched at various elevations in valleys cut by modern streams. The largest north slope river, the Colville, heads in the western Brooks Range and presently flows into Harrison Bay. Formerly, however, its course ran further east, through the present Kuparuk and Sagavanirktok drainages, and extensive early Pleistocene fluvial gravel sheets preserved in that area were probably deposited largely by the Colville. The change in course was a result of stream capture.

On the eastern coastal plain the mountains are much closer to the coastline, and a number of important rivers, most notably the Canning, have constructed large alluvial fans. Some of those include high proportions of Pleistocene glacial outwash. Drift sheets deposited during at least three distinct glaciations are well preserved upstream in several of the river valleys.

Extensive Wisconsinan eolian deposits are preserved on the coastal plain, especially west of the Colville River where a sheet of stabilized linear dunes covers an area larger than 11,000 km^2. Studies of these deposits and related fluvial sediments have allowed the division of Wisconsin and Holocene time into several periods of contrasting paleoclimate. The first period, ending at about 36 ka, was drier than at present, but still moist enough to allow ice wedges and organic soils to form south of the active dunefield. The second period, 36 to 13.5 ka, was dominated by eolian sediment transport, and characterized also by a lack of preserved organic soils. Northeasterly winds carried material from eastern outwash fans to be deposited in sand wedges over much of the coastal plain, in the western dunefield, and in a loess blanket still farther to the southwest. Aridity was especially severe after 28 ka. A moister period beginning at about 13.5 ka is marked by an increase in birch pollen and the reestablishment of through-flowing streams. By 12 ka the dunes were stabilized, and organic soils and ice wedges were forming across the coastal plain. During a fourth period, however, from 11 to 8 ka, a sheet of eolian sand blanketed the older linear dunes. Summers were warmer and drier than now, but streams were still through-flowing. The present, relatively moist climatic regime began at about 8 ka.

The part of the Gubik Formation lying beneath the Beaufort continental shelf has been profiled seismically and sampled in a number of shallow cores from the inner shelf and one from the outer shelf. In general, the submerged deposits are thicker, more dominantly marine, and more continuous laterally than those exposed onshore. The ages and depositional environments of the offshore deposits are not as well known, however, owing to a paucity of dated samples in crucial areas, and to ambiguities of interpretation in the areas that have been cored.

High-resolution seismic reflection profiles from the middle and outer Beaufort shelf show the Gubik Formation deposits there to be composed mainly of a progradational sequence of offshore-thickening wedge-shaped strata. The wedges are inferred to be dominantly marine because of their lateral persistence and acoustic homogeneity, and because probably correlative deposits cored beneath the inner and outer shelf are dominantly marine. Individual wedges, usually separated by relatively minor disconformities, have been grouped into several composite wedge units bounded by strongly reflective, laterally persistent disconformities. These surfaces are generally quite flat, and are interpreted to record erosion during transgressions following major glacioeustatic sea-level lowstands. Seaward termination depths of the disconformities may record the sea-level minima attained during such events.

The youngest composite wedge deposit on the shelf, unit A, has a basal disconformity that terminates seaward at depths near 110 m below present sea level. A late Wisconsin age proposed for this surface in earlier reports is tentatively revised here to early Wisconsin, based on dates obtained from a borehole on the Canadian outer shelf. Unit A in this revised model would be predominantly middle Wisconsin in age.

Underlying unit A is unit E, which thickens from a few meters locally near shore to more than 60 m beneath some parts of the outer shelf. The basal disconformity of unit E terminates seaward at about 127 m below present sea level. It appears to correlate with the base of the Leffingwell Lagoon unit, a marine deposit that has been cored beneath the inner shelf between Prudhoe Bay and the Canning River. The immediately overlying deposit, the Maguire Islands unit, is also dominantly marine, and its basal disconformity appears to correlate with a surface internal to unit E. A third, very thin, marine deposit, the Cross Island unit, overlies the Maguire Islands unit. Its top, at the sea floor on the inner shelf, probably coincides with the top of unit E.

Two conflicting age interpretations have been presented for the core units, but both are tentative because no samples from the cores have been reliably dated. Micropaleontologic reports have correlated the Leffingwell Lagoon, Maguire Islands, and Cross Island units with the Wainwrightian, Pelukian, and Simpsonian transgressions, respectively, whereas the seismically defined unit

E, which appears to comprise all three units, has been hypothesized to correlate with oxygen isotope stage 5, and so to include no Wainwrightian deposits.

Subsequent to the Simpsonian transgression there was an important erosional event on the Beringian Platform that probably removed Simpsonian and older deposits from the shelf locally to create Harrison and Prudhoe Bays and possibly some others. These bays are floored by 2 to 10 m of Holocene marine deposits that may be underlain in places by thin deposits of one or more earlier transgressions.

Throughout most of Gubik time, much of the North Beringian Platform was tectonically stable because it overlies a largely stable bedrock platform at depth. This stable bedrock is absent beneath the shelf and coastal plain east of the Canning River, and in that area, thrust faults rooted beneath the Brooks Range extend beneath the continental margin. Above those thrusts the entire Cenozoic sedimentary section, including Gubik deposits, has been extensively folded and faulted. The major structural elements are northeast-trending, east-plunging detachment anticlines separated by contemporaneous synformal subbasins. Tear faults and normal faults are common near the west margins of the region underlain by these features, and the terrane is also seismogenic. An earthquake with a magnitude of 5.3 originated at shallow depth beneath the shelf in 1968 (Biswas and Gedney, 1978).

The Gubik Formation bears a wealth of information on the late Cenozoic depositional, paleoclimatic, paleontologic, and sea-level history of the Arctic. The studies summarized here have elucidated some framework aspects of that history, but important elements are still unknown. Future research should concentrate on coring the deposits of the middle and outer shelf, and on more extensive sampling and analysis of key outcrops on the coastal plain.

REFERENCES CITED

Aharon, P., Chappell, J., and Compston, W., 1980, Stable isotope and sea-level data from New Guinea support Antarctic ice-surge theory of ice ages: Nature, v. 283, p. 649–654.

Andrews, J. T., Shilts, W. W., and Miller, G. H., 1983, Multiple deglaciations of the Hudson Bay lowlands, Canada, since deposition of the Missinaibi (last-interglacial?) Formation: Quaternary Research, v. 19, no. 1, p. 18–37.

Berg, T. E., and Black, R. F., 1966, Preliminary measurements of growth of non-sorted polygons, Victoria Land, Antarctica, in Tedrow, J.F.C., ed., Antarctic soils and soil-forming processes: American Geophysical Union Antarctic Research Series, v. 8, p. 61–108.

Berger, A. L., 1978, Long-term variations of caloric insolation resulting from the earth's orbital elements: Quaternary Research, v. 9, p. 139–167.

Biswas, N., and Gedney, L., 1978, Seismotectonic studies of northeast and western Alaska: Fairbanks, University of Alaska Geophysical Institute Administrative Report, 45 p.

Black, R. F., 1951, Eolian deposits of Alaska: Arctic, v. 4, no. 2, p. 89–111.

—— , 1964, Gubik Formation of Quaternary age in northern Alaska: U.S. Geological Survey Professional Paper 302-C, p. 59–91.

—— , 1969, Thaw depression and thaw lakes, a review: Biuletyn Peryglacjalny, v. 18, p. 131–150.

—— , 1976, Periglacial features indicative of permafrost; Ice and soil wedges: Quaternary Research, v. 6, no. 1, p. 3–26.

Black, R. F., and Barksdale, W. L., 1949, Oriented lakes of northern Alaska: Journal of Geology, v. 57, no. 2, p. 105–118.

Black, R. F., and Berg, T. E., 1963, Hydrothermal regimen of patterned ground, Victoria Land, Antarctica: International Association of Scientific Hydrology, Commission of Snow and Ice, Publication no. 61, p. 121–127.

Bloom, A. L., Broecker, W. S., Chappell, J.M.A., Matthews, R. K., and Mesolella, K. J., 1974, Quaternary sea level fluctuations on a tectonic coast; New ^{230}Th/^{234}U dates from the Huon Peninsula, New Guinea: Quaternary Research, v. 4, p. 185.

Brewer, M. C., 1958, The thermal regime of an arctic lake: EOS American Geophysical Union Transactions, v. 39, p. 278–284.

Brigham, J. K., 1984, Marine stratigraphy and amino acid geochronology of the Gubik Formation, western Arctic Coastal Plain, Alaska: U.S. Geological Survey Circular 934, p. 5–9.

—— , 1985, Marine stratigraphy and amino acid geochronology of the Gubik Formation, western Arctic Coastal Plain, Alaska [Ph.D. thesis]: Boulder, University of Colorado, 316 p.

Brigham, J. K., and Miller, G. H., 1983, Paleotemperature estimates of the Alaskan Arctic Coastal Plain during the last 1,250,000 years; Fourth International Conference on Permafrost, Fairbanks, July 18–22, 1983, Proceedings: Washington, D.C., National Academy Press, p. 80–85.

Britton, M. E., 1957, Vegetation of the Arctic tundra, in Hansen, H. P., ed., Arctic biology: Corvallis, Oregon State University, p. 67–130.

Broecker, W. S., 1975, Floating glacial ice caps in the Arctic Ocean: Science, v. 188, p. 1116–1118.

Broecker, W. S., Thurber, D. L., Goddard, J., Ku, T. L., Matthews, R. K., and Mesolella, K. J., 1968, Milankovitch hypothesis supported by precise dating of coral reefs and deep-sea sediments: Science, v. 159, p. 297.

Brouwers, E. M., Marincovich, L., Jr., and Hopkins, D. M., 1984, Paleoenvironmental record of Pleistocene transgressive events preserved at Skull Cliff, northern Alaska: U.S. Geological Survey Circular 934, p. 9–12.

Brown, J., 1965, Radiocarbon dating, Barrow, Alaska: Arctic, v. 18, no. 1, p. 36–48.

Brown, J., Everett, K. R., Webber, P. J., MacLean, S. F., and Murray, D. F., 1980, The coastal tundra at Barrow, in Brown, J., and others, eds., An arctic ecosystem, the coastal tundra at Barrow, Alaska: Stroudsburg, Pennsylvania, Dowden, Hutchinson, and Ross, p. 1–29.

Carson, C. E., 1968, Radiocarbon dating of lacustrine strands in Arctic Alaska: Arctic, v. 21, no. 1, p. 12–26.

Carson, C. E., and Hussey, K. M., 1960, Hydrodynamics in three Arctic lakes: Journal of Geology, v. 68, no. 6, p. 585–600.

—— , 1962, The oriented lakes of Arctic Alaska: Journal of Geology, v. 70, no. 4, p. 417–439.

—— , 1963, The oriented lakes of Arctic Alaska, a reply: Journal of Geology, v. 71, no. 4, p. 532–533.

Carter, L. D., 1981, A Pleistocene sand sea on the Alaskan Arctic Coastal Plain: Science, v. 211, no. 4480, p. 381–383.

—— , 1983a, Cenozoic glacial and glaciomarine deposits of the central North Slope, Alaska, in Thorson, R. M., and Hamilton, T. D., eds., Glaciation in Alaska; Extended abstracts from a workshop: Alaska Quaternary Center, University of Alaska Museum Occasional Paper no. 2, p. 17–21.

—— , 1983b, A Pleistocene sand desert in Arctic Alaska [abs.]: U.S. Geological Survey Circular 911, p. 36.

—— , 1983c, Fossil sand wedges on the Alaskan Arctic Coastal Plain and their paleoenvironmental significance; Fourth International Conference on Permafrost, Fairbanks, July 18–22, 1983, Proceedings: Washington, D.C., National Academy Press, p. 109–114.

Carter, L. D., and Galloway, J. P., 1982, Terraces of the Colville River Delta region, Alaska, *in* Coonrad, W. L., ed., The United States Geological Survey in Alaska; Accomplishments during 1980: U.S. Geological Survey Circular 844, p. 49–51.

——, 1985, Engineering geologic maps of northern Alaska, Harrison Bay Quadrangle: U.S. Geological Survey Open-File Report 85-256, 49 p., scale 1:250,000, 2 sheets.

——, 1986, Engineering-geologic maps of northern Alaska, Umiat Quadrangle: U.S. Geological Survey Open-File Report 86-335, scale 1:250,000, 2 sheets.

Carter, L. D., and Robinson, S. W., 1981, Minimum age of beach deposits north of Teshekpuk Lake, Arctic Coastal Plain, *in* Albert, N.R.D., and Hudson, T., eds., The United States Geological Survey in Alaska; Accomplishments during 1979: U.S. Geological Survey Circular 823-B, p. B8–B9.

Carter, L. D., Marincovich, L., Jr., Brouwers, E. M., and Forester, R. M., 1979, Paleogeography of a Pleistocene coastline, Alaskan Arctic Coastal Plain, *in* Blean, K. M., and Williams, J. R., eds., The United States Geological Survey in Alaska; Accomplishments during 1978: U.S. Geological Survey Circular 804–B, p. B39–B41.

Carter, L. D., Forester, R. M., and Nelson, R. E., 1984, Mid Wisconsin through early Holocene changes in seasonal climate in northern Alaska: American Quaternary Association Eighth Biennial Meeting, Program with Abstracts, 13–15 August, 1984, p. 20–22.

Carter, L. D., O'Neil, J. R., and Stipp, J. J., 1985, High sea level along the Alaskan arctic coast about 70 or 80 ka; Evidence for an Antarctic icesurge?: Arctic Land-Sea Interactions, 14th Arctic Workshop, November 6–8, 1985, p. 22–24.

Carter, L. D., Brigham-Grette, J., and Hopkins, D. M., 1986a, Late Cenozoic marine transgressions of the Alaskan Arctic Coastal Plain, *in* Heginbottom, J. A., and Vincent, J. S., eds., Correlation of Quaternary deposits and events around the margin of the Beaufort Sea; Contributions from a joint Canadian-American workshop, April, 1984: Geological Survey of Canada Open-File Report 1237, p. 21–26.

Carter, L. D., Brigham-Grette, J., Marincovich, L, Jr., Pease, V. L., and Hillhouse, J. W., 1986b, Late Cenozoic Arctic Ocean sea ice and terrestrial paleoclimate: Geology, v. 14, p. 675–678.

Carter, L. D., Ferrians, O. J., Jr., and Galloway, J. P., 1986c, Engineering-geologic maps of northern Alaska coastal plain and foothills of the Arctic National Wildlife Refuge: U.S. Geological Survey Open-File Report 86-334, scale 1:250,000, 2 sheets.

Chamberlain, E. J., 1979, Overconsolidated sediments in the Beaufort Sea: The Northern Engineer, v. 10, no. 3, p. 24–29.

Chamberlain, E. J., and Gow, A. J., 1979, Effect of freezing and thawing on the permeability and structure of soils: Engineering Geology, v. 13, nos. 1–4, p. 73–92.

Chamberlain, E. J., Sellmann, P. V., Blouin, S. E., Hopkins, D. M., and Lewellen, R. I., 1978, Engineering properties of subsea permafrost in the Prudhoe Bay region of the Beaufort Sea: Third International Conference on Permafrost, Edmonton, Alberta, Canada, July, 1978, Proceedings, p. 629–635.

Chappell, J., 1974, Geology of coral terraces, Huon Peninsula, New Guinea; A study of Quaternary movements and sea-level changes: Geological Society of America Bulletin, v. 84, p. 553–570.

Chappell, J., and Shackleton, N. J., 1986, Oxygen isotopes and sea level: Nature, v. 324, p. 137–140.

Clark, D. L., 1982, Origin, nature, and world climate effect of Arctic Ocean ice cover: Nature, v. 300, p. 321–325.

Coulter, H. W., Hussey, K. M., and O'Sullivan, J. B., 1960, Radiocarbon dates relating to the Gubik Formation, northern Alaska: U.S. Geological Survey Professional Paper 400-B, p. B350–351.

Craig, J. D., and Thrasher, G. P., 1982, Environmental geology of Harrison Bay, northern Alaska: U.S. Geological Survey Open-File Report 82-85, 25 p.

Cronin, T. M., 1983, Rapid sea level and climate changes; Evidence from continental and island margins: Quaternary Science Review, v. 1, p. 177–214.

Cronin, T. M., Szabo, B. J., Ager, T. A., Hazel, J. E., and Owens, J. P., 1981, Quaternary climates and sea levels of the U.S. Atlantic Coastal Plain: Science, v. 211, p. 233–240.

Cronin, T. M., Ager, T. A., Szabo, B. J., Rosholt, J., and Shaw, E. G., 1984, Cold climates-high sea level; Interglacial deposits of the North Carolina Coastal Plain: American Quaternary Association Eighth Biennial Meeting, Program and Abstracts, 13–15 August, 1984, p. 28.

Damuth, J. E., 1975, Echo character of the western equatorial Atlantic floor and its relationship to the dispersal and distribution of terrigenous sediments: Marine Geology, v. 18, p. 17–45.

Davies, O., 1981, A review of Wilson's theory that the Last Interglacial ended with an ice-surge, and the South African evidence therefore: Annals of the Natal Museum, v. 24, p. 701–720.

Denton, G. H., and Hughes, T. J., 1983, Milankovitch theory of ice ages; Hypothesis of ice-sheet linkage between regional insolation and global climate: Quaternary Research, v. 20, no. 2, p. 125–144.

Dinter, D. A., 1982, Holocene marine sediments on the middle and outer continental shelf of the Beaufort Sea north of Alaska: U.S. Geological Survey Map I–1182–B, 5 p., 1 fig., 2 map sheets.

——, 1985, Quaternary sedimentation of the Alaskan Beaufort shelf; Influence of regional tectonics, fluctuating sea levels, and glacial sediment sources: Tectonophysics, v. 114, p. 133–161.

Fairbanks, R. G., and Matthews, R. K., 1978, The marine oxygen isotope record in Pleistocene coral, Barbados, West Indies: Quaternary Research, v. 10, p. 181–196.

Fillon, R. H., and Williams, D. F., 1983, Glacial evolution of the Plio-Pleistocene; Role of continental and Arctic Ocean ice sheets: Palaeogeography, Palaeoclimatology, Palaeoecology, v. 42, p. 7–33.

Giterman, R. E., Sher, A. V., and Matthews, J. V., Jr., 1982, Comparison of the development of steppe-tundra environments in west and east Beringia; Pollen and macrofossil evidence from key sections, *in* Hopkins, D. M., Matthews, J. V., Jr., Schweger, C. E., and Young, J. P., eds., Paleoecology of Beringia: New York, Academic Press, p. 43–76.

Gladenkov, Y. B., 1981, Marine Plio-Pleistocene of Iceland and problem of its correlation: Quaternary Research, v. 15, no. 1, p. 18–23.

Grantz, A., and May, S. D., 1983, Geologic framework and petroleum potential of the United States Chukchi shelf north of Point Hope, Alaska: American Association of Petroleum Geologists Bulletin, v. 67, p. 474.

Grantz, A., Dinter, D. A., Hill, E. R., May, S. D., McMullin, R. H., Phillips, R. L., and Reimnitz, E., 1982, Geologic framework, hydrocarbon potential, and environmental conditions for exploration and development of proposed oil and gas lease sale 87 in the Beaufort and northeast Chukchi Seas; A summary report: U.S. Geological Survey Open-file Report 82–482, 73 p.

Grantz, A., Dinter, D. A., and Biswas, N. N., 1983, Map cross-sections and chart showing Late Quaternary faults, folds, and earthquakes epicenters on the Alaskan Beaufort shelf: U.S. Geological Survey Miscellaneous Investigations Series Map I–1182C, scale 1:500,000, 3 sheets.

Grantz, A., Dinter, D. A., and Culotta, R., 1987, Structure of the continental shelf north of the Arctic National Wildlife Refuge, *in* Bird, L. J., and Magoon, L. B., eds., Petroleum geology of the northern part of the Arctic National Wildlife Refuge, northeastern Alaska: U.S. Geological Survey Bulletin 1778, p. 271–276.

Hamilton, T. D., 1981, Multiple moisture sources in the Brooks Range glacial record; Tenth Annual Arctic Workshop, March 12–14, 1981, Proceedings: Boulder, University of Colorado, Institute of Arctic and Alpine Research, p. 16–18.

——, 1986, Late Cenozoic glaciation of the central Brooks Range, *in* Hamilton, T. D., Reed, K. M., and Thorson, R. M., eds., Glaciation in Alaska; The geologic record: Anchorage, Alaska Geological Society, p. 9–50.

Hodgson, D. A., 1982, Surficial materials and geomorphological processes, Western Sverdrup and adjacent islands, District of Franklin: Geological Survey of Canada Paper 81-9, 37 p.

Hopkins, D. M., 1967, Quaternary marine transgressions in Alaska, *in* Hopkins, D. M., ed., the Bering Land Bridge: Stanford, California, Stanford University Press, p. 47–90.

——, 1972, The paleogeography and climatic history of Beringia during late Cenozoic time: Inter-Nord, v. 12, p. 121–150.

——, 1982a, Abortive glaciations at high latitudes indicated by glaciomarine deposits, Gubik Formation, northern Alaska: Geological Society of America Abstracts with Programs, v. 14, no. 7, p. 518.

——, 1982b, Aspects of the paleogeography of Beringia during the late Pleistocene, in Hopkins, D. M., Matthews, J. V., Jr., Schweger, C. E., and Young, S. B., eds., Paleoecology of Beringia: New York, Academic Press, p. 3–28.

Hopkins, D. M., and Hartz, R. W., 1978, Coastal morphology, coastal erosion, and barrier island of the Beaufort Sea, Alaska: U.S. Geological Survey Open-File Report 78–1063, 54 p.

Hopkins, D. M., and Robinson, S. W., 1979, Radiocarbon dates from the Beaufort and Chukchi Sea coasts, in Blean, K. M., and Williams, J. R., eds., The United States Geological Survey in Alaska; Accomplishments during 1978: U.S. Geological Survey Circular 804-B, B44–B47.

Hopkins, D. M., McDougall, K., and Brouwers, E., 1981a, Microfossil studies of Pelukian and Flaxman deposits, Alaska coast of the Beaufort Sea, in Smith, P. A., Hartz, R. W., and Hopkins, D. M., Offshore permafrost studies and shoreline history as an aid to predicting offshore permafrost conditions: U.S. National Oceanic and Atmospheric Administration, Environmental Assessment of the Alaskan Continental Shelf, Annual Report, Task D-9, Research Unit 204 and 473, April 1979 to March 1980, Appendix G, p. 64–71.

Hopkins, D. M., Robinson, S. W., and Buckley, J., 1981b, Radiocarbon dates from the Beaufort and Chukchi Sea coasts (1979–1980), in NOAA, Environmental Assessment of the Alaskan Continental Shelf, Annual Reports, Principal Investigators, IV (Hazards), p. 203–220.

Hussey, K. M., and Michelson, R. W., 1966, Tundra relief features near Point Barrow, Alaska: Arctic, v. 19, p. 162–184.

Lachenbruch, A. H., 1962, Mechanics of thermal contraction cracks and ice-wedge polygons in permafrost: Geological Society of America Special Paper 70, 69 p.

Leffingwell, E. de K., 1915, Ground-ice wedges; The dominant form of ground ice on the north coast of Alaska: Journal of Geology, v. 23, p. 635–654.

——, 1919, The Canning River region, northern Alaska: U.S. Geological Survey Professional Paper 109, 251 p.

Lewellen, R. I., 1972, Studies on the fluvial environment, Arctic Coastal Plain Province, northern Alaska: Littleton, Colorado (published privately), 2 v., 282 p.

Livingston, D. A., Bryan, K., Jr., and Leahy, R. G., 1958, Effects of an arctic environment on the origin and development of freshwater lakes: Limnology and Oceanography, v. 3, p. 194–214.

MacCarthy, G. R., 1958, Glacial boulders on the Arctic coast of Alaska: Arctic, v. 11, p. 70–85.

McCulloch, D. S., 1967, Quaternary geology of the Alaskan shore of Chukchi Sea, in Hopkins, D. M., ed., The Bering Land Bridge: Stanford, California, Stanford University Press, p. 91–120.

McDougall, K., Brouwers, E., and Smith, P. A., 1986, Micropaleontology and sedimentology of the PB Borehole series, Prudhoe Bay, Alaska: U.S. Geological Survey Bulletin 1598, 62 p.

Mix, A. C., and Ruddiman, W. F., 1984, Oxygen-isotope analyses and Pleistocene ice volumes: Quaternary Research, v. 21, p. 1–20.

Morris, R. H., 1957, Reconnaissance study of the Marsh anticline, northern Alaska: U.S. Geological Survey Open-File Report, OF57-76, 6 p.

Morrissey, L. A., 1979, Succession of plant communities in response to thaw-lake activity on the Arctic Coastal Plain, Alaska [M.S. thesis]: San Jose, California, Sn Jose State University, Department of Geography, 71 p.

Mowatt, T. C., and Naidu, A. S., 1974, Gravels from the Alaska continental shelf, Beaufort Sea, Arctic Ocean; Petrologic character and implications for sediment source and transport: Alaska Division of Geological and Geophysical Surveys Open-File Report 43, 70 p.

Nelson, R. E., 1981, Paleoenvironments during deposition of a section of the Gubik Formation exposed along the lower Colville River, North Slope, in Albert, N.R.D., and Hudson, T., eds., The United States Geological Survey in Alaska; Accomplishments during 1979: U.S. Geological Survey Circular 823-B, p. B9–B11.

——, 1982, Late Quaternary environments of the western Arctic Slope of Alaska [Ph.D. thesis]: Seattle, University of Washington, 146 p.

Nelson, R. E., and Carter, L. D., 1985, Pollen analysis of a part of the Gubik Formation, Arctic Coastal Plain, Alaska: Quaternary Research, v. 24, p. 295–306.

O'Sullivan, J. B., 1961, Quaternary geology of the Arctic Coastal Plain, northern Alaska [Ph.D. thesis]: Ames, Iowa State University of Science and Technology, 191 p.

O'Sullivan, J. B., and Hussey, K. M., 1960, Noneolian origin for silts of the Arctic Slope, Alaska [abs.]: Geological Society of America Bulletin, v. 71, no. 12, pt. 2, p. 1940.

Péwé, T. L., 1959, Sand-wedge polygons (tesselations) in the McMurdo Sound Region, Antarctica; A progress report: American Journal of Science, v. 257, p. 545–552.

Rawlinson, S. E., 1986, Late Cenozoic geology of the Arctic Coastal Plain between the Colville and Canning Rivers, in Heginbottom, J. A., and Vincent, J. S., eds., Correlation of Quaternary deposits and events around the margin of the Beaufort Sea; Contributions from a joint Canadian-American workshop, April 1984: Geological Survey of Canada Open-file Report 1237, p. 30–33.

Reimnitz, E., Kempema, E., Ross, R., and Minkler, P., 1980, Overconsolidated surficial deposits on the Beaufort Sea Shelf: U.S. Geological Survey Open-File Report 80–2010, 37 p.

Reiser, H. N., Brosgé, W. P., Dutro, J. T., Jr., and Detterman, R. L., 1971, Preliminary geologic map, Mt. Michelson quadrangle, Alaska: U.S. Geological Survey Open-file Report 71–0237, scale 1:200,000, 2 sheets.

Repenning, C. A., 1983, New evidence for the age of the Gubik Formation, Alaskan North Slope: Quaternary Research, v. 19, no. 3, p. 356–372.

Repenning, C. A., Brouwers, E. M., Carter, L. D., Marincovich, L., Jr., and Ager, T. A., 1987, The Beringian ancestry of Phenacomys (Rodentia; Cricetidae) and the beginning of the modern Arctic Ocean borderland biota: U.S. Geological Survey Bulletin 1687, 31 p.

Rodeick, C. A., 1975, The origin, distribution, and depositional history of gravel deposits on the Beaufort Sea continental shelf, Alaska [M.S. thesis]: California, San Jose State University, 87 p.

——, 1979, The origin, distribution, and depositional history of gravel deposits on the Beaufort Sea continental shelf, Alaska: U.S. Geological Survey Open-file Report 79–234, 87 p.

Ruddiman, W. F., and McIntyre, A., 1979, Warmth of the subpolar North Atlantic Ocean during northern hemisphere ice-sheet growth: Science, v. 204, p. 173–175.

Schneider, K. B., and Faro, J. B., 1975, Effects of sea ice on sea otters: Journal of Mammology, v. 56, no. 1, p. 91–101.

Sellmann, P. V., and Brown, J., 1973, Stratigraphy and diagenesis of perennially frozen sediments in the Barrow, Alaska, region, in International Conference on Permafrost, 2nd, North American Contribution, Yakutsk, U.S.S.R.: National Academy of Sciences, p. 171–181.

Sellmann, P. V., and Chamberlain, E. J., 1979, Permafrost beneath the Beaufort Sea; Near Prudhoe Bay, Alaska: 11th Annual Offshore Technology Conference, Houston, Texas, April 1979, Proceedings, Paper OTC 3527, p. 1481–1493.

Sellmann, P. V., Brown, J., Lewellen, R. I., McKim, H., and Merry, C., 1975, The classification and geomorphic implications of thaw lakes on the Arctic Coastal Plain, Alaska: U.S. Army Cold Regions Research and Engineering Laboratory Research Report 344, 21 p.

Shackleton, N. J., 1987, Oxygen isotopes, ice volume, and sea level: Quaternary Science Reviews, v. 6, p. 183–190.

Shackleton, N. J., and Opdyke, N. D., 1973, Oxygen isotope and paleomagnetic stratigraphy of equatorial Pacific core V28-238; Oxygen isotope temperature and ice volumes on a 10^5 and 10^6 year scale: Quaternary Research, v. 3, p. 39–55.

——, 1977, Oxygen isotope and palaeomagnetic evidence for early Northern Hemisphere glaciation: Nature, v. 270, p. 216–219.

Shackleton, N. J., and 16 others, 1984, Oxygen isotope calibration of the onset of ice-rafting and history of glaciation in the North Atlantic region: Nature,

v. 307, p. 620–623.

Sher, A. V., and others, 1979, Late Cenozoic of the Kolyma lowland, Pacific Science Congress, 14th, Tour Guide 11: Moscow, USSR, Academy of Sciences, 115 p.

Smith, P. A., 1985a, Late Quaternary geology of the Beaufort Sea inner shelf near Prudhoe Bay, *in* Bartsch-Winkler, S., and Reed, K. M., eds., The United States Geological Survey in Alaska; Accomplishments during 1983: U.S. Geological Survey Circular 945, p. 100–103.

—— , 1985b, Late Cenozoic stratigraphy of the Beaufort Sea inner shelf near Prudhoe Bay, Alaska; Abstracts of the 14th Arctic Workshop, Arctic Land-Sea Interaction, November, 1985: Dartmouth, Nova Scotia, Bedford Institute of Oceanography, p. 25–28.

Williams, J. R., 1979, Stratigraphy of the Gubik Formation at Skull Cliff, northern Alaska, *in* Johnson, K. M., and Williams, J. R., eds., The United States Geological Survey in Alaska; Accomplishments during 1978: U.S. Geological Survey Circular 804–B, p. 31–33.

—— , 1983a, Engineering-geologic maps of northern Alaska, Meade River Quadrangle: U.S. Geological Survey Open-File Report 83–294, 29 p., scale 1:250,000.

—— , 1983b, Engineering-geologic maps of northern Alaska, Wainwright Quadrangle: U.S. Geological Survey Open-File Report 83–457, 28 p., scale 1:250,000.

Williams, J. R., and Yeend, W. E., 1979, Deep thaw lake basins of the inner Arctic Coastal Plain, Alaska, *in* Johnson, K. M., and Williams, J. R., eds., The United States Geological Survey in Alaska; Accomplishments during 1978: U.S. Geological Survey Circular 804–B, p. B35–B37.

Williams, J. R., Yeend, W., Carter, L. D., and Hamilton, T. D., 1977, Preliminary surficial deposits map of National Petroleum Reserve—Alaska: U.S. Geological Survey Open-File Report 77–868, scale 1:500,000, 2 sheets.

Wolf, S. C., Reimnitz, E., and Barnes, P. W., 1985a, Pleistocene and Holocene seismic stratigraphy between the Canning River and Prudhoe Bay, Beaufort Sea, Alaska: U.S. Geological Survey Open-File Report 85–549, 50 p.

—— , 1985b, Seismic stratigraphy of late Quaternary inner-shelf from Prudhoe Bay to Demarcation Point, Alaska; Abstracts of the 14th Arctic Workshop, Arctic Land-Sea Interaction, November 1985: Dartmouth, Nova Scotia, Bedford Institute of Oceanography, p. 33–36.

Wolfe, J. A., 1985, Distribution of major vegetational types during the Tertiary, *in* Sondquist, E. T., and Broecker, W. A., eds., The carbon cycle and atmospheric CO_2; Natural variations, Archean to present: American Geophysical Union Monograph 32, p. 357–375.

MANUSCRIPT ACCEPTED BY THE SOCIETY JANUARY 8, 1988

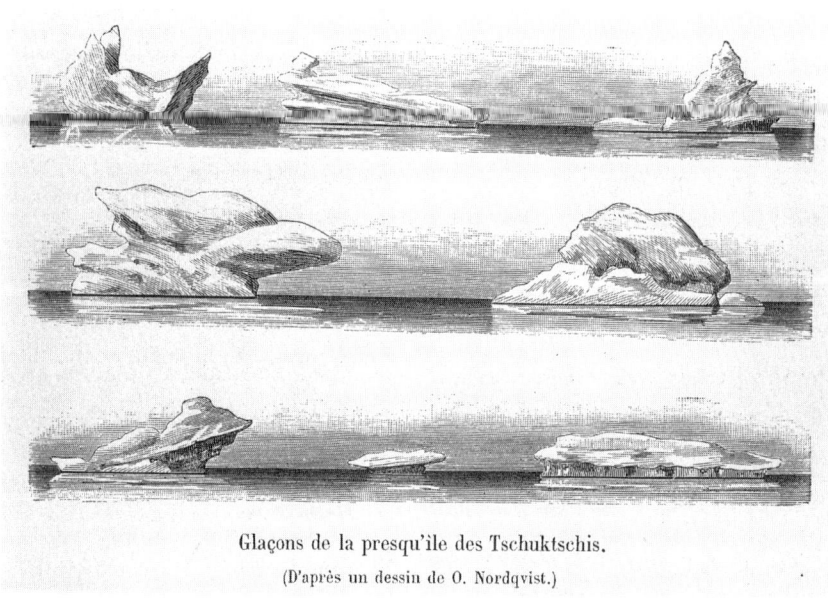

Glaçons de la presqu'île des Tschuktschis.
(D'après un dessin de O. Nordqvist.)

From A. E. Nordenskjold, 1885, Voyage de la *Vega* Autour de l'Asie et de l'Europe [1878–1879], (translated from Swedish by Charles Rabot and Charles Lallemond), Vol. 1: Paris, Libraire Hachette et cie, p. 407.

Chapter 26

The late Neogene and Quaternary stratigraphy of the Canadian Beaufort continental shelf

S. M. Blasco
Geological Survey of Canada, P.O. Box 1006, Dartmouth, Nova Scotia B2Y 4A2, Canada
G. Fortin
H. R. Seismic Interpretation Services, Ltd., 66 Lanctot St., Hull, Quebec J8Y 1B6, Canada
P. R. Hill
Hill Geoscience Research, Ltd., 70 Neptune Ct, Suite 220 Dartmouth, Nova Scotia B2Y 4M9, Canada
M. J. O'Connor
M. J. O'Connor and Associates, Ltd., 201, 1144 - 29 Ave., N.E., Calgary, Alberta T2E 7P1, Canada
J. Brigham-Grette
Department of Geology and Geography, University of Massachusetts, Amherst, Massachusetts 01003

INTRODUCTION

This compilation of the late Neogene and Quaternary geology of the Canadian Beaufort continental shelf is the result of a nine-year cooperative effort between the Geological Survey of Canada and the Canadian Beaufort Sea oil industry. At depths beyond 100 m below seabed the deeper, more generalized stratigraphy is based on the interpretation of the first two seconds of conventional deep multichannel seismic reflection data (on an approximately 5-km grid) correlated with the shallow sections of several exploration wells (Fortin, 1990). The detailed surficial geology of the upper 100 m of sediment below seabed is based on the interpretation of some 15,000 line km of high-resolution, analogue, and shallow digital multichannel seismic reflection data, including boomer, small airgun, airgun array, and Flexichoc sources (Hunter and Blasco, 1980; Quinn and others, 1987). These shallow profiles were correlated with sedimentological, chronological, biostratigraphic and geotechnical analyses of more than 300 sediment cores recovered from the sea floor across the shelf using conventional gravity, piston, and wireline sampling techniques (Le Tirant, 1979). Sampling procedures included both continuous and interval coring, and sampled depths varied from less than 1 m to more than 100 m below seabed. Limited shallow-borehole well-log information, including velocity, density, and resistivity measurements, were also incorporated (Stirbys, 1990).

Physiography

The Canadian Beaufort continental shelf (Fig. 1) covers an area of 50,000 km^2 and stretches some 500 km from the United States border at 141°W to the entrance of Amundsen Gulf at 128°W. In general, the shelf forms a shallow, uniformly low-gradient, low-relief, flat, broad plain between 68°N and 71.5°N. The shelf break occurs between the 60- and 100-m isobaths. The area is divided into three distinct physiographic regions: the narrow western shelf adjacent to the U.S. border, the Mackenzie Trough, and the broad eastern shelf. The narrow western shelf is less than 60 km wide by 80 km long and slopes seaward with gradients of less than 0.05 degrees (0.08 percent). The adjacent Mackenzie Trough, a major, partially infilled, linear, northwest-trending depression, is approximately 80 km wide by 150 km long. Relative to adjacent areas, the central trough has a bathymetric relief of 100 m, and seaward-dipping gradients in excess of 1.5 degrees (0.24 percent). East of the trough, the broad, shallow eastern shelf is 350 km in length, up to 150 km wide, and slopes evenly seaward with an average gradient of 0.03 degrees (0.06 percent). The smooth relief of this part of the shelf is interrupted by cross-shelf, north trending, partially infilled to infilled linear troughs (such as the Ikit and Kugmallit Troughs). At the shelf break, gradients increase to more than 2 to 6 degrees (3 to 10 percent) as the shelf slopes northwad into the Canada Basin and eastward into Amundsen Gulf.

BACKGROUND

Based on the correlation of deep seismic reflection sections with sedimentological and biostratigraphic analyses of cuttings, including the interpretation of geophysical logs from several ex-

---

Blasco, S. M., Fortin, G., Hill, P. R., O'Connor, M. J., and Brigham-Grette, J., 1990, The late Neogene and Quaternary stratigraphy of the Canadian Beaufort continental shelf, *in* Grantz, A., Johnson, L., and Sweeney, J. F., eds., The Arctic Ocean region: Boulder, Colorado, Geological Society of America, The Geology of North America, v. L.

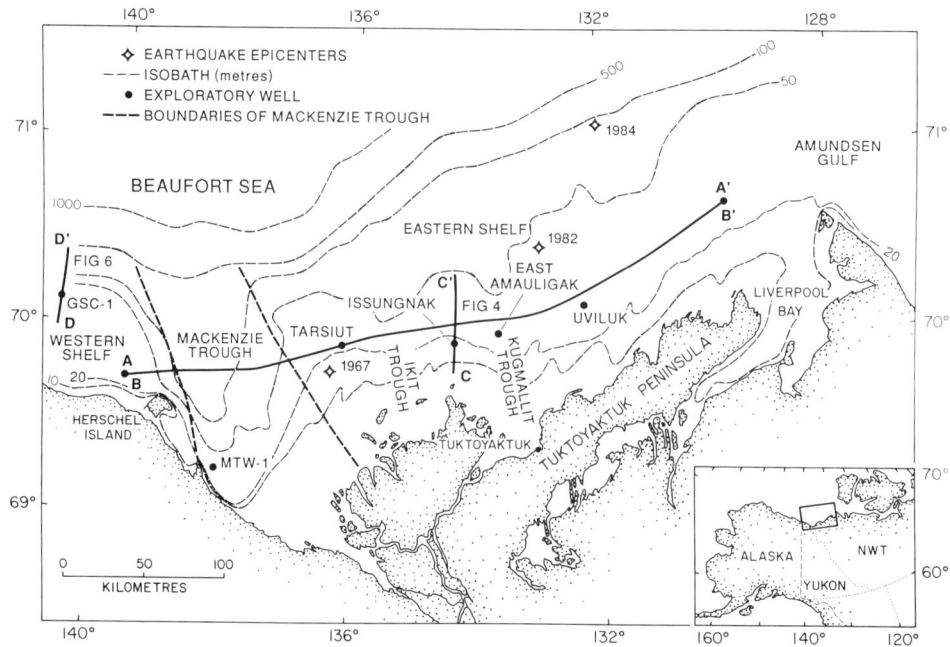

Figure 1. Canadian Beaufort Sea continental shelf showing earthquake epicenters, selected exploratory wells, and locations of Figures 3 to 6. Dashed lines show the boundary of Mackenzie Trough.

ploration wells drilled on the central shelf, Dixon and others (1984), McNeil and others (1982), Jones and others (1980), and Dixon and Snowdon (1979) established a broad stratigraphic framework for the late Neogene to Quaternary succession. However, only limited cuttings and well-log data have been recovered from the upper few hundred meters of exploration wells. Deep multichannel seismic data lack resolution in the same near-surface zone. As a result, the nature of the shallow Quaternary strata remains poorly defined. In addition, the highly terrigenous nature of sedimentation and the monotony of microfauna and flora through the late Neogene and Quaternary makes the chronological subdivision of this succession ambiguous at present.

By integrating the useful deeper exploratory-well data and deep reflection seismic profiles with high-resolution shallow seismic and borehole data acquired for regional, engineering, and site survey evaluations, Fortin (1990) attempted to more clearly define the late Neogene and Quaternary stratigraphy of the shelf.

Previous work on the surficial seabed geology (less than 100 m below sea floor) of the Canadian Beaufort continental shelf has been mostly limited to papers and publications on specific aspects of the shelf geology. O'Connor (1980), described a seismostratigraphic model for the upper 100 m of sediment for the central eastern shelf, and Hill and others (1985) developed a sea-level curve for these same sediments over the past 27,000 years. Shearer (1971) discussed the stratigraphic nature and origin of the Mackenzie Canyon (now Trough). Pelletier (1975, 1980, 1984, 1987) described the shallow stratigraphy, surface sediment distribution and seabed geomorphology. The depositional environments of Holocene sediments are described by Vilks and others (1979). Research is continuing on the surficial geology of the western shelf (J. Brigham-Grette and others, written communication, 1989), Mackenzie Trough (Blasco and others, 1989), and the eastern shelf (P. R. Hill and others, written communication, 1989).

Stratigraphic and Structural Setting

Geographically, the present Beaufort continental shelf occupies the central portion of the late Mesozoic to Cenozoic Beaufort-Mackenzie structural basin. This basin was initiated as a major sedimentary depocenter by tectonic events related to the opening or foundering of the Canada Basin between 130 and 80 Ma (Sweeney, 1985; Grantz and others, 1979, this volume). Upper Cretaceous to Holocene clastics were deposited as thick, offlapping prograding deltaic sequences of sandstone and mudstone, on a rapidly subsiding basement of faulted early Mesozoic and Paleozoic rocks (Willumsen and Cote, 1982; Hea and others, 1980; Young and others, 1976). Syndepositional listric faulting and shale diapirism of underconsolidated sediments occurred. Subsidence and eustatic changes in sea level resulted in the deposition of several major deltaic to marine wedges, of which the Pliocene-Pleistocene Iperk and overlying Shallow Bay Sequences are the most recent (Dixon and Dietrich, this volume; Dietrich and others, 1985; Dixon and others, 1984). This late Mesozoic and Cenozoic deltaic succession reaches a maximum thickness of 12,000 m north of the present Mackenzie Delta (Dixon and Dietrich, this volume).

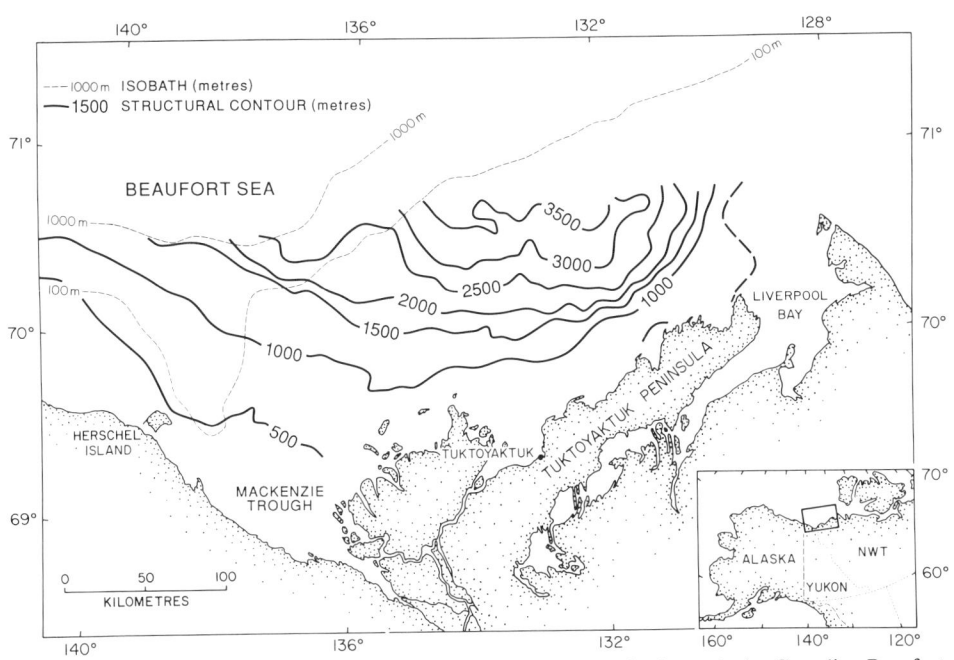

Figure 2. Structural contour map of the late Miocene unconformity beneath the Canadian Beaufort Shelf.

POST–LATE MIOCENE TO LATE PLEISTOCENE STRATIGRAPHY

Sediments of the Tertiary deltaic sequences of the Beaufort-Mackenzie Basin (Akpak and Mackenzie Bay) and older strata were significantly eroded during a period of uplift and/or eustatic lowering of sea level during the late Miocene (Dixon and Dietrich, this volume; Dixon and others 1984; McNeil and others, 1982; Bujak and Davies, 1981). Strata and structural features are truncated at a well-defined angular unconformity to disconformity, which marks the last major tectonic disruption of the Beaufort-Mackenzie Basin. Overlying sediments of the Iperk and Shallow Bay Sequences are largely undeformed (Fortin, 1990; Dietrich and others, 1985). Post-Neogene strata appear to form a largely continuous succession. No major unconformities are evident, although significant disconformities must exist where the sequence pinches out at the basin margins. The late Miocene unconformity appears as a high-amplitude event on shallow and deep multichannel seismic reflection profiles and has been regionally mapped across the shelf (Fig. 2) by Fortin (1990). In excess of 3,500 m of post–late Miocene sediments have been deposited on the shelf at the present depocenter of the Beaufort-Mackenzie Basin, located northeast of the Kugmallit Trough (Fig. 1). An east-west cross section of the shelf, in water depths of approximately 30 to 50 m (Fig. 3), illustrates the smooth, well-defined nature of this erosional unconformity and bowl-shaped character of the basin. In the plane of this section, more than 3,000 m of infill has occurred. The late Neogene and Quaternary succession above the unconformity thins significantly to less than 200 m at the Canada–U.S. border to the west and toward the Amundsen Gulf to the east. This sediment infill constitutes the seismostratigraphic Iperk and Shallow Bay Sequences of the Beaufort-Mackenzie Basin.

The Iperk Sequence, as defined by Dietrich and others (1985) is Pliocene (latest Miocene?) to Pleistocene in age. From base to top, the sequence consists of a prograded succession of deep-water basinal mudstones that grade upward into slope and outer- to mid-shelf fine-grained sediments. These sediments, in turn, grade upward and landward into Pleistocene outer- to inner-shelf interbedded clays, silts, and sands and non-marine alluvium (Dixon and others, 1984; McNeil and others, 1982; Jones and others, 1980; Dixon and Snowdon, 1979). The type section for the Iperk is described by Jones and others (1980). Fortin (1990), Sykora (1984), Willumsen and Cote (1982), and others refer to the Iperk as deltaic. Fortin (1990; Fig. 3) subdivides the Iperk into a Lower Iperk Sequence that prograded from a southeasterly direction, and an unconformable overlying Upper Iperk Sequence that prograded from a more southerly direction. The Lower Iperk Sequence consists of a wedge of basin infill sediments up to 1,600 m thick deposited on the late Miocene unconformity in the eastern and central area of the Beaufort-Mackenzie Basin. A progradational succession of four seismic facies has been identified within the Lower and Upper Iperk. Basal turbidite fills are overlain by basinal strata that grade upward and shoreward into a slope facies and overlying delta and shelf deposits. A major shift in sediment source area to the south resulted in deposition of the Upper Iperk Sequence over the Lower Iperk in the central and eastern basin, and directly upon the late Miocene unconformity in the western Beaufort (Fig. 3). A similar progradational to aggradational Upper Iperk succession of turbiditic, basinal, slope, and deltaic sediments more than 3,500 m thick (Fortin, 1990) infilled the Beaufort-Mackenzie Basin during the late Neogene and Quaternary. Delta-front and delta-plain sediments occur within the Pleistocene section of the Upper Iperk Sequence (Fig. 3; Fortin, 1990).

The Pliocene-Pleistocene boundary remains poorly defined in the Beaufort-Mackenzie Basin due to the lack of geochronologic or paleomagnetic data. Assuming the average sedimentation rate to be constant for the Neogene through Holocene sequence, an inferred 1.8-Ma Pliocene-Pleistocene boundary has been plotted on the east-west schematic cross section of Figure 3. There is a significant faunal change at this horizon, characterized by an upward increase in abundance of *Elphidium excavatum* (Dixon and others, 1984; McNeil and others, 1982). This change may reflect a major cooling of the Beaufort Sea at the Pliocene-Pleistocene boundary, and is tentatively used as a marker for this boundary. On this basis, an estimated total thickness of Quaternary sediments of 1,000 m may exist (Fortin, 1990). These strata thin to less than 100 m onshore and at the basin margins to the east and west. The sequence thickens to the basin center but thins again beneath the present shelf edge/slope and toward the Canada Basin.

Seismically, the younger Pleistocene section of the Upper Iperk Sequence consists predominantly of closely spaced, flat-lying, parallel, laterally discontinuous, moderate- to low-amplitude reflections typical of topset beds. Multiples and poor resolution mask more subtle elements of the seismic stratigraphy. Toward the shelf edge these reflections diverge into prograding shelf-edge clinoforms (Fortin, 1990; Dixon and others, 1984). Lithologically, the Pleistocene section consists of interbedded, poorly consolidated thin muds and thick sands, including some gravel layers. Even near the present shelf edge, sand units make up slightly more than 50 percent of the flat-lying strata to depths of 863 m (Dixon and Snowdon, 1979). Throughout the Pleistocene section, there is an alternation of sequences dominated by the *Elphidium excavatum* microfauna and sequences containing freshwater algae with lacustrine ostracods in a predominantly mixed, reworked matrix (Dixon and others, 1984; McNeil and others, 1982). These alternations may indicate oscillating delta-front to delta-plain (inner shelf to non-marine) conditions for the Upper Iperk Sequence.

Paleoenvironmentally, the Pleistocene sediment section of the Upper Iperk Sequence appears to be dominated by shallow water, low- to high-energy inner-shelf to non-marine delta plain conditions. During low or rising sea-level intervals, glacial melt-waters discharged sediments across broad, exposed, coastal outwash plains as far northward as the present shelf edge. During interglacial high sea-level stands, transgressive marine to brackish marine conditions predominated, with the associated deposition of thin, fine-grained sediments. Deposits representing glacial/interglacial cycles accumulated in the Beaufort-Mackenzie Basin throughout the Pleistocene (and possibly late Pliocene).

The Iperk Sequence is unconformably to conformably overlain by the Shallow Bay Sequence. This surficial sequence, as defined by Dietrich and others (1985), includes Holocene fine-grained marine sediments deposited on the shelf as a result of the last (late Wisconsinan) transgression.

NEOTECTONICS

The period of erosion associated with the late Miocene unconformity was followed by renewed subsidence of the Beaufort-Mackenzie Basin. The succession of overlying strata, from turbidite to basinal, slope and shelf/delta plain deposits, which

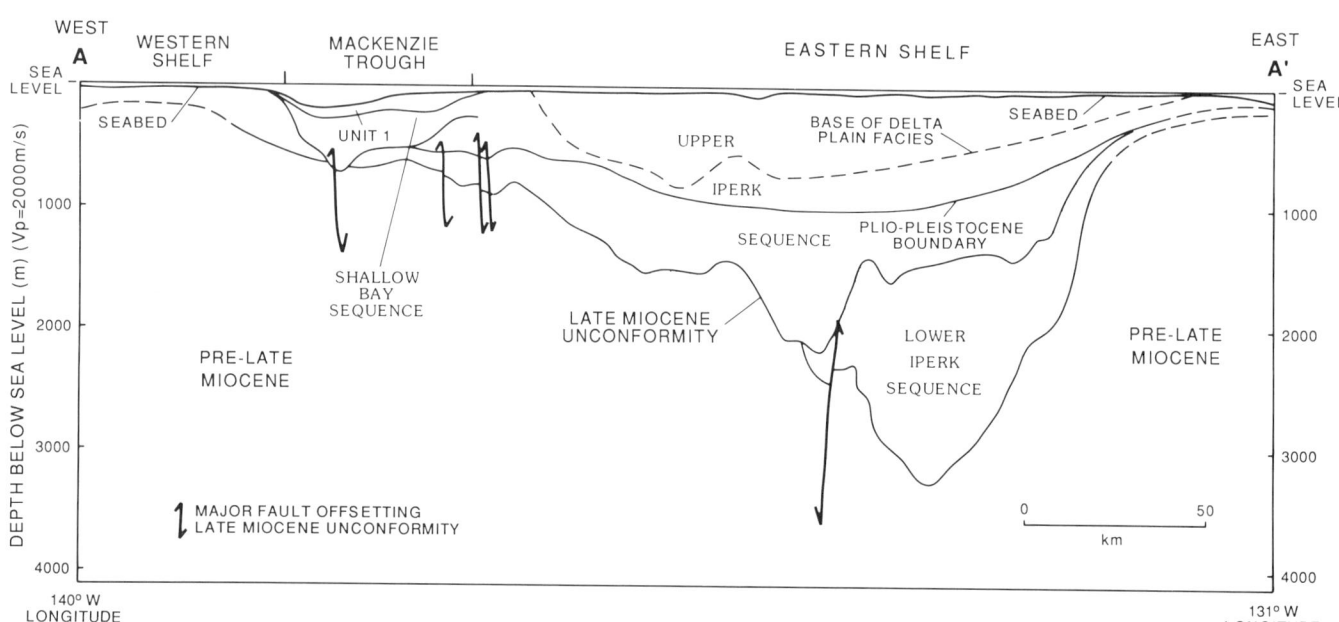

Figure 3. Schematic east-west cross section across the Beaufort Shelf showing late Neogene and Quaternary stratigraphy of the Beaufort Mackenzie Basin. For location, see Figure 1.

resulted in the present unusually shallow continental shelf, suggests that the basin has filled and that sedimentation has kept pace with subsidence. The late Neogene and Quaternary infill has experienced only minor deformation and displacement since the late Miocene. The complex high-angle normal-fault and normal listric growth-fault systems of earlier Tertiary age (J. R. Dietrich, written communication, 1985; Fortin, 1990) are mostly truncated by the late Miocene unconformity. Within the resolution of existing multichannel seismic reflection data, offsets of this unconformity are observed in only two areas (Fortin, 1990; Fig. 3). Vertical displacements of the unconformity, reaching from 50 to 150 m on high-angle normal faults (associated with the Eskimo Lakes fault zone: Dietrich, written communication, 1985) indicate continued Neogene down to the basin movement along the edge of the Arctic Platform. Fault traces observed on the sea floor of the eastern Beaufort shelf (Fortin, 1990) may be related to the same activity. Vertical offsets of 50 to 75 m along synthetic and antithetic listric growth faults are also observed on the late Miocene unconformity in the Tarsiut area (Figs. 1 and 3). Whether these post-Miocene displacements are related to continued activity associated with the Kaltag/Rapid Fault Array, syndepositional faulting, or deep-seated right-lateral regional wrenching (Fortin, 1990) is unknown. Faults from these two systems can be traced to within 200 m of the seabed where they appear to die out in flexure. Fortin (1990) also noted two shallow normal faults close to the sea floor near the eastern edge of the Mackenzie Trough (Fig. 3) and adjacent eastern shelf. These faults and others may be related to differential consolidation of surficial sediments.

The late Miocene unconformity has also been deformed by minor continued late Neogene uplift on underlying Tertiary anticlines and diapirs (Fortin, 1990). Several such structures within the Mackenzie Trough, the Tarsiut area, and the outer northeastern shelf have experienced uplift. The amplitude of folds on the unconformity may exceed 100 m, but deformation dies out in the overlying Quaternary section.

Earthquake activity in the Canadian Beaufort region is focused primarily within the Beaufort cluster (Atkinson and Charlwood, 1988) located beyond the current shelf edge in the southern Canada Basin (Pl. 2). Such seismicity, including events of magnitude greater than 5.0 on the Richter scale, are attributed by Basham (*in* Atkinson and Charlwood, 1988) to the crustal response of a large uncompensated sediment load along the continental slope. Only three earthquakes have been recorded in the shelf area between 1967 and 1985 (Fortin, 1990; Fig. 1). A magnitude-3.5 event in 1984 in the eastern Beaufort Sea may be related at depth to activity at the edge of the Arctic Platform, and a magnitude-3.4 event that occurred in 1967 in the Tarsuit area may be linked to the post-Miocene fault activity mentioned above. An isolated magnitude-2.0 event beneath the central shelf occurred in 1982. Lack of data on focal depths makes it difficult to relate seismicity to known faults or tectonic activity in the region.

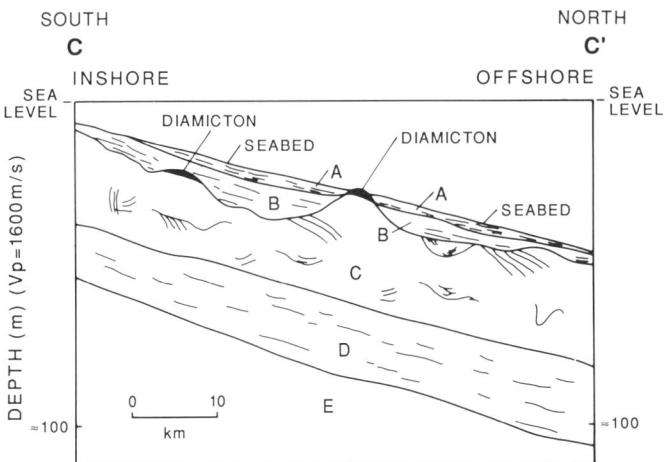

Figure 4. Schematic north-south cross section across the Beaufort Shelf north of Richards Island showing stratigraphy of the upper 100 m of sediment below seabed. Unit A is Holocene marine clay; Unit B is transgressive interbedded sand, silt, and clay; Unit C is a glaciofluvial outwash sand complex; Unit D is inner-shelf marine clays; and Unit E is an underlying glaciofluvial outwash sand. The top of Unit C forms a regional erosional unconformity with associated coarse lag deposits (diamicton). For location, see Figure 1.

LATE PLEISTOCENE–HOLOCENE HISTORY

Regional and well-site surveys for geohazards assessment and shallow and deep borehole sampling in support of foundation investigations for exploratory drilling islands provide a significant data base for defining the stratigraphy of the upper 100 m of sediment across the Beaufort shelf. An information gap of 100 to 300 m exists between the seabed data and the deep seismic and exploratory well data acquired for hydrocarbon exploration. As a result, the intervening mid- to late Pleistocene section is poorly defined. However, the similarity of seismostratigraphy and depositional environments between the known seabed discussed below and the deeper sediments discussed above suggests continuity in the geology through the unsampled zone. This remains to be proven, however. Minor hiatuses to major disconformities may exist in this section.

Eastern shelf

Figure 4 (modified after Blasco and others *in* Pelletier, 1987) illustrates a schematic north-south cross section of the upper 100 m of sediment across the central eastern shelf, north of Richards Island and the Tuktoyaktuk Peninsula. Figure 5 (modified after Blasco and others *in* Pelletier, 1987) presents a corresponding east-west schematic cross section in mid-shelf water depths from east of the Canada–U.S. border toward the Amundsen Gulf (140° to 131°W). In Figure 4, units E through C represent the uppermost succession of the Upper Iperk Sequence, while units B and A correspond to the Shallow Bay Sequence of Dietrich and others (1985).

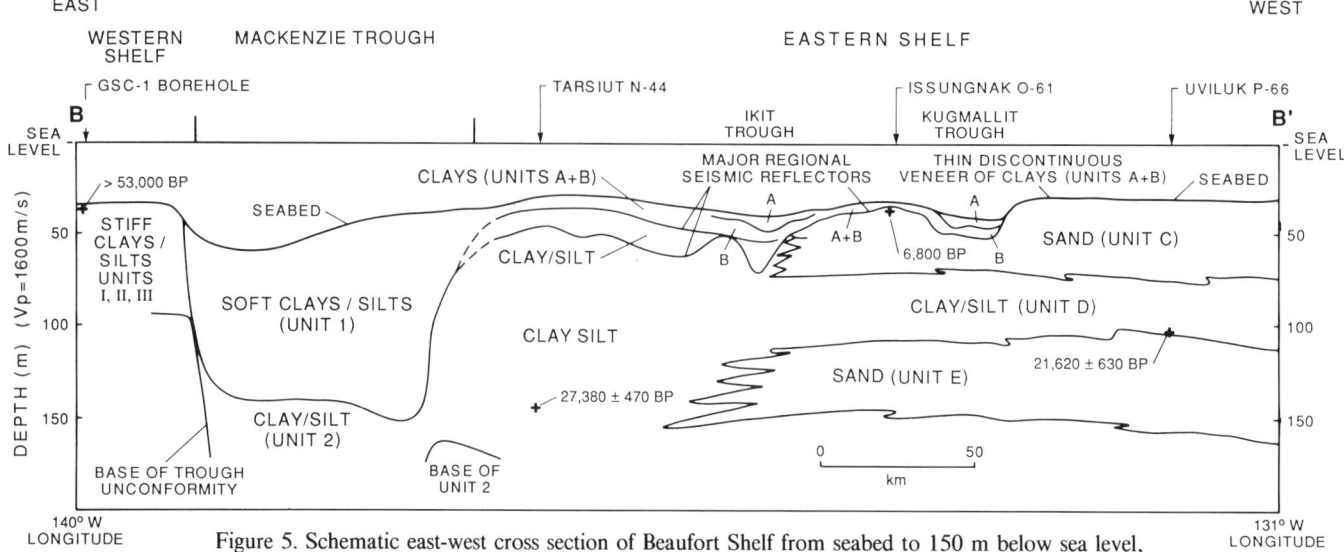

Figure 5. Schematic east-west cross section of Beaufort Shelf from seabed to 150 m below sea level, showing the variation in shallow stratigraphy and chronology for the eastern and western shelves and the Mackenzie Trough. For location, see Figure 1.

Little is known of unit E except that it appears to be a widespread, thick, medium- to fine-grained sand, the top of which can be mapped seismically as a weak, flat-lying discontinuous reflector across the central eastern shelf. To the west of approximately 136°W this unit undergoes a facies change to interbedded sand and silty sand intervals interlayered with much more dominant silt and clay muds. Northwest of Richards Island, unit E may be represented at the Tarsiut N44 well site by sandy interbeds 100 to 135 m below sea level. At 141 m below sea level at this site, Hill and others (1985) dated an in-situ fibrous peat sample at $27,380 + 470$ yr B.P. Within the peat, abundant, well-preserved desmids indicate a freshwater pond environment located beyond marine influence. Limited shallow seismic data suggest the zone associated with this sample, and the sandy interbeds, are characterized by prograded delta lobes, and biostratigraphic evidence indicates this unit was deposited under alternating subaerial delta plain and nearshore marine environments. Elsewhere on the eastern shelf, depositional environments associated with unit E become more distal and marine toward the Mackenzie Trough in the west, and toward the shelf edge in the north. To the east of Kugmallit Trough, seismic evidence suggests that unit E consists predominantly of sand but becomes interbedded with finer grained sediments.

Disconformably overlying the sand is unit D, an interbedded silt and clay unit, with an observed maximum thickness of more than 40 m on the central eastern shelf. Based on limited seismic and borehole evidence the unit appears to be distributed shelf wide. The top of the unit is not detected seismically, most likely due to a low impedance contrast at the contact with the overlying unit. A peaty mud sample, containing abundant coarse wood, herb, and root material, recovered from the bottom of unit D in contact with the sand at the Uviluk P66 wellsite, yielded a radiocarbon date of $21,260 \pm 630$ yr B.P. (Hill and others, 1985).

At the base of the sample, palynomorphs are nonexistent, but they increase in abundance upward. The assemblage becomes dominated by spruce, birch, alder and *Sphagnum* moss, with common freshwater *Pediastrum* and marine dinoflagellates. The organic matter and palynological evidence (Hill and others, 1985) are interpreted to represent a basal high-energy deltaic environment, probably associated with the top of the underlying sand, followed by an influx of marine waters. Seismic profiles suggest unit D represents delta-margin depositional conditions, and the probable shelf-wide distribution of unit D may indicate a broad inner shelf marine depositional environment.

Unit C consists of a massive, 40-m-thick, fine- to medium-grained sand with a low silt/clay content. East-west facies changes are similar to those in the underlying unit E sand. The unit grades westward into interbedded silt and clay muds with less common silty sand layers, and eastward into a more sand-dominated sequence with interbedded finer grained beds. This sand also becomes thicker and finer grained offshore on the central shelf. Scanning electron micrographs of quartz grains within this sand (Hill and Nadeau, 1984) reveal fracturing, pitting and abrasion—characteristics that suggest these sands were exposed to glacial, fluvial, littoral, and aeolian transport processes prior to and during final deposition on the shelf. Internally, this sand unit is seismically characterized by "cut and fill" structures, infilled channels and depressions, and progradational clinoforms (Fig. 4).

The upper surface of the sand is frequently identified by a well-defined, high-amplitude seismic reflection. This undulating, smooth seismic event can be mapped across the eastern shelf and represents an erosional unconformity, disconformity, or hiatus, depending on the location. Within unit C, seismic-borehole correlations at several sites (Hill and others, 1985) reveal a variety of deltaic depositional environments. Near the Issungnak 061 well site, 2- to 3-m-deep infilled depressions can be mapped just below the unconformity as shallow lake basins or channels. Deeper within unit C, localized, high-angle reflectors delineate laterally migrating channels. A peat sample recovered 7 m below the unconformity at this site (Hill and others, 1985) consisted of common fine wood fragments, charcoal, palynomorphs of spruce, birch, grass, *Sphagnum* spores, desmids, and reworked pre-Quaternary pollen. This assemblage is similar in composition to that found in sediment deposited above the present storm flood line of the Babbage River delta on the Yukon coast (Forbes, 1981 *in* Hill and others, 1985). This peat yielded a corrected date of 6,800 yr B.P. (Fig. 5). Similarly, at the East Amauligak site, a seismic profile shows a 3-m-thick, acoustically complex delta-top sequence below the unconformity but overlying clinoforms of a prograding delta lobe. Biostratigraphic evidence supports this interpretation. A 0.5-m-thick mossy peat interbedded with sand stringers was recovered from 2 m below the unconformity in the delta-top sequence. The abundance of well-preserved moss material, fine to coarse wood fragments, well-preserved palynomorphs and spores, including dwarf birch, *Polytrichum, Pediastrum, Cyperaceae* and other grasses, suggests a freshwater raised bog or ephemeral pond environment within the delta plain (Hill and others, 1985). Radiocarbon dates on the peat bracket the age of the sample between 8820 ± 100 and 7740 ± 90 yr B.P. However, the broad spatial distribution, uniform lithology, consistent thickness (40 m), and quartz grain characteristics of unit C would suggest the sand represents a broad coastal glacial outwash plain rather than prograded deltaic deposits, which tend to be spatially more discontinuous.

Overlying the well-defined regional seismic event at the top of unit C (Fig. 5) is unit B (O'Connor, 1980), a complex transitional sequence between units C and A. Unit B consists primarily of interbedded to interlayered thin beds of dense sand and silt, with thicker intervals of stiff silty clay. Unit B sediments may partially represent reworked older sediments of unit C and reflect depositional conditions associated with shallow-water, higher energy environments (less than 10 m). Unit B sediments were deposited during Holocene sea-level rise (Hill and others, 1985). Total thickness varies across the eastern shelf from 0 m in the east to more than 10 m in the west near the Mackenzie Trough (Fig. 5). These sediments infill small depressions (channels and lake basins) in the top of unit C as well as major valleys such as the Ikit and Kugmallit Troughs. Unit B grades upward into surficial unit A.

Unit A sediments consist of soft marine, silty clays recently deposited under lower energy conditions on the shelf (O'Connor, 1980) in water depths beyond 10 m. Fine-grained sediment outflow from the Mackenzie River, estimated at 85 million m^3/yr (Harper and Penland, 1990), represents the main source of unit A muds accumulating on the shelf. Similar in distribution to unit B, unit A sediments form a thin veneer less than a few centimeters thick on the eastern shelf to as much as 10 m thick, as depression infill, to the west in areas adjacent to the Mackenzie Trough. The contact between units A and B is probably conformable, consisting of a transition from stratified to transparent character in seismic records, and is detected in boreholes by subtle changes in lithology, density, stiffness, or shear strength. Major cross-shelf depressions such as the Ikit and Kugmallit Troughs are infilled with as much as 20 m of unit A. The combined thickness of units B and A may totally infill major cross-shelf valleys such as the Ikit Trough, particularly in shallow water.

The late Wisconsinan to Holocene history of the eastern shelf region, as defined by the above stratigraphy, is reasonably well constrained. Chronologic and biostratigraphic evidence (Hill and others, 1985) suggests that, in general, the upper 100 m of sediment across the eastern shelf is less than 27,000 years old, and that relative sea level has risen from a lowstand of −140 m or more, from about that time. Unit E may represent an early glaciofluvial outwash phase similar in character to unit C, but its age is not known. Units D and most of C were probably deposited under transgressive conditions between 27,000 yr B.P. and an undetermined time in the late Wisconsinan, perhaps close to the continental glacial maximum at 18,000 yr B.P. Fine-grained sediment of unit D was deposited under inner-shelf conditions, whereas unit C sand was probably deposited by a prograding delta and outwash system in advance of the late Wisconsinan ice sheet.

The incision of deep cross-shelf valleys into unit C sands is evidence for a second lowstand of sea level during the late Wisconsinan. Based on the maximum depth of erosion on the unconformity between Units B and C, the lowstand reached approximately 70 m below present sea level. It appears that the lowstand postdated deposition of the bulk of unit C. The upper part of unit C represents a broad glaciofluvial outwash plain related to the lowstand. Prolonged subaerial exposure with little or no sedimentation led to the development of a thermokarst topography, which is partially preserved as shallow basins and channels at the top of unit C.

From a sea-level lowstand of at least 70 m below present sea surface, rising waters have been transgressing the shelf to the present day. Advancing seas eroded and reworked the surface of unit C, leaving a well-defined regional seismic reflector. The deposition of high-energy inner-shelf sediments (unit B) accompanied coastal retreat. As water depths increased, sedimentation gave way to the deposition of lower energy marine clays (unit A) largely derived from the Mackenzie River.

Correlation with the onshore stratigraphy of Richards Island and the Tuktoyaktuk Peninsula is poorly constrained, and is the focus of present research. As it does to the east and west (Fig. 3), the Iperk Sequence pinches out landward to the south, implying that the above-described units E through A may also pinch out shoreward. The Holocene marine clay unit A is only found in depressions inside the 10-m isobath, and transgressive unit B stops at the present coastline. Onshore, on Richards Island, the Kidluit sand, Hooper clay, Kittigazuit sand, and Toker Point gravel succession are all described by Rampton (1988) and regarded as being of infinite radiocarbon age. If this is so, then the offshore equivalents of these deposits must underlie units E, D, and C, which are dated at less than 27,000 yr B.P. Offshore sand units E and C are similar sedimentologically and structurally to the Kidluit and Kittigazuit and may therefore represent more recent reworking and redeposition (by glaciofluvial processes) of these older onshore sediments.

Western shelf

High-resolution analogue, shallow seismic reflection profiles indicate that the Upper Iperk Sequence of the western shelf consists of a wedge-shaped cyclic succession of strata overlying the late Miocene unconformity (Meagher and Lewis, 1989; Fortin, 1990; Fig. 6). The thickness of the Upper Iperk increases from approximately 100 m near the coastline to greater than 700 m beneath the shelf break. Ten cycles are recognized in this thin, post–late Miocene wedge. Internal reflectors within each cycle are non-existent to parallel, low-amplitude events that dip and diverge slightly toward the shelf edge. Below the outer shelf, clinoforms or monoclines (truncated at the upper surface) suggest basinward shelf-edge progradation. The upper surface of several cycles is eroded and incised by channels and depressions that are, in turn, infilled with cut and fill deposits (Fig. 6). A high-amplitude, smooth to irregular unconformity truncates these channels and strata (Fig. 6). On the surfaces of three of the upper cycles the incised channels have a southeast-northwest orientation, suggesting ancient drainage patterns to the northwest, approximately normal to the present offshore-trending shelf gradient. With the exception of the nearshore, successively younger strata crop out on the sea floor toward the shelf edge (Fig. 6). On the western shelf, the Shallow Bay Sequence (Meagher and Lewis, 1990) exists only as a thin, discontinuous veneer of Holocene sediments resting unconformably on the older truncated Upper Iperk strata. Much of this veneer appears to be found within a shallow depression adjacent to the coast.

Limited borehole control exists for the succession of younger Iperk strata on the central to outer western shelf. This shallow sequence, to depths of 65 m below seabed, consists of overconsolidated, stiff to hard, homogeneous to laminated clays and silty clays with minor coarser grained thin layers or inclusions of sandy clay and gravel. The thin, discontinuous overlying Shallow Bay Sequence consists of softer, weakly laminated, organic-rich, sandy to silty mud and localized gravel deposits, all varying in thickness from 0 to 2 m across the shelf (Meagher and Lewis, 1990). Brigham-Grette and others (written communication, 1989) describe the seismostratigraphy, lithostratigraphy, biostratigraphy, and geochronology of a 52-m borehole located in 44 m of water on the outer shelf (borehole GSC-1, Figs. 1 and 6). The borehole penetrates seismostratigraphic units I, II, and III. Below 40 m, unit III consists of massive clay with exotic clasts of granitic and dolomitic composition. Similar clasts are found as a gravel lag on the seabed of the central shelf where the unit crops out. Ostracode and foraminifera assemblages within this unit suggest mid-shelf to upper continental slope depositional conditions and therefore a paleo–sea level approximately similar to present. A thermoluminescence (TL) date from 41 m, at the top of this unit, indicates an age range of 60,000 to 120,000 yr B.P. Amino acid alloisoleucine/isoleucine epimerization ratios on the foraminifer *Nonion depressulum* range from 0.058 at 48 m below seabed to 0.033 at 41 m, confirming the TL date and suggesting a late Pleistocene age for this unit. Brigham-Grette and others (written communication, 1989), however, suggest that unit III may be as old as 180,000 yr B.P.

Unit III is truncated, incised by a regional unconformity,

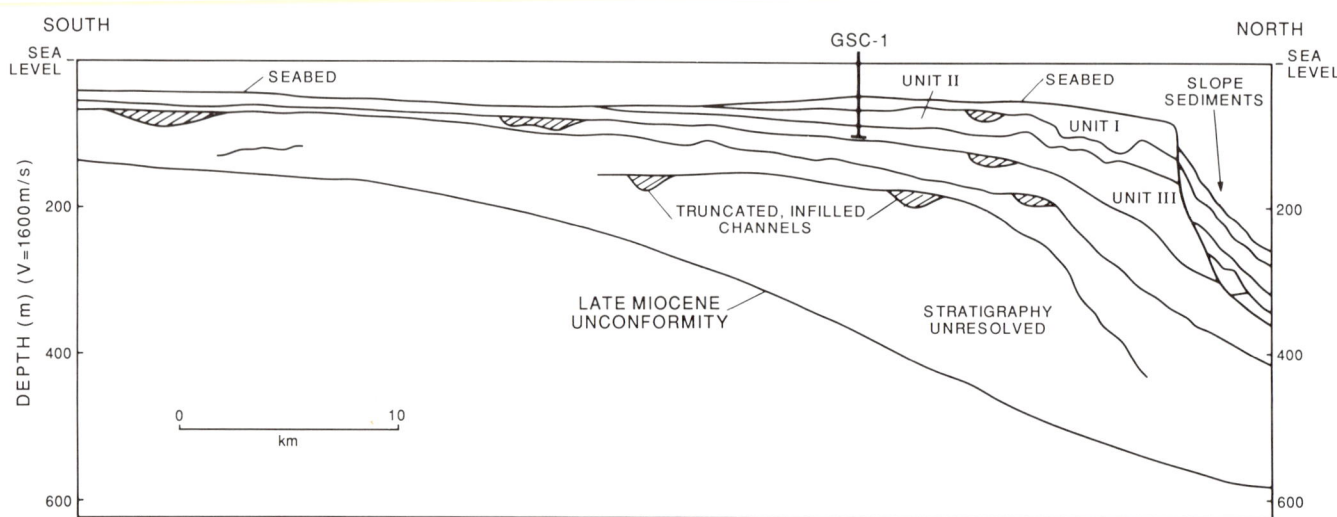

Figure 6. Schematic north-south cross section of the outer western Beaufort Shelf through GSC-1 borehole showing the late Miocene to Pleistocene accumulation of basinward-thickening cyclic sediment wedges. Many cycles are eroded and incised by infilled depressions and channels. Successively younger strata outcrop on the seabed toward the outer shelf. The present seabed is erosional, and seabed sediments of the outer shelf at the noted borehole location are older than 53,000 yr B.P. For location, see Figure 1.

and overlain by a 10- to 60-m-thick seismic unit II on the outer shelf (Fig. 6). This succeeding unit is represented in the borehole by a massive clay from 40 to 13 m, and is characterized by a paucity of palynomorphs and ostracodes, and almost total absence of foraminifera. The minor presence of ostracode species *Pteroloxa cumuloidea* implies very shallow or brackish-water depositional conditions. The massive nature of this clay unit and lack of microfauna and flora, in conjunction with TL dates of 78,000 to 117,000 yr B.P. at 32 m and 66,000 to 96,000 yr B.P. at 13 m suggest this unit may have been rapidly deposited not long after the deposition and erosion of the underlying sediments.

A similar major erosional unconformity separates unit II from overlying unit I in seismic profiles. Unit I consists of laminated silty clay that crops out on the outer-shelf seabed (Fig. 6). This youngest unit of the three described achieves a maximum thickness of 70 m on seismic profiles and is truncated at the seabed and at the shelf edge. The basal section of this seismic unit is exposed in the upper 13 m of the borehole referred to above. Biostratigraphic evidence indicates these sediments were deposited in a predominantly inner-shelf environment. Pollen evidence in terms of a relative abundance of *Betula* palynomorphs may also suggest that warming climate conditions, which were initiated at 22 m depth in the underlying unit II, continued to at least 9 m below seabed. AMS radiocarbon dating of small shell fragments recovered from 3 m and 4 m depth below seabed yielded dates of 29,000 ± 600 yr B.P. and 33,200 ± 600 yr B.P., respectively, both considered infinite ages due to modern carbon contamination (Polach and Golson, 1966; Stuvier, 1971). Thermoluminescence dating (Brigham-Grette and others, written communication, 1989) on sediments 5 m below seabed indicates a minimum age of >53,000 yr B.P., and an amino acid ratio of 0.023 on *Elphidium excavatum,* at a depth of approximately 2 m, confirms this but does not improve on the temporal resolution. Detailed paleomagnetic analyses of the borehole (Brigham-Grette and others, written communication, 1989) revealed no magnetic reversals in the 52-m core.

The interpretation of this stratigraphy is poorly constrained. If the younger limit on the above chronology is assumed, and the presence of the exotic erratic clasts is significant (Rodeick, 1979), then the borehole sequence described above represents deposition of the erratic-bearing glaciomarine Flaxman member of the Gubik Formation about 70,000 to 80,000 yr B.P. (Carter and others, 1986; Brigham, 1985), followed by subaerial exposure, erosion, and the rapid deposition of nearshore sediments under lower than present sea-level conditions, ending, at the latest, some 53,000 yr B.P. These sediments subsequently would have been exposed to erosion during the late Wisconsinan low sea-level stand. Reworked sediments, generated during the last transgression, form the discontinuous thin veneer of younger, probably late Wisconsinan–Holocene deposits on the shelf.

The late Neogene and Quaternary strata of the western shelf appear to consist of a succession of regressive/transgressive cycles that culminate below seabed with the early to mid-Wisconsinan (or older?) cycle. The link between this cyclic succession and glacial/interglacial cyclicity is unknown. Late Wisconsinan sediments are not present on the shelf, and the Holocene is represented primarily by thin discontinuous reworked deposits resting on a regional unconformity that truncates the described mid- to late Wisconsinan sediments offshore and older strata onshore.

The seismic stratigraphy of the western shelf is similar in character to the stratigraphy of the Alaskan Beaufort Shelf, as described by Dinter (1985) and Dinter and others (this volume). However, interpretations regarding the age and relations between late Quaternary sequences in these adjacent regions are significantly different. Future work will focus on resolving these correlation problems.

Mackenzie Trough

The Mackenzie Trough (Fig. 1) is an asymmetric, linear depression incised more than 400 m into the broad, flat continental shelf. This paleovalley is partially infilled by more than 300 m of Quaternary sediments (Blasco and others, 1989; O'Connor, 1989a; Fig. 3). On the outer shelf the feature disrupts the continuity of the flat seabed with a bathymetric deepening in excess of 100 m. In water depths of 20 m and less, the landward-shallowing trough is completely infilled with 150 m of sediment. The base of this infilled trough is defined by a high-amplitude, smooth, U-shaped, erosional seismic unconformity (O'Connor, 1989a; Figs. 3 and 7). In the central trough area, sediments below the late Miocene unconformity are incised by the base of the trough unconformity (Figs. 3 and 7). On the flanks of the trough this rising unconformity truncates regional northeasterly dipping strata of the Upper Iperk Sequence. These dipping strata are deformed and folded within the sidewall of the western flank. Regional continuity of reflections beneath the trough eliminates the possibility of fault control. The well-defined, smooth morphology of the trough base and the structure of adjacent strata do not support a graben, slump, or canyon origin but suggest the feature was excavated by the repeated action of ice tongues during the Pleistocene (Blasco and others, 1989; O'Connor, 1989a) although Shearer (1971) attributed the trough to the action of late Wisconsinan ice.

The exact stratigraphic position of the basal unconformity within the shallow sedimentary sequences of the adjacent western and eastern shelves is not clear (Blasco and others, 1989; Meagher and Lewis, 1990; O'Connor, 1989a). On the western shelf, correlation is possible with any of the high-amplitude, laterally continuous reflectors associated with the upper sediment cycles described above. On the outer western shelf at the core site described above, the most probable correlative reflector coincides with the event at the base of unit III, below the bottom of the core at approximately 60 m below seabed. Based on the age of unit III, the base of the trough unconformity would then be 60,000 to 120,000 yr B.P. in age, or possibly older. On the eastern flank, the base of the trough unconformity (Fig. 7) is identified as an irregular, high-amplitude event that intersects the eastern shelf at approximately 200 m below seabed and dips easterly in conformity

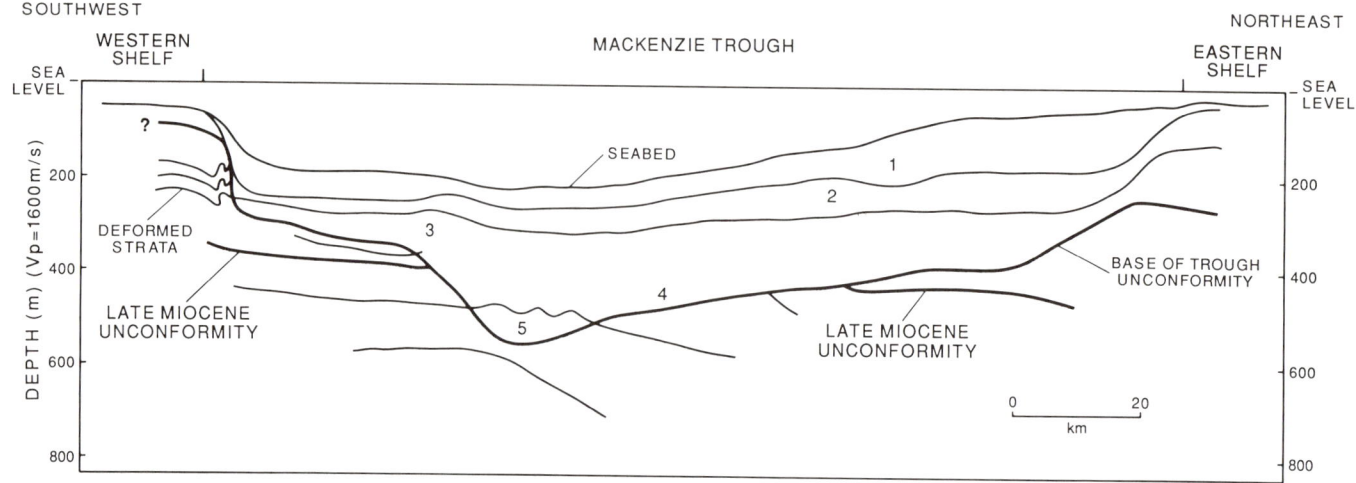

Figure 7. Schematic east-west cross section of the Mackenzie Trough, Canadian Beaufort Shelf, at approximately 70°N. The base of the trough is defined by a smooth, U-shaped erosional unconformity generated by an advancing ice tongue. Unit 5 may be a till; Units 4 and 2, glacial drift(?) deposits; Unit 3, a moraine or ice load deformation structure; and Unit 1, a subaqueous deltaic sequence overlain by transgressive sediments and recent marine clays. Unconformities at the tops of Units 4 and 2 are also smooth and trough-wide, and may have been generated by the action of successive ice advances.

with the regional trend (Fig. 7). Extrapolated known local Holocene sedimentation rates in this area of the eastern shelf suggest the unconformity must be older than 80,000 years. However, the age estimates of sediments at these depths on the western and eastern shelves are very poorly constrained, and are regarded as minimums. The age of the deepest excavation of the Mackenzie Trough is therefore inferred to be early Wisconsinan or earlier.

In terms of trough infill, five seismostratigraphic units with a composite thickness of more than 300 m have been identified above the basal unconformity (O'Connor, 1989a). These units are illustrated schematically on Figure 7. Occupying a narrow, V-shaped valley in the west-central section of the broad, flat trough base are unsampled sediments up to 70 m thick that have a chaotic, hummocky acoustic character. These sediments (unit 5) are overlain by acoustically massive to poorly stratified sand of unit 4. Up to 200 m thick, this unit rests directly on the basal unconformity over much of the trough. The contact between this sand and the overlying unit 2 is a poorly defined, trough-wide unconformity that also appears to be truncated against the rising base of trough unconformity on the western flank, but rises under the eastern shelf to dip conformably with regional bedding. The planar nature of this unconformity is interrupted by an internally structureless axial ridge (unit 3) with relief of approximately 30 m. Unit 2 is an acoustically unstratified, trough-wide silty clay with a thickness that varies from 40 to 60 m. Both the underlying sand and this silty clay are characterized by a paucity of microflora and fauna.

The upper surface of the unit 2 silty clay is well defined and can be mapped across the trough as a flat-lying to locally hummocky horizon. On the western flank this reflector intersects the rising base of trough unconformity, rises coincidentally with the basal unconformity, then truncates shallow strata to the present sea floor. These Upper Iperk sea-floor sediments (excluding the thin, discontinuous veneer of Shallow Bay sediments) are known only to be older than 53 ka (see above). As a result, the age of the unconformity at the top of unit 2 is largely unconstrained to the west. However, at the edge of the eastern shelf this same event rises and is mapped at about 40 m below seabed. Sediments at this depth are known to be late Wisconsinan in age (see above), implying that the unconformity at the top of unit 2 is late Wisconsinan in age.

Overlying this unconformity in the trough is unit 1. Borehole-seismic correlation indicates this unit has complex internal stratigraphy, consisting of basal prograded deltaic sediments (well-defined bottomset, foreset, and topset bedding), truncated at the upper surface by transgressive muds that are in turn overlain by thick, soft, recent marine clays up to 30 m thick. Unit 1 attains a maximum thickness of 125 m in the central trough area, pinches out on the eastern edge of the western shelf, and thins to less than 40 m on the eastern shelf. An 82-m-deep borehole (MTW-1, Fig. 1), collected in 45 m of water in the thickest section of unit 1, was deep enough to intersect the bottomset beds. Core stratigraphy and biostratigraphy have been described by Moran and others (1989) and Helenes and others (1990), respectively. Interbedded sands and clays and sands and silts of the bottomset and foreset beds between the base of the core at 82 m and 40 m below seabed are dominated by a pollen assemblage characterized by a high ratio of pre-Quaternary to Quaternary palynomorphs, and abundant herb pollen among a large marine algal population. The overlying silt topset and succeeding silt and clay transgressive units at 40 to 21 m below seabed are dominated by a relatively abundant terrestrial pollen assemblage of *Cyperaceae*, *Graminineae*, and *Sphagnum* with upwardly increasing *Pediastrum*.

The recent marine clays overlying this sequence are distinguished by abundant *Picea* above 21 m and an *Alnus* peak above 11.5 m. The trend in pollen stratigraphy suggests ameliorating climatic conditions from the base of the core to seabed. From a chronological perspective, the onshore pollen record of the Mackenzie delta (Ritchie, 1984) and the northern Yukon (Cwyner, 1982) suggests that *Picea* came into abundance in the region around 9,500 yr B.P. and *Alnus* about 6,800 yr B.P. Correlation with the pollen assemblages found in the 82-m borehole suggests that the upper 21 m or more of sediment is Holocene in age, and that the entire core is probably less than 14,000 years old. Unit 1 would be late Wisconsinan to Holocene in age, correlating well with the inferred late Wisconsinan age of the underlying unconformity at the top of unit 2.

Tentative interpretation of the above stratigraphy suggests the Mackenzie Trough was excavated to its present maximum depth by glacial ice during the early Wisconsinan, leaving a basal till deposit (unit 5). The thick sand (unit 4) was deposited with retreat of the early Wisconsinan ice. A second ice tongue may have advanced into the Mackenzie Trough during the mid- to late Wisconsinan (Hill and others, 1985), overriding, deforming, and partially eroding unit 4, to leave a well-defined trough-wide unconformity (contact between units 4 and 2). Contrary to this interpretation, Rampton (1982, 1988) and Hughes (1987) argued that late Wisconsinan ice did not extend beyond the position of the modern Mackenzie Delta. Beget (1987) determined that late Wisconsinan ice in the Mackenzie area was too thin to be very erosive and may have simply overridden preexisting sediments. Nevertheless, the above-mentioned ridge (unit 3) associated with the top of unit 4 may represent a deformation structure related to ice loading, or possibly a medial moraine. Unit 2 silty clays are possibly subglacial drift deposited by the oscillating/ablating ice. Retreat of this late Wisconsinan ice tongue was accompanied by (or followed by) deposition of the thick progradational subaqueous deltaic sequence of bottomset, foreset, and topset beds less than 14,000 years ago. Transgression followed, with the subsequent deposition of marine clays during much of the Holocene.

By definition, the Shallow Bay Sequence of Dietrich and others (1985) would correspond only to the surficial marine clay sediments of unit 1, with a maximum thickness of 30 m, as well as the underlying thin transgressive layer, which may also be mainly Holocene in age. The balance of the trough infill is, therefore, a younger part of the Upper Iperk Sequence, not Shallow Bay.

CORRELATION

The correlation of the eastern, western and Mackenzie Trough stratigraphy is poorly resolved. The marine clays and transgressive interbeds of units A and B, respectively, of the eastern shelf correlate in time with similar deposits of the upper part of unit 1 in the Mackenzie Trough, and with the discontinuous veneer of sediments on the western shelf. On the outer shelf these sediments may span the late Wisconsinan to present, while onshore they may only represent the past thousand years or less. These sediments compose the Shallow Bay Sequence. The late Wisconsinan unit C sands, (and laterally equivalent silts and clays) on the eastern shelf, may correlate or be slightly older than the deltaic sequence forming the lower part of unit 1 in the Mackenzie Trough. Equivalent sediments are not present on the western shelf except perhaps as part of a nearshore complex. If the Mackenzie Trough was excavated to its maximum depth in the early Wisconsinan, and seismic correlations are correct, then units D and E on the eastern shelf, units 2 through 5 in the Mackenzie Trough, and units I to III on the western shelf must all be of this age and younger. However, the exact interrelation of these units is unknown. If the Trough is older than the early Wisconsinan, then the correlation becomes even more tenuous.

SUMMARY

Sedimentation in the Cretaceous-Tertiary Beaufort-Mackenzie Basin continued in the late Neogene and Quaternary, following a period of major erosion during the late Miocene. At the basin depocenter, more than 3,500 m of clastic infill occurred as two successions of turbiditic, basinal, slope, and shelf/delta sediments. Quaternary sediments may reach a total thickness of more than 1,000 m and are composed principally of interlayered thick regressive delta plain/delta front sands and thin transgressive finer grained muds. Surficial sediments of the upper 100 m of the eastern shelf are less than 27,000 years old and are sand dominated to the east but become fine-grained toward the Mackenzie Trough. The Mackenzie Trough was excavated by ice tongues during the early and mid(?) to late Wisconsinan, and possibly by earlier glaciations. In excess of 300 m of Quaternary sediments partially infill the trough. The thick late Neogene and Quaternary sediment wedge pinches out toward both the east and west. Silty clay seabed sediments on the western shelf beneath thin, localized Holocene deposits are older than 53,000 yr B.P.

REFERENCES CITED

Atkinson, G. M., and Charlwood, R. G., 1988, Seismic hazard maps for northern and western Canadian offshore regions: Ottawa, Canada Oil and Gas Lands Administration special publication, March 1988, 110 p.

Beget, J., 1987, Low profile of the northwest Laurentide ice sheet: Arctic and Alpine Research, v. 19, no. 1, p. 81–88.

Blasco, S. M., Brigham-Grette, J., and Hill, P. R., 1989, Offshore constraints on the late Pleistocene glacial history at the mouth of the Mackenzie River, *in* Carter, L. D., Hamilton, T. D., and Galloway, J. P., eds., Late Cenozoic history of the interior basins of Alaska and the Yukon, United States Geological Survey Circular 1026, p. 15–17.

Brigham, J. K., 1985, Marine stratigraphy and amino acid geochronology of the Gubik formation, western Arctic coastal plain, Alaska: United States Geological Survey Open File Report 85-381, 218 p.

Bujak, J. P., and Davies, E. H., 1981, Neogene dinoflagellate cysts from the Hunt Dome Kopanoar M-13 well, Beaufort Sea, Canada: Canadian Petroleum Geology Bulletin, v. 29, p. 420–425.

Carter, L. D., Brigham-Grette, J., and Hopkins, D. M., 1986, Late Cenozoic marine transgressions of the Arctic Coastal Plain, *in* Correlation of Quaternary deposits and events around the margin of the Beaufort Sea; Contributions from a joint Canadian-American workshop, April, 1984: Geological Survey of Canada Open-File Report 1237, p. 21–26.

Cwynar, L. C., 1982, A late Quaternary vegetation history from Hanging Lake, northern Yukon: Ecological Monographs, v. 52, p. 1–24.

Dietrich, J. R., Dixon, J., and McNeil, D. H., 1985, Sequence analysis and nomenclature of upper Cretaceous to Holocene strata in the Beaufort-Mackenzie Basin: Geological Survey of Canada Paper 80-11, 11 p.

Dinter, D. A., 1985, Quaternary sedimentation of the Alaskan Beaufort shelf; Influence of regional tectonics, fluctuating sea levels and glacial sediment sources: Tectonophysics, v. 114, p. 133–161.

Dixon, J., McNeil, D. H., Dietrich, J. R., Bujak, J. P., and Davies, E. H., 1984, Geology and biostratigraphy of the Dome Gulf and others, Hunt Kopanoar M-13 well, Beaufort Sea: Geological Survey of Canada Paper 82-13, 28 p.

Dixon, J., and Snowdon, L. R., 1979, Geology and organic geochemistry of the Dome Hunt Nektoralik K-59 well, Beaufort Sea, in Current Research, Part C: Geological Survey of Canada Paper 79-1C, p. 85–90.

Fortin, G., 1990, Regional geological framework for the late Neogene/Quaternary strata beneath the Canadian Beaufort continental shelf: Geological Survey of Canada Open File Report, 180 p (in press).

Grantz, A., Eittreim, S., and Dinter, D. A., 1979, Geology and tectonic development of the continental margin north of Alaska: Tectonophysics, v. 59, p. 263–291.

Harper, J. R., and Penland, S., 1990, Beaufort Sea sediment dynamics: Geological Survey of Canada Open File Report, 206 p. (in press).

Hea, J. P., Arcuri, J., Campbell, G. R., Fuglem, M. D., O'Bertos, J. J., Smith, D. R., and Zayat, M., 1980, Post-Ellesmerian basins of Arctic Canada; Their depocentres, rates of sedimentation and petroleum potential, in Miall, A. D., ed., Facts and principles of world petroleum occurrences: Canadian Society of Petroleum Geologists Memoir 6, p. 447–488.

Helenes, H., Davies, E. H., and Bujak, J. P., 1990, Palynology and micropaleontology of the Mackenzie trough MTW-1 core, Canadian Beaufort Sea: Geological Survey of Canada Open File Report (in press).

Hill, P. R., Mudie, J. P., Moran, K., and Blasco, S. M., 1985, A sea-level curve for the Canadian Beaufort shelf: Canadian Journal of Earth Sciences, v. 22, p. 1383–1393.

Hill, P. R., and Nadeau, O. C., 1984, Grain-surface textures of late Wisconsinan sands from the Canadian Beaufort shelf: Journal of Sedimentary Petrology, v. 54, p. 1349–1357.

Hughes, O. L., 1987, Late Wisconsinan Laurentide glacial limits of northwestern Canada; The Tutsieta Lake and Kelly Lake phases: Geological Survey of Canada Paper 85-25, 19 p.

Hunter, J. A., and Blasco, S. M., 1980, High resolution marine geophysics in Canada, A review, in Eden, W. J., ed., Proceedings of the First Canadian Conference on Marine Geotechnical Engineering, April 1979: Calgary, Alberta, Canadian Geotechnical Society, p. 95–124.

Jones, P. B., Braches, J., and Lentin, J. K., 1980, The geology of the 1977 offshore hydrocarbon discoveries in the Beaufort-Mackenzie basin, N.W.T.: Bulletin of Canadian Petroleum Geology, v. 28, p. 81–102.

Le Tirant, P., 1979, Seabed reconnaissance and offshore soil mechanics for the installation of petroleum structures: Paris, Editions Technip, p. 133–217.

McNeil, D. H., Ioannides, N. S., and Dixon, J., 1982, Geology and biostratigraphy of the Dome Gulf et al. Ukalerk C-50 well, Beaufort Sea: Geological Survey of Canada Paper 80-32, 17 p.

Meagher, L., and Lewis, J. F., 1990, Upper Tertiary and Quaternary geology and morphology of the western Beaufort (Yukon) continental shelf and slope, Geological Survey of Canada Open File Report, 136 p. (in press).

Moran, K., Hill, P. R., and Blasco, S. M., 1989, Interpretation of piezocone penetration profiles in sediment from the Mackenzie trough Canadian Beaufort Sea: Journal of Sedimentary Petrology, v. 59 p. 88–97.

O'Connor, M. J., 1989a, Surficial geology of the Mackenzie trough: Geological Survey of Canada Open File Report, 188 p. (in press).

O'Connor, M. J., 1989b, An evaluation of the regional surficial geology of the southern Beaufort Sea: Geological Survey of Canada Open File Report, 188 p. (in press).

O'Connor, M. J., 1980, Development of a proposed model to account for the surficial geology of the southern Beaufort Sea: Geological Survey of Canada Open File Report no. 954, 128 p.

Pelletier, B. R., ed., 1987, Marine science atlas of the Beaufort Sea, geology and geophysics: Geological Survey of Canada Miscellaneous Report 40, 39 p.

Pelletier, B. R., ed., 1984, Marine science atlas of the Beaufort Sea, sediments: Geological Survey of Canada Miscellaneous Report 38, 27 p.

Pelletier, B. R., 1980, Review of surficial geology and engineering hazards in the Canadian offshore, in Proceedings of the First Canadian Conference on Marine Geotechnical Engineering, April 1979: Calgary, Alberta, Canadian Geotechnical Society, p. 6–46.

Pelletier, B. R., 1975, Sediment dispersal in the southern Beaufort Sea: Sydney, British Columbia, Environment Canada, Institute of Ocean Sciences Technical Report no. 25a, 80 p.

Polach, H. A., and Golson, J., 1966, Collection of specimens for radiocarbon dating and interpretation of results, Australian Institute of Aboriginal Studies, A.N.U., Canberra, manual no. 2, 42 p.

Quinn, F. J., Vigier, L., Poley, D. F., and Simpkin, P. G., 1987, Evaluation/calibration of marine sources for high-resolution seismic studies, Geological Survey of Canada Open-File Report 1520, 230 p.

Rampton, V. N., 1988, Quaternary geology of the Tuktoyaktuk coastlands, Northwest Territories: Geological Survey of Canada Memoir 423, 98 p., 1 map.

Rampton, V. N., 1982, Quaternary geology of the Yukon coastal plain: Geological Survey of Canada Bulletin 317, 49 p.

Ritchie, J. C., 1984, Past and present vegetation of the far northwest of Canada: Toronto, University of Toronto Press, 251 p.

Rodeick, C. A., 1979, The origin, distribution and depositional history of gravel deposits on the Beaufort Sea continental shelf, Alaska: United States Geological Survey Open File 79-234, 76 p.

Shearer, J. M., 1971, Preliminary interpretation of shallow seismic reflection profiles from west side of Mackenzie Bay, Beaufort Sea, in Report of activities, Part B: Geological Survey of Canada Paper 71-1, Part B, p. 131–138.

Stirbys, T., 1990, Acoustic/physical property correlation and downhole logging, in Notes from the workshop on geotechnical in-situ testing for the Canadian offshore, Jan 27–28, 1986, Dartmouth, Nova Scotia: Geological Survey of Canada Open File Report (in press).

Stuvier, M., 1971, Evidence for the variation of atmospheric carbon 14 content in the late Quaternary, in Turekian, K. K., ed., The late Cenozoic glacial ages: New Haven, Yale University Press, p. 69–70.

Sweeney, J., 1985, Comments about the age of the Canada basin: Tectonophysics, v. 114, p. 1–10.

Sykora, J. J., 1984, The Iperk deltaic sequence, Beaufort Sea; A regional sedimentological study using seismic and well data [abs.]: Calgary, Alberta, Canadian Society of Exploration Geophysicists–Canadian Geophysical Union National Convention, p. 50.

Vilks, G., Wagner, F.J.E., and Pelletier, B. R., 1979, The Holocene marine environment of the Beaufort Shelf: Geological Survey of Canada Bulletin 303, 43 p.

Willumsen, P. S., and Cote, R. P., 1982, Tertiary sedimentation in the southern Beaufort Sea, Canada, in Embry, A. F., and Balkwill, H. R., eds., Arctic Geology and Geophysics, Proceedings of the 3rd International Symposium on Arctic Geology: Canadian Society of Petroleum Geologists Memoir 8, p. 43–54.

Young, F. G., Myrh, D. W., and Yorath, C. J., 1976, Geology of the Beaufort-Mackenzie basin: Geological Survey of Canada Paper 76-11, 63 p.

Manuscript Accepted by the Society December 1, 1989

Chapter 27

Sedimentary basins and petroleum resource potential of the Arctic Ocean region

N. E. Haimila
ZI Consulting, Ltd., Box 909, Cocrane, Alberta T0L 0W0, Canada
C. E. Kirschner
U.S. Geological Survey, P.O. Box 154, Union, Washington 98592
W. W. Nassichuk
Geological Survey of Canada, 3303 33rd St. NW, Calgary, Alberta T2L 2A7, Canada
G. Ulmichek
U.S. Geological Survey, Box 25046, Denver Federal Center, Denver, Colorado 80225
R. M. Procter
Geological Survey of Canada, 3303 33rd St. NW, Calgary, Alberta T2L 2A7, Canada

INTRODUCTION

This chapter examines the petroleum potential of the sedimentary basins along the continental margins of the North American Plate in the Arctic Ocean region, including those beneath the continent itself and those beneath its fringing continental terraces. Basins within the Canadian Arctic Islands of North America and in the Baffin Bay regions are considered in other volumes of this series. The large petroleum potential of some of the sedimentary basins of the Arctic Ocean margin of the North American Plate, particularly those on the continental shelf, is already well established. The petroleum resource potential of the abyssal plains of the Arctic Ocean is poorly understood but is thought to represent only a minor portion of the total potential of the region.

The basins in the periphery of the Arctic Ocean Basin are mainly continental terrace wedges on foundered passive continental margins and successor basins on extended continental shelves. The Kronprins Christian Basin on the East Greenland Shelf is separated from European basins by the Mid-Atlantic Ridge north of Iceland (Fig. 1). The rest of the basins along the edge of the North American continent area, from east to west, are the Wandel Sea Basin in Greenland, the Lincoln Sea Basin, the various sub-basins of the Canadian Arctic Coastal Plain and Shelf, the Mackenzie Delta–Beaufort Sea Basin in Canada, and the Kaktovik Basin, the Demarcation Subbasin, the Dinkum Graben, and the Nuwuk Basin off Alaska. West of Alaska and north of Siberia the broad continental shelf contains upper Paleozoic–Mesozoic successor basins that are flanked seaward by younger shelf-margin basins. Between Alaska and the Lena River Delta in Siberia, where the Arctic Mid-Ocean Ridge impinges on the continent and marks the boundary between the Asian and North American Plates, the intrashelf-shelf basins include the offshore Colville Trough and Arctic Platform, Hanna Trough and Chukchi Platform, Hope Basin, Chaun Basin, and the East Siberian Basin.

Major discoveries extending from Prudhoe Bay through the Mackenzie Delta to the Sverdrup Basin in the Canadian Arctic Islands demonstrate that favorable conditions for the generation and entrapment of oil and gas are widespread in the Arctic Ocean region (Dixon and Dietrich, this volume; Nassichuk, 1983, 1987; Embry, 1989). Confidence in the probable occurrence of petroleum deposits in basins to the east and west of this demonstrated trend must be tempered with uncertainty because of lack of exploratory drilling and in some cases by very incomplete knowledge of their sedimentary sequences. Nevertheless, these distant basins, particularly those of northern Alaska, show considerable promise for future potential.

In the Mackenzie Delta–Canadian Beaufort Sea region about 240 exploratory wells have led to the discovery of 49 significant oil and gas discoveries, including the giant Amauligak oil field and the Parsons and Taglu gas fields. Almost 356×10^9 m^3 (12.6 TCF) of gas and 317×10^6 m^3 (2.0 billion barrels) of oil have been discovered. In addition, there is an estimated undiscovered potential (average expectation) of $1,577 \times 10^9$ m^3 (56 TCF) of gas and 843×10^6 m^3 (5.3 billion barrels) of oil. Onshore discoveries and potential are in rocks from Devonian to Tertiary age, whereas offshore potential is confined largely to Tertiary sequences. The resources appear to be concentrated in

Haimila, N. E., Kirschner, C. E., Nassichuk, W. W., Ulmichek, G., and Procter, R. M., 1990, Sedimentary basins and petroleum resource potential of the Arctic Ocean region, *in* Grantz, A., Johnson, L., and Sweeney, J. F., eds., The Arctic Ocean region: Boulder, Colorado, Geological Society of America, The Geology of North America, v. L.

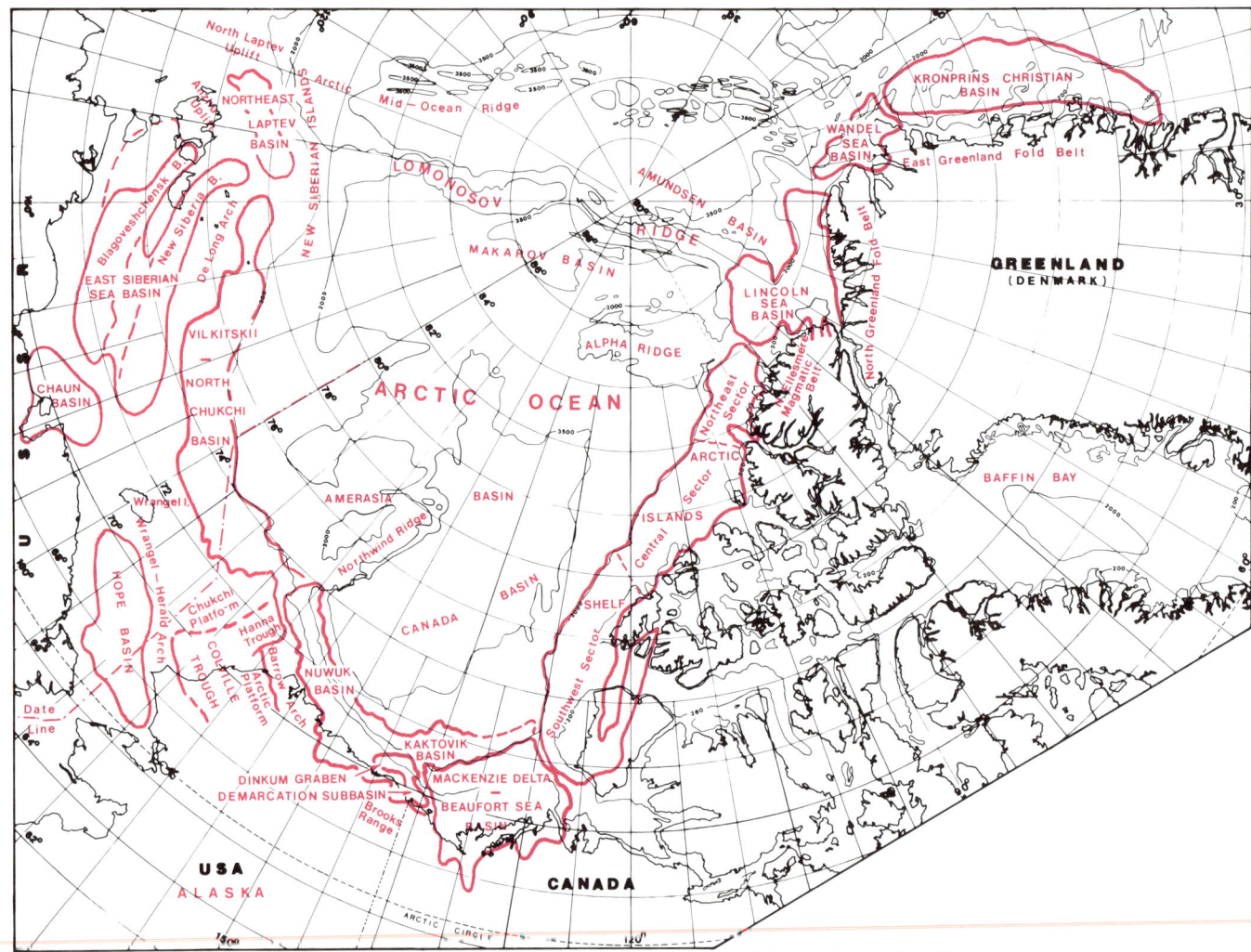

Figure 1. Sedimentary basins of the Arctic Ocean region of the North American Plate.

relatively few major trends. A largely unknown but important northern extension of the Canadian Beaufort Shelf is the portion of the Arctic Coastal Plain and Shelf, largely ice covered, that lies adjacent to the Arctic Islands. The extension of an arcuate trend of anticlinal features west from the recent Adlartok oil discovery near Herschel Island off the northern Yukon implies high potential for the western part of the Beaufort Sea across the northern Alaska Shelf.

In the Arctic Islands, about 90 exploratory wells have resulted in 15 significant discoveries, all of which are in Triassic Heiberg Sandstone in the Sverdrup Basin, except for one small oil discovery in Devonian carbonates on the southern margin of the basin. In total, about 425×10^9 m^3 (15 TCF) of gas and about 80×10^6 m^3 (500 million barrels) of oil have been discovered, including the giant Drake and Hecla gas fields and a major oil discovery at Cisco (about 32×10^6 m^3 or 200 million barrels). In addition, it is estimated that the undiscovered potential for the area is $2,200 \times 10^9$ m^3 (78 TCF) of gas and 685×10^6 m^3 (4.3 billion barrels) of oil (average expectation). Much of this remaining potential is expected to occur in upper Carboniferous and Permian rocks in the Sverdrup Basin.

The petroleum potential of the Arctic Platform of northern Alaska and several adjacent offshore basins is considered to be similar to that of the Mackenzie Delta–Canadian Beaufort Sea region. Source rocks, reservoir potential, and thermal maturity that led to the supergiant Prudhoe Bay Field as well as several significant discoveries in adjacent parts of central northern Alaska are present through most of the Arctic Platform and nearby offshore. In addition, the offshore basins contain a thick Brookian section, much of it within the oil generation window (Grantz and others, 1987; Grantz and May, 1987). Petroleum potential is probably greatest in the Arctic Platform, the Nuwuk and Kaktovik Basins, Hanna Trough, and the flanks of the Chukchi Platform. Parts of the region farther west are also prospective but lack definitive data.

Prospective petroleum basins in the Soviet portion of the Arctic Ocean region are very incompletely understood. The East Siberian Sea Basin is considered to have the highest potential, but

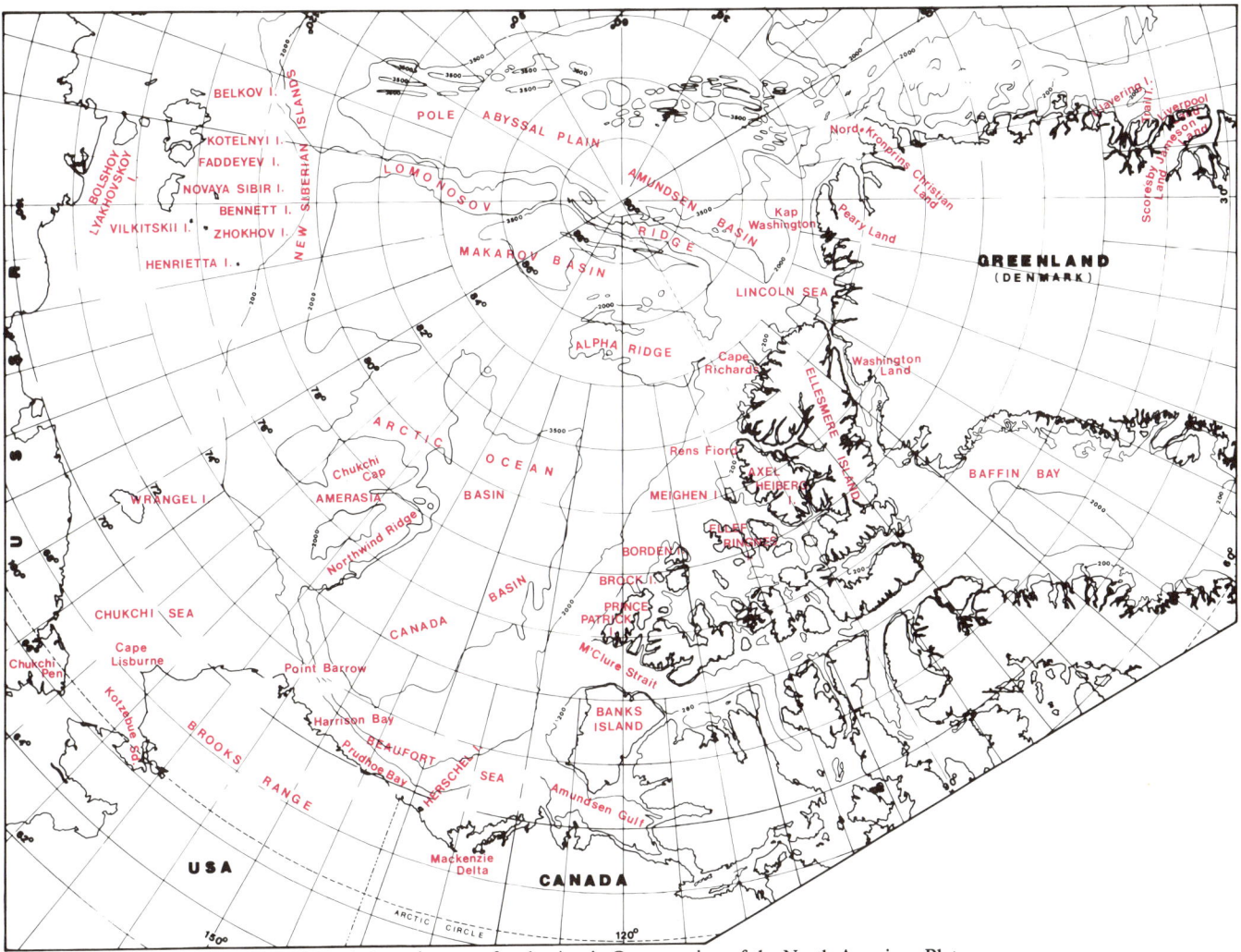

Figure 2. Location map for the Arctic Ocean region of the North American Plate.

like the Chaun and Hope Basins it probably is more likely to contain gas than oil due to the relatively thin and largely young sedimentary cover.

KRONPRINS CHRISTIAN BASIN

The geology of East Greenland has been well studied, and is described in numerous publications. The exhaustive works of Larsen (this volume), Haller (1971), Birkelund and others (1981), and the collection edited by Escher and Watt (1976) deserve special notice. However, due to its remoteness and the year-round presence of pack ice, the extensive continental shelf of northeastern Greenland remains one of the least known shelf areas in the world (Figs. 1 and 2).

During the past five years, important multichannel reflection seismic data (Larsen, 1984, and this volume) have added significantly to the data base. Unfortunately, seismic profiles are sparse north of 72°N, and few are available for the Kronprins Christian Basin. Accordingly, assessment of the petroleum potential of this largely unexplored basin depends on extrapolation of data from onshore and from analogous basins in northwestern Europe.

The Kronprins Christian Basin appears to be an offshore extension of the central East Greenland Rift. The basement is estimated to be about 10 km deep. The structural character of the basin is a series of half-grabens of Triassic-Jurassic age, overlain by lenticular downwarped Cretaceous and Tertiary strata; four or five north- to northeast-trending grabens, or systems of grabens, separated by structural highs, are known (Larsen, 1984). Westward-tilted half-grabens in a narrow strip offshore of Liverpool Land, south of the Kronprins Christian Basin, have been identified in seismic reflection profiles. The great depth to the basement may indicate the presence of Carboniferous–Lower Permian, and perhaps Devonian grabens at the base of the sedimentary cover. Although the structure of the northeastern Greenland shelf is poorly known, the tectonic style is similar to that known from onshore central East Greenland and northwestern Europe.

The basement of the northeastern Greenland shelf and ad-

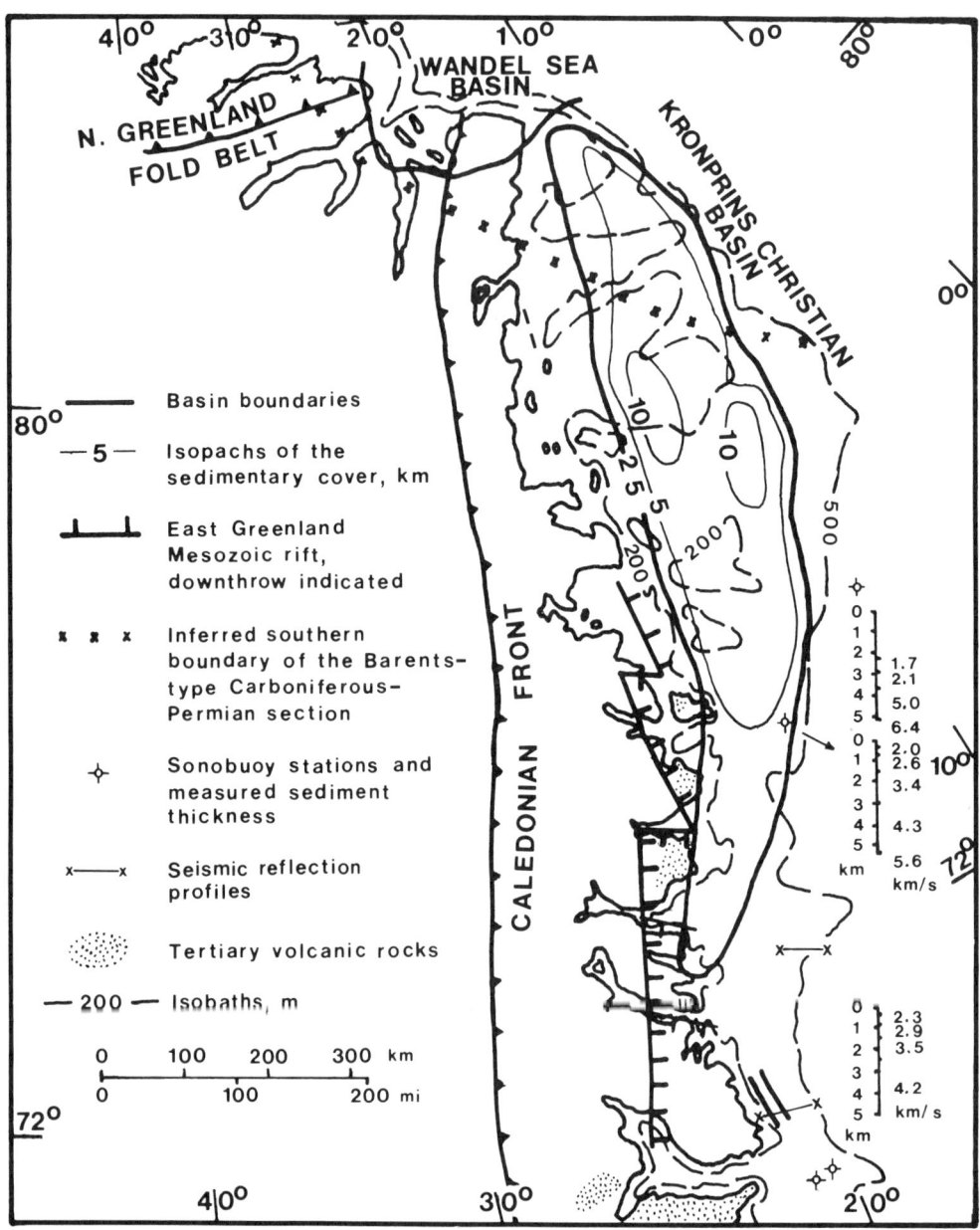

Figure 3. Sedimentary basins of the northeastern Greenland Shelf.

joining onshore areas consists of Late Proterozoic through Middle Ordovician rocks that were folded and metamorphosed during the Caledonian orogeny (Fig. 3). The post-Caledonian tectonic history of central East Greenland includes three successive rifting episodes that ended in Cretaceous time. The first rifting episode in the Caledonian fold belt occurred during Middle to Late Devonian time. Coarse clastic rocks are particularly prevalent. Some thinner clastic and marl layers were deposited in ephemeral limnic basins. Igneous activity was moderately intensive, particularly in the northern and southern margins of the trough. The entire sedimentary complex experienced significant folding and faulting during and immediately following deposition.

The second stage of rifting began in Early Carboniferous time; sedimentation appears to have begun during Namurian time and lasted until Early Permian time (Haller, 1971). The continental molasse complex that filled the rift shows depositional cyclicity and may be 5 to 6 km thick. Coarse sandstones and arkoses constitute the thickest part of each cycle, and are overlain by fine sandstones and black, partly bituminous lacustrine shales (Fig. 4). The whole molasse complex was faulted and folded, possibly during deposition, but certainly before Late Permian time.

Regional transgression of the sea during the relatively quiescent Late Permian time resulted in widespread deposition of marine rocks. As much as 300 m of Upper Permian deposits are known in central East Greenland. These rocks, the Foldvik Creek Formation, consist of conglomerates, reefy and argillaceous limestones, reddish sandstones, and bituminous dark shales.

Rifting in central East Greenland resumed at the beginning

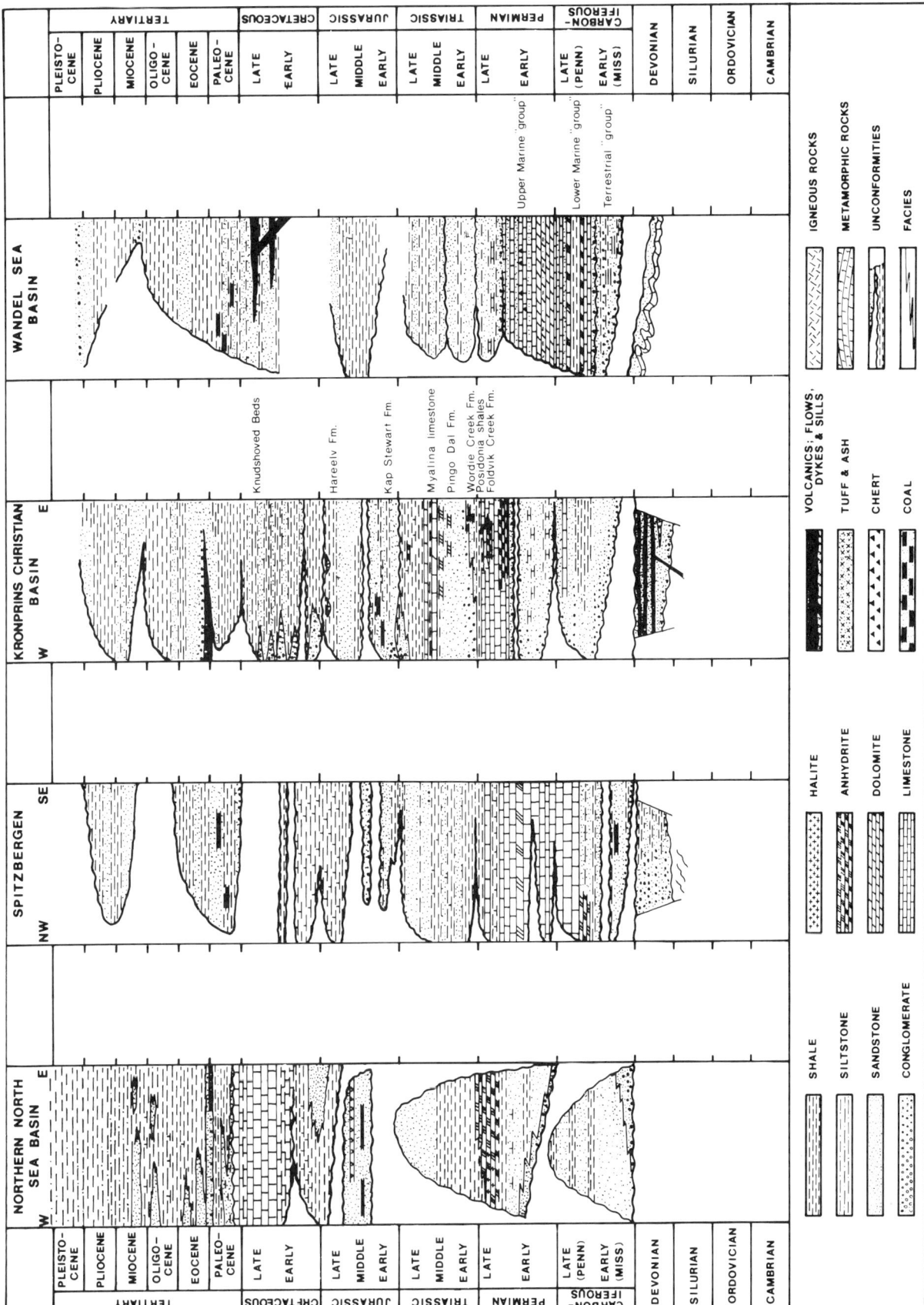

Figure 4. Schematic stratigraphic sequences of the North Sea, Spitzbergen, Kronprins Christian Basin, and Wandel Sea Basin.

of the Triassic. The Mesozoic rift extends for more than 600 km (Fig. 3) along strike. It consists of three main segments separated by transverse en echelon faults. The eastern boundary of the rift is located offshore; its precise position is uncertain. The most complete Triassic-Jurassic sequence in the East Greenland Rift is in the Jameson Land Basin. Dark and green marine shales with intercalations of coarse clastic rocks and minor limestones and evaporites (the Wordie Creek Formation) occur near the base of the Triassic succession (Fig. 4). The formation is overlain by as much as 900 m of mainly terrestrial clastic rocks of the Lower Triassic Pingo Dal Formation. The overlying Middle Triassic succession is dominated by gypsiferous shales with intercalations of sandstones, siltstones, and subordinate dolomites and limestones. Beds of black bituminous shales and limestones, known as the *Myalina* limestones, are conspicuous (Birkelund and Perch-Nielsen, 1976). The evaporitic unit grades upward into an Upper Triassic sequence composed mainly of marine mudstones and sandstones with minor dolomite and limestone. The Triassic sequence is capped by the Rhaetic-lower Liassic Kap Stewart Formation, a sequence of continental clastic strata with numerous coal fragments and with coal seams up to 15 m thick.

The lowest marine beds in the central East Greenland Rift are Hettangian in age, but continuous deposition appears to have begun later, during the Pliensbachian, and continued through middle Oxfordian time. A significant hiatus occurred from latest Toarcian through middle Bajocian time, and a main marine transgression followed in the Middle Jurassic. The two northern segments of the rift began to form in Middle Jurassic time and were superimposed on the older, pre-Triassic rocks. A restricted marine basin with about 100 m of black silty shales existed at the beginning of the transgression. The upper Oxfordian-lower Volgian section in central East Greenland includes black and gray shales intercalated with irregular lenses of sandstone derived from gravity flows.

Shales were deposited in relatively deep water, except in the northernmost portion of the rift where a nearshore sandy facies occurs. This complex is analogous to the Kimmeridgian shales of the North Sea. The top of the Jurassic sequence includes middle Volgian-Valanginian sandstones that probably reflect relatively strong tectonic activity, block-fault movements, and a concomitant rejuvenation of source areas. The Jurassic sequence in central East Greenland exceeds 2,000 m in thickness.

The western system of faults controls the distribution of Mesozoic rocks everywhere except on Mine Land, where Bathonian and Upper Jurassic sediments overstep the boundary fault of the graben. The only exposure of older rocks east of the rift is on Liverpool Land. The mid-Kimmeridgian tectonic event, prominent in the North Sea, caused significant faulting and slight folding in the East Greenland Rift.

As is apparent in the North Sea, the Early Cretaceous transgression produced strata that overstepped the tilted Jurassic blocks. The Lower Cretaceous deposits in central East Greenland are represented by open-marine facies bordered by coarse clastics along the ancient coastlines. The Ryazanian-Valanginian sequence is strongly transgressive, and in offshore facies is composed of shales and marls with limestone intercalations. Hauterivian and Barremian strata are absent, and dark Aptian shales and nearshore clastic strata rest unconformably on older strata. Dark gray and black Albian-Cenomanian shales with alternating sandstones reach significant thickness (to 1,000 m) and are also strongly transgressive. The rest of the Upper Cretaceous is represented by Turonian shales, sandstones, and conglomerates to 300 m thick, and Santonian-Campanian sandstones overlain by about 100 m of organic-rich black shales (the Knudshoved Beds). Despite a few prominent breaks in sedimentation, East Greenland was not tectonically active during the Cretaceous, and no significant Cretaceous differential movements along the Jurassic faults are known.

At the beginning of Tertiary time, strong basaltic volcanism occurred in the coastal area between 67°N and 73°30′N. South of 70°N these Tertiary plateau basalts obscure earlier sediments and the rift systems, but elsewhere an erosional surface can be seen beneath the basalt flows (Noe-Nygaard, 1976). Magmatic activity continued into Eocene time and was clearly related to the opening of the North Atlantic. East Greenland was strongly uplifted and eroded during the Tertiary. Near Liverpool Land, several kilometers of displacement along faults and flexures separate the shelf and onshore areas.

Petroleum potential

The tectonic and stratigraphic similarity between the East Greenland Rift and the North Sea Rift system suggests a comparably high petroleum potential for both areas. Both systems were formed before the opening of the North Atlantic, and at that time belonged to a single chain of Mesozoic basins situated more or less along the line of eventual separation (Vogt and others, 1981).

Several stratigraphic intervals in the sedimentary cover of eastern Greenland and the adjoining shelf could conceivably contain oil and gas source rocks. The Devonian section of central East Greenland is composed entirely of redbeds devoid of source rocks and lacking significant seal units. Black, partly bituminous shales occur in Carboniferous continental sequences on Trail Island and in northern Scoresby Land (Birkelund and Perch-Nielsen, 1981). They were deposited in limnic conditions and are interbedded with pebbly arkoses and sandstones.

Potential reservoir rocks are probably associated with Upper Permian reefs or reeflike banks. A comparable sequence is known to be productive in the Central Graben of the North Sea and in the southern part of the Northwest European Basin. Sandstones are also found in this interval. Black, often bituminous lagoonal *Posidonia* shales are good potential source rocks, and organic matter content sometimes reaches 2 to 5 percent (Surlyk and others, 1984). The basin facies to the east of the *Posidonia* shales also includes good potential oil source rocks.

Two intervals of arkosic nonmarine strata in the Triassic section probably include some reservoir sandstones. These occur in the Lower Triassic Pingo Dal Formation and the Rhaetic-lower Liassic Kap Stewart Formation, respectively. Some beds in the Kap-Stewart Formation might also be potential gas source rocks throughout the Kronprins Christian Basin. Bituminous shales with intercalations of limestones (the *Myalina* limestones) are known from the Middle Triassic section (Henderson, 1976). These may be a source for hydrocarbons in the southern half of the basin. Toward the north they grade into a more open-marine facies.

Dark, finely laminated silty shales at the base of the Middle Jurassic are present in all exposed sequences, and probably represent a period of quiescence and planation at the beginning of a large marine transgression. These shales can be considered to be a possible source for oil and gas. Undoubtedly the most important potential source rocks in the basin are the Upper Jurassic bituminous shales in the Hareelv Formation. These shales cover all the depressions on the northeastern Greenland shelf and, as in the North Sea, probably thicken in the rift structures.

The Jurassic sequence onshore in central East Greenland contains many sandstone horizons that can be considered as potential reservoir rocks. Significant development of marine sandstones probably occurs offshore in transgressive Lower Jurassic strata, in the Middle Jurassic, and at the base of the Upper Jurassic. Some sandstones, presumably of deep-water origin, may also be expected in and especially over the top of the black shales of the Hareelv Formation. The shales themselves may be considered as an important potential regional seat. Most of the sandstone facies known in the Cretaceous section onshore in central eastern Greenland have a nearshore origin, and thus it is difficult to predict their distribution offshore.

Potential reservoir rocks in the Cretaceous section of the Kronprins Christian Basin are much less well developed than those in the Jurassic section. Sandstones may be present in the basal, transgressive part of the Aptian-Cenomanian section and in the Turonian section. The organic-rich Santonian-Campanian Knudshoved black shales are potential source rocks in the post–Upper Jurassic sequence, but these shales may not have been buried deeply enough for even the initial stages of maturation to have occurred.

The major uncertainty regarding the petroleum potential of the Kronprins Christian Basin is the degree of maturation of organic matter in these rocks. Neither their depth of occurrence nor geothermal gradient are known. Several heat-flow measurements made on the continental slope and rise off East Greenland show values between 1.3 and 2.5 heat-flow units (Vogt and others, 1981), but these data are difficult to extrapolate to the shelf.

In the North Sea grabens, Kimmeridgian bituminous shales reach a maturation stage corresponding to the upper boundary of the "oil window" at depths of 3 to 3.5 km. No significant hydrocarbon accumulations have yet been found in areas where these shales occur at shallower depths. If the average geothermal gradient on the eastern Greenland shelf is about the same as in the North Sea, a similar minimum depth should be required for maturation of organic matter. The maximum thickness of the composite sedimentary sequence over the Upper Jurassic (Hareelv Formation) black shales in the Central East Greenland rift is about 2 km (Fig. 3), and most of it is composed of Lower Cretaceous–Cenomanian clastics. The Cretaceous rocks and the Kimmeridgian shales may be somewhat thicker in offshore grabens. Thus, the thickness of the Tertiary section over the rifts would appear to be the controlling factor in maturation of Upper Jurassic bituminous shales in grabens of the northeastern Greenland shelf, as it is in the North Sea. The intense igneous activity in Tertiary time, however, could have provided a higher heat flow and enhanced the maturation of source rocks even at reduced depths of burial.

The structural style of the East Greenland Rift system was formed during a tensional regime. Thus, trap types in the Kronprins Christian Basin might resemble those in the rift basins of the North Sea. Rotational fault blocks probably form the most important trap type.

The petroleum potential of the Kronprins Christian Basin is considered to be high because of the close similarity in structural style and geologic history with productive regions in the North Sea. Source rocks are present at several stratigraphic levels, but the most important are bituminous shales in the Upper Jurassic. Adequate reservoir rocks and seals are also likely to be present. The major uncertainty is the level of maturation of the Upper Jurassic bituminous shales. However, these shales are probably mature in parts of the down-faulted grabens. To conclude, the Kronprins Christian Basin might conceivably become a major oil-producing province. Additional data on the thickness of the Upper Jurassic and Cretaceous-Tertiary sequences and on the geothermal gradients are necessary to construct a more reliable model of petroleum generation and accumulation.

WANDEL SEA BASIN

The Wandel Sea Basin (Fig. 1) extends from the northeastern corner of Greenland to the continental slope. It is separated from the Lincoln Sea Basin by the aseismic and dominantly volcanic Morris Jesup Plateau. The Wandel Sea Basin in the offshore is probably contiguous with the Kronprins Christian Basin of East Greenland. The upper Paleozoic through Tertiary sediments of the Wandel Sea Basin overlie the folded, faulted, and metamorphosed rocks of the North Greenland fold belt in the north, the lower Paleozoic homoclinal platform to the south, and the Caledonian East Greenland fold belt along the eastern coast (Figs. 2, 3, and 5) (Dawes, 1976, and this volume).

The homoclinal wedge of lower Paleozoic sediments that overlies the Precambrian shield of Greenland thickens to the east, north, and northwest. These sediments were thrust toward the west during the Caledonian orogeny and the local Volvedal orogeny (Hakansson and Pedersen, 1982) during Late Silurian and Early Devonian time. In the north and northwest the gently northward-dipping lower Paleozoic sediments are mainly composed of platform carbonates. Northward, the intensity of deformation increases from steeply dipping symmetrical folds, to northward-overturned folds with south-dipping axial planes, to isoclinal folds overprinted by second and third folding phases. The intense folding is accompanied by northward-increasing metamorphism.

The North Greenland fold belt was deformed during the Late Devonian and/or Early Carboniferous Ellesmerian orogeny. Additional deformation occurred during Late Permian, Early Jurassic, Late Cretaceous, and middle Tertiary time.

The platform and deformed sequences are unconformably overlain by the transgressive Lower Carboniferous Terrestrial "group" (Dawes, 1976). The mainly continental rocks in this sequence are composed of dark conglomerate and sandstone with minor sandy and micaceous shales and local thin coal seams.

The Terrestrial "group" is succeeded by the transgressive Upper Carboniferous Lower Marine "group." A 10-m-thick conglomerate that disconformably overlies the continental beds is followed by approximately 600 m of alternating limestone and sandstone beds with minor marl and shale. Locally, accumulations of anhydrite may be found in the middle of the sequence. The limestones may contain small bank and patch reef deposits. The sandstones represent minor regressive cycles—some are cross-bedded, reddish, and contain plant remains. According to Dawes (1976), many of the shales, marls, and limestones are bituminous. The Lower Permian Upper Marine "group" generally includes about 500 m of sandstones and carbonates that rest unconformably on the Lower Marine "group."

Paleogeographic reconstructions of Haller (1971) and Johnson and others (1975) show that the Upper Permian sea north of Greenland and Svalbard supplied oceanic water for evaporite sedimentation in the Zechstein Basin through a narrow strait between the East Greenland and Scandinavian shelves. It is not clear how far to the south open-marine sediments, including bituminous layers, could have been deposited.

The Triassic in the Wandel Sea Basin is characterized by a 200-m-thick deltaic unit of shales and sandstones in its lower part and at least 400 m of deeper basinal, shaly sandstones in the upper part. Jurassic siltstones and shales crop out in northeastern Kronprins Christian Land. Cretaceous and Tertiary strata constitute a composite section more than 600 m thick. Cretaceous strata are mainly fine-grained dark sandstones up to 30 m thick alternating with shale units. The Tertiary section contains alternating sandstones and black shales interbedded with coal seams.

The composite section of upper Paleozoic, Mesozoic, and Tertiary sediments approximates 3,000 m in the onshore margin-

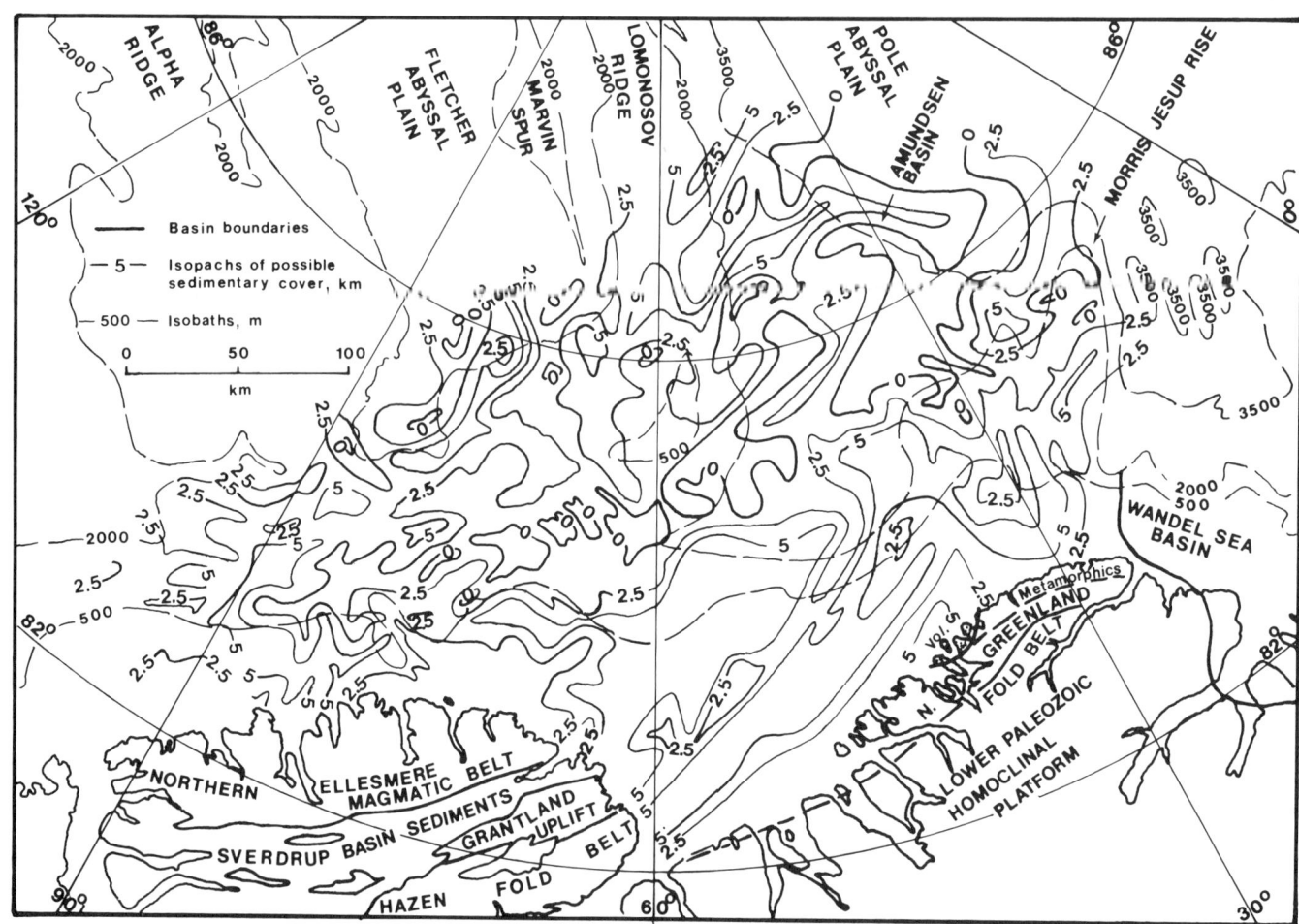

Figure 5. Possible sediment thicknesses in the Lincoln Sea area derived from depth-to-magnetic-source estimates (after Kovacs, 1982) and bathymetric depths (Plate 1, this volume).

al portions of the Wandel Sea Basin and probably exceeds that thickness in offshore areas.

Early Carboniferous sediments of the Wandel Sea Basin were affected by Early to middle Carboniferous faulting. Large-scale Late Permian and possibly Early Jurassic strike-slip faulting (Hakansson and Pedersen, 1982) may have been active along the northern side of the Wandel Sea Basin. Late Cretaceous and Tertiary strike-slip faulting along northwest-trending fault zones affected all previously deposited sediments and caused domes and extensional basins to form in the Wandel Sea Basin. Hakansson and Pedersen (1982) noted that a significant increase in heat flow in the central part of the Wandel Sea Basin in post-Paleocene time accompanied this deformation.

Petroleum Potential

According to Nassichuk (1983), the Wandel Sea Basin contains as much as 10 km (33,000 ft) of Carboniferous through Tertiary strata that are closely similar to those in the Sverdrup Basin. Clastic, carbonate, and evaporitic sequences in facies belts comparable to the Sverdrup Basin indicate that numerous source rocks and traps are probably available. Reservoir rocks are probable in coarse-clastic and carbonate units that might be sealed by evaporites and shale beds.

Geochemical analyses have been performed with encouraging results on a number of Wandel Sea sediments. One sample of upper Paleozoic limestone contained migrated hydrocarbons (Henderson, 1976). Source rocks can be anticipated in Upper Permian shale, Middle Triassic limestone, and two distinctive shaly Upper Jurassic units.

The portion of the Wandel Sea Basin that is buried under sufficient cover to form effective traps is relatively small. The shelf area extends only 50 to 100 km beyond the headlands of Peary Land and Kronprins Christian Land, where the potential source and reservoir rocks crop out. Conditions for hydrocarbon generation and accumulation might be more favorable in the southeast, where the basin is contiguous with the Kronprins Christian Basin. Because of the paucity of traps and the limited basin area, the potential of the Wandel Sea Basin must be considered low to moderate.

LINCOLN SEA BASIN

The Lincoln Sea Basin (Fig. 1), north of Greenland and Ellesmere Island, extends from the Morris Jesup Plateau in the east to where the Alpha Ridge impinges on the continental slope to the west. The shelf in this region is underlain by the seaward extension of the Hazen fold belt, the Northern Ellesmere magmatic belt, and parts of the Sverdrup Basin (Fig. 5) (Higgins and others, 1982).

The Hazen fold belt consists of numerous closely spaced isoclinal folds in lower Paleozoic flysch rocks. The fold limbs dip mainly to the northwest at very steep angles and have well-developed axial-plane cleavage. They were metamorphosed to sub-greenschist or greenschist facies prior to deposition of the overlying Carboniferous strata.

Within the Northern Ellesmere magmatic belt, Grenville basement rocks are overlain by Ordovician and Silurian shelf carbonates and volcanics that were intruded by Devonian plutons. The lower Paleozoic rocks were folded along arcuate northeasterly trends and metamorphosed to amphibolite grade.

The lower Paleozoic rocks of the Hazen fold belt and the Northern Ellesmere magmatic belt are unconformably overlain by varying thicknesses of Carboniferous to early Tertiary sediments of the Sverdrup Basin. The Sverdrup Basin appears to have undergone local deformation during Permian time, but the major period of disturbance was during the Eurekan orogeny, from Late Cretaceous to early Tertiary time. The Sverdrup Basin sediments appear to have been warped into open compressional folds. Along with the underlying metamorphosed rocks, Sverdrup Basin strata were affected by thrust faults that locally merge into strike-slip fault zones.

Seismic data are absent, but at least 30,000 km of aeromagnetic data are available from the Lincoln Sea Basin (Kovacs, 1982) and a few gravity data have also been collected. Extensive field geological mapping has been conducted in the onshore areas.

The magnetic basement between the Morris Jesup Plateau and the Lomonosov Ridge is characterized by a long linear graben that extends subparallel to the northern Greenland coast in a northeasterly direction (see Fig. 5, derived from Fig. 5 in Kovacs [1982]). Bordering the graben on the northwest is a complex ridge of en echelon horsts that separates the southern graben from a broader basin to the north that extends into the oceanic Amundsen Basin (Pole Abyssal Plain, Figs. 2 and 5). The magnetic basement in the two basins is approximately 10 km below the ocean surface. Because the water depths vary from 500 to 3,500 m, the sedimentary sequences are interpreted to be between 6.0 and 9.5 km thick in the grabens and between 1 and 4 km over the horsts.

Estimates of depth to magnetic basement indicate that, between the Lomonosov and Alpha Ridges, there is a complex structural realm characterized by randomly oriented horsts, grabens, and sub-basins (Kovacs, 1982, and Fig. 5). Sedimentary sequences might conceivably range from zero to 8.0 km in thickness.

The Hazen fold belt and the Northern Ellesmere magmatic belt are unconformably overlain by lacustrine and continental deposits of the Early Carboniferous Emma Fiord Formation at the base of the section in Sverdrup Basin (Fig. 6). The continental conglomerates and sandstones are overlain by a varied series of younger upper Paleozoic Sverdrup Basin strata (Mayr, 1976).

The upper Paleozoic section in the Sverdrup Basin is approximately 3,000 m thick in northern Ellesmere Island. Little can be said about the thickness or character of these strata offshore from Ellesmere Island in the Lincoln Sea.

A thin, but fairly complete Triassic section overlies the upper Paleozoic succession in the Sverdrup Basin in northern

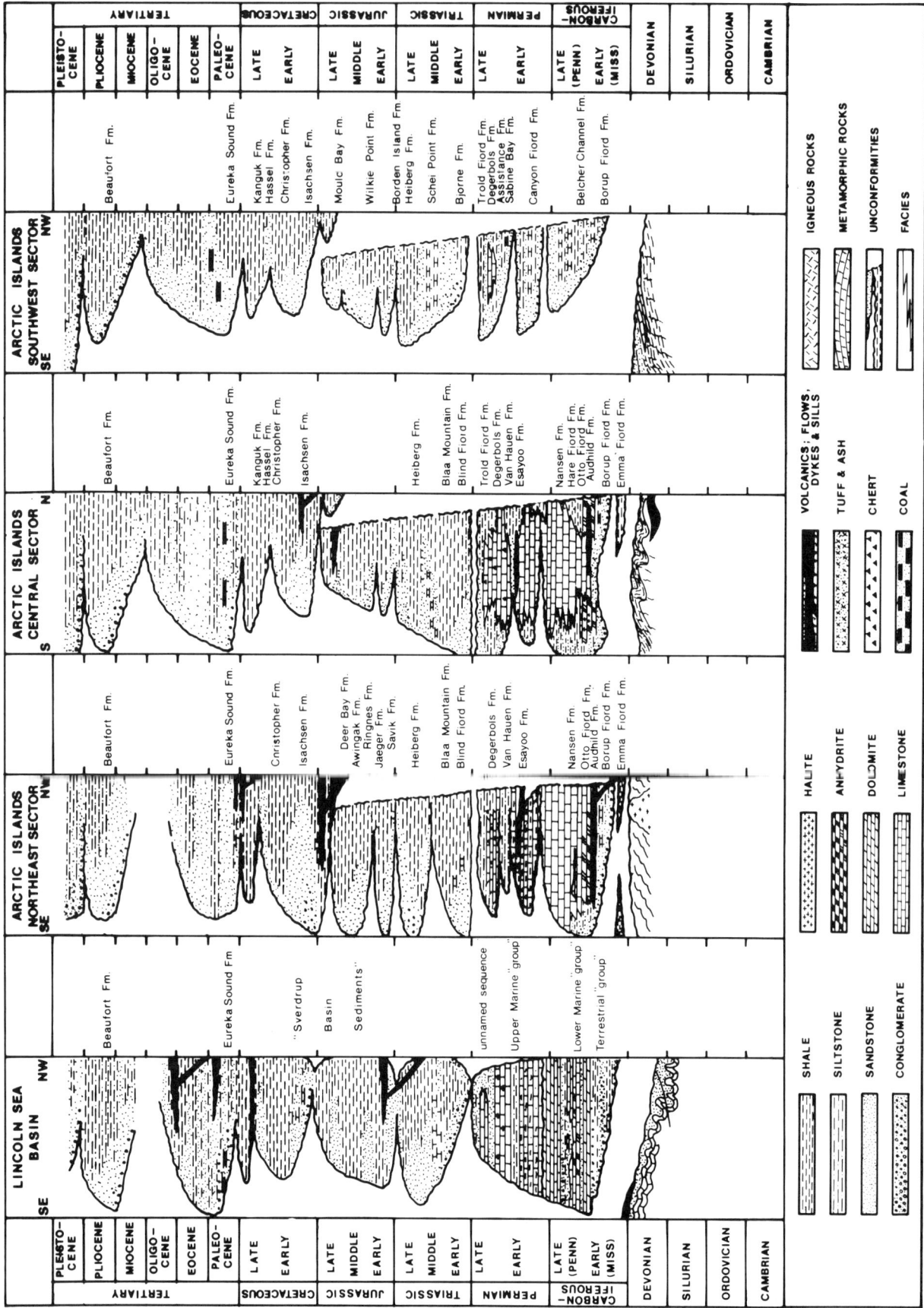

Figure 6. Schematic stratigraphic sequences of the Lincoln Sea Basin and northeast, central, and southwest sectors of the Arctic Island Shelf.

Ellesmere Island (Wilson, 1976) and comparable strata are present in North Greenland (Dawes, 1976). The Triassic sequence in both these areas represents a transgressive-regressive cycle. The lower formations are continental deltaic sediments, the middle formations are marine units, and the upper formations are prograding deltaic deposits. The Triassic sequences may vary from a few hundred kilometers thick near tectonic highs to nearly 1,000 m in sub-basins. Little can be said about the presence or nature of Triassic and younger strata in the Lincoln Sea Basin until seismic or drilling data are available.

An extinct spreading center may cross the Lincoln Sea Basin and impinge on the northern coast of Greenland between Morris Jesup Plateau and Lomonosov Ridge (Soper and others, 1982). Late Cretaceous(?) basic dike swarms (Dawes, 1976) cut through lower Paleozoic terranes of North Greenland, and 1,500 m of Tertiary lavas and tuffs crop out below thrusts in the Kap Washington area, along the northern coast of Greenland. The thermal event accompanying the emplacement of the Tertiary volcanics has important implications for the geochemical maturation of sediments in the Lincoln Sea Basin.

Petroleum potential

Through extrapolation from the Wandel Sea Basin in North Greenland and the Sverdrup Basin in northern Ellesmere Island, strata of comparable Carboniferous to Tertiary age may be present in the Lincoln Sea Basin. Many of the limestones, marls, and shales in the Upper Carboniferous section in North Greenland are bituminous, and migrated hydrocarbons and bitumen have been reported in this interval in both North Greenland (Henderson, 1976) and northern Ellesmere Island. Additional potential source rocks may occur in Permian basinal shales and limestone-clastic sequences. Most of the potential source rocks in the onshore upper Paleozoic successions are mature to overmature and rank as intermediate source rocks for oil or gas condensate.

Most of the predominantly shale formations in the Triassic and Jurassic sequences in the Sverdrup Basin onshore may contain beds that are potential prolific source rocks, and comparable strata probably occur in the Lincoln Sea Basin. In addition, the Lower and Upper Cretaceous formations in the Sverdrup Basin contain hydrocarbon-prone organic matter. The Cretaceous and younger units are usually geochemically immature except where they have been deeply buried (3,000 m or more [McMillan, 1982]), or where the Cretaceous-Tertiary thermal event has locally elevated maturation levels.

The grabens of the Lincoln Sea Basin probably preserve upper Paleozoic and Mesozoic sediments beneath a thick cover of Tertiary deposits. Reservoir and source rocks probably exist within these grabens. Throughout the basin, most of the grabens appear to have been formed during the various stages of the Eurekan orogeny, from Late Cretaceous to Tertiary time.

In the Amundsen Basin (Pole Abyssal Plain, Fig. 5) most of the ocean-floor spreading has occurred since the Oligocene. Because it is contiguous with the Amundsen Basin, most of the graben development and sediment infilling in the Lincoln Sea Basin between the Morris Jesup Plateau and the Lomonosov Ridge also must have occurred during post–mid-Tertiary time.

The area between the Lomonosov Ridge and the Alpha Ridge, in contrast with the area between the Morris Jesup Plateau and Lomonosov Ridge to the northeast, experienced graben development and sediment infilling slightly earlier in the Tertiary. The individual grabens in this area are much smaller than in the area to the northeast, and fewer have thick sedimentary sections. In the area between the Morris Jesup Plateau and the Lomonosov Ridge there is the potential for larger traps, but the timing of structural development, geochemical maturation, sediment infilling, and trap sealing is less favorable. The hydrocarbon potential for the Lincoln Sea Basin cannot be properly assessed because of the absence of critical data, but it is probably relatively low when compared with other basins of the Arctic Ocean region.

CANADIAN ARCTIC COASTAL PLAIN AND SHELF

The Canadian Arctic Coastal Plain and Shelf (Fig. 1) form a strip along the Arctic Ocean 150 to 200 km wide from Cape Richards at 83°N (Fig. 2) to Amundsen Gulf at 72°N. This area comprises about 270,000 km^2 of the offshore Arctic Ocean Basin.

Data for this region are mainly potential field geophysics comprising both extensive aeromagnetic surveys (Coles and Taylor, this volume) and gravity surveys (Sobczak and others, this volume). Seismic reflection data exist mainly on the coastal plain and the shelf off Banks Island. Recently, seismic reflection data have been obtained along the path of an ice island on the inner shelf north of Axel Heiberg Island and on the outer shelf north of Ellef Ringnes Island (Overton and others, 1989). Reconnaissance seismic refraction lines were shot on the shelf north of Ellef Ringnes Island (Hobson and Overton, 1967) and northwest of Brock Island (Overton, 1970; Berry and Barr, 1971). In 1985 and 1986 a seismic refraction grid was shot on the shelf north of Axel Heiberg and Meighen islands (Asudeh and others, 1989).

Well data are available only from the coastal plain. No wells have been drilled on the shelf due to the presence of the shifting polar ice pack. The geology and geophysics of the shelf have been summarized recently by Embry and others (1988) and Forsyth and others (1988).

Tectonic evolution and petroleum potential

Interpretation of the stratigraphy, structure, and petroleum potential of the Arctic continental shelf is based on the available geological and geophysical data and on the assumption that the Amerasia Basin formed in part by counterclockwise rotation and translation of Alaska and adjacent Siberia away from the Arctic Islands (i.e., it is a passive margin of rift origin). The major geologic events that shaped the geology of the margin are:

1. Lower Paleozoic sedimentation on the Arctic Platform and in the Franklinian Geosyncline, with subsequent deformation

of the latter in Silurian and Devonian time (Ellesmerian orogeny).

2. Formation of the Sverdrup Basin by rifting during Carboniferous and Early Permian time and subsequent thermal subsidence.

3. Opening of the Amerasia Basin by rifting and subsequent sea-floor spreading from Middle Jurassic to latest Cretaceous time.

4. Deformation of the northeastern portion of the Arctic Islands related to the opening of Labrador Sea and Baffin Bay in latest Cretaceous–early Tertiary time (Eurekan orogeny).

A number of regional unconformities developed in the Arctic Islands continental shelf region in response to these tectonic events, and the geologic evolution and petroleum potential of the area can be discussed in terms of six unconformity-bounded sequences: (a) lower Paleozoic, (b) upper Paleozoic–Lower Jurassic, (c) Middle Jurassic–lowest Cretaceous, (d) Lower Cretaceous, (e) Upper Cretaceous–lower Tertiary, (f) upper Tertiary. The general stratigraphy for the northern, central, and southern portions of the coastal plain and shelf is given in Figure 5. For summaries of upper Paleozoic and Mesozoic strata, respectively, in the adjacent Sverdrup Basin, see Davies and Nassichuk (1989) and Embry (1989).

Lower Paleozoic strata underlie the entire Canadian Arctic shelf but vary greatly in character along its length. Three zones are recognized, which allows the shelf to be divided into three sectors (Fig. 1). In the northeast sector, which extends from Cape Richards to Axel Heiberg Island, the lower Paleozoic rocks consist of highly deformed clastics, carbonates, and volcanics which are variably metamorphosed and intruded by igneous rocks. In the central sector, which extends from Axel Heiberg Island to northern Prince Patrick Island, the lower Paleozoic strata are folded and faulted argillaceous clastics and cherts. In the southwestern sector the lower Paleozoic strata consist mainly of gently deformed carbonates.

The petroleum potential of the lower Paleozoic strata along the margin is poor. In the northeastern and central sectors, these strata are too highly deformed and thermally altered to have any potential. In the southwestern sector, thermal maturation is still very high (>3.0 Ro), which suggests that only dry gas might be present.

Upper Paleozoic to Lower Jurassic strata along the continental margin were deposited on the northwest margin of the Sverdrup Basin and thus occur only in the area adjacent to central Prince Patrick Island and northward. The strata are truncated to progressively deeper levels northwestward across the shelf (Figs. 7 and 8), with Triassic and upper Paleozoic strata being preserved only along the inner shelf (Fig. 7). Upper Paleozoic strata consist mainly of shallow-water carbonates and clastics. Overlying Triassic strata are mainly shales and siltstones with a few sandstone-dominant intervals. The petroleum potential of upper Paleozoic to Jurassic strata in the Sverdrup Basin proper is significant, but the potential of this interval in the continental shelf is difficult to assess. Both reservoir and source strata are present (Embry, 1989; Embry and others, 1989), especially in the Triassic interval. Traps may occur along the subcrop belts of porous units where they are sealed by overlying Cretaceous shales. The thermal maturity of the strata varies from overmature (dry gas) in the northeast sector to mature (oil and gas) in the central sector. Overall, the potential of these strata is rated as fair to good, especially in the central sector.

Middle Jurassic to lowermost Cretaceous strata are absent along the landward margin of the shelf, but they may be present in grabens that formed during the initial rifting phase of the Amerasia Basin. Such grabens might be expected on the outer shelf and slope and might contain clastic rocks of fluvial, lacustrine, and possibly marine origin as well as volcanic rocks. Where such grabens are not too deeply buried by subsequent Cretaceous and Tertiary strata, the petroleum potential might be reasonable, but lack of data precludes any realistic assessment.

Lower Cretaceous strata are absent or very thin along the landward margin of the continental shelf but very likely occur in down-faulted areas on the continental shelf. Thick intervals of alternating sandstone-dominant and shale-dominant units (Fig. 6) would be expected. Volcanic strata and associated dikes and sills occur within this sequence in the northern portion of the shelf (Embry and Osadetz, 1988). Again, the petroleum potential of such inferred strata is difficult to assess. Overall, both reservoirs and source intervals may well be present, and the petroleum potential of the strata would be good in areas of favorable maturation.

Much of the continental shelf succession consists of thick Upper Cretaceous to lower Tertiary strata that were deposited during and/or following the opening of the Amerasia Basin. The lower strata consist of prodelta shales (Kanguk Formation) and are overlain by thick, sandstone-dominant clastics of deltaic origin (Eureka Sound Formation). Several depositional sequences equivalent to those identified in the Beaufort Sea likely compose the lower Tertiary succession. Thick Upper Cretaceous volcanics occur in the northeastern sector (Embry and Osadetz, 1988). These strata were deformed by the Eurekan orogeny, the intensity of deformation decreasing southwestward. High-amplitude folds and faults probably characterize the northeastern sector, with lower amplitude structures in the central sector. The strata in the southwestern sector are essentially undeformed and exhibit gentle seaward dips. The petroleum potential of these strata is rated as good; reservoirs, source intervals, and traps are potentially present in all three sectors. The central sector likely holds the greatest promise because the succession is only mildly deformed, free of volcanic rocks, and thick enough so that source strata are probably mature.

The uppermost sequence, which is present all along the shelf, consists of Miocene to Holocene deltaic clastics (the Beaufort Formation). The strata are undeformed and thicken gradually seaward. The petroleum potential of this succession is very low due to lack of source rock and structures and overall very low thermal maturity.

In summary, the Phanerozoic succession of the polar conti-

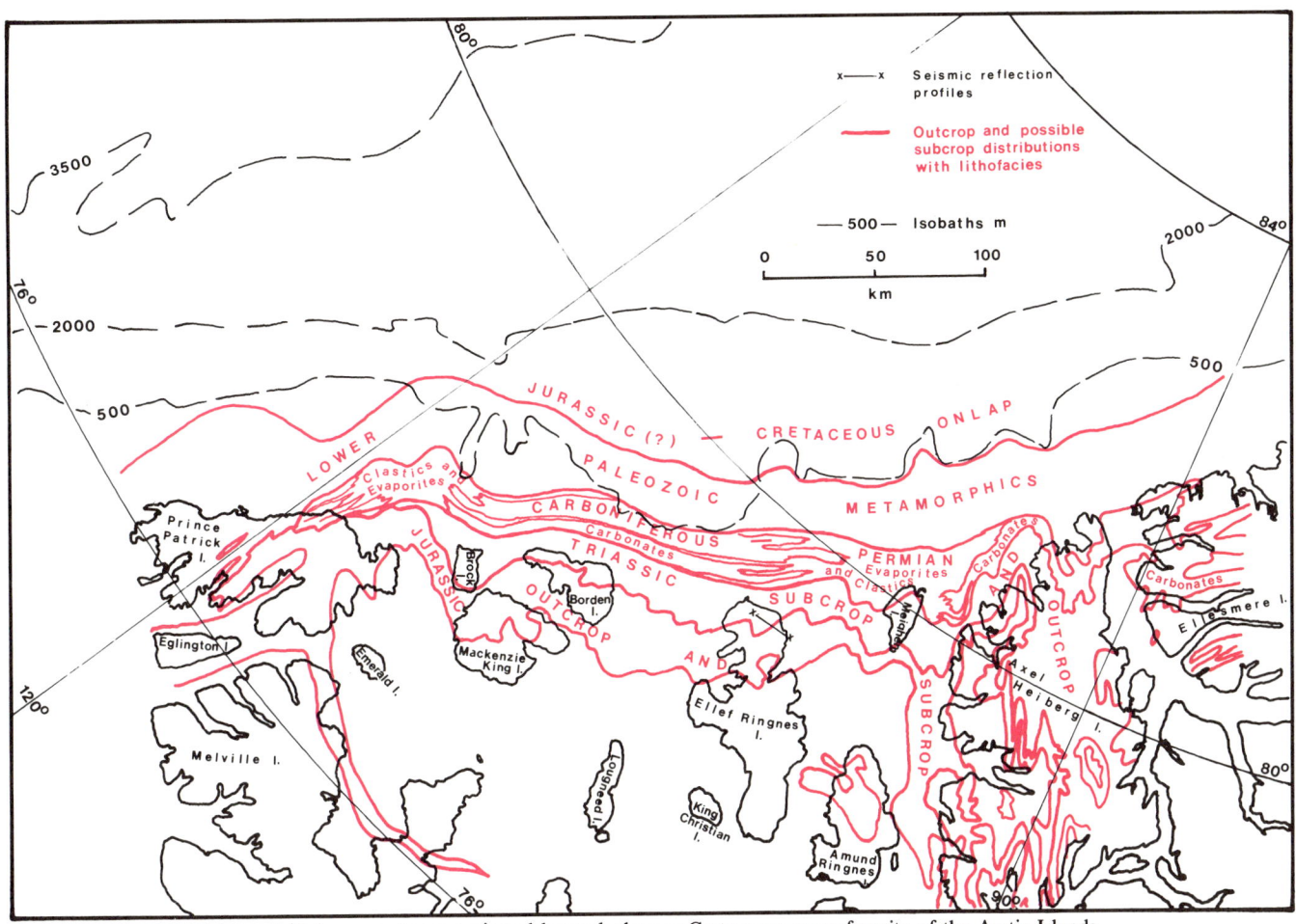

Figure 7. Subcrop patterns projected beneath the pre-Cretaceous unconformity of the Arctic Islands Shelf.

nental shelf consists of six major sequences that are separated from each other by regional unconformities of tectonic origin. The area of greatest petroleum potential occurs in the central sector of the shelf where gently deformed Cretaceous and Tertiary strata as much as 12 km thick underlie the outer shelf and upper Paleozoic–Triassic strata underlie Cretaceous strata along the inner shelf.

MACKENZIE DELTA–BEAUFORT SEA BASIN

The Mackenzie Delta–Beaufort Sea Basin extends in the offshore from Amundsen Gulf at 72°N to the Alaska-Yukon border at 141°W (Figs. 1 and 2). Mesozoic and Cenozoic sediments extend from near 68°N in the onshore areas of the Mackenzie Delta to the distal end of the delta's sedimentary cone north of 73°N.

Extensive geophysical data exist for the Mackenzie Delta–Beaufort Sea region. Gravity and aeromagnetic coverage extend into the offshore areas, and more than a hundred thousand kilometers of reflection seismic coverage exists for the onshore and offshore portions of the basin. The interpretations of the geophysical data have been verified by data from approximately 240 exploratory wells.

The geology and regional tectonics of the Canadian Beaufort Sea and adjacent land areas are covered in Dixon and Dietrich (this volume). A brief summary of the geology and structure is included here to serve as a basis for an evaluation of the hydrocarbon potential.

Along the southeast margin of the Mackenzie Delta–Beaufort Sea Basin, southwest of Amundsen Gulf, Proterozoic sedimentary and volcanic rocks are overlain by Cambrian through Devonian sedimentary strata. Following deposition of transgressive clastics and minor evaporites during the Cambrian, sedimentation during the rest of the lower Paleozoic was dominated by carbonate deposition (Fig. 9). During the Late Devonian, rare reefs developed locally; they were surrounded by bituminous basinal shales transitional upward into coarser clastics prograded from the Arctic Islands (Klovan and Embry, 1971). Carboniferous strata are not known to occur along the southeast flank of the Mackenzie Delta–Beaufort Sea Basin, but according to the Government of Canada's (Department of Indian and Northern Affairs) 1981 "Schedule of Wells for the Northwest Territories

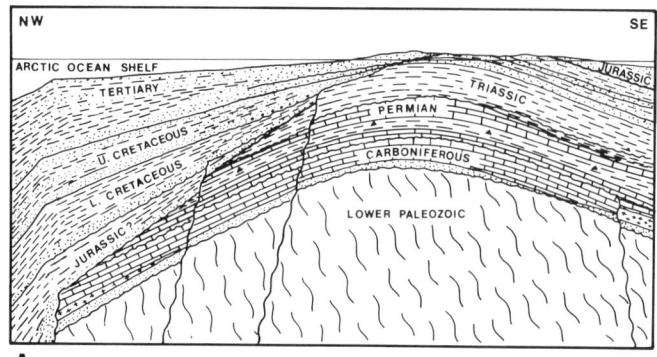

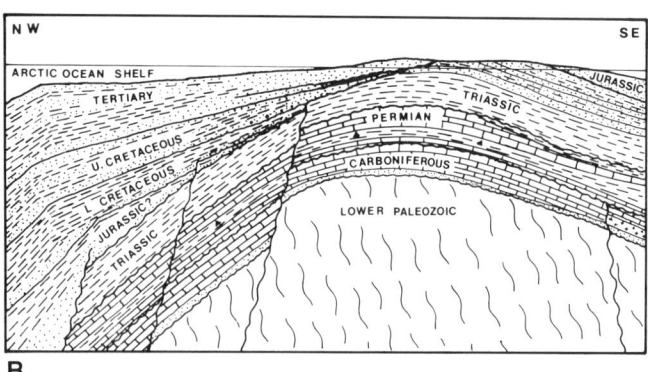

Figure 8. A. The Sverdrup Rim and Arctic Islands Shelf interpreted as a homocline that has been flexed and faulted. B. The Sverdrup Rim and Arctic Islands Shelf interpreted as an anticline that has been faulted.

and Yukon Territory," Permian clastics may have been encountered in delta wells west of 135°W.

Along the southwest margin of the basin the Precambrian and younger Neruokpuk Formation is variously overlain by Cambrian through Devonian basinal shales or Cambrian through Silurian marine limestones. The lower Paleozoic and Precambrian strata are unconformably overlain by transgressive Carboniferous sequences of conglomerates, sandstones, shales, and diachronous limestones. The Carboniferous strata are disconformably overlain by a regressive Permian sequence composed, in ascending order, of limestone, shale, and sandstone. Locally, limestone and shale of the Upper Triassic Shublik Formation unconformably overlie the Permian strata. Economic basement for liquid hydrocarbons in the cratonically deposited sediments around the margins of the Mackenzie Delta–Beaufort Sea Basin appears to rise from within the lower Paleozoic section in the east to within or above the Permian-Carboniferous section in the west.

Jurassic strata unconformably overlie Proterozoic through Triassic rocks around the margin of the Mackenzie Delta–Beaufort Sea Basin. Coarse-clastic rocks of Early and Middle Jurassic age lap onto the Paleozoic and Proterozoic sequences along the southeast margin of the basin. The Bug Creek Group contains nearshore clastic rocks, and the Kingak Formation represents relatively thicker argillaceous basinal rocks that thicken to the north away from the North American craton (Poulton, 1982).

The Jurassic succession consists of several transgressive-regressive megacycles (Dixon, 1982), with coarse-clastic rocks being introduced into the basin from both southeast and southwest hinterlands.

Five depositional sequences, or megacycles, prograded northward into the Mackenzie Delta–Beaufort Sea Basin during the Early Cretaceous. In each cycle a marine transgressive shale was overlain diachronously by delta-front sandstone and siltstone. In each megacycle, regional depositional breaks or subaerial unconformities bound the prograding clastic units. Generally, each megacycle extends farther into the basin than previously deposited sequences. By Late Cretaceous time the slope-shelf break between the delta-front sandstone and the prodelta shale facies had prograded beyond the present shoreline. The organically rich Boundary Creek and subsequent Smoking Hills sequences were deposited during this time (Dixon and Dietrich, this volume).

The deposition of the Fish River sequence followed during the Maastrichtian through mid-Paleocene, spanning the Cretaceous-Tertiary boundary. As much as 5,000 m of strata representing the Fish River sequence are preserved in its depocenter along the southwest margin of the basin.

From mid-Paleocene to Pleistocene time, seven more sequences were deposited in the Mackenzie Delta–Beaufort Sea Basin. They are, in ascending order, the Reindeer, Richards, Kopanoar, Kugmallit, Mackenzie Bay, Akpak, and Iperk sequences. The Shallow Bay sequence is currently being deposited above the glacial and interglacial deposits. The Upper Cretaceous to Holocene sediments in the Mackenzie Delta–Beaufort Sea Basin are at least 11,000 m thick seaward of the Mackenzie Delta.

Syndepositional tectonic events complicated the simplified depositional patterns presented here. The Jurassic and Early Cretaceous sedimentation occurred along the collapsing southeast margin of the Mackenzie Delta–Beaufort Sea Basin; the bounding Aklavik Arch Complex served as a local sediment source. The onlapping Jurassic and Early Cretaceous sediments are preserved on the down-to-basin fault blocks that are the sites of hydrocarbon traps.

Laramide faults displaying dextral offsets onshore have been traced offshore where antithetic faults and the probable juxtaposition of sedimentary facies reflect the structural complexities associated with lateral motion. The northeast-southwest compression accompanying the lateral motion has resulted in enhanced relief and possibly reverse faulting on the elongated diapiric structures in the offshore area of the southwestern Mackenzie Delta–Beaufort Sea Basin. In the adjacent onshore areas, this style of deformation is reflected in the thrust faults that have been located in Jurassic and Cretaceous strata.

The age and position of the diapiric structures and faults vary with the age of the underlying depocenters. The Paleocene diapirs lie outboard of the Maastrichtian to Paleocene Fish Creek sequence depocenter, subparallel to the southwest margin of the basin. Subsequent structures migrate to the northeast, and their axes rotate counterclockwise into north-northeast alignments, fol-

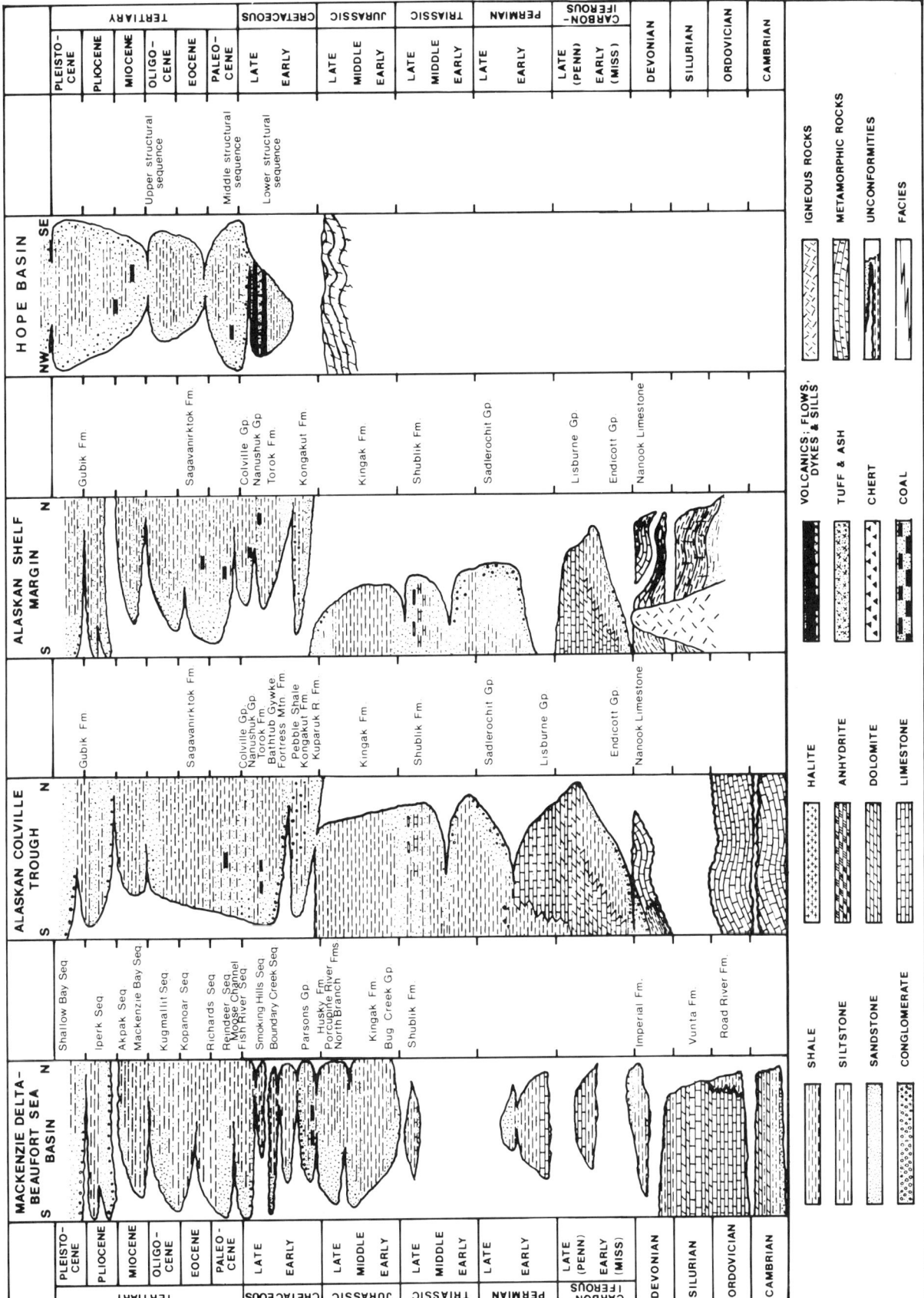

Figure 9. Schematic stratigraphic sequences of the Mackenzie Delta–Beaufort Sea Basin, the Alaskan Colville Trough, the Alaskan Shelf margin, and Hope Basin.

Figure 10. Map of the significant Mackenzie Delta–Beaufort Sea discoveries.

lowing the younger depositional trends (Willumsen and Cote, 1982). Some of the later faults are perpendicular to the associated diapirs. The diapiric structures are numerous in the Canadian portion of the Mackenzie Delta–Beaufort Sea Basin and extend both into the Alaskan Beaufort shelf and into the abyssal plain of the Canada Basin.

Petroleum potential

Exploration in the Mackenzie Delta–Beaufort Sea Basin began in 1958, but it was not until 1965 that the Reindeer D-27 well was completed in the Mackenzie Delta. The intensity of activity increased following the Prudhoe Bay discovery in Alaska, and oil was found in Lower Cretaceous sandstones in the Atkinson Point H-25 well in 1970. To 1988, approximately 240 wells had been drilled, resulting in the discovery of 49 significant hydrocarbon accumulations. Seventeen fields contain oil, 9 contain both oil and gas, and 23 contain gas (Fig. 10). Many of the fields require further delineation drilling and production testing to validate the size of the accumulations. Currently the Amauligak field, with estimated oil reserves of 80×10^6 m^3 (500 million barrels), and the Taglu field with estimated gas reserves of 85×10^9 m^3 (3 trillion cubic ft [TCF]) have the largest established reserves (Dixon and others, 1988).

Hydrocarbons with probable sources in Cretaceous sediments have been found in Devonian carbonate reservoirs in two wells. Other horizons yielding hydrocarbons include the Parsons Group sandstones in the first sequence above the Jurassic-Cretaceous Husky Formation; the Paleocene Moose Channel and Reindeer sequences; the Eocene Richards and Kopanoar sequences; the Oligocene Kugmallit sequence; and the Oligocene-Miocene Mackenzie Bay sequence.

Along the southeast margin of the basin, organic-rich and bituminous Devonian shales may constitute source rocks where they are still within the geochemically mature zone. In the west, Permian shale may be a fair source rock locally. The organic-rich shales and mudstones of the Kingak and Husky Formations are probably the sources of the reservoirs in the Parsons Group sandstones. Oils on the southeast margin of the basin were probably derived from the organic-rich mudstones and bituminous shales of the Upper Cretaceous Boundary Creek and Smoking Hills Formations.

The Tertiary sediments are terrestrially derived and should be gas-prone, with limited high-wax oil potential. The Tertiary section, however, produces unique oils and condensates that were derived from resin-rich organic material at lower than normal maturation levels (Snowdon, 1980). Oils of normal composition may have originated in deeper sequences and migrated up fault planes to accumulate in Tertiary traps.

The reservoirs that have been found to contain hydrocarbons, or may be found in the future, fall into several categories. Potential reservoirs exist in leached Paleozoic rocks at unconformities. In the Mesozoic and Tertiary sequences, potential reservoirs exist in each of the delta-front sandstones of the delta megacycles. Additional reservoirs may be found in channel sandstones of the delta-plain environments or in turbiditic sandstones of the prodelta slope environments.

Trapping mechanisms are provided by fault-bounded, rollover anticlines and tilted blocks; draping over, and truncations against, diapiric structures; and onlap onto existing structures. The marine shales within the section provide excellent seals for hydrocarbons in all of the trapping configurations. Because many of the structures are syndepositional, the sandstone reservoirs may not be fully developed over the tops of the prospective structural traps. Sandstone reservoirs may be best developed on the upslope side of ponding diapiric structures or on the downthrown side of listric faults.

Deltas are normally prolific hydrocarbon producers; the size of the fields is determined by the size of the structures and their drainage areas. Because the structures in the Mackenzie Delta–Beaufort Sea Basin are large, the potential for large individual accumulations is excellent.

The Mackenzie Delta–Beaufort Sea Basin is a relatively cool basin geochemically; the top of the normal "oil window" is very deep in the younger sedimentary section. Because the structures become younger oceanward (bringing over-pressured diapiric shale closer to the sea floor) and the top of the normal "oil window" gets deeper oceanward, the potential zone for finding oil becomes increasingly restricted offshore.

Reserves of about 0.238 to 0.317×10^9 m^3 (1.5 to 2.0 billion barrels [BBO]) of oil and 299 to 356×10^9 m^3 (10.9 to 12.6 TCf) of gas have already been found in the Mackenzie Delta–Beaufort Sea Basin (Dixon and others, 1988). The Geological Survey of Canada has recently completed an assessment of the region and has defined approximately 20 exploration plays (Dixon and others, 1988). In this assessment the expected values of the undiscovered resources are about three times the quantities of oil that have already been discovered and about five times the quantity of gas already discovered. The Mackenzie Delta–

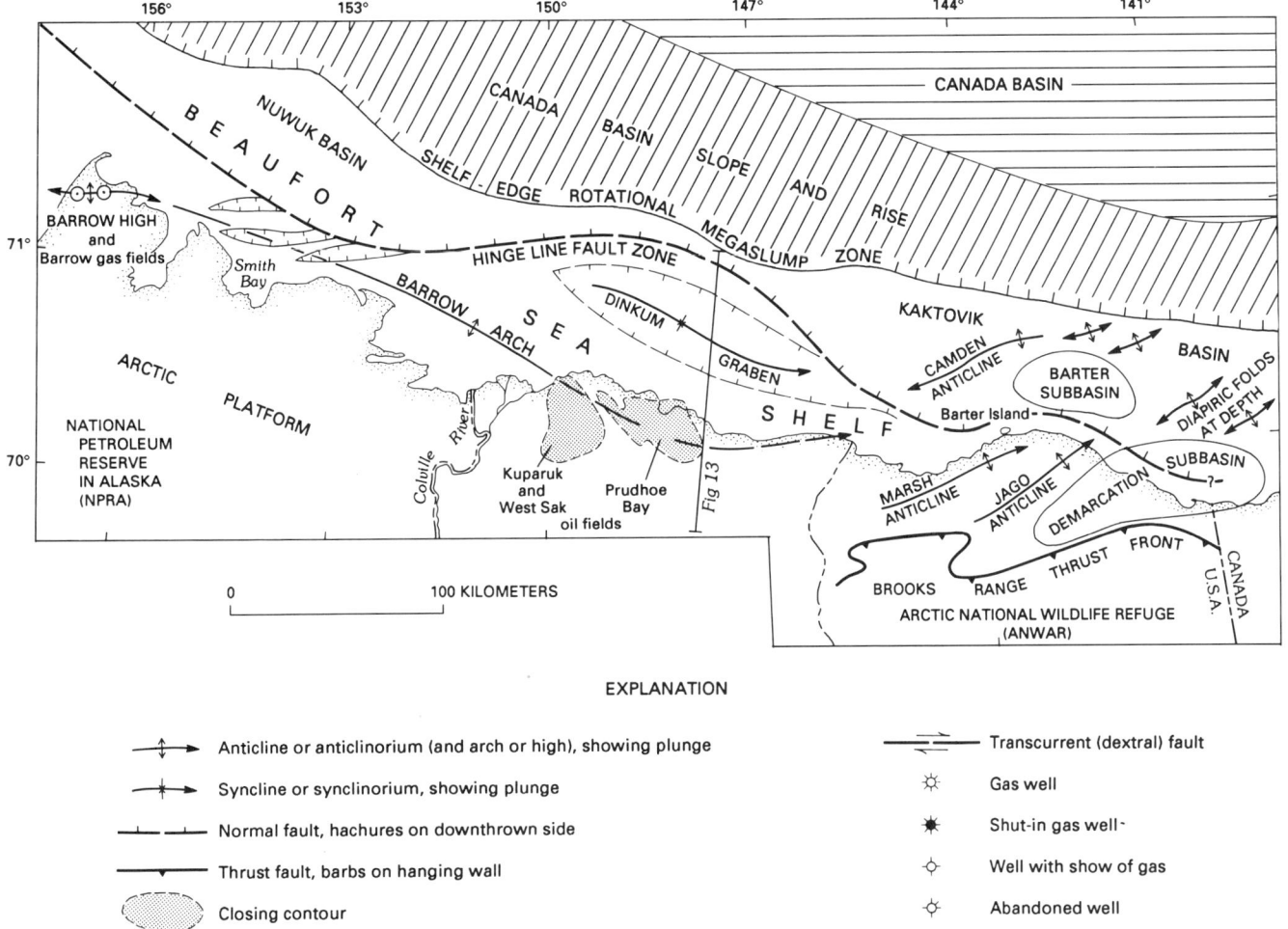

Figure 11. Geologic framework of the Beaufort Sea shelf north of the Arctic Platform and the eastern Brooks Range thrust front. Modified from Craig and others (1985). Includes explanation of map symbols on Figures 11, 14 to 16, and 19.

Beaufort Sea Basin has perhaps the greatest potential for oil and gas of all the basins in the Arctic Ocean region adjacent to the North American Plate.

NORTHERN ALASKA CONTINENTAL MARGIN

The Northern Alaska Continental Margin extends in the offshore from the Alaska-Yukon border at 141°W on the east to the International Date Line near 169°W on the west (Figs. 1 and 2). The region is very large and has diverse stratigraphic and structural habitats, and thus variable oil potential. For these reasons it is subdivided into three sections for discussion: (1) the Beaufort Sea shelf basins, (2) the Chukchi Sea shelf basins north of Herald Arch, and (3) the Chukchi Sea shelf–Hope Basin south of Herald Arch.

Beaufort Sea shelf basins

Introduction and regional tectonic elements. The Beaufort Sea shelf trends northwesterly over 600 km from the Canada–United States boundary, and averages about 75 km in width from the coastline on the south to the shelf edge of the Beaufort Sea slope and rise on the north (Fig. 11). The shelf edge and upper slope are the locus of a zone of listric rotational faults or megaslumps that drop the thick sedimentary prism of the shelf into the deep Canada Basin. The Barrow Arch approximately defines the southern margin of the Beaufort Sea shelf basins. In the central and western sectors of the shelf, structures are tensional in listric, down-to-the-north faults in the upper and younger part of the sedimentary prism, as in the Nuwuk and Kaktovik Basins. Structure is also tensional in graben and half-graben complexes beneath a regional unconformity of Early Cretaceous age, as in the Dinkum graben (Figs. 11 and 13). In the eastern sector of the shelf, north of the Arctic National Wildlife Refuge, anticlinal structures are compressional in detachment and diapiric anticlines, presumably in response to northward-directed compression from the Brooks Range thrust front. The Barter and the Demarcation subbasins are regionally synclinal and were downwarped contemporaneously with folding.

Stratigraphy. The stratigraphy of the offshore is interpreted from geophysical, mainly seismic, data and by analogy to onshore seismic, outcrop, and well data. The onshore data base is voluminous. Stratigraphic columns in recent industry and government publications are selected here to illustrate the onshore stratigraphy (Fig. 12).

Lerand (1973) divided the bedded rocks of western Arctic North America into three stratigraphic sequences: (1) the Franklinian, (2) the Ellesmerian, and (3) the Brookian–each of contrasting tectonic style, provenance terrane, and lithology.

The Franklinian sequence may range from Cambrian to Devonian in age. It is economic basement for petroleum exploration beneath the North Slope of Alaska and the offshore area. The rocks consist of slightly metamorphosed and folded lower Paleozoic (Ordovician to Silurian) graptolite-bearing argillite with thin beds of arenite, carbonate, and chert beneath a Late Devonian unconformity.

The Ellesmerian sequence of Mississippian to Early Cretaceous age rests unconformably on the eroded Franklinian basement (Figs. 12 and 14B). The rocks comprise a stable shelf clastic and carbonate sequence 0 to 5,000 m thick that was derived from a northerly provenance terrane named Barrovia by Tailleur (1973). Barrovia was rifted away from Arctic Alaska in Jurassic to Early Cretaceous time. The Ellesmerian rocks are time transgressive northerly on the Arctic Platform and they thin to 0 m on the Barrow Arch beneath the widespread Early Cretaceous unconformity at the base of the late Neocomian pebble shale unit (PSU). The PSU is generally a thin (0–700 m), low-velocity, organic shale–starved basin unit (Fig. 12) that marks the transition from Ellesmerian shelf rocks derived from the northerly source terranes of Barrovia to Brookian nonmarine and marine shale and graywacke flushed from the rising Brooks Range beginning in Late Jurassic time.

The Early Carboniferous transgressive sequence of clastic rocks that make up the Endicott Group begins with conglomerates that are transitional upward and northeastward into finer

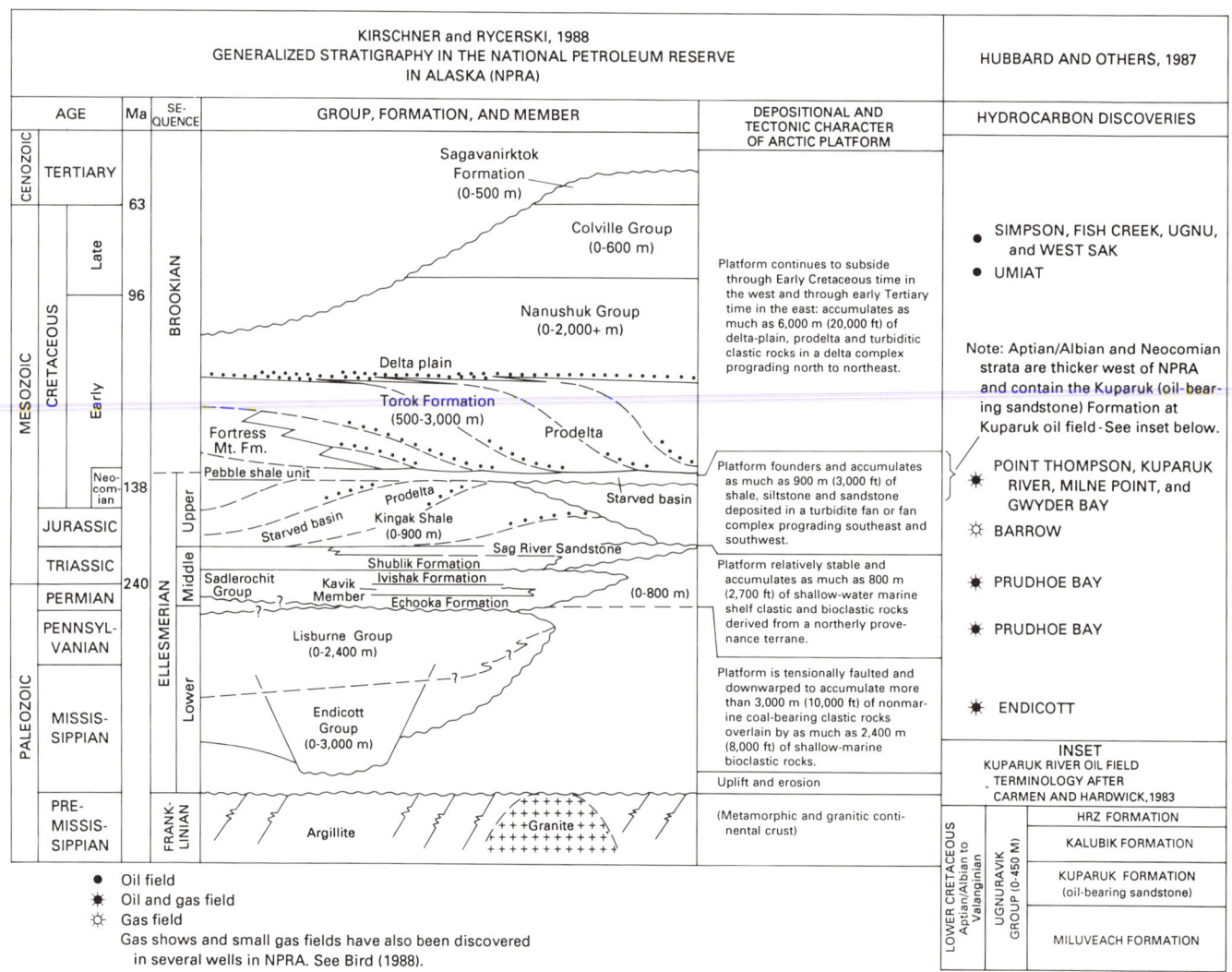

Figure 12. Generalized stratigraphy in National Petroleum Reserve in Alaska, showing interpreted environments of deposition for selected units, stratigraphic position of hydrocarbon discoveries, and Kuparuk River oil field terminology proposed by Carman and Hardwick (1983).

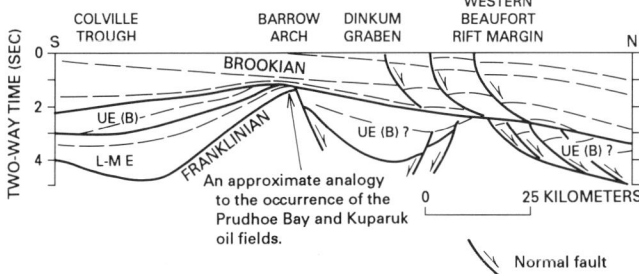

Figure 13. Schematic cross section showing stratigraphic and structural relations of the Brookian, upper Ellesmerian (UE[B]), lower and middle Ellesmerian (L-ME), and Franklinian sequences (and the position of the Prudhoe Bay and Kuparuk oil fields) beneath the North Slope and the Beaufort Shelf and Slope. Hubbard and others (1987) have proposed the name Beaufortian sequence (B) for the upper Ellesmerian strata of Jurassic to Early Cretaceous age, and interpret these strata to represent a failed rift sequence in the Dinkum graben and the North Slope. Grantz and May (this volume) refer to the presumed upper Ellesmerian strata in the Dinkum graben as the Dinkum sequence.

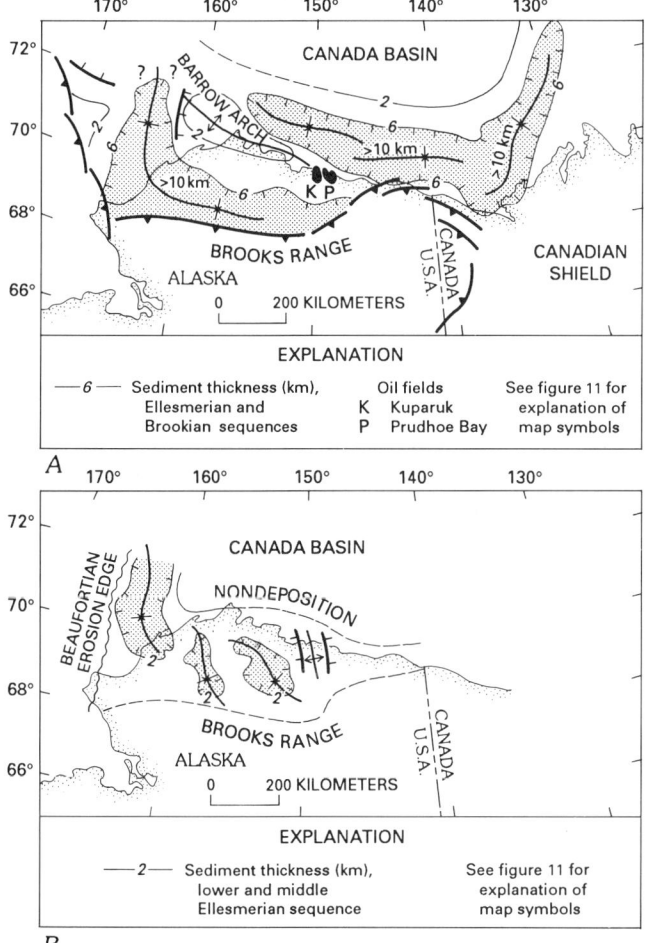

Figure 14. A. Generalized isopachous map of the combined Ellesmerian, Beaufortian, and Brookian sequences beneath Northern Alaska and its offshore, modified from Hubbard and others (1987). B. Generalized isopachous map of the Ellesmerian sequence beneath Northern Alaska and its offshore, modified from Hubbard and others (1987).

grained units. Endicott Group clastics grade upward into carbonates of the overlying Lisburne Group. The Lisburne Group consists of a diachronous series of cyclic carbonates deposited in alternating subtidal to open-marine environments. The Lisburne limestones and dolomites range in age from late Early Carboniferous in the southwest to Early Permian in the northeast. In surface exposures the Lisburne Group may be much as 2,000 m thick. The Lisburne Group culminates in an erosional surface over most of the North Slope, but local sedimentation may be transitional into major transgressive-regressive sequences of the Permian to Lower Triassic Sadlerochit Group, which attains a thickness of about 500 m. The initial deposits of the Sadlerochit are argillaceous and glauconitic sandstones. They grade upward into shallow-water marine shales with locally developed turbiditic siltstone and sandstone lenses. The shale units in turn grade upward into prograding sandstone and conglomerate. The conglomerates are coarsest to the northeast, near the present coastline. Beneath the present Colville Basin, the Sadlerochit Group is coeval with a sequence of siliceous shale.

The Sadlerochit Group is paraconformably to unconformably overlain by the Middle to Late Triassic Shublik Formation. The Shublik represents another transgressive-regressive cycle and is composed of calcareous shale, sandstone, bioclastic limestone, and phosphatic pellets. A Late Triassic to Early Jurassic quartz sandstone and siltstone up to 40 m thick transitionally overlies the Shublik Formation.

The broadly distributed gray to black shales and minor siltstones of the Kingak Shale overlie the sand or siltstone unit. The Kingak varies from a feather edge to 1,200 m in thickness. It generally thins to the north, in part by internal unconformities, and thickens to the south, in part by diachronous deposition. Its age ranges from earliest Jurassic to Early Cretaceous (Neocomian).

In the Kuparuk–Prudhoe Bay area the Kingak Shale is overlain, in part unconformably, by the 450-m-thick Ugnuravik Group of Carman and Hardwick (1983), which contains the Kaparuk River Formation oil-bearing sandstones of the Kuparuk oil field (Fig. 12). The Ugnuravik Group of Aptian/Albian and Neocomian age and the Kingak Shale of Jurassic age compose the Beaufortian sequence as defined by Hubbard and others (1987) (Figs. 13 and 15A), which is stratigraphically equivalent to the upper Ellesmerian of Kirschner and Rycerski (1988) and Grantz and May (this volume). The Ugnuravik Group is subdivided into four formations: in descending order, they are the HRZ, Kalubik, Kuparuk, and Miluveach Formations (Carman and Hardwick, 1983). The upper HRZ Formation is lithologically correlatable to the PSU of the National Petroleum Reserve in Alaska (NPRA; see Fig. 11 for location). The PSU is a black shale characterized by high radioactivity, subrounded quartz and chert grains, and shell and woody fragments. It was probably deposited in a marine anoxic environment. The HRZ Formation is one of the richest source rocks in northern Alaska. The Kalubik Formation is a brownish-gray to black silty mudstone containing nodular and disseminated pyrite and siderite bands. The Kuparuk

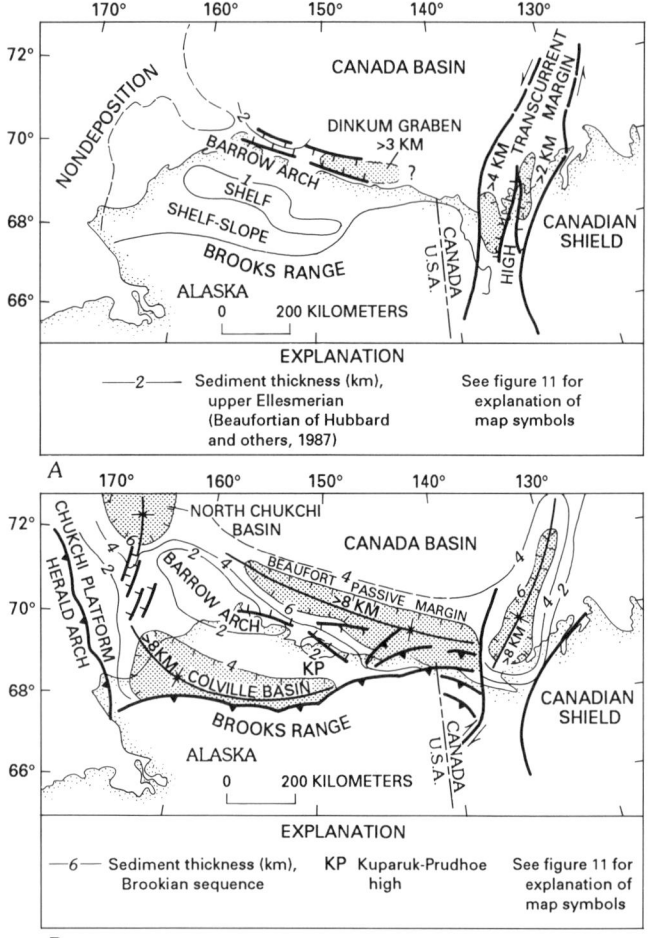

Figure 15. A. Generalized isopachous map of the Beaufortian sequence beneath Northern Alaska and its offshore, modified from Hubbard and others (1987). B. Generalized isopachous map of the Brookian sequence beneath Northern Alaska and its offshore, modified from Hubbard and others (1987).

Formation is a cyclic sequence of interbedded sandstone, siltstone, and mudstone. On the basis of microfauna, glauconite, bioturbation, and sedimentary structures, Carman and Hardwick (1983) interpret the formation to have been deposited in a shallow-marine environment. The basal Miluveach Formation consists of gray-brown to black silty mudstone that is micaceous and contains finely disseminated pyrite. It is noteworthy that the Kuparuk Formation sandstones are underlain by the black shales of the Kingak and Miluveach Formations and overlain by the black shales of the HRZ Formation, which in turn are overlain by deep-water turbidites of the basal Torok Formation. Also noteworthy is that the morphology of the Ugnuravik Group and the cyclic upward-coarsening sandstone strata in the Kuparuk Formation define characteristics very similar to those of a suprafan lobe deposited by turbidity currents in a submarine mid-fan environment.

A regional Lower Cretaceous unconformity of Hauterivian or early Barremian age, which lies between the Kuparuk and the overlying Kalubik Formation, is accompanied by down-to-basin faulting north of the Barrow Arch. It is the result of extensive erosion and has produced a complex subcrop pattern on the North Slope and beneath the Arctic Ocean continental terrace sedimentary wedge. The Lower Cretaceous unconformity in places truncates all formations down to, and including, the early Paleozoic rocks that constitute economic basement for petroleum.

The Brookian sequence includes all Cretaceous and Tertiary rocks derived from the Brooks Range. In the Aptian to Albian, conglomerates, sandstones, and shales were shed from the developing Brooks Range as the Fortress Mountain Formation and the Torok Formation. The sandstone units may have been deposited as turbidites and slope traction deposits. This sequence is about 8 km thick in the Colville Basin. It thins northerly over the Barrow Arch and thickens to about 8 km on the Beaufort passive margin (Fig. 15B).

The intertonguing shallow-marine sandstone, siltstone, shale, and conglomerate of the Nanushuk Group prograde basinward to transitionally overlie the Torok Formation. Upward, the Nanushuk Group is locally transitional into nonmarine sandstone and coal. Over the Barrow High, the Nanushuk Group is absent due to uplift and erosion, but within the Colville Basin to the southwest it may exceed 3,000 m in thickness. Fine-grained equivalents of the Nanushuk Group overlie the down-to-basin faults north of the Barrow Arch. The Nanushuk Group ranges in age from early Albian to late Cenomanian.

The Nanushuk Group is paraconformably to unconformably overlain by the Late Cretaceous Colville Group. Like the Mackenzie-Beaufort area, the depositional patterns developed in the Colville Group may mark the onset of a series of depositional megacycles. The marine shales at the base mark the initial marine transgression that is overlain by nonmarine clastics. An upper nonmarine unit progrades north and west over the Barrow Arch and into the Kaktovik Basin. North of the Barrow Arch the correlative sediments are probably fine-grained marine clastics.

The Colville Group is transitionally overlain by additional sequences of marine and nonmarine sediments of the Sagavanirktok Formation. These sediments consist of carbonaceous shale, sandstone, and conglomerate with interbeds of lignite. In the onshore areas this Tertiary section may be up to 3,000 m thick, but north of the Barrow Arch these sediments may thicken to more than 7,000 m.

Petroleum Potential. The play concepts and hydrocarbon trap configurations of Craig and others (1985) and the U.S. Geological Survey and the U.S. Minerals Management Service (1988) are summarized here for the Beaufort Sea shelf province. Eighteen exploratory wells were drilled in the province through 1987. Fifteen tested Ellesmerian plays and three tested Brookian plays. Most of the wells encountered minor to significant shows of oil and gas.

Source rocks in the Ellesmerian Sequence are organic carbon sapropelic oil-prone kerogens within the thermal oil window.

Total thickness of potential source rock is about 600 m. Source rocks in the Brookian Sequence are shales with about 1 percent TOC., Kerogens are terrestrial and gas prone, but much of the sequence is thermally immature. Reservoir rocks in the Ellesmerian are mainly mineralogically mature quartz-rich sandstone and, to some extent, carbonates. Reservoir rocks in the Brookian are immature and contaminated with clay and silt, but individual potential reservoir beds can be up to 200 m thick. The largest discovered oil field in Brookian sandstone is the West Sak heavy oil field, with about 40 BBO in place; in upper Ellesmerian sandstone is the Kuparuk oil field with about 6 BBO in place; in the Ellesmerian is the Prudhoe Bay oil field with about 23 BBO (sandstone reservoirs) and 3 BBO (carbonate reservoirs) in place.

In the Nuwuk Basin the potentially larger prospects are roll-over anticlines on listric faults in Brookian deltaic sandstone reservoirs, and fault-unconformity prospects in Ellesmerian sandstone reservoirs (Fig. 13). In the Dinkum graben failed-rift sequence, primarily fault traps may offer prospects in Jurassic to Early Cretaceous sandstone reservoirs. Along the trend of the Barrow Arch, relatively shallow prospects in PSU sandstone reservoirs, other smaller failed-rift sequences similar in style to the Dinkum graben, and a Prudhoe Bay–type accumulation may be present. Tests of the large Mukluk prospect north of the Colville River delta, however, which was a Prudhoe Bay–type play, failed to find an economic oil accumulation. In the Kaktovik Basin, as in the Nuwuk Basin, rollover anticlines on listric faults with Brookian sandstone reservoirs may be present, as well as compressional thrust-folds and diapir-driven anticlinal fold traps. In the Barter and Demarcation subbasins, primarily stratigraphically controlled sandstone wedges could be prospects. Although there are numerous play styles and prospects, a large oil accumulation will be necessary to be economic, because gas is currently not economic. An estimate of the mean probability for undiscovered recoverable oil on the Beaufort Sea shelf reported by the U.S. Geological Survey and the U.S. Minerals Management Service (1988) is 1.27 billion barrels.

Chukchi Sea shelf basins

Regional Tectonic Elements. The area of the Chukchi Sea discussed in this section is bounded on the south by the Herald Arch; on the west by 168°58′W (the USA-Russian Convention of 1867 line); on the north by the North Chukchi Basin, North Chukchi high, and Nuwuk Basin; and on the southeast by the northwest Alaska coastline. The total area is about 120,000 km² (Fig. 16). The data presented here are summarized mainly from Thurston and Theiss (1987), who in turn have mainly accepted previous geological interpretations of Grantz and May (1982, 1984). No wells have been drilled in this extensive offshore area, but the geology of the National Petroleum Reserve in Alaska (NPRA), southeast of the central Chukchi Basin, is reasonably well defined from previous exploration and offers a data base to aid seismic interpretation in the offshore.

The Herald Arch at the southern margin of the Chukchi

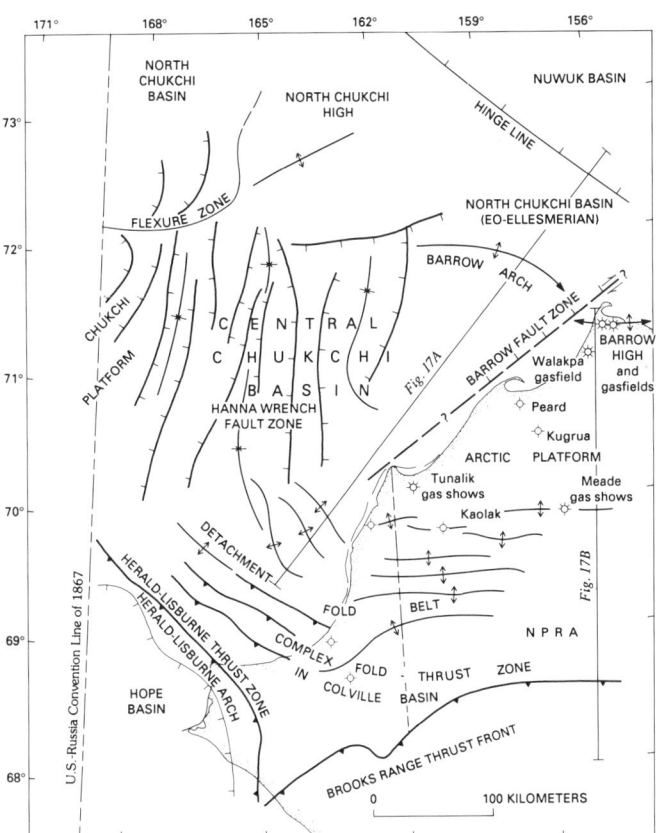

Figure 16. Geologic framework of the Chukchi Basin. Modified from Thurston and Theiss (1987).

Basin is a northwest-trending thrust belt of seismically opaque basement rocks probably comparable in style and lithologies to the Brooks Range thrust front. To the north a detachment fold belt in Brookian (Early Cretaceous) rocks also trends northwest, as a northwesterly extension of the detachment fold belt of the Colville Basin in NPRA. The detachment folds in Brookian sediments overlie mildly deformed Ellesmerian strata at depths in the range of 6 to 10 km (Figs. 17A and 17B). North of the fold belt is the central Chukchi Basin, which includes the Hanna wrench fault zone, a broad north-trending extensional (transtensional?) basin in a horst and graben complex. The basin is approximately square and about 200 km on a side. Brookian and Ellesmerian sedimentary fill above acoustic basement ranges from 6 to 12 km in the central basin area (Figs. 17A and 15B). The central Chukchi Basin is bordered on the west by the Chukchi Platform and on the east by the northern part of the Arctic Platform and the Barrow Arch. The thick Ellesmerian sequence of the central basin onlaps, wedges out, and is truncated beneath the Early Cretaceous unconformity at the base of the PSU along the western and eastern platform margins, and probably also to the north on the Barrow Arch and North Chukchi high, which are fundamentally northwesterly extensions of the onshore Arctic Platform (Profile 9E, Plate 9, this volume). The North Chukchi Basin and the

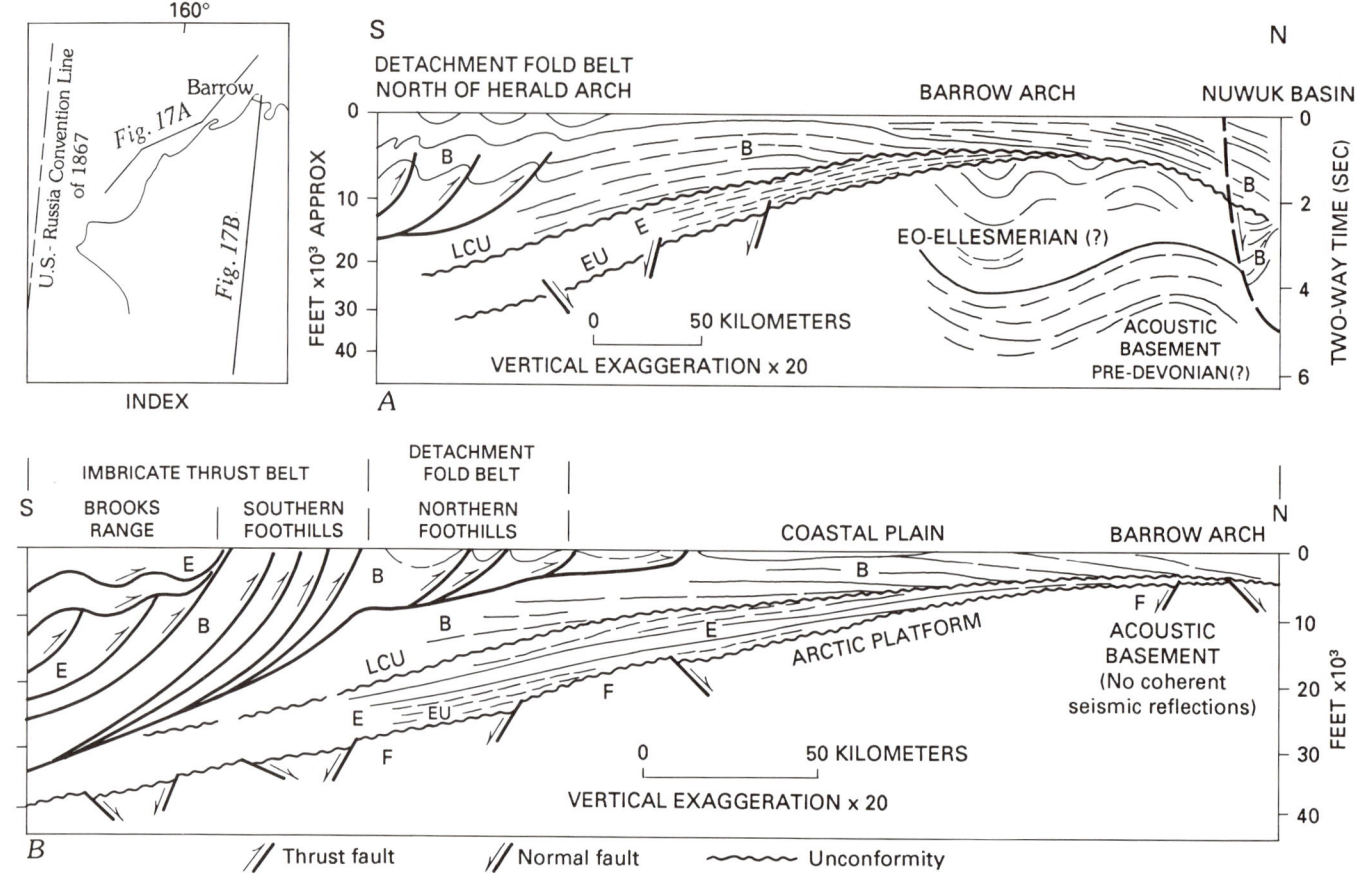

Figure 17. A. Modified from Grantz and others (1981) to show the coherent Eo-Ellesmerian sequence on the Barrow Arch in the northeast Chukchi Sea (Fig. 17A) in contrast to the acoustic basement with no coherent seismic reflections in the Franklinian sequence on the Arctic Platform in NPRA (Fig. 17B). B, Brookian sequence; E, Ellesmerian sequence; F, Franklinian sequence; LCU, Lower Cretaceous unconformity; EU, basal Ellesmerian unconformity.

Nuwuk Basin are the locus of a northward-thickening wedge of prograding Brookian rocks and large listric faults that downdrop the thick Brookian wedge toward the north.

Stratigraphy. In Figure 18 the seismic signature of the stratigraphy in the Chukchi Basin is modified from Thurston and Theiss (1987), and the sequence nomenclature from Grantz and May (1987). In NPRA three sequences are recognized: the Franklinian sequence, which is acoustically opaque and consists of strongly deformed and mildly metamorphosed sedimentary rocks of pre-Mississippian age; the Ellesmerian sequence of mature clastic and shelf carbonate rocks of Mississippian to Early Cretaceous age, derived from a northerly provenance terrane; and the Brookian sequence of immature graywacke and shale derived from the southerly provenance terrane of the Brooks Range. In comparison, four sequences may be present in the Chukchi Basin: a Franklinian(?) sequence that is seismically opaque, constitutes acoustic basement, and is presumed to be pre-Devonian in age; an Eo-Ellesmerian sequence of clastic and carbonate(?) rocks presumed to be of Devonian age but whose correlation to the Franklinian or older Ellesmerian sequences of NPRA is equivocal (Figs. 17A, and 18); and the Ellesmerian and Brookian sequences that can be reliably correlated to the same sequences in NPRA.

The top of the acoustic basement of the Franklinian sequence is clearly defined in seismic and well data in the onshore Arctic Platform, where basal Ellesmerian strata overlie steeply dipping metamorphosed clastic strata that are commonly argillite in the northwestern North Slope adjacent to the Chukchi Basin. In the offshore it is also clearly defined at shallow depths on the Chukchi platform and the North Chukchi high. However, in some areas of the central Chukchi Basin, where the structure is complex, acoustic basement is difficult to define and may be below the seismic panel at six seconds (two-way time) or more than 12 km deep (40,000 ft).

The Eo-Ellesmerian sequence is interpreted to include an upper clastic wedge up to 6 km thick overlying a carbonate(?) unit up to 3 km thick of Devonian(?) age (Figs. 17A and 18). The clastic unit progradationally downlaps the carbonate(?) unit (Fig. 18), and reflecting horizons diverge northwesterly, suggesting a provenance terrane to the northwest. The strata are mildly deformed and are unconformable beneath the Early Cretaceous unconformity at the base of the PSU unit in the area of the Barrow Arch northeast of the central Chukchi Basin. To the southwest the strata are downfaulted into the central Chukchi Basin, where they are interpreted to be unconformable beneath upper Ellesmerian strata (Fig. 17A), but their relation to lower Ellesmerian strata farther southwest is not interpretable from published seismic data. The Eo-Ellesmerian sequence is probably truncated by the PSU unconformity to the west and northwest on the Chukchi platform. On the east near the onshore portion of the Arctic Platform the Eo-Ellesmerian strata appear to be structurally juxtaposed to known Franklinian rocks along the northeast-trending Barrow fault zone (Fig. 16) that is subparallels to the Barrow sea valley and canyon. It is speculated that the Barrow fault zone is a major normal, baement-controlled transtensional fault with pre–Early Cretaceous throw of up to 9 km, based on the interpretation that the Eo-Ellesmerian rocks west of the fault zone are younger than the Franklinian rocks east of the fault zone. Even if the Eo-Ellesmerian is the same age as the Franklinian, the contrast in structural complexity and lithologies is so pronounced that a major tectonic discontinuity appears to be required to separate the gently folded, seismically coherent clastic and carbonate(?) Eo-Ellesmerian rocks of the Chukchi Basin from the complexly folded, seismically incoherent argillite Franklinian rocks of the Arctic Platform. Dextral transtensional movement is implied by the northeasterly offset of the Barrow arch from the Barrow high (Fig. 16) and by the need to accommodate the extension in the north-trending Hanna wrench-fault zone of the central Chukchi Basin. This interpretation necessarily, but questionably, implies that the Barrow fault zone could be a fundamental plate boundary of Paleozoic (pre-Mississippian) age between the basement rocks of the Chukchi Basin and the Franklinian basement rocks of the onshore Arctic Platform.

The Ellesmerian sequence of Early Cretaceous to Mississippian age is interpreted to be a platform sequence of carbonate and clastic rocks comparable to the Ellesmerian sequence of the Arctic Platform in NPRA. By jump correlation to the Tunalik, Peard, and Walakpa No. 2 wells, it is interpreted to be about 4.6 km thick west of the Tunalik well. It thins northward to zero on the south flank of the Barrow arch (Fig. 18A), and westward on the Chukchi platform. The Ellesmerian is time transgressive northward. Older Ellesmerian strata are Mississippian in age at the latitude of the Tunalik well and Jurassic to Early Cretaceous near their wedge edge on the north. Thinning is by basal onlap, wedging, internal unconformities, and overlap by the Early Cretaceous PSU. Ellesmerian formations on the Arctic Platform contain rich source rocks and good reservoir rocks, and probably will constitute the best play for a giant oil field in the Chukchi Basin.

The lower part of the Brookian sequence of Cretaceous age in the southern part of the Chukchi Basin consists of a basal sequence of clinoformal seismic reflectors that downlap northeasterly and merge with the top of the Early Cretaceous PSU. They represent distal marine beds of a prograding delta whose source terrain was in the Herald Arch and the now-founded Hope

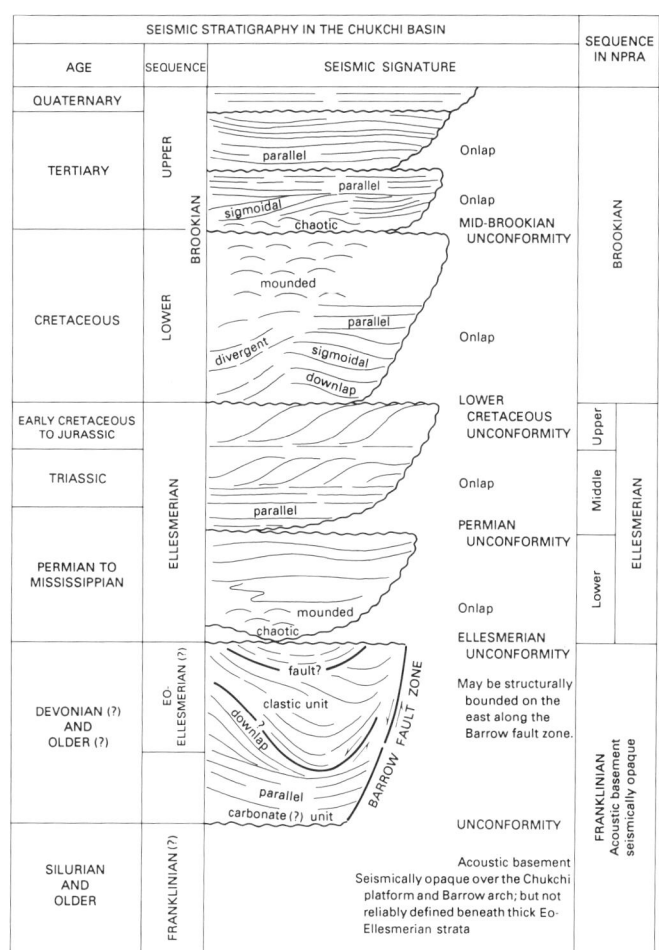

Figure 18. Seismic stratigraphy in the Chukchi Basin. Modified from Thurston and Theiss (1987) and Grantz and others (1987).

Basin basement rocks and are the offshore extension of the Torok Formation of NPRA. The clinoformal reflectors merge upward into a series of parallel reflectors that represent the topset marine and nonmarine strata of the delta and are the offshore extension of the Nanushuk Group of NPRA. North of the Herald arch, this part of the lower Brookian sequence is up to 6 km thick in a northeast-trending, structurally complex, thrust-fold and detachment-fold belt. The sequence thins northwesterly over the Chukchi platform and northeasterly over the Barrow arch, in large part by erosion beneath a middle Brookian unconformity. The lower Brookian sequence thickens rapidly northward in the North Chukchi Basin and northwestward in the Nuwuk Basin.

The upper part of the Brookian sequence, presumed to be mainly of Tertiary age, is represented by a thick sequence of low-velocity seismic refelctors that probably are thin-bedded, fine-grained, marine clastic rocks. Basal strata are unconformable on faulted and gently folded lower Brookian rocks. Sigmoidal downlapping reflectors are present in the basal strata, and chaotic reflectors are associated with faults and shale diapirs. The upper part of the Brookian sequence is confined to the Hanna Trough segment of the central Chukchi Basin, where it is about 12 km thick. It thickens northward into the North Chukchi Basin, where it is more than 5 km thick. From the Barrow arch it thickens northward into the Nuwuk Basin from 0 to at least 3 km thick (Profile 9E, Plate 9, this volume).

Petroleum potential. This discussion is summarized mainly from the work of Thurston and Theiss (1987) and Grantz and May (1987). The structure and stratigraphy in the Chukchi Basin is varied and complex, and the seismic data show diverse hydrocarbon play potential. No wells have been drilled in the offshore, but an industry program is expected to be initiated in 1989 (Oil and Gas Journal, March 27, 1989). In the adjacent onshore, two small gas fields are in production for the Barrow community, a small gas field was discovered at Walakpa, and a strong gas show was encountered in the Tunalik well, all in sandstone reservoirs in upper Ellesmerian strata. In the foothills detachment fold belt in NPRA, gas shows or small gas fields have been discovered at the Meade well, and other similar prospects to the east in Brookian rocks. Minor oil shows are also common in wells on the Barrow high and in the foothills, as at the Kaolak well, but no oil production has been established. Gas is currently not economic in this part of the Arctic, and a giant oil accumulation of the Prudhoe Bay type will probably be the type of play to be targeted in early exploration on the Chukchi Shelf.

The Prudhoe Bay oil field (Fig. 13) is a combination structural and stratigraphic trap with good reservoir beds in middle Ellesmerian sandstone that contain the major part of the oil reserves, although some additional reserves are also present in the underlying lower Ellesmerian carbonate rocks. Rich shale source rocks to charge the reservoir beds are in overlying, stratigraphically equivalent, and underlying strata. The overlying shale seal is the Early Cretaceous PSU. This play type may be found along the eastern flank of the Chukchi platform, where the unconformity at the base of the PSU truncates the Ellesmerian strata at depths within the oil window. Similar conditions may also be present along the south flank of the North Chukchi high. Within part of the Hanna wrench fault zone where lower Brookian and upper Ellesmerian strata are within the oil window, anticlines or domal structures would constitute a viable play of sufficient size to have giant oil reserves. In the deeper parts of the central Chukchi Basin, Ellesmerian rocks are now probably below the oil window. Listric fault plays may be present along the south margins of the North Chukchi Basin and the Nuwuk Basin (Profile 9E, Plate 9, this volume). Large listric faults produce rollover anticlines that could have reservoir targets within the oil window in Brookian and Ellesmerian(?) strata. However, reservoir quality and source rocks are unknowns. Detachment folds in early Brookian rocks in the northern part of the detachment fold belt constitute another distinctly different play, but the rocks are more likely to be gas than oil prone. Several test wells in NPRA in this type of play failed to discover economic accumulations, so this play is unlikely to be prospective for large oil reserves. Numerous types of fault traps in both Brookian and Ellesmerian rocks are likely to be present in the Hanna wrench fault zone of the central Chukchi Basin, but the complexity of the structures suggests that this type of play is more likely to have small prospects that could not be economically developed unless they were in proximity to a giant economically developed oil field.

The Eo-Ellesmerian strata of this report (lower Ellesmerian sequence of Thurston and Theiss, 1987; Franklinian of Grantz and others, 1987) present a play with reservoir and source-rock uncertainties. Although the strata could be tested, in the vicinity of the Barrow Arch, at depths theoretically now within the oil window, the relatively high seismic velocities may imply consolidation or low-grade metamorphism as the result of a Late Devonian orogenic episode. A stratigraphic test of this rock sequence seems most likely to yield valuable data bearing on the geologic history of the Arctic Platform in the Chukchi Sea, rather than revealing a sequence prospective for oil reserves.

A resource assessment by the U.S. Geological Survey and the U.S. Minerals Management Service (1988) estimates a 5 percent probability of 7.2 billion and a mean probability of 2.2 billion barrels of undiscovered recoverable oil in the United States Chukchi Basin. If source and reservoir rocks comparable to those in the Prudhoe Bay area Ellesmerian strata are present in the Chukchi Basin, present estimates of potential oil reserves could be grossly understated. Economic viability is the primary problem.

Hope Basin[1]

Regional tectonic elements. The Hope Basin trends about 700 km northwesterly beneath the Chukchi Sea from the western terminus of the Brooks Range and the north margin of the Seward Peninsula to Long Strait between Wrangel Island and the Chukotsk Peninsula of eastern Siberia (Figs. 1 and 2). Mainly the better-studied southeastern one-third of the basin is discussed here. A southeasterly salient of the Hope Basin is referred to as the Kotzebue subbasin (Fig. 19). The Hope Basin is extensional in a complex of mainly northwest-trending horsts and grabens or half-grabens. The east-trending Kotzebue arch separates the Hope Basin from the Kotzebue subbasin, which is a half-graben with a complex of normal faults along its south margin north of the Seward Peninsula uplift. Maximum sediment fill in the Hope Basin is about 3 sec (TWT) or about 4.5 km, but on average the basin fill is about 2.0 to 2.5 km thick. The character of the sediment fill in the Hope Basin is known only from seismic stratigraphic analysis. Two wells have been drilled in the Kotzebue subbasin and may offer insight as to the probable character of the sediments in the Hope Basin.

---

[1]In the Russian literature (Polkin, 1984), the Hope Basin has been referred to as the South Chukchi Basin. However, the name Hope Basin, which was applied to the basin by Grantz and others (1970), and extended to virtually the entire basin by Grantz and others (1975, 1981), has priority. As this is accepted usage in the North American literature, this feature is referred to as Hope Basin in this volume.

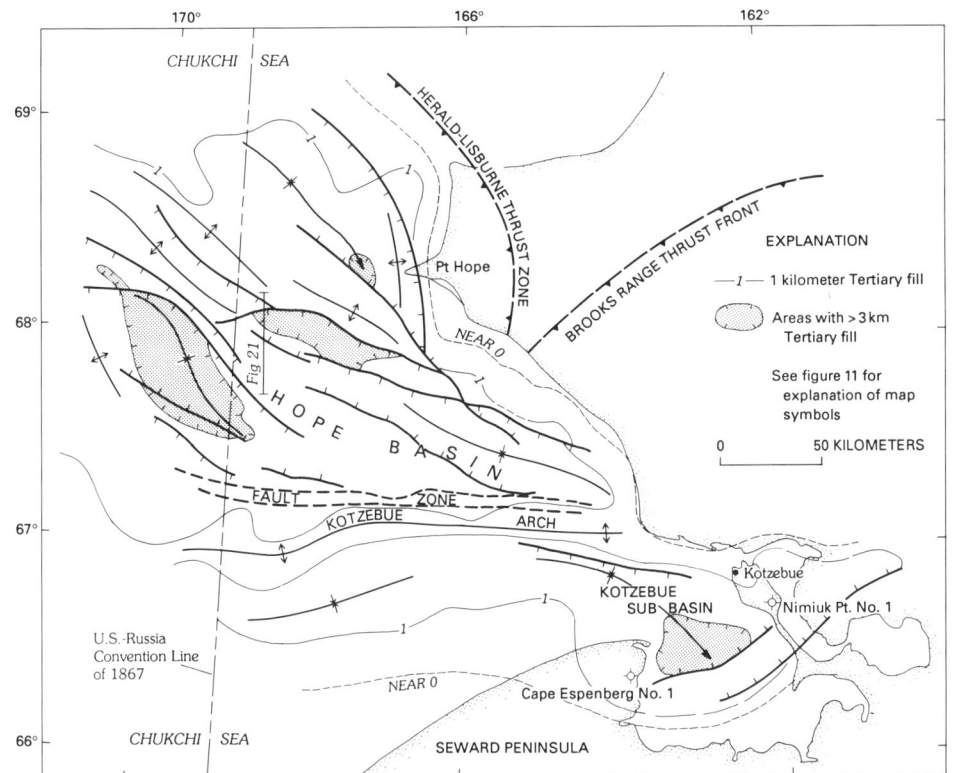

Figure 19. Simplified structure contour map of the Hope Basin and Kotzebue subbasin. Contours at one second and three seconds (two-way time) on top of acoustic basement. Modified from Tolson (1987) and Kirschner (1989).

Stratigraphy. Basement rocks of the eastern part of the Hope Basin are acoustically opaque and probably consist of complexly folded and metamorphosed Paleozoic or older sedimentary and igneous rocks similar to those exposed in the Brooks Range east of the basin and the Seward Peninsula south of the basin. Paleozoic(?) limestone and dolomite were drilled beneath Eocene volcanic and volcaniclastic rocks in both wells in the Kotzebue subbasin (Fig. 20). A lower structural sequence of the western Hope Basin, with V_p = 4.5 km/s, (Fig. 21), is tentatively identified as Lower Cretaceous (Polkin, 1984). This unit overlies folded basement (V_p = 6.1 km/s) but, judging from seismic reflections, it not itself folded. Its thickness reaches 1 to 1.5 km. On the basis of aeromagnetic data, volcanic rocks are widespread at the top of this section. This sequence has not been identified in the American portion of the Hope Basin (Grantz and others, 1975; Tolson, 1987); it is either absent or folded and not distinguished from the basement, which in this part of the basin, has velocities of 4.5 to 5.2 km/sec.

Tolson (1987) defined three Tertiary stratigraphic units based on his seismic reflection studies in the Hope Basin (Fig. 22). These are correlated to the Kotzebue subbasin well data in Figure 20. Unit I, of Eocene to Oligocene age, consists predominantly of volcanic and volcaniclastic rocks, conglomerate, sandstone, shale, and coal in the Cape Espenberg well. Its seismic signature in the Hope Basin commonly shows sigmoidal, clinoform, progradational beds typical of a delta system merging with parallel reflectors typical of basin plain deposition. The rocks were probably deposited in a nonmarine basin, but may be lacustrine or marine(?) in lows to the northwest. They were deposited unconformably on the basement rocks in topographic, locally fault bounded, depressions.

In the Kobuk River valley, about 170 km east of Kotzebue, nonmarine coal-bearing rocks are Late Cretaceous in age (Patton and Miller, 1968). Late Cretaceous (Maastrichtian) palynomorphs are also common in other nonmarine basins in Alaska (Kirschner, 1988), indicating extensional tectonism. Initiation of "Tertiary" basin formation began in latest Late Cretaceous time. It is therefore possible that the oldest rocks of Unit I, in the deeper parts of the Hope Basin, are Late Cretaceous in age.

Unit II consists of nonmarine conglomerate, sandstone, siltstone, and coal in the Cape Espenberg well. Its seismic signature shows concordant reflections typical of alluvial plain or paralic deposition. Unit II overlaps all of Unit I and intrabasinal highs and laps onto basement at the basin margins. Reflectors in Unit II are more continuous to the northwest and may indicate the unit is marginal marine in that area. Unit III consists of fine-grained sandstone, siltstone, and carbonaceous shale in the Cape Espenberg well. Its seismic signature shows low-amplitude parallel reflectors, suggesting a marine or lacustrine depositional environment. Continental and nearshore clastic rocks of Neogene and

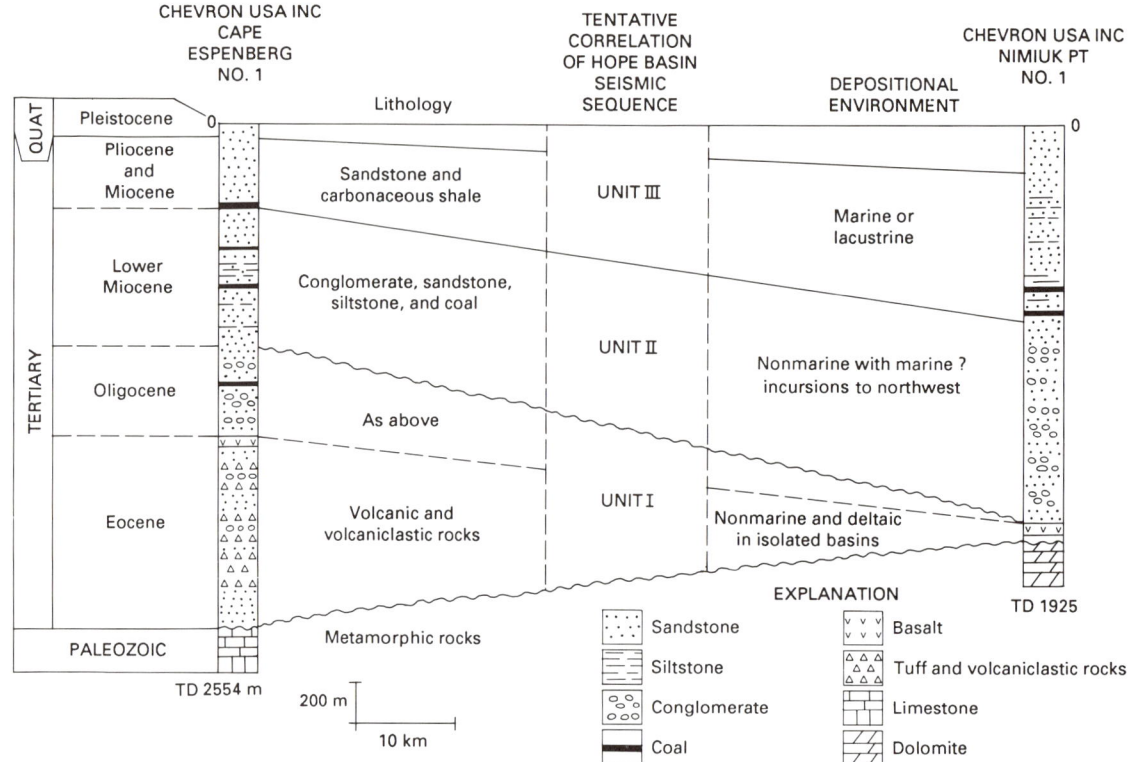

Figure 20. Correlation of the Chevron USA Inc., Cape Espenberg No. 1 and Nimiuk Pt. No. 1 wells of the Kotzebue subbasin, showing lithology and depositional environment correlated with seismic sequences of the Hope Basin. See Figure 19 for location of test wells. Modified from Tolson (1987) and Kirschner (1989).

Quaternary age are present in tectonic depressions along the northern shore of the Chukchi Peninsula. Judging from the character of seismic reflections, it appears that marine sediments deposited in quiet environments may predominate offshore, in the central part of Hope Basin (Eittreim and others, 1979).

Petroleum potential. Even though anticlinal traps, possibly developed by transtensional faulting, fault traps, and onlap over basement highs may offer prospects in the Hope Basin, the potential for source beds to generate oil appears slim. Both of the wells in the Kotzebue subbasin had low (1 to 2 percent) total organic carbon (TOC), and the rocks were immature. Thermal maturity could be reached in the 3,000- to 4,500-m range; if organically rich lacustrine or marine beds are present in the deeper parts of the basin, oil generation would be possible. However, the most likely hydrocarbon to be generated is gas, which is currently not economic in Arctic Alaska.

Resource estimates of undiscovered oil reported by the U.S. Geological Survey and the U.S. Minerals Management Service (1988) suggest a mean probability of 0.02 billion barrels of oil. Even if this amount of oil were found in one prospect, it would be uneconomic in the offshore Hope Basin. However, a small gas field onshore in proximity to a local community such as Kotzebue could be an economic benefit to that community, as the Barrow gas fields are to the Barrow community.

EASTERN SIBERIAN CONTINENTAL MARGIN

Chaun Basin

The rocks that compose the basement of the Chaun Basin (Fig. 1) are exposed onshore immediately to the south of the basin, where they fill the intermontane Rauchuan depression; they consist of strongly metamorphosed Devonian and less metamorphosed Carboniferous through Lower Jurassic rocks. The intermontane depression is filled with about 2,000 m of fine-grained Upper Jurassic clastic rocks with intervals of graded bedding overlain by about 500 m of tuffs which are also Upper Jurassic. The Valanginian (Lower Cretaceous) section consists of 1,300 to 2,000 m of clastic rocks, mainly fine-grained at the base of the section and coarsening upward. This sedimentary sequence is covered by 1,600 to 2,700 m of Lower Cretaceous volcanics, mainly lavas, and about 600 m of andesites, dacites, and basalts of Late Cretaceous and early Paleogene age. Klubov and Semenov (1973) reported that all sedimentary rocks in the Jurassic-Cretaceous sequence are slightly metamorphosed and diagenetically altered. The clayey sediments are altered into phyllites, and the sandstones are strongly silicified. Rocks with porosities of more than 5 percent were not found, and porosities usually do not exceed 1 to 3 percent. Permeabilities are usually 0.1 md or

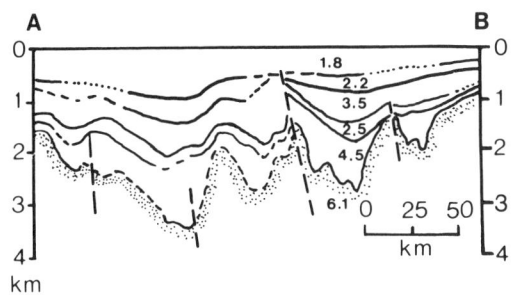
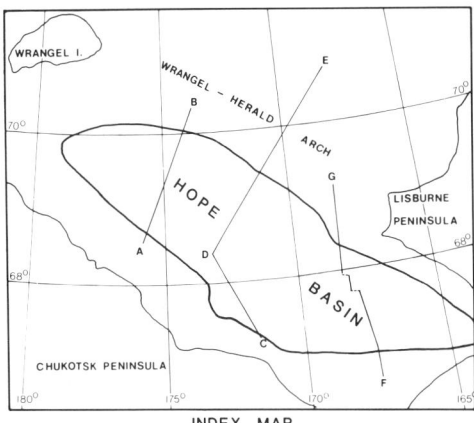
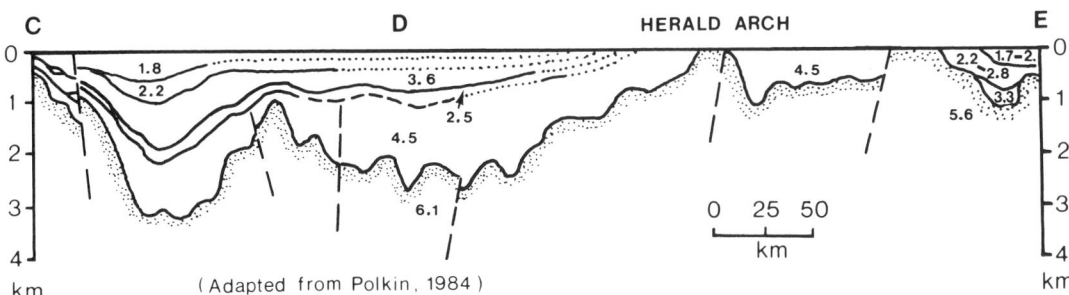
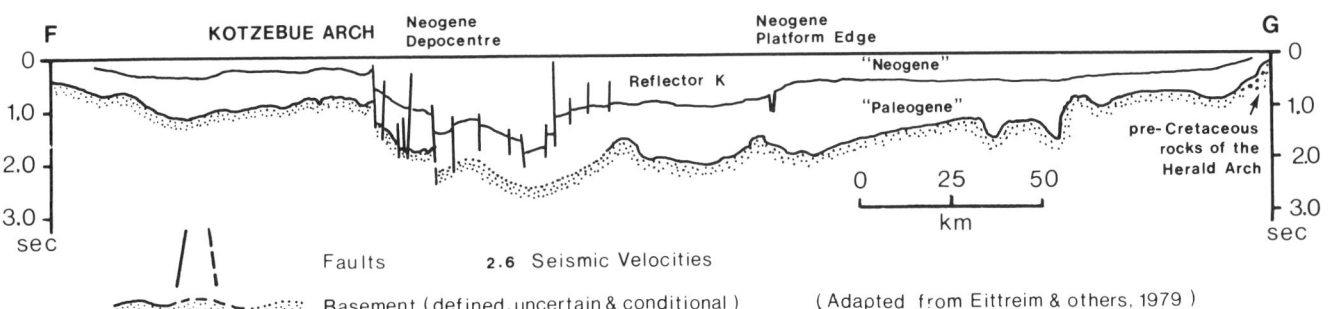

Figure 21. Line drawing showing typical structure and seismic signature of the lower (I), middle (II), and upper (III) seismic stratigraphic units in the central part of the Hope Basin. See Figure 19 for location of line. See Figure 20 for correlation of seismic units with strata in Cape Espenberg No. 1 and Nimiuk Point No. 1 test wells.

less. Most of the fractures are filled with calcite or quartz. The rocks have a very low bitumen content, and organic matter is overmature. The petroleum potential of the Mesozoic sequence is therefore considered negligible (Klubov and Semenov, 1973).

The onshore Jurassic and Cretaceous sequence of the Rauchuan depression is inferred to extend offshore, where it is covered by 2 to 3 km of Tertiary clastics (Fig. 23). The Tertiary section is probably analogous to the middle and upper sequences of Hope Basin. The underlying rocks are considered to be economic basement.

East Siberian Sea Basin

The structure of the East Siberian Sea Basin, which lies between the De Long Arch and Anzhu Uplift (Fig. 1), is poorly known due to an absence of seismic data. To the south lies a tectonic terrace covered by thin Cenozoic sediments. To the northeast, the basin may be separated from the Vilkitskii–North Chukchi Basin by a structural saddle connecting the Wrangel and De Long uplifts, but the existence of this structure has not been demonstrated.

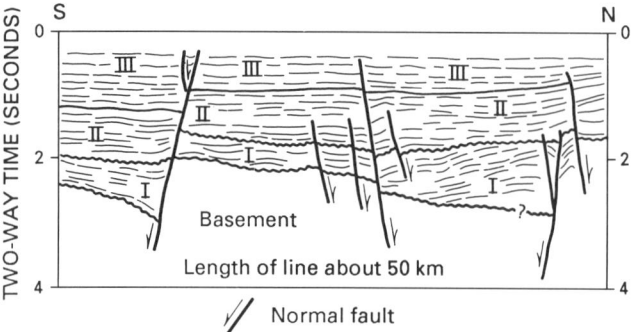

Figure 22. Line drawings of seismic reflection sections A-B, C-D-E, and F-G through the Hope Basin.

The present-day structure of exposed Paleozoic rocks on Kotelnyi Island of the New Siberian Islands, which lie just west of the basin, is characterized by two regional anticlinoria and two adjacent synclinoria that strike northwestward, parallel to facies zones in the Paleozoic rocks. These structures are about 30 to 60 km wide, and their observed length onshore is about 150 km. Middle Devonian to Mesozoic rocks outcrop in the synclinoria, and Ordovician to Lower Devonian rocks are exposed in the anticlinoria. This general type of tectonics probably continues eastward, beneath the East Siberian Sea Basin, although the intensity of deformation may be somewhat lower. Folding is generally Germanotype. Box folds with steep dips (20° to 50°) on the flanks predominate (Genin and others, 1977). Two systems of faults that strike north and northwest, with displacements of hundreds of meters, complicate the structure. The north-trending fault system is considered to be much younger and presumably formed in Late Cretaceous and Tertiary time (Kos'ko and Nepomiluyev, 1975). Block tectonics is strongly expressed, and two phases of faulting may be present, as seen on a seismic profile between Kotelnyi and Faddeyev islands (Fig. 24).

An interpretation of gravity and magnetic data (Vinogradov and others, 1974; Koś ko, 1984) suggests the presence of a regional east-west–striking arch (Anzhu Ridge of Fujita and Cook, this volume) that separates the East Siberian Sea Basin into two subbasins, the New Siberia Basin on the north and the Blagovshchensk Basin on the south. The arch extends from the northwestern corner of Wrangel Island to Novaya Sibir Island. On the southwestern shore of Novaya Sibir Island, a series of thrusts and steep to overturned folds has been mapped in Cretaceous rocks (Koś ko, 1984). It is possible that this thrust zone is a western continuation of the Herald-Wrangel thrust zone, and marks the boundary between the Arctic platform and the New Siberian–Chukchi fold belt. However, the thrust planes on Novaya Sibir Island dip north-northeast, as opposed to the southerly dip on the Herald-Wrangel arch, and the observed width of the zone is only about 2 km. Structural relations and even the existence of the central arch have yet to be demonstrated by seismic data.

The sedimentary section of the New Siberian Islands may trend east, beneath the New Siberian Sea Basin, and therefore offer some clues as to the stratigraphy of the basin. The pre–late Mesozoic rocks of the islands are thought to belong to a rigid massif in the New Siberian–Chukchi fold system (Khain, 1979), but Fujita and Cook (this volume) divide these rocks into five distinct lithotectonic terranes. The basement of the New Siberian massif is presumably analogous to the Middle to Late Proterozoic crystalline schists of Bolshoy Lyakhovskoy Island in the Oloy-Lyakhovskoy volcanic belt (the Lyakhov–South Anyui suture zone of Fujita and Cook, this volume).

Paleozoic rocks deposited in the northwest-striking Belkov-Nerpalakh trough overlie basement in the New Siberian Islands. The axial part of the trough, with relatively deep-water facies, is exposed in the southwestern part of the New Siberian Islands; the northeast flank of the trough, with shallow-water facies, is exposed in the northeastern part of the islands. The oldest exposed sedimentary rocks in the trough are a 500-m section of Middle to Upper Cambrian shales with intercalations of siltstones and limestones on Bennett Island (Fig. 13). Geophysical data suggest that these rocks increase in thickness to a few kilometers on Kotelnyi Island, where the section may include uppermost Proterozoic rocks (Volnov, 1975). The Ordovician to Middle Devonian section in the axial part of the trough consists of lutite with beds of pelitomorphic limestone and quartzose sandstone and zones of enriched organic matter (Kos'ko and others, 1975). These deep-water facies are analogous to those of the Central Taimyr Trough of north-central Siberia and the Franklinian sequence rocks of the Hazen Trough in the Canadian Arctic Islands. The Ordovician to Middle Devonian beds in the northeast flank of the trough consist of shallow-marine and lagoonal rocks, including thick sections of fossiliferous limestone and dolomite with local reefoid buildups.

The Ordovician to Middle Devonian sequence of the New Siberian Islands is overlain by 8,000 m of Upper Devonian to Lower Mississippian shale and siltstone with beds of sandstone, limestone, conglomerate, and basalt on the southwest that grade northeastward into a section of variegated clastics only 300 m thick that includes redbeds and limestone. Carboniferous carbonates and Lower Permian clastic rocks as much as a few hundred meters thick locally overlie the Devonian beds and are overlain unconformably by a section of Upper Permian shale. Triassic rocks, which are widespread in the New Siberian Islands, conformably overlie the Permian rocks. On Kotelnyi Island these rocks include Triassic green to black shales with some limestone in the lower part and thin sandstone layers in the upper part. Basalt flows are found at the base of the sequence, and tuffaceous material is present throughout the Lower Triassic (Preobrazhenskaya and others, 1975). The Triassic sequence, which is as much as 1,260 m thick, is overlain conformably by 200 to 300 m of Lower Jurassic rocks of similar composition. Middle and Upper Jurassic rocks are absent in exposures on the New Siberian Islands, but Upper Jurassic rocks, represented by fossils in redeposited concretions on the northern shore of Kotelnyi Island, may be present beneath the deeper parts of the adjoining East Siberian Sea Basin. Lower Cretaceous coal-bearing clastics and tuffs, which are about 200 m thick on the island, may also underlie the basin. Uppermost Upper Cretaceous and lower Tertiary terrestrial clastics with an admixture of volcanic material and lignites in the lower part of the section are 1,500 to 1,600 m thick on Novaya Sibir Island at the margin of the East Siberian Sea Basin. These rocks are characterized by a seismic velocity of 3.0 to 3.6 km/sec (Kos'ko, 1984). It is supposed that strata of analogous facies and age cover all of the East Siberian Sea Basin.

The general structural style of upper Mesozoic and Tertiary rocks in the East Siberian Sea Basin is likely to be similar to that of Hope Basin. Structures probably strike southeast, and deformation should be more intense in the lower and middle structural sequences. Significant folding and faulting have been observed in Paleogene and Neogene sediments on the northern shore of Novaya Sibir and Faddeyev islands (Trufanov and others, 1979). Some features of the distribution of Cretaceous and Tertiary sediments on the New Siberian Islands suggest (Kos'ko, 1984) that the lower structural sequence (Cretaceous?) is thin, and may even be absent, north of the central arch in the northern part of the basin. Total thickness of the late Mesozoic and Tertiary sedimentary cover may exceed 5 km in the deepest parts of the basin.

Petroleum potential of the intrashelf basins. In the absence of drilling data, the major factors controlling petroleum potential of the intrashelf basins of the East Siberian and Chukchi Seas can be evaluated only on the basis of a regional geologic

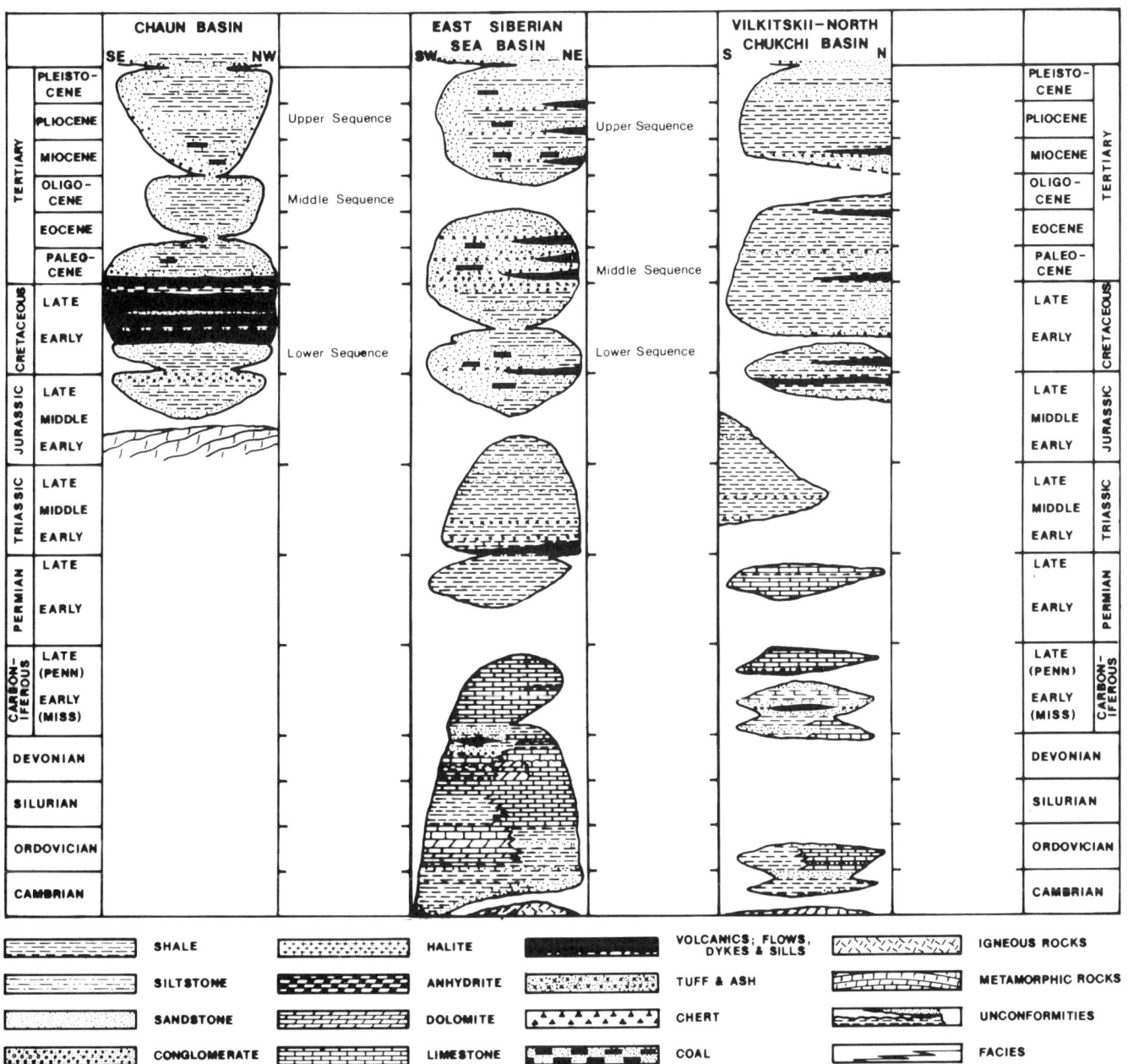

Figure 23. Schematic stratigraphic sequences of the Chaun, East Siberian Sea, and Vilkitskii–North Chukchi Basins.

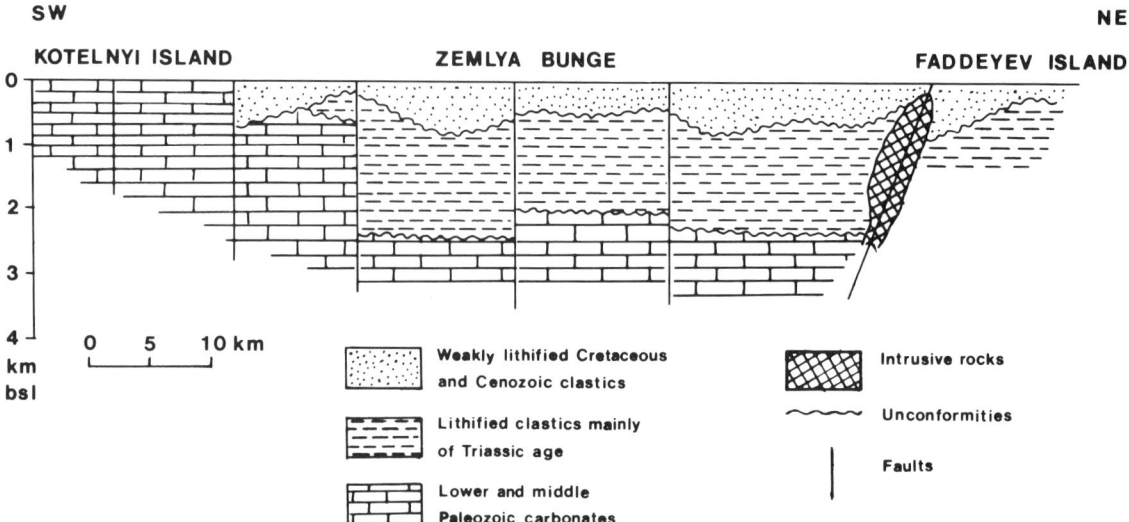

Figure 24. Cross section through the western part of the East Siberian Sea Basin. (Adapted from Genin and others, 1977.)

model. Thermal conditions in the sedimentary cover of the three basins are completely unknown. By analogy with areas to the east and southeast, the upper boundary of the "oil window" in the Hope Basin supposedly occurs at 2.5 to 3.0 km, and the lower boundary may be deep as 5 km (Grantz and May, 1984). The same deep interval for the "oil window" may be inferred for the geologically similar Chaun Basin. Therefore, only the lowermost parts of the sedimentary cover in these basins may reach maturity for oil generation. This part of the sedimentary succession comprises the lower structural sequence and in some areas the middle sequence (Chaun Basin and eastern Hope Basin). Both sequences are predominantly composed of terrestrial, partly coal-bearing rocks, with significant volcanics in the lower sequence. Such a facies composition implies gas-prone source rocks, but their ability to generate some oil cannot be completely discounted.

Generally, the same character of potential source rocks in the late Mesozoic and Tertiary sedimentary cover may be inferred for the East Siberian Sea Basin. During Tertiary time, however, the adjoining De Long Arch became an area of intense basaltic volcanism. It is not clear how this volcanic event would affect the thermal regime in the basin, but a higher heat flow and correspondingly higher position of the "oil window" in the section may be possible.

In the western part of the East Siberian Sea Basin, overlying the New Siberian massif, potential source rocks may be present in the Paleozoic and Triassic section. Two stratigraphic intervals are characterized by increased bitumen and organic matter content in exposures on Kotelnyi Island (Ivanof and Nepomiluyev, 1975). The first consists of Lower to Middle Devonian carbonates with an average concentration of dispersed bitumen of 0.01 to 0.07 percent. This is an order of magnitude higher than in all the underlying rocks. The supposed source rocks are deep-water and lagoonal back-reef shales and carbonates containing up to 3 to 5 percent of organic matter. Thick Upper Devonian clastics are almost devoid of bitumen except in the narrow zone near the contact with Middle Devonian rocks, but the sandstones may constitute reservoir units. The Devonian section, however, may contain potential source rocks everywhere in the East Siberian Sea Basin. Bituminous black shales and limestones in the Devonian section grade into deep-water facies of the Belkov-Nerpalakh Trough and its flanks on the southwest, but eastward they grade into light-colored shallow-water carbonates with a low content of bitumen and organic matter. The second interval of potential source rocks consists of black Triassic shales. These contain an average of 0.10 to 0.15 percent of bitumen, but in thin sandstone layers the concentration reaches 0.75 percent. The Triassic shales are considered to be the major potential source rock in the pre-Cretaceous section of the East Siberian Sea Basin.

The maturity of the Triassic rocks in the subsurface of the basin is difficult to predict. It depends largely on the thickness of the Jurassic overburden that was completely or partly removed by erosion in pre-Cretaceous time. It is likely that this overburden was not very thick on the New Siberian massif nor in all areas north of the Oloy-Lyakhovskoy belt (the Lyakov–South Anyui suture zone of Plate 10). Another factor is the degree to which the Triassic rocks were affected by a tectonic and thermal event associated with later Mesozoic folding in the New Siberian–Chukchi system. The effect of this event could be pronounced, especially in the southern part of the basin. There is a possibility, however, that in the western part of the basin, Triassic black shales are not overmature and could have generated oil and gas beneath the thick Tertiary cover inferred to overlie that part of the basin. Evaluation of Triassic rocks as a potential source for oil and gas in the eastern part of the basin depends on the interpretation of the basement tectonics. If this region is underlain by the Arctic Platform, Triassic rocks may be potential source rocks. If it is underlain by the New Siberian–Chukchi fold belt, this possibility should be rejected. A possible negative factor is the observation that the Triassic strata on Wrangel Island, on strike to the east of the East Siberian Sea Basin, are metamorphosed to greenschist facies (Cecile and Harrison, 1987).

Coarse clastics that can serve as reservoir rocks in Hope Basin are abundant in exposures of the lower and middle structural sequences and in wells around Kotzebue Sound (Eittreim and others, 1979). Seismic data suggest the presence of such rocks in Hope Basin, and they are probably also well developed in the intrashelf basins of the East Siberian Sea. The quality of these reservoir rocks in the predominantly, or even entirely, terrestrial sediments of these sequences may be rather poor, particularly in the lower sequence, which contains abundant volcanic material. In exposures on the New Siberian Islands, sandstones of this sequence are "dirty" and unevenly distributed. The sandstone units are not more than 6 m thick and constitute the lower parts of coal-bearing cycles (Preobrazhenskaya and others, 1975). Poorly sorted polymictic sands separated by clay and silt predominate in the middle sequence on the islands. Sands in the supposedly marine upper sequence, although less abundant, are of better quality. This sequence is considered to be a regional seal.

The overall petroleum potential of the intrashelf basins of the East Siberian and Chukchi Seas is considered moderate. Inadequacy of most potential source rocks and poor quality of reservoir rocks are negative factors. All three basins may be gas prone. The East Siberian Sea Basin may be more promising than the other two if potential Triassic source rocks are not overmature. Although reservoir rocks are probably absent in the Triassic section, oil generated in these beds could have migrated into overlying rocks along faults and fracture systems.

Shelf-margin basins of the East Siberian and Chukchi Seas

A Tertiary shelf-margin depression stretches along most of the outer shelf of the East Siberian and Chukchi Seas. The depression is separated by an uplift into two basins: the Vilkitskii–North Chukchi Basin[2] on the east and the Northeast Laptev Basin on the west (Fig. 1). Another uplift is supposedly present at approximately 160°E. On the south, the shelf-margin basins are bounded by the De Long arch and a system of adjoining structural terraces and saddles that separate these basins from the intrashelf basins of the East Siberian and Chukchi Seas. On the west, the shelf-margin depressions are terminated by the North Laptev uplift. On the east, the boundary is drawn along a tectonic hinge line at the east end of the North Chukchi Basin (Grantz and May, 1984).

The shelf-margin basins have been studied even less than the intrashelf basins. East of 176°W, the data base consists of several multichannel seismic reflection lines (Grantz and May, 1984,

1987), gravity data, and some single-channel seismic reflection and sonobuoy refraction profiles (Grantz and others, 1975, 1980). West of 176°W, the data base is restricted to gravimetric and aeromagnetic surveys, and most concepts on the geology of these basins are conjectural.

The shelf-margin basins are thought to have developed on the old basement of the Arctic (Hyperborean) Platform (Semenovich and others, 1973; Yegiazarov and others, 1977). The existence of a stable platform is proved, however, only on the shelf off Alaska, where late Paleozoic formations overlie folded and mildly metamorphosed Franklinian (early Paleozoic) basement. Exposed basement rocks on Wrangel Island and on Bolshoy Lyakhavskoy Island of the New Siberian Islands are most probably of Late Proterozoic age (Kos'ko and others, in prep.), which suggests that basement under this part of the Arctic Platform may be pre-Paleozoic.

By extrapolation from onshore Alaska one would expect that both the lower and upper Brookian sequences in the North Chukchi Basin would be mainly marine in character. Marine facies probably also dominate the young sedimentary section in the shelf-margin basins of the Chukchi and East Siberian shelves to the west.

The seismically observed sedimentary section of the eastern North Chukchi Basin includes the lower Brookian (largely post-Neocomian Cretaceous) and upper Brookian (largely Tertiary) sequence (Fig. 17). In the eastern corner of the basin the lower sequence attains a thickness of 7 km, and the upper sequence is more than 5 km thick (Grantz and May, 1984). South of the hinge line zone the thickness rapidly decreases onto the Chukchi platform of Grantz and May (1984). Faulting of the lower Brookian rocks has produced a structurally complex upper surface for this sequence. Only a few faults, however, penetrate into the upper Brookian sequence. The lowermost part of the upper Brookian sequence fills structural depressions in the surface of the lower sequence. Most of the upper Brookian sequence is essentially flat lying, with a slight northward dip. The presence of the Ellesmerian (Carboniferous to Neocomian) sequence beneath the Brookian rocks is inferred from seismic data in the eastern part of the North Chukchi Basin (Grantz and others, 1975, 1984). It seems probable, however, that this sequence thins westward in the basin from its depocenter in Hanna Trough as it does on the Chukchi Platform, which lies south of the basin and west of Hanna Trough.

Westward along the strike of the North Chukchi Basin, total thickness of the lower and upper Brookian sequences evidently decreases 5 to 6 km in the north-central East Siberian Sea and to about 3 km in the western part of the basin. This interpretation is based on magnetic and gravity measurements (Kosko, 1984). The great thickness of Brookian rocks in the easternmost part of the basin is apparently associated with rifting of the Chukchi Borderland away from the continent and filling of the rift by mainly lower Brookian sediments (Grantz and May, 1984). It is likely that westward from the rifted zone, the lower Brookian sequence is thinner, and the main portion of the basin fill is represented by

---

[2]The western part of this major shelf-margin depression is called the Vilkitskii Basin in recent Russian publications (Polkin, 1984; Kos'ko, 1984). Its eastern part is known as the North Chukchi Basin in American literature (Grantz and others, 1975, 1982a, b). We apply here the complex name to describe the whole basin, but in places, for convenience, we use the names North Chukchi and Vilkitskii for the eastern and western parts of the basin, respectively.

Upper Brookian sediments. This trend to thinner and younger sediments westward would also apply to the Northeast Laptev Basin, where gravimetric data suggest that the thickness of the late Mesozoic and Tertiary sedimentary cover does not exceed 3.0 to 3.5 km (Vinogradov, 1984).

Little is known about the extent and character of the pre-Brookian rocks in the shelf-margin basins west of the eastern part of the North Chukchi Basin. The thick Paleozoic to Triassic sequence of the New Siberian Islands and, possibly, of the intra-shelf East Siberian Sea Basin thins northeast, toward the De Long uplift, due to both stratal thinning and truncation of the upper beds. A thin lower to middle Paleozoic section may therefore underlie the northern edge of the Arctic Platform (Fig. 17A). All Paleozoic rocks are evidently folded beneath the Northeast Laptev Basin, which is superimposed on the northwest continuation of the Paleozoic Belkov-Nerpalakh Trough from the New Siberian Islands.

On Wrangel Island, Upper Silurian to Devonian clastic rocks and limestone with gypsum beds and volcanic rocks attain a thickness of 2,000 m. Carboniferous and Permian limestones and shales range in thickness from 700 to 900 m. The section thins, and becomes less complete from south to north across the island and its medial overthrust zone (Kameneva, 1975). Upper Paleozoic beds are thus absent on northern Wrangel Island and perhaps generally from the De Long Arch.

The presence of reservoir rocks in the Vilkitskii–North Chukchi Basin is conjectural. On the basis of the character of reflectors, Grantz and May (1984) concluded that the lower Brookian sequence of the North Chukchi Basin contains some coarse clastics. The upper Brookian sequence lacks strong reflectors and is evidently composed of predominantly clayey material. The source for coarse clastics for the Vilkitskii–North Chukchi Basin most probably was the Chukchi Platform and De Long Arch. Sediment from the continent probably did not reach the shelf-margin basins because they were separated from the continent by the Hope, Chaun, and East Siberian Sea basins and by structural platforms. Most of the coarse material derived from the continent would have been trapped in these basins. Unfortunately, the De Long uplift, which adjoins the Vilkitskii and western part of the North Chukchi Basins on the south, is covered by Paleozoic and Mesozoic carbonates, fine clastics, and Tertiary volcanics that would not provide abundant coarse detritus. If, however, the plutonic rocks of Herald Island, on the Chukchi Platform, are widespread, they might have supplied significant amounts of coarse detritus, and therefore the materials for potential reservoir rocks, to the basin.

The Northeast Laptev Basin, in turn, may be favorably situated to receive sands from the adjacent Anzhu and North Laptev uplifts. Intense Tertiary basalt volcanism on the De Long uplift suggests widespread distribution of volcanic material in sediments of the central and western parts of the Vilkitskii–North Chukchi Basin, which might have degraded the potential of Tertiary reservoir rocks in these parts of the basin.

The presence of shale diapirs with probable roots in the lower Brookian sequence of the eastern part of the North Chukchi Basin indicates overpressured conditions in the thick parts of this sequence. Such conditions develop where the absence of extensive reservoir beds leads to the restricted migration of liquids and gases from shaly formations, and indicate a lack of continuous coarse clastic beds in the lower Brookian sequence. The only important local source of coarse clastic material might have been the De Long uplift, but most of this area is covered by Paleozoic and Mesozoic carbonates, fine clastics, and Tertiary volcanics that would not provide abundant coarse material.

The structural style in the shelf-margin basins west of the eastern part of the North Chukchi Basin is poorly understood. Intense faulting found in the lower Brookian sequence in the eastern part of the basin is apparently associated with supposed rifting between the continent and the Chukchi Borderland (Grantz and May, 1984) and probably does not continue farther west. Some Soviet geologists infer the presence of a regional swell 2 to 3 km high along the outer, oceanward edge of the shelf-margin basins (Gaponenko, 1973; Khain, 1979). This marginal uplift, however, may result from an incorrect interpretation of magnetic and gravimetric data in the transition zone between the continental and oceanic crust. Seismic data indicate that such an uplift is absent from the continental margin east of the North Chukchi Basin but that a deep, low-amplitude sill may underlie the north margin of the basin itself. Without a marginal uplift, the main expected deformation in the Vilkitskii–North Chukchi Basin would be regional seaward-dipping monoclines and growth faults in the areas of the basin underlying the outer shelf and slope.

Shale diapirs represent another type of structural deformation in the late Mesozoic–Cenozoic sediments. Several of them have been mapped on the northeastern Chukchi Shelf (Grantz and others, 1975; Grantz and May, 1984). The inferred widespread distribution of thick, young, shaley sediments in the shelf-margin basins implies that diapirs may exist beneath much of the region.

Petroleum potential of the shelf-margin basins. The thermal history of the sedimentary cover of the shelf-margin basins is not known. Generally, moderate thermal gradients characteristic of passive margins could be interpreted, but the impact of the Tertiary volcanism on the heat flow is difficult to evaluate. As a rough approximation, it may be supported that the lower boundary of the "oil window" occurs at a depth of about 4 to 5 km in late Mesozoic and Tertiary sediments. Most older rocks, where present, are probably overmature.

Potential source rocks for oil and gas should exist in the predominantly shaly marine sediments of the shelf-margin basins, and a significant part of this sequence probably occurs in the "oil window" in the North Chukchi Basin. In the Vilkitskii and Northeast Laptev Basins, however, only the lowermost portion of the young sediments appears to be in the "oil window." These young sediments are thought to be predominantly terrestrial and they may lack good oil source rocks.

The occurrence of suitable reservoir rocks is likely to be a limiting factor for the accumulation of petroleum deposits in the shelf-margin basins. The lower Brookian sequence, derived from the Chukchi Platform and De Long Arch, is interpreted to contain coarse clastics in the eastern part of the North Chukchi Basin (Grantz and May, 1984). Westward, the sequence is probably thinner and more terrestrial, and the presence of good reservoir rocks is doubtful. A significant admixture of volcanic material in the late Paleogene to Neogene section may have reduced the quality of reservoirs in this part of the sedimentary cover.

The numerous listric normal faults and rotated fault blocks in the lower Brookian sequence of the eastern North Chukchi Basin provide favorable conditions for trapping oil and gas. The upper Brookian sequence of the same area, however, apparently lacks suitable traps. These sediments are predominantly monoclinal and are offset by only a few of the many faults that penetrate the lower Brookian sequence. These faults, moreover, have only limited displacements in the upper sequence (Grantz and May, 1984). Small traps may also be associated with relatively small shale diapirs (less than a few kilometers in diameters) of the North Chukchi Basin. West of the interpreted rift between the continental shelf and the Chukchi Borderland, structural conditions are probably similar to those in the upper Brookian sequence of the eastern part of the North Chukchi Basin, and a paucity of structural traps may be a problem. A possible exception is a regional uplift that supposedly occurs near 160°W that may have more favorable structural character.

Considering the available data and the proposed geologic model, structures in the lower Brookian sequence related to the rift in the eastern part of the North Chukchi Basin are the most promising exploration targets in the shelf-margin basins. The petroleum potential of the rest of the Vilkitskii–North Chukchi Basin, despite its large size, is rated moderate at best because of the inferred lack of reservoir rocks and traps. The potential of the Northeast Laptev Basin is considered to be low because of the thin and relatively young sedimentary cover (about 3 km).

SUMMARY AND CONCLUSIONS

The Kronprins Christian Basin is considered to have high petroleum potential because of its thick Carboniferous to Tertiary stratigraphic section, its tectonic similarities with the North Sea area, and because it was juxtaposed against the productive North Sea area prior to rifting along the Mid-Atlantic Ridge. The hostile climatic conditions and the year-round presence of pack ice will preclude exploration in this area in the near future.

The Wandel Sea Basin contains a thick Carboniferous to Tertiary sedimentary sequence similar to that of the Sverdrup Basin, with coarse clastic and carbonate reservoirs, evaporite and shale seal rocks, and numerous potential petroleum source rocks. Although it is a relatively small basin that has probably reached the oil window only in its southeast portion, there are reports of migrated hydrocarbons in Permian rocks on its west flank.

The Lincoln Sea Basin also contains a sedimentary sequence much like that of the Sverdrup Basin, with numerous potential petroleum source rocks and reservoirs in upper Paleozoic to Cretaceous marine strata. Reports of bitumen and possible migrated hydrocarbons in these strata in northern Greenland and northern Ellesmere Island provide some encouragement. Nevertheless, the potential of the Lincoln Sea Basin and the adjacent Wandel Sea Basin is thought to be considerably lower than that of the Kronprins Christian Basin.

The Northeast Sector of the Canadian Arctic Islands Shelf is similar to the western Lincoln Sea, but it is intruded by numerous dikes and sills. The limited interval in which hydrocarbons may be generated reduces the number of prospects in the area, and the hydrocarbon potential is low. The Central Sector of the Arctic Islands Shelf has had a varied geologic and tectonic history and contains numerous source and reservoir rocks. Its potential is rated very good. The Southwest Sector of the Arctic Islands Shelf is transitional between the Sverdrup Basin and the Mackenzie-Beaufort region. Its hydrocarbon potential, however, may be less than either of these surrounding areas because of fewer structures and a less varied stratigraphic section.

The Mackenzie Delta–Beaufort Sea Basin is considered to have some of the best potential of the North American Arctic Ocean basins, with substantial reserves already established. The Nuwuk and Kaktovik Basins of offshore Northern Alaska are also good prospects and are estimated to have a resource potential similar to that of the Mackenzie Delta–Beaufort Sea Basin. The portion of the Colville Basin that underlies the Chukchi Shelf is considered to have a resource potential approximately half as large as either the Mackenzie-Beaufort or offshore northern Alaska regions.

Of the intrashelf basins, the East Siberian Sea Basin is considered to have better hydrocarbon potential than either the Hope or Chaun Basins. All these basins are likely to be gas prone and appear to lack rich source rocks and good quality reservoirs. The Chaun and Hope Basins contain only late Mesozoic to Holocene sediments overlying a pre–Early Cretaceous basement. The shelf-margin basins extend westward from the Alaskan Nuwuk Basin but are thought to contain thinner sedimentary sections west of the Chukchi Borderland. Although source rocks are likely to be abundant, good quality reservoirs may be lacking in all but the Northeast Laptev Basin. Because of these factors the potential in these shelf-margin basins is considered to be less than the basins along the Alaskan coast.

REFERENCES CITED

Asudeh, I., Forsyth, D., Stephenson, R., Embry, A., Jackson, H. R., and White, D., 1988, 1985 seismic refraction survey indicates crustal structure: GEOS, v. 17, no. 4, p. 17–20.

——, 1989, Crustal structure of the Canadian polar margin, part 1: Canadian Journal of Earth Sciences (in press).

Berry, M. J., and Barr, K. G., 1971, A seismic refraction profile across the polar continental shelf of the Queen Elizabeth Islands: Canadian Journal of Earth Sciences, v. 8, p. 347–360.

Bird, K. J., 1988, Alaskan North Slope stratigraphic nomenclature and data summary for government-drilled wells, *in* Gyrc, G., ed., Geology and exploration of the National petroleum Reserve in Alaska, 1974 to 1982: U.S. Geological Survey Professional Paper 1399, p. 317–353.

Birkelund, T., and Perch-Nielsen, K., 1976, Late Paleozoic–Mesozoic evolution of central East Greenland, *in* Escher, A., and Watt, W. S., eds., Geology of Greenland: Copenhagen, Geological Survey of Greenland, p. 304–339.

Birkelund, T., Perch-Nielsen, K., Bridgewater, D., and Higgins, A. K., 1981, An outline of the geology of the Atlantic Coast of Greenland, *in* Nairn, A.E.M., and Stehli, F. G., eds., The ocean basins and margins; Volume 2, The North Atlantic: New York and London, Plenum Press, p. 125–159.

Carman, G. J., and Hardwick, P., 1983, Geology and regional setting of Kuparuk oil field, Alaska: American Association of Petroleum Geologists Bulletin, v. 67, no. 6, p. 1014–1031.

Cecile, M. P., and Harrison, J. C., 1987, Review of the geology of Wrangel Island, Chukchi, and east Siberian Sea, far northeastern Soviet Union: Geological Survey of Canada Open-File Report 1655, 109 p.

Craig, J. D., Sherwood, K. W., and Johnson, P. P., 1985, Geologic report for the Beaufort Sea planning area, Alaska; Regional geology, petroleum geology, environmental geology: Anchorage, Alaska, U.S. Minerals Management Service OCS Report MMS 85-0111, 192 p.

Davies, G. R., and Nassichuk, W. W., 1989, Carboniferous to Permian geology of the Sverdrup Basin, Canadian Arctic Archipelago, *in* Trettin, H. P., ed., Innuitian orogen and Arctic platform: Canada and Greenland: Geological Survey of Greenland, Geology of Canada, no. 3 (in press).

Dawes, P. R., 1976, Precambrian to Tertiary of northern Greenland, *in* Escher, A., and Watt, W. S., eds., Geology of Greenland: Copenhagen, Geological Survey of Greenland, p. 248–303.

Dixon, J., 1982, Upper Oxfordian to Albian geology, Mackenzie Delta, Arctic Canada, *in* Embry, A. F., and Balkwill, H. R., eds., Arctic geology and geophysics: Canadian Society of Petroleum Geologists Memoir 8, p. 29–42.

Dixon, J., Morrell, G. R., Dietrich, J. R., Procter, R. M., and Taylor, G. C., 1988, Petroleum resources of the Mackenzie Delta–Beaufort Sea: Geological Survey of Canada Open-File 1926, 74 p.

Eittreim, S., Grantz, A., and Whitney, O. T., 1979, Cenozoic sedimentation and tectonics of Hope Basin, southern Chukchi Sea, *in* Sisson, A., ed., The relationship of plate tectonics to Alaskan geology and resources: Alaska Geological Society Symposium Proceedings, no. 6, p. B-1–B-11.

Embry, A. F., 1988, Geological setting of the polar continental margin: GEOS, v. 17, no. 4, p. 9–11.

——, 1989, Mesozoic history of the Arctic Islands, *in* Trettin, H. P., ed., Innuitian orogen and Arctic platform; Canada and Greenland: Geological Survey of Canada Geology of Canada, no. 3 (in press).

Embry, A. F., and Osadetz, K. G., 1988, Stratigraphy and tectonic significance of Cretaceous volcanism in the Queen Elizabeth Islands, Canadian Arctic Archipelago: Canadian Journal of Earth Sciences, v. 25, p. 1209–1219.

Embry, A. F., Stephenson, R. A. and Forsyth, D. A., 1988, Geological setting; the Canadian polar margin: GEOS, v. 17, p. 9–11.

Embry, A. F., Powell, T., and Mayr, U., 1989, Resources; Petroleum, *in* Trettin, H. P., ed., Innuitian orogen and Arctic platform; Canada and Greenland: Geological Survey of Canada Geology of Canada, no. 3 (in press).

Escher, A., and Watt, W. S., editors, 1976, Geology of Greenland: Copenhagen, Geological Survey of Greenland, 603 p.

Forsyth, ., Broome, J., and Embry, A. F., 1988, Aeromagnetic, gravity and earthquake features; the Canadian polar margin: GEOS, v. 17, p. 12–16.

Gaponenko, G. I., 1973, Comparative assessment of oil and gas potential of poorly known offshore regions: Leningrad, USSR, Geofizicheskiye Metody Razoedki v Arktike, vyp. 8, p. 16–21 (in Russian).

Genin, B. L., Lipkov, L. Z., and Piskarev, A. L., 1977, Structure of the East Siberian Shelf basement; An example from the Novosibirsk Islands: Leningrad, USSR, Tektonika Arktiki, Skladchoty Fundament Shelfovykh Sedimentatsionnykh Basseynov, p. 86–97 (in Russian).

Grantz, A., and May, S. D., 1982, Rifting history and structural development of the continental margin north of Alaska, *in* Watkins, J. S., and Drake, C. L., eds., Studies in continental margin geology: American Association of Petroleum Geologists Memoir 34, p. 77–100.

——, 1984, Summary geologic report for Barrow Arch outer continental shelf (OCS) planning area, Chukchi Sea, Alaska: U.S. Geological Survey Open-File Report 84–395, 44 p.

——, 1987, Regional geology and petroleum potential of the United States Chukchi Shelf north of Point Hope, *in* Scholl, D. W., Grantz, A., and Vedder, J. G., eds., Geology and resource potential of the continental margin of western North America and adjacent ocean basins; Beaufort Sea to Baja California: Houston, Circum-Pacific Council for Energy and Mineral Resources, Earth Sciences Series no. 6, p. 37–58.

Grantz, A., Wolf, S. C., Breslau, L., Johnson, T. C., and Hanna, W. F., 1970, Reconnaissance geology of the Chukchi Sea as determined by acoustic and magnetic profiling, *in* Adkison, W. L., and Brosgé, M. M., eds., Proceedings of the geological seminar on the North Slope of Alaska: Los Angeles, American Association of Petroleum Geologists, Pacific Section, p. F1–F28.

Grantz, A., Holmes, M. L., and Kososki, B. A., 1975, Geologic framework of the Alaskan continental terrace in the Chukchi and Beaufort seas, *in* Yorath, C. J., Parker, E. R., and Glass, D. J., eds., Canada's continental margins and offshore petroleum exploration: Canadian Society of Petroleum Geologists Memoir 4, p. 669–700.

Grantz, A., Eittreim, S., and Whitney, O. T., 1981, Geology and physiography of the continental margin north of Alaska and implications for the origin of the Canada Basin, *in* Nairn, A.E.M., Churkin, M., Jr., and Stehli, F. G., eds., The ocean basins and margins; Volume 5, Geology of the Arctic Ocean Basin and its margins: New York and London, Plenum Press, p. 439–492.

Grantz, A., and 6 others, 1982a, Geologic framework, hydrocarbon potential and environmental conditions for exploration and development of proposed oil and gas lease sale 87 in Beaufort and Northeast Chukchi Seas; A summary report: U.S. Geological Survey Open-File Report 82–482, 80 p.

Grantz, A., and 6 others, 1982b, Geologic framework, hydrocarbon potential, and environmental conditions for exploration and development of proposed oil and gas lease sale 85 in the central and northern Chukchi Sea: U.S. Geological Survey Open-File Report 82–1053, 84 p.

Grantz, A., May, S. D., and Dinter, D. A., 1987, Regional geology and petroleum potential of the United States Beaufort and northeasternmost Chukchi seas, *in* Scholl, D. W., Grantz, A., and Vedder, J. G., eds., Geology and resource potential of the continental margin of western North America and adjacent ocean basins; Beaufort Sea to Baja California: Houston, Circum-Pacific Council for Energy and Mineral Resources, Earth Science Series no. 6, p. 17–35.

Hakansson, E., and Pedersen, S.A.S., 1982, Late Paleozoic to Tertiary tectonic evolution of the continental margin in North Greenland, *in* Embry, A. F., and Balkwill, H. R., eds., Arctic geology and geophysics: Canadian Society of Petroleum Geologists Memoir 8, p. 331–348.

Haller, J., 1971, Geology of the East Greenland Caledonides: London, Wiley Interscience, 381 p.

Henderson, G., 1976, Petroleum geology, *in* Escher, A., and Watt, W. S., eds., Geology of Greenland: Copenhagen, Geological Survey of Greenland, p. 488–505.

Higgins, A. K., Mayr, U., and Soper, N. J., 1982, Fold belts and metamorphic zones of northern Ellesmere Island and North Greenland, *in* Dawes, P. R., and Kerr, J. W., eds., Nares Strait and the drift of Greenland; A conflict in plate tectonics: Meddelelser om Grønland Geoscience 8-1982, p. 159–166.

Hubbard, R. J., Edrich, S. P., and Rattey, R. P., 1987, Geologic evolution and hydrocarbon habitat of the 'Arctic Alaska microplate,' *in* Tailleur, I., and Weimer, P., eds., Alaskan North Slope geology, Volume 2: Bakersfield, California, Society of Economic Paleontologists and Mineralogists, and Anchorage, Alaska Geological Society, p. 797–830.

Ivanov, V. L., and Nepomiluyev, V. F., 1975, New data on bitumen shows in Paleozoic and Triassic rocks of the Novosibirsk Islands: Leningrad, USSR, Geologiya i Poleznye Iskopayemye Novosibirskikh Ostrovov i Ostrova Wrangelya, p. 55–60 (in Russian).

Johnson, G. L., McMillan, N. J., and Egloff, J., 1975, East Greenland continental margin, in Yorath, C. J., Parker, E. R., and Glass, D. J., eds., Canada's continental margins and offshore petroleum exploration: Canadian Society of Petroleum Geologists Memoir 4, p. 205–224.

Kameneva, I., 1975, Pre-Mesozoic deposits of Wrangel Island: Leningrad, Avtoreferat dissertatsii na soiskanie uchenoi stepeni kandidata geologo-mineralogicheskikh nauk, 21 p. (in Russian).

Khain, V. Ye., 1979, Regional geotectonics, extra-alpine Asia and Australia: Moscow, Nedra, 356 p. (in Russian).

Kirschner, C. E., 1988, Map showing sedimentary basins of onshore and continental shelf areas, Alaska: U.S. Geological Survey Miscellaneous Investigations Series Map I-1873, scale 1:2,500,000.

—— , 1989, Interior basins of Alaska, in Plafker, G., Jones, D. L., and Berg, H. C., eds., The Cordilleran orogen; Alaska: Boulder, Colorado, Geological Society of America, The Geology of North America, v. G-1 (in press).

Kirschner, C. E., and Rycerski, B. A., 1988, Petroleum potential of representative stratigraphic and structural elements in the National Petroleum Reserve in Alaska, in Gryc, G., ed., Geology and exploration of the National Petroleum Reserve in Alaska, 1974 to 1982: U.S. Geological Survey Professional Paper 1399, p. 191–208.

Klovan, J. E., and Embry, A. F., 1971, Upper Devonian stratigraphy northeastern Banks Island, N.W.T.: Canadian Society of Petroleum Geologists Bulletin, v. 19, no. 4, p. 705–729.

Klubov, B. A., and Semenov, G. A., 1973, Oil and gas potential of the Rauchuan Depression: Magadan, USSR, Problemy Neftegazohashoti Severo–Vostika SSSR, p. 50–60 (in Russian).

Kos'ko, M. K., 1984, East Siberian Sea, in Gramberg, I. S., and Pogrebitskiy, Yu. Ye., eds., Geologic structure and economic minerals of the USSR; Volcanic 9, Seas of the Soviet Arctic: Leningrad, USSR, Nedra, p. 60–66 (in Russian).

Kos'ko, M. K. and Nepomiluev, V. F., 1975, A reconstruction of Paleozoic structural-formational zones in the region of Anzhu Island: Tektonika Arktiki, v. 1, p. 26–30 (in Russian).

Kos'ko, M. K., Sobolevskaya, R. F., Nepomiluyev, V. R., and Vol'nov, D. A., 1975, Cambrian to Middle Devonian deposits of the New Siberian Islands, in Vol'nov, D. A., and Ivanov, V. L., eds., Geology and guide fossils of the New Siberian Islands and Wrangel Island: Leningrad, NIIGA, p. 8–21 (in Russian).

Kovacs, L. C., 1982, Motion along Nares Strait recorded in the Lincoln Sea; Aeromagnetic evidence, in Dawes, P. R., and Kerr, J. S., eds., Nares Strait and the drift of Greenland; A conflict in plate tectonics: Meddelelser om Grønland Geoscience 8–1982, p. 275–290.

Larsen, H. C., 1984, Geology of the East Greenland Shelf, in Spencer, A. M., and 5 others, eds., Petroleum geology of the North European margin: London, Graham and Trotman, Ltd., p. 329–339.

Lerand, M., 1973, Beaufort Sea, in McCrossan, R. G., ed., The future petroleum resources of Canada—their geology and potential: Canadian Society of Petroleum Geologists Memoir 1, p. 315–386.

Mayr, U., 1976, Upper Paleozoic succession in the Yelverton area, northern Ellesmere Island, District of Franklin, in Report of activities, Part A: Geological Survey of Canada Paper 76–1A, p. 445–448.

McMillan, N. J., 1982, Nares Strait and the petroleum explorer, in Dawes, P. R., and Kerr, J. W., eds., Nares strait and the drift of Greenland; A conflict in plate tectonics: Meddelelser om Grønland Geoscience 8–1982, p. 355–361.

Nassichuk, W. W., 1983, Petroleum potential in Arctic North America: Cold Regions Science and Technology, v. 7, p. 51–88.

—— , 1987, Forty years of northern non-renewable resource development: Arctic, v. 40, no. 4, p. 274–284.

Noe-Nygaard, A., 1976, Tertiary igneous rocks between Shannon and Scoresby Sund, East Greenland, in Escher, A., and Watts, W. S., eds., Geology of Greenland: Geological Survey of Greenland, p. 387–402.

Overton, A., 1970, Seismic refraction surveys, western Queen Elizabeth Islands and continental margin: Canadian Journal of Earth Sciences, v. 7, p. 346–365.

Overton, A., Embry, A., Hunter, J., and Pullan, S., 1989, Seismic reflection profiling from an ice island along the continental shelf of the Canadian Arctic Archipelago, in Current research, Part D: Geological Survey of Canada Paper 89–1 (in press).

Patton, W. W., Jr., and Miller, T. P., 1988, Geologic map of the Selawik and southeast Baird Mountains Quadrangles, Alaska: U.S. Geological Survey Miscellaneous Geologic Investigations Map I–530, scale 1:250,000.

Polkin, Ya. I., 1984, Chukchi Sea, in Gramberg, I. S., and Pogrebitskiy, Yu. Ye., eds., Geologic structure and economic minerals of the USSR; Vol. 9, Seas of the Soviet Arctic: Leningrad, USSR, Nedra, p. 67–79 (in Russian).

Poulton, T. P., 1982, Paleogeographic and tectonic implications of the Lower and Middle Jurassic facies patterns in northern Yukon Territory and adjacent Northwest Territories, in Embry, A. F., and Balkwill, H. P., eds., Arctic geology and geophysics: Canadian Society of Petroleum Geologists Memoir 8, p. 13–27.

Preobrazhenskaya, E. N., and others, 1975, Mesozoic rocks of Kotelny Island: Leningrad, USSR, Geologiya i Poleznye Iskopayemye Novosibirskikh Ostrovov I Ostrova Vrangelya, p. 28–37 (in Russian).

Semenovich, V. V., Gramberg, I. S., and Nesterov, I. I., 1973, Oil and gas possibilities in the Soviet Arctic, in Pitcher, M. G., ed., Arctic geology: Tulsa, Oklahoma, American Association of Petroleum Geologists, p. 194–203.

Snowdon, L. R., 1980, Resinite; A potential petroleum source in the Upper Cretaceous/Tertiary of the Beaufort-Mackenzie Basin, in Miall, A. D., ed., Facts and principles of world petroleum occurrence: Canadian Society of Petroleum Geologists Memoir 6, p. 509–521.

Soper, N. J., Dawes, P. R., and Higgins, A. K., 1982, Cretaceous–Tertiary magmatic and tectonic events in North Greenland and the history of adjacent ocean basins, in Dawes, P. R., and Kerr, J. W., eds., Nares Strait and the drift of Greenland; A conflict in plate tectonics: Meddelelser om Grønland Geoscience 8–1982, p. 205–220.

Surlyk, F., and 5 others, 1984, The Permian basin of East Greenland, in Spencer, A. M., and 5 others, eds., Petroleum geology of the North European margin: London, Graham and Trotman, Ltd., p. 303–315.

Tailleur, I. L., 1973, Probable rift origin of Canada Basin, in Pitcher, M. F., ed., Arctic geology: American Association of Petroleum Geologists Memoir 19, p. 526–535.

Thurston, D. K., and Theiss, L. A., 1987, Geologic report for the Chukchi Sea planning area, Alaska; Regional geology, petroleum geology, and environmental geology: Anchorage, Alaska, U.S. Minerals Management Service OCS Report MMS 87-0046, 193 p.

Tolson, R. B., 1987, Structure and stratigraphy of the Hope Basin, southern Chukchi Sea, Alaska, in Scholl, D. W., Grantz, A., and Vedder, J. G., eds., Geology and resource potential of the continental margin of western North America and adjacent ocean basins; Beaufort Sea to Baja California: Houston, Circum-Pacific Council for Energy and Mineral Resources, Earth Sciences Series no. 6, p. 59–72.

Trufanov, G. V., Belousov, K. N., and Vakulenko, A. S., 1979, Stratigraphy of Cenozoic sediments of Novosibirsk Archipelago, in Kontinentalnye Tretichnye Tolshchi Severo–Vostochnoy Azii: Novosibirsk, USSR, p. 30–40 (in Russian).

U.S. Geological Survey and U.S. Minerals Management Service, 1988, National assessment of undiscovered conventional oil and gas resources: U.S. Geological Survey Open-File Report 88-373, 51 p.

Vinogradov, V. A., 1984, Laptev Sea, in Gramberg, I. S., and Pogrebitskiy, Yu. Ye., eds., Geologic structure and economic minerals of the USSR; Volume 9, Seas of the Soviet Arctic: Leningrad, USSR, Nedra, p. 50–59 (in Russian).

Vinogradov, V. A., and others, 1974, Tectonics of the East Arctic Shelf of the USSR: Leningrad, USSR, 144 p. (in Russian).

Vogt, P. R., Perry, P. R., Feden, R. H., Fleming, H. S., and Cherkis, N. Z., 1981, The Greenland–Norwegian Sea and Iceland environment; Geology and geophysics, in Nairn, A.E.M., Churkin, M., Jr., and Stehli, F. G., eds., The ocean basins and margins; Volume 5, The Arctic Ocean: New York and London, Plenum Press, p. 493–598.

Volnov, D. A., 1975, History of geologic development of the Novosibirsk Islands, in Geologiya i Poleznye Iskopayemye Novosibirskikh Ostrovov I Ostrova Wrangelya: Leningrad, USSR, p. 61–71 (in Russian).

Yegiazarov, B. Kh., and others, 1977, Tectonics and main features of ore distribution between the Pacific and Arctic mobile belts, *in* Tektonika Arktiki, Skladchatyy Fundament Shelfovykh Sedimentatsionnykh Basseynov: Leningrad, USSR, p. 132–141 (in Russian).

Willumsen, P. S., and Cote, R. P., 1982, Tertiary sedimentation in the southern Beaufort Sea, Canada, *in* Embry, A. F., and Balkwill, H. R., eds., Arctic geology and geophysics: Canadian Society of Petroleum Geologists Memoir 8, p. 43–53.

Wilson, D. G., 1976, Studies of Mesozoic stratigraphy, Tanquary Fiord to Yelverton Pass, northern Ellesmere Island, District of Franklin, *in* Report of activities, Part A: Geological Survey of Canada Paper 76–1A, p. 449–451.

MANUSCRIPT ACCEPTED BY THE SOCIETY JULY 26, 1989

Drilling rig on Arctic ice. From Blasco, S., Johnson, G. L., Mayer, L., and Thiede, J., 1987, Drilling will reveal important changes: Geotimes, v. 32, p. 8.

Printed in U.S.A.

Chapter 28

Gas hydrates of the Arctic Ocean region

Keith A. Kvenvolden and Arthur Grantz
U.S. Geological Survey, 345 Middlefield Road, Menlo Park, California 94025

INTRODUCTION

Sediments of the Arctic Ocean region may trap enormous quantities of natural gas in and beneath gas hydrates. These solid, ice-like substances, composed mainly of methane and water, are found in two distinct environments: (1) offshore, in sediment of the outer continental margin, and (2) onshore, in and below areas of thick permafrost. Most offshore gas-hydrate occurrences have been inferred from marine seismic-reflection records where an anomalous acoustic reflector correlates with the base of the gas-hydrate zone. Onshore, most gas-hydrate occurrences have been inferred from well-log responses. In only a few cases have gas hydrates actually been sampled. This chapter focuses on the known and inferred gas hydrates of the North American Arctic and estimates the amount of methane that may be associated with sediments in the Arctic Basin.

Composition and Crystallography

Natural gas is composed mostly of methane, which is often accompanied by hydrocarbons of higher molecular weight such as ethane, propane, and butanes, as well as inorganic gases such as nitrogen, carbon dioxide, and hydrogen sulfide. Under appropriate pressure and temperature conditions, often found in permafrost areas and in outer continental margin sediment, natural gas may interact with water to crystallize as a solid three-dimensional framework of water molecules that is stabilized by the included molecules of natural gas. This solid structure is called a gas hydrate (Davidson, 1973).

In gas hydrates, water crystallizes in the cubic crystallographic system rather than in the hexagonal system of normal ice. Two structures of the cubic lattice are possible. In structure I, the cages are arranged in body-centered packing and include small molecules such as methane, ethane, and nonhydrocarbons like carbon dioxide, hydrogen sulfide, and nitrogen. In structure II, diamond packing is present, and not only can molecules of the gases just mentioned be included in the cages, but significant quantities of propane and isobutane are also needed to occupy the larger cages in order to stabilize the structure. Only structure I gas hydrates are expected in nature unless the gas is relatively rich in propane and isobutane (Davidson and others, 1978). A more detailed discussion of the crystallography of natural gas hydrates is given by Hitchon (1974).

Pressure-Temperature Stability Fields

The established pressure-temperature equilibrium conditions (Fig. 1) for the formation of structure I gas hydrates (containing mainly methane) show that (1) higher pressures enable the gas hydrates to form at correspondingly higher temperatures, and (2) the components in the methane have an effect on the pressures and temperatures at which gas hydrates form. For example, ethane, propane, carbon dioxide, and hydrogen sulfide shift the methane equilibrium conditions to higher equilibrium temperatures at a given pressure. Nitrogen, on the other hand, shifts the methane equilibrium conditions to lower equilibrium temperatures at a given pressure; salinity shifts the equilibrium conditions in the same direction as does nitrogen because salt lowers the gas-hydrate decomposition temperatures. Shifts in the equilibrium phase boundary of gas hydrates tend to cancel each other due to the addition of other gases to methane and of salts to water. Unless the gas composition and salinity are known, a pure-water and pure-methane system provides the best first approximation for establishing the depth-temperature relation of naturally occurring gas hydrates (Claypool and Kaplan, 1974).

If geothermal gradients are superimposed on the gas-hydrate equilibrium phase diagram, the depth limits of gas hydrates can be predicted. Two arbitrary examples follow. Figure 2A shows the limits of the gas-hydrate zone in which permafrost is 600 m thick and there is sufficient methane to form gas hydrates. The geothermal gradient of 18°C/km within the permafrost changes at the base of the permafrost to 27°C/km, due to the difference in thermal conductivities of frozen and unfrozen sediment. The diagram indicates that gas hydrates in this example may occur in the permafrost between depths of about 200 and 600 m and below the permafrost between depths of 600 and about 1,000 m. Figure 2B shows the depth limits for gas hydrates in an offshore region where the water depth is 1,200 m and the geothermal gradient is

Kvenvolden, K. A., and Grantz, A., 1990, Gas hydrates of the Arctic Ocean region, *in* Grantz, A., Johnson, L., and Sweeney, J. F., eds., The Arctic Ocean region: Boulder, Colorado, Geological Society of America, The Geology of North America, v. L.

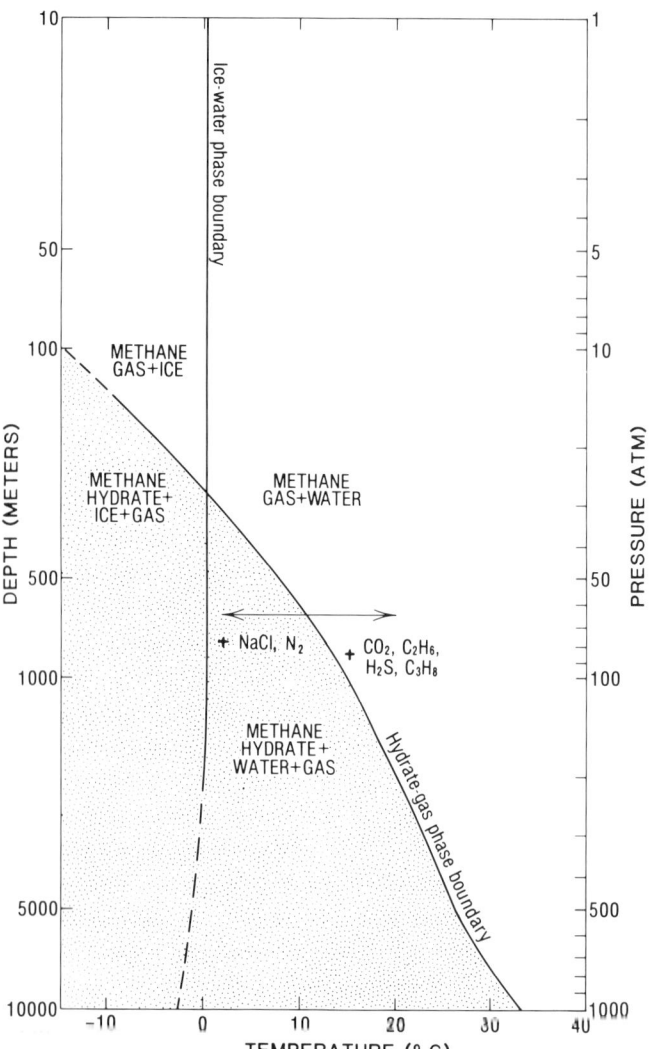

Figure 1. Phase diagram showing boundary between free methane gas (no pattern) and methane hydrate (pattern) for a pure-water and pure-methane system. Pressure is converted to depth assuming a lithostatic and hydrostatic pressure gradient of 0.1 atm/m. The diagram is useful for predicting depth-temperature relations for naturally occurring gas hydrates (modified from Kvenvolden and McMenamin, 1980).

50°C/km. There is no permafrost here, and the bottom water temperature is estimated to be about 1°C. In this example, gas hydrates may occur at subbottom depths between 0 and 250 m; where water depths are less than about 300 m, sediments cannot contain gas hydrates because the pressure is too low.

Gas-hydrate Formation

Besides the pressure-temperature conditions, methane-hydrate formation also requires that sufficient methane be present to stabilize the gas-hydrate structure. Methane is essentially condensed within the solid framework of water molecules so that the molar ratio of methane to water in a fully saturated structure I gas hydrate is nearly 1:6. Thus, at standard conditions, one volume of gas hydrate may contain up to about 164 volumes of methane (Davidson and others, 1978). At depths less than about 1,700 m, gas hydrates in sediment can have as much as six times more methane per unit volume than can be accommodated as free gas in the same space (Bily and Dick, 1974; Hunt, 1979). The source of methane for gas-hydrate formation may be either biogenic or thermogenic. Biogenic methane results from the microbial breakdown of organic matter in shallow sediment; thermogenic methane comes from the thermal alteration of organic matter in sediment at depth. Because gas hydrates occur in shallow sediment, biogenic sources are often implicated, especially for gas hydrates of outer continental margins (Kvenvolden and Barnard, 1983). Where gas migration pathways are available from deep within the sedimentary section, thermogenic gas may also form gas hydrates. In addition to serving as a kind of reservoir for methane, gas hydrates are also impermeable to free gas, so a layer of gas hydrate could trap free gas beneath it.

IDENTIFICATION OF GAS HYDRATES

Gas hydrates have been directly observed at only one location in the North American Arctic where a pressure-core barrel was successfully used for gas-hydrate recovery. On the other hand, gas hydrates have been inferred to be present in many areas (1) by use of well-logging methods, such as comparison of wire-line logs (caliper, gamma ray, spontaneous potential, resistivity, sonic, and neutron porosity) and measurements of gas in total mud-gas logs; and (2) by use of seismic-reflection methods.

Pressure-core Barrel

Proof that gas hydrates underlie permafrost was obtained in 1972 at the ARCO-EXXON N.W. Eileen State No. 2 well west of Prudhoe Bay (Collet and Kvenvolden, 1987). Two pressurized cores were successfully recovered and were maintained in the barrels at temperatures slightly above 0°C. After each sample of gas was removed from the pressurized core barrels, the valve was closed and pressures began to build toward the gas-hydrate equilibrium pressure. Pressure was maintained even after several samples of gas were withdrawn. This result could only have been caused by the decomposition of gas hydrate after each sample of gas was removed (Hunt, 1979). Additionally, down-hole well logs indicated that the depth of the gas-hydrate zone extended from 640 to 730 m in permeable sandstone that lies 60 m beneath the base of permafrost.

Wire-line Logs

When used in combination with each other, wire-line logs can be useful for detection and evaluation of gas-hydrate intervals, provided that extensive decomposition of gas hydrate has

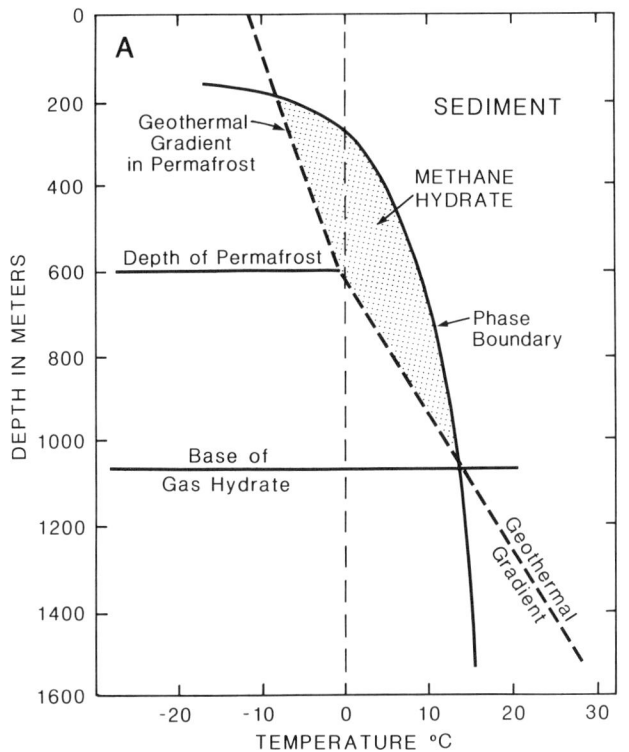
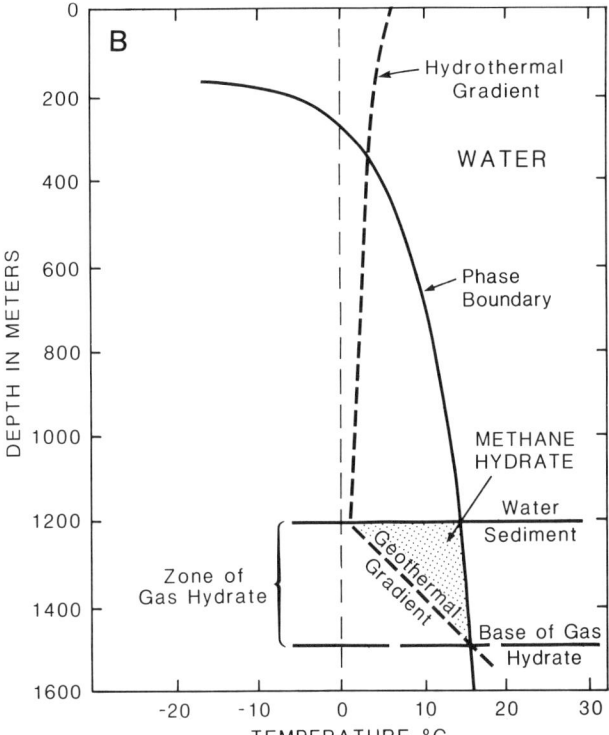

Figure 2. Examples of different depth-temperature zones for gas-hydrate occurrence. (A) conditions that are favorable for gas-hydrate formation where permafrost is present (after Bily and Dick, 1974; Collett, 1983). (B) conditions in which gas hydrates are stable in outer continental margin sediments (modified from Kvenvolden and McMenamin, 1980).

not taken place. Log characteristics expected for gas hydrates were summarized by Goodman (1980):

Caliper: overgauge hole through gas-hydrate zone.

Gamma ray: response in gas-hydrate zones is same as in nonhydrate zones, indicating sand-shale intervals.

Spontaneous potential: little deflection opposite gas-hydrate zones when compared to that in gas or water zones.

Resistivity (lat log): 10 to 100 ohm-m for gas-hydrate intervals compared to 1 to 10 ohm-m in water or free-gas zones.

Sonic velocity: high acoustic velocity (short travel times) in gas-hydrate intervals, with cycle skipping if decomposition has occurred.

Neutron porosity: crossplots give estimates of contents of gas, water, and gas hydrates.

Evaluation of gas hydrates by means of well logs is highly subjective, however. Gas-hydrate decomposition beyond the penetration depths of the logging tool, washouts, and the existence of gas and/or water along with gas hydrates will alter the log responses and may limit definitive analyses. Figure 3 illustrates the wire-line log responses in one of the gas-hydrate intervals in the N.W. Eileen State No. 2 well in Alaska. Whereas strong mud-gas shows suggested free gas in the formation, high resistivities and sonic velocities indicated ice or ice-like material. In com-

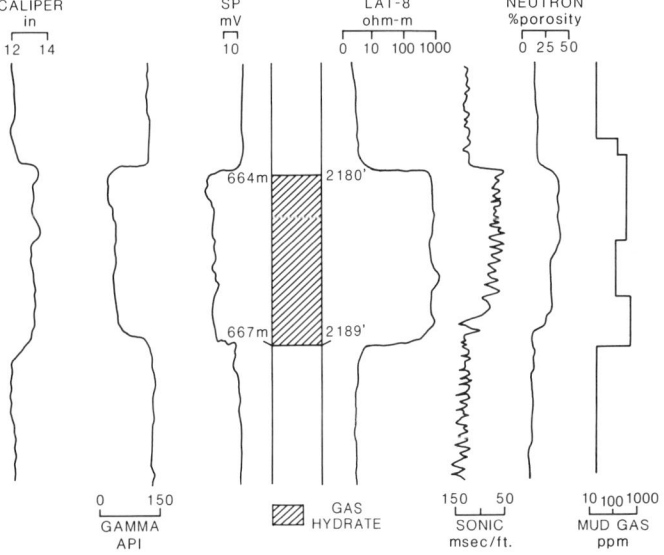

Figure 3. Comparison of wire-line logs (caliper, gamma-ray, spontaneous potential [SP], resistivity [LAT-8], sonic velocity, and neutron porosity) and total mud-gas log for a gas-hydrate-containing interval (664–667 m) in the ARCO-EXXON N.W. Eileen State No. 2 well on the North Slope of Alaska (modified from Collett, 1983).

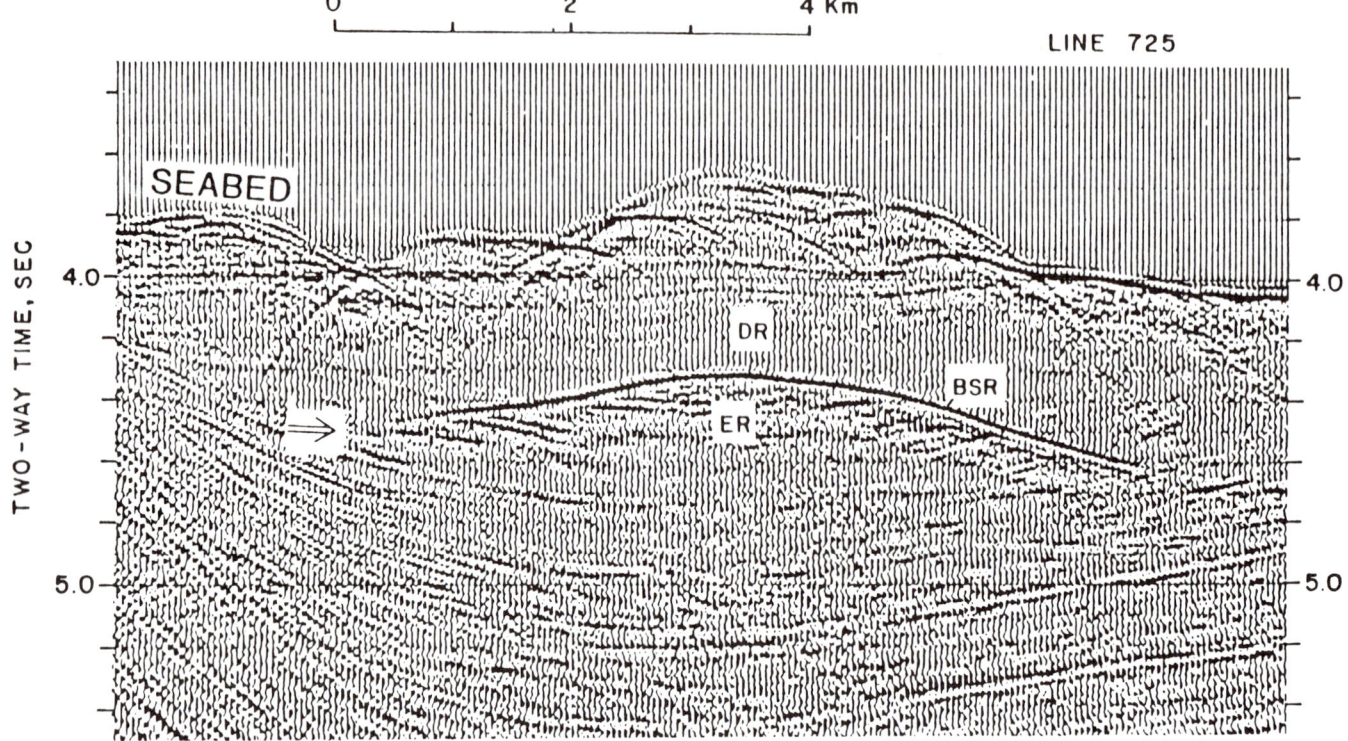

Figure 4. Multichannel seismic-reflection profile from offshore northern Alaska showing the anomalous acoustic reflector (BSR), which may mark the base of the zone of gas hydrate. (DR) diminished reflections thought to be caused by gas hydrates. (ER) enhanced reflections interpreted to represent sediment charged with gas that is trapped beneath the BSR (from Grantz and others, 1982a).

bination, the resistivity, sonic-velocity, and mud-gas logs pointed to the presence of gas hydrates (Collett and Kvenvolden, 1987).

Total Mud-gas Logs

The most pronounced characteristic of gas-hydrate-bearing zones is the significant amount of gas that is liberated as the gas hydrates decompose when their pressure-temperature equilibrium is altered by drilling (Bily and Dick, 1974). Total mud-gas logs record these intervals by showing a sharp increase in the amount of gas in the circulating mud. Figure 3 compares a total mud-gas log with the wire-line logs discussed above.

Seismic Surveys

Interpretation of onshore seismic data for the presence of gas hydrates has not been particularly successful because of the difficulty in distinguishing permafrost reflectors from gas-hydrate reflectors (Davidson and others, 1978). In offshore areas, however, seismic-reflection surveys have provided evidence for extensive gas-hydrate deposits in sediments of the outer continental margin under the Beaufort Sea off the northern coast of Alaska (Grantz and others, 1976) and Canada (Neave and others, 1978). Features observed on both single-channel and multichannel seismic-reflection profiles suggest that solid gas hydrates are present offshore of northern Alaska (Fig. 4). The most striking feature on the record is a strong seismic reflector that regionally lies 300 to more than 700 m beneath the sea floor. On average, the subseabottom depth of the reflector is proportional to the water depth. Generally, this reflector has been recognized only where water depths exceed 400 m, and it has been traced basinward to water depths as great as 2,800 m on some seismic lines. The increase in subseabottom depth is gradual, and locally the reflector is subparallel to the sea bed; thus, it has been called a bottom-simulating reflector, or BSR.

The BSR approximates the pressure-temperature boundary between methane hydrate above and free methane in water below. Accordingly, the reflector is interpreted to mark the boundary between an overlying region containing zones of solid gas hydrate and an underlying region containing free gas. Gas hydrate is thought to cement the zone immediately above the BSR and thereby to markedly diminish the amplitude of seismic reflectors that originate within that zone. The amplitude of the reflectors is decreased because cementation by the gas hydrate is thought to override original differences in acoustic impedance between the sedimentary layers. The zone of diminished reflectors

TABLE 1. PREDICTED INTERVALS OF GAS-HYDRATE OCCURRENCES IN THE ARCTIC OCEAN REGION

	Minimum Depth to Top of Gas Hydrate (m)	Maximum Depth to Bottom of Gas Hydrate (m)	Interval Thickness (m)	Reference
Offshore				
Alaska Beaufort Sea Shelf	?	300-700	300-700	Grantz and Dinter, 1980
Canadian Beaufort Sea Shelf	200*	1560*	1360	Weaver and Stewart, 1982
Sverdrup Basin	140	1270	1130	Judge, 1982
Onshore				
Mackenzie Delta				
East	190	1860	1670	Judge, 1982
West	340	730	390	Judge, 1982
Sverdrup Basin	140	1270	1130	Judge, 1982
Arctic Islands				
Western	140	1100	960	Judge, 1982
Eastern	140	960	820	Judge, 1982
Arctic Platform	140	1400	1260	Judge, 1982
Alaskan North Slope	177	1119	942	Collett, 1983

*Depth below mean sea level. All other depths are measured from the sea bottom or ground level.

(DR in Fig. 4) is irregular in areal distribution, but it typically lies just above the BSR and consists of the lower half, or less, of the supra-BSR section.

A reflection polarity opposite to that of the sea-floor reflection typifies the BSR, and a zone within which seismic-reflection amplitudes are strongly enhanced (ER in Fig. 4) always lies immediately beneath the BSR. Moreover, on some seismic profiles the apparent dip of seismic reflectors is seen to increase on entering the ER zone. These effects suggest that free gas may have accumulated in the ER zone, because even a few percent of free gas in pore water significantly decreases the seismic velocity of a sediment. Enhancement of reflectivity in the ER zone may have resulted from the differential accumulation of gas in the more permeable sedimentary layers. A velocity reduction beneath the BSR is consistent with all of the seismic phenomena noted above.

The amplitude of the BSR and the vertical extent of the ER zone are greatest beneath bathymetric highs. The bowing upward of the BSR (inferred base of gas hydrate) beneath these highs appears to create pseudoanticlines, which can act as structural traps for free gas (probably mainly methane) in the sediments below the BSR, and the cap is the gas-hydrate zone above the BSR. Conversely, the BSR and adjacent DR and ER zones are commonly weakest in amplitude at pseudosynclines beneath bathymetric lows. Migration of free gas beneath the BSR is suggested by a belt of exceptionally gassy Quaternary sediments recognized by D. A. Dinter (personal communication, 1985) on high-resolution seismic-reflection profiles that cross the outer Alaskan Beaufort Shelf. The gassy sediments lie near the landward edge of the basinward-dipping BSR. These observations suggest that free gas moves upslope, beneath the generally seaward-dipping BSR, and the gas is preferentially accumulated in pseudoanticlines and perhaps in other types of traps.

OCCURRENCES OF GAS HYDRATES

Gas hydrates have been identified both onshore and offshore in the North American Arctic. Table 1 summarizes the depth intervals of expected gas-hydrate occurrences in the Arctic Ocean region, and Figure 5 shows the locations of the areas where gas hydrates are believed to be present.

ONSHORE GAS HYDRATES

Mackenzie Delta

In 1972, Imperial Oil Limited drilled two exploratory wells (Fig. 6) in the MacKenzie Delta of the Northwest Territories of Canada (Bily and Dick, 1974). Log-response characteristics and formation tests in both the Mallik L-38 and Ivik J-26 wells indicated that gas hydrates are present. In the Mallik L-38 well, the total thickness of gas-hydrate-bearing sand was determined to be 99 m in an interval from 820 to 1,103 m; in the Ivik J-26, 25 m total of gas-hydrate-bearing sand was measured in an interval from 978 to 1,020 m. At both of these wells the gas hydrates occur beneath the base of the permafrost, and the composition of gas is more than 99 percent methane.

Possible gas-hydrate occurrences were listed by G. Hood in nine additional wells in the onshore and nearshore Mackenzie Delta in a depth interval ranging from 214 to 1,174 m (Arctic Petroleum Operators Association Drilling Subcommittee, 1980). The predicted depth limits (Table 1) of the methane-hydrate stability field in the east Mackenzie Delta are 190 to 1,860 m; in the west Mackenzie Delta these limits are 340 to 730 m (Judge, 1982).

Sverdrup Basin, Arctic Platform, and Arctic Islands

Davidson and others (1978) and Judge (1982) show that in

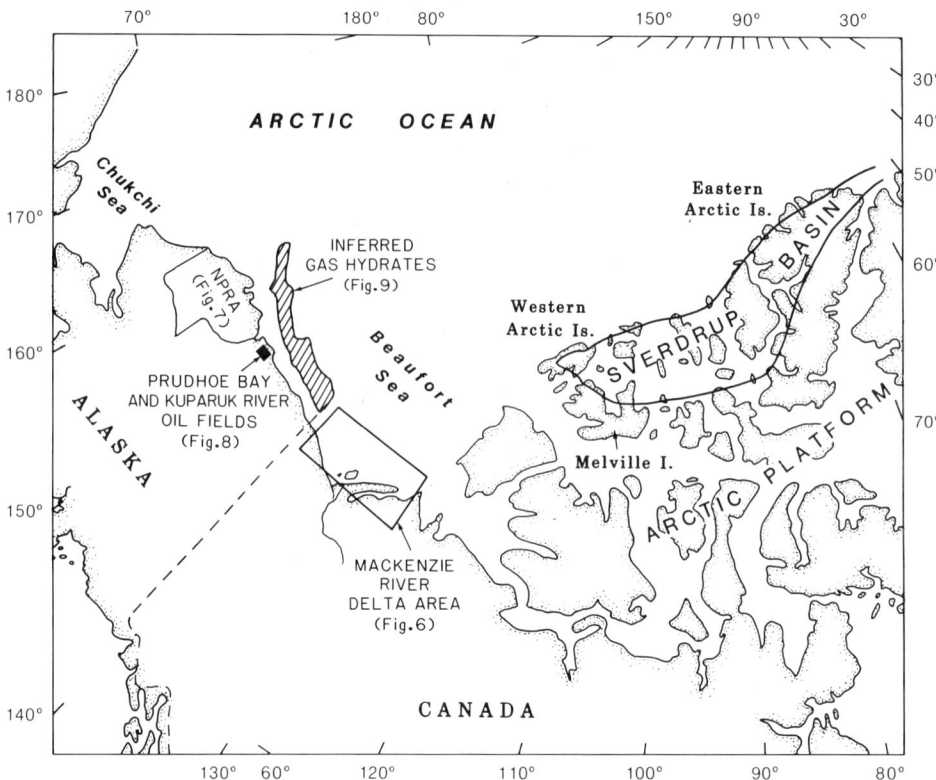

Figure 5. Map of the North American Arctic showing regions of probable gas-hydrate occurrence discussed in the text.

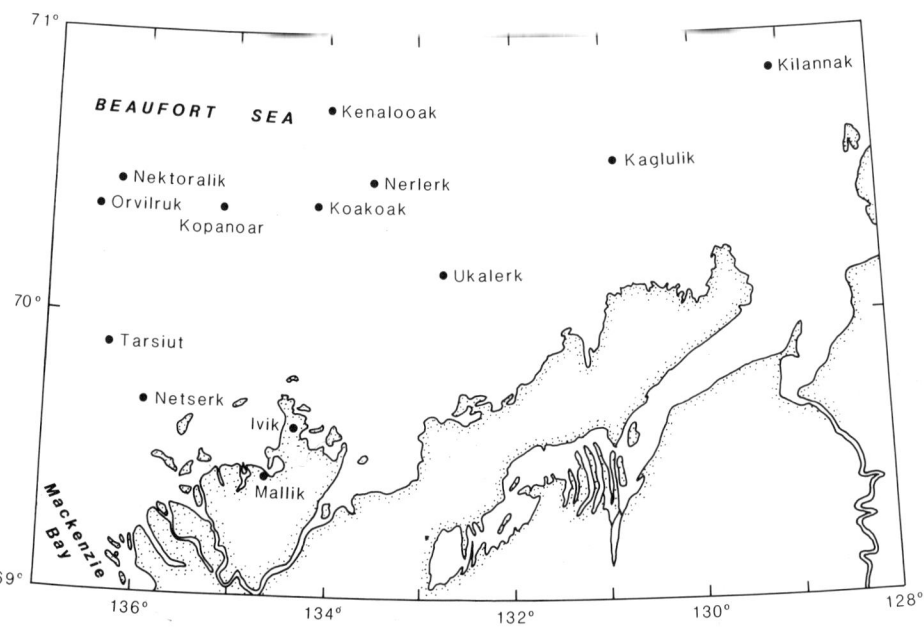

Figure 6. Map of the Mackenzie River Delta region showing locations of wells where the occurrences of gas hydrates have been identified through drilling, formation testing, and logging (modified from Bily and Dick [1974] and Weaver and Stewart [1982]).

11 wells in the central Sverdrup Basin the depth limits of the gas-hydrate stability field range from 140 to 1,270 m (Table 1). They do not differentiate between onshore and offshore wells, and the evidence for gas-hydrate occurrence is not given. These same authors indicate that three wells with possible gas hydrates are present on the Arctic Platform. In this region the predicted depth range of possible occurrence of methane hydrate is 140 m to 1,400 m (Table 1). Judge (1982) suggests that thicknesses of the zone of gas hydrate may be as great as 1,260 m to 2000 m.

In an extensive compilation of 151 wells drilled in the Arctic Islands, A. Judge and J. Jones (unpublished report, 1985) list depth intervals where gas hydrates are identified in down-hole logs from 103 wells. The depths of possible methane-hydrate occurrences in eight wells in the western and eastern Arctic Islands (Table 1) range from 140 m to 1,100 m (Judge, 1982). Earlier, Hitchon (1974) reported the detection of unusual gas flow, thought to be from gas hydrates, in a well on Melville Island at depths between 319 m and 727 m.

North Slope of Alaska

Gas hydrates have been inferred from well logs and drilling data to be present in the National Petroleum Reserve of Alaska (NPRA) and in the region of Prudhoe Bay. Galate and Goodman (1982) studied wire-line logs from 16 wells in the NPRA (Fig. 7) and reported that three of the wells showed what they called "significant" evidence for gas hydrates:

Well Name	Gas Hydrate Interval
East Simpson No. 1	303-308 m
South Meade No. 1	562-565 m
Tunalik No. 1	306-367 m

In addition, the logs from five wells (Fig. 7) had "weak" evidence for gas hydrates. Confirmation of the presence of gas hydrates was not obtained for any of these wells where "significant" or "weak" evidence for gas hydrates was found. The remaining wells (Fig. 7) showed no evidence for gas hydrates.

A study of wire-line logs from 125 wells in the Prudhoe Bay region of Alaska indicates possible gas hydrates in 33 of these wells (Collett, 1983). The depth intervals between which the occurrence of gas hydrates is inferred from well logs ranges from 128 to 1,090 m. The upper and lower depth limits for gas-hydrate stability are predicted to be 197 m and 1,119 m, respectively. Most of the gas hydrates appear to be geographically restricted to the Kuparuk River field to the west of Prudhoe Bay where gas hydrates were actually recovered at the N.W. Eileen State No. 2 well (Fig. 8). The Kuparuk River field likely contains as many as six laterally continuous, gas-hydrate-saturated sedimentary units.

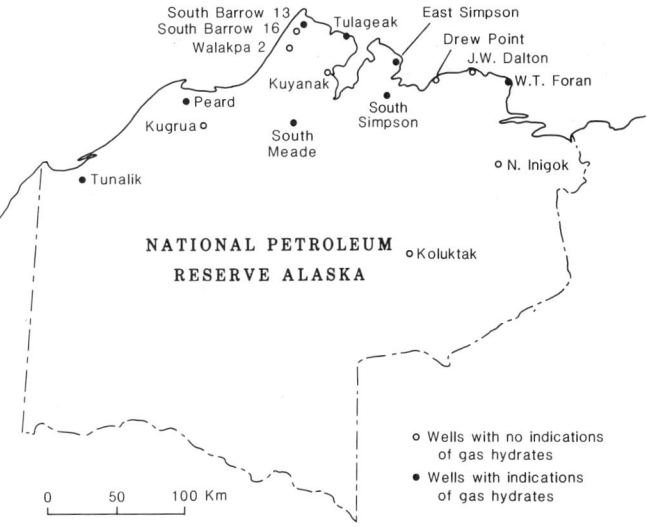

Figure 7. Map showing location of 16 wells in the National Petroleum Reserve of Alaska studied for presence of gas hydrates (modified from Galate and Goodman, 1982).

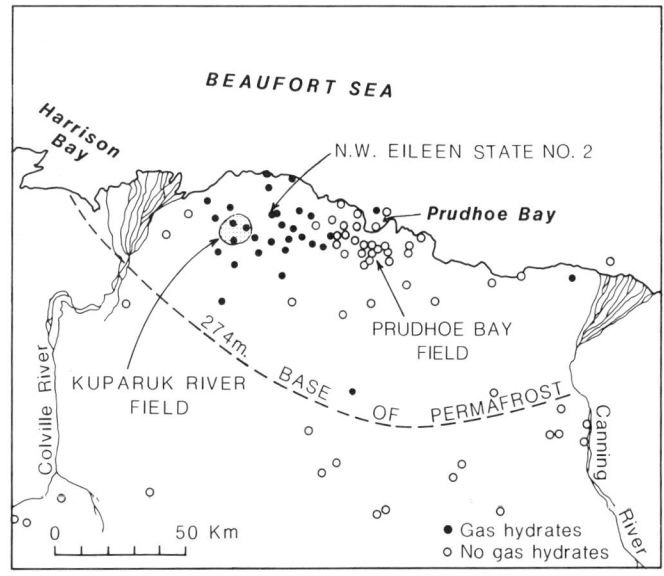

Figure 8. Map of wells examined for gas-hydrate occurrences in the Prudhoe Bay region of Alaska (modified from Collett, 1983).

OFFSHORE GAS HYDRATES

Beaufort Sea (Alaska and Canada)

The most extensive offshore occurrence of gas hydrates in the North American Arctic lies north of Alaska beneath the Beaufort Sea (Grantz and others, 1976; Grantz and Dinter, 1980;

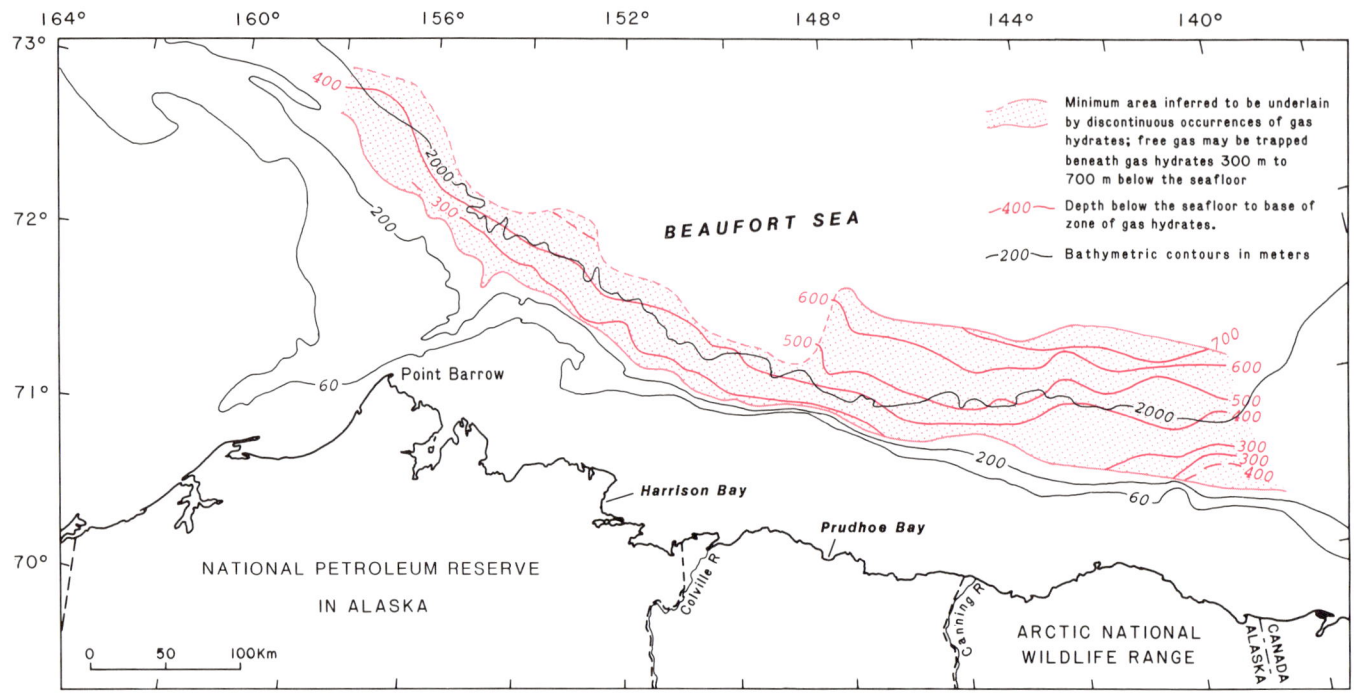

Figure 9. Map of the areal extent of the seismically inferred gas hydrates in sediment of the Alaskan Beaufort Sea (modified from Grantz and others, 1982a).

Grantz and others, 1982a). Seismic surveys show that the area of continental slope across which the seismically inferred gas hydrates occur exceeds 7,500 km^2 (Fig. 9) and may encompass a significant part of the Arctic Ocean basin where water is deeper than 400 to 600 m. The geothermal gradient has been predicted to be 50 ± 9°C/km on the basis of the depth of gas hydrates in this area (MacLeod, 1982). Drilling has not yet directly tested for gas hydrates in this region, so the presence of gas hydrates remains inferential.

Surveys of Neave and others (1978) suggest that gas hydrates are present in sediment under the Canadian Beaufort Sea. Northwest of the Mackenzie Delta in the Netserk well area (Fig. 6), low temperatures and gas were encountered in drill holes, and low sonic velocities were measured and interpreted to be caused by gas. Neave and others (1978) infer from this combination of evidence that gas hydrates are present and responsible for the observed gas.

Beaufort Sea Shelf

The presence of gas hydrates in the Mackenzie Delta-Beaufort Sea areas has been indicated by a detailed examination of good-quality down-hole logs from 161 wells. Gas hydrates have been identified in about 27 of the wells to depths in excess of 1,200 m both onshore and offshore (Judge, 1984; Judge and Jones, unpublished report, 1985). Weaver and Stewart (1982) discuss 10 wells (Fig. 6) where, on the basis of well-log interpretations, both permafrost and gas hydrates are believed to exist. Although these wells are technically offshore, the gas-hydrate occurrences are much like the onshore occurrences, discussed previously, in that they are associated with permafrost. The predicted intervals of gas-hydrate occurrences in four wells having the most convincing well-log evidence for gas hydrates follow:

Well Name	Predicted Interval (m below sea level)
Nerlerk	200–1,450
Koakoak	230–1,500
Ukalerk	250–1,480
Kopanoar	230–880

These intervals are predicted on the basis of a gas composition of more than 99 percent methane, which is the usual composition for gas in the upper 200 m of sediment in the Beaufort Sea. For six additional wells on the Beaufort Sea Shelf, Weaver and Stewart (1982) predicted the base of the gas-hydrate zone as follows:

Well Name	Predicted Base of Gas Hydrates (m below sea level)
Tarsiut	800
Orvilruk	800
Nektoralik	900-1,300
Kenalooak	1,200-1,560
Kaglulik	800+
Kilannak	700

Thus the predicted depth below sea level of the base of gas hydrates varies from 800 m in the western part to at least 1,500 m in the eastern part of this area of the Beaufort Shelf. The geothermal gradient below the permafrost is typically 30°C/km. Although gas hydrates are apparently common on the Beaufort Shelf, insufficient amounts of gas hydrates have been discovered to justify producing gas from these zones (Weaver and Stewart, 1982).

Sverdrup Basin

Gas hydrates have been identified by analyses of well logs and drilling histories in offshore wells in the Sverdrup Basin, although specific information regarding these offshore wells is currently not available. In this basin the depth interval of possible gas-hydrate occurrence in 11 wells is between 140 to 1,270 m (Table 1; Judge, 1982). In the offshore Panarctic Ten Sun Dome Jackson G-16 well, the mud-gas log showed gas kicks and gas-cut mud at depths between 523 and 600 m, indicating a possible gas-hydrate occurrence (Arctic Petroleum Operators Association Drilling Subcommittee, 1980).

ESTIMATE OF THE EXTENT OF GAS HYDRATES IN THE ARCTIC BASIN

Rough estimates of the extent of inferred gas hydrates and of the magnitude of the volume of gas that may be trapped in the inferred gas-hydrate zone and underlying zone of free gas in the Arctic Basin may be made by extrapolating from our knowledge of gas-hydrate occurrences north of Alaska. Approximately 75 percent of the multichannel and 60 percent of the single-channel seismic-reflection profiles of Grantz and others (1972, 1974, and 1982b) that cross areas of the Alaskan Beaufort and northeastern Chukchi Seas, having about 400 to 2,800 m of water depth, show a BSR, DR, ER, or other features suggestive of gas hydrates (Fig. 4). The seaward extent of the gas hydrates is not clear because the gas-hydrate reflectors, if present in deep water, would be essentially parallel to sedimentary layering and difficult to recognize. The thickness of the zone with gas hydrates, as inferred from the observed subseabed depth of the BSR, is 300 to 700 m or more. In general, only the lower half, or less, of this interval is believed to be occupied by the DR zone, which is inferred to actually contain the gas hydrates. To estimate the magnitude of the hydrate-related gas deposits of the Arctic Basin, we assumed that (1) the methane in gas hydrates in the Arctic Basin is mainly or entirely biogenic, (2) sediments sufficiently rich in organic matter to produce significant accumulations of gas hydrates are deposited only near the continental margins or off the mouths of major rivers, and (3) the inferred distribution of gas hydrates off Alaska is a reasonable guide to their distribution around the Arctic Basin.

The zone of gas-hydrate occurrences north of Alaska, as inferred from seismic-reflection data is about 80 km wide (Fig. 9). For our estimate, we consider that gas hydrates in the Arctic lie only within a belt 80 km seaward of the 400-m isobath, except off the mouths of the Mackenzie River of Canada and the Lena River of Siberia. Off these major rivers, which deliver abundant nutrients and organic matter to the Arctic Basin, we extended the zone to the 2,800-m isobath. The area thus defined is roughly 700,000 km^2. From their distribution off Alaska, we assume that only 75 percent of this area, or about 525,000 km^2, is underlain by gas hydrates. The interval above the BSR is 300 to 700 m thick, but the DR zone, which is inferred to contain the gas hydrates, occupies half or less of this interval. The average thickness of the sediments above the BSR is about 400 m, and we estimate that the DR zone occupies 10 percent of this interval, which yields an estimated average thickness of 40 m for the actual gas-hydrate zone. We arbitrarily take a minimum value of 30 percent as the average porosity of the sediment in the hydrate zone. One m^3 of gas-hydrate would yield, on decomposition, a maximum of 164 m^3 of methane gas at standard temperature and pressure (STP). Because it is unlikely that the gas hydrate is fully saturated, we assume a decomposition yield of 140 m^3 of methane. The product of these measurements, estimates, and assumptions gives a rough estimate of the volume of methane that might be tied up as gas hydrates in sediments beneath the Arctic Ocean.

(1) Area underlain by gas hydrates: $0.75 \times (7 \times 10^{11})$ m^2 = 5.25×10^{11} m^2. (2) Estimated average thickness of zone containing gas hydrates: 0.1×400 m = 40 m. (3) Estimated average porosity of gas-hydrate zone: 30%. (4) Yield: m^3 methane per m^3 methane gas hydrate = 140. (5) Total: 5.25×10^{11} m^2 × 40 m × $0.3 \times 140 = 8.8 \times 10^{14}$ = $\sim 10^{15}$ m^3 of methane STP.

This estimate is comparable to those for the gas-hydrate resources of the entire world ocean made by Trofimuk and others (1977) of 5 to 25×10^{15} m^3, and by McIver (1981) as adapted from Cherskiy and Makogon (1970) of 3.1×10^{15} m^3. The estimate is, however, about four orders of magnitude smaller than an estimate for the world ocean by Dobrynin and others (1981) of 7.6×10^{18} m^3.

We have not attempted to estimate the volume of free gas occupying the ER zone beneath the BSR, but that amount also appears to be large. Gas is presumably being added to the ER zone by some biogenic generation of new gas below the BSR, by breakdown of the gas hydrates within the DR zone where the geotherms are rising as a result of sea-floor aggradation, and possibly by leakage of deeper thermogenic gas. The free-gas buildup is presumably balanced by loss of gas to upslope migration and possibly by local leakage into or through the interval above the BSR. It is conceivable that the volume of free gas beneath the BSR is comparable to that estimated to be trapped in the overlying gas hydrates.

SUMMARY

Gas hydrates commonly occur in sediments of the North American Arctic. Onshore, gas hydrates have been identified through drilling and logging in the Canadian MacKenzie Delta, the Sverdrup Basin and Arctic Platform, the Arctic Islands, and the North Slope of Alaska. Offshore, gas hydrates have been identified on marine seismic records from the Alaskan and Canadian Beaufort Sea. Also, evidence for gas hydrates has been encountered in offshore wells on the Canadian Beaufort Shelf and the Sverdrup Basin.

The consequences of gas-hydrate deposits in sediments of this region are many. Some examples follow:

(1) Geothermal gradients are affected by gas hydrates; MacLeod (1982) used gas-hydrate information to estimate geothermal gradients of $50 \pm 9°C/km$ beneath the Alaskan Beaufort Sea, and Collett (1983) showed that geothermal gradients in the Prudhoe Bay region must be less than $37°C/km$ for gas hydrates to be stable.

(2) The movement of sediment as slumps and slides can possibly be triggered by the decomposition of gas hydrates and the resulting expansion or release of gas. Both permafrost and gas hydrates of the Canadian Beaufort Shelf are relict in nature and are currently degrading (Weaver and Stewart, 1982). In sediments beneath the Canadian Beaufort Sea, gas-hydrate decomposition may be responsible for gassy shallow sediments, high formation pressures, mud volcanoes on the sea floor, and sediment instability at the shelf edge (A. Judge, personal communication, 1984).

(3) Penetration of gas hydrates during drilling could be hazardous. Special procedures, including slow drilling rates and carefully controlled mud weights and temperatures have proven to be successful in wells located in the Canadian Beaufort Sea (Weaver and Stewart, 1982). Wells drilled in the Sverdrup Basin occasionally have encountered gas hydrates, but no adverse effects have been experienced in any of the recent drilling (L. Franklin, personal communication, 1985).

(4) Gas hydrates and the free gas associated with them may constitute a potential source of natural gas. Any resource estimate for gas hydrates must be highly speculative because there is insufficient knowledge about the actual distribution of gas hydrates within sediments. This chapter has pointed out, whenever possible, the predicted thickness of the zone in which gas hydrates would be stable. Although this zone is thick, ranging from 200 to about 1,700 m, the zone has not been shown to contain gas hydrates throughout. In contrast, evidence from the North Slope of Alaska (Collett, 1983), the Mackenzie Delta (Bily and Dick, 1974) and the Beaufort Shelf (Weaver and Stewart, 1982) all indicate that the gas-hydrate occurrences are limited to thin intervals within the predicted zone. Nevertheless, the amount of natural gas that could be contained in gas hydrates is enormous because gas hydrates concentrate the gas and are apparently present in large areas of the Arctic Ocean region. The amount of gas-hydrate resources in Alaska has been estimated to range from 10^{11} to 10^{14} m^3 (Potential Gas Committee, 1981); Davidson (1978) suggested that 10^{11} m^3 of gas-hydrate resources, in addition to conventional gas, might be present in the Mackenzie Delta area. We estimate that more than 10^{15} m^3 of methane may be present in gas hydrates in sediments of the margin of the Arctic Basin. Although the resource figures are large, so are the uncertainties. Until more information on gas-hydrate distributions is obtained, any resource estimates must be viewed as highly speculative.

REFERENCES CITED

Arctic Petroleum Operators Association Drilling Subcommittee, 1980, A review of oil industry experience with gas hydrates in exploratory drilling in the Canadian Arctic, in Scott, W. J., and Brown, R.J.E., eds., Proceedings, Symposium on Permafrost Geophysics, no. 5, 1978: National Research Council of Canada Technical Memorandum 128, p. 159–162.

Bily, C., and Dick, J.W.L., 1974, Naturally occurring gas hydrates in the Mackenzie Delta, N.W.T.: Canadian Petroleum Geology Bulletin, v. 32, p. 340–352.

Cherskiy, N. V., and Makogon, Yu. F., 1970, Solid gas; World reserves are enormous: Oil and Gas International, v. 10, no. 8, p. 82.

Claypool, G. E., and Kaplan, I. R., 1974, The origin and distribution of methane in marine sediments, in Kaplan, I. R., ed., Natural gases in marine sediments: New York, Plenum Press, p. 94–139.

Collett, T. S., 1983, Detection and evaluation of natural gas hydrates from well logs, Prudhoe Bay, Alaska [M.S. thesis]: Fairbanks, University of Alaska, 78 p.

Collett, T. S., and Kvenvolden, K. A., 1987, Evidence of naturally occurring gas hydrates on the North Slope of Alaska: U.S. Geological Survey Open-File Report 87-0255, 5 p..

Davidson, D. W., 1973, Clathrate hydrates, in Frank, F., ed., Water; A comprehensive treatise: New York, Plenum Press, v. 2, p. 115–234.

Davidson, D. W., El-Defrawy, M. K., Fuglem, M. O., and Judge, A. S., 1978, Natural gas hydrates in northern Canada, in Proceedings, Third International Conference on Permafrost, 1978: National Research Council of Canada, v. 1, p. 938–943.

Dobrynin, V. M., Korotajev, Yu. P., and Plyuschev, D. V., 1979, Gas hydrates; A possible energy source, in Meyer, R. F., ed., Long-term energy resources: Boston, Pitman Publishing Co., v. 1, p. 727–729.

Galate, J. W., and Goodman, M. A., 1982, Review and evaluation of evidence of insitu gas hydrates in the National Petroleum Reserve of Alaska: Report to the U.S. Geological Survey, Contract No. 14-08-0001-19148, 102 p.

Goodman, M. A., 1980, Insitu gas hydrates; Past experience and exploitation concepts: Proceedings, First International Gas Research Conference, Chicago, p. 376–391.

Grantz, A., and Dinter, D. A., 1980, Constraints of geologic processes on western Beaufort Sea oil developments: Oil and Gas Journal, v. 78, no. 18, p. 304–319.

Grantz, A., Holmes, M. L. Riley, D. C., and Wallace, S. L., 1972, Seismic reflection profiles; Part 1 of seismic, magnetic, and gravity profiles; Chukchi Sea and adjacent Arctic Ocean, 1972: U.S. Geological Survey Open-File Report, 19 sheets seismic reflection profiles, 2 maps.

Grantz, A., McHendrie, A. G., Nilsen, T. H., and Yorath, C. J., 1974, Seismic reflection profiles, 1973, on the continental shelf and slope between Bering Strait and Barrow, Alaska, and Mackenzie Bay, Canada: U.S. Geological Survey Open-File Report, 49 sheets seismic reflection profiles, 2 maps.

Grantz, A., Boucher, G., and Whitney, O. T., 1976, Possible solid gas hydrate and natural gas deposits beneath the continental slope of the Beaufort Sea, in The U.S. Geological Survey of Alaska; Accomplishments during 1975: U.S. Geological Survey Circular 733, p. 17.

Grantz, A., Dinter, D. A., Hill, E. R., May, S. D., McMullin, R. H., Phillips, R. L., and Reimnitz, E., 1982a, Geologic framework, hydrocarbon potential, and environmental conditions for exploration and development of proposed oil and gas lease sale 87 in the Beaufort and northeast Chukchi Seas: U.S. Geological Survey Open-File Report 82-482, 71 p.

Grantz, A., Mann, D. M., and May, S. D., 1982b, Tracklines of multichannel seismic-reflection data collected by the U.S. Geological Survey in the Beaufort and Chukchi Sea in 1977 for which profiles and stack tapes are available: U.S. Geological Survey Open-File Report 82-735, 1 map sheet with text.

Hitchon, B., 1974, Occurrence of natural gas hydrates in sedimentary basins, in Kaplan, I. R., ed., Natural gases in marine sediments: New York, Plenum Press, p. 195–225.

Hunt, J. M., 1979, Methane hydrates, in Hunt, J. M., ed., Petroleum geochemistry and geology: San Francisco, W. H. Freeman, p. 156–162.

Judge, A., 1982, Natural gas hydrates in Canada, in French, M. H., ed., Proceedings, Fourth Canadian Permafrost Conference, 1981: National Research Council of Canada, The Roger J. E. Brown Memorial Volume, p. 320–328.

—— , 1984, Natural gas hydrates in the Mackenzie Delta-Beaufort Sea areas of northern Canada: American Institute of Chemical Engineers, 1984 Winter National Meeting, Atlanta, Georgia, p. T-35.

Kvenvolden, K. A., and Barnard, L. A., 1983, Hydrates of natural gas in continental margins, in Watkins, J. S., and Drake, C. L., eds., Studies in continental margin geology: American Association of Petroleum Geologists Memoir 34, p. 631–640.

Kvenvolden, K. A., and McMenamin, M. A., 1980, Hydrates of natural gas; A review of their geologic occurrences: U.S. Geological Survey Circular 825, 11 p.

MacLeod, M. K., 1982, Gas hydrates in ocean bottom sediments: American Association of Petroleum Geologists Bulletin, v. 66, p. 2649–2662.

McIver, R. D., 1981, Gas hydrates, in Meyer, R. F., ed., Long-term energy resources: Boston, Pitman Publishing Co., v. 1, p. 713–726.

Neave, K. G., Judge, A. S., Hunter, J. A., and MacAulay, H. A., 1978, Offshore permafrost distribution in the Beaufort Sea as determined from temperature and seismic observations, in Current Research, pt. C: Geological Survey of Canada Paper 78-1C, p. 13–18.

Potential Gas Committee, 1981, Potential supply of natural gas in the United States (as of December 31, 1980): Golden, Colorado School of Mines, Potential Gas Agency, 119 p.

Trofimuk, A. A., Cherskiy, N. V., and Tsaryov, V. P., 1977, The role of the continental glaciation and hydrate formation on petroleum occurrence, in Meyer, R. F., ed., The future supply of nature-made petroleum and gas: New York, Pergamon Press, p. 919–926.

Weaver, J. S., and Stewart, J. M., 1982, *In situ* hydrates under the Beaufort Sea Shelf, *in* French, M. H., ed., Proceedings, Fourth Canadian Permafrost Conference, 1981: National Research Council of Canada, The Roger J. E. Brown Memorial Volume, p. 312–319.

MANUSCRIPT ACCEPTED BY THE SOCIETY NOVEMBER 3, 1986

ACKNOWLEDGMENTS

This work was done by the U.S. Geological Survey and was partially supported by the Morgantown Energy Technology Center, Morgantown, West Virginia, under U.S. Geological Survey/Department of Energy Interagency Agreement No. DE-AI21-83MC20422. This paper was reviewed by A. K. Cooper, T. S. Collett, P. McGuire, and L. P. Franklin.

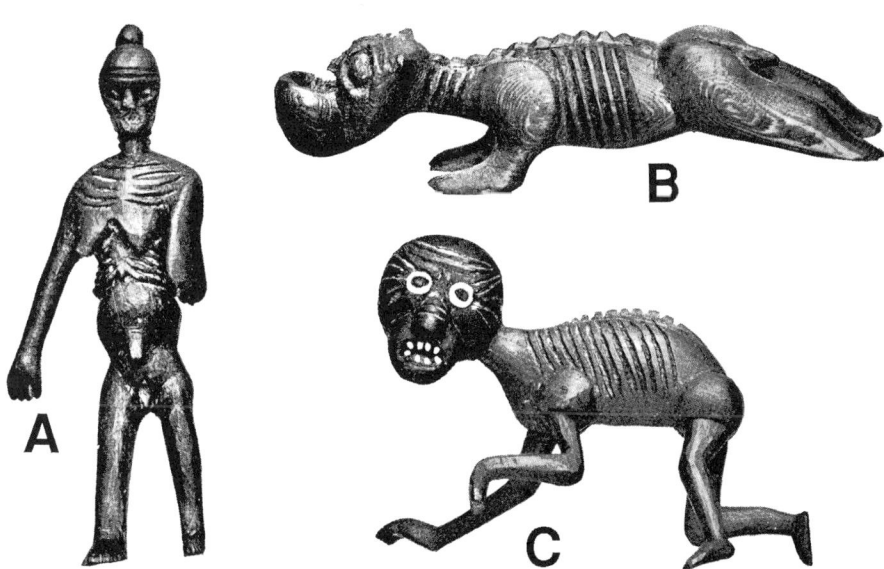

East Greenland tupileqs. A, uvissoq, a tupileq who is half man and half woman, and has a seal flipper and a dog foot; B, nerrisiaq, a thin animal with bear forelegs and an enormous undershot jaw; C, qitornaterut, part dog, part dead child. From T. Mathaisson, 1933, Prehistory of the Angmagssalik eskimos: Copenhagen, C. A. Reitzels Forlag, p. 142.

Printed in U.S.A.

Chapter 29

Offshore hard minerals

Peter B. Hale
Ocean Mining Division, Mineral Policy Sector, Energy, Mines and Resources Canada, 580 Booth Street, Ottawa, Ontario K1A 0E4, Canada

INTRODUCTION

Offshore mining for minerals such as barite, coal, calcium carbonate, gold, and tin is a well-established industry in many countries. Although there have been several attempts to develop mining systems to recover manganese nodules in water depths of 4,000 m, commercial mining is at present confined to shallow coastal waters.

Undersea mining for sub-surface deposits dates from at least the early 1600s and accounts for a significant proportion of the total mineral production in some countries. More than 100 undersea mines have been constructed worldwide; with few exceptions they began as onland mines that moved offshore after the onland sources were depleted (Austin, 1967).

In 1977, the last year for which comprehensive global production statistics are available, offshore non-fuel mineral production was worth about $460 million, with most of that coming from sand and gravel, tin, and calcium carbonate (Glasby, 1979). This valuation is conservative because numerous small operations go unreported and the Soviet Union does not make public its production statistics. The Soviet Union has, for several years, dredged cassiterite for tin in the Arctic Ocean, but we have no information regarding the level of production.

Most marine mining activity to date has taken place in temperate or tropical regions, yet the Arctic may host equally exciting mineral deposits, and both tin and sand and gravel are already mined there. The problems of mining in a region covered by ice for much of the year should not, however, be underestimated. New technologies will be required for exploration and mining if work is to be carried on during the long winter months, and the necessary infrastructure will have to be developed. Nevertheless, the Arctic is a frontier that in the future may yield significant quantities of a diverse range of minerals.

This chapter provides a framework for the discussion of offshore hard mineral resources in the Arctic. It includes a classification scheme and discussion of the major factors influencing exploitability of the resource. This is followed by an overview of previous and ongoing activitites and a discussion of development potential in the Arctic Ocean Basin.

Types of offshore hard-mineral resources

Marine hard-mineral resources can be divided into three general categories on the basis of their geographic distribution and physical characteristics: seawater minerals, continental shelf minerals, and deep-sea minerals. These minerals are present in solution within the water column, as consolidated deposits buried beneath or exposed at the seafloor, or as unconsolidated granular deposits.

Seawater. As an ore body, the oceans are unusual in that the minerals contained in the seawater are renewable resources. They are being replenished by river runoffs at a rate equal to or greater than the present scales of their commercial extraction (Wang and McKelvey, 1976). Five minerals are extracted commercially: deuterium (as a component of heavy water), magnesium, iodine, bromine, and sodium chloride. Fresh water is also extracted in desalinization plants.

The process for extracting most of the seawater minerals is simple; seawater is collected in shallow ponds where the sun evaporates the liquid, leaving a salt residue that can then be collected. This process is only successful in countries with hot, dry climates and little rainfall during the evaporating months, hence no such plants exist in the Arctic. Alternate means have been developed for the Arctic regions that rely on freezing to extract the salt from seawater. The brine is separated from the ice in successive freezing stages to obtain a sufficiently high concentration for evaporation using artificial heat (Armstrong and Miall, 1946). This process has been used in Sweden and the Soviet Union.

Currently there is no interest in extracting minerals from seawater in the North American Arctic and no activity of this kind, nor is the author aware of any Soviet involvement in this area. Given the unfavorable climate for evaporative techniques, and the fairly uniform distribution of minerals dissolved in seawater, there is little likelihood of seawater extraction plants being established in the Arctic.

Deep-sea minerals. Offshore prospecting has been underway since the early 1970s for deep-sea concentrations of manganese nodules in the Pacific, Atlantic, and Indian Oceans and for

Hale, P. B., 1990, Offshore hard minerals, *in* Grantz, A., Johnson, L., and Sweeney, J. F., eds., The Arctic Ocean region: Boulder, Colorado, Geological Society of America, The Geology of North America, v. L.

metalliferous muds in the Red Sea. In the case of the latter, work has reached the prototype mining phase (Amann, 1985). Polymetallic sulphide deposits associated with oceanic spreading centers were first discovered in 1978 in the eastern Pacific Ocean (21°N) off Mexico (CYAMEX, 1979). Since then additional occurrences have been discovered off the west coast of North America and along portions of the mid-Atlantic ridge. Because the deposits may be enriched in zinc, copper, manganese, cobalt, gold, and silver, they have attracted commercial interest and could be the object of exploration efforts by the turn of the century.

Holmes and Creager (1974) report finding manganese nodules and crusts in two grab samples from the Eastern Lena Valley of the Laptev Sea. One nodule with an iron-manganese crust and three smaller crusts were collected. The 2 to 3 mm thick crusts contain about 10 percent manganese and 22 percent iron. They occur in water depths of 45 to 55 m, which is one of the shallowest known occurrences of such material. Quartz and altered basalt fragments form the nuclei of these nodules and crusts. These fragments were probably deposited from floating ice that originated on the southwestern shore of the Laptev Sea. The presence of these crusts suggests that there is very little terrigenous influx to the area.

Nodules have not been reported in the Arctic Ocean Basin, but several workers have noted the presence of manganese micronodules encrusting foraminifera and other small particles in some regions (e.g., Clark and others, 1980; Herman and Hopkins, 1980). The substantial terrigenous influx to all deep-lying areas of the Arctic Ocean Basin would appear to preclude the formation of significant deep-water nodule deposits.

Commercially interesting deep-sea deposits have yet to be discovered in the Arctic. Even if significant concentrations of deep-sea minerals are discovered, the technology does not exist to mine such deposits, and they would be situated far from potential markets in a very difficult operating environment. Thus, it is unlikely that the Arctic Ocean will be a source of minerals from deep seabed deposits within the foreseeable future.

Shelf Minerals. The continental shelf mineral deposits occur on submerged offshore extensions of the land masses. The relatively shallow water depth associated with these deposits and their proximity to shore make them particularly attractive for exploration and development. The following consolidated minerals have been mined from the world's coastal regions over the years: barite (Alaska, USA) (Thompson and Smith, 1970; Stevens, 1970); iron (Newfoundland, Canada) (Rose and others, 1970); coal (Cape Breton Island, Canada) (Rose and others, 1970), (Japan) (Earney, 1980), (United Kingdom) (Austin, 1967); and tin (United Kingdom). However, in terms of the number of mining operations and value of production, the unconsolidated minerals are more important.

The unconsolidated mineral deposits occur in two groups: industrial minerals or placer minerals. The former are those in which all, or almost all, of the mined material is utilized, such as sand and gravel for construction and calcium carbonate for cement. In contrast, mining operations for placer minerals such as gold, rutile, and zircon retain only the heavy mineral fraction of the deposit and discard the rest, usually on the sea floor. Both types of unconsolidated deposits are commonly mined by dredging. Most industrial mineral operations employ self-propelled suction dredges. Placer minerals are usually mined with bucket ladder or cutter suction dredges, both of which have onboard processing.

Exploitability criteria

Unconsolidated minerals. In order to carry out an assessment of offshore hard-mineral resource potential it is necessary to consider both the likelihood of existence and exploitability. The term "resource" refers to any mineral concentration, the existence of which is reasonably assured and which is currently mineable at a profit or is perceived to be of economic interest within the foreseeable future. The term also encompasses as-yet-undiscovered deposits in favorable geologic settings. Quantified deposits that are presently recoverable at a profit are termed "reserves" (see Fig. 1). Documentation of all known or inferred mineral occurrences and their characteristics constitutes a resource inventory.

Sufficient information pertaining to the distribution of occurrences, their geologic characteristics (e.g., tonnage and grade), markets, means of extraction and transport, and associated costs of mining and processing are seldom available for offshore deposits and rarely for the Arctic, which has seen relatively little in the way of mineral exploration. Consequently, the approach adopted herein is to present a subjective assessment of resource potential that applies a few criteria concerning exploitability and emphasizes the level of certainty that a deposit exists. It is based on a systematic review of information from published and unpublished geological literature and verbal communication with government and industry geologists.

Commercial dredging operations worldwide excavate to a maximum depth below sea level of about 80 m. Larger dredges, capable of digging to greater depths, could be built, but this would involve additional expense and require time for both design and construction. Offshore mining for surficial materials within the next 10 to 20 years will, therefore, be confined to water depths of less than 100 m. Mineral occurrences below this depth should be considered long-term prospects rather than potential resources.

Adoption of the 100-m isobath as the maximum water depth for resource assessment excludes much of the Arctic from consideration (see Fig. 2). East of Point Barrow the geologic continental shelf of the Arctic Ocean extends to as much as 200 km offshore of the Canadian Arctic Islands. However, the 100 m isobath is relatively close to shore in all areas except the Foxe Basin, the Gulf of Boothia, Queen Maud Gulf, Coronation Gulf, and the Beaufort Sea, so consequently the total area shallower than 100 m is relatively small. West of Point Barrow, in contrast, vast expanses of water shallower than 100 m extend as much as 600 km offshore. Water depths in the Chukchi Sea, the East

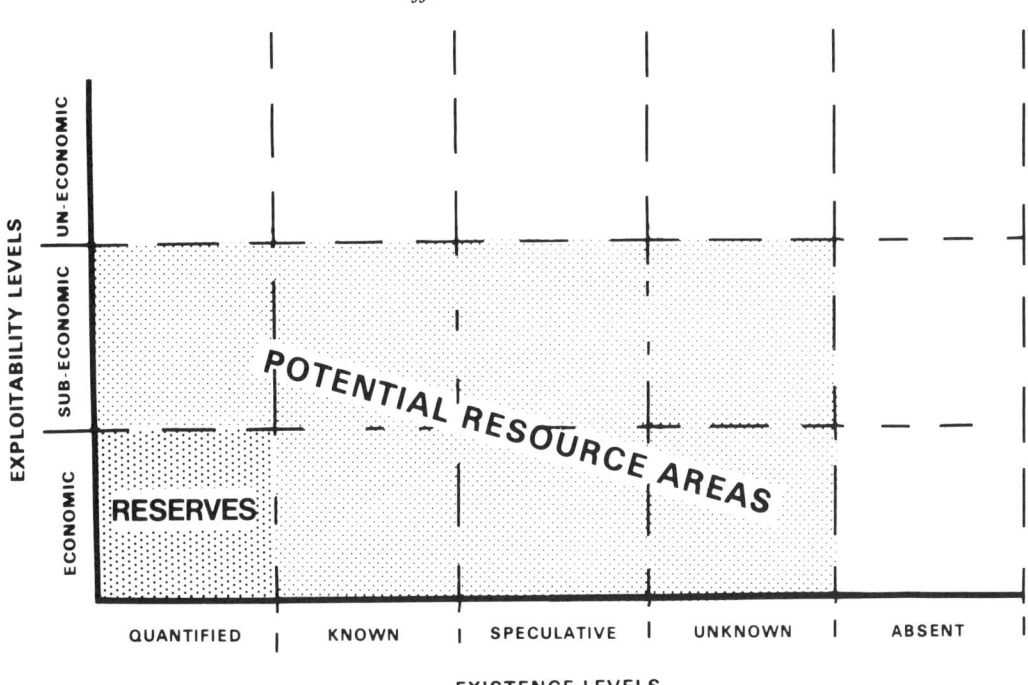

Figure 1. Conceptual representation of the relationship between existence, exploitability, resources, and reserves (from Hale, 1987).

Siberian Sea, and the Laptev Sea at no time exceed 100 m, and more than 50 percent of each is shallower than 50 m.

Ice imposes an enormous constraint on marine mineral exploration and mining operations in the Arctic. As of 1986, there had been no commercial dredging during the period of ice-cover in the Canadian or American Arctic. Limited available public information regarding Soviet Arctic dredging activities indicates that the Soviets have attempted to dredge year round in at least one instance. An operation was established to mine cassiterite from a placer deposit in Vankina Bay (see Fig. 4) on the Laptev Sea in 1974 (Anonymous, 1976).

The Soviet Union has investigated the feasibility of utilizing, in the Arctic, nuclear-powered dredges that could operate in isolated locations for as much as two years at a stretch. Such dredges could supply hot water to thaw the ice around a ship, thereby permitting year-round operations (Bakke, 1971; Livshits, 1973). Although the cost of constructing a nuclear-powered dredge is high relative to conventional dredges, such projects might cost one-third that of alternate onshore mines because there would be no need to build settlements, roads, mines, or permanent processing plants.

The fact that the Soviet Union has the largest fleet of nuclear-powered ice breakers in the world indicates that they have the capability to acquire dredges with similar powerplants, but there is no evidence that they have already done so. Although such dredges may be technically feasible, and their mining costs lower than those of comparable onshore mines in the high Arctic, they would still be costly propositions. A seabed deposit in the Arctic would, therefore, have to be of much higher grade than a seabed deposit elsewhere. Gold, platinum, chromite, and diamonds are the commodities most likely to be developed, owing to their high intrinsic value or strategic importance.

Nuclear-powered dredges may be the way of the future in the Arctic, but over the next 10 to 20 years, dredging will be confined to the open-water period. Bearing this in mind, a map was compiled to illustrate the average duration of open-water conditions in the Arctic for severe and light ice years (Fig. 3). The estimated duration of open water for each region (shown on the map in months) is conservative in that the estimates reflect the period during which ice was absent from the entire coastal area. Some portions of each region will experience longer periods of open water than indicated.

Thus far, Arctic dredging for tin and for sand and gravel has been confined to regions having open water for four months each year. It is unlikely that future conventional dredging operations will be established in regions having open water for less than four months a year, based on light ice-year statistics. This suggests that mineral deposits in much of the Arctic, with the exception of Lancaster Sound, Hudson Strait, Hudson Bay, the Beaufort Sea, the Chukchi Sea, the East Siberian Sea, and Laptev Sea, will not be developed with existing mining systems.

Consolidated minerals. Consolidated mineral deposits buried beneath the sea floor are typically mined from shore using traditional onland tunnelling techniques. However, as the distance offshore increases, the time required to transport workers and materials to and from the working face of the mine rises dramatically. It also becomes increasingly difficult to provide adequate ventilation. Thus there is a practical limit of about 7 km offshore for land-based tunnelling operations. Beyond that distance it may become necessary to construct artificial islands for access and ventilation. Sub-sea mining for this type of deposit will, therefore, usually be confined to a narrow coastal band.

Consolidated deposits exposed at the sea floor must be dislodged prior to shipment to shore. In the case of friable minerals, this is achieved by mechanical cutting devices such as cutter suction dredges. These disaggregate the material and lift it to a ship, which then transports the material to shore. For more resistant materials, it may be necessary to first break the rock into manageable pieces by drilling and blasting. Following this step, the material is lifted to the ship using a bucket ladder dredge or a clamshell bucket suspended from a cable. The latter system is capable of operating in greater water depths than the bucket ladder dredge, but cycle time increases markedly with increasing water depth, resulting in a decline in production capacity. The practical limit for this approach is approximately 100 m of water depth.

The short open-water season in the Arctic, coupled with a general lack of suitable infrastructure, particularly in the Western Hemisphere, imposes such severe constraints upon offshore mineral development that activities over the next 10 to 20 years will focus on the higher value placer minerals. Efforts to mine the industrial minerals will be limited to sand and gravel dredging in support of oil and gas exploration and development and the construction of coastal ports and settlements.

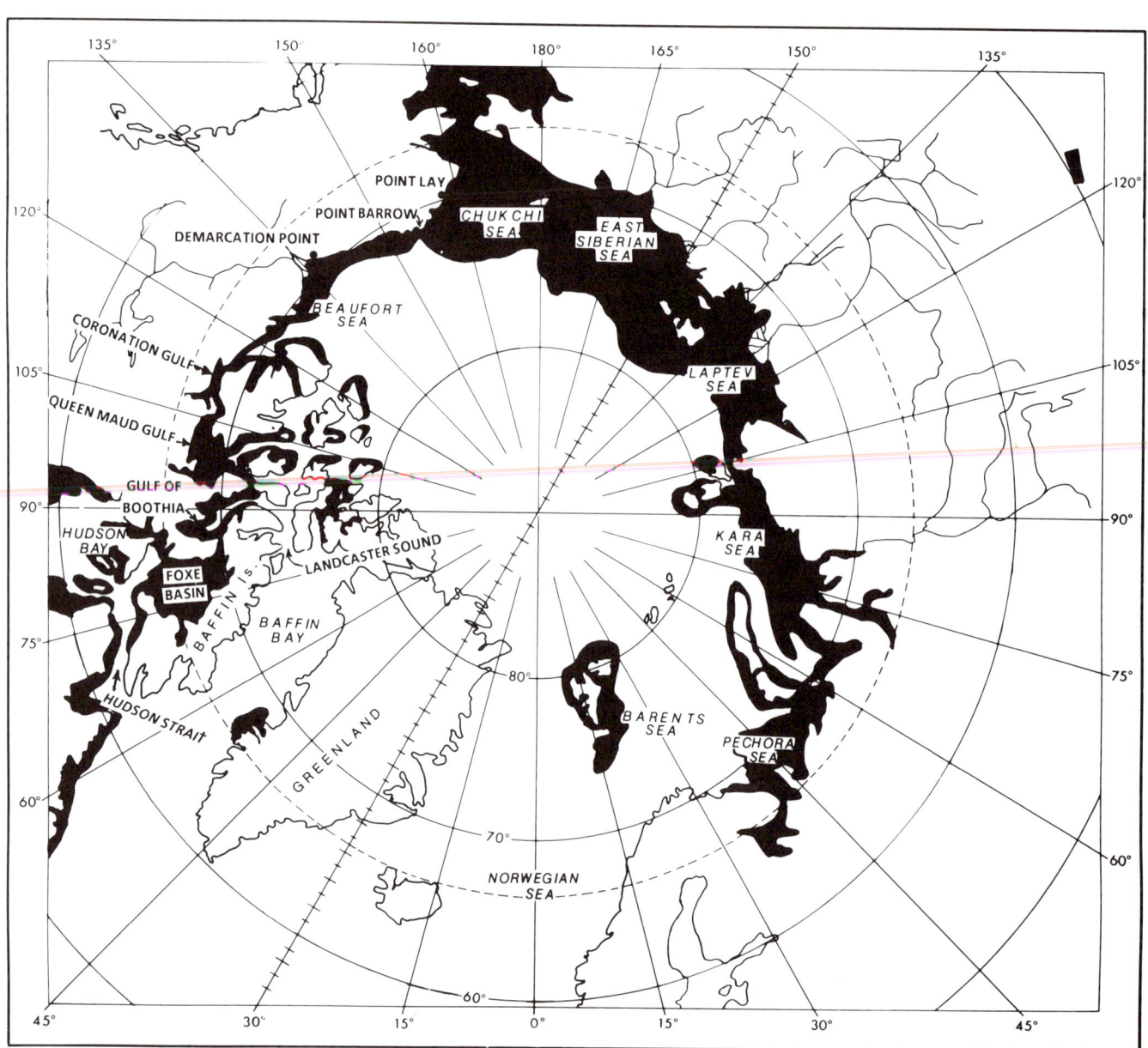

Figure 2. Map of the Arctic showing areas with water less than 100 m deep.

SHELF MINERALS

Consolidated surface and sub-surface mineral deposits

Consolidated mineral deposits exposed at the sea floor have been exploited on a limited basis worldwide. In each case an actively worked onland deposit was followed offshore. A case in point is the barite mining project near Petersburg, southeast Alaska (Thompson and Smith, 1970; Stevens, 1970). There have been no similar commercial ventures in the western Arctic, nor is there any evidence of such activities in the Soviet Arctic.

As of 1986 there were no undersea mines for either surface or sub-surface consolidated mineral deposits in the western Arctic. Two lead-zinc mines in the Canadian Arctic Islands (Little Cornwallis Island and Arctic Bay on Baffin Island) and one in Greenland are situated at the coast and could eventually extend beneath the sea (Fig. 4). The Soviet Union has opened several mines along the Arctic coast to recover coal, gold, and tin. Some of these mines may have tunnels extending under the sea. A chromium deposit has been identified near Fiskenasset, southwest Greenland (Miles and Wright, 1978); if developed, it could result in sub-sea mine workings.

There has been little exploration for offshore consolidated mineral deposits outside of those areas where they have been identified on land. There is a good likelihood that many consolidated mineral deposits await discovery, but only if they are of

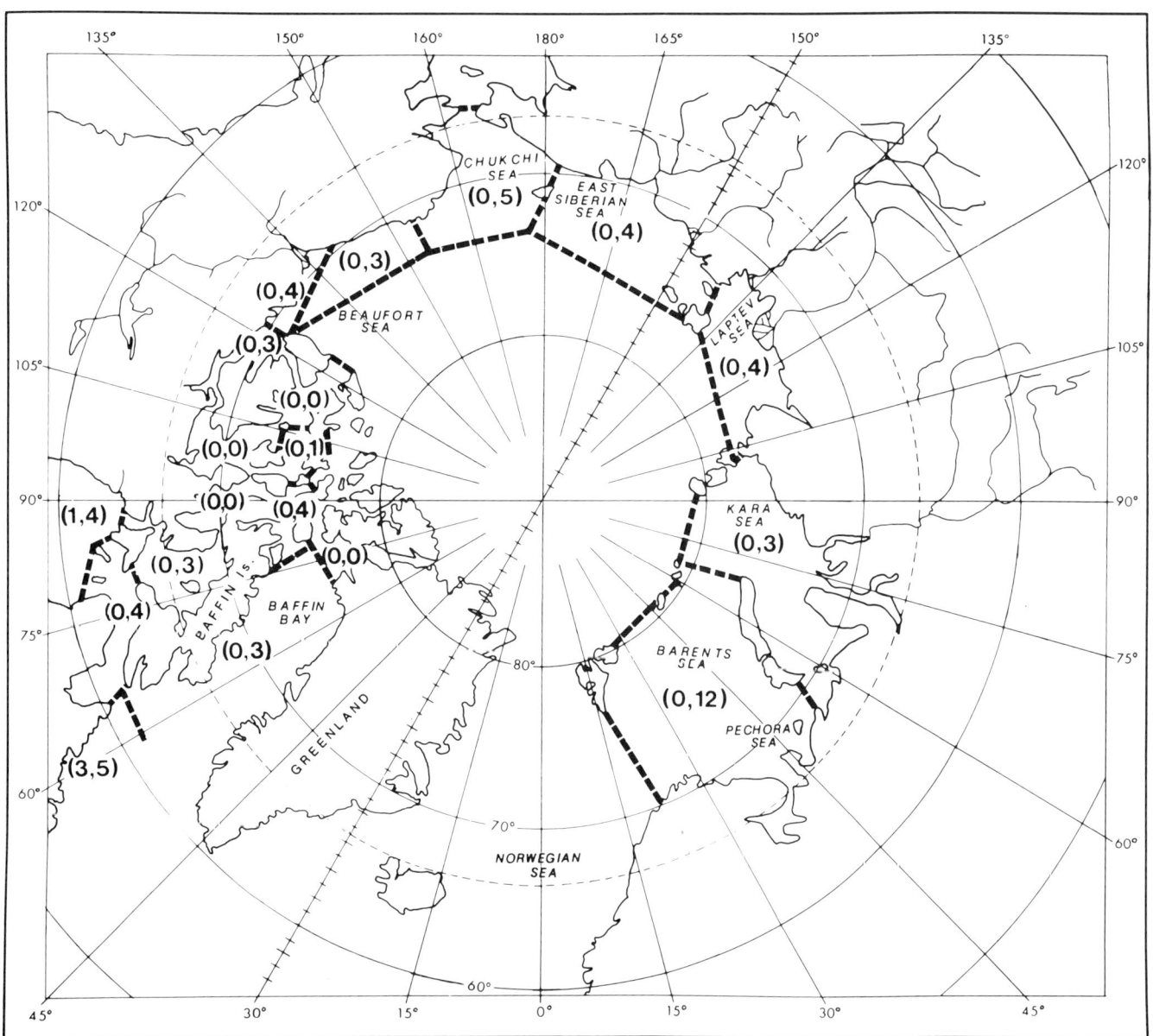

Figure 3. Map of the Arctic showing average duration in months (parentheses) of open water in severe and light ice years (adapted from Soviet Ministry of Defence, 1980).

exceptional tonnage and grade will they be viable to develop. Barring this, they would be unable to compete with mines in the south where the necessary infrastructure is in place and the costs of labor and production are much less.

Coal

Many of the world's continental shelves, including those in the Arctic Ocean Basin, were at one time above sea level, and some of these contain coal-bearing non-marine sedimentary rocks. The distribution of coal resources in the Arctic Ocean Basin is not well documented. There have been several investigations into the on-land distribution (e.g., Ricketts and Embry, 1986), but only a few researchers have addressed the question of offshore potential (e.g., Affolter and Stricker, 1987; Tailleur and Brosge, 1976; Wang and McKelvey, 1976). Figure 5 documents the distribution of known coal deposits in the Arctic. From this it is apparent that there are numerous deposits at or near the coast that could extend offshore. Such deposits are in the Canadian Arctic Archipelago, the Beaufort Sea, the Laptev Sea, the Kara Sea, the Barents Sea, and the Norwegian Sea.

The potential for coal offshore of Alaska was addressed in a recent paper by Affolter and Stricker (1987). On the basis of limited seismic data and onshore mud logs, they concluded that a coal-bearing formation, containing 300 billion metric tons of lignite, extends beneath the Beaufort Sea. The U.S. Chuckchi Sea is also thought to have coal resource potential in the North Slope area. Two trillion metric tons of subbituminous coal are speculated to exist north of Cape Lisburne, and additional deposits may

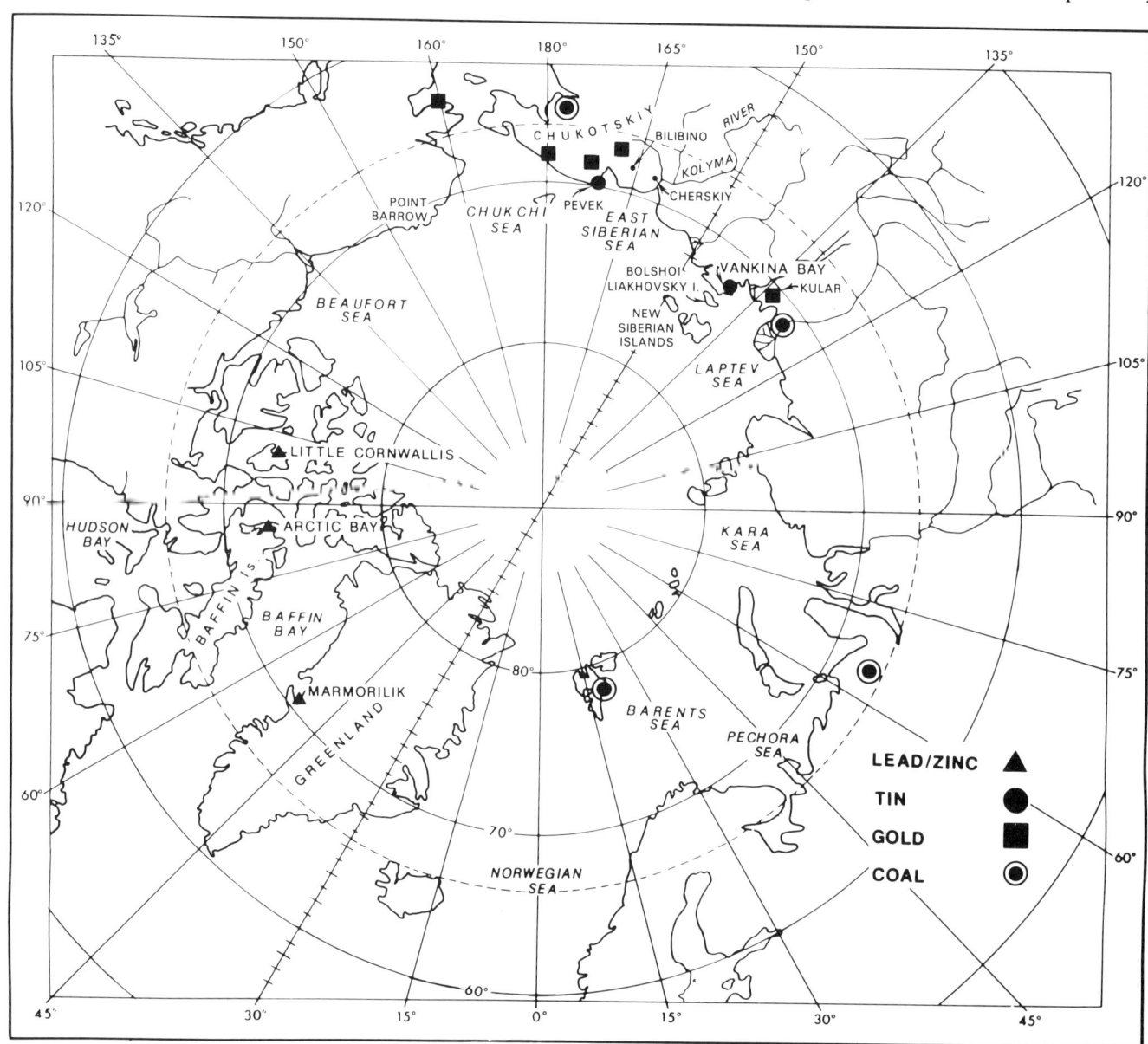

Figure 4. Map of the Arctic showing location of mines situated at, or close to, the coast (after Central Intelligence Agency, 1978).

occur in Hope Basin. Data were insufficient to evaluate the possible extent of the sub-sea coal deposits in the other areas.

The sparse information suggests that there is a good likelihood of sizable coal deposits existing in select offshore regions. It is premature to say whether or not these will be economical to mine. Additional seismic and drilling data are required to confirm the presence, extent, and quality of the deposits.

At present we can only speculate as to the mining scenarios that might be considered in the event that deposits are identified. Sub-surface deposits situated close to shore will probably be exploited first, using land-based technology. This type of operation would be relatively isolated from the harsh climate and could rely on stockpiling for shipping the material to market during the ice-free period. Coal deposits outcropping on the sea floor may be mined at a later time using powerful cutter-suction dredges similar to those already in use for channel dredging in coralline rock. Dredging operations would, however, be severely constrained by the short open-water season.

Ultimately, economics will dictate whether or not these offshore resources are developed; the technology exists or can be readily adapted to the situation. Given the lead time required for exploration and development, it is improbable that there will be marine mining for coal in the Arctic before the turn of the century.

Unconsolidated shelf mineral deposits

Soviet Union. Substantial hydrocarbon resources may exist in the Arctic Ocean offshore of the Soviet Union. At the present

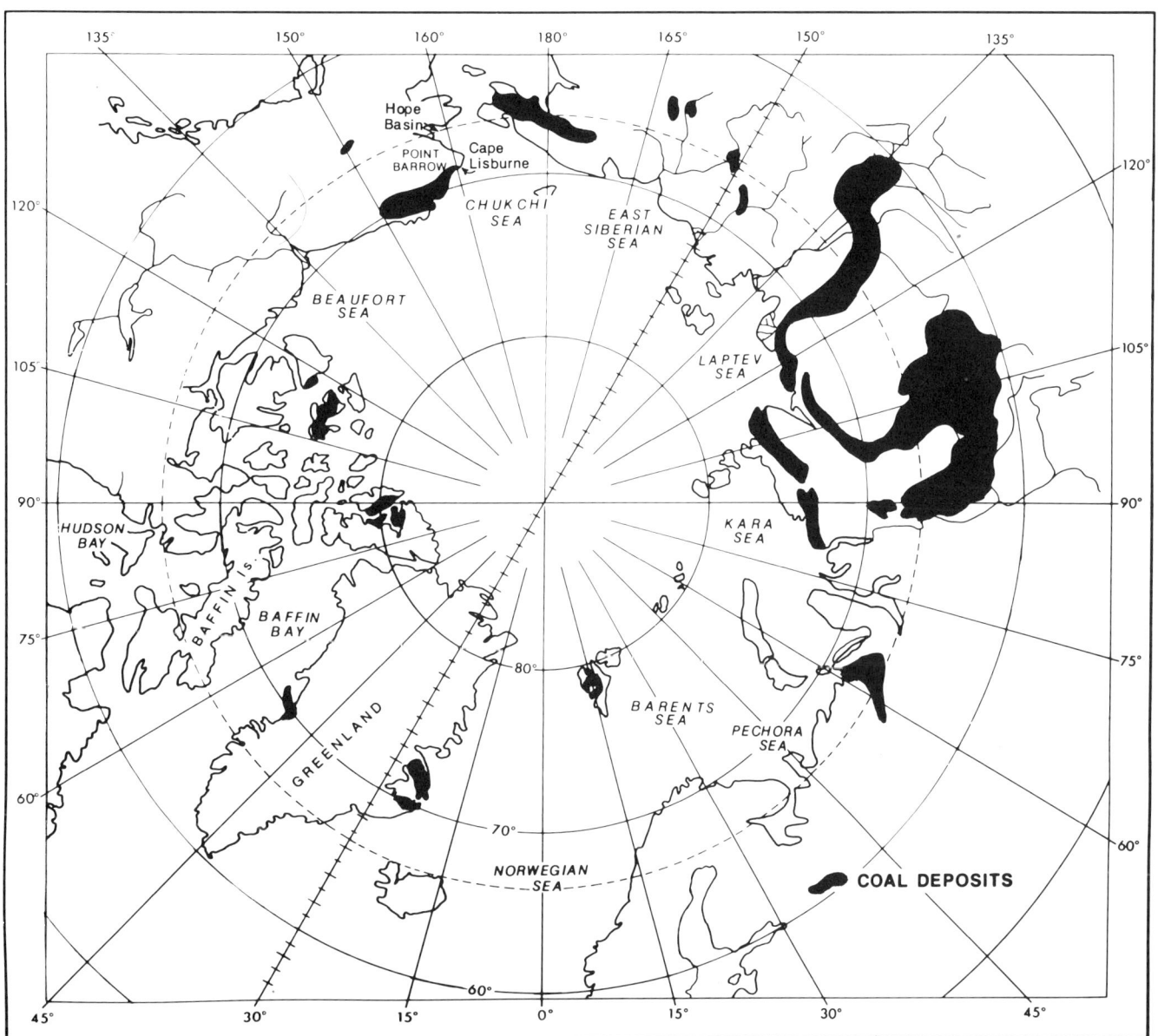

Figure 5. Map of the Arctic showing known coal deposits (after Affolter and Stricker, 1987; Central Intelligence Agency, 1978; Ricketts and Embry, 1986; Tailleur and Brosge, 1976).

TABLE 1. ARTIFICAL ISLANDS CONSTRUCTED IN THE CANADIAN BEAUFORT SEA*

Name of Island	Operator	Year Built	Status 1985	Water Depth (m)	Island Type	Volume of Material Required (thousand m³)	Locations of Source Material	Construction Method
Immerk	Esso	1972-73	Abandoned	3	Sacrifical Beach	38.0	Pit 1.2 km distant	Dredged and barged
Adgo F-28	Esso	1973	Abandoned	2	Silt Berm/Sandbag	46.2	Local	Dredged locally
Unark	Sun	1974	Abandoned	1.1	Silt Berm/Sandfill	28.0	Onshore, Ya Ya Lakes	Trucked over ice
Pelly	Sun	1974	Abandoned	2.7	Silt Berm/Sandfill	30.0	Local/Onshore, Ya Ya Lakes	Trucked over ice and dredged locally
Netserk B-44	Esso	1974	Abandoned	4.6	Barged Berm/Sandbag	307.7	32 km distant	Dredged and barged
Adgo P-25	Esso	1974	Abandoned	2	Silt Berm/Sandbag	35.0	Local	Dredged
Pullen	Esso	1974	Abandoned	1.5	Trucked Berm/Sandbag	61.2	Onshore, 104 km distant	Trucked over ice
Netserk F-40	Esso	1975	Abandoned	7	Barged Berm/Sandbag	310.0		Dredged
Adgo C-15	Esso	1975	Abandoned	2	Trucked Berm/Sandbag	35.0	Onshore	Trucked over ice
Ikattok	Esso	1975	Abandoned	2	Barged Berm/Sandbag	35.0		Dredged and barged
Adgo J-27	Esso	1976	Abandoned	2	Barged Berm/Sandbag	45.0		Dredged and barged
Sarpik	Esso	1976	Abandoned	3.5	Trucked Berm/Sandbag	75.0	Onshore	Trucked over ice
Kugmallit	Esso	1976	Abandoned	5.2	Barged Berm/Sandbag	240.0		Dredged
Arnak	Esso	1976	Abandoned	8.5	Sacrifical Beach	1250.0		Dredged
Kannerk	Esso	1976	Abandoned	8	Sacrifical Beach	1200.0	Local sand	Dredged
Isserk	Esso	1977	Abandoned	13	Sacrifical Beach	1920.0	Local sand/ Tuft Point	Dredged and barged
Issungnak	Esso	1978	Abandoned	20	Sacrifical Beach	4100.0	Local pits/ Tuft Point	Dredged and barged
Alerk	Esso	1980	Abandoned	12	Sacrifical Beach	1500.0	Local pits	Dredged
Tarsiut	Gulf/Dome	1980-81	Abandoned	21	Berm/Caisson	1800.0	3 pits, Ukalerk, S. Tarsiut and Herschel Island	Dredged and barged
W. Atkinson	Esso	1981-82	Abandoned	6	Sacrifical Beach	1000.0	Local pits	Dredged
Itoyok	Esso	1981-82	Abandoned	15	Sacrifical Beach	2600.0	Local pits	Dredged
Uviluk	Dome	1981-82	Abandoned	30	Berm/SSDC	1320.0	Pit 3 km distant	Dredged
E. Nerlerk	Dome	1982-83	Abandoned	45	Berm/SSDC	3500.0	Ukalerk pit/ local pits	Dredged and barged
Kadluk	Esso	1982-83	Abandoned	13	Berm/CRI (steel)	250.0	Alerk pit	Dredged
Kogyuk	Gulf	1983	Abandoned	30	Berm/SSDC	1260.0	Uviluk pit	Dredged
Amerk	Esso	1984	Construction	26	Berm/CRI	2060.0	Ukalerk/Issigak Kadluk pits	Dredged
Nipterk	Esso	1984	Construction	11.3	Sacrifical Beach	2600.0	Issigak or Ukalerk pits	Dredged
Adgo C-29	Esso	1984	Construction	2.8	Sandbag retained	88.0	Itiyok pit	Dredged and barged
Kaubvik	Esso	1984-85	Construction	18.6	Berm/CRI	379.0	Ukalerk or Issigak/Kadluk pit	Dredged
Minuk	Esso	1984-85	Construction	14.7	Sacrifical Beach	2700.0	Issigak/Kadluk or Ukalerk pit	Dredged

*Location of Islands shown in Figure 6.

time, exploration is underway in the Barents Sea and the Pechora Sea in water depths up to 100 m. Given the shallow water depths, artificial production islands may be constructed in the event that commercial fields are discovered. Such islands could be built using aggregates dredged from the sea floor.

The Chukotskiy region in eastern Siberia (Fig. 4) accounts for more than 57 percent of Soviet gold production, and it is increasing in importance (Meyerhoff, 1983). Most of the gold is derived from placer deposits that have been under development since the 1930s (Conquest, 1979). Many of these are situated along the Kolyma River, but some occur along the coast of the Chukchi Sea (see Fig. 4). Numerous coal-fired thermal electric and small nuclear power stations have been constructed in the regions of Pevek, Cherskiy, and Bilibino to provide the electric power necessary to support the gold mining enterprises. One can only surmise that the deposits are extensive and that production rates are appreciable, based on the presence of the power stations.

Gold is also mined from deposits close to the coast in the central Arctic at Kular (see Fig. 4). This is relatively close to an offshore cassiterite deposit that was discovered in the early 1970s in Vankina Bay, in the eastern Laptev Sea (see Fig. 4). The preliminary investigation of this deposit involved winter drilling

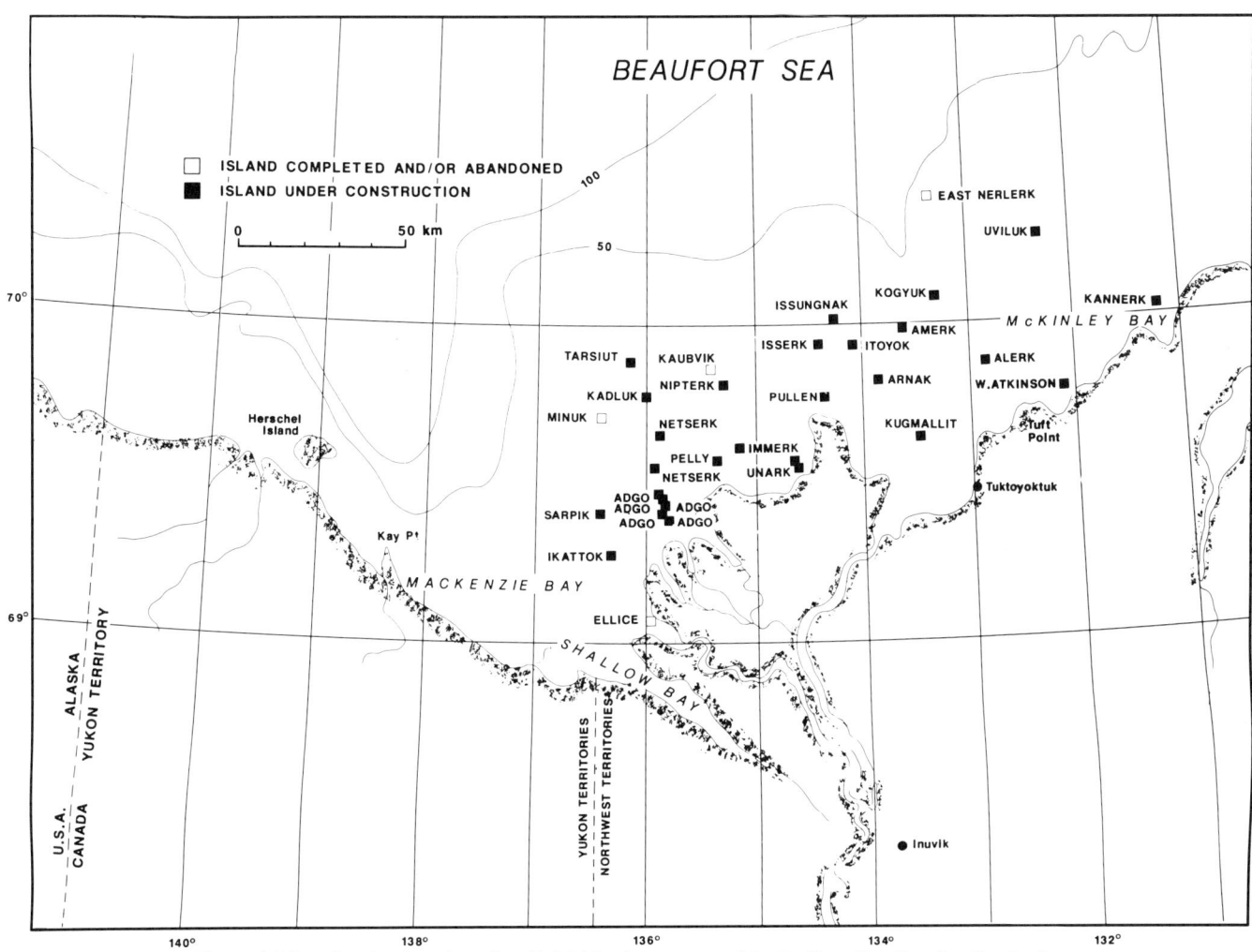

Figure 6. Map showing location of artificial islands constructed in the Canadian Beaufort Sea in the period 1972 to 1985. Once drilling activity is complete, the island is abandoned. Consequently, many of the islands no longer exist. See Table 1 for details.

through sea ice. A subsequent expedition from the Moscow Mining Institute drilled some 40 m into the deposit without reaching its lower limits. The cassiterite appears to lie directly on the bottom of Vankina Bay, only several tens of meters from the shoreline, and extends over a large area.

The Vankina discovery led to formation of the Northern Maritime Exploration and Development Enterprise (SEVMOR OLOVO) and the first Arctic offshore placer mining operation (circa 1972) (Anonymous, 1976; *Offshore,* November, 1971, p. 41; Livshits, 1973). Attempts were made in 1974 to mine the deposit during the winter using the *Gorniak,* a clamshell dredge with onboard processing equipment, and the submarine suction dredge *Malyutka.* The flotilla, with two steamers, a tanker, and a floating warehouse, was in place and occupied throughout the winter. However, the mineral recovery operation shut down in the fall and did not resume until the spring. Nuclear-powered dredges may be mining this deposit currently, but this has yet to be substantiated.

The Vankina deposit is not an isolated occurrence. Also rich in cassiterite are nearby Seliakhskaya Bay, adjacent on the south; Dimitry Laptev Strait, which lies between Bolshoi Liakhovsky Island of the New Siberian Islands and the mainland near Vankina Bay; the Cape Sviatoi Nos area of the mainland near the strait; and the southern part of Bolshoi Liakhovsky Island (Fig. 4). There also appears to be good potential for other placer minerals, including ilmenite-magnetite, rutile, zircon, and gold, in select areas proximal to the major rivers.

Published reports on the distribution and characteristics of placer deposits in the Soviet offshore are sparse. However, on the basis of information on Quaternary glaciation, sea-level history, and regional geology, it is possible to make some generalizations concerning these deposits. Most, if not all of them, occur in relatively shallow-water areas that were covered by a continental ice sheet during part of the Pleistocene epoch. Some of the deposits appear to be associated with drowned fluvial systems and may have formed during a former lower sea level. Others may be the result of contemporary coastal-marine processes, but the restricted open-water season and low wave-energy conditions suggest that this mechanism is relatively unimportant.

Canada. Dredging for aggregates to construct temporary artificial islands from which oil companies can drill exploration wells has been ongoing in the Canadian Beaufort Sea since 1972. The artificial islands provide a stable working base for the drill rigs and have sufficient size and mass to withstand ice loads and wave action, thereby enabling year-round operation. Conventional drill ships can only operate for about 110 days each year during the ice-free period.

As of the spring of 1985, twenty-eight islands had been constructed in water depths of 45 m or less in the Canadian Beaufort Sea (see Table 1 and Fig. 6). The islands have been built using a variety of construction materials and techniques. In the early 1970s they were constructed close to shore in water depths of only a few meters. It was a relatively simple matter to truck the sand and gravel for these islands from onshore borrow pits across ice roads. The islands required only a moderate quantity of material and could be built in a single winter season. The early artificial islands resembled inverted cones resting on the seafloor. The sand beaches around these islands absorbed the incoming wave energy, but in so doing they were rapidly eroded; thus, they were referred to as "sacrificial beach" islands.

As exploration moved into deeper water, the quantity of material needed to construct these sacrificial beach islands increased appreciably (see Fig. 7). An island constructed in 10 m of water, for example, requires about 1.4 million m^3 of material, whereas one in 20 m of water consumes in excess of 4.1 million m^3. Transportation of the construction aggregate to the building site also becomes more difficult. It therefore became necessary to develop offshore sources of aggregate that could be mined with dredges.

Suitable aggregate deposits in the eastern Beaufort Sea are hard to find. The most promising deposits of granular material are those associated with the sea-level minimum that predates the last marine transgression (see Chapter 28). These glacio-fluvial and coastal-marine sediments are commonly covered by 2 to 6 m of Holocene marine clays. Areas where the clays are absent present the best targets for aggregate mining. Transgressive units are also potential sources of aggregates. However, these lag-type deposits are often relatively thin and of small volume.

Even with some of the largest dredges in the world, it became difficult, if not impossible, to complete deeper water islands in a single ice-free season (see Fig. 8). In some instances the problem was compounded by local shortages of coarse aggregate, forcing the operators to dredge and haul from sources more than 150 km distant using hopper dredges.

The difficulty of locating sufficient nearby supplies of coarse aggregate and other problems led to development of new approaches to island construction that decreased the quantity of aggregate required and speeded up the construction process (Janson, 1983; Brakel, 1984). These goals were achieved through the use of caissons. The first island that was built using this technique

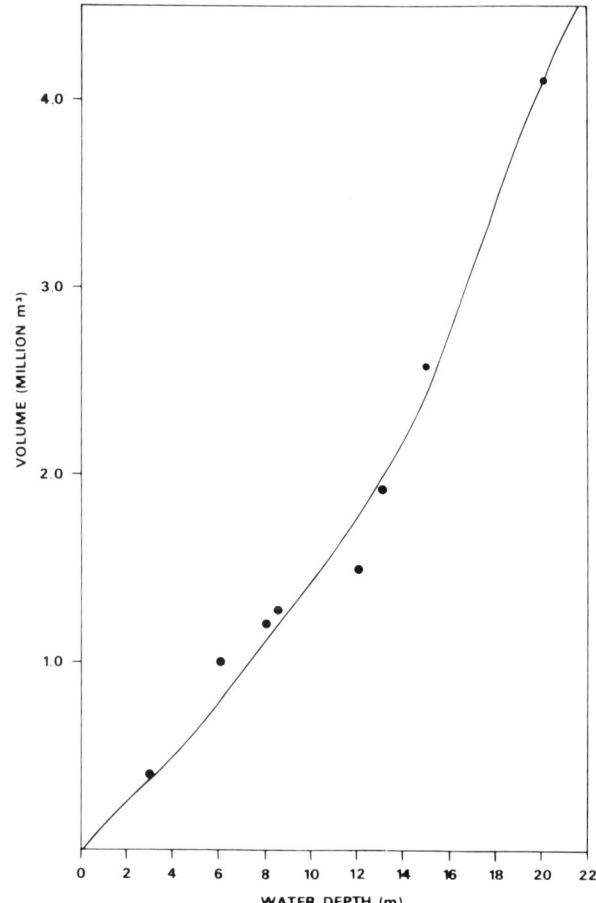

Figure 7. Graph showing the aggregate requirements for sacrificial beach-type islands as a function of water depth.

was Tarsiut (Fig. 6 and Table 1), a concrete caisson built in 1980–1981 in 21 m of water. Some 1.8 million m^3 of fill were dredged from the seafloor and pumped into the caisson. This was approximately one-quarter the volume that would have been needed to construct a comparable sacrificial beach island.

The construction of Tarsiut demonstrated the viability of the caisson approach and led to the design and construction of several different types of caissons using both concrete and steel. The caissons are generally set on a preconstructed sand berm and then ballasted with water or sand. Upon completion of drilling, the equipment and the ballast are removed, and the caisson is refloated for use at a new drilling location.

The use of caissons, in combination with other innovative systems designed to withstand the forces of ice and wave attack, has reduced the quantity of aggregate needed for exploratory drilling. In addition, petroleum geologists have, over the past two decades, acquired a good understanding of the regional potential for oil and gas reserves in the eastern Beaufort Sea. Thus the demand for marine aggregates to support petroleum exploration is expected to decline.

Oil and gas production in the Beaufort Sea, now in its initial stages, will require permanent man-made structures. A single production island could consume in excess of 20 million m^3 of sand and gravel, and there would be additional requirements for pipeline foundations and capping. The total quantity of granular material could approach 700 million m^3, with about 5 percent of this being gravel. The source for most of this material will likely be offshore.

Although there appears to be an ample supply of fine sand for petroleum resource–related construction projects anticipated in the near future, gravel is in relatively short supply (O'Connor and Associates, Ltd., 1983a, b). However, approximately 95 million m^3 of gravel have already been discovered near Herschel Island, the Issungnak and Isserk well sites (Fig. 6 and Table 1), and the west side of Banks Island. These deposits and additional ones that may be located should, with careful management, provide sufficient offshore aggregate to satisfy industry needs well into the future.

Extraction of the marine aggregate will not be an easy task. In some localities it will be necessary to dredge down to 20 m below the sea floor, using large-capacity stationary suction dredges capable of operating in water deeper than 20 m. In some cases, excavation will have to contend with sub-sea permafrost and sea ice.

Substantial quantities of marine aggregate may also be required for the construction of a major port at Kay Point, located in Mackenzie Bay (Fig. 6) in the Canadian Beaufort Sea. The Canadian Ministry of Transport and the U.S. government identify it as the only site in the western Arctic, including Alaska, that has potential as a commercial and military port capable of handling ships without draft restrictions.

The absence of commercial exploration for placer deposits in the Canadian Arctic offshore, coupled with a paucity of samples and the absence of appropriate placer deposit models for glaciated continental shelves, makes it difficult to assess placer potential. Nevertheless, coastal areas possessing suitable host rocks to yield detrital heavy minerals have been identified (Hale and McLaren, 1984; Miles and Wright, 1978). The minerals considered were chromite, tungsten, platinum-group metals, gold, and diamonds. Lower value minerals such as ilmenite or zircon were excluded on the grounds that even if such deposits were identified, they would be uneconomic to mine. Figure 9 shows that coastal regions with favorable on-land geology to produce placer deposits of various types are widely distributed. However, until sampling confirms the presence of such minerals in the offshore, the occurrences are speculative.

United States. Sand and gravel are the only commodities that appear to offer development potential off the Alaskan coast of the Chukchi and Beaufort Sea shelves from Point Lay to Demarkation Point. In Alaska, in contrast to Canada, the oil and gas industry has thus far been able to satisfy its aggregate requirements from onshore sites. Future mining of marine aggregates will depend on the nature and extent of offshore oil and gas development.

A generalized distribution pattern of surficial sediments on the inner shelf of the Beaufort Sea has been constructed from grab

Figure 8. Large sand and gravel dredge operating in the Canadian Beaufort Sea to construct artificial islands for oil and gas exploration (photograph courtesy of IHC Holland).

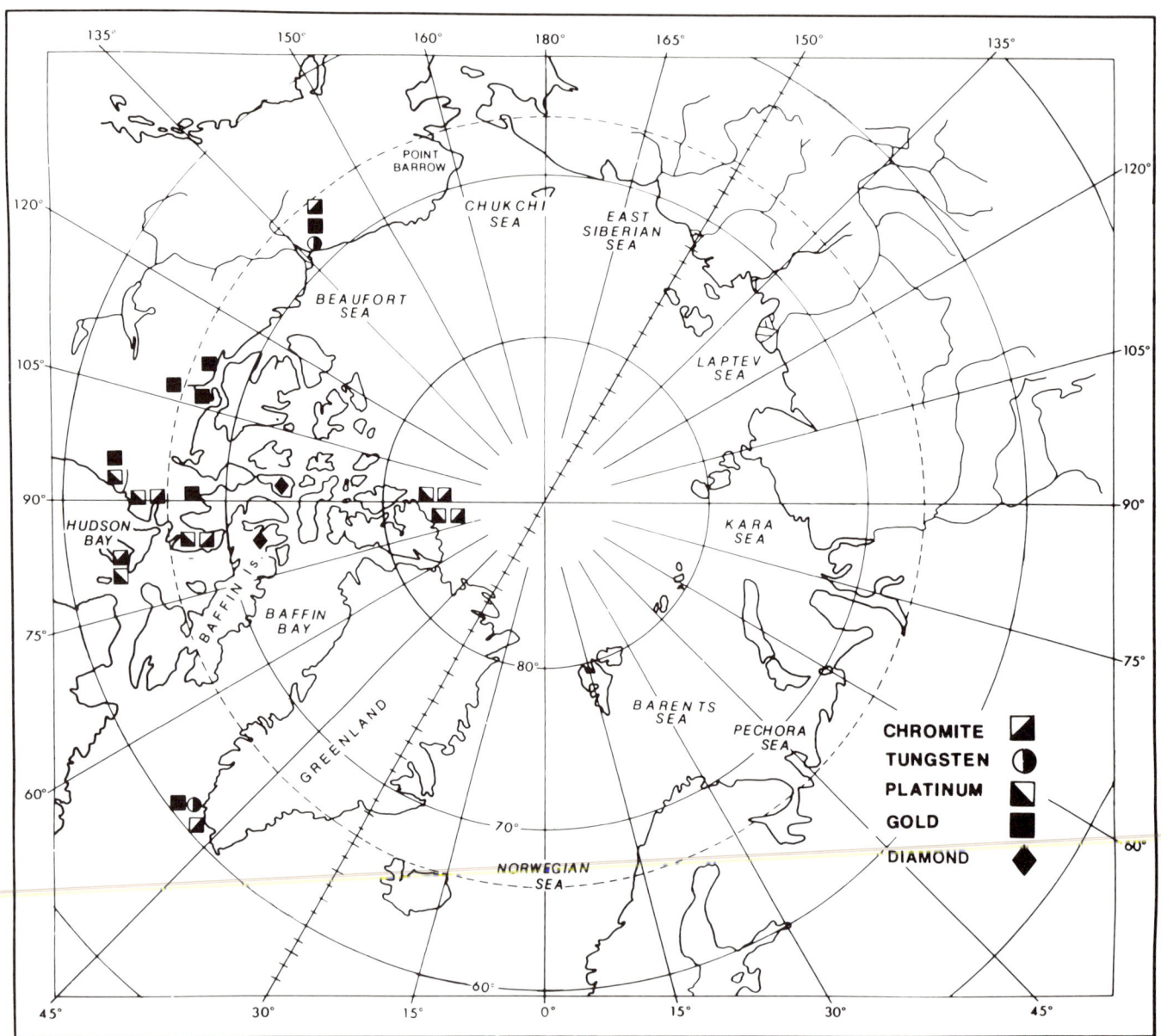

Figure 9. Possible marine placer occurrences in Arctic Canada and Greenland determined on the basis of favorable onland geology (after Hale and McLaren, 1984; Miles and Wright, 1978).

samples, short cores, and diving observations, supplemented by side-scan sonar and fathometer records (see Fig. 10). Data coverage is best in the lagoons and inner shelf region near Prudhoe Bay (Naidu, 1980; Barnes and others, 1979, 1980) and in Harrison Bay (Craig and Thrasher, 1982; Barnes and others, 1980). Surficial sediment distribution on the Beaufort shelf west of Harrison Bay, east of the Canning River, and on most of the outer shelf is poorly known. A thorough review of sediment sources, processes, and environmental consequences of offshore mining for sand and gravel is presented by Briggs (1983). Potential sites for mining of sand and gravel on the shelf include mid- and outer-shelf lag gravels, hydraulic bedforms, and buried gravels on the inner shelf, beaches, and barrier islands.

Relict surficial gravel. The presence of surficial gravel on the mid- to outer-shelf of the Alaskan Beaufort Sea has been noted by Barnes (1974), Mowatt and Naidu (1974), Rodeick (1979), and Reimnitz and others (1982). Gravel is especially prominent east of 145°W at depths between 50 and 70 m, with a secondary accumulation between 146°W and 149°W at water depths of 30 to 70 m. On the central portion of the shelf, the deposits form a thin cover (less than 0.10 m) overlying marine silt and clay, while those farther east may be several meters thick. These gravel accumulations have been interpreted as relict ice-rafted deposits formed early in the sea-level rise following the last glaciation (Mowatt and Naidu, 1974; Rodeick, 1979). Surficial gravel is also present on the inner shelf east of the Canning River (Reim-

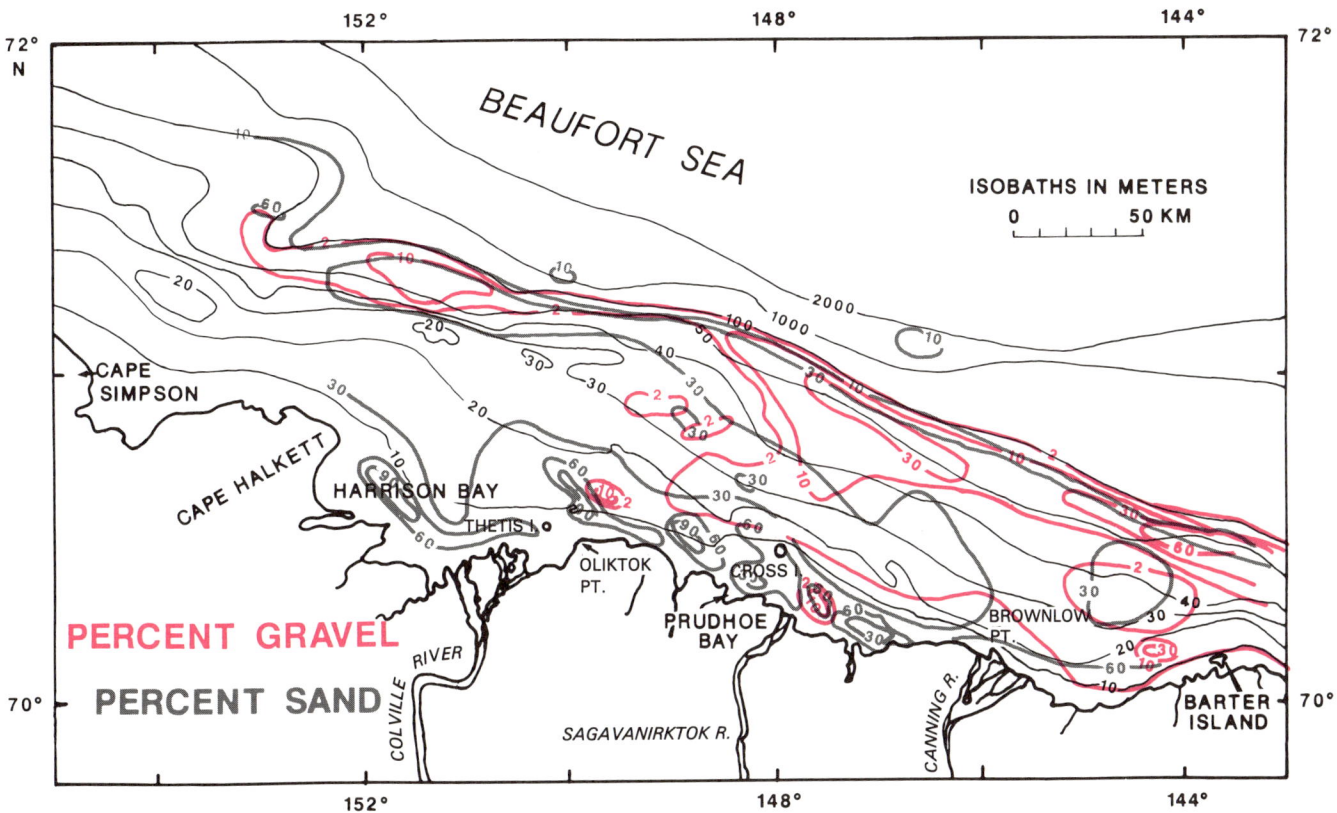

Figure 10. Percent of sand and gravel in surficial deposits, western Beaufort Sea (after Naidu, 1980; Barnes and others, 1979, 1980; Craig and Thrasher, 1982).

nitz and others, 1982), but thickness and lateral extent of mineable deposits have not been evaluated.

Active bed forms. Shoals and sand ridges in the stamukhi zone on the inner shelf between Harrison Bay and Sagavanirktok River to the east (see Dinter and others, this volume) have been extensively studied by Barnes, Reimitz, and coworkers (Reimnitz and Maurer, 1979; Barnes and others, 1980; Reimnitz and Kempema, 1983) and by Craig and Thrasher (1982). An area of active sand ridges in water depths of 10 m or less extends westward from Pingok Island, which lies about 20 km east-northeast of Oliktok Point, to beyond Thetis Island. Briggs (1983) estimates that about 1×10^5 m^3 of sand is available from these bodies. He likewise estimates 1×10^5 m^3 of sand each from Pacific Shoal and Finger Shoals, in western Harrison Bay, and 1×10^4 m^3 of gravel from an unnamed shoal lying about 5 km east of Thetis Island. Two large areas of sand and gravel, Weller Bank and Stamukhi Shoal, also lie near the 20 m isobath north of Harrison Bay. These shoals project 5 to 10 m above the surrounding sea floor and are believed to control the position of the stamukhi zone, the zone of intense grounding of sea-ice ridges (Reimnitz and Maurer, 1978; Barnes and others, 1980; Hopkins, 1981).

Sub-surface gravels. The distribution of sub-surface sand and gravel deposits is less well understood than that of the surficial deposits. No public documents are available for the area west of Harrison Bay, and coverage for the rest of the Alaskan Beaufort Sea is generally inadequate for quantifying estimates of sand and gravel resources, except for localized areas in Harrison Bay and in the vicinity of Prudhoe Bay.

Sub-surface sand and gravel west of Oliktok Point probably exist only in Pleistocene drainage channels, if at all. Information from proprietary and OCSEAP drilling programs in the Harrison Bay area verifies the fine-grained nature of the sub-surface sediments (Briggs, 1983). Between Oliktok Point and Prudhoe Bay, sand and gravel of outwash and alluvial origin are present beneath 0 to 10 m of Holocene marine silt and clay. Between Prudhoe Bay and Brownlow Point, alluvial and outwash gravels are present under a greater thickness (20 to 40 m) of fine-grained marine sediment. East of Brownlow Point, gravel is present at the surface on the inner shelf (Reimnitz and others, 1982) and is likely present at depth as well. Several paleovalleys containing gravels with a thin cover of fine-grained Holocene marine deposits may exist on the shelf north of Prudhoe Bay (Hopkins, 1979, 1981). Hopkins postulates that a former channel of the Sagavanirktok River underlies what is now Prudhoe Bay and turns westward beneath the shelf about 10 km north of the bay. Further discussion of this paleovalley can be found in Dinter and others (this volume).

Beaches and barrier islands. Beach deposits along the Beaufort Sea coast from Oliktok Point to the Canadian border tend to be thin and narrow, and contain only small amounts of sand and gravel. Beaches east of Prudhoe Bay consist primarily of a thin gravel veneer overlying silt and clay, while those farther west are predominantly sand. Beach material is derived largely from coastal bluff erosion, with only minor contributions from ice-push and longshore transport (Hopkins and Hartz, 1978).

Barrier islands in the Beaufort Sea form three northwest-trending chains: (1) Brownlow Point to Cross Island, (2) Prudhoe Bay to Thetis Island, and (3) Cape Simpson to Point Barrow. The origin of islands and the processes affecting them have been discussed by Reimnitz and others (1977) and Reimnitz and Maurer (1979). Most of the islands are constructional deposits of sand and gravel that are migrating southwestward from source areas that have since been largely destroyed by marine abrasion.

In summary, the distribution of sand and gravel along the north shore of Alaska is highly variable. Gravel is abundant in many regions, with the best sources being glacial outwash, alluvial deposits, or lag-type gravel deposits in the offshore. There are large volumes of sand in the numerous deltas and sand-ridge fields that could be exploited. Many of the barrier islands and spits contain large quantities of material, but most are isolated from their sources of supply and should not be mined (Williams, 1986).

If the current level of artificial island construction continues and there is further oil and gas exploration, the demand for sand and gravel will remain high. Although there are abundant on-land resources, high transportation costs may favor offshore mining in some localities.

THE FUTURE OF MARINE MINING IN THE ARCTIC OCEAN BASIN

Efforts in the next 10 to 20 years will concentrate on the consolidated and unconsolidated shelf mineral deposits situated close to shore in water depths of 100 m or less. No deep-sea mineral deposits have as yet been identified in the Arctic Ocean Basin. If such were to be found, however, the absence of appropriate mining technologies, coupled with weak metals markets and difficulties of working in the Arctic, would preclude their development for the foreseeable future.

Sub-sea mining of consolidated mineral deposits will be land based, using traditional tunnelling techniques. Should such deposits extend more than about 6 km offshore, then artificial islands would probably have to be constructed for ventilation and access.

Dredging activities for sand and gravel on the Arctic ocean shelves will keep pace with nearby offshore hydrocarbon development and other large coastal and offshore construction projects but will not become widespread in the Arctic. Dredges capable of operating through the ice could be designed and built, but it may be preferable to construct dredges with greater production capacities and confine activities to the ice-free season.

Numerous regions in the Arctic Ocean Basin possess favorable geology for placer deposits. At least one offshore tin placer has been brought into production in the Soviet Union, and other tin and gold placers may also be mined. It is premature to say whether there are exploitable placers in the North American Arctic.

REFERENCES CITED

Affolter, R. H., and Stricker, G. D., 1987, Offshore Alaska coal, in Scholl, D. W., Grantz, A., Vedder, J. G., eds., Geology and resource potential of the continental margin of western North America and adjacent ocean basins; Beaufort Sea to Baja California: Houston, Circum-Pacific Council for Energy and Mineral Resources, Earth Science Series 6, p. 635–643.

Amann, H., 1985, Development of Ocean Mining in the Red Sea: Journal of Marine Mining, v. 5, no. 2, p. 103–116.

Anonymous, 1976, Soviet Oceans Development: Washington, D.C., U.S. Government Printing Office, U.S. Government Committee on Commerce and National Ocean Policy Study, pursuant to senate resolution 222, 646 p.

Armstrong, E. F., and Miall, L. M., 1946, Raw Materials from the Sea: Brooklyn, New York, Chemical Publishing Co., 196 p.

Austin, C. F., 1967, In the Rock; A Logical Approach for Undersea Mining of Resources: Engineering and Mining Journal, v. 168, no. 8, p. 82–88.

Bakke, D. R., 1971, Russia Strengthens its Mining Program: Offshore, v. 31, no. 12, p. 34–38.

Barnes, P. W., 1974, Preliminary results of marine geologic studies off the northern coast of Alaska, in An ecological survey in the Beaufort Sea, WEBSEC 71–72, Department of Transportation: U.S. Coast Guard Oceanographic Report CG 373-64, p. 183–227.

Barnes, P. W., Reimnitz, E., Toimil, L. J., McDowell, D. M., and Maurer, D. K., 1979, Vibracores, Beaufort Sea, Alaska; Descriptions and preliminary interpretation: U.S. Geological Survey Open-File Report 79-351, 103 p.

Barnes, P. W., Reimnitz, E., and Ross, C. R., 1980, Nearshore surficial sediment textures; Beaufort Sea, Alaska, in Environmental assessment of the Alaskan continental shelf: NOAA/OCEAP Quarterly Report 2, p. 132–170.

Brakel, J., 1984, Dredging developments in the Canadian Arctic; Proceedings: American Society of Civil Engineers Dredging 1984 Conference, Clearwater Beach, Florida, November 14–16.

Briggs, S. R., 1983, Geology report for proposed Beaufort Sea OCS sand and gravel lease sale: U.S. Geological Survey Open-File Report 83-606, 25 p.

Central Intelligence Agency, 1978, Polar Regions Atlas: Washington, D.C., U.S. Government Printing Office, 66 p.

Clark, D. L., Whitman, R. R., Morgan, K. A., and Macker, S. D., 1980, Stratigraphy and glacial-marine sediments of the Amerasian Basin, central Arctic Ocean: Geological Society of America Special Paper 181, 57 p.

Conquest, R., 1979, Kolyma; The Arctic Death Camps: Oxford, Oxford University Press, 256 p.

Craig, J. D., and Thrasher, G. P., 1982, Environmental Geology of Harrison Bay, Northern Alaska: U.S. Geological Survey Open-File Report 82-35, 25 p.

CYAMEX, 1979, Massive Deep-Sea Sulfide Ore Deposits Discovered on East Pacific Rise: Nature, v. 277, p. 523–528.

Earney, F.C.F., 1980, Petroleum and Hard Minerals from the Sea: London, Edward Arnold Company, 291 p.

Glasby, G. P., 1979, Minerals from the Sea: Endeavor, New Series, Oxford, Pergamon Press, p. 82–85.

Hale, P. B., 1987, Canada's Offshore Non-Fuel Mineral Resources; Opportunities for Development: Journal of Marine Mining, v. 6, no. 2, p. 89–108.

Hale, P. B., and McLaren, P., 1984, A Preliminary Assessment of Unconsolidated Mineral Resources in the Canadian Offshore: Canadian Institute of Mining and Metallurgical Bulletin, v. 77, no. 869, p. 51–61.

Herman, Y., and Hopkins, D. M., 1980, Arctic Oceanic Climate in Late Cenozoic

Time: Science, v. 209, p. 557–562.
Holmes, M. L. and Creager, J. S., 1974, Holocene History of the Laptev Sea Continental Shelf, in Herman, Y., ed., Marine Geology and Oceanography of the Arctic Seas: New York, Springer-Verlag, p. 211–229.
Hopkins, D. M., 1979, Offshore permafrost studies, Beaufort Sea, in Environmental assessment of the Alaskan continental shelf: NOAA/OCSEAP Annual Report 16, p. 396–518.
—— , ed., 1981, Gravel sources and management options, in Norton, D. W., and Sackinger, W. M., eds., Beaufort Sea (Sale 71) synthesis report: Washington, D.C., U.S. Department of Commerce/U.S. Department of Interior, p. 169–178.
Hopkins, D. M., and Hartz, R. W., 1978, Coastal morphology, coastal erosion, and barrier islands of the Beaufort Sea, Alaska: U.S. Geological Survey Open File Report 78-1063, 54 p.
Janson, I.W.M., 1983, Artificial Island Construction in the Canadian Beaufort Sea: World Dredging Congress, April 19–22, Mandarin, Singapore, preprint.
Livshits, L., 1973, USSR's Seafloor Mining Experiments: Ocean Industry, v. 8, no. 4, p. 240.
Meyerhoff, A. A., 1983, The USSR Northern and Far Eastern Coasts; Petroleum Geology and Technology, Mining Activities, and Environmental Factors: Canada Department of Indian and Northern Affairs, unpublished report, 279 p.
Miles, T., and Wright, N.J.R., 1978, An Outline of Mineral Extraction in the Arctic: Polar Record, v. 19, no. 118, p. 11–38.
Mowatt, T. C., and Naidu, S., 1974, Gravels from the Alaskan continental shelf, Beaufort Sea, Arctic Ocean; Petrographic character and implications for sediment source and transport: Alaska Division of Geological and Geophysical Surveys Open-File Report AOF43, 40 p.
Naidu, A. S., 1980, Sources, transport pathways, depositional sites, and dynamics of sediments in the lagoon and shallow marine regions, northern Arctic Alaska: National Oceanic and Atmospheric Administration, Environmental Assessment of the Alaskan Continental Shelf, Principal Investigator's report for 1980, p. 3–94.
O'Connor and Associates Ltd., 1983a, An evaluation of the regional surficial geology of the southern Beaufort Sea: Unpublished report prepared for the Atlantic Geoscience Centre, Geological Survey of Canada, 188 p.
—— , 1983b, Regional inventory of offshore gravel prospects Canadian Beaufort Sea: Unpublished report prepared for Northern Renewable Resources Branch, Department of Indian and Northern Affairs, Canada, 63 p.
Reimnitz, E., and Kempema, E. W., 1983, Pack ice interaction with Stambukbi Shoal, Beaufort Sea, Alaska; Attachment H, in Barnes, P. W., Reimnitz, E., Hunter, R. E., Phillips, R. L., and Wolf, S. C., Geologic processes and hazards of the Beaufort and Chukchi Sea shelf and coastal regions; Environmental assessment of the Alaskan continent shelf: Boulder, Colorado, National Oceanographic and Atmospheric Administration, Annual Reports of principal investigators for the year ending March 1983, Attachment F, p. F1 to F24.
Reimnitz, E., and D. K. Maurer, 1979, Stamukhi shoals of the Arctic; Some observations from the Beaufort Sea: U.S. Geological Survey Open-File Report 78-666, 17 p.
Reimnitz, E., Barnes, P. W., Minkler, P. W., Rearic, D. M., Kempema, E. W., and Reiss, T., 1982, Marine Geological Investigations in the Beaufort Sea in 1981 and preliminary interpretations for region from the Canning River to the Canadian border: National Oceanic and Atmospheric Administration, Environmental Assessment of the Alaskan Continental Shelf, Principal Investigators Report for 1981, 46 p.
Reimnitz, E., Toimil, L. J., and Barnes, P. W., 1977, Stamukhi zone processes; implications for developing the Arctic offshore: Houston, Texas, Proceedings, Offshore Technology Conference, Paper OTC 2945, p. 513–518.
Ricketts, B. D. and Embry, A. F., 1986, Coal in the Canadian Arctic Archipelago; A potential resource: GEOS, v. 1, p. 16–18.
Rodeick, C. A., 1979, The origin, distribution, and depositional history of gravel deposits on the Beaufort Sea continental shelf, Alaska: U.S. Geological Survey Open-File Report 79-234, 87 p.
Rose, E. R., Sandford, B. V., and Hacquebard, P. A., 1970, Economic Minerals of southwestern Canada, in Douglas, R.J.W., ed., Geology and Economic Materials of Canada: Geological Survey of Canada, p. 307–364.
Soviet Ministry of Defence, 1980, Ocean Atlas; The Arctic Ocean: Leningrad, Chief Directorate of Navigation and Oceanography of the USSR, 184 p. (in Russian).
Stevens, J. F., 1970, Mining the Alaskan Seas: Ocean Industry, November, p. 47–50.
Tailleur, I. L., and Brosge, W. P., 1976, Coal Resources of Northern Alaska may be Nation's Largest: Proceedings, Focus on Alaska Coal Symposium, 1975, Fairbanks, Alaska, p. 219–226.
Thompson, R. M., and Smith, K. G., 1970, Undersea Lode Mining in Alaska: Proceedings, Offshore Technology Conference, Houston, Texas, Paper OTC 1312, p. 819–826.
Wang, F.F.H., and McKelvey, V. E., 1976, Marine Mineral Resources, in Govett, G.J.S., and Govett, M. H., eds., World Mineral Supplies Assessment and Perspective: New York, Elsevier Scientific Company, p. 221–286.
Williams, S. J., 1986, Sand and Gravel Deposits within the United States Exclusive Economic Zone; Resource Assessment and Uses: Annual Offshore Technology Conference, Houston, Texas, Paper OTC 5197, p. 377–386.

MANUSCRIPT ACCEPTED BY THE SOCIETY APRIL 12, 1988

1. Mouette tridactyle.   2. Pagophile blanche.
(*Larus tridactylus* L.)   (*Larus eburneus* Gmel.)

From A. E. Nordenskjold, 1885, Voyage de la *Vega* Autour de l'Asie et de l'Europe [1878–1879], (translated from Swedish by Charles Rabot and Charles Lallemond), Vol. 1: Paris, Libraire Hachette et Cie, p. 107.

Printed in U.S.A.

Chapter 30

Paleomagnetic and plate-tectonic constraints on the evolution of the Alaskan–eastern Siberian Arctic

William Harbert
Department of Earth and Planetary Science, University of Pittsburgh, Pittsburgh, Pennsylvania 15206
Leah Frei
Geophysics Department, Stanford University, Stanford, California 94305
Richard Jarrard and Susan Halgedahl
Lamont-Doherty Geological Observatory of Columbia University, Palisades, New York 10964
David Engebretson
Geology Department, Western Washington University, Bellingham, Washington 98225

INTRODUCTION

The tectonic development of the Arctic Basin is constrained by several independent sets of data. These include paleomagnetic Apparent Polar Wander Paths for the North American and Eurasian Plates, paleomagnetic data from Arctic Alaska, and magnetic isochrons in the Arctic, Atlantic, and Pacific Oceans. In this chapter we use each set of data to constrain plate-tectonic models describing the development of the Amerasia Basin, northern Alaska, and the northeast USSR. First, we use Apparent Polar Wander Paths for the Eurasian and North American Plates to show the existence of a gap between these two plates in the Arctic Basin region before the formation of oceanic crust in the North Atlantic and Arctic oceans (the Late Carboniferous to Early Cretaceous, about 310 to 120 Ma). We then review and present new paleomagnetic data from the North Slope of Alaska to constrain the timing and geometry of the opening of the Canada Basin. The new data shows that counterclockwise rotation of ~70° has occurred since Barremian time, providing strong evidence supporting a rotational opening of the Canada Basin. Next, we review plate-tectonic models describing rifting in the Arctic and North Atlantic Basins and correlate tectonic events in the Arctic Basin with these motions. We correlate periods of strong convergence between the continental plates from ~70 to ~56 Ma (Maastrichtian to Paleocene) with compressional deformation between the Chukotsk Peninsula and northern Alaska and movement along the Denali Fault. Transform motion between these plates from ~56 through 50 to 38 Ma (lower to upper Eocene) coincides with subsidence of the Bering Shelf and creation of a series of pull-apart basins along the Bering Margin. Finally, we review the oceanic plates interacting with the North American and Eurasian Plates. Motions of the oceanic plates coincide with magmatism in Alaska belts. Magmatic quiescence occurred throughout southwestern Alaska and the northeastern USSR during a period of plate reorganization from about 56 to 43 Ma, a period that began with extremely rapid northward motion of the Kula Plate, from about 74 to 56 Ma. For the discussion that follows, a brief review of the geologic framework is necessary (see also Plate 11). More detailed descriptions of these regions are presented in Fujita and others (this volume, Siberia), Grantz and others (ch. 22, this volume, Canada Basin), and Kristoffersen (this volume, Eurasia Basin).

REGIONAL GEOLOGICAL FRAMEWORK

The region of the Arctic Basin discussed in this paper may be divided into four parts; northeastern Siberia, Alaska, Canadian Arctic Islands, and the Amerasia Basin (Fig. 1).

Northeastern Siberia

The region north of the Kamchatka Peninsula and east of the Verkhoyansk complex has recently been interpreted as consisting of numerous tectonostratigraphic terranes (Arkhipov and others, 1981; Fujita and Newberry, 1982). The geology of the northeastern USSR records a complex history of Paleozoic and Mesozoic tectonic accretion (Parfenov and Natal'in, 1985; Green and others, 1986). The four main elements important to our analysis are (1) the Anyuy suture zone, (2) the Okhotsk-Chukotsk volcanogenic belt, (3) the Kolymo-Omolonsky "Kolymia" composite terrane, and (4) the Koryak volcanogenic and thrust belt, "Koryakia" composite terrane. The Anyuy Suture records the collision of the Eurasian and North American Plates during the late Early Cretaceous. The Okhotsk-Chukotsk volcanogenic belt defines the late Mesozoic geometry of the Eurasian Plate in the Bering Sea region. The Kolymia and Koryakia Terranes are allochthonous composite terranes that accreted to the

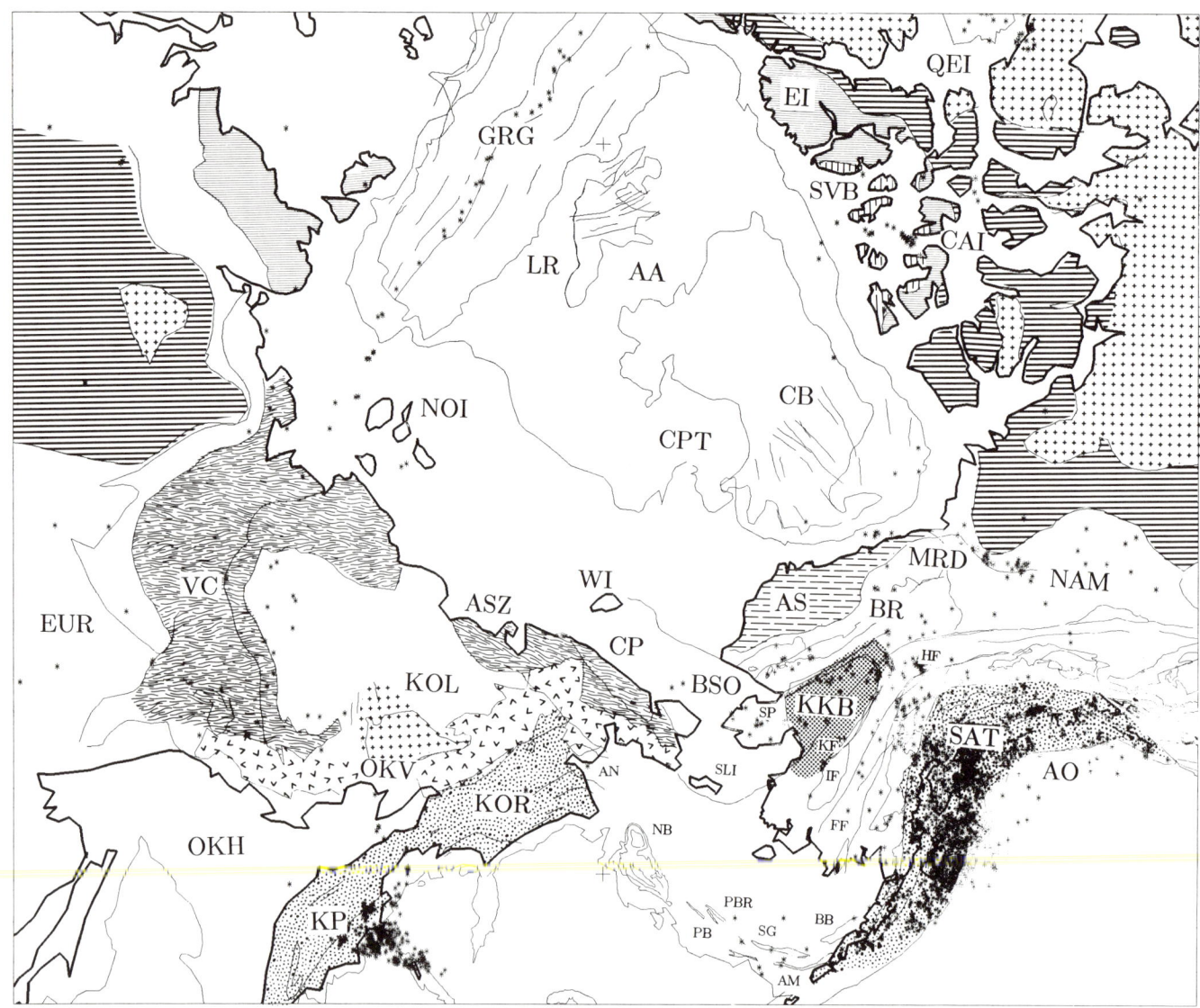

Figure 1. Simplified location map of the Bering sea region utilizing information presented in Nalivkin (1965), Belyi and others (1974), Patton and Tailleur (1977), Grantz and others (1979), Coney and others (1980), Fujita and Newberry (1983), and Parfenov and Natal'in (1985). The following abbreviations are used: AA, Alpha-Mendeleev Ridge Complex; AM, Amak Basin; AN, Anadyr Basin; AO, Alaska Orocline; AS, Arctic Slope; ASZ, Anyuy Suture Zone; BB, Bristol Bay Basin; BR, Brooks, Range; BSO, Bering Strait Orocline; CAI, Canadian Arctic Islands; CB, Canada Basin; CPT, Chukchi Plateau; CP, Chukotsk Peninsula; EI, Ellesmere Island; EUR, Eurasia Plate; FF, Farewell Fault System; GRG, Arctic mid-ocean Ridge; HF, Hines Creek Fault; IF, Iditarod Fault System; KF, Kaltag Fault System; KKB, Koyukuk-Kuskokwim Basins; KOL, Kolymo-Omolonsky "Kolymia" composite terrane; KOR, Koryak volcanogenic and thrust belt, "Koryakia" composite terrane; KP, Kamchatka Peninsula; LR, Lomonosov Ridge; MRD, Mackenzie River delta; NAM, North America Plate; NB, Navarin Basin; NOI, Novosibirsk Islands; OKH, Okhotsk Plate; OKV, Okhotsk-Chukotsk volcanogenic belt; PB, Pribilof Basin; PBR, Pribilof Ridge; QEI, Queen Elizabeth Islands; SAT, Tectonostratigraphic terranes to the south of the Jurassic flysch basin; SG, St George Basin; SLI, St. Lawrence Island; SP, Seward Peninsula; SVB, Sverdrup Basin; VC, Verkhoyansk Complex; WI, Wrangell Island.

Eurasian plate during the late Mesozoic (Zonenshain and others, 1987). Geographic terms used in this section are defined in Suslov (1961).

The Anyuy Fold Belt has been interpreted to be the suture zone between the Chukotsk Peninsula and Eurasian Plate. The suture extends from the northwest Chukotsk Peninsula to the Novosibirsk Islands. Collision occurred during the Late Jurassic to Neocomian (Tibilov, 1982; Parfenov and Natal'in, 1985; Parfenov, 1984), and the Anyuy Suture is overlapped by volcanic and plutonic rocks of the Okhotsk-Chukotsk Belt.

The Okhotsk-Chukotsk volcanogenic belt strikes northeastward along the northern Sea of Okhotsk, and southern Chukotsk Peninsula. This arc was active during the Aptian (?) to Late Cretaceous (Zaborovskaya and Nekrasov, 1977; Parfenov and Natal'in, 1985), and consists of an inner and outer zone. The arc has been interpreted to represent the Cretaceous margin of eastern Siberia (Shilo and others, 1974; Natal'in and Parfenov, 1983; Parfenov and Natal'in, 1985). It overlaps tectonostratigraphic terranes, such as the Kolymia composite terrane, and microplates that make up northeastern Asia, suggesting these fragments had accreted to the Eurasian plate by Late Cretaceous (Parfenov and Natal'in, 1985; Fujita and Newberry, 1982, 1983).

The Kolymo-Omolonsky massif or Kolyma block appears to have accreted to Eurasia at approximately 120 Ma. This collision resulted in formation of the Verkhoyansk-Kolymian orogenic belt of Early Cretaceous age (Zonenshain and others, 1987). Crust underlying the present-day Sea of Okhotsk, the "Okhotia terrane" of Zonenshain and others, may have accreted at 70 Ma.

Outboard of the Okhotsk-Chukotsk volcanic arc is a second volcanic belt, the Koryak zone (Mitrofanov and Sheludchemko, 1981). The Koryak zone consists of complexly folded and thrust ultramafic units, calc-alkaline volcanic deposits and mélange units (Filotova and others, 1980). Ophiolites of Late Jurassic to Cretaceous age are observed along some thrusts (Alekseyev, 1981; Filotova and others, 1980; Pevye, 1984). Thrusting occurred during the Middle Jurassic, Late Cretaceous, and late Eocene; however, the most intense deformation occurred between Cenomanian and early Paleocene (Danian; Kosygin and Parfenov, 1981; Pushcharovskiy and others, 1983). Some blocks of Paleozoic samples have been interpreted to contain Tethyian foraminifera, suggesting large horizontal displacements (Epshtein and others, 1985; Koltypin and Kononov, 1986). Accretion of tectonostratigraphic terranes in the Koryak Mountains occurred in the Late Cretaceous and early Tertiary (120 to 70 Ma, Zonenshain and others, 1987).

Alaska

Alaska is similar to eastern Siberia in that it consists of parautochthonous and allochthonous terranes that vary in age from Paleozoic to Cenozoic. Five major tectonic elements have been recognized: (1) allochthonous rocks in the Brooks Range and Seward Peninsula, (2) sedimentary rocks in the Koyukuk-Kuskokwim Basin, (3) the Ruby Geanticline, (4) the Late Jurassic flysch basin of the Alaska Range, and (5) tectonostratigraphic terranes to the south of the Jurassic flysch basin.

Paleozoic units exposed north of the Koyukuk Basin consist of limestones, dolomites, shales, sandstones, and conglomerates. They are believed to be parautochthonous to the North American plate (Churkin and others, 1979; Mayfield and others, 1983). North-directed overthrusting occurred in the Brooks Range between Middle Jurassic and Early Cretaceous (~110 to 160 Ma). The amount of shortening in the DeLong Mountains at the extreme western end of the Brooks Range is perhaps as much as 700 km (Mayfield and others, 1983). Continuity of lithology and structure suggests that the Chukotsk Peninsula, St. Lawrence Island, Seward Peninsula, northern Alaska, and the northern Bering Shelf have not had substantial differential motion since the Paleozoic Churkin, 1972, 1975; Patton and Tailleur, 1977; Churkin and Trexler, 1980).

South of the Brooks Range, the Koyukuk-Kuskokwim Basin is rimmed by ophiolites of Middle Jurassic to Early Cretaceous age (K-Ar ages between 164 and 138 Ma). The ophiolites exposed along the northern and southeastern margins dip toward the basin (Patton and others, 1977) and are thought to represent obducted oceanic crust on which the sediments of the Koyukuk-Kuskokwim Basin were deposited. Andesitic arc volcanism within the Koyukuk Basin occurred during the Neocomian, whereas infilling by orogenic sediments derived from the Brooks Range was restricted in time between the Albian and the Cenomanian (Patton, 1973). Bordering the Koyukuk Basin to the south is the Ruby Geanticline, a composite terrane of Paleozoic and Mesozoic age. As in the Brooks Range, the Ruby Geanticline is overthrust by ophiolitic units; however, deformation is less intense and no associated fold and thrust belt is observed.

To the south of the Ruby Geanticline, a flysch basin of Late Jurassic to Valanginian (Early Cretaceous) age borders the allochthonous Talkeetna Superterrane (Csejtey and others, 1982; Stone and others, 1982; Plumley and others, 1983; Moore and others, 1983; Hillhouse, 1987; Hillhouse and McWilliams, 1987). The flysch basin is dominantly composed of an intensely deformed lithic greywacke and argillite turbidite sequence. In the northeastern Talkeetna Mountains the deformed flysch is cut by andesite dikes with K-Ar ages of 97 Ma (Csejtey and others, 1982). The late Early Cretaceous age of intense deformation of the flysch is thought to represent the time of accretion of the southern terranes (Talkeetna Superterrane) to North America (Csejtey and others, 1982). Other major events in western Alaska are widespread calc-alkalic volcanism in the Koyukuk-Kuskokwim Basin and the Ruby Geanticline (~70 to 50 Ma) and widespread plutonism (~110 to 80 Ma) in the Ruby Geanticline, Koyukuk Basin, Seward Peninsula, and St. Lawrence Island (Burk, 1965; Hudson, 1983; Moll and Patton, 1984; Wallace and Engebretson, 1984).

Two large zones of arcuate geologic trends are exposed in the central-southern Alaska and Bering Strait regions. These are the Alaska and Bering Strait Oroclines (Carey, 1955; Patton and

Tailleur, 1977; Holmes and Creager, 1981). The Alaska Orocline is traced by the geometry of the Peninsular Terrane and numerous right-lateral strike-slip faults, including the Kaltag, Iditarod, and Farewell Faults and the Denali Fault System. Paleomagnetic evidence presented in Globerman and Coe (1984) supports the existence of the Alaska Orocline and suggests that southwestern Alaska has rotated 50° counterclockwise since the early Tertiary. Geologic mapping of the Denali fault system (an 'Oroclinal Fault' of Kosygin and Parfenov, 1981) and earlier work limits the timing of oroclinal deformation to between the Late Cretaceous and early Tertiary (Grantz, 1966; Hickman and others, 1978).

A second zone of oroclinal bending has been identified between the Seward and Chukotsk Peninsulas. Deflection of folds, Cordilleran trends, a Cretaceous plutonic belt, exposures of Paleozoic and Mesozoic units, and juxtaposition of dissimilar depositional facies along the western and southeastern margins of the Yukon-Koyukuk Basin suggest major post-Cenomanian structural shortening (Patton and Tailleur, 1977; Nilsen and Patton, 1984) and oroclinal deformation between the North American and Eurasian Plates.

Canadian Arctic Islands

Simply, this region consists of a series of large uplifted sedimentary basins separated by arches and uplifts, deposited on Precambrian crystalline basement forming the Canadian Arctic Islands. During the Lower Devonian, closure of the Iapetus Ocean resulted in uplift and arching in the eastern Canadian Arctic Islands region (Miall, 1986). The Franklinian phase of Upper Proterozoic–lower Paleozoic deposition was ended in the Late Devonian to Early Mississippian by the Ellesmerian Orogeny when, Franklinian-aged rocks were folded and thrust cratonward (Trettin and others, 1972; Miall, 1976; Balkwill, 1978; Balkwill and Bustin, 1980). Fragmentation of the Canadian Arctic occurred in two major deformational episodes, the Boreal episode and the Eurekan Orogeny. The Boreal episode was a prolonged intermittent event beginning shortly after the Ellesmerian Orogeny in the Mississippian and continuing until the Late Cretaceous (Kerr, 1978, 1981; Balkwill and others, 1983). Formation of extensional and strike-slip faults, local basement uplift, and creation of depositional basins occurred during this interval. The Sverdrup Basin, a deep structural depression about 1,200 km long and 400 km wide, was the dominant structural element of the Canadian Arctic Islands between the Early Carboniferous and Late Cretaceous. The Sverdrup Basin contains 12 km of upper Paleozoic and Mesozoic strata and has a present outcrop area of approximately 350,000 km^2 (Sweeney, 1977; Balkwill and Bustin, 1980; Balkwill and others, 1983).

The Eurekan Orogeny occurred during the latest Cretaceous (Campanian-Maestrichtian) and Tertiary time in the Queen Elizabeth Islands and Sverdrup Basin. This orogeny formed most of the fault-controlled channels of the southeast part of the Queen Elizabeth Islands (Kerr, 1978; Balkwill, 1978; Wynne and others, 1983; Balkwill and others, 1983; Hugon, 1983; Jackson, 1985; Jackson and Koppen, 1985; Srivastava, 1985; Kovacs and others, 1986). In the Sverdrup Basin, three phases of the orogeny have been identified. The first is a Late Cretaceous to late Paleocene phase of uplift and erosion, followed by a middle Eocene to early Miocene phase of compressive folding and faulting. The final phase of uplift and erosion of the northwestern Sverdrup rim occurred during the Miocene (Balkwill, 1978; Balkwill and others, 1983; Riediger and others, 1984).

Amerasia Basin

The Arctic Ocean Basin may be divided into the Eurasia and Amerasia Basins (Plate 1). Kristoffersen (this volume) reviews in detail the Arctic Mid-ocean Ridge. Weber and others (this volume) discuss the development of Lomonosov and Alpha Ridges. The principal bathymetric features in the Amerasia Basin are the Canada Bain, Alpha-Mendeleev Ridge Complex, and Chukchi Plateau. Each of these features is examined in detail in Grantz and others (ch. 22, this volume), and only the Canada Basin and Alpha-Mendeleev Ridge Complex are briefly described in this section.

Modelling of aeromagnetic data from the Canada Basin suggests that the basin consists of oceanic crust produced from an extinct spreading feature within the basin (Taylor and others, 1981; Vogt and others, 1979, 1982; Taylor and others, 1986). Magnetic isochrons within the basin (Plate 4) are of low amplitude but have been interpreted to consist of isochrons M25 to M15. On the basis of these identifications, depth to basement calculations, heat-flow measurements, and geologic evidence from the margin of the basin, spreading was thought to have occurred between 155 to 133 through 115 Ma (Vogt and others, 1982) or 118 to 79 Ma (Sweeney, 1985) between the Canadian Arctic Islands and the North Slope–Chukotka Terrane.

The Alpha-Mendeleev Ridge Complex stretches between Ellesmere Island in the Canadian Arctic to Wrangell Island in eastern Siberia. Magnetic anomaly patterns associated with the ridge are variable and not consistent with a typical oceanic spreading center. Heat-flow measurements from the ridge have been interpreted to suggest that no significant thermal events have affected the ridge during the last 100 m.y. (Taylor and others, 1986). Tuffaceous sediment of Maestrichtian and Eocene age have been recovered from two sites along the ridge (Clark, 1974; Clark and Morris, 1984; Mudie, 1986; see also Weber and others, this volume). The ridge has been interpreted to have formed between about 120 to 80 Ma, during the time of formation of the Canada Basin, but before sea-floor spreading along the Lomonosov Ridge (Sweeney and Weber, 1986; Taylor and others, 1986; Van Wagoner and others, 1986).

Using this brief outline of the geologic framework, we will now examine the relationships between paleomagnetic and plate-motion data for the North America and Eurasia Plates. Later we will use plate-motion data from the Pacific Basin to help explain the geologic development of the Alaskan-Siberian arctic. From magnetic isochrons in the Arctic and North Atlantic Oceans, we will see that a substantial gap existed between the North American and Eurasian Plates before the rotational opening of the Canada Basin.

LATE CARBONIFEROUS–EARLY TRIASSIC GEOMETRY OF THE NORTH AMERICA AND EURASIA PLATES

The relative position of the Eurasia and North America continents can be reconstructed using three different methods: (a) calculation of Euler poles from magnetic anomalies and fracture zones from intervening oceanic crust; (b) the overall regional shape of rifted continental margins; (c) overlapping of the Apparent Polar Wander Paths (APWP) from cratonic portions of the plates. The first and second methods are limited to reconstructions of the current tectonic cycle and do not take into account deformation of the continental margins during rifting. In this section we discuss the third method: reconstructions based on the fit of the APWPs of the Eurasian and North American continents. If the APWP of one continent is rotated about the correct Euler pole for the complete opening between the two continents, it will be congruent with the part of the APWP of the second continent that predates the displacement. This method determines the total amount of displacement and is not sensitive to deformation of the continental margin.

The continental plates surrounding the Arctic are the Eurasia, North America, and Greenland Plates. Because of the lack of paleomagnetic data from Greenland, we use the first method to reconstruct its position relative to North America using the Euler pole of Srivastava (1978), which is based on magnetic anomalies in the Labrador Sea.

In order to construct a well-defined APWP for Eurasia Frei and Cox (1987) evaluated the paleomagnetic data from cratonal Eurasia. In constructing the APWP, they did not use the paleomagnetic data from the Iberian Peninsula, which has rotated relative to the rest of cratonal Eurasia (Van der Voo, 1969), or data from the USSR, for which there is not enough information to permit evaluation by the methods used for the western European data. They followed the method of Irving and Irving (1982) to find the means for every 10 m.y. with a sliding time window of 30 m.y. The same method was applied to the paleomagnetic data from North America summarized by Gordon and others (1984). The two APWPs have minimal combined errors for the period 290 to 240 Ma. In order to check for the possibility that some displacement did take place between North America and Eurasia in the Late Permian or Early Triassic, and to determine the effect of using paleomagnetic APWP data from the USSR, Frei and Cox also used two different segments of the North America and Eurasia APWPs of Irving and Irving (1982). Irving and Irving (1982) used data from both Europe and the USSR to calculate a APWP for the Eurasia Plate.

Frei and Cox (1987) used an algorithm that searched for rotation poles and angles, producing the best fit for different segments of the APWPs. The segments of the APWPs they fit were: (a) the APWPs of Frei and Cox (1987) for the period 290 to 240 Ma; (b) the APWPs of Irving and Irving (1982) for Late Carboniferous to Permian; and (c) the APWPs of Irving and Irving for Triassic. Using each of these segments for each trial rotation pole, they found the angle of rotation that produced the minimum misfit between the APWPs. They plotted and contoured the misfit as a function of the rotation poles. The contours of the misfit approximate an ellipsoid with a large aspect ratio. The contours of the angles of rotation are approximately perpendicular to the long axis of the ellipsoid. Since the fit of the APWPs is not perfect for any of the segments because of experimental errors, the preferred reconstruction pole chosen was not the Euler pole that resulted in the best fit. The Euler pole chosen is located along the long axis of the ellipsoid and has a rotation angle that results in a geologically reasonable reconstruction. The following criteria were used in the evaluation: overlaps in the reconstructions should be located in areas that have undergone extension since the time of reconstruction, and similarly, gaps should correspond to compression. The amounts of extension and compression predicted by the reconstruction should be reasonable, and linear geologic features predating the opening of the North Atlantic and appearing on both sides of it should realign in the reconstructions. Based on these geological constraints, Frei and Cox (1987) prefer the Euler poles that fit the Late Carboniferous to Permian APWPs of Irving and Irving (1982). The rotation poles are listed in Table 1; the preferred reconstructions are shown in polar projection in Figures 2 and 3. Assuming the plates are rigid, the same Euler pole reconstructs the relative position of the plates in the North Atlantic, and in the Bering Sea area. In Figures 2 and 3, the North Slope–Chukotka Terrane has been rotated to close the Canada Basin (discussed in the following section), and allochtonous terranes of southern Alaska and northeastern Siberia have been removed.

In these reconstructions of the Bering Sea region, there is a large gap between the continental plates. Ocean crust from the Pacific Basin may have entered the Arctic Basin through this gap, which also suggests that at the time of these reconstructions, Alaska and Siberia would have been deforming separately, with no interaction. The size of the gap shown in the reconstructions could have been smaller if subduction was taking place in the Urals during the Permian and Early Triassic, as suggested by Zoneshain and others (1984). Extension east of the Ural Mountains (Rudkevich, 1976) has not been corrected for; such a correction would enlarge the gap between these two plates in the Alaskan-Siberian region.

This geometry suggests that subduction of an oceanic plate in a "Sinus Borealis" (Dietz and Holden, 1970) may have occurred until the geometry of the Eurasia and North America Plates was changed in the Arctic by the rotational opening of the Canada Basin during the Early Cretaceous, accretion of terranes, and opening of the Arctic and North Atlantic Oceans. Paleomagnetic data constraining the timing and style of the formation of the Canada Basin is presented in the following section.

TABLE 1. FINITE ROTATION POLES USED TO RECONSTRUCT THE POSITIONS
OF THE CONTINENTAL BLOCKS FROM PRESENT POSITIONS TO POSITION AT AGE T

Rotated continental block	Relative to	Age T of Reconstruction	Finite Rotation Pole		
			N Lat.	E Long.	CCW Rotation[1]
Greenland[2]	NA	76 Ma Chron 33	71.5	233.7	-11.04
Eurasia	NA	post 240 Ma	88.0	215.0	-42.0
	NA	post 220 Ma	80.0	230.0	-45.0
	NA	post 250 Ma	86.0	230.0	-44.0
North America[3]	HS	200 Ma	56.6	16.1	81.1
Greenland	HS	200 Ma*	52.3	25.4	74.3
Eurasia	HS	200 Ma*	32.7	38.1	51.8
	HS	200 Ma*	29.6	44.8	55.1
	HS	200 Ma*	30.9	40.8	51.8

Notes:
1. Counterclockwise rotations are positive (right-hand rule). Negative angles indicate clockwise rotation.
2. Srivastava, 1978.
3. Morgan, 1983.

*The rotation poles of Greenland and Eurasia relative to hot spots assume that there was no relative motion between Greenland and North America before 76 Ma, and no relative motion between Eurasia and North America before 200 Ma.

NA = North America.   HS = Hot spots.

PALEOMAGNETISM OF THE NORTH SLOPE AND THE OPENING OF THE CANADA BASIN

The tectonic history of the North Slope block has been a subject of debate since Carey (1955) cited this region as an example of possible oroclinal bending. Numerous models have been proposed on the basis of diverse geologic correlations between the North Slope and nearby regions: little or no motion of the North Slope since the Paleozoic (e.g., Churkin, 1970, 1973a,b; Herron and others, 1974; Churkin and Trexler, 1980); rifting of the North Slope from the Lomonosov Ridge in the Late Jurassic or Early Cretaceous (Dutro, 1981); dextral slip from a southerly location in the Canadian Yukon along a Tintina-Kaltag Fault System during the Early Cretaceous (Jones, 1980, 1982); approximately 70° of counterclockwise rotation away from the Canadian Arctic about a rotation pole in the Mackenzie River Delta in Late Jurassic or Early Cretaceous (e.g., Tailleur, 1969; Rickwood, 1970; Freeland and Dietz, 1973; Grantz and others, 1979; Taylor and others, 1981; Bee and others, 1984). Variations on these four models have also been proposed (see Lawer and Scotese, this volume, for a complete review).

Paleomagnetism can provide one means of testing models of oroclinal bending by comparing North Slope paleomagnetic poles to the APWP established for cratonic North America (e.g., Harrison and Lindh, 1982; Irving and Irving, 1982). However, the validity of a paleomagnetic test ultimately rests upon three fundamental criteria being satisfied by the samples: (1) that magnetic cleaning techniques (i.e., thermal and alternating-field [af] demagnetization) can isolate a direction of characteristic remanent magnetization (ChRM) free of contamination by other components (see Zijderveld, 1967, for a full discussion), (2) that the age of the ChRM is fairly well known, and (3) that the age of ChRM is relevant to the problem at hand. Timing of ChRM acquisition often may be constrained through a number of paleomagnetic tests, such as fold, reversal, and conglomerate tests.

On the Alaskan North Slope, locating rocks that satisfy these requirements has proved to be extremely challenging. The history of most rocks in the Brooks Range is complex, involving

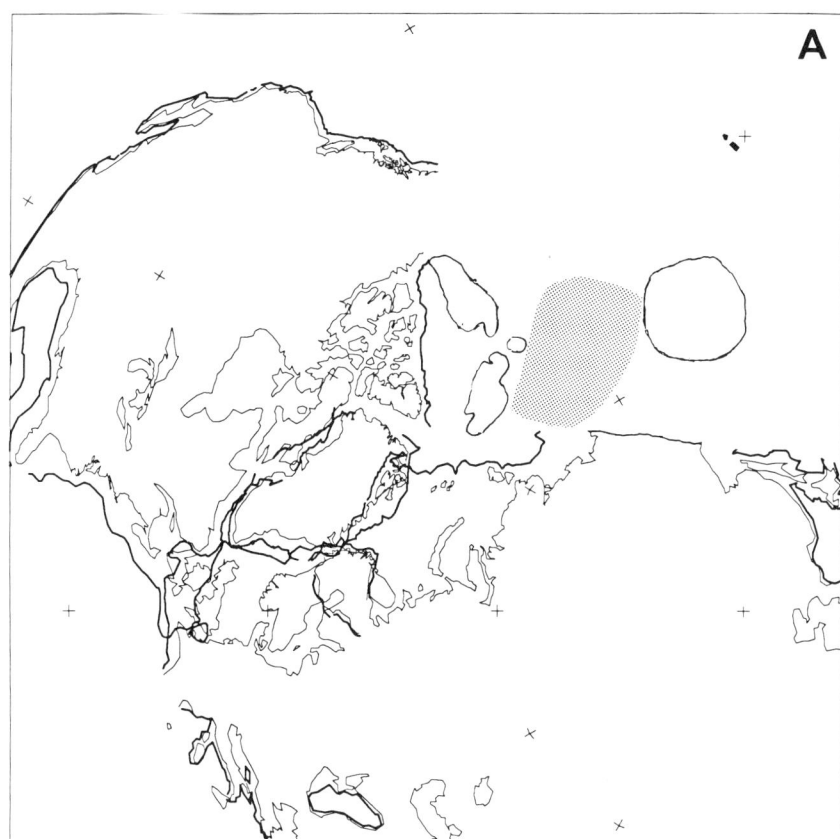

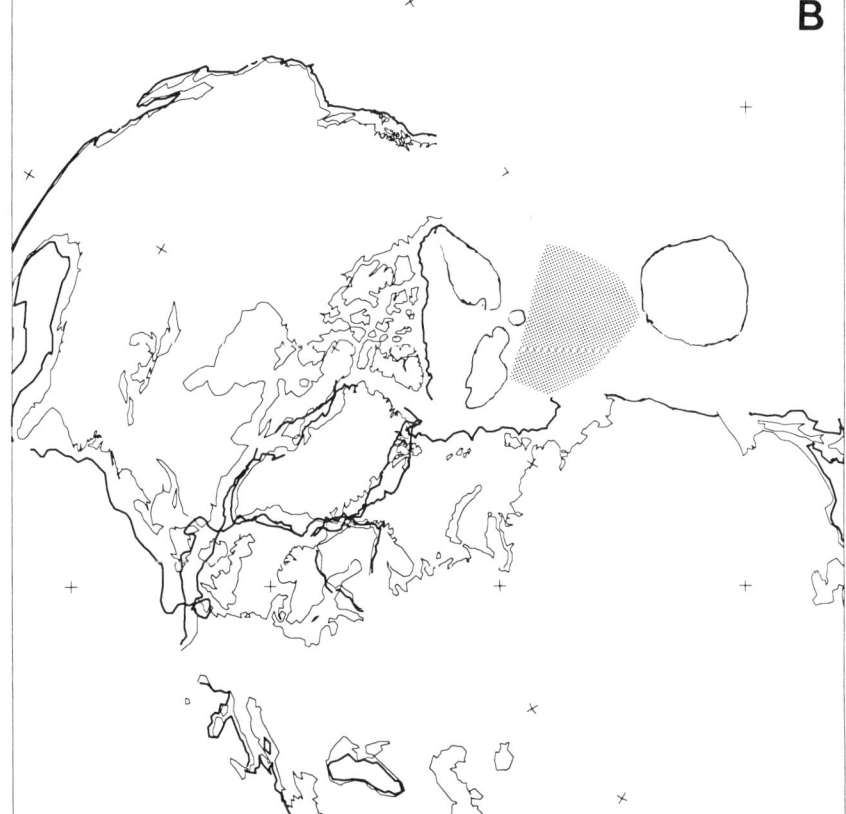

Figure 2. The reconstructions of the continental plates surrounding the Arctic in a fixed North America reference frame. In all reconstructions, the relative position of Greenland and North America is a result of the pole of Srivastava (1978). The relative position of Eurasia and North America is a result of the rotation poles that fit the APWPs. (A) The APWPs of Frei and Cox (1987) for 290 to 240 Ma. (B) The APWPs of Irving and Irving (1982) for the Late Carboniferous to Permian.

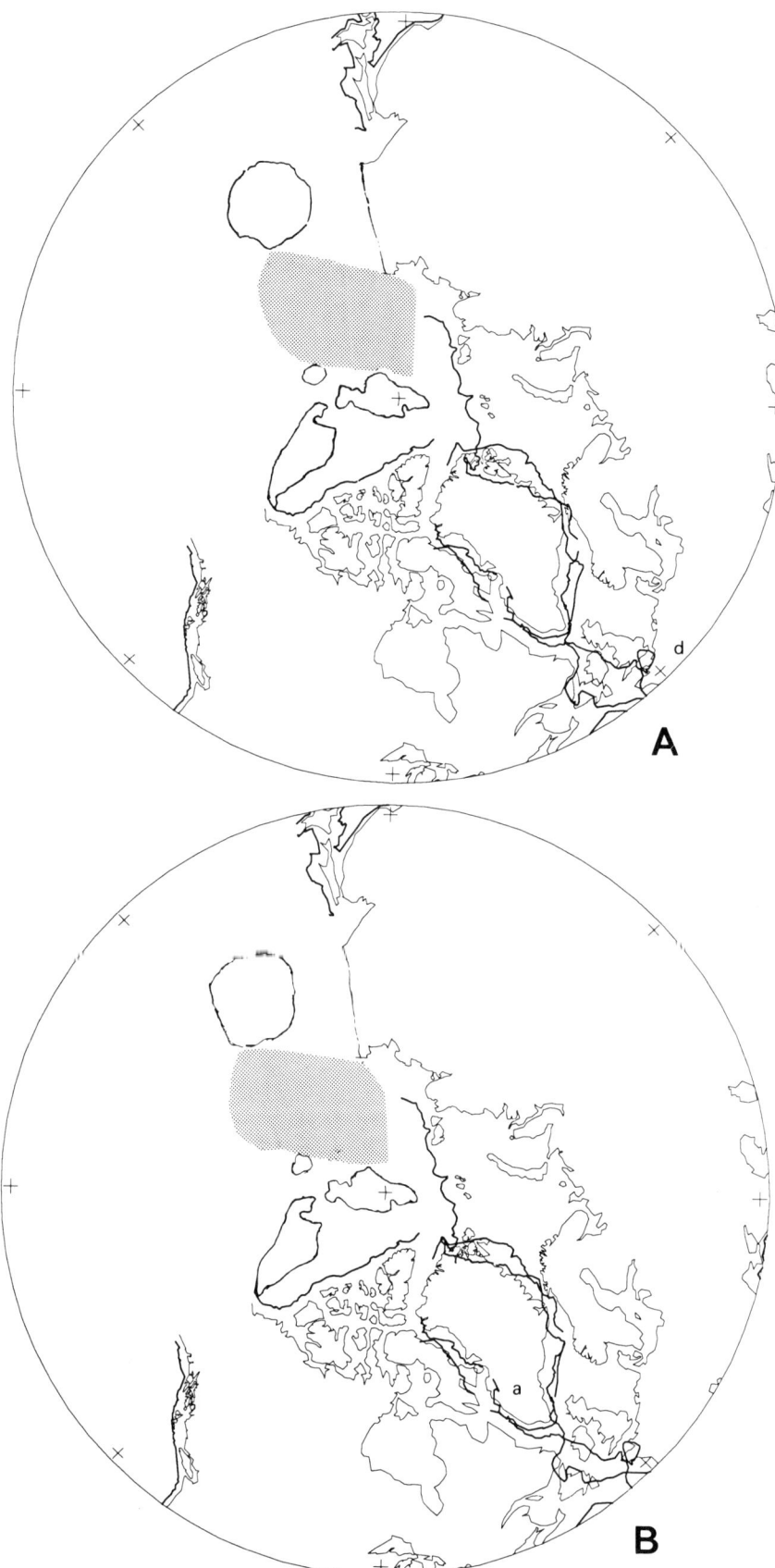

Figure 3. The reconstruction of the continental plates surrounding the Arctic. In all reconstructions, the relative position of Greenland and North America is a result of the pole of Srivastava (1978). The relative position of Eurasia and North America is a result of the rotation poles that fit the APWPs. (A) The APWPs of Frei and Cox (1987) for 290 to 240 Ma. (B) The APWPs of Irving and Irving (1982) for the Late Carboniferous to Permian. All the continental plates are then rotated to their position in a fixed hotspot reference frame, using the rotation pole of Morgan (1983), for North America at 200 Ma.

burial, thrusting, reheating, and fluid migration during the mid-Cretaceous Brookian Orogeny. Thermal alteration studies (Harris and others, 1983) show that reheating to 200°C was common throughout the Brooks Range thrust sheets. While 200°C may be far below the temperature for unblocking the remanence carried by fine-grained magnetite and hematite over laboratory time scales, prolonged heating to this temperature during 10^4 to 10^6 years in nature can be more than sufficient to reset magnetizations (Pullaiah and others, 1975; Dodson and McClelland-Brown, 1980; Halgedahl and others, 1980; Walton, 1980; Middleton and Schmidt, 1982). Also, orogenically triggered fluid migration may alter existing magnetic phases or cause precipitation of new ones; thus, even rocks exposed to conditions under which low-temperature thermal alteration indices are very low still may have been chemically remagnetized. Reset K-Ar ages of Devonian granites along the southern front of the Brooks Range place the main Brookian reheating event at about 100 to 120 Ma (Turner and others, 1979). The main phase of imbricate thrusting in the Brooks Range probably occurred prior to 100 to 120 Ma, accompanied by reheating of the lower thrust sheets during deep burial (Turner and others, 1979). Subsequent rapid erosion of the Brooks Range allowed isostatic rebound, initialization of the argon clocks, and blocking in of the reset magnetization directions. As a result, paleomagnetic studies of pre–mid-Cretaceous rocks from the Brooks Range have been plagued by thermal, and possibly chemical, remagnetization problems.

Outcrops of largely mid-Cretaceous and younger rocks along the Arctic Slope may have escaped resetting of magnetization during the Brookian Orogeny. Unfortunately, these rocks may be too young to have recorded the North Slope motion during the opening of the Canada Basin, and reversal tests of the mid-Cretaceous rocks are precluded by the long Cretaceous normal superchron. For these reasons, some of the most likely candidates for successful paleomagnetic studies may reside in pre-Cretaceous rocks in the subsurface of the northernmost North Slope. Such rocks are available in cores drilled in the North Slope.

PRE–95 Ma PALEOMAGNETIC DATA

The first paleomagnetic study of rocks from the Alaskan North Slope was conducted by Newman and others (1977), who reported results from Upper Devonian and Lower Mississippian sedimentary rocks from the Brooks Range. Their samples were collected on an east-west span of 1,000 km. They interpreted their results to indicate approximately 70° of counterclockwise rotation of the North Slope relative to the North American Craton. Unfortunately, they published no information regarding the number or location of sites, number of samples, magnetic cleaning techniques, fold or reversal tests, response of the samples to demagnetization, rock magnetic characteristics, or statistical analyses. Hillhouse and Grommé (1983) examined the unpublished Newman and others (1977) results and concluded that they failed the fold test.

Hillhouse and Grommé (1980, 1983) conducted a similar but independent study of upper Paleozoic rocks from 15 Brooks Range sites. As in the earlier study by Newman and others (1977), these rocks also failed the fold test, and their mean pole before tilt correction was not significantly different from the 100-m.y. mean pole for cratonic North America (Fig. 4A; Harrison and Lindh, 1982; Irving and Irving, 1982). Apparently, all primary magnetizations were reset by chemical alteration or reheating to moderate temperature for the duration of the orogeny. The data of Hillhouse and Grommé suggest that the North Slope has experienced little or no motion relative to North America since the mid-Cretaceous. However, some skewing of individual Brooks Range poles along a north-south direction (Fig. 4A) may have resulted from small-scale local tilting along east-west strike lines associated with rejuvenation of the Brookian Orogeny during the Late Cretaceous and Eocene (Porter, 1966; Mull, 1982).

To circumvent the reheating and remagnetization problem encountered in the Brooks Range, Hillhouse and Grommé (1983) studied two oriented cores from two NPRA wells: East Simpson No. 1 and East Simpson No. 2. Bulk treatment of the core from East Simpson No. 1 with 10 mT of peak demagnetizing alternating field gave a paleomagnetic direction not much different from that obtained before demagnetization; also, because of the large circle of confidence, the paleomagnetic direction could not be distinguished from either the present field at the wellsite or the Cretaceous direction for North America.

The East Simpson No. 2 core was more magnetically stable; although the results are difficult to interpret, magnetizations from this well may be the oldest yet obtained from the North Slope. About 10 m of core had been drilled at the wellsite, but only one downhole photograph was available for core orientation. The core consisted of steeply dipping (80° to 85°) black argillite with a distinctive reddened zone in the upper third of the core. Black and red zones give different pole positions, both of which are significantly different from the Paleozoic through Triassic APWP for cratonic North America. However, late Mesozoic remagnetization is strongly suspected in the less stable black zone (Hillhouse and Grommé, 1983; see their Fig. 4) since the circle of confidence about the paleomagnetic pole from this zone overlaps the Mesozoic portion of the North American APWP. However, contemporary VRM (Virtual Remnant Magnetization) cannot be ruled out. If hematite diagenesis occurred shortly after tilting, making the age of magnetization in the red zone Early Mississippian, then 30° to 40° of counterclockwise rotation relative to cratonic North America occurred; a substantially larger amount of rotation is implied if the remagnetization in the red zone is as young as Permo-Triassic. The uncertainty in the age of ChRM, lack of fold or reversal tests, and very limited core orientation data lead to substantial ambiguity in the interpretation of the East Simpson No. 2 paleomagnetic results.

Results leading to a very different interpretation has been reported by Witte (1982) and Witte and others (1987) from mid-Cretaceous (Albian-Cenomanian) sediments of the Nanushuk Group from the northwestern Arctic Slope. These sediments, derived from the uplifting Brooks Range, for the basal

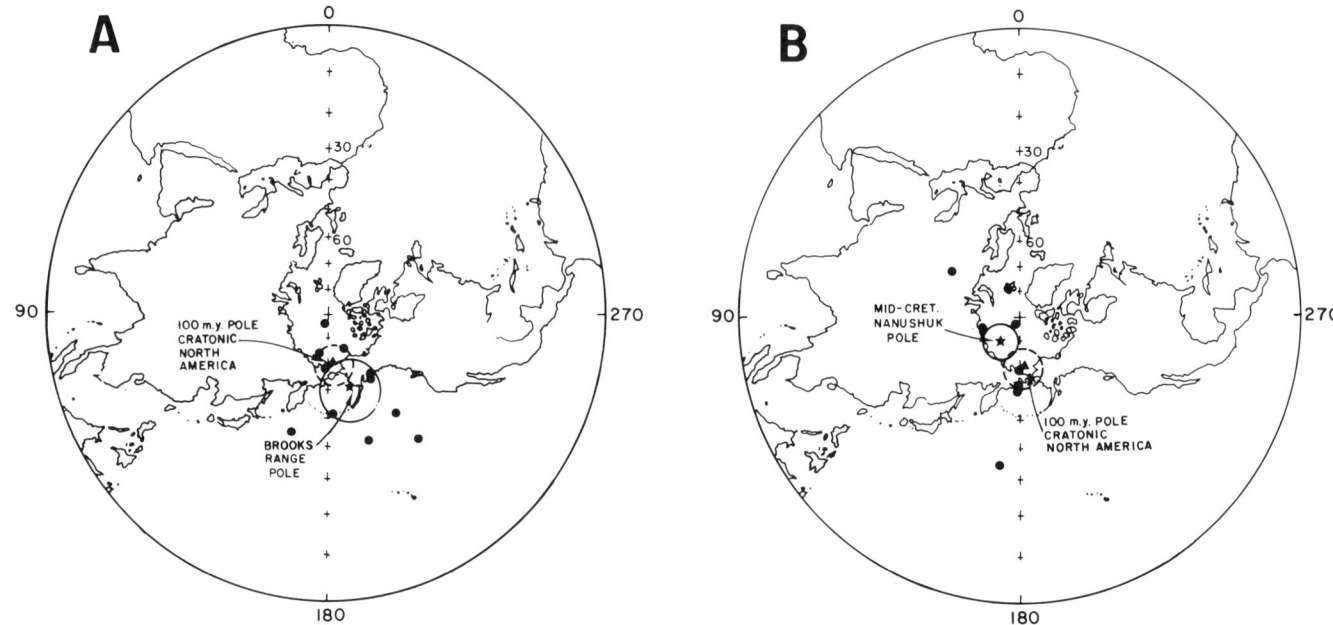

Figure 4. Paleomagnetic test of motion of the North Slope block with respect to cratonic North America during the last 100 m.y. Black dots are paleomagnetic pole positions for individual sites; star and enclosing solid circle are the mean and 95 percent confidence limits of all sites. Triangle and enclosing dashed circle are the paleomagnetic mean pole and 95 percent confidence limits for cratonic North America for 100 Ma (Harrison and Lindt, 1982). A: Paleomagnetic poles before tilt correction for Devonian sediments of the Brooks Range, thought to have been remagnetized at about 100 Ma (Hillhouse and Grommé, 1983). B: Paleomagnetic poles after tilt correction for sediments of the Nanushuk Group, deposited on the northwest Arctic Slope about 100 Ma (Witte, 1982). Note that both sets show skewed distributions of site poles, indicating that ovals of confidence would be more appropriate than the circular confidence limits assumed. Given the skewed distributions and the bracketing of the North American reference pole by the mean poles of A and B, these data suggest that the North Slope has undergone little or no significant motion with respect to cratonic North America since 100 Ma.

portion of a northeasterly prograding deltaic sequence of marine sands. They were probably deposited far enough from the Brooks Range to have escaped any reheating during the waning main phase of the Brookian Orogeny. Broad folding, which dies out northward under the Arctic Coastal Plain, occurred primarily in the Tertiary (Brosge and others, 1966); however, some folding may have been synchronous with deposition (Molenaar, 1983).

The Nanushuk was sampled at 144 localities in the extreme northwestern Brooks Range foothills. Owing to acquisition of spurious components during AF (Alternating Field) demagnetization (possibly a rotational remanent magnetization), thermal demagnetization was chosen as the most effective cleaning technique. Unfortunately, heating above 500°C resulted in irreversible changes in the magnetic properties due to chemical alteration (Witte, 1982). For this reason, it is unclear from the few vector diagrams presented by Witte (1982) whether ChRM directions were fully isolated. Within site, dip variations are generally too small for a diagnostic fold test, though at least one site clearly passes a fold test and one site fails. The combined mean of all characteristic magnetization directions from the Nanushuk does pass a fold test. However, there is significant north-south skewing of tilt-corrected site poles (Fig. 4B). This may indicate either (a) the presence of variable primary dip in these prodelta sediments (Witte, 1982; Witte and others, 1987) or (b) a small residual component of VRM acquired during the present normal polarity epoch that survived demagnetization. No reversal test is possible for these sediments, which were deposited during the Cretaceous normal superchron.

The mean pole position for the Nanushuk Group is displaced about 10° to the northwest relative to the mid-Cretaceous pole position for cratonic North America (Fig. 4B). According to the interpretation of Witte (1982) and Witte and others (1987), this difference indicates that either: (a) the sites have moved northward with respect to North America since 100 Ma from a location in the Pacific, or (b) the sites have undergone about 56° of site-centered rotation and have moved northward about 10° with respect to North America since 100 Ma. However, the difference in pole positions may not be significant in view of the overlap of the skewed distribution of Nanushuk paleomagnetic poles with the North American Cretaceous reference pole. An alternative interpretation is that both the Nanushuk and reset Brooks Range paleomagnetic poles indicate that the North Slope has experienced little motion with respect to cratonic North America since the mid-Cretaceous.

Recent paleomagnetic studies have been conducted on oriented drill core from the Kuparuk River Formation by Halgedahl and Jarrard (1987). The Kuparuk River Formation is a sequence of siltstones and fine-grained sandstones and is a major producing hydrocarbon reservoir on the North Slope. Deposition occurred in a shallow-marine environment during Early Cretaceous time; a Neocomian (Berriasian-Barremian) age has been assigned on the basis of pollen and dinoflagellates (Tabbert and Bennett, 1976). A regional erosional unconformity divides the formation into a lower member, thought to be mainly Valanginian in age, and an upper member that is mostly Hauterivian (Bennett, personal communication, 1986). The unconformity marks a sudden relative drop in sea level that may have been caused by crustal doming just prior to a rifting episode (Masterson and Paris, 1986). The lower member was derived from an unknown sediment source located to the north of the Kuparuk River field in its present location, that is, where the Canada Basin is now located (Carman and Hardwick, 1983; Masterson and Paris, 1986); thus the Kuparuk River Formation poses the sediment source problem encountered in the older, underlying rocks such as the Permo-Triassic Sadlerochit Group (Carman and Hardwick, 1983). The formation is cut by a system of numerous small-throw, northwest-southeast–trending normal faults that were active during deposition of the upper member and may have been generated by doming and rifting. Because it was deposited during the time of the M-sequence of magnetic isochrons, the Kuparuk River Formation should contain both normal and reversed polarities.

The cores examined by Halgedahl and Jarrard (1987) were drilled at three wells in the Kuparuk River oil filed on the North Slope. The core at one well was oriented only vertically, while cores from the other two wells were fully oriented with respect to geographic north. Between 90 and 150 m of virtually continuous core were available from each well, so that the formation was well represented in all three series of cores. The small dips in each of the two oriented cores were significantly different from each other, probably because of local normal faults. Core-orienting photographs were taken every 1.5 m downhole at the wellsite, and the overall reliability of the core-orienting surveys was established from three observed facts: (1) agreement of dip directions measured directly from the core with dip directions calculated from the dipmeter, (2) clustering of ChRM directions within each oriented core after correction of directions of individual samples (collected at random azimuths about the core axis) with the orienting log, and (3) good agreement between the paleomagnetic directions from the two oriented cores.

Much of the lower Kuparuk River Member (approximately the bottom half of the cored interval) revealed good magnetic stability characteristics, so that ChRM directions could be confidently isolated with AF and thermal demagnetization. Unfortunately, the upper member was much less stable, so that it was used only for a very tentative polarity assignment for defining a reversal stratigraphy. The dominant magnetic carrier was judged to be fine magnetite, on the basis of IRM (Isothermal Remanent Magnetization) acquisition curves and magnetic response at low temperatures (−196° to 20°C).

Reversal stratigraphy in the lower Kuparuk Member correlates quite well among the three cores and can be matched with chrons M14 to M11An (about 141 to 136 Ma) on the reversal time scale (Harland and others, 1982; Kent and Gradstein, 1985). Correlations in the much less magnetically stable upper member are highly tentative, although a polarity sequence that may represent chrons M11n to M9 is present. Reversal stratigraphy in the lower member of the Kuparuk River Formation is thus consistent with the Neocomian age assigned by Tabbert and Bennett (1976) on the basis of microfossils. It also strongly suggests that the characteristic remanence of the lower member has survived since the time of deposition, despite the upward migration of oil through the formation, which may have begun in the early Tertiary.

Paleomagnetic directions from the two oriented Kuparuk cores were determined mainly from the more stable lower member, most of which was of reversed polarity. Normal and reversed directions are approximately antipodal, but the small number of stable, normally magnetized samples makes a reversal test inconclusive. Correction for bedding attitude greatly improves the directional agreement between the two wells; however, a tilt test is also inconclusive since the dips are so small (2° to 6°) in the two oriented cores.

In view of the seemingly pervasive remagnetization problem on the North Slope, the possibility of remagnetization in the Kuparuk River Formation has been investigated. Since both polarities are present, it is unlikely that any remagnetization was triggered by the Brookian Orogeny, which largely coincided with the long mid-Cretaceous Normal Superchron. The most likely time of possible remagnetization was sometime in the Tertiary, when oil began to migrate upward through the section from the source rocks below. A Tertiary origin for the magnetization would require relatively substantial tilting (on the order of 15° or more to the south), Tertiary remagnetization, and a second tilting episode that would restore near-horizontal bedding attitudes. These hypothesized tilting episodes are unlikely, considering the conformable and nearly flat-lying Late Cretaceous through Tertiary stratigraphy shown on seismic sections and found in cores throughout the Kuparuk River field (Carman and Hardwick, 1983).

The mean paleomagnetic pole position for the Kuparuk River Formation both before and after bedding correction is significantly different from the APWP for cratonic North America from the Lower Cretaceous to the present day (Fig. 5A, Table 2). It is also quite far removed from the present-day magnetic pole in the Queen Elizabeth Islands. The paleolatitude derived from the mean inclination indicates that the North Slope has undergone little or no significant latitudinal displacement with respect to cratonic North American since the Kuparuk River Formation was deposited.

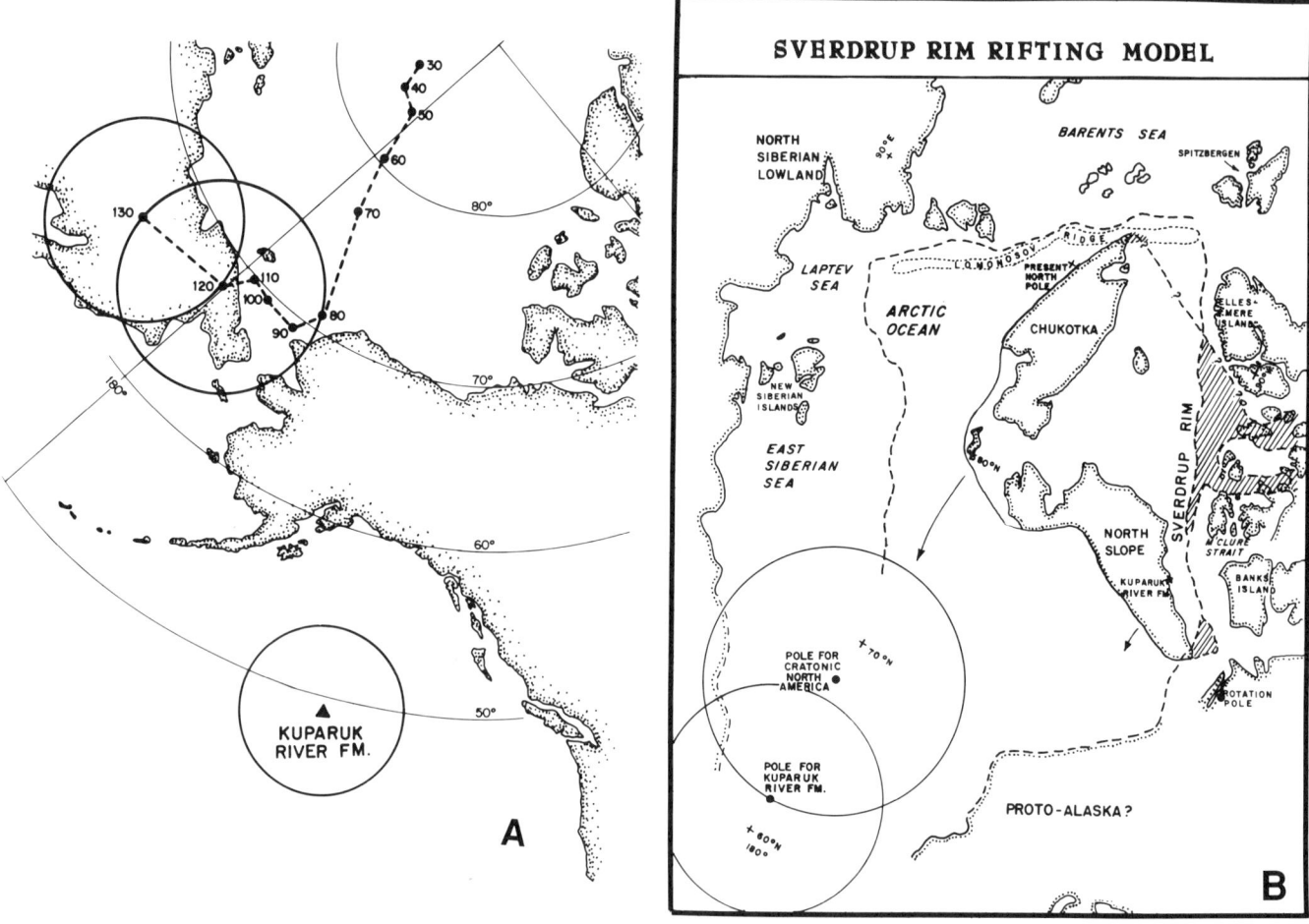

Figure 5. A: Comparison of the mean paleomagnetic pole for oriented cores of the Lower Cretaceous Kuparuk River Formation (Halgedahl and Jarrard, 1987) with the 30 to 130 Ma paleomagnetic polar path for cratonic North America (Harrison and Lindh, 1982). Note the significant difference between the two, indicating that the Alaskan North Slope has not remained in its current position with respect to cratonic North America since the Early Cretaceous. B: Earliest Cretaceous reconstruction of the Arctic region, assuming that the North Slope block was originally adjacent to the Sverdrup Rim of Arctic Canada (Tailleur, 1969, 1973), based on the finite rotation pole of Grantz and others (1979). Diagonal hachures indicate overlap of presumed continental crust. Pluses indicate present latitudes and longitudes of the North American reference frame used for the reconstruction. Note that the North Slope rotation implicit in this model brings the mean paleomagnetic pole for the Kuparuk River Formation into concordance with the reference pole for the same age from cratonic North America.

Assuming that the Kuparuk River Formation acquired its characteristic magnetization in Neocomian time, the only existing tectonic model compatible with the Kuparuk River pole position is that for approximately 66° of counterclockwise rotation of the North Slope away from Arctic Canada, about a rotation pole near the Mackenzie Delta (Fig. 5B), as hypothesized by Tailleur (1969), Grantz and others (1979) and other investigators. The reversal stratigraphy and pole position of the Kuparuk River Formation suggest that the North Slope was still adjacent to the Sverdrup Rim at about anomaly M11An time, or about 136 Ma. By this interpretation, rifting commenced shortly thereafter along the Canadian Arctic margin, with subsequent rotation of the North Slope as the Canada Basin opened. On the basis of remagnetized rocks from the Brooks Range (Fig. 4A), significant relative motion of the North Slope ceased shortly before about 100 Ma, when the North Slope block collided with the east-west oriented trench that was adjacent to what is now the Yukon-Koyukuk Basin.

POST–95 Ma PALEOMAGNETIC DATA

No North Slope paleomagnetic data have yet been reported for rocks younger than 95 Ma. However, data from adjacent

TABLE 2. PALEOMAGNETIC POLES FROM NORTHERN ALASKA

Locality	Formation	Rock Age	Proposed Age of ChRM (this paper)	No. of Sites (No. of Samples)	Lat.	Long.	k	95 or dp, dm	Tilt Corr*	Reference
E. Simpson #2 well, NPRA	Hematitic basement	pre-Miss.	<Devon.	(11)	39.2	157.5	218	4.3, 5.2	B	Hillhouse and Gromme, 1983
E. Simpson #2 well, NPRA	Argillite basement	pre-Miss.	<Devon.	(48)	57.4	154.7	11	11.1, 11.9	B	Hillhouse and Gromme, 1983
Kuparuk River wells	Kuparuk River	E. Cret.	E. Cret.	(89)	49.0	214.0	31	4.9, 5.2	A	Halgedahl and Jarrard, 1986
Brooks Range	Kanayut	L. Devon.	M. Cret.	11	59.0	197.0	16	12	B	Hillhouse and Gromme, 1983
NW Arctic Slope	Nanushuk	M. Cret.	M. Cret.	(98)	76.0	156.0	13	6.3	A	Witte, 1982
St. Matthew Is.	Unnamed volcanics	75 ± 2 Ma	75 ± 2 Ma	10	76.0	240.0	31	9	A	Wittbrodt, 1985
Yukon-Koyukuk	Unnamed sed.	m-L. Cret.	m-L. Cret. or Eoc.	12	85.0	132.0	17	11	A	Harris, 1985
Yukon-Koyukuk	Unnamed sed. and volc.	Cret.	Eocene	15	81.0	176.0	39	11, 12	B	Harris, 1985
Yukon-Koyukuk	Unnamed volcanics	Eocene	Eocene	3	55.0	213.0	5	62.0	A	Harris, 1985
E. Simpson #1 well, NPRA	Ivishak	E. Triassic	present?	(31)	66.5	240.2	9	21.2	B	Hillhouse and Gromme, 1983

*Pole position is before tilt correction (B) or after tilt correction (A).

regions may place limits on possible motions of the North Slope subsequent to 95 Ma. Various lines of evidence suggest that little or no substantial relative motion on a plate-tectonic scale has occurred between the North Slope, Seward Peninsula, and the Yukon-Koyukuk Basin since the Early Cretaceous main phase of the Brookian Orogeny. Paleomagnetic data suggesting significant amounts of northward motion must be reconciled with the present positions of these regions, as well as of any terranes that underlie the Bering Shelf.

Evidence for differential motion between part of Arctic Alaska and the North American craton subsequent to 90 Ma comes from St. Matthew Island, on the Bering Shelf (Wittbrodt, 1985). Andesitic flows and tuffs dated at about 75 Ma yield consistent directions as well as normal and reversed polarities that are approximately antipodal. Variations in tilt are not substantial enough for a diagnostic fold test. A plate-tectonic interpretation of paleomagnetic results from St. Matthew Island is dependent on whether the observed 10° average dip of formations on the island is primary or the result of subsequent tilting. If the dip is of primary origin, then the agreement of the mean paleomagnetic direction without tilt correction with the Late Cretaceous pole for North America indicates no relative motion of St. Matthew Island. In contrast, tilt correction assuming originally horizontal layering suggests about 10° of northward motion and some clockwise rotation of St. Matthew Island relative to cratonic North America since 75 Ma (Wittbrodt, 1985).

Paleomagnetic results from Cretaceous and Eocene rocks from the Navarin Basin (Van Alstine and Whitney, 1984) and the Yukon-Koyukuk (Harris, 1985a, 1985b) are also subject to several interpretations, depending on the timing of magnetization. Eocene flat-lying sediments in the Navarin Basin COST Well No. 1 yield a uniform reversed polarity and a paleolatitude that is not significantly different from that expected on the basis of the Eocene pole for North America (Van Alstine and Whitney, 1984). Underlying Campanian sediments, which dip approximately 30° to the north, are also reversely magnetized, and their mean inclination is not significantly different from that of the Eocene sediments before tilt correction. Application of a 30° tilt correction to the Campanian data leads to the interpretation that at least part of the Navarin Basin is an allochthonous terrane that has moved northward by about 30° at rates of greater than 100 mm/yr between the Campanian and the Eocene (Van Alstine and Whitney, 1984). However, an alternative and more straightforward interpretation is that the magnetization of the Cretaceous sediments was reset in the Eocene after tilting (Van Alstine, personal communication, 1986). Remagnetization also may be suggested by the lack of normal directions in the Campanian rocks, since the short Campanian stage includes both normal and reversed polarities.

In a very comprehensive study of the paleomagnetism of sedimentary and igneous rocks of the Yukon-Koyukuk province, Harris (1985a, 1985b) determined mean poles for Eocene, mid–Upper Cretaceous, and Lower Cretaceous formations. The Eocene paleomagnetic data are consistent with no motion of this region with respect to cratonic North America since the Eocene, but the lack of attitude indicators for most sites limits resolution of the Eocene data. Lower Cretaceous formations fail the fold test and yield a mean direction before tilt correction that is nearly identical with the predicted Eocene direction based on data from cratonic North America. A post-tilting Eocene remagnetization seems well established for these Lower Cretaceous formations (Harris, 1985a, 1985b).

In contrast, mid–Upper Cretaceous rocks from one of the five regions sampled by Harris (1985a; Nulato region) clearly pass the fold test. Both polarities of magnetization are observed at one site, which suggests a positive reversal test, although remagnetization circles were used to determine a final reversed-polarity direction due to a resistant secondary component. The presence of magnetite was indicated on the basis of Curie temperature. Calculations using the laboratory unblocking temperature spectra and paleotemperatures from vitrinite reflectance were performed to assess whether primary directions could have been thermally reset in nature at some later time. It was concluded that regional reheating could not have reset the Nulato magnetizations. It is important to note, however, that all time-temperature relations for magnetic unblocking developed to data apply only to single-domain particles. Whether the relations developed by Pullaiah and others (1975), Walton (1980), and others are appropriate to the Nulato rocks is unknown.

The Nulato region yields a tilt-corrected paleomagnetic direction statistically indistinguishable from the Eocene reset directions of the Lower Cretaceous units. If this magnetization was acquired in the mid–Late Cretaceous, then $19° \pm 10°$ of northward motion of Yukon-Koyukuk relative to cratonic North America is implied (Harris, 1985a, 1985b). Because the mid–Upper Cretaceous and Lower Cretaceous units studied are geographically separated, an alternative interpretation is that both were tilted and remagnetized in the Eocene, but not necessarily simultaneously. Whereas the older units were tilted and then remagnetized, the younger ones may have been remagnetized and then tilted.

Carey (1955) proposed that the Arctic, Canada, and Atlantic Basins had rotationally opened (creating Carey's "sphenochasm") together about a pivot point in the Gulf of Alaska. Tailleur (1969, 1973) later suggested that the Canada Basin had opened independently and earlier than the Arctic or Atlantic Basins. North Slope paleomagnetic data support the rotational model describing the opening of the Canada Basin. The opening of the Canada Basin beginning in the Neocomian fundamentally changed the plate geometry in the Arctic. Paleomagnetic data suggests that the North Slope was very near the geographic North Pole after rotation of the North Slope–Chukotka Terrane ended in the Aptian. An even larger change in plate configuration resulted from the opening of the North Atlantic and Eurasia Basins during the Late Cretaceous and Tertiary. Models describing the relative motions of these plates and resulting periods of deformation in eastern Siberia, Alaska, and the Canadian Arctic Islands are described in the following section. This section will show that rapid divergence in the North Atlantic in the Late Cretaceous and Paleocene resulted in convergence, uplift, erosion, and strike-slip faulting in the Alaskan and Canadian Arctic.

LATE CRETACEOUS AND TERTIARY PLATE MOTIONS IN THE NORTH ATLANTIC

In zones of continental plate convergence, the dominant tectonic style is one of widespread and complex compression (e.g., western China and the Tibetan Plateau [Molnar and Chen, 1983; Tapponnier and Molnar, 1977]). In zones of transform motion between plates (e.g., coastal California [Howell and others, 1980]), the dominant tectonic style is the development of pull-apart basins and local zones of compression along a long linear belt. In zones of divergence, the expected tectonic style is one of rifting. Alternation between these tectonic styles is to be expected if the motion between the North America and Eurasia Plates changed throughout geologic time. The relative motions of the Eurasia and North America Plates since the Cretaceous are recorded by magnetic anomalies (isochrons) and fracture zones in the North Atlantic and Arctic Oceans and in the Norwegian-Greenland and Labrador Seas (Plate 4). The geometry of the isochrons and fracture zones reflects the direction and rate of relative motion between these two plates. Pitman and Talwani (1972), Srivastava (1978), Kristoffersen (1978), Vink (1984), Karasik and others (1984), and others calculated relative motions of Eurasia and North America from the Late Cretaceous to the present. We will examine the models of Pitman and Talwani (1972), Srivastava (1978), Kristoffersen (1978), Vink (1984), Sirvastava (1985), and Srivastava and Tapscott (1986), referring to these as models PT, S-1, K, V, and S-2 respectively. The models of Srivastava (1985) and Srivastava and Tapscott (1986) are virtually identical, differing by a single total reconstruction pole. Stage poles and mean angular velocities during stages provide the basis for our estimates of the motion between Eurasia and North America as a function of time.

Pitman and Talwani (1972), model PT, calculated five total reconstruction poles in the North Atlantic for isochrons 5, 13, 21, 25, and 31, corresponding to ages of 9, 37, 48, 56, and 67 Ma, using the time scale of Harland and others (1982). Srivastava (1978), model S-1, identified isochrons 20 through 31 in the Labrador Sea and used relative motion poles from the North Atlantic and Norwegian-Greenland Sea to describe the relative movement of the Eurasia and North America Plates. Eight total reconstruction poles are given, corresponding to isochrons 13, 21, 24, 25, 31, 32, and 33 and the initial opening of the North Atlantic (37, 48, 53, 56, 67, 70, 76 and ~90 Ma). Kristoffersen (1978), model K, calculated the total rotation poles for his picks of anomalies 24, 33, 34 and initial opening of the Atlantic. To study an anomalous plateau in the Norwegian-Greenland Sea, Vink (1984), model V, used Norwegian-Greenland Sea data, triple-junction data south of Greenland, and Arctic data to calculate total reconstruction poles for North America, Greenland, and Eurasia for isochrons 23, 21, 20, 13, 6, and 5 (52, 48, 45, 37, 20, and 9 Ma) in an Iceland Hotspot fixed coordinate system. Using the absolute motion poles from Vink (1984) for North America and Eurasia, we calculated total reconstruction poles for the Eurasia Plate with respect to a fixed North America Plate.

Srivastava and Tapscott (1986) recalculated total reconstruction, and stage poles for 10, 20, 36, 50, 56, 59, 69, 80, 84, 95, and 105 Ma. The difference between the finite rotation poles presented in Srivastava (1985) and Srivastava and Tapscott (1986) is that the latter includes a 20-Ma total reconstruction pole. In this analysis, we will calculate linear velocities from the rotation poles given in Srivastava and Tapscott (1986) and refer to this as model S-2.

The relative velocity between the two plates depends critically on the identification of magnetic anomalies. Kristoffersen (1978) identified the anomaly numbered 31 by Pitman and Talwani (1972) as anomaly 33, and therefore the angular velocities produced by Kristoffersen's model are substantially smaller than those of Pitman and Talwani (1972). Srivastava (1978) agreed with Pitman and Talwani's (1972) identification of anomaly 31. In our reconstructions we have used all five models in order to assess the sensitivity of the reconstructions to the assumptions of the plate-tectonic models. Our reconstructions are for chrons 13, 21, 25, and 31 corresponding to 37, 48, 56, and 67 Ma.

The location of the boundary between the North America and Eurasia Plates at the time of interest must be known in order to determine the magnitude and direction of motion between Eurasia and Alaska from the relative motion poles. While the trend of the plate boundary we assume is important, the exact location of the boundary is not critical to the discussion that follows because the deformation associated with the convergence of these two mainly continental plates was undoubtedly not confined to a narrow suture but probably was distributed over a wide zone analogous to that caused by the convergence between Africa and Eurasia. We have used the South Anyuy suture discussed in Patton and Tailleur (1977), Fujita and Newberry (1982), and Harbert and others (1987).

The motion of Eurasia relative to North America is described by Figures 6 and 7, and the linear velocities are given in Table 3. Periods during which Eurasia was moving toward North America are interpreted as times of regional compression both along the boundary between the two plates and at points within both plates near the boundary. Similarly, periods during which Eurasia was moving away from North America are interpreted as times of regional extension, and periods during which the motion was parallel to the plate boundary are interpreted as periods of transform deformation. A combination of these motions is interpreted as periods of transpression or transtension (Harland, 1971).

Because the angle of relative motion between plates with respect to a plate boundary will be a crucial part of our interpretation, it is useful to define a specific angle beyond which transform motion becomes transpressive, an angle beyond which transpressive becomes compressive, and so on. Tectonic data listed in Harbert and others (1987) suggest that portions of plate boundaries generally considered to be transform may occur between plates with relative motion that is as much as 16° away from parallel.

In the Alaskan region, the azimuths of the motion of Eurasia relative to North America calculated from models PT and S-1 are similar but not identical. In both models, three distinct time intervals can be recognized (Figs. 7 and 8), each characterized by a different azimuth of Eurasia–North America relative motion and, presumably, a different deformational regime. From 67 to 57 Ma, the direction of motion of Eurasia relative to Alaska was east-southeast (Fig. 6, Table 3), producing sinistral transpression; from 56 to 49 Ma, the direction of motion in the model of PT was southeast, subparallel to the boundary between the two plates and therefore sinistral transform in character. In the model of S, two stage poles are given for the interval 56 to 49 Ma; for the period 56 to 54 Ma, relative motion was directed east-southeast as in the model of PT, but with a much higher (~60 mm/yr) rate of convergence; for the period 53 to 49 Ma, the relative motion vectors suggest that the boundary was dextral transform in character. In both models, northwest-directed relative motion characterizes the 48 to 38 Ma stage interval, suggesting a dominantly dextral transform boundary. From 37 to 0 Ma, the motion in both models was northeast, compressional. The main differences between results obtained using the plate models of S-1 and PT is that the latter yields rates of convergence decreasing from those of model PT from Late Cretaceous to present, whereas the former shows the highest rate of convergence occurring between 56 and 53 Ma, and a higher rate of convergence during the period of transform motion between 48 and 38 Ma (Fig. 7). The model of V is similar to that of PT and S-1. From 52 to 48 Ma, dextral transform motion is predicted, while at 48 Ma, dextral transform changes to dextral transpression. From 45 Ma to the present, compressional motion is predicted. In model V the highest rate of relative motion (24 mm/yr) occurs during the interval of dextral transform motion. Model S-2 also suggests three styles of interaction between the North America and Eurasia Plates in the Bering Sea region. Sinistral transpression of ~20 mm/yr between 105 and 56 Ma, dextral transform motion at 21 mm/yr between 56 and 50 Ma, and a final compressive stage. The main difference between models S-2 or V and model S-1 is the lower convergence rate and shorter time interval of dextral transform motion of the former models during the early Tertiary. Models S-2 and V suggest that this interval of motion ended by 50 or 48 Ma. The model produced using the rotation poles of Kristoffersen (1978) is much different. Only two stages are recognized. Linear velocities from 48 Ma to the present suggest dextral transpression motion, and from 67 to 49 Ma suggest sinistral transpression.

RELATION OF CONTINENTAL MOTIONS TO TECTONICS IN THE BERING SEA REGION

We will now consider in the light of plate motions the tectonic evolution of the Bering Shelf, including deformation in the Chukotsk–Seward Peninsula regions, movement along the Denali Fault, uplift and erosion of the western Brooks Range and Alaska Range during the early Tertiary, and counterclockwise rotation of western Alaska. We will see that a better fit to regional tectonics is provided by plate models PT, S-1, S-2, and V than by model K.

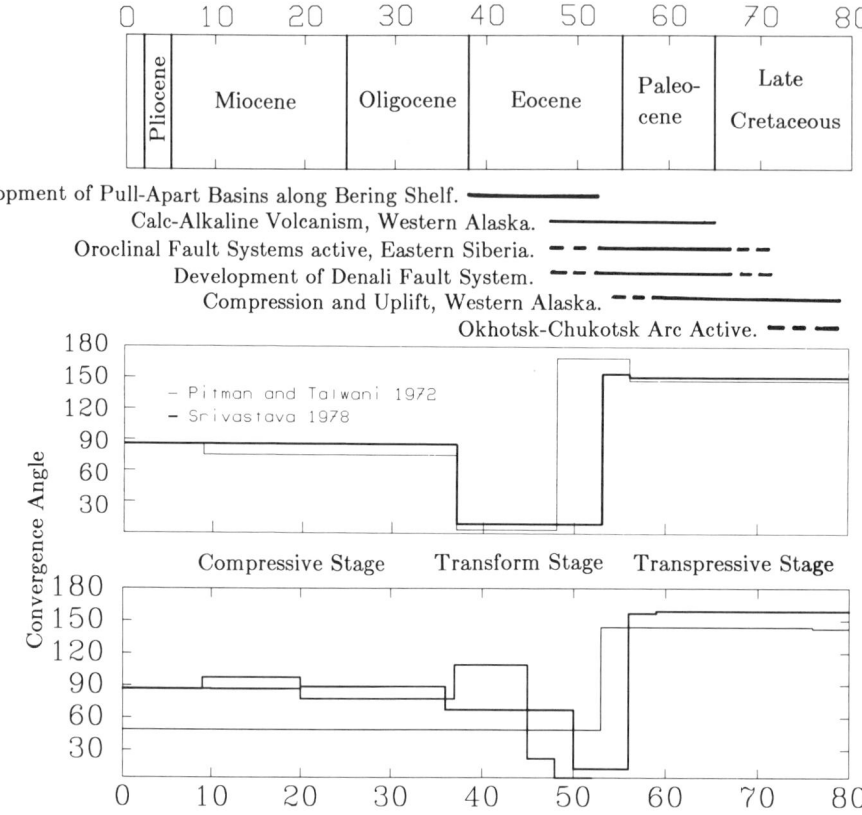

Figure 6. Angle of convergence between the Eurasia plate and the Bering Shelf margin. The oceanic crust of the Aleutian Basin is assumed to have been coupled to the Eurasia Plate after the formation of the Aleutian Arc at about 56 Ma. Linear velocity vectors are calculated for a point along the North America–Eurasia plate boundary near the St. George Basin (lat. 56°N, long. 193°E), using the models of Pitman and Talwani (1972), Srivastava (1978), Kristoffersen (1978), and Vink (1984) The angles describe the azimuth relative to the trend of the margin of the Bering Shelf at a point on the Eurasia Plate as seen in a North America fixed reference frame. A convergence angle of 0° describes perfect right-lateral transform motion of the Eurasia Plate relative to the margin of a stationary Bering Shelf. Events in the Bering Sea region are plotted above. Linear velocities are in mm/yr and convergence angles are in degrees east of north between the Eurasia and North America Plates.

Transpressive stage

In models PT, S-1, and S-2 the movement of the Eurasia Plate for the period 67 to 57 Ma is to the east-southeast, toward the North America Plate, at a rate of approximately 21 to 50 mm/yr (Fig. 7). The expected tectonic effect—west-northwest to east-southeast convergence between the cratons and compression between the respective accreted terranes—provides a plausible causal mechanism for the counterclockwise oroclinal bending of western Alaska during the early Tertiary, which was proposed by Carey (1955), elaborated by Freeland and Dietz (1973), and confirmed paleomagnetically by Globerman and Coe (1984). The regional compression may also have helped activate the Denali Fault system and other strike-slip fault systems in Alaska during the early Tertiary (Grantz, 1966; Freeland and Dietz, 1973) in a manner analogous to that of the activation of strike-slip faults in Asia by the collision of India with Asia. The timing of this compression agrees well with the late Mesozoic to early Tertiary compressive deformation of the Chukotsk Peninsula and northern Alaska (Patton and Tailleur, 1977; Nilsen and Patton, 1984), with uplift and retrograde metamorphism in the Seward Peninsula (Thurston, 1985), with the compression and thrusting in the southwest-central Brooks Range (Hitzman, 1983), with the initiation of the Eurekan Orogeny in the Canadian Arctic Islands, and with the formation of fault-controlled channels of the southeastern Queen Elizabeth Islands (Kerr, 1978; Balkwill, 1978; Balkwill and others, 1983; Jackson, 1985; Srivastava, 1985). In the Anyuy fold belt, this period of convergence may have initiated reactivation of the "oroclinal fault system" of Kosygin and Parfenov (1981) and produed compressional deformation in the

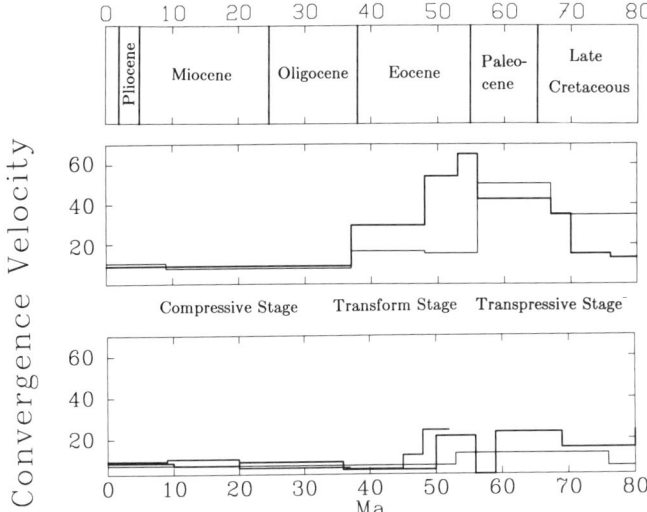

Figure 7. Rate of convergence velocity between the Eurasia Plate and The Bering Shelf (assumed fixed to the North America Plate). The oceanic crust of the Aleutian Basin is assumed to have been coupled to the Eurasian Plate. Note that the models of Srivastava (1978) and Vink (1984) predict relatively high rates of motion between the North America and Eurasia Plates along the Bering shelf margin during the early Eocene. The model of Pitman and Talwani (1972) predicts decreasing velocities through the Tertiary. The model of Kristoffersen (1978) predicts uniformly small velocities during the Late Cretaceous and Tertiary.

Anadyr, Anyuy, and Novasibirski regions. This period of convergence appears to have been accompanied by widespread early Tertiary uplift and erosion throughout western Alaska, as evidenced by (1) the general absence of Paleocene rocks in western Alaska in general (Burk, 1965), in the western Brooks Range (Grantz and others, 1979), and in the Canadian Arctic Islands (Kerr, 1981; Sobczak, 1982); (2) the presence of coarse conglomerates in the Paleocene Cantwell Formation of the Alaska Range (Wolfe and Wahrhaftig, 1968); and (3) the presence of coarse sediments in the Cook Inlet area in strata such as the Chickaloon Formation (Fisher and Magoon, 1978).

Transform stage

The motion of Eurasia relative to North America during the interval from ~56 through 50 to 38 Ma was approximately parallel to the Bering margin in models PT, S-1, and S-2, which suggests a dextral transform boundary during this interval. The motion was to the southeast from 56 to 54 Ma in model S-1 and to the east-southeast from 56 to 49 Ma in model PT. The motion changed to northwest at 53 Ma in model S-1 and at 48 Ma in model PT (Fig. 6). During the Paleocene the Aleutian subduction zone was probably initiated (Scholl and others, 1975; Rubinstone, 1984a,b), and as a result, a piece of Izanagi oceanic crust

TABLE 3. LINEAR VELOCITIES CALCULATED AT A POINT NEAR THE NAVARIN BASIN*

A_1	A_2	V	Strike	V_N	V_E
9	0	10.5	41.5	7.9	7.0
37	9	7.9	30.0	6.8	3.9
48	37	16.7	307.9	10.3	-13.2
56	48	15.5	137.6	-11.5	10.5
67	56	50.4	106.6	-14.4	48.3
83	67	34.7	106.6	-9.9	33.2

A_1	A_2	V	Strike	V_N	V_E
37	0	9.0	41.6	6.7	6.0
48	37	29.6	305.0	17.0	-24.2
53	48	54.0	305.9	31.7	-43.7
56	53	64.9	113.6	-26.0	59.4
67	56	42.6	110.7	-15.1	39.9
70	67	35.1	110.7	-12.4	32.8
76	70	15.2	110.8	-5.4	14.2
90	76	13.1	110.7	-4.7	12.3

A_1	A_2	V	Strike	V_N	V_E
53	0	7.9	6.7	7.8	0.9
76	53	14.2	93.1	-0.8	14.2
85	76	7.6	92.0	-0.3	7.6
90	85	23.6	94.1	-1.7	23.6

A_1	A_2	V	Strike	V_N	V_E
9	0	10.6	41.3	7.9	7.0
20	9	11.4	50.6	7.2	8.8
37	20	6.8	32.5	5.7	3.7
45	37	7.0	61.8	3.3	6.1
48	45	12.4	342.5	11.9	-3.7
52	48	23.9	309.4	15.2	-18.5

A_1	A_2	V	Strike	V_N	V_E
10	0	8.6	37.1	6.9	5.2
20	10	7.3	37.0	5.8	4.4
36	20	9.1	38.9	7.1	5.7
50	36	5.3	17.3	5.1	1.6
56	50	21.4	322.7	17.0	13.0
59	56	3.1	106.9	0.9	3.0
69	59	23.3	109.0	-7.6	22.0
80	69	15.8	109.0	-5.1	14.9
84	80	24.0	109.0	-7.8	22.7
95	84	10.6	109.0	-3.5	10.0
105	95	11.6	108.9	-3.8	11.0

*Models used for the opening of the North Atlantic are those of Pitman and Talwani (1972), Srivastava (1978), Kristoffersen (1978), Vink (1984), and Srivastava and Tapscott (1986). A1 and A2 show the stage ages over which this direction and rate of motion are calculated. V is magnitude of relative motion between North America and Eurasia in mm/yr. Strike is the azimuth of motion (positive to the east), and V_N and V_E are the northerly and easterly components of motion in mm/yr. Motions are calculated going forward in time from older to younger ages.

TABLE 4. LINEAR VELOCITIES OF OCEANIC PLATES
RELATIVE TO NORTH AMERICA PLATE AT
KODIAK ISLAND*

Site	
Kodiak Island	
Lat. 58°N	Long. 208°E

Pacific Plate		
Age(Ma)		Vector
from	to	azimuth	speed
0	5	334	72
5	9	319	54
9	17	320	53
17	28	327	52
28	37	331	46
37	43	343	49
*43	48	24	84
*48	66	35	99

Kula Plate		
Age(Ma)		Vector
from	to	azimuth	speed
43	48	359	206
48	56	3	213
56	61	20	124
61	66	12	146
66	74	6	158
74	85	347	167

Farallon Plate N.O.M.[1]		
Age(Ma)		Vector
from	to	azimuth	speed
*74	85	6	118
85	100	12	111
100	115	36	32
115	119	21	59
119	127	57	108
127	135	50	102
135	145	105	39
145	161	67	92
161	163	80	115
163	180	82	119

Farallon Plate S.O.M.[2]		
Age(Ma)		Vector
from	to	azimuth	speed
85	100	7	137
100	115	9	59
115	119	9	90

*Azimuth in degrees; speed in km/m.y.
[1]Farallon Plate velocity determined from isochrons north of the Mendocino Fracture Zone.
[2]Farallon Plate velocity determined from isochrons south of the Mendocino Fracture Zone.

was trapped in the Aleutian Basin (Cooper and others, 1976; Ben-Avraham and Cooper, 1981; Cooper and others, 1981). In the models of PT, S-1, and K, the Eurasia Plate has a large component of northward motion relative to North America during the ~50 to 38 Ma stage. Models S-2 and V predict lower velocity dextral transform motion ending between 48 and 50 Ma. The lack of marginal basins or extensional features along the Koryak-Kamchatka margin suggests that sutured oceanic crust trapped in the Aleutian Basin was coupled to the Eurasia plate after initiation of subduction along the Aleutian Arc.

While each basin along the Bering Shelf is unique and the evolution of each is complex, the general development of the basins suggests right-lateral transform motion along the Bering Shelf. The well-studied Neogene basins in western California (Blake and others, 1978; Graham and others, 1984) provide an interesting analogue. Model S-1 predicts linear velocities of ~50 to 30 mm/yr during the interval from 53 to 38 Ma. Models S-2 and V predict linear velocities of ~20 mm/yr from 56 to 50 or 48 Ma. These convergence values are comparable with the velocity of 55 mm/yr between the Pacific and North America Plates along the southern Californian coast today. Along the Californian coast, broad Paleogene bathymetric lows were replaced by deep localized Neogene basins after the onset of transform motion. The same pattern of basin evolution may well have occurred along the Bering Shelf. Broad bathymetric lows that existed during the Late Cretaceous and early Teritary were segmented and replaced by deep localized basins, such as the St. George Basin, during the middle Eocene to middle Oligocene (McLean, 1979; Turner and others, 1983, 1984a,b). If the analogy with Neogene basin development along western California is correct, sedimentation and facies patterns of increasing complexity would be expected during this interval of active wrench tectonics (Blake and others, 1978; Reading, 1980; Graham and others, 1984).

Compressive stage

From 37 to 0 Ma the motion of Eurasia relative to North America was directed to the northeast at a low rate (~10 mm/yr). An expected result is compressive deformation of sediments deposited within the pull-apart basins of the Bering Shelf. Models for the present-day plate boundary between the Eurasia and North America Plates have been presented in Chapman and Solomon (1976), Minster and Jordan (1978), and Savostin and Karasik (1981). Although intermediate microplates between the North America and Eurasia Plates have been proposed (Minster and others, 1974; Stone, 1982), the zones of present seismicity are usually interpreted to show that the present-day North America Plate extends nearly to the Verkhoyansk Mountains (Chapman and Solomon, 1976; Minster and Jordan, 1978; Savostin and Karasik, 1981). Recent extension-related volcanism (Moll and Patton, 1984) and sedimentary grabens in western Alaska (Lockhard, 1984) are not well understood in the context of compressive deformation.

The relative motions of the Eurasia and North America

Plates in the Arctic resulted in a major period of compressive deformation. In the following section we review models for plate motions of the oceanic plates in the Pacific Basin with respect to the North American Plate since the time of rifting of the North Slope–Chukotka Terrane away from the Canadian Arctic Islands. These models describe motions beginning in the Berriasian. It is important to review these motions because they play a dominant role in the plate tectonics of this region and because of the presumed presence of an island arc between the Izanagi and Farallon Plates. This arc may have collided with eastern Siberia and Alaska

LATE MESOZOIC AND CENOZOIC OCEANIC PLATE MOTIONS IN THE PACIFIC BASIN

Relative motion between the continental North American and the Pacific plates currently produces volcanism along the Kuril-Aleutian island arc and strike-slip deformation along the Queen Charlotte Fault and strike-slip along the extreme western Aleutian Arc west of Buldir Island (Scholl and others, 1975). Arc magmatism, quiescence, and strike-slip deformation are expected because the relative motion of oceanic plates (Izanagi, Kula, and Pacific) has changed with respect to the North America Plate. The Euler poles describing the relative motion of these oceanic plates with respect to North America and Eurasia have been described in Engebretson and others (1984, 1985).

Two major plate reorganizations are reflected in the oceanic plate motion vectors. The first began with a dramatic increase in the relative velocity of the Kula Plate with respect to North America at about 56 Ma, the result of rapid spreading on the Kula-Pacific Ridge. After spreading ceased on the Kula-Pacific Ridge (40 to 43 Ma), the Kula and Pacific Plates acted as a single composite plate (Byrne, 1979). The second plate reorganization resulted in a major change in motion of the composite Kula/Pacific Plate at about 43 Ma, as indicated by a sharp change in the trend of the hotspot-generated Emperor-Hawaii seamount chain (Dalrymple and others, 1977).

In summary, it is most likely that the plates interacting with Alaska were the Farallon prior to about 85 Ma, the Kula from then until the demise of the Kula-Pacific Ridge, and the composite Kula/Pacific Plate from then until the present. At about 85 Ma, there probably was an eastward jump of the ridge separating the ancestral Kula Plate (the "Izanagi" Plate) from the Farallon Plate. This ridge jump greatly enlarged the Kula Plate at the expense of the Farallon Plate, and probably caused the end of Farallon-Alaska interaction and the start of Kula-Alaska interaction (Engebretson and others, 1985). This scenario is emphasized in the following discussion, in which reconstructions of the Pacific Basin are presented for three ages.

56 Ma (chron 25)

The location of the Kula-Farallon boundary, which is not limited by marine data, during the Late Cretaceous and early

TABLE 5. LINEAR VELOCITIES OF OCEANIC PLATES RELATIVE TO FIXED EURASIA PLATE AT A SITE IN THE KORYAK MOUNTAINS[†]

Site	
Eastern Koryak Mtns.	
Lat. 62°N	Long. 175°E

Kula Plate			
Age(Ma)		Vector	
from	to	azimuth	speed
43	48	325	164
48	53	334	158
53	56	319	220
56	61	331	135
61	66	32	157
66	74	316	177
74	85	301	203

Izanagi Plate			
Age(Ma)		Vector	
from	to	azimuth	speed
*85	95	9	208
*95	100	16	222
*100	115	40	193
*115	119	32	192
*119	127	27	183
*127	135	23	266
*135	145	4	18

Farallon Plate N.O.M.[(1)]			
Age(Ma)		Vector	
from	to	azimuth	speed
*85	95	310	116
*95	100	317	94
*100	115	14	10
*115	119	328	37
*119	127	4	111
*127	135	357	107
*135	145	55	38
*145	161	28	75
*161	163	41	100
*163	180	41	108

Farallon Plate S.O.M.[(2)]			
Age(Ma)		Vector	
from	to	azimuth	speed
*85	95	305	131
*95	100	308	109
*100	115	293	24
*115	119	306	56

[†]Azimuth in degrees; speed in km/m.y.
*Asterisk indicates that either the Farallon or the Izanagi Plate could be present during these times.
[(1)]Farallon Plate velocity determined from isochrons north of the Mendocino Fracture Zone.
[(2)]Farallon Plate velocity determined from isochrons south of the Mendocino Fracture Zone.

Tertiary, is crucial to the present analysis. Engebretson and others (1985) adopted the interpretation of Wood and Davies (1982) that the Kula Plate broke from the ancestral Farallon Plate at about 85 Ma and that subsequent Kula-Pacific spreading produced the east-west magnetic lineations south of the Aleutian Trench. In northern Washington and British Columbia the presence of northwest-trending faults with large amounts of Cretaceous dextral motion suggests a tectonic driving force with a strong northward component. This style of deformation would be consistent with a Kula Plate that extended at least as far south as northern Washington in latest Cretaceous time. This observation prompted Engebretson and others (1985) to constrain the Kula-Farallon spreading center at 65 Ma to intersect the continental margin in southern Washington and to connect this control point to the Pacific-Farallon-Kula triple junction with a single great-circle ridge. Using the known Euler poles for Kula-Pacific and Farallon-Pacific motion to derive a pole for Kula-Farallon motion and assuming symmetrical spreading, Engebretson and others (1985) modelled the generation of oceanic lithosphere by Kula-Farallon spreading and found that the North America–Farallon–Kula triple junction ranged between northern California and northern Washington from 85 to 56 Ma.

Similarly, the location of the Kula-Pacific boundary is not constrained by ocean-floor data. We have followed Hilde and others (1977) in making the boundary a northwest-trending transform. In the model of Engebretson and others (1985) the trend of the transform (although not its location) is determined by the Euler pole for the Kula-Pacific motion. The assumption behind the Pacific boundary as drawn in Figure 8 is that the Pacific Plate was moving toward a subduction zone along its northwest boundary where, presumably, a slab attached to the plate was providing slab pull to drive the plate. This geometry is characteristic of all present plates having high velocities relative to hotspots (Gordon and others, 1978).

110 Ma (Albian, middle of Cretaceous Normal Superchron)

Although magnetic anomalies older than 85 Ma in the northwestern Pacific have been attributed to spreading between the Pacific Plate and an ancestral Kula Plate, Woods and Davies (1982) pointed out that there is no evidence that the post–85 Ma and pre–85 Ma plates were even continuous. They proposed that the older plate to the west be called the Izanagi Plate. The analysis of Engebretson and others (1984, 1985) supports this interpretation. In the reconstructions of Engebretson and others (1985), plates of pre–85 Ma age west of the ancestral Farallon Plate are referred to as the Izanagi Plate or plates.

Engebretson and others (1985) suggest the following plate geometry for the northern Pacific Basin prior to 85 Ma. To the east lay an ancestral Farallon Plate, including the northern segment that broke away at 85 Ma to form the Kula Plate. To the west lay the Izanagi Plate or plates. The following information is available concerning the nature of the boundaries between the three plates. The time of the reconstruction of Figure 8B, 110 Ma, lies within the Cretaceous normal polarity superchron (118 to 83 Ma), so no isochrons are available to mark the Izanagi, Farallon, or Pacific Plate boundaries. However, well-defined isochrons were produced by Pacific-Farallon spreading both before and after the Cretaceous Normal Superchron. So there is little doubt that the Pacific-Farallon boundary was a ridge at 110 Ma. The ridge's location was found by interpolation. The Pacific-Izanagi boundary produced a magnetic anomaly at the beginning of the Cretaceous Normal Superchron, which shows that it was a ridge at 119 Ma.

To investigate the nature of the Izanagi-Farallon boundary, velocity fields in a fixed hotspot reference frame were plotted for both plates. The two velocity fields converge along almost any boundary drawn between the Izanagi and Farallon Plates except for a short segment of boundary south of the Izanagi-Farallon rotation pole. Therefore, the boundary is dominantly convergent. To determine which of the two plates is subducting along this boundary, Engebretson and others (1985) examined the velocity of the Izanagi Plate in the hotspot reference frame and noted that it was high and directed toward the boundary, whereas that of the Farallon Plate in the vicinity of the boundary was low. Rapidly moving, present-day oceanic plates are all attached to downgoing slabs and are moving toward the trenches where the slabs are being subducted (Gordon and others, 1978), whereas present-day upper plates generally have low velocities relative to hotspots. Therefore, it seems likely that the Izanagi Plate was the subducting plate and the Farallon was the upper plate at the boundary between the two plates (see Fig. 8); although, as noted earlier, the location of this boundary is highly uncertain. The location of the Izanagi-Farallon boundary is not well determined and could lie well to the east of the position shown in Figure 8.

140 Ma (Berriasian, chron M14)

The Pacific-Izanagi and Pacific-Farallon boundaries are known to have been spreading centers at this time because of the presence on the Pacific Plate of magnetic anomalies produced along these ridges. Velocity fields for the Izanagi and Farallon

Figure 8. Reconstructions in a fixed hotspot reference frame for early Cretaceous (140 Ma), mid-Cretaceous (110 Ma) and Eocene (56 Ma) times. Double heavy lines: ridge boundaries between oceanic plates (dashed where inferred). Single heavy lines: transforms (dashed where inferred). Arows: motion of plates as determined from stage poles for the time intervals shown in parentheses; arrow length indicates 10 m.y. of motion. Dots: Yellowstone (Y) and Hawaiian (H) Hotspots. Diagonal shading: lithosphere that could be either Farallon or Kula Plate. Barbed arcs: island arc inferred from convergence of Farallon and Izanagi velocity vectors—solid barbs when arc was active, open barbs when inactive. Squares: Euler stage poles for oceanic plate pairs (PA-KU = Pacific-Kula; IZ-FA = Izanagi-Farallon) shown in present coordinates in fixed hotspot reference frame. NA, North America Plate; SA, South America Plate; EU, Eurasia Plate.

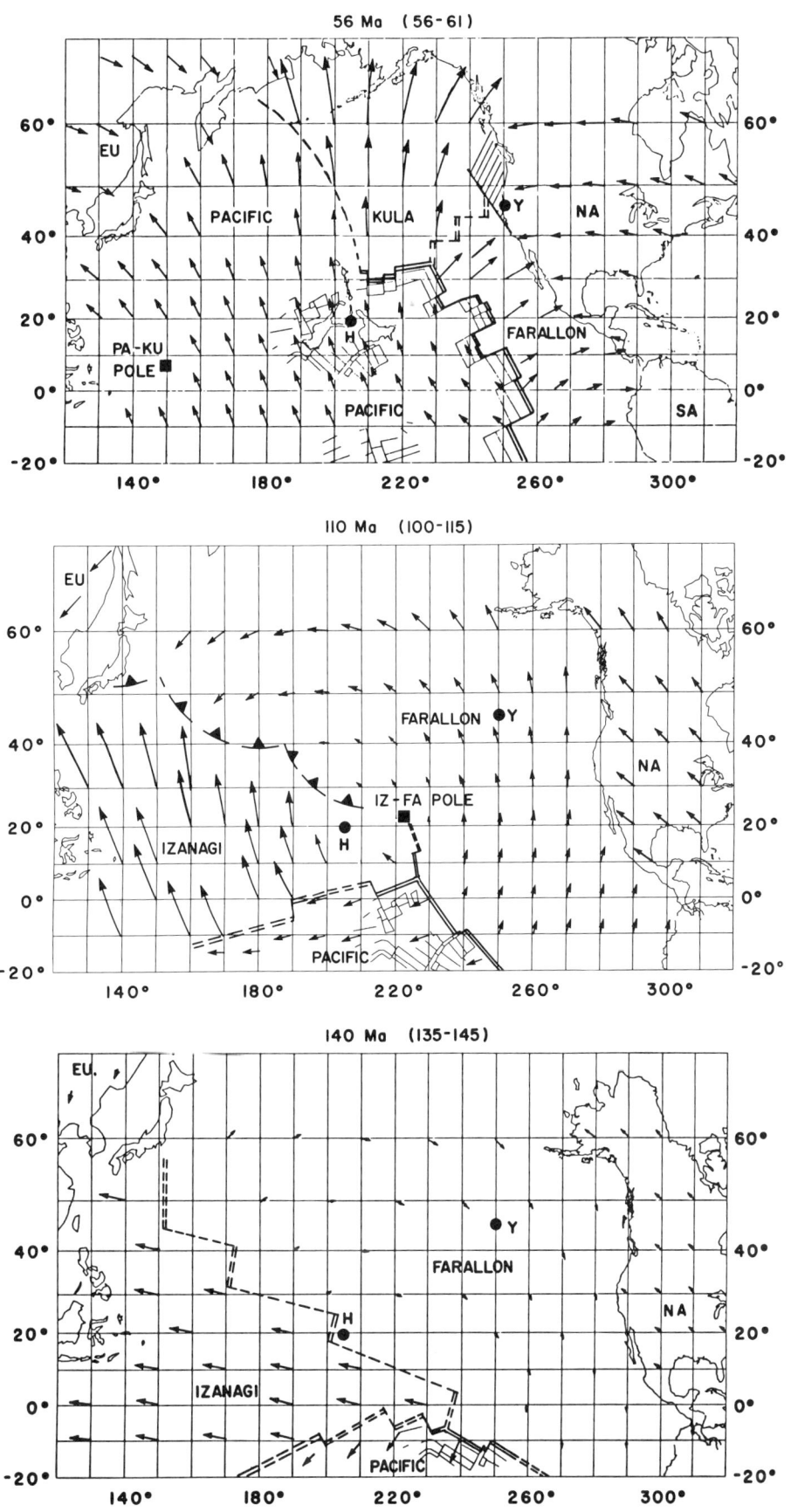

Plates in a fixed hotspot reference frame show that the motion of the two plates was oblique, which suggests that the Izanagi-Farallon boundary was dominantly transform in character. In going from the reconstruction for 140 Ma to that for 110 Ma, Engebretson and others (1985) were guided by a suggestion of Uyeda and Yamano (1984) that a subduction zone may originate along the locus of an earlier transform.

Comparison of the timing of magmatic events in southwestern Alaska with the timing of changes in motions of the oceanic plates that interacted with southern Alaska shows some clear coincidences: (1) major magmatism occurred in the Alaska Range, Kuskokwim Mountains, and Gulf of Alaska belts during a period of rapid north-northeastward motion of the Kula Plate from about 74 to 56 Ma, and (2) magmatic quiescence occurred throughout southwestern Alaska and the eastern Siberia during a period of plate reorganization from about 56 to 43 Ma, a period that began with extremely rapid northward motion of the Kula Plate (Wallace and Engebretson, 1984). The beginning of the formation of the Canada Basin between 155 and 133 Ma corresponds to a major change in the absolute motion of the Farallon Plate in the Arctic Basin. At 135 Ma the absolute motion of the Farallon Plate changes from motion toward the Canadian Arctic Islands to motion away from this margin. Hence, the formation of the Canada Basin may have been triggered by a change in the absolute motion of the Farallon Plate.

SUMMARY

Paleomagnetic and isochron data constrain tectonic models of the Arctic Basin. Apparent Polar Wander Paths from the Eurasia and North America Plates suggest that a substantial gap existed between these plates before the formation of the Canada Basin began in the Neocomian. Paleomagnetic data from oriented drill cores from the North Slope suggest that the North Slope was originally situated along the Sverdrup Rim (Halgedahl and Jarrard, 1986). Beginning at about Barremian time, the North Slope rifted away from Arctic Canada and formed the Canada Basin. The North Slope rotated approximately 70° about a rotation pole located in the Mackenzie River Delta. Motion ceased in the mid-Cretaceous, when collision between the North Slope and a trench to the south triggered the Brookian Orogeny and reset paleomagnetic pole positions of the thrust sheets to the Cretaceous pole for cratonic North America. Evidence for counterclockwise rotation of the North Slope from the Canadian Arctic is compatible with: (1) the apparent northerly sediment source of many of the late Paleozoic through Early Cretaceous rocks on the North Slope, and (2) the presence of an east-west-striking trench to the south near what is now the Yukon-Koyukuk Basin, and (3) continuity of the Brooks Range with the mid-Cretaceous suture zones in the northeastern USSR.

The relative motion between the North America and Eurasia Plates provides an explanation for the timing and style of some of the observed deformational events in the Bering Sea region. A period of strong convergence (~70 to ~50 Ma, Upper Cretaceous to middle Eocene) correlates well with compressional deformation in the Chukotsk Peninsula and northern Alaska responsible for the observed deflection in structural trends between northern Alaska, the Seward and Chukotsk Peninsulas, and uplift and erosion in the Sverdrup Basin and the Canadian Arctic Islands. The compression may have initiated movement along the Denali Fault and other fault systems in both Alaska and northeastern Siberia, and produced counterclockwise bending of western Alaska. Widespread erosion and deposition of formations such as the Cantwell and Chickaloon may have been caused by uplift related to Eurasia–North America convergence. Transtensional motion between the Eurasia and North America Plates (56 to 48 through 50 to 38 Ma, Eocene) provides an explanation for the observed subsidence of the Bering Shelf and development of a series of pull-apart basins along the Bering margin.

Motions of the oceanic plates in the Pacific Basin correlate with magmatism and magmatic quiescence in southwestern Alaska and northeastern USSR. The rotational opening of the Canada Basin correlates with a major change in North America–Farallon relative motion. At 140 Ma, the Farallon Plate was converging toward the North Slope–Chukotka–Canadian Arctic Islands margin. At 135 Ma the absolute motion changed to divergence away from the North America Plate. Both the overriding (North America) and underthrusting (Farallon) plates are moving in a roughly parallel direction, in the absolute reference frame the Farallon Plate was moving away from the North America–Farallon plate boundary. This change in Farallon–North America motion may have triggered rifting in the Canada Basin. Oceanic plate motions also suggest the presence of a poleward-moving island arc between the Farallon and Izanagi Plates in the Cretaceous.

REFERENCES CITED

Alekeseyev, E. S., 1981, The Kuyul' Serpentinite Mélange and the structure of the Talovsk-Mayna Zone (Koryak Highlands): Geotectonics, v. 26, p. 68–78.

Arkhipov, Y., Volkodav, V., Kamaletdinov, I. G., and Yan-Zhinshiv, V. A., 1981, Overthrust in the western part of the Verkhoyansk-Chukchi Folded Area: Geotectonics, v. 15, p. 148–161.

Balkwill, H. R., 1978, Evolution of Severdrup Basin, Arctic Canada: American Association of Petroleum Geologists Bulletin, v. 62, p. 1004–1028.

Balkwill, H. R., and Bustin, R. M., 1980, Late Phanerozoic structures, Canadian Arctic archipelago: Palaeogeography, Palaeoclimatology, Palaeocology, v. 30, p. 219–227.

Balkwill, H. R., and 7 others, 1983, Arctic North America and northern Greenland, in Moullade, M., and Narin, A.E.M., eds., The Phanerozoic geology of the world; II, The Mesozoic, B: The Netherlands, Elsevier, p. 1–31.

Bee, M., Johnson, S. H., and Chiburis, E. F., 1984, Marine seismic refraction study between Cape Simpson and Prudoe Bay, Alaska: Journal of Geophysical Research, v. 89, p. 6941–6960.

Belyi, V. F., Kotlyar, I. N., Milov, A. P., and Pavlov, P. P., 1974, On the late Mesozoic acidic volcanism in the east Asian system of volcanogenic belts: Geologiya i Geofizika, v. 15, p. 3–10. (in Russian).

Ben-Avraham, Z., and Cooper, A. K., 1981, Early evolution of the Bering Sea by collision of oceanic rises and North Pacific subduction zones: Geological Society of America Bulletin, v. 92, p. 485–495.

Blake, M. C., Jr., and 7 others, 1978, Neogene Basin Formation in relation to plate-tectonic evolution of San Andreas Fault System, California: American Association of Petroleum Geologists Bulletin, v. 62, p. 344–372.

Brosgé, W. P., Whittington, C. L., and Morris, R. H., 1966, Geology of the Umiat-Maybe Creek region, Alaska: U.S. Geological Survey Professional Paper 303-H, p. 501–638.

Burk, C. A., 1965, Geology of the Alaska Peninsula Island arc and continental margin: Geological Society of America Memoir 99, 250 p.

Byrne, T., 1979, Late Paleocene demise of the Kula-Pacific spreading center: Geology, v. 7, p. 341–344.

Carey, S. W., 1955, The orocline concept in geotectonics, Part 1: Papers and Proceedings of the Royal Society of Tasmania, v. 89, p. 255–288.

Carman, G. J., and Hardwick, P., 1983, Geology and regional setting of the Kuparuk oil field, Alaska: American Association of Petroleum Geologists Bulletin, v. 67, p. 1014–1031.

Chapman, M. E., and Solomon, S. C., 1976, North American–Eurasian plate boundary in northeastern Asia: Journal of Geophysical Research, v. 81, p. 921–930.

Churkin, M., Jr., 1970, Foldbelts of Alaska and Siberia and drift between North America and Asia, in Adkison, W. L., and Brosgé, M. M., eds., Geological Seminar on the North Slope of Alaska, Proceedings: Los Angeles, American Association of Petroleum Geologists, Pacific Section, p. G1–G17.

—— , 1972, Western boundary of the North American continental plate in Asia: Geological Society of America Bulletin, v. 83, p. 1027–1036.

—— , 1973a, Geologic concepts of Arctic Ocean Basin, in Pitcher, M. G., ed., Arctic Geology: American Association of Petroleum Geologists Memoir 19, p. 485–499.

—— , 1973b, Paleozoic and Precambrian rocks of Alaska and their role in its structural evolution: U.S. Geological Survey Professional Paper 740, 64 p.

—— , 1975, Basement rocks of Barrow Arch, Alaska, and Circum-Arctic Paleozoic mobile belt: American Association of Petroleum Geologists Bulletin, v. 59, p. 451–456.

Churkin, M., Jr., Nokelberg, W. J., and Huie, C., 1979, Collision-deformed Paleozoic continental margin, western Brooks Range, Alaska: Geology, v. 7, p. 379–383.

Churkin, M., Jr., and Trexler, J. H., Jr., 1980, Circum-Arctic plate accretion-isolating part of a Pacific plate to form the nucleus of the Arctic basin: Earth and Planetary Science Letters, v. 48, p. 356–362.

Clark, D. L., 1974, Late Mesozoic and early Cenozoic sediment cores from the Arctic ocean: Geology, v. 2, p. 41–44.

Clark, D. L., and Morris, Th. H., 1984, Cenozoic sedimentation patterns in the evolving Arctic Ocean; Canada Basin and Alpha-Chukchi region to Lomonosov Ridge, in Gramberg, I. S., and 5 others, eds., Arctic geology: International Geological Congress Colloquium 04 Reports, v. 4, p. 173–178.

Coney, P. J., Jones, D. L., and Monger, J.W.A., 1980, Cordilleran suspect terranes: Nature, v. 288, p. 329–333.

Cooper, A. K., Marlow, M. S., and Scholl, D. W., 1976, Mesozoic magnetic lineations in the Bering Sea marginal basin: Journal of Geophysical Research, v. 81, p. 1916–1934.

Cooper, A. K., Marlow, M. S., and Ben-Avraham, Z., 1981, Multichannel seismic evidence bearing on the origin of Bowers Ridge, Bering Sea: Geological Society of America Bulletin, v. 92, p. 474–484.

Csejtey, B., Jr., Cox, D. P., Evarts, R. C., Stricker, G. D., and Foster, H., 1982, The Cenozoic Denali Fault system and the Cretaceous accretionary development of southern Alaska: Journal of Geophysical Research, v. 87, p. 3741–3754.

Dalrymple, G. B., Claque, D. A., and Lamphere, M. A., 1977, Revised age for Midway volcano, Hawaiian volcanic chain: Earth and Planetary Science Letters, v. 37, p. 107–116.

Dietz, R. S., and Holden, J. C., 1970, The breakup of Pangea: Scientific American, v. 223, p. 30–41.

Dodson, M. H., and McClelland-Brown, E., 1980, Magnetic blocking temperatures during slow cooling: Journal of Geophysical Research, v. 85, p. 2625–2637.

Dutro, J. T., Jr., 1981, Geology of Alaska bordering the Arctic Ocean, in Nairn, A.E.M., Stehli, F. T., and Churkin, M., Jr., eds., The Ocean Basins and Margins, v. 5: New York, Plenum, p. 21–36.

Engebretson, D. C., Cox, A., and Gordon, R. G., 1984, Relative motions between oceanic plates of the Pacific Basin: Journal of Geophysical Research, v. 89, p. 10291–10310.

—— , 1985, Relative motions between oceanic and continental plates: Geological Society of America Special Paper 206, 59 p.

Epshtein, O. G., Terekhova, G. P., and Solovieva, M. N., 1985, The Paleozoic of the Koryak Range; Foraminifer fauna, biostratigraphy: Voprosy Mikropaleontologii, v. 27, p. 47–77 (English summary).

Filotova, N. I., Mazhenshteyn, F. A., Kuznetsova, N. A., and Smelovshaya, M. M., 1980, The structure of the junction zone between the Verkhoyansk-Chukchi and Koryak-Kamchatka regions based on data from Satellite Meteor-25: Geotectonics, v. 14, p. 398–406.

Fisher, M. A., and Magoon, L. B., 1978, Geologic framework of Lower Cook Inlet, Alaska: American Association of Petroleum Geologists Bulletin, v. 63, p. 373–402.

Freeland, G. L., and Dietz, R. S., 1973, Rotation history of Alaskan tectonic blocks: Tectonophysics, v. 18, p.379–389.

Frei, L. S., and Cox, A., 1987, Relative displacement between Eurasia and North America prior to the formation of oceanic crust in the North Atlantic: Tectonophysics, v. 142, p. 111–136.

Fujita, K., and Newberry, J. T., 1982, Tectonic evolution of northeastern Siberia and adjacent regions: Tectonophysics, v. 89, p. 337–357.

—— , 1983, Accretionary terranes and tectonic evolution of northeast Siberia, in Hashimoto, M., and Uyeda, S., eds., Accretion tectonics in the Circum-Pacific regions: Tokyo, Terra Scientific Publishing Company, p. 43–57.

Globerman, B. R., and Coe, R. S., 1984, Discordant declinations from "in place" Upper Cretaceous volcanics, southwest Alaska; Evidence for oroclinal bending: Geological Society of America Abstracts with Programs, v. 16, p. 286.

Gordon, R. G., Cox, A., and Harter, C. E., 1978, Absolute motion of an individual plate estimated from its ridge and trench boundaries: Nature, v. 274, p. 752–755.

Gordon, R. G., Cox, A., and O'Hare, S., 1984, Paleomagnetic Euler poles and the apparent polar wander and absolute motion of North America since the Carboniferous: Tectonics, v. 3, p. 499–537.

Graham, S. A., McCloy, C., Hitzman, M., Ward, R., and Turner, R., 1984, Basin evolution during change from convergent to transform continental margin in central California: American Association of Petroleum Geologists Bulletin, v. 68, p. 233–249.

Grantz, A., 1966, Strike-slip faults in Alaska [Ph.D. thesis]: Stanford, California, Stanford University, 82 p.

Grantz, A., Eittreim, S., and Dinter, D. A., 1979, Geology and tectonic development of the continental margin north of Alaska: Tectonophysics, v. 59, p. 263–291.

Green, A. R., Kaplan, A. A., and Vierbuchen, R. C., 1986, Circum-Arctic petroleum potential, in Halbouty, M. T., ed., Future petroleum provinces of the world: American Association of Petroleum Geologists Memoir 40, p. 101–130.

Helgedahl, S. L., and Jarrard, R. D., 1987, Paleomagnetism of the Kuparuk River Formation from oriented drillcore; Evidence for rotation of the North Slope block, in Tailleur, I. and Weimer, P., eds., Alaskan and North Slope geology, v. 2: Pacific Section Society of Economic Paleontologists and Mineralogists, p. 581–620.

Halgedahl, S. L., Day, R., and Fuller, M., 1980, The effect of cooling rate on the intensity of weak-field TRM in single-domain magnetite: Journal of Geophysical Research, v. 85, p. 3690–3698.

Harbert, W., Frei, L. S., Cox, A., and Engebretson, D. C., 1987, Relative motions between Eurasia and North America in the Bering Sea region: Tectonophysics, v. 134, p. 239–261.

Harland, W. B., 1971, Tectonic transpression in Caledonian Spitzbergen: Geological Magazine, v. 108, p. 27–42.

Harland, W. B., and 5 others, 1982, A geologic time scale: New York, Cambridge University Press, 131 p.

Harris, A. G., Ellersieck, I. F., Mayfield, C. F., and Tailleur, I. L., 1983, Thermal maturation values (conodont color alternation indices) for Paleozoic and Triassic rocks, Chandler Lake, Delong Mountains, Howare Pass, Killik River, Misheguk Mountain, and Point Hope Quadrangles, northwest Alaska, and subsurface NPRA: U.S. Geological Survey Open-File Report 83-505, 15 p.

Harris, R. A., 1985a, Paleomagnetism, geochronology, and paleotemperature of the Yukon-Koyukuk Province, Alaska [M. Sc. thesis]: Fairbanks, University of Alaska, 134 p.

—— , 1985b, Paleomagnetism, geochronology, and paleotemperature of the Yukon-Koyukuk Province, Alaska: EOS Transactions of the American Geophysical Union, v. 66, p. 1103.

Harrison, C.G.A., and Lindh, T., 1982, A polar wandering curve for North America during the Mesozoic and Cenozoic: Journal of Geophysical Research, v. 87, p. 1903–1920.

Herron, E. M., Dewey, J. F., and Pitman, W. C. III, 1974, Plate tectonic model for the evolution of the Arctic: Geology, v. 2, p. 377–380.

Hickman, R. G., Craddock, C., and Sherwood, K. W., 1978, The Denali Fault system and the tectonic development of southern Alaska: Tectonophysics, v. 47, p. 247–273.

Hilde, T.W.C., Uyeda, S., and Kroenke, L., 1977, Evolution of the western Pacific and its margin: Tectonophysics, v. 38, p. 145–165.

Hillhouse, J. S., 1987, Accretion in southern Alaska: Tectonophysics, v. 139, p. 107–122.

Hillhouse, J. W., and Grommé, S., 1980, Cretaceous overprint revealed by paleomagnetic study in the northern Brooks Range: U.S. Geological Survey Circular 844, p. 43–46.

—— , 1983, Paleomagnetic studies and the hypothetical rotation of Arctic Alaska: Journal of the Alaska Geological Society, v. 2, p. 27–39.

Hillhouse, J. W., and McWilliams, M. O., 1987, Application of paleomagnetism to accretionary tectonics and structural geology: Reviews of Geophysics, v. 25, p. 951–959.

Hitzman, M. W., 1983, Geology of the Cosmos Hills and its relationship to the Ruby Creek copper-cobalt deposit [Ph.D. thesis]: Stanford, California, Stanford University, 266 p.

Holmes, M. L., and Creager, J. S., 1981, The role of the Kaltag and Kobuk faults in the tectonic evolution of the Bering Sea region, in Hood, D. W., and Calder, J. A., eds., The eastern Bering Sea Shelf: Oceanography and Resources, v. 1, p. 293–302.

Howell, D. G., Crough, J. K., Greene, H. G., McCulloch, D. S., and Vedder, J. G., 1980, Basin development along the late Mesozoic and Cenozoic California margin; A plate tectonic margin and subduction oblique subduction and transform tectonics, in Ballance, P. F., and Reading, H. G., eds., Sedimentation in oblique-slip mobile zones: International Association of Sedimentologists Special Publication 4, p. 43–62.

Hudson, T., 1983, Calc-alkaline plutonism along the Pacific rim of southern Alaska: Geological Society of America Memoir 159, p. 159–169.

Hugon, H., 1983, Ellesmere-Greenland fold belt; Structural evidence for left-lateral shearing: Tectonophysics, v. 100, p. 215–225.

Irving, E., and Irving, G. A., 1982, Apparent polar wander paths Carboniferous through Cenozoic and the assembly of Gondwana: Geophysical Surveys, v. 5, p. 141–188.

Jackson, H. R., 1985, Nares Strait, a suture zone; Geophysical and geological implications: Tectonophysics, v. 114, p. 11–28.

Jackson, H. R., and Koppen, L., 1985, The Nares Strait gravity anomaly and its implications for crustal structure: Canadian Journal of Earth Science, v. 22, p. 1322–1328.

Jones, P. B., 1980, Evidence from Canada and Alaska on plate tectonic evolution of the Arctic Ocean Basin: Nature, v. 285, p. 215–217.

Jones, P. B., 1982, Mesozoic rifting in the western Arctic Ocean Basin and its relationship to Pacific sea-floor spreading, in Embry, A. F., and Balkwill, H. R., eds., Arctic Geology and Geophysics: Canadian Society of Petroleum Geologists Memoir 8, p. 83–99.

Karasik, A. M., Ustritsky, V. I., and Khramov, A. N., 1984, History of Arctic Ocean formation: Abstracts, 27th International Geological Congress, Moscow, v. 9, p. 245.

Kent, D. V., and Gradstein, F. M., 1985, A Cretaceous and Jurassic geochronology: Geological Society of America Bulletin, v. 96, p. 1419–1427.

Kerr, J. W., 1978, A plate tectonic contest in Arctic Canada, in Strangway, D. W., ed., The continental crust and its mineral deposits: Geological Association of Canada Special Paper 20, p. 457–486.

—— , 1981, Evolution of the Canadian Arctic Islands, A Transition between the Atlantic and Arctic oceans, in Nairn, A.E.M., Stehli, C. G., and Churkin, M., Jr., eds., The Arctic Ocean: New York, Plenum Press, p. 105–199.

Koltypin, A. V., and Kononov, M. V., 1986, Evolution of South Koriak Late Cretaceous-Paleogene Island arcs: Moskovskoe Obschchestov Ispytatelei Prirody Biulleten Otdel Geologischeskii, v. 61, p. 25–38. (in Russian)

Kosygin, Y. A., and Parfenov, L. M., 1981, Tectonics of the Soviet Far East, in Nairn, A. E., Churkin, M., and Stehli, F. G., eds., The ocean basins and margins: New York, Plenum Press, v. 5, p. 377–412.

Kovacs, L. C., Srivastava, S. P., and Jackson, H. R., 1986, Results from an aeromagnetic investigation of the Nares Strait region: Journal of Geodynamics, v. 6, p. 91–110.

Kristoffersen, Y., 1978, Sea floor spreading and the early opening of the North Atlantic: Earth and Planetary Science Letters, v. 38, p. 273–290.

Lockhard, A. B., 1984, A gravity survey of the central Seward Peninsula, Alaska: Abstracts and Program, Geological Society of America Cordilleran Section, v. 16, p. 319.

Masterson, W. D., and Paris, C. E., 1987, Depositional history and reservoir description of the Kuparuk River Formation, North Slope, Alaska, in Tailleur, I., and Weimer, P., eds., Alaskan and North Slope geology, v. 1: Pacific Section Society of Economic Paleontologists and Mineralogists, p. 95–107.

Mayfield, C. F., Tailleur, I. L., and Ellersieck, I., 1983, Stratigraphy, structure, and palinspastic synthesis of the western Brooks Range, northwestern Alaska: U.S. Geological Survey Open-File Report 83-779, 57 p.

McLean, H., 1979, Review of petroleum geology of Anadyr and Khatyrka basins, U.S.S.R.: American Association of Petroleum Geologists Bulletin, v. 63, p. 1467–1477.

Miall, A. D., 1976, Devonian geology of Banks Island, Arctic Canada, and its bearing on the tectonic development of the circum-Arctic region: Geological Society of America Bulletin, v. 87, p. 1599–1608.

—— , 1986, Effects of Caledonian tectonism in Arctic Canada: Geology, v. 14, p. 904–907.

Middleton, M. F., and Schmidt, P. W., 1982, Paleothermometry of the Sydney Basin: Journal of Geophysical Research, v. 87, p. 5351–5359.

Minster, J. B., and Jordon, T. H., 1978, Present-day plate motions: Journal of Geophysical Research, v. 83, p. 5331–5354.

Minster, J. B., Jordan, T. H., Molnar, P., and Haines, E., 1974, Numerical modeling of instantaneous plate tectonics: Geophysical Journal of the Royal Astronomical Society, v. 36, p. 541–576.

Mitrofanov, N. P., and Sheludchemko, S. D., 1981, Age of terrigenous deposits in the southwestern area of the central Koryak folded zone: Geologiya i Geofizika, v. 22, p. 128–131. (in Russian)

Molenaar, C. M., 1983, Depositional relations of Cretaceous and Lower Tertiary rocks, northeastern Alaska: American Association of Petroleum Geologists Bulletin, v. 67, p. 1066–1080.

Moll, E. J., and Patton, W. W., Jr., 1984, Volcanic history of the southern Yukon-Koyukuk depression; Evidence from the Unalakeet Quadrangle, Alaska: Geological Society of America Abstracts with Programs, v. 16, p. 322.

Molnar, P., and Chen, W., 1983, Focal depths and fault plane solutions of earthquakes under the Tibetan plateau: Journal of Geophysical Research, v. 88, p. 1180–1196.

Moore, J. C., and 5 others, 1983, Paleogene evolution of the Kodiak Islands, Alaska; Consequences of ridge-trench interaction in a more southerly latitude: Tectonics, v. 2, p. 265–293.

Morgan, W. J., 1983, Hotspot tracks and the early rifting of the Atlantic: Tectonophysics, v. 94, p. 123–139.

Mudie, P. J., Stoffyn-Egli, P., and van Wagoner, N. A., 1986, Geological constraints for tectonic models of the Alpha Ridge: Journal of Geodynamics, v. 6, p. 215–236.

Mull, C. G., 1982, Tectonic evolution and structural style of the Brooks Range, Alaska; An illustrated summary, in Powers, R. B., ed., Geologic studies of the Cordilleran thrust belt: Denver, Rocky Mountain Association of Geologists, p. 1–45.

Nalivkin, D. V., 1965, Geologic map of the Union of Soviet Socialist Republics: Ministry of the Geology of the U.S.S.R., 6 sheets, scale 1:5,000,000.

Natal'in, B. A., and Parfenov, L. M., 1983, Accretional and collisional eugeosynclinal folded systems of the northwestern Pacific rim, in Hashimoto, M., and Uyeda, S., eds., Accretion tectonics in the Circum-Pacific Regions: Tokyo, Terra Scientific Publishing Company, p. 59–68.

Newman, G. W., Mull, C. G., and Watkins, N. D., 1977, Northern Alaska paleomagnetism, plate rotation, and plate tectonics, in Sisson, A., ed., Relationship of Plate Tectonics to Alaskan Geology and Resources: Anchorage, Alaska Geological Society, p. C1–C7.

Nilsen, T. H., and Patton, W. W., Jr., 1984, Cretaceous fluvial to deep-marine deposits of the central Yukon-Koyukuk basin, Alaska: Accomplishments of the Geological Survey in Alaska During 1982, p. 37–40.

Parfenov, L. M., and Natal'in, B. A., 1984, Continental margins and oceanic archs of Mesozoic northeastern Asia: Novosibirsk, Academy of Sciences of the U.S.S.R., 190 p. (in Russian)

—— , 1985, Mesozoic accretion and collision tectonics of northeastern Asia, in Howell, D., ed., Tectonostratigraphic terranes of the Circum-Pacific region: Circum-Pacific Council for Energy and Mineral Resources Earth Science Series 1, p. 363–373.

Patton, W. W., Jr., 1973, Reconnaissance geology of the northern Yukon-Koyukuk Province, Alaska: U.S. Geological Survey Professional Paper 774-A, 17 p.

Patton, W. W., Jr., and Tailleur, I. L., 1977, Evidence in the Bering Strait region for differential movement between North America and Eurasia: Geological Society of America Bulletin, v. 88, p. 1298–1304.

Patton, W. W., Jr., Tailleur, I. L., Brosge, C. W., and Lamphere, M. A., 1977, Preliminary report on the ophiolites of northern and western Alaska, in Coleman, R. G., and Irwin, W. P., eds., North American ophiolites: Oregon Department of Geology and Mineral Industries Bulletin, v. 95, p. 51–58.

Pevye, A. A., 1984, Structure and structural position of ophiolites in the Koryak Uplands: Moscow, Academy of Sciences of the U.S.S.R., 99 p (in Russian).

Pitman, W. C., III, and Talwani, M., 1972, Sea-floor spreading in the North Atlantic: Geological Society of America Bulletin, v. 83, p. 619–649.

Plumley, P. W., Coe, R. S., and Byrne, T., 1983, Paleomagnetism of the Paleocene Ghost Rocks Formation, Prince William Terrane, Alaska: Tectonics, v. 2, p. 295–314.

Porter, S. C., 1966, Stratigraphy and deformation of Paleozoic section at Anaktuvuk Pass, central Brooks Range, Alaska: American Association of Petroleum Geologists Bulletin, v. 50, p. 952–980.

Pullaiah, G., Irving, E., Buchan, K. L., and Dunlop, D. J., 1975, Magnetization changes caused by burial and uplift: Earth and Planetary Science Letters, v. 28, p. 133–143.

Pushcharovskiy, Yu. M., and 6 others, 1983, Overthrusts and imbricate structures of the northwestern Pacific margin: Geotectonics, v. 17, p. 466–477.

Reading, H. G., 1980, Characteristics and recognition of strike-slip fault system, in Ballance, P. F., and Reading, H. G., eds., Sedimentation in oblique-slip mobil zones: International Association of Sedimentologists Special Publication 4, p. 1–43.

Reidiger, C. L., Bustin, R. M., and Rouse, G. E., 1984, New evidence for the chronology of the Eurekan Orogeny from south-central Ellesmere Island: Canadian Journal of Earth Sciences, v. 21, p. 1286–1295.

Rickwood, F. K., 1970, The Prudhoe Bay field, in Adkinson, W. L., and Brosgé, M. M., eds., Geological Seminar on the North Slope of Alaska, Proceedings: Los Angeles, American Association of Petroleum Geologists, Pacific Section, p. L1–L11.

Rubinstone, J. L., 1984a, Geology and geochemistry of early Tertiary submarine volcanic rocks of the Aleutian Islands, and their bearing on the development of the Aleutian Island Arc [Ph.D. thesis]: Ithaca, New York, Cornell University, 350 p.

—— , 1984b, Early Tertiary volcanism in the Aleutian Islands; Geochemical variations and tectonic implications: Geological Society of America Abstracts with Programs, v. 16, p. 331.

Rudkevich, M. K., 1976, The history and geodynamics of the development of the West Siberian Platform: Tectonophysics, v. 36, p. 275–287.

Savostin, L. A., and Karasik, A. M., 1981, Recent plate tectonics of the Arctic Basin and of northeastern Asia: Tectonophysics, v. 74, p. 111–145.

Scholl, D. W., Buffington, E. C., and Marlow, M. S., 1975, Plate tectonics and the structural evolution of the Aleutian-Bering Sea region, in Forbes, R. B., ed., Contributions to the geology of the Bering Sea basin and adjacent regions: Geological Society of America Special Paper 151, p. 1–32.

Shilo, N. A., Belyi, V. F., and Sidrov, A. A., 1974, The volcanic belts of east Asia and their relation to problems of tectonics, magmatism, and metallogeny: Geologiya i Geofizika, v. 15, p. 70–88. (in Russian)

Sobczak, L. W., 1982, Fragmentation of the Canadian Arctic Archipelago, Greenland, and surrounding oceans: Meddelser om Gronland, Geoscience, v. 8, p. 221–236.

Srivastava, S. P., 1978, Evolution of the Labrador Sea and its bearing on the early evolution of the North Atlantic: Geophysical Journal of the Royal Astronomical Society, v. 52, p. 313–357.

—— , 1985, Evolution of the Eurasian basin and its implications to the motion of Greenland along Nares Strait: Tectonophysics, v. 114, p. 29–53.

Srivastava, S. P., and Tapscott, C. R., 1986, Plate kinematics of the North Atlantic, in Vogt, P. R., and Tucholke, B. E., eds., The western North Atlantic region: Boulder, Colorado, Geological Society of America, The geology of North America, v. M, p. 379–404.

Stone, D. B., 1982, Present-day plate boundaries in Alaska and the Arctic: Journal of the Alaskan Geological Society, v. 3, p. 1–15.

Stone, D. B., Panuska, B. C., and Packer, D. R., 1982, Paleolatitudes versus time for southern Alaska: Journal of Geophysical Research, v. 87, p. 3697–3707.

Suslov, S. P., 1961, Physical Geography of Asiatic Russia: San Francisco, W. H. Freeman and Company, 594 p.

Sweeney, J. F., 1977, Subsidence of the Sverdrup Basin, Canadian Arctic Islands: Geological Society of America Bulletin, v. 88, p. 41–48.

—— , 1985, Comments about the age of the Canada Basin: Tectonophysics, v. 114, p. 1–10.

Sweeney, J. F., and Weber, J. R., 1986, Progress in understanding the age and origin of the Alpha Ridge, Arctic Ocean: Journal of Geodynamics, v. 6, p. 237–244.

Tabbert, R. L., and Bennett, J. E., 1976, Lower Cretaceous micro-plankton from the subsurface of Northern Alaska: Geoscience and Man, v. 15: Baton Rouge, Louisiana State University Press, p. 146.

Tailleur, I., 1969, Rifting speculation on the geology of Alaska's North Slope: Oil and Gas Journal, v. 67, p. 128–130.

—— , 1973, Probable rift origin of Canada Basin, Arctic Ocean, in Pitcher, M. G., ed., Arctic geology: American Association of Petroleum Geologists Memoir 19, p. 529–535.

Tapponnier, P., and Molnar, P., 1977, Active faulting and tectonics in China: Journal of Geophysical Research, v. 87, p. 2905–2930.

Taylor, P. T., Kovacs, L. C., Vogt, P. R., and Johnston, G. L., 1981, Detailed aeromagnetic investigation of the Arctic Basin, 2: Journal of Geophysical Research, v. 86, p. 6323–6333.

Taylor, A., Judge, A., and Allen, V., 1986, Terrestrial heat flow on project CESAR, Alpha Ridge, Arctic Ocean: Journal of Geodynamics, v. 6,

p. 137–176.

Thurston, S. P., 1985, Structure, petrology, and metamorphic history of the Nome Group blueschist terrane, Salmon Lake area, Seward Peninsula, Alaska: Geological Society of America Bulletin, v. 96, p. 600–617.

Tibilov, I. V., 1982, Tectonic thrust sheets in central Chukotka: Geologiya i Geofizika, v. 23, p. 70–75. (In Russian)

Trettin, H. P., and 7 others, 1972, The Innuitian Province, in Price, R. A., and Douglas, R.J.W., eds., Variations in Tectonic styles in Canada: Geological Association of Canada Special Paper 11, p. 83–179.

Turner, D. L., Forbes, R. B., and Dillon, J. T., 1979, K-Ar geochronology of the southwestern Brooks Range, Alaska: Canadian Journal of Earth Sciences, v. 16, p. 1789–1804.

Turner, R. F., and 5 others, 1983, Geological and operational summary of Norton Sound COST No. 1 well, Norton Sound, Alaska: U.S. Geological Survey Open-File Report 83-124, 164 p.

Turner, R. F., and 6 others, 1984a, Geological and operational summary of St. George Basin COST No. 2 well, Alaska: U.S. Geological Survey Open-File Report 84-18, 79 p.

Turner, R. F., and 5 others, 1984b, Geological and operational summary of Navarin Basin COST No. 1 well, Bering Sea, Alaska: U.S. Geological Survey Open-File Report 84-31, 245 p.

Uyeda, S., and Yamano, M., 1984, Softness of the lithosphere and change of plate motions due to collisions, in Howell, D. G., Jones, D. L., and Cox, A., eds., Proceedings of the Circum-Pacific Terrane Conference, Stanford: Stanford University Publications, Geological Sciences, v. 28, p. 195–196.

Van Alstine, D. R., and Whitney, J. W., 1984, Paleomagnetism of drillcore from the Navarin Basin COST No. 1 well; Implications for the accreted terrane history of the Bering Sea: EOS Transactions of the American Geophysical Union, v. 65, p. 869.

Van der Voo, R., 1969, Paleomagnetic evidence for the rotation of the Iberian Peninsula: Tectonophysics, v. 7, p. 5–56.

Van Wagoner, N. A., Williamson, M. C., Robinson, P. T., and Gibson, I. L., 1986, First samples of acoustic basement recovered from the Alpha Ridge, Arctic Ocean; New constraints for the origin of the ridge: Journal of Geodynamics, v. 6, p. 177–196.

Vink, G. E., 1984, A hotspot model for Iceland and the Voring Plateau: Journal of Geophysical Research, v. 89, p. 9949–9959.

Vogt, P. R., Taylor, P. T., Kovacs, L. C., and Johnson, G. L., 1979, Detailed aeromagnetic investigation of the Arctic Basin: Journal of Geophysical Research, v. 84, p. 1071–1089.

——, 1982, The Canada Basin; Aeromagnetic constraints on structure and evolution: Tectonophysics, v. 89, p. 295–336.

Wallace, W. K., and Engebretson, D. C., 1984, Relationships between plate motions and Late Cretaceous to Paleogene magmatism in southwestern Alaska: Tectonics, v. 3, p. 295–315.

Walton, D., 1980, Time-temperature relations in the magnetization of assemblies of single domain grains: Nature, v. 286, p. 245–247.

Wittbrodt, P. R., 1985, Paleomagnetism and petrology of St. Matthew Island, Bering Sea Alaska [M.Sc. thesis]: Fairbanks, University of Alaska, 107 p.

Witte, W. K., 1982, Paleomagnetism and paleogeography of Cretaceous northern Alaska [M. Sc. thesis]: Fairbanks, University of Alaska, 146 p.

Witte, W. K., Stone, D. B., and Mull, C. G., 1987, Paleomagnetism, paleobotany, and paleogeography of the Arctic slope, Alaska; in Tailleur, I., and Weimer, P., eds., Alaskan North Slope Geology, v. 2: Los Angeles, Society of Economic Paleontologists and Mineralogists, Pacific Section, p. 571–579.

Wolfe, J. A., and Wahrhaftig, C., 1968, The Cantwell Formation of the central Alaska Range: U.S. Geological Survey Bulletin 1294-A, p. A41–A46.

Woods, M. T., and Davies, G. F., 1982, Late Cretaceous genesis of the Kula plate: Earth and Planetary Science Letters, v. 58, p. 161–166.

Wynne, P. J., Irving, E., and Osadetz, K., 1983, Paleomagnetism of the Esayoo Formation (Permian) of northern Ellesmere Island; Possible clue to the solution of the Nares Strait dilemma: Tectonophysics, v. 100, p. 241–256.

Zaborovskaya, N. B., and Nekrasov, G. Ye, 1977, Tectonics and magmatism of the transition zone from the Yana-Kolyma Mesozoides to the Koryak-Kamchatka folded region: Geotectonics, v. 11, p. 62–72.

Zijderveld, J.D.A., 1967, AC demagnetization of rocks; Analysis of results, in Collinson, D. W., Creer, K. M., and Runcorn, S. K., eds., Methods in Paleomagnetism: New York, Elsevier, p. 254–286.

Zonenshain, L. P., and 5 others, 1984, Plate tectonic model of the south Urals development: Tectonophysics, v. 109, p. 95–135.

Zonenshain, L. P., Kononov, M. V., and Savostin, L. A., 1987, Pacific and Kula-Eurasia relative motions during the last 130 Ma and their bearing on orogenesis in northeast Asia, in Monger, J.W.H., and Franchcheteau, J., eds., Circum-Pacific Orogenic Belts and Evolution of the Pacific Ocean Basin: American Geophysical Union Geodynamics Series, v. 18, p. 29–47.

MANUSCRIPT ACCEPTED BY THE SOCIETY JANUARY 29, 1988

Lead in ice field, developed through the AIDJEX ice camp in the Beaufort Sea. Photo from Roy Wilkens.

Printed in U.S.A.

Chapter 31

A review of tectonic models for the evolution of the Canada Basin

L. A. Lawver and C. R. Scotese*
Institute for Geophysics, The University of Texas, 8701 N. MOPAC Boulevard, Austin, Texas 78759-8346

INTRODUCTION

The Arctic Ocean has a nearly continuous ice cover that makes collection of shipborne geological and geophysical data almost impossible. As late as 1907 (Mikkelsen, 1955), expeditions were still being sponsored to discover the elusive northern continent thought to occupy much of the region. Since the plate-tectonic revolution of the sixties, numerous theories concerning the tectonic origin of the Arctic Ocean, and the Canada Basin in particular (Fig. 1), have been proposed.

Tectonic models for the Canada Basin can be separated into three broad categories: oceanization of continental crust, entrapment of old oceanic crust, and the in situ formation of the oceanic crust by sea-floor spreading. The first category consists of the tectonic model originally suggested by Shatskiy in 1935 and later given prominence by Beloussov in the 1950s and 1960s (Shatskiy, 1935; Beloussov, 1970). They argued that the Canada Basin was a cratonic high that shed debris southward onto Arctic Canada and the north slope of Alaska, and that this high was later oceanized by mantle convection that eroded the root and caused the area to subside. Pogrebitskiy (1976) and Pushcharovskiy (1976) also invoked oceanization of continental crust to explain the formation of the Canada Basin, but Pogrebitskiy and others (1984) later explained the formation of the basin by a combination of lithospheric oceanization and granitization (endogenic differentiation).

The second category of models suggests that much of the Canada Basin resulted from entrapment of older oceanic crust (Churkin, 1970; Churkin and Trexler, 1980; Karasik and others, 1984). Early Mesozoic oceanic lithosphere, travelling northward on the Kula plate, was inserted into the Arctic and during the mid-Cretaceous was cut off from the Pacific by the suturing of North America, the Kolyma terrane, and Eurasia (Fig. 2). Others have suggested that only parts of the Canada and Makarov basins are composed of trapped oceanic crust of Paleozoic age (Jones, 1980; Rowley and others, 1985).

The tectonic models that make up the third category, in situ sea-floor spreading, can be subdivided four ways. The first subdivision consists of rotational models (Carey, 1955, 1958; Grantz, 1966; Hamilton, 1967, 1968, 1970; Tailleur, 1969; Tailleur and Snelson, 1969; Rickwood, 1970; Tailleur and Brosgé, 1970; Freeland and Dietz, 1973; Tailleur, 1973; Johnson and others, 1978; Sweeney and others, 1978; Grantz and others, 1979, 1981; Fujita and Newberry, 1982; Mair and Forsyth, 1982; Vogt and others, 1982; May and Grantz, 1983; Sweeney, 1983, 1985; Burke, 1984; Green and others, 1984; Harland and others, 1984; Embry, 1985; McWhae, 1986). The rotational model suggests that the Arctic Alaska block rotated away from the Canadian Arctic Islands about a pole near the Mackenzie Delta (Fig. 3). The second subdivision of in situ sea-floor spreading models (Fig. 4) is based on the assumption that the Alpha and Mendeleev ridges were once an active spreading center or formed parallel to a linear sea-floor spreading center (Johnson and Heezen, 1967; Beal, 1968; Vogt and Ostenso, 1970; Ostenso and Wold, 1971; Hall, 1970, 1973; Ostenso, 1974; Christie, 1979; Crane, 1987; Smith, 1987). This subdivision, characterized as the "Arctic Islands strike-slip" model, consists of scenarios predicting that the North Slope is a passive margin that rifted either from the Lomonosov Ridge or from the Alpha and Mendeleev ridges. In these models, the Canadian Arctic Islands were bounded by a left-lateral transform fault. The third subdivision of sea-floor spreading models can be characterized as the "Arctic Alaska strike-slip" model (Herron and others, 1974; Vogt and others, 1982; Metz and others, 1982; Rowley and others, 1985). In these models (Fig. 5), northeastern Siberia or the Chukchi Plateau rifts away from the Canadian Arctic Islands along a transform fault that parallels the margin of the Arctic Alaska. These models predict little or no motion of the Arctic Alaska block with respect to cratonic North America. Finally, the fourth subdivision is the model of the Canada Basin suggested by Jones (1980, 1982, 1983). His model

---

*Present address: Shell Development Co., Bellaire Research Center, P.O. Box 481, Houston, Texas 77001.

Lawver, L. A., and Scotese, C. R., 1990, A review of tectonic models for the evolution of the Canada Basin, *in* Grantz, A., Johnson, L., and Sweeney, J. F., eds., The Arctic Ocean region: Boulder, Colorado, Geological Society of America, The Geology of North America, v. L.

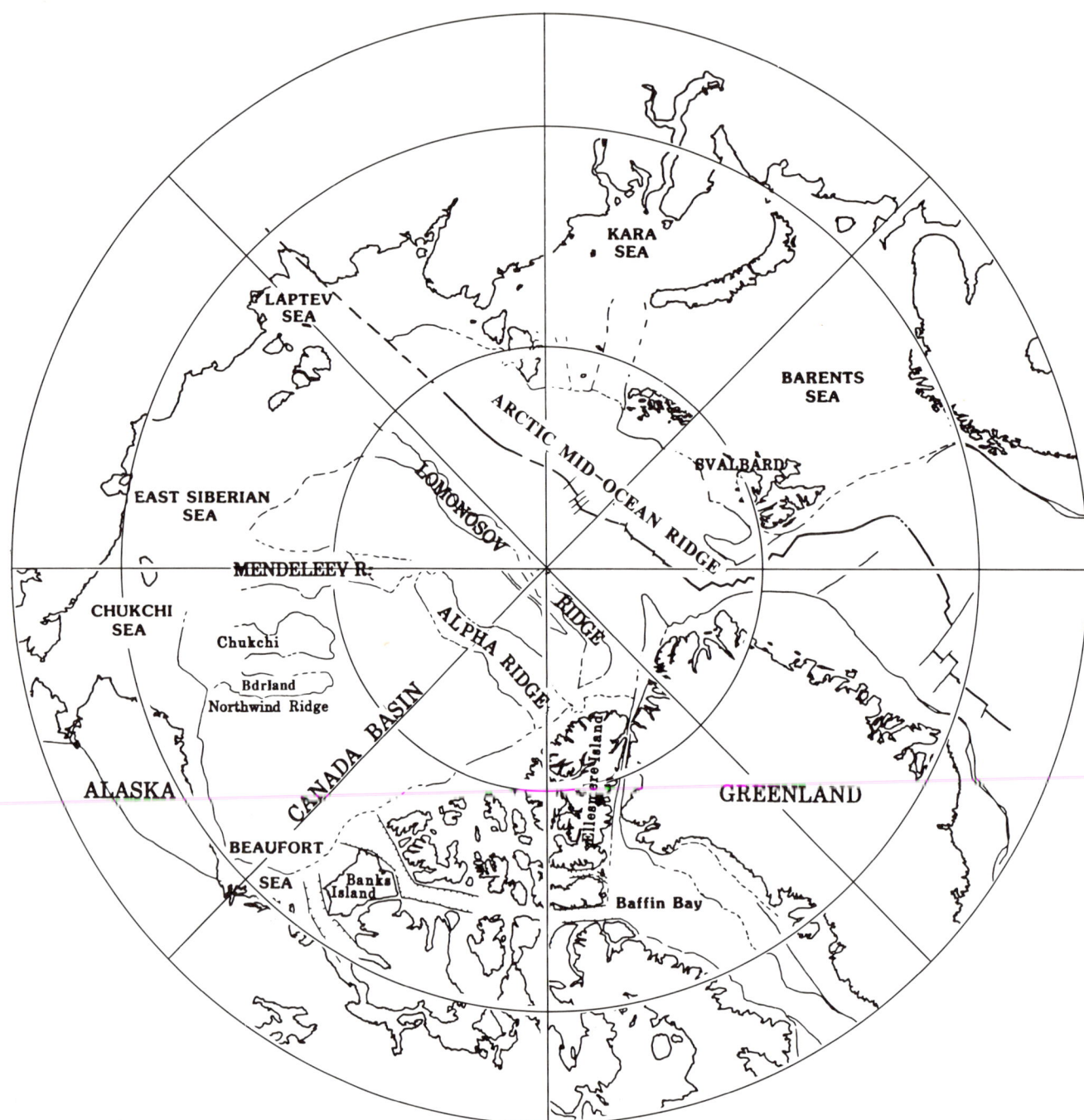

Figure 1. Location map of the Arctic Ocean region. Lightweight lines indicate outer continental margins, dashed where uncertain. Heavyweight line is the presently active sea-floor spreading ridge in the North Atlantic and Eurasia Basin. Hatchered lines in the Canadian Arctic Islands indicate grabenlike features that can be closed in reconstructions of the Arctic region. Bathymetric features taken from Perry and others (1985).

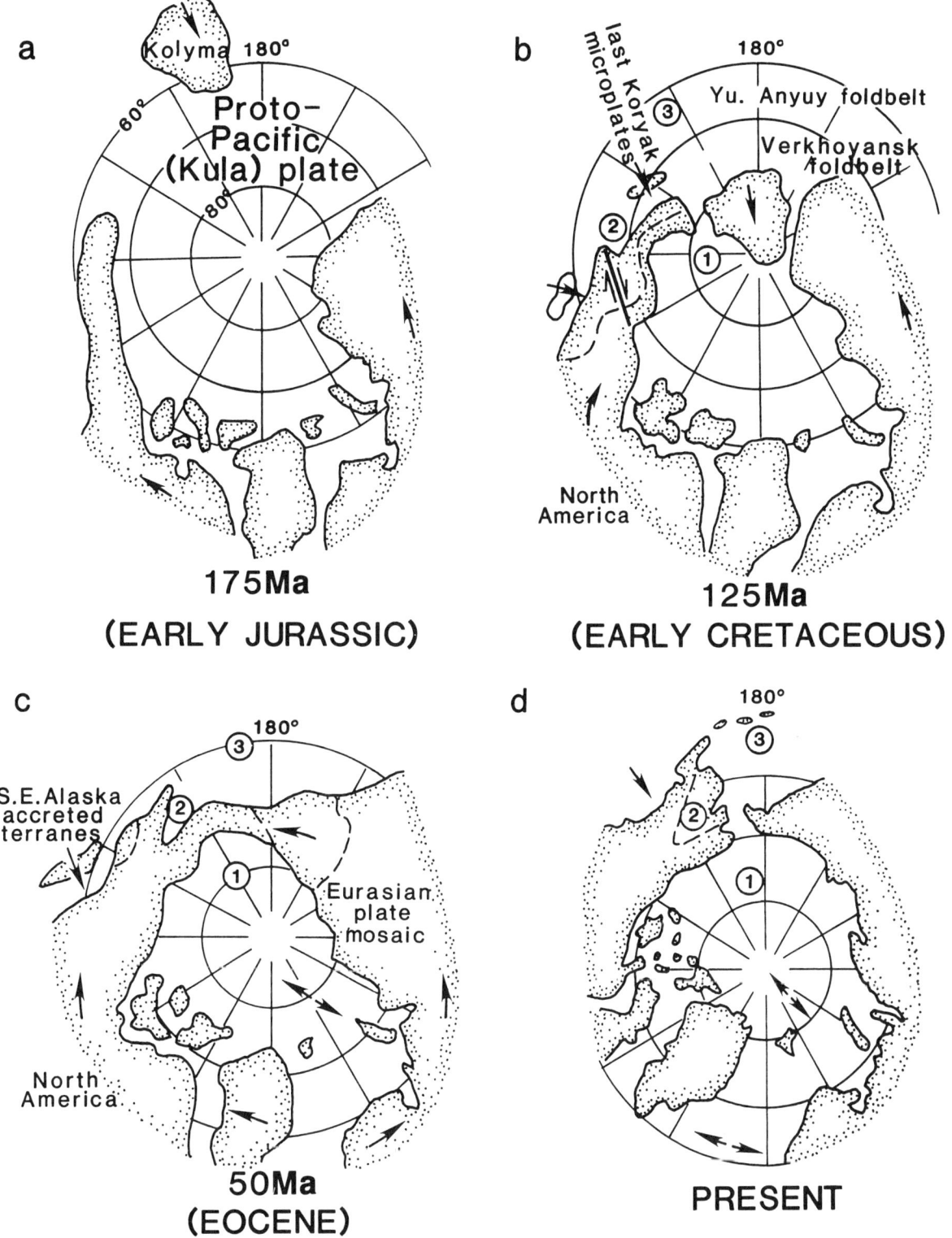

Figure 2. Entrapment-of-older-oceanic-crust model redrawn from Churkin and Trexler (1980). Paleogeographic reconstructions of the Arctic showing northward drift, collision, and accretion. Projection is flat polar, and shelf areas are not shown so that the land areas can be recognized. Maps are not intended to show rigorous geographic locations but rather the process of terrane accretion and Kula plate capture. (1) indicates trapped Canada Basin, (2) indicates trapped Yukon-Koyukuk region, and (3) indicates trapped Bering Sea.

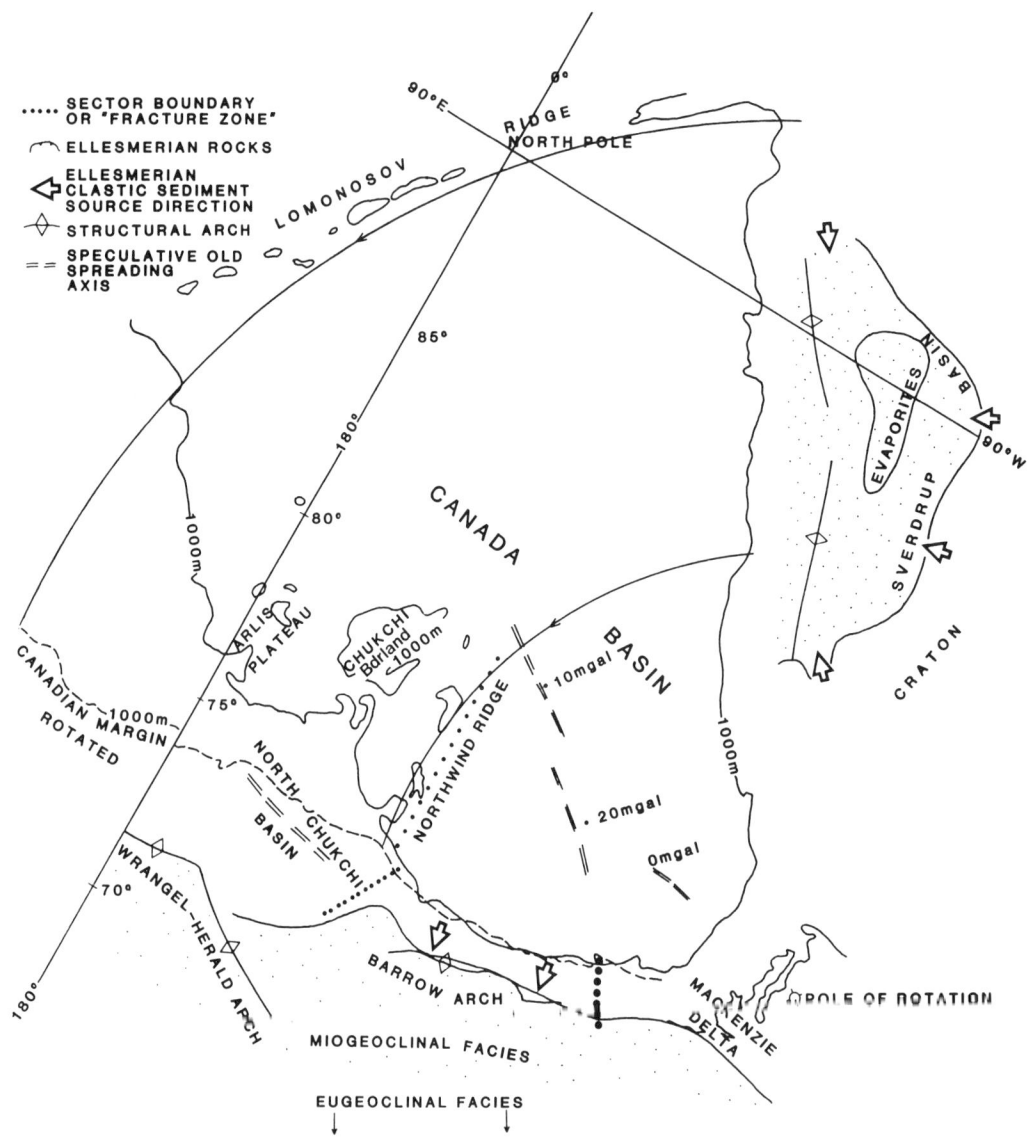

Figure 3. Rotational model for the development of the Canada Basin redrawn from Grantz and others (1979). The 1,000-m bathymetric contour from the Canadian side has been rotated 66° about a pole at 69.1°N, 130.5°W. The Lomonosov Ridge lies nearly on a small circle about the pole of rotation as does the Northwind Ridge. Hypothetical spreading center in the North Chukchi Basin indicates region from which Grantz and others (1979) suggest the Chukchi Borderland could have extended.

proposes a combination of trapped Paleozoic oceanic crust, dextral strike-slip movement along the North Slope margin, and sea-floor spreading along the Alpha Ridge.

The next section presents a chronological development of the tectonic models for the evolution of the Canada Basin, followed by a brief discussion of the tectonic setting of the Canada Basin in a global framework and the relevant bathymetric features of the Canada Basin, which must be dealt with by any model that has validity. These sections are followed by a discussion of the four main models that involve in situ sea-floor spread-

ing in the Canada Basin and the arguments for each model. The final section presents some of the problems inherent with each model.

HISTORICAL DEVELOPMENT

The first mobile model for the in situ formation of the Canada Basin was the rotational, or sphenochasm model of Carey (1955, 1958). Carey cited the bend in the trend from the Canadian Rockies and Coast Ranges through the Alaska Range

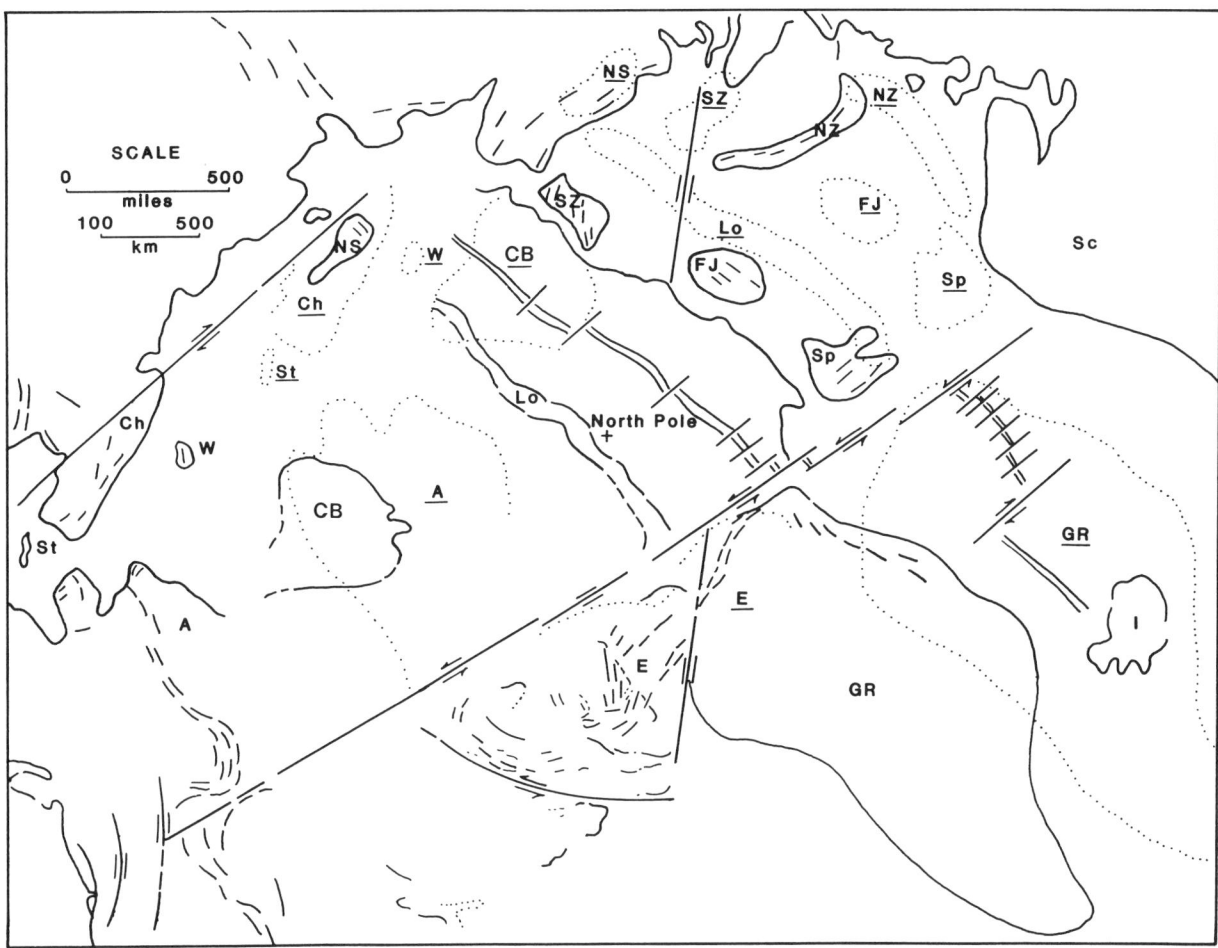

Figure 4. Figure illustrating the Arctic Islands strike-slip model redrawn from Dutro (1981) and showing the hypothetical development of the Arctic Ocean Basin and adjacent regions in post-Paleozoic time. A, northern Alaska; Ch, Chukchi Peninsula; CB, Chukchi Borderland; E, Ellesmere Island; FJ, Franz Josef Land; GR, Greenland; I, Iceland; Lo, Lomonosov Ridge; NS, New Siberian Islands; NZ, Novaya Zemlya; Sc, Scandinavia; Sp, Spitsbergen; St, St. Lawrence Island; SZ, Severna Zemlya; W, Wrangel Island. Dashed outlines with underlined letters indicate approximate positions during early Mesozoic time. Large arrows show directions of relative transport. Small arrows show relative transcurrent movements.

into the Alaska Peninsula and categorized the bend as an orocline. Grantz (1966) worked on the structure and tectonics of western Alaska and realized that the positions and trends of the strike-slip faults in western Alaska could be explained by a modification of Carey's (1958) oroclinal model. By 1967, it had been observed that there was a good paleogeographic fit between Arctic Alaska and Arctic Canada (Tailleur, 1973). Hamilton (1967, 1968) discussed the rotation of northern Alaska away from the Canadian Arctic Islands and felt that the rotational opening of the Canada Basin could be accommodated by the deflection of the Cordilleran front combined with strike-slip motion between Siberia and the Chukchi Shelf. In 1967, Tailleur presented a talk at the International Symposium on the Devonian System; he showed a slide of Arctic Alaska rotated clockwise about a pole south of the Mackenzie Delta that placed Early Mesozoic Alaska against Banks Island in the Canadian Arctic. His reconstruction juxtaposed the Devonian clastic wedges on the Amerasian continental edge with those in the Canadian Arctic Islands. Tailleur felt it was more likely that the Devonian clastic wedges had been shed off opposite flanks of a single linear uplift than off the southern flank of a 3,500-km-long semicircular uplift whose northern flank was an ocean deep. In August of 1967 at the Alaska Science Congress, Tailleur specified 30° to 40° of clockwise pivoting of Alaska about the northern end of the Canadian Rockies to restore "the counterclockwise drift suggested by Grantz and by Hamilton."

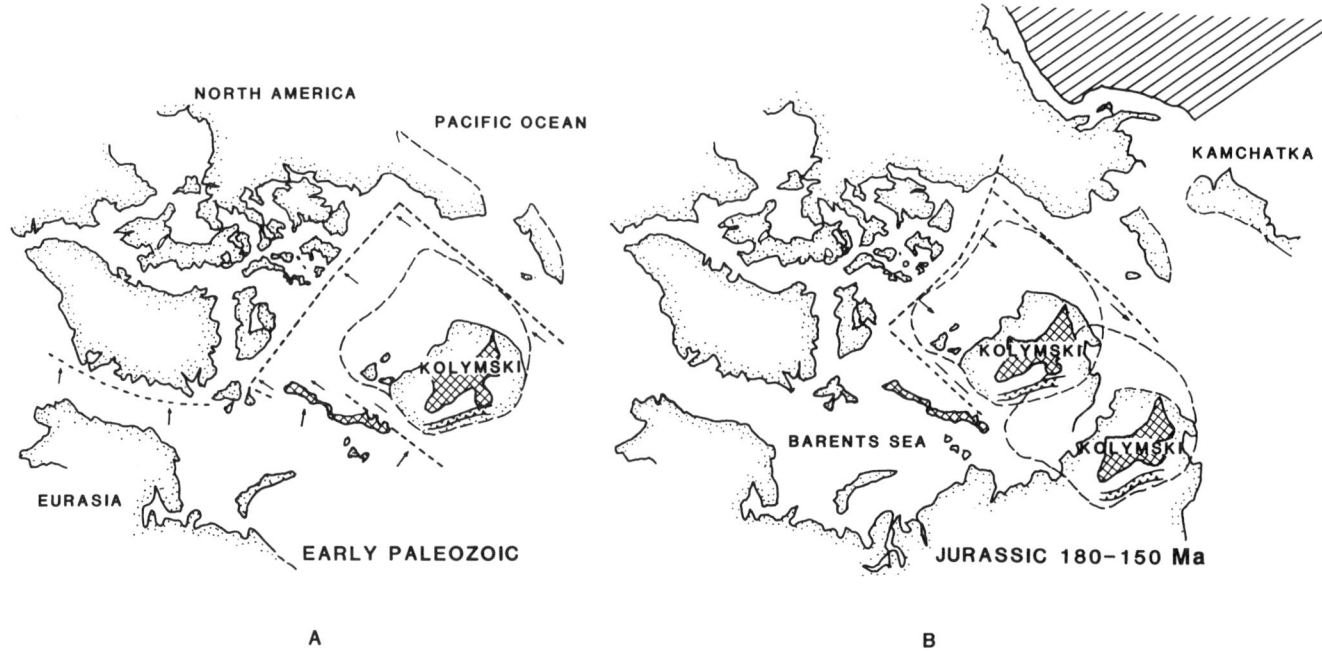

Figure 5. Figure redrawn from Herron and others (1974) showing the North Slope transform model. Heavy dashed lines with arrows show major plate boundaries and direction of movement relative to North America. (A) closure of proto-Amerasia Basin in early Paleozoic time. This motion culminated with mid-Paleozoic folding of Franklinian geoclinal sediments and shedding of clastic rocks onto Canadian Arctic Islands, Brooks Range, and Wrangel Island north of Chukotka. (B) opening of the Amerasia Basin during Jurassic magnetic quiet period, as Kolymski broke away from North America.

By 1969, Tailleur (1969) and Tailleur and Snelson (1969) described large-scale horizontal displacements in the Brooks Range and speculated that they could be explained if the Siberian-Chukchi shelf had drifted southeastward and that northern Alaska and the Arctic Islands had earlier rifted apart rotating open the Canada Basin. Tailleur (1969) showed a 30° rotational opening of the Canada Basin about a pole 500 km south of the Mackenzie Delta while Hamilton (1970) showed a rotational opening of the Canada Basin of about 50° about a pole that appears to be located 300 or 400 km south of the Mackenzie Delta. Hamilton's support for this model included the need for a northern source for the Carboniferous through Neocomian clastic rocks of northern Alaska and for an explanation of the bifurcating trends of the lower Paleozoic rocks in the northern Yukon Territory and in the Northwest Territories. He (Fig. 6 of Hamilton, 1970) was the first to show a model for the tectonic evolution of the Canada Basin and the Eurasia Basin.

Rickwood (1970) discussed the Prudhoe Bay field and concluded that the Canada Basin opened 67° about a pole of rotation located in the Mackenzie Delta. In the same symposium volume, Tailleur and Brosgé (1970) explained the geology of the North Slope in terms of a rotational opening of the Canada Basin between Neocomian and late Albian times. The timing of their model was based on changes in deposition observed in the geological record.

By 1970, the extension of the mid-ocean ridge in the Atlantic through the Norwegian-Greenland Sea and into the Eurasia Basin had been recognized and accepted as part of the global plate tectonics picture (Heezen and Ewing, 1961; Wilson, 1963; Vogt and others, 1970). Vogt and Ostenso (1970) inferred an age of 40 to 0 Ma for the Eurasia Basin from the Russian aeromagnetic data. They also inferred a sea-floor spreading origin for the Alpha and Mendeleev ridges, and an age for them of 60 to 40 Ma, but left the tectonic evolution of the Canada Basin undecided. Magnetic anomalies parallel to the Alpha Ridge had first been noticed by King and others (1966), and Ostenso (1962) had earlier noted the high-amplitude magnetic anomalies associated with the Alpha Ridge.

Churkin (1973, actually submitted in 1971) recognized that the Eurasia Basin was still active but that the rotational opening of the Canada Basin had to be much older. He used the model of Hamilton (1970) but concluded that the available data required opening of the modern Canada Basin (Late Jurassic or Early Cretaceous), subsidence of the deep Canada Basin (Late Cretaceous), and opening of the Eurasian Basin in connection with Cenozoic sea-floor spreading from the Arctic Mid-Ocean Ridge (Nansen-Gakkel Ridge).

In 1972, Pitman and Talwani (1972) published their paper on sea-floor spreading in the North Atlantic. This paper seems to have prompted speculation (Freeland and Dietz, 1973; Herron and others, 1974) on how to place the Canada Basin into a global framework. The location of the Pitman and Talwani (1972) pole of opening for North America–Eurasia (63.0°N, 157°E) for 63 Ma to present was used by Herron and others (1974) to explain the opening of the Eurasia Basin during the same time period. This work was prior to the identification of the sea-floor spreading anomalies by Karasik (1974). Linear magnetic anomalies had been first observed in the Eurasia Basin in 1968 (Karasik, 1968) while Vogt and others (1979) updated and confirmed Karasik's (1974) work with additional aeromagnetic data.

Freeland and Dietz (1973) used the ideas of Grantz (1966), Tailleur (1969), Tailleur and Brosgé (1970), Vogt and Ostenso (1970), and Pitman and Talwani (1972) to develop a model for the rotational history of Alaskan tectonic blocks. Freeland and Dietz (1973) also incorporated the translation of northeastern Siberia up against the Canadian Islands by strike-slip motion along the northern edge of Alaska and along the Lomonosov Ridge (Fig. 6). While Churkin (1973) assumed the Alpha Ridge to have been an active sea-floor spreading center, Freeland and Dietz (1973) ignored the Alpha and Mendeleev ridges since the strike-slip motion of the Siberian block rifting away from Arctic Canada cannot be reconciled with sea-floor spreading along the Alpha and Mendeleev ridges. While Freeland and Dietz (1973) incorporated the rotation of Alaska in their model, they in fact suggested the first major variation on the tectonic evolution of the Canada Basin.

For the Canada Basin, Herron and others (1974) postulated that during the early Paleozoic, the Kolymski block collided with Arctic Canada. Herron and others (1974) then modified the Freeland and Dietz (1973) idea to have all of the Kolymski block rifting away from Arctic Canada during the Jurassic on parallel strike-slip faults along the Lomonosov Ridge and along the North Slope of Alaska (Fig. 5). Their model was the first one to propose a tectonic history of the Canada Basin that did not include a rotational opening of the Canada Basin and did not result in passive margins on both Arctic Alaska and Arctic Canada. Because the pole of rotation for North America and Eurasia was located on the north coast of Greenland (81 Ma and 63 Ma; Pitman and Talwani, 1972), Herron and others (1974) postulated that the observed extension in the North Atlantic must have produced compression in the Canada Basin on the opposite side of the pole of rotation during the Cretaceous. This would have made the Alpha and Mendeleev ridges arc-related features rather than sea-floor spreading features as Vogt and others (1970) postulated. Vogt and Ostenso (1970) had earlier mentioned the possibility that the Alpha Ridge might be arc related, but their idea was based on a superficial resemblance between the Alpha Ridge and the Beata Ridge in the Caribbean, which was also believed to

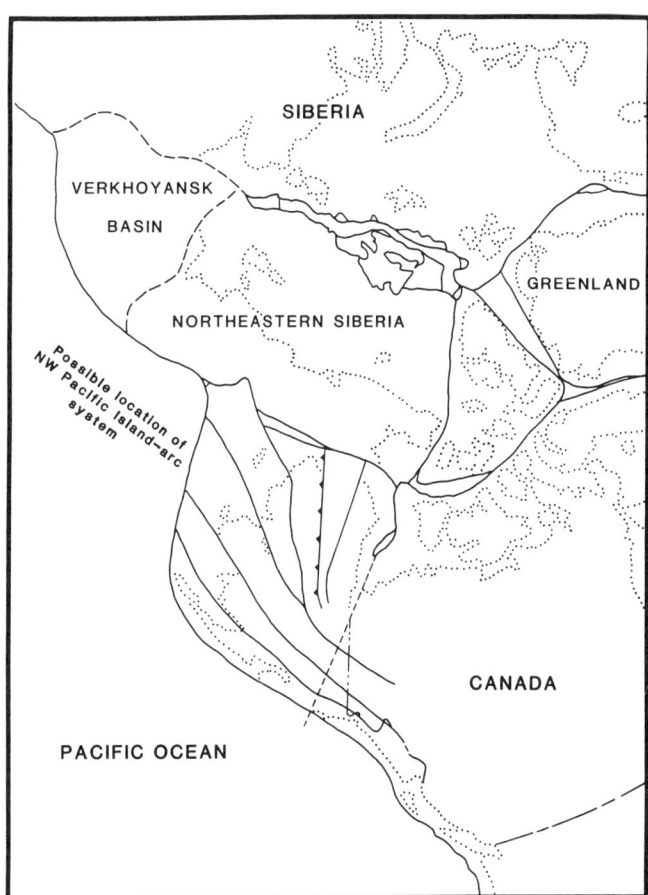

Figure 6. Tectonic reconstruction of the Canada Basin using the multi-block fanning model of Freeland and Dietz (1973). While Arctic Alaska is rotated against Banks Island, northeastern Siberia is translated away from Arctic Canada along transform faults parallel to the Lomonosov Ridge and the northern margin of Alaska.

be arc-related. Yorath and Norris (1975) presented a modification of the concepts of Herron and others (1974) that required extreme asymmetrical spreading from a spreading center that rifted the Kolymski block off Arctic Canada but then remained along Arctic Canada.

Sweeney and others (1978) used new geophysical data to support the Hamilton (1970) and Tailleur and Brosgé (1970) model for the rotational opening of the Canada Basin. De Laurier (1978) expanded the arguments by Herron and others (1974) and Clark (1975) that the Alpha and Mendeleev ridges could not have been produced by normal sea-floor spreading. De Laurier (1978) cited the age-versus-depth relationship of Parsons and Sclater (1977) on two separate points. The first implies that if the Alpha Ridge is at least 70 m.y. old (based on the age of silicoflagellates cored from its crest; Ling and others, 1973; Clark, 1974), then its relief should have decayed by 2,900 m to a minimum depth of 5,350 m and a total relief of not more than 1,000 m (as opposed to the 1,500 to 2,500 m of relief observed). The second point is, given the present relief that approximates an active but very slow spreading ridge, the present minimum depth of the Alpha Ridge, which ranges between 1,200 m and a saddle on the Mendeleev Ridge of just below 2,500 m, is well above the average depth for any active sea-floor spreading ridge.

Christie (1979) discussed the relationship of Svalbard to the Franklinian Geosyncline in the Canadian Arctic. He used the onshore geology to infer that these two features had been juxtaposed (Fig. 7) and that the Canada Basin opened with either spreading along the Alpha Ridge or spreading along a center parallel to the Alpha Ridge, resulting in transform fault motion along the Canadian Arctic. The Lomonosov Ridge, Arctic-Alaska, and "Bering Splinter" (part of Northeast Siberia) were all rifted margins. After the Canada Basin opened in the late Paleozoic or earliest Mesozoic, Cenozoic opening in the North Atlantic produced closure between the "Bering and Kolymski splinters" and Siberia so that the transform margin opposite to Arctic Canada was obscured.

Vogt and others (1979) found complex, sublinear, high-amplitude magnetic anomalies over the Alpha Ridge that correlate with topography and with free-air gravity data. In the northern Canada Basin, they found several prominent linear magnetic anomalies subparallel to the Alpha Ridge (Cordillera); which could not have been produced by sea-floor spreading along an axis parallel to either the Canadian continental margin (as Herron and others, 1974, suggested) or the Alpha Ridge (as Christie, 1979, suggested) but could be related to an axis parallel to the Northwind Ridge (Plate 4). Vogt and others (1982) further developed this model.

The first seismic reflection data from the continental margin north of Alaska was published by Eittreim and Grantz (1979) and Grantz and others (1979). Grantz and others (1979) concluded that the Arctic-Alaska margin was a passive margin of Atlantic type. In the west, the Chukchi sector is characterized by the deep late Mesozoic and Tertiary North Chukchi basins and the Chukchi Borderland (Continental Borderland). Grantz and others speculated that the Chukchi Borderland, which has continental affinities (Hunkins and others, 1962; Shaver and Hunkins, 1964), was rifted from the region of the North Chukchi Basin, and that the scattered continental fragments of the Chukchi Borderland would fit within the structurally deeper regions of the North Chukchi Basin. The linear Northwind Ridge could have functioned as a strike-slip fault as the Canada Basin opened and the Chukchi Borderland could be stretched and intruded continental crust (Plate 11).

Jones (1980) presented a new model, not classifiable with any of the previous models. In his model the Lomonosov Ridge can be considered a passive margin opposed by an indistinct passive margin in the deep Canada Basin. The remainder of the southern Canada Basin is old Paleozoic oceanic crust of uncertain origin. The sense of strike-slip motion along Arctic Alaska is opposite to that proposed by Vogt and others (1982) or Herron and others (1974). The sense of strike-slip motion along Arctic Canada is also opposite to that proposed by Christie (1979) and almost approximates a counterclockwise rotation of the Canada Basin as a block.

After Jones (1980), the more recent papers that discuss in situ formation of the Canada Basin have presented data and interpretations that support one of the four previous models or can be considered to be only slight modifications of the four. Of particular importance to our understanding of tectonic features in the Canada Basin have been the data presented from the CESAR (Canadian Expedition to Study the Alpha Ridge) study of the Alpha Ridge (Jackson and others, 1985). Even though they collected seismic refraction, heat flow, magnetics, gravity, and bathymetry data, they were able to conclude only that the Alpha Ridge is an oceanic plateau of problematic origin like the Ontong-Java and Manihiki plateaus of the Pacific (Forsyth and others, 1986). The data also support the earlier idea of Vogt and others (1979) that the Alpha and Mendeleev ridges were formed similar to the present-day Icelandic hotspot. Lawver and others (1983) suggested that the Alpha and Mendeleev ridges may have been formed by a hot spot that developed near the Siberian side. As the active ridge that opened the Canada Basin passed over the hot spot, the plume transferred to the Arctic Canada side. Their model would explain both the apparent necking of the Mendeleev Ridge near 81°N and the change in strike between the Alpha and Mendeleev ridges. Forsyth and others (1986) propose that the hot spot or plume that formed the Alpha Ridge continued under Greenland and may manifest itself presently as the Icelandic hotspot.

An important constraint on the movement of northern Alaska with respect to North America would be reliable paleomagnetic results. Newman and others (1977) determined paleopoles from Late Devonian and Mississippian strata from the Brooks Range and used paleomagnetic data from 12 major stratigraphic sections and an oriented core from Prudhoe Bay. They found the paleopoles to be "highly divergent" from coeval North American poles and to show a counterclockwise rotation of about 70° for a continental plate that included all of the North Slope and Brooks Range of Alaska and the adjacent Yukon Territory. Hillhouse and Grommé (1983), however, found that Upper Devonian and Mississippian sedimentary rocks in a large part of the Brooks Range had been remagnetized by a major episode of thrusting and folding during the Cretaceous, so they concluded that paleomagnetic results from the Brooks Range could not be used to confirm a rotational opening of the Canada Basin. They did report on two additional oriented cores taken from the Lower Triassic Ivishak Formation and the pre-Mississippian argillite from East Simpson no. 2, a National Petroleum Reserve-Alaska well on the coast about 250 km west-northwest of Prudhoe Bay. While the Lower Triassic Ivishak Formation core gave a poorly defined paleomagnetic pole of probable post-Triassic age, the other core, taken in the pre-Mississippian argillite, carried a stable magnetic component (in hematite) that probably originated during deposition of the overlying Mississippian red beds (Hillhouse and Grommé, 1983).

LATE PALEOZOIC: VARISCAN

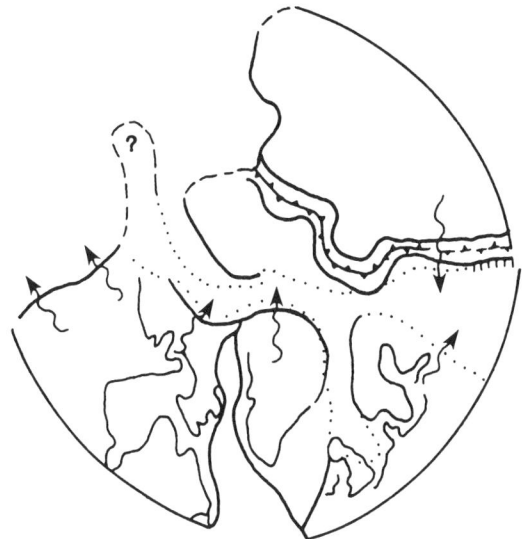

LATE PALEOZOIC–EARLIEST MESOZOIC: RIFTING

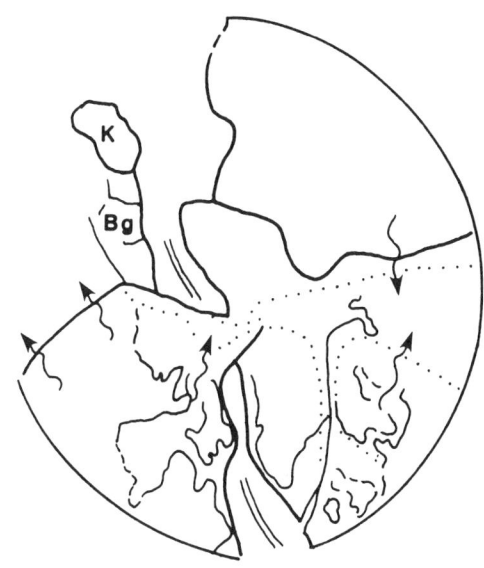

MID-TO LATE MESOZOIC: RIFTING

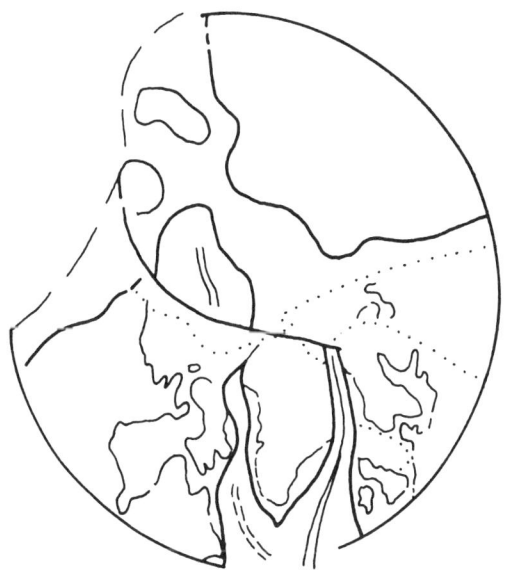

LATE CRETACEOUS–EARLY CENOZOIC: RIFTING, VOLCANISM

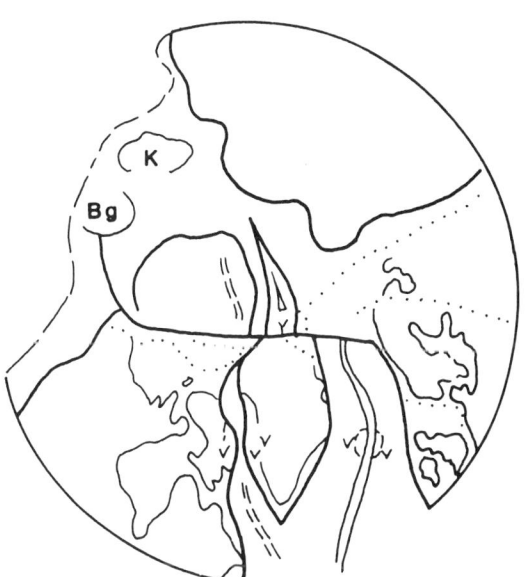

Figure 7. Figure redrawn from Christie (1979). Stages in a hypothetical reconstruction of continents of the Arctic region using an FPFP model for the evolution of the Canada Basin. Bg, Bering splinter; K, Kolymski splinter; dotted line indicates late Paleozoic–Mesozoic successor basin; double line indicates an active spreading center; dashed double line indicates "fossil spreading center"; wiggly arrow indicates direction of sedimentary transport.

They found that the hematite zone gives a pole consistent with large-scale counterclockwise rotation of Arctic Alaska.

Finally, Halgedahl and Jarrard (1987), undertook a paleomagnetic study using fully oriented drill cores from two ARCO wells in the Kuparuk River oil field, immediately west of Prudhoe Bay. Unlike the earlier studies, which were uncertain of the timing of the rotational opening of the Canada Basin, the ARCO study concentrated on the Kuparuk River formation, a Lower Cretaceous clastic shelf sequence of Valangian to Barremian age, which is possibly the youngest pre-emplacement formation on the North Slope. Their results are only compatible with the 70° counterclockwise rotation of the Arctic Alaska block away from Arctic Canada about a pole of rotation in the Mackenzie Delta. Furthermore, they conclude that the rotation began at approximately 130 Ma and ended no later than about 100 Ma, when collision between the Arctic Alaska block and the South Anyui-Yukon-Koyukuk trench triggered the Brookian orogeny.

Major aeromagnetic programs of the U.S. Navy were reported by Taylor and others (1981), Vogt and others (1981), and Vogt and others (1982). While Taylor and others (1981) interpreted the Canada Basin aeromagnetic results as indicating sea-floor spreading of Jurassic age (153 Ma to 127 Ma: DNAG timescale; Palmer, 1983) and supportive of a rotational opening of the Canada Basin, Vogt and others (1982, p. 333) reinterpreted the data and concluded that such questions (of tectonic evolution) "cannot be resolved with existing data, or even with more of the same." They suggest that using the tectonic models as guides, multiyear, multidisciplinary airlifted experiments deployed on ice flows will be needed to make major progress in our understanding of the tectonic evolution of the Canada Basin.

TECTONIC SETTING OF THE CANADA BASIN

In order to provide a proper framework to study the evolution of the Canada Basin, the North Atlantic and Eurasia basins must be closed, restoring North America and Eurasia to their predrift configuration. This exercise itself is not without controversy. Though numerous reconstructions of the North Atlantic have been proposed (Bullard and others, 1965; Sclater and others, 1977; Srivastava, 1978; Unternehr, 1982; Srivastava and Tapscott, 1986), most investigations have focused on the evolution of the Atlantic region, and little attention has been paid to the fit between North America and northeastern Eurasia. Indeed, most of these reconstructions require 1,000 to 2,000 km of east-to-west closure between Alaska and northeast Eurasia as a consequence of sea-floor spreading in the North Atlantic during the Tertiary. It is difficult to find evidence for compression of this magnitude.

Another unresolved problem is the fit of Greenland and North America, and the implied offset across the Nares Strait (Dawes and Kerr, 1982). Geological and structural arguments have been made suggesting that the offset along the Nares Strait fault is less than 50 km (Dawes and Kerr, 1982); however, complete closure of Baffin Bay and the Labrador Sea requires at least

TABLE 1. POLES OF ROTATION FOR PLATES WITH RESPECT TO NORTH AMERICA*

Continent	Latitude	Longitude	Angle
North America	0.00	0.00	0.00
Greenland	-50.07	6.29	7.74
Europe	-69.34	-33.20	23.61
Iberia	-74.43	176.23	49.76
Ellesmere Island	-68.72	77.34	11.36

*The reconstruction using these poles produces the framework for the Canada Basin shown in Figure 8.

250 km of sinistral strike-slip movement (Wilson, 1963; Johnson and Srivastava, 1982).

In an attempt to solve these problems, we propose the North Atlantic reconstruction illustrated in Figure 8. In this reassembly, North America and northeastern Eurasia are nearly contiguous. The closure between these regions, required by the opening of the North Atlantic and Eurasia basins, is about 500 km and can be accommodated by compression along the Delong Mountains in northwestern Alaska and in the Verkhoyansk foldbelt between Kolyma and Siberia. Greenland is fitted tightly against Baffin Island and Labrador. The offset along the Nares Strait fault is kept to a minimum by undeforming the Eurekan foldbelt and by unstretching the grabens in the Lawrence, Jones, and Viscount-Melville sounds. Also, in this reconstruction the Lomonosov Ridge has been rotated independently with respect to North America. Approximately 300 km of right-lateral displacement is required between the southern end of the Lomonosov Ridge and northernmost Ellesmere Island (Vogt and others, 1982). The poles of rotation used to produce the reconstruction illustrated in Figure 8 are listed in Table I.

TECTONIC FEATURES OF THE CANADA BASIN

The major tectonic features of the Canada Basin that must be accounted for in any tectonic model are the Alpha Ridge, the Mendeleev Ridge, the Chukchi Borderland, and the Northwind Ridge (Fig. 1). Most authors agree that the crust of the Chukchi Borderland and Northwind Ridge is stretched continental crust or transitional crust (Sweeney and others, 1978). These latter features are thought to be derived from either the North Chukchi Basin (Grantz and May, 1983) or from the continental margin adjacent to Banks Island (Metz and others, 1982; Mair and Forsyth, 1982; Vogt and others, 1982; Rowley and others, 1985).

More problematic are the Alpha and Mendeleev ridges, which have been interpreted to be: (1) an extinct spreading center (Johnson and Heezen, 1967; Beal, 1968; Vogt and Ostenso,

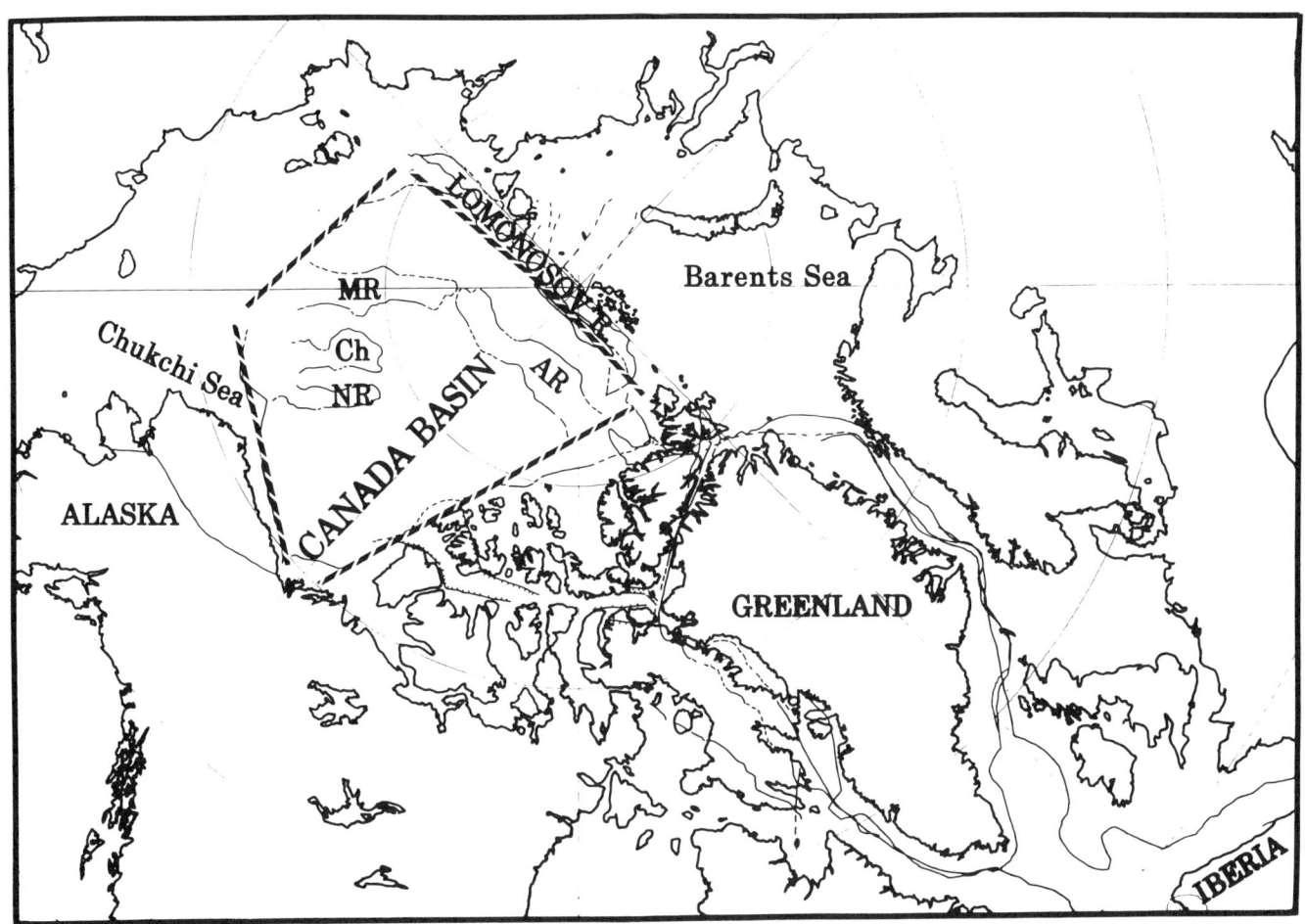

Figure 8. The Arctic region restored to its configuration prior to opening in the Eurasia Basin and Labrador Sea. Lightweight line in northern Alaska is the assumed boundary between Arctic Alaska, which moved as an independent piece, and the remainder of Alaska, which is not considered to have been involved in the tectonic evolution of the Canada Basin. MR, Mendeleev Ridge; Ch, Chukchi Borderland; NR, Northwind Escarpment; AR, Alpha Ridge.

1970; Ostenso and Wold, 1971; Hall, 1970, 1973; Christie, 1979; Jones, 1980); (2) a thin sliver of continental crust like the Lomonosov Ridge (Johnson and others, 1978); (3) a stretched fragment of continental or transitional crust (King and others, 1966; Kerr, 1980; Karasik and others, 1984; Crane, 1987); (4) an island arc (Herron and others, 1974; Taylor, 1978; Churkin and Trexler, 1980; Rowley and others, 1985); (5) a oceanic plateau (Vogt and others, 1981; Jackson and others, 1986); (6) a "hot spot" trace (Vogt and others, 1979; Lawver and others, 1983); (7) a "leaky transform" (Embry, 1985, and personal communication); or (8) the result of excess ridge axis volcanism, as in the case of Iceland (Vogt and others, 1982; Forsyth and others, 1986; Smith, 1987).

The presence of Late Cretaceous sediments along the axis of the Alpha Ridge indicates that if it was a spreading center, it was not active during the Tertiary. A Mesozoic age for spreading is also unlikely because the corrected depth to basement (2.5 km) is far too shallow, since a spreading center of Cretaceous age would have subsided to a depth of 4 to 5 km (DeLaurier, 1978). Recent results of the CESAR study indicate that the topography of the ridge is complex, unlike the Lomonosov Ridge (Jackson and Johnson, 1984). The axial valley of the Alpha Ridge is an elongate graben with a thick cover of sediments (>400 m). Samples dredged from the steep northeastern flank of the valley have been identified as vesicular alkali basalt (Van Wagoner and Robinson, 1985), indicating that at one time at least part of the ridge was very shallow. Though the evidence is not conclusive, recent discussions of the Alpha and Mendeleev ridges (Jackson and others, 1986; Smith, 1987) tend to favor an oceanic origin, similar to Iceland or the high-standing plateaus of the Pacific.

CLASSIFICATION SCHEME

As shown in Figure 8, the Canada Basin can be considered to have four sides: (1) Arctic Canada, (2) Arctic Alaska (also known as the North Slope of Alaska), (3) Siberia, and (4) either the Lomonosov Ridge or the Alpha and Mendeleev ridges. One of the most important features of the various models for the Canada Basin is the prediction that is made as to whether these margins have acted as passive or strike-slip boundaries. We have classified the tectonic models for the Canada Basin according to a scheme where (P) indicates a passive, extensional margin and (F) represents a strike-slip, transform margin (Table 2). The annotation (c) indicates the few cases where the margins have been characterized as compressive.

The four circum-Arctic margins can be classified as passive (P) or transform (F) boundaries in 16 different ways. The number of likely configurations, however, is less because geometry requires that each passive margin have a conjugate margin, eliminating PFFF, FPFF, FFPF, and FFFP. Two other possible configurations, PPPP or FFFF, seem highly unlikely. The model first proposed by Carey (1958) as the oroclinal bending model, and more recently referred to as the "rotational" model, would be classified as a PPPF, because in this model, a combined North Slope (P) and Siberian (P) block rotates away from Arctic Canada (P), along a transform fault formed by the Alpha and Mendeleev ridges or Lomonosov Ridge (F). Four of the probable ten models (PPPF, PPFP, PFPP, FPPP) are variations of the "rotational" model with the pivot point simply changed from the Mackenzie Delta to the other corners.

Many of the evolutionary models for the Canada Basin that have been proposed in the past two decades are contradictory. Most of the models assume the same boundaries as we show in Figure 8, although some consider Arctic Alaska to be continuous with the Siberian margin. A few of the models combine trapped oceanic crust with crust formed in situ, which leads to over simplification in order to place every model into the four boundary schemes. The chosen models generally address at least two of the four boundaries of the Canada Basin and are tabulated in Table 2.

Model A. Rotational (PPPF)

(Carey, 1955, 1958; Grantz, 1966; Hamilton, 1967, 1968; Tailleur, 1969; Tailleur and Snelson, 1969; Tailleur and Brosgé, 1970; Rickwood, 1970; Tailleur, 1973; Freeland and Dietz, 1973; Johnson and others, 1978; Sweeney and others, 1978; Grantz and others, 1979; Grantz and others, 1981; Mair and Forsyth, 1982; Sweeney and others, 1982; Vogt and others, 1982; May and Grantz, 1983; Sweeney, 1983; Burke, 1984; Green and others, 1984; Harland and others, 1984; Embry, 1985; Sweeney, 1985; McWhae, 1986).

A rotational opening of the Canada Basin was first proposed by Carey (1955) based on his concept of oroclinal bending; he later related it to plate tectonics. Hamilton (1968), Tailleur (1969), Tailleur and Brosgé (1970), following the suggestion of Grantz (1966), applied the concept of rotational opening of the Canada Basin to explain the change in provenance directions of North Slope sediments.

Prior to the uplift of the Brooks Range, sediments on the North Slope had a northern source and prograded southward. The tectonic land of the Innuitian foldbelt was the source for the clastic deposits on Wrangell Island and for the clastic wedge of the Endicott Group in northern Alaska (Tailleur and Brosgé, 1970). The prerifting phase of the Canada Basin was thought to coincide with 193 Ma diabase intrusives that were emplaced into a condensed sequence of Early and Middle Jurassic chert, limestone, and oil shale (Kingak). The "pebble shale" that unconformably overlies the Kingak shale was considered by Tailleur and Brosgé (1970) to indicate the last strong influence of the Innuitian landmass. They dated the rotational opening of the Canada Basin as Aptian-Albian (119 to 97 Ma), with a pole of rotation located approximately 500 km south of the Mackenzie Delta.

Rickwood (1970) produced a fit of the Barrow Arch section of the North Slope of Alaska to the Banks Island section of Arctic Canada in which he estimated that roughly 67° of rotational opening had taken place about a pole in the southern part of the Mackenzie Delta. He suggested that the opening of the Canada Basin was contemporaneous with the observed faulting along the margin that ranged in age from Late Neocomian to Barremian, just slightly older than the Tailleur and Brosgé (1970) estimate. Rickwood (1970) also pointed out that it was at this time that the Brooks Range began to rise, perhaps as a consequence of the opening.

Grantz and others (1979) rotated the 1,000 m isobaths by 66° about a pole at 69.1°N, 130.5°W and found that the coastlines from the Mackenzie delta west to the Northwind Escarpment fit well against the Canadian Arctic Islands (Fig. 3). The authors noted that the Lomonosov Ridge fell on a small circle about this pole of rotation. In the same study, Grantz and others (1979) summarized the depositional characteristics of the North Slope strata between the Mackenzie Delta and Camden Bay. West of Camden Bay, the northern source continued to shed debris, but waningly so through the Late Jurassic and the Neocomian. They concluded that initial rifting may have begun in the Mackenzie Delta region as early as the Middle Jurassic, but that actual opening of the Canada Basin was delayed until late Neocomian time.

Vogt and others (1982) suggested a similar scenario for the opening based on a fan-shaped set of magnetic anomalies in the Canada Basin (Taylor and others, 1981). In this model, the North Slope of Alaska first rotated away from Arctic Canada about a pole in the Mackenzie Delta, with a younger rift splitting the Chukchi Plateau away from Arctic Canada (Fig. 9).

Other workers have also preferred the rotational model (Sweeney and others, 1978, 1982; Mair and Forsyth, 1982; Burke, 1984; Green and others, 1984; Harland and others, 1984; Embry, 1985; McWhae, 1986). These models are similar in that they rift the Arctic Alaska block from along the margins of the

TABLE 2. CLASSIFICATION OF MODELS FOR THE OPENING OF THE CANADA BASIN
(The models listed all assume in situ formation of oceanic crust.)

Models by Author	Classification			
	Arctic	North Slope	Siberia	Lomonosov
Grantz (1966)	P	P	P	F
Hamilton (1967, 1968)	P	P	P	F
Tailleur (1969)	P	P	P	F
Tailleur and Snelson (1969)	P	P	P	F
Tailleur and Brosge (1970)	P	P	P	F
Tailleur (1973)	P	P	P	F
Freeland and Dietz (1973)	P	P	P	F
Sweeney and others (1978)	P	P	P	F
Johnson and others (1978)	P	P	-	F-P*
Grantz and others (1979)	P	P	P	F
Green and others (1986)	P	P	P	F
Sweeney (1982)	P	P	P	F
Vogt and others (1982)	P	P	-	F
May and Grantz (1983)	-	P	-	-†
Sweeney (1983)	-	P	-	-†
Burke (1984)	P	P	P	F
Harland and others (1984)	P	P	P	F
Embry (1985)	P	P	P	F
Sweeney (1985)	P	P	P	F
McWhae (1986)	P	P	P	F
Ostenso (1974)	P	P	F	P§
Christie (1979)	P	P	-	P
Crane (1987)	P	P	F	P
Smith (1987)	P	P	F	P
Herron and others (1974)	P	F	P	F(c)**
Vogt and others (1982)	P	F	-	F††
Metz and others (1982)	P	F	P	F
Rowley and others (1985)	P	F	-	(c)††
Jones (1980)	F	F	F	P§§
Jones (1983)	F	F	F	P

Classification: F = strike-slip faulting
P = passive
(c) = compressive

*F during early history (Cretaceous), in Tertiary opening of Makarov Basin is precursor to opening along Arctic Mid-Ocean Ridge.

†Classification of North Slope as passive margin consistent with PPPF and FPFP models.

§Implied from assignment of Alpha Ridge as Cretacesous spreading center.

**F during early history (Cretaceous), in Tertiary (c) due to opening of North Atlantic.

††Though similar to models by Herron and others (1974) and Metz and others (1982), in this model only the Chukchi Borderland rifts away from Arctic Canada.

§§In this model, part of the Canada Basin consists of trapped late Paleozoic ocean crust.

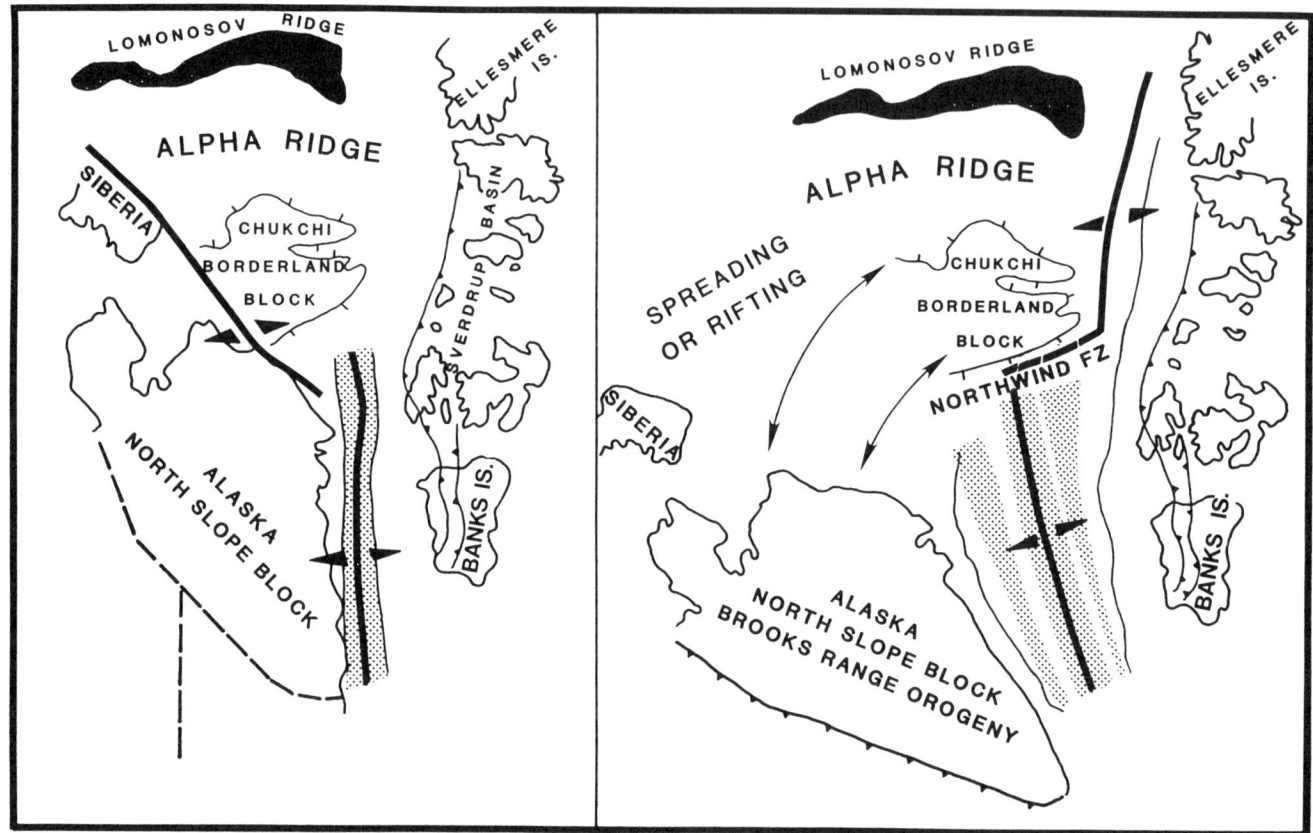

Figure 9. Variation on the rotational model redrawn from Vogt and others (1982). The initial rifting between the Canadian Arctic Islands and Arctic Alaska only extends between the Mackenzie Delta region and the Chukchi Borderland with the remainder of the extension occurring between the Chukchi Borderland and Alaska and Siberia as Hamilton (1970) suggested. At a later time (right-hand figure), the Chukchi Borderland block also begins to move away from Arctic Canada as Alaska continues to rotate away. While they show the Alpha Ridge in existence at the time of these scenarios, it is not essential to their hypothesis.

Canadian Arctic Islands; however, they differ in the exact timing of the motion and the presumed extent of the reconstructed "rotational" block.

Harland and others (1984) utilized the rotational model to explain the formation of the Canada Basin during the Late Jurassic to earliest Cretaceous. In their model, the North Slope of Alaska was originally located adjacent to Ellesmere Island–northern Greenland during the Middle Devonian. They suggest that at least 1,000 km of left-lateral strike-slip motion along Arctic Canada occurred before the late Carboniferous to bring the North Slope of Alaska into its predrift position. The existence of a major inactive strike-slip fault may have been the cause for the later rifting along the same boundary.

Embry (1985) noted four regional unconformities in Arctic Canada that he related to the tectonic development of the Canada Basin: (1) a Middle Jurassic unconformity, followed by the development of grabens (e.g., Eglinton graben) parallel to the future margin of the Canada Basin, related to the onset of rifting; (2) a Callovian (latest Middle Jurassic) unconformity, caused by a subsequent episode of rifting and graben development; (3) a widespread late Valangian and early Hauterivian (Early Cretaceous) unconformity that Embry (1985) relates to the onset of sea-floor spreading (during this later phase, subsidence rates along the Arctic margin increased rapidly and basalt flows appeared for the first time in the Mesozoic succession); and (4) the final stage (earliest Late Cretaceous), during which uplift occurred, was coincident with the final phase of volcanism and collision. Embry suggests that sea-floor spreading in the Canada Basin ceased at this time and that the continental margin began to undergo thermal subsidence.

Embry (1985) also suggests that the rotational model restores the continuity of predrift facies trends. The axis of deposition of predrift Mesozoic strata (Triassic-Hauterivian) crosses the Canadian Arctic Islands and is truncated by the con-

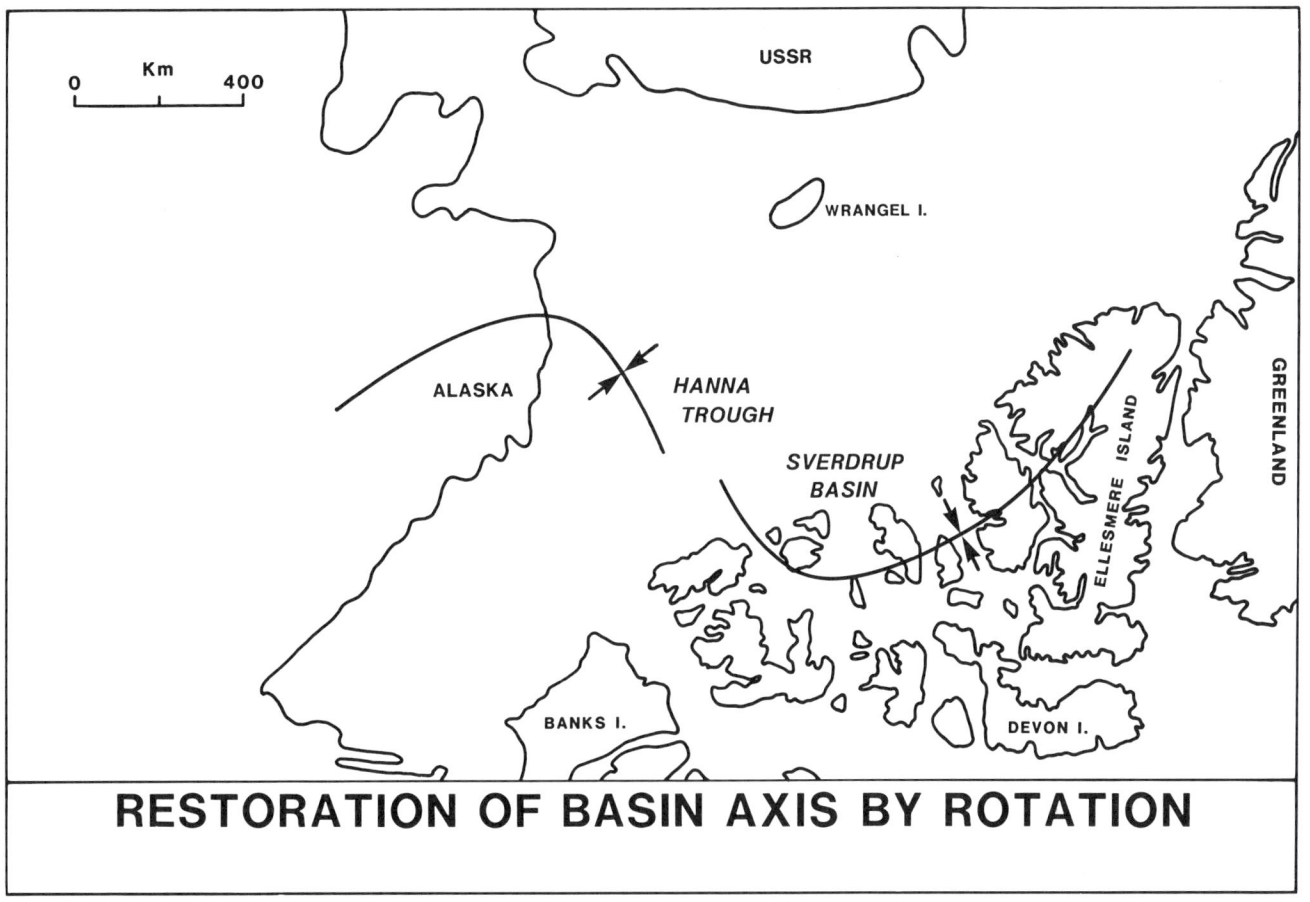

Figure 10. Provided by Embry (personal communication, 1986). The depocenter axis of the predrift Mesozoic strata can be traced through the Canadian Arctic Islands to where it is truncated perpendicular to the Canada Basin margin. Clockwise rotation of northern Alaska and adjacent northeastern Siberia about the pivot in the Mackenzie Delta restores this truncated axis with a similarly truncated basin axis on the Chukchi Shelf.

tinental margin in the vicinity of Banks Island. The rotation of the North Slope block restores this truncated basin axis (Hanna Trough) on the Chukchi Shelf (Fig. 10).

McWhae (1986) also advocates a rotational opening of the Canada Basin (between 125 and 85 Ma) about a pole in the Mackenzie Delta. McWhae (1986) suggests that when spreading ceased in the Canada Basin, movement along the Kaltag and associated strike-slip faults during the Late Cretaceous severed the North Slope of Alaska from the North American plate and it became part of the northeasterly moving Eurasian plate.

Though the rotational model has been popular until recently, paleomagnetic evidence documenting the rotation of the North Slope has been difficult to obtain. Earlier workers were frustrated by both the lack of suitable rock types (few red beds or volcanic rocks) and the presence of a pervasive Cretaceous overprint (Newman and others, 1977; Hillhouse and Grommé, 1983). The most recent effort by Halgedahl and Jarrard (1987), clearly supports the rotational model. From studying fully oriented drill cores from the North Slope, Halgedahl and Jarrard (1987) determined a pole position for the Valanginian (chrons M14 through M11; 138 to 133 Ma) section of the Kuparuk River Formation (49.1°N and 146.1°W). When compared with paleomagnetic poles for cratonic North America, the Kuparuk pole suggests significant relative motion between North America and the North Slope block. As illustrated in Figure 11, the rotational model is compatible with these new data.

Model B. Arctic Islands Strike-Slip (FPFP)

(Ostenso, 1974; Christie, 1979; Kerr, 1981; Dutro, 1981; Crane, 1987; Smith, 1987)

Model B, like the rotational model, also predicts that Arctic-Alaska is a passive margin; however, the conjugate margin is not the Canadian Arctic, but rather the Lomonosov Ridge or the

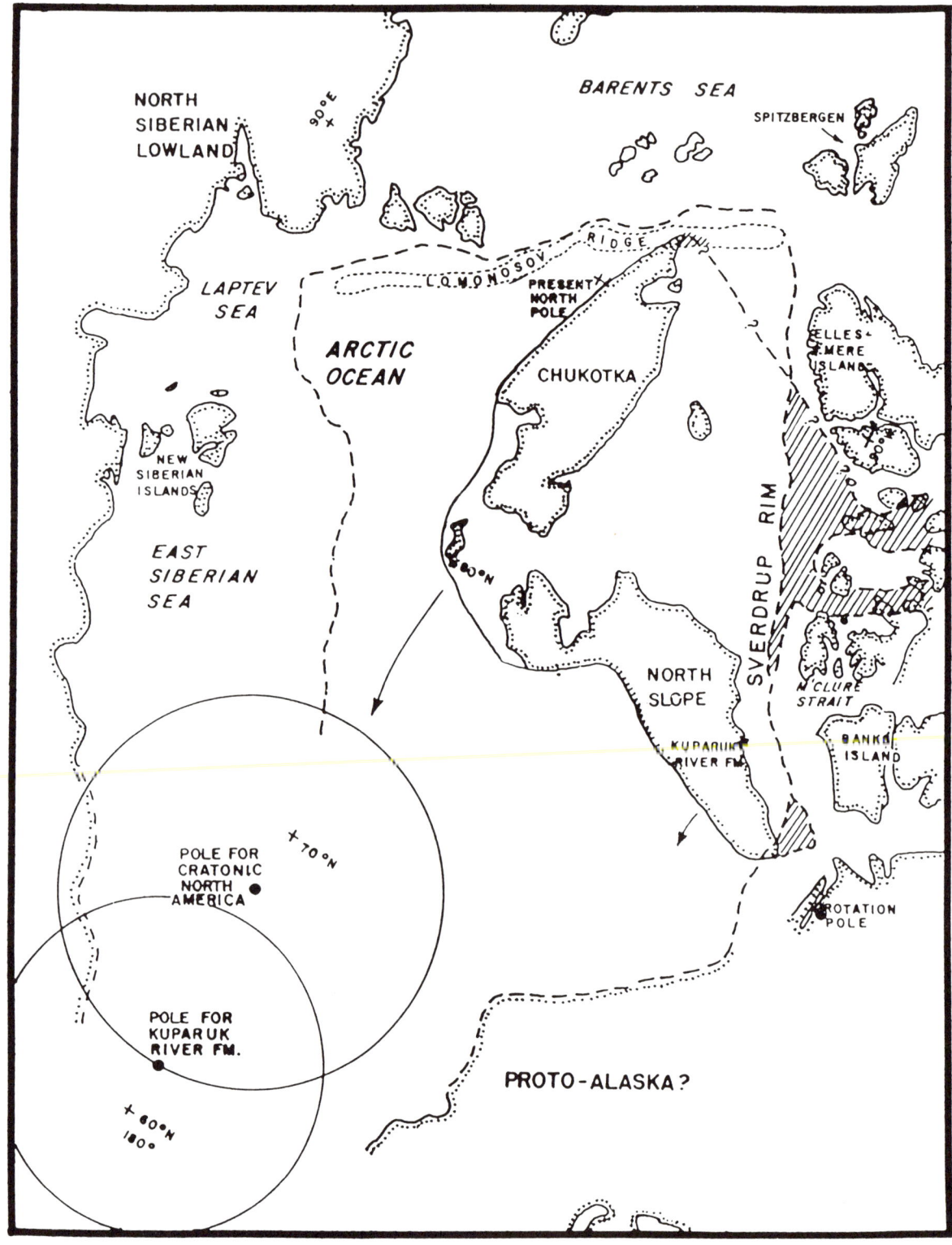

Figure 11. Taken from Halgedahl and Jarrard (1987). Comparisons of the mean Kuparuk River paleomagnetic pole to the 120-Ma pole for cratonic North America using the rotational (PPPF) model for the evolution of the Canada Basin.

Alpha and Mendeleev ridges. In this scenario, the Canadian Arctic margin acted as a left-lateral transform fault. Though strike-slip movement along the margin of the Arctic Islands was implicit in many of the early suggestions that the Alpha Ridge was a spreading center (Johnson and Heezen, 1967; Beal, 1968; Vogt and Ostenso, 1970; Ostenso and Wold, 1971; Hall, 1970, 1973), Christie (1979) was one of the first workers to use this framework to explain the tectonic development of the Canada Basin (Fig. 7).

Set in the context of a general discussion of the Franklinian orogenic belt, Christie's (1979) model suggests that during the late Paleozoic–earliest Mesozoic, rifting began in the Canada Basin either on, or parallel to, the Alpha and Mendeleev ridges. This opening produced a rifted margin along the Lomonosov Ridge, Arctic Alaska, and Bering Sea splinter, and resulted in transform motion along the margin of the Canadian Arctic (Fig. 7).

Dutro (1981) and Kerr (1981) supported the interpretation that the Canadian Arctic margin was bounded by a transform fault, noting that the margin is remarkably straight and might be an extension of the Kaltag/Porcupine fault system, as suggested by Yorath and Norris (1975). Kerr (1981) concluded that the Canada Basin is an ancient ocean basin that formed during a rifting episode in the late Paleozoic (Mississippian). Dutro (1981) indicates a substantial Canada Basin predating the early Mesozoic that was later enlarged by rifting during the Jurassic. The Alpha Ridge was considered by both of them to be the spreading center that created the basin (Fig. 4).

Recently, two similar models for the evolution of the Canada Basin have been proposed by Smith (1987) and Crane (1987). Both models use approximately the same tectonic elements and begin to open the Canada Basin at about the same time (150 Ma). In both Crane (1987) and Smith (1987), the Chukchi Borderland and Mendeleev Ridge are foundered continental fragments. Crane also considers the Alpha Ridge to be of continental origin; however, Smith is less certain and allows that the inclusion or exclusion of it would not "substantially" affect the major features of the reconstruction. The reconstructed positions of these fragments against the Lomonosov Ridge is somewhat tighter in the fit (Fig. 12) of Smith (1987), and the shape and extent of the North Slope and Chukotka blocks, in both models, are quite different. The North Slope block in the Crane (1987) model is larger, and includes Wrangel Island (Fig. 13). According to Smith, Wrangell Island is part of the Chukotka block, as is the Seward Peninsula. In Crane (1987), the Seward Peninsula is a separate block that travels independently of the North Slope and Chukotka terranes.

The tectonic scenario outlined by both models is very similar. The Canada Basin began to open in the Late Jurassic (150 Ma), as the North Slope terrane rifted away from the Alpha Ridge and the Chukotka terrane translated dextrally with respect to the Siberian margin. By the mid-Cretaceous the Chukchi Borderland and Mendeleev Ridge had been stretched and rifted away from the Lomonosov margin. The Canada Basin had finished spreading by 80 Ma (at the latest), and the focus of rifting shifted to the North Atlantic. Both Crane and Smith suggest that the Makarov Basin formed in the early Tertiary, and was a precursor to spreading along the Arctic Mid-Ocean Ridge. Halgedahl and Jarrard (1987) referred to this as the Lomonosov Ridge model in their paper.

Model C. Arctic-Alaska Transform (PFPF)

(Herron and others, 1974; Vogt and others, 1982; Metz and others, 1982; Rowley and others, 1985)

Model C is the converse of Model B; the assignment of passive and transform margins has been switched. In the resulting model, the Canadian Arctic is a passive margin, as is the Siberian shelf edge (including the Chukchi Borderland). Consequently, the North Slope margin and Lomonosov Ridge are the transform faults that bound the basin.

The most familiar model that falls into this category was proposed by Herron and others (1974). In their model, the Kolymski block collides with Arctic Canada during the early Paleozoic (Franklinian orogeny; Fig. 5). The same block rifts away during Middle Jurassic (187 to 163 Ma) with transform motion parallel to Arctic Alaska and the Lomonosov Ridge (Fig. 5). The Canada Basin was fully opened when the Kolymski block collided with Siberia along the Verkhoyansk fold belt in Early Cretaceous time. During the period 81 Ma to 63 Ma, the pole of opening between North America and Eurasia was in northern Greenland (Pitman and Talwani, 1972). Herron and others (1974) assumed that such a pole would necessitate compression north of Greenland and suggested that the compression was accommodated, in part, by subduction along the Alpha and Mendeleev ridges.

Recently, modified versions of Model C (PFPF) have been proposed (Vogt and others, 1982; Metz and others, 1982; Rowley and others, 1985). In these models, as in Herron and others (1974), the North Slope margin is a left-lateral strike-slip fault and the Canadian Arctic is a passive margin. However, the Chukchi Borderland, rather than the Kolymski block, is the terrane that rifts away from the Arctic Islands (Fig. 14). This interpretation is in best agreement with the trend of linear magnetic anomalies in the Canadian Basin (Vogt and others, 1982) and crustal structure inferred from seismic refraction studies (Mair and Lyons, 1981). Rowley and others (1985) take this model one step further and argue that the Canada Basin is, in effect, a back-arc basin that opened as a result of subduction to the west beneath the Alpha and Mendeleev ridges.

Model D. Yukon Strike Slip (FFFP)

Jones (1980, 1982, 1983) postulated a model for the development of the Canada Basin based on petroleum exploration data collected in the Mackenzie Delta region. He assumed that much of the crust in the Canada Basin was Paleozoic in age and was attached to Arctic Canada as part of the North American plate. The North Slope of Alaska and northeast Siberia formed a single

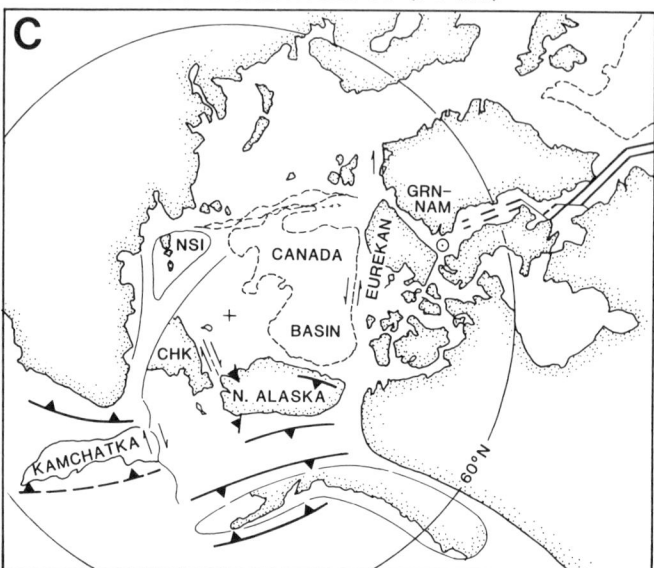

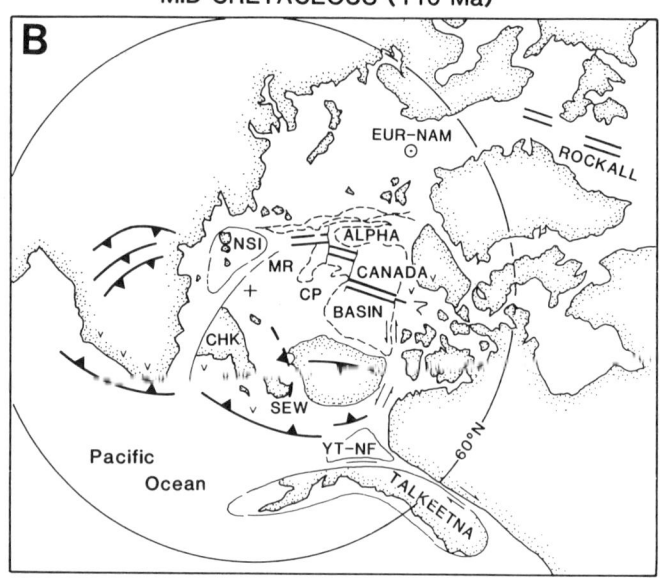

Figure 12. Figures redrawn from Smith (1987) illustrating a modification of the Arctic Islands strike-slip (FPFP) model. Ax, Axel Heiberg; CHK, Chukotka block; CP, Chukchi Borderland; ELL, Ellesmere; EUR-NAM, pole of opening for Eurasia-North America; GRN-NAM, pole of opening for Greenland-North America; MR, Mendeleev Ridge; NSI, New Siberian Islands; OM, Omolon block; PR, Prikolymsk block; YT-NF, Yukon-Koyukok block; SEW, Seward Peninsula. (A) reconstruction of the Canada Basin region at 150 Ma prior to the opening of the Canada Basin, (B) mid-Cretaceous reconstruction of the region showing active spreading occurring parallel to the Alpha Ridge. (C) Late Cretaceous reconstruction showing continued motion along strike-slip faults bordering the Canada Basin.

Figure 13. Figure redrawn from Crane (1987) showing his reconstruction of the Arctic region prior to opening in the Canada Basin. All the pieces shown are assumed by Crane (1987) to be continental in nature. WI, Wrangel Island.

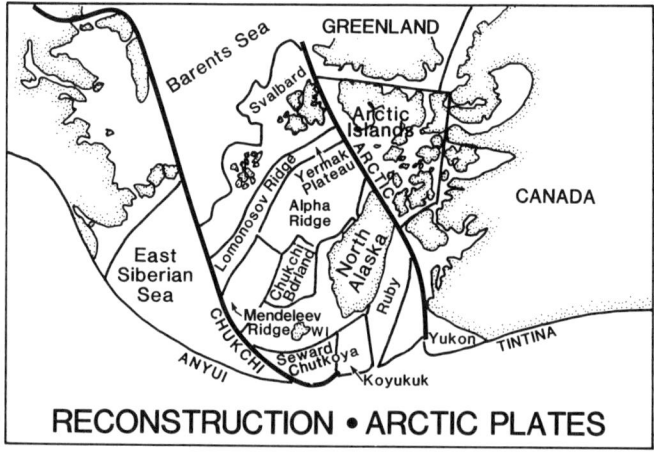

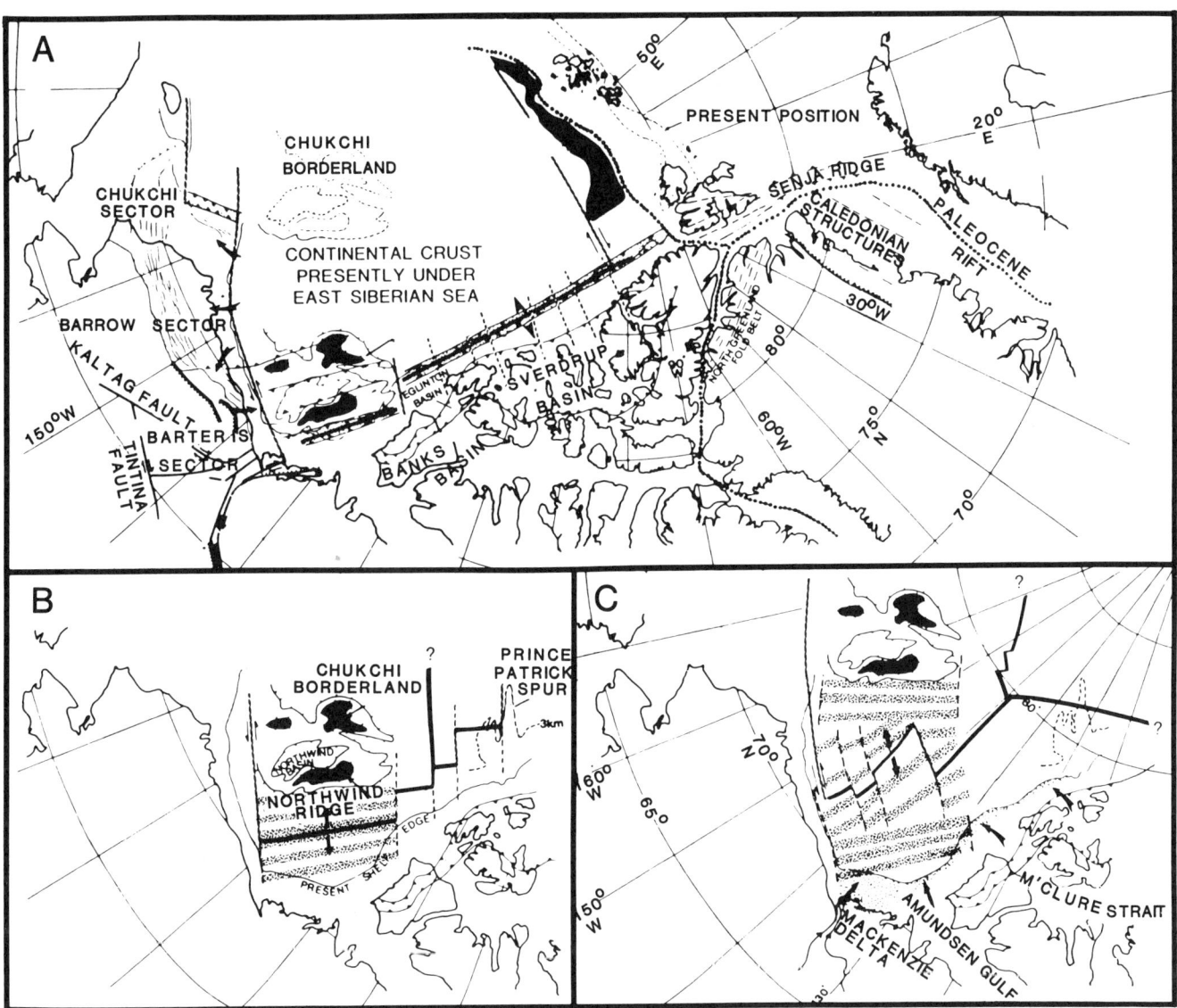

Figure 14. Modification of North Slope transform (PFPF) model redrawn from Vogt and others (1982). (A) Jurassic to Lower Cretaceous rifting breaks up Chukchi Borderland and detaches it from Kolyma Block, which begins to separate from the Canadian Arctic Islands along a line roughly paralleling the Banks-Eglinton-Sverdrup basins. At this time there is still southward sediment transport (arrows) into northern Alaska. (B) the first phase of spreading ends and the plate boundary begins to reorient itself and becomes extinct at time shown in (C).

terrane and were offset with respect to North America by a large right-lateral strike-slip fault that aligned the Tintina fault, the margin of the North Slope, and the Arctic margin of northeastern Siberia (Fig. 15).

During the Permo-Triassic the North Slope terrane translated northward (right-lateral motion) with respect to North America along this mega-fault zone (Fig. 15). Strike-slip motion continued, and during the Early Cretaceous the Makarov and northernmost half of the Canada Basin opened as Alaska continued to translate northward (Fig. 15). During the Late Cretaceous and early Tertiary, extension in the North Atlantic resulted in compression in Alaska, and the North Slope/northeastern Siberian block moved northeastward with respect to cratonic North America along a dextral strike-slip fault that ran along the Kaltag fault and margin of the Canadian Arctic Islands.

DISCUSSION

In the thirty years since Carey (1955) first discussed oroclinal bending and its implication for the opening of the Arctic Ocean, hundreds of papers have been written about the tectonics, marine geology, and marine geophysics of the Arctic region. Knowledge of the Arctic has increased tremendously but is still meager compared to most of the other oceans of the world. Of the three main modes of formation for the Canada Basin, oceanization of continental crust, entrapment of old Paleozoic oceanic crust, and in situ formation of Mesozoic or Cenozoic oceanic crust, only the last seems to have withstood the increased available data.

The seismic refraction results of Mair and Forsyth (1982) showed that while the crust of the Canada Basin may be covered with a thick sedimentary sequence, it is true oceanic crust. The entrapment of older oceanic crust (Churkin, 1970; Churkin and Trexler, 1980; Karasik and others, 1984) as shown in Figure 2 cannot be supported by the heat-flow data (Lachenbruch and Marshall, 1966; Lachenbruch, 1969; Langseth and Lachenbruch, this volume) (Plate 2) and the depth-to-basement calculations (Lawver and Baggeroer, 1983) since both suggest an age for the Canada Basin of Cretaceous or younger, consistent with the geology of the North Slope of Alaska (Brosgé and Tailleur, 1970) and the Canadian Arctic Islands (McWhae, 1986). Consequently, only the models for the tectonic evolution of the Arctic that suggest in situ formation of oceanic crust have been tabulated in Table 2.

For the first fifteen years after Carey's (1955) paper, virtually all models of the evolution of the Canada Basin relied exclusively on the surrounding land geology to produce tectonic models. It was not until the works of Beal (1968), Lachenbruch (1969), Hall (1970), and Vogt and Ostenso (1970) were published that much of the early geophysical data from the Canada Basin became widely available. Later aeromagnetic data (Vogt and others, 1979) produced new interpretations, but these were eventually termed inadequate to resolve the problem (Vogt and others, 1982). With the exception of the CESAR results (Jackson and others, 1986), which determined that the Alpha Ridge is not an abandoned spreading center but more probably is of oceanic plateau origin, no new data from the Canada Basin has resulted. Even some of the CESAR results remain ambiguous as to whether the Alpha Ridge is an oceanic plateau, a hot-spot trace similar to Iceland, or contains continental fragments (Sweeney and Weber, 1986).

Since the marine geological and geophysical data are unable to resolve the tectonic evolution of the Canada Basin, new data from the land and continental margins must be utilized. Two important contributions have been the multichannel seismic reflection results from the Beaufort and Chukchi seas (Grantz and others, 1979; Grantz and May, 1983) and paleomagnetic results from the North Slope (Newman and others, 1977; Hillhouse and Grommé, 1983; Halgedahl and Jarrard, 1987). Grantz and others (1979) concluded that the North Slope of Alaska has to be a rifted "Atlantic-type" continental margin with no evidence of strike-slip motion along the Alaskan continental margin. The paleomagnetic results (Halgedahl and Jarrard, 1987) are only compatible with a rotational opening of the Canada Basin.

Many authors have used depositional paleocurrents from the surrounding margins to support a rotational opening of the Canada Basin (Model A), particularly Tailleur and Brosgé (1970), Hamilton (1970), and Freeland and Dietz (1973). Objections to the rotational model have been raised by some, based on the fact that the depositional trends are east to west on both Arctic Alaska and the Canadian Arctic and rotation would produce opposing depositional directions (Churkin and Trexler, 1980). Others have objected that Arctic Alaska needs to be positioned closer to the northern Canadian Arctic Islands and that simply rotating Alaska into Banks Island does not place it close enough to Ellesmere Island (Crane, 1987). Smith (1987) points out that the geology of the pivot area in the Mackenzie Delta is not consistent with a rotational opening of the Canada Basin because Jurassic sediments prograded north and west toward the present-day position of Alaska, when they should have faced an open ocean. Supporters of the rotational model cite the paleomagnetic results of Halgedahl and Jarrard (1987) and the seismic reflection results of Grantz and others (1979) as support for the rotational model. They would reply that the depositional directions on the North Slope and Canadian Arctic Islands may not be of the same formation and that the prerift high may have had opposing depositional directions on different sides of it. Sweeney (1982) addresses the concern of Crane (1987) by suggesting that Arctic Alaska may have been against northern Ellesmere Island and Greenland during the Paleozoic, but in mid-Paleozoic time, Arctic Alaska was sheared sinistrally along the Canadian margin to its Jurassic prerotated position opposite Banks Island. Sweeney (1982) suggests that the cause for the major sinistral shear was the Middle Devonian collision of Siberia with Baltica and Arctic Alaska resulting in an almost 2,000-km displacement southwestward. Finally with respect to Smith (1987), the region of the Mackenzie Delta could have in fact been facing an extension of an open ocean in prerotation time, because the rotated Arctic Alaska block cannot be considered to have been very wide. Certainly the

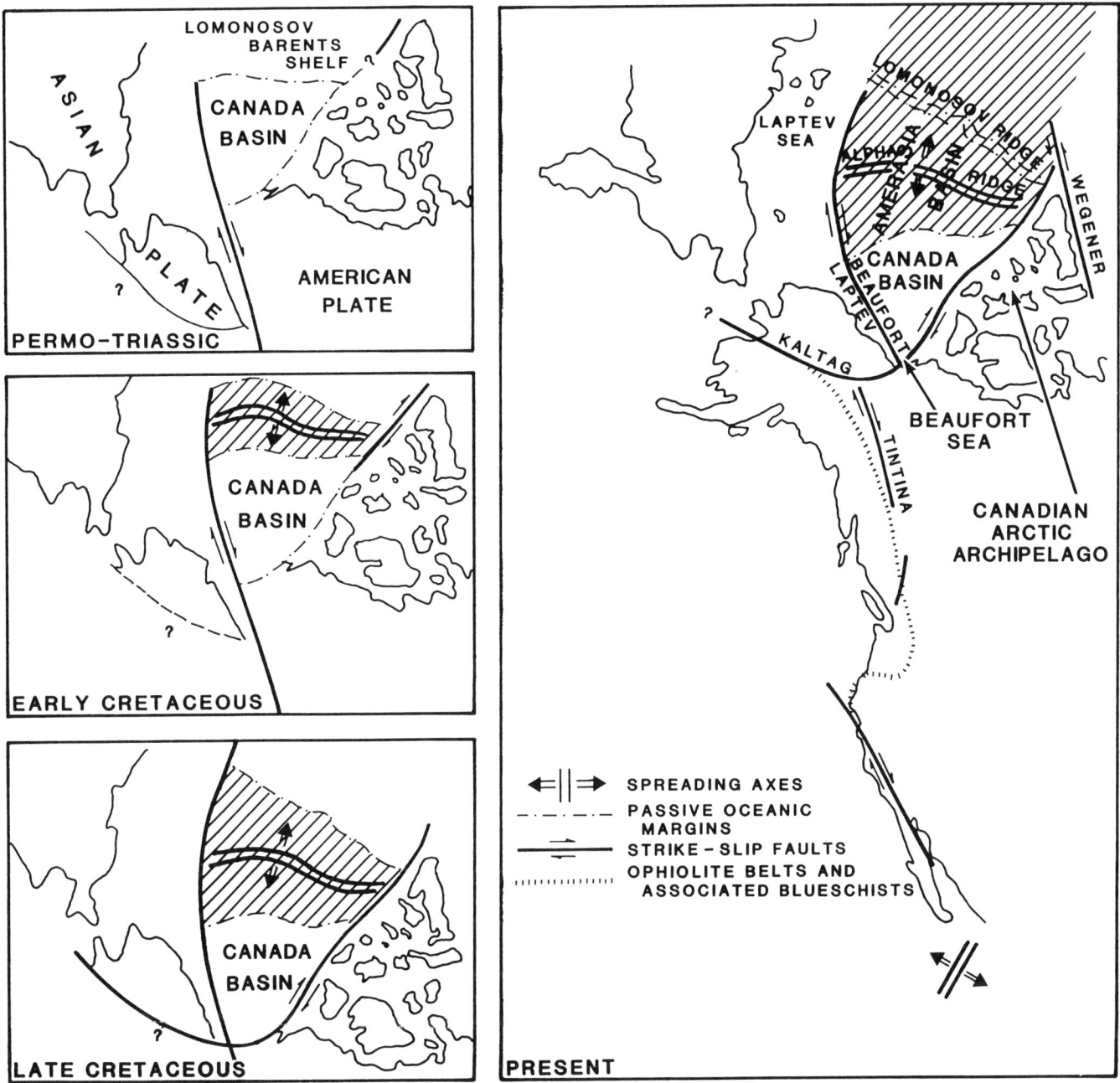

Figure 15. Yukon strike-slip (FFFP) model redrawn from Jones (1980). The evolution of the Amerasia Basin is shown with the associated displacements along the Tintina and Kaltag faults.

Yukon-Koyukuk region is presumably Jurassic or older trapped oceanic crust, just as Churkin and Trexler (1980) show it to have been in Figure 2.

Model B, which generally presumes a sea-floor spreading on or parallel to the Alpha and Mendeleev ridges, was suggested by Ostenso (1974), elaborated upon by Christie (1979), and used by Dutro (1981), Crane (1987), and Smith (1987). Their model solves the problem of the northern Ellesmere–Greenland source for North Slope Alaska while maintaining the North Slope as a passive Atlantic-type margin as Grantz and others (1979) requires. So little multichannel seismic reflection data is available along the Canadian Arctic margin that it cannot be classified as either passive or faulted on the basis of geophysical data. Perhaps the most difficult objections to overcome for this model are the

LOMONOSOV RIFTING MODEL

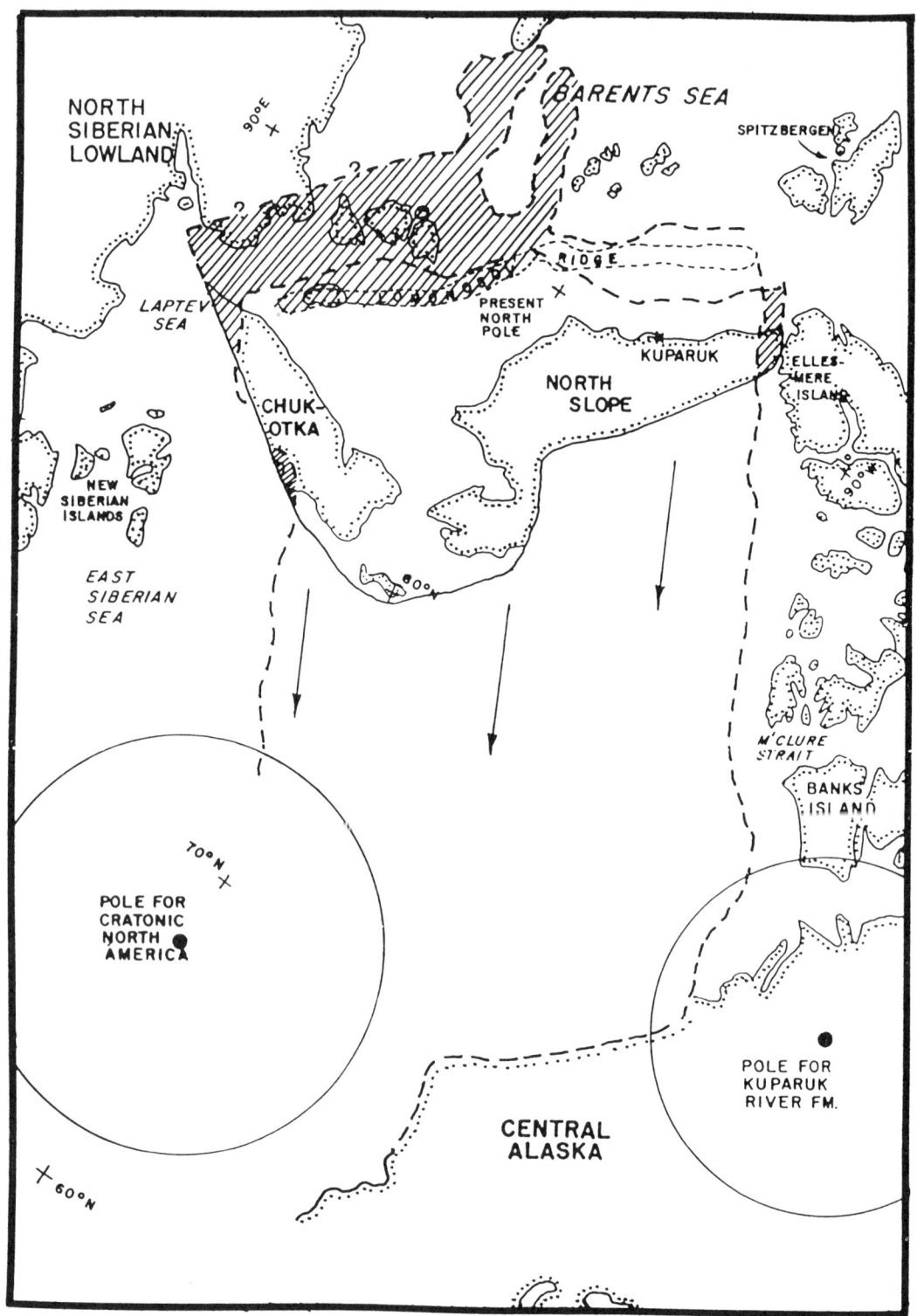

Figure 16. Taken from Halgedahl and Jarrard (1987). Comparisons of the mean Kuparuk River paleomagnetic pole to the 120-Ma pole for cratonic North America using the FPFP model for the evolution of the Canada Basin.

recent paleomagnetic results of Halgedahl and Jarrard (1987). Figure 16 indicates that the paleomagnetic pole for the Model B Early Cretaceous North Slope would not coincide at all with that for North America.

Model C, which was first suggested by Herron and others (1974) in order to explain the Early Cretaceous Verkhoyansk foldbelt, has since been discussed by many others including Vogt and others (1982). They suggest that the folding resulted from the collision of a piece (Kolymski Block) rifted off Arctic Canada that collided with Eurasia. Vogt and others (1982) believed the best fit to the magnetic lineations they found in the Canada Basin could only have been produced by a spreading ridge parallel to the Chukchi Borderland. Rowley and others (1985) believe that the North Slope of Alaska has not changed appreciably since Paleozoic time. It is difficult to reconcile the requirement of Model C for a strike-slip fault boundary along the North Slope of Alaska with the multichannel seismic reflection results of Grantz and others (1979). Halgedahl and Jarrard (1987) did not show the results of a fixed Alaska with respect to North America, but it is obvious that such a scenario would not agree with the paleomagnetic pole they found for the North Slope since a 70° counterclockwise rotation is required for it to be in agreement with the pole for North America.

Model D, suggested by Jones (1980, 1983), requires far greater offset on many of the faults in Alaska than can be documented by workers in northern Alaska. Even though Brosgé (personal communication, 1982) is often referenced for the continuation of the Kaltag fault into the Porcupine lineation of the Yukon, he agrees that there is no observeable field evidence to support such a continuation across the Yukon-Porcupine lowlands. Model D, the Yukon strike-slip model as used in Halgedahl and Jarrard's (1987) paleomagnetic study, produces a solution that cannot be rectified with the observed paleomagnetic data collected.

The question of timing for the opening of the Canada Basin has not been extensively dealt with in this chapter. Tailleur and Brosgé (1970) suggested rotational opening of Aptian and Albian age (119 Ma to 97 Ma). Lawver and Baggeroer (1983) suggested Late Neocomian to about Campanian (125 Ma to 80 Ma) based on heat flow–versus-age and depth-versus-age calculations. Finally Halgedahl and Jarrard (1987) have suggested an age of Hauterivian to Albian (130 Ma to 100 Ma) based on their paleomagnetic results. They constrain the beginning of rotation with their Kuparuk Formation results and they assume the age of the thrusting in the Brooks Range constrains the cessation of motion. Unfortunately, there are no absolute data to constrain the age better than the general time frame of mid to Late Cretaceous.

REFERENCES CITED

Beal, M. A., 1968, Bathymetry and structure of the Arctic Ocean [Ph.D. thesis]: Corvallis, Oregon State University, 204 p.

Beloussov, V. V., 1970, Against the hypothesis of ocean-floor spreading: Tectonophysics, v. 9, p. 489–511.

Brosgé, W. P., and Tailleur, I. L., 1970, Depositional history of northern Alaska, in Adkinson, W. L., and Brosgé, W. P., eds., Proceedings of the geological seminar on the North Slope of Alaska: American Association of Petroleum Geologists, Pacific Section, p. D1–D17.

Bullard, E. C., Everett, J. E., and Smith, A. G., 1965, The fit of the continents around the Atlantic; Symposium on continental drift: Philosophical Transactions of the Royal Society of London, v. 258A, no. 1088, p. 41–51.

Burke, K., 1984, Plate tectonic history of the Arctic: 27th International Geological Congress, Colloquium 4, p. 179–189.

Carey, S. W., 1955, The orocline concept in geotectonics: Royal Society of Tasmania Proceedings, v. 89, p. 255–288.

—— , 1958, The tectonic approach to continental drift, in Proceedings, Continental drift; A symposium, Hobart, March, 1956: Hobart, University of Tasmania, p. 177–355.

Christie, R. L.,1979, The Franklinian geosyncline in the Canadian Arctic and its relationship to Svalbard: Saertrykk av Norsk Polarinstitutt, Skrifter, v. 167, p. 263–314.

Churkin, M., Jr., 1970, Fold belts of Alaska and Siberia and drift between North America and Asia, in Adkison, W. L., and Brosgé, W. P., eds., Proceedings of the geological seminar on the North Slope of Alaska: American Association of Petroleum Geologists, Pacific Section, p. G1–G17.

—— , 1973, Geological concepts of Arctic Ocean Basin, in Fitcher, M. G., ed., Arctic geology: American Association of Petroleum Geologists Memoir 19, p. 485–499.

Churkin, M., Jr., and Trexler, J. H., Jr., 1980, Circum-Arctic plate accretion; Isolating part of a Pacific plate to form the nucleus of the Arctic Basin: Earth and Planetary Science Letters, v. 49, p. 356–362.

Clark, D. L., 1974, Late Mesozoic and Early Cenozoic sediment cores from the Arctic Ocean: Geology, v. 2, p. 41–44.

—— , 1975, Geological history of the Arctic Ocean Basin, in Yorath, C. S., Parker, E. R., and Glass, D. J., eds., Canada's Continental Margins and offshore petroleum exploration: Canadian Society of Petroleum Geologists Memoir 4, p. 501–523.

Crane, R. C., 1985, Arctic reconstruction from an Alaskan viewpoint [abs.]: American Association Petroleum Geologists, v. 69, p. 247.

—— , 1987, Arctic reconstruction from an Alaskan viewpoint, in Tailleur, I. L., and Weimer, P., eds., Alaskan North Slope Geology: Society of Economic Paleontologists and Mineralogists, Pacific Section, Special Publication 50, 769–784.

Dawes, R. F., and Kerr, J W., 1982, Nares Strait and the drift of Greenland; A conflict in plate tectonics: Meddelelser öm Grønland, Geological Science, v. 8, 392 p.

DeLaurier, J., 1978, Magnetic anomalies and the evolution of the Arctic, in Sweeney, J. F., ed., Arctic Geophysical Review: Ottawa, Canada, Earth Physics Branch, Department of Energy Mines and Resources, v. 45-4, p. 87–90.

Dutro, J. T., Jr., 1981, Geology of Alaska bordering the Arctic Ocean, in Nairn, A.E.M., Churkin, M., Jr., and Stehli, F. T., eds., The ocean basins and margins, v. 5, The Arctic Ocean: New York, Plenum, p. 21–36.

Eittreim, S., and Grantz, A., 1979, CDP Seismic sections of western Beaufort continental margin: Tectonophysics, v. 59, p. 251–262.

Embry, A. F., 1985, Mesozoic stratigraphy of Canadian Arctic Archipelago and implications for opening of Amerasian Basin [abs.]: American Association of Petroleum Geologists, v. 69, p. 253.

Forsyth, D. A., Asudeh, I., Green, A. G., and Jackson, H. R., 1986, Crustal structure of the northern Alpha Ridge beneath the Arctic Ocean: Nature, v. 322, p. 349–352.

Forsyth, D. A., Morel-a-l'Huissier, P., Asudsen, I., and Green, A. G., 1986, Alpha

Ridge and Iceland; Products of the same plume?: Journal of Geodynamics, v. 6, p. 197–214.

Freeland, G. L., and Dietz, R. S., 1973, Rotation and history of Alaskan tectonic blocks: Tectonophysics, v. 18, p. 379–390.

Fujita, K., and Newberry, J. T., 1982, Tectonic evolution of northeastern Siberia and adjacent regions: Tectonophysics, v. 89, p. 337–357.

Grantz, A., 1966, Strike-slip faults in Alaska: U.S. Geological Survey Open-File Report 267, p. 82.

Grantz, A., and May, S. D., 1983, Rifting history and structural development of the continental margin north of Alaska, in Watkins, J. S., and Drake, C., eds., Studies in continental margin geology: American Association of Petroleum Geologists Memoir 34, p. 77–100.

Grantz, A., Eittreim, S., and Dinter, D. A., 1979, Geology and tectonic development of the continental margin north of Alaska: Tectonophysics, v. 59, p. 263–291.

Grantz, A., Eittreim, S., and Whitney, O. T., 1981, Geology and physiography of the continental margin north of Alaska and implications for the origin of the Canada Basin, in Nairn, A.E.M., Churkin, M., and Stehli, F. T., eds., The ocean basins and margins, Volume 5, The Arctic Ocean: New York, Plenum, p. 439–492.

Green, A. R., Kaplan, A. A., and Vierbuchen, R. C., 1984, Circum-Arctic Petroleum Potential, in Halbouty, M. T., ed., Future Petroleum Provinces of the World: American Association Petroleum Geologists Memoir 40, p. 101–130.

Halgedahl, S., and Jarrard, R., 1987, Paleomagnetism of the Kuparuk River Formation from oriented drill core; Evidence for rotation of the North Slope block, in Tailleur, I. L., and Weimer, P., eds., Alaskan North Slope Geology: Society of Economic Paleontologists and Mineralogists, Pacific Section, Special Publication 50, p. 581–620.

Hall, J. K., 1970, Arctic Ocean geophysical studies; The Alpha Cordillera and Mendeleev Ridge: Palisades, New York, Lamont-Doherty Geological Observatory Technical Report CU-2-70, 125 p.

——, 1973, Geophysical evidence for ancient sea-floor spreading from Alpha Cordillera and Mendeleev Ridge, in Pitcher, M. G., ed., Arctic geology: American Association of Petroleum Geologists Memoir 19, p. 542–561.

Hamilton, W., 1967, Continental drift in the Arctic [abs.], in Symposium on Continental Drift, Montevideo, Uruquay, 16-19 October, 1967: Paris, UNESCO, International Union of Geological Sciences, p. 192–193.

——, 1968, Continental drift in the Arctic [abs.]: Geological Society of America Special Paper 121, p. 510.

——, 1970, The Uralides and the motion of the Russian and Siberian Platforms: Geological Society of America Bulletin, v. 81, p. 2553–2576.

Harland, W. B., Gaskell, B. A., Heafford, A. P., Lind, E. K., and Perlinns, P. F., 1984, Outline of Arctic post-Silurian continental displacements, in Petroleum geology of the North European Margin: Norwegian Petroleum Society, p. 137–148.

Heezen, B. C., and Ewing, M., 1961, The mid-oceanic ridge and its extension through the Arctic Basin, in Raasch, G. O., ed., Geology of the Arctic: Toronto, Ontario, University of Toronto Press, v. 1, p. 622–642.

Herron, E. M., Dewey, J. F., and Pitman, W. C., III, 1974, Plate tectonics model for the evolution of the Arctic: Geology, v. 2, p. 377–380.

Hillhouse, J. W., and Grommé, C. S., 1983, Paleomagnetic studies and the hypothetical rotation of Arctic Alaska: Journal of the Alaska Geological Society, v. 2, p. 27–40.

Hunkins, K., Herron, T., Kutschale, H., and Peter, G., 1962, Geophysical studies of the Chukchi Cap, Arctic Ocean: Journal of Geophysical Research, v. 67, p. 234–247.

Jackson, H. R., and Johnson, G. L., 1984, Structure and history of the Amerasian Basin: 27th International Geological Congress, Colloquium 4, p. 143–151.

Jackson, H. R., Mudie, P. J., and Blasco, S. M., 1985, Initial geological report on CESAR; The Canadian expedition to study the Alpha Ridge, Arctic Ocean: Geological Survey of Canada Paper 84-22, p. 177.

Jackson, H. R., Forsyth, D. A., and Johnson, G. L., 1986, Oceanic affinities of the Alpha Ridge, Arctic Ocean: Marine Geology, v. 73, p. 237–261.

Johnson, G. L., and Heezen, B. C., 1967, The Arctic Mid-Ocean Ridge: Nature, v. 215, p. 724–725.

Johnson, G. L., and Srivastava, S. P., 1982, The case for displacement along Nares Strait, in Dawes, P. R., and Kerr, J. W., eds., Nares Strait and the drift of Greenland; A conflict in plate tectonics: Meddelelser om Grønland, Geoscience 8, p. 365–368.

Johnson, G. L., Taylor, P. T., Vogt, P. R., and Sweeney, J. F., 1978, Arctic Basin morphology: Polarforschung, v. 48, p. 20–30.

Jones, P. R., 1980, Evidence from Canada and Alaska on plate tectonic evolution of the Arctic Ocean Basin: Nature, v. 285, p. 215–217.

——, 1982, Mesozoic rifting in the western Arctic Ocean basin and its relationship to Pacific seafloor spreading, in Embry, A. F., and Balkwill, H., eds., Arctic geology and geophysics: Calgary, Canadian Society of Petroleum Geologists, p. 83–99.

——, 1983, The Cordilleran connection; A link between Arctic and Pacific sea-floor spreading: Journal of the Alaskan Geological Society, v. 2, p. 41–54.

Karasik, A. M., 1968, Magnetic anomalies of the Gakkel Ridge and origin of the central Arctic Ocean: Geophysical Methods of Prospecting in the Arctic, v. 5, p. 8–19.

——, 1974, The Eurasian Basin of the northern Arctic Ocean in respect to plate tectonics in Lazurkin, V. M., Gramberg, I. S., and Ravich, M. G., eds., Problemy geologii polyarnykh oblastey Zemli: Sbornik Statey, Nauchno-Issledovatel'skaya Institut Geologii Arktika, Leningrad, p. 23–31. (in Russian)

Karasik, A. M., Ustritsky, V. I., and Khramov, A. N., 1984, History of the formation of the Arctic Ocean: 27th International Geological Congress, Colloquium 4, p. 179–189.

Kerr, J. W., 1980, A plate tectonic contrast in northern Canada: Geophysical Association of Canada Special Paper 20, p. 457–484.

——, 1981, Evolution of the Canadian Arctic Islands; A transition between the Atlantic and Arctic oceans, in Nairn, A.E.M., Churkin, M., Jr., and Stehli, F. G., eds., Ocean basins and margins; The Arctic Ocean, Volume 5: New York, Plenum, p. 105–199.

King, E. R., Zietz, I., and Alldredge, L. R., 1966, Magnetic data on the structure of the central Arctic region: Geological Society of America Bulletin, v. 77, p. 619–646.

Lachenbruch, A. H., 1969, Heat flow in the Arctic: Journal of the Arctic Institute of North America, v. 22, no. 3, p. 300–311.

Lachenbruch, A. H., and Marshall, B. V., 1966, Heat flow through the Arctic Ocean floor; The Canada Basin–Alpha Rise Boundary: Journal of Geophysical Research, v. 71, p. 1223–1248.

Lawver, L. A., and Baggeroer, A., 1983, A note on the age of the Canada Basin: Journal of the Alaskan Geological Society, v. 2, p. 57–66.

Lawver, L. A., Grantz, A., and Meinke, L., 1983, The tectonics of the Arctic Ocean, in Chryssostomidis, C., and Dyer, I., eds., Arctic Technology and Policy: Washington, D.C., Hemisphere Publishing Company, p. 147–158.

Ling, H. Y., McPherson, L. M., and Clark, D. L., 1973, Late Cretaceous (Maastrichtian?) silicoflagellates from the Alpha Cordillera of the Arctic Ocean: Science, v. 180, p. 1360–1361.

Mair, J. A., and Lyons, J. A., 1981, Crustal structure and velocity anisotrophy beneath the Beaufort Sea: Canadian Journal of Earth Sciences, v. 18, p. 724–741.

Mair, J. A., and Forsyth, D. A., 1982, Crustal structures of the Canada Basin near Alaska, the Lomonosov Ridge, and adjoining basins near the North Pole: Tectonophysics, v. 89, p. 239–253.

May, S. D., and Grantz, A., 1983, Origin of the Canada Basin as inferred from the seismic geology of offshore northern Alaska: Journal of the Alaskan Geological Society, v. 2, p. 9–16.

McWhae, J. R., 1986, Tectonic history of the North Pacific, Canadian Arctic, and Spitsbergen regions since Early Cretaceous time: American Association of Petroleum Geologists, v. 70, p. 430–450.

Metz, P. A., Egan, A., and Johansen, O., 1982, Landsat linear features and incipient rift system model for the origin of base metal and petroleum resources of northern Alaska, *in* Embry, A. F., and Balkwill, H. R., eds., Arctic geology and geophysics: Calgary, Canadian Society of Petroleum Geologists Memoir 8, p. 101–112,

Mikkelsen, E., 1955, Mirage in the Arctic: London, Rupert Hart-Davis, p. 9, 24–27, 88–89.

Newman, G. W., Mull, C. G., and Watkins, N. D., 1977, Northern Alaska paleomagnetism, plate rotation, and tectonics [abs.]: Anchorage, Alaska Geological Society Symposium, v. 1, p. 16–19.

Ostenso, N. A., 1962, Geophysical investigations of the Arctic Ocean basins: Madison, University of Wisconsin Polar Research Center, Research Report 62-4, 124 p.

—— , 1974, Arctic Ocean Margins, *in* Burk, C. A., and Drake, C. L., eds., The geology of continental margins: New York, Springer-Verlag, p. 753–763.

Ostenso, N. A., and Wold, R. J., 1971, Aeromagnetic survey of the Arctic Ocean; Techniques and interpretations: Marine Geophysical Research, v. 1, p. 178–219.

Palmer, A. R., compiler, 1983, The Decade of North American Geology 1983 Time Scale: Geology, v. 11, p. 503–504.

Parsons, B., and Sclater, J. G., 1977, An analysis of the variation of ocean floor bathymetry and heat flow with age: Journal of Geophysical Research, v. 84, p. 803–827.

Perry, R. K., Fleming, H. S., Weber, J. R., Kristoffersen, Y., Hall, J. K., Grantz, A., and Johnson, G. L., 1985, Bathymetry of the Arctic Ocean: Naval Research Laboratory, Acoustics Division, scale 1:4,704,075 at 78°N.

Pitman, W. C., III, and Talwani, M., 1972, Sea-floor spreading in the North Atlantic: Geological Society of America Bulletin, v. 83, p. 619–646.

Pogrebitskiy, Yu. Ye., 1976, The geodynamic system of the Arctic Ocean and its structural evolution: International Geology Review, v. 20, p. 1251–1266.

Pogrebitskiy, Yu. Ye., and 8 others, 1984, Endogenic differentiation of matter in the geodynamic system of the Arctic Ocean: 27th International Geological Congress, Colloquium 4, p. 13–29.

Pushcharovskiy, Yu. M., 1976, Tectonics of the Arctic Ocean Basin: Geotectonics, v. 10, p. 85–91.

Rickwood, F. K., 1970, The Prudhoe Bay Field, *in* Adkinson, W. L., and Brosgé, W. P., eds., Proceedings of the geological seminar on the North Slope of Alaska: American Association of Petroleum Geologists, Pacific Section, L1–L11.

Rowley, D. B., Lottes, A. L., and Ziegler, A. M., 1985, North America–Greenland–Eurasia relative motions; Implications for circum-Arctic tectonic reconstructions [abs.]: American Association of Petroleum Geologists Bulletin, v. 69, p. 303.

Sclater, J. G., Hellinger, S., and Tapscott, C., 1977, The paleobathymetry of the Atlantic Ocean from the Jurassic to the Present: Journal of Geology, v. 85, p. 509–552.

Shatskiy, N. S., 1935, On the tectonics of the Arctic (in Russian): The geology and mineral resources of the northern USSR Glavsenmorputi, 1st Geological Invitational Conference, Moscow, Translation, v. 1, p. 149–168.

Shaver, R., and Hunkins, K., 1964, Arctic Ocean geophysical studies; Chukchi Cap and Chukchi Abyssal Plain: Deep Sea Research, v. 11, p. 905–916.

Smith, D. G., 1985, Late Paleozoic to Cenozoic reconstructions of the Arctic [abs.]: American Association of Petroleum Geologists Bulletin, v. 69, p. 679.

—— , 1987, Late Paleozoic to Cenozoic reconstructions of the Arctic, *in* Tailleur, I. L., and Weimer, P., eds., Alaskan North Slope Geology: Society of Economic Paleontolgists and Mineralogists, Pacific Section, Special Publication 50, p. 785–796.

Srivastava, S. P., 1978, Evolution of the Labrador Sea and its bearing on the early evolution of the North Atlantic: Geophysical Journal of the Royal Astronomical Society, v. 52, p. 313–357.

Srivastava, S. P., and Tapscott, C. R., 1986, Plate kinematics of the North Atlantic, *in* Vogt, P. R., and Tucholke, B. E., eds., The western North Atlantic region: Boulder, Colorado, Geological Society of America, The geology of North America, v. M, p. 379–404.

Sweeney, J. F., 1978, Arctic Geophysical Review: Ottawa, Canada, Earth Physics Branch, Department of Energy, Mines, and Resources, v. 45, p. 108.

—— , 1982, Mid-Paleozoic travels of the Arctic-Alaska: Nature, v. 298, p. 647–649.

—— , 1983, Evidence for the origin of the Canada basin margin by rifting in the Early Cretaceous time: Journal of Alaskan Geological Society, v. 2, p. 17–23.

—— , 1985, Comments about the age of the Canada Basin: Tectonophysics, v. 114, p. 1–10.

Sweeney, J. F., and Weber, J. R., 1986, Progress in understanding the age and origin of the Alpha Ridge, Arctic Ocean: Journal of Geodynamics, v. 6, p. 237–244.

Sweeney, J. F., Irving, E., and Geuer, J. W., 1978, Evolution of the Arctic Basin, *in* Sweeney, J. F., ed., Arctic Geophysical Review: Ottawa, Canada, Earth Physics Branch, Department of Energy, Mines, and Resources, v. 45, no. 4, p. 91–100.

Sweeney, J. F., Weber, J. R., and Blasco, S. M., 1982, Continental ridges in the Arctic Ocean; LOREX constraints: Tectonophysics, v. 89, p. 217–237.

Tailleur, L. L., 1969, Rifting speculation of the geology of Alaska's North Slope: Oil and Gas Journal, v. 67, no. 39, p. 128–130.

—— , 1973, Probable rift origin of Canada Basin, Arctic Ocean, *in* Pitcher, M. G., ed., Arctic Geology: American Association of Petroleum Geologists Memoir 19, p. 526–535.

Tailleur, I. L., and Brosgé, W. P., 1970, Tectonic history of northern Alaska, *in* Adkison, W. L., and Brosgé, W. P., eds., Proceedings of the geological seminar on the North Slope of Alaska: American Association of Petroleum Geologists, Pacific Section, p. E1–E19.

Tailleur, I. L., and Snelson, S., 1969, Large-scale thrusting in northwestern Alaska; Possibly related to rifting of the Arctic Ocean [abs.]: Geological Society of America Special Paper 121, p. 569.

Taylor, P. T., 1978, Low-level aeromagnetic data across the western Arctic Basin [abs.]: EOS Transactions of the American Geophysical Union, v. 59, p. 268–269.

Taylor, P. T., Kovacs, L. C., Vogt, P. R., and Johnson, G. L., 1981, Detailed aeromagnetic investigation of the Arctic Basin, 2: Journal of Geophysical Research, v. 86, p. 6323–6333.

Unternehr, P., 1982, Etude structurale et cinematique de la mer de Norvege et du Groenland evolution du microcontinent de Jan Mayen [Ph.D. thesis]: Brest, France, Université de Bretagne Occidental, 228 p.

Van Wagoner, N. A., and Robinson, P. T., 1985, Petrology and geochemistry of a CESAR bedrock sample; Implications for the origin of the Alpha Ridge, *in* Jackson, R., Mudie, P. J., and Blasco, S. M., eds., Initial geological report on CESAR; The Canadian expedition to study the Alpha Ridge, Arctic Ocean: Geological Society of Canada Paper 84–22, p. 47–58.

Vogt, P. R., and Ostenso, N. A., 1970, Magnetic and gravity profiles across the Alpha Cordillera and their relation to Arctic sea-floor spreading: Journal of Geophysical Research, v. 75, p. 4925–4937.

Vogt, P. R., Ostenso, N. A., and Johnson, G. L., 1970, Magnetic and bathymetric data bearing on sea-floor spreading north of Iceland: Journal of Geophysical Research, v. 75, p. 903–920.

Vogt, P. R., Taylor, P. T., Kovacs, L. C., and Johnson, G. L., 1979, Detailed aeromagnetic investigations of the Arctic basin: Journal of Geophysical Research, v. 84, p. 1071–1089.

Vogt, P. R., Bernero, C., Kovacs, L., and Taylor, P., 1981, Structure and plate tectonic evolution of the marine Arctic as revealed by aeromagnetics: Oceanologica Acta, 26th International Geological Congress, Paris, Colloquium 4, p. 25–40.

Vogt, P. R., Taylor, P. T., Kovacs,, L. C., and Johnson, G. L., 1982, The Canada Basin; Aeromagnetic constraints on structure and evolution: Tectonophysics, v. 89, p. 295–336.

Wilson, J. T., 1963, Continental drift: Scientific American, v. 208, p. 86–100.

Yorath, C. J., and Norris, D. K., 1975, The tectonic development of the southern

Beaufort Sea and its relationship to the origin of the Arctic Ocean basin, *in* Yorath, C. J., Parker, E. R., and Glass, D. J., eds., Canada's Continental Margins and Offshore Petroleum Exploration: Canadian Society of Petroleum Geologists Memoir 4, p. 589–612.

MANUSCRIPT ACCEPTED BY THE SOCIETY SEPTEMBER 16, 1987

ACKNOWLEDGMENTS

Many people assisted us in the preparation of this manuscript. Ashton Embry and J. R. McWhae not only provided us with unpublished manuscripts but they also wrote synopses of their ideas on the evolution of the Canada Basin. David G. Smith, R. C. Crane, and Sue Halgedahl allowed us to use their manuscripts prior to publication. We thank Dave Rowley for his comments and for his unpublished reconstructions of the North Atlantic. Paul Weimer corrected a number of our errors concerning North Slope geography and geology. Warren Hamilton provided a critical review that was much appreciated. We also thank John Sclater and Jack Hillhouse for reviewing the manuscript. Cathy Mayes, Kyle Winn, and Debbie Lyle helped in typing, proof-reading, and assembling figures for the paper. Nancy Kelly redrafted the figures for use in this paper. This paper is contribution number 718 of the Institute for Geophysics of the University of Texas at Austin.

NOTE ADDED IN PROOF

This article was written as a review of the various tectonic models presented for the evolution of the Canada Basin. Since this article was written, there have not been many new models proposed. I [LAL] with Dietmar Müller, Shiri Srivastava, and Walter Roest have recently written an article concerning the tectonic history of the entire Arctic region. We show reconstructions for the polar region north of 55°N with North America held fixed. We use the model based on the rotational opening of the Canada Basin about a pole located near the Mackenzie Delta. We feel that such a model explains most of the known Arctic geology and produces the fewest contradictions. We emphasize that far more real data is needed before the tectonic evolution of the Canada Basin will be ascertained. Presently, all models are merely inspired guess work, as Dave Stone so eloquently put it in his recent paper "Paleogeography and rotations of Arctic Alaska—an unresolved problem" (Stone, 1989). Our paper on "The opening of the Arctic Ocean" should be published in early 1990; it shows our reconstructions for each 20-m.y. period for the northern polar region from 180 Ma to the present. We include in our recent paper poles of rotation for the northern plates, as well as a detailed look at the opening of the Greenland-Svalbard deep-water passage between the Arctic Ocean and the Atlantic.

Lawver, L. A., Müller, R. D., Srivastava, S. P., and Roest, W., 1990, The opening of the Arctic Ocean, *in* Bleil, U., ed., The geological history of the Polar Oceans; Arctic versus Antarctic: Amsterdam, Kluwer Academic Publishers (in press).

Stone, D. B., 1989, Paleogeography and rotations of Arctic Alaska; An unresolved problem, *in* Kissel, C., and Laj, C., eds., Paleomagnetic rotations and continental deformation: Amsterdam, Kluwer Academic Publishers, p. 343–364.

Courtesy of the Atlantic Richfield Company, New York. Reproduced from Jules Verne, 1874, The Fur Country (Seventy Degrees North Latitude): Boston, James R. Osgood and Company.

Printed in U.S.A.

Chapter 32

Summary

J. F. Sweeney
Geological Survey of Canada, 100 West Pender, Vancouver, British Columbia V6B 1R8, Canada
G. L. Johnson
Office of Naval Research, Arlington, Virginia 22217
A. Grantz
U.S. Geological Survey, 345 Middlefield Road, Menlo Park, California 94025

INTRODUCTION

As this volume makes clear, the last 15 years have seen a revolutionary increase in the amount and variety of geoscientific information retrieved from Arctic domains. While the new data have done much to improve the definition of major Arctic crustal and submarine features, it is evident that the latest results provide only modest new constraints on the evolution of the region.

The Eurasia Basin became part of the world ocean about 10 m.y. ago and it has had a significant impact on the Earth's climate system since that time. The history of this linkage is crucial to the study of global change through time. An understanding of past and present plate movements in the Arctic is needed to build accurate tectonic models of the world during the late Mesozoic and Cenozoic, which in turn, are highly relevant to resource exploration.

In this chapter we summarize the present knowledge of the north polar area from a geoscientific and an environmental point of view, assess some outstanding scientific problems, and pose research targets for the upcoming decade.

PRESENT KNOWLEDGE

The Lomonosov Ridge divides the Arctic sea floor into two broad regions, with respect to its morphology and in terms of our understanding of its tectonic evolution. The development of the Eurasia Basin is relatively well understood, but the evolution of the Amerasia Basin is ambiguous for three major reasons. First, the Amerasia Basin is isolated from the world ocean system so there are no obvious developmental ties between it and the major sea floors. Second, nearly half of the Amerasia Basin is composed of submarine ridges and plateaus that are themselves of enigmatic origin. Third, marine magnetic anomalies, indicative of the pattern of sea-floor generation in the large ocean basins, show no consistent regional trends in the Amerasia Basin.

Eurasia Basin and Norwegian-Greenland Sea

The Eurasia Basin has been expanding asymmetrically at slow rates (<2 cm/yr) about the Arctic Mid-Ocean Ridge since the early Paleogene (Vogt and others, 1979). The Norwegian-Greenland Sea has a similar history of slow opening about a more complex system of spreading ridges (Eldholm and others, this volume). Both ocean basins are part of the North Atlantic sea floor, which has opened about a sequence of pivots, the most recent at about 70°N, 130°E near the Lena River delta (Pitman and Talwani, 1972).

The initial opening of the Eurasia Basin separated the Lomonosov Ridge from the Eurasian continent and produced thermal and structural disturbances within the Amerasia Basin. The opening of the Norwegian-Greenland Sea likewise has carried small ridge-like fragments—the Jan Mayen Ridge (69°N, 8°W) and part of the Hovgaard Fracture Zone (78°N, 2°E)—away from the Greenland continental margin.

The age of the Eurasia Basin and the Norwegian-Greenland Sea is constrained by well-lineated marine magnetic anomalies. The oldest that can be identified with confidence is anomaly 24. In the Eurasia Basin, space exists for anomalies 25 to 28 on the deep sea floor beyond anomaly 24 (Vogt and others, 1979). In the Norwegian-Greenland Sea, oceanic crust is present up to 90 km landward of this anomaly (Eldholm and others, this volume; Larsen, this volume; Plate 4). Hence, these basins probably began to form in the interval between about 65 and 56 Ma (Palmer, 1983, time scale).

Early right-lateral shearing between Svalbard and Greenland became oblique pull-apart motion when the latter became part of the North American plate at about anomaly 13 time. This initiated a deep-water connection, the Spitzbergen Fracture Zone, between the Eurasia Basin and the Norwegian-Greenland Sea, that became an effective seaway by about anomaly 5 time (Eldholm and others, this volume; Kristoffersen, this volume).

Sweeney, J. F., Johnson, G. L., and Grantz, A., 1990, Summary, *in* Grantz, A., Johnson, G. L., and Sweeney, J. F., eds., The Arctic Ocean region: Boulder, Colorado, Geological Society of America, The Geology of North America, v. L.

The Arctic Mid-Ocean Ridge has typical spreading axis morphology, with a well-developed median valley more than 5,000 m deep in places and flanking rift mountains rising to within 2,200 m of the sea surface (Plate 1). Seismicity associated with the plate boundary is generated mainly by normal faulting with little evidence that offsets of the spreading axis, if they exist, are more than about 100 km (Fujita and others, this volume). Much larger offsets of the axis occur to the south along the Spitzbergen and western Jan Mayen fracture zones.

Seismic refraction profiles suggest that the Moho below the Eurasia Basin may possess significant relief, with several areas of anomalously thin (2 to 3 km) crust and abrupt changes in crustal thickness of as much as 3 km (Kristoffersen, this volume). Moho relief may have been created by sporadic bursts of crust-forming magmatic activity associated with a very slow spreading axis (Jackson and others, 1982). The refraction data are too sparse to suggest a symmetric pattern to the Moho relief, but the thickness of oceanic crust varies both along and across magnetic isochrons (Kristoffersen, this volume).

The northern part of the Yermak Plateau has particularly thick (18+ km) crust with a high P-wave velocity (5.0 to 7.2 km/s) and very positive magnetic intensity (>1,000 nT; Jackson and others, this volume; Coles and Taylor, this volume). The Morris Jesup Plateau has a similar magnetic signature. It has been suggested that the plateaus were formed during the Eocene and early Oligocene (magnetic anomaly 21 to 13 time) by a great Iceland-like volcanic effusion that straddled the accreting plate boundary near the Spitsbergen Fracture Zone. When magmatic activity declined, perhaps in response to a change in relative motion of the Greenland plate, the volcanic pile was split by continued spreading along the Arctic Mid-Ocean Ridge. The separated parts became the Yermak and Morris Jesup Plateaus (Dawes and Soper, 1973; Feden and others, 1979; Jackson and others, 1984; Kristoffersen, this volume).

Sediment cover in the Eurasia Basin varies from nearly zero along the active spreading axis to more than 3 km in Nansen Basin near continental Eurasia, and to more than 2 km in Amundsen Basin near the Lomonosov Ridge (Kristoffersen, this volume). Near the Laptev Shelf, sediments thicken to between 4 and 5 km (Plate 5).

In the Norwegian-Greenland Sea the thickest sediments lie close to the Barents Shelf where they are more than 2 km deep. Elsewhere, deposits are generally less than a kilometer thick and largely are absent near the accreting margin (Eldholm and others, this volume).

Lomonosov Ridge

The Lomonosov Ridge is a steep-sided, relatively flat-topped feature that rises about 3 km above the surrounding abyssal plains. Near the North Pole the ridge crust extends about 27 km below sea level and has a P-wave velocity structure similar to that determined across the Barents and Kara continental shelves (Forsyth and Mair, 1984). A 1- to 2-km-deep structural trough separates each end of the Lomonosov Ridge from the adjacent continental shelf. The trough near the New Siberian Islands is filled with sediments; the trough near Ellesmere Island is not (Plate 1; Kristoffersen, this volume).

The continental character of the Lomonosov Ridge is suggested by the correspondence of its geophysical properties with those of the Barents and Kara Shelves, and by the fact that the ridge was adjacent to these shelves before the Eurasia Basin opened (Weber and Sweeney, this volume).

A modern analogue to the Lomonosov Ridge, in size, morphology, and style of origin, may be Baja California and the continental slice west of the San Andreas fault in California. Like Baja, the Lomonosov Ridge could have resulted from the high-angle intersection of an active plate margin (Mid-Atlantic Ridge) with continental crust. Over the last 56 to 65 m.y., the Lomonosov Ridge has been transported to the middle of the Arctic Ocean by sea-floor spreading along the Arctic Mid-Ocean Ridge, as first suggested by Wilson (1963).

Amerasia Basin

The most popular concept to explain the opening of the Amerasia Basin is the wiper-blade retreat of continental blocks from polar Canada about a pivot near the Mackenzie River delta (Harbert and others, this volume; Lawver and Scotese, this volume). The present whereabouts of the drifted blocks, their extent, and their drift paths are open to question. Major features within the basin—the Chukchi Borderland and the Alpha-Mendeleev submarine ridge complex—may represent igneous outpourings that occurred during or shortly after Amerasia Basin formation. These features also may contain significant continental elements.

Canada Basin. The age of the Canada Basin is placed within the Cretaceous Period between about 130 and 80 Ma. Broad age constraints are provided by the initiation of continental breakup in polar North America during Hauterivian time (131 to 124 Ma) and by geophysical measurements from the Canada Basin.

Thermal cooling models of oceanic lithosphere indicate a Barremian to Campanian age (about 120 to 80 Ma) for the sea floor of the Canada Basin (Lawver and Baggeroer, 1983; Langseth and others, this volume). Near Alaska, depth-to-basement estimates suggest a similar range in sea-floor age (e.g., Baggeroer and Falconer, 1982), although there is some ambiguity about the level of the basement-sediment interface in the seismic refraction records; overlying sediments may be 6 to 9 km thick in the Canada Basin (Grantz and others, Chapter 22, this volume).

The age estimates suggest that the Canada Basin sea floor probably formed during the long period of normal geomagnetic polarity between about 118 and 84 Ma (Palmer, 1983, time scale). This may explain the apparent absence of characteristic magnetic stripes over the abyssal plain. The observed anomaly variations, which average about 200 nT across the southern part of the Canada Basin (Vogt and others, 1982), may reflect basement topography or structures within oceanic crust.

Moho depth below the Canada Basin is known near Alaska where the crust thins rapidly from about 19 km near the base of the continental slope to between 10 and 12 km beneath the continental rise (Mair and Lyons, 1981; Baggeroer and Falconer, 1982). Northwest of the Queen Elizabeth Islands, continental crust thins seaward from about 40 km at the coast to about 25 km below the outer shelf (Hobson and Overton, 1967; Asudeh and others, 1989). The crust is 10 to 15 km thick at the base of the continental slope near Prince Patrick Island (Berry and Barr, 1971).

Oceanic crustal velocities range from 2.7 to 7.7 km/s. Beneath the oceanic Moho, P-wave velocities average 8.2 km/s (Grantz and others, Chapter 22, this volume).

Alpha-Mendeleev ridge complex. The Alpha Ridge is 300 to 500 km wide with rugged topography as much as 3 km high that is approximately symmetric about a central axis. Near Canada, its crust appears from seismic refraction profiles to be 35 to 40 km thick below the axial region and 15 to 20 km thick below the north flank (Asudeh and others, 1988). Below the south flank, gravity models suggest a 10- to 15-km-thick ridge crust (Weber, 1986).

The oceanic character of the Alpha Ridge close to Canada is inferred by the resemblance of its geophysical properties to those of oceanic crust and major marine edifices such as Iceland and the Ontong-Java Plateau (Forsyth and others, 1986; Weber, 1986; Jackson and others, 1986). Highly altered bedrock dredge samples from the crestal region appear to be alkali basalt (Van Wagoner and others, 1986).

The western part of the Alpha Ridge has a smoother basement-sediment interface and a relatively subdued aeromagnetic signature compared with the ridge segment near Canada (Hunkins, 1961; Taylor and others, 1981). To the south, scanty bathymetric data suggest that the Mendeleev Ridge is less broad and rugged than the Alpha Ridge (Plate 1). Satellite magnetic measurements show that the Mendeleev Ridge contains far less magnetic material than does the Alpha Ridge (Taylor, 1983).

The apparent change in gross crustal properties to the west and south along the ridge complex may reflect regional trends in composition and structure, with more oceanic elements present close to Canada and more continental elements present close to the East Siberian Shelf. As the published measurements are few, this suggestion must be regarded as speculative.

Age constraints, based on thermal cooling models of ridge crust, biochronology of overlying sediments, and a very positive magnetic signature, apply only to the segment of the Alpha Ridge thought to be oceanic in nature (Weber and Sweeney, this volume). This part of the ridge is estimated to be Cretaceous in age, between about 120 and 80 Ma.

Makarov Basin. There are insufficient data to determine whether the Makarov Basin is equivalent to the Canada Basin in age and origin. East of about 160°W the Makarov Basin (Siberia Abyssal Plain) appears as a graben-like block downdropped between the steep bounding flanks of the Alpha and Lomonosov Ridges (Crary, 1954; Weber and Sweeney, 1985; Plate 1). A reversed refraction profile indicates that the underlying crust is about 14 km thick (Forsyth and Mair, 1984).

West of 160°W the Siberia Plain becomes much wider and has magnetic stripes that are discordant with the trend of the graben-like trough (Taylor and others, 1981; Plate 4). The cause of the magnetic anomalies is unknown. They could represent magnetic field reversals associated with an episode of sea-floor spreading (Taylor and others, 1981). Near the Lomonosov Ridge, magnetic stripes are associated with basement ridges and troughs (Overton, 1982).

The wider and shallower Wrangel Plain contains 3.5 to 6 km of sediment above a northward-rising ramp of basement rocks that appear to be highly deformed (Kutschale, 1966; Gramberg and Kulakov, 1975). What this basement structure signifies for the origin of the Wrangel Plain is unclear. The morphology and magnetic character of the Siberia Plain suggests that it may have been created by one or more episodes of extension directed obliquely to the direction of pull-apart expected from a Carey-style rotational opening of the Amerasia Basin.

Chukchi Borderland. The nature of the crust below the Chukchi Borderland is poorly constrained. Its subdued magnetic character and fault-block morphology resemble the continental Lomonosov Ridge. A crustal density model of the borderland is similar to the oceanic part of the Alpha Ridge near Canada (Hall, this volume).

The blocks of the Chukchi Borderland appear to have been rifted apart during or soon after the opening of the Amerasia Basin, before much of the overlying sediment was deposited (Hall, this volume). The relation between the presumed rifting and formation of the surrounding sea floor is moot. Major extensional structures of inferred latest Cretaceous–earliest Tertiary age transect the East Chukchi Shelf on line with the Borderland blocks, implying that Borderland morphology may have been disturbed well after its creation (Grantz and others, Chapter 16, this volume).

Continental margins

Norwegian-Greenland Sea. Crustal rock type and pre-rift structural history have been dominant influences in the structural style of continental breakup and subsequent formation of the continent-ocean transition in the Norwegian-Greenland Sea. Deformed rocks of the Caledonian orogen underlie the basement along the margin in Norway and in northeast and east Greenland (Eldholm and others, this volume; Larsen, this volume). During late Paleozoic time the crust in these regions was stretched, thinned, and blanketed with thick sediments. In the northern subregions a second period of crustal extension took place in Late Jurassic time, followed by further sedimentation. In contrast, little pre-rift stretching or other tectonism appears to have affected Precambrian crystalline rocks that form the basement along the continental margin in southeast Greenland (Larsen, this volume).

Continental breakup and sea-floor formation produced a broad zone of flexure across previously thinned continental crust below the margin in northeast and East Greenland and off Norway. It also produced a narrow zone of flexure across the abrupt transition from cratonic to oceanic crust in southeast Greenland. These zones now lie under 2 to 4 km of post-rift sediments.

Much thicker deposits cover the East Greenland margin, where rifting forces apparently decoupled continental and oceanic crust along a coast-parallel detachment, the East Greenland Escarpment. Crust along the seaward side of the detachment subsided rapidly, and the resulting half-graben received about 7 km of Paleogene sediments. The cause of the presumed decoupling is unclear. It may be linked to intense Paleogene activity along the Aegir Ridge that was then nearby, or it could be a pre-rift structure that was reactivated in Eocene time (Larsen, this volume).

Off Norway and much of Greenland, sea-floor formation began subaerially during the early Eocene. Between Greenland and Iceland, the accreting margin in what is now the Denmark Strait remained above sea level until the late Miocene, about magnetic anomaly 5 time. Just prior to this, at about anomaly 6 to 7 time, the continental margin of East Greenland was rejuvenated when its outer part, now the Jan Mayen Ridge, was split off by the westward jump of the spreading axis from the Aegir Ridge to what is now the Kolbeinsey Ridge (Larsen, this volume; Eldholm and others, this volume).

Eurasia Basin. Relatively little is known of the pre-rift history of continental margins in the Eurasia Basin. Basement below the Barents Shelf appears to be composed of Caledonian metamorphosed rocks in the west and Precambrian rocks of the Fennoscandian Shield in the east. Below the adjacent Kara Shelf, basement may also contain rocks deformed by Hercynian events (Eldholm and Talwani, 1977; Meyerhoff, 1980). Basement character below the Laptev Shelf is undetermined. The shelf is bordered on the west by a Hercynian foldbelt and on the east by the New Siberian Islands. The latter may be part of the Siberian platform or they may make up one or more allochthonous terranes (Fujita and Cook, this volume).

Sediments below the Barents margin are early Paleozoic to Tertiary in age and range in thickness from more than 4 km along the inner shelf (Timan-Pechora Basin) to 1 km or less at the shelf edge close to Svalbard. The entire shelf may have been subaerial for much of the Cenozoic: few Tertiary deposits are present, and near Svalbard, Late Cretaceous rocks are absent and presumably were eroded. Below the slope north of Svalbard, Tertiary sediments are up to 3 km thick (Eldholm and Talwani, 1977; Kristoffersen, this volume).

Below the Kara margin, sediments south and east of Novaya Zemlya (West Siberia Basin) range in age from Jurassic to Tertiary and are up to 3.5 km thick. North of Novaya Zemlya lies a broad trough filled with sediments of uncertain thickness and probable Jura-Cretaceous age. This sequence thins toward the shelf edge and is overlain by Late Cretaceous mafic volcanic rocks on Franz Josef Land. Tertiary rocks are unknown on Novaya Zemlya and Franz Josef Land but they may be more than 6 km thick below the adjacent continental slope (Eldholm and Talwani, 1977; Meyerhoff, 1980; Kristoffersen, this volume).

The active plate boundary comes ashore across the Laptev margin, which has experienced as much as 400 km of crustal stretching during the Tertiary (Kristoffersen, this volume). Earthquake focal depths along the plate boundary increase in depth from 1 to 2 km in the Eurasia Basin to about 5 km at the outer edge of the Laptev Shelf and 10 to 25 km near the Lena River delta. Focal mechanisms for shelf seismicity indicate mostly normal faulting; the largest events occur about 300 km west of the projected trend of the mid-ocean ridge (Fujita and others, this volume).

Basement below the Laptev Shelf is characterized by a large, triangle-shaped block bounded by a sequence of steep-sided grabens and horsts that transect the margin (Plate 11). Postrift sediments on the Laptev margin are as much as 12 km thick below the shelf and 4 to 5 km thick beneath the slope (Kristoffersen, this volume).

The sheared margin of northern Greenland is conjugate to the margin that faces the Norwegian-Greenland Sea between Norway and Svalbard. Across northern Greenland the continental shelf narrows, and the slope steepens eastward along a progressively younger continent-ocean transition. The changes in margin morphology presumably reflect the shorter history of cooling, subsidence, and crustal stretching across the margin as the active spreading axis is approached (Dawes, this volume).

Basement below the North Greenland shelf probably contains thinned Precambrian crystalline rocks below a thick (as much as 10 km) deformed lower Paleozoic sequence whose tectonic strike is subparallel with the trend of the margin. These units are overlain by as much as 7 km of upper Paleozoic to Tertiary sediments and volcanics (Dawes, this volume).

These rocks were sheared dextrally during the opening of the Eurasia Basin beginning about 65 to 56 Ma. The shelf is characterized by several prominent margin-parallel faults and, below the Lincoln Shelf, by large linear troughs filled with up to 10 km of nonmagnetic material, presumably sediments (Kovacs and Vogt, 1982; Dawes, this volume). The filling of these troughs probably postdates the opening of the Eurasia Basin. A substantial sediment budget is indicated for the North Greenland continental shelf by the great thickness (up to 6 km) of nonmagnetic material that overlies Tertiary (anomaly 13 age) basement below the Morris Jesup Plateau (Kovacs and Vogt, 1982).

Amerasia Basin. The character and composition of the Amerasia Basin margin is best known in North America where the continental shelf is relatively narrow and is linked structurally to onshore geology. In contrast, the geologic structure of the East Siberian Shelf is virtually unknown. Basement beneath this shelf, as determined from seismic refraction studies, consists of a 5.5 to 5.7 km/s folded layer, possibly sedimentary in character, over a 6.0 to 6.3 km/s crystalline layer (Demenitskaya and others, 1973). Estimates from aeromagnetic measurements over the East Siberian Shelf suggest that its crust may be 30 to 35 km thick, with basement rocks covered by 5 to 10 km of sediments concentrated into three basins that roughly parallel the continental margin. The most northerly basin is believed to be the westward extension of the North Chukchi Basin and therefore presumably is filled with Cretaceous and Cenozoic sediments. The other basins may contain older rocks but the geological constraints are few (Fujita and Cook, this volume).

The North American polar margin has a prebreakup history similar to the continental margin of northern Greenland. The main differences between the two are that in the Amerasia Basin the margin is at least 15 m.y. older and was probably formed by rifting as opposed to shearing.

Cratonic rocks may be absent below parts of the Canadian Beaufort Shelf but they are present and thin seaward elsewhere beneath the polar margin in Canada and Alaska (Dixon and Dietrich, this volume; Grantz and others, Chapter 16, this volume; Berry and Barr, 1971; Asudeh and others, 1989). These rocks are overlain by thick, early Paleozoic stratigraphic sequences that, except for the eastern Beaufort Sea area, were deformed and thermally altered in mid-Paleozoic time (Miall, 1976). In Canada the deformed belt extends from northern Greenland to Prince Patrick Island where it strikes west-northwest and is truncated at the continental margin (Sweeney and others, this volume).

Upper Paleozoic and Mesozoic strata, unconformable on these older rocks, are several kilometers thick below the North American shelf, except at Banks Island and the eastern Beaufort Sea where pre-Jurassic rocks are absent (Dixon and Dietrich, this volume).

Development of the present continental margin appears to have begun in Hauterivian time about 130 Ma, as indicated by a breakup unconformity along the Alaskan Beaufort Shelf and by uplift followed by rapid subsidence and normal faulting along the Canadian Beaufort Shelf. From Banks Island to northeastern Alaska a series of grabens and half-grabens initiated in Early Jurassic time underwent a renewed phase of extension during the late Early Cretaceous (Grantz and others, Chapter 16, this volume; Dixon and Dietrich, this volume).

To the northeast, regional extension is indicated by accelerated subsidence in the Sverdrup Basin beginning in the Hauterivian. In Barremian time, subsidence was accompanied by normal faulting and mafic magmatism that extended northwest of the basin along the present continental margin between Ellef Ringnes and Ellesmere Islands (Sweeney and others, this volume).

Basement rocks below the North American margin are unconformably covered by a clastic prism that is typically 3 to 5 km thick over the shelf. Gravity data suggest that post-breakup sediments may be quite thin over the mid-Paleozoic (Ellesmerian) structures between Borden and Prince Patrick Islands but could be up to 12 km thick below the Beaufort Shelf (Plate 3; Sobczak and others, this volume; Dixon and Dietrich, this volume; Sweeney and others, this volume).

Clastic sediments began to accumulate along the newly formed continental margin by Aptian-Albian time. Northwest of the Queen Elizabeth Islands, only Maastrichtian and younger post-breakup strata are known. Here there was substantial uplift and erosion of the inner continental shelf in Campanian-Maastrichtian time, perhaps related to the initial movements of Greenland relative to Canada during the opening of Labrador Sea–Baffin Bay. At this time, east-west rifting also may have taken place below the western Chukchi Shelf and Chukchi Borderland. Connections between these widely separated events are undetermined.

In early to middle Eocene time, when sea-floor spreading had just begun in the North Atlantic and Eurasia Basin, Greenland began to impinge upon and regionally deform continental crust in northeastern Canada. Contemporary north-directed thrusting, active today, also began in northeastern Alaska and nearby parts of the Beaufort-Mackenzie Basin (Grantz and others, Chapter 16, this volume; Dixon and Dietrich, this volume). At about this same time, parts of the Amerasia Basin sea floor appear to have been under tensional stress. Heat-flow anomalies near each end of the Alpha Ridge indicate possible Eocene thermal activity (Langseth and others, this volume).

Arctic marine environment

Knowledge of past Arctic Ocean environments is derived largely from the study of biotic remains from short seabed cores and from outcrops on the fringing landmasses. Sea-floor samples from the Alpha Ridge and rock samples from onshore document an ice-free, highly productive warm ocean during late Campanian to Eocene time, about 75 to 40 Ma, that was characterized by intense seasonal changes in flora and fauna (Thiede and others, this volume; Marincovich and others, this volume). Continental biotic diversity decreased during Campanian and Maastrichtian time, then apparently increased in late Paleocene and Eocene time (Marincovich and others, this volume).

Global extinction events at the close of Cretaceous time have been attributed to substantial volcanism, a significant marine regression, and reduced temperatures. An additional or alternative factor may have been a bolide impact that filled the Earth's atmosphere with sunlight-blocking debris.

The presence of relict Cretaceous Mollusk and Ostracode taxa within early Paleogene strata in northwestern Alaska implies that terminal Cretaceous extinction processes were only partly effective in the Arctic Ocean. These shallow-water biota were already adapted to relatively cool conditions and winter darkness. Marincovich and others (this volume) speculate that some high-latitude invertebrates were able to endure the terminal Cretaceous events that devastated most planktonic and nektonic organisms.

Species recovered from several circum-Arctic land areas indicate that temperate, possibly mild, conditions continued into Oligocene time in the Arctic Ocean (Marincovich and others, this volume). The north polar climate then seems to have entered a period of transition. Apparently coeval warm-to-mild temperate and cold-to-subfrigid species collected in widely separated Arctic coastal areas suggest that a north-south marine climatic zonation became well established during the Miocene (Marincovich and others, this volume). No Oligocene or Miocene material has been retrieved from the Arctic seabed (Thiede and others, this volume; Clark, this volume).

In Pliocene time the Arctic Ocean became distinctly colder, as indicated by cold-water biota from northern Alaska and Canada (Marincovich and others, this volume; Dinter and others, this volume). It now appears, from recently improved dating techniques, that the present ice-covered Arctic Ocean and associated glacial conditions evolved during late Pliocene time. The earliest ice-rafting is inferred, from seabed sediments cored in the central Arctic Ocean, to be at about 2.5 Ma (Thiede and others, this volume; Clark, this volume). The disappearance of ice-intolerant animals and the appearance of glacial deposits in northwestern Alaska suggest that the onset of ice cover began sometime after about 2.4 Ma (Dinter and others, this volume).

Studies of seismic stratigraphy on the Alaskan Beaufort Shelf have recorded six to eight Plio-Pleistocene marine transgressions thought to represent glacioeustatic sea-level changes related to fluctuating global ice volumes (Dinter and others, this volume).

All late Cenozoic deep-sea sediment cores from the Arctic Ocean document a cold, ice-covered Arctic Ocean that intermittently received large amounts of coarse, ice-rafted material from the fringing landmasses. Sedimentation rates in the Eurasia Basin are about 1 to 3 cm/kyr, whereas in the Amerasia Basin they are ten times less, about 1 to 3 mm/kyr (Thiede and others, this volume; Hall, this volume). The 1987 *Polarstern* cruise found that sediment-laden ice in the Eurasia Basin is much more prevalent than anticipated (Thiede, 1988). The debris presumably was entrained on the extensive shallow continental shelves north of the Soviet Union, particularly near the outflows of the Lena, Ob, and Yenisey Rivers. This may explain the higher sedimentation rates in the eastern Arctic Basin.

THE NEXT DECADE OF ARCTIC GEOSCIENCE

Knowledge of the paleoenvironmental and tectonic development of the north polar region remains primitive compared to what is known about the more accessible ocean basins. The chief impediments to data retrieval from the Arctic Ocean have been its ice cover, the expense and technical difficulty of operating in a frigid climate, lack of outstanding economic/political incentives, and limited international cooperation. This is gradually changing because of ongoing technical improvements and the increasing need of the world's scientific community to understand the place of the Arctic in both past and present global processes.

The Arctic clearly is sensitive to changes in global climate, but the role of the Arctic in effecting global climate change is unclear. Major progress in understanding and correlating boreal paleoenvironments will be achieved with more and deeper sampling of the Arctic seabed sediment column, with refined dating techniques for Arctic deep-sea sediment cores, and with improved local and regional marine stratigraphic correlation. The importance of the latter is emphasized by the differing interpretations of seismic stratigraphy on neighboring areas of the Beaufort Shelf by Dinter and others (this volume) and Blasco and others (this volume).

First-order paleoenvironmental questions in the Arctic include the timing and characteristics of boreal cooling and glaciation, the onset and history of the marine ice cover, the frequency and magnitude of late Paleogene climatic oscillations, the effect of a cold Arctic Ocean on global ocean circulation, and biotic responses to Arctic climatic fluctuations.

Several ambiguities of stratigraphic correlation should be resolved by systematic shallow seismic profiling over broad areas. Long, continuous cores recovered in grid fashion or along profiles are needed for stratigraphic correlation and solution of most of the paleoenvironmental problems. The retrieval of intact Holocene samples, the top few centimeters of seabed sediment, requires large box cores. Coring to 10-m depths is feasible now; coring to 50-m depths is possible from substantial floating platforms such as large ice-breakers that would be capable of maneuvering through much of the ice pack.

Studies seeking to understand the age and evolution of the oceanic Arctic Basin must center on the stratigraphy, structure and age of its continental margins, aseismic ridges, plateaus, borderland, and sediment-covered subbasins. Of equal importance are similar studies in the surrounding landmasses and continental shelves to determine the paleomagnetic history and present geodynamic state of the principal circum-Arctic terranes.

The tectonic questions begin with the structure, age, and evolution of the Amerasia Basin and its components. From a regional viewpoint, there is a clear need for potential field and bathymetric mapping. Large regions of the basin are virtually unexplored (e.g., Plates 2, 3, and 4). Simultaneous aerogravity and aeromagnetic measurements are now possible from long-range low-flying aircraft (L. Kovacs, personal communication, 1989), and these should be undertaken. Airborne bathymetric measurements cannot be made over ice-covered waters. It is a much-needed technical capability that should be pursued.

Airborne regional surveys should include detailed swaths at 1- to 2-km spacing, and multibeam bathymetric imaging over specific sea-floor targets in conjunction with multiparameter corridor studies. Primary targets are the Chukchi Borderland, central Canada Basin, and transects across the continent-ocean transition in Alaska and Canada.

The Chukchi Borderland is one of the least-studied large features in the Amerasia Basin. Knowledge of its composition and age would shed much light on its role in the development of the surrounding sea floor. Added to potential field and bathymetry surveys, corridor measurements should include crustal refraction and deep-penetrating reflection profiles, a grid of both heat-flow measurements and long (>10 m) sediment cores, and ultimately, ODP-type deep drilling to obtain very long (as much as 500 m), large-diameter continuous cores of sediment and basement.

The most significant artifact of the opening of the Amerasia Basin is the crust below the central Canada Basin. The opening mechanism is the key to understanding the evolution of the region. Critical needs are crustal seismic refraction and detailed deep seismic reflection profiling. This should be complimented by gridded heat-flow measurements and by a high-density potential field swath transecting the basin from Canada to the Chukchi Borderland. Deep drilling may be of limited value in this area because the sediment cover is thick and composed largely of turbidites.

Imprecise knowledge of the age and character of the continental margin around most of the Amerasia Basin and generally weak ties between offshore geophysical measurements and onshore outcrop and borehole data can be improved by multiparameter transects across several segments of the continent-ocean transition. Such corridors will identify major lateral changes in margin structure and assess possible conjugate connections between the margins of Arctic Alaska and the Queen Elizabeth Islands. Suggested transects are from the Barrow, Alaska, area, from Banks Island, and from Ellef Ringnes Island to the Canada Abyssal Plain. The desired techniques are those indicated previously, especially seismic refraction and reflection, detailed potential field surveys, gridded heat flow, and deep coring and deep drilling. On the shelf, deep drilling will be of singular importance in determining the time of continental breakup and the geodynamic history of the margin after breakup.

Regional gravity mapping is the greatest need in the Eurasia Basin. Detailed potential field measurements in swaths across the North Greenland margin and the Morris Jesup and Yermak Plateaus promise to yield significant results. Multiparameter corridors across the North Greenland margin at the Lincoln Shelf and near Morris Jesup Plateau would address two questions with major conceptual consequences: How does a sheared margin evolve through time? In what ways does this sheared margin differ from the presumed rifted margin of Amerasia Basin, given that both margins share a similar pre-breakup history and structure?

Other targets for swath-type multiparameter studies are the junction of the Alpha and Lomonosov Ridges with the continent north of Ellesmere Island and the Lincoln Sea, and the junction of the Arctic Mid-Ocean Ridge with the Laptev Shelf. Deep drilling of Arctic aseismic ridges, the continental shelves, and plateaus would define their stratigraphy and shallow basement composition, bracket their time of formation, and reveal their subsequent vertical motion history. Definitive tectonic and paleoenvironmental constraints will come primarily from the physical evidence that deep drilling and other direct sampling techniques provide.

As for the present geodynamic state of the Arctic, major seismicity is concentrated along the active plate boundary. Secondary intraplate activity is located mainly along the polar continental margin in North America (Plate 2; Fujita and others, this volume). The plate-margin seismicity needs to be studied with tomographic and dispersion techniques to assess elastic properties of the underlying oceanic crust and upper mantle, and to provide information about slow rifting processes, including the apparent lack of transform-fault activity along the Arctic Mid-Ocean Ridge. Three-dimensional modeling of reflected and regional phases will help to define the large-scale structure of major Arctic features.

To achieve these objectives and to understand the causes of intraplate activity, existing seismic stations in the circum-Arctic must be upgraded to IRIS (Incorporated Research Institutions for Seismology) standards (broadband, digital) and additional stations added, particularly in active intraplate areas, to improve first-motion resolution and to define the state of regional stress. In the active continental margin areas, short-term, high-quality local networks and ocean-bottom seismometers should be deployed to provide detailed information on the geometry and character of contemporary deformation. Ocean-bottom seismometers placed on the major aseismic ridges and borderlands would provide information about their structure and would detect any low-level seismic activity.

On the horizon

The logistical technologies and data acquisition methods proposed here are mostly proven or can be developed with relatively modest research effort within a few years. It is equally important to identify new techniques and capabilities that will take Arctic geoscientific research beyond what is now possible. Some specific future technologies with high scientific potential are:

1. procurement of an ice-breaker for scientific research capable of operating anywhere on the Arctic Ocean,

2. Ocean Drilling Program–type deep coring of Arctic marine sediments and basement rocks from a floating platform (e.g., an ice-breaker),

3. conversion of a nuclear submarine to an under-ice research platform,

4. deployment of remote buoys and a high-latitude communications satellite for seismic and environmental observations and high data rate telemetry out of the Arctic.

REFERENCES CITED

Asudeh, I., Green, A. G., and Forsyth, D. A., 1988, Canadian expedition to study the Alpha Ridge complex; Results of the seismic refraction survey: Geophysical Journal of the Royal Astronomical Society, v. 92, p. 283–301.

Asudeh, I., and 5 others, 1989, Crustal structure of the Canadian polar margin; Results of the 1985 seismic refraction survey: Canadian Journal of Earth Sciences, v. 26, p. 853–866.

Baggeroer, A. B., and Falconer, R., 1982, Array refraction profiles and crustal models of the Canada Basin: Journal of Geophysical Research, v. 87, p. 5461–5476.

Berry, M. J., and Barr, K. G., 1971, A seismic refraction profile across the polar continental shelf of the Queen Elizabeth Islands: Canadian Journal of Earth Sciences, v. 8, p. 347–360.

Crary, A. P., 1954, Bathymetric chart of the Arctic Ocean along the route of T-3, April 1952 to October 1953: Geological Society of America Bulletin, v. 65, p. 709–712.

Dawes, P. R., and Soper, N. J., 1973, Pre-Quaternary history of North Greenland, *in* Pitcher, M. G., ed., Arctic geology: American Association of Petroleum Geologists Memoir 19, p. 117–134.

Demenitskaya, R. M., Ivanov, S. S., and Volk, V. E., 1973, Crust of the Arctic seas of Eurasia: Tectonophysics, v. 20, p. 97–104.

Eldholm, O., and Talwani, M., 1977, Sediment distribution and structural framework of the Barents Sea: Geological Society of America Bulletin, v. 88, p. 1015–1029.

Feden, R. A., Vogt, P. R., and Fleming, H. S., 1979, Magnetic and bathymetric evidence for the "Yermak" hot spot northwest of Svalbard in the Arctic Basin: Earth and Planetary Science Letters, v. 44, p. 18–38.

Forsyth, D. A., and Mair, J. A., 1984, Crustal structure of the Lomonosov Ridge and the Fram and Makarov basins near the North Pole: Journal of Geophysical Research, v. 89, p. 473–481.

Forsyth, D. A., Morel-a-L'Huissier, P., Asudeh, I., and Green, A. G., 1986, Alpha Ridge and Iceland; Products of the same plume?: Journal of Geodynamics, v. 6, p. 197–214.

Gramberg, I. S., and Kulakov, Y. N., 1975, General geological structures and possible oil and gas provinces of the Arctic Basin, in Yorath, C. J., Parker, E. R., and Glass, D. J., eds., Canada's continental margins: Canadian Society of Petroleum Geologists Memoir 4, p. 525–529.

Hobson, G. D., and Overton, A., 1967, A seismic section of the Sverdrup Basin, Canadian Arctic Islands, in Musgrave, A. W., ed., Seismic refraction prospecting: Society of Exploration Geophysicists, p. 500–562.

Hunkins, K. L., 1961, Seismic studies of the Arctic Ocean floor, in Raasch, G. O., ed., Geology of the Arctic, Volume 1: Toronto, Ontario, University of Toronto Press, p. 645–665.

Jackson, H. R., Reid, I., and Falconer, R.H.K., 1982, Crustal structure near the Arctic Mid-Ocean Ridge: Journal of Geophysical Research, v. 87, p. 1773–1783.

Jackson, H. R., Johnson, G. L., Sundvor, E., and Myhre, A. M., 1984, The Yermak Plateau; Formed at a triple junction: Journal of Geophysical Research, v. 89, p. 3223–3232.

Jackson, H. R., Forsyth, D. A., and Johnson, G. L., 1986, Oceanic affinities of the Alpha Ridge, Arctic Ocean: Marine Geology, v. 73, p. 237–262.

Kovacs, L. C., and Vogt, P. R., 1982, Depth-to-magnetic source analysis of the Arctic Ocean region: Tectonophysics, v. 89, p. 255–294.

Kutchale, H. W., 1966, Arctic Ocean geophysical studies; The southern half of the Siberia Basin: Geophysics, v. 31, p. 683–710.

Lawver, L. A., and Baggeroer, A. B., 1983, A note on the age of the Canada Basin: Journal of the Alaska Geological Society, v. 2, p. 57–66.

Mair, J. A., and Lyons, J. A., 1981, Crustal structure and velocity anisotropy beneath the Beaufort Sea: Canadian Journal of Earth Sciences, v. 18, p. 724–741.

Meyerhoff, A. A., 1980, Petroleum basins of the Soviet Arctic: Geological Magazine, v. 117, p. 101–186.

Miall, A. D., 1976, Devonian geology of Banks Island, Arctic Canada, and its bearing on the tectonic development of the circum-Arctic region: Geological Society of America Bulletin, v. 87, p. 1599–1608.

Overton, A., 1982, A seismic reflection profile across the Lomonosov Ridge, central Arctic Ocean: Dallas, Texas, Society of Exploration Geophysicists 52nd Annual Meeting Technical Program, p. 87–89.

Palmer, A. R., 1983, The decade of North American geology 1983 geologic time scale: Geology, v. 11, p. 503–504.

Pitman, W. C., III, and Talwani, M., 1972, Sea-floor spreading in the North Atlantic: Geological Society of America Bulletin, v. 83, p. 619–646.

Taylor, P. T., 1983, Nature of the Canada Basin; Implications from satellite-derived magnetic anomaly data: Journal of the Alaska Geological Society, v. 2, p. 1–8.

Taylor, P. T., Kovacs, L. C., Vogt, P. R., and Johnson, G. L., 1981, Detailed aeromagnetic investigation of the Arctic Basin, 2: Journal of Geophysical Research, v. 86, p. 6323–6333.

Thiede, J., ed., 1988, Scientific cruise report of Arctic expedition ARK IV/3: Reports on Polar Research (AWI) 43, 237 p.

Van Wagoner, N. A., Williamson, M. -C., Robinson, P. T., and Gibson, I. L., 1986, First samples of acoustic basement recovered from the Alpha Ridge, Arctic Ocean; New constraints for the origin of the ridge: Journal of Geodynamics, v. 6, p. 177–196.

Vogt, P. R., Taylor, P. T., Kovacs, L. C., and Johnson, G. L., 1979, Detailed aeromagnetic investigation of the Arctic Basin: Journal of Geophysical Research, v. 84, p. 1071–1089.

—— , 1982, The Canada Basin; Aeromagnetic constraints on structure and evolution: Tectonophysics, v. 89, p. 295–336.

Weber, J. R., 1986, The Alpha Ridge; Gravity, seismic, and magnetic evidence for a homogeneous, mafic crust: Journal of Geodynamics, v. 6, p. 117–136.

Weber, J. R., and Sweeney, J. F., 1985, Reinterpretation of morphology and crustal structure in the central Arctic Ocean basin: Journal of Geophysical Research, v. 90, p. 663–677.

Wilson, J. T., 1963, Hypothesis of the Earth's behavior: Nature, v. 198, p. 925–929.

MANUSCRIPT ACCEPTED BY THE SOCIETY FEBRUARY 12, 1990
GEOLOGICAL SURVEY OF CANADA CONTRIBUTION NO. 36489

Index

[Italic page numbers indicate major references]

Abisko, Sweden, 79
acritarchs, 296
Admiralty Bay, 467
advection, vertical, 137
Aegir Ridge, 205, 206, 353, 361, 622
aeromagnetics, *316, 328, 344*
Aforica circinata, 466
aftershocks, 88, 90, 92, 95, 284
aggregates, marine, *560*
Aichilik River drainage, 469
AIDJEX. *See* Arctic Ice Dynamics Joint Experiment
airguns, 153
Airy model root system, 114
Aklavik Arch Complex, 516
Akpak sequence, *251*, 282, 516
Alaska, 16, *68, 70*, 79, 91, *105*, 232, 246, *257*, 301, 518, *545, 561*, 567, *569*, 579, 593, 597, 600, 604, 607, 609
    gravity anomalies, *105*
    northeastern, 284, *420*
    northern, 406, 582
    western, 467, 581
Alaska Basin, *395*
Alaska block, 612
Alaska plate, 245, 259
Alaska Range, 569, 581, 583, 588
Alaskan continental margin, *257*
    Arctic Platform, 259, *262*
    Barrow sector, *257, 275, 278*
    Barter Island sector, *257, 279*
    Canada Basin, 259, *270*
    Chukchi Borderland, 259, *270*
    Chukchi sector, *257, 270*
    geology, *259*
    model, *262*
    physiography, *257*
    stratigraphy, *259, 270*
    structure, *270*
    tectonic events, *259*
Alaskan continental shelf, *68, 70*
Alaskan–Eastern Siberian Arctic, *567*
Alaskan North Slope, *459*
Albian, *246*
Aleutian Arc, 81, 90, 585
Aleutian Basin, 584
Aleutian Benioff zone, 279
Aleutian Islands, 79
Aleutian-Kurile arc-arc junction, 91
algae, freshwater, 494
allochthons, 265
alluvium, 469, 472, 493
Alnus, 501
Alpha-Lomonosov complex, 309
Alpha-Mendeleev Ridge, 19, *307, 320, 330*, 429, 447, *570*, 620, *621*
Alpha Ridge, 3, 18, 24, 26, 63, 64, 71, *72*, 107, *108*, 114, 130, 140, *144, 167*, 227, 232, 235, 305, *307, 320*, 325, *328, 330*, *333, 382, 390*, 395, *398, 436*, 447, 453, 593, 598, 599, *600*, 602, 609, 612, *621*
    axial valley, 603
    bathymetry, *72*
    evolution hypothesis, *331*
    heat flow, *149*
    magnetic anomalies, *127*
    model, *326*
    seismic data, 159, *161*
    volcanic origin, *398*
Alpha Ridge Graben, 308
Amauligak oil field, 503, 518
Amauropsis, 413, 414
Amerasia Basin, 2, 3, 26, 63, *70*, 71, 75, 103, 136, 138, *140, 145, 157*, 305, 332, 337, 345, 348, 387, 430, 440, 447, 514, 567, *570, 619, 620*, 622, *624*
    bathymetry, *71*
    heat flow, *141, 145*
    models, 146, *394*
    provinces age, *145*
    seismic data, *157*
ammonites, 405
amphibole, 291
amphibolite, 296
Amundsen abyssal plain, 319
Amundsen Basin, 3, 63, *70*, 71, 108, 114, 139, *156*, 160, 212, 216, 218, 305, *312, 317, 320*, 365, *367, 371*, 511, 513, 620
    seismic data, *156*
Amundsen Gulf, 239, *242*, 270
Amundsen Gulf channel, 239
Anakturuk River, 469
Ancient Arctica, 301
Anderson Basin, 242, 247, 248
Anderson Plain, 239, 246
andesites, 528
anhydrite, 510
Anjou Islands, *290*
anomalies
    aeromagnetic, 105, 124
    Bouguer, 103, 106, 218, 344
    boundary, 345
    depth, *180*
    electrical conductivity, 317
    free-air, 22, 93, 101, *103*, 105, *109*, 114, 172, 180, 309, 319, 325, 326, 331, 344, 358
    gravity, 93, *94, 101, 105*, 114, 172, *180*, 232, 275, *299*, 309, 319, 326, 331, 358
    high-amplitude, 216, 372
    long-wavelength, 216, 328
    magnetic, *119*, 171, 172, 176, 180, 194, 202, 215, *216*, 232, 236, 285, 295, 298, *316*, 329, *330*, 345, 358, 371, 372, 384, *390, 398*, 400, 429, *448*, 571, *580*, 586, 598, 599, *600*, 609, *619*
    mid-ocean ridge elevation, 65
    POGO, 124
    sea-floor spreading, 185, 356
    short-wavelength, 328
anticlines, 518, 530
    asymmetric, 251
    diapiric, 245
    rollover, 391
Anyuy fold belt, 582
Anyuy suture zone, *567*
Anzhu Islands, *290*, 300
Anzhu Ridge, 298, *299*, 530
Apparent Polar Wander Paths (APWP), *567, 571*
APWP. *See* Apparent Polar Wander Paths
Aquitaine Basin, 413
archaemonads, 436
Arctic Basin, *14, 16*, 20, 29, 37, 63, 107, *284*, 305, 337, *403, 423*, 503, *567*, 580
    annual surface pressure, 40
    central, 48, *72, 449*
    eastern, *441*, 448
    evolution, *140*
    gas hydrates, *547*
    geological explorations, *21*
    geophysical explorations, *21*
    magnetic anomalies, *126*
    manganese nodules, 552
    marine mining, *564*
    paleoclimatic history, *403*
    paleogeographic history, *403*
    sediment cores, 38
Arctic Bay, 555
Arctic Data Buoy Program, 39
Arctic Foothills, 262, 266
Arctic Ice Dynamics Joint Experiment (AIDJEX), *25*, 50
Arctic Islands, 71, 246, 259, 285, 480, 486, *504*, 514, 515, 530
    gas hydrates, *543*
    margin, 245
    model, 593, *607*
    shelf, *535*
    unconformities, 514
Arctic land sites, heat-flow measurements, *134*
Arctic Mid-Ocean Ridge, 3, 20, 23, 27, 63, *65*, 70, 74, 81, *82*, 91, 97, 108, *114*, 180, 134, 138, 139, 156, 330, *351*, 365, *371*, 503, 620
    bathymetry, *65*
    continental extension, *372*
    magnetic anomaly, *127*
    seismicity, *82*
Arctic Ocean–North Sea Basin seaway, 408, *409*
Arctic Platform, 242, 243, *244*, 252, *253, 262*, 495, 503, *504*, 513, 520, 523, *524*

Brookian sequence, *263*, *266*, 273, 278
Dinkum succession, 263, *266*
Ellesmerian sequence, 263, *265*, 273, 274, 275
Franklinian sequence, *263*, 278
gas hydrates, *543*
hinge line, 243
stratigraphy, *263*
Arctic Red Formation, 252
Arctic Terrace Wedge, *227*, 230, *231*, 234, *235*
Arctica, 414, 419, *421*
arenite, 263, 520
argillites, 246, 263, 265, 275, *276*, 280, 520, 524, 575, 600
Argyromya, 412, 414
arkoses, 506
Arlis Gap, 71, 306, 309
Arlis Plateau, 3, 70, 289, 309, 337, *343*
ARLIS II, 16, *24*, 49, 71, 72, 107, 153, 158, 160, 212, 217, 305, 307, 308, *308*, 310, *332*, 337, 365, 366, 385
Artyk earthquake, 88
ash, volcanic, 295, 324
Astarte, 414
borealis, 468
leffingwelli, 464, 466
Asterigerina guerichi, 410
Atkinson Point, 247
well, 518
Atlantic Basin, 580
Atlantic–Greenland Sea corridor, 408
Aulocytheridea, 408
Axel Heiberg continental shelf, 28
Axel Heiberg Island, 18, 49, 69, 93, 228, 230, 231, 234, 236, 332, 399, 415

Babbage River delta, 497
Baffin, William, 11, 30
Baffin Bay, 11, *92*, 105, *108*, 113, 114, 211, 234, 285, 406, 427
gravity anomalies, *108*
seismicity, *92*
shelf, 111
Baffin Bay–Davis Strait, 37
Baffin Island, 9, 91, 555
Baffinicythere emarginata, 467
bairdiids, 407
Bakunella, 408
Baltic Sea, 37
Balyktakh suite, 294
Balyktakh synclinorium 294, 299
Banks Island, 70, 107, 113, 228, 232, 239, *242*, 245, 246, *247*, 259, 395, 597, 602, 604, 623
Banks Island Basin, 242, *246*, 247, 248, 249
Banks Island graben, 244
Barents Abyssal Plain, 3, 27, 70, *367*
Barents' Chart, 19
Barents continental shelf, 308, 330
Barents-Kara Sea, 373
margin, 375
Barents-Kara Shelf, 365

Barents Sea, 14, 18, 37, 63, 107, 109, 315, 351, 445, 446, 448, 556, 558
continental margin, 215, 220, 355, 622
Barents Shelf, 72, 103, 107, 113, *108*, 315, 353, 455, 622
barite, 552
mining project, 555
Barn Uplift, 240, 246
Barrow Arch, 105, 107, *262*, 519, 520, 522, 523, *525*
Barrow fault zone, *276*, *525*
Barrow high, 525, 526
Barrow sector, *257*, *275*, *278*, *282*
Barrow unit, 460
Barter Island, *257*, *279*, *282*, 284, 285, *420*
Barter Island subbasin, *282*, *284*, 523
Bartholomew's Chart, 19
Bartlett, Robert, 15
basalts, *181*, *192*, 206, 208, 216, 219, 221, 228, 293, *295*, 355, *375*, 385, 390, 423, 528, 530, 552, 603
basement
acoustic, 342, 353, 355, 393, 524
continental, 68
crystalline, 201, 301, 372, 570
granitic, 215
magnetic, *328*, *511*
oceanic, 146
volcanic, 192, 197
basins, 70, *140*, 166, 177, *194*, 204, 208, *242*, 263, 265, 270, *282*, 305, 354, 379, *429*, *503*, *584*
back-arc, 609
deep-sea, *448*
evolution, 220
fill, *319*
flysch, *569*
foreland, 266
formation, 192, 206
half-graben, 199
intrashelf, *531*, 535
margins, 379, *391*
predrift, 207
pull-apart, 567, 580, 584
rift, 188
sedimentary, 2, 106, 111, *213*, 218, 220, 397, *503*, 570
shelf, *519*
shelf-margin, *533*, *534*
See also specific basins
bathymetry, 3, *18*, *20*, 29, *63*, 108, 171, 176, *188*, 212, *230*, 232, *282*, *309*, 325, 331, *337*, 390, 445, 491, 499
Alpha Ridge, 72
Amerasia Basin, *71*
Arctic Mid-Ocean Ridge, 65
Eurasia Basin, *70*
Knipovitch Ridge, *65*
Kolbeinsey Ridge, *64*
Lomonosor Ridge, *71*
Mohns Ridge, 65
Bay Fiord, 414
beaches, *563*
ancient, 37

Beaufort cluster, 495
Beaufort Formation, 251, 421, 514
Beaufort-Mackenzie Basin, 245, *246*, 492, *493*, 501.
depositional sequences, *245*
See also Mackenzie-Beaufort Basin
Beaufort Ramp, 239
Beaufort Sea, 16, 18, 41, 50, 63, 91, 94, 105, 106, 107, 145, *239*, *251*, 381, 421, 464, 469, 515, 547, 552, *556*, 561, 562
basins, *519*, *520*
coast, 467, 468
continental margin, 245, 249, 243, *331*, 477
continental shelf, 69, 393, 459, 476, *491*, *495*, *498*
continental slope, 477
deposits, 478
gas hydrates, *545*, 548
gyre, 24, 25, 39, 446, 480
island chains, *564*
passive margin, 522
petroleum potential, *522*
shelf basins, *519*
shelf hydrates, *546*
shelf province, *522*
See also Canadian Beaufort Sea
Beaufort Shelf, 70, 107, 257, 259, *266*, 275, *276*, 385, 399, *486*, 562, 623, 624
composite units, 477, 480
core subunits, 482
Cross Island unit, *481*, 486
inner, 480, 483
Leffingwell Lagoon unit, *481*, 486
Maguire Islands unit, *481*, 486
marine sequences, *481*
middle, 477
outer, 477
wedge units, 477
Beaufort structural province, *484*, 485
Beaufort Terrace, 19
Beaufort western shelf, seismostratigraphic units, *498*
Beaufortian sequence, 266
bed forms, active, *563*
bedrock, 312, 323, 459
basaltic, 27
volcanic, 26
Beerenberg volcano, 175, 179
Belgica Bank, 211
Bel'kov Island, 290, 293, *294*, 298, 299
Bel'kov-Nerpalakh depression, 293, 294, 530, 532, 534
Bell Sea sediments, 468
Bennett complex, *295*
Bennett Island, 74, 290, *295*, 298, 530
Bennett terrane, *295*, 301
bentonite beds, 247, 282
Bering Sea, 37, 427, 466
continental motions, *581*
tectonics, *581*
Bering shelf, 579
Bering Splinter, 600, 609
Bering Strait, *11*, 15, *422*, 427, 429, 446, 464

Bering Strait Oroclines, 569
Bering, Vitus, 11
Beringian Platform, 487
Berri suite, 297
Betula, 499
Big River sub-basin, *242*
Bigbendian beds, *462*
Bigbendian transgression, 461, *462*, 485
biofacies, 440
biota, 468
    Atlantic-Arctic, 243
    cold-water, 624
    marine, 409, *410*
    shallow-water, 623
bioturbation, 313, 323
bitumen, 513
bituminous beds, 248
bivalves, 405, 414, *419*, *422*
Blagoveshchensk Basin, 298, *299*, *300*, 530, 533
Blethisa catenaria, 473
BLKS. *See* Blosseville Kyst Shelf
Blosseville Kyst Basin, *199*
    half-graben, *199*
Blosseville Kyst Shelf (BLKS), 192, *197*, 205
Bol'shoi Lyakhov Island, 96, 290, 291, *293*, 299, 530, 559
Bonnet Lake area, 285
Borden Island, 70, 232, 235
Borderland. *See* Chukchi Sea
Boreal episode, 570
Boreas Basin, *353*, 358
boreholes, *134*, 228, *481*, *482*, 497, 498
bottom currents, *74*, 174, 315, 323, 355, 375, 446, 448
bottom melting, 49
bottom photography, *323*
bottom waters, *138*, 428, *449*, 468
Boundary Creek Formation, 282, 518
Boundary Creek sequence, *247*, 516
brachiopods, 293, 297, 410
Brachycythere, 408, 413
Bravo, 16, 24
brine, 41
    formation, 428
British Mountains, 239, 263, 285
British Trans-Arctic Expedition, 124
Brito-Arctic Volcanic Province, 361
Brock Island, 27
bromine, 551
Brookian sequence, 263, *266*, 273, 276, 278, 520, *522*, *524*, 533, 534, 535, 573, 602
Brooks Range, 95, *105*, *262*, 270, 279, 398, 459, *469*, 472, 478, 483, 484, 486, 520, 522, 524, 526, *569*, 572, *575*, 581, 582, 598, *600*, 615
    eastern, 262
    glaciers, *469*
    northeastern, 262
Brooks Range Geanticline, 245, 247
Brooks Range orogen, 259, *262*, 279, 282
Brooks Range thrust sheets, 572
bryozoans, 297, 410

Buch Gulf region, 93
Bug Creek Group, 246, 516
Burustas suite, *292*
Bythocypris, 408

Cache Creek Uplift, 240, 246, 247
caissons, *560*
calving, iceberg, 440
Cambrian, 246
Camden Anticline, 279, 281, 282, *283*, 393, 477, 480, *484*
Camden Bay, 604
Cameron Island, 133
Campbell Uplift, 246
Canada, *68*, *70*, *93*, 232, 421, 459, 468, 475, 503, *560*, 599, 609, 615
    coast, 91
    northern, 103, *105*, *414*
Canada Abyssal Plain, 3, 70, *71*, 387, 391, 446
Canada Basin, 3, 24, 27, 63, *108*, 114, 130, 140, *141*, *146*, *160*, *164*, *167*, 227, 232, 234, 235, 244, 247, 257, 270, 285, *328*, 332, *333*, *379*, 381, 427, 429, *440*, 449, 492, 567, 570, 580, 588, *593*, 597, 606, *620*
    age, 394
    crust thickness, *382*
    crustal layer, *382*
    evolution, *593*
    evolutionary models, 604
    magnetic anomaly, 127
    models, *394*, 399, *593*, *596*, 604, 605
    Modern, 399
    morphology, *386*
    opening, *571*, 615
    origin, *394*
    physiography, *379*
    rotational model, *593*, *596*, 605
    rotational opening, 599
    seafloor, *386*
    sediment thickness, *385*
    sedimentation, *440*
    seismic-stratigraphic units, *385*
    seismicity, *160*, *164*, *393*
    solid earth, 379
    stratigraphy, *382*
    structure, *391*
    tectonics, *378*, *593*, *602*
Canada Basin Acoustic Reverberation Experiment (CANBAREX), 25
Canada Plain, 327
Canadian Archipelago, 37, 446. *See also* Canadian Arctic Archipelago
Canadian Arctic Archipelago, 11, 13, 133, 427, 556
Canadian Arctic coastal plain, *513*
Canadian Arctic coastal shelf, *513*, 514
    petroleum potential, *513*
    tectonic evolution, *513*
Canadian Arctic Expedition, 379
Canadian Arctic Islands, 259, 285, 480, 486, 530, 567, *570*, 582, *593*, 597, 604, 606, 612

    mines, 555
    shelf, 535
Canadian Arctic low, 609
Canadian Arctic margin, 113, *609*
Canadian Basin Acoustic Reverberation Study (CANBARX), 160
Canadian Beaufort continental shelf, 281, *491*
Canadian Beaufort Sea, 548, *560*
    gas hydrates, *545*
    See also Beaufort Sea
Canadian Beaufort Shelf, 548, 623
    See also Beaufort Shelf
Canadian Continental Rise, 71
Canadian Continental Slope, *70*
Canadian continental shelf, *68*, 282
Canadian Department of Energy, Mines, and Resources (EMR), 71, 305
Canadian Expedition to Study the Alpha Ridge (CESAR 83), 18, *26*, 72, 107, 134, 141, 160, 308, 309, *321*, 330, 332, *333*, 391, 430, 600, 603, 612
Canadian Hydrographic Service (CHS), 18, 20, 309
Canadian outer shelf, 477
Canadian polar margin, 227
    bathymetry, *230*
    gravity, 232
    heat flow, *234*
    magnetic field, 232
    seismic refraction, *230*
    sesmicity, *234*
Canning Basin, 277
Canning Displacement Zone, 105, *262*, 279, 393, 485
Canning Formation, *267*, 277, 282
Canning River, 263, *267*, 279, 459, *481*, 486
    alluvial fan, 472
    drainage, 469
Cannonball Formation, 409, 413, *415*, 423
Cannonball Sea, 419
Canoe Depression, 240
Canol Formation, 246
Cantwell Formation, 583
canyons, submarine, 285, 298, 395
Cape Burus Tas, 293
Cape Deceit Foramtion, 466
Cape Dyer, 108
Cape Espenberg well, *527*
Cape Lambton Uplift, 242, 245
Cape Lisburne, 556
Cape Pillar, 297
Cape Prince of Wales, 11
Cape Shalaurova, 299
Cape Simpson, 467, 468
Cape Svyatoi Nos, 299, 559
Cape Thompson, Alaska, 133
Cape Utes Drevyannikh Gor, 294
carbonates, 231, 246, 276, 279, *293*, 295, 296, 343, 397, 504, 509, 511, 514, *520*, 525, 530, 532, 534
    detrital, 54
    platform, 220

shelf, 194
Carboniferous, *246*, *297*, 358, *571*
Caribou Hills, 249
Carnwath Platform, 242
Carter Creek outcrop, *420*
cartographers, *6*, 28
cassiterite, 553, *558*
Cenozoic, *53*, *54*, 220, *245*, 375, *403*, *427*, *436*, *439*, *459*, *461*, *468*, *585*
Central Arctic Basin, 37
Central Range, *296*
Central Taimyr Trough, 530
Central Trough, 322, 323
cephalopods, 405
CESAR 83. See Canadian Expedition to Study the Alpha Ridge
CESAR cores, *6*, *323*, 331, *439*, 452
Cesar North Ridge, 26, 323, 331
Cesar South Ridge, 323, 332
Cesar Trough, 26, 323, 324, 326
  model, 325
chalk, 313
Chamaecyparis nootkaensis, 472
channels, 239, 480, 570, 582
  drainage, 563
  inter-island, 69
  marginal, 68
  submerged river, 69
  turbidity current, 70
Charlie Gap, 71, *343*
Chaun Basin, 503, *528*, *535*
Chekurian anticlinorium, 294
Cherskii Mountains, *87*, 91, 97
  seismicity, *87*
chert, 246, 263, 265, 266, 469, 483, 514, 520
Chickaloon Formation, 583
chitinozoans, 263
Chlamys, 421
chlorite, 343
Christopher Formation, 247
chromium deposits, 555
CHS. See Canadian Hydrographic Service
Chukchi Abyssal Plain, 3, *71*, 337, 342, *343*, 390,
Chukchi-Alpha Ridge, sedimentation, *440*
Chukchi Basin, *523*
  petroleum potential, *526*
  stratigraphy, *524*
  tectonics, *523*
Chukchi Borderland, 3, 257, *270*, 285, *337*, 379, 400, 535, 600, 602, 609, *620*, *621*, 624
  crust, 348
  geology, *343*
  model, 344, *347*
  physiography, *337*
  tectonic development, *345*
Chukchi Cap, *69*, 337, *342*, *345*
Chukchi continental shelf, 69, 105, 107, 113, 345, 390, 459
Chukchi hingeline, 533
Chukchi Peninsula, *95*, 528
Chukchi Plateau, *69*, 107, 108, 109, 124, 593
Chukchi Platform, 270, 274, 285, 299, 503, 504, 523, 524, 525, 526, 533, 534
Chukchi Rise, 337, *342*, *345*
Chukchi Sea, 63, 91, *95*, 105, 106, 276, 381, 446, *523*, 526, 547, 552, 556, 558
  coast, 468
  petroleum potential, *531*, *534*
  seismicity, *95*
  shelf basins, *523*, *533*
Chukchi sector, 257, *270*
Chukchi Shelf, 257, 259, 270, *275*, *276*, 285, 400
  northern, 265
Chukchi Trench, 344
Chukostskiy region, 558
Chukotka Peninsula, *301*
Chukotka terrane, 609
Chukotsk Peninsula, 569, *582*
Chukotsk-Seward Peninsula region, 581
Cibicides, 420
  tenellus, 420
circulation
  bottom-water, 428
  oceanic, 53
  surface-water, 428
  water, 406
  winter cyclonic, 439
Circum-Antarctic Current, 54
Cisco, 504
clastics, 220, 246, 247, 252, 439, 492, 514, 530, 533, 534
  marine, 194
clasts, 483, 498
clay, 55, 294, 367, 368, 482, 493, 497, *498*, 500, 562
claystone, 420
climate, *53*, *59*, 406, *427*, 436, *442*
  global, 406, 624
  interglacial, 54
Climatic Long-Range Interpretation, Mapping, and Prediction (CLIMAP) project, 39
Clinocardium
  californiense, 466
  ciliatum, 423
clinoforms, 494, 496, 498
coal, 246, 266, 292, 295, 436, 483, 522, 527, 552, 555, *556*
  brown, 294, 372
  seams, 510
Coastal Plain, 262, 263, 265, 279, 284, 421, *459*, 461, 466, 469, 476, 503, 576
  Alaskan, *459*, 461, 466, 469, 476, 503
Coastal Shelf, 503
coccoliths, 408, 443
coeloma, 420
College, Alaska, 79
Colville Basin, 266, 277, 279, 522, 535
Colville Delta, 267
Colville foreland basin, 262
Colville Group, 267, 277, *522*
Colville River, 262, *267*, 406, 410, *462*, 464, *469*, 486
  bluffs, 464
  delta, *279*, 465, 483
Colville Trough, 503
Colvillian transgression, 461, *462*
compression, 88, 93, 97, 220, 230, 285, 393, 516, 519, 580, 582, 602
conductivity, thermal, 29, *136*, 145
cones, 295
  alluvial, 289
conglomerates, 246, 247, 250, 265, 266, *297*, 462, 469, 506, 508, *510*, 511, 520, 522, 527, 530, 569
continental breakup, 235, 244, 259, 429, 620, 621
continental crust, models, 299
continental drift, 221
continental margin, 48, *65*, 91, 145, 171, 176, *188*, *208*, *211*, 219, *227*, 230, *251*, 257, 289, 351, *352*, 355, 358, *395*, 429, 449, *503*, 514, *519*, *528*, 539, *581*, 600, 602, 612, 619, *621*, 625
  age, *235*
  development, *243*
  origin, *235*
  physiographic regions, *239*
  passive, 107, 110
  rifted, 2
  sheared, 2
  structure, *234*, *251*
  tectonic history, *284*
  See also specific locations
continental plates, *571*
  convergence, *580*
  reconstruction, *571*
continental platforms, 20
continental rift, 218, *251*
continental rise, 70, 239, 257, 365, 379, 382, 387, 441, 509, 621
  sedimentary prisms, 2
continental shelf, 2, 15, 18, 28, 63, *65*, 75, 91, 107, 109, *185*, *188*, 203, *208*, 211, 212, 215, *227*, 265, 270, 279, 289, 295, *306*, 309, *459*, 476, *491*, 499, 503, 505, *513*
  inner, 68, 232, 235, 251, 291, 464, 466, 477, 480, 486, 514, 563
  insular, 191
  middle, 477, 485
  minerals, 551, *552*, *555*
  outer, 257, 477, 480, 485, 486
  progradation, 201
  Siberia, 83
  See also specific locations
continental slope, 70, *93*, 109, 178, 211, 213, 215, 239, 251, 257, 270, 289, 365, 441, 477, 509, 546
  See also specific locations
convergence, 257, 259, 262, 279, 283, 285, 439, 567, *580*, *582*
Cook Inlet area, 583
Cooperation Gap, 72, *309*
Coppermine arch, 242
corals, 293, 297, 408
Corbicula, 414

Corbula (Bicorbula), 419
cores, 398, *480*, *577*, 600, 602, 624
    Cesar, *323*, 331
    piston, 355
    sediment, 38, 343, 427
    stratigraphy, *481*, *428*
coring, *312*, *323*
    seabed, 24
Coriolis effect, 70, 446
Cornwallis Island, 133
Coronation Gulf region, 468, 480, 552
Coryphodon, 415
COST Well No. 1, 579
crabs, 419
Crassacythere, 413
cratons, 215
    North American, 516, 575, 579
Crenella, 419
Cretaceous, *245*, *247*, *408*
    Late, *580*
Cross Island unit, *480*, 483, 486
crust
    basaltic, 149
    continental, 70, 74, *110*, 130, 160, 179, 185, 188, 194, 199, 206, *215*, 218, 219, 221, 227, 231, 235, 320, 331, 345, 358, 372, 395, 400, 430, 593, 602
    lower, *382*
    magnetic, 218
    oceanic, 25, 26, *27*, 91, 97, 110, 113, 137, 156, 157, 165, 166, 177, 181, 182, 185, *188*, 192, 194, 197, 206, *207*, 219, 220, *230*, 243, 270, 315, 321, 332, 351, *353*, 361, *371*, 391, 399, 567, 570, 583, 593, *612*, 619
    stretching, 333
    structure, 96, 163, 315, *368*
    thickness, 97, *109*, 114, 127, 164, 270, 309, 320
    thin, 156, 215, 227, 235, 326, 620
    transitional, 602
    upper, 93, 94, 137, 181, 208, 215, 283, 320
    young, 171, 182
crystallography, *539*
currents, *446*
    bottom, 74, 174, 315, 323, 355, 375, 446, 448
    Circum-Antarctic, 54
    circumpolar, 406
    East Greenland, 19, 21, 63
    transpolar, *15*, 19, 26, 312, 375
    turbidity, 70, 71, 309, 342
    Vestspitsbergen, 21, *428*, 445
    West Spitzbergen, 21
cycles
    regressive-transgressive, 499, 513, 521
    transgressive-regressive, 265
Cyperaceae, 497, 500
cyprids, 407
Cyrena, 420
Cyrtodaria, 412, 414
    rutupiensis, 412, *414*, *419*
Cythere lutea, 467

cytherellids, 407
Cytheretta, 421
cytherids, 407, 413
Cytheromorpha, 413
Cytheropteron, 407, 421
Cytherura, 413

dacites, 528
Darnley Bay, 105
data
    aeromagnetic, *124*, 203, 232, 373, *384*, 391, 511, 517, 570, 598
    bathymetric, *18*, 20, 21, *71*, 305, 372
    geophysical, *449*
    gravity, 511
    paleomagnetic, *575*, *578*, 600, 612
    seismic, 480, 513
    solid earth, *379*
Davis Strait, 9, *108*, 113
    gravity anomalies, *108*
De Inventione Fortunata, 6
debris, 50, 199, 323, 440, 446, 465, 482, 593
Defence Research Board, Canada, *19*
deformation, 244, 245, 262, 276, *393*, 495, 509, 510, 513, 514, 567, 585, 586
    compressive, *582*, 588
deglaciation, *54*, 93, 234, 440, *442*, 453
DeLong Arch, 532, 533, 534
DeLong Islands, 290, *295*, 298, *300*
DeLong Mountains, 569, 602
DeLong uplift, *534*
deltas, 518
Demarcation subbasins, 282, 284, 503, 519, 523
Denali fault, 567, 570, 581, 582
Denmark Strait, 138, 192, 353, 355, 622
Denmark Strait Escarpment Zone, 192, *197*
Denmark Strait Ridge, 191, 192, *194*, 205, 206, 208
Dentalium, 419
depocenter, 199, 202, 243, 250, 251, 282, 484, 516
deposit cassiterite, *558*
deposition, 387
deposits
    aggregate, 560
    alluvial, *472*
    beach, 563
    Carboniferous, *297*
    clastic, 295
    coal, 556
    consolidated sub-surface mineral, *555*
    consolidated surface mineral, *555*
    eolian, 486
    failed rift, 263, *266*
    fluvial, *469*, *472*
    glacial, *469*
    Kogru River, 467
    marine, *459*, *462*, 482
    placer, 561

    polymetallic sulphide, 552
    pond, 473
    salt, 113
    sedimentary, 161
    subsurface, 407
    thaw lake, 468, *476*
    unconsolidated shelf mineral, *557*
    Wright Point, 467
depressions, 72, *88*, 174, 194, *199*, 240, 273, 293, 300, *342*, 353, 372, 496, 497, *499*, *533*, 570
    bathymetric, 172
    Bel'kov-Nerpalakh, 293, 294
    intermontane, *528*
    Nares Strait, 373
    Nerpalakh, 299
    nodal, 172, 175
    Rapid, 240, 244, 247, 399
    Shmidt, 300
    submarine, 213
    Turgai, 407
desalination, 43, 551
Deshayes, 464
detritus, *230*, 282, 387, 534
deuterium 551
Devonian, *246*
diabase, 296, 468, 483
diapirism, 492
diapirs, 72, *243*, *274*, 285, 516, *534*
diatoms, 53, 399, 436
Dickson Island, 15
dikes, 293
    andesite, 569
    gabbro, 285
    swarm, 188, *218*
Dinkum fault, 279
Dinkum graben, *266*, *275*, *278*, 285, 503, 519, 523
Dinkum horst, 279
Dinkum succession, 263, *266*, 277
dinoflagellate, 59, 313, 420, 452, 496
dinosaur bone deposit, 406
Diomede Islands, 11
disconformities, 486, 493
    basal, *477*, *480*, 486
Disko Island, 108, 113
displacements, 262, 284, 294, 495, 571
Dissacus, 415
Dmitri Laptev Strait, 290, *299*, 559
dolomites, 293, 468, 483, 508, 521, 527, 569
dolerites, 375
Drake gas field, 504
Dramkhedian suite, *297*
dredges, 560
    nuclear-powered, 553
dredging, *312*, *323*
    Arctic, 553
drift
    glacial, 468
    transpolar, 39
DSDP North Atlantic Leg, 49, 55
DSDP sites, *357*
dunes, *472*, *474*
    linear, 486
    longitudinal, 476
    parabolic, 476

pond, 473
dust, eolian, *447*
dykes, alkaline, 215, 217, 221

Eagle Plain Formation, 247
earthquakes, 79, *80*, 182, 220, 234, 262, 279, 284, 285, *300*, 309, *393*, *485*, 487, 495
   Artyk, 88
   compressional zone, 81
   data, 218
   epicenters, 19, 82, 83, 91, 172, 179, 220, 234, 262, 344, 393
   extensional zone, 81
   intraplate, *81*
   mechanism parameters, *82*
   Sakhalin, 89
   swarm, 82, 92, 93, 94
   wave trains, 368
East Amauligak site, 497
East Greenland, *491*, *505*
   continental margin, *188*, 449
   current, 19, 21, 63
   fold belt, 509
   rifting episodes, *506*
   tectonic history, 506
East Greenland Current, *428*, *446*
East Greenland Escarpment, 197, 201, 208, 622
East Greenland Margin, 206, 622
East Greenland Rift, 505, *508*
East Greenland Sea, 18
East Greenland Shelf, *185*, *207*, 503
   bathymetry, *188*
   Blossevilel Kyst Shelf, 192
   Denmark Strait Ridge, 192
   geologic provinces, *192*
   Liverpool Land Shelf, 192
   morphology, *191*
   physiography, *188*
   sea bed, 191
   Southeast Greenland Shelf and Rise, 192
   tectonic development, *205*
   tectonic realms, *205*, *207*
   transverse zones, *192*
East Jan Mayen Fracture Zone, 355
East Siberian Basin, 503, 504
   petroleum potential, *531*, *534*
East Siberian continental shelf, *69*, 71, 289, 298, *301*, 306, 309, 390, 400
East Siberian Sea, 63, *289*, 294, *298*, 446
   anomalies, *298*
   basin, *529*, 535
   shelf-margin basins, *533*
East Siberian Shelf, 622
East Simpson wells, 575, 600
East Teshekput well, 275
Eastern Arctic Basin, *441*, 448
Eastern Beaufort structural province, *484*
Eastern Siberian continental margin, *528*
   Chaun Basin, *528*
   East Siberian sea basin, *529*
   shelf-margin basins, *533*
Eastern Wedge Terrane, *477*, *480*

ebridians, 436
Eburneopecten, 413
echinoderms, 433
echograms, 18, 309, 320, 355
ecosystem, 60
effect
   lake, *134*
   ocean, *134*
Eggvin Bank, 64
elastics, 515
Eldorado, Saskatchewan, 134
Elesmere Island ice shelves, 446
Ellef Ringnes Island, 27, 70, 94, 107, 113, 228, 230, 232, *393*
Ellesmere Fracture Zone, 219
Ellesmere Island, 14, 15, 49, 93, 105, 107, 109, 213, 218, 220, *227*, 230, 232, 234, 325, 332, 413, *414*, 513, 606
   basin, *215*
   continental margin, 211, 234, 331
   continental shelf, 18, 28, *68*, 70, 145, 309
Ellesmerian orogeny, 228, 263, 570
Ellesmerian sequence, 263, *265*, 273, 274, 275, *276*, *520*, 522, *524*, 533
Elphidium excavatum, 494, 499
embayment, 390, 423, 472, 478
   marine, 194
Emma Fiord Formation, 511
EMR. *See* Canadian Department of Energy, Mines, and Resources
EMSD. *See* estimated magnetic source depth
endemism, 60
Endicott Group, *265*, *520*
energy, 37
Enhydra, 464
environment, depositional, *428*, *436*
Eo-Ellesmerian Sequence, 263, 524
Eocene, 452
epicentral distribution, *2*
erosion, 230, 235, 244, *265*, 273, *375*, 429, 494, 522, 570, *581*
erratics, 469
escarpment, *306*, 320, 340, 353, 354, 387
   transverse basement, *194*
Eschrichtius sp., 468
Eskimo Lakes Arch, 240, 243, 244, 246, 247
Eskimo Lakes fault zone, 495
estimated magnetic source depth (EMSD), 212, 216, 218, *219*
EUBEX. *See* Eurasia Basin Experiment
Eucytheridea, 413, 414
Euler pole, 571, 585, 586
Eurasia, *69*, *70*
   cratonal, 571
Eurasia Basin, 2, 3, *18*, *21*, 27, 29, 63, *70*, 81, 103, 108, *138*, *140*, *153*, *166*, 177, 178, 211, 216, 221, 224, 305, *365*, *598*, 602, 615, *619*, 622, 625
   bathymetry, *70*
   crust, 368
   marginal plateaus, *371*
   models, 371

   paleoenvironment, *375*
   physiography, *365*
   plate tectonics, *372*
   sea floor character, 26
   sediments, *365*
   seismic data, *153*
Eurasia Basin Experiment (EUBEX), 18
Eurasian continental margin, 449
Eurasian continental slope, *70*
Eurasian plate, 81, 97, 351, 567, 569, *571*, *580*, *582*
Eureka Sound Formation, 249, 253, 514
Eureka Sound Group, 409, 413, *414*, *415*
Eurekan orogeny, 228, *230*, 511, 514, *570*, 582
evaporites, 113, 397, 508, 515
evolution
   Alaskan Arctic, *567*
   Arctic Ocean basins, *140*
   Canada Basin, *593*
   eastern Siberian Arctic, *567*
   faunas, *452*
   geologic, *459*
   marine floras, *452*
   plate-tectonic, *429*
   tectonic, *301*, *513*
Ewing-Donn theory, 442
expeditions
   British polar, *12*, *18*, 124
   Canadian polar, *14*, *18*, *25*
   Fram, *15*, *21*
   High-Latitude Air, 15
   North Pole, 25
   Norwegian, *18*
   Phipps', *21*
   Soviet Russian polar, 14, *15*, *22*, 63, 305
   submarine, *16*
   Swedish polar, 14, *18*
   U.S. polar, *15*, *16*, *24*, 63
   See also Canadian Expedition to Study the Alpha Ridge
experiment, crustal refraction, 27
explorations
   Austrian, 14
   British, *12*
   ecological, *21*
   geophysical, *21*
   hydrographic, *14*
   marine mineral, 553
   polar geographic, *5*, *8*
   sea floor, *14*
   technology, 12
   U.S., *13*
explorers, 5
Extinct Axis, 206, 353

Faddeya Island, 290, *294*, 299, *300*, 531
Faeroe Islands, 353
Faeroe-Shetland Channel, 353, 448
Faeroe-Shetland Escarpment, 361
fan
   alluvial, *472*, 486
   submarine, 70
Farallon plate, 585, 586, 588

Farewell fault, 570
faults
 antithetic, 516
 blocks, 373
 detachment, 270, 283
 dip-slip, 90
 en echelon, 90, 508
 Eskimo Lakes, 495
 extensional, 285
 high-angle, 240, 372
 Kaltag, 570, 612, 615
 listric, 252, *274*, 492, 519, 523, 526, 535
 master, 393
 multistrand detachment, 279
 normal, 82, 83, 179, 229, 244, 257, *274*, 276, *278*, 283, 285, 294, 395, 485, 487, *495*, 526, 535, 577
 north-strking, 107
 Queen Charlotte, 585
 steep, 72
 step, 68
 strike-slip, 90, 294, 298, 485, 511, 570, 582, 597, 599, 606, 609, 612
 tear, 459, 485, 487
 thrust, 270, 511
 Tintina, 612
 transform, 64, 88, 171, 176, 221, 262, 275, 301, 353, 400, 593, *609*
 wrench, 274
faunas, 462
 bottom, 343
 evolution, *452*
 foraminifera, *453*
 shallow-water marine, *403*
 terrestrial vertebrate, 404
Faxe, Denmark, 419
feldspar, 313, 343
Fennoscandia, gravity anomalies, *106*
Fennoscandian Shield, 622
Finger Shoals, *563*
fiords, glaciated, 69
Fish Creek, *464*, 469
Fish River, 247
Fish River sequence, *248*, 282, 516
Fishcreekian transgression, 461, *464*, 485
fishes, 408
Fiskenassef, Greenland, 555
Flaxman Island, 263, 483
Flaxman Member, 466, *468*, 472, 483, 499
Fletcher Abyssal Plain, 400
Fletcher's Ice Island, *24*, 107, 124
floodplain, 469
flora
 evolution, *452*
 planktonic, 430, 443
flowlines, 180
flows
 andesitic, 579
 basalt, *295*, 298, 397, 530
 heat, *397*, *399*, 511
 high heat, 27, 88
 land heat, *134*
 lava, 357, 422

 turbidity, 390, 440
flysch, 263, 266, 282
focal mechanisms, *79*, *81*, *87*, *97*, 234, 393, 622
fold belt, detachment, 523, 526
folds, *484*
 box, 530
 detachment, 459, 526
 thrust, 270, *279*, 283, 284, *393*
Foldvik Creek Formation, 506
foraminifers, 447
 planktonic, 419
forcing, orbital, *54*, *59*, *442*
forest, coniferous, 464
foraminifera, *54*, *58*, *59*, *60*, 266, 295, 297, 313, 482
 arenaceous, 414, *452*
 benthic, 407, 408, 410, *418*, *412*, *433*
Fortress Mountain Formation, 266, 522
fossils, 293
 Arctic Ocean, *452*
 calcareous, *453*
Fox Hills Formation, 405
Foxe Basin, 552
Foxe's Polar Card, 19
Fram Basin, 432, 441
Fram expedition, *15*, *21*, *26*, 29, 63, 365. See also Fram I-IV
Fram I-IV, 82, 107, 153, 181, 366, 430, 443
Fram Strait, 18, 21, 39, 48, 375, 443, 445, 446, 448, 451
Franklin Bluffs, Alaska, 420
Franklinian Basin, 213, 218, *220*, 227
Franklinian Geosyncline, 513, 600
Franklinian orogeny, 246
Franklinian rocks, 275
Franklinian sequence, *263*, *278*, *520*, *524*
Franz Josef Land, 14, 375, 622

gap, abyssal, 343
Gari (Garum), 412, 413, 414
gas, 503, 504, 514, 518, 526, 528, 534, 535, 547, 548
 dry, 514
 fields, 503, 526
 natural, *539*, 548
 production, 561
 reserves, 518
gas hydrates, *145*, *539*, *543*, *548*
 formation, *540*
 heat flow, 145, 162
 identification, *540*
 offshore, *545*
 onshore, *543*
gastropods, 414, *422*
geochemistry, amino acid, 462, 466
geothermics, *133*, *317*, *329*
glaciation, 37, *355*, 375, 385, 422, 427, 439, *440*, *442*, 451, 476
glaciers, 68, 387, 442, 446, *469*
 calving, 442
 drift, 468
 history, *45*
 unloading, 93

glendonites, 439, 440
global climate, 406, 624
global ice, 468
gold, 555, *558*
gold rush, 9
grabens, 88, 166, 242, 263, 265, 266, 270, 274, 299, 332, 372, 375, 505, 509, 511, *513*, 519, 523, 526, 584, 602, 603
gradients
 geothermal, 539, 548
 thermal, 439
Graminineae, 500
granites, 215, 246, *275*, 291, 293, 468, 483
granodiorite, 291, 293
graptolites, 263, 293, 295
gravel, 294, 372, 460, 462, 464, *469*, *472*, *483*, 553, 561
 relict surficial, *562*
 sub-surface, *563*
gravimeter data, surface-ship, 105
gravity, *101*, *232*, *319*, *325*, *344*
 anomalies, *105*, 107, *108*, 109, 111, 227, *232*, 235, *299*
 highs, 105, 107, 109, 227, *232*, 235, *299*
 lows, 105, 107, 109, 111, 227, *299*
 measurements, 22
 satellite data, satellite, *103*
graywacke, 265, *275*, *276*, 280, 524, 569
Greenland, 11, 14, 49, *65*, *70*, 91, 97, *105*, *211*, 232, *361*, 398, 446, 503, 600, 602, 609, 622
 East. *See* East Greenland
 eastern, *91*
 gravity anomalies, *105*
 northern, 93, 606
 seismicity, *91*
 West, 406
Greenland Abyssal Plain, 70
Greenland Basin, *353*
 formation, *194*
 Southeast, 194, 206
Greenland Canadian Shield, *215*
Greenland continental margin, *208*, 355, 361, 619
 north. *See* North Greenland continental margin
Greenland continental shelf, *65*
Greenland Continental Slope, *70*
Greenland Escarpment, East. *See* East Greenland Escarpment
Greenland fold belt, North, 509
Greenland Fracture Zone, 70, *353*
Greenland Ice Cape, 13, 59, 106
Greenland Ice Sheet Project, 106
Greenland-Iceland-Faeroe transverse, *353*, 361
Greenland/North American plate, 351
Greenland plate, 571
Greenland Sea, 39, 48, 65, 213, 215, 351, *361*, 373, 448
 formation, 361
 model, 361
Greenland-Scotland Ridge, 427, 428, 429, 430, *448*

Greenland-Senja Fracture Zone, 353, *361*
Greenland Shelf
  East. *See* East Greenland Shelf
  northeastern, 505
Gromorian suite, *296*
Gubik deposits, 476
Gubik Formation, 270, 278, 410, 421, *423*, *459*, 485, 486, 499
  Barrow unit, 460
  Bigbendian transgression, *461*, *462*, *485*
  central coastal plain, *472*
  Colvillian transgression, *461*, *462*
  eastern coastal plain, *472*
  Fishcreekian transgression, 461, *464*, 485
  lithologic subdivisions, *460*
  marine deposits, *459*, *462*
  marine transgressions, *461*, 485
  Meade River unit, 460
  offshore, *476*
  onshore, *460*
  Pelukian transgression, 461, *467*
  Simpsonian transgression, 461, *468*, 486
  Skull Cliff unit, 460
  Wainwrightian transgression, 461, *467*, 485
  western coastal plain, *469*
Gulf Coast province, 413
Gulf of Alaska, 580, 588
Gulf of Boothia, 552
Gulf of Bothnia, 106
Gunsight Mountain glacial interval, 469
Gustaf-Lougheed Arch, 229, 232, 235
gypsum beds, 534

hadrosaurs, 407
Hadrynian Glenelg Formation, 245
half-graben, *199*, 244, 265, 266, 505, 519, 526, 622
Hall Land, 13
Hanna Trough, 107, 273, 395, 503, 504, 526, 533
Hanna wrench fault zone, *274*, 523, 526
Haplophragmoides, 420
  bonanzensis, 248
Harder Fjord fault zone, *221*
Hareely Formation, *509*
Harrison Bay, 467, 469, 472, 480, *483*, 562, *563*
Hauterivian breakup unconformity, 263, 265
Hazen fold belt, *511*
Hazen Trough, 246, 530
healdiids, 407
Hearne, Samuel, 12
heat flow, *134*, *136*, *138*, *145*, *181*, *232*, *317*, 320, 329, 331, *397*, *399*, 511
  Alpha Ridge, *149*
  Amerasia Basin, *141*, *145*
  gas hydrates, 145, 162
  high, 88, 234, 372, 393
  land, *134*
  marine, *136*, *138*

Mendeleev Ridge, *149*
  rate, 133
  transient, 136
heat
  flux, 43, 59, 133, 134
  gain, 59
  latent, 41
  loss, 59, 133
  radiative, 41
  sensible, 41
  transfer, 138
Hecla gas field, 504
Heiberg Sandstone, 504
hematite, 602
Henrietta Island, 290, *295*, 298
Henrietta terrane, *295*
Herald Arch, 523, 525
Herald Canyon, 71, 390
Herald Islands, 270, *296*, 534
Herald thrust, 95
Herald-Wrangel arch, 530
Herald-Wrangel thrust zone, 530
Herschel Arch, 281, 282, *283*
Herschel Island, 251, 561
Heterocyprideis, 413, 414, 421
Hiatella arctica, 462, 464, 466, *467*
highly radioactive zone, 266
highs, marginal, *355*, *362*
hills, abyssal, 441
hingeline, 113, 243, 273, 278, *285*, *395*, 533
history
  Arctic Ocean, 5, *451*
  geologic, 53
  glacial, 45
  paleoclimatic, *403*
  paleogeographic, *403*
  tectonic, *284*, *361*
Histriophoca fasciata, 468
Hobson's Choice, 18, *26*, 28
Hoidahl Dome, 246
Holocene, *247*, *446*, *495*
Home Bay, 93
Hope Basin, *299*, *300*, 503, *526*, *535*, 557
  basement rocks, 525
  petroleum potential, *528*
  stratigraphic units, *527*
horizons
  opaque, *356*
  sedimentary, 166
Hornsund Fault Zone, 113
horst, *199*, 270, 348, 372, 511, 523, 526
Horton Plain, 239
hot spot, 64, *74*, 149, *181*, 207, 216, 219, 332, 373, 399, 600
Hovgaard Fracture Zone, 358, *361*, 619
HRZ Formation, *521*
HRZ. *See* highly radioactive zone
Hudson, *26*
Hudson Bay Lowlands, 468
Hudson Bay region, 468
Hudson's Bay, 12, 37
Hudson's Strait, 9, 11
Hue Shale, 267, 277, 282
Hulahula River drainage, 469
Hunkins Seamount, *342*

Husavik Fault, *172*
Husky Formation, 244, 246, 247, 518
hydrocarbons, 2, 509, 511, *513*, 516, *518*, *535*, 539
hydrophone array, 154
hydrospheres, 2
Hyperborean platform, 301
Hypoxytoma, 413

ice, 26, *49*, 212, 323, 375, 443, 468, *469*, 472, 480, 501, 551, *552*, 560
  ablation, 41, 50
  acceleration, 46
  accretion, 41, 50
  advances, 469
  algae, 60
  brash, 37
  crystals, 37, 41
  discharge, 445
  displacements, *48*
  drift, *16*, 445
  extent, *39*
  fields, 37
  floes, 16, 24, *25*, 43
  formation, 37
  frazil, 37
  glacial, 25, 54, 55, 375, 468, 469, 501
  global, 468
  growth rates, 43
  heat flux, 43
  heat storage, 39
  high-latitude, 58
  models, 43
  motion, *39*, *49*
  multiyear, 41, 50
  new, 50
  particles, *48*
  perennial, 54
  platelets, 41
  production, 48
  properties, *41*
  rafting, *49*, *55*, 59, 355, 447, 451, 480, 624
  salinity, 41
  seasonal cycle, 37, *39*
  sediment-laden, 451
  shelf, 446
  shore-fast, *50*
  snow cover, 43
  solar radiation, 43
  streams, 375
  stress, 46
  thermal history, *43*
  thermodynamics, *41*
  thickness, 43, 50
  thin, 37, 50
  tongues, 499, 501
  transport, 446
  velocities, *39*, 46
  winter, 15, 37
ice cap, 375
ice cover, *37*, *53*, *54*, *79*, *133*, *442*, *449*, *503*, 624
  bipolar, 59
  climatic significance, *53*, *59*
  dynamics, 37

formation, *54*
geologic history, *53*
origin theories, *56*
structure, *37*
ice current, 39
ice islands, *16*, 18, *24*, *26*, *49*, 106, 134, *157*, 162, 300, *332*, *333*, 430
ice melt, 48
ice pack, 1, 13, 18, 19, 24, 27, *49*, *54*, 185, 239, 371, 381, *428*, 440, 445, *446*, 449, 505, 535
ice sheets, 466, 468, 486, 497
ice shields, *449*, 451
ice stations
   Canadian, 25, 63
   drifting, 15, *16*, *22*, 63, 309, *337*, 365, 381
   Soviet, *22*, 63, 309, *337*, 365, 381
   U.S., *24*, 63, 72, 82, *124*
ice wedge, 472, *473*, 486
Iceberg Bay Formation, *415*
icebergs, *26*, *49*, *54*, 387, *428*, 440, 443, *446*, 449, 468, 480
   calving, 440
   gouging, 342
   melting, 483
   plow marks, 445
Iceland, *109*, 172, 180, 182, 191, 353, 393
Iceland-Faeroe Ridge, 353, 355
Icelandic hot spot, 64, *74*, 207, 208
Icelandic Plateau, 171, 175, 180, 197, 201, *353*, *356*, 361
Icelandic shelf, 174
Icelandic spreading center, 188
icequake, swarms, 95
Iditarod fault, 570
Ikit Trough, 497
Ikpikpuk dunes, *472*, *476*
Ikpikpuk River, 469
illite, 343
ilmenite-magnetite, 559
Imperial Formation, 246, 252
Indigirka River, 289
Indigirka submarine valley, 69
inflow, deep-water, 439
Inkalinian suite, *296*
Inland Ice, 213
Inner Liverpool Land Basin, *201*
Integricardium, 412
interglacials, 449
inversion
   body-waver, 82, 83
   moment-tensor, 82, 83
invertebrates, marine, *422*
iodine, 551
Iperk sequence, *251*, 282, 492, *493*, 497, 516
   Lower, 493
   Upper, 493, 495, *498*, 501
Irik well, 251, 543
Irishak Formation, 600
iron, 552
ironstone, 247, 282
irradiation, solar, 50
Isachsen Formation, 245, 247
Isfjorden, 445

island arc, poleward-moving, 588
islands
   artificial, *560*
   barrier, *563*
   chains, *483*
   production, 561
Isserk well, 561
Issungnak well, 496, 561
Itkillik River, *469*
   glacial episodes, 469
Izanagi-Farallon boundary, 586
Izanagi plate, *586*

Jackson well, 547
Jago River drainage, 469
Jameson Land, 201
Jameson Land Basin, 508
Jan Mayen Fracture Zone, 64, 172, 174, 185, 192, 206, 352, 355, *361*
   East, *353*
   West, *174*, *353*
Jan Mayen hot spot, 64
Jan Mayen Island, 64, 74, 175, 179, 181, 353
Jan Mayen Ridge, 74, 109, 114, *202*, 355, 619
   block, *356*
Janusfjell Formation, 445
Japan, northeast, 89
Jeannette Island, 290, *295*, 298

Kadleroshilik, *481*
Kaesleria, 413
Kaktovik Basin, 262, 279, 282, 503, 504, 519, 522, 523, 535
Kaltag Fault, 570, 612, 615
Kaltag/Porcupine fault system, 609
Kaltag/Rapid Fault Array, 495
Kalubik Formation, *521*
Kamchatka
   Northeast Seismic Zone, *90*, 97
   northwestern, 90-
Kamik Formation, 247
Kangerdlugssuaq Escarpment Zone, 192, 197
Kangerdlugssuaq fiord, 192
Kanguk Formation, 247, 248, 253, 514
Kaolak well, 526
kaolinite, 343
Kap Brewseter, East Greenland, *420*
Kap Dalton, East Greenland, *420*
Kap Stewart Formation, 508, 509
Kap Washington Group, 217, 221, 373
Kapanoar sequence, *250*
Kaparuk River Formation, *521*
Kara continental shelf, 309
Kara margin, 622
Kara Sea, 37, 63, 315, 375, 446, 556
Kara shelf, 70, 103, 315, 330
Karaginskii Island, 89, 90
Karen Creek Sandstone, 265
Karmuk beds, *467*
Kay Point, 561
Kayak Formation, 246
Kayak Shale, 265
Kekiktuk Conglomerate, 265

Kekiktuk Formation, 246
Kenalooak well, 251
Kennedy Channel, 212
Khroma plate, 301
Killi Creek beds, *464*
Kimmeridgian shales, *509*
King Frederik VIII's Land, 68
King Island, 11
Kingak Formation, 246, 282, 516, 518
Kingak Shale, 265, *521*, 604
Knipovitch Ridge, 65, *74*, *175*, 180, 181, 351, *353*, 361
   bathymetry, *65*
   plate boundary, *175*
Kobuk River valley, 527
Kogru River, 467, 484
   deposits, 467
Kolbeinsey Ridge, *64*, *74*, 138, *172*, 179, 180, 181, 188, 202, 205, 351, 354
   bathymetry, *64*
   plate boundary, *172*
Kolyma River, 289, 390, 558
Kolyma submarine valley, *69*, 390
Kolymia, 297
Kolymia terrane, *567*, 593
Kolymo-Omolonsky massif, 569
Kolymski block, 599, *609*, 615
Kolymski splinters, 600
Kong Christian X's Land, 65
Kong Oscars Fiord, 192
   fracture zone, 192
   transverse fault zone, 201
Kopanoar sequence, 516, 518
Kopanoar well, 252
Koryak-Kamchatka margin, 584
Koryak zone, *569*
Koryakia terrane, *567*
Kotel'nyi Island, 96, 290, 293, *294*, 298, 299, 301, *539*, 532
Kotel'nyi terrane, *293*, 298, 299, *300*
Kotzebue Arch, *95*, 526
Kotzebue Sound, 95, 533
Kotzebue subbasin, *526*
Koyukuk-Kushokwim Basin, 569
Kresta Gulf, 95
Kronprins Christian Basin, 503, *505*, 511, *535*
   petroleum potential, *508*
Kronprins Christian Land, 68, 211, 212, 215
Kuekvan' River Valley, 95
Kugmallit delta, 251, 252
Kugmallit Formation, 250
Kugmallit sequence, *251*, 282, 516, 518
Kugmallit Trough, 240, 244, 246, 247, 493, 496, 497
Kukpowruk River, 462
Kula-Farallon boundary, 585
Kula-Farallon spreading center, 586
Kula-Pacific Ridge, *585*
Kula plate, 567, *585*, 558, 593
Kular, 558
Kuparuk gravel, 462, 469
Kuparuk oil field, 521, 523
Kuparuk River, 469
   oil field, 577, 602

Index

Kuparuk River Formation, 398, *577*, 602, 615
Kuril-Aleutian island arc, 585
Kurile arc, 81, 90
Kuskokwim Mountains, 588

Labrador Sea, 285, 373, 408, 571, 580
Lady Franklin Bay, 213
lakes, 136
laminae, carbonaceous, 410
Lamont-Doherty Geological Observatory (L-DGO), 107, 109
Lancaster Sound, 111, 427, 429
Laptev Sea, 63, 70, 289, 301, 446, 552, 553, 556, 558
 continental margin, 178, *622*
 continental slope, 178
 shelf, *69*, *81*, *82*, 97, 103, 219, 365, 366, 372, 375, 620, 622
 seismicity, *83*
Laramide Orogeny, 408
Larix, 469, 472
Laurentide ice, 468, 480
lavas, 203, 513
lebensspuren, 343
Leffingwell Lagoon unit, *481*, 486
Lena River, 71, 547
Lena River Delta, *83*, 372
 seismicity, *83*
Lena Trough, 19, 178, 179, 180, 212, 220, 224, 443, 448
Lena Valley, 552
Leptocythere, 407
lignite, 522, 556
LILS. See Liverpool Land Shelf
Limacina helcina, 447
limestones, 246, 293, 294, 297, 315, 407, 483, 506, 508, 511, 513, 516, 521, 527, 530, 532, 534, 569
Lincoln Sea, 63, 70, *91*, 212, 215, *218*, 221, 232, *234*, 535
 margin, *213*, *218*, *219*, 235
 seismicity, *91*
 shelf, 213, 232, 234
Lincoln Sea Basin, 218, 503, *511*, *535*
 petroleum potential, *513*
Lincoln Sea–Hazen Plateau High, 218
lineaments, 219, 221
lineations
 gravity, 399
 magnetic, 372
Lisburne Group, 246, 265, *521*
Lisburne Hills, Alaska, 95
Lisburne Peninsula, 263
lithosphere, 93, *146*, 203, 235, 368, 593, 620
lithostratigraphy, *55*, *324*
Little Cornallis Island, 555
Littorina squalidia, 464, 466
Liverpool Land, 508
Liverpool Land Escarpment, 201
Liverpool Land Shelf (LILS), 192, *201*, 205
loading, 208, 262
 sediment, 93
loams, 372

loess, *472*
Lofoten Basin, 353, 355
Lofoten Islands, 109, 113, 114, 352
logs
 wire-line, *540*
 mud-gas, *542*
Lomonosov Ridge, 3, 16, 18, 19, 24, 25, 26, 63, 64, *71*, 74, 91, 97, 107, *108*, 114, 126, 130, 138, *160*, 211, 219, 232, 236, 289, *305*, *309*, *315*, 319, 325, 328, *330*, *333*, 365, *372*, 375, 395, 400, 429, 432, 447, 599, *600*, 602, 604, 609, 619, 620
 age, *330*
 bathymetry, *71*
 origin, *330*
 seismic data, 159, *160*
Lomonosov Ridge Experiment (LOREX 79), 18, *25*, 71, 72, 107, 126, 134, 160, 305, 309, *312*, 319, 320, 332, 366, 430
Lomonosov Ridge–Makarov Basin area, *441*
London Basin, 412, 418, 423
Long Strait, 289, 526
LOREX. See Lomonosov Ridge Experiment
Low, A. P., 14
Lower Iperk sequence, 493
Lower Marine group, 510
Loxoconcha, 408, 413
lutite, 265, 266, 285, 313, 315, 343, 540
Lutkevichella, 408
Lyakhov Islands, *290*, 299, 300
Lyakhov–South Anyui suture zone, 301, 530, 532
Lyakhov terrane, 291, 298, 300

Mackenzie Bay, 561
Mackenzie Bay sequence, *251*, 282, 516, 518
Mackenzie-Beaufort Basin
 Akpak Sequences, *251*, 516
 Boundary Creek Sequences, *247*, 516
 depositional sequences, *516*
 Fish River Sequences, *248*, 516
 Iperk Sequences, *251*, 516
 Kopanoar Sequences, *250*, 516, 518
 Kugmallit Sequences, *251*, 516, 518
 Mackenzie Bay Sequences, *251*, 516, 518
 petroleum potential, *518*
 Reindeer Sequences, *249*, 516, 518
 Richards Sequences, *250*, 516, 518
 Shallow Bay Sequences, *251*, 516
 Smoking Hills Sequences, *247*, 516
Mackenzie Cone, 70, 17
Mackenzie Delta, 69, 70, 95, 107, 111, 113, 239, 245, 246, *247*, 257, 270, 332, 279, 283, 285, *393*, 395, 399, *420*, 440, 548, 572, 588, 598, 602, 604, 607
 gas hydrates, *543*

Mackenzie Delta–Beaufort Sea Basin, 503, *515*, *535*
Mackenzie River, 276, 279, 285, 399, 480, 547
Mackenzie River Basin, 71
Mackenzie River valley, 276, 279, 285, 399, 480
Mackenzie Trough, *239*, 251, 491, *495*, *499*
 seismostratigraphic units, *500*
macrofauna, 293
macrofossils, 469, 473
Magadan region, 88
magmatism, 215, 217, 585, 588
 hot spot, 216
magnesium, 551
Magnetic Satellite (Magsat), 329, 331
magnetic activity, levels, *119*
magnetic anomalies, *119*
 Arctic Basin, *126*
 Arctic Mid-Ocean Ridge, *127*
 Canada Basin, 127
magnetic field, Arctic, *119*
magnetic highs, 316
magnetic storm, 119, 124
magnetics, *180*, *232*
 satellite, *329*
magnetism, 12
magnetite, 580
magnetization, *579*
magnetometers, 126
magnetotellurics, *317*, *329*
Magsat. See Magnetic Satellite
Maguire Islands unit, *481*, 483, 486
Main Camp drift path, 317
mainshock, 88, 90
Makarov Basin, 3, 63, *70*, 71, 72, *108*, 114, 130, *164*, *166*, 305, *306*, *309*, *312*, 316, 317, *319*, *332*, 365, 382, *399*, 429, 432, 593, 609, *621*
 age, 33
 origin, *333*
 seismic data, *164*
Mallile well, 543
Malyi Lyakhov Island, 290, 291, 293
mammals, 474
 marine, *422*
manganese, 313, 551, 552
Manihiki Plateau, *331*
mantle, 160, 326
 plume, 182
 upper, *382*
maps
 American Geographical Society, 20
 Barents' circumpolar, 8
 Bartholomews Arctic Ocean, *19*
 bathymetric, 3, *18*, *20*, *21*, 64, 172, 188, *309*, 321, 351, 382
 Canadian Arctic Archipelago, 14
 CESAR central Arctic Ocean, *21*
 DRB, *19*
 Eardley's, *19*
 Eurasia Basin, *19*
 free-air gravity, 93, 325
 GEBCO, *20*, *21*
 magnetic anomaly, 321

Mercator's Arctic, *8*, *28*
National Geographic Society, *20*
Ruysch's polar basin, 8
satellite magnetic anomaly, 398
sea floor, *14*
Sobczak's Artic Ocean, *21*
Soviet, *19*
marbles, 296
Mare
  clausum, 6, *29*
  liberum, 12
  nostrum, 29
Margaret Formation, 415
margin
  basin, 379, *391*
  circum-Arctic, 604
  continental. *See* continental margin
  mid-Norwegian, 208
  Norwegian, 208
  passive, 107, 110, 188, 208, 234, 244, *351*, *391*, 399, 503, 522, 534, 593, 600, 604, 607, *609*, 613
  pull-apart, 244
  strike-slip, 604
  transform, 604
Marginal Ice Zone Experiment (MIZEX), 18
marine mining, *564*
marl, 510, 513
Marsh Anticline, 462, 466, *484*
Martin Creek Formation, 247
Martin Point, *95*
  seismicity, *95*
Marvin Seamounts, *72*, *320*, *332*
Marvin Spur, *72*, *306*, *302*, 331
Mason River Formation, 248, 249, 252
Matuyama Superchron, 466
McClure Island, 483
McClure Strait, 134, 230, 232, *235*
McGuire Foramtion, 247
McTavish Point, 467
Meade River unit, 460, 469
Meadwell, 526
measurements
  bathymetric, 320
  field intensity, 124
  gravity, 22, *106*, 309, 312, 320, 326
  heat flow, 23, 24, 133, *134*, *136*, 309, *329*, *344*, 397, 509, 570
  land heat-flow, *134*
  magnetotelluric, *345*
  marine heat-flow, *136*, *138*
  pendulum, 107
  refraction, 212, *275*, *385*
  sea-floor, 133, 136
  seismic, *153*, *309*, 320, 371, 381
  subsurface temperature, 133, 136
  surface gravity, 103, 105
  surface radar, 106
Mercator, Gerhard Kremer, *8*, *28*
megacycles
  depositional, 522
  transgressive-regressive, 516
megaslumps, 519
Meighen Island, *230*

melt pits, 50
melting, 50
  bottom, 49
meltwater, 38, 41, 43
Melville Bay, 11
Melville Island, 13, 231
Melville Island Group, 246
Melville Sound, 13
Mendeleev Abyssal Plain, 3, *71*, 108, 337, *343*, 379, 385, 390, 391, 393
Mendeleev Fracture zone, 72
Mendeleev Ridge, 3, 63, 70, *72*, 108, 130, 140, *144*, *307*, *320*, *330*, 344, 399, 593, 598, 599, 600, *602*, 609, *621*
  bathymetry, *72*
  heat flow, *149*
  seismic data, *161*
Mesozoic, *53*, *404*
  early, *404*
  late, *403*, *427*, *436*, *585*
metamorphism, 276, 291, 296, 510, 582
metasediments, 292
methane, *539*
methodology, *432*, *433*, *434*, *435*
microcontinents, 171, *356*
microearthquakes, 79, 93
microfossils, 246, 292, 313, 403, 414, *419*, *423*, 452
micronodules, 315
microphytoliths, 296
microrelief, 342
microseismicity, 95
Mid-Atlantic Ridge system, 20, 171, 182
Mid-Labrador Sea Ridge, 320
mid-Norwegian margin, 208
Mid-Oceanic Ridge (MORB), 181. *See also* Arctic Mid-Ocean Ridge
Midway Group, 418
milioliids, 452
Miluveach Formation, 521, *522*
Miluveach River, 462, 464
Mine Land, 508
minerals
  consolidated, 553
  continental shelf, 551, *552*, *555*
  deep-sea, *551*
  deposits, *555*, *557*
  industrial, 552
  offshore hard, *551*
  placer, 552
  seawater, 551
  unconsolidated, *552*
mines, lead-zinc, 555
mining
  aggregate, 560
  marine, *564*
  offshore, 552
  sub-sea, 554
Ministicoog Member, 249
Minto arch, 242
Miocene, *493*
  late, 452
miospores, 292
MIZEX. *See* Marginal Ice Zone Experiment

models
  Alaska continental margin, 262
  Alpha Ridge, *326*
  Amerasia Basin, 146, *394*
  Arctic Alaska strike-slip, 593
  Arctic Islands strike-slip, 593, *607*
  Arctic-Alaska Transform, *609*
  Canada Basin, *394*, 399, 612
  Cesar Trough, 325
  continental crust, 299
  continental crust oceanization, *593*
  crustal, 344
  crustal density, 319, 320
  density, 325
  dynamic-thermodynamic, *43*
  gravity-density, *326*
  Greenland Sea, 361
  LOREX gravity, 319, 320
  New Siberian Islands, 300
  oceanic crust entrapment, *593*
  oroclinal, 604
  plate tectonic, *581*
  rational, *593*, *596*, *604*, *612*
  rifted-rotational, *347*
  rifted-translational, *347*
  rotational rifting, 244, 399
  sea ice, *43*
  sea-floor spreading, *593*
  stochastic-kinematic, *48*
  tectonic, 262, *301*, *347*, *593*
  thermal evolution, 146
  translation (rotational), *347*
  velocity, 300
  Vøring Plateau, 356
  Yukon strike-slip, *609*
Mohns Ridge, *65*, *175*, 179, 180, 181, 188, 205, 351, 361
  bathymetry, *65*
  plate boundary, *175*
  spreading axis, 353
Moho, 320, 332, *382*, 621
Mohorovicic Discontinuity, 113
Mokka Formation, 415
molasse, 266
Molasse complex, 506
Molloy Ridge, 172, 178, 179, 352
mollusks, *419*, *421*, 464, 466
  fossil, 461
  marine, 403, 408, 409, *410*, *423*
Moma depression, 88
Moma rift system, 88, 97
monoclines, 498
Monotis, 404
Monster Formation, 247
monzonite, quartz, 246
Moose Channel Formation, 248, 282
Moose Channel sequence, 518
MORB, 181. *See also* Arctic Mid-Oceanic Ridge
morphology, *64*, *72*, 174, 179, 182, *191*, 257, 282, 309, 320, 330, 348, 351, 365, 371, 375, *386*, *395*, 427, 499, 620, 621
  sea floor, *14*
  seabed, 1

Morris Jesup Plateau, 3, 68, 69, 108, 109, 153, *156*, *212*, *216*, *219*, 221, 365, 371, *372*, 430, 620
  anomalies, *216*
  seismic data, *156*
Morris Jesup Rise, 448
motions
  continental, *581*
  plate, *91*, *580*, *585*
  strike-slip, 82, 83
Mould Bay, 94
Mount Goodenough Formation, 245, *247*, *282*
Mount Moore Formation, 409, 414, 415
mountains
  axial, 174, 176, 178
  rift, 620
  submarine, 16, 63, *71*, *305*
mud, 251, 323, 442, 496, 500
  black, *436*, 453
mud-gas logs, *542*
mudrock, 294, 295
mudstones, 250, 294, 295, 355, 415, 492, 493, 518
Muellerina, 421
Musculus, 423
Mya, 423
Myalina limestone, 508, 509
mylonite, 298

Nagssuqtoqidian mobile belt, 106
Nansen Basin, 3, 63, *70*, 107, *156*, 365, 375, 620
  seismic data, *156*
  seismic sequence, *367*
Nansen-Gakkel Ridge, *65*
Nansen Ridge, *178*, 179, 180, 181, 218, 449
  plate boundary, *178*
Nansen's Sill, 19
Nanuk Formation, 246
Nanushuk Group, 266, 277, *522*, *576*
Napoiak High, 240
nappes, *262*, 279
Nares Strait, 13, 14, *92*, 211, 213, 219, *221*, 232, 320, 373, 427, 429, 602
  channel, 232
  depression, 219, 373
  fault, 602
  lineament, 213
  seismicity, *92*
Naskhokian series, *296*
Natica clausa, 423
Natica janthostoma, 466
National Petroleum Reserve Alaska (NPRA), 105, 545
Natsek well, 249
Nautilus, 16, 71, 337
Navarin Basin, *579*
navigation, radio, *121*
NEAS. *See* Northeast Greenland Shelf
Neilonella, 419
Neogene
  early, *420*
  late, *422*, *441*, *491*
Neogloboquadrina pachyderma, 433, 435, 452, 453

neotectonics, *484*, *494*
Neptunea, 423
  lyrata leffingwelli, 462, 466
Neroukpuk Formation, 246, 516
Nerpalakh depression, 299
Netserk well, 546
New Siberian Basin, 298, *299*, *300*, 530
New Siberian-Chukchi fold system, 530, 532
New Siberian Islands, 14, 71, 83, 91, *95*, 289, *290*, 298, 300, *301*, *530*, 533, *534*, 620
  anomalies, *298*
  Bennet terrane, *295*
  Henrietta terrane, *295*
  Kotel'nyi terrane, *293*
  Lyakhov terrane, *291*
  model, 300
  Novaya Sibir' terrane, *294*
  seismicity, *95*
  terranes, *290*
  velocity model, 300
New Siberian massif, 530, *532*
New Siberian plate, 301
Newfoundland Fracture Zone, 374
Noatak-Kobuk valley system 390
nomenclature, Arctic marine, *3*
Nonion depressulum, 498
Nordenskiöld, *14*
Nordkapp Basin, 113
Norsemen, 6, 28
North American craton, 259, 395, 516, *575*, *579*
North American margin, 623
North American plate, 79, 81, 97, *171*, *182*, 289, 361, 375, 503, 567, 569, *571*, *580*, 582
  anomalies, *180*
  heatflow, *181*
  magnetics, *180*
  petrology, *181*
  seismicity, *179*
  spreading, 180
  velocity structure, *181*
North American polar margin, 27
North American shelf, 623
North America-Eurasia plate boundary, extension, 83
North America-Eurasian pole of rotation, 87, 88, 91, 97
North Atlantic
  plate motions, *580*
  reconstruction, *602*
North Atlantic Basin, 567, 602
North Atlantic Deep Water (NADW), *58*
North Atlantic Ocean, *428*, *432*, 448, 466, *580*, *599*
North Atlantic sea floor, 619
North Beringian Platform, *459*, 484, *485*, *487*
North Chukchi Basin, *107*, 113, *262*, *270*, 285, 400, 523, 526, *533*, *535*, 600, 602, 623
  seismic-stratigraphic units, *272*
North Chukchi high, 524, 526
North Dakota, 409, 413, *415*, 423
North-East Passage, 14

North Greenland continental margin, *211*
  geologic provinces, *213*
  physiographic provinces, *212*
  physiography, *212*
  tectonic development, *219*
  tectonic history, 220
North Greenland shelf, 622
North Issugnak well, 251, 252
North Laptev Uplift, *372*, 533
North Magnetic Pole, 13
North Polar Chart, *20*
North Pole, *101*, 134, 160, 166, 305, 309, 330, 337, 365, 436, 447
  expeditions, *25*
NORTH POLE series operations, 16, 22
North Sea, 351
North Sea Basin, *408*, 413, 420
North Sea Basin-North Atlantic connection, 419
North Sea Basin province, *413*
North Sea-Labrador Sea connection, 408
NORTH-series operations, 16, 22
North Shore, gas hydrates, *545*
North Slope, 95, 263, *265*, 275, *276*, 520, 521, 522, 524, 548, 556, 567, *575*, *588*, 593, 598, 602, 604, 612, *613*
  Alaskan, *459*
  Barrow Arch section, 604
  block, 607, 609
  paleomagnetism, *571*
  tectonic history, 571
  terrane, 612
North-West Passage, 13
Northeast Greenland Shelf (NEAS), 192, *202*, 205
Northeast Laptev Basin, 533, *534*
Northern Alaska continental margin, *519*
  Beaufort Sea shelf basins, *519*
  Chukchi Sea shelf basins, *519*, *523*
  Chukchi Sea shelf-Hope Basin, *519*, *526*
Northern Ellesmere magmatic belt, *511*
Northern Hemisphere, 427
  sea ice, *37*
Northern Maritime Exploration and Development Enterprise, 559
Northern Sea of Okhotsk, *90*
  seismicity, *90*
Northwest Canada Basin, 141
  abyssal plain, 144
Northwest Territories, 598
Northwind Abyssal Plain, 69, 337, *340*
Northwind Escarpment, 257, 270, 379, 391, 604
Northwind Ridge, 3, 69, 70, 71, 108, 257, 270, 337, *340*, 379, 600, 602
Northwind Sea Valley, 69
Norton Sound, 466
Norway, 109, 421

Norway Basin, 109, 139, 206, *353*, 361
Norwegian Basin, 428
Norwegian continental margin, 208, 449
Norwegian Current, 428, 449
Norwegian Sea, 556
 southern, *206*
Norwegian Sea Shelf, 114, 445
Norwegian-Greenland Sea, 2, 63, *64*, 103, 105, *108*, 113, *138*, 171, 175, 176, *181*, *351*, 420, *428*, 432, 443, 446, *448*, *580*, 598, *619*, *621*
 basins, 429
 central region, *353*
 defined, 351
 gravity anomalies, *108*
 northern region, 353
 paleoenvironments, *448*
 southern region, 353
 tectonic evolution, *358*
 tectonic history, *361*
Novaya Sibir' Island, 96, 290, 299, *530*
Novaya Sibir' terrane, *294*, 299, *300*
Novaya Zemlya, 13, 622
Novosibirsk complex, *294*
NPRA. *See* National Petroleum Reserve Alaska
Nucula (Nucula), 419
Nugssuaq, West Greenland, 419
Nulato region, *580*
Nulavik beds, 462
nutrients, 38
Nuwok Member, *420*
Nuwuk Basin, 275, 277, 279, 503, 504, 519, 523, 524, 526, 535
Nyeboe Land, 219

Ob' Bank, 215
Obik Sea, 436
Ocean Point, Alaska, 407, *409*, 464
 beds, *412*
oceans, world, 59, *404*, 420, 436, 439
ocean-to-continent transition (OCT), 194, *197*, 202, 203, 230
OCT. *See* ocean-to-continent transition
Odontaspis, 415
oil, 503, 504, 514, 518, 528, 534
 production, 561
 reserves, 518
 window, 518, 522, 526, *532*, 534
oil field, Kuparuk, 521, 523, 577, 602
Okhotsk-Chukotsk volcanogenic belt, 567
Okhotsk Plate, *88*, *97*
Okhotsk Sea, 37
Old Crow–Babbage depression, 240
Oloy-Lyakhorskoy volcanic belt, 530
Omoloi River, 87
Omolon massif, 405
ooze, 324, 355, 399, 453
 biogenic, 53
ophiolites, *569*
Orksut Formation, 246

orocline, 597
orthoquartzite, 483
ostracodes, 60, 297, 407, 408, 409, *410*, 413, 433, 453, 494
Ostrov Vrangelya. *See* Wrangel Island
otoliths, 415
Outer Liverpool Land Basin, *201*
oxygen isotopes
 ratios, 435
 stages, 443, 454
Ozernoi Peninsula, 90

Pachyaena, 415
Pacific Basin, plate motions, *585*
Pacific-Farallon boundary, 586
Pacific plates, 585
Pacific Shoal, 563
Paijenborchella, 407, 408
Palaeozoic, *220*
paleoceanography, *427*
paleocirculation, 53, 54
paleoclimates, *427*, *472*, 486
 marine, *403*
paleocurrents, *406*, 612
paleoenvironment, *375*, 414, *439*, *448*
Paleogene, *408*
 late, *420*
paleomagnetism, *398*, *571*, 579
paleopole, 395, 398, 399, 600
paleoshelf, 273
paleoshoreline, 395, 467
paleoslope, 194
paleosols, 473
paleotemperatures, 580
paleovalleys, 499, 563
palynomorphs, 266, 399, *410*, 527
Paracyprideis, 413
 similis, 412
 sp., 415
Paracypris, 408
Paris Basin, 413, 418
Parsons Group, 247
Parsons Group sandstone, 518
Parsons gas field, 503
Patellacythere, 408
PCSP. *See* Polar Continental Shelf Project
Peard Bay, 468
Peard well, 525
Peary, Robert E., 14
Peary Land, 213, *215*, 219, 220, 511
Pearya terrane, *227*
peat, 294, 472, 496, *497*
pebble shale unit, 265
pebbles, ice-rafted, *451*
Pechora Sea, 558
Pediastrum, 496, 497, 500
Peel Trough, 247
Pegtymel'skii Range, 95
pelagic realm, *442*
pelecypods, 293, 297
Pelukian beach, 483
Pelukian deposits, 485
Pelukian transgression, 461, *467*
Peninsular Terrane, 570
peridotite, 293

permafrost, 60, 133, *134*, 294, 464, *466*, 475, *539*, 547, 548
 sub-sea, 561
Permian, 246
petroleum, 308, *503*
 potential, *503*, *504*, *508*, *511*, *513*, *518*, *522*, *526*, *528*, *531*
 See also specific sites
petrology, *181*
Phacorhabdotus, 408
Phipps' expedition, *21*
phyllite, 246, 296, 528
physiography, *63*, *140*, *188*, *212*, *257*, *305*, *337*, *351*, *379*, *428*, *491*
phytoplankton, 321, 439, *452*
Picea, 469, 501
Pillar series, *297*
Pingo Dal Formation, 508
Pingok Island, 563
plains
 abyssal, *70*, 145, 289, *306*, 337, 343, 353, 365, *366*, 379, 382
 alluvial, 469
 central coastal, 472
 coastal, 257
 eastern coatal, 472
 western coastal, 469
plate boundary
 Knipovich Ridge, *175*
 Kolbeinsey Ridge, *172*
 Mohns Ridge, *175*
 Nansen Ridge, *178*
 Spitsbergen Transform, *176*
 West Jan Mayen Fracture Zone, *174*
plate geometry, *571*
plate motions, *91*, *580*, *585*
 oceanic, *585*
plateaus, 337, 342, *343*, 379
 marginal, 63, *69*, *371*
 submarine, 270, 619
 volcanic, 171
plates
 continental, *571*
 oceanic, *580*, *585*, *588*
 See also specific plates
platforms
 bedrock, 484
 carbonates, 220
 continental, 20
 homoclinal, 509
Pleistocene, *422*
 early, *411*, *441*, *453*
 late, *420*, *442*, *493*, *495*
Pliocene, middle, *453*
plume
 hot-spot, 399
 mantle, 295, 332
plutonism, 227, 569
plutons, 203, 234, 275, 511
POGO. *See* Polar Orbiting Geophysical Observatory
Point Barrow, 105, 107, 133, 275, 467, 468, 552
Polar Continental Shelf Project (PCSP), *18*, 105
Polar continental margin, 325

Polar Orbiting Geophysical
  Observatory (POGO), 329, 331
polar margin, *227*
polar oceans, northern, *427*
Polarstern, RV, *27*
pole of rotation, 259, 332, 391, 395,
  399, *598*, 602, 604
  North America–Eurasia, 87, 88,
    91, 97
poles
  Abyssal Plain, 3, 91, 511, 513
  Euler, 571, 585, 586
  paleomagnetic, 398, *576*, 607
  reconstruction, *580*
  rotation, 245, 571, 581, 586, 588
pollen, 294, 295, 313, 410, 420,
  452, 464, *466*, 469, 473, 485,
  486, 497, 501
polynyas, 41, 43
Polytrichum, 497
Populus, 469
Porcupine Plateau, 239
Porcupine River Formation, 246
porosity, 41, 145, 146, 317
porphyry
  basalt, 295
  diorite, 293
  granitic, 296
Portlandia arctica, 465
Posidonia Shales, 508
Precambrian, *245*
Pribilof Islands, 466
Prince Albert Homocline, 242
Prince Creek Formation, 407, 409,
  410
Prince Patrick Island, 27, 70, 94,
  228, 230, 231, 232, 234, 235
prisms, sedimentary, 2, 266, 270,
  275, 277, 279, 281, 384, 386,
  391, 393, 519
profiles
  aeromagnetic, 320, 344
  airgun-reflection, 162
  bathymetric, 282, 342
  central Beaufort Sea, *251*
  gravity, 28
  northeastern Beaufort Shelf, *253*
  reflection, 384, 486, 498
  refraction, 382
  salinity, 21
  seismic, *251*, 270, *274*, 277, 480,
    497
  seismic reflection, 27, 72, 161,
    212, 270, 275, 281, 384, *385*,
    391, 393, 395
  seismic refraction, 27, 28, *315*,
    320, 620
  southeast Beaufort Sea, *252*
  temperature, 21, 134
  velocity, *181*
  western Beaufort Sea, *251*
Project Chariot, 133
Proliv Longa. *See* Long Strait
proto-Canada Basin, 382, 395, *398*
proto-Gulf Stream, 406
protozoans, planktonic, 60
provinces
  geologic, *192*
  listric-normal fault, *274*

Prudhoe Bay, 134, 276, 469, 472,
  482, 518, 545, 548, 562, 600
  oil field, 504, 523, *526*, 598
pseudoescarpments, 197, *201*
pseudomorphs, 472
Pteroloxa cumuloidea, 499
Pterygocythereis vannieuwenhuisei,
  421
Put alluvium, 472
Put deposits, 472
Put outwash, 472
Putuligayuk River, 482
pycnocline, 38
pyrite, 522
pyroxenite, 293, 468
Pytheas, *5*, 28

quartz, 265, 266, 313, 343, 469, 552
quartzite, 246, 263, 296, 468
Quaternary, *449*, *491*
Queen Charlotte fault, 585
Queen Elizabeth Islands, 14, 69, 91,
  93, 105, *227*, 231, 331, 391,
  409, 414, 570, 582
Queen Maud Gulf, 552
quiescence, 585
  magmatic, 588

Rabilimis paramirabilis, 421, 466
radiation, solar, 37, 39, 41
radiolarians, 266
Rayleigh wave radiation, 90, 96
Rapid Creek Formation, 247
Rapid Depression, 240, 244, 247,
  399
Rapid Fault Array, 240
Rat River Formation, 247
Rauchuan depression, 529
reconstruction, North Atlantic, *602*
Red Formation, 247
redbeds, 508, 600
reefs, 508
reflections
  mantle, 160
  seismic, 27, 72, 153, 203, 276,
    312, *315*, *321*, 612
reflectors, *386*, 477, 496, 527, 534,
  542
  acoustic basement, 356
  bottom simulating, 162
  clinoformal, 525
  gas-hydrate, 547
  high-angle, 497
  hyperbolic, 384
  internal, 367
  seaward-dipping, 197, *355*, *357*
  sedimentary, *166*, 342
  seismic, 497, 525
  subbasalt, 355
  sub-basement, 185, 194, *206*
  subhorizontal, 312
  sub-seafloor, 480
refraction, seismic, 27, 72, *153*, 230,
  300, *325*, *344*, 515, 612
Reindeer Formation, 249, 282
Reindeer Island, *482*, 483
Reindeer sequence, 249, 282, 516,
  518
Reindeer well, 518

relief, oceanic, *64*
remagnetization, *577*, 579, 600
renewal, deep-water, 429
reserves, 552
  gas, 518
  oil, 518
reservoirs, 518
  carbonate, 523
  sandstone, 523, 526
Reshetnikova anticlinorium, 294
Resolute, Canada, 79
Resolute Bay, 133
Return Island, 483
Reykjanes Ridge, 64, 181, 188, *194*,
  205
rhyolites, 294
Richards Island, 239, 245, 250, 251,
  497
Richards sequence, *250*, 282, 516,
  518
Richardson Mountains, 246, 247,
  248, 262, 279, 285, 399
Richardson Trough, 246
ridges, *64*, *72*, 114, 166, 171, 17,
  178, *182*, *196*, 202, 285, *305*,
  337, 365, *400*
  aseismic, 2
  basement, 71, 178, 375
  ice-shore, 37
  J-anomaly, 375
  mid-ocean, *64*, 81, 130, 171, 320,
    351, *372*, 598
  pressure, 37
  sand, *563*
  spreading, 2
  submarine, 19, *71*, 270, *379*, 619
  volcanic, 353
rifting, 68, 93, 185, 194, 202, *205*,
  208, 244, 247, 257, *259*, *270*,
  278, *284*, 348, 375, 385, 387,
  391, *506*, 514, 567, 572, 580,
  599, 604, 609
  nonrotational, 398
  rotational, *395*
rifts
  Cenozoic, 207
  continental, 218, 257
  series, 259
  valley, 171, 176, 178, 180, 244,
    353, 366, 371
  valley axial, 176
  zone axial, 366
rise, continental, *70*, 239, 257, 365,
  379, 382, 387, 441, 509, 621
Robeson Channel, 215, 218, 219
rocks
  allochthonous, 569
  basement, 188, 300, 331, 511,
    523, 525, 527
  Brookian, *276*
  carbonate, 263, 265, 276
  clastic, 273, 525, 528, 598
  coal-bearing, 527
  continental, 510
  crystalline, 201, 215, 275, 622
  Ellesmerian, *276*
  felsic, 230
  flysch, 511
  Franklinian, *275*

granitic, 105, 315
ice-rafted, 343
igneous, 111, 234, *296*, 298, 332, 514, 527, 579
mafic, 230, 235
magmatic, 216
marine, 506
metabasic, 215
metamorphic, 276, 291, 298
metasedimentary, 230
opaque, *391*
platform, 228, 279
plutonic, 534, 569
remagnetized, 578
reservoir, *509*, 511, 523, 533, *534*
sedimentary, 2, 157, 202, 230, 263, 265, *296*, 298, 309, *385*, 399, 515, 524, 527, 528, 530, 556, 569, 575, 579, 600
source, *532*
terrigenous, 293
tholeiitic, 235
volcanic, 26, 27, 105, 215, 246, 263, 332, *380*, *399*, 515, 527, 534, 569
volcanic basaltic, 436
Romanzof Uplift, 240, *246*
Romanzov Mountains, 95
rotaliids, 452
rotational rifting hypothesis, 398, 400
Roundstonia, 413, 414, 421
Ruby Geanticline, *569*
rust, sialic, 215, 218
rutile, 559

Sadko Trough, 178
Sadlerochit Formation, 246
Sadlerochit Group, 265, *279*, *521*, 577
Sadlerochit Mountains, 263
Sag River Sandstone, 265
Sagavanirktok Formation, 267, 277, 278, *410*, *420*, 522
Sagavanirktok River, 469, 563
St. Anna Trough, 375
St. George Basin, 584
St. Lawrence Island, 569
St. Matthew Island, *579*
Sakhalin earthquakes, 89
Sakhalin Island, 89, 91
salinity, 41, *58*, 138, 405, 415, *428*, 539
salt, 41, 113, 551
sand, 460, 464, *472*, 493, 496, 497, 500, 553, 561, *563*
dune, 473
eolian, *476*
movement, *476*
wedges, *474*, 486
sandsheet, eolian, *476*
sandstones, 246, 247, 250, 265, 266, 281, 292, 294, 295, 296, 410, 415, 419, 420, 462, 469, 483, 492, 506, 508, *510*, 511, 518, 521, 522, 526, 527, 532, *533*, 569
Sannikov Strait, 290

Sargo Plateau, 337, *343*
Sarsicytheridea, 413, 414, 421
satellite, gravity data, *103*
scaphopod, 414, 419
scarp, *72*, 108, 163, 217, 273, 307, 323, 372, 379, 387, *391*, 465, 466, 467, 469
schists, *292*, *296*, 313
crystalline, 291, 292
mica, 9
Scoresbysund, Greenland, 79
Scoresby Land, 508
Scoresby Sund fiord, 192
Scoresby Sund Fracture Zone, 192
Scoresby Sund river system, *201*
Scorseby, William, 12
scouring, 312, 422
ice, 37
sediment, 37
Sea of Okhotsk, *89*, 91, 97, 569
Sea of Okhotsk plate, *89*
sea floors, north polar, 2
sea ice, 37, 421, *446*, 559, 560
sea otter remains, 464, 466
seabed morphology, 1
Seabee Formation, 267
seafloor, 2, *14*
seafloor, 24, 25, 95, 171, 182, 185, 192, *194*, 197, 205, *207*, 216, 244, 275, 330, 333, 355, *358*, *362*, *372*, 391, 395, 399, *420*, 429, 513, 514, *593*, 598, *599*, 602, 606, 613
seamounts, *72*, 166, *320*, 332, 342, 344, 353, 367
SEAS. *See* Southeast Greenland Shelf and Rise
seawater, *551*
minerals, 551
seaways, *405*, 427, 619
epicontinental, *405*
Second Canadian North Pole Expedition, 309
sedimentary basins, *503*
sedimentary environments, classification, 137
sedimentary prism, 2, 266, 270, 275, 277, 279, 281, *384*, 386, 391, 393, 519
sedimentation, 93, 107, 146, 160, 192, 197, 199, *201*, 208, *245*, 277, 284, *358*, 385, *386*, *440*, 494, 495, *501*, 510, 513, 515, 516, 521, 621
glacial marine, 440, 445
post-rift, 185, 202
rates, 68, 343, 367, *385*, 393, 435, 440, 443, 448, *449*, 500, 624
sediments, 49, *55*, *59*, 71, 107, 111, 137, 192, *201*, 208, 218, 228, 230, 234, 235, 245, 250, 252, 263, 266, *270*, 275, 291, 299, *309*, *312*, 320, *323*, 332, 342, *343*, 348, *353*, *365*, 375, *385*, 390, 391, 414, *419*, 421, *436*, 466, *495*, *499*, *509*, 535, 539, 548, *579*, 603, 622
accumulation, 53

amino-acid epimerization techniques, *435*
basement interface, 160
biogenic, 37
biostratigraphic data, *433*
clastic, 247, 262
composition, *446*
cores, 343, 427, 430, *432*, *433*, *434*, *435*, *440*, *442*, *449*, 453
cover, 234, 299, *432*, *449*
cross sections, *495*, *498*
deep-sea, 145
detrital, *446*
flux, *449*
glacial, 423
glacial marine, 53, 441
lithostratigraphic units, *433*
loading, 93
magnetostratigraphic data, *434*
marine, 2, *461*
oxygen-isotope ratios, 435
post-rift, 194, 197, 207, 208, 485
pre-rift, 199
radiocarbon ages, *435*
rift, 208
source, *446*
thickness, 72, *146*, 156, 165, 197, 301, *353*, 365, 372
transport, 387, *446*, 473
traps, 446
volcaniclastic, 194
Sedov, 15
seismic data
Alpha Ridge, 159, *161*
Amerasia Basin, *157*
Amundsen Basin, *156*
Canada Basin, *160*, *164*
Eurasia Basin, *153*
Lomonosov Ridge, 159, *160*
Makarov Basin, *164*
Mendeleev Ridge, *161*
Morris Jesup Plateau, *156*
Nansen Basin, *156*
Yermak Plateau, *156*
seismic stations, 79
seismic measurements, *153*, *309*, 320
seismic reflection, 27, 72, *153*, 203, *276*, *312*, *315*, *321*, 612
seismic refraction, 27, 72, *153*, 230, 300, *325*, 344, 515, 612
seismicity, 79, *81*, *91*, 105, 107, 113, *179*, 220, 221, *234*, 309, *344*, 372, *393*, 495, 620, 625
Arctic Mid-Ocean Ridge, *82*
Baffin Bay, *92*
Cherskii Mountains, *87*
Chukchi Sea, *95*
clusters, *93*
interplate, *82*
intraplate, *91*, 220
Laptev Sea shelf, *83*
Lena River Delta, *83*
Martin Point, *95*
Nares Strait, *92*
New Siberian Islands, *95*
Northern Sea of Okhotsk, *90*
seismology, *344*
seismometer, 154, 160
Selennyakh Range, *88*

642　Index

Seliakhskaya Bay, 559
Senja Fracture Zone, 113, *353*, 361, 448
Serripes groenlandicus, 423
Serripes zone, *423*
Seven Islands, 445
Severnaya Zemlya, 14
Seward Peninsula, 105, 466, 526, 569, 582, 609
Seward Peninsula Uplift, 526
Shaler Group, 245
shales, 231, 246, 247, 249, 252, 265, 266, 281, 285, 297, 445, 483, 506, *508*, 510, 513, 516, 581, 521, 522, 524, 526, 530, 532, 534, 569
　bituminous, *508*, 515, 518
　fragments, 445
　Kimmeridgian, *509*
　Kingak, *521*, 604
　pebble, 604
Shallow Bay sequence, *251*, 492, 493, *498*, 501, 516
shelf, continental. *See* continental shelf
Shelikhov, Bay, 89, *90*
ship research, *26*
Shmidt depression, 300
shoals, *563*
shortening, 569
　crustal, 230
Shublik Formation, 246, 265, 516, *521*
Shublik Mountains, 263, *279*
Siberia, *407*, 530
　continental shelf, 83
　eastern, *289*, 558, 588
　northeast, 81, 91, *567*, 593, 599
　tectonic evolution, *501*
　western, 405
Siberian Abyssal Plain, 3, *71*, 72, 306, 317, 332
Siberian Arctic (eastern), evolution, *567*
Siberian coast, 37
Siberian continental margin, 171, *289*, *301*
Siberian Plain, 621
Siberian Platform, 87, *301*
Siberian Prikolyma massif, 405
Siberian Sea, 553
Siberian Shelf, 609
Siberian shield, 405
Siku Formation, 247
silica, *436*
silicoflagellates, 53, 399, 436, 452
silt, 372, 462, 464, 468, 472, 482, 483, 496, 497, 562
siltstone, 281, 285, 294, 295, 407, 410, 420, 483, 514, 521, 522, 527, 530
Simpson Cover, 468
Simpson Lagoon, 484
Simpsonian transgressions, 461, *468*, 486
sinks, 46
Sinus Borealis, 571
Sitka, Alaska, 79
Skull Cliff, 462, *464*, 466, 468

Skull Cliff unit, 460, 464
slope, continental, 70, *93*, 109, 178, 211, 213, 215, 239, 251, 257, 270, 289, 365, 441, 477, 509, 546, 575
slumping, 322, 391, 548
Smith Bay, 467
Smoking Hills Formation, 518
Smoking Hills sequence, 247, 516
snow, 59
snowcover, 43, 473
snowfall, 41, 473
snowmelt, 43
sodium chlorite, 551
sonobuoy, 154, 212, 258, 281, 371
South Dakota, 409, 413, *415*, 423
Southeast Greenland Basin, 194, 206
Southeast Greenland Shelf and Rise (SEAS), 192, *194*, 204
Southern Greenland Sea, 37
Southern Hemisphere, 427
Soviet Arctic, 91
Soviet Northern Sea Route, 15
Soviet Union, *557*
Spar Fracture Zone, 64, *174*, 179, 192
sparkers, 153
Sphagnum, 496, 497, 500
spicules, sponge, 433, 453
spilite, 293
spillage, episodic, 138
Spitzbergen, 11, 12, 14, 82, 114, 352, 371
Spitsbergen Fracture Zone, 70, 179, 215, *219*, 224, 373, 375, 619, 620
Spitsbergen Transform, *176*, 181
　plate boundary, *176*
spores, 294, *295*, 313, 410
spreading
　asymmetric, *180*
　oblique, *180*
　rates, 171, 179, 180, 371
　sea-floor. *See* seafloor spreading
spreading axis, *332*
　extinct, 353
spreading center, 138, 140, 149, 188, 320, *332*, 361, 372, 400, 586, 593, 599, 603
　extinct, 171, 513,
spreading ridge, 353
Spy Island, 483
Stamukhi Shoal, 563
Station Alpha, 16, *24*, 64, 72, *308*, *320*, 381
Station Charlie, 16, *24*, 124, 321, 337, 340, 342
Station North Pole 15, 134
Station Tiksi, 96
stations
　drifting ice, 15, *16*, *22*, 29, 63, 72, 82, *124*, 153, *157*
　seismic, 79
Stockton Island, 483
Stolbovoi Island, 290, 291, 293
stones, ice-rafted, 467
Storkerson, Storker, *15*
Storkerson Bay well, 253
Storkerson Uplift, 242

Strand Fiord Formation, 230, 399
strandflat, 68
Strathcona Fiord, Ellesmere Island, 409, *414*
stratigraphy, 192, 202, 227, *245*, *247*, *259*, 262, *263*, *272*, *275*, *279*, *366*, *382*, *432*, *491*, *493*, *520*, *524*
　core, *481*, *428*
　reversal, *577*
　seismic, *477*, *480*, *483*
streams, *476*, *478*
　transpolar drift, 446
Strelka Anzhu, *295*, 299
stresses, *91*, *234*, *393*
　compressional, 95
　shear, 93
　wind, 50
structure
　conductivity, *316*, *328*
　gravity, *319*, *325*, 328
　magnetic, *316*, *328*
　seismic refraction, *315*, *325*, 328
sub-Arctic, 55, 60
subbasins, 242, 243, 513
　Barter Island, *282*, *284*, 523
　Demarcation, *282*, *284*, 503, 519, 523
　Kotzebue, *526*
　sedimentary, 281
　synformal, *484*
submarines, nuclear-powered, 18, 72, 305, 309, 337, 365
submersions, marine, 459
subsidence, 88, *192*, 194, 197, 199, 202, 207, 208, 228, 239, 266, 294, 362, 395, 436, 494, 514, 598, 623
　rate, 68
surveys
　aeromagnetic, *121*, 298, 328, 365, 372, 513
　gravimetric, *299*
　gravity, 513
　magnetic, 429
　Magnetotelluric, 300
　satellite, *124*
　seismic, 153, *542*, 546
　shipborne, *16*
Svalbard, 74, 107, 228, 355, 358, 361, 412, 413, *419*, 436, 441, *445*, 600
Svalbard Archipelago, 375, 445
Svalbard continental margin, 176
Svalbard Platform, 108
Svalbard shelf, 215
Svalbard Transform, 181
Sverdrup Basin, *110*, 213, 218, 220, 227, 229, 235, *285*, 315, *395*, 399, 504, *511*, 514, 548, *570*, 623
　gas hydrates, *543*, *547*
　rift zone, 285
Sverdrup Islands, 14, 475
Sverdrup Rim, 113, *228*, 231, 232, 234, *235*
swarms
　earthquake, 82, 92, 93, 94
　icequake, 95

syenite, 246
synclines, 296, 414
synclinoria, 530

T-3 ice station, 16, *24*, 49, 72, 124, 134, 141, 146, *157*, 162, 305, 309, *320*, 330, 381, 397, 430
T-3 Plateau, 337, *343*
Taglu gas field, 503, 518
Taimyr Peninsula, 293
Talkeetna Mountains, 569
Talkeetna Super terrane, 569
talus, 293
Tancredia, 412
Tarsiut island, *560*
Tarsiut area, 495
Tarsiut well, 496
tectonics, *243, 245*, 285
　development, *205, 219, 345, 398*
　evolution, *301, 330*, 354, *358, 372*
tectonism, 202
Tellinimera, 412
temperature, 41, 53, 133, *145*, 466, *539*, 623
　borehole, 133
　bottom-water, *138*
　surface water, 439
　transient surface, *136*
Ten Sun Dome well, 547
Tent Island Formation, 248, 282
Teredo, 419
Terrestrial group, *510*
Tertiary, *138, 580*
Teshekpuk Lake, 467
Tethys, 413
thermal evolution model, 146
Thetis Island, 483, 563
tholeiites, 295
Thoracosphaera
　arctica, 453
　heimii, 453
thrusting, imbricate, 575
Tiksi station, 96
tillites, 423
tin, 552, 553, 555
Tintina fault, 612
Tjörnes sequence, *422*
Tjørnes Fracture Zone, *172*, 179
Topagaruk well, 265, 276
Torok Formation, 266, *277*, 522, 525
Trachyleberis, 407
Trail Island, 508
transforms, slow-slipping, 171
transgressions, marine, 459, *461*
transition
　continent-ocean crustal, 93, 113
　ocean-to-continent (OCT), 194, *197*, 202, 203, 230, 356, 621
transport
　cross-latitude, 53
　ice, 445, *446*
　sediment, 445, *446*, 473
transpression, 581
transtension, 581
Transverse Zone, 192
Treaty of Tordesillas, 8
trench, *221*, 588, 602

Triassic, *246, 570*
trilobite remains, 295
triple junction
　Pacific-Farallon-Kula, 586
　rift-rift-shear, 332
troodontids, 407
troughs, *107*, 130, 163, 175, 178, 213, 219, 220, 228, 239, 244, 251 273, 289, 307, *309*, 312, 320, 331, *332*, 348, 365, 372, *477, 491*, 493, *499*, 506, *530*, 620, 621
Tsuga sp., 472
Tuapaktushak beds, *466*
tuffs, 294, 296, 513, 530, 579
Tuktoyaktuk Peninsula, 70, 239, 244, 246, 247, 252, 497
Tunallk well, 525, 526
tundra, 133, 485
Tununuk High, 240
turbidity, 246, 266, 267, 335, 367, 385, 387, 390, 432, *440*, 493
　currents, 70, 71, 309, 342
Turgai Depression, 407
Turgai Strait, 405, *407*, 423
Turrilina alsatica, 420
tyrranosaurids, 407

Ugnuravik gravel, *472*
Ugnuravik Group, *521*
unconformities, 518, 522, 606
　basal, 500
　erosional, 281
　Miocene, *495*, 499
uplift, 68, 86, 93, 188, 201, 221, *230*, 235, 244, 245, 257, *262*, 281, *495*, 526, 533, *534*, 570, 581, 582, 597, 606
Upper Iperk sequence, 493, 495, *498*, 501
Upper Marine Group, 510
upwelling, 53
　mid-ocean, 439
Ursus maritimus, 21, 60
Uviluk well, 496

Valanginian section, 528
Vallacerta siderea, 452
valley rift, 171, 176, 178, 180, 244, 353, 366, 371
Vankina Bay, 553, *558*
variations, magnetic, *329*
velocity fields, 586
velocities
　current, 315
　linear, *581*
　seismic, 300
Verkhoyansk fold belt, 602, 609
Verkhoyansk-Kolymian orogenic belt, 569
vertebrates, terrestrial, *403, 423*
Vesteralen Island, 114, 352
Vestspitsbergen Current, 428, 445
Victoria Fjord, 93, 213
Victoria Island, 239, 242
Victoria Land, Antarctica, 475
Vil'kitskii Basin, *299, 300*
Vil'kitskii Island, 290, *295*, 298

Vilkitskii–North Chukchi Basin, 533, *534*
volcanic centers, 215
volcanics, 113, 188, 194, 201, 204, 207, 215, 217, 246, 295, 301, 323, *399*, 511, 513, 514, 528, 534
　rift, 201
volcanism, 74, 88, 181, 197, *202*, 229, 295, *373*, 508, 532, 569, 585, 603, 623
　hot spot, 399
　intraplate, 373
volcanoes, 179
　active submarine, 342
　Beerenberg, 175, 179
Vorinin Trough, 375
Vøring marginal high, 361
Vøring Plateau, *109*, 114, 138, 353, 355, 449
　models, 356

Wainwrightian transgression, 461, *467*, 485
Walakpa Bay, 468
Walakpa beds, *467*
Walakpa gas field, 526
Walakpa well, 525
Wandel Sea, *215*, 375
Wandel Sea Basin, 213, *215*, 218, 220, 503, *509, 535*
　petroleum potential, *511*
Wandel Sea margin, *212, 215, 219*
Ward Hunt Ice Shelf, 26
waters
　bottom, *138*, 428, *449*, 468
　fresh, 551
　open, *553*
waves, 81, 90, 94, 218, 231, 331, 620
　Rayleigh, 90, 96
　seismic, 300
　shear, 156
　surface, 82, 94, 95, 96
　velocity, 244
wedges
　clastic, 194, 234, 524, 597
　continental terrace, 503
　homoclinal, 509
　ice, 472, *473*, 486
　marine, *477*
　sand, *474*, 486
　sandstone, 523
　sedimentary, 522
Wegener Fracture Zone, 291
wells
　Atkinson Point, 518
　Cape Espenberg, *527*
　COST No. 1, 579
　East Simpson, 575, 600
　East Teshekput, 275
　Irik, 543
　Isserk, 561
　Issungnak, 496, 561
　Jackson, 547
　Kaolak, 526
　Kenalooak, 251
　Kopanoar, 252
　Mallile, 543

Natsek, 249
Netserk, 546
North Issugnak, 251, 252
Peard, 525
Reindeer, 518
Storkerson Bay, 253
Tarsiut, 496
Ten Sun Dome, 547
Topagaruk, 265, 276
Tunallk, 525, 526
Uviluk, 496
Walakpa No. 2, 525
Weller Bank, 563
West Greenland. *See* Greenland, West
West Jan Mayen Fracture Zone, *353*
  plate boundary, *174*
West Sak oil field, 523
West Spitzbergen, current, 21
Western Beaufort structural province, *485*
Western High, 358
Western Interior Seaway, *405*, 423
Western Wedge Terrane, *477*, *480*

White Sea, 15, 106
White Uplift, 246
Wilkins, Sir Hubert, *15*, 16
wind stress, 50
Wordie Creek Formation, 508
world oceans, 59, *404*, 420, 436, 439
Wrangel Abyssal Plain, 3, 70, *71*, 306, *309*, 320, 621
Wrangel arch, 270
Wrangel Island, 15, 270, 289, *296*, *279*, *301*, 390, 533, *534*, 609
wrenching, 495
Wright Point, 467
  deposits, 467

xenoliths, 215

Yana River, 87, 105
Yermak H zone, 156
Yermak hot spot, 219, 373
Yermak Plateau, 3, *69*, 107, 108, 109, 114, 128, 153, *156*, 218, 219, 365, *371*, 430, 448, 620
  seismic data, *156*
Ymer, 212, 430
Yoner, 27
Yukon, northern, 95, 239, *240*, 244, *246*, 282
Yukon Coastal Plain, 239
Yukon-Koyukuk Basin, 570, *579*
Yukon Territory, northern, 263, 285, 399, 598

Zarya strait, 300
Zechstein Basin, 510
Zemlya Bunge, 290, 293, *294*, *299*, *300*, 301
Zhokhov Island, 290, *295*, 298
zircon, 559
zones
  continental rift, 372
  highly radioactive (HRZ), 266
  magnetic quiet, 358
  transverse, 192